# 2016/17

# THE DIRECTORY OF GRANT MAKING TRUSTS

24th edition

Gabriele Zagnojute, Rachel Cain, Denise Lillya, Ian Pembridge, Jennifer Reynolds

Additional research by Stuart Cole and Emma Weston

Published by the Directory of Social Change (Registered Charity no. 800517 in England and Wales)
Head office: Resource for London, 352 Holloway Rd, London N7 6PA
Northern office: Suite 103, 1 Old Hall Street, Liverpool L3 9HG
Tel: 08450 77 77 07

Visit www.dsc.org.uk to find out more about our books, subscription funding websites and training events. You can also sign up for e-newsletters so that you're always the first to hear about what's new.

The publisher welcomes suggestions and comments that will help to inform and improve future versions of this and all of our titles. Please give us your feedback by emailing publications@dsc.org.uk.

It should be understood that this publication is intended for guidance only and is not a substitute for professional or legal advice. No responsibility for loss occasioned as a result of any person acting or refraining from acting can be accepted by the authors or publisher.

First published by Charities Aid Foundation 1968
Second edition 1971
Third edition 1974
Fourth edition 1975
Fifth edition 1977
Sixth edition 1978
Seventh edition 1981
Eighth edition 1983
Ninth edition 1985
Tenth edition 1987
Eleventh edition 1989
Twelfth edition 1991
Thirteenth edition 1993
Fourteenth edition 1995
Fifteenth edition 1997
Sixteenth edition 1999
Seventeenth edition published by Directory of Social Change 2001
Eighteenth edition 2003
Nineteenth edition 2005
Twentieth edition 2007
Twenty-first edition 2010
Twenty-second edition 2012
Twenty-third edition 2014
Twenty-fourth edition 2015

Copyright © Directory of Social Change 2001, 2003, 2005, 2007, 2010, 2012, 2014, 2015

All rights reserved. No part of this book may be stored in a retrieval system or reproduced in any form whatsoever without prior permission in writing from the publisher. This book is sold subject to the condition that it shall not, by way of trade or otherwise, be lent, re-sold, hired out or otherwise circulated without the publisher's prior permission in any form of binding or cover other than that in which it is published, and without a similar condition including this condition being imposed on the subsequent purchaser.

The publisher and author have made every effort to contact copyright holders. If anyone believes that their copyright material has not been correctly acknowledged, please contact the publisher **who will be pleased to rectify the omission.**

The moral right of the author has been asserted in accordance with the Copyrights, Designs and Patents Act 1988.

ISBN 978 1 78482 004 6

**British Library Cataloguing in Publication Data**
A catalogue record for this book is available from the British Library

Cover design by Kate Bass
Text designed by Eugenie Dodd Typographics, London
Typeset by Marlinzo Services, Frome
Printed and bound in Great Britain by CPI Group, Croydon

# Contents

| | |
|---|---|
| Foreword | v |
| About the Directory of Social Change | vii |
| Introduction | ix |
| Acknowledgements | xii |
| How to use DGMT | xiii |
| A typical grant-making charity entry | xxi |
| The top 150 grant-makers by grant total | xxiii |
| Other publications and resources | xxv |

**INDEXES**

| | |
|---|---|
| Grant-makers by geographical area | 1 |
| Grant-makers by field of interest and type of beneficiary | 43 |
| Grant-makers by type of grant | 171 |

**REGISTER**

| | |
|---|---|
| The alphabetical register of grant-making charities | 253 |

# Foreword

It is hardly original to proclaim fundraising as a people business, but it remains true. Encouraging others to support our causes is an emotional business; it is about finding a narrative that captures the essence of the work we are trying to fund and the impact it will have, whatever we have put our shoulders to the wheel to fundraise for. Then we have to communicate it, as passionately and convincingly as we can.

Great fundraising needs great fundraisers, but, like other crafts, they also need the best tools: *The Directory of Grant Making Trusts* is a key part of any fundraiser toolkit. The temptation is to hit the internet as the default approach to research, but that can be a time-wasting and bottomless pit. Instead, here, in one book, all the work has been done for you. It is a treasure trove of information that helps a fundraiser unlock the impact that trusts and foundations can have on your cause. Trust and foundations are perhaps the quiet relation in the fundraising family. There is a process and formality about trust fundraising, with guidelines, applications and deadlines, but also tremendous opportunities, particularly for small and medium charities.

With much of fundraising, we invest heavily in search of answers to the key questions. Who are the right people to ask? What is the right time to ask? And what is the right thing to ask for? We test, learn, test again, then roll-out, and sometimes we fail several times before we succeed. Here is a book that gives the fundraiser the answers to these key questions about thousands of trusts, so they can focus on the best way to deploy this knowledge to raise more money for their cause. We do so knowing that this is the one area of fundraising where the donors have to give the money away. So there is an even greater incentive to carefully approach those who have clearly stated that they might support the project you are pitching.

And perhaps, best of all, it costs very little. There is the investment in the directory, time, certainly, and maybe paper and a stamp to start. Trust fundraising is a great equaliser: your success depends on the quality of what you do and how you do it rather than mass mailings, large events or high-profile brand partnerships.

So keep your copy close to hand and dust-free. Good luck!

**Paul Farthing MInstF**
**Director of Fundraising, NSPCC**

# About the Directory of Social Change

The Directory of Social Change (DSC) has a vision of an independent voluntary sector at the heart of social change. The activities of independent charities, voluntary organisations and community groups are fundamental to achieve social change. We exist to help these organisations and the people who support them to achieve their goals.

We do this by:

- providing practical tools that organisations and activists need, including online and printed publications, training courses, and conferences on a huge range of topics;
- acting as a 'concerned citizen' in public policy debates, often on behalf of smaller charities, voluntary organisations and community groups;
- leading campaigns and stimulating debate on key policy issues that affect those groups;
- carrying out research and providing information to influence policymakers.

DSC is the leading provider of information and training for the voluntary sector and publishes an extensive range of guides and handbooks covering subjects such as fundraising, management, communication, finance and law. We have a range of subscription-based websites containing a wealth of information on funding from grant-makers, companies and government sources. We run more than 300 training courses each year, including bespoke in-house training provided at the client's location. DSC conferences, many of which run on an annual basis, include the Charity Management Conference, the Charity Accountants' Conference and the Charity Law Conference. DSC's major annual event is Charityfair, which provides low-cost training on a wide variety of subjects.

For details of all our activities, and to order publications and book courses, go to www.dsc.org.uk, call 08450 777707 or email publications@dsc.org.uk.

# Introduction

Welcome to the 24th edition of *The Directory of Grant Making Trusts* (DGMT). This book covers just over 2,000 of the largest grant-making charities that give grants to UK organisations. The amounts given by individual funders listed in this guide generally range from around £40,000 annually, up to a staggering £670 million. The combined giving of all these grant-makers in the financial year covering 2013/14 totalled over £4.3 billion, of which nearly £4.25 million was given to organisations. The grant-total figure remains the same as in previous editions and, as before, includes significant funding from the Big Lottery Fund (and its Awards for All programme). The top 150 funders (by their individual grant totals) are listed at the end of this introduction and include the Big Lottery Fund, as well as more traditional grant-making charities.

The Charities Aid Foundation published the first edition of DGMT in 1968 and it has been researched and published by DSC since 2001. Over this time the title has gained a notable reputation as a comprehensive guide to UK grant-making charities and their funding policies. It is designed to provide a bridge between the grant-makers and fundraising communities in the UK. Today it is hard to imagine the difficulties which must have been encountered and the amount of time spent trying to obtain funds from these charities before DGMT brought together so many of them in one place.

DGMT remains a key source of information with each entry reflecting where possible the trustees' own view of policies, priorities and exclusions. DSC's other guides include independent, sometimes critical, comment on and analysis of funders' activities. DGMT does not. Rather, it is a concise and straight to the point guide to grant-making charities.

In the previous edition we noted a general improvement in the financial situation of the charities listed in the book and this seems to be a continuing trend. In the course of our research we looked at information contained in the annual reports and accounts mainly from 2013/14 and 2014 (occasionally 2014/15), as well as other resources, such as charities' websites, published guidelines or direct contact with funders. We have decided to concentrate on those grant-makers whose charitable activities generally have the potential to exceed £40,000 and not to include some of the smallest and exclusively local givers.

This edition features 70 new charities that have not been included before. Each of the entries gives a figure for the annual grant total and the amount given to organisations only. In many cases the two figures will match; however, where support is given to both organisations and individuals you will be able to see the difference. In some cases we were unable to determine the breakdown and both fields will show the same figure to reflect the charity's potential to give.

Even with some previously listed funders omitted, both the income and the assets of the organisations listed mark an increase from the previous edition and the total given in grants remained approximately the same. In addition, about 57% of all grant-makers have increased the total amount given in grants during the year compared with the previous edition. Nevertheless, despite the seemingly improving financial position, charity trustees remain uncertain and cautious about the ongoing impact of government welfare reforms and public spending cuts. They recognise the strain on charitable resources and the fact that the voluntary sector is largely stepping in to replace this diminishing statutory support.

Some of the key issues mentioned in the trustees' annual reports include: an increase in grant referrals from other organisations; a demand for support and advice projects to help people deal with changes to the benefits' system and coping with debt; an increase in demand for assistance from those directly affected by reductions in their benefit entitlement as well as from organisations and agencies helping individuals; and greater competition for funding.

Aside from these more obvious implications, the less obvious adverse impacts on the sector have also been highlighted: 'Many funders are reporting a drop in applications. It may be that cuts in public funding is reducing the income of third sector organisations, many of which received funding from central or local government and hence organisations' capacity and appetite for new initiatives. We have noticed a number of senior people moving on from local charities and with them experience may also be lost'. **The Hillingdon Community Trust Trustees' Report and Financial Statements 2013/14**

The competition for funding is fierce and not getting easier. Grant-makers continue to state that they are forced to decline many appeals, even the most eligible and deserving ones. In order to stand out from the crowd, fundraisers must not only have a worthy cause to promote but also a well-tailored appeal addressed to the right person – and this book will help you to achieve that.

We value the opinions of our readers on all aspects of our work including this directory. We are always looking to improve the guide and would welcome any feedback – positive or negative – which could be useful for future editions. Please contact us at: Research Team, Directory of Social Change, Suite 103, 1 Old Hall Street, Liverpool L3 9HG, telephone 0151 708 0136 or email us at: dgmt@dsc.org.uk with any comments you would like to make.

## The grant-making charities we have listed

This directory aims to include the majority of UK-based grant-makers that are capable of giving at least around £40,000 a year to organisations. Many of their trustees and/or staff are extremely helpful and we have accessed comprehensive information on current policies via their websites, published material or direct communication. However, not all are so open. Where we have found this to be the case and information is not readily available, the funder's details have been updated, where possible, using the information on the appropriate regulator's website. Grant-makers have been included in the index under the appropriate headings according to their own published guidelines/grant-making practices/annual reports. We have placed those for which we do not have such information available under what we believe are the most suitable categories based on the information available.

Some trustees continue to state their wish for their charity not to be included in this book. However, we believe that our guides provide an invaluable bridge between the charitable community and the rest of the voluntary sector, and that charities in receipt of public funds through tax relief should not attempt to draw a veil of secrecy over their activities, barring the most exceptional cases. Consequently, we have declined requests from grant-makers to be excluded from this directory. We are happy to explain the reasons why the organisation may not be awarding grants or accepting applications, and we think this is more helpful than letting the charity remain an obscure name in the sea of funders.

In general we have included:

- charities with a grant-making capacity of at least about £40,000 per year which make grants to charities and voluntary organisations, including Big Lottery Fund and its programme Awards for All (which operate like grant-making charities). Please note that while grant totals of some of the funders listed here could be below £40,000 in the given year, their grant-making activities either have the potential to exceed this amount or vary significantly each year.

We have excluded:

- grant-makers which fund individuals only;
- grant-makers which fund one organisation exclusively;
- grant-makers which generally have a grant-making capacity of less than £40,000 (smaller grant-making charities are included on www.trustfunding.org.uk);
- grant-makers which have ceased to exist or are being wound up with any remaining funds fully committed.

We continue to include grant-making charities which state that they do not respond to unsolicited applications. We believe that their inclusion benefits fundraisers by giving a broader overview of the grant-making community, and that the information could be important in supporting relationship fundraising activity. We feel it benefits the grant-makers in helping them to communicate that they do not wish to receive applications, which fundraisers might not know if they identified that particular grant-maker through other avenues. In this way we are working towards achieving one of our Great Giving campaign goals of reducing the number of ineligible applications that are submitted to very busy and often over-stretched grant-making charities (please visit www.dsc.org.uk for more information).

# Acknowledgements

We would like to thank Paul Farthing, Director of Fundraising at NSPCC, for contributing the foreword to this edition.

We would also like to thank all those trustees and staff of grant-making charities who strive to make their information openly available, and all those who help our research by responding to our communications and providing helpful comments.

# How to use DGMT

The directory starts with three indexes:

- grant-makers by geographical area;
- grant-makers by field of interest and type of beneficiary;
- grant-makers by grant type.

There is a listing of the top 150 grant-makers by grant total at the end of this Introduction. All of these are in alphabetical order.

Using these indexes, readers should end up with a shortlist of grant-makers whose funding policies match their needs.

## Grant-makers by geographical area

This index enables you to see which grant-makers will consider applications from a charity or project in a particular geographical area. It contains two separate listings:

**LIST OF GEOGRAPHICAL AREA HEADINGS**

This is a complete list of all the geographical area headings used in DGMT.

**LIST OF GRANT-MAKERS BY GEOGRAPHICAL AREA**

These pages list grant-makers under the geographical areas where they will consider funding.

## Grant-makers by field of interest and type of beneficiary

This index enables you to see which grant-makers are likely to fund projects doing a particular type of work to benefit a particular type of person. It lists grant-makers according to:

- the type of activity or work they are willing to fund – their 'fields of interest';
- who they want to benefit – their preferred 'beneficiaries'.

These pages contain two separate listings:

**CATEGORISATION OF FIELDS OF INTEREST AND TYPES OF BENEFICIARY**

This lists all of the headings used in DGMT to categorise fields of interest and types of beneficiary. This listing should help you match your project with one – or more – of the categories used. The page numbers relate to the second listing.

**LIST OF GRANT-MAKERS BY FIELD OF INTEREST AND TYPE OF BENEFICIARY**

These pages list grant-makers under the fields of interest and types of beneficiary they have indicated they have a preference for or might be willing to support.

The index is structured hierarchically. This means that the general heading comes first, followed by more specific subject areas. For example, 'Rights, law and conflict' is split into four sub-headings, including 'Citizen participation' and 'Conflict resolution'. Some of these are then split further. For example, under 'Conflict resolution' you can find further four categories, including 'Cross-border initiatives' and 'Peace and disarmament'.

So, if your project falls under a specific heading such as 'Cross border initiatives', it is also worth looking at the grant-makers which have expressed a general interest in funding 'Conflict resolution' and, above that, 'Rights, law and conflict'. Grant-makers might be interested in funding your project even if they have not specifically expressed a preference for a particular field as long as it falls within the broad area they are supporting.

**Grant-makers by type of grant**

This index enables you to see which grant-makers can consider making the types of grant you are looking for. Grant-makers are listed under the types of grant that they have indicated they are willing or are likely to make. These pages contain two separate listings:

**LIST OF GRANT TYPES**

This lists all of the headings used in DGMT to categorise grant types. Page numbers relate to the second listing.

**LIST OF GRANT-MAKERS BY GRANT TYPE**

These pages list grant-makers under the types of grant that they are expressly willing or likely to make.

**The largest grant-makers**

At the end of these sections, we have listed the largest 150 grant-makers by grant total in alphabetical order. Between them they account for around £3.7 billion, or about 85% of the funds available in the book. *Please do not* use this simply as a mailing list: these grant-makers cover a wide range of specialist interests and many of them will never fund your work.

We strongly recommend that you read each entry carefully and compile your own list of major grant-makers relevant to you. You can then set this list alongside the other lists generated from the other indexes in the directory. We believe this list should only be used as an effective way of ensuring that you do not omit any major grant-makers.

# How to use DGMT
## Key steps

**STEP 1**

Define the project, programme or work for which you are seeking funding.

**STEP 2**

Geographical area: find the area most local to your requirements. Note down the names of the grant-makers listed here.

**STEP 3**

Field of interest and type of beneficiary: identify the categories that match your project. Note down the names of the grant-makers listed here.

**STEP 4**

Type of grant: identify the type of grant you are looking for. Note down the names of the grant-makers listed here.

**STEP 5**

Compare the three lists of grant-makers to produce a list of those whose funding policies most closely match the characteristics of the project for which you are seeking funding.

**STEP 6**

If your list is too short you could include grant-makers that have a general interest in funding your area – while these may not define a specific field as a priority or preference they will consider applications as long as they fall within the broad category.

**STEP 7**

Look up entries for the grant-makers identified, study their details carefully and pay close attention to 'What is funded', 'What is not funded' and note the preferred way of communication or where further details may be found.

**STEP 8**

Look at the list of the top 150 grant-makers to make sure you do not miss any major funders. Look up entries for the grant-makers identified, study their details carefully and again pay particularly close attention to 'What is funded' and 'What is not funded'. Remember that these funders are likely to be more well-known and consequently over-subscribed.

# Checklist

**STEP 1** The following checklist will help you assemble the information you need.

- What is the geographical location of the people who will benefit from any funding received?
- What facilities or services will the funding provide?
- What are the characteristics which best describe the people who will benefit from any funding received?
- What type of grant are you looking for?

**EXAMPLE** *Funding is being sought for a project in North Wales to improve a community care centre for women in poverty*

- The geographical location is: United Kingdom → Wales → North Wales
- The service to be provided is: Community care
- The key characteristic of the people to benefit is that they are: Poor or on low incomes
- The type of grant being sought is: Development funding

**STEP 2** Look up the area where your project is based in the list of geographical area headings on page 2.

- Turn to the relevant pages in the list of grant-makers by geographical area and note down the names of the grant-makers which have stated that they will consider funding projects in your area.

**EXAMPLE** Look up the area most local to your requirements (North Wales) in the list of geographical area headings. Then turn to the relevant page in the list of grant-makers by geographical area and look up the names of the grant-makers listed under North Wales. You may want to look at the grant-makers listed under the broader region (Wales) as well. Note down the names so that they can be compared with the lists through the indexes by type of grant and by field of interest and type of beneficiary.

It is also worth looking at grant-makers listed under United Kingdom because a grant-maker listed under a more general heading may be just as willing to fund activity in a specific region as another which states that it has a specific interest in that region.

**STEP 3** Using the 'Field of interest and type of beneficiary' category on page 44, identify all the categories that match the project, programme or work for which you are seeking funding.

Turn to the relevant pages in the list of grant-makers by field of interest and type of beneficiary and look up the headings identified.

Note down the names of the grant-makers that appear under these headings so that you can compare them with the names identified through the indexes by geographical area and by type of grant.

**EXAMPLE** With a project to develop a community care centre, you will probably look first under the main heading 'Social welfare'. Under this heading you will find the sub-heading 'Community care services' and under this you will find the heading 'Services for women'. Note down the page numbers beside 'Community care services' and 'Services for women'. Grant-makers that have expressed an interest in funding services for women may represent your best prospects, but grant-makers with a more general interest in funding community care services might be as worth approaching – particularly if they like to fund projects in your area.

If you look under 'Beneficial groups' you will find 'People who are poor, on low incomes', which is under 'Social and economic circumstances' and 'Women', which is under 'Gender and relationships'. Note down these page numbers too.

**STEP 4** Look up the type of grant that you are seeking in 'Grant-makers by type of grant' on page 172.

Turn to the relevant pages in the list of grant-makers by type of grant and note down the names of the grant-makers which can consider giving the type of grant that you are seeking. Compare these names with those that you identified through the indexes by geographical area and by field of interest and type of beneficiary.

**EXAMPLE** Look up the type of grant you are seeking in the list of grant types (in this case 'Development funding'). Then turn to the relevant page of the list of grant-makers by type of grant and look at the names of the grant-makers listed under 'Development funding'. Note down the names of all these grant-makers.

**STEP 5** Compare the lists of charity names produced via steps 2, 3 and 4, and make a list of all the grant-makers which appear on more than one list. This will produce a list of grant-makers whose funding policies most closely match the characteristics of the project for which you are seeking funding.

**STEP 6** If the list turns out to be too short it can easily be adjusted.

**EXAMPLE** You will end up with a list of grant-makers most accurately matching your project criteria.

By going back to step 3, you could include the grant-makers which come under 'Social welfare', or, by going back to step 2, you could include grant-makers which will consider funding projects in Wales.

**STEP 7** Look up the entries for the grant-makers identified and study their details carefully, paying particular attention to 'Where funding can be given', 'What is funded' and 'What is not funded'.

If you feel that there is a good match between the characteristics of the project for which you require support and the funding policies of the grant-making charity identified, you could submit an application, making sure you choose appropriate means of doing so.

**STEP 8** Look at the list of the top 150 grant-makers.

Check that you have not missed any of the major funders because you have made your search too specific. Some of the largest foundations give to a wide range of organisations and projects, and they tend to give the largest grants. They are also the most over-subscribed.

Look up the entries for each grant-maker and study their details carefully, paying particular attention to 'Where funding can be given', 'What is funded' and 'What is not funded'. If you feel that there is a good match between the characteristics of the project for which you require support and the funding policies of the trust identified, you could submit an application.

Most importantly, make sure that there is a good reason for writing to any grant-maker that you select: do not just send off indiscriminate applications to the whole list!

# A typical grant-making charity entry

A complete entry should contain information under the headings listed below. An explanation of the information which should appear in these fields is given alongside.

**CC NO**
Charity registration number

**WHERE FUNDING CAN BE GIVEN**
The village, town, borough, parish or other geographical area the trust is prepared to fund

**WHAT IS FUNDED**
Details of the types of project or activity the trust plans to fund and groups it intends to ultimately benefit

**WHAT IS NOT FUNDED**
The types of projects or causes the trust does not fund, e.g. expeditions, scholarships

**SAMPLE GRANTS**
An example of grants given by the trust in the given financial year

**TRUSTEES**
Names of the trustees

**PUBLICATIONS**
Details of publications the trust has produced which may be of interest to grant-seekers

**WHO TO APPLY TO**
The name and address of the person to whom applications should be sent

## ■ The Fictitious Trust

**CC NO** 123456  **ESTABLISHED** 1993
**WHERE FUNDING CAN BE GIVEN** UK.
**WHO CAN BENEFIT** Charities benefitting children.
**WHAT IS FUNDED** Education and training.
**WHAT IS NOT FUNDED** Individuals.
**TYPE OF GRANT** One-off; capital; running costs.
**RANGE OF GRANTS** £250–£5,000.
**SAMPLE GRANTS** A school (£5,000); a university (£1,000); a school library (£800); a school (£600); a grammar school, a further education college and for classroom equipment (£500 each); a university appeal (£400); a wheelchair ramp (£250).
**FINANCES** Year 2014 Income £55,000 Grants £50,000 Grants to organisations £40,000 Assets £800,000
**TRUSTEES** Ernestine Papadopoulos, Chair; Samuel Akintola; Mary Brown; Alistair Johnson; Dr Angelique Kidjo; Prof. Miriam Masekela.
**PUBLICATIONS** The Fictitious Trust – The First 20 Years.
**OTHER INFORMATION** This grant-making charity recently merged with the Fictional Trust.
**HOW TO APPLY** Apply in writing to the address below. An sae should be enclosed if an acknowledgement is required.
**WHO TO APPLY TO** A Grant, Secretary, The Old Barn, Main Street, New Town ZC48 2QQ *Tel* 020 7123 4567 *Fax* 020 7123 4567 *email* grantsteam@fictitioustrust.co.uk *Website* www.fictitioustrust.co.uk

**ESTABLISHED**
Year established

**WHO CAN BENEFIT**
The types of organisations that can be supported

**TYPE OF GRANT**
The types of grant or loan the trust is prepared to give, e.g. one-off, recurring, project costs

**RANGE OF GRANTS**
The smallest, largest and typical size of grant normally given

**FINANCES**
The most recent financial information, including the total amount of grants given

**OTHER INFORMATION**
Any other information which might be useful to grant-seekers

**HOW TO APPLY**
Useful information to those preparing their grant application

xxi

# The top 150 grant-makers by grant total

This is a list of the largest 150 grant-makers by grant total in alphabetical order. Between them they account for around £3.7 billion, or about 85% of the funds available in the book. **Please do not** use this simply as a mailing list: these grant-makers cover a wide range of specialist interests and many of them will never fund your work.

We recommend that you read each entry carefully and compile your own list of major grant-makers relevant to you. You can use this list alongside the other lists generated from the indexes in the directory. We believe this is the most effective way of ensuring that you do not omit any major grant-makers.

The 29th May 1961 Charitable Trust
A. W. Charitable Trust
The Aberdeen Foundation
ABF The Soldiers' Charity
Achisomoch Aid Company Limited
Action Medical Research
Age UK
Aid to the Church in Need (UK)
Allchurches Trust Ltd
Amabrill Limited
Arthritis Research UK
Arts Council England
Arts Council of Northern Ireland
Arts Council of Wales
The Asda Foundation
The Baily Thomas Charitable Fund
The Bamford Charitable Foundation
BBC Children in Need
The Big Lottery Fund
Bloodwise
The Bloom Foundation
The Liz and Terry Bramall Foundation
British Gas (Scottish Gas) Energy Trust
British Heart Foundation (BHF)
The Burdett Trust for Nursing
The Derek Butler Trust
The Barrow Cadbury Trust

The Cadogan Charity
CAFOD
Christian Aid
The City Bridge Trust
The Clore Duffield Foundation
The Clothworkers' Foundation
Comic Relief
Community Foundation for Leeds
Co-operative Community Investment Foundation
Creative Scotland
Diabetes UK
The Dulverton Trust
Dunard Fund
The Dunhill Medical Trust
The John Ellerman Foundation
The Eranda Foundation
Euro Charity Trust
The Exilarch's Foundation
Esmée Fairbairn Foundation
The Fidelity UK Foundation
The Football Association National Sports Centre Trust
The Football Foundation
The Foyle Foundation
The Freemasons' Grand Charity
The Gatsby Charitable Foundation

Goldman Sachs Gives (UK)
The Goldsmiths' Company Charity
The Gosling Foundation Limited
The M and R Gross Charities Limited
The Hadley Trust
Paul Hamlyn Foundation
The Peter Harrison Foundation
The Headley Trust
The Health Foundation
The Helping Foundation
The Hintze Family Charity Foundation
Hospice UK
Impetus–The Private Equity Foundation
The Jerusalem Trust
The Elton John Aids Foundation (EJAF)
The Kay Kendall Leukaemia Fund
Kent Community Foundation
Keren Association Limited
Maurice and Hilda Laing Charitable Trust
The LankellyChase Foundation
The Leverhulme Trust
The Linbury Trust
Lloyds Bank Foundation for England and Wales
The Lolev Charitable Trust
The Trust for London

**xxiii**

The London Community Foundation
The London Marathon Charitable Trust Limited
John Lyon's Charity
Mayfair Charities Ltd
The Mercers' Charitable Foundation
The Monument Trust
Muslim Hands
The National Art Collections Fund
Nominet Charitable Foundation
Norfolk Community Foundation
The Northern Rock Foundation
The Northwood Charitable Trust
The Nuffield Foundation
Oxfam (GB)
The P. F. Charitable Trust
The Pears Family Charitable Foundation
The Jack Petchey Foundation
The Polonsky Foundation
The John Porter Charitable Trust
The Premier League Charitable Fund
The Prince of Wales's Charitable Foundation
Quartet Community Foundation
The Queen's Silver Jubilee Trust
Rachel Charitable Trust
The Rank Foundation Limited
The Sigrid Rausing Trust
The Robertson Trust
Rosetrees Trust
The Joseph Rowntree Charitable Trust
The Joseph Rowntree Foundation
Royal British Legion

Royal Masonic Trust for Girls and Boys
The Rufford Foundation
S. F. Foundation
The Sackler Trust
Sam and Bella Sebba Charitable Trust
Santander UK Foundation Limited
Foundation Scotland
Seafarers UK
The Shetland Charitable Trust
The Henry Smith Charity
The Sobell Foundation
The Souter Charitable Trust
St James's Place Foundation
The Stewards' Company Limited
The Stone Family Foundation
Stratford upon Avon Town Trust
The Bernard Sunley Charitable Foundation
Tearfund
The Tennis Foundation
Tesco Charity Trust
The Thompson Family Charitable Trust
The Sir Jules Thorn Charitable Trust
The Tudor Trust
Community Foundation Serving Tyne and Wear and Northumberland
The Underwood Trust
United Utilities Trust Fund
The Michael Uren Foundation
The Vodafone Foundation
Volant Charitable Trust
Voluntary Action Fund (VAF)
Wales Council for Voluntary Action
The Walker Trust

The Waterloo Foundation
The Wellcome Trust
The Garfield Weston Foundation
The Maurice Wohl Charitable Foundation
The Charles Wolfson Charitable Trust
The Wolfson Foundation
The Wood Family Trust
Youth Music
Youth United Foundation
The Zochonis Charitable Trust

# Other publications and resources

The following publications and resources may also be of interest to readers of DGMT. They are all available directly from the Directory of Social Change by ringing 08450 77 77 07 or visiting our website at www.dsc.org.uk.

**The Guide to Grants for Individuals in Need**

This best-selling funding guide gives details of a wide range of funds and other support available for the relief of individual poverty and hardship. It remains a key reference book for social workers, as well as the individuals themselves and those concerned with their welfare. It contains:

- Details on national and local charitable grant-makers which collectively give around £268 million a year towards the relief of individual poverty and hardship.
- Essential advice on applications for each source: eligibility; types of grants given; annual grant total; contact details.
- An example of how to make an effective application, and advice on finding the right sources to apply to.

**The Guide to Educational Grants**

This popular guide gives details on a wide range of funds and other support available to schoolchildren and students in need, up to and including first degree level. It is a key reference book for educational social workers, student welfare officers, teachers and advice agencies, and the individuals themselves and their families. It includes:

- Sources of funding for children and students up to and including first degree level from grant-makers that collectively give over £54 million each year.
- Essential advice and information on applications for each source including eligibility, types of grants given, annual grant total and contact details.
- An example of how to make an effective application, and advice on finding the right sources to apply to.

**The Guide to UK Company Giving**

This invaluable guide includes details of 400 companies in the UK that give a combined total of around £658 million in community contributions to voluntary and community organisations. It contains:

- Essential information on who to contact with each company.
- Detailed information on cash and in-kind donations, employee-led support, sponsorship, Charity of the Year partnerships and details of CSR programmes.
- A section containing essential details on 114 corporate charities.

**The Guide to the Major Trusts Volumes 1 & 2**
Directory of Social Change

The in-depth research and independent comment that these flagship titles offer has made them an essential reference guide for all fundraisers. These guides are the only source of independent critical analysis of grant-makers in practice.

Volume 1: concentrates on the 400 largest grant-makers that each give over £300,000 a year.

Volume 2: complements volume 1 to provide a further 1,100 grant-makers that each give between £30,000 and £300,000 each year.

**www.trustfunding.org.uk**

Packed with information on more than 4,500 UK grant-making charities, this successful and popular tool for fundraisers lists grant-makers that collectively give about £4.7 billion each year.

- Search by geographical area, name of grant-maker, type of grant or by keyword search.
- Choose to receive notification when information on a particular grant-makers are updated.
- Receive monthly bulletins that keep you informed of news and updates.

**www.grantsfor individuals.org.uk**

A Guide to Grants for Individuals in Need and The Educational Grants Directory come together in this database. It contains around 3,500 charities that give to individuals for educational and welfare purposes. Collectively they give over £362 million each year.

- Search by geographical area, name of the grant-maker, type of grant or by keyword search.
- Choose to receive notification when information on a particular grant-makers is updated.

**www.companygiving. org.uk**

This database contains almost 600 companies, including those featured in The Guide to UK Company Giving Entries contain full details on the various giving methods (cash donations, in-kind support, employee-led support, sponsorship, commercially-led support and Charity of the Year partnerships), and describe both what the company is prepared to fund and the organisations it has supported in the past.

- Search by geographical area, name of company, type of grant or keyword.
- Choose to receive notification when information on a particular company or companies is updated.

**www.government funding.org.uk**

This database is an essential tool for anyone looking for information on statutory funding. Continually updated, it provides details on over £2 billion of funding from local, regional, national and European sources.

- Receive notification of funding rounds before they open.
- Search by type of grant, e.g. small grants, loans and contracts.

DSC offers a wide range of specialist guides for fundraisers, providing essential tailored reference points for work in specific areas. For more details see our website www.dsc.org.uk

# Grant-makers by geographical area

This index contains two separate listings:

**Geographical area headings:** This lists all of the geographical area headings used in the DGMT.

Grant-makers by geographical area: This lists the trusts appearing in the DGMT under the geographical area for which they have expressed a funding preference.

# Grant-makers by geographical area

The index contains two separate listings:

Geographical area headings
This lists all of the geographical area headings used in DGMT.

Grant-makers by geographical area
This lists the trusts appearing in the DGMT under the geographical areas for which they have expressed a funding preference

## Type of place 4

- Financially developing countries 4

## Worldwide 5

- Europe 6
- Central Europe 6
- Eastern Europe 6
- Northern Europe 7
- Southern Europe 7
- Western Europe including the Republic of Ireland 7
- Asia 7
- Arabian Peninsula 8
- Central Asia 8
- Far East 8
- Middle East 8
- South Asia 9
- South East Asia 9
- Africa 9
- Central Africa 9
- East Africa 9
- Southern Africa 9
- West Africa 9
- America and the West Indies 9
- Caribbean, West Indies 9
- Central America 9
- North America 10
- South America 10
- Australasia 10

## United Kingdom 10
## UK 23
## England 23

- Greater London 28
  Barking and Dagenham 29
  Barnet 29
  Bexley 29
  Brent 29
  Bromley 29
  Camden 29
  City of London 29
  City of Westminster 29
  Croydon 29
  Ealing 29
  Enfield 29
  Greenwich 29
  Hackney 29
  Hammersmith and Fulham 30
  Haringey 30
  Harrow 30
  Havering 30
  Hillingdon 30
  Islington 30
  Kensington and Chelsea 30
  Lambeth 30

*Geographical area headings*

Lewisham 30
Merton 30
Newham 30
Redbridge 30
Richmond upon Thames 30
Southwark 30
Sutton 30
Tower Hamlets 30
Wandsworth 30

■ **South Eastern England 30**

Berkshire 31
Buckinghamshire 31
East Sussex 31
Hampshire 31
Isle of Wight 31
Kent 31
Oxfordshire 32
Surrey 32
West Sussex 32

■ **South Western England 32**

Avon 32
Cornwall and the Scilly Isles 32
Devon 33
Dorset 33
Gloucestershire 33
Somerset 33
Wiltshire 33

■ **West Midlands region 33**

Herefordshire 34
Shropshire 34
Staffordshire 34
Warwickshire 34
West Midlands 34
Worcestershire 34

■ **East Midlands 34**

Derbyshire 35
Leicestershire 35
Lincolnshire 35
Northamptonshire 35
Nottinghamshire 35

■ **Eastern England 35**

Bedfordshire 36

Cambridgeshire 36
Essex 36
Hertfordshire 36
Norfolk 36
Suffolk 36

■ **North West 36**

Cheshire 37
Cumbria 37
Greater Manchester 37
Lancashire 37
Merseyside 37

■ **Yorkshire and the Humber 38**

Humberside, East Riding 38
North Yorkshire 38
South Yorkshire 38
West Yorkshire 38

■ **North East 38**

Cleveland 39
Durham 39
Northumberland 39
Tyne & Wear 39

## Northern Ireland 39

## Scotland 39

Central 40
Grampian Region 40
Highlands & Islands 40
Lothians Region 40
Southern Scotland 40
Strathclyde 40
Tayside & Fife 40

## Wales 40

North Wales 41
Mid and West Wales 41
South Wales 41

## Channel Islands 41

## Isle of Man 41

3

## Type of place

### ■ Financially developing countries

The Pat Allsop Charitable Trust
Anglo American Group Foundation
The Ardwick Trust
The AS Charitable Trust
The Austin Bailey Foundation
The Balmore Trust
The Baring Foundation
The Bartlett Taylor Charitable Trust
The Bay Tree Charitable Trust
The John Beckwith Charitable Trust
The Bloom Foundation
P. G. and N. J. Boulton Trust
Buckland Charitable Trust
The Burden Trust
Burden's Charitable Foundation
The Arnold Burton 1998 Charitable Trust
Edward Cadbury Charitable Trust
Henry T. and Lucy B. Cadbury Charitable Trust
CAFOD (Catholic Agency for Overseas Development)
The Calpe Trust
The Canning Trust
The Casey Trust
Christadelphian Samaritan Fund
Christian Aid
Chrysalis Trust
The Coltstaple Trust
The Gershon Coren Charitable Foundation
Michael Cornish Charitable Trust
The Evan Cornish Foundation
The Cotton Trust
The Cumber Family Charitable Trust
Dromintee Trust
The Eagle Charity Trust
The Gilbert and Eileen Edgar Foundation
The Ellerdale Trust
The Ericson Trust
The ERM Foundation
Euro Charity Trust
The A. M. Fenton Trust
The Allan and Nesta Ferguson Charitable Settlement
The Forest Hill Charitable Trust
The Donald Forrester Trust
The Anna Rosa Forster Charitable Trust
The Four Winds Trust
The Jill Franklin Trust

The Fulmer Charitable Trust
The Fuserna Foundation
General Charitable Trust
The Galanthus Trust
The Generations Foundation
Global Care
The Green Hall Foundation
H. C. D. Memorial Fund
The Haramead Trust
Miss K. M. Harbinson's Charitable Trust
The Hasluck Charitable Trust
The Headley Trust
Philip Sydney Henman Deceased Will Trust
The Hilden Charitable Fund
R. G. Hills Charitable Trust
The Thomas J. Horne Memorial Trust
The Hunter Foundation
Ibrahim Foundation Ltd
The Innocent Foundation
The Jephcott Charitable Trust
The Cyril and Eve Jumbo Charitable Trust
The Kirby Laing Foundation
The Beatrice Laing Trust
Langley Charitable Trust
The William Leech Charity
The Linbury Trust
The Marie Helen Luen Charitable Trust
Paul Lunn-Rockliffe Charitable Trust
The Mahavir Trust
Mariapolis Limited
The Marr-Munning Trust
Mercury Phoenix Trust
T. & J. Meyer Family Foundation Limited
The Mirianog Trust
The Mizpah Trust
The Monatrea Charitable Trust
The Morel Charitable Trust
Frederick Mulder Charitable Trust
Muslim Hands
The Nazareth Trust Fund
Network for Social Change
Alice Noakes Memorial Charitable Trust
The Northern Rock Foundation
The Father O'Mahoney Memorial Trust
The Odin Charitable Trust
The Paget Charitable Trust
The Pears Family Charitable Foundation
The Pilkington Charities Fund
Estate of the Late Colonel W. W. Pilkington Will Trusts – The General Charity Fund
The Popocatepetl Trust
The David and Elaine Potter Foundation

The W. L. Pratt Charitable Trust
The Bishop Radford Trust
The Eleanor Rathbone Charitable Trust
The Reed Foundation
The Rhododendron Trust
The Sir Cliff Richard Charitable Trust
The River Farm Foundation
Rivers Foundation
Robyn Charitable Trust
The Rock Foundation
The Roddick Foundation
The Sir James Roll Charitable Trust
The Rufford Foundation
Ryklow Charitable Trust 1992
The Saga Charitable Trust
The Alan and Babette Sainsbury Charitable Fund
The SDL Foundation
The Shanti Charitable Trust
Rita and David Slowe Charitable Trust
The SMB Charitable Trust
The W. F. Southall Trust
The Peter Stebbings Memorial Charity
The Stone Family Foundation
The Gay and Keith Talbot Trust
The Lady Tangye Charitable Trust
C. B. and H. H. Taylor 1984 Trust
Tearfund
The C. Paul Thackray General Charitable Trust
The Loke Wan Tho Memorial Foundation
Thomson Reuters Foundation
The Tinsley Foundation
The Tisbury Telegraph Trust
The Tolkien Trust
The Tresillian Trust
UIA Charitable Foundation
Ulting Overseas Trust
The United Society for the Propagation of the Gospel
The Valentine Charitable Trust
The Van Neste Foundation
The Vardy Foundation
The Vodafone Foundation
War on Want
The Waterloo Foundation
The Westcroft Trust
The Harold Hyam Wingate Foundation
The Wood Family Trust
The Matthews Wrightson Charity Trust
The Wyndham Charitable Trust
Zephyr Charitable Trust

## Worldwide

4 Charity Foundation
A. W. Charitable Trust
The Aberdeen Foundation
The Acacia Charitable Trust
Aid to the Church in Need (UK)
The Alliance Family Foundation
The Altajir Trust
The Apax Foundation
The Ardwick Trust
Armenian General Benevolent Union London Trust
Arts Council of Northern Ireland
The Ashden Trust
The Associated Country Women of the World
The Scott Bader Commonwealth Limited
The Bagri Foundation
The C. Alma Baker Trust
The Andrew Balint Charitable Trust
The George Balint Charitable Trust
The Paul Balint Charitable Trust
The Bamford Charitable Foundation
The Barbour Foundation
The Beaverbrook Foundation
The Bestway Foundation
BHST
The Bertie Black Foundation
The Blandford Lake Trust
The Bloom Foundation
The Bonamy Charitable Trust
The Linda and Gordon Bonnyman Charitable Trust
The Breadsticks Foundation
The Brendish Family Foundation
British Institute at Ankara
The Consuelo and Anthony Brooke Charitable Trust
Edna Brown Charitable Settlement
The Noel Buxton Trust
The James Caan Foundation
Cable & Wireless Worldwide Foundation
The William A. Cadbury Charitable Trust
Calouste Gulbenkian Foundation – UK Branch
The Catholic Charitable Trust
The CH (1980) Charitable Trust
Charitworth Limited
Chaucer Foundation
Church of Ireland Priorities Fund
Closehelm Limited
The Vivienne and Samuel Cohen Charitable Trust
Col-Reno Ltd

Comic Relief
Coutts Charitable Foundation
The Craps Charitable Trust
Itzchok Meyer Cymerman Trust Ltd
The Daiwa Anglo-Japanese Foundation
The Wilfrid Bruce Davis Charitable Trust
The Davis Foundation
The Debman Benevolent Trust
The Delves Charitable Trust
The Djanogly Foundation
The DM Charitable Trust
The Dollond Charitable Trust
The Doughty Charity Trust
The Dulverton Trust
Dushinsky Trust Ltd
The James Dyson Foundation
eaga Charitable Trust
Edge Fund
The Edith Maud Ellis 1985 Charitable Trust
Entindale Ltd
The Ericson Trust
The ERM Foundation
The Estelle Trust
Euro Charity Trust
Famos Foundation Trust
The Farthing Trust
Federation of Jewish Relief Organisations
The Fidelity UK Foundation
Mejer and Gertrude Miriam Frydman Foundation
The Gatsby Charitable Foundation
The Great Britain Sasakawa Foundation
Philip and Judith Green Trust
N. and R. Grunbaum Charitable Trust
Paul Hamlyn Foundation
The Helen Hamlyn Trust
The Hathaway Trust
The Maurice Hatter Foundation
The Charles Hayward Foundation
The Headley Trust
The Christina Mary Hendrie Trust for Scottish and Canadian Charities
The Hospital Saturday Fund
The Reta Lila Howard Foundation
The Daniel Howard Trust
Human Relief Foundation
The Humanitarian Trust
The Huntingdon Foundation Limited
IBM United Kingdom Trust
Ibrahim Foundation Ltd
Interserve Employee Foundation Ltd
Investream Charitable Trust

The Ireland Fund of Great Britain
Irish Youth Foundation (UK) Ltd
The Jacobs Charitable Trust
JCA Charitable Foundation
Nick Jenkins Foundation
The Joffe Charitable Trust
The Elton John Aids Foundation
The J. E. Joseph Charitable Fund
The Josh Charitable Trust
The Bernard Kahn Charitable Trust
The Ian Karten Charitable Trust
The Kasner Charitable Trust
The Kennedy Charitable Foundation
Keren Association Limited
Kupath Gemach Chaim Bechesed Viznitz Trust
The Lambert Charitable Trust
Lancaster Foundation
Largsmount Ltd
The Lauffer Family Charitable Foundation
The Kennedy Leigh Charitable Trust
The Erica Leonard Trust
Joseph Levy Charitable Foundation
David and Ruth Lewis Family Charitable Trust
Jack Livingstone Charitable Trust
The Locker Foundation
Paul Lunn-Rockliffe Charitable Trust
Lord and Lady Lurgan Trust
The Sir Jack Lyons Charitable Trust
Marbeh Torah Trust
The Marchig Animal Welfare Trust
The Hilda and Samuel Marks Foundation
J. P. Marland Charitable Trust
The Marr-Munning Trust
Mayfair Charities Ltd
Melodor Limited
The Melow Charitable Trust
Mercaz Torah Vechesed Limited
Merchant Navy Welfare Board
The Merlin Magic Wand Children's Charity
The Esmé Mitchell Trust
The Henry Moore Foundation
Morgan Stanley International Foundation
The Miles Morland Foundation
The Mount Everest Foundation
Muslim Hands
MYR Charitable Trust

# Europe

Ner Foundation
NJD Charitable Trust
The Community Foundation for Northern Ireland
The Nuffield Foundation
The Father O'Mahoney Memorial Trust
Open Gate
The Ouseley Trust
Oxfam (GB)
Ambika Paul Foundation
The Payne Charitable Trust
Rosanna Pearson's 1987 Charity Trust
The Peltz Trust
The Polonsky Foundation
The John Porter Charitable Trust
The Porter Foundation
The Puri Foundation
The Queen Anne's Gate Foundation
Rachel Charitable Trust
The Joseph and Lena Randall Charitable Trust
The Joseph Rank Trust
The Rayne Trust
Ridgesave Limited
Robyn Charitable Trust
Rowanville Ltd
William Arthur Rudd Memorial Trust
Raymond and Beverly Sackler 1988 Foundation
The Ruzin Sadagora Trust
Saint Sarkis Charity Trust
Sam and Bella Sebba Charitable Trust
The Samworth Foundation
SEM Charitable Trust
The Archie Sherman Cardiff Foundation
The Archie Sherman Charitable Trust
Shlomo Memorial Fund Limited
The Shoe Zone Trust
The Sino-British Fellowship Trust
The Sobell Foundation
Sodexo Foundation
The Solo Charitable Settlement
Songdale Ltd
R. H. Southern Trust
Rosalyn and Nicholas Springer Charitable Trust
St James's Trust Settlement
The Steinberg Family Charitable Trust
The Stephen Barry Charitable Trust
Sir Halley Stewart Trust
The Adrienne and Leslie Sussman Charitable Trust
The Tajtelbaum Charitable Trust

The David Tannen Charitable Trust
C. B. and H. H. Taylor 1984 Trust
Tegham Limited
Tomchei Torah Charitable Trust
The True Colours Trust
The Tudor Trust
TVML Foundation
Trustees of Tzedakah
The United Society for the Propagation of the Gospel
The Vail Foundation
Veneziana Fund
The Scurrah Wainwright Charity
Webb Memorial Trust
The Norman Whiteley Trust
The HDH Wills 1965 Charitable Trust
The Maurice Wohl Charitable Foundation
The Charles Wolfson Charitable Trust
The Wolfson Family Charitable Trust
The Wolfson Foundation
The Wood Family Trust
The Zochonis Charitable Trust
Zurich Community Trust (UK) Limited

..........................................

■ **Europe**

Aid to the Church in Need (UK)
The Apax Foundation
Armenian General Benevolent Union London Trust
Arts Council of Northern Ireland
The Scott Bader Commonwealth Limited
The Andrew Balint Charitable Trust
The George Balint Charitable Trust
The Paul Balint Charitable Trust
The Blandford Lake Trust
British Institute at Ankara
The William A. Cadbury Charitable Trust
Calouste Gulbenkian Foundation – UK Branch
The Catholic Charitable Trust
Chaucer Foundation
Church of Ireland Priorities Fund
eaga Charitable Trust
Edge Fund
The Edith Maud Ellis 1985 Charitable Trust
The Ericson Trust
The Fidelity UK Foundation
The Maurice Hatter Foundation
The Headley Trust

The Hospital Saturday Fund
The Reta Lila Howard Foundation
IBM United Kingdom Trust
The Ireland Fund of Great Britain
Irish Youth Foundation (UK) Ltd
The Elton John Aids Foundation
The Kennedy Charitable Foundation
The Marchig Animal Welfare Trust
Merchant Navy Welfare Board
The Esmé Mitchell Trust
The Henry Moore Foundation
Morgan Stanley International Foundation
The Community Foundation for Northern Ireland
The Father O'Mahoney Memorial Trust
Open Gate
The Ouseley Trust
Oxfam (GB)
Rachel Charitable Trust
The Joseph Rank Trust
William Arthur Rudd Memorial Trust
Saint Sarkis Charity Trust
Sodexo Foundation
R. H. Southern Trust
C. B. and H. H. Taylor 1984 Trust
Veneziana Fund
Webb Memorial Trust
The Norman Whiteley Trust
The HDH Wills 1965 Charitable Trust

..........................................

■ **Central Europe**

The Scott Bader Commonwealth Limited
The Andrew Balint Charitable Trust
The George Balint Charitable Trust
The Paul Balint Charitable Trust
The Ericson Trust
The Maurice Hatter Foundation
The Headley Trust
The Father O'Mahoney Memorial Trust
The Norman Whiteley Trust

..........................................

■ **Eastern Europe**

Aid to the Church in Need (UK)
Armenian General Benevolent Union London Trust
British Institute at Ankara
The Ericson Trust

The Headley Trust
The Father O'Mahoney Memorial Trust
Open Gate
Oxfam (GB)
Saint Sarkis Charity Trust
Webb Memorial Trust

### ■ Northern Europe

Chaucer Foundation

### ■ Southern Europe

The Apax Foundation
The Scott Bader Commonwealth Limited
The Blandford Lake Trust
British Institute at Ankara
Merchant Navy Welfare Board
The Father O'Mahoney Memorial Trust
Open Gate
Oxfam (GB)
William Arthur Rudd Memorial Trust
Veneziana Fund

### ■ Western Europe including the Republic of Ireland

Arts Council of Northern Ireland
The Scott Bader Commonwealth Limited
The William A. Cadbury Charitable Trust
Calouste Gulbenkian Foundation – UK Branch
Church of Ireland Priorities Fund
Edge Fund
The Edith Maud Ellis 1985 Charitable Trust
The Hospital Saturday Fund
The Reta Lila Howard Foundation
The Ireland Fund of Great Britain
Irish Youth Foundation (UK) Ltd
The Kennedy Charitable Foundation
The Esmé Mitchell Trust
The Community Foundation for Northern Ireland
The Ouseley Trust
The Joseph Rank Trust
Sodexo Foundation
R. H. Southern Trust
C. B. and H. H. Taylor 1984 Trust
The HDH Wills 1965 Charitable Trust

### ■ Asia

4 Charity Foundation
A. W. Charitable Trust
The Aberdeen Foundation
The Acacia Charitable Trust
Aid to the Church in Need (UK)
The Alliance Family Foundation
The Altajir Trust
The Apax Foundation
The Ardwick Trust
The Ashden Trust
The Scott Bader Commonwealth Limited
The Bagri Foundation
The Andrew Balint Charitable Trust
The George Balint Charitable Trust
The Paul Balint Charitable Trust
The Bestway Foundation
BHST
The Bertie Black Foundation
The Blandford Lake Trust
The Bloom Foundation
The Bonamy Charitable Trust
The Breadsticks Foundation
The Brendish Family Foundation
British Institute at Ankara
Edna Brown Charitable Settlement
The James Caan Foundation
Cable & Wireless Worldwide Foundation
The CH (1980) Charitable Trust
Charitworth Limited
Chaucer Foundation
Closehelm Limited
The Vivienne and Samuel Cohen Charitable Trust
Col-Reno Ltd
The Craps Charitable Trust
Itzchok Meyer Cymerman Trust Ltd
The Daiwa Anglo-Japanese Foundation
The Wilfrid Bruce Davis Charitable Trust
The Davis Foundation
The Debmar Benevolent Trust
The Djanogly Foundation
The DM Charitable Trust
The Dollond Charitable Trust
The Doughty Charity Trust
Dushinsky Trust Ltd
Entindale Ltd
Euro Charity Trust
Famos Foundation Trust
Federation of Jewish Relief Organisations
Mejer and Gertrude Miriam Frydman Foundation
The Great Britain Sasakawa Foundation

N. and R. Grunbaum Charitable Trust
Paul Hamlyn Foundation
The Helen Hamlyn Trust
The Hathaway Trust
The Maurice Hatter Foundation
The Daniel Howard Trust
The Humanitarian Trust
The Huntingdon Foundation Limited
IBM United Kingdom Trust
Ibrahim Foundation Ltd
Investream Charitable Trust
JCA Charitable Foundation
Nick Jenkins Foundation
The Elton John Aids Foundation
The J. E. Joseph Charitable Fund
The Josh Charitable Trust
The Bernard Kahn Charitable Trust
The Ian Karten Charitable Trust
The Kasner Charitable Trust
Keren Association Limited
Kupath Gemach Chaim Bechesed Viznitz Trust
The Lambert Charitable Trust
Largsmount Ltd
The Lauffer Family Charitable Foundation
The Kennedy Leigh Charitable Trust
Joseph Levy Charitable Foundation
David and Ruth Lewis Family Charitable Trust
Jack Livingstone Charitable Trust
The Locker Foundation
Paul Lunn-Rockliffe Charitable Trust
The Sir Jack Lyons Charitable Trust
Marbeh Torah Trust
The Marchig Animal Welfare Trust
The Hilda and Samuel Marks Foundation
The Marr-Munning Trust
Mayfair Charities Ltd
Melodor Limited
The Melow Charitable Trust
Mercaz Torah Vecheshed Limited
Morgan Stanley International Foundation
MYR Charitable Trust
Ner Foundation
NJD Charitable Trust
The Father O'Mahoney Memorial Trust
Open Gate
Oxfam (GB)
Ambika Paul Foundation

7

The Payne Charitable Trust
The Peltz Trust
The Polonsky Foundation
The John Porter Charitable Trust
The Porter Foundation
The Puri Foundation
The Queen Anne's Gate Foundation
The Rayne Trust
Rowanville Ltd
The Ruzin Sadagora Trust
Sam and Bella Sebba Charitable Trust
The Archie Sherman Cardiff Foundation
The Archie Sherman Charitable Trust
Shlomo Memorial Fund Limited
The Shoe Zone Trust
The Sino-British Fellowship Trust
The Sobell Foundation
The Solo Charitable Settlement
Songdale Ltd
R. H. Southern Trust
Rosalyn and Nicholas Springer Charitable Trust
The Steinberg Family Charitable Trust
The Stephen Barry Charitable Trust
The Adrienne and Leslie Sussman Charitable Trust
The Tajtelbaum Charitable Trust
The David Tannen Charitable Trust
Tegham Limited
Tomchei Torah Charitable Trust
TVML Foundation
Trustees of Tzedakah
The Vail Foundation
The Maurice Wohl Charitable Foundation
The Charles Wolfson Charitable Trust
The Wolfson Family Charitable Trust
The Wolfson Foundation

■ **Arabian Peninsula**

The Scott Bader Commonwealth Limited

■ **Central Asia**

Paul Lunn-Rockliffe Charitable Trust

■ **Far East**

The Great Britain Sasakawa Foundation
The Sino-British Fellowship Trust

■ **Middle East**

4 Charity Foundation
A. W. Charitable Trust
The Aberdeen Foundation
The Acacia Charitable Trust
The Alliance Family Foundation
The Altajir Trust
The Ardwick Trust
The Andrew Balint Charitable Trust
The George Balint Charitable Trust
The Paul Balint Charitable Trust
BHST
The Bertie Black Foundation
The Blandford Lake Trust
The Bloom Foundation
The Bonamy Charitable Trust
British Institute at Ankara
Edna Brown Charitable Settlement
The CH (1980) Charitable Trust
Charitworth Limited
Closehelm Limited
The Vivienne and Samuel Cohen Charitable Trust
Col-Reno Ltd
The Craps Charitable Trust
Itzchok Meyer Cymerman Trust Ltd
The Davis Foundation
The Debmar Benevolent Trust
The Djanogly Foundation
The DM Charitable Trust
The Dollond Charitable Trust
The Doughty Charity Trust
Dushinsky Trust Ltd
Entindale Ltd
Famos Foundation Trust
Federation of Jewish Relief Organisations
Mejer and Gertrude Miriam Frydman Foundation
N. and R. Grunbaum Charitable Trust
The Hathaway Trust
The Maurice Hatter Foundation
The Daniel Howard Trust
The Humanitarian Trust
The Huntingdon Foundation Limited
IBM United Kingdom Trust
Investream Charitable Trust
JCA Charitable Foundation
The J. E. Joseph Charitable Fund
The Josh Charitable Trust
The Bernard Kahn Charitable Trust
The Ian Karten Charitable Trust
The Kasner Charitable Trust
Keren Association Limited
Kupath Gemach Chaim Bechesed Viznitz Trust
The Lambert Charitable Trust
Largsmount Ltd
The Lauffer Family Charitable Foundation
The Kennedy Leigh Charitable Trust
Joseph Levy Charitable Foundation
David and Ruth Lewis Family Charitable Trust
Jack Livingstone Charitable Trust
The Locker Foundation
The Sir Jack Lyons Charitable Trust
Marbeh Torah Trust
The Hilda and Samuel Marks Foundation
Mayfair Charities Ltd
Melodor Limited
The Melow Charitable Trust
Mercaz Torah Vechesed Limited
Morgan Stanley International Foundation
MYR Charitable Trust
Ner Foundation
NJD Charitable Trust
The Peltz Trust
The Polonsky Foundation
The John Porter Charitable Trust
The Porter Foundation
The Rayne Trust
Rowanville Ltd
The Ruzin Sadagora Trust
Sam and Bella Sebba Charitable Trust
The Archie Sherman Cardiff Foundation
The Archie Sherman Charitable Trust
Shlomo Memorial Fund Limited
The Sobell Foundation
The Solo Charitable Settlement
Songdale Ltd
Rosalyn and Nicholas Springer Charitable Trust
The Steinberg Family Charitable Trust
The Stephen Barry Charitable Trust
The Adrienne and Leslie Sussman Charitable Trust
The Tajtelbaum Charitable Trust

The David Tannen Charitable
 Trust
Tegham Limited
Tomchei Torah Charitable
 Trust
TVML Foundation
Trustees of Tzedakah
The Vail Foundation
The Maurice Wohl Charitable
 Foundation
The Charles Wolfson
 Charitable Trust
The Wolfson Family Charitable
 Trust
The Wolfson Foundation

## ■ South Asia

The Bagri Foundation
The Blandford Lake Trust
The Brendish Family
 Foundation
The James Caan Foundation
Cable & Wireless Worldwide
 Foundation
The Wilfrid Bruce Davis
 Charitable Trust
Euro Charity Trust
Paul Hamlyn Foundation
The Helen Hamlyn Trust
Ibrahim Foundation Ltd
Nick Jenkins Foundation
The J. E. Joseph Charitable
 Fund
The Lauffer Family Charitable
 Foundation
The Marr-Munning Trust
Ambika Paul Foundation
The Payne Charitable Trust
The Puri Foundation
The Archie Sherman Cardiff
 Foundation
R. H. Southern Trust

## ■ South East Asia

Chaucer Foundation
The Marr-Munning Trust
The Shoe Zone Trust
The Stephen Barry Charitable
 Trust

## ■ Africa

The Lauffer Family Charitable
 Foundation
Paul Lunn-Rockliffe Charitable
 Trust
The Marchig Animal Welfare
 Trust
The Marr-Munning Trust
Morgan Stanley International
 Foundation
The Nuffield Foundation

The Father O'Mahoney
 Memorial Trust
Open Gate
Oxfam (GB)
The Samworth Foundation
The Archie Sherman Cardiff
 Foundation
The Stephen Barry Charitable
 Trust
Sir Halley Stewart Trust
The True Colours Trust
The Tudor Trust
The Scurrah Wainwright Charity
The Wood Family Trust
The Zochonis Charitable Trust

## ■ Central Africa

The Dulverton Trust
The Stephen Barry Charitable
 Trust

## ■ East Africa

The Consuelo and Anthony
 Brooke Charitable Trust
The Noel Buxton Trust
The Dulverton Trust
Nick Jenkins Foundation
The Joffe Charitable Trust
The Lauffer Family Charitable
 Foundation
Paul Lunn-Rockliffe Charitable
 Trust
The Nuffield Foundation

## ■ Southern Africa

The Scott Bader
 Commonwealth Limited
The Noel Buxton Trust
The Estelle Trust
The Maurice Hatter Foundation
The Joffe Charitable Trust
The Lauffer Family Charitable
 Foundation
The Nuffield Foundation
The Archie Sherman Cardiff
 Foundation
The Scurrah Wainwright Charity

## ■ West Africa

The Joffe Charitable Trust
The Tudor Trust

## ■ America and the West Indies

Aid to the Church in Need (UK)
The Apax Foundation
The Ashden Trust
The Scott Bader
 Commonwealth Limited

The Beaverbrook Foundation
The Blandford Lake Trust
The Linda and Gordon
 Bonnyman Charitable Trust
The Catholic Charitable Trust
Chaucer Foundation
Col-Reno Ltd
The Hathaway Trust
The Maurice Hatter Foundation
The Christina Mary Hendrie
 Trust for Scottish and
 Canadian Charities
The Huntingdon Foundation
 Limited
The Jacobs Charitable Trust
Kupath Gemach Chaim
 Bechesed Viznitz Trust
The Lauffer Family Charitable
 Foundation
The Marchig Animal Welfare
 Trust
J. P. Marland Charitable Trust
The Henry Moore Foundation
MYR Charitable Trust
The Father O'Mahoney
 Memorial Trust
Open Gate
Oxfam (GB)
Rosanna Pearson's 1987
 Charity Trust
The Polonsky Foundation
SEM Charitable Trust
The Archie Sherman Cardiff
 Foundation
Shlomo Memorial Fund Limited
St James's Trust Settlement
The Stephen Barry Charitable
 Trust
TVML Foundation

## ■ Caribbean, West Indies

The Blandford Lake Trust
The Lauffer Family Charitable
 Foundation
The Marchig Animal Welfare
 Trust
The Father O'Mahoney
 Memorial Trust
Open Gate
Oxfam (GB)
Rosanna Pearson's 1987
 Charity Trust

## ■ Central America

The Blandford Lake Trust
The Marchig Animal Welfare
 Trust
The Father O'Mahoney
 Memorial Trust
Open Gate
Oxfam (GB)

## ■ North America

The Apax Foundation
The Scott Bader Commonwealth Limited
The Beaverbrook Foundation
The Linda and Gordon Bonnyman Charitable Trust
The Catholic Charitable Trust
Chaucer Foundation
Col-Reno Ltd
The Hathaway Trust
The Maurice Hatter Foundation
The Christina Mary Hendrie Trust for Scottish and Canadian Charities
The Huntingdon Foundation Limited
The Jacobs Charitable Trust
Kupath Gemach Chaim Bechesed Viznitz Trust
The Lauffer Family Charitable Foundation
The Marchig Animal Welfare Trust
J. P. Marland Charitable Trust
The Henry Moore Foundation
MYR Charitable Trust
The Polonsky Foundation
SEM Charitable Trust
Shlomo Memorial Fund Limited
St James's Trust Settlement
The Stephen Barry Charitable Trust

## ■ South America

Aid to the Church in Need (UK)
The Ashden Trust
The Blandford Lake Trust
The Marchig Animal Welfare Trust
The Father O'Mahoney Memorial Trust
Open Gate
Oxfam (GB)
The Stephen Barry Charitable Trust
TVML Foundation

## ■ Australasia

The C. Alma Baker Trust
The Josh Charitable Trust
The Lauffer Family Charitable Foundation
The Marchig Animal Welfare Trust
The Mount Everest Foundation
Open Gate
The Archie Sherman Cardiff Foundation
R. H. Southern Trust

## ■ United Kingdom

4 Charity Foundation
A. B. Grace Trust
The 1970 Trust
The 1989 Willan Charitable Trust
The 29th May 1961 Charitable Trust
A. W. Charitable Trust
The Aberbrothock Skea Trust
The Aberdeen Endowments Trust
The Aberdeen Foundation
The Aberdeenshire Educational Trust Scheme
ABF The Soldiers' Charity
Eric Abrams Charitable Trust
The Acacia Charitable Trust
Access Sport
The ACT Foundation
Action Medical Research
The Company of Actuaries' Charitable Trust Fund
The Adamson Trust
The Victor Adda Foundation
The Addleshaw Goddard Charitable Trust
The Adint Charitable Trust
The Adnams Charity
AF Trust Company
Age Scotland
Age UK
The AIM Foundation
The Sylvia Aitken Charitable Trust
The Al Fayed Charitable Foundation
The Alabaster Trust
D. G. Albright Charitable Trust
The Alchemy Foundation
Aldgate and All Hallows' Foundation
All Saints Educational Trust
Allchurches Trust Ltd
The H. B. Allen Charitable Trust
The Alliance Family Foundation
Alliance Trust Staff Foundation
Angus Allnatt Charitable Foundation
The Pat Allsop Charitable Trust
The Almond Trust
Almondsbury Charity
The Altajir Trust
Amabrill Limited
The Ammco Trust
Sir John and Lady Amory's Charitable Trust
Viscount Amory's Charitable Trust
The Ampelos Trust
The AMW Charitable Trust
Mary Andrew Charitable Trust
Anguish's Educational Foundation
The Animal Defence Trust

The Eric Anker-Petersen Charity
The Annandale Charitable Trust
Anpride Ltd
The Anson Charitable Trust
The Apax Foundation
The Appletree Trust
The John Apthorp Charity
The Arbib Foundation
The Archbishop's Council – The Church and Community Fund
The Architectural Heritage Fund
The Ardwick Trust
The Argentarius Foundation
The Argus Appeal
Armenian General Benevolent Union London Trust
The John Armitage Charitable Trust
The Armourers' and Brasiers' Gauntlet Trust
The Artemis Charitable Trust
Arthritis Research UK
Arts Council England
Arts Council of Wales (Cyngor Celfyddydau Cymru)
The AS Charitable Trust
ASCB Charitable Fund
The Ascot Fire Brigade Trust
The Asda Foundation
The Ashburnham Thanksgiving Trust
A. J. H. Ashby Will Trust
The Ashden Trust
The Ashley Family Foundation
The Ian Askew Charitable Trust
The Association of Colleges Charitable Trust
Asthma UK
AstonMansfield Charitable Trust
The Astor Foundation
The Astor of Hever Trust
The Atlas Fund
The Aurelius Charitable Trust
The Lord Austin Trust
Autonomous Research Charitable Trust
The John Avins Trust
The Avon and Somerset Police Community Trust
Awards for All
The Aylesford Family Charitable Trust
The Harry Bacon Foundation
The BACTA Charitable Trust
The Scott Bader Commonwealth Limited
Bag4Sport Foundation
The Austin Bailey Foundation
The Baily Thomas Charitable Fund
The Baird Trust

The Roy and Pixie Baker Charitable Trust
The Balcombe Charitable Trust
The Andrew Balint Charitable Trust
The George Balint Charitable Trust
The Paul Balint Charitable Trust
The Albert Casanova Ballard Deceased Trust
The Ballinger Charitable Trust
Balmain Charitable Trust
The Balmore Trust
The Balney Charitable Trust
The Baltic Charitable Fund
The Bamford Charitable Foundation
The Banbury Charities
The Band Trust
The Bank of Scotland Foundation
The Barbers' Company General Charities
The Barbour Foundation
The Barcapel Foundation
Barchester Healthcare Foundation
The Barclay Foundation
The Baring Foundation
The Barker-Mill Foundation
Lord Barnby's Foundation
Barnes Workhouse Fund
The Barnsbury Charitable Trust
The Barnstaple Bridge Trust
The Barnwood House Trust
The Misses Barrie Charitable Trust
Bartholomew Charitable Trust
The Bartlett Taylor Charitable Trust
The Paul Bassham Charitable Trust
The Bates Charitable Trust
The Battens Charitable Trust
The Louis Baylis (Maidenhead Advertiser) Charitable Trust
BBC Children in Need
BC Partners Foundation
The B-CH Charitable Trust
BCH Trust
The Bearder Charity
The James Beattie Charitable Trust
The Beaverbrook Foundation
The Beccles Town Lands Charity
The Beckett's and Sargeant's Educational Foundation
The Peter Beckwith Charitable Trust
The Bedfordshire and Hertfordshire Historic Churches Trust
The Bedfordshire and Luton Community Foundation

The Provincial Grand Lodge of Bedfordshire Charity Fund
The David and Ruth Behrend Fund
The Bellahouston Bequest Fund
The Bellinger Donnay Trust
The Benfield Motors Charitable Trust
The Benham Charitable Settlement
Michael and Leslie Bennett Charitable Trust
The Gerald Bentall Charitable Trust
The Bergne-Coupland Charity
Bergqvist Charitable Trust
The Berkshire Community Foundation
The Bernadette Charitable Trust
The Bertarelli UK Foundation
The Bestway Foundation
BHST
The Mason Bibby 1981 Trust
The Bideford Bridge Trust
The Big Lottery Fund
The Billmeir Charitable Trust
Percy Bilton Charity
The Bingham Trust
The Bintaub Charitable Trust
The Birmingham District Nursing Charitable Trust
The Birmingham Hospital Saturday Fund Medical Charity and Welfare Trust
Birmingham International Airport Community Trust
The Lord Mayor of Birmingham's Charity Birthday House Trust
The Michael Bishop Foundation
The Sydney Black Charitable Trust
The Bertie Black Foundation
Sir Alec Black's Charity
Isabel Blackman Foundation
The BlackRock (UK) Charitable Trust
The Blagrave Trust
The Blair Foundation
The Morgan Blake Charitable Trust
The Blanchminster Trust
The Blandford Lake Trust
The Sir Victor Blank Charitable Settlement
Blatchington Court Trust
Bloodwise
The Bloom Foundation
The Bluston Charitable Settlement
The Nicholas Boas Charitable Trust

The Marjory Boddy Charitable Trust
The Bonamy Charitable Trust
The John and Celia Bonham Christie Charitable Trust
The Charlotte Bonham-Carter Charitable Trust
The Linda and Gordon Bonnyman Charitable Trust
The Boodle & Dunthorne Charitable Trust
BOOST Charitable Trust
The Booth Charities
Boots Charitable Trust
The Bordon Liphook Haslemere Charity
The Oliver Borthwick Memorial Trust
The Boshier-Hinton Foundation
The Bothwell Charitable Trust
The Harry Bottom Charitable Trust
Sir Clive Bourne Family Trust
Bourneheights Limited
The Bower Trust
The Bowerman Charitable Trust
The Bowland Charitable Trust
The Frank Brake Charitable Trust
The William Brake Charitable Trust
The Tony Bramall Charitable Trust
The Liz and Terry Bramall Foundation
The Bramhope Trust
The Bransford Trust
The Breadsticks Foundation
The Breast Cancer Research Trust
The Brendish Family Foundation
The Harold and Alice Bridges Charity
Briggs Animal Welfare Trust
The Brighton District Nursing Association Trust
Bristol Archdeaconry Charity
The Bristol Charities
British Council for Prevention of Blindness (Save Eyes Everywhere)
The British Dietetic Association General and Education Trust Fund
British Gas (Scottish Gas) Energy Trust
British Heart Foundation
The British Humane Association
British Institute at Ankara
British Record Industry Trust
The Britten-Pears Foundation
The J. and M. Britton Charitable Trust

The Broderers' Charity Trust
The Consuelo and Anthony
    Brooke Charitable Trust
The Roger Brooke Charitable
    Trust
The David Brooke Charity
The Charles Brotherton Trust
Joseph Brough Charitable
    Trust
Miss Marion Broughton's
    Charitable Trust
Bill Brown 1989 Charitable
    Trust
Edna Brown Charitable
    Settlement
R. S. Brownless Charitable
    Trust
The T. B. H. Brunner
    Charitable Settlement
The Jack Brunton Charitable
    Trust
The Bruntwood Charity
Buckinghamshire Community
    Foundation
The Buckinghamshire Historic
    Churches Trust
The Buckinghamshire Masonic
    Centenary Fund
The Buffini Chao Foundation
The E. F. Bulmer Benevolent
    Fund
The Burden Trust
Burden's Charitable
    Foundation
The Burdett Trust for Nursing
The Burghley Family Trust
The Burry Charitable Trust
The Burton Breweries
    Charitable Trust
Consolidated Charity of Burton
    upon Trent
The Worshipful Company of
    Butchers General Charities
The Noel Buxton Trust
C. and F. Charitable Trust
The James Caan Foundation
Cable & Wireless Worldwide
    Foundation
Edward Cadbury Charitable
    Trust
Henry T. and Lucy B. Cadbury
    Charitable Trust
The Christopher Cadbury
    Charitable Trust
The Richard Cadbury
    Charitable Trust
The William A. Cadbury
    Charitable Trust
The Cadbury Foundation
The Barrow Cadbury Trust
The Edward and Dorothy
    Cadbury Trust
The George Cadbury Trust
The Cadogan Charity
Community Foundation for
    Calderdale

Callander Charitable Trust
Calouste Gulbenkian
    Foundation – UK Branch
The Cambridge Chrysalis Trust
The Cambridgeshire
    Community Foundation
The Cambridgeshire Historic
    Churches Trust
The Camelia Trust
The Campden Charities
    Trustee
The Frederick and Phyllis Cann
    Trust
The Canning Trust
Canoe Foundation
The H. and L. Cantor Trust
Cardy Beaver Foundation
The Carew Pole Charitable
    Trust
David William Traill Cargill
    Fund
The Carlton House Charitable
    Trust
The Carmelite Monastery Ware
    Trust
The Worshipful Company of
    Carmen Benevolent Trust
The Richard Carne Trust
The Carnegie Dunfermline
    Trust
The Carnegie Trust for the
    Universities of Scotland
The Carpenters' Company
    Charitable Trust
The Carr-Gregory Trust
The Carrington Charitable
    Trust
The Leslie Mary Carter
    Charitable Trust
Carter's Educational
    Foundation
Cash for Kids – Radio Clyde
Sir John Cass's Foundation
The Castang Foundation
The Catalyst Charitable Trust
The Catholic Trust for England
    and Wales
The Cattanach Charitable Trust
The Joseph and Annie Cattle
    Trust
The Thomas Sivewright Catto
    Charitable Settlement
The Wilfrid and Constance
    Cave Foundation
The Cayo Foundation
Elizabeth Cayzer Charitable
    Trust
The B. G. S. Cayzer Charitable
    Trust
The Cazenove Charitable Trust
Celtic Charity Fund
The Gaynor Cemlyn-Jones
    Trust
The CH (1980) Charitable
    Trust
The Amelia Chadwick Trust

Champneys Charitable
    Foundation
John William Chapman's
    Charitable Trust
The Charities Advisory Trust
Charitworth Limited
Chaucer Foundation
The Cheruby Trust
Cheshire Freemason's Charity
Chest, Heart and Stroke
    Scotland
The Chetwode Foundation
Child Growth Foundation
Children's Liver Disease
    Foundation
The Children's Research Fund
The Chippenham Borough
    Lands Charity
The Chipping Sodbury Town
    Lands Charity
CHK Charities Limited
The Chownes Foundation
The Christabella Charitable
    Trust
Christadelphian Samaritan
    Fund
Christian Aid
The Church Burgesses
    Educational Foundation
Church Burgesses Trust
Church of Ireland Priorities
    Fund
Church Urban Fund
The City Bridge Trust
The City Educational Trust
    Fund
CLA Charitable Trust
Stephen Clark 1957
    Charitable Trust
J. A. Clark Charitable Trust
The Hilda and Alice Clark
    Charitable Trust
The Roger and Sarah Bancroft
    Clark Charitable Trust
The Clarke Charitable
    Settlement
The Cleopatra Trust
The Clore Duffield Foundation
Closehelm Limited
The Clothworkers' Foundation
Richard Cloudesley's Charity
The Clover Trust
The Robert Clutterbuck
    Charitable Trust
Clydpride Ltd
The Francis Coales Charitable
    Foundation
The Coalfields Regeneration
    Trust
The John Coates Charitable
    Trust
The Cobtree Charity Trust Ltd
The Denise Cohen Charitable
    Trust
The Vivienne and Samuel
    Cohen Charitable Trust

*Grant-makers by geographical area*          **United Kingdom**

The R. and S. Cohen Foundation
The Colchester Catalyst Charity
John Coldman Charitable Trust
The Cole Charitable Trust
The Colefax Charitable Trust
John and Freda Coleman Charitable Trust
The Bernard Coleman Trust
The George Henry Collins Charity
The Sir Jeremiah Colman Gift Trust
Col-Reno Ltd
The Colt Foundation
Colwinston Charitable Trust
Colyer-Fergusson Charitable Trust
Comic Relief
The Comino Foundation
Community First (Landfill Communities Fund)
Community Foundation for Leeds
The Compton Charitable Trust
The Douglas Compton James Charitable Trust
The Congleton Inclosure Trust
The Congregational and General Charitable Trust
Martin Connell Charitable Trust
The Conservation Foundation
The Consolidated Charities for the Infirm – Merchant Taylors' Company
Gordon Cook Foundation
The Ernest Cook Trust
The Cooks Charity
The Catherine Cookson Charitable Trust
Harold and Daphne Cooper Charitable Trust
Mabel Cooper Charity
The Alice Ellen Cooper Dean Charitable Foundation
Co-operative Community Investment Foundation
The Marjorie Coote Animal Charity Trust
The Marjorie Coote Old People's Charity
The Helen Jean Cope Trust
The J. Reginald Corah Foundation Fund
The Gershon Coren Charitable Foundation
Michael Cornish Charitable Trust
Cornwall Community Foundation
The Duke of Cornwall's Benevolent Fund
The Cornwell Charitable Trust

The Sidney and Elizabeth Corob Charitable Trust
The Corona Charitable Trust
The Costa Family Charitable Trust
The Cotton Industry War Memorial Trust
The Cotton Trust
Country Houses Foundation
County Durham Community Foundation
The Augustine Courtauld Trust
Coutts Charitable Foundation
General Charity of Coventry
Coventry Building Society Charitable Foundation
The Sir Tom Cowie Charitable Trust
Dudley and Geoffrey Cox Charitable Trust
The Sir William Coxen Trust Fund
The Lord Cozens-Hardy Trust
The Craignish Trust
The Craps Charitable Trust
Michael Crawford Children's Charity
The Cray Trust
Creative Scotland
The Crerar Hotels Trust
The Crescent Trust
Cripplegate Foundation
The Violet and Milo Cripps Charitable Trust
The Cross Trust
The Croydon Relief in Need Charities
The Peter Cruddas Foundation
Cruden Foundation Ltd
The Ronald Cruickshanks Foundation
The Cuby Charitable Trust
Cullum Family Trust
Cumbria Community Foundation
The Cunningham Trust
The Harry Cureton Charitable Trust
D. J. H. Currie Memorial Trust
The Dennis Curry Charitable Trust
The Cwmbran Trust
Itzchok Meyer Cymerman Trust Ltd
D. C. R. Allen Charitable Trust
The D. G. Charitable Settlement
The D'Oyly Carte Charitable Trust
Roald Dahl's Marvellous Children's Charity
Daily Prayer Union Charitable Trust Limited
The Daiwa Anglo-Japanese Foundation
Baron Davenport's Charity

The Davidson Family Charitable Trust
Michael Davies Charitable Settlement
The Gwendoline and Margaret Davies Charity
The Hamilton Davies Trust
The Wilfrid Bruce Davis Charitable Trust
The Davis Foundation
The Henry and Suzanne Davis Foundation
The Dawe Charitable Trust
The De Brye Charitable Trust
Peter De Haan Charitable Trust
The Deakin Charitable Trust
William Dean Countryside and Educational Trust
Debenhams Foundation
The Debmar Benevolent Trust
The Delius Trust
The Dellal Foundation
The Delves Charitable Trust
The Denman Charitable Trust
The Dentons UKMEA LLP Charitable Trust
The Derbyshire Churches and Chapels Preservation Trust
Derbyshire Community Foundation
The J. N. Derbyshire Trust
Devon Community Foundation
The Devon Historic Churches Trust
The Duke of Devonshire's Charitable Trust
The Sandy Dewhirst Charitable Trust
The Laduma Dhamecha Charitable Trust
Diabetes UK
Alan and Sheila Diamond Charitable Trust
The Dibden Allotments Fund
The Gillian Dickinson Trust
The Digbeth Trust Limited
The Dinwoodie Settlement
Disability Aid Fund (The Roger and Jean Jefcoate Trust)
Dischma Charitable Trust
The Djanogly Foundation
The DLM Charitable Trust
The DM Charitable Trust
The Derek and Eileen Dodgson Foundation
The Dollond Charitable Trust
Dorset Community Foundation
The Dorset Historic Churches Trust
The Dorus Trust
The Doughty Charity Trust
Douglas Arter Foundation
R. M. Douglas Charitable Trust
The Drapers' Charitable Fund
Dromintee Trust

**13**

Duchy Health Charity Limited
The Dulverton Trust
The Dumbreck Charity
Dunard Fund
The Dunhill Medical Trust
The Dunn Family Charitable Trust
The W. E. Dunn Trust
The Charles Dunstone Charitable Trust
The Dyers' Company Charitable Trust
The James Dyson Foundation
eaga Charitable Trust
The Eagle Charity Trust
Audrey Earle Charitable Trust
The Earley Charity
Earls Colne and Halstead Educational Charity
East End Community Foundation
Eastern Counties Educational Trust Limited
The Sir John Eastwood Foundation
The Ebenezer Trust
The EBM Charitable Trust
The Ecology Trust
The Economist Charitable Trust
EDF Energy Trust
The Gilbert and Eileen Edgar Foundation
The Gilbert Edgar Trust
Edge Fund
Edinburgh & Lothian Trust Fund
Edinburgh Children's Holiday Fund
Edinburgh Trust No 2 Account
Educational Foundation of Alderman John Norman
Dr Edwards Bishop King's Fulham Endowment Fund
The W. G. Edwards Charitable Foundation
The Elephant Trust
The George Elias Charitable Trust
The Gerald Palmer Eling Trust Company
The Wilfred and Elsie Elkes Charity Fund
The Maud Elkington Charitable Trust
The John Ellerman Foundation
The Ellinson Foundation Ltd
The Edith Maud Ellis 1985 Charitable Trust
The Ellis Campbell Foundation
The Elmgrant Trust
The Elmley Foundation
Elshore Ltd
The Vernon N. Ely Charitable Trust
The Emerton-Christie Charity

EMI Music Sound Foundation
Engage Foundation
The Englefield Charitable Trust
The English Schools' Football Association
The Enkalon Foundation
Entindale Ltd
The Epigoni Trust
Epilepsy Research UK
The Equity Trust Fund
The Eranda Foundation
The Ericson Trust
The ERM Foundation
The Ernest Hecht Charitable Foundation
The Erskine Cunningham Hill Trust
Esh Foundation
The Essex and Southend Sports Trust
Essex Community Foundation
The Essex Fairway Charitable Trust
The Essex Heritage Trust
The Essex Youth Trust
The Estelle Trust
Euro Charity Trust
The Alan Evans Memorial Trust
Sir John Evelyn's Charity
The Eventhall Family Charitable Trust
The Everard Foundation
The Eveson Charitable Trust
The Beryl Evetts and Robert Luff Animal Welfare Trust Limited
The Exilarch's Foundation
The Expat Foundation
Extonglen Limited
The F. P. Limited Charitable Trust
Esmée Fairbairn Foundation
The Fairway Trust
Famos Foundation Trust
The Lord Faringdon Charitable Trust
Samuel William Farmer's Trust
The Thomas Farr Charity
The Farthing Trust
The Fassnidge Memorial Trust
The February Foundation
The John Feeney Charitable Bequest
The George Fentham Birmingham Charity
The A. M. Fenton Trust
Elizabeth Ferguson Charitable Trust Fund
The Fidelity UK Foundation
The Doris Field Charitable Trust
Field Family Charitable Trust
The Fifty Fund
Filey Foundation Ltd
Dixie Rose Findlay Charitable Trust

Finnart House School Trust
Firtree Trust
The Fishmongers' Company's Charitable Trust
Marc Fitch Fund
The Fitton Trust
The Earl Fitzwilliam Charitable Trust
The Ian Fleming Charitable Trust
The Joyce Fletcher Charitable Trust
Florence's Charitable Trust
The Flow Foundation
The Gerald Fogel Charitable Trust
The Football Association National Sports Centre Trust
The Football Association Youth Trust
The Football Foundation
The Forbes Charitable Foundation
Ford Britain Trust
The Oliver Ford Charitable Trust
Fordeve Limited
The Lady Forester Trust
Forever Manchester (The Community Foundation for Greater Manchester)
The Forman Hardy Charitable Trust
Gwyneth Forrester Trust
The Fort Foundation
The Lord Forte Foundation
The Foyle Foundation
The Isaac and Freda Frankel Memorial Charitable Trust
The Elizabeth Frankland Moore and Star Foundation
The Gordon Fraser Charitable Trust
The Hugh Fraser Foundation
The Joseph Strong Frazer Trust
The Fred and Maureen Charitable Trust
The Louis and Valerie Freedman Charitable Settlement
The Freemasons' Grand Charity
The Charles S. French Charitable Trust
The Anne French Memorial Trust
The Freshfield Foundation
The Freshgate Trust Foundation
The Friarsgate Trust
The Friends of Kent Churches
Friends of Wiznitz Limited
Friends Provident Charitable Foundation
The Frognal Trust

Grant-makers by geographical area United Kingdom

The Patrick & Helena Frost Foundation
Mejer and Gertrude Miriam Frydman Foundation
The Fulmer Charitable Trust
G. M. C. Trust
The Galbraith Trust
The Gale Family Charity Trust
Gamlen Charitable Trust
The Gamma Trust
The Gannochy Trust
The Ganzoni Charitable Trust
The Worshipful Company of Gardeners of London
The Samuel Gardner Memorial Trust
The Garnett Charitable Trust
The Garrick Charitable Trust
Garthgwynion Charities
Gatwick Airport Community Trust
The Robert Gavron Charitable Trust
Jacqueline and Michael Gee Charitable Trust
Sir Robert Geffery's Almshouse Trust
The General Nursing Council for England and Wales Trust
The Steven Gerrard Foundation
Get Kids Going
The David Gibbons Foundation
The Gibbs Charitable Trust
Simon Gibson Charitable Trust
The G. C. Gibson Charitable Trust
The Girdlers' Company Charitable Trust
The B. and P. Glasser Charitable Trust
Global Charities
Gloucestershire Community Foundation
The Gloucestershire Historic Churches Trust
Worshipful Company of Glovers of London Charitable Trust
The GNC Trust
The Godinton Charitable Trust
The Sydney and Phyllis Goldberg Memorial Charitable Trust
The Golden Bottle Trust
Golden Charitable Trust
The Goldsmiths' Arts Trust Fund
The Goldsmiths' Company Charity
The Golf Foundation Limited
The Golsoncott Foundation
Nicholas and Judith Goodison's Charitable Settlement
The Goodman Foundation

The Mike Gooley Trailfinders Charity
The Gosling Foundation Limited
The Gould Charitable Trust
The Grace Charitable Trust
The Graff Foundation
E. C. Graham Belford Charitable Settlement
The Grahame Charitable Foundation Limited
The Granada Foundation
Grand Charitable Trust of the Order of Women Freemasons
The Grange Farm Centre Trust
Grantham Yorke Trust
GrantScape
The J. G. Graves Charitable Trust
The Gordon Gray Trust
The Gray Trust
The Great Britain Sasakawa Foundation
The Great Stone Bridge Trust of Edenbridge
The Great Torrington Town Lands Charity
The Kenneth & Susan Green Charitable Foundation
The Green Hall Foundation
Philip and Judith Green Trust
The Greggs Foundation
The Gretna Charitable Trust
The Greys Charitable Trust
The Grimmitt Trust
The Grocers' Charity
The M. and R. Gross Charities Limited
The GRP Charitable Trust
N. and R. Grunbaum Charitable Trust
The Bishop of Guildford's Foundation
The Guildry Incorporation of Perth
The Walter Guinness Charitable Trust
The Gunter Charitable Trust
The Gur Trust
The Gurney Charitable Trust
Dr Guthrie's Association
The H. and M. Charitable Trust
The Hackney Parochial Charities
The Hadfield Trust
The Hadley Trust
The Hadrian Trust
The Alfred Haines Charitable Trust
E. F. and M. G. Hall Charitable Trust
The Edith Winifred Hall Charitable Trust
The Hamamelis Trust
Hamilton Wallace Trust

Paul Hamlyn Foundation
Sue Hammerson Charitable Trust
The Hampshire and Islands Historic Churches Trust
Hampshire and Isle of Wight Community Foundation
The Hampstead Wells and Campden Trust
Hampton Fuel Allotment
The W. A. Handley Charitable Trust
The Kathleen Hannay Memorial Charity
Harbo Charities Limited
The Harborne Parish Lands Charity
The Harbour Charitable Trust
The Harbour Foundation
The Harding Trust
William Harding's Charity
The Hare of Steep Charitable Trust
The Harebell Centenary Fund
The Harpur Trust
The Harris Charity
The Harris Family Charitable Trust
The Edith Lilian Harrison 2000 Foundation
The Peter Harrison Foundation
The Hartley Charitable Trust
The Alfred And Peggy Harvey Charitable Trust
Edward Harvist Trust
The Hasluck Charitable Trust
The Hathaway Trust
The Maurice Hatter Foundation
The M. A. Hawe Settlement
The Hawthorne Charitable Trust
The Dorothy Hay-Bolton Charitable Trust
The Charles Hayward Foundation
Headley-Pitt Charitable Trust
The Health Foundation
May Hearnshaw Charitable Trust
Heart of England Community Foundation
Heart Research UK
The Heathcoat Trust
The Heathside Charitable Trust
The Percy Hedley 1990 Charitable Trust
The Hedley Denton Charitable Trust
Hedley Foundation Limited
The H. J. Heinz Company Limited Charitable Trust
The Michael Heller Charitable Foundation
The Simon Heller Charitable Settlement
Help for Health

15

Help the Homeless Limited
The Helping Foundation
The Hemby Charitable Trust
The Christina Mary Hendrie
    Trust for Scottish and
    Canadian Charities
Henley Educational Trust
The G. D. Herbert Charitable
    Trust
Herefordshire Community
    Foundation
The Herefordshire Historic
    Churches Trust
The Heritage of London Trust
    Limited
The Hertfordshire Community
    Foundation
The Hesslewood Children's
    Trust (Hull Seamen's and
    General Orphanage)
Hexham and Newcastle
    Diocesan Trust (1947)
P. and C. Hickinbotham
    Charitable Trust
The Alan Edward Higgs Charity
Highcroft Charitable Trust
The Hilden Charitable Fund
The Derek Hill Foundation
The Hillingdon Community
    Trust
The Hillingdon Partnership
    Trust
R. G. Hills Charitable Trust
Hinchley Charitable Trust
The Lady Hind Trust (Lilian
    Frances Hind Bequest)
Stuart Hine Trust
The Hinrichsen Foundation
The Hintze Family Charity
    Foundation
The Hiscox Foundation
Hitchin Educational Foundation
The Henry C. Hoare Charitable
    Trust
The Hobson Charity Limited
Hockerill Educational
    Foundation
The Sir Julian Hodge
    Charitable Trust
The Jane Hodge Foundation
The J. G. Hogg Charitable
    Trust
The Holden Charitable Trust
The Hollands-Warren Fund
The Hollick Family Charitable
    Trust
The Holliday Foundation
The Dorothy Holmes Charitable
    Trust
P. H. Holt Foundation
The Edward Holt Trust
The Holywood Trust
The Homelands Charitable
    Trust
The Homestead Charitable
    Trust

The Mary Homfray Charitable
    Trust
The Hoover Foundation
Hope for Youth (NI)
Hopmarket Charity
The Antony Hornby Charitable
    Trust
The Horne Foundation
The Thomas J. Horne
    Memorial Trust
The Worshipful Company of
    Horners' Charitable Trusts
The Hornsey Parochial
    Charities
The Hospital of God at
    Greatham
The Hospital Saturday Fund
The Sir Joseph Hotung
    Charitable Settlement
House of Industry Estate
The Reta Lila Howard
    Foundation
The Daniel Howard Trust
James T. Howat Charitable
    Trust
The Hudson Foundation
The Huggard Charitable Trust
The Hull and East Riding
    Charitable Trust
Hulme Trust Estates
    (Educational)
The Humanitarian Trust
The Michael and Shirley Hunt
    Charitable Trust
The Albert Hunt Trust
The Hunter Foundation
Miss Agnes H. Hunter's Trust
The Huntingdon Foundation
    Limited
Huntingdon Freemen's Trust
Hurdale Charity Limited
The Nani Huyu Charitable Trust
The P. Y. N. and B. Hyams
    Trust
Hyde Charitable Trust (Youth
    Plus)
IBM United Kingdom Trust
Ibrahim Foundation Ltd
The Idlewild Trust
The Iliffe Family Charitable
    Trust
Impetus – The Private Equity
    Foundation
The Indigo Trust
The Ingram Trust
The Inlight Trust
The Inman Charity
Inner London Magistrates
    Court's Poor Box and
    Feeder Charity
The International Bankers
    Charitable Trust
Interserve Employee
    Foundation Ltd
The Inverforth Charitable Trust
    (ICT)

Investream Charitable Trust
The Ireland Fund of Great
    Britain
Irish Youth Foundation (UK)
    Ltd
The Ironmongers' Foundation
The Charles Irving Charitable
    Trust
The J. Isaacs Charitable Trust
The Isle of Anglesey Charitable
    Trust
The ITF Seafarers Trust
The J. & J. Benevolent
    Foundation
The J. & J. Charitable Trust
The J. A. R. Charitable Trust
The J. J. Charitable Trust
The JRSST Charitable Trust
C. Richard Jackson Charitable
    Trust
The Jacobs Charitable Trust
The Ruth and Lionel Jacobson
    Trust (Second Fund) No 2
Jaffe Family Relief Fund
John James Bristol Foundation
The Susan and Stephen
    James Charitable
    Settlement
The James Trust
The Jarman Charitable Trust
John Jarrold Trust
Jeffrey Charitable Trust
Rees Jeffreys Road Fund
Nick Jenkins Foundation
The Jenour Foundation
The Jerusalem Trust
The Jerwood Charitable
    Foundation
Jewish Child's Day
The Jewish Youth Fund
The Elton John Aids
    Foundation
Lillie Johnson Charitable Trust
The Johnson Foundation
The Johnnie Johnson Trust
The Johnson Wax Ltd
    Charitable Trust
The Joicey Trust
The Jones 1986 Charitable
    Trust
The Dezna Robins Jones
    Charitable Foundation
The Marjorie and Geoffrey
    Jones Charitable Trust
The Jordan Charitable
    Foundation
The Joron Charitable Trust
The J. E. Joseph Charitable
    Fund
The Lady Eileen Joseph
    Foundation
The Josephs Family Charitable
    Trust
The Josh Charitable Trust
Anton Jurgens Charitable Trust

Grant-makers by geographical area

The Bernard Kahn Charitable Trust
The Stanley Kalms Foundation
The Boris Karloff Charitable Foundation
The Ian Karten Charitable Trust
The Kasner Charitable Trust
The Kass Charitable Trust
The Michael and Ilse Katz Foundation
C. S. Kaufman Charitable Trust
The Kelly Family Charitable Trust
Kelsick's Educational Foundation
The Kay Kendall Leukaemia Fund
William Kendall's Charity (Wax Chandlers' Company)
The Kennel Club Charitable Trust
Kent Community Foundation
The Nancy Kenyon Charitable Trust
Keren Association Limited
E. and E. Kernkraut Charities Limited
The Peter Kershaw Trust
Keswick Hall Charity
The Kettering and District Charitable Medical Trust
The Ursula Keyes Trust
The Robert Kiln Charitable Trust
The King Henry VIII Endowed Trust – Warwick
The King/Cullimore Charitable Trust
Kingdom Way Trust
The Kingsbury Charity
The Mary Kinross Charitable Trust
Kirkley Poor's Land Estate
The Richard Kirkman Trust
Kirschel Foundation
Robert Kitchin (Saddlers' Company)
The Marina Kleinwort Charitable Trust
The Sir James Knott Trust
The Kobler Trust
The Kohn Foundation
The KPMG Foundation
The Kreditor Charitable Trust
The Kreitman Foundation
The Neil Kreitman Foundation
The Heinz, Anna and Carol Kroch Foundation
Kupath Gemach Chaim Bechesed Viznitz Trust
The Kyte Charitable Trust
Ladbrokes in the Community Charitable Trust
John Laing Charitable Trust

Christopher Laing Foundation
The Lambert Charitable Trust
Community Foundation for Lancashire (Former)
Community Foundations for Lancashire and Merseyside
Lancashire Environmental Fund Limited
Duchy of Lancaster Benevolent Fund
Lancaster Foundation
LandAid Charitable Trust
The Jack Lane Charitable Trust
The Allen Lane Foundation
The Langtree Trust
The LankellyChase Foundation
The R. J. Larg Family Charitable Trust
Largsmount Ltd
The Lark Trust
Laufer Charitable Trust
The Lauffer Family Charitable Foundation
The Kathleen Laurence Trust
The Edgar E. Lawley Foundation
The Herd Lawson and Muriel Lawson Charitable Trust
Lawson Beckman Charitable Trust
The Raymond and Blanche Lawson Charitable Trust
The Mason Le Page Charitable Trust
The Leach Fourteenth Trust
The David Lean Foundation
The Leathersellers' Company Charitable Fund
The Leche Trust
The Arnold Lee Charitable Trust
The William Leech Charity
The Lord Mayor of Leeds Appeal Fund
Leeds Building Society Charitable Foundation
Leicester and Leicestershire Historic Churches Preservation Trust
Leicestershire, Leicester and Rutland Community Foundation
The Kennedy Leigh Charitable Trust
Morris Leigh Foundation
P. Leigh-Bramwell Trust 'E'
The Erica Leonard Trust
The Mark Leonard Trust
The Leverhulme Trade Charities Trust
The Leverhulme Trust
Lord Leverhulme's Charitable Trust
Joseph Levy Charitable Foundation

United Kingdom

David and Ruth Lewis Family Charitable Trust
The John Spedan Lewis Foundation
The Sir Edward Lewis Foundation
John Lewis Partnership General Community Fund
The Lewis Ward Trust
LHR Airport Communities Trust
Liberum Foundation
Limoges Charitable Trust
Lincolnshire Churches Trust
Lincolnshire Community Foundation
The Lind Trust
The Linden Charitable Trust
The Enid Linder Foundation
The Ruth and Stuart Lipton Charitable Trust
The Lister Charitable Trust
The Frank Litchfield Charitable Trust
The Charles Littlewood Hill Trust
The Second Joseph Aaron Littman Foundation
The George John and Sheilah Livanos Charitable Trust
Liverpool Charity and Voluntary Services
Jack Livingstone Charitable Trust
The Elaine and Angus Lloyd Charitable Trust
Lloyd's Charities Trust
Lloyds Bank Foundation for England and Wales
Lloyds Bank Foundation for Northern Ireland
Lloyds Bank Foundation for the Channel Islands
Lloyds TSB Foundation for Scotland
Localtrent Ltd
Loftus Charitable Trust
The Lolev Charitable Trust
The Joyce Lomax Bullock Charitable Trust
The Trust for London
London Catalyst
The London Community Foundation
London Housing Foundation Ltd
The London Law Trust
London Legal Support Trust
The London Marathon Charitable Trust Limited
The William and Katherine Longman Trust
The Lord's Taverners
The Loseley and Guildway Charitable Trust
The Lowy Mitchell Foundation
The C. L. Loyd Charitable Trust

17

# United Kingdom

*Grant-makers by geographical area*

LSA Charitable Trust
The Marie Helen Luen Charitable Trust
Robert Luff Foundation Ltd
C. F. Lunoe Trust Fund
The Ruth and Jack Lunzer Charitable Trust
Lord and Lady Lurgan Trust
The Lyndhurst Trust
The Lynn Foundation
John Lyon's Charity
The Lyons Charitable Trust
The Sir Jack Lyons Charitable Trust
Sylvanus Lysons Charity
M. and C. Trust
The M. K. Charitable Trust
The E. M. MacAndrew Trust
The R. S. Macdonald Charitable Trust
The Macdonald-Buchanan Charitable Trust
The Mackay and Brewer Charitable Trust
The Mackintosh Foundation
The MacRobert Trust
The Ian Mactaggart Trust (The Mactaggart Second Fund)
James Madison Trust
The Magdalen and Lasher Charity (General Fund)
The Magen Charitable Trust
The Mageni Trust
The Brian Maguire Charitable Trust
Man Group plc Charitable Trust
The Manackerman Charitable Trust
Manchester Airport Community Trust Fund
The Manchester Guardian Society Charitable Trust
Lord Mayor of Manchester's Charity Appeal Trust
The Manifold Charitable Trust
The W. M. Mann Foundation
Maranatha Christian Trust
Marbeh Torah Trust
The Marcela Trust
The Marchig Animal Welfare Trust
The Stella and Alexander Margulies Charitable Trust
Market Harborough and The Bowdens Charity
The Marks Family Foundation
The Ann and David Marks Foundation
The Hilda and Samuel Marks Foundation
J. P. Marland Charitable Trust
The Michael Marsh Charitable Trust
The Marsh Christian Trust
Charity of John Marshall

Charlotte Marshall Charitable Trust
D. G. Marshall of Cambridge Trust
The Marshgate Charitable Settlement
Sir George Martin Trust
John Martin's Charity
The Dan Maskell Tennis Trust
The Mason Porter Charitable Trust
The Nancie Massey Charitable Trust
The Mathew Trust
The Matliwala Family Charitable Trust
The Matt 6.3 Charitable Trust
The Violet Mauray Charitable Trust
Mayfair Charities Ltd
The Robert McAlpine Foundation
McGreevy No 5 Settlement
D. D. McPhail Charitable Settlement
The Medlock Charitable Trust
The Melow Charitable Trust
Menuchar Limited
Mercaz Torah Vechesed Limited
The Mercers' Charitable Foundation
Merchant Navy Welfare Board
The Merchant Taylors' Company Charities Fund
The Merchant Venturers' Charity
The Merchants' House of Glasgow
The Merlin Magic Wand Children's Charity
The Mersey Docks and Harbour Company Charitable Fund
The Tony Metherell Charitable Trust
The Metropolitan Masonic Charity
The Mickel Fund
The Mickleham Trust
The Gerald Micklem Charitable Trust
The Masonic Province of Middlesex Charitable Trust
Middlesex Sports Foundation
Millennium Stadium Charitable Trust (Ymddiriedolaeth Elusennol Stadiwm y Mileniwm)
The Ronald Miller Foundation
The Millfield House Foundation
The Millfield Trust
The Millichope Foundation
The Mills Charity
The Clare Milne Trust

Milton Keynes Community Foundation Limited
The Edgar Milward Charity
The Peter Minet Trust
Minge's Gift and the Pooled Trusts
Minton Charitable Trust
The Mirianog Trust
The Laurence Misener Charitable Trust
The Mishcon Family Charitable Trust
The Misselbrook Trust
The Brian Mitchell Charitable Settlement
The Esmé Mitchell Trust
The MITIE Foundation
Keren Mitzvah Trust
The Mizpah Trust
Mobbs Memorial Trust Ltd
The Modiano Charitable Trust
Mole Charitable Trust
The Monatrea Charitable Trust
Monmouthshire County Council Welsh Church Act Fund
The Montague Thompson Coon Charitable Trust
The Monument Trust
The George A. Moore Foundation
The Henry Moore Foundation
John Moores Foundation
The Morel Charitable Trust
The Morgan Charitable Foundation
The Morgan Foundation
Morgan Stanley International Foundation
The Oliver Morland Charitable Trust
S. C. and M. E. Morland's Charitable Trust
The Morris Charitable Trust
The Willie and Mabel Morris Charitable Trust
The Peter Morrison Charitable Foundation
G. M. Morrison Charitable Trust
The Moshal Charitable Trust
The Moshulu Charitable Trust
The Moss Family Charitable Trust
Mosselson Charitable Trust
Mothercare Group Foundation
Moto in the Community British Motor Sports Training Trust
J. P. Moulton Charitable Foundation
The Mount Everest Foundation
Mrs Waterhouse Charitable Trust
The MSE Charity
The Mugdock Children's Trust
The Mulberry Trust

........
18

The Edith Murphy Foundation
Murphy-Neumann Charity Company Limited
The John R. Murray Charitable Trust
The Music Sales Charitable Trust
The Mutual Trust Group
MW (CL) Foundation
MYA Charitable Trust
MYR Charitable Trust
The Janet Nash Charitable Settlement
The National Art Collections Fund
The National Churches Trust
The National Express Foundation
The National Hockey Foundation
The National Manuscripts Conservation Trust
The Nationwide Foundation
The Worshipful Company of Needlemakers' Charitable Fund
The Neighbourly Charitable Trust
The James Neill Trust Fund
Nemoral Ltd
Ner Foundation
Nesswall Ltd
The New Appeals Organisation for the City and County of Nottingham
Newby Trust Limited
The Newcomen Collett Foundation
The Frances and Augustus Newman Foundation
Newpier Charity Ltd
Alderman Newton's Educational Foundation
The NFU Mutual Charitable Trust
The Chevras Ezras Nitzrochim Trust
NJD Charitable Trust
Alice Noakes Memorial Charitable Trust
The Noon Foundation
Norfolk Community Foundation
Normalyn Charitable Trust
The Norman Family Charitable Trust
The Normanby Charitable Trust
North West Cancer Research
The Northampton Municipal Church Charities
Northamptonshire Community Foundation
The Community Foundation for Northern Ireland
The Northern Rock Foundation
The Northumberland Village Homes Trust

The Northwood Charitable Trust
The Norton Foundation
The Norwich Town Close Estate Charity
The Norwood and Newton Settlement
The Notgrove Trust
The Nottingham General Dispensary
Nottinghamshire Community Foundation
The Nottinghamshire Historic Churches Trust
The Nuffield Foundation
O&G Schreiber Charitable Trust
The Oakley Charitable Trust
The Oakmoor Charitable Trust
The Odin Charitable Trust
The Ofenheim Charitable Trust
Oglesby Charitable Trust
Oizer Charitable Trust
Old Possum's Practical Trust
The John Oldacre Foundation
Open Gate
The Ouseley Trust
The Owen Family Trust
Oxfam (GB)
City of Oxford Charity
Oxfordshire Community Foundation
The P. F. Charitable Trust
The Paget Charitable Trust
Eleanor Palmer Trust
The Panacea Charitable Trust
The James Pantyfedwen Foundation
The Park Charitable Trust
The Samuel and Freda Parkinson Charitable Trust
Miss M. E. Swinton Paterson's Charitable Trust
The Patrick Charitable Trust
The Jack Patston Charitable Trust
Ambika Paul Foundation
The Payne Charitable Trust
The Harry Payne Fund
The Peacock Charitable Trust
The Susanna Peake Charitable Trust
The David Pearlman Charitable Foundation
Rosanna Pearson's 1987 Charity Trust
The Pedmore Sporting Club Trust Fund
The Dowager Countess Eleanor Peel Trust
The Peltz Trust
The Pennycress Trust
People's Postcode Trust
The Performing Right Society Foundation
B. E. Perl Charitable Trust

The Personal Assurance Charitable Trust
The Jack Petchey Foundation
The Petplan Charitable Trust
The Phillips and Rubens Charitable Trust
The Phillips Charitable Trust
The Phillips Family Charitable Trust
The David Pickford Charitable Foundation
The Bernard Piggott Charitable Trust
The Pilgrim Trust
The Elise Pilkington Charitable Trust
The Pilkington Charities Fund
The Austin and Hope Pilkington Trust
The Sir Harry Pilkington Trust Fund
Estate of the Late Colonel W. W. Pilkington Will Trusts – The General Charity Fund
Miss A. M. Pilkington's Charitable Trust
The DLA Piper Charitable Trust
The Platinum Trust
G. S. Plaut Charitable Trust Limited
Polden-Puckham Charitable Foundation
The George and Esme Pollitzer Charitable Settlement
The Pollywally Charitable Trust
The Polonsky Foundation
The Ponton House Trust
The John Porter Charitable Trust
The Porter Foundation
Porticus UK
The Portishead Nautical Trust
The Portrack Charitable Trust
The Mary Potter Convent Hospital Trust
The W. L. Pratt Charitable Trust
The William Price Charitable Trust
Sir John Priestman Charity Trust
The Primrose Trust
The Prince of Wales's Charitable Foundation
Princess Anne's Charities
Prison Service Charity Fund
The Privy Purse Charitable Trust
The Puri Foundation
The PwC Foundation
Mr and Mrs J. A. Pye's Charitable Settlement
Quartet Community Foundation
The Queen Anne's Gate Foundation

Queen Mary's Roehampton Trust
The Queen's Silver Jubilee Trust
Quercus Trust
R. S. Charitable Trust
The RVW Trust
The Monica Rabagliati Charitable Trust
Rachel Charitable Trust
The Racing Foundation
Racing Welfare
The Mr and Mrs Philip Rackham Charitable Trust
Richard Radcliffe Charitable Trust
The Radcliffe Trust
The Bishop Radford Trust
The Rank Foundation Limited
The Joseph Rank Trust
The Ratcliff Foundation
The E. L. Rathbone Charitable Trust
The Ravensdale Trust
The Rayden Charitable Trust
The Roger Raymond Charitable Trust
The Rayne Foundation
The Rayne Trust
The John Rayner Charitable Trust
The Sir James Reckitt Charity
Red Hill Charitable Trust
The C. A. Redfern Charitable Foundation
The Reed Foundation
Richard Reeve's Foundation
The Rest Harrow Trust
The Rhondda Cynon Taff Welsh Church Acts Fund
Daisie Rich Trust
The Sir Cliff Richard Charitable Trust
The Clive Richards Charity
The Violet M. Richards Charity
The Richmond Parish Lands Charity
Ridgesave Limited
The Sir John Ritblat Family Foundation
The River Farm Foundation
The River Trust
Rivers Foundation
Rix-Thompson-Rothenberg Foundation
Thomas Roberts Trust
The Robertson Trust
Edwin George Robinson Charitable Trust
Robyn Charitable Trust
The Rochester Bridge Trust
The Rofeh Trust
Rokach Family Charitable Trust
The Helen Roll Charitable Trust

The Sir James Roll Charitable Trust
Mrs L. D. Rope Third Charitable Settlement
The Rosca Trust
The Rose Foundation
The Cecil Rosen Foundation
Rosetrees Trust
The Rothermere Foundation
The Rothley Trust
The Roughley Charitable Trust
Mrs Gladys Row Fogo Charitable Trust
Rowanville Ltd
The Rowlands Trust
The Joseph Rowntree Charitable Trust
The Joseph Rowntree Foundation
Joseph Rowntree Reform Trust Limited
Royal Artillery Charitable Fund
Royal British Legion
Royal Docks Trust (London)
Royal Masonic Trust for Girls and Boys
The Royal Victoria Hall Foundation
William Arthur Rudd Memorial Trust
The Rugby Group Benevolent Fund Limited
The Russell Trust
The J. S. and E. C. Rymer Charitable Trust
Raymond and Beverly Sackler 1988 Foundation
The Sackler Trust
The Ruzin Sadagora Trust
The Saddlers' Company Charitable Fund
The Jean Sainsbury Animal Welfare Trust
The Sainsbury Family Charitable Trusts
The Saintbury Trust
The Salamander Charitable Trust
The Andrew Salvesen Charitable Trust
Sam and Bella Sebba Charitable Trust
Coral Samuel Charitable Trust
The Basil Samuel Charitable Trust
The Peter Samuel Charitable Trust
The Samworth Foundation
The Sandra Charitable Trust
Santander UK Foundation Limited
The Sants Charitable Trust
The Peter Saunders Trust
The Scarfe Charitable Trust
The Schapira Charitable Trust
The Schreib Trust

The Schreiber Charitable Trust
The Schuster Charitable Trust
Foundation Scotland
The Francis C. Scott Charitable Trust
The Frieda Scott Charitable Trust
Sir Samuel Scott of Yews Trust
The Sir James and Lady Scott Trust
Scottish Coal Industry Special Welfare Fund
The Scottish Power Energy People Trust
The Scottish Power Foundation
The Scouloudi Foundation
The SDL Foundation
The Searchlight Electric Charitable Trust
Leslie Sell Charitable Trust
Sellata Ltd
The Seneca Trust
SF Group Charitable Fund for Disabled People
The Cyril Shack Trust
The Jean Shanks Foundation
The Shanti Charitable Trust
ShareGift (The Orr Mackintosh Foundation)
The Shears Foundation
The Sheepdrove Trust
The Sheffield and District Hospital Services Charitable Fund
The Sheldon Trust
The Patricia and Donald Shepherd Charitable Trust
The Sylvia and Colin Shepherd Charitable Trust
The Archie Sherman Cardiff Foundation
The Archie Sherman Charitable Trust
The R. C. Sherriff Rosebriars Trust
The Shetland Charitable Trust
SHINE (Support and Help in Education)
The Bassil Shippam and Alsford Trust
The Shipwrights' Company Charitable Fund
The Shirley Foundation
Shlomo Memorial Fund Limited
The Shoe Zone Trust
The J. A. Shone Memorial Trust
The Barbara A. Shuttleworth Memorial Trust
The Mary Elizabeth Siebel Charity
David and Jennifer Sieff Charitable Trust
The Simmons & Simmons Charitable Foundation

The Huntly and Margery Sinclair Charitable Trust
The Sino-British Fellowship Trust
Six Point Foundation
The Skelton Bounty
The Charles Skey Charitable Trust
Skinners' Company Lady Neville Charity
Skipton Building Society Charitable Foundation
The John Slater Foundation
The Slaughter and May Charitable Trust
Sloane Robinson Foundation
The Mrs Smith and Mount Trust
The DS Smith Charitable Foundation
The Smith Charitable Trust
The Henry Smith Charity
The WH Smith Group Charitable Trust
Philip Smith's Charitable Trust
The R. C. Snelling Charitable Trust
The Sobell Foundation
Sodexo Foundation
Solev Co Ltd
The Solo Charitable Settlement
David Solomons Charitable Trust
Somerset Churches Trust
Songdale Ltd
The E. C. Sosnow Charitable Trust
The Souter Charitable Trust
The South Square Trust
The W. F. Southall Trust
Southdown Trust
R. H. Southern Trust
The Southover Manor General Education Trust
The Sovereign Health Care Charitable Trust
Spar Charitable Fund
Sparks Charity (Sport Aiding Medical Research For Kids)
Sparquote Limited
The Spear Charitable Trust
The Worshipful Company of Spectacle Makers' Charity
The Jessie Spencer Trust
The Ralph and Irma Sperring Charity
The Spielman Charitable Trust
Split Infinitive Trust
The Spoore, Merry and Rixman Foundation
Sported Foundation
Rosalyn and Nicholas Springer Charitable Trust
Springrule Limited
The Spurrell Charitable Trust

The Geoff and Fiona Squire Foundation
The St Hilda's Trust
St James's Trust Settlement
St James's Place Foundation
Sir Walter St John's Educational Charity
The St Laurence Relief In Need Trust
St Luke's College Foundation
St Michael's and All Saints' Charities Relief Branch (The Church Houses Relief in Need Charity)
St Monica Trust
St Peter's Saltley Trust
The Stanley Foundation Ltd
The Staples Trust
The Star Charitable Trust
The Peter Stebbings Memorial Charity
The Steel Charitable Trust
The Steinberg Family Charitable Trust
The Stephen Barry Charitable Trust
Sir Halley Stewart Trust
The Stewarts Law Foundation
The Leonard Laity Stoate Charitable Trust
The Stobart Newlands Charitable Trust
The Edward Stocks-Massey Bequest Fund
The Stoller Charitable Trust
M. J. C. Stone Charitable Trust
The Samuel Storey Family Charitable Trust
Peter Stormonth Darling Charitable Trust
Peter Storrs Trust
The Strangward Trust
Stratford upon Avon Town Trust
The W. O. Street Charitable Foundation
The Strowger Trust
The Sudborough Foundation
Suffolk Community Foundation
The Suffolk Historic Churches Trust
The Alan Sugar Foundation
The Bernard Sunley Charitable Foundation
Community Foundation for Surrey
The Sussex Community Foundation
The Sussex Historic Churches Trust
The Sutasoma Trust
Sutton Coldfield Charitable Trust
Swan Mountain Trust
The Swann-Morton Foundation

Swansea and Brecon Diocesan Board of Finance Limited
Swimathon Foundation
The John Swire (1989) Charitable Trust
The Swire Charitable Trust
The Hugh and Ruby Sykes Charitable Trust
The Charles and Elsie Sykes Trust
The Charity of Stella Symons
The Tajtelbaum Charitable Trust
The Talbot Trusts
The Talbot Village Trust
The Lady Tangye Charitable Trust
The David Tannen Charitable Trust
The Tanner Trust
The Lili Tapper Charitable Foundation
The Taurus Foundation
The Tay Charitable Trust
C. B. and H. H. Taylor 1984 Trust
The Connie and Albert Taylor Charitable Trust
The Taylor Family Foundation
A. P. Taylor Trust
The Tedworth Charitable Trust
Tees Valley Community Foundation
Tegham Limited
The Templeton Goodwill Trust
The Tennis Foundation
Tesco Charity Trust
The C. Paul Thackray General Charitable Trust
The Thistle Trust
The Thompson Family Charitable Trust
The Len Thomson Charitable Trust
The Sue Thomson Foundation
Thomson Reuters Foundation
The Sir Jules Thorn Charitable Trust
The Thornton Foundation
The Thousandth Man- Richard Burns Charitable Trust
The Three Guineas Trust
The Thriplow Charitable Trust
The Daniel Thwaites Charitable Trust
The Tisbury Telegraph Trust
The Tobacco Pipe Makers and Tobacco Trade Benevolent Fund
The Tolkien Trust
Tomchei Torah Charitable Trust
The Tompkins Foundation
Toras Chesed (London) Trust
Tottenham Grammar School Foundation

The Tower Hill Trust
The Towry Law Charitable Trust
The Toy Trust
Toyota Manufacturing UK Charitable Trust
Annie Tranmer Charitable Trust
The Constance Travis Charitable Trust
The Trefoil Trust
The Tresillian Trust
The Triangle Trust (1949) Fund
The True Colours Trust
Truedene Co. Ltd
The Truemark Trust
Truemart Limited
Trumros Limited
The Trusthouse Charitable Foundation
The James Tudor Foundation
Tudor Rose Ltd
The Tudor Trust
The Tufton Charitable Trust
Tuixen Foundation
The Douglas Turner Trust
The Florence Turner Trust
The G. J. W. Turner Trust
TVML Foundation
Two Ridings Community Foundation
Community Foundation Serving Tyne and Wear and Northumberland
Trustees of Tzedakah
UKI Charitable Foundation
Ulster Garden Villages Ltd
The Underwood Trust
The Union of Orthodox Hebrew Congregation
The UNITE Foundation
United Utilities Trust Fund
The Michael Uren Foundation
Uxbridge United Welfare Trust
The Vail Foundation
The Valentine Charitable Trust
The Valiant Charitable Trust
The Van Neste Foundation
Mrs Maud Van Norden's Charitable Foundation
The Vandervell Foundation
The Vardy Foundation
The Variety Club Children's Charity
Veneziana Fund
The William and Patricia Venton Charitable Trust
Victoria Homes Trust
The Nigel Vinson Charitable Trust
The William and Ellen Vinten Trust
The Vintners' Foundation
Vision Charity
Vivdale Ltd
The Vodafone Foundation
Voluntary Action Fund
Wade's Charity

The Scurrah Wainwright Charity
The Wakefield and Tetley Trust
Wakeham Trust
The Community Foundation in Wales
Wales Council for Voluntary Action
Robert and Felicity Waley-Cohen Charitable Trust
The Walker Trust
Wallace and Gromit's Children's Foundation
Sir Siegmund Warburg's Voluntary Settlement
The Ward Blenkinsop Trust
The Barbara Ward Children's Foundation
The Waterloo Foundation
G. R. Waters Charitable Trust 2000
Wates Family Enterprise Trust
The Wates Foundation
Blyth Watson Charitable Trust
John Watson's Trust
Waynflete Charitable Trust
Weatherley Charitable Trust
The Weavers' Company Benevolent Fund
Webb Memorial Trust
The David Webster Charitable Trust
The William Webster Charitable Trust
The James Weir Foundation
The Wellcome Trust
Welsh Church Fund – Dyfed area (Carmarthenshire, Ceredigion and Pembrokeshire)
The Welton Foundation
The West Derby Wastelands Charity
The Westminster Foundation
The Garfield Weston Foundation
The Barbara Whatmore Charitable Trust
The Whitaker Charitable Trust
The Colonel W. H. Whitbread Charitable Trust
The Melanie White Foundation Limited
White Stuff Foundation
The Whitecourt Charitable Trust
A. H. and B. C. Whiteley Charitable Trust
The Norman Whiteley Trust
The Whitley Animal Protection Trust
The Lionel Wigram Memorial Trust
The Felicity Wilde Charitable Trust
The William Barrow's Charity
The Charity of William Williams

The Kay Williams Charitable Foundation
The Williams Charitable Trust
Williams Serendipity Trust
The HDH Wills 1965 Charitable Trust
The Dame Violet Wills Will Trust
The Wilmcote Charitrust
Sumner Wilson Charitable Trust
David Wilson Foundation
The Wilson Foundation
J. and J. R. Wilson Trust
The Community Foundation for Wiltshire and Swindon
The Benjamin Winegarten Charitable Trust
The Harold Hyam Wingate Foundation
The Francis Winham Foundation
The James Wise Charitable Trust
The Michael and Anna Wix Charitable Trust
The Wixamtree Trust
The Maurice Wohl Charitable Foundation
The Charles Wolfson Charitable Trust
The Wolfson Family Charitable Trust
The Wolfson Foundation
The James Wood Bequest Fund
The Wood Family Trust
Wooden Spoon Society
The F. Glenister Woodger Trust
Woodroffe Benton Foundation
The Woodward Charitable Trust
Worcester Municipal Charities
The Worcestershire and Dudley Historic Churches Trust
The Wragge and Co Charitable Trust
The Diana Edgson Wright Charitable Trust
The Matthews Wrightson Charity Trust
Wychville Ltd
The Wyndham Charitable Trust
The Wyseliot Charitable Trust
The Xerox (UK) Trust
The Yapp Charitable Trust
The Yardley Great Trust
The W. Wing Yip and Brothers Foundation
Yorkshire and Clydesdale Bank Foundation
Yorkshire Building Society Charitable Foundation
The South Yorkshire Community Foundation

The Yorkshire Dales
    Millennium Trust
The Yorkshire Historic
    Churches Trust
The William Allen Young
    Charitable Trust
The John Kirkhope Young
    Endowment Fund
Youth Music
Youth United Foundation
The Marjorie and Arnold Ziff
    Charitable Foundation
Stephen Zimmerman
    Charitable Trust
The Zochonis Charitable Trust
Zurich Community Trust (UK)
    Limited

## UK

## England

The 1989 Willan Charitable
    Trust
A. W. Charitable Trust
The Aberdeen Foundation
ABF The Soldiers' Charity
The Addleshaw Goddard
    Charitable Trust
The Adnams Charity
AF Trust Company
Aldgate and All Hallows'
    Foundation
The H. B. Allen Charitable
    Trust
Alliance Trust Staff Foundation
Almondsbury Charity
Amabrill Limited
The Ammco Trust
Viscount Amory's Charitable
    Trust
Anguish's Educational
    Foundation
Anpride Ltd
The Archbishop's Council –
    The Church and Community
    Fund
The Argus Appeal
Arts Council England
The Ascot Fire Brigade Trust
The Asda Foundation
AstonMansfield Charitable
    Trust
The Lord Austin Trust
The John Avins Trust
The Avon and Somerset Police
    Community Trust
The Aylesford Family
    Charitable Trust
The Roy and Pixie Baker
    Charitable Trust
The Albert Casanova Ballard
    Deceased Trust
The Ballinger Charitable Trust
The Banbury Charities
The Barbour Foundation
Barchester Healthcare
    Foundation
Barnes Workhouse Fund
The Barnstaple Bridge Trust
The Barnwood House Trust
The Bates Charitable Trust
The Battens Charitable Trust
BCH Trust
The Bearder Charity
The James Beattie Charitable
    Trust
The Beccles Town Lands
    Charity
The Beckett's and Sargeant's
    Educational Foundation
The Bedfordshire and
    Hertfordshire Historic
    Churches Trust

The Bedfordshire and Luton
    Community Foundation
The Provincial Grand Lodge of
    Bedfordshire Charity Fund
The Bellinger Donnay Trust
The Benfield Motors Charitable
    Trust
The Bergne-Coupland Charity
Bergqvist Charitable Trust
The Berkshire Community
    Foundation
The Mason Bibby 1981 Trust
The Bideford Bridge Trust
The Bingham Trust
The Bintaub Charitable Trust
The Birmingham District
    Nursing Charitable Trust
Birmingham International
    Airport Community Trust
Birthday House Trust
The Michael Bishop
    Foundation
Isabel Blackman Foundation
The Blagrave Trust
The Blanchminster Trust
The Sir Victor Blank Charitable
    Settlement
The Bloom Foundation
The Nicholas Boas Charitable
    Trust
The Boodle & Dunthorne
    Charitable Trust
The Booth Charities
Boots Charitable Trust
The Bordon Liphook
    Haslemere Charity
The Boshier-Hinton Foundation
The Bothwell Charitable Trust
The Bowland Charitable Trust
The Frank Brake Charitable
    Trust
The Bramhope Trust
The Bransford Trust
The Harold and Alice Bridges
    Charity
The Brighton District Nursing
    Association Trust
Bristol Archdeaconry Charity
The Bristol Charities
British Council for Prevention
    of Blindness (Save Eyes
    Everywhere)
British Gas (Scottish Gas)
    Energy Trust
The J. and M. Britton
    Charitable Trust
The Consuelo and Anthony
    Brooke Charitable Trust
The Charles Brotherton Trust
Joseph Brough Charitable
    Trust
The Jack Brunton Charitable
    Trust
Buckinghamshire Community
    Foundation

The Buckinghamshire Historic Churches Trust
The Buckinghamshire Masonic Centenary Fund
The E. F. Bulmer Benevolent Fund
The Burghley Family Trust
The Burton Breweries Charitable Trust
Consolidated Charity of Burton upon Trent
The Worshipful Company of Butchers General Charities
Cable & Wireless Worldwide Foundation
The William A. Cadbury Charitable Trust
Community Foundation for Calderdale
The Cambridge Chrysalis Trust
The Cambridgeshire Community Foundation
The Cambridgeshire Historic Churches Trust
The Camelia Trust
The Campden Charities Trustee
The Frederick and Phyllis Cann Trust
Carter's Educational Foundation
Sir John Cass's Foundation
The Catholic Trust for England and Wales
The Joseph and Annie Cattle Trust
John William Chapman's Charitable Trust
Chaucer Foundation
Cheshire Freemason's Charity
The Chippenham Borough Lands Charity
The Chipping Sodbury Town Lands Charity
The Christabella Charitable Trust
Christadelphian Samaritan Fund
The Church Burgesses Educational Foundation
Church Burgesses Trust
Church Urban Fund
The City Bridge Trust
CLA Charitable Trust
The Hilda and Alice Clark Charitable Trust
The Clarke Charitable Settlement
Richard Cloudesley's Charity
The Coalfields Regeneration Trust
The Cobtree Charity Trust Ltd
The R. and S. Cohen Foundation
The Colchester Catalyst Charity

The Cole Charitable Trust
The Colefax Charitable Trust
John and Freda Coleman Charitable Trust
The George Henry Collins Charity
Colyer-Fergusson Charitable Trust
Community First (Landfill Communities Fund)
Community Foundation for Leeds
The Compton Charitable Trust
The Douglas Compton James Charitable Trust
The Congleton Inclosure Trust
The Consolidated Charities for the Infirm – Merchant Taylors' Company
The Catherine Cookson Charitable Trust
The Marjorie Coote Animal Charity Trust
The Marjorie Coote Old People's Charity
The Helen Jean Cope Trust
The J. Reginald Corah Foundation Fund
Cornwall Community Foundation
Country Houses Foundation
County Durham Community Foundation
General Charity of Coventry
Coventry Building Society Charitable Foundation
The Sir Tom Cowie Charitable Trust
The Sir William Coxen Trust Fund
Michael Crawford Children's Charity
Cripplegate Foundation
The Croydon Relief in Need Charities
Cumbria Community Foundation
The Harry Cureton Charitable Trust
D. J. H. Currie Memorial Trust
D. C. R. Allen Charitable Trust
Baron Davenport's Charity
The Hamilton Davies Trust
The Davis Foundation
The Henry and Suzanne Davis Foundation
The Denman Charitable Trust
The Dentons UKMEA LLP Charitable Trust
The Derbyshire Churches and Chapels Preservation Trust
Derbyshire Community Foundation
The J. N. Derbyshire Trust
Devon Community Foundation

The Devon Historic Churches Trust
The Dibden Allotments Fund
The Gillian Dickinson Trust
The Digbeth Trust Limited
Dischma Charitable Trust
The DM Charitable Trust
The Derek and Eileen Dodgson Foundation
Dorset Community Foundation
The Dorset Historic Churches Trust
The Doughty Charity Trust
Duchy Health Charity Limited
The Dulverton Trust
The Dumbreck Charity
The W. E. Dunn Trust
The James Dyson Foundation
The Earley Charity
Earls Colne and Halstead Educational Charity
East End Community Foundation
The Ebenezer Trust
The Economist Charitable Trust
The Gilbert and Eileen Edgar Foundation
Edinburgh Trust No 2 Account
Educational Foundation of Alderman John Norman
Dr Edwards Bishop King's Fulham Endowment Fund
The Elephant Trust
The Gerald Palmer Eling Trust Company
The Wilfred and Elsie Elkes Charity Fund
The Maud Elkington Charitable Trust
The Ellinson Foundation Ltd
The Ellis Campbell Foundation
The Elmgrant Trust
The Elmley Foundation
Elshore Ltd
The Vernon N. Ely Charitable Trust
The English Schools' Football Association
The Ernest Hecht Charitable Foundation
Esh Foundation
The Essex and Southend Sports Trust
Essex Community Foundation
The Essex Fairway Charitable Trust
The Essex Heritage Trust
The Essex Youth Trust
Sir John Evelyn's Charity
The Eventhall Family Charitable Trust
The Everard Foundation
The Eveson Charitable Trust
The Farthing Trust
The Fassnidge Memorial Trust

The John Feeney Charitable Bequest
The George Fentham Birmingham Charity
The A. M. Fenton Trust
Field Family Charitable Trust
The Fifty Fund
Finnart House School Trust
Firtree Trust
The Joyce Fletcher Charitable Trust
The Football Foundation
Ford Britain Trust
The Lady Forester Trust
Forever Manchester (The Community Foundation for Greater Manchester)
Gwyneth Forrester Trust
The Fort Foundation
The Joseph Strong Frazer Trust
The Fred and Maureen Charitable Trust
The Freemasons' Grand Charity
The Charles S. French Charitable Trust
The Anne French Memorial Trust
The Freshgate Trust Foundation
The Friends of Kent Churches
Friends of Wiznitz Limited
The Fulmer Charitable Trust
The Galbraith Trust
The Ganzoni Charitable Trust
The Worshipful Company of Gardeners of London
The Samuel Gardner Memorial Trust
The Garnett Charitable Trust
Gatwick Airport Community Trust
The General Nursing Council for England and Wales Trust
The David Gibbons Foundation
The Girdlers' Company Charitable Trust
The B. and P. Glasser Charitable Trust
Gloucestershire Community Foundation
The Gloucestershire Historic Churches Trust
The GNC Trust
The Godinton Charitable Trust
The Goldsmiths' Company Charity
The Goodman Foundation
A. B. Grace Trust
The Graff Foundation
E. C. Graham Belford Charitable Settlement
The Grahame Charitable Foundation Limited
The Granada Foundation

Grand Charitable Trust of the Order of Women Freemasons
The Grange Farm Centre Trust
Grantham Yorke Trust
The Gordon Gray Trust
The Gray Trust
The Great Stone Bridge Trust of Edenbridge
The Great Torrington Town Lands Charity
The Green Hall Foundation
The Greggs Foundation
The Grimmitt Trust
The M. and R. Gross Charities Limited
The Bishop of Guildford's Foundation
The Walter Guinness Charitable Trust
The Gur Trust
The Hackney Parochial Charities
The Hadfield Trust
The Hadrian Trust
The Alfred Haines Charitable Trust
E. F. and M. G. Hall Charitable Trust
The Hampshire and Islands Historic Churches Trust
Hampshire and Isle of Wight Community Foundation
The Hampstead Wells and Campden Trust
Hampton Fuel Allotment
The W. A. Handley Charitable Trust
The Harborne Parish Lands Charity
The Harbour Foundation
William Harding's Charity
The Harpur Trust
The Harris Charity
The Peter Harrison Foundation
The Hartley Charitable Trust
The Alfred And Peggy Harvey Charitable Trust
Edward Harvist Trust
The Maurice Hatter Foundation
The M. A. Hawe Settlement
The Dorothy Hay-Bolton Charitable Trust
The Health Foundation
Heart of England Community Foundation
The Heathcoat Trust
The Hedley Denton Charitable Trust
The Simon Heller Charitable Settlement
Help for Health
The Helping Foundation
The Hemby Charitable Trust
Henley Educational Trust

Herefordshire Community Foundation
The Herefordshire Historic Churches Trust
The Heritage of London Trust Limited
The Hertfordshire Community Foundation
The Hesslewood Children's Trust (Hull Seamen's and General Orphanage)
Hexham and Newcastle Diocesan Trust (1947)
The Alan Edward Higgs Charity
Highcroft Charitable Trust
The Hillingdon Community Trust
The Hillingdon Partnership Trust
R. G. Hills Charitable Trust
Stuart Hine Trust
The Hintze Family Charity Foundation
The Hiscox Foundation
Hitchin Educational Foundation
The Hollands-Warren Fund
The Hollick Family Charitable Trust
The Edward Holt Trust
Hopmarket Charity
The Antony Hornby Charitable Trust
The Worshipful Company of Horners' Charitable Trusts
The Hornsey Parochial Charities
The Hospital of God at Greatham
The Sir Joseph Hotung Charitable Settlement
House of Industry Estate
The Hudson Foundation
The Hull and East Riding Charitable Trust
Hulme Trust Estates (Educational)
The Huntingdon Foundation Limited
Huntingdon Freemen's Trust
Hurdale Charity Limited
The P. Y. N. and B. Hyams Trust
Hyde Charitable Trust (Youth Plus)
The Iliffe Family Charitable Trust
The Indigo Trust
Inner London Magistrates Court's Poor Box and Feeder Charity
Interserve Employee Foundation Ltd
The Charles Irving Charitable Trust
The J. Isaacs Charitable Trust
The ITF Seafarers Trust

**25**

The J. A. R. Charitable Trust
The J. J. Charitable Trust
C. Richard Jackson Charitable Trust
John James Bristol Foundation
The James Trust
The Jarman Charitable Trust
The Jerusalem Trust
Jewish Child's Day (JCD)
The Johnson Foundation
The Johnson Wax Ltd Charitable Trust
The J. E. Joseph Charitable Fund
The Stanley Kalms Foundation
The Boris Karloff Charitable Foundation
The Ian Karten Charitable Trust
The Michael and Ilse Katz Foundation
Kelsick's Educational Foundation
William Kendall's Charity (Wax Chandlers' Company)
Kent Community Foundation
The Peter Kershaw Trust
Keswick Hall Charity
The Ursula Keyes Trust
The King Henry VIII Endowed Trust – Warwick
The Kingsbury Charity
Kirkley Poor's Land Estate
Robert Kitchin (Saddlers' Company)
The Sir James Knott Trust
The KPMG Foundation
Community Foundation for Lancashire (Former)
Community Foundations for Lancashire and Merseyside
Duchy of Lancaster Benevolent Fund
The Jack Lane Charitable Trust
The Langtree Trust
The Herd Lawson and Muriel Lawson Charitable Trust
The Mason Le Page Charitable Trust
The Leach Fourteenth Trust
The William Leech Charity
The Lord Mayor of Leeds Appeal Fund
Leicester and Leicestershire Historic Churches Preservation Trust
Leicestershire, Leicester and Rutland Community Foundation
Morris Leigh Foundation
The Erica Leonard Trust
LHR Airport Communities Trust
Lincolnshire Churches Trust
Lincolnshire Community Foundation

The Ruth and Stuart Lipton Charitable Trust
Liverpool Charity and Voluntary Services
Lloyds Bank Foundation for England and Wales
The Lolev Charitable Trust
The Trust for London
London Catalyst
The London Community Foundation
London Housing Foundation Ltd (LHF)
London Legal Support Trust (LLST)
The London Marathon Charitable Trust Limited
The Lowy Mitchell Foundation
Lord and Lady Lurgan Trust
John Lyon's Charity
Sylvanus Lysons Charity
The Magdalen and Lasher Charity (General Fund)
Man Group plc Charitable Trust
Manchester Airport Community Trust Fund
The Manchester Guardian Society Charitable Trust
Lord Mayor of Manchester's Charity Appeal Trust
Market Harborough and The Bowdens Charity
The Ann and David Marks Foundation
The Michael Marsh Charitable Trust
Charity of John Marshall (Marshall's Charity)
John Martin's Charity
The Merchant Venturers' Charity
The Merlin Magic Wand Children's Charity
The Mersey Docks and Harbour Company Charitable Fund
The Metropolitan Masonic Charity
The Gerald Micklem Charitable Trust
The Masonic Province of Middlesex Charitable Trust (Middlesex Masonic Charity)
The Millfield House Foundation (MHF)
The Mills Charity
The Clare Milne Trust
Milton Keynes Community Foundation Limited
The Peter Minet Trust
Mobbs Memorial Trust Ltd
The Modiano Charitable Trust
John Moores Foundation (JMF)
The Morgan Foundation

Morgan Stanley International Foundation
The Moss Family Charitable Trust
Moto in the Community
The Music Sales Charitable Trust
MYA Charitable Trust
MYR Charitable Trust
The National Churches Trust
The Worshipful Company of Needlemakers' Charitable Fund
The Neighbourly Charitable Trust
The James Neill Trust Fund
Nemoral Ltd
The New Appeals Organisation for the City and County of Nottingham
The Newcomen Collett Foundation
Alderman Newton's Educational Foundation
The Noon Foundation
Norfolk Community Foundation
The Norman Family Charitable Trust
North West Cancer Research
The Northampton Municipal Church Charities
Northamptonshire Community Foundation
The Northern Rock Foundation
The Northumberland Village Homes Trust
The Norwich Town Close Estate Charity
The Norwood and Newton Settlement
The Notgrove Trust
The Nottingham General Dispensary
Nottinghamshire Community Foundation
The Nottinghamshire Historic Churches Trust
O&G Schreiber Charitable Trust
Oglesby Charitable Trust
Open Gate
The Ouseley Trust
City of Oxford Charity
Oxfordshire Community Foundation
The Paget Charitable Trust
Eleanor Palmer Trust
The Jack Patston Charitable Trust
The Payne Charitable Trust
The Harry Payne Fund
The Pedmore Sporting Club Trust Fund
People's Postcode Trust
The Jack Petchey Foundation

# England

Grant-makers by geographical area

The David Pickford Charitable Foundation
The Bernard Piggott Charitable Trust
The Pilkington Charities Fund
The Sir Harry Pilkington Trust Fund
Porticus UK
The Portishead Nautical Trust
The Mary Potter Convent Hospital Trust
The William Price Charitable Trust
Sir John Priestman Charity Trust
The Puri Foundation
Quartet Community Foundation
The Mr and Mrs Philip Rackham Charitable Trust
The Ravensdale Trust
Red Hill Charitable Trust
Richard Reeve's Foundation
The Richmond Parish Lands Charity
The Rochester Bridge Trust
The Rosca Trust
The Rose Foundation
Rosetrees Trust
The Rothermere Foundation
The Rothley Trust
The Roughley Charitable Trust
Royal British Legion
Royal Docks Trust (London)
The Royal Victoria Hall Foundation
The Rugby Group Benevolent Fund Limited
The J. S. and E. C. Rymer Charitable Trust
Raymond and Beverly Sackler 1988 Foundation
The Sackler Trust
The Basil Samuel Charitable Trust
The Samworth Foundation
The Sants Charitable Trust
The Francis C. Scott Charitable Trust
The Frieda Scott Charitable Trust
The Sir James and Lady Scott Trust
The Scottish Power Energy People Trust
The SDL Foundation
SF Group Charitable Fund for Disabled People
ShareGift (The Orr Mackintosh Foundation)
The Shears Foundation
The Sheldon Trust
The Sylvia and Colin Shepherd Charitable Trust
The R. C. Sherriff Rosebriars Trust

SHINE (Support and Help in Education)
The Shoe Zone Trust
The J. A. Shone Memorial Trust
The Mary Elizabeth Siebel Charity
The Simmons & Simmons Charitable Foundation
The Skelton Bounty
Skipton Building Society Charitable Foundation
The Slaughter and May Charitable Trust
The Mrs Smith and Mount Trust
The DS Smith Charitable Foundation
The R. C. Snelling Charitable Trust
The Sobell Foundation
Somerset Churches Trust
R. H. Southern Trust
The Southover Manor General Education Trust
Sparquote Limited
The Ralph and Irma Sperring Charity
The Spielman Charitable Trust
The Spoore, Merry and Rixman Foundation
Springrule Limited
The St Hilda's Trust
Sir Walter St John's Educational Charity
The St Laurence Relief In Need Trust
St Luke's College Foundation
St Michael's and All Saints' Charities Relief Branch
St Monica Trust
St Peter's Saltley Trust
The Leonard Laity Stoate Charitable Trust
The Edward Stocks-Massey Bequest Fund
The Strangward Trust
Stratford upon Avon Town Trust
The Strowger Trust
Suffolk Community Foundation
The Suffolk Historic Churches Trust
Community Foundation for Surrey
The Sussex Community Foundation
The Sussex Historic Churches Trust
Sutton Coldfield Charitable Trust
The Talbot Trusts
The Talbot Village Trust
The Tanner Trust
C. B. and H. H. Taylor 1984 Trust

The Connie and Albert Taylor Charitable Trust
The Taylor Family Foundation
A. P. Taylor Trust
Tees Valley Community Foundation
Tegham Limited
The C. Paul Thackray General Charitable Trust
Thomson Reuters Foundation
The Daniel Thwaites Charitable Trust
The Tobacco Pipe Makers and Tobacco Trade Benevolent Fund
Tottenham Grammar School Foundation
The Tower Hill Trust
Toyota Manufacturing UK Charitable Trust
Tuixen Foundation
The G. J. W. Turner Trust
Two Ridings Community Foundation
Community Foundation Serving Tyne and Wear and Northumberland
United Utilities Trust Fund
Uxbridge United Welfare Trust
The Valentine Charitable Trust
The Vintners' Foundation
Wade's Charity
The Scurrah Wainwright Charity
The Wakefield and Tetley Trust
Robert and Felicity Waley-Cohen Charitable Trust
The Walker Trust
The Barbara Ward Children's Foundation
The Wates Foundation
The William Webster Charitable Trust
The West Derby Wastelands Charity
A. H. and B. C. Whiteley Charitable Trust
The Norman Whiteley Trust
The William Barrow's Charity
The Charity of William Williams
The Dame Violet Wills Will Trust
The Wilmcote Charitrust
David Wilson Foundation
The Wilson Foundation
The Community Foundation for Wiltshire and Swindon
The Francis Winham Foundation
The F. Glenister Woodger Trust
Worcester Municipal Charities
The Worcestershire and Dudley Historic Churches Trust
The Yapp Charitable Trust
The Yardley Great Trust

27

The W. Wing Yip and Brothers
   Foundation
The South Yorkshire
   Community Foundation
The Yorkshire Dales
   Millennium Trust
The Yorkshire Historic
   Churches Trust
Youth Music
The Zochonis Charitable Trust

..........................................

■ **Greater London**

A. W. Charitable Trust
ABF The Soldiers' Charity
The Addleshaw Goddard
   Charitable Trust
Aldgate and All Hallows'
   Foundation
Alliance Trust Staff Foundation
Amabrill Limited
Anpride Ltd
AstonMansfield Charitable
   Trust
Barnes Workhouse Fund
The Bellinger Donnay Trust
Bergqvist Charitable Trust
The Bintaub Charitable Trust
The Sir Victor Blank Charitable
   Settlement
The Bloom Foundation
The Nicholas Boas Charitable
   Trust
British Council for Prevention
   of Blindness (Save Eyes
   Everywhere)
The Consuelo and Anthony
   Brooke Charitable Trust
The Worshipful Company of
   Butchers General Charities
The Campden Charities
   Trustee
Sir John Cass's Foundation
Chaucer Foundation
The City Bridge Trust
Richard Cloudesley's Charity
The R. and S. Cohen
   Foundation
The Consolidated Charities for
   the Infirm – Merchant
   Taylors' Company
Cripplegate Foundation
The Croydon Relief in Need
   Charities
The Dentons UKMEA LLP
   Charitable Trust
Dischma Charitable Trust
East End Community
   Foundation
Edinburgh Trust No 2 Account
Dr Edwards Bishop King's
   Fulham Endowment Fund
Elshore Ltd
The Vernon N. Ely Charitable
   Trust
Sir John Evelyn's Charity

The Fassnidge Memorial Trust
Field Family Charitable Trust
Finnart House School Trust
Firtree Trust
Ford Britain Trust
The Charles S. French
   Charitable Trust
Friends of Wiznitz Limited
The Worshipful Company of
   Gardeners of London
The Samuel Gardner Memorial
   Trust
The B. and P. Glasser
   Charitable Trust
The Goldsmiths' Company
   Charity
The Graff Foundation
The Grahame Charitable
   Foundation Limited
Grand Charitable Trust of the
   Order of Women
   Freemasons
The Grange Farm Centre Trust
The Greggs Foundation
The M. and R. Gross Charities
   Limited
The Gur Trust
The Hackney Parochial
   Charities
The Hampstead Wells and
   Campden Trust
Hampton Fuel Allotment
The Harbour Foundation
The Alfred And Peggy Harvey
   Charitable Trust
Edward Harvist Trust
The Maurice Hatter Foundation
The Health Foundation
The Simon Heller Charitable
   Settlement
The Helping Foundation
The Heritage of London Trust
   Limited
Highcroft Charitable Trust
The Hillingdon Community
   Trust
The Hillingdon Partnership
   Trust
The Hiscox Foundation
The Hollick Family Charitable
   Trust
The Antony Hornby Charitable
   Trust
The Worshipful Company of
   Horners' Charitable Trusts
The Hornsey Parochial
   Charities
The Sir Joseph Hotung
   Charitable Settlement
The Huntingdon Foundation
   Limited
Hurdale Charity Limited
The P. Y. N. and B. Hyams
   Trust
Hyde Charitable Trust (Youth
   Plus)

The Indigo Trust
Inner London Magistrates
   Court's Poor Box and
   Feeder Charity
The ITF Seafarers Trust
The J. A. R. Charitable Trust
The J. J. Charitable Trust
The Jerusalem Trust
Jewish Child's Day
The J. E. Joseph Charitable
   Fund
The Stanley Kalms Foundation
The Boris Karloff Charitable
   Foundation
William Kendall's Charity (Wax
   Chandlers' Company)
The Kingsbury Charity
Robert Kitchin (Saddlers'
   Company)
The Mason Le Page Charitable
   Trust
The Ruth and Stuart Lipton
   Charitable Trust
The Lolev Charitable Trust
The Trust for London
London Catalyst
The London Community
   Foundation
London Housing Foundation
   Ltd
London Legal Support Trust
The London Marathon
   Charitable Trust Limited
The Lowy Mitchell Foundation
John Lyon's Charity
Man Group plc Charitable
   Trust
The Metropolitan Masonic
   Charity
The Masonic Province of
   Middlesex Charitable Trust
The Peter Minet Trust
The Modiano Charitable Trust
Morgan Stanley International
   Foundation
The Music Sales Charitable
   Trust
MYA Charitable Trust
The Worshipful Company of
   Needlemakers' Charitable
   Fund
Nemoral Ltd
The Newcomen Collett
   Foundation
Eleanor Palmer Trust
People's Postcode Trust
The Jack Petchey Foundation
The David Pickford Charitable
   Foundation
Richard Reeve's Foundation
The Richmond Parish Lands
   Charity
The Rose Foundation
Royal Docks Trust (London)
The Royal Victoria Hall
   Foundation

The Basil Samuel Charitable Trust
ShareGift (The Orr Mackintosh Foundation)
SHINE (Support and Help in Education)
The Simmons & Simmons Charitable Foundation
The Slaughter and May Charitable Trust
The Mrs Smith and Mount Trust
Sir Walter St John's Educational Charity
The Taylor Family Foundation
A. P. Taylor Trust
Tegham Limited
Thomson Reuters Foundation
The Tobacco Pipe Makers and Tobacco Trade Benevolent Fund
Tottenham Grammar School Foundation
The Tower Hill Trust
Tuixen Foundation
Uxbridge United Welfare Trust
The Vintners' Foundation
The Wakefield and Tetley Trust
The Wates Foundation
The W. Wing Yip and Brothers Foundation

■ **Barking and Dagenham**
Ford Britain Trust

■ **Barnet**
The Bintaub Charitable Trust
The Consuelo and Anthony Brooke Charitable Trust
Elshore Ltd
Finnart House School Trust
Edward Harvist Trust
Highcroft Charitable Trust
Jewish Child's Day
John Lyon's Charity
Eleanor Palmer Trust
Tegham Limited

■ **Bexley**
Ford Britain Trust
The Alfred And Peggy Harvey Charitable Trust

■ **Brent**
Edward Harvist Trust
The Huntingdon Foundation Limited
The Kingsbury Charity
John Lyon's Charity
The W. Wing Yip and Brothers Foundation

■ **Bromley**
The Alfred And Peggy Harvey Charitable Trust

■ **Camden**
The Bloom Foundation
British Council for Prevention of Blindness (Save Eyes Everywhere)
The Consuelo and Anthony Brooke Charitable Trust
Sir John Cass's Foundation
The Grahame Charitable Foundation Limited
The Hampstead Wells and Campden Trust
Edward Harvist Trust
The Huntingdon Foundation Limited
The J. A. R. Charitable Trust
The Lowy Mitchell Foundation
John Lyon's Charity
Richard Reeve's Foundation

■ **City of London**
Aldgate and All Hallows' Foundation
Alliance Trust Staff Foundation
Sir John Cass's Foundation
The Dentons UKMEA LLP Charitable Trust
East End Community Foundation
The B. and P. Glasser Charitable Trust
The Hiscox Foundation
The Sir Joseph Hotung Charitable Settlement
John Lyon's Charity
The Modiano Charitable Trust
The Worshipful Company of Needlemakers' Charitable Fund
Richard Reeve's Foundation
The Simmons & Simmons Charitable Foundation
Thomson Reuters Foundation
The Tobacco Pipe Makers and Tobacco Trade Benevolent Fund
Tuixen Foundation
The Wakefield and Tetley Trust

■ **City of Westminster**
The Nicholas Boas Charitable Trust
The Consuelo and Anthony Brooke Charitable Trust
Sir John Cass's Foundation
The R. and S. Cohen Foundation
Dischma Charitable Trust
Edinburgh Trust No 2 Account

The Graff Foundation
The M. and R. Gross Charities Limited
Edward Harvist Trust
The Health Foundation
The Simon Heller Charitable Settlement
The Hollick Family Charitable Trust
The P. Y. N. and B. Hyams Trust
The J. J. Charitable Trust
The Jerusalem Trust
The Stanley Kalms Foundation
The Boris Karloff Charitable Foundation
The Ruth and Stuart Lipton Charitable Trust
John Lyon's Charity
Nemoral Ltd
The Basil Samuel Charitable Trust
ShareGift (The Orr Mackintosh Foundation)

■ **Croydon**
The Croydon Relief in Need Charities
The W. Wing Yip and Brothers Foundation

■ **Ealing**
John Lyon's Charity

■ **Enfield**
The Greggs Foundation

■ **Greenwich**
Sir John Cass's Foundation
Sir John Evelyn's Charity
Ford Britain Trust
The Alfred And Peggy Harvey Charitable Trust

■ **Hackney**
Sir John Cass's Foundation
East End Community Foundation
Friends of Wiznitz Limited
The Gur Trust
The Hackney Parochial Charities
The Harbour Foundation
The Hornsey Parochial Charities
Hurdale Charity Limited
The Lolev Charitable Trust
MYA Charitable Trust

## ■ Hammersmith and Fulham
Sir John Cass's Foundation
Dr Edwards Bishop King's Fulham Endowment Fund
John Lyon's Charity

## ■ Haringey
The Hornsey Parochial Charities
Tottenham Grammar School Foundation

## ■ Harrow
Amabrill Limited
The Samuel Gardner Memorial Trust
Edward Harvist Trust
John Lyon's Charity

## ■ Havering
Ford Britain Trust

## ■ Hillingdon
The Fassnidge Memorial Trust
The Hillingdon Community Trust
The Hillingdon Partnership Trust
A. P. Taylor Trust
Uxbridge United Welfare Trust

## ■ Islington
Sir John Cass's Foundation
Richard Cloudesley's Charity
Cripplegate Foundation
Richard Reeve's Foundation

## ■ Kensington and Chelsea
ABF The Soldiers' Charity
The Consuelo and Anthony Brooke Charitable Trust
The Campden Charities Trustee
Sir John Cass's Foundation
Grand Charitable Trust of the Order of Women Freemasons
John Lyon's Charity

## ■ Lambeth
Sir John Cass's Foundation
Sir Walter St John's Educational Charity

## ■ Lewisham
Sir John Cass's Foundation
Sir John Evelyn's Charity

The Alfred And Peggy Harvey Charitable Trust

## ■ Merton
The Vernon N. Ely Charitable Trust

## ■ Newham
AstonMansfield Charitable Trust
Sir John Cass's Foundation
East End Community Foundation
Ford Britain Trust
Morgan Stanley International Foundation
Royal Docks Trust (London)

## ■ Redbridge
Ford Britain Trust

## ■ Richmond upon Thames
Barnes Workhouse Fund
The Greggs Foundation
Hampton Fuel Allotment
The Richmond Parish Lands Charity

## ■ Southwark
The Sir Victor Blank Charitable Settlement
Sir John Cass's Foundation
The Alfred And Peggy Harvey Charitable Trust
The ITF Seafarers Trust
The Newcomen Collett Foundation
The Wakefield and Tetley Trust

## ■ Sutton
Firtree Trust

## ■ Tower Hamlets
Aldgate and All Hallows' Foundation
Sir John Cass's Foundation
East End Community Foundation
Morgan Stanley International Foundation
The Simmons & Simmons Charitable Foundation
The Tower Hill Trust
The Wakefield and Tetley Trust

## ■ Wandsworth
Sir John Cass's Foundation
Sir Walter St John's Educational Charity

## ■ South Eastern England
The Ammco Trust
The Argus Appeal
The Ascot Fire Brigade Trust
The Banbury Charities
The Bellinger Donnay Trust
Bergqvist Charitable Trust
The Berkshire Community Foundation
Isabel Blackman Foundation
The Blagrave Trust
The Bordon Liphook Haslemere Charity
The Frank Brake Charitable Trust
The Brighton District Nursing Association Trust
The Consuelo and Anthony Brooke Charitable Trust
Buckinghamshire Community Foundation
The Buckinghamshire Historic Churches Trust
The Buckinghamshire Masonic Centenary Fund
Chaucer Foundation
The Coalfields Regeneration Trust
The Cobtree Charity Trust Ltd
The Cole Charitable Trust
The Colefax Charitable Trust
John and Freda Coleman Charitable Trust
Colyer-Fergusson Charitable Trust
The Dibden Allotments Fund
The Derek and Eileen Dodgson Foundation
The Dulverton Trust
The Earley Charity
The Gilbert and Eileen Edgar Foundation
The Gerald Palmer Eling Trust Company
The Ellis Campbell Foundation
The Essex Fairway Charitable Trust
Ford Britain Trust
The Friends of Kent Churches
Gatwick Airport Community Trust
The GNC Trust
The Godinton Charitable Trust
The Great Stone Bridge Trust of Edenbridge
The Bishop of Guildford's Foundation
The Walter Guinness Charitable Trust

E. F. and M. G. Hall Charitable Trust
The Hampshire and Islands Historic Churches Trust
Hampshire and Isle of Wight Community Foundation
William Harding's Charity
The Peter Harrison Foundation
The Alfred And Peggy Harvey Charitable Trust
The Dorothy Hay-Bolton Charitable Trust
Henley Educational Trust
R. G. Hills Charitable Trust
Stuart Hine Trust
The Hollands-Warren Fund
The Antony Hornby Charitable Trust
Hyde Charitable Trust (Youth Plus)
The Iliffe Family Charitable Trust
The Johnson Wax Ltd Charitable Trust
Kent Community Foundation
The Leach Fourteenth Trust
The Erica Leonard Trust
LHR Airport Communities Trust
London Legal Support Trust
The Magdalen and Lasher Charity (General Fund)
The Gerald Micklem Charitable Trust
The Masonic Province of Middlesex Charitable Trust
Milton Keynes Community Foundation Limited
Mobbs Memorial Trust Ltd
City of Oxford Charity
Oxfordshire Community Foundation
The David Pickford Charitable Foundation
The William Price Charitable Trust
Red Hill Charitable Trust
The Rochester Bridge Trust
The Rothermere Foundation
The Rugby Group Benevolent Fund Limited
The Sants Charitable Trust
The SDL Foundation
The R. C. Sherriff Rosebriars Trust
The Mrs Smith and Mount Trust
The Southover Manor General Education Trust
The Spoore, Merry and Rixman Foundation
The St Laurence Relief In Need Trust
St Michael's and All Saints' Charities Relief Branch
Community Foundation for Surrey

The Sussex Community Foundation
The Sussex Historic Churches Trust
The Tanner Trust
The Taylor Family Foundation
The Wates Foundation
The William Barrow's Charity
The F. Glenister Woodger Trust

■ **Berkshire**

The Ascot Fire Brigade Trust
Bergqvist Charitable Trust
The Berkshire Community Foundation
The Colefax Charitable Trust
The Earley Charity
The Gilbert and Eileen Edgar Foundation
The Gerald Palmer Eling Trust Company
Henley Educational Trust
The Iliffe Family Charitable Trust
The Johnson Wax Ltd Charitable Trust
The SDL Foundation
The Spoore, Merry and Rixman Foundation
The St Laurence Relief In Need Trust
The Wates Foundation

■ **Buckinghamshire**

Bergqvist Charitable Trust
Buckinghamshire Community Foundation
The Buckinghamshire Historic Churches Trust
The Buckinghamshire Masonic Centenary Fund
William Harding's Charity
Hyde Charitable Trust (Youth Plus)
London Legal Support Trust
Milton Keynes Community Foundation Limited
Mobbs Memorial Trust Ltd
The Wates Foundation

■ **East Sussex**

The Argus Appeal
Isabel Blackman Foundation
The Brighton District Nursing Association Trust
The Consuelo and Anthony Brooke Charitable Trust
The Derek and Eileen Dodgson Foundation
Gatwick Airport Community Trust
Stuart Hine Trust

Hyde Charitable Trust (Youth Plus)
The Magdalen and Lasher Charity (General Fund)
The Rugby Group Benevolent Fund Limited
The Southover Manor General Education Trust
The Sussex Community Foundation
The Sussex Historic Churches Trust
The Wates Foundation

■ **Hampshire**

The Bordon Liphook Haslemere Charity
The Colefax Charitable Trust
John and Freda Coleman Charitable Trust
The Dibden Allotments Fund
The Ellis Campbell Foundation
Ford Britain Trust
The Walter Guinness Charitable Trust
The Hampshire and Islands Historic Churches Trust
Hampshire and Isle of Wight Community Foundation
Hyde Charitable Trust (Youth Plus)
The Johnson Wax Ltd Charitable Trust
LHR Airport Communities Trust
The Gerald Micklem Charitable Trust
The William Price Charitable Trust

■ **Isle of Wight**

Hampshire and Isle of Wight Community Foundation

■ **Kent**

The Frank Brake Charitable Trust
Chaucer Foundation
The Coalfields Regeneration Trust
The Cobtree Charity Trust Ltd
The Cole Charitable Trust
Colyer-Fergusson Charitable Trust
The Friends of Kent Churches
Gatwick Airport Community Trust
The Godinton Charitable Trust
The Great Stone Bridge Trust of Edenbridge
The Alfred And Peggy Harvey Charitable Trust
R. G. Hills Charitable Trust
The Hollands-Warren Fund

Hyde Charitable Trust (Youth Plus)
Kent Community Foundation
London Legal Support Trust
The David Pickford Charitable Foundation
The Rochester Bridge Trust
The Rothermere Foundation
The Rugby Group Benevolent Fund Limited
The William Barrow's Charity

■ **Oxfordshire**

The Banbury Charities
Bergqvist Charitable Trust
Henley Educational Trust
Hyde Charitable Trust (Youth Plus)
City of Oxford Charity
Oxfordshire Community Foundation
The Rugby Group Benevolent Fund Limited
The Sants Charitable Trust
St Michael's and All Saints' Charities Relief Branch
The Wates Foundation

■ **Surrey**

John and Freda Coleman Charitable Trust
Gatwick Airport Community Trust
The Bishop of Guildford's Foundation
The Alfred And Peggy Harvey Charitable Trust
Hyde Charitable Trust (Youth Plus)
The Erica Leonard Trust
London Legal Support Trust
The Masonic Province of Middlesex Charitable Trust
The R. C. Sherriff Rosebriars Trust
Community Foundation for Surrey
The Wates Foundation

■ **West Sussex**

The Argus Appeal
The Consuelo and Anthony Brooke Charitable Trust
The Derek and Eileen Dodgson Foundation
Gatwick Airport Community Trust
Hyde Charitable Trust (Youth Plus)
LHR Airport Communities Trust
The Southover Manor General Education Trust

The Sussex Community Foundation
The Sussex Historic Churches Trust
The Wates Foundation
The F. Glenister Woodger Trust

..........................................

■ **South Western England**

The H. B. Allen Charitable Trust
Almondsbury Charity
Viscount Amory's Charitable Trust
The Avon and Somerset Police Community Trust
The Albert Casanova Ballard Deceased Trust
The Barnstaple Bridge Trust
The Barnwood House Trust
The Battens Charitable Trust
The Bellinger Donnay Trust
The Bideford Bridge Trust
The Blagrave Trust
The Blanchminster Trust
Bristol Archdeaconry Charity
The Bristol Charities
The J. and M. Britton Charitable Trust
The Chippenham Borough Lands Charity
The Chipping Sodbury Town Lands Charity
The Hilda and Alice Clark Charitable Trust
Community First (Landfill Communities Fund)
Cornwall Community Foundation
The Denman Charitable Trust
Devon Community Foundation
The Devon Historic Churches Trust
Dorset Community Foundation
The Dorset Historic Churches Trust
Duchy Health Charity Limited
The Dulverton Trust
The Elmgrant Trust
The Joyce Fletcher Charitable Trust
The Fulmer Charitable Trust
The Garnett Charitable Trust
The David Gibbons Foundation
Gloucestershire Community Foundation
The Gloucestershire Historic Churches Trust
The GNC Trust
The Gordon Gray Trust
The Great Torrington Town Lands Charity
The Walter Guinness Charitable Trust
The Peter Harrison Foundation

The Heathcoat Trust
The Charles Irving Charitable Trust
John James Bristol Foundation
The Michael and Ilse Katz Foundation
The Jack Lane Charitable Trust
The Langtree Trust
The Leach Fourteenth Trust
Sylvanus Lysons Charity
The Merchant Venturers' Charity
The Clare Milne Trust
The Norman Family Charitable Trust
The Notgrove Trust
The Portishead Nautical Trust
Quartet Community Foundation
Somerset Churches Trust
The Ralph and Irma Sperring Charity
The Spielman Charitable Trust
St Luke's College Foundation
St Monica Trust
The Talbot Village Trust
The Tanner Trust
The Valentine Charitable Trust
The Wates Foundation
The Charity of William Williams
The Dame Violet Wills Will Trust
The Community Foundation for Wiltshire and Swindon

■ **Avon**

Almondsbury Charity
The Avon and Somerset Police Community Trust
Bristol Archdeaconry Charity
The Bristol Charities
The J. and M. Britton Charitable Trust
The Chipping Sodbury Town Lands Charity
The Denman Charitable Trust
John James Bristol Foundation
The Merchant Venturers' Charity
The Portishead Nautical Trust
Quartet Community Foundation
The Ralph and Irma Sperring Charity
The Spielman Charitable Trust
The Wates Foundation
The Dame Violet Wills Will Trust

■ **Cornwall and the Scilly Isles**

The Blanchminster Trust
Cornwall Community Foundation
Duchy Health Charity Limited
The Heathcoat Trust

The Michael and Ilse Katz
   Foundation
The Clare Milne Trust

■ **Devon**

The H. B. Allen Charitable
   Trust
Viscount Amory's Charitable
   Trust
The Albert Casanova Ballard
   Deceased Trust
The Barnstaple Bridge Trust
The Bideford Bridge Trust
Devon Community Foundation
The Devon Historic Churches
   Trust
The David Gibbons Foundation
The Great Torrington Town
   Lands Charity
The Heathcoat Trust
The Clare Milne Trust
St Luke's College Foundation
The Dame Violet Wills Will
   Trust

■ **Dorset**

The Battens Charitable Trust
Dorset Community Foundation
The Dorset Historic Churches
   Trust
The Talbot Village Trust
The Valentine Charitable Trust
The Wates Foundation
The Charity of William Williams

■ **Gloucestershire**

The Barnwood House Trust
Gloucestershire Community
   Foundation
The Gloucestershire Historic
   Churches Trust
The Gordon Gray Trust
The Charles Irving Charitable
   Trust
The Jack Lane Charitable Trust
The Langtree Trust
Sylvanus Lysons Charity
The Notgrove Trust
Quartet Community Foundation
St Monica Trust
The Wates Foundation

■ **Somerset**

The Avon and Somerset Police
   Community Trust
The Battens Charitable Trust
The Hilda and Alice Clark
   Charitable Trust
Quartet Community Foundation
Somerset Churches Trust
St Monica Trust
The Wates Foundation

■ **Wiltshire**

The Battens Charitable Trust
The Bellinger Donnay Trust
The Blagrave Trust
The Chippenham Borough
   Lands Charity
Community First (Landfill
   Communities Fund)
The Fulmer Charitable Trust
The Walter Guinness
   Charitable Trust
The Jack Lane Charitable Trust
St Monica Trust
The Community Foundation for
   Wiltshire and Swindon

..........................................

■ **West Midlands
   region**

The Lord Austin Trust
The John Avins Trust
The Aylesford Family
   Charitable Trust
The James Beattie Charitable
   Trust
The Birmingham District
   Nursing Charitable Trust
Birmingham International
   Airport Community Trust
The Michael Bishop
   Foundation
The Bransford Trust
The Charles Brotherton Trust
The E. F. Bulmer Benevolent
   Fund
The Burton Breweries
   Charitable Trust
Consolidated Charity of Burton
   upon Trent
The William A. Cadbury
   Charitable Trust
Christadelphian Samaritan
   Fund
The Clarke Charitable
   Settlement
The Coalfields Regeneration
   Trust
The Cole Charitable Trust
The George Henry Collins
   Charity
General Charity of Coventry
Coventry Building Society
   Charitable Foundation
Baron Davenport's Charity
The Digbeth Trust Limited
The Dulverton Trust
The Dumbreck Charity
The W. E. Dunn Trust
The Wilfred and Elsie Elkes
   Charity Fund
The Elmley Foundation
The Eveson Charitable Trust
The John Feeney Charitable
   Bequest
The George Fentham
   Birmingham Charity

Field Family Charitable Trust
The Lady Forester Trust
The GNC Trust
Grantham Yorke Trust
The Greggs Foundation
The Grimmitt Trust
The Alfred Haines Charitable
   Trust
The Harborne Parish Lands
   Charity
The Peter Harrison Foundation
Heart of England Community
   Foundation
Herefordshire Community
   Foundation
The Herefordshire Historic
   Churches Trust
The Alan Edward Higgs Charity
Hopmarket Charity
The Huntingdon Foundation
   Limited
The Jarman Charitable Trust
The King Henry VIII Endowed
   Trust – Warwick
The London Marathon
   Charitable Trust Limited
The Michael Marsh Charitable
   Trust
John Martin's Charity
Open Gate
The Payne Charitable Trust
The Harry Payne Fund
The Pedmore Sporting Club
   Trust Fund
People's Postcode Trust
The Bernard Piggott Charitable
   Trust
The Roughley Charitable Trust
The Rugby Group Benevolent
   Fund Limited
SF Group Charitable Fund for
   Disabled People
The Sheldon Trust
St Peter's Saltley Trust
Stratford upon Avon Town
   Trust
Sutton Coldfield Charitable
   Trust
C. B. and H. H. Taylor 1984
   Trust
The Connie and Albert Taylor
   Charitable Trust
The C. Paul Thackray General
   Charitable Trust
The G. J. W. Turner Trust
The Walker Trust
The Wilmcote Charitrust
Worcester Municipal Charities
The Worcestershire and
   Dudley Historic Churches
   Trust
The Yardley Great Trust
The W. Wing Yip and Brothers
   Foundation

**33**

## Herefordshire

The Elmley Foundation
The Eveson Charitable Trust
Herefordshire Community Foundation
The Herefordshire Historic Churches Trust
The Huntingdon Foundation Limited
St Peter's Saltley Trust
The C. Paul Thackray General Charitable Trust

## Shropshire

Baron Davenport's Charity
The Lady Forester Trust
The C. Paul Thackray General Charitable Trust
The Walker Trust

## Staffordshire

The Burton Breweries Charitable Trust
Consolidated Charity of Burton upon Trent
The Clarke Charitable Settlement
Baron Davenport's Charity
The Wilfred and Elsie Elkes Charity Fund
The Alfred Haines Charitable Trust
The Michael Marsh Charitable Trust
Open Gate
St Peter's Saltley Trust

## Warwickshire

The Aylesford Family Charitable Trust
Birmingham International Airport Community Trust
Baron Davenport's Charity
The Dumbreck Charity
Field Family Charitable Trust
The Alfred Haines Charitable Trust
Heart of England Community Foundation
The Alan Edward Higgs Charity
The King Henry VIII Endowed Trust – Warwick
The Michael Marsh Charitable Trust
The Harry Payne Fund
The Rugby Group Benevolent Fund Limited
Stratford upon Avon Town Trust

## West Midlands

The Lord Austin Trust
The John Avins Trust
The Aylesford Family Charitable Trust
The James Beattie Charitable Trust
The Birmingham District Nursing Charitable Trust
Birmingham International Airport Community Trust
The Charles Brotherton Trust
The William A. Cadbury Charitable Trust
Christadelphian Samaritan Fund
The Cole Charitable Trust
The George Henry Collins Charity
General Charity of Coventry
Baron Davenport's Charity
The Digbeth Trust Limited
The Dumbreck Charity
The Eveson Charitable Trust
The John Feeney Charitable Bequest
The George Fentham Birmingham Charity
Field Family Charitable Trust
Grantham Yorke Trust
The Greggs Foundation
The Grimmitt Trust
The Alfred Haines Charitable Trust
The Harborne Parish Lands Charity
Heart of England Community Foundation
The Alan Edward Higgs Charity
The Jarman Charitable Trust
The London Marathon Charitable Trust Limited
The Michael Marsh Charitable Trust
Open Gate
The Payne Charitable Trust
The Harry Payne Fund
The Bernard Piggott Charitable Trust
The Roughley Charitable Trust
The Sheldon Trust
St Peter's Saltley Trust
Sutton Coldfield Charitable Trust
C. B. and H. H. Taylor 1984 Trust
The W. Wing Yip and Brothers Foundation

## Worcestershire

Baron Davenport's Charity
The Dumbreck Charity
The Elmley Foundation
The Eveson Charitable Trust
Hopmarket Charity
The Michael Marsh Charitable Trust
John Martin's Charity
The Harry Payne Fund
St Peter's Saltley Trust
The C. Paul Thackray General Charitable Trust
Worcester Municipal Charities
The Worcestershire and Dudley Historic Churches Trust

## East Midlands

The Bates Charitable Trust
The Beckett's and Sargeant's Educational Foundation
The Bergne-Coupland Charity
Bergqvist Charitable Trust
The Bingham Trust
The Michael Bishop Foundation
Boots Charitable Trust
The Burghley Family Trust
The Burton Breweries Charitable Trust
The Frederick and Phyllis Cann Trust
Carter's Educational Foundation
Chaucer Foundation
The Clarke Charitable Settlement
The Coalfields Regeneration Trust
The Compton Charitable Trust
The Douglas Compton James Charitable Trust
The Helen Jean Cope Trust
The J. Reginald Corah Foundation Fund
Coventry Building Society Charitable Foundation
The Derbyshire Churches and Chapels Preservation Trust
Derbyshire Community Foundation
The J. N. Derbyshire Trust
The Dulverton Trust
The W. E. Dunn Trust
The Maud Elkington Charitable Trust
The Everard Foundation
The Fifty Fund
Ford Britain Trust
The GNC Trust
The Gray Trust
The Peter Harrison Foundation
The Hartley Charitable Trust
Hyde Charitable Trust (Youth Plus)
Leicester and Leicestershire Historic Churches Preservation Trust

34

Leicestershire, Leicester and
  Rutland Community
  Foundation
Lincolnshire Churches Trust
Lincolnshire Community
  Foundation
The London Marathon
  Charitable Trust Limited
Market Harborough and The
  Bowdens Charity
The New Appeals Organisation
  for the City and County of
  Nottingham
Alderman Newton's
  Educational Foundation
The Northampton Municipal
  Church Charities
Northamptonshire Community
  Foundation
The Nottingham General
  Dispensary
Nottinghamshire Community
  Foundation
The Nottinghamshire Historic
  Churches Trust
Open Gate
The Paget Charitable Trust
The Jack Patston Charitable
  Trust
People's Postcode Trust
The Mary Potter Convent
  Hospital Trust
The Puri Foundation
The Rugby Group Benevolent
  Fund Limited
The Samworth Foundation
SF Group Charitable Fund for
  Disabled People
The Shoe Zone Trust
The Mary Elizabeth Siebel
  Charity
Toyota Manufacturing UK
  Charitable Trust
The G. J. W. Turner Trust
The Wates Foundation
The Wilmcote Charitrust
David Wilson Foundation
The Wilson Foundation

### ■ Derbyshire

The Clarke Charitable
  Settlement
The Helen Jean Cope Trust
The Derbyshire Churches and
  Chapels Preservation Trust
Derbyshire Community
  Foundation
Open Gate
The Samworth Foundation
SF Group Charitable Fund for
  Disabled People
Toyota Manufacturing UK
  Charitable Trust

### ■ Leicestershire

The Burghley Family Trust
The Burton Breweries
  Charitable Trust
The Helen Jean Cope Trust
The J. Reginald Corah
  Foundation Fund
The Maud Elkington Charitable
  Trust
The Everard Foundation
Leicester and Leicestershire
  Historic Churches
  Preservation Trust
Leicestershire, Leicester and
  Rutland Community
  Foundation
Market Harborough and The
  Bowdens Charity
Alderman Newton's
  Educational Foundation
Open Gate
The Paget Charitable Trust
The Jack Patston Charitable
  Trust
The Samworth Foundation
SF Group Charitable Fund for
  Disabled People
The Shoe Zone Trust
David Wilson Foundation

### ■ Lincolnshire

The Bergne-Coupland Charity
The Burghley Family Trust
Hyde Charitable Trust (Youth
  Plus)
Lincolnshire Churches Trust
Lincolnshire Community
  Foundation
The Rugby Group Benevolent
  Fund Limited

### ■ Northamptonshire

The Beckett's and Sargeant's
  Educational Foundation
Bergqvist Charitable Trust
The Burghley Family Trust
The Frederick and Phyllis Cann
  Trust
The Compton Charitable Trust
The Douglas Compton James
  Charitable Trust
The Maud Elkington Charitable
  Trust
Ford Britain Trust
The London Marathon
  Charitable Trust Limited
The Northampton Municipal
  Church Charities
Northamptonshire Community
  Foundation
The Wilson Foundation

### ■ Nottinghamshire

Boots Charitable Trust
Carter's Educational
  Foundation
Chaucer Foundation
The Helen Jean Cope Trust
The J. N. Derbyshire Trust
The Fifty Fund
The Gray Trust
The Hartley Charitable Trust
The New Appeals Organisation
  for the City and County of
  Nottingham
The Nottingham General
  Dispensary
Nottinghamshire Community
  Foundation
The Nottinghamshire Historic
  Churches Trust
Open Gate
The Mary Potter Convent
  Hospital Trust
The Puri Foundation
The Samworth Foundation
SF Group Charitable Fund for
  Disabled People
The Mary Elizabeth Siebel
  Charity
The Wates Foundation

### ■ Eastern England

The Adnams Charity
Anguish's Educational
  Foundation
The Beccles Town Lands
  Charity
The Bedfordshire and
  Hertfordshire Historic
  Churches Trust
The Bedfordshire and Luton
  Community Foundation
The Provincial Grand Lodge of
  Bedfordshire Charity Fund
Bergqvist Charitable Trust
The Burghley Family Trust
The Cambridgeshire
  Community Foundation
The Cambridgeshire Historic
  Churches Trust
The Christabella Charitable
  Trust
The Colchester Catalyst
  Charity
The Cole Charitable Trust
The Harry Cureton Charitable
  Trust
D. J. H. Currie Memorial Trust
The Dulverton Trust
Earls Colne and Halstead
  Educational Charity
The Ebenezer Trust
Educational Foundation of
  Alderman John Norman
The Essex and Southend
  Sports Trust

**35**

Essex Community Foundation
The Essex Heritage Trust
The Essex Youth Trust
The Farthing Trust
Ford Britain Trust
The Charles S. French
    Charitable Trust
The Anne French Memorial
    Trust
The Ganzoni Charitable Trust
The GNC Trust
The Grange Farm Centre Trust
The Harpur Trust
The Peter Harrison Foundation
The Hertfordshire Community
    Foundation
Hitchin Educational Foundation
House of Industry Estate
The Hudson Foundation
The Huntingdon Foundation
    Limited
Huntingdon Freemen's Trust
Hyde Charitable Trust (Youth
    Plus)
Kirkley Poor's Land Estate
LHR Airport Communities Trust
London Legal Support Trust
The Masonic Province of
    Middlesex Charitable Trust
The Mills Charity
The Music Sales Charitable
    Trust
The Neighbourly Charitable
    Trust
Norfolk Community Foundation
The Norwich Town Close
    Estate Charity
The Jack Patston Charitable
    Trust
The Jack Petchey Foundation
The Mr and Mrs Philip
    Rackham Charitable Trust
Red Hill Charitable Trust
The Rosca Trust
The Rugby Group Benevolent
    Fund Limited
The R. C. Snelling Charitable
    Trust
The Strangward Trust
Suffolk Community Foundation
The Suffolk Historic Churches
    Trust

■ **Bedfordshire**

The Bedfordshire and
    Hertfordshire Historic
    Churches Trust
The Bedfordshire and Luton
    Community Foundation
The Provincial Grand Lodge of
    Bedfordshire Charity Fund
Bergqvist Charitable Trust
The Harpur Trust
Hitchin Educational Foundation
House of Industry Estate

The Neighbourly Charitable
    Trust
The Rugby Group Benevolent
    Fund Limited

■ **Cambridgeshire**

The Burghley Family Trust
The Cambridgeshire
    Community Foundation
The Cambridgeshire Historic
    Churches Trust
The Cole Charitable Trust
The Harry Cureton Charitable
    Trust
The Farthing Trust
The Hudson Foundation
Huntingdon Freemen's Trust
The Jack Patston Charitable
    Trust
The Rugby Group Benevolent
    Fund Limited

■ **Essex**

The Christabella Charitable
    Trust
The Colchester Catalyst
    Charity
D. J. H. Currie Memorial Trust
Earls Colne and Halstead
    Educational Charity
The Ebenezer Trust
The Essex and Southend
    Sports Trust
Essex Community Foundation
The Essex Heritage Trust
The Essex Youth Trust
Ford Britain Trust
The Charles S. French
    Charitable Trust
The Grange Farm Centre Trust
The Huntingdon Foundation
    Limited
Hyde Charitable Trust (Youth
    Plus)
LHR Airport Communities Trust
London Legal Support Trust
The Jack Petchey Foundation
The Rosca Trust
The Rugby Group Benevolent
    Fund Limited

■ **Hertfordshire**

The Bedfordshire and
    Hertfordshire Historic
    Churches Trust
Bergqvist Charitable Trust
The Hertfordshire Community
    Foundation
Hitchin Educational Foundation
London Legal Support Trust
The Masonic Province of
    Middlesex Charitable Trust

■ **Norfolk**

The Adnams Charity
Anguish's Educational
    Foundation
Educational Foundation of
    Alderman John Norman
The Anne French Memorial
    Trust
Hyde Charitable Trust (Youth
    Plus)
Norfolk Community Foundation
The Norwich Town Close
    Estate Charity
The Mr and Mrs Philip
    Rackham Charitable Trust
The R. C. Snelling Charitable
    Trust

■ **Suffolk**

The Adnams Charity
The Beccles Town Lands
    Charity
The Anne French Memorial
    Trust
The Ganzoni Charitable Trust
Kirkley Poor's Land Estate
The Mills Charity
The Music Sales Charitable
    Trust
Suffolk Community Foundation
The Suffolk Historic Churches
    Trust

■ **North West**

A. W. Charitable Trust
The Addleshaw Goddard
    Charitable Trust
BCH Trust
The Mason Bibby 1981 Trust
The Booth Charities
The Bowland Charitable Trust
The Harold and Alice Bridges
    Charity
The Charles Brotherton Trust
The Camelia Trust
Cheshire Freemason's Charity
The Coalfields Regeneration
    Trust
The Congleton Inclosure Trust
Cumbria Community
    Foundation
The Hamilton Davies Trust
The Dulverton Trust
The Eventhall Family
    Charitable Trust
Forever Manchester (The
    Community Foundation for
    Greater Manchester)
The Fort Foundation
The Galbraith Trust
The GNC Trust
A. B. Grace Trust
The Granada Foundation
The Greggs Foundation

The Hadfield Trust
The Harris Charity
The Peter Harrison Foundation
The M. A. Hawe Settlement
The Helping Foundation
The Hemby Charitable Trust
The Edward Holt Trust
Hulme Trust Estates
The Johnson Foundation
The J. E. Joseph Charitable Fund
Kelsick's Educational Foundation
The Peter Kershaw Trust
The Ursula Keyes Trust
Community Foundation for Lancashire (Former)
Community Foundations for Lancashire and Merseyside
Duchy of Lancaster Benevolent Fund
The Herd Lawson and Muriel Lawson Charitable Trust
Liverpool Charity and Voluntary Services
Manchester Airport Community Trust Fund
The Manchester Guardian Society Charitable Trust
Lord Mayor of Manchester's Charity Appeal Trust
The Ann and David Marks Foundation
The Mersey Docks and Harbour Company Charitable Fund
John Moores Foundation
The Morgan Foundation
North West Cancer Research
The Northern Rock Foundation
Oglesby Charitable Trust
The Payne Charitable Trust
People's Postcode Trust
The Pilkington Charities Fund
The Sir Harry Pilkington Trust Fund
The Ravensdale Trust
The Francis C. Scott Charitable Trust
The Frieda Scott Charitable Trust
The Sir James and Lady Scott Trust
SHINE (Support and Help in Education)
The J. A. Shone Memorial Trust
The Skelton Bounty
The Edward Stocks-Massey Bequest Fund
The Daniel Thwaites Charitable Trust
United Utilities Trust Fund
The West Derby Wastelands Charity
The Norman Whiteley Trust

The W. Wing Yip and Brothers Foundation
The Yorkshire Dales Millennium Trust
The Zochonis Charitable Trust

■ **Cheshire**

Cheshire Freemason's Charity
The Congleton Inclosure Trust
The Hamilton Davies Trust
The Ursula Keyes Trust
John Moores Foundation

■ **Cumbria**

The Harold and Alice Bridges Charity
Cumbria Community Foundation
The Hadfield Trust
Kelsick's Educational Foundation
The Herd Lawson and Muriel Lawson Charitable Trust
The Northern Rock Foundation
The Payne Charitable Trust
The Francis C. Scott Charitable Trust
The Frieda Scott Charitable Trust
The Norman Whiteley Trust
The Yorkshire Dales Millennium Trust

■ **Greater Manchester**

A. W. Charitable Trust
The Addleshaw Goddard Charitable Trust
BCH Trust
The Booth Charities
The Camelia Trust
Cheshire Freemason's Charity
The Hamilton Davies Trust
Forever Manchester (The Community Foundation for Greater Manchester)
The Greggs Foundation
The Helping Foundation
The Edward Holt Trust
Hulme Trust Estates (Educational)
The J. E. Joseph Charitable Fund
The Peter Kershaw Trust
Duchy of Lancaster Benevolent Fund
Manchester Airport Community Trust Fund
The Manchester Guardian Society Charitable Trust
Lord Mayor of Manchester's Charity Appeal Trust
The Ann and David Marks Foundation

The Sir James and Lady Scott Trust
SHINE (Support and Help in Education)
The Skelton Bounty
The W. Wing Yip and Brothers Foundation
The Zochonis Charitable Trust

■ **Lancashire**

The Harold and Alice Bridges Charity
The Fort Foundation
The Galbraith Trust
A. B. Grace Trust
The Harris Charity
The M. A. Hawe Settlement
Community Foundation for Lancashire (Former)
Community Foundations for Lancashire and Merseyside
Duchy of Lancaster Benevolent Fund
John Moores Foundation
The Francis C. Scott Charitable Trust
The Skelton Bounty
The Edward Stocks-Massey Bequest Fund
The Daniel Thwaites Charitable Trust
The Yorkshire Dales Millennium Trust

■ **Merseyside**

The Mason Bibby 1981 Trust
The Charles Brotherton Trust
The Camelia Trust
Cheshire Freemason's Charity
The Hemby Charitable Trust
The Johnson Foundation
Community Foundation for Lancashire (Former)
Community Foundations for Lancashire and Merseyside
Duchy of Lancaster Benevolent Fund
Liverpool Charity and Voluntary Services
The Mersey Docks and Harbour Company Charitable Fund
John Moores Foundation
The Pilkington Charities Fund
The Sir Harry Pilkington Trust Fund
The Ravensdale Trust
The J. A. Shone Memorial Trust
The Skelton Bounty
The West Derby Wastelands Charity

37

## Yorkshire and the Humber

The Addleshaw Goddard Charitable Trust
The Bearder Charity
The Benfield Motors Charitable Trust
The Bergne-Coupland Charity
The Bramhope Trust
The Charles Brotherton Trust
The Jack Brunton Charitable Trust
Community Foundation for Calderdale
The Joseph and Annie Cattle Trust
John William Chapman's Charitable Trust
The Church Burgesses Educational Foundation
Church Burgesses Trust
The Coalfields Regeneration Trust
Community Foundation for Leeds
The Marjorie Coote Animal Charity Trust
The Marjorie Coote Old People's Charity
The Dulverton Trust
The A. M. Fenton Trust
The Freshgate Trust Foundation
The GNC Trust
The Green Hall Foundation
The Peter Harrison Foundation
The Hartley Charitable Trust
Help for Health
The Hesslewood Children's Trust (Hull Seamen's and General Orphanage)
The Hull and East Riding Charitable Trust
Duchy of Lancaster Benevolent Fund
The Lord Mayor of Leeds Appeal Fund
The James Neill Trust Fund
Open Gate
People's Postcode Trust
Sir John Priestman Charity Trust
The J. S. and E. C. Rymer Charitable Trust
The SDL Foundation
The Shears Foundation
The Sylvia and Colin Shepherd Charitable Trust
The Talbot Trusts
Two Ridings Community Foundation
Wade's Charity
The Scurrah Wainwright Charity
The South Yorkshire Community Foundation

The Yorkshire Dales Millennium Trust
The Yorkshire Historic Churches Trust

## Humberside, East Riding

The Bergne-Coupland Charity
The Joseph and Annie Cattle Trust
Help for Health
The Hesslewood Children's Trust (Hull Seamen's and General Orphanage)
The Hull and East Riding Charitable Trust
The J. S. and E. C. Rymer Charitable Trust

## North Yorkshire

The Charles Brotherton Trust
The Jack Brunton Charitable Trust
The Marjorie Coote Animal Charity Trust
Sir John Priestman Charity Trust
The Sylvia and Colin Shepherd Charitable Trust
Two Ridings Community Foundation
The Yorkshire Dales Millennium Trust

## South Yorkshire

John William Chapman's Charitable Trust
The Church Burgesses Educational Foundation
Church Burgesses Trust
The Marjorie Coote Old People's Charity
The Freshgate Trust Foundation
The James Neill Trust Fund
Open Gate
The SDL Foundation
The Talbot Trusts
The South Yorkshire Community Foundation

## West Yorkshire

The Addleshaw Goddard Charitable Trust
The Bearder Charity
The Benfield Motors Charitable Trust
The Bramhope Trust
The Charles Brotherton Trust
Community Foundation for Calderdale
Community Foundation for Leeds
The Green Hall Foundation
Duchy of Lancaster Benevolent Fund
The Lord Mayor of Leeds Appeal Fund
The Shears Foundation
Wade's Charity

## North East

The 1989 Willan Charitable Trust
The Roy and Pixie Baker Charitable Trust
The Ballinger Charitable Trust
The Barbour Foundation
The Benfield Motors Charitable Trust
Joseph Brough Charitable Trust
The Coalfields Regeneration Trust
The Catherine Cookson Charitable Trust
County Durham Community Foundation
The Sir Tom Cowie Charitable Trust
The Gillian Dickinson Trust
The Dulverton Trust
The Ellinson Foundation Ltd
Esh Foundation
The GNC Trust
E. C. Graham Belford Charitable Settlement
The Greggs Foundation
The Hadrian Trust
The W. A. Handley Charitable Trust
The Peter Harrison Foundation
The Hedley Denton Charitable Trust
Hexham and Newcastle Diocesan Trust (1947)
The Hospital of God at Greatham
The Sir James Knott Trust
The William Leech Charity
The Millfield House Foundation
The Northern Rock Foundation
The Northumberland Village Homes Trust
People's Postcode Trust
Sir John Priestman Charity Trust
The Rothley Trust
The Shears Foundation
The Sylvia and Colin Shepherd Charitable Trust
The St Hilda's Trust
Tees Valley Community Foundation
Community Foundation Serving Tyne and Wear and Northumberland

*Grant-makers by geographical area* — **Scotland**

The William Webster
  Charitable Trust

■ **Cleveland**

The Hadrian Trust
Hexham and Newcastle
  Diocesan Trust (1947)
The Hospital of God at
  Greatham
The Sir James Knott Trust
The Northern Rock Foundation
Tees Valley Community
  Foundation

■ **Durham**

Joseph Brough Charitable
  Trust
County Durham Community
  Foundation
The Sir Tom Cowie Charitable
  Trust
The Gillian Dickinson Trust
The Hadrian Trust
Hexham and Newcastle
  Diocesan Trust (1947)
The Hospital of God at
  Greatham
The Sir James Knott Trust
The William Leech Charity
The Northern Rock Foundation
Sir John Priestman Charity
  Trust
The Shears Foundation

■ **Northumberland**

Joseph Brough Charitable
  Trust
The Gillian Dickinson Trust
E. C. Graham Belford
  Charitable Settlement
The Hadrian Trust
The W. A. Handley Charitable
  Trust
Hexham and Newcastle
  Diocesan Trust (1947)
The Hospital of God at
  Greatham
The Sir James Knott Trust
The William Leech Charity
The Northern Rock Foundation
The Shears Foundation
The St Hilda's Trust
Community Foundation Serving
  Tyne and Wear and
  Northumberland

■ **Tyne & Wear**

Joseph Brough Charitable
  Trust
The Sir Tom Cowie Charitable
  Trust
The Gillian Dickinson Trust

The Ellinson Foundation Ltd
The Hadrian Trust
The W. A. Handley Charitable
  Trust
Hexham and Newcastle
  Diocesan Trust (1947)
The Hospital of God at
  Greatham
The Sir James Knott Trust
The William Leech Charity
The Northern Rock Foundation
Sir John Priestman Charity
  Trust
The Shears Foundation
The St Hilda's Trust
Community Foundation Serving
  Tyne and Wear and
  Northumberland

■ **Northern Ireland**

Church of Ireland Priorities
  Fund
The Enkalon Foundation
The Garnett Charitable Trust
The GNC Trust
The Goodman Foundation
The Peter Harrison Foundation
Hope for Youth (NI)
The Ian Karten Charitable
  Trust
Lloyds Bank Foundation for
  Northern Ireland
Lord and Lady Lurgan Trust
The Esmé Mitchell Trust
John Moores Foundation
The Community Foundation for
  Northern Ireland
Royal British Legion
The Sackler Trust
Ulster Garden Villages Ltd
Victoria Homes Trust

■ **Scotland**

The Aberbrothock Skea Trust
The Aberdeen Endowments
  Trust
The Aberdeenshire Educational
  Trust Scheme
Age Scotland
Alliance Trust Staff Foundation
The AMW Charitable Trust
The Baird Trust
The Bank of Scotland
  Foundation
Barchester Healthcare
  Foundation
The Bellahouston Bequest
  Fund
The Benfield Motors Charitable
  Trust
British Gas (Scottish Gas)
  Energy Trust

Miss Marion Broughton's
  Charitable Trust
Callander Charitable Trust
The Carnegie Dunfermline
  Trust
The Carnegie Trust for the
  Universities of Scotland
Cash for Kids – Radio Clyde
The Cattanach Charitable Trust
Chest, Heart and Stroke
  Scotland
The Coalfields Regeneration
  Trust
Martin Connell Charitable
  Trust
The Craignish Trust
The Cray Trust
Creative Scotland
The Crerar Hotels Trust
The Cross Trust
The Cunningham Trust
The Dulverton Trust
Edinburgh & Lothian Trust
  Fund
Edinburgh Children's Holiday
  Fund
The Ellis Campbell Foundation
The Erskine Cunningham Hill
  Trust
The Gannochy Trust
The GNC Trust
The Greggs Foundation
The Guildry Incorporation of
  Perth
Dr Guthrie's Association
The Peter Harrison Foundation
The Christina Mary Hendrie
  Trust for Scottish and
  Canadian Charities
The Holywood Trust
James T. Howat Charitable
  Trust
Miss Agnes H. Hunter's Trust
Jeffrey Charitable Trust
The Ian Karten Charitable
  Trust
The KPMG Foundation
The R. J. Larg Family
  Charitable Trust
LHR Airport Communities Trust
Lloyds TSB Foundation for
  Scotland
The R. S. Macdonald
  Charitable Trust
The Mackintosh Foundation
The W. M. Mann Foundation
The Nancie Massey Charitable
  Trust
The Mathew Trust
The Merchants' House of
  Glasgow
Morgan Stanley International
  Foundation
The Mugdock Children's Trust
The Northwood Charitable
  Trust

Miss M. E. Swinton Paterson's
   Charitable Trust
People's Postcode Trust
The Ponton House Trust
Porticus UK
The Robertson Trust
Rosetrees Trust
Mrs Gladys Row Fogo
   Charitable Trust
Royal British Legion
The Sackler Trust
Foundation Scotland
Scottish Coal Industry Special
   Welfare Fund
The Scottish Power Energy
   People Trust
The Shetland Charitable Trust
R. H. Southern Trust
The Templeton Goodwill Trust
The Len Thomson Charitable
   Trust
Voluntary Action Fund
John Watson's Trust
A. H. and B. C. Whiteley
   Charitable Trust
J. and J. R. Wilson Trust
The James Wood Bequest
   Fund
The John Kirkhope Young
   Endowment Fund

■ Central

Callander Charitable Trust
Mrs Gladys Row Fogo
   Charitable Trust
The James Wood Bequest
   Fund

■ Grampian Region

The Aberbrothock Skea Trust
The Aberdeen Endowments
   Trust
The Aberdeenshire Educational
   Trust Scheme
LHR Airport Communities Trust

■ Highlands & Islands

The Mackintosh Foundation
The Shetland Charitable Trust

■ Lothians Region

Alliance Trust Staff Foundation
The Benfield Motors Charitable
   Trust
Edinburgh & Lothian Trust
   Fund
Edinburgh Children's Holiday
   Fund
LHR Airport Communities Trust
The Ponton House Trust
Mrs Gladys Row Fogo
   Charitable Trust

The John Kirkhope Young
   Endowment Fund

■ Southern Scotland

Callander Charitable Trust
The Holywood Trust

■ Strathclyde

The Bellahouston Bequest
   Fund
Cash for Kids – Radio Clyde
The Greggs Foundation
LHR Airport Communities Trust
The Merchants' House of
   Glasgow
Morgan Stanley International
   Foundation
The Templeton Goodwill Trust
The James Wood Bequest
   Fund

■ Tayside & Fife

The Aberbrothock Skea Trust
Alliance Trust Staff Foundation
The Carnegie Dunfermline
   Trust
The Ellis Campbell Foundation
The Guildry Incorporation of
   Perth
The Northwood Charitable
   Trust

## Wales

Arts Council of Wales (Cyngor
   Celfyddydau Cymru)
The Asda Foundation
The Austin Bailey Foundation
Barchester Healthcare
   Foundation
Birthday House Trust
The Blandford Lake Trust
The Boodle & Dunthorne
   Charitable Trust
The Boshier-Hinton Foundation
The Bower Trust
British Gas (Scottish Gas)
   Energy Trust
Cable & Wireless Worldwide
   Foundation
The Cambridge Chrysalis Trust
The Catholic Trust for England
   and Wales
The Gaynor Cemlyn-Jones
   Trust
CLA Charitable Trust
The Coalfields Regeneration
   Trust
The Bernard Coleman Trust
Colwinston Charitable Trust
Michael Crawford Children's
   Charity

The Cwmbran Trust
D. C. R. Allen Charitable Trust
The Henry and Suzanne Davis
   Foundation
The DM Charitable Trust
The Dulverton Trust
The James Dyson Foundation
The Economist Charitable
   Trust
The Elephant Trust
The Ernest Hecht Charitable
   Foundation
Ford Britain Trust
Gwyneth Forrester Trust
The Joseph Strong Frazer Trust
The Fred and Maureen
   Charitable Trust
The Freemasons' Grand
   Charity
The General Nursing Council
   for England and Wales
   Trust
The Girdlers' Company
   Charitable Trust
The GNC Trust
The Goodman Foundation
The Greggs Foundation
The Peter Harrison Foundation
The Hintze Family Charity
   Foundation
The Jane Hodge Foundation
Interserve Employee
   Foundation Ltd
The J. Isaacs Charitable Trust
The Isle of Anglesey Charitable
   Trust
C. Richard Jackson Charitable
   Trust
The James Trust
The Dezna Robins Jones
   Charitable Foundation
The Ian Karten Charitable
   Trust
Keswick Hall Charity
The KPMG Foundation
Morris Leigh Foundation
Lloyds Bank Foundation for
   England and Wales
Lord and Lady Lurgan Trust
Charity of John Marshall
The Merlin Magic Wand
   Children's Charity
Millennium Stadium Charitable
   Trust (Ymddiriedolaeth
   Elusennol Stadiwm y
   Mileniwm)
Monmouthshire County Council
   Welsh Church Act Fund
The Morgan Foundation
The Moss Family Charitable
   Trust
Moto in the Community
The National Churches Trust
The Noon Foundation
North West Cancer Research

The Norwood and Newton
    Settlement
O&G Schreiber Charitable
    Trust
The Ouseley Trust
The James Pantyfedwen
    Foundation
The Payne Charitable Trust
People's Postcode Trust
The Bernard Piggott Charitable
    Trust
Porticus UK
The Rhondda Cynon Taff
    Welsh Church Acts Fund
Rosetrees Trust
Royal British Legion
The Sackler Trust
The Peter Saunders Trust
The Scottish Power Energy
    People Trust
Skipton Building Society
    Charitable Foundation
The DS Smith Charitable
    Foundation
The Sobell Foundation
R. H. Southern Trust
Sparquote Limited
Springrule Limited
The Leonard Laity Stoate
    Charitable Trust
The Strowger Trust
Swansea and Brecon Diocesan
    Board of Finance Limited
Toyota Manufacturing UK
    Charitable Trust
The Community Foundation in
    Wales
Wales Council for Voluntary
    Action
Robert and Felicity Waley-
    Cohen Charitable Trust
The Barbara Ward Children's
    Foundation
Welsh Church Fund – Dyfed
    area (Carmarthenshire,
    Ceredigion and
    Pembrokeshire)
A. H. and B. C. Whiteley
    Charitable Trust
The Yapp Charitable Trust

■ **North Wales**

The Blandford Lake Trust
The Gaynor Cemlyn-Jones
    Trust
The Isle of Anglesey Charitable
    Trust
The Morgan Foundation
North West Cancer Research
The Payne Charitable Trust
The Bernard Piggott Charitable
    Trust
Toyota Manufacturing UK
    Charitable Trust

■ **Mid and West Wales**

Swansea and Brecon Diocesan
    Board of Finance Limited
Welsh Church Fund – Dyfed
    area (Carmarthenshire,
    Ceredigion and
    Pembrokeshire)

■ **South Wales**

The Austin Bailey Foundation
The Cwmbran Trust
Ford Britain Trust
The Greggs Foundation
Monmouthshire County Council
    Welsh Church Act Fund
The Rhondda Cynon Taff
    Welsh Church Acts Fund
Swansea and Brecon Diocesan
    Board of Finance Limited

## Channel Islands

The Freemasons' Grand
    Charity
The Hampshire and Islands
    Historic Churches Trust
Lloyds Bank Foundation for the
    Channel Islands
Lord and Lady Lurgan Trust

## Isle of Man

The Freemasons' Grand
    Charity
Lord and Lady Lurgan Trust

# Grant-makers by field of interest and type of beneficiary

This index contains two separate listings:

**Categorisation of fields of interest and type of beneficiary:** This lists all of the headings used in the DGMT to categorise fields of interest and types of beneficiary.

**Grant-makers by field of interest and type of beneficiary:** This lists trusts under the fields of interest and types of beneficiary for which they have expressed a funding preference.

# Grant-makers by field of interest and type of beneficiary

*These pages contain two separate listings:*

Categorisation of fields of interest and type of beneficiary
This lists all of the headings used in the DGMT to categorise fields of interest and types of beneficiary

Grant-makers by field of interest and type of beneficiary
This lists trusts under the fields of interest and types of beneficiary for which they have expressed a funding preference

**Arts, culture, sport and recreation 51**
**Arts and culture 56**

**Access to the arts 58**

**Amateur and community arts 58**

**Art and culture of specific countries 58**

**Arts management, policy and planning 59**

**Combined arts 59**

**Crafts 59**

**Disability arts 59**

**Libraries 59**

**Literature 59**

**Museums and galleries 59**

**Performing arts 59**

**Dance 60**

**Music 60**

**Theatre 60**

**Visual arts 60**

**Fine art 60**

**Public art/sculpture 60**

**Heritage and the built environment 60**
**Arts and the environment 61**

**Landscape 62**

**Heritage 62**

**Maintenance and preservation of buildings 62**

**Religious buildings 63**

**Restoration and maintenance of inland waterways 63**

**Built environment – education and research 63**

**Humanities 63**
**Archaeology 63**

**History 63**

**International understanding 64**

**Philosophy and ethics 64**

*Fields of interest and type of beneficiary*

**Media and communications 64**

**Recreation and sport 64**
Parks and open spaces 65

Recreation facilities 65

Sports for people with a disability 65

Sports 65

**Development, housing and employment 66**
Community and economic development 68

Housing 70

Specific industries 70

**Education and training 71**
Higher education 78

Universities 78

Informal, continuing and adult education 78

Adult and community education 78

Vocational education and training 78

Integrated education 78

Management of schools 78

Particular subjects, curriculum development 79

Arts education and training 79

Business education 79

Citizenship, personal and social education 79

Construction industry education 80

Home economics and life skills education 80

Hospitality and leisure industry education 80

Language and literacy education 80

Legal education 80

Religious education 80

Science education 80

Sports education 80

Technology, engineering and computer education 80

Pre-school education 80

Primary and secondary school education 80

Faith schools 81

Public and independent schools 81

Special needs schools 81

State schools 81

Teacher training and development 81

**45**

## Environment and animals 81
Agriculture and fishing 84

Farming and food production 84

Forestry 84

Horticulture 84

Animal care 85

Animal conservation 85

Climate change 85

Countryside 85

Environmental education and research 86

Natural environment 86

Flora and fauna 87

Water resources 87

Wild places, wilderness 87

Pollution abatement and control 87

Sustainable environment 87

Energy issues 87

Loss of biodiversity 87

Transport 87

## General charitable purposes 88

## Health 96
Alternative and complementary medicine 103

Health care 103

Health training 104

Therapy 104

Medical equipment 104

Medical institutions 105

Nursing 105

Medical research and clinical treatment 105

History of medicine 107

Health education/ prevention/ development 107

Medical ethics 107

## Overseas aid/ projects 107

## Philanthropy and the voluntary sector 109
Voluntarism 109

Community participation 110

Voluntary sector capacity building 110

## Religious activities 110
Christianity 113

Christian causes 114

Christian churches 115

Christian social thought 115

Ecumenicalism 115

Missionary work, evangelism 115

Hinduism 116

Inter-faith activities 116

Islam 116

Judaism 116

Jewish causes, work 118

Orthodox Judaism 118

Religious understanding 118

**Rights, law and conflict 119**
Citizen participation 120

Conflict resolution 120

Cross border initiatives 120

Cross community work 120

Mediation 120

Peace and disarmament 120

Legal advice and services 120

Advice services 120

Legal issues 121

Rights, equality and justice 121

Human rights 121

Civil liberties 121

Cultural equity 121

Disability rights 121

Economic justice 121

Racial justice 122

Social justice 122

Women's rights 122

Young people's rights 122

**Science and technology 122**
Engineering/technology 122

Life sciences 122

Physical and earth sciences 123

**Social sciences, policy and research 123**
Economics 123

Political science 123

Social policy 123

**Social welfare 124**
Community care services 131

Services for and about children and young people 132

Services for and about older people 133

Services for and about vulnerable people/people who are ill 133

Services for carers 134

Services for victims of crime 134

Services for women 134

Activities and relationships between generations 134

47

Community centres and activities 134

Community and social centres 134

Community organisations 135

Community outings and holidays 135

Community transport 135

Emergency response 135

Armed forces 135

Lifeboat service 135

Relief assistance 135

Socially preventative schemes 136

Crime prevention 136

Family justice 136

Family planning 136

Prisons and penal reform 136

Substance abuse and education 136

## Beneficial groups 137
### Age 137

- Babies 137
- Children and young people 137
- Older people 143

### Class, group, occupation or former occupation 146

- Armed forces 146
- Arts, culture, sports and recreation 147
- Environment and agriculture 147
- Financial services 147
- Law 147
- Manufacturing and service industries 147
- Medicine and health 147
- Religion 147
- Science, technology and engineering 148

- Seafarers and ex-seafarers 148
- Sporting or social clubs (inc. Masons) 148
- Transport 148

### Disability 148

- People with a mental/mental health disability 148
- People with autism 148
- People with dyslexia 149
- People with learning difficulties 149
- People with a physical impairment 149
- People with a sensory impairment 149
- Hearing loss 150
- Sight loss 150

### Ethnicity 150

### Faith 150

- People of the Christian faith 153
- People of the Jewish faith 154

- People of the Muslim faith 156
- People of the Zoroastrian faith 156

### Gender and relationships 156

- Adopted or fostered children 156
- Bereaved 156
- Carers 156
- Families 156
- Gay and transgender people 156
- Orphans 156
- Parents 156
- Lone parents 156
- Women 156

### Ill health 157

- People with cardiovascular disorders 160
- People with haematological disorders 160
- People with glandular and endocrine disorders 160
- People with immune system disorders 160
- People with a mental disability 160
- People with musculoskeletal disorders 160
- People with neurological disorders 160
- People with oncological disorders 160
- People with respiratory disorders 161
- People with skin disorders 161
- People who are substance misusers 161
- Palliative care 161

### Nationality 161

- Asian 161
- Eastern European 161
- Southern European 161

### Social or economic circumstances 161

- People with an alternative lifestyle (inc. travellers) 165
- People who are educationally disadvantaged 165
- People who are homeless 165
- People who are housebound 166
- People who are unemployed 166
- Carers 166
- Migrants 166
- Offenders 166
- Ex-offenders 167
- Prisoners and their families 167
- Young people at risk of offending 167
- People who are poor, on low incomes 167
- Refugees and asylum seekers 168
- Victims, oppressed people 168

**49**

- **People who have suffered abuse, violence or torture** 169

- **Victims of crime** 169

- **Victims of disasters** 169

- **People suffering from famine** 169

- **People suffering injustice** 169

- **Victims of war or conflict** 169

## Arts, culture, sport and recreation

The 29th May 1961 Charitable Trust
The Aberdeen Endowments Trust
The Acacia Charitable Trust
Access Sport
The Victor Adda Foundation
Allchurches Trust Ltd
The H. B. Allen Charitable Trust
Angus Allnatt Charitable Foundation
The Ammco Trust
The AMW Charitable Trust
Andor Charitable Trust
The Eric Anker-Petersen Charity
The Architectural Heritage Fund
The Armourers' and Brasiers' Gauntlet Trust
Arts Council England
Arts Council of Northern Ireland
Arts Council of Wales (Cyngor Celfyddydau Cymru)
The Ove Arup Foundation
ASCB Charitable Fund
The Asda Foundation
A. J. H. Ashby Will Trust
The Ashden Trust
The Ashley Family Foundation
The Astor Foundation
The Astor of Hever Trust
The Aurelius Charitable Trust
Bag4Sport Foundation
The Bagri Foundation
The Baird Trust
The Roy and Pixie Baker Charitable Trust
The Ballinger Charitable Trust
The Balney Charitable Trust
The Band Trust
The Barbour Foundation
The Barcapel Foundation
Barchester Healthcare Foundation
The Baring Foundation
The Barker-Mill Foundation
Barnes Workhouse Fund
The Barnwood House Trust
BBC Children in Need
BC Partners Foundation
The Beaverbrook Foundation
The John Beckwith Charitable Trust
The Bedfordshire and Hertfordshire Historic Churches Trust
The Bellahouston Bequest Fund
Bergqvist Charitable Trust

The Bernadette Charitable Trust
The Bertarelli UK Foundation
The Big Lottery Fund (see also Awards for All)
Birmingham International Airport Community Trust
The BlackRock (UK) Charitable Trust
The Blagrave Trust
The Nicholas Boas Charitable Trust
The Boltini Trust
BOOST Charitable Trust
The Boshier-Hinton Foundation
The Bowerman Charitable Trust
The Liz and Terry Bramall Foundation
The Bramhope Trust
The Bransford Trust
The Harold and Alice Bridges Charity
British Institute at Ankara
British Record Industry Trust
The Britten-Pears Foundation
The Consuelo and Anthony Brooke Charitable Trust
The Rory and Elizabeth Brooks Foundation
Miss Marion Broughton's Charitable Trust
The Brownsword Charitable Foundation
The T. B. H. Brunner Charitable Settlement
The Buckinghamshire Historic Churches Trust
The Bulldog Trust Limited
The Arnold Burton 1998 Charitable Trust
Consolidated Charity of Burton upon Trent
The Derek Butler Trust
The James Caan Foundation
Edward Cadbury Charitable Trust
Peter Cadbury Charitable Trust
The Christopher Cadbury Charitable Trust
The G. W. Cadbury Charitable Trust
The William A. Cadbury Charitable Trust
The Barrow Cadbury Trust
The Edward and Dorothy Cadbury Trust
The George Cadbury Trust
Callander Charitable Trust
Calleva Foundation
Calouste Gulbenkian Foundation – UK Branch
The Cambridge Chrysalis Trust
The Cambridgeshire Historic Churches Trust

The Frederick and Phyllis Cann Trust
Canoe Foundation
The Richard Carne Trust
The Carnegie Dunfermline Trust
The Carpenters' Company Charitable Trust
The Carr-Gregory Trust
Carter's Educational Foundation
The Catalyst Charitable Trust
The Cayo Foundation
Elizabeth Cayzer Charitable Trust
The B. G. S. Cayzer Charitable Trust
The Gaynor Cemlyn-Jones Trust
The Amelia Chadwick Trust
The Chapman Charitable Trust
The Chetwode Foundation
The Chipping Sodbury Town Lands Charity
CHK Charities Limited
The City Bridge Trust
The City Educational Trust Fund
Stephen Clark 1957 Charitable Trust
J. A. Clark Charitable Trust
The Roger and Sarah Bancroft Clark Charitable Trust
The Cleopatra Trust
The Clore Duffield Foundation
The Clover Trust
The Robert Clutterbuck Charitable Trust
The Francis Coales Charitable Foundation
The Coalfields Regeneration Trust
The John Coates Charitable Trust
The Denise Cohen Charitable Trust
The Vivienne and Samuel Cohen Charitable Trust
The John S. Cohen Foundation
The R. and S. Cohen Foundation
The Bernard Coleman Trust
Colwinston Charitable Trust
Colyer-Fergusson Charitable Trust
Community First (Landfill Communities Fund)
The Congleton Inclosure Trust
The Congregational and General Charitable Trust
The Conservation Foundation
The Ernest Cook Trust
The Catherine Cookson Charitable Trust
The Helen Jean Cope Trust

51

## Arts, culture, sport and recreation

Michael Cornish Charitable Trust
The Evan Cornish Foundation
The Duke of Cornwall's Benevolent Fund
The Cotton Industry War Memorial Trust
Country Houses Foundation
The Sir Tom Cowie Charitable Trust
The Craignish Trust
The Craps Charitable Trust
The Cray Trust
Creative Scotland
The Crescent Trust
The Cross Trust
The Peter Cruddas Foundation
Cruden Foundation Ltd
The Cumber Family Charitable Trust
D. J. H. Currie Memorial Trust
The Cwmbran Trust
The D'Oyly Carte Charitable Trust
The Daiwa Anglo-Japanese Foundation
The Davidson Family Charitable Trust
Michael Davies Charitable Settlement
The Gwendoline and Margaret Davies Charity
The Hamilton Davies Trust
The Davis Foundation
The Henry and Suzanne Davis Foundation
Peter De Haan Charitable Trust
The De Laszlo Foundation
The Deakin Charitable Trust
The Delius Trust
The Denman Charitable Trust
The Dentons UKMEA LLP Charitable Trust
The Derbyshire Churches and Chapels Preservation Trust
The Devon Historic Churches Trust
The Sandy Dewhirst Charitable Trust
The Gillian Dickinson Trust
Dischma Charitable Trust
The Djanogly Foundation
Dorset Community Foundation
The Dorset Historic Churches Trust
The Dorus Trust
The Drapers' Charitable Fund
The Dulverton Trust
Dunard Fund
The Dyers' Company Charitable Trust
The Sir John Eastwood Foundation
The Gilbert and Eileen Edgar Foundation

Edinburgh Trust No 2 Account
Educational Foundation of Alderman John Norman
The Elephant Trust
The John Ellerman Foundation
The Ellis Campbell Foundation
The Elmgrant Trust
The Elmley Foundation
The Vernon N. Ely Charitable Trust
The Emerton-Christie Charity
The English Schools' Football Association
The Epigoni Trust
The Equity Trust Fund
The Eranda Foundation
The Ericson Trust
The Essex and Southend Sports Trust
The Essex Fairway Charitable Trust
The Essex Heritage Trust
The Alan Evans Memorial Trust
Esmée Fairbairn Foundation
The Fairway Trust
The Lord Faringdon Charitable Trust
Samuel William Farmer's Trust
The February Foundation
The John Feeney Charitable Bequest
The Fidelity UK Foundation
Fisherbeck Charitable Trust
The Fishmongers' Company's Charitable Trust
Marc Fitch Fund
The Joyce Fletcher Charitable Trust
The Follett Trust
The Football Association National Sports Centre Trust
The Football Association Youth Trust
The Football Foundation
The Donald Forrester Trust
The Fort Foundation
The Foyle Foundation
The Jill Franklin Trust
The Gordon Fraser Charitable Trust
The Hugh Fraser Foundation
The Joseph Strong Frazer Trust
The Freshgate Trust Foundation
Friends of Essex Churches Trust
The Friends of Kent Churches
The Frognal Trust
The Fuserna Foundation General Charitable Trust
The Galanthus Trust
The Galbraith Trust
Gamlen Charitable Trust
The Gamma Trust
The Gannochy Trust

## Fields of interest and type of beneficiary

The Samuel Gardner Memorial Trust
The Garnett Charitable Trust
The Garrick Charitable Trust
The Gatsby Charitable Foundation
Gatwick Airport Community Trust
The Robert Gavron Charitable Trust
Jacqueline and Michael Gee Charitable Trust
The Nigel Gee Foundation
The Generations Foundation
Get Kids Going
The Gibbs Charitable Trust
Simon Gibson Charitable Trust
The Girdlers' Company Charitable Trust
The Gloucestershire Historic Churches Trust
The GNC Trust
The Golden Bottle Trust
Golden Charitable Trust
The Goldsmiths' Arts Trust Fund
The Goldsmiths' Company Charity
The Golf Foundation Limited
The Golsoncott Foundation
Nicholas and Judith Goodison's Charitable Settlement
The Gosling Foundation Limited
The Granada Foundation
The Grange Farm Centre Trust
The J. G. Graves Charitable Trust
The Great Britain Sasakawa Foundation
The Kenneth & Susan Green Charitable Foundation
Greenham Common Community Trust Limited
The Greggs Foundation
The Greys Charitable Trust
The Grimmitt Trust
The Grocers' Charity
The Hadfield Trust
The Hadrian Trust
Paul Hamlyn Foundation
The Helen Hamlyn Trust
Sue Hammerson Charitable Trust
The Hampshire and Islands Historic Churches Trust
Hampshire and Isle of Wight Community Foundation
Hampton Fuel Allotment
The W. A. Handley Charitable Trust
The Kathleen Hannay Memorial Charity
Miss K. M. Harbinson's Charitable Trust

The Harbour Charitable Trust
The Harbour Foundation
The Harding Trust
William Harding's Charity
The Hare of Steep Charitable Trust (HOST)
The Harpur Trust
The Harris Charity
The Peter Harrison Foundation
The Hartley Charitable Trust
Edward Harvist Trust
The Maurice Hatter Foundation
The Hawthorne Charitable Trust
The Dorothy Hay-Bolton Charitable Trust
The Charles Hayward Foundation
The Headley Trust
Heart of England Community Foundation
The Heathside Charitable Trust
The Charlotte Heber-Percy Charitable Trust
The Percy Hedley 1990 Charitable Trust
Hedley Foundation Limited
The Michael Heller Charitable Foundation
The Simon Heller Charitable Settlement
The Hemby Charitable Trust
The Christina Mary Hendrie Trust for Scottish and Canadian Charities
Henley Educational Trust
Herefordshire Community Foundation
The Herefordshire Historic Churches Trust
The Heritage of London Trust Limited
The Hesslewood Children's Trust
The Derek Hill Foundation
The Hillingdon Community Trust
The Hillingdon Partnership Trust
R. G. Hills Charitable Trust
The Lady Hind Trust
The Hinduja Foundation
The Hinrichsen Foundation
The Hintze Family Charity Foundation
The Hiscox Foundation
The Henry C. Hoare Charitable Trust
The Hobson Charity Limited
The Hollick Family Charitable Trust
The Holliday Foundation
The Dorothy Holmes Charitable Trust
The Holst Foundation
P. H. Holt Foundation

The Holywood Trust
The Homestead Charitable Trust
The Mary Homfray Charitable Trust
Hope for Youth (NI)
The Antony Hornby Charitable Trust
The Horne Foundation
The Sir Joseph Hotung Charitable Settlement
The Reta Lila Howard Foundation
The Daniel Howard Trust
The Hull and East Riding Charitable Trust
Human Relief Foundation
Huntingdon Freemen's Trust
The Idlewild Trust
The Iliffe Family Charitable Trust
Incommunities Foundation
The Ingram Trust
The Inlight Trust
The Inverforth Charitable Trust (ICT)
Investream Charitable Trust
The Ireland Fund of Great Britain
Irish Youth Foundation (UK) Ltd (incorporating The Lawlor Foundation)
The Ironmongers' Foundation
The J. Isaacs Charitable Trust
The Isle of Anglesey Charitable Trust
The J. J. Charitable Trust
The Jabbs Foundation
The Jacobs Charitable Trust
John Jarrold Trust
The Jenour Foundation
The Jerusalem Trust
The Jerwood Charitable Foundation
The Jewish Youth Fund (JYF)
The Johnson Foundation
The Johnnie Johnson Trust
The Johnson Wax Ltd Charitable Trust
The Joicey Trust
The Marjorie and Geoffrey Jones Charitable Trust
The Jordan Charitable Foundation
The Joron Charitable Trust
The Cyril and Eve Jumbo Charitable Trust
Jusaca Charitable Trust
The Stanley Kalms Foundation
Karaviotis Foundation
The Boris Karloff Charitable Foundation
The Michael and Ilse Katz Foundation
The Kelly Family Charitable Trust

John Thomas Kennedy Charitable Foundation
Kent Community Foundation
The Robert Kiln Charitable Trust
The Marina Kleinwort Charitable Trust
The Sir James Knott Trust
The Kobler Trust
The Kohn Foundation
The Kreitman Foundation
The Neil Kreitman Foundation
The Kyte Charitable Trust
Ladbrokes in the Community Charitable Trust
Christopher Laing Foundation
The David Laing Foundation
The Kirby Laing Foundation
The Martin Laing Foundation
The Lambert Charitable Trust
Lancashire Environmental Fund Limited
Duchy of Lancaster Benevolent Fund
The Jack Lane Charitable Trust
The Langtree Trust
The R. J. Larg Family Charitable Trust
The Lark Trust
Laslett's (Hinton) Charity
The Lauffer Family Charitable Foundation
Mrs F. B. Laurence Charitable Trust
The Edgar E. Lawley Foundation
Lawson Beckman Charitable Trust
The Raymond and Blanche Lawson Charitable Trust
The David Lean Foundation
The Leathersellers' Company Charitable Fund
The Leche Trust
The William Leech Charity
Leicester and Leicestershire Historic Churches Preservation Trust
Leicestershire, Leicester and Rutland Community Foundation
The Kennedy Leigh Charitable Trust
Morris Leigh Foundation
The Lennox and Wyfold Foundation
The Leverhulme Trust
Lord Leverhulme's Charitable Trust
Joseph Levy Charitable Foundation
The Sir Edward Lewis Foundation
John Lewis Partnership General Community Fund
Liberum Foundation

53

The Limbourne Trust
Limoges Charitable Trust
The Linbury Trust
Lincolnshire Churches Trust
Lincolnshire Community Foundation
The Linden Charitable Trust
The Enid Linder Foundation
The Ruth and Stuart Lipton Charitable Trust
The Lister Charitable Trust
The Charles Littlewood Hill Trust
The Second Joseph Aaron Littman Foundation
Jack Livingstone Charitable Trust
The Elaine and Angus Lloyd Charitable Trust
The Charles Lloyd Foundation
Lloyd's Charities Trust
Lloyds Bank Foundation for Northern Ireland
The London Community Foundation
The London Marathon Charitable Trust Limited
The William and Katherine Longman Trust
The Lord's Taverners
The Lowy Mitchell Foundation
The C. L. Loyd Charitable Trust
The Ruth and Jack Lunzer Charitable Trust
Lord and Lady Lurgan Trust
The Lynn Foundation
John Lyon's Charity
The Sir Jack Lyons Charitable Trust
Sylvanus Lysons Charity
The E. M. MacAndrew Trust
The Mackintosh Foundation
The MacRobert Trust
The Mactaggart Third Fund
The Ian Mactaggart Trust
The Mageni Trust
The Brian Maguire Charitable Trust
Man Group plc Charitable Trust
Manchester Airport Community Trust Fund
The Manchester Guardian Society Charitable Trust
The Manifold Charitable Trust
The W. M. Mann Foundation
R. W. Mann Trust
The Manoukian Charitable Foundation
Maranatha Christian Trust
The Stella and Alexander Margulies Charitable Trust
Market Harborough and The Bowdens Charity
The Michael Marks Charitable Trust

The Marks Family Foundation
J. P. Marland Charitable Trust
The Marsh Christian Trust
Charity of John Marshall
Sir George Martin Trust
John Martin's Charity
The Dan Maskell Tennis Trust
The Nancie Massey Charitable Trust
The Mayfield Valley Arts Trust
The Medlock Charitable Trust
The Brian Mercer Charitable Trust
The Mercers' Charitable Foundation
The Merchant Taylors' Company Charities Fund
The Merchant Venturers' Charity
The Merchants' House of Glasgow
The Merlin Magic Wand Children's Charity
The Metropolitan Masonic Charity
The Mickel Fund
The Gerald Micklem Charitable Trust
Middlesex Sports Foundation
Millennium Stadium Charitable Trust (Ymddiriedolaeth Elusennol Stadiwm y Mileniwm)
The Ronald Miller Foundation
The Millichope Foundation
The Millward Charitable Trust
Milton Keynes Community Foundation Limited
The Peter Minet Trust
Minge's Gift and the Pooled Trusts
Minton Charitable Trust
The Laurence Misener Charitable Trust
The Brian Mitchell Charitable Settlement
The Esmé Mitchell Trust
The Modiano Charitable Trust
Monmouthshire County Council Welsh Church Act Fund
The Monument Trust
The George A. Moore Foundation
The Henry Moore Foundation
The Morel Charitable Trust
The Diana and Allan Morgenthau Charitable Trust
The Miles Morland Foundation
The Morris Charitable Trust
The Peter Morrison Charitable Foundation
Mosselson Charitable Trust
British Motor Sports Training Trust
The Mount Everest Foundation

Mrs Waterhouse Charitable Trust
The John R. Murray Charitable Trust
The Music Sales Charitable Trust
The National Art Collections Fund
The National Churches Trust
The National Express Foundation
The National Hockey Foundation
The National Manuscripts Conservation Trust
The NDL Foundation
Network for Social Change
Norfolk Community Foundation
The Normanby Charitable Trust
The Community Foundation for Northern Ireland
The Northern Rock Foundation
The Northwood Charitable Trust
The Norton Foundation
The Notgrove Trust
The Nottinghamshire Historic Churches Trust
The Oakdale Trust
The Oakley Charitable Trust
The Ofenheim Charitable Trust
Oglesby Charitable Trust
Old Possum's Practical Trust
The Ouseley Trust
The Owen Family Trust
The James Pantyfedwen Foundation
Miss M. E. Swinton Paterson's Charitable Trust
The Jack Patston Charitable Trust
The Pedmore Sporting Club Trust Fund
The Pell Charitable Trust
The Peltz Trust
People's Postcode Trust
The Performing Right Society Foundation
The Phillips and Rubens Charitable Trust
The Bernard Piggott Charitable Trust
The Pilgrim Trust
The Austin and Hope Pilkington Trust
The Sir Harry Pilkington Trust Fund
Estate of the Late Colonel W. W. Pilkington Will Trusts – The General Charity Fund
Polden-Puckham Charitable Foundation
The Polonsky Foundation
The John Porter Charitable Trust
The Porter Foundation

54

The Premier League Charitable Fund
The Prince of Wales's Charitable Foundation
The Puri Foundation
Mr and Mrs J. A. Pye's Charitable Settlement
Quartet Community Foundation
Quercus Trust
The RVW Trust
The Racing Foundation
The Radcliffe Trust
The Ragdoll Foundation
Ranworth Trust
The Ravensdale Trust
The Rayne Foundation
The Rayne Trust
The Reed Foundation
The Rhododendron Trust
The Rhondda Cynon Taff Welsh Church Acts Fund
The Sir Cliff Richard Charitable Trust
The Clive Richards Charity
The Richmond Parish Lands Charity
Rivers Foundation
Rix-Thompson-Rothenberg Foundation
The Robertson Trust
The Roddick Foundation
Mrs L. D. Rope Third Charitable Settlement
The Rose Foundation
The Rothley Trust
The Roughley Charitable Trust
The Rowlands Trust
The Joseph Rowntree Charitable Trust
Royal Docks Trust (London)
The Royal Victoria Hall Foundation
The Rubin Foundation
The J. S. and E. C. Rymer Charitable Trust
The Michael Sacher Charitable Trust
The Michael Harry Sacher Trust
Raymond and Beverly Sackler 1988 Foundation
The Sackler Trust
The Saddlers' Company Charitable Fund
The Alan and Babette Sainsbury Charitable Fund
The Saintbury Trust
The Salamander Charitable Trust
The Andrew Salvesen Charitable Trust
Coral Samuel Charitable Trust
The Basil Samuel Charitable Trust
The Peter Samuel Charitable Trust

The Sandhu Charitable Foundation
The Sands Family Trust
The Peter Saunders Trust
The Scarfe Charitable Trust
Schroder Charity Trust
The Frieda Scott Charitable Trust
The Sir James and Lady Scott Trust
Scottish Coal Industry Special Welfare Fund
The Scottish Power Foundation
The Scouloudi Foundation
The Shears Foundation
The Archie Sherman Charitable Trust
The R. C. Sherriff Rosebriars Trust
The Shetland Charitable Trust
The Bassil Shippam and Alsford Trust
The Shipwrights' Company Charitable Fund
David and Jennifer Sieff Charitable Trust
The Huntly and Margery Sinclair Charitable Trust
SITA Cornwall Trust Limited
Skinners' Company Lady Neville Charity
The N. Smith Charitable Settlement
The Stanley Smith UK Horticultural Trust
The Solo Charitable Settlement
Somerset Churches Trust
The E. C. Sosnow Charitable Trust
Spears-Stutz Charitable Trust
The Spero Foundation
The Spielman Charitable Trust
Split Infinitive Trust
The Spoore, Merry and Rixman Foundation
Sported Foundation
Rosalyn and Nicholas Springer Charitable Trust
St James's Trust Settlement
St James's Place Foundation
The Stanley Foundation Ltd
The Peter Stebbings Memorial Charity
The Steel Charitable Trust
Stevenson Family's Charitable Trust
The Stewarts Law Foundation
The Leonard Laity Stoate Charitable Trust
The Edward Stocks-Massey Bequest Fund
Peter Stormonth Darling Charitable Trust
The Suffolk Historic Churches Trust

The Sussex Community Foundation
The Sussex Historic Churches Trust
Sutton Coldfield Charitable Trust
The Suva Foundation Limited
Swimathon Foundation
The John Swire (1989) Charitable Trust
The Swire Charitable Trust
Sylvia Waddilove Foundation UK
The Connie and Albert Taylor Charitable Trust
A. P. Taylor Trust
The Tennis Foundation
The Thistle Trust
The Thompson Family Charitable Trust
The Sue Thomson Foundation
The Tinsley Foundation
The Tompkins Foundation
The Tower Hill Trust
Annie Tranmer Charitable Trust
The Trefoil Trust
The Tresillian Trust
The Douglas Turner Trust
Two Ridings Community Foundation
Community Foundation Serving Tyne and Wear and Northumberland
The Underwood Trust
The Michael Uren Foundation
The Valentine Charitable Trust
The Albert Van Den Bergh Charitable Trust
The Vardy Foundation
The Variety Club Children's Charity
Veneziana Fund
The Nigel Vinson Charitable Trust
Wade's Charity
Wakeham Trust
Wales Council for Voluntary Action
Robert and Felicity Waley-Cohen Charitable Trust
Sir Siegmund Warburg's Voluntary Settlement
The Ward Blenkinsop Trust
The Barbara Ward Children's Foundation
The Waterloo Foundation
Welsh Church Fund – Dyfed area (Carmarthenshire, Ceredigion and Pembrokeshire)
The Welton Foundation
The Wessex Youth Trust
The Westcroft Trust
The Garfield Weston Foundation

55

The Barbara Whatmore
   Charitable Trust
The Whitaker Charitable Trust
The Colonel W. H. Whitbread
   Charitable Trust
The Williams Charitable Trust
Williams Serendipity Trust
The HDH Wills 1965
   Charitable Trust
David Wilson Foundation
The Harold Hyam Wingate
   Foundation
The Wixamtree Trust
The Maurice Wohl Charitable
   Foundation
The Wolfson Family Charitable
   Trust
The Wolfson Foundation
Wooden Spoon Society
The Woodward Charitable
   Trust
The Worcestershire and
   Dudley Historic Churches
   Trust
The Matthews Wrightson
   Charity Trust
The Wyseliot Charitable Trust
The W. Wing Yip and Brothers
   Foundation
Yorkshire and Clydesdale Bank
   Foundation
The Yorkshire Dales
   Millennium Trust
The Yorkshire Historic
   Churches Trust
The William Allen Young
   Charitable Trust
Youth Music
Youth United Foundation
The Marjorie and Arnold Ziff
   Charitable Foundation
The Zochonis Charitable Trust

## Arts and culture

The Victor Adda Foundation
The H. B. Allen Charitable
   Trust
Angus Allnatt Charitable
   Foundation
Prefix Alpha Name
The AMW Charitable Trust
Andor Charitable Trust
The Eric Anker-Petersen
   Charity
The Armourers' and Brasiers'
   Gauntlet Trust
Arts Council England
Arts Council of Northern
   Ireland
Arts Council of Wales (Cyngor
   Celfyddydau Cymru)
The Ashden Trust
The Ashley Family Foundation
The Aurelius Charitable Trust
The Bagri Foundation

The Ballinger Charitable Trust
The Band Trust
The Barbour Foundation
Barchester Healthcare
   Foundation
The Baring Foundation
The Barnwood House Trust
BC Partners Foundation
The John Beckwith Charitable
   Trust
Bergqvist Charitable Trust
The Bernadette Charitable
   Trust
The Bertarelli UK Foundation
The Big Lottery Fund (see also
   Awards for All)
The Nicholas Boas Charitable
   Trust
The Boltini Trust
The Bowerman Charitable
   Trust
The Liz and Terry Bramall
   Foundation
The Bransford Trust
British Institute at Ankara
British Record Industry Trust
The Britten-Pears Foundation
The Rory and Elizabeth Brooks
   Foundation
The Brownsword Charitable
   Foundation
The T. B. H. Brunner
   Charitable Settlement
The Bulldog Trust Limited
The Derek Butler Trust
Edward Cadbury Charitable
   Trust
Peter Cadbury Charitable Trust
The Christopher Cadbury
   Charitable Trust
The G. W. Cadbury Charitable
   Trust
The William A. Cadbury
   Charitable Trust
The Edward and Dorothy
   Cadbury Trust
Calouste Gulbenkian
   Foundation – UK Branch
The Richard Carne Trust
The Carnegie Dunfermline
   Trust
The Cayo Foundation
Elizabeth Cayzer Charitable
   Trust
The Chetwode Foundation
CHK Charities Limited
J. A. Clark Charitable Trust
The Clore Duffield Foundation
The Francis Coales Charitable
   Foundation
The Denise Cohen Charitable
   Trust
The John S. Cohen Foundation
The R. and S. Cohen
   Foundation
Colwinston Charitable Trust

Colyer-Fergusson Charitable
   Trust
The Ernest Cook Trust
The Catherine Cookson
   Charitable Trust
The Cotton Industry War
   Memorial Trust
The Craignish Trust
The Cray Trust
Creative Scotland
The Cross Trust
The Cumber Family Charitable
   Trust
The D'Oyly Carte Charitable
   Trust
The Daiwa Anglo-Japanese
   Foundation
The Davidson Family
   Charitable Trust
Michael Davies Charitable
   Settlement
The Gwendoline and Margaret
   Davies Charity
The Davis Foundation
The Henry and Suzanne Davis
   Foundation
Peter De Haan Charitable
   Trust
The Deakin Charitable Trust
The Delius Trust
The Denman Charitable Trust
The Dentons UKMEA LLP
   Charitable Trust
The Djanogly Foundation
The Drapers' Charitable Fund
Dunard Fund
The Dyers' Company
   Charitable Trust
The Gilbert and Eileen Edgar
   Foundation
The Elephant Trust
The John Ellerman Foundation
The Elmley Foundation
The Emerton-Christie Charity
The Equity Trust Fund
The Eranda Foundation
The Ericson Trust
Esmée Fairbairn Foundation
The Lord Faringdon Charitable
   Trust
The John Feeney Charitable
   Bequest
The Fidelity UK Foundation
The Joyce Fletcher Charitable
   Trust
The Follett Trust
The Fort Foundation
The Foyle Foundation
The Gordon Fraser Charitable
   Trust
The Hugh Fraser Foundation
The Freshgate Trust
   Foundation
Gamlen Charitable Trust
The Samuel Gardner Memorial
   Trust

## Arts and culture

The Garnett Charitable Trust
The Garrick Charitable Trust
The Gatsby Charitable Foundation
Gatwick Airport Community Trust
The Robert Gavron Charitable Trust
Jacqueline and Michael Gee Charitable Trust
The Gibbs Charitable Trust
Simon Gibson Charitable Trust
The Girdlers' Company Charitable Trust
Golden Charitable Trust
The Goldsmiths' Arts Trust Fund
The Goldsmiths' Company Charity
The Golsoncott Foundation
Nicholas and Judith Goodison's Charitable Settlement
The Granada Foundation
The J. G. Graves Charitable Trust
The Great Britain Sasakawa Foundation
The Kenneth & Susan Green Charitable Foundation
The Greys Charitable Trust
The Grimmitt Trust
The Grocers' Charity
The Hadfield Trust
The Hadrian Trust
Paul Hamlyn Foundation
Sue Hammerson Charitable Trust
Hampton Fuel Allotment
The W. A. Handley Charitable Trust
Miss K. M. Harbinson's Charitable Trust
The Harbour Charitable Trust
The Harbour Foundation
The Harding Trust
The Hawthorne Charitable Trust
The Headley Trust
The Heathside Charitable Trust
The Michael Heller Charitable Foundation
The Simon Heller Charitable Settlement
The Christina Mary Hendrie Trust for Scottish and Canadian Charities
Henley Educational Trust
The Heritage of London Trust Limited
The Hesslewood Children's Trust
The Derek Hill Foundation
R. G. Hills Charitable Trust
The Lady Hind Trust
The Hinduja Foundation

The Hinrichsen Foundation
The Hintze Family Charity Foundation
The Hiscox Foundation
The Henry C. Hoare Charitable Trust
The Holliday Foundation
The Holst Foundation
The Holywood Trust
The Homestead Charitable Trust
Hope for Youth (NI)
The Antony Hornby Charitable Trust
The Horne Foundation
The Sir Joseph Hotung Charitable Settlement
The Reta Lila Howard Foundation
The Daniel Howard Trust
The Hull and East Riding Charitable Trust
Human Relief Foundation
The Idlewild Trust
The Ingram Trust
The Inverforth Charitable Trust (ICT)
Investream Charitable Trust
The Ireland Fund of Great Britain
The Ironmongers' Foundation
The J. J. Charitable Trust
The Jabbs Foundation
The Jacobs Charitable Trust
John Jarrold Trust
The Jenour Foundation
The Jerwood Charitable Foundation
The Cyril and Eve Jumbo Charitable Trust
The Stanley Kalms Foundation
Karaviotis Foundation
The Boris Karloff Charitable Foundation
The Michael and Ilse Katz Foundation
John Thomas Kennedy Charitable Foundation
The Robert Kiln Charitable Trust
The Marina Kleinwort Charitable Trust
The Kobler Trust
The Kohn Foundation
The Neil Kreitman Foundation
Christopher Laing Foundation
The Kirby Laing Foundation
The Martin Laing Foundation
The Lark Trust
The Lauffer Family Charitable Foundation
The Leathersellers' Company Charitable Fund
The Leche Trust
The Kennedy Leigh Charitable Trust

Morris Leigh Foundation
The Leverhulme Trust
Lord Leverhulme's Charitable Trust
The Limbourne Trust
Limoges Charitable Trust
The Linbury Trust
The Linden Charitable Trust
The Enid Linder Foundation
The Ruth and Stuart Lipton Charitable Trust
The Charles Littlewood Hill Trust
The Second Joseph Aaron Littman Foundation
Jack Livingstone Charitable Trust
The Charles Lloyd Foundation
Lloyds Bank Foundation for Northern Ireland
The William and Katherine Longman Trust
The Ruth and Jack Lunzer Charitable Trust
Lord and Lady Lurgan Trust
John Lyon's Charity
The Sir Jack Lyons Charitable Trust
Sylvanus Lysons Charity
The Mackintosh Foundation
The MacRobert Trust
The Ian Mactaggart Trust
The Mageni Trust
The Brian Maguire Charitable Trust
Man Group plc Charitable Trust
The Manchester Guardian Society Charitable Trust
The Manifold Charitable Trust
The Michael Marks Charitable Trust
John Martin's Charity
The Nancie Massey Charitable Trust
The Brian Mercer Charitable Trust
The Mercers' Charitable Foundation
The Merchant Venturers' Charity
The Merchants' House of Glasgow
Millennium Stadium Charitable Trust (Ymddiriedolaeth Elusennol Stadiwm y Mileniwm)
The Millward Charitable Trust
Minge's Gift and the Pooled Trusts
The Brian Mitchell Charitable Settlement
The Esmé Mitchell Trust
The Modiano Charitable Trust
The Monument Trust
The Henry Moore Foundation

**57**

The Morel Charitable Trust
The Diana and Allan
    Morgenthau Charitable
    Trust
The John R. Murray Charitable
    Trust
The Music Sales Charitable
    Trust
The National Art Collections
    Fund
The National Manuscripts
    Conservation Trust
Network for Social Change
The Normanby Charitable Trust
The Community Foundation for
    Northern Ireland
The Northwood Charitable
    Trust
The Notgrove Trust
The Oakdale Trust
The Oakley Charitable Trust
The Ofenheim Charitable Trust
Oglesby Charitable Trust
Old Possum's Practical Trust
The Ouseley Trust
The Owen Family Trust
The James Pantyfedwen
    Foundation
The Pell Charitable Trust
The Peltz Trust
The Performing Right Society
    Foundation
The Phillips and Rubens
    Charitable Trust
The Bernard Piggott Charitable
    Trust
The Pilgrim Trust
The Austin and Hope
    Pilkington Trust
The Sir Harry Pilkington Trust
    Fund
Estate of the Late Colonel
    W. W. Pilkington Will Trusts
    – The General Charity Fund
The Polonsky Foundation
The John Porter Charitable
    Trust
The Porter Foundation
The Prince of Wales's
    Charitable Foundation
Mr and Mrs J. A. Pye's
    Charitable Settlement
Quercus Trust
The RVW Trust
The Radcliffe Trust
The Ragdoll Foundation
Ranworth Trust
The Ravensdale Trust
The Rayne Foundation
The Rhododendron Trust
The Clive Richards Charity
Rix-Thompson-Rothenberg
    Foundation
The Robertson Trust
The Roddick Foundation
The Rose Foundation

The Roughley Charitable Trust
The Rowlands Trust
Royal Docks Trust (London)
The Royal Victoria Hall
    Foundation
The Rubin Foundation
The Michael Sacher Charitable
    Trust
The Michael Harry Sacher
    Trust
Raymond and Beverly Sackler
    1988 Foundation
The Sackler Trust
The Alan and Babette
    Sainsbury Charitable Fund
The Andrew Salvesen
    Charitable Trust
Coral Samuel Charitable Trust
The Basil Samuel Charitable
    Trust
The Sands Family Trust
The Scarfe Charitable Trust
Schroder Charity Trust
The Frieda Scott Charitable
    Trust
The Archie Sherman Charitable
    Trust
The R. C. Sherriff Rosebriars
    Trust
The Shetland Charitable Trust
The Bassil Shippam and
    Alsford Trust
David and Jennifer Sieff
    Charitable Trust
Skinners' Company Lady
    Neville Charity
The N. Smith Charitable
    Settlement
The E. C. Sosnow Charitable
    Trust
Spears-Stutz Charitable Trust
Rosalyn and Nicholas Springer
    Charitable Trust
The Stanley Foundation Ltd
Stevenson Family's Charitable
    Trust
The Stewarts Law Foundation
The John Swire (1989)
    Charitable Trust
Sylvia Waddilove Foundation
    UK
A. P. Taylor Trust
The Thistle Trust
The Sue Thomson Foundation
The Trefoil Trust
The Underwood Trust
The Albert Van Den Bergh
    Charitable Trust
The Vardy Foundation
Veneziana Fund
Wakeham Trust
Robert and Felicity Waley-
    Cohen Charitable Trust
Sir Siegmund Warburg's
    Voluntary Settlement
The Ward Blenkinsop Trust

The Waterloo Foundation
The Wessex Youth Trust
The Barbara Whatmore
    Charitable Trust
The Whitaker Charitable Trust
The Williams Charitable Trust
The Harold Hyam Wingate
    Foundation
The Wolfson Foundation
The Woodward Charitable
    Trust
The Wyseliot Charitable Trust
The William Allen Young
    Charitable Trust
The Marjorie and Arnold Ziff
    Charitable Foundation
The Zochonis Charitable Trust

## Access to the arts

Barchester Healthcare
    Foundation
The Big Lottery Fund (see also
    Awards for All)
The Chetwode Foundation
Creative Scotland
Gamlen Charitable Trust
Paul Hamlyn Foundation
The Heritage of London Trust
    Limited
Lloyds Bank Foundation for
    Northern Ireland

## Amateur and community arts

The Ashden Trust
Calouste Gulbenkian
    Foundation – UK Branch
The Ericson Trust
The Joyce Fletcher Charitable
    Trust
The Horne Foundation
The Community Foundation for
    Northern Ireland
The Oakdale Trust
The James Pantyfedwen
    Foundation
The Ragdoll Foundation
Wakeham Trust

## Art and culture of specific countries

The Baring Foundation
Calouste Gulbenkian
    Foundation – UK Branch
Creative Scotland
The Great Britain Sasakawa
    Foundation

## Arts management, policy and planning

The Eric Anker-Petersen Charity
Creative Scotland
Miles Trust for the Putney and Roehampton Community
The Peter Moores Foundation
The Scottish Arts Council

## Combined arts

The Joyce Fletcher Charitable Trust

## Crafts

The Ernest Cook Trust
The Girdlers' Company Charitable Trust
The Ironmongers' Foundation
Minge's Gift and the Pooled Trusts
The Community Foundation for Northern Ireland
The Radcliffe Trust

## Disability arts

The A. B. Charitable Trust
Barchester Healthcare Foundation
The Barnwood House Trust
Creative Scotland
The Jungels-Winkler Charitable Foundation
Lloyds Bank Foundation for Northern Ireland
Rix-Thompson-Rothenberg Foundation

## Libraries

Barchester Healthcare Foundation
The Barnwood House Trust
The Big Lottery Fund (see also Awards for All)
The Francis Coales Charitable Foundation
Colwinston Charitable Trust
Creative Scotland
The J. G. Graves Charitable Trust
Paul Hamlyn Foundation
The Heritage of London Trust Limited
The Second Joseph Aaron Littman Foundation
Lloyds Bank Foundation for Northern Ireland

The John R. Murray Charitable Trust
The Pilgrim Trust
Rix-Thompson-Rothenberg Foundation

## Literature

The Joyce Fletcher Charitable Trust
The Follett Trust
The Garrick Charitable Trust
The John R. Murray Charitable Trust
The Sue Thomson Foundation

## Museums and galleries

The Victor Adda Foundation
The Armourers' and Brasiers' Gauntlet Trust
The Aurelius Charitable Trust
The Christopher Cadbury Charitable Trust
The Clore Duffield Foundation
The Francis Coales Charitable Foundation
The John S. Cohen Foundation
The Cumber Family Charitable Trust
The Djanogly Foundation
The Joyce Fletcher Charitable Trust
The Girdlers' Company Charitable Trust
Golden Charitable Trust
The J. G. Graves Charitable Trust
The Heritage of London Trust Limited
The Leche Trust
Jack Livingstone Charitable Trust
The Manifold Charitable Trust
The Henry Moore Foundation
The John R. Murray Charitable Trust
The National Art Collections Fund
The National Manuscripts Conservation Trust
The Pilgrim Trust
The Radcliffe Trust
Raymond and Beverly Sackler 1988 Foundation
Spears-Stutz Charitable Trust

## Performing arts

Angus Allnatt Charitable Foundation
British Record Industry Trust
Colwinston Charitable Trust
Creative Scotland
Dunard Fund
Henley Educational Trust
Skinners' Company Lady Neville Charity
Spears-Stutz Charitable Trust
Sylvanus Lysons Charity
The Bernard Piggott Charitable Trust
The Bertarelli UK Foundation
The Boltini Trust
The Boris Karloff Charitable Foundation
The Britten-Pears Foundation
The Charles Lloyd Foundation
The Davis Foundation
The Deakin Charitable Trust
The Delius Trust
The Derek Butler Trust
The Equity Trust Fund
The Eric Anker-Petersen Charity
The Fort Foundation
The Freshgate Trust Foundation
The Garrick Charitable Trust
The Gatsby Charitable Foundation
The Gibbs Charitable Trust
The Girdlers' Company Charitable Trust
The Gordon Fraser Charitable Trust
The Harding Trust
The Hinrichsen Foundation
The Holst Foundation
The Hugh Fraser Foundation
The John S. Cohen Foundation
The Joyce Fletcher Charitable Trust
The Kohn Foundation
The Leche Trust
The Mackintosh Foundation
The MacRobert Trust
The Merchants' House of Glasgow
The Michael and Ilse Katz Foundation
The Millward Charitable Trust
The Northwood Charitable Trust
The Oakdale Trust
The Ouseley Trust
The Pell Charitable Trust
The Performing Right Society Foundation
The RVW Trust
The Radcliffe Trust
The Richard Carne Trust
The Rowlands Trust
The Royal Victoria Hall Foundation
The Sands Family Trust
The Whitaker Charitable Trust
The Williams Charitable Trust

## Dance

The Girdlers' Company Charitable Trust

## Music

Angus Allnatt Charitable Foundation
The Boltini Trust
British Record Industry Trust
The Britten-Pears Foundation
The Derek Butler Trust
The Deakin Charitable Trust
The Delius Trust
Dunard Fund
The Joyce Fletcher Charitable Trust
The Hugh Fraser Foundation
The Freshgate Trust Foundation
The Gatsby Charitable Foundation
The Hinrichsen Foundation
The Holst Foundation
The Michael and Ilse Katz Foundation
The Leche Trust
The Charles Lloyd Foundation
Sylvanus Lysons Charity
The Mackintosh Foundation
The MacRobert Trust
The Oakdale Trust
The Ouseley Trust
The Performing Right Society Foundation
The RVW Trust
The Radcliffe Trust
The Rowlands Trust
The Whitaker Charitable Trust

## Theatre

The Bernard Piggott Charitable Trust
The Bertarelli UK Foundation
The Equity Trust Fund
The Eric Anker-Petersen Charity
The Gatsby Charitable Foundation
The Gibbs Charitable Trust
The Leche Trust
The Mackintosh Foundation
The Royal Victoria Hall Foundation
The Williams Charitable Trust

## Visual arts

Colwinston Charitable Trust
Creative Scotland
Dunard Fund

The Gilbert and Eileen Edgar Foundation
The Elephant Trust
The Joyce Fletcher Charitable Trust
The Gordon Fraser Charitable Trust
The Brian Mercer Charitable Trust
The Henry Moore Foundation
The National Art Collections Fund

## Fine art

The Gilbert and Eileen Edgar Foundation
The Henry Moore Foundation
The National Art Collections Fund

## Public art/sculpture

The Henry Moore Foundation

## Heritage and the built environment

Allchurches Trust Ltd
The Architectural Heritage Fund
Arts Council of Wales (Cyngor Celfyddydau Cymru)
The Ove Arup Foundation
A. J. H. Ashby Will Trust
The Baird Trust
The Balney Charitable Trust
The Band Trust
The Barbour Foundation
The Barcapel Foundation
The Beaverbrook Foundation
The Bedfordshire and Hertfordshire Historic Churches Trust
The Bellahouston Bequest Fund
The Bernadette Charitable Trust
Birmingham International Airport Community Trust
The Harold and Alice Bridges Charity
Miss Marion Broughton's Charitable Trust
The T. B. H. Brunner Charitable Settlement
The Buckinghamshire Historic Churches Trust
The Bulldog Trust Limited
The Arnold Burton 1998 Charitable Trust
The Cambridgeshire Historic Churches Trust
The Frederick and Phyllis Cann Trust
The Carpenters' Company Charitable Trust
The Chipping Sodbury Town Lands Charity
The City Educational Trust Fund
The Francis Coales Charitable Foundation
The John S. Cohen Foundation
Colyer-Fergusson Charitable Trust
The Congregational and General Charitable Trust
The Conservation Foundation
The Catherine Cookson Charitable Trust
The Duke of Cornwall's Benevolent Fund
Country Houses Foundation
The Cumber Family Charitable Trust
The Henry and Suzanne Davis Foundation
The Derbyshire Churches and Chapels Preservation Trust

The Devon Historic Churches Trust
The Dorset Historic Churches Trust
The Drapers' Charitable Fund
The Dulverton Trust
The Gilbert and Eileen Edgar Foundation
Edinburgh Trust No 2 Account
The Elephant Trust
The Ellis Campbell Foundation
The Ericson Trust
The Essex Fairway Charitable Trust
The Essex Heritage Trust
The Alan Evans Memorial Trust
The Fairway Trust
The John Feeney Charitable Bequest
Fisherbeck Charitable Trust
The Fishmongers' Company's Charitable Trust
Marc Fitch Fund
The Jill Franklin Trust
The Gordon Fraser Charitable Trust
The Freshgate Trust Foundation
Friends of Essex Churches Trust
The Friends of Kent Churches
The Frognal Trust
The Galanthus Trust
The Gannochy Trust
The Samuel Gardner Memorial Trust
The Girdlers' Company Charitable Trust
The Gloucestershire Historic Churches Trust
The Goldsmiths' Company Charity
The Golsoncott Foundation
The Gosling Foundation Limited
The Greys Charitable Trust
The Grocers' Charity
The Hadrian Trust
The Hampshire and Islands Historic Churches Trust
The W. A. Handley Charitable Trust
The Harbour Foundation
The Maurice Hatter Foundation
The Charles Hayward Foundation
The Headley Trust
The Michael Heller Charitable Foundation
The Simon Heller Charitable Settlement
The Herefordshire Historic Churches Trust
The Heritage of London Trust Limited

The Hillingdon Partnership Trust
The Hiscox Foundation
The Sir Joseph Hotung Charitable Settlement
The Daniel Howard Trust
The Idlewild Trust
The Iliffe Family Charitable Trust
Investream Charitable Trust
The Ironmongers' Foundation
The Jerusalem Trust
The Jordan Charitable Foundation
John Thomas Kennedy Charitable Foundation
The Robert Kiln Charitable Trust
The Langtree Trust
Laslett's (Hinton) Charity
Mrs F. B. Laurence Charitable Trust
The Raymond and Blanche Lawson Charitable Trust
The Leche Trust
Leicester and Leicestershire Historic Churches Preservation Trust
The Kennedy Leigh Charitable Trust
Limoges Charitable Trust
The Linbury Trust
Lincolnshire Churches Trust
The Charles Littlewood Hill Trust
The Charles Lloyd Foundation
John Lyon's Charity
Manchester Airport Community Trust Fund
The Manifold Charitable Trust
The Michael Marks Charitable Trust
Charity of John Marshall
The Mercers' Charitable Foundation
The Gerald Micklem Charitable Trust
Minton Charitable Trust
The Laurence Misener Charitable Trust
The Esmé Mitchell Trust
The Monument Trust
Mrs Waterhouse Charitable Trust
The John R. Murray Charitable Trust
The National Churches Trust
The Normanby Charitable Trust
The Northern Rock Foundation
The Nottinghamshire Historic Churches Trust
The Owen Family Trust
The James Pantyfedwen Foundation
Miss M. E. Swinton Paterson's Charitable Trust

The Jack Patston Charitable Trust
The Pilgrim Trust
The Prince of Wales's Charitable Foundation
Mr and Mrs J. A. Pye's Charitable Settlement
The Radcliffe Trust
The Robertson Trust
Mrs L. D. Rope Third Charitable Settlement
The Roughley Charitable Trust
Royal Docks Trust (London)
The J. S. and E. C. Rymer Charitable Trust
The Peter Samuel Charitable Trust
Schroder Charity Trust
The Shears Foundation
The Shetland Charitable Trust
SITA Cornwall Trust Limited
The Stanley Smith UK Horticultural Trust
Somerset Churches Trust
Stevenson Family's Charitable Trust
Peter Stormonth Darling Charitable Trust
The Suffolk Historic Churches Trust
The Sussex Historic Churches Trust
The Connie and Albert Taylor Charitable Trust
The Michael Uren Foundation
Veneziana Fund
Welsh Church Fund – Dyfed area (Carmarthenshire, Ceredigion and Pembrokeshire)
The Barbara Whatmore Charitable Trust
The Colonel W. H. Whitbread Charitable Trust
The Wolfson Foundation
The Worcestershire and Dudley Historic Churches Trust
The Yorkshire Dales Millennium Trust
The Yorkshire Historic Churches Trust
The Marjorie and Arnold Ziff Charitable Foundation

## Arts and the environment

The Carpenters' Company Charitable Trust
The Conservation Foundation
The Samuel Gardner Memorial Trust
The Headley Trust
The Leche Trust

Manchester Airport Community
   Trust Fund
The Monument Trust
The Shetland Charitable Trust
The Stanley Smith UK
   Horticultural Trust
The Marjorie and Arnold Ziff
   Charitable Foundation

## Landscape

The Conservation Foundation
The Samuel Gardner Memorial
   Trust
Manchester Airport Community
   Trust Fund
The Stanley Smith UK
   Horticultural Trust
The Marjorie and Arnold Ziff
   Charitable Foundation

## Heritage

The Architectural Heritage
   Fund
Arts Council of Wales (Cyngor
   Celfyddydau Cymru)
A. J. H. Ashby Will Trust
Birmingham International
   Airport Community Trust
The T. B. H. Brunner
   Charitable Settlement
The Arnold Burton 1998
   Charitable Trust
The Carpenters' Company
   Charitable Trust
The Francis Coales Charitable
   Foundation
The Henry and Suzanne Davis
   Foundation
The Elephant Trust
The Ericson Trust
The Essex Fairway Charitable
   Trust
The Essex Heritage Trust
The John Feeney Charitable
   Bequest
The Fishmongers' Company's
   Charitable Trust
Marc Fitch Fund
The Freshgate Trust
   Foundation
The Frognal Trust
The Samuel Gardner Memorial
   Trust
The Goldsmiths' Company
   Charity
The Gosling Foundation
   Limited
The Grocers' Charity
The W. A. Handley Charitable
   Trust
The Maurice Hatter Foundation
The Headley Trust

The Michael Heller Charitable
   Foundation
The Simon Heller Charitable
   Settlement
The Ironmongers' Foundation
The Langtree Trust
The Leche Trust
The Linbury Trust
The Manifold Charitable Trust
The Gerald Micklem Charitable
   Trust
The Laurence Misener
   Charitable Trust
The Esmé Mitchell Trust
The Monument Trust
Mrs Waterhouse Charitable
   Trust
The John R. Murray Charitable
   Trust
The Normanby Charitable Trust
The Northern Rock Foundation
The Owen Family Trust
Miss M. E. Swinton Paterson's
   Charitable Trust
The Pilgrim Trust
The Radcliffe Trust
The Robertson Trust
Mrs L. D. Rope Third
   Charitable Settlement
The Peter Samuel Charitable
   Trust
The Shears Foundation
Peter Stormonth Darling
   Charitable Trust
The Connie and Albert Taylor
   Charitable Trust
Veneziana Fund
The Wolfson Foundation
The Worcestershire and
   Dudley Historic Churches
   Trust

## Maintenance and preservation of buildings

The Architectural Heritage
   Fund
The Baird Trust
The Bedfordshire and
   Hertfordshire Historic
   Churches Trust
The Bellahouston Bequest
   Fund
The Bernadette Charitable
   Trust
Miss Marion Broughton's
   Charitable Trust
The Buckinghamshire Historic
   Churches Trust
The Cambridgeshire Historic
   Churches Trust
The Carpenters' Company
   Charitable Trust

The City Educational Trust
   Fund
The Francis Coales Charitable
   Foundation
Colyer-Fergusson Charitable
   Trust
The Congregational and
   General Charitable Trust
The Conservation Foundation
The Duke of Cornwall's
   Benevolent Fund
The Derbyshire Churches and
   Chapels Preservation Trust
The Devon Historic Churches
   Trust
The Dorset Historic Churches
   Trust
The Dulverton Trust
Edinburgh Trust No 2 Account
The Ellis Campbell Foundation
The Essex Heritage Trust
The Alan Evans Memorial Trust
The Fishmongers' Company's
   Charitable Trust
The Jill Franklin Trust
Friends of Essex Churches
   Trust
The Friends of Kent Churches
The Girdlers' Company
   Charitable Trust
The Gloucestershire Historic
   Churches Trust
The Greys Charitable Trust
The Grocers' Charity
The Hadrian Trust
The Hampshire and Islands
   Historic Churches Trust
The Headley Trust
The Herefordshire Historic
   Churches Trust
The Jordan Charitable
   Foundation
Laslett's (Hinton) Charity
Leicester and Leicestershire
   Historic Churches
   Preservation Trust
Lincolnshire Churches Trust
The Charles Lloyd Foundation
Manchester Airport Community
   Trust Fund
The Manifold Charitable Trust
Charity of John Marshall
   (Marshall's Charity)
The Monument Trust
The National Churches Trust
The Nottinghamshire Historic
   Churches Trust
The James Pantyfedwen
   Foundation
Miss M. E. Swinton Paterson's
   Charitable Trust
The Jack Patston Charitable
   Trust
The Pilgrim Trust
The Prince of Wales's
   Charitable Foundation

Royal Docks Trust (London)
Somerset Churches Trust
The Suffolk Historic Churches Trust
The Sussex Historic Churches Trust
The Connie and Albert Taylor Charitable Trust
The Michael Uren Foundation
Welsh Church Fund – Dyfed area (Carmarthenshire, Ceredigion and Pembrokeshire)
The Worcestershire and Dudley Historic Churches Trust
The Yorkshire Historic Churches Trust

## Religious buildings

The Architectural Heritage Fund
The Bedfordshire and Hertfordshire Historic Churches Trust
The Bellahouston Bequest Fund
The Bernadette Charitable Trust
Miss Marion Broughton's Charitable Trust
The Buckinghamshire Historic Churches Trust
The Cambridgeshire Historic Churches Trust
The Francis Coales Charitable Foundation
Colyer-Fergusson Charitable Trust
The Congregational and General Charitable Trust
The Derbyshire Churches and Chapels Preservation Trust
The Devon Historic Churches Trust
The Dorset Historic Churches Trust
The Alan Evans Memorial Trust
The Fishmongers' Company's Charitable Trust
The Jill Franklin Trust
Friends of Essex Churches Trust
The Friends of Kent Churches
The Girdlers' Company Charitable Trust
The Gloucestershire Historic Churches Trust
The Grocers' Charity
The Hadrian Trust
The Hampshire and Islands Historic Churches Trust
The Headley Trust
The Herefordshire Historic Churches Trust

Laslett's (Hinton) Charity
Lincolnshire Churches Trust
The Charles Lloyd Foundation
The Manifold Charitable Trust
Charity of John Marshall (Marshall's Charity)
The Monument Trust
The National Churches Trust
The Nottinghamshire Historic Churches Trust
The James Pantyfedwen Foundation
The Jack Patston Charitable Trust
The Pilgrim Trust
The Prince of Wales's Charitable Foundation
Somerset Churches Trust
The Suffolk Historic Churches Trust
The Sussex Historic Churches Trust
Welsh Church Fund – Dyfed area (Carmarthenshire, Ceredigion and Pembrokeshire)
The Yorkshire Historic Churches Trust

## Restoration and maintenance of inland waterways

The Carpenters' Company Charitable Trust
The Gerald Micklem Charitable Trust

## Built environment – education and research

The Ove Arup Foundation
The Frederick and Phyllis Cann Trust
The Carpenters' Company Charitable Trust
The Gannochy Trust
The Worcestershire and Dudley Historic Churches Trust

## Humanities

The Aurelius Charitable Trust
British Institute at Ankara
The Barrow Cadbury Trust
Calouste Gulbenkian Foundation – UK Branch
The Gaynor Cemlyn-Jones Trust
The Francis Coales Charitable Foundation
The Denise Cohen Charitable Trust
The Daiwa Anglo-Japanese Foundation
Edinburgh Trust No 2 Account
Marc Fitch Fund
The Golsoncott Foundation
The Great Britain Sasakawa Foundation
The Sir Joseph Hotung Charitable Settlement
The Inlight Trust
The Robert Kiln Charitable Trust
The Neil Kreitman Foundation
The Linbury Trust
The Michael Marks Charitable Trust
The Mount Everest Foundation
The Peltz Trust
Polden-Puckham Charitable Foundation
The Sir Cliff Richard Charitable Trust
Mrs L. D. Rope Third Charitable Settlement
The Rothley Trust
The Joseph Rowntree Charitable Trust
The Tinsley Foundation
The Westcroft Trust
The W. Wing Yip and Brothers Foundation

## Archaeology

Marc Fitch Fund
The Robert Kiln Charitable Trust

## History

The Gaynor Cemlyn-Jones Trust
The Francis Coales Charitable Foundation
Marc Fitch Fund

63

## International understanding

The Barrow Cadbury Trust
Calouste Gulbenkian Foundation – UK Branch
The Daiwa Anglo-Japanese Foundation
Edinburgh Trust No 2 Account
The Great Britain Sasakawa Foundation
The Mount Everest Foundation
The Rothley Trust
The Tinsley Foundation
The Westcroft Trust
The W. Wing Yip and Brothers Foundation

## Philosophy and ethics

The Inlight Trust
Polden-Puckham Charitable Foundation
The Sir Cliff Richard Charitable Trust
Mrs L. D. Rope Third Charitable Settlement
The Joseph Rowntree Charitable Trust

## Media and communications

The Eric Anker-Petersen Charity
The J. J. Charitable Trust
Paul Hamlyn Foundation
The Sir Joseph Hotung Charitable Settlement
The David Lean Foundation
The Roddick Foundation

## Recreation and sport

Access Sport
Angus Allnatt Charitable Foundation
ASCB Charitable Fund
The Asda Foundation
A. J. H. Ashby Will Trust
Bag4Sport Foundation
The Barnwood House Trust
BBC Children in Need
The John Beckwith Charitable Trust
The Bellahouston Bequest Fund
The Big Lottery Fund (see also Awards for All)
Birmingham International Airport Community Trust
The Blagrave Trust
BOOST Charitable Trust
Canoe Foundation
The Carnegie Dunfermline Trust
Carter's Educational Foundation
The Chetwode Foundation
The Chipping Sodbury Town Lands Charity
The Clover Trust
The Robert Clutterbuck Charitable Trust
The Coalfields Regeneration Trust
The Bernard Coleman Trust
Community First
The Congleton Inclosure Trust
Michael Cornish Charitable Trust
The Cray Trust
D. J. H. Currie Memorial Trust
The Cwmbran Trust
The Hamilton Davies Trust
The Sir John Eastwood Foundation
The Vernon N. Ely Charitable Trust
The English Schools' Football Association
The Essex and Southend Sports Trust
The Fairway Trust
The February Foundation
The John Feeney Charitable Bequest
The Football Association National Sports Centre Trust
The Football Association Youth Trust
The Football Foundation
The Joseph Strong Frazer Trust
Gatwick Airport Community Trust

The Robert Gavron Charitable Trust
The Generations Foundation
Get Kids Going
The Girdlers' Company Charitable Trust
The Golf Foundation Limited
The Granada Foundation
The Grange Farm Centre Trust
The J. G. Graves Charitable Trust
Hampton Fuel Allotment
The Harpur Trust
The Harris Charity
The Peter Harrison Foundation
The Dorothy Hay-Bolton Charitable Trust
Hedley Foundation Limited
Henley Educational Trust
The Heritage of London Trust Limited
The Holywood Trust
The Johnnie Johnson Trust
The Boris Karloff Charitable Foundation
The Kelly Family Charitable Trust
The Kreitman Foundation
The Kyte Charitable Trust
Lancashire Environmental Fund Limited
The William Leech Charity
The London Marathon Charitable Trust Limited
The Lord's Taverners
John Lyon's Charity
The Dan Maskell Tennis Trust
The Brian Mercer Charitable Trust
The Merchant Taylors' Company Charities Fund
The Merchant Venturers' Charity
The Gerald Micklem Charitable Trust
Middlesex Sports Foundation
Millennium Stadium Charitable Trust (Ymddiriedolaeth Elusennol Stadiwm y Mileniwm)
Minton Charitable Trust
The Morel Charitable Trust
British Motor Sports Training Trust
The National Express Foundation
The National Hockey Foundation
The Community Foundation for Northern Ireland
The Northern Rock Foundation
The Pedmore Sporting Club Trust Fund
People's Postcode Trust
The Premier League Charitable Fund

The Puri Foundation
Quartet Community Foundation
The Racing Foundation
The Richmond Parish Lands Charity
The Robertson Trust
Royal Docks Trust (London)
The Saddlers' Company Charitable Fund
The Peter Saunders Trust
The Shears Foundation
The Shetland Charitable Trust
The Shipwrights' Company Charitable Fund
The Huntly and Margery Sinclair Charitable Trust
SITA Cornwall Trust Limited
Sported Foundation
Peter Stormonth Darling Charitable Trust
Swimathon Foundation
The Connie and Albert Taylor Charitable Trust
A. P. Taylor Trust
The Tennis Foundation
The Thompson Family Charitable Trust
The Tower Hill Trust
The Wessex Youth Trust
David Wilson Foundation
Wooden Spoon Society
The William Allen Young Charitable Trust
Youth United Foundation

## Parks and open spaces

Community First
The John Feeney Charitable Bequest
The J. G. Graves Charitable Trust
The Heritage of London Trust Limited
Lancashire Environmental Fund Limited
The Merchant Venturers' Charity
SITA Cornwall Trust Limited
The Tower Hill Trust

## Recreation facilities

The Carnegie Dunfermline Trust
Carter's Educational Foundation
The Chipping Sodbury Town Lands Charity
Community First (Landfill Communities Fund)

The John Feeney Charitable Bequest
The Football Association National Sports Centre Trust
The Granada Foundation
The J. G. Graves Charitable Trust
Hampton Fuel Allotment
The Peter Harrison Foundation
Henley Educational Trust
The Heritage of London Trust Limited
Lancashire Environmental Fund Limited
The Merchant Venturers' Charity
The Community Foundation for Northern Ireland
The Northern Rock Foundation
SITA Cornwall Trust Limited
The Tower Hill Trust
Wooden Spoon Society

## Sports for people with a disability

The Barnwood House Trust
The Blagrave Trust
BOOST Charitable Trust
The Football Association National Sports Centre Trust
Get Kids Going
The Peter Harrison Foundation
The Dorothy Hay-Bolton Charitable Trust
Henley Educational Trust
The London Marathon Charitable Trust Limited
The Lord's Taverners
The Dan Maskell Tennis Trust
The Brian Mercer Charitable Trust
The Gerald Micklem Charitable Trust
Minton Charitable Trust
The Community Foundation for Northern Ireland
Wooden Spoon Society

## Sports

A. J. H. Ashby Will Trust
Access Sport
Angus Allnatt Charitable Foundation
BOOST Charitable Trust
British Motor Sports Training Trust
D. J. H. Currie Memorial Trust
Henley Educational Trust

## Development, housing and employment

Millennium Stadium Charitable Trust (Ymddiriedolaeth Elusennol Stadiwm y Mileniwm)
Minton Charitable Trust
Peter Stormonth Darling Charitable Trust
Swimathon Foundation
The Boris Karloff Charitable Foundation
The Chetwode Foundation
The Clover Trust
The Cwmbran Trust
The English Schools' Football Association
The Football Association National Sports Centre Trust
The Football Association Youth Trust
The Football Foundation
The Golf Foundation Limited
The Huntly and Margery Sinclair Charitable Trust
The John Beckwith Charitable Trust
The Kyte Charitable Trust
The London Marathon Charitable Trust Limited
The Lord's Taverners
The Merchant Taylors' Company Charities Fund
The National Hockey Foundation
The Peter Harrison Foundation
The Racing Foundation
The Richmond Parish Lands Charity
The Saddlers' Company Charitable Fund
The Shipwrights' Company Charitable Fund
The Sir John Eastwood Foundation
The Tennis Foundation
The Thompson Family Charitable Trust
The Vernon N. Ely Charitable Trust
Wooden Spoon Society

ABF The Soldiers' Charity
The ACT Foundation
The AIM Foundation
The Ajahma Charitable Trust
The H. B. Allen Charitable Trust
Anglo American Group Foundation
The Archbishop's Council – The Church and Community Fund
The Asda Foundation
The Ashden Trust
The Ashley Family Foundation
The Ashmore Foundation
The Associated Country Women of the World
AstonMansfield Charitable Trust
The Scott Bader Commonwealth Limited
The Balmore Trust
The Balney Charitable Trust
The Band Trust
The Bank of Scotland Foundation
The Barbour Foundation
The Baring Foundation
Barnes Workhouse Fund
The Barnwood House Trust
BC Partners Foundation
The Bedfordshire and Luton Community Foundation
The Berkeley Charitable Foundation
The Bestway Foundation
The Big Lottery Fund (see also Awards for All)
Birmingham International Airport Community Trust
The BlackRock (UK) Charitable Trust
The Blagrave Trust
Boots Charitable Trust
The Oliver Borthwick Memorial Trust
The Liz and Terry Bramall Foundation
The Bramhope Trust
The Broderers' Charity Trust
The Consuelo and Anthony Brooke Charitable Trust
R. S. Brownless Charitable Trust
The Brownsword Charitable Foundation
Buckinghamshire Community Foundation
The Burghley Family Trust
Henry T. and Lucy B. Cadbury Charitable Trust
The Cadbury Foundation

The Barrow Cadbury Trust
CAFOD (Catholic Agency for Overseas Development)
Community Foundation for Calderdale
Calouste Gulbenkian Foundation – UK Branch
The Carpenters' Company Charitable Trust
CHK Charities Limited
Chrysalis Trust
Church Urban Fund
The City Bridge Trust
The Cleopatra Trust
The Clothworkers' Foundation
The Coalfields Regeneration Trust
The Cole Charitable Trust
John and Freda Coleman Charitable Trust
The Coltstaple Trust
Colyer-Fergusson Charitable Trust
The Consolidated Charities for the Infirm – Merchant Taylors' Company
The Cooks Charity
Mabel Cooper Charity
The Evan Cornish Foundation
The Cotton Industry War Memorial Trust
Coutts Charitable Foundation
Dudley and Geoffrey Cox Charitable Trust
Michael Crawford Children's Charity
The Cray Trust
The Cumber Family Charitable Trust
Cumbria Community Foundation
Baron Davenport's Charity
The Sandy Dewhirst Charitable Trust
The Diageo Foundation
The Digbeth Trust Limited
Dorset Community Foundation
The Dorus Trust
The Drapers' Charitable Fund
The Dulverton Trust
The Dyers' Company Charitable Trust
The Ebenezer Trust
The Economist Charitable Trust
The Gilbert Edgar Trust
The Edith Maud Ellis 1985 Charitable Trust
The Englefield Charitable Trust
The Epigoni Trust
Essex Community Foundation
Sir John Evelyn's Charity
The Expat Foundation
Esmée Fairbairn Foundation
The Allan and Nesta Ferguson Charitable Settlement

The Football Association
  National Sports Centre
  Trust
The Football Foundation
Ford Britain Trust
The Oliver Ford Charitable
  Trust
The Donald Forrester Trust
Friends Provident Charitable
  Foundation
The Patrick & Helena Frost
  Foundation
The Fuserna Foundation
  General Charitable Trust
The G. D. Charitable Trust
The Gatsby Charitable
  Foundation
Gatwick Airport Community
  Trust
The Robert Gavron Charitable
  Trust
Jacqueline and Michael Gee
  Charitable Trust
The G. C. Gibson Charitable
  Trust
The Girdlers' Company
  Charitable Trust
Gloucestershire Community
  Foundation
Grand Charitable Trust of the
  Order of Women
  Freemasons
GrantScape
Greenham Common
  Community Trust Limited
The Greggs Foundation
The Grimmitt Trust
The Grocers' Charity
The Hadfield Trust
Hampshire and Isle of Wight
  Community Foundation
Hampton Fuel Allotment
The W. A. Handley Charitable
  Trust
The Kathleen Hannay
  Memorial Charity
The Haramead Trust
The Harborne Parish Lands
  Charity
The Harbour Foundation
William Harding's Charity
The Hare of Steep Charitable
  Trust (HOST)
The Harpur Trust
The Edith Lilian Harrison 2000
  Foundation
The Alfred And Peggy Harvey
  Charitable Trust
The Hasluck Charitable Trust
The Charles Hayward
  Foundation
May Hearnshaw Charitable
  Trust
Heart of England Community
  Foundation
Help the Homeless Limited

The Hemby Charitable Trust
The Christina Mary Hendrie
  Trust for Scottish and
  Canadian Charities
Philip Sydney Henman
  Deceased Will Trust
Herefordshire Community
  Foundation
The Hertfordshire Community
  Foundation
The Alan Edward Higgs Charity
The Hilden Charitable Fund
The Hillingdon Community
  Trust
The Hillingdon Partnership
  Trust
The Lady Hind Trust
The Hiscox Foundation
The Henry C. Hoare Charitable
  Trust
The Hollick Family Charitable
  Trust
The Edward Holt Trust
The Mary Homfray Charitable
  Trust
Sir Harold Hood's Charitable
  Trust
Hope for Youth (NI)
The Thomas J. Horne
  Memorial Trust
The Worshipful Company of
  Horners' Charitable Trusts
The Hospital of God at
  Greatham
James T. Howat Charitable
  Trust
The Huggard Charitable Trust
Human Relief Foundation
The Hunter Foundation
Miss Agnes H. Hunter's Trust
Hyde Charitable Trust (Youth
  Plus)
Impetus – The Private Equity
  Foundation (Impetus – PEF)
Incommunities Foundation
The Innocent Foundation
The International Bankers
  Charitable Trust
Investream Charitable Trust
The Ireland Fund of Great
  Britain
Irish Youth Foundation (UK)
  Ltd (incorporating The
  Lawlor Foundation)
The Isle of Anglesey Charitable
  Trust
John James Bristol Foundation
The Jarman Charitable Trust
John Jarrold Trust
JCA Charitable Foundation
Rees Jeffreys Road Fund
Nick Jenkins Foundation
The Joffe Charitable Trust
The Johnson Foundation
The Johnson Wax Ltd
  Charitable Trust

The Joicey Trust
The Jordan Charitable
  Foundation
The Joron Charitable Trust
The Cyril and Eve Jumbo
  Charitable Trust
Anton Jurgens Charitable Trust
Jusaca Charitable Trust
John Thomas Kennedy
  Charitable Foundation
Kent Community Foundation
Kingdom Way Trust
The Kingsbury Charity
The Mary Kinross Charitable
  Trust
Robert Kitchin (Saddlers'
  Company)
The Sir James Knott Trust
The KPMG Foundation
The Heinz, Anna and Carol
  Kroch Foundation (HACKF)
John Laing Charitable Trust
Maurice and Hilda Laing
  Charitable Trust
The Beatrice Laing Trust
The Lambert Charitable Trust
Community Foundations for
  Lancashire and Merseyside
Duchy of Lancaster Benevolent
  Fund
LandAid Charitable Trust
The Jack Lane Charitable Trust
The Allen Lane Foundation
The R. J. Larg Family
  Charitable Trust
Laslett's (Hinton) Charity
Mrs F. B. Laurence Charitable
  Trust
Lawson Beckman Charitable
  Trust
The Raymond and Blanche
  Lawson Charitable Trust
The Leathersellers' Company
  Charitable Fund
The William Leech Charity
Leeds Building Society
  Charitable Foundation
Leicestershire, Leicester and
  Rutland Community
  Foundation
The Lennox and Wyfold
  Foundation
The Mark Leonard Trust
David and Ruth Lewis Family
  Charitable Trust
The Sir Edward Lewis
  Foundation
John Lewis Partnership
  General Community Fund
LHR Airport Communities Trust
Liberum Foundation
Lincolnshire Community
  Foundation
The Linden Charitable Trust
Lindenleaf Charitable Trust
Lloyd's Charities Trust

**67**

Lloyds Bank Foundation for England and Wales
Lloyds Bank Foundation for Northern Ireland
Lloyds TSB Foundation for Scotland
The Trust for London
The London Community Foundation
London Housing Foundation Ltd
The Lotus Foundation
Paul Lunn-Rockliffe Charitable Trust
C. F. Lunoe Trust Fund
John Lyon's Charity
The Mackintosh Foundation
The Mactaggart Third Fund
Manchester Airport Community Trust Fund
Lord Mayor of Manchester's Charity Appeal Trust
The W. M. Mann Foundation
R. W. Mann Trust
Market Harborough and The Bowdens Charity
The Hilda and Samuel Marks Foundation
Charlotte Marshall Charitable Trust
The Mathew Trust
The Matliwala Family Charitable Trust
The Medlock Charitable Trust
The Merchant Venturers' Charity
The Merchants' House of Glasgow
T. & J. Meyer Family Foundation Limited
The Mickel Fund
The Mickleham Trust
The Millfield House Foundation
The Mills Charity
Milton Keynes Community Foundation Limited
The Peter Minet Trust
The Mirianog Trust
The MITIE Foundation
Monmouthshire County Council Welsh Church Act Fund
The Monument Trust
The George A. Moore Foundation
John Moores Foundation (JMF)
The Morgan Charitable Foundation
The Morgan Foundation
Morgan Stanley International Foundation
The Morris Charitable Trust
Vyoel Moshe Charitable Trust
Mothercare Group Foundation
Moto in the Community
Muslim Hands
The National Churches Trust

The Nationwide Foundation
The Worshipful Company of Needlemakers' Charitable Fund
The NFU Mutual Charitable Trust
Nominet Charitable Foundation
Norfolk Community Foundation
The Community Foundation for Northern Ireland
The Northern Rock Foundation
The Norton Foundation
The Norwich Town Close Estate Charity
Nottinghamshire Community Foundation
Oizer Charitable Trust
The Harry Payne Fund
People's Postcode Trust
The Phillips and Rubens Charitable Trust
The Phillips Charitable Trust
The Pilgrim Trust
The Pilkington Charities Fund
The Premier League Charitable Fund
The Puebla Charitable Trust
The PwC Foundation
Ranworth Trust
The Eleanor Rathbone Charitable Trust
The Sigrid Rausing Trust
The Rayne Foundation
Eva Reckitt Trust Fund
Rivers Foundation
The Robertson Trust
Mrs L. D. Rope Third Charitable Settlement
The Joseph Rowntree Charitable Trust
Royal British Legion
Royal Docks Trust (London)
The Saddlers' Company Charitable Fund
The Saga Charitable Trust
The Sandhu Charitable Foundation
The Sants Charitable Trust
The Peter Saunders Trust
Foundation Scotland
Scottish Coal Industry Special Welfare Fund
The Scottish Power Energy People Trust
The Scottish Power Foundation
The SDL Foundation
The Seneca Trust
The Shanti Charitable Trust
The Sheldon Trust
SITA Cornwall Trust Limited
The Mrs Smith and Mount Trust
Sodexo Foundation
The Spero Foundation
The Spielman Charitable Trust
St James's Trust Settlement

St James's Place Foundation
St Monica Trust
The Stanley Foundation Ltd
The Peter Stebbings Memorial Charity
Sir Halley Stewart Trust
The Edward Stocks-Massey Bequest Fund
The Sussex Community Foundation
Sutton Coldfield Charitable Trust
The Hugh and Ruby Sykes Charitable Trust
C. B. and H. H. Taylor 1984 Trust
The Tresillian Trust
The Douglas Turner Trust
Community Foundation Serving Tyne and Wear and Northumberland
UIA Charitable Foundation
Ulster Garden Villages Ltd
The Nigel Vinson Charitable Trust
The Vodafone Foundation
Volant Charitable Trust
Voluntary Action Fund (VAF)
The Scurrah Wainwright Charity
Wakeham Trust
The Community Foundation in Wales
Wales Council for Voluntary Action
War on Want
The Waterloo Foundation
The Wates Foundation
The Welton Foundation
The Westminster Foundation
The Wixamtree Trust
The Wood Family Trust
Woodroffe Benton Foundation
The Woodward Charitable Trust
Yorkshire and Clydesdale Bank Foundation
The Yorkshire Dales Millennium Trust
Zurich Community Trust (UK) Limited

## Community and economic development

The AIM Foundation
The Archbishop's Council – The Church and Community Fund
The Asda Foundation
The Ashley Family Foundation
The Ashmore Foundation
The Balmore Trust
The Bank of Scotland Foundation

The Baring Foundation
The Barnwood House Trust
BC Partners Foundation
The Bedfordshire and Luton Community Foundation
The Bestway Foundation
Birmingham International Airport Community Trust
The Blagrave Trust
Boots Charitable Trust
The Liz and Terry Bramall Foundation
The Consuelo and Anthony Brooke Charitable Trust
The Brownsword Charitable Foundation
Buckinghamshire Community Foundation
The Cadbury Foundation
The Barrow Cadbury Trust
Community Foundation for Calderdale
Calouste Gulbenkian Foundation – UK Branch
CHK Charities Limited
Church Urban Fund
The Coalfields Regeneration Trust
The Cole Charitable Trust
Colyer-Fergusson Charitable Trust
The Evan Cornish Foundation
Coutts Charitable Foundation
Dudley and Geoffrey Cox Charitable Trust
The Cray Trust
The Cumber Family Charitable Trust
Cumbria Community Foundation
The Diageo Foundation
The Digbeth Trust Limited
The Dulverton Trust
The Economist Charitable Trust
The Edith Maud Ellis 1985 Charitable Trust
Essex Community Foundation
Esmée Fairbairn Foundation
The Allan and Nesta Ferguson Charitable Settlement
The Football Association National Sports Centre Trust
The Football Foundation
Ford Britain Trust
Friends Provident Charitable Foundation
The Patrick & Helena Frost Foundation
The Gatsby Charitable Foundation
Gatwick Airport Community Trust
The Robert Gavron Charitable Trust

The G. C. Gibson Charitable Trust
Gloucestershire Community Foundation
GrantScape
The Grimmitt Trust
The Grocers' Charity
The Hadfield Trust
The W. A. Handley Charitable Trust
The Kathleen Hannay Memorial Charity
The Edith Lilian Harrison 2000 Foundation
Heart of England Community Foundation
Help the Homeless Limited
The Christina Mary Hendrie Trust for Scottish and Canadian Charities
Philip Sydney Henman Deceased Will Trust
Herefordshire Community Foundation
The Hertfordshire Community Foundation
The Alan Edward Higgs Charity
The Hilden Charitable Fund
The Hillingdon Community Trust
The Hillingdon Partnership Trust
The Hiscox Foundation
The Henry C. Hoare Charitable Trust
Hope for Youth (NI)
James T. Howat Charitable Trust
Human Relief Foundation
The Hunter Foundation
Miss Agnes H. Hunter's Trust
Hyde Charitable Trust (Youth Plus)
The Innocent Foundation
The International Bankers Charitable Trust
The Isle of Anglesey Charitable Trust
JCA Charitable Foundation
Rees Jeffreys Road Fund
Nick Jenkins Foundation
The Joffe Charitable Trust
The Johnson Foundation
The Johnson Wax Ltd Charitable Trust
The Cyril and Eve Jumbo Charitable Trust
The Mary Kinross Charitable Trust
Robert Kitchin (Saddlers' Company)
The KPMG Foundation
Community Foundations for Lancashire and Merseyside
LandAid Charitable Trust
The Allen Lane Foundation

The R. J. Larg Family Charitable Trust
The William Leech Charity
Leeds Building Society Charitable Foundation
The Lennox and Wyfold Foundation
The Mark Leonard Trust
David and Ruth Lewis Family Charitable Trust
John Lewis Partnership General Community Fund
LHR Airport Communities Trust
Liberum Foundation
The Linden Charitable Trust
Lindenleaf Charitable Trust
Lloyds Bank Foundation for England and Wales
Lloyds TSB Foundation for Scotland
The Trust for London
The London Community Foundation
The Lotus Foundation
John Lyon's Charity
The Mactaggart Third Fund
Lord Mayor of Manchester's Charity Appeal Trust
The W. M. Mann Foundation
The Hilda and Samuel Marks Foundation
The Mathew Trust
The Matliwala Family Charitable Trust
The Merchants' House of Glasgow
T. & J. Meyer Family Foundation Limited
The Mickleham Trust
The Millfield House Foundation (MHF)
Milton Keynes Community Foundation Limited
The Peter Minet Trust
The MITIE Foundation
Monmouthshire County Council Welsh Church Act Fund
The George A. Moore Foundation
John Moores Foundation
The Morris Charitable Trust
Vyoel Moshe Charitable Trust
Mothercare Group Foundation
The National Churches Trust
The Nationwide Foundation
The NFU Mutual Charitable Trust
Nominet Charitable Foundation
The Community Foundation for Northern Ireland
The Northern Rock Foundation
The Norwich Town Close Estate Charity
The Harry Payne Fund
People's Postcode Trust
The Pilkington Charities Fund

69

## Housing

*Fields of interest and type of beneficiary*

The Premier League Charitable Fund
The Puebla Charitable Trust
Ranworth Trust
The Eleanor Rathbone Charitable Trust
The Sigrid Rausing Trust
Rivers Foundation
The Robertson Trust
The Joseph Rowntree Charitable Trust
Royal Docks Trust (London)
The Saga Charitable Trust
Foundation Scotland
The Scottish Power Foundation
The Shanti Charitable Trust
The Sheldon Trust
SITA Cornwall Trust Limited
Sodexo Foundation
The Spero Foundation
The Stanley Foundation Ltd
The Peter Stebbings Memorial Charity
Sir Halley Stewart Trust
The Edward Stocks-Massey Bequest Fund
Sutton Coldfield Charitable Trust
The Hugh and Ruby Sykes Charitable Trust
C. B. and H. H. Taylor 1984 Trust
The Tresillian Trust
Community Foundation Serving Tyne and Wear and Northumberland
The Vodafone Foundation
Volant Charitable Trust
Voluntary Action Fund (VAF)
The Scurrah Wainwright Charity
Wakeham Trust
The Community Foundation in Wales
Wales Council for Voluntary Action
The Wates Foundation
The Welton Foundation
The Westminster Foundation
The Woodward Charitable Trust
Yorkshire and Clydesdale Bank Foundation
The Yorkshire Dales Millennium Trust

## Housing

The H. B. Allen Charitable Trust
The Balney Charitable Trust
The Band Trust
The Barbour Foundation
The Barnwood House Trust
The Oliver Borthwick Memorial Trust

Henry T. and Lucy B. Cadbury Charitable Trust
The Carpenters' Company Charitable Trust
The Clothworkers' Foundation
The Cole Charitable Trust
John and Freda Coleman Charitable Trust
The Coltstaple Trust
The Consolidated Charities for the Infirm – Merchant Taylors' Company
Mabel Cooper Charity
The Evan Cornish Foundation
Michael Crawford Children's Charity
The Cumber Family Charitable Trust
Baron Davenport's Charity
The Ebenezer Trust
The Gilbert Edgar Trust
The Oliver Ford Charitable Trust
The Patrick & Helena Frost Foundation
The Girdlers' Company Charitable Trust
Greenham Common Community Trust Limited
Hampton Fuel Allotment
The W. A. Handley Charitable Trust
The Haramead Trust
The Harborne Parish Lands Charity
The Harpur Trust
The Alfred And Peggy Harvey Charitable Trust
The Charles Hayward Foundation
May Hearnshaw Charitable Trust
Help the Homeless Limited
The Hilden Charitable Fund
The Lady Hind Trust
The Edward Holt Trust
Sir Harold Hood's Charitable Trust
The Thomas J. Horne Memorial Trust
The Hospital of God at Greatham
The Huggard Charitable Trust
Hyde Charitable Trust (Youth Plus)
Irish Youth Foundation (UK) Ltd (incorporating The Lawlor Foundation)
John James Bristol Foundation
The Jarman Charitable Trust
Anton Jurgens Charitable Trust
Kingdom Way Trust
The Kingsbury Charity
The Sir James Knott Trust
The Heinz, Anna and Carol Kroch Foundation (HACKF)

John Laing Charitable Trust
Maurice and Hilda Laing Charitable Trust
The Beatrice Laing Trust
The Lambert Charitable Trust
LandAid Charitable Trust
Laslett's (Hinton) Charity
The Raymond and Blanche Lawson Charitable Trust
Leeds Building Society Charitable Foundation
The Mark Leonard Trust
The Sir Edward Lewis Foundation
Lloyds Bank Foundation for Northern Ireland
The Trust for London
The London Community Foundation
London Housing Foundation Ltd
John Lyon's Charity
The Mackintosh Foundation
Charlotte Marshall Charitable Trust
The Mickleham Trust
The Mills Charity
The Mirianog Trust
The Monument Trust
The Morgan Charitable Foundation
The Nationwide Foundation
The Norton Foundation
Oizer Charitable Trust
The Phillips and Rubens Charitable Trust
The Pilgrim Trust
The Rayne Foundation
Eva Reckitt Trust Fund
Mrs L. D. Rope Third Charitable Settlement
Royal British Legion
The Scottish Power Energy People Trust
The Seneca Trust
St James's Place Foundation
St Monica Trust
The Sussex Community Foundation
Community Foundation Serving Tyne and Wear and Northumberland
Ulster Garden Villages Ltd
Woodroffe Benton Foundation

## Specific industries

The Broderers' Charity Trust
The Clothworkers' Foundation
The Cooks Charity
The Cotton Industry War Memorial Trust
Cumbria Community Foundation
The Drapers' Charitable Fund

## Education and training

The Oliver Ford Charitable Trust
The Worshipful Company of Horners' Charitable Trusts
JCA Charitable Foundation
The Leathersellers' Company Charitable Fund
The Mark Leonard Trust
C. F. Lunoe Trust Fund
The Merchants' House of Glasgow
The Worshipful Company of Needlemakers' Charitable Fund
The Phillips Charitable Trust
The Saddlers' Company Charitable Fund
Scottish Coal Industry Special Welfare Fund

The 1989 Willan Charitable Trust
Aberdeen Asset Management Charitable Foundation
The Aberdeen Endowments Trust
The Aberdeen Foundation
The Aberdeenshire Educational Trust Scheme
ABF The Soldiers' Charity
The Acacia Charitable Trust
Access Sport
The Company of Actuaries' Charitable Trust Fund
The Addleshaw Goddard Charitable Trust
AF Trust Company
Aldgate and All Hallows' Foundation
All Saints Educational Trust
Allchurches Trust Ltd
The H. B. Allen Charitable Trust
The Alliance Family Foundation
Angus Allnatt Charitable Foundation
The Pat Allsop Charitable Trust
Almondsbury Charity
The Altajir Trust
The Ammco Trust
Viscount Amory's Charitable Trust
The AMW Charitable Trust
Anglo American Group Foundation
Anguish's Educational Foundation
The Apax Foundation
The John Apthorp Charity
The Arbib Foundation
The Ardwick Trust
The John Armitage Charitable Trust
The Armourers' and Brasiers' Gauntlet Trust
Arts Council of Wales (Cyngor Celfyddydau Cymru)
A. J. H. Ashby Will Trust
The Ashmore Foundation
The Associated Country Women of the World
The Association of Colleges Charitable Trust
The Astor of Hever Trust
The Lord Austin Trust
Autonomous Research Charitable Trust
The Scott Bader Commonwealth Limited
The Bagri Foundation
The Baily Thomas Charitable Fund

The Roy and Pixie Baker Charitable Trust
The Balcombe Charitable Trust
The Balfour Beatty Charitable Trust
The George Balint Charitable Trust
The Bamford Charitable Foundation
The Banbury Charities
The Band Trust
The Barbour Foundation
The Baring Foundation
Barnes Workhouse Fund
Bay Charitable Trust
BBC Children in Need
BC Partners Foundation
BCH Trust
The Beckett's and Sargeant's Educational Foundation
The John Beckwith Charitable Trust
The Bellahouston Bequest Fund
The Berkeley Charitable Foundation
The Ruth Berkowitz Charitable Trust
The Berkshire Community Foundation
The Bernadette Charitable Trust
The Bestway Foundation
The Big Lottery Fund (see also Awards for All)
The Bintaub Charitable Trust
The Sydney Black Charitable Trust
The BlackRock (UK) Charitable Trust
The Blagrave Trust
The Blanchminster Trust
The Blandford Lake Trust
Blatchington Court Trust
Bloodwise
The Bloom Foundation
The Bluston Charitable Settlement
The Nicholas Boas Charitable Trust
BOOST Charitable Trust
The Booth Charities
Boots Charitable Trust
The Harry Bottom Charitable Trust
The Bowland Charitable Trust
The Liz and Terry Bramall Foundation
The Bramhope Trust
The Bransford Trust
The Breadsticks Foundation
The Brendish Family Foundation
Bridgepoint Charitable Trust
The Bristol Charities

**71**

## Education and training

The British & Foreign School Society
British Record Industry Trust
The Britten-Pears Foundation
The J. and M. Britton Charitable Trust
The Consuelo and Anthony Brooke Charitable Trust
The Rory and Elizabeth Brooks Foundation
The Charles Brotherton Trust
The Brownsword Charitable Foundation
Brushmill Ltd
The Buffini Chao Foundation
The Bulldog Trust Limited
Burden's Charitable Foundation
The Clara E. Burgess Charity
The Burghley Family Trust
The Burry Charitable Trust
The Arnold Burton 1998 Charitable Trust
Consolidated Charity of Burton upon Trent
The Derek Butler Trust
The James Caan Foundation
Cable & Wireless Worldwide Foundation
Edward Cadbury Charitable Trust
The G. W. Cadbury Charitable Trust
The William A. Cadbury Charitable Trust
The Cadbury Foundation
The Edward and Dorothy Cadbury Trust
CAFOD (Catholic Agency for Overseas Development)
Calleva Foundation
Calouste Gulbenkian Foundation – UK Branch
The Cambridge Chrysalis Trust
The Campden Charities Trustee
The Frederick and Phyllis Cann Trust
The Carlton House Charitable Trust
The Richard Carne Trust
The Carnegie Trust for the Universities of Scotland
The Carpenters' Company Charitable Trust
The Carr-Gregory Trust
Carter's Educational Foundation
Sir John Cass's Foundation
The Elizabeth Casson Trust
The Catalyst Charitable Trust
Catholic Foreign Missions (CFM)
The B. G. S. Cayzer Charitable Trust
Celtic Charity Fund

The Gaynor Cemlyn-Jones Trust
The Amelia Chadwick Trust
Charitworth Limited
The Charter 600 Charity
The Worshipful Company of Chartered Accountants General Charitable Trust
The Cheruby Trust
The Chetwode Foundation
The Chipping Sodbury Town Lands Charity
CHK Charities Limited
Chrysalis Trust
The Church Burgesses Educational Foundation
Church Burgesses Trust
The City Bridge Trust
The City Educational Trust Fund
J. A. Clark Charitable Trust
The Roger and Sarah Bancroft Clark Charitable Trust
The Cleopatra Trust
The Clore Duffield Foundation
The Robert Clutterbuck Charitable Trust
Clydpride Ltd
The Coalfields Regeneration Trust
The John Coates Charitable Trust
The Denise Cohen Charitable Trust
The Vivienne and Samuel Cohen Charitable Trust
The John S. Cohen Foundation
The R. and S. Cohen Foundation
John and Freda Coleman Charitable Trust
Colyer-Ferguson Charitable Trust
The Comino Foundation
The Douglas Compton James Charitable Trust
The Congleton Inclosure Trust
Gordon Cook Foundation
The Cooks Charity
The Catherine Cookson Charitable Trust
The Helen Jean Cope Trust
The J. Reginald Corah Foundation Fund
Michael Cornish Charitable Trust
The Evan Cornish Foundation
The Duke of Cornwall's Benevolent Fund
The Corona Charitable Trust
The Sir Tom Cowie Charitable Trust
Dudley and Geoffrey Cox Charitable Trust
The Lord Cozens-Hardy Trust
The Craignish Trust

The Craps Charitable Trust
The Cray Trust
Criffel Charitable Trust
The Cross Trust
The Peter Cruddas Foundation
Cruden Foundation Ltd
The Ronald Cruickshanks Foundation
The Cuby Charitable Trust
Cullum Family Trust
The Cumber Family Charitable Trust
The Cwmbran Trust
Daily Prayer Union Charitable Trust Limited
The Daiwa Anglo-Japanese Foundation
Oizer Dalim Trust
The Davidson Family Charitable Trust
Michael Davies Charitable Settlement
The Hamilton Davies Trust
The Davis Foundation
The Henry and Suzanne Davis Foundation
The Deakin Charitable Trust
William Dean Countryside and Educational Trust
The Desmond Foundation
The Sandy Dewhirst Charitable Trust
The Diageo Foundation
The Dibden Allotments Fund
Dischma Charitable Trust
The Djanogly Foundation
The DM Charitable Trust
Dorset Community Foundation
The Dorus Trust
The Double 'O' Charity Ltd
The Drapers' Charitable Fund
Dromintee Trust
The Royal Foundation of the Duke and Duchess of Cambridge and Prince Harry
The Dyers' Company Charitable Trust
The James Dyson Foundation
Earls Colne and Halstead Educational Charity
East End Community Foundation
Eastern Counties Educational Trust Limited
The Sir John Eastwood Foundation
The Ebenezer Trust
The Economist Charitable Trust
The Gilbert and Eileen Edgar Foundation
Edinburgh Trust No 2 Account
Educational Foundation of Alderman John Norman
Edupoor Limited
The Elephant Trust

**Education and training**

The George Elias Charitable Trust
The Ellinson Foundation Ltd
The Ellis Campbell Foundation
The Elmgrant Trust
EMI Music Sound Foundation
The Epigoni Trust
The Eranda Foundation
The ERM Foundation
The Ernest Hecht Charitable Foundation
Esh Foundation
The Essex Youth Trust
Euro Charity Trust
Sir John Evelyn's Charity
The Exilarch's Foundation
The Expat Foundation
Extonglen Limited
The F. P. Limited Charitable Trust
Esmée Fairbairn Foundation
The Fairway Trust
Famos Foundation Trust
The Lord Faringdon Charitable Trust
Samuel William Farmer's Trust
The Farthing Trust
The February Foundation
Federation of Jewish Relief Organisations
The George Fentham Birmingham Charity
The Allan and Nesta Ferguson Charitable Settlement
The Doris Field Charitable Trust
Filey Foundation Ltd
Finnart House School Trust
Fisherbeck Charitable Trust
The Fishmongers' Company's Charitable Trust
The Ian Fleming Charitable Trust
The Joyce Fletcher Charitable Trust
Florence's Charitable Trust
The Follett Trust
The Football Association National Sports Centre Trust
The Football Foundation
The Forbes Charitable Foundation
Ford Britain Trust
The Oliver Ford Charitable Trust
The Forest Hill Charitable Trust
The Donald Forrester Trust
The Fort Foundation
The Lord Forte Foundation
The Foyle Foundation
The Jill Franklin Trust
The Hugh Fraser Foundation
The Joseph Strong Frazer Trust

The Louis and Valerie Freedman Charitable Settlement
The Freemasons' Grand Charity
The Freshfield Foundation
The Freshgate Trust Foundation
The Friarsgate Trust
Friends of Wiznitz Limited
The Patrick & Helena Frost Foundation
Mejer and Gertrude Miriam Frydman Foundation
The Fuserna Foundation
General Charitable Trust
The Galanthus Trust
The Gale Family Charity Trust
Gamlen Charitable Trust
The Samuel Gardner Memorial Trust
The Garnett Charitable Trust
The Garrick Charitable Trust
The Gatsby Charitable Foundation
The Robert Gavron Charitable Trust
Jacqueline and Michael Gee Charitable Trust
The Nigel Gee Foundation
Sir Robert Geffery's Almshouse Trust
The G. C. Gibson Charitable Trust
The Girdlers' Company Charitable Trust
The GNC Trust
The Golden Bottle Trust
The Goldman Sachs Charitable Gift Fund (UK)
Goldman Sachs Gives (UK)
The Goldsmiths' Company Charity
The Golsoncott Foundation
Nicholas and Judith Goodison's Charitable Settlement
The Gosling Foundation Limited
The Granada Foundation
Grantham Yorke Trust
The J. G. Graves Charitable Trust
The Great Britain Sasakawa Foundation
The Great Stone Bridge Trust of Edenbridge
The Kenneth & Susan Green Charitable Foundation
Greenham Common Community Trust Limited
The Greggs Foundation
The Grimmitt Trust
The Grocers' Charity
The M. and R. Gross Charities Limited

The Guildry Incorporation of Perth
The Gur Trust
The H. and M. Charitable Trust
H. C. D. Memorial Fund
The Hadrian Trust
Paul Hamlyn Foundation
The Helen Hamlyn Trust
Sue Hammerson Charitable Trust
Hampshire and Isle of Wight Community Foundation
Hampton Fuel Allotment
The W. A. Handley Charitable Trust
The Kathleen Hannay Memorial Charity
The Haramead Trust
Miss K. M. Harbinson's Charitable Trust
Harbo Charities Limited
The Harbour Charitable Trust
The Harbour Foundation
William Harding's Charity
The Hare of Steep Charitable Trust (HOST)
The Harebell Centenary Fund
The Harpur Trust
The Harris Charity
The Edith Lilian Harrison 2000 Foundation
Edward Harvist Trust
The Hathaway Trust
The Maurice Hatter Foundation
The Headley Trust
May Hearnshaw Charitable Trust
Heart of England Community Foundation
The Heathcoat Trust
The Heathside Charitable Trust
The Charlotte Heber-Percy Charitable Trust
The Percy Hedley 1990 Charitable Trust
Hedley Foundation Limited
The Michael Heller Charitable Foundation
The Simon Heller Charitable Settlement
The Helping Foundation
The Hemby Charitable Trust
The Christina Mary Hendrie Trust for Scottish and Canadian Charities
Henley Educational Trust
Philip Sydney Henman Deceased Will Trust
Herefordshire Community Foundation
The Hertfordshire Community Foundation
Hesed Trust
The Hesslewood Children's Trust

73

**Education and training**  *Fields of interest and type of beneficiary*

Hexham and Newcastle Diocesan Trust (1947)
P. and C. Hickinbotham Charitable Trust
The Alan Edward Higgs Charity
Highcroft Charitable Trust
The Hilden Charitable Fund
The Hillingdon Community Trust
R. G. Hills Charitable Trust
The Lady Hind Trust
The Hinduja Foundation
The Hinrichsen Foundation
The Hintze Family Charity Foundation
The Hiscox Foundation
Hitchin Educational Foundation
The Henry C. Hoare Charitable Trust
The Hobson Charity Limited
Hockerill Educational Foundation
The Sir Julian Hodge Charitable Trust
The Jane Hodge Foundation
The Holden Charitable Trust
The Hollick Family Charitable Trust
The Holliday Foundation
The Dorothy Holmes Charitable Trust
P. H. Holt Foundation
The Mary Homfray Charitable Trust
Sir Harold Hood's Charitable Trust
The Hoover Foundation
Hope for Youth (NI)
The Hope Trust
The Horizon Foundation
The Antony Hornby Charitable Trust
The Horne Foundation
The Worshipful Company of Horners' Charitable Trusts
The Hornsey Parochial Charities
Hospice UK
The Sir Joseph Hotung Charitable Settlement
House of Industry Estate
The Reta Lila Howard Foundation
The Daniel Howard Trust
James T. Howat Charitable Trust
Hulme Trust Estates
Human Relief Foundation
The Humanitarian Trust
The Hunter Foundation
Miss Agnes H. Hunter's Trust
The Huntingdon Foundation Limited
Huntingdon Freemen's Trust
Hurdale Charity Limited
The Nani Huyu Charitable Trust

Hyde Charitable Trust (Youth Plus)
IBM United Kingdom Trust
Ibrahim Foundation Ltd
The Idlewild Trust
The Iliffe Family Charitable Trust
Impetus – The Private Equity Foundation
Incommunities Foundation
The International Bankers Charitable Trust
The Inverforth Charitable Trust (ICT)
Investream Charitable Trust
The Ireland Fund of Great Britain
Irish Youth Foundation (UK) Ltd (incorporating The Lawlor Foundation)
The Ironmongers' Foundation
The J. Isaacs Charitable Trust
The Isle of Anglesey Charitable Trust
The J. & J. Benevolent Foundation
The J. & J. Charitable Trust
The J. A. R. Charitable Trust
The J. J. Charitable Trust
The Jabbs Foundation
C. Richard Jackson Charitable Trust
The Ruth and Lionel Jacobson Trust (Second Fund) No 2
John James Bristol Foundation
The Susan and Stephen James Charitable Settlement
John Jarrold Trust
Jay Education Trust
JCA Charitable Foundation
Rees Jeffreys Road Fund
Nick Jenkins Foundation
The Jephcott Charitable Trust
The Jerusalem Trust
The Jerwood Charitable Foundation
The Jewish Youth Fund (JYF)
The Johnson Foundation
The Johnson Wax Ltd Charitable Trust
The Joicey Trust
The Dezna Robins Jones Charitable Foundation
The Marjorie and Geoffrey Jones Charitable Trust
The Joron Charitable Trust
The J. E. Joseph Charitable Fund
The Cyril and Eve Jumbo Charitable Trust
Anton Jurgens Charitable Trust
Jusaca Charitable Trust
The Bernard Kahn Charitable Trust
The Stanley Kalms Foundation

The Ian Karten Charitable Trust
The Kass Charitable Trust (KCT)
C. S. Kaufman Charitable Trust
Kelsick's Educational Foundation
John Thomas Kennedy Charitable Foundation
Kent Community Foundation
Keren Association Limited
E. and E. Kernkraut Charities Limited
The Peter Kershaw Trust
Keswick Hall Charity
The Robert Kiln Charitable Trust
The Mary Kinross Charitable Trust
Kirkley Poor's Land Estate
Kirschel Foundation
Robert Kitchin (Saddlers' Company)
The Sir James Knott Trust
The Kobler Trust
The Kohn Foundation
Kollel and Co. Limited
The KPMG Foundation
The Kreditor Charitable Trust
The Kreitman Foundation
The Neil Kreitman Foundation
Kupath Gemach Chaim Bechesed Viznitz Trust
The Kyte Charitable Trust
John Laing Charitable Trust
Maurice and Hilda Laing Charitable Trust
The David Laing Foundation
The Kirby Laing Foundation
The Beatrice Laing Trust
The Lambert Charitable Trust
Community Foundations for Lancashire and Merseyside
Duchy of Lancaster Benevolent Fund
LandAid Charitable Trust
The Jack Lane Charitable Trust
The Allen Lane Foundation
Langdale Trust
Langley Charitable Trust
The R. J. Larg Family Charitable Trust
Largsmount Ltd
The Lauffer Family Charitable Foundation
Mrs F. B. Laurence Charitable Trust
The Law Society Charity
The Edgar E. Lawley Foundation
Lawson Beckman Charitable Trust
The David Lean Foundation
The Leathersellers' Company Charitable Fund

The Leche Trust
The Arnold Lee Charitable Trust
Leicestershire, Leicester and Rutland Community Foundation
The Kennedy Leigh Charitable Trust
Morris Leigh Foundation
The Leigh Trust
P. Leigh-Bramwell Trust 'E'
The Lennox and Wyfold Foundation
The Mark Leonard Trust
The Leverhulme Trade Charities Trust
The Leverhulme Trust
Lord Leverhulme's Charitable Trust
Joseph Levy Charitable Foundation
David and Ruth Lewis Family Charitable Trust
The John Spedan Lewis Foundation
The Sir Edward Lewis Foundation
John Lewis Partnership General Community Fund
The Lewis Ward Trust
LHR Airport Communities Trust
Liberum Foundation
The Limbourne Trust
Limoges Charitable Trust
The Linbury Trust
Lincolnshire Community Foundation
Lindale Educational Foundation
The Linden Charitable Trust
The Ruth and Stuart Lipton Charitable Trust
The Lister Charitable Trust
The Charles Littlewood Hill Trust
The Second Joseph Aaron Littman Foundation
The Elaine and Angus Lloyd Charitable Trust
Lloyd's Charities Trust
Lloyds Bank Foundation for Northern Ireland
Lloyds TSB Foundation for Scotland
Localtrent Ltd
Loftus Charitable Trust
The Trust for London
The London Community Foundation
The London Law Trust
The William and Katherine Longman Trust
The Lord's Taverners
The Lotus Foundation
The Lower Green Foundation
The Lowy Mitchell Foundation

The C. L. Loyd Charitable Trust
LSA Charitable Trust
The Marie Helen Luen Charitable Trust
The Henry Lumley Charitable Trust
Paul Lunn-Rockliffe Charitable Trust
C. F. Lunoe Trust Fund
The Ruth and Jack Lunzer Charitable Trust
Lord and Lady Lurgan Trust
The Lyndhurst Trust
The Lynn Foundation
John Lyon's Charity
The Lyons Charitable Trust
The Sir Jack Lyons Charitable Trust
M. and C. Trust
The M. K. Charitable Trust
The Madeline Mabey Trust
The E. M. MacAndrew Trust
The Macdonald-Buchanan Charitable Trust
The Mackintosh Foundation
The MacRobert Trust
The Ian Mactaggart Trust
James Madison Trust
The Magdalen and Lasher Charity (General Fund)
The Magen Charitable Trust
The Mahavir Trust
Malbin Trust
The Mallinckrodt Foundation
Man Group plc Charitable Trust
The Manackerman Charitable Trust
The Manchester Guardian Society Charitable Trust
The Manifold Charitable Trust
The W. M. Mann Foundation
R. W. Mann Trust
The Manoukian Charitable Foundation
Maranatha Christian Trust
Marbeh Torah Trust
The Stella and Alexander Margulies Charitable Trust
Mariapolis Limited
Market Harborough and The Bowdens Charity
The Ann and David Marks Foundation
The Hilda and Samuel Marks Foundation
J. P. Marland Charitable Trust
The Marr-Munning Trust
The Michael Marsh Charitable Trust
The Marsh Christian Trust
Charlotte Marshall Charitable Trust
D. G. Marshall of Cambridge Trust

The Marshgate Charitable Settlement
Sir George Martin Trust
John Martin's Charity
The Nancie Massey Charitable Trust
The Mathew Trust
The Matliwala Family Charitable Trust
The Mayfield Valley Arts Trust
The Robert McAlpine Foundation
The Medlock Charitable Trust
Melodor Limited
The Melow Charitable Trust
Mercaz Torah Vechesed Limited
The Mercers' Charitable Foundation
The Merchant Taylors' Company Charities Fund
The Merchant Venturers' Charity
The Merchants' House of Glasgow
The Metropolitan Masonic Charity
T. & J. Meyer Family Foundation Limited
The Mickel Fund
The Mickleham Trust
The Gerald Micklem Charitable Trust
Millennium Stadium Charitable Trust (Ymddiriedolaeth Elusennol Stadiwm y Mileniwm)
The Ronald Miller Foundation
The Millfield Trust
The Millichope Foundation
The Edgar Milward Charity
The Peter Minet Trust
Minge's Gift and the Pooled Trusts
Minton Charitable Trust
The Laurence Misener Charitable Trust
The Brian Mitchell Charitable Settlement
The MITIE Foundation
Keren Mitzvah Trust
The Mizpah Trust
The Modiano Charitable Trust
Mole Charitable Trust
Monmouthshire County Council Welsh Church Act Fund
The George A. Moore Foundation
The Henry Moore Foundation
John Moores Foundation (JMF)
The Morel Charitable Trust
The Morgan Foundation
Morgan Stanley International Foundation

The Diana and Allan
   Morgenthau Charitable
   Trust
The Miles Morland Foundation
The Morris Charitable Trust
The Peter Morrison Charitable
   Foundation
G. M. Morrison Charitable
   Trust
The Moshal Charitable Trust
Vyoel Moshe Charitable Trust
Mosselson Charitable Trust
Mothercare Group Foundation
Moto in the Community
J. P. Moulton Charitable
   Foundation
The MSE Charity
The Music Sales Charitable
   Trust
Muslim Hands
The Mutual Trust Group
MW (CL) Foundation
MW (GK) Foundation
MW (HO) Foundation
MW (RH) Foundation
The National Express
   Foundation
The NDL Foundation
The Worshipful Company of
   Needlemakers' Charitable
   Fund
Ner Foundation
Newby Trust Limited
The Newcomen Collett
   Foundation
Alderman Newton's
   Educational Foundation
The NFU Mutual Charitable
   Trust
Nominet Charitable Foundation
The Noon Foundation
Norfolk Community Foundation
The Normanby Charitable Trust
The Northampton Municipal
   Church Charities
Northamptonshire Community
   Foundation
The Community Foundation for
   Northern Ireland
The Northumberland Village
   Homes Trust
The Norton Foundation
The Norton Rose Charitable
   Foundation
The Norwich Town Close
   Estate Charity
The Notgrove Trust
The Nuffield Foundation
The Father O'Mahoney
   Memorial Trust
The Oakley Charitable Trust
Oglesby Charitable Trust
Oizer Charitable Trust
Old Possum's Practical Trust
Open Gate

The O'Sullivan Family
   Charitable Trust
The Owen Family Trust
City of Oxford Charity
The James Pantyfedwen
   Foundation
The Park Charitable Trust
The Park House Charitable
   Trust
Ambika Paul Foundation
The Susanna Peake Charitable
   Trust
The Dowager Countess
   Eleanor Peel Trust
The Peltz Trust
The Performing Right Society
   Foundation
The Jack Petchey Foundation
The Phillips and Rubens
   Charitable Trust
The Bernard Piggott Charitable
   Trust
The Pilgrim Trust
The Pollywally Charitable Trust
The Polonsky Foundation
The Ponton House Trust
The Popocatepetl Trust
The John Porter Charitable
   Trust
The Porter Foundation
Porticus UK
The David and Elaine Potter
   Foundation
The Praebendo Charitable
   Foundation
The Premier League Charitable
   Fund
The William Price Charitable
   Trust
Sir John Priestman Charity
   Trust
The Prince of Wales's
   Charitable Foundation
The Puri Foundation
The PwC Foundation
Mr and Mrs J. A. Pye's
   Charitable Settlement
Quartet Community Foundation
The Queen Anne's Gate
   Foundation
The Queen's Silver Jubilee
   Trust
The Racing Foundation
Richard Radcliffe Charitable
   Trust
The Radcliffe Trust
The Rank Foundation Limited
Ranworth Trust
The Rashbass Family Trust
The Ravensdale Trust
The Rayne Foundation
Eva Reckitt Trust Fund
Red Hill Charitable Trust
The Reed Foundation
Richard Reeve's Foundation
Reuben Foundation

The Clive Richards Charity
The Violet M. Richards Charity
The Richmond Parish Lands
   Charity
Ridgesave Limited
Rivers Foundation
Rix-Thompson-Rothenberg
   Foundation
The Robertson Trust
Robyn Charitable Trust
The Roddick Foundation
The Sir James Roll Charitable
   Trust
Mrs L. D. Rope Third
   Charitable Settlement
The Rose Foundation
The Rothermere Foundation
The Rothley Trust
The Roughley Charitable Trust
Rowanville Ltd
The Rowland Family
   Foundation
The Rowlands Trust
Royal British Legion
Royal Docks Trust (London)
Royal Masonic Trust for Girls
   and Boys
The Royal Victoria Hall
   Foundation
Ryklow Charitable Trust 1992
The J. S. and E. C. Rymer
   Charitable Trust
The Michael Harry Sacher
   Trust
The Saddlers' Company
   Charitable Fund
Erach and Roshan Sadri
   Foundation
The Saga Charitable Trust
The Saintbury Trust
The Salamander Charitable
   Trust
The Andrew Salvesen
   Charitable Trust
Sam and Bella Sebba
   Charitable Trust
Coral Samuel Charitable Trust
The Basil Samuel Charitable
   Trust
The Samworth Foundation
The Sandhu Charitable
   Foundation
The Sands Family Trust
Santander UK Foundation
   Limited
The Sants Charitable Trust
The Schreiber Charitable Trust
Schroder Charity Trust
The Scottish Power Foundation
The Scouloudi Foundation
The SDL Foundation
The Seneca Trust
The Jean Shanks Foundation
The Shears Foundation
The Sheepdrove Trust

The Archie Sherman Cardiff Foundation
The Archie Sherman Charitable Trust
SHINE (Support and Help in Education)
The Bassil Shippam and Alsford Trust
The Shoe Zone Trust
David and Jennifer Sieff Charitable Trust
The Simmons & Simmons Charitable Foundation
The Sino-British Fellowship Trust
The John Slater Foundation
The Slaughter and May Charitable Trust
Sloane Robinson Foundation
The DS Smith Charitable Foundation
The WH Smith Group Charitable Trust
The Stanley Smith UK Horticultural Trust
Philip Smith's Charitable Trust
The R. C. Snelling Charitable Trust
Sodexo Foundation
The Solo Charitable Settlement
Songdale Ltd
The E. C. Sosnow Charitable Trust
The South Square Trust
Southdown Trust
R. H. Southern Trust
The Southover Manor General Education Trust
Sparquote Limited
The Spero Foundation
The Spielman Charitable Trust
Split Infinitive Trust
The Spoore, Merry and Rixman Foundation
Rosalyn and Nicholas Springer Charitable Trust
The Geoff and Fiona Squire Foundation
St James's Trust Settlement
St James's Place Foundation
Sir Walter St John's Educational Charity
St Luke's College Foundation
St Peter's Saltley Trust
The Stanley Foundation Ltd
The Peter Stebbings Memorial Charity
Stevenson Family's Charitable Trust
The Stewarts Law Foundation
M. J. C. Stone Charitable Trust
Peter Stormonth Darling Charitable Trust
Peter Storrs Trust

Stratford upon Avon Town Trust
The W. O. Street Charitable Foundation
The Sudborough Foundation Sueberry Ltd
The Alan Sugar Foundation
The Sussex Community Foundation
The Adrienne and Leslie Sussman Charitable Trust
The Sutasoma Trust
Sutton Coldfield Charitable Trust
The Suva Foundation Limited
The Swann-Morton Foundation
The John Swire (1989) Charitable Trust
The Hugh and Ruby Sykes Charitable Trust
Sylvia Waddilove Foundation UK
The David Tannen Charitable Trust
C. B. and H. H. Taylor 1984 Trust
The Connie and Albert Taylor Charitable Trust
Tesco Charity Trust
The C. Paul Thackray General Charitable Trust
The Thales Charitable Trust
The Thompson Family Charitable Trust
The Sue Thomson Foundation
Thomson Reuters Foundation
The Thornton Trust
The Thousandth Man- Richard Burns Charitable Trust
The Thriplow Charitable Trust
The Tobacco Pipe Makers and Tobacco Trade Benevolent Fund
The Tolkien Trust
Tomchei Torah Charitable Trust
The Tompkins Foundation
Toras Chesed (London) Trust
The Tory Family Foundation
Tottenham Grammar School Foundation
The Tower Hill Trust
The Towry Law Charitable Trust
Toyota Manufacturing UK Charitable Trust
Annie Tranmer Charitable Trust
The Tresillian Trust
Truedene Co. Ltd
Trumros Limited
The James Tudor Foundation
TVML Foundation
Community Foundation Serving Tyne and Wear and Northumberland
UIA Charitable Foundation
Ulting Overseas Trust

The UNITE Foundation
The Michael Uren Foundation
Uxbridge United Welfare Trust
The Vardy Foundation
The Variety Club Children's Charity
Roger Vere Foundation
The Nigel Vinson Charitable Trust
The William and Ellen Vinten Trust
The Vintners' Foundation
Volant Charitable Trust
Voluntary Action Fund (VAF)
Wakeham Trust
Wales Council for Voluntary Action
The Walker Trust
The Ward Blenkinsop Trust
The Barbara Ward Children's Foundation
The Waterloo Foundation
Wates Family Enterprise Trust
The Wates Foundation
John Watson's Trust
The Weavers' Company Benevolent Fund
Webb Memorial Trust
The James Weir Foundation
The Welton Foundation
The Wessex Youth Trust
The Garfield Weston Foundation
The Barbara Whatmore Charitable Trust
The Whitaker Charitable Trust
The Colonel W. H. Whitbread Charitable Trust
The Norman Whiteley Trust
The William Barrow's Charity
The Charity of William Williams
The Williams Charitable Trust
Williams Serendipity Trust
The HDH Wills 1965 Charitable Trust
David Wilson Foundation
The Wilson Foundation
The Harold Hyam Wingate Foundation
The Winton Charitable Foundation
The Michael and Anna Wix Charitable Trust
The Wixamtree Trust
The Maurice Wohl Charitable Foundation
The Charles Wolfson Charitable Trust
The Wolfson Family Charitable Trust
The Wolfson Foundation
The Wood Family Trust
Woodroffe Benton Foundation
The Woodward Charitable Trust
Worcester Municipal Charities

The Matthews Wrightson
   Charity Trust
Wychdale Ltd
The Yapp Charitable Trust
The W. Wing Yip and Brothers
   Foundation
Yorkshire and Clydesdale Bank
   Foundation
Yorkshire Building Society
   Charitable Foundation
The John Kirkhope Young
   Endowment Fund
Youth Music
Youth United Foundation
The Marjorie and Arnold Ziff
   Charitable Foundation
The Zochonis Charitable Trust

## Higher education

AF Trust Company
The Alliance Family Foundation
The Altajir Trust
Bloodwise
The Harry Bottom Charitable
   Trust
The Rory and Elizabeth Brooks
   Foundation
The Carlton House Charitable
   Trust
The Carnegie Trust for the
   Universities of Scotland
The City Educational Trust
   Fund
The John S. Cohen Foundation
Dudley and Geoffrey Cox
   Charitable Trust
The Essex Youth Trust
The February Foundation
The Football Association
   National Sports Centre
   Trust
The Hugh Fraser Foundation
The Joseph Strong Frazer Trust
The Gatsby Charitable
   Foundation
Paul Hamlyn Foundation
The Harris Charity
Henley Educational Trust
The Hesslewood Children's
   Trust
Hulme Trust Estates
The Nani Huyu Charitable Trust
Rees Jeffreys Road Fund
The Ian Karten Charitable
   Trust
The Leche Trust
The Leverhulme Trade
   Charities Trust
The Sir Jack Lyons Charitable
   Trust
James Madison Trust
The Mahavir Trust
The Nuffield Foundation
The Polonsky Foundation

Mr and Mrs J. A. Pye's
   Charitable Settlement
Richard Reeve's Foundation
The Robertson Trust
The South Square Trust
Stevenson Family's Charitable
   Trust
The Thriplow Charitable Trust
Webb Memorial Trust
The Wilson Foundation
The Winton Charitable
   Foundation
The John Kirkhope Young
   Endowment Fund

## Universities

Paul Hamlyn Foundation
The Trust for London
The Peter Minet Trust
John Moores Foundation (JMF)

## Informal, continuing and adult education

The Association of Colleges
   Charitable Trust
The Big Lottery Fund (see also
   Awards for All)
The Blagrave Trust
Boots Charitable Trust
The Cadbury Foundation
John and Freda Coleman
   Charitable Trust
Dudley and Geoffrey Cox
   Charitable Trust
The Royal Foundation of the
   Duke and Duchess of
   Cambridge and Prince Harry
The Essex Youth Trust
The Hugh Fraser Foundation
The Freemasons' Grand
   Charity
The Gatsby Charitable
   Foundation
The Girdlers' Company
   Charitable Trust
Paul Hamlyn Foundation
The Harris Charity
The Hillingdon Community
   Trust
Hope for Youth (NI)
The Nani Huyu Charitable Trust
Hyde Charitable Trust (Youth
   Plus)
The Jerwood Charitable
   Foundation
The Ian Karten Charitable
   Trust
The Allen Lane Foundation
The Trust for London
The Lower Green Foundation
The Mahavir Trust

The Mathew Trust
The Millichope Foundation
The Peter Minet Trust
John Moores Foundation (JMF)
The MSE Charity
The Community Foundation for
   Northern Ireland
The Nuffield Foundation
Richard Reeve's Foundation
Royal British Legion
The Wilson Foundation
Youth United Foundation

## Adult and community education

Paul Hamlyn Foundation
The Trust for London
The Peter Minet Trust
John Moores Foundation (JMF)

## Vocational education and training

John and Freda Coleman
   Charitable Trust
Dudley and Geoffrey Cox
   Charitable Trust
The Hugh Fraser Foundation
The Freemasons' Grand
   Charity
The Gatsby Charitable
   Foundation
The Girdlers' Company
   Charitable Trust
The Harris Charity
Hope for Youth (NI)
Hyde Charitable Trust (Youth
   Plus)
The Jerwood Charitable
   Foundation
The Ian Karten Charitable
   Trust
The Allen Lane Foundation
The Lower Green Foundation
The Nuffield Foundation

## Integrated education

The Essex Youth Trust
Hope for Youth (NI)
The Lord's Taverners

## Management of schools

Calouste Gulbenkian
   Foundation – UK Branch

The Nuffield Foundation

## Particular subjects, curriculum development

All Saints Educational Trust
Angus Allnatt Charitable Foundation
The Altajir Trust
Arts Council of Wales (Cyngor Celfyddydau Cymru)
The Big Lottery Fund (see also Awards for All)
British Record Industry Trust
The Britten-Pears Foundation
The Derek Butler Trust
Calouste Gulbenkian Foundation – UK Branch
The Richard Carne Trust
The Elizabeth Casson Trust
Catholic Foreign Missions (CFM)
The Gaynor Cemlyn-Jones Trust
Church Burgesses Trust
The Clore Duffield Foundation
The Deakin Charitable Trust
The James Dyson Foundation
The Ellis Campbell Foundation
EMI Music Sound Foundation
The Ian Fleming Charitable Trust
The Joyce Fletcher Charitable Trust
The Lord Forte Foundation
Mejer and Gertrude Miriam Frydman Foundation
Gamlen Charitable Trust
The Samuel Gardner Memorial Trust
The Gatsby Charitable Foundation
The Girdlers' Company Charitable Trust
The Golsoncott Foundation
Nicholas and Judith Goodison's Charitable Settlement
The J. G. Graves Charitable Trust
Paul Hamlyn Foundation
The Headley Trust
The Michael Heller Charitable Foundation
Hesed Trust
Hexham and Newcastle Diocesan Trust (1947)
The Hinrichsen Foundation
Hockerill Educational Foundation
The Hope Trust
Hyde Charitable Trust (Youth Plus)

IBM United Kingdom Trust
The Idlewild Trust
The International Bankers Charitable Trust
The J. J. Charitable Trust
Jay Education Trust
The Jerusalem Trust
Keren Association Limited
The Robert Kiln Charitable Trust
Kollel and Co. Limited
Kupath Gemach Chaim Bechesed Viznitz Trust
Maurice and Hilda Laing Charitable Trust
Largsmount Ltd
The Law Society Charity
The Lord's Taverners
C. F. Lunoe Trust Fund
The Lyndhurst Trust
Mercaz Torah Vechesed Limited
The Henry Moore Foundation
The MSE Charity
The Nuffield Foundation
Old Possum's Practical Trust
The Performing Right Society Foundation
The Pilgrim Trust
Sir John Priestman Charity Trust
The Racing Foundation
Richard Radcliffe Charitable Trust
The Radcliffe Trust
The Sir James Roll Charitable Trust
Mrs L. D. Rope Third Charitable Settlement
The Royal Victoria Hall Foundation
The South Square Trust
St Luke's College Foundation
St Peter's Saltley Trust
Ulting Overseas Trust
The William and Ellen Vinten Trust
The Norman Whiteley Trust
The Winton Charitable Foundation
Youth Music

## Arts education and training

Angus Allnatt Charitable Foundation
Arts Council of Wales (also known as Cyngor Celfyddydau Cymru)
British Record Industry Trust
The Britten-Pears Foundation
The Derek Butler Trust
Calouste Gulbenkian Foundation – UK Branch

The Richard Carne Trust
The Gaynor Cemlyn-Jones Trust
The Clore Duffield Foundation
The Deakin Charitable Trust
The James Dyson Foundation
EMI Music Sound Foundation
The Ian Fleming Charitable Trust
The Joyce Fletcher Charitable Trust
Gamlen Charitable Trust
The Samuel Gardner Memorial Trust
The Golsoncott Foundation
Nicholas and Judith Goodison's Charitable Settlement
Paul Hamlyn Foundation
The Headley Trust
The Hinrichsen Foundation
The Idlewild Trust
The Robert Kiln Charitable Trust
The Henry Moore Foundation
The Performing Right Society Foundation
The Pilgrim Trust
The Radcliffe Trust
The Royal Victoria Hall Foundation
The South Square Trust
Youth Music

## Business education

The Ellis Campbell Foundation
The Gatsby Charitable Foundation
The International Bankers Charitable Trust
The MSE Charity

## Citizenship, personal and social education

The Big Lottery Fund (see also Awards for All)

## Construction industry education

C. F. Lunoe Trust Fund

## Home economics and life skills education

All Saints Educational Trust
The Girdlers' Company Charitable Trust

## Hospitality and leisure industry education

The Lord Forte Foundation

## Language and literacy education

The Headley Trust
Hyde Charitable Trust
The J. J. Charitable Trust
Old Possum's Practical Trust

## Legal education

Gamlen Charitable Trust
The Law Society Charity

## Religious education

All Saints Educational Trust
The Altajir Trust
Catholic Foreign Missions (CFM)
Church Burgesses Trust
Mejer and Gertrude Miriam Frydman Foundation
The Girdlers' Company Charitable Trust
Hesed Trust
Hexham and Newcastle Diocesan Trust (1947)
Hockerill Educational Foundation
The Hope Trust
Jay Education Trust
The Jerusalem Trust
Keren Association Limited
Kollel and Co. Limited
Kupath Gemach Chaim Bechesed Viznitz Trust
Maurice and Hilda Laing Charitable Trust
Largsmount Ltd
The Lyndhurst Trust

Mercaz Torah Vechesed Limited
Sir John Priestman Charity Trust
St Luke's College Foundation
St Peter's Saltley Trust
Ulting Overseas Trust
The Norman Whiteley Trust

## Science education

The Gatsby Charitable Foundation
The J. G. Graves Charitable Trust
The Michael Heller Charitable Foundation
The Nuffield Foundation
The Racing Foundation
Mrs L. D. Rope Third Charitable Settlement
The William and Ellen Vinten Trust
The Winton Charitable Foundation

## Sports education

The Girdlers' Company Charitable Trust
The Lord's Taverners

## Technology, engineering and computer education

The James Dyson Foundation
The Gatsby Charitable Foundation
The Headley Trust
The Michael Heller Charitable Foundation
IBM United Kingdom Trust
Richard Radcliffe Charitable Trust
The Sir James Roll Charitable Trust
The William and Ellen Vinten Trust

## Pre-school education

BBC Children in Need
Carter's Educational Foundation
The Football Association National Sports Centre Trust
Hampton Fuel Allotment
The Hemby Charitable Trust

Henley Educational Trust
The Hesslewood Children's Trust
Mr and Mrs J. A. Pye's Charitable Settlement
Richard Reeve's Foundation

## Primary and secondary school education

The Alliance Family Foundation
The Ammco Trust
A. J. H. Ashby Will Trust
The Baily Thomas Charitable Fund
BBC Children in Need
The Blandford Lake Trust
The Harry Bottom Charitable Trust
The Bristol Charities
The Cadbury Foundation
Calouste Gulbenkian Foundation – UK Branch
Carter's Educational Foundation
The Catalyst Charitable Trust
The J. J. Charitable Trust
Dudley and Geoffrey Cox Charitable Trust
The Hamilton Davies Trust
The Deakin Charitable Trust
The Dibden Allotments Fund
Earls Colne and Halstead Educational Charity
Eastern Counties Educational Trust Limited
The Ellis Campbell Foundation
The ERM Foundation
The February Foundation
The Joyce Fletcher Charitable Trust
The Football Association National Sports Centre Trust
The Forbes Charitable Foundation
The Joseph Strong Frazer Trust
Mejer and Gertrude Miriam Frydman Foundation
The Gatsby Charitable Foundation
The Girdlers' Company Charitable Trust
Paul Hamlyn Foundation
Hampton Fuel Allotment
The Harris Charity
The Headley Trust
Henley Educational Trust
The Hesslewood Children's Trust
The Hornsey Parochial Charities
Hulme Trust Estates (Educational)

*Fields of interest and type of beneficiary*  **Environment and animals**

The Nani Huyu Charitable Trust
The Ian Karten Charitable Trust
The Peter Kershaw Trust
The Leche Trust
The Mark Leonard Trust
LHR Airport Communities Trust
The Charles Littlewood Hill Trust
The Lord's Taverners
The Gerald Micklem Charitable Trust
The Newcomen Collett Foundation
The Nuffield Foundation
The Owen Family Trust
City of Oxford Charity
The Jack Petchey Foundation
Mr and Mrs J. A. Pye's Charitable Settlement
Richard Reeve's Foundation
Rix-Thompson-Rothenberg Foundation
The Robertson Trust
The South Square Trust
The Colonel W. H. Whitbread Charitable Trust
The Wilson Foundation

### Faith schools

The Alliance Family Foundation
Mejer and Gertrude Miriam Frydman Foundation
The Owen Family Trust

### Public and independent schools

The Headley Trust
The Leche Trust
The Nuffield Foundation
The Owen Family Trust

### Special needs schools

The Ammco Trust
The Baily Thomas Charitable Fund
Eastern Counties Educational Trust Limited
The Ellis Campbell Foundation
The Joyce Fletcher Charitable Trust
The Forbes Charitable Foundation
The Girdlers' Company Charitable Trust
The Ian Karten Charitable Trust
The Lord's Taverners

The Gerald Micklem Charitable Trust
Rix-Thompson-Rothenberg Foundation

### State schools

The Deakin Charitable Trust
The Mark Leonard Trust
Richard Reeve's Foundation

### Teacher training and development

The City Educational Trust Fund
Hockerill Educational Foundation
The Nuffield Foundation

### Environment and animals

The 1970 Trust
A. J. H. Ashby Will Trust
The Aberbrothock Skea Trust
The AIM Foundation
The Alborada Trust
The H. B. Allen Charitable Trust
The AMW Charitable Trust
Anglo American Group Foundation
The Animal Defence Trust
The Ardwick Trust
The John Armitage Charitable Trust
The Ashden Trust
The Associated Country Women of the World
The Astor Foundation
The Astor of Hever Trust
Autonomous Research Charitable Trust
The Harry Bacon Foundation
The Scott Bader Commonwealth Limited
The C. Alma Baker Trust
The Balcombe Charitable Trust
The Balney Charitable Trust
The Barbour Foundation
Lord Barnby's Foundation
BC Partners Foundation
The Bellahouston Bequest Fund
The Bergne-Coupland Charity
The Berkeley Charitable Foundation
The Big Lottery Fund (see also Awards for All)
Birmingham International Airport Community Trust
The BlackRock (UK) Charitable Trust
The Blair Foundation
The Body Shop Foundation
The Bothwell Charitable Trust
The Brendish Family Foundation
Bridgepoint Charitable Trust
Briggs Animal Welfare Trust
The J. and M. Britton Charitable Trust
The Bromley Trust
The Consuelo and Anthony Brooke Charitable Trust
Edward Cadbury Charitable Trust
The Christopher Cadbury Charitable Trust
The G. W. Cadbury Charitable Trust
The William A. Cadbury Charitable Trust
The Cadbury Foundation

81

# Environment and animals

The Edward and Dorothy
  Cadbury Trust
CAFOD (Catholic Agency for
  Overseas Development)
Calleva Foundation
Calouste Gulbenkian
  Foundation – UK Branch
The Cambridge Chrysalis Trust
The Frederick and Phyllis Cann
  Trust
The Leslie Mary Carter
  Charitable Trust
The Wilfrid and Constance
  Cave Foundation
The Gaynor Cemlyn-Jones
  Trust
The Chapman Charitable Trust
CHK Charities Limited
The City Bridge Trust
CLA Charitable Trust
Clark Bradbury Charitable
  Trust
J. A. Clark Charitable Trust
The Roger and Sarah Bancroft
  Clark Charitable Trust
The Robert Clutterbuck
  Charitable Trust
The John Coates Charitable
  Trust
The John S. Cohen Foundation
John Coldman Charitable Trust
Colyer-Fergusson Charitable
  Trust
The Conservation Foundation
The Ernest Cook Trust
The Catherine Cookson
  Charitable Trust
Mabel Cooper Charity
Co-operative Community
  Investment Foundation
The Marjorie Coote Animal
  Charity Trust
The Helen Jean Cope Trust
The Gershon Coren Charitable
  Foundation
The Duke of Cornwall's
  Benevolent Fund
The Craignish Trust
The Craps Charitable Trust
The Cray Trust
The Crescent Trust
The Ronald Cruickshanks
  Foundation
The Cumber Family Charitable
  Trust
D. J. H. Currie Memorial Trust
The Dennis Curry Charitable
  Trust
The D'Oyly Carte Charitable
  Trust
The Davis Foundation
Peter De Haan Charitable
  Trust
William Dean Countryside and
  Educational Trust
The Delves Charitable Trust

Dischma Charitable Trust
The Dorus Trust
The Royal Foundation of the
  Duke and Duchess of
  Cambridge and Prince Harry
The Dulverton Trust
The Dumbreck Charity
Dunard Fund
The Dunn Family Charitable
  Trust
eaga Charitable Trust
Audrey Earle Charitable Trust
The Sir John Eastwood
  Foundation
The EBM Charitable Trust
The Ecology Trust
Edinburgh Trust No 2 Account
The John Ellerman Foundation
The Ellis Campbell Foundation
The Epigoni Trust
The Ericson Trust
The ERM Foundation
Esh Foundation
The Alan Evans Memorial Trust
The Beryl Evetts and Robert
  Luff Animal Welfare Trust
  Limited
The Matthew Eyton Animal
  Welfare Trust
Esmée Fairbairn Foundation
The Lord Faringdon Charitable
  Trust
Samuel William Farmer's Trust
The Fishmongers' Company's
  Charitable Trust
The Oliver Ford Charitable
  Trust
The Donald Forrester Trust
The Anna Rosa Forster
  Charitable Trust
The Gordon Fraser Charitable
  Trust
The Hugh Fraser Foundation
The Louis and Valerie
  Freedman Charitable
  Settlement
The Freshfield Foundation
The Fuserna Foundation
General Charitable Trust
The G. D. Charitable Trust
The Galanthus Trust
The Gannochy Trust
The Worshipful Company of
  Gardeners of London
The Garnett Charitable Trust
The Gatsby Charitable
  Foundation
Gatwick Airport Community
  Trust
The Generations Foundation
The Girdlers' Company
  Charitable Trust
The GNC Trust
The Golden Bottle Trust
The Gosling Foundation
  Limited

GrantScape
The Gordon Gray Trust
The Green Room Charitable
  Trust
Greenham Common
  Community Trust Limited
The Greggs Foundation
H. C. D. Memorial Fund
The Hadfield Trust
The Hadrian Trust
The Doris Louise Hailes
  Charitable Trust
The Hamamelis Trust
Hampshire and Isle of Wight
  Community Foundation
The Kathleen Hannay
  Memorial Charity
Miss K. M. Harbinson's
  Charitable Trust
The Harbour Foundation
The Harebell Centenary Fund
The Hawthorne Charitable
  Trust
The Headley Trust
The Charlotte Heber-Percy
  Charitable Trust
The Percy Hedley 1990
  Charitable Trust
The G. D. Herbert Charitable
  Trust
The Hillingdon Community
  Trust
The Hillingdon Partnership
  Trust
R. G. Hills Charitable Trust
The Henry C. Hoare Charitable
  Trust
The Hobson Charity Limited
The J. G. Hogg Charitable
  Trust
The Dorothy Holmes Charitable
  Trust
The Homestead Charitable
  Trust
The Mary Homfray Charitable
  Trust
The Reta Lila Howard
  Foundation
The Michael and Shirley Hunt
  Charitable Trust
The Idlewild Trust
The Iliffe Family Charitable
  Trust
The Ingram Trust
The Innocent Foundation
The Isle of Anglesey Charitable
  Trust
The J. J. Charitable Trust
The Jabbs Foundation
John Jarrold Trust
JCA Charitable Foundation
Rees Jeffreys Road Fund
The Jenour Foundation
The Jephcott Charitable Trust
The Johnson Wax Ltd
  Charitable Trust

The Marjorie and Geoffrey Jones Charitable Trust
The Jordan Charitable Foundation
The Kennel Club Charitable Trust
The Ernest Kleinwort Charitable Trust
The Sir James Knott Trust
Ladbrokes in the Community Charitable Trust
John Laing Charitable Trust
Christopher Laing Foundation
The Martin Laing Foundation
Lancashire Environmental Fund Limited
Duchy of Lancaster Benevolent Fund
The Jack Lane Charitable Trust
The Lauffer Family Charitable Foundation
Mrs F. B. Laurence Charitable Trust
The Raymond and Blanche Lawson Charitable Trust
The Leach Fourteenth Trust
The Leathersellers' Company Charitable Fund
The Leche Trust
Leicestershire, Leicester and Rutland Community Foundation
The Lennox and Wyfold Foundation
The Mark Leonard Trust
Lord Leverhulme's Charitable Trust
David and Ruth Lewis Family Charitable Trust
The John Spedan Lewis Foundation
The Sir Edward Lewis Foundation
John Lewis Partnership General Community Fund
LHR Airport Communities Trust
The Limbourne Trust
Limoges Charitable Trust
The Linbury Trust
Lincolnshire Community Foundation
The Lister Charitable Trust
The Frank Litchfield Charitable Trust
The Charles Littlewood Hill Trust
The London Community Foundation
The William and Katherine Longman Trust
The Lotus Foundation
The C. L. Loyd Charitable Trust
LSA Charitable Trust
The Lynn Foundation
The Lyons Charitable Trust

The R. S. Macdonald Charitable Trust
The Macdonald-Buchanan Charitable Trust
The Mackay and Brewer Charitable Trust
The Mackintosh Foundation
The MacRobert Trust
The Mactaggart Third Fund
The Ian Mactaggart Trust
The Mahavir Trust
Manchester Airport Community Trust Fund
The Manifold Charitable Trust
R. W. Mann Trust
The Marcela Trust
The Marchig Animal Welfare Trust
Market Harborough and The Bowdens Charity
The Michael Marks Charitable Trust
Marmot Charitable Trust
The Marsh Christian Trust
Sir George Martin Trust
The Medlock Charitable Trust
The Mercers' Charitable Foundation
T. & J. Meyer Family Foundation Limited
The Mickel Fund
Millennium Stadium Charitable Trust (Ymddiriedolaeth Elusennol Stadiwm y Mileniwm)
The Ronald Miller Foundation
The Millichope Foundation
The Millward Charitable Trust
The Peter Minet Trust
The Mirianog Trust
The Misselbrook Trust
The Montague Thompson Coon Charitable Trust
The Monument Trust
The George A. Moore Foundation
The Morel Charitable Trust
The Morris Charitable Trust
The Peter Morrison Charitable Foundation
Moto in the Community
Mrs Waterhouse Charitable Trust
Frederick Mulder Charitable Trust
The Edith Murphy Foundation
Network for Social Change
The NFU Mutual Charitable Trust
Alice Noakes Memorial Charitable Trust
Nominet Charitable Foundation
Norfolk Community Foundation
The Community Foundation for Northern Ireland

The Sir Peter O'Sullevan Charitable Trust
The Oakdale Trust
The Oakley Charitable Trust
The Ofenheim Charitable Trust
Oglesby Charitable Trust
The John Oldacre Foundation
Open Gate
The Owen Family Trust
The Paget Charitable Trust
The Panton Trust
The Samuel and Freda Parkinson Charitable Trust
The Jack Patston Charitable Trust
The Peacock Charitable Trust
The Susanna Peake Charitable Trust
People's Postcode Trust
The Persula Foundation
The Petplan Charitable Trust
The Phillips Charitable Trust
The Pilgrim Trust
The Elise Pilkington Charitable Trust
Estate of the Late Colonel W. W. Pilkington Will Trusts – The General Charity Fund
Polden-Puckham Charitable Foundation
The John Porter Charitable Trust
The Porter Foundation
The Primrose Trust
The Prince of Wales's Charitable Foundation
Princess Anne's Charities
The PwC Foundation
Mr and Mrs J. A. Pye's Charitable Settlement
Quartet Community Foundation
The Racing Foundation
The Joseph Rank Trust
The Sigrid Rausing Trust
The Reed Foundation
The Rhododendron Trust
The River Farm Foundation
The Robertson Trust
The Rochester Bridge Trust
The Roddick Foundation
The Roughley Charitable Trust
The Rowlands Trust
Royal Docks Trust (London)
The Rufford Foundation
Ryklow Charitable Trust 1992
The Michael Harry Sacher Trust
The Jean Sainsbury Animal Welfare Trust
The Saintbury Trust
The Salamander Charitable Trust
The Basil Samuel Charitable Trust
The Peter Samuel Charitable Trust

83

# Agriculture and fishing

The Sandra Charitable Trust
The Scarfe Charitable Trust
Schroder Charity Trust
The Scottish Power Foundation
The Scouloudi Foundation
Seafarers UK
SEM Charitable Trust
The Shears Foundation
The Sheepdrove Trust
The Sylvia and Colin Shepherd Charitable Trust
The Shetland Charitable Trust
The Shipwrights' Company Charitable Fund
David and Jennifer Sieff Charitable Trust
SITA Cornwall Trust Limited
Skinners' Company Lady Neville Charity
The John Slater Foundation
Ruth Smart Foundation
The SMB Charitable Trust
The DS Smith Charitable Foundation
The N. Smith Charitable Settlement
The Stanley Smith UK Horticultural Trust
Philip Smith's Charitable Trust
The R. C. Snelling Charitable Trust
The Sobell Foundation
Sodexo Foundation
The South Square Trust
The W. F. Southall Trust
R. H. Southern Trust
The Spero Foundation
The Staples Trust
The Steel Charitable Trust
Stevenson Family's Charitable Trust
The Andy Stewart Charitable Foundation
The Stewarts Law Foundation
The Leonard Laity Stoate Charitable Trust
The Edward Stocks-Massey Bequest Fund
M. J. C. Stone Charitable Trust
The Stone Family Foundation
The Adrienne and Leslie Sussman Charitable Trust
The Swann-Morton Foundation
The Swire Charitable Trust
Sylvia Waddilove Foundation UK
C. B. and H. H. Taylor 1984 Trust
The Connie and Albert Taylor Charitable Trust
Tearfund
The C. Paul Thackray General Charitable Trust
The Loke Wan Tho Memorial Foundation
The Three Guineas Trust

Toyota Manufacturing UK Charitable Trust
Annie Tranmer Charitable Trust
The Tresillian Trust
Community Foundation Serving Tyne and Wear and Northumberland
The Underwood Trust
The Michael Uren Foundation
The Valentine Charitable Trust
The Albert Van Den Bergh Charitable Trust
The William and Patricia Venton Charitable Trust
Roger Vere Foundation
Wales Council for Voluntary Action
The Waterloo Foundation
The David Webster Charitable Trust
The Garfield Weston Foundation
The Barbara Whatmore Charitable Trust
The Whitaker Charitable Trust
The Colonel W. H. Whitbread Charitable Trust
The Whitley Animal Protection Trust
The HDH Wills 1965 Charitable Trust
J. and J. R. Wilson Trust
The Wixamtree Trust
The Maurice Wohl Charitable Foundation
The Wolfson Family Charitable Trust
Woodroffe Benton Foundation
The Woodward Charitable Trust
The Diana Edgson Wright Charitable Trust
Yorkshire and Clydesdale Bank Foundation
Yorkshire Building Society Charitable Foundation
The Yorkshire Dales Millennium Trust
Youth United Foundation
Zephyr Charitable Trust

## Agriculture and fishing

The Scott Bader Commonwealth Limited
The C. Alma Baker Trust
The Chapman Charitable Trust
CLA Charitable Trust
The Ecology Trust
The John Ellerman Foundation
Esmée Fairbairn Foundation
The Fishmongers' Company's Charitable Trust

The Oliver Ford Charitable Trust
The Worshipful Company of Gardeners of London
The Gatsby Charitable Foundation
The Headley Trust
The Innocent Foundation
The J. J. Charitable Trust
JCA Charitable Foundation
The Mark Leonard Trust
The Frank Litchfield Charitable Trust
LSA Charitable Trust
The MacRobert Trust
Manchester Airport Community Trust Fund
The NFU Mutual Charitable Trust
The John Oldacre Foundation
The PwC Foundation
Mr and Mrs J. A. Pye's Charitable Settlement
Quartet Community Foundation
The Peter Samuel Charitable Trust
Seafarers UK
The Stanley Smith UK Horticultural Trust
The Stewarts Law Foundation
The Waterloo Foundation
The Garfield Weston Foundation

## Farming and food production

CLA Charitable Trust
The Gatsby Charitable Foundation
The Innocent Foundation
LSA Charitable Trust
The NFU Mutual Charitable Trust
Mr and Mrs J. A. Pye's Charitable Settlement

## Forestry

CLA Charitable Trust
The Headley Trust
Manchester Airport Community Trust Fund
The Peter Samuel Charitable Trust

## Horticulture

CLA Charitable Trust
The Oliver Ford Charitable Trust
The Worshipful Company of Gardeners of London

Fields of interest and type of beneficiary — Countryside

The Gatsby Charitable Foundation
LSA Charitable Trust
The MacRobert Trust
The Stanley Smith UK Horticultural Trust

## Animal care

The Alborada Trust
The Animal Defence Trust
The Ashden Trust
The Astor Foundation
The Harry Bacon Foundation
The Bellahouston Bequest Fund
Briggs Animal Welfare Trust
The Wilfrid and Constance Cave Foundation
The Gaynor Cemlyn-Jones Trust
The Robert Clutterbuck Charitable Trust
The Marjorie Coote Animal Charity Trust
The Dumbreck Charity
The Sir John Eastwood Foundation
The EBM Charitable Trust
The Beryl Evetts and Robert Luff Animal Welfare Trust Limited
The Matthew Eyton Animal Welfare Trust
The Anna Rosa Forster Charitable Trust
The Doris Louise Hailes Charitable Trust
The J. G. Hogg Charitable Trust
The Michael and Shirley Hunt Charitable Trust
The Jenour Foundation
The Kennel Club Charitable Trust
David and Ruth Lewis Family Charitable Trust
The William and Katherine Longman Trust
The Lyons Charitable Trust
The R. S. Macdonald Charitable Trust
The Mackay and Brewer Charitable Trust
The Marchig Animal Welfare Trust
The Millward Charitable Trust
The Edith Murphy Foundation
Alice Noakes Memorial Charitable Trust
The Sir Peter O'Sullevan Charitable Trust
Open Gate
The Paget Charitable Trust
The Samuel and Freda Parkinson Charitable Trust

The Persula Foundation
The Petplan Charitable Trust
The Phillips Charitable Trust
The Elise Pilkington Charitable Trust
The Racing Foundation
The Joseph Rank Trust
The Jean Sainsbury Animal Welfare Trust
David and Jennifer Sieff Charitable Trust
The John Slater Foundation
Ruth Smart Foundation
The Andy Stewart Charitable Foundation
The Adrienne and Leslie Sussman Charitable Trust
The William and Patricia Venton Charitable Trust
J. and J. R. Wilson Trust
The Diana Edgson Wright Charitable Trust
Yorkshire Building Society Charitable Foundation

## Animal conservation

A. J. H. Ashby Will Trust
The Scott Bader Commonwealth Limited
Birmingham International Airport Community Trust
The Body Shop Foundation
The Brendish Family Foundation
The Wilfrid and Constance Cave Foundation
The Gaynor Cemlyn-Jones Trust
The Chapman Charitable Trust
Clark Bradbury Charitable Trust
The Robert Clutterbuck Charitable Trust
The John S. Cohen Foundation
The Conservation Foundation
The Marjorie Coote Animal Charity Trust
The Cumber Family Charitable Trust
William Dean Countryside and Educational Trust
The Dumbreck Charity
The Sir John Eastwood Foundation
The Iliffe Family Charitable Trust
The Lister Charitable Trust
The Lotus Foundation
The Marchig Animal Welfare Trust
The Mirianog Trust
The Oakdale Trust
The Owen Family Trust

The Paget Charitable Trust
The Samuel and Freda Parkinson Charitable Trust
The Jack Patston Charitable Trust
The Primrose Trust
The PwC Foundation
Mr and Mrs J. A. Pye's Charitable Settlement
The Joseph Rank Trust
The Rhododendron Trust
The Rufford Foundation
Ryklow Charitable Trust 1992
The Michael Harry Sacher Trust
The Jean Sainsbury Animal Welfare Trust
SITA Cornwall Trust Limited
Ruth Smart Foundation
The Albert Van Den Bergh Charitable Trust
The David Webster Charitable Trust
The Garfield Weston Foundation
The Diana Edgson Wright Charitable Trust

## Climate change

The Ashden Trust
The Scott Bader Commonwealth Limited
The Chapman Charitable Trust
The John Ellerman Foundation
Esmée Fairbairn Foundation
The Mark Leonard Trust
Frederick Mulder Charitable Trust
The PwC Foundation
Mr and Mrs J. A. Pye's Charitable Settlement
The Joseph Rank Trust
SEM Charitable Trust
The Stewarts Law Foundation
The Three Guineas Trust
The Waterloo Foundation
The Garfield Weston Foundation

## Countryside

The Aberbrothock Skea Trust
The Astor Foundation
The Scott Bader Commonwealth Limited
The Big Lottery Fund (see also Awards for All)
The Blair Foundation
The Bothwell Charitable Trust
The Cadbury Foundation
The Chapman Charitable Trust
CHK Charities Limited
CLA Charitable Trust

85

Colyer-Fergusson Charitable Trust
The Ernest Cook Trust
D. J. H. Currie Memorial Trust
The D'Oyly Carte Charitable Trust
The Dunn Family Charitable Trust
The John Ellerman Foundation
The Ellis Campbell Foundation
The Alan Evans Memorial Trust
Esmée Fairbairn Foundation
The Freshfield Foundation
The Galanthus Trust
The Gannochy Trust
The Girdlers' Company Charitable Trust
The Green Room Charitable Trust
The Greggs Foundation
The Idlewild Trust
The Leche Trust
LHR Airport Communities Trust
Manchester Airport Community Trust Fund
Sir George Martin Trust
The Mirianog Trust
The Pilgrim Trust
Estate of the Late Colonel W. W. Pilkington Will Trusts – The General Charity Fund
The PwC Foundation
Mr and Mrs J. A. Pye's Charitable Settlement
Quartet Community Foundation
The Joseph Rank Trust
The Rufford Foundation
Ryklow Charitable Trust 1992
Schroder Charity Trust
The Shears Foundation
SITA Cornwall Trust Limited
Skinners' Company Lady Neville Charity
The Stewarts Law Foundation
The Connie and Albert Taylor Charitable Trust
The Valentine Charitable Trust
The Waterloo Foundation
The David Webster Charitable Trust
The Garfield Weston Foundation
The Colonel W. H. Whitbread Charitable Trust
Woodroffe Benton Foundation
Zephyr Charitable Trust

## Environmental education and research

The Ardwick Trust
The Ashden Trust
The Scott Bader Commonwealth Limited

The Big Lottery Fund (see also Awards for All)
Birmingham International Airport Community Trust
The Body Shop Foundation
The Cadbury Foundation
The Chapman Charitable Trust
The J. J. Charitable Trust
The Conservation Foundation
The Ernest Cook Trust
The Dennis Curry Charitable Trust
The Davis Foundation
William Dean Countryside and Educational Trust
The Dulverton Trust
The Dunn Family Charitable Trust
eaga Charitable Trust
The John Ellerman Foundation
Esmée Fairbairn Foundation
The Green Room Charitable Trust
The Greggs Foundation
The Mark Leonard Trust
LHR Airport Communities Trust
Manchester Airport Community Trust Fund
The Marchig Animal Welfare Trust
Marmot Charitable Trust
The Mirianog Trust
Network for Social Change
Nominet Charitable Foundation
The Community Foundation for Northern Ireland
Oglesby Charitable Trust
Estate of the Late Colonel W. W. Pilkington Will Trusts – The General Charity Fund
The Porter Foundation
The PwC Foundation
Quartet Community Foundation
The Joseph Rank Trust
The Rufford Foundation
The Saintbury Trust
The Shears Foundation
The Stanley Smith UK Horticultural Trust
The Sobell Foundation
The Spero Foundation
The Staples Trust
The Stewarts Law Foundation
The Waterloo Foundation
The David Webster Charitable Trust
The Garfield Weston Foundation
The Woodward Charitable Trust

## Natural environment

A. J. H. Ashby Will Trust
The Ashden Trust
The Scott Bader Commonwealth Limited
The Balney Charitable Trust
BC Partners Foundation
The Blair Foundation
Bridgepoint Charitable Trust
The Christopher Cadbury Charitable Trust
The Cadbury Foundation
The Chapman Charitable Trust
Clark Bradbury Charitable Trust
The Robert Clutterbuck Charitable Trust
The Conservation Foundation
The Ernest Cook Trust
Mabel Cooper Charity
The Dennis Curry Charitable Trust
The D'Oyly Carte Charitable Trust
The Davis Foundation
William Dean Countryside and Educational Trust
The Dulverton Trust
The Dunn Family Charitable Trust
The John Ellerman Foundation
The Ericson Trust
Esmée Fairbairn Foundation
The Galanthus Trust
The Gannochy Trust
The Girdlers' Company Charitable Trust
The Gordon Gray Trust
The Green Room Charitable Trust
The Headley Trust
The Ingram Trust
The Isle of Anglesey Charitable Trust
The J. J. Charitable Trust
The Jabbs Foundation
The Marjorie and Geoffrey Jones Charitable Trust
The Lauffer Family Charitable Foundation
LHR Airport Communities Trust
The Charles Littlewood Hill Trust
Manchester Airport Community Trust Fund
The Marchig Animal Welfare Trust
Sir George Martin Trust
The Medlock Charitable Trust
The Mercers' Charitable Foundation
T. & J. Meyer Family Foundation Limited

Millennium Stadium Charitable Trust (Ymddiriedolaeth Elusennol Stadiwm y Mileniwm)
The Peter Minet Trust
The Mirianog Trust
The Oakdale Trust
The Owen Family Trust
The Jack Patston Charitable Trust
Estate of the Late Colonel W. W. Pilkington Will Trusts – The General Charity Fund
Polden-Puckham Charitable Foundation
The PwC Foundation
Mr and Mrs J. A. Pye's Charitable Settlement
Quartet Community Foundation
The Joseph Rank Trust
The Sigrid Rausing Trust
The Rhododendron Trust
The Roughley Charitable Trust
The Rufford Foundation
Ryklow Charitable Trust 1992
The Saintbury Trust
The Peter Samuel Charitable Trust
Schroder Charity Trust
SITA Cornwall Trust Limited
The Stanley Smith UK Horticultural Trust
Stevenson Family's Charitable Trust
The Stewarts Law Foundation
The Valentine Charitable Trust
The Waterloo Foundation
The David Webster Charitable Trust
The Garfield Weston Foundation
Woodroffe Benton Foundation
Zephyr Charitable Trust

### Flora and fauna

A. J. H. Ashby Will Trust
The Blair Foundation
The J. J. Charitable Trust
Mabel Cooper Charity
The Dulverton Trust
Manchester Airport Community Trust Fund
The Marchig Animal Welfare Trust
The Mercers' Charitable Foundation
The Jack Patston Charitable Trust
The Peter Samuel Charitable Trust
The Stanley Smith UK Horticultural Trust
The Valentine Charitable Trust

### Water resources

The Headley Trust

### Wild places, wilderness

The Dulverton Trust
The Girdlers' Company Charitable Trust

### Pollution abatement and control

BC Partners Foundation
Esmée Fairbairn Foundation
Marmot Charitable Trust
Mr and Mrs J. A. Pye's Charitable Settlement
Quartet Community Foundation
SITA Cornwall Trust Limited
The Ashden Trust
The Big Lottery Fund (see also Awards for All)
The Chapman Charitable Trust
The Garfield Weston Foundation
The Green Room Charitable Trust
The John Ellerman Foundation
The Joseph Rank Trust
The Mark Leonard Trust
The PwC Foundation
The Saintbury Trust
The Scott Bader Commonwealth Limited
The Sigrid Rausing Trust
The Stewarts Law Foundation
The Waterloo Foundation
Woodroffe Benton Foundation
Zephyr Charitable Trust

### Sustainable environment

The 1970 Trust
The AIM Foundation
The Ashden Trust
The Associated Country Women of the World
The Scott Bader Commonwealth Limited
BC Partners Foundation
The Big Lottery Fund (see also Awards for All)
The Body Shop Foundation
The Cadbury Foundation
Calouste Gulbenkian Foundation – UK Branch
The Chapman Charitable Trust
J. A. Clark Charitable Trust
The Dunn Family Charitable Trust
eaga Charitable Trust
The Ecology Trust
The John Ellerman Foundation
Esmée Fairbairn Foundation
The Freshfield Foundation
The Gannochy Trust
The Generations Foundation
The Green Room Charitable Trust
The Greggs Foundation
The J. J. Charitable Trust
John Laing Charitable Trust
The Mark Leonard Trust
LHR Airport Communities Trust
Manchester Airport Community Trust Fund
Marmot Charitable Trust
Nominet Charitable Foundation
The Community Foundation for Northern Ireland
Open Gate
People's Postcode Trust
Polden-Puckham Charitable Foundation
The PwC Foundation
Mr and Mrs J. A. Pye's Charitable Settlement
Quartet Community Foundation
The Joseph Rank Trust
The Sigrid Rausing Trust
The Roughley Charitable Trust
The Rufford Foundation
The Saintbury Trust
SITA Cornwall Trust Limited
The Staples Trust
The Stewarts Law Foundation
The Stone Family Foundation
The Waterloo Foundation
The David Webster Charitable Trust
The Garfield Weston Foundation
Woodroffe Benton Foundation
Zephyr Charitable Trust

### Energy issues

The 1970 Trust
eaga Charitable Trust
LHR Airport Communities Trust

### Loss of biodiversity

The Rufford Foundation

### Transport

The 1970 Trust
The Scott Bader Commonwealth Limited

## General charitable purposes

The Big Lottery Fund (see also Awards for All)
The Chapman Charitable Trust
The J. J. Charitable Trust
The Green Room Charitable Trust
The Hillingdon Community Trust
Rees Jeffreys Road Fund
The PwC Foundation
Quartet Community Foundation
The Joseph Rank Trust
The Rochester Bridge Trust
Seafarers UK
The Shipwrights' Company Charitable Fund
The Stewarts Law Foundation
The Garfield Weston Foundation

The 101 Foundation
The 1989 Willan Charitable Trust
The 29th May 1961 Charitable Trust
A. B. Grace Trust
A. W. Charitable Trust
The Aberdeen Foundation
ABF The Soldiers' Charity
The Acacia Charitable Trust
The Addleshaw Goddard Charitable Trust
The Adnams Charity
The Adrian Swire Charitable Trust
The Sylvia Aitken Charitable Trust
The Al Fayed Charitable Foundation
D. G. Albright Charitable Trust
Allchurches Trust Ltd
The H. B. Allen Charitable Trust
The Alliance Family Foundation
Alliance Trust Staff Foundation
The Almond Trust
Almondsbury Charity
AM Charitable Trust
The Amalur Foundation Limited
Sir John and Lady Amory's Charitable Trust
The Ampelos Trust
Andor Charitable Trust
Mary Andrew Charitable Trust
The Annandale Charitable Trust
Anpride Ltd
The Anson Charitable Trust
The Arbib Foundation
The Ardeola Charitable Trust
The Ardwick Trust
The Argentarius Foundation
The John Armitage Charitable Trust
The Armourers' and Brasiers' Gauntlet Trust
The Ascot Fire Brigade Trust
The Asda Foundation
The Ashburnham Thanksgiving Trust
The Ashworth Charitable Trust
The Ian Askew Charitable Trust
The Astor Foundation
The Atlas Fund
The Lord Austin Trust
Autonomous Research Charitable Trust
Awards for All (see also the Big Lottery Fund)
The Aylesford Family Charitable Trust
The BACTA Charitable Trust

The Scott Bader Commonwealth Limited
The Bagri Foundation
The Balfour Beatty Charitable Trust
The Andrew Balint Charitable Trust
The George Balint Charitable Trust
The Paul Balint Charitable Trust
The Albert Casanova Ballard Deceased Trust
Balmain Charitable Trust
The Balney Charitable Trust
The Bamford Charitable Foundation
The Banbury Charities
The Band Trust
The Bank of Scotland Foundation
The Barbour Foundation
The Barham Charitable Trust
The Barker-Mill Foundation
Lord Barnby's Foundation
The Barnsbury Charitable Trust
The Barnstaple Bridge Trust
The Misses Barrie Charitable Trust
The Bartlett Taylor Charitable Trust
The Paul Bassham Charitable Trust
The Batchworth Trust
The Battens Charitable Trust
The Bay Tree Charitable Trust
The Louis Baylis (Maidenhead Advertiser) Charitable Trust
BBC Children in Need
BC Partners Foundation
BCH Trust
The Bearder Charity
The James Beattie Charitable Trust
The Beaverbrook Foundation
The Beccles Town Lands Charity
The Becker Family Charitable Trust
The Peter Beckwith Charitable Trust
The Bedfordshire and Luton Community Foundation
The Provincial Grand Lodge of Bedfordshire Charity Fund
Beefy's Charity Foundation
The David and Ruth Behrend Fund
The Bellinger Donnay Trust
The Benfield Motors Charitable Trust
The Benham Charitable Settlement
Maurice and Jacqueline Bennett Charitable Trust

*Fields of interest and type of beneficiary* — **General charitable purposes**

Michael and Leslie Bennett Charitable Trust
The Gerald Bentall Charitable Trust
The Bergne-Coupland Charity
The Berkeley Charitable Foundation
The Ruth Berkowitz Charitable Trust
The Berkshire Community Foundation
The Bernadette Charitable Trust
The Bertarelli UK Foundation
The Bideford Bridge Trust
The Big Lottery Fund (see also Awards for All)
The Billmeir Charitable Trust
The Bingham Trust
The Lord Mayor of Birmingham's Charity
Birthday House Trust
The Michael Bishop Foundation
The Bertie Black Foundation
Isabel Blackman Foundation
The BlackRock (UK) Charitable Trust
The Blair Foundation
The Morgan Blake Charitable Trust
Blakemore Foundation
The Sir Victor Blank Charitable Settlement
The Bloom Foundation
The Bluston Charitable Settlement
The Marjory Boddy Charitable Trust
The Boltini Trust
The Bonamy Charitable Trust
The John and Celia Bonham Christie Charitable Trust
The Charlotte Bonham-Carter Charitable Trust
The Linda and Gordon Bonnyman Charitable Trust
The Boodle & Dunthorne Charitable Trust
The Booth Charities
Boots Charitable Trust
The Bordon Liphook Haslemere Charity
The Bothwell Charitable Trust
The Bower Trust
The Bowerman Charitable Trust
The Bowland Charitable Trust
The Frank Brake Charitable Trust
The William Brake Charitable Trust
The Liz and Terry Bramall Foundation
The Bramhope Trust
The Bransford Trust

The Brendish Family Foundation
Bridgepoint Charitable Trust
The Bristol Charities
The British Humane Association
The J. and M. Britton Charitable Trust
The Consuelo and Anthony Brooke Charitable Trust
The Roger Brooke Charitable Trust
The David Brooke Charity
Joseph Brough Charitable Trust
Bill Brown 1989 Charitable Trust
Edna Brown Charitable Settlement
The Brownsword Charitable Foundation
The T. B. H. Brunner Charitable Settlement
The Jack Brunton Charitable Trust
The Bruntwood Charity
The Buckinghamshire Masonic Centenary Fund
Buckland Charitable Trust
The Buffini Chao Foundation
The Bulldog Trust Limited
The Burden Trust
Burden's Charitable Foundation
The Clara E. Burgess Charity
Consolidated Charity of Burton upon Trent
The Derek Butler Trust
Cable & Wireless Worldwide Foundation
Edward Cadbury Charitable Trust
Peter Cadbury Charitable Trust
The Christopher Cadbury Charitable Trust
The G. W. Cadbury Charitable Trust
The Richard Cadbury Charitable Trust
The Edward and Dorothy Cadbury Trust
The George Cadbury Trust
The Cadogan Charity
Community Foundation for Calderdale
Callander Charitable Trust
Calleva Foundation
The Cambridge Chrysalis Trust
The Camelia Trust
The Frederick and Phyllis Cann Trust
The Canning Trust
The H. and L. Cantor Trust
Cardy Beaver Foundation
The Carew Pole Charitable Trust

David William Traill Cargill Fund
The Carlton House Charitable Trust
The Carmelite Monastery Ware Trust
The Carpenters' Company Charitable Trust
The Carrington Charitable Trust
The Casey Trust
The Catalyst Charitable Trust
The Joseph and Annie Cattle Trust
The Thomas Sivewright Catto Charitable Settlement
The Wilfrid and Constance Cave Foundation
The Cayo Foundation
The B. G. S. Cayzer Charitable Trust
The Cazenove Charitable Trust
The CBD Charitable Trust
The Gaynor Cemlyn-Jones Trust
The Amelia Chadwick Trust
The Chapman Charitable Trust
The Charities Advisory Trust
Charitworth Limited
The Charter 600 Charity
The Worshipful Company of Chartered Accountants General Charitable Trust
Chaucer Foundation
The Cheruby Trust
Cheshire Freemason's Charity
The Chetwode Foundation
The Childs Charitable Trust
The Chippenham Borough Lands Charity
The Chipping Sodbury Town Lands Charity
CHK Charities Limited
The Chownes Foundation
Christian Aid
Chrysalis Trust
Church Burgesses Trust
The CIBC World Markets Children's Miracle Foundation
Stephen Clark 1957 Charitable Trust
The Hilda and Alice Clark Charitable Trust
The Roger and Sarah Bancroft Clark Charitable Trust
The Cleopatra Trust
Closehelm Limited
The Clothworkers' Foundation
The Clover Trust
The Robert Clutterbuck Charitable Trust
Clydpride Ltd
The Coalfields Regeneration Trust

**89**

## General charitable purposes

*Fields of interest and type of beneficiary*

The John Coates Charitable Trust
The Cobalt Trust
The Cobtree Charity Trust Ltd
The John S. Cohen Foundation
John Coldman Charitable Trust
The Cole Charitable Trust
The Colefax Charitable Trust
John and Freda Coleman Charitable Trust
The George Henry Collins Charity
The Sir Jeremiah Colman Gift Trust
Community Foundation for Leeds
The Compton Charitable Trust
The Douglas Compton James Charitable Trust
The Congleton Inclosure Trust
Martin Connell Charitable Trust
The Catherine Cookson Charitable Trust
Mabel Cooper Charity
The Alice Ellen Cooper Dean Charitable Foundation
Co-operative Community Investment Foundation
The Helen Jean Cope Trust
The Gershon Coren Charitable Foundation
Michael Cornish Charitable Trust
The Evan Cornish Foundation
Cornwall Community Foundation
The Duke of Cornwall's Benevolent Fund
The Cornwell Charitable Trust
The Sidney and Elizabeth Corob Charitable Trust
The Cotton Industry War Memorial Trust
County Durham Community Foundation
The Augustine Courtauld Trust
Coutts Charitable Foundation
General Charity of Coventry
Coventry Building Society Charitable Foundation
The Sir Tom Cowie Charitable Trust
Cowley Charitable Foundation
Dudley and Geoffrey Cox Charitable Trust
The Lord Cozens-Hardy Trust
The Craignish Trust
The Craps Charitable Trust
The Cray Trust
The Crescent Trust
Cripplegate Foundation
The Croydon Relief in Need Charities
Cruden Foundation Ltd

The Ronald Cruickshanks Foundation
The Cuby Charitable Trust
Cullum Family Trust
D. J. H. Currie Memorial Trust
The Dennis Curry Charitable Trust
The Cwmbran Trust
Itzchok Meyer Cymerman Trust Ltd
D. C. R. Allen Charitable Trust
The D. G. Charitable Settlement
Oizer Dalim Trust
Michael Davies Charitable Settlement
The Gwendoline and Margaret Davies Charity
The Hamilton Davies Trust
The Wilfrid Bruce Davis Charitable Trust
The Davis Foundation
The Henry and Suzanne Davis Foundation
The De Brye Charitable Trust
Peter De Haan Charitable Trust
The De Laszlo Foundation
Debenhams Foundation
The Dellal Foundation
The Delves Charitable Trust
The Dentons UKMEA LLP Charitable Trust
Derbyshire Community Foundation
The Desmond Foundation
Devon Community Foundation
The Duke of Devonshire's Charitable Trust
The Sandy Dewhirst Charitable Trust
The Laduma Dhamecha Charitable Trust
The Diageo Foundation
Alan and Sheila Diamond Charitable Trust
The Dibden Allotments Fund
The Gillian Dickinson Trust
Dischma Charitable Trust
The Djanogly Foundation
The DLM Charitable Trust
The Dollond Charitable Trust
Dorset Community Foundation
The Dorus Trust
The Double 'O' Charity Ltd
R. M. Douglas Charitable Trust
The Drapers' Charitable Fund
Dromintee Trust
The Duis Charitable Trust
The Royal Foundation of the Duke and Duchess of Cambridge and Prince Harry
The Dulverton Trust
The Dumbreck Charity
The Dunn Family Charitable Trust

The W. E. Dunn Trust
The Charles Dunstone Charitable Trust
Mildred Duveen Charitable Trust
The Dyers' Company Charitable Trust
The James Dyson Foundation
The Eagle Charity Trust
Audrey Earle Charitable Trust
The Earley Charity
The Sir John Eastwood Foundation
The Ebenezer Trust
The Economist Charitable Trust
The Gilbert and Eileen Edgar Foundation
The Gilbert Edgar Trust
Edinburgh & Lothian Trust Fund
Edinburgh Trust No 2 Account
The George Elias Charitable Trust
The Wilfred and Elsie Elkes Charity Fund
The Maud Elkington Charitable Trust
The Ellerdale Trust
The Edith Maud Ellis 1985 Charitable Trust
The Vernon N. Ely Charitable Trust
The Emerton-Christie Charity
Engage Foundation
The Englefield Charitable Trust
The Epigoni Trust
The Erskine Cunningham Hill Trust
Essex Community Foundation
The Estelle Trust
Joseph Ettedgui Charitable Foundation
The Eventhall Family Charitable Trust
The Everard Foundation
The Exilarch's Foundation
The Expat Foundation
The William and Christine Eynon Charity
The Fairstead Trust
The Fairway Trust
Famos Foundation Trust
The Lord Faringdon Charitable Trust
The Thomas Farr Charity
The Farthing Trust
The Fassnidge Memorial Trust
The A. M. Fenton Trust
The Fidelity UK Foundation
The Doris Field Charitable Trust
Field Family Charitable Trust
Filey Foundation Ltd
Dixie Rose Findlay Charitable Trust

90

Fisherbeck Charitable Trust
The Earl Fitzwilliam Charitable Trust
The Joyce Fletcher Charitable Trust
Florence's Charitable Trust
The Flow Foundation
The Gerald Fogel Charitable Trust
The Forbes Charitable Foundation
The Forest Hill Charitable Trust
Forever Manchester (The Community Foundation for Greater Manchester)
Gwyneth Forrester Trust
The Donald Forrester Trust
The Isaac and Freda Frankel Memorial Charitable Trust
The Elizabeth Frankland Moore and Star Foundation
The Gordon Fraser Charitable Trust
The Hugh Fraser Foundation
The Joseph Strong Frazer Trust
The Fred and Maureen Charitable Trust
The Louis and Valerie Freedman Charitable Settlement
The Michael and Clara Freeman Charitable Trust
The Freemasons' Grand Charity
The Charles S. French Charitable Trust
The Anne French Memorial Trust
The Freshgate Trust Foundation
The Friarsgate Trust
Friends of Wiznitz Limited
The Frognal Trust
The Patrick & Helena Frost Foundation
The Fulmer Charitable Trust
The Fuserna Foundation
General Charitable Trust
G. M. C. Trust
The Galbraith Trust
The Gale Family Charity Trust
Gamlen Charitable Trust
The Gamma Trust
The Ganzoni Charitable Trust
The Worshipful Company of Gardeners of London
The Garrick Charitable Trust
Garthgwynion Charities
The Gatsby Charitable Foundation
Gatwick Airport Community Trust
The Nigel Gee Foundation
Sir Robert Geffery's Almshouse Trust
Simon Gibson Charitable Trust

The G. C. Gibson Charitable Trust
Global Charities
Worshipful Company of Glovers of London Charitable Trust
The Godinton Charitable Trust
The Golden Bottle Trust
The Goldsmiths' Company Charity
The Mike Gooley Trailfinders Charity
The Gosling Foundation Limited
The Gould Charitable Trust
The Graff Foundation
E. C. Graham Belford Charitable Settlement
Grand Charitable Trust of the Order of Women Freemasons
Grantham Yorke Trust
GrantScape
The J. G. Graves Charitable Trust
The Gray Trust
The Great Stone Bridge Trust of Edenbridge
The Great Torrington Town Lands Charity
The Kenneth & Susan Green Charitable Foundation
The Green Hall Foundation
The Green Room Charitable Trust
Greenham Common Community Trust Limited
The Gretna Charitable Trust
The Greys Charitable Trust
The Grimmitt Trust
The Grocers' Charity
The GRP Charitable Trust
The Bishop of Guildford's Foundation
The Walter Guinness Charitable Trust
The Gunter Charitable Trust
The Gurney Charitable Trust
The H. and M. Charitable Trust
H. and T. Clients Charitable Trust
The Edith Winifred Hall Charitable Trust
Hamilton Wallace Trust
Sue Hammerson Charitable Trust
Hampshire and Isle of Wight Community Foundation
The Hampstead Wells and Campden Trust
Hampton Fuel Allotment
The W. A. Handley Charitable Trust
The Kathleen Hannay Memorial Charity

The Doughty Hanson Charitable Foundation
The Haramead Trust
Miss K. M. Harbinson's Charitable Trust
Harbo Charities Limited
The Harborne Parish Lands Charity
The Harbour Charitable Trust
The Harbour Foundation
William Harding's Charity
The Hare of Steep Charitable Trust (HOST)
The Harebell Centenary Fund
The Hargrave Foundation
The Harpur Trust
The Harris Family Charitable Trust
The Edith Lilian Harrison 2000 Foundation
The Hartley Charitable Trust
Edward Harvist Trust
The Hasluck Charitable Trust
The Hathaway Trust
The Maurice Hatter Foundation
The M. A. Hawe Settlement
The Hawthorne Charitable Trust
The Charles Hayward Foundation
Headley-Pitt Charitable Trust
May Hearnshaw Charitable Trust
Heart of England Community Foundation
The Heathcoat Trust
The Heathside Charitable Trust
The Charlotte Heber-Percy Charitable Trust
The Percy Hedley 1990 Charitable Trust
The Hedley Denton Charitable Trust
The Michael Heller Charitable Foundation
The Simon Heller Charitable Settlement
The Helping Foundation
The Hemby Charitable Trust
The Christina Mary Hendrie Trust for Scottish and Canadian Charities
Philip Sydney Henman Deceased Will Trust
The G. D. Herbert Charitable Trust
Herefordshire Community Foundation
The Hertfordshire Community Foundation
P. and C. Hickinbotham Charitable Trust
The Alan Edward Higgs Charity
The Hilden Charitable Fund
The Hillingdon Partnership Trust

**General charitable purposes**  *Fields of interest and type of beneficiary*

R. G. Hills Charitable Trust
Hinchley Charitable Trust
The Lady Hind Trust
The Hintze Family Charity Foundation
The Hiscox Foundation
The Henry C. Hoare Charitable Trust
The Hobson Charity Limited
The Sir Julian Hodge Charitable Trust
The Jane Hodge Foundation
The J. G. Hogg Charitable Trust
The Hollick Family Charitable Trust
The Holliday Foundation
The Dorothy Holmes Charitable Trust
P. H. Holt Foundation
The Homestead Charitable Trust
The Mary Homfray Charitable Trust
The Horizon Foundation
The Antony Hornby Charitable Trust
The Worshipful Company of Horners' Charitable Trusts
The Hornsey Parochial Charities
The Hospital of God at Greatham
The Sir Joseph Hotung Charitable Settlement
House of Industry Estate
The Daniel Howard Trust
James T. Howat Charitable Trust
The Hudson Foundation
The Huggard Charitable Trust
The Hull and East Riding Charitable Trust
The Michael and Shirley Hunt Charitable Trust
The Albert Hunt Trust
Huntingdon Freemen's Trust
The Hutton Foundation
The Nani Huyu Charitable Trust
The P. Y. N. and B. Hyams Trust
Ibrahim Foundation Ltd
The Iliffe Family Charitable Trust
Impetus – The Private Equity Foundation
Incommunities Foundation
The Indigo Trust
The Ingram Trust
The Inman Charity
Interserve Employee Foundation Ltd
The Inverforth Charitable Trust (ICT)
Investream Charitable Trust

The Ireland Fund of Great Britain
The Ironmongers' Foundation
The Charles Irving Charitable Trust
The J. Isaacs Charitable Trust
The Isle of Anglesey Charitable Trust
The J. & J. Benevolent Foundation
The J. & J. Charitable Trust
The Jabbs Foundation
C. Richard Jackson Charitable Trust
John James Bristol Foundation
The Susan and Stephen James Charitable Settlement
The Jarman Charitable Trust
John Jarrold Trust
Jay Education Trust
Nick Jenkins Foundation
The Jenour Foundation
The Jephcott Charitable Trust
Lillie Johnson Charitable Trust
The Johnson Wax Ltd Charitable Trust
The Joicey Trust
The Jones 1986 Charitable Trust
The Dezna Robins Jones Charitable Foundation
The Marjorie and Geoffrey Jones Charitable Trust
The Muriel Jones Foundation
The Jordan Charitable Foundation
The Joron Charitable Trust
The Lady Eileen Joseph Foundation
The Josephs Family Charitable Trust
The Josh Charitable Trust
The Cyril and Eve Jumbo Charitable Trust
Anton Jurgens Charitable Trust
The Bernard Kahn Charitable Trust
The Stanley Kalms Foundation
The Boris Karloff Charitable Foundation
The Kasner Charitable Trust
The Kass Charitable Trust (KCT)
The Michael and Ilse Katz Foundation
William Kendall's Charity (Wax Chandlers' Company)
John Thomas Kennedy Charitable Foundation
The Kennedy Charitable Foundation
Kent Community Foundation
The Nancy Kenyon Charitable Trust
Keren Association Limited

E. and E. Kernkraut Charities Limited
The Ursula Keyes Trust
The King Henry VIII Endowed Trust – Warwick
The King/Cullimore Charitable Trust
Kingdom Way Trust
The Richard Kirkman Trust
Robert Kitchin (Saddlers' Company)
The Ernest Kleinwort Charitable Trust
The Sir James Knott Trust
The Kobler Trust
Kollel and Co. Limited
The Kreitman Foundation
The Neil Kreitman Foundation
The Kyte Charitable Trust
Ladbrokes in the Community Charitable Trust
The K. P. Ladd Charitable Trust
John Laing Charitable Trust
Christopher Laing Foundation
The David Laing Foundation
The Kirby Laing Foundation
The Martin Laing Foundation
Community Foundation for Lancashire (Former)
Community Foundations for Lancashire and Merseyside
Duchy of Lancaster Benevolent Fund
The Jack Lane Charitable Trust
Langdale Trust
Langley Charitable Trust
The Langtree Trust
The LankellyChase Foundation
Laufer Charitable Trust
The Lauffer Family Charitable Foundation
Mrs F. B. Laurence Charitable Trust
The Kathleen Laurence Trust
The Edgar E. Lawley Foundation
The Herd Lawson and Muriel Lawson Charitable Trust
Lawson Beckman Charitable Trust
The Raymond and Blanche Lawson Charitable Trust
The Leach Fourteenth Trust
The Leathersellers' Company Charitable Fund
The Arnold Lee Charitable Trust
The William Leech Charity
The Lord Mayor of Leeds Appeal Fund
Leeds Building Society Charitable Foundation
Leicestershire, Leicester and Rutland Community Foundation

Fields of interest and type of beneficiary — General charitable purposes

The Kennedy Leigh Charitable Trust
Morris Leigh Foundation
The Leigh Trust
P. Leigh-Bramwell Trust 'E'
The Lennox and Wyfold Foundation
The Erica Leonard Trust
The Mark Leonard Trust
The Leverhulme Trade Charities Trust
Lord Leverhulme's Charitable Trust
David and Ruth Lewis Family Charitable Trust
The Sir Edward Lewis Foundation
John Lewis Partnership General Community Fund
Liberum Foundation
Limoges Charitable Trust
The Linbury Trust
Lincolnshire Community Foundation
The Lind Trust
The Linden Charitable Trust
Lindenleaf Charitable Trust
The Enid Linder Foundation
The Ruth and Stuart Lipton Charitable Trust
The Lister Charitable Trust
The Frank Litchfield Charitable Trust
The Second Joseph Aaron Littman Foundation
The George John and Sheilah Livanos Charitable Trust
Liverpool Charity and Voluntary Services (LCVS)
Jack Livingstone Charitable Trust
The Elaine and Angus Lloyd Charitable Trust
Lloyd's Charities Trust
Lloyds Bank Foundation for Northern Ireland
Lloyds Bank Foundation for the Channel Islands
Localtrent Ltd
The Locker Foundation
The Joyce Lomax Bullock Charitable Trust
The London Community Foundation
The William and Katherine Longman Trust
The Loseley and Guildway Charitable Trust
The Lower Green Foundation
The Lowy Mitchell Foundation
The C. L. Loyd Charitable Trust
The Henry Lumley Charitable Trust
Paul Lunn-Rockliffe Charitable Trust
Lord and Lady Lurgan Trust

The Lynn Foundation
The Lyons Charitable Trust
The E. M. MacAndrew Trust
The Macdonald-Buchanan Charitable Trust
The Mackay and Brewer Charitable Trust
The Mackintosh Foundation
The MacRobert Trust
The Mactaggart Third Fund
The Ian Mactaggart Trust
The Magen Charitable Trust
The Mageni Trust
The Brian Maguire Charitable Trust
The Mahavir Trust
Malbin Trust
The Mallinckrodt Foundation
Man Group plc Charitable Trust
The Manackerman Charitable Trust
The Manchester Guardian Society Charitable Trust
Lord Mayor of Manchester's Charity Appeal Trust
The Manifold Charitable Trust
The W. M. Mann Foundation
R. W. Mann Trust
Maranatha Christian Trust
Marbeh Torah Trust
The Marcela Trust
The Stella and Alexander Margulies Charitable Trust
Market Harborough and The Bowdens Charity
The Marks Family Foundation
The Ann and David Marks Foundation
The Hilda and Samuel Marks Foundation
J. P. Marland Charitable Trust
The Michael Marsh Charitable Trust
The Marsh Christian Trust
Charlotte Marshall Charitable Trust
D. G. Marshall of Cambridge Trust
Sir George Martin Trust
John Martin's Charity
The Mason Porter Charitable Trust
The Matt 6.3 Charitable Trust
The Violet Mauray Charitable Trust
Mazars Charitable Trust
The Robert McAlpine Foundation
McGreevy No 5 Settlement
The Medlock Charitable Trust
Melodor Limited
The Melow Charitable Trust
The Brian Mercer Charitable Trust

The Mercers' Charitable Foundation
Merchant Navy Welfare Board
The Merchant Taylors' Company Charities Fund
The Merchant Venturers' Charity
The Merchants' House of Glasgow
The Metropolitan Masonic Charity
The Mickel Fund
The Gerald Micklem Charitable Trust
The Masonic Province of Middlesex Charitable Trust
Millennium Stadium Charitable Trust (Ymddiriedolaeth Elusennol Stadiwm y Mileniwm)
Hugh and Mary Miller Bequest Trust
The Ronald Miller Foundation
The Millichope Foundation
The Mills Charity
The Millward Charitable Trust
Milton Keynes Community Foundation Limited
The Edgar Milward Charity
The Peter Minet Trust
Minge's Gift and the Pooled Trusts
Minton Charitable Trust
The Mirianog Trust
The Laurence Misener Charitable Trust
The Misselbrook Trust
The Brian Mitchell Charitable Settlement
The Esmé Mitchell Trust
The MITIE Foundation
Keren Mitzvah Trust
The Mizpah Trust
Mobbs Memorial Trust Ltd
The Modiano Charitable Trust
Mole Charitable Trust
The Monatrea Charitable Trust
The Monument Trust
The Moonpig Foundation
The George A. Moore Foundation
John Moores Foundation (JMF)
The Morgan Charitable Foundation
The Morgan Foundation
The Diana and Allan Morgenthau Charitable Trust
The Oliver Morland Charitable Trust
The Miles Morland Foundation
The Morris Charitable Trust
The Willie and Mabel Morris Charitable Trust
The Peter Morrison Charitable Foundation

93

**General charitable purposes**  *Fields of interest and type of beneficiary*

G. M. Morrison Charitable Trust
The Moshal Charitable Trust
Vyoel Moshe Charitable Trust
Brian and Jill Moss Charitable Trust
The Moss Family Charitable Trust
Moto in the Community
The Mulberry Trust
The Music Sales Charitable Trust
Muslim Hands
The Janet Nash Charitable Settlement
The NDL Foundation
The Worshipful Company of Needlemakers' Charitable Fund
The James Neill Trust Fund
Ner Foundation
Network for Social Change
Newpier Charity Ltd
Norfolk Community Foundation
Normalyn Charitable Trust
The Norman Family Charitable Trust
The Normanby Charitable Trust
Northamptonshire Community Foundation
The Northwood Charitable Trust
The Notgrove Trust
Nottinghamshire Community Foundation
O&G Schreiber Charitable Trust
The Oakmoor Charitable Trust
The Odin Charitable Trust
The Ofenheim Charitable Trust
Oglesby Charitable Trust
Oizer Charitable Trust
Oxfordshire Community Foundation
The P. F. Charitable Trust
The Paget Charitable Trust
Panahpur
The James Pantyfedwen Foundation
The Paphitis Charitable Trust
The Paragon Trust
The Samuel and Freda Parkinson Charitable Trust
Miss M. E. Swinton Paterson's Charitable Trust
The Patrick Charitable Trust
The Peacock Charitable Trust
The Susanna Peake Charitable Trust
Rosanna Pearson's 1987 Charity Trust
The Dowager Countess Eleanor Peel Trust
The Pell Charitable Trust
The Pennycress Trust

The Personal Assurance Charitable Trust
The Persula Foundation
The Pharsalia Charitable Trust
The Phillips and Rubens Charitable Trust
The Phillips Family Charitable Trust
The David Pickford Charitable Foundation
The Bernard Piggott Charitable Trust
The Pilkington Charities Fund
The Sir Harry Pilkington Trust Fund
Miss A. M. Pilkington's Charitable Trust
The DLA Piper Charitable Trust
G. S. Plaut Charitable Trust Limited
The George and Esme Pollitzer Charitable Settlement
The Pollywally Charitable Trust
Edith and Ferdinand Porjes Charitable Trust
The John Porter Charitable Trust
The Porter Foundation
The Portrack Charitable Trust
The W. L. Pratt Charitable Trust
The Premier League Charitable Fund
Premierquote Ltd
The Primrose Trust
Princess Anne's Charities
Prison Service Charity Fund
The Privy Purse Charitable Trust
The Puebla Charitable Trust
The PwC Foundation
The Pyne Charitable Trust
Quartet Community Foundation
The Queen's Silver Jubilee Trust
R. J. M. Charitable Trust
The Monica Rabagliati Charitable Trust
Rachel Charitable Trust
The Mr and Mrs Philip Rackham Charitable Trust
The Rainford Trust
The Joseph and Lena Randall Charitable Trust
The Rank Foundation Limited
The Joseph Rank Trust
The Rashbass Family Trust
The Ratcliff Foundation
The Ravensdale Trust
The Roger Raymond Charitable Trust
The John Rayner Charitable Trust
The Sir James Reckitt Charity
The C. A. Redfern Charitable Foundation

The Reed Foundation
The Rest Harrow Trust
Reuben Foundation
The Rhododendron Trust
The Rhondda Cynon Taff Welsh Church Acts Fund
Daisie Rich Trust
The Clive Richards Charity
The Richmond Parish Lands Charity
The Sir John Ritblat Family Foundation
The River Farm Foundation
Rivers Foundation
The Robertson Trust
Robyn Charitable Trust
The Rochester Bridge Trust
The Rofeh Trust
Rokach Family Charitable Trust
The Helen Roll Charitable Trust
The Sir James Roll Charitable Trust
The Gerald Ronson Foundation
Mrs L. D. Rope Third Charitable Settlement
The Rosca Trust
The Rose Foundation
The Rothermere Foundation
The Rothley Trust
The Rowland Family Foundation
The Rowlands Trust
Royal Artillery Charitable Fund
The Rubin Foundation
William Arthur Rudd Memorial Trust
The Rugby Group Benevolent Fund Limited
The Russell Trust
The J. S. and E. C. Rymer Charitable Trust
The Michael Sacher Charitable Trust
The Michael Harry Sacher Trust
The Saddlers' Company Charitable Fund
The Alan and Babette Sainsbury Charitable Fund
The Saintbury Trust
The Salamander Charitable Trust
The Andrew Salvesen Charitable Trust
Sam and Bella Sebba Charitable Trust
Coral Samuel Charitable Trust
The Basil Samuel Charitable Trust
The M. J. Samuel Charitable Trust
The Samworth Foundation
The Sandhu Charitable Foundation
The Sands Family Trust

The Sants Charitable Trust
The Peter Saunders Trust
The Schmidt-Bodner Charitable Trust
The Schreib Trust
The Schuster Charitable Trust
Foundation Scotland
The Frieda Scott Charitable Trust
The Scottish Power Foundation
The Scouloudi Foundation
The SDL Foundation
The Searchlight Electric Charitable Trust
The Cyril Shack Trust
The Shanti Charitable Trust
ShareGift (The Orr Mackintosh Foundation)
The Sheepdrove Trust
The Sheldon Trust
The Patricia and Donald Shepherd Charitable Trust
The Sylvia and Colin Shepherd Charitable Trust
The Archie Sherman Charitable Trust
The Barnett and Sylvia Shine No 2 Charitable Trust
The Shoe Zone Trust
David and Jennifer Sieff Charitable Trust
Silver Family Charitable Trust
The Huntly and Margery Sinclair Charitable Trust
The Charles Skey Charitable Trust
Skipton Building Society Charitable Foundation
The John Slater Foundation
The Slaughter and May Charitable Trust
Rita and David Slowe Charitable Trust
The SMB Charitable Trust
The DS Smith Charitable Foundation
The N. Smith Charitable Settlement
The Smith Charitable Trust
The WH Smith Group Charitable Trust
Philip Smith's Charitable Trust
The R. C. Snelling Charitable Trust
Social Business Trust (Scale-Up)
Sodexo Foundation
The Solo Charitable Settlement
The South Square Trust
The W. F. Southall Trust
Spar Charitable Fund
Sparquote Limited
The Spear Charitable Trust
Spears-Stutz Charitable Trust

The Worshipful Company of Spectacle Makers' Charity
The Jessie Spencer Trust
The Ralph and Irma Sperring Charity
The Spielman Charitable Trust
Split Infinitive Trust
Rosalyn and Nicholas Springer Charitable Trust
The Spurrell Charitable Trust
The Geoff and Fiona Squire Foundation
The St Hilda's Trust
St James's Trust Settlement
The Star Charitable Trust
The Peter Stebbings Memorial Charity
The Steel Charitable Trust
The Steinberg Family Charitable Trust
The Stephen Barry Charitable Trust
C. E. K. Stern Charitable Trust
Stevenson Family's Charitable Trust
The Andy Stewart Charitable Foundation
Sir Halley Stewart Trust
The Stewarts Law Foundation
The Leonard Laity Stoate Charitable Trust
The Edward Stocks-Massey Bequest Fund
The Stoller Charitable Trust
M. J. C. Stone Charitable Trust
The Samuel Storey Family Charitable Trust
Peter Storrs Trust
Stratford upon Avon Town Trust
The Strowger Trust
Suffolk Community Foundation
The Alan Sugar Foundation
The Bernard Sunley Charitable Foundation
Community Foundation for Surrey
The Sussex Community Foundation
The Adrienne and Leslie Sussman Charitable Trust
The Sutasoma Trust
Sutton Coldfield Charitable Trust
The Suva Foundation Limited
The Swann-Morton Foundation
Swansea and Brecon Diocesan Board of Finance Limited
The John Swire (1989) Charitable Trust
The Swire Charitable Trust
The Hugh and Ruby Sykes Charitable Trust
The Charles and Elsie Sykes Trust

Sylvia Waddilove Foundation UK
The Charity of Stella Symons
The Talbot Village Trust
The Lady Tangye Charitable Trust
The Tanner Trust
The Lili Tapper Charitable Foundation
The Taurus Foundation
The Tay Charitable Trust
C. B. and H. H. Taylor 1984 Trust
The Tedworth Charitable Trust
Tees Valley Community Foundation
The Templeton Goodwill Trust
The Thales Charitable Trust
The Loke Wan Tho Memorial Foundation
The Thompson Family Charitable Trust
Thomson Reuters Foundation
The Thornton Foundation
The Thousandth Man- Richard Burns Charitable Trust
The Daniel Thwaites Charitable Trust
The Tisbury Telegraph Trust
The Tobacco Pipe Makers and Tobacco Trade Benevolent Fund
The Tolkien Trust
Tomchei Torah Charitable Trust
The Tower Hill Trust
The Toy Trust
Annie Tranmer Charitable Trust
The Constance Travis Charitable Trust
The Tresillian Trust
The Truemark Trust
Truemart Limited
The Trusthouse Charitable Foundation
The Tudor Trust
Tuixen Foundation
The Douglas Turner Trust
The Florence Turner Trust
The G. J. W. Turner Trust
TVML Foundation
Two Ridings Community Foundation
Community Foundation Serving Tyne and Wear and Northumberland
The Udlington Trust
UKI Charitable Foundation
The Michael Uren Foundation
The Vail Foundation
The Valentine Charitable Trust
The Valiant Charitable Trust
The Albert Van Den Bergh Charitable Trust
Mrs Maud Van Norden's Charitable Foundation

95

The Vandervell Foundation
The Vardy Foundation
The Variety Club Children's Charity
Roger Vere Foundation
Victoria Homes Trust
The Nigel Vinson Charitable Trust
Virgin Atlantic Foundation
The Vodafone Foundation
Volant Charitable Trust
Voluntary Action Fund (VAF)
Wade's Charity
The Wakefield and Tetley Trust
The Community Foundation in Wales
Robert and Felicity Waley-Cohen Charitable Trust
The Ward Blenkinsop Trust
G. R. Waters Charitable Trust 2000
Blyth Watson Charitable Trust
Waynflete Charitable Trust
Weatherley Charitable Trust
The Weavers' Company Benevolent Fund
The William Webster Charitable Trust
The Weinstein Foundation
The James Weir Foundation
The Joir and Kato Weisz Foundation
Welsh Church Fund – Dyfed area (Carmarthenshire, Ceredigion and Pembrokeshire)
The Welton Foundation
The Wessex Youth Trust
The West Derby Wastelands Charity
The Garfield Weston Foundation
The Melanie White Foundation Limited
White Stuff Foundation
The Whitecourt Charitable Trust
A. H. and B. C. Whiteley Charitable Trust
The Lionel Wigram Memorial Trust
The Kay Williams Charitable Foundation
The Williams Charitable Trust
Williams Serendipity Trust
The HDH Wills 1965 Charitable Trust
The Dame Violet Wills Will Trust
The Wilmcote Charitrust
Sumner Wilson Charitable Trust
David Wilson Foundation
The Community Foundation for Wiltshire and Swindon

The Harold Hyam Wingate Foundation
The Winton Charitable Foundation
The James Wise Charitable Trust
The Michael and Anna Wix Charitable Trust
The Wixamtree Trust
The Maurice Wohl Charitable Foundation
The Charles Wolfson Charitable Trust
The James Wood Bequest Fund
The F. Glenister Woodger Trust
Woodroffe Benton Foundation
The Woodward Charitable Trust
The Wragge and Co Charitable Trust
The Diana Edgson Wright Charitable Trust
The Matthews Wrightson Charity Trust
Wychdale Ltd
Wychville Ltd
The Wyndham Charitable Trust
The Yardley Great Trust
The W. Wing Yip and Brothers Foundation
Yorkshire Building Society Charitable Foundation
The South Yorkshire Community Foundation
The William Allen Young Charitable Trust
The Marjorie and Arnold Ziff Charitable Foundation
Stephen Zimmerman Charitable Trust
The Zochonis Charitable Trust
The Zolfo Cooper Foundation
Zurich Community Trust (UK) Limited

# Health

The 1970 Trust
The 1989 Willan Charitable Trust
The Aberbrothock Skea Trust
ABF The Soldiers' Charity
Access Sport
The ACT Foundation
Action Medical Research
The Company of Actuaries' Charitable Trust Fund
The Adamson Trust
The Victor Adda Foundation
The Adint Charitable Trust
Age UK
The AIM Foundation
The Sylvia Aitken Charitable Trust
The Ajahma Charitable Trust
The Al Fayed Charitable Foundation
The Alchemy Foundation
The H. B. Allen Charitable Trust
The Alliance Family Foundation
The Pat Allsop Charitable Trust
Almondsbury Charity
The Ammco Trust
The Andrew Anderson Trust
Andor Charitable Trust
Anglo American Group Foundation
The Appletree Trust
The Arbib Foundation
The Ardwick Trust
The John Armitage Charitable Trust
The Armourers' and Brasiers' Gauntlet Trust
The Artemis Charitable Trust
Arthritis Research UK
The Ashmore Foundation
The Associated Country Women of the World
Astellas European Foundation
Asthma UK
The Astor Foundation
The Astor of Hever Trust
The Lord Austin Trust
Autonomous Research Charitable Trust
The John Avins Trust
The Harry Bacon Foundation
The Scott Bader Commonwealth Limited
The Baily Thomas Charitable Fund
The Baker Charitable Trust
The Roy and Pixie Baker Charitable Trust
The Balcombe Charitable Trust
The George Balint Charitable Trust
The Albert Casanova Ballard Deceased Trust
The Ballinger Charitable Trust

# Health

The Band Trust
The Barbers' Company General Charities
The Barbour Foundation
The Barcapel Foundation
Barchester Healthcare Foundation
The Barclay Foundation
The Baring Foundation
Barnes Workhouse Fund
The Barnwood House Trust
The Misses Barrie Charitable Trust
Bartholomew Charitable Trust
The Bartlett Taylor Charitable Trust
The Batchworth Trust
BBC Children in Need
BC Partners Foundation
The B-CH Charitable Trust
The John Beckwith Charitable Trust
The Peter Beckwith Charitable Trust
Beefy's Charity Foundation
The Bellahouston Bequest Fund
Bergqvist Charitable Trust
The Berkeley Charitable Foundation
The Ruth Berkowitz Charitable Trust
The Berkshire Community Foundation
The Bernadette Charitable Trust
The Bestway Foundation
The Mason Bibby 1981 Trust
The Big Lottery Fund
The Billmeir Charitable Trust
The Bintaub Charitable Trust
The Birmingham District Nursing Charitable Trust
The Birmingham Hospital Saturday Fund Medical Charity and Welfare Trust
Sir Alec Black's Charity
The BlackRock (UK) Charitable Trust
The Morgan Blake Charitable Trust
Bloodwise
The Bloom Foundation
The Marjory Boddy Charitable Trust
BOOST Charitable Trust
The Booth Charities
Boots Charitable Trust
The Boshier-Hinton Foundation
The Bothwell Charitable Trust
The Harry Bottom Charitable Trust
P. G. and N. J. Boulton Trust
Sir Clive Bourne Family Trust
The Bowerman Charitable Trust

The Tony Bramall Charitable Trust
The Liz and Terry Bramall Foundation
The Bramhope Trust
The Breadsticks Foundation
The Breast Cancer Research Trust
The Brendish Family Foundation
Bridgepoint Charitable Trust
The Brighton District Nursing Association Trust
British Council for Prevention of Blindness (Save Eyes Everywhere)
The British Dietetic Association General and Education Trust Fund
British Heart Foundation
The British Humane Association
The J. and M. Britton Charitable Trust
The David Brooke Charity
The Rory and Elizabeth Brooks Foundation
The Charles Brotherton Trust
Miss Marion Broughton's Charitable Trust
Bill Brown 1989 Charitable Trust
Edna Brown Charitable Settlement
R. S. Brownless Charitable Trust
The Brownsword Charitable Foundation
Buckland Charitable Trust
The Bulldog Trust Limited
The Burden Trust
Burden's Charitable Foundation
The Burdett Trust for Nursing
The Clara E. Burgess Charity
The Burry Charitable Trust
The Arnold Burton 1998 Charitable Trust
The Derek Butler Trust
Cable & Wireless Worldwide Foundation
Edward Cadbury Charitable Trust
Henry T. and Lucy B. Cadbury Charitable Trust
Peter Cadbury Charitable Trust
The William A. Cadbury Charitable Trust
The Cadbury Foundation
The Edward and Dorothy Cadbury Trust
The George Cadbury Trust
CAFOD (Catholic Agency for Overseas Development)
Callander Charitable Trust
Calleva Foundation

The Carr-Gregory Trust
The Carrington Charitable Trust
The Elizabeth Casson Trust
The Castang Foundation
The Catalyst Charitable Trust
The Wilfrid and Constance Cave Foundation
The Cayo Foundation
The B. G. S. Cayzer Charitable Trust
Celtic Charity Fund
The Gaynor Cemlyn-Jones Trust
The Amelia Chadwick Trust
Champneys Charitable Foundation
The Chapman Charitable Trust
The Charities Advisory Trust
The Charter 600 Charity
Cheshire Freemason's Charity
Chest, Heart and Stroke Scotland
Child Growth Foundation
Children's Liver Disease Foundation
The Children's Research Fund
CHK Charities Limited
The Chownes Foundation
Chrysalis Trust
Church Burgesses Trust
The City Bridge Trust
Stephen Clark 1957 Charitable Trust
J. A. Clark Charitable Trust
The Roger and Sarah Bancroft Clark Charitable Trust
The Clarke Charitable Settlement
The Cleopatra Trust
The Clothworkers' Foundation
Richard Cloudesley's Charity
The Clover Trust
The Robert Clutterbuck Charitable Trust
The Coalfields Regeneration Trust
The John Coates Charitable Trust
The Denise Cohen Charitable Trust
The Vivienne and Samuel Cohen Charitable Trust
The Colchester Catalyst Charity
John Coldman Charitable Trust
The Cole Charitable Trust
The Bernard Coleman Trust
The Colt Foundation
Colyer-Fergusson Charitable Trust
The Congleton Inclosure Trust
The Consolidated Charities for the Infirm – Merchant Taylors' Company

# Health

The Catherine Cookson Charitable Trust
Harold and Daphne Cooper Charitable Trust
Mabel Cooper Charity
The Marjorie Coote Old People's Charity
The Helen Jean Cope Trust
The J. Reginald Corah Foundation Fund
The Gershon Coren Charitable Foundation
Michael Cornish Charitable Trust
The Evan Cornish Foundation
The Cotton Trust
Coutts Charitable Foundation
Dudley and Geoffrey Cox Charitable Trust
The Sir William Coxen Trust Fund
The Lord Cozens-Hardy Trust
The Craps Charitable Trust
Michael Crawford Children's Charity
The Cray Trust
The Crerar Hotels Trust
Criffel Charitable Trust
The Violet and Milo Cripps Charitable Trust
The Peter Cruddas Foundation
Cruden Foundation Ltd
The Cumber Family Charitable Trust
Cumbria Community Foundation
The Cunningham Trust
The Harry Cureton Charitable Trust
The Cwmbran Trust
The D'Oyly Carte Charitable Trust
Roald Dahl's Marvellous Children's Charity
Baron Davenport's Charity
The Davidson Family Charitable Trust
Michael Davies Charitable Settlement
The Wilfrid Bruce Davis Charitable Trust
The De Brye Charitable Trust
The Deakin Charitable Trust
Debenhams Foundation
The Delves Charitable Trust
The Denman Charitable Trust
The Dentons UKMEA LLP Charitable Trust
The J. N. Derbyshire Trust
The Desmond Foundation
The Sandy Dewhirst Charitable Trust
Diabetes UK
The Dinwoodie Settlement
Disability Aid Fund (The Roger and Jean Jefcoate Trust)

Dischma Charitable Trust
The Djanogly Foundation
The Derek and Eileen Dodgson Foundation
Dorset Community Foundation
The Dorus Trust
The Double 'O' Charity Ltd
Douglas Arter Foundation
Dromintee Trust
Duchy Health Charity Limited
The Royal Foundation of the Duke and Duchess of Cambridge and Prince Harry
The Dumbreck Charity
The Dunhill Medical Trust
The Dunn Family Charitable Trust
The W. E. Dunn Trust
The Dyers' Company Charitable Trust
The James Dyson Foundation
The Sir John Eastwood Foundation
The Ebenezer Trust
The EBM Charitable Trust
The Gilbert and Eileen Edgar Foundation
The Gilbert Edgar Trust
Edinburgh Trust No 2 Account
Educational Foundation of Alderman John Norman
The George Elias Charitable Trust
The Gerald Palmer Eling Trust Company
The John Ellerman Foundation
The Emerton-Christie Charity
Engage Foundation
The Englefield Charitable Trust
The Epigoni Trust
Epilepsy Research UK
The Eranda Foundation
Esh Foundation
Sir John Evelyn's Charity
The Eventhall Family Charitable Trust
The Eveson Charitable Trust
The Exilarch's Foundation
The F. P. Limited Charitable Trust
The Lord Faringdon Charitable Trust
Samuel William Farmer's Trust
The Farthing Trust
Federation of Jewish Relief Organisations
The A. M. Fenton Trust
Elizabeth Ferguson Charitable Trust Fund
The Fidelity UK Foundation
The Doris Field Charitable Trust
Dixie Rose Findlay Charitable Trust
The Fishmongers' Company's Charitable Trust

The Fitton Trust
The Ian Fleming Charitable Trust
Florence's Charitable Trust
The Follett Trust
The Oliver Ford Charitable Trust
The Forest Hill Charitable Trust
The Lady Forester Trust
The Forman Hardy Charitable Trust
The Donald Forrester Trust
The Anna Rosa Forster Charitable Trust
The Fort Foundation
The Forte Charitable Trust
The Elizabeth Frankland Moore and Star Foundation
The Jill Franklin Trust
The Hugh Fraser Foundation
The Joseph Strong Frazer Trust
The Louis and Valerie Freedman Charitable Settlement
The Freemasons' Grand Charity
The Freshfield Foundation
The Freshgate Trust Foundation
The Friarsgate Trust
The Frognal Trust
The Patrick & Helena Frost Foundation
Mejer and Gertrude Miriam Frydman Foundation
The Fuserna Foundation General Charitable Trust
G. M. C. Trust
The Galanthus Trust
The Gamma Trust
The Ganzoni Charitable Trust
The Garnett Charitable Trust
Garthgwynion Charities
The Gatsby Charitable Foundation
The Robert Gavron Charitable Trust
Jacqueline and Michael Gee Charitable Trust
The Nigel Gee Foundation
The General Nursing Council for England and Wales Trust
The Generations Foundation
The David Gibbons Foundation
Simon Gibson Charitable Trust
The G. C. Gibson Charitable Trust
The Girdlers' Company Charitable Trust
The B. and P. Glasser Charitable Trust
The GNC Trust
The Sydney and Phyllis Goldberg Memorial Charitable Trust

## Health

The Golden Bottle Trust
Golden Charitable Trust
The Goldman Sachs Charitable Gift Fund (UK)
Goldman Sachs Gives (UK)
The Goldsmiths' Company Charity
The Goodman Foundation
The Mike Gooley Trailfinders Charity
Grand Charitable Trust of the Order of Women Freemasons
The Gordon Gray Trust
The Green Hall Foundation
Greenham Common Community Trust Limited
The Greggs Foundation
The Grimmitt Trust
The Grocers' Charity
The H. and M. Charitable Trust
H. C. D. Memorial Fund
The Doris Louise Hailes Charitable Trust
E. F. and M. G. Hall Charitable Trust
The Hamamelis Trust
The Helen Hamlyn Trust
Sue Hammerson Charitable Trust
Hampshire and Isle of Wight Community Foundation
The Hampstead Wells and Campden Trust
Hampton Fuel Allotment
The W. A. Handley Charitable Trust
The Kathleen Hannay Memorial Charity
The Doughty Hanson Charitable Foundation
The Haramead Trust
Miss K. M. Harbinson's Charitable Trust
Harbo Charities Limited
The Harborne Parish Lands Charity
The Harbour Charitable Trust
The Harbour Foundation
The Harding Trust
The Hare of Steep Charitable Trust
The Harebell Centenary Fund
The Hargrave Foundation
The Harris Family Charitable Trust
The Edith Lilian Harrison 2000 Foundation
The Hartley Charitable Trust
The Alfred And Peggy Harvey Charitable Trust
Edward Harvist Trust
The Hasluck Charitable Trust
The Hathaway Trust
The Maurice Hatter Foundation

The Hawthorne Charitable Trust
The Dorothy Hay-Bolton Charitable Trust
The Headley Trust
The Health Foundation
May Hearnshaw Charitable Trust
Heart of England Community Foundation
Heart Research UK
The Heathcoat Trust
The Heathside Charitable Trust
The Charlotte Heber-Percy Charitable Trust
The Percy Hedley 1990 Charitable Trust
Hedley Foundation Limited
The H. J. Heinz Company Limited Charitable Trust
The Michael Heller Charitable Foundation
The Simon Heller Charitable Settlement
Help for Health
The Hemby Charitable Trust
The Christina Mary Hendrie Trust for Scottish and Canadian Charities
The G. D. Herbert Charitable Trust
Herefordshire Community Foundation
The Hertfordshire Community Foundation
The Hesslewood Children's Trust (Hull Seamen's and General Orphanage)
P. and C. Hickinbotham Charitable Trust
The Alan Edward Higgs Charity
The Hilden Charitable Fund
R. G. Hills Charitable Trust
The Lady Hind Trust (Lilian Frances Hind Bequest)
The Hinduja Foundation
The Hintze Family Charity Foundation
The Hiscox Foundation
The Henry C. Hoare Charitable Trust
The Hobson Charity Limited
The Sir Julian Hodge Charitable Trust
The Jane Hodge Foundation
The Hollands-Warren Fund
The Hollick Family Charitable Trust
The Holliday Foundation
The Dorothy Holmes Charitable Trust
The Edward Holt Trust
The Homelands Charitable Trust
The Homestead Charitable Trust

The Mary Homfray Charitable Trust
Sir Harold Hood's Charitable Trust
The Hoover Foundation
The Hope Trust
Hopmarket Charity
The Antony Hornby Charitable Trust
The Thomas J. Horne Memorial Trust
The Worshipful Company of Horners' Charitable Trusts
The Hornsey Parochial Charities
Hospice UK
The Hospital of God at Greatham
The Hospital Saturday Fund
House of Industry Estate
The Hudson Foundation
The Huggard Charitable Trust
The Hull and East Riding Charitable Trust
Human Relief Foundation
The Humanitarian Trust
The Albert Hunt Trust
Miss Agnes H. Hunter's Trust
Huntingdon Freemen's Trust
Hurdale Charity Limited
The Hutton Foundation
The Nani Huyu Charitable Trust
The Iliffe Family Charitable Trust
Incommunities Foundation
The Ingram Trust
The Inman Charity
The Innocent Foundation
Investream Charitable Trust
The Ireland Fund of Great Britain
The Charles Irving Charitable Trust
The J. Isaacs Charitable Trust
The J. & J. Benevolent Foundation
The J. & J. Charitable Trust
The Jabbs Foundation
C. Richard Jackson Charitable Trust
The Ruth and Lionel Jacobson Trust (Second Fund) No 2
John James Bristol Foundation
The Susan and Stephen James Charitable Settlement
The Jarman Charitable Trust
John Jarrold Trust
Jeffrey Charitable Trust
Nick Jenkins Foundation
The Jenour Foundation
The Jephcott Charitable Trust
Jewish Child's Day
The Elton John Aids Foundation
Lillie Johnson Charitable Trust

**99**

The Johnson Foundation
The Johnnie Johnson Trust
The Johnson Wax Ltd Charitable Trust
The Joicey Trust
The Jones 1986 Charitable Trust
The Dezna Robins Jones Charitable Foundation
The Marjorie and Geoffrey Jones Charitable Trust
The Jordan Charitable Foundation
The Joron Charitable Trust
The J. E. Joseph Charitable Fund
The Lady Eileen Joseph Foundation
The Josephs Family Charitable Trust
The Cyril and Eve Jumbo Charitable Trust
Anton Jurgens Charitable Trust
Jusaca Charitable Trust
The Bernard Kahn Charitable Trust
The Stanley Kalms Foundation
Karaviotis Foundation
The Ian Karten Charitable Trust
The Kass Charitable Trust
The Michael and Ilse Katz Foundation
The Kelly Family Charitable Trust
The Kay Kendall Leukaemia Fund
John Thomas Kennedy Charitable Foundation
The Kennedy Charitable Foundation
Kent Community Foundation
The Peter Kershaw Trust
The Kettering and District Charitable Medical Trust
The Ursula Keyes Trust
The Kingsbury Charity
The Mary Kinross Charitable Trust
Kirkley Poor's Land Estate
The Richard Kirkman Trust
Kirschel Foundation
The Ernest Kleinwort Charitable Trust
The Sir James Knott Trust
The Kobler Trust
The Kohn Foundation
Kollel and Co. Limited
The Kreditor Charitable Trust
The Kreitman Foundation
The Neil Kreitman Foundation
The Heinz, Anna and Carol Kroch Foundation
The Kyte Charitable Trust
Ladbrokes in the Community Charitable Trust

The K. P. Ladd Charitable Trust
Maurice and Hilda Laing Charitable Trust
Christopher Laing Foundation
The David Laing Foundation
The Kirby Laing Foundation
The Beatrice Laing Trust
The Lambert Charitable Trust
The Jack Lane Charitable Trust
Langdale Trust
Langley Charitable Trust
The LankellyChase Foundation
The R. J. Larg Family Charitable Trust
Laslett's (Hinton) Charity
The Lauffer Family Charitable Foundation
Mrs F. B. Laurence Charitable Trust
The Kathleen Laurence Trust
The Edgar E. Lawley Foundation
Lawson Beckman Charitable Trust
The Raymond and Blanche Lawson Charitable Trust
The Mason Le Page Charitable Trust
The Leach Fourteenth Trust
The Leathersellers' Company Charitable Fund
The Arnold Lee Charitable Trust
The William Leech Charity
Leeds Building Society Charitable Foundation
Leicestershire, Leicester and Rutland Community Foundation
The Kennedy Leigh Charitable Trust
The Leigh Trust
P. Leigh-Bramwell Trust 'E'
The Lennox and Wyfold Foundation
Lord Leverhulme's Charitable Trust
Joseph Levy Charitable Foundation
David and Ruth Lewis Family Charitable Trust
The Sir Edward Lewis Foundation
John Lewis Partnership General Community Fund
The Lewis Ward Trust
Lifeline 4 Kids
The Limbourne Trust
Limoges Charitable Trust
The Linbury Trust
Lincolnshire Community Foundation
The Linden Charitable Trust
The Enid Linder Foundation

The Ruth and Stuart Lipton Charitable Trust
The Lister Charitable Trust
The Frank Litchfield Charitable Trust
The Charles Littlewood Hill Trust
The George John and Sheilah Livanos Charitable Trust
Jack Livingstone Charitable Trust
The Elaine and Angus Lloyd Charitable Trust
Lloyds Bank Foundation for Northern Ireland
Lloyds Bank Foundation for the Channel Islands
Lloyds TSB Foundation for Scotland
The Locker Foundation
Loftus Charitable Trust
The Lolev Charitable Trust
The Trust for London
London Catalyst
The London Community Foundation
London Housing Foundation Ltd
The London Law Trust
The William and Katherine Longman Trust
The Lord's Taverners
The Loseley and Guildway Charitable Trust
The Lotus Foundation
The Lower Green Foundation
The Lowy Mitchell Foundation
The C. L. Loyd Charitable Trust
The Marie Helen Luen Charitable Trust
Robert Luff Foundation Ltd
The Henry Lumley Charitable Trust
Paul Lunn-Rockliffe Charitable Trust
Lord and Lady Lurgan Trust
The Lynn Foundation
The Lyons Charitable Trust
M. and C. Trust
The M. K. Charitable Trust
The Madeline Mabey Trust
The E. M. MacAndrew Trust
The R. S. Macdonald Charitable Trust
The Macdonald-Buchanan Charitable Trust
The Mackay and Brewer Charitable Trust
The Mackintosh Foundation
The MacRobert Trust
The Mactaggart Third Fund
The Ian Mactaggart Trust
The Brian Maguire Charitable Trust
The Mahavir Trust
Malbin Trust

100

The Mallinckrodt Foundation
The Manackerman Charitable Trust
The Manchester Guardian Society Charitable Trust
The W. M. Mann Foundation
R. W. Mann Trust
The Manoukian Charitable Foundation
Maranatha Christian Trust
The Marcela Trust
The Stella and Alexander Margulies Charitable Trust
Market Harborough and The Bowdens Charity
The Marks Family Foundation
The Ann and David Marks Foundation
The Hilda and Samuel Marks Foundation
J. P. Marland Charitable Trust
The Michael Marsh Charitable Trust
The Marsh Christian Trust
Charlotte Marshall Charitable Trust
D. G. Marshall of Cambridge Trust
The Marshgate Charitable Settlement
Sir George Martin Trust
John Martin's Charity
The Mason Porter Charitable Trust
The Nancie Massey Charitable Trust
The Matliwala Family Charitable Trust
The Violet Mauray Charitable Trust
The Robert McAlpine Foundation
D. D. McPhail Charitable Settlement
The Medlock Charitable Trust
Mercaz Torah Vechesed Limited
The Brian Mercer Charitable Trust
The Mercers' Charitable Foundation
Merchant Navy Welfare Board
The Merchant Taylors' Company Charities Fund
The Merchant Venturers' Charity
Mercury Phoenix Trust
The Tony Metherell Charitable Trust
The Metropolitan Masonic Charity
T. & J. Meyer Family Foundation Limited
The Mickel Fund
The Mickleham Trust

The Gerald Micklem Charitable Trust
Hugh and Mary Miller Bequest Trust
The Ronald Miller Foundation
The Millichope Foundation
The Mills Charity
The Millward Charitable Trust
The Clare Milne Trust
The Peter Minet Trust
Minge's Gift and the Pooled Trusts
Minton Charitable Trust
The Laurence Misener Charitable Trust
The Mishcon Family Charitable Trust
The Misselbrook Trust
Keren Mitzvah Trust
Monmouthshire County Council Welsh Church Act Fund
The Montague Thompson Coon Charitable Trust
The Monument Trust
The George A. Moore Foundation
The Morel Charitable Trust
The Morgan Charitable Foundation
The Morgan Foundation
Morgan Stanley International Foundation
The Diana and Allan Morgenthau Charitable Trust
The Morris Charitable Trust
The Willie and Mabel Morris Charitable Trust
The Peter Morrison Charitable Foundation
G. M. Morrison Charitable Trust
Vyoel Moshe Charitable Trust
Brian and Jill Moss Charitable Trust
The Moss Family Charitable Trust
Mosselson Charitable Trust
Mothercare Group Foundation
Moto in the Community
J. P. Moulton Charitable Foundation
The Edwina Mountbatten & Leonora Children's Foundation
Mrs Waterhouse Charitable Trust
The Edith Murphy Foundation
Murphy-Neumann Charity Company Limited
The Music Sales Charitable Trust
Muslim Hands
The Janet Nash Charitable Settlement
The NDL Foundation

The Neighbourly Charitable Trust
Ner Foundation
Network for Social Change
The New Appeals Organisation for the City and County of Nottingham
Newby Trust Limited
The Frances and Augustus Newman Foundation
The Chevras Ezras Nitzrochim Trust
Nominet Charitable Foundation
The Noon Foundation
Norfolk Community Foundation
The Normanby Charitable Trust
Northamptonshire Community Foundation
The Community Foundation for Northern Ireland
The Northwood Charitable Trust
The Norton Foundation
The Norton Rose Charitable Foundation
The Notgrove Trust
The Nottingham General Dispensary
Nottinghamshire Community Foundation
The Nuffield Foundation
The Father O'Mahoney Memorial Trust
The Oakdale Trust
The Oakley Charitable Trust
The Ofenheim Charitable Trust
Oglesby Charitable Trust
Oizer Charitable Trust
The Olga Charitable Trust
The O'Sullivan Family Charitable Trust
The Owen Family Trust
The Paget Charitable Trust
The Paphitis Charitable Trust
The Park Charitable Trust
The Samuel and Freda Parkinson Charitable Trust
The Harry Payne Fund
The Peacock Charitable Trust
The Susanna Peake Charitable Trust
The Pedmore Sporting Club Trust Fund
The Dowager Countess Eleanor Peel Trust
The Peltz Trust
People's Postcode Trust
The Personal Assurance Charitable Trust
The Pharsalia Charitable Trust
The Phillips and Rubens Charitable Trust
The Bernard Piggott Charitable Trust
The Pilkington Charities Fund

The Austin and Hope
  Pilkington Trust
The Sir Harry Pilkington Trust
  Fund
Estate of the Late Colonel
  W. W. Pilkington Will Trusts
  – The General Charity Fund
The DLA Piper Charitable Trust
G. S. Plaut Charitable Trust
  Limited
The John Porter Charitable
  Trust
The Porter Foundation
The J. E. Posnansky Charitable
  Trust
The Mary Potter Convent
  Hospital Trust
The Praebendo Charitable
  Foundation
The Premier League Charitable
  Fund
Sir John Priestman Charity
  Trust
The Prince of Wales's
  Charitable Foundation
Princess Anne's Charities
Prison Service Charity Fund
The PwC Foundation
Mr and Mrs J. A. Pye's
  Charitable Settlement
The Queen Anne's Gate
  Foundation
Queen Mary's Roehampton
  Trust
Quothquan Trust
The Monica Rabagliati
  Charitable Trust
The Mr and Mrs Philip
  Rackham Charitable Trust
Richard Radcliffe Charitable
  Trust
The Joseph Rank Trust
Ranworth Trust
The Rashbass Family Trust
The Ravensdale Trust
The Rayne Foundation
The John Rayner Charitable
  Trust
The C. A. Redfern Charitable
  Foundation
The Reed Foundation
The Rest Harrow Trust
Reuben Foundation
The Rhondda Cynon Taff
  Welsh Church Acts Fund
The Violet M. Richards Charity
The Richmond Parish Lands
  Charity
The River Farm Foundation
Thomas Roberts Trust
The Robertson Trust
Edwin George Robinson
  Charitable Trust
Robyn Charitable Trust
The Roddick Foundation
The Rosca Trust

The Rose Foundation
The Cecil Rosen Foundation
Rosetrees Trust
The Rothley Trust
The Roughley Charitable Trust
Mrs Gladys Row Fogo
  Charitable Trust
The Rowland Family
  Foundation
The Rowlands Trust
The J. S. and E. C. Rymer
  Charitable Trust
The Michael Sacher Charitable
  Trust
The Michael Harry Sacher
  Trust
Raymond and Beverly Sackler
  1988 Foundation
The Sackler Trust
The Saga Charitable Trust
The Alan and Babette
  Sainsbury Charitable Fund
The Saintbury Trust
The Salamander Charitable
  Trust
The Andrew Salvesen
  Charitable Trust
Sam and Bella Sebba
  Charitable Trust
Coral Samuel Charitable Trust
The Basil Samuel Charitable
  Trust
The Peter Samuel Charitable
  Trust
The Sandhu Charitable
  Foundation
The Sandra Charitable Trust
The Sants Charitable Trust
The Scarfe Charitable Trust
The Schreiber Charitable Trust
Schroder Charity Trust
Sir Samuel Scott of Yews
  Trust
The Scouloudi Foundation
The Seneca Trust
The Jean Shanks Foundation
The Shanti Charitable Trust
The Shears Foundation
The Sheepdrove Trust
The Sheffield and District
  Hospital Services
  Charitable Fund
The Sylvia and Colin Shepherd
  Charitable Trust
The Archie Sherman Cardiff
  Foundation
The Bassil Shippam and
  Alsford Trust
The Shirley Foundation
The Shoe Zone Trust
The Barbara A. Shuttleworth
  Memorial Trust
David and Jennifer Sieff
  Charitable Trust
The Huntly and Margery
  Sinclair Charitable Trust

The John Slater Foundation
The Slaughter and May
  Charitable Trust
The SMB Charitable Trust
The Mrs Smith and Mount
  Trust
The N. Smith Charitable
  Settlement
The Henry Smith Charity
The WH Smith Group
  Charitable Trust
The R. C. Snelling Charitable
  Trust
The Sobell Foundation
Sodexo Foundation
The Solo Charitable
  Settlement
David Solomons Charitable
  Trust
The E. C. Sosnow Charitable
  Trust
The South Square Trust
R. H. Southern Trust
The Sovereign Health Care
  Charitable Trust
Sparks Charity (Sport Aiding
  Medical Research For Kids)
Sparquote Limited
The Worshipful Company of
  Spectacle Makers' Charity
The Spero Foundation
The Spielman Charitable Trust
Split Infinitive Trust
Rosalyn and Nicholas Springer
  Charitable Trust
The Geoff and Fiona Squire
  Foundation
St James's Trust Settlement
St James's Place Foundation
St Michael's and All Saints'
  Charities Relief Branch
St Monica Trust
The Stanley Foundation Ltd
The Peter Stebbings Memorial
  Charity
The Steel Charitable Trust
The Steinberg Family
  Charitable Trust
Stevenson Family's Charitable
  Trust
The Andy Stewart Charitable
  Foundation
Sir Halley Stewart Trust
The Leonard Laity Stoate
  Charitable Trust
The Stoller Charitable Trust
M. J. C. Stone Charitable Trust
Peter Stormonth Darling
  Charitable Trust
The Strangward Trust
The Strawberry Charitable
  Trust
The W. O. Street Charitable
  Foundation
The Strowger Trust
Sueberry Ltd

The Sussex Community Foundation
The Adrienne and Leslie Sussman Charitable Trust
The Suva Foundation Limited
Swan Mountain Trust
The Swann-Morton Foundation
The John Swire (1989) Charitable Trust
The Swire Charitable Trust
The Hugh and Ruby Sykes Charitable Trust
The Charles and Elsie Sykes Trust
Sylvia Waddilove Foundation UK
The Charity of Stella Symons
The Tajtelbaum Charitable Trust
The Gay and Keith Talbot Trust
The Talbot Trusts
C. B. and H. H. Taylor 1984 Trust
The Connie and Albert Taylor Charitable Trust
A. P. Taylor Trust
Tesco Charity Trust
The C. Paul Thackray General Charitable Trust
Thackray Medical Research Trust
The Thales Charitable Trust
The Loke Wan Tho Memorial Foundation
The Thompson Family Charitable Trust
The Len Thomson Charitable Trust
The Sir Jules Thorn Charitable Trust
The Thornton Trust
The Thousandth Man- Richard Burns Charitable Trust
The Three Guineas Trust
The Tolkien Trust
The Tompkins Foundation
The Tory Family Foundation
The Towry Law Charitable Trust
The Toy Trust
Toyota Manufacturing UK Charitable Trust
Annie Tranmer Charitable Trust
The Trefoil Trust
The Tresillian Trust
The True Colours Trust
Trumros Limited
The James Tudor Foundation
The Douglas Turner Trust
Community Foundation Serving Tyne and Wear and Northumberland
UKI Charitable Foundation
The Ulverscroft Foundation
The Underwood Trust
The Michael Uren Foundation
The Valentine Charitable Trust
The Albert Van Den Bergh Charitable Trust
The Variety Club Children's Charity
Roger Vere Foundation
The Vintners' Foundation
Virgin Atlantic Foundation
Vision Charity
Volant Charitable Trust
Voluntary Action Fund (VAF)
The Wakefield and Tetley Trust
Wales Council for Voluntary Action
Robert and Felicity Waley-Cohen Charitable Trust
The Walker Trust
Wallace and Gromit's Children's Foundation
The Ward Blenkinsop Trust
The Barbara Ward Children's Foundation
The Waterloo Foundation
The Wates Foundation
Blyth Watson Charitable Trust
Weatherley Charitable Trust
The Weinstein Foundation
The James Weir Foundation
The Wellcome Trust
The Welton Foundation
The Wessex Youth Trust
The Westcroft Trust
The Garfield Weston Foundation
The Melanie White Foundation Limited
The Felicity Wilde Charitable Trust
The Will Charitable Trust
The Kay Williams Charitable Foundation
The Williams Charitable Trust
Williams Serendipity Trust
The Harold Hyam Wingate Foundation
The Winton Charitable Foundation
The Michael and Anna Wix Charitable Trust
The Wixamtree Trust
The Maurice Wohl Charitable Foundation
The Charles Wolfson Charitable Trust
The Wolfson Family Charitable Trust
The Wolfson Foundation
The Wood Family Trust
The Woodward Charitable Trust
The Wragge and Co Charitable Trust
The Matthews Wrightson Charity Trust
Wychdale Ltd
The Wyseliot Charitable Trust
The Xerox (UK) Trust
The Yapp Charitable Trust
The W. Wing Yip and Brothers Foundation
Yorkshire and Clydesdale Bank Foundation
Yorkshire Building Society Charitable Foundation
The William Allen Young Charitable Trust
The John Kirkhope Young Endowment Fund
Zephyr Charitable Trust
The Marjorie and Arnold Ziff Charitable Foundation
The Zochonis Charitable Trust
Zurich Community Trust (UK) Limited

## Alternative and complementary medicine

The AIM Foundation
The Scott Bader Commonwealth Limited
Edna Brown Charitable Settlement
Disability Aid Fund (The Roger and Jean Jefcoate Trust)
The Hospital Saturday Fund
The Joseph Rank Trust
The Roughley Charitable Trust

## Health care

The 1970 Trust
The Aberbrothock Skea Trust
The ACT Foundation
The Alchemy Foundation
Almondsbury Charity
The Artemis Charitable Trust
The Scott Bader Commonwealth Limited
The George Balint Charitable Trust
The Barbers' Company General Charities
The Barclay Foundation
The Barnwood House Trust
The Big Lottery Fund
The Birmingham District Nursing Charitable Trust
Sir Alec Black's Charity
The Boshier-Hinton Foundation
The Harry Bottom Charitable Trust
The Tony Bramall Charitable Trust
The Breadsticks Foundation
Edna Brown Charitable Settlement
The Burdett Trust for Nursing
The William A. Cadbury Charitable Trust

**103**

The Cadbury Foundation
The Carrington Charitable Trust
The Elizabeth Casson Trust
The Catalyst Charitable Trust
The Amelia Chadwick Trust
Cheshire Freemason's Charity
Chest, Heart and Stroke Scotland
The Chownes Foundation
The Clarke Charitable Settlement
The Congleton Inclosure Trust
Mabel Cooper Charity
The Marjorie Coote Old People's Charity
Dudley and Geoffrey Cox Charitable Trust
The Sir William Coxen Trust Fund
The D'Oyly Carte Charitable Trust
Baron Davenport's Charity
Michael Davies Charitable Settlement
The Deakin Charitable Trust
The Dentons UKMEA LLP Charitable Trust
The Dinwoodie Settlement Disability Aid Fund (The Roger and Jean Jefcoate Trust)
The Dunhill Medical Trust
The Gilbert Edgar Trust
The Eranda Foundation
The Eveson Charitable Trust
Elizabeth Ferguson Charitable Trust Fund
The Lady Forester Trust
The Forte Charitable Trust
The Hugh Fraser Foundation
The Freemasons' Grand Charity
The Freshfield Foundation
The Freshgate Trust Foundation
G. M. C. Trust
The Ganzoni Charitable Trust
The Gatsby Charitable Foundation
The General Nursing Council for England and Wales Trust
The Generations Foundation
Simon Gibson Charitable Trust
The Girdlers' Company Charitable Trust
The Goldsmiths' Company Charity
The Gordon Gray Trust
The Green Hall Foundation
The W. A. Handley Charitable Trust
The Harris Family Charitable Trust
The Health Foundation
The Hemby Charitable Trust

The Hesslewood Children's Trust (Hull Seamen's and General Orphanage)
The Hintze Family Charity Foundation
The Hollands-Warren Fund
The Homelands Charitable Trust
Sir Harold Hood's Charitable Trust
The Thomas J. Horne Memorial Trust
Hospice UK
The Hospital Saturday Fund
Human Relief Foundation
Huntingdon Freemen's Trust
The Jarman Charitable Trust
The Joicey Trust
The Jordan Charitable Foundation
The Ian Karten Charitable Trust
The Kass Charitable Trust
The Peter Kershaw Trust
The Kettering and District Charitable Medical Trust
The Ernest Kleinwort Charitable Trust
Langdale Trust
Laslett's (Hinton) Charity
Lifeline 4 Kids
The Charles Littlewood Hill Trust
Lloyds Bank Foundation for Northern Ireland
The Trust for London
The Lord's Taverners
Lord and Lady Lurgan Trust
The MacRobert Trust
Market Harborough and The Bowdens Charity
John Martin's Charity
The Mason Porter Charitable Trust
The Robert McAlpine Foundation
The Tony Metherell Charitable Trust
Brian and Jill Moss Charitable Trust
The Frances and Augustus Newman Foundation
The Nottingham General Dispensary
The Nuffield Foundation
The Owen Family Trust
The Park Charitable Trust
The Samuel and Freda Parkinson Charitable Trust
The Mary Potter Convent Hospital Trust
Sir John Priestman Charity Trust
The Prince of Wales's Charitable Foundation

Mr and Mrs J. A. Pye's Charitable Settlement
Richard Radcliffe Charitable Trust
The Joseph Rank Trust
Ranworth Trust
The Rayne Foundation
Reuben Foundation
The Violet M. Richards Charity
Thomas Roberts Trust
The Rose Foundation
The Sackler Trust
The Saga Charitable Trust
The Saintbury Trust
The Sheepdrove Trust
The Sheffield and District Hospital Services Charitable Fund
David Solomons Charitable Trust
The E. C. Sosnow Charitable Trust
The South Square Trust
St James's Place Foundation
Stevenson Family's Charitable Trust
The Strawberry Charitable Trust
The Tajtelbaum Charitable Trust
The Connie and Albert Taylor Charitable Trust
The Trefoil Trust
The True Colours Trust
Trumros Limited
The Variety Club Children's Charity
Wallace and Gromit's Children's Foundation
Blyth Watson Charitable Trust
The Westcroft Trust
The Wixamtree Trust
The Charles Wolfson Charitable Trust
The Xerox (UK) Trust
The Yapp Charitable Trust

## Health training

The Barbers' Company General Charities
The Dinwoodie Settlement
The Nuffield Foundation

## Therapy

The Artemis Charitable Trust
The Elizabeth Casson Trust
The Trust for London

## Medical equipment

The Barnwood House Trust
Sir Alec Black's Charity

Mabel Cooper Charity
The Green Hall Foundation
The Jordan Charitable Foundation
The Ian Karten Charitable Trust
Lifeline 4 Kids
The Lord's Taverners
The Frances and Augustus Newman Foundation
The Saga Charitable Trust

## Medical institutions

The Aberbrothock Skea Trust
The George Balint Charitable Trust
The Birmingham District Nursing Charitable Trust
Sir Alec Black's Charity
The Harry Bottom Charitable Trust
The Carrington Charitable Trust
The Catalyst Charitable Trust
The Amelia Chadwick Trust
Cheshire Freemason's Charity
Chest, Heart and Stroke Scotland
The Chownes Foundation
The Clarke Charitable Settlement
Mabel Cooper Charity
The Marjorie Coote Old People's Charity
Dudley and Geoffrey Cox Charitable Trust
The Sir William Coxen Trust Fund
Baron Davenport's Charity
Michael Davies Charitable Settlement
The Deakin Charitable Trust
The Dunhill Medical Trust
The Gilbert Edgar Trust
The Eveson Charitable Trust
Elizabeth Ferguson Charitable Trust Fund
The Hugh Fraser Foundation
The Freemasons' Grand Charity
The Ganzoni Charitable Trust
The Girdlers' Company Charitable Trust
The Gordon Gray Trust
The Green Hall Foundation
The Homelands Charitable Trust
Sir Harold Hood's Charitable Trust
The Thomas J. Horne Memorial Trust
Hospice UK
The Jarman Charitable Trust

The Peter Kershaw Trust
The Ernest Kleinwort Charitable Trust
Lloyds Bank Foundation for Northern Ireland
Lord and Lady Lurgan Trust
The Mason Porter Charitable Trust
The Robert McAlpine Foundation
The Tony Metherell Charitable Trust
The Nottingham General Dispensary
The Owen Family Trust
Sir John Priestman Charity Trust
Richard Radcliffe Charitable Trust
The Rayne Foundation
The Rose Foundation
The Sackler Trust
The Sheffield and District Hospital Services Charitable Fund
St James's Place Foundation
The Tajtelbaum Charitable Trust
The Connie and Albert Taylor Charitable Trust
Blyth Watson Charitable Trust

## Nursing

The Barbers' Company General Charities
The Birmingham District Nursing Charitable Trust
The General Nursing Council for England and Wales Trust
The Health Foundation
The Kass Charitable Trust

## Medical research and clinical treatment

The 1989 Willan Charitable Trust
The Aberbrothock Skea Trust
Action Medical Research
Age UK
The Alchemy Foundation
The Alliance Family Foundation
The Pat Allsop Charitable Trust
Anglo American Group Foundation
The Arbib Foundation
The Armourers' and Brasiers' Gauntlet Trust
Arthritis Research UK
Astellas European Foundation
Asthma UK

The Astor Foundation
The Astor of Hever Trust
The Baily Thomas Charitable Fund
The Baker Charitable Trust
The Barbers' Company General Charities
The Barclay Foundation
The John Beckwith Charitable Trust
Bergqvist Charitable Trust
The Ruth Berkowitz Charitable Trust
The Bestway Foundation
Bloodwise
BOOST Charitable Trust
P. G. and N. J. Boulton Trust
The Breast Cancer Research Trust
British Council for Prevention of Blindness (Save Eyes Everywhere)
British Heart Foundation
The Charles Brotherton Trust
The Brownsword Charitable Foundation
Buckland Charitable Trust
The Burry Charitable Trust
The Arnold Burton 1998 Charitable Trust
The Derek Butler Trust
Peter Cadbury Charitable Trust
Calleva Foundation
The Castang Foundation
The Cayo Foundation
The B. G. S. Cayzer Charitable Trust
The Gaynor Cemlyn-Jones Trust
The Charities Advisory Trust
Cheshire Freemason's Charity
Chest, Heart and Stroke Scotland
Child Growth Foundation
Children's Liver Disease Foundation
The Children's Research Fund
CHK Charities Limited
The Clarke Charitable Settlement
The Clothworkers' Foundation
The Bernard Coleman Trust
The Colt Foundation
The Cotton Trust
Dudley and Geoffrey Cox Charitable Trust
The Sir William Coxen Trust Fund
Cruden Foundation Ltd
The Cunningham Trust
Roald Dahl's Marvellous Children's Charity
Michael Davies Charitable Settlement
The Denman Charitable Trust
Diabetes UK

The Dinwoodie Settlement
The Dunhill Medical Trust
The Dunn Family Charitable Trust
The James Dyson Foundation
The EBM Charitable Trust
The Gilbert Edgar Trust
Epilepsy Research UK
The Eranda Foundation
The Eveson Charitable Trust
Elizabeth Ferguson Charitable Trust Fund
The Fishmongers' Company's Charitable Trust
The Ian Fleming Charitable Trust
The Follett Trust
The Anna Rosa Forster Charitable Trust
The Hugh Fraser Foundation
The Joseph Strong Frazer Trust
The Freemasons' Grand Charity
The Frognal Trust
G. M. C. Trust
The Garnett Charitable Trust
Garthgwynion Charities
The Gatsby Charitable Foundation
The Girdlers' Company Charitable Trust
The Sydney and Phyllis Goldberg Memorial Charitable Trust
Golden Charitable Trust
The Mike Gooley Trailfinders Charity
The Gordon Gray Trust
The Hamamelis Trust
The W. A. Handley Charitable Trust
The Hargrave Foundation
The Health Foundation
Heart Research UK
The Simon Heller Charitable Settlement
The Sir Julian Hodge Charitable Trust
The Jane Hodge Foundation
The Homelands Charitable Trust
Sir Harold Hood's Charitable Trust
The Hope Trust
The Antony Hornby Charitable Trust
The Hospital Saturday Fund
Miss Agnes H. Hunter's Trust
The Jabbs Foundation
Jeffrey Charitable Trust
The Elton John Aids Foundation
The Jones 1986 Charitable Trust
The Jordan Charitable Foundation

The Stanley Kalms Foundation
Karaviotis Foundation
The Ian Karten Charitable Trust
The Kass Charitable Trust
The Kay Kendall Leukaemia Fund
The Peter Kershaw Trust
The Kettering and District Charitable Medical Trust
The Mary Kinross Charitable Trust
The Ernest Kleinwort Charitable Trust
The Kohn Foundation
Kollel and Co. Limited
The LankellyChase Foundation
The William Leech Charity
The Leigh Trust
The Enid Linder Foundation
The Charles Littlewood Hill Trust
The London Law Trust
The Lower Green Foundation
The Marie Helen Luen Charitable Trust
Robert Luff Foundation Ltd
Lord and Lady Lurgan Trust
The Madeline Mabey Trust
The R. S. Macdonald Charitable Trust
The Mackintosh Foundation
The W. M. Mann Foundation
The Manoukian Charitable Foundation
The Marcela Trust
The Marshgate Charitable Settlement
The Nancie Massey Charitable Trust
The Robert McAlpine Foundation
D. D. McPhail Charitable Settlement
The Brian Mercer Charitable Trust
The Mercers' Charitable Foundation
Mercury Phoenix Trust
The Tony Metherell Charitable Trust
The Millward Charitable Trust
Mothercare Group Foundation
The Frances and Augustus Newman Foundation
The Northwood Charitable Trust
The Nottingham General Dispensary
The Nuffield Foundation
The Oakdale Trust
Oglesby Charitable Trust
The Owen Family Trust
The Dowager Countess Eleanor Peel Trust

Estate of the Late Colonel W. W. Pilkington Will Trusts – The General Charity Fund
The DLA Piper Charitable Trust
Mr and Mrs J. A. Pye's Charitable Settlement
Queen Mary's Roehampton Trust
The Monica Rabagliati Charitable Trust
The Mr and Mrs Philip Rackham Charitable Trust
Ranworth Trust
The Rayne Foundation
The Violet M. Richards Charity
The Robertson Trust
Edwin George Robinson Charitable Trust
Rosetrees Trust
Mrs Gladys Row Fogo Charitable Trust
The Rowlands Trust
Raymond and Beverly Sackler 1988 Foundation
The Sackler Trust
The Alan and Babette Sainsbury Charitable Fund
The Andrew Salvesen Charitable Trust
The Peter Samuel Charitable Trust
Sir Samuel Scott of Yews Trust
The Jean Shanks Foundation
The Sheepdrove Trust
The Bassil Shippam and Alsford Trust
The Shirley Foundation
The SMB Charitable Trust
The N. Smith Charitable Settlement
The Henry Smith Charity
The South Square Trust
Sparks Charity (Sport Aiding Medical Research For Kids)
The Worshipful Company of Spectacle Makers' Charity
The Spielman Charitable Trust
The Geoff and Fiona Squire Foundation
St James's Place Foundation
The Andy Stewart Charitable Foundation
Sir Halley Stewart Trust
Swan Mountain Trust
The Swann-Morton Foundation
The John Swire (1989) Charitable Trust
The Charles and Elsie Sykes Trust
Sylvia Waddilove Foundation UK
The Connie and Albert Taylor Charitable Trust
The Len Thomson Charitable Trust

Fields of interest and type of beneficiary — Overseas aid/projects

The Sir Jules Thorn Charitable Trust
The Towry Law Charitable Trust (Castle Educational Trust)
The Trefoil Trust
Trumros Limited
The Ulverscroft Foundation
The Michael Uren Foundation
The Variety Club Children's Charity
Roger Vere Foundation
The Vintners' Foundation
Vision Charity
Weatherley Charitable Trust
The Wellcome Trust
The Felicity Wilde Charitable Trust
The Will Charitable Trust
The Kay Williams Charitable Foundation
The Williams Charitable Trust
The Harold Hyam Wingate Foundation
The Winton Charitable Foundation
The Charles Wolfson Charitable Trust
Wychdale Ltd
The W. Wing Yip and Brothers Foundation
The John Kirkhope Young Endowment Fund

## History of medicine

The Scott Bader Commonwealth Limited
Edna Brown Charitable Settlement
The Joseph Rank Trust
Thackray Medical Research Trust
The Wellcome Trust

## Health education/ prevention/ development

The AIM Foundation
The Alchemy Foundation
The Associated Country Women of the World
The Scott Bader Commonwealth Limited
The Big Lottery Fund
BOOST Charitable Trust
The Tony Bramall Charitable Trust
The British Dietetic Association General and Education Trust Fund
Edna Brown Charitable Settlement

The Derek Butler Trust
Henry T. and Lucy B. Cadbury Charitable Trust
Chest, Heart and Stroke Scotland
The Colt Foundation
The Marjorie Coote Old People's Charity
The Cotton Trust
Disability Aid Fund (The Roger and Jean Jefcoate Trust)
The Gilbert Edgar Trust
The John Ellerman Foundation
The Hope Trust
The Hospital Saturday Fund
Human Relief Foundation
The Innocent Foundation
The Kelly Family Charitable Trust
The Enid Linder Foundation
Lloyds Bank Foundation for Northern Ireland
The Trust for London
Mercury Phoenix Trust
The Community Foundation for Northern Ireland
The Joseph Rank Trust
The Violet M. Richards Charity
The Rosca Trust
The Roughley Charitable Trust
The Saga Charitable Trust
The Wellcome Trust

## Medical ethics

The Scott Bader Commonwealth Limited
Edna Brown Charitable Settlement
The Joseph Rank Trust
The Wellcome Trust

## Overseas aid/ projects

The Acacia Charitable Trust
Aid to the Church in Need (UK)
The Alchemy Foundation
The H. B. Allen Charitable Trust
The Pat Allsop Charitable Trust
The Andrew Anderson Trust
The Associated Country Women of the World
The Scott Bader Commonwealth Limited
The Bagri Foundation
The Austin Bailey Foundation
The Balmore Trust
The Baring Foundation
The Bartlett Taylor Charitable Trust
The John Beckwith Charitable Trust
The Bernadette Charitable Trust
The Bestway Foundation
The Big Lottery Fund (see also Awards for All)
The BlackRock (UK) Charitable Trust
The Blandford Lake Trust
The Bloom Foundation
The Boltini Trust
The Breadsticks Foundation
The Brendish Family Foundation
British Council for Prevention of Blindness (Save Eyes Everywhere)
The Consuelo and Anthony Brooke Charitable Trust
Buckland Charitable Trust
The Burden Trust
Burden's Charitable Foundation
The Calpe Trust
Catholic Foreign Missions (CFM)
The Cheruby Trust
Christadelphian Samaritan Fund
Christian Aid
Stephen Clark 1957 Charitable Trust
The Cleopatra Trust
The Clover Trust
The Vivienne and Samuel Cohen Charitable Trust
The Coltstaple Trust
Comic Relief
The Gershon Coren Charitable Foundation
Michael Cornish Charitable Trust
The Evan Cornish Foundation
The Cotton Trust
The Craps Charitable Trust

107

Criffel Charitable Trust
The Cumber Family Charitable Trust
The Delves Charitable Trust
The Diageo Foundation
Dischma Charitable Trust
The Dorus Trust
The Eagle Charity Trust
The Gilbert Edgar Trust
The Epigoni Trust
The Ericson Trust
The ERM Foundation
The Estelle Trust
Euro Charity Trust
The Expat Foundation
The Farthing Trust
The Allan and Nesta Ferguson Charitable Settlement
The Forest Hill Charitable Trust
The Donald Forrester Trust
The Anna Rosa Forster Charitable Trust
The Four Winds Trust
The Elizabeth Frankland Moore and Star Foundation
The Freshfield Foundation
The G. D. Charitable Trust
The Galanthus Trust
The Generations Foundation
Global Care
The GNC Trust
The Golden Bottle Trust
The Goodman Foundation
The Grimmitt Trust
H. C. D. Memorial Fund
The Helen Hamlyn Trust
The Doughty Hanson Charitable Foundation
The Haramead Trust
Miss K. M. Harbinson's Charitable Trust
The Harbour Foundation
The Hartley Charitable Trust
The Hasluck Charitable Trust
The Hathaway Trust
The Hawthorne Charitable Trust
The Dorothy Hay-Bolton Charitable Trust
The Charles Hayward Foundation
The Headley Trust
The Charlotte Heber-Percy Charitable Trust
The Simon Heller Charitable Settlement
Philip Sydney Henman Deceased Will Trust
Hesed Trust
Hexham and Newcastle Diocesan Trust (1947)
The Hilden Charitable Fund
R. G. Hills Charitable Trust
The Hinduja Foundation
Hockerill Educational Foundation

The Hollick Family Charitable Trust
Sir Harold Hood's Charitable Trust
The Thomas J. Horne Memorial Trust
Human Relief Foundation
The Michael and Shirley Hunt Charitable Trust
The Hunter Foundation
Ibrahim Foundation Ltd
The Indigo Trust
The Innocent Foundation
Investream Charitable Trust
The J. J. Charitable Trust
The James Trust
John Jarrold Trust
The Jerusalem Trust
The Joffe Charitable Trust
The Elton John Aids Foundation (EJAF)
The Joron Charitable Trust
The Cyril and Eve Jumbo Charitable Trust
Jusaca Charitable Trust
John Thomas Kennedy Charitable Foundation
The K. P. Ladd Charitable Trust
Maurice and Hilda Laing Charitable Trust
The David Laing Foundation
The Kirby Laing Foundation
The Martin Laing Foundation
The Beatrice Laing Trust
Lancaster Foundation
Mrs F. B. Laurence Charitable Trust
Lawson Beckman Charitable Trust
The William Leech Charity
The Erica Leonard Trust
David and Ruth Lewis Family Charitable Trust
The Linbury Trust
The Lister Charitable Trust
Lloyd's Charities Trust
Lloyds Bank Foundation for Northern Ireland
Lloyds TSB Foundation for Scotland
Localtrent Ltd
The Lotus Foundation
Paul Lunn-Rockliffe Charitable Trust
Lord and Lady Lurgan Trust
The Lyndhurst Trust
The Madeline Mabey Trust
The Mackintosh Foundation
The Mactaggart Third Fund
The Mahavir Trust
The Manoukian Charitable Foundation
Maranatha Christian Trust
The Ann and David Marks Foundation

The Marr-Munning Trust
The Marsh Christian Trust
The Marshgate Charitable Settlement
The Matliwala Family Charitable Trust
The Gerald Micklem Charitable Trust
The Millfield Trust
The Millichope Foundation
The Millward Charitable Trust
The Mirianog Trust
The Brian Mitchell Charitable Settlement
The Mizpah Trust
The Moonpig Foundation
The Morel Charitable Trust (The Morel Trust)
The Morgan Charitable Foundation
The Diana and Allan Morgenthau Charitable Trust
The Miles Morland Foundation
The Morris Charitable Trust
Vyoel Moshe Charitable Trust
The Moshulu Charitable Trust
Mothercare Group Foundation
The Edwina Mountbatten & Leonora Children's Foundation
Frederick Mulder Charitable Trust
The Music Sales Charitable Trust
Muslim Hands
National Committee of the Women's World Day of Prayer for England and Wales and Northern Ireland
The Nazareth Trust Fund
Network for Social Change
The Norton Rose Charitable Foundation
The Father O'Mahoney Memorial Trust
Oizer Charitable Trust
The Olga Charitable Trust
Open Gate
The Paget Charitable Trust
The Park House Charitable Trust
The Susanna Peake Charitable Trust
Rosanna Pearson's 1987 Charity Trust
The Persson Charitable Trust
The Pilkington Charities Fund Estate of the Late Colonel W. W. Pilkington Will Trusts – The General Charity Fund
The Popocatepetl Trust
The W. L. Pratt Charitable Trust
The Prince of Wales's Charitable Foundation

Ranworth Trust
The Eleanor Rathbone
   Charitable Trust
Eva Reckitt Trust Fund
The Reed Foundation
The Rhododendron Trust
Rivers Foundation
Robyn Charitable Trust
Ryklow Charitable Trust 1992
The Saga Charitable Trust
The Salamander Charitable
   Trust
The Basil Samuel Charitable
   Trust
The Sandhu Charitable
   Foundation
The Scouloudi Foundation
The Shanley Charitable Trust
The Shanti Charitable Trust
The Archie Sherman Cardiff
   Foundation
The Shoe Zone Trust
The N. Smith Charitable
   Settlement
The Souter Charitable Trust
The W. F. Southall Trust
The Spurrell Charitable Trust
The Staples Trust
The Peter Stebbings Memorial
   Charity
The Steinberg Family
   Charitable Trust
Sir Halley Stewart Trust
The Stewarts Law Foundation
The Leonard Laity Stoate
   Charitable Trust
The Stobart Newlands
   Charitable Trust
The Stone Family Foundation
The Sutasoma Trust
The Gay and Keith Talbot Trust
The Tanner Trust
C. B. and H. H. Taylor 1984
   Trust
Tearfund
The C. Paul Thackray General
   Charitable Trust
Thackray Medical Research
   Trust
The Loke Wan Tho Memorial
   Foundation
The Thornton Trust
The Tinsley Foundation
The Tisbury Telegraph Trust
The Tolkien Trust
The Toy Trust
The Constance Travis
   Charitable Trust
The Tresillian Trust
The True Colours Trust
Truemart Limited
The Douglas Turner Trust
UIA Charitable Foundation
Ulting Overseas Trust
The Valentine Charitable Trust

The Albert Van Den Bergh
   Charitable Trust
The Van Neste Foundation
The Vardy Foundation
Virgin Atlantic Foundation
The Vodafone Foundation
Volant Charitable Trust
War on Want
The Waterloo Foundation
The Westcroft Trust
Williams Serendipity Trust
The HDH Wills 1965
   Charitable Trust
The Wixamtree Trust
The Maurice Wohl Charitable
   Foundation
The Wood Family Trust
The Matthews Wrightson
   Charity Trust
Zurich Community Trust (UK)
   Limited

## Philanthropy and the voluntary sector

Consolidated Charity of Burton
   upon Trent
The Edward and Dorothy
   Cadbury Trust
Chaucer Foundation
The Digbeth Trust Limited
Samuel William Farmer's Trust
Gatwick Airport Community
   Trust
The Hadrian Trust
The Hartley Charitable Trust
The Hemby Charitable Trust
The Dorothy Holmes Charitable
   Trust
The Hull and East Riding
   Charitable Trust
John Thomas Kennedy
   Charitable Foundation
The William Leech Charity
The London Law Trust
Lord Mayor of Manchester's
   Charity Appeal Trust
R. W. Mann Trust
The Peter Minet Trust
The Moonpig Foundation
The MSE Charity
Wakeham Trust
Waynflete Charitable Trust
The Westcroft Trust

## Voluntarism

The Big Lottery Fund (see also
   Awards for All)
Calouste Gulbenkian
   Foundation – UK Branch
The Peter Cruddas Foundation
Esmée Fairbairn Foundation
Gatwick Airport Community
   Trust
Heart of England Community
   Foundation
The Hemby Charitable Trust
John Thomas Kennedy
   Charitable Foundation
Maurice and Hilda Laing
   Charitable Trust
The William Leech Charity
The Mark Leonard Trust
Lloyds Bank Foundation for
   Northern Ireland
The London Community
   Foundation
London Housing Foundation
   Ltd (LHF)
The London Law Trust
Lord Mayor of Manchester's
   Charity Appeal Trust
Milton Keynes Community
   Foundation Limited
The Jack Petchey Foundation

Mrs L. D. Rope Third Charitable Settlement
The Slaughter and May Charitable Trust
Voluntary Action Fund (VAF)
Wakeham Trust
Wales Council for Voluntary Action
Waynflete Charitable Trust
Youth United Foundation

## Community participation

The Big Lottery Fund (see also Awards for All)
Calouste Gulbenkian Foundation – UK Branch
The Hemby Charitable Trust
Maurice and Hilda Laing Charitable Trust
The Mark Leonard Trust
The London Law Trust
The Jack Petchey Foundation
The Slaughter and May Charitable Trust
Wakeham Trust

## Voluntary sector capacity building

The Digbeth Trust Limited
The Hadrian Trust
Paul Hamlyn Foundation
The Trust for London
The London Community Foundation
The MSE Charity
The Northern Rock Foundation
Voluntary Action Fund (VAF)
Wales Council for Voluntary Action
The Wates Foundation
Waynflete Charitable Trust
The Westcroft Trust

## Religious activities

The Acacia Charitable Trust
Adenfirst Ltd
The Alabaster Trust
All Saints Educational Trust
The Almond Trust
Almondsbury Charity
The Altajir Trust
Altamont Ltd
AM Charitable Trust
The Anchor Foundation
Andor Charitable Trust
Anpride Ltd
The Archer Trust
The Ardwick Trust
The Armourers' and Brasiers' Gauntlet Trust
The AS Charitable Trust
The Ashburnham Thanksgiving Trust
The Austin Bailey Foundation
The Baird Trust
The Baker Charitable Trust
The Andrew Balint Charitable Trust
The George Balint Charitable Trust
The Balney Charitable Trust
BCH Trust
Bear Mordechai Ltd
Beauland Ltd
The Becker Family Charitable Trust
The Bellahouston Bequest Fund
Michael and Leslie Bennett Charitable Trust
The Ruth Berkowitz Charitable Trust
BHST
Miss Jeanne Bisgood's Charitable Trust
The Sydney Black Charitable Trust
The Bertie Black Foundation
The Blandford Lake Trust
The Sir Victor Blank Charitable Settlement
The Bonamy Charitable Trust
Salo Bordon Charitable Trust
The Harry Bottom Charitable Trust
P. G. and N. J. Boulton Trust
Sir Clive Bourne Family Trust
The Bowerman Charitable Trust
Bristol Archdeaconry Charity
The Burden Trust
The Arnold Burton 1998 Charitable Trust
C. and F. Charitable Trust
The H. and L. Cantor Trust
Carlee Ltd

The Carmelite Monastery Ware Trust
The Catalyst Charitable Trust
The Catholic Charitable Trust
The B. G. S. Cayzer Charitable Trust
The CH (1980) Charitable Trust
The Worshipful Company of Chartered Accountants General Charitable Trust
The Chownes Foundation
The Christabella Charitable Trust
The Hilda and Alice Clark Charitable Trust
The Clarke Charitable Settlement
Closehelm Limited
The Clover Trust
Clydpride Ltd
The Denise Cohen Charitable Trust
The Vivienne and Samuel Cohen Charitable Trust
John Coldman Charitable Trust
Col-Reno Ltd
The Congregational and General Charitable Trust
Harold and Daphne Cooper Charitable Trust
The Helen Jean Cope Trust
The Gershon Coren Charitable Foundation
The Duke of Cornwall's Benevolent Fund
The Sidney and Elizabeth Corob Charitable Trust
The Corona Charitable Trust
The Craps Charitable Trust
Criffel Charitable Trust
The Cuby Charitable Trust
The Cumber Family Charitable Trust
The Cwmbran Trust
Daily Prayer Union Charitable Trust Limited
Oizer Dalim Trust
The De Brye Charitable Trust
The Deakin Charitable Trust
The Debmar Benevolent Trust
The Dellal Foundation
The Derbyshire Churches and Chapels Preservation Trust
The Desmond Foundation
The Sandy Dewhirst Charitable Trust
Alan and Sheila Diamond Charitable Trust
The DM Charitable Trust
The Ebenezer Trust
The Gilbert and Eileen Edgar Foundation
The George Elias Charitable Trust

**Religious activities**

The Gerald Palmer Eling Trust Company
Ellador Ltd
The Ellinson Foundation Ltd
The Edith Maud Ellis 1985 Charitable Trust
Elshore Ltd
The Ernest Hecht Charitable Foundation
The Erskine Cunningham Hill Trust
The Eventhall Family Charitable Trust
The F. P. Limited Charitable Trust
Famos Foundation Trust
The Farthing Trust
The Gerald Fogel Charitable Trust
Fordeve Limited
The Forest Hill Charitable Trust
The Forman Hardy Charitable Trust
The Four Winds Trust
The Isaac and Freda Frankel Memorial Charitable Trust
The Anne French Memorial Trust
Friends of Essex Churches Trust
The Gale Family Charity Trust
The Gamma Trust
The Ganzoni Charitable Trust
Jacqueline and Michael Gee Charitable Trust
The Gibbs Charitable Trust
The B. and P. Glasser Charitable Trust
Golden Charitable Trust
The Grace Charitable Trust
The Grahame Charitable Foundation Limited
Philip and Judith Green Trust
The Greys Charitable Trust
The GRP Charitable Trust
N. and R. Grunbaum Charitable Trust
The Gur Trust
The Hackney Parochial Charities
Sue Hammerson Charitable Trust
Harbo Charities Limited
The Hathaway Trust
The Maurice Hatter Foundation
Headley-Pitt Charitable Trust
The Herefordshire Historic Churches Trust
P. and C. Hickinbotham Charitable Trust
Highcroft Charitable Trust
Hinchley Charitable Trust
The Hinduja Foundation
Stuart Hine Trust
The Henry C. Hoare Charitable Trust

Hockerill Educational Foundation
Matthew Hodder Charitable Trust
The Sir Julian Hodge Charitable Trust
The Dorothy Holmes Charitable Trust
The Homelands Charitable Trust
The Homestead Charitable Trust
The Mary Homfray Charitable Trust
The Hope Trust
The Daniel Howard Trust
The Huggard Charitable Trust
The Humanitarian Trust
The Huntingdon Foundation Limited
The Hutton Foundation
The P. Y. N. and B. Hyams Trust
Ibrahim Foundation Ltd
The Inlight Trust
The J. & J. Benevolent Foundation
The J. & J. Charitable Trust
The J. A. R. Charitable Trust
The Jacobs Charitable Trust
The Ruth and Lionel Jacobson Trust (Second Fund) No 2
The Susan and Stephen James Charitable Settlement
The James Trust
John Jarrold Trust
The Jenour Foundation
The Jewish Youth Fund (JYF)
The Joicey Trust
The Joron Charitable Trust
The J. E. Joseph Charitable Fund
Jusaca Charitable Trust
The Bernard Kahn Charitable Trust
The Stanley Kalms Foundation
Karaviotis Foundation
The Kasner Charitable Trust
The Kass Charitable Trust (KCT)
The Michael and Ilse Katz Foundation
C. S. Kaufman Charitable Trust
John Thomas Kennedy Charitable Foundation
The Kennedy Charitable Foundation
The Nancy Kenyon Charitable Trust
Keswick Hall Charity
The Kobler Trust
The Kreditor Charitable Trust
Kupath Gemach Chaim Bechesed Viznitz Trust

The Kyte Charitable Trust
The K. P. Ladd Charitable Trust
The Lambert Charitable Trust
Langdale Trust
The R. J. Larg Family Charitable Trust
Largsmount Ltd
Laslett's (Hinton) Charity
The Lauffer Family Charitable Foundation
Mrs F. B. Laurence Charitable Trust
The Herd Lawson and Muriel Lawson Charitable Trust
Lawson Beckman Charitable Trust
The Arnold Lee Charitable Trust
The William Leech Charity
The Kennedy Leigh Charitable Trust
P. Leigh-Bramwell Trust 'E'
Joseph Levy Charitable Foundation
The Sir Edward Lewis Foundation
Lincolnshire Churches Trust
Lindale Educational Foundation
The Ruth and Stuart Lipton Charitable Trust
The Charles Littlewood Hill Trust
The Second Joseph Aaron Littman Foundation
Jack Livingstone Charitable Trust
The Elaine and Angus Lloyd Charitable Trust
Localtrent Ltd
The Lolev Charitable Trust
The Lowy Mitchell Foundation
The C. L. Loyd Charitable Trust
The Lyndhurst Trust
The Sir Jack Lyons Charitable Trust
Sylvanus Lysons Charity
M. and C. Trust
The M. K. Charitable Trust
The Macdonald-Buchanan Charitable Trust
The Magen Charitable Trust
The Mahavir Trust
Malbin Trust
The Manackerman Charitable Trust
Marbeh Torah Trust
Mariapolis Limited
The Marks Family Foundation
The Hilda and Samuel Marks Foundation
The Michael Marsh Charitable Trust
The Marsh Christian Trust

111

## Religious activities

Charlotte Marshall Charitable Trust
Sir George Martin Trust
John Martin's Charity
The Mason Porter Charitable Trust
The Matt 6.3 Charitable Trust
The Violet Mauray Charitable Trust
Melodor Limited
The Merchant Taylors' Company Charities Fund
The Metropolitan Masonic Charity
The Ronald Miller Foundation
The Millfield Trust
The Millward Charitable Trust
The Laurence Misener Charitable Trust
The Mishcon Family Charitable Trust
Keren Mitzvah Trust
The Mizpah Trust
The Modiano Charitable Trust
Mole Charitable Trust
Monmouthshire County Council Welsh Church Act Fund
The Diana and Allan Morgenthau Charitable Trust
The Oliver Morland Charitable Trust
S. C. and M. E. Morland's Charitable Trust
The Morris Charitable Trust
The Peter Morrison Charitable Foundation
The Moshal Charitable Trust
The Moshulu Charitable Trust
Brian and Jill Moss Charitable Trust
The Moss Family Charitable Trust
Mosselson Charitable Trust
The Music Sales Charitable Trust
MW (CL) Foundation
MW (GK) Foundation
MW (HO) Foundation
MW (RH) Foundation
MYA Charitable Trust
The Worshipful Company of Needlemakers' Charitable Fund
Nemoral Ltd
Ner Foundation
Nesswall Ltd
The New Appeals Organisation for the City and County of Nottingham
NJD Charitable Trust
The Norwood and Newton Settlement
The Notgrove Trust
The Nottinghamshire Historic Churches Trust

O&G Schreiber Charitable Trust
The Ogle Christian Trust
The Ouseley Trust
The Owen Family Trust
The Paget Charitable Trust
Panahpur
The Park Charitable Trust
The Jack Patston Charitable Trust
The Payne Charitable Trust
The Harry Payne Fund
The Peltz Trust
B. E. Perl Charitable Trust
The Phillips Family Charitable Trust
The David Pickford Charitable Foundation
G. S. Plaut Charitable Trust Limited
The George and Esme Pollitzer Charitable Settlement
Edith and Ferdinand Porjes Charitable Trust
The J. E. Posnansky Charitable Trust
The Praebendo Charitable Foundation
Premishlaner Charitable Trust
The William Price Charitable Trust
The Pyne Charitable Trust
Quothquan Trust
R. J. M. Charitable Trust
R. S. Charitable Trust
The Rashbass Family Trust
The Rest Harrow Trust
The Rhondda Cynon Taff Welsh Church Acts Fund
The Sir Cliff Richard Charitable Trust
The Sir John Ritblat Family Foundation
The River Trust
The Rock Foundation
The Rofeh Trust
The Sir James Roll Charitable Trust
The Michael Sacher Charitable Trust
The Michael Harry Sacher Trust
The Ruzin Sadagora Trust
The Salamander Charitable Trust
The M. J. Samuel Charitable Trust
The Peter Samuel Charitable Trust
The Sants Charitable Trust
The Scarfe Charitable Trust
The Annie Schiff Charitable Trust
The Schmidt-Bodner Charitable Trust
The Schreib Trust

The Schreiber Charitable Trust
The Searchlight Electric Charitable Trust
The Seedfield Trust
Sellata Ltd
The Seneca Trust
The Cyril Shack Trust
The Shanti Charitable Trust
The Archie Sherman Cardiff Foundation
The Bassil Shippam and Alsford Trust
David and Jennifer Sieff Charitable Trust
The SMB Charitable Trust
The R. C. Snelling Charitable Trust
The Solo Charitable Settlement
Songdale Ltd
The E. C. Sosnow Charitable Trust
The W. F. Southall Trust
Rosalyn and Nicholas Springer Charitable Trust
St Peter's Saltley Trust
C. E. K. Stern Charitable Trust
The Leonard Laity Stoate Charitable Trust
The Strawberry Charitable Trust
Sueberry Ltd
The Suffolk Historic Churches Trust
The Alan Sugar Foundation
The Sussex Historic Churches Trust
The Adrienne and Leslie Sussman Charitable Trust
Sutton Coldfield Charitable Trust
Swansea and Brecon Diocesan Board of Finance Limited
The Lady Tangye Charitable Trust
The Lili Tapper Charitable Foundation
Tegham Limited
The C. Paul Thackray General Charitable Trust
The Thornton Trust
The Tisbury Telegraph Trust
Tomchei Torah Charitable Trust
The Tory Family Foundation
Truemart Limited
Trumros Limited
The Tufton Charitable Trust
UKI Charitable Foundation
Ulting Overseas Trust
The Van Neste Foundation
Vivdale Ltd
The Weinstein Foundation
The Joir and Kato Weisz Foundation
The Westcroft Trust

*Fields of interest and type of beneficiary* — **Christianity**

The Whitecourt Charitable Trust
The Norman Whiteley Trust
Dame Violet Wills Charitable Trust
The Benjamin Winegarten Charitable Trust
The Michael and Anna Wix Charitable Trust
The James Wood Bequest Fund
Woodlands Green Ltd
The Matthews Wrightson Charity Trust
Wychdale Ltd
Yankov Charitable Trust
The Yorkshire Historic Churches Trust
Stephen Zimmerman Charitable Trust

## Christianity

Aid to the Church in Need (UK)
The Alabaster Trust
The Alexis Trust
Allchurches Trust Ltd
The Almond Trust
Almondsbury Charity
Viscount Amory's Charitable Trust
The Anchor Foundation
The Andrew Anderson Trust
Andrews Charitable Trust
The John Apthorp Charity
The Archbishop's Council – The Church and Community Fund
The Archer Trust
The Armourers' and Brasiers' Gauntlet Trust
The AS Charitable Trust
The Ashburnham Thanksgiving Trust
The Baird Trust
The Balney Charitable Trust
The Bates Charitable Trust
Miss Jeanne Bisgood's Charitable Trust
The Sydney Black Charitable Trust
The Blandford Lake Trust
The Harry Bottom Charitable Trust
P. G. and N. J. Boulton Trust
The Bowland Charitable Trust
The Liz and Terry Bramall Foundation
Bristol Archdeaconry Charity
The T. B. H. Brunner Charitable Settlement
Buckingham Trust
The Burden Trust
Henry T. and Lucy B. Cadbury Charitable Trust

The William A. Cadbury Charitable Trust
The Cambridgeshire Historic Churches Trust
The Carpenters' Company Charitable Trust
The Catholic Charitable Trust
Catholic Foreign Missions
The Catholic Trust for England and Wales
The Childs Charitable Trust
The Christabella Charitable Trust
Church Burgesses Trust
Church Urban Fund
The Hilda and Alice Clark Charitable Trust
The Roger and Sarah Bancroft Clark Charitable Trust
The Clarke Charitable Settlement
Richard Cloudesley's Charity
The Clover Trust
John Coldman Charitable Trust
The Congregational and General Charitable Trust
The Costa Family Charitable Trust
Criffel Charitable Trust
The Cumber Family Charitable Trust
Daily Prayer Union Charitable Trust Limited
The Dulverton Trust
The Dyers' Company Charitable Trust
The Edith Maud Ellis 1985 Charitable Trust
The Englefield Charitable Trust
The Erskine Cunningham Hill Trust
The Fairway Trust
The Farthing Trust
Firtree Trust
Fisherbeck Charitable Trust
The Forest Hill Charitable Trust
The Forman Hardy Charitable Trust
The Forte Charitable Trust
The Four Winds Trust
The Anne French Memorial Trust
The Gale Family Charity Trust
The Gamma Trust
The Ganzoni Charitable Trust
The Gibbs Charitable Trust
The Girdlers' Company Charitable Trust
Global Care
Golden Charitable Trust
The Grace Charitable Trust
Philip and Judith Green Trust
The Greys Charitable Trust
E. F. and M. G. Hall Charitable Trust

The W. A. Handley Charitable Trust
Headley-Pitt Charitable Trust
Hesed Trust
Hexham and Newcastle Diocesan Trust (1947)
P. and C. Hickinbotham Charitable Trust
Hinchley Charitable Trust
Stuart Hine Trust
The Hintze Family Charity Foundation
Hockerill Educational Foundation
The Homelands Charitable Trust
The Homestead Charitable Trust
Sir Harold Hood's Charitable Trust
The Hope Trust
The Hutton Foundation
The J. A. R. Charitable Trust
The James Trust
The Jarman Charitable Trust
The Jerusalem Trust
The Kennedy Charitable Foundation
The King Henry VIII Endowed Trust – Warwick
Kingdom Way Trust
The K. P. Ladd Charitable Trust
Maurice and Hilda Laing Charitable Trust
The Kirby Laing Foundation
The Beatrice Laing Trust
Lancaster Foundation
Langdale Trust
Langley Charitable Trust
Laslett's (Hinton) Charity
The Herd Lawson and Muriel Lawson Charitable Trust
The William Leech Charity
P. Leigh-Bramwell Trust 'E'
The Lind Trust
Lindale Educational Foundation
The Charles Littlewood Hill Trust
The Elaine and Angus Lloyd Charitable Trust
The Charles Lloyd Foundation
The Lyndhurst Trust
Sylvanus Lysons Charity
Mariapolis Limited
The Marsh Christian Trust
Charity of John Marshall
Charlotte Marshall Charitable Trust
The Marshgate Charitable Settlement
Sir George Martin Trust
John Martin's Charity
The Mason Porter Charitable Trust

**113**

The Matt 6.3 Charitable Trust
The Mercers' Charitable Foundation
The Merchant Taylors' Company Charities Fund
The Millfield Trust
The Edgar Milward Charity
The Mizpah Trust
Monmouthshire County Council Welsh Church Act Fund
The Oliver Morland Charitable Trust
S. C. and M. E. Morland's Charitable Trust
The Moshulu Charitable Trust
Mrs Waterhouse Charitable Trust
National Committee of the Women's World Day of Prayer for England and Wales and Northern Ireland
The Nazareth Trust Fund
The New Appeals Organisation for the City and County of Nottingham
The Norwood and Newton Settlement
The Nottinghamshire Historic Churches Trust
The Ogle Christian Trust
The Ouseley Trust
The Owen Family Trust
The Paget Charitable Trust
The Panacea Charitable Trust
Panahpur
The James Pantyfedwen Foundation
The Park House Charitable Trust
Miss M. E. Swinton Paterson's Charitable Trust
The Jack Patston Charitable Trust
The Payne Charitable Trust
The Persson Charitable Trust
The David Pickford Charitable Foundation
The Bernard Piggott Charitable Trust
The Praebendo Charitable Foundation
The William Price Charitable Trust
Sir John Priestman Charity Trust
The Pyne Charitable Trust
Quothquan Trust
The Bishop Radford Trust
The Rank Foundation Limited
The Sir James Reckitt Charity
The Rhondda Cynon Taff Welsh Church Acts Fund
The Sir Cliff Richard Charitable Trust
The Clive Richards Charity
The River Trust

The Rock Foundation
Mrs L. D. Rope Third Charitable Settlement
Saint Sarkis Charity Trust
The Salamander Charitable Trust
The Sants Charitable Trust
The Scarfe Charitable Trust
The Seedfield Trust
The Shanti Charitable Trust
The Bassil Shippam and Alsford Trust
The J. A. Shone Memorial Trust
The SMB Charitable Trust
The Souter Charitable Trust
The W. F. Southall Trust
St Peter's Saltley Trust
The Stewards' Company Limited (incorporating the J. W. Laing Trust and the J. W. Laing Biblical Scholarship Trust)
Sir Halley Stewart Trust
The Leonard Laity Stoate Charitable Trust
The Stobart Newlands Charitable Trust
The Sussex Historic Churches Trust
Swansea and Brecon Diocesan Board of Finance Limited
The Lady Tangye Charitable Trust
C. B. and H. H. Taylor 1984 Trust
Tearfund
The C. Paul Thackray General Charitable Trust
The Thornton Trust
The Tisbury Telegraph Trust
The Tolkien Trust
The Tory Family Foundation
The Tufton Charitable Trust
Ulting Overseas Trust
The United Society for the Propagation of the Gospel
The Van Neste Foundation
The Vardy Foundation
The Westcroft Trust
The Whitecourt Charitable Trust
The Norman Whiteley Trust
Dame Violet Wills Charitable Trust
The James Wood Bequest Fund
The Worcestershire and Dudley Historic Churches Trust
The Matthews Wrightson Charity Trust
The Yorkshire Historic Churches Trust

## Christian causes

The Alexis Trust
The Almond Trust
The Andrew Anderson Trust
The Archer Trust
The Ashburnham Thanksgiving Trust
The Baird Trust
The Blandford Lake Trust
Bristol Archdeaconry Charity
The Carpenters' Company Charitable Trust
Church Burgesses Trust
Church Urban Fund
The Englefield Charitable Trust
The Farthing Trust
Firtree Trust
The Forest Hill Charitable Trust
The Forte Charitable Trust
The Four Winds Trust
The Anne French Memorial Trust
The Gibbs Charitable Trust
The Girdlers' Company Charitable Trust
Global Care
Stuart Hine Trust
The Jerusalem Trust
Maurice and Hilda Laing Charitable Trust
Langdale Trust
The Herd Lawson and Muriel Lawson Charitable Trust
The William Leech Charity
Sir George Martin Trust
National Committee of the Women's World Day of Prayer for England and Wales and Northern Ireland
The Nazareth Trust Fund
The Norwood and Newton Settlement
The Owen Family Trust
The Paget Charitable Trust
The Panacea Charitable Trust
The Park House Charitable Trust
The Payne Charitable Trust
The Sir Cliff Richard Charitable Trust
The River Trust
Mrs L. D. Rope Third Charitable Settlement
The Salamander Charitable Trust
The Seedfield Trust
The Shanti Charitable Trust
The J. A. Shone Memorial Trust
The Stewards' Company Limited (incorporating the J. W. Laing Trust and the J. W. Laing Biblical Scholarship Trust)
The Stobart Newlands Charitable Trust

Tearfund
The Tufton Charitable Trust
The Vardy Foundation
The Whitecourt Charitable Trust

## Christian churches

Aid to the Church in Need (UK)
Almondsbury Charity
Viscount Amory's Charitable Trust
The Archbishop's Council – The Church and Community Fund
The Baird Trust
The Balney Charitable Trust
The Bates Charitable Trust
Miss Jeanne Bisgood's Charitable Trust
The Sydney Black Charitable Trust
The T. B. H. Brunner Charitable Settlement
Henry T. and Lucy B. Cadbury Charitable Trust
The William A. Cadbury Charitable Trust
The Cambridgeshire Historic Churches Trust
The Catholic Charitable Trust
Catholic Foreign Missions (CFM)
The Catholic Trust for England and Wales
Church Burgesses Trust
The Hilda and Alice Clark Charitable Trust
The Roger and Sarah Bancroft Clark Charitable Trust
Richard Cloudesley's Charity
The Congregational and General Charitable Trust
The Edith Maud Ellis 1985 Charitable Trust
The Erskine Cunningham Hill Trust
The Four Winds Trust
The Anne French Memorial Trust
The Gale Family Charity Trust
The Gibbs Charitable Trust
The Girdlers' Company Charitable Trust
The Greys Charitable Trust
E. F. and M. G. Hall Charitable Trust
The W. A. Handley Charitable Trust
Headley-Pitt Charitable Trust
Hexham and Newcastle Diocesan Trust (1947)
P. and C. Hickinbotham Charitable Trust
Stuart Hine Trust

The Homelands Charitable Trust
Sir Harold Hood's Charitable Trust
The J. A. R. Charitable Trust
The Jarman Charitable Trust
The Kennedy Charitable Foundation
The King Henry VIII Endowed Trust – Warwick
Laslett's (Hinton) Charity
Lindale Educational Foundation
The Charles Lloyd Foundation
Sylvanus Lysons Charity
Charity of John Marshall (Marshall's Charity)
Charlotte Marshall Charitable Trust
Monmouthshire County Council Welsh Church Act Fund
The Oliver Morland Charitable Trust
S. C. and M. E. Morland's Charitable Trust
Mrs Waterhouse Charitable Trust
The Nazareth Trust Fund
The New Appeals Organisation for the City and County of Nottingham
The Norwood and Newton Settlement
The Nottinghamshire Historic Churches Trust
The Ogle Christian Trust
The Ouseley Trust
The Owen Family Trust
Miss M. E. Swinton Paterson's Charitable Trust
The Bernard Piggott Charitable Trust
The William Price Charitable Trust
Sir John Priestman Charity Trust
The Bishop Radford Trust
The Sir James Reckitt Charity
The Clive Richards Charity
Mrs L. D. Rope Third Charitable Settlement
Saint Sarkis Charity Trust
The W. F. Southall Trust
The Leonard Laity Stoate Charitable Trust
The Sussex Historic Churches Trust
The Lady Tangye Charitable Trust
C. B. and H. H. Taylor 1984 Trust
The Thornton Trust
The Tolkien Trust
The Westcroft Trust
The Norman Whiteley Trust

The James Wood Bequest Fund
The Worcestershire and Dudley Historic Churches Trust
The Yorkshire Historic Churches Trust

## Christian social thought

The Carpenters' Company Charitable Trust
The Jerusalem Trust
Sir Halley Stewart Trust

## Ecumenicalism

The Carpenters' Company Charitable Trust
The Gibbs Charitable Trust
Mariapolis Limited
Mrs L. D. Rope Third Charitable Settlement

## Missionary work, evangelism

The Armourers' and Brasiers' Gauntlet Trust
P. G. and N. J. Boulton Trust
The Carpenters' Company Charitable Trust
Daily Prayer Union Charitable Trust Limited
The Fairway Trust
The Farthing Trust
The Four Winds Trust
Philip and Judith Green Trust
Stuart Hine Trust
Hockerill Educational Foundation
The Jerusalem Trust
Maurice and Hilda Laing Charitable Trust
Lancaster Foundation
The Moshulu Charitable Trust
National Committee of the Women's World Day of Prayer for England and Wales and Northern Ireland
The Nazareth Trust Fund
The Ogle Christian Trust
The Owen Family Trust
Panahpur
The Payne Charitable Trust
The Persson Charitable Trust
The Rank Foundation Limited
The Sir Cliff Richard Charitable Trust
The Rock Foundation
The Seedfield Trust

The J. A. Shone Memorial Trust
The Stewards' Company Limited (incorporating the J. W. Laing Trust and the J. W. Laing Biblical Scholarship Trust)
The Thornton Trust
The United Society for the Propagation of the Gospel
The Norman Whiteley Trust
Dame Violet Wills Charitable Trust

## Hinduism

The Carpenters' Company Charitable Trust

## Inter-faith activities

All Saints Educational Trust
The Astor of Hever Trust
The Bowerman Charitable Trust
The Carpenters' Company Charitable Trust
The Edith Maud Ellis 1985 Charitable Trust
The Joseph Strong Frazer Trust
The Anne French Memorial Trust
Joseph Levy Charitable Foundation
The C. L. Loyd Charitable Trust
The Mahavir Trust
The Community Foundation for Northern Ireland
The Harry Payne Fund
The Rofeh Trust
The Sir James Roll Charitable Trust
The Michael Sacher Charitable Trust
Sir Halley Stewart Trust
Roger Vere Foundation

## Islam

The Altajir Trust
The Carpenters' Company Charitable Trust
Euro Charity Trust
The Matliwala Family Charitable Trust
Muslim Hands

## Judaism

4 Charity Foundation
A. W. Charitable Trust
Eric Abrams Charitable Trust

The Acacia Charitable Trust
Achisomoch Aid Company Limited
Adenfirst Ltd
The Adint Charitable Trust
The Alliance Family Foundation
Altamont Ltd
AM Charitable Trust
Amabrill Limited
Andor Charitable Trust
Anpride Ltd
The Ardwick Trust
The Baker Charitable Trust
The Andrew Balint Charitable Trust
The George Balint Charitable Trust
The Paul Balint Charitable Trust
Bay Charitable Trust
BCH Trust
Bear Mordechai Ltd
Beauland Ltd
The Becker Family Charitable Trust
Maurice and Jacqueline Bennett Charitable Trust
Michael and Leslie Bennett Charitable Trust
The Ruth Berkowitz Charitable Trust
BHST
The Bintaub Charitable Trust
The Bertie Black Foundation
The Sir Victor Blank Charitable Settlement
The Bluston Charitable Settlement
The Bonamy Charitable Trust
Salo Bordon Charitable Trust
Sir Clive Bourne Family Trust
Bourneheights Limited
Edna Brown Charitable Settlement
Brushmill Ltd
The Arnold Burton 1998 Charitable Trust
C. and F. Charitable Trust
The H. and L. Cantor Trust
Carlee Ltd
The Carlton House Charitable Trust
The Carpenters' Company Charitable Trust
The CH (1980) Charitable Trust
Charitworth Limited
The Clore Duffield Foundation
Closehelm Limited
Clydpride Ltd
The Denise Cohen Charitable Trust
The Vivienne and Samuel Cohen Charitable Trust
Col-Reno Ltd

Harold and Daphne Cooper Charitable Trust
The Gershon Coren Charitable Foundation
The Sidney and Elizabeth Corob Charitable Trust
The Corona Charitable Trust
The Craps Charitable Trust
The Cuby Charitable Trust
Itzchok Meyer Cymerman Trust Ltd
Oizer Dalim Trust
The Davidson Family Charitable Trust
The Davis Foundation
The Debmar Benevolent Trust
The Dellal Foundation
The Desmond Foundation
Alan and Sheila Diamond Charitable Trust
The Djanogly Foundation
The DM Charitable Trust
The Dollond Charitable Trust
The Doughty Charity Trust
Dushinsky Trust Ltd
The George Elias Charitable Trust
Ellador Ltd
The Ellinson Foundation Ltd
Elshore Ltd
Entindale Ltd
The Esfandi Charitable Foundation
The Eventhall Family Charitable Trust
The Exilarch's Foundation
Extonglen Limited
Famos Foundation Trust
Finnart House School Trust
The Gerald Fogel Charitable Trust
Fordeve Limited
The Isaac and Freda Frankel Memorial Charitable Trust
Friends of Boyan Trust
Friends of Wiznitz Limited
Mejer and Gertrude Miriam Frydman Foundation
Jacqueline and Michael Gee Charitable Trust
The B. and P. Glasser Charitable Trust
Golden Charitable Trust
The Grahame Charitable Foundation Limited
The M. and R. Gross Charities Limited
The GRP Charitable Trust
N. and R. Grunbaum Charitable Trust
The Gur Trust
Harbo Charities Limited
The Hathaway Trust
The Maurice Hatter Foundation
The Heathside Charitable Trust

The Simon Heller Charitable Settlement
The Helping Foundation
Highcroft Charitable Trust
The Holden Charitable Trust
The Daniel Howard Trust
The Humanitarian Trust
The Huntingdon Foundation Limited
Hurdale Charity Limited
The P. Y. N. and B. Hyams Trust
Investream Charitable Trust
The J. & J. Benevolent Foundation
The J. & J. Charitable Trust
The Jacobs Charitable Trust
The Ruth and Lionel Jacobson Trust (Second Fund) No 2
The Susan and Stephen James Charitable Settlement
Jay Education Trust
JCA Charitable Foundation
Jewish Child's Day (JCD)
The Jewish Youth Fund (JYF)
The Joron Charitable Trust
The J. E. Joseph Charitable Fund
The Josephs Family Charitable Trust
Jusaca Charitable Trust
The Bernard Kahn Charitable Trust
The Stanley Kalms Foundation
Karaviotis Foundation
The Kasner Charitable Trust
The Kass Charitable Trust (KCT)
The Michael and Ilse Katz Foundation
C. S. Kaufman Charitable Trust
Keren Association Limited
E. and E. Kernkraut Charities Limited
Kirschel Foundation
The Kobler Trust
The Kohn Foundation
Kollel and Co. Limited
The Kreditor Charitable Trust
Kupath Gemach Chaim Bechesed Viznitz Trust
The Kyte Charitable Trust
The Lambert Charitable Trust
Largsmount Ltd
The Lauffer Family Charitable Foundation
Lawson Beckman Charitable Trust
The Arnold Lee Charitable Trust
The Kennedy Leigh Charitable Trust
Morris Leigh Foundation

Joseph Levy Charitable Foundation
The Ruth and Stuart Lipton Charitable Trust
The Second Joseph Aaron Littman Foundation
Jack Livingstone Charitable Trust
Localtrent Ltd
The Locker Foundation
Loftus Charitable Trust
The Lolev Charitable Trust
The Lowy Mitchell Foundation
The Ruth and Jack Lunzer Charitable Trust
The Sir Jack Lyons Charitable Trust
M. and C. Trust
The M. K. Charitable Trust
The Magen Charitable Trust
Malbin Trust
The Manackerman Charitable Trust
Marbeh Torah Trust
The Stella and Alexander Margulies Charitable Trust
The Marks Family Foundation
The Ann and David Marks Foundation
The Hilda and Samuel Marks Foundation
The Violet Mauray Charitable Trust
Mayfair Charities Ltd
Melodor Limited
The Melow Charitable Trust
Menuchar Limited
Mercaz Torah Vechesed Limited
The Laurence Misener Charitable Trust
The Mishcon Family Charitable Trust
Keren Mitzvah Trust
The Modiano Charitable Trust
Mole Charitable Trust
The Diana and Allan Morgenthau Charitable Trust
The Peter Morrison Charitable Foundation
The Moshal Charitable Trust
Vyoel Moshe Charitable Trust
Brian and Jill Moss Charitable Trust
Mosselson Charitable Trust
The Mutual Trust Group
MW (CL) Foundation
MW (GK) Foundation
MW (HO) Foundation
MW (RH) Foundation
MYA Charitable Trust
MYR Charitable Trust
Nemoral Ltd
Ner Foundation
Nesswall Ltd

Newpier Charity Ltd
The Chevras Ezras Nitzrochim Trust
NJD Charitable Trust
Normalyn Charitable Trust
O&G Schreiber Charitable Trust
Oizer Charitable Trust
The Park Charitable Trust
The David Pearlman Charitable Foundation
The Pears Family Charitable Foundation
The Peltz Trust
B. E. Perl Charitable Trust
The Phillips and Rubens Charitable Trust
The Phillips Family Charitable Trust
G. S. Plaut Charitable Trust Limited
The George and Esme Pollitzer Charitable Settlement
The Pollywally Charitable Trust
Edith and Ferdinand Porjes Charitable Trust
The John Porter Charitable Trust
The J. E. Posnansky Charitable Trust
Premierquote Ltd
Premishlaner Charitable Trust
R. J. M. Charitable Trust
R. S. Charitable Trust
Rachel Charitable Trust
The Rayden Charitable Trust
The Rayne Trust
The Rest Harrow Trust
Reuben Foundation
Ridgesave Limited
The Sir John Ritblat Family Foundation
Rokach Family Charitable Trust
The Gerald Ronson Foundation
Rowanville Ltd
The Rubin Foundation
S. F. Foundation
The Ruzin Sadagora Trust
Sam and Bella Sebba Charitable Trust
The M. J. Samuel Charitable Trust
The Peter Samuel Charitable Trust
The Schapira Charitable Trust
The Annie Schiff Charitable Trust
The Schmidt-Bodner Charitable Trust
The Schreib Trust
The Schreiber Charitable Trust
The Searchlight Electric Charitable Trust
Sellata Ltd
The Seneca Trust
The Cyril Shack Trust

## Jewish causes, work

The Archie Sherman Cardiff
  Foundation
The Archie Sherman Charitable
  Trust
Shlomo Memorial Fund Limited
David and Jennifer Sieff
  Charitable Trust
Six Point Foundation
The Sobell Foundation
Solev Co Ltd
The Solo Charitable
  Settlement
Songdale Ltd
The E. C. Sosnow Charitable
  Trust
Sparquote Limited
Spears-Stutz Charitable Trust
Rosalyn and Nicholas Springer
  Charitable Trust
Springrule Limited
The Steinberg Family
  Charitable Trust
C. E. K. Stern Charitable Trust
The Strawberry Charitable
  Trust
Sueberry Ltd
The Alan Sugar Foundation
The Adrienne and Leslie
  Sussman Charitable Trust
The Tajtelbaum Charitable
  Trust
The David Tannen Charitable
  Trust
The Lili Tapper Charitable
  Foundation
Tegham Limited
Tomchei Torah Charitable
  Trust
Toras Chesed (London) Trust
Truedene Co. Ltd
Truemart Limited
Trumros Limited
Tudor Rose Ltd
Trustees of Tzedakah
The Union of Orthodox Hebrew
  Congregation
The Vail Foundation
Vivdale Ltd
The Weinstein Foundation
The Joir and Kato Weisz
  Foundation
The Benjamin Winegarten
  Charitable Trust
The Harold Hyam Wingate
  Foundation
The Michael and Anna Wix
  Charitable Trust
The Maurice Wohl Charitable
  Foundation
The Charles Wolfson
  Charitable Trust
The Wolfson Family Charitable
  Trust
Woodlands Green Ltd
Wychdale Ltd
Wychville Ltd

Yankov Charitable Trust
The Marjorie and Arnold Ziff
  Charitable Foundation
Stephen Zimmerman
  Charitable Trust

## Jewish causes, work

Altamont Ltd
The Arnold Burton 1998
  Charitable Trust
Ellador Ltd
N. and R. Grunbaum
  Charitable Trust
The Hathaway Trust
The J. & J. Charitable Trust
The Susan and Stephen
  James Charitable
  Settlement
The Kyte Charitable Trust
The Lambert Charitable Trust
Malbin Trust
The Modiano Charitable Trust
The Peltz Trust
Sellata Ltd
Rosalyn and Nicholas Springer
  Charitable Trust

## Orthodox Judaism

Achisomoch Aid Company
  Limited
Amabrill Limited
The Becker Family Charitable
  Trust
Bourneheights Limited
C. and F. Charitable Trust
The Doughty Charity Trust
Extonglen Limited
Friends of Boyan Trust
The Helping Foundation
The J. & J. Benevolent
  Foundation
The Lolev Charitable Trust
Mayfair Charities Ltd
Mercaz Torah Vechesed
  Limited
MW (CL) Foundation
MW (GK) Foundation
MW (HO) Foundation
MW (RH) Foundation
Ner Foundation
Newpier Charity Ltd
O&G Schreiber Charitable
  Trust
Oizer Charitable Trust
Rowanville Ltd
Sparquote Limited
C. E. K. Stern Charitable Trust
Tegham Limited
Vivdale Ltd

## Religious understanding

The Carpenters' Company
  Charitable Trust
The Doughty Charity Trust
The Gilbert and Eileen Edgar
  Foundation
The Anne French Memorial
  Trust
Ibrahim Foundation Ltd
Keswick Hall Charity
The Kennedy Leigh Charitable
  Trust
Joseph Levy Charitable
  Foundation
The Noon Foundation
Quothquan Trust

## Rights, law and conflict

The 1970 Trust
ABF The Soldiers' Charity
The Ajahma Charitable Trust
The Alchemy Foundation
The AS Charitable Trust
The Ashworth Charitable Trust
The Associated Country Women of the World
The Bank of Scotland Foundation
The Baring Foundation
The Barnwood House Trust
The Big Lottery Fund
The Body Shop Foundation
British Gas (Scottish Gas) Energy Trust
The Bromley Trust
The William A. Cadbury Charitable Trust
The Barrow Cadbury Trust
CAFOD (Catholic Agency for Overseas Development)
Calouste Gulbenkian Foundation – UK Branch
The Calpe Trust
Celtic Charity Fund
The Charities Advisory Trust
J. A. Clark Charitable Trust
The Evan Cornish Foundation
The Violet and Milo Cripps Charitable Trust
The Daiwa Anglo-Japanese Foundation
The Davis Foundation
The Henry and Suzanne Davis Foundation
The Dentons UKMEA LLP Charitable Trust
The Dulverton Trust
Dunard Fund
EDF Energy Trust
Edge Fund
The Edith Maud Ellis 1985 Charitable Trust
The Ericson Trust
Esmée Fairbairn Foundation
The Farthing Trust
The Allan and Nesta Ferguson Charitable Settlement
The Jill Franklin Trust
Friends Provident Charitable Foundation
The Fuserna Foundation
General Charitable Trust
The G. D. Charitable Trust
Gamlen Charitable Trust
The Robert Gavron Charitable Trust
The Hadley Trust
Paul Hamlyn Foundation
The Helen Hamlyn Trust
The Maurice Hatter Foundation

The Charles Hayward Foundation
Heart of England Community Foundation
The Hilden Charitable Fund
The Henry C. Hoare Charitable Trust
Hope for Youth (NI)
The Sir Joseph Hotung Charitable Settlement
Human Relief Foundation
The Michael and Shirley Hunt Charitable Trust
The Hunter Foundation
The Indigo Trust
The Ireland Fund of Great Britain
Irish Youth Foundation (UK) Ltd
The JRSST Charitable Trust
The Joffe Charitable Trust
Kent Community Foundation
Robert Kitchin (Saddlers' Company)
Community Foundations for Lancashire and Merseyside
The Allen Lane Foundation
The LankellyChase Foundation
The Law Society Charity
The Kennedy Leigh Charitable Trust
The Leigh Trust
The Lennox and Wyfold Foundation
The Mark Leonard Trust
Joseph Levy Charitable Foundation
Lloyds Bank Foundation for England and Wales
Lloyds Bank Foundation for Northern Ireland
Lloyds TSB Foundation for Scotland
The Trust for London
The London Community Foundation
London Legal Support Trust
John Lyon's Charity
The Sir Jack Lyons Charitable Trust
M. and C. Trust
The Mactaggart Third Fund
The Ian Mactaggart Trust
Mariapolis Limited
Marmot Charitable Trust
The Ronald Miller Foundation
The Millfield House Foundation
John Moores Foundation
The Miles Morland Foundation
S. C. and M. E. Morland's Charitable Trust
Muslim Hands
The Nationwide Foundation
Network for Social Change
The Noon Foundation
Norfolk Community Foundation

The Community Foundation for Northern Ireland
The Northern Rock Foundation
The Nuffield Foundation
The Harry Payne Fund
The Pears Family Charitable Foundation
People's Postcode Trust
The Persula Foundation
Estate of the Late Colonel W. W. Pilkington Will Trusts – The General Charity Fund
Polden-Puckham Charitable Foundation
The Polonsky Foundation
The David and Elaine Potter Foundation
Quartet Community Foundation
The Monica Rabagliati Charitable Trust
The Eleanor Rathbone Charitable Trust
The Sigrid Rausing Trust
Eva Reckitt Trust Fund
The Roddick Foundation
The Joseph Rowntree Charitable Trust
Joseph Rowntree Reform Trust Limited
The Alan and Babette Sainsbury Charitable Fund
Sam and Bella Sebba Charitable Trust
Santander UK Foundation Limited
The Scottish Power Energy People Trust
The Simmons & Simmons Charitable Foundation
The Slaughter and May Charitable Trust
The W. F. Southall Trust
The Staples Trust
The Gay and Keith Talbot Trust
Thomson Reuters Foundation
The Tinsley Foundation
The Tresillian Trust
UIA Charitable Foundation
United Utilities Trust Fund
The Nigel Vinson Charitable Trust
Voluntary Action Fund
The Scurrah Wainwright Charity
War on Want
Webb Memorial Trust
The Westcroft Trust
The Wolfson Family Charitable Trust
The Wood Family Trust
The Woodward Charitable Trust
Worcester Municipal Charities
The Xerox (UK) Trust
Yorkshire and Clydesdale Bank Foundation
Youth United Foundation

## Citizen participation

The Bromley Trust
The Barrow Cadbury Trust
The Ericson Trust
The Henry C. Hoare Charitable Trust
The Michael and Shirley Hunt Charitable Trust
The Hunter Foundation
The Indigo Trust
The Joffe Charitable Trust
The Leigh Trust
The Lennox and Wyfold Foundation
Lloyds TSB Foundation for Scotland
The London Community Foundation
The Nuffield Foundation
People's Postcode Trust
The Joseph Rowntree Charitable Trust
Joseph Rowntree Reform Trust Limited
Thomson Reuters Foundation
The Tinsley Foundation
The Nigel Vinson Charitable Trust
Webb Memorial Trust
The Wood Family Trust
Youth United Foundation

## Conflict resolution

The A. S. Charitable Trust
The William A. Cadbury Charitable Trust
The Barrow Cadbury Trust
Calouste Gulbenkian Foundation – UK Branch
The Charities Advisory Trust
J. A. Clark Charitable Trust
The Daiwa Anglo-Japanese Foundation
The Dulverton Trust
The Edith Maud Ellis 1985 Charitable Trust
The Ericson Trust
Esmée Fairbairn Foundation
The Allan and Nesta Ferguson Charitable Settlement
The Hadley Trust
Hope for Youth (NI)
Human Relief Foundation
The Ireland Fund of Great Britain
Irish Youth Foundation (UK) Ltd
The Allen Lane Foundation
The Kennedy Leigh Charitable Trust
Mariapolis Limited
Marmot Charitable Trust
John Moores Foundation

S. C. and M. E. Morland's Charitable Trust
The Noon Foundation
The Community Foundation for Northern Ireland
The Harry Payne Fund
The Pears Family Charitable Foundation
People's Postcode Trust
Polden-Puckham Charitable Foundation
The Polonsky Foundation
The Eleanor Rathbone Charitable Trust
The Joseph Rowntree Charitable Trust
The W. F. Southall Trust
Thomson Reuters Foundation
The Tresillian Trust
The Westcroft Trust
The Woodward Charitable Trust

## Cross border initiatives

Calouste Gulbenkian Foundation – UK Branch
Hope for Youth (NI)
Irish Youth Foundation (UK) Ltd

## Cross community work

The William A. Cadbury Charitable Trust
The Barrow Cadbury Trust
The Daiwa Anglo-Japanese Foundation
Esmée Fairbairn Foundation
The Hadley Trust
Hope for Youth (NI)
Irish Youth Foundation (UK) Ltd
John Moores Foundation
The Noon Foundation
The Pears Family Charitable Foundation
The Eleanor Rathbone Charitable Trust
The Woodward Charitable Trust

## Mediation

The Charities Advisory Trust
The Ireland Fund of Great Britain

## Peace and disarmament

The AS Charitable Trust
The Charities Advisory Trust
J. A. Clark Charitable Trust
The Edith Maud Ellis 1985 Charitable Trust
The Allan and Nesta Ferguson Charitable Settlement
S. C. and M. E. Morland's Charitable Trust
The Harry Payne Fund

## Legal advice and services

The Bank of Scotland Foundation
The Big Lottery Fund
British Gas (Scottish Gas) Energy Trust
The Dentons UKMEA LLP Charitable Trust
EDF Energy Trust
Friends Provident Charitable Foundation
Community Foundations for Lancashire and Merseyside
The Law Society Charity
Lloyds Bank Foundation for England and Wales
Lloyds Bank Foundation for Northern Ireland
The London Community Foundation
London Legal Support Trust
John Moores Foundation
The Nationwide Foundation
The Community Foundation for Northern Ireland
The Northern Rock Foundation
The Nuffield Foundation
The David and Elaine Potter Foundation
Quartet Community Foundation
Eva Reckitt Trust Fund
Santander UK Foundation Limited
The Scottish Power Energy People Trust
The Simmons & Simmons Charitable Foundation
The Slaughter and May Charitable Trust
Thomson Reuters Foundation
United Utilities Trust Fund
Worcester Municipal Charities

## Advice services

The Bank of Scotland Foundation
The Big Lottery Fund

*Fields of interest and type of beneficiary* — **Economic justice**

British Gas (Scottish Gas) Energy Trust
EDF Energy Trust
Friends Provident Charitable Foundation
Community Foundations for Lancashire and Merseyside
Lloyds Bank Foundation for England and Wales
Lloyds Bank Foundation for Northern Ireland
The London Community Foundation
John Moores Foundation
The Community Foundation for Northern Ireland
The Northern Rock Foundation
Quartet Community Foundation
Eva Reckitt Trust Fund
Santander UK Foundation Limited
The Scottish Power Energy People Trust
United Utilities Trust Fund
Worcester Municipal Charities

## Legal issues

The Dentons UKMEA LLP Charitable Trust
The Law Society Charity
The Nationwide Foundation
The Nuffield Foundation
Eva Reckitt Trust Fund

## Rights, equality and justice

The 1970 Trust
The Ajahma Charitable Trust
The Associated Country Women of the World
The Barnwood House Trust
The Body Shop Foundation
The Bromley Trust
The Barrow Cadbury Trust
Calouste Gulbenkian Foundation – UK Branch
Celtic Charity Fund
The Henry and Suzanne Davis Foundation
Dunard Fund
The Ericson Trust
The Farthing Trust
The Allan and Nesta Ferguson Charitable Settlement
The G. D. Charitable Trust
The Robert Gavron Charitable Trust
Paul Hamlyn Foundation
The Helen Hamlyn Trust
The Maurice Hatter Foundation
The Charles Hayward Foundation

Heart of England Community Foundation
The Hilden Charitable Fund
Hope for Youth (NI)
The Sir Joseph Hotung Charitable Settlement
Human Relief Foundation
The Michael and Shirley Hunt Charitable Trust
The Indigo Trust
The JRSST Charitable Trust
The Joffe Charitable Trust
Kent Community Foundation
Robert Kitchin (Saddlers' Company)
The Allen Lane Foundation
The LankellyChase Foundation
The Law Society Charity
The Kennedy Leigh Charitable Trust
The Leigh Trust
The Mark Leonard Trust
Joseph Levy Charitable Foundation
Lloyds Bank Foundation for England and Wales
Lloyds TSB Foundation for Scotland
The London Community Foundation
John Lyon's Charity
The Millfield House Foundation
John Moores Foundation
Network for Social Change
The Noon Foundation
The Community Foundation for Northern Ireland
The Nuffield Foundation
People's Postcode Trust
The Persula Foundation
Estate of the Late Colonel W. W. Pilkington Will Trusts – The General Charity Fund
Polden-Puckham Charitable Foundation
The David and Elaine Potter Foundation
The Monica Rabagliati Charitable Trust
The Eleanor Rathbone Charitable Trust
Eva Reckitt Trust Fund
The Roddick Foundation
The Joseph Rowntree Charitable Trust
Joseph Rowntree Reform Trust Limited
The Alan and Babette Sainsbury Charitable Fund
The Staples Trust
The Gay and Keith Talbot Trust
Thomson Reuters Foundation
The Tinsley Foundation
Voluntary Action Fund
Webb Memorial Trust
The Westcroft Trust

The Xerox (UK) Trust

## Human rights

The 1970 Trust
The Ajahma Charitable Trust
The Body Shop Foundation
The Bromley Trust
Dunard Fund
The Farthing Trust
The Robert Gavron Charitable Trust
The Helen Hamlyn Trust
The Maurice Hatter Foundation
The Indigo Trust
The Kennedy Leigh Charitable Trust
John Lyon's Charity
Polden-Puckham Charitable Foundation
The Monica Rabagliati Charitable Trust
The Roddick Foundation
The Gay and Keith Talbot Trust
Thomson Reuters Foundation
The Tinsley Foundation
The Westcroft Trust

## Civil liberties

The 1970 Trust
The Bromley Trust
Human Relief Foundation
The Joseph Rowntree Charitable Trust
Joseph Rowntree Reform Trust Limited
The Tinsley Foundation

## Cultural equity

Calouste Gulbenkian Foundation – UK Branch
The Ericson Trust
Paul Hamlyn Foundation
The Kennedy Leigh Charitable Trust
The Leigh Trust
John Lyon's Charity

## Disability rights

The Barnwood House Trust
Calouste Gulbenkian Foundation – UK Branch
The G. D. Charitable Trust
Thomson Reuters Foundation
The Xerox (UK) Trust

## Economic justice

The Allan and Nesta Ferguson Charitable Settlement

Lloyds Bank Foundation for
England and Wales
Eva Reckitt Trust Fund
The Joseph Rowntree
Charitable Trust
Thomson Reuters Foundation
The Tinsley Foundation
Webb Memorial Trust

## Racial justice

Celtic Charity Fund
The Ericson Trust
The Farthing Trust
The Hilden Charitable Fund
The Kennedy Leigh Charitable Trust
The Leigh Trust
Joseph Levy Charitable Foundation
The Noon Foundation
The Joseph Rowntree Charitable Trust
The Tinsley Foundation

## Social justice

The Leigh Trust
Network for Social Change
Joseph Rowntree Reform Trust Limited
Thomson Reuters Foundation
The Tinsley Foundation
Webb Memorial Trust
The Xerox (UK) Trust

## Women's rights

The Associated Country Women of the World
Polden-Puckham Charitable Foundation
The Staples Trust
Thomson Reuters Foundation

## Young people's rights

Calouste Gulbenkian Foundation – UK Branch
Hope for Youth (NI)
The Mark Leonard Trust
The Xerox (UK) Trust

## Science and technology

The 1970 Trust
The Aberdeen Endowments Trust
The Armourers' and Brasiers' Gauntlet Trust
Astellas European Foundation
The Big Lottery Fund
The Carlton House Charitable Trust
The John Coates Charitable Trust
The Ernest Cook Trust
The Evan Cornish Foundation
The Cray Trust
The Davis Foundation
William Dean Countryside and Educational Trust
The Dunn Family Charitable Trust
The James Dyson Foundation
The Gilbert and Eileen Edgar Foundation
The Beryl Evetts and Robert Luff Animal Welfare Trust Limited
The Gamma Trust
The Gatsby Charitable Foundation
The GNC Trust
The Golden Bottle Trust
The Granada Foundation
Paul Hamlyn Foundation
The Harbour Foundation
The Simon Heller Charitable Settlement
The Indigo Trust
John Thomas Kennedy Charitable Foundation
The Kohn Foundation
The Kennedy Leigh Charitable Trust
The Lennox and Wyfold Foundation
The Leverhulme Trust
The John Spedan Lewis Foundation
The Limbourne Trust
The Lowy Mitchell Foundation
The MacRobert Trust
The W. M. Mann Foundation
The Michael Marks Charitable Trust
The Nancie Massey Charitable Trust
The Ronald Miller Foundation
The NFU Mutual Charitable Trust
Nominet Charitable Foundation
The Nuffield Foundation
Open Gate
The Petplan Charitable Trust
Mrs L. D. Rope Third Charitable Settlement
The Rowlands Trust
The Michael Sacher Charitable Trust
Raymond and Beverly Sackler 1988 Foundation
The Sackler Trust
The Alan and Babette Sainsbury Charitable Fund
The Andrew Salvesen Charitable Trust
David and Jennifer Sieff Charitable Trust
The Stanley Smith UK Horticultural Trust
The Edward Stocks-Massey Bequest Fund
The Thales Charitable Trust
The Thompson Family Charitable Trust
The Vodafone Foundation
The Waterloo Foundation
The Wellcome Trust
The Winton Charitable Foundation
The Wolfson Family Charitable Trust
The Wolfson Foundation
Yorkshire and Clydesdale Bank Foundation
The John Kirkhope Young Endowment Fund

## Engineering/ technology

The 1970 Trust
The Armourers' and Brasiers' Gauntlet Trust
The Ernest Cook Trust
The James Dyson Foundation
Paul Hamlyn Foundation
The Indigo Trust
Open Gate
The Thales Charitable Trust
The Vodafone Foundation

## Life sciences

The Big Lottery Fund
The Ernest Cook Trust
The Davis Foundation
William Dean Countryside and Educational Trust
The Dunn Family Charitable Trust
The Beryl Evetts and Robert Luff Animal Welfare Trust Limited
The Gatsby Charitable Foundation
The John Spedan Lewis Foundation
The Limbourne Trust
The Michael Marks Charitable Trust

The Petplan Charitable Trust
The Andrew Salvesen
 Charitable Trust
The Stanley Smith UK
 Horticultural Trust
The Thompson Family
 Charitable Trust
The Waterloo Foundation
The Wellcome Trust

## Physical and earth sciences

The Armourers' and Brasiers'
 Gauntlet Trust
The NFU Mutual Charitable
 Trust
Mrs L. D. Rope Third
 Charitable Settlement
The John Kirkhope Young
 Endowment Fund

## Social sciences, policy and research

Age UK
The Bergne-Coupland Charity
British Institute at Ankara
Callander Charitable Trust
The Cayo Foundation
Itzchok Meyer Cymerman Trust
 Ltd
The Daiwa Anglo-Japanese
 Foundation
The Davis Foundation
eaga Charitable Trust
The Gilbert Edgar Trust
The Elmgrant Trust
The Gatsby Charitable
 Foundation
The Robert Gavron Charitable
 Trust
The Hadley Trust
The Harbour Foundation
The Maurice Hatter Foundation
The Hinduja Foundation
The Allen Lane Foundation
The LankellyChase Foundation
The Leverhulme Trust
Joseph Levy Charitable
 Foundation
The Trust for London
London Housing Foundation
 Ltd
James Madison Trust
The Millfield House Foundation
Monmouthshire County Council
 Welsh Church Act Fund
The Nuffield Foundation
The Polonsky Foundation
Porticus UK
The David and Elaine Potter
 Foundation
The Sigrid Rausing Trust
Eva Reckitt Trust Fund
The Joseph Rowntree
 Charitable Trust
The Joseph Rowntree
 Foundation
The Steel Charitable Trust
The Sutasoma Trust
The UNITE Foundation
The Nigel Vinson Charitable
 Trust
War on Want
Webb Memorial Trust
The Wellcome Trust

## Economics

Age UK

## Political science

The Gatsby Charitable
 Foundation
The Maurice Hatter Foundation
The Allen Lane Foundation
James Madison Trust
The Sigrid Rausing Trust
The Joseph Rowntree
 Charitable Trust
The Joseph Rowntree
 Foundation

## Social policy

Age UK
The Cayo Foundation
The Davis Foundation
The Gilbert Edgar Trust
The Gatsby Charitable
 Foundation
The Robert Gavron Charitable
 Trust
The Maurice Hatter Foundation
The Hinduja Foundation
Joseph Levy Charitable
 Foundation
The Trust for London
London Housing Foundation
 Ltd
Monmouthshire County Council
 Welsh Church Act Fund
The Nuffield Foundation
Porticus UK
The Sigrid Rausing Trust
Eva Reckitt Trust Fund
The Joseph Rowntree
 Foundation
The UNITE Foundation
The Wellcome Trust

## Social welfare

The 1970 Trust
The 1989 Willan Charitable Trust
The 29th May 1961 Charitable Trust
Aberdeen Asset Management Charitable Foundation
The Aberdeen Foundation
ABF The Soldiers' Charity
The Acacia Charitable Trust
Access Sport
The ACT Foundation
The Company of Actuaries' Charitable Trust Fund
The Adamson Trust
The Addleshaw Goddard Charitable Trust
The Adint Charitable Trust
Age Scotland
Age UK
The Sylvia Aitken Charitable Trust
The Ajahma Charitable Trust
The Alborada Trust
The Alchemy Foundation
Alliance Trust Staff Foundation
The Pat Allsop Charitable Trust
The Almond Trust
Almondsbury Charity
Altamont Ltd
Amabrill Limited
The Ammco Trust
Viscount Amory's Charitable Trust
The AMW Charitable Trust
The Andrew Anderson Trust
Andrews Charitable Trust
The Apax Foundation
The Appletree Trust
The John Apthorp Charity
The Arbib Foundation
The Archbishop's Council – The Church and Community Fund
The Archer Trust
The Ardwick Trust
The Argus Appeal
The John Armitage Charitable Trust
The Armourers' and Brasiers' Gauntlet Trust
The Artemis Charitable Trust
The Ashworth Charitable Trust
The Associated Country Women of the World
AstonMansfield Charitable Trust
The Astor Foundation
The Lord Austin Trust
The Avon and Somerset Police Community Trust
Awards for All
The Scott Bader Commonwealth Limited
The Austin Bailey Foundation

The Roy and Pixie Baker Charitable Trust
The Balcombe Charitable Trust
The Balfour Beatty Charitable Trust
The Paul Balint Charitable Trust
The Albert Casanova Ballard Deceased Trust
The Ballinger Charitable Trust
The Balmore Trust
The Band Trust
The Barbour Foundation
The Barcapel Foundation
Barchester Healthcare Foundation
The Barclay Foundation
Lord Barnby's Foundation
Barnes Workhouse Fund
The Barnwood House Trust
Bartholomew Charitable Trust
The Bartlett Taylor Charitable Trust
The Batchworth Trust
The Bates Charitable Trust
BBC Children in Need
BCH Trust
The John Beckwith Charitable Trust
The Peter Beckwith Charitable Trust
The Bedfordshire and Luton Community Foundation
The Bellahouston Bequest Fund
Bergqvist Charitable Trust
The Berkeley Charitable Foundation
The Bernadette Charitable Trust
The Bestway Foundation
The Mason Bibby 1981 Trust
The Big Lottery Fund
The Birmingham District Nursing Charitable Trust
The Sydney Black Charitable Trust
The BlackRock (UK) Charitable Trust
The Blagrave Trust
The Morgan Blake Charitable Trust
The Blanchminster Trust
The Blandford Lake Trust
The Bloom Foundation
The Bluston Charitable Settlement
The Boltini Trust
The Booth Charities
Boots Charitable Trust
Salo Bordon Charitable Trust
The Bothwell Charitable Trust
P. G. and N. J. Boulton Trust
The Bowerman Charitable Trust

The Liz and Terry Bramall Foundation
The Bramhope Trust
The Bridging Fund Charitable Trust
The Brighton District Nursing Association Trust
The Bristol Charities
The British Humane Association
The Bromley Trust
The David Brooke Charity
The Rory and Elizabeth Brooks Foundation
Bill Brown 1989 Charitable Trust
The Bruntwood Charity
Brushmill Ltd
Buckland Charitable Trust
The E. F. Bulmer Benevolent Fund
The Burden Trust
The Clara E. Burgess Charity
The Arnold Burton 1998 Charitable Trust
The Burton Breweries Charitable Trust
Consolidated Charity of Burton upon Trent
The Worshipful Company of Butchers General Charities
The Noel Buxton Trust
The James Caan Foundation
Edward Cadbury Charitable Trust
The G. W. Cadbury Charitable Trust
The William A. Cadbury Charitable Trust
The Barrow Cadbury Trust
The Edward and Dorothy Cadbury Trust
CAFOD (Catholic Agency for Overseas Development)
Calleva Foundation
Calouste Gulbenkian Foundation – UK Branch
The Calpe Trust
The Cambridgeshire Community Foundation
The Campden Charities Trustee
The Carr-Gregory Trust
The Leslie Mary Carter Charitable Trust
Carter's Educational Foundation
The Casey Trust
The Cattanach Charitable Trust
The Wilfrid and Constance Cave Foundation
The Cayo Foundation
Celtic Charity Fund
The Amelia Chadwick Trust
The Chapman Charitable Trust

## Social welfare

John William Chapman's Charitable Trust
Charitworth Limited
The Charter 600 Charity
The Cheruby Trust
Cheshire Freemason's Charity
The Chipping Sodbury Town Lands Charity
CHK Charities Limited
The Chownes Foundation
Christadelphian Samaritan Fund
Chrysalis Trust
Church Urban Fund
The City Bridge Trust
Stephen Clark 1957 Charitable Trust
Clark Bradbury Charitable Trust
The Roger and Sarah Bancroft Clark Charitable Trust
The Cleopatra Trust
Closehelm Limited
The Clothworkers' Foundation
Richard Cloudesley's Charity
The Clover Trust
The Robert Clutterbuck Charitable Trust
The Coalfields Regeneration Trust
The John Coates Charitable Trust
The Denise Cohen Charitable Trust
The Vivienne and Samuel Cohen Charitable Trust
The R. and S. Cohen Foundation
The Cole Charitable Trust
The Coltstaple Trust
Colyer-Fergusson Charitable Trust
Comic Relief
Community Foundation for Leeds
The Douglas Compton James Charitable Trust
The Congleton Inclosure Trust
The Consolidated Charities for the Infirm – Merchant Taylors' Company
The Cooks Charity
The Helen Jean Cope Trust
The J. Reginald Corah Foundation Fund
The Gershon Coren Charitable Foundation
Michael Cornish Charitable Trust
The Evan Cornish Foundation
Cornwall Community Foundation
The Duke of Cornwall's Benevolent Fund
The Corona Charitable Trust
The Cotton Trust

County Durham Community Foundation
Coutts Charitable Foundation
The Sir Tom Cowie Charitable Trust
The Lord Cozens-Hardy Trust
The Craps Charitable Trust
Michael Crawford Children's Charity
The Crerar Hotels Trust
Criffel Charitable Trust
The Violet and Milo Cripps Charitable Trust
The Croydon Relief in Need Charities
Cruden Foundation Ltd
The Ronald Cruickshanks Foundation
Cullum Family Trust
Cumbria Community Foundation
D. J. H. Currie Memorial Trust
The Cwmbran Trust
Itzchok Meyer Cymerman Trust Ltd
Oizer Dalim Trust
Baron Davenport's Charity
The Davidson Family Charitable Trust
The Hamilton Davies Trust
The Davis Foundation
The De Brye Charitable Trust
Peter De Haan Charitable Trust
Debenhams Foundation
The Debmar Benevolent Trust
The Denman Charitable Trust
Derbyshire Community Foundation
The J. N. Derbyshire Trust
The Desmond Foundation
The Sandy Dewhirst Charitable Trust
The Dibden Allotments Fund
Disability Aid Fund (The Roger and Jean Jefcoate Trust)
Dischma Charitable Trust
The Djanogly Foundation
The DM Charitable Trust
The Derek and Eileen Dodgson Foundation
Dorset Community Foundation
The Dorus Trust
The Double 'O' Charity Ltd
R. M. Douglas Charitable Trust
The Drapers' Charitable Fund
The Royal Foundation of the Duke and Duchess of Cambridge and Prince Harry
The Dulverton Trust
The Dumbreck Charity
The W. E. Dunn Trust
The James Dyson Foundation
The Eagle Charity Trust
East End Community Foundation

Eastern Counties Educational Trust Limited
The Ebenezer Trust
The EBM Charitable Trust
The Gilbert and Eileen Edgar Foundation
The Gilbert Edgar Trust
Edge Fund
Edinburgh & Lothian Trust Fund
Edinburgh Children's Holiday Fund
Edinburgh Trust No 2 Account
Edupoor Limited
Dr Edwards Bishop King's Fulham Endowment Fund
The W. G. Edwards Charitable Foundation
The George Elias Charitable Trust
The Gerald Palmer Eling Trust Company
The Maud Elkington Charitable Trust
The Ellerdale Trust
The John Ellerman Foundation
The Edith Maud Ellis 1985 Charitable Trust
The Elmgrant Trust
The Emerton-Christie Charity
Engage Foundation
The Englefield Charitable Trust
The Enkalon Foundation
The Epigoni Trust
The Eranda Foundation
The Ericson Trust
The Ernest Hecht Charitable Foundation
Esh Foundation
Essex Community Foundation
Euro Charity Trust
Sir John Evelyn's Charity
The Eventhall Family Charitable Trust
The Eveson Charitable Trust
The Exilarch's Foundation
The Expat Foundation
Extonglen Limited
Esmée Fairbairn Foundation
The Fairway Trust
Famos Foundation Trust
The Lord Faringdon Charitable Trust
Samuel William Farmer's Trust
The Fassnidge Memorial Trust
The February Foundation
Federation of Jewish Relief Organisations
The George Fentham Birmingham Charity
Elizabeth Ferguson Charitable Trust Fund
The Doris Field Charitable Trust
Field Family Charitable Trust
Filey Foundation Ltd

**125**

Dixie Rose Findlay Charitable Trust
Fisherbeck Charitable Trust
The Fishmongers' Company's Charitable Trust
The Fitton Trust
The Ian Fleming Charitable Trust
Florence's Charitable Trust
The Football Association National Sports Centre Trust
The Forbes Charitable Foundation
Ford Britain Trust
The Oliver Ford Charitable Trust
The Forest Hill Charitable Trust
The Lady Forester Trust
Forever Manchester (The Community Foundation for Greater Manchester)
The Forman Hardy Charitable Trust
The Donald Forrester Trust
The Fort Foundation
The Jill Franklin Trust
The Gordon Fraser Charitable Trust
The Hugh Fraser Foundation
The Joseph Strong Frazer Trust
The Freemasons' Grand Charity
The Freshgate Trust Foundation
Friends of Boyan Trust
The Patrick & Helena Frost Foundation
The Fuserna Foundation General Charitable Trust
The G. D. Charitable Trust
Gamlen Charitable Trust
The Gamma Trust
The Gannochy Trust
The Ganzoni Charitable Trust
Garthgwynion Charities
The Gatsby Charitable Foundation
The Nigel Gee Foundation
The Generations Foundation
The Steven Gerrard Foundation
The David Gibbons Foundation
The Gibbs Charitable Trust
Simon Gibson Charitable Trust
The Girdlers' Company Charitable Trust
The B. and P. Glasser Charitable Trust
The Sydney and Phyllis Goldberg Memorial Charitable Trust
The Goldman Sachs Charitable Gift Fund (UK)
Goldman Sachs Gives (UK)
The Goldsmiths' Company Charity

The Goodman Foundation
The Mike Gooley Trailfinders Charity
The Gosling Foundation Limited
Grand Charitable Trust of the Order of Women Freemasons
Grantham Yorke Trust
The Gordon Gray Trust
The Kenneth & Susan Green Charitable Foundation
The Green Hall Foundation
The Greggs Foundation
The Bishop of Guildford's Foundation
The Guildry Incorporation of Perth
The Gur Trust
Dr Guthrie's Association
The H. and M. Charitable Trust
H. C. D. Memorial Fund
The Hackney Parochial Charities
The Hadfield Trust
The Hadley Trust
The Hadrian Trust
The Alfred Haines Charitable Trust
E. F. and M. G. Hall Charitable Trust
Hampshire and Isle of Wight Community Foundation
The Hampstead Wells and Campden Trust
Hampton Fuel Allotment
The W. A. Handley Charitable Trust
The Kathleen Hannay Memorial Charity
The Haramead Trust
Miss K. M. Harbinson's Charitable Trust
Harbo Charities Limited
The Harborne Parish Lands Charity
The Harbour Charitable Trust
The Harbour Foundation
William Harding's Charity
The Hargrave Foundation
The Harpur Trust
The Harris Charity
The Edith Lilian Harrison 2000 Foundation
The Peter Harrison Foundation
The Alfred And Peggy Harvey Charitable Trust
The Hasluck Charitable Trust
The Dorothy Hay-Bolton Charitable Trust
The Charles Hayward Foundation
The Headley Trust
May Hearnshaw Charitable Trust

Heart of England Community Foundation
The Heathcoat Trust
The Charlotte Heber-Percy Charitable Trust
Hedley Foundation Limited
The H. J. Heinz Company Limited Charitable Trust
The Helping Foundation
The Hemby Charitable Trust
The Christina Mary Hendrie Trust for Scottish and Canadian Charities
Henley Educational Trust
Philip Sydney Henman Deceased Will Trust
The G. D. Herbert Charitable Trust
The Hertfordshire Community Foundation
The Hesslewood Children's Trust (Hull Seamen's and General Orphanage)
P. and C. Hickinbotham Charitable Trust
The Alan Edward Higgs Charity
The Hilden Charitable Fund
The Hillingdon Community Trust
The Lady Hind Trust
The Hinduja Foundation
The Hiscox Foundation
The Henry C. Hoare Charitable Trust
The Hobson Charity Limited
The J. G. Hogg Charitable Trust
The Dorothy Holmes Charitable Trust
P. H. Holt Foundation
The Holywood Trust
The Homelands Charitable Trust
The Homestead Charitable Trust
Sir Harold Hood's Charitable Trust
The Hoover Foundation
Hope for Youth (NI)
The Hope Trust
Hopmarket Charity
The Horizon Foundation
The Antony Hornby Charitable Trust
The Horne Foundation
The Thomas J. Horne Memorial Trust
The Hornsey Parochial Charities
The Hospital of God at Greatham
The Reta Lila Howard Foundation
James T. Howat Charitable Trust
The Hudson Foundation

*Fields of interest and type of beneficiary*  **Social welfare**

The Huggard Charitable Trust
The Hull and East Riding Charitable Trust
Human Relief Foundation
The Humanitarian Trust
The Michael and Shirley Hunt Charitable Trust
The Albert Hunt Trust
Miss Agnes H. Hunter's Trust
Huntingdon Freemen's Trust
The Nani Huyu Charitable Trust
Hyde Charitable Trust (Youth Plus)
Ibrahim Foundation Ltd
Impetus – The Private Equity Foundation
Incommunities Foundation
The Inman Charity
Inner London Magistrates Court's Poor Box and Feeder Charity
The Innocent Foundation
The Inverforth Charitable Trust
Investream Charitable Trust
The Ireland Fund of Great Britain
Irish Youth Foundation (UK) Ltd
The Charles Irving Charitable Trust
The J. Isaacs Charitable Trust
The Isle of Anglesey Charitable Trust
The ITF Seafarers Trust
The J. & J. Benevolent Foundation
The Jabbs Foundation
The Ruth and Lionel Jacobson Trust (Second Fund) No 2
Jaffe Family Relief Fund
John James Bristol Foundation
The Jarman Charitable Trust
Jeffrey Charitable Trust
Rees Jeffreys Road Fund
The Jenour Foundation
Jewish Child's Day
Lillie Johnson Charitable Trust
The Johnson Foundation
The Johnnie Johnson Trust
The Johnson Wax Ltd Charitable Trust
The Jones 1986 Charitable Trust
The Cyril and Eve Jumbo Charitable Trust
Anton Jurgens Charitable Trust
The Kass Charitable Trust
The Michael and Ilse Katz Foundation
The Kelly Family Charitable Trust
Kelsick's Educational Foundation
William Kendall's Charity (Wax Chandlers' Company)
Kent Community Foundation

The Nancy Kenyon Charitable Trust
The Peter Kershaw Trust
The Kingsbury Charity
The Mary Kinross Charitable Trust
Kirkley Poor's Land Estate
Kirschel Foundation
The Ernest Kleinwort Charitable Trust
The Sir James Knott Trust
Kollel and Co. Limited
The KPMG Foundation
The Kreditor Charitable Trust
The Kreitman Foundation
The Neil Kreitman Foundation
The Heinz, Anna and Carol Kroch Foundation
The Kyte Charitable Trust
Ladbrokes in the Community Charitable Trust
John Laing Charitable Trust
Maurice and Hilda Laing Charitable Trust
Christopher Laing Foundation
The David Laing Foundation
The Beatrice Laing Trust
The Lambert Charitable Trust
Community Foundation for Lancashire (Former)
Community Foundations for Lancashire and Merseyside
Lancashire Environmental Fund Limited
Duchy of Lancaster Benevolent Fund
Lancaster Foundation
LandAid Charitable Trust
The Allen Lane Foundation
Langdale Trust
Langley Charitable Trust
The Langtree Trust
The LankellyChase Foundation
The R. J. Larg Family Charitable Trust
The Lark Trust
Laslett's (Hinton) Charity
The Lauffer Family Charitable Foundation
Mrs F. B. Laurence Charitable Trust
The Kathleen Laurence Trust
The Edgar E. Lawley Foundation
The Herd Lawson and Muriel Lawson Charitable Trust
Lawson Beckman Charitable Trust
The Raymond and Blanche Lawson Charitable Trust
The William Leech Charity
Leeds Building Society Charitable Foundation
The Kennedy Leigh Charitable Trust
The Leigh Trust

The Lennox and Wyfold Foundation
The Mark Leonard Trust
The Leverhulme Trade Charities Trust
Lord Leverhulme's Charitable Trust
Joseph Levy Charitable Foundation
David and Ruth Lewis Family Charitable Trust
John Lewis Partnership General Community Fund
Liberum Foundation
The Limbourne Trust
The Linbury Trust
The Lind Trust
Lindenleaf Charitable Trust
The Enid Linder Foundation
The Lister Charitable Trust
The Charles Littlewood Hill Trust
The Second Joseph Aaron Littman Foundation
Jack Livingstone Charitable Trust
The Elaine and Angus Lloyd Charitable Trust
Lloyd's Charities Trust
Lloyds Bank Foundation for England and Wales
Lloyds Bank Foundation for Northern Ireland
Lloyds Bank Foundation for the Channel Islands
Lloyds TSB Foundation for Scotland
The Trust for London
London Catalyst
The London Community Foundation
London Housing Foundation Ltd
The London Marathon Charitable Trust Limited
The Lord's Taverners
The Loseley and Guildway Charitable Trust
The Lotus Foundation
The C. L. Loyd Charitable Trust
The Marie Helen Luen Charitable Trust
The Henry Lumley Charitable Trust
Paul Lunn-Rockliffe Charitable Trust
The Lynn Foundation
John Lyon's Charity
The Lyons Charitable Trust
Sylvanus Lysons Charity
M. and C. Trust
The Madeline Mabey Trust
The E. M. MacAndrew Trust
The R. S. Macdonald Charitable Trust

**127**

The Macdonald-Buchanan Charitable Trust
The Mackintosh Foundation
The MacRobert Trust
The Mactaggart Third Fund
The Ian Mactaggart Trust
The Magdalen and Lasher Charity
The Magen Charitable Trust
The Brian Maguire Charitable Trust
The Mahavir Trust
Malbin Trust
Man Group plc Charitable Trust
Manchester Airport Community Trust Fund
The Manchester Guardian Society Charitable Trust
Lord Mayor of Manchester's Charity Appeal Trust
The Manifold Charitable Trust
R. W. Mann Trust
The Manoukian Charitable Foundation
Maranatha Christian Trust
Marbeh Torah Trust
The Stella and Alexander Margulies Charitable Trust
Mariapolis Limited
Market Harborough and The Bowdens Charity
The Ann and David Marks Foundation
The Hilda and Samuel Marks Foundation
The Marr-Munning Trust
The Michael Marsh Charitable Trust
The Marsh Christian Trust
Charlotte Marshall Charitable Trust
Sir George Martin Trust
John Martin's Charity
The Nancie Massey Charitable Trust
The Matliwala Family Charitable Trust
The Violet Mauray Charitable Trust
The Robert McAlpine Foundation
The Medlock Charitable Trust
Melodor Limited
The Melow Charitable Trust
The Mercers' Charitable Foundation
Merchant Navy Welfare Board
The Merchant Taylors' Company Charities Fund
The Merchant Venturers' Charity
The Merchants' House of Glasgow

The Mersey Docks and Harbour Company Charitable Fund
The Tony Metherell Charitable Trust
The Metropolitan Masonic Charity
The Mickel Fund
The Mickleham Trust
The Gerald Micklem Charitable Trust
Middlesex Sports Foundation
Millennium Stadium Charitable Trust (Ymddiriedolaeth Elusennol Stadiwm y Mileniwm)
The Ronald Miller Foundation
The Millichope Foundation
The Mills Charity
The Millward Charitable Trust
Milton Keynes Community Foundation Limited
The Peter Minet Trust
The Laurence Misener Charitable Trust
The Mishcon Family Charitable Trust
Monmouthshire County Council Welsh Church Act Fund
The Monument Trust
The George A. Moore Foundation
John Moores Foundation
The Morel Charitable Trust
The Morgan Charitable Foundation
The Morgan Foundation
Morgan Stanley International Foundation
S. C. and M. E. Morland's Charitable Trust
The Morris Charitable Trust
G. M. Morrison Charitable Trust
Vyoel Moshe Charitable Trust
The Moss Family Charitable Trust
Mosselson Charitable Trust
Mothercare Group Foundation
Moto in the Community
J. P. Moulton Charitable Foundation
Mrs Waterhouse Charitable Trust
The Mugdock Children's Trust
The Edith Murphy Foundation
Murphy-Neumann Charity Company Limited
Muslim Hands
The Mutual Trust Group
MW (CL) Foundation
MW (GK) Foundation
MW (HO) Foundation
MW (RH) Foundation
MYA Charitable Trust

The Janet Nash Charitable Settlement
The National Express Foundation
The Nationwide Foundation
The Worshipful Company of Needlemakers' Charitable Fund
Nemoral Ltd
Ner Foundation
The New Appeals Organisation for the City and County of Nottingham
Newby Trust Limited
Newpier Charity Ltd
The NFU Mutual Charitable Trust
The Chevras Ezras Nitzrochim Trust
Nominet Charitable Foundation
The Noon Foundation
Norfolk Community Foundation
The Normanby Charitable Trust
The Northampton Municipal Church Charities
Northamptonshire Community Foundation
The Community Foundation for Northern Ireland
The Northern Rock Foundation
The Northmoor Trust
The Northumberland Village Homes Trust
The Norton Foundation
The Norton Rose Charitable Foundation
The Norwich Town Close Estate Charity
The Nottingham General Dispensary
Nottinghamshire Community Foundation
The Nuffield Foundation
The Father O'Mahoney Memorial Trust
The Oakdale Trust
The Oakley Charitable Trust
The Ofenheim Charitable Trust
Old Possum's Practical Trust
The Olga Charitable Trust
Open Gate
The O'Sullivan Family Charitable Trust
The Owen Family Trust
The Paget Charitable Trust
Eleanor Palmer Trust
The Panacea Charitable Trust
The Paphitis Charitable Trust
The Park Charitable Trust
The Park House Charitable Trust
Miss M. E. Swinton Paterson's Charitable Trust
The Harry Payne Fund
The Peacock Charitable Trust

*Fields of interest and type of beneficiary* — Social welfare

The Pears Family Charitable Foundation
The Pedmore Sporting Club Trust Fund
People's Postcode Trust
The Personal Assurance Charitable Trust
The Jack Petchey Foundation
The Phillips Charitable Trust
The Phillips Family Charitable Trust
The Bernard Piggott Charitable Trust
The Pilgrim Trust
The Elise Pilkington Charitable Trust
The Pilkington Charities Fund
The Austin and Hope Pilkington Trust
The Sir Harry Pilkington Trust Fund
Estate of the Late Colonel W. W. Pilkington Will Trusts – The General Charity Fund
The DLA Piper Charitable Trust
G. S. Plaut Charitable Trust Limited
The Pollywally Charitable Trust
The John Porter Charitable Trust
The Porter Foundation
Porticus UK
The Portishead Nautical Trust
The J. E. Posnansky Charitable Trust
The Mary Potter Convent Hospital Trust
The Praebendo Charitable Foundation
The Premier League Charitable Fund
Sir John Priestman Charity Trust
Princess Anne's Charities
The Puebla Charitable Trust
The Puri Foundation
The PwC Foundation
Mr and Mrs J. A. Pye's Charitable Settlement
Quartet Community Foundation
Queen Mary's Roehampton Trust
The Queen's Silver Jubilee Trust
Quothquan Trust
R. S. Charitable Trust
The Monica Rabagliati Charitable Trust
The Racing Foundation
The Rainford Trust
The Rank Foundation Limited
The Joseph Rank Trust
Ranworth Trust
The Rashbass Family Trust
The E. L. Rathbone Charitable Trust

The Eleanor Rathbone Charitable Trust
The Sigrid Rausing Trust
The Ravensdale Trust
The Rayne Foundation
The Rayne Trust
The Sir James Reckitt Charity
Eva Reckitt Trust Fund
The C. A. Redfern Charitable Foundation
The Reed Foundation
The Rest Harrow Trust
The Rhododendron Trust
The Rhondda Cynon Taff Welsh Church Acts Fund
The Sir Cliff Richard Charitable Trust
The Richmond Parish Lands Charity
Ridgesave Limited
The River Farm Foundation
Rivers Foundation
Rix-Thompson-Rothenberg Foundation
Thomas Roberts Trust
The Robertson Trust
Robyn Charitable Trust
The Roddick Foundation
The Sir James Roll Charitable Trust
Mrs L. D. Rope Third Charitable Settlement
The Rosca Trust
The Cecil Rosen Foundation
The Rothley Trust
The Roughley Charitable Trust
The Rowland Family Foundation
The Rowlands Trust
The Joseph Rowntree Foundation
Royal British Legion
Royal Docks Trust (London)
Royal Masonic Trust for Girls and Boys
Ryklow Charitable Trust 1992
The Michael Harry Sacher Trust
Erach and Roshan Sadri Foundation
The Saga Charitable Trust
Saint Sarkis Charity Trust
The Saintbury Trust
The Salamander Charitable Trust
The Andrew Salvesen Charitable Trust
Sam and Bella Sebba Charitable Trust
Coral Samuel Charitable Trust
The Basil Samuel Charitable Trust
The Peter Samuel Charitable Trust
The Sandhu Charitable Foundation

The Sandra Charitable Trust
Santander UK Foundation Limited
The Sants Charitable Trust
The Schreiber Charitable Trust
Schroder Charity Trust
Foundation Scotland
The Francis C. Scott Charitable Trust
The Frieda Scott Charitable Trust
The Sir James and Lady Scott Trust
Scottish Coal Industry Special Welfare Fund
The Scottish Power Energy People Trust
The Scottish Power Foundation
The Scouloudi Foundation
The SDL Foundation
Seafarers UK (King George's Fund for Sailors)
Leslie Sell Charitable Trust
Sellata Ltd
The Seneca Trust
The Shanley Charitable Trust
The Shears Foundation
The Sheffield and District Hospital Services Charitable Fund
The Sheldon Trust
The Sylvia and Colin Shepherd Charitable Trust
The Archie Sherman Cardiff Foundation
The Archie Sherman Charitable Trust
The Shetland Charitable Trust
The Bassil Shippam and Alsford Trust
The Shipwrights' Company Charitable Fund
The Shoe Zone Trust
The J. A. Shone Memorial Trust
The Barbara A. Shuttleworth Memorial Trust
The Mary Elizabeth Siebel Charity
David and Jennifer Sieff Charitable Trust
The Simmons & Simmons Charitable Foundation
Six Point Foundation
The Skelton Bounty
Skinners' Company Lady Neville Charity
The Slaughter and May Charitable Trust
The SMB Charitable Trust
The Mrs Smith and Mount Trust
The N. Smith Charitable Settlement
The Henry Smith Charity
Philip Smith's Charitable Trust

The R. C. Snelling Charitable Trust
The Sobell Foundation
Social Business Trust (Scale-Up)
Sodexo Foundation
The Solo Charitable Settlement
Songdale Ltd
The E. C. Sosnow Charitable Trust
The Souter Charitable Trust
The South Square Trust
The W. F. Southall Trust
R. H. Southern Trust
Spar Charitable Fund
Sparquote Limited
Spears-Stutz Charitable Trust
The Spielman Charitable Trust
Rosalyn and Nicholas Springer Charitable Trust
The St Hilda's Trust
St James's Place Foundation
The St Laurence Relief In Need Trust
St Michael's and All Saints' Charities Relief Branch
St Monica Trust
The Stanley Foundation Ltd
The Peter Stebbings Memorial Charity
The Steel Charitable Trust
Stevenson Family's Charitable Trust
The Stewarts Law Foundation
The Leonard Laity Stoate Charitable Trust
M. J. C. Stone Charitable Trust
The Stone Family Foundation
Stratford upon Avon Town Trust
The W. O. Street Charitable Foundation
Sueberry Ltd
Suffolk Community Foundation
The Alan Sugar Foundation
Community Foundation for Surrey
The Sussex Community Foundation
The Sutasoma Trust
Sutton Coldfield Charitable Trust
Swan Mountain Trust
The Swann-Morton Foundation
The John Swire (1989) Charitable Trust
The Swire Charitable Trust
The Tajtelbaum Charitable Trust
The Gay and Keith Talbot Trust
The Lady Tangye Charitable Trust
The David Tannen Charitable Trust
The Tanner Trust

C. B. and H. H. Taylor 1984 Trust
The Connie and Albert Taylor Charitable Trust
The Taylor Family Foundation
The Tedworth Charitable Trust
Tesco Charity Trust
The C. Paul Thackray General Charitable Trust
The Len Thomson Charitable Trust
The Sue Thomson Foundation
The Sir Jules Thorn Charitable Trust
The Tisbury Telegraph Trust
The Tobacco Pipe Makers and Tobacco Trade Benevolent Fund
The Tolkien Trust
Tomchei Torah Charitable Trust
The Tompkins Foundation
Toras Chesed (London) Trust
The Tory Family Foundation
The Towry Law Charitable Trust
The Toy Trust
Annie Tranmer Charitable Trust
The Trefoil Trust
The Triangle Trust (1949) Fund
The True Colours Trust
Truemart Limited
Trumros Limited
The James Tudor Foundation
Tudor Rose Ltd
The Tudor Trust
The Douglas Turner Trust
TVML Foundation
Two Ridings Community Foundation
Community Foundation Serving Tyne and Wear and Northumberland
Trustees of Tzedakah
UIA Charitable Foundation
Ulster Garden Villages Ltd
The Underwood Trust
Uxbridge United Welfare Trust
The Valentine Charitable Trust
The Valiant Charitable Trust
The Albert Van Den Bergh Charitable Trust
The Van Neste Foundation
The Vardy Foundation
The Variety Club Children's Charity
The William and Patricia Venton Charitable Trust
Roger Vere Foundation
Victoria Homes Trust
Virgin Atlantic Foundation
The Vodafone Foundation
Volant Charitable Trust
Voluntary Action Fund
Wade's Charity
The Wakefield and Tetley Trust
Wakeham Trust

The Community Foundation in Wales
Wales Council for Voluntary Action
The Ward Blenkinsop Trust
The Barbara Ward Children's Foundation
The Waterloo Foundation
Wates Family Enterprise Trust
The Wates Foundation
Blyth Watson Charitable Trust
John Watson's Trust
The Weavers' Company Benevolent Fund
The Weinstein Foundation
The James Weir Foundation
The Wessex Youth Trust
The West Derby Wastelands Charity
The Westcroft Trust
The Westminster Foundation
The Garfield Weston Foundation
The Melanie White Foundation Limited
White Stuff Foundation
The Lionel Wigram Memorial Trust
The Felicity Wilde Charitable Trust
The Will Charitable Trust
The William Barrow's Charity
The Charity of William Williams
Williams Serendipity Trust
The HDH Wills 1965 Charitable Trust
David Wilson Foundation
The Wilson Foundation
J. and J. R. Wilson Trust
The Community Foundation for Wiltshire and Swindon
The Francis Winham Foundation
The James Wise Charitable Trust
The Michael and Anna Wix Charitable Trust
The Wixamtree Trust
The Maurice Wohl Charitable Foundation
The Charles Wolfson Charitable Trust
The Wolfson Foundation
The Wood Family Trust
Woodlands Green Ltd
Woodroffe Benton Foundation
The Woodward Charitable Trust
Worcester Municipal Charities
The Wragge and Co Charitable Trust
The Diana Edgson Wright Charitable Trust
The Matthews Wrightson Charity Trust
The Wyseliot Charitable Trust

*Fields of interest and type of beneficiary* — **Community care services**

The Yapp Charitable Trust
The Yardley Great Trust
Yorkshire and Clydesdale Bank Foundation
Yorkshire Building Society Charitable Foundation
The South Yorkshire Community Foundation
The Yorkshire Dales Millennium Trust
The William Allen Young Charitable Trust
Youth United Foundation
Zephyr Charitable Trust
The Marjorie and Arnold Ziff Charitable Foundation
The Zochonis Charitable Trust
Zurich Community Trust (UK) Limited

## Community care services

The 1989 Willan Charitable Trust
Age Scotland
Age UK
The Archer Trust
The Artemis Charitable Trust
The Astor Foundation
The Avon and Somerset Police Community Trust
The Barcapel Foundation
Barchester Healthcare Foundation
The Barnwood House Trust
BBC Children in Need
The Bernadette Charitable Trust
The Birmingham District Nursing Charitable Trust
The David Brooke Charity
The Rory and Elizabeth Brooks Foundation
The Burton Breweries Charitable Trust
The Noel Buxton Trust
The Barrow Cadbury Trust
Calouste Gulbenkian Foundation – UK Branch
Carter's Educational Foundation
The Casey Trust
The Cayo Foundation
D. J. H. Currie Memorial Trust
Baron Davenport's Charity
The Hamilton Davies Trust
Disability Aid Fund (The Roger and Jean Jefcoate Trust)
The Dulverton Trust
The Dumbreck Charity
The Gilbert Edgar Trust
Edinburgh Children's Holiday Fund
The Eveson Charitable Trust

Esmée Fairbairn Foundation
The Fairway Trust
Samuel William Farmer's Trust
The Fassnidge Memorial Trust
The February Foundation
Elizabeth Ferguson Charitable Trust Fund
Field Family Charitable Trust
The Forbes Charitable Foundation
The Oliver Ford Charitable Trust
The Jill Franklin Trust
The Gordon Fraser Charitable Trust
The Freshgate Trust Foundation
The Ganzoni Charitable Trust
The Gatsby Charitable Foundation
The Girdlers' Company Charitable Trust
The Gosling Foundation Limited
The Gordon Gray Trust
The Green Hall Foundation
Dr Guthrie's Association
The Hadrian Trust
The Alfred Haines Charitable Trust
The W. A. Handley Charitable Trust
The Harbour Charitable Trust
The Harris Charity
The Edith Lilian Harrison 2000 Foundation
The Peter Harrison Foundation
The Alfred And Peggy Harvey Charitable Trust
The Dorothy Hay-Bolton Charitable Trust
The Charles Hayward Foundation
Heart of England Community Foundation
Hedley Foundation Limited
The H. J. Heinz Company Limited Charitable Trust
The Hemby Charitable Trust
The Christina Mary Hendrie Trust for Scottish and Canadian Charities
Henley Educational Trust
Philip Sydney Henman Deceased Will Trust
The Hesslewood Children's Trust (Hull Seamen's and General Orphanage)
The Hillingdon Community Trust
The Hiscox Foundation
The Henry C. Hoare Charitable Trust
The Holywood Trust
Hope for Youth (NI)
Hopmarket Charity

The Horizon Foundation
The Thomas J. Horne Memorial Trust
The Hornsey Parochial Charities
The Reta Lila Howard Foundation
The Hudson Foundation
The Huggard Charitable Trust
The Hull and East Riding Charitable Trust
Miss Agnes H. Hunter's Trust
Huntingdon Freemen's Trust
Hyde Charitable Trust (Youth Plus)
Irish Youth Foundation (UK) Ltd
The J. Isaacs Charitable Trust
The Isle of Anglesey Charitable Trust
The Ruth and Lionel Jacobson Trust (Second Fund) No 2
John James Bristol Foundation
Jeffrey Charitable Trust
Jewish Child's Day
Lillie Johnson Charitable Trust
The Johnnie Johnson Trust
The Jones 1986 Charitable Trust
The Kelly Family Charitable Trust
Kelsick's Educational Foundation
The Mary Kinross Charitable Trust
Kirschel Foundation
The KPMG Foundation
John Laing Charitable Trust
Community Foundations for Lancashire and Merseyside
Duchy of Lancaster Benevolent Fund
Lancaster Foundation
LandAid Charitable Trust
The Allen Lane Foundation
The Langtree Trust
The Lark Trust
The Lauffer Family Charitable Foundation
The Edgar E. Lawley Foundation
The Herd Lawson and Muriel Lawson Charitable Trust
The Mark Leonard Trust
Lord Leverhulme's Charitable Trust
The Lind Trust
The Lister Charitable Trust
Lloyds Bank Foundation for Northern Ireland
Lloyds Bank Foundation for the Channel Islands
London Catalyst
The Lord's Taverners
The Lotus Foundation
John Lyon's Charity

131

The Lyons Charitable Trust
The R. S. Macdonald Charitable Trust
The Mackintosh Foundation
The MacRobert Trust
The Mahavir Trust
Mariapolis Limited
Sir George Martin Trust
The Nancie Massey Charitable Trust
The Violet Mauray Charitable Trust
The Merchants' House of Glasgow
The Gerald Micklem Charitable Trust
Middlesex Sports Foundation
The Millichope Foundation
Monmouthshire County Council Welsh Church Act Fund
The Monument Trust
John Moores Foundation
The Mugdock Children's Trust
The National Express Foundation
The Northern Rock Foundation
The Nottingham General Dispensary
The Nuffield Foundation
The Paget Charitable Trust
The Paphitis Charitable Trust
Miss M. E. Swinton Paterson's Charitable Trust
The Pears Family Charitable Foundation
The Jack Petchey Foundation
The Bernard Piggott Charitable Trust
The Pilgrim Trust
G. S. Plaut Charitable Trust Limited
The Portishead Nautical Trust
The Mary Potter Convent Hospital Trust
Mr and Mrs J. A. Pye's Charitable Settlement
The Monica Rabagliati Charitable Trust
The Rank Foundation Limited
The Rayne Foundation
The Reed Foundation
The Rhondda Cynon Taff Welsh Church Acts Fund
The Richmond Parish Lands Charity
Rix-Thompson-Rothenberg Foundation
The Robertson Trust
Mrs L. D. Rope Third Charitable Settlement
The Rothley Trust
The Roughley Charitable Trust
The Rowlands Trust
Royal British Legion
Ryklow Charitable Trust 1992

The Michael Harry Sacher Trust
The Saintbury Trust
The Andrew Salvesen Charitable Trust
The Sandra Charitable Trust
The Francis C. Scott Charitable Trust
The Scottish Power Energy People Trust
Seafarers UK (King George's Fund for Sailors)
Leslie Sell Charitable Trust
The Shears Foundation
The Sheldon Trust
The Shipwrights' Company Charitable Fund
The Mary Elizabeth Siebel Charity
David and Jennifer Sieff Charitable Trust
St Monica Trust
The Tajtelbaum Charitable Trust
The Connie and Albert Taylor Charitable Trust
The Taylor Family Foundation
The Tedworth Charitable Trust
The True Colours Trust
The William and Patricia Venton Charitable Trust
Victoria Homes Trust
Wade's Charity
Wakeham Trust
John Watson's Trust
The Weavers' Company Benevolent Fund
The Westcroft Trust
The Felicity Wilde Charitable Trust
The Will Charitable Trust
David Wilson Foundation
The Wilson Foundation
J. and J. R. Wilson Trust
The Francis Winham Foundation
Woodroffe Benton Foundation
The Marjorie and Arnold Ziff Charitable Foundation

## Services for and about children and young people

The 1989 Willan Charitable Trust
The Artemis Charitable Trust
The Barcapel Foundation
BBC Children in Need
The Bernadette Charitable Trust
The David Brooke Charity
The Burton Breweries Charitable Trust
The Noel Buxton Trust

Calouste Gulbenkian Foundation – UK Branch
Carter's Educational Foundation
The Casey Trust
The Cayo Foundation
Baron Davenport's Charity
The Dulverton Trust
The Dumbreck Charity
The Gilbert Edgar Trust
Edinburgh Children's Holiday Fund
The Eveson Charitable Trust
Esmée Fairbairn Foundation
The Fairway Trust
Samuel William Farmer's Trust
Elizabeth Ferguson Charitable Trust Fund
Field Family Charitable Trust
The Gordon Fraser Charitable Trust
The Freshgate Trust Foundation
The Ganzoni Charitable Trust
The Gatsby Charitable Foundation
The Girdlers' Company Charitable Trust
The Gosling Foundation Limited
The Green Hall Foundation
Dr Guthrie's Association
The Alfred Haines Charitable Trust
The Harbour Charitable Trust
The Harris Charity
The Edith Lilian Harrison 2000 Foundation
The Peter Harrison Foundation
The Alfred And Peggy Harvey Charitable Trust
Hedley Foundation Limited
The H. J. Heinz Company Limited Charitable Trust
The Christina Mary Hendrie Trust for Scottish and Canadian Charities
Henley Educational Trust
Philip Sydney Henman Deceased Will Trust
The Hesslewood Children's Trust (Hull Seamen's and General Orphanage)
The Henry C. Hoare Charitable Trust
The Holywood Trust
Hope for Youth (NI)
The Reta Lila Howard Foundation
Miss Agnes H. Hunter's Trust
Hyde Charitable Trust (Youth Plus)
Irish Youth Foundation (UK) Ltd
The Ruth and Lionel Jacobson Trust (Second Fund) No 2

Jeffrey Charitable Trust
Jewish Child's Day (JCD)
Lillie Johnson Charitable Trust
The Johnnie Johnson Trust
The Kelly Family Charitable Trust
Kelsick's Educational Foundation
The Mary Kinross Charitable Trust
The KPMG Foundation
John Laing Charitable Trust
Lancaster Foundation
LandAid Charitable Trust
The Langtree Trust
The Lauffer Family Charitable Foundation
The Mark Leonard Trust
Lord Leverhulme's Charitable Trust
The Lind Trust
The Lister Charitable Trust
The Lord's Taverners
John Lyon's Charity
The Lyons Charitable Trust
The R. S. Macdonald Charitable Trust
The MacRobert Trust
Mariapolis Limited
Sir George Martin Trust
The Nancie Massey Charitable Trust
The Violet Mauray Charitable Trust
The Merchants' House of Glasgow
Middlesex Sports Foundation
The Monument Trust
The Mugdock Children's Trust
The National Express Foundation
The Northern Rock Foundation
The Nuffield Foundation
The Paget Charitable Trust
The Paphitis Charitable Trust
The Pears Family Charitable Foundation
The Jack Petchey Foundation
The Bernard Piggott Charitable Trust
The Portishead Nautical Trust
Mr and Mrs J. A. Pye's Charitable Settlement
The Monica Rabagliati Charitable Trust
The Rank Foundation Limited
The Rhondda Cynon Taff Welsh Church Acts Fund
The Richmond Parish Lands Charity
The Rothley Trust
Royal British Legion
Ryklow Charitable Trust 1992
The Andrew Salvesen Charitable Trust
The Sandra Charitable Trust

The Francis C. Scott Charitable Trust
Seafarers UK (King George's Fund for Sailors)
Leslie Sell Charitable Trust
The Shears Foundation
The Shipwrights' Company Charitable Fund
The Connie and Albert Taylor Charitable Trust
The Taylor Family Foundation
The Tedworth Charitable Trust
Victoria Homes Trust
Wade's Charity
John Watson's Trust
The Weavers' Company Benevolent Fund
The Felicity Wilde Charitable Trust
David Wilson Foundation
The Wilson Foundation

## Services for and about older people

Age Scotland
Age UK
Barchester Healthcare Foundation
The Birmingham District Nursing Charitable Trust
D. J. H. Currie Memorial Trust
Baron Davenport's Charity
Disability Aid Fund (The Roger and Jean Jefcoate Trust)
The Dumbreck Charity
The Eveson Charitable Trust
Samuel William Farmer's Trust
The Fassnidge Memorial Trust
Field Family Charitable Trust
The Girdlers' Company Charitable Trust
The Green Hall Foundation
The Alfred Haines Charitable Trust
The Edith Lilian Harrison 2000 Foundation
The Alfred And Peggy Harvey Charitable Trust
The Charles Hayward Foundation
The Christina Mary Hendrie Trust for Scottish and Canadian Charities
The Hiscox Foundation
The Henry C. Hoare Charitable Trust
The Hudson Foundation
The Ruth and Lionel Jacobson Trust (Second Fund) No 2
John James Bristol Foundation
The Herd Lawson and Muriel Lawson Charitable Trust
Mariapolis Limited
Sir George Martin Trust

The Nancie Massey Charitable Trust
The Merchants' House of Glasgow
G. S. Plaut Charitable Trust Limited
The Rowlands Trust
The Andrew Salvesen Charitable Trust
Seafarers UK (King George's Fund for Sailors)
The Mary Elizabeth Siebel Charity
The Tajtelbaum Charitable Trust
The Connie and Albert Taylor Charitable Trust
The William and Patricia Venton Charitable Trust
J. and J. R. Wilson Trust
The Francis Winham Foundation
Woodroffe Benton Foundation

## Services for and about vulnerable people/people who are ill

The 1989 Willan Charitable Trust
The Archer Trust
The Artemis Charitable Trust
Barchester Healthcare Foundation
The Barnwood House Trust
The Birmingham District Nursing Charitable Trust
The Dumbreck Charity
Samuel William Farmer's Trust
The Forbes Charitable Foundation
The Oliver Ford Charitable Trust
The Jill Franklin Trust
The Freshgate Trust Foundation
The Girdlers' Company Charitable Trust
The Green Hall Foundation
The Hadrian Trust
The Alfred And Peggy Harvey Charitable Trust
The Thomas J. Horne Memorial Trust
Huntingdon Freemen's Trust
Irish Youth Foundation (UK) Ltd
The Ruth and Lionel Jacobson Trust (Second Fund) No 2
Jeffrey Charitable Trust
John Laing Charitable Trust
The Allen Lane Foundation
The Lark Trust
John Lyon's Charity

133

The Mugdock Children's Trust
The Nottingham General Dispensary
G. S. Plaut Charitable Trust Limited
The Portishead Nautical Trust
The Mary Potter Convent Hospital Trust
The Rothley Trust
The Rowlands Trust
The Andrew Salvesen Charitable Trust
The Connie and Albert Taylor Charitable Trust
The True Colours Trust
The Westcroft Trust
The Will Charitable Trust
Woodroffe Benton Foundation

## Services for carers

The Astor Foundation
The Eveson Charitable Trust
The Girdlers' Company Charitable Trust
Hedley Foundation Limited
The Ruth and Lionel Jacobson Trust (Second Fund) No 2
The Northern Rock Foundation
Rix-Thompson-Rothenberg Foundation
The Will Charitable Trust

## Services for victims of crime

The Girdlers' Company Charitable Trust

## Services for women

The Barrow Cadbury Trust
The Northern Rock Foundation
The Reed Foundation

## Activities and relationships between generations

BBC Children in Need
The Kelly Family Charitable Trust
Mariapolis Limited

## Community centres and activities

Barchester Healthcare Foundation
The Barnwood House Trust
BBC Children in Need
The J. & J. Benevolent Foundation
The Barrow Cadbury Trust
The Hamilton Davies Trust
Disability Aid Fund (The Roger and Jean Jefcoate Trust)
Eastern Counties Educational Trust Limited
The Gilbert Edgar Trust
Dr Edwards Bishop King's Fulham Endowment Fund
Samuel William Farmer's Trust
The George Fentham Birmingham Charity
Field Family Charitable Trust
The Football Association National Sports Centre Trust
The Gannochy Trust
The Mike Gooley Trailfinders Charity
The Alfred Haines Charitable Trust
The W. A. Handley Charitable Trust
Hedley Foundation Limited
The Hemby Charitable Trust
The Hillingdon Community Trust
P. H. Holt Foundation
The Holywood Trust
The Horne Foundation
The Hornsey Parochial Charities
James T. Howat Charitable Trust
Hyde Charitable Trust (Youth Plus)
The Innocent Foundation
The J. Isaacs Charitable Trust
The Isle of Anglesey Charitable Trust
Rees Jeffreys Road Fund
Jewish Child's Day
The Jones 1986 Charitable Trust
Community Foundations for Lancashire and Merseyside
Lancashire Environmental Fund Limited
Duchy of Lancaster Benevolent Fund
The Edgar E. Lawley Foundation
Lord Leverhulme's Charitable Trust
Jack Livingstone Charitable Trust

Lloyds Bank Foundation for Northern Ireland
Lloyds Bank Foundation for the Channel Islands
London Catalyst
The London Marathon Charitable Trust Limited
The Lord's Taverners
John Lyon's Charity
The Mackintosh Foundation
The Michael Marsh Charitable Trust
John Martin's Charity
The Gerald Micklem Charitable Trust
Middlesex Sports Foundation
Monmouthshire County Council Welsh Church Act Fund
John Moores Foundation
Mothercare Group Foundation
The Northern Rock Foundation
The Owen Family Trust
The Pilgrim Trust
The Rhododendron Trust
The Richmond Parish Lands Charity
The Robertson Trust
The Sir James Roll Charitable Trust
The Rothley Trust
The Roughley Charitable Trust
Royal Docks Trust (London)
The Saintbury Trust
Foundation Scotland
The Frieda Scott Charitable Trust
The Sheldon Trust
The Archie Sherman Cardiff Foundation
Skinners' Company Lady Neville Charity
Wade's Charity
Wakeham Trust
The Westcroft Trust
The Wilson Foundation
The Yorkshire Dales Millennium Trust

## Community and social centres

The Gilbert Edgar Trust
Samuel William Farmer's Trust
The Horne Foundation
James T. Howat Charitable Trust
Hyde Charitable Trust (Youth Plus)
The J. Isaacs Charitable Trust
Lancashire Environmental Fund Limited
Duchy of Lancaster Benevolent Fund
John Lyon's Charity

*Fields of interest and type of beneficiary*  **Relief assistance**

The Gerald Micklem Charitable Trust
Monmouthshire County Council Welsh Church Act Fund
John Moores Foundation
The Northern Rock Foundation
The Owen Family Trust
The Rhododendron Trust
Wakeham Trust

### Community organisations

The Barrow Cadbury Trust
Disability Aid Fund (The Roger and Jean Jefcoate Trust)
The Holywood Trust
James T. Howat Charitable Trust
Hyde Charitable Trust (Youth Plus)
The Innocent Foundation
The J. & J. Benevolent Foundation
Lancashire Environmental Fund Limited
Duchy of Lancaster Benevolent Fund
Jack Livingstone Charitable Trust
The London Marathon Charitable Trust Limited
John Moores Foundation
The Rothley Trust
Foundation Scotland
Skinners' Company Lady Neville Charity
Wakeham Trust

### Community outings and holidays

The Alfred Haines Charitable Trust
Hedley Foundation Limited
The Holywood Trust
Middlesex Sports Foundation
Wakeham Trust

### Community transport

Rees Jeffreys Road Fund
The Lord's Taverners

### Emergency response

Bergqvist Charitable Trust
The Blandford Lake Trust
The Boltini Trust

P. G. and N. J. Boulton Trust
Christadelphian Samaritan Fund
Clark Bradbury Charitable Trust
The Robert Clutterbuck Charitable Trust
The Dulverton Trust
Edinburgh Trust No 2 Account
The Gibbs Charitable Trust
The Gosling Foundation Limited
The Alfred Haines Charitable Trust
The W. A. Handley Charitable Trust
Miss K. M. Harbinson's Charitable Trust
The Hiscox Foundation
The Hobson Charity Limited
The Thomas J. Horne Memorial Trust
The Inverforth Charitable Trust
Mrs F. B. Laurence Charitable Trust
The William Leech Charity
The Lennox and Wyfold Foundation
The Charles Littlewood Hill Trust
Lloyds Bank Foundation for Northern Ireland
The Loseley and Guildway Charitable Trust
The Madeline Mabey Trust
The MacRobert Trust
The Mahavir Trust
Man Group plc Charitable Trust
The Marr-Munning Trust
The Laurence Misener Charitable Trust
Monmouthshire County Council Welsh Church Act Fund
The George A. Moore Foundation
John Moores Foundation
The Father O'Mahoney Memorial Trust
The Phillips Charitable Trust
Queen Mary's Roehampton Trust
The Sigrid Rausing Trust
The Rhododendron Trust
The Robertson Trust
The Sir James Roll Charitable Trust
The Rothley Trust
The Rowlands Trust
Royal British Legion
The SMB Charitable Trust
Stevenson Family's Charitable Trust
The Gay and Keith Talbot Trust
The Lady Tangye Charitable Trust

The Tisbury Telegraph Trust
Roger Vere Foundation
The Westcroft Trust
Woodroffe Benton Foundation

### Armed forces

The Robert Clutterbuck Charitable Trust
Edinburgh Trust No 2 Account
The Gosling Foundation Limited
The W. A. Handley Charitable Trust
The Hiscox Foundation
The Hobson Charity Limited
The Inverforth Charitable Trust
Mrs F. B. Laurence Charitable Trust
The William Leech Charity
The Charles Littlewood Hill Trust
Queen Mary's Roehampton Trust
The Rowlands Trust

### Lifeboat service

Mrs F. B. Laurence Charitable Trust
The Phillips Charitable Trust

### Relief assistance

Bergqvist Charitable Trust
The Boltini Trust
P. G. and N. J. Boulton Trust
Christadelphian Samaritan Fund
The Dulverton Trust
The Gibbs Charitable Trust
The Alfred Haines Charitable Trust
The W. A. Handley Charitable Trust
Miss K. M. Harbinson's Charitable Trust
The Madeline Mabey Trust
The Mahavir Trust
The Marr-Munning Trust
John Moores Foundation
The Father O'Mahoney Memorial Trust
The Sigrid Rausing Trust
The Rhododendron Trust
The Rothley Trust
The SMB Charitable Trust
Stevenson Family's Charitable Trust
The Gay and Keith Talbot Trust
The Lady Tangye Charitable Trust
The Tisbury Telegraph Trust

**135**

Roger Vere Foundation
The Westcroft Trust

## Socially preventative schemes

The 1970 Trust
The Avon and Somerset Police Community Trust
BBC Children in Need
The Bowerman Charitable Trust
The Bromley Trust
The Noel Buxton Trust
The G. W. Cadbury Charitable Trust
The Barrow Cadbury Trust
The Cayo Foundation
The Evan Cornish Foundation
The Violet and Milo Cripps Charitable Trust
The Hamilton Davies Trust
The Ericson Trust
The Peter Harrison Foundation
The Charles Hayward Foundation
Heart of England Community Foundation
Hedley Foundation Limited
The Hemby Charitable Trust
The Henry C. Hoare Charitable Trust
Sir Harold Hood's Charitable Trust
The Hope Trust
The Michael and Shirley Hunt Charitable Trust
Hyde Charitable Trust (Youth Plus)
Impetus – The Private Equity Foundation
Irish Youth Foundation (UK) Ltd
The Jabbs Foundation
Jewish Child's Day
The Kelly Family Charitable Trust
The Mary Kinross Charitable Trust
The KPMG Foundation
Community Foundations for Lancashire and Merseyside
The Allen Lane Foundation
The Leigh Trust
The Mark Leonard Trust
Lloyds Bank Foundation for Northern Ireland
London Housing Foundation Ltd
The Lotus Foundation
John Lyon's Charity
Charlotte Marshall Charitable Trust

The Merchant Taylors' Company Charities Fund
The Monument Trust
Mothercare Group Foundation
The National Express Foundation
The Nuffield Foundation
The Oakdale Trust
The Pilgrim Trust
The Portishead Nautical Trust
The Robertson Trust
Saint Sarkis Charity Trust
The Saintbury Trust
Swan Mountain Trust
The Weavers' Company Benevolent Fund

## Crime prevention

The 1970 Trust
BBC Children in Need
The Bromley Trust
The Barrow Cadbury Trust
The Cayo Foundation
The Peter Harrison Foundation
The Charles Hayward Foundation
Heart of England Community Foundation
Hedley Foundation Limited
The Hemby Charitable Trust
The Henry C. Hoare Charitable Trust
Sir Harold Hood's Charitable Trust
The Michael and Shirley Hunt Charitable Trust
Hyde Charitable Trust (Youth Plus)
The Mary Kinross Charitable Trust
The KPMG Foundation
The Leigh Trust
The Mark Leonard Trust
Lloyds Bank Foundation for Northern Ireland
London Housing Foundation Ltd
John Lyon's Charity

## Family justice

BBC Children in Need
The Charles Hayward Foundation
Heart of England Community Foundation
John Lyon's Charity
The Nuffield Foundation

## Family planning

BBC Children in Need
The G. W. Cadbury Charitable Trust
John Lyon's Charity
The Monument Trust

## Prisons and penal reform

The Bowerman Charitable Trust
The Bromley Trust
The Noel Buxton Trust
The Barrow Cadbury Trust
The Evan Cornish Foundation
The Violet and Milo Cripps Charitable Trust
The Ericson Trust
The Charles Hayward Foundation
The Michael and Shirley Hunt Charitable Trust
The Mary Kinross Charitable Trust
The Allen Lane Foundation
The Leigh Trust
London Housing Foundation Ltd
The Monument Trust
The Oakdale Trust
Saint Sarkis Charity Trust
Swan Mountain Trust

## Substance abuse and education

The Hope Trust
The Michael and Shirley Hunt Charitable Trust
The Leigh Trust
The Lotus Foundation
Charlotte Marshall Charitable Trust
The Merchant Taylors' Company Charities Fund
The Portishead Nautical Trust
The Robertson Trust

## Beneficial groups

### Age

**■ Babies**

The 1989 Willan Charitable Trust
Children's Liver Disease Foundation
The G. D. Charitable Trust
Lifeline 4 Kids (Handicapped Children's Aid Committee)
The Edwina Mountbatten & Leonora Children's Foundation (formerly The Edwina Mounbatten Trust)
The Francis C. Scott Charitable Trust

**■ Children and young people**

The 1989 Willan Charitable Trust
The Aberbrothock Skea Trust
Aberdeen Asset Management Charitable Foundation
Access Sport
The ACT Foundation
The Adamson Trust
The Adint Charitable Trust
The Al Fayed Charitable Foundation
Aldgate and All Hallows' Foundation
Alliance Trust Staff Foundation
Angus Allnatt Charitable Foundation
The Pat Allsop Charitable Trust
Viscount Amory's Charitable Trust
The AMW Charitable Trust
Anglo American Group Foundation
Anguish's Educational Foundation
The Armourers' and Brasiers' Gauntlet Trust
A. J. H. Ashby Will Trust
The Associated Country Women of the World
The Astor Foundation
The Astor of Hever Trust
The Lord Austin Trust
Autonomous Research Charitable Trust
The Scott Bader Commonwealth Limited
The Balfour Beatty Charitable Trust
The Albert Casanova Ballard Deceased Trust
The Ballinger Charitable Trust
The Balmore Trust

The Barbour Foundation
The Barcapel Foundation
The Barclay Foundation
The Baring Foundation
Barnes Workhouse Fund
The Louis Baylis (Maidenhead Advertiser) Charitable Trust
BBC Children in Need
The B-CH Charitable Trust
The John Beckwith Charitable Trust
Beefy's Charity Foundation
The Bellinger Donnay Trust
The Benfield Motors Charitable Trust
The Gerald Bentall Charitable Trust
Bergqvist Charitable Trust
The Berkeley Charitable Foundation
The Ruth Berkowitz Charitable Trust
Percy Bilton Charity
The Sydney Black Charitable Trust
The BlackRock (UK) Charitable Trust
The Blagrave Trust
The Bloom Foundation
The Nicholas Boas Charitable Trust
The Boltini Trust
BOOST Charitable Trust
The Bothwell Charitable Trust
The Bowland Charitable Trust
The Bramhope Trust
The Bransford Trust
The Breadsticks Foundation
The Brendish Family Foundation
Bridgepoint Charitable Trust
The British Dietetic Association General and Education Trust Fund
British Record Industry Trust
The Britten-Pears Foundation
The Bromley Trust
The Consuelo and Anthony Brooke Charitable Trust
The David Brooke Charity
The Charles Brotherton Trust
The Brownsword Charitable Foundation
The Bruntwood Charity
The Buffini Chao Foundation
The Clara E. Burgess Charity
The Burghley Family Trust
The Burton Breweries Charitable Trust
The Noel Buxton Trust
The James Caan Foundation
The William A. Cadbury Charitable Trust
The Barrow Cadbury Trust
Calleva Foundation

Calouste Gulbenkian Foundation – UK Branch
The H. and L. Cantor Trust
Carter's Educational Foundation
The Casey Trust
Cash for Kids – Radio Clyde
The Cattanach Charitable Trust
The Joseph and Annie Cattle Trust
The Cayo Foundation
The CBD Charitable Trust
Celtic Charity Fund
The Worshipful Company of Chartered Accountants General Charitable Trust (also known as CALC)
Chaucer Foundation
Cheshire Freemason's Charity
The Chetwode Foundation
Children's Liver Disease Foundation
The Children's Research Fund
The Church Burgesses Educational Foundation
Church Urban Fund
The CIBC World Markets Children's Miracle Foundation
The City Bridge Trust
The Cleopatra Trust
The Clore Duffield Foundation
The Clothworkers' Foundation
The Clover Trust
The Robert Clutterbuck Charitable Trust
The John Coates Charitable Trust
The Vivienne and Samuel Cohen Charitable Trust
John Coldman Charitable Trust
John and Freda Coleman Charitable Trust
The Bernard Coleman Trust
Colyer-Fergusson Charitable Trust
Comic Relief
The Comino Foundation
The Douglas Compton James Charitable Trust
Gordon Cook Foundation
The Ernest Cook Trust
The Cooks Charity
The Catherine Cookson Charitable Trust
The J. Reginald Corah Foundation Fund
The Gershon Coren Charitable Foundation
Michael Cornish Charitable Trust
The Evan Cornish Foundation
The Duke of Cornwall's Benevolent Fund
The Corona Charitable Trust
The Cotton Trust

137

Dudley and Geoffrey Cox Charitable Trust
The Craps Charitable Trust
Michael Crawford Children's Charity
The Crerar Hotels Trust
Criffel Charitable Trust
The Cross Trust
The Peter Cruddas Foundation
Cullum Family Trust
The Cumber Family Charitable Trust
Cumbria Community Foundation
D. J. H. Currie Memorial Trust
Roald Dahl's Marvellous Children's Charity
Daily Prayer Union Charitable Trust Limited
Oizer Dalim Trust
Baron Davenport's Charity
The Hamilton Davies Trust
The Davis Foundation
The De Brye Charitable Trust
Peter De Haan Charitable Trust
William Dean Countryside and Educational Trust
The Desmond Foundation
The Sandy Dewhirst Charitable Trust
The Dibden Allotments Fund
Dischma Charitable Trust
The Djanogly Foundation
Dorset Community Foundation
The Dorus Trust
Douglas Arter Foundation
The Drapers' Charitable Fund
Dromintee Trust
The Duis Charitable Trust
The Royal Foundation of the Duke and Duchess of Cambridge and Prince Harry
The Dulverton Trust
The Dumbreck Charity
The Charles Dunstone Charitable Trust
The Dyers' Company Charitable Trust
Earls Colne and Halstead Educational Charity
Eastern Counties Educational Trust Limited
The Sir John Eastwood Foundation
The Ebenezer Trust
The EBM Charitable Trust
The Economist Charitable Trust
The Gilbert and Eileen Edgar Foundation
The Gilbert Edgar Trust
Edinburgh Children's Holiday Fund
Edinburgh Trust No 2 Account

Educational Foundation of Alderman John Norman
Dr Edwards Bishop King's Fulham Endowment Fund
The Wilfred and Elsie Elkes Charity Fund
The Maud Elkington Charitable Trust
The Ellerdale Trust
The Ellis Campbell Foundation
EMI Music Sound Foundation
The Englefield Charitable Trust
The English Schools' Football Association
The Epigoni Trust
The Ernest Hecht Charitable Foundation
The Erskine Cunningham Hill Trust
Esh Foundation
The Essex Youth Trust
Joseph Ettedgui Charitable Foundation
Sir John Evelyn's Charity
The Eventhall Family Charitable Trust
The Eveson Charitable Trust
The Exilarch's Foundation
The Expat Foundation
Esmée Fairbairn Foundation
The Fairway Trust
Samuel William Farmer's Trust
The George Fentham Birmingham Charity
The A. M. Fenton Trust
The Allan and Nesta Ferguson Charitable Settlement
Elizabeth Ferguson Charitable Trust Fund
The Doris Field Charitable Trust
Field Family Charitable Trust
Dixie Rose Findlay Charitable Trust
The Joyce Fletcher Charitable Trust
The Football Association National Sports Centre Trust
Ford Britain Trust
The Lady Forester Trust
The Donald Forrester Trust
The Fort Foundation
The Forte Charitable Trust
The Gordon Fraser Charitable Trust
The Hugh Fraser Foundation
The Joseph Strong Frazer Trust
The Louis and Valerie Freedman Charitable Settlement
The Freemasons' Grand Charity
The Friarsgate Trust
Friends of Wiznitz Limited
The Frognal Trust

The Patrick & Helena Frost Foundation
Mejer and Gertrude Miriam Frydman Foundation
The Fuserna Foundation General Charitable Trust
The Gale Family Charity Trust
Gamlen Charitable Trust
The Gannochy Trust
The Garrick Charitable Trust
The Gatsby Charitable Foundation
Gatwick Airport Community Trust
The Robert Gavron Charitable Trust
Sir Robert Geffery's Almshouse Trust
The Generations Foundation
The Steven Gerrard Foundation
Get Kids Going
Simon Gibson Charitable Trust
The G. C. Gibson Charitable Trust
The Girdlers' Company Charitable Trust
Global Care
Global Charities
The GNC Trust
The Golf Foundation Limited
The Mike Gooley Trailfinders Charity
The Gosling Foundation Limited
Grand Charitable Trust of the Order of Women Freemasons
Grantham Yorke Trust
The Gordon Gray Trust
The Green Hall Foundation
Greenham Common Community Trust Limited
The Greggs Foundation
The Grimmitt Trust
The Grocers' Charity
The Bishop of Guildford's Foundation
The Gur Trust
Dr Guthrie's Association
The H. and M. Charitable Trust
The Hackney Parochial Charities
The Hadfield Trust
The Hadrian Trust
E. F. and M. G. Hall Charitable Trust
The Helen Hamlyn Trust
Sue Hammerson Charitable Trust
Hampton Fuel Allotment
The W. A. Handley Charitable Trust
The Kathleen Hannay Memorial Charity
The Doughty Hanson Charitable Foundation

Children and young people

The Haramead Trust
Harbo Charities Limited
The Harbour Charitable Trust
The Harbour Foundation
William Harding's Charity
The Hare of Steep Charitable Trust (HOST)
The Harebell Centenary Fund
The Harris Charity
The Harris Family Charitable Trust
The Edith Lilian Harrison 2000 Foundation
The Peter Harrison Foundation
The Hartley Charitable Trust
The Alfred And Peggy Harvey Charitable Trust
Edward Harvist Trust (The Harvist Estate)
The Hasluck Charitable Trust
The Hathaway Trust
The M. A. Hawe Settlement
The Hawthorne Charitable Trust
The Dorothy Hay-Bolton Charitable Trust
The Headley Trust
The Health Foundation
May Hearnshaw Charitable Trust
Heart of England Community Foundation
The Heathcoat Trust
The Charlotte Heber-Percy Charitable Trust
The Percy Hedley 1990 Charitable Trust
Hedley Foundation Limited
The Helping Foundation
The Hemby Charitable Trust
The Christina Mary Hendrie Trust for Scottish and Canadian Charities
Henley Educational Trust
Philip Sydney Henman Deceased Will Trust
The G. D. Herbert Charitable Trust
Herefordshire Community Foundation
Hesed Trust
The Hesslewood Children's Trust (Hull Seamen's and General Orphanage)
P. and C. Hickinbotham Charitable Trust
The Alan Edward Higgs Charity
The Hilden Charitable Fund
The Derek Hill Foundation
The Hillingdon Partnership Trust
R. G. Hills Charitable Trust
Hinchley Charitable Trust
The Lady Hind Trust
The Hiscox Foundation
Hitchin Educational Foundation

The Hobson Charity Limited
The Sir Julian Hodge Charitable Trust
The Jane Hodge Foundation
The Holden Charitable Trust
The Hollick Family Charitable Trust
The Holliday Foundation
The Dorothy Holmes Charitable Trust
The Holywood Trust
The Homelands Charitable Trust
The Homestead Charitable Trust
The Mary Homfray Charitable Trust
Sir Harold Hood's Charitable Trust
Hope for Youth (NI)
Hopmarket Charity
The Horizon Foundation
The Horne Foundation
The Thomas J. Horne Memorial Trust
The Hornsey Parochial Charities
Hospice UK
House of Industry Estate
The Reta Lila Howard Foundation
The Huggard Charitable Trust
The Hull and East Riding Charitable Trust
Hulme Trust Estates (Educational)
The Humanitarian Trust
The Albert Hunt Trust
The Hunter Foundation
Miss Agnes H. Hunter's Trust
The Huntingdon Foundation Limited
Huntingdon Freemen's Trust
Hurdale Charity Limited
Hyde Charitable Trust (Youth Plus)
Ibrahim Foundation Ltd
The Idlewild Trust
The Iliffe Family Charitable Trust
Impetus – The Private Equity Foundation (Impetus – PEF)
Incommunities Foundation
The Ingram Trust
Inner London Magistrates Court's Poor Box and Feeder Charity
The International Bankers Charitable Trust
The Inverforth Charitable Trust (ICT)
Investream Charitable Trust
The Ireland Fund of Great Britain

Irish Youth Foundation (UK) Ltd (incorporating The Lawlor Foundation)
The Ironmongers' Foundation
The Charles Irving Charitable Trust
The J. Isaacs Charitable Trust
The J. & J. Charitable Trust
The J. J. Charitable Trust
C. Richard Jackson Charitable Trust
The Jacobs Charitable Trust
The Ruth and Lionel Jacobson Trust (Second Fund) No 2
John James Bristol Foundation
The James Trust
The Jarman Charitable Trust
John Jarrold Trust
Jay Education Trust
Jeffrey Charitable Trust
Nick Jenkins Foundation
The Jenour Foundation
The Jephcott Charitable Trust
Jewish Child's Day (JCD)
The Jewish Youth Fund (JYF)
Lillie Johnson Charitable Trust
The Johnson Foundation
The Johnnie Johnson Trust
The Johnson Wax Ltd Charitable Trust
The Joicey Trust
The Jones 1986 Charitable Trust
The Dezna Robins Jones Charitable Foundation
The Marjorie and Geoffrey Jones Charitable Trust
The Joron Charitable Trust
The J. E. Joseph Charitable Fund
The Josephs Family Charitable Trust
The Cyril and Eve Jumbo Charitable Trust
Anton Jurgens Charitable Trust
The Bernard Kahn Charitable Trust
The Kass Charitable Trust (KCT)
The Michael and Ilse Katz Foundation
C. S. Kaufman Charitable Trust
The Kelly Family Charitable Trust
Kelsick's Educational Foundation
John Thomas Kennedy Charitable Foundation
The Nancy Kenyon Charitable Trust
The Peter Kershaw Trust
The Ursula Keyes Trust
The Robert Kiln Charitable Trust

**139**

The Mary Kinross Charitable Trust
Kirkley Poor's Land Estate
The Richard Kirkman Trust
Robert Kitchin (Saddlers' Company)
The Ernest Kleinwort Charitable Trust
The Sir James Knott Trust
The Kobler Trust
The KPMG Foundation
The Kreditor Charitable Trust
The Heinz, Anna and Carol Kroch Foundation (HACKF)
Ladbrokes in the Community Charitable Trust
The K. P. Ladd Charitable Trust
John Laing Charitable Trust
Maurice and Hilda Laing Charitable Trust
Christopher Laing Foundation
The David Laing Foundation
The Kirby Laing Foundation
The Martin Laing Foundation
The Beatrice Laing Trust
The Lambert Charitable Trust
Community Foundations for Lancashire and Merseyside
Duchy of Lancaster Benevolent Fund
Lancaster Foundation
LandAid Charitable Trust
The Jack Lane Charitable Trust
Langdale Trust
Langley Charitable Trust
The Langtree Trust
The R. J. Larg Family Charitable Trust
Laslett's (Hinton) Charity
The Lauffer Family Charitable Foundation
Mrs F. B. Laurence Charitable Trust
The Kathleen Laurence Trust
The Edgar E. Lawley Foundation
The Raymond and Blanche Lawson Charitable Trust
The Leach Fourteenth Trust
The David Lean Foundation
The Leathersellers' Company Charitable Fund
Leeds Building Society Charitable Foundation
Leicestershire, Leicester and Rutland Community Foundation
The Leigh Trust
P. Leigh-Bramwell Trust 'E'
The Mark Leonard Trust
The Leverhulme Trade Charities Trust
Lord Leverhulme's Charitable Trust

Joseph Levy Charitable Foundation
David and Ruth Lewis Family Charitable Trust
The John Spedan Lewis Foundation
John Lewis Partnership General Community Fund
The Lewis Ward Trust
Liberum Foundation
Lifeline 4 Kids
The Limbourne Trust
Limoges Charitable Trust
The Lind Trust
Lindale Educational Foundation
The Linden Charitable Trust
Lindenleaf Charitable Trust
The Enid Linder Foundation
The Lister Charitable Trust
The Frank Litchfield Charitable Trust
The Charles Littlewood Hill Trust
The Second Joseph Aaron Littman Foundation
The George John and Sheilah Livanos Charitable Trust
Jack Livingstone Charitable Trust
The Elaine and Angus Lloyd Charitable Trust
Lloyd's Charities Trust
Lloyds Bank Foundation for England and Wales
Lloyds Bank Foundation for Northern Ireland
Lloyds TSB Foundation for Scotland
Localtrent Ltd
The Locker Foundation
Loftus Charitable Trust
The Lolev Charitable Trust
London Catalyst
The London Law Trust
The William and Katherine Longman Trust
The Lord's Taverners
The Loseley and Guildway Charitable Trust
The Lotus Foundation
The Lower Green Foundation
The C. L. Loyd Charitable Trust
The Henry Lumley Charitable Trust
Paul Lunn-Rockliffe Charitable Trust
C. F. Lunoe Trust Fund
The Ruth and Jack Lunzer Charitable Trust
Lord and Lady Lurgan Trust
The Lynn Foundation
John Lyon's Charity
The Lyons Charitable Trust
The Sir Jack Lyons Charitable Trust

Sylvanus Lysons Charity
M. and C. Trust
The M. K. Charitable Trust
The Madeline Mabey Trust
The R. S. Macdonald Charitable Trust
The Macdonald-Buchanan Charitable Trust
The Mackintosh Foundation
The MacRobert Trust
The Magdalen and Lasher Charity (General Fund)
The Magen Charitable Trust
The Mageni Trust
The Brian Maguire Charitable Trust
The Mahavir Trust
Malbin Trust
The Mallinckrodt Foundation
Man Group plc Charitable Trust
The Manackerman Charitable Trust
Manchester Airport Community Trust Fund
The Manchester Guardian Society Charitable Trust
The Manifold Charitable Trust
R. W. Mann Trust
The Manoukian Charitable Foundation
Maranatha Christian Trust
The Stella and Alexander Margulies Charitable Trust
Mariapolis Limited
The Marks Family Foundation
The Ann and David Marks Foundation
The Michael Marsh Charitable Trust
The Marsh Christian Trust
Charlotte Marshall Charitable Trust
D. G. Marshall of Cambridge Trust
The Marshgate Charitable Settlement
Sir George Martin Trust
John Martin's Charity
The Nancie Massey Charitable Trust
The Matliwala Family Charitable Trust
The Violet Mauray Charitable Trust
The Robert McAlpine Foundation
McGreevy No 5 Settlement
D. D. McPhail Charitable Settlement
Melodor Limited
Mercaz Torah Vechesed Limited
The Mercers' Charitable Foundation

The Merchant Taylors' Company Charities Fund
The Merlin Magic Wand Children's Charity
The Metropolitan Masonic Charity
T. & J. Meyer Family Foundation Limited
The Mickleham Trust
The Gerald Micklem Charitable Trust
Middlesex Sports Foundation
Millennium Stadium Charitable Trust (Ymddiriedolaeth Elusennol Stadiwm y Mileniwm)
The Millfield House Foundation (MHF)
The Millfield Trust
The Millichope Foundation
The Mills Charity
The Millward Charitable Trust
The Edgar Milward Charity
The Peter Minet Trust
Minton Charitable Trust
The Mishcon Family Charitable Trust
The Misselbrook Trust
The MITIE Foundation
Keren Mitzvah Trust
Mobbs Memorial Trust Ltd
The Modiano Charitable Trust
Mole Charitable Trust
Monmouthshire County Council Welsh Church Act Fund
The Montague Thompson Coon Charitable Trust
The Monument Trust
The Moonpig Foundation
The George A. Moore Foundation
John Moores Foundation
The Morgan Charitable Foundation
The Morgan Foundation
Morgan Stanley International Foundation
The Miles Morland Foundation
The Morris Charitable Trust
The Peter Morrison Charitable Foundation
G. M. Morrison Charitable Trust
Vyoel Moshe Charitable Trust
The Moss Family Charitable Trust
Mosselson Charitable Trust
Mothercare Group Foundation
Moto in the Community
The Edwina Mountbatten & Leonora Children's Foundation
The Mugdock Children's Trust
The Mulberry Trust
The Edith Murphy Foundation

Murphy-Neumann Charity Company Limited
The Music Sales Charitable Trust
Muslim Hands
The National Express Foundation
The National Hockey Foundation
The Nazareth Trust Fund
The Newcomen Collett Foundation
The NFU Mutual Charitable Trust
Nominet Charitable Foundation
Norfolk Community Foundation
The Normanby Charitable Trust
Northamptonshire Community Foundation
The Northern Rock Foundation
The Northumberland Village Homes Trust
The Norton Foundation
The Norton Rose Charitable Foundation
The Notgrove Trust
Nottinghamshire Community Foundation
The Nuffield Foundation
The Oakley Charitable Trust
Oizer Charitable Trust
Old Possum's Practical Trust
The Olga Charitable Trust
Open Gate
The O'Sullivan Family Charitable Trust
The Paphitis Charitable Trust
Miss M. E. Swinton Paterson's Charitable Trust
Ambika Paul Foundation
The Harry Payne Fund
The Peacock Charitable Trust
The Susanna Peake Charitable Trust
The Pears Family Charitable Foundation
The Pedmore Sporting Club Trust Fund
The Persula Foundation
The Jack Petchey Foundation
The Phillips Charitable Trust
The Pilkington Charities Fund
The Austin and Hope Pilkington Trust
The Platinum Trust
G. S. Plaut Charitable Trust Limited
The Ponton House Trust
The Popocatepetl Trust
The Portishead Nautical Trust
The Praebendo Charitable Foundation
The Premier League Charitable Fund
The William Price Charitable Trust

Sir John Priestman Charity Trust
The Prince of Wales's Charitable Foundation
Princess Anne's Charities
The Puri Foundation
Mr and Mrs J. A. Pye's Charitable Settlement
The Queen's Silver Jubilee Trust
Quothquan Trust
The Monica Rabagliati Charitable Trust
The Ragdoll Foundation
The Rank Foundation Limited
The Joseph Rank Trust
The Rashbass Family Trust
The Ravensdale Trust
The Rayne Foundation
The Rayne Trust
The John Rayner Charitable Trust
The Sir James Reckitt Charity
Eva Reckitt Trust Fund
Red Hill Charitable Trust
The Reed Foundation
Richard Reeve's Foundation
The Rhondda Cynon Taff Welsh Church Acts Fund
The Clive Richards Charity
The Richmond Parish Lands Charity
The Robertson Trust
Robyn Charitable Trust
Mrs L. D. Rope Third Charitable Settlement
The Rosca Trust
The Rothley Trust
The Rowland Family Foundation
Royal Docks Trust (London)
Royal Masonic Trust for Girls and Boys
Ryklow Charitable Trust 1992
The Saga Charitable Trust
The Alan and Babette Sainsbury Charitable Fund
The Saintbury Trust
The Salamander Charitable Trust
The Andrew Salvesen Charitable Trust
Sam and Bella Sebba Charitable Trust
The Basil Samuel Charitable Trust
The Sandhu Charitable Foundation
The Sandra Charitable Trust
Santander UK Foundation Limited
The Sants Charitable Trust
Schroder Charity Trust
The Francis C. Scott Charitable Trust

# Children and young people

The Sir James and Lady Scott Trust
The Scouloudi Foundation
Leslie Sell Charitable Trust
The Seneca Trust
The Shears Foundation
The Patricia and Donald Shepherd Charitable Trust
The Sylvia and Colin Shepherd Charitable Trust
The R. C. Sherriff Rosebriars Trust
SHINE (Support and Help in Education)
The Bassil Shippam and Alsford Trust
The Shipwrights' Company Charitable Fund
The Shoe Zone Trust
The Barbara A. Shuttleworth Memorial Trust
David and Jennifer Sieff Charitable Trust
Skipton Building Society Charitable Foundation
The Slaughter and May Charitable Trust
Sloane Robinson Foundation
The Henry Smith Charity
The WH Smith Group Charitable Trust
Philip Smith's Charitable Trust
The R. C. Snelling Charitable Trust
The Sobell Foundation
Sodexo Foundation
The Solo Charitable Settlement
The E. C. Sosnow Charitable Trust
The South Square Trust
Southdown Trust
The Southover Manor General Education Trust
Spar Charitable Fund
Sparquote Limited
The Spero Foundation
The Spielman Charitable Trust
The Spoore, Merry and Rixman Foundation
The Spurrell Charitable Trust
The Geoff and Fiona Squire Foundation
St James's Trust Settlement
St James's Place Foundation
Sir Walter St John's Educational Charity
The St Laurence Relief In Need Trust
The Peter Stebbings Memorial Charity
The Steinberg Family Charitable Trust
C. E. K. Stern Charitable Trust
The Andy Stewart Charitable Foundation

Sir Halley Stewart Trust
The Leonard Laity Stoate Charitable Trust
The Edward Stocks-Massey Bequest Fund
The Stoller Charitable Trust
The Strawberry Charitable Trust
The W. O. Street Charitable Foundation
The Strowger Trust
The Sudborough Foundation
Sueberry Ltd
The Alan Sugar Foundation
The Bernard Sunley Charitable Foundation
The Swann-Morton Foundation
Sylvia Waddilove Foundation UK
The Charity of Stella Symons
The Talbot Trusts
The Lili Tapper Charitable Foundation
The Connie and Albert Taylor Charitable Trust
The Taylor Family Foundation
A. P. Taylor Trust
The Tedworth Charitable Trust
Tesco Charity Trust
The Thales Charitable Trust
The Sue Thomson Foundation
The Thornton Trust
The Thousandth Man- Richard Burns Charitable Trust
The Daniel Thwaites Charitable Trust
The Tolkien Trust
The Tompkins Foundation
Toras Chesed (London) Trust
The Tory Family Foundation
The Toy Trust
Toyota Manufacturing UK Charitable Trust
Annie Tranmer Charitable Trust
The Trefoil Trust
The Tresillian Trust
The True Colours Trust
Trumros Limited
The Douglas Turner Trust
TVML Foundation
Community Foundation Serving Tyne and Wear and Northumberland
The UNITE Foundation
The Valentine Charitable Trust
The Albert Van Den Bergh Charitable Trust
The Vardy Foundation
The Variety Club Children's Charity
Victoria Homes Trust
The William and Ellen Vinten Trust
The Vintners' Foundation
Virgin Atlantic Foundation
Volant Charitable Trust

Voluntary Action Fund (VAF)
Wade's Charity
Wales Council for Voluntary Action
Robert and Felicity Waley-Cohen Charitable Trust
Wallace and Gromit's Children's Foundation
The Barbara Ward Children's Foundation
The Waterloo Foundation
Wates Family Enterprise Trust
The Wates Foundation
John Watson's Trust
The Weavers' Company Benevolent Fund
The Welton Foundation
The Wessex Youth Trust
The West Derby Wastelands Charity
The Westminster Foundation
The Garfield Weston Foundation
The Barbara Whatmore Charitable Trust
White Stuff Foundation
The Felicity Wilde Charitable Trust
The William Barrow's Charity
The Charity of William Williams
Williams Serendipity Trust
The HDH Wills 1965 Charitable Trust
David Wilson Foundation
The Wilson Foundation
The Community Foundation for Wiltshire and Swindon
The Wixamtree Trust
The Maurice Wohl Charitable Foundation
The Charles Wolfson Charitable Trust
The Wolfson Family Charitable Trust
The Wood Family Trust
Wooden Spoon Society
The Woodward Charitable Trust
The Wragge and Co Charitable Trust
The Matthews Wrightson Charity Trust
The Yapp Charitable Trust
Yorkshire and Clydesdale Bank Foundation
Yorkshire Building Society Charitable Foundation
The John Kirkhope Young Endowment Fund
Youth Music
Youth United Foundation
The Marjorie and Arnold Ziff Charitable Foundation
The Zochonis Charitable Trust
Zurich Community Trust (UK) Limited

Fields of interest and type of beneficiary — Older people

## ■ Older people

The ACT Foundation
Age Scotland
Age UK
Sir John and Lady Amory's Charitable Trust
Viscount Amory's Charitable Trust
The AMW Charitable Trust
The Argus Appeal
The Lord Austin Trust
Autonomous Research Charitable Trust
The Baker Charitable Trust
The Ballinger Charitable Trust
The Balney Charitable Trust
The Barbour Foundation
Barchester Healthcare Foundation
The Barclay Foundation
The Baring Foundation
Barnes Workhouse Fund
The Louis Baylis (Maidenhead Advertiser) Charitable Trust
The Beaverbrook Foundation
The Bellinger Donnay Trust
The Benfield Motors Charitable Trust
The Gerald Bentall Charitable Trust
The Mason Bibby 1981 Trust
Percy Bilton Charity
Birmingham International Airport Community Trust
Miss Jeanne Bisgood's Charitable Trust
The BlackRock (UK) Charitable Trust
The Morgan Blake Charitable Trust
The Bothwell Charitable Trust
P. G. and N. J. Boulton Trust
The Bramhope Trust
The British Dietetic Association General and Education Trust Fund
The Britten-Pears Foundation
The Consuelo and Anthony Brooke Charitable Trust
The David Brooke Charity
The Charles Brotherton Trust
Miss Marion Broughton's Charitable Trust
The Brownsword Charitable Foundation
The Burghley Family Trust
The William A. Cadbury Charitable Trust
The H. and L. Cantor Trust
The Joseph and Annie Cattle Trust
The Worshipful Company of Chartered Accountants General Charitable Trust
CHK Charities Limited
The City Bridge Trust

The Cleopatra Trust
The Clore Duffield Foundation
The Clothworkers' Foundation
The Clover Trust
The Robert Clutterbuck Charitable Trust
The John Coates Charitable Trust
The Vivienne and Samuel Cohen Charitable Trust
Colyer-Fergusson Charitable Trust
Comic Relief
The Consolidated Charities for the Infirm – Merchant Taylors' Company
The Catherine Cookson Charitable Trust
The Marjorie Coote Old People's Charity
The Gershon Coren Charitable Foundation
The Evan Cornish Foundation
The Duke of Cornwall's Benevolent Fund
The Corona Charitable Trust
The Cotton Industry War Memorial Trust
The Cotton Trust
Dudley and Geoffrey Cox Charitable Trust
The Craps Charitable Trust
The Crerar Hotels Trust
Criffel Charitable Trust
The Cumber Family Charitable Trust
Cumbria Community Foundation
D. J. H. Currie Memorial Trust
Oizer Dalim Trust
Baron Davenport's Charity
The Davis Foundation
The De Brye Charitable Trust
William Dean Countryside and Educational Trust
The Desmond Foundation
The Sandy Dewhirst Charitable Trust
Dischma Charitable Trust
The Djanogly Foundation
The Derek and Eileen Dodgson Foundation
Dorset Community Foundation
The Dorus Trust
Douglas Arter Foundation
The Drapers' Charitable Fund
The Dulverton Trust
The Dumbreck Charity
The Dunhill Medical Trust
The Sir John Eastwood Foundation
The Ebenezer Trust
The Economist Charitable Trust
The Gilbert and Eileen Edgar Foundation

The W. G. Edwards Charitable Foundation
The Wilfred and Elsie Elkes Charity Fund
The Maud Elkington Charitable Trust
The Englefield Charitable Trust
The Epigoni Trust
The Ericson Trust
The Ernest Hecht Charitable Foundation
The Erskine Cunningham Hill Trust
Esh Foundation
Sir John Evelyn's Charity
The Eventhall Family Charitable Trust
The Eveson Charitable Trust
The Expat Foundation
Esmée Fairbairn Foundation
The Fairway Trust
The Lord Faringdon Charitable Trust
Samuel William Farmer's Trust
The Fassnidge Memorial Trust
The A. M. Fenton Trust
Field Family Charitable Trust
Dixie Rose Findlay Charitable Trust
The Football Association National Sports Centre Trust
The Lady Forester Trust
The Donald Forrester Trust
The Hugh Fraser Foundation
The Joseph Strong Frazer Trust
The Freemasons' Grand Charity
The Friarsgate Trust
The Frognal Trust
The Patrick & Helena Frost Foundation
The Fuserna Foundation General Charitable Trust
The G. D. Charitable Trust
The Gale Family Charity Trust
Gatwick Airport Community Trust
The David Gibbons Foundation
The Girdlers' Company Charitable Trust
The GNC Trust
The Gosling Foundation Limited
Grand Charitable Trust of the Order of Women Freemasons
The Gordon Gray Trust
The Green Hall Foundation
Greenham Common Community Trust Limited
The Greggs Foundation
The Grimmitt Trust
The Grocers' Charity
The Bishop of Guildford's Foundation

143

The Guildry Incorporation of
   Perth
The H. and M. Charitable Trust
The Hadfield Trust
The Hadrian Trust
The Alfred Haines Charitable
   Trust
E. F. and M. G. Hall Charitable
   Trust
The Helen Hamlyn Trust
Sue Hammerson Charitable
   Trust
Hampton Fuel Allotment
The W. A. Handley Charitable
   Trust
The Kathleen Hannay
   Memorial Charity
The Doughty Hanson
   Charitable Foundation
The Haramead Trust
Harbo Charities Limited
The Harbour Charitable Trust
The Harbour Foundation
William Harding's Charity
The Hare of Steep Charitable
   Trust (HOST)
The Harebell Centenary Fund
The Harris Family Charitable
   Trust
The Edith Lilian Harrison 2000
   Foundation
The Alfred And Peggy Harvey
   Charitable Trust
Edward Harvist Trust
The Hasluck Charitable Trust
The Hathaway Trust
The M. A. Hawe Settlement
The Dorothy Hay-Bolton
   Charitable Trust
The Charles Hayward
   Foundation
The Headley Trust
The Health Foundation
May Hearnshaw Charitable
   Trust
Heart of England Community
   Foundation
The Heathcoat Trust
The Charlotte Heber-Percy
   Charitable Trust
The Percy Hedley 1990
   Charitable Trust
The Helping Foundation
The Hemby Charitable Trust
The Christina Mary Hendrie
   Trust for Scottish and
   Canadian Charities
The G. D. Herbert Charitable
   Trust
Herefordshire Community
   Foundation
Hesed Trust
The Hillingdon Partnership
   Trust
R. G. Hills Charitable Trust
The Lady Hind Trust

The Hiscox Foundation
The Hobson Charity Limited
The Sir Julian Hodge
   Charitable Trust
The Jane Hodge Foundation
The Hollick Family Charitable
   Trust
The Dorothy Holmes Charitable
   Trust
The Edward Holt Trust
The Homestead Charitable
   Trust
The Mary Homfray Charitable
   Trust
Hopmarket Charity
The Thomas J. Horne
   Memorial Trust
The Hornsey Parochial
   Charities
Hospice UK
House of Industry Estate
The Hudson Foundation
The Huggard Charitable Trust
The Hull and East Riding
   Charitable Trust
The Albert Hunt Trust
Miss Agnes H. Hunter's Trust
Huntingdon Freemen's Trust
The Iliffe Family Charitable
   Trust
Incommunities Foundation
The Inman Charity
Investream Charitable Trust
The Ireland Fund of Great
   Britain
The Charles Irving Charitable
   Trust
The J. Isaacs Charitable Trust
The J. & J. Charitable Trust
C. Richard Jackson Charitable
   Trust
The Ruth and Lionel Jacobson
   Trust (Second Fund) No 2
John James Bristol Foundation
The Jarman Charitable Trust
John Jarrold Trust
The Jenour Foundation
The Johnson Foundation
The Johnson Wax Ltd
   Charitable Trust
The Joicey Trust
The Jones 1986 Charitable
   Trust
The Dezna Robins Jones
   Charitable Foundation
The Marjorie and Geoffrey
   Jones Charitable Trust
The Joron Charitable Trust
The J. E. Joseph Charitable
   Fund
The Cyril and Eve Jumbo
   Charitable Trust
Anton Jurgens Charitable Trust
The Bernard Kahn Charitable
   Trust

The Kass Charitable Trust
   (KCT)
The Michael and Ilse Katz
   Foundation
John Thomas Kennedy
   Charitable Foundation
The Peter Kershaw Trust
The Ursula Keyes Trust
Kirkley Poor's Land Estate
The Richard Kirkman Trust
Robert Kitchin (Saddlers'
   Company)
The Ernest Kleinwort
   Charitable Trust
The Sir James Knott Trust
The Kreditor Charitable Trust
The Heinz, Anna and Carol
   Kroch Foundation
Kupath Gemach Chaim
   Bechesed Viznitz Trust
Ladbrokes in the Community
   Charitable Trust
The K. P. Ladd Charitable
   Trust
John Laing Charitable Trust
Christopher Laing Foundation
The David Laing Foundation
The Kirby Laing Foundation
The Martin Laing Foundation
The Beatrice Laing Trust
The Lambert Charitable Trust
Duchy of Lancaster Benevolent
   Fund
The Jack Lane Charitable Trust
The Allen Lane Foundation
Langdale Trust
The R. J. Larg Family
   Charitable Trust
Laslett's (Hinton) Charity
Mrs F. B. Laurence Charitable
   Trust
The Kathleen Laurence Trust
The Edgar E. Lawley
   Foundation
The Herd Lawson and Muriel
   Lawson Charitable Trust
The Raymond and Blanche
   Lawson Charitable Trust
The Mason Le Page Charitable
   Trust
The Leach Fourteenth Trust
The Leathersellers' Company
   Charitable Fund
Leeds Building Society
   Charitable Foundation
Leicestershire, Leicester and
   Rutland Community
   Foundation
P. Leigh-Bramwell Trust 'E'
The Leverhulme Trade
   Charities Trust
Joseph Levy Charitable
   Foundation
David and Ruth Lewis Family
   Charitable Trust

144

*Fields of interest and type of beneficiary* — **Older people**

John Lewis Partnership General Community Fund
The Linden Charitable Trust
The Frank Litchfield Charitable Trust
The George John and Sheilah Livanos Charitable Trust
Jack Livingstone Charitable Trust
Lloyds Bank Foundation for England and Wales
Lloyds Bank Foundation for Northern Ireland
Lloyds TSB Foundation for Scotland
The Locker Foundation
Loftus Charitable Trust
The Lolev Charitable Trust
London Catalyst
The William and Katherine Longman Trust
The Lotus Foundation
Paul Lunn-Rockliffe Charitable Trust
C. F. Lunoe Trust Fund
Lord and Lady Lurgan Trust
The Lynn Foundation
M. and C. Trust
The Macdonald-Buchanan Charitable Trust
The Mackintosh Foundation
The Magdalen and Lasher Charity (General Fund)
The Mahavir Trust
Man Group plc Charitable Trust
The Manchester Guardian Society Charitable Trust
R. W. Mann Trust
The Stella and Alexander Margulies Charitable Trust
Mariapolis Limited
The Marks Family Foundation
The Ann and David Marks Foundation
The Michael Marsh Charitable Trust
The Marsh Christian Trust
Charlotte Marshall Charitable Trust
Sir George Martin Trust
John Martin's Charity
The Nancie Massey Charitable Trust
The Matliwala Family Charitable Trust
The Violet Mauray Charitable Trust
The Robert McAlpine Foundation
D. D. McPhail Charitable Settlement
Mercaz Torah Vechesed Limited
The Mercers' Charitable Foundation
The Merchant Taylors' Company Charities Fund
The Merchants' House of Glasgow
The Mersey Docks and Harbour Company Charitable Fund
The Tony Metherell Charitable Trust
The Metropolitan Masonic Charity
T. & J. Meyer Family Foundation Limited
The Mickleham Trust
The Gerald Micklem Charitable Trust
Millennium Stadium Charitable Trust (Ymddiriedolaeth Elusennol Stadiwm y Mileniwm)
The Millfield House Foundation (MHF)
The Millfield Trust
The Mills Charity
The Millward Charitable Trust
The Peter Minet Trust
The Mirianog Trust
The Mishcon Family Charitable Trust
The Misselbrook Trust
The MITIE Foundation
Keren Mitzvah Trust
Mobbs Memorial Trust Ltd
The Modiano Charitable Trust
Monmouthshire County Council Welsh Church Act Fund
The George A. Moore Foundation
The Morgan Charitable Foundation
The Morgan Foundation
The Morris Charitable Trust
G. M. Morrison Charitable Trust
Vyoel Moshe Charitable Trust
The Moss Family Charitable Trust
Mosselson Charitable Trust
The Mulberry Trust
The Edith Murphy Foundation
Murphy-Neumann Charity Company Limited
Muslim Hands
Nominet Charitable Foundation
Norfolk Community Foundation
The Normanby Charitable Trust
Northamptonshire Community Foundation
The Northern Rock Foundation
The Northwood Charitable Trust
The Notgrove Trust
Nottinghamshire Community Foundation
The Nuffield Foundation
The Oakley Charitable Trust
Oizer Charitable Trust
Miss M. E. Swinton Paterson's Charitable Trust
The Harry Payne Fund
The Susanna Peake Charitable Trust
The Pedmore Sporting Club Trust Fund
The Dowager Countess Eleanor Peel Trust
The Persula Foundation
The Phillips and Rubens Charitable Trust
The Elise Pilkington Charitable Trust
The Pilkington Charities Fund
The Austin and Hope Pilkington Trust
G. S. Plaut Charitable Trust Limited
Porticus UK
The Praebendo Charitable Foundation
Sir John Priestman Charity Trust
Quothquan Trust
The Rank Foundation Limited
The Joseph Rank Trust
The Rashbass Family Trust
The Ravensdale Trust
The Rayne Foundation
The Rayne Trust
The John Rayner Charitable Trust
The Sir James Reckitt Charity
The Violet M. Richards Charity
The Richmond Parish Lands Charity
The Robertson Trust
The Rosca Trust
The Cecil Rosen Foundation
Mrs Gladys Row Fogo Charitable Trust
The Rowland Family Foundation
The Rowlands Trust
The Saintbury Trust
The Salamander Charitable Trust
The Andrew Salvesen Charitable Trust
The Sandhu Charitable Foundation
Santander UK Foundation Limited
Schroder Charity Trust
The Sir James and Lady Scott Trust
The Scouloudi Foundation
The Sylvia and Colin Shepherd Charitable Trust
The R. C. Sherriff Rosebriars Trust
The Barnett and Sylvia Shine No 2 Charitable Trust
The Shoe Zone Trust

145

The Mary Elizabeth Siebel Charity
Six Point Foundation
Skipton Building Society Charitable Foundation
The Slaughter and May Charitable Trust
The Henry Smith Charity
The WH Smith Group Charitable Trust
Philip Smith's Charitable Trust
The R. C. Snelling Charitable Trust
The Sobell Foundation
Sodexo Foundation
The Solo Charitable Settlement
The Sovereign Health Care Charitable Trust
Sparquote Limited
The Spero Foundation
The Spielman Charitable Trust
The Spurrell Charitable Trust
The St Laurence Relief In Need Trust
St Monica Trust
The Stanley Foundation Ltd
The Peter Stebbings Memorial Charity
Sir Halley Stewart Trust
The Alan Sugar Foundation
The Bernard Sunley Charitable Foundation
Sylvia Waddilove Foundation UK
The Charity of Stella Symons
The Tajtelbaum Charitable Trust
The Talbot Trusts
The Lili Tapper Charitable Foundation
The Connie and Albert Taylor Charitable Trust
A. P. Taylor Trust
Tesco Charity Trust
The Thousandth Man- Richard Burns Charitable Trust
The Tolkien Trust
Toras Chesed (London) Trust
Annie Tranmer Charitable Trust
The Tresillian Trust
Trumros Limited
The Trusthouse Charitable Foundation
The Douglas Turner Trust
Community Foundation Serving Tyne and Wear and Northumberland
The Valiant Charitable Trust
The Albert Van Den Bergh Charitable Trust
The Van Neste Foundation
The William and Patricia Venton Charitable Trust
Voluntary Action Fund (VAF)
Wade's Charity

Wales Council for Voluntary Action
The Welton Foundation
The West Derby Wastelands Charity
The Westminster Foundation
The Garfield Weston Foundation
Williams Serendipity Trust
The HDH Wills 1965 Charitable Trust
J. and J. R. Wilson Trust
The Community Foundation for Wiltshire and Swindon
The Francis Winham Foundation
The James Wise Charitable Trust
The Michael and Anna Wix Charitable Trust
The Wixamtree Trust
The Maurice Wohl Charitable Foundation
The Charles Wolfson Charitable Trust
Woodroffe Benton Foundation
The Wragge and Co Charitable Trust
The Matthews Wrightson Charity Trust
The Wyseliot Charitable Trust
The Xerox (UK) Trust
The Yapp Charitable Trust
Yorkshire and Clydesdale Bank Foundation
Yorkshire Building Society Charitable Foundation
The Marjorie and Arnold Ziff Charitable Foundation
Zurich Community Trust (UK) Limited

## Class, group, occupation or former occupation

■ **Armed forces**

ABF The Soldiers' Charity
The Ammco Trust
The Armourers' and Brasiers' Gauntlet Trust
ASCB Charitable Fund
The Balney Charitable Trust
The Baltic Charitable Fund
The BlackRock (UK) Charitable Trust
Chaucer Foundation
The Robert Clutterbuck Charitable Trust
The Royal Foundation of the Duke and Duchess of Cambridge and Prince Harry
The Dulverton Trust
Edinburgh Trust No 2 Account

The Erskine Cunningham Hill Trust
The Donald Forrester Trust
The Fuserna Foundation General Charitable Trust
The Girdlers' Company Charitable Trust
The Mike Gooley Trailfinders Charity
The Gosling Foundation Limited
Sue Hammerson Charitable Trust
The W. A. Handley Charitable Trust
The Hawthorne Charitable Trust
The Charlotte Heber-Percy Charitable Trust
The Christina Mary Hendrie Trust for Scottish and Canadian Charities
The Hiscox Foundation
The Hobson Charity Limited
The Inman Charity
The Inverforth Charitable Trust (ICT)
The Michael and Ilse Katz Foundation
The Peter Kershaw Trust
The Richard Kirkman Trust
The Ernest Kleinwort Charitable Trust
The Sir James Knott Trust
The Beatrice Laing Trust
Duchy of Lancaster Benevolent Fund
Mrs F. B. Laurence Charitable Trust
The Raymond and Blanche Lawson Charitable Trust
John Lewis Partnership General Community Fund
The Charles Littlewood Hill Trust
The Henry Lumley Charitable Trust
Paul Lunn-Rockliffe Charitable Trust
The Macdonald-Buchanan Charitable Trust
The MacRobert Trust
The Laurence Misener Charitable Trust
The George A. Moore Foundation
The Peter Morrison Charitable Foundation
G. M. Morrison Charitable Trust
The Prince of Wales's Charitable Foundation
Princess Anne's Charities
Queen Mary's Roehampton Trust
The Rowlands Trust

146

Royal Artillery Charitable Fund
Royal British Legion
Seafarers UK (King George's Fund for Sailors)
The WH Smith Group Charitable Trust
Philip Smith's Charitable Trust
Sodexo Foundation
The Charity of Stella Symons
The Trefoil Trust
The Michael Uren Foundation
The Albert Van Den Bergh Charitable Trust
The Westminster Foundation

■ **Arts, culture, sports and recreation**

The Baring Foundation
BOOST Charitable Trust
The Bransford Trust
British Record Industry Trust
The Britten-Pears Foundation
The Richard Carne Trust
The Equity Trust Fund
Esmée Fairbairn Foundation
The Follett Trust
The Goldsmiths' Company Charity
Paul Hamlyn Foundation
The Derek Hill Foundation
The Hinrichsen Foundation
The Holst Foundation
The Horne Foundation
The Daniel Howard Trust
The Ironmongers' Foundation
The J. J. Charitable Trust
The Jerwood Charitable Foundation
Karaviotis Foundation
The Boris Karloff Charitable Foundation
The Marina Kleinwort Charitable Trust
The David Laing Foundation
The Kirby Laing Foundation
The David Lean Foundation
The Leathersellers' Company Charitable Fund
The Leche Trust
Limoges Charitable Trust
The Linbury Trust
The Linden Charitable Trust
The Enid Linder Foundation
Lord and Lady Lurgan Trust
The Lynn Foundation
The Sir Jack Lyons Charitable Trust
The Mageni Trust
The Mayfield Valley Arts Trust
The Brian Mercer Charitable Trust
The Merchants' House of Glasgow

Millennium Stadium Charitable Trust (Ymddiriedolaeth Elusennol Stadiwm y Mileniwm)
The Millward Charitable Trust
The Esmé Mitchell Trust
The Henry Moore Foundation
The Diana and Allan Morgenthau Charitable Trust
The RVW Trust
The Racing Foundation
Racing Welfare
The Rayne Foundation
The Royal Victoria Hall Foundation

■ **Environment and agriculture**

The C. Alma Baker Trust
Sir Alec Black's Charity
The Fishmongers' Company's Charitable Trust
The Girdlers' Company Charitable Trust
JCA Charitable Foundation
The Joicey Trust
The Kennel Club Charitable Trust
The Mark Leonard Trust
The John Spedan Lewis Foundation
The Frank Litchfield Charitable Trust
LSA Charitable Trust
The NFU Mutual Charitable Trust
The Racing Foundation
Racing Welfare
The Yorkshire Dales Millennium Trust

■ **Financial services**

The Company of Actuaries' Charitable Trust Fund
The Worshipful Company of Chartered Accountants General Charitable Trust
The International Bankers Charitable Trust
Mrs F. B. Laurence Charitable Trust

■ **Law**

The Addleshaw Goddard Charitable Trust
Gamlen Charitable Trust
The Law Society

■ **Manufacturing and service industries**

The Clothworkers' Foundation
The Cotton Industry War Memorial Trust
Florence's Charitable Trust
The Leathersellers' Company Charitable Fund
The Leverhulme Trade Charities Trust
C. F. Lunoe Trust Fund
Minge's Gift and the Pooled Trusts
The Rugby Group Benevolent Fund Limited

■ **Medicine and health**

The John Avins Trust
The B-CH Charitable Trust
Bloodwise
The British Dietetic Association General and Education Trust Fund
British Heart Foundation
The Dinwoodie Settlement
The General Nursing Council for England and Wales Trust
The Michael Heller Charitable Foundation
The Simon Heller Charitable Settlement
The Ursula Keyes Trust
The Leverhulme Trade Charities Trust
John Lewis Partnership General Community Fund
The Enid Linder Foundation
The Edwina Mountbatten & Leonora Children's Foundation
The Rayne Foundation
The Sandra Charitable Trust

■ **Religion**

All Saints Educational Trust
The Ashburnham Thanksgiving Trust
The Bellahouston Bequest Fund
Catholic Foreign Missions (CFM)
The Anne French Memorial Trust
Hesed Trust
Hexham and Newcastle Diocesan Trust (1947)
Hockerill Educational Foundation
Sir Harold Hood's Charitable Trust

The Hope Trust
The James Trust
Keswick Hall Charity
Maurice and Hilda Laing Charitable Trust
Langley Charitable Trust
The Lyndhurst Trust
Sylvanus Lysons Charity
Charity of John Marshall
Sir John Priestman Charity Trust
The Bishop Radford Trust
Swansea and Brecon Diocesan Board of Finance Limited
Ulting Overseas Trust
The James Wood Bequest Fund

### ■ Science, technology and engineering

The Colt Foundation
The Michael Heller Charitable Foundation
The Simon Heller Charitable Settlement
The Leverhulme Trade Charities Trust
Scottish Coal Industry Special Welfare Fund
The William and Ellen Vinten Trust
The Winton Charitable Foundation

### ■ Seafarers and ex-seafarers

The Baltic Charitable Fund
The H. and M. Charitable Trust
The W. A. Handley Charitable Trust
The ITF Seafarers Trust
The Sir James Knott Trust
Mrs F. B. Laurence Charitable Trust
Limoges Charitable Trust
The MacRobert Trust
The Mersey Docks and Harbour Company Charitable Fund
The Shipwrights' Company Charitable Fund

### ■ Sporting or social clubs (inc. Masons)

The Provincial Grand Lodge of Bedfordshire Charity Fund
Cheshire Freemason's Charity
The Freemasons' Grand Charity

Grand Charitable Trust of the Order of Women Freemasons

### ■ Transport

The Baltic Charitable Fund
The Worshipful Company of Carmen Benevolent Trust
The Erskine Cunningham Hill Trust
Dixie Rose Findlay Charitable Trust
The Donald Forrester Trust
The Gosling Foundation Limited
The ITF Seafarers Trust
The Joicey Trust
Mrs F. B. Laurence Charitable Trust
The George John and Sheilah Livanos Charitable Trust
Merchant Navy Welfare Board
The Merchants' House of Glasgow
The Phillips Charitable Trust
Seafarers UK (King George's Fund for Sailors)
The Shipwrights' Company Charitable Fund

### Disability

### ■ People with a mental/mental health disability

The 1989 Willan Charitable Trust
The Aberbrothock Skea Trust
The Adamson Trust
The Baily Thomas Charitable Fund
The Joseph and Annie Cattle Trust
The J. Reginald Corah Foundation Fund
Douglas Arter Foundation
The Drapers' Charitable Fund
The Dumbreck Charity
The W. E. Dunn Trust
Eastern Counties Educational Trust Limited
The EBM Charitable Trust
The Eveson Charitable Trust
Esmée Fairbairn Foundation
The Forbes Charitable Foundation
Ford Britain Trust
The Oliver Ford Charitable Trust
The Jill Franklin Trust
The Hugh Fraser Foundation
The Joseph Strong Frazer Trust

The Freemasons' Grand Charity
The Gatsby Charitable Foundation
The Robert Gavron Charitable Trust
Simon Gibson Charitable Trust
The Girdlers' Company Charitable Trust
The Gosling Foundation Limited
The Grocers' Charity
The Alfred Haines Charitable Trust
The J. J. Charitable Trust
Kelsick's Educational Foundation
Lloyds Bank Foundation for England and Wales
The Dan Maskell Tennis Trust
The Tony Metherell Charitable Trust
Murphy-Neumann Charity Company Limited
The Neighbourly Charitable Trust
The Northern Rock Foundation
The Nottingham General Dispensary
The Nuffield Foundation
The Susanna Peake Charitable Trust
The Platinum Trust
The Ponton House Trust
Mr and Mrs J. A. Pye's Charitable Settlement
The Richmond Parish Lands Charity
Rix-Thompson-Rothenberg Foundation
The Robertson Trust
The Rowlands Trust
The Saddlers' Company Charitable Fund
The Shirley Foundation
The Mrs Smith and Mount Trust
David Solomons Charitable Trust
St James's Place Foundation
The Strangward Trust
The Three Guineas Trust
Vision Charity
The Barbara Ward Children's Foundation
The Will Charitable Trust
The Xerox (UK) Trust

### ■ People with autism

The Girdlers' Company Charitable Trust
The Shirley Foundation
The Three Guineas Trust

Fields of interest and type of beneficiary — People with a sensory impairment

### ■ People with dyslexia

The Joseph and Annie Cattle Trust
The J. J. Charitable Trust
Vision Charity

### ■ People with learning difficulties

The Aberbrothock Skea Trust
The Baily Thomas Charitable Fund
The J. Reginald Corah Foundation Fund
Douglas Arter Foundation
The Drapers' Charitable Fund
The Dumbreck Charity
The W. E. Dunn Trust
Eastern Counties Educational Trust Limited
The EBM Charitable Trust
The Eveson Charitable Trust
Esmée Fairbairn Foundation
The Forbes Charitable Foundation
Ford Britain Trust
The Oliver Ford Charitable Trust
The Jill Franklin Trust
The Hugh Fraser Foundation
The Joseph Strong Frazer Trust
The Freemasons' Grand Charity
The Gatsby Charitable Foundation
The Robert Gavron Charitable Trust
Simon Gibson Charitable Trust
The Gosling Foundation Limited
The Grocers' Charity
The Alfred Haines Charitable Trust
Kelsick's Educational Foundation
Lloyds Bank Foundation for England and Wales
The Dan Maskell Tennis Trust
The Tony Metherell Charitable Trust
Murphy-Neumann Charity Company Limited
The Neighbourly Charitable Trust
The Northern Rock Foundation
The Nottingham General Dispensary
The Nuffield Foundation
The Susanna Peake Charitable Trust
The Platinum Trust
The Ponton House Trust
The Richmond Parish Lands Charity

Rix-Thompson-Rothenberg Foundation
The Robertson Trust
The Rowlands Trust
The Saddlers' Company Charitable Fund
The Mrs Smith and Mount Trust
St James's Place Foundation
The Will Charitable Trust
The Xerox (UK) Trust

### ■ People with a physical impairment

The 1989 Willan Charitable Trust
The Aberbrothock Skea Trust
The Adamson Trust
The Ajahma Charitable Trust
The De Brye Charitable Trust
The Dibden Allotments Fund
Douglas Arter Foundation
The Drapers' Charitable Fund
The Dumbreck Charity
The W. E. Dunn Trust
The EBM Charitable Trust
The Emerton-Christie Charity
The Eveson Charitable Trust
Esmée Fairbairn Foundation
The Follett Trust
Ford Britain Trust
The Donald Forrester Trust
The Jill Franklin Trust
The Hugh Fraser Foundation
The Freemasons' Grand Charity
The Frognal Trust
The Gatsby Charitable Foundation
The Robert Gavron Charitable Trust
Simon Gibson Charitable Trust
The Girdlers' Company Charitable Trust
The Gosling Foundation Limited
The Grocers' Charity
H. C. D. Memorial Fund
The Hadley Trust
The Hadrian Trust
The Alfred Haines Charitable Trust
Lloyds Bank Foundation for England and Wales
The R. S. Macdonald Charitable Trust
The Dan Maskell Tennis Trust
The Tony Metherell Charitable Trust
Murphy-Neumann Charity Company Limited
The Neighbourly Charitable Trust
The Northern Rock Foundation

The Nottingham General Dispensary
The Susanna Peake Charitable Trust
The Dowager Countess Eleanor Peel Trust
The Platinum Trust
The Ponton House Trust
Mr and Mrs J. A. Pye's Charitable Settlement
Richard Radcliffe Charitable Trust
The Richmond Parish Lands Charity
The Robertson Trust
Mrs L. D. Rope Third Charitable Settlement
The Rowlands Trust
Royal Docks Trust (London)
The Saddlers' Company Charitable Fund
St James's Place Foundation
The Strangward Trust
The Xerox (UK) Trust

### ■ People with a sensory impairment

Blatchington Court Trust
British Council for Prevention of Blindness (Save Eyes Everywhere)
The Charities Advisory Trust
The De Brye Charitable Trust
The Wilfred and Elsie Elkes Charity Fund
The Eveson Charitable Trust
The Joseph Strong Frazer Trust
The Frognal Trust
The Girdlers' Company Charitable Trust
The Dorothy Hay-Bolton Charitable Trust
Lillie Johnson Charitable Trust
The John Spedan Lewis Foundation
The R. S. Macdonald Charitable Trust
The Dan Maskell Tennis Trust
The Brian Mercer Charitable Trust
The Tony Metherell Charitable Trust
The Peter Morrison Charitable Foundation
The Northwood Charitable Trust
Richard Radcliffe Charitable Trust
The Worshipful Company of Spectacle Makers' Charity
The Ulverscroft Foundation
The Michael Uren Foundation
Vision Charity
The Will Charitable Trust

## Hearing loss

The Wilfred and Elsie Elkes Charity Fund
The Eveson Charitable Trust
The Joseph Strong Frazer Trust
The Girdlers' Company Charitable Trust
The Northwood Charitable Trust

## Sight loss

Blatchington Court Trust
British Council for Prevention of Blindness (Save Eyes Everywhere)
The De Brye Charitable Trust
The Wilfred and Elsie Elkes Charity Fund
The Eveson Charitable Trust
The Joseph Strong Frazer Trust
The Frognal Trust
The Girdlers' Company Charitable Trust
The R. S. Macdonald Charitable Trust
The Brian Mercer Charitable Trust
The Worshipful Company of Spectacle Makers' Charity
The Ulverscroft Foundation
The Michael Uren Foundation
Vision Charity
The Will Charitable Trust

## Ethnicity

The Billmeir Charitable Trust
The British Dietetic Association General and Education Trust Fund
The Barrow Cadbury Trust
The Cheruby Trust
The Evan Cornish Foundation
The Davis Foundation
Dorset Community Foundation
The Englefield Charitable Trust
The Football Association National Sports Centre Trust
The Gamma Trust
Greenham Common Community Trust Limited
The Hadrian Trust
Sue Hammerson Charitable Trust
Hampton Fuel Allotment
The Harris Family Charitable Trust
The Hasluck Charitable Trust
The Hillingdon Partnership Trust
The Hinduja Foundation

The Hollick Family Charitable Trust
The Homestead Charitable Trust
The Mary Homfray Charitable Trust
House of Industry Estate
John Jarrold Trust
The Joicey Trust
The Cyril and Eve Jumbo Charitable Trust
The LankellyChase Foundation
Leicestershire, Leicester and Rutland Community Foundation
Lloyds Bank Foundation for England and Wales
Lloyds TSB Foundation for Scotland
London Catalyst
R. W. Mann Trust
The Ann and David Marks Foundation
The Marsh Christian Trust
Millennium Stadium Charitable Trust (Ymddiriedolaeth Elusennol Stadiwm y Mileniwm)
The Millfield House Foundation (MHF)
John Moores Foundation (JMF)
The Morris Charitable Trust
The Noon Foundation
Norfolk Community Foundation
The Normanby Charitable Trust
Northamptonshire Community Foundation
The Northern Rock Foundation
The Harry Payne Fund
The Jack Petchey Foundation
The Rashbass Family Trust
The Eleanor Rathbone Charitable Trust
The Sigrid Rausing Trust
The Alan and Babette Sainsbury Charitable Fund
The Shoe Zone Trust
David and Jennifer Sieff Charitable Trust
Rita and David Slowe Charitable Trust
Sparquote Limited
The Spero Foundation
The Sussex Community Foundation
Community Foundation Serving Tyne and Wear and Northumberland
The Valentine Charitable Trust
Voluntary Action Fund (VAF)
The Wixamtree Trust
The Woodward Charitable Trust

## Faith

4 Charity Foundation
A. W. Charitable Trust
Eric Abrams Charitable Trust
The Acacia Charitable Trust
Achisomoch Aid Company Limited
Adenfirst Ltd
The Adint Charitable Trust
Aid to the Church in Need (UK)
The Alabaster Trust
The Alexis Trust
All Saints Educational Trust
The Alliance Family Foundation
The Almond Trust
The Altajir Trust
Altamont Ltd
Amabrill Limited
The AMW Charitable Trust
The Anchor Foundation
The Andrew Anderson Trust
Andrews Charitable Trust
Anpride Ltd
The Ashburnham Thanksgiving Trust
The Baker Charitable Trust
The George Balint Charitable Trust
The Balney Charitable Trust
Bay Charitable Trust
BCH Trust
Bear Mordechai Ltd
Beauland Ltd
The Benfield Motors Charitable Trust
The Ruth Berkowitz Charitable Trust
The Billmeir Charitable Trust
The Sir Victor Blank Charitable Settlement
The Bonamy Charitable Trust
Salo Bordon Charitable Trust
The Harry Bottom Charitable Trust
P. G. and N. J. Boulton Trust
Sir Clive Bourne Family Trust
Bourneheights Limited
The Bramhope Trust
Bristol Archdeaconry Charity
Edna Brown Charitable Settlement
Buckingham Trust
The Buckinghamshire Historic Churches Trust
The Burghley Family Trust
The Arnold Burton 1998 Charitable Trust
C. and F. Charitable Trust
Henry T. and Lucy B. Cadbury Charitable Trust
The William A. Cadbury Charitable Trust
The H. and L. Cantor Trust
Carlee Ltd
Catholic Foreign Missions (CFM)

The Catholic Trust for England and Wales
The CH (1980) Charitable Trust
Charitworth Limited
The Cheruby Trust
The Childs Charitable Trust
The Christabella Charitable Trust
The Roger and Sarah Bancroft Clark Charitable Trust
The Clore Duffield Foundation
Closehelm Limited
Richard Cloudesley's Charity
The Clover Trust
Clydpride Ltd
The Vivienne and Samuel Cohen Charitable Trust
Col-Reno Ltd
The Congregational and General Charitable Trust
The Gershon Coren Charitable Foundation
Michael Cornish Charitable Trust
The Duke of Cornwall's Benevolent Fund
The Sidney and Elizabeth Corob Charitable Trust
The Corona Charitable Trust
The Costa Family Charitable Trust
The Craps Charitable Trust
The Cuby Charitable Trust
The Cumber Family Charitable Trust
Itzchok Meyer Cymerman Trust Ltd
Daily Prayer Union Charitable Trust Limited
Oizer Dalim Trust
The Davidson Family Charitable Trust
The Davis Foundation
The Debmar Benevolent Trust
The Dellal Foundation
The Desmond Foundation
The Sandy Dewhirst Charitable Trust
The Djanogly Foundation
The DM Charitable Trust
The Dollond Charitable Trust
Dorset Community Foundation
The Doughty Charity Trust
Dushinsky Trust Ltd
The George Elias Charitable Trust
Ellador Ltd
The Ellinson Foundation Ltd
The Edith Maud Ellis 1985 Charitable Trust
Elshore Ltd
The Englefield Charitable Trust
Entindale Ltd
The Esfandi Charitable Foundation

Euro Charity Trust
The Exilarch's Foundation
Extonglen Limited
Federation of Jewish Relief Organisations
Finnart House School Trust
The Gerald Fogel Charitable Trust
The Forte Charitable Trust
The Four Winds Trust
The Isaac and Freda Frankel Memorial Charitable Trust
Friends of Boyan Trust
Friends of Wiznitz Limited
Mejer and Gertrude Miriam Frydman Foundation
The Gamma Trust
The B. and P. Glasser Charitable Trust
Global Care
The GNC Trust
The Grahame Charitable Foundation Limited
The M. and R. Gross Charities Limited
The GRP Charitable Trust
The Gur Trust
The Kathleen Hannay Memorial Charity
Harbo Charities Limited
The Hathaway Trust
The Maurice Hatter Foundation
The Heathside Charitable Trust
The Simon Heller Charitable Settlement
The Helping Foundation
Hesed Trust
Hexham and Newcastle Diocesan Trust (1947)
Highcroft Charitable Trust
Hinchley Charitable Trust
Stuart Hine Trust
The Hintze Family Charity Foundation
Hockerill Educational Foundation
The Sir Julian Hodge Charitable Trust
The Jane Hodge Foundation
The Holden Charitable Trust
Sir Harold Hood's Charitable Trust
The Hope Trust
The Daniel Howard Trust
The Humanitarian Trust
The Huntingdon Foundation Limited
Hurdale Charity Limited
The Hutton Foundation
The P. Y. N. and B. Hyams Trust
Ibrahim Foundation Ltd
The Inlight Trust
Investream Charitable Trust
The J. & J. Benevolent Foundation

The J. & J. Charitable Trust
The J. A. R. Charitable Trust
The Jacobs Charitable Trust
The Ruth and Lionel Jacobson Trust (Second Fund) No 2
The Susan and Stephen James Charitable Settlement
The James Trust
Jay Education Trust
JCA Charitable Foundation
The Jerusalem Trust
Jewish Child's Day (JCD)
The Jewish Youth Fund (JYF)
The Joron Charitable Trust
The J. E. Joseph Charitable Fund
The Josephs Family Charitable Trust
Jusaca Charitable Trust
The Bernard Kahn Charitable Trust
The Stanley Kalms Foundation
Karaviotis Foundation
The Kasner Charitable Trust
The Michael and Ilse Katz Foundation
C. S. Kaufman Charitable Trust
The Kennedy Charitable Foundation
Keren Association Limited
E. and E. Kernkraut Charities Limited
Keswick Hall Charity
Kingdom Way Trust
Kirschel Foundation
The Kobler Trust
The Kohn Foundation
Kollel and Co. Limited
The Kreditor Charitable Trust
Kupath Gemach Chaim Bechesed Viznitz Trust
The Kyte Charitable Trust
Maurice and Hilda Laing Charitable Trust
The Lambert Charitable Trust
Duchy of Lancaster Benevolent Fund
Lancaster Foundation
Largsmount Ltd
Laufer Charitable Trust
The Lauffer Family Charitable Foundation
The Herd Lawson and Muriel Lawson Charitable Trust
Lawson Beckman Charitable Trust
The Arnold Lee Charitable Trust
The Kennedy Leigh Charitable Trust
Morris Leigh Foundation
The Lennox and Wyfold Foundation

Lord Leverhulme's Charitable Trust
Joseph Levy Charitable Foundation
David and Ruth Lewis Family Charitable Trust
Lincolnshire Churches Trust
The Lind Trust
Lindale Educational Foundation
The Ruth and Stuart Lipton Charitable Trust
The Second Joseph Aaron Littman Foundation
Jack Livingstone Charitable Trust
The Charles Lloyd Foundation
Localtrent Ltd
The Locker Foundation
Loftus Charitable Trust
The Lolev Charitable Trust
The Lowy Mitchell Foundation
The C. L. Loyd Charitable Trust
The Ruth and Jack Lunzer Charitable Trust
The Lyndhurst Trust
The Sir Jack Lyons Charitable Trust
Sylvanus Lysons Charity
M. and C. Trust
The M. K. Charitable Trust
The Macdonald-Buchanan Charitable Trust
The Magen Charitable Trust
The Mahavir Trust
Malbin Trust
The Mallinckrodt Foundation
The Manackerman Charitable Trust
Maranatha Christian Trust
Marbeh Torah Trust
The Stella and Alexander Margulies Charitable Trust
Mariapolis Limited
The Marks Family Foundation
The Ann and David Marks Foundation
The Hilda and Samuel Marks Foundation
The Marsh Christian Trust
Charity of John Marshall (Marshall's Charity)
Charlotte Marshall Charitable Trust
The Marshgate Charitable Settlement
John Martin's Charity
The Mason Porter Charitable Trust
The Matliwala Family Charitable Trust
The Matt 6.3 Charitable Trust
The Violet Mauray Charitable Trust
Mayfair Charities Ltd
Melodor Limited

The Melow Charitable Trust
Menuchar Limited
Mercaz Torah Vechesed Limited
The Mercers' Charitable Foundation
The Metropolitan Masonic Charity
The Millfield Trust
The Millward Charitable Trust
The Edgar Milward Charity
The Laurence Misener Charitable Trust
The Mishcon Family Charitable Trust
Keren Mitzvah Trust
The Mizpah Trust
The Modiano Charitable Trust
Mole Charitable Trust
The Morgan Charitable Foundation
The Diana and Allan Morgenthau Charitable Trust
The Oliver Morland Charitable Trust
S. C. and M. E. Morland's Charitable Trust
The Peter Morrison Charitable Foundation
The Moshal Charitable Trust
Vyoel Moshe Charitable Trust
Brian and Jill Moss Charitable Trust
The Moss Family Charitable Trust
The Mulberry Trust
Muslim Hands
The Mutual Trust Group
MW (CL) Foundation
MW (GK) Foundation
MW (HO) Foundation
MW (RH) Foundation
MYA Charitable Trust
MYR Charitable Trust
National Committee of the Women's World Day of Prayer for England and Wales and Northern Ireland
The Nazareth Trust Fund
Nemoral Ltd
Ner Foundation
Nesswall Ltd
The Chevras Ezras Nitzrochim Trust
NJD Charitable Trust
Normalyn Charitable Trust
The Northampton Municipal Church Charities
The Norwood and Newton Settlement
The Notgrove Trust
O&G Schreiber Charitable Trust
The Ogle Christian Trust
Oizer Charitable Trust

The Ouseley Trust
The Owen Family Trust
The Panacea Charitable Trust
The Park Charitable Trust
The Park House Charitable Trust
Miss M. E. Swinton Paterson's Charitable Trust
The Payne Charitable Trust
The David Pearlman Charitable Foundation
The Pears Family Charitable Foundation
B. E. Perl Charitable Trust
The Persson Charitable Trust
The Phillips and Rubens Charitable Trust
The Phillips Family Charitable Trust
The David Pickford Charitable Foundation
G. S. Plaut Charitable Trust Limited
The Pollywally Charitable Trust
Porticus UK
The J. E. Posnansky Charitable Trust
Premishlaner Charitable Trust
Sir John Priestman Charity Trust
Quothquan Trust
R. J. M. Charitable Trust
R. S. Charitable Trust
Rachel Charitable Trust
The Bishop Radford Trust
The Joseph Rank Trust
The Rayden Charitable Trust
The Rayne Trust
The Sir James Reckitt Charity
The Rest Harrow Trust
The Rhondda Cynon Taff Welsh Church Acts Fund
The Clive Richards Charity
Ridgesave Limited
The Sir John Ritblat Family Foundation
The Gerald Ronson Foundation
Rowanville Ltd
The Rubin Foundation
S. F. Foundation
The Ruzin Sadagora Trust
Erach and Roshan Sadri Foundation
Sam and Bella Sebba Charitable Trust
The M. J. Samuel Charitable Trust
The Annie Schiff Charitable Trust
The Schmidt-Bodner Charitable Trust
The Schreib Trust
The Schreiber Charitable Trust
The Searchlight Electric Charitable Trust
Sellata Ltd

The Seneca Trust
The Cyril Shack Trust
The Archie Sherman Charitable Trust
The Bassil Shippam and Alsford Trust
Shlomo Memorial Fund Limited
David and Jennifer Sieff Charitable Trust
Six Point Foundation
Rita and David Slowe Charitable Trust
The SMB Charitable Trust
Solev Co Ltd
The Solo Charitable Settlement
Songdale Ltd
The E. C. Sosnow Charitable Trust
Sparquote Limited
Rosalyn and Nicholas Springer Charitable Trust
Springrule Limited
St Luke's College Foundation
The Steinberg Family Charitable Trust
C. E. K. Stern Charitable Trust
The Stewards' Company Limited (incorporating the J. W. Laing Trust and the J. W. Laing Biblical Scholarship Trust)
Sir Halley Stewart Trust
The Stobart Newlands Charitable Trust
The Strawberry Charitable Trust
The Sussex Community Foundation
The Adrienne and Leslie Sussman Charitable Trust
Swansea and Brecon Diocesan Board of Finance Limited
The Tajtelbaum Charitable Trust
The David Tannen Charitable Trust
The Lili Tapper Charitable Foundation
C. B. and H. H. Taylor 1984 Trust
The Thornton Trust
Tomchei Torah Charitable Trust
The Tompkins Foundation
Toras Chesed (London) Trust
Truedene Co. Ltd
Truemart Limited
Trumros Limited
Tudor Rose Ltd
The Tufton Charitable Trust
Community Foundation Serving Tyne and Wear and Northumberland
Trustees of Tzedakah

The Union of Orthodox Hebrew Congregation
The United Society for the Propagation of the Gospel
The Vail Foundation
The Valentine Charitable Trust
The Vardy Foundation
Vivdale Ltd
The Weinstein Foundation
Dame Violet Wills Charitable Trust
The Benjamin Winegarten Charitable Trust
The Harold Hyam Wingate Foundation
The Wixamtree Trust
The Maurice Wohl Charitable Foundation
The Charles Wolfson Charitable Trust
The Wolfson Family Charitable Trust
Woodlands Green Ltd
The Worcestershire and Dudley Historic Churches Trust
Wychdale Ltd
Wychville Ltd
Yankov Charitable Trust
The Marjorie and Arnold Ziff Charitable Foundation
Stephen Zimmerman Charitable Trust

..........................................

■ **People of the Christian faith**

Aid to the Church in Need (UK)
The Alexis Trust
All Saints Educational Trust
The Almond Trust
The AMW Charitable Trust
The Anchor Foundation
The Andrew Anderson Trust
Andrews Charitable Trust
The Ashburnham Thanksgiving Trust
The Balney Charitable Trust
The Benfield Motors Charitable Trust
The Harry Bottom Charitable Trust
P. G. and N. J. Boulton Trust
Bristol Archdeaconry Charity
Buckingham Trust
Henry T. and Lucy B. Cadbury Charitable Trust
The William A. Cadbury Charitable Trust
Catholic Foreign Missions (CFM)
The Catholic Trust for England and Wales
The Childs Charitable Trust
The Christabella Charitable Trust

The Roger and Sarah Bancroft Clark Charitable Trust
Richard Cloudesley's Charity
The Clover Trust
The Congregational and General Charitable Trust
Michael Cornish Charitable Trust
The Costa Family Charitable Trust
The Cumber Family Charitable Trust
Daily Prayer Union Charitable Trust Limited
The Edith Maud Ellis 1985 Charitable Trust
The Englefield Charitable Trust
The Forte Charitable Trust
The Four Winds Trust
The Gamma Trust
Global Care
Hesed Trust
Hexham and Newcastle Diocesan Trust (1947)
Hinchley Charitable Trust
Stuart Hine Trust
The Hintze Family Charity Foundation
Hockerill Educational Foundation
Sir Harold Hood's Charitable Trust
The Hope Trust
The Hutton Foundation
The J. A. R. Charitable Trust
The James Trust
The Jerusalem Trust
The Kennedy Charitable Foundation
Kingdom Way Trust
Maurice and Hilda Laing Charitable Trust
Lancaster Foundation
The Herd Lawson and Muriel Lawson Charitable Trust
Lincolnshire Churches Trust
The Lind Trust
Lindale Educational Foundation
The Charles Lloyd Foundation
The Lyndhurst Trust
Sylvanus Lysons Charity
The Mallinckrodt Foundation
Maranatha Christian Trust
Mariapolis Limited
The Marsh Christian Trust
Charity of John Marshall (Marshall's Charity)
Charlotte Marshall Charitable Trust
The Marshgate Charitable Settlement
John Martin's Charity
The Mason Porter Charitable Trust
The Matt 6.3 Charitable Trust

**153**

The Mercers' Charitable Foundation
The Millfield Trust
The Edgar Milward Charity
The Mizpah Trust
The Oliver Morland Charitable Trust
S. C. and M. E. Morland's Charitable Trust
The Mulberry Trust
National Committee of the Women's World Day of Prayer for England and Wales and Northern Ireland
The Nazareth Trust Fund
The Norwood and Newton Settlement
The Ogle Christian Trust
The Ouseley Trust
The Owen Family Trust
The Panacea Charitable Trust
The Park House Charitable Trust
Miss M. E. Swinton Paterson's Charitable Trust
The Payne Charitable Trust
The Persson Charitable Trust
The David Pickford Charitable Foundation
G. S. Plaut Charitable Trust Limited
Porticus UK
Sir John Priestman Charity Trust
Quothquan Trust
The Bishop Radford Trust
The Joseph Rank Trust
The Sir James Reckitt Charity
The Rhondda Cynon Taff Welsh Church Acts Fund
The Clive Richards Charity
The Bassil Shippam and Alsford Trust
The SMB Charitable Trust
The Stewards' Company Limited (incorporating the J. W. Laing Trust and the J. W. Laing Biblical Scholarship Trust)
The Stobart Newlands Charitable Trust
Swansea and Brecon Diocesan Board of Finance Limited
C. B. and H. H. Taylor 1984 Trust
The Thornton Trust
The Tufton Charitable Trust
The United Society for the Propagation of the Gospel
Dame Violet Wills Charitable Trust
The Worcestershire and Dudley Historic Churches Trust

# ■ People of the Jewish faith

4 Charity Foundation
A. W. Charitable Trust
Eric Abrams Charitable Trust
The Acacia Charitable Trust
Achisomoch Aid Company Limited
Adenfirst Ltd
The Adint Charitable Trust
The Alliance Family Foundation
Altamont Ltd
Amabrill Limited
Anpride Ltd
The Baker Charitable Trust
The George Balint Charitable Trust
Bay Charitable Trust
BCH Trust
Bear Mordechai Ltd
Beauland Ltd
The Ruth Berkowitz Charitable Trust
The Sir Victor Blank Charitable Settlement
The Bonamy Charitable Trust
Salo Bordon Charitable Trust
Sir Clive Bourne Family Trust
Bourneheights Limited
Edna Brown Charitable Settlement
The Arnold Burton 1998 Charitable Trust
C. and F. Charitable Trust
The H. and L. Cantor Trust
Carlee Ltd
The CH (1980) Charitable Trust
Charitworth Limited
The Cheruby Trust
The Clore Duffield Foundation
Closehelm Limited
Clydpride Ltd
The Vivienne and Samuel Cohen Charitable Trust
Col-Reno Ltd
The Gershon Coren Charitable Foundation
The Sidney and Elizabeth Corob Charitable Trust
The Corona Charitable Trust
The Craps Charitable Trust
Itzchok Meyer Cymerman Trust Ltd
Oizer Dalim Trust
The Davidson Family Charitable Trust
The Davis Foundation
The Debmar Benevolent Trust
The Dellal Foundation
The Djanogly Foundation
The DM Charitable Trust
The Dollond Charitable Trust
The Doughty Charity Trust
Dushinsky Trust Ltd

The George Elias Charitable Trust
Ellador Ltd
The Ellinson Foundation Ltd
Elshore Ltd
Entindale Ltd
The Esfandi Charitable Foundation
The Exilarch's Foundation
Extonglen Limited
Federation of Jewish Relief Organisations
Finnart House School Trust
The Gerald Fogel Charitable Trust
The Isaac and Freda Frankel Memorial Charitable Trust
Friends of Boyan Trust
Friends of Wiznitz Limited
Mejer and Gertrude Miriam Frydman Foundation
The B. and P. Glasser Charitable Trust
The Grahame Charitable Foundation Limited
The M. and R. Gross Charities Limited
The GRP Charitable Trust
The Gur Trust
Harbo Charities Limited
The Hathaway Trust
The Maurice Hatter Foundation
The Heathside Charitable Trust
The Simon Heller Charitable Settlement
The Helping Foundation
Highcroft Charitable Trust
The Holden Charitable Trust
The Daniel Howard Trust
The Humanitarian Trust
The Huntingdon Foundation Limited
Hurdale Charity Limited
The P. Y. N. and B. Hyams Trust
Investream Charitable Trust
The J. & J. Benevolent Foundation
The J. & J. Charitable Trust
The Jacobs Charitable Trust
The Ruth and Lionel Jacobson Trust (Second Fund) No 2
The Susan and Stephen James Charitable Settlement
Jay Education Trust
JCA Charitable Foundation
Jewish Child's Day (JCD)
The Jewish Youth Fund (JYF)
The Joron Charitable Trust
The J. E. Joseph Charitable Fund
The Josephs Family Charitable Trust
Jusaca Charitable Trust

154

*Fields of interest and type of beneficiary* — **People of the Jewish faith**

The Bernard Kahn Charitable Trust
The Stanley Kalms Foundation
Karaviotis Foundation
The Kasner Charitable Trust
The Michael and Ilse Katz Foundation
C. S. Kaufman Charitable Trust
Keren Association Limited
E. and E. Kernkraut Charities Limited
Kirschel Foundation
The Kobler Trust
The Kohn Foundation
Kollel and Co. Limited
The Kreditor Charitable Trust
Kupath Gemach Chaim Bechesed Viznitz Trust
The Kyte Charitable Trust
The Lambert Charitable Trust
Largsmount Ltd
Laufer Charitable Trust
The Lauffer Family Charitable Foundation
Lawson Beckman Charitable Trust
The Arnold Lee Charitable Trust
The Kennedy Leigh Charitable Trust
Morris Leigh Foundation
Joseph Levy Charitable Foundation
David and Ruth Lewis Family Charitable Trust
The Ruth and Stuart Lipton Charitable Trust
The Second Joseph Aaron Littman Foundation
Jack Livingstone Charitable Trust
Localtrent Ltd
The Locker Foundation
Loftus Charitable Trust
The Lolev Charitable Trust
The Lowy Mitchell Foundation
The Ruth and Jack Lunzer Charitable Trust
The Sir Jack Lyons Charitable Trust
M. and C. Trust
The M. K. Charitable Trust
The Magen Charitable Trust
Malbin Trust
The Manackerman Charitable Trust
Marbeh Torah Trust
The Stella and Alexander Margulies Charitable Trust
The Marks Family Foundation
The Ann and David Marks Foundation
The Hilda and Samuel Marks Foundation

The Violet Mauray Charitable Trust
Mayfair Charities Ltd
Melodor Limited
The Melow Charitable Trust
Menuchar Limited
Mercaz Torah Vechesed Limited
The Laurence Misener Charitable Trust
The Mishcon Family Charitable Trust
Keren Mitzvah Trust
The Modiano Charitable Trust
Mole Charitable Trust
The Morgan Charitable Foundation
The Diana and Allan Morgenthau Charitable Trust
The Peter Morrison Charitable Foundation
The Moshal Charitable Trust
Vyoel Moshe Charitable Trust
Brian and Jill Moss Charitable Trust
The Moss Family Charitable Trust
The Mutual Trust Group
MW (CL) Foundation
MW (GK) Foundation
MW (HO) Foundation
MW (RH) Foundation
MYA Charitable Trust
MYR Charitable Trust
Nemoral Ltd
Ner Foundation
Nesswall Ltd
The Chevras Ezras Nitzrochim Trust
NJD Charitable Trust
Normalyn Charitable Trust
O&G Schreiber Charitable Trust
Oizer Charitable Trust
The Park Charitable Trust
The David Pearlman Charitable Foundation
The Pears Family Charitable Foundation
B. E. Perl Charitable Trust
The Phillips and Rubens Charitable Trust
The Phillips Family Charitable Trust
G. S. Plaut Charitable Trust Limited
The Pollywally Charitable Trust
The J. E. Posnansky Charitable Trust
Premishlaner Charitable Trust
R. J. M. Charitable Trust
R. S. Charitable Trust
Rachel Charitable Trust
The Rayden Charitable Trust
The Rayne Trust

The Rest Harrow Trust
Ridgesave Limited
The Sir John Ritblat Family Foundation
The Gerald Ronson Foundation
Rowanville Ltd
The Rubin Foundation
S. F. Foundation
The Ruzin Sadagora Trust
Sam and Bella Sebba Charitable Trust
The M. J. Samuel Charitable Trust
The Annie Schiff Charitable Trust
The Schmidt-Bodner Charitable Trust
The Schreib Trust
The Schreiber Charitable Trust
The Searchlight Electric Charitable Trust
Sellata Ltd
The Seneca Trust
The Cyril Shack Trust
The Archie Sherman Charitable Trust
Shlomo Memorial Fund Limited
David and Jennifer Sieff Charitable Trust
Six Point Foundation
Solev Co Ltd
The Solo Charitable Settlement
Songdale Ltd
The E. C. Sosnow Charitable Trust
Sparquote Limited
Rosalyn and Nicholas Springer Charitable Trust
Springrule Limited
The Steinberg Family Charitable Trust
C. E. K. Stern Charitable Trust
The Strawberry Charitable Trust
The Adrienne and Leslie Sussman Charitable Trust
The Tajtelbaum Charitable Trust
The David Tannen Charitable Trust
The Lili Tapper Charitable Foundation
Tomchei Torah Charitable Trust
Toras Chesed (London) Trust
Truedene Co. Ltd
Truemart Limited
Trumros Limited
Tudor Rose Ltd
Trustees of Tzedakah
The Union of Orthodox Hebrew Congregation
The Vail Foundation
Vivdale Ltd
The Weinstein Foundation

**155**

The Benjamin Winegarten
    Charitable Trust
The Harold Hyam Wingate
    Foundation
The Maurice Wohl Charitable
    Foundation
The Charles Wolfson
    Charitable Trust
The Wolfson Family Charitable
    Trust
Woodlands Green Ltd
Wychdale Ltd
Wychville Ltd
Yankov Charitable Trust
The Marjorie and Arnold Ziff
    Charitable Foundation
Stephen Zimmerman
    Charitable Trust

■ **People of the
Muslim faith**

The Altajir Trust
Euro Charity Trust
Ibrahim Foundation Ltd
The Matliwala Family
    Charitable Trust
Muslim Hands

■ **People of the
Zoroastrian faith**

Erach and Roshan Sadri
    Foundation

## Gender and relationships

■ **Adopted or fostered
children**

The Girdlers' Company
    Charitable Trust
Hampton Fuel Allotment
The Hemby Charitable Trust
Hyde Charitable Trust (Youth
    Plus)
Anton Jurgens Charitable Trust
John Lyon's Charity

■ **Bereaved**

Baron Davenport's Charity
The Hemby Charitable Trust
Sylvanus Lysons Charity

■ **Carers**

The Alchemy Foundation
The Dulverton Trust
Esmée Fairbairn Foundation

The Fishmongers' Company's
    Charitable Trust
The Hugh Fraser Foundation
The Girdlers' Company
    Charitable Trust
The Headley Trust
The Hemby Charitable Trust
Anton Jurgens Charitable Trust
Lloyds Bank Foundation for
    England and Wales
London Catalyst
John Lyon's Charity
Norfolk Community Foundation
The Olga Charitable Trust
The Harry Payne Fund (formerly
    The Harry Payne Trust)
Rix-Thompson-Rothenberg
    Foundation
The True Colours Trust

■ **Families**

Children's Liver Disease
    Foundation
Hampton Fuel Allotment
The Headley Trust
Philip Sydney Henman
    Deceased Will Trust
Hyde Charitable Trust (Youth
    Plus)
Inner London Magistrates
    Court's Poor Box and
    Feeder Charity
The Jephcott Charitable Trust
The Kelly Family Charitable
    Trust
Maurice and Hilda Laing
    Charitable Trust
The Beatrice Laing Trust
The Lauffer Family Charitable
    Foundation
The Leverhulme Trade
    Charities Trust
The Limbourne Trust
The Lister Charitable Trust
Lloyds Bank Foundation for
    England and Wales
Lloyds Bank Foundation for
    Northern Ireland
London Catalyst
The Lotus Foundation
Paul Lunn-Rockliffe Charitable
    Trust
Sylvanus Lysons Charity
The R. S. Macdonald
    Charitable Trust
Malbin Trust
Mariapolis Limited
Charlotte Marshall Charitable
    Trust
The Monument Trust
The Mulberry Trust
The Harry Payne Fund
Porticus UK
Quothquan Trust
Ryklow Charitable Trust 1992

The Scottish Power Energy
    People Trust

■ **Gay and
transgender people**

The Baring Foundation
The Allen Lane Foundation
The Sigrid Rausing Trust
Voluntary Action Fund (VAF)
The Wragge and Co Charitable
    Trust

■ **Orphans**

The Clara E. Burgess Charity
The De Brye Charitable Trust
The Girdlers' Company
    Charitable Trust
Philip Sydney Henman
    Deceased Will Trust
Kollel and Co. Limited
Muslim Hands

■ **Parents**

The Girdlers' Company
    Charitable Trust
The Hemby Charitable Trust
Philip Sydney Henman
    Deceased Will Trust
Hyde Charitable Trust (Youth
    Plus)
Inner London Magistrates
    Court's Poor Box and
    Feeder Charity
The Kelly Family Charitable
    Trust
Lloyds Bank Foundation for
    England and Wales
Lloyds Bank Foundation for
    Northern Ireland
John Lyon's Charity
Mothercare Group Foundation
Quothquan Trust
The Tedworth Charitable Trust

■ **Lone parents**

The Girdlers' Company
    Charitable Trust
The Hemby Charitable Trust
Hyde Charitable Trust (Youth
    Plus)
John Lyon's Charity
Quothquan Trust

■ **Women**

The 1970 Trust
The Ajahma Charitable Trust
The Associated Country
    Women of the World

Fields of interest and type of beneficiary | Ill health

The Scott Bader Commonwealth Limited
The Balmore Trust
The Baring Foundation
The Barrow Cadbury Trust
The Clothworkers' Foundation
Michael Cornish Charitable Trust
Baron Davenport's Charity
The Freemasons' Grand Charity
The Hadrian Trust
Philip Sydney Henman Deceased Will Trust
P. and C. Hickinbotham Charitable Trust
The Hilden Charitable Fund
The Horizon Foundation
The Hull and East Riding Charitable Trust
The Ireland Fund of Great Britain
The Jephcott Charitable Trust
The Kelly Family Charitable Trust
The Peter Kershaw Trust
The Mary Kinross Charitable Trust
Maurice and Hilda Laing Charitable Trust
The Beatrice Laing Trust
The Allen Lane Foundation
The LankellyChase Foundation
Lloyds Bank Foundation for Northern Ireland
London Catalyst
The Lotus Foundation
The Henry Lumley Charitable Trust
The Monument Trust
Mosselson Charitable Trust
Oxfam (GB)
The Harry Payne Fund
The Pilgrim Trust
The Eleanor Rathbone Charitable Trust
The Sigrid Rausing Trust
Eva Reckitt Trust Fund
The Reed Foundation
The Staples Trust
A. P. Taylor Trust
The Tresillian Trust
The Vodafone Foundation
Volant Charitable Trust

## Ill health

The Aberbrothock Skea Trust
The Acacia Charitable Trust
The Sylvia Aitken Charitable Trust
The AMW Charitable Trust
Anglo American Group Foundation
The Appletree Trust
Arthritis Research UK

Asthma UK
The Lord Austin Trust
Autonomous Research Charitable Trust
The John Avins Trust
The Baker Charitable Trust
The Barbour Foundation
The Barcapel Foundation
The Barnwood House Trust
The B-CH Charitable Trust
Beefy's Charity Foundation
The Benfield Motors Charitable Trust
The Ruth Berkowitz Charitable Trust
The Billmeir Charitable Trust
The BlackRock (UK) Charitable Trust
The Blagrave Trust
The Morgan Blake Charitable Trust
Bloodwise
BOOST Charitable Trust
The Tony Bramall Charitable Trust
The Bramhope Trust
The Bransford Trust
The Breast Cancer Research Trust
Bridgepoint Charitable Trust
The British Dietetic Association General and Education Trust Fund
British Heart Foundation
The Charles Brotherton Trust
R. S. Brownless Charitable Trust
The Bruntwood Charity Buckingham Trust
The E. F. Bulmer Benevolent Fund
The Clara E. Burgess Charity
The Burry Charitable Trust
The Derek Butler Trust
Peter Cadbury Charitable Trust
Callander Charitable Trust
The Cayo Foundation
Celtic Charity Fund
Champneys Charitable Foundation
The Cheruby Trust
Child Growth Foundation
The Children's Research Fund
The City Bridge Trust
The Clover Trust
The Robert Clutterbuck Charitable Trust
Colyer-Fergusson Charitable Trust
The Consolidated Charities for the Infirm – Merchant Taylors' Company
The Gershon Coren Charitable Foundation
Michael Cornish Charitable Trust

Coutts Charitable Foundation
The Sir William Coxen Trust Fund
The Craps Charitable Trust
Michael Crawford Children's Charity
The Cray Trust
Criffel Charitable Trust
The Violet and Milo Cripps Charitable Trust
The Cumber Family Charitable Trust
The Cwmbran Trust
Roald Dahl's Marvellous Children's Charity
The Sandy Dewhirst Charitable Trust
Diabetes UK
The Dorus Trust
Dromintee Trust
Duchy Health Charity Limited
The W. E. Dunn Trust
Eastern Counties Educational Trust Limited
The Gilbert Edgar Trust
The Wilfred and Elsie Elkes Charity Fund
The Ellerdale Trust
The Emerton-Christie Charity
Engage Foundation
The Englefield Charitable Trust
Epilepsy Research UK
Sir John Evelyn's Charity
The Exilarch's Foundation
Esmée Fairbairn Foundation
The February Foundation
The A. M. Fenton Trust
Dixie Rose Findlay Charitable Trust
The Ian Fleming Charitable Trust
Florence's Charitable Trust
The Follett Trust
The Forte Charitable Trust
The Jill Franklin Trust
The Hugh Fraser Foundation
Mejer and Gertrude Miriam Frydman Foundation
The Fuserna Foundation General Charitable Trust
The Gamma Trust
Garthgwynion Charities
The Gatsby Charitable Foundation
The Generations Foundation
The David Gibbons Foundation
The Girdlers' Company Charitable Trust
The B. and P. Glasser Charitable Trust
Global Charities
The Gosling Foundation Limited
The J. G. Graves Charitable Trust

157

Greenham Common Community Trust Limited
The Greggs Foundation
The Grimmitt Trust
The Bishop of Guildford's Foundation
The Hadley Trust
The Doris Louise Hailes Charitable Trust
The Helen Hamlyn Trust
Sue Hammerson Charitable Trust
Hampton Fuel Allotment
The W. A. Handley Charitable Trust
The Kathleen Hannay Memorial Charity
Harbo Charities Limited
The Harris Family Charitable Trust
The Edith Lilian Harrison 2000 Foundation
The Peter Harrison Foundation
The Hasluck Charitable Trust
The Hathaway Trust
The Hawthorne Charitable Trust
The Charles Hayward Foundation
May Hearnshaw Charitable Trust
Heart of England Community Foundation
Heart Research UK
The Heathside Charitable Trust
The Charlotte Heber-Percy Charitable Trust
The Percy Hedley 1990 Charitable Trust
Hedley Foundation Limited
The Michael Heller Charitable Foundation
The Simon Heller Charitable Settlement
Help for Health
The Hemby Charitable Trust
Herefordshire Community Foundation
P. and C. Hickinbotham Charitable Trust
R. G. Hills Charitable Trust
The Lady Hind Trust
The Hintze Family Charity Foundation
The Hobson Charity Limited
The Sir Julian Hodge Charitable Trust
The Jane Hodge Foundation
The Hollands-Warren Fund
The Dorothy Holmes Charitable Trust
The Edward Holt Trust
The Homestead Charitable Trust
Sir Harold Hood's Charitable Trust

The Hope Trust
The Antony Hornby Charitable Trust
The Worshipful Company of Horners' Charitable Trusts
Hospice UK
The Hospital of God at Greatham
The Hospital Saturday Fund
The Hull and East Riding Charitable Trust
Human Relief Foundation
The Humanitarian Trust
The Albert Hunt Trust
Miss Agnes H. Hunter's Trust
Huntingdon Freemen's Trust
Hurdale Charity Limited
The Hutton Foundation
The Ingram Trust
The Inman Charity
The Inverforth Charitable Trust
Investream Charitable Trust
The Ireland Fund of Great Britain
Irish Youth Foundation (UK) Ltd (incorporating The Lawlor Foundation)
The Charles Irving Charitable Trust
The J. & J. Benevolent Foundation
The J. & J. Charitable Trust
The Ruth and Lionel Jacobson Trust (Second Fund) No 2
John James Bristol Foundation
The Susan and Stephen James Charitable Settlement
The Jarman Charitable Trust
Jeffrey Charitable Trust
Nick Jenkins Foundation
The Jenour Foundation
The Jephcott Charitable Trust
Jewish Child's Day
The Elton John Aids Foundation
Lillie Johnson Charitable Trust
The Johnson Foundation
The Johnson Wax Ltd Charitable Trust
The Jones 1986 Charitable Trust
The Dezna Robins Jones Charitable Foundation
The Joron Charitable Trust
The Josephs Family Charitable Trust
Anton Jurgens Charitable Trust
Jusaca Charitable Trust
Karaviotis Foundation
The Ian Karten Charitable Trust
The Kass Charitable Trust
The Michael and Ilse Katz Foundation

The Kay Kendall Leukaemia Fund
John Thomas Kennedy Charitable Foundation
The Kennedy Charitable Foundation
The Peter Kershaw Trust
The Kettering and District Charitable Medical Trust
The Ursula Keyes Trust
The Mary Kinross Charitable Trust
The Ernest Kleinwort Charitable Trust
The Kobler Trust
The Kohn Foundation
The Heinz, Anna and Carol Kroch Foundation
Maurice and Hilda Laing Charitable Trust
Christopher Laing Foundation
The Kirby Laing Foundation
The Beatrice Laing Trust
Duchy of Lancaster Benevolent Fund
The Allen Lane Foundation
Langdale Trust
Langley Charitable Trust
The LankellyChase Foundation
The R. J. Larg Family Charitable Trust
The Lauffer Family Charitable Foundation
The Kathleen Laurence Trust
The Edgar E. Lawley Foundation
Lawson Beckman Charitable Trust
The Raymond and Blanche Lawson Charitable Trust
The Mason Le Page Charitable Trust
The Leach Fourteenth Trust
Leeds Building Society Charitable Foundation
Leicestershire, Leicester and Rutland Community Foundation
The Kennedy Leigh Charitable Trust
The Leigh Trust
P. Leigh-Bramwell Trust 'E'
The Lennox and Wyfold Foundation
Lord Leverhulme's Charitable Trust
Joseph Levy Charitable Foundation
The Lewis Ward Trust
The Limbourne Trust
Limoges Charitable Trust
The Linbury Trust
The Linden Charitable Trust
The Enid Linder Foundation
The Ruth and Stuart Lipton Charitable Trust

The Lister Charitable Trust
The Frank Litchfield Charitable Trust
The Charles Littlewood Hill Trust
The George John and Sheilah Livanos Charitable Trust
Jack Livingstone Charitable Trust
The Elaine and Angus Lloyd Charitable Trust
Lloyds Bank Foundation for Northern Ireland
Lloyds TSB Foundation for Scotland
The Locker Foundation
Loftus Charitable Trust
The Lolev Charitable Trust
The William and Katherine Longman Trust
The Loseley and Guildway Charitable Trust
The Lower Green Foundation
The Lowy Mitchell Foundation
The C. L. Loyd Charitable Trust
The Marie Helen Luen Charitable Trust
Robert Luff Foundation Ltd
The Henry Lumley Charitable Trust
Lord and Lady Lurgan Trust
The Lynn Foundation
John Lyon's Charity
The Lyons Charitable Trust
M. and C. Trust
The M. K. Charitable Trust
The E. M. MacAndrew Trust
The R. S. Macdonald Charitable Trust
The Mackay and Brewer Charitable Trust
The Mackintosh Foundation
The Mageni Trust
The Brian Maguire Charitable Trust
The Mahavir Trust
Malbin Trust
The Manackerman Charitable Trust
The Manchester Guardian Society Charitable Trust
R. W. Mann Trust
The Manoukian Charitable Foundation
Maranatha Christian Trust
The Stella and Alexander Margulies Charitable Trust
The Marsh Christian Trust
Charlotte Marshall Charitable Trust
D. G. Marshall of Cambridge Trust
Sir George Martin Trust
John Martin's Charity
The Nancie Massey Charitable Trust

The Matliwala Family Charitable Trust
D. D. McPhail Charitable Settlement
The Brian Mercer Charitable Trust
The Mercers' Charitable Foundation
The Merchants' House of Glasgow
Mercury Phoenix Trust
The Merlin Magic Wand Children's Charity
The Tony Metherell Charitable Trust
The Metropolitan Masonic Charity
T. & J. Meyer Family Foundation Limited
The Mickleham Trust
The Gerald Micklem Charitable Trust
The Ronald Miller Foundation
The Millichope Foundation
The Mills Charity
The Millward Charitable Trust
Minge's Gift and the Pooled Trusts
The Laurence Misener Charitable Trust
The Misselbrook Trust
The Brian Mitchell Charitable Settlement
Keren Mitzvah Trust
Monmouthshire County Council Welsh Church Act Fund
The Montague Thompson Coon Charitable Trust
The Monument Trust
The George A. Moore Foundation
John Moores Foundation
The Morel Charitable Trust
The Diana and Allan Morgenthau Charitable Trust
The Morris Charitable Trust
The Willie and Mabel Morris Charitable Trust
The Peter Morrison Charitable Foundation
G. M. Morrison Charitable Trust
Moto in the Community
J. P. Moulton Charitable Foundation
The Mugdock Children's Trust
The Edith Murphy Foundation
The Chevras Ezras Nitzrochim Trust
The Noon Foundation
Norfolk Community Foundation
The Northern Rock Foundation
The Northwood Charitable Trust

The Norton Rose Charitable Foundation
The Owen Family Trust
The Panacea Charitable Trust
The Park Charitable Trust
Miss M. E. Swinton Paterson's Charitable Trust
The Pedmore Sporting Club Trust Fund
People's Postcode Trust
The Pilgrim Trust
G. S. Plaut Charitable Trust Limited
The Pollywally Charitable Trust
The Mary Potter Convent Hospital Trust
Sir John Priestman Charity Trust
Mr and Mrs J. A. Pye's Charitable Settlement
Quothquan Trust
Richard Radcliffe Charitable Trust
The Ravensdale Trust
The John Rayner Charitable Trust
Eva Reckitt Trust Fund
The Violet M. Richards Charity
Thomas Roberts Trust
The Robertson Trust
The Rowlands Trust
The Saga Charitable Trust
The Saintbury Trust
The Andrew Salvesen Charitable Trust
The Basil Samuel Charitable Trust
The Sandhu Charitable Foundation
Schroder Charity Trust
The Scouloudi Foundation
The Seneca Trust
Rita and David Slowe Charitable Trust
The Mrs Smith and Mount Trust
The WH Smith Group Charitable Trust
Sodexo Foundation
The Solo Charitable Settlement
The Sovereign Health Care Charitable Trust
Sparquote Limited
The Spielman Charitable Trust
Split Infinitive Trust
St James's Place Foundation
Sir Halley Stewart Trust
The Leonard Laity Stoate Charitable Trust
The Sussex Community Foundation
Swan Mountain Trust
The Talbot Trusts
C. B. and H. H. Taylor 1984 Trust

The Connie and Albert Taylor
    Charitable Trust
Tesco Charity Trust
The C. Paul Thackray General
    Charitable Trust
Thackray Medical Research
    Trust
The Thornton Trust
The Tompkins Foundation
The Tory Family Foundation
The True Colours Trust
Trumros Limited
The James Tudor Foundation
The Douglas Turner Trust
The Valentine Charitable Trust
The Variety Club Children's
    Charity
The Vintners' Foundation
Volant Charitable Trust
Voluntary Action Fund (VAF)
Wallace and Gromit's
    Children's Foundation
The Weinstein Foundation
The Welton Foundation
The Garfield Weston
    Foundation
White Stuff Foundation
The Lionel Wigram Memorial
    Trust
The Will Charitable Trust
The HDH Wills 1965
    Charitable Trust
The James Wise Charitable
    Trust
The Michael and Anna Wix
    Charitable Trust
The Wixamtree Trust
The Charles Wolfson
    Charitable Trust
The Wolfson Family Charitable
    Trust
Woodroffe Benton Foundation
The Woodward Charitable
    Trust
The Wragge and Co Charitable
    Trust
The Matthews Wrightson
    Charity Trust
The Wyseliot Charitable Trust
The Xerox (UK) Trust
Yorkshire and Clydesdale Bank
    Foundation
Yorkshire Building Society
    Charitable Foundation
The John Kirkhope Young
    Endowment Fund
Zurich Community Trust (UK)
    Limited

■ **People with cardiovascular disorders**

British Heart Foundation
The Girdlers' Company
    Charitable Trust
Heart Research UK
The Park Charitable Trust

■ **People with haematological disorders**

Roald Dahl's Marvellous
    Children's Charity
The Kay Kendall Leukaemia
    Fund

■ **People with glandular and endocrine disorders**

Child Growth Foundation
Diabetes UK
The Girdlers' Company
    Charitable Trust

■ **People with immune system disorders**

Anglo American Group
    Foundation
The Derek Butler Trust
The Elton John Aids
    Foundation
Maurice and Hilda Laing
    Charitable Trust
Lloyds Bank Foundation for
    Northern Ireland
The Mackintosh Foundation
Mercury Phoenix Trust
John Moores Foundation
The True Colours Trust

■ **People with a mental disability**

Eastern Counties Educational
    Trust Limited
The Hugh Fraser Foundation
The Fuserna Foundation
General Charitable Trust
The Gatsby Charitable
    Foundation
The Girdlers' Company
    Charitable Trust
The Hadley Trust
The Peter Harrison Foundation
Miss Agnes H. Hunter's Trust
The Charles Irving Charitable
    Trust
The Ian Karten Charitable
    Trust
The Beatrice Laing Trust
The Allen Lane Foundation
The LankellyChase Foundation
John Lyon's Charity

The Mercers' Charitable
    Foundation
Norfolk Community Foundation
The Northern Rock Foundation
The Pilgrim Trust
Mr and Mrs J. A. Pye's
    Charitable Settlement
The Mrs Smith and Mount
    Trust

■ **People with musculoskeletal disorders**

Arthritis Research UK
Miss Agnes H. Hunter's Trust
The Montague Thompson
    Coon Charitable Trust

■ **People with neurological disorders**

Roald Dahl's Marvellous
    Children's Charity
The Wilfred and Elsie Elkes
    Charity Fund
Epilepsy Research UK
Dixie Rose Findlay Charitable
    Trust
The Forte Charitable Trust
The Girdlers' Company
    Charitable Trust
The R. S. Macdonald
    Charitable Trust
The Owen Family Trust

■ **People with oncological disorders**

Bloodwise
The Breast Cancer Research
    Trust
Peter Cadbury Charitable Trust
The Girdlers' Company
    Charitable Trust
Miss Agnes H. Hunter's Trust
The Kay Kendall Leukaemia
    Fund
The Mackintosh Foundation
The Brian Mercer Charitable
    Trust
The Tony Metherell Charitable
    Trust
The Owen Family Trust
The Park Charitable Trust
The Will Charitable Trust

### ■ People with respiratory disorders

Asthma UK
The Girdlers' Company Charitable Trust

### ■ People with skin disorders

The Lewis Ward Trust

### ■ People who are substance misusers

Celtic Charity Fund
Esmée Fairbairn Foundation
The Hope Trust
The Leigh Trust
John Lyon's Charity
The Mercers' Charitable Foundation
The Misselbrook Trust
John Moores Foundation
Norfolk Community Foundation
The Northern Rock Foundation
The Robertson Trust
The Vintners' Foundation
The Woodward Charitable Trust

### ■ Palliative care

Peter Cadbury Charitable Trust
The Girdlers' Company Charitable Trust
The Peter Harrison Foundation
Hedley Foundation Limited
The Mugdock Children's Trust
Norfolk Community Foundation
Richard Radcliffe Charitable Trust
St James's Place Foundation
The Connie and Albert Taylor Charitable Trust
The True Colours Trust
Trumros Limited
The James Tudor Foundation
The Xerox (UK) Trust

## Nationality

### ■ Asian

Matliwala Family Charitable Trust
Sino-British Fellowship Trust
The W. Wing Yip and Brothers Foundation

### ■ Eastern European

Armenian General Benevolent Union London Trust
The Manoukian Charitable Foundation
Saint Sarkis Charity Trust

### ■ Southern European

Calouste Gulbenkian Foundation – UK Branch

## Social or economic circumstances

The 1970 Trust
The 1989 Willan Charitable Trust
The 29th May 1961 Charitable Trust
The Aberdeen Foundation
Access Sport
The ACT Foundation
The Addleshaw Goddard Charitable Trust
The Sylvia Aitken Charitable Trust
The Ajahma Charitable Trust
The Alchemy Foundation
The Alliance Family Foundation
The Pat Allsop Charitable Trust
Sir John and Lady Amory's Charitable Trust
Andrews Charitable Trust
The Appletree Trust
The John Apthorp Charity
The Archer Trust
The Argus Appeal
The Ashden Trust
AstonMansfield Charitable Trust
The Lord Austin Trust
Autonomous Research Charitable Trust
The Scott Bader Commonwealth Limited
The George Balint Charitable Trust
The Bank of Scotland Foundation
The Barbour Foundation
The Baring Foundation
Barnes Workhouse Fund
BBC Children in Need
The Bellahouston Bequest Fund
The Bellinger Donnay Trust
The Benfield Motors Charitable Trust
Bergqvist Charitable Trust
The Berkeley Charitable Foundation
The Billmeir Charitable Trust
Percy Bilton Charity

The BlackRock (UK) Charitable Trust
The Blagrave Trust
The Morgan Blake Charitable Trust
The Boltini Trust
Boots Charitable Trust
The Oliver Borthwick Memorial Trust
P. G. and N. J. Boulton Trust
The Bramhope Trust
The Breadsticks Foundation
The Bridging Fund Charitable Trust
The Bromley Trust
R. S. Brownless Charitable Trust
Buckingham Trust
The E. F. Bulmer Benevolent Fund
Consolidated Charity of Burton upon Trent
The Worshipful Company of Butchers General Charities
The Noel Buxton Trust
Henry T. and Lucy B. Cadbury Charitable Trust
The William A. Cadbury Charitable Trust
The Barrow Cadbury Trust
CAFOD (Catholic Agency for Overseas Development)
Callander Charitable Trust
The Calpe Trust
The Campden Charities Trustee
The Cayo Foundation
The Charities Advisory Trust
The Worshipful Company of Chartered Accountants General Charitable Trust
Chaucer Foundation
The Cheruby Trust
Cheshire Freemason's Charity
The Chetwode Foundation
CHK Charities Limited
Christadelphian Samaritan Fund
Christian Aid
Chrysalis Trust
Church Urban Fund
The City Bridge Trust
CLA Charitable Trust
The Cleopatra Trust
The Clore Duffield Foundation
Closehelm Limited
The Clothworkers' Foundation
Richard Cloudesley's Charity
The Clover Trust
The Vivienne and Samuel Cohen Charitable Trust
The R. and S. Cohen Foundation
The Coltstaple Trust
Colyer-Fergusson Charitable Trust

Comic Relief
The Consolidated Charities for the Infirm – Merchant Taylors' Company
The Cooks Charity
The Helen Jean Cope Trust
Michael Cornish Charitable Trust
The Evan Cornish Foundation
The Duke of Cornwall's Benevolent Fund
The Cotton Trust
Coutts Charitable Foundation
The Craps Charitable Trust
Michael Crawford Children's Charity
The Crerar Hotels Trust
Criffel Charitable Trust
The Violet and Milo Cripps Charitable Trust
The Cumber Family Charitable Trust
Cumbria Community Foundation
The Cwmbran Trust
The Davis Foundation
The Dawe Charitable Trust
The Sandy Dewhirst Charitable Trust
Disability Aid Fund (The Roger and Jean Jefcoate Trust)
Dorset Community Foundation
The Dorus Trust
The Double 'O' Charity Ltd
The Doughty Charity Trust
The Drapers' Charitable Fund
Dromintee Trust
The Duis Charitable Trust
The Royal Foundation of the Duke and Duchess of Cambridge and Prince Harry
The W. E. Dunn Trust
Eastern Counties Educational Trust Limited
The Ebenezer Trust
The EBM Charitable Trust
The Gilbert and Eileen Edgar Foundation
The Gilbert Edgar Trust
Edge Fund
Dr Edwards Bishop King's Fulham Endowment Fund
The George Elias Charitable Trust
The Wilfred and Elsie Elkes Charity Fund
The Ellerdale Trust
The Ellinson Foundation Ltd
The Edith Maud Ellis 1985 Charitable Trust
The Ellis Campbell Foundation
The Emerton-Christie Charity
Engage Foundation
The Englefield Charitable Trust
The Enkalon Foundation
The Epigoni Trust

The Ericson Trust
The ERM Foundation
The Ernest Hecht Charitable Foundation
Esh Foundation
Euro Charity Trust
Sir John Evelyn's Charity
The Eveson Charitable Trust
The Exilarch's Foundation
The Expat Foundation
Esmée Fairbairn Foundation
The George Fentham Birmingham Charity
The Doris Field Charitable Trust
The Fifty Fund
Fisherbeck Charitable Trust
The Fishmongers' Company's Charitable Trust
The Ian Fleming Charitable Trust
The Follett Trust
The Anna Rosa Forster Charitable Trust
The Jill Franklin Trust
The Hugh Fraser Foundation
The Freemasons' Grand Charity
Friends Provident Charitable Foundation
The Patrick & Helena Frost Foundation
The Fuserna Foundation
General Charitable Trust
The G. D. Charitable Trust
Gamlen Charitable Trust
The Gannochy Trust
Garthgwynion Charities
The Gatsby Charitable Foundation
The Robert Gavron Charitable Trust
The Generations Foundation
The Steven Gerrard Foundation
The David Gibbons Foundation
The Girdlers' Company Charitable Trust
Global Care
Global Charities
The GNC Trust
The Goldman Sachs Charitable Gift Fund (UK)
Goldman Sachs Gives (UK)
The Goodman Foundation
The J. G. Graves Charitable Trust
The Greggs Foundation
The Grocers' Charity
The Bishop of Guildford's Foundation
H. C. D. Memorial Fund
The Hackney Parochial Charities
The Hadley Trust
The Alfred Haines Charitable Trust

Paul Hamlyn Foundation
The Helen Hamlyn Trust
Sue Hammerson Charitable Trust
Hampton Fuel Allotment
The W. A. Handley Charitable Trust
The Kathleen Hannay Memorial Charity
The Haramead Trust
The Harbour Foundation
William Harding's Charity
The Edith Lilian Harrison 2000 Foundation
The Peter Harrison Foundation
Edward Harvist Trust
The Hasluck Charitable Trust
The Hathaway Trust
The Charles Hayward Foundation
The Headley Trust
May Hearnshaw Charitable Trust
Heart of England Community Foundation
The Charlotte Heber-Percy Charitable Trust
Hedley Foundation Limited
The Michael Heller Charitable Foundation
The Simon Heller Charitable Settlement
Help for Health
Help the Homeless Limited
The Hemby Charitable Trust
Henley Educational Trust
Philip Sydney Henman Deceased Will Trust
Herefordshire Community Foundation
The Hesslewood Children's Trust (Hull Seamen's and General Orphanage)
Hexham and Newcastle Diocesan Trust (1947)
P. and C. Hickinbotham Charitable Trust
Highcroft Charitable Trust
The Hilden Charitable Fund
R. G. Hills Charitable Trust
The Lady Hind Trust
The Hiscox Foundation
The Hobson Charity Limited
The Holden Charitable Trust
The Mary Homfray Charitable Trust
Sir Harold Hood's Charitable Trust
Hope for Youth (NI)
Hopmarket Charity
The Horizon Foundation
The Horne Foundation
The Thomas J. Horne Memorial Trust
The Hornsey Parochial Charities

The Hospital of God at Greatham
House of Industry Estate
The Daniel Howard Trust
The Huggard Charitable Trust
Human Relief Foundation
The Humanitarian Trust
The Michael and Shirley Hunt Charitable Trust
The Albert Hunt Trust
The Hunter Foundation
Miss Agnes H. Hunter's Trust
The Huntingdon Foundation Limited
Huntingdon Freemen's Trust
Hurdale Charity Limited
Hyde Charitable Trust
Ibrahim Foundation Ltd
Impetus – The Private Equity Foundation
Incommunities Foundation
The Ingram Trust
Investream Charitable Trust
The Ireland Fund of Great Britain
Irish Youth Foundation (UK) Ltd (incorporating The Lawlor Foundation)
The Charles Irving Charitable Trust
The J. & J. Benevolent Foundation
The J. A. R. Charitable Trust
The J. J. Charitable Trust
C. Richard Jackson Charitable Trust
Jaffe Family Relief Fund
The James Trust
The Jarman Charitable Trust
John Jarrold Trust
Jay Education Trust
The Jenour Foundation
The Jephcott Charitable Trust
The Joffe Charitable Trust
The Elton John Aids Foundation
The Johnson Foundation
The Johnson Wax Ltd Charitable Trust
The Joicey Trust
The Jones 1986 Charitable Trust
The Joron Charitable Trust
The J. E. Joseph Charitable Fund
The Lady Eileen Joseph Foundation
The Josephs Family Charitable Trust
The Cyril and Eve Jumbo Charitable Trust
Anton Jurgens Charitable Trust
Jusaca Charitable Trust
The Bernard Kahn Charitable Trust
The Kass Charitable Trust

The Michael and Ilse Katz Foundation
The Kelly Family Charitable Trust
William Kendall's Charity (Wax Chandlers' Company)
John Thomas Kennedy Charitable Foundation
The Nancy Kenyon Charitable Trust
Keren Association Limited
E. and E. Kernkraut Charities Limited
The Peter Kershaw Trust
Kingdom Way Trust
The Mary Kinross Charitable Trust
The Richard Kirkman Trust
Kirschel Foundation
The Sir James Knott Trust
The Kohn Foundation
The KPMG Foundation
The Kreditor Charitable Trust
The Heinz, Anna and Carol Kroch Foundation
Kupath Gemach Chaim Bechesed Viznitz Trust
John Laing Charitable Trust
Maurice and Hilda Laing Charitable Trust
The Kirby Laing Foundation
The Martin Laing Foundation
The Beatrice Laing Trust
Community Foundations for Lancashire and Merseyside
Duchy of Lancaster Benevolent Fund
Lancaster Foundation
LandAid Charitable Trust
The Jack Lane Charitable Trust
The Allen Lane Foundation
Langley Charitable Trust
The LankellyChase Foundation
The R. J. Larg Family Charitable Trust
Largsmount Ltd
Laslett's (Hinton) Charity
Mrs F. B. Laurence Charitable Trust
The Law Society Charity
The Edgar E. Lawley Foundation
Lawson Beckman Charitable Trust
The Raymond and Blanche Lawson Charitable Trust
The Leach Fourteenth Trust
The Leathersellers' Company Charitable Fund
Leeds Building Society Charitable Foundation
Leicestershire, Leicester and Rutland Community Foundation
The Kennedy Leigh Charitable Trust

The Leigh Trust
The Lennox and Wyfold Foundation
The Mark Leonard Trust
Joseph Levy Charitable Foundation
David and Ruth Lewis Family Charitable Trust
John Lewis Partnership General Community Fund
Liberum Foundation
The Limbourne Trust
The Linbury Trust
The Enid Linder Foundation
The Lister Charitable Trust
The Frank Litchfield Charitable Trust
The Second Joseph Aaron Littman Foundation
The Elaine and Angus Lloyd Charitable Trust
Lloyd's Charities Trust
Lloyds Bank Foundation for England and Wales
Lloyds Bank Foundation for Northern Ireland
Lloyds TSB Foundation for Scotland
Localtrent Ltd
Loftus Charitable Trust
London Catalyst
London Housing Foundation Ltd
London Legal Support Trust
The William and Katherine Longman Trust
The Lord's Taverners
The Loseley and Guildway Charitable Trust
The Lotus Foundation
The Lowy Mitchell Foundation
The C. L. Loyd Charitable Trust
LSA Charitable Trust
The Marie Helen Luen Charitable Trust
The Henry Lumley Charitable Trust
Paul Lunn-Rockliffe Charitable Trust
The Lynn Foundation
John Lyon's Charity
Sylvanus Lysons Charity
M. and C. Trust
The M. K. Charitable Trust
The E. M. MacAndrew Trust
The R. S. Macdonald Charitable Trust
The Mackintosh Foundation
The Magdalen and Lasher Charity (General Fund)
The Magen Charitable Trust
The Mahavir Trust
Malbin Trust
Man Group plc Charitable Trust

163

The Manackerman Charitable
  Trust
Manchester Airport Community
  Trust Fund
The Manchester Guardian
  Society Charitable Trust
Lord Mayor of Manchester's
  Charity Appeal Trust
The Manifold Charitable Trust
R. W. Mann Trust
The Manoukian Charitable
  Foundation
Maranatha Christian Trust
Marbeh Torah Trust
Mariapolis Limited
Marmot Charitable Trust
The Marr-Munning Trust
The Michael Marsh Charitable
  Trust
The Marsh Christian Trust
Charlotte Marshall Charitable
  Trust
D. G. Marshall of Cambridge
  Trust
John Martin's Charity
The Mathew Trust
The Matliwala Family
  Charitable Trust
Mayfair Charities Ltd
Melodor Limited
The Melow Charitable Trust
Mercaz Torah Vechesed
  Limited
The Mercers' Charitable
  Foundation
The Merchant Taylors'
  Company Charities Fund
The Merchants' House of
  Glasgow
The Merlin Magic Wand
  Children's Charity
The Mersey Docks and
  Harbour Company
  Charitable Fund
The Metropolitan Masonic
  Charity
T. & J. Meyer Family
  Foundation Limited
The Mickleham Trust
The Gerald Micklem Charitable
  Trust
Middlesex Sports Foundation
Millennium Stadium Charitable
  Trust (Ymddiriedolaeth
  Elusennol Stadiwm y
  Mileniwm)
The Ronald Miller Foundation
The Millfield House Foundation
The Millichope Foundation
The Mills Charity
The Peter Minet Trust
Minge's Gift and the Pooled
  Trusts
The Mirianog Trust
The Brian Mitchell Charitable
  Settlement

Keren Mitzvah Trust
The Mizpah Trust
The Modiano Charitable Trust
Monmouthshire County Council
  Welsh Church Act Fund
The Monument Trust
John Moores Foundation
The Morel Charitable Trust
The Morgan Charitable
  Foundation
The Morgan Foundation
The Miles Morland Foundation
The Morris Charitable Trust
The Peter Morrison Charitable
  Foundation
G. M. Morrison Charitable
  Trust
Vyoel Moshe Charitable Trust
The Moss Family Charitable
  Trust
J. P. Moulton Charitable
  Foundation
The Mulberry Trust
The Edith Murphy Foundation
Murphy-Neumann Charity
  Company Limited
Muslim Hands
The Nationwide Foundation
Network for Social Change
The NFU Mutual Charitable
  Trust
The Chevras Ezras Nitzrochim
  Trust
Nominet Charitable Foundation
The Noon Foundation
Norfolk Community Foundation
Northamptonshire Community
  Foundation
The Northern Rock Foundation
The Northmoor Trust
The Norton Foundation
The Norton Rose Charitable
  Foundation
The Nuffield Foundation
The Odin Charitable Trust
Oglesby Charitable Trust
Old Possum's Practical Trust
The Olga Charitable Trust
Oxfam (GB)
The Harry Payne Fund
The Peacock Charitable Trust
People's Postcode Trust
The Persula Foundation
The Pilgrim Trust
The Elise Pilkington Charitable
  Trust
The Pilkington Charities Fund
The Pollywally Charitable Trust
The Popocatepetl Trust
Porticus UK
The Portishead Nautical Trust
The W. L. Pratt Charitable
  Trust
Sir John Priestman Charity
  Trust
The Puebla Charitable Trust

The Puri Foundation
Mr and Mrs J. A. Pye's
  Charitable Settlement
The Queen Anne's Gate
  Foundation
Quothquan Trust
The Eleanor Rathbone
  Charitable Trust
The Sigrid Rausing Trust
The Ravensdale Trust
The Rayne Foundation
The Rayne Trust
The Sir James Reckitt Charity
Eva Reckitt Trust Fund
The Reed Foundation
The Rhondda Cynon Taff
  Welsh Church Acts Fund
The Richmond Parish Lands
  Charity
Ridgesave Limited
The River Farm Foundation
Thomas Roberts Trust
The Robertson Trust
Mrs L. D. Rope Third
  Charitable Settlement
The Rowland Family
  Foundation
The Rowlands Trust
The Joseph Rowntree
  Charitable Trust
Royal Docks Trust (London)
Ryklow Charitable Trust 1992
Erach and Roshan Sadri
  Foundation
The Saga Charitable Trust
The Alan and Babette
  Sainsbury Charitable Fund
Saint Sarkis Charity Trust
The Saintbury Trust
The Salamander Charitable
  Trust
Sam and Bella Sebba
  Charitable Trust
The Basil Samuel Charitable
  Trust
The Sandhu Charitable
  Foundation
The Sandra Charitable Trust
Santander UK Foundation
  Limited
Schroder Charity Trust
The Sir James and Lady Scott
  Trust
Scottish Coal Industry Special
  Welfare Fund
The Scottish Power Energy
  People Trust
The Scouloudi Foundation
The SDL Foundation
The Seedfield Trust
The Shanley Charitable Trust
The Shipwrights' Company
  Charitable Fund
The Shoe Zone Trust
The Simmons & Simmons
  Charitable Foundation

164

Six Point Foundation
Rita and David Slowe Charitable Trust
The Mrs Smith and Mount Trust
The Sobell Foundation
Social Business Trust (Scale-Up)
Sodexo Foundation
The Solo Charitable Settlement
The E. C. Sosnow Charitable Trust
R. H. Southern Trust
The Sovereign Health Care Charitable Trust
Sparquote Limited
Spears-Stutz Charitable Trust
The Spero Foundation
The Spielman Charitable Trust
Split Infinitive Trust
The St Hilda's Trust
St James's Place Foundation
Sir Walter St John's Educational Charity
The St Laurence Relief In Need Trust
Sir Halley Stewart Trust
The Leonard Laity Stoate Charitable Trust
The Stone Family Foundation
The Alan Sugar Foundation
The Bernard Sunley Charitable Foundation
The Sussex Community Foundation
Sutton Coldfield Charitable Trust
Swan Mountain Trust
The Swann-Morton Foundation
Sylvia Waddilove Foundation UK
C. B. and H. H. Taylor 1984 Trust
Tegham Limited
The C. Paul Thackray General Charitable Trust
Thomson Reuters Foundation
The Thornton Trust
The Tinsley Foundation
The Tolkien Trust
The Tory Family Foundation
The Toy Trust
Annie Tranmer Charitable Trust
The Tresillian Trust
The Triangle Trust (1949) Fund
The Douglas Turner Trust
TVML Foundation
Community Foundation Serving Tyne and Wear and Northumberland
UIA Charitable Foundation
UKI Charitable Foundation
The Underwood Trust
The UNITE Foundation

The United Society for the Propagation of the Gospel
Uxbridge United Welfare Trust
The Valentine Charitable Trust
The Vardy Foundation
The Variety Club Children's Charity
The Vintners' Foundation
The Vodafone Foundation
Volant Charitable Trust
Voluntary Action Fund (VAF)
The Scurrah Wainwright Charity
The Wakefield and Tetley Trust
Wakeham Trust
Wales Council for Voluntary Action
Wates Family Enterprise Trust
The Wates Foundation
John Watson's Trust
The Weavers' Company Benevolent Fund
Webb Memorial Trust
The Welton Foundation
The West Derby Wastelands Charity
The Westcroft Trust
The Westminster Foundation
The Garfield Weston Foundation
The Barbara Whatmore Charitable Trust
White Stuff Foundation
The Norman Whiteley Trust
The Lionel Wigram Memorial Trust
The Will Charitable Trust
The Charity of William Williams
Williams Serendipity Trust
The HDH Wills 1965 Charitable Trust
The Community Foundation for Wiltshire and Swindon
The Benjamin Winegarten Charitable Trust
The James Wise Charitable Trust
The Michael and Anna Wix Charitable Trust
The Wixamtree Trust
The Maurice Wohl Charitable Foundation
The Charles Wolfson Charitable Trust
The Wood Family Trust
Wooden Spoon Society
Woodlands Green Ltd
Woodroffe Benton Foundation
The Woodward Charitable Trust
Worcester Municipal Charities
The Wragge and Co Charitable Trust
The Matthews Wrightson Charity Trust
The Wyseliot Charitable Trust
The Yapp Charitable Trust

The Yardley Great Trust
Yorkshire and Clydesdale Bank Foundation
Yorkshire Building Society Charitable Foundation
Youth Music
Zephyr Charitable Trust
Zurich Community Trust (UK) Limited

■ **People with an alternative lifestyle (inc. travellers)**

The Allen Lane Foundation
The Odin Charitable Trust

■ **People who are educationally disadvantaged**

The Barrow Cadbury Trust
Eastern Counties Educational Trust Limited
The Ellis Campbell Foundation
Gamlen Charitable Trust
The Girdlers' Company Charitable Trust
Global Care
H. C. D. Memorial Fund
The Hadley Trust
The Hathaway Trust
Miss Agnes H. Hunter's Trust
The KPMG Foundation
The Kreditor Charitable Trust
The Beatrice Laing Trust
Community Foundations for Lancashire and Merseyside
John Lyon's Charity
The Manifold Charitable Trust
The Marr-Munning Trust
The Simmons & Simmons Charitable Foundation
The UNITE Foundation
The Wates Family Enterprise Trust

■ **People who are homeless**

The 29th May 1961 Charitable Trust
The Ashden Trust
The Berkeley Charitable Foundation
The Oliver Borthwick Memorial Trust
Henry T. and Lucy B. Cadbury Charitable Trust
The Charities Advisory Trust
CHK Charities Limited
Christian Aid
The Coltstaple Trust
The Dawe Charitable Trust

165

The Drapers' Charitable Fund
The Gilbert Edgar Trust
The Wilfred and Elsie Elkes Charity Fund
The Ellinson Foundation Ltd
The Ericson Trust
Esh Foundation
The Eveson Charitable Trust
Esmée Fairbairn Foundation
Fisherbeck Charitable Trust
The Fishmongers' Company's Charitable Trust
The Hugh Fraser Foundation
The Freemasons' Grand Charity
The G. D. Charitable Trust
The Girdlers' Company Charitable Trust
Global Care
The Bishop of Guildford's Foundation
The Alfred Haines Charitable Trust
Hampton Fuel Allotment
The Harbour Foundation
The Peter Harrison Foundation
The Charlotte Heber-Percy Charitable Trust
Help the Homeless Limited
The Hilden Charitable Fund
Sir Harold Hood's Charitable Trust
The Horne Foundation
The Thomas J. Horne Memorial Trust
Hyde Charitable Trust
Incommunities Foundation
The Ingram Trust
John Laing Charitable Trust
Maurice and Hilda Laing Charitable Trust
The Beatrice Laing Trust
London Housing Foundation Ltd
The Lotus Foundation
The Marie Helen Luen Charitable Trust
Paul Lunn-Rockliffe Charitable Trust
John Lyon's Charity
The Mackintosh Foundation
The Mirianog Trust
The Monument Trust
The Edith Murphy Foundation
Network for Social Change
Norfolk Community Foundation
The Odin Charitable Trust
The Persula Foundation
The Pilgrim Trust
The Portishead Nautical Trust
The Robertson Trust
Mrs L. D. Rope Third Charitable Settlement
Erach and Roshan Sadri Foundation

The Mrs Smith and Mount Trust
The Sobell Foundation
The Matthews Wrightson Charity Trust

■ **People who are housebound**

Elise Pilkington Charitable Trust

■ **People who are unemployed**

CHK Charities Limited
The Enkalon Foundation
The Hasluck Charitable Trust
Miss Agnes H. Hunter's Trust
Incommunities Foundation
The KPMG Foundation
The Lotus Foundation
Paul Lunn-Rockliffe Charitable Trust
John Lyon's Charity
The Marr-Munning Trust
The Mathew Trust
Vyoel Moshe Charitable Trust
The Pilgrim Trust
The Elise Pilkington Charitable Trust
The Simmons & Simmons Charitable Foundation
The UNITE Foundation
Wates Family Enterprise Trust

■ **Carers**

Disability Aid Fund (The Roger and Jean Jefcoate Trust)
The Jill Franklin Trust
Hampton Fuel Allotment
Hedley Foundation Limited
Help for Health
The Joron Charitable Trust
The Richard Kirkman Trust
The Martin Laing Foundation
The Leach Fourteenth Trust
John Lewis Partnership General Community Fund
The Lord's Taverners
M. and C. Trust
The E. M. MacAndrew Trust
The Gerald Micklem Charitable Trust
St James's Place Foundation
The Will Charitable Trust
The Woodward Charitable Trust

■ **Migrants**

The 29th May 1961 Charitable Trust 29th May 1961 Charitable Trust
The Barrow Cadbury Trust and the Barrow Cadbury Fund
The Manoukian Charitable Foundation
The Marr-Munning Trust

■ **Offenders**

The 29th May 1961 Charitable Trust
The Alchemy Foundation
The Bromley Trust
The Noel Buxton Trust
The William A. Cadbury Charitable Trust
The Barrow Cadbury Trust
The Chetwode Foundation
The Cooks Charity
The Evan Cornish Foundation
The Violet and Milo Cripps Charitable Trust
The Drapers' Charitable Fund
Esmée Fairbairn Foundation
The Jill Franklin Trust
The Gatsby Charitable Foundation
The Robert Gavron Charitable Trust
The Girdlers' Company Charitable Trust
The Hadley Trust
Paul Hamlyn Foundation
The Helen Hamlyn Trust
The Peter Harrison Foundation
The Hasluck Charitable Trust
The Charles Hayward Foundation
The Hilden Charitable Fund
Sir Harold Hood's Charitable Trust
The Michael and Shirley Hunt Charitable Trust
The J. J. Charitable Trust
C. Richard Jackson Charitable Trust
The KPMG Foundation
The Beatrice Laing Trust
The Allen Lane Foundation
The Law Society Charity
The Mark Leonard Trust
The William and Katherine Longman Trust
Paul Lunn-Rockliffe Charitable Trust
John Lyon's Charity
The Mercers' Charitable Foundation
The Monument Trust
The Nuffield Foundation
The Odin Charitable Trust
The Pilgrim Trust

*Fields of interest and type of beneficiary* — **People who are poor, on low incomes**

The Portishead Nautical Trust
The Rhondda Cynon Taff Welsh Church Acts Fund
Saint Sarkis Charity Trust
Swan Mountain Trust
The Triangle Trust (1949) Fund
The Underwood Trust
The Weavers' Company Benevolent Fund

■ **Ex-offenders**

The 29th May 1961 Charitable Trust
Esmée Fairbairn Foundation
The Girdlers' Company Charitable Trust
Paul Hamlyn Foundation
John Lyon's Charity
The Mercers' Charitable Foundation
The Odin Charitable Trust
The Weavers' Company Benevolent Fund

■ **Prisoners and their families**

The Noel Buxton Trust
The Odin Charitable Trust
The Weavers' Company Benevolent Fund

■ **Young people at risk of offending**

The Gatsby Charitable Foundation
Paul Hamlyn Foundation
The Peter Harrison Foundation
The Mark Leonard Trust
The Nuffield Foundation
The Portishead Nautical Trust
The Rhondda Cynon Taff Welsh Church Acts Fund
The Weavers' Company Benevolent Fund

■ **People who are poor, on low incomes**

The 1989 Willan Charitable Trust
The 29th May 1961 Charitable Trust
The Ajahma Charitable Trust
The Alliance Family Foundation
The Pat Allsop Charitable Trust
Sir John and Lady Amory's Charitable Trust
The Appletree Trust
The Archer Trust

AstonMansfield Charitable Trust
The George Balint Charitable Trust
The Bellahouston Bequest Fund
The Bellinger Donnay Trust
The Benfield Motors Charitable Trust
P. G. and N. J. Boulton Trust
The Bridging Fund Charitable Trust
Buckingham Trust
The E. F. Bulmer Benevolent Fund
The Worshipful Company of Butchers General Charities
The Barrow Cadbury Trust
CAFOD (Catholic Agency for Overseas Development)
The Worshipful Company of Chartered Accountants General Charitable Trust
The Chetwode Foundation
Christian Aid
Church Urban Fund
CLA Charitable Trust
Closehelm Limited
The R. and S. Cohen Foundation
Michael Crawford Children's Charity
The Double 'O' Charity Ltd
The Doughty Charity Trust
The Drapers' Charitable Fund
Eastern Counties Educational Trust Limited
The EBM Charitable Trust
The ERM Foundation
Euro Charity Trust
The Eveson Charitable Trust
The George Fentham Birmingham Charity
The Fifty Fund
The Fishmongers' Company's Charitable Trust
The Hugh Fraser Foundation
Gamlen Charitable Trust
The David Gibbons Foundation
The Girdlers' Company Charitable Trust
Global Care
The Goldman Sachs Charitable Gift Fund (UK)
Goldman Sachs Gives (UK)
The J. G. Graves Charitable Trust
The Grocers' Charity
The Bishop of Guildford's Foundation
H. C. D. Memorial Fund
The Hadley Trust
Sue Hammerson Charitable Trust
Hampton Fuel Allotment

The W. A. Handley Charitable Trust
The Harbour Foundation
The Edith Lilian Harrison 2000 Foundation
Edward Harvist Trust
The Hasluck Charitable Trust
The Hathaway Trust
May Hearnshaw Charitable Trust
The Charlotte Heber-Percy Charitable Trust
The Michael Heller Charitable Foundation
The Simon Heller Charitable Settlement
Henley Educational Trust
Herefordshire Community Foundation
The Hesslewood Children's Trust (Hull Seamen's and General Orphanage)
Hexham and Newcastle Diocesan Trust (1947)
Highcroft Charitable Trust
R. G. Hills Charitable Trust
The Lady Hind Trust
The Holden Charitable Trust
The Mary Homfray Charitable Trust
Hopmarket Charity
The Hornsey Parochial Charities
The Daniel Howard Trust
The Hunter Foundation
The Huntingdon Foundation Limited
Huntingdon Freemen's Trust
Hurdale Charity Limited
Hyde Charitable Trust
Incommunities Foundation
The J. & J. Benevolent Foundation
The J. A. R. Charitable Trust
Jaffe Family Relief Fund
The James Trust
John Jarrold Trust
Jay Education Trust
The Jephcott Charitable Trust
The Johnson Foundation
The Joicey Trust
The Jones 1986 Charitable Trust
The Joron Charitable Trust
The J. E. Joseph Charitable Fund
The Josephs Family Charitable Trust
The Cyril and Eve Jumbo Charitable Trust
Anton Jurgens Charitable Trust
Jusaca Charitable Trust
The Bernard Kahn Charitable Trust
The Kass Charitable Trust

**167**

William Kendall's Charity (Wax Chandlers' Company)
John Thomas Kennedy Charitable Foundation
The Nancy Kenyon Charitable Trust
Keren Association Limited
E. and E. Kernkraut Charities Limited
The Peter Kershaw Trust
The Kohn Foundation
The Kreditor Charitable Trust
The Heinz, Anna and Carol Kroch Foundation
Kupath Gemach Chaim Bechesed Viznitz Trust
Maurice and Hilda Laing Charitable Trust
The Kirby Laing Foundation
The Beatrice Laing Trust
Community Foundations for Lancashire and Merseyside
Duchy of Lancaster Benevolent Fund
The Jack Lane Charitable Trust
Largsmount Ltd
Laslett's (Hinton) Charity
The Edgar E. Lawley Foundation
Lawson Beckman Charitable Trust
The Leathersellers' Company Charitable Fund
The Kennedy Leigh Charitable Trust
David and Ruth Lewis Family Charitable Trust
The Enid Linder Foundation
The Frank Litchfield Charitable Trust
Localtrent Ltd
Loftus Charitable Trust
London Catalyst
The Lowy Mitchell Foundation
LSA Charitable Trust
The Marie Helen Luen Charitable Trust
The Henry Lumley Charitable Trust
Paul Lunn-Rockliffe Charitable Trust
The Lynn Foundation
John Lyon's Charity
The M. K. Charitable Trust
The E. M. MacAndrew Trust
The Mackintosh Foundation
The Magdalen and Lasher Charity (General Fund)
The Magen Charitable Trust
The Mahavir Trust
The Manackerman Charitable Trust
The Manoukian Charitable Foundation
Marbeh Torah Trust
Mariapolis Limited

The Marr-Munning Trust
The Michael Marsh Charitable Trust
Mayfair Charities Ltd
Melodor Limited
The Melow Charitable Trust
Mercaz Torah Vechesed Limited
The Merchants' House of Glasgow
The Metropolitan Masonic Charity
T. & J. Meyer Family Foundation Limited
The Gerald Micklem Charitable Trust
The Mills Charity
The Mirianog Trust
Keren Mitzvah Trust
The Mizpah Trust
Monmouthshire County Council Welsh Church Act Fund
The Morel Charitable Trust
The Morris Charitable Trust
Vyoel Moshe Charitable Trust
The Edith Murphy Foundation
Muslim Hands
Norfolk Community Foundation
The Northmoor Trust
The Odin Charitable Trust
The Olga Charitable Trust
Oxfam (GB)
The Elise Pilkington Charitable Trust
The Pollywally Charitable Trust
The Portishead Nautical Trust
Sir John Priestman Charity Trust
The Puebla Charitable Trust
The Puri Foundation
Quothquan Trust
The Rhondda Cynon Taff Welsh Church Acts Fund
The Richmond Parish Lands Charity
Mrs L. D. Rope Third Charitable Settlement
The Rowland Family Foundation
The Rowlands Trust
The Joseph Rowntree Charitable Trust
Royal Docks Trust (London)
The Sandra Charitable Trust
The Scottish Power Energy People Trust
The Seedfield Trust
The Shanley Charitable Trust
The Simmons & Simmons Charitable Foundation
R. H. Southern Trust
Spears-Stutz Charitable Trust
Tegham Limited
The Thornton Trust
The Tinsley Foundation
UKI Charitable Foundation

The UNITE Foundation
Uxbridge United Welfare Trust
The West Derby Wastelands Charity
The Barbara Whatmore Charitable Trust
The Norman Whiteley Trust
The Benjamin Winegarten Charitable Trust
The Maurice Wohl Charitable Foundation
Woodlands Green Ltd
The Matthews Wrightson Charity Trust

■ **Refugees and asylum seekers**

The 29th May 1961 Charitable Trust
The Bromley Trust
The Barrow Cadbury Trust
The Charities Advisory Trust
The Edith Maud Ellis 1985 Charitable Trust
The Ericson Trust
The Jill Franklin Trust
H. C. D. Memorial Fund
The Harbour Foundation
The Hilden Charitable Fund
The KPMG Foundation
The Allen Lane Foundation
The Leigh Trust
M. and C. Trust
The Mackintosh Foundation
Network for Social Change
The Odin Charitable Trust
The Pilgrim Trust
The Sigrid Rausing Trust
The Reed Foundation
The Alan and Babette Sainsbury Charitable Fund
Six Point Foundation

■ **Victims, oppressed people**

The 1970 Trust
The Alchemy Foundation
Bergqvist Charitable Trust
The Bromley Trust
The Barrow Cadbury Trust
CAFOD (Catholic Agency for Overseas Development)
The Charities Advisory Trust
Christadelphian Samaritan Fund
Christian Aid
The Coltstaple Trust
The Follett Trust
The Anna Rosa Forster Charitable Trust
The Jill Franklin Trust
The Freemasons' Grand Charity

The Girdlers' Company
    Charitable Trust
Global Care
The Charles Hayward
    Foundation
The Charlotte Heber-Percy
    Charitable Trust
The Hemby Charitable Trust
P. and C. Hickinbotham
    Charitable Trust
Hope for Youth (NI)
The Horizon Foundation
The Thomas J. Horne
    Memorial Trust
The Michael and Shirley Hunt
    Charitable Trust
Hyde Charitable Trust
The Ireland Fund of Great
    Britain
Irish Youth Foundation (UK)
    Ltd (incorporating The
    Lawlor Foundation)
The Jarman Charitable Trust
The Elton John Aids
    Foundation
The Kelly Family Charitable
    Trust
The Heinz, Anna and Carol
    Kroch Foundation
Duchy of Lancaster Benevolent
    Fund
The Allen Lane Foundation
The LankellyChase Foundation
The Law Society Charity
The Leathersellers' Company
    Charitable Fund
The Kennedy Leigh Charitable
    Trust
The Leigh Trust
The Loseley and Guildway
    Charitable Trust
The Lotus Foundation
The R. S. Macdonald
    Charitable Trust
Marmot Charitable Trust
The Marr-Munning Trust
Monmouthshire County Council
    Welsh Church Act Fund
The Morel Charitable Trust
Vyoel Moshe Charitable Trust
Muslim Hands
Network for Social Change
The Norton Rose Charitable
    Foundation
Oxfam (GB)
The Portishead Nautical Trust
The W. L. Pratt Charitable
    Trust
The Sigrid Rausing Trust
The Sir James Reckitt Charity
Eva Reckitt Trust Fund
The Joseph Rowntree
    Charitable Trust
Ryklow Charitable Trust 1992
Six Point Foundation
The Tinsley Foundation

The Tresillian Trust
The Westcroft Trust
Woodroffe Benton Foundation
The Woodward Charitable
    Trust

■ **People who have suffered abuse, violence or torture**

The Girdlers' Company
    Charitable Trust
Global Care
The Charlotte Heber-Percy
    Charitable Trust
The Hemby Charitable Trust
P. and C. Hickinbotham
    Charitable Trust
Hyde Charitable Trust
The Kelly Family Charitable
    Trust
The Heinz, Anna and Carol
    Kroch Foundation
Duchy of Lancaster Benevolent
    Fund
The Allen Lane Foundation
The Lotus Foundation
The R. S. Macdonald
    Charitable Trust
The Portishead Nautical Trust
The Sigrid Rausing Trust
Ryklow Charitable Trust 1992
The Woodward Charitable
    Trust

■ **Victims of crime**

The Girdlers' Company
    Charitable Trust
The Hemby Charitable Trust
The Heinz, Anna and Carol
    Kroch Foundation
Ryklow Charitable Trust 1992

■ **Victims of disasters**

Bergqvist Charitable Trust
Christadelphian Samaritan
    Fund
Christian Aid
The Follett Trust
The Freemasons' Grand
    Charity
The Leathersellers' Company
    Charitable Fund
The Loseley and Guildway
    Charitable Trust
Monmouthshire County Council
    Welsh Church Act Fund
Muslim Hands
The Norton Rose Charitable
    Foundation
Oxfam (GB)
The W. L. Pratt Charitable
    Trust

The Sir James Reckitt Charity
Woodroffe Benton Foundation

■ **People suffering from famine**

The Alchemy Foundation
Bergqvist Charitable Trust
CAFOD (Catholic Agency for
    Overseas Development)
Christadelphian Samaritan
    Fund
The Coltstaple Trust
The Anna Rosa Forster
    Charitable Trust
Global Care
Oxfam (GB)
Ryklow Charitable Trust 1992

■ **People suffering injustice**

The Charities Advisory Trust
Global Care
The Michael and Shirley Hunt
    Charitable Trust
The Allen Lane Foundation
The Law Society Charity
The Leigh Trust
Network for Social Change
The Sigrid Rausing Trust
The Joseph Rowntree
    Charitable Trust

■ **Victims of war or conflict**

CAFOD (Catholic Agency for
    Overseas Development)
Global Care
Hope for Youth (NI)
The Heinz, Anna and Carol
    Kroch Foundation
The Kennedy Leigh Charitable
    Trust
Marmot Charitable Trust
Vyoel Moshe Charitable Trust
Muslim Hands
Oxfam (GB)

# Grant-makers by type of grant

This index contains two separate listings:

**List of types of grant:** This lists all the headings used in the DGMT to categorise types of grant.

**Grant-makers by type of grant:** This lists trusts under the types of grant for which they have expressed a funding preference.

# Grant-makers by type of grant

*These pages contain two separate listings*

*List of type of grants*
This lists all of the headings used in the DGMT to categorise types of grants

*Grant-makers by type of grant*
This lists trusts under the types of grants for which they have expressed a funding preference

## Type of support 173

### Capital support 173

- Building/renovation 173

- Collections and acquisitions 179

- Computer systems and equipment 185

- Equipment 191

- Vehicles 198

### Core support 204

- Contributions to statutory funding 204

- Core costs 205

- Development funding 208

- Salaries 221

- Strategic funding 223

### Project support 236

- Full project funding 236

- Seed funding 243

### Campaigning 249

### Loan finance 250

## Type of support

### Capital support

#### ■ Building/renovation

The 1970 Trust
The 1989 Willan Charitable Trust
The 29th May 1961 Charitable Trust
A. W. Charitable Trust
The Aberbrothock Skea Trust
The Aberdeen Endowments Trust
The Aberdeenshire Educational Trust Scheme
Access Sport
Achisomoch Aid Company Limited
The ACT Foundation
Action Medical Research
The Victor Adda Foundation
The Adint Charitable Trust
The Adnams Charity
The Adrian Swire Charitable Trust
Age UK
Aid to the Church in Need (UK)
The Sylvia Aitken Charitable Trust
The Al Fayed Charitable Foundation
Allchurches Trust Ltd
The H. B. Allen Charitable Trust
The Alliance Family Foundation
Angus Allnatt Charitable Foundation
The Pat Allsop Charitable Trust
Altamont Ltd
The Ammco Trust
Viscount Amory's Charitable Trust
The AMW Charitable Trust
The Andrew Anderson Trust
Mary Andrew Charitable Trust
Anglo American Group Foundation
Anguish's Educational Foundation
Anpride Ltd
The Appletree Trust
The Arbib Foundation
The Archer Trust
The Architectural Heritage Fund
The Ardwick Trust
The Argus Appeal
The Artemis Charitable Trust
Arts Council England
Arts Council of Northern Ireland
Arts Council of Wales (Cyngor Celfyddydau Cymru)
The Ove Arup Foundation

The AS Charitable Trust
The Ascot Fire Brigade Trust
The Asda Foundation
The Ashden Trust
The Ashworth Charitable Trust
The Ian Askew Charitable Trust
The Associated Country Women of the World
The Association of Colleges Charitable Trust
Astellas European Foundation
The Astor Foundation
The Astor of Hever Trust
The Aurelius Charitable Trust
The John Avins Trust
The Bagri Foundation
The Austin Bailey Foundation
The Baily Thomas Charitable Fund
The Baird Trust
The Baker Charitable Trust
The Balcombe Charitable Trust
The Albert Casanova Ballard Deceased Trust
The Ballinger Charitable Trust
The Balmore Trust
The Balney Charitable Trust
The Baltic Charitable Fund
The Bamford Charitable Foundation
The Banbury Charities
The Barbers' Company General Charities
The Barnsbury Charitable Trust
The Barnstaple Bridge Trust
The Misses Barrie Charitable Trust
The Bartlett Taylor Charitable Trust
The Paul Bassham Charitable Trust
The Batchworth Trust
The Bates Charitable Trust
The Battens Charitable Trust
The Bay Tree Charitable Trust
The B-CH Charitable Trust
The Bearder Charity
The James Beattie Charitable Trust
The Beaverbrook Foundation
The Beccles Town Lands Charity
The Becker Family Charitable Trust
The Beckett's and Sargeant's Educational Foundation
The John Beckwith Charitable Trust
The Peter Beckwith Charitable Trust
The Bedfordshire and Hertfordshire Historic Churches Trust
The Provincial Grand Lodge of Bedfordshire Charity Fund

The David and Ruth Behrend Fund
The Bellahouston Bequest Fund
The Bellinger Donnay Trust
The Benfield Motors Charitable Trust
The Benham Charitable Settlement
Maurice and Jacqueline Bennett Charitable Trust
The Gerald Bentall Charitable Trust
The Bergne-Coupland Charity
Bergqvist Charitable Trust
The Bernadette Charitable Trust
The Mason Bibby 1981 Trust
The Bideford Bridge Trust
The Billmeir Charitable Trust
Percy Bilton Charity
The Bingham Trust
The Bintaub Charitable Trust
The Birmingham District Nursing Charitable Trust
The Birmingham Hospital Saturday Fund Medical Charity and Welfare Trust
Birmingham International Airport Community Trust
The Lord Mayor of Birmingham's Charity
Miss Jeanne Bisgood's Charitable Trust
The Michael Bishop Foundation
The Blair Foundation
The Morgan Blake Charitable Trust
The Blandford Lake Trust
The Sir Victor Blank Charitable Settlement
The Bluston Charitable Settlement
The Marjory Boddy Charitable Trust
The Bonamy Charitable Trust
The John and Celia Bonham Christie Charitable Trust
The Charlotte Bonham-Carter Charitable Trust
Boots Charitable Trust
The Bordon Liphook Haslemere Charity
The Oliver Borthwick Memorial Trust
The Bothwell Charitable Trust
The Harry Bottom Charitable Trust
The Bower Trust
The Bowerman Charitable Trust
The Bowland Charitable Trust
The Frank Brake Charitable Trust

The William Brake Charitable Trust
The Tony Bramall Charitable Trust
The Bramhope Trust
The Harold and Alice Bridges Charity
The Brighton District Nursing Association Trust
The British Humane Association
The J. and M. Britton Charitable Trust
The Broderers' Charity Trust
The Roger Brooke Charitable Trust
The David Brooke Charity
The Charles Brotherton Trust
Joseph Brough Charitable Trust
Miss Marion Broughton's Charitable Trust
Edna Brown Charitable Settlement
The Jack Brunton Charitable Trust
Buckinghamshire Community Foundation
The Buckinghamshire Historic Churches Trust
The Bulldog Trust Limited
The E. F. Bulmer Benevolent Fund
The Burghley Family Trust
The Burry Charitable Trust
The Arnold Burton 1998 Charitable Trust
The Burton Breweries Charitable Trust
Consolidated Charity of Burton upon Trent
The Worshipful Company of Butchers General Charities
Henry T. and Lucy B. Cadbury Charitable Trust
The Christopher Cadbury Charitable Trust
The G. W. Cadbury Charitable Trust
The Richard Cadbury Charitable Trust
The Edward and Dorothy Cadbury Trust
The George Cadbury Trust
CAFOD (Catholic Agency for Overseas Development)
Community Foundation for Calderdale
Callander Charitable Trust
Calleva Foundation
The Cambridgeshire Historic Churches Trust
The Campden Charities Trustee
The Canning Trust

The Carew Pole Charitable Trust
Carlee Ltd
The Carlton House Charitable Trust
The Carmelite Monastery Ware Trust
The Worshipful Company of Carmen Benevolent Trust
The Carnegie Dunfermline Trust
The Carpenters' Company Charitable Trust
The Carrington Charitable Trust
The Leslie Mary Carter Charitable Trust
Cash for Kids – Radio Clyde
The Catholic Charitable Trust
The Catholic Trust for England and Wales
The Joseph and Annie Cattle Trust
The Thomas Sivewright Catto Charitable Settlement
The Wilfrid and Constance Cave Foundation
Elizabeth Cayzer Charitable Trust
The B. G. S. Cayzer Charitable Trust
The Cazenove Charitable Trust
Celtic Charity Fund
The Chapman Charitable Trust
John William Chapman's Charitable Trust
The Charities Advisory Trust
Charitworth Limited
The Charter 600 Charity
The Cheruby Trust
Cheshire Freemason's Charity
The Chetwode Foundation
The Childs Charitable Trust
The Chippenham Borough Lands Charity
The Chipping Sodbury Town Lands Charity
The Chownes Foundation
Christadelphian Samaritan Fund
Christian Aid
Chrysalis Trust
The Church Burgesses Educational Foundation
Church Burgesses Trust
The City Bridge Trust
Stephen Clark 1957 Charitable Trust
The Hilda and Alice Clark Charitable Trust
The Roger and Sarah Bancroft Clark Charitable Trust
The Clarke Charitable Settlement
The Cleopatra Trust
The Clore Duffield Foundation

Closehelm Limited
The Clothworkers' Foundation
Richard Cloudesley's Charity
The Clover Trust
The Robert Clutterbuck Charitable Trust
Clydpride Ltd
The Francis Coales Charitable Foundation
The Coalfields Regeneration Trust
The John Coates Charitable Trust
The Cobtree Charity Trust Ltd
The Denise Cohen Charitable Trust
The Vivienne and Samuel Cohen Charitable Trust
The John S. Cohen Foundation
The R. and S. Cohen Foundation
The Colchester Catalyst Charity
The Colefax Charitable Trust
John and Freda Coleman Charitable Trust
The George Henry Collins Charity
The Sir Jeremiah Colman Gift Trust
The Coltstaple Trust
Colwinston Charitable Trust
Colyer-Fergusson Charitable Trust
Community First
The Compton Charitable Trust
The Congleton Inclosure Trust
Martin Connell Charitable Trust
The Conservation Foundation
Mabel Cooper Charity
The Alice Ellen Cooper Dean Charitable Foundation
The Marjorie Coote Animal Charity Trust
The Marjorie Coote Old People's Charity
The Helen Jean Cope Trust
The J. Reginald Corah Foundation Fund
The Gershon Coren Charitable Foundation
The Duke of Cornwall's Benevolent Fund
The Cornwell Charitable Trust
The Sidney and Elizabeth Corob Charitable Trust
The Corona Charitable Trust
The Costa Family Charitable Trust
The Cotton Industry War Memorial Trust
Country Houses Foundation
County Durham Community Foundation
General Charity of Coventry

174

Coventry Building Society Charitable Foundation
Dudley and Geoffrey Cox Charitable Trust
The Sir William Coxen Trust Fund
The Lord Cozens-Hardy Trust
The Craignish Trust
The Craps Charitable Trust
Michael Crawford Children's Charity
The Cray Trust
The Crerar Hotels Trust
The Crescent Trust
Cripplegate Foundation
The Violet and Milo Cripps Charitable Trust
The Cross Trust
Cruden Foundation Ltd
The Ronald Cruickshanks Foundation
The Cumber Family Charitable Trust
Cumbria Community Foundation
The Dennis Curry Charitable Trust
The Cwmbran Trust
Itzchok Meyer Cymerman Trust Ltd
The D. G. Charitable Settlement
Baron Davenport's Charity
The Davidson Family Charitable Trust
Michael Davies Charitable Settlement
The Gwendoline and Margaret Davies Charity
The Hamilton Davies Trust
The Wilfrid Bruce Davis Charitable Trust
The Dawe Charitable Trust
The De Brye Charitable Trust
The Deakin Charitable Trust
William Dean Countryside and Educational Trust
The Debmar Benevolent Trust
The Dellal Foundation
The Delves Charitable Trust
The Denman Charitable Trust
The Dentons UKMEA LLP Charitable Trust
The Derbyshire Churches and Chapels Preservation Trust
Derbyshire Community Foundation
The J. N. Derbyshire Trust
The Desmond Foundation
The Devon Historic Churches Trust
The Duke of Devonshire's Charitable Trust
The Sandy Dewhirst Charitable Trust

The Laduma Dhamecha Charitable Trust
The Dibden Allotments Fund
The Digbeth Trust Limited
The Dinwoodie Settlement
Dischma Charitable Trust
The DLM Charitable Trust
The Derek and Eileen Dodgson Foundation
The Dollond Charitable Trust
The Dorset Historic Churches Trust
The Dorus Trust
The Doughty Charity Trust
The Drapers' Charitable Fund
The Duis Charitable Trust
The Dumbreck Charity
Dunard Fund
The Dunn Family Charitable Trust
The W. E. Dunn Trust
Dushinsky Trust Ltd
The Dyers' Company Charitable Trust
The Eagle Charity Trust
The Earley Charity
Earls Colne and Halstead Educational Charity
Eastern Counties Educational Trust Limited
The Sir John Eastwood Foundation
The EBM Charitable Trust
The Gilbert and Eileen Edgar Foundation
Edinburgh Trust No 2 Account
The W. G. Edwards Charitable Foundation
The Elephant Trust
The George Elias Charitable Trust
The Gerald Palmer Eling Trust Company
The Wilfred and Elsie Elkes Charity Fund
The Maud Elkington Charitable Trust
The Ellerdale Trust
The John Ellerman Foundation
The Ellinson Foundation Ltd
The Ellis Campbell Foundation
The Vernon N. Ely Charitable Trust
The Emerton-Christie Charity
The Englefield Charitable Trust
The Enkalon Foundation
Entindale Ltd
The Epigoni Trust
The Equity Trust Fund
The Ericson Trust
The Erskine Cunningham Hill Trust
Essex Community Foundation
The Essex Fairway Charitable Trust
The Essex Heritage Trust

The Essex Youth Trust
Euro Charity Trust
Sir John Evelyn's Charity
The Eventhall Family Charitable Trust
The Everard Foundation
The Eveson Charitable Trust
The Beryl Evetts and Robert Luff Animal Welfare Trust Limited
The Exilarch's Foundation
The F. P. Limited Charitable Trust
The Fairway Trust
The Lord Faringdon Charitable Trust
The Fassnidge Memorial Trust
The February Foundation
The George Fentham Birmingham Charity
The A. M. Fenton Trust
The Allan and Nesta Ferguson Charitable Settlement
The Fidelity UK Foundation
The Doris Field Charitable Trust
The Ian Fleming Charitable Trust
The Football Association National Sports Centre Trust
The Football Association Youth Trust
The Football Foundation
The Oliver Ford Charitable Trust
The Forest Hill Charitable Trust
The Forman Hardy Charitable Trust
Gwyneth Forrester Trust
The Forte Charitable Trust
The Foyle Foundation
The Isaac and Freda Frankel Memorial Charitable Trust
The Elizabeth Frankland Moore and Star Foundation
The Gordon Fraser Charitable Trust
The Hugh Fraser Foundation
The Joseph Strong Frazer Trust
The Louis and Valerie Freedman Charitable Settlement
The Charles S. French Charitable Trust
The Freshfield Foundation
The Friarsgate Trust
Friends of Essex Churches Trust
The Friends of Kent Churches
The Frognal Trust
The Patrick & Helena Frost Foundation
The Fulmer Charitable Trust
G. M. C. Trust
The Gale Family Charity Trust

175

The Gamma Trust
The Gannochy Trust
The Samuel Gardner Memorial Trust
The Garnett Charitable Trust
The Gatsby Charitable Foundation
Gatwick Airport Community Trust
The Robert Gavron Charitable Trust
Sir Robert Geffery's Almshouse Trust
The Gibbs Charitable Trust
Simon Gibson Charitable Trust
The G. C. Gibson Charitable Trust
The Girdlers' Company Charitable Trust
The B. and P. Glasser Charitable Trust
Global Care
Global Charities
Gloucestershire Community Foundation
The Gloucestershire Historic Churches Trust
Worshipful Company of Glovers of London Charitable Trust
The GNC Trust
The Godinton Charitable Trust
The Sydney and Phyllis Goldberg Memorial Charitable Trust
The Golden Bottle Trust
The Goldsmiths' Company Charity
The Golsoncott Foundation
The Mike Gooley Trailfinders Charity
The Gosling Foundation Limited
The Gould Charitable Trust
The Grace Charitable Trust
A. B. Grace Trust
E. C. Graham Belford Charitable Settlement
The Grahame Charitable Foundation Limited
The Granada Foundation
Grand Charitable Trust of the Order of Women Freemasons
The Grange Farm Centre Trust
The J. G. Graves Charitable Trust
The Gray Trust
The Great Stone Bridge Trust of Edenbridge
The Green Hall Foundation
Greenham Common Community Trust Limited
The Greggs Foundation
The Gretna Charitable Trust
The Grimmitt Trust

The Grocers' Charity
The M. and R. Gross Charities Limited
The GRP Charitable Trust
The Guildry Incorporation of Perth
The Walter Guinness Charitable Trust
The Gur Trust
Dr Guthrie's Association
The H. and M. Charitable Trust
H. C. D. Memorial Fund
The Hackney Parochial Charities
The Hadfield Trust
The Hadley Trust
The Edith Winifred Hall Charitable Trust
The Hampshire and Islands Historic Churches Trust
Hampton Fuel Allotment
The Doughty Hanson Charitable Foundation
The Peter Harrison Foundation
Edward Harvist Trust
Headley-Pitt Charitable Trust
The Hedley Denton Charitable Trust
The H. J. Heinz Company Limited Charitable Trust
Help the Homeless Limited
The Herefordshire Historic Churches Trust
The Heritage of London Trust Limited
The Hesslewood Children's Trust (Hull Seamen's and General Orphanage)
The Horne Foundation
Incommunities Foundation
The Charles Irving Charitable Trust
The Ian Karten Charitable Trust
The Kingsbury Charity
The Mary Kinross Charitable Trust
The Sir James Knott Trust
John Laing Charitable Trust
Maurice and Hilda Laing Charitable Trust
The Beatrice Laing Trust
The Lark Trust
The William Leech Charity
Leicester and Leicestershire Historic Churches Preservation Trust
The Erica Leonard Trust
LHR Airport Communities Trust
Lifeline 4 Kids
Lincolnshire Churches Trust
The Charles Lloyd Foundation
Lloyds Bank Foundation for Northern Ireland
Man Group plc Charitable Trust

Charity of John Marshall
The Mersey Docks and Harbour Company Charitable Fund
The Tony Metherell Charitable Trust
Mobbs Memorial Trust Ltd
The Montague Thompson Coon Charitable Trust
The Moss Family Charitable Trust
Mosselson Charitable Trust
The Edwina Mountbatten & Leonora Children's Foundation
Mrs Waterhouse Charitable Trust
The Mugdock Children's Trust
The Mulberry Trust
The Edith Murphy Foundation
The Music Sales Charitable Trust
Muslim Hands
The Mutual Trust Group
The Janet Nash Charitable Settlement
The National Hockey Foundation
The Nationwide Foundation
The Worshipful Company of Needlemakers' Charitable Fund
The Neighbourly Charitable Trust
The James Neill Trust Fund
Nemoral Ltd
The Chevras Ezras Nitzrochim Trust
The Noon Foundation
Norfolk Community Foundation
The Norman Family Charitable Trust
The Normanby Charitable Trust
The Northampton Municipal Church Charities
The Northumberland Village Homes Trust
The Northwood Charitable Trust
The Norton Foundation
The Norwich Town Close Estate Charity
The Norwood and Newton Settlement
The Notgrove Trust
Nottinghamshire Community Foundation
The Nottinghamshire Historic Churches Trust
The Father O'Mahoney Memorial Trust
The Sir Peter O'Sullevan Charitable Trust
The Oakdale Trust
The Oakley Charitable Trust
The Oakmoor Charitable Trust

The Odin Charitable Trust
The Ofenheim Charitable Trust
Oglesby Charitable Trust
Oizer Charitable Trust
The John Oldacre Foundation
Open Gate
The Owen Family Trust
Oxfam (GB)
Oxfordshire Community Foundation
The P. F. Charitable Trust
The Paget Charitable Trust
The Panacea Charitable Trust
The James Pantyfedwen Foundation
The Paragon Trust
The Park House Charitable Trust
The Samuel and Freda Parkinson Charitable Trust
The Patrick Charitable Trust
The Jack Patston Charitable Trust
The Susanna Peake Charitable Trust
The Pedmore Sporting Club Trust Fund
The Dowager Countess Eleanor Peel Trust
The Pennycress Trust
The Performing Right Society Foundation
The Personal Assurance Charitable Trust
The Persson Charitable Trust
The Jack Petchey Foundation
The Petplan Charitable Trust
The Phillips and Rubens Charitable Trust
The Phillips Charitable Trust
The Phillips Family Charitable Trust
The Bernard Piggott Charitable Trust
The Pilgrim Trust
The Pilkington Charities Fund
The Austin and Hope Pilkington Trust
The Sir Harry Pilkington Trust Fund
The DLA Piper Charitable Trust
The Platinum Trust
The George and Esme Pollitzer Charitable Settlement
Edith and Ferdinand Porjes Charitable Trust
The John Porter Charitable Trust
The Porter Foundation
The Portishead Nautical Trust
The Portrack Charitable Trust
The J. E. Posnansky Charitable Trust
Premierquote Ltd
Premishlaner Charitable Trust

The William Price Charitable Trust
Sir John Priestman Charity Trust
The Primrose Trust
The Prince of Wales's Charitable Foundation
Prison Service Charity Fund
The Privy Purse Charitable Trust
The Puebla Charitable Trust
The Puri Foundation
Mr and Mrs J. A. Pye's Charitable Settlement
Quartet Community Foundation
Queen Mary's Roehampton Trust
The Queen's Silver Jubilee Trust
R. S. Charitable Trust
The Monica Rabagliati Charitable Trust
Rachel Charitable Trust
The Mr and Mrs Philip Rackham Charitable Trust
Richard Radcliffe Charitable Trust
The Radcliffe Trust
The Ragdoll Foundation
The Rainford Trust
The Joseph and Lena Randall Charitable Trust
The Rank Foundation Limited
The Ratcliff Foundation
The Eleanor Rathbone Charitable Trust
The Sigrid Rausing Trust
The Ravensdale Trust
The Rayden Charitable Trust
The Roger Raymond Charitable Trust
The Rayne Foundation
The Rayne Trust
The Sir James Reckitt Charity
Red Hill Charitable Trust
The C. A. Redfern Charitable Foundation
The Reed Foundation
Richard Reeve's Foundation
The Rest Harrow Trust
Reuben Foundation
The Rhododendron Trust
The Rhondda Cynon Taff Welsh Church Acts Fund
The Clive Richards Charity
The Richmond Parish Lands Charity
Ridgesave Limited
The Sir John Ritblat Family Foundation
Thomas Roberts Trust
The Robertson Trust
The Rochester Bridge Trust
The Rock Foundation
The Rofeh Trust
Rokach Family Charitable Trust

The Helen Roll Charitable Trust
The Sir James Roll Charitable Trust
The Rosca Trust
The Rose Foundation
The Cecil Rosen Foundation
The Rothermere Foundation
The Rothley Trust
The Roughley Charitable Trust
Rowanville Ltd
The Rowlands Trust
Royal Artillery Charitable Fund
Royal British Legion
Royal Docks Trust (London)
Royal Masonic Trust for Girls and Boys
The Royal Victoria Hall Foundation
The Rubin Foundation
The Russell Trust
The J. S. and E. C. Rymer Charitable Trust
The Michael Sacher Charitable Trust
The Michael Harry Sacher Trust
Raymond and Beverly Sackler 1988 Foundation
The Sackler Trust
The Ruzin Sadagora Trust
The Saddlers' Company Charitable Fund
The Saga Charitable Trust
The Jean Sainsbury Animal Welfare Trust
The Alan and Babette Sainsbury Charitable Fund
The Sainsbury Family Charitable Trusts
Sam and Bella Sebba Charitable Trust
The Basil Samuel Charitable Trust
The M. J. Samuel Charitable Trust
The Peter Samuel Charitable Trust
The Samworth Foundation
The Sandra Charitable Trust
The Scarfe Charitable Trust
The Schapira Charitable Trust
The Schmidt-Bodner Charitable Trust
The Schreib Trust
The Schreiber Charitable Trust
The Schuster Charitable Trust
Foundation Scotland
The Francis C. Scott Charitable Trust
The Frieda Scott Charitable Trust
Scottish Coal Industry Special Welfare Fund
The Scouloudi Foundation

**177**

Seafarers UK (King George's Fund for Sailors)
The Seedfield Trust
Leslie Sell Charitable Trust
ShareGift (The Orr Mackintosh Foundation)
The Shears Foundation
The Sheffield and District Hospital Services Charitable Fund
The Patricia and Donald Shepherd Charitable Trust
The Archie Sherman Cardiff Foundation
The Archie Sherman Charitable Trust
The Shetland Charitable Trust
SHINE (Support and Help in Education)
The Barnett and Sylvia Shine No 2 Charitable Trust
The Bassil Shippam and Alsford Trust
The Shipwrights' Company Charitable Fund
The Shirley Foundation
Shlomo Memorial Fund Limited
The J. A. Shone Memorial Trust
The Mary Elizabeth Siebel Charity
David and Jennifer Sieff Charitable Trust
The Huntly and Margery Sinclair Charitable Trust
The Sino-British Fellowship Trust
SITA Cornwall Trust Limited
The Skelton Bounty
The Charles Skey Charitable Trust
Sloane Robinson Foundation
The SMB Charitable Trust
The Mrs Smith and Mount Trust
The N. Smith Charitable Settlement
The Henry Smith Charity
The Stanley Smith UK Horticultural Trust
The Solo Charitable Settlement
Somerset Churches Trust
The E. C. Sosnow Charitable Trust
The South Square Trust
The W. F. Southall Trust
The Southover Manor General Education Trust
The Sovereign Health Care Charitable Trust
Sparquote Limited
The Spear Charitable Trust
The Worshipful Company of Spectacle Makers' Charity
The Jessie Spencer Trust

The Ralph and Irma Sperring Charity
The Spielman Charitable Trust
Springrule Limited
The Spurrell Charitable Trust
The Geoff and Fiona Squire Foundation
St James's Trust Settlement
St James's Place Foundation
St Michael's and All Saints' Charities Relief Branch
The Stanley Foundation Ltd
The Staples Trust
The Steel Charitable Trust
The Steinberg Family Charitable Trust
The Stephen Barry Charitable Trust
The Stewards' Company Limited (incorporating the J. W. Laing Trust and the J. W. Laing Biblical Scholarship Trust)
The Leonard Laity Stoate Charitable Trust
The Stobart Newlands Charitable Trust
The Edward Stocks-Massey Bequest Fund
The Stoller Charitable Trust
M. J. C. Stone Charitable Trust
The Samuel Storey Family Charitable Trust
Peter Stormonth Darling Charitable Trust
The Strangward Trust
Stratford upon Avon Town Trust
The W. O. Street Charitable Foundation
The Sudborough Foundation
The Bernard Sunley Charitable Foundation
The Sussex Historic Churches Trust
Sutton Coldfield Charitable Trust
The Swann-Morton Foundation
Swansea and Brecon Diocesan Board of Finance Limited
The John Swire (1989) Charitable Trust
The Swire Charitable Trust
The Hugh and Ruby Sykes Charitable Trust
The Charles and Elsie Sykes Trust
Sylvia Waddilove Foundation UK
The Charity of Stella Symons
The Talbot Trusts
The Talbot Village Trust
The Lady Tangye Charitable Trust
The David Tannen Charitable Trust

The Tanner Trust
The Lili Tapper Charitable Foundation
The Tay Charitable Trust
A. P. Taylor Trust
Tearfund
The Tedworth Charitable Trust
Tees Valley Community Foundation
The Templeton Goodwill Trust
Tesco Charity Trust
The C. Paul Thackray General Charitable Trust
The Thistle Trust
The Loke Wan Tho Memorial Foundation
The Thompson Family Charitable Trust
The Sir Jules Thorn Charitable Trust
The Thornton Foundation
The Thornton Trust
The Three Guineas Trust
The Thriplow Charitable Trust
The Daniel Thwaites Charitable Trust
The Tinsley Foundation
The Tobacco Pipe Makers and Tobacco Trade Benevolent Fund
The Tolkien Trust
Tomchei Torah Charitable Trust
The Tompkins Foundation
The Tory Family Foundation
Tottenham Grammar School Foundation
The Tower Hill Trust
The Towry Law Charitable Trust (also known as the Castle Educational Trust)
The Toy Trust
The Constance Travis Charitable Trust
The Triangle Trust (1949) Fund
The True Colours Trust
Truedene Co. Ltd
The Truemark Trust
Truemart Limited
Trumros Limited
The Trusthouse Charitable Foundation
Tudor Rose Ltd
The Tudor Trust
The Tufton Charitable Trust
The Douglas Turner Trust
The Florence Turner Trust
The G. J. W. Turner Trust
Community Foundation Serving Tyne and Wear and Northumberland
Trustees of Tzedakah
Ulster Garden Villages Ltd
The Underwood Trust
The Union of Orthodox Hebrew Congregation

The United Society for the
  Propagation of the Gospel
Uxbridge United Welfare Trust
The Van Neste Foundation
The Vandervell Foundation
The Vardy Foundation
The Variety Club Children's
  Charity
Veneziana Fund
The Nigel Vinson Charitable
  Trust
The William and Ellen Vinten
  Trust
Vision Charity
Vivdale Ltd
Voluntary Action Fund
Wade's Charity
The Community Foundation in
  Wales
Wales Council for Voluntary
  Action
War on Want
Sir Siegmund Warburg's
  Voluntary Settlement
The Ward Blenkinsop Trust
G. R. Waters Charitable Trust
  2000
The Wellcome Trust
The Westminster Foundation
The Charity of William Williams
The Kay Williams Charitable
  Foundation
The Community Foundation for
  Wiltshire and Swindon
The Maurice Wohl Charitable
  Foundation
The Charles Wolfson
  Charitable Trust
The Wolfson Family Charitable
  Trust
The Worcestershire and
  Dudley Historic Churches
  Trust
Wychville Ltd
Yorkshire Building Society
  Charitable Foundation
The Yorkshire Historic
  Churches Trust
The Zochonis Charitable Trust
Zurich Community Trust (UK)
  Limited

■ Collections and
  acquisitions

The 1970 Trust
The 1989 Willan Charitable
  Trust
The 29th May 1961 Charitable
  Trust
A. W. Charitable Trust
The Aberbrothock Skea Trust
The Aberdeen Endowments
  Trust
Achisomoch Aid Company
  Limited

The ACT Foundation
Action Medical Research
The Company of Actuaries'
  Charitable Trust Fund
The Victor Adda Foundation
The Adint Charitable Trust
The Adrian Swire Charitable
  Trust
Aid to the Church in Need (UK)
The Sylvia Aitken Charitable
  Trust
The Al Fayed Charitable
  Foundation
Aldgate and All Hallows'
  Foundation
Allchurches Trust Ltd
The H. B. Allen Charitable
  Trust
The Alliance Family Foundation
The Pat Allsop Charitable Trust
Altamont Ltd
The Ammco Trust
Viscount Amory's Charitable
  Trust
The AMW Charitable Trust
Mary Andrew Charitable Trust
Anguish's Educational
  Foundation
The Animal Defence Trust
The Eric Anker-Petersen
  Charity
Anpride Ltd
The Appletree Trust
The Arbib Foundation
The Archer Trust
The Architectural Heritage
  Fund
The Ardwick Trust
The Argus Appeal
The Armourers' and Brasiers'
  Gauntlet Trust
Arts Council England
Arts Council of Northern
  Ireland
Arts Council of Wales (Cyngor
  Celfyddydau Cymru)
The Ove Arup Foundation
The AS Charitable Trust
The Ascot Fire Brigade Trust
The Ashden Trust
The Ashley Family Foundation
The Ashworth Charitable Trust
The Ian Askew Charitable Trust
The Associated Country
  Women of the World
The Association of Colleges
  Charitable Trust
Astellas European Foundation
Asthma UK
The Astor Foundation
The Astor of Hever Trust
The Aurelius Charitable Trust
The John Avins Trust
The Avon and Somerset Police
  Community Trust
The Bagri Foundation

The Austin Bailey Foundation
The Baird Trust
The Baker Charitable Trust
The Balcombe Charitable Trust
The Albert Casanova Ballard
  Deceased Trust
The Ballinger Charitable Trust
The Balmore Trust
The Balney Charitable Trust
The Baltic Charitable Fund
The Bamford Charitable
  Foundation
The Banbury Charities
The Barbers' Company General
  Charities
The Barbour Foundation
Barchester Healthcare
  Foundation
The Barnsbury Charitable Trust
The Barnstaple Bridge Trust
The Misses Barrie Charitable
  Trust
Bartholomew Charitable Trust
The Bartlett Taylor Charitable
  Trust
The Paul Bassham Charitable
  Trust
The Batchworth Trust
The Bates Charitable Trust
The Battens Charitable Trust
The Bay Tree Charitable Trust
The B-CH Charitable Trust
The Bearder Charity
The James Beattie Charitable
  Trust
The Beaverbrook Foundation
The Beccles Town Lands
  Charity
The Becker Family Charitable
  Trust
The Beckett's and Sargeant's
  Educational Foundation
The Peter Beckwith Charitable
  Trust
The Provincial Grand Lodge of
  Bedfordshire Charity Fund
The David and Ruth Behrend
  Fund
The Bellahouston Bequest
  Fund
The Bellinger Donnay Trust
The Benfield Motors Charitable
  Trust
The Benham Charitable
  Settlement
Maurice and Jacqueline
  Bennett Charitable Trust
The Gerald Bentall Charitable
  Trust
The Bergne-Coupland Charity
Bergqvist Charitable Trust
The Bernadette Charitable
  Trust
BHST
The Mason Bibby 1981 Trust
The Bideford Bridge Trust

179

The Billmeir Charitable Trust
The Bingham Trust
The Bintaub Charitable Trust
The Birmingham District Nursing Charitable Trust
The Birmingham Hospital Saturday Fund Medical Charity and Welfare Trust
The Lord Mayor of Birmingham's Charity
Miss Jeanne Bisgood's Charitable Trust
The Michael Bishop Foundation
The Blair Foundation
The Morgan Blake Charitable Trust
The Blandford Lake Trust
The Sir Victor Blank Charitable Settlement
The Bluston Charitable Settlement
The Bonamy Charitable Trust
The John and Celia Bonham Christie Charitable Trust
The Charlotte Bonham-Carter Charitable Trust
Boots Charitable Trust
The Bordon Liphook Haslemere Charity
The Oliver Borthwick Memorial Trust
The Bothwell Charitable Trust
The Harry Bottom Charitable Trust
The Bower Trust
The Bowerman Charitable Trust
The Bowland Charitable Trust
The Frank Brake Charitable Trust
The William Brake Charitable Trust
The Tony Bramall Charitable Trust
The Bramhope Trust
The Harold and Alice Bridges Charity
The Brighton District Nursing Association Trust
British Gas (Scottish Gas) Energy Trust
British Heart Foundation
The British Humane Association
The J. and M. Britton Charitable Trust
The Broderers' Charity Trust
The Roger Brooke Charitable Trust
The David Brooke Charity
The Charles Brotherton Trust
Joseph Brough Charitable Trust
Miss Marion Broughton's Charitable Trust

Edna Brown Charitable Settlement
The Jack Brunton Charitable Trust
Buckinghamshire Community Foundation
The Bulldog Trust Limited
The E. F. Bulmer Benevolent Fund
The Burghley Family Trust
The Burry Charitable Trust
The Arnold Burton 1998 Charitable Trust
The Burton Breweries Charitable Trust
Consolidated Charity of Burton upon Trent
The Worshipful Company of Butchers General Charities
The Noel Buxton Trust
Henry T. and Lucy B. Cadbury Charitable Trust
The Christopher Cadbury Charitable Trust
The G. W. Cadbury Charitable Trust
The Richard Cadbury Charitable Trust
The Edward and Dorothy Cadbury Trust
The George Cadbury Trust
CAFOD (Catholic Agency for Overseas Development)
Community Foundation for Calderdale
Callander Charitable Trust
The Canning Trust
The Carew Pole Charitable Trust
Carlee Ltd
The Carlton House Charitable Trust
The Carmelite Monastery Ware Trust
The Worshipful Company of Carmen Benevolent Trust
The Carnegie Dunfermline Trust
The Carpenters' Company Charitable Trust
The Carrington Charitable Trust
The Leslie Mary Carter Charitable Trust
The Elizabeth Casson Trust
The Catholic Charitable Trust
The Catholic Trust for England and Wales
The Joseph and Annie Cattle Trust
The Thomas Sivewright Catto Charitable Settlement
The Wilfrid and Constance Cave Foundation
Elizabeth Cayzer Charitable Trust

The B. G. S. Cayzer Charitable Trust
The Cazenove Charitable Trust
Celtic Charity Fund
The Chapman Charitable Trust
John William Chapman's Charitable Trust
The Charities Advisory Trust
Charitworth Limited
The Charter 600 Charity
The Cheruby Trust
Cheshire Freemason's Charity
The Chetwode Foundation
The Childs Charitable Trust
The Chippenham Borough Lands Charity
The Chipping Sodbury Town Lands Charity
The Chownes Foundation
The Christabella Charitable Trust
Christadelphian Samaritan Fund
Christian Aid
The Church Burgesses Educational Foundation
Church Burgesses Trust
The City Educational Trust Fund
Stephen Clark 1957 Charitable Trust
J. A. Clark Charitable Trust
The Hilda and Alice Clark Charitable Trust
The Roger and Sarah Bancroft Clark Charitable Trust
The Clarke Charitable Settlement
The Cleopatra Trust
The Clore Duffield Foundation
Closehelm Limited
The Clothworkers' Foundation
The Clover Trust
The Robert Clutterbuck Charitable Trust
Clydpride Ltd
The John Coates Charitable Trust
The Cobtree Charity Trust Ltd
The Denise Cohen Charitable Trust
The Vivienne and Samuel Cohen Charitable Trust
The John S. Cohen Foundation
The R. and S. Cohen Foundation
The Colchester Catalyst Charity
The Colefax Charitable Trust
John and Freda Coleman Charitable Trust
The George Henry Collins Charity
The Sir Jeremiah Colman Gift Trust
The Coltstaple Trust

180

Colwinston Charitable Trust
Colyer-Ferguson Charitable Trust
Community First
The Compton Charitable Trust
The Congleton Inclosure Trust
Martin Connell Charitable Trust
The Conservation Foundation
The Consolidated Charities for the Infirm – Merchant Taylors' Company
Mabel Cooper Charity
The Alice Ellen Cooper Dean Charitable Foundation
The Marjorie Coote Animal Charity Trust
The Marjorie Coote Old People's Charity
The Helen Jean Cope Trust
The J. Reginald Corah Foundation Fund
The Gershon Coren Charitable Foundation
The Duke of Cornwall's Benevolent Fund
The Cornwell Charitable Trust
The Sidney and Elizabeth Corob Charitable Trust
The Corona Charitable Trust
The Costa Family Charitable Trust
The Cotton Industry War Memorial Trust
The Cotton Trust
County Durham Community Foundation
The Augustine Courtauld Trust
General Charity of Coventry
Coventry Building Society Charitable Foundation
Dudley and Geoffrey Cox Charitable Trust
The Sir William Coxen Trust Fund
The Lord Cozens-Hardy Trust
The Craignish Trust
The Craps Charitable Trust
Michael Crawford Children's Charity
The Cray Trust
Creative Scotland
The Crescent Trust
The Violet and Milo Cripps Charitable Trust
The Cross Trust
The Croydon Relief in Need Charities
Cruden Foundation Ltd
The Ronald Cruickshanks Foundation
The Cumber Family Charitable Trust
Cumbria Community Foundation

The Dennis Curry Charitable Trust
The Cwmbran Trust
Itzchok Meyer Cymerman Trust Ltd
The D. G. Charitable Settlement
Daily Prayer Union Charitable Trust Limited
The Daiwa Anglo-Japanese Foundation
The Davidson Family Charitable Trust
Michael Davies Charitable Settlement
The Gwendoline and Margaret Davies Charity
The Wilfrid Bruce Davis Charitable Trust
The Dawe Charitable Trust
The De Brye Charitable Trust
The Deakin Charitable Trust
The Debmar Benevolent Trust
The Delius Trust
The Dellal Foundation
The Delves Charitable Trust
The Denman Charitable Trust
The Dentons UKMEA LLP Charitable Trust
Derbyshire Community Foundation
The J. N. Derbyshire Trust
The Desmond Foundation
Devon Community Foundation
The Duke of Devonshire's Charitable Trust
The Sandy Dewhirst Charitable Trust
The Laduma Dhamecha Charitable Trust
The Dibden Allotments Fund
The Digbeth Trust Limited
The Dinwoodie Settlement
Dischma Charitable Trust
The DLM Charitable Trust
The Derek and Eileen Dodgson Foundation
The Dollond Charitable Trust
The Doughty Charity Trust
Douglas Arter Foundation
The Drapers' Charitable Fund
The Duis Charitable Trust
The Dumbreck Charity
Dunard Fund
The Dunn Family Charitable Trust
The W. E. Dunn Trust
Dushinsky Trust Ltd
The Dyers' Company Charitable Trust
The Eagle Charity Trust
The Earley Charity
Earls Colne and Halstead Educational Charity
East End Community Foundation

Eastern Counties Educational Trust Limited
EDF Energy Trust
The Gilbert and Eileen Edgar Foundation
Edinburgh & Lothian Trust Fund
Edinburgh Trust No 2 Account
The W. G. Edwards Charitable Foundation
The Elephant Trust
The George Elias Charitable Trust
The Gerald Palmer Eling Trust Company
The Wilfred and Elsie Elkes Charity Fund
The Ellerdale Trust
The Ellinson Foundation Ltd
The Ellis Campbell Foundation
The Elmley Foundation
The Vernon N. Ely Charitable Trust
The Emerton-Christie Charity
EMI Music Sound Foundation
The Englefield Charitable Trust
The Enkalon Foundation
Entindale Ltd
The Epigoni Trust
The Equity Trust Fund
The Ericson Trust
The Erskine Cunningham Hill Trust
Essex Community Foundation
The Essex Fairway Charitable Trust
The Essex Heritage Trust
Euro Charity Trust
Sir John Evelyn's Charity
The Eventhall Family Charitable Trust
The Everard Foundation
The Beryl Evetts and Robert Luff Animal Welfare Trust Limited
The Exilarch's Foundation
The F. P. Limited Charitable Trust
The Fairway Trust
The Lord Faringdon Charitable Trust
The Fassnidge Memorial Trust
The George Fentham Birmingham Charity
The A. M. Fenton Trust
The Allan and Nesta Ferguson Charitable Settlement
The Fidelity UK Foundation
The Doris Field Charitable Trust
Field Family Charitable Trust
The Ian Fleming Charitable Trust
The Football Association National Sports Centre Trust

The Football Foundation
The Oliver Ford Charitable Trust
The Forest Hill Charitable Trust
Forever Manchester (The Community Foundation for Greater Manchester)
The Forman Hardy Charitable Trust
Gwyneth Forrester Trust
The Forte Charitable Trust
The Four Winds Trust
The Foyle Foundation
The Isaac and Freda Frankel Memorial Charitable Trust
The Elizabeth Frankland Moore and Star Foundation
The Jill Franklin Trust
The Gordon Fraser Charitable Trust
The Hugh Fraser Foundation
The Joseph Strong Frazer Trust
The Louis and Valerie Freedman Charitable Settlement
The Charles S. French Charitable Trust
The Freshfield Foundation
The Friarsgate Trust
Friends Provident Charitable Foundation
The Frognal Trust
The Patrick & Helena Frost Foundation
The Fulmer Charitable Trust
The Gale Family Charity Trust
The Gamma Trust
The Gannochy Trust
The Samuel Gardner Memorial Trust
The Garnett Charitable Trust
Garthgwynion Charities
The Gatsby Charitable Foundation
Gatwick Airport Community Trust
The Robert Gavron Charitable Trust
Sir Robert Geffery's Almshouse Trust
The Gibbs Charitable Trust
Simon Gibson Charitable Trust
The G. C. Gibson Charitable Trust
The Girdlers' Company Charitable Trust
The B. and P. Glasser Charitable Trust
Global Care
Global Charities
Gloucestershire Community Foundation
Worshipful Company of Glovers of London Charitable Trust
The GNC Trust

The Godinton Charitable Trust
The Sydney and Phyllis Goldberg Memorial Charitable Trust
The Golden Bottle Trust
The Goldsmiths' Arts Trust Fund
The Goldsmiths' Company Charity
The Mike Gooley Trailfinders Charity
The Gosling Foundation Limited
The Gould Charitable Trust
The Grace Charitable Trust
A. B. Grace Trust
E. C. Graham Belford Charitable Settlement
The Grahame Charitable Foundation Limited
The Granada Foundation
Grand Charitable Trust of the Order of Women Freemasons
The Grange Farm Centre Trust
The Gray Trust
The Great Stone Bridge Trust of Edenbridge
Greenham Common Community Trust Limited
The Gretna Charitable Trust
The Grocers' Charity
The M. and R. Gross Charities Limited
The GRP Charitable Trust
The Guildry Incorporation of Perth
The Walter Guinness Charitable Trust
The Gur Trust
Dr Guthrie's Association
The H. and M. Charitable Trust
H. C. D. Memorial Fund
The Hackney Parochial Charities
The Hadfield Trust
The Alfred Haines Charitable Trust
Hamilton Wallace Trust
Paul Hamlyn Foundation
The Doughty Hanson Charitable Foundation
Edward Harvist Trust
Headley-Pitt Charitable Trust
The Hedley Denton Charitable Trust
The H. J. Heinz Company Limited Charitable Trust
Help the Homeless Limited
The Herefordshire Historic Churches Trust
The Heritage of London Trust Limited
Hitchin Educational Foundation
The Hoover Foundation

The Charles Irving Charitable Trust
The Kennel Club Charitable Trust
The Kingsbury Charity
The Lark Trust
Leicester and Leicestershire Historic Churches Preservation Trust
The Erica Leonard Trust
The Leverhulme Trust
LHR Airport Communities Trust
The Charles Lloyd Foundation
Robert Luff Foundation Ltd
The Lyndhurst Trust
Sylvanus Lysons Charity
Man Group plc Charitable Trust
Lord Mayor of Manchester's Charity Appeal Trust
Charity of John Marshall
The Mersey Docks and Harbour Company Charitable Fund
The Tony Metherell Charitable Trust
Mobbs Memorial Trust Ltd
The Montague Thompson Coon Charitable Trust
The Henry Moore Foundation
The Moss Family Charitable Trust
Mosselson Charitable Trust
The Mount Everest Foundation
The Edwina Mountbatten & Leonora Children's Foundation
Mrs Waterhouse Charitable Trust
The Mugdock Children's Trust
The Mulberry Trust
The Edith Murphy Foundation
The Music Sales Charitable Trust
Muslim Hands
The Mutual Trust Group
The Janet Nash Charitable Settlement
The National Art Collections Fund
The National Churches Trust
National Committee of the Women's World Day of Prayer for England and Wales and Northern Ireland
The National Hockey Foundation
The National Manuscripts Conservation Trust
The Nationwide Foundation
The Worshipful Company of Needlemakers' Charitable Fund
The Neighbourly Charitable Trust
The James Neill Trust Fund

182

Nemoral Ltd
The Newcomen Collett Foundation
The Chevras Ezras Nitzrochim Trust
The Noon Foundation
The Norman Family Charitable Trust
The Normanby Charitable Trust
The Northampton Municipal Church Charities
The Northmoor Trust
The Northumberland Village Homes Trust
The Northwood Charitable Trust
The Norton Foundation
The Norwich Town Close Estate Charity
The Nottingham General Dispensary
Nottinghamshire Community Foundation
The Nottinghamshire Historic Churches Trust
The Father O'Mahoney Memorial Trust
The Sir Peter O'Sullivan Charitable Trust
The Oakdale Trust
The Oakley Charitable Trust
The Oakmoor Charitable Trust
The Odin Charitable Trust
The Ofenheim Charitable Trust
The Ogle Christian Trust
Oizer Charitable Trust
The John Oldacre Foundation
Open Gate
The Ouseley Trust
The Owen Family Trust
Oxfam (GB)
Oxfordshire Community Foundation
The P. F. Charitable Trust
The Paget Charitable Trust
The Panacea Charitable Trust
The James Pantyfedwen Foundation
The Paragon Trust
The Park House Charitable Trust
The Samuel and Freda Parkinson Charitable Trust
The Patrick Charitable Trust
The Jack Patston Charitable Trust
The Harry Payne Fund
The Susanna Peake Charitable Trust
The Pedmore Sporting Club Trust Fund
The Pennycress Trust
The Performing Right Society Foundation
The Personal Assurance Charitable Trust

The Persson Charitable Trust
The Persula Foundation
The Jack Petchey Foundation
The Petplan Charitable Trust
The Phillips and Rubens Charitable Trust
The Phillips Charitable Trust
The Phillips Family Charitable Trust
The David Pickford Charitable Foundation
The Bernard Piggott Charitable Trust
The Pilgrim Trust
The Austin and Hope Pilkington Trust
The Sir Harry Pilkington Trust Fund
The DLA Piper Charitable Trust
The Platinum Trust
The George and Esme Pollitzer Charitable Settlement
The Ponton House Trust
Edith and Ferdinand Porjes Charitable Trust
The John Porter Charitable Trust
The Porter Foundation
The Portishead Nautical Trust
The Portrack Charitable Trust
The J. E. Posnansky Charitable Trust
Premierquote Ltd
Premishlaner Charitable Trust
The William Price Charitable Trust
Sir John Priestman Charity Trust
The Primrose Trust
The Prince of Wales's Charitable Foundation
Prison Service Charity Fund
The Privy Purse Charitable Trust
The Puebla Charitable Trust
The Puri Foundation
The Queen's Silver Jubilee Trust
R. S. Charitable Trust
The RVW Trust
The Monica Rabagliati Charitable Trust
Rachel Charitable Trust
The Mr and Mrs Philip Rackham Charitable Trust
Richard Radcliffe Charitable Trust
The Radcliffe Trust
The Ragdoll Foundation
The Rainford Trust
The Joseph and Lena Randall Charitable Trust
The Ratcliff Foundation
The Eleanor Rathbone Charitable Trust
The Sigrid Rausing Trust

The Ravensdale Trust
The Rayden Charitable Trust
The Roger Raymond Charitable Trust
The Rayne Foundation
The Rayne Trust
The Sir James Reckitt Charity
The C. A. Redfern Charitable Foundation
The Reed Foundation
Richard Reeve's Foundation
The Rest Harrow Trust
Reuben Foundation
The Rhododendron Trust
The Rhondda Cynon Taff Welsh Church Acts Fund
The Clive Richards Charity
The Richmond Parish Lands Charity
Ridgesave Limited
The Sir John Ritblat Family Foundation
The River Trust
Thomas Roberts Trust
The Robertson Trust
The Rochester Bridge Trust
The Rock Foundation
The Rofeh Trust
Rokach Family Charitable Trust
The Helen Roll Charitable Trust
The Sir James Roll Charitable Trust
The Rosca Trust
The Cecil Rosen Foundation
The Rothermere Foundation
The Rothley Trust
The Roughley Charitable Trust
Mrs Gladys Row Fogo Charitable Trust
Rowanville Ltd
The Rowlands Trust
Royal Artillery Charitable Fund
Royal British Legion
Royal Docks Trust (London)
Royal Masonic Trust for Girls and Boys
The Royal Victoria Hall Foundation
The Rubin Foundation
The Russell Trust
The J. S. and E. C. Rymer Charitable Trust
The Michael Sacher Charitable Trust
The Michael Harry Sacher Trust
Raymond and Beverly Sackler 1988 Foundation
The Sackler Trust
The Ruzin Sadagora Trust
The Saddlers' Company Charitable Fund
The Saga Charitable Trust
The Jean Sainsbury Animal Welfare Trust

The Alan and Babette
    Sainsbury Charitable Fund
The Sainsbury Family
    Charitable Trusts
Sam and Bella Sebba
    Charitable Trust
The Basil Samuel Charitable
    Trust
The M. J. Samuel Charitable
    Trust
The Peter Samuel Charitable
    Trust
The Samworth Foundation
The Sandra Charitable Trust
The Scarfe Charitable Trust
The Schapira Charitable Trust
The Schmidt-Bodner Charitable
    Trust
The Schreib Trust
The Schreiber Charitable Trust
The Schuster Charitable Trust
Foundation Scotland
The Francis C. Scott Charitable
    Trust
The Frieda Scott Charitable
    Trust
Scottish Coal Industry Special
    Welfare Fund
The Scouloudi Foundation
The Seedfield Trust
Leslie Sell Charitable Trust
ShareGift (The Orr Mackintosh
    Foundation)
The Sheepdrove Trust
The Sheffield and District
    Hospital Services
    Charitable Fund
The Sheldon Trust
The Patricia and Donald
    Shepherd Charitable Trust
The Archie Sherman Cardiff
    Foundation
The Archie Sherman Charitable
    Trust
The R. C. Sherriff Rosebriars
    Trust
The Shetland Charitable Trust
SHINE (Support and Help in
    Education)
The Barnett and Sylvia Shine
    No 2 Charitable Trust
The Bassil Shippam and
    Alsford Trust
The Shipwrights' Company
    Charitable Fund
The Shirley Foundation
Shlomo Memorial Fund Limited
The J. A. Shone Memorial
    Trust
David and Jennifer Sieff
    Charitable Trust
The Huntly and Margery
    Sinclair Charitable Trust
The Sino-British Fellowship
    Trust
SITA Cornwall Trust Limited

The Skelton Bounty
The Charles Skey Charitable
    Trust
Skipton Building Society
    Charitable Foundation
The SMB Charitable Trust
The Mrs Smith and Mount
    Trust
The N. Smith Charitable
    Settlement
The Stanley Smith UK
    Horticultural Trust
The Solo Charitable
    Settlement
The E. C. Sosnow Charitable
    Trust
The Souter Charitable Trust
The South Square Trust
The W. F. Southall Trust
The Sovereign Health Care
    Charitable Trust
Sparquote Limited
The Spear Charitable Trust
The Worshipful Company of
    Spectacle Makers' Charity
The Jessie Spencer Trust
The Ralph and Irma Sperring
    Charity
The Spielman Charitable Trust
The Spoore, Merry and Rixman
    Foundation
Springrule Limited
The Spurrell Charitable Trust
The Geoff and Fiona Squire
    Foundation
St James's Trust Settlement
St James's Place Foundation
Sir Walter St John's
    Educational Charity
St Michael's and All Saints'
    Charities Relief Branch
The Stanley Foundation Ltd
The Steel Charitable Trust
The Steinberg Family
    Charitable Trust
The Stephen Barry Charitable
    Trust
The Leonard Laity Stoate
    Charitable Trust
The Edward Stocks-Massey
    Bequest Fund
The Stoller Charitable Trust
M. J. C. Stone Charitable Trust
The Samuel Storey Family
    Charitable Trust
Peter Stormonth Darling
    Charitable Trust
The Strangward Trust
The Sudborough Foundation
The Bernard Sunley Charitable
    Foundation
The Sussex Historic Churches
    Trust
The Swann-Morton Foundation
Swansea and Brecon Diocesan
    Board of Finance Limited

The John Swire (1989)
    Charitable Trust
The Swire Charitable Trust
The Hugh and Ruby Sykes
    Charitable Trust
The Charles and Elsie Sykes
    Trust
The Charity of Stella Symons
The Talbot Trusts
The Talbot Village Trust
The Lady Tangye Charitable
    Trust
The David Tannen Charitable
    Trust
The Tanner Trust
The Lili Tapper Charitable
    Foundation
The Tay Charitable Trust
A. P. Taylor Trust
Tearfund
The Tedworth Charitable Trust
The Templeton Goodwill Trust
Tesco Charity Trust
The C. Paul Thackray General
    Charitable Trust
The Thistle Trust
The Loke Wan Tho Memorial
    Foundation
The Thompson Family
    Charitable Trust
The Thornton Foundation
The Thornton Trust
The Three Guineas Trust
The Thriplow Charitable Trust
The Daniel Thwaites Charitable
    Trust
The Tinsley Foundation
The Tobacco Pipe Makers and
    Tobacco Trade Benevolent
    Fund
The Tolkien Trust
Tomchei Torah Charitable
    Trust
The Tompkins Foundation
The Tory Family Foundation
Tottenham Grammar School
    Foundation
The Tower Hill Trust
The Towry Law Charitable Trust
    (also known as the Castle
    Educational Trust)
The Toy Trust
The Constance Travis
    Charitable Trust
The True Colours Trust
Truedene Co. Ltd
The Truemark Trust
Truemart Limited
Trumros Limited
Tudor Rose Ltd
The Tudor Trust
The Tufton Charitable Trust
The Douglas Turner Trust
The Florence Turner Trust
The G. J. W. Turner Trust
Trustees of Tzedakah

Ulster Garden Villages Ltd
The Ulverscroft Foundation
The Underwood Trust
The Union of Orthodox Hebrew Congregation
The United Society for the Propagation of the Gospel
Uxbridge United Welfare Trust
The Van Neste Foundation
The Vandervell Foundation
The Vardy Foundation
Veneziana Fund
The Nigel Vinson Charitable Trust
The William and Ellen Vinten Trust
The Vintners' Foundation
Vision Charity
Vivdale Ltd
Wade's Charity
The Scurrah Wainwright Charity
Wakeham Trust
The Community Foundation in Wales
Wales Council for Voluntary Action
War on Want
The Ward Blenkinsop Trust
G. R. Waters Charitable Trust 2000
The Wellcome Trust
The Charity of William Williams
The Kay Williams Charitable Foundation
The Maurice Wohl Charitable Foundation
The Wolfson Family Charitable Trust
The Wragge and Co Charitable Trust
Wychville Ltd
The Xerox (UK) Trust
Yorkshire Building Society Charitable Foundation
The Zochonis Charitable Trust
Zurich Community Trust (UK) Limited

........................................

## ■ Computer systems and equipment

The 1970 Trust
The 1989 Willan Charitable Trust
The 29th May 1961 Charitable Trust
A. W. Charitable Trust
The Aberbrothock Skea Trust
The Aberdeen Endowments Trust
The Aberdeenshire Educational Trust Scheme
Achisomoch Aid Company Limited
The ACT Foundation
Action Medical Research

The Company of Actuaries' Charitable Trust Fund
The Victor Adda Foundation
The Adint Charitable Trust
The Adrian Swire Charitable Trust
Age Scotland
Age UK
Aid to the Church in Need (UK)
The Sylvia Aitken Charitable Trust
The Al Fayed Charitable Foundation
Aldgate and All Hallows' Foundation
Allchurches Trust Ltd
The H. B. Allen Charitable Trust
The Alliance Family Foundation
Angus Allnatt Charitable Foundation
The Pat Allsop Charitable Trust
Altamont Ltd
The Ammco Trust
Viscount Amory's Charitable Trust
The AMW Charitable Trust
Mary Andrew Charitable Trust
Anguish's Educational Foundation
The Animal Defence Trust
Anpride Ltd
The Appletree Trust
The Archer Trust
The Ardwick Trust
The Argus Appeal
The Armourers' and Brasiers' Gauntlet Trust
The Artemis Charitable Trust
Arts Council England
Arts Council of Northern Ireland
Arts Council of Wales (Cyngor Celfyddydau Cymru)
The Ove Arup Foundation
The AS Charitable Trust
The Ascot Fire Brigade Trust
The Ashden Trust
The Ashley Family Foundation
The Ashworth Charitable Trust
The Ian Askew Charitable Trust
The Associated Country Women of the World
The Association of Colleges Charitable Trust
Astellas European Foundation
Asthma UK
The Astor Foundation
The Astor of Hever Trust
The Aurelius Charitable Trust
The John Avins Trust
The Avon and Somerset Police Community Trust
Bag4Sport Foundation
The Bagri Foundation
The Austin Bailey Foundation

The Baily Thomas Charitable Fund
The Baker Charitable Trust
The Balcombe Charitable Trust
The Albert Casanova Ballard Deceased Trust
The Ballinger Charitable Trust
The Balmore Trust
The Balney Charitable Trust
The Baltic Charitable Fund
The Bamford Charitable Foundation
The Banbury Charities
The Barbers' Company General Charities
The Barbour Foundation
Barchester Healthcare Foundation
The Barnsbury Charitable Trust
The Barnstaple Bridge Trust
The Barnwood House Trust
The Misses Barrie Charitable Trust
Bartholomew Charitable Trust
The Bartlett Taylor Charitable Trust
The Paul Bassham Charitable Trust
The Batchworth Trust
The Bates Charitable Trust
The Battens Charitable Trust
The Bay Tree Charitable Trust
The B-CH Charitable Trust
The Bearder Charity
The James Beattie Charitable Trust
The Beaverbrook Foundation
The Beccles Town Lands Charity
The Becker Family Charitable Trust
The Beckett's and Sargeant's Educational Foundation
The John Beckwith Charitable Trust
The Peter Beckwith Charitable Trust
The Provincial Grand Lodge of Bedfordshire Charity Fund
The David and Ruth Behrend Fund
The Bellahouston Bequest Fund
The Bellinger Donnay Trust
The Benfield Motors Charitable Trust
The Benham Charitable Settlement
Maurice and Jacqueline Bennett Charitable Trust
The Gerald Bentall Charitable Trust
The Bergne-Coupland Charity
Bergqvist Charitable Trust
The Bernadette Charitable Trust

**185**

BHST
The Mason Bibby 1981 Trust
The Bideford Bridge Trust
The Billmeir Charitable Trust
Percy Bilton Charity
The Bingham Trust
The Bintaub Charitable Trust
The Birmingham District Nursing Charitable Trust
The Birmingham Hospital Saturday Fund Medical Charity and Welfare Trust
Birmingham International Airport Community Trust
The Lord Mayor of Birmingham's Charity
Miss Jeanne Bisgood's Charitable Trust
The Michael Bishop Foundation
The Blair Foundation
The Morgan Blake Charitable Trust
The Blandford Lake Trust
The Sir Victor Blank Charitable Settlement
Bloodwise
The Bluston Charitable Settlement
The Bonamy Charitable Trust
The John and Celia Bonham Christie Charitable Trust
The Charlotte Bonham-Carter Charitable Trust
Boots Charitable Trust
The Bordon Liphook Haslemere Charity
The Oliver Borthwick Memorial Trust
The Bothwell Charitable Trust
The Harry Bottom Charitable Trust
The Bower Trust
The Bowerman Charitable Trust
The Bowland Charitable Trust
The Frank Brake Charitable Trust
The William Brake Charitable Trust
The Tony Bramall Charitable Trust
The Bramhope Trust
The Harold and Alice Bridges Charity
The Brighton District Nursing Association Trust
British Gas (Scottish Gas) Energy Trust
British Heart Foundation
The British Humane Association
The J. and M. Britton Charitable Trust
The Broderers' Charity Trust

The Roger Brooke Charitable Trust
The David Brooke Charity
The Charles Brotherton Trust
Joseph Brough Charitable Trust
Miss Marion Broughton's Charitable Trust
Edna Brown Charitable Settlement
The Jack Brunton Charitable Trust
Buckinghamshire Community Foundation
The Bulldog Trust Limited
The E. F. Bulmer Benevolent Fund
The Burghley Family Trust
The Burry Charitable Trust
The Arnold Burton 1998 Charitable Trust
The Burton Breweries Charitable Trust
Consolidated Charity of Burton upon Trent
The Worshipful Company of Butchers General Charities
The Noel Buxton Trust
Henry T. and Lucy B. Cadbury Charitable Trust
The Christopher Cadbury Charitable Trust
The G. W. Cadbury Charitable Trust
The Richard Cadbury Charitable Trust
The Edward and Dorothy Cadbury Trust
The George Cadbury Trust
CAFOD (Catholic Agency for Overseas Development)
Community Foundation for Calderdale
Callander Charitable Trust
Calleva Foundation
The Campden Charities Trustee
The Canning Trust
The Carew Pole Charitable Trust
Carlee Ltd
The Carlton House Charitable Trust
The Carmelite Monastery Ware Trust
The Worshipful Company of Carmen Benevolent Trust
The Carnegie Dunfermline Trust
The Carpenters' Company Charitable Trust
The Carrington Charitable Trust
The Leslie Mary Carter Charitable Trust
Sir John Cass's Foundation

The Elizabeth Casson Trust
The Castang Foundation
The Catholic Charitable Trust
The Catholic Trust for England and Wales
The Joseph and Annie Cattle Trust
The Thomas Sivewright Catto Charitable Settlement
The Wilfrid and Constance Cave Foundation
The B. G. S. Cayzer Charitable Trust
The Cazenove Charitable Trust
Celtic Charity Fund
The Chapman Charitable Trust
John William Chapman's Charitable Trust
The Charities Advisory Trust
Charitworth Limited
The Charter 600 Charity
The Cheruby Trust
Cheshire Freemason's Charity
The Chetwode Foundation
The Childs Charitable Trust
The Chippenham Borough Lands Charity
The Chipping Sodbury Town Lands Charity
The Chownes Foundation
The Christabella Charitable Trust
Christadelphian Samaritan Fund
Christian Aid
The Church Burgesses Educational Foundation
Church Burgesses Trust
Church Urban Fund
The City Bridge Trust
The City Educational Trust Fund
Stephen Clark 1957 Charitable Trust
J. A. Clark Charitable Trust
The Hilda and Alice Clark Charitable Trust
The Roger and Sarah Bancroft Clark Charitable Trust
The Clarke Charitable Settlement
The Cleopatra Trust
The Clore Duffield Foundation
Closehelm Limited
The Clothworkers' Foundation
Richard Cloudesley's Charity
The Clover Trust
The Robert Clutterbuck Charitable Trust
Clydpride Ltd
The Coalfields Regeneration Trust
The John Coates Charitable Trust
The Cobtree Charity Trust Ltd

The Denise Cohen Charitable Trust
The Vivienne and Samuel Cohen Charitable Trust
The John S. Cohen Foundation
The R. and S. Cohen Foundation
The Colchester Catalyst Charity
The Colefax Charitable Trust
John and Freda Coleman Charitable Trust
The George Henry Collins Charity
The Sir Jeremiah Colman Gift Trust
The Coltstaple Trust
Colwinston Charitable Trust
Colyer-Fergusson Charitable Trust
Comic Relief
The Comino Foundation
The Compton Charitable Trust
The Congleton Inclosure Trust
Martin Connell Charitable Trust
The Consolidated Charities for the Infirm – Merchant Taylors' Company
The Ernest Cook Trust
Mabel Cooper Charity
The Alice Ellen Cooper Dean Charitable Foundation
The Marjorie Coote Animal Charity Trust
The Marjorie Coote Old People's Charity
The Helen Jean Cope Trust
The J. Reginald Corah Foundation Fund
The Gershon Coren Charitable Foundation
The Duke of Cornwall's Benevolent Fund
The Cornwell Charitable Trust
The Sidney and Elizabeth Corob Charitable Trust
The Corona Charitable Trust
The Costa Family Charitable Trust
The Cotton Industry War Memorial Trust
The Augustine Courtauld Trust
General Charity of Coventry
Coventry Building Society Charitable Foundation
Dudley and Geoffrey Cox Charitable Trust
The Sir William Coxen Trust Fund
The Lord Cozens-Hardy Trust
The Craignish Trust
The Craps Charitable Trust
Michael Crawford Children's Charity
The Cray Trust

Creative Scotland
The Crerar Hotels Trust
The Crescent Trust
Cripplegate Foundation
The Violet and Milo Cripps Charitable Trust
The Cross Trust
The Croydon Relief in Need Charities
Cruden Foundation Ltd
The Ronald Cruickshanks Foundation
The Cumber Family Charitable Trust
Cumbria Community Foundation
The Dennis Curry Charitable Trust
The Cwmbran Trust
Itzchok Meyer Cymerman Trust Ltd
The D. G. Charitable Settlement
Daily Prayer Union Charitable Trust Limited
The Daiwa Anglo-Japanese Foundation
Baron Davenport's Charity
The Davidson Family Charitable Trust
Michael Davies Charitable Settlement
The Gwendoline and Margaret Davies Charity
The Wilfrid Bruce Davis Charitable Trust
The Dawe Charitable Trust
The De Brye Charitable Trust
The Deakin Charitable Trust
William Dean Countryside and Educational Trust
The Debmar Benevolent Trust
The Dellal Foundation
The Delves Charitable Trust
The Denman Charitable Trust
The Dentons UKMEA LLP Charitable Trust
Derbyshire Community Foundation
The J. N. Derbyshire Trust
The Desmond Foundation
Devon Community Foundation
The Duke of Devonshire's Charitable Trust
The Sandy Dewhirst Charitable Trust
The Laduma Dhamecha Charitable Trust
Diabetes UK
The Dibden Allotments Fund
The Digbeth Trust Limited
The Dinwoodie Settlement
Dischma Charitable Trust
The DLM Charitable Trust
The Derek and Eileen Dodgson Foundation

The Dollond Charitable Trust
The Dorus Trust
The Doughty Charity Trust
Douglas Arter Foundation
The Drapers' Charitable Fund
The Duis Charitable Trust
The Dulverton Trust
The Dumbreck Charity
The Dunn Family Charitable Trust
The W. E. Dunn Trust
Dushinsky Trust Ltd
The Dyers' Company Charitable Trust
The Eagle Charity Trust
The Earley Charity
Earls Colne and Halstead Educational Charity
East End Community Foundation
Eastern Counties Educational Trust Limited
The Sir John Eastwood Foundation
The EBM Charitable Trust
EDF Energy Trust
The Gilbert and Eileen Edgar Foundation
Edinburgh & Lothian Trust Fund
Edinburgh Trust No 2 Account
The W. G. Edwards Charitable Foundation
The Elephant Trust
The George Elias Charitable Trust
The Gerald Palmer Eling Trust Company
The Wilfred and Elsie Elkes Charity Fund
The Maud Elkington Charitable Trust
The Ellerdale Trust
The John Ellerman Foundation
The Ellinson Foundation Ltd
The Ellis Campbell Foundation
The Elmley Foundation
The Vernon N. Ely Charitable Trust
The Emerton-Christie Charity
EMI Music Sound Foundation
The Englefield Charitable Trust
The Enkalon Foundation
Entindale Ltd
The Epigoni Trust
The Equity Trust Fund
The Ericson Trust
The Erskine Cunningham Hill Trust
Essex Community Foundation
The Essex Fairway Charitable Trust
The Essex Youth Trust
Euro Charity Trust
Sir John Evelyn's Charity

The Eventhall Family Charitable Trust
The Everard Foundation
The Eveson Charitable Trust
The Beryl Evetts and Robert Luff Animal Welfare Trust Limited
The Exilarch's Foundation
The F. P. Limited Charitable Trust
The Fairway Trust
The Lord Faringdon Charitable Trust
The Fassnidge Memorial Trust
The George Fentham Birmingham Charity
The A. M. Fenton Trust
The Allan and Nesta Ferguson Charitable Settlement
The Fidelity UK Foundation
The Doris Field Charitable Trust
Field Family Charitable Trust
The Ian Fleming Charitable Trust
The Football Association National Sports Centre Trust
The Oliver Ford Charitable Trust
The Forest Hill Charitable Trust
Forever Manchester (The Community Foundation for Greater Manchester)
The Forman Hardy Charitable Trust
Gwyneth Forrester Trust
The Forte Charitable Trust
The Four Winds Trust
The Isaac and Freda Frankel Memorial Charitable Trust
The Elizabeth Frankland Moore and Star Foundation
The Jill Franklin Trust
The Gordon Fraser Charitable Trust
The Hugh Fraser Foundation
The Joseph Strong Frazer Trust
The Louis and Valerie Freedman Charitable Settlement
The Charles S. French Charitable Trust
The Freshfield Foundation
The Friarsgate Trust
Friends Provident Charitable Foundation
The Frognal Trust
The Patrick & Helena Frost Foundation
The Fulmer Charitable Trust
The Gale Family Charity Trust
The Gamma Trust
The Gannochy Trust
The Samuel Gardner Memorial Trust

The Garnett Charitable Trust
Garthgwynion Charities
The Gatsby Charitable Foundation
Gatwick Airport Community Trust
The Robert Gavron Charitable Trust
Sir Robert Geffery's Almshouse Trust
The Gibbs Charitable Trust
Simon Gibson Charitable Trust
The G. C. Gibson Charitable Trust
The Girdlers' Company Charitable Trust
The B. and P. Glasser Charitable Trust
Global Care
Global Charities
Gloucestershire Community Foundation
Worshipful Company of Glovers of London Charitable Trust
The GNC Trust
The Sydney and Phyllis Goldberg Memorial Charitable Trust
The Golden Bottle Trust
The Goldsmiths' Arts Trust Fund
The Goldsmiths' Company Charity
The Golsoncott Foundation
The Mike Gooley Trailfinders Charity
The Gosling Foundation Limited
The Gould Charitable Trust
The Grace Charitable Trust
A. B. Grace Trust
E. C. Graham Belford Charitable Settlement
The Grahame Charitable Foundation Limited
The Granada Foundation
Grand Charitable Trust of the Order of Women Freemasons
The Grange Farm Centre Trust
The J. G. Graves Charitable Trust
The Gray Trust
The Great Stone Bridge Trust of Edenbridge
The Green Hall Foundation
Greenham Common Community Trust Limited
The Greggs Foundation
The Gretna Charitable Trust
The Grocers' Charity
The M. and R. Gross Charities Limited
The GRP Charitable Trust

The Guildry Incorporation of Perth
The Walter Guinness Charitable Trust
The Gur Trust
Dr Guthrie's Association
The H. and M. Charitable Trust
H. C. D. Memorial Fund
The Hackney Parochial Charities
The Hadfield Trust
The Hadley Trust
The Alfred Haines Charitable Trust
The Edith Winifred Hall Charitable Trust
Hamilton Wallace Trust
Paul Hamlyn Foundation
Hampton Fuel Allotment
The Doughty Hanson Charitable Foundation
Edward Harvist Trust
Headley-Pitt Charitable Trust
The Hedley Denton Charitable Trust
The H. J. Heinz Company Limited Charitable Trust
Help the Homeless Limited
Philip Sydney Henman Deceased Will Trust
The Hesslewood Children's Trust (Hull Seamen's and General Orphanage)
Hitchin Educational Foundation
The Hoover Foundation
The Horne Foundation
IBM United Kingdom Trust
Jewish Child's Day
The Ian Karten Charitable Trust
The Kennel Club Charitable Trust
The Kettering and District Charitable Medical Trust
The Kingsbury Charity
The Mary Kinross Charitable Trust
The Sir James Knott Trust
John Laing Charitable Trust
Maurice and Hilda Laing Charitable Trust
The Beatrice Laing Trust
The Lark Trust
The William Leech Charity
The Erica Leonard Trust
The Leverhulme Trust
LHR Airport Communities Trust
Lifeline 4 Kids
The Charles Lloyd Foundation
Lloyds Bank Foundation for England and Wales
Lloyds Bank Foundation for Northern Ireland
The Lord's Taverners
Robert Luff Foundation Ltd
The Lyndhurst Trust

Sylvanus Lysons Charity
Man Group plc Charitable Trust
Manchester Airport Community Trust Fund
Lord Mayor of Manchester's Charity Appeal Trust
The Mersey Docks and Harbour Company Charitable Fund
The Tony Metherell Charitable Trust
Mobbs Memorial Trust Ltd
The Montague Thompson Coon Charitable Trust
The Moss Family Charitable Trust
Mosselson Charitable Trust
The Mount Everest Foundation
The Edwina Mountbatten & Leonora Children's Foundation
Mrs Waterhouse Charitable Trust
The Mugdock Children's Trust
The Mulberry Trust
The Edith Murphy Foundation
The Music Sales Charitable Trust
Muslim Hands
The Mutual Trust Group
The Janet Nash Charitable Settlement
The National Churches Trust
The Worshipful Company of Needlemakers' Charitable Fund
The Neighbourly Charitable Trust
The James Neill Trust Fund
Nemoral Ltd
The Newcomen Collett Foundation
The Chevras Ezras Nitzrochim Trust
Nominet Charitable Foundation
The Noon Foundation
Norfolk Community Foundation
The Norman Family Charitable Trust
The Normanby Charitable Trust
The Northampton Municipal Church Charities
The Northmoor Trust
The Northumberland Village Homes Trust
The Northwood Charitable Trust
The Norton Foundation
The Norwich Town Close Estate Charity
The Notgrove Trust
The Nottingham General Dispensary
Nottinghamshire Community Foundation

The Father O'Mahoney Memorial Trust
The Sir Peter O'Sullevan Charitable Trust
The Oakdale Trust
The Oakley Charitable Trust
The Oakmoor Charitable Trust
The Odin Charitable Trust
The Ofenheim Charitable Trust
The Ogle Christian Trust
Oizer Charitable Trust
The John Oldacre Foundation
Open Gate
The Ouseley Trust
The Owen Family Trust
Oxfam (GB)
Oxfordshire Community Foundation
The P. F. Charitable Trust
The Paget Charitable Trust
The Panacea Charitable Trust
The James Pantyfedwen Foundation
The Paragon Trust
The Park House Charitable Trust
The Samuel and Freda Parkinson Charitable Trust
The Patrick Charitable Trust
The Jack Patston Charitable Trust
The Harry Payne Fund
The Susanna Peake Charitable Trust
The Pedmore Sporting Club Trust Fund
The Dowager Countess Eleanor Peel Trust
The Pennycress Trust
The Performing Right Society Foundation
The Personal Assurance Charitable Trust
The Persson Charitable Trust
The Persula Foundation
The Jack Petchey Foundation
The Petplan Charitable Trust
The Phillips and Rubens Charitable Trust
The Phillips Charitable Trust
The Phillips Family Charitable Trust
The David Pickford Charitable Foundation
The Bernard Piggott Charitable Trust
The Pilkington Charities Fund
The Austin and Hope Pilkington Trust
The Sir Harry Pilkington Trust Fund
The DLA Piper Charitable Trust
The Platinum Trust
The George and Esme Pollitzer Charitable Settlement
The Ponton House Trust

Edith and Ferdinand Porjes Charitable Trust
The John Porter Charitable Trust
The Porter Foundation
The Portishead Nautical Trust
The Portrack Charitable Trust
The J. E. Posnansky Charitable Trust
Premierquote Ltd
Premishlaner Charitable Trust
The William Price Charitable Trust
Sir John Priestman Charity Trust
The Primrose Trust
The Prince of Wales's Charitable Foundation
Prison Service Charity Fund
The Privy Purse Charitable Trust
The Puebla Charitable Trust
The Puri Foundation
Mr and Mrs J. A. Pye's Charitable Settlement
Quartet Community Foundation
Queen Mary's Roehampton Trust
The Queen's Silver Jubilee Trust
R. S. Charitable Trust
The RVW Trust
The Monica Rabagliati Charitable Trust
Rachel Charitable Trust
The Mr and Mrs Philip Rackham Charitable Trust
Richard Radcliffe Charitable Trust
The Radcliffe Trust
The Ragdoll Foundation
The Rainford Trust
The Joseph and Lena Randall Charitable Trust
The Rank Foundation Limited
The Ratcliff Foundation
The Eleanor Rathbone Charitable Trust
The Sigrid Rausing Trust
The Ravensdale Trust
The Rayden Charitable Trust
The Roger Raymond Charitable Trust
The Rayne Foundation
The Rayne Trust
The Sir James Reckitt Charity
The C. A. Redfern Charitable Foundation
The Reed Foundation
Richard Reeve's Foundation
The Rest Harrow Trust
Reuben Foundation
The Rhododendron Trust
The Rhondda Cynon Taff Welsh Church Acts Fund
The Clive Richards Charity

**189**

The Richmond Parish Lands Charity
Ridgesave Limited
The Sir John Ritblat Family Foundation
The River Trust
Thomas Roberts Trust
The Robertson Trust
The Rochester Bridge Trust
The Rock Foundation
The Rofeh Trust
Rokach Family Charitable Trust
The Helen Roll Charitable Trust
The Sir James Roll Charitable Trust
The Rosca Trust
The Cecil Rosen Foundation
The Rothermere Foundation
The Rothley Trust
The Roughley Charitable Trust
Mrs Gladys Row Fogo Charitable Trust
Rowanville Ltd
The Rowlands Trust
The Joseph Rowntree Charitable Trust
Royal Artillery Charitable Fund
Royal British Legion
Royal Docks Trust (London)
Royal Masonic Trust for Girls and Boys
The Royal Victoria Hall Foundation
The Rubin Foundation
The Russell Trust
The J. S. and E. C. Rymer Charitable Trust
The Michael Sacher Charitable Trust
The Michael Harry Sacher Trust
Raymond and Beverly Sackler 1988 Foundation
The Sackler Trust
The Ruzin Sadagora Trust
The Saddlers' Company Charitable Fund
The Saga Charitable Trust
The Jean Sainsbury Animal Welfare Trust
The Alan and Babette Sainsbury Charitable Fund
The Sainsbury Family Charitable Trusts
Sam and Bella Sebba Charitable Trust
The Basil Samuel Charitable Trust
The M. J. Samuel Charitable Trust
The Peter Samuel Charitable Trust
The Samworth Foundation
The Sandra Charitable Trust

Santander UK Foundation Limited
The Scarfe Charitable Trust
The Schapira Charitable Trust
The Schmidt-Bodner Charitable Trust
The Schreib Trust
The Schreiber Charitable Trust
The Schuster Charitable Trust
Foundation Scotland
The Francis C. Scott Charitable Trust
The Frieda Scott Charitable Trust
Sir Samuel Scott of Yews Trust
Scottish Coal Industry Special Welfare Fund
The Scouloudi Foundation
Seafarers UK (King George's Fund for Sailors)
The Seedfield Trust
Leslie Sell Charitable Trust
ShareGift (The Orr Mackintosh Foundation)
The Shears Foundation
The Sheepdrove Trust
The Sheffield and District Hospital Services Charitable Fund
The Sheldon Trust
The Patricia and Donald Shepherd Charitable Trust
The Archie Sherman Cardiff Foundation
The Archie Sherman Charitable Trust
The R. C. Sherriff Rosebriars Trust
The Shetland Charitable Trust
SHINE (Support and Help in Education)
The Barnett and Sylvia Shine No 2 Charitable Trust
The Bassil Shippam and Alsford Trust
The Shirley Foundation
Shlomo Memorial Fund Limited
The J. A. Shone Memorial Trust
The Mary Elizabeth Siebel Charity
David and Jennifer Sieff Charitable Trust
The Huntly and Margery Sinclair Charitable Trust
The Sino-British Fellowship Trust
The Skelton Bounty
The Charles Skey Charitable Trust
Skipton Building Society Charitable Foundation
Sloane Robinson Foundation
The SMB Charitable Trust

The Mrs Smith and Mount Trust
The N. Smith Charitable Settlement
The Henry Smith Charity
The Stanley Smith UK Horticultural Trust
The Sobell Foundation
The Solo Charitable Settlement
The E. C. Sosnow Charitable Trust
The Souter Charitable Trust
The South Square Trust
The W. F. Southall Trust
The Southover Manor General Education Trust
The Sovereign Health Care Charitable Trust
Sparquote Limited
The Spear Charitable Trust
The Worshipful Company of Spectacle Makers' Charity
The Jessie Spencer Trust
The Ralph and Irma Sperring Charity
The Spielman Charitable Trust
The Spoore, Merry and Rixman Foundation
Springrule Limited
The Spurrell Charitable Trust
The Geoff and Fiona Squire Foundation
St James's Trust Settlement
St James's Place Foundation
Sir Walter St John's Educational Charity
St Michael's and All Saints' Charities Relief Branch
The Stanley Foundation Ltd
The Staples Trust
The Steel Charitable Trust
The Steinberg Family Charitable Trust
The Stephen Barry Charitable Trust
The Stewards' Company Limited (incorporating the J. W. Laing Trust and the J. W. Laing Biblical Scholarship Trust)
The Leonard Laity Stoate Charitable Trust
The Stobart Newlands Charitable Trust
The Edward Stocks-Massey Bequest Fund
The Stoller Charitable Trust
M. J. C. Stone Charitable Trust
The Samuel Storey Family Charitable Trust
Peter Stormonth Darling Charitable Trust
The Strangward Trust
Stratford upon Avon Town Trust

190

The W. O. Street Charitable Foundation
The Sudborough Foundation
The Bernard Sunley Charitable Foundation
The Sussex Historic Churches Trust
Sutton Coldfield Charitable Trust
The Swann-Morton Foundation
Swansea and Brecon Diocesan Board of Finance Limited
The John Swire (1989) Charitable Trust
The Swire Charitable Trust
The Hugh and Ruby Sykes Charitable Trust
The Charles and Elsie Sykes Trust
The Charity of Stella Symons
The Talbot Trusts
The Talbot Village Trust
The Lady Tangye Charitable Trust
The David Tannen Charitable Trust
The Tanner Trust
The Lili Tapper Charitable Foundation
The Tay Charitable Trust
A. P. Taylor Trust
Tearfund
The Tedworth Charitable Trust
Tees Valley Community Foundation
The Templeton Goodwill Trust
Tesco Charity Trust
The C. Paul Thackray General Charitable Trust
The Thistle Trust
The Loke Wan Tho Memorial Foundation
The Thompson Family Charitable Trust
The Sir Jules Thorn Charitable Trust
The Thornton Foundation
The Thornton Trust
The Three Guineas Trust
The Thriplow Charitable Trust
The Daniel Thwaites Charitable Trust
The Tinsley Foundation
The Tobacco Pipe Makers and Tobacco Trade Benevolent Fund
The Tolkien Trust
Tomchei Torah Charitable Trust
The Tompkins Foundation
The Tory Family Foundation
Tottenham Grammar School Foundation
The Tower Hill Trust

The Towry Law Charitable Trust (also known as the Castle Educational Trust)
The Toy Trust
The Constance Travis Charitable Trust
The Triangle Trust (1949) Fund
The True Colours Trust
Truedene Co. Ltd
The Truemark Trust
Truemart Limited
Trumros Limited
Tudor Rose Ltd
The Tudor Trust
The Tufton Charitable Trust
The Douglas Turner Trust
The Florence Turner Trust
The G. J. W. Turner Trust
Community Foundation Serving Tyne and Wear and Northumberland
Trustees of Tzedakah
Ulster Garden Villages Ltd
The Ulverscroft Foundation
The Underwood Trust
The Union of Orthodox Hebrew Congregation
The United Society for the Propagation of the Gospel
Uxbridge United Welfare Trust
The Van Neste Foundation
The Vandervell Foundation
The Vardy Foundation
The Variety Club Children's Charity
Veneziana Fund
The Nigel Vinson Charitable Trust
The William and Ellen Vinten Trust
The Vintners' Foundation
Vision Charity
Vivdale Ltd
Wade's Charity
The Scurrah Wainwright Charity
Wakeham Trust
The Community Foundation in Wales
Wales Council for Voluntary Action
War on Want
The Ward Blenkinsop Trust
G. R. Waters Charitable Trust 2000
The Wellcome Trust
The Westminster Foundation
The Charity of William Williams
The Kay Williams Charitable Foundation
The Community Foundation for Wiltshire and Swindon
The Maurice Wohl Charitable Foundation
The Charles Wolfson Charitable Trust

The Wolfson Family Charitable Trust
The Wragge and Co Charitable Trust
Wychville Ltd
The Xerox (UK) Trust
Yorkshire Building Society Charitable Foundation
The Zochonis Charitable Trust
Zurich Community Trust (UK) Limited

■ Equipment

The 1970 Trust
The 1989 Willan Charitable Trust
The 29th May 1961 Charitable Trust
A. W. Charitable Trust
The Aberbrothock Skea Trust
The Aberdeen Endowments Trust
The Aberdeenshire Educational Trust Scheme
Access Sport
Achisomoch Aid Company Limited
The ACT Foundation
Action Medical Research
The Company of Actuaries' Charitable Trust Fund
The Victor Adda Foundation
The Adint Charitable Trust
The Adnams Charity
The Adrian Swire Charitable Trust
Age Scotland
Age UK
Aid to the Church in Need (UK)
The Sylvia Aitken Charitable Trust
The Al Fayed Charitable Foundation
Aldgate and All Hallows' Foundation
Allchurches Trust Ltd
The H. B. Allen Charitable Trust
The Alliance Family Foundation
Angus Allnatt Charitable Foundation
The Pat Allsop Charitable Trust
Altamont Ltd
The Ammco Trust
Viscount Amory's Charitable Trust
The AMW Charitable Trust
The Anchor Foundation
The Andrew Anderson Trust
Mary Andrew Charitable Trust
Anglo American Group Foundation
Anguish's Educational Foundation
The Animal Defence Trust

191

The Eric Anker-Petersen
    Charity
Anpride Ltd
The Appletree Trust
The Arbib Foundation
The Archer Trust
The Ardwick Trust
The Argus Appeal
The Armourers' and Brasiers'
    Gauntlet Trust
The Artemis Charitable Trust
Arts Council England
Arts Council of Northern
    Ireland
Arts Council of Wales (Cyngor
    Celfyddydau Cymru)
The Ove Arup Foundation
The AS Charitable Trust
ASCB Charitable Fund
The Ascot Fire Brigade Trust
The Asda Foundation
The Ashden Trust
The Ashley Family Foundation
The Ashworth Charitable Trust
The Ian Askew Charitable Trust
The Associated Country
    Women of the World
The Association of Colleges
    Charitable Trust
Astellas European Foundation
Asthma UK
The Astor Foundation
The Astor of Hever Trust
The Aurelius Charitable Trust
The John Avins Trust
The Avon and Somerset Police
    Community Trust
The BACTA Charitable Trust
Bag4Sport Foundation
The Bagri Foundation
The Austin Bailey Foundation
The Baily Thomas Charitable
    Fund
The Baird Trust
The Baker Charitable Trust
The Balcombe Charitable Trust
The Albert Casanova Ballard
    Deceased Trust
The Ballinger Charitable Trust
The Balmore Trust
The Balney Charitable Trust
The Baltic Charitable Fund
The Bamford Charitable
    Foundation
The Banbury Charities
The Barbers' Company General
    Charities
The Barbour Foundation
Barchester Healthcare
    Foundation
The Barnsbury Charitable Trust
The Barnstaple Bridge Trust
The Barnwood House Trust
The Misses Barrie Charitable
    Trust
Bartholomew Charitable Trust

The Bartlett Taylor Charitable
    Trust
The Paul Bassham Charitable
    Trust
The Batchworth Trust
The Bates Charitable Trust
The Battens Charitable Trust
The Bay Tree Charitable Trust
The B-CH Charitable Trust
The Bearder Charity
The James Beattie Charitable
    Trust
The Beaverbrook Foundation
The Beccles Town Lands
    Charity
The Becker Family Charitable
    Trust
The Beckett's and Sargeant's
    Educational Foundation
The John Beckwith Charitable
    Trust
The Peter Beckwith Charitable
    Trust
The Provincial Grand Lodge of
    Bedfordshire Charity Fund
The David and Ruth Behrend
    Fund
The Bellahouston Bequest
    Fund
The Bellinger Donnay Trust
The Benfield Motors Charitable
    Trust
The Benham Charitable
    Settlement
Maurice and Jacqueline
    Bennett Charitable Trust
The Gerald Bentall Charitable
    Trust
The Bergne-Coupland Charity
Bergqvist Charitable Trust
The Bernadette Charitable
    Trust
BHST
The Mason Bibby 1981 Trust
The Bideford Bridge Trust
The Billmeir Charitable Trust
Percy Bilton Charity
The Bingham Trust
The Bintaub Charitable Trust
The Birmingham District
    Nursing Charitable Trust
The Birmingham Hospital
    Saturday Fund Medical
    Charity and Welfare Trust
Birmingham International
    Airport Community Trust
The Lord Mayor of
    Birmingham's Charity
Miss Jeanne Bisgood's
    Charitable Trust
The Michael Bishop
    Foundation
Sir Alec Black's Charity
The Blair Foundation
The Morgan Blake Charitable
    Trust

The Blandford Lake Trust
The Sir Victor Blank Charitable
    Settlement
Bloodwise
The Bluston Charitable
    Settlement
The Bonamy Charitable Trust
The John and Celia Bonham
    Christie Charitable Trust
The Charlotte Bonham-Carter
    Charitable Trust
Boots Charitable Trust
The Bordon Liphook
    Haslemere Charity
The Oliver Borthwick Memorial
    Trust
The Bothwell Charitable Trust
The Harry Bottom Charitable
    Trust
The Bower Trust
The Bowerman Charitable
    Trust
The Bowland Charitable Trust
The Frank Brake Charitable
    Trust
The William Brake Charitable
    Trust
The Tony Bramall Charitable
    Trust
The Bramhope Trust
The Harold and Alice Bridges
    Charity
The Bridging Fund Charitable
    Trust
The Brighton District Nursing
    Association Trust
British Heart Foundation
The British Humane
    Association
The J. and M. Britton
    Charitable Trust
The Broderers' Charity Trust
The Roger Brooke Charitable
    Trust
The David Brooke Charity
The Charles Brotherton Trust
Joseph Brough Charitable
    Trust
Miss Marion Broughton's
    Charitable Trust
Edna Brown Charitable
    Settlement
The Jack Brunton Charitable
    Trust
Buckinghamshire Community
    Foundation
The Bulldog Trust Limited
The E. F. Bulmer Benevolent
    Fund
The Burghley Family Trust
The Burry Charitable Trust
The Arnold Burton 1998
    Charitable Trust
The Burton Breweries
    Charitable Trust

Consolidated Charity of Burton upon Trent
The Worshipful Company of Butchers General Charities
The Noel Buxton Trust
Henry T. and Lucy B. Cadbury Charitable Trust
The Christopher Cadbury Charitable Trust
The G. W. Cadbury Charitable Trust
The Richard Cadbury Charitable Trust
The Barrow Cadbury Trust
The Edward and Dorothy Cadbury Trust
The George Cadbury Trust
CAFOD (Catholic Agency for Overseas Development)
Community Foundation for Calderdale
Callander Charitable Trust
Calleva Foundation
The Campden Charities Trustee
The Canning Trust
The Carew Pole Charitable Trust
Carlee Ltd
The Carlton House Charitable Trust
The Carmelite Monastery Ware Trust
The Worshipful Company of Carmen Benevolent Trust
The Carnegie Dunfermline Trust
The Carpenters' Company Charitable Trust
The Carrington Charitable Trust
The Leslie Mary Carter Charitable Trust
Sir John Cass's Foundation
The Elizabeth Casson Trust
The Castang Foundation
The Catholic Charitable Trust
The Catholic Trust for England and Wales
The Joseph and Annie Cattle Trust
The Thomas Sivewright Catto Charitable Settlement
The Wilfrid and Constance Cave Foundation
Elizabeth Cayzer Charitable Trust
The B. G. S. Cayzer Charitable Trust
The Cazenove Charitable Trust
Celtic Charity Fund
The Gaynor Cemlyn-Jones Trust
Champneys Charitable Foundation
The Chapman Charitable Trust

John William Chapman's Charitable Trust
The Charities Advisory Trust
Charitworth Limited
The Charter 600 Charity
The Cheruby Trust
Cheshire Freemason's Charity
The Chetwode Foundation
Children's Liver Disease Foundation
The Childs Charitable Trust
The Chippenham Borough Lands Charity
The Chipping Sodbury Town Lands Charity
The Chownes Foundation
The Christabella Charitable Trust
Christadelphian Samaritan Fund
Christian Aid
Chrysalis Trust
The Church Burgesses Educational Foundation
Church Burgesses Trust
Church Urban Fund
The City Bridge Trust
The City Educational Trust Fund
Stephen Clark 1957 Charitable Trust
J. A. Clark Charitable Trust
The Hilda and Alice Clark Charitable Trust
The Roger and Sarah Bancroft Clark Charitable Trust
The Clarke Charitable Settlement
The Cleopatra Trust
The Clore Duffield Foundation
Closehelm Limited
Richard Cloudesley's Charity
The Clover Trust
The Robert Clutterbuck Charitable Trust
Clydpride Ltd
The Coalfields Regeneration Trust
The John Coates Charitable Trust
The Cobtree Charity Trust Ltd
The Denise Cohen Charitable Trust
The Vivienne and Samuel Cohen Charitable Trust
The John S. Cohen Foundation
The R. and S. Cohen Foundation
The Colchester Catalyst Charity
The Colefax Charitable Trust
John and Freda Coleman Charitable Trust
The George Henry Collins Charity

The Sir Jeremiah Colman Gift Trust
The Coltstaple Trust
Colwinston Charitable Trust
Colyer-Fergusson Charitable Trust
Comic Relief
The Comino Foundation
Community First
The Compton Charitable Trust
The Congleton Inclosure Trust
Martin Connell Charitable Trust
The Conservation Foundation
The Consolidated Charities for the Infirm – Merchant Taylors' Company
The Ernest Cook Trust
Mabel Cooper Charity
The Alice Ellen Cooper Dean Charitable Foundation
The Marjorie Coote Animal Charity Trust
The Marjorie Coote Old People's Charity
The Helen Jean Cope Trust
The J. Reginald Corah Foundation Fund
The Gershon Coren Charitable Foundation
The Duke of Cornwall's Benevolent Fund
The Cornwell Charitable Trust
The Sidney and Elizabeth Corob Charitable Trust
The Corona Charitable Trust
The Costa Family Charitable Trust
The Cotton Industry War Memorial Trust
The Cotton Trust
County Durham Community Foundation
General Charity of Coventry
Coventry Building Society Charitable Foundation
Dudley and Geoffrey Cox Charitable Trust
The Sir William Coxen Trust Fund
The Lord Cozens-Hardy Trust
The Craignish Trust
The Craps Charitable Trust
Michael Crawford Children's Charity
The Cray Trust
Creative Scotland
The Crerar Hotels Trust
The Crescent Trust
Cripplegate Foundation
The Violet and Milo Cripps Charitable Trust
The Cross Trust
The Croydon Relief in Need Charities
Cruden Foundation Ltd

.........
**193**

The Ronald Cruickshanks Foundation
The Cumber Family Charitable Trust
Cumbria Community Foundation
The Cunningham Trust
The Dennis Curry Charitable Trust
The Cwmbran Trust
Itzchok Meyer Cymerman Trust Ltd
The D. G. Charitable Settlement
Daily Prayer Union Charitable Trust Limited
The Daiwa Anglo-Japanese Foundation
Baron Davenport's Charity
The Davidson Family Charitable Trust
Michael Davies Charitable Settlement
The Gwendoline and Margaret Davies Charity
The Hamilton Davies Trust
The Wilfrid Bruce Davis Charitable Trust
The Dawe Charitable Trust
The De Brye Charitable Trust
The Deakin Charitable Trust
William Dean Countryside and Educational Trust
The Debmar Benevolent Trust
The Dellal Foundation
The Delves Charitable Trust
The Denman Charitable Trust
The Dentons UKMEA LLP Charitable Trust
The Derbyshire Churches and Chapels Preservation Trust
Derbyshire Community Foundation
The J. N. Derbyshire Trust
The Desmond Foundation
Devon Community Foundation
The Devon Historic Churches Trust
The Duke of Devonshire's Charitable Trust
The Sandy Dewhirst Charitable Trust
The Laduma Dhamecha Charitable Trust
Diabetes UK
The Dibden Allotments Fund
The Digbeth Trust Limited
The Dinwoodie Settlement
Disability Aid Fund (The Roger and Jean Jefcoate Trust)
Dischma Charitable Trust
The DLM Charitable Trust
The Derek and Eileen Dodgson Foundation
The Dollond Charitable Trust

The Dorset Historic Churches Trust
The Dorus Trust
The Doughty Charity Trust
The Drapers' Charitable Fund
The Duis Charitable Trust
The Dulverton Trust
The Dumbreck Charity
Dunard Fund
The Dunn Family Charitable Trust
The W. E. Dunn Trust
Dushinsky Trust Ltd
The Dyers' Company Charitable Trust
The Eagle Charity Trust
The Earley Charity
Earls Colne and Halstead Educational Charity
East End Community Foundation
Eastern Counties Educational Trust Limited
The Sir John Eastwood Foundation
The EBM Charitable Trust
EDF Energy Trust
The Gilbert and Eileen Edgar Foundation
Edinburgh & Lothian Trust Fund
Edinburgh Children's Holiday Fund
Edinburgh Trust No 2 Account
The W. G. Edwards Charitable Foundation
The Elephant Trust
The George Elias Charitable Trust
The Gerald Palmer Eling Trust Company
The Wilfred and Elsie Elkes Charity Fund
The Maud Elkington Charitable Trust
The Ellerdale Trust
The John Ellerman Foundation
The Ellinson Foundation Ltd
The Ellis Campbell Foundation
The Elmley Foundation
The Vernon N. Ely Charitable Trust
The Emerton-Christie Charity
EMI Music Sound Foundation
The Englefield Charitable Trust
The English Schools' Football Association
The Enkalon Foundation
Entindale Ltd
The Epigoni Trust
The Equity Trust Fund
The Ericson Trust
The Erskine Cunningham Hill Trust
The Essex and Southend Sports Trust

Essex Community Foundation
The Essex Fairway Charitable Trust
The Essex Heritage Trust
The Essex Youth Trust
Euro Charity Trust
Sir John Evelyn's Charity
The Eventhall Family Charitable Trust
The Everard Foundation
The Eveson Charitable Trust
The Beryl Evetts and Robert Luff Animal Welfare Trust Limited
The Exilarch's Foundation
The F. P. Limited Charitable Trust
The Fairway Trust
The Lord Faringdon Charitable Trust
The Fassnidge Memorial Trust
The George Fentham Birmingham Charity
The A. M. Fenton Trust
The Allan and Nesta Ferguson Charitable Settlement
The Fidelity UK Foundation
The Doris Field Charitable Trust
Field Family Charitable Trust
The Ian Fleming Charitable Trust
The Football Association National Sports Centre Trust
The Football Association Youth Trust
The Football Foundation
Ford Britain Trust
The Oliver Ford Charitable Trust
The Forest Hill Charitable Trust
Forever Manchester (The Community Foundation for Greater Manchester)
The Forman Hardy Charitable Trust
Gwyneth Forrester Trust
The Forte Charitable Trust
The Four Winds Trust
The Foyle Foundation
The Isaac and Freda Frankel Memorial Charitable Trust
The Elizabeth Frankland Moore and Star Foundation
The Jill Franklin Trust
The Gordon Fraser Charitable Trust
The Hugh Fraser Foundation
The Joseph Strong Frazer Trust
The Louis and Valerie Freedman Charitable Settlement
The Charles S. French Charitable Trust
The Freshfield Foundation

The Friarsgate Trust
Friends Provident Charitable Foundation
The Frognal Trust
The Patrick & Helena Frost Foundation
The Fulmer Charitable Trust
G. M. C. Trust
The Gale Family Charity Trust
The Gamma Trust
The Gannochy Trust
The Samuel Gardner Memorial Trust
The Garnett Charitable Trust
Garthgwynion Charities
The Gatsby Charitable Foundation
Gatwick Airport Community Trust
The Robert Gavron Charitable Trust
Sir Robert Geffery's Almshouse Trust
Get Kids Going
The Gibbs Charitable Trust
Simon Gibson Charitable Trust
The G. C. Gibson Charitable Trust
The Girdlers' Company Charitable Trust
The B. and P. Glasser Charitable Trust
Global Care
Global Charities
Gloucestershire Community Foundation
Worshipful Company of Glovers of London Charitable Trust
The GNC Trust
The Sydney and Phyllis Goldberg Memorial Charitable Trust
The Golden Bottle Trust
The Goldsmiths' Arts Trust Fund
The Goldsmiths' Company Charity
The Golf Foundation Limited
The Golsoncott Foundation
The Mike Gooley Trailfinders Charity
The Gosling Foundation Limited
The Gould Charitable Trust
The Grace Charitable Trust
A. B. Grace Trust
E. C. Graham Belford Charitable Settlement
The Grahame Charitable Foundation Limited
The Granada Foundation
Grand Charitable Trust of the Order of Women Freemasons
The Grange Farm Centre Trust

The J. G. Graves Charitable Trust
The Gray Trust
The Great Stone Bridge Trust of Edenbridge
The Green Hall Foundation
Greenham Common Community Trust Limited
The Greggs Foundation
The Gretna Charitable Trust
The Grimmitt Trust
The Grocers' Charity
The M. and R. Gross Charities Limited
The GRP Charitable Trust
The Guildry Incorporation of Perth
The Walter Guinness Charitable Trust
The Gur Trust
Dr Guthrie's Association
The H. and M. Charitable Trust
H. C. D. Memorial Fund
The Hackney Parochial Charities
The Hadfield Trust
The Hadley Trust
The Alfred Haines Charitable Trust
The Edith Winifred Hall Charitable Trust
Hamilton Wallace Trust
The Hampshire and Islands Historic Churches Trust
Hampton Fuel Allotment
The Doughty Hanson Charitable Foundation
The Peter Harrison Foundation
Edward Harvist Trust
Headley-Pitt Charitable Trust
The Hedley Denton Charitable Trust
The H. J. Heinz Company Limited Charitable Trust
Help the Homeless Limited
Philip Sydney Henman Deceased Will Trust
The Herefordshire Historic Churches Trust
The Heritage of London Trust Limited
The Hesslewood Children's Trust (Hull Seamen's and General Orphanage)
Hitchin Educational Foundation
The Hoover Foundation
The Horne Foundation
IBM United Kingdom Trust
Jewish Child's Day
The Ian Karten Charitable Trust
The Kennel Club Charitable Trust
The Kettering and District Charitable Medical Trust
The Kingsbury Charity

The Mary Kinross Charitable Trust
The Sir James Knott Trust
John Laing Charitable Trust
Maurice and Hilda Laing Charitable Trust
The Beatrice Laing Trust
The Lark Trust
The William Leech Charity
Leicester and Leicestershire Historic Churches Preservation Trust
The Erica Leonard Trust
The Leverhulme Trust
LHR Airport Communities Trust
Lifeline 4 Kids
The Charles Lloyd Foundation
Lloyds Bank Foundation for England and Wales
Lloyds Bank Foundation for Northern Ireland
The Lord's Taverners
Robert Luff Foundation Ltd
The Lyndhurst Trust
Sylvanus Lysons Charity
Man Group plc Charitable Trust
Lord Mayor of Manchester's Charity Appeal Trust
Charity of John Marshall
The Dan Maskell Tennis Trust
The Mersey Docks and Harbour Company Charitable Fund
The Tony Metherell Charitable Trust
Mobbs Memorial Trust Ltd
The Montague Thompson Coon Charitable Trust
The Moss Family Charitable Trust
Mosselson Charitable Trust
The Mount Everest Foundation
The Edwina Mountbatten & Leonora Children's Foundation
Mrs Waterhouse Charitable Trust
The Mugdock Children's Trust
The Mulberry Trust
The Edith Murphy Foundation
The Music Sales Charitable Trust
Muslim Hands
The Mutual Trust Group
The Janet Nash Charitable Settlement
The National Hockey Foundation
The Worshipful Company of Needlemakers' Charitable Fund
The Neighbourly Charitable Trust
The James Neill Trust Fund
Nemoral Ltd

The Newcomen Collett Foundation
The Frances and Augustus Newman Foundation
The Chevras Ezras Nitzrochim Trust
The Noon Foundation
Norfolk Community Foundation
The Norman Family Charitable Trust
The Normanby Charitable Trust
The Northampton Municipal Church Charities
The Northmoor Trust
The Northumberland Village Homes Trust
The Northwood Charitable Trust
The Norton Foundation
The Norwich Town Close Estate Charity
The Notgrove Trust
The Nottingham General Dispensary
Nottinghamshire Community Foundation
The Nottinghamshire Historic Churches Trust
The Father O'Mahoney Memorial Trust
The Sir Peter O'Sullivan Charitable Trust
The Oakdale Trust
The Oakley Charitable Trust
The Oakmoor Charitable Trust
The Odin Charitable Trust
The Ofenheim Charitable Trust
The Ogle Christian Trust
Oizer Charitable Trust
The John Oldacre Foundation
Open Gate
The Owen Family Trust
Oxfam (GB)
Oxfordshire Community Foundation
The P. F. Charitable Trust
The Paget Charitable Trust
The Panacea Charitable Trust
The James Pantyfedwen Foundation
The Paragon Trust
The Park House Charitable Trust
The Samuel and Freda Parkinson Charitable Trust
The Patrick Charitable Trust
The Jack Patston Charitable Trust
The Harry Payne Fund
The Susanna Peake Charitable Trust
The Pedmore Sporting Club Trust Fund
The Dowager Countess Eleanor Peel Trust
The Pennycress Trust

The Performing Right Society Foundation
The Personal Assurance Charitable Trust
The Persson Charitable Trust
The Persula Foundation
The Jack Petchey Foundation
The Petplan Charitable Trust
The Phillips and Rubens Charitable Trust
The Phillips Charitable Trust
The Phillips Family Charitable Trust
The David Pickford Charitable Foundation
The Bernard Piggott Charitable Trust
The Pilkington Charities Fund
The Austin and Hope Pilkington Trust
The Sir Harry Pilkington Trust Fund
The DLA Piper Charitable Trust
The Platinum Trust
The George and Esme Pollitzer Charitable Settlement
The Ponton House Trust
Edith and Ferdinand Porjes Charitable Trust
The John Porter Charitable Trust
The Porter Foundation
The Portishead Nautical Trust
The Portrack Charitable Trust
The J. E. Posnansky Charitable Trust
Premierquote Ltd
Premishlaner Charitable Trust
The William Price Charitable Trust
Sir John Priestman Charity Trust
The Primrose Trust
The Prince of Wales's Charitable Foundation
Prison Service Charity Fund
The Privy Purse Charitable Trust
The Puebla Charitable Trust
The Puri Foundation
Mr and Mrs J. A. Pye's Charitable Settlement
Quartet Community Foundation
Queen Mary's Roehampton Trust
The Queen's Silver Jubilee Trust
Quothquan Trust
R. S. Charitable Trust
The RVW Trust
The Monica Rabagliati Charitable Trust
Rachel Charitable Trust
The Mr and Mrs Philip Rackham Charitable Trust

Richard Radcliffe Charitable Trust
The Radcliffe Trust
The Ragdoll Foundation
The Rainford Trust
The Joseph and Lena Randall Charitable Trust
The Rank Foundation Limited
The Ratcliff Foundation
The Eleanor Rathbone Charitable Trust
The Sigrid Rausing Trust
The Ravensdale Trust
The Rayden Charitable Trust
The Roger Raymond Charitable Trust
The Rayne Foundation
The Rayne Trust
The Sir James Reckitt Charity
Red Hill Charitable Trust
The C. A. Redfern Charitable Foundation
The Reed Foundation
Richard Reeve's Foundation
The Rest Harrow Trust
Reuben Foundation
The Rhododendron Trust
The Rhondda Cynon Taff Welsh Church Acts Fund
The Clive Richards Charity
The Richmond Parish Lands Charity
Ridgesave Limited
The Sir John Ritblat Family Foundation
The River Trust
Thomas Roberts Trust
The Robertson Trust
The Rochester Bridge Trust
The Rock Foundation
The Rofeh Trust
Rokach Family Charitable Trust
The Helen Roll Charitable Trust
The Sir James Roll Charitable Trust
Mrs L. D. Rope Third Charitable Settlement
The Rosca Trust
The Cecil Rosen Foundation
The Rothermere Foundation
The Rothley Trust
The Roughley Charitable Trust
Mrs Gladys Row Fogo Charitable Trust
Rowanville Ltd
The Rowlands Trust
The Joseph Rowntree Charitable Trust
Royal Artillery Charitable Fund
Royal British Legion
Royal Docks Trust (London)
Royal Masonic Trust for Girls and Boys
The Royal Victoria Hall Foundation

The Rubin Foundation
The Russell Trust
The J. S. and E. C. Rymer Charitable Trust
The Michael Sacher Charitable Trust
The Michael Harry Sacher Trust
Raymond and Beverly Sackler 1988 Foundation
The Sackler Trust
The Ruzin Sadagora Trust
The Saddlers' Company Charitable Fund
The Saga Charitable Trust
The Jean Sainsbury Animal Welfare Trust
The Alan and Babette Sainsbury Charitable Fund
The Sainsbury Family Charitable Trusts
Sam and Bella Sebba Charitable Trust
The Basil Samuel Charitable Trust
The M. J. Samuel Charitable Trust
The Peter Samuel Charitable Trust
The Samworth Foundation
The Sandra Charitable Trust
Santander UK Foundation Limited
The Scarfe Charitable Trust
The Schapira Charitable Trust
The Schmidt-Bodner Charitable Trust
The Schreib Trust
The Schreiber Charitable Trust
The Schuster Charitable Trust
Foundation Scotland
The Francis C. Scott Charitable Trust
The Frieda Scott Charitable Trust
Scottish Coal Industry Special Welfare Fund
The Scouloudi Foundation
Seafarers UK (King George's Fund for Sailors)
The Seedfield Trust
Leslie Sell Charitable Trust
ShareGift (The Orr Mackintosh Foundation)
The Shears Foundation
The Sheepdrove Trust
The Sheffield and District Hospital Services Charitable Fund
The Sheldon Trust
The Patricia and Donald Shepherd Charitable Trust
The Archie Sherman Cardiff Foundation
The Archie Sherman Charitable Trust

The R. C. Sherriff Rosebriars Trust
The Shetland Charitable Trust
SHINE (Support and Help in Education)
The Barnett and Sylvia Shine No 2 Charitable Trust
The Bassil Shippam and Alsford Trust
The Shipwrights' Company Charitable Fund
The Shirley Foundation
Shlomo Memorial Fund Limited
The J. A. Shone Memorial Trust
The Mary Elizabeth Siebel Charity
David and Jennifer Sieff Charitable Trust
The Huntly and Margery Sinclair Charitable Trust
The Sino-British Fellowship Trust
SITA Cornwall Trust Limited
The Skelton Bounty
The Charles Skey Charitable Trust
Skipton Building Society Charitable Foundation
Sloane Robinson Foundation
The SMB Charitable Trust
The Mrs Smith and Mount Trust
The N. Smith Charitable Settlement
The Henry Smith Charity
The Stanley Smith UK Horticultural Trust
The Sobell Foundation
The Solo Charitable Settlement
The E. C. Sosnow Charitable Trust
The Souter Charitable Trust
The South Square Trust
The W. F. Southall Trust
The Southover Manor General Education Trust
The Sovereign Health Care Charitable Trust
Sparks Charity (Sport Aiding Medical Research For Kids)
Sparquote Limited
The Spear Charitable Trust
The Worshipful Company of Spectacle Makers' Charity
The Jessie Spencer Trust
The Ralph and Irma Sperring Charity
The Spielman Charitable Trust
The Spoore, Merry and Rixman Foundation
Sported Foundation
Springrule Limited
The Spurrell Charitable Trust

The Geoff and Fiona Squire Foundation
St James's Trust Settlement
St James's Place Foundation
Sir Walter St John's Educational Charity
St Michael's and All Saints' Charities Relief Branch
The Stanley Foundation Ltd
The Staples Trust
The Steel Charitable Trust
The Steinberg Family Charitable Trust
The Stephen Barry Charitable Trust
The Stewards' Company Limited (incorporating the J. W. Laing Trust and the J. W. Laing Biblical Scholarship Trust)
The Leonard Laity Stoate Charitable Trust
The Stobart Newlands Charitable Trust
The Edward Stocks-Massey Bequest Fund
The Stoller Charitable Trust
M. J. C. Stone Charitable Trust
The Samuel Storey Family Charitable Trust
Peter Stormonth Darling Charitable Trust
The Strangward Trust
Stratford upon Avon Town Trust
The W. O. Street Charitable Foundation
The Sudborough Foundation
The Bernard Sunley Charitable Foundation
The Sussex Historic Churches Trust
Sutton Coldfield Charitable Trust
The Swann-Morton Foundation
Swansea and Brecon Diocesan Board of Finance Limited
Swimathon Foundation
The John Swire (1989) Charitable Trust
The Swire Charitable Trust
The Hugh and Ruby Sykes Charitable Trust
The Charles and Elsie Sykes Trust
The Charity of Stella Symons
The Talbot Trusts
The Talbot Village Trust
The Lady Tangye Charitable Trust
The David Tannen Charitable Trust
The Tanner Trust
The Lili Tapper Charitable Foundation
The Tay Charitable Trust

197

A. P. Taylor Trust
Tearfund
The Tedworth Charitable Trust
Tees Valley Community Foundation
The Templeton Goodwill Trust
Tesco Charity Trust
The C. Paul Thackray General Charitable Trust
Thackray Medical Research Trust
The Thistle Trust
The Loke Wan Tho Memorial Foundation
The Thompson Family Charitable Trust
The Sir Jules Thorn Charitable Trust
The Thornton Foundation
The Thornton Trust
The Three Guineas Trust
The Thriplow Charitable Trust
The Daniel Thwaites Charitable Trust
The Tinsley Foundation
The Tobacco Pipe Makers and Tobacco Trade Benevolent Fund
The Tolkien Trust
Tomchei Torah Charitable Trust
The Tompkins Foundation
The Tory Family Foundation
Tottenham Grammar School Foundation
The Tower Hill Trust
The Towry Law Charitable Trust (also known as the Castle Educational Trust)
The Toy Trust
The Constance Travis Charitable Trust
The Triangle Trust (1949) Fund
The True Colours Trust
Truedene Co. Ltd
The Truemark Trust
Truemart Limited
Trumros Limited
The Trusthouse Charitable Foundation
The James Tudor Foundation
Tudor Rose Ltd
The Tudor Trust
The Tufton Charitable Trust
The Douglas Turner Trust
The Florence Turner Trust
The G. J. W. Turner Trust
Community Foundation Serving Tyne and Wear and Northumberland
Trustees of Tzedakah
Ulster Garden Villages Ltd
The Ulverscroft Foundation
The Underwood Trust
The Union of Orthodox Hebrew Congregation

The United Society for the Propagation of the Gospel
Uxbridge United Welfare Trust
The Van Neste Foundation
The Vandervell Foundation
The Vardy Foundation
The Variety Club Children's Charity
Veneziana Fund
The Nigel Vinson Charitable Trust
The William and Ellen Vinten Trust
The Vintners' Foundation
Vision Charity
Vivdale Ltd
Voluntary Action Fund
Wade's Charity
The Scurrah Wainwright Charity
Wakeham Trust
The Community Foundation in Wales
Wales Council for Voluntary Action
War on Want
Sir Siegmund Warburg's Voluntary Settlement
The Ward Blenkinsop Trust
G. R. Waters Charitable Trust 2000
Weatherley Charitable Trust
The Wellcome Trust
The Westminster Foundation
The Charity of William Williams
The Kay Williams Charitable Foundation
The Community Foundation for Wiltshire and Swindon
The Maurice Wohl Charitable Foundation
The Charles Wolfson Charitable Trust
The Wolfson Family Charitable Trust
The Worcestershire and Dudley Historic Churches Trust
The Wragge and Co Charitable Trust
Wychville Ltd
The Xerox (UK) Trust
Yorkshire Building Society Charitable Foundation
The Zochonis Charitable Trust
Zurich Community Trust (UK) Limited

.......................................

■ Vehicles

The 1970 Trust
The 1989 Willan Charitable Trust
The 29th May 1961 Charitable Trust
A. W. Charitable Trust
The Aberbrothock Skea Trust

The Aberdeen Endowments Trust
The Aberdeenshire Educational Trust Scheme
Achisomoch Aid Company Limited
The ACT Foundation
Action Medical Research
The Company of Actuaries' Charitable Trust Fund
The Victor Adda Foundation
The Adint Charitable Trust
The Adrian Swire Charitable Trust
Age UK
Aid to the Church in Need (UK)
The Sylvia Aitken Charitable Trust
The Al Fayed Charitable Foundation
Aldgate and All Hallows' Foundation
Allchurches Trust Ltd
The H. B. Allen Charitable Trust
The Alliance Family Foundation
Angus Allnatt Charitable Foundation
The Pat Allsop Charitable Trust
Altamont Ltd
The Ammco Trust
Viscount Amory's Charitable Trust
The AMW Charitable Trust
Mary Andrew Charitable Trust
Anguish's Educational Foundation
The Animal Defence Trust
Anpride Ltd
The Appletree Trust
The Archer Trust
The Ardwick Trust
The Argus Appeal
The Armourers' and Brasiers' Gauntlet Trust
The Artemis Charitable Trust
Arts Council England
Arts Council of Northern Ireland
Arts Council of Wales (Cyngor Celfyddydau Cymru)
The Ove Arup Foundation
The AS Charitable Trust
The Ascot Fire Brigade Trust
The Ashden Trust
The Ashley Family Foundation
The Ashworth Charitable Trust
The Ian Askew Charitable Trust
The Association of Colleges Charitable Trust
Astellas European Foundation
Asthma UK
The Astor Foundation
The Astor of Hever Trust
The Aurelius Charitable Trust
The John Avins Trust

198

The Avon and Somerset Police Community Trust
The Bagri Foundation
The Austin Bailey Foundation
The Baily Thomas Charitable Fund
The Baker Charitable Trust
The Balcombe Charitable Trust
The Albert Casanova Ballard Deceased Trust
The Ballinger Charitable Trust
The Balmore Trust
The Balney Charitable Trust
The Baltic Charitable Fund
The Bamford Charitable Foundation
The Banbury Charities
The Barbers' Company General Charities
The Barbour Foundation
Barchester Healthcare Foundation
The Barnsbury Charitable Trust
The Barnstaple Bridge Trust
The Barnwood House Trust
The Misses Barrie Charitable Trust
Bartholomew Charitable Trust
The Bartlett Taylor Charitable Trust
The Paul Bassham Charitable Trust
The Batchworth Trust
The Bates Charitable Trust
The Battens Charitable Trust
The Bay Tree Charitable Trust
The B-CH Charitable Trust
The Bearder Charity
The James Beattie Charitable Trust
The Beaverbrook Foundation
The Beccles Town Lands Charity
The Becker Family Charitable Trust
The Beckett's and Sargeant's Educational Foundation
The John Beckwith Charitable Trust
The Peter Beckwith Charitable Trust
The Provincial Grand Lodge of Bedfordshire Charity Fund
The David and Ruth Behrend Fund
The Bellahouston Bequest Fund
The Bellinger Donnay Trust
The Benfield Motors Charitable Trust
The Benham Charitable Settlement
Maurice and Jacqueline Bennett Charitable Trust
The Gerald Bentall Charitable Trust

The Bergne-Coupland Charity
Bergqvist Charitable Trust
The Bernadette Charitable Trust
BHST
The Mason Bibby 1981 Trust
The Bideford Bridge Trust
The Billmeir Charitable Trust
Percy Bilton Charity
The Bingham Trust
The Bintaub Charitable Trust
The Birmingham District Nursing Charitable Trust
Birmingham International Airport Community Trust
The Lord Mayor of Birmingham's Charity
Miss Jeanne Bisgood's Charitable Trust
The Michael Bishop Foundation
The Blair Foundation
The Morgan Blake Charitable Trust
The Blandford Lake Trust
The Sir Victor Blank Charitable Settlement
The Bluston Charitable Settlement
The Bonamy Charitable Trust
The John and Celia Bonham Christie Charitable Trust
The Charlotte Bonham-Carter Charitable Trust
Boots Charitable Trust
The Bordon Liphook Haslemere Charity
The Oliver Borthwick Memorial Trust
The Bothwell Charitable Trust
The Harry Bottom Charitable Trust
The Bower Trust
The Bowerman Charitable Trust
The Bowland Charitable Trust
The Frank Brake Charitable Trust
The William Brake Charitable Trust
The Tony Bramall Charitable Trust
The Bramhope Trust
The Harold and Alice Bridges Charity
The Brighton District Nursing Association Trust
The British Humane Association
The J. and M. Britton Charitable Trust
The Broderers' Charity Trust
The Roger Brooke Charitable Trust
The David Brooke Charity
The Charles Brotherton Trust

Joseph Brough Charitable Trust
Miss Marion Broughton's Charitable Trust
Edna Brown Charitable Settlement
The Jack Brunton Charitable Trust
Buckinghamshire Community Foundation
The Bulldog Trust Limited
The E. F. Bulmer Benevolent Fund
The Burghley Family Trust
The Burry Charitable Trust
The Arnold Burton 1998 Charitable Trust
The Burton Breweries Charitable Trust
Consolidated Charity of Burton upon Trent
The Worshipful Company of Butchers General Charities
The Noel Buxton Trust
Henry T. and Lucy B. Cadbury Charitable Trust
The Christopher Cadbury Charitable Trust
The G. W. Cadbury Charitable Trust
The Richard Cadbury Charitable Trust
The Edward and Dorothy Cadbury Trust
The George Cadbury Trust
CAFOD (Catholic Agency for Overseas Development)
Community Foundation for Calderdale
Callander Charitable Trust
Calleva Foundation
The Campden Charities Trustee
The Canning Trust
The Carew Pole Charitable Trust
Carlee Ltd
The Carlton House Charitable Trust
The Carmelite Monastery Ware Trust
The Worshipful Company of Carmen Benevolent Trust
The Carnegie Dunfermline Trust
The Carpenters' Company Charitable Trust
The Carrington Charitable Trust
The Leslie Mary Carter Charitable Trust
The Catholic Charitable Trust
The Catholic Trust for England and Wales
The Joseph and Annie Cattle Trust

**199**

The Thomas Sivewright Catto
    Charitable Settlement
The Wilfrid and Constance
    Cave Foundation
The B. G. S. Cayzer Charitable
    Trust
The Cazenove Charitable Trust
Celtic Charity Fund
The Gaynor Cemlyn-Jones
    Trust
The Chapman Charitable Trust
John William Chapman's
    Charitable Trust
The Charities Advisory Trust
Charitworth Limited
The Charter 600 Charity
The Cheruby Trust
Cheshire Freemason's Charity
The Chetwode Foundation
The Childs Charitable Trust
The Chippenham Borough
    Lands Charity
The Chipping Sodbury Town
    Lands Charity
The Chownes Foundation
The Christabella Charitable
    Trust
Christadelphian Samaritan
    Fund
Christian Aid
The Church Burgesses
    Educational Foundation
Church Burgesses Trust
Church Urban Fund
Stephen Clark 1957
    Charitable Trust
J. A. Clark Charitable Trust
The Hilda and Alice Clark
    Charitable Trust
The Roger and Sarah Bancroft
    Clark Charitable Trust
The Clarke Charitable
    Settlement
The Cleopatra Trust
The Clore Duffield Foundation
Closehelm Limited
The Clothworkers' Foundation
Richard Cloudesley's Charity
The Clover Trust
The Robert Clutterbuck
    Charitable Trust
Clydpride Ltd
The Coalfields Regeneration
    Trust
The John Coates Charitable
    Trust
The Cobtree Charity Trust Ltd
The Denise Cohen Charitable
    Trust
The Vivienne and Samuel
    Cohen Charitable Trust
The John S. Cohen Foundation
The R. and S. Cohen
    Foundation
The Colchester Catalyst
    Charity

The Colefax Charitable Trust
John and Freda Coleman
    Charitable Trust
The George Henry Collins
    Charity
The Sir Jeremiah Colman Gift
    Trust
The Coltstaple Trust
Colwinston Charitable Trust
Community First
The Compton Charitable Trust
The Congleton Inclosure Trust
Martin Connell Charitable
    Trust
The Consolidated Charities for
    the Infirm – Merchant
    Taylors' Company
The Ernest Cook Trust
Mabel Cooper Charity
The Alice Ellen Cooper Dean
    Charitable Foundation
The Marjorie Coote Animal
    Charity Trust
The Marjorie Coote Old
    People's Charity
The Helen Jean Cope Trust
The J. Reginald Corah
    Foundation Fund
The Gershon Coren Charitable
    Foundation
The Duke of Cornwall's
    Benevolent Fund
The Cornwell Charitable Trust
The Sidney and Elizabeth
    Corob Charitable Trust
The Corona Charitable Trust
The Costa Family Charitable
    Trust
The Cotton Industry War
    Memorial Trust
The Cotton Trust
The Augustine Courtauld Trust
General Charity of Coventry
Coventry Building Society
    Charitable Foundation
Dudley and Geoffrey Cox
    Charitable Trust
The Sir William Coxen Trust
    Fund
The Lord Cozens-Hardy Trust
The Craignish Trust
The Craps Charitable Trust
Michael Crawford Children's
    Charity
The Cray Trust
Creative Scotland
The Crerar Hotels Trust
The Crescent Trust
Cripplegate Foundation
The Violet and Milo Cripps
    Charitable Trust
The Cross Trust
The Croydon Relief in Need
    Charities
Cruden Foundation Ltd

The Ronald Cruickshanks
    Foundation
The Cumber Family Charitable
    Trust
Cumbria Community
    Foundation
The Dennis Curry Charitable
    Trust
The Cwmbran Trust
Itzchok Meyer Cymerman Trust
    Ltd
The D. G. Charitable
    Settlement
Daily Prayer Union Charitable
    Trust Limited
Baron Davenport's Charity
The Davidson Family
    Charitable Trust
Michael Davies Charitable
    Settlement
The Gwendoline and Margaret
    Davies Charity
The Wilfrid Bruce Davis
    Charitable Trust
The Dawe Charitable Trust
The De Brye Charitable Trust
The Deakin Charitable Trust
William Dean Countryside and
    Educational Trust
The Debmar Benevolent Trust
The Dellal Foundation
The Delves Charitable Trust
The Denman Charitable Trust
The Dentons UKMEA LLP
    Charitable Trust
Derbyshire Community
    Foundation
The J. N. Derbyshire Trust
The Desmond Foundation
The Duke of Devonshire's
    Charitable Trust
The Sandy Dewhirst Charitable
    Trust
The Laduma Dhamecha
    Charitable Trust
The Dibden Allotments Fund
The Digbeth Trust Limited
The Dinwoodie Settlement
Dischma Charitable Trust
The DLM Charitable Trust
The Derek and Eileen Dodgson
    Foundation
The Dollond Charitable Trust
The Dorus Trust
The Doughty Charity Trust
Douglas Arter Foundation
The Drapers' Charitable Fund
The Duis Charitable Trust
The Dulverton Trust
The Dumbreck Charity
Dunard Fund
The Dunn Family Charitable
    Trust
The W. E. Dunn Trust
Dushinsky Trust Ltd

The Dyers' Company Charitable Trust
The Eagle Charity Trust
The Earley Charity
Earls Colne and Halstead Educational Charity
Eastern Counties Educational Trust Limited
The Sir John Eastwood Foundation
The EBM Charitable Trust
The Gilbert and Eileen Edgar Foundation
Edinburgh & Lothian Trust Fund
Edinburgh Trust No 2 Account
The W. G. Edwards Charitable Foundation
The Elephant Trust
The George Elias Charitable Trust
The Gerald Palmer Eling Trust Company
The Wilfred and Elsie Elkes Charity Fund
The Maud Elkington Charitable Trust
The Ellerdale Trust
The Ellinson Foundation Ltd
The Ellis Campbell Foundation
The Elmley Foundation
The Vernon N. Ely Charitable Trust
The Emerton-Christie Charity
The Englefield Charitable Trust
The English Schools' Football Association
The Enkalon Foundation
Entindale Ltd
The Epigoni Trust
The Equity Trust Fund
The Ericson Trust
The Erskine Cunningham Hill Trust
Essex Community Foundation
The Essex Fairway Charitable Trust
The Essex Youth Trust
Euro Charity Trust
Sir John Evelyn's Charity
The Eventhall Family Charitable Trust
The Everard Foundation
The Eveson Charitable Trust
The Beryl Evetts and Robert Luff Animal Welfare Trust Limited
The Exilarch's Foundation
The F. P. Limited Charitable Trust
The Fairway Trust
The Lord Faringdon Charitable Trust
The Fassnidge Memorial Trust
The George Fentham Birmingham Charity

The A. M. Fenton Trust
The Allan and Nesta Ferguson Charitable Settlement
The Fidelity UK Foundation
The Doris Field Charitable Trust
Field Family Charitable Trust
The Ian Fleming Charitable Trust
The Football Association National Sports Centre Trust
The Football Association Youth Trust
Ford Britain Trust
The Oliver Ford Charitable Trust
The Forest Hill Charitable Trust
Forever Manchester (The Community Foundation for Greater Manchester)
The Forman Hardy Charitable Trust
Gwyneth Forrester Trust
The Forte Charitable Trust
The Four Winds Trust
The Isaac and Freda Frankel Memorial Charitable Trust
The Elizabeth Frankland Moore and Star Foundation
The Jill Franklin Trust
The Gordon Fraser Charitable Trust
The Hugh Fraser Foundation
The Joseph Strong Frazer Trust
The Louis and Valerie Freedman Charitable Settlement
The Charles S. French Charitable Trust
The Freshfield Foundation
The Friarsgate Trust
The Frognal Trust
The Patrick & Helena Frost Foundation
The Fulmer Charitable Trust
The Gale Family Charity Trust
The Gamma Trust
The Gannochy Trust
The Samuel Gardner Memorial Trust
The Garnett Charitable Trust
Garthgwynion Charities
The Gatsby Charitable Foundation
Gatwick Airport Community Trust
The Robert Gavron Charitable Trust
Sir Robert Geffery's Almshouse Trust
Get Kids Going
The Gibbs Charitable Trust
Simon Gibson Charitable Trust
The G. C. Gibson Charitable Trust

The Girdlers' Company Charitable Trust
The B. and P. Glasser Charitable Trust
Global Care
Gloucestershire Community Foundation
Worshipful Company of Glovers of London Charitable Trust
The GNC Trust
The Sydney and Phyllis Goldberg Memorial Charitable Trust
The Golden Bottle Trust
The Goldsmiths' Arts Fund
The Goldsmiths' Company Charity
The Golsoncott Foundation
The Mike Gooley Trailfinders Charity
The Gosling Foundation Limited
The Gould Charitable Trust
The Grace Charitable Trust
A. B. Grace Trust
E. C. Graham Belford Charitable Settlement
The Grahame Charitable Foundation Limited
The Granada Foundation
Grand Charitable Trust of the Order of Women Freemasons
The Grange Farm Centre Trust
The J. G. Graves Charitable Trust
The Gray Trust
The Great Stone Bridge Trust of Edenbridge
The Green Hall Foundation
Greenham Common Community Trust Limited
The Greggs Foundation
The Gretna Charitable Trust
The Grimmitt Trust
The Grocers' Charity
The M. and R. Gross Charities Limited
The GRP Charitable Trust
The Guildry Incorporation of Perth
The Walter Guinness Charitable Trust
The Gur Trust
Dr Guthrie's Association
The H. and M. Charitable Trust
H. C. D. Memorial Fund
The Hackney Parochial Charities
The Hadfield Trust
The Hadley Trust
The Alfred Haines Charitable Trust

**201**

The Edith Winifred Hall Charitable Trust
Hamilton Wallace Trust
Paul Hamlyn Foundation
Hampton Fuel Allotment
The Doughty Hanson Charitable Foundation
Edward Harvist Trust
Headley-Pitt Charitable Trust
The Hedley Denton Charitable Trust
The H. J. Heinz Company Limited Charitable Trust
Help the Homeless Limited
The Hesslewood Children's Trust (Hull Seamen's and General Orphanage)
Hitchin Educational Foundation
The Hoover Foundation
The Horne Foundation
The Charles Irving Charitable Trust
Jewish Child's Day Foundation
The Ian Karten Charitable Trust
The Kennel Club Charitable Trust
The Kettering and District Charitable Medical Trust
The Kingsbury Charity
The Mary Kinross Charitable Trust
The Sir James Knott Trust
John Laing Charitable Trust
Maurice and Hilda Laing Charitable Trust
The Beatrice Laing Trust
The Lark Trust
The William Leech Charity
The Erica Leonard Trust
LHR Airport Communities Trust
Lifeline 4 Kids
The Charles Lloyd Foundation
Lloyds Bank Foundation for England and Wales
Lloyds Bank Foundation for Northern Ireland
The Lord's Taverners
The Lyndhurst Trust
Sylvanus Lysons Charity
Man Group plc Charitable Trust
Lord Mayor of Manchester's Charity Appeal Trust
The Mersey Docks and Harbour Company Charitable Fund
The Tony Metherell Charitable Trust
Mobbs Memorial Trust Ltd
The Montague Thompson Coon Charitable Trust
The Moss Family Charitable Trust
Mosselson Charitable Trust
The Mount Everest Foundation

The Edwina Mountbatten & Leonora Children's Foundation
Mrs Waterhouse Charitable Trust
The Mugdock Children's Trust
The Mulberry Trust
The Edith Murphy Foundation
The Music Sales Charitable Trust
Muslim Hands
The Mutual Trust Group
The Janet Nash Charitable Settlement
The National Churches Trust
The Worshipful Company of Needlemakers' Charitable Fund
The Neighbourly Charitable Trust
The James Neill Trust Fund
Nemoral Ltd
The Newcomen Collett Foundation
The Chevras Ezras Nitzrochim Trust
The Noon Foundation
The Norman Family Charitable Trust
The Normanby Charitable Trust
The Northampton Municipal Church Charities
The Northmoor Trust
The Northumberland Village Homes Trust
The Northwood Charitable Trust
The Norton Foundation
The Norwich Town Close Estate Charity
The Notgrove Trust
The Nottingham General Dispensary
Nottinghamshire Community Foundation
The Father O'Mahoney Memorial Trust
The Sir Peter O'Sullevan Charitable Trust
The Oakdale Trust
The Oakley Charitable Trust
The Oakmoor Charitable Trust
The Odin Charitable Trust
The Ofenheim Charitable Trust
The Ogle Christian Trust
Oizer Charitable Trust
The John Oldacre Foundation
Open Gate
The Ouseley Trust
The Owen Family Trust
Oxfam (GB)
Oxfordshire Community Foundation
The P. F. Charitable Trust
The Paget Charitable Trust
The Panacea Charitable Trust

The James Pantyfedwen Foundation
The Paragon Trust
The Park House Charitable Trust
The Samuel and Freda Parkinson Charitable Trust
The Patrick Charitable Trust
The Jack Patston Charitable Trust
The Harry Payne Fund
The Susanna Peake Charitable Trust
The Pedmore Sporting Club Trust Fund
The Dowager Countess Eleanor Peel Trust
The Pennycress Trust
The Performing Right Society Foundation
The Personal Assurance Charitable Trust
The Persson Charitable Trust
The Persula Foundation
The Jack Petchey Foundation
The Petplan Charitable Trust
The Phillips and Rubens Charitable Trust
The Phillips Charitable Trust
The Phillips Family Charitable Trust
The David Pickford Charitable Foundation
The Bernard Piggott Charitable Trust
The Pilkington Charities Fund
The Austin and Hope Pilkington Trust
The Sir Harry Pilkington Trust Fund
The DLA Piper Charitable Trust
The Platinum Trust
The George and Esme Pollitzer Charitable Settlement
The Ponton House Trust
Edith and Ferdinand Porjes Charitable Trust
The John Porter Charitable Trust
The Porter Foundation
The Portishead Nautical Trust
The Portrack Charitable Trust
The J. E. Posnansky Charitable Trust
Premierquote Ltd
Premishlaner Charitable Trust
The William Price Charitable Trust
Sir John Priestman Charity Trust
The Primrose Trust
The Prince of Wales's Charitable Foundation
Prison Service Charity Fund
The Privy Purse Charitable Trust

The Puebla Charitable Trust
The Puri Foundation
Mr and Mrs J. A. Pye's Charitable Settlement
Queen Mary's Roehampton Trust
The Queen's Silver Jubilee Trust
R. S. Charitable Trust
The RVW Trust
The Monica Rabagliati Charitable Trust
Rachel Charitable Trust
The Mr and Mrs Philip Rackham Charitable Trust
Richard Radcliffe Charitable Trust
The Radcliffe Trust
The Rainford Trust
The Joseph and Lena Randall Charitable Trust
The Rank Foundation Limited
The Ratcliff Foundation
The Eleanor Rathbone Charitable Trust
The Sigrid Rausing Trust
The Ravensdale Trust
The Rayden Charitable Trust
The Roger Raymond Charitable Trust
The Rayne Foundation
The Rayne Trust
The Sir James Reckitt Charity
The C. A. Redfern Charitable Foundation
The Reed Foundation
Richard Reeve's Foundation
The Rest Harrow Trust
Reuben Foundation
The Rhododendron Trust
The Rhondda Cynon Taff Welsh Church Acts Fund
The Clive Richards Charity
The Richmond Parish Lands Charity
Ridgesave Limited
The Sir John Ritblat Family Foundation
The River Trust
Thomas Roberts Trust
The Robertson Trust
The Rochester Bridge Trust
The Rock Foundation
The Rofeh Trust
Rokach Family Charitable Trust
The Helen Roll Charitable Trust
The Sir James Roll Charitable Trust
Mrs L. D. Rope Third Charitable Settlement
The Rosca Trust
The Cecil Rosen Foundation
The Rothermere Foundation
The Rothley Trust
The Roughley Charitable Trust

Rowanville Ltd
The Rowlands Trust
Royal Artillery Charitable Fund
Royal British Legion
Royal Docks Trust (London)
Royal Masonic Trust for Girls and Boys
The Royal Victoria Hall Foundation
The Rubin Foundation
The Russell Trust
The J. S. and E. C. Rymer Charitable Trust
The Michael Sacher Charitable Trust
The Michael Harry Sacher Trust
The Sackler Trust
The Ruzin Sadagora Trust
The Saddlers' Company Charitable Fund
The Saga Charitable Trust
The Jean Sainsbury Animal Welfare Trust
The Alan and Babette Sainsbury Charitable Fund
The Sainsbury Family Charitable Trusts
Sam and Bella Sebba Charitable Trust
The Basil Samuel Charitable Trust
The M. J. Samuel Charitable Trust
The Peter Samuel Charitable Trust
The Samworth Foundation
The Sandra Charitable Trust
Santander UK Foundation Limited
The Scarfe Charitable Trust
The Schapira Charitable Trust
The Schmidt-Bodner Charitable Trust
The Schreib Trust
The Schreiber Charitable Trust
The Schuster Charitable Trust
Foundation Scotland
The Francis C. Scott Charitable Trust
The Frieda Scott Charitable Trust
Scottish Coal Industry Special Welfare Fund
The Scouloudi Foundation
Seafarers UK (King George's Fund for Sailors)
The Seedfield Trust
Leslie Sell Charitable Trust
ShareGift (The Orr Mackintosh Foundation)
The Shears Foundation
The Sheepdrove Trust
The Sheffield and District Hospital Services Charitable Fund

The Patricia and Donald Shepherd Charitable Trust
The Archie Sherman Cardiff Foundation
The Archie Sherman Charitable Trust
The R. C. Sherriff Rosebriars Trust
The Shetland Charitable Trust
SHINE (Support and Help in Education)
The Barnett and Sylvia Shine No 2 Charitable Trust
The Bassil Shippam and Alsford Trust
The Shipwrights' Company Charitable Fund
The Shirley Foundation
Shlomo Memorial Fund Limited
The J. A. Shone Memorial Trust
David and Jennifer Sieff Charitable Trust
The Huntly and Margery Sinclair Charitable Trust
The Sino-British Fellowship Trust
The Skelton Bounty
The Charles Skey Charitable Trust
The SMB Charitable Trust
The Mrs Smith and Mount Trust
The N. Smith Charitable Settlement
The Henry Smith Charity
The Stanley Smith UK Horticultural Trust
The Sobell Foundation
The Solo Charitable Settlement
The E. C. Sosnow Charitable Trust
The Souter Charitable Trust
The South Square Trust
The W. F. Southall Trust
The Southover Manor General Education Trust
The Sovereign Health Care Charitable Trust
Sparquote Limited
The Spear Charitable Trust
The Worshipful Company of Spectacle Makers' Charity
The Jessie Spencer Trust
The Ralph and Irma Sperring Charity
The Spielman Charitable Trust
Springrule Limited
The Spurrell Charitable Trust
The Geoff and Fiona Squire Foundation
St James's Trust Settlement
St James's Place Foundation
Sir Walter St John's Educational Charity

St Michael's and All Saints'
    Charities Relief Branch
The Stanley Foundation Ltd
The Staples Trust
The Steel Charitable Trust
The Steinberg Family
    Charitable Trust
The Stephen Barry Charitable
    Trust
The Stewards' Company
    Limited (incorporating the
    J. W. Laing Trust and the
    J. W. Laing Biblical
    Scholarship Trust)
The Leonard Laity Stoate
    Charitable Trust
The Stobart Newlands
    Charitable Trust
The Edward Stocks-Massey
    Bequest Fund
The Stoller Charitable Trust
M. J. C. Stone Charitable Trust
The Samuel Storey Family
    Charitable Trust
Peter Stormonth Darling
    Charitable Trust
The Strangward Trust
Stratford upon Avon Town
    Trust
The W. O. Street Charitable
    Foundation
The Sudborough Foundation
The Bernard Sunley Charitable
    Foundation
The Sussex Historic Churches
    Trust
Sutton Coldfield Charitable
    Trust
The Swann-Morton Foundation
Swansea and Brecon Diocesan
    Board of Finance Limited
Swimathon Foundation
The John Swire (1989)
    Charitable Trust
The Swire Charitable Trust
The Hugh and Ruby Sykes
    Charitable Trust
The Charles and Elsie Sykes
    Trust
The Charity of Stella Symons
The Talbot Trusts
The Talbot Village Trust
The Lady Tangye Charitable
    Trust
The David Tannen Charitable
    Trust
The Tanner Trust
The Lili Tapper Charitable
    Foundation
The Tay Charitable Trust
A. P. Taylor Trust
Tearfund
The Tedworth Charitable Trust
Tees Valley Community
    Foundation
The Templeton Goodwill Trust

Tesco Charity Trust
The C. Paul Thackray General
    Charitable Trust
The Thistle Trust
The Loke Wan Tho Memorial
    Foundation
The Thompson Family
    Charitable Trust
The Sir Jules Thorn Charitable
    Trust
The Thornton Foundation
The Thornton Trust
The Three Guineas Trust
The Thriplow Charitable Trust
The Daniel Thwaites Charitable
    Trust
The Tinsley Foundation
The Tobacco Pipe Makers and
    Tobacco Trade Benevolent
    Fund
The Tolkien Trust
Tomchei Torah Charitable
    Trust
The Tompkins Foundation
The Tory Family Foundation
Tottenham Grammar School
    Foundation
The Tower Hill Trust
The Towry Law Charitable Trust
    (also known as the Castle
    Educational Trust)
The Constance Travis
    Charitable Trust
The Triangle Trust (1949) Fund
The True Colours Trust
Truedene Co. Ltd
The Truemark Trust
Truemart Limited
Trumros Limited
The Trusthouse Charitable
    Foundation
Tudor Rose Ltd
The Tudor Trust
The Tufton Charitable Trust
The Douglas Turner Trust
The Florence Turner Trust
The G. J. W. Turner Trust
Community Foundation Serving
    Tyne and Wear and
    Northumberland
Trustees of Tzedakah
Ulster Garden Villages Ltd
The Ulverscroft Foundation
The Union of Orthodox Hebrew
    Congregation
The United Society for the
    Propagation of the Gospel
Uxbridge United Welfare Trust
The Van Neste Foundation
The Vandervell Foundation
The Vardy Foundation
The Variety Club Children's
    Charity
Veneziana Fund
The Nigel Vinson Charitable
    Trust

The William and Ellen Vinten
    Trust
The Vintners' Foundation
Vision Charity
Vivdale Ltd
Wade's Charity
The Scurrah Wainwright Charity
The Community Foundation in
    Wales
Wales Council for Voluntary
    Action
War on Want
The Ward Blenkinsop Trust
G. R. Waters Charitable Trust
    2000
The Westminster Foundation
The Kay Williams Charitable
    Foundation
The Community Foundation for
    Wiltshire and Swindon
The Maurice Wohl Charitable
    Foundation
The Charles Wolfson
    Charitable Trust
The Wolfson Family Charitable
    Trust
The Wragge and Co Charitable
    Trust
Wychville Ltd
The Xerox (UK) Trust
Yorkshire Building Society
    Charitable Foundation
The Zochonis Charitable Trust
Zurich Community Trust (UK)
    Limited

## Core support

### ■ Contributions to statutory funding

The 1970 Trust
The 29th May 1961 Charitable
    Trust
The Aberdeen Endowments
    Trust
The Sylvia Aitken Charitable
    Trust
The Archer Trust
The Ardwick Trust
The Ashden Trust
The Ashworth Charitable Trust
Lord Barnby's Foundation
The Paul Bassham Charitable
    Trust
The Bellinger Donnay Trust
The Bingham Trust
The Tony Bramall Charitable
    Trust
Miss Marion Broughton's
    Charitable Trust
Edna Brown Charitable
    Settlement
Buckinghamshire Community
    Foundation

The G. W. Cadbury Charitable Trust
The Campden Charities Trustee
The Worshipful Company of Carmen Benevolent Trust
The Cattanach Charitable Trust
The Charities Advisory Trust
Christian Aid
The City Educational Trust Fund
Colyer-Fergusson Charitable Trust
The Ernest Cook Trust
The Alice Ellen Cooper Dean Charitable Foundation
General Charity of Coventry
Cruden Foundation Ltd
The Cwmbran Trust
The D. G. Charitable Settlement
Dorset Community Foundation
The Double 'O' Charity Ltd
The W. E. Dunn Trust
Earls Colne and Halstead Educational Charity
The Vernon N. Ely Charitable Trust
The Essex Fairway Charitable Trust
The Doris Field Charitable Trust
The Fifty Fund
The Football Foundation
The Oliver Ford Charitable Trust
The Garrick Charitable Trust
The Girdlers' Company Charitable Trust
Global Care Foundation
The Goldsmiths' Company Charity
The Grange Farm Centre Trust
The Great Stone Bridge Trust of Edenbridge
Greenham Common Community Trust Limited
The Hadrian Trust
The W. A. Handley Charitable Trust
Headley-Pitt Charitable Trust
Mothercare Group Foundation
Muslim Hands
The Northmoor Trust
The Odin Charitable Trust
The Owen Family Trust
The Mary Potter Convent Hospital Trust
The Prince of Wales's Charitable Foundation
The Mr and Mrs Philip Rackham Charitable Trust
The Ragdoll Foundation
The Joseph and Lena Randall Charitable Trust

The E. L. Rathbone Charitable Trust
The Ravensdale Trust
The Rayne Trust
The Rest Harrow Trust
The Rhododendron Trust
The Rosca Trust
Sir Samuel Scott of Yews Trust
The St Laurence Relief In Need Trust
C. B. and H. H. Taylor 1984 Trust
Tesco Charity Trust
The Tobacco Pipe Makers and Tobacco Trade Benevolent Fund
Tottenham Grammar School Foundation
The Tower Hill Trust
War on Want
The Norman Whiteley Trust

.........................................

■ Core costs
The 29th May 1961 Charitable Trust
ABF The Soldiers' Charity
The Adint Charitable Trust
The AIM Foundation
The Ajahma Charitable Trust
The Alchemy Foundation
The H. B. Allen Charitable Trust
The Almond Trust
The Ammco Trust
The Anchor Foundation
The Andrew Anderson Trust
Anglo American Group Foundation
The Archbishop's Council – The Church and Community Fund
The Ardwick Trust
The Armourers' and Brasiers' Gauntlet Trust
The Asda Foundation
The Ashley Family Foundation
The Ian Askew Charitable Trust
The Astor Foundation
The Lord Austin Trust
The Aylesford Family Charitable Trust
Bag4Sport Foundation
The Baily Thomas Charitable Fund
The Baker Charitable Trust
The Balmore Trust
The Barham Charitable Trust
Lord Barnby's Foundation
Barnes Workhouse Fund
The Paul Bassham Charitable Trust
BBC Children in Need
The Bedfordshire and Luton Community Foundation

The Bellahouston Bequest Fund
The Bellinger Donnay Trust
The Gerald Bentall Charitable Trust
The Berkeley Charitable Foundation
The Berkshire Community Foundation
The Bingham Trust
Miss Jeanne Bisgood's Charitable Trust
The Sydney Black Charitable Trust
Sir Alec Black's Charity
The Blagrave Trust
The Marjory Boddy Charitable Trust
The Body Shop Foundation
The Harry Bottom Charitable Trust
The Bower Trust
The Breadsticks Foundation
The Breast Cancer Research Trust
The Brighton District Nursing Association Trust
The British Dietetic Association General and Education Trust Fund
British Gas (Scottish Gas) Energy Trust
British Record Industry Trust
The J. and M. Britton Charitable Trust
The Bromley Trust
The Charles Brotherton Trust
Buckinghamshire Community Foundation
The E. F. Bulmer Benevolent Fund
The Clara E. Burgess Charity
Consolidated Charity of Burton upon Trent
Peter Cadbury Charitable Trust
The William A. Cadbury Charitable Trust
The Cadbury Foundation
The Barrow Cadbury Trust
The Calpe Trust
The Cambridgeshire Community Foundation
The Camelia Trust
The Campden Charities Trustee
The Richard Carne Trust
Carter's Educational Foundation
The Casey Trust
Cash for Kids – Radio Clyde
The Cattanach Charitable Trust
The Chapman Charitable Trust
Chrysalis Trust
The City Bridge Trust
Stephen Clark 1957 Charitable Trust

**205**

The Robert Clutterbuck
    Charitable Trust
The Cobtree Charity Trust Ltd
The Cole Charitable Trust
John and Freda Coleman
    Charitable Trust
The Sir Jeremiah Colman Gift
    Trust
The Colt Foundation
Comic Relief
Community First
The Congleton Inclosure Trust
Gordon Cook Foundation
The Ernest Cook Trust
Harold and Daphne Cooper
    Charitable Trust
The Alice Ellen Cooper Dean
    Charitable Foundation
The J. Reginald Corah
    Foundation Fund
Michael Cornish Charitable
    Trust
County Durham Community
    Foundation
The Augustine Courtauld Trust
Cripplegate Foundation
The Peter Cruddas Foundation
Cruden Foundation Ltd
Cullum Family Trust
The Cumber Family Charitable
    Trust
The Cwmbran Trust
Roald Dahl's Marvellous
    Children's Charity
The Gwendoline and Margaret
    Davies Charity
The Hamilton Davies Trust
William Dean Countryside and
    Educational Trust
Devon Community Foundation
The Dibden Allotments Fund
Disability Aid Fund (The Roger
    and Jean Jefcoate Trust)
The Djanogly Foundation
The Derek and Eileen Dodgson
    Foundation
Dorset Community Foundation
The Double 'O' Charity Ltd
The Drapers' Charitable Fund
The Dulverton Trust
The Dunhill Medical Trust
The W. E. Dunn Trust
The Charles Dunstone
    Charitable Trust
The Ebenezer Trust
Edge Fund
The Ellerdale Trust
The John Ellerman Foundation
The Elmgrant Trust
The Elmley Foundation
The Englefield Charitable Trust
Epilepsy Research UK
Esh Foundation
The Essex and Southend
    Sports Trust

The Essex Fairway Charitable
    Trust
The Essex Youth Trust
Joseph Ettedgui Charitable
    Foundation
The Eveson Charitable Trust
The Expat Foundation
Esmée Fairbairn Foundation
Famos Foundation Trust
The February Foundation
The George Fentham
    Birmingham Charity
Field Family Charitable Trust
The Fifty Fund
Gwyneth Forrester Trust
The Donald Forrester Trust
The Fort Foundation
The Forte Charitable Trust
The Foyle Foundation
The Freemasons' Grand
    Charity
The Patrick & Helena Frost
    Foundation
The Fuserna Foundation
General Charitable Trust
Gamlen Charitable Trust
The Garrick Charitable Trust
The Gibbs Charitable Trust
Simon Gibson Charitable Trust
The G. C. Gibson Charitable
    Trust
The Girdlers' Company
    Charitable Trust
Gloucestershire Community
    Foundation
The Goldsmiths' Company
    Charity
The Golsoncott Foundation
Nicholas and Judith
    Goodison's Charitable
    Settlement
The Gosling Foundation
    Limited
The Great Britain Sasakawa
    Foundation
The Greggs Foundation
H. C. D. Memorial Fund
The Hadfield Trust
The Hadley Trust
The Hadrian Trust
Paul Hamlyn Foundation
Hampshire and Isle of Wight
    Community Foundation
The Kathleen Hannay
    Memorial Charity
The Haramead Trust
The Harborne Parish Lands
    Charity
William Harding's Charity
The Harebell Centenary Fund
The Harpur Trust
The Peter Harrison Foundation
The Hartley Charitable Trust
The Dorothy Hay-Bolton
    Charitable Trust
The Headley Trust

May Hearnshaw Charitable
    Trust
Heart of England Community
    Foundation
Heart Research UK
The Percy Hedley 1990
    Charitable Trust
The Hedley Denton Charitable
    Trust
The Helping Foundation
The Hemby Charitable Trust
Henley Educational Trust
Herefordshire Community
    Foundation
The Herefordshire Historic
    Churches Trust
The Hertfordshire Community
    Foundation
The Alan Edward Higgs Charity
The Hilden Charitable Fund
The Hillingdon Community
    Trust
Hinchley Charitable Trust
The Lady Hind Trust
The Hintze Family Charity
    Foundation
The Holst Foundation
The Edward Holt Trust
The Holywood Trust
The Homelands Charitable
    Trust
The Homestead Charitable
    Trust
The Mary Homfray Charitable
    Trust
Sir Harold Hood's Charitable
    Trust
The Worshipful Company of
    Horners' Charitable Trusts
The Hospital of God at
    Greatham
The Hospital Saturday Fund
House of Industry Estate
The Huggard Charitable Trust
The Hull and East Riding
    Charitable Trust
The Albert Hunt Trust
The Hunter Foundation
Miss Agnes H. Hunter's Trust
Ibrahim Foundation Ltd
The Innocent Foundation
The Inverforth Charitable Trust
Irish Youth Foundation (UK)
    Ltd (incorporating The
    Lawlor Foundation)
The Isle of Anglesey Charitable
    Trust
The ITF Seafarers Trust
John James Bristol Foundation
The James Trust
Nick Jenkins Foundation
The Jephcott Charitable Trust
The Jerusalem Trust
The Joffe Charitable Trust
The Elton John Aids
    Foundation

The Joicey Trust
The Jordan Charitable
    Foundation
The Joron Charitable Trust
Jusaca Charitable Trust
The Boris Karloff Charitable
    Foundation
The Kass Charitable Trust
The Kelly Family Charitable
    Trust
The Kennel Club Charitable
    Trust
Kent Community Foundation
The Peter Kershaw Trust
Keswick Hall Charity
The Robert Kiln Charitable
    Trust
The King/Cullimore Charitable
    Trust
Kingdom Way Trust
The Mary Kinross Charitable
    Trust
The Sir James Knott Trust
The Neil Kreitman Foundation
The Heinz, Anna and Carol
    Kroch Foundation
The K. P. Ladd Charitable
    Trust
Community Foundations for
    Lancashire and Merseyside
The Allen Lane Foundation
The LankellyChase Foundation
The Lark Trust
Mrs F. B. Laurence Charitable
    Trust
The Edgar E. Lawley
    Foundation
The Leach Fourteenth Trust
The Leathersellers' Company
    Charitable Fund
The William Leech Charity
Leicestershire, Leicester and
    Rutland Community
    Foundation
The Kennedy Leigh Charitable
    Trust
The Leigh Trust
The Lennox and Wyfold
    Foundation
The Erica Leonard Trust
The Leverhulme Trust
Joseph Levy Charitable
    Foundation
The Sir Edward Lewis
    Foundation
Lincolnshire Community
    Foundation
Lindale Educational
    Foundation
The Frank Litchfield Charitable
    Trust
The Charles Littlewood Hill
    Trust
The Second Joseph Aaron
    Littman Foundation

Lloyds Bank Foundation for
    England and Wales
Lloyds Bank Foundation for
    Northern Ireland
Lloyds TSB Foundation for
    Scotland
The Trust for London
London Catalyst
The London Community
    Foundation
London Housing Foundation
    Ltd
The Lowy Mitchell Foundation
The Henry Lumley Charitable
    Trust
John Lyon's Charity
The R. S. Macdonald
    Charitable Trust
The Mackintosh Foundation
The MacRobert Trust
The W. M. Mann Foundation
R. W. Mann Trust
Market Harborough and The
    Bowdens Charity
The Marks Family Foundation
The Ann and David Marks
    Foundation
The Hilda and Samuel Marks
    Foundation
Marmot Charitable Trust
The Marr-Munning Trust
The Marsh Christian Trust
John Martin's Charity
The Nancie Massey Charitable
    Trust
The Mathew Trust
The Matliwala Family
    Charitable Trust
The Matt 6.3 Charitable Trust
Mayfair Charities Ltd
The Medlock Charitable Trust
The Mercers' Charitable
    Foundation
The Merchant Taylors'
    Company Charities Fund
The Merchant Venturers'
    Charity
Mercury Phoenix Trust
The Tony Metherell Charitable
    Trust
The Mickel Fund
The Gerald Micklem Charitable
    Trust
Middlesex Sports Foundation
The Millfield House Foundation
The Clare Milne Trust
The Esmé Mitchell Trust
The Modiano Charitable Trust
Mole Charitable Trust
Monmouthshire County Council
    Welsh Church Act Fund
The George A. Moore
    Foundation
John Moores Foundation
The Morgan Charitable
    Foundation

The Morgan Foundation
The Oliver Morland Charitable
    Trust
G. M. Morrison Charitable
    Trust
Mothercare Group Foundation
The Mugdock Children's Trust
Frederick Mulder Charitable
    Trust
Murphy-Neumann Charity
    Company Limited
National Committee of the
    Women's World Day of
    Prayer for England and
    Wales and Northern Ireland
The National Express
    Foundation
The National Hockey
    Foundation
The Nationwide Foundation
The Nazareth Trust Fund
The Neighbourly Charitable
    Trust
Network for Social Change
The Frances and Augustus
    Newman Foundation
Norfolk Community Foundation
Normalyn Charitable Trust
The Northern Rock Foundation
The Northmoor Trust
The Notgrove Trust
The Oakdale Trust
The Oakley Charitable Trust
The Odin Charitable Trust
Open Gate
The Owen Family Trust
The P. F. Charitable Trust
The Paget Charitable Trust
The Payne Charitable Trust
The Harry Payne Fund
The Peacock Charitable Trust
The Dowager Countess
    Eleanor Peel Trust
The Pennycress Trust
The Pilgrim Trust
The Pilkington Charities Fund
Estate of the Late Colonel
    W. W. Pilkington Will Trusts
    – The General Charity Fund
Polden-Puckham Charitable
    Foundation
The Pollywally Charitable Trust
The Mary Potter Convent
    Hospital Trust
The David and Elaine Potter
    Foundation
Princess Anne's Charities
Mr and Mrs J. A. Pye's
    Charitable Settlement
Queen Mary's Roehampton
    Trust
The Racing Foundation
The Ravensdale Trust
The Rayne Trust
The John Rayner Charitable
    Trust

The Sir James Reckitt Charity
The Rhododendron Trust
The Richmond Parish Lands Charity
Rivers Foundation
The Helen Roll Charitable Trust
The Rosca Trust
Mrs Gladys Row Fogo Charitable Trust
The Joseph Rowntree Charitable Trust
Royal British Legion
The Saddlers' Company Charitable Fund
The Alan and Babette Sainsbury Charitable Fund
The Saintbury Trust
Santander UK Foundation Limited
The Frieda Scott Charitable Trust
The Sir James and Lady Scott Trust
Seafarers UK (King George's Fund for Sailors)
The Sheldon Trust
SHINE (Support and Help in Education)
The Shirley Foundation
The Simmons & Simmons Charitable Foundation
SITA Cornwall Trust Limited
The Charles Skey Charitable Trust
Rita and David Slowe Charitable Trust
The Mrs Smith and Mount Trust
The Sobell Foundation
Social Business Trust (Scale-Up)
The Souter Charitable Trust
R. H. Southern Trust
The Sovereign Health Care Charitable Trust
The Jessie Spencer Trust
Sported Foundation
The St Hilda's Trust
Sir Walter St John's Educational Charity
The St Laurence Relief In Need Trust
The Staples Trust
The Peter Stebbings Memorial Charity
The Steel Charitable Trust
The Samuel Storey Family Charitable Trust
Peter Storrs Trust
Stratford upon Avon Town Trust
Sutton Coldfield Charitable Trust
Swimathon Foundation

Sylvia Waddilove Foundation UK
The Charity of Stella Symons
The Talbot Trusts
The Sue Thomson Foundation
The Sir Jules Thorn Charitable Trust
The Tisbury Telegraph Trust
The Tolkien Trust
The Tompkins Foundation
The Towry Law Charitable Trust (also known as the Castle Educational Trust)
The Constance Travis Charitable Trust
The Triangle Trust (1949) Fund
The Trusthouse Charitable Foundation
The James Tudor Foundation
The Tudor Trust
Tuixen Foundation
The Douglas Turner Trust
Two Ridings Community Foundation
United Utilities Trust Fund
The Valentine Charitable Trust
The Valiant Charitable Trust
The Vandervell Foundation
Volant Charitable Trust
Voluntary Action Fund
The Scurrah Wainwright Charity
The Wakefield and Tetley Trust
Sir Siegmund Warburg's Voluntary Settlement
The Barbara Ward Children's Foundation
The Waterloo Foundation
The Wates Foundation
Waynflete Charitable Trust
The Weavers' Company Benevolent Fund
Webb Memorial Trust
The James Weir Foundation
Welsh Church Fund – Dyfed area (Carmarthenshire, Ceredigion and Pembrokeshire)
The Westminster Foundation
The Whitaker Charitable Trust
White Stuff Foundation
The Norman Whiteley Trust
The Whitley Animal Protection Trust
The Lionel Wigram Memorial Trust
The William Barrow's Charity
Dame Violet Wills Charitable Trust
The Dame Violet Wills Will Trust
David Wilson Foundation
The Wilson Foundation
The Community Foundation for Wiltshire and Swindon
The Harold Hyam Wingate Foundation

The Wixamtree Trust
The Wolfson Family Charitable Trust
The Wood Family Trust
Wooden Spoon Society
Woodroffe Benton Foundation
The Woodward Charitable Trust
Worcester Municipal Charities
The Matthews Wrightson Charity Trust
The Wyndham Charitable Trust
The Yapp Charitable Trust
The Yardley Great Trust
The South Yorkshire Community Foundation
The John Kirkhope Young Endowment Fund
Youth Music
Youth United Foundation
Stephen Zimmerman Charitable Trust
Zurich Community Trust (UK) Limited

..................................

■ **Development funding**

The 101 Foundation
The 1970 Trust
The 1989 Willan Charitable Trust
The 29th May 1961 Charitable Trust
A. W. Charitable Trust
The Aberbrothock Skea Trust
The Aberdeen Foundation
ABF The Soldiers' Charity
Eric Abrams Charitable Trust
The Acacia Charitable Trust
Access Sport
Achisomoch Aid Company Limited
The ACT Foundation
Action Medical Research
The Company of Actuaries' Charitable Trust Fund
The Adamson Trust
The Victor Adda Foundation
The Addleshaw Goddard Charitable Trust
Adenfirst Ltd
The Adint Charitable Trust
The Adnams Charity
The Adrian Swire Charitable Trust
AF Trust Company
Age Scotland
Age UK
Aid to the Church in Need (UK)
The Sylvia Aitken Charitable Trust
The Ajahma Charitable Trust
The Al Fayed Charitable Foundation
The Alabaster Trust

Grant-makers by types of grant — Development funding

The Alborada Trust
D. G. Albright Charitable Trust
The Alchemy Foundation
Aldgate and All Hallows' Foundation
The Alexis Trust
All Saints Educational Trust
Allchurches Trust Ltd
The H. B. Allen Charitable Trust
The Alliance Family Foundation
Angus Allnatt Charitable Foundation
The Pat Allsop Charitable Trust
The Almond Trust
Almondsbury Charity
The Altajir Trust
Altamont Ltd
AM Charitable Trust
The Ammco Trust
Viscount Amory's Charitable Trust
The Ampelos Trust
The AMW Charitable Trust
The Anchor Foundation
The Andrew Anderson Trust
Andor Charitable Trust
Mary Andrew Charitable Trust
Andrews Charitable Trust
Anglo American Group Foundation
Anguish's Educational Foundation
The Eric Anker-Petersen Charity
The Annandale Charitable Trust
Anpride Ltd
The Anson Charitable Trust
The Apax Foundation
The Appletree Trust
The Arbib Foundation
The Archbishop's Council – The Church and Community Fund
The Archer Trust
The Architectural Heritage Fund
The Ardeola Charitable Trust
The Argentarius Foundation
The Argus Appeal
Armenian General Benevolent Union London Trust
The Armourers' and Brasiers' Gauntlet Trust
The Artemis Charitable Trust
Arts Council England
Arts Council of Northern Ireland
Arts Council of Wales (Cyngor Celfyddydau Cymru)
The Ove Arup Foundation
The AS Charitable Trust
The Ascot Fire Brigade Trust
The Ashburnham Thanksgiving Trust

A. J. H. Ashby Will Trust
The Ashden Trust
The Ashley Family Foundation
The Ian Askew Charitable Trust
The Associated Country Women of the World
The Association of Colleges Charitable Trust
Astellas European Foundation
Asthma UK
AstonMansfield Charitable Trust
The Astor Foundation
The Astor of Hever Trust
The Aurelius Charitable Trust
The Avon and Somerset Police Community Trust
Awards for All (see also the Big Lottery Fund)
The Aylesford Family Charitable Trust
The Harry Bacon Foundation
The BACTA Charitable Trust
The Scott Bader Commonwealth Limited
The Bagri Foundation
The Austin Bailey Foundation
The Baily Thomas Charitable Fund
The Baird Trust
The Baker Charitable Trust
The Roy and Pixie Baker Charitable Trust
The Balcombe Charitable Trust
The Albert Casanova Ballard Deceased Trust
The Ballinger Charitable Trust
Balmain Charitable Trust
The Balmore Trust
The Balney Charitable Trust
The Baltic Charitable Fund
The Bamford Charitable Foundation
The Banbury Charities
The Band Trust
The Bank of Scotland Foundation
The Barbers' Company General Charities
The Barbour Foundation
The Barcapel Foundation
Barchester Healthcare Foundation
The Barclay Foundation
The Barham Charitable Trust
The Baring Foundation
The Barker-Mill Foundation
Lord Barnby's Foundation
Barnes Workhouse Fund
The Barnsbury Charitable Trust
The Barnwood House Trust
The Misses Barrie Charitable Trust
Bartholomew Charitable Trust
The Bartlett Taylor Charitable Trust

The Paul Bassham Charitable Trust
The Batchworth Trust
The Bates Charitable Trust
The Battens Charitable Trust
Bay Charitable Trust
The Bay Tree Charitable Trust
The Louis Baylis (Maidenhead Advertiser) Charitable Trust
BBC Children in Need
BC Partners Foundation
The B-CH Charitable Trust
BCH Trust
Bear Mordechai Ltd
The Bearder Charity
The James Beattie Charitable Trust
Beauland Ltd
The Beaverbrook Foundation
The Beccles Town Lands Charity
The Becker Family Charitable Trust
The Beckett's and Sargeant's Educational Foundation
The John Beckwith Charitable Trust
The Peter Beckwith Charitable Trust
The Bedfordshire and Luton Community Foundation
The Provincial Grand Lodge of Bedfordshire Charity Fund
Beefy's Charity Foundation
The David and Ruth Behrend Fund
The Bellahouston Bequest Fund
The Bellinger Donnay Trust
The Benfield Motors Charitable Trust
The Benham Charitable Settlement
Maurice and Jacqueline Bennett Charitable Trust
Michael and Leslie Bennett Charitable Trust
The Bergne-Coupland Charity
The Berkeley Charitable Foundation
The Ruth Berkowitz Charitable Trust
The Berkshire Community Foundation
The Bernadette Charitable Trust
The Bertarelli UK Foundation
The Bestway Foundation
BHST
The Mason Bibby 1981 Trust
The Bideford Bridge Trust
The Big Lottery Fund (see also Awards for All)
The Billmeir Charitable Trust
The Bingham Trust
The Bintaub Charitable Trust

**209**

## Development funding

The Birmingham District Nursing Charitable Trust
The Birmingham Hospital Saturday Fund Medical Charity and Welfare Trust
Birmingham International Airport Community Trust
The Lord Mayor of Birmingham's Charity Birthday House Trust
The Michael Bishop Foundation
The Bertie Black Foundation
Isabel Blackman Foundation
The BlackRock (UK) Charitable Trust
The Blagrave Trust
The Blair Foundation
The Morgan Blake Charitable Trust
Blakemore Foundation
The Blanchminster Trust
The Blandford Lake Trust
The Sir Victor Blank Charitable Settlement
Blatchington Court Trust
Bloodwise
The Bloom Foundation
The Bluston Charitable Settlement
The Nicholas Boas Charitable Trust
The Marjory Boddy Charitable Trust
The Body Shop Foundation
The Bonamy Charitable Trust
The John and Celia Bonham Christie Charitable Trust
The Charlotte Bonham-Carter Charitable Trust
The Linda and Gordon Bonnyman Charitable Trust
The Booth Charities
Boots Charitable Trust
Salo Bordon Charitable Trust
The Bordon Liphook Haslemere Charity
The Oliver Borthwick Memorial Trust
The Boshier-Hinton Foundation
The Bothwell Charitable Trust
The Harry Bottom Charitable Trust
P. G. and N. J. Boulton Trust
Sir Clive Bourne Family Trust
Bourneheights Limited
The Bower Trust
The Bowerman Charitable Trust
The Bowland Charitable Trust
The Frank Brake Charitable Trust
The William Brake Charitable Trust
The Tony Bramall Charitable Trust

The Liz and Terry Bramall Foundation
The Bramhope Trust
The Bransford Trust
The Breadsticks Foundation
The Brendish Family Foundation
Bridgepoint Charitable Trust
The Harold and Alice Bridges Charity
Briggs Animal Welfare Trust
The Brighton District Nursing Association Trust
Bristol Archdeaconry Charity
The Bristol Charities
British Council for Prevention of Blindness (Save Eyes Everywhere)
The British Dietetic Association General and Education Trust Fund
British Gas (Scottish Gas) Energy Trust
British Heart Foundation
The British Humane Association
British Institute at Ankara
British Record Industry Trust
The J. and M. Britton Charitable Trust
The Broderers' Charity Trust
The Bromley Trust
The Consuelo and Anthony Brooke Charitable Trust
The Roger Brooke Charitable Trust
The David Brooke Charity
The Rory and Elizabeth Brooks Foundation
The Charles Brotherton Trust
Joseph Brough Charitable Trust
Miss Marion Broughton's Charitable Trust
Bill Brown 1989 Charitable Trust
Edna Brown Charitable Settlement
R. S. Brownless Charitable Trust
The Brownsword Charitable Foundation
The T. B. H. Brunner Charitable Settlement
The Bruntwood Charity
Brushmill Ltd
Buckingham Trust
Buckinghamshire Community Foundation
The Buckinghamshire Masonic Centenary Fund
Buckland Charitable Trust
The Bulldog Trust Limited
The E. F. Bulmer Benevolent Fund
The Burden Trust

Burden's Charitable Foundation
The Burdett Trust for Nursing
The Clara E. Burgess Charity
The Burghley Family Trust
The Burry Charitable Trust
The Arnold Burton 1998 Charitable Trust
The Burton Breweries Charitable Trust
Consolidated Charity of Burton upon Trent
The Worshipful Company of Butchers General Charities
The Derek Butler Trust
The Noel Buxton Trust
C. and F. Charitable Trust
The James Caan Foundation
Edward Cadbury Charitable Trust
Henry T. and Lucy B. Cadbury Charitable Trust
Peter Cadbury Charitable Trust
The Christopher Cadbury Charitable Trust
The G. W. Cadbury Charitable Trust
The Richard Cadbury Charitable Trust
The William A. Cadbury Charitable Trust
The Cadbury Foundation
The Barrow Cadbury Trust
The Edward and Dorothy Cadbury Trust
The George Cadbury Trust
The Cadogan Charity
CAFOD (Catholic Agency for Overseas Development)
Community Foundation for Calderdale
Callander Charitable Trust
Calleva Foundation
Calouste Gulbenkian Foundation – UK Branch
The Cambridge Chrysalis Trust
The Cambridgeshire Community Foundation
The Camelia Trust
The Campden Charities Trustee
The Canning Trust
The H. and L. Cantor Trust
Cardy Beaver Foundation
The Carew Pole Charitable Trust
David William Traill Cargill Fund
Carlee Ltd
The Carlton House Charitable Trust
The Carmelite Monastery Ware Trust
The Worshipful Company of Carmen Benevolent Trust
The Richard Carne Trust

The Carnegie Dunfermline Trust
The Carnegie Trust for the Universities of Scotland
The Carpenters' Company Charitable Trust
The Carrington Charitable Trust
The Leslie Mary Carter Charitable Trust
The Casey Trust
Cash for Kids – Radio Clyde
Sir John Cass's Foundation
The Elizabeth Casson Trust
The Castang Foundation
The Catalyst Charitable Trust
The Catholic Charitable Trust
Catholic Foreign Missions
The Catholic Trust for England and Wales
The Cattanach Charitable Trust
The Joseph and Annie Cattle Trust
The Thomas Sivewright Catto Charitable Settlement
The Wilfrid and Constance Cave Foundation
The Cayo Foundation
Elizabeth Cayzer Charitable Trust
The B. G. S. Cayzer Charitable Trust
The Cazenove Charitable Trust
The CBD Charitable Trust
Celtic Charity Fund
The Gaynor Cemlyn-Jones Trust
The CH (1980) Charitable Trust
The Amelia Chadwick Trust
The Chapman Charitable Trust
John William Chapman's Charitable Trust
The Charities Advisory Trust
Charitworth Limited
The Charter 600 Charity
The Worshipful Company of Chartered Accountants General Charitable Trust
Chaucer Foundation
The Cheruby Trust
Cheshire Freemason's Charity
The Chetwode Foundation
Child Growth Foundation
The Childs Charitable Trust
The Chipping Sodbury Town Lands Charity
CHK Charities Limited
The Chownes Foundation
The Christabella Charitable Trust
Christadelphian Samaritan Fund
Christian Aid
Chrysalis Trust

The Church Burgesses Educational Foundation
Church Burgesses Trust
Church Urban Fund
The CIBC World Markets Children's Miracle Foundation
The City Bridge Trust
The City Educational Trust Fund
CLA Charitable Trust
Stephen Clark 1957 Charitable Trust
J. A. Clark Charitable Trust
The Hilda and Alice Clark Charitable Trust
The Roger and Sarah Bancroft Clark Charitable Trust
The Clarke Charitable Settlement
The Cleopatra Trust
The Clore Duffield Foundation
The Clothworkers' Foundation
Richard Cloudesley's Charity
The Clover Trust
The Robert Clutterbuck Charitable Trust
Clydpride Ltd
The Coalfields Regeneration Trust
The John Coates Charitable Trust
The Cobalt Trust
The Cobtree Charity Trust Ltd
The Denise Cohen Charitable Trust
The Vivienne and Samuel Cohen Charitable Trust
The John S. Cohen Foundation
The R. and S. Cohen Foundation
John Coldman Charitable Trust
The Cole Charitable Trust
The Colefax Charitable Trust
John and Freda Coleman Charitable Trust
The Bernard Coleman Trust
The Sir Jeremiah Colman Gift Trust
Col-Reno Ltd
The Colt Foundation
The Coltstaple Trust
Colwinston Charitable Trust
Colyer-Fergusson Charitable Trust
Comic Relief
The Comino Foundation
Community Foundation for Leeds
The Compton Charitable Trust
The Congleton Inclosure Trust
Martin Connell Charitable Trust
The Conservation Foundation

The Consolidated Charities for the Infirm – Merchant Taylors' Company
Gordon Cook Foundation
The Ernest Cook Trust
The Cooks Charity
The Catherine Cookson Charitable Trust
Harold and Daphne Cooper Charitable Trust
Mabel Cooper Charity
The Alice Ellen Cooper Dean Charitable Foundation
The Marjorie Coote Animal Charity Trust
The Marjorie Coote Old People's Charity
The Helen Jean Cope Trust
The J. Reginald Corah Foundation Fund
The Gershon Coren Charitable Foundation
The Evan Cornish Foundation
The Duke of Cornwall's Benevolent Fund
The Cornwell Charitable Trust
The Sidney and Elizabeth Corob Charitable Trust
The Corona Charitable Trust
The Costa Family Charitable Trust
The Cotton Industry War Memorial Trust
The Cotton Trust
County Durham Community Foundation
The Augustine Courtauld Trust
General Charity of Coventry
Coventry Building Society Charitable Foundation
Cowley Charitable Foundation
Dudley and Geoffrey Cox Charitable Trust
The Sir William Coxen Trust Fund
The Lord Cozens-Hardy Trust
The Craignish Trust
The Craps Charitable Trust
Michael Crawford Children's Charity
The Cray Trust
Creative Scotland
The Crerar Hotels Trust
The Crescent Trust
Cripplegate Foundation
The Violet and Milo Cripps Charitable Trust
The Cross Trust
The Croydon Relief in Need Charities
The Peter Cruddas Foundation
Cruden Foundation Ltd
The Ronald Cruickshanks Foundation
The Cuby Charitable Trust

**211**

The Cumber Family Charitable Trust
Cumbria Community Foundation
D. J. H. Currie Memorial Trust
The Dennis Curry Charitable Trust
The Cwmbran Trust
Itzchok Meyer Cymerman Trust Ltd
The D. G. Charitable Settlement
The D'Oyly Carte Charitable Trust
Roald Dahl's Marvellous Children's Charity
Daily Prayer Union Charitable Trust Limited
Oizer Dalim Trust
Baron Davenport's Charity
The Davidson Family Charitable Trust
Michael Davies Charitable Settlement
The Gwendoline and Margaret Davies Charity
The Wilfrid Bruce Davis Charitable Trust
The Davis Foundation
The Henry and Suzanne Davis Foundation
The Dawe Charitable Trust
The De Brye Charitable Trust
Peter De Haan Charitable Trust
The De Laszlo Foundation
The Deakin Charitable Trust
The Debmar Benevolent Trust
The Dellal Foundation
The Delves Charitable Trust
The Denman Charitable Trust
The Dentons UKMEA LLP Charitable Trust
Derbyshire Community Foundation
The J. N. Derbyshire Trust
The Desmond Foundation
Devon Community Foundation
The Duke of Devonshire's Charitable Trust
The Sandy Dewhirst Charitable Trust
The Laduma Dhamecha Charitable Trust
Diabetes UK
The Diageo Foundation
Alan and Sheila Diamond Charitable Trust
The Digbeth Trust Limited
The Dinwoodie Settlement
Dischma Charitable Trust
The Djanogly Foundation
The DLM Charitable Trust
The DM Charitable Trust
The Derek and Eileen Dodgson Foundation

The Dollond Charitable Trust
Dorset Community Foundation
The Dorus Trust
The Double 'O' Charity Ltd
The Doughty Charity Trust
Douglas Arter Foundation
R. M. Douglas Charitable Trust
The Drapers' Charitable Fund
Dromintee Trust
Duchy Health Charity Limited
The Duis Charitable Trust
The Royal Foundation of the Duke and Duchess of Cambridge and Prince Harry
The Dulverton Trust
The Dumbreck Charity
Dunard Fund
The Dunhill Medical Trust
The Dunn Family Charitable Trust
The W. E. Dunn Trust
The Charles Dunstone Charitable Trust
Dushinsky Trust Ltd
Mildred Duveen Charitable Trust
The Dyers' Company Charitable Trust
The James Dyson Foundation
The Eagle Charity Trust
Audrey Earle Charitable Trust
The Earley Charity
Earls Colne and Halstead Educational Charity
East End Community Foundation
Eastern Counties Educational Trust Limited
The Sir John Eastwood Foundation
The Ebenezer Trust
The EBM Charitable Trust
EDF Energy Trust
The Gilbert and Eileen Edgar Foundation
The Gilbert Edgar Trust
Edge Fund
Edinburgh & Lothian Trust Fund
Edinburgh Children's Holiday Fund
Edinburgh Trust No 2 Account
Educational Foundation of Alderman John Norman
Edupoor Limited
The Elephant Trust
The George Elias Charitable Trust
The Gerald Palmer Eling Trust Company
The Wilfred and Elsie Elkes Charity Fund
The Maud Elkington Charitable Trust
Ellador Ltd
The Ellerdale Trust

The John Ellerman Foundation
The Ellinson Foundation Ltd
The Ellis Campbell Foundation
The Elmgrant Trust
The Elmley Foundation
Elshore Ltd
The Vernon N. Ely Charitable Trust
The Emerton-Christie Charity
Engage Foundation
The Englefield Charitable Trust
The English Schools' Football Association
The Enkalon Foundation
Entindale Ltd
The Epigoni Trust
The Equity Trust Fund
The Ericson Trust
The Erskine Cunningham Hill Trust
The Essex and Southend Sports Trust
Essex Community Foundation
The Essex Fairway Charitable Trust
The Essex Heritage Trust
The Essex Youth Trust
Joseph Ettedgui Charitable Foundation
Euro Charity Trust
The Alan Evans Memorial Trust
Sir John Evelyn's Charity
The Eventhall Family Charitable Trust
The Eveson Charitable Trust
The Beryl Evetts and Robert Luff Animal Welfare Trust Limited
The Exilarch's Foundation
The Matthew Eyton Animal Welfare Trust
The F. P. Limited Charitable Trust
Esmée Fairbairn Foundation
The Fairstead Trust
The Fairway Trust
Famos Foundation Trust
The Lord Faringdon Charitable Trust
Samuel William Farmer's Trust
The Thomas Farr Charity
The Farthing Trust
The Fassnidge Memorial Trust
The February Foundation
Federation of Jewish Relief Organisations
The John Feeney Charitable Bequest
The George Fentham Birmingham Charity
The A. M. Fenton Trust
The Allan and Nesta Ferguson Charitable Settlement
Elizabeth Ferguson Charitable Trust Fund
The Fidelity UK Foundation

The Doris Field Charitable Trust
Field Family Charitable Trust
Filey Foundation Ltd
Dixie Rose Findlay Charitable Trust
Finnart House School Trust
Firtree Trust
Fisherbeck Charitable Trust
The Fishmongers' Company's Charitable Trust
Marc Fitch Fund
The Fitton Trust
The Earl Fitzwilliam Charitable Trust
The Ian Fleming Charitable Trust
The Joyce Fletcher Charitable Trust
Florence's Charitable Trust
The Flow Foundation
The Gerald Fogel Charitable Trust
The Follett Trust
The Football Association National Sports Centre Trust
The Football Association Youth Trust
The Football Foundation
The Forbes Charitable Foundation
Ford Britain Trust
The Oliver Ford Charitable Trust
Fordeve Limited
The Forest Hill Charitable Trust
The Lady Forester Trust
Forever Manchester (The Community Foundation for Greater Manchester)
The Forman Hardy Charitable Trust
Gwyneth Forrester Trust
The Donald Forrester Trust
The Anna Rosa Forster Charitable Trust
The Forte Charitable Trust
The Lord Forte Foundation
The Four Winds Trust
The Foyle Foundation
The Isaac and Freda Frankel Memorial Charitable Trust
The Elizabeth Frankland Moore and Star Foundation
The Jill Franklin Trust
The Gordon Fraser Charitable Trust
The Hugh Fraser Foundation
The Joseph Strong Frazer Trust
The Fred and Maureen Charitable Trust
The Louis and Valerie Freedman Charitable Settlement

The Michael and Clara Freeman Charitable Trust
The Freemasons' Grand Charity
The Charles S. French Charitable Trust
The Anne French Memorial Trust
The Freshfield Foundation
The Freshgate Trust Foundation
The Friarsgate Trust
Friends of Boyan Trust
Friends of Wiznitz Limited
Friends Provident Charitable Foundation
The Frognal Trust
The Patrick & Helena Frost Foundation
Mejer and Gertrude Miriam Frydman Foundation
The Fulmer Charitable Trust
The Fuserna Foundation General Charitable Trust
The G. D. Charitable Trust
G. M. C. Trust
The Galbraith Trust
The Gale Family Charity Trust
Gamlen Charitable Trust
The Gamma Trust
The Gannochy Trust
The Ganzoni Charitable Trust
The Worshipful Company of Gardeners of London
The Samuel Gardner Memorial Trust
The Garnett Charitable Trust
The Garrick Charitable Trust
Garthgwynion Charities
The Gatsby Charitable Foundation
Gatwick Airport Community Trust
The Robert Gavron Charitable Trust
Jacqueline and Michael Gee Charitable Trust
The Nigel Gee Foundation
Sir Robert Geffery's Almshouse Trust
The General Nursing Council for England and Wales Trust
The Generations Foundation
The Steven Gerrard Foundation
The Gibbs Charitable Trust
Simon Gibson Charitable Trust
The G. C. Gibson Charitable Trust
The Girdlers' Company Charitable Trust
The B. and P. Glasser Charitable Trust
Global Care
Global Charities

Gloucestershire Community Foundation
Worshipful Company of Glovers of London Charitable Trust
The GNC Trust
The Godinton Charitable Trust
The Sydney and Phyllis Goldberg Memorial Charitable Trust
The Golden Bottle Trust
Golden Charitable Trust
The Goldsmiths' Arts Trust Fund
The Goldsmiths' Company Charity
The Golf Foundation Limited
The Golsoncott Foundation
Nicholas and Judith Goodison's Charitable Settlement
The Mike Gooley Trailfinders Charity
The Gosling Foundation Limited
The Gould Charitable Trust
The Grace Charitable Trust
A. B. Grace Trust
The Graff Foundation
E. C. Graham Belford Charitable Settlement
The Grahame Charitable Foundation Limited
The Granada Foundation
Grand Charitable Trust of the Order of Women Freemasons
The Grange Farm Centre Trust
Grantham Yorke Trust
The Gordon Gray Trust
The Gray Trust
The Great Britain Sasakawa Foundation
The Great Stone Bridge Trust of Edenbridge
The Great Torrington Town Lands Charity
The Kenneth & Susan Green Charitable Foundation
The Green Hall Foundation
The Green Room Charitable Trust
Philip and Judith Green Trust
Greenham Common Community Trust Limited
The Greggs Foundation
The Gretna Charitable Trust
The Greys Charitable Trust
The Grimmitt Trust
The Grocers' Charity
The M. and R. Gross Charities Limited
The GRP Charitable Trust
N. and R. Grunbaum Charitable Trust

The Bishop of Guildford's Foundation
The Guildry Incorporation of Perth
The Walter Guinness Charitable Trust
The Gunter Charitable Trust
The Gur Trust
The Gurney Charitable Trust
Dr Guthrie's Association
The H. and M. Charitable Trust
H. C. D. Memorial Fund
The Hackney Parochial Charities
The Hadfield Trust
The Hadley Trust
The Hadrian Trust
The Alfred Haines Charitable Trust
E. F. and M. G. Hall Charitable Trust
The Edith Winifred Hall Charitable Trust
The Hamamelis Trust
Hamilton Wallace Trust
Paul Hamlyn Foundation
The Helen Hamlyn Trust
Sue Hammerson Charitable Trust
Hampshire and Isle of Wight Community Foundation
The Hampstead Wells and Campden Trust
Hampton Fuel Allotment
The W. A. Handley Charitable Trust
The Kathleen Hannay Memorial Charity
The Doughty Hanson Charitable Foundation
The Haramead Trust
Miss K. M. Harbinson's Charitable Trust
Harbo Charities Limited
The Harborne Parish Lands Charity
The Harbour Charitable Trust
The Harbour Foundation
The Harding Trust
William Harding's Charity
The Hare of Steep Charitable Trust (HOST)
The Harebell Centenary Fund
The Harpur Trust
The Harris Charity
The Harris Family Charitable Trust
The Edith Lilian Harrison 2000 Foundation
The Hartley Charitable Trust
The Alfred And Peggy Harvey Charitable Trust
The Hathaway Trust
The Maurice Hatter Foundation
The M. A. Hawe Settlement

The Hawthorne Charitable Trust
The Dorothy Hay-Bolton Charitable Trust
The Charles Hayward Foundation
The Headley Trust
Headley-Pitt Charitable Trust
May Hearnshaw Charitable Trust
Heart of England Community Foundation
Heart Research UK
The Heathcoat Trust
The Heathside Charitable Trust
The Charlotte Heber-Percy Charitable Trust
The Percy Hedley 1990 Charitable Trust
The Hedley Denton Charitable Trust
Hedley Foundation Limited
The H. J. Heinz Company Limited Charitable Trust
The Michael Heller Charitable Foundation
The Simon Heller Charitable Settlement
Help for Health
Help the Homeless Limited
The Helping Foundation
The Hemby Charitable Trust
The Christina Mary Hendrie Trust for Scottish and Canadian Charities
Henley Educational Trust
Philip Sydney Henman Deceased Will Trust
The G. D. Herbert Charitable Trust
Herefordshire Community Foundation
The Herefordshire Historic Churches Trust
The Heritage of London Trust Limited
The Hertfordshire Community Foundation
Hesed Trust
The Hesslewood Children's Trust (Hull Seamen's and General Orphanage)
Hexham and Newcastle Diocesan Trust (1947)
P. and C. Hickinbotham Charitable Trust
The Alan Edward Higgs Charity
Highcroft Charitable Trust
The Hilden Charitable Fund
The Derek Hill Foundation
The Hillingdon Community Trust
The Hillingdon Partnership Trust
R. G. Hills Charitable Trust
Hinchley Charitable Trust

The Lady Hind Trust
The Hinduja Foundation
Stuart Hine Trust
The Hinrichsen Foundation
The Hintze Family Charity Foundation
The Hiscox Foundation
Hitchin Educational Foundation
The Henry C. Hoare Charitable Trust
The Hobson Charity Limited
Hockerill Educational Foundation
The Sir Julian Hodge Charitable Trust
The Jane Hodge Foundation
The J. G. Hogg Charitable Trust
The Holden Charitable Trust
The Hollands-Warren Fund
The Hollick Family Charitable Trust
The Holliday Foundation
The Dorothy Holmes Charitable Trust
The Holst Foundation
P. H. Holt Foundation
The Edward Holt Trust
The Holywood Trust
The Homelands Charitable Trust
The Homestead Charitable Trust
The Mary Homfray Charitable Trust
Sir Harold Hood's Charitable Trust
The Hoover Foundation
Hope for Youth (NI)
The Hope Trust
Hopmarket Charity
The Horizon Foundation
The Antony Hornby Charitable Trust
The Horne Foundation
The Thomas J. Horne Memorial Trust
The Worshipful Company of Horners' Charitable Trusts
The Hornsey Parochial Charities
The Hospital of God at Greatham
The Hospital Saturday Fund
The Sir Joseph Hotung Charitable Settlement
House of Industry Estate
The Reta Lila Howard Foundation
The Daniel Howard Trust
James T. Howat Charitable Trust
The Hudson Foundation
The Huggard Charitable Trust
The Hull and East Riding Charitable Trust

214

Hulme Trust Estates (Educational)
Human Relief Foundation
The Humanitarian Trust
The Michael and Shirley Hunt Charitable Trust
The Albert Hunt Trust
The Hunter Foundation
Miss Agnes H. Hunter's Trust
The Huntingdon Foundation Limited
Huntingdon Freemen's Trust
Hurdale Charity Limited
The Hutton Foundation
The Nani Huyu Charitable Trust
The P. Y. N. and B. Hyams Trust
Hyde Charitable Trust (Youth Plus)
IBM United Kingdom Trust
Ibrahim Foundation Ltd
The Idlewild Trust
The Iliffe Family Charitable Trust
Impetus – The Private Equity Foundation
Incommunities Foundation
The Indigo Trust
The Ingram Trust
The Inlight Trust
The Inman Charity
Inner London Magistrates Court's Poor Box and Feeder Charity
The Innocent Foundation
Interserve Employee Foundation Ltd
The Inverforth Charitable Trust
Investream Charitable Trust
The Ireland Fund of Great Britain
Irish Youth Foundation (UK) Ltd (incorporating The Lawlor Foundation)
The Ironmongers' Foundation
The Charles Irving Charitable Trust
The J. Isaacs Charitable Trust
The Isle of Anglesey Charitable Trust
The ITF Seafarers Trust
The J. & J. Benevolent Foundation
The J. & J. Charitable Trust
The J. A. R. Charitable Trust
The J. J. Charitable Trust
The JRSST Charitable Trust
The Jabbs Foundation
C. Richard Jackson Charitable Trust
The Jacobs Charitable Trust
The Ruth and Lionel Jacobson Trust (Second Fund) No 2
Jaffe Family Relief Fund
John James Bristol Foundation

The Susan and Stephen James Charitable Settlement
The James Trust
The Jarman Charitable Trust
Jay Education Trust
JCA Charitable Foundation
Jeffrey Charitable Trust
Rees Jeffreys Road Fund
Nick Jenkins Foundation
The Jenour Foundation
The Jephcott Charitable Trust
The Jerusalem Trust
Jewish Child's Day
The Jewish Youth Fund
The Joffe Charitable Trust
The Elton John Aids Foundation
Lillie Johnson Charitable Trust
The Johnson Foundation
The Johnnie Johnson Trust
The Johnson Wax Ltd Charitable Trust
The Joicey Trust
The Jones 1986 Charitable Trust
The Dezna Robins Jones Charitable Foundation
The Marjorie and Geoffrey Jones Charitable Trust
The Muriel Jones Foundation
The Jordan Charitable Foundation
The Joron Charitable Trust
The J. E. Joseph Charitable Fund
The Lady Eileen Joseph Foundation
The Josephs Family Charitable Trust
The Josh Charitable Trust
The Cyril and Eve Jumbo Charitable Trust
Anton Jurgens Charitable Trust
Jusaca Charitable Trust
The Bernard Kahn Charitable Trust
The Stanley Kalms Foundation
Karaviotis Foundation
The Boris Karloff Charitable Foundation
The Ian Karten Charitable Trust
The Kasner Charitable Trust
The Kass Charitable Trust
The Michael and Ilse Katz Foundation
C. S. Kaufman Charitable Trust
The Kelly Family Charitable Trust
Kelsick's Educational Foundation
The Kay Kendall Leukaemia Fund

William Kendall's Charity (Wax Chandlers' Company)
John Thomas Kennedy Charitable Foundation
The Kennedy Charitable Foundation
The Kennel Club Charitable Trust
Kent Community Foundation
The Nancy Kenyon Charitable Trust
Keren Association Limited
E. and E. Kernkraut Charities Limited
The Peter Kershaw Trust
Keswick Hall Charity
The Ursula Keyes Trust
The King/Cullimore Charitable Trust
Kingdom Way Trust
The Kingsbury Charity
The Mary Kinross Charitable Trust
Kirkley Poor's Land Estate
The Richard Kirkman Trust
Kirschel Foundation
Robert Kitchin (Saddlers' Company)
The Ernest Kleinwort Charitable Trust
The Marina Kleinwort Charitable Trust
The Kobler Trust
The Kohn Foundation
Kollel and Co. Limited
The KPMG Foundation
The Kreditor Charitable Trust
The Kreitman Foundation
The Neil Kreitman Foundation
The Heinz, Anna and Carol Kroch Foundation
Kupath Gemach Chaim Bechesed Viznitz Trust
The Kyte Charitable Trust
The K. P. Ladd Charitable Trust
John Laing Charitable Trust
Maurice and Hilda Laing Charitable Trust
Christopher Laing Foundation
The David Laing Foundation
The Kirby Laing Foundation
The Martin Laing Foundation
The Beatrice Laing Trust
The Lambert Charitable Trust
Community Foundation for Lancashire (Former)
Community Foundations for Lancashire and Merseyside
Duchy of Lancaster Benevolent Fund
Lancaster Foundation
The Jack Lane Charitable Trust
The Allen Lane Foundation
Langdale Trust
Langley Charitable Trust

The LankellyChase Foundation
The R. J. Larg Family Charitable Trust
Largsmount Ltd
The Lark Trust
Laslett's (Hinton) Charity
Laufer Charitable Trust
The Lauffer Family Charitable Foundation
Mrs F. B. Laurence Charitable Trust
The Kathleen Laurence Trust
The Law Society Charity
The Edgar E. Lawley Foundation
The Herd Lawson and Muriel Lawson Charitable Trust
Lawson Beckman Charitable Trust
The Raymond and Blanche Lawson Charitable Trust
The Mason Le Page Charitable Trust
The Leach Fourteenth Trust
The David Lean Foundation
The Leathersellers' Company Charitable Fund
The Arnold Lee Charitable Trust
The William Leech Charity
The Lord Mayor of Leeds Appeal Fund
Leicestershire, Leicester and Rutland Community Foundation
The Kennedy Leigh Charitable Trust
Morris Leigh Foundation
The Leigh Trust
P. Leigh-Bramwell Trust 'E'
The Lennox and Wyfold Foundation
The Erica Leonard Trust
The Mark Leonard Trust
The Leverhulme Trade Charities Trust
The Leverhulme Trust
Joseph Levy Charitable Foundation
David and Ruth Lewis Family Charitable Trust
The John Spedan Lewis Foundation
The Sir Edward Lewis Foundation
John Lewis Partnership General Community Fund
LHR Airport Communities Trust
Liberum Foundation
The Limbourne Trust
Limoges Charitable Trust
The Linbury Trust
Lincolnshire Churches Trust
Lincolnshire Community Foundation
The Lind Trust

Lindale Educational Foundation
The Linden Charitable Trust
Lindenleaf Charitable Trust
The Enid Linder Foundation
The Ruth and Stuart Lipton Charitable Trust
The Lister Charitable Trust
The Frank Litchfield Charitable Trust
The Charles Littlewood Hill Trust
The Second Joseph Aaron Littman Foundation
The George John and Sheilah Livanos Charitable Trust
Liverpool Charity and Voluntary Services
Jack Livingstone Charitable Trust
The Elaine and Angus Lloyd Charitable Trust
The Charles Lloyd Foundation
Lloyd's Charities Trust
Lloyds Bank Foundation for England and Wales
Lloyds Bank Foundation for Northern Ireland
Lloyds Bank Foundation for the Channel Islands
Lloyds TSB Foundation for Scotland
Localtrent Ltd
The Locker Foundation
Loftus Charitable Trust
The Lolev Charitable Trust
The Joyce Lomax Bullock Charitable Trust
The Trust for London
London Catalyst
The London Community Foundation
London Housing Foundation Ltd
The London Law Trust
London Legal Support Trust
The William and Katherine Longman Trust
The Loseley and Guildway Charitable Trust
The Lotus Foundation
The Lower Green Foundation
The Lowy Mitchell Foundation
The C. L. Loyd Charitable Trust
LSA Charitable Trust
The Marie Helen Luen Charitable Trust
Robert Luff Foundation Ltd
The Henry Lumley Charitable Trust
Paul Lunn-Rockliffe Charitable Trust
C. F. Lunoe Trust Fund
The Ruth and Jack Lunzer Charitable Trust
Lord and Lady Lurgan Trust

The Lyndhurst Trust
The Lynn Foundation
John Lyon's Charity
The Lyons Charitable Trust
The Sir Jack Lyons Charitable Trust
Sylvanus Lysons Charity
M. and C. Trust
The M. K. Charitable Trust
The Madeline Mabey Trust
The E. M. MacAndrew Trust
The R. S. Macdonald Charitable Trust
The Macdonald-Buchanan Charitable Trust
The Mackay and Brewer Charitable Trust
The Mackintosh Foundation
The MacRobert Trust
The Mactaggart Third Fund
The Ian Mactaggart Trust
The Magen Charitable Trust
The Mageni Trust
The Brian Maguire Charitable Trust
The Mahavir Trust
Malbin Trust
The Mallinckrodt Foundation
Man Group plc Charitable Trust
The Manackerman Charitable Trust
Manchester Airport Community Trust Fund
The Manchester Guardian Society Charitable Trust
Lord Mayor of Manchester's Charity Appeal Trust
The Manifold Charitable Trust
The W. M. Mann Foundation
R. W. Mann Trust
The Manoukian Charitable Foundation
Maranatha Christian Trust
Marbeh Torah Trust
The Marchig Animal Welfare Trust
The Stella and Alexander Margulies Charitable Trust
Mariapolis Limited
Market Harborough and The Bowdens Charity
The Michael Marks Charitable Trust
The Marks Family Foundation
The Ann and David Marks Foundation
The Hilda and Samuel Marks Foundation
J. P. Marland Charitable Trust
Marmot Charitable Trust
The Marr-Munning Trust
The Michael Marsh Charitable Trust
The Marsh Christian Trust

Charlotte Marshall Charitable Trust
D. G. Marshall of Cambridge Trust
The Marshgate Charitable Settlement
John Martin's Charity
The Mason Porter Charitable Trust
The Nancie Massey Charitable Trust
The Mathew Trust
The Matliwala Family Charitable Trust
The Matt 6.3 Charitable Trust
The Violet Mauray Charitable Trust
The Mayfield Valley Arts Trust
McGreevy No 5 Settlement
D. D. McPhail Charitable Settlement
The Medlock Charitable Trust
Melodor Limited
The Melow Charitable Trust
Menuchar Limited
Mercaz Torah Vechesed Limited
The Brian Mercer Charitable Trust
The Mercers' Charitable Foundation
The Merchant Taylors' Company Charities Fund
The Merchant Venturers' Charity
The Merchants' House of Glasgow
Mercury Phoenix Trust
The Mersey Docks and Harbour Company Charitable Fund
The Tony Metherell Charitable Trust
The Metropolitan Masonic Charity
T. & J. Meyer Family Foundation Limited
The Mickel Fund
The Mickleham Trust
The Gerald Micklem Charitable Trust
The Masonic Province of Middlesex Charitable Trust
Middlesex Sports Foundation
Millennium Stadium Charitable Trust (Ymddiriedolaeth Elusennol Stadiwm y Mileniwm)
Hugh and Mary Miller Bequest Trust
The Ronald Miller Foundation
The Millfield Trust
The Millichope Foundation
The Mills Charity
The Millward Charitable Trust
The Clare Milne Trust

Milton Keynes Community Foundation Limited
The Edgar Milward Charity
The Peter Minet Trust
Minge's Gift and the Pooled Trusts
Minton Charitable Trust
The Mirianog Trust
The Laurence Misener Charitable Trust
The Mishcon Family Charitable Trust
The Misselbrook Trust
The Brian Mitchell Charitable Settlement
The Esmé Mitchell Trust
The MITIE Foundation
Keren Mitzvah Trust
The Mizpah Trust
Mobbs Memorial Trust Ltd
The Modiano Charitable Trust
Mole Charitable Trust
The Monatrea Charitable Trust
Monmouthshire County Council Welsh Church Act Fund
The Montague Thompson Coon Charitable Trust
The Monument Trust
The Moonpig Foundation
The George A. Moore Foundation
The Henry Moore Foundation
The Morel Charitable Trust
The Morgan Charitable Foundation
The Morgan Foundation
Morgan Stanley International Foundation
The Diana and Allan Morgenthau Charitable Trust
The Oliver Morland Charitable Trust
S. C. and M. E. Morland's Charitable Trust
The Morris Charitable Trust
The Willie and Mabel Morris Charitable Trust
The Peter Morrison Charitable Foundation
The Moshal Charitable Trust
Vyoel Moshe Charitable Trust
The Moshulu Charitable Trust
Brian and Jill Moss Charitable Trust
The Moss Family Charitable Trust
Mosselson Charitable Trust
The Mount Everest Foundation
The Edwina Mountbatten & Leonora Children's Foundation
Mrs Waterhouse Charitable Trust
The Mugdock Children's Trust
The Mulberry Trust

Frederick Mulder Charitable Trust
The Edith Murphy Foundation
Murphy-Neumann Charity Company Limited
The Music Sales Charitable Trust
Muslim Hands
The Mutual Trust Group
MW (CL) Foundation
MW (GK) Foundation
MW (HO) Foundation
MW (RH) Foundation
MYA Charitable Trust
The Janet Nash Charitable Settlement
The National Churches Trust
The National Manuscripts Conservation Trust
The Nationwide Foundation
The Worshipful Company of Needlemakers' Charitable Fund
The Neighbourly Charitable Trust
The James Neill Trust Fund
Nemoral Ltd
Nesswall Ltd
The New Appeals Organisation for the City and County of Nottingham
Newby Trust Limited
The Newcomen Collett Foundation
Newpier Charity Ltd
The Chevras Ezras Nitzrochim Trust
NJD Charitable Trust
Alice Noakes Memorial Charitable Trust
Nominet Charitable Foundation
The Noon Foundation
Normalyn Charitable Trust
The Norman Family Charitable Trust
The Normanby Charitable Trust
The Northampton Municipal Church Charities
The Community Foundation for Northern Ireland
The Northern Rock Foundation
The Northmoor Trust
The Northumberland Village Homes Trust
The Northwood Charitable Trust
The Norton Foundation
The Norwich Town Close Estate Charity
The Nottingham General Dispensary
Nottinghamshire Community Foundation
The Nottinghamshire Historic Churches Trust
The Nuffield Foundation

O&G Schreiber Charitable Trust
The Father O'Mahoney Memorial Trust
The Sir Peter O'Sullevan Charitable Trust
The Oakdale Trust
The Oakmoor Charitable Trust
The Odin Charitable Trust
The Ofenheim Charitable Trust
The Ogle Christian Trust
Oizer Charitable Trust
Old Possum's Practical Trust
The John Oldacre Foundation
The Olga Charitable Trust
Open Gate
The O'Sullivan Family Charitable Trust
The Ouseley Trust
The Owen Family Trust
Oxfam (GB)
Oxfordshire Community Foundation
The P. F. Charitable Trust
The Paget Charitable Trust
The Panacea Charitable Trust
Panahpur
The Panton Trust
The Paphitis Charitable Trust
The Paragon Trust
The Park Charitable Trust
The Park House Charitable Trust
The Samuel and Freda Parkinson Charitable Trust
Miss M. E. Swinton Paterson's Charitable Trust
The Patrick Charitable Trust
The Jack Patston Charitable Trust
Ambika Paul Foundation
The Payne Charitable Trust
The Harry Payne Fund
The Peacock Charitable Trust
The Susanna Peake Charitable Trust
The Pears Family Charitable Foundation
Rosanna Pearson's 1987 Charity Trust
The Pedmore Sporting Club Trust Fund
The Dowager Countess Eleanor Peel Trust
The Pell Charitable Trust
The Peltz Trust
The Pennycress Trust
People's Postcode Trust
The Performing Right Society Foundation
B. E. Perl Charitable Trust
The Personal Assurance Charitable Trust
The Persson Charitable Trust
The Persula Foundation
The Jack Petchey Foundation

The Petplan Charitable Trust
The Pharsalia Charitable Trust
The Phillips and Rubens Charitable Trust
The Phillips Charitable Trust
The Phillips Family Charitable Trust
The David Pickford Charitable Foundation
The Pilgrim Trust
The Elise Pilkington Charitable Trust
The Pilkington Charities Fund
The Austin and Hope Pilkington Trust
The Sir Harry Pilkington Trust Fund
Estate of the Late Colonel W. W. Pilkington Will Trusts – The General Charity Fund
Miss A. M. Pilkington's Charitable Trust
The DLA Piper Charitable Trust
The Platinum Trust
G. S. Plaut Charitable Trust Limited
Polden-Puckham Charitable Foundation
The George and Esme Pollitzer Charitable Settlement
The Polonsky Foundation
The Ponton House Trust
Edith and Ferdinand Porjes Charitable Trust
The John Porter Charitable Trust
The Porter Foundation
Porticus UK
The Portrack Charitable Trust
The J. E. Posnansky Charitable Trust
The Mary Potter Convent Hospital Trust
The David and Elaine Potter Foundation
The Praebendo Charitable Foundation
The Premier League Charitable Fund
Premierquote Ltd
Premishlaner Charitable Trust
Sir John Priestman Charity Trust
The Primrose Trust
The Prince of Wales's Charitable Foundation
Princess Anne's Charities
Prison Service Charity Fund
The Privy Purse Charitable Trust
The Puebla Charitable Trust
The Puri Foundation
Mr and Mrs J. A. Pye's Charitable Settlement
Quartet Community Foundation

The Queen Anne's Gate Foundation
The Queen's Silver Jubilee Trust
Quercus Trust
Quothquan Trust
R. J. M. Charitable Trust
R. S. Charitable Trust
The RVW Trust
The Monica Rabagliati Charitable Trust
Rachel Charitable Trust
The Racing Foundation
The Mr and Mrs Philip Rackham Charitable Trust
Richard Radcliffe Charitable Trust
The Radcliffe Trust
The Bishop Radford Trust
The Ragdoll Foundation
The Rainford Trust
The Joseph and Lena Randall Charitable Trust
The Joseph Rank Trust
Ranworth Trust
The Ratcliff Foundation
The E. L. Rathbone Charitable Trust
The Eleanor Rathbone Charitable Trust
The Sigrid Rausing Trust
The Ravensdale Trust
The Rayden Charitable Trust
The Roger Raymond Charitable Trust
The Rayne Foundation
The Rayne Trust
The Sir James Reckitt Charity
Eva Reckitt Trust Fund
The C. A. Redfern Charitable Foundation
The Reed Foundation
Richard Reeve's Foundation
The Rest Harrow Trust
Reuben Foundation
The Rhododendron Trust
Daisie Rich Trust
The Clive Richards Charity
The Violet M. Richards Charity
The Richmond Parish Lands Charity
Ridgesave Limited
The Sir John Ritblat Family Foundation
The River Trust
Rivers Foundation
Thomas Roberts Trust
The Robertson Trust
Robyn Charitable Trust
The Rochester Bridge Trust
The Rock Foundation
The Roddick Foundation
The Rofeh Trust
Rokach Family Charitable Trust
The Helen Roll Charitable Trust

218

The Sir James Roll Charitable Trust
The Rosca Trust
The Cecil Rosen Foundation
Rosetrees Trust
The Rothermere Foundation
The Roughley Charitable Trust
Mrs Gladys Row Fogo Charitable Trust
Rowanville Ltd
The Rowlands Trust
The Joseph Rowntree Charitable Trust
The Joseph Rowntree Foundation
Royal Artillery Charitable Fund
Royal British Legion
Royal Docks Trust (London)
Royal Masonic Trust for Girls and Boys
The Royal Victoria Hall Foundation
The Rubin Foundation
William Arthur Rudd Memorial Trust
The Russell Trust
Ryklow Charitable Trust 1992
The J. S. and E. C. Rymer Charitable Trust
S. F. Foundation
The Michael Sacher Charitable Trust
The Michael Harry Sacher Trust
The Sackler Trust
The Ruzin Sadagora Trust
The Saddlers' Company Charitable Fund
The Saga Charitable Trust
The Jean Sainsbury Animal Welfare Trust
The Alan and Babette Sainsbury Charitable Fund
The Sainsbury Family Charitable Trusts
Saint Sarkis Charity Trust
The Saintbury Trust
The Salamander Charitable Trust
The Andrew Salvesen Charitable Trust
Sam and Bella Sebba Charitable Trust
Coral Samuel Charitable Trust
The Basil Samuel Charitable Trust
The M. J. Samuel Charitable Trust
The Peter Samuel Charitable Trust
The Samworth Foundation
The Sandra Charitable Trust
The Sands Family Trust
Santander UK Foundation Limited
The Peter Saunders Trust

The Scarfe Charitable Trust
The Schapira Charitable Trust
The Annie Schiff Charitable Trust
The Schmidt-Bodner Charitable Trust
The Schreib Trust
The Schreiber Charitable Trust
Schroder Charity Trust
The Schuster Charitable Trust
Foundation Scotland
The Francis C. Scott Charitable Trust
The Frieda Scott Charitable Trust
Sir Samuel Scott of Yews Trust
Scottish Coal Industry Special Welfare Fund
The Scouloudi Foundation
The SDL Foundation
Seafarers UK (King George's Fund for Sailors)
The Searchlight Electric Charitable Trust
The Seedfield Trust
Sellata Ltd
SEM Charitable Trust
The Seneca Trust
The Cyril Shack Trust
The Jean Shanks Foundation
The Shanti Charitable Trust
ShareGift (The Orr Mackintosh Foundation)
The Shears Foundation
The Sheepdrove Trust
The Sheffield and District Hospital Services Charitable Fund
The Sheldon Trust
The Patricia and Donald Shepherd Charitable Trust
The Sylvia and Colin Shepherd Charitable Trust
The Archie Sherman Cardiff Foundation
The Archie Sherman Charitable Trust
The R. C. Sherriff Rosebriars Trust
The Shetland Charitable Trust
SHINE (Support and Help in Education)
The Barnett and Sylvia Shine No 2 Charitable Trust
The Bassil Shippam and Alsford Trust
The Shipwrights' Company Charitable Fund
The Shirley Foundation
Shlomo Memorial Fund Limited
The J. A. Shone Memorial Trust
The Barbara A. Shuttleworth Memorial Trust

The Mary Elizabeth Siebel Charity
David and Jennifer Sieff Charitable Trust
Silver Family Charitable Trust
The Simmons & Simmons Charitable Foundation
The Huntly and Margery Sinclair Charitable Trust
The Sino-British Fellowship Trust
SITA Cornwall Trust Limited
Six Point Foundation
The Skelton Bounty
The Charles Skey Charitable Trust
Skipton Building Society Charitable Foundation
The John Slater Foundation
The Slaughter and May Charitable Trust
Rita and David Slowe Charitable Trust
Ruth Smart Foundation
The SMB Charitable Trust
The Mrs Smith and Mount Trust
The DS Smith Charitable Foundation
The N. Smith Charitable Settlement
The Smith Charitable Trust
The Henry Smith Charity
The WH Smith Group Charitable Trust
The Stanley Smith UK Horticultural Trust
Philip Smith's Charitable Trust
The R. C. Snelling Charitable Trust
The Sobell Foundation
Solev Co Ltd
The Solo Charitable Settlement
David Solomons Charitable Trust
Songdale Ltd
The E. C. Sosnow Charitable Trust
The Souter Charitable Trust
The South Square Trust
The W. F. Southall Trust
R. H. Southern Trust
The Sovereign Health Care Charitable Trust
Spar Charitable Fund
Sparks Charity (Sport Aiding Medical Research For Kids)
Sparquote Limited
Spears-Stutz Charitable Trust
The Jessie Spencer Trust
The Spero Foundation
The Ralph and Irma Sperring Charity
The Spielman Charitable Trust

The Spoore, Merry and Rixman Foundation
Sported Foundation
Rosalyn and Nicholas Springer Charitable Trust
Springrule Limited
The Spurrell Charitable Trust
The Geoff and Fiona Squire Foundation
The St Hilda's Trust
St James's Trust Settlement
Sir Walter St John's Educational Charity
St Michael's and All Saints' Charities Relief Branch
The Stanley Foundation Ltd
The Staples Trust
The Star Charitable Trust
The Peter Stebbings Memorial Charity
The Steinberg Family Charitable Trust
The Stephen Barry Charitable Trust
C. E. K. Stern Charitable Trust
Stevenson Family's Charitable Trust
The Stewards' Company Limited (incorporating the J. W. Laing Trust and the J. W. Laing Biblical Scholarship Trust)
Sir Halley Stewart Trust
The Stobart Newlands Charitable Trust
The Edward Stocks-Massey Bequest Fund
The Stoller Charitable Trust
M. J. C. Stone Charitable Trust
The Samuel Storey Family Charitable Trust
Peter Stormonth Darling Charitable Trust
Peter Storrs Trust
The Strangward Trust
Stratford upon Avon Town Trust
The Strawberry Charitable Trust
The W. O. Street Charitable Foundation
The Sudborough Foundation
Sueberry Ltd
Suffolk Community Foundation
The Suffolk Historic Churches Trust
The Alan Sugar Foundation
The Sussex Historic Churches Trust
The Adrienne and Leslie Sussman Charitable Trust
The Sutasoma Trust
Swan Mountain Trust
The Swann-Morton Foundation
Swansea and Brecon Diocesan Board of Finance Limited

The John Swire (1989) Charitable Trust
The Swire Charitable Trust
The Hugh and Ruby Sykes Charitable Trust
The Charles and Elsie Sykes Trust
Sylvia Waddilove Foundation UK
The Charity of Stella Symons
The Tajtelbaum Charitable Trust
The Talbot Trusts
The Lady Tangye Charitable Trust
The David Tannen Charitable Trust
The Tanner Trust
The Lili Tapper Charitable Foundation
The Taurus Foundation
The Tay Charitable Trust
C. B. and H. H. Taylor 1984 Trust
The Connie and Albert Taylor Charitable Trust
A. P. Taylor Trust
Tearfund
The Tedworth Charitable Trust
Tees Valley Community Foundation
Tegham Limited
The Templeton Goodwill Trust
Tesco Charity Trust
The C. Paul Thackray General Charitable Trust
Thackray Medical Research Trust
The Thistle Trust
The Loke Wan Tho Memorial Foundation
The Thompson Family Charitable Trust
The Len Thomson Charitable Trust
The Sir Jules Thorn Charitable Trust
The Thornton Foundation
The Thornton Trust
The Thousandth Man- Richard Burns Charitable Trust
The Three Guineas Trust
The Thriplow Charitable Trust
The Daniel Thwaites Charitable Trust
The Tinsley Foundation
The Tisbury Telegraph Trust
The Tobacco Pipe Makers and Tobacco Trade Benevolent Fund
The Tolkien Trust
Tomchei Torah Charitable Trust
The Tompkins Foundation
Toras Chesed (London) Trust
The Tory Family Foundation

Tottenham Grammar School Foundation
The Tower Hill Trust
The Towry Law Charitable Trust (also known as the Castle Educational Trust)
Annie Tranmer Charitable Trust
The Constance Travis Charitable Trust
The Trefoil Trust
The Tresillian Trust
The Triangle Trust (1949) Fund
The True Colours Trust
Truedene Co. Ltd
The Truemark Trust
Truemart Limited
Trumros Limited
The Trusthouse Charitable Foundation
The James Tudor Foundation
Tudor Rose Ltd
The Tudor Trust
The Tufton Charitable Trust
Tuixen Foundation
The Douglas Turner Trust
The Florence Turner Trust
The G. J. W. Turner Trust
Two Ridings Community Foundation
Community Foundation Serving Tyne and Wear and Northumberland
Trustees of Tzedakah
UKI Charitable Foundation
Ulster Garden Villages Ltd
The Ulverscroft Foundation
The Underwood Trust
The Union of Orthodox Hebrew Congregation
The UNITE Foundation
The United Society for the Propagation of the Gospel
United Utilities Trust Fund
Uxbridge United Welfare Trust
The Vail Foundation
The Valentine Charitable Trust
The Valiant Charitable Trust
The Albert Van Den Bergh Charitable Trust
The Van Neste Foundation
Mrs Maud Van Norden's Charitable Foundation
The Vandervell Foundation
The Vardy Foundation
The Variety Club Children's Charity
Roger Vere Foundation
Victoria Homes Trust
The Nigel Vinson Charitable Trust
The William and Ellen Vinten Trust
The Vintners' Foundation
The Virgin Foundation (Virgin Unite)
Vivdale Ltd

Volant Charitable Trust
Wade's Charity
The Scurrah Wainwright Charity
The Wakefield and Tetley Trust
Wakeham Trust
The Community Foundation in Wales
Wales Council for Voluntary Action
Robert and Felicity Waley-Cohen Charitable Trust
The Walker Trust
Wallace and Gromit's Children's Foundation
War on Want
Sir Siegmund Warburg's Voluntary Settlement
The Ward Blenkinsop Trust
The Barbara Ward Children's Foundation
G. R. Waters Charitable Trust 2000
The Wates Foundation
Blyth Watson Charitable Trust
John Watson's Trust
Waynflete Charitable Trust
The Weavers' Company Benevolent Fund
The David Webster Charitable Trust
The Weinstein Foundation
The James Weir Foundation
The Joir and Kato Weisz Foundation
The Wellcome Trust
Welsh Church Fund – Dyfed area (Carmarthenshire, Ceredigion and Pembrokeshire)
The Welton Foundation
The Wessex Youth Trust
The West Derby Wastelands Charity
The Westcroft Trust
The Westminster Foundation
The Garfield Weston Foundation
The Barbara Whatmore Charitable Trust
The Whitaker Charitable Trust
The Colonel W. H. Whitbread Charitable Trust
The Melanie White Foundation Limited
White Stuff Foundation
The Whitecourt Charitable Trust
A. H. and B. C. Whiteley Charitable Trust
The Norman Whiteley Trust
The Whitley Animal Protection Trust
The Lionel Wigram Memorial Trust
The Felicity Wilde Charitable Trust

The Will Charitable Trust
The Charity of William Williams
The Kay Williams Charitable Foundation
The Williams Charitable Trust
Williams Serendipity Trust
The HDH Wills 1965 Charitable Trust
Dame Violet Wills Charitable Trust
The Dame Violet Wills Will Trust
The Wilmcote Charitrust
Sumner Wilson Charitable Trust
David Wilson Foundation
The Wilson Foundation
J. and J. R. Wilson Trust
The Community Foundation for Wiltshire and Swindon
The Benjamin Winegarten Charitable Trust
The Harold Hyam Wingate Foundation
The Francis Winham Foundation
The Winton Charitable Foundation
The James Wise Charitable Trust
The Michael and Anna Wix Charitable Trust
The Wixamtree Trust
The Maurice Wohl Charitable Foundation
The Charles Wolfson Charitable Trust
The James Wood Bequest Fund
The Wood Family Trust
The F. Glenister Woodger Trust
Woodlands Green Ltd
Woodroffe Benton Foundation
The Woodward Charitable Trust
Worcester Municipal Charities
The Worcestershire and Dudley Historic Churches Trust
The Wragge and Co Charitable Trust
The Diana Edgson Wright Charitable Trust
The Matthews Wrightson Charity Trust
Wychdale Ltd
Wychville Ltd
The Wyndham Charitable Trust
The Wyseliot Charitable Trust
The Xerox (UK) Trust
Yankov Charitable Trust
The Yardley Great Trust
The W. Wing Yip and Brothers Foundation
The South Yorkshire Community Foundation

The Yorkshire Dales Millennium Trust
The William Allen Young Charitable Trust
The John Kirkhope Young Endowment Fund
Youth Music
Youth United Foundation
Zephyr Charitable Trust
The Marjorie and Arnold Ziff Charitable Foundation
Stephen Zimmerman Charitable Trust
The Zochonis Charitable Trust
The Zolfo Cooper Foundation

■ **Salaries**

The 29th May 1961 Charitable Trust
ABF The Soldiers' Charity
The AIM Foundation
The Alchemy Foundation
The Almond Trust
The Anchor Foundation
Anglo American Group Foundation
The Archbishop's Council – The Church and Community Fund
The Ardwick Trust
The Armourers' and Brasiers' Gauntlet Trust
The Ashley Family Foundation
The Ian Askew Charitable Trust
The Associated Country Women of the World
AstonMansfield Charitable Trust
The Aylesford Family Charitable Trust
The Baily Thomas Charitable Fund
The Baker Charitable Trust
Lord Barnby's Foundation
Barnes Workhouse Fund
The Paul Bassham Charitable Trust
BBC Children in Need
The Bedfordshire and Luton Community Foundation
The Berkshire Community Foundation
The Bingham Trust
The Blagrave Trust
The Boshier-Hinton Foundation
The Bower Trust
The Breadsticks Foundation
The Breast Cancer Research Trust
The Brighton District Nursing Association Trust
The British Dietetic Association General and Education Trust Fund
British Heart Foundation

**221**

British Record Industry Trust
The J. and M. Britton
    Charitable Trust
The Charles Brotherton Trust
Buckinghamshire Community
    Foundation
The E. F. Bulmer Benevolent
    Fund
The Clara E. Burgess Charity
Peter Cadbury Charitable Trust
The Cadbury Foundation
The Cambridgeshire
    Community Foundation
The Camelia Trust
The Campden Charities
    Trustee
The Richard Carne Trust
Cash for Kids – Radio Clyde
The Cattanach Charitable Trust
The Chippenham Borough
    Lands Charity
Church Urban Fund
The City Bridge Trust
The Sir Jeremiah Colman Gift
    Trust
The Colt Foundation
Colwinston Charitable Trust
The Ernest Cook Trust
The Alice Ellen Cooper Dean
    Charitable Foundation
Michael Cornish Charitable
    Trust
County Durham Community
    Foundation
Cripplegate Foundation
The Peter Cruddas Foundation
The Cunningham Trust
Roald Dahl's Marvellous
    Children's Charity
The Hamilton Davies Trust
The J. N. Derbyshire Trust
Devon Community Foundation
The Dibden Allotments Fund
The Digbeth Trust Limited
Disability Aid Fund (The Roger
    and Jean Jefcoate Trust)
The Derek and Eileen Dodgson
    Foundation
Dorset Community Foundation
The Drapers' Charitable Fund
The Dunhill Medical Trust
Eastern Counties Educational
    Trust Limited
The Ellerdale Trust
The John Ellerman Foundation
Epilepsy Research UK
The Essex Fairway Charitable
    Trust
The Essex Youth Trust
Joseph Ettedgui Charitable
    Foundation
The Eveson Charitable Trust
Esmée Fairbairn Foundation
Field Family Charitable Trust
Ford Britain Trust
The Donald Forrester Trust

The Foyle Foundation
The Gordon Fraser Charitable
    Trust
The Freemasons' Grand
    Charity
The Fuserna Foundation
General Charitable Trust
Gamlen Charitable Trust
The Garrick Charitable Trust
The Gibbs Charitable Trust
Simon Gibson Charitable Trust
The Girdlers' Company
    Charitable Trust
The Goldsmiths' Company
    Charity
The Golsoncott Foundation
The Greggs Foundation
The Hadfield Trust
The Hadley Trust
The Hadrian Trust
Paul Hamlyn Foundation
Hampshire and Isle of Wight
    Community Foundation
The Harborne Parish Lands
    Charity
William Harding's Charity
The Harebell Centenary Fund
The Harpur Trust
The Peter Harrison Foundation
May Hearnshaw Charitable
    Trust
Heart of England Community
    Foundation
Heart Research UK
The Percy Hedley 1990
    Charitable Trust
The Helping Foundation
Herefordshire Community
    Foundation
P. and C. Hickinbotham
    Charitable Trust
The Alan Edward Higgs Charity
The Hilden Charitable Fund
The Lady Hind Trust
Stuart Hine Trust
The Hintze Family Charity
    Foundation
The Edward Holt Trust
The Holywood Trust
Sir Harold Hood's Charitable
    Trust
The Worshipful Company of
    Horners' Charitable Trusts
The Hospital of God at
    Greatham
The Hunter Foundation
Miss Agnes H. Hunter's Trust
The Innocent Foundation
Irish Youth Foundation (UK)
    Ltd (incorporating The
    Lawlor Foundation)
The JRSST Charitable Trust
Rees Jeffreys Road Fund
Nick Jenkins Foundation
The Elton John Aids
    Foundation

The Joicey Trust
Jusaca Charitable Trust
The Boris Karloff Charitable
    Foundation
The Kelly Family Charitable
    Trust
William Kendall's Charity (Wax
    Chandlers' Company)
The Kennel Club Charitable
    Trust
The Peter Kershaw Trust
Keswick Hall Charity
Kingdom Way Trust
The Mary Kinross Charitable
    Trust
The Sir James Knott Trust
The K. P. Ladd Charitable
    Trust
Community Foundations for
    Lancashire and Merseyside
LandAid Charitable Trust
The Allen Lane Foundation
The Edgar E. Lawley
    Foundation
The Leach Fourteenth Trust
The Leathersellers' Company
    Charitable Fund
Leicestershire, Leicester and
    Rutland Community
    Foundation
The Leigh Trust
The Leverhulme Trust
Joseph Levy Charitable
    Foundation
The Sir Edward Lewis
    Foundation
Lincolnshire Community
    Foundation
Lloyds Bank Foundation for
    England and Wales
Lloyds Bank Foundation for
    Northern Ireland
Lloyds TSB Foundation for
    Scotland
The Trust for London
London Catalyst
The London Community
    Foundation
The Lotus Foundation
John Lyon's Charity
The R. S. Macdonald
    Charitable Trust
The MacRobert Trust
The W. M. Mann Foundation
R. W. Mann Trust
Market Harborough and The
    Bowdens Charity
The Marks Family Foundation
The Marsh Christian Trust
John Martin's Charity
The Nancie Massey Charitable
    Trust
The Mathew Trust
The Robert McAlpine
    Foundation

The Mercers' Charitable Foundation
The Mickel Fund
The Gerald Micklem Charitable Trust
The Millfield House Foundation
The Clare Milne Trust
The Edgar Milward Charity
The Mirianog Trust
The Esmé Mitchell Trust
The Modiano Charitable Trust
John Moores Foundation
The Morgan Charitable Foundation
Mothercare Group Foundation
The Mugdock Children's Trust
The National Hockey Foundation
The Nazareth Trust Fund
Network for Social Change
The Frances and Augustus Newman Foundation
Normalyn Charitable Trust
The Northampton Municipal Church Charities
The Northern Rock Foundation
The Northmoor Trust
The Nuffield Foundation
The Oakdale Trust
The Odin Charitable Trust
The Paget Charitable Trust
The Harry Payne Fund
People's Postcode Trust
The Pilgrim Trust
The Pilkington Charities Fund
Estate of the Late Colonel W. W. Pilkington Will Trusts – The General Charity Fund
Polden-Puckham Charitable Foundation
Princess Anne's Charities
The Racing Foundation
The Rainford Trust
The Rayne Trust
The Rhododendron Trust
The Roddick Foundation
The Joseph Rowntree Charitable Trust
Joseph Rowntree Reform Trust Limited
Royal British Legion
The Saddlers' Company Charitable Fund
The Saintbury Trust
Santander UK Foundation Limited
The Frieda Scott Charitable Trust
The Sir James and Lady Scott Trust
The Scottish Power Energy People Trust
Seafarers UK (King George's Fund for Sailors)
The Sheldon Trust

SHINE (Support and Help in Education)
The Shirley Foundation
Rita and David Slowe Charitable Trust
The Mrs Smith and Mount Trust
Social Business Trust (Scale-Up)
David Solomons Charitable Trust
R. H. Southern Trust
Sported Foundation
The St Hilda's Trust
St James's Place Foundation
Sir Walter St John's Educational Charity
The St Laurence Relief In Need Trust
The Steel Charitable Trust
Sir Halley Stewart Trust
Stratford upon Avon Town Trust
The Talbot Trusts
The Connie and Albert Taylor Charitable Trust
The Three Guineas Trust
The Thriplow Charitable Trust
The Tolkien Trust
The Tompkins Foundation
The Constance Travis Charitable Trust
The Triangle Trust (1949) Fund
The Trusthouse Charitable Foundation
The James Tudor Foundation
The Tudor Trust
The Douglas Turner Trust
Two Ridings Community Foundation
United Utilities Trust Fund
The Valiant Charitable Trust
Volant Charitable Trust
Voluntary Action Fund
The Scurrah Wainwright Charity
The Wakefield and Tetley Trust
Sir Siegmund Warburg's Voluntary Settlement
The Barbara Ward Children's Foundation
The Waterloo Foundation
The Wates Foundation
Waynflete Charitable Trust
The Westminster Foundation
The Whitaker Charitable Trust
White Stuff Foundation
The Norman Whiteley Trust
The Whitley Animal Protection Trust
The Lionel Wigram Memorial Trust
Dame Violet Wills Charitable Trust
David Wilson Foundation
The Community Foundation for Wiltshire and Swindon

The Wixamtree Trust
The Wood Family Trust
The Woodward Charitable Trust
The Matthews Wrightson Charity Trust
The Yapp Charitable Trust
The Yardley Great Trust
The South Yorkshire Community Foundation
The John Kirkhope Young Endowment Fund
Youth Music
Zurich Community Trust (UK) Limited

## ■ Strategic funding

The 1970 Trust
The 1989 Willan Charitable Trust
The 29th May 1961 Charitable Trust
A. W. Charitable Trust
The Aberbrothock Skea Trust
The Aberdeen Foundation
ABF The Soldiers' Charity
Eric Abrams Charitable Trust
The Acacia Charitable Trust
Achisomoch Aid Company Limited
The ACT Foundation
Action Medical Research
The Company of Actuaries' Charitable Trust Fund
The Adamson Trust
The Victor Adda Foundation
The Addleshaw Goddard Charitable Trust
Adenfirst Ltd
The Adint Charitable Trust
The Adnams Charity
The Adrian Swire Charitable Trust
AF Trust Company
Age Scotland
Age UK
Aid to the Church in Need (UK)
The Sylvia Aitken Charitable Trust
The Alabaster Trust
The Alborada Trust
D. G. Albright Charitable Trust
The Alchemy Foundation
Aldgate and All Hallows' Foundation
The Alexis Trust
All Saints Educational Trust
Allchurches Trust Ltd
The H. B. Allen Charitable Trust
The Alliance Family Foundation
Angus Allnatt Charitable Foundation
The Pat Allsop Charitable Trust
The Almond Trust

223

Almondsbury Charity
The Altajir Trust
Altamont Ltd
AM Charitable Trust
The Ammco Trust
Viscount Amory's Charitable Trust
The Ampelos Trust
The AMW Charitable Trust
The Anchor Foundation
The Andrew Anderson Trust
Andor Charitable Trust
Mary Andrew Charitable Trust
Anglo American Group Foundation
Anguish's Educational Foundation
The Eric Anker-Petersen Charity
The Annandale Charitable Trust
Anpride Ltd
The Anson Charitable Trust
The Apax Foundation
The Appletree Trust
The Archbishop's Council – The Church and Community Fund
The Archer Trust
The Architectural Heritage Fund
The Ardwick Trust
The Argentarius Foundation
The Argus Appeal
Armenian General Benevolent Union London Trust
The Armourers' and Brasiers' Gauntlet Trust
The Artemis Charitable Trust
Arts Council England
Arts Council of Northern Ireland
Arts Council of Wales (Cyngor Celfyddydau Cymru)
The Ove Arup Foundation
The AS Charitable Trust
The Ascot Fire Brigade Trust
The Asda Foundation
The Ashburnham Thanksgiving Trust
A. J. H. Ashby Will Trust
The Ashden Trust
The Ashley Family Foundation
The Ian Askew Charitable Trust
The Associated Country Women of the World
The Association of Colleges Charitable Trust
Astellas European Foundation
Asthma UK
The Astor Foundation
The Astor of Hever Trust
The Aurelius Charitable Trust
The Avon and Somerset Police Community Trust
Awards for All

The Aylesford Family Charitable Trust
The Harry Bacon Foundation
The Scott Bader Commonwealth Limited
Bag4Sport Foundation
The Bagri Foundation
The Austin Bailey Foundation
The Baily Thomas Charitable Fund
The Baird Trust
The Baker Charitable Trust
The Roy and Pixie Baker Charitable Trust
The Balcombe Charitable Trust
The Albert Casanova Ballard Deceased Trust
The Ballinger Charitable Trust
Balmain Charitable Trust
The Balmore Trust
The Balney Charitable Trust
The Baltic Charitable Fund
The Bamford Charitable Foundation
The Banbury Charities
The Band Trust
The Barbers' Company General Charities
The Barbour Foundation
The Barcapel Foundation
Barchester Healthcare Foundation
The Barclay Foundation
The Baring Foundation
The Barker-Mill Foundation
Lord Barnby's Foundation
Barnes Workhouse Fund
The Barnsbury Charitable Trust
The Barnwood House Trust
The Misses Barrie Charitable Trust
Bartholomew Charitable Trust
The Bartlett Taylor Charitable Trust
The Paul Bassham Charitable Trust
The Bates Charitable Trust
The Battens Charitable Trust
Bay Charitable Trust
The Bay Tree Charitable Trust
The Louis Baylis (Maidenhead Advertiser) Charitable Trust
BBC Children in Need
BC Partners Foundation
The B-CH Charitable Trust
Bear Mordechai Ltd
The Bearder Charity
The James Beattie Charitable Trust
Beauland Ltd
The Beaverbrook Foundation
The Beccles Town Lands Charity
The Becker Family Charitable Trust

The Beckett's and Sargeant's Educational Foundation
The John Beckwith Charitable Trust
The Peter Beckwith Charitable Trust
The Bedfordshire and Luton Community Foundation
The Provincial Grand Lodge of Bedfordshire Charity Fund
The David and Ruth Behrend Fund
The Bellahouston Bequest Fund
The Bellinger Donnay Trust
The Benfield Motors Charitable Trust
The Benham Charitable Settlement
Maurice and Jacqueline Bennett Charitable Trust
Michael and Leslie Bennett Charitable Trust
The Gerald Bentall Charitable Trust
The Bergne-Coupland Charity
Bergqvist Charitable Trust
The Berkeley Charitable Foundation
The Ruth Berkowitz Charitable Trust
The Berkshire Community Foundation
The Bernadette Charitable Trust
The Bestway Foundation
BHST
The Mason Bibby 1981 Trust
The Bideford Bridge Trust
The Big Lottery Fund (see also Awards for All)
The Billmeir Charitable Trust
The Bingham Trust
The Bintaub Charitable Trust
The Birmingham District Nursing Charitable Trust
The Birmingham Hospital Saturday Fund Medical Charity and Welfare Trust
The Lord Mayor of Birmingham's Charity Birthday House Trust
The Michael Bishop Foundation
The Bertie Black Foundation
Isabel Blackman Foundation
The BlackRock (UK) Charitable Trust
The Blagrave Trust
The Blair Foundation
The Morgan Blake Charitable Trust
Blakemore Foundation
The Blanchminster Trust
The Blandford Lake Trust

The Sir Victor Blank Charitable Settlement
Blatchington Court Trust
Bloodwise
The Bluston Charitable Settlement
The Nicholas Boas Charitable Trust
The Body Shop Foundation
The Bonamy Charitable Trust
The John and Celia Bonham Christie Charitable Trust
The Charlotte Bonham-Carter Charitable Trust
The Booth Charities
Boots Charitable Trust
Salo Bordon Charitable Trust
The Bordon Liphook Haslemere Charity
The Oliver Borthwick Memorial Trust
The Boshier-Hinton Foundation
The Bothwell Charitable Trust
The Harry Bottom Charitable Trust
P. G. and N. J. Boulton Trust
Sir Clive Bourne Family Trust
Bourneheights Limited
The Bower Trust
The Bowerman Charitable Trust
The Bowland Charitable Trust
The Frank Brake Charitable Trust
The William Brake Charitable Trust
The Tony Bramall Charitable Trust
The Liz and Terry Bramall Foundation
The Bramhope Trust
The Bransford Trust
The Breadsticks Foundation
Bridgepoint Charitable Trust
The Harold and Alice Bridges Charity
Briggs Animal Welfare Trust
The Brighton District Nursing Association Trust
Bristol Archdeaconry Charity
The Bristol Charities
British Council for Prevention of Blindness (Save Eyes Everywhere)
The British Dietetic Association General and Education Trust Fund
British Gas (Scottish Gas) Energy Trust
British Heart Foundation
The British Humane Association
British Institute at Ankara
British Record Industry Trust
The J. and M. Britton Charitable Trust

The Broderers' Charity Trust
The Bromley Trust
The Consuelo and Anthony Brooke Charitable Trust
The Roger Brooke Charitable Trust
The David Brooke Charity
The Rory and Elizabeth Brooks Foundation
Joseph Brough Charitable Trust
Miss Marion Broughton's Charitable Trust
Bill Brown 1989 Charitable Trust
Edna Brown Charitable Settlement
R. S. Brownless Charitable Trust
The Brownsword Charitable Foundation
The T. B. H. Brunner Charitable Settlement
The Bruntwood Charity
Brushmill Ltd
Buckingham Trust
Buckinghamshire Community Foundation
The Bulldog Trust Limited
The E. F. Bulmer Benevolent Fund
The Burden Trust
Burden's Charitable Foundation
The Burdett Trust for Nursing
The Clara E. Burgess Charity
The Burghley Family Trust
The Burry Charitable Trust
The Arnold Burton 1998 Charitable Trust
The Burton Breweries Charitable Trust
Consolidated Charity of Burton upon Trent
The Worshipful Company of Butchers General Charities
The Derek Butler Trust
The Noel Buxton Trust
C. and F. Charitable Trust
Cable & Wireless Worldwide Foundation
Edward Cadbury Charitable Trust
Henry T. and Lucy B. Cadbury Charitable Trust
Peter Cadbury Charitable Trust
The Christopher Cadbury Charitable Trust
The G. W. Cadbury Charitable Trust
The Richard Cadbury Charitable Trust
The William A. Cadbury Charitable Trust
The Cadbury Foundation
The Barrow Cadbury Trust

The Edward and Dorothy Cadbury Trust
The George Cadbury Trust
The Cadogan Charity
CAFOD (Catholic Agency for Overseas Development)
Community Foundation for Calderdale
Callander Charitable Trust
Calleva Foundation
Calouste Gulbenkian Foundation – UK Branch
The Calpe Trust
The Cambridge Chrysalis Trust
The Cambridgeshire Community Foundation
The Campden Charities Trustee
The Canning Trust
The H. and L. Cantor Trust
Cardy Beaver Foundation
The Carew Pole Charitable Trust
David William Traill Cargill Fund
Carlee Ltd
The Carlton House Charitable Trust
The Carmelite Monastery Ware Trust
The Worshipful Company of Carmen Benevolent Trust
The Richard Carne Trust
The Carnegie Dunfermline Trust
The Carnegie Trust for the Universities of Scotland
The Carpenters' Company Charitable Trust
The Carrington Charitable Trust
The Leslie Mary Carter Charitable Trust
The Casey Trust
Cash for Kids – Radio Clyde
Sir John Cass's Foundation
The Elizabeth Casson Trust
The Castang Foundation
The Catalyst Charitable Trust
The Catholic Charitable Trust
Catholic Foreign Missions
The Catholic Trust for England and Wales
The Cattanach Charitable Trust
The Joseph and Annie Cattle Trust
The Thomas Sivewright Catto Charitable Settlement
The Wilfrid and Constance Cave Foundation
The Cayo Foundation
Elizabeth Cayzer Charitable Trust
The B. G. S. Cayzer Charitable Trust
The Cazenove Charitable Trust

The CBD Charitable Trust
Celtic Charity Fund
The CH (1980) Charitable Trust
The Amelia Chadwick Trust
The Chapman Charitable Trust
John William Chapman's Charitable Trust
The Charities Advisory Trust
Charitworth Limited
The Charter 600 Charity
The Worshipful Company of Chartered Accountants General Charitable Trust
Chaucer Foundation
The Cheruby Trust
Cheshire Freemason's Charity
The Chetwode Foundation
The Childs Charitable Trust
The Chipping Sodbury Town Lands Charity
CHK Charities Limited
The Chownes Foundation
The Christabella Charitable Trust
Christadelphian Samaritan Fund
Christian Aid
Chrysalis Trust
The Church Burgesses Educational Foundation
Church Burgesses Trust
Church Urban Fund
The CIBC World Markets Children's Miracle Foundation
The City Bridge Trust
The City Educational Trust Fund
CLA Charitable Trust
Stephen Clark 1957 Charitable Trust
J. A. Clark Charitable Trust
The Hilda and Alice Clark Charitable Trust
The Roger and Sarah Bancroft Clark Charitable Trust
The Clarke Charitable Settlement
The Cleopatra Trust
The Clore Duffield Foundation
The Clothworkers' Foundation
Richard Cloudesley's Charity
The Clover Trust
The Robert Clutterbuck Charitable Trust
Clydpride Ltd
The Coalfields Regeneration Trust
The John Coates Charitable Trust
The Cobalt Trust
The Cobtree Charity Trust Ltd
The Denise Cohen Charitable Trust

The Vivienne and Samuel Cohen Charitable Trust
The John S. Cohen Foundation
The R. and S. Cohen Foundation
John Coldman Charitable Trust
The Cole Charitable Trust
The Colefax Charitable Trust
John and Freda Coleman Charitable Trust
The Bernard Coleman Trust
The George Henry Collins Charity
The Sir Jeremiah Colman Gift Trust
Col-Reno Ltd
The Colt Foundation
The Coltstaple Trust
Colwinston Charitable Trust
Colyer-Fergusson Charitable Trust
Comic Relief
Community First
Community Foundation for Leeds
The Compton Charitable Trust
The Congleton Inclosure Trust
Martin Connell Charitable Trust
The Conservation Foundation
The Consolidated Charities for the Infirm – Merchant Taylors' Company
Gordon Cook Foundation
The Ernest Cook Trust
The Cooks Charity
The Catherine Cookson Charitable Trust
Harold and Daphne Cooper Charitable Trust
Mabel Cooper Charity
The Alice Ellen Cooper Dean Charitable Foundation
The Marjorie Coote Animal Charity Trust
The Marjorie Coote Old People's Charity
The Helen Jean Cope Trust
The J. Reginald Corah Foundation Fund
The Gershon Coren Charitable Foundation
The Evan Cornish Foundation
The Cornwell Charitable Trust
The Sidney and Elizabeth Corob Charitable Trust
The Corona Charitable Trust
The Costa Family Charitable Trust
The Cotton Industry War Memorial Trust
The Cotton Trust
County Durham Community Foundation
The Augustine Courtauld Trust
General Charity of Coventry

Coventry Building Society Charitable Foundation
Cowley Charitable Foundation
Dudley and Geoffrey Cox Charitable Trust
The Sir William Coxen Trust Fund
The Lord Cozens-Hardy Trust
The Craignish Trust
The Craps Charitable Trust
Michael Crawford Children's Charity
The Cray Trust
Creative Scotland
The Crerar Hotels Trust
The Crescent Trust
Cripplegate Foundation
The Violet and Milo Cripps Charitable Trust
The Cross Trust
The Croydon Relief in Need Charities
Cruden Foundation Ltd
The Ronald Cruickshanks Foundation
The Cuby Charitable Trust
The Cumber Family Charitable Trust
Cumbria Community Foundation
D. J. H. Currie Memorial Trust
The Dennis Curry Charitable Trust
The Cwmbran Trust
Itzchok Meyer Cymerman Trust Ltd
The D. G. Charitable Settlement
The D'Oyly Carte Charitable Trust
Roald Dahl's Marvellous Children's Charity
Daily Prayer Union Charitable Trust Limited
Oizer Dalim Trust
Baron Davenport's Charity
The Davidson Family Charitable Trust
Michael Davies Charitable Settlement
The Gwendoline and Margaret Davies Charity
The Wilfrid Bruce Davis Charitable Trust
The Henry and Suzanne Davis Foundation
The Dawe Charitable Trust
The De Brye Charitable Trust
Peter De Haan Charitable Trust
The De Laszlo Foundation
The Deakin Charitable Trust
The Debmar Benevolent Trust
The Dellal Foundation
The Delves Charitable Trust
The Denman Charitable Trust

226

The Dentons UKMEA LLP Charitable Trust
Derbyshire Community Foundation
The J. N. Derbyshire Trust
The Desmond Foundation
Devon Community Foundation
The Duke of Devonshire's Charitable Trust
The Sandy Dewhirst Charitable Trust
The Laduma Dhamecha Charitable Trust
The Diageo Foundation
Alan and Sheila Diamond Charitable Trust
The Dibden Allotments Fund
The Digbeth Trust Limited
The Dinwoodie Settlement
Dischma Charitable Trust
The DM Charitable Trust
The Derek and Eileen Dodgson Foundation
The Dollond Charitable Trust
Dorset Community Foundation
The Double 'O' Charity Ltd
The Doughty Charity Trust
Douglas Arter Foundation
R. M. Douglas Charitable Trust
The Drapers' Charitable Fund
Dromintee Trust
Duchy Health Charity Limited
The Duis Charitable Trust
The Royal Foundation of the Duke and Duchess of Cambridge and Prince Harry
The Dulverton Trust
The Dumbreck Charity
Dunard Fund
The Dunhill Medical Trust
The Dunn Family Charitable Trust
The W. E. Dunn Trust
The Charles Dunstone Charitable Trust
Dushinsky Trust Ltd
Mildred Duveen Charitable Trust
The Dyers' Company Charitable Trust
The James Dyson Foundation
The Eagle Charity Trust
Audrey Earle Charitable Trust
The Earley Charity
Earls Colne and Halstead Educational Charity
East End Community Foundation
Eastern Counties Educational Trust Limited
The Sir John Eastwood Foundation
The Ebenezer Trust
The EBM Charitable Trust
EDF Energy Trust

The Gilbert and Eileen Edgar Foundation
The Gilbert Edgar Trust
Edinburgh & Lothian Trust Fund
Edinburgh Trust No 2 Account
Educational Foundation of Alderman John Norman
Edupoor Limited
The Elephant Trust
The George Elias Charitable Trust
The Gerald Palmer Eling Trust Company
The Wilfred and Elsie Elkes Charity Fund
Ellador Ltd
The Ellerdale Trust
The John Ellerman Foundation
The Ellinson Foundation Ltd
The Edith Maud Ellis 1985 Charitable Trust
The Ellis Campbell Foundation
The Elmgrant Trust
The Elmley Foundation
Elshore Ltd
The Vernon N. Ely Charitable Trust
The Emerton-Christie Charity
Engage Foundation
The Englefield Charitable Trust
The English Schools' Football Association
The Enkalon Foundation
Entindale Ltd
The Epigoni Trust
The Equity Trust Fund
The Ericson Trust
The Erskine Cunningham Hill Trust
Essex Community Foundation
The Essex Fairway Charitable Trust
The Essex Heritage Trust
The Essex Youth Trust
Joseph Ettedgui Charitable Foundation
Euro Charity Trust
The Alan Evans Memorial Trust
Sir John Evelyn's Charity
The Eventhall Family Charitable Trust
The Eveson Charitable Trust
The Beryl Evetts and Robert Luff Animal Welfare Trust Limited
The Exilarch's Foundation
The Matthew Eyton Animal Welfare Trust
The F. P. Limited Charitable Trust
Esmée Fairbairn Foundation
The Fairstead Trust
The Fairway Trust
Famos Foundation Trust

The Lord Faringdon Charitable Trust
Samuel William Farmer's Trust
The Thomas Farr Charity
The Farthing Trust
The Fassnidge Memorial Trust
The February Foundation
Federation of Jewish Relief Organisations
The John Feeney Charitable Bequest
The George Fentham Birmingham Charity
The A. M. Fenton Trust
The Allan and Nesta Ferguson Charitable Settlement
Elizabeth Ferguson Charitable Trust Fund
The Fidelity UK Foundation
The Doris Field Charitable Trust
Field Family Charitable Trust
Filey Foundation Ltd
Dixie Rose Findlay Charitable Trust
Finnart House School Trust
Firtree Trust
Fisherbeck Charitable Trust
The Fishmongers' Company's Charitable Trust
The Fitton Trust
The Earl Fitzwilliam Charitable Trust
The Ian Fleming Charitable Trust
The Joyce Fletcher Charitable Trust
Florence's Charitable Trust
The Flow Foundation
The Gerald Fogel Charitable Trust
The Follett Trust
The Football Association National Sports Centre Trust
The Football Foundation
The Forbes Charitable Foundation
Ford Britain Trust
The Oliver Ford Charitable Trust
Fordeve Limited
The Forest Hill Charitable Trust
The Lady Forester Trust
Forever Manchester (The Community Foundation for Greater Manchester)
The Forman Hardy Charitable Trust
Gwyneth Forrester Trust
The Donald Forrester Trust
The Anna Rosa Forster Charitable Trust
The Forte Charitable Trust
The Lord Forte Foundation
The Four Winds Trust

**227**

The Foyle Foundation
The Isaac and Freda Frankel Memorial Charitable Trust
The Elizabeth Frankland Moore and Star Foundation
The Jill Franklin Trust
The Gordon Fraser Charitable Trust
The Hugh Fraser Foundation
The Joseph Strong Frazer Trust
The Fred and Maureen Charitable Trust
The Louis and Valerie Freedman Charitable Settlement
The Michael and Clara Freeman Charitable Trust
The Freemasons' Grand Charity
The Charles S. French Charitable Trust
The Anne French Memorial Trust
The Freshfield Foundation
The Freshgate Trust Foundation
The Friarsgate Trust
Friends of Boyan Trust
Friends of Wiznitz Limited
Friends Provident Charitable Foundation
The Frognal Trust
The Patrick & Helena Frost Foundation
Mejer and Gertrude Miriam Frydman Foundation
The Fulmer Charitable Trust
The G. D. Charitable Trust
G. M. C. Trust
The Galbraith Trust
The Gale Family Charity Trust
Gamlen Charitable Trust
The Gamma Trust
The Gannochy Trust
The Ganzoni Charitable Trust
The Worshipful Company of Gardeners of London
The Samuel Gardner Memorial Trust
The Garnett Charitable Trust
The Garrick Charitable Trust
Garthgwynion Charities
The Gatsby Charitable Foundation
Gatwick Airport Community Trust
The Robert Gavron Charitable Trust
The Nigel Gee Foundation
Sir Robert Geffery's Almshouse Trust
The General Nursing Council for England and Wales Trust
The Generations Foundation
The Gibbs Charitable Trust

Simon Gibson Charitable Trust
The G. C. Gibson Charitable Trust
The Girdlers' Company Charitable Trust
The B. and P. Glasser Charitable Trust
Global Care
Global Charities
Gloucestershire Community Foundation
Worshipful Company of Glovers of London Charitable Trust
The GNC Trust
The Sydney and Phyllis Goldberg Memorial Charitable Trust
The Golden Bottle Trust
Golden Charitable Trust
The Goldsmiths' Arts Trust Fund
The Goldsmiths' Company Charity
The Golf Foundation Limited
The Golsoncott Foundation
Nicholas and Judith Goodison's Charitable Settlement
The Mike Gooley Trailfinders Charity
The Gosling Foundation Limited
The Gould Charitable Trust
The Grace Charitable Trust
A. B. Grace Trust
The Graff Foundation
E. C. Graham Belford Charitable Settlement
The Grahame Charitable Foundation Limited
The Granada Foundation
Grand Charitable Trust of the Order of Women Freemasons
The Grange Farm Centre Trust
Grantham Yorke Trust
The Gordon Gray Trust
The Gray Trust
The Great Britain Sasakawa Foundation
The Great Stone Bridge Trust of Edenbridge
The Great Torrington Town Lands Charity
The Green Hall Foundation
The Green Room Charitable Trust
Philip and Judith Green Trust
Greenham Common Community Trust Limited
The Greggs Foundation
The Gretna Charitable Trust
The Greys Charitable Trust
The Grimmitt Trust
The Grocers' Charity

The M. and R. Gross Charities Limited
The GRP Charitable Trust
The Bishop of Guildford's Foundation
The Guildry Incorporation of Perth
The Walter Guinness Charitable Trust
The Gunter Charitable Trust
The Gur Trust
The Gurney Charitable Trust
Dr Guthrie's Association
The H. and M. Charitable Trust
H. C. D. Memorial Fund
The Hackney Parochial Charities
The Hadfield Trust
The Hadley Trust
The Hadrian Trust
The Alfred Haines Charitable Trust
E. F. and M. G. Hall Charitable Trust
The Edith Winifred Hall Charitable Trust
The Hamamelis Trust
Hamilton Wallace Trust
Paul Hamlyn Foundation
The Helen Hamlyn Trust
Sue Hammerson Charitable Trust
Hampshire and Isle of Wight Community Foundation
The Hampstead Wells and Campden Trust
Hampton Fuel Allotment
The W. A. Handley Charitable Trust
The Kathleen Hannay Memorial Charity
The Doughty Hanson Charitable Foundation
The Haramead Trust
Miss K. M. Harbinson's Charitable Trust
Harbo Charities Limited
The Harborne Parish Lands Charity
The Harbour Charitable Trust
The Harbour Foundation
The Harding Trust
William Harding's Charity
The Hare of Steep Charitable Trust
The Harebell Centenary Fund
The Harpur Trust
The Harris Charity
The Harris Family Charitable Trust
The Edith Lilian Harrison 2000 Foundation
The Hartley Charitable Trust
The Alfred And Peggy Harvey Charitable Trust
The Hathaway Trust

228

*Grant-makers by types of grant* — **Strategic funding**

The Maurice Hatter Foundation
The M. A. Hawe Settlement
The Hawthorne Charitable Trust
The Dorothy Hay-Bolton Charitable Trust
The Charles Hayward Foundation
The Headley Trust
Headley-Pitt Charitable Trust
The Health Foundation
May Hearnshaw Charitable Trust
Heart of England Community Foundation
Heart Research UK
The Heathcoat Trust
The Heathside Charitable Trust
The Charlotte Heber-Percy Charitable Trust
The Percy Hedley 1990 Charitable Trust
The Hedley Denton Charitable Trust
Hedley Foundation Limited
The H. J. Heinz Company Limited Charitable Trust
The Michael Heller Charitable Foundation
The Simon Heller Charitable Settlement
Help for Health
The Helping Foundation
The Hemby Charitable Trust
The Christina Mary Hendrie Trust for Scottish and Canadian Charities
Henley Educational Trust
Philip Sydney Henman Deceased Will Trust
The G. D. Herbert Charitable Trust
Herefordshire Community Foundation
The Heritage of London Trust Limited
The Hertfordshire Community Foundation
Hesed Trust
The Hesslewood Children's Trust (Hull Seamen's and General Orphanage)
Hexham and Newcastle Diocesan Trust (1947)
P. and C. Hickinbotham Charitable Trust
The Alan Edward Higgs Charity
Highcroft Charitable Trust
The Hilden Charitable Fund
The Derek Hill Foundation
The Hillingdon Community Trust
The Hillingdon Partnership Trust
R. G. Hills Charitable Trust
Hinchley Charitable Trust

The Lady Hind Trust
The Hinduja Foundation
Stuart Hine Trust
The Hintze Family Charity Foundation
The Hiscox Foundation
Hitchin Educational Foundation
The Henry C. Hoare Charitable Trust
The Hobson Charity Limited
Hockerill Educational Foundation
The Sir Julian Hodge Charitable Trust
The Jane Hodge Foundation
The J. G. Hogg Charitable Trust
The Holden Charitable Trust
The Hollands-Warren Fund
The Hollick Family Charitable Trust
The Holliday Foundation
The Dorothy Holmes Charitable Trust
The Holst Foundation
P. H. Holt Foundation
The Holywood Trust
The Homelands Charitable Trust
The Homestead Charitable Trust
The Mary Homfray Charitable Trust
Sir Harold Hood's Charitable Trust
The Hoover Foundation
Hope for Youth (NI)
The Hope Trust
Hopmarket Charity
The Horizon Foundation
The Antony Hornby Charitable Trust
The Horne Foundation
The Thomas J. Horne Memorial Trust
The Worshipful Company of Horners' Charitable Trusts
The Hornsey Parochial Charities
The Hospital of God at Greatham
The Hospital Saturday Fund
The Sir Joseph Hotung Charitable Settlement
House of Industry Estate
The Reta Lila Howard Foundation
The Daniel Howard Trust
James T. Howat Charitable Trust
The Hudson Foundation
The Huggard Charitable Trust
The Hull and East Riding Charitable Trust
Hulme Trust Estates (Educational)

Human Relief Foundation
The Humanitarian Trust
The Michael and Shirley Hunt Charitable Trust
The Albert Hunt Trust
The Hunter Foundation
Miss Agnes H. Hunter's Trust
The Huntingdon Foundation Limited
Huntingdon Freemen's Trust
Hurdale Charity Limited
The Hutton Foundation
The Nani Huyu Charitable Trust
The P. Y. N. and B. Hyams Trust
Hyde Charitable Trust
Ibrahim Foundation Ltd
The Idlewild Trust
The Iliffe Family Charitable Trust
Impetus – The Private Equity Foundation
Incommunities Foundation
The Indigo Trust
The Ingram Trust
The Inlight Trust
The Inman Charity
Inner London Magistrates Court's Poor Box and Feeder Charity
The Innocent Foundation
Interserve Employee Foundation Ltd
The Inverforth Charitable Trust
Investream Charitable Trust
The Ireland Fund of Great Britain
Irish Youth Foundation (UK) Ltd (incorporating The Lawlor Foundation)
The Ironmongers' Foundation
The Charles Irving Charitable Trust
The J. Isaacs Charitable Trust
The Isle of Anglesey Charitable Trust
The ITF Seafarers Trust
The J. & J. Benevolent Foundation
The J. & J. Charitable Trust
The J. A. R. Charitable Trust
The J. J. Charitable Trust
The JRSST Charitable Trust
The Jabbs Foundation
C. Richard Jackson Charitable Trust
The Jacobs Charitable Trust
The Ruth and Lionel Jacobson Trust (Second Fund) No 2
Jaffe Family Relief Fund
John James Bristol Foundation
The Susan and Stephen James Charitable Settlement
The James Trust
The Jarman Charitable Trust

**229**

John Jarrold Trust
Jay Education Trust
JCA Charitable Foundation
Jeffrey Charitable Trust
Rees Jeffreys Road Fund
Nick Jenkins Foundation
The Jenour Foundation
The Jephcott Charitable Trust
The Jerusalem Trust
Jewish Child's Day
The Jewish Youth Fund
The Joffe Charitable Trust
The Elton John Aids Foundation
Lillie Johnson Charitable Trust
The Johnson Foundation
The Johnnie Johnson Trust
The Johnson Wax Ltd Charitable Trust
The Joicey Trust
The Jones 1986 Charitable Trust
The Dezna Robins Jones Charitable Foundation
The Marjorie and Geoffrey Jones Charitable Trust
The Muriel Jones Foundation
The Jordan Charitable Foundation
The J. E. Joseph Charitable Fund
The Lady Eileen Joseph Foundation
The Josephs Family Charitable Trust
The Josh Charitable Trust
The Cyril and Eve Jumbo Charitable Trust
Anton Jurgens Charitable Trust
Jusaca Charitable Trust
The Bernard Kahn Charitable Trust
The Stanley Kalms Foundation
Karaviotis Foundation
The Boris Karloff Charitable Foundation
The Ian Karten Charitable Trust
The Kasner Charitable Trust
The Kass Charitable Trust
The Michael and Ilse Katz Foundation
C. S. Kaufman Charitable Trust
The Kelly Family Charitable Trust
Kelsick's Educational Foundation
The Kay Kendall Leukaemia Fund
William Kendall's Charity (Wax Chandlers' Company)
John Thomas Kennedy Charitable Foundation
The Kennedy Charitable Foundation

The Kennel Club Charitable Trust
Kent Community Foundation
The Nancy Kenyon Charitable Trust
Keren Association Limited
E. and E. Kernkraut Charities Limited
The Peter Kershaw Trust
The Ursula Keyes Trust
The King/Cullimore Charitable Trust
Kingdom Way Trust
The Kingsbury Charity
The Mary Kinross Charitable Trust
Kirkley Poor's Land Estate
The Richard Kirkman Trust
Kirschel Foundation
Robert Kitchin (Saddlers' Company)
The Ernest Kleinwort Charitable Trust
The Marina Kleinwort Charitable Trust
The Sir James Knott Trust
The Kobler Trust
The Kohn Foundation
Kollel and Co. Limited
The KPMG Foundation
The Kreditor Charitable Trust
The Kreitman Foundation
The Neil Kreitman Foundation
The Heinz, Anna and Carol Kroch Foundation
Kupath Gemach Chaim Bechesed Viznitz Trust
The Kyte Charitable Trust
The K. P. Ladd Charitable Trust
John Laing Charitable Trust
Maurice and Hilda Laing Charitable Trust
Christopher Laing Foundation
The David Laing Foundation
The Kirby Laing Foundation
The Martin Laing Foundation
The Beatrice Laing Trust
The Lambert Charitable Trust
Community Foundation for Lancashire
Community Foundations for Lancashire and Merseyside
Duchy of Lancaster Benevolent Fund
Lancaster Foundation
The Jack Lane Charitable Trust
The Allen Lane Foundation
Langdale Trust
Langley Charitable Trust
The LankellyChase Foundation
The R. J. Larg Family Charitable Trust
Largsmount Ltd
The Lark Trust
Laslett's (Hinton) Charity

Laufer Charitable Trust
The Lauffer Family Charitable Foundation
Mrs F. B. Laurence Charitable Trust
The Kathleen Laurence Trust
The Law Society Charity
The Edgar E. Lawley Foundation
The Herd Lawson and Muriel Lawson Charitable Trust
Lawson Beckman Charitable Trust
The Raymond and Blanche Lawson Charitable Trust
The Leach Fourteenth Trust
The David Lean Foundation
The Leathersellers' Company Charitable Fund
The Arnold Lee Charitable Trust
The William Leech Charity
The Lord Mayor of Leeds Appeal Fund
Leicestershire, Leicester and Rutland Community Foundation
The Kennedy Leigh Charitable Trust
Morris Leigh Foundation
The Leigh Trust
P. Leigh-Bramwell Trust 'E'
The Lennox and Wyfold Foundation
The Erica Leonard Trust
The Mark Leonard Trust
The Leverhulme Trade Charities Trust
Joseph Levy Charitable Foundation
David and Ruth Lewis Family Charitable Trust
The John Spedan Lewis Foundation
The Sir Edward Lewis Foundation
John Lewis Partnership General Community Fund
LHR Airport Communities Trust
Liberum Foundation
The Limbourne Trust
Limoges Charitable Trust
The Linbury Trust
Lincolnshire Churches Trust
Lincolnshire Community Foundation
The Lind Trust
Lindale Educational Foundation
The Linden Charitable Trust
Lindenleaf Charitable Trust
The Enid Linder Foundation
The Ruth and Stuart Lipton Charitable Trust
The Lister Charitable Trust

The Frank Litchfield Charitable Trust
The Charles Littlewood Hill Trust
The Second Joseph Aaron Littman Foundation
The George John and Sheilah Livanos Charitable Trust
Liverpool Charity and Voluntary Services
Jack Livingstone Charitable Trust
The Elaine and Angus Lloyd Charitable Trust
The Charles Lloyd Foundation
Lloyd's Charities Trust
Lloyds Bank Foundation for England and Wales
Lloyds Bank Foundation for Northern Ireland
Lloyds Bank Foundation for the Channel Islands
Lloyds TSB Foundation for Scotland
Localtrent Ltd
The Locker Foundation
Loftus Charitable Trust
The Lolev Charitable Trust
The Joyce Lomax Bullock Charitable Trust
The Trust for London
London Catalyst
The London Community Foundation
London Housing Foundation Ltd
The London Law Trust
London Legal Support Trust
The William and Katherine Longman Trust
The Loseley and Guildway Charitable Trust
The Lotus Foundation
The Lower Green Foundation
The Lowy Mitchell Foundation
The C. L. Loyd Charitable Trust
LSA Charitable Trust
The Marie Helen Luen Charitable Trust
Robert Luff Foundation Ltd
The Henry Lumley Charitable Trust
Paul Lunn-Rockliffe Charitable Trust
C. F. Lunoe Trust Fund
The Ruth and Jack Lunzer Charitable Trust
Lord and Lady Lurgan Trust
The Lyndhurst Trust
The Lynn Foundation
John Lyon's Charity
The Lyons Charitable Trust
The Sir Jack Lyons Charitable Trust
Sylvanus Lysons Charity
M. and C. Trust

The M. K. Charitable Trust
The Madeline Mabey Trust
The E. M. MacAndrew Trust
The R. S. Macdonald Charitable Trust
The Macdonald-Buchanan Charitable Trust
The Mackay and Brewer Charitable Trust
The Mackintosh Foundation
The MacRobert Trust
The Ian Mactaggart Trust
The Magen Charitable Trust
The Mageni Trust
The Brian Maguire Charitable Trust
The Mahavir Trust
Malbin Trust
The Mallinckrodt Foundation
Man Group plc Charitable Trust
The Manackerman Charitable Trust
Manchester Airport Community Trust Fund
The Manchester Guardian Society Charitable Trust
Lord Mayor of Manchester's Charity Appeal Trust
The Manifold Charitable Trust
The W. M. Mann Foundation
R. W. Mann Trust
The Manoukian Charitable Foundation
Maranatha Christian Trust
Marbeh Torah Trust
The Marchig Animal Welfare Trust
Mariapolis Limited
Market Harborough and The Bowdens Charity
The Michael Marks Charitable Trust
The Marks Family Foundation
The Ann and David Marks Foundation
The Hilda and Samuel Marks Foundation
J. P. Marland Charitable Trust
Marmot Charitable Trust
The Marr-Munning Trust
The Michael Marsh Charitable Trust
The Marsh Christian Trust
Charlotte Marshall Charitable Trust
D. G. Marshall of Cambridge Trust
The Marshgate Charitable Settlement
John Martin's Charity
The Mason Porter Charitable Trust
The Mathew Trust
The Matliwala Family Charitable Trust

The Matt 6.3 Charitable Trust
The Violet Mauray Charitable Trust
The Mayfield Valley Arts Trust
The Robert McAlpine Foundation
McGreevy No 5 Settlement
D. D. McPhail Charitable Settlement
The Medlock Charitable Trust
Melodor Limited
The Melow Charitable Trust
Menuchar Limited
Mercaz Torah Vechesed Limited
The Brian Mercer Charitable Trust
The Mercers' Charitable Foundation
The Merchant Taylors' Company Charities Fund
The Merchant Venturers' Charity
The Merchants' House of Glasgow
Mercury Phoenix Trust
The Mersey Docks and Harbour Company Charitable Fund
The Tony Metherell Charitable Trust
The Metropolitan Masonic Charity
T. & J. Meyer Family Foundation Limited
The Mickel Fund
The Mickleham Trust
The Gerald Micklem Charitable Trust
The Masonic Province of Middlesex Charitable Trust
Middlesex Sports Foundation
Millennium Stadium Charitable Trust (Ymddiriedolaeth Elusennol Stadiwm y Mileniwm)
Hugh and Mary Miller Bequest Trust
The Ronald Miller Foundation
The Millfield Trust
The Millichope Foundation
The Mills Charity
The Millward Charitable Trust
The Clare Milne Trust
Milton Keynes Community Foundation Limited
The Edgar Milward Charity
The Peter Minet Trust
Minge's Gift and the Pooled Trusts
Minton Charitable Trust
The Mirianog Trust
The Laurence Misener Charitable Trust
The Mishcon Family Charitable Trust

231

The Misselbrook Trust
The Brian Mitchell Charitable Settlement
The Esmé Mitchell Trust
Keren Mitzvah Trust
The Mizpah Trust
Mobbs Memorial Trust Ltd
The Modiano Charitable Trust
Mole Charitable Trust
The Monatrea Charitable Trust
Monmouthshire County Council Welsh Church Act Fund
The Montague Thompson Coon Charitable Trust
The Monument Trust
The Moonpig Foundation
The George A. Moore Foundation
The Morel Charitable Trust
The Morgan Charitable Foundation
The Morgan Foundation
Morgan Stanley International Foundation
The Diana and Allan Morgenthau Charitable Trust
The Oliver Morland Charitable Trust
S. C. and M. E. Morland's Charitable Trust
The Morris Charitable Trust
The Willie and Mabel Morris Charitable Trust
The Peter Morrison Charitable Foundation
The Moshal Charitable Trust
Vyoel Moshe Charitable Trust
The Moshulu Charitable Trust
Brian and Jill Moss Charitable Trust
The Moss Family Charitable Trust
Mosselson Charitable Trust
The Mount Everest Foundation
The Edwina Mountbatten & Leonora Children's Foundation
Mrs Waterhouse Charitable Trust
The Mugdock Children's Trust
The Mulberry Trust
Frederick Mulder Charitable Trust
The Edith Murphy Foundation
Murphy-Neumann Charity Company Limited
The Music Sales Charitable Trust
Muslim Hands
The Mutual Trust Group
MW (CL) Foundation
MW (GK) Foundation
MW (HO) Foundation
MW (RH) Foundation
MYA Charitable Trust

The Janet Nash Charitable Settlement
The National Churches Trust
The National Hockey Foundation
The National Manuscripts Conservation Trust
The Worshipful Company of Needlemakers' Charitable Fund
The Neighbourly Charitable Trust
The James Neill Trust Fund
Nemoral Ltd
Nesswall Ltd
Network for Social Change
Newby Trust Limited
The Newcomen Collett Foundation
Newpier Charity Ltd
Alderman Newton's Educational Foundation
The Chevras Ezras Nitzrochim Trust
NJD Charitable Trust
Alice Noakes Memorial Charitable Trust
The Noon Foundation
The Norman Family Charitable Trust
The Normanby Charitable Trust
The Northampton Municipal Church Charities
The Community Foundation for Northern Ireland
The Northern Rock Foundation
The Northmoor Trust
The Northumberland Village Homes Trust
The Northwood Charitable Trust
The Norton Foundation
The Norwich Town Close Estate Charity
The Norwood and Newton Settlement
The Nottingham General Dispensary
Nottinghamshire Community Foundation
The Nottinghamshire Historic Churches Trust
O&G Schreiber Charitable Trust
The Father O'Mahoney Memorial Trust
The Sir Peter O'Sullevan Charitable Trust
The Oakdale Trust
The Oakley Charitable Trust
The Oakmoor Charitable Trust
The Odin Charitable Trust
The Ofenheim Charitable Trust
The Ogle Christian Trust
Oizer Charitable Trust
Old Possum's Practical Trust

The John Oldacre Foundation
The Olga Charitable Trust
Open Gate
The Ouseley Trust
The Owen Family Trust
Oxfam (GB)
Oxfordshire Community Foundation
The P. F. Charitable Trust
The Paget Charitable Trust
The Panacea Charitable Trust
Panahpur
The Panton Trust
The Paphitis Charitable Trust
The Paragon Trust
The Park Charitable Trust
The Park House Charitable Trust
The Samuel and Freda Parkinson Charitable Trust
Miss M. E. Swinton Paterson's Charitable Trust
The Patrick Charitable Trust
The Jack Patston Charitable Trust
Ambika Paul Foundation
The Payne Charitable Trust
The Harry Payne Fund
The Susanna Peake Charitable Trust
The Pears Family Charitable Foundation
Rosanna Pearson's 1987 Charity Trust
The Pedmore Sporting Club Trust Fund
The Dowager Countess Eleanor Peel Trust
The Pell Charitable Trust
The Peltz Trust
The Pennycress Trust
The Performing Right Society Foundation
B. E. Perl Charitable Trust
The Personal Assurance Charitable Trust
The Persson Charitable Trust
The Persula Foundation
The Jack Petchey Foundation
The Petplan Charitable Trust
The Pharsalia Charitable Trust
The Phillips and Rubens Charitable Trust
The Phillips Charitable Trust
The Phillips Family Charitable Trust
The David Pickford Charitable Foundation
The Pilgrim Trust
The Elise Pilkington Charitable Trust
The Pilkington Charities Fund
The Austin and Hope Pilkington Trust
The Sir Harry Pilkington Trust Fund

Estate of the Late Colonel
   W. W. Pilkington Will Trusts
   – The General Charity Fund
Miss A. M. Pilkington's
   Charitable Trust
The DLA Piper Charitable Trust
The Platinum Trust
G. S. Plaut Charitable Trust
   Limited
Polden-Puckham Charitable
   Foundation
The George and Esme Pollitzer
   Charitable Settlement
The Pollywally Charitable Trust
The Polonsky Foundation
The Ponton House Trust
Edith and Ferdinand Porjes
   Charitable Trust
The John Porter Charitable
   Trust
The Porter Foundation
Porticus UK
The Portrack Charitable Trust
The J. E. Posnansky Charitable
   Trust
The Mary Potter Convent
   Hospital Trust
The David and Elaine Potter
   Foundation
The Praebendo Charitable
   Foundation
The Premier League Charitable
   Fund
Premierquote Ltd
Premishlaner Charitable Trust
Sir John Priestman Charity
   Trust
The Primrose Trust
The Prince of Wales's
   Charitable Foundation
Princess Anne's Charities
Prison Service Charity Fund
The Privy Purse Charitable
   Trust
The Puebla Charitable Trust
The Puri Foundation
Mr and Mrs J. A. Pye's
   Charitable Settlement
Quartet Community Foundation
The Queen Anne's Gate
   Foundation
Queen Mary's Roehampton
   Trust
The Queen's Silver Jubilee
   Trust
Quercus Trust
Quothquan Trust
R. J. M. Charitable Trust
R. S. Charitable Trust
The RVW Trust
The Monica Rabagliati
   Charitable Trust
Rachel Charitable Trust
The Racing Foundation
The Mr and Mrs Philip
   Rackham Charitable Trust

Richard Radcliffe Charitable
   Trust
The Radcliffe Trust
The Bishop Radford Trust
The Ragdoll Foundation
The Rainford Trust
The Joseph and Lena Randall
   Charitable Trust
The Joseph Rank Trust
Ranworth Trust
The Ratcliff Foundation
The Eleanor Rathbone
   Charitable Trust
The Sigrid Rausing Trust
The Ravensdale Trust
The Rayden Charitable Trust
The Roger Raymond Charitable
   Trust
The Rayne Foundation
The Rayne Trust
The Sir James Reckitt Charity
Eva Reckitt Trust Fund
The C. A. Redfern Charitable
   Foundation
The Reed Foundation
Richard Reeve's Foundation
Reuben Foundation
The Rhododendron Trust
Daisie Rich Trust
The Sir Cliff Richard Charitable
   Trust
The Clive Richards Charity
The Violet M. Richards Charity
The Richmond Parish Lands
   Charity
Ridgesave Limited
The Sir John Ritblat Family
   Foundation
The River Trust
Rivers Foundation
Thomas Roberts Trust
The Robertson Trust
Robyn Charitable Trust
The Rochester Bridge Trust
The Rock Foundation
The Roddick Foundation
The Rofeh Trust
Rokach Family Charitable Trust
The Helen Roll Charitable
   Trust
The Sir James Roll Charitable
   Trust
The Rosca Trust
The Cecil Rosen Foundation
Rosetrees Trust
The Rothermere Foundation
The Roughley Charitable Trust
Mrs Gladys Row Fogo
   Charitable Trust
Rowanville Ltd
The Rowlands Trust
The Joseph Rowntree
   Charitable Trust
Joseph Rowntree Reform Trust
   Limited
Royal Artillery Charitable Fund

Royal British Legion
Royal Docks Trust (London)
Royal Masonic Trust for Girls
   and Boys
The Rubin Foundation
William Arthur Rudd Memorial
   Trust
The Russell Trust
Ryklow Charitable Trust 1992
The J. S. and E. C. Rymer
   Charitable Trust
S. F. Foundation
The Michael Sacher Charitable
   Trust
The Michael Harry Sacher
   Trust
The Sackler Trust
The Ruzin Sadagora Trust
The Saga Charitable Trust
The Jean Sainsbury Animal
   Welfare Trust
The Alan and Babette
   Sainsbury Charitable Fund
The Sainsbury Family
   Charitable Trusts
Saint Sarkis Charity Trust
The Saintbury Trust
The Andrew Salvesen
   Charitable Trust
Sam and Bella Sebba
   Charitable Trust
Coral Samuel Charitable Trust
The Basil Samuel Charitable
   Trust
The M. J. Samuel Charitable
   Trust
The Peter Samuel Charitable
   Trust
The Samworth Foundation
The Sandra Charitable Trust
The Sands Family Trust
Santander UK Foundation
   Limited
The Peter Saunders Trust
The Scarfe Charitable Trust
The Schapira Charitable Trust
The Annie Schiff Charitable
   Trust
The Schmidt-Bodner Charitable
   Trust
The Schreib Trust
The Schreiber Charitable Trust
Schroder Charity Trust
The Schuster Charitable Trust
Foundation Scotland
The Francis C. Scott Charitable
   Trust
Scottish Coal Industry Special
   Welfare Fund
The Scouloudi Foundation
Seafarers UK (King George's
   Fund for Sailors)
The Searchlight Electric
   Charitable Trust
The Seedfield Trust
Sellata Ltd

SEM Charitable Trust
The Seneca Trust
The Cyril Shack Trust
The Jean Shanks Foundation
The Shanti Charitable Trust
ShareGift (The Orr Mackintosh Foundation)
The Shears Foundation
The Sheepdrove Trust
The Sheffield and District Hospital Services Charitable Fund
The Sheldon Trust
The Patricia and Donald Shepherd Charitable Trust
The Sylvia and Colin Shepherd Charitable Trust
The Archie Sherman Cardiff Foundation
The Archie Sherman Charitable Trust
The R. C. Sherriff Rosebriars Trust
The Shetland Charitable Trust
SHINE (Support and Help in Education)
The Barnett and Sylvia Shine No 2 Charitable Trust
The Bassil Shippam and Alsford Trust
The Shipwrights' Company Charitable Fund
The Shirley Foundation
Shlomo Memorial Fund Limited
The J. A. Shone Memorial Trust
The Barbara A. Shuttleworth Memorial Trust
The Mary Elizabeth Siebel Charity
David and Jennifer Sieff Charitable Trust
The Simmons & Simmons Charitable Foundation
The Huntly and Margery Sinclair Charitable Trust
The Sino-British Fellowship Trust
SITA Cornwall Trust Limited
Six Point Foundation
The Skelton Bounty
Skipton Building Society Charitable Foundation
The John Slater Foundation
Rita and David Slowe Charitable Trust
Ruth Smart Foundation
The SMB Charitable Trust
The Mrs Smith and Mount Trust
The DS Smith Charitable Foundation
The N. Smith Charitable Settlement
The Smith Charitable Trust
The Henry Smith Charity

The WH Smith Group Charitable Trust
The Stanley Smith UK Horticultural Trust
Philip Smith's Charitable Trust
The R. C. Snelling Charitable Trust
The Sobell Foundation
Solev Co Ltd
The Solo Charitable Settlement
David Solomons Charitable Trust
Songdale Ltd
The E. C. Sosnow Charitable Trust
The Souter Charitable Trust
The South Square Trust
The W. F. Southall Trust
R. H. Southern Trust
Spar Charitable Fund
Sparquote Limited
The Spear Charitable Trust
Spears-Stutz Charitable Trust
The Jessie Spencer Trust
The Spero Foundation
The Ralph and Irma Sperring Charity
The Spielman Charitable Trust
The Spoore, Merry and Rixman Foundation
Rosalyn and Nicholas Springer Charitable Trust
Springrule Limited
The Spurrell Charitable Trust
The St Hilda's Trust
St James's Trust Settlement
Sir Walter St John's Educational Charity
St Michael's and All Saints' Charities Relief Branch
The Stanley Foundation Ltd
The Staples Trust
The Star Charitable Trust
The Steinberg Family Charitable Trust
The Stephen Barry Charitable Trust
C. E. K. Stern Charitable Trust
Stevenson Family's Charitable Trust
The Stewards' Company Limited (incorporating the J. W. Laing Trust and the J. W. Laing Biblical Scholarship Trust)
The Stobart Newlands Charitable Trust
The Edward Stocks-Massey Bequest Fund
The Stoller Charitable Trust
M. J. C. Stone Charitable Trust
The Samuel Storey Family Charitable Trust
Peter Stormonth Darling Charitable Trust

Peter Storrs Trust
The Strangward Trust
Stratford upon Avon Town Trust
The Strawberry Charitable Trust
The W. O. Street Charitable Foundation
The Sudborough Foundation
Sueberry Ltd
Suffolk Community Foundation
The Suffolk Historic Churches Trust
The Alan Sugar Foundation
The Sussex Historic Churches Trust
The Adrienne and Leslie Sussman Charitable Trust
The Sutasoma Trust
Swan Mountain Trust
The Swann-Morton Foundation
Swansea and Brecon Diocesan Board of Finance Limited
Swimathon Foundation
The John Swire (1989) Charitable Trust
The Swire Charitable Trust
The Hugh and Ruby Sykes Charitable Trust
The Charles and Elsie Sykes Trust
The Charity of Stella Symons
The Tajtelbaum Charitable Trust
The Lady Tangye Charitable Trust
The David Tannen Charitable Trust
The Tanner Trust
The Lili Tapper Charitable Foundation
The Taurus Foundation
The Tay Charitable Trust
C. B. and H. H. Taylor 1984 Trust
The Connie and Albert Taylor Charitable Trust
A. P. Taylor Trust
Tearfund
The Tedworth Charitable Trust
Tees Valley Community Foundation
Tegham Limited
The Templeton Goodwill Trust
Tesco Charity Trust
The C. Paul Thackray General Charitable Trust
Thackray Medical Research Trust
The Thistle Trust
The Loke Wan Tho Memorial Foundation
The Thompson Family Charitable Trust
The Len Thomson Charitable Trust

*Grant-makers by types of grant* — **Strategic funding**

The Sir Jules Thorn Charitable Trust
The Thornton Foundation
The Thornton Trust
The Thousandth Man- Richard Burns Charitable Trust
The Thriplow Charitable Trust
The Daniel Thwaites Charitable Trust
The Tinsley Foundation
The Tisbury Telegraph Trust
The Tobacco Pipe Makers and Tobacco Trade Benevolent Fund
The Tolkien Trust
Tomchei Torah Charitable Trust
The Tompkins Foundation
Toras Chesed (London) Trust
The Tory Family Foundation
Tottenham Grammar School Foundation
The Tower Hill Trust
The Towry Law Charitable Trust (also known as the Castle Educational Trust)
Annie Tranmer Charitable Trust
The Constance Travis Charitable Trust
The Trefoil Trust
The Tresillian Trust
The Triangle Trust (1949) Fund
The True Colours Trust
Truedene Co. Ltd
The Truemark Trust
Truemart Limited
Trumros Limited
The Trusthouse Charitable Foundation
Tudor Rose Ltd
The Tudor Trust
The Tufton Charitable Trust
The Douglas Turner Trust
The Florence Turner Trust
The G. J. W. Turner Trust
Two Ridings Community Foundation
Community Foundation Serving Tyne and Wear and Northumberland
Trustees of Tzedakah
The Udlington Trust
UKI Charitable Foundation
Ulster Garden Villages Ltd
The Ulverscroft Foundation
The Underwood Trust
The Union of Orthodox Hebrew Congregation
The United Society for the Propagation of the Gospel
United Utilities Trust Fund
Uxbridge United Welfare Trust
The Vail Foundation
The Valentine Charitable Trust
The Valiant Charitable Trust

The Albert Van Den Bergh Charitable Trust
The Van Neste Foundation
Mrs Maud Van Norden's Charitable Foundation
The Vandervell Foundation
The Vardy Foundation
The Variety Club Children's Charity
Veneziana Fund
Roger Vere Foundation
Victoria Homes Trust
The Nigel Vinson Charitable Trust
The William and Ellen Vinten Trust
The Vintners' Foundation
The Virgin Foundation
Vivdale Ltd
Wade's Charity
The Scurrah Wainwright Charity
Wakeham Trust
The Community Foundation in Wales
Wales Council for Voluntary Action
Robert and Felicity Waley-Cohen Charitable Trust
The Walker Trust
Wallace and Gromit's Children's Foundation
War on Want
Sir Siegmund Warburg's Voluntary Settlement
The Ward Blenkinsop Trust
The Barbara Ward Children's Foundation
G. R. Waters Charitable Trust 2000
The Wates Foundation
Blyth Watson Charitable Trust
John Watson's Trust
Waynflete Charitable Trust
The Weavers' Company Benevolent Fund
The David Webster Charitable Trust
The Weinstein Foundation
The James Weir Foundation
The Joir and Kato Weisz Foundation
The Wellcome Trust
Welsh Church Fund – Dyfed area (Carmarthenshire, Ceredigion and Pembrokeshire)
The Welton Foundation
The Wessex Youth Trust
The West Derby Wastelands Charity
The Westcroft Trust
The Westminster Foundation
The Garfield Weston Foundation
The Barbara Whatmore Charitable Trust

The Whitaker Charitable Trust
The Colonel W. H. Whitbread Charitable Trust
The Melanie White Foundation Limited
White Stuff Foundation
The Whitecourt Charitable Trust
A. H. and B. C. Whiteley Charitable Trust
The Norman Whiteley Trust
The Whitley Animal Protection Trust
The Lionel Wigram Memorial Trust
The Felicity Wilde Charitable Trust
The Charity of William Williams
The Kay Williams Charitable Foundation
The Williams Charitable Trust
Williams Serendipity Trust
The HDH Wills 1965 Charitable Trust
Dame Violet Wills Charitable Trust
The Dame Violet Wills Will Trust
The Wilmcote Charitrust
Sumner Wilson Charitable Trust
David Wilson Foundation
The Wilson Foundation
J. and J. R. Wilson Trust
The Community Foundation for Wiltshire and Swindon
The Benjamin Winegarten Charitable Trust
The Harold Hyam Wingate Foundation
The Francis Winham Foundation
The Winton Charitable Foundation
The James Wise Charitable Trust
The Michael and Anna Wix Charitable Trust
The Wixamtree Trust
The Maurice Wohl Charitable Foundation
The Charles Wolfson Charitable Trust
The James Wood Bequest Fund
The Wood Family Trust
Wooden Spoon Society
The F. Glenister Woodger Trust
Woodlands Green Ltd
Woodroffe Benton Foundation
The Woodward Charitable Trust
Worcester Municipal Charities
The Worcestershire and Dudley Historic Churches Trust

**235**

**Project support**

The Wragge and Co Charitable Trust
The Diana Edgson Wright Charitable Trust
The Matthews Wrightson Charity Trust
Wychdale Ltd
Wychville Ltd
The Wyndham Charitable Trust
The Wyseliot Charitable Trust
The Xerox (UK) Trust
Yankov Charitable Trust
The Yardley Great Trust
The W. Wing Yip and Brothers Foundation
The South Yorkshire Community Foundation
The Yorkshire Dales Millennium Trust
The William Allen Young Charitable Trust
The John Kirkhope Young Endowment Fund
Youth Music
Zephyr Charitable Trust
The Marjorie and Arnold Ziff Charitable Foundation
Stephen Zimmerman Charitable Trust
The Zochonis Charitable Trust
The Zolfo Cooper Foundation

## Project support

■ **Full project funding**

The 101 Foundation
The 1970 Trust
The 1989 Willan Charitable Trust
The 29th May 1961 Charitable Trust
A. W. Charitable Trust
The Aberbrothock Skea Trust
The Aberdeen Endowments Trust
The Aberdeen Foundation
ABF The Soldiers' Charity
Achisomoch Aid Company Limited
The ACT Foundation
Action Medical Research
The Victor Adda Foundation
The Addleshaw Goddard Charitable Trust
The Adint Charitable Trust
The Adrian Swire Charitable Trust
Age UK
Aid to the Church in Need (UK)
The Sylvia Aitken Charitable Trust
The Ajahma Charitable Trust
The Al Fayed Charitable Foundation

Aldgate and All Hallows' Foundation
Allchurches Trust Ltd
The H. B. Allen Charitable Trust
The Alliance Family Foundation
Alliance Trust Staff Foundation
Angus Allnatt Charitable Foundation
The Pat Allsop Charitable Trust
Altamont Ltd
The Ammco Trust
The AMW Charitable Trust
The Anchor Foundation
Mary Andrew Charitable Trust
Andrews Charitable Trust
Anglo American Group Foundation
Anguish's Educational Foundation
The Eric Anker-Petersen Charity
Anpride Ltd
The Appletree Trust
The Arbib Foundation
The Archer Trust
The Argus Appeal
The Armourers' and Brasiers' Gauntlet Trust
The Artemis Charitable Trust
Arthritis Research UK
Arts Council England
Arts Council of Northern Ireland
Arts Council of Wales (Cyngor Celfyddydau Cymru)
The Ove Arup Foundation
The AS Charitable Trust
The Ascot Fire Brigade Trust
The Ashden Trust
The Ashmore Foundation
The Ashworth Charitable Trust
The Ian Askew Charitable Trust
The Associated Country Women of the World
The Association of Colleges Charitable Trust
Astellas European Foundation
AstonMansfield Charitable Trust
The Astor Foundation
The Astor of Hever Trust
The Aurelius Charitable Trust
The BACTA Charitable Trust
The Scott Bader Commonwealth Limited
The Bagri Foundation
The Austin Bailey Foundation
The Baily Thomas Charitable Fund
The Baird Trust
The Baker Charitable Trust
The Balcombe Charitable Trust
The Balfour Beatty Charitable Trust

The Andrew Balint Charitable Trust
The Albert Casanova Ballard Deceased Trust
The Ballinger Charitable Trust
The Balmore Trust
The Balney Charitable Trust
The Baltic Charitable Fund
The Bamford Charitable Foundation
The Banbury Charities
The Barbers' Company General Charities
The Barnsbury Charitable Trust
The Misses Barrie Charitable Trust
Bartholomew Charitable Trust
The Bartlett Taylor Charitable Trust
The Paul Bassham Charitable Trust
The Batchworth Trust
The Bates Charitable Trust
The Battens Charitable Trust
The Bay Tree Charitable Trust
The B-CH Charitable Trust
The Bearder Charity
The James Beattie Charitable Trust
The Beaverbrook Foundation
The Beccles Town Lands Charity
The Becker Family Charitable Trust
The Beckett's and Sargeant's Educational Foundation
The John Beckwith Charitable Trust
The Peter Beckwith Charitable Trust
The Bedfordshire and Luton Community Foundation
The Provincial Grand Lodge of Bedfordshire Charity Fund
Beefy's Charity Foundation
The David and Ruth Behrend Fund
The Bellahouston Bequest Fund
The Bellinger Donnay Trust
The Benfield Motors Charitable Trust
The Benham Charitable Settlement
Maurice and Jacqueline Bennett Charitable Trust
The Bergne-Coupland Charity
The Berkeley Charitable Foundation
The Bernadette Charitable Trust
The Bertarelli UK Foundation
BHST
The Mason Bibby 1981 Trust
The Bideford Bridge Trust
The Billmeir Charitable Trust

........

**236**

The Bingham Trust
The Bintaub Charitable Trust
The Birmingham District Nursing Charitable Trust
The Birmingham Hospital Saturday Fund Medical Charity and Welfare Trust
Birmingham International Airport Community Trust
The Lord Mayor of Birmingham's Charity
The Michael Bishop Foundation
The Blair Foundation
The Morgan Blake Charitable Trust
The Blandford Lake Trust
The Sir Victor Blank Charitable Settlement
The Bluston Charitable Settlement
The Body Shop Foundation
The Bonamy Charitable Trust
The John and Celia Bonham Christie Charitable Trust
The Charlotte Bonham-Carter Charitable Trust
Boots Charitable Trust
The Bordon Liphook Haslemere Charity
The Oliver Borthwick Memorial Trust
The Boshier-Hinton Foundation
The Bothwell Charitable Trust
The Harry Bottom Charitable Trust
The Bower Trust
The Bowerman Charitable Trust
The Bowland Charitable Trust
The Frank Brake Charitable Trust
The William Brake Charitable Trust
The Tony Bramall Charitable Trust
The Bramhope Trust
The Harold and Alice Bridges Charity
The Brighton District Nursing Association Trust
The British & Foreign School Society
The British Humane Association
British Institute at Ankara
The J. and M. Britton Charitable Trust
The Broderers' Charity Trust
The Consuelo and Anthony Brooke Charitable Trust
The Roger Brooke Charitable Trust
The David Brooke Charity
The Charles Brotherton Trust

Joseph Brough Charitable Trust
Miss Marion Broughton's Charitable Trust
Edna Brown Charitable Settlement
Buckinghamshire Community Foundation
The Buckinghamshire Masonic Centenary Fund
The Bulldog Trust Limited
The E. F. Bulmer Benevolent Fund
The Burghley Family Trust
The Burry Charitable Trust
The Arnold Burton 1998 Charitable Trust
The Burton Breweries Charitable Trust
Consolidated Charity of Burton upon Trent
The Worshipful Company of Butchers General Charities
The Noel Buxton Trust
Cable & Wireless Worldwide Foundation
Henry T. and Lucy B. Cadbury Charitable Trust
The Christopher Cadbury Charitable Trust
The G. W. Cadbury Charitable Trust
The Edward and Dorothy Cadbury Trust
CAFOD (Catholic Agency for Overseas Development)
Community Foundation for Calderdale
Callander Charitable Trust
Calleva Foundation
The Calpe Trust
The Cambridge Chrysalis Trust
The Cambridgeshire Community Foundation
The Camelia Trust
The Campden Charities Trustee
The Canning Trust
The Carew Pole Charitable Trust
Carlee Ltd
The Carlton House Charitable Trust
The Carmelite Monastery Ware Trust
The Worshipful Company of Carmen Benevolent Trust
The Carnegie Dunfermline Trust
The Carpenters' Company Charitable Trust
The Carrington Charitable Trust
The Leslie Mary Carter Charitable Trust
Cash for Kids – Radio Clyde

Sir John Cass's Foundation
The Elizabeth Casson Trust
The Castang Foundation
The Catholic Charitable Trust
The Catholic Trust for England and Wales
The Cattanach Charitable Trust
The Joseph and Annie Cattle Trust
The Thomas Sivewright Catto Charitable Settlement
The Wilfrid and Constance Cave Foundation
The B. G. S. Cayzer Charitable Trust
The Cazenove Charitable Trust
Celtic Charity Fund
The Chapman Charitable Trust
John William Chapman's Charitable Trust
The Charities Advisory Trust
Charitworth Limited
The Charter 600 Charity
The Cheruby Trust
Cheshire Freemason's Charity
The Chetwode Foundation
The Childs Charitable Trust
The Chipping Sodbury Town Lands Charity
CHK Charities Limited
The Chownes Foundation
The Christabella Charitable Trust
Christadelphian Samaritan Fund
Christian Aid
Chrysalis Trust
The Church Burgesses Educational Foundation
Church Burgesses Trust
Church of Ireland Priorities Fund
Church Urban Fund
The CIBC World Markets Children's Miracle Foundation
The City Bridge Trust
The City Educational Trust Fund
Stephen Clark 1957 Charitable Trust
J. A. Clark Charitable Trust
The Hilda and Alice Clark Charitable Trust
The Roger and Sarah Bancroft Clark Charitable Trust
The Clarke Charitable Settlement
The Cleopatra Trust
The Clore Duffield Foundation
Closehelm Limited
Richard Cloudesley's Charity
The Clover Trust
The Robert Clutterbuck Charitable Trust
Clydpride Ltd

# Full project funding

The Coalfields Regeneration Trust
The John Coates Charitable Trust
The Cobtree Charity Trust Ltd
The Denise Cohen Charitable Trust
The Vivienne and Samuel Cohen Charitable Trust
The John S. Cohen Foundation
The R. and S. Cohen Foundation
The Colefax Charitable Trust
John and Freda Coleman Charitable Trust
The George Henry Collins Charity
The Coltstaple Trust
Colwinston Charitable Trust
Colyer-Fergusson Charitable Trust
Comic Relief
The Comino Foundation
The Compton Charitable Trust
The Congleton Inclosure Trust
Martin Connell Charitable Trust
The Conservation Foundation
The Consolidated Charities for the Infirm – Merchant Taylors' Company
Gordon Cook Foundation
The Ernest Cook Trust
The Cooks Charity
Mabel Cooper Charity
The Alice Ellen Cooper Dean Charitable Foundation
The Marjorie Coote Animal Charity Trust
The Marjorie Coote Old People's Charity
The Helen Jean Cope Trust
The J. Reginald Corah Foundation Fund
The Gershon Coren Charitable Foundation
The Cornwell Charitable Trust
The Sidney and Elizabeth Corob Charitable Trust
The Corona Charitable Trust
The Costa Family Charitable Trust
The Cotton Industry War Memorial Trust
The Cotton Trust
County Durham Community Foundation
The Augustine Courtauld Trust
General Charity of Coventry
Coventry Building Society Charitable Foundation
Dudley and Geoffrey Cox Charitable Trust
The Sir William Coxen Trust Fund
The Lord Cozens-Hardy Trust

The Craignish Trust
The Craps Charitable Trust
Michael Crawford Children's Charity
The Cray Trust
Creative Scotland
The Crerar Hotels Trust
The Crescent Trust
Cripplegate Foundation
The Violet and Milo Cripps Charitable Trust
The Cross Trust
The Croydon Relief in Need Charities
Cruden Foundation Ltd
The Ronald Cruickshanks Foundation
Cullum Family Trust
Cumbria Community Foundation
The Dennis Curry Charitable Trust
The Cwmbran Trust
Itzchok Meyer Cymerman Trust Ltd
The D. G. Charitable Settlement
The D'Oyly Carte Charitable Trust
Roald Dahl's Marvellous Children's Charity
Daily Prayer Union Charitable Trust Limited
The Daiwa Anglo-Japanese Foundation
Baron Davenport's Charity
The Davidson Family Charitable Trust
Michael Davies Charitable Settlement
The Gwendoline and Margaret Davies Charity
The Wilfrid Bruce Davis Charitable Trust
The Dawe Charitable Trust
The De Brye Charitable Trust
Peter De Haan Charitable Trust
The Deakin Charitable Trust
Debenhams Foundation
The Debmar Benevolent Trust
The Delius Trust
The Dellal Foundation
The Delves Charitable Trust
The Denman Charitable Trust
The Dentons UKMEA LLP Charitable Trust
Derbyshire Community Foundation
The J. N. Derbyshire Trust
The Desmond Foundation
The Sandy Dewhirst Charitable Trust
The Laduma Dhamecha Charitable Trust
Diabetes UK

The Diageo Foundation
The Gillian Dickinson Trust
The Digbeth Trust Limited
The Dinwoodie Settlement
Dischma Charitable Trust
The Djanogly Foundation
The DLM Charitable Trust
The Derek and Eileen Dodgson Foundation
The Dollond Charitable Trust
The Dorus Trust
The Doughty Charity Trust
The Drapers' Charitable Fund
The Royal Foundation of the Duke and Duchess of Cambridge and Prince Harry
The Dumbreck Charity
Dunard Fund
The Dunhill Medical Trust
The Dunn Family Charitable Trust
The W. E. Dunn Trust
Dushinsky Trust Ltd
The Dyers' Company Charitable Trust
The James Dyson Foundation
eaga Charitable Trust
The Eagle Charity Trust
The Earley Charity
Earls Colne and Halstead Educational Charity
East End Community Foundation
The EBM Charitable Trust
The Economist Charitable Trust
EDF Energy Trust
The Gilbert and Eileen Edgar Foundation
Edinburgh & Lothian Trust Fund
Edinburgh Children's Holiday Fund
Edinburgh Trust No 2 Account
Edupoor Limited
The Elephant Trust
The George Elias Charitable Trust
The Gerald Palmer Eling Trust Company
The Wilfred and Elsie Elkes Charity Fund
The Maud Elkington Charitable Trust
The Ellerdale Trust
The John Ellerman Foundation
The Ellinson Foundation Ltd
The Elmley Foundation
The Vernon N. Ely Charitable Trust
The Emerton-Christie Charity
The Englefield Charitable Trust
The English Schools' Football Association
The Enkalon Foundation
Entindale Ltd

238

The Epigoni Trust
Epilepsy Research UK
The Equity Trust Fund
The Ericson Trust
The ERM Foundation
The Erskine Cunningham Hill Trust
Esh Foundation
Essex Community Foundation
The Essex Fairway Charitable Trust
The Essex Youth Trust
Euro Charity Trust
Sir John Evelyn's Charity
The Eventhall Family Charitable Trust
The Eveson Charitable Trust
The Beryl Evetts and Robert Luff Animal Welfare Trust Limited
The Exilarch's Foundation
The F. P. Limited Charitable Trust
The Fairway Trust
The Lord Faringdon Charitable Trust
Samuel William Farmer's Trust
The Thomas Farr Charity
The Fassnidge Memorial Trust
Federation of Jewish Relief Organisations
The George Fentham Birmingham Charity
The A. M. Fenton Trust
The Allan and Nesta Ferguson Charitable Settlement
The Doris Field Charitable Trust
The Fifty Fund
Filey Foundation Ltd
Firtree Trust
Fisherbeck Charitable Trust
The Fishmongers' Company's Charitable Trust
The Fitton Trust
The Earl Fitzwilliam Charitable Trust
The Ian Fleming Charitable Trust
The Joyce Fletcher Charitable Trust
The Flow Foundation
The Gerald Fogel Charitable Trust
The Follett Trust
The Football Association National Sports Centre Trust
The Football Association Youth Trust
The Football Foundation
The Forbes Charitable Foundation
The Oliver Ford Charitable Trust
The Forest Hill Charitable Trust

The Lady Forester Trust
Forever Manchester (The Community Foundation for Greater Manchester)
The Forman Hardy Charitable Trust
Gwyneth Forrester Trust
The Forte Charitable Trust
The Four Winds Trust
The Foyle Foundation
The Isaac and Freda Frankel Memorial Charitable Trust
The Elizabeth Frankland Moore and Star Foundation
The Jill Franklin Trust
The Gordon Fraser Charitable Trust
The Hugh Fraser Foundation
The Joseph Strong Frazer Trust
The Fred and Maureen Charitable Trust
The Louis and Valerie Freedman Charitable Settlement
The Michael and Clara Freeman Charitable Trust
The Freemasons' Grand Charity
The Charles S. French Charitable Trust
The Anne French Memorial Trust
The Freshfield Foundation
The Freshgate Trust Foundation
The Friarsgate Trust
Friends of Boyan Trust
Friends Provident Charitable Foundation
The Frognal Trust
The Fulmer Charitable Trust
The Fuserna Foundation General Charitable Trust
The G. D. Charitable Trust
The Gale Family Charity Trust
The Gamma Trust
The Gannochy Trust
The Ganzoni Charitable Trust
The Worshipful Company of Gardeners of London
The Samuel Gardner Memorial Trust
The Garnett Charitable Trust
Garthgwynion Charities
The Gatsby Charitable Foundation
The Robert Gavron Charitable Trust
The Nigel Gee Foundation
Sir Robert Geffery's Almshouse Trust
The General Nursing Council for England and Wales Trust
The Gibbs Charitable Trust
Simon Gibson Charitable Trust

The G. C. Gibson Charitable Trust
The Girdlers' Company Charitable Trust
The B. and P. Glasser Charitable Trust
Global Care
Global Charities
Gloucestershire Community Foundation
Worshipful Company of Glovers of London Charitable Trust
The GNC Trust
The Godinton Charitable Trust
The Sydney and Phyllis Goldberg Memorial Charitable Trust
The Golden Bottle Trust
The Goldman Sachs Charitable Gift Fund (UK)
Goldman Sachs Gives (UK)
The Goldsmiths' Arts Trust Fund
The Goldsmiths' Company Charity
The Golf Foundation Limited
The Mike Gooley Trailfinders Charity
The Gosling Foundation Limited
The Gould Charitable Trust
The Grace Charitable Trust
A. B. Grace Trust
The Graff Foundation
E. C. Graham Belford Charitable Settlement
The Grahame Charitable Foundation Limited
The Granada Foundation
Grand Charitable Trust of the Order of Women Freemasons
The Grange Farm Centre Trust
Grantham Yorke Trust
The Gordon Gray Trust
The Gray Trust
The Great Stone Bridge Trust of Edenbridge
The Great Torrington Town Lands Charity
The Kenneth & Susan Green Charitable Foundation
The Green Hall Foundation
Philip and Judith Green Trust
Greenham Common Community Trust Limited
The Greggs Foundation
The Gretna Charitable Trust
The Grimmitt Trust
The Grocers' Charity
The M. and R. Gross Charities Limited
The GRP Charitable Trust
N. and R. Grunbaum Charitable Trust

**239**

The Bishop of Guildford's Foundation
The Guildry Incorporation of Perth
The Walter Guinness Charitable Trust
The Gunter Charitable Trust
The Gur Trust
The Gurney Charitable Trust
Dr Guthrie's Association
The H. and M. Charitable Trust
H. C. D. Memorial Fund
The Hackney Parochial Charities
The Hadfield Trust
The Hadley Trust
The Hadrian Trust
The Alfred Haines Charitable Trust
E. F. and M. G. Hall Charitable Trust
The Edith Winifred Hall Charitable Trust
The Hamamelis Trust
Hamilton Wallace Trust
Paul Hamlyn Foundation
The Hampshire and Islands Historic Churches Trust
The Doughty Hanson Charitable Foundation
The Peter Harrison Foundation
The Dorothy Hay-Bolton Charitable Trust
Headley-Pitt Charitable Trust
The Hedley Denton Charitable Trust
The H. J. Heinz Company Limited Charitable Trust
The Heritage of London Trust Limited
Hitchin Educational Foundation
The Mary Homfray Charitable Trust
The Hoover Foundation
IBM United Kingdom Trust
Interserve Employee Foundation Ltd
The Jerwood Charitable Foundation
The Kingsbury Charity
The Heinz, Anna and Carol Kroch Foundation
The Lark Trust
The Leche Trust
Morris Leigh Foundation
The Erica Leonard Trust
LHR Airport Communities Trust
Liverpool Charity and Voluntary Services
The Charles Lloyd Foundation
The Lowy Mitchell Foundation
James Madison Trust
Man Group plc Charitable Trust

The Mersey Docks and Harbour Company Charitable Fund
The Tony Metherell Charitable Trust
The Brian Mitchell Charitable Settlement
The MITIE Foundation
The Montague Thompson Coon Charitable Trust
The Moss Family Charitable Trust
Mosselson Charitable Trust
The Mount Everest Foundation
The Edwina Mountbatten & Leonora Children's Foundation
Mrs Waterhouse Charitable Trust
The Mugdock Children's Trust
The Mulberry Trust
The Edith Murphy Foundation
The Music Sales Charitable Trust
Muslim Hands
The Mutual Trust Group
The Janet Nash Charitable Settlement
The National Churches Trust
National Committee of the Women's World Day of Prayer for England and Wales and Northern Ireland
The National Express Foundation
The National Manuscripts Conservation Trust
The Worshipful Company of Needlemakers' Charitable Fund
The Neighbourly Charitable Trust
The James Neill Trust Fund
Nemoral Ltd
The Frances and Augustus Newman Foundation
The Chevras Ezras Nitzrochim Trust
The Noon Foundation
Norfolk Community Foundation
Normalyn Charitable Trust
The Norman Family Charitable Trust
The Normanby Charitable Trust
The Community Foundation for Northern Ireland
The Northern Rock Foundation
The Northmoor Trust
The Northumberland Village Homes Trust
The Northwood Charitable Trust
The Norton Foundation
The Norwich Town Close Estate Charity

The Nottingham General Dispensary
Nottinghamshire Community Foundation
The Nottinghamshire Historic Churches Trust
The Nuffield Foundation
O&G Schreiber Charitable Trust
The Father O'Mahoney Memorial Trust
The Sir Peter O'Sullevan Charitable Trust
The Oakdale Trust
The Oakmoor Charitable Trust
The Odin Charitable Trust
The Ofenheim Charitable Trust
The Ogle Christian Trust
Oglesby Charitable Trust
Oizer Charitable Trust
The John Oldacre Foundation
The Olga Charitable Trust
Open Gate
The Ouseley Trust
The Owen Family Trust
Oxfam (GB)
City of Oxford Charity
Oxfordshire Community Foundation
The P. F. Charitable Trust
The Paget Charitable Trust
Eleanor Palmer Trust
The Panacea Charitable Trust
The Paragon Trust
The Park House Charitable Trust
The Samuel and Freda Parkinson Charitable Trust
The Patrick Charitable Trust
The Jack Patston Charitable Trust
The Susanna Peake Charitable Trust
The Pedmore Sporting Club Trust Fund
The Dowager Countess Eleanor Peel Trust
The Pennycress Trust
The Performing Right Society Foundation
The Personal Assurance Charitable Trust
The Persson Charitable Trust
The Persula Foundation
The Jack Petchey Foundation
The Petplan Charitable Trust
The Phillips and Rubens Charitable Trust
The Phillips Charitable Trust
The Phillips Family Charitable Trust
The David Pickford Charitable Foundation
The Pilgrim Trust
The Pilkington Charities Fund

240

The Austin and Hope
    Pilkington Trust
The Sir Harry Pilkington Trust
    Fund
The DLA Piper Charitable Trust
The Platinum Trust
Polden-Puckham Charitable
    Foundation
The George and Esme Pollitzer
    Charitable Settlement
The Ponton House Trust
Edith and Ferdinand Porjes
    Charitable Trust
The John Porter Charitable
    Trust
The Porter Foundation
The Portrack Charitable Trust
The J. E. Posnansky Charitable
    Trust
The Mary Potter Convent
    Hospital Trust
The David and Elaine Potter
    Foundation
Premierquote Ltd
Premishlaner Charitable Trust
Sir John Priestman Charity
    Trust
The Primrose Trust
The Prince of Wales's
    Charitable Foundation
Prison Service Charity Fund
The Privy Purse Charitable
    Trust
The Puebla Charitable Trust
The Puri Foundation
Mr and Mrs J. A. Pye's
    Charitable Settlement
Quartet Community Foundation
Queen Mary's Roehampton
    Trust
The Queen's Silver Jubilee
    Trust
Quothquan Trust
R. S. Charitable Trust
The RVW Trust
The Monica Rabagliati
    Charitable Trust
Rachel Charitable Trust
The Racing Foundation
The Mr and Mrs Philip
    Rackham Charitable Trust
Richard Radcliffe Charitable
    Trust
The Radcliffe Trust
The Ragdoll Foundation
The Rainford Trust
The Joseph and Lena Randall
    Charitable Trust
The Rank Foundation Limited
The Ratcliff Foundation
The Eleanor Rathbone
    Charitable Trust
The Sigrid Rausing Trust
The Ravensdale Trust
The Rayden Charitable Trust

The Roger Raymond Charitable
    Trust
The Rayne Foundation
The Rayne Trust
The Sir James Reckitt Charity
Red Hill Charitable Trust
The C. A. Redfern Charitable
    Foundation
The Reed Foundation
Richard Reeve's Foundation
Reuben Foundation
The Rhododendron Trust
The Sir Cliff Richard Charitable
    Trust
The Clive Richards Charity
The Richmond Parish Lands
    Charity
Ridgesave Limited
The Sir John Ritblat Family
    Foundation
The River Trust
Thomas Roberts Trust
The Robertson Trust
The Rochester Bridge Trust
The Rock Foundation
The Rofeh Trust
Rokach Family Charitable Trust
The Helen Roll Charitable
    Trust
The Sir James Roll Charitable
    Trust
Mrs L. D. Rope Third
    Charitable Settlement
The Rosca Trust
The Rose Foundation
The Cecil Rosen Foundation
Rosetrees Trust
The Rothermere Foundation
The Roughley Charitable Trust
Mrs Gladys Row Fogo
    Charitable Trust
Rowanville Ltd
The Rowlands Trust
The Joseph Rowntree
    Charitable Trust
The Joseph Rowntree
    Foundation
Joseph Rowntree Reform Trust
    Limited
Royal Artillery Charitable Fund
Royal Docks Trust (London)
Royal Masonic Trust for Girls
    and Boys
The Royal Victoria Hall
    Foundation
The Rubin Foundation
The Russell Trust
The J. S. and E. C. Rymer
    Charitable Trust
The Michael Sacher Charitable
    Trust
The Michael Harry Sacher
    Trust
Raymond and Beverly Sackler
    1988 Foundation
The Sackler Trust

The Ruzin Sadagora Trust
Erach and Roshan Sadri
    Foundation
The Saga Charitable Trust
The Jean Sainsbury Animal
    Welfare Trust
The Alan and Babette
    Sainsbury Charitable Fund
The Sainsbury Family
    Charitable Trusts
The Salamander Charitable
    Trust
Sam and Bella Sebba
    Charitable Trust
The Basil Samuel Charitable
    Trust
The M. J. Samuel Charitable
    Trust
The Peter Samuel Charitable
    Trust
The Samworth Foundation
The Sandra Charitable Trust
Santander UK Foundation
    Limited
The Peter Saunders Trust
The Scarfe Charitable Trust
The Schapira Charitable Trust
The Schmidt-Bodner Charitable
    Trust
The Schreib Trust
The Schreiber Charitable Trust
The Schuster Charitable Trust
Foundation Scotland
The Francis C. Scott Charitable
    Trust
The Frieda Scott Charitable
    Trust
The Sir James and Lady Scott
    Trust
Scottish Coal Industry Special
    Welfare Fund
The Scottish Power Energy
    People Trust
The Scottish Power Foundation
The Scouloudi Foundation
Seafarers UK (King George's
    Fund for Sailors)
The Seedfield Trust
Leslie Sell Charitable Trust
The Jean Shanks Foundation
ShareGift (The Orr Mackintosh
    Foundation)
The Shears Foundation
The Sheepdrove Trust
The Sheffield and District
    Hospital Services
    Charitable Fund
The Sheldon Trust
The Patricia and Donald
    Shepherd Charitable Trust
The Archie Sherman Cardiff
    Foundation
The Archie Sherman Charitable
    Trust
The R. C. Sherriff Rosebriars
    Trust

The Shetland Charitable Trust
SHINE (Support and Help in Education)
The Barnett and Sylvia Shine No 2 Charitable Trust
The Bassil Shippam and Alsford Trust
The Shipwrights' Company Charitable Fund
The Shirley Foundation
Shlomo Memorial Fund Limited
The J. A. Shone Memorial Trust
The Mary Elizabeth Siebel Charity
David and Jennifer Sieff Charitable Trust
The Huntly and Margery Sinclair Charitable Trust
The Sino-British Fellowship Trust
Six Point Foundation
The Skelton Bounty
The Charles Skey Charitable Trust
Skipton Building Society Charitable Foundation
The Slaughter and May Charitable Trust
The SMB Charitable Trust
The Mrs Smith and Mount Trust
The N. Smith Charitable Settlement
The Henry Smith Charity
The Stanley Smith UK Horticultural Trust
The Sobell Foundation
Social Business Trust (Scale-Up)
Sodexo Foundation
The Solo Charitable Settlement
The E. C. Sosnow Charitable Trust
The Souter Charitable Trust
The South Square Trust
The W. F. Southall Trust
The Sovereign Health Care Charitable Trust
Sparks Charity (Sport Aiding Medical Research For Kids)
Sparquote Limited
The Spear Charitable Trust
The Worshipful Company of Spectacle Makers' Charity
The Jessie Spencer Trust
The Ralph and Irma Sperring Charity
The Spielman Charitable Trust
The Spoore, Merry and Rixman Foundation
Springrule Limited
The Spurrell Charitable Trust
The Geoff and Fiona Squire Foundation

The St Hilda's Trust
St James's Trust Settlement
St James's Place Foundation
Sir Walter St John's Educational Charity
St Michael's and All Saints' Charities Relief Branch
St Monica Trust
St Peter's Saltley Trust
The Stanley Foundation Ltd
The Staples Trust
The Peter Stebbings Memorial Charity
The Steinberg Family Charitable Trust
The Stephen Barry Charitable Trust
The Stewards' Company Limited (incorporating the J. W. Laing Trust and the J. W. Laing Biblical Scholarship Trust)
Sir Halley Stewart Trust
The Stobart Newlands Charitable Trust
The Edward Stocks-Massey Bequest Fund
The Stoller Charitable Trust
M. J. C. Stone Charitable Trust
The Samuel Storey Family Charitable Trust
Peter Stormonth Darling Charitable Trust
The Strangward Trust
The W. O. Street Charitable Foundation
The Sudborough Foundation
Suffolk Community Foundation
The Sussex Historic Churches Trust
Sutton Coldfield Charitable Trust
The Swann-Morton Foundation
Swansea and Brecon Diocesan Board of Finance Limited
The John Swire (1989) Charitable Trust
The Swire Charitable Trust
The Hugh and Ruby Sykes Charitable Trust
The Charles and Elsie Sykes Trust
The Charity of Stella Symons
The Lady Tangye Charitable Trust
The David Tannen Charitable Trust
The Tanner Trust
The Lili Tapper Charitable Foundation
The Tay Charitable Trust
A. P. Taylor Trust
Tearfund
The Tedworth Charitable Trust
Tees Valley Community Foundation

The Templeton Goodwill Trust
Tesco Charity Trust
The C. Paul Thackray General Charitable Trust
The Thales Charitable Trust
The Thistle Trust
The Loke Wan Tho Memorial Foundation
The Thompson Family Charitable Trust
The Sue Thomson Foundation
Thomson Reuters Foundation
The Sir Jules Thorn Charitable Trust
The Thornton Foundation
The Thornton Trust
The Three Guineas Trust
The Thriplow Charitable Trust
The Daniel Thwaites Charitable Trust
The Tinsley Foundation
The Tisbury Telegraph Trust
The Tobacco Pipe Makers and Tobacco Trade Benevolent Fund
The Tolkien Trust
Tomchei Torah Charitable Trust
The Tompkins Foundation
The Tory Family Foundation
Tottenham Grammar School Foundation
The Tower Hill Trust
The Towry Law Charitable Trust (also known as the Castle Educational Trust)
The Toy Trust
Toyota Manufacturing UK Charitable Trust
The Constance Travis Charitable Trust
The Triangle Trust (1949) Fund
The True Colours Trust
Truedene Co. Ltd
The Truemark Trust
Truemart Limited
Trumros Limited
The Trusthouse Charitable Foundation
Tudor Rose Ltd
The Tudor Trust
The Tufton Charitable Trust
The Douglas Turner Trust
The Florence Turner Trust
The G. J. W. Turner Trust
Community Foundation Serving Tyne and Wear and Northumberland
Trustees of Tzedakah
UIA Charitable Foundation
Ulster Garden Villages Ltd
The Ulverscroft Foundation
The Underwood Trust
The Union of Orthodox Hebrew Congregation
The UNITE Foundation

Grant-makers by types of grant — Seed funding

The United Society for the
    Propagation of the Gospel
Uxbridge United Welfare Trust
The Van Neste Foundation
The Vandervell Foundation
The Vardy Foundation
The Variety Club Children's
    Charity
Veneziana Fund
The Nigel Vinson Charitable
    Trust
The William and Ellen Vinten
    Trust
The Vintners' Foundation
The Virgin Foundation
Vivdale Ltd
Voluntary Action Fund
Wade's Charity
The Scurrah Wainwright Charity
The Community Foundation in
    Wales
Wales Council for Voluntary
    Action
The Walker Trust
War on Want
The Ward Blenkinsop Trust
The Waterloo Foundation
G. R. Waters Charitable Trust
    2000
The Wates Foundation
Webb Memorial Trust
The Westminster Foundation
The Kay Williams Charitable
    Foundation
The Maurice Wohl Charitable
    Foundation
The Charles Wolfson
    Charitable Trust
The Worcestershire and
    Dudley Historic Churches
    Trust
The Wragge and Co Charitable
    Trust
Wychville Ltd
The Xerox (UK) Trust
The Yapp Charitable Trust
The Zochonis Charitable Trust
Zurich Community Trust (UK)
    Limited

## ■ Seed funding

The 1970 Trust
The 1989 Willan Charitable
    Trust
The 29th May 1961 Charitable
    Trust
A. W. Charitable Trust
The Aberbrothock Skea Trust
The Aberdeen Endowments
    Trust
The Aberdeenshire Educational
    Trust Scheme
ABF The Soldiers' Charity
Achisomoch Aid Company
    Limited

Action Medical Research
The Victor Adda Foundation
The Addleshaw Goddard
    Charitable Trust
The Adint Charitable Trust
The Adrian Swire Charitable
    Trust
Age Scotland
Age UK
Aid to the Church in Need (UK)
The Sylvia Aitken Charitable
    Trust
The Al Fayed Charitable
    Foundation
Aldgate and All Hallows'
    Foundation
All Saints Educational Trust
Allchurches Trust Ltd
The Alliance Family Foundation
Angus Allnatt Charitable
    Foundation
The Pat Allsop Charitable Trust
The Almond Trust
Altamont Ltd
The Ammco Trust
Viscount Amory's Charitable
    Trust
The AMW Charitable Trust
The Anchor Foundation
Mary Andrew Charitable Trust
Anguish's Educational
    Foundation
The Eric Anker-Petersen
    Charity
Anpride Ltd
The Appletree Trust
The Arbib Foundation
The Archer Trust
The Ardwick Trust
The Argus Appeal
The Armourers' and Brasiers'
    Gauntlet Trust
The Artemis Charitable Trust
Arts Council England
Arts Council of Northern
    Ireland
Arts Council of Wales (Cyngor
    Celfyddydau Cymru)
The Ove Arup Foundation
The AS Charitable Trust
The Ascot Fire Brigade Trust
The Ashden Trust
The Ashworth Charitable Trust
The Ian Askew Charitable Trust
The Associated Country
    Women of the World
The Association of Colleges
    Charitable Trust
Astellas European Foundation
AstonMansfield Charitable
    Trust
The Astor Foundation
The Astor of Hever Trust
The Aurelius Charitable Trust
The Scott Bader
    Commonwealth Limited

The Bagri Foundation
The Austin Bailey Foundation
The Baily Thomas Charitable
    Fund
The Baird Trust
The Baker Charitable Trust
The Balcombe Charitable Trust
The Albert Casanova Ballard
    Deceased Trust
The Ballinger Charitable Trust
The Balmore Trust
The Balney Charitable Trust
The Baltic Charitable Fund
The Bamford Charitable
    Foundation
The Banbury Charities
The Barbers' Company General
    Charities
The Barnsbury Charitable Trust
The Misses Barrie Charitable
    Trust
Bartholomew Charitable Trust
The Bartlett Taylor Charitable
    Trust
The Paul Bassham Charitable
    Trust
The Batchworth Trust
The Bates Charitable Trust
The Battens Charitable Trust
The Bay Tree Charitable Trust
The B-CH Charitable Trust
The Bearder Charity
The James Beattie Charitable
    Trust
The Beaverbrook Foundation
The Beccles Town Lands
    Charity
The Becker Family Charitable
    Trust
The Beckett's and Sargeant's
    Educational Foundation
The John Beckwith Charitable
    Trust
The Peter Beckwith Charitable
    Trust
The Provincial Grand Lodge of
    Bedfordshire Charity Fund
The David and Ruth Behrend
    Fund
The Bellahouston Bequest
    Fund
The Bellinger Donnay Trust
The Benfield Motors Charitable
    Trust
The Benham Charitable
    Settlement
Maurice and Jacqueline
    Bennett Charitable Trust
The Bergne-Coupland Charity
The Bernadette Charitable
    Trust
BHST
The Mason Bibby 1981 Trust
The Bideford Bridge Trust
The Billmeir Charitable Trust
The Bingham Trust

243

# Seed funding

The Bintaub Charitable Trust
The Birmingham District Nursing Charitable Trust
The Birmingham Hospital Saturday Fund Medical Charity and Welfare Trust
Birmingham International Airport Community Trust
The Lord Mayor of Birmingham's Charity
The Michael Bishop Foundation
The Blair Foundation
The Morgan Blake Charitable Trust
The Blandford Lake Trust
The Sir Victor Blank Charitable Settlement
The Bluston Charitable Settlement
The Nicholas Boas Charitable Trust
The Body Shop Foundation
The Bonamy Charitable Trust
The John and Celia Bonham Christie Charitable Trust
The Charlotte Bonham-Carter Charitable Trust
Boots Charitable Trust
The Bordon Liphook Haslemere Charity
The Oliver Borthwick Memorial Trust
The Boshier-Hinton Foundation
The Bothwell Charitable Trust
The Harry Bottom Charitable Trust
The Bower Trust
The Bowerman Charitable Trust
The Bowland Charitable Trust
The Frank Brake Charitable Trust
The William Brake Charitable Trust
The Tony Bramall Charitable Trust
The Bramhope Trust
The Brighton District Nursing Association Trust
The British Humane Association
British Institute at Ankara
The J. and M. Britton Charitable Trust
The Broderers' Charity Trust
The Roger Brooke Charitable Trust
The David Brooke Charity
The Charles Brotherton Trust
Joseph Brough Charitable Trust
Miss Marion Broughton's Charitable Trust
Edna Brown Charitable Settlement

Buckinghamshire Community Foundation
The Bulldog Trust Limited
The E. F. Bulmer Benevolent Fund
The Burghley Family Trust
The Burry Charitable Trust
The Arnold Burton 1998 Charitable Trust
The Burton Breweries Charitable Trust
Consolidated Charity of Burton upon Trent
The Worshipful Company of Butchers General Charities
The Noel Buxton Trust
Henry T. and Lucy B. Cadbury Charitable Trust
The Christopher Cadbury Charitable Trust
The G. W. Cadbury Charitable Trust
The Richard Cadbury Charitable Trust
The Edward and Dorothy Cadbury Trust
The George Cadbury Trust
CAFOD (Catholic Agency for Overseas Development)
Community Foundation for Calderdale
Callander Charitable Trust
Calleva Foundation
Calouste Gulbenkian Foundation – UK Branch
The Calpe Trust
The Campden Charities Trustee
The Canning Trust
The Carew Pole Charitable Trust
Carlee Ltd
The Carlton House Charitable Trust
The Carmelite Monastery Ware Trust
The Worshipful Company of Carmen Benevolent Trust
The Carnegie Dunfermline Trust
The Carpenters' Company Charitable Trust
The Carrington Charitable Trust
The Leslie Mary Carter Charitable Trust
Cash for Kids – Radio Clyde
Sir John Cass's Foundation
The Elizabeth Casson Trust
The Castang Foundation
The Catholic Charitable Trust
The Catholic Trust for England and Wales
The Cattanach Charitable Trust
The Joseph and Annie Cattle Trust

The Thomas Sivewright Catto Charitable Settlement
The Wilfrid and Constance Cave Foundation
The B. G. S. Cayzer Charitable Trust
The Cazenove Charitable Trust
Celtic Charity Fund
The Chapman Charitable Trust
John William Chapman's Charitable Trust
The Charities Advisory Trust
Charitworth Limited
The Charter 600 Charity
The Cheruby Trust
Cheshire Freemason's Charity
The Chetwode Foundation
The Childs Charitable Trust
The Chipping Sodbury Town Lands Charity
CHK Charities Limited
The Chownes Foundation
The Christabella Charitable Trust
Christadelphian Samaritan Fund
Christian Aid
Chrysalis Trust
The Church Burgesses Educational Foundation
Church Burgesses Trust
Church of Ireland Priorities Fund
Church Urban Fund
The City Bridge Trust
The City Educational Trust Fund
Stephen Clark 1957 Charitable Trust
J. A. Clark Charitable Trust
The Hilda and Alice Clark Charitable Trust
The Roger and Sarah Bancroft Clark Charitable Trust
The Clarke Charitable Settlement
The Cleopatra Trust
The Clore Duffield Foundation
Closehelm Limited
Richard Cloudesley's Charity
The Clover Trust
The Robert Clutterbuck Charitable Trust
Clydpride Ltd
The Coalfields Regeneration Trust
The John Coates Charitable Trust
The Cobtree Charity Trust Ltd
The Denise Cohen Charitable Trust
The Vivienne and Samuel Cohen Charitable Trust
The John S. Cohen Foundation
The R. and S. Cohen Foundation

## Seed funding

The Colchester Catalyst Charity
The Colefax Charitable Trust
John and Freda Coleman Charitable Trust
The George Henry Collins Charity
The Sir Jeremiah Colman Gift Trust
The Coltstaple Trust
Colwinston Charitable Trust
Colyer-Fergusson Charitable Trust
Comic Relief
The Comino Foundation
The Compton Charitable Trust
The Congleton Inclosure Trust
Martin Connell Charitable Trust
The Conservation Foundation
The Consolidated Charities for the Infirm – Merchant Taylors' Company
The Ernest Cook Trust
The Cooks Charity
Mabel Cooper Charity
The Alice Ellen Cooper Dean Charitable Foundation
The Marjorie Coote Animal Charity Trust
The Marjorie Coote Old People's Charity
The Helen Jean Cope Trust
The J. Reginald Corah Foundation Fund
The Gershon Coren Charitable Foundation
The Cornwell Charitable Trust
The Sidney and Elizabeth Corob Charitable Trust
The Corona Charitable Trust
The Costa Family Charitable Trust
The Cotton Industry War Memorial Trust
County Durham Community Foundation
The Augustine Courtauld Trust
General Charity of Coventry
Coventry Building Society Charitable Foundation
Dudley and Geoffrey Cox Charitable Trust
The Sir William Coxen Trust Fund
The Lord Cozens-Hardy Trust
The Craignish Trust
The Craps Charitable Trust
Michael Crawford Children's Charity
The Cray Trust
Creative Scotland
The Crerar Hotels Trust
The Crescent Trust
Cripplegate Foundation

The Violet and Milo Cripps Charitable Trust
The Cross Trust
The Croydon Relief in Need Charities
Cruden Foundation Ltd
The Ronald Cruickshanks Foundation
Cumbria Community Foundation
The Dennis Curry Charitable Trust
The Cwmbran Trust
Itzchok Meyer Cymerman Trust Ltd
The D. G. Charitable Settlement
Roald Dahl's Marvellous Children's Charity
Daily Prayer Union Charitable Trust Limited
The Daiwa Anglo-Japanese Foundation
Baron Davenport's Charity
The Davidson Family Charitable Trust
Michael Davies Charitable Settlement
The Gwendoline and Margaret Davies Charity
The Hamilton Davies Trust
The Wilfrid Bruce Davis Charitable Trust
The Dawe Charitable Trust
The De Brye Charitable Trust
The Deakin Charitable Trust
The Debmar Benevolent Trust
The Dellal Foundation
The Delves Charitable Trust
The Denman Charitable Trust
The Dentons UKMEA LLP Charitable Trust
Derbyshire Community Foundation
The J. N. Derbyshire Trust
The Desmond Foundation
Devon Community Foundation
The Duke of Devonshire's Charitable Trust
The Sandy Dewhirst Charitable Trust
The Laduma Dhamecha Charitable Trust
Diabetes UK
The Dibden Allotments Fund
The Digbeth Trust Limited
Disability Aid Fund (The Roger and Jean Jefcoate Trust)
Dischma Charitable Trust
The DLM Charitable Trust
The Derek and Eileen Dodgson Foundation
The Dollond Charitable Trust
The Dorus Trust
The Doughty Charity Trust
Douglas Arter Foundation

The Drapers' Charitable Fund
The Duis Charitable Trust
The Dulverton Trust
The Dumbreck Charity
Dunard Fund
The Dunn Family Charitable Trust
The W. E. Dunn Trust
Dushinsky Trust Ltd
The Dyers' Company Charitable Trust
The Eagle Charity Trust
The Earley Charity
Earls Colne and Halstead Educational Charity
East End Community Foundation
Eastern Counties Educational Trust Limited
The EBM Charitable Trust
EDF Energy Trust
The Gilbert and Eileen Edgar Foundation
Edinburgh & Lothian Trust Fund
Edinburgh Trust No 2 Account
The Elephant Trust
The George Elias Charitable Trust
The Gerald Palmer Eling Trust Company
The Wilfred and Elsie Elkes Charity Fund
The Maud Elkington Charitable Trust
The Ellerdale Trust
The John Ellerman Foundation
The Ellinson Foundation Ltd
The Edith Maud Ellis 1985 Charitable Trust
The Elmley Foundation
The Vernon N. Ely Charitable Trust
The Emerton-Christie Charity
The Englefield Charitable Trust
The English Schools' Football Association
The Enkalon Foundation
Entindale Ltd
The Epigoni Trust
The Equity Trust Fund
The Ericson Trust
The ERM Foundation
The Erskine Cunningham Hill Trust
Essex Community Foundation
The Essex Fairway Charitable Trust
The Essex Heritage Trust
The Essex Youth Trust
Euro Charity Trust
Sir John Evelyn's Charity
The Eventhall Family Charitable Trust
The Eveson Charitable Trust

245

The Beryl Evetts and Robert
  Luff Animal Welfare Trust
  Limited
The Exilarch's Foundation
The Expat Foundation
The F. P. Limited Charitable
  Trust
The Fairway Trust
The Lord Faringdon Charitable
  Trust
The Fassnidge Memorial Trust
The George Fentham
  Birmingham Charity
The A. M. Fenton Trust
The Allan and Nesta Ferguson
  Charitable Settlement
The Doris Field Charitable
  Trust
The Ian Fleming Charitable
  Trust
The Football Association
  National Sports Centre
  Trust
The Football Foundation
The Oliver Ford Charitable
  Trust
The Forest Hill Charitable Trust
Forever Manchester (The
  Community Foundation for
  Greater Manchester)
The Forman Hardy Charitable
  Trust
Gwyneth Forrester Trust
The Forte Charitable Trust
The Four Winds Trust
The Foyle Foundation
The Isaac and Freda Frankel
  Memorial Charitable Trust
The Elizabeth Frankland Moore
  and Star Foundation
The Jill Franklin Trust
The Gordon Fraser Charitable
  Trust
The Hugh Fraser Foundation
The Joseph Strong Frazer Trust
The Louis and Valerie
  Freedman Charitable
  Settlement
The Freemasons' Grand
  Charity
The Charles S. French
  Charitable Trust
The Freshfield Foundation
The Freshgate Trust
  Foundation
The Friarsgate Trust
Friends Provident Charitable
  Foundation
The Frognal Trust
The Fulmer Charitable Trust
The Gale Family Charity Trust
The Gamma Trust
The Gannochy Trust
The Samuel Gardner Memorial
  Trust
The Garnett Charitable Trust

The Garrick Charitable Trust
Garthgwynion Charities
The Gatsby Charitable
  Foundation
Gatwick Airport Community
  Trust
The Robert Gavron Charitable
  Trust
Sir Robert Geffery's
  Almshouse Trust
The Gibbs Charitable Trust
Simon Gibson Charitable Trust
The G. C. Gibson Charitable
  Trust
The Girdlers' Company
  Charitable Trust
The B. and P. Glasser
  Charitable Trust
Global Care
Global Charities
Gloucestershire Community
  Foundation
Worshipful Company of
  Glovers of London
  Charitable Trust
The GNC Trust
The Godinton Charitable Trust
The Sydney and Phyllis
  Goldberg Memorial
  Charitable Trust
The Golden Bottle Trust
The Goldman Sachs Charitable
  Gift Fund (UK)
Goldman Sachs Gives (UK)
The Goldsmiths' Arts Trust
  Fund
The Goldsmiths' Company
  Charity
The Mike Gooley Trailfinders
  Charity
The Gosling Foundation
  Limited
The Gould Charitable Trust
The Grace Charitable Trust
A. B. Grace Trust
E. C. Graham Belford
  Charitable Settlement
The Grahame Charitable
  Foundation Limited
The Granada Foundation
Grand Charitable Trust of the
  Order of Women
  Freemasons
The Grange Farm Centre Trust
The Gordon Gray Trust
The Gray Trust
The Great Stone Bridge Trust
  of Edenbridge
The Green Hall Foundation
Greenham Common
  Community Trust Limited
The Greggs Foundation
The Gretna Charitable Trust
The Grocers' Charity
The M. and R. Gross Charities
  Limited

The GRP Charitable Trust
The Bishop of Guildford's
  Foundation
The Guildry Incorporation of
  Perth
The Walter Guinness
  Charitable Trust
The Gunter Charitable Trust
The Gur Trust
Dr Guthrie's Association
The H. and M. Charitable Trust
H. C. D. Memorial Fund
The Hackney Parochial
  Charities
The Hadfield Trust
The Hadley Trust
The Hadrian Trust
The Alfred Haines Charitable
  Trust
The Edith Winifred Hall
  Charitable Trust
Hamilton Wallace Trust
Paul Hamlyn Foundation
The Doughty Hanson
  Charitable Foundation
The Peter Harrison Foundation
The Dorothy Hay-Bolton
  Charitable Trust
Headley-Pitt Charitable Trust
The Health Foundation
The Hedley Denton Charitable
  Trust
The H. J. Heinz Company
  Limited Charitable Trust
The Heritage of London Trust
  Limited
The Hesslewood Children's
  Trust (Hull Seamen's and
  General Orphanage)
P. and C. Hickinbotham
  Charitable Trust
Hitchin Educational Foundation
The Hoover Foundation
John Jarrold Trust
Rees Jeffreys Road Fund
The Kingsbury Charity
The Sir James Knott Trust
The Langtree Trust
The Lark Trust
The William Leech Charity
Morris Leigh Foundation
The Erica Leonard Trust
Lord Leverhulme's Charitable
  Trust
LHR Airport Communities Trust
Liverpool Charity and Voluntary
  Services
The Charles Lloyd Foundation
Man Group plc Charitable
  Trust
Sir George Martin Trust
The Matt 6.3 Charitable Trust
The Mersey Docks and
  Harbour Company
  Charitable Fund

The Tony Metherell Charitable Trust
The Montague Thompson Coon Charitable Trust
The Moss Family Charitable Trust
Mosselson Charitable Trust
The Mount Everest Foundation
The Edwina Mountbatten & Leonora Children's Foundation
Mrs Waterhouse Charitable Trust
The Mugdock Children's Trust
The Mulberry Trust
The Edith Murphy Foundation
The Music Sales Charitable Trust
Muslim Hands
The Mutual Trust Group
The Janet Nash Charitable Settlement
The National Churches Trust
National Committee of the Women's World Day of Prayer for England and Wales and Northern Ireland
The National Hockey Foundation
The National Manuscripts Conservation Trust
The Worshipful Company of Needlemakers' Charitable Fund
The Neighbourly Charitable Trust
The James Neill Trust Fund
Nemoral Ltd
Network for Social Change
The Newcomen Collett Foundation
The Chevras Ezras Nitzrochim Trust
The Noon Foundation
Normalyn Charitable Trust
The Norman Family Charitable Trust
The Normanby Charitable Trust
The Northampton Municipal Church Charities
The Community Foundation for Northern Ireland
The Northern Rock Foundation
The Northmoor Trust
The Northumberland Village Homes Trust
The Northwood Charitable Trust
The Norton Foundation
The Norwich Town Close Estate Charity
The Nottingham General Dispensary
Nottinghamshire Community Foundation

The Nottinghamshire Historic Churches Trust
The Father O'Mahoney Memorial Trust
The Sir Peter O'Sullevan Charitable Trust
The Oakdale Trust
The Oakmoor Charitable Trust
The Odin Charitable Trust
The Ofenheim Charitable Trust
The Ogle Christian Trust
Oglesby Charitable Trust
Oizer Charitable Trust
The John Oldacre Foundation
The Olga Charitable Trust
Open Gate
The Ouseley Trust
The Owen Family Trust
Oxfam (GB)
Oxfordshire Community Foundation
The P. F. Charitable Trust
The Paget Charitable Trust
The Panacea Charitable Trust
The Paragon Trust
The Park House Charitable Trust
The Samuel and Freda Parkinson Charitable Trust
The Patrick Charitable Trust
The Jack Patston Charitable Trust
The Susanna Peake Charitable Trust
The Pedmore Sporting Club Trust Fund
The Dowager Countess Eleanor Peel Trust
The Pennycress Trust
The Performing Right Society Foundation
The Personal Assurance Charitable Trust
The Persson Charitable Trust
The Persula Foundation
The Jack Petchey Foundation
The Petplan Charitable Trust
The Phillips and Rubens Charitable Trust
The Phillips Charitable Trust
The Phillips Family Charitable Trust
The David Pickford Charitable Foundation
The Pilgrim Trust
The Pilkington Charities Fund
The Austin and Hope Pilkington Trust
The Sir Harry Pilkington Trust Fund
The DLA Piper Charitable Trust
The Platinum Trust
Polden-Puckham Charitable Foundation
The George and Esme Pollitzer Charitable Settlement

The Ponton House Trust
Edith and Ferdinand Porjes Charitable Trust
The John Porter Charitable Trust
The Porter Foundation
The Portrack Charitable Trust
The J. E. Posnansky Charitable Trust
The Mary Potter Convent Hospital Trust
The David and Elaine Potter Foundation
Premierquote Ltd
Premishlaner Charitable Trust
Sir John Priestman Charity Trust
The Primrose Trust
The Prince of Wales's Charitable Foundation
Prison Service Charity Fund
The Privy Purse Charitable Trust
The Puebla Charitable Trust
The Puri Foundation
Mr and Mrs J. A. Pye's Charitable Settlement
Quartet Community Foundation
Queen Mary's Roehampton Trust
The Queen's Silver Jubilee Trust
Quothquan Trust
R. S. Charitable Trust
The RVW Trust
The Monica Rabagliati Charitable Trust
Rachel Charitable Trust
The Mr and Mrs Philip Rackham Charitable Trust
Richard Radcliffe Charitable Trust
The Radcliffe Trust
The Ragdoll Foundation
The Rainford Trust
The Joseph and Lena Randall Charitable Trust
The Rank Foundation Limited
The Ratcliff Foundation
The Eleanor Rathbone Charitable Trust
The Sigrid Rausing Trust
The Ravensdale Trust
The Rayden Charitable Trust
The Roger Raymond Charitable Trust
The Rayne Foundation
The Rayne Trust
The Sir James Reckitt Charity
The C. A. Redfern Charitable Foundation
The Reed Foundation
Richard Reeve's Foundation
Reuben Foundation
The Rhododendron Trust

The Sir Cliff Richard Charitable Trust
The Clive Richards Charity
The Richmond Parish Lands Charity
Ridgesave Limited
The Sir John Ritblat Family Foundation
The River Trust
Thomas Roberts Trust
The Robertson Trust
The Rochester Bridge Trust
The Rock Foundation
The Rofeh Trust
Rokach Family Charitable Trust
The Helen Roll Charitable Trust
The Sir James Roll Charitable Trust
The Rosca Trust
The Cecil Rosen Foundation
Rosetrees Trust
The Rothermere Foundation
The Roughley Charitable Trust
Mrs Gladys Row Fogo Charitable Trust
Rowanville Ltd
The Rowlands Trust
The Joseph Rowntree Charitable Trust
The Joseph Rowntree Foundation
Joseph Rowntree Reform Trust Limited
Royal Artillery Charitable Fund
Royal Docks Trust (London)
Royal Masonic Trust for Girls and Boys
The Royal Victoria Hall Foundation
The Rubin Foundation
The Russell Trust
The J. S. and E. C. Rymer Charitable Trust
The Michael Sacher Charitable Trust
The Michael Harry Sacher Trust
The Sackler Trust
The Ruzin Sadagora Trust
The Saddlers' Company Charitable Fund
Erach and Roshan Sadri Foundation
The Saga Charitable Trust
The Jean Sainsbury Animal Welfare Trust
The Alan and Babette Sainsbury Charitable Fund
The Sainsbury Family Charitable Trusts
Sam and Bella Sebba Charitable Trust
The Basil Samuel Charitable Trust

The M. J. Samuel Charitable Trust
The Peter Samuel Charitable Trust
The Samworth Foundation
The Sandra Charitable Trust
Santander UK Foundation Limited
The Scarfe Charitable Trust
The Schapira Charitable Trust
The Schmidt-Bodner Charitable Trust
The Schreib Trust
The Schreiber Charitable Trust
The Schuster Charitable Trust
Foundation Scotland
The Francis C. Scott Charitable Trust
The Frieda Scott Charitable Trust
Scottish Coal Industry Special Welfare Fund
The Scouloudi Foundation
Seafarers UK (King George's Fund for Sailors)
The Seedfield Trust
Leslie Sell Charitable Trust
The Jean Shanks Foundation
ShareGift (The Orr Mackintosh Foundation)
The Shears Foundation
The Sheepdrove Trust
The Sheffield and District Hospital Services Charitable Fund
The Sheldon Trust
The Patricia and Donald Shepherd Charitable Trust
The Archie Sherman Cardiff Foundation
The Archie Sherman Charitable Trust
The R. C. Sherriff Rosebriars Trust
The Shetland Charitable Trust
SHINE (Support and Help in Education)
The Barnett and Sylvia Shine No 2 Charitable Trust
The Bassil Shippam and Alsford Trust
The Shipwrights' Company Charitable Fund
The Shirley Foundation
Shlomo Memorial Fund Limited
The J. A. Shone Memorial Trust
The Mary Elizabeth Siebel Charity
David and Jennifer Sieff Charitable Trust
The Huntly and Margery Sinclair Charitable Trust
The Sino-British Fellowship Trust
The Skelton Bounty

The Charles Skey Charitable Trust
Skipton Building Society Charitable Foundation
The SMB Charitable Trust
The Mrs Smith and Mount Trust
The N. Smith Charitable Settlement
The Henry Smith Charity
The Stanley Smith UK Horticultural Trust
The Sobell Foundation
The Solo Charitable Settlement
The E. C. Sosnow Charitable Trust
The Souter Charitable Trust
The South Square Trust
The W. F. Southall Trust
The Sovereign Health Care Charitable Trust
Sparquote Limited
The Spear Charitable Trust
The Jessie Spencer Trust
The Ralph and Irma Sperring Charity
The Spielman Charitable Trust
The Spoore, Merry and Rixman Foundation
Springrule Limited
The Spurrell Charitable Trust
The Geoff and Fiona Squire Foundation
The St Hilda's Trust
St James's Trust Settlement
Sir Walter St John's Educational Charity
St Michael's and All Saints' Charities Relief Branch
The Stanley Foundation Ltd
The Staples Trust
The Peter Stebbings Memorial Charity
The Steinberg Family Charitable Trust
The Stephen Barry Charitable Trust
The Stewards' Company Limited (incorporating the J. W. Laing Trust and the J. W. Laing Biblical Scholarship Trust)
Sir Halley Stewart Trust
The Stobart Newlands Charitable Trust
The Edward Stocks-Massey Bequest Fund
The Stoller Charitable Trust
M. J. C. Stone Charitable Trust
The Samuel Storey Family Charitable Trust
Peter Stormonth Darling Charitable Trust
The Strangward Trust

Stratford upon Avon Town Trust
The W. O. Street Charitable Foundation
The Sudborough Foundation
The Sussex Historic Churches Trust
The Swann-Morton Foundation
Swansea and Brecon Diocesan Board of Finance Limited
Swimathon Foundation
The John Swire (1989) Charitable Trust
The Swire Charitable Trust
The Hugh and Ruby Sykes Charitable Trust
The Charles and Elsie Sykes Trust
The Charity of Stella Symons
The Lady Tangye Charitable Trust
The David Tannen Charitable Trust
The Tanner Trust
The Lili Tapper Charitable Foundation
The Tay Charitable Trust
A. P. Taylor Trust
Tearfund
The Tedworth Charitable Trust
Tees Valley Community Foundation
The Templeton Goodwill Trust
Tesco Charity Trust
The C. Paul Thackray General Charitable Trust
The Thistle Trust
The Loke Wan Tho Memorial Foundation
The Thompson Family Charitable Trust
The Sue Thomson Foundation
The Sir Jules Thorn Charitable Trust
The Thornton Foundation
The Thornton Trust
The Three Guineas Trust
The Thriplow Charitable Trust
The Daniel Thwaites Charitable Trust
The Tinsley Foundation
The Tisbury Telegraph Trust
The Tobacco Pipe Makers and Tobacco Trade Benevolent Fund
The Tolkien Trust
Tomchei Torah Charitable Trust
The Tompkins Foundation
The Tory Family Foundation
Tottenham Grammar School Foundation
The Tower Hill Trust
The Towry Law Charitable Trust (also known as the Castle Educational Trust)

The Constance Travis Charitable Trust
The Triangle Trust (1949) Fund
The True Colours Trust
Truedene Co. Ltd
The Truemark Trust
Truemart Limited
Trumros Limited
Tudor Rose Ltd
The Tudor Trust
The Tufton Charitable Trust
Tuixen Foundation
The Douglas Turner Trust
The Florence Turner Trust
The G. J. W. Turner Trust
Community Foundation Serving Tyne and Wear and Northumberland
Trustees of Tzedakah
Ulster Garden Villages Ltd
The Ulverscroft Foundation
The Underwood Trust
The Union of Orthodox Hebrew Congregation
The United Society for the Propagation of the Gospel
Uxbridge United Welfare Trust
The Van Neste Foundation
The Vandervell Foundation
The Vardy Foundation
The Variety Club Children's Charity
Veneziana Fund
The Nigel Vinson Charitable Trust
The William and Ellen Vinten Trust
The Vintners' Foundation
Vivdale Ltd
Wade's Charity
The Scurrah Wainwright Charity
Wakeham Trust
The Community Foundation in Wales
Wales Council for Voluntary Action
War on Want
The Ward Blenkinsop Trust
G. R. Waters Charitable Trust 2000
The Wates Foundation
The Kay Williams Charitable Foundation
The Maurice Wohl Charitable Foundation
The Charles Wolfson Charitable Trust
The Worcestershire and Dudley Historic Churches Trust
The Wragge and Co Charitable Trust
Wychville Ltd
The Xerox (UK) Trust
The Zochonis Charitable Trust

Zurich Community Trust (UK) Limited

## Campaigning

The 1970 Trust
A. W. Charitable Trust
ABF The Soldiers' Charity
Access Sport
Action Medical Research
The Adamson Trust
The Addleshaw Goddard Charitable Trust
The Adint Charitable Trust
Age Scotland
Age UK
Aid to the Church in Need (UK)
The Alborada Trust
The H. B. Allen Charitable Trust
The Ammco Trust
The AMW Charitable Trust
Anglo American Group Foundation
Arts Council England
Arts Council of Wales (Cyngor Celfyddydau Cymru)
The AS Charitable Trust
The Ashden Trust
The Associated Country Women of the World
Asthma UK
The Avon and Somerset Police Community Trust
The Balcombe Charitable Trust
The Barnsbury Charitable Trust
The Bergne-Coupland Charity
The BlackRock (UK) Charitable Trust
The Morgan Blake Charitable Trust
The Blandford Lake Trust
The Bluston Charitable Settlement
The Body Shop Foundation
The Harry Bottom Charitable Trust
The Broderers' Charity Trust
The Roger Brooke Charitable Trust
The David Brooke Charity
Miss Marion Broughton's Charitable Trust
The Brownsword Charitable Foundation
Henry T. and Lucy B. Cadbury Charitable Trust
The Edward and Dorothy Cadbury Trust
CAFOD (Catholic Agency for Overseas Development)
Calouste Gulbenkian Foundation – UK Branch
The Carmelite Monastery Ware Trust

**249**

The B. G. S. Cayzer Charitable Trust
Celtic Charity Fund
The Charities Advisory Trust
Christian Aid
Church Urban Fund
Stephen Clark 1957 Charitable Trust
J. A. Clark Charitable Trust
The Cobalt Trust
The Coltstaple Trust
Colwinston Charitable Trust
Comic Relief
The Compton Charitable Trust
Martin Connell Charitable Trust
The Conservation Foundation
The Cooks Charity
The Marjorie Coote Animal Charity Trust
Michael Cornish Charitable Trust
The Corona Charitable Trust
The Costa Family Charitable Trust
Dudley and Geoffrey Cox Charitable Trust
The Craignish Trust
The Craps Charitable Trust
The Crescent Trust
The Violet and Milo Cripps Charitable Trust
The D. G. Charitable Settlement
Peter De Haan Charitable Trust
The De Laszlo Foundation
The Dellal Foundation
The Dollond Charitable Trust
Dorset Community Foundation
The Drapers' Charitable Fund
The Dulverton Trust
The Elephant Trust
The Ellerdale Trust
The John Ellerman Foundation
Entindale Ltd
The Erskine Cunningham Hill Trust
Essex Community Foundation
Esmée Fairbairn Foundation
The Allan and Nesta Ferguson Charitable Settlement
Elizabeth Ferguson Charitable Trust Fund
The Doris Field Charitable Trust
The Hugh Fraser Foundation
The Freshfield Foundation
The Gatsby Charitable Foundation
Global Care
The Great Britain Sasakawa Foundation
The Green Hall Foundation
The Guildry Incorporation of Perth

H. C. D. Memorial Fund
The Hadley Trust
Paul Hamlyn Foundation
The Doughty Hanson Charitable Foundation
The Dorothy Hay-Bolton Charitable Trust
The Health Foundation
Hospice UK
The Indigo Trust
Rees Jeffreys Road Fund
The Lotus Foundation
The Millfield House Foundation
S. C. and M. E. Morland's Charitable Trust
Mrs Waterhouse Charitable Trust
Frederick Mulder Charitable Trust
The National Churches Trust
The Neighbourly Charitable Trust
Nemoral Ltd
Network for Social Change
The Noon Foundation
The Norman Family Charitable Trust
The Northern Rock Foundation
The Northwood Charitable Trust
The Norton Foundation
The Sir Peter O'Sullevan Charitable Trust
The Oakmoor Charitable Trust
The Ofenheim Charitable Trust
Oxfam (GB)
The Park Charitable Trust
The Personal Assurance Charitable Trust
The Persula Foundation
The Jack Petchey Foundation
The Petplan Charitable Trust
The Pilgrim Trust
The Pilkington Charities Fund
Polden-Puckham Charitable Foundation
The David and Elaine Potter Foundation
The Prince of Wales's Charitable Foundation
The Puebla Charitable Trust
Quartet Community Foundation
Queen Mary's Roehampton Trust
The Queen's Silver Jubilee Trust
Rachel Charitable Trust
The Sigrid Rausing Trust
The Rayne Foundation
The Reed Foundation
Reuben Foundation
The Helen Roll Charitable Trust
The Joseph Rowntree Charitable Trust

The Joseph Rowntree Foundation
Joseph Rowntree Reform Trust Limited
Royal British Legion
The Rubin Foundation
S. F. Foundation
The Michael Harry Sacher Trust
The Alan and Babette Sainsbury Charitable Fund
Sam and Bella Sebba Charitable Trust
ShareGift (The Orr Mackintosh Foundation)
The Shears Foundation
The Sheepdrove Trust
The Barbara A. Shuttleworth Memorial Trust
The Slaughter and May Charitable Trust
The Souter Charitable Trust
Springrule Limited
The Swann-Morton Foundation
Swansea and Brecon Diocesan Board of Finance Limited
The C. Paul Thackray General Charitable Trust
Thomson Reuters Foundation
The Tobacco Pipe Makers and Tobacco Trade Benevolent Fund
The Tolkien Trust
The Triangle Trust (1949) Fund
The Tudor Trust
The Douglas Turner Trust
Trustees of Tzedakah
The Ulverscroft Foundation
The Underwood Trust
The United Society for the Propagation of the Gospel
The Vardy Foundation
Wales Council for Voluntary Action
G. R. Waters Charitable Trust 2000
The Wates Foundation

## Loan finance

The ACT Foundation
The Architectural Heritage Fund
The Bridging Fund Charitable Trust
The British Dietetic Association General and Education Trust Fund
The Burton Breweries Charitable Trust
The Cambridgeshire Historic Churches Trust
The Coalfields Regeneration Trust
The Dawe Charitable Trust

The Edith Maud Ellis 1985
    Charitable Trust
The February Foundation
The Hathaway Trust
The Maurice Hatter Foundation
The Helping Foundation
Nick Jenkins Foundation
The Joffe Charitable Trust
John Thomas Kennedy
    Charitable Foundation
Christopher Laing Foundation
The William Leech Charity
Marbeh Torah Trust
Charity of John Marshall
The Edward Stocks-Massey
    Bequest Fund
Ulster Garden Villages Ltd

# The alphabetical register of grant-making charities

This section lists the individual entries for the grant-making charities.

## ■ The 101 Foundation

**CC NO** 1146808    **ESTABLISHED** 2012
**WHERE FUNDING CAN BE GIVEN** UK.
**WHO CAN BENEFIT** Registered charities.
**WHAT IS FUNDED** General charitable purposes, with a particular interest in children and young people.
**SAMPLE GRANTS Previous beneficiaries have included:** Shooting Star Chase (£300,000); Make-A-Wish Foundation (£200,000); Great Ormond Street Hospital (£100,000); The Pepper Foundation (£80,000); Boxing Academy (£30,000); and Brighton and Hove Parents and Children's Group (£9,000).
**FINANCES** Year 2013/14 Income £102,818 Grants £90,000 Grants to organisations £90,000
**TRUSTEES** Angela Dawes; David Dawes; Coutts & Co.
**OTHER INFORMATION** The foundation was established by David and Angela Dawes, who won £101 million on the EuroMillions lottery in October 2011.
**HOW TO APPLY** Apply in writing to the correspondent.
**WHO TO APPLY TO** Coutts & Co, Trustee Department, 440 Strand, London WC2R 0QS *Tel.* 020 7663 6826 *email* couttscharities@coutts.com

## ■ The 1970 Trust

**SC NO** SC008788    **ESTABLISHED** 1970
**WHERE FUNDING CAN BE GIVEN** UK
**WHO CAN BENEFIT** Charities which support disadvantaged minorities.
**WHAT IS FUNDED** The trust states it supports small UK charities 'doing innovative, educational, or experimental work' in the following fields: civil liberties (e.g. freedom of information; constitutional reform; humanising work; children's welfare); the public interest in the face of vested interest groups (such as the advertising, alcohol, road, war, pharmaceuticals, and tobacco industries); disadvantaged minorities, multiracial work, prison reform; new economics and intermediate technology; public transport, pedestrians, bicycling, road crash prevention, traffic-calming, low-energy lifestyles; and preventative health.
**WHAT IS NOT FUNDED** No support is given for larger charities, those with religious connections, or individuals (except in rare cases – and then only through registered charities or educational bodies). No support to central or local government agencies.
**TYPE OF GRANT** Usually one to three years; sometimes longer.
**RANGE OF GRANTS** £1,000–£2,000
**SAMPLE GRANTS Previous beneficiaries have included:** Scarman Trust; Roadpeace; Public Interest Research Centre; Earth Resources; Parents for Children; Parent to Parent; Slower Speeds Trust; Prisoners' Wives; Pesticide Action Network; BackCare; and Shelter Winter Night.
**FINANCES** Year 2013/14 Income £19,862 Grants £200,000 Grants to organisations £200,000
**TRUSTEE** David Rennie.
**HOW TO APPLY** Apply writing to the correspondent. Proposals should be summarised on one page with one or two more pages of supporting information. The trust states that it regrettably only has time to reply to the very few applications it is able to fund.
**WHO TO APPLY TO** David Rennie, Trustee, 12 St Catherine Street, Cupar, Fife KY15 4HN *Tel.* 01334 653777 *email* enquiries@pagan.co.uk

## ■ The 1989 Willan Charitable Trust

**CC NO** 802749    **ESTABLISHED** 1989
**WHERE FUNDING CAN BE GIVEN** Worldwide, but in practice mainly the north east of England.
**WHO CAN BENEFIT** Registered charities for the benefit of children; people with disabilities; carers; volunteers; refugees; and offenders.
**WHAT IS FUNDED** Grants are given to: advance the education of children and help children in need; benefit people with physical or mental disabilities and alleviate hardship and distress either generally or individually; and further medical research.
**WHAT IS NOT FUNDED** The website gives the following information: Note that grants will not be available to fund: individuals; statutory organisations including schools or activities eligible for public funding; trips abroad; and projects focused on heritage and the environment, religion and the promotion of faith, scientific and/or medical research (unless these address deprivation and/or enrich local communities and improve local quality of life). Applicants that do not provide feedback on previous awards from the 1989 Willan Charitable Trust within the required timescale will not generally be considered for further funding.
**RANGE OF GRANTS** £500–£10,000
**SAMPLE GRANTS Previous beneficiaries have included:** SAFC Foundation and Cancer Connexions (£10,000 each); Amble Multi Agency Crime Prevention Initiative (£6,000); Durham City Centre Youth Project, The Children's Society and the Calvert Trust (£5,000 each); Chester le Street Youth Centre (£4,000); Different Strokes North East, Northern Roots and People and Drugs (£3,000 each); Leukaemia Research and Coast Video Club (£2,000 each); Northumberland Mountain Rescue and the Association of British Poles (£1,000 each); and Healthwise and Newcastle Gang Show (£500).
**FINANCES** Year 2013/14 Income £542,659 Grants £527,381 Grants to organisations £522,381 Assets £17,228,716
**TRUSTEES** Francis A. Chapman; Alex Ohlsson; Willan Trustee Ltd.
**HOW TO APPLY** Apply in writing to the correspondent at the Community Foundation Serving Tyne and Wear. Refer to the very helpful website for full details before making application.
**WHO TO APPLY TO** Community Foundation Tyne and Wear and Northumberland, 9th Floor, Cale Cross House, 156 Pilgrim Street, Newcastle upon Tyne NE1 6SU *Tel.* 0191 222 0945 *Fax* 0191 230 0689 *email* mp@communityfoundation.org.uk

## ■ The 29th May 1961 Charitable Trust

**CC NO** 200198    **ESTABLISHED** 1961
**WHERE FUNDING CAN BE GIVEN** UK, with a special interest in the Warwickshire/Birmingham/Coventry area.
**WHO CAN BENEFIT** Charitable organisations in the UK. People who are socially disadvantaged may be favoured.
**WHAT IS FUNDED** General charitable purposes across a broad spectrum, including: art, leisure and youth; health; social welfare; education and training; homelessness and housing; offenders; and conservation and protection.
**WHAT IS NOT FUNDED** Non-registered charities and individuals.

**TYPE OF GRANT** One-off, recurring and some spread over two to three years. Grants are given for capital and revenue purposes.
**RANGE OF GRANTS** £500–£250,000, but the great majority are less than £10,000.
**SAMPLE GRANTS** Abbeyfields West Midlands, Birmingham Settlement, Castel Froma, Crisis, Coventry Cyrenians, Federation of London Youth Clubs, Heart of England Community Foundation, Hope 4 Rugby, Life Path Trust, Macmillan Cancer Support, Monte San Martino Trust, NACRO, St Basil's Centre, Scope, The Connection at St Martins, University of Warwick, Coventry and Warwickshire Awards Trust, Warwickshire Association of Youth Clubs and World Monuments Fund.
**FINANCES** Year 2013/14 Income £3,416,822 Grants £5,321,835 Grants to organisations £5,321,835 Assets £110,357,632
**TRUSTEES** Vanni Emanuele Treves; Andrew C. Jones; Elizabeth Rantzen; Paul Varney.
**OTHER INFORMATION** Full details of grants awarded are shown in a separate report entitled Grants Awarded 2013/14 which is available from the charity at its correspondent address.
**HOW TO APPLY** To the secretary in writing, enclosing in triplicate the most recent annual report and accounts. Trustees normally meet in February, May, August and November. Due to the large number of applications received, they cannot be acknowledged.
**WHO TO APPLY TO** Vanni Emanuele Treves, Trustee, Ryder Court, 14 Ryder Street, London SW1Y 6QB *Tel.* 020 7024 9034 *email* enquiries@29may1961charity.org.uk

## ■ 4 Charity Foundation
**CC NO** 1077143  **ESTABLISHED** 1999
**WHERE FUNDING CAN BE GIVEN** UK and Israel.
**WHO CAN BENEFIT** Jewish charities and causes.
**WHAT IS FUNDED** Religious activities and education.
**SAMPLE GRANTS** Previous grants include those to: the American Jewish Joint Distribution Committee (£78,000); the Millennium Trust (£66,000); Keren Yehoshua V'Yisroel (£43,000); Project Seed (£35,000); World Jewish Relief (£29,000); Menorah Grammar School (£27,000); British Friends of Jaffa Institute (£23,000); Friends of Mir (£19,000); Heichal Hatorah Foundation (£15,000); Chai Life Line Cancer Care (£12,000); Jewish Care (£11,000); and British Friends of Ezer Mizion (£10,000).
**FINANCES** Year 2013/14 Income £7,036,092 Grants £1,136,112 Grants to organisations £1,136,112 Assets £15,506,302
**TRUSTEES** Jacob Schimmel; Marc Schimmel; D. Rabson; Anna Schimmel.
**HOW TO APPLY** This trust does not respond to unsolicited applications.
**WHO TO APPLY TO** Jacob Schimmel, Trustee, Suite 137, Devonshire House, 582 Honeypot Lane, Stanmore, Middlesex HA7 1JS *Tel.* 020 8732 5560 *email* four4charities@gmail.com

# A

## ■ A. W. Charitable Trust
**CC NO** 283322 **ESTABLISHED** 1961
**WHERE FUNDING CAN BE GIVEN** London, Gateshead, Manchester and Salford; Israel.
**WHO CAN BENEFIT** Jewish educational and religious organisations; registered charities.
**WHAT IS FUNDED** General charitable purposes.
**SAMPLE GRANTS Previous beneficiaries have included:** TET; Asser Bishvil Foundation; Chevras Oneg Shabbos-Yomtov; Friends of Mir; CML; Tomchei Shabbos Manchester; British Friends of Kupat Hair; Purim Fund; Beenstock Home; and Zoreya Tzedokos.
**FINANCES** Year 2013/14 Income £14,023,015 Grants £4,198,977 Grants to organisations £4,198,977 Assets £115,836,595
**TRUSTEES** Rabbi Aubrey Weis; Rachel Weis; Sir Weis.
**HOW TO APPLY** Apply in writing to the correspondent. The trust considers 'all justified applications for support of educational establishments, places of worship and other charitable activities'. Each application and request is considered on its own merit.
**WHO TO APPLY TO** Rabbi Aubrey Weis, Trustee, 1 Allandale Court, Waterpark Road, Manchester M7 4JL *Tel.* 0161 740 0116

## ■ The Aberbrothock Skea Trust (formerly known as Aberbrothock Charitable Trust)
**SC NO** SC039202 **ESTABLISHED** 1971/2008
**WHERE FUNDING CAN BE GIVEN** East of Scotland, north of the Firth of Tay.
**WHO CAN BENEFIT** Organisations benefitting the community with charitable status.
**WHAT IS FUNDED** Children/young people; disability; environment/conservation; hospitals/hospices; and medical research are all considered.
**WHAT IS NOT FUNDED** The geographical restriction is strictly adhered to. Applications from outside the area, and/or from individuals, will not be considered.
**TYPE OF GRANT** One-off, including project, research, capital and core costs.
**RANGE OF GRANTS** Up to £2,500.
**SAMPLE GRANTS Previous beneficiaries have included:** Colon Cancer Care, Dundee Heritage Trust, International League of Horses, Kids Out, Princess Royal Trust and Red Cross.
**FINANCES** Year 2013/14 Income £131,690 Grants £110,000 Grants to organisations £110,000
**TRUSTEES** Mr G. McNicol; Mrs A. T. L. Grant; Mr D. Dunlop; Mr E. Steven; Mr I. Townsend; Lady F. Fraser.
**OTHER INFORMATION** Although the income remains around the same, the grant total changes every year.
**HOW TO APPLY** Apply in writing to the correspondent. The trustees meet to consider grants in March, July and December.
**WHO TO APPLY TO** The Trustees, Thorntons Law LLP, Brothockbank House, Arbroath, Angus DD11 1NE *Tel.* 01241 872683

## ■ Aberdeen Asset Management Charitable Foundation
**SC NO** SC042597 **ESTABLISHED** 2011
**WHERE FUNDING CAN BE GIVEN** UK and overseas where the company has a presence.
**WHO CAN BENEFIT** Registered charities and non-profit organisations.
**WHAT IS FUNDED** Education, social welfare, children and young people.
**WHAT IS NOT FUNDED** The foundation does not support political causes, parties or organisations or charities with a religious focus.
**FINANCES** Year 2012/13 Income £557,500 Grants £682,000 Grants to organisations £682,000 Assets £683,000
**TRUSTEES** Anne Richards; Paul Aggett; Gary Marshall; Samantha Walker; Hugh Young.
**OTHER INFORMATION** The 2012/13 accounts were the latest available at the time of writing.
**HOW TO APPLY** Application forms are available to download from the foundation's page on the company's website. Completed application forms should be emailed to the foundation for consideration.
**WHO TO APPLY TO** Anne Richards, Trustee, 10 Queen's Terrace, Aberdeen AB10 1YG *Tel.* 01224 631999 *Fax* 01224 647010 *email* foundation.uk@aberdeen-asset.com *Website* www.aberdeen-asset.com/aam.nsf/foundation/home

## ■ The Aberdeen Endowments Trust
**SC NO** SC010507 **ESTABLISHED** 1909
**WHERE FUNDING CAN BE GIVEN** The former City and Royal Burgh of Aberdeen (i.e. pre-1975)
**WHO CAN BENEFIT** Persons of organisations which belong to the former City and Royal Burgh of Aberdeen.
**WHAT IS FUNDED** Education and the arts. The main purpose of the trust is to give financial assistance to individuals for educational purposes.
**WHAT IS NOT FUNDED** No grants are given to people or organisations from outside the former City and Royal Burgh of Aberdeen.
**RANGE OF GRANTS** Average grant is less than £1,000.
**FINANCES** Year 2013 Income £952,000 Grants £600,000 Grants to organisations £600,000
**OTHER INFORMATION** The grant total is for individuals and organisations; we have no breakdown for these.
**HOW TO APPLY** Application forms are available from the correspondent. The Benefactions Committee of the trust, which makes financial awards, normally meets nine or ten times a year.
**WHO TO APPLY TO** David Murdoch, Clerk, 19 Albert Street, Aberdeen AB25 1QF *Tel.* 01224 640194

## ■ The Aberdeen Foundation
**CC NO** 1151506
**WHERE FUNDING CAN BE GIVEN** UK and Israel; overseas including Chile and USA.
**WHO CAN BENEFIT** Charitable organisations.
**WHAT IS FUNDED** General charitable purposes; education and training; social welfare.
**FINANCES** Year 2013/14 Income £60,184,814 Grants £3,626,239 Grants to organisations £3,626,239 Assets £53,060,381
**TRUSTEES** Irwin Weiler; Albert Friedberg; Derek Zissman; Nancy Friedberg.

OTHER INFORMATION Grants made during the year totalled just over £3.6 million. A list of beneficiaries was not included in the 2013/14 accounts.
HOW TO APPLY Apply in writing to the correspondent. Detailed enquiries are made into all applications received and all grants are approved by the trustees.
WHO TO APPLY TO Derek Zissman, Trustee, 6 Lyttelton Road, London N2 0EF *Tel.* 020 7722 1906 *email* aberdeenfoundation@gmail.com

## ■ The Aberdeenshire Educational Trust Scheme

SC NO SC028382   ESTABLISHED 1999
WHERE FUNDING CAN BE GIVEN The former county of Aberdeen.
WHO CAN BENEFIT Individuals in education, schools and further education centres, as well as to clubs and other organisations.
WHAT IS FUNDED Providing and maintaining playing fields and other sports facilities including equipment; schools and further education centres to assist in providing special equipment; clubs, societies and organisations which include amongst their activities work of an educational nature; schools and organisations to assist education in art, music and drama; individuals and bodies to undertake educational experiments and research which will be for the benefit of people belonging to Aberdeen County. Help may also be given towards 'regional and national enterprises of an educational nature'.
RANGE OF GRANTS Small grants of £200–£230.
SAMPLE GRANTS Grants for individuals to attend school trips (Maximum awarded: £230); Grants to individuals going to study at further education institutes (Maximum awarded: £200)
FINANCES *Year* 2013/14 *Income* £92,000
*Grants* £51,000 *Grants to organisations* £51,000 *Assets* £3,203,000
TRUSTEES Isobel Davidson; Jean Dick; Susie Lyon
HOW TO APPLY Apply via a form available from the correspondent. Full guidelines are also available upon request from the trust.
WHO TO APPLY TO The Correspondent, Aberdeenshire Council, Woodhill House, Westburn Road, Aberdeen AB16 5GB

## ■ ABF The Soldiers' Charity

CC NO 1146420   ESTABLISHED 1944
WHERE FUNDING CAN BE GIVEN Worldwide.
WHO CAN BENEFIT Support and benefit of people serving, or who have served, in the British Army, or their families/dependants.
WHAT IS FUNDED Supporting individuals through the Regimental and Corps Benevolence Funds, and other military and national charities which look after the needs of the serving and retired army community.
TYPE OF GRANT One-off grants.
SAMPLE GRANTS Combat Stress (£365,000); Regular Forces Employment Association and SSAFA (£205,000 each); Erskine Hospital (£150,000); Alabare Care and Support (£30,000); Armed Forces and Veterans Launchpad in Newcastle and Community Self Build Agency, Bristol (£25,000 each); My Daddy is a Soldier Adventures (£2,000).
FINANCES *Year* 2013/14 *Income* £14,454,275
*Grants* £7,934,140 *Grants to organisations* £2,931,752 *Assets* £45,563,222
TRUSTEES Maj. Gen. George Kennedy; Stephen Clark; Guy Davies; Maj. Gen. Peter Sheppard; Brig. Andrew Freemantle; Allison M. Gallico; Damien Francis; Maj. Richard Davis; Paul Hearn; Maj. Gen. Malcolm Wood; Glenn Haughton; Mary Fagan.
OTHER INFORMATION £3.3 million went to charities; £5.3 million was awarded for the benefit of individuals.
HOW TO APPLY Individual cases should be referred initially to the appropriate Corps or Regimental Association. Charities should apply in writing and enclose the latest annual report and accounts. Also refer to the charity's website for current eligibility criteria and application processes. Initial telephone enquiries are welcome.
WHO TO APPLY TO Roger Musson, Director of Finance and Resources, Mountbarrow House, 6–20 Elizabeth Street, London SW1W 9RB *Tel.* 0845 241 4820 *Fax* 0845 241 4821 *email* rmusson@soldierscharity.org *Website* www.soldierscharity.org

## ■ The Acacia Charitable Trust

CC NO 274275   ESTABLISHED 1977
WHERE FUNDING CAN BE GIVEN UK and Israel.
WHO CAN BENEFIT Registered charities.
WHAT IS FUNDED Educational and medical charities in the UK. Jewish charities, both in the UK and the State of Israel.
WHAT IS NOT FUNDED Individuals.
TYPE OF GRANT Core and project costs will be considered.
RANGE OF GRANTS Up to £36,000, although most for under £5,000.
SAMPLE GRANTS The Jewish Museum (£36,500); World Jewish Relief (£6,000); Spanish and Portuguese Jews' Congregation (£3,700); Jewish Care, (£2,800); Community Security Trust, Parayhouse School (£2,000 each); Norwood Children's Home (£1,000); NSPCC (£500); Royal Academy of Arts (£150); Wormwood Scrubbs Pony Centre, Shelter (£100 each).
FINANCES *Year* 2013/14 *Income* £66,849
*Grants* £67,618 *Grants to organisations* £67,618 *Assets* £1,821,291
TRUSTEES Kenneth Rubens; Angela Gillian Rubens; Simon Rubens; Paul Rubens.
HOW TO APPLY Apply in writing to the correspondent.
WHO TO APPLY TO The Secretary, C/o H. W. Fisher and Co, Acre House, 11–15 William Road, London NW1 3ER *Tel.* 020 7486 1884 *email* acacia@dircon.co.uk

## ■ Access Sport

CC NO 1104687   ESTABLISHED 2004
WHERE FUNDING CAN BE GIVEN Throughout the UK.
WHO CAN BENEFIT Children and young people; disability; socially and economically disadvantaged people.
WHAT IS FUNDED Promotion of health 'by increasing sport participation opportunities for young people in the UK through local sports clubs in order to tackle social exclusion, inactivity and obesity, particularly in disadvantaged areas'.
TYPE OF GRANT One-off and ongoing grants to organisations.
FINANCES *Year* 2013/14 *Income* £858,771
*Grants* £273,867 *Grants to organisations* £273,867 *Assets* £230,992
TRUSTEES Fraser Hardie; John Sarsby; Michael Allen; Neil Robinson; Neil Goulden; Grace

# Achisomoch

Clancey; Tina Kokkinos; Phil Veasey; Timothy Jones; Greg Searle; Keith Wishart; Mark Donnelly.

**HOW TO APPLY** Contact details for each of the projects can be found on the trust's website. General enquiries should be directed to the correspondent.

**WHO TO APPLY TO** Sue Wheeler, Correspondent, 3 Durham Yard, Teesdale Street, London E2 6QF *Tel.* 020 7993 9883 *email* mark.hardie@accesssport.co.uk *Website* www.accesssport.co.uk

## ■ Achisomoch Aid Company Limited

**CC NO** 278387  **ESTABLISHED** 1979
**WHERE FUNDING CAN BE GIVEN** UK and overseas.
**WHO CAN BENEFIT** Jewish religious charities.
**WHAT IS FUNDED** The advancement of religion in accordance with the Jewish faith.
**SAMPLE GRANTS Previous beneficiaries have included:** the Ah Trust, Beis Malka Trust, Chevras Maoz Ladol, Comet Charities Ltd, Davis Elias Charitable Trust, Havenpoint Ltd, Heritage Retreats, Jewish Educational Trust, Lolev Charitable Trust, Menorah Primary School, Michlala Jerusalem College, SOFT, Tomchei Cholim Trust and Yad Eliezer – Israel.
**FINANCES** *Year* 2013/14 *Income* £11,257,478 *Grants* £10,878,223 *Grants to organisations* £10,878,223 *Assets* £3,722,137
**TRUSTEES** Jack Emanuel; Yitzchock Katz; Michael Hockenbroch.
**OTHER INFORMATION** The following information about how the trust operates is given on the its website: 'Achisomoch is a charity voucher agency – it is like a bank. You open an account with us and then pay money into the account. You are given a cheque (voucher) book and can then make (charitable) payments by using these vouchers. As a charity in its own right, we can reclaim the tax rebate under Gift Aid to increase the money in your account and available for distribution to charities. Donations, via vouchers can be made only to registered charities. You get regular statements and can arrange to speak to client services for any help or special instructions.'
**HOW TO APPLY** Apply in writing to the correspondent.
**WHO TO APPLY TO** Mark Katz, Trustee, 26 Hoop Lane, London NW11 8BU *Tel.* 020 8731 8988 *email* admin@achisomoch.org *Website* www.achisomoch.org

## ■ The ACT Foundation

**CC NO** 1068617  **ESTABLISHED** 1998
**WHERE FUNDING CAN BE GIVEN** UK and overseas.
**WHO CAN BENEFIT** Health, welfare and housing.
**WHAT IS FUNDED** Grants generally fall into the following areas: building – funding modifications to homes, schools, hospices, etc.; equipment – provision of specialised wheelchairs, other mobility aids and equipment including medical equipment to assist independent living; financial assistance – towards the cost of short-term respite breaks at a registered respite centre. Projects that intend to be a platform for continuing services will be expected to demonstrate sustainability. ACT would be concerned to be a sole funder of projects that require ongoing support.
**WHAT IS NOT FUNDED** The foundation will not make grants: to replace statutory funding; to pay for work that has already commenced or equipment already purchased or on order; towards the operating costs of other charities except in connection with setting up new services; to charities that have not been registered for at least three years; for projects which promote a particular religion or faith; to community centres and youth clubs except where those served are in special need of help (e.g. the elderly or persons with special needs); to local authorities; to umbrella or grant-making organisations except where they undertake special assessments not readily available from the foundation's own resources; to universities and colleges, and grant-maintained, private or local education authority schools or their PTAs, except if those schools are for students with special needs; for costs associated with political or publicity campaigns.
**SAMPLE GRANTS** Whizz-Kidz (£110,000); Autism West Midlands (£100,000); Treloar Trust (£75,000); First Step Trust (£47,000); Core Arts (£25,000); Hollybank Trust (£12,000); Surrey Care Trust (£7,000).
**FINANCES** *Year* 2013/14 *Income* £17,852,560 *Grants* £715,487 *Grants to organisations* £357,000 *Assets* £59,521,051
**TRUSTEES** Paul Nield; John J. O'Sullivan; Michael Street; Christine Erwood; Robert F. White; Denis Taylor; Russell Meadows; Andrew Ross; Colin Clarkson.
**OTHER INFORMATION** The grant total was divided almost 50/50 between individuals and organisations.
**HOW TO APPLY** The foundation's website provides detailed information on the application process and applicants are advised to visit the website in the first instance. It states: 'Application by registered charities and overseas charitable organisations has to be by way of letter on the organisation's headed paper and should: give a brief description of your organisation including any statutory or voluntary registration; provide a summary of the work you plan to undertake with the grant, together with a cost breakdown, plans and/or specification if available and a summary of the key milestones for the work; provide information on why you need to do this work and what would happen if you were unable to do it; give details of any other UK-based support received or pledged for your project; specify what you expect the results of the work to be and the number of beneficiaries helped; tell us how you plan to evaluate whether the work achieved its goals; tell us if the work will require capital and/or on-going operational funding and if so how you plan to meet these costs. In addition you need to attach the following financial information to the letter: a cashflow projection of income and expenditure budget for the work; details of any income already raised for the work and income outstanding and where you plan to raise it from; your latest annual report and accounts. You can apply for a grant at any time and for any amount, **however at the time of sending your application to us, you must confirm your acceptance of our Grant Terms & Conditions by signing at the bottom of the page and enclosing a copy with your application.** Trustees meet four times a year but procedures exist to give approvals between meeting dates if necessary. We do not publish the dates of trustees' meetings. We will send you an acknowledgement letter within one week of receiving your application. If your proposal is either in an unacceptable form, or ineligible, or a low priority, we will tell you in this letter. We will assess all acceptable applications and we

may contact you for further information and/or make a personal visit. In the case of charitable bodies we may also ask for a presentation. We aim to make decisions on grants of up to £50,000 within one month of receiving your application. Decisions on grants over £50,000 can take up to three months. If the application is for an emergency you may request a faster timescale and we will do our best to assist.'

WHO TO APPLY TO James Kerr, Grants Manager, 61 Thames Street, Windsor, Berkshire SL4 1QW *Tel.* 01753 753900 *Fax* 01753 753901 *email* info@theactfoundation.co.uk *Website* www.theactfoundation.co.uk

## ■ Action Medical Research

CC NO 208701   ESTABLISHED 1952
WHERE FUNDING CAN BE GIVEN UK.
WHO CAN BENEFIT University departments, hospitals and research institutes for specific research projects.
WHAT IS FUNDED Research focusing on child health including problems affecting pregnancy, childbirth, babies, children and young people. Within this a broad spectrum of research is supported with the objective of preventing disease and disability and of alleviating physical disability.
WHAT IS NOT FUNDED The charity does not provide grants towards: service provision or audit studies; grants purely for higher education, e.g. BSc/MSc/PhD course fees and subsistence costs; grants for medical or dental electives; grants for work undertaken outside the UK; any indirect costs such as administrative or other overheads imposed by the university or other institution; costs associated with advertising and recruitment; 'top up' funding for work supported by other funding bodies; costs to attend conferences and meetings (current Action Medical Research grant holders may apply separately); grants to other charities – applications would normally come directly from research teams and projects need to be passed through Action Medical Research's scientific peer review system; grants for research into complementary/alternative medicine; grants on how best to train clinical staff; grants for psychosocial aspects of treatment; grants on social research, family relationships or socioeconomic research; grants for very basic research with little likelihood of clinical impact within the short to medium term. Applicants based in core funded units can apply but need to demonstrate added value.
TYPE OF GRANT Research comprising: project grants and Research Training Fellowship scheme.
RANGE OF GRANTS The average award is about £80,000. It is unusual to fund projects over £150,000 in their entirety.
SAMPLE GRANTS Department of Pharmacology and Sir William Dunn School of Pathology both at the University of Oxford (£200,000 each); University of Manchester and St Mary's Hospital Manchester (£134,000); Molecular Immunology Unit, Institute of Child Health, London (£106,000); Royal College of Obstetricians and Gynaecologists, London (£5,000).
FINANCES *Year* 2013 *Income* £7,929,189 *Grants* £3,005,170 *Grants to organisations* £3,005,170 *Assets* £8,308,585
TRUSTEES Valerie Remington-Hobbs; Prof. Sarah Bray; Charles Jackson; Mark Gardiner; Philip Hodkinson; Esther Alderson; Caroline Hume-Kendall; Nick Peters; Rachel Molho; Luke Bordewich.

PUBLICATIONS Newsletter; medical conditions leaflets.
HOW TO APPLY Full details of applying for both project and research grants are given on the charity's website together with current closing dates. Read the guidelines (given in the general section of this entry) before making application online.
WHO TO APPLY TO Martin Richardson, Vincent House, 31 North Parade, Horsham, West Sussex RH12 2DP *Tel.* 01403 210406 *Fax* 01403 210541 *email* info@action.org.uk *Website* www.action.org.uk

## ■ The Company of Actuaries' Charitable Trust Fund

CC NO 280702   ESTABLISHED 1980
WHERE FUNDING CAN BE GIVEN UK and overseas, with a preference for the City of London.
WHO CAN BENEFIT Charitable organisations and individuals involved in, or training for, a career in actuary.
WHAT IS FUNDED Support for people who are elderly or who have disabilities; charities helping children and young people; those involved in treating medical conditions or funding medical research; other worthy charities, such as those working with people who are in need.
WHAT IS NOT FUNDED The propagation of religious or political beliefs; the maintenance of historic buildings or for conservation. The trustees do not usually support an organisation which has received a grant from the fund in the previous 24 months.
RANGE OF GRANTS £500–£5,000, with larger amounts given where liverymen have a significant connection.
SAMPLE GRANTS Royal Society (£54,000); Children's Liver Disease Foundation and Narcolepsy UK (£5,000 each); Guildhall School of Music and Drama (£4,500); The Brainwave Centre Limited (£3,500); East Anglia Children's Hospices (£2,500); Edmonton Sea Cadets and The Holst Birthplace Trust (£2,000 each); Action Medical Research, Independence at Home and Lakelands Hospice (£1,000 each); Auditory Verbal and Birmingham Centre for Art Therapies £500 each).
FINANCES *Year* 2013/14 *Income* £234,500 *Grants* £234,500 *Grants to organisations* £234,500 *Assets* £363,483
TRUSTEES Michael Turner; Sally Bridgeland; Geraldine Kaye; Michael Pomery; Alan Smith; George Yoxhall.
HOW TO APPLY Apply on the form which can be downloaded from the fund's website.
WHO TO APPLY TO Patrick O'Keeffe, Honorary Almoner, Broomyhurst, Shobley, Ringwood, Hampshire BH24 3HT *Tel.* 01425 472810 *email* almoner.cact@btinternet.com *Website* www.companyofactuaries.co.uk/ charitabletrust

## ■ The Adamson Trust

SC NO SC016517   ESTABLISHED 1946
WHERE FUNDING CAN BE GIVEN UK, but preference will be given to requests on behalf of Scottish children.
WHO CAN BENEFIT Children under 18 with a physical or mental disability, both groups and individuals.
WHAT IS FUNDED Assistance with holidays – grants may be given to the parent(s) of children or as

block grants; for example, to the special needs unit of a school.
TYPE OF GRANT Usually one-off.
SAMPLE GRANTS **Previous beneficiaries have included:** Barnardo's Dundee Family Support Team, Children's Hospice Association Scotland, Lady Hoare Trust for Physically Disabled Children, Hopscotch Holidays, Over the Wall Gang Group, Peak Holidays, React, Scotland Yard Adventure Centre, Sense Scotland, Special Needs Adventure Play Ground and Scottish Spina Bifida Association.
FINANCES Year 2013/14 Income £75,638 Grants £80,000 Grants to organisations £80,000
TRUSTEE Information not available.
OTHER INFORMATION Around £80,000 is given in grants each year to both organisations and individuals.
HOW TO APPLY Apply in writing to the correspondent. For organisations a copy of the latest audited accounts should be included together with details of the organisation, the number of children who would benefit and the proposed holiday. For individuals evidence is required from a professional health or social worker.
WHO TO APPLY TO Edward Elworthy, Correspondent, PO Box 26334, Crieff, Perthshire PH7 9AB email edward@elworthy.net Website www.theadamsontrust.co.uk

■ **The Victor Adda Foundation**
CC NO 291456   ESTABLISHED 1984
WHERE FUNDING CAN BE GIVEN UK, but in practice Greenwich.
WHO CAN BENEFIT Charitable organisations.
WHAT IS FUNDED This trust mainly supports the Fan Museum in Greenwich.
SAMPLE GRANTS The Fan Museum Trust (£30,000); and Genizah Research Unit (£4,000).
FINANCES Year 2013/14 Income £80,435 Grants £34,000 Grants to organisations £34,000 Assets £1,525,075
TRUSTEES Helene Alexander; Susannah Alexander; Jeremy Hawes; Linda Estelle.
HOW TO APPLY Apply in writing to the correspondent. Only successful applications are notified of a decision.
WHO TO APPLY TO Kleinwort Benson Trustees Limited, c/o Kleinwort Benson Trustees Ltd, 14 St George Street, London W1S 1FE Tel. 020 3207 7091

■ **The Addleshaw Goddard Charitable Trust**
CC NO 286887   ESTABLISHED 1983
WHERE FUNDING CAN BE GIVEN Greater London, Manchester and Leeds.
WHO CAN BENEFIT The legal profession and general charitable purposes.
WHAT IS FUNDED The charity states that it makes grants to: promote general charitable purposes in the City of London, especially education, health and poverty-related causes; promote charitable objects connected with the legal profession, and help individuals in need in that profession; advance legal education in all its aspects as far as it is a charitable cause.
RANGE OF GRANTS £100–£18,000
SAMPLE GRANTS Bleakholt Animal Sanctuary – Manchester (£17,500); St Joseph's Hospice – London and Martin House Children's Hospital – Leeds (£15,000 each); Habitat for Humanity (£8,500); The Lowry Centre Trust (£500); and Wykebeck Primary School (£300).
FINANCES Year 2013/14 Income £64,054 Grants £66,156 Grants to organisations £66,156 Assets £146,531
TRUSTEES Bruce Lightbody; Jonathan Cheney; Monica Burch; Lisa Rodgers; Pervinder Kaur; Christopher Noel.
HOW TO APPLY Apply in writing to the correspondent.
WHO TO APPLY TO Christopher Noel, Trustee, Addleshaw Goddard LLP, 100 Barbirolli Square, Manchester M2 3AB Tel. 020 7788 5504 Fax 0161 934 6060 email christopher.noel@addleshawgoddard.com

■ **Adenfirst Ltd**
CC NO 291647   ESTABLISHED 1984
WHERE FUNDING CAN BE GIVEN Worldwide.
WHO CAN BENEFIT Jewish organisations only.
WHAT IS FUNDED Jewish causes related to education, medical care, relief of poverty and the advancement of religion.
RANGE OF GRANTS £0–£35,000
SAMPLE GRANTS Previously: Beis Aaron Trust (£30,000); Ezer Vehatzolo and Kahal Chassidim Wiznitz (£20,000 each); and Beis Rochel D'Satmar, Lolev Charitable Trust and Mercaz Hatorah Belz Machnovke (£10,000 each).
FINANCES Year 2013 Income £167,842 Grants £99,000 Grants to organisations £99,000 Assets £1,500,439
TRUSTEES Mrs H. F. Bondi; Leonard Bondi; Mrs R. Cymerman; Sylvia Cymerman; Ian Heitner; Michael Cymerman; Sarah Heitner.
OTHER INFORMATION Latest accounts available from the Charity Commission were for 2011.
HOW TO APPLY Apply in writing to the correspondent.
WHO TO APPLY TO Leonard Bondi, Trustee, C/O 479 Holloway Road, London N7 6LE Tel. 020 7272 2255

■ **The Adint Charitable Trust**
CC NO 265290   ESTABLISHED 1973
WHERE FUNDING CAN BE GIVEN Worldwide, in practice UK.
WHO CAN BENEFIT Registered charities.
WHAT IS FUNDED Health and social welfare.
WHAT IS NOT FUNDED Individuals.
TYPE OF GRANT One-off grants and recurrent grants for more than three years are considered, for capital costs (including buildings) and core costs.
RANGE OF GRANTS £50–£15,000. Grants are usually for £10,000 and £5,000.
SAMPLE GRANTS ABF – The Soldiers Charity, Blind Veterans UK, British Red Cross, Cancer Research UK, Samaritans, Scope and Shelter (£10,000 each); British Lung Foundation, Elizabeth Fitzroy Support, Limbless Association and Royal London Society for Blind People (£5,000 each); Noah's Ark Children's Hospice (£1,000).
FINANCES Year 2013/14 Income £229,146 Grants £301,000 Grants to organisations £301,000 Assets £7,357,892
TRUSTEES Anthony Edwards; Margaret Edwards; Douglas Oram; Brian Pate.
HOW TO APPLY Apply in writing to the correspondent. Each applicant should make its own case in the way it considers best, but the application should include full details of the applicant charity. The trust states that it cannot enter into correspondence and unsuccessful applicants will not be notified.

WHO TO APPLY TO Douglas Oram, Trustee, Suite 42, 571 Finchley Road, London NW3 7BN email adintct@gmail.com

## ■ The Adnams Charity

**CC NO** 1000203 **ESTABLISHED** 1990
**WHERE FUNDING CAN BE GIVEN** Within a 25-mile radius of St Edmund's Church, Southwold.
**WHO CAN BENEFIT** Small local projects.
**WHAT IS FUNDED** General charitable purposes. The charity gives support to a wide variety of organisations including those involved with health and social welfare, education, recreation, the arts, environment and conservation and historic buildings.
**WHAT IS NOT FUNDED** The charity does not normally make grants to religious organisations or private clubs unless they can demonstrate that the purpose of the grant is for something of clear public benefit, accessible to all. It does not provide raffle prizes or sponsorship of any kind. No grants are made to individuals. However, public bodies and charities may apply on behalf of individuals. Grants are not made in successive years.
**TYPE OF GRANT** The trustees prefer applications for specific items. Grants are generally of a one-off nature. The trustees are reluctant to give grants to cover ongoing running costs, although in very exceptional circumstances they may do so.
**RANGE OF GRANTS** Normally £100–£2,500.
**SAMPLE GRANTS** Fen Park Primary School (£1,400); Prisoners' Education Trust (£1,500); Leeway Domestic Violence and Abuse Service (£850); Handicapped Children's Action Group (£750); The Poetry Trust (£1,250); Woodton Playing Field Association (£1,300); Horham and Athelington Village Hall (£500); Southwold Museum (£2,500); East Coast Hospice (£10,000).
**FINANCES** Year 2013/14 Income £74,540 Grants £62,381 Grants to organisations £62,381 Assets £14,860
**TRUSTEES** Jonathan Adnams, Chair; Lizzy Cantwell; Guy Heald; Emma Hibbert; Melvyn Horn; Simon Loftus; Andy Wood; Alison Kibble; Ann Cross.
**OTHER INFORMATION** 63 grants were made in 2013/14.
**HOW TO APPLY** Application forms are available on request to the Charity Administrator. Grants are considered at quarterly meetings, in January, April, July and October. Application deadlines usually fall in the previous month and are listed on the charity's website.
**WHO TO APPLY TO** Rebecca Abrahall, Charity Administrator, Adnams plc, Sole Bay Brewery, East Green, Southwold, Suffolk IP18 6JW Tel. 01502 727200 email charity@adnams.co.uk Website www.adnams.co.uk/charity

## ■ The Adrian Swire Charitable Trust

**CC NO** 800493 **ESTABLISHED** 1988
**WHERE FUNDING CAN BE GIVEN** UK and overseas.
**WHO CAN BENEFIT** Charitable organisations.
**WHAT IS FUNDED** General charitable purposes.
**RANGE OF GRANTS** Up to £60,000.
**SAMPLE GRANTS** The Brain Tumour Charity (£60,000); The Mango Tree (£35,000); Crisis Skylight Oxford (£25,000); Young Musicians Symphony Orchestra – YMSO (£17,500); Ashmolean Museum, European Squirrel Initiative and Wings for Warriors (£10,000 each); Royal Air Force Benevolent Fund (£5,500); Friends of Shakespeare's Church and Warwickshire Association of Youth Clubs (£2,500 each); Spitfire Society and Wantage Choral Society (£1,000 each).
**FINANCES** Year 2013 Income £773,058 Grants £536,050 Grants to organisations £536,050 Assets £22,375,210
**TRUSTEES** Merlin Swire; Sir Martin Dunne; Lady Judith Swire; Martha Allfrey; Richard Leonard; Samuel Swire.
**OTHER INFORMATION** Grants of less than £1,000 each totalled £4,300.
**HOW TO APPLY** Apply in writing to the correspondent explaining how the funds would be used and what would be achieved.
**WHO TO APPLY TO** Sarah Irving, Correspondent, Swire House, 59 Buckingham Gate, London SW1E 6AJ Tel. 020 7834 7717 email Sarah.Irving@jssldn.co.uk

## ■ AF Trust Company

**CC NO** 1060319 **ESTABLISHED** 1996
**WHERE FUNDING CAN BE GIVEN** England.
**WHO CAN BENEFIT** Higher education institutions.
**WHAT IS FUNDED** Charitable purposes connected with the provision of higher education.
**WHAT IS NOT FUNDED** Individuals.
**SAMPLE GRANTS** University of Nottingham (£76,000); University of Reading (£60,000); University of Exeter (£8,000); and other institutions (£6,000).
**FINANCES** Year 2013/14 Income £806,507 Grants £150,000 Grants to organisations £150,000 Assets £364,394
**TRUSTEES** Martin Wynne-Jones; Andrew Connolly; David Leah; Carol Wright.
**OTHER INFORMATION** The income figure also relates to funds used to lease buildings from educational establishments and then enter into lease-back arrangements rather than indicating the size of funds available.
**HOW TO APPLY** Apply in writing to the correspondent. However, unsolicited applications are only accepted from higher education institutions within England.
**WHO TO APPLY TO** Paul Welch, Secretary, 34 Chapel Street, Thatcham RG18 4QL

## ■ Age Scotland

**SC NO** SC010100 **ESTABLISHED** 2009
**WHERE FUNDING CAN BE GIVEN** Scotland.
**WHO CAN BENEFIT** Groups for the benefit and welfare of older people.
**WHAT IS FUNDED** Organising special outings or event, purchasing equipment, producing and distributing information, attending/running and event which will benefit older people, start-up costs for new groups, training costs, developing a substantial new project.
**WHAT IS NOT FUNDED** Statutory authorities; commercial organisations; individuals.
**TYPE OF GRANT** Capital; one-off; seed funding start-up costs.
**RANGE OF GRANTS** Up to £10,000.
**SAMPLE GRANTS** Nithsdale Walking Works (£6,500); Volunteer Centre East Lothian (£4,000); Grampian Hospitals Arts Trust (£3,000); Gordon Forum for the Arts (£2,500); Strange Theatre (£2,300); Third Age Computer Fun (£2,000); Penpont Friendship Club (£1,000).
**FINANCES** Year 2013/14 Income £3,968,486 Grants £152,603 Grants to organisations £152,603 Assets £1,631,636

# Age

**TRUSTEES** Paul Adams; George Foulkes; Tom O'Connell; Sue Holloway; Suzanne Munday; Brendan McCormack; Dorry McLaughlin; Alasdair Rutherford; Glenda Watt; Prof. John Williams; Ken Nicholson; Pennie Taylor.
**PUBLICATIONS** A wide range of fact sheets are available on money matters, health and well-being, travel and lifestyle, home and care, and work and learning. Research reports are also published on a number of topics. See the website for full details.
**OTHER INFORMATION** In 2013/14 grants were given to 130 organisations.
**HOW TO APPLY** Applicants are requested to call the freephone telephone number or visit the website for details of current grant programmes and how to apply.
**WHO TO APPLY TO** Katie Docherty, Head of Charity Services, Causewayside House, 160 Causewayside, Edinburgh EH9 1PR *Tel.* 0800 470 8090 *Website* www.ageuk.org.uk/scotland

## ■ Age UK
**CC NO** 1128267   **ESTABLISHED** 1977
**WHERE FUNDING CAN BE GIVEN** UK and overseas
**WHO CAN BENEFIT** Independently constituted, not-for-profit organisations that are accessible to all people in later life. Research organisations.
**WHAT IS FUNDED** The charity administers a variety of grant programmes aimed at organisations working to make life better for older people by addressing people's immediate needs or tackling the root causes of problems they are experiencing. Research grants, designed to increase understanding of the ageing process, of what it means to grow old and the implications for society and the economy, are also made.
**WHAT IS NOT FUNDED** Individuals.
**TYPE OF GRANT** Capital; one-off; running costs; salaries; and start-up costs. Funding is available for up to three years.
**FINANCES** *Year* 2013/14 *Income* £166,629,000 *Grants* £12,589,000 *Grants to organisations* £12,589,000 *Assets* £27,293,000
**TRUSTEES** Dianne Jeffrey, Chair; Dr Bernadette Fuge; Jeremy Greenhalgh; Timothy Hammond; Chris Hughes; Simon Waugh; David Hunter; John Briers; Nick Wilkinson
**PUBLICATIONS** A wide range of fact sheets are available on money matters, health and well-being, travel and lifestyle, home and care and work and learning. Research reports are also published on a number of topics. See the website for full details.
**OTHER INFORMATION** Total grants figure relates to UK charities. There are also extensive grant-making programmes overseas, amounting to £11 million in 2013/14, which are not covered here.
**HOW TO APPLY** For further information on general grant programmes currently open to applications, contact the Grants Team. Applicants interested in research funding should contact the Research Department at Tavis House, 1–6 Tavistock Square, London WC1H 9NA or email research@ageuk.org.uk.
**WHO TO APPLY TO** Grants Unit, Tavis House, 1–6 Tavistock Square, London WC1H 9NA *Tel.* 0800 169 8787 *email* contact@ageuk.org.uk *Website* www.ageuk.org.uk

## ■ Aid to the Church in Need (UK)
**CC NO** 1097984   **ESTABLISHED** 1947
**WHERE FUNDING CAN BE GIVEN** Eastern Europe, Africa, Russia, Asia and South America.
**WHO CAN BENEFIT** Persecuted and suffering Christians, especially Roman Catholics, Russian Orthodox and refugees.
**WHAT IS FUNDED** Religion and pastoral projects.
**WHAT IS NOT FUNDED** Private individuals with schooling; medical or living expenses.
**TYPE OF GRANT** Buildings, capital, core costs, endowment, one-off, project, running costs, salaries and start-up costs.
**FINANCES** *Year* 2013 *Income* £7,589,989 *Grants* £5,434,196 *Grants to organisations* £5,434,196 *Assets* £1,963,843
**TRUSTEES** John Marsden; Lord David Alton; Philipp Habsburg-Lothringen; Graham Hutton; Lisa Sanchez-Corea Simpson.
**PUBLICATIONS** 'Persecuted and Forgotten – A Report on Christians Oppressed for their Faith'
**OTHER INFORMATION** Note: the focus of this charity is the church overseas and that individuals without the backing as required may not apply for funding.
**HOW TO APPLY** Applicants are directed, where possible, to the charity's website where the criteria, guidelines and application process are posted. All applications by individuals must have the backing of a Catholic Bishop or religious superior.
**WHO TO APPLY TO** The Trustees, 12–14 Benhill Avenue, Sutton, Surrey SM1 4DA *Tel.* 020 8642 8668 *email* acn@acnuk.org *Website* www.acnuk.org

## ■ The AIM Foundation
**CC NO** 263294   **ESTABLISHED** 1971
**WHERE FUNDING CAN BE GIVEN** Worldwide, in practice UK.
**WHO CAN BENEFIT** Charitable organisations.
**WHAT IS FUNDED** Healthcare, community development, youth, environmental matters and other charitable activities particularly related to influencing long-term social change.
**WHAT IS NOT FUNDED** Individuals.
**TYPE OF GRANT** Revenue grants: core costs and salaries.
**RANGE OF GRANTS** Up to £135,000.
**SAMPLE GRANTS** New Economics Foundation (£135,000); The Impetus Trust (£50,000); ChildLine NSPCC (£35,000); Health Empowerment Through Nutrition (£20,000); Network for Social Change and The Children's Society (£15,000 each); Wells for India (£10,000); Families in Focus and Freedom from Torture (£5,000 each); Amnesty International (£3,000).
**FINANCES** *Year* 2012/13 *Income* £301,478 *Grants* £393,000 *Grants to organisations* £393,000 *Assets* £10,036,794
**TRUSTEES** Ian Marks; Angela Marks; Nicolas Marks; Joanna Pritchard-Barrett; Caroline Marks; Philippa Bailey.
**OTHER INFORMATION** The latest accounts available at the time of writing (June 2015) were those for 2012/13.
**HOW TO APPLY** It cannot be stressed enough that this foundation 'is proactive in its approach' and does not wish to receive applications. Unsolicited requests for assistance will not be responded to under any circumstance.

WHO TO APPLY TO Sean Grinsted, Francis Clark LLP, Vantage Point, Woodwater Park, Pynes Hill, Exeter EX2 5FD *Tel.* 01392 667000 *email* sean.grinsted@francisclark.co.uk

## ■ The Sylvia Aitken Charitable Trust

**SC NO** SC010556    **ESTABLISHED** 1985
**WHERE FUNDING CAN BE GIVEN** UK, with a preference for Scotland.
**WHO CAN BENEFIT** Registered medical research and welfare charities, and any small local groups – particularly in Scotland.
**WHAT IS FUNDED** General charitable purposes, with a preference for medical and welfare organisations.
**WHAT IS NOT FUNDED** Individuals.
**SAMPLE GRANTS** Previous grant beneficiaries have included: Association for International Cancer Research, Barn Owl Trust, British Lung Foundation, British Stammering Association, the Roy Castle Lung Cancer Foundation, Disabled Living Foundation, Epilepsy Research Trust, Friends of the Lake District, Motor Neurone Disease Association, Network for Surviving Stalking, Royal Scots Dragoon Guards Museum Trust, Sense Scotland, Scottish Child Psychotherapy Trust, Tall Ships Youth Trust, Tenovus Scotland, Wood Green Animal Shelters and Young Minds.
**FINANCES** *Year* 2013/14 *Income* £93,101 *Grants* £300,000 *Grants to organisations* £300,000
**TRUSTEE** Information not available
**HOW TO APPLY** Apply in writing to the correspondent. Applicants should outline the charity's objectives and current projects for which funding may be required. The trustees meet at least twice a year, usually in March/April and September/October.
**WHO TO APPLY TO** The Trustees, Fergusons Chartered Accountants, 24 Woodside, Houston, Renfrewshire PA6 7DD *Tel.* 01505 610412

## ■ The Ajahma Charitable Trust

**CC NO** 273823    **ESTABLISHED** 1977
**WHERE FUNDING CAN BE GIVEN** UK and overseas.
**WHO CAN BENEFIT** Registered charities.
**WHAT IS FUNDED** Development, health, disability, poverty, women's issues, family planning, human rights and social need.
**WHAT IS NOT FUNDED** Large organisations with a turnover above £4 million will not normally be considered; applications with any sort of religious bias; applications which support animal rights/welfare, the arts, medical research, buildings, equipment, local groups or overseas projects where the charity income is less than £500,000 a year. Applications for grants or sponsorship for individuals will not be supported.
**TYPE OF GRANT** Core and running costs, projects and salaries.
**SAMPLE GRANTS** Prisoners Abroad and Pump Aid (£50,000 each); Disability Rights UK and The Size of Wales (£25,000 each); Advocacy for Older People in Greenwich (£9,000); Jan Trust, Safer London Fund and Tender (£6,000 each); Age UK Kensington and Chelsea (£4,500); Headway Groups (£3,500).
**FINANCES** *Year* 2013/14 *Income* £82,228 *Grants* £235,075 *Grants to organisations* £235,075 *Assets* £2,792,760

**TRUSTEES** Jennifer Sheridan; Elizabeth Simpson; James Sinclair Taylor; Carole Pound; Roger Paffard.
**HOW TO APPLY** The trustees have reviewed their grant-making criteria and will now pro-actively seek and select organisations to which they wish to award grants; they will no longer consider unsolicited applications.
**WHO TO APPLY TO** Suzanne Hunt, 275 Dover House Road, London SW15 5BP *Tel.* 020 8788 5388

## ■ The Al Fayed Charitable Foundation

**CC NO** 297114    **ESTABLISHED** 1987
**WHERE FUNDING CAN BE GIVEN** Not defined, in practice, mainly the UK.
**WHO CAN BENEFIT** Mainly children and young people and health.
**WHAT IS FUNDED** Registered charities.
**TYPE OF GRANT** One-off and recurring.
**RANGE OF GRANTS** £1,000–£850,000
**SAMPLE GRANTS** Shooting Star (Chase) (£360,500); West Heath (£222,000); Francis House and Zoe's Place (£180,000 each); Facing the World (£118,000); Action on Hearing Loss (£100,000); Lotus Children's Centre (£80,000); WSPA (£35,000); SPANA and Chelsea and Westminster Hospital (£5,000 each); Kent, Surrey and Sussex Air Ambulance (£2,000); Chernobyl Children (£1,000).
**FINANCES** *Year* 2013 *Income* £1,668,342 *Grants* £1,568,922 *Grants to organisations* £1,562,922 *Assets* £76,999
**TRUSTEES** Mohamed Al-Fayed; Camilla Fayed; Heini Fayed.
**OTHER INFORMATION** In 2013, £6,000 was given in grants to individuals.
**HOW TO APPLY** Apply in writing to the correspondent including the following: name and contact details; an overview of why you are seeking funding; a breakdown of funds sought and a stamped addressed envelope.
**WHO TO APPLY TO** Kate Lovell, 55 Park Lane, London W1K 1QE *email* acf@alfayed.com *Website* www.alfayed.com/philanthropy.aspx

## ■ The Alabaster Trust

**CC NO** 1050568    **ESTABLISHED** 1995
**WHERE FUNDING CAN BE GIVEN** UK and overseas.
**WHO CAN BENEFIT** Organisations benefitting evangelical Christian organisations.
**WHAT IS FUNDED** General charitable purposes, particularly the advancement of the Christian faith.
**WHAT IS NOT FUNDED** Individuals.
**FINANCES** *Year* 2013/14 *Income* £51,000 *Grants* £37,409 *Grants to organisations* £37,409 *Assets* £70,978
**TRUSTEES** Jill Kendrick; Graham Kendrick; Abigail Sheldrake; Amy Waterman; Miriam Kendrick; Tamsin Kendrick.
**HOW TO APPLY** Apply in writing to the correspondent. The trustees meet to consider grants quarterly, usually in March, June, September and December.
**WHO TO APPLY TO** John Caladine, Trust Administrator, Chantry House, 22 Upperton Road, Eastbourne, East Sussex BN21 1BF *Tel.* 01323 644579 *email* john@caladine.co.uk

## ■ The Alborada Trust

**CC NO** 1091660    **ESTABLISHED** 2001
**WHERE FUNDING CAN BE GIVEN** Worldwide.
**WHO CAN BENEFIT** Charitable organisations.
**WHAT IS FUNDED** Veterinary causes in the United Kingdom and Ireland with activities primarily devoted to the welfare of animals and/or in their associated research. Projects throughout the world associated with the relief of poverty, human suffering, sickness or ill health.
**RANGE OF GRANTS** £20,000–£245,000
**SAMPLE GRANTS** The Langford Trust for Animal Health and Welfare (£200,000); University of Cambridge – Africa Project (£155,000); The Cambridge Foundation (£146,000); Alzheimer's Society (£109,000); University of Cambridge – Lectureship (£67,000); Animal Health Trust (£50,000); Brooke Hospital for Animals (£38,500); Irish Injured Jockeys (£21,000).
**FINANCES** Year 2013 Income £170,774 Grants £787,135 Grants to organisations £787,135 Assets £12,724,024
**TRUSTEES** Eva Rausing; David Way; Roland Lerner; James Nicholson; Robert Goff.
**HOW TO APPLY** This trust does not accept unsolicited applications.
**WHO TO APPLY TO** Jamie Matheson, Fladgate Fielder LLP, 16 Great Queen Street, London WC2 5DG *Tel.* 020 3036 7308 *Website* www.alboradatrust.com

## ■ D. G. Albright Charitable Trust

**CC NO** 277367    **ESTABLISHED** 1978
**WHERE FUNDING CAN BE GIVEN** UK, with a preference for Gloucestershire.
**WHO CAN BENEFIT** Registered charities.
**WHAT IS FUNDED** General charitable purposes.
**WHAT IS NOT FUNDED** Individuals.
**TYPE OF GRANT** One-off and recurrent.
**RANGE OF GRANTS** £300–£4,000
**SAMPLE GRANTS** The Shop at Bromesberrow and Westonbirt Arboretum Appeal (£5,000 each); Bromesberrow Parochial Church Council (£3,000); The Family Haven – Gloucester (£2,000); Hope for Tomorrow, Independent Age, Livability and Smile Support and Care (£1,000 each); War Memorials Trust (£500).
**FINANCES** Year 2013/14 Income £45,985 Grants £51,500 Grants to organisations £51,500 Assets £1,466,348
**TRUSTEES** Hon. Dr Gilbert Greenall; Richard Wood.
**HOW TO APPLY** Apply in writing to the correspondent.
**WHO TO APPLY TO** Richard Wood, Trustee, Old Church School, Hollow Street, Great Somerford, Chippenham, Wiltshire SN15 5JD *Tel.* 01249 720760 *email* richardandpennyw@btinternet.com

## ■ The Alchemy Foundation

**CC NO** 292500    **ESTABLISHED** 1985
**WHERE FUNDING CAN BE GIVEN** UK and overseas.
**WHO CAN BENEFIT** Community projects; voluntary organisations; registered charities.
**WHAT IS FUNDED** The focus is on The Alchemist Scheme (funding the costs of fundraisers assigned to other charities to assist with their fundraising efforts), water projects in financially developing countries, disability (particularly mobility, access, helplines and communications), social welfare (inner city community projects, disaffected youth, family mediation, homelessness), personal reform, penal reform (work with prisoners, especially young prisoners, and their families), medical research and aid (especially in areas of blindness and disfigurement), individual enterprise (by helping Raleigh International and similar organisations to give opportunities to young people according to need) and respite for carers.
**WHAT IS NOT FUNDED** Organisations exclusive to one faith or political belief.
**TYPE OF GRANT** Capital; revenue; one-off; salaries.
**SAMPLE GRANTS** A list of beneficiaries was not available.
**FINANCES** Year 2013/14 Income £303,571 Grants £272,716 Grants to organisations £272,716 Assets £2,774,401
**TRUSTEES** Dr Jemima Stilgoe; Holly Stilgoe; Jack Stilgoe; Rufus Stilgoe; Richard Stilgoe; Alex Armitage; Andrew Murison; Annabel Stilgoe; Esther Rantzen; Joseph Stilgoe; Tony Elias.
**HOW TO APPLY** Apply in writing to the correspondent.
**WHO TO APPLY TO** Richard Stilgoe, Trustee, Trevereux Manor, Limpsfield Chart, Oxted, Surrey RH8 0TL *Tel.* 01883 730600

## ■ Aldgate and All Hallows' Foundation (formerly Aldgate and All Hallows' Barking Exhibition Foundation)

**CC NO** 312500    **ESTABLISHED** 1893
**WHERE FUNDING CAN BE GIVEN** City of London and the London borough of Tower Hamlets.
**WHO CAN BENEFIT** Children or young people under the age of 25 who are: permanent residents of London Borough of Tower Hamlets or the City of London; in full-time education or studying for a recognised qualification, and who are; from disadvantaged backgrounds or areas of high deprivation in the two London boroughs mentioned above. Governors can also offer support to young people beyond school years who are in financial need, maybe while they are undertaking undergraduate or postgraduate studies. Such beneficiaries, or their parents or guardians, must have resided or been employed in the area for at least three years.
**WHAT IS FUNDED** The foundation is particularly keen to encourage and support: projects initiated by schools that enhance the National Curriculum; projects aimed at improving literacy and numeracy; projects aimed at promoting the study of science, mathematics and the arts; projects which attract match funding; projects which test out new ideas. Priority will be given to projects that are not yet part of a school's or organisation's regular activities; to developments that are strategic, such as practical initiatives seeking to address the root causes of problems, and those that have the potential to influence policy and practice more widely. The foundation may also from time to time initiate new projects that do not fall into the priority areas for grant-making to enable governors to explore ground-breaking or emergent fields of educational practice.
**WHAT IS NOT FUNDED** Equipment or teachers' salaries that are the responsibility of education authorities; youth groups; supplementary schools or mother tongue teaching; the purchase, repair or furnishing of buildings; conferences or seminars; stage, film, publication or video production costs; performances or exhibitions; retrospective requests (i.e. any activity that has already taken place); requests to substitute for the withdrawal or reduction of statutory funding; general fundraising campaigns or appeals.

RANGE OF GRANTS Up to £45,000.
SAMPLE GRANTS Wilton's Music Hall (£50,000); Adab Trust (£40,000); Rich Mix (£35,000); School Funding Network Ltd (£21,000); Box Clever Theatre Company (£20,000); and Ben Johnson Primary School (£11,000).
FINANCES Year 2013 Income £73,267 Grants £288,535 Grants to organisations £244,535 Assets £7,670,984
TRUSTEES Mr D. Ross; Robin Hazlewood; Cllr Denise Jones; David Mash; Revd Bertrand Olivier; John Hall; Graham Forbes; William Hamilton-Hinds; Marianne Fredericks; Billy Whitbread; Paul James; Susan Knowles; Cllr Sirajul Islam; Revd Laura Burgess; Kevin Everett.
OTHER INFORMATION The 2012 grant total includes £39,000 given in grants to individuals.
HOW TO APPLY Initial enquiries should be sent to the foundation. These must include the following information: information about your school or organisation including an outline of its current activities, its legal status, aims, brief history, details of staffing levels, management structure and composition of the management committee; an outline description of, and timetable for, the project for which funding is being sought, including information about who will be involved in and/or benefit from the project; details of the aims and outcomes for the project, including information about how you will monitor and evaluate the project; a detailed budget for the project; information about any other sources of income and partnership funding for the project. Enquiries from organisations should be accompanied by a copy of your organisation's governing document, most recent annual report and (audited) accounts, a contact name, address, email address and telephone number. Schools do not have to provide a copy of their governing document or annual accounts.
WHO TO APPLY TO Richard Foley, Clerk and Chief Executive, 31 Jewry Street, London EC3N 2EY Tel. 020 7488 2518 Fax 020 7488 2519 email aldgateandallhallows@sirjohncass.org Website www.aldgateallhallows.org.uk

■ **The Alexis Trust**
CC NO 262861    ESTABLISHED 1971
WHERE FUNDING CAN BE GIVEN UK and overseas.
WHO CAN BENEFIT Individuals and organisations.
WHAT IS FUNDED Support for a variety of causes, principally Christian missionary projects.
WHAT IS NOT FUNDED No grants for building appeals, or to individuals for education.
TYPE OF GRANT One-off, project and some recurring costs will be considered.
SAMPLE GRANTS Barnabas Fund (£2,000); Universities and Colleges Christian Fellowship (£1,700); Mission Aviation Fellowship, SGM Lifewords and Tearfund (£1,000 each).
FINANCES Year 2013/14 Income £46,662 Grants £39,902 Grants to organisations £32,252 Assets £529,872
TRUSTEES Prof. Duncan Vere; Chris Harwood; Elisabeth Harwood; Vera Vere.
OTHER INFORMATION There were 101 grants made to organisations totalling £32,000 and 69 grants to individuals totalling £7,500.
HOW TO APPLY Apply in writing to the correspondent, although the trust states that most of the funds are regularly committed.
WHO TO APPLY TO Prof. Duncan Vere, Trustee, 14 Broadfield Way, Buckhurst Hill, Essex IG9 5AG Tel. 020 8504 6872 email duncan.vere@talktalk.net

■ **All Saints Educational Trust**
CC NO 312934    ESTABLISHED 1978
WHERE FUNDING CAN BE GIVEN UK and overseas.
WHO CAN BENEFIT Ultimately, persons who are or intend to become engaged as teachers or in other capacities connected with education, in particular home economics and religious subjects, and those who teach or intend to teach in multicultural areas.
WHAT IS FUNDED Primarily, the training of Christian teachers. Its main purposes is to: help increase the number of new teachers with Qualified Teacher Status; improve the skills and qualifications of experienced teachers; encourage research that can assist teachers in their work; support specifically the teaching of religious studies and home economics and related areas – such as the promotion of public health and nutrition, both at home and overseas.
WHAT IS NOT FUNDED General or core funds of any organisation; public appeals; school buildings, equipment or supplies (except library resources); the establishment of new departments in universities and colleges; general bursary funds of other organisations.
TYPE OF GRANT One-off, project or annual grants for a limited period. Funding may be given for more than three years. Preference will be given to 'pump-priming' projects.
SAMPLE GRANTS Previously: National Association of Teachers in Home Economics, Southwark Cathedral Education Centre, British Nutrition Foundation, Design and Technology Association, Sheffield Hallam University, Wulugu – Ghana, Scripture Union, Christian Education Movement and the Soil Association.
FINANCES Year 2013/14 Income £549,810 Grants £209,000 Grants to organisations £139,000 Assets £11,016,766
TRUSTEES Diane McCrea; Revd Canon Peter Hartley; Revd Dr Keith Riglin; David J. Trillo; Dorothy Garland; Barbara E. Harvey; Dr Augur Pearce; Prof. Anthony R. Leeds; The Ven. Stephan J. Welch; Stephanie Valentine; Joanna Moriarty; Frances M. Smith; Anna E. Cumbers; Michael C. Jacob; Stephen Brooker; Nicola Sylvester.
OTHER INFORMATION 1n 2013/14 grants to organisations (Corporate Awards) totalled £139,000, with £70,000 going to individuals in scholarships and bursaries.
HOW TO APPLY For applications from organisations (not individuals): applicants are invited to discuss their ideas informally with the clerk before making an application. In some cases, a 'link trustee' is appointed to assist the organisation in preparing the application and who will act in a liaison role with the trust. Completed applications are put before the awards committee in April/May, with final decisions made in June. Application forms are available on the trust's website, either in interactive or printable form.
WHO TO APPLY TO Mr K. D. Mitchell, Clerk to the Trust, Knightrider House, 30–32 Knightrider Street, London EC4V 5JT Tel. 020 3440 5691 email aset@aset.org.uk Website www.aset.org.uk

■ **Allchurches Trust Ltd**
CC NO 263960    ESTABLISHED 1972
WHERE FUNDING CAN BE GIVEN UK.
WHO CAN BENEFIT Churches, church establishments, religious charities and charities preserving UK heritage.

**WHAT IS FUNDED** Promotion of the Christian religion and contributions to the funds of other charitable institutions.
**WHAT IS NOT FUNDED** Charities with political associations; national charities; individuals; appeals for running costs and salaries. Applications cannot be considered from the same recipient twice in one year or in two consecutive years.
**TYPE OF GRANT** Primarily one-off.
**RANGE OF GRANTS** Usually £100–£5,000.
**SAMPLE GRANTS** Beachy Head Chaplaincy Team; Better Together Trust; Bingham Methodist Church, Nottingham; East Cheshire Area Quaker Meeting; First Comber Presbyterian Church, County Down; Guildford Cathedral; Holy Trinity Church – Nailsea; Totland Methodist Church; and Waen Congregational Chapel.
**FINANCES** Year 2013 Income £5,406,000 Grants £9,955,000 Grants to organisations £9,955,000 Assets £411,637,000
**TRUSTEES** Michael Chamberlain; The Right Revd Nigel Stock; Sir Philip Mawer; Christopher Smith; The Venerable Annette Cooper; Denise Wilson; David Christie; Sir Laurence Magnus; Michael Arlington.
**OTHER INFORMATION** Income is derived from its wholly owned subsidiary company Ecclesiastical Insurance Office plc.
**HOW TO APPLY** Applications should ideally be submitted online via the trust's website.
**WHO TO APPLY TO** Rachael Hall, Beaufort House, Brunswick Road, Gloucester GL1 1JZ *Tel.* 01452 873189 *email* atl@ecclesiastical.com *Website* www.allchurches.co.uk

## ■ The H. B. Allen Charitable Trust
**CC NO** 802306 **ESTABLISHED** 1985
**WHERE FUNDING CAN BE GIVEN** Worldwide.
**WHO CAN BENEFIT** Registered charities in the UK.
**WHAT IS FUNDED** General charitable purposes including: blindness; children and young people; churches; people with disabilities; education/schools; environment, wildlife and animals; general community, hospices; housing/homeless; mental health; museums/galleries/heritage and overseas/international.
**WHAT IS NOT FUNDED** Individuals; organisations which are not UK-registered charities; gap year students (even if payable to a registered charity). No initial funding to newly established charities.
**TYPE OF GRANT** One-off and recurrent up to three years, revenue and capital including core costs.
**RANGE OF GRANTS** Mainly £5,000–£25,000.
**SAMPLE GRANTS** Landmark Trust (£250,000); St Michael and All Angels Church Bedford Park (£150,000); Cambridge University – Clinical medicine equipment (£100,000); Grange Park Opera (£60,000); Heron Corn Mill (£50,000); Pitt Rivers Museum (£45,000); Wildlife Conservation Research Unit (£40,000); Salisbury Cathedral and Trinity Church, Ossett (£35,000 each); Axminster Heritage Limited, The Sobriety Project, Young Offenders Scheme and Skeletal Cancer Action Trust (£25,000 each); Cure Parkinson's Trust and The Orton Trust (£10,000 each); Books Abroad and The Gurkha Welfare Trust (£5,000 each); Combat Stress and Practical Action (£2,500 each).
**FINANCES** Year 2013 Income £1,438,805 Grants £1,521,000 Grants to organisations £1,521,000 Assets £38,597,511
**TRUSTEES** Helen Ratcliffe; Peter Shone.
**HOW TO APPLY** Apply in writing to the correspondent including a copy of the organisation's latest annual report and accounts. Applications should be submitted by post, not email, although enquiries prior to any application can be made by email. Read the trust's application guidelines available from its helpful and concise website. Note the following comments from the trustees: 'Applicants should note that, at their main annual meeting, which takes place in the first few months of each year, the trustees consider applications received up to 31st December the previous year but do not carry them forward. Having regard for the time of year when this meeting takes place, it makes sense for applications to be made as late as possible in the calendar year so that the information they contain is most up to date when the trustees meet. It would be preferable, from all points of view, if applications were made only in the last quarter of the calendar year. Applications should be addressed to the correspondent by name and sent to the address shown. The trustees receive a very substantial number of appeals each year. It is not their practice to acknowledge appeals, and they prefer not to enter into correspondence with applicants other than those to whom grants are being made or from whom further information is required. Only successful applicants are notified of the outcome of their application.' Visit the trust's website where 'Guidelines for applicants' gives a comprehensive review of what the trustees regard as priority, not a priority and ineligible.
**WHO TO APPLY TO** Peter Shone, Trustee, Homefield, Chidden Holt, Hambledon, Waterlooville, Hampshire PO7 4TG *Tel.* 023 9263 2406 *email* mail@hballencт.org.uk *Website* www.hballencт.org.uk

## ■ The Alliance Family Foundation
**CC NO** 258721 **ESTABLISHED** 1968
**WHERE FUNDING CAN BE GIVEN** UK and Israel.
**WHO CAN BENEFIT** Organisations, particularly Jewish causes, benefitting young people and people disadvantaged by poverty.
**WHAT IS FUNDED** The relief of poverty and advancement of religion, education and medical knowledge.
**RANGE OF GRANTS** Up to £50,000.
**SAMPLE GRANTS** Jordan River Village (£177,000); Tel Aviv University Alzheimer's Research (£63,000); University of Manchester and Weizmann Institute Israel (£50,000); Alzheimer's clinical trials – Cognition Health (£44,000); Jewish Community Secondary School Trust (£31,000).
**FINANCES** Year 2013/14 Income £701,754 Grants £967,160 Grants to organisations £723,689 Assets £28,780,040
**TRUSTEES** Lord David Alliance; Graham Alliance; Sara Esterkin; Joshua Alliance.
**OTHER INFORMATION** £243,000 was distributed to individuals.
**HOW TO APPLY** Apply in writing to the trustees.
**WHO TO APPLY TO** The Trustees, Spencer House, 27 St James's Place, London SW1A 1NR *email* aff@alliance.me

## ■ Alliance Trust Staff Foundation
**SC NO** SC044113 **ESTABLISHED** 2013
**WHERE FUNDING CAN BE GIVEN** Dundee, Edinburgh and City of London.
**WHO CAN BENEFIT** Registered charities and community groups.
**WHAT IS FUNDED** General charitable purposes, children and young people.

RANGE OF GRANTS Up to £5,000.
SAMPLE GRANTS Streetwork – Edinburgh (£5,000); Baytree Centre, Dundee Disabled Children's Association, Links Park Community Trust and Action for Children Scotland (£2,000 each).
FINANCES Year 2014 Grants £29,000 Grants to organisations £29,000
TRUSTEES Ramsay Urquhart, Chair; Jack Willis; James Brown; Sinead Lennon; Ann McLeod; Stuart McMaster; Alvina Menzies; Kerry Moores; Kathryn Taylor.
OTHER INFORMATION This is the charitable foundation of Alliance Trust plc, an investment, savings and wealth management company. The foundation's income derives from Alliance Trust employees' fundraising activities and match funding from the company.
HOW TO APPLY Apply in writing to the correspondent.
WHO TO APPLY TO Jack Willis, Secretary, Alliance Trust plc, 8 West Marketgait, Dundee DD1 1QN Tel. 01382 321000 Fax 01382 321185 email contact@alliancetrust.co.uk Website investor.alliancetrust.co.uk/ati/investorrelations/staff-foundation

### ■ Angus Allnatt Charitable Foundation
CC NO 1019793    ESTABLISHED 1993
WHERE FUNDING CAN BE GIVEN UK.
WHO CAN BENEFIT Young people.
WHAT IS FUNDED This trust makes grants to organisations which offer opportunities for young musicians aged 13 to 25 or which provide water-based activities for those up to the age of 20.
WHAT IS NOT FUNDED Individuals; organisations which use music primarily for therapeutic or social purposes.
TYPE OF GRANT One-off for specific needs or start-up costs. Funding is available for up to one year.
RANGE OF GRANTS £250–£1,000 with a maximum of £2,000.
FINANCES Year 2013/14 Income £14,727 Grants £40,000 Grants to organisations £40,000
TRUSTEES David Briggs; Rodney Dartnall; Marian Durban; Andrew Hutchison, Shahareen Hilmy.
HOW TO APPLY Apply in writing to the correspondent. The trustees meet three times a year to consider applications. The trust has no staff and no telephone. Appeals falling outside the guidelines will not be considered.
WHO TO APPLY TO Marian Durban, Trustee, 62 Westfield Way, Charlton Heights, Wantage, Oxfordshire OX12 7EP Tel. 01235 223250 email m.durban1@ntlworld.com

### ■ The Almond Trust
CC NO 328583    ESTABLISHED 1990
WHERE FUNDING CAN BE GIVEN UK and worldwide.
WHO CAN BENEFIT Mostly individuals or organisations of which the trustees have personal knowledge, particularly those benefitting Christians and evangelists.
WHAT IS FUNDED Support of evangelical Christian projects, Christian evangelism, and advancement of Scripture.
TYPE OF GRANT Largely recurrent.
RANGE OF GRANTS Up to £12,000. The average grant in 2009–10 was £4,586.
SAMPLE GRANTS Lawyers' Christian Fellowship and St Mary's Warbleton PCC (£10,000 each); Christians in Sport, Christian Prison Resources Ministries Haggai Institute (£2,500 each); Friends International and Jews for Jesus (£2,000 each).
FINANCES Year 2013/14 Income £56,332 Grants £53,200 Grants to organisations £53,200 Assets £53,829
TRUSTEES Sir Jeremy Cooke; Jonathan Cooke; Lady Cooke.
OTHER INFORMATION The grant total includes five payments totalling £8,800, which were given to individuals.
HOW TO APPLY Apply in writing to the correspondent, but note that the trust states it rarely responds to uninvited applications.
WHO TO APPLY TO Sir Jeremy Cooke, Trustee, 19 West Square, London SE11 4SN Tel. 020 7587 5167

### ■ Almondsbury Charity
CC NO 202263    ESTABLISHED 1963
WHERE FUNDING CAN BE GIVEN The parish of Almondsbury as it existed in 1892, i.e. Almondsbury, Patchway, Easter Compton and parts of Pilning and Bradley Stoke North.
WHO CAN BENEFIT Organisations, churches, schools and individuals in the beneficiary area.
WHAT IS FUNDED Grants are made to both individuals and organisations in the parish of Almondsbury for educational purposes and the relief of those who are in need or in ill health. Grants are also made to repair and maintain the fabric of local churches and to further the religious and charitable work of the Church of England in the area.
TYPE OF GRANT Capital; one-off; recurrent.
RANGE OF GRANTS Between £500 and £5,000.
SAMPLE GRANTS St Peter's Church Pilning (£10,000); Almondsbury Old School Hall and Patchway Minibus (£5,000 each); Southern Brooks Community Partnership (£2,500); Patchway Community Association (£2,000); Stoke Lodge Primary School (£1,700); St Peter's Hospice (£1,500); Patchway Community College (£1,200); Four Towns Play Association (£1,000); Coniston Primary School (£700); Patchway Festival (£500); St Chad's Church (£400); Almondsbury Cricket Club (£300).
FINANCES Year 2013/14 Income £69,371 Grants £55,907 Grants to organisations £48,122 Assets £2,314,028
TRUSTEES Alan Gaydon; Ivor Humphries; Revd Howard Jameson; Lewis Gray; Alan Bamforth; Diane Wilson; Revd Philip Rowe; Sheila Futon; Jane Jones; Lucy Hamid; Revd Roger Ducker; Ben Walker.
OTHER INFORMATION The grant total for 2013/14 includes the total of £7,800 which was distributed in grants to individuals.
HOW TO APPLY Applications should be made in writing to the correspondent on a form which can be downloaded from the charity's website. The trustees meet six times each year and applications must be received at least two weeks before a meeting, the dates of which are published on the trust's website.
WHO TO APPLY TO Peter Orford, Wayside, Shepperdine Road, Oldbury Naite, Bristol BS35 1RJ Tel. 01454 415346 email peter.orford@gmail.com Website www.almondsburycharity.org.uk/almondsbury

## ■ The Altajir Trust

**CC NO** 284116  **ESTABLISHED** 1982
**WHERE FUNDING CAN BE GIVEN** UK and Arab or Islamic states.
**WHO CAN BENEFIT** Individuals and organisations.
**WHAT IS FUNDED** Support for exhibitions, publications, educational activities and other programmes related to Islamic culture and Muslim-Christian relations. The focus for activities is on: funding exhibitions and other events as well as publications and lectures to make aspects of Islamic culture and history better known to a wider audience in the United Kingdom; contributing through grants to the cost of conservation of Islamic artefacts and manuscripts in the United Kingdom and to assisting conservation in Muslim countries; supporting the production of a history of the Gulf (18th century to 1981) by a team of international scholars for the furtherance of international understanding of this region; funding, through grants, charitable and academic institutions assisting in rebuilding societies in the Islamic world after conflict; providing scholarships to students from the Arab world to study at British universities before returning to their own countries.
**RANGE OF GRANTS** Up to £60,000.
**SAMPLE GRANTS** University of York – Lectureship (£58,000); British Council – Chevening Scholarships (£6,000); University of Sterling – Scholarships (£2,500).
**FINANCES** Year 2013 Income £587,617 Grants £66,510 Grants to organisations £66,510 Assets £300,366
**TRUSTEES** Prof. Alan Jones, Chair; Prof. Roger Williams; Dr Charles Tripp; Dr Noel Brehony.
**OTHER INFORMATION** The trust also gave a further £201,500 in student support and £58,500 in support for events and publications.
**HOW TO APPLY** Make application on a form available from the trust's website. The trustees meet about four times a year. Applications can be submitted at any time but may have to await the next trustees' meeting for a decision. However, they will all be acknowledged when received and an indication of the time frame for a decision will be given. Note: applications should be printed and signed before being sent to the trust.
**WHO TO APPLY TO** The Trustees, 11 Elvaston Place, London SW7 5QG Tel. 020 7581 3522 Fax 020 7584 1977 email awitrust@tiscali.co.uk Website www.altajirtrust.org.uk

## ■ Altamont Ltd

**CC NO** 273971  **ESTABLISHED** 1977
**WHERE FUNDING CAN BE GIVEN** Worldwide.
**WHO CAN BENEFIT** Organisations benefitting Jewish people.
**WHAT IS FUNDED** Jewish charitable purposes.
**FINANCES** Year 2013/14 Income £39,719 Grants £0 Grants to organisations £0 Assets £566,322
**TRUSTEES** David Last; Henry Last; Mrs H. Kon; Mrs S. Adler; Gina Wiesenfeld.
**OTHER INFORMATION** In the previous year the charity had an income of £16,000 and a total expenditure of £101,000 and the trust's income and expenditure fluctuates from year to year. For this reason we have retained this entry here as we consider it is likely that funds will be available in future years.
**HOW TO APPLY** Apply in writing to the correspondent.
**WHO TO APPLY TO** David Last, Trustee, 18 Green Walk, London NW4 2AJ Tel. 020 8457 8760

## ■ AM Charitable Trust

**CC NO** 256283  **ESTABLISHED** 1968
**WHERE FUNDING CAN BE GIVEN** UK and overseas.
**WHO CAN BENEFIT** Registered charities; Jewish organisations.
**WHAT IS FUNDED** General charitable purposes, including medical, welfare, arts and conservation causes.
**WHAT IS NOT FUNDED** Individuals.
**TYPE OF GRANT** Certain charities are supported for more than one year, although no commitment is usually given to the recipients.
**RANGE OF GRANTS** Mainly smaller amounts to non-Jewish organisations.
**SAMPLE GRANTS** The Wallace Collection (£75,000); Youth Aliyah – Child Rescue and British ORT (£15,000 each); Friends of the Hebrew University of Jerusalem and Jerusalem Foundation (£10,000 each); Cancer Research Campaign (£3,000); British Heart Foundation (£2,000); Blond McIndoe Research Foundation (£1,500); Royal Academy of Music (£1,000); Alzheimer's Research Trust (£500); Crimestoppers Trust (£200).
**FINANCES** Year 2013/14 Income £159,888 Grants £135,000 Grants to organisations £135,000
**TRUSTEE** Kleinwort Benson Trustees Ltd.
**HOW TO APPLY** We understand from previous research that donations are decided periodically by the trustee having regard to the wishes of the settlor, and unsolicited appeals are considered as well as causes which have already been supported. Only successful applicants are notified of the trustee's decision. Certain charities are supported for more than one year, although no commitment is usually given to the recipients.
**WHO TO APPLY TO** The Correspondent, Kleinwort Benson Trustees Ltd, 14 St George Street, London W1S 1FE Tel. 020 3207 7091

## ■ Amabrill Limited

**CC NO** 1078968  **ESTABLISHED** 2000
**WHERE FUNDING CAN BE GIVEN** UK with a preference for north west London.
**WHO CAN BENEFIT** Jewish charities.
**WHAT IS FUNDED** The advancement of education and religious practice in accordance with the teachings of the Orthodox Jewish faith; and social welfare.
**SAMPLE GRANTS** Previous beneficiaries have included: Kahal Chassidim Bobov; YMER; BFON Trust; Beth Hamedrash Elyon Golders Green Ltd; Friends of Shekel Hakodesh Ltd; Friends of Mir and Parsha Ltd; Cosmon Belz Ltd; United Talmudical Academy; British Friends of Mosdos Tchernobel; Mayfair Charities Ltd; Friends of Toldos Avrohom Yitzchok; Achisomoch Aid Company; the Gertner Charitable Trust; and Higher Talmudical Education Ltd.
**FINANCES** Year 2013/14 Income £2,636,788 Grants £3,043,975 Grants to organisations £3,043,975 Assets £3,117,506
**TRUSTEES** Charles Lerner; Frances R. Lerner; Irving Lerner; Israel Grossnass.
**OTHER INFORMATION** A list of grants was not included in the most recent accounts.
**HOW TO APPLY** Apply in writing to the correspondent. Appeal letters are received from, and personal visits made by representatives of Jewish

charitable, religious and educational institutions. These requests are then considered by the trustees and grants are made in accordance with the trustees' decisions.

**WHO TO APPLY TO** Charles Lerner, Trustee, 1 Golder's Manor Drive, London NW11 9HU *Tel.* 020 8455 6785 *email* mail@venittandgreaves.com

## ■ The Amalur Foundation Limited

**CC NO** 1090476  **ESTABLISHED** 2002
**WHERE FUNDING CAN BE GIVEN** Worldwide.
**WHO CAN BENEFIT** Charitable organisations.
**WHAT IS FUNDED** General charitable purposes.
**SAMPLE GRANTS** Previously: Absolute Return for Kids (£110,000); St Patrick's Catholic Church (£50,000); Prostate Research Campaign UK (£10,000); Brain Tumour Research Campaign (£5,500); Breakthrough Breast Cancer (£3,000); and the Extra Care Charitable Trust (£2,000).
**FINANCES** *Year* 2013/14 *Income* £0 *Grants* £100,000 *Grants to organisations* £100,000
**TRUSTEES** Claudia Garuti; David Way; Helen Mellor.
**OTHER INFORMATION** Charity Commission record. Accounts had been received at the Commission but due to the low income, had not been published.
**HOW TO APPLY** We have been informed by the correspondent that the charity's income is diminishing and that it does not have a long-term future. While the trustees have funds available, they are pleased to consider applications. Applications should be made to the correspondent in writing please.
**WHO TO APPLY TO** David Way, Trustee, Fladgate LLP, 16 Great Queen Street, London WC2B 5DG *Tel.* 020 3036 7000

## ■ The Ammco Trust

**CC NO** 327962  **ESTABLISHED** 1988
**WHERE FUNDING CAN BE GIVEN** Oxfordshire and adjoining counties.
**WHO CAN BENEFIT** Small local charities and charitable projects based in the area of benefit.
**WHAT IS FUNDED** Disability, health, medical, special needs education, ex-services, sport and arts/heritage.
**WHAT IS NOT FUNDED** Individuals; students; research.
**TYPE OF GRANT** One-off.
**RANGE OF GRANTS** Usually up to £2,000, except in exceptional circumstances.
**SAMPLE GRANTS** **Previous beneficiaries have included:** BEWSA, Contact a Family Oxford, DEBRA Berkshire, Dorothy House Hospice Care Wiltshire, Live Music Now!, Oxford Children's Hospital Campaign, Pathway Workshop Oxford, Riding for the Disabled Association Abingdon Group and Wellbeing of Women.
**FINANCES** *Year* 2013/14 *Income* £53,891 *Grants* £49,235 *Grants to organisations* £49,235 *Assets* £1,544,304
**TRUSTEES** Esther Lewis; Rowena Vickers; Nicholas Cobbold.
**HOW TO APPLY** Apply in writing to the correspondent; there are no application forms. Applications are considered at any time. An sae is appreciated.
**WHO TO APPLY TO** Esther Lewis, Glebe Farm, Hinton Waldrist, Faringdon, Oxfordshire SN7 8RX *Tel.* 01865 820269

## ■ Sir John and Lady Amory's Charitable Trust

**CC NO** 203970  **ESTABLISHED** 1961
**WHERE FUNDING CAN BE GIVEN** UK, with a preference for Devon and the South West.
**WHO CAN BENEFIT** Local organisations, plus a few UK-wide charities.
**WHAT IS FUNDED** General charitable purposes, including education, health and welfare.
**TYPE OF GRANT** One-off grants for capital expenditure.
**RANGE OF GRANTS** Up to £10,000. Generally for under £5,000.
**SAMPLE GRANTS** Twyford Trust (£10,000); and Knightshayes Garden Trust (£8,000).
**FINANCES** *Year* 2013/14 *Income* £285,970 *Grants* £66,038 *Grants to organisations* £64,638 *Assets* £2,140,384
**TRUSTEES** Sir Ian Heathcoat Amory; Lady Heathcoat Amory; William Heathcoat Amory.
**OTHER INFORMATION** Twyford Trust (£10,000); and Knightshayes Garden Trust (£8,000). A further £1,400 was given to individuals.
**HOW TO APPLY** Apply in writing to the correspondent.
**WHO TO APPLY TO** The Trustees, The Island, Lowman Green, Tiverton, Devon EX16 4LA *Tel.* 01884 254899 *email* charities@lowman.co.uk

## ■ Viscount Amory's Charitable Trust

**CC NO** 204958  **ESTABLISHED** 1962
**WHERE FUNDING CAN BE GIVEN** UK, primarily in Devon.
**WHO CAN BENEFIT** Charities benefitting people from different family situations, clergy, ex-service and service people, people with disabilities, people disadvantaged by poverty, homeless people and people living in rural areas are also considered. Particular favour is given to young adults and older people.
**WHAT IS FUNDED** The income is employed mostly in the field of youth service and elderly people particularly to help a number of charitable objects with which the trust has been associated for a number of years, mostly within the county of Devon, including education and training for children and young people. Conservation and heritage causes are also considered.
**WHAT IS NOT FUNDED** Individuals from outside South West England.
**TYPE OF GRANT** Usually one-off including capital (including building) costs. Grants for up to three years will be considered.
**RANGE OF GRANTS** £1,000–£95,000; typically for £5,000 or less.
**SAMPLE GRANTS** Rona Sailing Project (£95,000); Blundells School (£40,000); Exeter Cathedral School (£25,000); Devon Community Foundation (£15,000); Tiverton Museum of Mid Devon Life (£10,500); King's College and Queen's College (£5,500 each); Magdalen Court School and Sunningmead Community Association (£5,000 each).
**FINANCES** *Year* 2013/14 *Income* £432,836 *Grants* £332,322 *Grants to organisations* £324,523 *Assets* £12,395,457
**TRUSTEES** Sir Ian Heathcoat Amory; Catherine Cavender.
**HOW TO APPLY** Apply in writing to the correspondent, giving general background information, total costs involved, amount raised so far and details of applications to other organisations.
**WHO TO APPLY TO** Secretary to the Trustees, The Island, Lowman Green, Tiverton, Devon

EX16 4LA  *Tel.* 01884 254899  *email* office@vact.org.uk  *Website* www.vact.org.uk

## ■ The Ampelos Trust
**CC NO** 1048778   **ESTABLISHED** 1995
**WHERE FUNDING CAN BE GIVEN** UK.
**WHO CAN BENEFIT** Registered charities.
**WHAT IS FUNDED** General charitable purposes.
**TYPE OF GRANT** Usually one-off.
**SAMPLE GRANTS** Shelter (£25,000); Handel House Trust, Little Hearts Matter and RNIB (£10,000 each); National Clinical Group (£6,000); and AIDS Life Cycle and Kingston C.A.B. (£1,000 each).
**FINANCES** Year 2012/13 Income £131,155 Grants £80,650 Grants to organisations £80,650 Assets £491,906
**TRUSTEES** Ruth Rendell; Ann Marie Witt; MMH. Trustees Limited.
**HOW TO APPLY** The 2013/14 annual report states: 'Since the trustees anticipate being able to identify sufficient potential recipients to whom to distribute the income of the trust, the trustees do not wish to receive unsolicited applications for grants.'
**WHO TO APPLY TO** Philip Hitchinson, Secretary, c/o Menzies LLP, Ashcombe House, 5 The Crescent, Leatherhead, Surrey KT22 8DY  *Tel.* 01372 360130  *email* phitchinson@menzies.co.uk

## ■ The AMW Charitable Trust
**SC NO** SC006959   **ESTABLISHED** 1974
**WHERE FUNDING CAN BE GIVEN** Scotland only, with a priority for the West of Scotland.
**WHO CAN BENEFIT** Charitable organisations.
**WHAT IS FUNDED** A broad range of activity is supported including those connected with religion, education, culture, poverty, sickness, disability, social welfare, older people and young adults.
**WHAT IS NOT FUNDED** No grants for individuals, or to organisations outside Scotland.
**SAMPLE GRANTS** Previous beneficiaries have included: The Dixon Community, Girl Guiding School, Kelvingrove Refurb Appeal, Lifeboats of the Cycle Appeal, Friends of Glasgow Humane Society, MND Scotland, Maryhill Parish Church, Aberlour Child Care Trust, Dystonia Society, Glasgow School of Arts, Momentum, Hansel Foundation and Muscular Dystrophy Campaign.
**FINANCES** Year 2013/14 Income £168,327 Grants £100,000 Grants to organisations £100,000
**TRUSTEE** Mr M. McColl
**HOW TO APPLY** Apply in writing to the correspondent. Appeals are not acknowledged and the trust only advises successful applicants.
**WHO TO APPLY TO** Ms M. McColl, Trustee, c/o KPMG LLP, 191 West George Street, Glasgow G2 2LJ  *Tel.* 0141 226 5511

## ■ The Anchor Foundation
**CC NO** 1082485   **ESTABLISHED** 2000
**WHERE FUNDING CAN BE GIVEN** UK and occasionally overseas.
**WHO CAN BENEFIT** Christian charities.
**WHAT IS FUNDED** Social inclusion, particularly through ministries of healing and the arts. Organisations with a number of projects operating are advised to choose a single project for their application.
**WHAT IS NOT FUNDED** Individuals and rarely for building work.
**TYPE OF GRANT** Applications for capital and revenue funding are considered. Only in very exceptional circumstances will grants be given for building work. It is not the normal practice of the charity to support the same project for more than three years (projects which have had three years funding may apply again two years from the payment of the last grant).
**RANGE OF GRANTS** Up to £10,000. Mostly for £5,000 or less.
**SAMPLE GRANTS** Bishop Gwynne College, Finns Place and REAP (£7,500 each); Children of Hope, Epiphany, Good News Family Care Homes Ltd, Foolproof Creative Arts and The Street Life Trust (£5,000 each); CURE International UK and Rope (£4,000 each); The Pennytrip Project and Toybox (£3,000 each); Niger Outreach Work (£1,000).
**FINANCES** Year 2013/14 Income £201,224 Grants £234,216 Grants to organisations £234,216 Assets £6,675,266
**TRUSTEES** Revd Michael Mitton; Revd Robin Anker-Petersen; Nina Anker-Petersen; Sue Mayfield.
**HOW TO APPLY** An initial application form can be completed online at the Anchor Foundation website. Full guidelines for applicants are also available online. If the trustees decide they are interested in your application you will be contacted and asked to send further relevant information such as a project budget and your annual accounts. **Do not send these with your application form.** Also note that applications should not be sent to the registered office in Nottingham. Applications are considered at twice yearly trustee meetings in April and November and need to be received by 31 January and 31 July each year. The foundation regrets that applications cannot be acknowledged. Successful applicants will be notified as soon as possible after trustees' meetings – usually before the end of May or the end of November. Unsuccessful applicants may re-apply after twelve months.
**WHO TO APPLY TO** Wenna Thompson, P.O. Box 21107, Alloa FK12 5WA  *Tel.* 0115 950 0055  *email* secretary@theanchorfoundation.org.uk  *Website* www.theanchorfoundation.org.uk

## ■ The Andrew Anderson Trust
**CC NO** 212170   **ESTABLISHED** 1954
**WHERE FUNDING CAN BE GIVEN** UK and overseas.
**WHO CAN BENEFIT** Organisations benefitting: Christians and evangelists; at risk groups; carers; people with disabilities; people disadvantaged by poverty; socially isolated people; and victims of abuse, crime and domestic violence.
**WHAT IS FUNDED** Grants to evangelical organisations and churches, small grants to health, disability and social welfare causes.
**WHAT IS NOT FUNDED** Individuals should not apply for travel or education.
**RANGE OF GRANTS** Usually under £1,000.
**SAMPLE GRANTS** Previously: Aycliffe Evangelical Church, Christian Medical Fellowship, Concern Worldwide, Emmanuel Baptist Church – Sidmouth, Fellowship of Independent Evangelical Churches, Good Shepherd Mission, Kenward Trust, Latin Link, Proclamation Trust, Rehoboth Christian Centre – Blackpool, Scientific Exploration Society, St Ebbe's PCC – Oxford, St Helen's Church – Bishopsgate, TNT Ministries, Trinity Baptist Church – Gloucester, Whitefield Christian Trust, Weald Trust and Worldshare.

**FINANCES** Year 2013/14 Income £367,607 Grants £307,900 Grants to organisations £307,900 Assets £11,870,799
**TRUSTEES** Revd Andrew Robertson Anderson; Anne Alexander Anderson; Margaret Lillian Anderson.
**HOW TO APPLY** The trust has previously stated that 'we prefer to honour existing commitments and initiate new ones through our own contacts rather than respond to applications'.
**WHO TO APPLY TO** Revd Andrew Robertson Anderson, Trustee, 1 Cote House Lane, Bristol BS9 3UW Tel. 0117 962 1588 email enquiries@pjecharteredaccountants.co.uk

## ■ Andor Charitable Trust

**CC NO** 1083572    **ESTABLISHED** 2000
**WHERE FUNDING CAN BE GIVEN** UK and overseas.
**WHO CAN BENEFIT** Charitable organisations.
**WHAT IS FUNDED** Health, the arts, Jewish and general charitable purposes.
**RANGE OF GRANTS** Mostly £2,000–£5,000.
**SAMPLE GRANTS** The Bobath Centre for Children with Cerebral Palsy (£3,000); Art in Healthcare (£2,000); Anne Frank Trust UK, Award for Young Musicians, Classical Opera, Depaul UK, Donmar Warehouse Projects Limited (£1,000 each).
**FINANCES** Year 2013/14 Income £92,558 Grants £140,900 Grants to organisations £140,900 Assets £3,176,146
**TRUSTEES** David Rothenberg; Nicholas Lederer; Claire Walford; Karen Andor.
**HOW TO APPLY** Apply in writing to the correspondent.
**WHO TO APPLY TO** David Rothenberg, Trustee, c/o Blick Rothenberg Chartered Accountants, 16 Great Queen Street, Covent Garden, London WC2B 5AH Tel. 020 7544 8865 email robin@blickrothenberg.com

## ■ Andrews Charitable Trust

**CC NO** 243509    **ESTABLISHED** 1965
**WHERE FUNDING CAN BE GIVEN** UK and overseas.
**WHO CAN BENEFIT** Charities and community groups.
**WHAT IS FUNDED** Social welfare and Christian causes.
**SAMPLE GRANTS** Restored (£85,000); 2nd Chance and Carers Worldwide (£25,000 each); Christian Initiative Trust (£20,000); Ekklesia (£16,000); Dementia Adventure (£7,500); Advantage Africa (£5,000).
**FINANCES** Year 2013 Income £599,945 Grants £183,750 Grants to organisations £183,750 Assets £10,695,092
**TRUSTEES** Michael Robson; David Westgate; Nicholas Wright; Helen Battrick; Paul Heal; Alastair Page; Elizabeth Hughes; Chris Chapman; Marcus Olliffe; Ami Davis; Alison Kelly.
**HOW TO APPLY** The trust's website states: 'Our experience of taking unsolicited proposals has not been fun. In 2014, we rejected 99% of applications we received! To reduce the time and hassle for all concerned we have decided not to accept proposals. We will instead use our extensive network to feed us organisations that meet our very specific criteria. When we do approach an organisation, we will initially ask for a simple 2–3 page summary of the idea and how it meets our objectives. This will be shared with all our trustees and so it needs to clearly communicate the need, the idea and its potential. If this is of interest to us then we will arrange a time to meet. At this point, the due diligence documents we require are things that organisations should already have on hand, including a business or strategic plan, financials, organisation chart, donor/investor list, leadership and board member CV.'
**WHO TO APPLY TO** Ms Sian Edwards, Director, The Clockhouse, Bath Hill, Keynsham, Bristol BS31 1HL Tel. 0117 946 1834 email info@andrewscharitabletrust.org.uk Website www.andrewscharitabletrust.org.uk

## ■ Anglo American Group Foundation

**CC NO** 1111719    **ESTABLISHED** 2005
**WHERE FUNDING CAN BE GIVEN** United Kingdom and overseas (priority countries include Brazil, Peru, Chile, Colombia, China, UK, Zimbabwe, Botswana, Namibia and the Democratic Republic of Congo amongst others).
**WHO CAN BENEFIT** Charitable organisations.
**WHAT IS FUNDED** Education, international development, health/HIV, environment and London-based community development.
**WHAT IS NOT FUNDED** Organisations which are not registered charities.
**TYPE OF GRANT** Support to ongoing projects by organisations.
**RANGE OF GRANTS** £23,000–£197,000 plus £75,000 in grants under £20,000.
**SAMPLE GRANTS** Pro Mujer Inc (£167,000); Leonard Cheshire Disability (£155,000); the Royal Academy of Engineering (£150,000); Engineers Without Borders (£125,000); the Terrance Higgins Trust (£104,000); the Cambridge Foundation (£100,000); WaterAid (£84,000); the Prince's Trust (£71,000); Care International (£60,000); the Connection at St Martin's (£51,000); Diamond Development Initiative International, Institute for Human Rights and Business (£50,000 each); International Women's Health Coalition (£46,000); the London Community Foundation (£43,000); Body and Soul (£40,000); Keeping Kids Company (£35,000); Engineering Development Trust (£31,000); Sentebale (£30,000); Kriel Orphanage (£29,000); Action for Brazil Children, the National AIDS Trust, St Andrew's Youth Club (£25,000 each); and the Samaritans (£23,000).
**FINANCES** Year 2013 Income £1,449,895 Grants £1,600,445 Grants to organisations £1,600,445 Assets £366,511
**TRUSTEES** Angela Bromfield; Ian Botha; Duncan Wanblad; Jonathan Samuel.
**OTHER INFORMATION** The foundation was established in 2005 by Anglo American plc, a large multinational mining company.
**HOW TO APPLY** Applicants are invited to contact the trust directly. The trustees meet quarterly.
**WHO TO APPLY TO** Erica Shinnie, Correspondent, Anglo American plc, 20 Carlton House Terrace, London SW1Y 5AN Tel. 020 7968 8727 email aagf@angloamerican.com Website www.angloamericangroupfoundation.org

## ■ Anguish's Educational Foundation

**CC NO** 311288    **ESTABLISHED** 1605
**WHERE FUNDING CAN BE GIVEN** Norwich and the parishes of Costessey, Hellesdon, Catton, Sprowston, Thorpe St Andrew and Corpusty.
**WHO CAN BENEFIT** Residents of the area of benefit under the age of 25.
**WHAT IS FUNDED** School clothing, school trips, books/equipment, sports and musical training,

grants for fees/maintenance at university/ tertiary education.
**SAMPLE GRANTS** Clover Hill Infant and Nursery School (£28,000); Parkside Community Trust and The Virtual School for Children in Care (£10,000 each); Norfolk and Norwich Scope Association (£8,000); FACE (£4,000); Lakenham Pre-School Playgroup (£3,000); The Chermond Trust (£1,100).
**FINANCES** Year 2013/14 Income £876,578 Grants £595,006 Grants to organisations £115,500 Assets £19,851,667
**TRUSTEES** Roy Blower; Philip Blanchflower; Iain Brooksby; Brenda Ferris; David Fullman; Heather Tyrrell; Geoffrey Loades; Pamela Scutter; Jeanne Southgate; Jeremy Hooke; Amy Stammers; Peter Shields; Michael Flynn.
**OTHER INFORMATION** In 2013/14 grants were given mainly to individuals (£489,500). A total of £115,500 was given to organisations.
**HOW TO APPLY** Apply in writing to the correspondent. Applications from other charities are considered at two meetings in a year. Applications from individuals are considered at seven meetings throughout the year. Individuals are usually invited to the office for an informal interview.
**WHO TO APPLY TO** David Walker, Clerk to the Trustees, 1 Woolgate Court, St Benedict's Street, Norwich NR2 4AP Tel. 01603 621023 email david.walker@norwichcharitabletrusts.org.uk

## ■ The Animal Defence Trust
**CC NO** 263095   **ESTABLISHED** 1971
**WHERE FUNDING CAN BE GIVEN** UK.
**WHO CAN BENEFIT** UK organisations benefitting animals.
**WHAT IS FUNDED** Capital projects for animal welfare/ protection.
**TYPE OF GRANT** Usually one-off payments.
**SAMPLE GRANTS** Brooke Hospital for Animals and Compassion in World Farming (£3,000 each); Plymouth Spay Team Coalition and Sebakwe Black Rhino Trust (£2,000 each); Care4cats, Cat Rescue, Help in Suffering, Hope Rescue, Les Amis des Chats and Pennine Pen Animal Rescue (£1,500 each).
**FINANCES** Year 2013/14 Income £59,863 Grants £73,500 Grants to organisations £73,500 Assets £1,367,882
**TRUSTEES** Marion Saunders; Carole Bowles; Richard J. Vines; Jenny Wheadon.
**HOW TO APPLY** Apply on a form which together with guidelines can be downloaded from the trust's website.
**WHO TO APPLY TO** Alan Meyer, Secretary, Horsey Lightly, 50 Broadway, London SW1H 0RG Tel. 020 7222 8844 email ameyer@horseylightly.com Website www.animaldefencetrust.org

## ■ The Eric Anker-Petersen Charity
**CC NO** 1061428   **ESTABLISHED** 1997
**WHERE FUNDING CAN BE GIVEN** UK.
**WHO CAN BENEFIT** Charitable causes in the fields of screen and stage.
**WHAT IS FUNDED** Grants are made towards the conservation of classic films.
**WHAT IS NOT FUNDED** Individuals; non-charitable purposes.
**SAMPLE GRANTS** Theatrical Ladies Guild, and Imperial War Museum for the following films: The British Atomic Trials at Maralinga,
Everybody's Business, The Women's Portion and for the book: This Film is Dangerous.
**FINANCES** Year 2013/14 Income £4,610 Grants £35,000 Grants to organisations £35,000
**TRUSTEES** George Duncan; Christopher Sokol; David Long.
**OTHER INFORMATION** Grants usually total about £35,000 a year.
**HOW TO APPLY** Apply in writing to the correspondent. The trust has previously wished to emphasise that it is always looking for projects to support which meet its criteria, outlined above.
**WHO TO APPLY TO** David Long, Trustee, 8–10 New Fetter Lane, London EC4A 1RS Tel. 020 7203 5096 email grainne.feeney@charlesrussell.co.uk

## ■ The Annandale Charitable Trust
**CC NO** 1049193   **ESTABLISHED** 1995
**WHERE FUNDING CAN BE GIVEN** UK.
**WHO CAN BENEFIT** Major charities.
**WHAT IS FUNDED** General charitable purposes.
**SAMPLE GRANTS** Unicef (£13,000); Bowel Cancer UK, (£5,000); Earl Mountbatten Hospice, International Animal Rescue, Meru and West Yorkshire Dog Rescue (£3,000 each); Equibuddy and The Legacy Rainbow House (£2,000).
**FINANCES** Year 2013/14 Income £254,433 Grants £305,800 Grants to organisations £305,800 Assets £11,980,358
**TRUSTEES** Carole Duggan; HSBC. Trust Company (UK) Ltd.
**HOW TO APPLY** The trustees have previously stated that they have an ongoing programme of funding for specific charities and all funds are fully committed.
**WHO TO APPLY TO** HSBC Trust Company UK Limited, Second Floor, 1 The Forum, Parkway, Whiteley, Fareham PO15 7PA Tel. 023 8072 3344 email charitable.trusts@hsbc.com

## ■ Anpride Ltd
**CC NO** 288978   **ESTABLISHED** 1984
**WHERE FUNDING CAN BE GIVEN** London and Israel.
**WHO CAN BENEFIT** Registered charities.
**WHAT IS FUNDED** Advancement of the Jewish faith and general charitable purposes.
**WHAT IS NOT FUNDED** Grants to state-aided institutions will generally not be considered and no grants are given to individuals.
**FINANCES** Year 2013/14 Income £154,978 Grants £58,766 Grants to organisations £58,766 Assets £165,000
**TRUSTEES** Chaim Benedikt; Golda Benedikt.
**HOW TO APPLY** Apply in writing to the correspondent.
**WHO TO APPLY TO** Golda Benedikt, Trustee and Secretary, 99 Geldeston Road, London E5 8RS Tel. 020 8806 1011

## ■ The Anson Charitable Trust
**CC NO** 1111010   **ESTABLISHED** 2005
**WHERE FUNDING CAN BE GIVEN** UK.
**WHO CAN BENEFIT** Charitable organisations and individuals.
**WHAT IS FUNDED** General charitable purposes, there is a preference for work with children and older people. Health and medical research causes are also supported.
**RANGE OF GRANTS** £100–£30,000
**SAMPLE GRANTS** New Horizon Youth Centre (£30,000); Royal Opera House Foundation

(£15,500); The Pace Centre (£12,000); Brill Village Community, Bucks Agri Association, The Sixteen Limited and Trail Blazers (£5,000 each); British Wireless for the Blind Fund and Changing Faces (£3,000 each); Breast Cancer Campaign and The British Stammering Association (£2,000 each); Autistica and Bipolar UK (£1,000 each); British Red Cross (£100).
FINANCES Year 2013/14 Income £225,000 Grants £281,013 Grants to organisations £281,013 Assets £598,079
TRUSTEES George Anson; Kirsty Anson; Lady Pauncefort-Duncombe.
HOW TO APPLY Apply in writing to the correspondent.
WHO TO APPLY TO George Anson, Trustee, The Lilies, High Street, Weedon, Aylesbury, Buckinghamshire HP22 4NS Tel. 01296 640331 email ansonctrust@btinternet.com

■ **The Apax Foundation**
CC NO 1112845        ESTABLISHED 2006
WHERE FUNDING CAN BE GIVEN UK and overseas.
WHO CAN BENEFIT Registered charities and community groups.
WHAT IS FUNDED Social welfare and education.
RANGE OF GRANTS Up to £215,000.
SAMPLE GRANTS Impetus – the Private Equity Foundation (£215,000); Schwab Foundation for Social Enterprise (£102,000); Emmaus Norwich, INSEAD (£100,000 each); Mosiac (£86,000); Trickle Up (£50,000); Finanzierungsagentur fur Social Entrepreneurship (£42,000); Bridges Ventures USA (£32,000); Shivia Finance (£25,000); Pilotlight (£18,000); and Crisis UK (£13,500).
FINANCES Year 2013/14 Income £566,979 Grants £951,996 Grants to organisations £951,996 Assets £17,845,921
TRUSTEES Ronald Cohen, Chair; Peter Englander; Martin Halusa; David Marks; John Megrue; Michael Phillips; Simon Cresswell; Mitch Truwit; Shashank Singh.
OTHER INFORMATION 'The Apax Foundation is the formal channel for Apax Partners' charitable giving and receives a percentage of the firm's profits and carried interest.'
HOW TO APPLY Apply in writing to the correspondent.
WHO TO APPLY TO David Marks, Trustee, Apax Partners, 33 Jermyn Street, London SW1Y 6DN Tel. 020 7872 6300 email foundation@apax.com Website www.apax.com/responsibility/apax-foundation

■ **The Appletree Trust**
SC NO SC004851        ESTABLISHED 1982
WHERE FUNDING CAN BE GIVEN Preference for Scotland and particularly the north east Fife district.
WHO CAN BENEFIT Charitable organisations, particularly in the city of Edinburgh and the north east Fife district.
WHAT IS FUNDED Disability, health causes, relief of poverty, cancer research
WHAT IS NOT FUNDED Individuals.
TYPE OF GRANT Capital, buildings, project, research. Grants can be for up to two years.
SAMPLE GRANTS Previous grant beneficiaries included: 1st St Andrews Boys' Brigade, Alzheimer Scotland, Arthritis Care In Scotland, the Broomhouse Centre, Children's Hospice Association, Discovery Camps Trust, Home Start East Fife, Marie Curie Cancer Care, PDSA, Prince and Princess of Wales Hospice, RNID, the Salvation Army, Scottish Motor Neurone Disease Association and Scottish Spina Bifida Association.
FINANCES Year 2013/14 Income £36,303 Grants £33,000 Grants to organisations £33,000
TRUSTEE The Royal Bank of Scotland plc.
HOW TO APPLY Apply in writing to the correspondent. The trustees usually meet to consider grants in April.
WHO TO APPLY TO The Royal Bank of Scotland plc, Trust and Estate Services, Eden Lakeside, Chester Business Park, Wrexham Road, Chester CH4 9QT

■ **The John Apthorp Charity (formerly Summary Limited)**
CC NO 1102472        ESTABLISHED 2004
WHERE FUNDING CAN BE GIVEN UK, with a preference for Hertfordshire.
WHO CAN BENEFIT Charitable organisations.
WHAT IS FUNDED Education, religion and social welfare.
RANGE OF GRANTS Up to £50,000.
SAMPLE GRANTS Walton and Frinton Yacht Club (£50,000); Radlett PCC (£30,000); North London Hospice (£27,000); Tay Foundation (£25,000); Radlett Art Society, RAFT, Herts Aid, Earthworks, Young Enterprise, Radlett Light Opera Society and Isabel Hospice (£10,000 each); Coram Voice (£6,000); Wavelength and Samaritans (£5,000 each); and the Tall Ships Youth Trust (£3,000).
FINANCES Year 2013 Income £416,107 Grants £397,300 Grants to organisations £397,300 Assets £11,388,680
TRUSTEES John Apthorp; Duncan Apthorp; Justin Apthorp; Kate Arnold.
HOW TO APPLY Apply in writing to the correspondent.
WHO TO APPLY TO John Apthorp, Trustee, The Field House Farm, 29 Newlands Avenue, Radlett, Hertfordshire WD7 8EJ Tel. 01923 855727

■ **The Arbib Foundation**
CC NO 296358        ESTABLISHED 1987
WHERE FUNDING CAN BE GIVEN UK.
WHO CAN BENEFIT Registered charities and local organisations with charitable purposes.
WHAT IS FUNDED Social welfare, medical, education and children's welfare In particular to maintain the River and Rowing Museum in the Thames Valley for the education of the general public in the history, geography and ecology of the Thames Valley and the River Thames, with some donations for general purposes.
WHAT IS NOT FUNDED Individuals.
TYPE OF GRANT Recurrent and single donations.
RANGE OF GRANTS £100–£125,000
SAMPLE GRANTS Cancer Research UK and the River and Rowing Museum Foundation (£50,000 each); Alfred Dunhill Foundation and the Barbados Community Foundation (£25,000 each); CLIC Sargent and Sandy Lane Charitable Trust (£10,000 each); Kidscancer (£5,000); Mary How Trust and Reeds School (£1,000 each); Henley Youth Festival (£500).
FINANCES Year 2013/14 Income £239,614 Grants £335,287 Grants to organisations £335,287 Assets £281,263
TRUSTEES Sir Martyn Arbib; Lady Arbib; Annabel Nicoll.
HOW TO APPLY Apply in writing to the correspondent, although note the trustees have stressed that grants are largely made to organisations with

which the trustees have a connection, and therefore unsolicited applications are unlikely to be successful.
**WHO TO APPLY TO** Paula Doraisamy, 61 Grosvenor Street, London W1K 3JE *Tel.* 020 3011 1100 *email* admin@61grosvenorstreet.com

■ **The Archbishop's Council – The Church and Community Fund**
**CC NO** 1074857   **ESTABLISHED** 1915
**WHERE FUNDING CAN BE GIVEN** England (unless applying from a chaplaincy within the Diocese in Europe).
**WHO CAN BENEFIT** Churches; parish, deanery or diocesan projects; community organisations; charities. Organisations have sufficiently strong Anglican (Church of England) links.
**WHAT IS FUNDED** Charitable work of the Church of England, primarily church and community projects. Support is especially given to initiatives which: engage with the whole community; support innovative use of resources; help transform areas of greatest need and opportunity; encourage spiritual and numerical growth.
**WHAT IS NOT FUNDED** Projects that: seek to expand locally rather than be replicated in other areas; do not have a track record of success or growth; only suit a unique local situation and environment; are essentially insular and inward looking; are primarily about maintaining the nation's architectural heritage; are primarily about liturgical reordering; concern restoration works to bells or organs; are research projects or personal grants; cover the repayment of debts or overdrafts; are not directly connected with the Church of England, ecumenical or other faith; are partnerships in which the Church of England element is small and projects which are predominantly secular in nature; cover anything for which the Church Commissioners' funds or diocesan core funding are normally available, including stipend support; feasibility studies (the fund is able to offer limited support towards the preliminary costs of projects, for example professional fees, but where a grants is awarded at this stage, no further funding will be available for the main body of the work). Application guidelines gives detailed further examples of what work would not be funded.
**TYPE OF GRANT** One-off and recurring for up to three years; capital and core costs; salaries.
**RANGE OF GRANTS** £10,000–£20,000; larger awards may be considered.
**SAMPLE GRANTS** Projects supported are listed online. **Most recent beneficiaries included**: All Saints Landmark Centre, Centre for Theology and Community and Luton Town Centre Chaplaincy (£20,000 each); St Mary Magdalene (£19,100); Christ Church Walton Breck (£17,000); St Francis of Assisi and Way4ward (£12,000 each); All Saints Centre – All Saints Youth Project (£11,000); Building Bridges Burnley and Telford Christian Council (£10,000 each).
**FINANCES** *Year* 2013 *Income* £9,000 *Grants* £442,000 *Grants to organisations* £442,000 *Assets* £19,051
**TRUSTEES** Richard Hopgood; The Very Revd Peter Bradley; Revd Andy Salmon; Susan Pope; Revd Nicholas Papadopulos.
**OTHER INFORMATION** This fund an excepted charity but its trustee, the Archbishop's Council, is registered under the above number. Brief accounting details for the fund were included in the notes to the accounts for the Archbishops' Council, of which the fund is a subsidiary. In 2014 the charity's grant-making strategy was due to be reviewed; therefore funding priorities may change. Details were not yet given at the time of writing (June 2015). Potential applicants are advised to consult the website or the correspondent for the most up-to-date changes.
**HOW TO APPLY** Full details of how to apply can be found on the fund's website and applicants are advised to refer to these before applying. If you feel that your project meets the aims of the funding themes and match the criteria detailed in the guidelines, then complete the eligibility quiz and an online application. The website states: 'The CCF endeavours to contact applicants within two weeks of receipt of their application. Applicants will be notified if; there are items missing from their application, an application is complete and ready for review at the next Committee meeting or an applicant is ineligible to apply due to failing to meet specific criteria.' You can only re-apply once two years have passed after the original application. See the website for latest deadlines.
**WHO TO APPLY TO** Hayley Corker, Grants Officer, Archbishop's Council, Church House, Great Smith Street, London SW1P 3AZ *Tel.* 07825 759520 or 020 7898 1000 (Archbishop's Council) *email* ccf@churchofengland.org *Website* www.ccfund.org.uk

■ **The Archer Trust**
**CC NO** 1033534   **ESTABLISHED** 1994
**WHERE FUNDING CAN BE GIVEN** Worldwide.
**WHO CAN BENEFIT** Voluntary organisations, especially those which make good use of volunteers or are located in areas of high unemployment or disadvantage. Preference is given to smaller organisations. Support is given to projects both in the UK and overseas, but for overseas projects only via UK charities.
**WHAT IS FUNDED** Provision of aid and support to a defined group of needy or deserving people, such as people with mental or physical disabilities or people who are otherwise disadvantaged; Christian causes.
**WHAT IS NOT FUNDED** Individuals (including for gap years); conservation or heritage projects; environmental causes; conversion for disability access; animal charities or research.
**RANGE OF GRANTS** Usually £250–£3,000.
**SAMPLE GRANTS** The Sycamore Project (£3,000); Basildon Resource Centre, Caris Camden, Cricklewood Homeless Concern, Ferndale Skate Park Limited, Support Line, The Upper Room and Westbourne Park Family Centre (£2,000 each); Beds Garden Carers and Church Army (£1,500 each); Angels International and Merseyside Youth Challenge Trust (£1,000 each).
**FINANCES** *Year* 2013/14 *Income* £110,540 *Grants* £65,395 *Grants to organisations* £65,395 *Assets* £1,934,602
**TRUSTEES** Catherine Archer; Lyn Packman; James Archer; Michael Baker.
**HOW TO APPLY** Apply in writing to the correspondent. Unsuccessful applicants will not receive a response, even if an sae is enclosed. Applications are considered twice a year, usually in March and September.
**WHO TO APPLY TO** The Secretary, Bourne House, Wadesmill, Ware, Hertfordshire SG12 0TT *Tel.* 01920 462312 *Website* www.archertrust.org.uk

## ■ The Architectural Heritage Fund
**CC NO** 266780 **ESTABLISHED** 1973
**WHERE FUNDING CAN BE GIVEN** UK (excluding the Channel Islands and the Isle of Man).
**WHO CAN BENEFIT** Registered charities; social enterprises; charitable incorporated organisations. Organisations must have charitable status.
**WHAT IS FUNDED** Support is given in the form of grants, loans, advice and information for the preservation and sustainable re-use of historic buildings. Grants may be given for purposes including project viability studies and project development. Up to date information on the grants and support available can be found on the fund's website.
**WHAT IS NOT FUNDED** Applications from private owners or developers; religious buildings in use or projects only involving routine maintenance; buildings which are not listed, scheduled as an ancient monument or in a Conservation Area. Each of the fund's grants and loan programmes have specific criteria which can be found in their respective guidance notes on the fund's website.
**TYPE OF GRANT** Loans; feasibility study grants; project development grants; refundable and non-refundable grants.
**RANGE OF GRANTS** Grants up to £25,000; loans up to £500,000 (more in exceptional circumstances).
**SAMPLE GRANTS** Berwick Community Trust; Edinburgh Printmakers; Llanelli Railway Goods Shed Trust; The Cleveland Pools Trust; The Arkwright Society Ltd; The National Trust for Scotland; The Sheffield General Cemetery Trust; Turner's House Trust; Waltham Forest Cinema Trust; Youthscape.
**FINANCES** Year 2013/14 Income £1,026,787 Grants £662,340 Grants to organisations £662,340 Assets £13,046,835
**TRUSTEES** Merlin Waterson, Chair; Myra Barnes; Roy Dantzic; Elizabeth Davidson; Kate Dickson; John Duggan; Rita Harkin; Michael Hoare; Richard Keen; Philip Kirby; Douglas Reid; John Townsend.
**OTHER INFORMATION** In addition to the amount given in grants, £2.36 million was disbursed in loans.
**HOW TO APPLY** Detailed notes for applicants for loans and feasibility studies are supplied with the application forms, all of which are available from the fund's website. The trustees meet in March, June, September and December; application deadlines for each meeting are published on the website, along with information about any funds that are currently fully committed or closed to application.
**WHO TO APPLY TO** Regional Project Support Officers, 15 Whitehall, London SW1A 2DD Tel. 020 7925 0199 Fax 020 7930 0295 email ahf@ahfund.org.uk Website www.ahfund.org.uk

## ■ The Ardeola Charitable Trust
**CC NO** 1124380 **ESTABLISHED** 2008
**WHERE FUNDING CAN BE GIVEN** Worldwide.
**WHO CAN BENEFIT** Registered charities.
**WHAT IS FUNDED** General charitable purposes, although the main beneficiary each year is Target Ovarian Cancer.
**SAMPLE GRANTS** Target Ovarian Cancer (£330,000); Durham University (£150,000); St Francis Hospice (£120,000); Royal National Theatre (£50,000).
**FINANCES** Year 2013/14 Income £1,987,145 Grants £650,075 Grants to organisations £650,075 Assets £3,887,556
**TRUSTEES** Graham Barker; Joanna Barker; Coutts & Co.; Prof. John Mark Cornwall; William Hiscocks.
**HOW TO APPLY** Apply in writing to the correspondent, although potential applicants should note that the trust's main beneficiary is connected with the trustees.
**WHO TO APPLY TO** The Trustees, Coutts & Co, Trustee Dept., 440 Strand, London WC2R 0QS Tel. 020 7753 1000 email couttscharities@coutts.com

## ■ The Ardwick Trust
**CC NO** 266981 **ESTABLISHED** 1975
**WHERE FUNDING CAN BE GIVEN** UK, Israel and financially developing countries.
**WHO CAN BENEFIT** Institutions and registered charities (mainly UK charities) benefitting people of all ages.
**WHAT IS FUNDED** To support Jewish welfare, along with a wide range of non-Jewish causes to include social welfare, health, education (especially special schools), elderly people, conservation and the environment, child welfare, disability and medical research. In general most of the largest grants go to Jewish organisations, with most of the smaller grants to non-Jewish organisations.
**WHAT IS NOT FUNDED** Individuals.
**TYPE OF GRANT** One-off or recurrent grants up to two years. Capital, including buildings, research and start-up costs.
**RANGE OF GRANTS** Mostly under £1,000.
**SAMPLE GRANTS** British Friends of the Hebrew University, Jewish Care, Nightingale Hammerson and Technion UK (£2,000 each); Langdon Foundation, Norwood, United Jewish Israel Appeal and World Jewish Relief (£1,000 each). Less than £1,000: Cancer Vaccine Institute, Carers UK, ChildHope, Children in Crisis, Combat Stress, Deafblind UK, Epilepsy Research UK, Food Lifeline, Friends of Regents Opera, Jumbulance Trust, Lepra, Let's Face It, Mercy Ships, New Israel Fund, Plan UK, Samaritans, Save the Children Fund, Scope, Sightsavers.
**FINANCES** Year 2013/14 Income £81,719 Grants £64,300 Grants to organisations £64,300 Assets £1,229,856
**TRUSTEES** Janet Bloch; Dominic Flynn; Judith Portrait.
**HOW TO APPLY** Apply in writing to the correspondent.
**WHO TO APPLY TO** Janet Bloch, Trustee, c/o Knox Cropper, 24 Petworth Road, Haslemere, Surrey GU27 2HR Tel. 01428 652788 email haslemere@knoxcropper.com

## ■ The Argentarius Foundation
**CC NO** 1079980 **ESTABLISHED** 2000
**WHERE FUNDING CAN BE GIVEN** UK.
**WHO CAN BENEFIT** Charitable organisations.
**WHAT IS FUNDED** General charitable purposes.
**SAMPLE GRANTS** No details available.
**FINANCES** Year 2013/14 Income £374 Grants £200,000 Grants to organisations £200,000
**TRUSTEES** Emily Marbach; Judy Jackson; Anna Josse.
**OTHER INFORMATION** Basic information taken from the Charity Commission website. Accounting documents had been received but were not published due to the foundation's low income.

## The Argus Appeal

**CC NO** 1013647  **ESTABLISHED** 1992
**WHERE FUNDING CAN BE GIVEN** Sussex.
**WHO CAN BENEFIT** Registered charities.
**WHAT IS FUNDED** Relief in need, older people.
**RANGE OF GRANTS** Up to £17,000.
**SAMPLE GRANTS** The Martlets (£4,270); The Dame Vera Lynn Trust (£3,000); Sussex Beacon (£2,000); St Michael's (£1,300); St Catherine's, Relate (£1,000 each); Lions Club of Chichester (£250).
**FINANCES** Year 2013/14 Income £167,514 Grants £83,813 Grants to organisations £59,475 Assets £335,095
**TRUSTEES** Elsa Gillio; David Goldin; Roger French; Sue Addis; Lucy Pearce; Dawn Sweeney; Michael Gilson
**OTHER INFORMATION** The grant total includes £59,400 to 45 organisations and £24,300 to individuals.
**HOW TO APPLY** Apply in writing to the correspondent.
**WHO TO APPLY TO** Elsa Gillio, Trustee, Argus House, Crowhurst Road, Hollingbury, Brighton BN1 8AR Tel. 01273 544465 email elsa.gillio@theargus.co.uk Website www.theargus.co.uk/argusappeal

## Armenian General Benevolent Union London Trust

**CC NO** 282070  **ESTABLISHED** 1981
**WHERE FUNDING CAN BE GIVEN** UK and overseas.
**WHO CAN BENEFIT** Armenian individuals and organisations.
**WHAT IS FUNDED** The purpose of the trust is to advance education among Armenians, particularly those in the UK, and to promote the study of Armenian history, literature, language, culture and religion.
**WHAT IS NOT FUNDED** Projects of a commercial nature.
**SAMPLE GRANTS** Previously: The Armenian Church Trust (£5,000) and the RP Musical for Remembrance Concert (£1,500). A further £4,000 was given under the grant category 'Education' to K Tahta Armenian Sunday School.
**FINANCES** Year 2013 Income £151,745 Grants £192,684 Grants to organisations £4,000 Assets £4,571,353
**TRUSTEES** Dr Berge Azadian; Berge Setrakian; Aris Atamian; Noushig Yakoubian Setrakian; Assadour Guzelian; Tro Manoukian; Arline Medazoumian; Armine Afrikian.
**OTHER INFORMATION** The only grant to an organisation in this financial year was £4,000 to K Tahta Armenian Sunday School. The remaining amount was given in grants and loans to students. Although the total of grants to organisations was very small, it could well be more in the future (as it has been in previous years).
**HOW TO APPLY** Apply in writing to the correspondent. Applications are considered all year around.
**WHO TO APPLY TO** Dr Berge Azadian, Trustee, 51c Parkside, Wimbledon Common, London SW19 5NE

**HOW TO APPLY** Apply in writing to the correspondent.
**WHO TO APPLY TO** Philip Goodman, Goodman and Co, 14 Basing Hill, London NW11 8TH Tel. 020 8458 0955 email philip@goodmanandco.com

## The John Armitage Charitable Trust

**CC NO** 1079688  **ESTABLISHED** 2000
**WHERE FUNDING CAN BE GIVEN** England and Wales.
**WHO CAN BENEFIT** Institutions and registered charities.
**WHAT IS FUNDED** Medical, relief in need, education, religion, environment, general charitable purposes.
**SAMPLE GRANTS** Bryan Adams Foundation, Canterbury Cathedral Trust and Winston Churchill Memorial Trust (£100,000 each); Russian Revival Project (£60,000); Redress, Shine and Youth Sport Trust (£36,000 each); Hop Skip Jump (£30,000); Fishmongers Company Charitable Trust and New Horizon Youth (£24,000 each); Kensington and Chelsea Foundation (£18,000); Gloucestershire Wildlife Trust (£12,000); The Foundation of Prince William and Prince Harry (£3,000).
**FINANCES** Year 2013/14 Income £13,617 Grants £1,681,800 Grants to organisations £1,681,800 Assets £47,005,593
**TRUSTEES** John Armitage; Catherine Armitage; William Francklin; Celina Francklin.
**HOW TO APPLY** Applications received by the trust are 'reviewed by the trustees and grants awarded at their discretion'.
**WHO TO APPLY TO** John Armitage, Trustee, c/o Sampson West, 12–14 Mitre House, London EC3A 5BU Tel. 020 7404 5040 Fax 020 7831 1098 email finance@sampsonwest.co.uk

## The Armourers' and Brasiers' Gauntlet Trust

**CC NO** 279204  **ESTABLISHED** 1979
**WHERE FUNDING CAN BE GIVEN** UK, with some preference for London.
**WHO CAN BENEFIT** Charitable organisations.
**WHAT IS FUNDED** The objectives of the trust are: support for education and research in materials science and technology and for basic science in schools; encouragement of the understanding and preservation of historic armour; encouragement of the armourers' trade in the armed services; encouragement of professional excellence in the training of young officers in the Royal Armoured Corps. It also considers appeals in the following overall categories: community, social care and armed forces; children, youth and general education; medical and health; medical and health; art, arms and armour; Christian mission.
**WHAT IS NOT FUNDED** In general grants are not made to organisation or groups which are not registered charities; in response to applications for the benefit of individuals; to organisations or groups whose main object is to fund or support other charitable bodies; which are in direct relief of, or will lead to, a reduction of financial support from public funds; to charities with a turnover in excess of £500,000; to charities which spend over 10% of their income on fundraising activities; towards general maintenance, repair or restoration of buildings, including ecclesiastical buildings, unless there is a connection with the Armourers and Brasiers' Company, or unless of outstanding importance to the national heritage; to appeals for charitable sponsorship from individuals.
**TYPE OF GRANT** 'Regular annual grants are not a policy of the trust at present, but charities can still apply for grants on an annual basis.'

RANGE OF GRANTS The trustees prefer to make grants to smaller and less well-known charitable organisations rather than to those with a high public profile. Over 100 such charities receive grants each year.
SAMPLE GRANTS Youth Action for Change International (£1,800); Coeliac UK (£1,500); Association of Visitors to Immigration Detainees, City of London Police, Widows' and Orphans' Fund, DEC Philippines Appeal, First Aid Nursing Yeomanry, Inns of Court and City Yeomanry, Keep Out – The Crime Diversion Scheme, Kingston Bereavement Service, Royal British Legion and Sheriffs' and Recorder's Fund (£500 each).
FINANCES Year 2013/14 Income £493,849 Grants £265,314 Grants to organisations £194,444 Assets £6,907,613
TRUSTEES Prof. William Bonfield; Dr Simon Archer; Col. David Davies; Sir Timothy Ruggles-Brise; Edward Pitt; Anthony Pontifex.
OTHER INFORMATION Grants of £71,000 were made to 98 individuals.
HOW TO APPLY Apply in writing to the correspondent, with a copy of the latest annual report and audited accounts. Applications are considered quarterly. For full guidelines, visit the trust's website.
WHO TO APPLY TO Peter Bateman, Armourers' Hall, 81 Coleman Street, London EC2R 5BJ *Tel.* 020 7374 4000 *Fax* 020 7606 7481 *email* clerk@armourersandbrasiers.co.uk *Website* www.armourersandbrasiers.co.uk

■ **The Artemis Charitable Trust**

CC NO 291328    ESTABLISHED 1985
WHERE FUNDING CAN BE GIVEN UK.
WHO CAN BENEFIT Registered charities benefitting parents, counsellors and psychotherapists.
WHAT IS FUNDED Counselling, psychotherapy, parenting, and human relationship training.
WHAT IS NOT FUNDED Individuals; organisations which are not registered charities.'
TYPE OF GRANT Recurring.
SAMPLE GRANTS Chester University – Primary Care Psychological Services (£160,000); Chichester Festival Theatre (£17,000); Coaching Inside and Out (£5,000).
FINANCES Year 2013 Income £49,849 Grants £182,400 Grants to organisations £182,400 Assets £1,522,971
TRUSTEES Richard Evans; Dawn Bergin; David Evans; Mark Evans; Wendy Evans Menke.
HOW TO APPLY 'Applicants should be aware that most of the trust's funds are committed to a number of major ongoing projects and that spare funds available to meet new applications are very limited.'
WHO TO APPLY TO Richard Evans, Trustee, Brook House, Quay Meadow, Bosham, West Sussex PO18 8LY *Tel.* 01243 573475 *email* ritchie80@outlook.com

■ **Arthritis Research UK**

CC NO 207711    ESTABLISHED 1936
WHERE FUNDING CAN BE GIVEN Mainly UK.
WHO CAN BENEFIT Mostly universities.
WHAT IS FUNDED Research into the cause and cure of arthritis and related musculoskeletal diseases.
WHAT IS NOT FUNDED Applications for welfare and social matters will not be considered.
TYPE OF GRANT One-off, project, recurring, running costs, and salaries. Programme support is for five years; project grants are usually for three years.
FINANCES Year 2013/14 Income £37,016,000 Grants £17,871,000 Grants to organisations £17,871,000 Assets £141,660,000
TRUSTEES Charles Maisey, Chair; Joe Carlebach; Dr Sylvie Jackson; Prof. Sir Patrick Sissons; Mike Pringle; Paul Rowen; Tom Hayhoe; Prof. David Isenberg; Prof. David Marsh; Prof. Jonathan Cohen; Dr Rodger Macmillan; Karin Hogsander; Juliette Scott; Phillip Gray.
HOW TO APPLY Application forms and guidelines are available from the Arthritis Research UK website. Although the application process has strict criteria, the procedure is clearly explained on the charity's website.
WHO TO APPLY TO Joanne Turner, Grants Team, Copeman House, St Mary's Court, St Mary's Gate, Chesterfield, Derbyshire S41 7TD *Tel.* 0300 790 0400 *Fax* 0300 790 0401 *email* enquiries@arthritisresearchuk.org *Website* www.arthritisresearchuk.org

■ **Arts Council England**

CC NO 1036733    ESTABLISHED 1994
WHERE FUNDING CAN BE GIVEN England.
WHO CAN BENEFIT Organisations and individuals.
WHAT IS FUNDED Developing, sustaining and promoting the arts. There are four areas in which the council makes awards: artists and creative professionals; libraries; museums; organisations.
SAMPLE GRANTS Projects covered a wide range of the arts, libraries and museums from theatre to digital art, reading to dance, music to literature, crafts to collections.
FINANCES Year 2013/14 Income £694,662,000 Grants £612,273,623 Grants to organisations £612,273,623 Assets £155,002,000
TRUSTEES Alistair Spalding; Jon Cook; Rosemary Squire; Nicholas Kenyon; Sheila Healy; Peter Phillips; Joe Docherty; David Joseph; Nazo Moosa; Dr Maria Balshaw; Veronica Wadley; Matthew Bowcock; Sir Peter Bazalgette.
PUBLICATIONS The council produces various publications and information sheets concerning the arts. These are available on its website.
OTHER INFORMATION The assets figure given here refers to free reserves held at the end of the year.
HOW TO APPLY The council's website stresses that it is important to read the guidelines for each grant programme carefully before making an application or expression of interest. We would advise that potential applicants phone and speak to a member of the enquiries team if any clarification of the process, or your organisation's eligibility is required.
WHO TO APPLY TO Enquiries Team, The Hive, 49 Lever Street, Manchester M1 1FN *Tel.* 0845 300 6200 *email* enquiries@artscouncil.org.uk *Website* www.artscouncil.org.uk

■ **Arts Council of Northern Ireland**

ESTABLISHED 1995
WHERE FUNDING CAN BE GIVEN UK and Ireland (but projects must benefit people of Northern Ireland).
WHO CAN BENEFIT Artists; arts organisations; individuals.
WHAT IS FUNDED The Arts Council of Northern Ireland (ACNI) is the development and funding agency for the arts in Northern Ireland. it distributes public money and National Lottery funds to

develop and deliver a wide variety of arts projects, events and initiatives across Northern Ireland.
**SAMPLE GRANTS** BEAM Creative Network (£31,000); Ulster Orchestra Society (£15,000); Waterside Theatre Company Ltd (£12,000); Arts Care (£10,000); Play Resource Warehouse (£8,000); and In Your Space (NI) Ltd (£4,000).
**FINANCES** Year 2013/14 Grants £13,028,957 Grants to organisations £13,028,957
**TRUSTEES** Damien Coyle; William Montgomery; Prof. Ian Montgomery; Prof. Paul Seawright; Janine Walker; Brian Sore; Bob Collins; David Alderdice; Anna Carragher; Noelle McAlinden; Katherine McCloskey; Paul Mullan; Conor Shields; Nisha Tandon; Eibhlín Ní Dhochartaigh; Dr Siun Hanrahan; Dr Leon Litvack.
**HOW TO APPLY** Guidelines and full details of how to apply can be found at the Arts Council of Northern Ireland website.
**WHO TO APPLY TO** The Arts Development Department, MacNeice House, 77 Malone Road, Belfast BT9 6AQ *Tel.* 028 9038 5200 *email* info@artscouncil-ni.org *Website* www.artscouncil-ni.org

## ■ Arts Council of Wales (also known as Cyngor Celfyddydau Cymru)

**CC NO** 1034245      **ESTABLISHED** 1994
**WHERE FUNDING CAN BE GIVEN** Wales.
**WHO CAN BENEFIT** Arts organisations and individuals based in Wales.
**WHAT IS FUNDED** Arts activities and projects based in or mainly in Wales.
**WHAT IS NOT FUNDED** Individuals; organisations not meeting the eligibility criteria.
**TYPE OF GRANT** Both recurrent and one-off grants.
**SAMPLE GRANTS** Clwyd Theatr Cymru (£1.6 million); Aberystwyth Arts Centre (£560,000); Arad Goch (£378,000); Oriel Davies Gallery (£230,000); NoFit State Community Circus Ltd (£200,000); Artes Mundi Prize Limited (£147,500); Artis Community Cymuned (£205,500); Arts Care Limited (£132,500); Pontardawe Arts Centre (£63,000); Oriel Myrddin Trust (£47,000); Ty Cerdd – Music Centre Wales (£10,000).
**FINANCES** Year 2013/14 Income £52,843,000 Grants £32,231,000 Grants to organisations £32,009,055
**TRUSTEES** Prof. Dai Smith; Emma Evans; Dr John Geraint; Margaret Jervis; Osi Rhys Osmond; Alan Watkin; Prof. Gerwyn Wiliams; John Williams; Dr Kate Woodward; Marian Jones; Richard Turner; Dr Lesley Hodgson; Michael Griffiths; Melanie Hawthorne; Andrew Miller.
**OTHER INFORMATION** £222,000 was awarded to individuals/creative professionals.
**HOW TO APPLY** By applying online on council's website www.artscouncilofwales.org.uk. The council offers assistance to those without access to a computer or having any other difficulties in completing the application online. Any enquiries should be communicated via email, telephone, SMS (07797800504 ) or by post to the correspondent. The 'Apply for Funding' section on the website provides funding advice and guidelines for artists in Wales. This includes advice not only on the funding available from Arts Council of Wales, but also funding available for the arts from other sources. Creative professionals and organisations who have received funding from the council should read carefully the guidelines for using its logos.

**WHO TO APPLY TO** The Grants Team, Bute Place, Cardiff CF10 5AL *Tel.* 0845 873 4900 *email* info@artscouncilofwales.org.uk *Website* www.artscouncilofwales.org.uk

## ■ The Ove Arup Foundation

**CC NO** 328138      **ESTABLISHED** 1989
**WHERE FUNDING CAN BE GIVEN** UK and overseas.
**WHO CAN BENEFIT** Organisations benefitting research workers and designers.
**WHAT IS FUNDED** Education and research in matters related to the built environment, particularly if related to multi-disciplinary design, through educational institutions and charities.
**WHAT IS NOT FUNDED** Individuals, including students.
**TYPE OF GRANT** Research and project, including start-up and feasibility costs. They can be one-off or recurrent.
**RANGE OF GRANTS** Up to £57,000.
**SAMPLE GRANTS** The University of Edinburgh (£57,000); Useful Simple Projects Ltd (£25,000); BCAA, MADE, The University of Queensland (£10,000 each); University College London (£6,000); and the Anglo Danish Society (£2,000).
**FINANCES** Year 2013/14 Income £241,653 Grants £119,568 Grants to organisations £119,568 Assets £3,454,455
**TRUSTEES** Caroline Cole; Richard Haryott; Duncan Michael; Andrew Chan; Joanna Kennedy; Gregory Hodkinson; Terry Hill.
**HOW TO APPLY** Application forms are available to download from the foundation's website.
**WHO TO APPLY TO** John Ward, Correspondent, Ove Arup and Partners, 13 Fitzroy Street, London W1T 4BQ *Tel.* 020 7636 1531 *email* ovarfound@arup.com *Website* www.theovearupfoundation.com

## ■ The AS Charitable Trust

**CC NO** 242190      **ESTABLISHED** 1965
**WHERE FUNDING CAN BE GIVEN** UK and financially developing countries.
**WHO CAN BENEFIT** Preference for charities in which the trust has special interest, knowledge of or association with. Christian organisations will benefit. Support may go to victims of famine, man-made or natural disasters, and war.
**WHAT IS FUNDED** The trust is sympathetic to projects which combine the advancement of the Christian religion with Christian lay leadership, development in financially developing countries, peacemaking and reconciliation, or other areas of social concern.
**WHAT IS NOT FUNDED** Grants to individuals or large charities are very rare. Such applications are discouraged.
**RANGE OF GRANTS** Up to £26,600, often in multiple gifts to the one charity.
**SAMPLE GRANTS** GRACE (£26,600 in ten gifts); Salem Scotland (£12,500); Lambeth Partnership, Christian International Peace Service and Dorothy Kerin Trust (£2,500 each); CMS limited, Scripture Gift Mission and Salt-7 Trust Limited (£1,000 each).
**FINANCES** Year 2013/14 Income £359,101 Grants £51,118 Grants to organisations £51,118 Assets £12,745,535
**TRUSTEES** Caroline Eady; George Calvocoressi; Simon Sampson.
**OTHER INFORMATION** The most recent accounts available from the Charity Commission at the time of writing were for 2009/10. 2010/11 accounts were 633 days late.

HOW TO APPLY Apply in writing to the correspondent.
WHO TO APPLY TO George Calvocoressi, Trustee, Bix Bottom Farm, Henley-on-Thames, Oxfordshire RG9 6BH

## ■ ASCB Charitable Fund
CC NO 1123854    ESTABLISHED 2008
WHERE FUNDING CAN BE GIVEN UK
WHO CAN BENEFIT Individual sports people, sports unions and associations and garrisons/units of the army.
WHAT IS FUNDED Annual grants to sports unions and associations; capital project grants for sports equipment/infrastructure; Army Sports Lottery Grants.
TYPE OF GRANT Annual grants and capital grants.
RANGE OF GRANTS Up to £270,000, Mostly £20,000 or less.
SAMPLE GRANTS Motor Sports Association – 4 wheel (£27,000); Golf Association (£19,000); Football Association (£10,000); Mountaineering Association (£6,000); Army Rugby Union (£5,400); Water-skiing and Wakeboarding Association (£3,500); Army Hockey Association (£2,000); and 3 Para (£800).
FINANCES Year 2013/14 Income £4,637,054 Grants £822,718 Grants to organisations £822,718 Assets £8,322,260
TRUSTEES Brig. J. Orr; David Rowe; Maj. Gen. G. Berragan; Brig. B. Bathurst; Richard Davis; Lt. Col K. Bennett; Richard Stanford; Brig. Stephen Potter; WO1 Carl Burnett; WO1 Brendan Reese.
HOW TO APPLY Apply in writing to the organisation. Applications for annual grants to sports unions and associations should be made in January/February, for capital projects in March and September and at any time for Army Sports Lottery grants.
WHO TO APPLY TO Maj. Gen. Christopher Elliott, Army Sport Control Board, ROOM G08, Mackenzie Building, Fox Lines, Queens Avenue, Aldershot GU11 2LB  Tel. 01252 787062  email accountant@ascb.uk.com

## ■ The Asda Foundation
CC NO 1124268    ESTABLISHED 2008
WHERE FUNDING CAN BE GIVEN England and Wales.
WHO CAN BENEFIT Registered charities and voluntary sector organisations.
WHAT IS FUNDED Sport and recreation; community development; general charitable purposes.
WHAT IS NOT FUNDED Expeditions; sponsorship of charitable activities by people other than Asda colleagues.
RANGE OF GRANTS £1,000–£100,000
SAMPLE GRANTS Run For All (£110,000); the Trussell Trust (£80,000); FareShare (£40,000); Age UK – Community Project (£20,000); Community Development Fund (£15,000); Leeds Rugby (£9,000); Yorkshire Cancer Centre (£7,500); the Freedom Centre – Community Project (£4,900); Playful Leeds (£2,000); and All Saints Landmark Centre (£1,000).
FINANCES Year 2013 Income £8,574,248 Grants £8,077,823 Grants to organisations £8,077,823 Assets £5,757,487
TRUSTEES David Wickert; Ann Marie Rocks; John Cookman; Jim Jefcoate; Helen Milford; Dominic Birch; Alison Seabrook; Munazah Dar; Lisa Smith; Gerald Oppenheim; Lorraine Jackson; Lynne Tooms.
OTHER INFORMATION The Asda Foundation is Asda's charitable trust. It supplements the good causes that colleagues support locally, as well as a number of bigger ad-hoc projects in local communities. It also manages all funds raised for national charities and monies raised in Asda House.
HOW TO APPLY In the first instance, contact your local store or depot with your proposal/application. This will then be passed on to the trustees who will make a final decision. There is an eligibility tool and 'store locator' on the website.
WHO TO APPLY TO Julie Ward, Foundation Manager, Asda Stores Ltd, Asda House, Great Wilson Street, Leeds LS11 5AD  Tel. 0113 243 5435  Website www.asdafoundation.org

## ■ The Ashburnham Thanksgiving Trust
CC NO 249109    ESTABLISHED 1965
WHERE FUNDING CAN BE GIVEN UK and worldwide.
WHO CAN BENEFIT Individuals and organisations benefitting Christians and evangelists.
WHAT IS FUNDED Only Christian work already known to the trustees is supported, particularly evangelical overseas missionary work.
WHAT IS NOT FUNDED Buildings.
RANGE OF GRANTS Generally under £5,000.
SAMPLE GRANTS New Destiny Trust (£6,300); Genesis Arts Trust (£3,000); Interserve (£2,000); Relationships Foundation (£1,000). Grants of under £1,000 included: Advantage Africa, Arts Centre Group, Epilepsy Society, Freedom in Christ Ministries, London City Mission, Mercy Ships UK, Release International, Servants with Jesus, Titus Trust and Trinity Fellowship.
FINANCES Year 2013/14 Income £226,249 Grants £143,881 Grants to organisations £143,881
TRUSTEES Edward Bickersteth; Robert Bickersteth; Dr Charles Warren.
HOW TO APPLY Note: The trustees state they are fully committed to supporting existing beneficiaries and otherwise proactive in their grant-making and so do not accept unsolicited applications, nor do they respond to such applications.
WHO TO APPLY TO The Charity Secretary, Agmerhurst House, Kitchenham Road, Ashburnham, Battle, East Sussex TN33 9NB  email att@lookingforward.biz

## ■ A. J. H. Ashby Will Trust
CC NO 803291    ESTABLISHED 1990
WHERE FUNDING CAN BE GIVEN UK, especially Lea Valley area of Hertfordshire.
WHO CAN BENEFIT Charitable organisations, sports clubs and schools.
WHAT IS FUNDED Wildlife, particularly birds; heritage; education projects; and children.
WHAT IS NOT FUNDED Individuals; students.
TYPE OF GRANT One-off and recurrent.
SAMPLE GRANTS RSPB (£25,000 in four grants); Portland Bird Observatory (£10,000); The Hertfordshire Groundwork Trust and Wildwood Trust (£2,000 each); and Poplar Harca (£1,000).
FINANCES Year 2013/14 Income £570,700 Grants £40,324 Grants to organisations £40,324 Assets £1,295,516
TRUSTEE HSBC. Trust Company (UK) Ltd.
HOW TO APPLY Apply in writing to the correspondent.

## ■ The Ashden Trust

**CC NO** 802623  **ESTABLISHED** 1989
**WHERE FUNDING CAN BE GIVEN** UK and overseas.
**WHO CAN BENEFIT** Registered charities.
**WHAT IS FUNDED** Programme areas: Sustainable Development – International and UK; Sustainable Regeneration; People at Risk; Arts and Sustainability; Social Investment Fund; Low Carbon Fund. These include the natural environment and wildlife.
**WHAT IS NOT FUNDED** The trustees generally do not make grants in response to unsolicited applications. However, see 'How to Apply'.
**TYPE OF GRANT** Primarily project.
**SAMPLE GRANTS** Original Beans Company (£90,000 over two years); Carbon Tracker (£30,000); Manchester Veg People (£28,000); Global Action Plan (£25,000); New Opportunities and Horizons Ltd (NOAH) (£20,000); Médecins Sans Frontières and Mortlake Community Trust (£5,000 each).
**FINANCES** Year 2013/14  Income £1,605,129  Grants £1,287,823  Grants to organisations £1,287,823  Assets £33,485,723
**TRUSTEES** Sarah Butler-Sloss; Robert Butler-Sloss; Judith Portrait.
**OTHER INFORMATION** The trust is one of the Sainsbury Family Charitable Trusts which share a common administration. An application to one is taken as an application to all.
**HOW TO APPLY** The 2013/14 annual report states: 'Proposals to The Ashden Trust are generally invited by the trustees or initiated at their request. Unsolicited applications are not encouraged unless they are aligned with trustees' interests. The trustees prefer to support innovative schemes that can be successfully replicated or become self-sustaining.' The website states: 'The trustees take a proactive approach to the work they wish to support, employing a range of specialist staff and advisers to research their areas of interest and bring forward suitable proposals. It should therefore be understood that the majority of unsolicited proposals we receive will be unsuccessful.' **We would advise potential applicants to read carefully the Q&A section on the trust's website before making application.**
**WHO TO APPLY TO** Alan Bookbinder, Director, The Peak, 5 Wilton Road, London SW1V 1AP  *Tel.* 020 7410 0330  *Fax* 020 7410 0332  *email* ashdentrust@sfct.org.uk  *Website* www.ashdentrust.org.uk

## ■ The Ashley Family Foundation

**CC NO** 288099  **ESTABLISHED** 1985
**WHERE FUNDING CAN BE GIVEN** Mostly Wales, other areas considered.
**WHO CAN BENEFIT** Charitable organisations, including registered charities, unincorporated organisations, or community groups with a constitution or terms of reference and a charitable purpose.
**WHAT IS FUNDED** The foundation has a strong commitment to art and design and also to Wales, particularly Powys, where the Ashley business was first established. As a guide, the foundation for the past few years has had a policy of giving half its funds to Welsh projects.

**WHO TO APPLY TO** Sandra Hill, Trust Manager, HSBC Trust Company (UK) Ltd, Trust Services, Norwich House, Nelson Gate, Commercial Road, Southampton SO15 1GX  *Tel.* 023 8072 2243

Support is given in areas in which the family have a connection such as helping the communities of Mid Wales that supported the growth of the Laura Ashley business. The trustees focus on the following priorities: support of charitable textiles projects, including small scale community textiles initiatives; support for the arts; support for projects which seek to strengthen rural communities in Wales, especially in Mid Wales.
**WHAT IS NOT FUNDED** The foundation does not generally fund: individuals; business ventures; overseas projects; projects falling within the field of religion; dance related projects; direct funding towards schools; or retrospective work.
**TYPE OF GRANT** Core funding; salaries; running costs; project costs; one-off, but funding for up to three years will be considered.
**RANGE OF GRANTS** £500–£35,000
**SAMPLE GRANTS** St John's Cymru Wales (£50,000); Fine Cell Work (£30,000 in total); Music in Hospitals (£13,000); Crossroads Mid and West Wales and Royal School of Needlework (£10,000); Rhayader YMCA (£9,300); Mid Wales Opera (£7,500); Farms For City Children (£5,500); Powys Provincial and Chair Eisteddfod (£5,000); Crisis (£3,500 in total); Carno Community Council and North Powys Youth Band (£3,200 each); Cwm Harry (£1,000); Aberystwyth 50 + Forum (£200); Rock and Roll Public Library (£95).
**FINANCES** Year 2012/13  Income £219,958  Grants £318,345  Grants to organisations £318,345  Assets £11,539,694
**TRUSTEES** Martyn C. Gowar, Chair; Jane Ashley; Emma Shuckburgh; Prof. Oriana Baddeley; Prof. Sue Timney; Michael Hodgson; Jeremy McIlroy; Anita George.
**OTHER INFORMATION** The 2012/13 accounts were the latest available at the time of writing (June 2015). Grants were made to 56 organisations.
**HOW TO APPLY** There is a two stage application process. Applications can be made throughout the year and are assessed in line with the guidelines available from the foundation's website. The final decision is made by the trustees during meetings held three times a year. The website states: 'Due to the economic downturn we are receiving an unprecedented increase in requests. We are therefore changing our long held policy of replying to all requests. If you have submitted a stage one proposal and have not heard within eight weeks assume you have been unsuccessful.'
**WHO TO APPLY TO** Mia Duddridge, Correspondent, 6 Trull Farm Buildings, Trull, Tetbury, Gloucestershire GL8 8SQ  *Tel.* 0303 040 1005  *email* info@ashleyfamilyfoundation.org.uk  *Website* www.ashleyfamilyfoundation.org.uk

## ■ The Ashmore Foundation

**CC NO** 1122351  **ESTABLISHED** 2007
**WHERE FUNDING CAN BE GIVEN** Worldwide.
**WHO CAN BENEFIT** Registered charities and voluntary organisations.
**WHAT IS FUNDED** Community and economic development; education and training; health.
**TYPE OF GRANT** One-off and multi-year grants for projects of up to three years.
**RANGE OF GRANTS** £1,000–£500,000
**SAMPLE GRANTS** STARS Foundation (£499,000); Manav Seva Santhan (£65,000); Save the Children, IDEP Foundation (£50,000 each); CASA (£45,000); KEDV (£35,000); Lend a Hand India (£30,000); ABC Trust (£20,000); United

Way India (£10,000); and Afghan Action (£1,000).

**FINANCES** Year 2013 Income £240,000 Grants £846,000 Grants to organisations £846,000 Assets £6,068,000

**TRUSTEES** Mark Coombs; James Carleton; Marlon Balroop; Samuel Rickard; Robert Rainey; Nadine Cotrell; Helen Mackay; Samantha Pope; Mythili Orton; Christoph Hoffman.

**HOW TO APPLY** The foundation does not accept unsolicited applications. They source new partners through recommendations from experts, existing partners, suggestions from Ashmore staff and detailed research by the foundation team.

**WHO TO APPLY TO** The Trustees, Ashmore Group, 5th Floor, 61 Aldwych, London WC2B 4AE Tel. 020 3077 6153 email foundation@ashmoregroup.org Website www.ashmorefoundation.org

## ■ The Ashworth Charitable Trust

**CC NO** 1045492    **ESTABLISHED** 1995

**WHERE FUNDING CAN BE GIVEN** UK and worldwide, with some preference for certain specific needs in Honiton, Ottery St Mary, Sidmouth and Wonford Green surgery, Exeter.

**WHO CAN BENEFIT** Registered UK charities. Individuals subject to meeting specific geographical and cause criteria, see What section.

**WHAT IS FUNDED** General charitable purposes. Particular emphasis is given to support for the Ironbridge Gorge Museum Trust and to humanitarian projects. Individuals living in the areas covered by the medical practices and social services in Honiton, Ottery St Mary, Sidmouth and Wonford Green surgery, Exeter. Such grants are to be paid for particularly acute needs and humanitarian projects either to other charities or to individuals.

**WHAT IS NOT FUNDED** Research-based charities; animal charities; 'heritage charities' such as National Trust or other organisations whose aim is the preservation of a building, museum, library and so on (with the exception of the Ironbridge Gorge Museum); 'faith-based' charities, unless the project is for primarily humanitarian purposes and is neither exclusive to those of that particular faith or evangelical in its purpose. Grants to individuals are strictly limited to the geographical area and purpose specified on the trust's website. Individuals are generally excluded including gap year funding, travel overseas for charity work and medical treatment. Professionals representing individuals are also excluded, unless they are applying from a registered charity.

**RANGE OF GRANTS** Usually £500–£3,000.

**SAMPLE GRANTS** Ironbridge Gorge Museum Trust and Hospiscare Exeter (£5,000 each); Burma Assist, Community Housing Aid and Refugee Support (Devon) Limited (£3,000 each); Ace Africa, Anaphylaxis Campaign, Disability Law Service, Moray Fresh Start (£2,000 each); Housing for the Homeless and Welfare Association (£1,500 each); Blind in Business (£1,000).

**FINANCES** Year 2013/14 Income £145,861 Grants £122,344 Grants to organisations £121,049 Assets £4,544,660

**TRUSTEES** Ian Miles; Sharareh Rouhipour; Katherine Gray; Hoshmand Rouhipour; Kian Golestani; Wendi Cunningham Momen.

**OTHER INFORMATION** £1,300 was given to four individuals from the Doctors' and Social Services Fund.

**HOW TO APPLY** All applications must be made online. No hard copies will be considered. Read the guidelines on the trust's website before making application. You will need the following information to hand to fill out the application form: contact details of a referee for your charity. Ensure they have been pre-advised, as the trustees may need to contact them when considering your application; a full set of your most recent audited accounts; concise details of your project (less than 300 words). The trustees meet twice a year in May and November. Applications should be submitted by the middle of March or the middle of September respectively. Note that the trustees are unable to enter into any discussions regarding funding, successful or otherwise, as there are no funds designated for this purpose. Note: Irrespective of an applicant's sphere of operation, whether it be at a local, national or international level, it is a pre-requisite of any funding by the trust that the applicant must have charitable status in the United Kingdom, namely that it must have a charity registration number and that that such status should be capable of verification by its regulator. The trust is unable to accept applications from individuals or professionals representing individuals.

**WHO TO APPLY TO** Mandy Walsom, Foot Anstey, Senate Court, Southernhay Gardens, Exeter EX1 1NT Tel. 01392 411221 Fax 01392 685220 email ashworthtrust@btinternet.com Website www.ashworthtrust.org

## ■ The Ian Askew Charitable Trust

**CC NO** 264515    **ESTABLISHED** 1972

**WHERE FUNDING CAN BE GIVEN** UK, with a preference for Sussex, and overseas.

**WHO CAN BENEFIT** Charitable organisations.

**WHAT IS FUNDED** General charitable purposes; education; health research; particularly mental health; preservation of ancient buildings; and the maintenance and conservation of woodlands belonging to the trust.

**RANGE OF GRANTS** Most grants are for £500 or less.

**SAMPLE GRANTS** The South of England Agricultural Society (£7,000 in two grants); The Sussex Heritage Trust (£2,500); The Landmark Trust, The Sussex Historic Churches Trust and War Memorial Trust (£1,000 each).

**FINANCES** Year 2013/14 Income £419,705 Grants £128,475 Grants to organisations £128,475 Assets £17,094,755

**TRUSTEES** John Hecks; Cleone Pengelley; Richard Lewis; Rory Askew; James Rank.

**OTHER INFORMATION** Grants to 215 charitable organisations totalled £129,000, excluding all support costs. Grants of £18,500 were made from the Conservation fund and £4,200 from the Educational sub fund.

**HOW TO APPLY** Apply in writing to the correspondent. Applications are considered every other month.

**WHO TO APPLY TO** The Trustees, c/o Baker Tilly, 18 Mount Ephraim Road, Tunbridge Wells, Kent TN1 1ED Tel. 01892 511944 email paul.hodge@bakertilly.co.uk

## ■ The Associated Country Women of the World

**CC NO** 290367 **ESTABLISHED** 1933
**WHERE FUNDING CAN BE GIVEN** Overseas.
**WHO CAN BENEFIT** Local projects and established organisations benefitting women and /or children in rural communities.
**WHAT IS FUNDED** Projects that are mainly ran by women and directly benefit women and/or children in connection with: literacy, health education, nutrition and home economics, agricultural training and development, income generating activities, water and sanitation, civic consciousness/community involvement.
**WHAT IS NOT FUNDED** The organisation does not provide funding to individuals, NGOs/SHGs not registered or registered for less than two years, emergency relief work, motor vehicles, items of large mechanical equipment, the purchase of land and capital infrastructure projects. Funding only available for projects taking place in the same country where the organisation is registered and directly benefit women and children in those countries.
**TYPE OF GRANT** One-off grants for projects for organisations.
**RANGE OF GRANTS** £5,001–£10,000
**SAMPLE GRANTS** Previously: Integrated Prevention of Female Infanticide and HIV/AIDS Project (Phase 3) – India (£84,000); My Name is Woman – South Africa (£6,000); Vocational Skills Development Tailoring – Uganda and Rain Water Harvesting – Sri Lanka (£5,000 each); and Facilities of Water Supply and Sanitation to End Disease and Poverty – Bangladesh and Rural Women Livelihood Development Project – Cambodia (£4,000 each).
**FINANCES** Year 2013 Income £620,371 Grants £109,809 Grants to organisations £109,809 Assets £2,635,376
**TRUSTEES** Alison Burnett; Ruth Shanks Am; Margaret Yetman; Henrietta Schoeman; Angela Njeazeh; Maybel Moyo; Prof. Momtaz Begum; HRH. Princess Azizah Iskandar; Sheila Needham; Margaret Sullivan; Beverly Earnhart; Dotsie Gordon.
**PUBLICATIONS** Working with Women Worldwide. (Visit the trust's website for a full list of publications.)
**OTHER INFORMATION** Processing of the application and the approval of a grant usually takes around ten months.
**HOW TO APPLY** Application forms can be downloaded from the organisation's website. In addition to the application form, it is necessary to provide a copy of a valid registration certificate for the applicant's organisation and an itemised budget.
**WHO TO APPLY TO** The Trustees, 24 Tufton Street, London SW1P 3RB *Tel.* 020 7799 3875 *email* info@acww.org.uk *Website* www.acww.org.uk

## ■ The Association of Colleges Charitable Trust

**CC NO** 1040631 **ESTABLISHED** 1994
**WHERE FUNDING CAN BE GIVEN** UK.
**WHO CAN BENEFIT** Further education establishments
**WHAT IS FUNDED** Further education. The charitable trust is responsible for administering two programmes. The largest of these is the Beacon Awards, which provide monetary grants to award-winning initiatives within further education colleges. The other scheme is the AoC Gold Awards for Further Education Alumni, which reward former members of further education colleges who have since excelled in their chosen field or profession.
**WHAT IS NOT FUNDED** Individuals.
**RANGE OF GRANTS** £3,000–£5,000
**SAMPLE GRANTS** Loughbrough College (£5,000 for AQA – College/School Partnerships); Chichester College (£5,000 for City and Guilds – Staff Development in FE); Grimsby Institute (£3,000 for UCAS HE in FE); Northbrook College Sussex (£3,000 for Jardine Loyd Thompson – Health and Community Care)
**FINANCES** Year 2013/14 Income £259,519 Grants £214,977 Grants to organisations £214,977 Assets £191,198
**TRUSTEES** Alice Thiagaraj; Peter Brophy; David Forrester; John Bingham; Martin Doel; Carole Stott; Dame Pat Bacon, Jane Samuels; Simon Francis; Shahida Aslam.
**HOW TO APPLY** See the trust's website for further information.
**WHO TO APPLY TO** Alice Thiagaraj, Managing Trustee, 2–5 Stedham Place, London WC1A 1HU *Tel.* 020 7034 9917 *email* alice_thiagaraj@aoc.co.uk *Website* www.aoc.co.uk

## ■ Astellas European Foundation

**CC NO** 1036344 **ESTABLISHED** 1993
**WHERE FUNDING CAN BE GIVEN** Worldwide.
**WHO CAN BENEFIT** Scientific research institutes; universities; research workers; medical professionals.
**WHAT IS FUNDED** The areas of interest of the foundation are: committing long-term support to basic medical and related scientific programmes through organisations such as the Société Internationale D'Urologie; supporting selected short, medium and long-term projects, aimed at integrating basic science and clinical research through interdisciplinary projects; providing facilities, promoting or sponsoring the exchange of ideas and views through lectures and discussions of an educational or cultural nature; promoting, assisting or otherwise supporting charitable institutions aimed at serving good causes.
**FINANCES** Year 2013/14 Income £53,175 Grants £262,467 Grants to organisations £262,467 Assets £16,419,919
**TRUSTEES** Kenneth Jones; Dr Patrick Errard; Yoshirou Miyokawa; Dr Ayad Abdulahad.
**OTHER INFORMATION** The sum of £552,000 was given in direct scientific support, with donations to charities totalling £262,500.
**HOW TO APPLY** Apply in writing to the correspondent.
**WHO TO APPLY TO** The Trustees, 2000 Hillswood Drive, Chertsey, Surrey KT16 0RS *Tel.* 020 3379 8000

## ■ Asthma UK

**CC NO** 802364 **ESTABLISHED** 1990
**WHERE FUNDING CAN BE GIVEN** UK.
**WHO CAN BENEFIT** Research organisations; universities; medical and academic professionals; people suffering from asthma.
**WHAT IS FUNDED** Research into and the provision of information and education on asthma and allied respiratory disorders. The focus of 2014–17 strategy is on reducing 'the risk of life threatening asthma attacks' with 'key to this will being ending the complacency about asthma'. There are a number of funding schemes available, including research projects, fellowships, studentships, support to academics

and research centres, commissioned research and innovation grants. The website states: 'We will continue to fund world-class laboratory-based research. In addition, we will support more clinical research that has a practical application and the potential to bring about health benefits within five years. We will support the growth of the asthma research community in the UK by helping promising researchers become established in their career. We will also explore possibilities to collaborate with other research organisations to increase the amount of funding available for asthma research.'

**TYPE OF GRANT** Project grants; research; fellowships and studentships; up to five years.

**SAMPLE GRANTS** Grants awarded included projects at: University of Leicester, University of Manchester and University of Sheffield (£97,000 each; four years); King's College London (£50,000; one year); University of Edinburgh (£50,000; 18 months); Imperial College London (£46,000; 18 months); Royal Brompton (£39,000; one year). Examples of current work supported are also given on the charity's website.

**FINANCES** Year 2013/14 Income £9,315,000 Grants £629,000 Grants to organisations £629,000 Assets £5,622,000

**TRUSTEES** June Coppel; Jane Tozer; Barbara Herts; David Steeds; John Lelliott; Dr Anne Thomson; Dr Iain Small; Prof. Jurgen Schwarze; Dr Robert Wilson; Mary Leadbeater; Matthew Smith; Martin Sinclair; Kate Clarke; John Garbutt.

**OTHER INFORMATION** The charity supports research, campaigns for good asthma care and supports people in risk of asthma attacks. In 2013/14 charitable activities totalled £5.4 million, which consisted of: advice and support (£2.35 million); improving care (£1.65 million); research (£1.4 million). Research grants 'charged in the year' totalled £629,000.

**HOW TO APPLY** The charity invites research proposals through its website and through the research professional press. The next funding call should be in autumn 2015. According to the annual report for 2013/14, 'the selection of research projects for funding is through an established peer review system which includes lay reviewers, in accordance with the guidelines of the Association of Medical Research Charities'. To learn more about awards available, applicants are invited to see the website and contact the Research Team at research@asthma.org.uk.

**WHO TO APPLY TO** Harriet Jones, Director of Finance and Resources, 18 Mansell Street, London E1 8AA Tel. 020 7786 4900 Fax 020 7488 0882 email info@asthma.org.uk Website www.asthma.org.uk

## ■ Aston–Mansfield Charitable Trust

**CC NO** 208155  **ESTABLISHED** 1930
**WHERE FUNDING CAN BE GIVEN** The borough of Newham.
**WHO CAN BENEFIT** Organisations.
**WHAT IS FUNDED** 'The objects of the charity are to develop the community wealth of East London and promote a diverse and inclusive society in which all are free to participate. ... Aston-Mansfield's Seed Grants, a small funding programme aimed at newly formed or completely unfunded groups, is a new initiative launched in April 2011. Groups can apply for up to a maximum of £400.'

**WHAT IS NOT FUNDED** Revenue funding for salaries and maintenance is unlikely to be given. No national appeals and no grants are given to individuals.

**TYPE OF GRANT** Capital (including buildings), feasibility studies, one-off, project and research. Funding of one year or less will be considered.

**FINANCES** Year 2013/14 Income £561,059 Grants £630,679 Grants to organisations £630,679 Assets £13,837,524

**TRUSTEES** Christopher C. Keen, Chair; Andrew F. West; Bernard A. Tyler; Stephen M. Wright; Revd Paul Regan.

**HOW TO APPLY** For Seed Grants applicants should see the trust's website where all information is posted. Applicants for all other grants should apply in writing to the correspondent.

**WHO TO APPLY TO** Eileen Da-Silva, Accountant, Durning Hall, Earlham Grove, Forest Gate, London E7 9AB Tel. 020 3740 8114 email eileen.da-silva@aston-mansfield.org.uk Website www.aston-mansfield.org.uk

## ■ The Astor Foundation

**CC NO** 225708  **ESTABLISHED** 1963
**WHERE FUNDING CAN BE GIVEN** UK.
**WHO CAN BENEFIT** Medical research organisations and registered charities. Children and youth groups, people who have disabilities, the countryside, the arts, sport, carers groups and animal welfare.
**WHAT IS FUNDED** Medical research in its widest sense, favouring research on a broad front rather than in specialised fields. In addition to its medical connection, the foundation has also supported initiatives for children and youth groups, people with disabilities, the countryside, the arts, sport, carers groups and animal welfare.
**WHAT IS NOT FUNDED** Individuals; salaries. Grants are given to registered charities only.
**TYPE OF GRANT** Preference for assistance with the launching and initial stages of new projects and filling in gaps/shortfalls.
**RANGE OF GRANTS** £500–£45,000; generally £500–£2,500.
**SAMPLE GRANTS** University College London Medical School (£16,000); Help the Hospices (£4,000); Independence at Home (£4,500); Reading YMCA and St John Ambulance Kent (£3,000 each); St Bride's Church (£2,500); The A21 Campaign (£2,000); BAAF and Brittle Bone Society (£1,000 each).
**FINANCES** Year 2013/14 Income £117,473 Grants £113,500 Grants to organisations £113,500 Assets £3,801,142
**TRUSTEES** Robert Astor, Chair; the Hon. Tania Astor; Lord Latymer; Charles Astor; Dr Howard Swanton; Prof. John Cunningham.
**HOW TO APPLY** There are no deadline dates or application forms. Applications should be in writing to the correspondent and must include accounts and an annual report if available. The trustees meet twice yearly, usually in October and April. If the appeal arrives too late for one meeting it will automatically be carried over for consideration at the next. An acknowledgement will be sent on receipt of an appeal. No further communication will be entered into unless the trustees raise any queries regarding the appeal, or unless the appeal is subsequently successful.
**WHO TO APPLY TO** Lisa Rothwell-Orr, Secretary, PO Box 168, Bideford EX39 6WB Tel. 07901 737488 email astor.foundation@gmail.com

## ■ The Atlas Fund

**CC NO** 278030
**WHERE FUNDING CAN BE GIVEN** UK
**WHO CAN BENEFIT** Registered charities; churches; schools.
**WHAT IS FUNDED** General charitable purposes.
**RANGE OF GRANTS** Up to around £10,000.
**SAMPLE GRANTS** Kings School Foundation (£6,000) National Trust (£5,000); Friends of Canterbury Cathedral and St Margaret's church – Ockley (£3,000 each); British Red Cross, Dragon School Trust Limited and Royal Academy of Arts (£2,000 each); Ashmolean Museum and Wychwood Project (£1,000 each).
**FINANCES** Year 2013/14 Income £76,010 Grants £56,000 Grants to organisations £56,000 Assets £1,974,672
**TRUSTEES** Lady Hester Touche; William Touche; Sir Anthony Touche; Helen Hofmann.
**HOW TO APPLY** Apply in writing to the correspondent.
**WHO TO APPLY TO** Lady Hester Touche, Trustee, Stane House, Ockley, Dorking, Surrey RH5 5TQ Tel. 01306 627397 email toucheockley@btinternet.com

## ■ The Aurelius Charitable Trust

**CC NO** 271333   **ESTABLISHED** 1975
**WHERE FUNDING CAN BE GIVEN** UK.
**WHO CAN BENEFIT** Registered charities; historic societies; museums/galleries; academic institutions.
**WHAT IS FUNDED** Conservation/preservation of culture inherited from the past; the dissemination of knowledge, particularly in the humanities field; research or publications.
**WHAT IS NOT FUNDED** Individuals.
**TYPE OF GRANT** Seed-corn or completion funding not otherwise available, usually one-off.
**RANGE OF GRANTS** Generally £500–£3,000.
**SAMPLE GRANTS** College of Arms (£6,000); Imperial War Museum Foundation (£5,000); Cumberland and Westmorland Antiquarian and Archaeological Society (£4,000); British The National Museum of the Royal Navy and The Wildlife Trust BCN (£3,000 each); Cornwall Heritage Group and British Academy (£2,000 each); Institute of Archaeology (£1,000).
**FINANCES** Year 2013/14 Income £90,782 Grants £75,500 Grants to organisations £75,500 Assets £2,401,174
**TRUSTEES** William Wallis; Philip Haynes.
**HOW TO APPLY** Apply in writing to the correspondent. Donations are generally made on the recommendation of the trust's board of advisors. Unsolicited applications will only be responded to if an sae is included. The trustees meet twice a year.
**WHO TO APPLY TO** Philip Haynes, Trustee, Briarsmead, Old Road, Buckland, Betchworth, Surrey RH3 7DU Tel. 01737 842186 email philip.haynes@tiscali.co.uk

## ■ The Lord Austin Trust

**CC NO** 208394   **ESTABLISHED** 1937
**WHERE FUNDING CAN BE GIVEN** Birmingham and its immediate area.
**WHO CAN BENEFIT** Hospitals, medical institutions and charities in England, restricted to: local charities based in Birmingham and West Midlands; and national organisations (but not their provincial branches).
**WHAT IS FUNDED** Emphasis on the welfare of children, the care of older people, medical institutions and research.
**WHAT IS NOT FUNDED** Individuals.
**TYPE OF GRANT** One-off.
**RANGE OF GRANTS** Up to £10,000.
**SAMPLE GRANTS** Previously: Birmingham St Mary's Hospice (£5,000); City of Birmingham Symphony Orchestra (£4,500); Acorns Children's Hospice Trust (£3,000); Tamworth Nursery (Special Needs) (£2,500); Saltley Neighbourhood Pensioner's Centre and Queen Elizabeth Hospital Birmingham (£2,000 each); Children's Heart Foundation (£1,500); and All Saints Youth Project, Army Benevolent Fund, Avoncroft Museum, Broadening Choices for Older People and St Martins Centre for Health and Healing (£1,000 each).
**FINANCES** Year 2013/14 Income £104,961 Grants £100,850 Grants to organisations £100,850 Assets £3,386,865
**TRUSTEES** James Fea; Rodney Kettel; Anthony Andrews.
**OTHER INFORMATION** In 2013/14 grants were given to 80 organisations.
**HOW TO APPLY** Apply in writing to the correspondent, including a set of recent accounts. The trustees meet twice a year in or around May and November to consider grants.
**WHO TO APPLY TO** Chrissy Norgrove, c/o SGH Martineau, 1 Colmore Square, Birmingham B4 6AA Tel. 0800 763 1000 email christine.norgrove@sghmartineau.com

## ■ Autonomous Research Charitable Trust

**CC NO** 1137503   **ESTABLISHED** 2010
**WHERE FUNDING CAN BE GIVEN** UK, mainly London, and Africa.
**WHO CAN BENEFIT** Registered charities.
**WHAT IS FUNDED** Projects which further the following objectives: 'To help disadvantaged people get a step up in life; to empower people to improve the quality of their lives; to focus our resources upon a small number of key partner charities – both in London and abroad – where we feel we can make a difference and establish long-term relationships.'
**SAMPLE GRANTS** One Degree – The Adnan Jaffery Educational Trust (£125,000); Dress for Success and Smart Works (£50,000 each); The One Fund (£6,500); Cardiac Risk in the Young and Little Hearts Matter (£2,500 each); Child of Hope and Mary Pollock Trust (£1,500 each).
**FINANCES** Year 2013/14 Income £399,051 Grants £288,163 Grants to organisations £288,163 Assets £283,566
**TRUSTEES** Graham Stuart; Britta Schmidt; Nathalie Garner; Neeta Atkar.
**HOW TO APPLY** Apply in writing to the correspondent.
**WHO TO APPLY TO** Reena Bhudia, Moore Stephens, 150 Aldersgate Street, London EC1A 4AB Tel. 020 7334 9191 email reena.bhudia@moorestephens.com

## ■ The John Avins Trust

**CC NO** 217301   **ESTABLISHED** 1931
**WHERE FUNDING CAN BE GIVEN** Birmingham and district.
**WHO CAN BENEFIT** Hospitals and medical charities. Also, certain non-medical charities named in the will of John Avins.

**WHAT IS FUNDED** Medical, including research and administration in the medical field.
**WHAT IS NOT FUNDED** Applications are only considered from medical charities working to the benefit of individuals living in or near to Birmingham.
**RANGE OF GRANTS** Generally between £1,000 to £3,000.
**SAMPLE GRANTS** Focus Birmingham (£3,000); Birmingham Centre for Arts Therapies and Whizz-Kidz (£2,500); Acorns (£2,400); Birmingham St Mary's Hospice (£2,000); Vitalise (£1,700); Birmingham Royal Ballet (£1,000).
**FINANCES** Year 2013/14 Income £56,819 Grants £47,100 Grants to organisations £38,000 Assets £1,440,559
**TRUSTEES** Vimal Chandar Sharma; Fiona Collins; David Cox; Mr J. Millward; John Russell.
**OTHER INFORMATION** During the year, one grant under £1,000 was given (£500). The charity gave £9,000 towards science scholarships, paid through the University of Birmingham, and for the Eliza Avins Music Scholarship.
**HOW TO APPLY** Application forms are available from the correspondent. The trustees meet annually, or more often if required.
**WHO TO APPLY TO** Christine Norgrove, Secretary, c/o SGH Martineau LLP, 1 Colmore Square, Birmingham B4 6AA Tel. 0800 763 2000 email christine.norgrove@sghmartineau.com

■ **The Avon and Somerset Police Community Trust**

**CC NO** 1076770   **ESTABLISHED** 1999
**WHERE FUNDING CAN BE GIVEN** The Avon and Somerset Constabulary area.
**WHO CAN BENEFIT** Organisations.
**WHAT IS FUNDED** The trustees favour projects that: promote safety and quality of life in the Avon and Somerset Constabulary area; through the prevention of crime and disorder, protect young people, people who are vulnerable and older people from criminal acts; advance education, including that related to alcohol, drugs, solvent abuse, community relations and responsible citizenship.
**WHAT IS NOT FUNDED** Individuals including students; expeditions; bursaries or scholarships; replacement of statutory funding; building works; projects that fall outside the constabulary's geographical area; further applications within three years.
**RANGE OF GRANTS** Usually up to £3,000.
**SAMPLE GRANTS** Bobby Van Scheme (£54,500); Hartcliffe and Withywood Angling Club, Stand Against Violence, The National Smelting Co Amateur Boxing Club, Henbury Football Club and Priory Community Association (£1,000 each); Sandford Scouts (£880); Wolverhampton Playing Fields and Thornbury Sea Cadets (£600 each); Oasis Community Club (£500); and Clevedon YMCA and Bath and North East Somerset Youth Offending Team (£250 each).
**FINANCES** Year 2013/14 Income £339,869 Grants £413,747 Grants to organisations £413,747 Assets £538,005
**TRUSTEES** Mary Prior; Lady Gass; Paul Hooper; Beatrice Salter; Dame Janet Trotter; Sean Connolly; Allen Bell; Patricia Hunt; Nick Gargan; Sue Mountstevens.
**OTHER INFORMATION** The grant total includes funds used to run the trust's own projects and initiatives.
**HOW TO APPLY** Application forms are available to download, together with criteria and guidelines, on the website. For further information about the trust or advice on obtaining or completing the trust's application form contact the Trust Manager. The trustees meet quarterly to consider the business of the trust and approve grants in accordance with the trust's aims and objectives. Grants in support of major projects are routinely reviewed and awarded by the trustees at the commencement of each financial year at their April meeting. All other grants are considered on their merit, having met the criteria for a grant as set out in the trust's aims and objectives.
**WHO TO APPLY TO** Tracey Clegg, Trust Manager, PO Box 37, Valley Road, Portishead, Bristol BS20 8QJ Tel. 01275 816240 Fax 01275 816129 email tracey.clegg@avonandsomerset.police.uik Website www.avonandsomerset.police.uk

■ **Awards for All (see also the Big Lottery Fund)**

**WHERE FUNDING CAN BE GIVEN** UK.
**WHO CAN BENEFIT** Community groups; clubs; societies; registered charities; exempt or excepted charities registered with the Inland Revenue in England; parish or town councils; schools; health bodies; companies limited by guarantee; non-registered not-for-profit organisations. Applicant organisation will generally be organised to the extent of having a constitution, a bank account and a set of accounts (unless a new organisation).
**WHAT IS FUNDED** This is one of the Big Lottery Fund programmes focusing on helping local communities, small organisations and grassroots groups. Community, health, educational and environmental projects are all supported.
**WHAT IS NOT FUNDED** See specific details applicable for each of the regions.
**TYPE OF GRANT** Here are some of the things that a grant could be spent on: publicity materials; venue hire; computers; research costs; transport costs; volunteers' expenses; updating equipment for health and safety reasons; refurbishment; training; sessional staff; fees to hire equipment; educational toys and games.
**RANGE OF GRANTS** England: £300–£10,000; Northern Ireland: £500–£10,000; Scotland: £500–£10,000; Wales: £500–£5,000.
**SAMPLE GRANTS** Ballybogey Over 50's Club, Fire in Babylon and St Polycarp's Catholic Primary School (£10,000 each); Church of the Nativity Guide Unit (£8,400); Youth Highland (£8,000); The Scottish Association of Writers (£7,600); Glasgow Disability Sport (£7,500); Myaware (£6,000); Age NI (£5,800); Kilkeel Community Association (£5,100); Ceredigion People First and Sew 'n' Grow (£5,000 each); Neath Division Girl Guiding and The Organic Growers of Bothwell (£4,900 each); Slievenaman Women's Institute (£3,900); C.A.S.M. Carers of Alcohol and Substance Misuse (£2,400); Anglesey Guide Association (£2,000); Dorchester Youth Extra (£1,900); Tregunnor Social Club (£1,400); Peacock Close Social Club (£1,000); Top Glass (£800); St Monans Community Choir (£600); Cambrian Art Society, Hampden Park in Bloom and Loans Gala Committee (£500 each).
**OTHER INFORMATION** For details on the Big Lottery Fund also see the separate entry. The amount

given through the scheme appears to be included in the overall total distributed by the Big Lottery Fund. The grant search facility available on the website shows that in the 2013/14 period there were about 6,830 awards made totalling around £51.8 million, allocated as follows: England (£39.4 million in 4,772 awards); Scotland (£8.7 million in 1,241 awards); Wales (£2.7 million in 704 awards); Northern Ireland (£960,000 in 114 awards). The annual report for the Big Lottery Fund notes that 88% of the overall awards (which totalled £670 million) 'went to projects valued at £10,000 or less'; this may include other programmes as well as Awards for All.

**HOW TO APPLY** All information, application forms and guidelines are available online. If you need further support or have any questions get in touch with the organisation. Note that there are separate offices for each region and you should contact the most appropriate one – see details on the website. Note that *Awards for All England* applications take around eight weeks to assess; therefore it is recommended that applications are submitted four months in advance of anticipated project start date. Appeals to *Awards for All Northern Ireland* will normally take around three or four months to decide.

**WHO TO APPLY TO** See the main body for details, c/o Big Lottery Fund, 1 Plough Place, London EC4A 1DE *Tel.* 0845 410 2030 *email* enquiries@biglotteryfund.org.uk *Website* www.awardsforall.org.uk

## ■ The Aylesford Family Charitable Trust

**CC NO** 328299          **ESTABLISHED** 1989
**WHERE FUNDING CAN BE GIVEN** West Midlands and Warwickshire.
**WHO CAN BENEFIT** Registered charities.
**WHAT IS FUNDED** General charitable purposes.
**WHAT IS NOT FUNDED** Individuals.
**TYPE OF GRANT** Recurrent; one-off.
**RANGE OF GRANTS** Usually £100 to £5,000.
**SAMPLE GRANTS** St James GPT (£5,000); Charlie Waller Memorial Trust (£1,100); National Garden School and Tusk (£1,000 each); Age UK Solihull, NW First Responders and Troop Aid (£500 each); Go Sober (£350); Dyslexia Action, Farm Africa, Fetlor Youth Club, Motability and Samaritans – Birmingham (£300 each); Cancer Research UK, Dogs Trust, Kings School – Gloucester and Operation New World (£250 each); SSAFA and St John Ambulance (£200).
**FINANCES** Year 2013/14 Income £50,293 Grants £48,050 Grants to organisations £48,050 Assets £1,801,030
**TRUSTEES** Lord Charles Aylesford; Lady Aylesford.
**OTHER INFORMATION** In 2013/14 grants were made to 110 organisations.
**HOW TO APPLY** Apply in writing to the correspondent at any time.
**WHO TO APPLY TO** The Trustees, Packington Hall, Meriden, Warwickshire CV7 7HF *Tel.* 01676 522020 *email* kevin@packingtonestate.co.uk

## ■ The Harry Bacon Foundation

CC NO 1056500 ESTABLISHED 1996
WHERE FUNDING CAN BE GIVEN UK.
WHO CAN BENEFIT Registered charities.
WHAT IS FUNDED Particularly health/medical charities and animal welfare. The same charities are generally supported every year at the request of the founder.
RANGE OF GRANTS Around £6,000.
SAMPLE GRANTS RNLI, Imperial Cancer Research, British Heart Foundation, PDSA, Parkinson's Disease Society, the Arthritis and Rheumatism Council for Research, Donkey Sanctuary and World Horse Welfare.
FINANCES Year 2013/14 Income £106,592 Grants £75,000 Grants to organisations £75,000
TRUSTEE NatWest Bank plc.
HOW TO APPLY Apply in writing to the correspondent. The trustees meet regularly to consider applications.
WHO TO APPLY TO The Trust Manager, NatWest Trust Services, 5th Floor, Trinity Quay 2, Avon Street, Bristol BS2 0PT *Tel.* 05516 577371 *email* nwb.charities@natwest.com

## ■ The BACTA Charitable Trust

CC NO 328668 ESTABLISHED 1991
WHERE FUNDING CAN BE GIVEN UK.
WHO CAN BENEFIT UK-registered charities.
WHAT IS FUNDED Generally to support causes recommended to it by members of the British Amusement Catering Trade Association (BACTA).
WHAT IS NOT FUNDED Overseas charities; religious purposes.
TYPE OF GRANT Long-term support (usually two to three years) to a specific project or charity and small one-off donations.
SAMPLE GRANTS Rays of Sunshine (£56,000); British Lung Foundation (£1,100); London Care Partnership (£400).
FINANCES Year 2013/14 Income £55,651 Grants £57,462 Grants to organisations £57,462 Assets £34,191
TRUSTEES John Stergides; Mark Horwood; Jimmy Thomas; Stephen Hawkins; Michael Green; Jonathan Lauder; David Anderson Orton.
HOW TO APPLY Requests for information about the trust's long-term partnerships should be addressed to the correspondent.
WHO TO APPLY TO Pru Kemball, Administration Assistant, 134–136 Buckingham Palace Road, London SW1W 9SA *Tel.* 020 7730 6444 *email* pru@bacta.org.uk *Website* www.bacta.org.uk

## ■ The Scott Bader Commonwealth Limited

CC NO 206391 ESTABLISHED 1951
WHERE FUNDING CAN BE GIVEN UK, Eire, Canada, France, South Africa, Croatia, Dubai, USA, Czech Republic, Sweden, Spain and China.
WHO CAN BENEFIT Charitable organisations.
WHAT IS FUNDED Education and training; relief of poverty; overseas aid; conservation; economic development; children and young people.
WHAT IS NOT FUNDED No support is given for charities concerned with animals; individual sponsorships; travel and adventure schemes; arts projects; any form of advertising; medical research and equipment; sports clubs; general charitable appeals; construction/renovation/maintenance of buildings.
TYPE OF GRANT One-off and funding over a period (3–5 years).
RANGE OF GRANTS Local Fund: £1,000–£5,000. Central Fund: Up to £25,000.
SAMPLE GRANTS The Prince's Trust, Northampton (£5,000); Livability (£3,000); Family Support Link, Wellingborough (£2,500); Tall Ships Youth Trust (£1,800); Beanstalk (£700); and the Children's Aid Team, Northamptonshire (£500).
FINANCES Year 2013 Income £199,033,000 Grants £155,000 Grants to organisations £155,000 Assets £41,508,000
TRUSTEES Andrew Radford; Syed Hayat; Julie Rogers; Anne Atkinson-Clark; Les Norwood; Jacquie Findlay; Barry Mansfield; Christian Caulier.
OTHER INFORMATION Grants were made totalling £155,000 of which £33,000 was given in the UK. £14,900 of the UK grant total was given through the nomination scheme whereby staff of Scott Bader can nominate a charity of their choice.
HOW TO APPLY Assessment criteria are available to download from the website. Application forms are available on request by post or email. Deadlines for the large project funding are available on the website. Applications for the Small International fund are accepted all year round. Applications for local funds should be made to the local office.
WHO TO APPLY TO Sue Carter, Commonwealth Secretary, Scott Bader Company Ltd, Wollaston Hall, Wollaston, Nr Wellingborough, Northants NN29 7RL *Tel.* 01933 666755 *email* commonwealth_office@scottbader.com *Website* www.scottbader.com

## ■ Bag4Sport Foundation

CC NO 1146920 ESTABLISHED 2012
WHERE FUNDING CAN BE GIVEN UK
WHO CAN BENEFIT Sports clubs; schools; youth organisations; individuals.
WHAT IS FUNDED Sport.
RANGE OF GRANTS Up to £500.
FINANCES Year 2012/13 Income £34,843 Grants £6,837 Grants to organisations £6,837 Assets -£1,599
TRUSTEES Andrew Trusler; Steven Taylor; John Matthews; David Bousfield.
OTHER INFORMATION The 2012/13 accounts were the latest available at the time of writing (June 2015).
HOW TO APPLY Apply on a form available to download, together with guidelines, from the website, providing as much detail as possible, and returning either by email to foundation@bag4sport.co.uk or by post to the correspondent address given in this entry.
WHO TO APPLY TO Andrew Trusler, Trustee, Unit 2a Roundway Business Park, Hopton Industrial Estate, Devizes, Wiltshire SN10 2HU *Tel.* 01380 728780 *email* andy@bag4sport.co.uk *Website* www.bag4sport.co.uk

## ■ The Bagri Foundation

**CC NO** 1000219     **ESTABLISHED** 1990
**WHERE FUNDING CAN BE GIVEN** Worldwide.
**WHO CAN BENEFIT** Organisations and individuals.
**WHAT IS FUNDED** General charitable purposes.
**SAMPLE GRANTS** London Business School (£200,000).
**FINANCES** Year 2013/14 Income £166,427 Grants £345,634 Grants to organisations £345,634 Assets £14,079,180
**TRUSTEES** Lord Bagri; Hon. A. Bagri; Lady Bagri; Hon. Mrs A. Bagri.
**OTHER INFORMATION** No breakdown of the total grants figure was available from the accounts.
**HOW TO APPLY** The foundation's website states: 'Please note, the Bagri Foundation's work is focused on a limited number of projects at any one time and it does not accept unsolicited requests for financial assistance.'
**WHO TO APPLY TO** D. M. Beaumont, Correspondent, 80 Cannon Street, London EC4N 6EJ *Tel.* 020 7280 0000 *email* enquiries@bagrifoundation.org *Website* bagrifoundation.org

## ■ The Austin Bailey Foundation

**CC NO** 514912     **ESTABLISHED** 1984
**WHERE FUNDING CAN BE GIVEN** Swansea and worldwide.
**WHO CAN BENEFIT** Churches; overseas aid organisations; local organisations.
**WHAT IS FUNDED** The foundation was set up to give approximately 25% of its income towards the advancement of religion by supporting the activities of local churches, 25% to relief agencies in poorer nations and 50% to local charities or branches of national charities to help older people, people with disabilities and families or children who are otherwise in need.
**WHAT IS NOT FUNDED** Individuals.
**TYPE OF GRANT** Core costs; salaries; start-up costs. One-off, up to three years.
**RANGE OF GRANTS** Up to £10,000.
**SAMPLE GRANTS** Y-Care International (£3,000); The Family Centre, Bonymaen, Swansea (£2,000); St Teilo's Church, Caereithin, Swansea (£1,500); Bishop Benjamin Vaughan (£1,000); Holy Trinity Church, Sketty (£800); Excellent Development (£500); African Revival, Amantani UK, Feed the Minds and Village Water (£400 each); and School Aid UK (£250).
**FINANCES** Year 2013/14 Income £56,980 Grants £62,588 Grants to organisations £62,588 Assets £682,396
**TRUSTEES** Clive Bailey; Sandra Morton; The Venerable Robert Williams; Penny Ryan; Revd Jonathan Davies.
**OTHER INFORMATION** Because of the fewer applications sometimes received within the local churches category, the trustees at their discretion can allocate additional funds to overseas charities.
**HOW TO APPLY** Apply in writing to the correspondent. Applications are considered in May, September and December. Applications under the local charity or church category from groups based outside the local area will only be considered if they demonstrate a strong local involvement. Applications under the overseas category must be from a UK-based charity. An application form is available at the foundation's website.
**WHO TO APPLY TO** Clive Bailey, Trustee, 64 Bosworth Road, Barnet EN5 5LP *Tel.* 020 8449 4321 *email* localcharities@austinbaileyfoundation.org *Website* www.austinbaileyfoundation.org

## ■ The Baily Thomas Charitable Fund

**CC NO** 262334     **ESTABLISHED** 1970
**WHERE FUNDING CAN BE GIVEN** UK.
**WHO CAN BENEFIT** Community groups, support groups and organisations benefitting people affected by learning disability. Applications will only be considered from voluntary organisations which are registered charities or are associated with a registered charity. Schools and PTAs and Industrial and Provident Societies can also apply. The fund does not currently accept appeals from Community Interest Companies.
**WHAT IS FUNDED** The trustees restrict their remit to learning disability. This can include residential facilities; respite; sheltered accommodation; crafts and music; support to volunteers; special schools and special needs education; care in the community; day centres; holidays and outings; play schemes; and research.
**WHAT IS NOT FUNDED** Grants are not normally awarded to individuals. The following areas are unlikely to receive funding: hospices; minibuses except those for residential and/or day care services for people who have learning disabilities; conductive education projects; swimming and hydro-therapy pools; advocacy projects; arts and theatre projects; physical disabilities unless accompanied by significant learning disabilities; grants for acquired brain injury unless the resulting learning disabilities occur early in the developmental period (i.e. birth, infancy or childhood), impacting on brain maturation and development and learning in childhood.
**TYPE OF GRANT** Capital and revenue. Loans may be made in certain circumstances. Grants are usually one-off.
**RANGE OF GRANTS** £250 to £130,000.
**SAMPLE GRANTS** Queen's University Belfast (£123,500); Development Trust and The JPK Sussex Project (£100,000 each); Rix-Thompson-Rothenberg Foundation (£70,000); Avon Riding Centre for the Disabled, Ferring Country Centre and The Hextol Foundation (£30,000 each).
**FINANCES** Year 2013/14 Income £1,968,766 Grants £2,976,278 Grants to organisations £2,976,278 Assets £87,867,006
**TRUSTEES** Prof. Sally-Ann Cooper; Prof. Anne Farmer; Suzanne Jane Marriott; Kenneth Young.
**OTHER INFORMATION** Beneficiaries receiving £25,000 or more were listed in the accounts. There were 291 grants made in total in 2013/14.
**HOW TO APPLY** Meetings of the trustees are usually held in April and October each year and applicants are advised to visit the charity's website for details of current deadlines. The website states that late applications will not be considered. If your application is considered under the Small Grants procedure then this will be reviewed by the trustees ahead of the usual meetings. Following the meeting all applicants are contacted formally to advise on the status of their application. Feel free to submit your application whenever you are ready, rather than waiting for the deadline. Applications must be made online via the charity's website from which the following information is taken:
'**General applications** Funding is normally considered for capital and revenue costs and for both specific projects and for general running/core costs. Grants are awarded for amounts from £250 and depend on a number of factors including the purpose, the total funding requirement and the potential sources of other funds including, in some cases, matching funding. Normally one-off grants are awarded but

exceptionally a new project may be funded over two or three years, subject to satisfactory reports of progress. Grants should normally be taken up within one year of the issue of the grant offer letter which will include conditions relating to the release of the grant. The following areas of work normally fall within the fund's policy: capital building/renovation/ refurbishment works for residential, nursing and respite care, and schools; employment schemes including woodwork, crafts, printing and horticulture; play schemes and play therapy schemes; day and social activities centres including building costs and running costs; support for families, including respite schemes; independent living schemes; support in the community schemes; Snoezelen rooms.'

'**Research applications** We generally direct our limited funds towards the initiation of research so that it can progress to the point at which there is sufficient data to support an application to one of the major funding bodies. Applications will only be considered from established research workers and will be subject to normal professional peer review procedures. Applications, limited to 5 pages with the type no smaller than Times New Roman 12, should be in the form of a scientific summary with a research plan to include a brief background and a short account of the design of the study and number of subjects, the methods of assessment and analysis, timetable, main outcomes and some indication of other opportunities arising from the support of such research. A detailed budget of costs should be submitted together with a justification for the support requested. Details should be included of any other applications for funding which have been made to other funders and their outcomes, if known. The fund does not contribute towards university overheads. A one page curriculum vitae will be required for each of the personnel actually carrying out the study and for their supervisor together with a note of the total number of their peer reviewed publications and details of the 10 most significant publications. Evidence may be submitted of the approval of the ethics committee of the applicant to the study and approval of the university for the application to the fund. An 80 word lay summary should also be submitted with the scientific summary. Any papers submitted in excess of those stipulated above will not be passed to the research committee for consideration. Before submitting a full application, researchers may submit a one page summary of the proposed study so that the trustees may indicate whether they are prepared to consider a full application.'

**WHO TO APPLY TO** Ann Cooper, Secretary to the Trustees, c/o TMF Management (UK) Ltd, 400 Capability Green, Luton LU1 3AE *Tel.* 01582 439205 *email* info@bailythomas.org.uk *Website* www.bailythomas.org.uk

## ■ The Baird Trust

**SC NO** SC016549    **ESTABLISHED** 1873
**WHERE FUNDING CAN BE GIVEN** Scotland.
**WHO CAN BENEFIT** Generally, the Church of Scotland.
**WHAT IS FUNDED** The trust is chiefly concerned with supporting the repair and refurbishment of the churches and halls belonging to the Church of Scotland. It also endows parishes and gives help to the Church of Scotland in its work.
**TYPE OF GRANT** One-off for capital and revenue.

**SAMPLE GRANTS** Airth Parish Church, Bellshill West Parish Church, Canisbay Church of Scotland, Church of Scotland Board Ministry, Coltness Memorial Church – Newmains, Kinross Parish Church, Kinnaird Church – Dundee, Lodging House Mission, London Road Church – Edinburgh, Newmachar Parish Church, St Andrew's Erskine Parish Church, St Michael's Parish Church – Edinburgh, Scottish Churches House and South Parish Church – East Kilbride.
**FINANCES** *Year* 2013 *Income* £391,138 *Grants* £250,000 *Grants to organisations* £250,000
**TRUSTEES** Lieut. Col. Charles Ball; Hon. Mary Coltman; Maj. J. Erskine; Revd Dr Johnston McKay; Alan Borthwick; Dr Alison Elliot; Luke Borwick; Walter Barbour; Lieut. Col. Richard Callander.
**HOW TO APPLY** An application form can be completed online or by paper copy and submitted to the secretary.
**WHO TO APPLY TO** Iain Mowat, Secretary, 182 Bath Street, Glasgow G2 4HG *Tel.* 0141 332 0476 *Fax* 0141 331 0874 *email* info@bairdtrust.org.uk *Website* www.bairdtrust.org.uk

## ■ The Baker Charitable Trust

**CC NO** 273629    **ESTABLISHED** 1977
**WHERE FUNDING CAN BE GIVEN** UK and overseas.
**WHO CAN BENEFIT** Registered charities including the headquarters of national organisations.
**WHAT IS FUNDED** Priority is given to charities concerned with the welfare of Jewish, elderly and disabled people; neurological research; and people with diabetes and epilepsy. Preference is given to charities in which the trust has special interest, knowledge or association.
**WHAT IS NOT FUNDED** Individuals; non-registered charities.
**TYPE OF GRANT** Core costs.
**RANGE OF GRANTS** £250–£10,000; typical grant £500–£3,000.
**SAMPLE GRANTS** **Previous beneficiaries have included:** British Council Shaare Zedek Medical Centre, Chai Cancer Care, Community Security Trust, Disabled Living Foundation, Friends of Magen David Adom in Great Britain, Hillel Foundation, Institute of Jewish Policy Research, Jewish Care; Jewish Women's Aid, Marie Curie Cancer Care, National Society for Epilepsy, Norwood; United Jewish Israel Appeal, St John's Hospice, United Synagogue, Winged Fellowship and World Jewish Relief.
**FINANCES** *Year* 2013/14 *Income* £61,718 *Grants* £49,610 *Grants to organisations* £49,610 *Assets* £1,364,908
**TRUSTEES** Dr Harvey Baker; Dr Adrienne Baker.
**HOW TO APPLY** Apply in writing to the correspondent. The trustees meet to consider applications in January, April, July and October.
**WHO TO APPLY TO** Dr Harvey Baker, Trustee, 16 Sheldon Avenue, Highgate, London N6 4JT *Tel.* 020 8340 5760 *email* harbaker@doctors.org.uk

## ■ The Roy and Pixie Baker Charitable Trust

**CC NO** 1101988    **ESTABLISHED** 1995
**WHERE FUNDING CAN BE GIVEN** North East of England.
**WHO CAN BENEFIT** Charitable organisations.
**WHAT IS FUNDED** Medical research, education, heritage, relief in need.
**TYPE OF GRANT** One-off and recurrent.

**RANGE OF GRANTS** Up to £10,000.
**SAMPLE GRANTS** Daft and a Brush (£5,000); Dementia Care Partnership, the Urology Foundation (£2,000); Evening Chronicle Sunshine Fund (£500), Percy Park Youth Trust (£5,000); Northumberland Clubs for Young People, Nunnykirk Centre for Dyslexia (£3,000 each); Ateres Girls' High School (£2,500), National Trust Seaton Delaval Hall (£5,000); Cathedral Church of St Nicholas (£4,500); Literary and Philosophical Society, Tyne Rivers Trust (£2,000 each), North East Help Link (£1,500)
**FINANCES** Year 2013/14 Income £73,336 Grants £50,000 Grants to organisations £50,000 Assets £3,072,582
**TRUSTEES** Tony Glenton; George Straker; Lesley Caisley; David Irvin; Bill Dryden.
**HOW TO APPLY** Apply in writing to the correspondent, providing full back up information. Trustees' meetings are held yearly. The trustees require a receipt from the donee in respect of each grant.
**WHO TO APPLY TO** The Trustees, c/o Ryecroft Glenton, 32 Portland Terrace, Newcastle upon Tyne NE2 1QP *Tel.* 0191 281 1292 *email* bakercharitabletrust@ryecroft-glenton.co.uk

## ■ The C. Alma Baker Trust

**CC NO** 1113864   **ESTABLISHED** 1981
**WHERE FUNDING CAN BE GIVEN** UK and overseas, particularly New Zealand.
**WHO CAN BENEFIT** Individuals or scientific research institutions benefitting young adults, farmers, academics, research workers and students.
**WHAT IS FUNDED** The trust makes grants for agricultural research and scholarships for students of agriculture wishing to attend a University or Technical Institute. The trust also supports travel likely to benefit agriculture and, in particular, travel between the UK and New Zealand, together with grants for educational purposes and general charitable donations.
**WHAT IS NOT FUNDED** General education grants.
**TYPE OF GRANT** Range of grants, though normally one-off annual grants.
**SAMPLE GRANTS** Maori Language Teachers Scholarship at Waikato University NZ (£8,600); Worshipful Company of Farmers (£2,000); Royal Agricultural Society of the Commonwealth and Royal Smithfield Club (£1,000 each).
**FINANCES** Year 2013/14 Income £1,346,376 Grants £126,574 Grants to organisations £126,574 Assets £9,539,719
**TRUSTEES** Charles Boyes; Roger Moore; Simon Taylor; David Heneage Wynne-Finch.
**PUBLICATIONS** Limestone Downs Annual Report in New Zealand.
**OTHER INFORMATION** The trust's main asset is Limestone Downs, a sheep and beef property in the North Island, New Zealand utilised for new ideas and development in agriculture to be explored and debated in a working farm environment.
**HOW TO APPLY** Apply in writing to the correspondent.
**WHO TO APPLY TO** Jane O'Beirne, Company Secretary, 20 Hartford Road, Huntingdon, Cambridgeshire PE29 3QH *Tel.* 01480 411331 *email* wba@wbalaw.co.uk *Website* www.calmabakertrust.co.uk

## ■ The Balcombe Charitable Trust

**CC NO** 267172   **ESTABLISHED** 1975
**WHERE FUNDING CAN BE GIVEN** UK and overseas.
**WHO CAN BENEFIT** Registered charities benefitting children and young adults, students, at risk groups, people with disabilities, people disadvantaged by poverty, socially isolated people, and people who are sick.
**WHAT IS FUNDED** Education; the environment; health and welfare.
**TYPE OF GRANT** One-off and recurrent grants.
**RANGE OF GRANTS** £5,000–£100,000
**SAMPLE GRANTS** Action Aid (£164,000); Raleigh International (£45,000); Age UK (£41,000); The Haven (£22,000); St Mungo's (£20,000); The 999 Club Trust and The Cambodian Children's Charity (£10,000 each); Freedom from Torture (£2,500).
**FINANCES** Year 2013/14 Income £478,010 Grants £395,982 Grants to organisations £395,982 Assets £27,699,037
**TRUSTEES** Mr R. A. Kreitman; Patricia M. Kreitman; Nicholas Brown.
**HOW TO APPLY** Apply in writing to the correspondent.
**WHO TO APPLY TO** Jonathan Prevezer, c/o Citroen Wells, Devonshire House, 1 Devonshire Street, London W1W 5DR *Tel.* 020 7304 2000 *email* jonathan.prevezer@citroenwells.co.uk

## ■ The Balfour Beatty Charitable Trust

**CC NO** 1127453   **ESTABLISHED** 2009
**WHERE FUNDING CAN BE GIVEN** UK.
**WHO CAN BENEFIT** Registered charities.
**WHAT IS FUNDED** Children and young people.
**RANGE OF GRANTS** Up to £100,000.
**SAMPLE GRANTS** Barnardo's (£100,000); the Prince's Trust (£100,000); Action for Children (£80,000); and the Thomas Coram Foundation (£80,000).
**FINANCES** Year 2013 Income £246,790 Grants £360,000 Grants to organisations £360,000 Assets £78,865
**TRUSTEES** Mark Peters; Paul Raby.
**HOW TO APPLY** The trustees work together with the Balfour Beatty Community Engagement Working Group (CEWG) to identify suitable charities to support.
**WHO TO APPLY TO** The Trustees, Company Secretarial Department, Balfour Beatty Ltd, 130 Wilton Road, London SW1V 1 LQ *Tel.* 020 7216 6800 *email* bbfutures@balfourbeatty.com *Website* www.balfourbeatty.com

## ■ The Andrew Balint Charitable Trust

**CC NO** 273691   **ESTABLISHED** 1961
**WHERE FUNDING CAN BE GIVEN** UK; Israel; Hungary and Romania.
**WHO CAN BENEFIT** Charitable organisations; Jewish organisations.
**WHAT IS FUNDED** General charitable causes; health, elderly, ex-service people, Jewish faith, and disability organisations.
**TYPE OF GRANT** One off and recurring.
**RANGE OF GRANTS** £100–£20,000
**SAMPLE GRANTS** Previously, Nightingale House (£20,000); Former Employee Trust and Hungarian Senior Citizens (£6,000 each); Jewish Care (£5,000); United Jewish Israel Appeal and Toth Gabor £5,000 each); The Board of Deputies of British Jews and World

Jewish Relief (£500 each); British Friends of Children's Town (£250).
**FINANCES** Year 2013/14 Income £21,149 Grants £45,000 Grants to organisations £45,000
**TRUSTEES** Dr Gabriel Balint-Kurti; Angela Balint; Roy Balint-Kurti; Daniel Balint-Kurti.
**OTHER INFORMATION** The Andrew Balint Charitable Trust, The George Balint Charitable Trust, The Paul Charitable Trust and the Trust for Former Employees of Balint Companies are jointly administered. They have some trustees in common and are independent in other matters. Accounts had been received at the Commission but because of the low income were not published.
**HOW TO APPLY** Applications should be made in writing to the correspondent.
**WHO TO APPLY TO** David Kramer, Correspondent, c/o Carter Backer Winter, Enterprise House, 21 Buckle Street, London E1 8NN *Tel.* 020 7309 3800 *email* david.kramer@cbw.co.uk

## ■ The George Balint Charitable Trust

**CC NO** 267482 **ESTABLISHED** 1961
**WHERE FUNDING CAN BE GIVEN** UK; Israel; Hungary.
**WHO CAN BENEFIT** Charitable organisations; individuals.
**WHAT IS FUNDED** General; education; medical care and research; Jewish.
**RANGE OF GRANTS** £200–£20,000
**SAMPLE GRANTS** United Jewish Israel Appeal (£20,000); Former Employees Trust (£4,200); Hungarian Senior Citizens (£3,700); North London Hospice, and Neviot Olam Institution (£1,000 each); London Soup Kitchen (£450); Hartsbourne Ladies Charity Committee (£200).
**FINANCES** Year 2013/14 Income £717,635 Grants £43,154 Grants to organisations £43,154 Assets £1,546,595
**TRUSTEES** Dr Andrew Balint; George Rothschild; Dr Marc Balint.
**OTHER INFORMATION** 'The George Balint Charitable Trust, the Paul Balint Charitable Trust and The Charitable Trust for Former Employees of Balint Companies operate from the same premises and are jointly administered. They have some trustees in common and are independent in all other matters.'
**HOW TO APPLY** Apply in writing to the correspondent.
**WHO TO APPLY TO** David Kramer, Correspondent, c/o Carter Backer Winter, Enterprise House, 21 Buckle Street, London E1 8NN *Tel.* 020 7309 3800 *email* balintcharitabletrust@gmail.com

## ■ The Paul Balint Charitable Trust

**CC NO** 273690 **ESTABLISHED** 1977
**WHERE FUNDING CAN BE GIVEN** UK; Hungary; Israel.
**WHO CAN BENEFIT** Charitable organisations.
**WHAT IS FUNDED** General charitable purposes; medical research; education; elderly assistance; relief of poverty.
**FINANCES** Year 2013/14 Income £502 Grants £35,000 Grants to organisations £35,000.
**TRUSTEES** Dr Andrew Balint; Dr Gabriel Balint-Kurti; Dr Marc Balint; Paul Balint.
**OTHER INFORMATION** The Andrew Balint Charitable Trust, The George Balint Charitable Trust, The Paul Balint Charitable Trust and the Trust for Former Employees of Balint Companies are jointly administered. They have some trustees in common and are independent in other matters.
**HOW TO APPLY** Apply in writing to the correspondent.
**WHO TO APPLY TO** Dr Andrew Balint, Trustee, 15 Portland Court, 101 Hendon Lane, London N3 3SH *Tel.* 020 8346 1266 *email* balintcharitabletrust@gmail.com

## ■ The Ballinger Charitable Trust

**CC NO** 1121739 **ESTABLISHED** 1994
**WHERE FUNDING CAN BE GIVEN** North east England, Tyne and Wear.
**WHO CAN BENEFIT** Registered charities only.
**WHAT IS FUNDED** The focus of the Ballinger Charitable Trust is currently to support projects in the North East of England, principally by providing funds that: support the health, development and well-being of young people; support the elderly; to improve the quality of life for people and communities; promote cultural/arts projects based in the North East of England.
**WHAT IS NOT FUNDED** Individuals; sponsorships.
**SAMPLE GRANTS** St Mary's Cathedral (£325,500); Dementia Care (£167,500); Alzheimer's Society (£167,000); Bernard Gilpin Primary School (£85,000); Keyfund (£64,000); Thomas Walling School (£38,000); St Cuthbert's Care (£30,000); Seven Stories (£25,000); Newcastle Society for the Blind (£15,000); Contact a Family (£5,000); Age UK, Leonard Cheshire Disability and The People's Kitchen (£2,500 each).
**FINANCES** Year 2013 Income £2,815,003 Grants £1,361,642 Grants to organisations £1,361,642 Assets £26,532,731
**TRUSTEES** Diana Ballinger; John Flynn; Andrew Ballinger; Nicola Crowther.
**HOW TO APPLY** The following information is taken from the trust's website: **Amounts up to £5,000** – A letter will suffice and will be acknowledged as soon as possible. **Amounts over £5,000** – Complete the initial application form and submit via the website. You will be contacted shortly afterwards to either: issue you with a unique user name and password giving access to the full application form, (note these details may be used for one full application only) or advise that your initial application has been unsuccessful.
**WHO TO APPLY TO** Nicola Crowther, Trustee, PO Box 166, Ponteland, Newcastle upon Tyne NE20 2BL *email* info@ballingercharitabletrust.org.uk *Website* www.ballingercharitabletrust.org.uk

## ■ Balmain Charitable Trust

**CC NO** 1079972 **ESTABLISHED** 1998
**WHERE FUNDING CAN BE GIVEN** UK.
**WHO CAN BENEFIT** Charitable organisations.
**WHAT IS FUNDED** General charitable purposes.
**RANGE OF GRANTS** Mostly £1,000–£2,000.
**SAMPLE GRANTS** British Red Cross Society (£7,000); The Suzy Lamplugh Trust (£6,000); Second Chance (£5,000); Conservation Zambesi, Crisis UK and Ewe and You and (£2,000 each); Taunton Choral Society (£1,000); Queen's Royal Hussars Charity (£500).
**FINANCES** Year 2013/14 Income £113,858 Grants £472,385 Grants to organisations £472,385 Assets £2,841,750
**TRUSTEES** Leonora D. Balmain; Stewart Balmain; Andrew Tappin; David Ashworth.
**OTHER INFORMATION** Many of the beneficiaries are supported year after year.

**HOW TO APPLY** Applications should be made in writing to the correspondent.
**WHO TO APPLY TO** The Correspondent, c/o Rutter and Alhusen, 2 Longmead, Shaftesbury, Dorset SP7 8PL *email* mail@rutterandallhusen.com

## ■ The Balmore Trust

**SC NO** SC008930 **ESTABLISHED** 1980
**WHERE FUNDING CAN BE GIVEN** Financially developing countries and UK, with a preference for Strathclyde.
**WHO CAN BENEFIT** Organisations.
**WHAT IS FUNDED** Two-thirds of grants are given to overseas projects and the remainder to local projects in the UK, working in the areas of education, health, alleviation of poverty and community development. Grant giving in the UK is concentrated mainly in the Glasgow area and favours families, teenagers, and women's aid groups. Overseas, the trust has close connections with community development programmes in India (Kolkata, Rajasthan and Kerala), Burma and Africa (Kenya, South Africa, Swaziland, Lesotho and Namibia).
**WHAT IS NOT FUNDED** Individuals.
**SAMPLE GRANTS** **Previous beneficiaries have included:** Church House – Bridgeton, Daynes Education Fund – South Africa, East Dunbartonshire Women's Aid, Family Action in Rogerfield and Easterhouse, Friends of CINI – India, Glasgow Children's Holiday Scheme, Humura Child Care Family – Uganda, Inverclyde Youth for Christ Reality at Work, Mission Aviation Fellowship, the Village Storytelling Centre – Pollok and Wells for India – Rajasthan.
**FINANCES** *Year* 2013/14 *Income* £36,788 *Grants* £29,648 *Grants to organisations* £29,648
**TRUSTEES** Mr J. Riches; Mr G. Burns; J. Eldridge; B. Holman; Ms R. Jarvis; Ms R. Riches.
**PUBLICATIONS** Newsletter available on website
**OTHER INFORMATION** The Balmore Trust distributes the profits of the Coach House charity craft shop as well as other donations. The trust's policy in grant-making is increasingly to build on partnerships already established.
**HOW TO APPLY** The trust is run entirely voluntarily and the trust states that it is unlikely that money will be available for new applicants, unless they have a personal link with the trust or its shop, the Coach House charity craft shop.
**WHO TO APPLY TO** The Secretary, Viewfield, Balmore, Torrance, Glasgow G64 4AE *Tel.* 01360 620742 *email* mailto@balmoretrust.org.uk *Website* www.balmoretrust.org.uk

## ■ The Balney Charitable Trust

**CC NO** 288575 **ESTABLISHED** 1983
**WHERE FUNDING CAN BE GIVEN** UK, with a preference for north Buckinghamshire and north Bedfordshire.
**WHO CAN BENEFIT** Individuals and registered charities.
**WHAT IS FUNDED** The furtherance of any religious and charitable purposes in connection with the parishes of Chicheley, North Crawley and the SCAN Group i.e. Sherington, Astwood, Hardmead and churches with a Chester family connection; the provision of housing for persons in needy circumstances; agriculture, forestry and armed service charities; care of older people and people who are sick and/or have disabilities.
**WHAT IS NOT FUNDED** Local community organisations; individuals outside north Buckinghamshire and north Bedfordshire.
**TYPE OF GRANT** Start-up costs, capital grants (including contributions to building projects, e.g. local churches) and research. Funding for up to three years will be considered.
**RANGE OF GRANTS** £25–£5,000
**SAMPLE GRANTS** Previously: St Lawrence Church – Chicheley (£7,500); National Trust – Montecute House (£7,000 in two grants); Queen Alexandra Hospital Home (£5,000); CHIT, Combat Stress, Motor Neurone Disease Association and St Luke's Hospital for the Clergy (£2,000 each); Emmaus Village – Carlton, Help for Heroes, MS Therapy Centre and Tree Aid – Ghana Village Tree Enterprise (£1,000 each); and Fun 4 Young People (£500).
**FINANCES** *Year* 2013/14 *Income* £175,652 *Grants* £47,485 *Grants to organisations* £47,485 *Assets* £879,452
**TRUSTEES** Ian Townsend; Robert Ruck-Keene; Jill Heaton.
**HOW TO APPLY** Apply in writing to the correspondent. Applications are acknowledged if an sae is enclosed, otherwise if the charity has not received a reply within six weeks the application has not been successful.
**WHO TO APPLY TO** Helen Chapman, Secretary to the Trustees, Hill Farm, North Crawley Road, Newport Pagnell, Buckinghamshire MK16 9HQ *Tel.* 07790 000217 *email* balney.charity@virginmedia.com

## ■ The Baltic Charitable Fund

**CC NO** 279194 **ESTABLISHED** 1979
**WHERE FUNDING CAN BE GIVEN** UK, with a preference for the City of London.
**WHO CAN BENEFIT** Registered charities benefitting residents of the City of London, seafarers, fishermen, and ex-service and service people.
**WHAT IS FUNDED** Registered charities only which must be connected with the City of London, shipping or the military forces.
**WHAT IS NOT FUNDED** Advertising; charity dinners.
**TYPE OF GRANT** One-off.
**RANGE OF GRANTS** £300–£36,000
**SAMPLE GRANTS** Sailors' Society (£10,000); Seavision (£6,600) Bletchley Park Trust (£2,500); Operation New World (£1,000); and Movember (£300).
**FINANCES** *Year* 2013/14 *Income* £82,750 *Grants* £33,431 *Grants to organisations* £33,431 *Assets* £2,306,093
**TRUSTEE** The directors of the Baltic Exchange Limited.
**HOW TO APPLY** Unsolicited applications are not considered.
**WHO TO APPLY TO** Clive Weston, Secretary to the Trustee, The Baltic Exchange, 38 St Mary Axe, London EC3A 8BH *Tel.* 020 7623 5501

## ■ The Bamford Charitable Foundation

**CC NO** 279848 **ESTABLISHED** 1979
**WHERE FUNDING CAN BE GIVEN** UK and overseas but mainly within a 40-mile radius of Rocester.
**WHO CAN BENEFIT** Mainly local organisations.
**WHAT IS FUNDED** General charitable purposes.
**TYPE OF GRANT** One-off.
**FINANCES** *Year* 2013/14 *Income* £155,833 *Grants* £3,260,778 *Grants to organisations* £3,260,778 *Assets* £2,374,944

**TRUSTEES** The Lord Bamford; Lady C. Bamford.
**HOW TO APPLY** Apply in writing to the correspondent. 'Successful applicants are required to demonstrate to the trustees that the receipt of the grant is wholly necessary to enable them to fulfil their own objectives.'
**WHO TO APPLY TO** Mr D. G. Garnett, Correspondent, c/o J. C. Bamford Excavators Ltd, Lakeside Works, Denstone Road, Rocester, Uttoxeter ST14 5JP *Tel.* 01889 593140

## ■ The Banbury Charities

**CC NO** 201418   **ESTABLISHED** 1961
**WHERE FUNDING CAN BE GIVEN** Banbury or its immediate environs.
**WHO CAN BENEFIT** Individuals and groups.
**WHAT IS FUNDED** General charitable purposes.
**WHAT IS NOT FUNDED** Debts; ongoing expenses.
**TYPE OF GRANT** One-off grants.
**RANGE OF GRANTS** Up to £35,000.
**SAMPLE GRANTS** Banbury Welfare Trust (£35,000); Banbury Rugby Union Football Club (£30,000); Katherine House Hospice (£10,500); Age UK Oxfordshire and Style Acre (£10,000 each); St Laurence Church (£6,000); Anjai Dance Company and St Leonard's Church of England Primary School (£5,000 each); Banbury Sailing Club (£4,000); Rotary Young Musician and Sunshine Centre (£1,000 each).
**FINANCES** *Year* 2014 *Income* £418,628 *Grants* £292,517 *Grants to organisations* £204,137 *Assets* £5,558,492
**TRUSTEES** Fred Blackwell; Valerie Fisher; Helen Madeiros; Judy May; Julia Colegrave; Keiron Mallon; Martin Humphris; Nigel Morris; Angela Heritage; Jamie Briggs; Janet Justice; Colin Clarke.
**OTHER INFORMATION** The Banbury Charities are The Bridge Estate, Lady Arran's Charity, Banbury Arts and Educational Charity, Banbury Sick Poor Fund, Banbury Almshouse Charity, Banbury Recreation Charity, Banbury Poor Trust and the Banbury Welfare Trust. About one-third of the grant total is given to individuals.
**HOW TO APPLY** Apply ii writing to the correspondent.
**WHO TO APPLY TO** Nigel Yeadon, Clerk to the Trustees, 36 West Bar, Banbury, Oxfordshire OX16 9RU *Tel.* 01295 251234

## ■ The Band Trust

**CC NO** 279802   **ESTABLISHED** 1976
**WHERE FUNDING CAN BE GIVEN** UK.
**WHO CAN BENEFIT** Registered UK charities.
**WHAT IS FUNDED** A very wide range of general charitable purposes; army and veterans; children and young people; disability; disadvantaged individuals; education and arts; older people; nursing care.
**WHAT IS NOT FUNDED** Unsolicited appeals; individuals directly; political activities; commercial ventures or publications; retrospective grants or loans; direct replacement of statutory funding or activities that are primarily the responsibility of central or local government.
**TYPE OF GRANT** One-off and recurring.
**RANGE OF GRANTS** £1,500–£60,000
**SAMPLE GRANTS** Maggie's (£60,000); Jewish Museum (£36,000); Beanstalk and Royal National Theatre (£30,000 each); The Duke of Edinburgh's Award, Trinity Winchester and Winchester Cathedral Trust (£20,000 each); Prison Reform Trust (£16,000); Armonico Consort (£15,000); Depaul UK (£12,000); Leonard Cheshire Disability and Resurgo Trust (£10,000 each); W11 Opera Rural Community (£7,500); Clean Up, Contact the Elderly and Rural Community Council of Essex (£5,000 each); NSPCC (£3,400 in a number of grants); Chelsea Old Church PCC (£1,500); British Library, Crohn's and Colitis UK and The Southbank Centre (£1,000 each); Florence Nightingale Foundation (£900); Breast Cancer Haven (£250).
**FINANCES** *Year* 2013/14 *Income* £1,024,886 *Grants* £816,668 *Grants to organisations* £816,668 *Assets* £27,411,231
**TRUSTEES** The Hon. Nicholas Wallop; The Hon. Nicholas Wallop; Richard Mason; Bruce Streather; Victoria Wallop.
**OTHER INFORMATION** The grant total consists of 74 donations (£768,500) and scholarships (£50,000).
**HOW TO APPLY** The trustees identify potential recipients themselves and the accounts state that 'the trustees do not wish to receive unsolicited applications for grants'. The website adds: 'Due to the increase in postage costs The Band Trust will not acknowledge unsolicited applications.' **Only** make applications if you have been specifically invited to do so by submitting an application to the trustee with whom you have been in contact, together with a copy of their latest report and accounts. The trustees meet to consider applications regularly during the year.
**WHO TO APPLY TO** Richard Mason, Trustee, c/o Moore Stephens, 150 Aldersgate Street, London EC1A 4AB *Tel.* 020 7334 9191 *email* richard.mason@moorestephens.com *Website* www.bandtrust.co.uk

## ■ The Bank of Scotland Foundation

**SC NO** SC032942   **ESTABLISHED** 2002
**WHERE FUNDING CAN BE GIVEN** Scotland.
**WHO CAN BENEFIT** Registered charities; community groups; local organisations.
**WHAT IS FUNDED** Developing and improving local communities; financial literacy and financial inclusion. The foundation operates the following programmes: small grants (£1,000–£10,000); medium grants (10,000–£25,000); large grants (£50,000–£100,000). According to the accounts for 2013 the foundation may also provide Volunteering Grants (£1,000–£2,000) 'to fund new or existing projects that are aimed at increasing community volunteering'.
**WHAT IS NOT FUNDED** Discriminatory, political or religious organisations; animal charities; medical research; individuals; advertising or sponsorship.
**RANGE OF GRANTS** £1,000–£100,000
**SAMPLE GRANTS** Alzheimer Scotland – Forget-me-not project (£16,200); Citizens Advice West Lothian (£15,400); Breast Cancer Care Scotland, Sick Kids Friends Foundation and St Columba's Hospice (£10,000 each); Parent to Parent (£9,200); Wigtownshire Community Transport (£8,100); Changing Faces Scotland (£7,500); Upward Mobility Ltd (£7,200); Reidvale Adventure Play Association (£5,600); Parkhead Youth Project (£5,500); Deaf Action (£5,000); Almond Mains Initiative (£4,000); Hearts and Minds (£2,400); Burntisland Playgroup (£1,500). Recipient of larger grants were not listed in the accounts.
**FINANCES** *Year* 2013 *Income* £1,397,917 *Grants* £1,334,341 *Grants to organisations* £1,334,341 *Assets* £11,926

TRUSTEES Kate Guthrie; Jim Coyle; Sarah Deas; Paul Grice; Robin Bulloch; Ed Smith.

OTHER INFORMATION The foundation also has a Matched Giving Programme whereby Lloyds Banking Group colleagues can receive matched funding for their charitable activities. Support was allocated between the two main focus areas: developing and improving local communities (nearly £1.3 million in 63 grants, including £675,500 in matched funding); money advice and financial literacy (£53,000 in six grants).

HOW TO APPLY Application forms are available from the foundation's website, where detailed criteria and guidelines are also posted. Appeals for small and medium grants can be made once every 12 months and for large grants can be submitted only after two years have passed from the receipt of an award. Unsuccessful organisations should wait one year before trying again. The submission deadlines for each programme may vary – see the website for most up-to-date information.

WHO TO APPLY TO Lorraine O'Neill, Finance and Grants Manager, The Mound, Edinburgh EH1 1YZ Tel. 0131 655 2599 email enquiries@bankofscotlandfoundation.co.uk Website www.bankofscotlandfoundation.org

■ **The Barbers' Company General Charities**

CC NO 265579   ESTABLISHED 1973
WHERE FUNDING CAN BE GIVEN UK.
WHO CAN BENEFIT Organisations and individuals.
WHAT IS FUNDED General charitable purposes, including medical education and nursing.
WHAT IS NOT FUNDED Unsolicited applications.
RANGE OF GRANTS £1,000–£50,000
SAMPLE GRANTS Royal College of Surgeons (£40,000); Phyliss Tuckwell Hospice (£22,000); The Guildhall School Trust (£6,500); Epsom College and Reeds School (£5,000 each); St Giles Cripplegate, Treloars and The Guildhall School Trust (£1,000 each).
FINANCES Year 2013/14 Income £143,570 Grants £161,863 Grants to organisations £161,863 Assets £1,530,918
TRUSTEE The Barbers Company.
HOW TO APPLY Visit the 'How to Apply' section on the Barbers' Company's website.
WHO TO APPLY TO The Clerk, Barber-Surgeons' Hall, 1A Monkwell Square, Wood Street, London EC2Y 5BL Tel. 020 7606 0741 email clerk@barberscompany.org Website barberscompany.org.uk

■ **The Barbour Foundation**

CC NO 328081   ESTABLISHED 1988
WHERE FUNDING CAN BE GIVEN Mainly Tyne and Wear, Northumberland and South Tyneside.
WHO CAN BENEFIT The trust likes to support local organisations dealing with community welfare, housing and social deprivation. Also supports local branches of national charities.
WHAT IS FUNDED Grants are awarded to support the foundation's objectives, which are: relief of patients suffering from any form of illness or disease, promotion of research into causes of such illnesses; furtherance of education; preservation of buildings and countryside of environmental, historical or architectural interest; relief of people in need; disaster relief (in England or overseas).

WHAT IS NOT FUNDED Requests from outside the geographical area; individual applications, unless backed by a particular charitable organisation; capital grants for building projects.
TYPE OF GRANT Core costs, start-up costs, full project costs. Funding for up to one year will be considered.
SAMPLE GRANTS Theatre Royal Newcastle (£50,000); Prince's Countryside Fund (£32,000); Grace House North East (£20,000); Calvert Trust – Kielder and Target Ovarian Cancer (£10,000 each); Cleveland Housing Advice Centre, Crisis Christmas Appeal, Rainbow Trust and Trinity Church (£5,000 each); Age UK and Wallsend Boys' Club (£3,000 each); Diabetes UK, Great North Festival Company, Meningitis Trust, Place2Be and Veterans at Ease (£2,000 each); Northern Children's Book Festival, Northumberland Wildlife Trust, South Tyneside Women's Aid and Washington Mind (£1,000 each).
FINANCES Year 2013/14 Income £1,736,048 Grants £572,191 Grants to organisations £572,191 Assets £12,094,108
TRUSTEES Dame Margaret Barbour, Chair; Helen Barbour; Helen Tavroges.
OTHER INFORMATION In 2013/14 grants were awarded in the following categories: community welfare; youth/children; medical; disability; elderly; conservation/horticultural; heritage/museums; service charities; the arts; housing/homeless; maritime; animal welfare; special appeals; education; deprivation. 532 organisations were awarded grants over the year. Grant total includes £4,791 paid in goods to the foundation by J Barbour and Sons Ltd.
HOW TO APPLY Applications should be made in writing to Mrs A Harvey, PO Box 21, Guisborough, Cleveland, TS14 8YH. The application should include full back-up information, a statement of accounts and the official charity number of the applicant. Grants of £500 or over are considered at trustee meetings three to four times each year, while grants for less than £500 are considered at monthly meetings. The trust always receives more applications than it can support. Even if a project fits its policy priority areas, it may not be possible to make a grant.
WHO TO APPLY TO Mr A. Harvey, J. Barbour and Sons Ltd, Simonside, South Shields, Tyne and Wear NE34 9PD Tel. 0191 427 4217 email admin@ryecroft-glenton.co.uk Website www.barbour.com

■ **The Barcapel Foundation**

SC NO SC009211   ESTABLISHED 1964
WHERE FUNDING CAN BE GIVEN Mainly Scotland, also other parts of the UK.
WHO CAN BENEFIT Charitable organisations.
WHAT IS FUNDED The foundation's three priority areas are health, heritage and youth, as described on their website: 'Health – the foundation supports all aspects of health, a wide ranging remit acknowledging that health is a state of complete physical, mental and social well-being and not merely the absence of disease or infirmity; Heritage – the original financiers of the foundation had a keen interest in our heritage, specifying that one of the foundation's aims was the preservation and beautification of historic properties. The foundation continues to support the built environment and will support our literary and artistic heritage as well as architectural; Youth – the development of people is one of the principal objectives of the Foundation. Whilst

charitable giving can be used to alleviate problems it can also be used to empower people and this is particularly true of the young.'

**WHAT IS NOT FUNDED** Individual applications for travel or similar; organisations or individuals engaged in promoting religious or political beliefs; applications for funding costs of feasibility studies or similar. Support is unlikely to be given for local charities whose work takes place outside the British Isles.

**RANGE OF GRANTS** Up to £100,000.

**SAMPLE GRANTS** Place2Be (£35,000); National Galleries of Scotland (£25,000); Prince and Princess of Wales Hospice (£20,000); Homeopathic Trust for Research and Education, Edinburgh Art Festival and The Scottish Book Trust (£15,000 each); Arkwright Scholarships Trust (£12,000); Jubilee Sailing Trust, National Star College, National Youth Theatre, South Ayrshire Befriending Project, The Teapot Trust and Woodland Trust (£10,000 each).

**FINANCES** Year 2013 Income £194,939 Grants £700,000 Grants to organisations £700,000

**TRUSTEES** Robert Wilson; Amanda Richards; Jed Wilson; Clement Wilson; Niall Scott.

**OTHER INFORMATION** Accounts were not available so grant total has been estimated based on the foundation's total expenditure of £842,000 in 2013. Sample beneficiaries were provided on the foundation's website.

**HOW TO APPLY** A preliminary application form can be downloaded from the foundation's website, to be returned by post with a covering letter and a copy of annual accounts. Applicants are advised to ensure that their interests, aims and objectives are compatible with those of the foundation. Applications are not accepted by email. After assessment by the secretary and director, the trust will contact eligible applicants for further information, before applications are reviewed at trustee meetings in May and November and deadlines are published on the website.

**WHO TO APPLY TO** Mia McCartney, The Mews, Skelmorlie Castle, Skelmorlie, Ayrshire PA17 5EY Tel. 01475 521616 email admin@barcapelfoundation.org Website www.barcapelfoundation.org

■ **Barchester Healthcare Foundation**

**CC NO** 1083272    **ESTABLISHED** 2000
**WHERE FUNDING CAN BE GIVEN** England, Scotland and Wales.
**WHO CAN BENEFIT** Individuals; small community groups; charities.
**WHAT IS FUNDED** Older people and other adults (18 plus) with a physical or mental disability whose health and/or social care needs cannot be met by the statutory public sector or by the individual. 'Our mission is to make a difference to the lives of older people and other adults with a physical or mental disability, supporting practical solutions that lead to increased personal independence, self-sufficiency and dignity.' The trust's website states that in 2015 'applications that combat loneliness and enable people to be active and engaged will receive our highest priority'.
**WHAT IS NOT FUNDED** Grants will not be made to community groups and small charities for: retrospective funding; groups that have received a grant in the last three years; core/ running costs or salaries or financial support to general projects; indirect services such as help lines, newsletters, leaflets or research; major building projects or large capital projects; training of staff and volunteers. The trustees reserve the right to put a cap on grants to a single charity (including all of its branches) in any one year.

**TYPE OF GRANT** One-off costs towards activities, outings, equipment, etc.

**RANGE OF GRANTS** Up to £5,000.

**SAMPLE GRANTS** Pannal Village Hall and Radnorshire Healthy Friendships (£3,000 each); Arts Together, Shopmobility Stockport and Slough Furniture Project (£2,000 each); Live Music Now (£1,500); St Leonard's Day Centre (£1,400); Harmony Therapy Trust, Ledbury Poetry Festival, Queens Park Bangladesh Association and The Caring Codgers (£1,000).

**FINANCES** Year 2013 Income £224,000 Grants £102,000 Grants to organisations £51,000 Assets £113,000

**TRUSTEES** Chris Vellenoweth; Mike Parsons; Janice Robinson; Lesley Flory; Pauline Houchin; David Walden; Dr Jackie Morris; Andrew Cozens.

**OTHER INFORMATION** The overall grant total includes 106 grants awarded to individuals, totalling £51,000. Grants were awarded to 52 organisations, 30 of which were for under £1,000 and totalled £15,000 altogether and 22 of which were for £1,000 and over, totalling £36,000.

**HOW TO APPLY** Application can be made via the foundation's website. A decision usually takes approximately ten weeks from the date of application. All applications supported by Barchester Healthcare staff will be given priority.

**WHO TO APPLY TO** Jon Hather, Correspondent, Suite 201, The Chambers, 2nd Floor, Design Centre East, Chelsea Harbour, London SW10 0XF Tel. 0800 328 3328 email info@bhcfoundation.org.uk Website www.bhcfoundation.org.uk

■ **The Barclay Foundation**

**CC NO** 803696    **ESTABLISHED** 1990
**WHERE FUNDING CAN BE GIVEN** UK.
**WHO CAN BENEFIT** Registered charities; hospitals; universities and individuals.
**WHAT IS FUNDED** The charitable objectives of the foundation are to fund: medical research; young people; people with disabilities; the sick; and the disadvantaged.
**TYPE OF GRANT** Projects and one-off grants. Some recurrent.
**RANGE OF GRANTS** £1,000–£1.2 million.
**SAMPLE GRANTS** Great Ormond Street Hospital (£1.05 million in total); University of Oxford (£147,500); Chain of Hope (£50,000); Make a Wish Foundation (£36,000 in total); Comic Relief and Duke of Edinburgh's International Award Foundation (£10,000 each); Friends of the National Libraries (£5,000); RAF Benevolent Fund (£3,000); Alzheimer's Society (£2,000); The Fashion and Textile Children's Trust (£1,000).
**FINANCES** Year 2014 Income £1,365,255 Grants £1,326,500 Grants to organisations £1,314,500 Assets £20,491
**TRUSTEES** Sir David Barclay; Sir Frederick Barclay; Aidan Barclay; Howard Barclay.
**OTHER INFORMATION** Grants were made to nine organisations in 2014. Two individuals received grants totalling £12,000.
**HOW TO APPLY** Applications should be in writing, clearly outlining the details of the proposed project, (for medical research, as far as possible in lay terms). The total cost and duration should be stated; also the amount, if

any, which has already been raised. Following an initial screening, applications are selected according to their merits, suitability and funds available. Visits are usually made to projects where substantial funds are involved. The foundation welcomes reports as to progress and requires these on the completion of a project.

**WHO TO APPLY TO** Michael Seal, Correspondent, 2nd Floor, 14 St George Street, London W1S 1FE *Tel.* 020 7915 0915 *email* mseal@ellerman.co.uk

## ■ The Barham Charitable Trust

**CC NO** 1129728        **ESTABLISHED** 2009
**WHERE FUNDING CAN BE GIVEN** UK and worldwide.
**WHO CAN BENEFIT** Charitable organisations.
**WHAT IS FUNDED** General charitable purposes.
**SAMPLE GRANTS** Previously: Medical Aid for Palestinians; The British Shalom Salaam Trust; War on Want; National Schizophrenia; Galilee Foundation; The Cambridge Foundation and IMET2000.
**FINANCES** Year 2013/14 *Income* £69,325 *Grants* £65,000 *Grants to organisations* £65,000
**TRUSTEES** Dr John Barham; Dr Eugenia Metaxa-Barham; Coutts & Co.
**OTHER INFORMATION** The accounts for 2013/14 had been received at the Charity Commission but had not been published online.
**HOW TO APPLY** Apply in writing to the correspondent.
**WHO TO APPLY TO** The Trustees, Coutts & Co, 440 Strand, London WC2R 0QS *Tel.* 020 7663 6825 *email* couttscharities@coutts.com

## ■ The Baring Foundation

**CC NO** 258583        **ESTABLISHED** 1969
**WHERE FUNDING CAN BE GIVEN** UK and overseas (UK charities working with NGO partners in financially developing countries), with a special interest in London, Merseyside, Cornwall and Devon.
**WHO CAN BENEFIT** Charitable organisations; UK charities working with NGO partners in financially developing countries.
**WHAT IS FUNDED** Arts – 'engaging the talent, experience and enthusiasm of older people in the creative arts' (grants are currently made by invitation only); LGBTI rights and gender in sub-Saharan Africa; (it is expected that most grants will be given directly to African civil society organisations); strengthening of the voluntary sector and supporting the development of social welfare legal advice (note that this programme is being replaced) and broad interest in the independence of the voluntary sector. Check the foundation's website for the current status and availability of programmes in these areas. The foundation's website states: 'We are an independent foundation working to improve the quality of life of people experiencing disadvantage and discrimination.'
**WHAT IS NOT FUNDED** Appeals or charities set up to support statutory organisations; animal welfare charities; grant-maintained, private or local education authority schools or their PTAs; individuals. Specific programmes may have further specific exclusions – see the guidelines for details.
**RANGE OF GRANTS** £750–£494,500
**SAMPLE GRANTS** STVS Advice Provider programme (£494,500); STVS Advice Strategic grants (£290,000); Africa Educational Trust and Arts Council England (£250,000 each); Arts Council Northern Ireland (£150,000); StreetInvest (£131,000); Youth Access (£100,000); Public Law Project (£80,000); Advice UK (£56,000); Comic Relief (£50,000); Anti Trafficking and Labour Exploitation Unit (£30,00); Cambridge House (£24,000); Centre for Mental Health (£20,000); Fair Money Advice (£17,000); Voluntary Arts Network (£10,000); ABF The Soldiers' Charity and Protimos Educational Trust (£5,000 each); Spinal Research (£2,500); Women and Children First (£2,000); Winston Churchill Memorial Trust (£750). **Most recent awards made in 2015 are listed online**: Luminate (£75,000); Live Music Now Ltd (£60,000); ALLFM (£20,000); Equality and Diversity Forum and University of Manchester (£5,000 each); Overseas Development Institute (£500).
**FINANCES** Year 2013 *Income* £2,516,063 *Grants* £2,111,782 *Grants to organisations* £2,111,782 *Assets* £65,008,369
**TRUSTEES** David Elliott; Dr Robert Berkeley; Amanda Jordan; Mark Baring; Myles Wickstead; Katherine Garrett-Cox; Shauneen Lambe; Janet Morrison; Andrew Hind; Lucy de Groot; Dr Dhanjayan Sriskandarajah; Edward Brown; Marie Staunton; Francois Matarasso.
**PUBLICATIONS** Various reports connected with its work are available from the foundation's website.
**OTHER INFORMATION** Note that international development programme has closed and from 2015 is replaced by initiatives with focus on LGBTI and gender in sub-Saharan Africa. Further details are due to be published on the foundation's website. The 'Strengthening the Voluntary Sector' programme has also closed and will have a new focus from 2015 – the details were not yet given on the website at the time of writing (June 2015). During the year a total of 37 grants were given.
**HOW TO APPLY** Application forms are available via the foundation's website. Potential applicants should carefully read the website for current guidelines and application deadlines prior to requesting any support. The website notes: 'Due to the high volume of enquiries received by the Foundation, we regret that we are not able to reply to unsolicited correspondence or grant applications that do not satisfy the guidelines for our programmes.'
**WHO TO APPLY TO** David Cutler, Director, 60 London Wall, London EC2M 5TQ *Tel.* 020 7767 1348 *email* baring.foundation@uk.ing.com *Website* www.baringfoundation.org.uk

## ■ The Barker-Mill Foundation (formerly known as the Peter Barker-Mill Memorial Charity)

**CC NO** 1045479        **ESTABLISHED** 1995
**WHERE FUNDING CAN BE GIVEN** UK, with a preference for South West Hampshire, including Southampton.
**WHO CAN BENEFIT** Charitable organisations; local groups; schools; individuals.
**WHAT IS FUNDED** General charitable purposes, including arts and culture, community facilities and conservation.
**TYPE OF GRANT** One-off or recurrent.
**RANGE OF GRANTS** Generally up to £5,000.
**SAMPLE GRANTS** Some recent projects supported are listed on the foundation's website. **Beneficiaries have included**: The Waterfall Trust (£5,000); Alive Activities Limited (£3,000); Hampshire Air Ambulance (£2,000); SCRATCH (£2,900); National Trust (£2,500); Life

Education Wessex and Romsey Young Carers (£1,000 each); Little Saints Community Pre-School (£800); British American Football Association (£350); Operation Wallacea (£150).
FINANCES Grants £238,000 Grants to organisations £238,000
TRUSTEES Christopher Gwyn-Evans; Tim Jobling; Richard Moyse.
OTHER INFORMATION About 80 grants are awarded each year. At the time of writing (June 2015) this was the latest information available; the foundation has not submitted its accounts since 2011/12. The foundation remains active and in the past grants have totalled about £238,000 on average.
HOW TO APPLY Application forms should be completed online on the foundation's website. You should wait at least one year before re-applying. Appeals should provide information on your organisation, purposes of funding required, the amount sought and how much has been raised so far.
WHO TO APPLY TO Christopher Gwyn-Evans, Trustee, c/o Longdown Management Ltd, The Estate Office, Longdown, Marchwood, Southampton SO40 4UH Tel. 023 8029 2107 email info@barkermillfoundation.com Website www.barkermillfoundation.com

## ■ The Barleycorn Trust

CC NO 296386 ESTABLISHED 1987
WHERE FUNDING CAN BE GIVEN UK and overseas.
WHO CAN BENEFIT Christian; relief of poverty; ill health; older people; young people.
WHAT IS FUNDED The advancement of the Christian faith, furtherance of religious or secular education, the encouragement of missionary activity, relief in need and welfare.
WHAT IS NOT FUNDED Building projects; gap year projects.
RANGE OF GRANTS £250–£15,000
SAMPLE GRANTS Kidz Klub Leeds (£13,000); Human Values Foundation (£4,000); City Gate Community Projects and Off the Fence (£2,000 each); Brighton and Hove City Mission (£1,300); and Breadline, Christians in Entertainment, Excellent, National Talking Newspapers, Royal National Mission to Deep Sea Fisherman and Village Water (£500 each).
FINANCES Year 2013 Income £40,990 Grants £36,050 Grants to organisations £36,050 Assets £1,268,190
TRUSTEES Helen Hazelwood; Sally Beckwith.
HOW TO APPLY Apply in writing to the correspondent, on no more than two sides of A4 including financial details of the proposed project. Special grants in addition to the trust's regular commitments are discussed by the trustees, based on specific needs. All grant-making decisions are taken at trustees' meetings.
WHO TO APPLY TO Helen Hazelwood, Trustee, PO Box 472, Sutton SM1 9NZ email partners@tudorjohn.co.uk

## ■ Lord Barnby's Foundation

CC NO 251016 ESTABLISHED 1966
WHERE FUNDING CAN BE GIVEN UK.
WHO CAN BENEFIT Registered charities.
WHAT IS FUNDED General charitable purposes.
WHAT IS NOT FUNDED Individuals.
TYPE OF GRANT One-off, capital (including buildings), project, research. Funding is up to two years.

RANGE OF GRANTS Grants range from £500–£10,000; but are generally for £1,000–£2,000.
SAMPLE GRANTS Countryside Learning, Farms for City Children and Game and Wildlife Conservation Trust (£10,000 each); Skiing with Heroes (£5,000); Crimestoppers, Emerge, Evelina Children's Hospital and Samaritans (£2,000 each); Streets of Growth (£1,000); All Saints Holbeton PCC and CRISIS (£500 each); Cancer Research UK (£250).
FINANCES Year 2013/14 Income £209,475 Grants £219,200 Grants to organisations £219,200 Assets £5,190,637
TRUSTEES Hon. George Lopes; Countess Peel; Sir Michael Farquhar; Algy Smith-Maxwell; Laura Greenall.
HOW TO APPLY Applications will only be considered if received in writing accompanied by a set of the latest accounts. Applicants do not need to send an sae. Appeals are considered three times a year, in February, June and November.
WHO TO APPLY TO Jane Lethbridge, Secretary, PO Box 71, Plymstock, Plymouth PL8 2YP email nlethbridge@btinternet.com

## ■ Barnes Workhouse Fund

CC NO 200103 ESTABLISHED 1970
WHERE FUNDING CAN BE GIVEN Ancient parish of Barnes only (SW13 postal district in London).
WHO CAN BENEFIT Charitable organisations benefitting local residents and local individuals.
WHAT IS FUNDED The fund makes grants to organisations who can demonstrate that their activities will benefit some of the inhabitants of its area of benefit. Grants are also made to individuals through referral agencies for educational purposes and for the relief of hardship.
WHAT IS NOT FUNDED National organisations.
TYPE OF GRANT Capital, core costs, one-off, project, running costs, recurring costs, salaries and start-up costs.
RANGE OF GRANTS Organisational grants up to £40,000, most below £10,000. Welfare grants for individuals are generally limited to up to £350 per year for up to three years.
SAMPLE GRANTS Castelnau Centre Project (£40,000); Richmond Citizens Advice (£35,000); Richmond Crossroads Care (£13,500); Mortlake Community Association (£12,000); Barnes Community Arts Centre (£10,700); Lowther Primary School (£6,800); Relate (£5,000); Richmond Mencap (£3,300); Richmond Adult Community College (£3,100); Brentford F.C. Community Sports Trust and Castelnau Young Voices (£1,000 each); Queen's Road Hostel – Richmond (£250).
FINANCES Year 2013 Income £614,752 Grants £218,214 Grants to organisations £190,971 Assets £9,400,598
TRUSTEES Caroline Kelsall; Carolyn Rampton; Deborah Ferreira; John Brocklebank; Karine Pengelley; Tim Besley; Lucy Hine; Paul Hodgins; John Story.
OTHER INFORMATION The grant total includes £27,200 given to individuals. Grants were made to 27 organisations in 2013, two of which were for capital purposes. 63 individuals received grants for the relief of poverty and a further 23 for educational purposes.
HOW TO APPLY Organisations should apply using the online form on the fund's website, or in writing to the fund's Director, and are advised to first read the eligibility guidelines on the website. Applications from organisations are considered

at trustee meetings in January, March, May, July, September and November each year. Applications must be received by the 6th of the month preceding a meeting to be considered.

**WHO TO APPLY TO** Miranda Ibbetson, Clerk to the Trustees, PO Box 665, Richmond, London TW10 6YL  *Tel.* 020 8241 3994 *email* mibbetson@barnesworkhousefund.org.uk *Website* www.barnesworkhousefund.org.uk

## ■ The Barnsbury Charitable Trust

**CC NO** 241383   **ESTABLISHED** 1964
**WHERE FUNDING CAN BE GIVEN** UK, but no local charities outside Oxfordshire.
**WHO CAN BENEFIT** Charitable organisations.
**WHAT IS FUNDED** General charitable purposes.
**WHAT IS NOT FUNDED** Individuals.
**RANGE OF GRANTS** £15–£10,000
**SAMPLE GRANTS** Oxford Chamber Music Festival (£10,000); Oxfordshire Historic Churches Trust and Oxfordshire Victoria County History Trust;(£7,500); Abingdon Museum Friends, Friends of Dorchester Abbey and Friends of St Michael Clifton (£5,000 each); Abingdon Bridge and PCC of St Mary's, Witney (£2,500 each); Oxford Citizens Advice and Oxfordshire Preservation Trust (£1,000 each); Oxfordshire Museum (£100).
**FINANCES** *Year* 2013/14  *Income* £97,836 *Grants* £91,316  *Grants to organisations* £91,316  *Assets* £3,597,762
**TRUSTEES** Hugo Brunner; Mary Brunner; Timothy Yates.
**HOW TO APPLY** Apply in writing to the correspondent.
**WHO TO APPLY TO** Hugo Brunner, Trustee, 26 Norham Road, Oxford OX2 6SF  *Tel.* 01865 316431 *email* hmrbrunner@gmail.com

## ■ The Barnstaple Bridge Trust

**CC NO** 201288   **ESTABLISHED** 1961
**WHERE FUNDING CAN BE GIVEN** Barnstaple and surrounding area.
**WHO CAN BENEFIT** The policy of the trustees is to consider grant applications from local charitable and amenity groups within the area of benefit; national organisations providing support to individuals or groups within the area of benefit; and individuals within the area of benefit, deserving and in need.
**WHAT IS FUNDED** General charitable purposes; grants are made to a wide range of causes, including welfare, older people and young people, health and medical, schools and sport.
**WHAT IS NOT FUNDED** Individuals, other than on referral through a caring agency.
**TYPE OF GRANT** Capital including buildings, core costs, one-off, project, research, running costs, recurring costs and start-up costs will be considered. Funding may be given for up to one year.
**SAMPLE GRANTS** North Devon Hospice Care (£9,000); Go North Devon and Westcountry Projects (£6,000 each); North Devon Citizens Advice and Children's Hospice (£4,000 each); Relate and Barnstaple Poverty Action Group (£3,000 each); North Devon Samaritans, Braunton CC, Pilton CC, Barnstaple Tennis Club, St Francis Chichester, Barnstaple RFC Juniors, Hamish Thompson, North Devon Scouts and Guides Gang Show, Alfie Huxtable, Torridge Home Start, Citizens Advice, Learning Difficulties, Two Moors Festival and Motor Neurone disease (£1,000 each).

**FINANCES** *Year* 2014  *Income* £346,189 *Grants* £118,584  *Grants to organisations* £118,584  *Assets* £4,854,261
**TRUSTEES** David Trueman; Valerie Elkin; Graham Lofthouse; James Waldron; Stephen Upcott; Suzanne Haywood; Keith Luckhurst; Amanda Isaac; Julie Hunt; Karen Trigger; Elizabeth Davies; Graham Townsend; Richard Knight; David Wright.
**HOW TO APPLY** Apply in writing to the correspondent. The trustees meet quarterly on the first Tuesday of March, June, September and December.
**WHO TO APPLY TO** Peter Laurie, Chamberlain, 7 Bridge Chambers, The Strand, Barnstaple, Devon EX31 1HB  *Tel.* 01271 343995 *email* chamberlain@barumbridgetrust.org *Website* www.barumbridgetrust

## ■ The Barnwood House Trust

**CC NO** 218401   **ESTABLISHED** 1972
**WHERE FUNDING CAN BE GIVEN** Gloucestershire.
**WHO CAN BENEFIT** Gloucestershire-based charitable organisations whose services seek to improve the quality of life of local people with long-term disabilities. Local individuals who have a long term disability, low income and a specific need for which state provision is not available. Small groups in Gloucestershire communities for activities where at least one participant has a disability. Village halls wishing to make adaptations for people with disabilities.
**WHAT IS FUNDED** Improving the quality of life of people in Gloucestershire with disabilities and mental health challenges, as well as hardship or distress. The trust also provides relief of persons in need by providing housing or other accommodation, care nursing and attention. Grants for individuals fall into the categories of either well-being or opportunities. Grants are awarded to organisations providing activities, services, holidays or play schemes to improve the lives of people with disabilities or mental health challenges. Small Sparks grants are given to small groups of people for shared activities which are inclusive of people with disabilities or mental health challenges. Grants are also given to village halls to improve accessibility.
**WHAT IS NOT FUNDED** People or organisations outside Gloucestershire. Specific exclusions and criteria apply to each of the grants programmes for individuals, as well as the Small Sparks grants, which are published on the trust's website.
**TYPE OF GRANT** Small grants to organisations and grants to individuals. Project costs, start-up costs, capital costs.
**RANGE OF GRANTS** Small grants of up to £1,000 for organisations; no limit specified for holidays and play schemes. Individual well-being grants range between £50 and £750, while the average opportunity grant is £850.
**SAMPLE GRANTS Previous beneficiaries have included:** Consortium of Mental Health Day Support Providers (£305,000); Crossroads Care – Cheltenham and Tewkesbury, Independence Trust and People and Places in Gloucestershire (£30,000 each); Whitefriars Sailing Club (£27,500); Stroke Association (£25,000); Forest of Dean Citizen's Advice Bureau and Hop, Skip and Jump (Cotswold) (£18,000 each); Art Shape LTD, Barnwood Residents Association and Watershed Riding for the Disabled (£10,000 each).
**FINANCES** *Year* 2013  *Income* £3,506,328 *Grants* £546,376  *Grants to organisations* £132,594  *Assets* £81,294,519

TRUSTEES John Colquhoun; James Davidson; Anne Cadbury; David A. Acland; Annabella Scott; Jonathan Carr; Prof. Clair Chilvers; Andrew North; Jonathan Harvie; Suzanne Beech; Dr Jean Waters.
PUBLICATIONS *Strategic Framework 2011–2021; ten-year investment plan.*
OTHER INFORMATION The trust has created a ten year strategic plan called You're Welcome, working towards welcoming and inclusive communities in Gloucestershire. Grants were awarded to 69 organisations in 2013. 12 Small Sparks grants were also awarded during the year, totalling £2,680. The overall grant total includes grants of £281,000 awarded to 722 individuals.
HOW TO APPLY Application forms are available to download from the trust's website. For any queries or to talk through your idea before applying, contact Gail Rodway, Grants Manager, on 01452 611292 or email gail.rodway@barnwoodtrust.org. More specific information about applying for village hall adaptations or individual grants are given on the trust's website.
WHO TO APPLY TO Gail Rodway, Grants Manager, Ullenwood Manor Farm, Ullenwood, Cheltenham GL53 9QT *Tel.* 01452 614429 *email* sally.byng@barnwoodtrust.org *Website* www.barnwoodtrust.org

## ■ The Misses Barrie Charitable Trust

CC NO 279459　　　ESTABLISHED 1979
WHERE FUNDING CAN BE GIVEN UK.
WHO CAN BENEFIT Registered charities.
WHAT IS FUNDED General charitable purposes in particular medical/health causes.
WHAT IS NOT FUNDED Individuals.
TYPE OF GRANT Mainly one-off.
RANGE OF GRANTS Average £1,000–£5,000.
SAMPLE GRANTS RNLI (£25,000); Scottish Chamber Orchestra and University of Oxford Institute of Molecular Medicine (£10,000 each); Canine Partners and The Berwickshire Maritime Trust (£5,000 each); Highland Hospice (£3,000); Dogs for the Disabled, Glasgow City Mission, Hearts and Minds, The Shakespeare Hospice and The Willow Trust (£2,000 each); Douglas Bader Foundation and The Gordon Russell Trust (£1,500 each); South Croydon Day Centre, Steer Right and Wheelpower (£1,000 each); The Boys' Brigade (£500).
FINANCES *Year* 2013/14 *Income* £246,951 *Grants* £244,950 *Grants to organisations* £244,950 *Assets* £6,484,848
TRUSTEES John A. Carter; Robin Stuart Ogg; Rachel Fraser.
HOW TO APPLY Apply in writing to the correspondent accompanied by up to date accounts or financial information. The trustees meet three times a year, in April, August and December. 'The trustees regret that due to the large number of unsolicited applications for grants received each week they are not able to notify those which are unsuccessful.'
WHO TO APPLY TO John A. Carter, Trustee, Raymond Carter and Co, 14A High Street, Reigate, Surrey RH2 9AY *Tel.* 01737 248065 *email* john@raymondcarter.co.uk

## ■ Bartholomew Charitable Trust

CC NO 1063797　　　ESTABLISHED 1997
WHERE FUNDING CAN BE GIVEN UK.
WHO CAN BENEFIT Registered charities only, for the benefit of people who are sick, have disabilities or are terminally ill.
WHAT IS FUNDED Particularly respite care, hospices, rehabilitation centres and cancer research. Hospices are supported in preference to nursing homes.
WHAT IS NOT FUNDED Individuals.
SAMPLE GRANTS Previous beneficiaries have included: Marie Curie Memorial Trust (£26,000); St Christopher's Hospice (£25,000); League of the Helping Hand (£500); and Springfield Boy's Club, The Quaker Tapestry, REMAP, Royal Marsden Cancer Campaign and Diabetes UK (£250).
FINANCES *Year* 2013/14 *Income* £19,086 *Grants* £40,000 *Grants to organisations* £40,000
TRUSTEES Julian Berry; Simon Berry; Rita Berry; Charlotte Irwin.
OTHER INFORMATION Due to the low income accounts were not available to view on the Charity Commission's website and based on previous years we estimate the grant total to be around £40,000.
HOW TO APPLY We had previously been informed that due to lack of funds no new requests for grants will be considered by the trustees until further notice.
WHO TO APPLY TO Julian Berry, Trustee, Goddards Farm, Ardingly Road, Lindfield, Haywards Heath, West Sussex RH16 2QX *email* charity@bartholomew.co.uk

## ■ The Bartlett Taylor Charitable Trust

CC NO 285249　　　ESTABLISHED 1982
WHERE FUNDING CAN BE GIVEN Preference for West Oxfordshire.
WHO CAN BENEFIT Registered charities; individuals (social welfare and education).
WHAT IS FUNDED General charitable purposes, with grants given in the following categories: (a) international charities; (b) UK national charities – medical; UK national charities – educational; (c) local organisations – community projects; local organisations – medical; local organisations – other; (d) individuals – educational; individuals – relief.
RANGE OF GRANTS £100–£1,000
SAMPLE GRANTS There was no list of beneficiaries available.
FINANCES *Year* 2013/14 *Income* £83,727 *Grants* £46,159 *Grants to organisations* £46,159 *Assets* £2,291,387
TRUSTEES Richard Bartlett; Gareth Alty; Katherine Bradley; Brenda Cook; James W. Dingle; Rosemary Warner; Ms S. Boyd; Jonathan Smith.
HOW TO APPLY Apply in writing to the correspondent. The trustees meet bi-monthly. It is the policy of the trustees to consider all applications for grants from national and local charities, individuals for educational and social assistance and other organisations of a charitable or social nature, with a preference for providing grants for the relief of local needs (West Oxfordshire). Note that the website states: 'Requests from individuals will only be considered with relevant back up information from a recognised source, and where relevant, evidence of income and expenditure.'

**WHO TO APPLY TO** Gareth Alty, Trustee, John Welch and Stammers, Solicitors, 24 Church Green, Witney, Oxfordshire OX28 4AT *Tel.* 01993 703941 *email* info@btctrust.org.uk *Website* www.btctrust.org.uk

■ **The Paul Bassham Charitable Trust**

**CC NO** 266842 **ESTABLISHED** 1973
**WHERE FUNDING CAN BE GIVEN** UK, mainly Norfolk.
**WHO CAN BENEFIT** UK-registered charities.
**WHAT IS FUNDED** General charitable purposes. Preference given to Norfolk charitable causes; if funds permit, other charities with national coverage will be considered.
**WHAT IS NOT FUNDED** Individuals; unregistered organisations.
**RANGE OF GRANTS** £1,000–£20,000. Average grant between £1,000–£5,000.
**SAMPLE GRANTS** Norwich Theatre Royal (£120,000); Norfolk Flood Appeal and South Creake War Memorial Institute (£10,000 each); Earlham Scout Group, Norfolk Can Inspire and Rescue Wooden Boats (£5,000 each); Build Charity, Connects and Co., Cromer Skate Park and Dilham Pre-School (£2,000 each); Somerton Village Hall and Wroxham Signalbox Trust (£1,000 each).
**FINANCES** *Year* 2013/14 *Income* £373,993 *Grants* £541,400 *Grants to organisations* £541,400 *Assets* £12,200,226
**TRUSTEES** Alexander Munro; Richard Lovett; Graham Tuttle; Patrick Harris.
**HOW TO APPLY** Only in writing to the correspondent – no formal application forms issued. Telephone enquiries are not invited because of administrative costs. The trustees meet quarterly to consider general applications.
**WHO TO APPLY TO** Richard Lovett, Trustee, c/o Howes Percival, The Guildyard, 51 Colegate, Norwich NR3 1DD *Tel.* 01603 762103

■ **The Batchworth Trust**

**CC NO** 245061 **ESTABLISHED** 1965
**WHERE FUNDING CAN BE GIVEN** Worldwide.
**WHO CAN BENEFIT** Major UK and international charities.
**WHAT IS FUNDED** General charitable purposes, medical, humanitarian aid, social welfare.
**WHAT IS NOT FUNDED** Individuals.
**RANGE OF GRANTS** £1,000–£25,000
**SAMPLE GRANTS** The Francis Crick Institute and Disaster Emergency Committee Philippines (£30,000 each); Clinical Neuroscience (University of Oxford Development Trust) (£26,000); International Red Cross (£20,000); Copenhagen Youth Project and SENSE (£15,000 each); Castle Douglas IT Centre, Crisis, Cure Parkinson's and Pimlico Opera (£10,000 each); Books Abroad (£5,000); Full Circle (£3,000); Orchestra of the City (£2,000).
**FINANCES** *Year* 2013/14 *Income* £398,907 *Grants* £388,696 *Grants to organisations* £388,696 *Assets* £12,553,681
**TRUSTEE** Lockwell Trustees Limited.
**HOW TO APPLY** Apply in writing to the correspondent. An sae should be included if a reply is required.
**WHO TO APPLY TO** Martin R. Neve, Administrative Executive, Reeves and Co LLP, Griffin House, 135 High Street, Crawley RH10 1DQ *Tel.* 01293 776411 *email* martin.neve@reeves.co

■ **The Battens Charitable Trust**

**CC NO** 293500
**WHERE FUNDING CAN BE GIVEN** There is a preference for Somerset, North and West Dorset.
**WHO CAN BENEFIT** Registered charities; local organisations.
**WHAT IS FUNDED** General charitable purposes.
**RANGE OF GRANTS** Mostly up to £5,000.
**SAMPLE GRANTS** Dorset Wildlife Trust (£13,500); LV Streetwise Safety Centre (£10,000); Citizens Advice, Dorset and Somerset Air Ambulance and RSPB (£5,000 each).
**FINANCES** *Year* 2013/14 *Income* £756,084 *Grants* £95,065 *Grants to organisations* £94,715 *Assets* £742,306
**TRUSTEES** Rupert Vaughan; Stuart Allen; Raymond Edwards; Robert Randall
**OTHER INFORMATION** In 2013/14 grants were made to 158 different causes, the majority of which were of less than £5,000. During the year, £350 was given in grants to individuals.
**HOW TO APPLY** Apply in writing to the correspondent.
**WHO TO APPLY TO** Kelly Payne, c/o Battens Solicitors, Mansion House, 54–58 Princes Street, Yeovil, Somerset BA20 1EP *Tel.* 01935 846237 *email* kelly.payne@battens.co.uk

■ **Bay Charitable Trust**

**CC NO** 1060537 **ESTABLISHED** 1997
**WHERE FUNDING CAN BE GIVEN** UK and overseas
**WHO CAN BENEFIT** Jewish organisations.
**WHAT IS FUNDED** 'The objectives of the charity are to give charity for the relief of poverty and the advancement of traditions of the Orthodox Jewish Religion and the study of Torah.'
**FINANCES** *Year* 2014 *Income* £600,000 *Grants* £661,896 *Grants to organisations* £661,896 *Assets* £375,141
**TRUSTEES** Ian M. Kreditor; Michael Lisser.
**OTHER INFORMATION** The grant total includes awards made to individuals.
**HOW TO APPLY** Apply in writing to the correspondent.
**WHO TO APPLY TO** Ian Kreditor, Trustee, 21 Woodlands Close, London NW11 9QR *Tel.* 020 8810 4321

■ **The Bay Tree Charitable Trust**

**CC NO** 1044091 **ESTABLISHED** 1994
**WHERE FUNDING CAN BE GIVEN** UK and overseas.
**WHO CAN BENEFIT** Charitable organisations.
**WHAT IS FUNDED** Development work.
**WHAT IS NOT FUNDED** Individuals.
**RANGE OF GRANTS** Up to £30,000.
**SAMPLE GRANTS** Médecins Sans Frontières UK (£30,000); Combat Stress (£20,000); Age UK, Children of the Andes, Housing for Women (£5,000 each).
**FINANCES** *Year* 2013 *Income* £148,369 *Grants* £111,150 *Grants to organisations* £111,150 *Assets* £3,886,960
**TRUSTEES** Ian Benton; Emma Benton; Paul Benton.
**HOW TO APPLY** All appeals should be by letter containing the following: aims and objectives of the charity; nature of appeal; total target if for a specific project; contributions received against target; registered charity number; any other relevant factors. Letters should be accompanied by a set of the charitable organisation's latest report and full accounts.
**WHO TO APPLY TO** The Trustees, PO Box 53983, London SW15 1VT

## ■ The Louis Baylis (Maidenhead Advertiser) Charitable Trust

**CC NO** 210533   **ESTABLISHED** 1962
**WHERE FUNDING CAN BE GIVEN** UK but mainly Berkshire, Buckinghamshire and Oxfordshire, with a preference for Maidenhead.
**WHO CAN BENEFIT** Local charities; national charities are also considered, but greater proportion is given to local causes (in 2013/14 local – 85% regional – 9% national – 6%).
**WHAT IS FUNDED** General charitable purposes, with some preference for children and young people, older individuals and disadvantaged people.
**WHAT IS NOT FUNDED** Individuals.
**RANGE OF GRANTS** £1,000–£25,000
**SAMPLE GRANTS** Some of the grant recipients were named in the accounts. **Beneficiaries included**: Maidenhead Citizens Advice (£25,000); People to Places (£24,500); RBWM Sports and Sports Aid Bursary (£8,000); Maidenhead Carnival (£6,000); Maidenhead Christmas Lights Appeal, Maidenhead Heritage Centre, Maidenhead Town Centre Partnership and Marlow Rowing Club (£5,000 each); Thames Hospice Care (£4,000); Rotary Club of Maidenhead Thames (£2,500); British Forces Foundation, Great Ormond Street Hospital, Open Kitchen and Thames Valley and Chiltern Air Ambulance Service (£2,000 each); Nordon Farm Centre for the Arts (£1,500); Berkshire Masonic Charity, Berkshire Masons Children's Panto Outing, Ordon Farm Festival Chorus and Sue Ryder Homes (£1,000 each).
**FINANCES** Year 2013/14 Income £4,272,850 Grants £264,140 Grants to organisations £264,140 Assets £13,989,296
**TRUSTEES** John Robertson; Peter Sands; Peter Murcott; Patricia Lattimer.
**OTHER INFORMATION** In 2013/14 grants were made to 136 beneficiaries, including £14,700 to 11 national charities, £25,000 to 16 regional institutions and £224,500 to 109 local charities and organisations. Smaller grant applications are encouraged. The trust states that it was 'established to safeguard the newspaper, The Maidenhead Advertiser, from all outside influence and provide for the newspaper's continuance as part of the civic and social life of the community it serves'.
**HOW TO APPLY** Application forms are available to download on the website and should be returned to the trust by email or post. The trustees meet twice a year to consider grants. The Trust Administrator attends the trust's offices, normally on Monday and Wednesday, and applicants are encouraged to visit the offices and speak to the administrator.
**WHO TO APPLY TO** Andrew Chitty, Correspondent, 78 Queen Street, Maidenhead, Berkshire SL6 I. HY *Tel.* 01628 678290 *email* lbctrust@baylismedia.co.uk *Website* baylis-trust.org.uk

## ■ BBC Children in Need

**CC NO** 802052/SC039557 **ESTABLISHED** 1989
**WHERE FUNDING CAN BE GIVEN** UK (including the Channel Islands and the Isle of Man).
**WHO CAN BENEFIT** Voluntary projects; community groups; registered charities; not-for-profit organisations; churches; schools.
**WHAT IS FUNDED** Children and young people under the age of 18 experiencing disadvantage through illness, distress, abuse or neglect, any kind of disability, behavioural or psychological difficulties, are living in poverty or experiencing situations of deprivation. The charity's vision is ' that every child in the UK has a safe, happy and secure childhood and the chance to reach their potential'. The charity offers support through: Main Grants Programme (up to £10,000 a year for up to three years); Small Grants Programme (up to £10,000 a year for one year); Emergency Essentials (administered on behalf of Buttle UK 'to meet the most basic needs of children and young people living with acute poverty and deprivation', grants are available to individuals and families); Fun and Friendship programme ('for the social and friendship needs of disabled young people'); Positive Destinations (in collaboration with the Hunter Foundation 'for young people not in employment, education or training').
**WHAT IS NOT FUNDED** Relief of statutory responsibility; applications from local government or NHS bodies; projects outside the UK; the promotion of religion. There are further exclusions related to specific areas and circumstances of the project. All are detailed in the helpful A-Z application guidelines online.
**TYPE OF GRANT** Capital expenditure; projects; salaries; recurrent grants; project related core expenditure but not the organisation running costs.
**RANGE OF GRANTS** Generally up to £100,000.
**SAMPLE GRANTS** The accounts give a full list specific grant recipients, but gave details of a few and further examples of giving are detailed online. **Beneficiaries have included**: Classical Cuties (£10,000); Ballons; Bede Youth Adventure Project; Bright Sparks; Bobath Therapy Centre; Buttle UK; Cancer Focus Northern Ireland; Celebrating Glasgow; Claire House; Code 7; Down Syndrome Trust; Haven House; Headway; Jessie May Trust; Julia's House; Llamau; Pedal Power; Playskill; SHINE Health Academy; St Crispin's After School Club; Stracharron Hospice; Studio 3 Arts; The Kings Foundation; The Yard Adventure centre; Umbrella PALS Project; Whizz-Kidz NI; Zoe's Place.
**FINANCES** Year 2013/14 Income £55,564,000 Grants £40,550,000 Grants to organisations £40,550,000 Assets £50,871,000
**TRUSTEES** Phil Hodkinson; Danny Cohen; Charlotte Moore; Peter McBride; Stevie Spring; Bob Shennan; Luke Mayhew; Ralph Rivera; Donalda Mackinnon; Gillian Sheldon; Matthew James; Joanna Berry; Anne Bulford.
**OTHER INFORMATION** During the year a total of 1,192 grants were made. About 71% of awards were made in England, followed by London and South East and the North (22% each), Central areas of the country (17%), Scotland (115), South West (10%) and Northern Ireland, Wales and elsewhere in the UK (6% each). Support through Emergence Essential fund totalled £2.1 million. Grants were given in the fields of: poverty and deprivation (36%); disability (21%); marginalised groups (14%); distress (11%); illness (8%); abuse/neglect (6%); behavioural difficulties (4%).
**HOW TO APPLY** Straightforward application forms and excellent guidelines are available from the charity's website. Requests should be made online. If you have a general enquiry, are unsure about anything you have read or are looking for support regarding your application contact the charity via phone or email. You can also contact your local regional or national office. For applications to the Main Grants Programme there are three deadlines per year and a two-stage process. All applicants need to complete an 'Initial Application' form considered within to three weeks. After this assessment successful applicants are invited to make a full application and unsuccessful appeals can be notified

immediately. For applications to the Small Grants Programme there are five application dates throughout the year with a shortened period of consideration.
WHO TO APPLY TO Sheila Malley, Director of Grant-Making and Policy, PO Box 1000, London W12 7WJ *Tel.* 0345 609 0015 *email* pudsey@bbc.co.uk *Website* www.bbc.co.uk/pudsey

■ **BC Partners Foundation**
CC NO 1136956    ESTABLISHED 2010
WHERE FUNDING CAN BE GIVEN UK.
WHO CAN BENEFIT Registered charities in the UK and worldwide.
WHAT IS FUNDED General charitable purposes.
RANGE OF GRANTS Up to £100,000.
SAMPLE GRANTS Private Equity Foundation (£104,000); BCPF Inc (£67,000); the Latymer Foundation (£40,000); Over the Wall (£31,000); Vocal Futures (£16,000); the Samson Centre (£10,000); Great Ormond Street Hospital (£8,000); Royal Opera House (£6,000); Music as Therapy (£5,000); Macmillan, C-R-Y (£1,900 each); and the Shakespeare Globe Trust (£1,000).
FINANCES *Year* 2013 *Income* £611,917 *Grants* £403,811 *Grants to organisations* £403,811 *Assets* £372,348
TRUSTEES Nikos Stathopolous; Joseph Cronley; Lorna Parker; Michael Pritchard; Richard Kunzer; Cedric Dubourdieu.
OTHER INFORMATION This is the foundation of private equity firm BC Partners.
HOW TO APPLY Apply in writing to the correspondent.
WHO TO APPLY TO The Trustees, BC Partners Limited, 40 Portman Square, London W1H 6DA *Tel.* 020 7009 4800 *email* bcpfoundation@bcpartners.com *Website* www.bcpartners.com/about-us/bcp-foundation.aspx

■ **BCH Trust**
CC NO 1138652    ESTABLISHED 2010
WHERE FUNDING CAN BE GIVEN UK.
WHO CAN BENEFIT Mainly Jewish organisations; schools.
WHAT IS FUNDED General charitable purposes with a stated interest in education, social welfare, the Jewish faith and disability.
SAMPLE GRANTS Manchester Senior Girls School (£67,000); Chesed L'Yisroel (£11,000); Prestwich Cost Shop (£4,000); Tashbar (£1,300).
FINANCES *Year* 2013/14 *Income* £187,446 *Grants* £84,158 *Grants to organisations* £84,158 *Assets* £199,547
TRUSTEES Benny Stone; Charles Bernstein; Yossef Bowden.
HOW TO APPLY Apply in writing to the correspondent.
WHO TO APPLY TO Benny Stone, Trustee, 59 Kings Road, Prestwich, Manchester M25 0LQ *Tel.* 0161 773 0512 *email* mail@bchtrust.org

■ **Bear Mordechai Ltd**
CC NO 286806    ESTABLISHED 1982
WHERE FUNDING CAN BE GIVEN Worldwide.
WHO CAN BENEFIT Individuals; small local projects; national organisations benefitting Jewish people.
WHAT IS FUNDED Jewish charities.
TYPE OF GRANT One-off and recurrent costs.
SAMPLE GRANTS Yad Yemin (£65,000); Chochmas Lev (£59,000); Shomrei Hachomos (£40,000); Tradton Limited (£30,000); Peninei Torah

(£20,000); Sellata (£15,000); Tevini Total (£7,000); and Tomchei shabbos Trust (£400).
FINANCES *Year* 2013/14 *Income* £349,167 *Grants* £306,220 *Grants to organisations* £306,220 *Assets* £1,206,115
TRUSTEES Chaim Benedikt; Eliezer Benedikt; Yechiel Benedikt.
HOW TO APPLY Apply in writing to the correspondent.
WHO TO APPLY TO Yechiel Benedikt, Trustee, 40 Fountayne Road, London N16 7DT

■ **The Bearder Charity**
CC NO 1010529    ESTABLISHED 1992
WHERE FUNDING CAN BE GIVEN Calderdale.
WHO CAN BENEFIT Registered charities and individuals.
WHAT IS FUNDED General charitable purposes, particularly the arts, infrastructure support and development, education and training and community facilities and services.
RANGE OF GRANTS Up to £5,000.
SAMPLE GRANTS Calderdale Smart Move (£3,000); Macmillan Cancer Support (2,000); Alpha House (£1,500); Alzheimer's Society, Eureka Children's Museum, Illingworth Cricket Club (£1,000 each); Waring Green Community Association (£500); Sowerby Bridge Fire and Water (£250).
FINANCES *Year* 2013/14 *Income* £137,510 *Grants* £204,799 *Grants to organisations* £37,000 *Assets* £3,791,047
TRUSTEES Richard Smithies; David Normanton; Trevor Simpson; Leyland Smith; Brendan Mowforth.
OTHER INFORMATION The grant total includes £76,300 that was given to individuals.
HOW TO APPLY Apply in writing to the correspondent, detailing requirements and costings. Trustee board meetings are held six times a year.
WHO TO APPLY TO Richard Smithies, Trustee, 5 King Street, Brighouse, West Yorkshire HD6 1NX *Tel.* 01484 710571 *email* bearders@btinternet.com *Website* www.bearder-charity.org.uk

■ **The James Beattie Charitable Trust**
CC NO 265654    ESTABLISHED 1961
WHERE FUNDING CAN BE GIVEN Wolverhampton area.
WHO CAN BENEFIT Local projects and organisations; hospitals; churches and schools benefitting the people of Wolverhampton.
WHAT IS FUNDED General charitable purposes.
WHAT IS NOT FUNDED Individuals; organisations outside the West Midlands, or exclusive organisations (e.g. all-white or all-Asian groups).
TYPE OF GRANT Grants awarded for capital including buildings, core costs, project research, running costs, salaries and start-up costs. Grants may be one-off or recurring and funding for a single project may be available for less than one year to more than three.
SAMPLE GRANTS Barnardo's, James Beattie House, Cottage Homes, Marie Curie Cancer Care, St Chad's – Pattingham, St Martin's School, Whizz-Kidz, Wolverhampton Grammar School and YMCA.
FINANCES *Year* 2013/14 *Income* £36,325 *Grants* £107,240 *Grants to organisations* £107,240 *Assets* £3,310,834
TRUSTEES Jane Redshaw; Michael Redshaw; Kenneth Dolman; Susannah Norbury.
OTHER INFORMATION In 2013/14 grants were made to 82 organisations. Donations made ranged between £375 and £10,000 and were made

largely to local charities or local branches of national charities.
**HOW TO APPLY** Apply in writing to the correspondent, including accounts.
**WHO TO APPLY TO** The Trustees, PO Box 12, Bridgnorth, Shropshire WV15 5LQ

## ■ Beauland Ltd
**CC NO** 511374  **ESTABLISHED** 1981
**WHERE FUNDING CAN BE GIVEN** Worldwide, with some preference for the Manchester area.
**WHO CAN BENEFIT** To benefit Jewish people and those in need.
**WHAT IS FUNDED** Educational institutions (including adult education) and institutions for the relief of poverty.
**SAMPLE GRANTS** Yesamach Levav Trust (£60,000); UTA (£50,000); ABC Trust, Beis Rochel, Cozmon Belz and CMZ (£20,000 each); Yetev Lev (£10,000); Yeshivas Shaarei Torah (£7,000); Rosecare (£5,000); Yesoiday Hatorah School (£1,000).
**FINANCES** Year 2013/14 Income £803,486 Grants £297,650 Grants to organisations £297,650 Assets £6,259,315
**TRUSTEES** Henry Neumann; Miriam Friedlander; Hannah Rosemann; Janet Bleier; Rebecca Delange; Maurice Neumann; Pinchas Neumann; E. Neumann; Esther Henry.
**OTHER INFORMATION** The grant total includes a number of grants of less than £1,000 each and totalling just over £2,000.
**HOW TO APPLY** Apply in writing to the correspondent.
**WHO TO APPLY TO** Maurice Neumann, Trustee, 32 Stanley Road, Salford M7 4ES

## ■ The Beaverbrook Foundation
**CC NO** 310003  **ESTABLISHED** 1954
**WHERE FUNDING CAN BE GIVEN** UK and Canada.
**WHO CAN BENEFIT** Registered charities, mainly headquarters organisations or national charities.
**WHAT IS FUNDED** The object of this foundation include: the erection or improvement of the fabric of any church building; the purchase of books, papers, manuscripts or works of art; care of the aged or infirm in the UK. One of the areas that the foundation has concentrated on over the past twenty years has been supporting small charitable projects and over that time the foundation has donated to more than 400 charities.
**WHAT IS NOT FUNDED** Non-registered charities
**TYPE OF GRANT** One-off capital grants.
**RANGE OF GRANTS** Generally between £1,000–£5,000.
**SAMPLE GRANTS** National Motor Museum – Beaulieu (£44,000); Battle of Britain Memorial Trust (£30,000); Blond McIndoe Research Foundation (£25,000); BASMOM and Key 4 Life Donation (£10,000 each); Elephant Family and Saint and Sinners Trust (£2,000 each); Help for Heroes (£300). There were a number of other grants for under £2,000 each, totalling £37,000.
**FINANCES** Year 2013/14 Income £39,309 Grants £209,650 Grants to organisations £209,650 Assets £12,434,760
**TRUSTEES** Lord Beaverbrook; Lady Beaverbrook; Hon. Laura Levi; John Kidd; Hon. Maxwell Aitken.
**OTHER INFORMATION** The grant total includes over £37,000 of grants under £2,000 each.
**HOW TO APPLY** There is an online application form at the foundation's website.
**WHO TO APPLY TO** Ms Ford, Correspondent, Third Floor, 11/12 Dover Street, London W1S 4LJ Tel. 020 7042 9435 email jane@beaverbrookfoundation.org Website www.beaverbrookfoundation.org

## ■ The Beccles Town Lands Charity
**CC NO** 210714  **ESTABLISHED** 1544
**WHERE FUNDING CAN BE GIVEN** Beccles only.
**WHO CAN BENEFIT** Organisations and individuals in Beccles.
**WHAT IS FUNDED** General charitable purposes. Note that it is likely that funds belonging to the charity represent permanent endowment and in that case, the assets figure is not the amount available for grant-giving.
**WHAT IS NOT FUNDED** Applications from outside, or not for the benefit of, Beccles and its inhabitants will not be considered.
**SAMPLE GRANTS** Abbeyfield Residential Home; Beccles Church; Beccles Citizens Advice; Beccles Mayor's Appeal; St Luke's Community Centre and Salvation Army.
**FINANCES** Year 2012/13 Income £156,178 Grants £82,559 Grants to organisations £43,000 Assets £4,642,823
**TRUSTEES** James Hartley; Montagu Pitkin; Kenneth Leggett; Gillian Campbell; Gordon Hickman; Jennifer Langeskov; Keith Gregory; Jane Seppings; Robert Seppings.
**OTHER INFORMATION** The 2012/13 accounts were the latest available at the time of writing (June 2015).
**HOW TO APPLY** Apply in writing to the correspondent. Full details of how to apply are given on the charity's very informative and helpful website and you are advised to refer to grant-making criteria before making application. The website also states: 'If you deliver your letter by hand ensure that it is placed in the trust's letter-box, and not in the one for Beccles museum, which shares the same building. This is especially important when the museum is closed in the winter months.'
**WHO TO APPLY TO** Robert Peck, Secretary, Leman House, Ballygate, Beccles, Suffolk NR34 9ND Website becclestownlandscharity.org.uk

## ■ The Becker Family Charitable Trust
**CC NO** 1047968  **ESTABLISHED** 1995
**WHO CAN BENEFIT** Registered charities.
**WHAT IS FUNDED** General charitable purposes, particularly Orthodox Jewish organisations.
**SAMPLE GRANTS** Previous beneficiaries have included: Keren Shabbas, Lolev CT, Menora Grammar School, Torah Temima and WST.
**FINANCES** Year 2012/13 Income £338,235 Grants £37,825 Grants to organisations £37,825 Assets £629,321
**TRUSTEES** Allan Becker; Ruth Becker; Deanna Fried.
**OTHER INFORMATION** The 2012/13 accounts were the latest available at the time of writing (June 2015).
**HOW TO APPLY** Apply in writing to the correspondent. However, note that the trust has previously stated that its funds were fully committed.
**WHO TO APPLY TO** Allan Becker, Trustee, 33 Sinclair Grove, London NW11 9JH

## ■ The Beckett's and Sargeant's Educational Foundation

**CC NO** 309766    **ESTABLISHED** 1986
**WHERE FUNDING CAN BE GIVEN** The borough of Northampton.
**WHO CAN BENEFIT** Church schools, and individuals under 25 years of age and in need of financial assistance, and either a resident in the borough or attending schools or full-time courses of education at any further education establishment in the borough, or a former pupil of All Saints' Middle School for at least two years.
**WHAT IS FUNDED** Education.
**WHAT IS NOT FUNDED** Part-time courses.
**RANGE OF GRANTS** Up to £40,000.
**SAMPLE GRANTS** Moulton College (£3,000); Friends of All Saints' Music (£1,300); Thorplands Primary School (£1,000); and St John the Baptist (£450).
**FINANCES** Year 2014 Income £190,175 Grants £123,616 Grants to organisations £5,750 Assets £3,087,568
**TRUSTEES** Philip Saunderson; Richard Pestell; Philip Larratt; The Ven. Richard Ormston; David Smith; Hilary Spenceley; Margaret Pickard; Andrew Cowling; Richard Lambert; Helen Gompertz; David McConkey.
**OTHER INFORMATION** The 2012 grant total includes £88,000 that was given to 134 individuals.
**HOW TO APPLY** Apply on a form available from the correspondent. Applications are considered four times a year, usually in February/March, May, September and December.
**WHO TO APPLY TO** Angela Moon, Grants Subcommittee Clerk, Hewitsons LLP, Elgin House, Billing Road, Northampton NN1 5AU Tel. 01604 233211 email angelamoon@hewitsons.com

## ■ The John Beckwith Charitable Trust

**CC NO** 800276    **ESTABLISHED** 1987
**WHERE FUNDING CAN BE GIVEN** UK and overseas.
**WHO CAN BENEFIT** Registered charities.
**WHAT IS FUNDED** General charitable purposes with a preference for: sports programmes for young people; education; children's charities; medical research; the arts; and charities involved with overseas aid.
**TYPE OF GRANT** Capital, one-off and recurring.
**SAMPLE GRANTS** Great Ormond Street Children's Charity (£30,000); David Ross Foundation (£28,000); RNIB (£10,000); LandAid Charitable Trust and Whiteley Homes Trust (£5,000 each); British Heart Foundation, Changing Faces, NSPCC, RSPCA and Sightsavers (£1,000 each); and Smile Train (£500).
**FINANCES** Year 2013/14 Income £369,426 Grants £163,899 Grants to organisations £163,899 Assets £1,261,810
**TRUSTEES** Sir John Beckwith; Heather Beckwith; Christopher Meech.
**HOW TO APPLY** Apply in writing to the correspondent.
**WHO TO APPLY TO** Ms Sally Holder, Correspondent, 124 Sloane Street, London SW1X 9BW Tel. 020 7225 2250 email info@beckwithlondon.com

## ■ The Bedfordshire and Hertfordshire Historic Churches Trust

**CC NO** 1005697    **ESTABLISHED** 1991
**WHERE FUNDING CAN BE GIVEN** Bedfordshire, Hertfordshire and that part of Barnet within the Diocese of St Albans.
**WHO CAN BENEFIT** Those entrusted with the upkeep of places of active Christian worship.
**WHAT IS FUNDED** Work to ensure that places of active Christian worship are maintained in a structurally sound and weatherproof condition.
**WHAT IS NOT FUNDED** Individuals.
**TYPE OF GRANT** One-off and buildings. Funding may be given for one year or less.
**RANGE OF GRANTS** £1,000–£15,000
**SAMPLE GRANTS** St John the Apostle RC – Sundon Park (£10,000); All Saints – Leighton Buzzard (£8,000); St Mary – Stocking Pelham (£5,000); St Andrew – Little Berkhemsted (£1,000).
**FINANCES** Year 2013/14 Income £269,418 Grants £170,000 Grants to organisations £170,000 Assets £249,688
**TRUSTEES** Stuart Russell; Richard Genochio; Jim May; Dr Christopher Green; P. Lepper; William Masterson; Madline Russell; Judith Howard; Nico Rodenburg.
**OTHER INFORMATION** Annual income comes from member subscription and from the annual 'Bike 'n Hike' event. The trust also acts as a distributive agent for church grants made by the Wixamtree Trust and Waste Recycling Environmental Ltd.
**HOW TO APPLY** Initial enquiries should be made to the Grants Secretary. Applications can only be made by members of the trust.
**WHO TO APPLY TO** Archie Russell, Grants Secretary and Trustee, Wychbrook, 31 Ivel Gardens, Biggleswade, Bedfordshire SG18 0AN Tel. 01767 312966 email grants@bedshertshct.org.uk Website www.bedshertshct.org.uk

## ■ The Bedfordshire and Luton Community Foundation

**CC NO** 1086516    **ESTABLISHED** 2001
**WHERE FUNDING CAN BE GIVEN** The county of Bedfordshire and the borough of Luton.
**WHO CAN BENEFIT** The grant schemes aim to assist community voluntary organisations and groups in Bedfordshire and Luton in new or exciting projects that can help make a positive difference in the local community.
**WHAT IS FUNDED** The foundation is dedicated to improving the quality of community life of those in Bedfordshire and Luton and in particular those in special need by reason of disability, age, financial or other disadvantage. The foundation manages a number of grants programmes awarding a range of grants for such causes. The foundation's aims include community purposes such as advancement of education, protection of physical and mental health and relief of poverty.
**WHAT IS NOT FUNDED** Criteria for each of the foundation's grants programmes are available on the website.
**SAMPLE GRANTS** Luton Borough Council (£64,500); Rampage Carnival Club (£10,000); Luton Sixth Form College (£9,800); UpRising Leadership (£7,400); Full House Theatre (£6,900); Luton Rape Crisis (£5,300); The Hope Trust – Bed Food Bank (£4,700); Team Luton Swimming Club (£4,400); 9th Harpenden Scout Group

(£3,800); Calibre Audio Library and Tilehouse Counselling (£3,000 each); Dunstable and District Citizens Advice and Livability (£2,500 each); Dagnall Village Hall (£1,800); Bedfordshire Carers (£1,000); Autism Bedfordshire and Riseley Community Theatre (£500 each); Brickhill Parish Council (£240); Dunstable Concert Ensemble and The Haywood Club (£200 each).
**FINANCES** *Year* 2013/14 *Income* £1,227,180 *Grants* £739,942 *Grants to organisations* £739,942 *Assets* £1,455,422
**TRUSTEES** Janet Ridge; Malcolm Newman; Clifton Ibbett; Wendi Momen; Geoff Lambert; Andy Rayment; Keith Rawlings; Steve Leverton.
**OTHER INFORMATION** The foundation manages a number of schemes that change regularly, therefore check its website for details of up to date schemes.
**HOW TO APPLY** Application forms for the various funds are available from the website. If applicants wish to apply for more than one fund at the same time, they must first contact the foundation. The panel meets six times a year and applicants should ensure their application is submitted at least three months before the funds are needed.
**WHO TO APPLY TO** Mark West, Chief Executive, The Old School, Southill Road, Cardington MK44 3SX *Tel.* 01234 834930 *email* administrator@blcf.org.uk *Website* www.blcf.org.uk

## ■ Beefy's Charity Foundation

**CC NO** 1151516
**WHERE FUNDING CAN BE GIVEN** UK.
**WHO CAN BENEFIT** Chronically ill children and young people.
**WHAT IS FUNDED** General charitable purposes, particularly health.
**WHAT IS NOT FUNDED** Individuals.
**TYPE OF GRANT** One-off, up to three years.
**SAMPLE GRANTS** Batten Disease Family Association, Brain Tumour Research and Support Across Yorkshire, Cardiac Risk in the Young, Juvenile Diabetes Research Foundation and Leukaemia and Lymphoma Research.
**FINANCES** *Year* 2013/14 *Income* £144,207 *Grants* £80,000 *Grants to organisations* £80,000 *Assets* £60,347
**TRUSTEES** Douglas Osborne; Naynesh Desai; Paul Monk.
**HOW TO APPLY** Apply in writing to the correspondent. The trustees will make grants to selected charities who can demonstrate: public benefit; independent peer review of research; infrastructure to manage and supervise the project supported; adequate reporting on the progress and outcomes resulting from the project supported; and compliance with relevant legislation, regulations and good practice.
**WHO TO APPLY TO** The Trustees, DDO Solicitors, 36 Upper Brook Street, London W1K 7QJ *Tel.* 020 7499 5353 *email* info@beefysfoundation.org *Website* www.beefysfoundation.org

## ■ The David and Ruth Behrend Fund

**CC NO** 261567 **ESTABLISHED** 1969
**WHERE FUNDING CAN BE GIVEN** UK.
**WHO CAN BENEFIT** Registered charities.
**WHAT IS FUNDED** General charitable purposes. The fund only gives funding to charities known to the settlors.
**RANGE OF GRANTS** Up to £16,000.
**SAMPLE GRANTS** Merseyside Development Foundation (£14,000); Liverpool Homeless Football Club and Merseyside Play Action Council (£2,000 each); and Merseyside Holiday Service, Sanctuary Family Support, Sal 4 Kids, Save the Children and Sheila Kay Fund (£1,000 each).
**FINANCES** *Year* 2013/14 *Income* £81,320 *Grants* £87,811 *Grants to organisations* £87,811 *Assets* £1,450,510
**TRUSTEE** Liverpool Charity and Voluntary Services.
**HOW TO APPLY** The trustees state that they do not respond to unsolicited applications. 'The charity only makes grants to charities already known to the settlors as this is a personal charitable trust.'
**WHO TO APPLY TO** The Secretary, 151 Dale Street, Liverpool L2 2AH *Tel.* 0151 227 5177 *Website* www.merseytrusts.org.uk

## ■ The Bellahouston Bequest Fund

**SC NO** SC011781 **ESTABLISHED** 1888
**WHERE FUNDING CAN BE GIVEN** Glasgow and district, but not more than five miles beyond the Glasgow city boundary (churches only).
**WHO CAN BENEFIT** Churches and registered charities in Glasgow or within five miles especially those benefitting Protestant evangelical denominations and clergy of such churches, as well as people disadvantaged by poverty.
**WHAT IS FUNDED** The trust supports a wide variety of causes. Its main priority is to help build, expand and repair Protestant evangelical churches or places of religious worship, as well as supporting the clergy of these churches. It further states that it is set up to give grants to charities for the relief of poverty or disease and to organisations concerned with promotion of the Protestant religion, education, and conservation of places of historical and artistic significance. It will consider social welfare causes generally and also animal welfare and sport and recreation.
**RANGE OF GRANTS** Usually between £1,000 and £5,000.
**SAMPLE GRANTS** Previous beneficiaries have included: 119th Glasgow Boys' Brigade, Airborne Initiative, Ballieston Community Care, Bellahouston Academy, Calvay Social Action Group, Citizens' Theatre, Church of Scotland, Colquhoun Trust, Crosshill Evangelical Church, Dalmarnock After School Care, Erskine Hospital, Girlguiding Scotland, House for an Art Lover, Kelvingrove Refurbishment Appeal, Maryhill Parish Church, William McCunn's Trust, Northwest Women's Centre, Pearce Institute, Prince and Princess of Wales Hospice, Shawlands United Reformed Church, St Paul's Parish Council, Strathclyde Youth Club Association, University of Strathclyde and Williamwood Parish Church.
**FINANCES** *Year* 2013/14 *Income* £192,780 *Grants* £100,000 *Grants to organisations* £100,000
**TRUSTEES** Peter C. Paisley; Peter L. Fairley; Andrew Primrose; Donald Blair; Graeme Kidd.

**HOW TO APPLY** Application forms are available from the trust for church applications only. Other charitable organisations can apply in writing to the correspondent. The trustees meet to consider grants in March, July, October and December.
**WHO TO APPLY TO** Edward Barry, Mitchells Roberton Solicitors, George House, 36 North Hanover Street, Glasgow G1 2AD *Tel.* 0141 552 3422 *email* emb@mitchells-roberton.co.uk

## ■ The Benfield Motors Charitable Trust

**CC NO** 328149   **ESTABLISHED** 1989
**WHERE FUNDING CAN BE GIVEN** Worldwide with preferences for north east England, Cumbria and Leeds.
**WHO CAN BENEFIT** Neighbourhood-based community projects and national schemes.
**WHAT IS FUNDED** Grants are given in the areas of social welfare; community development; work which supports children, young people and the elderly, local hospitals and hospices; Christian activities and the arts.
**TYPE OF GRANT** One-off or recurrent.
**RANGE OF GRANTS** Mostly under £1,000, with some larger grants reaching between £5,000 and £40,000.
**SAMPLE GRANTS** Traidcraft (£15,000); Live Theatre (£20,000); Metro Kids Africa (£16,000); Keyfund (£10,000); Newcastle Royal Grammar School (£9,000); Newcastle Cathedral Trust (£6,000); British Red Cross and Happy Days (£2,000 each); Dyslexia North East (£550).
**FINANCES** *Year* 2013/14  *Income* £238,755  *Grants* £184,703  *Grants to organisations* £184,703  *Assets* £351,908
**TRUSTEES** John Squires, Chair; Malcolm Squires; Stephen Squires; Lynn Squires.
**HOW TO APPLY** Apply in writing to the correspondent. The trustees' meet twice a year, this is usually in May and November with applications needing to be received by the beginning of April or October respectively.
**WHO TO APPLY TO** Lynn Squires, Trustee, c/o Benfield Motor Group, Asama Court, Newcastle Business Park, Newcastle upon Tyne NE4 7YD *Tel.* 0191 226 1700 *email* charitabletrust@ benfieldmotorgroup.com

## ■ The Benham Charitable Settlement

**CC NO** 239371   **ESTABLISHED** 1964
**WHERE FUNDING CAN BE GIVEN** UK, with very strong emphasis on Northamptonshire.
**WHO CAN BENEFIT** Registered charities.
**WHAT IS FUNDED** The trust's policy is to make a large number of relatively small grants to groups working in many charitable fields, including charities involved in medical research, disability, elderly people, children and young people, disadvantaged people, overseas aid, missions to seamen, the welfare of ex-servicemen, wildlife, the environment, and the arts. The trust also supports the Church of England, and the work of Christian mission throughout the world. Special emphasis is placed upon those churches and charitable organisations within the county of Northamptonshire [especially as far as new applicants are concerned].
**WHAT IS NOT FUNDED** Individuals.
**TYPE OF GRANT** One-off and recurring grants will be considered.
**RANGE OF GRANTS** Mostly between £400–£700, with some larger grants up to £40,000.
**SAMPLE GRANTS** Northamptonshire Association of Youth Clubs (£40,000); William Wilberforce Trust and Zimbabwe A National Emergency (£6,000 each); St Andrew's Church, Park Walk (£4,000); Age UK Northampton (£700); AIDS Trust and Anglo Peruvian Children's Charity (£600 each); Animals in Need Northampton and British Trust for Ornithology (£500 each); and League of Friends (£250).
**FINANCES** *Year* 2013/14  *Income* £244,544  *Grants* £161,000  *Grants to organisations* £161,000  *Assets* £6,305,235
**TRUSTEES** Mrs M. M. Tittle; Lady Hutton; David Tittle; Revd J. A. Nickols.
**OTHER INFORMATION** The majority of grants range from £400–£700.
**HOW TO APPLY** In recent years the trust has not been considering new applications. Enquiries should be made to the correspondent before making application.
**WHO TO APPLY TO** The Secretary, 1 Virginia Drive, Virginia Water, Surrey GU25 4NR

## ■ Michael and Leslie Bennett Charitable Trust

**CC NO** 1047611   **ESTABLISHED** 1995
**WHERE FUNDING CAN BE GIVEN** UK
**WHO CAN BENEFIT** Charitable organisations, mostly Jewish organisations.
**WHAT IS FUNDED** The trust supports a range of general charitable purposes, with a preference for Jewish organisations.
**RANGE OF GRANTS** Up to £10,000, many under £1,000.
**SAMPLE GRANTS** World Jewish Relief (£8,000 total, in three grants); Chai Cancer Care (£6,000 total, in two grants); UJIA (£6,000 total, in two grants); Community Security Trust and Norwood (£3,000 each); Magen David Adom (£1,500); Royal National Theatre Company and The Perse School (£1,000 each). A further 22 grants were made for less than £1,000 each, totalling £5,200.
**FINANCES** *Year* 2013/14  *Income* £56,461  *Grants* £34,660  *Grants to organisations* £34,660  *Assets* £299,351
**TRUSTEES** Michael Bennett; Lesley V. Bennett.
**HOW TO APPLY** Apply in writing to the correspondent.
**WHO TO APPLY TO** Michael Bennett, Trustee, Bedegars Lea, Kenwood Close, London NW3 7JL *Tel.* 020 8458 4945

## ■ Bergqvist Charitable Trust

**CC NO** 1015707   **ESTABLISHED** 1992
**WHERE FUNDING CAN BE GIVEN** Buckinghamshire and neighbouring counties.
**WHO CAN BENEFIT** Registered charities and community organisations.
**WHAT IS FUNDED** Education; medical health; environment; and disaster and famine relief.
**WHAT IS NOT FUNDED** Individuals; non-registered charities; animal causes.
**TYPE OF GRANT** One-off and recurrent grants.
**SAMPLE GRANTS** Abracadabra; British Epilepsy Association; British Heart Foundation; Church Urban Fund; Generation Trust for medical research; PACE; Sight Savers International; Stoke Mandeville Hospital.
**FINANCES** *Year* 2013/14  *Income* £44,077  *Grants* £47,625  *Grants to organisations* £47,625  *Assets* £1,851,624

**TRUSTEES** Patricia Bergqvist; Philip Bergqvist; Sophia Bergqvist.
**HOW TO APPLY** Apply in writing to the correspondent.
**WHO TO APPLY TO** Mrs Patricia Bergqvist, Trustee, Moat Farm, Water Lane, Ford, Aylesbury, Buckinghamshire HP17 8XD *Tel.* 01296 748560 *email* tsaukltd@gmail.com

## ■ The Berkeley Charitable Foundation

**CC NO** 1152596     **ESTABLISHED** 2011
**WHERE FUNDING CAN BE GIVEN** England and Wales.
**WHO CAN BENEFIT** Registered charities and community groups.
**WHAT IS FUNDED** General charitable purposes, education, health, social welfare, the environment and community development. The foundation has a particular interest in organisations working with people who are homeless.
**FINANCES** *Year* 2013/14 *Income* £3,294,954 *Grants* £1,744,167 *Grants to organisations* £1,744,167 *Assets* £976,000
**TRUSTEES** Anthony Pidgley; Charmaine Young; Robert Perrins; Wendy Pritchard.
**OTHER INFORMATION** The foundation was established by Anthony Pidgley founder and chair of the Berkeley Group, a British housebuilding company based in Surrey.
**HOW TO APPLY** The foundation has stated that it very rarely makes unsolicited donations; however, organisations can write to the correspondent if they believe there is a partnership that could be explored.
**WHO TO APPLY TO** Charmaine Young, Trustee, The Berkeley Group plc, Berkeley House, 19 Portsmouth Road, Cobham, Surrey KT11 1JG *Tel.* 020 7720 2600 *email* info@berkeleyfoundation.org.uk *Website* www.berkeleyfoundation.org.uk

## ■ The Ruth Berkowitz Charitable Trust

**CC NO** 1111673     **ESTABLISHED** 2005
**WHERE FUNDING CAN BE GIVEN** UK and overseas.
**WHO CAN BENEFIT** Charitable organisations.
**WHAT IS FUNDED** Youth; medical research; education; Jewish causes, including education and community.
**RANGE OF GRANTS** £2,000–£50,000
**SAMPLE GRANTS** National Jewish Chaplaincy Board and World Jewish Relief (£50,000 each); Community Security Trust (£40,000); Marie Curie Cancer Care (£35,000); Magen David Adom UK (£25,000); United Synagogue (£20,000); Jewish Women's Aid (£10,000); British Friends of Gesher (£5,000); and Camp Simcha (£4,000).
**FINANCES** *Year* 2013/14 *Income* £86,394 *Grants* £485,500 *Grants to organisations* £485,600 *Assets* £3,040,911
**TRUSTEES** Philip Beckman; Brian Beckman.
**HOW TO APPLY** The trustees stated in their annual report that the trust is not reactive they will 'generally only make grants to charities that are known to them and will not normally respond to unsolicited requests for assistance. There is no application form.'
**WHO TO APPLY TO** The Trustees, 25/26 Enford Street, London W1H 1DW

## ■ The Berkshire Community Foundation

**CC NO** 294220     **ESTABLISHED** 1985
**WHERE FUNDING CAN BE GIVEN** Berkshire (the unitary authorities of Bracknell, Reading, Slough, Windsor and Maidenhead, West Berkshire and Wokingham).
**WHO CAN BENEFIT** Voluntary organisations or groups established for charitable purposes; individual children up to the age of 18 (or 25 for those with learning/physical disabilities).
**WHAT IS FUNDED** The foundation manages a number of different funds. Grants are made to support groups aiding disadvantaged individuals, in particular in the fields of education, mental and physical health and the relief of poverty.
**WHAT IS NOT FUNDED** Medical research or equipment; sponsorship or one off events; individuals over the age of 18 (except those up to 25 for those with learning/physical disabilities); organisations that primarily support plants or animal welfare; building improvements/projects or capital appeals (unless flood damaged); overseas travel/expeditions; promotion of religious or political causes; statutory work (in educational institutions or replacing statutory funding); projects benefitting those outside the county; retrospective funding (exception of flood fund); organisations that are regional or national charities (unless locally led and run); organisations that have substantial unrestricted funds.
**TYPE OF GRANT** Capital and core costs; salaries; projects; one-off and up to three years; unrestricted funding.
**RANGE OF GRANTS** In 2013/14 average grant was £2,800.
**SAMPLE GRANTS** Awards were made through various funds including: Local Giving (£212,500); General (£49,000); Give A Child A Chance (£47,500); Autodata (£30,000); Sage (£13,700); NHS West Respite (£10,000); Herongate (£9,800); Surviving Winter (£7,000); Adviza Partnership (£6,300); BCF Flood Recovery Fund (£3,000); BCF Staff Giving (£400). **Beneficiaries included**: Creativity in Sport (£24,000); Berkshire Citizens Advice (£17,500); Berkshire Autistic Society (£15,000); Slough Homeless Our Concern (£12,000); Britwell Youth and Community Project (£10,000); Elizabeth Fry Approved Premises (£6,700); Sebastian's Action Trust (£5,000); Life Education Centres (£2,500); Age UK Berkshire (£1,900); Thatcham Neighbourhood Wardens (£1,100); Free Legal Advice Group (£500); ABC to Read (£50).
**FINANCES** *Year* 2013/14 *Income* £1,247,985 *Grants* £730,643 *Grants to organisations* £730,643 *Assets* £8,497,201
**TRUSTEES** Susie Tremlett; David Seward; Dick Taylor; Chris Barrett; Torquil Montague-Johnstone; Ramesh Kukar; Lady Catherine Stevenson; Jane Wates; Sue Ormiston; Christine Weston; Antony Wood; H. Storey; Sean Taylor; Nick Burrows; David Oram; Gordon Anderson.
**OTHER INFORMATION** The foundation supported 197 groups and 23 individuals. The grant total figure includes awards to both organisations and individuals.
**HOW TO APPLY** Full details of how to apply to the specific funding streams can be found on the foundation's website. Note that organisations are required to submit audited accounts for the past three financial years and their governing document. The website reminds: 'Potential applicants are strongly advised to speak to the

grants team to confirm their eligibility before submitting their request for funding.'
**WHO TO APPLY TO** Andrew Middleton, Chief Executive, 100 Longwater Avenue, Green Park, Reading RG2 6GP *Tel.* 0118 930 3021 *email* grants@berkshirecf.org *Website* www.berkshirecf.org

## ■ The Bertarelli UK Foundation
**CC NO** 1140189 **ESTABLISHED** 2011
**WHERE FUNDING CAN BE GIVEN** UK.
**WHO CAN BENEFIT** Charities and community groups.
**WHAT IS FUNDED** General charitable purposes.
**RANGE OF GRANTS** £87,000
**SAMPLE GRANTS** Stoke-on-Trent Theatres Trust (£87,000).
**FINANCES** *Year* 2013 *Income* £92,645 *Grants* £87,000 *Grants to organisations* £87,000
**TRUSTEES** Ernesto Bertarelli; Donata Bertarelli; Maria Bertarelli; Kirsty Bertarelli.
**OTHER INFORMATION** This is the charitable foundation of the Bertarelli family and the vehicle for their philanthropy in the UK. The family has a number of business interests, most notably in the pharmaceutical industry and property investments. Waypoint Corporate Services Ltd is also one of their companies. The family's wealth is estimated at around £7.4 billion.
**HOW TO APPLY** Apply in writing to the correspondent.
**WHO TO APPLY TO** Mark Bolland, c/o Waypoint Corporate Services Ltd, 1 Curzon Street, London W1J 5HD *Tel.* 020 7016 4000 *email* Mark.Bolland@waypointcapital.net

## ■ The Bestway Foundation
**CC NO** 297178 **ESTABLISHED** 1987
**WHERE FUNDING CAN BE GIVEN** UK and overseas.
**WHO CAN BENEFIT** Registered charities; unregistered organisations; overseas charitable bodies; individuals; educational establishments.
**WHAT IS FUNDED** Education and training; social welfare; health; medical causes; overseas aid; poverty reduction in Pakistan; provision of scholarships. Some preference to people of Indian, Pakistani, Bangladeshi or Sri Lankan origin.
**WHAT IS NOT FUNDED** Trips/travel abroad.
**TYPE OF GRANT** The majority of the grants are made on an annual basis.
**RANGE OF GRANTS** £500–£100,000
**SAMPLE GRANTS** Dyslexia Action (£100,000); Crimestoppers (£34,000); British Pakistan Foundation (£33,000); The Duke of Edinburgh's Award (£16,900); Asian Women's Resource Centre (£10,000); The Graham Layton Trust (£5,000); SSAFA (£2,000); Wines and Spirits Trades Benevolent Society (£1,000); Need 2 Know Education (£600); Harefield Hospital Re-Beat Club (£500).
**FINANCES** *Year* 2013/14 *Income* £648,106 *Grants* £399,820 *Grants to organisations* £243,741 *Assets* £7,034,971
**TRUSTEES** Mohammed Sheikh; Abdul Bhatti; Adalat Chaudhary; Sir Mohammed Pervez; Zameer Choudrey; Dawood Pervez; Rizwan Pervez; Arshad Chaudhary.
**OTHER INFORMATION** All trustees of this foundation are directors and shareholders of Bestway (Holdings) Limited, the parent company of Bestway Cash and Carry Limited. In 2013/14 awards were made to 17 organisations and 34 individuals. The grant total includes £243,500 given to organisations in the UK and £156,000 awarded to foreign charities and individuals.

**HOW TO APPLY** Applications may be made in writing to the correspondent, enclosing an sae. Appeals are normally considered in March/April. The foundation has previously noted that telephone calls are not invited.
**WHO TO APPLY TO** Mohammed Sheikh, Trustee, Bestway (Holdings) Ltd, Abbey Road, London NW10 7BW *Tel.* 020 8453 1234 *email* zulfikaur.wajid-hasan@bestway.co.uk *Website* www.bestwaygroup.co.uk/responsibility/bestway-foundation

## ■ BHST
**CC NO** 1004327 **ESTABLISHED** 1991
**WHERE FUNDING CAN BE GIVEN** UK and Israel.
**WHO CAN BENEFIT** Jewish organisations and individuals.
**WHAT IS FUNDED** Jewish charitable purposes.
**RANGE OF GRANTS** Usually £300–£7,400.
**SAMPLE GRANTS** Adath Yisroel Burial Society (£64,000); Easy Chasnea (£7,000); Shulum Berger Association (£3,000); United Talmudical Association (£2,500); and Beis Rochel (£1,600).
**FINANCES** *Year* 2013/14 *Income* £353,502 *Grants* £102,742 *Grants to organisations* £19,553 *Assets* £25,778
**TRUSTEES** Solomon Laufer; Pinchas Ostreicher; Joshua Sternlicht.
**OTHER INFORMATION** A total of £83,200 was given in student grants.
**HOW TO APPLY** Apply in writing to the correspondent.
**WHO TO APPLY TO** Solomon Laufer, Trustee, c/o Cohen Arnold and Co., New Burlington House, 1075 Finchley Road, London NW11 0PU *Tel.* 020 8731 0777 *Fax* 020 8731 0778 *email* mail@cohenarnold.com

## ■ The Mason Bibby 1981 Trust
**CC NO** 283231 **ESTABLISHED** 1981
**WHERE FUNDING CAN BE GIVEN** Merseyside and other areas where the company has or had a presence.
**WHO CAN BENEFIT** Priority to elderly people and employees and ex-employees of J Bibby and Sons plc (since renamed Barloworld plc).
**WHAT IS FUNDED** The main area of interest is elderly people but applications are considered from other groups, particularly from areas in which the company has a presence.
**WHAT IS NOT FUNDED** Apart from employees and ex-employees of J Bibby and Sons plc, applications are considered from registered charities only.
**RANGE OF GRANTS** £200–£3,500
**SAMPLE GRANTS** Age Concern Liverpool (£2,200); Liverpool Personal Service Society (£1,500); Macmillan Cancer Support and Salvation Army, Liverpool and North West (£1,000 each); Hoylake Cottage Hospital and Alzheimer's Society – Liverpool and Sefton (£800 each); Independent Age and Queenscourt Hospice (£400 each); and Friends of the Elderly, Help Link Community Support and Henshaws Society for Blind People North West (£200 each).
**FINANCES** *Year* 2013/14 *Income* £87,416 *Grants* £75,818 *Grants to organisations* £40,900 *Assets* £2,548,997
**TRUSTEES** John Wood; Dorothy Fairclough; Stephen Bowman; John McPheat; Alan Gresty; Peter Blocksidge; Lindsey Stead.
**OTHER INFORMATION** Donations are also made to employees and ex-employees. Grants to individuals for the year 2013/14 totalled £35,000.

**HOW TO APPLY** Apply in writing to the correspondent. The trustees meet half yearly. Applications are only acknowledged if a grant is agreed.
**WHO TO APPLY TO** Dorothy Fairclough, Trustee, c/o Rathbone Brothers and Co. Ltd, Port of Liverpool Building, Pier head, Liverpool L3 1NW email steve.bilbao@rathbones.com

## ■ The Bideford Bridge Trust

**CC NO** 204536    **ESTABLISHED** 1973
**WHERE FUNDING CAN BE GIVEN** Bideford, Devon and its neighbourhood.
**WHO CAN BENEFIT** Charities and individuals.
**WHAT IS FUNDED** Grants are dictated by the scheme of the trust, which maintains that the following grants should be made: to encourage education; to encourage poor people to become more self-sufficient by assisting them in business start-up schemes; to individual applications for charitable assistance (such as on the grounds of poverty or ill health); to clubs, organisations and charities; to assist people with disabilities living in the Parish of Bideford.
**WHAT IS NOT FUNDED** Computer purchases for individuals. Political donations.
**TYPE OF GRANT** Core and recurring costs.
**SAMPLE GRANTS** Business Start-Ups (M Lillis/Torridge Training Service) (£123,500); Bideford Film Society (£30,000); Bideford Amateur Rowing Club and East the Water Stepping Stones (£10,000 each); Appledore Charitable Community Trust and Bideford Methodist Church (£5,000 each); Bideford Town Band (£2,000); South West Family Support (£100).
**FINANCES** Year 2013/14 Income £798,383 Grants £559,890 Grants to organisations £559,890 Assets £15,197,426
**TRUSTEES** Mr P. Christie; William Isaac; Mrs E. Junkison; E. Hubber; Oliver Chope; Angus Harper; David Howell; David Dark; Philip Pester, Mr S. Ellis; Mr M. Langmead.
**HOW TO APPLY** Apply in writing to the correspondent.
**WHO TO APPLY TO** Mr P. R. Sims, Steward, 24 Bridgeland Street, Bideford, Devon EX39 2QB Tel. 01237 473122

## ■ The Big Lottery Fund (see also Awards for All)

**ESTABLISHED** 2004
**WHERE FUNDING CAN BE GIVEN** UK, also overseas.
**WHO CAN BENEFIT** Charitable organisations; statutory bodies; local groups; large national institutions; social enterprises.
**WHAT IS FUNDED** BIG runs a range of different programmes aimed at improving communities and people's lives. Some are UK-wide and others specific to each region. New programmes are introduced from time to time, and others close. Potential applicants are advised to check the fund's website for up-to-date information on current and upcoming programmes. There are also international funding programmes. The website states: 'Our money goes to community groups and projects that improve health, education and the environment.'
**WHAT IS NOT FUNDED** There will be specific and detailed conditions for each separate programme – see specific details.
**RANGE OF GRANTS** £300–£500,000
**SAMPLE GRANTS** Details of projects supported can be find online. **Beneficiaries included**: University of Warwick (£6.9 million); Addaction (£4.7 million); The Older People's Advocacy Alliance – UK (£1 million); Grampian Women's Aid (£783,500); NHS Lanarkshire (£701,000); Action for Children (£668,500); Volunteer Development Scotland Limited (£554,500); ChildHope UK (£504,000); The British Red Cross Society (£499,500); Women's Rape And Sexual Abuse Centre (Cornwall) Ltd (£476,000); UpRising Leadership (£427,500); Sensory Trust (£370,000); London Play (£348,000); Headway Suffolk Ltd (£266,500); SOS Polonia (£229,500); The Wooden Canal Boat Society (£169,000); Learning Library (£130,000); Trees for Life (£50,000); Challenge Wales (£41,000); Age Concern Isle of Wight (£20,000); Vista (£19,200); 1st Barrhead Scout Group, Bowel Cancer UK, Buckingham Primary School, Eckington Parish Church Hall, Encounters Arts Initiative, Getting Better Together Ltd, Russian Soul and Voice 4 Children (£10,000 each); Children England (£7,000); St Clare's Hospice (£6,700); The Sawmills Development Association (£3,100); Kinship Care Northern Ireland Ltd (£2,700); Emsworth Day Out Scheme (£1,200); East Ren Baby Friends (£900); Chippenham Rugby Football Club Limited (£500).
**FINANCES** Year 2013/14 Income £756,640,000 Grants £670,000 Grants to organisations £670,000 Assets £465,245,000
**TRUSTEES** The following are the board members: Peter Ainsworth; Tony Burton; Nat Sloane; Frank Hewitt; Sir Adrian Webb; Maureen McGinn; Dr Astrid Bonfield; David Isaac; Elizabeth Passey; Perdita Fraser; Natalie Campbell; Rachael Robathan.
**OTHER INFORMATION** BIG distributes money from the National Lottery to good causes as well as non-Lottery funding on behalf of public bodies, for example the Department for Education and the Office for Civil Society. The organisation's website gives extensive information on the background of the funds, support available, application procedures and so on, which is also subject to change. It would not be practicable to replicate all the details here and potential applicants are advised to study the helpful website to learn more about the funder. The 'Introduction and summary' section of the annual report states: 'In 2013/14 we received £662 million from the National Lottery and we made £670 million in grant awards to over 12,000 projects across the United Kingdom. Over 90 per cent of our funds went directly to the voluntary and community sector. We also appreciate the importance of the small and the local – 88 percent of our awards went to projects valued at £10,000 or less.' The project search facility given on the website indicates that in the period from 31 March 2013 to 31 March 2014 there were 8,187 projects awarded totalling nearly £232.5 million. The assets figure refers to 'total assets' (as named in the accounts). For the Awards for All programme also see the separate entry.
**HOW TO APPLY** Note there are different regional offices and contact details for England, Northern Ireland, Scotland and Wales (see the website for full details). All application forms and guidelines are given on the charity's website. If you need further guidance you can also call the BIG advice line at 0345 4 10 20 30.
**WHO TO APPLY TO** See 'How to apply', 1 Plough Place, London EC4A 1DE Tel. 020 7211 1800 or 0300 500 5050 Fax 020 7211 1750 email general.enquiries@biglotteryfund.org.uk Website www.biglotteryfund.org.uk

## ■ The Billmeir Charitable Trust

**CC NO** 208561 **ESTABLISHED** 1956

**WHERE FUNDING CAN BE GIVEN** UK, with a preference for the Surrey area, specifically Elstead, Tilford, Farnham and Frensham.

**WHO CAN BENEFIT** Charitable organisations.

**WHAT IS FUNDED** General charitable purposes. About a quarter of the grants are for health and medical causes and many are given to charities in Surrey.

**RANGE OF GRANTS** £500–£12,000

**SAMPLE GRANTS** Reed's School – Cobham (£12,000); Marlborough College (£8,000); The Watts Gallery and Tilford and Rushmoor Tennis Club (£10,000 each); Old Kiln Museum Trust and Woodlarks Campsite Trust (£5,000 each); Elstead United Reformed Church (£3,000); Cancer Vaccine and Crohn's and Colitis UK (£2,000 each); Give It Your Max (£500).

**FINANCES** Year 2013/14 Income £293,876 Grants £123,500 Grants to organisations £123,500 Assets £5,168,825

**TRUSTEES** Max Whitaker; Suzanne Marriott; Jason Whitaker.

**HOW TO APPLY** The trust states that unsolicited applications are not welcome and they are very rarely successful.

**WHO TO APPLY TO** Reena Bhudia, Correspondent, Moore Stephens, 150 Aldersgate Street, London EC1A 4AB Tel. 020 7334 9191 email reena.bhudia@moorestephens.com

## ■ Percy Bilton Charity

**CC NO** 1094720 **ESTABLISHED** 1962

**WHERE FUNDING CAN BE GIVEN** UK.

**WHO CAN BENEFIT** Large grants are only available to registered charities. Unregistered organisations can apply for a small grant but a reference from another charity, Council for Voluntary Service or the local authority youth service will be required.

**WHAT IS FUNDED** Projects working with disadvantaged and underprivileged young people (under 25), people with disabilities (physical or learning disabilities or mental health problems) and/or older people (aged over 60).

**WHAT IS NOT FUNDED** Running expenses for the organisation or individual projects; salaries, training costs or office equipment/furniture; projects for general community use e.g. community centre and church halls; disability access to community buildings; publication costs e.g. printing/distributing promotional and information leaflets; projects that have been completed; items that have already been purchased; provision of disability facilities in schemes mainly for the able-bodied; general funding/circularised appeals; pre-schools or playgroups (other than predominantly for children with disabilities); play schemes/ summer schemes; holidays or expeditions for individuals or groups; trips, activities or events; community sports/play area facilities; consumables (e.g. stationery, and arts and crafts materials); refurbishment or repair of places of worship/church halls; research projects; mainstream pre-schools, schools, colleges and universities (other than special schools); welfare funds for individuals; hospital/medical equipment; and works to premises not used primarily by the eligible groups.

**TYPE OF GRANT** One-off.

**RANGE OF GRANTS** Grants to individuals: up to £200; small grants to organisations: up to £500 towards furnishing and equipment for small projects; main funding single grants for capital expenditure: in excess of £2,000.

**SAMPLE GRANTS** Children's Trust – Surrey (£10,500); Bradbury Fields – Liverpool (£6,000); Heritage House Day care Centre – Norfolk and Vision 21 – Cardiff (£5,000 each); Aspire – Hereford (£4,000); Options for Life – West Midlands (£3,000); Cambridgeshire Mencap and Options for Supported Living – Liverpool (£2,000 each); Headway East London, Kent Friendz, Making A Difference – Tameside and Wirral Toy Library (£500 each); Blyth Star Enterprises – Northumberland and All Souls Clubhouse – London (£400 each); Stairways – Ivybridge (£300)

**FINANCES** Year 2013/14 Income £661,594 Grants £616,011 Grants to organisations £417,816 Assets £22,885,600

**TRUSTEES** Miles A. Bilton, Chair; James R. Lee; Stefan J. Paciorek; Kim Lansdown; Hayley Bilton.

**OTHER INFORMATION** Assistance is also given on a one-off basis to individuals and families who fall within the following categories: older people on a low income and people with physical or learning disabilities or mental health problems. All applications for individuals to be sent in by the relevant social worker on local or health authority headed notepaper. Grants to 190 organisations were made totalling £417,000 under both small and large grants programmes. An additional £155,000 was awarded to individuals and £44,000 was spent on over 2,000 food parcels distributed nationally.

**HOW TO APPLY** The charity's website gives the following guidance on making an application: 'Large grants (£2,000 and over) Please apply on your organisation's headed notepaper giving or attaching the following information. 1–6 must be provided in all cases and 7 as applicable to your appeal: 1. A summary outlining the amount you are requesting and what the funding is for. 2. A brief history of your Charity, its objectives and work. 3. Description of the project and what you intend to achieve. 4. A copy of your most recent Annual Report and audited accounts. 5. Details of funds already raised and other sources that you have approached. 6. Proposals to monitor and evaluate the project. 7. Any other relevant information that will help to explain your application. The following additional information that applies to your appeal: Building/ Refurbishment appeals: A statement of all costs involved. Please itemise major items and professional fees; confirmation that the project has on-going revenue funding; confirmation that all planning and other consents and building regulations approvals have been obtained; details of ownership of the premises and if leased, the length of the unexpired term; timetable of construction/refurbishment and anticipated date of completion. Equipment appeals: An itemised list of all equipment with estimate of costs. Please obtain at least 2 competitive estimates except where this is not practicable e.g. specialised equipment; when you plan to purchase the equipment. Contribution towards purchase of minibuses: Please note that minibuses can only be considered if used to transport older and/or disabled people with mobility problems. Please give details of provision made for insurance, tax and maintenance etc. We require confirmation that your organisation can meet future running costs. Small grants (up to £500) Please apply on your organisation's headed notepaper with the following information: brief details about your organisation and its work; a copy of your most recent annual accounts; outline of the project and its principal aims; breakdown of the cost of item/s required; the organisation's bank account name to which the cheque should be made payable if a grant is approved. (We cannot make cheques payable to individuals); if your organisation is not a registered charity, please supply a reference from a registered charity with whom you work or from the local Voluntary Service Council.'

WHO TO APPLY TO Tara Smith, Charity Administrator, Bilton House, 7 Culmington Road, Ealing, London W13 9NB *Tel.* 020 8579 2829 *Fax* 020 8579 3650 *email* TSmithPBCharity@aol.com *Website* www.percybiltoncharity.org.uk

## ■ The Bingham Trust

CC NO 287636   ESTABLISHED 1977
WHERE FUNDING CAN BE GIVEN Buxton and district.
WHO CAN BENEFIT Organisations and individuals.
WHAT IS FUNDED Community needs, churches, the arts and educational needs.
WHAT IS NOT FUNDED Generally, limited to the town of Buxton and district.
TYPE OF GRANT One-off, capital including buildings, project, running costs, salaries and start-up costs. Funding is for up to three years.
RANGE OF GRANTS Up to £5,000.
SAMPLE GRANTS Good News Family Care (£50,000); Buxton Community School (£13,000); Mission Direct (£6,000); Peaks and Dales Advocacy (£5,400); Blythe House Hospice, Fun 2 Do and Kinder Choir (£5,000 each); Buxton Cricket Club and Buxton Festival (£2,000 each); Plantlife (£500); Vitalise (£340); and Funny Wonders (£250).
FINANCES *Year* 2013/14 *Income* £190,959 *Grants* £174,204 *Grants to organisations* £135,467 *Assets* £4,458,619
TRUSTEES Eric Butterley; Christine McMullen; Roger Horne; Helen Mirtle; Alexandra Hurst.
OTHER INFORMATION In 2013/14 the trust distributed 45 grants to organisations. Grants to organisations totalled £135,000, while approximately £39,000 was distributed to individuals.
HOW TO APPLY Refer to the trust's very helpful and clear guidelines available together with an application form from its website.
WHO TO APPLY TO Roger Horne, Trustee, Unit 1, Tongue Lane Industrial Estate, Dew Pond Lane, Buxton, Derbyshire SK17 7LN *Tel.* 01298 600591 *email* binghamtrust@aol.com *Website* www.binghamtrust.org.uk

## ■ The Birmingham District Nursing Charitable Trust

CC NO 215652   ESTABLISHED 1960
WHERE FUNDING CAN BE GIVEN Within a 20-mile radius of the Council House in Birmingham.
WHO CAN BENEFIT Local organisations benefitting medical professionals. Grants may be made to local branches of national organisations.
WHAT IS FUNDED Medical or nursing organisations; convalescent homes; convalescent homes or rest homes for nurses or other medical or nursing institution; amenities for patients or nursing staff of Birmingham Domiciliary Nursing Service; amenities for patients or nursing staff of any state hospital.
WHAT IS NOT FUNDED No grants are given to individuals.
TYPE OF GRANT One-off and recurrent.
RANGE OF GRANTS £500–£3,000
SAMPLE GRANTS Age UK Birmingham, Birmingham PHAB Camps, Focus Birmingham, Freedom from Torture, Vitalise Skylarks (£3,000 each); Acorns Children's Hospice, Birmingham, Careers Advice and Resources Establishment Sandwell, Primrose Hospice Cancer Help, Shakespeare Hospice, St Mary's Hospice, St Giles Hospice (£2,500 each); Motor Neurone Disease Association (£2,000); Walsall Carers Centre (£1,750); Better Understanding of Dementia in Sandwell, Ex Cathedra (£1,000 each).
FINANCES *Year* 2013/14 *Income* £69,982 *Grants* £61,950 *Grants to organisations* £61,950 *Assets* £1,909,438
TRUSTEES Mr H. W. Tuckey; Mrs T. Cull; Dr P. Mayer; S. Reynolds; A. H. Jones; Dr M. Honeyman; Prof. F. Irvine
HOW TO APPLY Apply in writing to the correspondent with a copy of the latest accounts. Applications should be sent in August/September. The trustees meet to consider grants in the first week of November.
WHO TO APPLY TO Mr M. Parr, c/o Shakespeare Putsman, Somerset House, 37 Temple Street, Birmingham B2 5DJ *Tel.* 0121 237 3000 *email* matthew.parr@shakespeares.co.uk

## ■ Birmingham International Airport Community Trust

CC NO 1071176   ESTABLISHED 1998
WHERE FUNDING CAN BE GIVEN The areas affected by the airport's operation (East Birmingham, Solihull and parts of north Warwickshire).
WHO CAN BENEFIT Established local charities.
WHAT IS FUNDED Areas of work the trust supports are: environment improvement and heritage conservation; bringing the community closer together through facilities for sport, recreation and other leisure-time activities; improving awareness of environmental issues or environmental education and training activities; encouraging and protecting wildlife. It describes the types of projects it wishes to support as including community centres, community groups, sports, playgroups, schools, youth clubs, scouts, gardens/parks, environment, music and churches. Work should benefit a substantial section of the community rather than less inclusive groups, although work with older people or people with special needs is positively encouraged.
WHAT IS NOT FUNDED The following are not eligible for grants: individuals; projects which have already been carried out or paid for; organisations which have statutory responsibilities e.g. hospitals, surgeries, clinics, schools, etc. unless the project is clearly not a statutory responsibility. Grants are not normally recurrent, or given towards the purchase of land or buildings.
TYPE OF GRANT Grants may be for capital or revenue projects, although the trust will not commit to recurrent or running costs, such as salaries.
RANGE OF GRANTS Generally up to £3,000.
SAMPLE GRANTS 298th Birmingham Brownies/Rangers Pack; Age Concern – Castle Bromwich; Blakenhale Infant School; Chelmsley Town Football Club; Coleshill Bell Ringers; Coleshill Town Football Club; George Fentham Endowed School; Hatchford Brook Youth; Community Centre; Lane Baptist Free Church.
FINANCES *Year* 2013/14 *Income* £75,251 *Grants* £68,319 *Grants to organisations* £68,319 *Assets* £8,327

**TRUSTEES** Cllr Michael Wood; Cllr Michael Robinson; Cllr Martin Hewings; Paul Orton; Andrew Holding; Edward Richards; Margaret Kennett; James Dunlop Williams; Cllr Majid Mahmood.
**HOW TO APPLY** The trust gives the following information: 'To apply, you must contact us to receive an application form. This allows us to discuss with you whether or not your proposal meets the trust fund criteria and how to maximise your chances of making a successful application. Please be aware that the trustees meet twice a year in April and October and that there are deadlines in February and August respectively for the receipt of completed applications. Late applications cannot be considered.' Full guidelines are available from the trust's page on the company's website, along with specific deadline dates, which are usually towards the end of the months stated.
**WHO TO APPLY TO** Andrew Holding, Trustee, Birmingham International Airport Ltd, Diamond House, Birmingham B26 3QJ *Tel.* 0121 767 7448 *email* community@birminghamairport.co.uk *Website* www.birminghamairport.co.uk

■ **The Lord Mayor of Birmingham's Charity**
**CC NO** 1036968  **ESTABLISHED** 1994
**WHERE FUNDING CAN BE GIVEN** UK. There may be a preference for Birmingham.
**WHO CAN BENEFIT** Charities determined by the Lord Mayor at the commencement of term of office.
**WHAT IS FUNDED** Beneficiaries are determined by the Lord Mayor prior to taking up office. Three or four charities/voluntary organisations are usually selected at the beginning of the year.
**WHAT IS NOT FUNDED** Charities working outside the area of Birmingham.
**TYPE OF GRANT** One-off.
**SAMPLE GRANTS** Acorns Children's Hospice Trust, Guide Dogs for the Blind Association. SSAFA WMC and The Salvation Army (£16,000 each); Malaya, Borneo and FE Veterans Association (£5,000); ABF The Soldiers Charity and Listening Books (£100 each).
**FINANCES** *Year* 2013/14 *Income* £45,504 *Grants* £70,686 *Grants to organisations* £70,686 *Assets* £113,452
**TRUSTEES** Lord Mayor of Birmingham; Deputy Lord Mayor of Birmingham; Jim Whorwood; John Alden; Michael Wilkes; John Cotton; Anita Ward; Mike Sharpe; Randall Brew.
**HOW TO APPLY** Apply in writing to the correspondent. Although the beneficiaries are often predetermined, applications can be sent in January/February for the new Lord Mayor to consider.
**WHO TO APPLY TO** Leigh Nash, Secretary to the Trustees, Development Section, Room 403, 4th Floor, Council House, Birmingham B1 1BB *Tel.* 0121 303 2691 *email* leigh_nash@birmingham.gov.uk *Website* www.birmingham.gov.uk

■ **Birthday House Trust**
**CC NO** 248028  **ESTABLISHED** 1966
**WHERE FUNDING CAN BE GIVEN** England and Wales.
**WHO CAN BENEFIT** Charitable organisations and individuals.
**WHAT IS FUNDED** General charitable purposes.
**WHAT IS NOT FUNDED** Individuals; non-charitable organisations.
**TYPE OF GRANT** One-off and recurrent.
**SAMPLE GRANTS** Druk White Lotus School (£25,000); The Ecology Trust (£8,500); The Public Memorial Appeal (£5,000); Standing Voice (£2,000); Street Hope (£500).
**FINANCES** *Year* 2013/14 *Income* £168,564 *Grants* £51,271 *Grants to organisations* £51,271 *Assets* £7,086,749
**TRUSTEE** The Dickinson Trust Limited and Rathbone Trust Company Limited.
**OTHER INFORMATION** The main work of this trust is engaged with the running of a residential home for people who are elderly in Midhurst, West Sussex.
**HOW TO APPLY** Apply in writing to the correspondent, including an sae. No application forms are issued and there is no deadline. Only successful applicants are acknowledged.
**WHO TO APPLY TO** Anina Cheng, Trust Administrator, Millbank Financial Services Limited, 4th Floor, Swan House, 17–19 Stratford Place, London W1C 1BQ *Tel.* 020 7907 2100 *email* charity@mfs.co.uk

■ **Miss Jeanne Bisgood's Charitable Trust**
**CC NO** 208714  **ESTABLISHED** 1963
**WHERE FUNDING CAN BE GIVEN** UK, overseas and locally in Bournemouth and Dorset, especially Poole.
**WHO CAN BENEFIT** Registered charities.
**WHAT IS FUNDED** General charitable purposes. Main grants have been and will be concentrated on the following categories: (a) operating under Roman Catholic auspices; (b) operating in Poole, Bournemouth and the county of Dorset; (c) national (not local) charities concerned with older people.
**WHAT IS NOT FUNDED** Individuals and non-registered charities.
**TYPE OF GRANT** One-off, capital and recurring.
**RANGE OF GRANTS** £25–£2,500
**SAMPLE GRANTS** Previous beneficiaries from the general fund have included: Apex Trust, ITDG, Horder Centre for Arthritis, Impact, St Barnabas' Society, St Francis Leprosy Guild, Sight Savers International and YMCA.
**FINANCES** *Year* 2013/14 *Income* £191,847 *Grants* £189,000 *Grants to organisations* £189,000 *Assets* £6,531,740
**TRUSTEES** Jeanne Bisgood; Patrick Bisgood; Paula Schulte.
**OTHER INFORMATION** The trust operates a sub-fund – the Bertram Fund from which grants are usually made anonymously.
**HOW TO APPLY** Apply in writing to the correspondent, quoting the UK registration number and registered name of the charity. Accounts no longer need to be submitted along with the application as the trust can obtain them from the Charity Commission. Applications should NOT be made directly to the Bertram Fund. Applications for capital projects 'should provide brief details of the main purposes, the total target and the current state of the appeal'. The trustees regret that they are unable to acknowledge appeals. The trustees normally meet in late February/early March and September.
**WHO TO APPLY TO** Jeanne Bisgood, Trustee, Flat 12 Waters Edge, Brudenell Road, Poole BH13 7NN *Tel.* 01202 708460 *email* bisgoodchtr123@btinternet.com

## ■ The Michael Bishop Foundation

**CC NO** 297627    **ESTABLISHED** 1987
**WHERE FUNDING CAN BE GIVEN** Worldwide with a preference for Birmingham and the Midlands.
**WHO CAN BENEFIT** Registered charities.
**WHAT IS FUNDED** Arts, health, child welfare, education and religion.
**SAMPLE GRANTS** Glendonbrook Foundation (£632,000); Acorn Recovery Project (£300,000); Royal Collection Trust (£212,000); Focus (£100,000); Kaleidoscope (£10,000); Melbourne Parish Church (£2,500 each); Westminster Medical School Research Trust (£500).
**FINANCES** Year 2013/14 Income £741,792 Grants £1,536,746 Grants to organisations £1,536,746 Assets £20,363,201
**TRUSTEES** Grahame Elliott; Baron Glendonbrook of Bowdon; John Voulson; Martin Ritchie.
**HOW TO APPLY** Apply in writing to the correspondent.
**WHO TO APPLY TO** Charlotte Newall, Correspondent, Staunton House, Ashby-de-la-Zouch, Leicestershire LE65 1RW Tel. 01530 564388 email peter.francis@bdo.co.uk

## ■ The Sydney Black Charitable Trust

**CC NO** 219855    **ESTABLISHED** 1949
**WHERE FUNDING CAN BE GIVEN** UK.
**WHO CAN BENEFIT** Charitable organisations.
**WHAT IS FUNDED** Youth organisations, religious, medical and other institutions, such as those helping people who are disadvantaged.
**TYPE OF GRANT** One-off grants for core support, equipment and vehicles.
**RANGE OF GRANTS** £300–£2,134
**SAMPLE GRANTS** Unspecified institutions in support of the aged and the poor (£17,000); Endever Youth Club Merton (£10,000); unspecified institutions in support of religion (£5,700); unspecified institutions in support of prisoners and captives (£2,300); unspecified institutions in support of education and children (£8,000).
**FINANCES** Year 2013/14 Income £58,473 Grants £53,129 Grants to organisations £53,129 Assets £3,309,942
**TRUSTEES** Jennifer Crabtree; Hilary Dickenson; Stephen Crabtree; Philip Crabtree.
**OTHER INFORMATION** In 2001 The Edna Black Charitable Trust and The Cyril Black Charitable Trust were incorporated into this trust. Grants are generally in the region of £125 and £250 each.
**HOW TO APPLY** Applications should be made in writing to the correspondent.
**WHO TO APPLY TO** Jennifer Crabtree, Trustee, 30 Welford Place, London SW19 5AJ

## ■ The Bertie Black Foundation

**CC NO** 245207    **ESTABLISHED** 1965
**WHERE FUNDING CAN BE GIVEN** UK; Israel.
**WHO CAN BENEFIT** Registered charities.
**WHAT IS FUNDED** The foundation's objects are: the relief and assistance of people who are in need, the advancement of education and religion, and other charitable purposes. Particular support is given to Jewish causes.
**SAMPLE GRANTS** Previous beneficiaries have included: I Rescue (£50,000); Magen David Adom (£47,000 in three grants); Alyn Hospital (£49,000 in two grants); Emunah (£38,000); Laniardo Hospital and Shaare Zedek (£25,000 each); Friends of Israel Sports Centre for Disabled (£20,000); Child Resettlement Trust (£10,000 in four grants); Norwood (£7,600 in four grants); and Hope (£5,200 in four grants).
**FINANCES** Year 2013/14 Income £110,580 Grants £144,018 Grants to organisations £144,018 Assets £3,214,756
**TRUSTEES** Isabelle Seddon; Doris Black; Carolyn Black; Harry Black; Ivor Seddon.
**OTHER INFORMATION** Grants were made to 33 organisations in 2013/14 of which seven received £5,000. The largest grant was £90,000.
**HOW TO APPLY** The trust has previously stated that it 'supports causes known to the trustees' and that they 'do not respond to unsolicited requests'.
**WHO TO APPLY TO** Harry Black, Trustee, Abbots House, 13 Beaumont Gate, Shenley Hill, Radlett, Hertfordshire WD7 7AR Tel. 01923 850096 email sonneborn@btconnect.com

## ■ Isabel Blackman Foundation

**CC NO** 313577    **ESTABLISHED** 1966
**WHERE FUNDING CAN BE GIVEN** Hastings and St Leonards-on-Sea.
**WHO CAN BENEFIT** Charities and other organisations; individuals.
**WHAT IS FUNDED** General charitable purposes, including education, social welfare, people who are elderly or have disabilities, health, churches, youth organisations, environment, culture and recreation.
**WHAT IS NOT FUNDED** Note only applications from Hastings and St Leonards-on-Sea are considered.
**TYPE OF GRANT** One-off; capital costs.
**RANGE OF GRANTS** Up to £50,000.
**SAMPLE GRANTS** St Michael's Hospice – new extension (£50,000); Age UK – Isabel Blackman Centre (£22,000); Little Ridge Community Primary School (£6,000); Salvation Army (£4,000); Cystic Fibrosis Trust and Ore Community Centre (£3,000 each); RSPCA – Bluebell Ridge (£2,500); Fire Fighters Charity and Guide Dogs for the Blind Association (£2,000 each); Lupus UK (£1,500); Carers Wellbeing Initiative (£1,200); Parkwood 6th Form (£750); Grass Roots Open Writers (£350); 7th Hastings Scout Group – New Beaver Colony (£100).
**FINANCES** Year 2013/14 Income £289,796 Grants £214,693 Grants to organisations £191,664 Assets £5,352,544
**TRUSTEES** Denis Jukes; Patricia Connolly; Margaret Haley; John Lamplugh; Evelyn Williams; Christine Deacon.
**OTHER INFORMATION** The grant total includes grants made to individuals, which were comprised of 31 educational grants totalling £22,500 and one social welfare grant of £500. Grants were awarded to 50 organisations.
**HOW TO APPLY** Apply in writing to the correspondent. The trustees meet bi-monthly to consider applications.
**WHO TO APPLY TO** John Lamplugh, Secretary, Stonehenge, 13 Laton Road, Hastings, East Sussex TN34 2ES Tel. 01424 431756

## ■ The BlackRock (UK) Charitable Trust

**CC NO** 1065447 **ESTABLISHED** 1999
**WHERE FUNDING CAN BE GIVEN** UK.
**WHO CAN BENEFIT** Charitable organisations.
**WHAT IS FUNDED** General charitable purposes.
**SAMPLE GRANTS** BlackRock Community Action Team, British Red Cross, Changing Faces, Eating Disorders Association and Cross, Ovarian Cancer Action and Women in Prison.
**FINANCES** Year 2013 Income £1,201 Grants £1,000 Grants to organisations £1,000
**TRUSTEES** Richard Royds; Andrew Johnston; Elizabeth Tracey; Peter Walker; BlackRock Group Limited.
**HOW TO APPLY** 'The trustees invite staff, clients and business associates of BlackRock Investment Management (UK) Limited to submit applications for grants to a registered charity of their choice.' Other appeals would usually be declined.
**WHO TO APPLY TO** Agnieszka Caban, Correspondent, BlackRock, 12 Throgmorton Avenue, London EC2N 2DL *Tel.* 020 7743 3000

## ■ The Blagrave Trust (formerly The Herbert and Peter Blagrave Charitable Trust)

**CC NO** 277074 **ESTABLISHED** 1978
**WHERE FUNDING CAN BE GIVEN** South of England with a preference for Hampshire, Wiltshire and Berkshire.
**WHO CAN BENEFIT** Registered charities only working in the geographical areas stated. Particular preference is given to those working in deprived areas, including isolated rural communities lacking transport links and employment opportunities. Applications for joint work and partnerships with other grant-makers are also welcomed.
**WHAT IS FUNDED** Primarily charities that work with children and young people. The areas that are funded are: working to reduce the numbers of NEET young people; outdoor education, with a developmental purpose; supporting disadvantaged and vulnerable young people. The trust's website states that is currently not accepting applications in the latter category as it is currently refining its work in this area, but applicants should check the website for updates. Particular focus is given to transition years, either between primary and secondary school, or between leaving school and beginning adult life. Applications are also welcomed for working with young people with disabilities or special needs, providing they fit into the above categories. The trust looks carefully at how work is monitored and prefers to fund charities which ensure that young people have input into the development, monitoring and improvement of activities. The website states that: 'we work to add value to our grants where we can, for example through supporting thematic learning, monitoring and evaluation, sector collaboration, expansion of proven initiatives or the piloting of new ideas'.
**WHAT IS NOT FUNDED** Capital grants or building projects; grants for more than 20% of a charity's total turnover; general recreational or social activities; work outside the counties specified above; grants for periods shorter than three years and one-off initiatives that cannot demonstrate sustained impact.

**TYPE OF GRANT** Funding is given for three year periods and no less. One-off and recurrent; core costs; project costs; evaluations or pilots; unrestricted funding.
**RANGE OF GRANTS** Between £10,000 and £100,000.
**SAMPLE GRANTS** Winchester Cathedral Trust (£200,000); Barnardo's (£61,300); Community First Wiltshire (£44,000); SkillForce and Young Epilepsy (£40,000 each); Future First (£25,000); Berkshire Carers (£20,000); Changing Tunes (£19,000); Injured Jockeys Fund (£15,000); Multiple Sclerosis Society and Youth Clubs Hampshire and Isle of Wight (£10,000 each); Queen Elizabeth Foundation for Disabled People (£5,000).
**FINANCES** Year 2013/14 Income £1,589,502 Grants £1,255,153 Grants to organisations £1,255,153 Assets £35,977,365
**TRUSTEES** Julian Whately; Timothy Jackson-Stops; Sir Paul Neave; Diana Leat.
**OTHER INFORMATION** 44 grants were made to organisations in 2013/14. The trust is also working in partnership with community foundations in the beneficiary areas and made grants of £72,500 each to Berkshire Community Foundation, Hampshire and Isle of Wight Community Foundation and The Community Foundation for Wiltshire and Swindon, and a grant of £100,000 to Sussex Community Foundation.
**HOW TO APPLY** Initial applications should be made by completing the outline proposal form on the website, with a brief description of the project in fewer than 200 words. The trust will then contact applicants within one month to inform them whether their application is to receive further consideration and, if so, to discuss further details. Applicants who are eligible at this stage will then be required to complete a full application form, which is brought to trustees for review at a meeting in March, July or November. Full funding guidelines and criteria are provided on the trust's website.
**WHO TO APPLY TO** Jo Wells, Executive Director, c/o Rathbone Trust Company Limited, 1 Curzon Street, London W1J 5FB *Tel.* 020 7399 0370 *email* grants@blagravetrust.org *Website* www.blagravetrust.org

## ■ The Blair Foundation

**CC NO** 801755 **ESTABLISHED** 1989
**WHERE FUNDING CAN BE GIVEN** UK, particularly southern England and Scotland; overseas.
**WHO CAN BENEFIT** Organisations, particularly disability and wildlife groups.
**WHAT IS FUNDED** General charitable purposes, especially conservation and protection of the environment; improving disability access to wildlife areas; and medical charities.
**WHAT IS NOT FUNDED** Charities that have objectives which the trustees consider harmful to the environment are not supported.
**RANGE OF GRANTS** Up to £12,000.
**SAMPLE GRANTS** Previous beneficiaries have included: Ayrshire Wildlife Services (£12,000); King's School – Canterbury and Ayrshire Fiddler Orchestra (£10,000 each); Scottish National Trust (£7,000); Home Farm Trust (£5,000); CHAS (£2,000); Penny Brohn Cancer Care (£1,500); Ro-Ro Sailing Project and Sustrans (£1,000 each).
**FINANCES** Year 2013/14 Income £14,446 Grants £65,000 Grants to organisations £65,000
**TRUSTEES** Robert Thornton; Jennifer Thornton; Graham Healy.

**OTHER INFORMATION** Accounts were received at the Charity Commission but due to the charity's low income, were not published online.
**HOW TO APPLY** Apply in writing to the correspondent, for consideration at trustees' meetings held at least once a year. A receipt for donations is requested from all donees.
**WHO TO APPLY TO** The Trustees, Smith and Williamson, 1 Bishops Wharf, Walnut Tree Close, Guildford, Surrey GU1 4RA *Tel.* 01483 407100

## ■ Blakemore Foundation

**CC NO** 1015938     **ESTABLISHED** 1992
**WHERE FUNDING CAN BE GIVEN** England and Wales
**WHO CAN BENEFIT** The trust supports local and national charitable organisations.
**WHAT IS FUNDED** General charitable purposes.
**WHAT IS NOT FUNDED** Salaries; national charities (unless directly requested by an employee of A. F. Blakemore); individuals, including students; organisations outside England and Wales; overseas appeals; expeditions or overseas travel; sponsorship and marketing promotions; endowment funds; political donations.
**TYPE OF GRANT** One-off.
**RANGE OF GRANTS** Up to £200.
**SAMPLE GRANTS Previous beneficiaries have included:** Foundation for Conductive Education; St Andrew's Church – Biggleswade and Wenlock Poetry Festival.
**FINANCES** *Year* 2013/14 *Income* £172,516 *Grants* £68,857 *Grants to organisations* £68,857 *Assets* £51,687
**TRUSTEES** Peter Blakemore; Gwendoline Blakemore; Ita McAuley.
**HOW TO APPLY** Applications should be made on a form available to download from the trust's website, along with criteria and guidelines. The foundation's Community Affairs Officer may be contacted for further information.
**WHO TO APPLY TO** Kate Senter, Community Affairs Officer, A. F. Blakemore and Sons Ltd, Longacre, Willenhall WV13 2JP *Tel.* 0121 568 2910 *email* ksenter@afblakemore.com *Website* www.afblakemore.com

## ■ The Blanchminster Trust

**CC NO** 202118     **ESTABLISHED** 1421
**WHERE FUNDING CAN BE GIVEN** The parishes of Bude, Stratton and Poughill (i.e. the former urban district of Bude-Stratton on 31 March 1974).
**WHO CAN BENEFIT** Organisations or individuals residing in the area of benefit and showing proof of financial need.
**WHAT IS FUNDED** Charities working in the fields of education, community aid or social welfare, as well as locally resident individuals in need in such areas.
**WHAT IS NOT FUNDED** Applications from Bude-Stratton only will be considered. For educational applications, students who have at least one parent resident in the beneficiary area or are current or recent past pupils of Budehaven School may be eligible.
**TYPE OF GRANT** Cash grant or equipment, or a loan of cash or equipment. Funding will be considered for one year or less.
**SAMPLE GRANTS** Sound Waves South West (£11,000 in total); Stratton Play Area Regeneration Committee (£10,000); Marhamchurch Village Hall (£5,000); Stratton Primary School (£7,000); St Michael and All Angels Church (£5,500); Bude Nippers (£5,000); Bude Jujitsu Club (£4,000); Bude Cricket Club (£3,000); Pathfields (£800); Bude Youth Centre (£500); Bude After School Club (£300).
**FINANCES** *Year* 2013 *Income* £510,022 *Grants* £317,391 *Grants to organisations* £64,880 *Assets* £10,620,922
**TRUSTEES** Christopher Cornish; John Gardiner; Wilfred Keat; Valerie Newman; Chris Nichols; Gordon Rogers; Byron Rowlands; Julia Shepherd; Leonard Tozer; Owen May; Ian Whitfield; Michael Worden; Christine Bilsland.
**OTHER INFORMATION** 18 organisations received grants in 2013/14.
**HOW TO APPLY** Apply in writing to the correspondent. Organisations are also required to provide the latest annual accounts and an updated financial statement. Applicants may be called for an informal interview by the relevant committee. A recommendation is then made to the full board of trustees who make the final decision. Applications are considered at monthly meetings. All applications are acknowledged. Guidelines and criteria are available to view on the trust's website.
**WHO TO APPLY TO** Mrs J. E. Bunning, The Clerk to the Trustees, Blanchminster Building, 38 Lansdown Road, Bude, Cornwall EX23 8EE *Tel.* 01288 352851 *email* office@blanchminster.plus.com *Website* www.blanchminster.org.uk

## ■ The Blandford Lake Trust

**CC NO** 1069630     **ESTABLISHED** 1998
**WHERE FUNDING CAN BE GIVEN** North Wales and overseas.
**WHO CAN BENEFIT** Registered charities.
**WHAT IS FUNDED** Overseas development, church outreach work, Christian youth work, educational resources.
**SAMPLE GRANTS** Previously: Operation Smile (£37,000); Send a Cow (£10,500); Responding to Conflict (£10,000); Traidcraft (£8,000); Mission Aviation Fellowship (£5,000); and Christian Solidarity Worldwide (£2,000).
**FINANCES** *Year* 2014 *Income* £1,070 *Grants* £150,000 *Grants to organisations* £150,000
**TRUSTEES** Lucy Lake; Richard Lake; Jonathan Lake; Mathew Lake.
**OTHER INFORMATION** Accounts were received at the Commission but not published due to the charity's low income. We have estimated the grant total.
**HOW TO APPLY** Apply in writing to the correspondent including budgets and accounts. Only applications from eligible bodies will be acknowledged.
**WHO TO APPLY TO** Lucy Lake, The Courts, Park Street, Denbigh, Denbighshire LL16 3DE *Tel.* 01745 813174

## ■ The Sir Victor Blank Charitable Settlement

**CC NO** 1084187     **ESTABLISHED** 2000
**WHERE FUNDING CAN BE GIVEN** Worldwide
**WHO CAN BENEFIT** Jewish organisations and other registered charities.
**WHAT IS FUNDED** Jewish causes and general charitable purposes.
**SAMPLE GRANTS** Oxford Philomusica (£35,000); United Jewish Israel Appeal (£25,000); Well-being for Women (£13,000); Community Security Trust and Norwood Ravenswood

# Blatchington

(£15,000 each); Forward Thinking and Holocaust Education Trust (£10,000 each); Hop, Skip and Jump and Nightingale Hammerson (£5,000 each); University of Nottingham (£2,500); The Holocaust Centre (£2,000); Listening Books and The Throat Cancer Foundation (£1,000 each).

**FINANCES** Year 2013/14 Income £37,136 Grants £203,650 Grants to organisations £203,650 Assets £2,082,801

**TRUSTEES** Sir Maurice Blank; Lady Sylvia Blank; Simon Blank.

**OTHER INFORMATION** Other grants of less than £1,000 totalled nearly £11,000.

**HOW TO APPLY** Apply in writing to the correspondent.

**WHO TO APPLY TO** The Trustees, c/o Wilkins Kennedy, Bridge House, London Bridge, London SE1 9QR Tel. 020 7403 1877 email enquiries@sirvictorblankcharitablesettlement.com

## ■ Blatchington Court Trust

**CC NO** 306350     **ESTABLISHED** 1966

**WHERE FUNDING CAN BE GIVEN** UK, preference for Sussex.

**WHO CAN BENEFIT** Charities and other bodies in the field of education, training and personal development for the under 30 age group who are visually impaired. Grants are also made to individuals with a visual impairment in Sussex.

**WHAT IS FUNDED** To provide funding for the education of children and young people under 30 years of age with visual impairment. The trust's grants programme awards funding for: the provision of recreational and leisure facilities (or contributions towards such facilities), which enable vision impaired people to develop their physical, mental and moral capacities; any voluntary or charitable organisation approved by the trustees, the objects of which include the promotion of education, training and/or employment of vision impaired young people and their general well-being in pursuance of all the foregoing.

**WHAT IS NOT FUNDED** Applications for grants for research or salaries of workers in sister charities are not favoured.

**TYPE OF GRANT** One-off capital grants.

**RANGE OF GRANTS** Most under £3,000.

**FINANCES** Year 2013/14 Income £506,077 Grants £96,029 Grants to organisations £45,200 Assets £12,455,563

**TRUSTEES** Richard Martin, Chair; Alison Acason; Daniel Ellman-Brown; Georgina James; Roger Jones; Stephen Pavey; Anna Hunter; Jonathan Wilson; Martin Reith Murdoch.

**OTHER INFORMATION** The grant total includes 155 grants awarded to individuals, totalling £50,800.

**HOW TO APPLY** Applications should be made on a form available from the correspondent and downloaded from the trust's website, and should include costed proposals and confirm that any other finance required is in place or promised. For further information, applicants should contact Alison Evans by telephone on 01273 727222 or by email at alison@blatchingtoncourt.org.uk

**WHO TO APPLY TO** Alison Evans, Executive Manager, 6A Hove Park Villas, Hove, East Sussex BN3 6HW Tel. 01273 727222 Fax 01273 722144 email info@blatchingtoncourt.org.uk Website www.blatchingtoncourt.org.uk

## ■ Bloodwise (previously known as Leukaemia and Lymphoma Research)

**CC NO** 216032/SC037529     **ESTABLISHED** 1960

**WHERE FUNDING CAN BE GIVEN** UK.

**WHO CAN BENEFIT** Hospitals; university medical centres; medical professionals; academics; medical research projects.

**WHAT IS FUNDED** Research into leukaemia, lymphoma and related conditions. The charity supports specialist programmes, clinical trials, research projects and academic training and career development.

**TYPE OF GRANT** Equipment; feasibility studies; recurring costs; research; salaries.

**RANGE OF GRANTS** £2,000–£3 million.

**SAMPLE GRANTS** University of Birmingham (£3.7 million); University of Oxford (£3.3 million); University of Newcastle (£2 million); Institute of Cancer Research (£1.6 million); Derriford Combined Laboratories (£219,000); Addenbrookes Hospital (£129,000); The Babraham Institute (£120,000); London Hammersmith (£45,000); The University of Manchester (£33,000); St James's University Hospital (£2,000).

**FINANCES** Year 2013/14 Income £21,656,000 Grants £23,032,000 Grants to organisations £23,032,000 Assets £11,348,000

**TRUSTEES** Peter Burrell; Mike Williams; Maria Clarke; John Reeve; Lesley Lee; Charles Metcalfe; Jeremy Bird; Pelham Allen; Suzanna Floyd; Simon Guild; Michael Prescott.

**OTHER INFORMATION** Awards were made to 25 institutions. Most of the awards were made in the South East (49%), followed by Midlands (15%). According to the charity's website, following the most recent funding round in February 2015 a total of 16 awards were made totalling approximately £9 million.

**HOW TO APPLY** All applications for all forms of funding must be submitted via the fund's online application system. See the website for details on the application and decision process as well as submission deadlines. The website notes: 'Every year we receive more than 200 applications for funding from researchers at universities and hospitals across the UK. We only support the most original and innovative research, which will truly benefit patients affected by leukaemia, lymphoma, myeloma and related blood disorders.' Note: 'Applicants for all specialist programmes [and some of career development awards] **must** contact the Research Director, Professor Chris Bunce via Sara Darling at sdarling@beatingbloodcancers.org.uk or on 020 7405 0101, before any application can be considered.' Applicants for clinical trial awards 'are asked to contact the Research Office, via Emil Kazounis at ekazounis@beatingbloodcancers.org.uk, before any application can be considered'.

**WHO TO APPLY TO** Catherine Gilman, Chief Executive and Company Secretary, 39–40 Eagle Street, London WC1R 4TH Tel. 020 7405 0101 email info@beatbloodcancers.org Website www.beatbloodcancers.org

## ■ The Bloom Foundation

**CC NO** 1140213     **ESTABLISHED** 2011

**WHERE FUNDING CAN BE GIVEN** Camden, Israel and financially developing countries.

**WHO CAN BENEFIT** Organisations.

**WHAT IS FUNDED** General charitable purposes, including: health; education; social welfare; children; and Jewish organisations.

**RANGE OF GRANTS** Most grants appear to be of less than £5,000, though a number of larger grants are also made.

**SAMPLE GRANTS** Albion in the Community (£321,500); Optimus Foundation (£125,000); Action Aid (£105,000); Jewish Care and Lancing College (£100,000 each); Save the Children (£80,000); World Jewish Relief (£75,000); Kick 4 Life (£50,000); Soft Power Education (£28,000); Missing People and St Mungo's (£25,000 each); Elem – Youth in Distress (£15,000); St Vincent's Foundation (£5,000).

**FINANCES** Year 2013/14 Income £2,886,612 Grants £2,727,387 Grants to organisations £2,727,387 Assets £302,578

**TRUSTEES** Marc Sugarman; Adam Franks; Tony Bloom; Linda Bloom; Marcelle Lester.

**OTHER INFORMATION** Recipients of 'smaller' grants received a total of £670,500. Grants were distributed for the following purposes: Welfare (£917,000); Education (£853,000); Healthcare/ awareness (£841,500); Other (£108,500); Sport (£7,500).

**HOW TO APPLY** Apply in writing to the correspondent, although potential applicants should note that the foundation's annual report also states that 'the trustees have selected a number of projects which they wish to support, and have been guided in this by a committee of staff members of Star Lizard Consulting Ltd'.

**WHO TO APPLY TO** Marcelle Lester, Trustee, c/o Star Lizard Consulting Ltd, Iceworks, 34–36 Jamestown Road, London NW1 7BY email info@thebloomfoundation.com

## ■ The Bluston Charitable Settlement

**CC NO** 256691     **ESTABLISHED** 1968
**WHERE FUNDING CAN BE GIVEN** Mostly UK.
**WHO CAN BENEFIT** Registered charities, particularly Jewish organisations.
**WHAT IS FUNDED** General charitable purposes, particularly education, welfare and medical.
**WHAT IS NOT FUNDED** Individuals.
**RANGE OF GRANTS** £5,000 to £100,000.
**SAMPLE GRANTS** Shaarei Torah Fund (£75,000); British Friends of Bet Medrash Gevoha, (£50,000); (£40,000); Norwood (£30,000); Gateshead Talmudical College and The Langdon Foundation (£25,000 each); Holocaust Educational Trust (£20,000); Camden Physiotherapy Unit and Jewish Council for Racial Equality (£10,000 each); Maccabi GB (£5,000).
**FINANCES** Year 2013/14 Income £778,857 Grants £667,500 Grants to organisations £667,500 Assets £8,511,158
**TRUSTEES** Daniel Dover; Martin Paisner.
**OTHER INFORMATION** The trust has a list of regular beneficiaries.
**HOW TO APPLY** Apply in writing to the correspondent. The trustees meet annually in the spring.
**WHO TO APPLY TO** Martin Paisner, Trustee, c/o Prism Gift Fund, 20 Gloucester Place, London W1U 8HA Tel. 020 7486 7760 email info@prismthegiftfund.co.uk

## ■ The Nicholas Boas Charitable Trust

**CC NO** 1073359     **ESTABLISHED** 1998
**WHERE FUNDING CAN BE GIVEN** Worldwide.
**WHO CAN BENEFIT** Educational institutions, charities and other organisations connected with the arts.
**WHAT IS FUNDED** Education, performing and visual arts.
**TYPE OF GRANT** One-off.
**SAMPLE GRANTS** IMS Prussia Cove, English National Opera, Gabrieli Consort, Music Theatre Wales, Bampton Opera, Opera Danube, Ryedale Festival, Oxford Lieder Festival, Solent Music Festival, Tresanton Festival, Peasmarsh Festival, Wye Valley Festival, Leeds Lieder Festival. Small grants were also made to 22 young musicians to fund travel to auditions, vocal coaching, masterclasses.
**FINANCES** Year 2013/14 Income £32,326 Grants £39,474 Grants to organisations £39,474 Assets £390,653
**TRUSTEES** Robert Boas; Christopher Boas; Helena Boas; Elizabeth Boas.
**OTHER INFORMATION** Grants include travel scholarships for students of architecture.
**HOW TO APPLY** Apply in writing to the correspondent.
**WHO TO APPLY TO** Robert Boas, Trustee, 22 Mansfield Street, London W1G 9NR Tel. 020 7436 0344 email boas22million@btinternet.com Website www.nicholasboastrust.org.uk

## ■ The Marjory Boddy Charitable Trust

**CC NO** 1091356     **ESTABLISHED** 2002
**WHERE FUNDING CAN BE GIVEN** UK, with a preference for North West England.
**WHO CAN BENEFIT** Organisations and individuals.
**WHAT IS FUNDED** General charitable purposes.
**SAMPLE GRANTS** Brathay Trust, Motability, Nightingale House Hospice – Wrexham, Chance to Shine, the Christie Charitable Fund and Chester Mystery Plays.
**FINANCES** Year 2013/14 Income £108,679 Grants £93,000 Grants to organisations £93,000 Assets £3,149,877
**TRUSTEES** Revd Canon Christopher Samuels; Edward Walton; Richard Raymond.
**HOW TO APPLY** Apply in writing to the correspondent.
**WHO TO APPLY TO** Karen Welch, Correspondent, c/o Cullimore Dutton Solicitors, 20 White Friars, Chester CH1 1XS Tel. 01244 356789 Fax 01244 312582 email info@cullimoredutton.co.uk

## ■ The Body Shop Foundation

**CC NO** 802757     **ESTABLISHED** 1990
**WHERE FUNDING CAN BE GIVEN** UK and overseas.
**WHO CAN BENEFIT** Organisations at the forefront of social and environmental change; groups with little hope of conventional funding; projects working to increase public awareness.
**WHAT IS FUNDED** Grants are given to innovative, grassroots organisations working in the field of human and civil rights, and environmental and animal protection.
**WHAT IS NOT FUNDED** As the majority of applications come from projects nominated by staff, the foundation does not ask for public applications or nominations. Nor does it: sponsor individuals; fund sporting activities or the arts; sponsor or support fundraising events, receptions or conferences.

**TYPE OF GRANT** One-off and recurring grants.
**RANGE OF GRANTS** £3,000–£60,000
**SAMPLE GRANTS** Foundation for Australia's Most Endangered Species Ltd, Australia (£62,000); Orangutan Foundation, Indonesia (£42,000); 1001 Fontaines Pour Demain, Cambodia (£30,000); International Gender Studies Centre (£23,000); Environmental Investigation Agency (£15,000); Book-Cycle, UK (£6,400); the Foodbank, Worthing (£5,000); Centro Canino, Spain (£4,800); Seeds of Diversity, Canada (£3,800); Look Good, Feel Better and New Zealand (£3,700 each).
**FINANCES** Year 2013/14 Income £1,523,675 Grants £903,483 Grants to organisations £903,483 Assets £644,887
**TRUSTEES** Andrew Radford; Bhupendra Mistry; Paul Sanderson, R. Godfrey; Andrew Wade; Jason Matthews; Mark Davies; Jill Cochrane; Guy Culquhoun; Paolo Sala.
**OTHER INFORMATION** Grants were given to 206 organisations in 2013/14.
**HOW TO APPLY** The foundation does not accept unsolicited applications. The trustees research projects which meet their funding criteria and only then invite organisations to make an application.
**WHO TO APPLY TO** Lisa Jackson, Correspondent, The Body Shop, Watersmead Business Park, Littlehampton, West Sussex BN17 6LS *Tel.* 01903 844039 *email* bodyshopfoundation@thebodyshop.com *Website* thebodyshopfoundation.org

## ■ The Boltini Trust

**CC NO** 1123129    **ESTABLISHED** 2008
**WHERE FUNDING CAN BE GIVEN** UK, with a particular focus on Surrey and West Sussex. Some international support.
**WHO CAN BENEFIT** Charitable organisations.
**WHAT IS FUNDED** General including education, medical, disaster relief, international development, music and the disadvantaged.
**WHAT IS NOT FUNDED** Individuals.
**SAMPLE GRANTS** The Sussex Community Foundation (£200,000); The Britten – Pears Foundation and Worldwide Volunteering for Young People (£20,000 each); Music Theatre Wales (£15,000); Breast Cancer Haven (£7,500); Church Housing Trust, Reach Volunteering and Samaritans (£5,000 each); Prospect Burma (£3,500); Beachy Head Chaplaincy Team and The Blood Pressure Association (£2,500 each).
**FINANCES** Year 2013/14 Income £695,666 Grants £642,843 Grants to organisations £642,843 Assets £9,840,327
**TRUSTEES** Anthony Bolton; Sarah Bolton; James Nelson; Emma Nelson; Oliver Bolton; Benjamin Bolton.
**HOW TO APPLY** Initial enquiries should be made in writing to the correspondent. The trustees meet twice a year to consider applications. Successful applicants may be visited.
**WHO TO APPLY TO** Anthony Bolton, Trustee, Woolbeding Glebe, Woolbeding, Midhurst, West Sussex GU29 9RR *email* boltinitrust@gmail.com

## ■ The Bonamy Charitable Trust

**CC NO** 326424    **ESTABLISHED** 1983
**WHERE FUNDING CAN BE GIVEN** UK and overseas, with a preference for North-West England.
**WHO CAN BENEFIT** Charitable organisations.
**WHAT IS FUNDED** Jewish causes and general charitable purposes.
**RANGE OF GRANTS** Up to £17,000.
**SAMPLE GRANTS** South Manchester Synagogue (£25,000); The Fed (£10,000); King David School (£6,000); Agudat Ahavat Israel Synagogue (£2,000).
**FINANCES** Year 2013 Income £163,603 Grants £110,884 Grants to organisations £110,884 Assets £403,194
**TRUSTEES** Mr M. Moryoussef; James Moryoussef; Robert Moryoussef.
**OTHER INFORMATION** The total grant figure includes amounts for both individuals and organisations.
**HOW TO APPLY** Apply in writing to the correspondent.
**WHO TO APPLY TO** Mr M. Moryoussef, Trustees, Flat 2, Forrest Hills, South Downs Road, Bowdon, Altrincham, Cheshire WA14 3HD *Tel.* 01706 345868

## ■ The Charlotte Bonham-Carter Charitable Trust

**CC NO** 292839    **ESTABLISHED** 1985
**WHERE FUNDING CAN BE GIVEN** UK, with some emphasis on Hampshire.
**WHO CAN BENEFIT** Registered charities.
**WHAT IS FUNDED** General charitable purposes which were of particular concern to Lady Charlotte Bonham-Carter during her lifetime or are within the county of Hampshire. 'The trustees continue to support a core number of charities to whom they have made grants in the past as well as reviewing all applications received and making grants to new charities within their grant-giving criteria.'
**WHAT IS NOT FUNDED** Individuals; non-registered charities.
**TYPE OF GRANT** One-off grants.
**RANGE OF GRANTS** £500–£10,000
**SAMPLE GRANTS** National Trust (£10,000); Ashmolean Museum of Art and Archaeology (£8,000); Royal Academy Schools (£4,000); Providence Row (£3,000); Chelsea Physic Garden (£2,000); Cavell Nurses' Trust, Cherubim Music Trust, Demand, The Furniture History Society and The Old Vic (£1,000 each); Plant Heritage (£500).
**FINANCES** Year 2013/14 Income £135,573 Grants £97,775 Grants to organisations £97,775 Assets £4,835,682
**TRUSTEES** Sir Matthew Farrer; David Bonham-Carter; Eliza Bonham-Carter; Georgina Nayler.
**HOW TO APPLY** Apply in writing to the correspondent. There are no application forms. The application should include details of the funds required, funds raised so far and the timescale involved. The trust states that: 'unsolicited general applications are unlikely to be successful and only increase the cost of administration. The trustees meet in January and July; applications need to be received by May or November.'
**WHO TO APPLY TO** Jenny Cannon, Correspondent, Chelwood, Rectory Road, East Carleton, Norwich NR14 8HT *Tel.* 01508 571230

## ■ The Linda and Gordon Bonnyman Charitable Trust

**CC NO** 1123441    **ESTABLISHED** 2008
**WHERE FUNDING CAN BE GIVEN** UK and the USA.
**WHO CAN BENEFIT** Registered charities.
**WHAT IS FUNDED** General charitable purposes.
**SAMPLE GRANTS** Hospice in the Weald £15,000); Aspire Fundraising, Blond McIndoe Research Foundation and Reach Volunteering (£5,000 each);

**FINANCES** Year 2013/14 Income £8,468
Grants £160,000 Grants to organisations £160,000
**TRUSTEES** James Gordon Bonnyman; Linda Bonnyman; James Wallace Taylor Bonnyman.
**OTHER INFORMATION** Accounts were received at the Charity Commission but not published online due to the charity's low income.
**HOW TO APPLY** Apply in writing to the correspondent.
**WHO TO APPLY TO** Linda Bonnyman, Trustee, Ely Grange, Bells Yew Green Road, Frant, Tunbridge Wells, East Sussex TN3 9DY *Tel.* 01732 450744 *email* da@csw-uk.com

## ■ The Boodle & Dunthorne Charitable Trust

**CC NO** 1077748 **ESTABLISHED** 1999
**WHERE FUNDING CAN BE GIVEN** UK.
**WHO CAN BENEFIT** Registered charities and voluntary organisations.
**WHAT IS FUNDED** General charitable purposes.
**TYPE OF GRANT** One-off.
**RANGE OF GRANTS** £250–£55,000
**SAMPLE GRANTS** Shining Faces in India (£55,000); Rainbow Trust (£48,500); The Message Trust (£15,000).
**FINANCES** Year 2013/14 Income £206,172 Grants £149,540 Grants to organisations £149,540 Assets £444,759
**TRUSTEES** Nicholas Wainwright; Michael Wainwright.
**OTHER INFORMATION** Established in 1999 this is the charitable trust of Boodles, a family jewellers based in North West England.
**HOW TO APPLY** Apply in writing to the correspondent.
**WHO TO APPLY TO** Nicholas Wainwright, Correspondent, Boodle & Dunthorne, 35 Lord Street, Liverpool L2 9SQ *Tel.* 0151 224 0580

## ■ BOOST Charitable Trust

**CC NO** 1111961 **ESTABLISHED** 2005
**WHERE FUNDING CAN BE GIVEN** UK and overseas; 'the principal focus is in the UK but is extended to other countries where there are areas of significant disadvantage'.
**WHO CAN BENEFIT** Registered charities; not-for-profit organisations involved in sports and aiding individuals with disabilities or socially and economically disadvantaged people.
**WHAT IS FUNDED** Advancement of health; sports and physical education; assistance to people with disabilities, special needs and otherwise disadvantaged individuals whose sporting talents have been overlooked.
**WHAT IS NOT FUNDED** Only charities or non-profit making organisations with a focus on sport can be supported.
**TYPE OF GRANT** One-off and up to one year; scholarships; inter-continental cultural exchanges, visits and partnerships; projects. The majority awards are larger grants for long term initiatives.
**RANGE OF GRANTS** Up to £19,400; small awards – under £500.
**SAMPLE GRANTS** Boccia England (£19,400); Southwark City Tennis Club (£9,800); Cumbria Youth Alliance, Swaziland and Westminster Befriend A Family (£9,000 each); CP Sport – Football (£6,000); Plymouth College and Wheelpower (£5,000 each); Amputee Games/Limbpower (£4,000); Disability Snowsport UK (£2,000); Be Strong Project (£900). Small awards totalled £12,900.

**FINANCES** Year 2012/13 Income £72,587 Grants £107,954 Grants to organisations £107,954 Assets £1,138,724
**TRUSTEES** Robert Houston; Rachel Booth; Alurie Dutton; Oliver Bartrum.
**OTHER INFORMATION** The trust aims to **B**uild **O**n **O**verlooked **S**porting **T**alent. All of its activities, are designed to 'champion the disabled and disadvantaged and to inspire them to overcome their challenges through the power of sport'. There were at least 15 awards made during the year. At the time of writing (June 2015) this was the latest information available.
**HOW TO APPLY** Applicants should send or email a letter (no more than two sides of A4) outlining the following: name of the organisation; main activities and beneficiaries; why they need funding; details of the project and approximate funding requirements. The trustees meet quarterly to consider grants and it may take up to two months to proceed the appeal. You may be awarded a small grant (up to £500) or your proposal may be taken for further consideration for larger awards. The website notes: 'The Trust receives many more requests for funding than we are able to support, and we regret that we have to turn down many good proposals even though they meet our criteria.'
**WHO TO APPLY TO** Lucy Till, Correspondent, 5 St Bride Street, London EC4A 4AS *Tel.* 020 7078 1955 *email* lucy.till@boostct.org *Website* www.boostct.org

## ■ The Booth Charities

**CC NO** 221800 **ESTABLISHED** 1963
**WHERE FUNDING CAN BE GIVEN** Salford.
**WHO CAN BENEFIT** Organisations supporting the inhabitants of the City of Salford, especially older people.
**WHAT IS FUNDED** General charitable purposes; relief in need; social welfare; education; health; aid to older people, including payments of pensions and provision of almshouses; facilities for recreation and leisure.
**TYPE OF GRANT** Capital and revenue funding; salaries; one-off and up to three years.
**RANGE OF GRANTS** £100–£30,500; small grants up to £1,500.
**SAMPLE GRANTS** RECLAIM Project Ltd (£30,500); Macmillan Cancer Support (£20,000); The Magnus Mowat Bursary (£15,000); Ordsall Community Allotment Society (£12,500); The Manchester YMCA and Wood Street Mission (£10,000 each); St Michael's and All Angels Parochial Church Council (£9,900); Salford Mayoral Appeal and The Prince's Trust Fairbridge Programme (£5,000 each); Seedley and Langworthy in Bloom (£3,000); Elizabeth Prout Centre (£2,500); Age UK Salford (£800); Salford Cathedral Youth Group (£750); University of Salford (£500); Height Veterans Bowling Club and Manchester University Guild of Change Ringers (£100 each).
**FINANCES** Year 2012/13 Income £964,000 Grants £320,630 Grants to organisations £319,140 Assets £31,783,000
**TRUSTEES** William Whittle; David Tully; Richard Kershaw; Edward Hunt; Roger Weston; Michael Prior; John Willis; Alan Dewhurst; Richard Fildes; Jonathan Shelmerdine.
**OTHER INFORMATION** At the time of writing (June 2015) this was the latest information available. The charity consists of Humphrey Booth the Elder's Charity and the Charity of Humphrey Booth the Grandson. According to the latest accounts, the trustees had set a budget

distribution of £540,000 for 2013/14. The charity provides both responsive and accredited grants. Awards to 19 individuals totalled £1,500. Grant were allocated as follows: relief of distress and sickness (14 awards); educational facilities (6 awards); recreation and leisure (7 awards); other (10 awards); relief of older, infirm or poor people (25 awards).

**HOW TO APPLY** Applications may be made in writing to the correspondent.

**WHO TO APPLY TO** Jonathan Aldersley, Clerk to the Trustees, c/o Butcher and Barlow LLP, 3 Royal Mews, Gadbrook Road, Northwich, Cheshire CW9 7UD *Tel.* 01606 334309 *email* jaldersley@butcher-barlow.co.uk

## ■ Boots Charitable Trust

**CC NO** 1045927   **ESTABLISHED** 1971

**WHERE FUNDING CAN BE GIVEN** Nottinghamshire and Nottingham.

**WHO CAN BENEFIT** Charitable organisations benefitting people who live in Nottinghamshire.

**WHAT IS FUNDED** Health: community healthcare such as community healthcare services, home care, after care, relief of people who have disabilities, a medical condition and continuing care; and health education and prevention by promoting knowledge and awareness of specific diseases and medical conditions. Lifelong learning: helping people of any age to achieve their educational potential, supporting supplementary schools, literacy and numeracy projects, community education, vocational/restart education for the unemployed and alternative education for excluded school pupils. Community development: helping groups to organise and respond to problems and needs in their communities or networks. This could include groups such as Councils for Voluntary Services and self-help groups. Social care including: personal social services – organisations assisting individuals or families to overcome social deprivation, such as people who are homeless or have disabilities and their carers, lone parent and childcare groups and other family support groups; social preventive schemes – activities preventing crime, dropping out and general delinquency and providing other social care outreach work, social health and safety awareness schemes and so on; and community social activity – activities to promote social engagement for vulnerable people, mitigating against isolation and loneliness. 'We are especially interested in projects with the capacity to deliver significant impact and which reach the greatest number of people.'

**WHAT IS NOT FUNDED** Projects benefitting people outside Nottinghamshire; individuals; organisations which are not registered charities and which have income or expenditure of more than £5,000 per year; charities seeking funds to redistribute to other charities; projects for which there is a legal statutory obligation or which replace statutory funding.

**RANGE OF GRANTS** Up to £10,000.

**SAMPLE GRANTS** Groundwork Greater Nottingham (£15,000); Base 51 and Newark and Nottinghamshire Child Bereavement and Loss Centre and Survivors Helping Each Other (£10,000 each); Home Start Newark (£8,200); Age UK Nottinghamshire and Pintsize Theatre Limited (£7,000 each); Bassetlaw CVS (£6,300); Malt Cross Trust Company, Spring Nottingham and St Ann's Allotments (£5,000 each).

**FINANCES** *Year* 2013/14 *Income* £272,827 *Grants* £250,205 *Grants to organisations* £250,205 *Assets* £273

**TRUSTEES** Oonagh Turnbull; Alison Hands; Judith Lyons; Richard Burbidge; Helen Jeremiah; Michael Bradshaw; Lavinia Moxley

**OTHER INFORMATION** The trust made 40 grants totalling £250,000 during the year.

**HOW TO APPLY** Application forms and guidelines are available from the trust's website or can be requested by post. Completed forms should be sent to the correspondent with the latest annual report and accounts. For applications over £2,000 the deadlines are on the 7th of February, April, June, August, October and December. These applications take between two and four months to process. There is no deadline for applications under £2,000, and these take between one and two months to be processed.

**WHO TO APPLY TO** Caroline Ward, Correspondent, Boots UK Limited, 1698 Melton Road, Rearsby, Leicester LE7 4YR *Tel.* 0115 959 1285 *email* Julie.Lawrence@boots.co.uk *Website* www.boots-uk.com/corporate_social_responsibility/community/boots-charitable-trust.aspx

## ■ Salo Bordon Charitable Trust

**CC NO** 266439   **ESTABLISHED** 1973

**WHERE FUNDING CAN BE GIVEN** UK and worldwide.

**WHO CAN BENEFIT** Organisations, primarily Jewish.

**WHAT IS FUNDED** Religious education and social welfare.

**SAMPLE GRANTS** Previous beneficiaries have included: Agudas Israel Housing Association Ltd, Baer Hatorah, Beth Jacob Grammar School, Brisk Yeshivas, Golders Green Beth Hamedrash Congregation Jaffa Institute, Jewish Learning Exchange, London Academy of Jewish Studies, Society of Friends of Torah and WST Charity.

**FINANCES** *Year* 2013/14 *Income* £152,856 *Grants* £218,482 *Grants to organisations* £218,482 *Assets* £7,342,738

**TRUSTEES** Marcel Bordon; Salo Bordon; Lilly Bordon.

**HOW TO APPLY** Apply in writing to the correspondent.

**WHO TO APPLY TO** Marcel Bordon, Trustee, 39 Gresham Gardens, London NW11 8PA *Tel.* 020 8458 6622

## ■ The Bordon Liphook Haslemere Charity (formerly The Bordon and Liphook Charity)

**CC NO** 1032428   **ESTABLISHED** 1994

**WHERE FUNDING CAN BE GIVEN** Bordon, Liphook, Haslemere and surrounding areas, Hampshire.

**WHO CAN BENEFIT** Organisations and individuals.

**WHAT IS FUNDED** General charitable purposes.

**WHAT IS NOT FUNDED** Non-priority loans.

**TYPE OF GRANT** Cash or loan.

**SAMPLE GRANTS** British Kidney Patient Association; Breast Cancer Campaign; British Red Cross; Bordon Day Care Unit; Bordon Infants School; Cranstoun Drug Services Crossways Counselling; East Hants Advocacy Scheme (EHAS); Senior Luncheon Club Liphook (SCLC); St Francis Church; St John Ambulance; Stroke Association and Weyford County Junior School.

**FINANCES** *Year* 2013 *Income* £148,235 *Grants* £100,000 *Grants to organisations* £100,000

*Alphabetical register of grant-making charities* — **Bothwell**

**TRUSTEES** Toni Shaw; Jennie Vernon-Smith; Seona Rivett; Alison Bedford; Alan Finn; Michael Gallagher; Vanessa Moss.
**OTHER INFORMATION** Although the accounts were received by the Commission, they had not been published online. The annual report and accounts published on the funder's website was for the previous year. We estimate the total grants awarded in 2013 to be in the region of £100,000.
**HOW TO APPLY** Apply on a form available to download, together with criteria and guidelines, from the website. Alternatively, applicants can request forms to be sent out by post.
**WHO TO APPLY TO** Sue Nicholson, Correspondent, Room 29, The Forest Centre, Bordon, Hampshire GU35 0TN *Tel.* 01420 477787 *email* info@blhcharity.co.uk *Website* www.blhcharity.co.uk

## ■ The Oliver Borthwick Memorial Trust

**CC NO** 256206   **ESTABLISHED** 1968
**WHERE FUNDING CAN BE GIVEN** UK.
**WHO CAN BENEFIT** Registered charities benefitting homeless people and people disadvantaged by poverty. In particular the trustees welcome applications from small but viable charities in disadvantaged inner-city areas.
**WHAT IS FUNDED** Currently the main areas of interest are to provide shelter and help for homeless people.
**WHAT IS NOT FUNDED** Individuals, including people working temporarily overseas for a charity where the request is for living expenses; applications relating to health, disability and those from non-registered charitable organisations.
**TYPE OF GRANT** Mainly one-off.
**RANGE OF GRANTS** £2,000–£5,000
**SAMPLE GRANTS** Basildon Community Resource Centre, Christian Action and Response in Society (CARIS) – Camden, Clock Tower Sanctuary – Brighton, Homeless Care, The Porch, St Mary-le-Bow Young Homeless Project and Winchester Churches Night Shelter (£5,000 each); Deptford Reach and Slough Homeless Our Concern (£3,000); The Upper Room (£2,000).
**FINANCES** *Year* 2013/14 *Income* £51,785 *Grants* £48,000 *Grants to organisations* £48,000 *Assets* £1,240,055
**TRUSTEES** David Scott; James MacDonald; The Earl Bathurst; John Toth; Andrew Impey; Sebastian Cresswell-Turner; Virginia Buckley.
**OTHER INFORMATION** Grants were awarded to 11 organisations during the year.
**HOW TO APPLY** Apply in writing to the correspondent. Letters should be set out on a maximum of two sides of A4, giving full details of the project with costs, who the project will serve and the anticipated outcome of the project. Meetings take place once a year in May. Applications should be received no later than April.
**WHO TO APPLY TO** Anthony Blake, 2B Vicarage Drive, London SW14 8RX *Tel.* 020 8876 0582 *email* tblake@charaplus.co.uk

## ■ The Boshier-Hinton Foundation

**CC NO** 1108886   **ESTABLISHED** 2005
**WHERE FUNDING CAN BE GIVEN** England and Wales.
**WHO CAN BENEFIT** Charitable organisations; hospices; schools.

**WHAT IS FUNDED** Work with children and adults with special educational or other needs.
**WHAT IS NOT FUNDED** No repeat grants are made within two years.
**TYPE OF GRANT** One-off grants.
**RANGE OF GRANTS** £250–£20,000. Generally around £1,000–£2,000.
**SAMPLE GRANTS** Cumbria Wheelchair Sport Club (£4,500); Brainwave (£3,000); 4 Sight, Acorns Children's Hospice, Asthma UK, Autism Wessex, Children's Air Ambulance, Cirdan Sailing Trust, Connect, Good Rock Foundation, Hope House Children's Hospice, Living Options Devon, Tourettes Action and Young and Free (£2,000 each); Dyslexia Action and Life Education Centres Thames Valley (£1,000 each); Movement Foundation (£750); Mid-Staffordshire Mencap (£500).
**FINANCES** *Year* 2013/14 *Income* £497,633 *Grants* £265,740 *Grants to organisations* £265,740 *Assets* £1,327,847
**TRUSTEES** Thea Boshier, Chair; Dr Peter Boshier; Colin Flint; Janet Beale.
**HOW TO APPLY** The foundation accepts applications for grants in writing and via electronic communication, using a grant application form, which includes some notes for guidance, and is regularly monitored and updated. The application form can be downloaded from the website. The foundation welcomes informal email enquiries prior to the submission of a formal application.
**WHO TO APPLY TO** Dr Peter Boshier, Trustee, Yeomans, Aythorpe Roding, Great Dunmow, Essex CM6 1PD *Tel.* 01245 231032 *email* boshierhinton@yahoo.co.uk *Website* www.boshierhintonfoundation.org.uk

## ■ The Bothwell Charitable Trust

**CC NO** 299056   **ESTABLISHED** 1987
**WHERE FUNDING CAN BE GIVEN** England, particularly the South East.
**WHO CAN BENEFIT** Registered charities and hospices benefitting carers, people with disabilities and people disadvantaged by poverty.
**WHAT IS FUNDED** General charitable purposes in particular, health, disability and research.
**WHAT IS NOT FUNDED** Animal charities; overseas causes; individuals; charities not registered with the Charity Commission.
**TYPE OF GRANT** Core costs, running costs and research grants, for one year or less.
**RANGE OF GRANTS** Usually £1,000 or £2,000.
**SAMPLE GRANTS** **Previous beneficiaries have included:** Arthritis Research UK, Blackthorn Trust, British Heart Foundation, ECHO International Health Services Ltd, Friends of the Elderly, Invalid Children's Aid Nationwide, Leukaemia Research Fund (£2,000 each); and Brain Research Trust, British Trust for Conservation Volunteers, Childlink Adoption Society, Multiple Sclerosis Society and Riding for the Disabled Association (£1,000 each).
**FINANCES** *Year* 2013/14 *Income* £197,897 *Grants* £228,000 *Grants to organisations* £228,000 *Assets* £4,432,512
**TRUSTEES** Paul L. James; Crispian M. P. Howard; Theresa McGregor.
**HOW TO APPLY** Apply in writing to the correspondent. Distributions are usually made in February or March each year.
**WHO TO APPLY TO** Paul Leonard James, Trustee, 25 Ellenbridge Way, South Croydon CR2 0EW *Tel.* 020 8657 6884 *email* jillandpauljames@uwclub.net

321

# Bottom

## ■ The Harry Bottom Charitable Trust

**CC NO** 204675  **ESTABLISHED** 1960
**WHERE FUNDING CAN BE GIVEN** UK, with a preference for Yorkshire and Derbyshire.
**WHO CAN BENEFIT** Registered charities.
**WHAT IS FUNDED** The trust states that support is divided roughly equally between religion, education and medical causes. Within these categories grants are given to: religion – small local appeals and cathedral appeals; education – universities and schools; and medical – equipment for hospitals and charities concerned with disability.
**WHAT IS NOT FUNDED** Individuals.
**RANGE OF GRANTS** £250-£35,000
**SAMPLE GRANTS** University of Sheffield (£90,000); Yorkshire Baptist Association (£30,000); Sheffield Mencap (£3,000); Sheffield Royal Society for the Blind (£2,000).
**FINANCES** Year 2013/14 Income £248,152 Grants £183,826 Grants to organisations £183,826 Assets £5,991,602
**TRUSTEES** Helen Woolley; Derek Handforth; Prof. Andrew Rawlinson.
**HOW TO APPLY** Apply in writing to the correspondent at any time enclosing your most recent set of annual accounts.
**WHO TO APPLY TO** John Hinsley, c/o Westons, Chartered Accountants, 1 Vincent House, 149 Solly Street, Sheffield S1 4BB *Tel.* 0114 273 8341

## ■ P. G. and N. J. Boulton Trust

**CC NO** 272525  **ESTABLISHED** 1976
**WHERE FUNDING CAN BE GIVEN** Worldwide.
**WHO CAN BENEFIT** Organisations with whom the trustees have existing commitments/special interest.
**WHAT IS FUNDED** Christian missionary work; disaster and poverty relief; medical research and healthcare; disability relief and care of elderly.
**WHAT IS NOT FUNDED** Individuals; environment and conservation; culture and heritage; sport and leisure; animal welfare; church building repairs.
**RANGE OF GRANTS** up to £18,500.
**SAMPLE GRANTS** Vision for China (£18,500); New Life Centre (£10,000); Shalom Christian Trust (£6,000); Just Care (£4,000); Longcroft Christian Trust (£1,000); Other donations of £1,000 or less totalled £4,000.
**FINANCES** Year 2013/14 Income £141,567 Grants £43,500 Grants to organisations £43,500 Assets £4,061,903
**TRUSTEES** Andrew L. Perry; Shirley Perry; Peter H. Stafford; Margaret Jardine-Smith.
**HOW TO APPLY** Note the following statement from the trust's website: 'We are currently undergoing a long term review of our policies and this means that in practice, we are currently only making donations to organisations to whom we have an existing commitment. This unfortunately means that any new requests for funding at the present time will almost certainly be unsuccessful.'
**WHO TO APPLY TO** Andrew L. Perry, Trustee, PO Box 72, Wirral CH28 9AE *email* info@boultontrust.org.uk *Website* www.boultontrust.org.uk

## ■ Sir Clive Bourne Family Trust

**CC NO** 290620  **ESTABLISHED** 1984
**WHERE FUNDING CAN BE GIVEN** UK.
**WHO CAN BENEFIT** Individuals and institutions benefitting Jewish people.
**WHAT IS FUNDED** The trustees favour Jewish causes. A number of health and medical charities (particularly relating to cancer) have also benefitted.
**SAMPLE GRANTS** Prostate Action (£25,500); Jewish Care (£15,000); Mossbourne Community Academy (£10,000); Norwood Ravenswood (£5,500); World Jewish Relief (£5,000); Chabad Lubavitch Centre (£4,000); Lifeline 4 Kids and Jewish Women's Aid (£500 each).
**FINANCES** Year 2013/14 Income £98,345 Grants £93,021 Grants to organisations £93,021 Assets £4,305,131
**TRUSTEES** Lady Joy Bourne; Katie Cohen; Lucy Furman; Claire Lefton; Merryl Flitterman.
**HOW TO APPLY** Apply in writing to the correspondent.
**WHO TO APPLY TO** Janet Bater, Correspondent, Gardiner House, 6B Hemnall Street, Epping, Essex CM16 4LW *Tel.* 01992 560500 *email* jbater@seabourne-group.com

## ■ Bourneheights Limited

**CC NO** 298359  **ESTABLISHED** 1984
**WHERE FUNDING CAN BE GIVEN** UK
**WHO CAN BENEFIT** Orthodox Jewish organisations and registered charities.
**WHAT IS FUNDED** Orthodox Jewish organisations and registered charities.
**SAMPLE GRANTS** Previous beneficiaries have included: Moreshet Hatorah, Mercaz Torah Vahesed Ltd, BFOT, Belz Synagogue, Telz Academy Trust, Gevurath Ari Academy, UTA, Toreth Emeth, Olam Chesed Yiboneh, Before Trust, Heaven Point, Yeshivas Avas Torah and Lubavitch Mechina.
**FINANCES** Year 2012/13 Income £1,478,108 Grants £518,274 Grants to organisations £518,274 Assets £6,673,463
**TRUSTEES** Chaskel Rand; Esther Rand; Erno Berger; Yechiel Chersky; Schloime Rand.
**OTHER INFORMATION** These were the latest accounts available at the time of writing (June 2015).
**HOW TO APPLY** Apply in writing to the correspondent.
**WHO TO APPLY TO** Schloime Rand, Trustee, Flat 10, Palm Court, Queen Elizabeth's Walk, London N16 5XA *Tel.* 020 8809 7398

## ■ The Bower Trust

**CC NO** 283025  **ESTABLISHED** 1981
**WHERE FUNDING CAN BE GIVEN** Wales and Africa.
**WHO CAN BENEFIT** Generally, registered charities.
**WHAT IS FUNDED** Charities connected with Africa and charities with activities in Wales.
**WHAT IS NOT FUNDED** No personal sponsorships. Generally the trustees are not interested in regional requests from charities.
**RANGE OF GRANTS** Usually less than £1,000.
**SAMPLE GRANTS** National Trust (£7,500); Llanilltyd Fawr in Flower (£3,500); and Aride Island Trust, SCF Syria and Virtual Doctor Zambia (£2,000 each).
**FINANCES** Year 2013/14 Income £42,794 Grants £36,074 Grants to organisations £36,074 Assets £912,929
**TRUSTEES** Tina Benfield; Jack Benfield; Robert Benfield; Graham Benfield.
**OTHER INFORMATION** In 2013/14 grants were given to 39 charities.
**HOW TO APPLY** Apply in writing to the correspondent. The trustees meet quarterly to consider grants.
**WHO TO APPLY TO** Graham Benfield, Trustee, Old Rosedew House, Colhugh Street, Llantwit Major CF61 1RF

## ■ The Bowerman Charitable Trust

**CC NO** 289446  **ESTABLISHED** 1984
**WHERE FUNDING CAN BE GIVEN** UK, with a preference for West Sussex.
**WHO CAN BENEFIT** Registered charities.
**WHAT IS FUNDED** Church; the arts; medical; youth; social welfare; rehabilitation of offenders; general charitable purposes.
**TYPE OF GRANT** One-off.
**SAMPLE GRANTS** SCOPE (£30,000); Royal Academy of Music (£12,000); The Liver Group and Titus Trust (£5,000 each); Royal Philharmonic Society (£1,000).
**FINANCES** Year 2013/14 Income £193,282 Grants £176,152 Grants to organisations £153,953 Assets £17,639,061
**TRUSTEES** David Bowerman; Anna Downham; Clarice Bowerman; Janet Taylor; Julyan Capper; Katharine Bowerman; Michael Follis.
**HOW TO APPLY** The trustees have previously stated that they are 'bombarded' with applications and unsolicited applications will not be considered.
**WHO TO APPLY TO** David Bowerman, Trustee, Champs Hill, Coldwatham, Pulborough, West Sussex RH20 1LY Tel. 01798 831205

## ■ The Bowland Charitable Trust

**CC NO** 292027  **ESTABLISHED** 1985
**WHERE FUNDING CAN BE GIVEN** North west England.
**WHO CAN BENEFIT** Individuals, institutions and registered charities benefitting, in general, children and young adults.
**WHAT IS FUNDED** Young people, education and general charitable purposes.
**SAMPLE GRANTS** United Learning (£500,000); University of York (£250,000); General Assembly of Unitarian and Free Christian Churches (£166,000 each); Lowther Castle and Garden Trust (£12,500); Prisoners' Education Trust (£2,000).
**FINANCES** Year 2013/14 Income £365,714 Grants £1,168,111 Grants to organisations £1,168,111 Assets £11,184,817
**TRUSTEES** Tony Cann; Ruth A. Cann; Carole Fahy; Hugh D. Turner.
**HOW TO APPLY** The charity invites applications for funding of projects from individuals, institutions and charitable organisations. The applications are made directly to the trustees, who meet regularly to assess them.
**WHO TO APPLY TO** Carole Fahy, Trustee, Activhouse, Philips Road, Blackburn, Lancashire BB1 5RD Tel. 01254 290433 email carole.fahy@cannco.co.uk

## ■ The Frank Brake Charitable Trust

**CC NO** 1023245  **ESTABLISHED** 1993
**WHERE FUNDING CAN BE GIVEN** Kent
**WHO CAN BENEFIT** Registered charities.
**WHAT IS FUNDED** General charitable purposes.
**SAMPLE GRANTS** Parkinson's Disease Society of the UK (£35,000); Motor Neurone Disease Association and NSPCC (£10,000 each); Home Start Ashford (£5,000); Children with Special Needs and The Prostate Cancer Charity (£2,000 each); BLISS (£1,000).
**FINANCES** Year 2013/14 Income £1,131,954 Grants £444,033 Grants to organisations £444,033 Assets £7,271,512
**TRUSTEES** Philip Wilson; Michael Trigg; Michelle Leveridge; Richard Brake.
**OTHER INFORMATION** The charity had given a commitment to the Kent Multiple Sclerosis Therapy Centre, Butterfly Appeal to match funds raised before the end of 2013 subject to a minimum contribution of £100,000 and a maximum contribution of £500,000. During the year the charity fulfilled its commitment by paying £349,000 to the Butterfly Appeal having already paid £151,000 in the previous year. The £349,000 is included in the grant total.
**HOW TO APPLY** Apply in writing to the correspondent.
**WHO TO APPLY TO** Michael Trigg, Trustee, c/o Gill Turner Tucker, Colman House, King Street, Maidstone, Kent ME14 1JE Tel. 01622 759051 email michael.trigg@gillturnertucker.com

## ■ The William Brake Charitable Trust

**CC NO** 1023244  **ESTABLISHED** 1984
**WHERE FUNDING CAN BE GIVEN** UK, with a preference for Kent.
**WHO CAN BENEFIT** Registered charities.
**WHAT IS FUNDED** General charitable purposes.
**RANGE OF GRANTS** £1,000–£50,000
**SAMPLE GRANTS** **Previous beneficiaries have included:** Aurora Tsunami Orphanage; Canterbury Cathedral Development; Mike Collingwood Memorial Fund; Cancer Research UK; The Duke of Edinburgh's Award; The Ecology Trust; Elimination of Leukaemia Fund; Friends of St Peter's Hospital Chertsey; League of Remembrance; Maidstone Mencap Charitable Trust; RNLI; Whitely Fund for Nature; Wooden Spoon Society.
**FINANCES** Year 2013/14 Income £119,942 Grants £368,250 Grants to organisations £368,250 Assets £9,978,212
**TRUSTEES** Philip Wilson; Deborah Isaac; Penelope Lang; Michael Trigg.
**HOW TO APPLY** The 2013/14 accounts note that, 'the charity invites applications from the William Brake family for funding of worthy registered charities each year, with a particular emphasis on local charities where the family know the charity's representative.'
**WHO TO APPLY TO** Michael Trigg, Trustee, c/o Colman House, King Street, Maidstone, Kent ME14 1JE Tel. 01622 759051 email michael.trigg@gillturnertucker.com

## ■ The Tony Bramall Charitable Trust

**CC NO** 1001522  **ESTABLISHED** 1990
**WHERE FUNDING CAN BE GIVEN** UK, with some preference for Yorkshire.
**WHO CAN BENEFIT** Local charities within Yorkshire and national medical institutions.
**WHAT IS FUNDED** Medical research, ill health and social welfare.
**RANGE OF GRANTS** Usually £1,000–£5,000.
**SAMPLE GRANTS** British Heart Foundation, British Red Cross – Typhoon Appeal and The Prince's Trust (£5,000 each); The Sick Children's Trust (£3,000); Air Ambulance and Leeds Samaritans (£2,500 each); Care for Casualties (£250).
**FINANCES** Year 2013/14 Income £151,969 Grants £189,600 Grants to organisations £189,600 Assets £4,435,359
**TRUSTEES** Tony Bramall; Karen Bramall Odgen; Melanie Foody; Geoffrey Tate; Anna Bramall.
**HOW TO APPLY** Apply in writing to the correspondent.
**WHO TO APPLY TO** The Trustees, 12 Cardale Court, Beckwith Head Road, Harrogate, North Yorkshire HG3 1RY Tel. 01423 535300 email alison.lockwood@bramallproperties.co.uk

## ■ The Liz and Terry Bramall Foundation

**CC NO** 1121670  **ESTABLISHED** 2007
**WHERE FUNDING CAN BE GIVEN** UK, in practice mainly Yorkshire.
**WHO CAN BENEFIT** Charitable organisations; churches.
**WHAT IS FUNDED** Support of the Christian faith; promotion of urban or rural regeneration in areas of social and economic deprivation; relief of sickness and the advancement of health; education; arts and culture.
**RANGE OF GRANTS** £1,000–£355,000
**SAMPLE GRANTS** West Yorkshire Playhouse (£355,000); University of Leeds (£244,000); Skelmanthorpe Brass Band (£130,000); Yorkshire Sculpture Park (£100,000); Wakefield Cathedral (£42,000); Ovarian Cancer Action (£25,000); The Anthony Nolan Trust (£18,100); St Gemma's Hospice (£16,000); Trinity Church Ossett (£10,000); Unique (£5,000); Woodlands Trust (£3,000); The Shack (£1,000).
**FINANCES** Year 2013/14 Income £2,094,283 Grants £5,212,972 Grants to organisations £5,212,972 Assets £110,968,371
**TRUSTEES** Terence Bramall; Elizabeth Bramall; Suzannah Allard; Rebecca Bletcher; Rachel Tunnicliffe; Anthony Sharp.
**OTHER INFORMATION** The trustees' annual report for 2013/14 states: 'The grant making policy of the charity is being developed and but it will include small donations (on application) to causes within the objectives and also larger long term projects. The plan for the future is to donate as much as possible, to deserving applicants, to a level that broadly matches the annual income received ... In the short term additional spend, over and above the current level of income, will be required to bring the free reserves to the target levels.' During the year more than 132 awards were made.
**HOW TO APPLY** Applications can be made in writing to the correspondent. The foundation has stated that 'unsolicited requests from national charities will generally only be considered if there is some public benefit to the Yorkshire region'.
**WHO TO APPLY TO** Dr Terence Bramall, Trustee, c/o Raworths LLP, Eton House, 89 Station Parade, Harrogate, North Yorkshire HG1 1HF *Tel.* 01423 566666

## ■ The Bransford Trust

**CC NO** 1106554  **ESTABLISHED** 2004
**WHERE FUNDING CAN BE GIVEN** Preference for the West Midlands.
**WHO CAN BENEFIT** Registered charities; hospices; educational establishments.
**WHAT IS FUNDED** General charitable purposes, particularly arts and music, education of young people both in Worcestershire and from disadvantaged backgrounds, social welfare and alleviation of sickness.
**RANGE OF GRANTS** Up to £120,000.
**SAMPLE GRANTS** St Richards Hospice (£120,000); Sing UK (£95,500); Acorns Children's Hospice (£40,000); Three Choirs Festival (£25,000); Young Enterprise and The Prince's Trust (£15,000); Bewdley Youth Cafe (£10,000); County Air Ambulance (£7,000); Worcester Arts Workshop (£5,000); Severn Valley Railway Charitable Trust (£2,500). Other grants under £5,000 totalled £40,500.
**FINANCES** Year 2013/14 Income £711,328 Grants £479,568 Grants to organisations £479,568 Assets £14,421,457
**TRUSTEES** Arthur Neil; Colin Kinnear; Brenda Kinnear; John Carver.
**HOW TO APPLY** Applications can be made in writing to the correspondent. The trustees meet twice a year – in July/August and December/January. In order to cut down on costs only successful applicants are notified.
**WHO TO APPLY TO** Julia Kirkham, Correspondent, c/o Bransford Facilities Management, 6 Edgar Street, Worcester WR1 2LR *Tel.* 01684 310259 *email* julia@bransford-facilities.co.uk

## ■ The Breadsticks Foundation

**CC NO** 1125396  **ESTABLISHED** 2008
**WHERE FUNDING CAN BE GIVEN** UK, Africa and Asia.
**WHO CAN BENEFIT** Charities and community groups.
**WHAT IS FUNDED** Healthcare and education, particularly young people and disadvantaged adults.
**WHAT IS NOT FUNDED** Individuals; animals; medical research; capital and building projects. It will not fund faith-based programmes unless they work with beneficiaries from all faiths.
**TYPE OF GRANT** Core funding; project funding.
**SAMPLE GRANTS** Hope and Homes for Children (£180,000); Freedom from Torture and Riders for Health (£150,000 each); St Mungo's Community Housing Association (£70,000); Brighton Oasis Project (£45,000); Zisize Education Trust (£32,000); Class Act (£10,000).
**FINANCES** Year 2013/14 Income £3,146 Grants £956,941 Grants to organisations £956,941 Assets £395,597
**TRUSTEES** Beatrix Payne, Chair; Dr Kirsty Le Doare; Dr Paul Ballantyne; Beatrice Roberts; Trevor Macy.
**HOW TO APPLY** Applications are by invitation only, and unsolicited applications will not be considered.
**WHO TO APPLY TO** Beatrix Payne, Trustee, 35 Canonbury Square, London N1 2AN *Tel.* 020 7288 0667 *email* breadsticksfoundation@gmail.com *Website* www.breadsticksfoundation.org

## ■ The Breast Cancer Research Trust (BCRT)

**CC NO** 272214  **ESTABLISHED** 1961
**WHERE FUNDING CAN BE GIVEN** UK.
**WHO CAN BENEFIT** Recognised cancer centres or research institutions – specific units in teaching hospitals or universities.
**WHAT IS FUNDED** Clinical and translational research and laboratory projects in the field of the prevention, early diagnosis and treatment of breast cancer.
**WHAT IS NOT FUNDED** Students.
**TYPE OF GRANT** Project; research; core costs; salaries; up to a term of three years (reviewed annually).
**SAMPLE GRANTS** King's College London (£49,000); Mount Vernon Hospital, Southampton University and University of South Manchester (£40,000 each); Nottingham University (£39,000); Breakthrough Breast Cancer – The Institute of Cancer Research (£25,000); University of Reading (£8,000); Charing Cross Hospital (£3,900).

FINANCES Year 2013/14 Income £58,738 Grants £244,900 Grants to organisations £244,900 Assets £221,693
TRUSTEES Dame Vera Lynn; Prof. Charles Coombes; Virginia Lewis-Jones; Bob Potter; Prof. Trevor Powles; R. M. Rainsbury; Dr Margaret Spittle.
OTHER INFORMATION Note the following stated in the accounts for 2013/14: 'It is now felt that, following the prudence of the Trustees over the last few years, there will be a period of consolidation to allow the reserves to return to their former level, with a consequent reduction in grants in the year 2014/2015.' During the year eight grants were made.
HOW TO APPLY Application forms are available only from the trust's website. Awards are made once or twice a year. Note that seven copies of the form are required. All appeals are assessed by a peer group.
WHO TO APPLY TO Rosemary Sutcliffe, Executive Administrator, PO Box 861, Bognor Regis, West Sussex PO21 9HW Tel. 01243 583143 Fax 01243 583143 email bcrtrust@bt.internet.com Website www.breastcancerresearchtrust.org.uk

■ **The Brendish Family Foundation**
CC NO 1079065    ESTABLISHED 2000
WHERE FUNDING CAN BE GIVEN UK and overseas, with a preference for India.
WHO CAN BENEFIT The foundation was established in 2000 for general charitable purposes.
WHAT IS FUNDED General charitable purposes often with a preference for children's charities.
SAMPLE GRANTS The Game and Wildlife Conservation Trust (£20,000); Child in Need Institute – India (£10,000); The Busoga Trust (£3,500); and £100 spent in awards of less than £1,000.
FINANCES Year 2013/14 Income £252,740 Grants £33,600 Grants to organisations £33,600 Assets £1,537,855
TRUSTEES Graham Chambers; Susan Brendish; Clayton Brendish; Nathan Brendish; Natalie Brendish; Claire Brendish.
HOW TO APPLY Apply in writing to the correspondent.
WHO TO APPLY TO Natalie Brendish, Trustee, 1 Saffron Wharf, 20 Shad Thames, London SE1 2YG email nbrendish@hotmail.com

■ **Bridgepoint Charitable Trust (formerly Bridgepoint Inspire)**
CC NO 1134525    ESTABLISHED 2010
WHERE FUNDING CAN BE GIVEN UK and Europe.
WHO CAN BENEFIT Registered charities.
WHAT IS FUNDED General charitable purposes, especially education, health, environment and children. The trust aims to help 'where its donation can make a meaningful difference'.
RANGE OF GRANTS Up to £64,000.
SAMPLE GRANTS Wunder Stiftung (£64,000); Fryshuset and Teens and Toddlers (£50,000 each); other donations below £25,000 (£27,500).
FINANCES Year 2013 Income £180,070 Grants £203,303 Grants to organisations £203,303 Assets £628,960
TRUSTEES Michael Walton; James Murray; Ruth McIntosh; P. R. Gunner; Jamie Wyatt; David Hankin; Emma Watford; Stefanie Arensmann; Mathew Legg; Vincent-Gael Baudet.
OTHER INFORMATION The trust is linked to the international private equity firm, Bridgepoint. It also operates an employee matched funding scheme (matching donations below £10,000 totalled £11,600).
HOW TO APPLY Applications may be made in writing to the correspondent.
WHO TO APPLY TO David Hankin, Secretary, Bridgepoint, 30 Warwick Street, London W1B 5AL Tel. 020 7432 3500 Website www.bridgepoint.eu

■ **The Harold and Alice Bridges Charity**
CC NO 236654    ESTABLISHED 1963
WHERE FUNDING CAN BE GIVEN South Cumbria and North Lancashire (as far south as Preston)
WHO CAN BENEFIT Organisations supporting to children, young adults, older people and village activities.
WHAT IS FUNDED General charitable purposes, particularly young people, elderly people and supporting village capital projects.
WHAT IS NOT FUNDED Individuals.
TYPE OF GRANT The trustees prefer mainly capital projects which have an element of self-help.
RANGE OF GRANTS Usually £500–£5,000.
SAMPLE GRANTS Opportunity Sports Foundation and Stainton Institute (£5,000 each); Legacy Rainbow House (£3,000); Burnside Brass Band, Bleasdale Parish Hall, Dalton Community Association, Kirkby Lonsdale Bowling Club and Singleton Village Hall (£2,000 each); Kepple Lane Park Trust (£1,000); Ingleton Cricket Club (£500).
FINANCES Year 2013/14 Income £122,335 Grants £102,800 Grants to organisations £102,800 Assets £3,508,049
TRUSTEES Richard N. Hardy; Irene Greenwood.
HOW TO APPLY Refer to the charity's website for full application details including a downloadable form. The trustees meet three times a year to discuss and approve grant applications and review finances. Cheques are sent out to those successful applicants within days of each meeting.
WHO TO APPLY TO Richard N. Hardy, Trustee, Linder Myers, 21–23 Park Street, Lytham FY8 5LU Tel. 0844 984 6001 email david.hinchliffe@lindermyers.co.uk Website www.haroldandalicebridgescharity.co.uk

■ **The Bridging Fund Charitable Trust**
CC NO 1119171    ESTABLISHED 2007
WHERE FUNDING CAN BE GIVEN UK
WHO CAN BENEFIT Charitable organisations that help individuals in need.
WHAT IS FUNDED Social welfare and the relief of poverty.
WHAT IS NOT FUNDED Running costs; individuals.
FINANCES Year 2013 Income £16,126 Grants £300,000 Grants to organisations £300,000
TRUSTEES Debbie Cockrill; David Reeds; Mike Richardson; Rosemary Mackay; Gordon Hayes; Rosemary Williamson.
HOW TO APPLY Apply in writing to the correspondent.
WHO TO APPLY TO Debbie Cockrill, Trustee, PO Box 3106, Lancing, West Sussex BN15 5BL Tel. 01903 750008 email info@bridgingfund.org

## ■ Briggs Animal Welfare Trust

**CC NO** 276459 **ESTABLISHED** 1978
**WHERE FUNDING CAN BE GIVEN** UK and overseas.
**WHO CAN BENEFIT** Charities concerned with animal welfare, particularly animals in distress caused by man including wildlife.
**WHAT IS FUNDED** Although the original objects of the trust were general, but with particular support for animal welfare, the trust's policy is to support only animal welfare causes.
**TYPE OF GRANT** Ongoing grants.
**RANGE OF GRANTS** £1,000–£2,000
**SAMPLE GRANTS** There are five named beneficiaries in the trust deed: RSPCA, Reystede Animal Sanctuary Ringmer, Brooke Hospital for Animals Cairo, Care of British Columbia House and the Society for the Protection of Animals in North Africa.
**FINANCES** Year 2013/14 Income £183 Grants £13,000 Grants to organisations £13,000
**TRUSTEES** Louise Hartnett; Adrian Schouten.
**OTHER INFORMATION** Accounts were received by the Charity Commission but were not available to view.
**HOW TO APPLY** Apply in writing to the correspondent.
**WHO TO APPLY TO** Louise Hartnett, Trustee, Little Champions Farm, Maplehurst Road, West Grinstead, Horsham, West Sussex RH13 6RN

## ■ Bristol Archdeaconry Charity

**CC NO** 1058853 **ESTABLISHED** 1996
**WHERE FUNDING CAN BE GIVEN** Archdeaconry of Bristol and the surrounding area including the Deanery of Kingswood in South Gloucestershire, and the Benefice of Marshfield with Cold Ashton and Tormarton with West Littleton.
**WHO CAN BENEFIT** Registered charities; religious bodies; individuals.
**WHAT IS FUNDED** Religious and other charitable purposes of the Church of England in the area of benefit. The accounts state: 'Grants should generally be associated with church-based ministry and community projects in U.P.A. parishes, and made wherever possible by way of start-up funding.'
**TYPE OF GRANT** One-off and recurrent; capital costs; projects; start-up costs.
**RANGE OF GRANTS** £1,000–£60,000
**SAMPLE GRANTS** Bristol Diocesan Board of finance (£60,000); Bristol Cathedral (£20,000); Christ Church Downend (£11,300); Parish of Bishopston and St Andrews (£10,000); Frenchay (£7,500); St Mary's Almondsbury (£5,000); St Barnabas' Warmley (£2,000); Kingswood Team Ministry (£1,700); St Aidan with St George (£1,000).
**FINANCES** Year 2013 Income £140,576 Grants £171,075 Grants to organisations £171,075 Assets £3,535,999
**TRUSTEES** Roger Metcalfe; Peter Woolf; Timothy Thom; Anthony Brown; David Worthington; The Ven. Christine Froude; Stephen Gisby; Oliver Home.
**OTHER INFORMATION** In 2013 grants were given to 22 institutions. The accounts state: 'The policy adopted in respect of grant making is that, ideally, the proportion of annual income to be dealt with as regular grants should not be more than 65% with the balance dealt with either as grants for specific purposes or retained as accumulated funds.'
**HOW TO APPLY** Applications may be made in writing to the correspondent. The trustees meet two or three times a year.

**WHO TO APPLY TO** Philippa Drewett, Clerk, All Saints Centre, 1 All Saints Court, Bristol BS1 1JN Tel. 0117 929 2709

## ■ The Bristol Charities

**CC NO** 1109141 **ESTABLISHED** 1960
**WHERE FUNDING CAN BE GIVEN** In practice the City of Bristol, North Somerset and South Gloucestershire; mainly within a 10-mile radius of Bristol city centre.
**WHO CAN BENEFIT** Educational and religious establishments; community organisations; individuals.
**WHAT IS FUNDED** Educational assistance to schools and educational charities (via Barry Theo Jones Fund). A great part of support is given to individual beneficiaries for the relief of sickness and need and supporting carers, especially women.
**RANGE OF GRANTS** Up to £66,000.
**SAMPLE GRANTS** The accounts list recipients of grants over £1,000. **Beneficiaries included**: Bristol Grammar School (£66,000 in two grants); Colston's School (£5,600); Red Maids' School (£5,200); Badminton School (£3,200); Bristol Steiner School (£2,000); St Stephen's Church (£1,800).
**FINANCES** Year 2013/14 Income £1,486,934 Grants £235,695 Grants to organisations £117,564 Assets £26,876,389
**TRUSTEES** David Watts; Susan Hampton; Sonia Mills; Kamala Das; Andrew Hillman; Laura Claydon; John Webster; Anthony Harris; Paul Staples; Richard Gore; Dr Ros Kennedy; Michelle Meredith; Dudley Lewis.
**OTHER INFORMATION** The charity also provides housing and day care services for older people. Note that the assets figure relates to consolidated amount; the charity assets totalled £12.6 million. The grant total consist of £232,500 in regular grants and £3,300 defined as 'winter support grant' awards to individuals totalled around £118,000.
**HOW TO APPLY** Application forms are available to download from the charity's website, together with full criteria and guidelines.
**WHO TO APPLY TO** Lorraine Chapman, Grants Administrator, 17 St Augustine's Parade, Bristol BS1 4UL Tel. 0117 930 0301 Fax 0117 925 3824 email info@bristolcharities.org.uk or lorraine.chapman@bristolcharities.org.uk Website www.bristolcharities.org.uk

## ■ The British and Foreign School Society

**CC NO** 314286
**WHERE FUNDING CAN BE GIVEN** UK and overseas
**WHO CAN BENEFIT** UK-registered charities.
**WHAT IS FUNDED** Advancing educational opportunity in the UK and financially developing countries.
**WHAT IS NOT FUNDED** Grants are not normally made to support special events such as conferences or seminars or for expeditions and overseas travel; grants are not normally made for endowments or scholarships; grants are not normally made for projects for which the main requirement is funding for transport. Organisations whose sole purpose is to raise funds and who are not themselves involved in the provision of charitable services will not normally be considered for funding.
**TYPE OF GRANT** One-off and recurring.
**RANGE OF GRANTS** Up to £35,000.

SAMPLE GRANTS The Sabre Charitable Trust (£40,000 in two grants); The British Asian Trust (£35,000); Fresh Start Foundation (£28,000); Baynards Zambia Trust (£25,000); Teens and Toddlers (£19,500); Disability and Development Partners (£15,400); Resolve International (£10,200); Chance for Childhood (£7,500); Chhahari Schools (£4,000).
FINANCES Year 2014 Income £752,886 Grants £630,082 Grants to organisations £630,082 Assets £21,961,688
TRUSTEES Graham Kingsley; David Swain; Professor Steve Hodkinson; Revd David Tennant; Brian York; Stephen King; Stephen Ross; Dr Emily Tomlinson; Dr Jaz Saggu; Stephen Wordsworth; Dr Ben Ramm; E. J. Weale; Peter Miller.
OTHER INFORMATION Grants from 'other funds' administered by the society amounted to an additional £12,900. The society no longer makes grants to individuals.
HOW TO APPLY There is an online application form. Applications from charitable organisations which meet the grant criteria are considered by the grants committee, which normally meets quarterly. Refer to the society's website for more details, including deadline dates.
WHO TO APPLY TO Belinda Lawrance, Correspondent, Maybrook House, Godstone Road, Caterham, Surrey CR3 6RE Tel. 01883 331177 email enquiries@bfss.org.uk. Website www.bfss.org.uk

## ■ British Council for Prevention of Blindness (Save Eyes Everywhere)

CC NO 270941 ESTABLISHED 1976
WHERE FUNDING CAN BE GIVEN Worldwide.
WHO CAN BENEFIT Organisations benefitting people with sight loss; research bodies; medical professionals, research workers and scientists in the field.
WHAT IS FUNDED According to the website, funding is given for 'research, including fellowships, which has the potential to make breakthroughs in understanding and treating currently incurable eye diseases, and operational research to determine the best methods of preventing blindness'. Barrie Jones Fellowships are 'awarded to UK-based Fellows who carry out research in a developing country' and Sir John Wilson Fellowships are 'awarded to students from developing countries who come to the UK to carry out research'. Research Mentorship Awards are given 'to foster research and training links between low-income country institutions (hospitals/universities) and UK universities/NHS Trusts'.
WHAT IS NOT FUNDED Individual welfare of blind people; completion of an existing project when previous funding has ended; unless in exceptional circumstances – laboratory-based research of a basic molecular or cell biological nature.
TYPE OF GRANT Fellowships; funding for studentships; research grants over one, two or three years.
RANGE OF GRANTS Research grants up to £60,000.
SAMPLE GRANTS International Centre for Eye Health (£75,000 in two grants); Boulter Fellowship Awards (£41,000); Institute of Ophthalmology (£14,500); Frimley Park Hospital (£13,300).
FINANCES Year 2013/14 Income £493,326 Grants £247,869 Grants to organisations £247,869 Assets £676,720
TRUSTEE BCPB. Management Ltd.

OTHER INFORMATION The grant total refers to 'grants paid during the year' the accounts state that 'grants awarded in the year' totalled £143,500, with further sum due within one year.
HOW TO APPLY Application forms are accessible on the charity's website. See online for full guidelines and submission deadlines (most recently applications had to be made by October).
WHO TO APPLY TO Stephen Silverton, Fundraising Director, 4 Bloomsbury Square, London WC1A 2RP Tel. 020 7404 7114 email info@bcpb.org Website www.bcpb.org

## ■ The British Dietetic Association General and Education Trust Fund

CC NO 282553 ESTABLISHED 1981
WHERE FUNDING CAN BE GIVEN UK.
WHO CAN BENEFIT Organisations; individuals; recognised associations; groups of people engaged in dietetic research and associated activities.
WHAT IS FUNDED Education, research and other purposes related to the science of dietetics.
WHAT IS NOT FUNDED Buying buildings; expenses for postgraduate qualifications; support dietetic students in training; conference attendance, unless the attendee is presenting a poster, a lecture, leading a workshop, etc. and the conference will promote the science of dietetics or dietetic practice. Projects which are 'too local and funding is sought to fund activities which should be supported by another organisation' are unlikely to be funded.
TYPE OF GRANT Projects; research; one-off and recurring costs up to three years; salaries; start-up costs; interest-free loans; running costs.
SAMPLE GRANTS The accounts note that 'the trustees considered five bids for development, research or educational activities over 2013/14'. Full details of grant recipients were not listed.
FINANCES Year 2013/14 Income £51,844 Grants £39,415 Grants to organisations £39,415 Assets £1,650,305
TRUSTEES Peter Brindley; William Seddon; Michele Mackintosh; Prof. Martin Wiseman; Sian O'Shea.
OTHER INFORMATION There were three research grants made. The trust also makes national awards to recognise excellence in the field of dietetics.
HOW TO APPLY Application forms can be downloaded from the trust's website. They should be submitted at least six weeks before the trustees' meeting – mid-March for the May meeting and mid-September for the November meeting. Supporting documentation is welcome. Full and detailed guidelines are given online.
WHO TO APPLY TO The Secretary to the Trustees, 5th Floor, Charles House, 148–149 Great Charles Street, Queensway, Birmingham B3 3HT Tel. 0121 200 8080 Fax 0121 200 8081 email info@bda.uk.com Website www.bda.uk.com/about/trustfund/home

## ■ British Gas (Scottish Gas) Energy Trust

**CC NO** 1106218  **ESTABLISHED** 2004
**WHERE FUNDING CAN BE GIVEN** England, Scotland and Wales.

**WHO CAN BENEFIT** Charities and other voluntary sector organisations; charitable advice agencies; current domestic customers of British Gas or Scottish Gas. Organisations must operate or serve people in the main regions of the trust's operation.

**WHAT IS FUNDED** Relief in need for individuals and families; agencies providing money and debt prevention advice and education, often with a particular fuel poverty emphasis. The main aim of the fund is to address health problems that are exacerbated by fuel poverty. There is also the British Gas Energy Trust Healthy Homes Fund which will fund charities and other voluntary organisations, both large and small, across Great Britain 'to work with local partners, to deliver projects which will assist low-income and vulnerable households and demonstrate a positive health impact'. The programme is especially looking for new and innovative ideas.

**WHAT IS NOT FUNDED** Fines for criminal offences; educational or training needs; debts to central government departments; medical equipment, aids and adaptations; holidays; business debts; catalogues; credit cards; personal loans; deposits for secure accommodation; overpayment of benefits. British Gas Energy Trust Healthy Homes Fund: any measure for which funding for social and environmental energy obligations is already available, including ECO and Warm Home Discount programmes; debt write off (application referrals can be made to the BGET main fund to assist eligible households); activities outside Great Britain.

**TYPE OF GRANT** One-off grants for individuals; one-off and recurrent, capital and revenue grants for organisations.

**SAMPLE GRANTS** Bradford and Airedale Citizen Advice Bureau; Bristol Debt Advice Centre; Local Solutions – Liverpool; Manchester Citizen Advice Bureau; Money Matters Money Advice Centre – Glasgow; Riverside Advice Centre – Cardiff; Shelter Norwich; Speakeasy Advice Centre – Cardiff; St Ann's Advice Group – Nottingham.

**FINANCES** *Year* 2013 *Income* £18,175,810 *Grants* £8,542,573 *Grants to organisations* £1,207,394 *Assets* £12,862,584

**TRUSTEES** Stephen Harrap; Gillian Tishler; Maria Wardrobe; Imelda Redmond; Andrew Brown; John Kolm-Murray.

**OTHER INFORMATION** The majority of grants are given to individuals and families (over £5 million in 2013). During the year a total of 18 organisations received funding totalling over £1.2 million. The trust is administered by Charis Grants and funded solely by the British Gas.

**HOW TO APPLY** Funding rounds for organisations are normally publicised on the trust's website and in its newsletter. Applications from individuals should be made by post using a form available from the trust's website. Successful applicant cannot re-apply for a period of two years; unsuccessful applicants can re-apply if their circumstances change. Completed applications for British Gas Energy Trust Healthy Homes Fund should be returned via email to BGETHealthyHomes@charisgrants.com. The most recent application deadline was at the beginning of July and successful charities were informed in September.

**WHO TO APPLY TO** The Trustees, 3rd Floor, Midgate House, Midgate, Peterborough PE1 1TN *Tel.* 01733 421060 *Fax* 01733 421021 *email* bget@charisgrants.com *Website* www.britishgasenergytrust.org.uk

## ■ British Heart Foundation (BHF)

**CC NO** 225971  **ESTABLISHED** 1961
**WHERE FUNDING CAN BE GIVEN** Unrestricted, in practice UK.

**WHO CAN BENEFIT** Organisations; research bodies; educational and medical institutions; academics; medical professionals; students.

**WHAT IS FUNDED** Medical research into all aspects of heart disease. There are a range of awards available, all schemes being detailed on the foundation's website.

**WHAT IS NOT FUNDED** Applications are accepted only from appropriately qualified individuals.

**TYPE OF GRANT** Projects; research; programmes; fellowship grants; salaries.

**RANGE OF GRANTS** Unrestricted.

**SAMPLE GRANTS** University of Oxford (£13.3 million in ten grants); King's College London (£10.1 million in four grants); University of Glasgow (£5.7 million in four grants); University of Birmingham (£2.6 in two grants); Medical Research Council (£1.5 million); ASH England and University of Hull (£700,000 each).

**FINANCES** *Year* 2013/14 *Income* £275,100,000 *Grants* £116,700,000 *Grants to organisations* £116,700,000 *Assets* £121,500,000

**TRUSTEES** Prof. Kay-Tee Khaw; Roger Pilgrim; Philip Yea; Sir C. Edwards; Lance Trevellyan; Richard Hytner; Dr Simon Ray; Prof. Robert Lechler; Dr Evan Harris; Andrew Balfour; Prof. Nishi Chaturvedi Dr Robert Easton; Prof. Anna Dominicza; Prof. Liam Smeeth.

**OTHER INFORMATION** In 2013/14 a total of 207 new research grants were awarded. Over 60% of the overall expenditure was for research grants in 2013/14. The grant total consists of £113.5 million in research and £3.2 million in prevention and care.

**HOW TO APPLY** Detailed and helpful criteria, guidelines, forms and application procedure are all fully explained on the foundation's website. You will need to prepare a detailed research proposal. Some appeals may be submitted in paper and others will need to be made using an online system. If you need any help or advice with your application, the foundation is happy to help. There are no deadlines (unless exceptionally stated for specific rounds). All appeals go through a peer review stage.

**WHO TO APPLY TO** Dr Debora Prince, Company Secretary, Greater London House, 180 Hampstead Road, London NW1 7AW *Tel.* 020 7554 0070 *Fax* 020 7554 0100 *email* research@bhf.org.uk or supporterservices@bhf.org.uk *Website* www.bhf.org.uk

## ■ The British Humane Association

**CC NO** 207120  **ESTABLISHED** 1922
**WHERE FUNDING CAN BE GIVEN** UK.

**WHO CAN BENEFIT** Charities directly involved in humanitarian activities; charities distributing grants to individuals; charities providing relief of poverty or sickness, or benefit to the community.

**WHAT IS FUNDED** Humanitarian activities; social welfare; community development.

**TYPE OF GRANT** One-off, capital and recurring grants will be considered.
**RANGE OF GRANTS** £2,000–£15,000
**SAMPLE GRANTS** St John of Jerusalem Eye Hospital (£15,000); St John Australia (£12,000); Send a Cow, St John Zimbabwe, Writers in Prison (£10,000 each); Duke of Edinburgh Wales (£8,000); Zoe Carrs Education Trust (£7,000); Gloucester Action for Asylum Seekers (£6,000); Conquest Art, London School of Hygiene and Tropical Medicine (£2,000 each).
**FINANCES** Year 2013 Income £137,817 Grants £127,500 Grants to organisations £127,500 Assets £4,421,438
**TRUSTEES** Dr John Breen; David Eldridge; Benedict Campbell-Johnston; Rachel Campbell-Johnston; Duncan Cantlay; Philip Gee; John Huntington-Whiteley; Anthony Chignell; Michael Nemko.
**HOW TO APPLY** Applications not considered. The charity's 2013 trustees' report states: 'The primary aim of the company, which is a registered charity, is the promotion of benevolence for the good of humanity and the community, through grant making. The directors of the Association have decided, that in order to increase the amount available for grant distribution to beneficiaries, they will transfer funds to other charitable organisations, which have in place systems for identifying and assisting deserving cases in need. By so doing, they will not duplicate selection processes and the resultant costs. It is the intention that any one or more of the directors will examine requests for assistance received and submit a proposal to the board to award a one-off, set period or continuing grant to anybody, which has applied for assistance.'
**WHO TO APPLY TO** Henry Grant, Company Secretary, The Cottage, New Road, Cutnall Green, Droitwich WR9 0PQ Tel. 01299 851588

## ■ British Institute at Ankara
**CC NO** 313940    **ESTABLISHED** 1948
**WHERE FUNDING CAN BE GIVEN** UK, Turkey and the Black Sea region.
**WHO CAN BENEFIT** British and UK-resident students and academics of archaeology and associated fields.
**WHAT IS FUNDED** Research focused on Turkey and the Black Sea littoral in all academic disciplines within the arts, humanities and social sciences.
**SAMPLE GRANTS** University College London (£20,000); University of Liverpool (£12,000); Newcastle University and the University of Kent (£5,000 each).
**FINANCES** Year 2013/14 Income £701,405 Grants £180,207 Grants to organisations £47,862 Assets £423,109
**TRUSTEES** Sir David Logan; Dr Aylin Orbasli; Prof. Stephen Mitchell; Dr Simon Corcoran; Dr Neil Macdonald; Anthony Sheppard; Jill Sindall; William Park; Prof. John Haldon; Shahina Farid; Dr Claire Norton; Dr Gulnur Aybet; Dr Peter Sarris. Dr Deniz Kandiyoti.
**PUBLICATIONS** Anatolian Studies and Anatolian Archaeology. Both annual publications.
**OTHER INFORMATION** In 2013/14 £133,000 was given to individuals.
**HOW TO APPLY** Initial enquiries regarding potential applications are welcomed. Full details can be found on the institute's website.
**WHO TO APPLY TO** Claire McCafferty, The British Academy, 10 Carlton House Terrace, London SW1Y 5AH Tel. 020 7969 5204 email biaa@britac.ac.uk Website www.biaa.ac.uk

## ■ British Record Industry Trust
**CC NO** 1000413    **ESTABLISHED** 1989
**WHERE FUNDING CAN BE GIVEN** Worldwide, in practice UK.
**WHO CAN BENEFIT** Registered charities benefitting young people involved in the arts, particularly music; schools.
**WHAT IS FUNDED** The trust's mission is 'to encourage young people in the exploration and pursuit of educational, cultural or therapeutic benefits emanating from music'. There is an ongoing commitment to the BRIT School for Performing Arts and Technology and Nordoff-Robbins Music Therapy but other appropriate good causes are also assisted.
**WHAT IS NOT FUNDED** Scholarships or grants to individuals; capital funding projects; unregistered charities; grants outside the UK.
**TYPE OF GRANT** One-off and recurring grants; capital and core costs; salaries; projects; unrestricted funding.
**RANGE OF GRANTS** £750–£350,000
**SAMPLE GRANTS** BRIT School for Performing Arts and Technology (£350,000); Nordoff Robbins Music Therapy (£300,000); Warchild (£55,500); Creative Access (£40,000); Drugscope (£30,000); Chickenshed Theatre (£6,000); Midi Music Company (£5,000); Company Music Theatre (£4,500); Text Santa (£1,900); Withycombe Raleigh (£750).
**FINANCES** Year 2013 Income £976,565 Grants £799,852 Grants to organisations £799,852 Assets £8,317,575
**TRUSTEES** John Deacon; John Craig; Andy Cleary; Jonathan Morrish; Rob Dickins; Tony Wadsworth; David Kassner; Geoff Taylor; Korda Marshall; David Sharpe; William Rowe; David Munns; Margaret Crowe; Angela Watts; Simon Paul; Thomas Presswell.
**OTHER INFORMATION** During the year a total of 12 awards were made. The accounts note: 'After meeting the larger commitments of the BRIT School and Nordoff Robbins, if possible, it is the Trustees' policy to make a number of smaller donations to various charities.'
**HOW TO APPLY** Applications should be made using an online system on the trust's website. The information given there states: 'Please note that The BRIT Trust is only able to consider applications from fellow organisations with a charitable status. ... Note that applications are only considered annually at a Trust meeting in September – all applications should be received by The Trust no later than August and should be for projects planned for the following year.'
**WHO TO APPLY TO** Jenny Clarke, Riverside Building, County Hall, Westminster Bridge Road, London SE1 7JA Tel. 020 7803 1351 email jenny.clarke@bpi.co.uk Website www.brittrust.co.uk

## ■ The Britten-Pears Foundation (The Britten Pears Library)
**CC NO** 295595    **ESTABLISHED** 1986
**WHERE FUNDING CAN BE GIVEN** UK, with a preference for East Anglia and Suffolk in particular.
**WHO CAN BENEFIT** Registered charities; arts organisations, including opera companies, orchestras and music ensembles; individual performers, authors and scholars; institutions with charitable objectives; UK-based commissioning bodies; local organisations.
**WHAT IS FUNDED** The foundation 'continues to support causes that were dear to Benjamin Britten and Peter Pears' – musical, local and pacifist causes – and offers: Britten Awards for

'projects that promote the music of Benjamin Britten in areas of the world where it is less well known', in South America, Asia, Eastern Europe or Africa (exceptionally student productions of Britten's chamber operas taking place in territories other than those listed above may be considered provided they are student-led and financed and not part of their formal education programme); support to new, substantial music commissions; local grants within the vicinity of Aldeburgh (within 20 miles, especially Orford, Snape and Blythburgh) for grassroots projects in a range of fields and activities 'that promote the vitality of community life', with preference for causes involving young people, good environmental practice or environment and local amenities. The foundation's objectives include the promotion of Britten's and Pears' legacy worldwide. The Grants Panel will look more favourably on applications that can demonstrate that the work will receive more than one performance and will be looking to support composers who have demonstrated a real gift for their craft or a recognised potential and for a partnership of composer and performer/s that impresses them as a significant project.

**WHAT IS NOT FUNDED** Grants of a capital nature (including those for instrumental purchase or restoration); ongoing running costs; retrospective awards; tuition fees; rehearsal fees; performance costs; recordings; educational or non-musical projects; applications for support for performances or recordings of the works of Benjamin Britten, of whose estate it is the beneficiary; subsidy for works by Britten which, in the estate's view, need further promotion can be sought from the Britten Estate Limited.

**TYPE OF GRANT** One-off and recurring; projects. Partnership funding will be considered, though the foundation will wish to be a major contributor in all cases. Matching funding will not be a condition of grant.

**RANGE OF GRANTS** Up to £40,000.

**SAMPLE GRANTS** English Touring Opera (£40,000); Russian National Orchestra (£35,000); Isango Ensemble – Noye's Fludde (£10,000); British Youth Opera (£7,000); Britten's Children and Scottish Chamber Orchestra (£5,000 each); Birmingham Contemporary Music Group (£4,000); The Opera Group (£2,800); Disability Arts On (£2,000); International Guitar Foundation and Nottingham Philharmonic Orchestra (£1,500 each); Aldeburgh Jubilee Hall and Framlingham Tennis Club (£1,000 each). Grants under £1,000 totalled 7,900.

**FINANCES** Year 2013 Income £3,500,703 Grants £854,830 Grants to organisations £854,830 Assets £22,136,493

**TRUSTEES** Andrew Fane; Philip Ramsbottom; Dr Sally Irvine; Dr Colin Matthews; Ghislaine Kenyon; Nicholas Prettejohn; Sybella Zisman; Edward Blakeman; Janis Susskind; Caroline Brazier; Penelope Heath.

**OTHER INFORMATION** During the year a total of 81 grants were made. Grants were allocated as follows: Aldeburgh Music (£365,000); centenary grants (£359,500); one-off grants (£70,750); Britten 100 Awards (£47,000); Local Community Fund grants (£12,300). As conditions and criteria vary across the three types of funding, applicants are advised to read the website carefully before applying.

**HOW TO APPLY** Full and most up-to-date details of how to apply, including application forms, guidelines, criteria and deadlines, can be found on the foundation's website. Applications for commissions and local grants should be made using an application form available online. Applications for commissions should be returned by email by 30 March and 14 September and for local grants – by 9 February and 7 September. To apply for the Britten awards applicants should send an email to r.jarman@brittenpears.org with a brief outline of the project, works to be performed, dates and places of the performance, performers involved and associated educational activities. Applicants will then be contacted with a request for further information or an indication that the project cannot be assisted.

**WHO TO APPLY TO** Amanda Arnold, Company Secretary, The Red House, Golf Lane, Aldeburgh, Suffolk IP15 5PZ *Tel.* 01728 451700 *email* grants@brittenpears.org or enquiries@brittenpears.org *Website* www.brittenpears.org

## ■ The J. and M. Britton Charitable Trust

**CC NO** 1081979  **ESTABLISHED** 1996

**WHERE FUNDING CAN BE GIVEN** Mainly Bristol and the former county of Avon.

**WHO CAN BENEFIT** General charitable purposes; education.

**WHAT IS FUNDED** Local charities such as hospital appeals and other charities that the trustees are involved in.

**WHAT IS NOT FUNDED** Individuals; non-registered charities.

**RANGE OF GRANTS** Up to £10,000.

**SAMPLE GRANTS** Alabare £10,000; Into University, John Wesley's Chapel (£5,000 each); British Zoological Society (£4,000); St John's Church (£3,000); Carers' Support Centre, Home Start (£2,000 each); Teenage Cancer Trust (£1,000); (An undisclosed number of smaller grants of £1,000 or less for charitable and educational purposes totalled £35,300).

**FINANCES** Year 2013/14 Income £103,340 Grants £75,450 Grants to organisations £75,450 Assets £3,030,346

**TRUSTEES** Robert Bernays; R. Bernays; Lady Merrison; Alison Bernays.

**HOW TO APPLY** Apply in writing to the correspondent enclosing an sae. Charities can apply at any time, but the trust makes distributions twice a year, usually in May and November.

**WHO TO APPLY TO** Mr R. E. J. Bernays, Trustee, Kilcot House, Lower Kilcot, Hillesley, Wotton-Under-Edge, Gloucestershire GL12 7RL *Tel.* 01454 238571

## ■ The Bromley Trust

**CC NO** 801875  **ESTABLISHED** 1989

**WHERE FUNDING CAN BE GIVEN** Worldwide.

**WHO CAN BENEFIT** UK-registered charities only. The trust is happy to work with other charities and particularly encourages crossover between the different funding streams and focus areas. Overseas projects and organisations can be assisted through a UK body only.

**WHAT IS FUNDED** Prevention of violations of human rights, helping help victims of torture, refugees, people suffering from oppression and those who have been falsely imprisoned, assisting those who have suffered severe bodily or mental harm through no fault of their own (and, if need be, their dependants); Prison Reform within the UK with particular emphasis on the reduction of re-offending; protection of the world's fauna and flora and prevention of destruction of the environment for wildlife and for mankind worldwide.

**WHAT IS NOT FUNDED** Individuals; expeditions; scholarships, although in certain cases the trust supports research that falls within its aims (but always through a registered charity); statutory authorities or charities whose main source of funding is via statutory agencies; overseas development or disaster relief; local conservation projects or charities that work with single species; drug rehabilitation or housing programmes.

**TYPE OF GRANT** For one year or recurrent; unrestricted grants; occasionally one-off awards; core funding; salaries; start-up costs. It is the trust's policy to give larger amounts to fewer charities rather than to spread income over a large number of small grants.

**RANGE OF GRANTS** £400–£20,000

**SAMPLE GRANTS** Ashden Awards, Landlife, Prison Reform Trust and Redress Trust (£20,000 each); Imperial War Museum (£15,000); Butler Trust £(13,000); Room 2 Heal (£12,500); Barnardo's, Council for Assisting Refugee Academics, Inquest, Marine Biological Conservation, Save Brasil, Transition Streets and Wave Trust (£10,000 each); Koestler Awards Trust (£8,000); Animb (£7,500); Birdlife Human Rights, Detention Forum and Zahid Mubarek Trust (£5,000 each); The Clink (£400).

**FINANCES** Year 2013/14 Income £722,228 Grants £726,000 Grants to organisations £726,000 Assets £17,092,192

**TRUSTEES** Bryan Blamey; Dr Judith Brett; Peter Edwards; Jean Ritchie; Anthony Roberts; Anne-Marie Edgell; Nigel Dyson.

**PUBLICATIONS** A range of publications supported by the trust are listed on its website.

**OTHER INFORMATION** Support was allocated as follows: human rights (£315,000 in 28 grants); prison reform and prison awards (£231,500 in 21 grants); sustainability and conservation (£180,000 in 17 grants).

**HOW TO APPLY** The website states: 'Please note that we will not be accepting new grant applications until further notice. This includes responding to e-mails and phone enquiries concerning new applications. We will announce the re-opening of the new grant applications programme on the web site as soon as possible.' Normally application forms are available from the trust's website and can be returned via email. Appeals should not generally exceed eight to ten pages. All charities are visited before a grant is made. There are no deadlines; however, the trust has warned that 'due to the current funding environment its application process is taking longer than previously described' – appeals are ordinarily acknowledged immediately but notification that your application has progressed to the next stage may take up to three months and confirmation of a visit may take up to six months, as all applications need to be approved at the bi-annual meetings. Full criteria, guidelines and application process are detailed on the website. The trust states that you should not request a specific amount because the size of its grants is made at the discretion of trustees. If you have applied before (either successfully or unsuccessfully), the trust asks that you do not re-apply.

**WHO TO APPLY TO** Teresa Elwes, Grants Executive, Studio 7, 2 Pinchin Street, Whitechapel, London E1 1SA Tel. 020 7481 4899 email info@thebromleytrust.org.uk Website www.thebromleytrust.org.uk

■ **The Consuelo and Anthony Brooke Charitable Trust**

**CC NO** 1150569

**WHERE FUNDING CAN BE GIVEN** UK and overseas, particularly Barnet, Camden, City of Westminster, East Sussex, Kensington and Chelsea, West Sussex and Uganda.

**WHO CAN BENEFIT** Charitable organisations.

**WHAT IS FUNDED** General charitable purposes; education and training; arts and culture; the environment; economic and community development; children and young people; older people.

**FINANCES** Year 2013/14 Income £72,885 Grants £69,000 Grants to organisations £69,000

**TRUSTEES** Carol Consuelo Brooke; Anthony Brooke; Charlotte Eade; Alexander Brooke.

**HOW TO APPLY** Apply in writing to the correspondent.

**WHO TO APPLY TO** Anthony Brooke, Trustee, 20 Caroline Place, London W2 4AN Tel. 07802 796416 email anthonylbrooke@btinternet.com

■ **The David Brooke Charity**

**CC NO** 283658     **ESTABLISHED** 1961

**WHERE FUNDING CAN BE GIVEN** UK with a preference for the north so that recipients can be visited.

**WHO CAN BENEFIT** Registered charities and voluntary and community-based groups, especially those concerned with disadvantaged young people.

**WHAT IS FUNDED** Groups supporting disadvantaged young people, older people and medical organisations.

**TYPE OF GRANT** Long-term support.

**RANGE OF GRANTS** Up to £6,000.

**SAMPLE GRANTS** Arthritis Research Campaign and Child Action North West (£3,000) each; RSPB (£2,500); Samaritans (£2,000); East Lancashire Guides and East Lancashire Guides (£1,500 each); and Guide Dogs for the Blind (£300).

**FINANCES** Year 2013/14 Income £43,250 Grants £23,700 Grants to organisations £23,700 Assets £2,655,152

**TRUSTEES** David Rusman; Nigel Brooke; Matthew Brooke; James Brooke.

**OTHER INFORMATION** £12,350 was awarded in total to organisations for children and young people; and £11,350 was awarded in total to other organisations.

**HOW TO APPLY** The correspondent stated that the charity's annual income is not for general distribution as it is committed to a limited number of charities on a long-term basis.

**WHO TO APPLY TO** Nigel Brooke, Trustee, Fairways, 17 Mill Lane, Great Harwood, Blackburn, Lancashire BB6 7UQ email nigel.brooke@tiscali.co.uk

■ **The Rory and Elizabeth Brooks Foundation**

**CC NO** 1111587     **ESTABLISHED** 2005

**WHERE FUNDING CAN BE GIVEN** Worldwide.

**WHO CAN BENEFIT** Charitable organisations.

**WHAT IS FUNDED** The main objects of the charity are to promote and advance education, medical research, healthcare, community care and arts and culture.

**FINANCES** Year 2013/14 Income £300,177 Grants £396,620 Grants to organisations £396,620 Assets £226,357

**TRUSTEES** Elizabeth Brooks; Roderick Brooks; David Way.

**OTHER INFORMATION** A list of beneficiaries was unavailable, but the total amount was shared between 20 organisations.
**HOW TO APPLY** Apply in writing to the correspondent.
**WHO TO APPLY TO** Mary Nuttall, Grand Buildings, One Strand, Trafalgar Square, London WC2N 5HR *Tel.* 020 7024 2200 *email* MNUTTALL@MMLCAPITAL.COM

## ■ The Charles Brotherton Trust

**CC NO** 227067  **ESTABLISHED** 1940
**WHERE FUNDING CAN BE GIVEN** The cities of Birmingham, Leeds, Liverpool, Wakefield, York and Bebington in the borough of Wirral.
**WHO CAN BENEFIT** Charitable organisations.
**WHAT IS FUNDED** 'The charity is principally directed to encourage young people to improve their own lives by taking advantage of educational opportunities and organised recreational activities. The charity is also empowered to help improve the standard of living of the elderly and disabled people and relieve the suffering caused by illness.'
**WHAT IS NOT FUNDED** Grants to registered charities and recognised bodies only. No grants are given to individuals.
**TYPE OF GRANT** Recurrent.
**RANGE OF GRANTS** £100–£6,000. Mostly £250 or less.
**SAMPLE GRANTS** University of Leeds Brotherton Library (£6,000); University of Leeds (£3,000); Brotherton Park – Dibbinsdale Nature Centre (£500); Salvation Army, Shaftesbury Youth Club (£250 each); Birmingham City Mission, Queen Alexandra College (£200 each); Age Concern Leeds (£150); Sailors' Children's' Society (£100).
**FINANCES** *Year* 2013/14 *Income* £81,879 *Grants* £62,675 *Grants to organisations* £62,675 *Assets* £1,775,486
**TRUSTEES** C. Brotherton-Ratcliffe; D. Ratcliffe-Brotherton.
**HOW TO APPLY** Apply in writing to the correspondent. The application should clearly show the organisation's activities, geographical area of operations, and for what the funds are required. Applications should be accompanied by the organisation's most recent set of accounts. There is no formal application form and applications are not acknowledged. Grants are considered by the trustees at the start of the trust's accounting year in April, and a single payment made to successful applicants in October. (Scholarships are available to students on scientific courses at the universities of Leeds, Liverpool, Birmingham and York, but applications for these must be made to the university in question, not to the above correspondent.)
**WHO TO APPLY TO** The Secretary, PO Box 374, Harrogate, North Yorkshire HG1 4YW *email* admin@charlesbrothertontrust.com *Website* www.charlesbrothertontrust.com

## ■ Bill Brown 1989 Charitable Trust

**CC NO** 801756  **ESTABLISHED** 1989
**WHERE FUNDING CAN BE GIVEN** UK, preference for South England.
**WHO CAN BENEFIT** Charities registered in the UK.
**WHAT IS FUNDED** Research into blindness, medical research, deaf and blind people, elderly, people with disabilities, general welfare and hospices.
**WHAT IS NOT FUNDED** Individuals; animal welfare; small/local charitable causes; wildlife or environmental charities; building maintenance; regional branches of national charitable organisations or religious charities.
**TYPE OF GRANT** Mainly recurrent.
**RANGE OF GRANTS** Mostly of £7,500, but up to £75,000.
**SAMPLE GRANTS** Charities Aid Foundation Trust (£75,000); Macmillan Cancer Support and Salvation Army (£15,000 each); GLMW Scout County Chalfont Development Fund (£11,000); Alzheimer's Society, Cancer Research UK, Contact the Elderly, Crohn's and Colitis UK, St Christopher's Hospice (£7,500 each); Barnardo's, NCH Action for Children, Richmond Borough Mind (£3,750 each).
**FINANCES** *Year* 2013/14 *Income* £361,027 *Grants* £194,000 *Grants to organisations* £194,000 *Assets* £13,972,817
**TRUSTEES** G. S. Brown; A. J. Barnett.
**HOW TO APPLY** Apply in writing containing the following: aims and objectives of the charity; nature of appeal; total target if for a specific project; contributions received against target; registered charity number; any other relevant factors. Appeals should be accompanied by a set of the organisation's latest report and full accounts. The trustees meet to consider applications in mid-June and December; applications should be received by the end of May and October to be considered at the respective meeting. Only successful applicants will be notified.
**WHO TO APPLY TO** The Trustees, BM BOX 4567, London WC1N 3XX *email* aanother@phb.co.uk *Website* www.billbrowncharity.org

## ■ R. S. Brownless Charitable Trust

**CC NO** 1000320  **ESTABLISHED** 1990
**WHERE FUNDING CAN BE GIVEN** Mainly UK and occasionally overseas.
**WHO CAN BENEFIT** Organisations working with children, young adults and people with disabilities.
**WHAT IS FUNDED** Accommodation and housing, education, job creation and voluntary work.
**WHAT IS NOT FUNDED** Grants are rarely given to individuals for educational projects or to education or conservation causes or overseas aid.
**TYPE OF GRANT** Usually one-off; sometimes annual.
**RANGE OF GRANTS** Up to £2,000 (occasionally more); usually £100–£500.
**SAMPLE GRANTS** Previous beneficiaries have included: Alzheimer's Society, Camp Mohawk, Casa Allianza UK, Crisis, Foundation for Study of Infant Deaths, Prader-Willi Foundation, St Andrew's Hall, UNICEF, Wargrave PCC and Witham on the Hill PCC. No details of 2013/14 beneficiaries were provided by the trust.
**FINANCES** *Year* 2013/14 *Income* £56,464 *Grants* £50,745 *Grants to organisations* £50,745 *Assets* £1,447,874
**TRUSTEES** Frances Plummer; Philippa Nicolai.
**HOW TO APPLY** Apply in writing to the correspondent. The trustees meet twice a year, but in special circumstances will meet at other times. The trust is unable to acknowledge all requests.
**WHO TO APPLY TO** Philippa Nicolai, Trustee, Hennerton Holt, Hennerton, Wargrave, Reading RG10 8PD *Tel.* 0118 940 4029

# The Brownsword Charitable Foundation

**CC NO** 1012615 **ESTABLISHED** 1992
**WHERE FUNDING CAN BE GIVEN** The city of Bath, principally but not exclusively.
**WHO CAN BENEFIT** Charitable organisations, preferably in the city of Bath.
**WHAT IS FUNDED** General charitable purposes, with particular focus on children and young people, older people, the arts, community and neighbourhood work, physical and learning disabilities, educational projects and medical projects.
**TYPE OF GRANT** One-off grants to organisations.
**RANGE OF GRANTS** £200–£35,000
**SAMPLE GRANTS** Cancer Research (£35,000); Iford Arts (£5,000); Merchant Venturers, Dartington Hall, and Trust Friends of the RUH (£1,000 each); SEKSA (£500); RNLI (£250); Penny Brohn Cancer Care, and The Grateful Society (£200 each).
**FINANCES** Year 2013 Income £214,460 Grants £44,150 Grants to organisations £44,150 Assets £9,398,538
**TRUSTEES** Christina Brownsword; Andrew Brownsword; Robert Calleja.
**HOW TO APPLY** Apply in writing to the correspondent.
**WHO TO APPLY TO** Nicholas Burrows, Correspondent, 4 Queen Square, Bath BA1 2HA *Tel.* 01225 339661

# The T. B. H. Brunner Charitable Settlement

**CC NO** 260604 **ESTABLISHED** 1969
**WHERE FUNDING CAN BE GIVEN** UK with some preference for Oxfordshire.
**WHO CAN BENEFIT** Registered charities and individuals.
**WHAT IS FUNDED** Church of England preservation projects and other charities dealing with historical preservation, both local to Oxfordshire and nationally; the arts; music; and general charitable purposes.
**RANGE OF GRANTS** £100–£3,000
**SAMPLE GRANTS** Friends of Dorchester Abbey (£8,000 in two grants); Institute of Economic Affairs and Peppard Church of England Primary School (£2,500 each); Oxfordshire Victoria Country House Trust (£2,000); Rotherfield Greys PCC (£1,500); British Suzuki Insitute (£1,000); Listening Library and York Minster Fund (£500); Cothill House Appeal (£250); Moorfields Eye Hospital (£100).
**FINANCES** Year 2013/14 Income £58,038 Grants £50,750 Grants to organisations £50,750 Assets £2,108,340
**TRUSTEES** Timothy Brunner; Helen Brunner; Dr Imogen Brunner.
**OTHER INFORMATION** Grants were made to 53 organisations during the year.
**HOW TO APPLY** Apply in writing to the correspondent.
**WHO TO APPLY TO** Timothy Brunner, Trustee, Flat 4, 2 Inverness Gardens, London W8 4RN *Tel.* 020 7727 6277 *email* p.roberts@robco.uk.com

# The Jack Brunton Charitable Trust

**CC NO** 518407 **ESTABLISHED** 1986
**WHERE FUNDING CAN BE GIVEN** North Riding area of Yorkshire prior to the 1974 boundary changes
**WHO CAN BENEFIT** Registered charities for the benefit of the population of the rural villages and towns within the beneficial area.
**WHAT IS FUNDED** General charitable purposes.
**WHAT IS NOT FUNDED** 'Grants to individuals or out of area applicants are only made in very rare and exceptional circumstances.'
**TYPE OF GRANT** One-off for capital costs.
**RANGE OF GRANTS** Between £100 and £40,000.
**SAMPLE GRANTS** York Minster (£55,000); James Cook Hospital (£10,000); Girl Guiding and Kirby Fleetham Village Hall (£5,000 each); Ocean Youth Trust and Stokesley Cricket Club (3,000 each); Asthma Relief and Relate (£2,000 each); Barnardo's (£1,500); Doorways Youth Project, East Cleveland Youth Housing, Just the Job, Mind (£1,000 each).
**FINANCES** Year 2013/14 Income £142,570 Grants £129,560 Grants to organisations £129,560 Assets £4,951,676
**TRUSTEES** Joan Brunton; Jonathan Brunton; Edward Marquis; Derek Noble; James Lumb; Dr Clair Hurst.
**OTHER INFORMATION** In 2013/14 grants were given to 45 organisations.
**HOW TO APPLY** Apply in writing to the correspondent including full details of costings if relevant.
**WHO TO APPLY TO** David Swallow, Correspondent, Commercial House, 10 Bridge Road, Stokesley, North Yorkshire TS9 5AA *Tel.* 01642 711407 *email* margaretc@swallco.co.uk

# The Bruntwood Charity

**CC NO** 1135777 **ESTABLISHED** 2010
**WHERE FUNDING CAN BE GIVEN** UK, mainly in the areas charities in each of the four areas where the company has a presence.
**WHO CAN BENEFIT** Registered charities.
**WHAT IS FUNDED** General charitable purposes and social welfare, especially with regards to children and disability causes. The charity focuses on fundraising for five charities: Claire House Children's Hospice – Liverpool; Onside and the Factory Youth Zone – Manchester; St Gemma's Hospice – Leeds; Whizz-Kidz – Birmingham.
**RANGE OF GRANTS** £2,300–£40,000
**SAMPLE GRANTS** Onside – Manchester (£40,000); Factory Youth Zone – Manchester (£30,000); Clare House (£8,000); Prince's Trust – Birmingham (£6,000); Whizz-Kidz (£4,000); and St Martens House (£2,300).
**FINANCES** Year 2012/13 Income £64,887 Grants £90,345 Grants to organisations £90,345 Assets £25,903
**TRUSTEES** Katharine Vokes; Sally Hill; Kathryn Graham; Jane Williams; Peter Crowther.
**OTHER INFORMATION** This is the charity of Bruntwood Ltd, a company which owns and manages commercial property and offices space in Birmingham, Leeds, Manchester and Liverpool. At the time of writing (June 2015) this was the latest information available.
**HOW TO APPLY** The charity states that 'as their funds are fully committed they do not seek unsolicited requests for funding'.
**WHO TO APPLY TO** Sally Hill, Trustee, Bruntwood Ltd, City Tower, Piccadilly Plaza, Manchester M1 4BT *Tel.* 0161 237 3883

## ■ Brushmill Ltd

**CC NO** 285420     **ESTABLISHED** 1982
**WHERE FUNDING CAN BE GIVEN** Worldwide.
**WHO CAN BENEFIT** Organisations benefitting Jewish people.
**WHAT IS FUNDED** Jewish charitable purposes, education and social welfare.
**SAMPLE GRANTS Previous beneficiaries have included:** Bais Rochel, Friends of Yeshivas Shaar Hashomaim and Holmleigh Trust.
**FINANCES** Year 2013/14 Income £326,305 Grants £326,300 Grants to organisations £326,300 Assets £34,223
**TRUSTEES** Mr C. Getter, Chair; Mr J. Weinberger; Mrs E. Weinberger.
**OTHER INFORMATION** A list of beneficiaries was not available.
**HOW TO APPLY** Apply in writing to the correspondent.
**WHO TO APPLY TO** Mrs M. Getter, Secretary, 76 Fairholt Road, London N16 5HN *email* mail@cohenarnold.com

## ■ Buckingham Trust

**CC NO** 237350     **ESTABLISHED** 1962
**WHERE FUNDING CAN BE GIVEN** UK and worldwide.
**WHO CAN BENEFIT** Charitable organisations and churches.
**WHAT IS FUNDED** Advancement of religion (including missionary activities); relief of people disadvantaged by poverty and older people or those who are ill.
**TYPE OF GRANT** One-off and recurrent grants.
**RANGE OF GRANTS** Up to £104,000.
**SAMPLE GRANTS** Battle Methodist Church (£104,500); Titus Trust (£81,300); Grace Church (£28,000); Cure International (£25,400); The Manor Prep School (£6,000); New Life Church (£4,300); Marine Research (£2,100); Godalming Baptist (£2,000); Roding Valley Church (£1,500); Christians in Sport (£1,100).
**FINANCES** Year 2013/14 Income £293,073 Grants £386,941 Grants to organisations £372,381 Assets £734,029
**TRUSTEES** Richard Foot; Tina Clay.
**OTHER INFORMATION** Preference is given to charities of which the trustees have personal interest, knowledge, or association. The trust acts mainly as an agency charity acting on behalf of other donors. The grant total also includes £14,600 in grants to individuals.
**WHO TO APPLY TO** The Trustees, Foot Davson, 17 Church Road, Tunbridge Wells, Kent TN1 1LG *Tel.* 01892 774774

## ■ Buckinghamshire Community Foundation

**CC NO** 1073861     **ESTABLISHED** 1998
**WHERE FUNDING CAN BE GIVEN** Buckinghamshire.
**WHO CAN BENEFIT** Voluntary and community groups.
**WHAT IS FUNDED** Community development. Visit the foundation's website for details of up-to-date schemes.
**WHAT IS NOT FUNDED** Organisations outside the beneficial area; individuals; religious or political organisations; animal welfare or to statutory organisations (with the exception of Parish Councils).
**RANGE OF GRANTS** £5,000–£960,000
**SAMPLE GRANTS** Community First Endowment Match (£962,883); Prevention Matters (£150,000); Kop Hill Climb (£55,500); South Bucks Education Fund (£50,000); Big Local Marsh and Micklefield (£34,000); Community Philanthropy (£30,000); Oving Community Fund (£20,000); North Bucks Fund (£15,000); Martin Baker Fund (£10,000); Bucks CC Social Opportunity Fund, Salter (£5,000).
**FINANCES** Year 2013/14 Income £1,750,555 Grants £582,773 Grants to organisations £582,773 Assets £5,103,110
**TRUSTEES** Peter Keen; David Sumpter; Roy Collis; Simon Deans; Colin Hayfield; Munir Hussain; The Countess Howe; Graham Corney; Linda Clegg; Carl Etholen.
**HOW TO APPLY** In the first instance, an 'expression of interest' form available from the Foundation's website, where criteria and guidelines are also posted.
**WHO TO APPLY TO** Richard Dickson, Foundation House, 119A Bicester Road, Aylesbury, Buckinghamshire HP19 9BA *Tel.* 01296 330134 *Fax* 01296 330158 *email* info@buckscf.org.uk *Website* www.buckscf.org.uk

## ■ The Buckinghamshire Historic Churches Trust

**CC NO** 206471     **ESTABLISHED** 1957
**WHERE FUNDING CAN BE GIVEN** The county or archdeaconry of Buckingham.
**WHO CAN BENEFIT** Parochial church councils or trustees of Christian churches and chapels, including Baptist, Anglican, Methodist and Catholic.
**WHAT IS FUNDED** The preservation, repair, maintenance and upkeep of the fabric of churches or chapels in Buckinghamshire. Grants are made to churches and chapels embarking upon restoration.
**WHAT IS NOT FUNDED** Repairs to bells, bell frames, bell chambers, window glass, organs, furnishings; work on heating, lighting, decoration, churchyard maintenance. Churches and chapels not in use for public worship are not supported.
**TYPE OF GRANT** One-off.
**RANGE OF GRANTS** £500–£20,000
**SAMPLE GRANTS** St Mary Ludgershall (£20,000); St Mary the Virgin Long Crendon (£15,000); Baptist Church Princes Risborough (£14,000); St James the Less Dorney, (£10,000 each); All Saints Bisham, Former Methodist Church Wolverton, St Mary Cold Brayfield, St Mary Farnham Royal (£5,000 each); St Dunstan Monks Risborough (£4,000); St Nicholas Ickford (£2,000); St John, Ashley Green (£500).
**FINANCES** Year 2013/14 Income £92,607 Grants £95,500 Grants to organisations £95,500 Assets £827,287
**TRUSTEES** Sir Henry Aubrey-Fletcher; Caroline Abel-Smith; Cherry Aston; Rupert Carington; Revd Canon Herbert Cavell-Northam; Ann Cutcliffe; Roger Evans; Hon Jenefer Farncombe; Andrew Finn-Kelcey; Jennifer Moss; Timothy Oliver; Francis Robinson; Mary Villiers; Rt Revd Alan Wilson; Mary Saunders; Marilynne Morgan.
**OTHER INFORMATION** In 2012/13 grants were given to 11 churches.
**HOW TO APPLY** An application form is available from the correspondent.
**WHO TO APPLY TO** Mrs Penny Keens, Hon. Secretary, C/O Community Impact Bucks, 6 Centre Parade, Place Farm Way, Monks Risborough, Princes Risborough HP27 9JS *Tel.* 01844 274162 *email* penny@pkeens.plus.com *Website* www.bucks-historic-churches.org

## ■ The Buckinghamshire Masonic Centenary Fund

**CC NO** 1007193  **ESTABLISHED** 1991
**WHERE FUNDING CAN BE GIVEN** Buckinghamshire.
**WHO CAN BENEFIT** Individuals and registered charities, including hospitals and hospices, schools and nurseries, youth groups, residential homes, nursing and day care centres, charities for people with disabilities, victim support charities, ex-service charities.
**WHAT IS FUNDED** General charitable purposes in Buckinghamshire. Grants may be given to non-Masonic charitable causes with a strong Buckinghamshire connection. Charities that work with individuals in Buckinghamshire or those that have connections to surrounding areas as well as Buckinghamshire will be considered. Grants may be given to individuals in need if referred through a welfare or health agency.
**WHAT IS NOT FUNDED** National charities; general running costs.
**TYPE OF GRANT** Grants are given for specific projects or facilities, rather than general appeals or core costs.
**RANGE OF GRANTS** Up to £15,000.
**SAMPLE GRANTS** Wendover Community Library (£4,200); High Wycombe Amateur Boxing Club (£3,600); Search Dogs Bucks (£2,800); Action 4 Youth and Chesham Cricket Club (£2,600 each); Aylesbury Project (£2,500); Denham ATC (£1,200); Wycombe Talking Newspapers (£600); Slough Mayoral Charity (£500); International Scout Jamboree – St Peter and St Paul Lodge (£250).
**FINANCES** Year 2013/14 Income £36,921 Grants £29,646 Grants to organisations £29,646 Assets £717,419
**TRUSTEES** Clifford Drake; Michael Stimson; Robert Wharton.
**OTHER INFORMATION** 19 grants were made in 2013/14. The fund receives its income solely from the Buckinghamshire Freemasons.
**HOW TO APPLY** Apply in writing to the correspondent, concisely setting out the aims and objectives of the organisation, along with the latest annual report and audited accounts. Details should be supplied of the specific facilities or projects for which funding is sought, as well as a budget and forecast of how the required total will be raised. Guidelines are given on the fund's website. The trustees meet three or four times a year to consider applications and meeting dates are published on the website. Applications should be sent at least two weeks before a meeting.
**WHO TO APPLY TO** Peter Carey, Correspondent, 46 Parklands, Great Linford, Milton Keynes, Buckinghamshire MK14 5DZ Tel. 01908 605997 email peterrcarey@gmail.com Website www.buckspgl.org

## ■ The Buffini Chao Foundation

**CC NO** 1111022  **ESTABLISHED** 2005
**WHERE FUNDING CAN BE GIVEN** England and Wales.
**WHO CAN BENEFIT** Charitable organisations.
**WHAT IS FUNDED** General charitable purposes, especially organisations working in the field of education and with children.
**RANGE OF GRANTS** Up to £50,000.
**SAMPLE GRANTS** The Community Foundation Surrey (£30,000); Suburban Hockey (£20,000); Build Africa, Kaine Management Limited for Yes You Can school mentoring project and Tonbridge School (£10,000 each); and London Children's Ballet – Dancer sponsorship (£4,500).
**FINANCES** Year 2013/14 Income £79,632 Grants £106,024 Grants to organisations £106,024 Assets £5,277,671
**TRUSTEES** Deborah Buffini; Damon Buffini; Maria Hindmarsh; Sue Gutierrez.
**HOW TO APPLY** Apply in writing to the correspondent.
**WHO TO APPLY TO** Deborah Buffini, Trustee, 77 Mount Ephraim Road, Tunbridge Wells, Kent TN4 8BS Tel. 01892 701801

## ■ The Bulldog Trust Limited

**CC NO** 1123081  **ESTABLISHED** 1983
**WHERE FUNDING CAN BE GIVEN** Worldwide, with a preference for the South of England.
**WHO CAN BENEFIT** Charitable organisations.
**WHAT IS FUNDED** General charitable purposes.
**WHAT IS NOT FUNDED** Individuals; unsolicited applications.
**RANGE OF GRANTS** £10,000 to £100,000.
**SAMPLE GRANTS** Caius House (£100,000); British Paraorchestra (£30,000); Campaign for Drawing (£20,000); Team UP (£28,000); Arts Together and North London Cares (£18,000 each) Sydney Children's Hospitals (£17,000); The Hailer Foundation (£15,000); Apollo Music Projects (£12,000); Dance United and Find a Cure (£10,000 each).
**FINANCES** Year 2013/14 Income £1,169,503 Grants £517,768 Grants to organisations £517,768 Assets £10,080,593
**TRUSTEES** Martin Riley; Brian Smouha; Charles Hoare; Hamish McPherson; Kim Hoare; Alex Williams.
**HOW TO APPLY** The trust regrets that unsolicited applications cannot be accepted.
**WHO TO APPLY TO** Mary Gunn, Correspondent, 2 Temple Place, London WC2R 3BD Tel. 020 7240 6044 email info@bulldogtrust.org Website www.bulldogtrust.org

## ■ The E. F. Bulmer Benevolent Fund

**CC NO** 214831  **ESTABLISHED** 1938
**WHERE FUNDING CAN BE GIVEN** Herefordshire.
**WHO CAN BENEFIT** Organisations, former employees of H P Bulmer Holdings plc or its subsidiaries and individuals.
**WHAT IS FUNDED** Organisations benefitting people who are sick or disadvantaged by poverty. Former employees of H P Bulmer Holdings plc and individuals who are in need.
**WHAT IS NOT FUNDED** Large UK charities and those from outside Herefordshire are unlikely to be supported.
**TYPE OF GRANT** One-off for capital (including buildings), core costs, feasibility studies, project, research, running costs, salaries and start-up costs. Funding may be given for up to three years.
**RANGE OF GRANTS** Up to £10,000.
**SAMPLE GRANTS** Bulmer Foundation (£10,000); British Red Cross Hereford and Worcester (£6,000); Yeleni Support Centre For Cancer and Chronic Illness (£5,000); Herefordshire Community Foundation (£4,100); Acorns Children's Hospice, Combat Stress, Family Drug Support, Hereford Deaf Children's Society, Marie Curie Cancer Care (£3,000 each).
**FINANCES** Year 2013/14 Income £383,452 Grants £234,885 Grants to organisations £151,129 Assets £13,136,075

**Burden** — Alphabetical register of grant-making charities

**TRUSTEES** Richard Bulmer; Edward Bulmer; Jocelyn Wood; Andrew Patten; Hannah Lort-Phillips.

**OTHER INFORMATION** The grant total includes £28,000 to HP Bulmer pensioners pension supplement. £26,000 to pensioners of H P Bulmer Holdings plc or its subsidiaries and £18,000 to other individuals.

**HOW TO APPLY** Apply in writing to the correspondent, although a voluntary application form is available and will be sent if requested. Applications should be accompanied by a copy of the latest report and accounts. The administrator is very happy to discuss applications by e-mail or telephone prior to the application being submitted. The trustees usually meet four times a year. Smaller groups who may have difficulty in receiving support from large national trusts are normally given priority. More detailed information on applying for grants is available on the fund's website

**WHO TO APPLY TO** James Greenfield, Correspondent, Fred Bulmer Centre, Wall Street, Hereford, Herefordshire HR4 9HP *Tel.* 01432 271293 *email* efbulmer@gmail.com *Website* www.efbulmer.co.uk

···········································

## ■ The Burden Trust

**CC NO** 235859   **ESTABLISHED** 1913

**WHERE FUNDING CAN BE GIVEN** UK and overseas.

**WHO CAN BENEFIT** Charitable organisations; hospitals; retirement homes; schools and training institutions.

**WHAT IS FUNDED** Medical research, hospitals, retirement homes, schools and training institutions, homes and care for young and people in need. The trust operates with an adherence to the tenets and principles of the Church of England.

**WHAT IS NOT FUNDED** Individuals.

**TYPE OF GRANT** Recurring and one-off. Grants are not automatic and must be applied for annually.

**SAMPLE GRANTS** Langham Research Scholarships and Trinity College Bristol (£20,000); Easton Families Project (£18,000); Oxford Centre for Mission Studies (£16,000); Union Biblical Seminary, Pune (£14,000); Crisis Centre Ministries (£12,000); Changing Tunes (£6,000); Wheels Project (£4,000); Barton Camp (£3,000); Alive (£2,500).

**FINANCES** *Year* 2013/14 *Income* £141,303 *Grants* £138,000 *Grants to organisations* £138,000 *Assets* £4,404,343

**TRUSTEES** Anthony Miles; Dr Joanna Bacon; Robert Bernays; Colin Havill; Prof. Andrew Halestrap; Prof. Gordon Stirrat.

**HOW TO APPLY** Via the online form available on the trust's website by 31 March each year in preparation for the trustee meeting in June. Once an online application is submitted the trustees will make further contact before the June meeting if they want a full application.

**WHO TO APPLY TO** Patrick O'Conor, Secretary, 51 Downs Park West, Westbury Park, Bristol BS6 7QL *Tel.* 0117 962 8611 *email* p.oconor@netgates.co.uk *Website* www.burdentrustbristol.co.uk

···········································

## ■ Burden's Charitable Foundation

**CC NO** 273185   **ESTABLISHED** 1977

**WHERE FUNDING CAN BE GIVEN** UK, but mostly overseas, with special interest in Sub-Saharan Africa.

**WHO CAN BENEFIT** Registered charities; community organisations.

**WHAT IS FUNDED** The charity's objectives outlined in the accounts state: 'There are no formal restrictions on the charitable activities that can be supported, but the Trustees' main activities currently embrace the prevention and relief of acute, poverty, substantially through the medium of education and healthcare and most especially in countries such as those of sub-Saharan Africa.'

**WHAT IS NOT FUNDED** Individuals; loans. Our research suggests that causes which rarely or never benefit include: animal welfare (except in less developed countries); arts and museums; political activities; most medical research; preservation of historic buildings and monuments; individual educational grants; sport, except sport for people with disabilities.

**TYPE OF GRANT** One-off or, exceptionally, more than one year; capital; project, research; running costs; salaries; start-up funding.

**RANGE OF GRANTS** £3,000–£49,000

**SAMPLE GRANTS** Previous beneficiaries have included: Build-it (£49,000); The Message Trust (£20,000); REAP (£11,000); Kings World Trust India and Wuluga (£10,000 each); Tenovus (£5,000); Zagalona Workshop (£3,000).

**FINANCES** *Grants* £250,000 *Grants to organisations* £250,000

**TRUSTEES** Arthur Burden; Godfrey Burden; Hilary Perkins; Sally Schofield; Anthony Burden; Prof. A. D. Burden; Timothy Burden.

**OTHER INFORMATION** At the time of writing (June 2015) this was the latest information available. The foundation has not submitted its accounts since 2011/12. In the past grants have totalled over £250,000 a year on average, with over £60,000 given in the UK and over £180,000 overseas.

**HOW TO APPLY** Applications may be made in writing to the correspondent, accompanied by the most recent, audited annual report and accounts. You should also give the outline of your business plan, where relevant, and brief details of the project. The trustees usually meet in March, June, September and December.

**WHO TO APPLY TO** Arthur Burden, Trustee, St George's House, 215–219 Chester Road, Manchester M15 4JE *Tel.* 0161 832 4901 *email* burdenscharitablefoundation@gmail.com

···········································

## ■ The Burdett Trust for Nursing

**CC NO** 1089849   **ESTABLISHED** 2001

**WHERE FUNDING CAN BE GIVEN** Mostly UK.

**WHO CAN BENEFIT** Nurses and other healthcare professionals involved in innovative projects.

**WHAT IS FUNDED** The trust makes grants to support the nursing contribution to health care. The trust's website states three key priority areas: *Building nursing research capacity* – 'supporting clinical nursing research and research addressing policy, leadership development and delivery of nursing care'; *Building nurse leadership capacity* – 'supporting nurses in their professional development to create a cadre of excellent nursing and allied health professionals who will become leaders of the future and foster excellence and capacity-building in advancing the nursing profession'; *Supporting Local Nurse-led Initiatives* – 'supporting nurse-led initiatives that make a difference at local level and are focused explicitly on improving care for patients and users of services'. Details on the current grant programmes can be found on the trust's website.

**WHAT IS NOT FUNDED** Consult the relevant programme guidance for information on the funding criteria.

**TYPE OF GRANT** Usually one-off, although up to three years will be considered.
**RANGE OF GRANTS** Up to £400,000.
**SAMPLE GRANTS** International Council of Nurses (£407,000 in partnership funding); C3 Collaborating for Health (£300,000); Junius S Morgan Benevolent Fund (£250,000 towards a small grants programme for nurses in hardship); Age UK/NHS Confederation/Local Government Association (£200,000); De Montfort University (£158,000); Winston Churchill Memorial Trust (£120,000 in partnership funding); Kings College Hospital NHS Foundation Trust (£62,500); Florence Nightingale Foundation (£50,000 in partnership funding); St Christopher's Hospice (£39,500); Breast Cancer Care (£22,000); Cambodian Nurse Conference (£3,100); Tenovus (£1,000).
**FINANCES** Year 2013 Income £1,606,330 Grants £3,688,085 Grants to organisations £3,321,057 Assets £71,943,344
**TRUSTEES** Alan Gibbs, Chair; Dame Christine Beasley; Jack Gibbs; Bill Gordon; Andrew Martin-Smith; Lady Henrietta St George; Eileen Sills; Jo Webber; Evy Hambro; David Sines.
**OTHER INFORMATION** The grants total above refers to funds committed in the year. During 2013 grants to individuals totalled £367,000, of which £150,000 was given in bursaries to 53 individuals.
**HOW TO APPLY** See the trust's website for information on the current grant programmes and details on how to apply.
**WHO TO APPLY TO** Shirley Baines, Charity Grants Director, Rathbone Trust Company Ltd, 1 Curzon Street, London W1J 5FB *Tel.* 020 7399 0102 *Fax* 020 7399 0050 *email* administrator@btfn.org.uk *Website* www.btfn.org.uk

## ■ The Clara E. Burgess Charity

**CC NO** 1072546    **ESTABLISHED** 1998
**WHERE FUNDING CAN BE GIVEN** UK and overseas.
**WHO CAN BENEFIT** Registered charities benefitting children.
**WHAT IS FUNDED** Children and young people; facilities of and assistance for education, health and physical well-being. Preference may be given to younger children under the age of ten who have lost one or both parents.
**WHAT IS NOT FUNDED** Non-registered charities.
**TYPE OF GRANT** One-off and recurrent (up to three years); capital and core costs; salaries; projects; research; start-up costs.
**RANGE OF GRANTS** £500–£10,000
**SAMPLE GRANTS** **Previous beneficiaries have included:** Adoption UK, Operation Orphan, Positive Action on Cancer and Rucksack (£10,000 each); Smile Train (£7,500); Autism Initiatives (£5,500); Douglas Bader Foundation, Play Train, Richard House, Sign Post and The Dyslexia Research Trust (£5,000 each); Friends of Castle Wood School (£4,000); International Refugee Trust (£3,500); Nelson's Journey and Toybox (£3,000 each); Campus Children's Holidays (£2,900); Dove Service and Royal Horticultural Society (£2,000 each); Goodwill Children's Homes (£1,500); Human Farleigh Hospice and Mentor Link (£500 each).
**FINANCES** Year 2013/14 Income £264,473 Grants £295,500 Grants to organisations £295,500
**TRUSTEE** The Royal Bank of Scotland plc.
**OTHER INFORMATION** In 2013/14 the charity had a total charitable expenditure of £492,000. At the time of writing (June 2015) the latest accounts for were not published by the Charity

Commission. In the previous years, grants amounted to about 60% of the overall expenditure; therefore it is likely that grants totalled about £295,500. Each year about 50–60 awards are made.
**HOW TO APPLY** Applications can be made in writing to the correspondent and are considered in January and July.
**WHO TO APPLY TO** The Trust Section Manager, c/o RBS Trust Administration, Eastwood House, Glebe Road, Chelmsford, Essex CM1 1RS *Tel.* 01245 292453

## ■ The Burry Charitable Trust

**CC NO** 281045    **ESTABLISHED** 1961
**WHERE FUNDING CAN BE GIVEN** UK, with a preference for Highcliffe and the surrounding and further areas.
**WHO CAN BENEFIT** Charities, voluntary groups and other not-for-profit organisations.
**WHAT IS FUNDED** Medicine, health, disability and welfare.
**WHAT IS NOT FUNDED** Individuals; students.
**RANGE OF GRANTS** £250–£25,000
**SAMPLE GRANTS** Hordle Church of England School (£25,000); Oakhaven Hospital Trust (£11,500); Mobility Trust (£5,600); Diverse Abilities Plus (£5,000 each); Canine Partners and Salvation Army, Not Forgotten Association (£5,000 each); Salvation Army, Canine Partners, Wessex Heartbeat (£2,500 each); New Forest Mencap (£1,000); Ability Net (£500); Sway Welfare Aid Group (£250).
**FINANCES** Year 2013/14 Income £57,573 Grants £76,670 Grants to organisations £76,670 Assets £932,018
**TRUSTEES** Robert Burry; Adrian Osman; Judith Knight; James Lapage.
**HOW TO APPLY** **This trust states that it does not respond to unsolicited applications.**
**WHO TO APPLY TO** Robert J. Burry, Trustee, 261 Lymington Road, Highcliffe, Christchurch, Dorset BH23 5EE *Tel.* 01425 277661 *email* sarahteague@hoburne.com

## ■ The Arnold Burton 1998 Charitable Trust

**CC NO** 1074633    **ESTABLISHED** 1998
**WHERE FUNDING CAN BE GIVEN** Worldwide.
**WHO CAN BENEFIT** Jewish charities.
**WHAT IS FUNDED** Medical research, education, social welfare and heritage.
**WHAT IS NOT FUNDED** Individuals.
**RANGE OF GRANTS** £100–£40,000
**SAMPLE GRANTS** Garsington Opera Ltd (£40,000); Donisthorpe Hall, Harrogate Hebrew Congregation and Leeds Jewish Welfare Board (£20,000 each); Corda (£10,000); West Oxfordshire Citizen's Advice Bureau and Gladrags Community Costume Resource (£5,0000 each); Yorkshire Cancer Centre Appeal and The Jewish Museum (£1,000 each); Mental Health Foundation and Woolf Institute (£500 each); Act in Teens and The Samaritans (£250 each); British Heart Foundation and Wetherby in Bloom (£100 each).
**FINANCES** Year 2013/14 Income £172,399 Grants £183,350 Grants to organisations £183,350 Assets £5,983,866
**TRUSTEES** Mark Burton; Jeremy Burton; Nicholas Burton.

**HOW TO APPLY** Apply in writing to the trust managers. Unsuccessful appeals will not necessarily be acknowledged.
**WHO TO APPLY TO** The Trust Managers, c/o Trustee Management Ltd, 19 Cookridge Street, Leeds LS2 3AG *Tel.* 0113 243 6466

## ■ Consolidated Charity of Burton upon Trent

**CC NO** 239072   **ESTABLISHED** 1981
**WHERE FUNDING CAN BE GIVEN** The former county borough of Burton upon Trent and the parishes of Branston, Stretton and Outwoods.
**WHO CAN BENEFIT** Individuals, and organisations that benefit people in need, who live in the beneficial area.
**WHAT IS FUNDED** General charitable purposes.
**WHAT IS NOT FUNDED** Salaries.
**RANGE OF GRANTS** Up to £19,000.
**SAMPLE GRANTS** **Sport Recreation and Leisure**: East Staffordshire Powerchair Football Club (£5,000); ESBC Sports Development (£1,500); Able Too Forum (£1,081); Winshill Parish FC (£500). **Education and Youth Development**: Burton and District Art Council (£1,000). **Voluntary Groups**: Branston Village Hall (£3,500); Carver Road Community Centre and Burton and District Mind (£3,000 each); East Staffordshire CVS (£2,500); Little Theatre Company (£2,000). **Faith**: The Parish of our lady of the Most Holy Rosary (£1,000). **Health Social Welfare and Care**: Burton and District Stroke Club and Happy Days Children's Charity (£1,000 each); Sailors Children's Charity (£240). **Voluntary Groups**: Branston Village Hall (£3,500); Carver Road Community Centre and Burton and District Mind (£3,000 each); East Staffordshire CVS (£2,500); Little Theatre Company (£2,000). **Faith**: The Parish of our lady of the Most Holy Rosary (£1,000). **Health Social Welfare and Care**: Burton and District Stroke Club and Happy Days Children's Charity (£1,000 each); Sailors Children's Charity (£240).
**FINANCES** *Year* 2013/14 *Income* £497,234 *Grants* £143,710 *Grants to organisations* £55,142 *Assets* £12,357,459
**TRUSTEES** Valerie Burton; Gwendoline Fosterl; Cllr Beryl Toon; John Peach; Marie Lorain Nash; Peter Davies; Margaret Heather; Cllr Dennis Fletcher; Patricia Ackroyd; Gerald Hamilton; Cllr Elizabeth Staples; Ben Robinson; Cllr David Clegg Leese; Revd Robert Styles; Cllr Leonard Milner; George Faragher; Geoffrey Brown; Sandra Phillips.
**OTHER INFORMATION** £89,000 of the grant total was distributed to individuals.
**HOW TO APPLY** Application forms can be downloaded from the trust's website. Applications for grants from organisations are considered by the main committee which meets three times a year. Meeting dates and deadlines are available published along with the application form and guidelines.
**WHO TO APPLY TO** Mr J. P. Southwell, Clerk to the Trustees, Dains LLP, 1st Floor, Gibraltar House, Crown Square, First Avenue, Burton-on-Trent *Tel.* 01283 527067 *email* clerk@consolidatedcharityburton.org.uk *Website* www.consolidatedcharityburton.org.uk

## ■ The Worshipful Company of Butchers General Charities

**CC NO** 257928   **ESTABLISHED** 1969
**WHERE FUNDING CAN BE GIVEN** City of London or its adjacent boroughs.
**WHO CAN BENEFIT** Organisations benefitting people in need.
**WHAT IS FUNDED** The charity aims to: provide relief to people who are in conditions of need, hardship, or distress; further its broad remit of charitable giving through grants to appropriate groups and organisations.
**WHAT IS NOT FUNDED** The committee does not fund groups which it considers have large financial reserves.
**RANGE OF GRANTS** Up to £22,000.
**SAMPLE GRANTS** Teach First (£16,000); Barts and the London Trust (£15,000); Poppy Factory (£2,000); British Red Cross (£550); and United Guilds (£500).
**FINANCES** *Year* 2013/14 *Income* £77,892 *Grants* £38,737 *Grants to organisations* £37,717 *Assets* £1,806,034
**TRUSTEE** The members of the court of the Worshipful Company of Butchers.
**OTHER INFORMATION** 'The principal purpose of the Charities Committee is to provide ongoing financial support to TWO chosen charities for a period of three years.' The Charity currently supports Barts Hospital and Teach First. This support will come to an end on 31 December 2017. Note: other organisations are also supported, albeit on a lesser scale.
**HOW TO APPLY** Apply in writing to the correspondent. 'Whilst there is an annual review, it is anticipated that applications from other groups/organisations will not be considered during the fixed three year period. Applications for the next three year period will be invited from new organisations from 1 July 2016.'
**WHO TO APPLY TO** The Chair of the Charities Committee, Butchers Hall, 87 Bartholomew Close, London EC1A 7EB *Tel.* 020 7600 4106 *email* clerk@butchershall.com *Website* www.butchershall.com

## ■ The Derek Butler Trust

**CC NO** 1081995   **ESTABLISHED** 2000
**WHERE FUNDING CAN BE GIVEN** Worldwide, in practice UK.
**WHO CAN BENEFIT** Institutions; hospices; charitable organisations.
**WHAT IS FUNDED** The Charity has wide objects but since its inception, in line with Mr Butler's particular concerns and interests, the trustees have pursued three particular objects for the public benefit: cancer research and general palliative care; music and music education, including postgraduate level; HIV/AIDS Relief and education.
**RANGE OF GRANTS** Usually up to £10,000–£2,515,000.
**SAMPLE GRANTS** The Digestive Disorders Foundation (£2,515,547); Countess of Munster Musical Trust (£1,000,000); Trinity Laban Conservatoire of Music and Drama, The Guildhall School Trust (£500,000 each); British Library; Holidays for Carers (£20,000); St Luke's Hospice Harrow (£15,000); Great Western Air Ambulance Charity, Cancer Research (£10,000 each); Royal Academy of Music Scholarship Award (£9,000); Guildhall School of Music and Drama, Guildford Cathedral Choir School (£5,000); The Wigmore Hall Trust (£1,700)

**FINANCES** Year 2013/14 Income £37,937 Grants £5,855,266 Grants to organisations £5,855,266 Assets £570,895

**TRUSTEES** Bernard W. Dawson; Donald F. Freeman; Revd Michael Fuller; Hilary A. E. Guest.

**OTHER INFORMATION** Grants were made during the year totalling £402,000, which included £58,000 in awards through the Derek Butler London Prize.

**HOW TO APPLY** Apply in writing to the correspondent. 'The trustees continue to seek new charities to which they can make suitable donations.'

**WHO TO APPLY TO** James McLean, Trustee, c/o Underwood Solicitors LLP, 40 Welbeck Street, London W1G 8LN Tel. 020 7526 6000 email enquiries@underwoodco.com Website www.thederekbutlertrust.org.uk

## ■ The Noel Buxton Trust

**CC NO** 220881     **ESTABLISHED** 1919

**WHERE FUNDING CAN BE GIVEN** UK, eastern and southern Africa.

**WHO CAN BENEFIT** Registered charities, although grants are not made to large popular national charities or in response to general appeals. Smaller local bodies and less popular causes are preferred.

**WHAT IS FUNDED** Welfare of children in disadvantaged families and children in care; prevention of crime, especially among young people; the rehabilitation of prisoners and the welfare of their families; education and development in eastern and southern Africa.

**WHAT IS NOT FUNDED** In addition to the specific exclusions of each programme, grants are not made for: academic research; advice centres; animal charities including those running sanctuaries, rescue or adoption services; the arts for their own sake; buildings; conferences; counselling for individuals; expeditions, exchanges, holidays, study tours, visits; housing and homelessness; human rights; HIV/AIDS programmes; grants are not made to INDIVIDUALS for any purpose; Northern Ireland; organisations set up primarily to treat medical conditions, physical disabilities or mental health issues; playgrounds; prizes; race relations; contribution to a specific salaried post; schools, including school infrastructure and teaching equipment; vehicles; victims of crime (except those affected by domestic violence and victims involved with restorative justice projects); videos and IT.

**TYPE OF GRANT** One-off or recurrent. Not for buildings or salaries.

**RANGE OF GRANTS** £1,000–£5,000. Most grants are for £1,000–£2,000 or less.

**SAMPLE GRANTS** Family Rights Group, Forum for Community Change and Development, SPANA, (£5,000 each); Feltham Community Chaplaincy Trust, Haven Hampton Trust, House Project (£3,000 each); Norfolk and Norwich Families' House, Jubilee Action, Survive (£2,000 each); Consequences, Music In Prisons – Irene Taylor Trust (£1,000).

**FINANCES** Year 2013 Income £113,870 Grants £110,742 Grants to organisations £110,742 Assets £2,683,004

**TRUSTEES** Simon Buxton; Jo Tunnard; John Littlewood; Brendan Gormley; Emma Compton-Burnett; Katie Aston; Katie Buxton.

**HOW TO APPLY** Visit the trust's website for guidance on how to apply to each programme.

**WHO TO APPLY TO** The Trustees, PO Box 520, Fleet, Hampshire GU51 9GX Website www.noelbuxtontrust.org.uk

## ■ C. and F. Charitable Trust
**CC NO** 274529 **ESTABLISHED** 1977
**WHERE FUNDING CAN BE GIVEN** UK and overseas.
**WHO CAN BENEFIT** Orthodox Jewish charities.
**WHAT IS FUNDED** Relief of poverty amongst the Jewish Community; the furtherance of the Jewish education and religion.
**WHAT IS NOT FUNDED** Registered charities only.
**SAMPLE GRANTS** Previous beneficiaries have included: Community Council of Gateshead, Ezras Nitrochim, Gur Trust, Kollel Shaarei Shlomo, SOFT and Yetev Lev Jerusalem Trust.
**FINANCES** Year 2013/14 Income £153,155 Grants £111,100 Grants to organisations £111,100 Assets £1,187,910
**TRUSTEES** Fradel Kaufman; Simon Kaufman.
**PUBLICATIONS** An analysis of charitable donations is published separately in a document entitled 'C and F Charitable Trust – Schedule of Charitable Donations'. Copies are available on written request to the correspondent.
**HOW TO APPLY** Apply in writing to the correspondent.
**WHO TO APPLY TO** The Trustees, 50 Keswick Street, Gateshead, Tyne and Wear NE8 1TQ

## ■ The James Caan Foundation
**CC NO** 1136617 **ESTABLISHED** 2010
**WHERE FUNDING CAN BE GIVEN** UK and Pakistan.
**WHO CAN BENEFIT** Organisations and individuals.
**WHAT IS FUNDED** The objects of the foundation are broadly social welfare and education in the UK and Caan's native Pakistan.
**RANGE OF GRANTS** £250–£16,400
**SAMPLE GRANTS** Muslim Hands (£16,400); Media Trust (£6,000); University of the Arts London (£4,500); Magic Bus, Ubuntu Education Fund, Shooting Stars, Arts for India (£1,000 each); Speed of Sight (£500); PayPal donations (£250).
**FINANCES** Year 2013/14 Income £51,635 Grants £31,630 Grants to organisations £31,630 Assets £230,324
**TRUSTEES** James Caan; Deepak Jalan; Hanah Caan.
**HOW TO APPLY** Apply in writing to the correspondent.
**WHO TO APPLY TO** Hanah Caan, Trustee, Hamilton Bradshaw, 60 Grosvenor Street, London W1K 3HZ Tel. 020 7399 6700 email HC@HBPE.COM Website www.thejcf.co.uk

## ■ Cable & Wireless Worldwide Foundation
**CC NO** 1144008 **ESTABLISHED** 2011
**WHERE FUNDING CAN BE GIVEN** UK and India.
**WHO CAN BENEFIT** Registered charities and community groups.
**WHAT IS FUNDED** General charitable purposes.
**FINANCES** Year 2012/13 Income £597 Grants £100,000 Grants to organisations £100,000
**TRUSTEES** Philip Davis; Steward Rix.
**OTHER INFORMATION** Established in 2011, the foundation is the charity of Cable & Wireless a large multinational communications company. The 2012/13 accounts were the latest available at the time of writing (June 2015). Full accounts were not available due to the foundation's low income and the grant total has therefore been estimated based on previous grant-making.
**HOW TO APPLY** Apply in writing to the correspondent.
**WHO TO APPLY TO** Tracy O'Brien, Correspondent, Cable & Wireless Communications plc, Worldwide House, Western Road, Bracknell, Berkshire RG12 1RW Tel. 01344 713000 email foundation@cwc.com

## ■ Edward Cadbury Charitable Trust
**CC NO** 227384 **ESTABLISHED** 1945
**WHERE FUNDING CAN BE GIVEN** Worldwide, in practice mainly UK with a preference for the Midlands region.
**WHO CAN BENEFIT** Registered charities.
**WHAT IS FUNDED** General charitable purposes, including: conservation and the environment; arts and culture; community projects and integration; compassionate support; ecumenical mission and interfaith relations; education and training; research. 'The Trust usually makes grants which vary in size between £500 and £5,000. These are normally awarded on a one-off basis for a specific purpose or part of a project. Larger grants are occasionally made on an exceptional basis where the purpose is particularly apposite to the Trust's interests.'
**TYPE OF GRANT** Usually one-off grants for a specific purpose or part of a project.
**RANGE OF GRANTS** £250–£1 million. Generally £500–£5,000.
**SAMPLE GRANTS** Trinity Christian Centre – Rowheath Pavilion, Bournville (£200,000); Arthritis Research UK (£25,000); City of Birmingham Symphony Orchestra Centre (£20,000); Emmaus UK (£15,000); Community Service Volunteers (£10,000); Elgar School of Music (£5,000); British Red Cross Society (£2,500); All Saints Youth Project, Kings Heath (£2,000); Autism West Midlands (£1,500); Centre for Enterprise, Markets and Ethics (£1,000).
**FINANCES** Year 2013/14 Income £943,662 Grants £619,732 Grants to organisations £619,732 Assets £35,819,900
**TRUSTEES** Andrew Littleboy; Charles R. Gillett; Nigel Cadbury; Hugh Marriott; Dr William Southall.
**OTHER INFORMATION** Grants given were broken-down as follows: Art and Culture (£37,300); Community Projects and Integration (£366,600); Compassionate Support (£39,500); Conservation and Environment (£79,200); Interfaith and Multifaith Relations (£5,000); Research (£26,300); Education and Training (£103,200).
**HOW TO APPLY** The Edward Cadbury Charitable Trust only makes grants to registered charities and not to individuals. An application for funding may be made at any time and should be submitted in writing to the Trust Manager either by post or email. Trustees request that the letter of application should provide a clear and concise description of the project for which the funding is required as well as the outcomes and benefits that it is intended to achieve. They also require an outline budget and explanation of how the project is to be funded initially and in the future together with the latest annual report and accounts for the charity. Applications for funding are generally considered within a three month timescale. Note that applications which fall outside the trust's stated areas of interest may not be considered or acknowledged. Before awarding a grant, trustees assess applications against the trust's objectives and the Charity Commission's public benefit guidelines to check

that public benefit criteria are met. The trust usually makes grants which vary in size between £500 and £5,000. These are normally awarded on a one-off basis for a specific purpose or part of a project. Larger grants are occasionally made on an exceptional basis.
WHO TO APPLY TO Sue Anderson, Trust Manager, Rokesley, University of Birmingham, Bristol Road, Selly Oak, Birmingham B29 6QF *Tel.* 0121 472 1838 *Fax* 0121 472 1838 *email* ecadburytrust@btconnect.com *Website* www.edwardcadburytrust.org.uk

### ■ The Christopher Cadbury Charitable Trust

CC NO 231859 ESTABLISHED 1922
WHERE FUNDING CAN BE GIVEN UK, with a strong preference for the Midlands.
WHO CAN BENEFIT Registered charities.
WHAT IS FUNDED To support approved charities by annual contribution. The trustees have drawn up a schedule of commitments covering charities which they have chosen to support.
WHAT IS NOT FUNDED Individuals.
RANGE OF GRANTS £200–£10,500
SAMPLE GRANTS Fircroft College and Island Conservation Society UK (£10,500 each); Playthings Past Museum Trust (£7,500); Devon Wildlife Trust, and Norfolk Wildlife Trust (£6,000 each); Bower Trust, R A and V B Reekie Charitable Trust, R V J Cadbury Charitable Trust, Sarnia Charitable Trust (£3,000 each); Survival International (£1,000); and Avoncroft Arts Society, Selly Oak Nursery School (£500 each).
FINANCES *Year* 2013/14 *Income* £82,569 *Grants* £66,450 *Grants to organisations* £66,450 *Assets* £2,236,498
TRUSTEES Roger Cadbury; Tim Peet; Dr James Cadbury; Tina Benfield; Virginia Reekie; Peter Cadbury.
HOW TO APPLY Unsolicited applications are unlikely to be successful.
WHO TO APPLY TO Sarah Moss, B. D. O. Stoy Howard, 125 Colmore Row, Birmingham B3 3SD *Tel.* 0121 265 7288

### ■ The G. W. Cadbury Charitable Trust

CC NO 231861 ESTABLISHED 1922
WHERE FUNDING CAN BE GIVEN Worldwide.
WHO CAN BENEFIT Organisations benefitting at-risk groups, people disadvantaged by poverty, and socially isolated people.
WHAT IS FUNDED General charitable purposes.
WHAT IS NOT FUNDED Individuals; non-registered charities; scholarships.
RANGE OF GRANTS Under £1,000 to £35,000.
SAMPLE GRANTS Colston's Primary School (£35,000); Pacific Northwest Ballet – USA (£30,000); Gender and Development Network (£10,000); British Pregnancy Advisory Service (£6,000); Compassion in Dying (£5,000); Brook (£4,000); Birmingham Royal Ballet (£2,000); and Swaledale Friends (£1,000).
FINANCES *Year* 2013/14 *Income* £229,039 *Grants* £205,954 *Grants to organisations* £205,954 *Assets* £6,662,191
TRUSTEES Jennifer Boal; Jessica Woodroffe; Peter Boal; Lyndall Boal; Nick Woodroffe; Caroline Woodroffe.
OTHER INFORMATION Grants were split between the UK (£94,600) and the USA (£111,300).
HOW TO APPLY Apply in writing to the correspondent.

WHO TO APPLY TO The Trust Administrator, B. D. O. Stoy Hayward, 125 Colmore Row, Birmingham B3 3SD *Tel.* 0121 265 7288

### ■ The Richard Cadbury Charitable Trust

CC NO 224348 ESTABLISHED 1948
WHERE FUNDING CAN BE GIVEN UK, but mainly Birmingham, Coventry and Worcester.
WHO CAN BENEFIT Organisations with charitable status.
WHAT IS FUNDED Community centres and village halls; libraries and museums; counselling; crime prevention; play schemes; gay and lesbian rights; racial equality, discrimination and relations; social advocacy; health care; hospices and rehabilitation centres; cancer and prenatal research; health promotion; and health-related volunteer schemes. Grants also for accommodation and housing; infrastructure support and development; conservation and environment; and religion.
WHAT IS NOT FUNDED Running costs; core funding.
TYPE OF GRANT One-off and capital costs.
RANGE OF GRANTS £250–£1,000
SAMPLE GRANTS Previous beneficiaries have included: Barnardo's, Centrepoint, Marie Curie Cancer Centre and RNLI (£1,000 each); Birmingham Settlement, Dodford Children's Holiday Farm and NSPCC (£750 each); LEPRA and VSO (£500 each); ESO (£400); Worcester Live and Youth at Risk – Nottingham (£300 each); and Sandwell Asian Development Association and St David's Church – Selly Oak (£250 each).
FINANCES *Year* 2013/14 *Income* £18,799 *Grants* £44,000 *Grants to organisations* £44,000
TRUSTEES Richard Cadbury; Margaret Eardley; David Slora; Jacqueline Slora; Lucy Cadbury-Hamood.
HOW TO APPLY Apply in writing to the correspondent giving reasons why a grant is needed and including a copy of the latest accounts if possible. Meetings are held in February, June and October. Unsolicited applications are not accepted.
WHO TO APPLY TO Margaret Eardley, Trustee, 26 Randall Road, Kenilworth, Warwickshire CV8 1JY *Tel.* 01926 857793 *email* margaret@eardley2.orangehome.co.uk

### ■ The William A. Cadbury Charitable Trust

CC NO 213629 ESTABLISHED 1923
WHERE FUNDING CAN BE GIVEN West Midlands, especially Birmingham and to a lesser extent, UK, Ireland and overseas.
WHO CAN BENEFIT Organisations serving Birmingham and the West Midlands; organisations whose work has a national significance; organisations outside the West Midlands where the trust has well-established links; organisations in Northern Ireland, and UK-based charities working overseas. UK bodies legally exempt from registration with the Charity Commission can apply and small grants are occasionally made to unregistered groups in the West Midlands.
WHAT IS FUNDED Birmingham and the West Midlands: *community action* – community based and organised schemes (which may be centred on a place of worship) aimed at solving local problems and improving the quality of life of community members; *vulnerable groups* –

vulnerable groups include the elderly, children and young people, people with disabilities, asylum seekers and similar minorities; *advice, mediation and counselling* – applicants must be able to point to the rigorous selection, training and monitoring of front line staff (particularly in the absence of formal qualifications) as well as to the overall need for the service provided; *education and training* – trustees are particularly interested in schemes that help people of working age develop new skills in order to re-enter the jobs market; *environment and conservation* – projects which address the impact of climate change and projects to preserve buildings and installations of historic importance and local interest; *medical and healthcare* – covers hospices, self-help groups and some medical research which must be based in and be of potential benefit to the West Midlands; *the arts* – music, drama and the visual arts, museums and art galleries. United Kingdom: *the Religious Society of Friends* – support for groups with a clear Quaker connection and support for the work of the Religious Society of Friends in the UK; *penal affairs* – restorative justice, prison based projects and work with ex-offenders aimed at reducing re-offending. Ireland: *peace and reconciliation*. International development: *Africa* – the international development programme is concentrated on West Africa and work to reduce poverty on a sustainable basis in both rural and urban communities – schemes that help children access education are also supported; *Asia and Eastern Europe; South America.*' Note: The international development programme is heavily oversubscribed and unsolicited applications are unlikely to be successful.

**WHAT IS NOT FUNDED** The trust supports charitable organisations based in the UK. If you do not have a UK base, are not a registered with the Charity Commission or are applying as an individual the tust will not be able to help you. Review the Grant Programmes page on the trust's website in order to establish whether your project qualifies for support. Grants are normally awarded on a one-off basis and repeat applications are not usually considered within two years of an award.

**TYPE OF GRANT** Specific grant applications are favoured. Grants are generally one-off or for projects of one year or less. The trust will consider applications for core costs as well as for development/project funding. Grants are not usually awarded on an annual basis, except to a small number of charities for revenue costs.

**RANGE OF GRANTS** Small grants up to £2,000; large grants usually range from £10,000–£20,000 with an occasional maximum of £50,000.

**SAMPLE GRANTS** Concern Universal (£90,000); Britain Yearly Meeting – Religious Society of Friends (£25,000); St Richard's Hospice (£20,000); Artrix Arts Centre and Court Based Personal Support (£15,000 each); Birmingham Churches Together and Prisoners Education Trust (£10,000 each); Clooney Soccer School, HOOPS Birmingham (£8,000 each); Garden Organic (£5,750); Peoples Bureau of Education and Training (£4,000).

**FINANCES** Year 2013/14 *Income* £929,305 *Grants* £750,750 *Grants to organisations* £750,750 *Assets* £29,732,055

**TRUSTEES** Victoria Salmon; Rupert Cadbury; Katherine van Hagen Cadbury; Margaret Salmon; Sarah Stafford; Adrian Thomas; John Penny; Sophy Blandy; Janine Cobain.

**PUBLICATIONS** Policy statement and guidelines for applicants.

**OTHER INFORMATION** Grants were divided between the following areas: International Development (£133,250); Ireland (£22,000); Society of Friends (£51,500); Penal Affairs (£29,300); West Midlands Advice, Mediation, Counselling (£61,750); Community Action (£72,050); Environment and Conservation (£24,000);.

**HOW TO APPLY** Grant applications can be submitted on-line (preferred) or by post. Applications are considered by trustees on a regular basis and small grants (up to a maximum of £2000) are awarded monthly. The trustees meet in May and November to award approximately twenty large grants at each meeting, ranging in value from £10,000 to £20,000 with an occasional maximum of £50,000. The cut-off for applications to the May meeting is early March while for November the cut-off is early September. A detailed outline of the application process is available on the trust's website.

**WHO TO APPLY TO** Carolyn Bettis, Trust Administrator, Rokesley, University of Birmingham, Bristol Road, Selly Oak, Birmingham B29 6QF *Tel.* 0121 472 1464 *email* info@wa-cadbury.org.uk *Website* www.wa-cadbury.org.uk

## ■ The Cadbury Foundation

**CC NO** 1050482  **ESTABLISHED** 1994
**WHERE FUNDING CAN BE GIVEN** UK and Africa, particularly in areas where the company has operations.
**WHO CAN BENEFIT** Registered charities and voluntary organisations.
**WHAT IS FUNDED** Education and enterprise, poverty and homelessness, the environment and international development.
**RANGE OF GRANTS** Between £5,000 and £100,000.
**SAMPLE GRANTS** Charities Aid Foundation (£105,000); British Paralympic Association (£100,000); National Grocer Benevolent Fund (£75,000); Northside Partnership (£50,000); Tembisa Child Welfare (£30,000); the Achimota Trust (£25,000); Groundworth South Trust (£15,000); Mondelēz UK Holdings and Services – Ghana Wells, Trinity Homeless Project, Disaster Emergency Committee (£10,000 each); and Bournville Village Trust (£5,000).
**FINANCES** Year 2013 *Income* £784,357 *Grants* £435,174 *Grants to organisations* £435,174 *Assets* £194,338
**TRUSTEES** Jonathan Horrell; Diane Tomlinson; Neil Chapman; David Oliver; Vinzenz Gruber; Michael Huggins; Sonia Farrell; Mary Barnard; Eoin Kellet.
**OTHER INFORMATION** The Cadbury Foundation was set up in 1935 in recognition of the company founders George and Richard Cadbury and their investment in the welfare of their employees and wider communities. In 2010 Kraft Foods Inc. gained control of Cadbury plc. In 2012 Kraft Foods Inc. was split into Kraft Food Group plc and Mondelēz which now funds the Cadbury Foundation.
**HOW TO APPLY** The foundations actively seeks out projects to support and therefore cannot accept any unsolicited requests for funding.
**WHO TO APPLY TO** Ms Louise Ayling, Correspondent, Mondelēz UK, Unit 3, Sanderson Road, Uxbridge Business Park, Uxbridge. UB8 1DH *Tel.* 01895 615000 *email* louise.ayling@mdlz.com

## ■ The Barrow Cadbury Trust

**CC NO** 1115476 **ESTABLISHED** 1920

**WHERE FUNDING CAN BE GIVEN** UK and overseas, with a preference for Birmingham and the Black Country (Wolverhampton, Dudley, West Bromwich, Smethwick or Sandwell).

**WHO CAN BENEFIT** Charities; voluntary organisations; preferably grassroots community groups and user-led projects. You do not have to be a registered charity but should have a formal structure and governing documents.

**WHAT IS FUNDED** Criminal justice; migration; poverty and exclusion; social justice. There is a particular interest in the following themes: 'supporting the independence and diversity of the voluntary sector; addressing gender-based disadvantage; addressing disadvantage based on race and ethnicity; funding groups, projects and programmes in Birmingham and the Black Country'. See the website for schemes available.

**WHAT IS NOT FUNDED** Activities that central or local government is responsible for; animal welfare; arts and cultural projects; capital costs for building, refurbishment and outfitting; endowment funds; fundraising events or activities; general appeals; general health; individuals; housing; learning disability; medical research or equipment; mental health; children under 16 and older people; physical disability; the promotion of religion or belief systems; schools; sponsorship or marketing appeals; unsolicited international projects. The trust will not normally consider funding the following areas unless they are part of a broader project: counselling drug and alcohol services (unless under criminal justice programme); environmental projects (unless under the poverty and inclusion programme); homelessness and destitution (unless for those leaving the criminal justice system or in relation to the migration programme); IT training; sporting activities. Colleges and universities can only apply under the policy and research funding streams.

**TYPE OF GRANT** Projects; recurring costs; running expenditure; start-up funding.

**RANGE OF GRANTS** Grassroots grant generally £15,000–£50,000 per year.

**SAMPLE GRANTS** Detailed examples of previously funded projects are available on the trust's website. **Beneficiaries have included**: Anawim (£75,000 over two years); Refugee and Migrant Centre (£65,500 in two years); City United (£60,000 over three years); Kalayaan and Piers Road new Communities Centre (£60,000 over two years each); Detention Action (£60,000 over three years); Clinks: Going for Gold (£51,000 over 18 months); Migrant Voice (£51,000 in two years); ShareAction (£50,000 in two years); UK Feminista (£33,500 over two years); Birmingham YMCA (£32,000 over two years); Localise West Midlands (£30,000 in one year); Women for Refugee Women (£30,000 in two years); St Margaret's Community Trust (£30,000 in three years); Birmingham Citizens Advice (£15,000 over 18 months).

**FINANCES** Year 2013/14 Income £2,791,000 Grants £3,143,395 Grants to organisations £3,143,395 Assets £70,514,000

**TRUSTEES** Ruth Cadbury; Anna Southall; Erica Cadbury; Nicola Cadbury; Tamsin Rupprechter; Gordon Mitchell; Harry Serle; Helen Cadbury; Jack Serle; Steven Skakel.

**PUBLICATIONS** A number of publications and reports are published on the trust's website.

**OTHER INFORMATION** The annual report for 2013/14 notes that 'the trust values its historical roots within Quaker ways of working and tradition of social and penal reform'. In 2013/14 awards were distributed as follows: migration (£923,500); criminal justice (£858,500); resources and resilience (£849,500); philanthropy and other (£512,000). The trust is also engaged in social investment, research, influencing public policy and raising awareness of issues in the field of its interest. During the year there were 122 awards made.

**HOW TO APPLY** The trust's website states: 'If you have an idea for a project you would like us to consider funding, please complete our enquiry form.' If invited to complete a full application form you should do so via the Application Portal, available online. You may also get in touch with the Grant Administrator to discuss your eligibility. The trust reminds: 'We are usually able to respond to enquiries within 10 working days, but it may take up to four months for us to assess a full application once you have submitted it. Please bear this in mind when planning your start date.'

**WHO TO APPLY TO** Asma Aroui, Grants Administrator, Kean House, 6 Kean Street, London WC2B 4AS Tel. 020 7632 9260 (switchboard) Fax 020 7632 9061 email info@barrowcadbury.org.uk or general@barrowcadbury.org.uk Website www.barrowcadbury.org.uk

## ■ The Edward and Dorothy Cadbury Trust

**CC NO** 1107327 **ESTABLISHED** 1928

**WHERE FUNDING CAN BE GIVEN** Preference for the West Midlands area.

**WHO CAN BENEFIT** Registered charities.

**WHAT IS FUNDED** The trust continues to support, where appropriate, the interests of the founders and the particular charitable interests of the trustees. Grants are grouped under six main headings: arts and culture; community projects and integration; compassionate support; education and training; conservation and environment; and research. 'As a matter of good practice, trustees undertake a programme of visits to organisations where a grant of high value has been made or the activity is of particular interest to the trust in terms of future development. This has proved helpful in building up positive relationships with grantees and providing networking opportunities.'

**WHAT IS NOT FUNDED** Individuals.

**TYPE OF GRANT** Ongoing funding commitments rarely considered.

**RANGE OF GRANTS** Usually £500–£2,500, with occasional larger grants made.

**SAMPLE GRANTS** Breast Cancer Unit, Worcester (£15,000); Age UK Bromsgrove and District (£6,000); Acorns Children's Hospice, Cerebral Palsy Midlands, Cotteridge Day Centre (£5,000 each); Cure Leukaemia, Disasters Emergency Committee, Elgar Foundation, Macmillan Cancer Support Birmingham, Selly Oak Quaker Meeting (£1,000 each): British Heart Foundation, Motor Neurone Disease Association, Special Olympics West Midlands – Ski Group (£750 each); Birmingham Festival Choral Society, British Library, Garden Organic (£500 each).

**FINANCES** Year 2013/14 Income £172,658 Grants £126,629 Grants to organisations £126,629 Assets £6,576,448

**TRUSTEES** Philippa Ward; Susan Anfilogoff; Julia Gillett; Julie Cadbury.

**HOW TO APPLY** The following is taken from the trust's helpful website: 'An application for funding may be made at any time and should be submitted in writing to the Trust Manager either by post or email. Trustees request that the letter of application should provide a clear and concise description of the project for which the funding is required as well as the outcomes and benefits that it is intended to achieve. They also require an outline budget and explanation of how the project is to be funded initially and in the future together with the latest annual report and accounts for the charity. Applications for funding are generally considered within a three month timescale. Please note that applications which fall outside the Trust's stated areas of interest may not be considered or acknowledged.'
**WHO TO APPLY TO** Susan Anderson, Company Secretary/Trust Manager, Rokesley, Bristol Road, Selly Oak, Birmingham B29 6QF *Tel.* 0121 472 1838 *email* e-dcadburytrust@btconnect.com *Website* www.e-dcadburytrust.org.uk

## ■ The George Cadbury Trust

**CC NO** 1040999 **ESTABLISHED** 1924
**WHERE FUNDING CAN BE GIVEN** Preference for the West Midlands, Hampshire and Gloucestershire.
**WHO CAN BENEFIT** UK-based charities.
**WHAT IS FUNDED** General charitable purposes.
**WHAT IS NOT FUNDED** Individuals for projects, courses of study, expeditions or sporting tours; overseas appeals.
**RANGE OF GRANTS** £1,000–£25,000
**SAMPLE GRANTS** Dean and Chapter Gloucester Cathedral for the Dorothea Hoyland Choral Scholarship (£25,000); Birmingham Royal Ballet (£20,000); Acorns Children's Hospice, Performances Birmingham Limited (£10,000 each); Age UK Warwickshire, Hepatitis C Trust (£5,000); Cheltenham YMCA, National Trust (£3,000 each); Actors' Benevolent Fund, RNLI (£2,000 each); Royal Hospital for Neuro-disability, Tewkesbury Sea Cadets (£1,000 each).
**FINANCES** *Year* 2013/14 *Income* £437,794 *Grants* £328,465 *Grants to organisations* £328,465 *Assets* £12,507,800
**TRUSTEES** Anne L. K. Cadbury; Robin N. Cadbury; Sir Adrian Cadbury; Roger V. J. Cadbury; A. Jane Cadbury.
**HOW TO APPLY** Apply in writing to the correspondent to be considered quarterly. Note that very few new applications are supported due to ongoing and alternative commitments.
**WHO TO APPLY TO** Sarah Moss, B. D. O. Stoy Hayward, 125 Colmore Row, Birmingham B3 3SD *Tel.* 0121 265 7288

## ■ The Cadogan Charity

**CC NO** 247773 **ESTABLISHED** 1966
**WHERE FUNDING CAN BE GIVEN** Worldwide. In practice UK, with a preference for charities operating or based in London or Scotland.
**WHO CAN BENEFIT** Registered charities.
**WHAT IS FUNDED** General charitable purposes, in particular social welfare, medical research, services charities, animal welfare, education and conservation and the environment.
**WHAT IS NOT FUNDED** Individuals.
**TYPE OF GRANT** Support is usually given over one to two years, although some one-off grants may be made.
**RANGE OF GRANTS** Up to £300,000.
**SAMPLE GRANTS** St George's Cathedral, Perth (£445,000); Culford School (£100,000); Battle of Britain Memorial Trust (£50,000); Alzheimer's Research Trust (£37,000); Home of Horse Racing Trust (£25,000); Samaritans (£20,000); Royal Ballet School and Scotland Uplands Appeal (£10,000 each) Guard's Museum; Animal Health Trust (£5,000 each); World Sight Foundation (£4,000); Epilepsy Research Foundation and Family Holiday Association (£1,000 each).
**FINANCES** *Year* 2013/14 *Income* £2,305,797 *Grants* £2,652,580 *Grants to organisations* £2,652,580 *Assets* £48,476,619
**TRUSTEES** Earl Cadogan; Countess Cadogan; Viscount Chelsea; Lady Anna Thomson; The Hon. William Cadogan.
**OTHER INFORMATION** The charity was created with a gift from Cadogan Holdings Company in 1985.
**HOW TO APPLY** Apply in writing to the correspondent. However, note that we have received information stating that the trust's funds are fully committed until 2016.
**WHO TO APPLY TO** Mr P. M. Loutit, Secretary, The Cadogan Group, 18 Cadogan Gardens, London SW3 2RP *Tel.* 020 7730 4567

## ■ CAFOD (Catholic Agency for Overseas Development)

**CC NO** 285776 **ESTABLISHED** 1962
**WHERE FUNDING CAN BE GIVEN** Predominantly overseas, with some funding to partners in England and Wales.
**WHO CAN BENEFIT** Poorer communities overseas and victims of famine, disasters or war.
**WHAT IS FUNDED** Long-term development work with some of the world's poorest communities. In almost all cases work overseas is planned and run by local people. Programmes include education and skills training, human rights promotion, healthcare, HIV/AIDS, safe water, agriculture and small businesses. Immediate help for people affected by emergencies such as wars and natural disasters is also funded, as is the analysis of the causes of underdevelopment and campaigns on behalf of the world's poor. All programmes seek to promote gender equality. In England and Wales CAFOD's Development Education Fund makes small grants to local or national groups with young people and adults for projects developing education and campaigning on global justice.
**WHAT IS NOT FUNDED** Individuals; organisations whose aims are primarily political.
**TYPE OF GRANT** Partnership, programme and project.
**FINANCES** *Year* 2013/14 *Income* £51,287,000 *Grants* £26,199,000 *Grants to organisations* £26,199,000 *Assets* £31,152,000
**TRUSTEES** Rt. Revd John Arnold; Rt. Revd John Sherrington; Mary Ney; Fr Jim O'Keefe; Joanne Rule; Dominic Jermey; Margaret Mwaniki; Catherine Newman; Dr Hugo Slim; John Darley; Jan Wilkinson; Megan Russell.
**OTHER INFORMATION** During the year, 581 grants were distributed for the following purposes: Disaster relief (£10.3 million); Sustainable livelihoods (£5.9 million); Human rights (£3.5 million); Health (£2 million); HIV/AIDS (£1.8 million); Economic advocacy (£1.3 million); Conflict resolution (£917,000); Education (£397,000).
**HOW TO APPLY** Organisations and groups in England and Wales can apply for development education grants, which support initiatives educating about

and campaigning for global justice. Criteria, guidelines and details of the application process for Development Education Fund grants can be found on the CAFOD website. For further information, contact the Education Fund Co-ordinator by telephone 0207 095 5317 or by email deved@cafod.org.uk.

**WHO TO APPLY TO** Education Fund Co-ordinator, Romero House, 55 Westminster Bridge Road, London SE1 7JB *Tel.* 020 7733 7900 *Fax* 020 7274 9630 *email* cafod@cafod.org.uk *Website* www.cafod.org.uk

## ■ Community Foundation for Calderdale

**CC NO** 1002722    **ESTABLISHED** 1991

**WHERE FUNDING CAN BE GIVEN** Calderdale, with ability to manage funds outside this area.

**WHO CAN BENEFIT** Constituted voluntary, community and faith groups, run for and by local people and registered charities working in Calderdale.

**WHAT IS FUNDED** General charitable purposes. Each scheme has different criteria but priority tends to be given to projects which: achieve outstanding community impact; help people living in communities identified as being particularly disadvantaged; benefit people from black and minority ethnic communities; help people with special needs; benefit older people; and/or benefit young people under the age of 19.

**TYPE OF GRANT** Revenue, capital, one-off.

**RANGE OF GRANTS** £100–£40,000, depending on the scheme.

**SAMPLE GRANTS** Northorpe Hall Child and Family Trust (£34,800); Incredible Edible Todmorden (£25,000); Healthy Minds (£23,000); Working Wonders (£22,000); Calderdale Smartmove (£18,500); Square Chapel Trust (£11,000); Age UK Calderdale and Kirklees (£6,100); Calderdale British Muslim Association (£5,000); Samaritans of Halifax and Calderdale (£3,000); Arden Road Community Hub (£1,500); The Old Library Group (£600).

**FINANCES** *Year* 2013/14 *Income* £934,171 *Grants* £540,942 *Grants to organisations* £488,729 *Assets* £9,680,309

**TRUSTEES** Russell Earnshaw; Juliet Chambers; Roger Moore; Stuart Rumney; Wim Batist; Susannah Hammond; Lee Kenny; Andrew Banks; Amanda Garrard; Claire O'Connor; Christopher Harris.

**OTHER INFORMATION** Grants made in 2013/14 were split between 349 individuals (£52,200) and 97 organisations.

**HOW TO APPLY** The foundation's website has details of the grant schemes currently being administered. Application packs for all of the programmes are available to download from the website. Alternatively, contact the foundation directly and they will send a pack in the post. If you wish to discuss your project before applying, the grants team are happy to answer any queries. The foundation also runs a monthly drop-in, where groups can go for advice and support on their applications. **Note:** All applications to CFFC for grant aid from its general fund will now be assessed for their suitability for the Calderdale Social Impact Fund. This may result in your organisation being offered a loan from the Calderdale Social Impact Fund rather than a grant.

**WHO TO APPLY TO** Danni Bailey, Senior Grants Administrator, The 1855 Building (first floor), Discovery Road, Halifax HX1 2NG *Tel.* 01422 349700 *Fax* 01422 350017 *email* enquiries@cffc.co.uk *Website* www.cffc.co.uk

## ■ Callander Charitable Trust

**SC NO** SC016609    **ESTABLISHED** 1972

**WHERE FUNDING CAN BE GIVEN** Primarily Scotland, but also other parts of the UK

**WHO CAN BENEFIT** Charitable organisations.

**WHAT IS FUNDED** General charitable purposes.

**WHAT IS NOT FUNDED** Individuals; non-registered charities.

**SAMPLE GRANTS** According the Scottish Charity Regulator website, the trust focuses its grant-making in the following areas: the furtherance of and advancement of religion, education, training, instruction and culture; the promotion of spiritual, moral, intellectual, social and physical well-being; the relief or prevention of poverty, misery, neglect, suffering, disease, sickness, infirmary, age, distress, physical and mental handicap and/or need. We estimate that around £70,000 was made in grants (estimate based on income and expenditure, as no exact figures were provided by the trust). A list of beneficiaries was not available.

**FINANCES** *Year* 2013/14 *Income* £78,401 *Grants* £70,000 *Grants to organisations* £70,000

**TRUSTEE** No information available.

**OTHER INFORMATION** Total expenditure in 2013/14 was £77,401. We estimate that around £70,000 was made in grants (estimate based on income and expenditure, as no exact figures were provided by the trust).

**HOW TO APPLY** Apply in writing to the correspondent.

**WHO TO APPLY TO** The Secretary, Anderson Strathern LLP, 1 Rutland Court, Edinburgh EH3 8EY

## ■ Calleva Foundation

**CC NO** 1078808    **ESTABLISHED** 1999

**WHERE FUNDING CAN BE GIVEN** UK and worldwide.

**WHO CAN BENEFIT** Charitable organisations.

**WHAT IS FUNDED** Grants were categorised as follows: social services; children's holidays; overseas/international relief; education; arts and culture; medical research; and animal welfare.

**SAMPLE GRANTS** No sample available. **Beneficiary categories include**: education and academic research (£807,000); social services (£56,000); environment (£42,000); overseas/International relief (£31,000); medical research (£26,000); children's holidays (£16,000); animal welfare/other (£3,000).

**FINANCES** *Year* 2013 *Income* £3,750,000 *Grants* £981,031 *Grants to organisations* £981,031 *Assets* £2,162,941

**TRUSTEES** Stephen Butt; Caroline Butt.

**HOW TO APPLY** This trust does not accept unsolicited applications.

**WHO TO APPLY TO** The Trustees, PO Box 22554, London W8 5GN *email* contactcalleva@btopenworld.com

# Calouste

## ■ Calouste Gulbenkian Foundation – UK Branch

**ESTABLISHED** 1956

**WHERE FUNDING CAN BE GIVEN** UK and the Republic of Ireland.

**WHO CAN BENEFIT** Registered charities or tax exempt organisations.

**WHAT IS FUNDED** The foundation's UK Branch Strategy 2014/2019 focuses on four areas of work: Transitions in later life – 'To increase knowledge about transitions in later life and secure more appropriate responses to the issues they create for older people' Sharing the stage – 'To widen participation in performing arts practice, and identify and support models of best practice and originality in the field' Valuing the Ocean – 'To make connections and build relationships designed to help protect our oceans' Creating the conditions – 'We have a cross-cutting priority which is to create the conditions for change by promoting social innovation, strengthening civil society and working to advance our own and others' philanthropic practice'. The foundation's support is largely proactive, though some support is available for a small number of exceptional projects that meet the foundation's priorities.

**WHAT IS NOT FUNDED** Work that does not have a direct benefit in the UK or the Republic of Ireland; individuals; curriculum based activities in statutory education; student grants or scholarships for tuition and maintenance; vocational training; teaching or research posts or visiting fellowships; educational resources and equipment; gap year activities; group or individual visits abroad, including to Portugal; core services and standard provisions; routine information and advice services; capital costs for housing or the purchase, construction, repair or furnishing of buildings; equipment, including vehicles, IT, or musical instruments; scientific or medical research; medicine or related therapies such as complementary medicine, hospices, counselling and therapy; promoting religion or a belief system; website development; sports; holidays of any sort; animal welfare; loans; retrospective grants; the payment of deficits or loans; the replacement of statutory funding; capital, endowment or widely-distributed appeals. Historically the foundation has supported arts-related applications (arts, arts and science and arts education); however, these will no longer be accepted unless they meet the foundation's current aims.

**TYPE OF GRANT** Generally one-off grants, occasionally recurring for a maximum of three years.

**SAMPLE GRANTS** Recent beneficiaries listed on the foundation's website have included: Independent Age (£300,000); New Economics Foundation (£216,000); Pig Shed Trust (£180,000); Shoreditch Town Hall (£150,000); National Endowment for Science, Technology and the Arts – NESTA (£60,000); Organisation for Economic Co-operation and Development – OECD (£45,000); Streetwise Opera (£28,000); North Music Trust (£20,000); King's College London (£19,000); Thames Estuary Partnership (£15,000); Ocean Recovery Alliance (£10,000); The Age of No Retirement – AMBT Ltd (£7,000); The Legal Education Foundation (£6,000).

**FINANCES** Year 2014 Grants £1,623,750 Grants to organisations £1,623,750

**TRUSTEE** The foundation's board of administration is based in Lisbon. The UK resident trustee is Martin Essayan.

**PUBLICATIONS** The UK Branch commissions and publishes a number of reports and books connected with its programmes of work.

**OTHER INFORMATION** The foundation, which was established in Portugal, is headquartered in Lisbon and has offices in Paris and London. During the year, 42 projects were supported.

**HOW TO APPLY** Ordinarily, applications are only accepted for projects through the foundation's open fund; however, at the time of writing, the open fund had temporarily been suspended and open calls for proposals for some of the foundation's other funding strands had been recently undertaken. Refer to the website for details of areas where the foundation is currently accepting applications.

**WHO TO APPLY TO** Andrew Barnett, Director, 50 Hoxton Square, London N1 6PB *Tel.* 020 7012 1400 *Fax* 020 7739 1961 *email* info@gulbenkian.org.uk *Website* www.gulbenkian.org.uk

## ■ The Cambridge Chrysalis Trust

**CC NO** 1151614

**WHERE FUNDING CAN BE GIVEN** England and Wales.

**WHO CAN BENEFIT** Charitable organisations.

**WHAT IS FUNDED** General charitable purposes; education; arts and culture; the environment and conservation. Although the trust's Charity Commission record states that 'its primary activity until 2027 is the accumulation of funds through investment. However, the trust also considers grant applications from registered charities'.

**SAMPLE GRANTS** Wildlife Trust BCN (£13,200).

**FINANCES** Year 2013/14 Income £121,451 Grants £13,233 Grants to organisations £13,233 Assets £161,571

**TRUSTEES** Dr Cathryn Downing; Prof. John Daugman.

**HOW TO APPLY** Apply in writing to the correspondent. The trust's annual report for 2013/14 states the following: 'The trust considers grant applications from registered charities. These will be scored on five factors: the degree of match between the candidate project's objectives and those of the trust; the importance of the candidate project; the likelihood of the project achieving its goals; the strategic value of the grant to the project; and the relative cost of the grant. The trust asks applicants to outline the importance of their project on the international, national and regional levels and to provide evidence that will assist the trustees in determining the likelihood that the project will succeed at each of these levels. Applicants are also encouraged to indicate what level of funding would be significant to the project and whether matching funds are available.'

**WHO TO APPLY TO** Dr Cathryn Downing, Trustee, 9 Bell Lane, Fenstanton, Huntingdon, Cambridgeshire PE28 9JX *Tel.* 01480 462021 *email* cathryn.downing@gmail.com

## ■ The Cambridgeshire Community Foundation

**CC NO** 1103314   **ESTABLISHED** 2003

**WHERE FUNDING CAN BE GIVEN** Cambridgeshire and Peterborough

**WHO CAN BENEFIT** Voluntary and charitable groups.

**WHAT IS FUNDED** Community projects seeking to tackle a need or disadvantage. The foundation administers a number of funds. For up-to-date details, see its website. 'The majority of grants

(71%) awarded are for small sums (less than £3,000) to volunteer led groups that are improving the quality of life for local people who face disadvantage. Through one fund the Foundation is able to offer support to larger scale capital projects that are enhancing public amenities, but the majority of grants fund revenue costs.'

**TYPE OF GRANT** One-off.

**RANGE OF GRANTS** The majority of the grants awarded are for small amounts of between £500–£5,000.

**SAMPLE GRANTS** Details of individual beneficiaries and amounts paid are not included in the foundation's accounts. Only one grant included details: Fredericks Foundation (£130,000) (registered charity 1086562) for Fredericks Cambridgeshire, a micro loan fund for Cambridgeshire. Grants paid are listed according to 'theme' and include the following: Community Assets (£1,392,500); Social inclusion (£95,300); Education and skills (£74,000); Community cohesion (£42,000); Disability and chronic ill health (£36,300); Economic hardship (£33,500); Homelessness (£22,200); Improved green spaces (£20,000); Help limit climate change (£5,000).

**FINANCES** Year 2013/14 Income £2,942,381 Grants £1,982,462 Grants to organisations £1,836,850 Assets £4,573,973

**TRUSTEES** Jane Darlington; John Bridge; Mick Leggett; Sam Weller; William Dastur; Richard Barnwell; Richard Barnwell; Christopher Belcher; Catherine Stewart; Philip Woolner; Robert Satchwell.

**OTHER INFORMATION** Grants to 33 individuals totalled £4,950.

**HOW TO APPLY** Detailed information regarding eligibility for funding is available through the very helpful 'Grant Application Decision Matrix' found on the foundation's website online application forms are available on the foundation's website. Applicants are urged to complete the 'Grant Application Decision Matrix' before application.

**WHO TO APPLY TO** Jane Darlington, Chief Executive, The Quorum, Barnwell Road, Cambridge CB3 8RE *Tel.* 01223 410535 *email* info@cambscf.org.uk *Website* www.cambscf.org.uk

## ■ The Camelia Trust

**CC NO** 1081074  **ESTABLISHED** 2000

**WHERE FUNDING CAN BE GIVEN** Liverpool and Manchester.

**WHO CAN BENEFIT** Charitable organisations.

**WHAT IS FUNDED** General charitable purposes.

**RANGE OF GRANTS** Up to £6,000.

**SAMPLE GRANTS** Deafblind UK, Motor Neurone Disease Association and Redeeming your Communities (£2,000 each); Tall Ships Youth Trust £1,200); Bluecoat Display Centre, Clare House Children's Hospice and Personal Support Unit (£1,000 each); and British Wireless for the Blind Fund and Ten Ten Theatre (£500 each).

**FINANCES** Year 2013/14 Income £45,712 Grants £31,532 Grants to organisations £31,532 Assets £861,584

**TRUSTEES** Jennifer Sykes, Prudence Gillett; David Sykes; Michael Taxman.

**HOW TO APPLY** Apply in writing to the correspondent.

**WHO TO APPLY TO** Michael Taxman, Trustee, Blankstone Sington Limited, 10th Floor, Walker House, Exchange Flags, Liverpool L2 3YL *Tel.* 0151 236 8200 *email* m_taxman@blankstonesington.co.uk

## ■ The Campden Charities Trustee

**CC NO** 1104616  **ESTABLISHED** 1629

**WHERE FUNDING CAN BE GIVEN** The former parish of Kensington, London; a north-south corridor, roughly from north of the Fulham Road to the north of Ladbroke Grove (a map can be viewed on the website).

**WHO CAN BENEFIT** Individuals and non-statutory not-for-profit organisations which refer and support individuals.

**WHAT IS FUNDED** There are four main areas for grant-making: assisting people of working age to obtain employment through grants for course fees, travel, equipment and childcare; supporting university students; helping older people, including with grants towards the replacement of household appliances, local social activities, courses and debt advice; supporting non-profit organisations that help with the charity's work with individuals.

**WHAT IS NOT FUNDED** UK charities or charities outside Kensington, unless they are of significant benefit to Kensington residents; schemes or activities which are generally regarded as the responsibility of the statutory authorities; UK fundraising appeals; environmental projects unless connected with education or social need; medical research or equipment; animal welfare; advancement of religion or religious groups, unless they offer non-religious services to the community; commercial and business activities; endowment appeals; projects of a political nature; retrospective capital grants.

**TYPE OF GRANT** One-off and recurrent. Pensions to older people, grants in cash or in kind to relieve need, bursaries and grants to Kensington-based organisations.

**RANGE OF GRANTS** £1,000 to £128,000.

**SAMPLE GRANTS** Westway Community Transport (£128,000); Nucleus Legal Advice Centre (£74,000); NOVA (£57,000); Earls Court YMCA (£14,000); Prospects Kensington (£9,000); Age UK – Kensington and Chelsea (£5,000); Hestia Housing (£2,000); Ethiopian Women's Environment Group and Rugby Portobello Trust (£1,000 each).

**FINANCES** Year 2013/14 Income £2,969,744 Grants £1,893,564 Grants to organisations £401,951 Assets £126,346,304

**TRUSTEES** Revd Gillean Craig, Chair; David Banks; Elisabeth Brockmann; Dr Chris Calman; Dr Kit Davis; Robert Atkinson; Susan Lockhart; Tim Martin; Terry Myers; Ben Pilling; Michael Finney; Richard Walker-Arnott; Ms M. Rodkina; Sam Berwick; Ms J. Mills; Mr T. Harvey-Samuel.

**OTHER INFORMATION** During the year, the charity gave six 'partnership' grants totalling £349,000. Nineteen 'referral' grants amounted to £53,000. An additional £1.5 million was given in grants to individuals.

**HOW TO APPLY** The following information is taken from the website: 'We are trying to target our resources where they can be of the most direct benefit to financially disadvantaged individuals. **We therefore do not receive unsolicited applications from organisations.** However, the Charities officers are eager to meet with colleagues from other not-for-profit organisations to explore ways in which we can work together to help individuals to end dependency on benefits or improve a low wage. We make incentive payments to any not-for-profit non-statutory organisations that successfully refer individuals and families to us. The best way to show us that you are working with the people that we want to help is to refer individuals to us

and at the same time you will benefit your organisation. **Referrals:** Non-statutory not-for-profit organisations that are working directly with low-income residents of Kensington are eligible to receive £1,000 for each individual or family that they refer successfully (i.e. each individual or family that is awarded a grant or pension).'
**WHO TO APPLY TO** Chris Stannard, Chief Executive Officer, Studios 3 & 4, 27a Pembridge Villas, London W11 3EP *Tel.* 020 7243 0551 or 020 7313 3797 *Website* www.campdencharities.org.uk

## ■ The Frederick and Phyllis Cann Trust

**CC NO** 1087863 **ESTABLISHED** 1998
**WHERE FUNDING CAN BE GIVEN** Northamptonshire.
**WHO CAN BENEFIT** The Trust Deed names seven charities, but trustees are prepared to consider other charities that fall within the charitable objects of the trust.
**WHAT IS FUNDED** The main objects of the trust are animal welfare, welfare of children and safety at sea.
**RANGE OF GRANTS** Up to £20,000.
**SAMPLE GRANTS** Northgate School (£20,000); The Salvation Army (£10,000); Museum of Leathercraft (£5,000); Animal in Need, Dogs for the Disabled (£3,000 each); Asthma Relies (£2,000); Mission to Seafarers (£1,500); Muir Maxwell (£1,000); Amber Trust (£750).
**FINANCES** *Year* 2013/14 *Income* £117,786 *Grants* £89,250 *Grants to organisations* £89,250 *Assets* £2,260,936
**TRUSTEES** Michael Percival; David Sharp; Keith Panter; Philip Saunderson; Christopher Toller; Laura Steedman.
**OTHER INFORMATION** Grants were made to 27 organisations.
**HOW TO APPLY** Apply in writing to the correspondent.
**WHO TO APPLY TO** Mrs Angela Moon, c/o Hewitsons, Elgin House, Billing Road, Northampton NN1 5 AU *Tel.* 01604 233233 *email* angelamoon@hewitsons.com

## ■ The H. and L. Cantor Trust

**CC NO** 220300 **ESTABLISHED** 1959
**WHERE FUNDING CAN BE GIVEN** UK, with some preference for Sheffield.
**WHO CAN BENEFIT** Registered charities, particularly Jewish organisations; schools; hospitals.
**WHAT IS FUNDED** General charitable purposes; Jewish causes.
**TYPE OF GRANT** One-off; capital costs; project funding.
**RANGE OF GRANTS** Up to £15,000; mostly around £100.
**SAMPLE GRANTS** **Previous beneficiaries have included:** Brain Research Trust; Delamere Forest School Ltd; I Rescue; Jewish Child's Day; PDSA – Sheffield and World Cancer Research; Sense; Shaare Zedek UK; Sheffield Jewish Congregation and Centre; Sheffield Jewish Welfare Organisation.
**FINANCES** *Year* 2013/14 *Income* £14,195 *Grants* £76,500 *Grants to organisations* £76,500
**TRUSTEES** Lily Cantor; Nicholas Jeffrey.
**OTHER INFORMATION** The trust had a total expenditure of £117,500. The 2013/14 accounts were not required to be published due to low income. Based on the patterns of previous giving it is likely that grants totalled about £76,500. Note that financial figures vary each year.
**HOW TO APPLY** Applications may be made in writing to the correspondent. Bear in mind that our research has noted that unsolicited applications are not generally invited.
**WHO TO APPLY TO** Lilly Cantor, Trustee, Flat 3, Ivy Park Court, 35 Ivy Park Road, Sheffield S10 3LA *Tel.* 0114 230 6354 *email* nicholasjeffrey@hotmail.com

## ■ Cardy Beaver Foundation

**CC NO** 265763 **ESTABLISHED** 1973
**WHERE FUNDING CAN BE GIVEN** UK with preference for Berkshire.
**WHO CAN BENEFIT** National and local registered charities.
**WHAT IS FUNDED** General charitable purposes.
**RANGE OF GRANTS** Usually under £5,000.
**SAMPLE GRANTS** **Previous beneficiaries have included:** Cancer Research UK, Watermill Theatre Appeal, Wallingford Museum, NSPCC, Berkshire Blind Society, Adventure Dolphin, St Peter's PCC, Church House Trust, RNLI and Asthma Relief, Julia's House, Elizabeth Foundation, Com Exchange – Newbury and Pangbourne Fete.
**FINANCES** *Year* 2013/14 *Income* £138,142 *Grants* £109,000 *Grants to organisations* £109,000 *Assets* £3,042,314
**TRUSTEES** John James; Mary Cardy; Sandra Rice.
**HOW TO APPLY** Apply in writing to the correspondent.
**WHO TO APPLY TO** John James, Trustee, Clifton House, 17 Reading Road, Pangbourne, Berkshire RG8 7LU *Tel.* 0118 961 4260 *email* jjames@valewest.com

## ■ The Carew Pole Charitable Trust

**CC NO** 255375 **ESTABLISHED** 1968
**WHERE FUNDING CAN BE GIVEN** UK, in practice, mainly Cornwall.
**WHO CAN BENEFIT** Donations normally made only to registered charities, but applications will be considered from individuals for non-full-time education purposes.
**WHAT IS FUNDED** General charitable purposes principally in Cornwall. In the case of support to churches and village halls, donations are in practice only made to those in the immediate vicinity to Antony House, Torpoint or to those with connections to the Carew Pole Family.
**WHAT IS NOT FUNDED** The trustees do not support applications from individuals for full-time education.
**RANGE OF GRANTS** Up to £15,000.
**SAMPLE GRANTS** Antony Parish Church (£11,000); Royal Academy and Tate St Ives (£10,000 each); HFT (£5,000); National Maritime Museum (£2,500); Grant Piano Project for Truro Cathedral (£2,000); Carefree (£1,000); Countryside Learning (£500); and Cornwall Music Festival (£200).
**FINANCES** *Year* 2013/14 *Income* £93,567 *Grants* £57,200 *Grants to organisations* £57,200 *Assets* £2,134,720
**TRUSTEES** Tremayne Carew Pole; James Kitson; James Williams.
**OTHER INFORMATION** In 2013/14 grants were given to 37 organisations.
**HOW TO APPLY** Application forms are available from the trust. The trustees consider and approve major donations in November each year, while other smaller appeals are considered, and donations made, throughout the year.

WHO TO APPLY TO Paul Cressy, Correspondent, The Antony Estate Office, Antony, Torpoint, Cornwall PL11 3AB *Tel.* 01752 815303

## ■ David William Traill Cargill Fund

SC NO SC012703  ESTABLISHED 1939
WHERE FUNDING CAN BE GIVEN UK, with a preference for the West of Scotland.
WHO CAN BENEFIT Registered charities.
WHAT IS FUNDED General charitable purposes, particularly religious causes, medical charities, education and help for older people.
WHAT IS NOT FUNDED Individuals.
TYPE OF GRANT One-off and recurrent.
SAMPLE GRANTS Previous beneficiaries have included: City of Glasgow Society of Social Service; Colquhoun Bequest Fund for Incurables; Crathie Opportunity Holidays; Glasgow and West of Scotland Society for the Blind; Glasgow City Mission; Greenock Medical Aid Society; North Glasgow Community Forum; Scottish Maritime Museum – Irvine; Scottish Episcopal Church; Scottish Motor Neurone Disease Association; Lead Scotland; Three Towns Blind Bowling/Social Club.
FINANCES Year 2012/13 Income £297,301 Grants £238,147 Grants to organisations £238,147
TRUSTEES A. C. Fyfe; W. G. Peacock; Norman Fyfe; Mirren Elizabeth Graham.
OTHER INFORMATION At the time of writing (June 2015) this was the latest information available. The OSCR record shows that out of the total expenditure of £256,500, 'grants and donations' totalled £238,000.
HOW TO APPLY Applications may be made in writing to the correspondent, supported by up-to-date accounts. The trustees meet quarterly.
WHO TO APPLY TO Norman Fyfe, Trustee, c/o Miller Beckett and Jackson Solicitors, 190 St Vincent Street, Glasgow G2 5SP

## ■ Carlee Ltd

CC NO 282873  ESTABLISHED 1981
WHERE FUNDING CAN BE GIVEN Worldwide.
WHO CAN BENEFIT Talmudic scholars and Jewish people.
WHAT IS FUNDED The advancement of religion in accordance with the Orthodox Jewish faith; the relief of poverty; general charitable purposes.
SAMPLE GRANTS Previous beneficiaries have included: Antryvale Ltd, Asos Chesed, Egerton Road Building Fund, Glasgow Kollel, HTVC, Rav Chesed Trust, Tevini, Union of Hebrew Congregations, YHS and YHTC.
FINANCES Year 2013/14 Income £157,008 Grants £175,600 Grants to organisations £175,600 Assets £78,327
TRUSTEES Hershel Grunhut; Pearl Grunhut; Bernard Dor Stroh; Blima Stroh.
HOW TO APPLY Apply in writing to the correspondent.
WHO TO APPLY TO The Secretary, 32 Pagent Road, London N16 5NQ

## ■ The Carmelite Monastery Ware Trust

CC NO 298379  ESTABLISHED 1987
WHERE FUNDING CAN BE GIVEN UK with preference for Ware
WHO CAN BENEFIT Registered charities and churches.
WHAT IS FUNDED Religious and other charitable work carried out in Ware for the benefit of the public.
SAMPLE GRANTS Previous beneficiaries have included: Association of British Carmels' Cardinal Hume Centre Trust; Catholic Aid Fund for Overseas Development; Catholic Housing Aid Society; Emmaus UK; Hertfordshire Community Trust; Medical Foundation for the Care of Victims of Torture; Passage Day Centre; Shelter; and Sion Evangelisation Centre for National Training.
FINANCES Year 2013/14 Income £25,525 Grants £22,516 Grants to organisations £22,516 Assets £307,267
TRUSTEES Sister Patricia McGee; Sister Susan Morrell; Sister Margaret Prickett; Sister Mary Bosworth-Smith.
HOW TO APPLY Apply in writing to the correspondent.
WHO TO APPLY TO Sister Mary Bosworth-Smith, Bursar, Carmelite Monastery, Ware, Hertfordshire SG12 ODT *email* warecarmel@btinternet.com *Website* www.warecarmel.com

## ■ The Worshipful Company of Carmen Benevolent Trust

CC NO 1050893  ESTABLISHED 1995
WHERE FUNDING CAN BE GIVEN City of London and UK.
WHO CAN BENEFIT Charitable organisations
WHAT IS FUNDED Objects of relieving necessitous past or present Liverymen or Freemen of the Company, its employees and servants, or those connected with transport in the UK. The trust is also allowed to made grants to any charitable fund in the City of London or elsewhere.
RANGE OF GRANTS £100–£11,500
SAMPLE GRANTS Widow and Dependant of Deceased Liveryntan (£11,500); The No Way Trust (£4,000); City of London Freemen's School (£3,500); Lord Mayor's Appeal 2014 (£3,000); Hackney Carriage Drivers (£2,500); Family Holidays Association, The Connection St Martin-in-the-Fields (£1,000); Clapton Common Boys' Club, Housing the Homeless, West London Day Centre, Young and Inspired (£500); Summer Dreams (£200).
FINANCES Year 2013/14 Income £273,959 Grants £59,676 Grants to organisations £59,676 Assets £1,708,265
TRUSTEES Telfer Saywell; Michael Power; Mary Bonar; M. Simpkin; Robert Russett; Richard Pollitzer; Neil Coles.
OTHER INFORMATION In 2031/14 five individuals received a total of £2,065.
HOW TO APPLY Apply in writing to the correspondent.
WHO TO APPLY TO Chris Godbold, Five Kings House, 1 Queen Street Place, London EC4R 1QS *Tel.* 020 7489 8289 *email* carmenbentrust@hotmail.com *Website* www.thecarmen.co.uk

## ■ The Richard Carne Trust

CC NO 1115903  ESTABLISHED 2006
WHERE FUNDING CAN BE GIVEN UK.
WHO CAN BENEFIT Registered charities; arts institutions; educational establishments; individuals; theatrical groups or musical groups in the early stages of their careers.
WHAT IS FUNDED Children and young people in the performing arts, especially music and theatre. A number of selected charities are supported on an ongoing basis.
TYPE OF GRANT One-off and recurrent.
RANGE OF GRANTS Up to £50,000 to organisations.

SAMPLE GRANTS **Previous beneficiaries have included:** Royal College of Music (£30,000); Trinity Laban Conservatoire of Dance and Music (£16,000); Royal Welsh College of Music and Drama (£15,000); ChamberStudio (£5,500); Classical Opera Company and Theatre 503 (£5,000 each); Red Handed Theatre Company (£3,000); British Isles Music Festival (£2,000); National Children's Wind Orchestra of Great Britain and Orion Symphony Orchestra (£1,000 each); Brodowski Quartet (£500).

FINANCES Year 2013 Income £19,266 Grants £147,000 Grants to organisations £147,000

TRUSTEES Kleinwort Benson Trustees Ltd; Philip Carne; Marjorie Carne.

OTHER INFORMATION The trust had a total expenditure of £186,500. The 2012/13 accounts were not required to be published due to low income. Based on the patterns of previous giving it is likely that awards totalled about £147,000. About 30 awards are made annually.

HOW TO APPLY The trust has previously notes that it is the policy of trustees 'to consider all written appeals received, but only successful applications are notified of the trustees' decision'. Applications are considered at the annual meeting, normally in June.

WHO TO APPLY TO Christopher Gilbert, Correspondent, c/o Kleinwort Benson Trustees Ltd, 14 St George Street, London W1S 1FE Tel. 020 3207 7356

## ■ The Carnegie Dunfermline Trust

SC NO SC015710    ESTABLISHED 1903

WHERE FUNDING CAN BE GIVEN Dunfermline and Rosyth.

WHO CAN BENEFIT Registered charities and schools.

WHAT IS FUNDED The trust's website states: 'The Trust funds projects, activities and schemes with social, community, educational, cultural, sport and recreational purposes for the benefit of those within the defined geographic area of the operation of the Trust. We look for proposals that are innovative and far reaching together with those that particularly impact on young people. We are also interested in active partnerships where organisations decide to work together and adopt a joint approach. Start-up funding is offered on a one-off basis.' Additional guidelines are available for schools.

WHAT IS NOT FUNDED Individuals; closed groups (with the exception of those catering for specialist needs); political, military or sectarian bodies; activities out of the geographic scope of the trust; medical organisations; routine running or salary costs; costs which are the responsibility of a government body.

TYPE OF GRANT Principally single grants and capital funding. Pump priming and start-up funding is offered on a one off basis.

RANGE OF GRANTS Typical grant between £300 and £10,000.

SAMPLE GRANTS Primary Schools Sports Festivals (£5,500); Carnegie Swimming Club (£2,500); West Fife Woodlands Group, 4th Dunfermline Boys' Brigade (£2,000); Fife Festival of Music, Fresh Air Festival (£1,000 each).

FINANCES Year 2013 Income £608,552 Grants £113,638 Grants to organisations £113,638

TRUSTEES Andrew Croxford; Dr David Fraser; Claire Gemmell; Angus Hogg; Jane Livingstone; William Livingstone; Janet McCauslin; Keith Punler; Dr Ruth Ray; Fiona Robertson; J. Douglas Scott; David Walker; Robin Watson; Ian M. Wilson; David Fleetwood; Cllr Alice Callaghan; Cllr Willie Campbell; Cllr Mike Shirkie; Nora Rundell.

HOW TO APPLY Application forms can be downloaded from the trust's website. The trust provides the following additional information: 'Trustees meet every two months and applications can be submitted at any time. Application forms are available from the website or from the office and initial discussion with the Grants Officer is encouraged. Where possible applications will be acknowledged and further information may be sought. Once all the necessary background is available the application will be considered by the appropriate assessing trustee in the first instance who will decide if a grant under delegated powers is applicable, if it should go to the board, or if it is not suitable to progress. When a grant is awarded the recipient will be notified in writing with any related terms and conditions which will include the take up of the grant within a twenty four month period. If an application is unsuccessful, the trust is unlikely to consider a further application within twelve months.'

WHO TO APPLY TO Elaine Stewart, Grants Officer, Andrew Carnegie House, Pittencrieff Street, Dunfermline KY12 8AW Tel. 01383 749789 Fax 01383 749799 email grants@carnegietrust.com Website www.andrewcarnegie.co.uk

## ■ The Carnegie Trust for the Universities of Scotland

SC NO SC015600    ESTABLISHED 1901

WHERE FUNDING CAN BE GIVEN Scotland.

WHO CAN BENEFIT The 15 Universities of Scotland, their staff and students.

WHAT IS FUNDED The enrichment of the scholarly capability of Scotland's Universities and assistance for people of limited means to benefit from higher education. The trust operates a number of funding streams to achieve this, which are: fee support for Scottish students unable to fund their course at a Scottish University; Vacation Scholarships for undergraduates who have a talent and an interest for research; bursaries to cover the cost of tuition fees of one year of postgraduate study at a Scottish university; Scholarships for PhD study; Research Incentive Grants to fund high-quality research in any academic field; Collaborative Research Grants to encourage academic researchers to initiate joint research projects to the benefit of Scottish universities as a whole; the Centenary Professorship scheme to support visits to Scotland from leading international researchers.

WHAT IS NOT FUNDED See the website for exclusions of individual schemes.

TYPE OF GRANT Funding for projects of value to the Scottish universities, with wide discretion on what is allowable; scholarships; professorships; bursaries.

SAMPLE GRANTS University of Aberdeen; University of Dundee; University of Glasgow; University of Strathclyde.

FINANCES Year 2013/14 Income £2,873,367 Grants £2,431,078 Grants to organisations £2,431,078 Assets £73,639,315

TRUSTEES Prof. Anne Glover; Louise Adams; The Lady Balfour of Burleigh; Richard Burns Esq.; Sir John Grant; Lord Kerr of Kinlochard; Eileen Mackay; Iain Macmillan; Judith Sischy; Ian Sword; Ed Weeple; Lord Wilson of Tillyorn;

Principals of the Universities of Scotland (ex officio); The First Minister (ex officio); The Lord Provosts of Edinburgh and Glasgow (ex officio).
**OTHER INFORMATION** The grant total above includes funding given both to Universities and to individuals.
**HOW TO APPLY** Details of the various schemes operated by the trust are available from its website.
**WHO TO APPLY TO** The Secretary, Andrew Carnegie House, Pittencrieff Street, Dunfermline, Fife KY12 8AW *Tel.* 01383 724990 *Fax* 01383 749799 *email* admin@carnegie-trust.org *Website* www.carnegie-trust.org

## ■ The Carpenters' Company Charitable Trust

CC NO 276996          ESTABLISHED 1978
**WHERE FUNDING CAN BE GIVEN** UK. Mainly Greater London.
**WHO CAN BENEFIT** Individuals and schools, colleges, universities and other charitable organisations promoting the craft of carpentry and individuals within the building craft.
**WHAT IS FUNDED** Charitable causes benefitting from grants include organisations supporting older, homeless or young people, people with disabilities, children, education, medical causes and museums. Craft causes receive a high priority when awards are considered.
**WHAT IS NOT FUNDED** Grants are not normally made to individual churches or cathedrals, or to educational establishments having no association to the Carpenters' Company. No grants (except educational grants) are made to individual applicants. Funds are usually only available to charities registered with the Charity Commission or exempt from registration.
**SAMPLE GRANTS** Building Crafts College (£722,110); Carpenters and Docklands Centre (25,000); Carpenters Primary School (£10,200); and Institute of Carpenters (£6,000).
**FINANCES** *Year* 2013/14 *Income* £1,101,071 *Grants* £845,297 *Grants to organisations* £845,297 *Assets* £23,531,986
**TRUSTEES** Peter A. Luton; Michael Matthews; Michael I. Montague-Smith; Guy Morton-Smith.
**OTHER INFORMATION** The Trust's grants are broken-down as follows: Craft activities (£741,600); City of London (£15,000); Religious organisations (£1,000); Youth and children's organisations (£40,000); Miscellaneous (£20,800).
**HOW TO APPLY** Applications should be sent to the trust's administrator. Application forms are available on the trust's website. Application should be submitted by 1 June.
**WHO TO APPLY TO** The Clerk, Carpenters' Hall, 1 Throgmorton Avenue, London EC2N 2JJ *Tel.* 020 7588 7001 *email* info@carpentersco.com *Website* www.carpentersco.com/charitable_ccct.php

## ■ The Carr-Gregory Trust

CC NO 1085580          ESTABLISHED 2001
**WHERE FUNDING CAN BE GIVEN** London and Bristol.
**WHO CAN BENEFIT** Charitable organisations.
**WHAT IS FUNDED** Education, particularly the performing arts and social welfare.
**WHAT IS NOT FUNDED** Individuals.
**RANGE OF GRANTS** There is no specified grant range; however, grants to previous beneficiaries should be used as a guide.
**SAMPLE GRANTS** National Theatre (£20,000); Royal Academy of Music (£10,000); Alzheimer's Research UK (£5,000); Diana Award (£3,500); Macular Society, Prisoners' Education Trust and Penny Brohn Cancer Care (£2,000 each); Beating Bowel Cancer, Help the Hospices and Stroke Association (£1,000 each); and The Salvation Army and St Mungo's (£500 each).
**FINANCES** *Year* 2013 *Income* £109,064 *Grants* £77,490 *Grants to organisations* £77,490 *Assets* £445,194
**TRUSTEES** Russ Carr; Heather Wheelhouse; Linda Carr; Hannah Nicholls.
**OTHER INFORMATION** Grants were made to 46 organisations and totalled £77,500.
**HOW TO APPLY** Apply in writing to the correspondent and should not exceed two A4 pages.
**WHO TO APPLY TO** Russ Carr, Trustee, 56 Pembroke Road, Clifton, Bristol BS8 3DT

## ■ The Carrington Charitable Trust

CC NO 265824          ESTABLISHED 1973
**WHERE FUNDING CAN BE GIVEN** UK with a preference for Buckinghamshire.
**WHO CAN BENEFIT** Registered charities.
**WHAT IS FUNDED** General charitable purposes.
**WHAT IS NOT FUNDED** Individuals; non-registered charities.
**RANGE OF GRANTS** Up to £15,000, mostly for smaller amounts.
**SAMPLE GRANTS** Grenadier Guards – Colonel's Fund (£15,000); Hope and Homes for Children (£5,000); Garsington Opera (£3,400); Bledlow PCC Holy Trinity Church (£1,000); Blind Veterans UK and Hospice of St Francis (£500 each); Aylesbury Grammar School Foundation (£250); ACT Breast Cancer and Chiltern Open Air Museum (£50 each); Bucks Archaeological Society (£12).
**FINANCES** *Year* 2013/14 *Income* £94,196 *Grants* £48,133 *Grants to organisations* £48,133 *Assets* £5,460,248
**TRUSTEES** Rt Hon. Lord Carrington; Mr J. A. Cloke; Rt Hon. V. Carrington.
**HOW TO APPLY** Applications should be made in writing to the correspondent.
**WHO TO APPLY TO** Jeffrey Cloke, Trustee, c/o Cloke and Co, 475 Salisbury House, London Wall, London EC2M 5QQ *Tel.* 020 7638 8992 *email* jeff@cloke.co.uk

## ■ The Leslie Mary Carter Charitable Trust

CC NO 284782          ESTABLISHED 1982
**WHERE FUNDING CAN BE GIVEN** UK, with a preference for Norfolk, Suffolk and North Essex.
**WHO CAN BENEFIT** Registered charities.
**WHAT IS FUNDED** The preferred areas for grant-giving are conservation/environment and welfare causes. Other applications will be considered but acknowledgements may not always be sent. Trustees prefer well thought-out applications for larger gifts, than many applications for smaller grants.
**WHAT IS NOT FUNDED** Individuals.
**TYPE OF GRANT** Capital including buildings, core costs, one-off, project, research, running costs and recurring costs will be considered.
**RANGE OF GRANTS** Grants generally range from £500–£5,000, but larger grants are sometimes considered.
**SAMPLE GRANTS** Norfolk Wildlife Trust (£15,000); Animal Health Trust, St Elizabeth Hospice, St

Helena Hospice (£10,000 each); British Heart Foundation, Combat Stress, East Anglia's Children's Hospices, RNIB Talking Books (£5,000 each); Barn Owl Trust, Bat Conservation Trust, Friends of the Earth (£2,000 each); Natural History Museum, Suffolk Owl Sanctuary, Suzy Lamplugh Trust (£1,000); People's Trust for Endangered Species, East Suffolk Association for the Blind (£500).

**FINANCES** Year 2013/14 Income £135,241 Grants £118,500 Grants to organisations £118,500 Assets £3,491,156

**TRUSTEES** Sam Wilson; Leslie Carter; Martyn Carr.

**HOW TO APPLY** Apply in writing to the correspondent. Telephone calls are not welcome. There is no need to enclose an sae unless applicants wish to have materials returned. Applications made outside the preferred areas for grant-giving will be considered, but acknowledgements may not always be sent.

**WHO TO APPLY TO** Sam Wilson, Trustee, c/o Birketts, 24–26 Museum Street, Ipswich IP1 1HZ Tel. 01473 232300

## ■ Carter's Educational Foundation

**CC NO** 528161     **ESTABLISHED** 1888

**WHERE FUNDING CAN BE GIVEN** The ancient parish of Wilford.

**WHO CAN BENEFIT** The trust supports the South Wilford Endowed Church of England School. It may also give grants to individuals under 25 living in the ancient parish and organisations for such people, with a broadly educational nature, operating within the beneficial area of the ancient parish of Wilford, Nottingham, including Wilford Village, Silverdale, Compton Acres, part of West Bridgford mainly west of Loughborough Road, and parts of the south of the Meadows.

**WHAT IS FUNDED** Education.

**WHAT IS NOT FUNDED** People and organisations outside the ancient parish of Wilford, Nottingham or any organisation based outside that area.

**RANGE OF GRANTS** £300–£80,000

**SAMPLE GRANTS** Extra teaching staff (£80,000); educational grants to young people (£37,435); educational awards (£7,406); St Saviours Church (£7,000); Hoods Basketball Club (£750).

**FINANCES** Year 2014 Income £304,658 Grants £132,028 Grants to organisations £132,028 Assets £6,560,646

**TRUSTEES** Paula Hammond; Robert Stanley; Madeleine Cox; Roy Nettleship; Raymond Hutchins; Robert Baxter; Roger Steel.

**OTHER INFORMATION** Grants to individuals totalled £44,181.

**HOW TO APPLY** The following information is provided by the foundation: 'Subject to the availability of funds, grants to voluntary charitable organisations in the ancient parish are normally considered at the same time as educational grants for individuals and awarded on the basis of the school year. Trustees meet four times a year however letters of application should be with the clerk to the foundation before 31 May. Letters should identify the base for the organisation's work, outline the nature of the activities involved and the approximate number of young people participating from the ancient parish. If this is the first application from your organisation, please give full details and include a copy of your latest accounts. Applications must be made in writing.'

**WHO TO APPLY TO** Sally Morrant, The Clerk to the Trustees, Pennine House, 8 Stanford Street, Nottingham NG1 7BQ Tel. 0115 958 6262 Website www.wilford-carters-education.org.uk

## ■ The Casey Trust

**CC NO** 1055726     **ESTABLISHED** 1996

**WHERE FUNDING CAN BE GIVEN** UK and financially developing countries.

**WHO CAN BENEFIT** Registered (or UK affiliate) charities benefitting children. The trust works with established UK charities.

**WHAT IS FUNDED** Children and young people. The trust is particularly interested in supporting new projects, 'start-up or bold new initiatives that might not have happened without its participation'. Note that projects must be exclusively concerned with children or young people. The latest accounts state that 'the trustees will concentrate their efforts in specific sectors where funding requirements at particular levels will make a real difference'.

**WHAT IS NOT FUNDED** Individual applicants requesting funds to continue studies or travel; unregistered organisations; projects that are not exclusively for children.

**TYPE OF GRANT** Capital and core costs; project funding; start-up costs; up to three years.

**RANGE OF GRANTS** £1,000–£12,500; average grant was £2,150.

**SAMPLE GRANTS** Raw Material (£12,500); World Monuments Fund (£11,000); Buttle UK (£2,500); Acorns (£2,400); The Children's Adventure Farm Trust (£2,300); Lifelites (£2,100); Malaika Kids UK, Motability and Sightsavers (£2,000 each); Street Child – Liberia (£1,800); Perthes Association (£1,600); Sunny Days Children's Fund (£1,500); Edinburgh Young Carers Project and St Luke's Cares (£1,000 each).

**FINANCES** Year 2012/13 Income £160,029 Grants £88,220 Grants to organisations £88,220 Assets £3,097,941

**TRUSTEES** Kenneth Howard; Benjamin Shorten; Sam Howard; Alex Krikler.

**OTHER INFORMATION** At the time of writing (June 2015) this was the latest information available – 2013/14 accounts were overdue. Awards were made to 41 institutions.

**HOW TO APPLY** Appeals may be made in writing to the correspondent, providing a brief outline of your work and project for which the money is required as well as a clear budget and a recent set of accounts, if possible. However, bear in mind that the trust is not reactive and the trustees will not be able to respond to the majority of requests for assistance – in order to both reduce costs and administration they will respond mainly to those charitable institutions known to them. The trustees meet four times a year and will only notify unsuccessful applicants if an sae is enclosed.

**WHO TO APPLY TO** Kenneth Howard, Trustee, 27 Arkwright Road, London NW3 6BJ Tel. 020 7435 9601 email kchoward1@mac.com Website www.caseytrust.org

## ■ Cash for Kids – Radio Clyde

**SC NO** SC003334     **ESTABLISHED** 1984

**WHERE FUNDING CAN BE GIVEN** Radio Clyde transmission area, i.e. Inverclyde, Argyll and Bute, Dumfries and Galloway, East Ayrshire, South Ayrshire, North Ayrshire, East Dunbartonshire, West Dunbartonshire, Renfrewshire, East Renfrewshire, Glasgow City

Council, North Lanarkshire and South Lanarkshire.

**WHO CAN BENEFIT** Organisations benefitting children and young adults up to the age of 16 disadvantaged through: illness, distress, abuse or neglect; any kind of disability; behavioural or psychological difficulties; living in poverty or situations of deprivation.

**WHAT IS FUNDED** Children and young adults up to the age of 16 disadvantaged through: illness, distress, abuse or neglect; any kind of disability; behavioural or psychological difficulties; living in poverty or situations of deprivation. Organisations benefitting this group. Grants, Christmas presents, food, pantomime trips, clothing and other support is given to children via social work departments and through community and voluntary groups.

**WHAT IS NOT FUNDED** Trips or projects abroad; medical treatment/research; unspecified expenditure; deficit funding or repayment of loans; retrospective funding (projects taking place before the grant award date); projects unable to start within six months of the grant award date; distribution to another/other organisation/s; general appeals or endowment funds; relief of statutory responsibility; the promotion of religion. No funding for capital expenditure except in very special circumstances that must be made clear at the time of applying. Organisations whose administration costs exceed 15% of total expenditure will not be supported.

**SAMPLE GRANTS** Previous beneficiaries have included: Aberlour Bridges Project – Royston: supporting children affected by addiction; and Centre for Under 5s Toy Library: supporting children with physical disabilities through a novel 'Toys on the Road' mobile library.

**FINANCES** Year 2013 Income £1,147,621 Grants £1,028,170 Grants to organisations £1,028,170

**TRUSTEES** Mr J. Brown; Ewan Hunter; Ian Grabiner; Lord Jack McConnell; Sir Tom Hunter; Brenda Ritchie.

**HOW TO APPLY** Application forms and guidelines are available from the charity's website.

**WHO TO APPLY TO** Trust Administrator, Radio Clyde, 3 South Avenue, Clydebank Business Park, Glasgow G81 2RX Tel. 0141 204 1025 Fax 0141 565 2370 email lesley.cashforkids@radioclyde.com Website www.clydecashforkids.com

## ■ Sir John Cass's Foundation

**CC NO** 312425 **ESTABLISHED** 1748
**WHERE FUNDING CAN BE GIVEN** The inner London boroughs – Camden, Greenwich, Hackney, Hammersmith and Fulham, Islington, Kensington and Chelsea, Lambeth, Lewisham, Newham, Southwark, Tower Hamlets, Wandsworth, Westminster and the City of London.

**WHO CAN BENEFIT** Individuals; schools; organisations. The foundation will only consider proposals from schools and organisations that benefit: children or young people under the age of 25, who are permanent residents of named inner London boroughs (Camden, Greenwich, Hackney, Hammersmith and Fulham, Islington, Kensington and Chelsea, Lambeth, Lewisham, Newham, Southwark, Tower Hamlets, Wandsworth, Westminster and the City of London), and from disadvantaged backgrounds or areas of high deprivation.

**WHAT IS FUNDED** Education, especially of people in financial need. The foundation has four areas of focus for grant-giving: widening participation in further and higher education; truancy, exclusion and behaviour management; prisoner education; new initiatives.

**WHAT IS NOT FUNDED** Projects that do not meet a foundation priority; holiday projects, school journeys, trips abroad or exchange visits; supplementary schools or mother tongue teaching; independent schools; youth and community groups, or projects taking place in these settings; pre-school and nursery education; general fundraising campaigns or appeals; costs for equipment or salaries that are the statutory responsibility of education authorities; costs to substitute for the withdrawal or reduction of statutory funding; costs for work or activities that have already taken place prior to the grant application; costs already covered by core funding or other grants; capital costs, that are exclusively for the purchase, repair or furnishing of buildings, purchase of vehicles, computers, sports equipment or improvements to school grounds.

**TYPE OF GRANT** Recurrent for individuals; project, recurrent or one-off support for groups, organisations and schools. Funding may be given for up to three years.

**RANGE OF GRANTS** Usually £5,000–£75,000.

**SAMPLE GRANTS** Share Foundation (£77,000); Sir John Cass's Foundation Secondary School (£71,500 in three grants); Baker Dearing Trust (£70,000); Goldsmiths College (£43,000); British Academy (£40,000); University of the Arts (£35,000); Spitalfields Music (£12,000); Royal London Society (£7,500); Royal London Society for Blind People (£5,500); Institute of Education (£4,000).

**FINANCES** Year 2013/14 Income £6,171,294 Grants £1,024,893 Grants to organisations £814,019 Assets £129,356,426

**TRUSTEES** Kevin Everett; HH. Judge Brian Barker; Graham Forbes; Helen Meixner; Alderman Dr Ray Ellis; Prof. Michael Thorne; Revd Laura Jorgensen; Revd Trevor Critchlow; Paul Bloomfield; Jennifer Mosley; Sophie Fernandes.

**OTHER INFORMATION** Grants were made to 32 organisations in 2013/14. Grants to individuals totalled £211,000.

**HOW TO APPLY** The foundation operates a two stage application process – an initial enquiry and a full application stage. At stage 1, applicants are required to complete and submit the initial enquiry form which is available from the foundation's website and on request from the correspondent. The form asks for outline information about your proposed project; information about how the project meets the foundation's priorities; a summary of the project that includes the following information: the aims of the project including outputs and outcomes, how the project will be delivered; the duration of the project, including when and where it will take place; and a budget covering project costs. Enquiries will then be considered and applicants informed of the decision taken within three weeks. Successful stage 1 applicants will be invited to proceed to Stage 2 and submit a full application. A copy of the stage 2 guidelines will be sent to you at that time. This form should be completed and submitted with copies of the memorandum and articles of association (or constitution) of your organisation, together with the latest annual report and accounts. On receipt of your application foundation staff may meet with you as part of the assessment process. The grants committee meets in March, June and November each year. It normally takes between two and four months from receipt of a full application until a decision is made. All applicants will be sent formal notification of the outcome of their applications within two weeks of the committee decision. Those who are offered a grant will be sent a formal offer letter and copies of the foundation's standard terms and conditions of grant. Copies of the standard terms and conditions of grant are available on the foundation's website. Additional conditions are sometimes included depending on the nature of the grant. All applications are assessed on merit. If your application is refused you can apply again twelve months after the date you submitted your last application.

**WHO TO APPLY TO** Tony Mullee, Clerk/Chief Executive, 31 Jewry Street, London EC3N 2EY *Tel.* 020 7480 5884 *email* contactus@sirjohncass.org *Website* www.sirjohncass.org

## ■ The Elizabeth Casson Trust

**CC NO** 227166  **ESTABLISHED** 1930
**WHERE FUNDING CAN BE GIVEN** Worldwide.
**WHO CAN BENEFIT** Occupational therapy schools/departments; individual occupational therapists.
**WHAT IS FUNDED** The training and development of occupational therapists. Ongoing support is given to Oxford Brookes University.
**WHAT IS NOT FUNDED** Anything other than occupational therapy education and training.
**TYPE OF GRANT** Research projects and courses/travel bursaries that will benefit the profession as well as the individual.
**RANGE OF GRANTS** £400–£30,000
**SAMPLE GRANTS Beneficiaries have included:** Fit to Work Project (£30,000); Scholarship at Tufts University (£18,700); Combat Stress, Multiple Sclerosis Trust, Resurge Africa and UK Occupational Therapy Research Foundation (a total of £11,500); College of Occupational Therapy and Ugandan Association of Occupational Therapists (£1,000 each); Oxford Research Group (£400).
**FINANCES** *Year* 2013/14 *Income* £217,376 *Grants* £118,000 *Grants to organisations* £118,000
**TRUSTEES** Carolyn Rutland; Juliet Croft; Dr Peter Agulnik; Geoffrey Paine; Rosemary Hallam; Bernard Davies; Sally Townsend; Dr David Parker; Mark Drasdo; Prof. Elizabeth Turner.
**OTHER INFORMATION** At the time of writing (June 2015) the latest information available. Full accounts for 2014/15 were not published by the Charity Commission. During the year the trust had a total charitable expenditure of £134,000. The trust supports both individuals and organisations and the allocations vary annually. Lately most support has been given to individuals; however, in the past significant support has been given to institutions. Based on the most recent giving we estimate that about £118,000 was given in grants to individuals and organisations.
**HOW TO APPLY** Applications can be made using the trust's application form which can be obtained from the website.
**WHO TO APPLY TO** Caroline Gray, Secretary to the Trustees, Corner House, Cote, Bampton, Oxfordshire OX18 2EG *Tel.* 01993 850716 *email* ec.trust@btinternet.com *Website* www.elizabethcassontrust.org.uk

## ■ The Castang Foundation

**CC NO** 1003867  **ESTABLISHED** 1991
**WHERE FUNDING CAN BE GIVEN** UK.
**WHO CAN BENEFIT** Registered charities.
**WHAT IS FUNDED** Research into neurodevelopmental disorders in children.
**RANGE OF GRANTS** £600–£134,400
**SAMPLE GRANTS Research project funding** – Foetal growth restriction research (£134,400); Infantile spasms (£43,000); Nutrition study (£23,000); Prevention of drooling project (£20,000); Fatigue and stress PhD student funding (£11,200). **Conferences and Seminars** – Developmental disorders (£10,300); Hypoxic Ischemic Encephalopathy (£700). **Lecture grants** – European Academy of Childhood Disability (£600).
**FINANCES** *Year* 2013/14 *Income* £88,339 *Grants* £248,231 *Grants to organisations* £248,231 *Assets* £2,004,128
**TRUSTEES** Mr I. A. Burman; Mr M. B. Glynn, Mr M. Bax.
**OTHER INFORMATION** In 2013/14 the foundation had a total expenditure of £317,618.
**HOW TO APPLY** Apply in writing to the correspondent.
**WHO TO APPLY TO** Ian Burman, Laytons, 50 Victoria Embankment, London EC4Y 0LS *Tel.* 020 7842 8000 *email* ian.burnham@laytons.com *Website* www.castangfoundation.net

## ■ The Catalyst Charitable Trust

**CC NO** 1001962  **ESTABLISHED** 1990
**WHERE FUNDING CAN BE GIVEN** Mainly Suffolk and Essex.
**WHO CAN BENEFIT** Registered charities; churches; schools; hospitals.
**WHAT IS FUNDED** General charitable purposes. This trust has an interest in supporting small charities in the Suffolk/Essex area, particularly churches, schools and hospitals.
**RANGE OF GRANTS** £500–£10,000
**SAMPLE GRANTS** Oundle School Foundation (£10,000); The Shakespeare Globe Trust (£7,000); The Suffolk Foundation (£4,000); Bildeston Parish Council (£2,000); Bildeston Primary School PTFA, Friends of Holy Innocents Church – Lamarsh (£1,000); Friends of St Barnabas Church – Alphamstone and Lindsey PCC (£500 each).
**FINANCES** *Year* 2012/13 *Income* £37,500 *Grants* £38,000 *Grants to organisations* £34,000 *Assets* £10,740
**TRUSTEES** Gillian Buckle; James Buckle; Louise Somerset; Charles Course.
**OTHER INFORMATION** At the time of writing (June 2015) this was the latest information available. During the year 18 awards were made to institutions. A total of £4,000 was given to individuals.
**HOW TO APPLY** Apply in writing to the correspondent, although beneficiaries are normally selected through personal contact.
**WHO TO APPLY TO** Penny Andrews, Buckle Farms, Dairy Farm Office, Dairy Road, Semer, Ipswich IP7 6RA

## ■ The Catholic Charitable Trust

**CC NO** 215553  **ESTABLISHED** 1935
**WHERE FUNDING CAN BE GIVEN** America and Europe.
**WHO CAN BENEFIT** Traditional Catholic organisations.
**WHAT IS FUNDED** The traditional teachings of the Roman Catholic faith. The trust's income is usually fully committed.

**WHAT IS NOT FUNDED** The trust does not normally support a charity unless it is known to the trustees. Grants are not made to individuals.
**RANGE OF GRANTS** £1,500–£16,000
**SAMPLE GRANTS** Society of Saint Pius X – England (£16,000); Missio, White Fathers (£5,000 each); Little Sisters of the Poor (£3,000); Holy Cross Parish Fulham (£2,000); Cardinal Hume Centre (£1,000).
**FINANCES** Year 2013 Income £70,260 Grants £58,108 Grants to organisations £58,108 Assets £2,138,220
**TRUSTEES** John C. Vernor-Miles; Wilfrid E. Vernor-Miles; David P. Orr.
**HOW TO APPLY** Applications can only be accepted from registered charities and should be in writing to the correspondent. The trust does not normally support a charity unless it is known to the trustees. In order to save administration costs replies are not sent to unsuccessful applicants. For the most part funds are fully committed.
**WHO TO APPLY TO** Wilfrid Miles, Trustee, c/o Hunters, 9 New Square, London WC2A 3QN Tel. 020 7412 0050

## ■ Catholic Foreign Missions (CFM)

**CC NO** 249252  **ESTABLISHED** 1941
**WHERE FUNDING CAN BE GIVEN** UK and overseas.
**WHO CAN BENEFIT** Overseas missions; Catholic bodies; charities; clergy and missionaries.
**WHAT IS FUNDED** Catholic faith; charitable and voluntary missions in any part of the world; education and training and welfare of clergy and missionaries; overseas aid. The accounts state: 'Grants are made principally to support active and retired Catholic missionaries, seminarians in training for the Catholic priesthood and the building of seminaries and houses of residence in mission territories.'
**RANGE OF GRANTS** £3,500–£735,000
**SAMPLE GRANTS** Congregation of the Mission – Province of Paris (£735,000); Congregation of the Mission – General Curia-Rome (£188,000); Congregation of the Mission – Province of Toulouse (£131,500); Congregation of the Mission – Province of Ireland (£26,500); Oeuvre du Bienheureux Perboyre (£24,000); Mission Bikoro (£3,500).
**FINANCES** Year 2012/13 Income £707,230 Grants £1,108,695 Grants to organisations £1,108,695 Assets £17,893,166
**TRUSTEES** Revd Bernard Meade; Revd Desmond Beirne; Revd Jean-Marie Lesbats; Revd Philip Walshe; Revd Philippe Lamblin; Revd Kieran Magovern; Revd Eric Ravoux; Revd Eric Saint-Sevin.
**OTHER INFORMATION** At the time of writing (June 2015) this was the latest information available. During the year six missions were supported.
**HOW TO APPLY** Our research suggests that external applications are not considered, as the funds are fully committed.
**WHO TO APPLY TO** Revd Bernard Meade, Secretary, c/o Pothecary Witham Weld, 70 St George's Square, London SW1V 3RD Tel. 020 7821 8211

## ■ The Catholic Trust for England and Wales

**CC NO** 1097482  **ESTABLISHED** 1968
**WHERE FUNDING CAN BE GIVEN** England and Wales.
**WHO CAN BENEFIT** Roman Catholic organisations.
**WHAT IS FUNDED** The advancement of the Roman Catholic religion in England and Wales.
**WHAT IS NOT FUNDED** Individuals; local projects or projects not immediately advancing the Roman Catholic religion in England and Wales.
**SAMPLE GRANTS** CARITAS Social Action Network (£181,300); Catholic Chaplain in Higher Education, Catholic Voices (£20,000 each); National Board of Catholic Women (£10,000); National Council of Lay Associations (£7,000); Lisbonian Society (£5,000); National Conference of Priests (£800).
**FINANCES** Year 2013 Income £4,640,673 Grants £244,150 Grants to organisations £244,150 Assets £15,599,122
**TRUSTEES** Rt Revd Malcolm McMahon; Richard King; Revd John Nelson; Michael Prior; Dr Elizabeth Walmsley; William Moyes; Nigel Newton; Edward Poyser.
**HOW TO APPLY** Apply in writing to the correspondent. The trust has stated previously that it does not respond to unsolicited applications.
**WHO TO APPLY TO** Revd Marcus Stock, Secretary, 39 Eccleston Square, London SW1V 1BX Tel. 020 7901 4810 email secretariat@cbcew.org.uk Website www.catholicchurch.org.uk

## ■ The Cattanach Charitable Trust

**SC NO** SC020902  **ESTABLISHED** 1992
**WHERE FUNDING CAN BE GIVEN** Scotland.
**WHO CAN BENEFIT** The trust will fund charities registered either in Scotland or in England for work done exclusively in Scotland. 'Organisations should be registered with the Office of the Scottish Charity Regulator, or, if registered with the Charity Commission, should be in the process of registering with OSCR.'
**WHAT IS FUNDED** 'The Cattanach Trust seeks applications for projects which support children from pre-birth to three years old, who are affected by levels of relative deprivation. There is good evidence that supporting children during the first years of a child's life has the greatest positive impact on their developmental progress. Good quality services improve not only a child's life during these years, but also have substantial benefits into adolescence and adulthood. Projects should be working from a strengths based model; the existing and potential strengths of the child, the family and the community should be recognised and should form the basis of the work. Projects must actively involve the parent(s)/main carers of the children. The trust's view is that prioritising this age group values children in Scotland appropriately, and will make a significant contribution to Scotland's National Outcome.'
**WHAT IS NOT FUNDED** Individuals; hospices and palliative care; appliances for illness or disability; organisations concerned with specific diseases; or animal charities.
**TYPE OF GRANT** The trust prefers to make grants which contribute substantially to smaller-scale projects.
**RANGE OF GRANTS** Mostly £3,600–£24,000.
**SAMPLE GRANTS** One Parent Families Scotland, Shelter Scotland (£60,000 each); Breastfeeding Network (£50,000); Geeza Break, Glasgow City Mission (£33,000); Dr Bell's Family Centre (£20,000); Dumfries Toy Library (£14,500);

Barnardo's Paisley, Home Start Glasgow South, Multi-Cultural Family Base (£10,000 each); Edinburgh Woman's Aid (£5,000); PRYDE Kilwinning (£4,000).
**FINANCES** Year 2013 Income £524,321 Grants £746,965 Grants to organisations £746,965 Assets £16,772,343
**TRUSTEES** Anne Houston; Euan Davidson; Duncan McEachran; Alastair Wilson; Rachel Lewis; Janet Barr; Steven Murray; Andrew Millington.
**HOW TO APPLY** Applications should be made via a form which can be completed online or downloaded from the trust's website. The trust does not normally accept hand-written applications – phone if you do not have access to a computer. The trust no longer has application deadlines, but works on a rolling programme. Trust meetings are listed on its website and you should allow around ten weeks for your application to reach a meeting.
**WHO TO APPLY TO** Alison Campbell, 136 Lower Granton Road, Edinburgh EH5 1EX Tel. 0131 557 2052 email alison@cattanach.org.uk Website www.cattanach.org.uk

## ■ The Joseph and Annie Cattle Trust

**CC NO** 262011  **ESTABLISHED** 1970
**WHERE FUNDING CAN BE GIVEN** Worldwide, with a preference for Hull and East Yorkshire.
**WHO CAN BENEFIT** Organisations and individuals. 'The aged, disabled and underprivileged are assisted wherever possible as are children suffering from dyslexia. Financial assistance is provided as far as possible by supporting institutions specialising in these areas.'
**WHAT IS FUNDED** General charitable purposes.
**WHAT IS NOT FUNDED** The trust **only** works with charitable bodies or statutory authorities and it does not provide grants directly to individuals.
**TYPE OF GRANT** One-off, capital, recurring and interest-free loans are considered.
**RANGE OF GRANTS** Up to £15,000.
**SAMPLE GRANTS Previous beneficiaries have included:** Sobriety Project (£15,000); Dyslexia Action (£14,000); Anlaby Park Methodist Church and Prince's Trust (£5,000 each); Hull and East Riding Institution for the Blind (£3,000); Bath Institute of Medical Engineering and Ocean Youth Trust (£2,000 each); and Age UK East Riding, Longhill Primary School and Prison Fellowship (£1,000 each).
**FINANCES** Year 2013/14 Income £367,095 Grants £319,065 Grants to organisations £319,065 Assets £8,640,452
**TRUSTEES** Paul Edwards; Michael Gyte; Christopher Munday; S. C. Jowers.
**OTHER INFORMATION** No details of 2013/14 beneficiaries were included in the trust's Charity Commission record.
**HOW TO APPLY** The following information is taken from the trust's website: 'There are two main types of application that we are looking to support: Firstly, there are applications by charitable or statutory bodies on behalf of individuals or families. The application form available through this web page must be completed by the charitable organisation/ statutory body concerned and not the individual/ family. Supporting papers should be attached where necessary. Secondly, there are applications for projects and work with the groups of people who are outlined in our key objective [see 'Where funding can be given', 'Who can benefit' and 'What is not funded'].

Please submit full details to the address shown below including the following: the charitable organisation including contact details and the latest financial statements; projects/work successfully completed to date that support the current application. Please outline work already carried out in the Hull & East Riding area. Because we will request that our grants are used exclusively in the Hull & East Riding area please identify how your organisation will guarantee this is achieved; the project/work together with detailed costings and supporting information. (e.g. estimates/planning permission etc.); identify other grants received or currently being considered by other bodies; how the grant is to be spent. In considering applications the trustees may require further information so please remember it is in your interests to give as much detail as possible. Application forms should be printed, **completed in handwriting** and sent to the correspondent by post or fax.'
**WHO TO APPLY TO** Roger Waudby, Correspondent, PO Box 23, Patrington, Hull HU12 0WF Tel. 01964 671742 Fax 01964 671742 email rogerwaudby@hotmail.co.uk Website www.jacattletrust.co.uk

## ■ The Thomas Sivewright Catto Charitable Settlement

**CC NO** 279549  **ESTABLISHED** 1979
**WHERE FUNDING CAN BE GIVEN** Unrestricted (for UK-based registered charities).
**WHO CAN BENEFIT** Registered charities only.
**WHAT IS FUNDED** General charitable purposes.
**WHAT IS NOT FUNDED** Non-registered charities; expeditions; travel bursaries; or unsolicited applications from churches of any denomination. Grants are unlikely to be considered in the areas of community care, playschemes and drug abuse, or for local branches of national organisations.
**RANGE OF GRANTS** Up to £14,000.
**SAMPLE GRANTS** Royal College of Music, and Royal Conservatoire of Scotland (£12,000 each); Platform 51, and World YWCA (£5,000 each); Disasters Emergency Committee (£3,000); Brain Research Trust, Multiple Sclerosis Society, and Strongbones Children's Charitable Trust (£1,000 each); ActionAid, Arthritis Research UK, Kidney Research UK, National Autistic Society, Wiltshire Air Ambulance Charitable Trust, Deafness Research UK, Mind, Prisoners' Advice Service, Action on Elder Abuse (£500 each).
**FINANCES** Year 2013/14 Income £177,357 Grants £115,153 Grants to organisations £115,153 Assets £8,933,746
**TRUSTEES** Lord Catto; Olivia Marchant; Zoe Richmond-Watson.
**HOW TO APPLY** Apply in writing to the correspondent, including an sae.
**WHO TO APPLY TO** The Secretary to the Trustees, PO Box 47408, London N21 1YW

## ■ The Wilfrid and Constance Cave Foundation

**CC NO** 241900  **ESTABLISHED** 1965
**WHERE FUNDING CAN BE GIVEN** UK, with preference for Berkshire, Cornwall, Devon, Dorset, Hampshire, Oxfordshire, Somerset, Warwickshire and Wiltshire.
**WHO CAN BENEFIT** Registered charities. Mainly local charities or charities which the trustees have

personal knowledge of, interest in, or association with are considered.

WHAT IS FUNDED General charitable purposes including conservation, animal welfare, health and social welfare.

WHAT IS NOT FUNDED Individuals.

TYPE OF GRANT Buildings, core costs, one-off, project, research, and running costs. Grants may be given for up to three years.

RANGE OF GRANTS £1,000–£50,000

SAMPLE GRANTS Oxford Museum of Children's Literature (£50,000); North Devon Hospice (£11,000); Thames Rivers Restoration Trust and The Farmer's Club Pinnacle Award (£7,000); Royal Agricultural Benevolent Institution (£6,000); Clowns Playbus and Moorland Mousie Trust (£5,000 each); Motor Neurones Disease Association and Theatre Royal Plymouth and 1st Exmoor Scout Group (£5,000); Exmoor Search and Rescue and The Children's Hospital South West (£3,000 each); Dyslexia Action (£2,000); Alcombe Food Cupboard and Tykes – Teignmouth Players (£1,000 each).

FINANCES Year 2013/14 Income £140,312 Grants £165,250 Grants to organisations £165,250 Assets £4,340,376

TRUSTEES Toni Jones; Jacqueline Archer; Mark Pickin; Nicola Thompson; Glyn Howells; Francois Jones; Janet Pickin; Melanie Waterworth; Roy Walker; William Howells; Matthew Pickin; Emily Pickin.

HOW TO APPLY Apply in writing to the correspondent a month before the trustees' meetings held twice each year, in May and October.

WHO TO APPLY TO The Secretary, New Lodge Farm, Drift Road, Winkfield, Windsor SL4 4QQ email tcf@eamo.co.uk

## ■ The Cayo Foundation

CC NO 1080607　　ESTABLISHED 1999

WHERE FUNDING CAN BE GIVEN UK.

WHO CAN BENEFIT Registered charities.

WHAT IS FUNDED General charitable purposes; medical research; crime prevention; children and young people.

TYPE OF GRANT Grants and loans.

RANGE OF GRANTS £1,000–£125,000

SAMPLE GRANTS A list of beneficiaries was not included in the latest accounts. **Previous beneficiaries have included:** NSPCC (£125,000); Disability Foundation, PACT and The Royal Opera House (£25,000 each); Prince's Foundation (£20,000); Wessex Youth Trust (£10,000); Christian Blind Mission (£6,000); Wellbeing of Women (£3,000); Institute for Policy Research and Royal Humane Society (£2,500 each); Sue Ryder Care – St John's Hospice (£1,000).

FINANCES Year 2012/13 Income £1,088,180 Grants £1,204,971 Grants to organisations £1,204,971 Assets £1,583,658

TRUSTEES Angela McCarville; Stewart Harris.

OTHER INFORMATION At the time of writing (June 2015) this was the latest information available Awards were made to 59 organisations. During the year the foundation also funded the expenses of a veteran's transition review (£49,000).

HOW TO APPLY Applications can be made in writing to the correspondent.

WHO TO APPLY TO Angela McCarville, Trustee, 7 Cowley Street, London SW1P 3NB Tel. 020 7248 6700

## ■ Elizabeth Cayzer Charitable Trust

CC NO 1059265　　ESTABLISHED 1996

WHERE FUNDING CAN BE GIVEN UK.

WHO CAN BENEFIT Museums, galleries and other arts organisations and projects.

WHAT IS FUNDED Funds are used in promoting activities related to art, including education, restoration, research, conservation and conferences and exhibitions.

SAMPLE GRANTS Elias Ashmole Trust; Dulwich Picture Gallery; the National Gallery and Sir John Soane's Museum.

FINANCES Year 2013/14 Income £113,389 Grants £117,500 Grants to organisations £117,500 Assets £4,652,263

TRUSTEES The Hon. Elizabeth Gilmour; Diana Lloyd; Dominic Gibbs.

OTHER INFORMATION This charity was established by The Honourable Elizabeth Gilmour, who has made significant donations to the charity since 1996. In formulating policy the trustees have taken into account the wishes of the Settlor, which are that the assets of the charity should be used in supporting and promoting activities relating to art.

HOW TO APPLY Note the following statement taken from the charity's 2013/14 accounts: 'The trustees identify the projects and organisations they wish to support and so do not consider grants to people or organisations who apply speculatively. The trust also has a policy of not responding to any correspondence unless it relates to grants it has agreed to make or to the general management of the trust.'

WHO TO APPLY TO The Hon. Elizabeth Gilmour, Trustee, The Cayzer Trust Company Limited, Cayzer House, 30 Buckingham Gate, London SW1E 6NN Tel. 020 7802 8080 email admin@cayzertrust.com

## ■ The B. G. S. Cayzer Charitable Trust

CC NO 286063　　ESTABLISHED 1982

WHERE FUNDING CAN BE GIVEN UK.

WHO CAN BENEFIT Registered charities.

WHAT IS FUNDED General charitable purposes.

WHAT IS NOT FUNDED Organisations outside the UK.

SAMPLE GRANTS Heritage and conservation (£90,000); medical research, treatment and care and people with disabilities (£14,250); religious activities (£11,000); education and training (£5,500); relief of poverty (£5,000); arts and culture (£1,200).

FINANCES Year 2013/14 Income £115,632 Grants £126,950 Grants to organisations £126,950 Assets £1,377,797

TRUSTEES Mr P. R. Davies; Mrs M. Buckley; Mrs A. M. Hunter; Mrs R. N. Leslie.

HOW TO APPLY The trust tends to support only people/projects known to the Cayzer family or the trustees. Unsolicited appeals will not be supported.

WHO TO APPLY TO Mrs Sonia Barry, Trust Administrator, The Cayzer Trust Company Limited, Cayzer House, 30 Buckingham Gate, London SW1E 6NN Tel. 020 7802 8439 email admin@cayzertrust.com

## ■ The Cazenove Charitable Trust

**CC NO** 1086899 **ESTABLISHED** 1969
**WHERE FUNDING CAN BE GIVEN** UK.
**WHO CAN BENEFIT** Charitable organisations. The trust primarily supports fundraising activities by employees and ex-employees of JP Morgan Cazenove and Cazenove Capital Management via a matched giving scheme.
**WHAT IS FUNDED** General charitable purposes.
**SAMPLE GRANTS** Alzheimer's Research and The Huguenot Heritage Centre (£5,000 each); Goodenough College, King's Medical Research Trust, London Catalyst, The '999' Club, The Marine Society, The Sixteen Ltd and Trinity Hospice (£2,500 each); Marie Curie Cancer Care, St Margaret Lothbury Church and Welsh Guards Afghanistan Appeal (£1,000 each).
**FINANCES** Year 2014 Income £79,162 Grants £49,767 Grants to organisations £49,767 Assets £2,763,842
**TRUSTEES** David Mayhew; Edward Harley; Michael Wentworth-Stanley; Michael Power; Lucinda Napier.
**OTHER INFORMATION** In 2014 60 grants were made. Grants of less than £1,000 each totalled £19,300.
**HOW TO APPLY** This trust does not respond to unsolicited applications.
**WHO TO APPLY TO** Edward Harley, Trustee, Cazenove, 12 Moorgate, London EC2R 6DA *Tel.* 020 3479 0102

## ■ The CBD Charitable Trust

**CC NO** 1136702 **ESTABLISHED** 2010
**WHERE FUNDING CAN BE GIVEN** Worldwide.
**WHO CAN BENEFIT** Registered charities, particularly organisations benefitting children and young people.
**WHAT IS FUNDED** General charitable purposes; children and young people.
**RANGE OF GRANTS** £100–£152,000
**SAMPLE GRANTS** **Previous beneficiaries have included:** British Red Cross; Crisis; Earthway; Hope Community Village; Interdependence Project; Martlets Hospice; Oxfam; Self Help Africa; Unity Church New York.
**FINANCES** Year 2014/15 Income £122,665 Grants £120,000 Grants to organisations £120,000
**TRUSTEES** Coutts & Co.; Ingrid Scott.
**OTHER INFORMATION** The 2014/15 accounts were not required to be published due to low income. The trust had a total expenditure of about £122,500 and in the past about 98% of the overall amount has been distributed in grants. Based on the previous giving patterns it is likely that grants totalled about £120,000. On average about 50 awards are made annually.
**HOW TO APPLY** Applications may be made in writing to the correspondent.
**WHO TO APPLY TO** c/o Coutts & Co., Trustee Department, 440 Strand, London WC2R 0QS *Tel.* 020 7663 6825 *email* couttscharities@coutts.com

## ■ Celtic Charity Fund

**SC NO** SC024648 **ESTABLISHED** 1995
**WHERE FUNDING CAN BE GIVEN** Worldwide but with a preference for Scotland and Ireland.
**WHO CAN BENEFIT** Charitable organisations.
**WHAT IS FUNDED** Health, education, homelessness, employability and social welfare.
**SAMPLE GRANTS** No details regarding individual grant beneficiaries are provided.
**FINANCES** Year 2013/14 Income £1,676,966 Grants £309,852 Grants to organisations £309,852
**TRUSTEES** Chris Traynor; Peter Lawwell; Gavin Kelly; Eric Riley; Adrian Filby.
**HOW TO APPLY** Application forms are available to download from the website. Closing dates for applications are 30 June and 31 December.
**WHO TO APPLY TO** Jane Maguire, Celtic Football Club, Celtic Park, Glasgow G40 3RE *Tel.* 0141 551 4262 *email* janemaguire@celticfc.co.uk *Website* www.celticfc.net

## ■ The Gaynor Cemlyn-Jones Trust

**CC NO** 1039164 **ESTABLISHED** 1994
**WHERE FUNDING CAN BE GIVEN** North Wales and Anglesey.
**WHO CAN BENEFIT** Registered charities; educational and religious bodies.
**WHAT IS FUNDED** Conservation and protection of general public amenities, historic or public interests in Wales; medical research; protection and welfare of animals and birds; study and promotion of music, especially operatic performance; activities and requirements of religious and educational bodies. Preference for projects in the local area.
**WHAT IS NOT FUNDED** Individuals; non-charitable organisations.
**TYPE OF GRANT** One-off; capital costs.
**RANGE OF GRANTS** £1,000–£10,200
**SAMPLE GRANTS** Bangor University (£10,200); Bryn Terfel Foundation (£3,000); Sir Henry Jones Memorial (£1,000).
**FINANCES** Year 2013/14 Income £238,554 Grants £14,150 Grants to organisations £14,150 Assets £1,113,482
**TRUSTEES** Janet Lea; Eryl Jones; Colin Wickens.
**OTHER INFORMATION** There were three grants made in 2013/14. Note that the charitable spending is normally higher and in the previous five years have totalled £48,000 per year on average.
**HOW TO APPLY** Apply in writing to the correspondent.
**WHO TO APPLY TO** Colin Wickens, Trustee, 122 Llanrwst Road, Bae Colwyn, Conwy LL28 5UT *Tel.* 01492 530677 *email* colin.wickens@quiltercheviot.com

## ■ The CH (1980) Charitable Trust

**CC NO** 279481 **ESTABLISHED** 1980
**WHERE FUNDING CAN BE GIVEN** UK and Israel.
**WHO CAN BENEFIT** Jewish organisations.
**WHAT IS FUNDED** Jewish causes.
**WHAT IS NOT FUNDED** 'There is no facility for processing applications from individuals for financial support, and these cannot be considered.'
**RANGE OF GRANTS** £500 to £102,000.
**SAMPLE GRANTS** Oxford Centre for Hebrew and Jewish Studies (£102,000); The Jerusalem Foundation (£31,000); West London Synagogue (£3,900); Israel Diaspora Trust (£3,000); B'nai B'rith Hillel Foundation (£1,000); Israel Guide Dogs for the Blind (£500).
**FINANCES** Year 2013/14 Income £125,745 Grants £141,400 Grants to organisations £141,400 Assets £1,325,543
**TRUSTEE** Kleinwort Benson Trustees Limited.
**HOW TO APPLY** 'Unsolicited appeals are considered as well as causes which have already been supported. Only successful applicants are notified of the Trustee's decision. There is no

facility for processing applications from individuals for financial support, and these cannot be considered.'
**WHO TO APPLY TO** The Correspondent, Kleinwort Benson Trustees Ltd, 14 St George Street, London W1S 1FE *Tel.* 020 3207 7000

## ■ The Amelia Chadwick Trust
**CC NO** 213795 **ESTABLISHED** 1960
**WHERE FUNDING CAN BE GIVEN** UK, especially Merseyside.
**WHO CAN BENEFIT** Neighbourhood-based community projects, some UK organisations.
**WHAT IS FUNDED** General charitable purposes including education, health, the arts, social welfare and the environment.
**WHAT IS NOT FUNDED** Individuals.
**TYPE OF GRANT** Mostly recurring.
**RANGE OF GRANTS** £100–£35,600
**SAMPLE GRANTS** Merseyside Development Foundation (£35,600); Liverpool PSS (£12,500); Save the Children (£10,000); European Play-Work Association (£9,000); Médecins Sans Frontières, Unicef (£6,000 each); Catalyst Housing Ltd, Claire House, Liverpool Dyslexia Association, Royal Liverpool Philharmonic Society (£2,000 each): Birkenhead YMCA, Oxfam, Wirral Women and Children's Aid (£1,000 each)
**FINANCES** *Year* 2013/14 *Income* £140,815 *Grants* £137,640 *Grants to organisations* £136,640 *Assets* £4,357,579
**TRUSTEES** Liverpool Charity and Voluntary Services; Ruth Behrend; Caroline Dawson.
**OTHER INFORMATION** Grants under £1,000 were listed by the trust as 'other grants'. In total £1,000 was given in 'other grants' by the trust.
**HOW TO APPLY** All donations are made through Liverpool Charity and Voluntary Services. Grants are only made to charities known to the trustees, and unsolicited applications are not considered.
**WHO TO APPLY TO** The Trustees, c/o Liverpool Charity and Voluntary Services, 151 Dale Street, Liverpool L2 2AH *Tel.* 0151 227 5177 *email* info@lcvs.org.uk

## ■ Champneys Charitable Foundation
**CC NO** 1114429 **ESTABLISHED** 2006
**WHERE FUNDING CAN BE GIVEN** UK.
**WHO CAN BENEFIT** Charitable organisations.
**WHAT IS FUNDED** Health, medical and disability causes.
**RANGE OF GRANTS** Up to £27,000.
**SAMPLE GRANTS** Variety Club (£27,000); Breast Cancer Care (£20,000); Target Ovarian Cancer (£18,000); and Ataxia Foundation (£2,000).
**FINANCES** *Year* 2013/14 *Income* £74,153 *Grants* £72,247 *Grants to organisations* £69,275 *Assets* £45,841
**TRUSTEES** Dorothy Purdew; Stephen Purdew; Michael Hawkins.
**OTHER INFORMATION** Grants are also given to individuals. In 2013/14 this totalled £3,000.
**HOW TO APPLY** Apply in writing to the correspondent.
**WHO TO APPLY TO** Dorothy Purdew, Trustee, Henlow Grange, Henlow, Bedfordshire SG16 6DB *Tel.* 01462 810712 *email* charity@champneys.co.uk *Website* www.champneys.com

## ■ The Chapman Charitable Trust
**CC NO** 232791 **ESTABLISHED** 1963
**WHERE FUNDING CAN BE GIVEN** London, south-east and eastern England, North Wales. National charities are also supported.
**WHO CAN BENEFIT** Any recognised charity, but mainly those charities in which the late settlor had, or the trustees have, a personal interest or concern.
**WHAT IS FUNDED** General charitable purposes. Main areas supported are social services, culture and recreation, education and research, health, environment and heritage.
**WHAT IS NOT FUNDED** The trust does not make grants to individuals, to overseas charities, to local branches of national charities, for animal welfare, for sports tours, for research expeditions or for sponsored adventure holidays.
**RANGE OF GRANTS** Mostly £1,000–£2,000, up to £20,000.
**SAMPLE GRANTS** Pesticide Action Network UK (£20,000); Action for Children, Aldeburgh Music, Fragile X Society, Methodist Homes for the Aged (£12,000 each); Ambitious about Autism, A Rocha – transform Norwood Green wasteland into green space (£6,000 each); British Film Institute (£4,000); Action for Kids – training young people with disabilities; Asthma UK – research and support (£2,000 each); Countryside Learning, Standing Together Against Domestic Violence (£1,500 each).
**FINANCES** *Year* 2013/14 *Income* £272,835 *Grants* £265,000 *Grants to organisations* £265,000 *Assets* £7,622,229
**TRUSTEES** Roger Chapman; Richard Chapman; Bruce Chapman; Guy Chapman; Bryony Chapman.
**OTHER INFORMATION** There were 68 grants of £1,000 each made to organisations.
**HOW TO APPLY** Apply in writing at any time. The trustees currently meet to consider grants twice a year at the end of September and in March. They receive a large number of applications and regret that they cannot acknowledge receipt of them. The absence of any communication for six months would mean that an application must have been unsuccessful.
**WHO TO APPLY TO** Roger S. Chapman, Trustee, Crouch Chapman, 62 Wilson Street, London EC2A 2BU *Tel.* 020 7782 0007 *email* cct@rpgcrouchchapman.co.uk *Website* www.chapmancharitabletrust.org.uk

## ■ John William Chapman's Charitable Trust
**CC NO** 223002 **ESTABLISHED** 1942
**WHERE FUNDING CAN BE GIVEN** The borough of Doncaster.
**WHO CAN BENEFIT** Individuals or other bodies assisting individuals in need.
**WHAT IS FUNDED** Relief in need.
**WHAT IS NOT FUNDED** The trust's funds are to be used for the relief of hardship and distress but will not be given for payments in respect of council tax, income tax or where public funds are available for the relief of that hardship. Grants are not given for large, national appeals.
**RANGE OF GRANTS** Up to £12,000.
**SAMPLE GRANTS** Safe@last (£12,000); Barnardo's Young Carers' Project (£5,000 each); Doncaster Communities Live at Home Scheme (£1,000).
**FINANCES** *Year* 2013/14 *Income* £186,294 *Grants* £65,598 *Grants to organisations* £27,106 *Assets* £3,727,652

TRUSTEES Victoria Ferres; Michael Gornall; Mark Hunter; David Kirk; Lady Catherine Neill.
OTHER INFORMATION The 2013/14 grant total includes £38,000 that was given to individuals.
HOW TO APPLY Application forms are available to download, together with criteria and guidelines, on the website.
WHO TO APPLY TO Rosemarie Sharp, Secretary, c/o Jordans Solicitors, 4 Priory Place, Doncaster DN1 1BP *email* info@chapmantrust.org

## ■ The Charities Advisory Trust

CC NO 1040487    ESTABLISHED 1994
WHERE FUNDING CAN BE GIVEN UK and overseas.
WHO CAN BENEFIT Any charitable purpose is considered, but generally the trust is proactive.
WHAT IS FUNDED General charitable purposes, particularly: income generation projects; homelessness; museums; cancer research and treatment; peace and reconciliation; and refugees.
WHAT IS NOT FUNDED In previous years, trustees have rarely responded to unsolicited applications for projects of which they have no knowledge. In such cases where support is given, the amounts are usually £200 or less. The trust considers any applications for funds but primarily work with charities with whom they have developed a programme to deliver the outcomes they seek. They very rarely give grants to individuals or large fundraising charities.
TYPE OF GRANT Buildings, capital, core costs, endowments, interest-free loans; one-off, project, research, running costs, recurring costs, salaries and start-up costs. Funding is available for up to and over three years.
RANGE OF GRANTS £11,100–£102,400
SAMPLE GRANTS Ikamva Labantu (£102,400); SURF Survivors Fund (£80,900); FARE (£47,600); Moorfield Eye Charity (£41,000); Africa Educational Trust (£35,400); Leket (£17,500); Sightcare International (£26,600); Kunyanja Private Secondary School (£15,600); Médecins Sans Frontières (£12,300); Rural Literacy (£12,100); Sahabhagi (£11,100).
FINANCES *Year* 2013/14 *Income* £1,172,081 *Grants* £625,804 *Grants to organisations* £625,804 *Assets* £3,155,207
TRUSTEES Prof. Cornelia Navari; Brij Bhasin; David Russell; Leila Mac Tavish Mohamed.
HOW TO APPLY The trustees are pro-active in looking for causes to support. They are though 'happy for charities to keep us informed of developments, as we do change our support as new solutions to needs emerge.' **Unsolicited applications for projects of which the trust know nothing are rarely responded to.** 'To apply, simply send details of your proposal (no more than two pages in length) in the form of a letter. You might try to include the following information: the aims and objectives of your organisation; the project for which you need money; who benefits from the project and how; breakdown of the costs and total estimated costs; how much money you need from us; other funding secured for the project a summary of your latest annual accounts. If we refuse you it is not because your project is not worthwhile – it is because we do not have sufficient funds, or it is simply outside our current area of interest.'
WHO TO APPLY TO Dame Hilary Blume, Director, Radius Works, Back Lane, London NW3 1HL *Tel.* 020 7794 9835 *Fax* 020 7431 3739 *email* people@charitiesadvisorytrust.org.uk *Website* www.charitiesadvisorytrust.org.uk

## ■ Charitworth Limited

CC NO 286908    ESTABLISHED 1983
WHERE FUNDING CAN BE GIVEN Worldwide, mainly UK and Israel.
WHO CAN BENEFIT Charitable organisations.
WHAT IS FUNDED Religious, educational and charitable purposes. In practice, mainly Jewish causes.
TYPE OF GRANT One-off and recurring.
RANGE OF GRANTS Up to around £150,000.
SAMPLE GRANTS No details of 2013/14 beneficiaries were included in the Charity Commission record. Previous beneficiaries have included: Zichron Nahum; British Friends of Tshernobil; Cosmon Belz; Chevras Maoz Ladal; Dushinsky Trust; Centre for Torah Education Trust; Finchley Road Synagogue; Friends of Viznitz; Beer Yaakov; and Beis Soroh Schneirer.
FINANCES *Year* 2013/14 *Income* £897,940 *Grants* £1,605,100 *Grants to organisations* £1,605,100 *Assets* £24,268,886
TRUSTEES David Halpern; Reilly Halpern; Sidney Halpern; Samuel J. Halpern.
HOW TO APPLY Apply in writing to the correspondent.
WHO TO APPLY TO David Halpern, Trustee, Cohen Arnold and Co., New Burlington House, 1075 Finchley Road, London NW11 0PU *Tel.* 020 8731 0777 *Fax* 020 8731 0778 *email* dh@dominionltd.net

## ■ The Charter 600 Charity

CC NO 1051146    ESTABLISHED 1994
WHERE FUNDING CAN BE GIVEN UK and occasionally overseas.
WHO CAN BENEFIT Registered charities. Community-based, grass-roots organisations.
WHAT IS FUNDED General charitable purposes, with particular emphasis on education, social and medical welfare support for young people and communities.
WHAT IS NOT FUNDED Applications for charitable grants will only be accepted when put forward by a member of the Mercers' Company.
RANGE OF GRANTS Up to £2,500.
SAMPLE GRANTS A Way Out, Cherished Memories Support Group, Gunton Baptist Church, Library Project in Aru Congo, Plough Arts Centre and School Aid (£1,500 each); Becs Big Bike Ride; Blind Sailing, Disaway; and East Sussex Association of Blind and Partially Sighted People (£1,000 each); and Beaford Village Hall and Christian Evangelical Centre (£500 each).
FINANCES *Year* 2013/14 *Income* £54,970 *Grants* £36,550 *Grants to organisations* £36,550 *Assets* £1,126,809
TRUSTEE The Mercers Company.
HOW TO APPLY The charity does not consider unsolicited applications.
WHO TO APPLY TO Mr M. McGregor, The Clerk, Mercers' Hall, Ironmongers Lane, London EC2V 8HE *Website* www.mercers.co.uk

## ■ The Worshipful Company of Chartered Accountants General Charitable Trust (also known as CALC)

CC NO 327681    ESTABLISHED 1988
WHERE FUNDING CAN BE GIVEN UK.
WHO CAN BENEFIT Registered charities; voluntary organisations.
WHAT IS FUNDED General charitable causes; relief of poverty; education and training; religion; causes which are associated with accountancy, the

profession, the City or the Livery. At least one theme directly or indirectly of relevance to the work of the profession (chosen by the master on their appointment in October of each year). Other recommendations and proposals put to the trustees by members of the Livery are also considered.

**RANGE OF GRANTS** £2,100–£50,000
**SAMPLE GRANTS** Major beneficiaries included: MyBnk (£50,000); Place2Be (£15,000); Guildhall School of Music and Drama (£10,000); SBS Association and 47 Squadron of the Royal Air Force (£7,100); St Paul's and St Mark's Youth Project (£3,000); The Lord Mayor's Appeal 2014 (£2,500); City of London Academy (£2,300); Harrow and Wembley Sea Cadets (£2,100).
**FINANCES** Year 2013/14 Income £143,421 Grants £110,435 Grants to organisations £110,435 Assets £1,628,961
**TRUSTEES** Richard Dyson; Richard Green; Adam Broke; Nigel Turnbull; Richard Battersby; Andrew Popham; William Fowle; David Illingworth.
**OTHER INFORMATION** The grant total includes support for bursary and scholarship funds.
**HOW TO APPLY** Applications must be sponsored by a liveryman of the company.
**WHO TO APPLY TO** Peter Lusty, Clerk, c/o Hampton City Services, Hampton House, High Street, East Grinstead, West Sussex RH19 3AW Tel. 01342 319038 email peterlusty@btconnect.com

■ **Chaucer Foundation**
**CC NO** 1153423  **ESTABLISHED** 2013
**WHERE FUNDING CAN BE GIVEN** Communities in which Chaucer Syndicates Ltd operates; London, Nottingham and Whitstable, USA, Northern Europe, Singapore.
**WHO CAN BENEFIT** Local projects; charities which are either active in communities local to Chaucer Syndicates Ltd or have some relevance to the insurance sector; other local charities and communities.
**WHAT IS FUNDED** General charitable purposes, especially supporting disadvantaged individuals and in particular projects 'that help young people from disadvantaged backgrounds achieve their full potential'. The foundation also supports Chaucer Syndicates Ltd employees' charitable endeavours.
**SAMPLE GRANTS** Prince's Trust (£50,000); Royal British Legion (£5,000).
**FINANCES** Year 2013 Income £218,612 Grants £55,000 Grants to organisations £55,000 Assets £155,507
**TRUSTEES** Jessica Stephenson; Kevin Iles; Michael Dickinson; Robert Stuchbery; Susan Helson; Virginia Williams.
**OTHER INFORMATION** Note that the latest set accounts were prepared for the period from June to December 2013 (the foundation was established in 2013). The accounts note: 'The charitable company did not start operating fully until January 2014 and as such these financial statements show minimal activity.' The foundation has a four-year Charity of the Year commitment to the Prince's trust (currently in its third year) and had a three-year support arrangement with the Royal British Legion (ended 2013).
**HOW TO APPLY** According to the website, 'organisations may apply for grants at any time' and 'applications for foundation funding are reviewed and approved on a quarterly basis by the Chaucer Foundation Board'.

**WHO TO APPLY TO** Kate Shallcross, Secretary, Chaucer Syndicates Ltd, Plantation Place, 30 Fenchurch Street, London EC3M AD Tel. 020 7397 9700 email enquiries@chaucer-foundation.org.uk Website www.chaucer-foundation.org.uk

■ **The Cheruby Trust**
**CC NO** 327069  **ESTABLISHED** 1986
**WHERE FUNDING CAN BE GIVEN** UK and worldwide.
**WHO CAN BENEFIT** Registered charities.
**WHAT IS FUNDED** Welfare; education; general; Jewish causes; overseas aid. UK and worldwide.
**RANGE OF GRANTS** £100–£6,000
**SAMPLE GRANTS** World Jewish Relief (£6,000); Alzheimer's Society, British Humanitarian Aid, Mind and Save the Children (£5,000 each); Family Action (£3,500); Amnesty International, APT Enterprise Development and Indian Rural Health Trust (£3,000 each); Breadline Africa, ChildHope and Crisis at Christmas (£2,000 each); SANE, WaterAid and Winston's Wish (£1,000 each); London Listening Books (£200).
**FINANCES** Year 2013/14 Income £82,537 Grants £86,050 Grants to organisations £86,050 Assets £43,652
**TRUSTEES** Alison Corob; Laura Corob; Christopher Cook; Sheila Wechsler; Tricia Corob.
**HOW TO APPLY** Apply in writing to the correspondent.
**WHO TO APPLY TO** Sheila Wechsler, Trustee, 62 Grosvenor Street, London W1K 3JF Tel. 020 7499 4301

■ **Cheshire Freemason's Charity (formerly Cheshire Provincial Fund of Benevolence)**
**CC NO** 219177  **ESTABLISHED** 1963
**WHERE FUNDING CAN BE GIVEN** Cheshire and parts of Greater Manchester and Merseyside.
**WHO CAN BENEFIT** Individuals and organisations benefitting Masons and their families.
**WHAT IS FUNDED** The relief of Masons and their dependants, Masonic charities and other charities, especially medical.
**SAMPLE GRANTS** Previous beneficiaries have included: Children's Cancer Support Group, Mencap, Wirral Autistic Society, Bollington and Macclesfield Sea Cadets and Cathedral Road Kids Project.
**FINANCES** Year 2013/14 Income £221,358 Grants £154,892 Grants to organisations £77,692 Assets £4,217,774
**TRUSTEES** Alan Glazier; Peter Carroll; Stephen Kinsey; Eric McConnell; Ivor Henry; Leyland Preston; David Littlewood.
**OTHER INFORMATION** Grants made in 2013/14 are divided between Masonic institutions (£77,200) and non-Masonic Individuals and Charities (£77,692).
**HOW TO APPLY** Apply in writing to the correspondent.
**WHO TO APPLY TO** Christopher Renshaw, 92 Nuttall Lane, Ramsbottom, Bury, Lancashire BL0 9JZ Tel. 01706 823850 email enquiries@cheshiremasons.co.uk

■ **Chest, Heart and Stroke Scotland**
**SC NO** SC018761  **ESTABLISHED** 1990
**WHERE FUNDING CAN BE GIVEN** Scotland.
**WHO CAN BENEFIT** The Charity's website describes the charity mission as: 'To improve the quality

of life for people in Scotland affected by chest, heart and stroke illness, through medical research, influencing public policy, advice and information and support in the Academics, research workers and medical professionals living and working in Scotland.'

**WHAT IS FUNDED** 'Chest Heart & Stroke Scotland improves the quality of life for people in Scotland affected by chest, heart and stroke illness, through medical research, influencing public policy, advice and information, and support in the community' Medical research into all aspects of the aetiology, diagnosis, prevention, treatment and social impact of chest, heart and stroke illness. Applications directly relating to improvements in patient care, quality of life and health promotion are particularly welcomed. Particular medical focus for the Charity is on Coronary heart disease, stroke, and chest illness. 'We fund research into all aspects of prevention, diagnosis, treatment, rehabilitation and the social impact of chest heart and stroke illness. We provide care and support throughout Scotland for people affected by these conditions, as well as their families and other carers. More than 1,200 people affected by stroke, especially those with communication problems, benefit from our main community service, the Community Support Service and 800 volunteers help operate it locally.'

**WHAT IS NOT FUNDED** Research projects involving animals are not funded or research studies whose primary focus is lung or other cancers.

**TYPE OF GRANT** Research fellowships, project grants, travel and equipment grants, career development awards, research secondments, and student electives. Funding may be given for up to three years.

**RANGE OF GRANTS** Research grants up to £120,000.

**SAMPLE GRANTS** Information naming individual beneficiaries with the exception of research grants was unavailable from the Charity. Research grants were awarded to the following institutions during the year: Western General Hospital (£85,000); University of Aberdeen (£60,000); Glasgow Royal Infirmary (£48,000); University of Edinburgh (£76,000); University of Glasgow (£37,000); University of Strathclyde (£25,300); Glasgow Royal Infirmary (£14,300).

**FINANCES** Year 2013/14 Income £6,302,065 Grants £993,699 Grants to organisations £993,699

**TRUSTEE** No information was available.

**HOW TO APPLY** Contact the correspondent for further details of how to apply or visit the website where criteria, guidelines and application process are posted.

**WHO TO APPLY TO** Research Manager, Third Floor, Roseberry House, 9 Haymarket Terrace, Edinburgh EH12 5EZ Tel. 0131 225 6963 email research@chss.org.uk Website www.chss.org.uk

## ■ The Chetwode Foundation

**CC NO** 265950         **ESTABLISHED** 1973

**WHERE FUNDING CAN BE GIVEN** Nottinghamshire, Leicestershire and Derby with occasional grants elsewhere in UK.

**WHO CAN BENEFIT** Registered charities only.

**WHAT IS FUNDED** General charitable purposes with a preference for the disadvantaged and young people.

**WHAT IS NOT FUNDED** Individuals; national charities; organisations outside the UK.

**RANGE OF GRANTS** Up to £15,000.

**SAMPLE GRANTS** Framework Nottingham (£12,000); Greater Nottingham Groundwork Trust (£10,000); The Vineyard Arches Trust (£7,700); Tythby and Cropwell Butler PCC (£3,000); and Beds Garden Carers; Homestart Newark, NSPCC and Think Children (£1,000 each).

**FINANCES** Year 2013/14 Income £194,659 Grants £60,399 Grants to organisations £60,399 Assets £1,975,728

**TRUSTEES** John Ellis; Russell Price.

**HOW TO APPLY** Application forms are available to download from the website or by contacting the trust via email or post. The application form is basic, with the majority of detail to be included in a written statement outlining the project on no more than two sides of A4. Consult the application guidelines for an idea of what the trustees want to see. Applications can be submitted at any time and the trust aims to acknowledge all relevant applications within four weeks. If you are unsuccessful at the initial assessment you will be informed within eight weeks of receipt of your application. Multiple grants over successive years will only be considered in exceptional circumstances.

**WHO TO APPLY TO** John Ellis, Trustee, Samworth Brothers (Holdings) Ltd, Chetwode House, 1 Samworth Way, Leicester Road, Melton Mowbray LE13 1GA Tel. 01664 414500 email info@thechetwodefoundation.co.uk Website www.thechetwodefoundation.co.uk

## ■ Child Growth Foundation

**CC NO** 274325         **ESTABLISHED** 1977

**WHERE FUNDING CAN BE GIVEN** UK.

**WHO CAN BENEFIT** Institutions researching child/adult growth disorders, and people with such diseases.

**WHAT IS FUNDED** Research into the causes and cure of growth disorders in children within the area of benefit and to publish the results of such research. The conditions covered by the foundation are: Turner syndrome; Russell Silver syndrome/intrauterine growth retardation; bone dysplasia; sots syndrome; premature sexual maturity; growth/multiple pituitary hormone deficiency.

**TYPE OF GRANT** Research.

**RANGE OF GRANTS** Up to £7,500.

**SAMPLE GRANTS** University College London Butler/Tollerfield (£7,500); University of Birmingham Dias (£5,600); Loughborough University (£4,700).

**FINANCES** Year 2013/14 Income £86,891 Grants £13,073 Grants to organisations £13,073 Assets £289,854

**TRUSTEES** Nick Child; Russell Chaplin; Rachel Pidcock; Linda Washington; Mark Coyle; Sue Davies; Nikos Tzvadis; Kevin Kirk; Simon Lane.

**HOW TO APPLY** Apply in writing to the correspondent.

**WHO TO APPLY TO** Russell Chaplin, 13 Chestnut Avenue, Edgware, Middlesex HA8 7RA Tel. 020 8912 0720 email jenny.child@childgrowthfoundation.org Website www.childgrowthfoundation.org

## ■ Children's Liver Disease Foundation

**CC NO** 1067331         **ESTABLISHED** 1998

**WHERE FUNDING CAN BE GIVEN** UK.

**WHO CAN BENEFIT** Organisations benefitting children (up to the age of 18) with liver disease.

**WHAT IS FUNDED** Clinical and laboratory-based research and social research which looks at topics such as how to improve quality of life.

**WHAT IS NOT FUNDED** The charity does not accept applications from organisations whose work is not associated with paediatric liver disease. No grants are given to individuals, whether medical professionals or patients. No grants for travel or personal education. No grants for general appeals.

**TYPE OF GRANT** Research and project (maximum three years). Occasionally medical equipment.

**RANGE OF GRANTS** Small grant programme: up to £5,000.

**SAMPLE GRANTS** Birmingham Children's Hospital (£30,000); Coventry University (£74,600); University College London (£164,600). **Previous beneficiaries have included:** King's College Hospital; University of Birmingham; University College Medical School.

**FINANCES** Year 2013/14 Income £828,605 Grants £276,348 Grants to organisations £276,348 Assets £1,004,795

**TRUSTEES** Thomas Ross; David Tildesley; Mairi Everard; Kellie Charge; Nicholas Budd; Georgina Sugden; Theresa Martin.

**PUBLICATIONS** Research priorities for 2011–14 are available to download from the website.

**HOW TO APPLY** Applicants are strongly advised to look at the relevant pages on the Children's Liver Disease Foundation website where further information and application forms are available.

**WHO TO APPLY TO** Alison Taylor, Correspondent, 36 Great Charles Street, Queensway, Birmingham B3 3JY *Tel.* 0121 212 3839 *Fax* 0121 212 4300 *email* info@childliverdisease.org *Website* www.childliverdisease.org

## ■ The Children's Research Fund

**CC NO** 226128   **ESTABLISHED** 1962
**WHERE FUNDING CAN BE GIVEN** UK.
**WHO CAN BENEFIT** Research bodies; institutes of child health; university child health departments; medical institutions.
**WHAT IS FUNDED** Promoting, encouraging and fostering research into all aspects of diseases in children, child health and prevention of illness in children. Support of research centres and research units by grants to academic institutions, hospitals and other bodies with similar aims and objects to the fund. Support after the first year is dependent on receipt of a satisfactory report.
**WHAT IS NOT FUNDED** Capital projects.
**TYPE OF GRANT** Research; one-off and recurrent.
**RANGE OF GRANTS** £700–£100,000
**SAMPLE GRANTS** 2013/14 beneficiaries: Orthopaedic Conference (£700) **Previous beneficiaries have included:** UCL Institute of Child Health (£100,000); British Association of Paediatric Surgeons and The Peninsula Foundation (£30,000 each); Dubai – War Damaged Children (£9,600); The Not Forgotten Association (£3,000); Alder Hey Children's Hospital (£2,100); Coming Home (£2,000).
**FINANCES** Year 2013/14 Income £28,516 Grants £725 Grants to organisations £725 Assets £1,152,623
**TRUSTEES** Hugo Greenwood; Gerald Inkin; Hugh Greenwood; Elizabeth Theobald; Prof. David Lloyd.
**OTHER INFORMATION** Only one beneficiary was named as having received a grant in 2013/14. 'Grant funding of activities' amounted to £725 and 'support costs' were reported as totalling £6,600. Note that the charity's charitable expenditure varies annually and in the previous four years has totalled about 133,000 per year on average.
**HOW TO APPLY** Applicants from child health research units and university departments are invited to send in an initial outline of their proposal; if it is eligible they will then be sent an application form. Applications are normally considered in March and November. The charity has a website; however, at the time of writing (June 2015) it did not appear to be functioning.
**WHO TO APPLY TO** The Trustees, 6 Scarthill Property, New Lane, Aughton, Ormskirk L39 4UD *Tel.* 01695 420928 *email* childrensresearchfund@btinternet.com *Website* www.childrensresearchfund.org.uk

## ■ The Childs Charitable Trust

**CC NO** 234618   **ESTABLISHED** 1962
**WHERE FUNDING CAN BE GIVEN** Worldwide.
**WHO CAN BENEFIT** Christian UK-registered charities.
**WHAT IS FUNDED** Christian activity at home and overseas, especially the furtherance of the Christian Gospel.
**TYPE OF GRANT** One-off and recurrent. Preference for large-scale project grants.
**RANGE OF GRANTS** £2,500–£27,000
**SAMPLE GRANTS** Orphaids UK (£27,500); Outreach UK (£24,000); Cross Teach (£16,000); Off the Fence (£10,000); OxTrad (£6,000); Daylight Prison Trust and Wycliffe (£5,000 each); Mission Direct (£4,000); Bible Society and Interserve (£3,000 each); Esther Benjamin Trust (£2,500).
**FINANCES** Year 2012/13 Income £500,175 Grants £551,310 Grants to organisations £549,810 Assets £9,198,646
**TRUSTEES** Andrew Griffiths; John Harris; Steve Puttock; Chris Large
**OTHER INFORMATION** The 2012/13 accounts were the latest available at the time of writing.
**HOW TO APPLY** The trustees are currently reviewing their funding criteria and have therefore taken the decision not to fund any further projects until 2016. Check the trust's website for the latest information.
**WHO TO APPLY TO** Melanie Churchyard, Secretary, 3 Cornfield Terrace, Eastbourne, East Sussex BN21 4NN *Tel.* 01323 417944 *email* info@childstrust.org *Website* childscharitabletrust.org

## ■ The Chippenham Borough Lands Charity

**CC NO** 270062   **ESTABLISHED** 1990
**WHERE FUNDING CAN BE GIVEN** Chippenham parish.
**WHO CAN BENEFIT** Individuals or community/charitable organisations which benefit the people of the Parish of Chippenham. Individuals must be living within the Parish of Chippenham at the date of application, and for a minimum of two years immediately prior to applying.
**WHAT IS FUNDED** The charity's income can be used by, or for the benefit of, the inhabitants of the Parish of Chippenham for: relief of the aged, sick, disabled or poor; provision of facilities for recreation or other leisure time occupation; the advancement of education; the promotion of any other charitable purpose.
**WHAT IS NOT FUNDED** Individual adult sportsmen/woman; direct subsidy to local authorities; religious organisations (except for projects involving substantial non-denominational use for

community benefit); retrospective applications; first degrees.
**RANGE OF GRANTS** Usually £100–£25,000.
**SAMPLE GRANTS** The Rise Trust (£25,200); Relate Mid Wilts (£17,200); Wiltshire Citizens Advice (£15,000); Schools Social Fund (£12,000); North Wilts Holiday Club (£10,000); Chippenham Town Council, St Nicholas' School (£6,000 each); Springboard Opportunity Group (£3,000); 1st Chippenham Scouts (£2,000); Chippenham Rotary Club and Inner Wheel (£1,500); Frogwell Special Needs Unit (£1,200).
**FINANCES** Year 2013/14 Income £470,379 Grants £245,917 Grants to organisations £245,917 Assets £13,780,845
**TRUSTEES** Desna Allen; Graham Bone; Jenny Budgell; Jan Morgan; Ian Humphrey; Mark Allum; Huw Thomas; Philip Cozens; Roger Hammor; Teresa Hutton; Michael Stone.
**OTHER INFORMATION** In 2013/14 a total of £215,600 was given to 83 organisations. The remainder went to individuals.
**HOW TO APPLY** Apply via a form available from the correspondent, either via an agency or self-referral.
**WHO TO APPLY TO** Philip Tansley, Jubilee Building, 32 Market Place, Chippenham, Wiltshire SN15 3HP *Tel.* 01249 658180 *Fax* 01249 446048 *email* pam@cblc.org.uk *Website* www.cblc.org.uk

## ■ The Chipping Sodbury Town Lands Charity

**CC NO** 236364 **ESTABLISHED** 1977
**WHERE FUNDING CAN BE GIVEN** The parishes of Chipping Sodbury and Old Sodbury.
**WHO CAN BENEFIT** Individuals and organisations.
**WHAT IS FUNDED** The trust gives grants for relief-in-need and educational purposes, and also other purposes within Sodbury, including the provision of leisure facilities.
**TYPE OF GRANT** Buildings, capital, one-off and recurring costs will be considered.
**RANGE OF GRANTS** £500–£43,000
**SAMPLE GRANTS** Old Sodbury Football Club – new pavilion (£43,000); Chipping Sodbury Endowed School (17,500); Old Sodbury Village Hall repairs (£9,000); Sodbury Town Council Play scheme (£4,000); Old Sodbury School (£3,000); St John the Baptist Nativity Celebration (£1,000); Chipping Sodbury Music Society (£500).
**FINANCES** Year 2013 Income £360,414 Grants £127,186 Grants to organisations £95,887 Assets £8,867,873
**TRUSTEES** Paul Tily; David Shipp; Bill Ainsley; Michelle Cook; Wendy Whittle; Colin Hatfield; Jim Elsworth; Bryan Seymour; Paul Robins.
**OTHER INFORMATION** In 2013 grants totalling £31,299 were made to individuals.
**HOW TO APPLY** Apply in writing to the correspondent. The trustees meet on the third week of each month except August.
**WHO TO APPLY TO** Nicola Gideon, Clerk, Town Hall, 57–59 Broad Street, Chipping Sodbury, Bristol, South Gloucestershire BS37 6AD *Tel.* 01454 852223 *email* nicola.gideon@chippingsodburytownhall.co.uk

## ■ CHK Charities Limited

**CC NO** 1050900 **ESTABLISHED** 1995
**WHERE FUNDING CAN BE GIVEN** Worldwide, in practice mainly UK with a preference for national and West Midlands charities.
**WHO CAN BENEFIT** Registered charities.
**WHAT IS FUNDED** Artistic causes; conservation/preservation; countryside matters; care of the elderly; crime prevention; people with disabilities; drug prevention and treatment; education; employment and job creation; general medical research; general welfare and social problems; homeless and housing; hospices; hospitals; population control; research into blindness; research into deafness; youth care; general charitable causes.
**WHAT IS NOT FUNDED** The following will not normally be considered for funding: organisations not registered as charities or those that have been registered for less than a year; pre-school groups; out of school play schemes including pre-school and holiday schemes; 'bottomless pits' and unfocused causes; very small and narrowly specialised activities; community centres; local authorities; umbrella or grant-making organisations; universities and colleges and grant maintained private or local education authority schools or their PTAs, except if these schools are for students with special needs; individuals or charities applying on behalf of individuals; general requests for donations; professional associations and training of professionals; projects which are abroad even though the charity is based in the UK; expeditions or overseas travel; 'campaigning organisations' or Citizens Advice projects providing legal advice; community transport projects; general counselling projects, except those in areas of considerable deprivation and with a clearly defined client group.
**TYPE OF GRANT** One-off; conditionally renewable; large grants (over £25,000).
**RANGE OF GRANTS** Up to £100,000 but generally £3,000–£20,000.
**SAMPLE GRANTS** Fair Shares and the Royal Shakespeare Company (£100,000 each); Pace Centre (£50,000); Coram Life Education (£25,000); Campaign to Protect Rural England (£20,000); Police Rehabilitation Trust (£15,000); Anchor House and the Royal Ballet School (£10,000 each); Fight for Sight (£5,000); Garden Organic and Theodora Children's Trust (£3,000 each); Garsington Opera Ltd (£1,000).
**FINANCES** Year 2013/14 Income £2,784,325 Grants £2,240,410 Grants to organisations £2,240,410 Assets £92,252,591
**TRUSTEES** Charlotte Percy; Joanna Prest; Katherine Lloyd; Lucy Morris; Rupert Prest; Serena Acland; Susanna Peake; Edward Peake; Diana Acland.
**OTHER INFORMATION** This trust has a very useful website that should be referred to when considering making an application.
**HOW TO APPLY** The following information is taken from the trust's website: 'Preference is given to National or West Midlands charities, and the organization will normally be based within the United Kingdom. The trustees do not require applicants to use a special application form, but suggest that the following guidelines be used: Applications should be no longer than four A4 sides, and should incorporate a short (half page) summary. Applications should also include a detailed budget for the project and the applicant's most recent audited accounts. If those accounts show a significant surplus or deficit of income, please explain how this has

arisen. Applications should: state clearly who they are, what they do and whom they seek to help; give the applicant's status, e.g., registered charity; confirm that the organisation has a Child Protection Policy (where appropriate) and that Criminal Record Bureau checks are carried out on all staff working with children; describe clearly the project for which the grant is sought answering the following questions: What is the aim of the project and why is it needed? What practical results will it produce? How many people will benefit from it? What stage has the project reached so far? How will you ensure that it is cost-effective?; if the request is for a salary, enclose a job description; explain how the project will be monitored, evaluated and how its results will be disseminated; state what funds have already been raised for the project, and name any other sources of funding applied for; explain where on-going funding (if required) will be obtained when the Charity's grant has been used; if the request is for revenue funding for a specific item, please state the amount needed; please keep the application as simple as possible and avoid the use of technical terms, acronyms and jargon. If you are sending videos or CD Roms, please provide a stamped address envelope so that they may be returned.'

**WHO TO APPLY TO** Scott Rice, Kleinwort Benson Trustees Ltd, 14 St George Street, London W1S 1FE *Tel.* 020 3207 7232 *email* scott.rice@kleinwortbenson.com *Website* www.chkcharities.co.uk

■ **The Chownes Foundation**

**CC NO** 327451  **ESTABLISHED** 1987

**WHERE FUNDING CAN BE GIVEN** UK, priority is given to charities based in Sussex, particularly in mid Sussex.

**WHO CAN BENEFIT** Organisations and individuals.

**WHAT IS FUNDED** The advancement of religion, the advancement of education among the young, the amelioration of social problems, and the relief of poverty amongst older people and the former members of Sound Diffusion plc who lost their pensions when the company went into receivership. Preference will be given to projects where a donation may have some meaningful impact on an identified need rather than simply being absorbed into a larger funding requirement. Applications from smaller charities whose aims mirror those of the founder, Paul Stonor, will be favoured.

**TYPE OF GRANT** One-off, recurrent, buildings, capital, core costs, research and running costs. Funding is available for up to and over three years.

**RANGE OF GRANTS** Up to £17,000.

**SAMPLE GRANTS** Relief of hardship of former employees of Sound Diffusion (five grants totalling £17,000); Age Unlimited (£7,500); St Catherine's Hospice, St Peter and St James Hospice (£3,000 each) Amnesty International (£2,500); Mencap, NSPCC (£1,000 each).

**FINANCES** *Year* 2013/14 *Income* £20,233 *Grants* £80,000 *Grants to organisations* £80,000

**TRUSTEES** Mrs U. Hazeel; The Rt Revd S. Ortiger; M. Woolley.

**OTHER INFORMATION** The full accounts were not available on the Charity Commission website due to the foundation's low income. The grant total has therefore been estimated based on grant-making in previous years.

**HOW TO APPLY** Apply in writing to the correspondent.

**WHO TO APPLY TO** Sylvia Spencer, Trust Secretary, The Courtyard, Beeding Court, Shoreham Road, Steyning, West Sussex BN44 3TN *Tel.* 01903 816699 *email* sylvia@russellnew.com

■ **The Christabella Charitable Trust**

**CC NO** 800610  **ESTABLISHED** 1988

**WHERE FUNDING CAN BE GIVEN** General but mainly Essex and surrounding areas.

**WHO CAN BENEFIT** Registered charities, local organisations and individuals.

**WHAT IS FUNDED** Christian causes are much favoured and there are several local organisations regularly supported including St Francis Church in West Horndon and Viz-a-Viz's evangelical work. The trustees prefer 'seed corn' funding of projects involving volunteers. Normally only one or two additional projects of special interest to the trust are supported each year.

**WHAT IS NOT FUNDED** No support is given for UK-wide or international charities. Applications for grants towards general running costs or building refurbishment are very unlikely to be supported.

**TYPE OF GRANT** The trust prefer 'seed corn' funding of projects involving volunteers.

**RANGE OF GRANTS** Up to £20,000.

**SAMPLE GRANTS** National Garden Scheme; St Francis Church and Viz-a-Viz. Details of individual grant totals were omitted from the 2013/14 trust report.

**FINANCES** *Year* 2014 *Income* £360,467 *Grants* £40,045 *Grants to organisations* £40,045 *Assets* £6,042,789

**TRUSTEES** Ernest Munroe; Christine Turner; Richard Hilburn; Ian Elliot; Robert Folwell.

**OTHER INFORMATION** This trust's primary objective is to maintain the charity's property at Barnards Farm in West Horndon as the house of the National Malus Collection, to allow the general public access on various published dates each year and for use by other charitable organisations.

**HOW TO APPLY** Apply in writing to the correspondent, from whom an application form is available.

**WHO TO APPLY TO** Robert Folwell, Trustee, 3 Burses Way, Hutton, Brentwood, ESSEX CM13 2PL *Tel.* 01277 514056 *Fax* 01268 776400 *email* bobfolwell@hotmail.com *Website* www.barnardsfarm.eu/christabella.htm

■ **Christadelphian Samaritan Fund**

**CC NO** 1004457  **ESTABLISHED** 1991

**WHERE FUNDING CAN BE GIVEN** UK and overseas.

**WHO CAN BENEFIT** Registered charities.

**WHAT IS FUNDED** Preference is given to human causes and aid to financially developing countries.

**WHAT IS NOT FUNDED** Individuals; non-registered charities.

**TYPE OF GRANT** Single donations.

**RANGE OF GRANTS** £1,000 to £8,300.

**SAMPLE GRANTS** MSF – Sudan Appeal (£6,400); British Red Cross – Hurricane Sandy Appeal and UNICEF – West Africa and Syria (£5,000 each); and British Red Cross – Turkey Earthquake Appeal (£2,000).

**FINANCES** *Year* 2013/14 *Income* £109,496 *Grants* £82,091 *Grants to organisations* £82,091 *Assets* £80,625

**TRUSTEES** K. H. A. Smith; David Ensell; William Moss; John Buckler; Roger Miles; Pauline Bromage; Elizabeth Briley.

**HOW TO APPLY** Apply in writing to the correspondent.

**WHO TO APPLY TO** Mr K. H. A. Smith, Treasurer, Westhaven House, Arleston Way, Shirley, Solihull, West Midlands B90 4LH *Tel.* 0121 713 7100

...................................................

## ■ Christian Aid

**CC NO** 1105851 **ESTABLISHED** 1945
**WHERE FUNDING CAN BE GIVEN** Mainly financially developing countries. Limited assistance for development education projects in the UK.
**WHO CAN BENEFIT** Councils of Churches; other ecumenical bodies, development and relief groups; UN agencies which benefit at risk groups; people disadvantaged by poverty; homeless people; refugees; immigrants; socially isolated people; victims of famine, man-made or natural disasters, and war.
**WHAT IS FUNDED** Organisations which work with the world's poorest people and communities. Funding is given to partner organisations only.
**WHAT IS NOT FUNDED** Individuals; political causes; organisations whose aims are primarily political are not eligible for grants.
**TYPE OF GRANT** Project.
**SAMPLE GRANTS** UK Department for International Development (£16.2 million); European Commission (£5.5 million); Irish Aid (£3.7 million); ICCO (£385,000); Jersey Overseas Aid Commission (£360,000); Comic Relief (£187,000); United States Agency for International Development (£59,000); Guernsey Overseas Aid Commission (£20,000).
**FINANCES** *Year* 2013/14 *Income* £103,604,000 *Grants* £31,459,000 *Grants to organisations* £31,459,000 *Assets* £28,034,000
**TRUSTEES** Dr Rowan Williams; Jennifer Cormack; Wilton Powell; Rt Revd John Davies; Bala Gnanapragasam; Brian Risdale; Alexis Chapman; Alastair Redfern; Revd Bob Fyffe; Dr Charlotte Seymore-Smith; Carloyn Gray; Morag Mylne; Thomas Hinton; Paul Spray; Trevor Williams; Alan McDonald; Victoria Hardman; Carla Stent; Mervyn McCullagh.
**OTHER INFORMATION** Other smaller organisations received grants of £4.2 million in total and other governments and public authorities received £506,000.
**HOW TO APPLY** Initial approaches by potential partner organisations should be made in writing.
**WHO TO APPLY TO** Martin Birch, Director of Finance and Operations, 35–41 Lower Marsh, London SE1 7RL *Tel.* 020 7620 4444 *email* info@christian-aid.org *Website* www.christianaid.org.uk

...................................................

## ■ Chrysalis Trust

**CC NO** 1133525 **ESTABLISHED** 2010
**WHERE FUNDING CAN BE GIVEN** North East of England, UK national organisations providing benefit across the UK, overseas.
**WHO CAN BENEFIT** Charities, community groups and educational projects.
**WHAT IS FUNDED** General charitable purposes, education, social welfare
**WHAT IS NOT FUNDED** Research – academic or medical; holidays or outings; arts or entertainment activities; animal welfare; general appeals.
**TYPE OF GRANT** One-off grants to support capital costs and core funding.
**RANGE OF GRANTS** £1,000–£10,000
**SAMPLE GRANTS** Build it International, Greggs Foundation (£10,000 each); Barnardo's (£8,000); Zambia Orphans of Aids (£6,050); Hope and Homes for Children (£5,000); Huntington's Disease Association (£4,000); Village Water (£3,500); Seeds for Africa (£3,000); The Woodfuel Centre (£2,000); Key Project (£1,000).
**FINANCES** *Year* 2013/14 *Income* £152,035 *Grants* £63,529 *Grants to organisations* £63,529 *Assets* £1,695,285
**TRUSTEES** Mark Price Evans; Sarah Evans; Andrew Playle; Alba Lewis.
**HOW TO APPLY** The trust provides the following helpful information on its website: '**Application Checklist** There is no application form. Outline your project on no more than 4 A4 sides using the following checklist: what is the name of your organisation and what is your charitable registration number if you have one?; what does your organisation do?; who are you helping, how many and how?; how many staff and volunteers do you have?; which statutory and voluntary organisations do you have links with, if any?; how much money do you need? [e.g., a contribution of £X towards a total budget of £Y]. Where will the balance of the funds required come from? what do you need the money for?; when do you need the money?; have you applied to other sources? If so, give details and outcomes; who is your key contact regarding this application and what are their contact details (including telephone, email and mailing address)? Attach: a 250 word summary of your proposal; the contact details of two organisations or individuals able to provide a reference on your behalf; a copy of your latest audited annual report and accounts or a copy of your most recent bank statement if you do not have accounts; a budget for the project for which the application is made; a do not attach any unnecessary documentation. Applications should then be submitted preferably by email; if necessary, applications may be sent by post. **What will happen next?** You will receive an acknowledgement that your application has been received. Applications are considered by the Trustees twice a year – usually in June and December, however, applications for amounts less than £1,001 may be considered sooner. We may contact you by telephone or email to discuss your application or to arrange a visit. We aim to let applicants know whether or not their application has been successful within two weeks of the trustees meeting at which the application is being considered. **What are the terms and conditions of a grant?** Successful applicants will be asked to sign a simple grant agreement setting out their obligations in relation to the grant. Grants must be used for the purposes outlined in the application. If the project is unable to go ahead as planned we are happy to consider variations as to how the money is to be spent, however, the money must not be used for any other purposes without our agreement. It must be returned if the project does not go ahead. Recipients of a grant will be required to provide a report on the funded project to the trustees within 3 months of receiving the grant.'
**WHO TO APPLY TO** Sarah Evans, Trustee, Piper Close House, Aydon Road, Corbridge, Northumberland NE45 5PW *email* info@chrysalis-trust.co.uk *Website* www.chrysalis-trust.co.uk

## ■ The Church Burgesses Educational Foundation

**CC NO** 529357 **ESTABLISHED** 1963
**WHERE FUNDING CAN BE GIVEN** Sheffield.
**WHO CAN BENEFIT** Individuals and schools benefitting children and young adults.
**WHAT IS FUNDED** Church schools, independent schools, junior schools, language schools, primary and secondary schools, special schools, tertiary and higher education, and youth organisations. Also funded are bursaries, fees, scholarships, and the purchase of books.
**WHAT IS NOT FUNDED** Non-Sheffield residents
**TYPE OF GRANT** Core costs, one-off and running costs. Funding may be given for up to three years.
**SAMPLE GRANTS Previous beneficiaries have included:** Dyslexia Institute, the Flower Estate Community Association, Pitstop, Sheffield County Guide Association, Sheffield YMCA, South Yorkshire and Hallam Clubs for Young People, Whirlow Hall Farm Trust and Wybourn Youth Trust.
**FINANCES** Year 2013 Income £258,654 Grants £335,003 Grants to organisations £211,030 Assets £145,082
**TRUSTEES** Revd S. A. P. Hunter; Mrs B. R. Hickman; Mr D. Stanley; Mr W. Thomas; Prof. D. Luscombe; David Brooker; Cllr John Campbell; Mrs Susan Bain
**OTHER INFORMATION** In 2013 grants were made in the following categories: Church Schools Grant (£29,500); Donations to Youth Organisations (£9,500); Individual Grants for Education (£101,000); Special Individual Grants (£23,000); Special Grants (£55,200); Church-based youth work (£81,700); Music in the City (£35,100).
**HOW TO APPLY** On forms available to download, together with criteria and guidelines, from the website. The trustees meet four times a year. Initial telephone calls are welcome.
**WHO TO APPLY TO** Mr G. J. Smallman, Law Clerk, 3rd Floor, Fountain Precinct, Balm Green, Sheffield S1 2JA Tel. 0114 267 5594 Fax 0114 276 3176 email sheffieldchurchburgesses@wrigleys.co.uk Website www.sheffieldchurchburgesses.org.uk

## ■ Church Burgesses Trust

**CC NO** 221284 **ESTABLISHED** 1554
**WHERE FUNDING CAN BE GIVEN** Sheffield.
**WHO CAN BENEFIT** Voluntary organisations, registered charities and churches in Sheffield.
**WHAT IS FUNDED** Ecclesiastical purposes, education, and other charitable purposes.
**WHAT IS NOT FUNDED** Individuals. 'Individuals under 25 can apply to the Church Burgesses Educational Foundation for specific educational help'
**TYPE OF GRANT** One-off and recurring.
**RANGE OF GRANTS** £200 to £165,400.
**SAMPLE GRANTS** Parish support grants (£165,400); St Cuthbert's Fir Vale (£100,000); St Matthew's Carver Street (£50,000); St Peter Project and St Oswald (£27,700); Mission and Development coordinator (£35,000); St John's Park Church Army (£24,000); St Thomas Crookes Eden project Fir Vale (£19,600); University of Sheffield Chaplaincy (£16,600); Whirlow Grange spirituality centre (£16,600); Whirlow Grange spirituality centre part-time worker (£10,000); Voluntary Action Sheffield (£7,000); Cavendish Centre for Cancer Care (£6,000); Theadora's Children's Trust (£3,000); Whizz-Kidz (£2,500);

St Timothy's Scouts (£1,000); Happy Days Children's Charity (£500); Friends of Ruskin Park (£250).
**FINANCES** Year 2013 Income £2,091,656 Grants £191,182 Grants to organisations £191,182 Assets £35,880,179
**TRUSTEES** D. F. Booker; Revd S. A. P. Hunter; Nicholas J. A. Hutton; Julie Banham; Peter W. Lee; J. F. W. Peters; Prof. G. D. Sims; Ian G. Walker; Mike R. Woffenden; D. Stanley; B. R. Hickman; Mrs S. Bain.
**PUBLICATIONS** We of Our Bounty – a history of the Sheffield Church Burgesses.
**OTHER INFORMATION** The trust's website is very useful and should be referred to. 13 individuals were awarded clergy work experience grants or support grants. The total cost of the individual grants was not provided, and so is included in the grant totals.
**HOW TO APPLY** 'It is the policy of the Trust in its grant making to support charitable causes in Sheffield, Sheffield Cathedral and the Sheffield city Anglican parishes to the maximum possible extent that its income allows. The Trust favours pump priming grants and Is keen to be an enabler, rather than a long term funder, of new projects. The Trust invites applications from Anglican parishes, from individuals involved In Christian work of a wide variety of types and from charities both national and local, involved in general charitable work within the Trust's geographical area of remit.' Details of how to apply for grants are available from the trust's website.
**WHO TO APPLY TO** Godfrey J. Smallman, Law Clerk, Sheffield Church Burgesses Trust, 3rd Floor, Fountain Precinct, Balm Green, Sheffield S1 2JA Tel. 0114 267 5594 Fax 0114 276 3176 email godfrey.smallman@wrigleys.co.uk Website www.sheffieldchurchburgesses.org.uk

## ■ Church of Ireland Priorities Fund

**ESTABLISHED** 1980
**WHERE FUNDING CAN BE GIVEN** Ireland.
**WHO CAN BENEFIT** Projects within the Church of Ireland.
**WHAT IS FUNDED** Ministry; retirement; education; community; areas of need; outreach initiatives; innovative ministry in a rural context.
**WHAT IS NOT FUNDED** Projects which are still at the planning stage; recurrent grant aiding; salaries; financing debts; funding for cathedrals and churches; routine renovations and repairs. The committee make the following choices whilst considering applications: people not buildings; new projects rather than recurrent expenditure; mission and outreach rather than maintenance; projects and programmes rather than structure.
**RANGE OF GRANTS** €2,000-€65,000
**SAMPLE GRANTS** The Church Of Ireland Theological Institute (€65,000); The House of Bishops (€40,000); Diocese of Connor (€26,000); Icon Community – Dublin and Glendalough (€20,000); Dunboyne Union (€15,000); Beacon Ministries Limited (€7,500); Armagh Diocesan Council (€6,500); Brandon Grammar School – Cork (€5,000); Clonmel Union of Parishes (€3,000); St Mary's Church – Killarney (€2,000).
**FINANCES** Year 2014 Income £548,471 Grants £571,489 Grants to organisations £571,489
**TRUSTEE** No information was available.
**OTHER INFORMATION** All the financial information is in euros.

**HOW TO APPLY** Application forms are available, together with criteria and guidelines, from the fund's website. Applications must be made by 31 October each year. Applications are considered in February and approved in March.
**WHO TO APPLY TO** Mrs Sylvia Simpson, Organiser, Church of Ireland House, Church Avenue, Rathmines, Dublin 6 *Tel.* 00353 (0) 1 4125607 *email* priorities@ireland.anglican.org *Website* www.priorities.ireland.anglican.org

## ■ Church Urban Fund
**CC NO** 297483 **ESTABLISHED** 1988
**WHERE FUNDING CAN BE GIVEN** The most deprived areas of England.
**WHO CAN BENEFIT** Local faith-based groups and activists working to help individuals, families and communities of people living in deprived neighbourhoods in England.
**WHAT IS FUNDED** The fund will support projects that: tackle major problems in their area, such as poverty, unemployment, disaffected youth, lack of community facilities, loneliness and isolation, or housing and homelessness; equip local communities to address local needs and issues and encourage people to take control of their lives; empower the faith community to take an active role in wider community development, particularly through interfaith and ecumenical developments; are innovative, will make a practical impact and can develop partnerships with other agencies.
**WHAT IS NOT FUNDED** The fund's website states that it will not fund the following: 'projects outside England; individuals; projects not directly tackling profound poverty; projects without faith links; organisations with an annual turnover of over £150,000; salary costs, except where there is a significant increase in hours in order to expand an existing project or begin new work; core costs; repeated activities; work that has already been completed or started; campaigning and fundraising activity; revenue and capital for national voluntary/community organisations and public and private sector organisations; activities open only to church members; evangelistic activity not part of a response to poverty; clergy stipends including church army posts; general repairs and refurbishment; and general appeals.' Those that fall outside the priority groups, which are: offenders/ex-offenders; refugees and asylum seekers; deprived young people aged 14–19 years; homelessness; and substance misuse are unlikely to be funded. The fund is also unable to fund health and well-being projects, general family work, or work addressing shorter term aspects of poverty such as food banks.
**TYPE OF GRANT** Capital, project and revenue funding for up to three years.
**RANGE OF GRANTS** £100–£5,000
**SAMPLE GRANTS** All Saints Hanley, The Bridge Pregnancy Crisis, Community Money Advice, Faith Drama Productions Project, Freedom Trust, Housing Justice, Reading Refugee Support Group and Sussex Pathways (£5,000 each); Bristol Inter Faith Group, Church Action on Poverty and Keeping Health in Mind (£4,500 each) Youth Project @ Apostles and Cuthbert's (£4,200); St Andrew's Community Network (£4,000).
**FINANCES** *Year* 2013 *Income* £4,157,000 *Grants* £330,000 *Grants to organisations* £330,000 *Assets* £3,446,000
**TRUSTEES** Andrew Dorton; Revd Canon Denise Poole; Revd Christopher Chessun; Derek Twine;

Patrick Coldstream; Canon Paul Hackwood; Revd David Walker; Brian Carroll; Marnie Woodward; John Iles.
**PUBLICATIONS** The trust has produced a detailed and helpful grants policy and procedure manual and applicants are advised to read this before making an application. The manual is available from the trust's website. The trust also publishes excellent reports on a wide range of issues related to poverty and deprivation. These are also available on the website.
**HOW TO APPLY** Before making an application it is recommended you read through the guidance manual to establish eligibility. Applicants should then contact their local Diocesan Link Officer (contact details on website). An application form should then be completed and returned to the link officer (with budget and accounts) who will then review it and forward it on to the fund for final assessment. The fund aims to give a decision on application within a month of receipt.
**WHO TO APPLY TO** Revd Canon Paul Hackwood, Church House, 27 Great Smith Street, Westminster, London SW1P 3AZ *Tel.* 020 7898 1090 *email* enquiries@cuf.org.uk *Website* www.cuf.org.uk

## ■ The CIBC World Markets Children's Miracle Foundation
**CC NO** 1105094 **ESTABLISHED** 2004
**WHERE FUNDING CAN BE GIVEN** UK and the Netherlands.
**WHO CAN BENEFIT** Registered charities.
**WHAT IS FUNDED** Children affected by disability, illness, social deprivation or life-limiting conditions.
**WHAT IS NOT FUNDED** Individuals; political or advocacy groups; private schools and groups that limit their activities to benefitting persons of a designated ethnic or religious affiliation; endowments, funds given permanently to a foundation so it may produce its own income for grant-making purposes; multi-year projects or commitments; charities with an annual income over £5 million.
**TYPE OF GRANT** One-off large grants for projects, core costs and capital costs.
**RANGE OF GRANTS** £1,000–£380,000
**SAMPLE GRANTS** CHICKS (£380,000); the PACE Centre (£250,000); Haven House Children's Hospice, Rainbow Trust Children's Charity and Rays of Sunshine (£63,000 each); Honeypot (£28,000); and Homestart Greenwich, Roald Dahl's Marvellous Children's Charity, the Sick Children's Trust, Tommy's and Wellchild (£1,000 each).
**FINANCES** *Year* 2013/14 *Income* £526,265 *Grants* £851,000 *Grants to organisations* £851,000 *Assets* £703,196
**TRUSTEES** Mark Beels; Howard Redgwell; Helen Hayes; Martin Autotte; Andrew Ryde; Paul Weideman.
**HOW TO APPLY** In the past the foundation has chosen its charities for the year through funding requests that are accepted only in January. Check the foundation's website for the latest details. All applications should be made by email. If this is not possible contact Howard Redgwell. All applicants should read the eligibility guidelines and must also send; a brief presentation/document detailing the charity's background and activities; last year's accounts filed with the Charity Commission; a very short memo (up to one A4 page) detailing how the

funds raised by CIBC will be used, and the potential need for non-financial assistance from CIBC and its staff. Charities may be invited to make presentations to the trustees.
**WHO TO APPLY TO** Howard Redgwell, Trustee, Canadian Imperial Bank of Commerce, 150 Cheapside, London EC2V 6ET *Tel.* 020 7234 6000 *email* ukchildrensmiracle@cibc.co.uk *Website* www.cibc.com/ca/miracleday/international/childrens-foundation.html

## ■ The City Bridge Trust

**CC NO** 1035628        **ESTABLISHED** 1995
**WHERE FUNDING CAN BE GIVEN** Greater London.
**WHO CAN BENEFIT** Charitable organisations whose activities benefit the people of Greater London.
**WHAT IS FUNDED** Arts, culture, recreation and sports; community development; mental health; environment; older people; disability; voluntary sector.
**WHAT IS NOT FUNDED** Political parties; political lobbying; non-charitable activities; and work which does not benefit the inhabitants of Greater London. The trust does not fund: individuals; grant-making bodies to make grants on its behalf; schools, PTAs, universities or other educational establishments (except where they are undertaking ancillary charitable activities specifically directed towards one of the agreed priority areas); medical or academic research; churches or other religious bodies where the monies will be used for religious purposes; hospitals; projects which have already taken place or building work which has already been completed; statutory bodies; profit making organisations (except social enterprises); and charities established outside the UK. Grants will not usually be given to: work where there is statutory responsibility to provide funding; organisations seeking funding to replace cuts by statutory authorities, except where that funding was explicitly time-limited and for a discretionary (non-statutory) purpose; organisations seeking funding to top up on under-priced contracts; and work where there is significant public funding available (including funding from sports governing bodies).
**TYPE OF GRANT** Grants for either running costs or capital costs. Grants for running costs are made for one to three years. Projects of an exceptionally strategic nature may make an application for a further two years, a maximum of five years in all.
**RANGE OF GRANTS** No minimum amount but applications over £55,000 need to be accompanied by a detailed proposal. Large grants to small organisations are unlikely to be made.
**SAMPLE GRANTS** National Army Museum (£150,000); Wac Arts (£120,000); Age UK – Enfield (£97,500); Community Focus (£90,000); Advice UK (£75,000); British Wheelchair Sports Foundation (£71,000); English Folkdance and Song Society (£50,000) Beyond Youth CIC (£38,000); Ealing Music Therapy (£26,500); Angel Shed Theatre Company (£24,000); Holy Trinity Church Tooting (£15,000); DASH (£6,000).
**FINANCES** *Year* 2013/14 *Income* £40,900,000 *Grants* £19,700,000 *Grants to organisations* £19,700,000 *Assets* £1,023,900,000
**TRUSTEE** The Corporation of the City of London.
**OTHER INFORMATION** The City Bridge Trust is the grant-making arm of the Bridge House Estates charity whose prime objective is the provision and maintenance of the four bridges across the Thames into the City of London.
**HOW TO APPLY** Applications are made through the trust's website. Applications will have to set up an online account using an email address. The following supporting documents should be submitted: detailed proposal: for all funding requests of £5,000 or more; job description(s): for all requests that ask for funding towards a postholder; monitoring framework: all requests; signed, audited or independently examined accounts: you do not need to include these if they are available on the Charity Commission website; draft accounts for your most recent financial year: if your audited or examined accounts are not ready; a financial forecast for your current financial year; a budget for your next financial year if your next financial year is due to start within four months of your submission of this application.
**WHO TO APPLY TO** Jenna Rigley, Budget Division, City of London, PO Box 270, Guildhall, London EC2P 2EJ *Website* www.citybridgetrust.org.uk/cbt

## ■ The City Educational Trust Fund

**CC NO** 290840        **ESTABLISHED** 1967
**WHERE FUNDING CAN BE GIVEN** Generally Greater London.
**WHO CAN BENEFIT** Institutions in London benefitting young adults, research workers, students and teachers.
**WHAT IS FUNDED** A variety of educational groups and institutions to promote study, teaching and training in areas such as science, technology, business management, commerce, biology, ecology and the cultural arts.
**WHAT IS NOT FUNDED** Individuals.
**TYPE OF GRANT** One-off, ongoing and fixed period grants.
**RANGE OF GRANTS** Up to £60,000.
**SAMPLE GRANTS** City University teaching and learning in Mathematics project (£60,000); Spitalfields Festival – towards running costs (£45,000); Wilton's Music Hall refurbishment (£25,000); St Paul's Cathedral School – towards choristers boarding costs (£15,000); Dr Johnson's House – towards running costs (£8,750); City of London Symphonia – towards costs of a music education project (£5,000).
**FINANCES** *Year* 2014 *Income* £130,774 *Grants* £158,750 *Grants to organisations* £158,750 *Assets* £3,390,560
**TRUSTEE** The Corporation of London.
**HOW TO APPLY** Apply in writing to the correspondent. Guidelines are available from the trust.
**WHO TO APPLY TO** Mr Steven Reynolds, c/o Corporation of London, PO Box 270, Guildhall, London EC2P 2EJ *Tel.* 020 7332 1382 *email* laura.yeo@cityoflondon.gov.uk *Website* www.cityoflondon.gov.uk

## ■ CLA Charitable Trust

**CC NO** 280264        **ESTABLISHED** 1980
**WHERE FUNDING CAN BE GIVEN** England and Wales only.
**WHO CAN BENEFIT** Small local projects, innovative projects and newly established projects, where a grant can make a 'real contribution to the success of the project'.
**WHAT IS FUNDED** To promote education about the countryside for young people from towns and cities and those who are disadvantaged; to provide facilities for those with disabilities, who

have learning difficulties or who are in some way disadvantaged to enjoy the benefits of the countryside; to support the advancement of education in agriculture, horticulture and conservation for disadvantaged people, particularly the young.

**WHAT IS NOT FUNDED** Individuals; sensory gardens; community allotments; state funded schools or other institutions. Projects which are based on horticultural activities must be able to demonstrate that they provide training to a recognised qualification for the participants. The website states: 'The Trustees do not normally grant money for core funding or make limited contributions to a much larger project. They prefer to fund specific capital purchases or a discrete part of a project with which the Trust can be identified. The Trustees are unlikely to approve grants to charities or organisations with substantial incoming resources as they prefer to support smaller projects and organisations to which our limited funding will be crucial. We do not normally give a second grant to a recipient within a minimum of two years of the first or last award.'

**TYPE OF GRANT** Specific projects or items rather than for ongoing running costs.

**RANGE OF GRANTS** Up to £10,000 but typically £1,000–£4,000.

**SAMPLE GRANTS** Farms for City Children (£10,000); Harper Adams University Scholarships (£4,000); Bendrigg Trust (£2,700); Magdalen Trust, Rhubarb Farm and Twycross Zoo (£2,000 each); Springs – Nottingham (£1,500); Yorkshire Wildlife Trust (£1,300); Lambourn RDA and Nancy Oldfield Trust (£1,000 each); Bursary for Tall Ships Youth Trust (£900).

**FINANCES** Year 2013/14 Income £54,196 Grants £53,671 Grants to organisations £53,671 Assets £304,891

**TRUSTEES** Sir Henry Aubrey-Fletcher; Hugh Duberly; Neil Mainwaring; Bridget Biddell; John Homfray.

**HOW TO APPLY** Apply in writing (preferably by email) with details of your organisation, the project for which funding is required, costings, timing, sources of other funding and any other information which you think will help the trustees in their decision. The trustees usually meet in February, May, August and November.

**WHO TO APPLY TO** Peter Geldart, Director, Hopbine Farm, Main Street, Ossington, Newark NG23 6LJ Tel. 020 7235 0511 email charitabletrust@cla.org.uk Website www.cla.org.uk

■ **Stephen Clark 1957 Charitable Trust**

**CC NO** 258690   **ESTABLISHED** 1969
**WHERE FUNDING CAN BE GIVEN** UK with some preference for Bath and Somerset.
**WHO CAN BENEFIT** Registered charities.
**WHAT IS FUNDED** The trust's priorities are 'to make donations to charities in respect of the preservation, embellishment, maintenance, improvement or development of any monuments, churches or other buildings', but also general charitable purposes. The trust prefers local charities to national ones.
**WHAT IS NOT FUNDED** Animal charities; individuals.
**TYPE OF GRANT** One-off.
**RANGE OF GRANTS** Up to £32,000, but usually under £3,000.
**SAMPLE GRANTS** BIHT (£32,400); Bath Industrial Heritage Trust (£7,000); Holbume Museum (£5,700); Iford Arts (£1,600); Elenore Mechin

Fleury and Microloan Foundation (£1,000 each); Médecins Sans Frontières (£500); Afghan Aid and Target Tuberculosis (£300 each); Alzheimer's Research UK and Music Alive (£200 each); Send a Cow (£130); Bristol Children's Help Society and St John Ambulance (£100).

**FINANCES** Year 2013 Income £98,153 Grants £86,663 Grants to organisations £86,663 Assets £2,572,831

**TRUSTEES** Dr Marianna Clark; Mary Lovell; Alice Clark.

**HOW TO APPLY** Apply in writing to the correspondent. Note, replies are not usually made to unsuccessful applications. Include sae for reply.

**WHO TO APPLY TO** Dr Marianna Clark, Trustee, 16 Lansdown Place East, Bath BA1 5ET

■ **Clark Bradbury Charitable Trust**

**CC NO** 1129841   **ESTABLISHED** 2009
**WHERE FUNDING CAN BE GIVEN** UK and overseas with a preference for Cambridgeshire.
**WHO CAN BENEFIT** Registered charities.
**WHAT IS FUNDED** To provide support to charities involved in environmental conservation and in educating the public about the environment; to provide support to charities helping people with disabilities to experience the outdoors; to respond to specific world crises.
**TYPE OF GRANT** Usually one-off.
**RANGE OF GRANTS** £385–£10,000
**SAMPLE GRANTS** Bedfordshire Cambridgeshire Northamptonshire Wildlife Trust (£4,000); the Woodland Trust (£10,000); RSPB (£5,000); Norfolk Wildlife Trust (£2,500); Plantlife (£2,000); Little Ouse Headwaters Project (£1,600); Cambridge Past Present and Future (£1,000); Walsham Le Willows Wild Wood (£400).
**FINANCES** Year 2013/14 Income £48,064 Grants £59,551 Grants to organisations £59,551 Assets £43,787
**TRUSTEES** Dr Mike Clarke; Dr Jane Bradbury; Robin Hodgkinson; Prof. Elizabeth Morris.
**HOW TO APPLY** Apply in writing to the correspondent, via email.
**WHO TO APPLY TO** Dr Mike Clark, Trustee, Brownscroft, Stackhouse, Giggleswick, Settle, North Yorkshire BD24 0DN Tel. 01729 825140 email contact@cbct.org.uk Website www.cbct.org.uk

■ **J. A. Clark Charitable Trust**

**CC NO** 1010520   **ESTABLISHED** 1992
**WHERE FUNDING CAN BE GIVEN** UK, with a preference for South West England.
**WHO CAN BENEFIT** Charitable organisations for the benefit of the general public.
**WHAT IS FUNDED** Health, education, peace, preservation of the earth and the arts
**RANGE OF GRANTS** £2500–£50,000
**SAMPLE GRANTS** Kwendo Kor (£50,000); SEHER (£30,000); Conflicts Forum (£20,000); Tanzanear (£16,000); Crossway Foundation (£15,000); Ground Work (£13,000); Syrian Appeal (£11,600); City Masters, Marginal Voices, Microloan Foundation (£10,000 each); Bridge of Hope Foundation (£8,400); Christian Aid (£5,000); Centralian Senior College (£2,500).
**FINANCES** Year 2013 Income £706,478 Grants £500,754 Grants to organisations £500,754 Assets £19,787,895
**TRUSTEE** William Pym.

HOW TO APPLY This trust does not respond to unsolicited applications.
WHO TO APPLY TO Jackie Morgan, Secretary, PO Box 1704, Glastonbury, Somerset BA16 0YB

## ■ The Hilda and Alice Clark Charitable Trust

CC NO 211513  ESTABLISHED 1960
WHERE FUNDING CAN BE GIVEN UK and overseas, with preference for Somerset.
WHO CAN BENEFIT Religious Society of Friends, registered charities and individuals. Preference is given to local appeals.
WHAT IS FUNDED General charitable purposes with particular reference to: Religious Society of Friends and associated bodies; charities connected with Somerset; education.
WHAT IS NOT FUNDED Students.
TYPE OF GRANT Recurrent grants..
RANGE OF GRANTS Mostly £200–£5,000.
SAMPLE GRANTS Scottish Heritage Buildings (£300,000); Quaker Peace and Social Witness (£16,000); Oxfam (£12,000); Hickman Retirement Home (£10,000); Society for the Protection of Ancient Buildings (£6,000); Bart's and The Lonson School of Medicine (£5,000); Family Meditation Lothian (£4,000); Campaign to Protect Rural England (£2,000); National Youth Orchestra of Great Britain; Shelter Scotland (£500); Bumblebee Conservation Trust (£300).
FINANCES Year 2013 Income £327,611 Grants £573,301 Grants to organisations £560,151 Assets £8,313,862
TRUSTEES Mary Lovell; Alice Clark; Martin Lovell; Caroline Gould; Roger Goldby; Robert Robertson.
PUBLICATIONS Grants to 86 individuals totalled £26,600
HOW TO APPLY Apply in writing to the correspondent.
WHO TO APPLY TO The Secretary, c/o KPMG, 100 Temple Street, Bristol BS1 1AG Tel. 0117 905 4000 email angela.southern@clarks.com

## ■ The Roger and Sarah Bancroft Clark Charitable Trust

CC NO 290916  ESTABLISHED 1953
WHERE FUNDING CAN BE GIVEN Street, Somerset.
WHO CAN BENEFIT There is a preference given to the Society of Friends (Quakers) and to children and young adults.
WHAT IS FUNDED General charitable purposes and Quaker causes.
WHAT IS NOT FUNDED Only registered charities are considered.
RANGE OF GRANTS £1,000–£22,000
SAMPLE GRANTS Britain Yearly Meeting (£22,000 in total); Greenbank Swimming Pool (£15,000); UK Friends of Hope Flowers and Medical Aid for Palestinians (£10,000 each); Ulster Quaker Social Committee (£9,000); Crispin Hall and Red Brick Building Centre Ltd (£3,000 each); West Wiltshire and East Somerset Area Meeting (£2,000); Scholarships for Street Kids, Sightsavers International and West Somerset Area Quaker Meeting (£1,000 each).
FINANCES Year 2013 Income £82,696 Grants £82,000 Grants to organisations £82,000 Assets £2,244,180
TRUSTEES Richard Clark; Thomas Clark; Martin Lovell; Alice Clark; Susannah Clark.

HOW TO APPLY Apply in writing to the correspondent by 30 September. The trustees meet in December each year.
WHO TO APPLY TO Lynette Cooper, Correspondent, 40 High Street, Somerset BA16 0EQ email lynette.cooper@clarks.com

## ■ The Clarke Charitable Settlement

CC NO 702980  ESTABLISHED 1990
WHERE FUNDING CAN BE GIVEN Staffordshire and Derbyshire.
WHO CAN BENEFIT Funding may be considered for Christians, research workers and medical professionals.
WHAT IS FUNDED The advancement of Christian religion, medical research and hospices.
RANGE OF GRANTS Most grants are for under £5,000, although they can be for much more.
SAMPLE GRANTS Bruswick Youth Club, Church of Holy Angels, Derbyshire Community Foundation (£5,000 each); Air Ambulance Service, Bowel Cancer Research, Charles Hayward Air Ambulance, Derby Cathedral (£1,000 each); Douglas Macmillan Hospice, Meningitis Trust, Teenage Cancer Trust (£500 each); Animal Health Trust, British Heart Foundation, Donna Louise Children's Hospice (£200 each); Alzheimer's Society Christian Aid, Lichfield Cathedral Flower Guild, Macmillan Cancer Support, Spinal Research, The Gurkha Welfare Trust (£100 each).
FINANCES Year 2013/14 Income £183,948 Grants £37,500 Grants to organisations £37,500 Assets £2,210,240
TRUSTEES Lady Hilda Clarke; Sally Hayward; Mary MacGregor; Jane Gerard-Pearse.
HOW TO APPLY Apply in writing to the correspondent, although the trust has previously stated that support is only given to charities known to the trustees or the Clarke family.
WHO TO APPLY TO Mary MacGregor, Longmoor Point, Wood Street, Catfield, GREAT YARMOUTH, Norfolk Tel. 01692 580240

## ■ The Cleopatra Trust

CC NO 1004551  ESTABLISHED 1990
WHERE FUNDING CAN BE GIVEN Mainly UK.
WHO CAN BENEFIT Registered charities with a national focus.
WHAT IS FUNDED General charitable purposes; health and disability.
WHAT IS NOT FUNDED Individuals.
RANGE OF GRANTS £500–£26,000
SAMPLE GRANTS Maggie Keswick Jencks Cancer Caring Centres Trust (26,000); PSP Association (£10,000); AHOY Centre and Project Luanga (£10,000 each); Wellington College (£1,800); and Centrepoint Soho, Children's Trust and St Barnabas Hospice (£1,000 each).
FINANCES Year 2013 Income £37,638 Grants £71,591 Grants to organisations £71,591 Assets £3,566,117
TRUSTEES Bettine Bond; Charles Peacock; Dr Clare Peacock.
OTHER INFORMATION 14 grants were made to organisations in 2013.
HOW TO APPLY Apply in writing to the correspondent.
WHO TO APPLY TO Charles Peacock, Trustee, Charities Aid Foundation, 25 Kings Hill Avenue, Kings Hill, West Malling ME19 4TA Tel. 01732 520028

## ■ The Clore Duffield Foundation

**CC NO** 1084412   **ESTABLISHED** 2000

**WHERE FUNDING CAN BE GIVEN** UK, the larger grants go to London-based institutions.

**WHO CAN BENEFIT** Institutions and registered charities, particular emphasis on supporting children, young people and society's more vulnerable individuals.

**WHAT IS FUNDED** Main grants programme, mainly in the fields of museums, galleries and heritage sites (particularly for learning spaces), the arts, education, health, social care and disability and Jewish charities with interests in any of these areas.

**WHAT IS NOT FUNDED** Potential applicants should note that their organisation must be a registered charity to be eligible. The foundation does not fund projects retrospectively and will not support applications from the following: individuals; general appeals and circulars. It should also be noted that the following are funded only very rarely: projects outside the UK; staff posts; local branches of national charities; academic or project research; conference costs.

**TYPE OF GRANT** Capital grants.

**SAMPLE GRANTS** Jewish Community Centre (£25 million); Tate (£500,000); University Church of St Mary the Virgin (£215,000); Said Business School (£150,000); Bristol Old Vic and Historic Royal Palaces (£100,000 each); Ashmolean Museum and National Museums Liverpool (£50,000 each); Greenhouse (£10,000); Newcastle University (£7,000); Dylan Thomas Centre (£4,000); Ryedale Book Festival (£2,500).

**FINANCES** Year 2013 Income £659,977 Grants £29,752,177 Grants to organisations £29,752,177 Assets £51,230,073

**TRUSTEES** Dame Vivien Dufflied; Richard Oldfield; Caroline Deletra; David Harrel; Michael Trask; James Harding; Melanie Clore; Jeremy Sandelson.

**HOW TO APPLY** Refer to the foundation's guidance leaflet which can be downloaded from its website. You are invited to contact the foundation, before making application if you have any queries regarding criteria set or the process itself.

**WHO TO APPLY TO** Sally Bacon, Executive Director, Studio 3, Chelsea Manor Studios, Flood Street, London SW3 5SR Tel. 020 7351 6061 email info@cloreduffield.org.uk Website www.cloreduffield.org.uk

## ■ Closehelm Limited

**CC NO** 291296   **ESTABLISHED** 1983

**WHERE FUNDING CAN BE GIVEN** UK and Israel.

**WHO CAN BENEFIT** Individuals and institutions benefitting Jewish people and people disadvantaged by poverty.

**WHAT IS FUNDED** The advancement of religion in accordance with the Jewish faith; the relief of poverty; and general charitable purposes.

**RANGE OF GRANTS** up to £117,600.

**SAMPLE GRANTS** Zaks (£117,600); D Sassoon (£3,000); Beenstock Home(£1,700); Friends of Karlin Stolin, Friends of Mir, Chanichel Yesivas Jewish Teacher (£500 each); Keren Shabbos (£200); Chinuch Atsmai (£325).

**FINANCES** Year 2013/14 Income £190,090 Grants £207,289 Grants to organisations £124,716 Assets £2,460,465

**TRUSTEES** Mr A. Van Praagh; Hanna Grosberg; Henrietta Van Praagh.

**OTHER INFORMATION** Grants totalling £83,000 were given to individuals and £124,700 to organisations in 2013/14.

**HOW TO APPLY** Apply in writing to the correspondent.

**WHO TO APPLY TO** Mr A. Van Praagh, Trustee, 30 Armitage Road, London NW11 8RD Tel. 020 8201 8688

## ■ The Clothworkers' Foundation

**CC NO** 274100   **ESTABLISHED** 1977

**WHERE FUNDING CAN BE GIVEN** UK.

**WHO CAN BENEFIT** Charitable organisations.

**WHAT IS FUNDED** Alcohol and substance misuse; people with disabilities; disadvantaged young people; domestic and sexual violence; disadvantaged minority communities older people; homelessness; prisoners and ex-offenders; visual impairment.

**WHAT IS NOT FUNDED** Overheads; training; volunteer expenses; rent; lease of property or equipment; websites; databases/software; professional fees; hospices; projects to create or refurbish charity shops; events; projects that have already been declined for funding by the foundation; grant-making organisations; general mailings; medical research or equipment; emergency appeals; overseas work, even if the charity is registered in the UK; political projects; IT equipment, which will only be used by staff or volunteers; arts or education projects unless they work exclusively with people from the eligible groups described; schools, colleges or universities unless they work exclusively with people with disabilities or people with learning difficulties; students or any individuals other that professional conservators; organisations with an annual income of more than £15 million; organisations that have received a grant in the last five years; work to satisfy the requirements of the Disability Discrimination Act; and organisations that promote a particular religion or only provide services to people of a particular faith.

**TYPE OF GRANT** Capital; one-off; occasionally recurring for more than three years.

**RANGE OF GRANTS** Main grants: grants of up to £100,000 (larger grants awarded on very rare occasions). Average grant size of £20,000, grants size is relative to project size – smaller projects usually receive smaller grants and vice versa. Small grants: grants of between £500 and £10,000 for capital costs.

**SAMPLE GRANTS** Kibbleworks (£200,000); Deafblind Scotland (£85,000); Action Mental Health (£25,000); Unseen (£24,000); Gibside School (£15,000); Islington Boat Club (£20,000); Rainbow Film Society (£10,000); Birmingham Asian Resource Centre (£8,000); Swale Action to End Domestic Abuse (£3,000); Health Action Charity Organisation (£1,300).

**FINANCES** Year 2013 Income £34,453,917 Grants £5,537,815 Grants to organisations £5,537,815 Assets £133,321,867

**TRUSTEES** Anne Luttman-Johnson; Richard Jonas; Dr Carolyn Boulter; Michael Jarvis; Melville Haggard; Michael Howell; Joanna Dodd; Thomas Clark; Andrew Clark; Alexander Nelson; John Wake; Dr Lucy Rawson.

**OTHER INFORMATION** The sample grants were awarded in 2015.

**HOW TO APPLY** Refer to the foundation's very helpful and detailed guidelines on how to apply for either main or small grants, which can be downloaded from the foundation's website.

**WHO TO APPLY TO** Andrew Blessley, Chief Executive, Clothworkers' Hall, Dunster Court, Mincing Lane,

London EC3R 7AH *Tel.* 020 7623 7041
*email* foundation@clothworkers.co.uk
*Website* www.clothworkers.co.uk

## ■ Richard Cloudesley's Charity

**CC NO** 205959  **ESTABLISHED** 1517
**WHERE FUNDING CAN BE GIVEN** Ancient parish of Islington, London
**WHO CAN BENEFIT** Voluntary and charitable organisations. Individuals are assisted through the trust's welfare fund.
**WHAT IS FUNDED** Church of England churches, health and welfare. The Charity only provides funding for the following topics – **Health:** to organisations operating in the area of benefit working with people who are poor and in ill health; **Welfare:** to individuals who live in the area of benefit who are poor and in ill health; **Churches:** to Church of England churches in the ancient parish of St Mary, Islington
**TYPE OF GRANT** One-off grants are preferred; the vast majority of grants are free of restrictions. Grants for capital, core, recurring, running and start-up costs will be considered, as will grants for buildings, feasibility studies, project, research and salaries.
**RANGE OF GRANTS** Up to £45,000.
**SAMPLE GRANTS** Hope Church Islington – St David (£45,000); St Jude and St Paul, Mildmay Grove (£25,000); St Mary's, Islington (£10,000); Help on Your Doorstep, Islington Giving, Islington Law Centre(£35,000); Asylum Aid; Disability Action in Islington, Islington Carers Hub (£5,000); St Mungo's Broadway, The Manna (£3,000).
**FINANCES** *Year* 2013/14 *Income* £1,552,167 *Grants* £559,472 *Grants to organisations* £558,272 *Assets* £44,673,524
**TRUSTEE** Richard Cloudesley Trustee Limited
**OTHER INFORMATION** The grant total figure includes an amount of £1,200, paid to individuals.
**HOW TO APPLY** Health Grants: The Charity has asked the Cripplegate Foundation to work with local organisations that will make an impact for the funds available. The fund is not open to applications at this time. Church Grants: Visit the Spring Round 2015 web page for details of how to apply. The closing date for applications is **Monday 27 April 2015 at 5.00pm**. If you have any questions about the Church Grants funding programme or an application which you would like to make, please contact the Charity
**WHO TO APPLY TO** Melanie Griffiths, Director, Office 1.1, Resource for London, 356 Holloway Road, London N7 6PA *Tel.* 020 7697 4094
*email* info@richardcloudesleycharity.org.uk
*Website* www.richardcloudesleycharity.org.uk

## ■ The Clover Trust

**CC NO** 213578  **ESTABLISHED** 1961
**WHERE FUNDING CAN BE GIVEN** UK, and occasionally overseas, with a slight preference for West Dorset.
**WHO CAN BENEFIT** Registered charities. 'The Trustees prefer to make regular donations to a designated selection of recipients and intend to continue with this policy for the foreseeable future.'
**WHAT IS FUNDED** Older people, young people, Catholicism, health, disability.
**TYPE OF GRANT** Up to three years.
**RANGE OF GRANTS** £2,000–£35,000
**SAMPLE GRANTS** Friends of Children in Romania (£35,000); Farms for City Children (£12,000); The AIDIS Trust, Brain Wave, Children with Cancer (£8,000 each); Bridport Stroke Club, DEMAND, Orchard Vale Trust (£4,000 each); Essex Association of Boys' Clubs, Fight for sight (£3,000 each); Orchard Vale Trust, The Can Care support group (£2,000 each).
**FINANCES** *Year* 2013 *Income* £187,069 *Grants* £189,250 *Grants to organisations* £189,250 *Assets* £4,660,626
**TRUSTEES** Sara Woodhouse; Nicholas Haydon; Benedict Woodhouse; Charlotte Morrison.
**HOW TO APPLY** 'The Trustees prefer to make regular donations to a designated selection of recipients and intend to continue with this policy for the foreseeable future.'
**WHO TO APPLY TO** Jeremy Major, Smith and Williams LLP, Old Library Chambers, 21 Chipper Street, Salisbury, Wiltshire SP1 1BG *Tel.* 01722 411881 *email* jeremycb.major@smith.williamson.co.uk

## ■ The Robert Clutterbuck Charitable Trust

**CC NO** 1010559  **ESTABLISHED** 1992
**WHERE FUNDING CAN BE GIVEN** UK, with preference for Cheshire and Hertfordshire.
**WHO CAN BENEFIT** Registered charities and other organisations with a charitable focus.
**WHAT IS FUNDED** Personnel within the armed forces and ex-servicemen and women; sport and recreational facilities for young people benefitting Cheshire and Hertfordshire; the welfare, protection and preservation of domestic animal life benefitting Cheshire and Hertfordshire; natural history and wildlife; other charities associated with the counties of Cheshire and Hertfordshire; charities which have particular appeal to the founder, Robert Clutterbuck.
**WHAT IS NOT FUNDED** Individuals.
**TYPE OF GRANT** Specific items and projects rather than running costs. One-off.
**RANGE OF GRANTS** £1,000–£3,000
**SAMPLE GRANTS** Royal Star and Garter (an unusually high grant of £75,000); Claire House Hospice (£3,500); Barn Owl Trust, Blind Veterans UK, Dogs Trust, Dyspraxia Foundation, Gurkha Welfare Trust Mountain Training Trust, Seashsell Trust and World Society for Protection of animals (£1,000 each); and Bedfordshire Wildlife Trust (£900).
**FINANCES** *Year* 2013/14 *Income* £548,327 *Grants* £120,744 *Grants to organisations* £120,744 *Assets* £1,816,977
**TRUSTEES** Roger Pincham; Ian Pearson; Lucy Pitman.
**HOW TO APPLY** Apply in writing to the correspondent. There are no application forms. Applicants should write to the secretary giving details of what is proposed and of your current financial position. The deadlines for the rounds of applications are 30 June and 31 December in each year. The trustees generally meet in March and September. The trustees will not normally consider appeals from charities within two years of a previous grant being approved.
**WHO TO APPLY TO** George Wolfe, Secretary, 28 Brookfields, Calver, Hope Valley, Derbyshire S32 3XB *Tel.* 01433 631308 *email* secretary@clutterbucktrust.org.uk *Website* www.clutterbucktrust.org.uk

## ■ Clydpride Ltd

**CC NO** 295393  **ESTABLISHED** 1982
**WHERE FUNDING CAN BE GIVEN** UK.
**WHO CAN BENEFIT** Individuals and institutions benefitting Jewish people and people disadvantaged by poverty.
**WHAT IS FUNDED** Advancement of the Orthodox Jewish faith; relief of poverty; general charitable purposes. The main focus is to support the 'renaissance of religious study and to alleviate the plight of poor scholars'.
**SAMPLE GRANTS** Achiezer; Achisomoch Aid Company; Beis Chinuch Lebonos; Beis Soroh Scheneirer Seminary; Bnei Braq Hospital; Comet Charities Limited; EM Shasha Foundation; Friends of Mir; Gevurath Ari Torah Academy Trust; Mosdos Tchernobil; Notzar Chesed; Seed; Society of Friends of Torah; and Telz Talmudical Academy Trust.
**FINANCES** Year 2013 Income £2,687,177 Grants £195,835 Grants to organisations £195,835 Assets £20,796,483
**TRUSTEES** L. Faust; M. H. Linton; A. Faust.
**OTHER INFORMATION** A list of grant beneficiaries was not included in the trust's accounts. However, we know that the grant total comprised: £126,000 to educational institutions to support the advancement of religion through education; £50,000 for the relief of poverty; £20,000 which was donated to institutions that benefit the Jewish community.
**HOW TO APPLY** The charity considers all grant requests from organisations that fall within the criteria of the charity's objects. The trustees' policy is to award grants on the basis of educational, religious or charitable need, subject to the general objects of the charity and cash resources available.
**WHO TO APPLY TO** Mr L. Faust, Trustee, c/o Rayner Essex Accountants, Tavistock House South, Tavistock Square, London WC1H 9LG *Tel.* 020 8731 7744

## ■ Co-operative Community Investment Foundation

**CC NO** 1093028  **ESTABLISHED** 2000
**WHERE FUNDING CAN BE GIVEN** UK.
**WHO CAN BENEFIT** Registered charities and community groups.
**WHAT IS FUNDED** General charitable purposes; environment; community development; young people.
**WHAT IS NOT FUNDED** The Co-operative Membership Community Fund generally excludes: groups other than community, self-help and voluntary groups; the core activities of auxiliary groups; non-charitable purposes (although a group does not have to be a registered charity); overseas activities; grant or loan schemes; religious worship; core activities of statutory services; improvements to property not owned by the applicant; party political activity; individual sponsorship; cadets.
**TYPE OF GRANT** One-off grants.
**RANGE OF GRANTS** Up to £350,000.
**SAMPLE GRANTS** British Film Academy (£350,000); Oval House, Prince's Trust, Prince's Trust Cymru, Royal Exchange (£280,000 each); Envision (£73,000); Buglife (£25,000).
**FINANCES** Year 2013 Income £3,389,678 Grants £4,605,531 Grants to organisations £4,605,531 Assets £14,045,905
**TRUSTEES** Robert Haber; Jennifer Barnes; Herbert Daybell; David Pownall; Andrew Donkin; David Smith; David Morrow.

**HOW TO APPLY** Applications can usually be made online; however, the following was taken from the foundation website: 'Unfortunately, we are not accepting applications to The Community Fund for the time being. The charity's trustees are currently looking at the best way to develop the scheme and to continue to support local communities in the future. Please accept our apologies for any inconvenience this has caused you, but watch this space for updates and future funding opportunities. If you have already submitted an application and have received a confirmation email with a case number, your application will be considered before 31 December 2014 and we will email you with an outcome as soon as possible. If you have any questions, please contact either the helpline team on **0844 262 4001**, or email **community.fund@co-operative.coop**.'
**WHO TO APPLY TO** Clare Oakley, Correspondent, The Co-operative Group, 1 Angel Square, Manchester M60 0AG *Tel.* 0161 834 1212 *Website* www.co-operative.coop/join-the-revolution/our-plan/keeping-communities-thriving/funds-and-foundations

## ■ The Francis Coales Charitable Foundation

**CC NO** 270718  **ESTABLISHED** 1975
**WHERE FUNDING CAN BE GIVEN** UK, with a preference for Bedfordshire, Buckinghamshire, Hertfordshire and Northamptonshire.
**WHO CAN BENEFIT** Old buildings open to the public, usually churches. Organisations involved in archaeological research and related causes.
**WHAT IS FUNDED** Repair and restoration of buildings, monuments, etc.; archaeological research with preference to Buckinghamshire, Bedfordshire, Northamptonshire and Hertfordshire.
**WHAT IS NOT FUNDED** In respect of buildings, assistance is only given towards fabric repairs, but not to 'domestic' items such as heating, lighting, wiring, installation of facilities, etc.
**TYPE OF GRANT** Largely one-off.
**SAMPLE GRANTS Previous beneficiaries have included:** Paulerspury – Northants, Upton – Bucks and Ivinghoe – Beds (£2,500 each); Wingrave – Bucks and Hockliffe – Beds (£2,000 each); Alpheton – Suffolk and Cransley – Northants (£1,000 each); Tibenham – Norfolk and Laindon – Essex (£750 each); Harlaxton Series (£500); and Church Monuments Soc. (£250).
**FINANCES** Year 2012/13 Income £117,246 Grants £86,087 Grants to organisations £86,087 Assets £3,970,206
**TRUSTEES** Martin Stuchfield; Guy Harding; Revd Brian Wilcox; Ian Barnett; Matthew Saunders.
**OTHER INFORMATION** 31grants were made totalling £86,087.
**HOW TO APPLY** Application forms can be downloaded from the foundation's website. Trustees normally meet three times a year to consider grants. 'In respect of a building or contents, include a copy of the relevant portion only of the architect's (or conservator's) specification showing the actual work proposed. Photographs illustrating this are a necessity, and only in exceptional circumstances will an application be considered without supporting photographs here. It is of help if six copies of any supporting documentation are submitted in order that each trustee may have a copy in advance of the meeting.'

WHO TO APPLY TO Trevor Parker, Correspondent, The Bays, Hillcote, Bleadon Hill, Weston-super-Mare, Somerset BS24 9JS *Tel.* 01934 814009 *email* fccf45@hotmail.com *Website* franciscoales.co.uk

## ■ The Coalfields Regeneration Trust

CC NO 1074930  ESTABLISHED 1999
WHERE FUNDING CAN BE GIVEN Coalfield and former coalfield communities in England (North West and North East, Yorkshire, West Midlands and East Midlands, Kent), Scotland (West and East) and Wales.
WHO CAN BENEFIT Community and voluntary organisations who are working to tackle problems at grass-roots level within coalfield communities.
WHAT IS FUNDED Welfare of coalfield communities.
WHAT IS NOT FUNDED Individuals; private businesses; statutory bodies; national organisations; parish, town and community councils; organisations with total annual income (from all sources) above £100,000; organisations that the trust believes are in a poor financial position or whose financial management systems are not in good order; friends of groups where the end beneficiary will clearly be a statutory body; pigeon (flying) clubs; organisations not established in the UK.
TYPE OF GRANT Usually one-off grants.
RANGE OF GRANTS Up to £200,000.
SAMPLE GRANTS Aylesham Neighbourhood Project (£210,000); Haswell and District Mencap Society – The Community Anchor (£98,000); Derbyside Rural Community Council – Wheels to Work (£89,000); The Cornforth Partnership – The Reach project (£75,000); Nottinghamshire Independent Domestic Abuse Link Workers (£66,000); Stoke-on-Trent and District Gingerbread Centre Ltd – Peer Mentoring (£37,000); St John's Church – A Building in Which to Serve Our Community (£10,000); Mansfield and Dukeries Irish Association – Luncheon Club (£5,000); City of Durham Air Cadets – Achieving Duke of Edinburgh's Awards (£3,800); Thornycroft Art Club – Christmas Tree Exhibition (£520).
FINANCES Year 2013/14 *Income* £15,188,000 *Grants* £1,709,000 *Grants to organisations* £1,709,000 *Assets* £26,721,000
TRUSTEES Nicholas Wilson; Peter McNestry; Vernon Jones; Dawn Davies; Fran Walker; Roger Owen; Michael Clapham; Thomas McAughtrie; William Skilki; Terrence O'Neill; Robert Young.
OTHER INFORMATION The trust provides advice, support and financial assistance to community and voluntary organisations who are working to tackle problems at grass-roots level within coalfield communities. It is closely connected with the areas it serves, operating through a network of staff based at offices located within coalfield regions themselves.
HOW TO APPLY Application details are different for each programme. The trust has produced very comprehensive information booklets that should be read before applying to any fund. Applicants are advised to contact their regional manager before making an application, details of which are also on the website. The staff will be able to advise on the trust's application process and an appointment can be made with a member of the development team to discuss the application in more detail.

WHO TO APPLY TO Louise Dyson, Head of Finance and Corporate Services, 1 Waterside Park, Valley Way, Wombwell, Barnsley S73 0BB *Tel.* 01226 272810 *email* info@coalfields-regen.org.uk *Website* www.coalfields-regen.org.uk

## ■ The John Coates Charitable Trust

CC NO 262057  ESTABLISHED 1969
WHERE FUNDING CAN BE GIVEN UK, mainly southern England.
WHO CAN BENEFIT Institutions either national or of personal or local interest to one or more of the trustees.
WHAT IS FUNDED Preference is given to education, arts and culture, children, environment and health.
WHAT IS NOT FUNDED Grants are given to individuals only in exceptional circumstances.
TYPE OF GRANT Capital and recurring.
RANGE OF GRANTS £1,000–£10,000
SAMPLE GRANTS Action on Addiction, British Heart Foundation, Cambridge King's College School Appeal, Royal Botanic Gardens, Kew (£10,000 each); British Stammering Association, Country Holidays for Inner City Kids, (£5,000 each); Independent Parental Special Education Advice, Motability, Rose Theatre, Kingston (£3,000); Exmoor Search and Rescue, Yes Outdoors (£2,000 each); The Bumblebee Conservation Trust (£1,000).
FINANCES Year 2013/14 *Income* £727,613 *Grants* £470,000 *Grants to organisations* £470,000 *Assets* £12,271,209
TRUSTEES Gillian McGregor; Rebecca Lawes; Phyllida Youngman; Catharine Kesley; Claire Cartledge.
OTHER INFORMATION The trust made grants totalling £470,000 to 85organisations in 2013/14.
HOW TO APPLY Apply in writing to the correspondent. Note that the trust does not invite phone calls; any communication should be made in writing. Small local charities are visited by the trust. It is the trust's policy to request a post-grant report detailing how a donation has been spent for any single donation over £15,000.
WHO TO APPLY TO Rebecca Lawes, Trustee, 3 Grange Road, Cambridge CB3 9AS *Tel.* 01223 301354

## ■ The Cobalt Trust

CC NO 1096342  ESTABLISHED 2002
WHERE FUNDING CAN BE GIVEN UK and overseas.
WHO CAN BENEFIT Registered charities known to the trustees.
WHAT IS FUNDED General charitable purposes.
TYPE OF GRANT Capital and revenue grants over three years.
SAMPLE GRANTS Impetus Trust (£169,000); EVPA (£26,000); Streets Limited (£14,000); Enable Ethiopia and Tree Aid (£12,000 each); Rose trees Trust and Money for Madagascar (£10,000 each); Beat – Eating Disorders Association (£5,000); Wherever the Need (£1,000); Red Squirrel Survival Trust (£500); Wessex MS Therapy Centre (£100); and Bath RSPB (£50). Many of the beneficiaries were supported on a recurrent basis.
FINANCES Year 2013/14 *Income* £21,020 *Grants* £300,000 *Grants to organisations* £300,000
TRUSTEES Stephen Dawson; Brigitte Dawson.

**OTHER INFORMATION** Full accounts were not available for 2013/14 due to the trust's low income. The grant total has been estimated based on grant-making in previous years.
**HOW TO APPLY** The trustees do not respond to unsolicited applications
**WHO TO APPLY TO** Stephen Dawson, Trustee, 17 New Row, London WC2N 4LA *Tel.* 07720 345880

## ■ The Cobtree Charity Trust Ltd
**CC NO** 208455  **ESTABLISHED** 1951
**WHERE FUNDING CAN BE GIVEN** Maidstone and district.
**WHO CAN BENEFIT** Registered charities.
**WHAT IS FUNDED** The maintenance and development of Cobtree Manor Estate, and other general charitable purposes in the Maidstone and district area.
**WHAT IS NOT FUNDED** Individuals; non-registered charities; charities outside Maidstone and district.
**TYPE OF GRANT** Largely recurrent.
**RANGE OF GRANTS** Average £700–£11,500.
**SAMPLE GRANTS** Blackthorn Trust (£11,500); Ulcombe Church (£10,000); Bearsted and Thurnham Bowling Club (£5,000); All Saints Church – Maidstone and Cheshire Homes, Staplehurst (£3,750 each); Age Concern – Maidstone, Demelza House Children's Hospice (£1,500 each); British Wireless For The Blind (£1,000); Boys' Brigade – North West Kent, Maidstone Day Centre; (£700).
**FINANCES** Year 2013/14 *Income* £161,844 *Grants* £106,820 *Grants to organisations* £106,820 *Assets* £6,081,200
**TRUSTEES** R. J. Corben; J. Fletcher; L. J. Martin; R. N. Hext; D. T. B. Wigg; S. W. L. Brice; M. Lawrence; S. Beck
**HOW TO APPLY** Apply in writing to the correspondent. The trustees meet quarterly.
**WHO TO APPLY TO** Colin Mills, c/o Larkings (S.E.) LLP, Cornwallis House, Pudding Lane, Maidstone, Kent ME14 1NH *Tel.* 01622 754033 *Website* thecobtreecharitytrust.co.uk

## ■ The Denise Cohen Charitable Trust
**CC NO** 276439  **ESTABLISHED** 1977
**WHERE FUNDING CAN BE GIVEN** UK.
**WHO CAN BENEFIT** Registered charities.
**WHAT IS FUNDED** Jewish causes; education; health and welfare of older people; people, including children, who are ill; humanities; arts and culture.
**RANGE OF GRANTS** £160 to £8,000.
**SAMPLE GRANTS** Chai Cancer Care (£8,000); Nightingale Hammerson (£5,200); Youth Aliyah – Child Rescue (£5,000); Jewish Woman's Aid (£1,000); Community Security Trust (£3,000); British Friends of Herzog Hospitality and Royal British Legion (£1,000 each); Jewish Book Council, Macmillan Cancer Support (£500 each); United Jewish Israel Appeal (£250); Chicken Soup Shelter (£160).
**FINANCES** Year 2013/14 *Income* £36,447 *Grants* £67,592 *Grants to organisations* £67,592 *Assets* £1,453,098
**TRUSTEES** Denise Cohen; Martin Paisner; Sara Cohen.
**HOW TO APPLY** Apply in writing to the correspondent incorporating full details of the charity for which funding is requested. No acknowledgements will be sent out to unsuccessful applicants.

**WHO TO APPLY TO** Martin Paisner, Trustee, Berwin Leighton and Paisner, Adelaide House, London Bridge, London EC4R 9HA *Tel.* 020 3400 1000

## ■ The Vivienne and Samuel Cohen Charitable Trust
**CC NO** 255496  **ESTABLISHED** 1965
**WHERE FUNDING CAN BE GIVEN** UK and Israel.
**WHO CAN BENEFIT** Charitable organisations.
**WHAT IS FUNDED** Jewish causes; education; health; medical; culture; general charitable purposes.
**WHAT IS NOT FUNDED** Individuals.
**RANGE OF GRANTS** Up to £14,000.
**SAMPLE GRANTS** Ariel (£14,000); Mosaica (£6,000); Friends of S H Hospital and World Jewish Relief (£5,000 each); Chug Ha'amakim and Jewish Care (£3,000 each); The Spiro Ark, University College London, University Jewish Chaplaincy Board (£2,000 each); Chai Cancer Care, Hamifal, Disabled Living Foundation, Educational Children's Hospital (£1,000 each); Other (195 grants all of less than £1,000).
**FINANCES** Year 2013/14 *Income* £462,640 *Grants* £126,399 *Grants to organisations* £126,399 *Assets* £3,926,008
**TRUSTEES** Jonathan Lauffer; Gershon Cohen; Michael Ben-Gershon; Dr Vivienne Cohen; Gideon Lauffer.
**OTHER INFORMATION** 195 of the 235 grants made were under £1,000. These grants totalled £43,300.
**HOW TO APPLY** Apply in writing only, to the correspondent.
**WHO TO APPLY TO** Dr Vivienne Cohen, Trustee, Clayton Start and Co, 5th Floor, Charles House, 108–110 Finchley Road, London NW3 5JJ *Tel.* 020 7431 4200 *email* csco@claytonstark.co.uk

## ■ The John S. Cohen Foundation
**CC NO** 241598  **ESTABLISHED** 1965
**WHERE FUNDING CAN BE GIVEN** Worldwide, in practice mainly UK.
**WHO CAN BENEFIT** Registered charities.
**WHAT IS FUNDED** General charitable purposes but particularly education, music and the arts and the environment, both built and natural.
**TYPE OF GRANT** One-off and recurring.
**RANGE OF GRANTS** £100–£25,000
**SAMPLE GRANTS** Royal Opera House (£25,000), Friends of The National Libraries, National Gallery (£20,000 each); English Heritage Foundation, Royal National Theatre (£15,000); National Youth Choirs, Watts Gallery (£10,000); British Film Institute, Royal Air Force Museum (£5,000); University of Oxford Development Trust (£3,500); Shelter, University of Oxford Development Trust (£2,000); Royal Philharmonic Society (£1,000); National Holocaust Centre (£500); Federation of British Artists (£250); Liberal Jewish Synagogue (£100).
**FINANCES** Year 2013/14 *Income* £539,172 *Grants* £400,658 *Grants to organisations* £400,658 *Assets* £7,225,980
**TRUSTEES** Dr David Cohen; Imogen Cohen; Olivia Cohen; Veronica Cohen.
**HOW TO APPLY** Apply in writing to the correspondent.
**WHO TO APPLY TO** Diana Helme, Foundation Administrator, PO Box 21277, London W9 2YH *Tel.* 020 7286 6921

## ■ The R. and S. Cohen Foundation

**CC NO** 1078225  **ESTABLISHED** 1999
**WHERE FUNDING CAN BE GIVEN** Worldwide.
**WHO CAN BENEFIT** Educational, theatrical, operatic, medical and Jewish charitable organisations.
**WHAT IS FUNDED** Education and relief in need.
**TYPE OF GRANT** One-off and recurrent.
**SAMPLE GRANTS** UJIA (£50,000); Design Museum (£40,000); Muscular Dystrophy, Royal National Institute for the Blind (£25,000 each); Jewish Care (£20,000); Tel-Aviv University Trust (£15,000); British Museum (£13,000); New Israel Fund (£8,000); Tate Foundation (£5,000); Royal Academy of the Arts (£4,500); WLS Charitable Fund (£1,200).
**FINANCES** Year 2013 Income £6,598 Grants £1,700,000 Grants to organisations £1,700,000
**TRUSTEES** Lady Sharon Harel-Cohen; Sir Ronald Cohen; Tamara Harel-Cohen; David Marks; Jonathan Harel-Cohen.
**OTHER INFORMATION** Full accounts were not available on the Charity Commission website due to the low income of the foundation. The grant total has therefore been estimated based on previous years' grant-making.
**HOW TO APPLY** Apply in writing to the correspondent.
**WHO TO APPLY TO** Martin Dodd, 42 Portland Place, London W1B 1NB

## ■ Col-Reno Ltd

**CC NO** 274896  **ESTABLISHED** 1977
**WHERE FUNDING CAN BE GIVEN** UK and Israel.
**WHO CAN BENEFIT** Religious and educational institutions benefitting children, young adults, students and Jewish people.
**WHAT IS FUNDED** Jewish religion and education.
**RANGE OF GRANTS** Mostly under £2,000.
**SAMPLE GRANTS** Society of Friends of the Torah (£17,000); Lubavitch of Liverpool (£9,900); Friends of the Small Communities (£4,000); Yad Aliezer Trust (£2,000); Yeshiva Gedola Lubavitch London (£1,700); Chabad of Wimbledon (£1,250); Zionist Federation (£1,000); Laniado UK (£800); and Hospital Kosher Meals Service (£200).
**FINANCES** Year 2013–14 Income £109,551 Grants £71,802 Grants to organisations £71,802 Assets £1,137,297
**TRUSTEES** Martin Stern; Alan Stern; Keith Davis; Rhona Davis; Chaim Stern; Libbie Goldstein.
**HOW TO APPLY** Apply in writing to the correspondent.
**WHO TO APPLY TO** Martin Stern, Trustee, 10 Hampshire Court, 9 Brent Street, London NW4 2EW Tel. 020 8202 7013

## ■ The Colchester Catalyst Charity

**CC NO** 228352  **ESTABLISHED** 1959
**WHERE FUNDING CAN BE GIVEN** North east Essex.
**WHO CAN BENEFIT** Health organisations.
**WHAT IS FUNDED** Provision of support by direct contributions to health organisations for specific and well-designed projects in order to improve healthcare.
**WHAT IS NOT FUNDED** General funding; staff or running costs (usually); retrospective funding. The charity is unable to consider applications for any item where there is an obligation for provision by a statutory authority.
**TYPE OF GRANT** One-off.
**SAMPLE GRANTS** **Previous beneficiaries have included:** Essex University (£28,000); Opportunities through Technology (£19,500) SCANS (£10,000); Chariot Community Buses (£7,000) The Ark Centre, TCVS, Halstead Day Centre (£5,000 each); Leonard Cheshire Homes (£3,000); St Helena Hospice (£2,500); Colchester Hospital Unit (£1,000).
**FINANCES** Year 2013/14 Income £364,310 Grants £365,679 Grants to organisations £139,479 Assets £10,170,220
**TRUSTEES** P. Fitt, Chair; C. Hayward; Dr E. Hall; Dr M. P. Hickman; A. W. Livesley; M. F. Pertwee; Dr T. P. Rudra; Dr N. J. Busfield.
**OTHER INFORMATION** Grants were divided as follows: Charities (£139,479); Special Individual Needs (£88,124); Equipment Pools (£3,737); Respite Care (£134,339).
**HOW TO APPLY** The application procedure varies for the different grants, full instructions can be obtained on the trust's website. Alternatively applicants may call or email the trust for further information on the application procedure. If you have any other questions regarding the application process, contact the charity on 01206 323420 or by email on info@colchestercatalyst.co.uk.
**WHO TO APPLY TO** Peter Fitt, Company Secretary, 7 Coast Road, West Mersea, Colchester CO5 8QE Tel. 01206 752545 email info@colchestercatalyst.co.uk Website www.colchestercatalyst.co.uk

## ■ John Coldman Charitable Trust

**CC NO** 1050110  **ESTABLISHED** 1995
**WHERE FUNDING CAN BE GIVEN** UK, with a preference for Edenbridge in Kent.
**WHO CAN BENEFIT** Registered charities.
**WHAT IS FUNDED** General charitable purposes, particularly community and Christian groups and UK organisations whose work benefits the community, such as children's and medical charities and schools.
**RANGE OF GRANTS** £250 upwards.
**SAMPLE GRANTS** Chiddingstone Church of England School (£50,000); Prince's Trust, NSPCC (£20,000 each); Celtic FC Charity Fund (£15,000); National Gardens Scheme (£11,400); African Promise (£13,400); St Peter's Church, Hever (£10,000); The Sick Children's Trust (£5,000); Cancer Research UK, Darent Valley Hospital Charity Fund, The Gurkha Welfare Trust (£1,000 each); Movember (£250).
**FINANCES** Year 2014 Income £27,300 Grants £209,548 Grants to organisations £209,548 Assets £928,879
**TRUSTEES** John Coldman; Graham Coldman; Charles Warner.
**OTHER INFORMATION** During 2011–12 an additional £35,000 went towards the running of the Holcot Residential Centre, which operates as a hostel, holiday centre and community centre for the use of young people and others.
**HOW TO APPLY** Apply in writing to the correspondent.
**WHO TO APPLY TO** Charles Warner, Trustee, Lockskinners Farmhouse, Chiddingstone, Edenbridge, Kent TN8 7NA email johncoldman@benfieldpartners.com

## ■ The Cole Charitable Trust

**CC NO** 264033  **ESTABLISHED** 1972
**WHERE FUNDING CAN BE GIVEN** Greater Birmingham, Kent and Cambridge.
**WHO CAN BENEFIT** Registered charities.
**WHAT IS FUNDED** General charitable purposes, including: social welfare; housing/homelessness; community and environmental

development; opportunities for young people; promotion of improved quality of life; and personal or community empowerment.

**WHAT IS NOT FUNDED** Large building appeals; animal welfare charities; research or further education; individuals.

**TYPE OF GRANT** Small capital or project grants; normally one-off; core costs.

**RANGE OF GRANTS** £300–£1,000, occasionally more.

**SAMPLE GRANTS** Hope Projects (£15,000); Kent Multiple Sclerosis (£3,000); Emmaus – Medway (£2,000); Citizens Advise Bureau Swale and Sittingbourne, Coventry Central Foodbank, Midlands Arts Centre, Samaritans Birmingham and Tiny Tim's Children's Centre (£1,000 each); Carers Sandwell (£800); Rusthall Community and Youth Project (£700); Age UK Bromsgrove and District, Big Brum Theatre in Education, Sandwell Asian Development Association, Scouts Group 1st Bilston, Solihull Action Through Advocacy and West Midlands Disability Swimming Squad (£500 each).

**FINANCES** Year 2013/14 Income £155,111 Grants £72,125 Grants to organisations £72,125 Assets £3,766,499

**TRUSTEES** Andy Cole; George Cole; James Cole; Jont Cole; Tim Cole; Tom Cole; Ann Frewin; Karen Hebron; Ranjit Sondhi.

**OTHER INFORMATION** Grants were made to 90 organisations in 2013/14.

**HOW TO APPLY** Applications should be made on a form available to download from the website, along with guidance and criteria. Application forms should be returned with a one page letter outlining the project and the why the grant is needed. A copy of latest accounts should be attached unless these are not already available to view on the Charity Commission website. The trust prefers to receive applications electronically. The trustees meet to consider applications twice a year usually in April/May and October/November, applications should be received six weeks before the meeting and precise deadlines are available on the website. Applicants will be notified of the outcome in writing within six weeks of the meeting.

**WHO TO APPLY TO** Lise Jackson, PO Box 955, Haslingfield, Cambridge CB23 1WX *Tel.* 01223 871676 *email* thecoletrust@gmail.com *Website* www.colecharitabletrust.org.uk

■ **The Colefax Charitable Trust**

**CC NO** 1017285    **ESTABLISHED** 1993

**WHERE FUNDING CAN BE GIVEN** Hampshire and Berkshire.

**WHO CAN BENEFIT** Registered charities.

**WHAT IS FUNDED** General charitable purposes.

**WHAT IS NOT FUNDED** Individuals.

**SAMPLE GRANTS** A list of beneficiaries was not included in the trust's annual report. **Previous beneficiaries have included:** Church on the Heath, Homestart, Jumbulance, Living Paintings Trust, Newbury District OAP Association, Newbury Spring Festival, Prospect Educational Trust, Reading Voluntary Action, Reliance Cancer Foundation, Southend Residents' Association and Watership Brass.

**FINANCES** Year 2013/14 Income £327,809 Grants £53,703 Grants to organisations £53,703 Assets £13,967,886

**TRUSTEES** J. E. Heath; H. J. Krohn.

**HOW TO APPLY** 'The trustees decide jointly which charitable institutions are to receive donations from the trust. No invitations are sought from eligible institutions.'

**WHO TO APPLY TO** Hans Krohn, Trustee, Westbrook House, St Helens Gardens, The Pitchens, Wroughton, Wiltshire SN4 0RU *Tel.* 01635 200415 *email* newbury@griffins.co.uk

■ **John and Freda Coleman Charitable Trust**

**CC NO** 278223    **ESTABLISHED** 1979

**WHERE FUNDING CAN BE GIVEN** Hampshire and Surrey and surrounding areas.

**WHO CAN BENEFIT** Education and training centres.

**WHAT IS FUNDED** The trust's Charity Commission record aims to provide: 'small grants to organisations helping young people to obtain the skills they need for both work and life. Principal donations are currently directed to organisations in Surrey and Hampshire focused on providing practical training, skills and support where the education system is not enabling young people to reach their full potential.'

**WHAT IS NOT FUNDED** Students.

**TYPE OF GRANT** Loans not given. Grants to 'kick start' relevant projects, capital costs other than buildings and core costs are all considered. Recurrent grants are given.

**RANGE OF GRANTS** Up to £20,000.

**SAMPLE GRANTS** Surrey SATRO (£35,000); Surrey Care Trust (£10,000); Guildford YMCA (£6,000); Reigate and Redhill YMCA and Second Change (£3,000 each); Lifetrain Trust (£1,000); and The Vine Project (£750).

**FINANCES** Year 2013–14 Income £39,194 Grants £66,750 Grants to organisations £66,750

**TRUSTEES** Paul Coleman; Jeanette Bird; Brian Coleman; Nicole Coleman.

**HOW TO APPLY** Apply in writing to the correspondent via post or email. Telephone calls are welcome.

**WHO TO APPLY TO** Jeanette Bird, Trustee, 3 Gasden Drive, Witley, Godalming, Surrey GU8 5QQ *Tel.* 01428 681333 *email* questrum.holdings@gmail.com

■ **The Bernard Coleman Trust**

**CC NO** 1075731    **ESTABLISHED** 1999

**WHERE FUNDING CAN BE GIVEN** Worldwide.

**WHO CAN BENEFIT** Charitable organisations.

**WHAT IS FUNDED** 'The objects of the charity are to provide coaching facilities to young sportsmen and sportswomen and to give donations to other similar sporting charities and grants to sporting clubs and associations. It also makes grants to medical services and to youth projects.'

**RANGE OF GRANTS** £200–£16,000

**SAMPLE GRANTS** Downside Fisher Youth Club, Surrey Cricket Board for The Wisden City Cup (£16,000 each); Arundel Castle Cricket Foundation, the Surrey Care Trust, Royal Hospital for Neuro-disability (£5,000); UCL Hospitals Charitable Foundation (£3,000).

**FINANCES** Year 2013/14 Income £147,521 Grants £112,281 Grants to organisations £112,281 Assets £363,457

**TRUSTEES** Bernard Coleman; Derek Newton; James Fairclough; Michael Courtness; Joyce Coleman.

**HOW TO APPLY** Apply in writing to the correspondent.

**WHO TO APPLY TO** Sheila Stewart, The Secretary, 5 Ravenswood Close, Cobham, Surrey KT11 3AQ *Tel.* 01932 866508 *email* sheilastew@live.co.uk

## ■ The George Henry Collins Charity

**CC NO** 212268  **ESTABLISHED** 1959
**WHERE FUNDING CAN BE GIVEN** Within a 25-mile radius of Birmingham city centre.
**WHO CAN BENEFIT** Local charitable organisations and local branches of registered national charities in Birmingham.
**WHAT IS FUNDED** General charitable purposes, but the relief of illness, infirmity, old age or loneliness take preference.
**WHAT IS NOT FUNDED** Individuals.
**TYPE OF GRANT** One-off project funding.
**RANGE OF GRANTS** Between £250 and £1,000. Most grants were of £500.
**SAMPLE GRANTS** Birmingham St Mary's Hospice (£1,000); St Anne's Hostel (£750); Bishop Latimer United Church, Carrs Lane Counselling, Spinal Injuries Association and Stambermill Scout Group (£500 each); Beanstalk, Sailors Children's Association, Sandwell Asian Development Association and Warwickshire Social Inclusion Partnership (£250 each).
**FINANCES** Year 2013/14 Income £58,825 Grants £49,450 Grants to organisations £49,450 Assets £1,830,132
**TRUSTEES** Anthony Collins; Sally Botteley; Andrew Waters; Roger Otto; Peter Coggan.
**OTHER INFORMATION** Around 100 grants were made in 2013/14.
**HOW TO APPLY** Apply in writing to the correspondent. The trustees usually meet in March, July and November.
**WHO TO APPLY TO** Chrissy Norgrove, Clerk to the Trustees, c/o SGH Martineau LLP, 1 Colmore Square, Birmingham B4 6AA *Tel.* 0870 763 1000 *email* christine.norgrove@sghmartineau.com

## ■ The Sir Jeremiah Colman Gift Trust

**CC NO** 229553  **ESTABLISHED** 1920
**WHERE FUNDING CAN BE GIVEN** UK, with a preference for Hampshire, especially Basingstoke.
**WHO CAN BENEFIT** Projects with well-established needs for support; the trust has already established priority beneficiaries.
**WHAT IS FUNDED** Advancement of education and literary scientific knowledge; moral and social improvement of people; maintenance of churches of the Church of England and gifts and offerings to the churches; financial assistance to past and present employees/members of Sir Jeremiah Colman at Gatton Park or other institutions associated with Sir Jeremiah Colman.
**WHAT IS NOT FUNDED** Individuals requiring support for personal education; individual families for welfare purposes.
**RANGE OF GRANTS** £1,000–£20,000
**SAMPLE GRANTS** The Nehemiah Project (£20,000); Alpha International (£15,000); Northants Medical (£10,000); PACT (£5,500); Depaul Night Stop, St Leonard's – Oakley with Wooton (£5,000 each); Sailors Society (£3,800); Wessex Counselling Service (£3,000); Bible Society; Hope for the Future; The Centre for Social Justice (£2,000 each); Depaul Night Stop, National Autistic Society, Smile Support and Care, Spinal Injuries Association (£1,000).
**FINANCES** Year 2013/14 Income £155,100 Grants £155,700 Grants to organisations £155,700 Assets £6,173,901
**TRUSTEES** Michael Colman; Judith Colman; Oliver Colman; Cynthia Colman; Jeremiah Colman; Sue Colman.
**OTHER INFORMATION** Grants made totalling £155,700, comprised of £63,400 in 'annual donations' 'extra donations' accounted for £2,000; grants to 'new appeals' totalled £45,400; 'long term' grants totalled £43,000.
**HOW TO APPLY** The trust states the unsolicited applications are unwelcome.
**WHO TO APPLY TO** Sir Michael Colman, Malshanger, Basingstoke, Hampshire RG23 7EY *Tel.* 01256 780252

## ■ The Colt Foundation

**CC NO** 277189  **ESTABLISHED** 1978
**WHERE FUNDING CAN BE GIVEN** UK.
**WHO CAN BENEFIT** Universities and research establishments benefitting research workers and students taking higher degrees.
**WHAT IS FUNDED** Research projects at universities and other independent research institutions into occupational and environmental health.
**WHAT IS NOT FUNDED** General funds of another charity; individuals; overseas projects.
**TYPE OF GRANT** Research, project.
**RANGE OF GRANTS** £20,000–£100,000
**SAMPLE GRANTS** University of Edinburgh (£76,000); Deafness Research UK (£68,000); City University (£43,000); University of Oxford (£42,000); University of Southampton (£28,000); Imperial College, Queen University of London (£15,000 each); Royal Society of Medicine (£3,000); Inhaled Particles XI (£3,000); and British Occupational Health Research Foundation (£600).
**FINANCES** Year 2013 Income £507,574 Grants £527,896 Grants to organisations £527,896 Assets £18,042,916
**TRUSTEES** Jerome O'Hea; Claire Gilchrist; Patricia Lebus; Peter O'Hea; Alan O'Hea; Prof. David Coggon; Natasha Heydon; Prof. Sir Anthony Taylor.
**OTHER INFORMATION** Grants were made to 20 organisations in 2013/14.
**HOW TO APPLY** The foundation provided the following information on its website: 'The trustees meet twice a year to review applications, in the spring and in the autumn, and applications normally need to be received at the beginning of April and October to be considered at the meetings. Applicants can submit a single sheet lay summary at any time during the year prior to working on a full application, so that advice can be given on whether the work is likely to fall within the remit of the foundation. The trustees are particularly keen to fund research that is likely to make a difference to government policy or working practices. **What needs to be in an application?** Applications should contain sufficient information for the Scientific Advisers to be able to comment, and should include a lay summary for the trustees' first appraisal. This lay summary is essential as the majority of the trustees do not have a medical or scientific background. This summary will help them in their decision between the different applications under consideration. Applications are not expected to exceed 3,000 words, excluding references, the lay summary and justification of resources. Brief CVs, not exceeding two sides of A4 paper, should be attached for each of the major applicants. Please read the following questions carefully and bear them in mind when preparing your application: what is the work you would like to do? Explain the background and its

relevance for occupational health; explain the specific research question and why it is important; what are you proposing to do to answer the research question? Why do you think this is the right approach? How will it answer the research question? What potential problem (e.g. biases) do you see with this study design, and how will they be addressed?; what do you think will be the potential ultimately to influence policy or practice for the benefit of workers or the wider public? Who else is doing or has done work in the same area, and how will your work complement theirs?; what resources will you need to do the work, and to what extent are these resources already available? How much money do you need to complete the work? You will need to demonstrate that the study is good value for money; who will do the work, and how much time will each of the people, including yourself as PI, involved devote to it?; how long will the work take and when do you plan to start? Applications involving research on people and/or on human tissues must receive the approval of an ethics committee. As a charity, the Colt Foundation will only pay the Directly Incurred Costs of a project, together with some categories of necessary Directly Attributable Costs. Universities are reimbursed by HEFCE for the majority of Directly Attributable and Indirect Costs. In addition to funding, the foundation takes a continuing interest in its research projects and holds annual review meetings. The trustees may appoint an external assessor to report on project progress. Grants are not made to the general funds of other charities, or directly to individuals, or to projects based outside the UK. Details of recent projects supported are shown on the website under 'Projects'. Applicants are advised to visit the foundation's helpful website.

**WHO TO APPLY TO** Jacqueline Douglas, Director, New Lane, Havant, Hampshire PO9 2LY *Tel.* 023 9249 1400 *email* jackie.douglas@uk.coltgroup.com *Website* www.coltfoundation.org.uk

## ■ The Coltstaple Trust

**CC NO** 1085500 **ESTABLISHED** 2001
**WHERE FUNDING CAN BE GIVEN** Worldwide.
**WHO CAN BENEFIT** Charitable organisations.
**WHAT IS FUNDED** The relief of persons in need, poverty or distress in financially developing countries and the relief of people who are homeless or in housing need in the UK or any other part of the world.
**TYPE OF GRANT** Recurrent.
**SAMPLE GRANTS** Oxfam (£150,000); St Mungo's (£30,000); Opportunity International (£80,000); Emmaus UK (£30,000).
**FINANCES** Year 2013/14 *Income* £231,972 *Grants* £290,000 *Grants to organisations* £290,000 *Assets* £5,718,665
**TRUSTEES** Lord Oakeshott of Seagrove Bay; Lord Stoneham of Droxford; Elaine Colville; Dr Philippa Oakeshott.
**HOW TO APPLY** The trustees intend to continue providing grants in a similar way to the recent past while retaining flexibility as to the timing and scale of grants.
**WHO TO APPLY TO** Lord Oakeshott of Seagrove Bay, Trustee, Oakeshott, 2 Queen Anne's Gate Buildings, Dartmouth Street, London SW1H 9BP *Tel.* 020 7647 6701 *email* carolyn.nichols@olimproperty.co.uk

## ■ Colwinston Charitable Trust

**CC NO** 1049189 **ESTABLISHED** 1995
**WHERE FUNDING CAN BE GIVEN** Mostly Wales.
**WHO CAN BENEFIT** UK-registered charities.
**WHAT IS FUNDED** The trustees seek to support charitable organisations working in the fields of opera/music theatre, classical music, and the visual arts. They will also consider specific project proposals for the assistance of libraries and archives. Opera/music theatre – the trust aims to widen the opportunities to enjoy and appreciate performances of opera and music theatre, especially by assisting organisations to develop new audiences for performances of the highest quality; classical music – the trust aims to widen the opportunities to enjoy and to appreciate traditional classical music, and is especially interested to support projects that deliver high quality performances to areas where provision is limited; visual arts – the trust aims to widen the opportunities to enjoy and to be stimulated by the visual arts, to foster creative endeavour and to help develop new audiences; and libraries and archives – the trust will consider applications for specific projects but are unlikely to support capital projects. 'The trust is especially interested in *exceptional* projects that demonstrate *excellence* in terms of the creative ambition of the project, the quality of the artistic product, the calibre of the participating artists, and the value of the artistic experience for audiences and/or participants.'
**WHAT IS NOT FUNDED** Retrospective funding; non-registered charities.
**RANGE OF GRANTS** Generally grants up to £50,000. Majority in the range of £5,000 to £15,000.
**SAMPLE GRANTS** Welsh National Opera (£165,000); Gregynog Festival (£60,000); Mousetrap Productions Ltd (£54,000); The Aloud Charity and Artes Mundi (£50,000 each); Mid Wales Opera (£45,000); National Museum Wales (£30,000); Llandaff Cathedral (£25,000); Paintings in Hospitals (£20,000); Arts & Business Cymru (£10,000); Oriel Davies Gallery (£10,000); Presteigne Festival of Music and the Arts (£7,500); Young Musicians of Dyfed (£5,000); Musicfest Aberystwyth (£2,500).
**FINANCES** Year 2013/14 *Income* £605,109 *Grants* £558,900 *Grants to organisations* £558,900 *Assets* £1,489,993
**TRUSTEES** Mathew Prichard; Robert Maskrey; Martin Tinney; Sian Williams.
**OTHER INFORMATION** The trust derives its income from the royalties from the West End production of *The Mousetrap*, the Agatha Christie play, which opened in 1952.
**HOW TO APPLY** Full and detailed guidelines and an application form are available on the trust's website. 'In the first instance, and prior to sending any application to the trust, organisations should make contact with the Consultant Director, preferably by email, supplying a brief summary of the project and indicating the grant level being sought.' The trustees meet twice yearly (usually March and November) to consider applications and to make decisions on grants.
**WHO TO APPLY TO** Christopher Bliss, c/o Rawlinson and Hunter, 8th Floor, 6 New Street Square, London EC4A 3AQ *Tel.* 020 7842 2000 *email* colwinston.trust@ntlworld.com *Website* www.colwinston.org.uk

## ■ Colyer-Fergusson Charitable Trust

**CC NO** 258958  **ESTABLISHED** 1969
**WHERE FUNDING CAN BE GIVEN** Kent.
**WHO CAN BENEFIT** Registered charities
**WHAT IS FUNDED** Social welfare and education of young people.
**WHAT IS NOT FUNDED** The trust only funds projects that meet its funding policies. Applications will only be considered if they have a strong focus on meeting the needs of 'young people with poverty of opportunity'. The trustees cannot support applications from: Individuals – unless they are made via one of the trust's referral partners as part of its 'Hardship Awards' programme; national charities receiving widespread support; statutory bodies; hospitals and health authorities; medical care, medical equipment or medical research; academic research, scholarships or bursaries; animal charities; the promotion of religion; The restoration or conservation of buildings; work outside Kent; endowment appeals; work that has already taken place i.e. retrospective funding; round-robin, widely circulated appeals
**TYPE OF GRANT** One-off, recurring, capital, core, running and start-up costs will all be considered, as will salaries, buildings, project and research costs. Funding may be given for up to three years.
**RANGE OF GRANTS** Up to £40,000.
**SAMPLE GRANTS** Kent Community Foundation (£40,000); KWES Kent Woodland Employment Scheme, Tilmanstone Miners Welfare Institute and Recreation Ground (£20,000 each); Swale Action To End Domestic Abuse, Church in Hope Street (£15,000 each); Strood Community Project (£12,500); Shoreham Village School Fund (£10,000); Ashford Counselling Service (£9,100); Catching Lives (£8,000).
**FINANCES** Year 2013/14 Income £462,460 Grants £264,338 Grants to organisations £264,338 Assets £18,852,139
**TRUSTEES** Nicholas Fisher; Robert North; Ruth Murphy; Rosalind Riley; James Thorne; Barbara Long.
**OTHER INFORMATION** The 2013/14 grant total includes the 'Trustees Discretionary Awards' comprising 19 grants, totalling £33,500. The total is also inclusive of 42 'Hardship Awards' totalling £16,242.
**HOW TO APPLY** Full guidance and application forms are available on the trust's website.
**WHO TO APPLY TO** Colyer Fergusson, Hogarth House, 34 Paradise Road, Richmond, Surrey TW9 1SE Tel. 020 8948 3388 email grantadmin@cfct.org.uk Website www.cfct.org.uk

## ■ Comic Relief

**CC NO** 326568  **ESTABLISHED** 1985
**WHERE FUNDING CAN BE GIVEN** UK and overseas (mainly sub-Saharan Africa).
**WHO CAN BENEFIT** UK-registered charities; voluntary organisations; self-help groups.
**WHAT IS FUNDED** The charity's UK and international grant-making strategy is based on five themes. **Better Futures:** improving the lives of vulnerable young people in the UK, and enabling some of the world's poorest people to gain access to vital services such as health and education; **Healthier Finances:** tackling financial poverty, and enabling economic resilience in families and communities, as well as supporting enterprise and employment; **Safer Lives:** reducing violence, abuse and exploitation; **Stronger Communities:** empowering people, organisations and networks to play an effective role in their communities and society, as well as nurturing talent and leadership; **Fairer Society:** helping people overcome inequality and have a say in decisions that affect their lives, whoever and wherever they are.
**WHAT IS NOT FUNDED** Individuals; medical research or hospitals; churches or other religious bodies where the monies will be used for religious purposes; work where there is statutory responsibility to provide funding; projects where the work has already taken place; statutory bodies, such as local authorities or Primary Care Trusts or organisations seeking funding to replace cuts by statutory bodies; profit-making organisations, except social enterprises; organisations who hold free reserves equivalent to the amount applied for may be turned down. The charity is also unable to fund minibuses.
**TYPE OF GRANT** Capital or revenue. One-off or spread over up to three years.
**RANGE OF GRANTS** Grants average between £25,000 and £40,000, and rarely exceed this upper limit.
**FINANCES** Year 2013/14 Income £84,424,000 Grants £84,604,000 Grants to organisations £84,604,000 Assets £113,415,000
**TRUSTEES** Michael Harris; Colin Howes; Sir Lenny Henry; Richard Curtis; Timothy Davie; Theo Sowa; Harry Cayton; Daniel Cohen; Diana Barran; Tristia Clarke; Priscilla Snowball; Suzi Aplin; Robert Webb; Peter Salmon; Saul Klein.
**PUBLICATIONS** Essential Information for applicants; Grants Strategy.
**OTHER INFORMATION** The grant total includes £27.6 million in UK grants and £57 million in international grants.
**HOW TO APPLY** Applications are made online via the charity's website, where full guidance is also provided. Potential applicants must register and complete Stage 1 of the process, an initial proposal. Applicants are shortlisted from those successfully completing Stage 1.
**WHO TO APPLY TO** Judith McNeill, Grants Director, 1st Floor, 89 Albert Embankment, London SE1 7TP Tel. 020 7820 2000 email ukgrants@comicrelief.com Website www.comicrelief.com

## ■ The Comino Foundation

**CC NO** 312875  **ESTABLISHED** 1971
**WHERE FUNDING CAN BE GIVEN** UK.
**WHO CAN BENEFIT** Organisations benefitting young adults and academics.
**WHAT IS FUNDED** Support of educational activities which encourage and enable individuals and groups to motivate and empower themselves, progressively develop their potential for the benefit of themselves and others, and encourage a culture which affirms and celebrates both achievement and responsible practice in industry and commerce.
**WHAT IS NOT FUNDED** The foundation currently gives consideration only to grant applications that provide evidence showing that the new proposal will have an extremely close fit to existing work. It has a wide range of established longer-term funding commitments and has limited capacity to make further grants. It does not fund any research or activities.
**TYPE OF GRANT** One-off.
**RANGE OF GRANTS** Up to 56,000.
**SAMPLE GRANTS** Ideas Foundation (£56,000); RSA Tipton Academy (£50,000); Potential Plus UK (£41,000); Local Solutions – Liverpool (£35,000); Sheffield Hallam University

(£16,000); Potential Trust (£12,000); Enabling Enterprise (£5,000); The Army Cadet Force Association, Foundation for Science and Technology (£3,000 each).

**FINANCES** Year 2013/14 Income £232,454 Grants £509,568 Grants to organisations £509,568 Assets £4,243,115

**TRUSTEES** Mrs A. Comino-James; David Perry; James Westhead.

**OTHER INFORMATION** The trust meets these aims through its patented GRASP approach, which offers a structure for thinking in a results-driven manner through a greater pattern, design and method of thinking. Most of the funds are given towards centres which promote the GRASP approach. Further information on this can be gathered from a leaflet prepared from the trust or on their extensive website.

**HOW TO APPLY** All funding proposals and applications should be sent to the correspondent. A detailed account of how to apply is available on the foundation's website.

**WHO TO APPLY TO** Anthony Derbyshire, Correspondent, c/o Firs House, Bilby, Retford, Nottinghamshire DN22 8JB Tel. 01777 711141 email anthony.darbyshire@cominofoundation. org.uk Website www.cominofoundation.org.uk

■ **Community First (Landfill Communities Fund)**

**CC NO** 288117 **ESTABLISHED** 1983

**WHERE FUNDING CAN BE GIVEN** Wiltshire and Swindon

**WHO CAN BENEFIT** Charities; community organisations; parish or town councils.

**WHAT IS FUNDED** Community, built heritage and environmental projects in the vicinity of landfill sites and / or landfill operator depots.

**WHAT IS NOT FUNDED** If you wish to apply for a Landfill Communities Fund grant, your project will need to find 11.386% of the total grant applied for from a contributing Third Party (a source other than LCF money or the applicant). See document below on contributing third parties.

**TYPE OF GRANT** Project costs.

**RANGE OF GRANTS** Up to £60,000.

**SAMPLE GRANTS** Marlborough Golf Club (£60,000); Swindon Old Town Community Centre (£50,000); Wiltshire Music Centre (£36,000); Kintbury Skate Park (£29,500); Purton Institute and Village Hall (£18,500); Burbage and Easton Royal Cricket Club, Mere Skate Park (£15,000 each); Archaeology of Wessex Gallery (£10,000).

**FINANCES** Year 2013/14 Income £2,303,448 Grants £510,466 Grants to organisations £510,466 Assets £1,497,784

**TRUSTEES** Jane James; Piers Dibbin; Dr Martin Hamer; Brian Clake; Edward Heard; Jane Rowell; Geraldine McKibbin; Anthony Pooley; Peter Duke.

**OTHER INFORMATION** in 2013/14 nine grants were provided for 'Community Transport Development Grants' (£21,400); forty-seven grants were paid to 'Landfill Communities Fund Grants' (£510,466).

**HOW TO APPLY** In the first instance download and complete the expression of interest form from the website then email to grants@communityfirst.org.uk. If you have been advised that your project is eligible for LCF funding, then download and complete the application form from the website and submit with supporting documents as specified in the form.

**WHO TO APPLY TO** Community First, Unit C2 Brecon Business Centre, Hopton Park, Devizes, Wiltshire SN10 2EY Tel. 01380 722475 email reception@communityfirst.org.uk Website www.communityfirst.org.uk

■ **Community Foundation for Leeds**

**CC NO** 1096892 **ESTABLISHED** 2005

**WHERE FUNDING CAN BE GIVEN** Leeds.

**WHO CAN BENEFIT** Community and voluntary groups; registered charities; not-for-profit organisations; social enterprises. Priority is given to 'groups that benefit people living in economically or socially deprived areas of Leeds, and/or those supporting vulnerable groups'.

**WHAT IS FUNDED** General charitable purposes; social welfare; community work.

**WHAT IS NOT FUNDED** Projects that have already taken place; projects where there is statutory responsibility to provide funding; deficit funding (direct replacement of statutory obligation or public funding or repayment of loans); projects primarily for the advancement of religion or politics; projects from regional or local offices of a national organisation (unless you can show that you are independently managed); small contributions towards larger appeals; profit-making organisations (except social enterprises); animals (The Mars Fund will support animal welfare projects) or plants, unless the project directly benefits people; applications for the benefit of an individual (other than for the Ideas that Change Lives and Looked After Children programmes); research projects; overseas work and travel; groups that have had a previous grant which has not been managed satisfactorily; projects outside Leeds apart from grants made via the Bradford District Community Fund or Henry Smith Charity; sponsorship, fundraising events or advertising; large national charities except for independent local branches working for local people.

**TYPE OF GRANT** Capital and core costs.

**RANGE OF GRANTS** Usually from below £1,000 to £50,000.

**SAMPLE GRANTS** Grants were made from the following funds: Jimbo's (£1.2 million); The Henry Smith Charity (£1.2 million); Sport Relief (£196,000); Transition Fund (£138,000); Leeds Winter Fuel (£54,000); Local Giving Grants (£24,000); Ideas That Change Lives (£20,000); Leeds Tradesmen's Trust (£19,000); Grassroots Grants (£16,000).

**FINANCES** Year 2013/14 Income £2,794,000 Grants £3,208,000 Grants to organisations £3,208,000 Assets £20,454,000

**TRUSTEES** Andrew Wriglesworth; Rachel Hannan; Steve Rogers; Helen Thomson; Jonathan Morgan; Catherine Mahoney; Hanif Malik; Martin Allison.

**OTHER INFORMATION** The foundation runs a number of grant schemes that change frequently. Consult the foundation's website for details of current programmes and their deadlines. Each scheme tends to have a different criteria and size of award. The exclusions listed are given as general areas where the foundation cannot provide help. A total of 511 grants were made to approximately 393 community groups and charities.

**HOW TO APPLY** The foundation's website has full details of grant schemes currently administered and the application procedure. Most applications should now be made using an

online system. Alternative arrangements can be made upon request at grants@leedscf.org.uk.
**WHO TO APPLY TO** Carlos Chavez, Grants and Community Manager, 1st Floor, 51A St Paul's Street, Leeds LS1 2TE *Tel.* 0113 242 2426 *email* sally-anne@leedscf.org.uk *Website* www.leedscf.org.uk

## ■ The Compton Charitable Trust
**CC NO** 280404        **ESTABLISHED** 1980
**WHERE FUNDING CAN BE GIVEN** Northamptonshire.
**WHO CAN BENEFIT** Charitable organisations, with a preference for those with a connection to the family estates of the Marquess of Northampton as well as those which the Marquess is a patron of.
**WHAT IS FUNDED** General charitable purposes.
**RANGE OF GRANTS** £200–£3,000
**SAMPLE GRANTS** Oxhill Church (£3,000); Castle Ashby PCC (£1,500); Grand Charity (£1,300); Royal British Legion, Poppy Appeal (£200).
**FINANCES** *Year* 2013/14 *Income* £184,072 *Grants* £5,950 *Grants to organisations* £5,950 *Assets* £615,001
**TRUSTEES** Marquess of Northampton; Lady Pamela Northampton; Earl Daniel Compton.
**OTHER INFORMATION** 'The amount paid out in grants is lower than Trust's total income for the year, following the receipt of a claim made for Gift Aid during the year.' Income prior to Gift Aid was £2,118 for 2013/14. While the expenditure in 2013/14 was lower than usual, over the previous four years grants to organisations totalled an average of £212,000 (£320,000 – 2012/13).
**HOW TO APPLY** Apply in writing to the correspondent. Unsolicited applications are considered, but are usually unsuccessful.
**WHO TO APPLY TO** The Trustees, Rathbone Trust Company Limited, 4th Floor, 1 Curzon Street, London W1J 5FB *Tel.* 020 7399 0000

## ■ The Douglas Compton James Charitable Trust
**CC NO** 1091125        **ESTABLISHED** 2002
**WHERE FUNDING CAN BE GIVEN** Northamptonshire.
**WHO CAN BENEFIT** Registered charities. Some preference is given for Masonic charities.
**WHAT IS FUNDED** General charitable purposes; education; social welfare.
**TYPE OF GRANT** One-off and recurrent.
**RANGE OF GRANTS** Up to £27,000.
**SAMPLE GRANTS** *Previous beneficiaries have included:* Provincial Grand Charity (£27,000); NHS Bedford Hospital (£12,000); Corby Women's Centre (£9,100); Lakeland Day Care Hospice and Cransley Hospital (£5,000 each); Kettering General Hospital Charity Fund and Newton in the Willows (£3,000 each); and Life Education Northamptonshire Limited, Wellingborough All Saints Scouts, Lakeland Day Care Hospice and Deafblind UK (£2,000 each).
**FINANCES** *Year* 2013/14 *Income* £105,186 *Grants* £131,238 *Grants to organisations* £131,238 *Assets* £5,155,100
**TRUSTEES** Ian Clarke; John Humphrey; Richard Ongley.
**OTHER INFORMATION** A list of individual beneficiaries was absent from the trustees report for 2013/14.
**HOW TO APPLY** Apply in writing to the correspondent.
**WHO TO APPLY TO** Louise Davies, Montague House, Chancery Lane, Thrapston, Northamptonshire NN14 4LN *Tel.* 01832 732161 *email* louise.davies@vshlaw.co.uk

## ■ The Congleton Inclosure Trust
**CC NO** 244136        **ESTABLISHED** 1795
**WHERE FUNDING CAN BE GIVEN** The town of Congleton and the parishes of Hulme Walfield and Newbold with Astbury.
**WHO CAN BENEFIT** Local organisations; UK organisations with projects in the area.
**WHAT IS FUNDED** The relief of poverty or sickness; the provision of support for recreational, leisure or educational facilities; charitable purposes which are helpful to residents in the area.
**WHAT IS NOT FUNDED** Individuals outside the beneficial area; organisations not benefitting exclusively the people in the area of benefit.
**TYPE OF GRANT** Buildings, capital, core costs, feasibility studies, salaries and start-up costs will be considered. Funding may be given for up to one year.
**RANGE OF GRANTS** Up to £7,000.
**SAMPLE GRANTS** St Mary's Primary School (£7,000); Ruby's Fund (5,500) Crossroads Care (£2,500); Astbury Mere Trust and Congleton Community Projects (£2,000 each); Dane Valley Swimming Club (£1,000); and Electric Picture House (£150).
**FINANCES** *Year* 2013 *Income* £59,725 *Grants* £68,490 *Grants to organisations* £68,490 *Assets* £2,129,454
**TRUSTEES** Kenneth Wainwright; John Beardmore; Janet Goodier; Revd Canon David Taylor; David Boon; Revd Jonathan Sharples; John Davies; Peter Boon; Douglas Gibbons; John Hulse; David Newman; Janet Hollins.
**OTHER INFORMATION** The trust is willing to provide funding for core costs and capital costs.
**HOW TO APPLY** Application forms are available from the correspondent. The trustees meet in January, April, July and October. Applications should be submitted by the first day of the month in which the trustees meet.
**WHO TO APPLY TO** Jo Money, Clerk, PO Box 138, Congleton, Cheshire CW12 3SZ *Tel.* 01260 273180 *email* info@congletoninclosuretrust.org.uk *Website* www.congletoninclosuretrust.org.uk

## ■ The Congregational & General Charitable Trust
**CC NO** 297013        **ESTABLISHED** 1987
**WHERE FUNDING CAN BE GIVEN** UK.
**WHO CAN BENEFIT** Protestant churches and community projects, in particular those associated with United Reformed and Congregational denominations.
**WHAT IS FUNDED** Funds for building or property projects to churches and charities of the United Reformed and Congregational denominations or other Protestant churches; church community projects seeking funding towards their capital costs.
**TYPE OF GRANT** One-off for property projects and capital costs.
**RANGE OF GRANTS** £1,000–£10,000
**SAMPLE GRANTS** Details of grant recipients were not included in the accounts.
**FINANCES** *Year* 2013 *Income* £963,000 *Grants* £142,000 *Grants to organisations* £142,000 *Assets* £24,296,000
**TRUSTEES** Revd Arnold Harrison; Robert Wade; Margaret Atkinson; Robert Copleton; Revd

William Adams; Revd Pamela Ward; Stephen Wood; Stuart Young; Gordon Pullan.
**OTHER INFORMATION** The trust's accounts provide financial details for the nine-month period until 31 December 2013. Additional figures are given for the following three months (grants totalled £73,000). The website suggests that 37 awards were made in 2013.
**HOW TO APPLY** Applications should be made using a form which can be downloaded from the trust's website. 'The website notes: 'When sending your application please attach any supporting documentation – such as your church's or organisation's accounts, the project's accounts, appeal leaflets or project literature – along with your signed application form.' The closing dates for applications are 31 January and 31 July each year.
**WHO TO APPLY TO** Julie Porter, Trust Administrator, c/o Congregational & General Insurance, Currer House, Currer Street, Bradford BD1 5BA *Tel.* 01274 700700 *email* trust@congregational.co.uk *Website* www.congregational.co.uk

## ■ Martin Connell Charitable Trust
**SC NO** SC009842      **ESTABLISHED** 1972
**WHERE FUNDING CAN BE GIVEN** Scotland.
**WHO CAN BENEFIT** Scottish-based local charities.
**WHAT IS FUNDED** General charitable purposes.
**WHAT IS NOT FUNDED** Individuals.
**FINANCES** *Year* 2013/14 *Income* £283,679 *Grants* £307,000 *Grants to organisations* £307,000
**HOW TO APPLY** Apply in writing to the correspondent.
**WHO TO APPLY TO** The Trustees, Maclay Murray and Spens LLP, 1 George Square, Glasgow G2 1AL *Tel.* 0330 222 0050

## ■ The Conservation Foundation
**CC NO** 284656      **ESTABLISHED** 1982
**WHERE FUNDING CAN BE GIVEN** Throughout the UK and overseas projects.
**WHO CAN BENEFIT** Individuals and organisations involved in environmental and conservation projects throughout the UK and overseas.
**WHAT IS FUNDED** Creation, management and support towards environmental and conservation orientated projects.
**RANGE OF GRANTS** £150–£1,500
**SAMPLE GRANTS** A list of specific beneficiaries was not given in the accounts; however, as the funder's website provides, the following currently operating projects are sponsored: Wessex Watermarks Awards (ranging from £150 to £1,500), Young Scientists for rainforests (grants in the range of £1,000).
**FINANCES** *Year* 2013/14 *Income* £185,301 *Grants* £120,730 *Grants to organisations* £120,730 *Assets* £229,757
**TRUSTEES** David Shreeve; William Moloney; Prof. David Bellamy; Libby Kinmonth; Lindsay Dunn; Dorothy Harris.
**OTHER INFORMATION** Information about the foundation's current projects can be found on its website.
**HOW TO APPLY** Application details for specific awards are outlined on the foundation's website. General enquiries can also be directed to the correspondent.

**WHO TO APPLY TO** William Moloney, Trustee, 1 Kensington Gore, London SW7 2AR *Tel.* 020 7591 3111 *Fax* 020 7591 3110 *email* info@conservationfoundation.co.uk *Website* www.conservationfoundation.co.uk

## ■ The Consolidated Charities for the Infirm – Merchant Taylors' Company
**CC NO** 214266      **ESTABLISHED** 1960
**WHERE FUNDING CAN BE GIVEN** Lewisham, Southwark, Tower Hamlets, Hackney and environs; occasionally Greater London. National grants made in exceptional cases.
**WHO CAN BENEFIT** Charitable organisations.
**WHAT IS FUNDED** Relief of need; people with disabilities; infirm, older people and children; sheltered housing and residential care homes. Preference is given to work taking place in, or benefitting the people of, the London Boroughs of Lewisham; Southwark; Tower Hamlets; Hackney; and their environs, and, more occasionally, elsewhere in Greater London. Exceptionally, work which is national in scope may receive funding, especially where it benefits members or ex-members of Her Majesty's Armed Forces, or has some connection to tailoring or clothing.
**WHAT IS NOT FUNDED** As a matter of policy, the trustees do not usually contribute to: 'Bricks and mortar', although they will consider contributing to the fitting out or refurbishment of new or existing buildings; medical research; funds for 'on-granting' to third-party charities or individuals; generalised appeals; very large charities, except occasionally in support of localised work in the trustees' geographical area of interest; Individual applicants.
**RANGE OF GRANTS** £2,000–£72,000
**SAMPLE GRANTS** Ranyard Charitable Trust (£72,000); Crossroads Greenwich and Lewisham (£40,000); Jubilee Sailing Trust (£25,000); Body and Soul (£18,700); Mudchute City Farm (£15,000); Bellingham Community Project (£10,000); Calibre Audio Library, Cure Parkinson's (£5,000 each); First Aid Nursing Yeomanry, Quaker Social Action (£3,000 each) Place2Be (£2,000)
**FINANCES** *Year* 2013 *Income* £486,595 *Grants* £555,131 *Grants to organisations* £555,131 *Assets* £11,523,602
**TRUSTEES** Johnny Armstrong; Duncan Eggar; Peter Magill; Rupert Bull; Simon Bass.
**HOW TO APPLY** Apply via a form available to download, together with criteria and guidelines, from the website. The charity states that emailed enquiries are preferred and responded to quickest.
**WHO TO APPLY TO** David Atkinson, Merchant Taylors' Hall, 30 Threadneedle Street, London EC2R 8JB *Tel.* 020 7450 4440 *email* DAtkinson@merchant-taylors.co.uk *Website* www.merchant-taylors.co.uk

## ■ Gordon Cook Foundation
**SC NO** SC017455      **ESTABLISHED** 1974
**WHERE FUNDING CAN BE GIVEN** UK.
**WHO CAN BENEFIT** National curriculum agencies in the four home nations; Local Education Authorities; universities; colleges; schools and clusters of schools; voluntary organisations.
**WHAT IS FUNDED** The foundation is dedicated to the advancement of all aspects of education and

training which are likely to promote character development and citizenship. In recent years the foundation has adopted the term 'values education' to denote the wide range of activity it seeks to support. More details are available from the website.

**WHAT IS NOT FUNDED** Individuals are unlikely to be funded.

**TYPE OF GRANT** One-off and recurring for projects and research. Funding may be given for more than three years.

**RANGE OF GRANTS** In previous years, between £5,000 and £15,000.

**SAMPLE GRANTS Previous beneficiaries have included:** Tan Dance (£15,000); Five Nations (£9,000); and R.H.E.T and Association of Directors Education in Scotland (£5,000 each).

**FINANCES** Year 2013/14 Income £297,842 Grants £388,370 Grants to organisations £388,370

**TRUSTEES** Anne Harper; David Adams; Gavin Ross; Dr D. Sutherland; James Anderson.

**HOW TO APPLY** The foundation's website states that it operates a pro-active grant-making policy and actively seeks partnerships with other charities in order to develop its mission. The foundation does not normally invite or respond to unsolicited applications.

**WHO TO APPLY TO** The Foundation Secretary, 3 Chattan Place, Aberdeen AB10 6RB Tel. 01224 571010 email gordoncook@btconnect.com Website www.gordoncook.org

## ■ The Ernest Cook Trust

**CC NO** 1146629      **ESTABLISHED** 1952
**WHERE FUNDING CAN BE GIVEN** UK

**WHO CAN BENEFIT** Charitable or not-for-profit organisations working through education or training.

**WHAT IS FUNDED** Grants are given for educational work only, focusing on children and young people in the fields of countryside and environment, the arts, science and literacy and numeracy.

**WHAT IS NOT FUNDED** Applicants must represent either registered charities or not-for-profit organisations. Grants are normally awarded on an annual basis and will not be awarded retrospectively. Grants are not made to pre-school groups; individuals; agricultural colleges; independent schools or local authorities; for building work; infrastructure or refurbishment work; for youth work; social support; therapy and medical treatment; including projects using the arts; environment or literacy and numeracy for these purposes; for projects related to sports; outward bound type activities or recreation; for overseas projects; for wildlife trusts and for farming and wildlife advisory groups other than those which are based in counties in which the ECT owns land (Buckinghamshire, Dorset, Gloucestershire, Leicestershire and Oxfordshire).

**TYPE OF GRANT** Conditional; annual; one-off. Project; research; salaries; and start-up costs. Funding may be given for up to three years.

**RANGE OF GRANTS** £1,000–£10,000

**SAMPLE GRANTS** Canterbury Cathedral and Opera North (£10,000 each); Watts Gallery (£8,000); Conservation Volunteers Northern Ireland (£7,000); Edward Peake Middle School (£5,000); Read for Life CIC (£4,000); and Making Places (£2,000).

**FINANCES** Year 2013/14 Income £4,029,851 Grants £1,800,050 Grants to organisations £1,800,050 Assets £130,435,307

**TRUSTEE** This charity has been given a dispensation by the Charity Commission from publishing the names of its trustees.

**HOW TO APPLY** The ECT aims to have a 'light-touch' application process with a view to enabling small regional or local organisations to apply for support. All applicant organisations must be based and working in the UK and should be either state schools, registered charities or other recognised not-for-profit organisations. It is very important, however, to read the list of restrictions below before applying. There are no application forms. All applicants are asked to post a covering letter on the official headed paper of the applicant organisation (letters from schools must be signed by the headteacher) and also include: up to two additional sheets of A4 describing the organisation, outlining the project and specifying its educational elements and the way in which it fits in with the interests of the ECT; a simple budget for the project, outlining the way in which the grant would be spent; a list of any other funding applications; the latest annual report and accounts for the organisation (schools are not required to send one) Do not send further supporting material or e-mail applications, which are not accepted.

**WHO TO APPLY TO** The Trustees, Fairford Park, Fairford, Gloucestershire GL7 4JH Tel. 01285 712492 email admin@ernestcooktrust.org.uk Website www.ernestcooktrust.org.uk

## ■ The Cooks Charity

**CC NO** 297913      **ESTABLISHED** 1987
**WHERE FUNDING CAN BE GIVEN** UK, especially City of London.

**WHO CAN BENEFIT** Charities and individuals within the City of London

**WHAT IS FUNDED** Projects concerned with catering.

**WHAT IS NOT FUNDED** Individuals. Applicants outside the City of London (except in exceptional circumstances, when close proximity to London is required.)

**RANGE OF GRANTS** £500 to £65,000.

**SAMPLE GRANTS** Academy of Culinary Arts (£65,000); Springboard and FareShare (£25,000 each); Hackney Community College (£24,000); Treloar Trust, Jamie Oliver Foundation and Bridge Project (£15,000 each); The Worshipful Company of Cooks of London Apprenticeship Programme (£8,800); Crisis Skylight Cafe (£3,500); SSAFA (£500).

**FINANCES** Year 2013/14 Income £194,988 Grants £196,720 Grants to organisations £196,720 Assets £4,942,129

**TRUSTEES** Peter Wright, Bev Puxley; Oliver Goodinge.

**HOW TO APPLY** Apply in writing to the correspondent. Applications are considered in spring and autumn. 'When making awards to individuals, the Trustees are required to take into account the financial means of the beneficiaries and their parents or guardians.'

**WHO TO APPLY TO** Peter Wilkinson, Correspondent, 18 Solent Drive, Warsash, Southampton SO31 9HB email clerk@cookslivery.org.uk Website www.cookslivery.org.uk

## ■ The Catherine Cookson Charitable Trust

**CC NO** 272895     **ESTABLISHED** 1977

**WHERE FUNDING CAN BE GIVEN** UK, with some preference for the North East of England.

**WHO CAN BENEFIT** Charitable organisations, including those benefitting children and young people, individuals with disabilities and older people.

**WHAT IS FUNDED** General charitable purposes, including: education; advancement of religion; environment and animals; arts and culture; health.

**RANGE OF GRANTS** Mostly £1,000 or less. A few large grants are made.

**SAMPLE GRANTS** Larger grant beneficiaries included: Live Theatre Limited (£200,000); Cancer Research UK (£100,000); Percy Hedley Foundation (£75,000); Dame Allan's School (£70,000); Bubble Appeal (£50,000); Jesmond Library (£25,000); Derwenthaugh Boat Station and St Michael's Hospice (£20,000 each); Alzheimer's Research UK and Wildfowl and Wetlands Trust (£5,000 each). Smaller grant beneficiaries included: Seaton Sluice Community Association and St Paul's Church – Branxton (£2,000 each); Clowns in the Sky and Kelly Hendry School of Irish Dancing (£1,500 each); Lewin of Greenwich Organisation, Muscular Dystrophy Campaign and Northumbria Blood Bikes (£1,000 each); Wavelength Charity Ltd (£600); Hexham Book Festival and Samaritans (£500 each); Bringing Words to Life Ltd and Huntington's Disease Association (£250 each); Northern Ballet Leeds (£200); Burniston and Clough Village Hall and St Luke's Hospice Plymouth (£100 each).

**FINANCES** Year 2013/14 Income £1,159,145 Grants £974,510 Grants to organisations £974,510 Assets £28,249,361

**TRUSTEES** Peter Magnay; David Hawkins; Hugo Marshall; Jack Ravenscroft; Daniel Sallows.

**OTHER INFORMATION** There were a total of 184 awards made.

**HOW TO APPLY** Applications can be made in writing to the correspondent.

**WHO TO APPLY TO** Peter Magnay, Trustee, Thomas Magnay and Co, 8 St Mary's Green, Whickham, Newcastle upon Tyne NE16 4DN *Tel.* 0191 488 7159 *email* enquiries@thomasmagnay.co.uk

## ■ Harold and Daphne Cooper Charitable Trust

**CC NO** 206772     **ESTABLISHED** 1962

**WHERE FUNDING CAN BE GIVEN** UK.

**WHO CAN BENEFIT** National charities.

**WHAT IS FUNDED** Medical research, health and Jewish charities.

**WHAT IS NOT FUNDED** Individuals.

**TYPE OF GRANT** Small one-off grants and ongoing support for capital (buildings considered), project and research. Core costs and running costs are considered.

**SAMPLE GRANTS** Jewish Care (£45,000); Action Against Cancer (£20,000); and Macmillan Cancer Support (£5,000).

**FINANCES** Year 2013/14 Income £83,278 Grants £62,000 Grants to organisations £62,000 Assets £2,698,376

**TRUSTEES** Judith Portrait; Timothy Roter; Abigail Roter; Dominic Roter.

**HOW TO APPLY** Apply in writing to the correspondent; applications are not acknowledged.

**WHO TO APPLY TO** Alison Burton, Trust Administrator, c/o Portrait Solicitors, 21 Whitefriars Street, London EC4Y 8JJ *Tel.* 020 7092 6984 *email* alison.burton@portraitsolicitors.com

## ■ Mabel Cooper Charity

**CC NO** 264621     **ESTABLISHED** 1972

**WHERE FUNDING CAN BE GIVEN** UK, with a possible interest in South Devon.

**WHO CAN BENEFIT** Registered charities.

**WHAT IS FUNDED** General charitable purposes. Preference is given to projects with low overheads.

**WHAT IS NOT FUNDED** Individuals.

**RANGE OF GRANTS** £5,000–£10,000

**SAMPLE GRANTS** Devon Air Ambulance (£10,000); Alzheimer's Research UK, Crisis, Cancer Research, Macmillan Cancer Support, St Luke's Hospice and St Peter's Hospice (£5,000 each); Rowcroft House Foundation, Salvation Army, and Shelter (£2,500 each); CLIC Sargent and Future Trees Trust (£1,000 each).

**FINANCES** Year 2013/14 Income £90,509 Grants £71,000 Grants to organisations £71,000 Assets £3,680,872

**TRUSTEES** Alison Barrett; Joan Harbottle; Ian Harbottle; David John Harbottle.

**OTHER INFORMATION** Grants were awarded to 18 organisations.

**HOW TO APPLY** The trustees state that they do not welcome, or reply to, unsolicited applications.

**WHO TO APPLY TO** Ian Harbottle, Trustee, Middle Manor, Lascot Hill, Wedmore BS28 4AF *Tel.* 01934 712102

## ■ The Alice Ellen Cooper Dean Charitable Foundation

**CC NO** 273298     **ESTABLISHED** 1977

**WHERE FUNDING CAN BE GIVEN** Worldwide, with a preference for UK charities in Dorset and west Hampshire.

**WHO CAN BENEFIT** Registered charities.

**WHAT IS FUNDED** Health; humanitarian causes; social disadvantage; education; religion; community; arts and culture; amateur sport; disability.

**WHAT IS NOT FUNDED** Individuals; non-UK-registered charitable entities.

**TYPE OF GRANT** One-off and recurring.

**RANGE OF GRANTS** £1,000–£60,000

**SAMPLE GRANTS** Sheltered Work Opportunities Project (£60,000); British Red Cross – South Sudan Crisis Appeal (£25,000) Age UK Dorchester (£10,000); Contact the Elderly (£7,500); Christ Church Creekmoor (£6,000); The Alcohol Education Trust (£5,000); Widehorizons Outdoor Education Trust (£4,000); Epilepsy Society (£3,000); Clothing Solutions for Disabled People (£2,000); The Douglas Bader Foundation (£1,000).

**FINANCES** Year 2013/14 Income £1,076,512 Grants £850,000 Grants to organisations £850,000 Assets £27,277,897

**TRUSTEES** John Bowditch; Linda Bowditch; Rupert Edwards; Douglas Neville-Jones; Emma Blackburn.

**HOW TO APPLY** Apply in writing to the correspondent. The foundation considers applications for funding of projects and appeals from local and national charitable bodies registered with the Charity Commission. Applicants are asked to provide a summary of the project together with costings, financial accounts and details of fundraising activities.

**WHO TO APPLY TO** Rupert Edwards, Trustee, Edwards and Keeping, Unity Chambers, 34 High East

Street, Dorchester, Dorset DT1 1HA *Tel.* 01305 251333 *Fax* 01305 251465 *email* office@edwardsandkeeping.co.uk

## ■ The Marjorie Coote Animal Charity Trust

**CC NO** 208493  **ESTABLISHED** 1954
**WHERE FUNDING CAN BE GIVEN** Worldwide.
**WHO CAN BENEFIT** Registered charities.
**WHAT IS FUNDED** The care and protection of horses, dogs and other animals and birds. It is the policy of the trustees to concentrate on research into animal health problems and on the protection of species, whilst continuing to apply a small proportion of the income to general animal welfare, including sanctuaries.
**WHAT IS NOT FUNDED** Individuals.
**TYPE OF GRANT** One-off and recurrent.
**RANGE OF GRANTS** Grants are usually in the range of £250–£20,000.
**SAMPLE GRANTS Regular grants (£60,800 in 18 grants)** Beneficiaries included: Animal Health Trust (£20,000); PDSA Sheffield (£10,000); RSPCA Sheffield (£7,500); Friends of Conservation and Brooke Hospital for Animals (£3,000 each); Devon Wildlife Trust and Sheffield Wildlife Trust (£1,000 each); Tusk Trust and Wildfowl and Wetlands (£500 each).
**One-off grants (£35,800 in 30 grants)** Beneficiaries included: Support Dogs (£10,000); Royal Veterinary College Animal Care Trust, The Horse Trust (£5,000 each); Rarebreeds Survival Trust (£2,000); Alberts Horse Sanctuary (£1,500); Cheetah Conservation Fund and Hull Animal Welfare Trust (£1,000 each); International Fund for Animal Welfare and Rainforest Concern (£500 each); Suffolk Owl Sanctuary and West Yorkshire Dog Rescue (£250 each).
**FINANCES** *Year* 2013/14 *Income* £136,805 *Grants* £96,500 *Grants to organisations* £96,500 *Assets* £3,726,585
**TRUSTEES** James Neill; Jill P. Holah; Lady Neill; Mrs S. E. Browne; Mrs N. C. Baguley.
**HOW TO APPLY** Apply in writing to the correspondent. Applications should reach the correspondent during September for consideration in October/November. Appeals received at other times of the year are deferred until the following autumn unless they require consideration for an urgent one-off grant for a specific project.
**WHO TO APPLY TO** Jill Holah, Trustee, End Cottage, Terrington, York YO60 6PU *email* j.holah@mcacharity.org.uk

## ■ The Marjorie Coote Old People's Charity

**CC NO** 226747  **ESTABLISHED** 1958
**WHERE FUNDING CAN BE GIVEN** South Yorkshire.
**WHO CAN BENEFIT** Established charitable organisations in the area of jurisdiction.
**WHAT IS FUNDED** Work benefitting older people.
**WHAT IS NOT FUNDED** Individuals.
**RANGE OF GRANTS** Up to £25,000.
**SAMPLE GRANTS** St Luke's Capital Appeal (£25,000); Age UK Sheffield, Cavendish Cancer Care, St Luke's Hospice (£15,000 each); Sheffield Dial-A-Ride, Voluntary Action Sheffield (£10,000 each); Age UK Rotherham (£7,000); Age UK Barnsley (£3,000); The Broomgrove Trust and The ExtraCare Charitable Trust (£2,500 each); St Wilfrid's Centre and Trinity Day Care Trust (£1,000 each); Deafblind UK and The British

Polio Fellowship (£500 each); The Almshouse Association (£200).
**FINANCES** *Year* 2013/14 *Income* £116,909 *Grants* £115,200 *Grants to organisations* £115,200 *Assets* £3,273,241
**TRUSTEES** Sir Hugh Neill; Mrs J. A. Lee; Lady Neill; Mr N. Hutton; Mrs C. J. Lawrenson.
**HOW TO APPLY** Apply in writing to the correspondent during May. Appeals received at other times of the year are deferred unless for an urgent grant for a specific one-off project.
**WHO TO APPLY TO** Lady Neill, Trustee, Barn Cottage, Lindrick Common, Worksop, Nottinghamshire S81 8BA *Tel.* 01909 562806 *email* neillcharities@me.com

## ■ The Helen Jean Cope Trust

**CC NO** 1125937  **ESTABLISHED** 1998
**WHERE FUNDING CAN BE GIVEN** Mostly Leicestershire, but also Derbyshire and Nottinghamshire.
**WHO CAN BENEFIT** Registered charities only.
**WHAT IS FUNDED** General charitable purposes, supporting single projects.
**WHAT IS NOT FUNDED** Individuals; non-registered charities.
**TYPE OF GRANT** Generally single projects. Capital and core costs. Unrestricted funding. Replacement of statutory funding.
**RANGE OF GRANTS** £500 to £5,000.
**SAMPLE GRANTS** Anthony Nolan Trust, Bradgate Park Trust, Steps, Twenty Twenty (£5,000 each); Marie Curie Cancer Care (£4,000); Charnwood Toys, Derbyshire Leicestershire Rutland Air Ambulance, Peter Le Marchant Trust, 1st Rothley Scout Group (£2,500 each); Nottingham Music School, Shepshed Volunteer Centre, St Peter's Church Redmile, Veronica House Project(£1,000 each); Selston Music Festival, St Botolph's Church Shepshed, (£500).
**FINANCES** *Year* 2013 *Income* £97,232 *Grants* £120,730 *Grants to organisations* £120,730 *Assets* £4,260,589
**TRUSTEES** J. M. Carrington; Lindsay Brydson; Graham Freckelton; Alan Roberts
**HOW TO APPLY** An online application is available from the trust's website. For details of what information should be included in the application see the website.
**WHO TO APPLY TO** J. M. Carrington, Secretary, 1 Woodgate, Loughborough, Leicestershire LE11 2TY *Tel.* 01509 218298 *email* helenjeancope@btconnect.com *Website* www.thehelenjeancopecharity.co.uk

## ■ The J. Reginald Corah Foundation Fund

**CC NO** 220792  **ESTABLISHED** 1953
**WHERE FUNDING CAN BE GIVEN** Leicestershire and Rutland.
**WHO CAN BENEFIT** Charitable organisations. However, particular favour is given to hosiery firms carrying out their business in the city or county of Leicester and Rutland.
**WHAT IS FUNDED** General charitable purposes, particularly for the benefit of employees and ex-employees of hosiery firms carrying on business in the city or county of Leicester and Rutland
**WHAT IS NOT FUNDED** Applications from individuals are not considered unless made by, or supported by, a recognised charitable organisation.
**TYPE OF GRANT** One-off and recurrent.
**RANGE OF GRANTS** Up to £10,000.

SAMPLE GRANTS LCOS (£10,100); Leicester Children's Holiday Centre (£5,500); Leicestershire and Rutland Air Ambulance Service (£7,000). A detailed list was of 2013/14 beneficiaries was omitted from the trust's report. **Previous beneficiaries have included:** LOROS and In Kind (£2,000 each); SSAFA (£1,700); Family Action Leicester and Army Benevolent Fund (£1,600); and Leicester Scouts Council (£1,500).
FINANCES *Year* 2013/14 *Income* £117,127 *Grants* £92,600 *Grants to organisations* £92,600 *Assets* £4,725,713
TRUSTEES David Corah; Roger Bowder; Geoffrey Makings.
OTHER INFORMATION In 2013/14 grants were given to 76 organisations.
HOW TO APPLY Apply in writing to the correspondent. The trustees meet about every two months.
WHO TO APPLY TO The Trustees, c/o Shakespeares LLP, Two Colton Square, Leicester LE1 1QH *Tel.* 0116 257 6129 *email* gsmfambus@btconnect.com

## ■ The Gershon Coren Charitable Foundation (also known as The Muriel and Gus Coren Charitable Foundation)
CC NO 257615  ESTABLISHED 1968
WHERE FUNDING CAN BE GIVEN UK and financially developing countries.
WHO CAN BENEFIT Charitable organisations, particularly Jewish organisations.
WHAT IS FUNDED General charitable purposes; social welfare; Jewish causes.
RANGE OF GRANTS £500–£40,000
SAMPLE GRANTS Gategi Village Self Help Group (£90,000); Centre for Jewish Life (£15,000); Hobrifa, Jewish Blind and Disabled, Jewish Care, Magen David Adom UK and Nightingale Hammerson (£5,000 each); B'nai B'rith UK and British Friends of Migdal Ohr (£3,000 each); Jewish Renaissance and Kisharon (£2,000 each);(£1,000 each); British Blind Sport, CPRE, Friends of the Sick and the Royal British Legion (£1,000 each); and National Trust (£500).
FINANCES *Year* 2013–14 *Income* £185,811 *Grants* £211,000 *Grants to organisations* £211,000 *Assets* £2,611,294
TRUSTEES Walter Stanton; Anthony Coren; Muriel Coren.
HOW TO APPLY Apply in writing to the correspondent.
WHO TO APPLY TO Muriel Cohen, Trustee, 5 Golders Park Close, London NW11 7QR *email* graham.weinberg@mhllp.co.uk

## ■ Michael Cornish Charitable Trust
CC NO 1107890  ESTABLISHED 2005
WHERE FUNDING CAN BE GIVEN Nationwide and overseas, with preference of Lincolnshire.
WHO CAN BENEFIT Registered charities. Individuals are supported only in exceptional circumstances. Preference for charities in the Lincolnshire area and charities involving children.
WHAT IS FUNDED General charitable purposes, including: advancement of health; education; community and youth support; overseas aid.
TYPE OF GRANT Most grants are awarded to registered charities, but grants to individuals for worthy causes or in exceptional circumstances may be considered. Capital grants. Unrestricted funding.

RANGE OF GRANTS Average grant between £100–£20,000.
SAMPLE GRANTS Christian Partners in Africa (£20,000); Christian Partners in Africa, Hill Holt Wood (£10,000); RNLI (£5,000); Hope UK, Lincolnshire Bomber Command Memorial (£2,500 each); Salvation Army (£2,000); Barnardo's, Brain Tumour UK, Chernobyl Children in Need, Grantham Foodbank, RNLI – Africa Lifeguard Training, The Children's HIV Association, The Prince's Trust, The Samaritans, War Memorials Trust; (£1,000 each); Bransby Rest Home for Horses, Guide Dogs for the Blind (£500 each); Cancer Research UK, Save the children (£250 each).
FINANCES *Year* 2013/14 *Income* £1,416,338 *Grants* £157,526 *Grants to organisations* £157,526 *Assets* £15,913,315
TRUSTEES Michael Cornish; Susan Cornish; Richard Vigar.
OTHER INFORMATION The trustees meet quarterly.
HOW TO APPLY Apply in writing to the correspondent.
WHO TO APPLY TO Mrs Cridland, 15 Newland, Lincoln, Lincolnshire LN1 1XG *Tel.* 01522 531341 *email* phillipa.cridland@wrightvigar.co.uk

## ■ The Evan Cornish Foundation
CC NO 1112703  ESTABLISHED 2005
WHERE FUNDING CAN BE GIVEN UK and financially developing countries.
WHO CAN BENEFIT Charitable organisations.
WHAT IS FUNDED Education; older people; health; human rights; social and economic inequality; prisons.
WHAT IS NOT FUNDED The foundation is unable to support the following activities: religious activities; animal welfare; individuals/gap year students; political activities; medical research; and holiday club providers.
TYPE OF GRANT One-off.
RANGE OF GRANTS £500–£20,000
SAMPLE GRANTS St Luke's Hospice (£20,000); Goldigger Trust (£11,500); Photovoice (£10,000); St John of Jerusalem Eye Hospital (£8,500); Alzheimer's Society (£7,000); Deafblind UK (£5,000); Africa Educational Trust, Chernobyl Children in Need, Health Poverty Action (£3,000 each); Disability and Development Partners, Positive Action On Cancer (£2,000); InterCare Medical Aid (£1,000); St Columba Activity Group (£500).
FINANCES *Year* 2013/14 *Income* £502,982 *Grants* £879,947 *Grants to organisations* £879,947 *Assets* £12,612,824
TRUSTEES Rachel Cornish; Barbara Ward; Sally Cornish.
HOW TO APPLY The trustees will consider applications as well as seeking out causes to support. They have a three step application process which can be found on the foundation's website. First time applicants should complete the standard application form. Applicants who wish to apply again should complete the re-application form, which can also be found on the foundation's website. Applicants can re-apply for additional funding one year from the date of the last grant; however, a one-year progress report must be provided. Recipients of support are expected to provide feedback on the use of any grant and the achievements from it, through a six month update and a one-year progress report. See the foundation's website for up-to-date application deadlines and make sure you apply during a correct round for your project – appeals for overseas and UK projects are accepted at different times.

WHO TO APPLY TO Rachel Cornish, Trustee, The Innovation Centre, 217 Portobello, Sheffield S1 4DP *Tel.* 0114 224 2230 *email* contactus@evancornishfoundation.org.uk *Website* www.evancornishfoundation.org.uk

## ■ Cornwall Community Foundation

CC NO 1099977    ESTABLISHED 2003
WHERE FUNDING CAN BE GIVEN Cornwall and the Isles of Scilly
WHO CAN BENEFIT Local projects in Cornwall and the Isles of Scilly that engage local people in making their communities better places to live. This includes groups, projects and individuals.
WHAT IS FUNDED Community-based causes.
WHAT IS NOT FUNDED Funding is **not** given for the following: profit-making organisations; statutory/public sector organisations such as health authorities, schools, hospitals, parish or town councils; grant-making organisations or bodies which fundraise or distribute grants on behalf of other organisations; regional offices of national bodies if they are not independent, i.e. you must have your own local accounts and management committee; groups whose beneficiaries are not people; projects that help only one individual; groups that have had a previous grant which has not been managed satisfactorily; works or equipment already committed, bought or completed (including trips); projects where beneficiaries live outside Cornwall or the Isles of Scilly; unspecified expenditure; projects primarily for the advancement of religion or politics.
RANGE OF GRANTS £300–£91,000
SAMPLE GRANTS The Frederick Foundation (£91,000); Goonhilly Wind Farm Community Fund (£48,000); Wellbeing and Prevention (£27,700), Winter Fuel Payments Fund (£21,000); The Lord and Lady St Levan Fund (£19,000); Caradon Area Community Fund (£11,500); Lord Lieutenant's Fund for Youth (£8,500); Benefitting Older People (£3,000); The Cornwall Crimebeat Fund (£1,100); Albert Van Den Bergh/Jane Hartley Fund (£320)
FINANCES *Year* 2013 *Income* £1,116,378 *Grants* £641,629 *Grants to organisations* £641,629 *Assets* £2,916,052
TRUSTEES The Hon Evelyn Boscawen; The Lady Mary Holborow; Jane Hartley; James Williams; Margaret Bickford-Smith; Daphne Skinnard; John Ede; Bishop Tim Thornton; Lady George; Tim Smith; Elaine Hunt; Mark Mitchell; Thomas Varcoe; Charles Reynolds; Nicola Marquis.
HOW TO APPLY Applications should be made via a form available from the foundation. For general information about grants contact the grants team (tel.: 01566 779333 or e-mail: grants@cornwallfoundation.com). Criteria, guidelines and application process are also posted on the foundation's website.
WHO TO APPLY TO Carolyn Boyce, Suite 1, Sheers Barton Barns, Lawhitton, Launceston, Cornwall PL15 9NJ *Tel.* 01566 779333 *email* office@cornwallfoundation.com *Website* www.cornwallfoundation.com

## ■ The Duke of Cornwall's Benevolent Fund

CC NO 269183    ESTABLISHED 1975
WHERE FUNDING CAN BE GIVEN UK, with a number of grants made in the Cornwall area.
WHO CAN BENEFIT Charitable organisations.

WHAT IS FUNDED The relief of people in need of assistance because of sickness, poverty or age; the provision of almshouses, homes of rest, hospitals and convalescent homes; the advancement of education; the advancement of the arts and religion; and the preservation for the benefit of the public of lands and buildings.
WHAT IS NOT FUNDED Individuals.
TYPE OF GRANT One-off.
RANGE OF GRANTS Typically under £5,000 each.
SAMPLE GRANTS Rare Breeds Survival Trust (£8,000), Cornwall Red Squirrel Project, Dartmoor Search Rescue, Leonard Cheshire Disability (£5,000 each); Home Start Exeter (£2,730); Sea Sanctuary (£4,400); Cornwall Heritage Group, Dutton Davis Tennis Club, Sailors Children's Society, The Churches Conservation Trust (£2,000); Blackwater Village Trust, Hearing Dogs for Death People, Penwith Volunteer Bureau, St Austell Sea Cadets (£1,000).
FINANCES *Year* 2013/14 *Income* £63,980 *Grants* £98,299 *Grants to organisations* £98,299 *Assets* £3,772,031
TRUSTEES Bertie Ross; The Hon. James Leigh-Pemberton.
HOW TO APPLY Apply in writing to the correspondent.
WHO TO APPLY TO Terry Cotter, 10 Buckingham Gate, London SW1E 6LA *Tel.* 020 7834 7346

## ■ The Cornwell Charitable Trust

CC NO 1012467    ESTABLISHED 1992
WHERE FUNDING CAN BE GIVEN The UK with a preference for the south west of England, in particular, Cornwall.
WHO CAN BENEFIT Registered charities.
WHAT IS FUNDED General charitable purposes, funding projects and individuals specifically and primarily in the Cornwall area.
WHAT IS NOT FUNDED No support is given for travel, expeditions or university grants.
TYPE OF GRANT Project and capital grants.
RANGE OF GRANTS Up to £50,000 – the majority are for £1,000 or less.
SAMPLE GRANTS Community House St Buryan (£50,000); The Zacchaeus 2000 Trust (£20,000); Fearless Choices Young Actors Project (£5,000); Independent Diplomatic Inc (£3,000); Hayle Youth Project and Stand Proud (£2,000 each); and Cornwall Hospice Care, Cornwall Air Ambulance Trust and Prisoners of Conscience Appeal Fund (£1,000 each).
FINANCES *Year* 2013/14 *Income* £110,715 *Grants* £100,078 *Grants to organisations* £100,078 *Assets* £1,290,723
TRUSTEES David Cornwell; Valerie Cornwell; Matthew Bennett; Mark Bailey.
OTHER INFORMATION In 2013/14 grants were given to 53 organisations, the majority of which were for under £1,000.
HOW TO APPLY Apply in writing to the correspondent.
WHO TO APPLY TO Mark Bailey, Trustee, Devonshire House, 1 Devonshire Street, London W1W 5DR *Tel.* 020 7304 2000 *email* cw@citroenwells.co.uk

## ■ The Sidney and Elizabeth Corob Charitable Trust

**CC NO** 266606    **ESTABLISHED** 1973
**WHERE FUNDING CAN BE GIVEN** UK.
**WHO CAN BENEFIT** Charitable organisations.
**WHAT IS FUNDED** General charitable purposes, including: education; arts; welfare; Jewish causes.
**WHAT IS NOT FUNDED** Individuals or non-registered charities.
**RANGE OF GRANTS** Up to £90,000.
**SAMPLE GRANTS** University College of London £380,000 in two grants); Oxford Centre for Hebrew and Jewish Studies (£50,000); Chief Rabbinate Trust, Norwood and Technion UK (£5,000 only); Anglo-Israel Association, Community Service Trust and JAMI (£2,500 each); and Chai Cancer Care (£2,000).
**FINANCES** Year 2013/14 Income £161,236 Grants £180,576 Grants to organisations £180,576 Assets £221,953
**TRUSTEES** Alison Corob; Elizabeth Corob; Christopher Cook; Joseph Hajnal; Sheila Wechsler; Stephen Wiseman.
**OTHER INFORMATION** Various grants of under £2,000 each totalled £21,000.
**HOW TO APPLY** Apply in writing to the correspondent. The trustees meet at regular intervals.
**WHO TO APPLY TO** The Trustees, c/o Corob Holdings, 62 Grosvenor Street, London W1K 3JF Tel. 020 7499 4301

## ■ The Corona Charitable Trust

**CC NO** 1064320    **ESTABLISHED** 1997
**WHERE FUNDING CAN BE GIVEN** UK and overseas.
**WHO CAN BENEFIT** Jewish organisations.
**WHAT IS FUNDED** Jewish religious education and relief in need, particularly for older and younger people.
**SAMPLE GRANTS** **Previous beneficiaries have included:** Menorah Foundation School, the ZSV Trust, Ahavas Shalom Charity Fund, WST Charity Limited, and Edgware Jewish Primary School.
**FINANCES** Year 2013/14 Income £35,250 Grants £73,123 Grants to organisations £73,123 Assets £14,093
**TRUSTEES** Abraham Levy; Alison Levy; Ben Levy.
**HOW TO APPLY** Apply in writing to the correspondent.
**WHO TO APPLY TO** The Trustees, 16 Mayfield Gardens, Hendon, London NW4 2QA Tel. 020 7405 3041 email cct@coronaoverseas.co.uk

## ■ The Costa Family Charitable Trust (formerly the Morgan Williams Charitable Trust)

**CC NO** 221604    **ESTABLISHED** 1964
**WHERE FUNDING CAN BE GIVEN** UK
**WHO CAN BENEFIT** Christian organisations.
**WHAT IS FUNDED** Charities with which the trustees have some connection.
**SAMPLE GRANTS** Alpha International (£250,000); VSO (£12,000); Pentecost Festival (£10,000); the Chase Trust and the Philo Trust (£5,000 each); British Museum (£2,000); and the Wallace Collection (£1,000).
**FINANCES** Year 2013/14 Income £960 Grants £500,000 Grants to organisations £500,000
**TRUSTEES** Kenneth Costa; Ann Costa.
**OTHER INFORMATION** Full accounts were not available for 2013/14 and the grant total has therefore been estimated based on previous years' grant-making.
**HOW TO APPLY** The trust states that only charities personally connected with the trustees are supported and absolutely no applications are either solicited or acknowledged.
**WHO TO APPLY TO** Kenneth Costa, Trustee, 43 Chelsea Square, London SW3 6LH Tel. 07785 467441

## ■ The Cotton Industry War Memorial Trust

**CC NO** 242721    **ESTABLISHED** 1947
**WHERE FUNDING CAN BE GIVEN** UK.
**WHO CAN BENEFIT** Individuals and organisations.
**WHAT IS FUNDED** This trust makes grants to all aspects of aid and assistance to employees, former employees and students of the textile industry.
**RANGE OF GRANTS** Up to £42,300.
**SAMPLE GRANTS** Lancashire Textile Manufacturers' Association (£42,300); Children's Adventure Farm Trust (£30,000); Seashell Trust (£26,100); Samuel Crompton Fellowship Award (£12,000); the Society of Dyers and Colourists (£10,000); Manchester Art Gallery (£6,200); Bradford Textile Society (£1,500); Hearing Dogs for Deaf People (£1,500).
**FINANCES** Year 2013/14 Income £322,257 Grants £124,596 Grants to organisations £123,396 Assets £6,662,041
**TRUSTEES** Peter Booth; Christopher Trotter; Prof. Albert Lockett; Keith Garbett; Peter Reid; Philip Roberts; John Ward; Dr Michael Glover; George Pope
**OTHER INFORMATION** The grants figure includes three grants to individuals totalling £1,200.
**HOW TO APPLY** Apply in writing to the correspondent. The trust meets at least four times a year to consider requests for funds and grants.
**WHO TO APPLY TO** Peter Booth, Stables Barn, Coldstones Farm, Bewerley, HARROGATE, North Yorkshire HG3 5BJ Tel. 01423 711205 email ciwmt@btinternet.com

## ■ The Cotton Trust

**CC NO** 1094776    **ESTABLISHED** 1956
**WHERE FUNDING CAN BE GIVEN** UK and overseas.
**WHO CAN BENEFIT** UK-registered charities.
**WHAT IS FUNDED** Relief of suffering; elimination and control of disease; people who have disabilities and disadvantaged people.
**WHAT IS NOT FUNDED** Grants are only given to UK-registered charities that have been registered for at least one year.
**TYPE OF GRANT** Grants are primarily awarded for capital expenditure for specific projects or items of specialist equipment. A limited number of grants are awarded for running costs where the grant will provide direct support for a clearly identifiable charitable project.
**RANGE OF GRANTS** Usually £250–£2,000.
**SAMPLE GRANTS** **Previous beneficiaries have included:** Leicester Charity Link (£30,500); Merlin (£25,000); Camfed (£15,000); Earl Shilton Social Institute, British Red Cross, Save The Children and Concern Worldwide (£5,000 each); Cecily's Fund and the Queen Alexandra Hospital Home (£2,000 each); Computer Aid International, Health Poverty Action and Resolve International (£1,000 each); Special Toys Educational Postal Service, Strongbones Children's Charitable Trust and Inter Care (£500

each); Orcadia Creative Learning Centre (£250); and the Leysian Mission (£10).

**FINANCES** Year 2013/14 Income £206,059 Grants £218,119 Grants to organisations £218,119 Assets £6,662,128

**TRUSTEES** Joanne Congdon; Erica Cotton; Tenney Cotton.

**OTHER INFORMATION** A total of £218,100 was made in grants to 93 organisations in 2013/14.

**HOW TO APPLY** Apply in writing to the correspondent. According to the trustees' report for 2011/12, trustees reach decisions on applications by taking into accounts the following: 'how effective the grant is expected to be towards fulfilling a charity's stated objective; the size of the grant requested in relation to the stated overall project and/or capital costs; and the financial standing of the charity as presented in its latest report and accounts with respect to: the extent of the applicant's exclusively charitable expenditure in relation to its annual income; the extent of expenditure on fundraising and management as a proportion of the charity's annual income; and the level of a charity's free and restricted reserves against its annual spending on charitable activities.'

**WHO TO APPLY TO** Joanne Burgess, Trustee, PO Box 6895, Earl Shilton, Leicester LE9 8ZE Tel. 01455 440917

## ■ Country Houses Foundation

**CC NO** 1111049        **ESTABLISHED** 2005

**WHERE FUNDING CAN BE GIVEN** England.

**WHO CAN BENEFIT** Registered charities; building preservation trusts; private owners.

**WHAT IS FUNDED** The preservation of buildings of historic or architectural significance together with their gardens and grounds, for the public benefit. 'We aim to give grants for repairs and restoration work required to prevent loss or damage to historic buildings located in England, their gardens, grounds and any outbuildings. We would normally expect your building to be listed, scheduled, or in the case of a garden included in the English Heritage Register of Parks and Gardens. However, we may also make grants to projects which involve an unlisted building of sufficient historic or architectural significance or importance if it is within a conservation area.'

**WHAT IS NOT FUNDED** 'As a general rule we do not offer grants for the following: Buildings and structures which have been the subject of recent purchase and where the cost of works for which grant is sought should have been recognized in the purchase price paid. Projects which do not principally involve the repair or conservation of a historic building or structure; Churches and chapels unless now or previously linked to a country house or estate; Alterations and improvements, and repairs to non historic fabric or services; Routine maintenance and minor repairs; General running costs; Demolition unless agreed as part of a repair and conservation programme; Rent, loan or mortgage payments; Conservation of furniture, fittings and equipment except where they are themselves of historic or architectural significance, have a historic relationship with the site, are relevant to the project, and can be secured long term from sale or disposal; Work carried out before a grant offer has been made in writing and accepted.'

**RANGE OF GRANTS** £2,500 to £76,500.

**SAMPLE GRANTS** Abberley Hall (£76,500); St Barts Chapel (£75,000); St Giles House (£50,000); Forcett Hall (£42,000); Copped Hall (£34,400); Castle Drogo (£30,000); Severndroog Castle (£27,500); Leiston Abbey (£22,500); Caerhays Castle (£19,500); Scampston Hall – Glasshouse (£15,000); Blithfield Hall Orangery (£10,000); Heritage Funding Directory (£2,500).

**FINANCES** Year 2013/14 Income £362,176 Grants £631,645 Grants to organisations £631,645 Assets £12,802,961

**TRUSTEES** Oliver Pearcey; Nicholas Barber; Michael Clifton; Norman Hudson; Christopher Taylor; Sir John Parsons; Mary King.

**HOW TO APPLY** Refer to the foundation's very helpful website for full information on how to make an application. Pre-Application Forms can be completed online, or in a hard copy and returned by post. The foundation tries to respond to within 28 days of receipt. If a project fits the criteria then a unique reference number will be issued which must be quoted on the Full Application Form. Applications can be made at any time.

**WHO TO APPLY TO** David Price, Company Secretary, The Manor, Sheephouse Farm, Uley Road, Dursley, Gloucestershire GL11 5AD Tel. 0845 402 4102 Fax 0845 402 4103 email david@countryhousesfoundation.org.uk Website www.countryhousesfoundation.org.uk

## ■ County Durham Community Foundation

**CC NO** 1047625        **ESTABLISHED** 1995

**WHERE FUNDING CAN BE GIVEN** County Durham, Darlington and surrounding areas.

**WHO CAN BENEFIT** Community and voluntary organisations that are of a charitable, educational, philanthropic or benevolent nature.

**WHAT IS FUNDED** Projects working to create opportunity and to combat the issues of social disadvantage and exclusion in communities. Grants are made under five main themes: Aspiring; Healthier; Greener; Safer; and Inclusive. The foundation typically supports projects working in the following areas: children and young people; vulnerable people; older people; self-help groups; community regeneration; environmental improvement; health and well-being; educational projects; and capacity and skills development.

**WHAT IS NOT FUNDED** Regional or local offices of national organisations (unless it can be demonstrated that they operate independently); 'arms-length' public sector organisations; party political activity; commercial ventures; organisations that have the sole purpose of benefitting or relieving animals or plants; the advancement of religion/faith; feasibility or other investigative studies; general contributions to large appeals (specific stand-alone items, however, can be funded); groups that hold more than one year's running costs as unrestricted free reserves (unless this can be justified); improvements to land or buildings not open or accessible for the general public; groups restricted by membership other than that associated with the objects of the group itself where this is necessary for the safety/well-being of disadvantaged users and undertaken for charitable purposes; deficit or retrospective funding; sponsored events; prizes or incentives; contingency amounts. The foundation will not normally fund the following: statutory bodies (unless it can be proven that the project is community-led, will benefit the whole community and is not a statutory responsibility; medical research and equipment; multi-annual grants;

school projects (unless the project involves the wider community); the construction or purchase of premises and freehold or leasehold land rights; the purchase of minibuses and other vehicles; multiple IT equipment; salaries (unless it is for a few hours which will make a large contribution to the project); overseas travel. If your project falls under the 'not normally' funded criteria, contact the foundation before submitting your application. Individual funds may have their own exclusions to consider.

**TYPE OF GRANT** Various depending on funding criteria.

**RANGE OF GRANTS** Some funds award grants up to £5,000. The average grant size is £3,000.

**FINANCES** Year 2013/14 Income £4,612,427 Grants £2,449,795 Grants to organisations £2,449,795 Assets £11,565,377

**TRUSTEES** Mark I'Anson, Chair; Michele Armstrong; Duncan Barrie; Ada Burns; Paul Chandler; George Garlick; Andrew Martell; David Martin; Lady Nicholson; Gerry Osborne; Ruth Thompson; David Watson.

**PUBLICATIONS** Newsletter, information leaflets, grant guidelines and application forms.

**HOW TO APPLY** Applications to all but three funds (the Banks Community Fund, ESF Community Grant and Surviving Winter each have their own bespoke application forms) can be made using the online standard application form, of which there is a Part A and Part B. The foundation states the following on its website: 'We mix-and-match applications to the most appropriate fund behind the scenes, so you don't need to worry about which fund is right for you.' Detailed guidelines are available to download from the website and should be read before an application is started.

**WHO TO APPLY TO** Barbara Gubbins, Chief Executive, Victoria House, Whitfield Court, St John's Road, Meadowfield Industrial Estate, Durham DH7 8XL Tel. 0191 378 6340 email info@cdcf.org.uk Website www.cdcf.org.uk

## ■ The Augustine Courtauld Trust

**CC NO** 226217 **ESTABLISHED** 1956
**WHERE FUNDING CAN BE GIVEN** UK, with a preference for Essex.

**WHO CAN BENEFIT** Registered charities.

**WHAT IS FUNDED** General charitable purposes, but mostly organisations in Essex working with young people who are disadvantaged and conservation. Exploration of the Arctic and Antarctic regions are also supported. Preference is given to charities which the trust has a special interest in, knowledge of, or, association with.

**WHAT IS NOT FUNDED** Individuals; churches for fabric repairs or maintenance.

**TYPE OF GRANT** One-off grants for projects and core costs, which may be made for multiple years if an application is submitted for each year.

**RANGE OF GRANTS** £500–£9,000. Normally in the range of £500–£2,000.

**SAMPLE GRANTS** Gino Watkins Memorial Trust (£9,000); The Friends of Essex Churches Trust (£8,000); Essex Boys' and Girls' Clubs (£6,000); and Cirdan Sailing Trust (£5,000); Marie Curie Cancer Care and Rural Community Council of Essex (£2,500 each); Essex Playing Fields Association and Philippines Typhoon Appeal (£1,000 each); and Barrow Farm Riding for the Disabled, Brentwood Catholic Children's Society, Chain Reaction Theatre Company and Voice for the Child in Care (£500 each).

**FINANCES** Year 2013–14 Income £49,742 Grants £56,500 Grants to organisations £56,500 Assets £1,448,393

**TRUSTEES** Revd A. C. Courtauld, Chair; John P. Petre; Julien Courtauld; Derek Fordham; Anthony Denison-Smith.

**OTHER INFORMATION** This trust was founded in 1956 by Augustine Courtauld, an Arctic explorer who was proud of his Essex roots. His charitable purpose was simple: 'My idea is to make available something that will do some good.'

**HOW TO APPLY** Applications must be submitted via the online form on the trust's website. Written applications will not be accepted.

**WHO TO APPLY TO** Bruce Ballard, Clerk, Birkett Long Solicitors, Number One, Legg Street, Chelmsford, Essex CM1 1JS Tel. 01245 453800 email bruce.ballard@birkettlong.co.uk Website www.augustinecourtauldtrust.org

## ■ Coutts Charitable Foundation

**CC NO** 1150784 **ESTABLISHED** 2013
**WHERE FUNDING CAN BE GIVEN** UK and overseas.

**WHO CAN BENEFIT** Charitable organisations.

**WHAT IS FUNDED** General charitable purposes, particularly the relief of poverty, health and community and economic development.

**RANGE OF GRANTS** £10,000–£95,000

**SAMPLE GRANTS** Lien Aid (£95,000); Ranthambhore Foundation (£45,000); Ashden Trust (£30,000); Connection at St Martins (£17,000); and City Gateway (£10,000).

**FINANCES** Year 2013/14 Income £642,216 Grants £197,113 Grants to organisations £197,113 Assets £445,103

**TRUSTEES** Sir Christopher Geidt; Ian Ewart; Lord Waldegrave of North Hill; Nicholas Tapner; Alexander Classen; Leslie Gent; Shirley Tang; Michael Morley; Shivaashish Gupta; Andrew Sumner; Dr Linda Yueh.

**OTHER INFORMATION** Grants to five organisations totalled £197,000 during the year.

**HOW TO APPLY** Apply in writing to the correspondent via an application form available to download on the foundation's website. The foundation's website states the following: 'The Coutts Foundation takes a proactive approach to identifying its grantees. We prefer to fund organisations where our funding can be catalytic – either testing a new idea or helping scale a tested programme. The foundation does not accept unsolicited proposals for funding. However, we welcome information about organisations that fit our funding priorities and approach.'

**WHO TO APPLY TO** Kay Boland, Correspondent, Coutts & Co., Strand, 440 London WC2R 0QS Tel. 020 7957 2822 email coutts.foundation@coutts.com Website www.coutts.com/foundation

## ■ General Charity of Coventry

**CC NO** 216235 **ESTABLISHED** 1983
**WHERE FUNDING CAN BE GIVEN** Within the boundary of the City of Coventry.

**WHO CAN BENEFIT** People who are in need, children, young and older people, people with physical or mental disabilities, people in need of social or health care and organisations that would benefit such people in the City of Coventry.

**WHAT IS FUNDED** Welfare; general charitable purposes; health; research; education and training. The Charity describes its objectives as follows: 'Relief in Need in relieving either generally or individually persons resident in the

City of Coventry who are in conditions of need, hardship or distress.'; 'The payment of pensions to a maximum of 650 persons, over the age of 60, resident in the City of Coventry.'; 'Donations to local institutions or organisations which provide or undertake to provide items, services or facilities for persons in need living within the City of Coventry.'; 'Grants to Coventry persons for advancement of Education and Research.'

**WHAT IS NOT FUNDED** No grants are given to organisations outside Coventry, or for holidays unless of a recuperative nature.

**RANGE OF GRANTS** Up to £66,000.

**SAMPLE GRANTS** Coventry Sports Foundation (£66,000); grants for relief-in-need purposes (£52,000); David Scott's Coventry Jubilee Community Care Trust (£45,000); University of Warwick Medical Research (£40,000); Coventry Boys' Club (£30,000); Enterprise Club for Disabled People (£20,000); Alzheimer's Society (£15,000); Tiny Tim's Children's Centre (£10,000); Coventry Citizens Advice (£6,000); Coventry City Mission (£5,000); Coventry Rugby Community Foundation (£4,000); Hereward College (£2,500); Zoe's Place Baby Hospice (£1,300)

**FINANCES** Year 2013 Income £1,373,866 Grants £645,689 Grants to organisations £585,689 Assets £9,358,028

**TRUSTEES** Richard Smith; David Mason; Michael Harris; Edna Eaves; Margaret Lancaster; Terence McDonnell; William Thomson; Cllr Nigel Lee; David Evans; Terry Proctor; Dr Caroline Rhodes; Cllr Marcus Lapsa; Edward Curtis; Cllr Catherine Miks; Vivian Kershaw; Cllr Ram Lakha; Julia McNaney; Cllr Gary Crookes.

**OTHER INFORMATION** Grants to individuals were included in the grant total for 2013; however, the number and total amounts given to individuals is not disclosed in the charity accounts. Based on limited information, grants to individuals appear to total in the region of £60,000. The 'grant total to organisations' reflects this approximation.

**HOW TO APPLY** Apply in writing to the correspondent. Applications are not accepted directly from the general public for relief in need (individuals).

**WHO TO APPLY TO** Mrs V. Tosh, Clerk to the Trustees, General Charities Office, Old Bablake, Hill Street, Coventry CV1 4AN Tel. 024 7622 2769 email cov.genchar@virgin.net

## ■ Coventry Building Society Charitable Foundation

**CC NO** 1072244  **ESTABLISHED** 1998
**WHERE FUNDING CAN BE GIVEN** The Midlands.
**WHO CAN BENEFIT** Registered charities.
**WHAT IS FUNDED** A wide range of causes based, or active, in the Midlands, with a preference for smaller local charities.
**WHAT IS NOT FUNDED** No grants can be given outside the Midlands area. The following are not eligible for support: large charities which enjoy national coverage; charities with no base within the branch area; charities with an annual donated income in excess of £250,000; charities with assets over £500,000; projects requiring ongoing commitment; large capital projects; maintenance or building works for buildings, gardens or playgrounds; major fundraising; projects which are normally the responsibility of other organisations such as NHS and local authorities; sponsorship of individuals; requests from individuals; replacing funds which were the responsibility of another body; educational institutions, unless for the relief of disadvantage; promotion of religious, political or military causes; sporting clubs or organisations, unless for the relief of disadvantage; medical research or equipment; more than one donation to the same organisation in a year – further applications will be considered after a period of three years; animal welfare.

**TYPE OF GRANT** One-off.
**RANGE OF GRANTS** Up to £35,000, but, generally £1,000–£10,000.
**SAMPLE GRANTS** Heart of England Community Foundation (£35,000); Gloucestershire Community Foundation (£13,000); Swindon and Wiltshire Community Foundation (£8,700); Quartet Community Foundation (£7,200); Leicestershire and Rutland Community Foundation and Northamptonshire Community Foundation (£2,600 each); and Somerset Community Foundation, South Yorkshire Community Foundation and Staffordshire Community Foundation (£1,700).
**FINANCES** Year 2013 Income £106,813 Grants £102,120 Grants to organisations £102,120 Assets £5,229
**TRUSTEES** Emma Brodie; Anna Cuskin.
**HOW TO APPLY** Applications can be made online through the community foundation for your area. In order to do this choose the area closest to where your charity operates from the table at the bottom of the Coventry Building Society Charitable Foundation website and click on the relevant link. This will take you to go to the community foundation website for your area. From here, you will be able to find out more about your local community foundation and all of the information that you'll need to apply for a grant.
**WHO TO APPLY TO** Alison Readman, Correspondent, Coventry Building Society, Oak Tree Court, Binley Business Park, Binley, Coventry CV3 2UN Tel. 024 7643 5231 email alison.readman@thecoventry.co.uk Website www.coventrybuildingsociety.co.uk/your-society/community.aspx#tabs-3

## ■ The Sir Tom Cowie Charitable Trust

**CC NO** 1096936  **ESTABLISHED** 2003
**WHERE FUNDING CAN BE GIVEN** City of Sunderland and County Durham.
**WHO CAN BENEFIT** Organisations benefitting young people, older people, the infirm and disabled, poor or needy people due to social and/or economic circumstances.
**WHAT IS FUNDED** General charitable purposes.
**RANGE OF GRANTS** Usually up to £20,000.
**SAMPLE GRANTS** Fund Bursary, St Mark's Community Association (£20,000 each); Hendon Young People's Project (£15,500); All Saints Catholic VA Primary School, Wolsingham and Wear Valley Agricultural Society (£10,000 each); Asthma Relief, Guide Dogs (£5,000 each); The Lambton Run (£2,500); Blind Veterans UK (£1,500) SCOPE Laverno Sunderland (£1,000); Outward Bound Trust (£500); SHINE (£200).
**FINANCES** Year 2013/14 Income £135,598 Grants £134,573 Grants to organisations £134,573 Assets £5,239,147
**TRUSTEES** Peter Blackett; David Gray; Lady Diana Cowie.
**HOW TO APPLY** Apply in writing to the correspondent.

# Cowley

WHO TO APPLY TO Loraine Maddison, Estate Office, Broadwood Hall, Lanchester, Durham DH7 0TN *Tel.* 01207 529663 *email* lorraine@sirtomcowie.com *Website* www.stcct.co.uk

## ■ Cowley Charitable Foundation

CC NO 270682     ESTABLISHED 1973
WHERE FUNDING CAN BE GIVEN Worldwide, with some preference for south Buckinghamshire and the Aylesbury area.
WHO CAN BENEFIT Registered charities.
WHAT IS FUNDED General charitable purposes.
WHAT IS NOT FUNDED Non-registered charities; individuals; causes supposed to be serviced by public funds; causes with a scope considered to be too narrow.
TYPE OF GRANT One-off donations for development, capital projects and project funding.
RANGE OF GRANTS £500 to £5,000.
SAMPLE GRANTS Sarla and Tau Zero (£5,000); National Gallery (£3,000); Age UK (£2,000); Children With Cancer UK (£1,000); London Shakespeare Workout, Trinity Hospice and YMCA (£500).
FINANCES *Year* 2013/14 *Income* £33,990 *Grants* £33,200 *Grants to organisations* £33,200 *Assets* £934,979
TRUSTEES 140 Trustee Co. Ltd; Harriet Cullen.
HOW TO APPLY The trust has states that unsolicited applications are unlikely to be supported and that the trustees carry out their own research into charities.
WHO TO APPLY TO The Secretary, 140 Trustee Co. Ltd, 2nd Floor, 17 Grosvenor Gardens, London SW1W 0BD *Tel.* 020 7834 9797 *email* info@140trustee.com

## ■ Dudley and Geoffrey Cox Charitable Trust

CC NO 277761     ESTABLISHED 1979
WHERE FUNDING CAN BE GIVEN UK.
WHO CAN BENEFIT Organisations benefitting children and young adults; former employees of Haymills; at-risk groups; people who are disadvantaged by poverty and socially isolated people.
WHAT IS FUNDED The trust seeks to support projects which are not widely known, and therefore likely to be inadequately funded. Grants fall into four main categories: education – schools, colleges and universities; medicine – hospitals, associated institutions and medical research; welfare – primarily to include former Haymills staff, people in need, or who are otherwise distressed or disadvantaged; and youth – support for schemes to assist in the education, welfare and training of young people.
WHAT IS NOT FUNDED No personal applications will be considered unless endorsed by a university, college or other appropriate authority.
RANGE OF GRANTS £2,000 to £40,000.
SAMPLE GRANTS Merchant Taylors School Geoffrey Cox Scholarships (£40,000); Action Medical Research, Royal College of Physicians, (£5,000 each); MS Society, Prostate Cancer Research (£4,000 each); Parkinson's Disease Society, Royal College of Surgeons, Scouts (£3,000 each); Motability (£2,000).
FINANCES *Year* 2013/14 *Income* £253,200 *Grants* £289,500 *Grants to organisations* £289,500 *Assets* £7,664,625

TRUSTEES Ian Ferres; Bill Underwood; Peter Watkins; John Sharpe; John Wosner; Michael Boyle.
OTHER INFORMATION Grants were broken down as follows: Medical (£86,000); Educational (£42,300); Youth and Welfare (£161,200).
HOW TO APPLY Apply in writing to the correspondent. The trustees meet at least twice a year.
WHO TO APPLY TO David Atkinson, c/o Merchant Taylors' Company, 30 Threadneedle Street, London EC2R 8JB *Tel.* 020 7450 4440 *email* mdear@merchant-taylors.co.uk

## ■ The Sir William Coxen Trust Fund

CC NO 206936     ESTABLISHED 1940
WHERE FUNDING CAN BE GIVEN England.
WHO CAN BENEFIT Hospitals or charitable institutions.
WHAT IS FUNDED Orthopaedic work, particularly in respect of children.
WHAT IS NOT FUNDED Individuals or non-charitable institutions.
TYPE OF GRANT One-off grants and research fellowships.
SAMPLE GRANTS Royal National Orthopaedic Hospital (10,500 in two grants); Action for Kids, Action Medical Research for Children, Air Ambulance (£5,000 each); Perthes Association (£4,000); Osteopathic Centre for Children and Stagecoach Charitable Trust (£3,000 each).
FINANCES *Year* 2013/14 *Income* £114,678 *Grants* £100,000 *Grants to organisations* £100,000 *Assets* £2,527,325
TRUSTEES John Stuttard; Michael Savory; Michael Bear; John Garbutt; Andrew Parmley.
OTHER INFORMATION Grants were made to 19 organisations.
HOW TO APPLY Apply in writing to the correspondent who has guidelines available.
WHO TO APPLY TO Natasha Dogra, Correspondent, The Town Clerk's Office, City of London, PO Box 270, Guildhall, London EC2P 2EJ *Tel.* 020 7332 1434 *email* natasha.dogra@cityoflondon.gov.uk

## ■ The Lord Cozens-Hardy Trust

CC NO 264237     ESTABLISHED 1972
WHERE FUNDING CAN BE GIVEN Merseyside and Norfolk.
WHO CAN BENEFIT Registered charities.
WHAT IS FUNDED General charitable purposes with a particular interest in supporting medical, health, education and welfare causes.
WHAT IS NOT FUNDED Individuals.
TYPE OF GRANT One-off and recurrent.
RANGE OF GRANTS Up to £15,000, mostly for smaller amounts of £1,000 or less.
SAMPLE GRANTS University of East Anglia (£15,000); Brain Research trust (£10, 000); Poppy Centre Trust (£7,500); Action for Children; Home-Start-Norwich, Woodlands Hospice Charitable Trust (£5,000 each); The National Search and Rescue Dogs Association (£2,000); Blind Veterans UK, Liverpool School of tropical Medicine, Prostate Cancer UK, Royal National Institute for Deaf People, Shelter, The Prince's Trust (£1,000).
FINANCES *Year* 2013/14 *Income* £122,286 *Grants* £90,500 *Grants to organisations* £90,500 *Assets* £3,119,277
TRUSTEES J. E. V. Phelps; Mrs L. F. Phelps; J. Ripman.

**HOW TO APPLY** Apply in writing to the correspondent. Applications are reviewed quarterly.
**WHO TO APPLY TO** The Trustees, PO Box 28, Holt, Norfolk NR25 7WH email Justin.ripman@millsreeve.com

## ■ The Craignish Trust
**SC NO** SC016882   **ESTABLISHED** 1961
**WHERE FUNDING CAN BE GIVEN** UK, with a preference for Scotland.
**WHO CAN BENEFIT** Charitable organisations.
**WHAT IS FUNDED** Education; the arts; heritage; culture; science; environmental protection and improvement
**WHAT IS NOT FUNDED** Running costs are not normally supported.
**TYPE OF GRANT** Project grants.
**RANGE OF GRANTS** £500–£7,500
**SAMPLE GRANTS Previous beneficiaries have included:** Art in Healthcare, Boilerhouse Theatre Company Ltd, Butterfly Conservation – Scotland, Cairndow Arts Promotions, Centre for Alternative Technology, Edinburgh International Book Festival, Edinburgh Royal Choral Union, Friends of the Earth Scotland, Human Rights Watch Charitable Trust and Soil Association Scotland.
**FINANCES** Year 2013/14 Income £131,372 Grants £190,000 Grants to organisations £190,000
**TRUSTEES** Ms M. Matheson; J. Roberts; Ms C. Younger.
**OTHER INFORMATION** The grant total is an approximation, based on the previous year's grant total being 85% of the trust's annual expenditure.
**HOW TO APPLY** There is no formal application form; applicants should write to the correspondent. Details of the project should be included together with a copy of the most recent audited accounts.
**WHO TO APPLY TO** The Trustees, c/o Geoghegan and Co, 6 St Colme Street, Edinburgh EH3 6AD

## ■ The Craps Charitable Trust
**CC NO** 271492   **ESTABLISHED** 1976
**WHERE FUNDING CAN BE GIVEN** UK, Israel.
**WHO CAN BENEFIT** Charitable organisations, particularly Jewish organisations.
**WHAT IS FUNDED** General charitable purposes.
**RANGE OF GRANTS** Up to £25,000.
**SAMPLE GRANTS** British Technion Society (£25,000); Jewish Care (£20,000); Nightingale – Home for Aged Jews, The Friends of The Jerusalem Botanical Gardens (£16,000 each); Jerusalem Foundation (£14,000); Ben-Gurion University Foundation, British Friends of Herzog Hospital (£4,000 each); Freedom from Torture, The United Jewish Israel Appeal (£3,000 each); Motor Neurone Disease Association, Save the Children (£2,000 each); Anglo Israel Association, Amnesty International, Friends of the Royal Botanic Gardens Kew, National Theatre, Shelter (£1,000 each).
**FINANCES** Year 2013/14 Income £186,484 Grants £182,500 Grants to organisations £182,500 Assets £4,190,006
**TRUSTEES** Caroline Dent; Jonathan Dent; Louisa Dent.
**HOW TO APPLY** Apply in writing to the correspondent.
**WHO TO APPLY TO** The Trustees, Grant Thornton, Chartered Accountants, 202 Silbury Boulevard, Milton Keynes MK9 1LW Tel. 01908 660666

## ■ Michael Crawford Children's Charity
**CC NO** 1042211   **ESTABLISHED** 1994
**WHERE FUNDING CAN BE GIVEN** Throughout England and Wales.
**WHO CAN BENEFIT** Children and young people especially those disadvantaged by poverty and/or illness, organisations benefitting such people.
**WHAT IS FUNDED** Relief of sickness; prevention and relief of poverty.
**TYPE OF GRANT** Grants to individuals and institutions.
**SAMPLE GRANTS** The Sick Children's Trust (£50,000).
**FINANCES** Year 2012/13 Income £640,034 Grants £30,000 Grants to organisations £30,000 Assets £4,922,205
**TRUSTEES** Alan Clark; Michael Crawford; Kenneth Dias; Natasha Macaller.
**OTHER INFORMATION** The 2012/13 accounts were the latest available at the time of writing (June 2015).
**HOW TO APPLY** Apply in writing to the correspondent.
**WHO TO APPLY TO** Kenneth Dias, Trustee, Regina House, 124 Finchley Road, London NW3 5JS Tel. 020 7433 2400

## ■ The Cray Trust
**SC NO** SC005592   **ESTABLISHED** 1976
**WHERE FUNDING CAN BE GIVEN** Mainly the east of Scotland.
**WHO CAN BENEFIT** Charitable organisations and community groups in Scotland.
**WHAT IS FUNDED** General charitable purposes, including: education; health; community development; arts and culture; participation in sports; ill health; disability; relief of poverty.
**WHAT IS NOT FUNDED** No support is given for political appeals and large UK or international charities. No grants are given to individuals.
**TYPE OF GRANT** One-off grants.
**RANGE OF GRANTS** Usually under £1,000.
**SAMPLE GRANTS Previous beneficiaries have included:** Charitable Assets Trust; Canine Partners; Equibuddy; Equine Grass Sickness Fund; Princess Royal Trust for Carers; Alzheimer's Scotland; Cherish India; Backup Trust; Barnardo's Scotland; the Priory Church; and Rainbow RDA.
**FINANCES** Year 2013/14 Income £56,046 Grants £60,000 Grants to organisations £60,000
**HOW TO APPLY** This trust does not accept unsolicited applications. The correspondent has stated that the trust already has more beneficiaries than it can handle.
**WHO TO APPLY TO** The Trustees, c/o Springfords Accountants, Dundas House, Westfield Park, Eskbank, Edinburgh EH22 3FB

## ■ Creative Scotland
**ESTABLISHED** 2010
**WHERE FUNDING CAN BE GIVEN** Scotland.
**WHO CAN BENEFIT** Organisations and individuals.
**WHAT IS FUNDED** Creative Scotland is a public body that, through a range of programmes, distributes funding from the Scottish government and The National Lottery. It supports the arts, screen and creative industries across the whole of Scotland by 'helping others to develop great ideas and bring them to life'.

**WHAT IS NOT FUNDED** Many programmes have their own specific exclusions, more details of which are available on the Creative Scotland website. In general, the following cannot apply: individuals not based in Scotland; students in full-time education at the date of the project start; individuals working in the museum or heritage sector (unless it can be demonstrated that the main benefit of the project will be to an area supported by Creative Scotland); professional development funding for academics and other education professionals.

**SAMPLE GRANTS** Royal Lyceum Theatre Company (£1.2 million); Centre for the Moving Image (£750,000); Sistema Scotland (£400,000); Theatre Cryptic (£247,000); Glasgow Sculpture Studios (£166,500); Red Note Ensemble (£82,000); Highland Print Studio (£70,000); engage Scotland (£30,000).

**FINANCES** Year 2014/15 Income £88,152,698 Grants £84,853,444 Grants to organisations £84,853,444

**TRUSTEES** Steve Grimmond; Prof. Robin Macpherson; Dr Gary West; Ruth Wishart; Barclay Price; Fergus Muir; May Miller; Richard Scott; Sandra Gunn; Richard Findlay.

**OTHER INFORMATION** Creative Scotland assumed the responsibilities and function of the Scottish Arts Council in 2010. For a complete list and details of each funding programme that Creative Scotland operates visit the website. The figures above were taken from the organisation's Summary Budget 2014/15. The grant total includes funding awarded to individuals during the year.

**HOW TO APPLY** For information on the various funding programmes available, visit the Creative Scotland website.

**WHO TO APPLY TO** Janine Hunt, Director of Operations, 249 West George Street, Glasgow G2 4QE Tel. 0845 603 6000 email enquiries@creativescotland.com Website www.creativescotland.com

........

## ■ The Crerar Hotels Trust (formerly the North British Hotel Trust)

**CC NO** 221335 **ESTABLISHED** 1903
**WHERE FUNDING CAN BE GIVEN** Scotland.
**WHO CAN BENEFIT** Mainly registered charities.
**WHAT IS FUNDED** General charitable purposes, mainly welfare, health, older people and people with disabilities.
**WHAT IS NOT FUNDED** Individuals.
**TYPE OF GRANT** Capital, revenue and project funding.
**RANGE OF GRANTS** £200–£25,000
**SAMPLE GRANTS** Hospitality Industry Trust Scotland (£25,000); Children 1st (£20,000); Children's Hospice Association Scotland (£17,700); The Movement for Non-Mobile Children — Whizz-Kidz (£15,000); Cancer Link Aberdeen &. North, Macmillan Cancer Support (£10,000 each); Scottish Autism (£6,000); Discovery Camps Trust (£3,000); St Columba's Cathedral, Citizens Theatre Limited (£1,000); Action on Hearing Loss Scotland (£500); Cullonden/Smithton Senior Citizens Club (£200).
**FINANCES** Year 2013/14 Income £430,439 Grants £407,020 Grants to organisations £407,020 Assets £10,582,916
**TRUSTEES** Patrick Crerar; Graham Brown; Jeanette Crerar; Mike Still; James Barrack; John Williams; Claire Smith; Tarquin de Burgh.
**HOW TO APPLY** Application forms are available from the correspondent.

**WHO TO APPLY TO** Patrick Crerar, Clerk, c/o Crerar Management Limited, 1 Queen Charlotte Lane, Edinburgh EH6 6BL Tel. 0843 050 2020 email crerarhotelstrust@samuelston.com

........

## ■ The Crescent Trust

**CC NO** 327644 **ESTABLISHED** 1987
**WHERE FUNDING CAN BE GIVEN** UK.
**WHO CAN BENEFIT** Charitable organisations.
**WHAT IS FUNDED** The arts; heritage; ecology.
**TYPE OF GRANT** One-off and recurrent.
**RANGE OF GRANTS** £100–£11,000
**SAMPLE GRANTS** Public Monuments and Sculpture Association (£11,000); The Watts Gallery (£10,000); The Eternal Baroque Publication (£4,000); Chalke Valley History Trust (£2,500); Countryside Alliance (£500); Save the Children (£250); and Salisbury Hospice (£100).
**FINANCES** Year 2013–14 Income £144,909 Grants £43,692 Grants to organisations £43,692 Assets £473,435
**TRUSTEES** John Tham; Richard Lascelles.
**HOW TO APPLY** The trustees state that they do not respond to unsolicited applications.
**WHO TO APPLY TO** Christine Akehurst, Correspondent, 9 Queripel House, 1 Duke of York Square, London SW3 4LY Tel. 020 7730 5420 email mail@thecrescenttrust.co.uk

........

## ■ Criffel Charitable Trust

**CC NO** 1040680 **ESTABLISHED** 1994
**WHERE FUNDING CAN BE GIVEN** UK and overseas.
**WHO CAN BENEFIT** Registered charities, churches and schools.
**WHAT IS FUNDED** The advancement of Christianity and the relief of poverty, sickness and other needs.
**WHAT IS NOT FUNDED** Individuals.
**TYPE OF GRANT** Up to three years.
**RANGE OF GRANTS** Up to £53,000.
**SAMPLE GRANTS** Advancement of Christianity (£73,000); Relief of Sickness (£16,500); Relief of the Poor and Needy (£19,000); Miscellaneous (£1,000). Included in the above list is a grant to Four Oaks Methodist Church (£53,000); Action Centres UK (£5,000). All other non-specified donations were reported to be under £2,000.
**FINANCES** Year 2013/14 Income £104,122 Grants £109,850 Grants to organisations £109,850 Assets £1,805,459
**TRUSTEES** Jim Lees; Joy Harvey; Juliet Lees.
**HOW TO APPLY** The trust states that 'unsolicited applications are declined on each of two applications and shredded on a third application.'
**WHO TO APPLY TO** The Trustees, Ravenswood Lodge, 1a Wentworth Road, Sutton Coldfield B74 2SG Tel. 0121 308 1575

........

## ■ Cripplegate Foundation

**CC NO** 207499 **ESTABLISHED** 1891
**WHERE FUNDING CAN BE GIVEN** London borough of Islington and part of the City of London.
**WHO CAN BENEFIT** Charitable organisations, schools and organisations working with schools and individuals.
**WHAT IS FUNDED** Grants which aim to improve the quality of life in the area of benefit and provide opportunities for local residents. All of the foundation's work is informed by the following programme objectives: financial inclusion and

capability; advice and access to services; supporting families; investing in young people; mental health and well-being; and confronting isolation. At the time of writing, a new grants programme was under development.

**WHAT IS NOT FUNDED** At the time of writing, a new grants programme was under development. The following exclusions applied to the main grants programme in its previous form and we have kept them as a general guide to activities the foundation is likely not to fund: national charities or organisations outside the area of benefit; schemes or activities which would relieve central or local government of their statutory responsibilities; grants to replace cuts in funding made by the local authority or others; medical research or equipment; national fundraising appeals; advancement of religion unless the applicant also offers non-religious services to the community; animal welfare; retrospective grants; commercial or business activities; grants for events held in the church of St Giles-without-Cripplegate; grants to organisations recruiting volunteers in south Islington for work overseas. Note that exclusions for the new grants programme may differ from those listed here.

**TYPE OF GRANT** Grants for core costs, project funding, salary costs and capital costs, up to three years.

**RANGE OF GRANTS** Main grants ranged between £15,000 and £45,000.

**SAMPLE GRANTS** The Claremont Project and Solace Women's Aid (£45,000 each); Freightliners Farm Ltd (£32,000); Chance UK (£26,000); Culpeper Community Garden (£20,000); Islington Community Theatre (£16,500); Caspari Foundation (£14,800).

**FINANCES** Year 2013 Income £2,255,672 Grants £921,405 Grants to organisations £814,027 Assets £34,981,390

**TRUSTEE** Cripplegate Foundation Limited – Sole Corporate Trustee

**OTHER INFORMATION** The grants totals above (which do not take into account support, pro-activity and research costs) include funds administered by the foundation on behalf of other charities. Excluding support and other costs, 19 Cripplegate main grants made during the year amounted to £316,500. For more details of the funds administered by the foundation, including Islington Council's Community Chest and Richard Cloudesley's Charity, see Cripplegate's helpful website. Excluding support costs, grants to individuals amounted to £107,500 during the year.

**HOW TO APPLY** At the time of writing (June 2015) the foundation's main grants scheme was closed and a new grants programme was under development. If you wish to be kept informed of the development of the programme, send an email to grants@cripplegate.org.uk. Alternatively, visit the website for updates.

**WHO TO APPLY TO** Kristina Glenn, Director, 13 Elliott's Place, Islington, London N1 8HX *Tel.* 020 7288 6940 *email* grants@cripplegate.org.uk *Website* www.cripplegate.org

■ **The Violet and Milo Cripps Charitable Trust**

**CC NO** 289404   **ESTABLISHED** 1984
**WHERE FUNDING CAN BE GIVEN** UK.
**WHO CAN BENEFIT** Charitable organisations.
**WHAT IS FUNDED** Prison and human rights.

**SAMPLE GRANTS** Previous beneficiaries have included: Lancaster University, the Prison Advice and Care Trust, Dorothy House Hospice Care, Frank Langford Charitable Trust and Trinity Hospice.

**FINANCES** Year 2013/14 Income £506,261 Grants £530,600 Grants to organisations £530,600 Assets £658,895

**TRUSTEES** Richard Linenthal; Anthony Newhouse; Jennifer Beattie.

**HOW TO APPLY** The trust states that unsolicited applications will not receive a response.

**WHO TO APPLY TO** The Trustees, Wedlake Bell, 52 Bedford Row, London WC1R 4LR

■ **The Cross Trust**

**SC NO** SC008620   **ESTABLISHED** 1943
**WHERE FUNDING CAN BE GIVEN** Scotland.
**WHO CAN BENEFIT** Individuals and organisations.
**WHAT IS FUNDED** About 80% of the grants are given to individuals for educational purposes (including travel for their courses). Grants to organisations are normally made for music, drama or outdoor activities to benefit young people.

**WHAT IS NOT FUNDED** Retrospective applications.
**TYPE OF GRANT** Normally one-off, occasionally for longer periods.

**SAMPLE GRANTS** Previous beneficiaries have included: Grants to organisations in excess of £2,000 were: Perth Festival of Fine Arts (£10,000); Perth Theatre and Concert Hall, Out of the Blue Arts and Education Trust (£5,000 each); Byre Theatre (£2,000). Grants to individuals ranged from £500 to just over £2,000 with the largest of these in support of: Fine art, music, law, history and nursing.

**FINANCES** Year 2013/14 Income £203,410 Grants £120,000 Grants to organisations £120,000

**TRUSTEES** Beppo Buchanan-Smith; Hannah Buchanan-Smith; Prof. R. H. MacDougall; Clair Meredith; Dougal Philip; Mark Webster.

**OTHER INFORMATION** We estimate grants to be in the region of £120,000 for 2013/14. Grants are made to both individuals and organisations.

**HOW TO APPLY** Application forms and guidance notes are available from the correspondent. Deadlines for applications as follows: University and college courses and other studies: 1 Feb, 7 June and 30 Aug Vacation studies in the arts: 1 April Medical elective studies abroad: 1 April, 30 Sept and 31 Dec John Fife travel awards: 1st Organisations: 1 Feb and 16 Aug

**WHO TO APPLY TO** Kathleen Carnegie, McCash and Hunter Solicitors, 25 South Methven Street, Perth PH1 5ES *Tel.* 01738 620451 *email* kathleencarnegie@mccash.co.uk *Website* www.thecrosstrust.org.uk

■ **The Croydon Relief in Need Charities**

**CC NO** 810114   **ESTABLISHED** 1962
**WHERE FUNDING CAN BE GIVEN** The borough of Croydon.
**WHO CAN BENEFIT** Local charities and individuals.
**WHAT IS FUNDED** General charitable purposes; health; social welfare.
**TYPE OF GRANT** Recurrent.
**RANGE OF GRANTS** Up to £50,000.
**SAMPLE GRANTS** Home-Start Croydon (£20,000); Marie Curie Cancer Care (£19,000); Croydon Mencap (£15,900) Nordoff-Robbins Music

Therapy for St Giles School (£12,000); Selsdon Centre Trust (£8,000); Alzheimer's Society (£5,500); Family Focus (£5,000); Missing People, Happy Days Children's Charity, Kazzum Arts Project (£2,000); A-T Society (£250).

FINANCES Year 2013 Income £146,106 Grants £134,844 Grants to organisations £131,886 Assets £24,561

TRUSTEES Noel Hepworth; Lynda Talbot; Mrs C. Trower; Alan Galer; Diana Harries; Diana Hemmings; Caroline Melrose; Christopher Clementi; Revd Canon Colin Boswell; John Tough; John Tough; Gail Winter; Deborah Knight; Martin Evans.

OTHER INFORMATION Grants were made to two individuals totalling £3,000.

HOW TO APPLY Apply in writing to the correspondent. Guidelines and criteria are available to view on the website.

WHO TO APPLY TO Mr W. Rymer, Clerk, Elis David Almshouses, Duppas Hill Terrace, Croydon CR0 4BT Tel. 020 8774 9382 email billrymer@croydonalmshousecharities.org.uk Website www.croydonalmshousecharities.org.uk

■ **The Peter Cruddas Foundation**

CC NO 1117323  ESTABLISHED 2006

WHERE FUNDING CAN BE GIVEN UK, with a particular interest in London.

WHO CAN BENEFIT Registered charities.

WHAT IS FUNDED The foundation gives priority to programmes calculated to help disadvantaged young people to pursue their education (including vocational) and more generally develop their potential whether through sport or recreation, voluntary programmes or otherwise. Preference is given to the support of projects undertaken by charitable organisations for the benefit of those young people, but consideration will also be given in appropriate circumstances to applications for individual support. The foundation adopts a priority funding programme scheme that is available to be scrutinised on the web site. The programmes are subject to trustee review at any time. In addition to financial funding given by the foundation, it also provides mentoring support to many organisations through the foundation administrator's experience in the third sector.

TYPE OF GRANT One-off and recurrent grants for capital and revenue costs.

RANGE OF GRANTS £200–£236,000

SAMPLE GRANTS Royal Opera House Foundation (£236,000); Crimestoppers (£80,000); The Heart Cells Foundation, and The Presidents Club Charitable Trust (£15,000 each); Royal Ballet School (£10,000); Great Ormond Street Hospital Children's Charity (£5,000); Chickenshed Theatre (£2,000); Action Adventure (£1,800); Zambezi River Challenge (£600); Southern 50 Challenge, and St John Ambulance Wiltshire (£500 each).

FINANCES Year 2013/14 Income £513,105 Grants £366,657 Grants to organisations £366,657 Assets £88,517

TRUSTEES Lord David Young, Chair; Peter Cruddas; Martin Paisner.

OTHER INFORMATION No grants were given to individuals.

HOW TO APPLY Application forms are available to download from the foundation's website. The foundation provides guidance on how to complete the application form, also available on the website.

WHO TO APPLY TO Stephen Cox, Correspondent, 133 Houndsditch, London EC3A 7BX Tel. 020 3003 8360 Fax 020 3003 8580 email s.cox@pcfoundation.org.uk Website www.petercruddasfoundation.org.uk

■ **Cruden Foundation Ltd**

SC NO SC004987  ESTABLISHED 1956

WHERE FUNDING CAN BE GIVEN Mainly Scotland.

WHO CAN BENEFIT Registered charities.

WHAT IS FUNDED General charitable purposes.

WHAT IS NOT FUNDED Individuals.

TYPE OF GRANT Recurrent and one-off.

RANGE OF GRANTS Up to £18,000.

SAMPLE GRANTS Edinburgh International Festival (£17,500); St Columba's Hospice (£11,000); Marie Curie Cancer Care (£10,000); Festival City Theatres Trust (£7,500); Scottish Cancer Foundation (£3,000); Scottish Seabird Centre (£2,500); Gurkha Welfare Trust (£2,000); Open Door (£1,500); and the Factory Skatepark, Bobath Scotland, Corstorphine Trust, NSPCC Scotland and Dyslexia Action (£1,000 each).

FINANCES Year 2013/14 Income £489,299 Grants £336,490 Grants to organisations £336,490

TRUSTEES J. C. Rafferty, Chair; M. R. A. Matthews; J. G. Mitchell; A. Johnston; M. J. Rowley; D. D. Walker; K. D. Reid.

HOW TO APPLY Apply in writing to the correspondent, accompanied by most recent accounts.

WHO TO APPLY TO Mr M. J. Rowley, Secretary, Baberton House, Juniper Green, Edinburgh EH14 3HN

■ **The Ronald Cruickshanks Foundation**

CC NO 296075  ESTABLISHED 1987

WHERE FUNDING CAN BE GIVEN UK, with some preference for Folkestone, Faversham and the surrounding area.

WHO CAN BENEFIT Individuals and organisations, including various local churches.

WHAT IS FUNDED General charitable purposes, particularly for the benefit of people in financial and other need within the beneficial area.

TYPE OF GRANT Recurrent.

RANGE OF GRANTS £250–£9,000

SAMPLE GRANTS Demelza House Children's Hospice (£9,500); Holy Trinity Church and Jesuit Missions (4,000 each); St Augustine's Centre (£2,000); Independent Age, Kent Lupus Group, Prostate Cancer UK and Shepway Citizens Advice (£1,000 each); Action for Kids and Hospice in the Weald (£500 each); and Kent Crimestoppers (£250).

FINANCES Year 2013/14 Income £27,722 Grants £186,600 Grants to organisations £186,600 Assets £1,467,438

TRUSTEES Susan Cloke; Ian Cloke; Jan Schilder.

HOW TO APPLY Apply in writing to the correspondent. Applications should be received by the end of September for consideration on a date coinciding closely with the anniversary of the death of the founder, which was 7 December.

WHO TO APPLY TO Ian Cloke, Trustee, 34 Cheriton Gardens, Folkestone, Kent CT20 2AX Tel. 01303 251742 email ian@iancloke.co.uk

## ■ The Cuby Charitable Trust

**CC NO** 328585 **ESTABLISHED** 1990
**WHERE FUNDING CAN BE GIVEN** UK; overseas.
**WHO CAN BENEFIT** Registered charities.
**WHAT IS FUNDED** Jewish causes.
**SAMPLE GRANTS** A list of grants was not provided with the accounts to indicate the size or number of beneficiaries during the year. No information on previous beneficiaries is currently available.
**FINANCES** Year 2012/13 Income £70,000 Grants £79,974 Grants to organisations £79,974 Assets £305,123
**TRUSTEES** C. Cuby; Sidney Cuby; Jonathan Cuby; Raquel Talmor.
**OTHER INFORMATION** The 2012/13 accounts were the latest available at the time of writing (June 2015). A list of grant beneficiaries was included not with the accounts.
**HOW TO APPLY** Apply in writing to the correspondent.
**WHO TO APPLY TO** Sidney Cuby, Trustee, 16 Mowbray Road, Edgware HA8 8JQ Tel. 020 7563 6868

## ■ Cullum Family Trust

**CC NO** 1117056 **ESTABLISHED** 2006
**WHERE FUNDING CAN BE GIVEN** UK.
**WHO CAN BENEFIT** Registered charities and institutions.
**WHAT IS FUNDED** Social welfare; education; general charitable purposes.
**TYPE OF GRANT** One off and up to two years funding.
**RANGE OF GRANTS** £500–£70,000
**SAMPLE GRANTS** City University (£70,000); Cancer Research (£5,500); RADA (£550).
**FINANCES** Year 2013/14 Income £1,341,819 Grants £79,709 Grants to organisations £79,709 Assets £26,859,731
**TRUSTEES** Ann Cullum; Claire Cullum; Peter Cullum; Simon Cullum.
**OTHER INFORMATION** The trust offers full project funding and will fund core and capital costs.
**HOW TO APPLY** Apply in writing to the correspondent.
**WHO TO APPLY TO** Peter Cullum, Trustee, Wealden Hall, Parkfield, Sevenoaks TN15 0HX

## ■ The Cumber Family Charitable Trust

**CC NO** 291009 **ESTABLISHED** 1985
**WHERE FUNDING CAN BE GIVEN** Worldwide, with a preference for financially developing countries and Berkshire and Oxfordshire.
**WHO CAN BENEFIT** Charitable organisations.
**WHAT IS FUNDED** General charitable purposes, with preference being given to overseas projects, housing and welfare, children, youth and education, medical and disability and environment.
**WHAT IS NOT FUNDED** Individuals are not usually supported. Individuals with local connections and who are personally known to the trustees are occasionally supported.
**TYPE OF GRANT** One-off grants.
**RANGE OF GRANTS** £200–£8,000
**SAMPLE GRANTS** Helen and Douglas House and Oxford Radcliffe Hospitals Charitable Trust (£2,000 each); Marcham with Garford Youth and Children's Minister (£1,500); Arts for All, Azafady, Barnardo's, Children of Choba, Excellent Development, Footsteps Foundation Tanzania (UK) Trust and WaterAid (£1,000 each); Cued Speech and The Who Cares? Trust (£500 each); and 1st White Knights Brownies (£250).
**FINANCES** Year 2013/14 Income £37,884 Grants £45,751 Grants to organisations £45,751 Assets £665,369
**TRUSTEES** William Cumber; Mary Tearney; Alec Davey; Margaret Freeman; Julia Mearns.
**HOW TO APPLY** Applications must be sent in paper format and not via email. There is no formal application; however, the trust has provided guidelines which can be found on the trust's website. Applications must be sent to the secretary. The trustees meet twice a year to consider applications, usually in March and November. Applications need to be made at least a month before the meeting date. First time applicants must provide a copy of the latest annual report and accounts.
**WHO TO APPLY TO** Mary Tearney, Trustee, Manor Farm, Mill Road, Marcham, Abingdon OX13 6NZ Tel. 01865 391327 email mary.tearney@hotmail.co.uk Website www.cumberfamilycharitabletrust.org.uk

## ■ Cumbria Community Foundation

**CC NO** 1075120 **ESTABLISHED** 1999
**WHERE FUNDING CAN BE GIVEN** Cumbria.
**WHO CAN BENEFIT** Community and voluntary groups; individuals.
**WHAT IS FUNDED** Improving the quality of the community life of people in Cumbria, and in particular those in need by reason of disability, age, low-income or other disadvantage.
**WHAT IS NOT FUNDED** Animal welfare; contact boxing (unless the application is to Comic Relief); deficit funding; general large appeals; medical research; non-Cumbrian projects; sponsored events; activities which are usually the responsibility of statutory bodies; activities that have already happened; applications for funds from which you have had a grant in the past 12 months. Statutory bodies are ineligible to apply to most funds. Individual funds may be subject to their own exclusions. See the website for more information.
**TYPE OF GRANT** One off and recurring.
**RANGE OF GRANTS** Generally under £10,000.
**SAMPLE GRANTS** Cumbria Youth Alliance and Howgill Family Centre (£50,000 each); Disability Association Carlisle and Eden – DaCE (£22,000); Maryport Amateur Rugby League Club (£15,000); Hunsonby Swimming Club (£14,900); Age UK South Lakeland (£8,000); British Red Cross (£6,100); Friends of Tebay Church (£6,000); Copeland Occupational and Social Centre – COSC, West Cumbria Rape Crisis Ltd – WCRC and Workington Heritage Group Ltd – WHG (£5,000 each).
**FINANCES** Year 2013/14 Income £3,388,142 Grants £1,949,403 Grants to organisations £1,938,654 Assets £9,771,328
**TRUSTEES** Ian Brown; Rob Cairns; David Brown; James Airey; Tony Burbridge; Robin Burgess; Tim Cartmell; Mike Casson; Tom Foster; Cath Giel; Jane Humphries; Tim Knowles; Adam Naylor Willie Slavin; Sarah Snyder; Chris Tomlinson OBE; John Whittle; Diane Wood; Valerie Young.
**OTHER INFORMATION** During the year 251 grants were made, of which 19 grants totalling £10,700 were awarded to individuals. A number of grants, ranging from £6,000 to £150,000, were made in support of six partnerships through the Neighbourhood Care Independence Programme. Grants were also made in partnership with Age UK organisations as part of the Winter Warmth Appeal.

**HOW TO APPLY** Each fund is subject to its own criteria, which are detailed on the individual webpages of each. Most funds share the same online application form, with the foundation deciding the fund to which your application is most suited. Applications are subject to deadline dates which can be found, along with further guidelines, on the website.
**WHO TO APPLY TO** Andrew Beeforth, Director, Dovenby Hall, Dovenby, Cockermouth, Cumbria CA13 0PN *Tel.* 01900 825760 *email* enquiries@cumbriafoundation.org *Website* www.cumbriafoundation.org

## ■ The Cunningham Trust

**SC NO** SC013499 **ESTABLISHED** 1984
**WHERE FUNDING CAN BE GIVEN** Scotland.
**WHO CAN BENEFIT** Mostly universities, also individuals.
**WHAT IS FUNDED** Academic research in the field of medicine and zoology.
**WHAT IS NOT FUNDED** Grants are unlikely to be made available to non-regular beneficiaries.
**TYPE OF GRANT** Revenue and project funding for up to two years.
**SAMPLE GRANTS** Aberdeen University – Department of Zoology, Aberdeen University – Department of Ophthalmology, Department of Biomedical Sciences, Edinburgh University's Centre of Tropical Veterinary Medicine and St Andrew's University – School of Biomedical Sciences.
**FINANCES** *Year* 2013/14 *Income* £257,447 *Grants* £240,362 *Grants to organisations* £240,362
**TRUSTEES** Dr D. Corner; A. C. Caithness; Dr D. M. Greenhough.
**HOW TO APPLY** All applications must be submitted on the standard form.
**WHO TO APPLY TO** Kim Falconer, Correspondent, Murray Donald Drummond Cook LLP, Kinburn Castle, St Andrews, Fife KY16 9DR *email* kfalconer@murraydonald.co.uk

## ■ The Harry Cureton Charitable Trust

**CC NO** 1106206 **ESTABLISHED** 2005
**WHERE FUNDING CAN BE GIVEN** The area covered by Peterborough and Stamford hospitals.
**WHO CAN BENEFIT** Individuals and organisations.
**WHAT IS FUNDED** Medical causes; health; relief of sickness.
**RANGE OF GRANTS** £900–£11,000
**SAMPLE GRANTS** Paediatric Occupational Therapy (£11,000); Headway Cambridgeshire (£3,000); The Hodgson Centre Surgery (£2,400); The Grange Medical Centre (£2,000); New Sheepmarket Surgery (£1,200); Minster Medical Practice (£900).
**FINANCES** *Year* 2012/13 *Income* £94,802 *Grants* £39,572 *Grants to organisations* £18,687 *Assets* £3,266,663
**TRUSTEES** Nick Monsell; Simon Richards; Nick Plumb; Christopher Banks.
**OTHER INFORMATION** The 2012/13 accounts were the latest available at the time of writing (June 2015). Grants to individuals totalled £21,000. The proportions available for organisations and individuals are not set and vary each year.
**HOW TO APPLY** Application forms are available to download via the website. Grants are administered by the Cambridgeshire Community Foundation.
**WHO TO APPLY TO** Jane Darlington, c/o Cambridgeshire Community Foundation, The Quorum, Barnwell Road, Cambridge CB5 8RE *Tel.* 01223 410535 *email* hcct@cambscf.org.uk *Website* www.harrycureton.org.uk

## ■ D. J. H. Currie Memorial Trust

**CC NO** 802971 **ESTABLISHED** 1990
**WHERE FUNDING CAN BE GIVEN** Essex.
**WHO CAN BENEFIT** Registered charities.
**WHAT IS FUNDED** General charitable purposes. The trust continues to support causes which the founder had an interest in, including charities supporting people with disabilities (particularly children), conservation of the countryside, homes for older people and sporting activities in Essex.
**WHAT IS NOT FUNDED** Individuals.
**SAMPLE GRANTS** Previous beneficiaries have included: Alcohelp; Autism Anglia; Braintree Emergency Night Shelter; Braintree Women's Aid; Finchingfield Guildhall; Holy Family Catholic Church; Little Heath School; St Luke's Hospice; Tabor Centre; The Sea Cadets; Transplant Sport UK.
**FINANCES** *Year* 2013/14 *Income* £61,917 *Grants* £34,000 *Grants to organisations* £34,000
**TRUSTEE** NatWest Trust Services.
**OTHER INFORMATION** At the time of writing (June 2015) the 2013/14 accounts were not yet published by the Charity Commission. Over the past few years the trust has been allocating higher proportion of the overall expenditure in grants. On average about 56% of the expenditure has been awarded in grants. Based on the previous giving patterns it is likely that grants totalled at least £34,000.
**HOW TO APPLY** Applications should be made in writing to the correspondent. The trustees consider appeals in June each year and all requests should be submitted by the end of May. The latest set of annual report and accounts should be enclosed with the application. No recipient may benefit more than once every four years.
**WHO TO APPLY TO** The Trustees, c/o NatWest Trust Services, Ground Floor, Eastwood House, Glebe Road, Chelmsford CM1 1RS *Tel.* 01245 292445 *email* nwb.charities@natwest.com

## ■ The Dennis Curry Charitable Trust

**CC NO** 263952 **ESTABLISHED** 1971
**WHERE FUNDING CAN BE GIVEN** UK.
**WHO CAN BENEFIT** Charitable organisations.
**WHAT IS FUNDED** General charitable purposes, with a particular interest in conservation/environment and education. Occasional support is given to churches and cathedrals.
**RANGE OF GRANTS** £500–£25,000
**SAMPLE GRANTS** Durrel Wildlife Conservation Trust (£25,000) Galapagos Durrel Wildlife Conservation Trust (£25,000); WildCRU (£20,000); Galapagos Conservation Trust (£10,000); South Georgia Heritage Trust (£5,000); University of Glasgow Trinidad Expedition (£2,000); and Médecins Sans Frontières (£1,000); and The Open Spaces Society (£500).
**FINANCES** *Year* 2013/14 *Income* £83,652 *Grants* £75,811 *Grants to organisations* £75,811 *Assets* £3,687,119

TRUSTEES P. A. Curry; Anabel Sylvia Curry; Margaret Curry-Jones; Patricia Rosemary Edmund.
HOW TO APPLY Applications should be made in writing to the correspondent.
WHO TO APPLY TO Nigel Armstrong, Secretary to the Trust, Alliotts, Imperial House, 15 Kingsway, London WC2B 6UN *Tel.* 020 7240 9971 *email* denniscurryscharity@alliotts.com

## ■ The Cwmbran Trust

CC NO 505855   ESTABLISHED 1976
WHERE FUNDING CAN BE GIVEN Cwmbran.
WHO CAN BENEFIT Local groups.
WHAT IS FUNDED Grants are made to provide social amenities, for the advancement of education and the relief of poverty and sickness in the urban area of Cwmbran town. Particular support is given to local groups for older people and people with disabilities.
WHAT IS NOT FUNDED Causes outside Cwmbran; organisational running costs.
RANGE OF GRANTS £100 to £25,000.
SAMPLE GRANTS **Beneficiaries include**: Glen Liwyd Scout Group (£5,600); C Sensory Garden (£12,000); Lucas Girling Sports Association (£10,000); Cwmbran Community Council (£1,500); Parkside Resident's Association (£175) Grants to individuals included funding for the following items: Mobility scooter; shower room (£1,500 each); Bunk beds and mattresses, Household equipment (£400 each); Removal of stairlift (£100).
FINANCES *Year* 2013 *Income* £98,568 *Grants* £65,250 *Grants to organisations* £19,500 *Assets* £2,351,480
TRUSTEE Ken Maddox, John Cunningham, David Bassett, Anna Price and C. Thomas, Dean Horsell.
OTHER INFORMATION The grant total in 2013 includes £19,500 donated to 33 individuals.
HOW TO APPLY Apply in writing to the correspondent. Trustees usually meet five times a year in March, May, July, October and December. Where appropriate, applications are investigated by the grants research officer. When the trustees judge it would be helpful, applicants are invited to put their case to the trustees in person. Where an application has to be dealt with urgently, for example, because of the pressure of time or of need, trustees may be contacted by letter or telephone in order that an early decision may be made.
WHO TO APPLY TO K. L. Maddox, Arvin Meritor HVBS (UK) Ltd, H. V. B. S. (UK) Ltd, Grange Road, Cwmbran, Gwent NP44 3XU *Tel.* 01633 834040 *email* cwmbrantrust@arvinmeritor.com

## ■ Itzchok Meyer Cymerman Trust Ltd

CC NO 265090   ESTABLISHED 1972
WHERE FUNDING CAN BE GIVEN UK and Israel.
WHO CAN BENEFIT Registered charities and occasional small grants to individuals – both mainly of the Jewish faith.
WHAT IS FUNDED Advancement of the Orthodox Jewish faith; education; social welfare; relief of sickness; medical research; general charitable purposes.
TYPE OF GRANT Mostly recurrent.
RANGE OF GRANTS Up to £161,000.
SAMPLE GRANTS Russian Immigrant Aid Fund – advancement of religion/relief of poverty (£161,000); Ichud Mosdos Gur (£115,050); Yeshivat Kolel Breslov (£53,000); Beth Hamidrash Gur (£50,000); Collel Polen Kupath Ramban (£39,800); Telz Academy Trust (£35,000); Society of Friends of the Torah Ltd (£25,000)
FINANCES *Year* 2013/14 *Income* £864,166 *Grants* £691,220 *Grants to organisations* £691,220 *Assets* £11,035,898
TRUSTEES H. F. Bondi; M. D. Cymerman; S. Cymerman; S. Heitner; L. H. Bondi; Ian Heitner.
OTHER INFORMATION **Grants are split between the following areas:** Advancement of religion (£407,870); Relief of poverty (£138,850); Religious education (£124,100); Medical aid (£20,400).
HOW TO APPLY Apply in writing to the correspondent.
WHO TO APPLY TO Ian Heitner, Trustee, 497 Holloway Road, London N7 6LE *Tel.* 020 7272 2255

## ■ D. C. R. Allen Charitable Trust

CC NO 277293   ESTABLISHED 1979
WHERE FUNDING CAN BE GIVEN England and Wales.
WHO CAN BENEFIT Charitable organisations.
WHAT IS FUNDED General charitable purposes.
WHAT IS NOT FUNDED Individuals.
SAMPLE GRANTS Grants were given to 20 charities; however, a list of individual beneficiaries was unavailable.
FINANCES Year 2013/14 Income £1,733,912 Grants £177,500 Grants to organisations £177,500 Assets £3,776,118
TRUSTEES Julie Frusher; Martin Allen; Colin Allen.
OTHER INFORMATION A list of beneficiaries was unavailable.
HOW TO APPLY Apply in writing to the correspondent.
WHO TO APPLY TO Julie Frusher, Trustee, Estate Office, Edgcote House, Edgcote, Banbury, Oxfordshire OX17 1AG email robert.mcdonald@btinternet.com

## ■ The D. G. Charitable Settlement

CC NO 1040778   ESTABLISHED 1994
WHERE FUNDING CAN BE GIVEN UK.
WHO CAN BENEFIT Registered charities.
WHAT IS FUNDED General charitable purposes, mainly supporting a fixed list of charities.
RANGE OF GRANTS £500–£200,000
SAMPLE GRANTS Previous beneficiaries have included: Oxfam (£100,000); Crisis (£40,000); Great Ormond Street Hospital and Shelter (£25,000 each); Cancer Research UK, Environmental Investigation Agency Charitable Trust, Friends of the Earth and Reprieve UK (£10,000 each); Defend the Right to Protest, Media Standards Trust – Hacked Off and University of St Andrews (£5,000 each); Terrence Higgins Trust (£2,000).
FINANCES Year 2013/14 Income £1,120 Grants £350,000 Grants to organisations £350,000
TRUSTEES David Gilmour; Patrick Grafton-Green; Polly Samson.
OTHER INFORMATION The grant total has been estimated based on the charity's expenditure. During the year the charity had an expenditure totalling £365,000.
HOW TO APPLY This charity does not consider unsolicited applications.
WHO TO APPLY TO Joanna Nelson, Secretary, PO Box 62, Heathfield, East Sussex TN21 9ZF Tel. 01435 867604 email joanna.nelson@btconnect.com

## ■ The D'Oyly Carte Charitable Trust

CC NO 1112457   ESTABLISHED 1972
WHERE FUNDING CAN BE GIVEN UK.
WHO CAN BENEFIT Registered charities only, or where it is clear the objects of the appeal are for charitable purposes.
WHAT IS FUNDED Mainly the arts, medical/welfare charities and the environment.
WHAT IS NOT FUNDED The trust is unlikely to support the following: animal welfare; campaigning or lobbying projects; community transport organisations or services; conferences and seminars; exhibitions; expeditions and overseas travel; friend associations and PTAs; general appeals; individuals or applications for the benefit of one individual; large national charities enjoying wide support; local authorities and areas of work considered a statutory requirement; medical research; NHS hospitals for operational and building costs; projects taking place or benefitting people outside the UK; recordings and commissioning of new works; religious causes and activities; routine maintenance of religious buildings; salaries and positions, though the trustees will consider contributing to core operating costs of which they recognise general salary costs will be a part; support and rehabilitation from drug abuse or alcoholism; universities, colleges, schools, nurseries, playgroups (other than those for special needs children). The trustees do not consider requests from charities that have had an application turned down until two years have elapsed after the date of rejection.
TYPE OF GRANT Mainly one-off.
RANGE OF GRANTS Up to £20,000 but mostly £1,000–£5,000.
SAMPLE GRANTS Royal Academy of Dramatic Art – bursaries for undergraduates (£20,000); Somerset Community Foundation (£10,000); Music in Hospitals – concerts for people in hospice care (£5,400); Tommy's – reprint of a health publication (£5,000); Sing for Pleasure – scholarships for young conductors (£4,900); New Writing North – young writers workshops (£4,500); The Royal Opera House Foundation and St David's Hospice Care – Newport (£3,000 each); Story Door (£1,900); and Friends of Kent Churches (£250).
FINANCES Year 2013/14 Income £1,361,483 Grants £117,851 Grants to organisations £117,851 Assets £48,279,781
TRUSTEES Jeremy Pemberton, Chair; Francesca Radcliffe; Julia Sibley; Henry Freeland; Andrew Jackson; Michael O'Brien; Andrew Wimble.
OTHER INFORMATION Grants were made to 290 organisations in 2013/14.
HOW TO APPLY Potential applicants should write to the correspondent with an outline proposal of no more than two A4 pages. This should cover the work of the charity, its beneficiaries and the need for funding. Applicants qualifying for consideration will then be required to complete the trust's application form. The form should be returned with a copy of the latest annual report and accounts. Applications for specific projects should also include clear details of the need the intended project is designed to meet and an outline budget.
WHO TO APPLY TO Sarah Conley, Grants Administrator, 6 Trull Farm Buildings, Tetbury, Gloucestershire GL8 8SQ Tel. 020 3637 3003 email info@doylycartecharitabletrust.org Website www.doylycartecharitabletrust.org

## ■ Roald Dahl's Marvellous Children's Charity

CC NO 1137409   ESTABLISHED 1991
WHERE FUNDING CAN BE GIVEN UK.
WHO CAN BENEFIT Registered charities and individuals. In general, the charity aims to provide help to organisations where funds are not readily available. Preference for small or new organisations rather than long-established, large or national organisations.

**WHAT IS FUNDED** 'The charity makes grants to benefit children who have the following conditions. Neurology: acquired brain injury as the result of benign brain tumour, encephalitis, head injury, hydrocephalus, meningitis, stroke, neuro-degenerative conditions, defined as conditions in which there is progressive intellectual and/or neurological deterioration and rare and/or severe forms of epilepsy; Haematology: chronic debilitating blood diseases of childhood, excluding leukaemia and related disorders; conditions include: sickle cell anaemia, thalassaemia, haemolytic anaemia, bone marrow failure syndrome, haemophilia, thrombophilia and Von Willebrand's Disease. The charity primarily makes grants to benefit children (i.e. up to the 18th birthday). However, we may consider supporting young people between the ages of 18 and 25 (i.e. up to the 26th birthday) where a case can be made that they have specific needs associated with their medical condition. We are looking for applications that will clearly tackle the needs and challenges children face as a result of living with the conditions listed above. We are particularly interested in: pump-priming of new specialist Paediatric nursing posts, where there is an emphasis on community care, for a maximum of 2 years. We will only consider funding posts where the applicant organisation commits to taking over funding of the post for a minimum of 3 years after our grant ends; the provision of information and/or support to children and their families; specific projects within residential and day centres to benefit children within the above-mentioned criteria; small items of medical equipment, not available from statutory sources, to enable children to be cared for in their own homes; activities to disseminate good practice in support of children living with our priority conditions; other projects which specifically benefit children and young people within the above mentioned medical criteria may be considered. Although we prefer to fund specific projects, posts and activities, we will consider providing core funding particularly in the case of very small organisations.'
**WHAT IS NOT FUNDED** General appeals from large, well-established charities; national appeals for large building projects; arts projects; any organisations which do not have charitable status or exclusively charitable aims (other than NHS organisations under the charity's specialist nurses programme); statutory bodies (other than NHS organisations under the charity's specialist nurses programme); school or higher education fees; organisations outside the UK; organisations for people with blood disorders which are cancer related due to the relatively large number of charities helping in the oncological field.
**TYPE OF GRANT** One-off, start-up costs, salaries, projects for up to two years; the range is wide.
**RANGE OF GRANTS** Up to £21,000.
**SAMPLE GRANTS** Sickle Cell and Young Stroke Survivors (£21,760); UK Children's Neurological Research Campaign (£19,300); Reverse Rett (aka Rett Syndrome Research Trust UK) (£18,500); Brainbox (£12,000); Genetic Disorders UK (£11,000); Batten Disease Family Association, Encephalitis Society (£10,000 each); Kids Care (£9,300); Hope for Paediatric Epilepsy (£2,200); Royal Surrey County Hospital (£300).
**FINANCES** Year 2013/14 Income £868,730 Grants £468,335 Grants to organisations £404,035 Assets £1,460,757

**TRUSTEES** Felicity Dahl, Chair; Martin Goodwin; Roger Hills; Georgina Cannon; Virginia Myer; Graham Faulkner; Donald Sturrok.
**OTHER INFORMATION** The charity was established in 2010 to supersede the Roald Dahl Foundation following a strategic review, although the focus of the charity remains the same.
**HOW TO APPLY** Visit the charity's website for full and current information on how to apply.
**WHO TO APPLY TO** Dr Richard Piper, Chief Executive, 81a High Street, Great Missenden, Buckinghamshire HP16 0AL *Tel.* 01494 890465 *Fax* 01494 890459 *email* grants@marvellouschildrenscharity.org *Website* www.roalddahlcharity.org

## ■ Daily Prayer Union Charitable Trust Limited

**CC NO** 284857 **ESTABLISHED** 1983
**WHERE FUNDING CAN BE GIVEN** UK.
**WHO CAN BENEFIT** Christians and evangelists.
**WHAT IS FUNDED** Evangelical Christian purposes.
**RANGE OF GRANTS** £1,000–£7,000
**SAMPLE GRANTS Previous beneficiaries have included:** Monkton Combe School (£7,000); Jesus Lane Trust (£3,000); London City Mission and People International (£2,000 each); Interserve (£1,500); and AIM International (£1,000).
**FINANCES** Year 2013/14 Income £45,944 Grants £39,000 Grants to organisations £39,000 Assets £34,890
**TRUSTEES** Revd David Jackman; Revd Timothy Sterry; Anne Tompson; Elizabeth Bridger; Fiona Ashton; Dr Joanna Sudell; Giles Rawlinson; Revd Raymond Porter; Carolyn Ash.
**OTHER INFORMATION** Grants totalling £30,750 was shared between an undisclosed number of individuals. (2013/14).
**HOW TO APPLY** The trustees meet regularly to review applications for new grants and grants which are due for renewal.
**WHO TO APPLY TO** Clare Palmer, Secretary, 12 Weymouth Street, London W1W 5BY *email* dputrust@hotmail.co.uk

## ■ The Daiwa Anglo-Japanese Foundation

**CC NO** 299955 **ESTABLISHED** 1988
**WHERE FUNDING CAN BE GIVEN** UK, Japan.
**WHO CAN BENEFIT** Individuals and organisations (UK or Japanese) benefitting young adults, students and Japanese people – including schools, universities, grass roots and professional groups.
**WHAT IS FUNDED** The education of citizens of the UK and Japan in each other's culture, institutions, arts, and so on. Scholarships, bursaries and awards to enable students and academics in the UK and Japan to pursue their education abroad. Grants to charitable organisations and institutions promoting education in the UK or Japan, and research.
**WHAT IS NOT FUNDED** Daiwa Foundation Small Grants cannot be used for: general appeals; capital expenditure (e.g., building refurbishment, equipment acquisition, etc.); consumables (e.g., stationery, scientific supplies, etc.); school, college or university fees; research or study by an individual school/college/university student; salary costs or professional fees; commissions for works of art; retrospective grants; replacement of statutory funding; commercial

activities. Daiwa Foundation Awards cannot be used for: any project that does not involve both a British and a Japanese partner; general appeals; capital expenditure (e.g., building refurbishment, equipment acquisition, etc.); salary costs or professional fees; commissions for works of art; retrospective grants; commercial activities.
**TYPE OF GRANT** Outright or partnership grants, paid in sterling or Japanese yen. One-year funding.
**RANGE OF GRANTS** £5,000–£15,000 for collaborative projects; £1,000–£5,000 for small grants.
**SAMPLE GRANTS** Daiwa Adrian Prize (£44,000); The Royal Society-Daiwa Anglo-Japanese Foundation Joint Project Grants (£34,500); Keys of Change (£11,000); Asabi Shimbun (£10,000); AMI Theatre (£8,000); Kyoto University, Graduate School of Medicine (£5,000); City of Birmingham Symphony Orchestra (£4,000); 83rd Fife Explorer Scout Unit (£3,500); Cardiff University, School of Psychology, and Liverpool John Moores University Exhibition Research Centre (£3,000 each).
**FINANCES** Year 2013/14 Income £236,351 Grants £954,400 Grants to organisations £942,400 Assets £36,247,380
**TRUSTEES** Mami Mizutori; Lord Brittan; Sir Michael Perry; Sir Michael Perry; Merryn Somerset Webb; Sir Peter Williams; Andrew Smithers; Paul Dimond; Prof. Richard Bowring; Yusuke Kawamura; Masaki Orita; Shigeharu Suzuki; Prof. Hirotaka Takeuchi.
**OTHER INFORMATION** The total grants figure for 2013/14 includes £499,000 awarded as scholarships. Included in the total grants given are four grants made to individuals (£12,000).
**HOW TO APPLY** Application forms are available from the foundation's website. Details of deadlines and criteria for grants, awards and prizes, together with the relevant application forms and guidelines are available on the foundation's website. 'The next deadline for Daiwa Foundation Small Grant and Award Applications is 30th September 2015 for a decision by the end of November 2015'
**WHO TO APPLY TO** Jason James, Director General and Secretary, Daiwa Foundation, Japan House, 13/14 Cornwall Terrace, London NW1 4QP Tel. 020 7486 4348 Fax 020 7486 2914 email office@dajf.org.uk Website www.dajf.org.uk

■ **Oizer Dalim Trust**
**CC NO** 1045296 **ESTABLISHED** 1994
**WHERE FUNDING CAN BE GIVEN** UK and overseas.
**WHO CAN BENEFIT** Registered charities.
**WHAT IS FUNDED** To alleviate poverty and further education within the Orthodox Jewish community.
**FINANCES** Year 2013/14 Income £84,210 Grants £85,512 Grants to organisations £85,512 Assets £22,760
**TRUSTEES** Mordechai Cik; Maurice Freund; Moshe Cohen.
**OTHER INFORMATION** No beneficiary list was available within the annual report and accounts.
**HOW TO APPLY** Apply in writing to the correspondent.
**WHO TO APPLY TO** Mordechai Cik, Trustee, 68 Osbaldeston Road, London N16 7DR

■ **Baron Davenport's Charity**
**CC NO** 217307 **ESTABLISHED** 1930
**WHERE FUNDING CAN BE GIVEN** Birmingham and the West Midlands counties. Applicants must be within 60 miles of Birmingham Town Hall.
**WHO CAN BENEFIT** Almshouses, hospices and residential homes for older people; organisations benefitting children and young people; organisations supporting older people; individuals who meet specific criteria set-out by the charity.
**WHAT IS FUNDED** Children and young people under the age of 25; older people.
**WHAT IS NOT FUNDED** There are no exclusions, providing the applications come within the charity's objects and the applying organisation is based within the charity's beneficial area, or the organisation's project lies within or benefits people who live in the beneficial area.
**TYPE OF GRANT** One-off or annual grants; project funding; equipment costs; running costs.
**RANGE OF GRANTS** Grants are at the discretion of the trustees though most are for less than £6,000. Grants for organisations working with children and young people usually begin at around £200 and rarely exceed £1,000.
**SAMPLE GRANTS** Acorns Children's Hospice and Age Concern Birmingham (£10,000 each); Zoe's Place Trust (£9,000); Birmingham Children's Hospital Charity (£8,000); Little Sisters of the Poor (£7,500); St Andrew's House and Sir Baptist Hicks Almshouse Trust (£6,000 each).
**FINANCES** Year 2014 Income £1,315,657 Grants £1,169,441 Grants to organisations £714,834 Assets £33,239,318
**TRUSTEES** William Colacicchi; Christopher Hordern; Rob Prichard; Sue Ayres; Lisa Bryan; Alec Jones; Jon Warlow, Ex officio.
**OTHER INFORMATION** During the year, 2,109 grants were made, of which 461 were to organisations. Of these grants to organisations, 437 were of less than £6,000. A total of 1,648 grants, amounting to £454,500, were awarded to individuals.
**HOW TO APPLY** Applications should be made in writing to the correspondent, and accompanied by your organisation's latest accounts along with any project costs. They are considered twice a year, with distributions being made at the end of May/beginning of June and at the end November/beginning of December, and should be received at the charity's office by 15 March or 15 September respectively. All applications are acknowledged and those not within the charity's objects are advised. No more than one application should be submitted within twelve months. There are further guidelines on the website.
**WHO TO APPLY TO** Kate Slater, Charity Administrator, Portman House, 5–7 Temple Row West, Birmingham B2 5NY Tel. 0121 236 8004 Fax 0121 233 2500 email enquiries@barondavenportscharity.org Website www.barondavenportscharity.org

■ **The Davidson Family Charitable Trust**
**CC NO** 262937 **ESTABLISHED** 1971
**WHERE FUNDING CAN BE GIVEN** UK.
**WHO CAN BENEFIT** Mainly Jewish organisations.
**WHAT IS FUNDED** General charitable purposes.
**RANGE OF GRANTS** Up to £425,000.
**SAMPLE GRANTS** Peterhouse Development Fund and Youth Aliyah Child Rescue (£425,000 each); Friends of Israel Antiquities Authority

(£175,000); Bowel and Cancer Research (£102,500); Friends of Ezer Mizion (£25,000); United Synagogue (£11,700); Community Security Trust (£10,000); World Jewish Relief (£5,700); Shaare Zedek UK (£5,000); British Ort Foundation (£2,500); Starlight Children's Foundation (£1,500); Newham Allstar Sports Academy (£1,000).

**FINANCES** Year 2013/14 Income £937,668 Grants £1,414,593 Grants to organisations £1,414,593 Assets £257,312

**TRUSTEES** Gerald Davidson; Maxine Davidson; Eve Winer.

**HOW TO APPLY** Apply in writing to the correspondent.

**WHO TO APPLY TO** Eve Winer, Trustee, c/o Queen Anne Street Capital, 58 Queen Anne Street, London W1G 8HW Tel. 020 7224 1030 email ewiner@wolfeproperties.co.uk

## ■ Michael Davies Charitable Settlement

**CC NO** 1000574   **ESTABLISHED** 1990
**WHERE FUNDING CAN BE GIVEN** UK.
**WHO CAN BENEFIT** Charities.
**WHAT IS FUNDED** General charitable purposes.
**RANGE OF GRANTS** £1,000 to £10,000.
**SAMPLE GRANTS** Royal Society of Arts, North London Hospice, Modern Art Oxford, Hampstead Garden Suburb Fellowship (£10,000 each); Village Education Project Kilimanjaro (£5,000); Royal Parks Foundation (£2,000); Cycle to Cannes, Cycle Club Hackney, Juvenile Diabetes Research Foundation, Kids Company (£1,000 each).
**FINANCES** Year 2013/14 Income £105,516 Grants £92,000 Grants to organisations £92,000 Assets £843,345
**TRUSTEES** Michael Davies; Kenneth Hawkins.
**HOW TO APPLY** Apply in writing to the correspondent.
**WHO TO APPLY TO** Kenneth Hawkins, Trustee, HW Lee Associates, New Derwent House, 69/73 Theobalds Road, London WC1X 8TA Tel. 020 7025 4600

## ■ The Gwendoline and Margaret Davies Charity

**CC NO** 235589   **ESTABLISHED** 1934
**WHERE FUNDING CAN BE GIVEN** UK, with particular favour given to Wales.
**WHO CAN BENEFIT** Registered charities only. Welsh charities are particularly favoured.
**WHAT IS FUNDED** General charitable purposes, with special consideration given to the arts, health and young people. Organisations in the fields of education, medical research, community care services environment and faith activities may also be considered.
**WHAT IS NOT FUNDED** Grants are made to registered charities only.
**TYPE OF GRANT** Mainly one-off, occasionally recurrent for specific capital projects.
**RANGE OF GRANTS** £1,000 to £38,000.
**SAMPLE GRANTS** University of Wales (£37,000); David Device Memorial Institute (£38,000); Gregynog Festival (£10,000); Montgomeryshire Family Crisis Centre (£8,000); Age Concern Powys (£6,000); Oriel Davies Gallery, Royal Voluntary Service (£5,000 each); Caersws Village Hall, The National Deaf Children's Society (£2,000 each); Listening Books, Montgomeryshire Music Festival (£1,000 each).
**FINANCES** Year 2013/14 Income £322,642 Grants £181,308 Grants to organisations £181,308 Assets £7,841,358

**TRUSTEES** Lord David Davies; Dr David Lewis; Dr Denis Balsom; Dr Janet Lewis.
**HOW TO APPLY** The trustees consider appeals on an individual basis. There are no application forms as the trustees prefer to receive letters from applicants setting out the following information: whether the organisation is a registered charity; details of the reason for the application – the type of work and so on; the cost; how much has been raised so far towards the cost; the source of the sums raised; a copy of the last audited accounts if available; and any other information that the applicant may consider would help the application. Unsuccessful appeals are not informed unless an sae is enclosed.
**WHO TO APPLY TO** Susan Hamer, Secretary, The Offices, Plas Dolerw, Milford Road, Newtown, Powys SY16 2EH Tel. 01686 625228 email susan@daviescharities.freeserve.co.uk

## ■ The Hamilton Davies Trust

**CC NO** 1106123   **ESTABLISHED** 2004
**WHERE FUNDING CAN BE GIVEN** Salford City and Warrington. Irlam and Cadishead (in Salford) and Rixton with Glazebrook (in Warrington).
**WHO CAN BENEFIT** Sustainable projects which benefit the communities of Irlam, Cadishead and Rixton-with-Glazebrook.
**WHAT IS FUNDED** 'Youth – Supporting youth leaders and developing the youth movement with the aim of promoting links to education, sports and community initiatives and encouraging organised activities. Education – Adding value to existing provision and raising children's expectations. Sport – Sport is particularly important in the development of young people and the trust has supported projects by providing funds for equipment and kit, holiday programmes and competitions. Community – Support for the community by way of rebuilding and refurbishment of community buildings, supporting group work, festivals and enhancing communication between local facilities and residents.'
**WHAT IS NOT FUNDED** Applications for projects outside the beneficial area will not be considered.
**RANGE OF GRANTS** Up to £22,000.
**SAMPLE GRANTS** Manchester United Foundation (£22,000); Irlam and Cadishead Leisure Centre (£14,000); Refurbishment of Cadishead Sports JFC (£10,000); Salford City Council to fund Christmas lights for the area (£20,000); The Rotary Club of Irlam to 'match fund' the money they raise themselves (£11,000) Roof repair at Preston Hall, where the local Disabled Persons Group is based (£5,000).
**FINANCES** Year 2013/14 Income £1,236,620 Grants £146,907 Grants to organisations £146,907 Assets £8,198,834
**TRUSTEES** Neil McArthur; Graham Chisnall; Frank Cocker.
**OTHER INFORMATION** 17 Grants with a total value of £59,000 were awarded to 'Sport'; 27 Grants totalling £53,000 were awarded to 'Community'; 10 Grants with a total value of £25,000 were awarded to 'Education'; 6 Grants with totalling £6,000 were awarded to 'Youth'.
**HOW TO APPLY** For applications under £150, you simply need to send in a letter detailing: A brief outline of the project and its benefits; Who will be involved?; How many people will be involved?; Who will benefit?; How many will benefit?; What area will the project benefit?; The amount of financial support required?; Details of any other funding received or applied for If your

application is for £150 or over, simply download an application from the website.
**WHO TO APPLY TO** Mandy Coleman, General Manager, Hamilton Davies House, 117c Liverpool Road, Cadishead, Manchester M44 5BG *Tel.* 0161 222 4003 *email* info@hamiltondavies.org.uk *Website* www.hamiltondavies.org.uk

## ■ The Wilfrid Bruce Davis Charitable Trust

**CC NO** 265421 **ESTABLISHED** 1967
**WHERE FUNDING CAN BE GIVEN** UK, but mainly Cornwall; India.
**WHO CAN BENEFIT** Voluntary groups and registered charities.
**WHAT IS FUNDED** The trust presently concentrates on 'improving the quality of life for those who are physically disadvantaged and their carers'. The geographical area covered is almost exclusively Cornwall; however, the main thrust of the trust's activities is now focused on India.
**WHAT IS NOT FUNDED** Individuals.
**RANGE OF GRANTS** Generally around £1,000 to £10,000.
**SAMPLE GRANTS** Tikwonda Youth Organisation, Malawi (£62,000); Savitri Waney Charitable Trust (£51,000); Merlin Project and Guwahati Pain Clinic (£5,000 each); Cornwall Community Foundation (£2,000) Precious Lives Appeal and Jubilee Sailing Trust (£1,000 each).
**FINANCES** *Year* 2013/14 *Income* £99,063 *Grants* £151,238 *Grants to organisations* £151,238 *Assets* £93,283
**TRUSTEES** Wilfrid Davis; Doreen Davis; Diana Dickens; Christina Pierce.
**HOW TO APPLY** Unsolicited applications are generally not supported.
**WHO TO APPLY TO** Wilfrid Davis, Trustee, La Feock Grange, Feock, Truro, Cornwall TR3 6RG *Tel.* 01872 862795 *email* wbdfeock@aol.com

## ■ The Davis Foundation

**CC NO** 1152998 **ESTABLISHED** 2013
**WHERE FUNDING CAN BE GIVEN** England and Israel.
**WHO CAN BENEFIT** Organisations.
**WHAT IS FUNDED** Jewish causes; young people; older people; disability; citizenship; racial and religious harmony; public education in the areas of opera, music, the performing arts, horticulture, ecology and conservation; social inclusion; security, advice and training for religious-based schools and places of worship.
**FINANCES** *Year* 2013/14 *Income* £7,005,000 *Grants* £1,427,637 *Grants to organisations* £1,427,637 *Assets* £5,573,544
**TRUSTEES** Michael Davis; Barbara Davis; Sarah Davis.
**HOW TO APPLY** Apply in writing to the correspondent.
**WHO TO APPLY TO** Michael Davis, Trustee, 3 Beechworth Close, London NW3 7UT *Tel.* 07771 662693

## ■ The Henry and Suzanne Davis Foundation

**CC NO** 1153199
**WHERE FUNDING CAN BE GIVEN** England and Wales.
**WHO CAN BENEFIT** Charitable organisations and individuals.
**WHAT IS FUNDED** General charitable purposes; education and training; arts and culture; human rights.

**FINANCES** *Year* 2013/14 *Income* £155,000 *Grants* £100,000 *Grants to organisations* £100,000
**TRUSTEES** Robert Craig; Henry Davis; Suzanne Davis.
**OTHER INFORMATION** Grants totalled around £100,000. A list of beneficiaries was not available.
**HOW TO APPLY** Apply in writing to the correspondent.
**WHO TO APPLY TO** Robert Craig, Trustee, Howard Kennedy Fsi LLP, No. 1 London Bridge, London SE1 9BG *Tel.* 020 3755 5421 *email* robert.craig@howardkennedy.com

## ■ The Dawe Charitable Trust

**CC NO** 1060314 **ESTABLISHED** 1997
**WHERE FUNDING CAN BE GIVEN** Cambridgeshire, national, international.
**WHO CAN BENEFIT** Charitable organisations.
**WHAT IS FUNDED** Disadvantaged people and homelessness.
**RANGE OF GRANTS** £1,000–£100,000
**SAMPLE GRANTS** Previous beneficiaries have included: Prince's Trust (£50,000); St Theresa Charity and Manda Wilderness Agricultural Project (£5,000 each).
**FINANCES** *Year* 2013/14 *Income* £63,178 *Grants* £100,000 *Grants to organisations* £100,000 *Assets* £1,934,217
**TRUSTEES** Dr Peter Dawe; Mark Turner; David Kerr.
**HOW TO APPLY** The trustees do not actively solicit the making of grants or loans, but will consider applications on their merits. Apply in writing to the correspondent, outlining ideas and needs.
**WHO TO APPLY TO** Dr Peter Dawe, Trustee, 17A Broad Street, Ely, Cambridgeshire CB7 4AJ *Tel.* 0845 345 8999 *email* office@dawe.co.uk

## ■ The De Brye Charitable Trust

**CC NO** 326226 **ESTABLISHED** 1982
**WHERE FUNDING CAN BE GIVEN** United Kingdom.
**WHO CAN BENEFIT** Charitable organisations.
**WHAT IS FUNDED** General charitable purposes, preference may be given to the activities affecting the orphans, neglected children and children with physical disabilities, older people and the blind.
**TYPE OF GRANT** One-off grants to organisations.
**RANGE OF GRANTS** £1,000–£11,000
**SAMPLE GRANTS** Salisbury Cathedral (£11,000); Fauna and Flora International and The Stars Appeal (£10,000 each); BAAF (£8,000); Hampshire and Isle of Wight Air Ambulance, Siblings Together, Sparks (£5,000 each); Lessons for Life Foundation (£4,900); INSPIRE, Sierra Leonean Adventists Abroad (£1,000 each).
**FINANCES** *Year* 2013/14 *Income* £98,903 *Grants* £60,875 *Grants to organisations* £60,875 *Assets* £2,636,528
**TRUSTEES** Alexander de Brye; Jennifer de Brye; Phillip Sykes.
**HOW TO APPLY** Apply in writing to the correspondent.
**WHO TO APPLY TO** George Georghiou, Mercer and Hole, 72 London Road, St Albans, Hertfordshire AL1 1NS *Tel.* 01727 869141

## ■ Peter De Haan Charitable Trust

**CC NO** 1077005  **ESTABLISHED** 1999
**WHERE FUNDING CAN BE GIVEN** UK.
**WHO CAN BENEFIT** Charitable organisations.
**WHAT IS FUNDED** The trust has focused its activities on the areas of the arts, the environment and social welfare. The website states that 'the Trust operates under a venture philanthropy model, working closely with the organisations it supports financially and organisationally to increase their capacity and impact.'
**TYPE OF GRANT** Project grants or core costs.
**RANGE OF GRANTS** Mostly up to £20,000.
**SAMPLE GRANTS** Leicestershire and Rutland Wildlife Trust; National Youth Theatre; Old Vic New Voices; Yorkshire Wildlife Trust
**FINANCES** Year 2013/14 Income £509,000 Grants £664,000 Grants to organisations £107,000 Assets £7,649,000
**TRUSTEES** Peter Charles De Haan; Janette McKay; Dr Rob Stoneman; Opus Corporate Trustees Limited.
**OTHER INFORMATION** The trust's website states that it 'will not exist in perpetuity', but rather was founded in 1999 with the plan of having its reserves spent over a 20 year period. Until recently, a significant proportion of the trust's resources were directed towards its subsidiary, IdeasTap, which was a youth arts charity. Due to unconfirmed future funding for its operations, IdeasTap was due to close in July 2015. During 2013/14 arts programme grants to young adults totalled £576,000.
**HOW TO APPLY** The trust does not accept unsolicited applications; however, at the time of writing (June 2015) the trust's website stated that it would, from July 2015, be accepting applications from environmental organisations. Refer to the website for updates and more information.
**WHO TO APPLY TO** Simon Johnson, Finance Director, Wool Yard, 54 Bermondsey Street, London SE1 3UD Tel. 020 7232 5465 email sjohnson@pdhct.org.uk Website www.pdhct.org.uk

## ■ The De Laszlo Foundation

**CC NO** 327383  **ESTABLISHED** 1978
**WHERE FUNDING CAN BE GIVEN** UK and worldwide.
**WHO CAN BENEFIT** Arts organisations and registered charities.
**WHAT IS FUNDED** Promotion of the arts; general charitable purposes.
**SAMPLE GRANTS** The de Laszlo Archive Trust (£175,000); Technology Centre and iPads for The Treloar School for severely handicapped children, (£20,000) **Previous beneficiaries have included:** the De Laszlo Archive Trust (£188,000); Gordonstoun School Arts Centre (£20,000); Durham University and Royal Marsden (£10,000 each); Foundation for Liver Research (£8,000); Southampton University (£5,000); Federation of British Artists (£3,000); AGORA (£2,500); National Youth Orchestra (£1,500); Tate Foundation (£1,000); Cardboard Citizens (£500); and Chelsea Open Air Nursery School (£250).
**FINANCES** Year 2013/14 Income £484,014 Grants £400,686 Grants to organisations £400,686 Assets £2,206,663
**TRUSTEES** Damon de Laszlo, Chair; Lucy Birkbeck; Robert de Laszlo; William de Laszlo.
**OTHER INFORMATION** The foundation was set up to promote the advancement and promotion of education and interest in the visual arts with special reference to encouraging knowledge of the works of contemporary painters, in particular those of the late Philip de Laszlo.
**HOW TO APPLY** No grants are given to applicants whose applications are unsolicited.
**WHO TO APPLY TO** Christabel Wood, 5 Albany Courtyard, London W1J 0HF Tel. 020 7437 1982 email catalogue@delaszlo.com

## ■ The Deakin Charitable Trust

**CC NO** 258001  **ESTABLISHED** 1968
**WHERE FUNDING CAN BE GIVEN** Mainly Surrey with a preference for Woking.
**WHO CAN BENEFIT** Mainly local charities including hospices and various religious organisations, and students seeking to extend their music education.
**WHAT IS FUNDED** General charitable purposes.
**RANGE OF GRANTS** Generally £250–£500.
**SAMPLE GRANTS** Woking Hospice (£15,000); Chase Children's Hospice and Phyllis Tuckwell (£9,000 each); Macmillan Nurses and University of Surrey – prostate research (£500 each); ABF Soldiers Charity, Stagecoach and REACT (£400 each); and International Spinal Research, Livability and Mercy Ships (£300 each).
**FINANCES** Year 2013/14 Income £74,034 Grants £51,500 Grants to organisations £51,500 Assets £842,014
**TRUSTEES** Geraldine Lawson; Paul Deakin; William Hodgetts.
**HOW TO APPLY** Apply in writing to the correspondent.
**WHO TO APPLY TO** William Hodgetts, Trustee, Station House, Connaught Road, Brookwood, Woking GU24 0ER Tel. 01483 485444 email path@herbertprnell.com

## ■ William Dean Countryside and Educational Trust

**CC NO** 1044567  **ESTABLISHED** 1995
**WHERE FUNDING CAN BE GIVEN** Principally Cheshire; also Derbyshire, Lancashire, Staffordshire and the Wirral.
**WHO CAN BENEFIT** Individuals and organisations.
**WHAT IS FUNDED** The trust gives grants individuals and organisations in its immediate locality which promote education in natural history, ecology and the conservation of the natural environment. For example, wildlife trusts; schools for ecological and conservation projects; and parks and pleasure grounds for similar purposes.
**WHAT IS NOT FUNDED** Education is not funded, unless directly associated with one of the stated eligible categories.
**TYPE OF GRANT** Capital, core costs. One-off grants.
**RANGE OF GRANTS** £200–£15,000
**SAMPLE GRANTS** Cheshire Wildlife Trust (£15,000); Willoughbridge Garden Trust Dorothy Clive Garden, Eco-Schools Competition (£3,000 each); Staffordshire Wildlife Trust (£2,000); Crowton C of E primary School gardens, Marine Conservation Society, Wildfowl and Wetlands Trust (£1,000 each); Animal Rescue Sanctuary, Bollin Valley Partnership, Clean Rivers Trust (£500); British Hen Welfare Trust (£250), Norris Primary School (£200).
**FINANCES** Year 2012/13 Income £60,876 Grants £54,805 Grants to organisations £54,805 Assets £1,408,480
**TRUSTEES** John Ward; David Daniel; Margaret Williamson; David Crawford; Rebecca Franklin, Prof. David Parsons; W. Crawford

**HOW TO APPLY** Apply in writing to the correspondent. The Trustees meet four times each year in March, June, September and December when applications for grants are considered.
**WHO TO APPLY TO** Clare Amare, 5 The Parklands, Congleton, Cheshire CW12 3DS *Tel.* 01260 276970 *email* clare.amare@ellanet.co.uk

## ■ Debenhams Foundation

**CC NO** 1147682 **ESTABLISHED** 2012
**WHERE FUNDING CAN BE GIVEN** UK.
**WHO CAN BENEFIT** Registered charities and community organisations.
**WHAT IS FUNDED** Health; social welfare; breast cancer; children's charities.
**SAMPLE GRANTS** Debenhams Retirement Association (£74,000); BBC Children in Need (£72,000); Breakthrough Breast Cancer, Breast Cancer Campaign (£60,000 each); Pink Ribbon Foundation (£24,000); Retail Trust North (£19,000); NSPCC (£13,000); Marie Curie Cancer Care (£9,000); Wessex Cancer Trust (£500); and Children 1st Scotland (£100).
**FINANCES** *Year* 2013/14 *Income* £1,543,245 *Grants* £1,575,112 *Grants to organisations* £1,575,112 *Assets* £253,986
**TRUSTEES** Keith Markham; Nicola Zamblera; Patricia Skinner.
**OTHER INFORMATION** There were 30 grants made to organisations in 2013/14.
**HOW TO APPLY** Apply in writing to the correspondent for grant-giving or to the local store for community projects.
**WHO TO APPLY TO** Kate Thomas, Correspondent, Debenhams plc, 10 Brock Street, Regent's Place, London NW1 3FG *Tel.* 020 3549 6418 *email* kate.thomas@debenhams.com *Website* www.debenhams.com/webapp/wcs/stores/servlet/contentView?filepath=/DebenhamsUKSite/Static/footer_debenhams_supports_uk.xml&storeId=10701&langId=-1#slided

## ■ The Debmar Benevolent Trust

**CC NO** 283065 **ESTABLISHED** 1979
**WHERE FUNDING CAN BE GIVEN** UK and Israel.
**WHO CAN BENEFIT** Jewish organisations.
**WHAT IS FUNDED** Jewish charitable purposes.
**RANGE OF GRANTS** Up to £30,000, but mostly under £1,000.
**SAMPLE GRANTS** Beis Hamedrash Hachodosh; Chasdei Belz; Chevras Mauous Lador; Gevurath Ari; Telz Talmudical Academy; Friends of Assos Chesed; Pardes Chana; ATLIB, Bobov Institutions; Ohr Akiva Institute; Tomchei Shaarei Zion; Ponivitch Institutions; Yeshiva Shaarei Zion; Beis Yoel High School; Format Charity Trust; Manchester Kollel.
**FINANCES** *Year* 2012/13 *Income* £1,169,837 *Grants* £40,816 *Grants to organisations* £40,816 *Assets* £4,364,494
**TRUSTEES** David Olsberg; Jacob Halpern.
**OTHER INFORMATION** The 2012/13 accounts were the latest available at the time of writing (June 2013). The grant total was considerably lower than in previous years due to the fact that the company received fewer donations and was committed to make capital repayments off its bank loan. A list a grants was not provided in the trust's latest accounts.
**HOW TO APPLY** Apply in writing to the correspondent.
**WHO TO APPLY TO** David Olsberg, Trustee, 16 Stanley Road, Salford M7 4RW

## ■ The Delius Trust

**CC NO** 207324 **ESTABLISHED** 1935
**WHERE FUNDING CAN BE GIVEN** UK.
**WHO CAN BENEFIT** Registered charities and individuals.
**WHAT IS FUNDED** 'The trust promotes the music of Frederick Delius and of British composers born since 1860, by giving help towards the cost of performances, publications and recordings. In addition, assistance is occasionally offered to organisations and institutions active in this field. Priority is always given to the promotion of the works of Delius, especially those that are rarely performed.'
**WHAT IS NOT FUNDED** The trust will not usually make retrospective grants, nor does it consider support for capital projects. Grants are not generally made for individual performance, recording or publishing projects.
**RANGE OF GRANTS** £250 to £5,000.
**SAMPLE GRANTS** Delius Society (£30,000 over five years); Dutton Vocalion (£4,000); Epsom Symphony Orchestra (£2,000); English Music Festival (£1,000); North Yorks Moors Chamber Music Festival (£500); and Northern Lights Symphony Orchestra and William Alwyn Festival (£250 each).
**FINANCES** *Year* 2013 *Income* £83,334 *Grants* £78,655 *Grants to organisations* £78,655 *Assets* £2,380,126
**TRUSTEES** Musicians' Benevolent Fund (Representative: John Axon); David Lloyd-Jones; Martin Williams.
**HOW TO APPLY** Apply in writing for consideration by the trustees and the advisers. See the trust's website for further details. The trustees meet three times a year, in February, June and October. Applications should be received early in the month before each meeting. The trust will not usually make retrospective grants. There is no standard application form.
**WHO TO APPLY TO** Helen Faulkner, Secretary to the Trust, 7–11 Britannia Street, London WC1X 9JS *Tel.* 020 7239 9143 *email* deliustrust@mbf.org.uk *Website* www.delius.org.uk

## ■ The Dellal Foundation

**CC NO** 265506 **ESTABLISHED** 1973
**WHERE FUNDING CAN BE GIVEN** UK.
**WHO CAN BENEFIT** Registered charities only.
**WHAT IS FUNDED** Mostly 'the welfare and benefit of Jewish people'.
**WHAT IS NOT FUNDED** Individuals.
**TYPE OF GRANT** One-off.
**FINANCES** *Year* 2013/14 *Income* £0 *Grants* £72,672 *Grants to organisations* £72,672
**TRUSTEES** Edward Azouz; Guy Della; Jeffrey Azouz; Alexander Dellal.
**HOW TO APPLY** Apply in writing to the correspondent.
**WHO TO APPLY TO** S. Hosier, Correspondent, 25 Harley Street, London W1G 9BR *Tel.* 020 7299 1400

## ■ The Delves Charitable Trust

**CC NO** 231860 **ESTABLISHED** 1922
**WHERE FUNDING CAN BE GIVEN** UK and overseas.
**WHAT IS FUNDED** General charitable purposes. To support approved charities by annual subscriptions and donations.
**WHAT IS NOT FUNDED** The trust does not give sponsorships or personal educational grants.
**RANGE OF GRANTS** £1300 to £20,500.

SAMPLE GRANTS Médecins Sans Frontières (£20,800); Parkinson's UK (£17,800); British Heart Foundation (£16,200); Freedom From Torture (£14,500); Action Medical Research (£10,800); Alzheimer's Society (£10,500); Friendship Works (£10,000); Hospice in the Weald, Muscular Disease Society, Trees for Cities (£5,000 each); International Alert, WWF UK (£4,000 each); Survival International (£1,300).
FINANCES Year 2013/14 Income £254,995 Grants £207,324 Grants to organisations £207,324 Assets £7,954,331
TRUSTEES Elizabeth Breeze; John Breeze; George Breeze; Charles Breeze; William Breeze; Mark Breeze; Catharine Mackey.
HOW TO APPLY The trust does not accept unsolicited applications for funding.
WHO TO APPLY TO The Trust Administrator, Luminary Finance LLP, PO Box 135, Longfield, Kent DA3 8WF Tel. 01732 822114

## ■ The Denman Charitable Trust
CC NO 326532 ESTABLISHED 1983
WHERE FUNDING CAN BE GIVEN Bath, North-East Somerset, Bristol and Gloucestershire.
WHO CAN BENEFIT Organisations benefitting research workers, at-risk groups, people disadvantaged by poverty, and socially isolated people.
WHAT IS FUNDED Medical research; health; welfare; the arts.
WHAT IS NOT FUNDED Individuals; non-charitable organisations.
TYPE OF GRANT Pump priming rather than running costs.
RANGE OF GRANTS £100–£25,000. Mostly under £5,000.
SAMPLE GRANTS Bristol Old Vic (£25,000); Old Sodbury Football Club (£10,000); Creative Youth Network (£5,000); Bath Samaritans and Rework (£2,000 each); Avon Riding for the Disabled, The Rainbow Centre and Triple H Trust (£1,000 each).
FINANCES Year 2013/14 Income £58,634 Grants £91,306 Grants to organisations £91,306 Assets £38,065
TRUSTEES Arnold Denman; Dorothy Denman; David Marsh; Sue Blatchford; Joanna Denman.
HOW TO APPLY Apply in writing to the correspondent.
WHO TO APPLY TO Dorothy Denman, Trustee, c/o Steeple Group, PO Box 1881, Old Sodbury, Bristol BS37 6WS email dorothydenman@camers.org

## ■ The Dentons UKMEA LLP Charitable Trust
CC NO 1041204 ESTABLISHED 1994
WHERE FUNDING CAN BE GIVEN England and Wales
WHO CAN BENEFIT Normally registered charities.
WHAT IS FUNDED General charitable purposes with a preference for organisations with a legal connection, such as community law centres, or children's charities, medical charities or the arts. Preference is also given to organisations which have a connection with Denton Wilde Sapte LLP or are local to the company's offices.
WHAT IS NOT FUNDED Individuals; education and scholarships.
TYPE OF GRANT One-off and recurrent.
RANGE OF GRANTS Previously between £75 and £6,000, usually up to £2,000.
SAMPLE GRANTS Social Committee and Tower Project (£6,000 each); Alone In London, Depford Action Group for the Elderly (£3,000); Help for Heroes (£1,500); Inspirations (£1,000); Archway Project, Ragged School Museum and Trinity Hospital (£500 each); Walk the Walk (£250); and Cancer Research UK (£75).
FINANCES Year 2013/14 Income £93,765 Grants £89,240 Grants to organisations £89,240 Assets £19,341
TRUSTEES Mark Andrews; Virginia Glastonbury; Matthew Harvey and Brandon Ransley.
HOW TO APPLY Apply in writing to the correspondent. The trustees meet quarterly.
WHO TO APPLY TO Bernadette O'Sullivan, Correspondent, 1 One Fleet Place, London EC4M 7WS Tel. 020 7246 4843

## ■ The Derbyshire Churches and Chapels Preservation Trust
CC NO 1010953 ESTABLISHED 1992
WHERE FUNDING CAN BE GIVEN Derbyshire
WHO CAN BENEFIT Churches and chapels of any Christian denomination.
WHAT IS FUNDED The preservation, repair and improvement of Christian churches and chapels in Derbyshire.
TYPE OF GRANT One-off grants.
RANGE OF GRANTS £1,000–£5,000
SAMPLE GRANTS St Wystan – Repton (£7,500); Holy Trinity – Middleton by Wirksworth and St John Baptist – Chelmorton (£5,000 each); St Peter's – Hartshorne and Wirksworth URC (£4,000); St John Baptist – Dethick (£3,000); and All Saints – Bakewell, Holy Trinity – Milford, St Giles – Sandiacre and St Paul – Hasland (£2,000 each).
FINANCES Year 2013/14 Income £27,916 Grants £44,600 Grants to organisations £44,600 Assets £22,912
TRUSTEES Michael Millender; Dr Patrick Strange; Dr Christopher Conifer; Richard Fitz Herbert; Ben Roper.
OTHER INFORMATION In 2013/14 grants were made to ten churches and chapels.
HOW TO APPLY Application forms are available from the correspondent. Our research suggests that the grants panel meets quarterly. Any enquiries are preferred via phone or email.
WHO TO APPLY TO Michael Mallender, Trustee, 1 Greenhill, Wirksworth, Derbyshire DE4 4EN Tel. 01629 824904 Fax 01629 826390 email dccpt@dhbt.clara.net Website www.derbyshirehistoricbuildings.org.uk

## ■ Derbyshire Community Foundation
CC NO 1039485 ESTABLISHED 1996
WHERE FUNDING CAN BE GIVEN Derbyshire and the city of Derby.
WHO CAN BENEFIT Voluntary groups and volunteers and the people they work with in Derbyshire across a wide spectrum of activity tackling disadvantage and promoting quality of life.
WHAT IS FUNDED Community groups and voluntary organisations working to tackle disadvantage and improve quality of life. Likely priority themes are as follows: supporting families; getting back to work; health and well-being; young people; helping groups work; and creative community.
WHAT IS NOT FUNDED The foundation's general exclusions are: profit making organisations/businesses; medical equipment; animal charities; any project which promotes faith or involves the refurbishment/building of a place of

worship; statutory bodies – schools, hospitals, police, etc.; any project which directly replaces statutory obligations; projects which benefit people outside Derbyshire; any project which promotes a political party; retrospective funding (grants for activities which have already taken place); sponsored events. Specific programs may have additional exclusions.

**TYPE OF GRANT** Usually one-off, though depending on the programme and donor's wishes, the trust may give more than one grant to the same group for different projects or items. Capital, core costs, feasibility studies, research, running costs, salaries and start-up costs. Funding for up to one year will be considered.

**RANGE OF GRANTS** Mainly between £100 to £5,000; possibly more for managed programmes depending on their criteria.

**SAMPLE GRANTS** Derby Quad (£30,000); Jonathan Vickers Fine Art Award Residency (£17,500); Beckett School Garden Project Phase II (£14,000); Repton Foundation Student Bursary and Sinfonia Viva (£10,000 each); PARC (£9,700); Beckett School Garden Project Phase I (£7,600); and Doe Hill Country Park (£7,000).

**FINANCES** Year 2013/14 Income £576,421 Grants £342,594 Grants to organisations £342,594 Assets £6,831,557

**TRUSTEES** Arthur Blackwood; Robin Wood; Michael Hall; Lucy Palmer; David Coleman; Nicholas Mirfin; David Walker; Matthew Montague; Louise Pinder; Nicola Phillips; Peter Pimm; Philip Boxham.

**HOW TO APPLY** The grants team are always willing to discuss applications before they are formally submitted; this saves both the applicant and the foundation time. Call them on: 01773 514850. The foundation offers several different funds, each with a specific focus or set of criteria. Visit the foundation's website for full details of the current grant programmes and the relevant application documents. Applicants should download and complete the appropriate application form from the website and send it to the correspondent. Applications are passed to a member of the grants team for assessment and to prepare all of the information ready to present to the award making panel. During this time, applicants are likely to be contacted by the grants team for an informal chat about their application and their group, which helps the foundation to understand the background of the project and gives the best chance of a successful bid. Applicants will be informed of the decision date for their application and are invited to call the grants team or check the website to find out the decision two days after the panel date. You will also receive the panel decision in writing within two weeks of the panel date. The foundation states that it is willing to provide full, honest feedback on all decisions and is happy to discuss any outcome with applicants.

**WHO TO APPLY TO** Rachael Grime, Correspondent, Foundation Derbyshire, Unit 2 Heritage Business Centre, Derby Road, Belper, Derbyshire DE56 1SW Tel. 01773 525860 email hello@foundationderbyshire.org Website www.derbyshirecommunityfoundation.co.uk

## ■ The J. N. Derbyshire Trust

**CC NO** 231907  **ESTABLISHED** 1944
**WHERE FUNDING CAN BE GIVEN** Mainly Nottingham and Nottinghamshire.
**WHO CAN BENEFIT** Organisations with charitable status.

**WHAT IS FUNDED** General charitable purposes, including: the promotion of health; the development of physical improvement; the advancement of education; and the relief of poverty, distress and sickness. Local charities receive preferential consideration.

**WHAT IS NOT FUNDED** No grants are given to individuals. Costs of study are not supported.

**TYPE OF GRANT** Buildings, capital, core costs, project, research, recurring and running costs, salaries, and start-up costs will be considered. Funding may be given for up to three years.

**RANGE OF GRANTS** Up to £15,000.

**SAMPLE GRANTS** Norfolk and Norwich NHS Foundation (£15,000); Walesby Forest Scout Camp (£10,000); Elizabeth Finn Care (£7,500); Greenway Community Centre (£5,000); Broxtowe Women's Project Limited and NSPCC (£3,000 each); Action for ME and Rutland House School for Parents (£2,500 each); Emmanuel House (£2,300); and the Salvation Army (£2,100).

**FINANCES** Year 2013/14 Income £194,707 Grants £173,644 Grants to organisations £173,644 Assets £5,207,405

**TRUSTEES** Andora Carver; Sidney Christophers; Peter Moore; Lucy Whittle; Charles George; Belinda Lawrie.

**HOW TO APPLY** Application forms are available from the correspondent. Applications can be made at any time but trustees usually only meet to consider them twice a year in March and September. Details of the project are required. A reply is only given to unsuccessful applicants if they enclose an sae.

**WHO TO APPLY TO** Amy Taylor, Secretary, The Poynt, 45 Wollaton Street, Nottingham NG1 5FW Tel. 0115 948 9400 email amy.taylor@bakertilly.co.uk

## ■ The Desmond Foundation (formerly known as the RD Crusaders Foundation)

**CC NO** 1014352  **ESTABLISHED** 1992
**WHERE FUNDING CAN BE GIVEN** Worldwide.
**WHO CAN BENEFIT** Charitable organisations, with a preference towards Jewish organisations.
**WHAT IS FUNDED** The relief of poverty and sickness, particularly among children.
**TYPE OF GRANT** One-off grants.
**RANGE OF GRANTS** Up to £250,000 (2013).
**SAMPLE GRANTS** Norwood (£250,000); World Jewish Relief (£137,000); United Jewish Israel Appeal (£100,000); Fight for Sight (£50,000); Variety, the Children's Charity (£21,000); Presidents Club Charitable Trust (£17,500); Well Being of Women (£15,000); Clinton Foundation and the Holocaust Education Trust and RNIB (£10,000 each); Chai Cancer Care, the Disability Foundation and Duchenne Children's Trust (£5,000 each); and Lawnfest and Walk the Walk (£1,00 each).

**FINANCES** Year 2013 Income £769,492 Grants £780,239 Grants to organisations £780,239 Assets £58,422

**TRUSTEES** Richard Desmond; Northern & Shell Services Limited; Northern & Shell Media Group Limited.

**HOW TO APPLY** Apply in writing to the correspondent. All grant requests are considered and awards made are based on the merits of each proposal.

**WHO TO APPLY TO** Allison Racher, Correspondent, Northern & Shell Media Group Ltd, The Northern & Shell Building, 10 Lower Thames Street, London EC3R 6EN *Tel.* 020 8612 7760 *email* allison.racher@express.co.uk

## ■ Devon Community Foundation

**CC NO** 1057923  **ESTABLISHED** 1996
**WHERE FUNDING CAN BE GIVEN** Devon
**WHO CAN BENEFIT** Voluntary and community groups.
**WHAT IS FUNDED** Support primarily for voluntary and community organisations, particularly those working to relieve the effects of poverty and disadvantage.
**WHAT IS NOT FUNDED** Individuals (except the Devonian Fund); previously funded projects that have outstanding evaluations; large projects where a small grant would not make a difference; more than one application to the same fund in a 12 month period; Organisations that are regional or national charities (unless locally led and run); organisations that have substantial unrestricted funds (i.e. more than one year's running costs); statutory bodies; organisations or activities that primarily support animals or plants; organisations which are not constituted; grant-making organisations; organisations that are for personal profit or are commercial; building works; capital purchases over £1000; overseas travel; consultancy fees or feasibility studies; promoting political or religious beliefs; sponsorship and/or fundraising events; never 100% of the project costs; projects directly benefitting areas outside Devon.
**TYPE OF GRANT** Predominantly one-off small grants for projects. Running costs and start-up costs will be considered. Funding may be given for up to one year, and very occasionally for two years.
**RANGE OF GRANTS** £1,000–£30,000
**SAMPLE GRANTS** Grow 4 Good South West Limited (£35,000); Exeter YMCA (£23,000); Cornwall Community Foundation (£22,500); Young Devon (£15,000); Plymouth Cricket Club, Shout it Out Learning Project and Time Out For All (£5,000 each); Coast Net and Community Housing Aid (£4,500); Plymouth Foodbank (£2,000); and Devon and Cornwall Refugee Support, Play Torbay and Tavistock Street Pastors (£1,000 each).
**FINANCES** *Year* 2013/14 *Income* £1,385,419 *Grants* £712,736 *Grants to organisations* £712,736 *Assets* £4,557,719
**TRUSTEES** Mike Bull; Steve Hindley; Robin Barlow; Caroline Marks; Nigel Arnold; John Glasby; James Cross; Christine Allison; Caroline Harlow; Rt Reverend Robert Atwell Bishop of Exeter.
**OTHER INFORMATION** There were various grants under £1,000 but these were not listed in the accounts.
**HOW TO APPLY** The foundation's website has details of the grant schemes currently being administered and how to apply. The website also has a 'grant alert sign-up' which emails information about new grant programmes as they are available.
**WHO TO APPLY TO** Martha Wilkinson, Chief Executive, The Factory, Leat Street, Tiverton, Devon EX16 5LL *Tel.* 01884 235887 *email* info@devoncf.com *Website* www.devoncf.com

## ■ The Devon Historic Churches Trust

**CC NO** 265594  **ESTABLISHED** 1973
**WHERE FUNDING CAN BE GIVEN** Devon and diocese of Exeter.
**WHO CAN BENEFIT** Churches and chapels.
**WHAT IS FUNDED** The trust gives grants/loans for 'the preservation, repair, maintenance, improvement and upkeep of churches in the County of Devon.'
**WHAT IS NOT FUNDED** Redundant churches/chapels, bells, plumbing, disability facilities and routine maintenance.
**TYPE OF GRANT** Grants.
**RANGE OF GRANTS** £1000–£5,000
**SAMPLE GRANTS** St Andrew's Church, South Tawton, St Andrew's Church, Hittisleigh (£5,000 each); St Michael's Church, Trusham, St Mary's Church, Crode (£3,000 each); South Molton Methodist Church, St Giles Church, Kimlington (£2,000 each); St Andrew's Church, Colebrook, St Mary's Church, Clyst St Lawrence (£1,500 each); St John the Baptist Church, Membury (£1,000); St John the Baptist Church, Bovey (£500).
**FINANCES** *Year* 2013/14 *Income* £194,296 *Grants* £72,500 *Grants to organisations* £72,500 *Assets* £1,316,874
**TRUSTEES** Hugh Harrison; Lady Anne Boles; Carol Plumstead; Lt Cdr Christopher Tuke; The Earl of Devon; Lt Col James Michie; Judith Kauntze; Rosemary Howell; Lee Martin; Lady Burnell-Nugent; The Revd Dr David Keep; Philip Tuckett; John Mills; Hendrik Vollers; Charlie Hutchings; Jon Rawlings.
**HOW TO APPLY** Apply in writing to the correspondent. The trustees meet quarterly to receive reports from officers and committees and to consider grant applications.
**WHO TO APPLY TO** John Malleson, Dolphins, Popes Lane, Colyford, Colyton EX24 6QR *Tel.* 01297 553666 *email* contact@devonhistoricchurches.co.uk *Website* www.devonhistoricchurches.co.uk

## ■ The Duke of Devonshire's Charitable Trust

**CC NO** 213519  **ESTABLISHED** 1949
**WHERE FUNDING CAN BE GIVEN** UK.
**WHO CAN BENEFIT** UK-registered charities only.
**WHAT IS FUNDED** General charitable purposes.
**WHAT IS NOT FUNDED** According to the website, the trust: 'will not normally consider any funding request made within 12 months of the outcome of a previously unsuccessful application or 5 years of a successful one. This is to ensure that the trust can assist as wide a spread of worthwhile organisations as possible'; 'only considers applications from UK registered charities and your registration number is required (unless you have exempt status as a church, educational establishment, hospital, etc.)'; 'does not typically fund projects outside the UK, even if the organisation is a registered charity within Britain'; 'is not able to accept applications from individuals or for individual research or study. This includes gap year activities, study trips, fundraising expeditions and sponsorship'; 'does not normally make funding commitments over several years – grants made are typically for a single year with few exceptions'; 'does not normally fund specific salaries and positions. This is primarily because grants are single-year commitments and the trustees would not wish a specific job

to become unsustainable'; '[will not usually] consider making a grant to organisations who cannot demonstrate significant progress with fundraising, so please bear this in mind when considering the timing of your application'; '[will not consider applications] until all the information we have requested has been being provided. Please keep your answers concise and avoid including protracted Mission Statements, jargon and acronyms. Failure to do so may result in your application being overlooked.'

**TYPE OF GRANT** Capital costs.
**RANGE OF GRANTS** £100–34,000; typically £250–£10,000.
**SAMPLE GRANTS** Chatsworth House Trust (£34,000); Bradford Diocesan (£21,000); Barts and the London Charity (£10,000); Heart of Staveley Ltd (£7,500); Royal National Lifeboat Institution (£5,000); Sense (£3,000); Safe and Sound – Derby (£2,000); SPARKS (£1,000); Matlock Mencap (£500); Netherthorpe School (£100).
**FINANCES** Year 2013/14 Income £244,758 Grants £232,792 Grants to organisations £232,792 Assets £11,838,245
**TRUSTEES** Duke of Devonshire; Duchess of Devonshire; Earl of Burlington; Sir Richard Beckett.
**OTHER INFORMATION** Grants were made to 132 organisations.
**HOW TO APPLY** Application forms are available on the trust's website, along with guidelines and details of current application deadlines. It is noted: 'The Trustees take a range of considerations into account, including such factors as previous grants, costs, available resources, sustainability of the project, and the viability of your fundraising plan. This list is not exhaustive and while the Trustees aim to support as many good projects and organisations as possible, it is unfortunately not possible to provide funding to all applicants. ... If your organization is not successful this time, you will receive a confirmation by e-mail (or where no e-mail address is provided, by post) and you will be reminded that you should not apply again within a 12 month period.' Do not include any additional information which is not required as to do so will harm your application. The trustees meet three-four times a year.
**WHO TO APPLY TO** Mollie Moseley, Chatsworth, Bakewell, Derbyshire DE45 1PP Tel. 01246 565437 Website www.ddct.org.uk

■ **The Sandy Dewhirst Charitable Trust**
**CC NO** 279161   **ESTABLISHED** 1979
**WHERE FUNDING CAN BE GIVEN** UK, with a strong preference for East and North Yorkshire.
**WHO CAN BENEFIT** Charitable organisations and individuals connected with I J Dewhirst Holdings Limited.
**WHAT IS FUNDED** General charitable purposes; social welfare; community.
**SAMPLE GRANTS** Sargent Cancer Care for Children (£10,000); Help for Heroes (£5,000); Salvation Army, the Army Benevolent Fund and Yorkshire Air Ambulance (£3,000 each); Action Medical Research (£2,000); Driffield Town Cricket and Recreation Club (£1,500); St Catherine's Hospice, Hull Sea Cadets and All Saints Church – Nafferton (£500 each).
**FINANCES** Year 2013/14 Income £23,828 Grants £40,000 Grants to organisations £40,000
**TRUSTEES** Paul Howell; Timothy Dewhirst.

**HOW TO APPLY** The trust does not accept unsolicited applications.
**WHO TO APPLY TO** Louise Cliffe, Correspondent, Addleshaw Goddard, 100 Barbirolli Square, Manchester M2 3AB Tel. 0161 934 6373 email louise.cliffe@addleshawgoddard.com

■ **The Laduma Dhamecha Charitable Trust**
**CC NO** 328678   **ESTABLISHED** 1990
**WHERE FUNDING CAN BE GIVEN** UK and overseas
**WHO CAN BENEFIT** Charitable organisations.
**WHAT IS FUNDED** General charitable purposes including the relief of sickness and education in rural areas.
**FINANCES** Year 2013/14 Income £349,261 Grants £258,287 Grants to organisations £258,287 Assets £1,744,127
**TRUSTEES** K. R. Dhamecha; S. R. Dhamecha; P. K. Dhamecha.
**OTHER INFORMATION** The trust received £300,000 from Dhamecha Foods Limited.
**HOW TO APPLY** Apply in writing to the correspondent.
**WHO TO APPLY TO** Pradip Dhamecha, Trustee, The Dhamecha Group, 2 Hathaway Close, Stanmore, Middlesex HA7 3NR Tel. 020 8903 8181 email info@dhamecha.com

■ **Diabetes UK**
**CC NO** 215199   **ESTABLISHED** 1934
**WHERE FUNDING CAN BE GIVEN** UK.
**WHO CAN BENEFIT** Organisations which benefit people with diabetes.
**WHAT IS FUNDED** To promote and fund research into the causes and effects of diabetes, and the treatment and alleviation of the effects of diabetes to minimise the potential serious complications that can arise.
**TYPE OF GRANT** Equipment, fellowships, research grants, small grants, and studentships will be considered.
**RANGE OF GRANTS** Up to £850,000.
**SAMPLE GRANTS** King's College London (£857,000); Imperial College (£539,000); University of Dundee (£514,000); University of Bristol (£275,000); University of Bristol (£275,000); University of Glasgow (£266,000); University of Oxford (£258,000); Queen's University, Belfast (£238,000); University of Southampton (£193,000); University of Ulster (£162,000); University of Warwick (£153,000); and Peninsular Medical School (£130,000).
**FINANCES** Year 2013 Income £38,840,000 Grants £6,055,000 Grants to organisations £6,055,000 Assets £17,760,000
**TRUSTEES** Peter Dixon; Noah Franklin; Julian Baust; Dr Robert Young; Halima Khan; Prof. David Williams; Helen McCallum; James McCall; Gareth Hoskin; Janice Watson.
**OTHER INFORMATION** Grants to institutions in 2013 were broken down as follows: Care and treatment: £2.6 million Cause and prevention and cure: £3.4 million.
**HOW TO APPLY** Potential applicants are first advised to read the 'General guidelines for research grant applicants' on the charity's website. Information on the application process and deadlines for each specific scheme is also available on the website or by contacting the trust directly.

WHO TO APPLY TO Siobhan O'Shea, Correspondent, 10 Parkway, London NW1 7AA *Tel.* 020 7424 1000 *email* info@diabetes.org.uk *Website* www.diabetes.org.uk

## ■ The Diageo Foundation
CC NO 1014681   ESTABLISHED 1992
WHERE FUNDING CAN BE GIVEN There is a focus on Africa, Latin America, Asia and Eastern Europe.
WHO CAN BENEFIT Global or local NGOs.
WHAT IS FUNDED Community projects. To be eligible for funding from the Diageo Foundation, projects must fall within one of the four key focus areas: Skills for Life; Water of Life; Local Communities; Disaster Relief. There are further guidelines available from Diageo's website.
WHAT IS NOT FUNDED Organisations which are not registered charities; individuals; loans, business finance or endowment funds; medical charities or hospitals; promotion of religion; animal welfare; expeditions or overseas travel; political organisations; advertising; product donations; capital projects (e.g. buildings).
RANGE OF GRANTS Up to £50,000. Payments are usually over a period of one to three years.
SAMPLE GRANTS Desnoes and Geddes Foundation (£266,500); Barbados Community College (£70,000); British Council India (£50,000); Fundacion Televisa – Mexico (£25,000); New Entrepreneurs Foundation (£20,000); City Gateway (£15,000); Samanthran Trust (£5,200); Sports for Special Needs (£1,500).
FINANCES Year 2013/14 *Income* £803,917 *Grants* £1,416,844 *Grants to organisations* £1,416,844 *Assets* £1,064,891
TRUSTEES William Bullard; Geoffrey Thomas Bush; James Crampton; Georgie Passalaris.
OTHER INFORMATION More than 30 grants were made during the year.
HOW TO APPLY Apply in writing to the correspondent. There is additional guidelines information available to from the Diageo website, which should be read before an application is started.
WHO TO APPLY TO Lynne Smethurst, Correspondent, Diageo plc, Lakeside Drive, Park Royal, London NW10 7HQ *Tel.* 020 8978 6000 *email* diageofoundation@diageo.com *Website* www.diageo.com

## ■ Alan and Sheila Diamond Charitable Trust
CC NO 274312   ESTABLISHED 1977
WHERE FUNDING CAN BE GIVEN UK.
WHO CAN BENEFIT Registered charities only, particularly Jewish charities.
WHAT IS FUNDED Jewish causes and general charitable purposes.
WHAT IS NOT FUNDED Individuals.
RANGE OF GRANTS Up to £14,000.
SAMPLE GRANTS Magen David Adom (£14,000); Dementia UK (£8,600); Norwood (£7,500); Anglo Israel Association (£5,800); Youth Aliyah Child Rescue (£5,500); Chai Cancer Centre (£4,000); British WIZO (£3,300); Western Marble Arch Synagogue (£2,600); Fight for Sight (£2,500); and British School of Osteopathy, Holocaust Educational Trust and The Stuart Young Foundation (£2,000 each).
FINANCES Year 2013/14 *Income* £104,611 *Grants* £76,624 *Grants to organisations* £76,624 *Assets* £1,827,433
TRUSTEES Alan Diamond, Chair; Sheila Diamond; Jonathan Kropman; Kate Goldberg.

HOW TO APPLY The trust states that it will not consider unsolicited applications. No preliminary telephone calls. There are no regular trustees' meetings. The trustees frequently decide how the funds should be allocated. The trustees have their own guidelines, which are not published.
WHO TO APPLY TO Carla Hobby, Correspondent, Mazars LLP, 8 New Fields, 2 Stinsford Road, Nuffield, Poole, Dorset BH17 0NF *Tel.* 01202 680777 *email* carla.hobby@mazars.co.uk

## ■ The Dibden Allotments Fund
CC NO 255778   ESTABLISHED 1995
WHERE FUNDING CAN BE GIVEN Hythe, Fawley and Marchwood.
WHO CAN BENEFIT Grants can be made to individuals as well as organisations, including students and unemployed people.
WHAT IS FUNDED To relieve need, hardship or distress, and to invest in the community's future. Grants are awarded to individuals in need, to voluntary and charitable organisations, and to schemes benefitting children, particularly under-fives, older people and young people.
WHAT IS NOT FUNDED Grants will not be awarded to a church or other religious group to promote religion, fund religious activities or to support activities which are only available to members of the church or religious group.
RANGE OF GRANTS Up to £23,000.
SAMPLE GRANTS Handy Trust (£23,000); 14th New Forest East Scouts (£14,000); Waterside Ecumenical Project (£13,500); Choices Advocacy (£8,000); Planet Kids (£4,500); Relate Solent (£2,000); Waterside Amateur Boxing Club (£1,800); Marchwood Junior School and Waterside Gateway (£1,000 each); and Hythe Voluntary Car Group (£500).
FINANCES Year 2013/14 *Income* £391,516 *Grants* £264,122 *Grants to organisations* £93,828 *Assets* £9,499,989
TRUSTEES Judith Saxby; Maureen Maclean; Pat Hedges; Peter Parrott; Chris Harrison; Rosemary Dash; Jill Tomlin; Declan English; Alan Alvey.
HOW TO APPLY Application forms are available to download, together with criteria and guidelines, from the website. A third party, such as social services, teachers, and so on, must support applications from individuals.
WHO TO APPLY TO Valerie Stewart, Correspondent, 7 Drummond Court, Prospect Place, Hythe, Hampshire SO45 6HD *Tel.* 023 8084 1305 *email* dibdenallotments@btconnect.com *Website* www.daf-hythe.org.uk

## ■ The Gillian Dickinson Trust
CC NO 1094362   ESTABLISHED 2002
WHERE FUNDING CAN BE GIVEN County Durham, Northumberland and Tyne and Wear.
WHO CAN BENEFIT Registered charities, museums, and arts and theatre groups.
WHAT IS FUNDED Arts and general charitable purposes.
WHAT IS NOT FUNDED Individuals.
TYPE OF GRANT One-off or capital grants.
RANGE OF GRANTS Up to £50,000.
SAMPLE GRANTS National Glass Centre (£50,000); Durham University – Library Project (£40,000); Hexham Book Festival (£27,000); Tyneside Cinema – Northern Stars (£20,000); Live Theatre, The Samling Foundation (£15,000); Artichoke Trust (£10,000); Theatre Royal – Shakespeare Foundation (£6,000); Hexham

# Digbeth

Abbey Festival of Music and Arts, Northern Stage and Piano for the North Foundation – Young Pianist of the North (£5,000 each); and Greyscale Theatre Limited (£1,800).
**FINANCES** Year 2013/14 Income £71,907 Grants £199,551 Grants to organisations £199,551 Assets £2,283,071
**TRUSTEES** Alexander Dickinson; Piers Dickinson; Adrian Gifford; James Ramsbotham.
**OTHER INFORMATION** Grants were made to 12 organisations.
**HOW TO APPLY** Application forms are available to download from the website, where criteria and guidelines are also posted. Applications should be kept short (less than 500 words) and should only include attachments where the applicant considers them absolutely necessary for the purposes of the application. If the trustees need to see any documents (for example financial statements) they will request them.
**WHO TO APPLY TO** Mary Waugh, Correspondent, c/o Dickinson Dees LLP, One Trinity Gardens, Broad Chare, Newcastle upon Tyne NE1 2HF email grants@gilliantrust.org.uk Website www.gilliandickinsontrust.org.uk

## ■ The Digbeth Trust Limited

**CC NO** 517343    **ESTABLISHED** 1984
**WHERE FUNDING CAN BE GIVEN** West Midlands, principally Birmingham.
**WHO CAN BENEFIT** Smaller local, new and emerging voluntary and community groups, particularly those addressing exclusion and disadvantage.
**WHAT IS FUNDED** The trust manages a number of grant programmes that are generally targeted by area or theme, or both. See its website for current schemes.
**WHAT IS NOT FUNDED** General appeals, capital core costs, medical research, project running costs and grants for individuals.
**TYPE OF GRANT** One-off grants to enable groups to access specialist advice and services.
**SAMPLE GRANTS** Body, Mind and Spirit Partnership (£179,000); and AFCAR (£9,600).
**FINANCES** Year 2013/14 Income £412,927 Grants £188,816 Grants to organisations £188,816 Assets £37,641
**TRUSTEES** Dr David Williams-Massinda; Graham Mitchell; Nigel Potter; Christopher Burrows; Mark Lynes; Daina Anderson; Mark Peters; Adrian Middleton; Jeanette Burrows.
**OTHER INFORMATION** Grants were made to two organisations.
**HOW TO APPLY** The trust welcomes direct contact with groups. Application forms and guidance notes are available for the programmes it manages (this changes from time to time). Development worker support is offered to eligible groups.
**WHO TO APPLY TO** Guy Kibbler, Operations Manager, Unit F1 The Arch 48–52, Floodgate Street, Birmingham B5 5SL Tel. 0121 753 0706 email info@digbethtrust.org.uk Website www.digbethtrust.org.uk

## ■ The Dinwoodie Settlement

**CC NO** 255495    **ESTABLISHED** 1968
**WHERE FUNDING CAN BE GIVEN** UK.
**WHO CAN BENEFIT** Organisations benefitting academics and postgraduate research workers.
**WHAT IS FUNDED** Postgraduate medical education centres (PMCs) and research fellowships for suitably qualified medical practitioners of registrar status in general medicine or general surgery.
**WHAT IS NOT FUNDED** Anything falling outside the main areas of work referred to above. The trustees do not expect to fund consumable or equipment costs or relieve the NHS of its financial responsibilities.
**TYPE OF GRANT** Building projects will be considered. The trust's funds can be committed for three years when supporting major projects.
**RANGE OF GRANTS** Maximum of £1 million towards no more than one postgraduate medical centre project in an area. No more than the salary of two research workers in any one year.
**SAMPLE GRANTS** Christie NHS Trust (£250,000); Wrightington Wigan and Leigh NHS Trust (£195,017); Medway NHS Foundation Trust (£42,000); Medical Research Council (£14,500).
**FINANCES** Year 2012/13 Income £4,250,792 Grants £321,512 Grants to organisations £321,512 Assets £4,158,334
**TRUSTEES** William Fairbairn; John Black; Christian Webster; Rodney Fisher; Dr John Gibson.
**OTHER INFORMATION** The 2012/3 accounts were the latest available at the time of writing.
**HOW TO APPLY** The trustees state they are proactive rather than reactive in their grant-giving. Negotiating for new PMCs and monitoring their construction invariably takes a number of years.
**WHO TO APPLY TO** The Clerk to the Trustees, The Corn Exchange, Baffins Lane, Chichester, West Sussex PO19 1GE Tel. 01243 786111

## ■ Disability Aid Fund (The Roger and Jean Jefcoate Trust)

**CC NO** 1096211    **ESTABLISHED** 2002
**WHERE FUNDING CAN BE GIVEN** Buckinghamshire.
**WHO CAN BENEFIT** The following statement from the fund's 2013/14 accounts explains its grant-making strategy: 'We support a few carefully selected local, regional and small national disability and healthcare charities for older people in Buckinghamshire and Milton Keynes and adjacent counties, sometimes more widely if a trustee knows the charity. We look for strong support from charity service users and volunteers, and only modest expenditure on fundraising and administration.'
**WHAT IS FUNDED** People with physical, mental or multiple disabilities or hearing or visual impairment.
**TYPE OF GRANT** Building and refurbishment, equipment, training and general costs.
**RANGE OF GRANTS** £2,000–£25,000
**SAMPLE GRANTS** Canine Partners, Ashby (£25,000); Pace Centre, Aylesbury (£10,000); Carers Bucks, Aylesbury (£6,000); BBWOT, Oxford (£5,200); Lin Berwick Trust, ME Research UK, Wildfowl and Wetland Trust (£5,000 each); Multiple Sclerosis Trust (£4,000); Sensory Trust (£3,000); and the Carers Trust (£2,000).
**FINANCES** Year 2013/14 Income £185,856 Grants £120,204 Grants to organisations £120,204 Assets £4,126,305
**TRUSTEES** Vivien Dinning, Chair; Roger Jefcoate; Valerie Henchoz; Rosemary McCloskey; Carol Wemyss.
**HOW TO APPLY** Information provided by the fund: 'if you think that your charity might fit our remit telephone Roger Jefcoate on 01296 715466 weekdays before 7pm to discuss your proposal. You may then be invited to submit a written application summarising your request on just one side of paper, with minimal supporting

information like a single sheet general leaflet or a magazine article; do not send your annual review, we would ask for that if we need it. We would normally only consider a further request after two years, and then only by invitation.'
**WHO TO APPLY TO** Roger Jefcoate, Trustee, 2 Copse Gate, Winslow, Buckingham MK18 3HX *Tel.* 01296 715466

■ **Dischma Charitable Trust**
**CC NO** 1077501     **ESTABLISHED** 1999
**WHERE FUNDING CAN BE GIVEN** Worldwide, with a strong preference for London and the south east of England.
**WHO CAN BENEFIT** Charitable organisations.
**WHAT IS FUNDED** General charitable purposes, with a preference for education, arts and culture, conservation and human and animal welfare.
**WHAT IS NOT FUNDED** Medical research charities.
**RANGE OF GRANTS** £500–£5,000
**SAMPLE GRANTS** British Association for Adoption and Fostering (£5,000); Forward (£4,000); Epic Arts (£3,000); Theatre Centre Ltd (£2,800); Women and Children First (£2,000); Book Aid International and Chickenshed Theatre (£1,500 each); Contact the Elderly and CSV (£1,000 each); and Bumblebee Conservation Trust (£500).
**FINANCES** Year 2013 *Income* £126,242 *Grants* £103,955 *Grants to organisations* £103,955 *Assets* £5,054,167
**TRUSTEES** Simon Robertson; Edward Robertson; Lorna Robertson Timmis; Virginia Robertson; Selina Robertson; Arabella Brooke.
**OTHER INFORMATION** Grants were made to 69 organisations.
**HOW TO APPLY** The trustees meet half-yearly to review applications for funding. Only successful applicants are notified of the trustees' decision. Certain charities are supported annually, although no commitment is given.
**WHO TO APPLY TO** Linda Cousins, Secretary, Rathbones, 1 Curzon Street, London W1J 5FB *Tel.* 020 7399 0820 *email* linda.cousins@rathbones.com

■ **The Djanogly Foundation**
**CC NO** 280500     **ESTABLISHED** 1980
**WHERE FUNDING CAN BE GIVEN** UK and overseas, mainly Israel.
**WHO CAN BENEFIT** Registered charities, schools and universities.
**WHAT IS FUNDED** Developments in medicine; education; social welfare; the arts; welfare of older and younger people; Jewish charities.
**RANGE OF GRANTS** £15–£250,000
**SAMPLE GRANTS** University of Nottingham (£250,000); Great Ormond Street Children's Hospital (£100,000); Nottingham City Academy (£81,000); Israel Philharmonic Orchestra (£63,000); Jewish Care (£13,000); Nottingham Playhouse (£10,000); National Portrait Gallery and Norwood (£5,000 each); Community Security Trust (£2,000); and the Jewish Book Society (£1,000).
**FINANCES** Year 2013/14 *Income* £127,388 *Grants* £752,961 *Grants to organisations* £752,961 *Assets* £6,707,909
**TRUSTEES** Harry Djanogly; Michael S. Djanogly; Carol Djanogly.
**OTHER INFORMATION** Grants were made to 45 organisations.

**HOW TO APPLY** Apply in writing to the correspondent. 'The charity achieves its objectives receiving and evaluating grant applications.'
**WHO TO APPLY TO** Christopher Sills, Secretary, 3 Angel Court, London SW1Y 6QF *Tel.* 020 7930 9845

■ **The DLM Charitable Trust**
**CC NO** 328520     **ESTABLISHED** 1990
**WHERE FUNDING CAN BE GIVEN** UK, especially the Oxford area.
**WHO CAN BENEFIT** Organisations benefitting: children; young adults; older people; medical professionals, nurses and doctors; and people with head and other injuries, heart disease or blindness.
**WHAT IS FUNDED** Charities operating in Oxford and the surrounding areas, particularly charities working in the fields of: arts, culture and recreation; religious buildings; self-help groups; the conservation of historic buildings; memorials; monuments and waterways; schools; community centres and village halls; parks; various community services and other charitable purposes.
**WHAT IS NOT FUNDED** Individuals.
**TYPE OF GRANT** Feasibility studies, one-off, research, recurring costs, running costs and start-up costs. Funding of up to three years will be considered.
**SAMPLE GRANTS** Ley Community (£20,000); See Saw (£16,000); Stillbirth and Neonatal Death Charity (£10,000); Brainwave (£5,000); RNIB (£4,000); Prison Phoenix Trust (£3,000); Action for Blind People (£2,500); Footsteps Foundation and Talking Newspaper (£2,000 each); and Calibre Audio Centre (£1,000).
**FINANCES** Year 2013/14 *Income* £157,843 *Grants* £105,000 *Grants to organisations* £105,000 *Assets* £6,044,165
**TRUSTEES** Jeffrey Alan Cloke; Dr Eric Anthony de la Mare; Jennifer Elizabeth Pyper; Philippa Sawyer.
**OTHER INFORMATION** Grants were made to 36 organisations.
**HOW TO APPLY** Apply in writing to the correspondent. The trustees meet in February, July and November to consider applications.
**WHO TO APPLY TO** Jeffrey Cloke, Trustee, c/o Cloke and Co, 475 Salisbury House, London Wall, London EC2M 5QQ *Tel.* 020 7638 8992 *email* jeff@cloke.co.uk

■ **The DM Charitable Trust**
**CC NO** 1110419     **ESTABLISHED** 2005
**WHERE FUNDING CAN BE GIVEN** UK and Israel.
**WHO CAN BENEFIT** Jewish registered charities.
**WHAT IS FUNDED** Social welfare and education.
**FINANCES** Year 2013/14 *Income* £264,093 *Grants* £237,700 *Grants to organisations* £237,700 *Assets* £4,374,405
**TRUSTEES** Stephen Goldberg, Chair; David Cohen; Patrice Klein.
**OTHER INFORMATION** A list beneficiaries was not available.
**HOW TO APPLY** Apply in writing to the correspondent.
**WHO TO APPLY TO** Stephen Goldberg, Trustee, Sutherland House, 70–78 West Hendon Broadway, London NW9 7BT *Tel.* 020 8457 3258

# ■ The Derek and Eileen Dodgson Foundation

**CC NO** 1018776　　**ESTABLISHED** 1993
**WHERE FUNDING CAN BE GIVEN** In practice, Brighton and Hove.
**WHO CAN BENEFIT** Individuals and organisations.
**WHAT IS FUNDED** Welfare of older people.
**SAMPLE GRANTS** Age Concern; Grace Eyre Foundation; Brighton, Hove and Adur Social Services; Hove YMCA; and Sussex Probation Services.
**FINANCES** Year 2013/14 Income £116,156 Grants £63,896 Grants to organisations £63,896 Assets £2,137,252
**TRUSTEES** Christopher Butler; Peter Goldsmith; Roy Prater; Ed Squires; Natasha Glover; Georgina Reed.
**HOW TO APPLY** Apply in writing to the correspondent. The trustees meet quarterly, or more frequently if necessary to assess grant applications.
**WHO TO APPLY TO** Ian Dodd, Clerk, 8 Locks Hill, Portslade, Brighton and Hove, East Sussex BN41 2LB *Tel.* 01273 419802 *email* ianwdodd@gmail.com

# ■ The Dollond Charitable Trust

**CC NO** 293459　　**ESTABLISHED** 1986
**WHERE FUNDING CAN BE GIVEN** UK and Israel.
**WHO CAN BENEFIT** Jewish organisations.
**WHAT IS FUNDED** Jewish communities; general charitable purposes.
**RANGE OF GRANTS** Typically £5,000–£10,000.
**SAMPLE GRANTS** Grants made to organisations during the year were broken down as follows: 23 grants for education and training (£510,000); 43 grants for religious education (£420,000); 15 grants for disability (£391,000); 44 grants for the relief of poverty (£360,000); 24 grants for medical, health and sickness (£174,000); eight grants for religious activities (£43,000).
**FINANCES** Year 2013/14 Income £1,828,524 Grants £1,896,850 Grants to organisations £1,896,850 Assets £38,648,803
**TRUSTEES** Adrian Dollond; Jeffrey Milston; Melissa Dollond; Brian Dollond; Rina Dollond.
**OTHER INFORMATION** 'Although the constitution of the charity is broadly based, the trustees have adopted a policy of principally assisting the Jewish communities in Britain and Israel. The trustees aim to maximise the grants that it pays taking into account the return on its investments and likely infrastructure projects.'
**HOW TO APPLY** Apply in writing to the correspondent.
**WHO TO APPLY TO** Jeffrey Milston, Trustee, 19 Ridge Hill, London NW11 8PN *Tel.* 020 8905 5354

# ■ Dorset Community Foundation (formerly known as Community Foundation for Bournemouth, Dorset and Poole)

**CC NO** 1122113　　**ESTABLISHED** 2007
**WHERE FUNDING CAN BE GIVEN** The county of Dorset, including the unitary authorities of Bournemouth and Poole.
**WHO CAN BENEFIT** Local organisations.
**WHAT IS FUNDED** Community; social welfare; education; health; the relief of poverty.
**WHAT IS NOT FUNDED** Each fund has different criteria, consult the website for up to date eligibility.
**RANGE OF GRANTS** £50–£40,500. Average grant range is between £1,000 and £5,000.
**SAMPLE GRANTS** Future Roots (£18,000); Island Community Action (£14,000); Colehill and Wimborne Youth Community Centre (£7,500); Sturminster Newton Amateur Boxing Club (£7,000); Stalbridge Hall (£5,000); Moving On (£3,000); Transition Town Christchurch (£2,100); Life Education Wessex (£1,500); Poole Young Carers (£1,000); Westbourne Aware (£500); Age Concern Blanford (£250); and The Footprints Project (£100).
**FINANCES** Year 2013/14 Income £743,303 Grants £658,439 Grants to organisations £658,439 Assets £1,433,249
**TRUSTEES** Christopher Beale; Ashley Rowlands; Gwyn Bates; Christopher Morle; Gordon Page; Richard Cossey; Christopher Mills; Jeffrey Hart; Henry Digby.
**HOW TO APPLY** Contact the foundation for details of up-to-date programmes. An online contact form is available on the site. Information regarding criteria and eligibility for each individual fund can be found on the foundation's website. For any further advice and guidance contact the grants team on 01202 292255 or email grants@dorsetcf.org. According to the foundation's website, most of the grant schemes, unless otherwise stated, require the completion of an online application form. This is a two stage application, which should then be posted to the grants team along with the following documentation: 'a signed copy of your organisation's rules/constitution/governing document; a copy of your last year's accounts (or any other year's accounts this will be specified on the application); a copy of your safeguarding: child protection/vulnerable persons policy (if appropriate); quotes (as appropriate); a list of your management committee/trustee names with any relationships to one another and cheque signatories identified; and any other material you consider relevant to your application (please do not send material you want returned) e.g. leaflets, flyers, press cuttings.'
**WHO TO APPLY TO** Ashley Rowlands, Trustee, Abchurch Chambers, Dorset, Bournemouth BH1 2LN *Tel.* 01202 292255 *email* Philanthropy@dorsetcf.org *Website* www.dorsetcommunityfoundation.org

# ■ The Dorset Historic Churches Trust

**CC NO** 282790　　**ESTABLISHED** 1960
**WHERE FUNDING CAN BE GIVEN** Dorset
**WHO CAN BENEFIT** Churches.
**WHAT IS FUNDED** Grants or Loans towards the cost of restoring Dorset Church buildings are made in order to maintain the structure, and on some occasions other items of significant historical and architectural interest, in good repair.
**WHAT IS NOT FUNDED** According to the trust's website they will not consider: routine maintenance and decoration; works in the churchyard; heating and electrical maintenance; new buildings or extensions; new furniture or fittings; new bells or new bell frames; replacement or repair of organs; and clocks or sound-systems.
**TYPE OF GRANT** One-off grants.
**RANGE OF GRANTS** Governed by funds available and by need.
**SAMPLE GRANTS** Miton Abbey (£10,000); Bloxworth (£6,000); Uploders Methodist and Melbury Abbas (£5,000 each); Winterbourne Strickland and Ryme Intrinseca (£4,000 each); Poyntingdon (£3,000); Lychett Minster (£2,000);

Okeford Fitzpaine (£1,000); and Dorchester St Peter (£500).
FINANCES Year 2013/14 Income £141,809 Grants £101,500 Grants to organisations £101,500 Assets £498,287
TRUSTEES Simon Pomeroy; James Sabben-Clare; Capt. Nigel Thimbleby; Barry De Morgan; Andrew Boggis; Peter Hodgkins; Anthony Yeatman; Elizabeth Ashmead; Revd Canon Woods; Col. Jeremy Selfe; Susan Bruce-Payne; Robert Fox; Timothy Connor; Mike Crossley; Susan Smith.
HOW TO APPLY Applications are to be made to the Deanery Representative of the trust in the area in which the church is located, on a form available to download, together with criteria and guidelines, from the website.
WHO TO APPLY TO Elizabeth Ashmead, Trustee, The Old Forge, Frome St Quintin, Dorchester DT2 0HG Tel. 01935 83548 email grantssecretary@dhct.org.uk Website www.dorsethistoricchurchestrust.co.uk

■ **The Dorus Trust**
CC NO 328724    ESTABLISHED 1990
WHERE FUNDING CAN BE GIVEN Mainly UK but sometimes overseas.
WHO CAN BENEFIT Registered UK charities.
WHAT IS FUNDED General charitable purposes.
WHAT IS NOT FUNDED Individuals.
TYPE OF GRANT Projects and one-off grants. Funding for one year or less.
RANGE OF GRANTS £2500–£8,000
SAMPLE GRANTS DEBRA and St Raphael's Hospice (£8,000 each); Home Start – Merton and Practical Action (£7,000 each); Crisis UK (£6,000); Action for ME and Switchback (£5,000 each); Landmark Trust (£4,000); Exeter University (£3,000); and the Game and Wildlife Conservation Trust and The Big Splash (£2,500 each).
FINANCES Year 2013 Income £37,320 Grants £58,000 Grants to organisations £58,000 Assets £3,426,488
TRUSTEES Bettine Bond; Charles Peacock; Sarah Peacock.
HOW TO APPLY This trust no longer accepts applications.
WHO TO APPLY TO Charles Peacock, Trustee, c/o Charities Aid Foundation, 25 Kings Hill Avenue, Kings Hill, West Malling ME19 4TA Tel. 01732 520028

■ **The Double 'O' Charity Ltd**
CC NO 271681    ESTABLISHED 1976
WHERE FUNDING CAN BE GIVEN UK and overseas.
WHO CAN BENEFIT Registered charities and individuals.
WHAT IS FUNDED Primarily, grants towards the relief of poverty, preservation of health and the advancement of education. However, the charity considers all requests for aid.
WHAT IS NOT FUNDED Individuals towards their education or for their involvement in overseas charity work.
TYPE OF GRANT Preferably one-off.
RANGE OF GRANTS Up to £300,000.
SAMPLE GRANTS Meher Baba (£299,000); Spirit of Recovery (£100,000); Richmond Bridge Friendship Club (£31,000); The National Association for People Abused in Childhood (£27,000); Livewire Youth (£11,000); CAST (£7,500); MJ Choir (£5,000); Cornwall Project (£3,000); Winchester Project (£2,000); Clifton Practice (£1,700); LookAhead (£500); and The Vineyard Project (£200).
FINANCES Year 2013/14 Income £520,268 Grants £488,463 Grants to organisations £486,863 Assets £52,026
TRUSTEES Peter Townshend; Rachel Fuller.
OTHER INFORMATION Grants were made to 12 organisations in 2013/14.
HOW TO APPLY Apply in writing to the correspondent.
WHO TO APPLY TO The Trustees, c/o 4 Friars Lane, Richmond, Surrey TW9 1NL Tel. 020 8940 8171

■ **The Doughty Charity Trust**
CC NO 274977    ESTABLISHED 1977
WHERE FUNDING CAN BE GIVEN England, Israel.
WHO CAN BENEFIT Jewish organisations benefitting people who are disadvantaged by poverty or who are sick.
WHAT IS FUNDED Orthodox Jewish religious education; relief of poverty.
TYPE OF GRANT One-off grants.
RANGE OF GRANTS Up to £50,000.
SAMPLE GRANTS Beth Hayeled School (£50,000); Beis Sorah Schneirer School and West Hendon (Elyon) School (£40,000); SOFT (£37,000); and Sinai Synagogue (£22,000).
FINANCES Year 2013 Income £384,020 Grants £411,706 Grants to organisations £411,706 Assets £73,319
TRUSTEES G. Halibard; M. Halibard.
HOW TO APPLY Apply in writing to the correspondent.
WHO TO APPLY TO Gerald Halibard, Trustee, 22 Ravenscroft Avenue, London NW11 0WY Tel. 020 8209 0500

■ **Douglas Arter Foundation**
CC NO 201794    ESTABLISHED 1960
WHERE FUNDING CAN BE GIVEN UK, with preference for Bristol, Somerset and Gloucestershire.
WHO CAN BENEFIT Registered charities whose principal activity is to assist people with physical or mental disabilities.
WHAT IS FUNDED Principally in respect of specific projects on behalf of people with mental or physical disabilities.
WHAT IS NOT FUNDED Support is not given for overseas projects; general community projects*; individuals; general education projects*; religious and ethnic projects*; projects for unemployment and related training schemes*; projects on behalf of offenders and ex-offenders; projects concerned with the abuse of drugs and/or alcohol; wildlife and conservation schemes*; and general restoration and preservation of buildings, purely for historical and/or architectural. (* If these projects are mainly or wholly for the benefit of people who have disabilities then they may be considered.) Ongoing support is not given, and grants are not usually given for running costs, salaries, research and items requiring major funding. Loans are not given.
TYPE OF GRANT One-off for specific projects. Ongoing, research, core funding and major funding appeals are not supported.
RANGE OF GRANTS Usually between £250–£2,500.
SAMPLE GRANTS Chescombe Trust – Bristol, Climbing Out – Westbury, Cornwall Blind Association – Truro and Meningitis Now – Stroud (£1,000 each); NeuroMuscular Centre – Winsford, Shine – Peterborough, Support Dogs – Sheffield and Tiny Tim's Children's Centre – Coventry (£500

each); MS Therapy Centre – Berkshire and Alzheimer's Bristol (£250 each).
**FINANCES** Year 2014 Income £110,532 Grants £75,250 Grants to organisations £79,850 Assets £2,864,391
**TRUSTEES** Geoffrey Arter; John Gurney; Peter Broderick; John Hudd; Peter Yardley.
**HOW TO APPLY** The trust does not have an official application form. Appeals should be made in writing to the secretary. Telephone calls are not welcome. The trust asks that the following is carefully considered before submitting an application – appeals must: be from registered charities; include a copy of the latest audited accounts available (for newly registered charities a copy of provisional accounts showing estimated income and expenditure for the current financial year); show that the project is 'both feasible and viable' and, if relevant, give the starting date of the project and the anticipated date of completion; include the estimated cost of the project, together with the appeal's target-figure and details of what funds have already been raised and any fundraising schemes for the project. The trustees state that 'where applicable, due consideration will be given to evidence of voluntary and self-help (both in practical and fundraising terms) and to the number of people expected to benefit from the project'. They also comment that their decision is final and 'no reason for a decision, whether favourable or otherwise, need be given' and that 'the award and acceptance of a grant will not involve the trustees in any other commitment'. Whilst appeals are dealt with on an ongoing basis, to cut down costs appeals will not be acknowledged unless they are successful in being awarded a grant. The trustees meet four times a year in the first weeks of March, June, September and December and successful applicants only, will be notified and sent cheques for grants by the second weekend of the relevant month.
**WHO TO APPLY TO** Belinda Arter, Secretary, Fern Villa, Melksham Road, Patterdown, Chippenham, Wiltshire SN15 2NR Tel. 01249 448252 email dafbristol.aol.com

## ■ R. M. Douglas Charitable Trust
**CC NO** 248775 **ESTABLISHED** 1966
**WHERE FUNDING CAN BE GIVEN** UK, with a preference for Staffordshire.
**WHO CAN BENEFIT** Registered charities already in receipt of support from the trust.
**WHAT IS FUNDED** The relief of poverty (including provision of pensions), especially for present and past employees (and their families) of Robert M Douglas (Contractors) Ltd; general charitable purposes, especially in the parish of St Mary – Dunstall.
**TYPE OF GRANT** Mostly small grants; buildings; capital and core costs; one-off and recurring expenditure; research.
**RANGE OF GRANTS** Typically £200–£500.
**SAMPLE GRANTS** A list beneficiaries was not included in the latest accounts. **Previous grant recipients have included**: Bible Explorer; British Red Cross; Burton Graduate Medical College; Four Oaks Methodist Church; Lichfield Diocesan Urban Fund; St Giles Hospice – Lichfield; SAT-7 Trust; John Taylor High School – Barton in Needwood.
**FINANCES** Year 2013/14 Income £328,021 Grants £46,977 Grants to organisations £38,000 Assets £1,502,345

**TRUSTEES** Juliet Lees, Jonathan Douglas; Murray Lees.
**OTHER INFORMATION** In 2013/14 a total of 35 grants were made to organisations. In addition nearly £9,000 was given to individuals.
**HOW TO APPLY** The annual report for 2013/14 states: 'The trustees' policy is to support individuals and institutions already in receipt of annual grants out of the assets of the charity, together with other charitable causes known to the trustees. Funding is not available for other beneficiaries and accordingly new applications cannot be considered.'
**WHO TO APPLY TO** Juliet Lees, Trustee, c/o Geens Ltd, 68 Liverpool Road, Stoke-on-Trent ST4 1BG Tel. 01782 847952 email info@geens.co.uk

## ■ The Drapers' Charitable Fund
**CC NO** 251403 **ESTABLISHED** 1959
**WHERE FUNDING CAN BE GIVEN** UK, with a special interest in the City and adjacent parts of London and Moneymore and Draperstown in Northern Ireland.
**WHO CAN BENEFIT** Registered or exempt charities.
**WHAT IS FUNDED** General charitable purposes including: social welfare; education; heritage; the arts; prisoner support; Northern Ireland; textile conservation.
**WHAT IS NOT FUNDED** Grants are not usually made for: individuals; schools, colleges and universities (except in certain circumstances); churches; almshouses; animal welfare; medical research/relief, hospitals or medical centres; children's disabilities, physical disabilities or medical conditions; holidays or general respite care; organisations that are not registered charities, unless exempt from registration; funds that replace or subsidise statutory funding; local branches of national charities, associations or movements; work that has already taken place; general appeals or circulars; loans or business finance.
**TYPE OF GRANT** Most grants are one-off payments but occasionally multi-year grants are awarded.
**RANGE OF GRANTS** Mostly for £10,000 or less.
**SAMPLE GRANTS** Bancroft's School (£75,000); Industrial Trust (£70,000); Kirkham Grammar School (£53,000); Centre of the Cell (£42,000); Pembroke College – Cambridge (£35,000); Poppy Factory, Shannon Trust and St Anne's College – Oxford (£25,000 each); Boxing Academy, Fields in Trust and Futureversity (£15,000 each); Baytree Centre, Fine Cell Work and Shelter from the Storm (£10,000 each); Living Paintings, Somerset Sight and Unicorn Theatre (£8,000 each).
**FINANCES** Year 2013/14 Income £2,046,178 Grants £1,708,940 Grants to organisations £1,708,940 Assets £49,375,825
**TRUSTEE** The Drapers' Company.
**HOW TO APPLY** We would advise that for full details of the application process and the trust's current priorities, applicants refer to the trust's website. The Charities Committee meets five times a year to review all applications which fall within the current priorities for funding. The charity aims to deal with each application within three months of its being received. Applications can be made at any time during the year. Applicants should complete the 'application summary sheet' (available to download from the website) and submit it together with a document on proposed funding. This should include detailed information about the organisation and the project/activity to be funded; full costings and project budget for the proposed work for

which the grant is requested, or the organisation's income and expenditure budget for the current year (whichever is appropriate); and the most recent audited financial statements and trustees report. Applications should be submitted by post only.
**WHO TO APPLY TO** Andy Mellows, Head of Charities, The Drapers' Company, Drapers' Hall, Throgmorton Avenue, London EC2N 2DQ *Tel.* 020 7588 5001 *Fax* 020 7628 1988 *email* charities@thedrapers.co.uk *Website* www.thedrapers.co.uk

### ■ Dromintee Trust
**CC NO** 1053956   **ESTABLISHED** 1996
**WHERE FUNDING CAN BE GIVEN** Worldwide.
**WHO CAN BENEFIT** Charitable organisations.
**WHAT IS FUNDED** People in need by reason of age, illness, disability or socio-economic circumstances; for charitable purposes connected with children's welfare; the advancement of health and education; research into rare diseases and disorders, in particular metabolic disorders; and for general charitable purposes.
**TYPE OF GRANT** One-off and recurrent.
**RANGE OF GRANTS** Up to £151,000.
**SAMPLE GRANTS** Light for the Blind – India (£100,000); CAFOD and Diocese of Nottingham (£50,000 each); Consolata Fathers (£30,000); InterCare (£20,000); and Consolata Fathers, John Boakye Mensah – two grants (£10,000 each).
**FINANCES** Year 2013/14 *Income* £445,580 *Grants* £280,000 *Grants to organisations* £280,000 *Assets* £1,419,190
**TRUSTEES** Hugh Murphy; Margaret Murphy; Mary Murphy; Patrick Hugh Murphy; Robert Smith; Paul Tiernan; Joseph Murphy.
**HOW TO APPLY** Apply in writing to the correspondent.
**WHO TO APPLY TO** Hugh Murphy, Trustee, 1 Westmoreland Avenue, Thurmaston, Leicester LE4 8PH *Tel.* 0116 260 3877 *email* dromineetrust@gmail.com

### ■ Duchy Health Charity Limited
**CC NO** 271957   **ESTABLISHED** 1976
**WHERE FUNDING CAN BE GIVEN** Cornwall.
**WHO CAN BENEFIT** NHS organisations or registered charities.
**WHAT IS FUNDED** Health care; relief of sickness; medical research; projects and schemes that improve health, well-being, the provision of health care and help people with health issues.
**WHAT IS NOT FUNDED** Individuals; applications that duplicate an existing provision.
**TYPE OF GRANT** Project costs; capital and revenue expenditure; equipment and services.
**RANGE OF GRANTS** £5,000–£120,000; generally up to £25,000.
**SAMPLE GRANTS** The Merlin Project (£120,000); Cornwall Age UK (£24,500); CRCC – dementia network (£19,800); Pentreath (£15,500); Cosgarne Hall (£14,000); Cornwall Partnership NHS Trust (£10,000); Penhaligons Friends (£9,600); Sound Waves (£5,000); Carefree (£2,000); Roseland Surgeries Patients Group (£1,000); Cornwall Arts Centre Trust (£500).
**FINANCES** Year 2013/14 *Income* £196,864 *Grants* £265,484 *Grants to organisations* £265,484 *Assets* £4,787,366
**TRUSTEES** Barbara Vann; Dr John Hyslop; Carol O'Brien; Ian Pawley; Mary Grigg; Richard Robinson; Sally-Jane Coode; Richard Sowerby;

Mary Vyvyan; Tim Guy; Scott Bennett; Pamela Clements; Caroline Dunstan; Jennifer Doble; Graham Murdoch; Mark Williams.
**OTHER INFORMATION** There were 19 awards made.
**HOW TO APPLY** Application forms can be downloaded from the charity's website. They can be submitted online (preferably) or via post. Applicants should provide a business plan (if possible), details of any other funding partners and an up to date set of accounts. The Grant Committee meets quarterly. Applications need to be submitted at least three weeks before a meeting (for most up to date information on when the meetings are held see the charity's website – 'events' section).
**WHO TO APPLY TO** Richard Robinson, Secretary, Robinson Reed Layton, Peat House, Newham Road, Truro, Cornwall TR1 2DP *Tel.* 01872 276116 or 01209 715198 *email* info@duchyhealthcharity.org or robin1674son@btinternet.com *Website* www.duchyhealthcharity.org

### ■ The Duis Charitable Trust
**CC NO** 800487   **ESTABLISHED** 1987
**WHO CAN BENEFIT** Children, medical, general charitable purposes.
**WHAT IS FUNDED** The trust makes grants benefitting groups largely concerned with children and Jewish causes, although this incorporates support of social welfare, education, capital library and hospital appeals.
**SAMPLE GRANTS** Norwood Ravenswood, Great Ormond Street Hospital, BINOH Norwood Childcare, Dulwich Picture Gallery, National Playing Fields, Down's Syndrome Association, Joint Jewish Charitable Trust, Hillel Special Purposes Fund, Breakaway Charity Committee, Children's Wish Foundation and Jewish Care.
**FINANCES** Year 2013/14 *Income* £18,509 *Grants* £11,000 *Grants to organisations* £11,000
**TRUSTEE** Jayne Steiner and Cheryl Davis.
**HOW TO APPLY** Apply in writing to the correspondent.
**WHO TO APPLY TO** Jayne Steiner, Trustee, 16 Ranulf Road, London NW2 2DE *email* cheryl@prn.org.uk

### ■ The Royal Foundation of the Duke and Duchess of Cambridge and Prince Harry
**CC NO** 1132048   **ESTABLISHED** 2009
**WHERE FUNDING CAN BE GIVEN** UK and overseas.
**WHO CAN BENEFIT** Registered charities.
**WHAT IS FUNDED** Currently: veterans and military families; disadvantaged children and young people; conservation and sustainable development.
**RANGE OF GRANTS** Up to £950,000.
**SAMPLE GRANTS** PEAS (£953,000); Fields in Trust (£458,000); Glasgow Life and Place 2 Be (£100,000 each); Action on Addiction (£95,000); Skillforce (£71,500); Greenhouse Charity and Greenhouse Schools (£56,500 each); Community Service Volunteers (£55,000); EPIC Partners (£5,000); The Evidence Centre (£4,000).
**FINANCES** Year 2013 *Income* £3,887,009 *Grants* £1,954,613 *Grants to organisations* £1,954,613 *Assets* £5,187,959
**TRUSTEES** Anthony James Lowther-Pinkerton; Guy Monson; Sir David Manning; Edward Harley; Lord Janvrin; Baroness Shackleton.

**OTHER INFORMATION** Grants were made to 20 organisations in 2013/14.

**HOW TO APPLY** To apply for an Endeavour Fund grant email a proposal no longer than four sides of A4 with the following criteria in mind: For distributing any size of grant: The applicants and/or beneficiaries should be wounded, injured or sick (including psychological illness) servicemen or women. They may or may not have been injured or become ill whilst on active duty but must have been in service at the time; The activity must be either a sporting or adventurous challenge and must represent a significant challenge for the applicant; Applicants should be able to demonstrate clear outcomes from the activity and should have the formal backing of their medical or rehabilitation team. For the Development and Venture grants: The activity must contribute to personal recovery and must contribute to a successful transition to civilian life; The activity must contribute to raising awareness of wounded, injured and sick servicemen and women; The activity must contribute to inspiring others, either other wounded, injured or sick servicemen and women, or members of the community, such as schoolchildren; There must be a clear and credible plan both for raising awareness and inspiring others; The applicant must demonstrate an ability to secure additional funding for the activity. **Currently the foundation is unable to accept unsolicited requests for support apart from through this fund.**

**WHO TO APPLY TO** Susan Stafford, St James's Palace, London SW1A 1BS *Tel.* 020 7101 2963 *email* info@royalfoundation.com *Website* www.royalfoundation.com

## ■ The Dulverton Trust

**CC NO** 1146484   **ESTABLISHED** 1949
**WHERE FUNDING CAN BE GIVEN** Unrestricted. Mainly UK in practice. Limited support to parts of Africa.
**WHO CAN BENEFIT** Registered charities.
**WHAT IS FUNDED** Youth opportunities; general welfare; preservation; Africa (usually Kenya and Uganda); peace and humanitarian support.
**WHAT IS NOT FUNDED** The following are not funded: individuals; museums, galleries, libraries, exhibition centres and heritage attractions; individual churches and other historic buildings; individual schools, colleges, universities or other educational establishments; hospices, hospitals, nursing or residential care homes; activities outside the stated geographical scope; charities whose main beneficiaries live within Greater London or in Northern Ireland. The following are rarely funded: regional charities that are affiliated with a national body; health, medicine and medical conditions including drug and alcohol addiction; therapy and counselling; specific support for people with disabilities; the arts and sport (except where used as a means of achieving a funding priority); animal welfare; expeditions; research; conferences; salaries; major building projects; endowments.
**TYPE OF GRANT** Project and one-off funding. Also capital and core costs. Funding is rarely given for more than one year.
**RANGE OF GRANTS** £5,000–£90,000
**SAMPLE GRANTS** Teens and Toddlers (£90,000); Amref UK (£84,000); The Brilliant Club (£75,000); Depaul UK (£60,000); Portsmouth D-Day Museum Trust (£50,000); Wildscreen (£40,000); Royal National Children's Foundation (£30,000); Encompass (£26,000); Uprising (£25,000); Wilderness Foundation UK (£10,000); Oakfield (£5,000).
**FINANCES** *Year* 2013/14 *Income* £3,539,384 *Grants* £3,109,526 *Grants to organisations* £3,109,526 *Assets* £81,107,143
**TRUSTEES** Christopher Willis; Sir John Kemp-Welch; Dr Catherine Willis; The Lord Dulverton; Tara Douglas-Home; Dame Mary Richardson; Richard Howard; The Rt Hon Earl of Grey Gowrie; Sir Malcolm Rifkind; The Lord Hemphill.
**HOW TO APPLY** Read the guidelines carefully and then complete the eligibility quiz on the trust's website. If your organisation passes the eligibility quiz you will be provided with a link to the e-application form. The trustees meet in February, June and October to discuss proposals. There are no deadlines or dates and the selection process can take between three and six months. All rejected applications will receive notification and an outline explanation for the rejection will usually be given. Applications under consideration for a grant will normally receive a visit from one of the trust's staff who will subsequently report to the trustees. Following the trustees' meeting successful applicants will be notified by email. If you wish to make initial enquiries, establish eligibility, discuss time scales or need to seek further guidance about an application, telephone the trust's office on 020 7495 7852. **Note: The trust has asked us to emphasise that they do not accept applications via post. You should apply only through the trust's website.**
**WHO TO APPLY TO** Anna de Pulford, Grants and Administration Manager, 5 St James's Place, London SW1A 1NP *Tel.* 020 7629 9121 *email* grants@dulverton.org *Website* www.dulverton.org

## ■ The Dumbreck Charity

**CC NO** 273070   **ESTABLISHED** 1976
**WHERE FUNDING CAN BE GIVEN** Worldwide, especially the west Midlands.
**WHO CAN BENEFIT** Charitable organisations. New applications are restricted to Midlands organisations.
**WHAT IS FUNDED** Animal welfare and conservation; children's welfare; people who are elderly or who have mental or physical disabilities; medical causes; general charitable purposes.
**WHAT IS NOT FUNDED** Individuals.
**TYPE OF GRANT** Recurring and one-off grants.
**RANGE OF GRANTS** £500–£5,000, but mainly for amounts under £1,000.
**SAMPLE GRANTS** Three Choirs Festival Association and Save the Children – Philippines Emergency Appeal (£5,000 each); Friends of Pershore Abbey and the Oesophageal Patients Association (£2,000 each); Ackers Trust, Dogs for the Disabled, Maggs Day Centre and Redwing Horse Sanctuary (£1,000 each); and Academy Chamber Orchestra, The Barn Owl Trust Focus Birmingham and the Trussell Trust (£500 each).
**FINANCES** *Year* 2013/14 *Income* £145,415 *Grants* £123,500 *Grants to organisations* £123,500 *Assets* £4,260,660
**TRUSTEES** Chris Hordern; Hugh Carslake; Jane Uloth; Judith Melling.
**HOW TO APPLY** Apply in writing to the correspondent. The trustees meet annually in April/May. Unsuccessful applications will not be acknowledged. In general, priority is given to applications from the Midlands counties.
**WHO TO APPLY TO** Mrs P. Spragg, Correspondent, c/o PS Accounting, 41 Sycamore Drive, Hollywood,

Birmingham B47 5QX *email* psaccounting@hotmail.co.uk

## ■ Dunard Fund

**CC NO** 295790   **ESTABLISHED** 1986
**WHERE FUNDING CAN BE GIVEN** In practice UK with a particular interest in Scotland.
**WHAT IS FUNDED** Principally to the training for and performance of classical music at the highest standard and to education and display of the visual arts, also at international standard. A small percentage of the fund is dedicated to environmental, humanitarian and architectural projects.
**WHAT IS NOT FUNDED** Grants are only given to charities recognised in Scotland or charities registered in England and Wales.
**TYPE OF GRANT** The trustees prefer to engage with recipients to enable long-term development of projects and initiatives which have major and lasting significance; they are therefore less inclined to provide one-off donations.
**RANGE OF GRANTS** £500–£500,000
**SAMPLE GRANTS** Dumfries House – Adam Bridge International (£400,000); Festival Cities Theatre Trust (£250,000); Royal Albert Hall and Royal Scottish National Opera (£200,000 each); Refuge (£125,000); Royal Opera House (£75,000); Glasgow School of Art (£30,000); Royal Botanic Gardens Edinburgh (£20,000); The Landmark Trust (£10,000); and Royal Chelsea Hospital (£1,000).
**FINANCES** *Year* 2013/14 *Income* £18,596,168 *Grants* £2,590,775 *Grants to organisations* £2,590,775 *Assets* £22,330,921
**TRUSTEES** Carol Colburn Grigor; Dr Catherine Colburn Høgel; Erik Colburn Høgel; Colin Liddell; Peter Thielfeldt.
**OTHER INFORMATION** The charity is also registered with the Office of the Scottish Charity Regulator.
**HOW TO APPLY** No grants are given to unsolicited applications.
**WHO TO APPLY TO** Carol Colburn Grigor, Trustee, 4 Royal Terrace, Edinburgh EH7 5AB *Tel.* 0131 556 4043 *email* annette.brash@tiscali.co.uk

## ■ The Dunhill Medical Trust

**CC NO** 1140372   **ESTABLISHED** 1951
**WHERE FUNDING CAN BE GIVEN** UK
**WHO CAN BENEFIT** Registered charities particularly those benefitting older people and academic institutions undertaking medical research.
**WHAT IS FUNDED** Care of older people, including rehabilitation and palliative care; research into the causes and treatments of disease, disability and frailty related to ageing.
**WHAT IS NOT FUNDED** Organisations based outside the United Kingdom or whose work primarily benefits people outside the United Kingdom; research staff based outside the UK; sponsorship of individuals; sponsorship of charitable events; providing clinical services or equipment that, in the opinion of the trust, would more appropriately be provided by the National Health Service or other statutory bodies; hospices (revenue or capital costs); travel or conference fees (except where these items are an integral part of a project); new or replacement vehicles (unless an integral part of a community based development); general maintenance; continuation/replacement funding where a project or post has previously been supported from statutory sources (or similar).
**TYPE OF GRANT** Project grants to research groups, as well as some grants for salaries and building or equipment costs for specific projects.
**RANGE OF GRANTS** Up to £1 million.
**SAMPLE GRANTS** Aston University (£110,000); Hope Park Trust and St John's Hospital – Bath (£100,000 each); Simeon Care for the Elderly (£55,500); University of Liverpool (£42,000); Vitalise (£34,500); King's College – London (£27,500); Magpie Dance (£10,500); Cornwall Blind and Partially Sighted Association (£7,500); Harrow Citizens Advice (£3,200).
**FINANCES** *Year* 2013/14 *Income* £3,165,498 *Grants* £3,198,414 *Grants to organisations* £3,198,414 *Assets* £108,142,431
**TRUSTEES** Kay Glendenning; Prof. Sir Roger Boyle; John Ransford; The Right Revd Christopher Chessun; Prof. Martin Severs; Prof. James McEwen; Mr R. E. Perry; Prof. Roderick Hay; Prof. Peter Lansley; Helen Davies.
**OTHER INFORMATION** Grant-making was split as follows: research and research related grants (£2.5 million); services and care for older people (£413,500); building grants – accommodation for older people (£290,500). Grants were made to 65 organisations in 2013/14.
**HOW TO APPLY** Applicants for Research Grants should complete the appropriate online application form on the trust's website. Applicants to the General Grants programme are asked to provide an initial outline (approximately two sides of A4) by post or email, including the following information: a brief description of the organisation and its status (e.g. whether it is a registered charity); who you are and what you do within the organisation; a description of the project for which funding is being sought, where it will take place and who it will involve; an outline of who will benefit from the work and why; the key outcomes and timescales; the total cost of the project/work and the specific amount being applied for from the trust. Outline applications for all programmes can be submitted at any time and those which are eligible will be invited to submit a formal application. The formal application requirements differ depending upon the type of grant being applied for and applicants are strongly advised to visit the trust's website before making an application to ensure that they have all the relevant information. Full applications are considered by the Grants and Research Committee which meets quarterly (normally in February, May, July and November). The committee makes recommendations on whether applications should be supported and decisions are then referred to the board of trustees for approval at their quarterly meetings (normally held in March, June, September and December). Successful applicants are normally notified within two weeks of the meeting. Generally, decisions are made within three to four months. At the time of writing (June 2015) the Research Training Fellowships are closed to new applications. Check the website for the latest information.
**WHO TO APPLY TO** Claire Large, Administrative Director, 3rd Floor, 16–18 Marshalsea Road, London SE1 1HL *Tel.* 020 7403 3299 *email* admin@dunhillmedical.org.uk *Website* www.dunhillmedical.org.uk

## ■ The Dunn Family Charitable Trust

**CC NO** 297389  **ESTABLISHED** 1987
**WHERE FUNDING CAN BE GIVEN** UK, with a strong preference for Nottinghamshire.
**WHO CAN BENEFIT** General charitable purposes including organisations benefitting people with multiple sclerosis, environmental charities and medical charities.
**WHAT IS FUNDED** Charities working in the fields of health facilities and buildings; support to voluntary and community organisations; MS research; conservation; bird sanctuaries and ecology.
**WHAT IS NOT FUNDED** Only organisations known to the trustees are supported. No grants are given to individuals.
**TYPE OF GRANT** Core costs and one-off; funding for one year or less will be considered.
**RANGE OF GRANTS** £100–£5,000
**SAMPLE GRANTS** Oakes Trust (£4,500); Nottingham Multiple Sclerosis Therapy Centre Ltd (£4,000); St Luke's Hospice and Support Dogs (£3,000 each); Peter Le Marchant Trust (£2,500); Edwalton Parish Church, RSPB and Seafarers UK (£2,000 each); Rainbow Children's Hospice (£1,500); and Malt Cross Trust Company and Nottinghamshire Wildlife Trust (£1,000 each).
**FINANCES** Year 2013/14 *Income* £71,424 *Grants* £53,000 *Grants to organisations* £53,000 *Assets* £1,959,290
**TRUSTEES** Graham Dunn; Jacky Dunn; Lisa Dunn; Nigel Dunn; Peter Dunn; Richard Dunn.
**HOW TO APPLY** Apply in writing to the correspondent.
**WHO TO APPLY TO** Jacky Chester, Rushcliffe Estates Ltd, Tudor House, 13–15 Rectory Road, West Bridgford, Nottingham NG2 6BE *Tel.* 0115 945 5300 *email* jrc@rushcliffe.co.uk

## ■ The W. E. Dunn Trust

**CC NO** 219418  **ESTABLISHED** 1958
**WHERE FUNDING CAN BE GIVEN** Midlands.
**WHO CAN BENEFIT** Charitable organisations and individuals.
**WHAT IS FUNDED** The general policy of the trust is to benefit people who are sick or in need and live in the Midlands, particularly Warwickshire, Staffordshire, Shropshire or Worcestershire and surrounding areas. It is the policy of the trustees to determine at the first meeting of the trustees for the year beginning 5 April how much will be available for grants. When the amount available for grants for the coming year has been calculated the trustees determine how this total shall be divided between: needy individuals for purposes other than further education; students for further educational purposes; and to charitable organisations.
**WHAT IS NOT FUNDED** No grants are given to settle or reduce debts already incurred.
**TYPE OF GRANT** Buildings, capital, core costs, one-off, project and start-up costs. All funding is for up to three years.
**RANGE OF GRANTS** Up to £3,000.
**SAMPLE GRANTS** Real Deal – Birmingham (£3,000); Abbots Morton Bell Tower Appeal, Acorns and Grove Residential Home (£2,000 each); and Air Ambulance Service, Bag Books, Blesma, Motability, National Youth Choirs, Target Ovarian Cancer and Wildlife Trust – Staffordshire (£1,000 each).
**FINANCES** Year 2013/14 *Income* £330,283 *Grants* £170,272 *Grants to organisations* £105,300 *Assets* £4,870,530
**TRUSTEES** David Corney; Leita Smethurst; Christopher King; Rachel Hardy.
**OTHER INFORMATION** The grant total in 2011/12 includes 358 grants to individuals totalling £56,000 and £92,000 given to 139 organisations.
**HOW TO APPLY** There is a detailed policy statement on the making of grants and guidance notes and model application for sponsoring bodies making application for a grant for an individual. Potential applicants are advised to contact the correspondent for copies of these documents in order to make an appropriate and relevant application. Generally, applications should be in writing to the correspondent giving the name and address, some idea of the income/outgoings and any other necessary particulars of the grantee. Organisations should always enclose accounts. Grants to individuals are considered every week; grants to organisations, every three or four months.
**WHO TO APPLY TO** David Corney, Trustee, The Trust Office, 30 Bentley Heath Cottages, Tilehouse Green Lane, Knowle, Solihull B93 9EL *Tel.* 01564 773407 *email* wedunn@tiscali.co.uk

## ■ The Charles Dunstone Charitable Trust

**CC NO** 1085955  **ESTABLISHED** 2001
**WHERE FUNDING CAN BE GIVEN** UK and overseas.
**WHO CAN BENEFIT** Registered charities.
**WHAT IS FUNDED** General charitable purposes.
**WHAT IS NOT FUNDED** The trustees do not normally make grants to individuals.
**SAMPLE GRANTS** Prince's Trust (£275,000); Media for Development (£100,000); St Giles Trust (£80,000); Norfolk Community Foundation (£52,000); Dance United and Priors Court (£50,000 each); Uppingham School (£27,000); Blue Marine Foundation, Get Connected and Switchback (£25,000 each); and Sky Badger (£10,000).
**FINANCES** Year 2013/14 *Income* £229,872 *Grants* £1,438,949 *Grants to organisations* £1,438,949 *Assets* £6,177,230
**HOW TO APPLY** Proposals are generally invited by the trustees or initiated at their request. Unsolicited applications are not encouraged and are unlikely to be successful. The trustees prefer to support innovative schemes that can be successfully replicated or become self-sustaining.
**WHO TO APPLY TO** The Trustees, H. W. Fisher and Company, 11–15 William Road, London NW1 3ER *Tel.* 020 7388 7000 *email* jtrent@hwfisher.co.uk

## ■ Dushinsky Trust Ltd

**CC NO** 1020301  **ESTABLISHED** 1992
**WHERE FUNDING CAN BE GIVEN** Mainly Israel.
**WHO CAN BENEFIT** Jewish and Israeli charities.
**WHAT IS FUNDED** Alleviation of poverty and the furtherance of Orthodox Jewish education.
**SAMPLE GRANTS** **Previous beneficiaries have included:** United Institutes of Dushinsky, Minchat Yitzchok Institutions and Ish Lerehu Fund.
**FINANCES** Year 2013 *Income* £499,304 *Grants* £489,032 *Grants to organisations* £489,302 *Assets* £11,229
**TRUSTEES** S. Reisner; Z. Levine; M. Schischa.
**HOW TO APPLY** The trust does not accept unsolicited applications.

WHO TO APPLY TO Simon Reisner, Secretary, 23 Braydon Road, London N16 6QL  Tel. 020 8802 7144

## ■ Mildred Duveen Charitable Trust

CC NO 1059355   ESTABLISHED 1996
WHERE FUNDING CAN BE GIVEN Worldwide.
WHO CAN BENEFIT Charitable organisations.
WHAT IS FUNDED General charitable purposes.
RANGE OF GRANTS £500–£10,000
SAMPLE GRANTS Missing People (£10,000); Almeida Theatre and Masterclass Trust (£5,000 each); Charlie Waller Memorial Trust (£3,300); Whittington Babies (£2,500); Three Wings Trust, St John's College and Hearing Dogs for Deaf People (£2,000 each); Combat Stress, Lingfield and District RDA, Old Meeting URC Bedworth and The Firefighters Charity (£1,000 each); Centrepoint (£750); and ACT (Prostate Cancer Charity), Cruse Bereavement Care, Shooting Start and The Rainbow Centre for Children (£500 each).
FINANCES Year 2013/14 Income £22,395 Grants £70,000 Grants to organisations £70,000
TRUSTEES Peter Holgate; Adrian Houstoun; Peter Loose; John Shelford.
HOW TO APPLY Apply in writing to the correspondent.
WHO TO APPLY TO Peter Holgate, Trustee, Devonshire House, 60 Goswell Road, London EC1M 7AD  Tel. 020 7566 4000 email pholgate@kingstonsmith.co.uk

## ■ The Dyers' Company Charitable Trust

CC NO 289547   ESTABLISHED 1984
WHERE FUNDING CAN BE GIVEN UK.
WHO CAN BENEFIT Hospices; churches; registered charities; schools; universities.
WHAT IS FUNDED General charitable purposes.
WHAT IS NOT FUNDED Individuals or international charities.
TYPE OF GRANT One-off and long-standing.
RANGE OF GRANTS Up to £70,000 but typically £500–£5,000.
SAMPLE GRANTS Archbishop Tenison's School (£70,000); University of Manchester (£10,000); Swan Sanctuary (£4,000); Combat Stress (£3,000); British Association of Performing Arts Medicine (£2,500); St Peter's Hospice – Bristol and Wasdale Mountain Rescue (£2,000 each); Young Bristol (£1,500); Above and Beyond and Association for Post Natal Illness (£1,000 each); Royal British Legion Poppy Appeal (£500).
FINANCES Year 2013/14 Income £1,233,385 Grants £484,022 Grants to organisations £484,022 Assets £642,145
TRUSTEE The Dyers Company.
OTHER INFORMATION The trust also funds a bursary for a school in Norwich.
HOW TO APPLY The company's website provides information regarding applications and states the following: 'Please note that as a matter of policy, the company does not accept unsolicited applications.'
WHO TO APPLY TO The Clerk of the Dyers, Dyer's Hall, Dowgate Hill, London EC4R 2ST  Tel. 020 7236 7197 Website www.dyerscompany.co.uk

## ■ The James Dyson Foundation

CC NO 1099709   ESTABLISHED 2003
WHERE FUNDING CAN BE GIVEN UK, local community around the Dyson company's UK headquarters, in Malmesbury, Wiltshire.
WHO CAN BENEFIT Registered charities and educational institutions.
WHAT IS FUNDED Educational institutions working in the field of design, technology and engineering; charities carrying out medical or scientific research; projects which aid the local community around Dyson, in Malmesbury, Wiltshire.
TYPE OF GRANT One-off and recurrent.
RANGE OF GRANTS Up to £230,000.
SAMPLE GRANTS Postgraduate Bursaries (£230,000); US Education Programme (£211,000); James Dyson Award (£106,000); Royal College of Art (£100,000); D&T Association CPD Project (£70,500); Malmesbury Schools Project (£24,000); Malaysia/Singapore Education Programme (£23,000); Japan Education Programme (£16,000); and Local Community and Education Fund (£11,000).
FINANCES Year 2013 Income £1,109,813 Grants £943,501 Grants to organisations £943,501 Assets £617,059
TRUSTEES Sir James Dyson; Lady Deirdre Dyson; Valerie West; Prof. Sir Christopher Frayling.
HOW TO APPLY Applications in writing on headed paper to the correspondent. Organisations can also apply through the 'get in touch' section of the foundation's website.
WHO TO APPLY TO Kevin Walker, Correspondent, Dyson Group plc, Tetbury Hill, Malmesbury, Wiltshire SN16 0RP  Tel. 01666 828416 email jamesdysonfoundation@dyson.com Website www.jamesdysonfoundation.com

## ■ eaga Charitable Trust

**CC NO** 1088361    **ESTABLISHED** 2001
**WHERE FUNDING CAN BE GIVEN** UK and European Union.
**WHO CAN BENEFIT** Organisations and institutions benefitting research workers, academics and medical professionals.
**WHAT IS FUNDED** The trust provides grants for work that helps towards the understanding of fuel poverty and helps to address its causes and effects.
**WHAT IS NOT FUNDED** No grants for: personal support of individuals in need; general fundraising appeals; capital works; retrospective funding; energy advice provision materials; maintenance of websites; local energy efficiency/warm homes initiatives.
**TYPE OF GRANT** One-off for projects and research, including reasonable overhead costs. Funding is available for up three years.
**RANGE OF GRANTS** The trust does not have minimum or maximum grant levels but it does encourage the co-funding of projects where appropriate. Average grant can go up to £25,000–£30,000.
**SAMPLE GRANTS** NatCen Social Research (£29,000); Future Climate (£22,800); The Children's Society (£21,000); Richard Moore and Energy Audit Company (£16,000); Changeworks (£14,700); EBX Ltd (£10,000); University of York (£4,700); and University of Leicester (£800).
**FINANCES** Year 2013/14 Income £33,346 Grants £119,273 Grants to organisations £119,273 Assets £591,619
**TRUSTEES** William Baker; Anne Toms; Elizabeth Gore; Pedro Guertler; Dr Eldin Fahmy; Prof. Christine Liddell; David Kidney.
**OTHER INFORMATION** Grants were made to eight organisations in 2013/14.
**HOW TO APPLY** Application forms and detailed guidance on the application process are available on the trust's website. Potential applicants are encouraged to contact the trust's manager, Naomi Brown at an early stage to discuss whether their ideas are likely to fall within the trust's areas of interest.
**WHO TO APPLY TO** Dr Naomi Brown, Trust Manager, PO Box 225, Kendal LA9 9DR *Tel.* 01539 736477 *email* eagact@aol.com *Website* www.eagacharitabletrust.org

## ■ The Eagle Charity Trust

**CC NO** 802134    **ESTABLISHED** 1989
**WHERE FUNDING CAN BE GIVEN** UK, in particular Manchester, and overseas.
**WHO CAN BENEFIT** UK, international and local charities.
**WHAT IS FUNDED** General charitable purposes including welfare and overseas aid.
**TYPE OF GRANT** One-off, with no commitment to providing ongoing funding.
**RANGE OF GRANTS** £500–£2,000
**SAMPLE GRANTS** Oxfam – Darfur and Chad (£2,500); Médecins Sans Frontières, UNICEF and Shelter (£2,000 each); British Red Cross – Bangladesh and Macmillan Cancer Support (£1,500 each); Amnesty International, Sight Savers International and Samaritans (£1,000 each); and Turning Point, Claire House and WaterAid (£500 each).
**FINANCES** Year 2013 Income £43,664 Grants £36,500 Grants to organisations £36,500 Assets £1,226,442
**TRUSTEES** Laura Gifford; Daphne Gifford; Elizabeth Williams; Sarah Nowakowski; Robert Gifford.
**OTHER INFORMATION** Grants were made to 33 organisations.
**HOW TO APPLY** Apply in writing to the correspondent. However, note that unsolicited applications are not invited.
**WHO TO APPLY TO** The Trustees, c/o Nairne Son and Green, 477 Chester Road, Cornbrook, Manchester M16 9HF *Tel.* 0161 872 1701

## ■ Audrey Earle Charitable Trust

**CC NO** 290028    **ESTABLISHED** 1984
**WHERE FUNDING CAN BE GIVEN** UK.
**WHO CAN BENEFIT** Registered charities.
**WHAT IS FUNDED** General charitable purposes, with some preference for animal welfare and conservation charities.
**TYPE OF GRANT** Mostly recurrent.
**RANGE OF GRANTS** Grants made were of £2,600 in July 2013 and £1,700 in January 2014.
**SAMPLE GRANTS** Age UK, Animal Health Trust, British Red Cross Society, Oxfam, PDSA, Redwing Horse Sanctuary, Royal British Legion, The Salvation Army (£4,200 in two grants each); Shire Horse Society (£1,700).
**FINANCES** Year 2013/14 Income £97,260 Grants £94,050 Grants to organisations £94,050 Assets £6,387,579
**TRUSTEES** Paul Andrew Sheils; Roger James Weetch.
**HOW TO APPLY** Apply in writing to the correspondent; however, the trust tends to support the same beneficiaries year after year and, therefore, it appears unlikely that new applications will receive support.
**WHO TO APPLY TO** Paul Sheils, Trustee, Bedford House, 21A John Street, London WC1N 2BF *Tel.* 020 7400 7770 *email* info@moonbeever.com

## ■ The Earley Charity

**CC NO** 244823    **ESTABLISHED** 1820
**WHERE FUNDING CAN BE GIVEN** The Ancient Liberty of Earley (i.e. the central eastern and southern part of Reading, Earley and Lower Earley, northern Shinfield, Winnersh, Sonning and Lower Caversham).
**WHO CAN BENEFIT** Individuals in need and charitable and community organisations.
**WHAT IS FUNDED** To give aid to: the relief of distress and sickness; the relief of people who are elderly, disabled or living in poverty; the provision and support (with the object of improving the conditions of life in the interests of social welfare) of facilities for recreation and other leisure time occupation; the provision and support of educational facilities; and any other charitable purpose for the benefit of the community.
**WHAT IS NOT FUNDED** The charity does not fund the following: postgraduate education; general running/living costs; core costs; open-ended salaries; general appeals; religious activities; national organisations operating in the area of benefit without a local office; general public sector appeals (apart from in a few very exceptional cases); applications from outside

the area of benefit; individuals who are planning to move out of the area of benefit; individuals who have been awarded a grant within the last two years; and individuals who have received three grants in the past.
TYPE OF GRANT One-off, project and start-up costs. Funding is available for up to one year.
RANGE OF GRANTS Up to £47,000.
SAMPLE GRANTS Beneficiaries include: Age UK – Reading (£47,000); Kilnsea Preschool (£28,000); Community Savings and Loans and Reading Community Welfare Rights Unit (£10,000 each); Reading Community Network (£5,000); Reading Sea Cadets (£2,500); East Reading Festival (£2,000); The Befriending Forum (£1,600); Reading Festival Chorus (£1,500); 1st Whitley Wood Brownies (£600); and the Older Person's Shared Sports Equipment Fund (£200).
FINANCES Year 2013 Income £113,377 Grants £555,579 Grants to organisations £306,582 Assets £13,160,445
TRUSTEES Robert Ames; Dr Christopher Sutton; Dr Deborah Jenkins; Miryam Eastwell; Philip Hooper; Lesley Owen; Bobbie Richardson; Richard Rodway.
HOW TO APPLY Application forms are available from the correspondent or to download, together with criteria and guidelines, on the website; applications are considered at any time. No response is given to applicants from outside the beneficial area. Telephone calls or emails are welcome from applicants who wish to check their eligibility.
WHO TO APPLY TO Jane Wittig, Clerk to the Trustees, The Liberty of Earley House, Strand Way, Lower Earley, Reading, Berkshire RG6 4EA Tel. 0118 975 5663 email ec@earleycharity.org.uk Website www.earleycharity.org.uk

## ■ Earls Colne and Halstead Educational Charity
CC NO 310859    ESTABLISHED 1975
WHERE FUNDING CAN BE GIVEN The catchment area of the former Earls Colne and Halstead grammar schools.
WHO CAN BENEFIT Organisations for the furtherance of education, individuals and local schools.
WHAT IS FUNDED Furtherance of the education of local children and young adults.
RANGE OF GRANTS Up to £10,000.
SAMPLE GRANTS Hedingham School (£5,000); Honywood School (£4,000); Richard de Clare School (£2,600); Ramsey School (£2,500); Richard De Clare School (£1,700); and Earls Colne School (£1,200).
FINANCES Year 2013–14 Income £51,474 Grants £60,066 Grants to organisations £47,296 Assets £1,325,895
TRUSTEES The Ramsey Academy (£9,800); St Peter's Coggeshall (£5,000); Holy Trinity PS. (£4,500); Honywood School (£4,400); Ramsey School (£2,200); and Holy Trinity School (£1,200).
OTHER INFORMATION In 2013/14 individuals received £12,770.
HOW TO APPLY Apply in writing to the correspondent.
WHO TO APPLY TO Martyn Woodward, Clerk to the Trustees, St Andrew's House, 2 Mallows Field, Halstead, Essex CO9 2LN Tel. 01787 479960 email earlscolnehalstead.edcharity@yahoo.co.uk Website www.echec.org.uk

## ■ East End Community Foundation (formerly the St Katharine and Shadwell Trust)
CC NO 1147789    ESTABLISHED 1990
WHERE FUNDING CAN BE GIVEN The London boroughs of Tower Hamlets, Hackney and City of London.
WHO CAN BENEFIT Voluntary and community organisations. Some grants may be made to statutory organisations such as schools.
WHAT IS FUNDED Community development; education; employment and training.
WHAT IS NOT FUNDED Individuals.
TYPE OF GRANT Capital, revenue and full project funding.
RANGE OF GRANTS £250–£10,000
SAMPLE GRANTS Docklands Youth Services (£11,300); Island Advice (£10,000); Lincoln Area Regeneration Group (£9,000); Splash Youth Activities (£6,000); Bethnal Green Academy (£5,000); Foodcycle (£3,000); Skills Enterprise (£1,200); Teviot Action Group (£1,000); East London Chinese Community Centre (£800); Island House Craft Club (£500); Creative Unity Steel Band (£200).
FINANCES Year 2013/14 Income £2,603,227 Grants £319,712 Grants to organisations £319,712 Assets £17,824,246
TRUSTEES Sister Christine Frost; Gabrielle Harrington; Howard Dawber; Mark Gibson; Ian Fisher; Eric Sorensen; Duke Chifiero; Manali Trivedi; Hamza Yusuf.
OTHER INFORMATION Grants were made to 119 organisations in 2013/14.
HOW TO APPLY See the foundation's website for details of up-to-date schemes.
WHO TO APPLY TO Tracey Walsh, Director, Jack Dash House, 2 Lawn House Close, London E14 9YQ Tel. 020 7345 4444 email admin@eastendcf.org Website www.eastendcf.org

## ■ Eastern Counties Educational Trust Limited
CC NO 310038    ESTABLISHED 1922
WHERE FUNDING CAN BE GIVEN Preference for Essex, Suffolk, Norfolk, Cambridgeshire and Hertfordshire.
WHO CAN BENEFIT Those with special educational needs, particularly those under 25 who have emotional and behavioural difficulties.
WHAT IS FUNDED Activities, projects or equipment which will assist the above.
WHAT IS NOT FUNDED Individuals. Normally no grants are given for recurring costs.
TYPE OF GRANT One-off grants.
RANGE OF GRANTS Up to £20,000.
SAMPLE GRANTS Red Balloon of the Air (£20,000); North Cambridge Academy (£19,300); The College of West Anglia (£15,600); University of Hertfordshire (£10,000); Norwood (£5,000); Avenues East and Happy Days (£4,500 each); Romsey Mill (£4,100); Tilehouse Counselling and Castledon Special School (£4,000 each); Autism Anglia (£3,500); Keep Out – Crime Diversion Scheme and Lexden Springs Special School (£2,000 each); and Dame Vera Lynn Trust (£1,500).
FINANCES Year 2013/14 Income £122,181 Grants £100,535 Grants to organisations £100,535 Assets £3,513,506
TRUSTEES Deborah Reed; Mr L. Lepper; Mr H. Anderson; Deborah Reed; Lady Singleton; Miss J. S. Clark; Diana Forrow.
HOW TO APPLY An application form should be obtained from the correspondent. This provides

details of information to be submitted with it. Unsuccessful applicants will not be informed unless an sae is provided.
**WHO TO APPLY TO** Mr A. Corin, Company Secretary, Brook Farm, Wet Lane, Boxted, Colchester CO4 5TN *Tel.* 01206 273295 *email* ahcorin@aol.com

## ■ The Sir John Eastwood Foundation
**CC NO** 235389 **ESTABLISHED** 1964
**WHERE FUNDING CAN BE GIVEN** UK, but mainly Nottinghamshire in practice.
**WHO CAN BENEFIT** Local organisations.
**WHAT IS FUNDED** General charitable purposes including children with special needs, older people and people with disabilities.
**WHAT IS NOT FUNDED** Individuals.
**TYPE OF GRANT** One-off projects and longer term funding.
**RANGE OF GRANTS** £250–£24,000
**SAMPLE GRANTS** Warsop Youth Club (£315,000); John Eastwood Hospice Trust (£50,000); Nottinghamshire Hospice (£24,000); The Oaklands (£15,000); Newark and Nottinghamshire Agricultural Society and Nottingham Hospitals Charity (£10,000 each); and Air Ambulance, Amantani UK Trust, Disabilities Living Centre, Macmillan Cancer Support and Mansfield Street Pastors (£5,000 each).
**FINANCES** *Year* 2013/14 *Income* £318,749 *Grants* £603,951 *Grants to organisations* £603,951 *Assets* £8,191,941
**TRUSTEES** Diana Cottingham; Constance Mudford; Gordon Raymond; Valerie Hardingham; David Marriott.
**OTHER INFORMATION** The grant total included a grant of £315,000 made to enable a local charity to purchase a freehold property from Sir John Eastwood Foundation's trading subsidiary company, Adam Eastwood and Sons Limited.
**HOW TO APPLY** Apply in writing to the correspondent.
**WHO TO APPLY TO** David Marriott, Trustee, PO Box 9803, Mansfield NG18 9FT *email* sirjohneastwoodfoundation@talktalk.net

## ■ The Ebenezer Trust
**CC NO** 272574 **ESTABLISHED** 1976
**WHERE FUNDING CAN BE GIVEN** UK and overseas.
**WHO CAN BENEFIT** Registered charities.
**WHAT IS FUNDED** Advancement of the evangelical tenets of the Christian faith.
**WHAT IS NOT FUNDED** Individuals.
**TYPE OF GRANT** One-off grants; core costs; capital costs; unrestricted funding.
**RANGE OF GRANTS** Up to around £10,000, in practice, between £500 and £5,000.
**SAMPLE GRANTS** Samaritan's Purse (£53,000); Holy Trinity Church – Sofia (£19,000); TEAR Fund (£7,000); World Team (£6,000); Christ Church – Stock (£5,400); Barnabas Fund (£3,000); Alpha Partners (£2,000); Livability (£1,000); Salvation Army (£500); Treasures in Heaven Trust (£300); Open Doors (£50).
**FINANCES** *Year* 2013/14 *Income* £47,000 *Grants* £132,763 *Grants to organisations* £132,763 *Assets* £578,346
**TRUSTEES** Nigel Davey; Ruth Davey.
**OTHER INFORMATION** Grants were made to 52 organisations in 2013/14.
**HOW TO APPLY** The trust states that they 'are most unlikely to consider unsolicited requests for grants'.
**WHO TO APPLY TO** Nigel Davey, Trustee, Longwood Lodge, Whites Hill, Stock, Ingatestone CM4 9QB *Tel.* 01277 829893

## ■ The EBM Charitable Trust
**CC NO** 326186 **ESTABLISHED** 1982
**WHERE FUNDING CAN BE GIVEN** UK.
**WHO CAN BENEFIT** Charitable organisations.
**WHAT IS FUNDED** General charitable purposes; animal welfare and research; youth development; social welfare.
**TYPE OF GRANT** Recurring and one-off.
**RANGE OF GRANTS** £5,000–£200,000
**SAMPLE GRANTS** British Racing School (£200,000); Community Links (£115,000); Second Chance (£100,000); Marie Curie Cancer Care (£50,000); Action for Kids (£30,000); Autistica (£35,000); Dogs for the Disabled (£10,000); the Queen Elizabeth Foundation (£6,000); Orchid and SPARKS (£5,000 each).
**FINANCES** *Year* 2013/14 *Income* £1,249,195 *Grants* £1,065,000 *Grants to organisations* £1,065,000 *Assets* £48,653,289
**TRUSTEES** Richard Moore; Michael Macfadyen; Stephen Hogg; Francis Moore; Lucy Forsyth.
**OTHER INFORMATION** The trust manages two funds, the general fund and the Fitz' fund. The Fitz' fund was established following the death of Cyril Fitzgerald, one of the original trustees of the charity who left the residue of his estate to the trust. The money is held as a designated fund for animal charities.
**HOW TO APPLY** The trustees have previously stated: 'Unsolicited applications are not requested as the trustees prefer to support donations to charities whose work they have researched and which is in accordance with the wishes of the settlor. The trustees do not tend to support research projects as research is not a core priority but there are exceptions. The trustees' funds are fully committed. The trustees receive a very high number of grant applications which are mostly unsuccessful.'
**WHO TO APPLY TO** Martin Pollock, Moore Stephens, 150 Aldersgate Street, London EC1A 4AB *Tel.* 020 7334 9191

## ■ The Ecology Trust
**CC NO** 1099222 **ESTABLISHED** 2003
**WHERE FUNDING CAN BE GIVEN** Mainly UK and Europe.
**WHO CAN BENEFIT** Registered charities working on ecological and environmental initiatives, particularly, in the areas of agriculture, energy, and climate change.
**WHAT IS FUNDED** Support is given to projects that prevent environmental degradation and that change values and attitudes, both amongst the public and with people in positions of power. In general the trust seeks to address the causes of the environmental crisis that we face, and to tackle these, rather than to make the consequences of this crisis easier to live with.
**WHAT IS NOT FUNDED** The trust is unlikely to make grants to the following kinds of projects: work that has already taken place; part of general appeals or circulars; outward-bound courses, expeditions and overseas travel; capital projects (i.e. buildings and refurbishment costs); conservation of already well-supported species or of non-native species; and furniture, white

goods, computer, paint, timber and scrap recycling projects.
TYPE OF GRANT One-off and recurring grants for project and core costs.
RANGE OF GRANTS Up to £30,000.
SAMPLE GRANTS School Food Matters (£45,000); Canopy (£43,000); Jikalahari – The Network for Riau Forest Rescue and Samdhana Institute (£31,000); Campaign for Better Transport Trust (£27,000); Salvia (£23,000); SEO Birdlife (£13,000); Amics de la Terra and GEN-GOB Eivissa (£9,000 each); Sociedad de Historia Natural de Baleares (£3,000).
FINANCES Year 2013/14 Income £524,648 Grants £261,577 Grants to organisations £261,577 Assets £357,087
TRUSTEES Benjamin Goldsmith; Charles Filmer; Alexander Goldsmith.
HOW TO APPLY Apply in writing to the correspondent.
WHO TO APPLY TO Jon Cracknell, Hon. Secretary, Unicorn Administration Ltd, 30–36 King Street, Maidenhead SL6 1NA Tel. 01797 222773 email heather@jmgfoundation.org

## ■ The Economist Charitable Trust
CC NO 293709   ESTABLISHED 1986
WHERE FUNDING CAN BE GIVEN England and Wales.
WHO CAN BENEFIT Charitable organisations.
WHAT IS FUNDED General charitable purposes; education and training; economic and community development; children and young people; older people; people with disabilities.
FINANCES Year 2013/14 Income £118,761 Grants £98,383 Grants to organisations £98,383 Assets £21,941
TRUSTEES Ada Simkins; Kiran Malik; Daniel Franklin; Cecelia Block.
OTHER INFORMATION The trust is the corporate charity of The Economist Newspaper Ltd, a multinational media company specialising in international business and world affairs.
HOW TO APPLY Apply in writing to the correspondent. A simple letter plus latest report and accounts is preferred. A telephone call to clarify specific queries is welcomed, call 020 7576 8546. Applications can be made at any time.
WHO TO APPLY TO Matthew Hanratty, Correspondent, The Economist Group, 25 St James's Street, London SW1A 1HG Tel. 020 7576 8546 email mathewhanratty@economist.com Website www.economist.com

## ■ EDF Energy Trust (EDFET)
CC NO 1099446   ESTABLISHED 1996
WHERE FUNDING CAN BE GIVEN UK.
WHO CAN BENEFIT Individuals and families and voluntary and not-for-profit organisations.
WHAT IS FUNDED The trust offers two types of grants: individual grants – to cover the payment of gas and electricity debts and other essential household debts or costs (applicants must be EDF Energy account holders); and organisational grants – for organisations working in the field of money advice, debt counselling or energy efficiency advice.
WHAT IS NOT FUNDED No grants for: fines for criminal offences; educational or training needs; debts to central government departments; medical equipment, aids and adaptations; holidays; business debts; catalogues; credit cards; personal loans; deposits for secure accommodation; or overpayment of benefits.
TYPE OF GRANT Contracts and full project funding for up to three years.
RANGE OF GRANTS Up to £20,000.
SAMPLE GRANTS Bristol Debt Advice Centre, East London Financial Inclusion (£20,000 each); Brixton Advice Centre (£18,300); Money Advice Plus – East Sussex (£18,100); Thanet District Citizens Advice (£17,000); Brighton and Hove Citizens Advice (£13,800)
FINANCES Year 2013 Income £3,015,533 Grants £1,944,208 Grants to organisations £378,796 Assets £1,186,597
TRUSTEES Denice Fennell; Vic Szewczyk; Tim Cole; Brian Cole; Bob Richardson; Richard Sykes; David Hawkes.
HOW TO APPLY Organisational grants: It is advisable to contact the foundation for further information on future grant programmes and deadlines. Individual grants: applications can be submitted throughout the year. Applications must be made on a standard application form, which can be downloaded from the website, obtained from local advice centres such as citizen's advice bureau or by writing to the trust. The trust also has an online application form, accessible via the website.
WHO TO APPLY TO The Trustees, Freepost RLXG-RBYJ-USXE, EDF Energy, PO Box 42, Peterborough PE3 8XH Tel. 01733 421021 Fax 01733 421020 email edfet@charisgrants.com Website www.edfenergytrust.org.uk

## ■ The Gilbert and Eileen Edgar Foundation
CC NO 241736   ESTABLISHED 1965
WHERE FUNDING CAN BE GIVEN UK.
WHO CAN BENEFIT Charitable organisations.
WHAT IS FUNDED General charitable purposes with preference towards: medical research; care and support; fine arts; education in the fine arts; religion; recreation.
WHAT IS NOT FUNDED Grants for education in the fine arts are made by way of scholarships awarded by academies.
TYPE OF GRANT One-off and longer term projects.
RANGE OF GRANTS Usually £250–£9,000.
SAMPLE GRANTS Royal College of Music – Junior Scholarship (£9,000); Royal Academy of Arts – Scholarship (£6,000); Royal Academy of Dramatic Art – Scholarship (£5,000); Missing People, Prostate Cancer Research Centre and The Trinity Sailing Trust (£1,000 each); and the Down's Syndrome Association, Fight for Sight, Havens Christian Hospice and Marine Conservation Society (£500 each).
FINANCES Year 2013/14 Income £99,000 Grants £71,750 Grants to organisations £71,750 Assets £1,877,780
TRUSTEES Simon Gentilli; Adam Gentilli.
OTHER INFORMATION Grants were made to 88 organisations in 2013/14.
HOW TO APPLY Apply in writing to the correspondent.
WHO TO APPLY TO Adam Gentilli, Trustee, Greville Mount, Milcote, Stratford-upon-Avon, Warwickshire CV37 8AB email trustee@milcote.uk

## ■ The Gilbert Edgar Trust
CC NO 213630   ESTABLISHED 1955
WHERE FUNDING CAN BE GIVEN Predominantly UK, but also overseas.
WHO CAN BENEFIT Registered charities; voluntary organisations; educational or cultural bodies benefitting children, medical professionals and research workers.

**WHAT IS FUNDED** Charities which the trustees find worthwhile will be supported, especially in the area of social welfare. Grants have been given in the following categories: children; deaf/blind individuals; people with mental and physical disabilities; drug abuse; homelessness; hospices; medical cause; overseas aid; research; social needs; young people; other purposes. The annual report states: 'The work of the charities supported has included providing treatment for people who are drug or alcohol dependent, providing help for people with learning disabilities, people who are homeless and children suffering from cruelty. It also has included providing medical help and emergency support abroad.'

**TYPE OF GRANT** Modest awards; occasionally larger one-off grants.

**RANGE OF GRANTS** Mostly £500–£1,500.

**SAMPLE GRANTS** British Red Cross, Mind, NSPCC and Shelter (£1,500 each); Macmillan Cancer Support, National Institute of Conductive Education and Prostate Cancer UK (£1,000 each); Camphill Communities, Hospice of St Francis, National Autistic Society, Prisoners Abroad, Robert Owen Communities, Sense and St John Ambulance (£500 each); Worshipful Company of Clockmakers (£100).

**FINANCES** Year 2013/14 Income £72,886 Grants £34,100 Grants to organisations £34,100 Assets £1,023,253

**TRUSTEES** Simon Gentilli; Adam Gentilli; Dr Richard Solomons.

**OTHER INFORMATION** During the year 50 awards were made to organisations. The grant total refers to 'grants payable in the year' (including 'prior grants withdrawn/not taken up' amounting to £1,500).

**HOW TO APPLY** Applications can be made in writing to the correspondent, providing with a copy of a brochure/flyer describing your work. According to the annual report, 'the trustees review the beneficiaries and from time to time amendments are made to the list'.

**WHO TO APPLY TO** Simon Gentilli, Trustee, Barnwell House, Skirmett Road, Fingest, Oxon RG9 6TH

■ **Edge Fund**

ESTABLISHED 2012

**WHERE FUNDING CAN BE GIVEN** UK.

**WHO CAN BENEFIT** Registered charities; CICs, social enterprises and community groups.

**WHAT IS FUNDED** Social, economic and environmental justice.

**FINANCES** Year 2012/13 Grants £33,692 Grants to organisations £33,692

**OTHER INFORMATION** Edge Fund was established in April 2012 by a group of philanthropists aiming to achieve a different funding model from traditional donor-led philanthropy. The fund is not a registered charity, but in September 2012 decided on the Community Benefit Society legal form. We took the grant total from information contained on the fund's website.

**HOW TO APPLY** Check the fund's website for current information on open rounds and deadlines.

**WHO TO APPLY TO** Sophie Pritchard, Co-ordinator, 13–15 Stockwell Road, London SW9 9AU Tel. 0300 123 1965 email info@edgefund.org.uk Website edgefund.org.uk

■ **Edinburgh and Lothian Trust Fund (formerly known as EVOT)**

SC NO SC031561    ESTABLISHED 1868

**WHERE FUNDING CAN BE GIVEN** Edinburgh and the Lothians.

**WHO CAN BENEFIT** Organisations and individuals. Priority is given to local charitable organisations so that a national organisation will be required to indicate need and a local presence in Edinburgh and the Lothians according to the agreed policy.

**WHAT IS FUNDED** Social welfare. Priority will be given to organisations which combat inequalities and promote voluntary action.

**WHAT IS NOT FUNDED** The trust does not normally accept applications from the following: organisations with a turnover of more than £200,000; organisations with significant liquid reserves; national organisations, (unless their grant is for a specific project meeting a local need in Edinburgh and the Lothians, and where there is an independent local committee and accounts so that the responsibility is with the local initiative. In this case the financial restrictions above will apply to the local unit.); commercial organisations or purpose; statutory agencies; schools and colleges. The trust does not normally provide grants for the following: salaries or similar; all core property costs, such as new buildings, property repairs, extensions, alterations, property rental, rates, etc.; educational and adventure type projects, holidays or day visits; arts, environmental or sports activities, except where a significant social service or therapeutic intent is the main aim; travel and transport (except as part of core volunteer expenses); disbursement to other agencies; general appeals.

**TYPE OF GRANT** One-off and recurrent for a maximum of three years.

**RANGE OF GRANTS** £1,000–£2,000

**SAMPLE GRANTS** Community Foundation for Planetary Healing, Edinburgh's Got Soul and West Lothian Financial Inclusion Network (£2,000 each); Pakistan Society Advice and Information Services (£1,700); Almonds Mains Initiative, Edinburgh Speakability Group and Scottish Disability Golf Partnership (£1,500 each); Community One Stop Shop (£1,300); Amica Pregnancy Crisis Centre (£1,000).

**FINANCES** Year 2013/4 Income £137,749 Grants £93,065 Grants to organisations £34,030 Assets £4,347,729

**TRUSTEES** Joan Fraser; Mike Gilbert; Sandra Blake; Peter Raistrick; Beverley Klein; Ella Simpson; Gordon Castrell; Janette Scappaticcio.

**OTHER INFORMATION** Grants were made to 18 organisations during the year.

**HOW TO APPLY** On forms available to download, together with guidelines and criteria, on the fund's website.

**WHO TO APPLY TO** Janette Scappaticcio, Trust Administrator, 14 Ashley Place, Edinburgh EH6 5PX Tel. 0131 555 9100 email janettescappaticco@evoc.org.uk Website www.evoc.org.uk

■ **Edinburgh Children's Holiday Fund**

SC NO SC010312    ESTABLISHED 1912

**WHERE FUNDING CAN BE GIVEN** Edinburgh and the Lothians.

**WHO CAN BENEFIT** Children.

**WHAT IS FUNDED** Grants are awarded to charitable and voluntary organisations that are concerned with children's welfare and provide holidays for children who are disadvantaged.
**WHAT IS NOT FUNDED** No grants directly to individuals.
**TYPE OF GRANT** One-off grants.
**SAMPLE GRANTS** Acorn Christian Centre, Castleview Primary School, Children 1st, Drug Prevention Group, Forthview Primary School, Mother's Union Holiday Scheme, the Roses Charitable Trust, Scottish Spina Bifida Association, Stepping Stones and Uphill Ski Club.
**FINANCES** Year 2012/13 Income £64,827 Grants £50,000 Grants to organisations £50,000
**OTHER INFORMATION** The grant total has been estimated based on the fund's total expenditure.
**HOW TO APPLY** Application forms are available from the correspondent. The trustees meet to consider grants in January and May. Applications should be sent in mid-December and mid-April respectively.
**WHO TO APPLY TO** The Trustees, c/o Bryce Wilson and Co., Granite House, 18 Alva Street, Edinburgh EH2 4QG Tel. 0131 225 5111

## ■ Edinburgh Trust No 2 Account
**CC NO** 227897     **ESTABLISHED** 1959
**WHERE FUNDING CAN BE GIVEN** UK and worldwide.
**WHO CAN BENEFIT** Registered charities only.
**WHAT IS FUNDED** Education; armed services; scientific expeditions.
**WHAT IS NOT FUNDED** Individuals and non-registered charities.
**TYPE OF GRANT** Unrestricted funding.
**RANGE OF GRANTS** Usually £1,000–£3,000.
**SAMPLE GRANTS** Edwina Mountbatten Trust (£2,800); The Award Scheme, King Edward VII Hospital for Officers, The Federation of London Youth Clubs, Outward Bound Trust, Royal Common Ex-serviceman's League, Royal Marines General Fund, Seafarers UK (£2,000 each); Burma Star Association, The Cutty Sark Trust (£1,500); and Intelligence Corp Association, Royal Airforce Benevolent Fund (£1,000).
**FINANCES** Year 2013/14 Income £112,041 Grants £81,659 Grants to organisations £81,659 Assets £3,072,917
**TRUSTEES** Charles Woodhouse; Brian McGrath; Brigadier Archie Miller-Bakewell.
**OTHER INFORMATION** Grants were made to 80 organisations in 2013/14.
**HOW TO APPLY** Apply in writing to the correspondent.
**WHO TO APPLY TO** Trustees, The Duke of Edinburgh's Household, Buckingham Palace, London SW1A 1AA Tel. 020 7024 4107 email paul.hughes@royal.gsx.gov.uk

## ■ Educational Foundation of Alderman John Norman
**CC NO** 313105     **ESTABLISHED** 1962
**WHERE FUNDING CAN BE GIVEN** Norwich and Old Catton.
**WHO CAN BENEFIT** Individuals who are descendants of Alderman Norman, and organisations benefitting children, young adults and students.
**WHAT IS FUNDED** Primarily, the education of the descendants of Alderman Norman, but also young people, local schools and educational establishments in the area.
**WHAT IS NOT FUNDED** No applications from outside Norwich and Old Catton will be considered.
**RANGE OF GRANTS** £500–£5,000
**SAMPLE GRANTS** 1st Norwich Sea Scouts (£7,000); the Matthew Project and How Hill Trust (£5,000 each); East Norwich Youth Project, Norfolk Eating Disorders Association and Norfolk Archaeological Trust – St Benet's Abbey (£3,000 each); West Norwich Partnership and Your Future (£2,000 each); Norwich Cycle Speedway and Eaton Vale Scouts and Guides Activity Centre (£1,000 each); and Sewell Toy Library (£500).
**FINANCES** Year 2013/14 Income £256,268 Grants £222,979 Grants to organisations £64,563 Assets £7,139,051
**TRUSTEES** Revd Jonathan Boston; Roger Sandall; Dr Julia Leach; Revd Canon Martin Smith; Derek Armes; Tracey Hughes; Stephen Slack; Christopher Brown; Francis Whymark; James Hawkins; Roy Hughes.
**OTHER INFORMATION** Grants were made to 18 organisations in 2013/14.
**HOW TO APPLY** Apply in writing to the correspondent. Grants to organisations are considered at the trustees' meeting in May/June. All applications should be made through the clerk.
**WHO TO APPLY TO** N. Saffell, Clerk, The Atrium, St George's Street, Norwich NR3 1AB Tel. 01603 629871 email nick.saffell@brown-co.com

## ■ Edupoor Limited
**CC NO** 1113785     **ESTABLISHED** 2006
**WHERE FUNDING CAN BE GIVEN** Worldwide.
**WHO CAN BENEFIT** Registered charities.
**WHAT IS FUNDED** The advancement in education and training through the world; the relief of poverty; old age; illness both mental and physical and the relief of persons suffering from any disability, general charitable purposes.
**FINANCES** Year 2013/14 Income £499,106 Grants £490,510 Grants to organisations £490,510 Assets £14,409
**TRUSTEES** Alan Shelton; Michael Shelton.
**HOW TO APPLY** Apply in writing to the correspondent.
**WHO TO APPLY TO** Michael Shelton, Flat 10, 125 Clapton Common, Stamford Hill, London E5 9AB Tel. 020 8800 0088

## ■ Dr Edwards Bishop King's Fulham Endowment Fund
**CC NO** 1113490     **ESTABLISHED** 1981
**WHERE FUNDING CAN BE GIVEN** Fulham: specifically the post code areas of SW6, part of W14 and part of W6.
**WHO CAN BENEFIT** Organisations or local groups that help people on low incomes who live in Fulham. Grants are also made to individuals in need.
**WHAT IS FUNDED** One-off projects and summer schemes.
**WHAT IS NOT FUNDED** 'The charity does not respond to general funding appeals but will consider matching funding raised from other sources, but not for any purpose for which statutory funding is available.'
**TYPE OF GRANT** Running costs, one off project grants.
**RANGE OF GRANTS** Generally up to £5,000 but higher awards would be considered.
**SAMPLE GRANTS** Hammersmith and Fulham Mind (£18,000); Furnish Community Furniture Store – new beds project (£12,000); Good Neighbour Service (£11,000); St Paul's Money Advice

(£10,000); Bishop Creighton House (£8,000); The Beef Kitchen (£5,700); Fulham Primary School (£3,500); Maggie's Cancer Care Centre (£3,000); The Honeypot Children's Charity (£2,000); and St John's Church (£700).

**FINANCES** Year 2013/14 Income £437,788 Grants £266,641 Grants to organisations £143,938 Assets £9,284,737

**TRUSTEES** Michael Clein; Carol Bailey; Lindsey Brock; Ronald Lawrence; Susan O'Neill; Revd Mark Osborne; Allen Smith; Cllr Adronie Alford; Charles Treloggan; Mrs B. Richards; Michael Waymouth.

**OTHER INFORMATION** Grants were made to 23 organisations in 2013/14.

**HOW TO APPLY** Application forms are available, together with criteria and guidelines, from the correspondent or the trust's website. The committee meets twice a year and applications must be received at least ten working days ahead of these dates. Details of scheduled committee meetings can be found on the fund's website.

**WHO TO APPLY TO** Jonathan Martin, Clerk to the Trustees, Percy Barton House, 33–35 Dawes Road, Fulham, London SW6 7DT Tel. 020 7386 9387 Fax 020 7610 2856 email clerk@debk.org.uk Website www.debk.org.uk

## ■ The W. G. Edwards Charitable Foundation

**CC NO** 293312  **ESTABLISHED** 1985
**WHERE FUNDING CAN BE GIVEN** UK.
**WHO CAN BENEFIT** Registered charities that assist in the care of older people.
**WHAT IS FUNDED** The provision of care for older people through existing charities.
**WHAT IS NOT FUNDED** Individuals. According to the trustees' report for 2012/13, 'beneficiaries must be established registered charities that assist with the care of old people ... the trustees consider than an older person is generally assumed to be over 60 years of age, but they will also look at projects for over 50s'.
**TYPE OF GRANT** Principally one-off capital projects. Trustees currently prefer to give towards a named item rather than into a pool building fund.
**RANGE OF GRANTS** £1,000 to £5,000.
**SAMPLE GRANTS** Music in Hospitals (£4,100); Heart of England Foundation Trust (£4,000); Rushmoor Healthy Living (£3,200); CharityAge UK – Suffolk (£3,000); Fatima Women's Association (£2,800); Contented Dementia Trust (£2,500); Blyth Star Enterprises (£2,000); Asthma Relief (£1,500); East Suffolk Association for the Blind (£1,000); and Ralli Hall Lunch and Social Club (£300).
**FINANCES** Year 2013/14 Income £107,859 Grants £95,207 Grants to organisations £95,207 Assets £3,245,190
**TRUSTEES** Gillian Shepherd Coates; Wendy Savage; Yewande Savage; William Mackie.
**OTHER INFORMATION** Grants were made to 43 organisations in 2013/14.
**HOW TO APPLY** The trust's website states that applications should be in writing to the correspondent, including: confirmation of charitable status (charity number on letterhead will suffice); brief details of the project; budget statement for the project; current fundraising achievements and proposals for future fundraising; items of expenditure within project costing approx. £1,000 to £5,000 – trustees currently prefer to give towards a named item rather than into a pool building fund; copy of latest accounts if available. There are no forms or deadlines for applications. If your project fulfils the foundation's policy criteria, your details will be passed on to the trustees for consideration at their next meeting. According to the trustees' report for 2012/13, 'beneficiaries must be established registered charities that assist with the care of old people ... the trustees consider than an older person is generally assumed to be over 60 years of age, but they will also look at projects for over 50s'.

**WHO TO APPLY TO** The Trustees, 19 Vincent Terrace, London N1 8HN Tel. 020 7837 7635 email helen@wgedwardscharitablefoundation.org.uk Website www.wgedwardscharitablefoundation.org.uk

## ■ The Elephant Trust

**CC NO** 269615  **ESTABLISHED** 1975
**WHERE FUNDING CAN BE GIVEN** England and Wales.
**WHO CAN BENEFIT** Individual artists, arts organisations and publications concerned with the visual arts.
**WHAT IS FUNDED** Visual arts; advancement of public education in all aspects of arts; development of artistic taste and knowledge; understanding and appreciation of the fine arts.
**WHAT IS NOT FUNDED** The following categories are not supported: arts festivals; group exhibitions; charities organising community projects; students; educational or other studies; residencies or research; symposia or conferences; publications or catalogues and projects taking place outside the UK.
**TYPE OF GRANT** One-off contributions to specific projects by individuals or organisations.
**RANGE OF GRANTS** Usually £2,000, but up to £10,000 may be considered.
**SAMPLE GRANTS** Camden Arts Centre and Triangle Arts Trust (£10,000 each); Hospitalfields Arts (£5,000); Culture and Sport Glasgow and Pallant House Gallery (£3,000 each); Wysing Arts Centre (£2,400); Grand Union Studios and University of Westminster (£2,000 each); Banner Repeater (£1,900); and Cove Park (£1,600).
**FINANCES** Year 2013/14 Income £115,597 Grants £117,051 Grants to organisations £59,517 Assets £3,221,583
**TRUSTEES** Prof. Dawn Ades; Antony Forwood; Rob Tufnell; Benjamin Cook; Elizabeth Carey-Thomas; Melissa Gronlund; Elizabeth Price; Antony Penrose.
**OTHER INFORMATION** Grants were made to 18 organisations and 28 individuals in 2013/14.
**HOW TO APPLY** Only postal applications will be accepted. Applications should include: synopsis of the project – single side of A4, 300 words maximum; budget – single side of A4, including total cost of the project, amount requested, details of other funding applications made and name and address of the recipient of grant if awarded; brief CV – one sheet of A4; visual material – still images, maximum of 8; DVDs are only accepted when artists are working with film/video; other material(e.g. catalogues, press cuttings, etc.) only if relevant and might help trustees in their consideration of application. Note that no materials will be returned. The trust's website states that 'priority is given to artists and small organisations and galleries who should submit well argued, imaginative proposals for making or producing new work or exhibitions'. If not contacted within six months, application has been unsuccessful.

WHO TO APPLY TO Ruth Rattenbury, Correspondent, Bridge House, 4 Borough High Street, London SE1 9QR Tel. 020 7403 1877 email ruth@elephanttrust.org.uk Website www.elephanttrust.org.uk

### ■ The George Elias Charitable Trust

CC NO 273993   ESTABLISHED 1977
WHERE FUNDING CAN BE GIVEN Some preference for Manchester.
WHO CAN BENEFIT Mostly Jewish organisations.
WHAT IS FUNDED Mainly Jewish causes. Some smaller donations are made to more general charitable causes, including educational needs, healthcare and the fight against poverty.
SAMPLE GRANTS Previous beneficiaries have included: UK Friends of Nadar Deiah (£50,000); Ahavat Shalom (£45,000); UJIA (£30,000); Hale and District Hebrew Congregation (£24,000); JEM (£5,000); South Manchester Mikva Trust (£4,000); British Friends of Rinat Aharon (£2,500); Moracha LTD (£1,000); Chai Lifeline Cancer Trust (£300); and Friends of the Sick (£100).
FINANCES Year 2013/14 Income £132,046 Grants £223,316 Grants to organisations £223,316 Assets £617,245
TRUSTEES Ernest Elias; Stephen Elias.
OTHER INFORMATION A list of beneficiaries was not included.
HOW TO APPLY Apply in writing to the correspondent. The trustees meet monthly.
WHO TO APPLY TO Stephen Elias, Trustee, Shaws Fabrics Ltd, 1 Ashley Road, Altrincham, Cheshire WA14 2DT Tel. 0161 928 7171 email textiles@kshaw.com

### ■ The Gerald Palmer Eling Trust Company

CC NO 1100869   ESTABLISHED 2003
WHERE FUNDING CAN BE GIVEN Berkshire.
WHO CAN BENEFIT Charitable organisations.
WHAT IS FUNDED Christian religion, particularly the Orthodox Church; medical research and the study of medicine; relief of sickness and poverty.
WHAT IS NOT FUNDED Individuals.
TYPE OF GRANT One-off.
RANGE OF GRANTS Up to £20,000.
SAMPLE GRANTS The Mary Hare Foundation (£20,000); Convent of the Annunciation (£10,000); Brainwave (£5,000); Bede House Association (£3,000); Fledglings Family Services (£2,000); The Bishop of Winches (£1,500); Berks' Healthcare Foundation NHS Trust (£500); and Hermitage Village Hall (£250).
FINANCES Year 2013/14 Income £1,324,122 Grants £273,918 Grants to organisations £273,918 Assets £77,775,516
TRUSTEES Desmond Harrison; Robin Broadhurst; James Gardiner; Kenneth McDiarmid.
OTHER INFORMATION The trust is responsible for the long term maintenance of the character and qualities of the Eling Estate, which is the principal asset of the original endowment, and the protection and sustenance of its environment. The sum of £1.1 million went towards running the estate during the year.
HOW TO APPLY Apply in writing to the correspondent.

WHO TO APPLY TO Jevan Booth, Company Secretary, Englefield Estate Office, Wellhouse, Hermitage, Thatcham, Berkshire RG19 9UF Tel. 01635 200268 email charities@elingestate.co.uk

### ■ The Wilfred and Elsie Elkes Charity Fund

CC NO 326573   ESTABLISHED 1984
WHERE FUNDING CAN BE GIVEN Staffordshire and especially Uttoxeter, including UK-wide charities benefitting the area.
WHO CAN BENEFIT Registered charities and organisations benefitting children and elderly people.
WHAT IS FUNDED Welfare of older people: organisations working with deaf people: and medical charities involved with deafness; Alzheimer's disease; Parkinson's disease and a range of other diseases; animal welfare; infrastructure development; charity or voluntary umbrella bodies; accommodation and housing; and community facilities and services.
WHAT IS NOT FUNDED Grants are normally made to organisations rather than to individuals.
TYPE OF GRANT Recurrent grants are given in a number of cases but more normally the grant is a one-off payment. Grants can be made for buildings, capital, core costs, project, research, running costs, salaries and start-up costs. Funding is available for up to and over three years.
RANGE OF GRANTS £500–£1,600
SAMPLE GRANTS Childhood Eye Cancer Trust; Father Hudson's Society; Breath of Life; Juvenile Diabetes Research and Somerset Rural Music School (£1,600 each); Stafford Churches Audio Magazine (£1,000); Rays of Sunshine Children's Charity, Cerebra and MedEquip4Kids (£800 each); Uttoxeter Methodist Church and Mad Hatter's Tea Party (£500 each).
FINANCES Year 2013/14 Income £65,681 Grants £67,900 Grants to organisations £67,900 Assets £655,741
TRUSTEE Royal Bank of Scotland plc.
HOW TO APPLY Apply in writing to the correspondent.
WHO TO APPLY TO The Trust Section Manager, RBS Trust and Estate Services, Eden Building, Lakeside, Chester Business Park, Wrexham Road, Chester CH4 9QT Tel. 01244 625810 email rbscharities@rbs.com

### ■ The Maud Elkington Charitable Trust

CC NO 263929   ESTABLISHED 1972
WHERE FUNDING CAN BE GIVEN Mainly Desborough, Northamptonshire and Leicestershire.
WHO CAN BENEFIT Registered charities, particularly local, and local branches of UK charities and individuals through established bodies such as NHS trusts.
WHAT IS FUNDED General charitable purposes including health and welfare, especially of older people, youth and community.
WHAT IS NOT FUNDED No grants directly to individuals.
TYPE OF GRANT One-off and recurrent.
SAMPLE GRANTS Nottinghamshire County Council; Leicester Grammar School – Bursary; Bromford Housing Association; Cynthia Spencer Hospice; Launde Abbey; Cancer Research UK; CARE Shangton; Multiple Sclerosis Society; Elizabeth Finn Care; Voluntary Action Northants; and Phoenix Furniture.

FINANCES Year 2013/14 Income £575,810
Grants £467,000 Grants to organisations
£467,000 Assets £24,746,871
TRUSTEES Roger Bowder, Chair; Michael Jones; Katherine Hall.
HOW TO APPLY Apply in writing to the correspondent. There is no application form or guidelines. The trustees meet every seven or eight weeks.
WHO TO APPLY TO Jenny Coleman, Correspondent, c/o Shakespeares LLP, Two Colton Square, Leicester LE1 1QH Tel. 0116 257 4645 email jenny.coleman@Shakespeares.co.uk

## ■ Ellador Ltd

CC NO 283202　　ESTABLISHED 1981
WHERE FUNDING CAN BE GIVEN UK and overseas.
WHO CAN BENEFIT Jewish people.
WHAT IS FUNDED The trust supports organisations benefitting Jewish people and also Jewish individuals.
FINANCES Year 2013/14 Income £67,005
Grants £100,653 Grants to organisations £100,653 Assets £527,841
TRUSTEES Joel Schreiber; Helen Schreiber; Rivka Schreiber; Mr J. Schreiber; Mr Y. Schreiber; Mrs S. Reisner; Mrs C. Hamburger; Mrs R. Benedikt.
HOW TO APPLY Apply in writing to the correspondent.
WHO TO APPLY TO Joel Schreiber, Trustee, 20 Ashtead Road, London E5 9BH Tel. 020 7242 3580 email mail@cohenarnold.com

## ■ The Ellerdale Trust

CC NO 1073376　　ESTABLISHED 1998
WHERE FUNDING CAN BE GIVEN Mainly Norfolk.
WHO CAN BENEFIT Local charitable organisations and some national charities which work with Norfolk children.
WHAT IS FUNDED Children; families; disability; ill health.
RANGE OF GRANTS £1,000–£30,000
SAMPLE GRANTS Action for Kids (£30,000); The Atrium Project (£25,000); Mind (£15,000); Prince's Trust (£10,000); Community Action Norwich and NANSA Family Centre (£6,000 each); BiPolar UK (£5,000); Eating Matters (£4,000); The Garage (£3,000); British Blind Sport and Home Start Breckland (£2,000 each); Mile Cross Phoenix Centre (£1,000).
FINANCES Year 2013/14 Income £470,258
Grants £209,500 Grants to organisations £209,500 Assets £6,000,592
TRUSTEES Alistair Macfarlane; P. C. Kurthausen; S. P. Moores.
HOW TO APPLY Apply in writing to the correspondent.
WHO TO APPLY TO Mary Adlard, Director of Grantmaking, The Parlour, The High Street, Ketteringham, Wymondham, Norfolk NR18 9RU Tel. 01603 813340 email mary.adlard@btconnect.com

## ■ The John Ellerman Foundation

CC NO 263207　　ESTABLISHED 1971
WHERE FUNDING CAN BE GIVEN Mainly UK; East and Southern Africa.
WHO CAN BENEFIT UK-registered charities which operate nationally or across England; local/regional charities should not apply.
WHAT IS FUNDED Welfare; environment; the arts.
WHAT IS NOT FUNDED 'Grants are not made for the following purposes: for or on behalf of individuals; individual hospitals and hospices; local branches of national organisations; mainstream education/establishments; purchase of vehicles; direct replacement of public funding, or deficit funding; drug or alcohol abuse; charities with an annual income less than £100,000; religious causes; friends of groups; medical research; conferences and seminars; sports and leisure facilities; domestic animal welfare; prisons and offenders; military museums at regimental/arm/corps level. The foundation will only consider applications from registered and exempt charities with a UK office. Most of our grants are for one and two years, but we will give grants for three years if a very strong case is made. Our minimum grant is £10,000. We aim to develop relationships with funded charities. We will only support charities that work – or have reach and impact – across England/UK. Those operating within a single locality, city, borough, county or region will not be considered. We believe other trusts and funders are better placed to help individuals and local or regional charities. For this reason also, applications operating exclusively in Wales, Scotland or Northern Ireland will NOT be considered.'
TYPE OF GRANT One-off and multi-year. Core costs, project, running costs, salaries, and start-up costs. Funding may be given for up to three years.
RANGE OF GRANTS £10,000–£40,000
SAMPLE GRANTS Fauna and Flora International (£150,000) – towards the costs of supporting community engagement in marine protection in Scotland; Blackpool Council/Grundy Art Gallery (£135,000) towards the salary of the Collections Officer; FareShare (£120,000) – towards the salary of the Chief Executive officer to develop their food distribution service; Hofesh Shechter Company (£116,000) – towards core costs; Carousel (£60,000) – towards the costs of a series of conferences and events; Shark Trust (£49,000) – towards core costs; University of Glasgow (£45,000) – towards the costs of the National Inventory Project; New Diorama Theatre (£30,000) – towards core costs; AVA (Against Violence and Abuse) (£21,500) – to fund a short film; Association of Charitable Foundations (£5,000) – towards core costs.
FINANCES Year 2013/14 Income £2,312,000
Grants £3,449,000 Grants to organisations £3,449,000 Assets £123,819,000
TRUSTEES Sarah Riddell, chair; Dominic Caldecott; Tim Glass; Brian Hurwitz; Hugh Raven; Diana Whitworth; Vivien Gould.
OTHER INFORMATION Grants were made to 45 organisations in 2013/14.
HOW TO APPLY Information taken from the foundation's website: 'If you are unsuccessful, we will ask you to wait for one year before you reapply. It is therefore important to make the best case you can at the first stage. The foundation encourages informal phone calls to discuss projects and eligibility before applications are submitted. Only one application per organisation can be considered at any one time. Stage 1 – Your first-stage application should include: 1. A description of what you are seeking funding for, on no more than two sides of A4. Please include: a brief summary of your organisation and relevant track record; where your work takes place, as we only support work with a national footprint; what you would like us to fund and why you are well placed to do this work and how your proposal fits our guidelines for this category. 2. A copy of your most recent annual accounts. If your accounts show a significant surplus or deficit, high or low

reserves, please explain this briefly. If the year-end date of your accounts is more than 10 months old, please include your latest management accounts. First stage applications can be submitted by post or email. Applications can be submitted at any time, unless you are applying for the museums and galleries fund. Applications are acknowledged and decisions made within 10 weeks. **Stage 2** – If we invite you to the second stage, we will ask for a more detailed application. Then we will arrange to meet you to find out more about your work. At this second stage we aim to make a decision within three months. If your application takes longer we will be in touch.'

**WHO TO APPLY TO** Barbra Mazur, Head of Grants, Suite 10, Aria House, 23 Craven Street, London WC2N 5NS *Tel.* 020 7930 8566 *email* enquiries@ellerman.org.uk *Website* www.ellerman.org.uk

## ■ The Ellinson Foundation Ltd

**CC NO** 252018 **ESTABLISHED** 1967
**WHERE FUNDING CAN BE GIVEN** Worldwide.
**WHO CAN BENEFIT** Organisations
**WHAT IS FUNDED** Hospitals, education and homelessness, usually with a Jewish teaching aspect.
**WHAT IS NOT FUNDED** Individuals.
**TYPE OF GRANT** Capital and recurring grants.
**RANGE OF GRANTS** Up to £140,00 but usually £1,000–£35,000.
**SAMPLE GRANTS** Kesser Yeshuva RP – (£140,000); Three Pillars (£20,000); Vaad Harobinim Tzeduka (£14,100); Kollel Ohel Torah (Jerusalem) (£12,000); British Friends of Meohr Bais Yaakov and British Friends of Rinat Aahron (£10,000 each); Friends of Ateres Moshe and Friends of Yeshivas Brink (£5,000 each); Zidkas Sholom – Israel (£1,200); Asser Bishivil (£1,000).
**FINANCES** *Year* 2013/14 *Income* £349,641 *Grants* £208,286 *Grants to organisations* £208,286 *Assets* £3,770,884
**TRUSTEES** A. Ellinson; A. Z. Ellinson; U. Ellinson.
**HOW TO APPLY** Apply in writing to the correspondent. However, the trust generally supports the same organisations each year and unsolicited applications are not welcome.
**WHO TO APPLY TO** The Trustees, Robson Laidler LLP, Fernwood House, Fernwood Road, Jesmond, Newcastle upon Tyne NE2 1TJ *Tel.* 0191 281 8191 *email* u.ellinson@gmail.com

## ■ The Edith Maud Ellis 1985 Charitable Trust

**CC NO** 292835 **ESTABLISHED** 1985
**WHERE FUNDING CAN BE GIVEN** UK, Ireland and overseas.
**WHO CAN BENEFIT** Grants are made to organisations that fall within following categories: UK-registered charities, NGOs and social enterprises with a turnover of less than £250,000; those who can demonstrate other sources of funding for their project; and innovative charities/projects not normally able to attract regular funding.
**WHAT IS FUNDED** Quaker work and witness; international peace and conflict resolution; interfaith and ecumenical understanding; community development work in the UK and overseas; work with asylum seekers and refugees including internally displaced people.
**WHAT IS NOT FUNDED** In general the trust does not support the following: core funding for organisations; individuals; infrastructure organisations; conferences or seminars; ongoing work; general appeals; educational bursaries; humanitarian relief appeals; and medical research and services.
**TYPE OF GRANT** Grants tend to be either: one-off; time limited in support; or; are given in the form of seed money for start-up projects. Usually small grants of up to £3000 (in exceptional circumstances larger grants may be given) or interest free loans of up to £5000 repayable over five years.
**RANGE OF GRANTS** Up to £3,000.
**SAMPLE GRANTS** Experiment with Light and Responding to Conflict (£3,000 each); Child Soldiers and UK Climate Outreach (£2,000 each); The Arbour (£1,800); Quaker Homeless Action and Their Furniture Today (£1,500 each); Community Projects Africa, Every Casualty and Farm Africa (£1,000 each); Carers Worldwide and Haringey Woman's Forum (£500).
**FINANCES** *Year* 2013/14 *Income* £41,397 *Grants* £87,240 *Grants to organisations* £87,240 *Assets* £1,254,325
**TRUSTEES** Michael Phipps; Jane Dawson; Elizabeth Cave; Nicholas Sims.
**HOW TO APPLY** According to the trust's website, 'applications should be received by the end of January, May and September, in order to be considered at one of the trustee meetings. It is sensible to get applications in well ahead of these dates. Late applicants will be considered in the next funding round. Successful applicants will be informed as soon as possible of the trustees' decisions. If you have not heard within one calendar month of the relevant closing date you should assume you have been unsuccessful. Successful applicants will be encouraged to contribute to our website in a variety of ways and may be approached to showcase the work of the trust.'
**WHO TO APPLY TO** Jacqueline Baily, Correspondent, Virtuosity Executive Support, 6 Westgate, Thirsk, North Yorkshire YO7 1QS *Tel.* 01845 574882 *email* jackie@virtuosity-uk.com *Website* www.theedithmellischaritabletrust.org

## ■ The Ellis Campbell Foundation

**CC NO** 802717 **ESTABLISHED** 1989
**WHERE FUNDING CAN BE GIVEN** London, Hampshire and Perthshire.
**WHO CAN BENEFIT** Organisations benefitting young disadvantaged people. Maintenance and preservation of buildings is also considered.
**WHAT IS FUNDED** Education of disadvantaged people under 25; preservation/protection/improvement of items of architectural/structural/horticultural/mechanical heritage; encouragement of community based projects.
**WHAT IS NOT FUNDED** Individuals. Other than the grants made annually over a period, no grants will be made more regularly than every other year. No funding for annual running costs.
**TYPE OF GRANT** Usually one-off funding, though grants may be given for over three to five years.
**RANGE OF GRANTS** Average grants of £2,000.
**SAMPLE GRANTS** Anvil Trust; Scottish Community Foundation; Prince's Trust; Bhutan Society; Meridian Trust Association; Hampshire Scouting; Hampshire Country Learning; Martin Sailing Project; Ro-Ro Sailing Project; and Wheatsheaf Trust.

# Elmgrant

FINANCES Year 2013 Income £53,995 Grants £68,000 Grants to organisations £68,000
TRUSTEES Michael Campbell, Chair; Linda Campbell; Jamie Campbell; Alexandra Andrews; Laura Montgomery.
OTHER INFORMATION The grant total has been estimated based on grant-making for previous years.
HOW TO APPLY Apply in writing to the correspondent. The trustees meet in April and November. Applications should be submitted before the preceding month and will only be acknowledged if they fall strictly within the trust's eligibility guidelines.
WHO TO APPLY TO Laura Montgomery, Trustee, c/o The Ellis Campbell Group, 10–12 Blandford Street, London W1U 4AZ email office@elliscampbell.co.uk

## ■ The Elmgrant Trust

CC NO 313398  ESTABLISHED 1936
WHERE FUNDING CAN BE GIVEN South West of England (Cornwall, Devon, Somerset, Dorset, Wiltshire and Gloucestershire).
WHO CAN BENEFIT Individuals and organisations.
WHAT IS FUNDED Projects which help to improve the quality of local life and welfare, particularly through arts, education and social sciences.
WHAT IS NOT FUNDED The following are not supported: large scale UK organisations; postgraduate study, overseas student grants, expeditions and travel and study projects overseas; counselling courses; promotion of religion; animal welfare; research; retrospective funding; renewed requests from the same (successful) applicant within a two-year period.
TYPE OF GRANT Primarily one-off, occasionally recurring (but not within a two-year period); core funding; project costs.
RANGE OF GRANTS Typically around £450 for organisations.
SAMPLE GRANTS Previous beneficiaries have included: Dartington International Summer School; Kinergy; Prison Phoenix Trust; Centre for the Spoken Word; Dawlish Gardens Trust; the Towersey Foundation; and the Daisy Garland and Guild of St Lawrence.
FINANCES Year 2013/14 Income £66,014 Grants £34,715 Grants to organisations £33,215 Assets £2,186,735
TRUSTEES Marian Ash; Sophie Young; Paul Elmhirst; Mark Sharman.
OTHER INFORMATION The grant total for 2013/14 includes 11 grants awarded to individuals, totalling £1,500. Grants were awarded to 81 organisations.
HOW TO APPLY Organisations should apply in writing to the correspondent, giving full contact details, a summary of the organisation and examples of its previous work, a copy of most recent accounts or a full budget, a description of the project for which a grant will be used and the amount requested. Guidance for applications from both organisations and individuals is provided on the trust's website. The trustees meet three times each year to award grants and applications should be received at least one calendar month before the meeting. Applicants will be notified whether their application has been shortlisted within six weeks and will be notified whether it has been successful within three weeks following a meeting.

WHO TO APPLY TO Amanda Critchlow, Secretary, The Elmhirst Centre, Dartington Hall, Totnes, Devon TQ9 6EL Tel. 01803 863160 email info@elmgrant.org.uk Website www.elmgrant.org.uk

## ■ The Elmley Foundation

CC NO 1004043  ESTABLISHED 1991
WHERE FUNDING CAN BE GIVEN Herefordshire and Worcestershire.
WHO CAN BENEFIT Individuals and organisations benefitting: actors and entertainment professionals; musicians; writers and poets; and textile workers and designers; students of the arts.
WHAT IS FUNDED Arts activity.
WHAT IS NOT FUNDED No grants for endowments, loans or general appeals.
TYPE OF GRANT Capital, core costs, contracts and full project funding. Funding of up to, and over, three years will be considered.
RANGE OF GRANTS £500–£30,000
SAMPLE GRANTS Meadow Arts (£12,500); Worcester Live Limited (£12,000); Ledbury Poetry Festival (£10,000); Presteigne Festival (£8,000); Worcester Cathedral (£5,000); Malvern Concert Club (£4,000); Malvern Theatre Players (£2,000); Kidderminster Chorale (£1,500); Alloy Workshop (£500); and University of Worcester (£250).
FINANCES Year 2013/14 Income £292,891 Grants £166,883 Grants to organisations £145,283 Assets £3,743,943
TRUSTEES Deborah Swallow; Diana Johnson; Sam White; Sally Luton.
OTHER INFORMATION Grants were made to 11 individuals and 34 organisations in 2013/14.
HOW TO APPLY Application forms, criteria and guidelines, for both the Small Grants Scheme and the Main Grants Scheme, are available to download on the website. Applicants for the Main Grants Scheme are strongly advised to contact the foundation before making a formal application. Applicants for the Small Grants Scheme should contact Cheryl Cooney at Community First on 01684 312739, or email cherylc@comfirst.org.uk
WHO TO APPLY TO Samuel Driver White, Secretary, West Aish, Morchard Bishop, Crediton, Devon EX17 6RX Tel. 01363 877433 email foundation@elmley.org.uk Website www.elmley.org.uk

## ■ Elshore Ltd

CC NO 287469  ESTABLISHED 1983
WHERE FUNDING CAN BE GIVEN Worldwide.
WHO CAN BENEFIT Jewish organisations.
WHAT IS FUNDED Advancement of religion and relief of poverty.
SAMPLE GRANTS Eminor Educational Centre (£26,000); Cosmon Belz (£20,000); Gur Trust and Marbe Torah Trust (£10,000 each).
FINANCES Year 2013/14 Income £73,455 Grants £62,022 Grants to organisations £62,022 Assets £35,817
TRUSTEES Hersz Lerner; Susan Yanofsky; Ahuva Lerner.
HOW TO APPLY Apply in writing to the correspondent.
WHO TO APPLY TO Hersz Lerner, Trustee, c/o Michael Pasha and Co., 220 The Vale, Golders Green, London NW11 8SR Tel. 020 8209 9880 email alecsudwarts@hotmail.com

## ■ The Vernon N. Ely Charitable Trust

**CC NO** 230033  **ESTABLISHED** 1962
**WHERE FUNDING CAN BE GIVEN** Worldwide, with a preference for London borough of Merton.
**WHO CAN BENEFIT** Charitable organisations.
**WHAT IS FUNDED** General charitable purposes, with a preference to the London borough of Merton and sports charities.
**WHAT IS NOT FUNDED** Individuals.
**RANGE OF GRANTS** Around £4,000.
**SAMPLE GRANTS** Age Concern, Cardiac Risk in the Young, Samaritans, London Sports Forum for Disabled People, Christchurch URC, Polka Children's Theatre and Community Housing Therapy (£4,000 each); British Tennis Foundation (£1,750); and West Barnes Singers and Sobell Hospice (£500 each).
**FINANCES** Year 2013/14 Income £66,955 Grants £74,750 Grants to organisations £74,750 Assets £1,979,127
**TRUSTEES** Derek Howorth; John Moyle; Richard Main.
**HOW TO APPLY** Apply in writing to the correspondent.
**WHO TO APPLY TO** Derek Howorth, Trustee, 13/15 Carteret Street, Westminster, London SW1H 9DG Tel. 020 7828 3156 email dph@helmores.co.uk

## ■ The Emerton-Christie Charity

**CC NO** 262837  **ESTABLISHED** 1971
**WHERE FUNDING CAN BE GIVEN** UK.
**WHO CAN BENEFIT** Registered charities only.
**WHAT IS FUNDED** General charitable purposes. Preference is given to assist older and younger people, particularly those with disabilities or who are disadvantaged. Arts and health charities are also supported.
**WHAT IS NOT FUNDED** Generally no grants are given to individuals; religious organisations; restoration or extension of buildings; start-up costs; animal welfare and research; cultural heritage; or environmental projects.
**TYPE OF GRANT** Donations for capital projects and/or income requirements.
**RANGE OF GRANTS** Usually up to £5,000.
**SAMPLE GRANTS** Trinity Laban Conservatoire of Music and Dance (£4,600); Action Medical Research, Centre for Sustainable Health, Disability North, Médecins Sans Frontières, Music in Detention, The Calvert Trust, The Life Centre and Trinity Hospice (£3,000 each); Papworth Trust (£2,400); Whizz-Kidz (£1,000); and BBACT (£500).
**FINANCES** Year 2013/14 Income £113,599 Grants £58,600 Grants to organisations £58,600 Assets £2,712,263
**TRUSTEES** Norman Walker; William Niekirk; Claire Mera-Nelson; Sally Walker.
**HOW TO APPLY** Apply in writing to the correspondent. A demonstration of need based on budgetary principles is required and applications will not be acknowledged unless accompanied by an sae. Trustees normally meet once a year in the autumn to select charities to benefit.
**WHO TO APPLY TO** The Trustees, c/o Cartmell Shepherd Solicitors, Viaduct House, Victoria Viaduct, Carlisle CA3 8EZ Tel. 01228 516666 email joanna.jeeves@cartmells.co.uk

## ■ EMI Music Sound Foundation

**CC NO** 1104027  **ESTABLISHED** 1996
**WHERE FUNDING CAN BE GIVEN** UK and Ireland
**WHO CAN BENEFIT** Individuals and organisations benefitting: children and young adults; musicians; music students; and music teachers.
**WHAT IS FUNDED** Non-specialist schools to fund music education; music students in full-time education to fund instrument purchase; music teachers to fund courses and training. Every year EMI Music Sound Foundation awards bursaries to students at seven music colleges in the UK and Ireland. These bursaries are distributed at each college's discretion, based on criteria provided by the foundation.
**WHAT IS NOT FUNDED** Applications from applicants based outside the United Kingdom and Ireland; non-school based community groups; applications for tuition fees and living expenses other than as described under the bursary awards section on the foundation's website; applications over £2000; independent music teachers; payment of staffing costs to cover the teaching of the national curriculum or peripatetic teaching costs; and retrospective grants.
**RANGE OF GRANTS** Maximum award £2,500 (for schools, individuals and music teachers).
**SAMPLE GRANTS** Royal Welsh College of Music and Drama (£10,000); Birmingham Conservatoire, Brighton Institute of Modern Music, Centre for Young Musicians, English National Opera, Irish World Music Centre, Royal Academy of Music, Royal Conservatoire of Scotland, Tech Music Schools – London (£5,000 each).
**FINANCES** Year 2013/4 Income £438,928 Grants £449,999 Grants to organisations £295,563 Assets £7,989,472
**TRUSTEES** Rupert Perry; David Hughes; Leslie Hill; Tony Wadsworth; James Beach; Paul Gambaccini; Christine Walter; Charles Ashcroft; Jo Hibbit; Keith Harris; Richard Lyttelton; Max Hole.
**OTHER INFORMATION** Grants to individuals totalled £154,500 and grants to organisations totalled £295,500.
**HOW TO APPLY** Application forms can be downloaded from the foundation's website. Guidance notes are also available regarding applications.
**WHO TO APPLY TO** Janie Orr, Chief Executive, EMI Group Ltd, Beaumont House, Avonmore Road, Kensington Village, London W14 8TS Tel. 020 7550 7898 email enquiries@musicsoundfoundation.com Website www.emimusicsoundfoundation.com

## ■ Engage Foundation

**ESTABLISHED** 2014
**WHERE FUNDING CAN BE GIVEN** UK – in the areas where OneFamily (previously known as Engage Mutual Assurance) operates.
**WHO CAN BENEFIT** Local community organisations and projects.
**WHAT IS FUNDED** A wide range of general charitable purposes and community causes. The foundation offers Community Awards of £5,000 and £25,000 for projects put forward by customers that want to improve their community. Assistance is also available through Personal Grants of up to £500 to help the company's customers in need. Beneficiaries are nominated by OneFamily (previously known as Engage Mutual Assurance) customers. Community projects are voted for by members of the public and those with the most votes are awarded.

# Englefield

*Alphabetical register of grant-making charities*

**WHAT IS NOT FUNDED** 'Support for commercial or profit making ventures; funding toward property bills (rent, mortgage payments, utility bills, maintenance costs, etc.); the sponsorship of an individual or team; financial contribution towards salaries (staffing costs on an hourly basis may be considered but only if this is necessary to achieve the project objectives, for example a music teacher to lead a music therapy group, or a builder to construct a sensory room); funding for 'paid for advertising' general contributions towards large appeals or fundraising (funding of standalone items may be considered, providing the use of these is not reliant on additional funds being raised, such as replacing a kitchen as part of a hospice renovation project); the promotion of political parties/groups; the advancement of religion/faith (although groups may be eligible for secular and inclusive community based activities, such as a food bank run by a local church); groups where membership costs are prohibitive – for instance a golf club with high membership costs that would prohibit certain members of the community from joining; overseas travel or activity outside the UK; regional or local offices of a national organisation (unless they can demonstrate that they operate independently); improvements to land or buildings that are not open or accessible for use by members of the community; contingency amounts; deficit or retrospective funding (for example, grants for activities or purchases that have already taken place); organisations that are for the sole relief or benefit of animals and plants; support for projects that have received substantial funding from another grant provider within 18 months prior to the date of your application.'

**RANGE OF GRANTS** Up to £5,000 and £25,000.

**SAMPLE GRANTS** Farnborough Fins and Witham Hill Gymnastics Club (£25,000 each); Acorn House – The Sick Children's Trust, Berwick and District friends of Dementia Active Mind and Body, Cambridge Breastfeeding Alliance, Extra-ordinary Exercise for the Neuromuscular Centre, Friends of Bude Sea Pool, Oakdale School, Resonate, Sensory Garden for All @ DAT Belfast, SMAE – Helping the Community to Connect, St Edward's Sensory Room, St Mary's Primary School Access for All, The Willow Trust and Woodlands Community Garden (£5,000 each); Forget-me-not! Alpha Project (£4,900); Stamford Bridge Community Swimming Pool (£2,100).

**FINANCES** Year 2014 Grants £122,037 Grants to organisations £122,037.

**OTHER INFORMATION** There is a helpful FAQ section online. In the coming five years the foundation seeks to distribute £5 million. The foundation is not a registered charity therefore there were no annual report and accounts. The website lists projects which have been supported, the latest being 2014 winners. During the year at least 122,000 was distributed to support various projects.

**HOW TO APPLY** Nominations for a project to support have to be made online on the foundation's website. Once your project suggestion has been accepted you will receive a confirmation. There are two rounds of awards during the year – check the website for most up to date details.

**WHO TO APPLY TO** The Online Community Executive, Hornbeam Park Avenue, Harrogate HG2 8XE *Tel.* 0800 169 4321 *email* foundation@engagemutual.com *Website* foundation.onefamily.com

## ■ The Englefield Charitable Trust

**CC NO** 258123   **ESTABLISHED** 1968

**WHERE FUNDING CAN BE GIVEN** Worldwide, in practice UK and local charities in Berkshire.

**WHO CAN BENEFIT** Mainly registered charities; some local schools and churches are supported.

**WHAT IS FUNDED** General charitable purposes but particularly charities working in the fields of: infrastructure development; religion; residential facilities and services; arts, culture and recreation; health; conservation; education and training; and various community facilities and services.

**WHAT IS NOT FUNDED** Individual applications for study or travel.

**TYPE OF GRANT** Buildings, capital, interest-free loans, research, running costs, salaries and start-up costs. Funding for one year or less will be considered.

**RANGE OF GRANTS** £100–£185,000

**SAMPLE GRANTS** Ufton Court Educational Trust (£100,000); Englefield PCC (£36,500); Thames Valley Chiltern Air Ambulance (£5,500); Trooper Potts VC Memorial Trust and Watermill Theatre (£5,000 each); Thrive and Corn Exchange Newbury (£3,000 each); 14–21 Time to Talk, Children's Trust and Church Housing Trust (£2,000 each); Christians Against Poverty, Andover Mind and British Horseracing Education (£1,000 each); Aldermaston Parish Hall (£500); and Volunteer Centre West Berks (£350).

**FINANCES** Year 2013/14 Income £482,349 Grants £417,789 Grants to organisations £417,789 Assets £14,096,166

**TRUSTEES** Catherine Haig; Elizabeth Benyon; Richard Benyon; Zoe Benyon; Melissa Owston; Richard Bampfylde; Richard Griffiths.

**OTHER INFORMATION** In 2013/14 the trust received 582 applications and made 151 grants.

**HOW TO APPLY** Apply in writing to the correspondent enclosing the latest accounts, stating the charity's registered number and the purpose for which the money is to be used. Applications are considered in March and September. Only applications going before the trustees will be acknowledged.

**WHO TO APPLY TO** Alexander Reid, Secretary, The Quantocks, North Street, Theale, Reading RG7 5EX *email* charity@englefield.co.uk

## ■ The English Schools' Football Association

**CC NO** 306003   **ESTABLISHED** 1904

**WHERE FUNDING CAN BE GIVEN** England.

**WHO CAN BENEFIT** Members of the association, and organisations benefitting children and young adults, sportspersons and teachers.

**WHAT IS FUNDED** Mental, moral and physical development of schoolchildren through association football. Assistance to teacher charities.

**WHAT IS NOT FUNDED** Grants are restricted to membership and teacher charities.

**FINANCES** Year 2013 Income £1,057,124 Grants £916,237 Grants to organisations £916,237 Assets £1,412,096

**TRUSTEES** Philip Harding; David Woollaston; Michael Coyne.

**HOW TO APPLY** Apply in writing to the correspondent.

**WHO TO APPLY TO** Michael Coyne, Trustee, 4 Parker Court, Staffordshire Technology Park, Stafford ST18 0WP *Tel.* 01785 785970 *email* office@efsa.co.uk *Website* www.esfa.co.uk

## ■ The Enkalon Foundation

**IR NO** XN62210  **ESTABLISHED** 1985
**WHERE FUNDING CAN BE GIVEN** Northern Ireland.
**WHO CAN BENEFIT** Grants made only to organisations for projects inside Northern Ireland.
**WHAT IS FUNDED** Improving the quality of life in Northern Ireland. Funding is given to cross-community groups, self-help, assistance to unemployed people and groups helping people who are disadvantaged.
**WHAT IS NOT FUNDED** Individuals, unless they are ex-employees. No grants are given outside Northern Ireland or for travel outside Northern Ireland. Normally grants are not made to playgroups or sporting groups outside the Antrim borough area or for medical research.
**TYPE OF GRANT** Mainly for starter finance, single projects or capital projects.
**RANGE OF GRANTS** Up to £6,000 maximum but usually between £500 and £1,000.
**SAMPLE GRANTS** Beneficiaries include: Antrim Borough Council – Old Courthouse Auditorium Seating (£88,000); Lyric Theatre – Belfast (£15,000); Macmillan Cancer Support – Antrim Area Hospital Palliative Care Unit Project (£10,000); Elisabeth Svendsen Trust for Children and Donkeys (£5,000); Antrim Citizens Advice (£4,000); Ulster Association of Youth Drama and Newlife Foundation for Disabled Children in NI (£2,000 each); Disability Action (NI) (£1,500); Art Ability (NI) Ltd (£1,000); Family Holiday Association – NI Project and Race Against Multiple Sclerosis – NI Ltd (£500 each); and The Crafts Class St Swithin's Church – Magherafelt (£200).
**FINANCES** Year 2013/14  Grants £150,000  Grants to organisations £150,000
**TRUSTEES** Raymond Milnes; Peter Dalton; Mark Patterson; Stephen Montgomery; John Wallace.
**OTHER INFORMATION** The foundation is not currently on the Northern Ireland Charity Commission website. The grant total is based on information on the foundation's website that states there is an annual budget for grant-making of £150,000 to £200,000.
**HOW TO APPLY** Apply in writing to the correspondent. There are no closing dates or application forms. Guidance notes are available from the foundation's website. Applications, by letter, should provide the following information: description of the organisation and a copy of the constitution and rules; proposed budget and details of the project; audited accounts (if available) or statement of accounts for the most recent; completed financial year and a copy of the latest annual report; details of charitable status; other sources of finance for the organisation at present and for the proposed project; experience and/or qualifications of staff and committee members; a list of officers and committee members; contact address and telephone number.
**WHO TO APPLY TO** Claire Cawley, Correspondent, 25 Randalstown Road, Antrim, Northern Ireland BT41 4LJ  Tel. 028 9446 3535  email info@enkelonfoundation.org  Website www.enkalonfoundation.org

## ■ Entindale Ltd

**CC NO** 277052  **ESTABLISHED** 1978
**WHERE FUNDING CAN BE GIVEN** UK and Israel.
**WHO CAN BENEFIT** Organisations benefitting Orthodox Jews.
**WHAT IS FUNDED** Orthodox Jewish charitable organisations.
**RANGE OF GRANTS** Up to £100,000; typically less than £10,000.
**SAMPLE GRANTS** British Friends of Rinat Aharon (£70,000); Tashbar of Edgware Primary School (£55,000); Yesamach Levav Trust (£17,000); Gateshead Talmudical College (£13,400); Rise and Shine Trust (£10,000); Friends of Ascent (£5,000); Jewish Teachers Training College (£3,900); Community Concern – London (£1,000); Tree of Life College (£700); Jewish Women's Aid (£500).
**FINANCES** Year 2013/14  Income £2,010,798  Grants £1,351,429  Grants to organisations £1,351,429
**TRUSTEES** Allan Becker; Barbara Bridgeman; Jonathan Hager.
**OTHER INFORMATION** Grants were made to 196 organisations in 2013/14.
**HOW TO APPLY** Apply in writing to the correspondent.
**WHO TO APPLY TO** J. Pearlman, 8 Highfield Gardens, London NW11 9HB  Tel. 020 8458 9266

## ■ The Epigoni Trust

**CC NO** 328700  **ESTABLISHED** 1990
**WHERE FUNDING CAN BE GIVEN** UK.
**WHO CAN BENEFIT** Registered UK charities.
**WHAT IS FUNDED** General charitable purposes.
**WHAT IS NOT FUNDED** Individuals.
**TYPE OF GRANT** Project and one-off. Funding for one year or less.
**RANGE OF GRANTS** £3,000–£17,000
**SAMPLE GRANTS** Pallant House Gallery (£17,500); Mondo Challenge Foundation (£10,000); and St Richard of Chichester Christian Care Association, Sussex Snowdrop Trust and Switchback (£5,000 each).
**FINANCES** Year 2013  Income £37,427  Grants £42,676  Grants to organisations £42,676  Assets £3,456,680
**TRUSTEES** Bettine Bond; Charles Peacock; Andrew Bond.
**HOW TO APPLY** This trust no longer accepts applications.
**WHO TO APPLY TO** Charles Peacock, Trustee, c/o Charities Aid Foundation, 25 Kings Hill Avenue, Kings Hill, West Malling ME19 4TA  Tel. 01732 520028

## ■ Epilepsy Research UK

**CC NO** 1100394  **ESTABLISHED** 1985
**WHERE FUNDING CAN BE GIVEN** UK.
**WHO CAN BENEFIT** Researchers conducting studies that will benefit people with epilepsy.
**WHAT IS FUNDED** 'Epilepsy Research UK annually invites applications for grants to support basic, clinical and scientific research work in the UK into the causes, treatment and prevention of epilepsy. We encourage applications on all aspects of epilepsy including basic and social science, clinical management and holistic management of patients.'
**TYPE OF GRANT** Projects, fellowship, research and equipment. Funding is for up to three years.
**RANGE OF GRANTS** Up to £150,000.
**SAMPLE GRANTS** University College London (£212,000); University of Oxford (£150,000); University of Bath and Cardiff University (£98,000 each); University of Bristol and Kings College London (£29,000); Birmingham Children's Hospital NHS Trust (£10,000).
**FINANCES** Year 2013/14  Income £1,153,133  Grants £625,697  Grants to organisations £625,697  Assets £1,660,850

TRUSTEES Dr Lina Nashef; Barrie Akin; Dr Helen Cross; Simon Lanyon; Mr H. Salmon; David Cameron; John Hirst; Prof. Matthew Walker; Graeme Sills; Mary Manning; Michael Kerr; Mark Rees; Mark Richarson; Judith Spencer-Gregson.
OTHER INFORMATION In 2013/14 a total of seven research grants were awarded.
HOW TO APPLY Application forms, together with criteria and guidelines, are available to download on the charity's website.
WHO TO APPLY TO Mr L. Slocombe, Correspondent, PO Box 3004, London W4 4XT *Tel.* 020 8995 4781 *email* info@eruk.org.uk *Website* www.epilepsyresearch.org.uk

## ■ The Equity Trust Fund

CC NO 328103          ESTABLISHED 1989
WHERE FUNDING CAN BE GIVEN UK.
WHO CAN BENEFIT Theatres, theatre companies and professional theatre performers in genuine need, with special reference to members, past and present, of the union Equity.
WHAT IS FUNDED Welfare and educational grants to individuals and work performed by theatres and theatre companies.
WHAT IS NOT FUNDED Non-professional performers; drama students; non-professional theatre companies; multi-arts venues; community projects; projects with no connection to the professional theatre.
TYPE OF GRANT Grants and loans.
RANGE OF GRANTS Up to £80,000.
SAMPLE GRANTS Dancers' Career Development (£80,000); New Theatre Royal – Portsmouth and Tara Arts – London (£5,000); Graeae Theatre Company (£4,600); Liverpool Actors Studio (£3,400); Stone Crabs (£1,500); and Actors' Centre, Orange Tree Theatre and Tricycle Centre (£1,000 each).
FINANCES *Year* 2013/14 *Income* £448,027 *Grants* £345,757 *Grants to organisations* £102,530 *Assets* £10,738,350
TRUSTEES Annie Bright; Barbara Hyslop; Harry Landis; Michael Branwell; Frank Hitchman; Frederick Pyne; Gillian Raine; Ian Talbot; Ian McGarry; James Bolam; John Worthy; Milton Johns; Josephine Tewson; Rosalind Shanks; David Cockayne; John Rubinstein; Glen Barnham; Oliver Davies; Robin Browne; Bryn Evans; Peggy Fraser.
OTHER INFORMATION A further £243,000 was given to 162 individuals for welfare and education.
HOW TO APPLY In the first instance call the office to ascertain if the application is relevant. Failing that, submit a brief letter outlining the application. A meeting takes place about every six to eight weeks. Ring for precise dates. Applications are required at least two weeks beforehand.
WHO TO APPLY TO Kaethe Cherney, Secretary, Plouviez House, 19–20 Hatton Place, London EC1N 8RU *Tel.* 020 7831 1926 *email* kaethe@equitycharitabletrust.org.uk *Website* www.equitycharitabletrust.org.uk

## ■ The Eranda Foundation

CC NO 255650          ESTABLISHED 1967
WHERE FUNDING CAN BE GIVEN UK and overseas.
WHO CAN BENEFIT Registered charities, schools, hospitals and universities.
WHAT IS FUNDED The promotion of original research, and the continuation of existing research into medicine and education, fostering of the arts, and promotion of social welfare.
WHAT IS NOT FUNDED Individuals.
TYPE OF GRANT Capital, project, running costs and recurring costs for up to three years.
RANGE OF GRANTS About £5,000–£150,000.
SAMPLE GRANTS Franklin D Roosevelt Four Freedoms Park – New York (£158,000); Peterson Institute for International Economics (£154,500); Forum for Jewish Leadership, Cancer Research UK and the Eden Project (£100,000 each); Exploring the Arts (£94,500); Fund for Refugees (£75,000); Prince's Foundation for Children and the Arts (£65,000); Young Vic (£50,000); Alzheimer's Drug Discovery Foundation (£31,000); St John of Jerusalem Eye Hospital (£30,000); Arabian School of Gymnastics (£20,000); National Association for Gifted Children (£16,000); London School of Economics (£10,000); and Friends of Africa Foundation (£5,000).
FINANCES *Year* 2013/14 *Income* £3,967,432 *Grants* £4,009,155 *Grants to organisations* £4,009,155 *Assets* £1,665,285
TRUSTEES Sir Evelyn de Rothschild; Renée Robeson; Jessica de Rothschild; Anthony de Rothschild; Sir Graham Hearne; Lady Lynn de Rothschild; Sir John Peace.
HOW TO APPLY Apply in writing to the correspondent. Trustees usually meet in March, July and November and applications should be received two months in advance.
WHO TO APPLY TO Evelyn de Rothschild, Trustee, PO Box 6226, Wing, Leighton Buzzard, Bedfordshire LU7 0XF *Tel.* 01296 689157 *email* eranda@btconnect.com

## ■ The Ericson Trust

CC NO 219762          ESTABLISHED 1962
WHERE FUNDING CAN BE GIVEN UK, financially developing countries, Eastern and Central Europe.
WHO CAN BENEFIT Registered charities only, benefitting: middle-aged and older people; researchers; people disadvantaged by poverty; ex-offenders and those at risk of offending; homeless people; immigrants and refugees.
WHAT IS FUNDED Older people; community projects/local interest groups, including arts; prisons, prison reform, mentoring projects, and research in this area; refugees; mental health; environmental projects and research; aid to financially developing countries only if supported and represented or initiated and administered by a UK-registered charity.
WHAT IS NOT FUNDED Individuals; non-registered charities. Applications from the following areas are generally not considered unless closely connected with one of the above: children's and young people's clubs, centres and so on; schools; charities dealing with illness or disability (except psychiatric); or religious institutions, except in their social projects.
TYPE OF GRANT Project grants.
RANGE OF GRANTS Up to £6,000, with average grants ranging from £1,000–£5,000.
SAMPLE GRANTS Action on Elder Abuse; Anti-Slavery International; Ashram International; Bhopal Medical Appeal; Headway East London; Howard League for Penal Reform; the Koestler Trust; Minority Rights Group; Psychiatric Rehabilitation Association; Quaker Social Action; the Rainforest Foundation; the Relatives and Residents Association; Tools for Self Reliance; and the Umalini Mary Brahma Charitable Trust.
FINANCES *Year* 2013/14 *Income* £19,626 *Grants* £43,000 *Grants to organisations* £43,000

TRUSTEES Valerie Barrow; Rebecca Cotton; Claudia Cotton.
HOW TO APPLY Unsolicited applications cannot be considered as the trust has no funds available for new applicants. The correspondent has stated: 'Our very limited funds and our loyalty to a small group of recipients means that by far most applicants however eligible in theory – are unsuccessful. This looks as if it will continue for the foreseeable future. We deplore the fact that some charities send us expensive brochures without contacting first by email. ... We are increasing worried by the waste of applicants' resources when they send expensive brochures at a time when we are unable to consider any new appeals and have, indeed, reduced some of our long standing grants due to the bad economic situation. It is particularly sad when we receive requests from small charities in Africa and Asia.'
WHO TO APPLY TO Claudia Cotton, Trustee, Flat 2, 53 Carleton Road, London N7 0ET email claudia.cotton@googlemail.com

### ■ The ERM Foundation
CC NO 1113415 ESTABLISHED 2006
WHERE FUNDING CAN BE GIVEN UK and overseas
WHO CAN BENEFIT Registered charities, social enterprises and schools.
WHAT IS FUNDED Environmental causes and sustainable development overseas via UK organisations. Environmental education projects in the UK and also supported.
FINANCES Year 2013/14 Income £248,041 Grants £32,000 Grants to organisations £32,000 Assets £188,000
TRUSTEES Tassilo Metternich-Sandor; Robin Bidwell; John Simonson; Ian Bailey; Sabine Hoefnagel.
OTHER INFORMATION This is the charitable foundation of Environmental Resources Management Ltd, a global provider of environmental, health, safety, risk and 'social' consulting services.
HOW TO APPLY Apply in writing to the correspondent.
WHO TO APPLY TO Shona King, Correspondent, ERM Group Holdings Ltd, Exchequer Court, 33 St Mary Axe, London EC3A 8AA email shona.king@erm.com Website www.erm.com/foundation

### ■ The Ernest Hecht Charitable Foundation
CC NO 1095850 ESTABLISHED 2002
WHERE FUNDING CAN BE GIVEN England and Wales.
WHO CAN BENEFIT Registered charities.
WHAT IS FUNDED 'People who are disadvantaged; the arts; education.'
WHAT IS NOT FUNDED Individuals; charities whose primary area of benefit is outside the UK.
SAMPLE GRANTS Action for the Blind; Action for Kids; Apex Works; Bede House; Bath Festivals; Book Aid International; Cardboard Citizens; Chickenshed Theatre; Child Bereavement; Chilean Earthquake Appeal; Dignity in Dying; Food Lifeline; Index on Censorship; Jewish Council for Racial Equality; Macmillan Cancer Support; Multiple Sclerosis Society; Notting Hill Housing Trust; RAF Benevolent Fund; Scottish Disability Golf Partnership; St John's Hospice; The Food Chain; Tranmere Community Project; University College London; The Wiener Library for the Study of the Holocaust and Genocide; Young Vic; and the YMCA.

FINANCES Year 2013 Income £127,004 Grants £115,278 Grants to organisations £115,248 Assets £499,463
TRUSTEES Ernest Hecht; Barb Jungr.
HOW TO APPLY Application forms are available from the foundation's website. The completed form should be emailed to the foundation along with copies of your two most recent audited accounts. There are no deadlines for applications, which are reviewed at regular intervals.
WHO TO APPLY TO Ms H. Townley, Correspondent, 843 Finchley Road, London NW11 8NA email info@ernesthechtcharitablefoundation.org Website ernesthechtcharitablefoundation.org

### ■ The Erskine Cunningham Hill Trust
SC NO SC001853 ESTABLISHED 1955
WHERE FUNDING CAN BE GIVEN Scotland.
WHO CAN BENEFIT Organisations registered in Scotland benefitting older people, young people, ex-service men and women, seamen, and the Church of Scotland.
WHAT IS FUNDED The Church of Scotland is the largest single focus of the trust's interest (50% of annual income). Other grants are restricted to charitable work in Scotland with older people; young people; ex-servicemen and women; seamen; Scottish interests; with priority given to charities administered by voluntary or honorary officials.
WHAT IS NOT FUNDED Individuals; charities outside Scotland.
TYPE OF GRANT Recurring grants to the Church of Scotland; one-off grants to individual Scottish charities.
RANGE OF GRANTS Approximately £1,000 each to individual charities.
SAMPLE GRANTS ChildLine and Cruse Bereavement Care, The Sailors' Family Society and Venture Trust.
FINANCES Year 2013/14 Income £53,708 Grants £50,000 Grants to organisations £50,000
TRUSTEES R. M. Maiden; Very Revd Dr A. McDonald; I. W. Grimmond; Very Revd J. Cairns; Very Revd A. McLellan; Dr A. Elliot; The Church of Scotland Trust.
HOW TO APPLY Apply in writing to the correspondent at the above address. An application form is available via email from the correspondent. There is a two-year time bar on repeat grants. The trustees do not consider applications from outside Scotland.
WHO TO APPLY TO Nicola Laing, Secretary, Stewardship and Finance Department, Church of Scotland Offices, 121 George Street, Edinburgh EH2 4YN Tel. 0131 225 5722 email nlaing@cofscotland.org.uk

### ■ The Esfandi Charitable Foundation
CC NO 1103095 ESTABLISHED 2004
WHERE FUNDING CAN BE GIVEN UK and overseas.
WHO CAN BENEFIT Charitable organisations.
WHAT IS FUNDED Jewish causes.
RANGE OF GRANTS Up to £250,000.
SAMPLE GRANTS Previous beneficiaries have included: Schlomo High School (£250,000); British Friends of Migdal Or (£60,000); Jewish Care and Jewish Community Secondary School Trust (£12,500); Naima Jewish Preparatory

School (£8,000); Royal National Theatre and Chief Rabbinate Trust (£5,000 each); British Friends of Gesher (£2,000); Western Marble Arch Synagogue (£1,500); and Norwood (£750).
**FINANCES** Grants £367,000 Grants to organisations £367,000
**TRUSTEES** Joseph Esfandi; Denise Esfandi.
**OTHER INFORMATION** The foundation has not submitted its accounts to the Charity Commission since 2011/12. This was the latest information available at the time of writing (June 2015). In the past on average about £367,000 has been given each year.
**HOW TO APPLY** Apply in writing to the correspondent.
**WHO TO APPLY TO** Joseph Esfandi, Trustee, 36 Park Street, London W1K 2JE Tel. 020 7629 6666

## ■ Esh Foundation

**CC NO** 1112040      **ESTABLISHED** 2005
**WHERE FUNDING CAN BE GIVEN** Cumbria, Durham, North Yorkshire and Northumberland.
**WHO CAN BENEFIT** Registered charities and community groups.
**WHAT IS FUNDED** Social welfare; environment; education and health; children and young people
**RANGE OF GRANTS** £1,000–£20,000
**SAMPLE GRANTS** County Durham Community Foundation and Eagles Community Foundation (£20,000 each); NUFC Foundation (£6,500); SAFC Foundation (£6,000); St Cuthbert's Hospice, Butterwick Hospice, Esh Winning AFC and Durham County Cricket Club (£5,000 each); and Avalunch Community Services and Artichoke Trust (£1,000 each).
**FINANCES** Year 2013 Income £141,687 Grants £91,272 Grants to organisations £91,272 Assets £60,011
**TRUSTEES** Brian Walker; Michael Hogan; Austin Donohoe; Karen Humble; Eric Morgan; John Flynn; Jack Lumsden; Dougie Emmerson; Ron Batty; Tony Carroll; Brian Manning.
**OTHER INFORMATION** This is the charitable foundation of the Esh Group, a civil engineering, construction and house building company based in County Durham. The company has committed to provide the foundation with £1 million over five years until 2017, subject to profits.
**HOW TO APPLY** Apply in writing to the correspondent. The trustees meet regularly to review applications and further support with the process is provided by the County Durham Community Foundation.
**WHO TO APPLY TO** Andrew Radcliffe, Correspondent, Esh Holdings Ltd, Esh House, Bowburn North Industrial Estate, Bowburn, Durham DH6 5PF Tel. 07976 077621 email enquiries@esh.uk.com

## ■ The Essex and Southend Sports Trust

**CC NO** 1092238      **ESTABLISHED** 2002
**WHERE FUNDING CAN BE GIVEN** Essex, Southend-on-Sea.
**WHO CAN BENEFIT** Charities, other not-for-profit organisations and individuals.
**WHAT IS FUNDED** Sports facilities, equipment, coaching and training.
**RANGE OF GRANTS** Up to £25,000.
**SAMPLE GRANTS** Centre of Cricketing Excellence – Southend and Southend United Community and Educational Trust (£25,000 each); Friends of Castledon School (£5,000); the Prince's Trust and Southend Rugby Club (£3,000 each);

Rettendon Cricket Club and Shoeburyness High School (£2,000 each); and South Essex District (£1,800).
**FINANCES** Year 2013/14 Income £423,536 Grants £96,644 Grants to organisations £96,644 Assets £4,515,960
**TRUSTEES** Joseph Sims; Linley Butler; Peter Butler.
**OTHER INFORMATION** Grants were made to 15 organisations in 2013/14.
**HOW TO APPLY** Contact the correspondent to enquire about making an application.
**WHO TO APPLY TO** Peter Butler, Trustee, Red House, Larks Lane, Great Waltham, Chelmsford CM3 1AD Tel. 01245 360385 email mail@easst.org.uk Website www.easst.org.uk

## ■ Essex Community Foundation

**CC NO** 1052061      **ESTABLISHED** 1996
**WHERE FUNDING CAN BE GIVEN** Essex, Southend and Thurrock
**WHO CAN BENEFIT** Any voluntary and community organisations, or any non-profit making organisation working for the benefit of people living in Essex, Southend and Thurrock. The foundation is particularly interested in small grass-roots groups.
**WHAT IS FUNDED** Support generally falls under the broad heading of social welfare. The foundation distributes grants through various funds. Information on current funds and their criteria is available on the foundation's website.
**WHAT IS NOT FUNDED** Political activities; statutory bodies undertaking their statutory obligations, including schools; general appeals; activities which support animal welfare; projects that operate outside Essex, or benefit non-Essex residents; retrospective funding.
**TYPE OF GRANT** Core costs/revenue costs, new or continuing projects, one-off initiatives and capital costs.
**RANGE OF GRANTS** £50–£100,000
**SAMPLE GRANTS** Cirdan Sailing Trust (£99,500); Relate (£57,000); 2nd Witham Boys' Brigade (£51,000); InterAct Chelmsford Ltd (£46,500); Homeless Action Resource Project (£19,000); Havens Hospice (£15,000); First Stop Centre (£11,500); Colchester Furniture Project (£11,000); and Huntingdon's Disease Association and Mistley Kids Club (£10,000 each).
**FINANCES** Year 2013/14 Income £4,143,270 Grants £2,030,774 Grants to organisations £2,030,774 Assets £29,188,558
**TRUSTEES** Peter Martin; Rhiannedd Pratley; Martin Hopkins; John Barnes; Jason Bartella; Peter Heap; Jacqueline Sully; Peter Blanc; Owen Richards; Kate Barker; Jonathan Minter; Lee Blissett; Rosemary Turner; Clare Ball.
**OTHER INFORMATION** The foundation administers a variety of funds which are subject to change and are likely to open and close throughout the year. Potential applicants are therefore advised to check the foundation's website for exact information on funds.
**HOW TO APPLY** Essex Community Foundation manages a number of funds, many of which are tailored to the individual wishes of the donors. Applicants should use the general applications forms (for either under or over £1,000), along with application guidelines. Applicants for Comic Relief, High Sherriff's Award, Red Nose Day or funding for individuals should use the specific application forms, also available from the foundation. Application forms are available from the foundation's office or can be downloaded from the website; they can be submitted at any

time throughout the year. The foundation welcomes initial enquires to discuss an application.

WHO TO APPLY TO The Grants Team, 121 New London Road, Chelmsford, Essex CM2 0QT Tel. 01245 355947 email general@essexcf.org.uk Website www.essexcommunityfoundation.org.uk

## ■ The Essex Fairway Charitable Trust

CC NO 1066858    ESTABLISHED 1997
WHERE FUNDING CAN BE GIVEN South east England, with a preference for Essex.
WHO CAN BENEFIT Registered charities, particularly those directly benefitting people in need. Small charities in south east England, particularly Essex, will be favoured.
WHAT IS FUNDED General charitable purposes.
WHAT IS NOT FUNDED Medical research; animal welfare; the environment; political or religious purposes; large UK charities; individuals.
TYPE OF GRANT One-off grants for capital and revenue costs and full project funding. Replacement of statutory funding also available.
SAMPLE GRANTS Awareness of Down's Syndrome; CHESS; East Essex District Scouts Council; Fair Haven Hospice; Farleigh Hospice; Felixstowe Youth Development Group; Hamelin Trust; Headway Essex; Anne Lloyd Memorial Trust; Macmillan Cancer Relief; Martha Trust; St Christopher's School; Stepney Children's Fund and St Patrick's Trust.
FINANCES Year 2013/14 Income £50,561 Grants £182,500 Grants to organisations £182,500 Assets £423,212
TRUSTEES P. W. George; Bruce Ballard.
PUBLICATIONS A full grants list is available on request to the trust.
OTHER INFORMATION In 2013 grants were made to 39 organisations.
HOW TO APPLY According to the Charity Commission website the trust '**now assists charities previously supported. Other applications will not be acknowledged.**'
WHO TO APPLY TO Bruce Ballard, c/o Birkett Long, Essex House, 42 Crouch Street, Colchester, Essex CO3 3HH Tel. 01206 217327

## ■ The Essex Heritage Trust

CC NO 802317    ESTABLISHED 1989
WHERE FUNDING CAN BE GIVEN Essex.
WHO CAN BENEFIT Any organisation, body or individual whose project will be to the benefit of the people of Essex.
WHAT IS FUNDED Grants to bodies or individuals undertaking specific work in accord with the objects of the trust, including publication or preservation of Essex history and restoration of monuments, significant structures, artefacts and church decorations and equipment.
WHAT IS NOT FUNDED No grants involving private property.
TYPE OF GRANT Mostly one-off grants for revenue and capital costs.
RANGE OF GRANTS £100–£10,000
SAMPLE GRANTS Canvey Island Town Council – enhancement works for Canvey Lake, Castle Hedingham Tennis – restoration of wall, Club Waltham Abbey Church – replacement of pipe organ and Dawn Sailing Barge Trust – restoration of tiller (£5,000 each); Safron Walden Museum – purchase of Anglo-Saxon gold ring (£4,000); St Peter and St Paul Church Foxearth – organ overhaul (£2,000); St Mary the Virgin, Farnham – conservation of stained glass panel (£1,500); Ashdon Windmill Trust Ltd – purchase of ash hurdles (£1,400); The Fry Art Gallery – painting acquisition (£600); and High Ongar Parish Council – wooden fingerpost (£400).
FINANCES Year 2013/14 Income £65,092 Grants £43,700 Grants to organisations £43,700 Assets £1,517,670
TRUSTEES Lord John Petre; Richard Wollaston; Mark Pertwee; Peter Mamelok; Dr James Bettley; Brian Moody; Susan Brice; Cllr Kay Twitchen; Jonathan Douglas-Hughes; Cllr Norman Hume.
PUBLICATIONS Annual newsletter.
HOW TO APPLY To apply for funding, complete the expression of interest form on the trust's website. They will then contact you with further instructions. The trustees meet three times a year to assess applications, in March, July and November.
WHO TO APPLY TO Sharon Hill, Correspondent, Cressing Temple, Witham Road, Braintree, Essex CM77 8PD Tel. 01376 585794 email mail@essexheritagetrust.co.uk Website www.essexheritagetrust.co.uk

## ■ The Essex Youth Trust

CC NO 225768    ESTABLISHED 1963
WHERE FUNDING CAN BE GIVEN Essex.
WHO CAN BENEFIT Beneficiaries include schools, youth clubs and organisations giving advice, help and information.
WHAT IS FUNDED The advancement of education for people under the age of 25 who are in need of assistance. Preference is given to those who are in need owing to 'being temporarily or permanently deprived of normal parental care or who are otherwise disadvantaged'. 'The trustees favour organisations which develop young people's physical, mental and spiritual capacities through active participation in sports and indoor and outdoor activities. As a result they are particularly supportive of youth clubs and other organisations which provide facilities for young people to take active part in an assortment of activities as well as single activity organisations.'
WHAT IS NOT FUNDED Individuals.
RANGE OF GRANTS Up to £25,000.
SAMPLE GRANTS Essex Boys' and Girls' Clubs (£66,000 in five grants); Cirdan Sailing Trust (£50,000 in two grants); Chain Reaction Theatre Company (£8,000); Chelmsford YMCA (£5,000); Ark Family Resource Centre and Colchester Institute (£3,000); Colchester Carers' Centre (£2,000); Basildon Community Resource Centre and Happy Days Children's Charity (£1,500 each); and Southview School (£800).
FINANCES Year 2013/14 Income £387,609 Grants £318,938 Grants to organisations £318,938 Assets £8,065,011
TRUSTEES Julien Courtauld; Revd Duncan Green; Claire Cottrell; William Robson; Julia Denison-Smith; Michael Dyer; Richard Wenley; Michael Biegel; Julie Rogers.
OTHER INFORMATION Grants were made to 40 organisations.
HOW TO APPLY Application forms are available from the correspondent. The trustees meet on a quarterly basis.
WHO TO APPLY TO Jonathan Douglas-Hughes, Correspondent, Gepp and Sons, 58 New London Road, Chelmsford, Essex CM2 0PA Tel. 01245 493939 email douglas-hughesj@gepp.co.uk

## ■ The Estelle Trust

**CC NO** 1101299 **ESTABLISHED** 2003
**WHERE FUNDING CAN BE GIVEN** UK and Zambia.
**WHO CAN BENEFIT** Organisations mostly in Zambia.
**WHAT IS FUNDED** Overseas aid and general charitable purposes.
**RANGE OF GRANTS** Up to £30,000.
**SAMPLE GRANTS** Zambia Orphans of Aids (£31,000); Project Luangwa (£16,000); Queen's College Cambridge (£7,000); International Rescue Committee (£5,000); Microloan (£3,800); African Lion and Environmental Research Trust (£3,500); ActionAid (£2,000); and Sight Savers, the Scottish National War Memorial and the Urology Foundation (£500 each).
**FINANCES** Year 2013/14 Income £56,829 Grants £103,381 Grants to organisations £103,381 Assets £1,272,685
**TRUSTEES** Nigel Farrow; Gerald Ornstein; Darren Wise; Rachel Lynch; Katherine Farrow; Imogen Abed; Sarah Davies.
**HOW TO APPLY** Apply in writing to the correspondent.
**WHO TO APPLY TO** Caroline Harvey, Correspondent, Fisher Phillips, 170 Finchley Road, London NW3 6BP Tel. 020 7483 6100

## ■ Joseph Ettedgui Charitable Foundation

**CC NO** 1139615 **ESTABLISHED** 2010
**WHERE FUNDING CAN BE GIVEN** UK and overseas.
**WHO CAN BENEFIT** Registered charities.
**WHAT IS FUNDED** General charitable purposes, with a preference for organisations working with children and young people, older people and people with disabilities.
**RANGE OF GRANTS** Up to £40,000.
**SAMPLE GRANTS** Debatemate; Imperial College; In Harmony Ltd; Salvation Army; St Mungo's; Teachfirst; ThamesReach; Ubuntu Education Fund.
**FINANCES** Year 2013/14 Income £156,735 Grants £125,000 Grants to organisations £125,000
**TRUSTEES** Isabel Ettedgui; Peter Ettedgui; Paul Ettedgui; Genevieve Ettedgui; Matilda Ettedgui; Coutts & Co.
**HOW TO APPLY** Apply in writing to the correspondent.
**WHO TO APPLY TO** Steve Harvey, Correspondent, c/o Trustee Dept, Coutts & Co, 440 Strand, London WC2R 0QS Tel. 020 7663 6814 email couttscharities@coutts.com

## ■ Euro Charity Trust

**CC NO** 1058460 **ESTABLISHED** 1996
**WHERE FUNDING CAN BE GIVEN** Worldwide, mainly India, Africa, Bangladesh and the UK.
**WHO CAN BENEFIT** Registered charities.
**WHAT IS FUNDED** The relief of poverty; to assist the vulnerable; to assist in the advancement of education in the UK and the rest of the world.
**RANGE OF GRANTS** Up to £1.25 million.
**SAMPLE GRANTS** Nathani Charitable Trust (£1.26 million); Maulana Hussain Ahmed Madani Charitable Society and Charitable Trust (£440,000); Anfar Foundation (£279,000); Anjuman-i-Islam (£219,000) Imadul Muslimeen (£204,000); and Mehboob Memorial Centre (£135,000).
**FINANCES** Year 2013 Income £2,131,239 Grants £2,527,194 Grants to organisations £2,495,983 Assets £326,695
**TRUSTEES** Nasir Awan; Abdul Malik; Abdul Alimahomed.
**OTHER INFORMATION** The trust receives the majority of its income from Euro Packaging Holdings Limited. A large proportion of the trust's grant-making is in India.
**HOW TO APPLY** Apply in writing to the correspondent.
**WHO TO APPLY TO** Nasir Awan, Trustee, Euro Packaging plc, 4 Woodbourne Road, Edgbaston, Birmingham B15 3HQ email info@eurocharity.org.uk

## ■ The Alan Evans Memorial Trust

**CC NO** 326263 **ESTABLISHED** 1979
**WHERE FUNDING CAN BE GIVEN** UK.
**WHO CAN BENEFIT** Registered charities only.
**WHAT IS FUNDED** Preservation of lands and tenements, of beauty or historic interest the natural aspect of features and animal and plant life.
**WHAT IS NOT FUNDED** Non-registered charities; general appeals.
**RANGE OF GRANTS** £400–£1,500
**SAMPLE GRANTS** Cathedral Church of the Holy Spirit – Guildford; the Church of Our Lord; St Mary and St Germaine – Selby Abbey; English Hedgerow Trust; Landmark Trust; Lincoln Cathedral; Peterborough Cathedral Development and Preservation Trust; Thatcham Charity; Wells Cathedral – Somerset; St Wilfrid's Church – Leeds; Wells Cathedral – Somerset; Zoological Society of London.
**FINANCES** Year 2013/14 Income £29,554 Grants £104,000 Grants to organisations £104,000
**TRUSTEES** David Halfhead; Deirdre Moss.
**OTHER INFORMATION** The grant total has been estimated based on previous years' grant-making.
**HOW TO APPLY** There is no formal application form, but appeals should be made in writing to the correspondent, stating why the funds are required, what funds have been promised from other sources (for example, English Heritage) and the amount outstanding. The trust has also stated previously that it would be helpful when making applications to provide a photograph of the project. The trustees normally meet four times a year, although in urgent cases decisions can be made between meetings. The trustees may wish to see the work undertaken out of the proceeds of the grant. Grant recipients might be asked to provide copies of receipts for expenditure.
**WHO TO APPLY TO** The Trustees, Withy King LLP, 34 Regent Circus, Swindon SN1 1PY Tel. 01793 847777 email aevans@withyking.co.uk

## ■ Sir John Evelyn's Charity

**CC NO** 225707 **ESTABLISHED** 1974
**WHERE FUNDING CAN BE GIVEN** Ancient parishes of St Nicholas Deptford and St Luke Deptford.
**WHO CAN BENEFIT** Registered charities benefitting the parishes of St Nicholas and St Luke's in Deptford, which relieve poverty, as well as advance education and community development.
**WHAT IS FUNDED** Pensions and grants to organisations working to relieve poverty, as well as advance education and community development.
**WHAT IS NOT FUNDED** Appeals from outside the area of benefit.
**TYPE OF GRANT** One-off grants and longer term grants.

SAMPLE GRANTS Armada Community Project (£46,000); Young People's Project (£17,500); Evelyn 190 Centre (£500).
FINANCES Year 2013 Income £71,980 Grants £64,769 Grants to organisations £64,519 Assets £2,788,704
TRUSTEES Kay Ingledew; Bridget Perry; Revd Jack Lucas; Janet Miller; Cllr Maureen O'Mara; Margaret Mythen; Revd Louise Cordington-Marshall; Maureen Vitler; Pat Greenwood.
OTHER INFORMATION Grants were made to four organisations.
HOW TO APPLY Apply in writing to the correspondent.
WHO TO APPLY TO Colette Saunders, Correspondent, Clerk's Office, Armada Court Hall, 21 Macmillan Street, Deptford, London SE8 3EZ Tel. 020 8694 8953

## ■ The Eventhall Family Charitable Trust

CC NO 803178  ESTABLISHED 1989
WHERE FUNDING CAN BE GIVEN UK with a preference for the north west of England.
WHO CAN BENEFIT Charitable organisations and individuals.
WHAT IS FUNDED General charitable purposes.
SAMPLE GRANTS Aish Hatorah, ChildLine, Clitheroe Wolves Football Club, Community Security Trust, Greibach Memorial, Guide Dogs for the Blind, Heathlands Village, International Wildlife Coalition, JJCT, MB Foundation Charity, Only Foals and Horses Sanctuary, Red Nose Day, RNLI, Sale Ladies Society, Shelter and South Manchester Synagogue.
FINANCES Year 2013/14 Income £141,512 Grants £225,437 Grants to organisations £225,437 Assets £3,889,759
TRUSTEES Julia Eventhall; David Eventhall.
HOW TO APPLY Apply in writing to the correspondent. Note, however, that previous research highlighted that the trust stated it only has a very limited amount of funds available.
WHO TO APPLY TO The Trustees, PO Box 490, Altrincham WA14 2ZT email efct@rectella.com

## ■ The Everard Foundation

CC NO 272248  ESTABLISHED 1976
WHERE FUNDING CAN BE GIVEN Leicestershire.
WHO CAN BENEFIT Local organisations of all sizes. Grants to UK-wide organisations must be to fund something tangibly local.
WHAT IS FUNDED General charitable purposes.
WHAT IS NOT FUNDED Individuals.
TYPE OF GRANT Capital costs.
RANGE OF GRANTS £100–£15,000
SAMPLE GRANTS Warning Zone – Leicester and Rutland Crimebeat (£16,500); National Army Museum Foundation (£7,500); Age UK Leicester and Rutland, Home-Start and the Scout Association (£5,000 each); Guide Association – Leicestershire and Leicestershire Cares (£2,500 each); ABF The Soldiers Charity (£1,000); Children's Society (£300); and Brewers Charitable Trust (£100).
FINANCES Year 2013/14 Income £112,387 Grants £69,220 Grants to organisations £69,220 Assets £3,140,259
TRUSTEES Richard Everard; Serena Richards; Simon Aitkinson; Charlotte Everard.
HOW TO APPLY Apply in writing to the correspondent.

WHO TO APPLY TO Richard Everard, Trustee, C/o Everards Brewery Ltd, Castle Acres, Everard Way, Enderby, Leicester LE19 1BY Tel. 0116 201 4307

## ■ The Eveson Charitable Trust

CC NO 1032204  ESTABLISHED 1994
WHERE FUNDING CAN BE GIVEN Herefordshire, Worcestershire and the county of West Midlands (covering Birmingham, Coventry, Dudley, Sandwell, Solihull, Walsall and Wolverhampton).
WHO CAN BENEFIT Registered charities.
WHAT IS FUNDED People with physical disabilities (including those who are blind or deaf); people with mental disabilities; hospitals and hospices; children who are in need, whether disadvantaged or with physical or mental disabilities; older people; homeless people; medical research into problems associated with any of these conditions.
WHAT IS NOT FUNDED Individuals, even if their request is submitted by a charitable organisation.
TYPE OF GRANT Capital and revenue, recurring and one-off.
RANGE OF GRANTS From a few hundred pounds to £150,000; average grant around £8,000.
SAMPLE GRANTS Acorns Children's Hospice Trust and Age UK Hereford and Localities (£55,000 each); Hereford Arts in Action (£30,000), towards music projects benefitting people with disabilities; Broadening Choices for Older People – Birmingham (£25,000), towards cost of new high dependency dementia care unit; St Paul's Hostel – Worcester (£20,000), towards counselling services for homeless people; Merton House Holiday Hotel Limited (£15,000); Haven – Wolverhampton (£7,500), towards services benefitting women in emergency accommodation; Music Therapy Works (£7,000) toward musical equipment; Action on Hearing Loss (£6,000) towards running costs in the area; and Worcester Action for Youth (£5,500), towards activities benefitting disadvantaged children.
FINANCES Year 2013/14 Income £1,260,413 Grants £1,950,887 Grants to organisations £1,950,887 Assets £69,981,343
TRUSTEES David Pearson, Martin Davies; Louise Woodhead; Bill Wiggin; Richard Mainwaring; Judi Millward.
OTHER INFORMATION Grants were made to 294 organisations in 2013/14.
HOW TO APPLY The following was taken from the 2013/14 trustee's report: 'The Trustees consider the making of grants at their quarterly meetings. Applications are only accepted if they are made on the Trust's standard form for Application for Support that can be obtained from the Administrator at the Trust's office in Gloucester. That form must be completed and returned (together with a copy of the latest accounts of the applying organisation) to the Trust's office at least six weeks before the meeting at which the application is to be considered to allow time for necessary assessment procedures including visits to the applicant if deemed appropriate. The policy of the Trustees is to make grants on an equal opportunities basis, regardless of gender, religion and ethnic background. Grants may be approved for capital or revenue purposes.'
WHO TO APPLY TO Alex Gay, Administrator, 45 Park Road, Gloucester GL1 1LP Tel. 01452 501352 email admin@eveson.plus.com

## ■ The Beryl Evetts and Robert Luff Animal Welfare Trust Limited

**CC NO** 283944  **ESTABLISHED** 1981
**WHERE FUNDING CAN BE GIVEN** UK.
**WHO CAN BENEFIT** Registered animal charities.
**WHAT IS FUNDED** Veterinary research and the care and welfare of animals.
**RANGE OF GRANTS** Up to £75,000 but typically £500–£3,500.
**SAMPLE GRANTS** Animal Health Trust (£75,000); Royal Veterinary College (£50,000); Nowzad Dogs, Orangutan Appeal and Red Squirrel Survival Trust (£3,500 each); Brooke Hospital for Animals (£2,000); Songbird Survival (£1,500); Eden Animal Rescue (£1,000); Lea Valley Riding for the Disabled Group (£800); Wellcat (£500).
**FINANCES** Year 2013/14 Income £176,475 Grants £182,500 Grants to organisations £182,500 Assets £4,613,381
**TRUSTEES** Jean Tomlinson; Sir Robert Johnson; Brian Nicholson; Revd Matthew Tomlinson; Richard Price; Melanie Condon; Lady Ruth Bodey.
**OTHER INFORMATION** Grants were made to 30 organisations in 2013/14.
**HOW TO APPLY** Apply in writing to the correspondent. Applications from organisations that the trust has never previously funded are considered; however, the trust has stated that it is very unlikely that grants of any higher than £5,000 are likely to be considered. Grants are made annually and administered in June.
**WHO TO APPLY TO** Richard Price, Trustee, Waters Edge, Ferry Lane, Moulsford, Wallingford, Oxfordshire OX10 9JF email rpjprice@gmail.com

## ■ The Exilarch's Foundation

**CC NO** 275919  **ESTABLISHED** 1978
**WHERE FUNDING CAN BE GIVEN** Mainly UK, occasionally overseas.
**WHO CAN BENEFIT** Jewish organisations and educational institutions.
**WHAT IS FUNDED** Education; medical; social welfare.
**RANGE OF GRANTS** Up to £3 million.
**SAMPLE GRANTS** Bar-Ilan University (£3,000,000); Royal Society of Medicine (£2,000,000); Redbridge School (£50,000); Birkbeck College (£300,000); Foundation for Relief and Reconciliation in the Middle East (£38,000); Spanish and Portuguese Jews' Congregation (£31,000); University Jewish Chaplaincy (£21,000); Chazak and The Yakar Educational Foundation (£20,000 each); Westminster Academy (£14,000); and Bet Yaakov of the Jersey Shore (£10,000).
**FINANCES** Year 2013 Income £5,408,809 Grants £5,693,270 Grants to organisations £5,693,270 Assets £59,739,987
**TRUSTEES** David Dangoor; Elie Dangoor; Robert Dangoor; Michael Dangoor; Dr Naim Dangoor.
**HOW TO APPLY** Apply in writing to the correspondent.
**WHO TO APPLY TO** Dr Naim Dangoor, Trustee, 4 Carlos Place, Mayfair, London W1K 3AW

## ■ The Expat Foundation

**CC NO** 1094041  **ESTABLISHED** 2002
**WHERE FUNDING CAN BE GIVEN** UK and overseas.
**WHO CAN BENEFIT** Registered charities and community groups.
**WHAT IS FUNDED** Education; social welfare; health; community development; young people; elderly people.
**WHAT IS NOT FUNDED** Individuals; animal welfare charities.
**TYPE OF GRANT** Capital, core and start-up costs. One-off and up to four years.
**RANGE OF GRANTS** £1,000–£75,000
**SAMPLE GRANTS** Kids Company (£75,000); LEAP Confronting Conflict (£50,000); Build it International (£47,500); University of Warwick (£26,500); Magic Me, Open Age, Room to Read (£10,000 each); Beat Bullying (£5,000); Ashanti Development (£4,000); and Ethiopiaid (£1,000).
**FINANCES** Year 2013/14 Income £216,044 Grants £347,034 Grants to organisations £347,034 Assets £889,222
**TRUSTEES** Ann Jacobs; John Barnsley; Patricia Wolfston; Paul Tuckwell; Janet Cummins; Gill Weavers.
**OTHER INFORMATION** Grants were given to 19 organisations in 2013/14.
**HOW TO APPLY** Apply in writing to the correspondent. Grant recipients must report on how the funds were spent.
**WHO TO APPLY TO** Patricia Wolfston, Chair, 127 Ellesmere Road, London NW10 1LG Tel. 020 3609 2105

## ■ Extonglen Limited

**CC NO** 286230  **ESTABLISHED** 1982
**WHERE FUNDING CAN BE GIVEN** UK and Israel
**WHO CAN BENEFIT** Orthodox Jewish organisations.
**WHAT IS FUNDED** Orthodox Jewish causes; education; and the relief of poverty.
**RANGE OF GRANTS** £3,000–£500,000
**SAMPLE GRANTS** Kol Halashon Education Programme (£470,000); Ahavas Chesed (£95,000); Pikuach Nefesh (£50,000); Kupath Gemach Chaim Bechesed Viznitz Trust (£40,000); British Friends of Nishmat Yisrael (£12,000); and Children's Town Charity (£3,600).
**FINANCES** Year 2013 Income £853,290 Grants £629,104 Grants to organisations £629,104 Assets £11,367,986
**TRUSTEES** Meir Levine; Mrs C. Levine; Isaac Katzenberg.
**HOW TO APPLY** Apply in writing to the correspondent.
**WHO TO APPLY TO** Mrs C. Levine, Trustee, New Burlington House, 1075 Finchley Road, London NW11 0PU Tel. 020 8731 0777 email ml@rowdeal.com

## ■ The William and Christine Eynon Charity

**CC NO** 1134334  **ESTABLISHED** 2010
**WHERE FUNDING CAN BE GIVEN** UK – There may be some preference for the Mid Glamorgan region of Wales.
**WHO CAN BENEFIT** Registered charities.
**WHAT IS FUNDED** General charitable purposes.
**FINANCES** Year 2013/14 Income £11,749 Grants £40,000 Grants to organisations £40,000
**TRUSTEES** William Eynon; Christine Eynon; Sophie Eynon; James Eynon.
**HOW TO APPLY** Apply in writing to the correspondent.
**WHO TO APPLY TO** William Eynon, Tusker House, Newton, Porthcawl CF36 5ST Tel. 01656 782312

## ■ The Matthew Eyton Animal Welfare Trust

**CC NO** 1003575   **ESTABLISHED** 1991
**WHERE FUNDING CAN BE GIVEN** England and Wales
**WHO CAN BENEFIT** Animal charities, mainly farm animal charities as opposed to wild or companion animals; vegetarians; and vegans.
**WHAT IS FUNDED** Animal charities; vegetarianism/veganism.
**TYPE OF GRANT** One-off.
**RANGE OF GRANTS** £100–£40,000
**SAMPLE GRANTS** PETA's Research and Educations Foundation (£40,000); RSPCA (£20,000); Compassion in World Farming Trust (£13,000); Lord Whiskey Animal Sanctuary and the Sustainable Trust Fund (£250); Animals Asia Foundation and the Greek Cat Society (£150 each); and Elephant Family and Society for Companion Animal Studies (£100).
**FINANCES** Year 2013/14 Income £43,801 Grants £75,258 Grants to organisations £75,258 Assets £45,930
**TRUSTEES** Audrey Eyton; Paul Flood.
**OTHER INFORMATION** Grants were made to 16 organisations in 2013/14.
**HOW TO APPLY** Apply in writing to the correspondent.
**WHO TO APPLY TO** The Trustees, Westgate House, 87 St Dunstan's Street, Canterbury, Kent CT2 8AE *Tel.* 01227 769321

## ■ The F. P. Limited Charitable Trust

**CC NO** 328737  **ESTABLISHED** 1990
**WHERE FUNDING CAN BE GIVEN** UK, with a possible preference for Greater Manchester.
**WHO CAN BENEFIT** Registered charities.
**WHAT IS FUNDED** Educational causes, schools, religious bodies and medical appeals. Most funds are given to regular beneficiaries.
**SAMPLE GRANTS** Donations were made to a variety of schools, religious institutions and medical appeals. Unfortunately a detailed list of beneficiaries was not available.
**FINANCES** Year 2013/14 Income £82,500 Grants £52,280 Grants to organisations £52,280 Assets £247,477
**TRUSTEES** Joshua Pine; Eli Pine.
**HOW TO APPLY** Apply in writing to the correspondent.
**WHO TO APPLY TO** Joshua Pine, Trustee, 14 Westfield Street, Salford M7 4NG Tel. 0161 834 0456 email ABURNETT@RPG.CO.UK

## ■ Esmée Fairbairn Foundation

**CC NO** 200051  **ESTABLISHED** 1961
**WHERE FUNDING CAN BE GIVEN** UK.
**WHO CAN BENEFIT** Organisations with charitable purposes.
**WHAT IS FUNDED** The Main Fund
The foundation's aims are to provide support to 'exceptional people with inspiring, workable ideas and organisations with latent or emerging models'. It states – 'we are prepared to fund where others do not and to confront issues that are unseen or unacknowledged'. Funding priorities for the next five years are: arts; children and young people; environment; social change; and food.
**Other funds:** In addition to the main fund (which accounts for about 80% of the overall expenditure) the foundation operates the following:
**The Esmée Fairbairn Collections Fund**
The three year programme (2013–16) 'aims to broaden access to, and use of, museum collections and focuses on time-limited collections work outside the scope of an organisation's core resources'. The website notes that 'the fund will be increased from £800,000 to £1 million per year in recognition of the strong demand and high number of good applications over the last three years'. The fund is run by the Museums Association and awards o museums, galleries and heritage organisations with two grant rounds per year. More information, including application guidelines, is available on the Museum Association website: www.museumsassociation.org/collections/18022011-esmee-fairbairn-collections-fund
**Finance Fund:** The £26 million fund 'invests in activities that aim to deliver both a financial return and a social benefit'. The average investment size is £390,000 with an average term of seven years. The website notes that 'social investments can take a variety of forms including loans, equity, quasi-equity (such as revenue participation agreements) and outcomes-based finance (such as Social Impact Bonds); Grants Plus – the programme provides a range of support to grant recipients alongside the main award.
**Grants Plus:** The programme provides a range of support to grant recipients alongside the main award. The website states: 'By identifying and providing the extra help an organisation might need at a difficult or opportune moment. We want to enable their work to have a greater impact, to make our money go further, and to make more of a difference as a Foundation. Examples of Grants Plus support include providing expert advice – e.g. on business planning, financial management, communications and evaluation. We have a pool of experts whose work we recommend, but also fund organisations directly to work with consultants they know and trust.'
**TASK Fund:** The foundation also makes grants from its TASK (Trustees' Areas of Special Knowledge) Fund to support organisations known to individual trustees.
**WHAT IS NOT FUNDED** The foundation does not support applications for: 'individuals or causes that will benefit only one person, including student grants or bursaries'; 'support for a general appeal or circular'; 'work that does not have a direct benefit in the UK'; 'the promotion of religion'; 'capital costs, including building work, renovations, and equipment', note that social investment can be provided for such expenditure; 'routine information and advice work'; 'work that is common to many parts of the UK', this includes mainstream activities of local organisations which are part of a wider network, services that are provided in similar ways in many locations (for example, hostels, night shelters, sports associations, playgroups and youth clubs) and general capacity building, professional development or employability skills; 'healthcare or related work such as medical research, complementary medicine, hospices, counselling and therapy, arts therapy, education about and treatment for drug and alcohol misuse'; 'work that is primarily the responsibility of central or local government, health trusts or health authorities. This includes residential, respite and day care, housing provision, individual schools, nurseries and colleges or a consortium of any of these, and vocational training'; 'the independent education sector'; 'animal welfare, zoos, captive breeding and animal rescue centres'; 'energy efficiency or waste reduction schemes such as recycling or renewable energy schemes unless they have exceptional social benefits'; 'recreational activities including outward bound courses and adventure experiences'; 'replacement or subsidising statutory income although the foundation will make rare exceptions where the level of performance has been exceptional and where the potential impact of the work is substantial'; 'retrospective funding'; 'work that is not legally charitable'; 'research' (can be funded very rarely).
**TYPE OF GRANT** Primarily core and project grants. Funding can be given for one to five years. The foundation also engages in social investment.
**RANGE OF GRANTS** In 2014 the average grant was £110,500.
**SAMPLE GRANTS Beneficiaries of grants from the Main Fund included**: IntoUniversity (£750,000 over five years); Teens and Toddlers (£387,500 over three years); CDI: Apps for Good (£319,500 over three years); Money Advice Trust (£300,000 over three years); Carers Trust (£255,000 over three years); Venture Scotland

(£188,000 over three years); Brook Young People (£177,000 over two years); Trust for London (£150,000 over two years); Centre for Contemporary Arts (£124,500 over three years); Khulisa UK (£115,000 over three years); After Adoption (£110,5000 over two years); Cumbria Wildlife Trust (£110,000 over three years); Disability Rights UK (£92,000 over two years); DigitalMe (£80,000 over two years); Magic Me (£69,000 over three years); You Make It (£60,000 over two years); FERN and Policy Exchange Ltd (£30,000 each); Ballet Lorent Ltd (£30,000 over two years); Northfield Ecocentre (£30,000 over three years); Arts 4 Dementia (£30,000 over four years); Demos Ltd (£27,500); ActOne ArtsBase (£20,000); Park Community Action (£20,000 over three years); Farm Carbon Cutting Toolkit (£19,900).

**FINANCES** *Year* 2014 *Income* £6,570,000 *Grants* £37,500,000 *Grants to organisations* £37,500,000 *Assets* £836,675,000

**TRUSTEES** James Hughes-Hallett; Tom Chandos; Beatrice Hollond; Thomas Hughes-Hallett; Kate Lampard; William Sieghart; John Fairbairn; Sir Jonathan Phillips; Sir David Bell; Joe Docherty; Eleanor Updale.

**OTHER INFORMATION** The foundation has a very informative website where further information, guidelines and examples of giving can be found. In 2014 there were a total of 440 grants awarded in the following categories: social change (£12.1 million in 128 awards); arts (£8.2 million in 88 awards); environment (£5.8 million in 40 awards); education and learning (£6.9 million in 33 awards); Food Strand (£2.5 million in 30 awards); TASKs (£1 million in 111 awards); Finance Fund Grants (£900,000 in ten awards); Grants Plus (£100,000).

**HOW TO APPLY** Follow these three steps: carefully read through the guidance notes, supported areas and exclusions; you may find it useful to take the online eligibility quiz before applying; if you are eligible you must create an account on the site and complete the online application form. Applications can be made at any time as funding decisions are made throughout the year. If your application is successful at first stage the foundation will contact you to invite you to make a second stage application and inform you of what further information is required. If your first stage application is unsuccessful you will be notified by email. The foundation has previously stated: 'You do not need to have matched funding in place before applying but where the total cost of the work you propose for funding is high you should indicate other sources of funding or specific plans to apply elsewhere.' Final decisions are made after careful 'assessment of the quality of the work proposed, the importance of the issue, the strength of your idea, the difference the work is likely to make and the match to at least one of the foundation's priorities'. Further guidance is available on the foundation's website.

**WHO TO APPLY TO** James Wragg, Director of Operations, Kings Place, 90 York Way, London N1 9AG *Tel.* 020 7812 3700 *Fax* 020 7812 3701 *email* info@esmeefairbairn.org.uk *Website* www.esmeefairbairn.org.uk

## ■ The Fairstead Trust

**CC NO** 1096359    **ESTABLISHED** 2003
**WHERE FUNDING CAN BE GIVEN** Worldwide.
**WHO CAN BENEFIT** UK-registered charities.
**WHAT IS FUNDED** General charitable purposes.
**RANGE OF GRANTS** £1,000–£30,000
**SAMPLE GRANTS** East Anglian Children's Hospices (£30,000); Grove House (£20,000); Paul's Cancer Centre and Family Links (£15,000 each); St Albans Cathedral Education Centre (£14,000); Afghan Connection, Castlehaven Community Association, The Archway Project, Hertfordshire Community Foundation and DEC East Africa Appeal (£10,000 each); Cley Memorial Hall Fund, Hillside Animal Sanctuary and Chance to Shine (£5,000 each); Hopefield Animal Sanctuary (£3,000); Smile Train (£1,500); and NNDRA (£1,000).

**FINANCES** *Year* 2013/14 *Income* £15,503 *Grants* £185,000 *Grants to organisations* £185,000

**TRUSTEES** Edward Cox; Wendy Cox; Lucinda Cox; Claire Mitchell.

**HOW TO APPLY** Apply in writing to the correspondent containing the following: aims and objectives of the charity; nature of appeal; total target if for a specific project; contributions received against target; registered charity number; any other relevant factors. Applications should be accompanied by full financial statements and the latest annual report.

**WHO TO APPLY TO** Anabelle Kalsi, 22 Chancery Lane, London WC2A 1LS *Tel.* 020 7430 7157 *email* charities@nqpltd.com

## ■ The Fairway Trust

**CC NO** 272227    **ESTABLISHED** 1976
**WHERE FUNDING CAN BE GIVEN** UK and worldwide.
**WHO CAN BENEFIT** Charities; universities; colleges; schools; religious organisations; youth clubs; museums; music and arts bodies.
**WHAT IS FUNDED** Educational causes; religious purposes; support of clubs and recreational facilities for children and young people; preservation and maintenance of buildings of particular interest; social welfare.
**WHAT IS NOT FUNDED** Our research suggests that grants are not made to medical charities.
**RANGE OF GRANTS** £650–£20,000
**SAMPLE GRANTS** Family Education Trust (£20,000); Thames Philharmonic Choir and Welsh National Opera (£3,000 each); Lucy Cavendish and Newnham College (£2,000 each); Combat Stress and Kids Out (£1,500 each); and The Art Fund and Fan Museum (£1,000 each).

**FINANCES** *Year* 2013/14 *Income* £34,154 *Grants* £40,650 *Grants to organisations* £40,650 *Assets* £43,504

**TRUSTEES** Janet Gudrun Grimstone; Kirsten Suenson-Taylor.

**OTHER INFORMATION** Grants were made to 14 organisations. The trust states that 'grants, gifts or interest-free loans to assist undergraduate and postgraduate students to continue their studies at universities and colleges within the United Kingdom and abroad' are also available.

**HOW TO APPLY** The trustees have an established list of charities which they support on a regular basis, therefore unsolicited applications are not generally considered. The trust has previously

stated that 'as funds and office resources are limited it cannot be guaranteed that unsolicited applications will be answered'.
**WHO TO APPLY TO** Janet Grimstone, Trustee, The Gate House, Coombe Wood Road, Kingston upon Thames, Surrey KT2 7JY

## ■ Famos Foundation Trust
**CC NO** 271211      **ESTABLISHED** 1976
**WHERE FUNDING CAN BE GIVEN** UK and Israel.
**WHO CAN BENEFIT** Small local projects and established organisations benefitting children, young adults, clergy and Jewish people.
**WHAT IS FUNDED** Education; religion; international organisations; general charitable purposes. The trust will consider funding: the advancement of the Jewish religion; synagogues; Jewish umbrella bodies; church schools; cultural and religious teaching and religious studies.
**TYPE OF GRANT** One-off, core costs and running costs. Funding is given for one year or less.
**RANGE OF GRANTS** Up to £5,000.
**SAMPLE GRANTS** Relief of poverty (£44,000); education (£23,000); Places of Worship (£15,500); medical (£10,000).
**FINANCES** Year 2013/14 Income £175,568 Grants £92,863 Grants to organisations £92,863 Assets £1,609,381
**TRUSTEES** Rabbi S. M. Kupetz; Fay Kupetz; Isaac Kupetz; Joseph Kupetz.
**OTHER INFORMATION** No list of beneficiaries available.
**HOW TO APPLY** Apply in writing to the correspondent, at any time. The trust does not accept telephone enquiries.
**WHO TO APPLY TO** Rabbi S. M. Kupetz, Trustee, 4 Hanover Gardens, Salford, Greater Manchester M7 4FQ *Tel.* 0161 740 5735 *email* bolsberg@taxprac.co.uk

## ■ The Lord Faringdon Charitable Trust
**CC NO** 1084690      **ESTABLISHED** 2000
**WHERE FUNDING CAN BE GIVEN** UK.
**WHO CAN BENEFIT** Registered charities only.
**WHAT IS FUNDED** Educational grants and scholarships; hospitals and the provision of medical treatment for people who are ill; purchase of antiques and artistic objects for museums and collections which have public access; care and assistance of people who are elderly or infirm; community and economic development and housing; development and assistance of arts and sciences, physical recreation and drama; research into matters of public interest; relief of poverty; support of matters of public interest; animal care and conservation; maintaining and improving the Faringdon Collection.
**WHAT IS NOT FUNDED** Individuals; non-registered charities.
**RANGE OF GRANTS** Up to £125,000 but generally £1,000–£5,000.
**SAMPLE GRANTS** Farringdon Collection Trust (£125,500); the New English Ballet and Greyhound Rescue (£5,000 each); Prospect Hospice (£3,500); Oxford Playhouse (£2,500); Operation New World (£2,000); Crimestoppers Trust (£1,500); and The Trussell Trust, West London Churches and Wiltshire Air Ambulance (£1,000 each).
**FINANCES** Year 2013/14 Income £206,356 Grants £240,710 Grants to organisations £240,710 Assets £8,760,144
**TRUSTEES** A. Forbes; The Hon J. Henderson; S. Maitland Robinson; Bernard Cazenove.
**OTHER INFORMATION** Grants to 85 organisations were made in 2013/14.
**HOW TO APPLY** Apply in writing to the correspondent. According to the trustees' report for 20113/14, 'grant applications are accepted from registered charities and other recognised bodies. All grant applications are required to provide information on the specific purpose and expected beneficiaries of the grants. This information helps the charity assess how its programme of discretionary grant-making achieves a spread of benefit.'
**WHO TO APPLY TO** Mrs S. Lander, Secretary to the Trustees, The Estate Office, Buscot Park, Faringdon SN7 8BU *Tel.* 01367 240786 *email* estbuscot@aol.com

## ■ Samuel William Farmer's Trust
**CC NO** 258459      **ESTABLISHED** 1929
**WHERE FUNDING CAN BE GIVEN** Mainly Wiltshire.
**WHO CAN BENEFIT** Registered charities benefitting children and older people.
**WHAT IS FUNDED** Residential facilities and services; infrastructure development; churches; hospices; healthcare; medical studies and research; conservation; environmental and animal sciences; education; various community facilities and services.
**TYPE OF GRANT** One-off and recurrent. Capital and core costs. Funding is given for up to three years.
**RANGE OF GRANTS** Up to £10,000 but generally £1,000–£2,500.
**SAMPLE GRANTS** The Friends of Westonbirt (£10,000); Wiltshire Air Ambulance Appeal (£7,000); Caudwell Children and Hope for Tomorrow (£2,500 each); Alive and Triumph over Phobia (£2,000 each); The Trussell Trust (£1,500); Cotswold Volunteers (£1,200); and Prospect Hospice and Positive Action on Cancer (£1,000 each).
**FINANCES** Year 2013 Income £86,179 Grants £75,220 Grants to organisations £75,220 Assets £2,447,840
**TRUSTEES** Bruce Waight; Jennifer Liddiard; Peter Fox-Andrews; Charles Brockis; Jean Simpson.
**OTHER INFORMATION** Grants were made to 34 organisations in 2013.
**HOW TO APPLY** Apply in writing to the correspondent. The trustees meet half-yearly. Trustees bring suggestions and applications for grants to their half yearly meetings. Grants must be formally approved before they are made. There must be at least three trustees present at a meeting for decisions to be made.
**WHO TO APPLY TO** Melanie Linden-Fermor, Correspondent, 71 High Street, Market Lavington, Devizes SN10 4AG *Tel.* 01380 813299

## ■ The Thomas Farr Charity
**CC NO** 328394      **ESTABLISHED** 1989
**WHERE FUNDING CAN BE GIVEN** UK, especially Nottinghamshire.
**WHO CAN BENEFIT** Registered charities only.
**WHAT IS FUNDED** General charitable purposes.
**WHAT IS NOT FUNDED** Individuals.
**TYPE OF GRANT** Capital costs; core costs; start-up costs. Unrestricted.

RANGE OF GRANTS Up to £60,000 but generally £1,000–£5,000.
SAMPLE GRANTS University of Nottingham (£60,000); School of Artisan Food (£25,000); Nottinghamshire Hospice (£10,000); Nottinghamshire Historic Churches Trust and Treetops Hospice (£5,000 each); Recycling Ollerton and Boughton (£4,000); Radford Visiting Scheme (£3,000); Relate Nottinghamshire (£2,000); Scope (£1,500); and the Royal Voluntary Service and Zone Youth Project (£1,000 each).
FINANCES Year 2013/14 Income £316,547 Grants £329,928 Grants to organisations £329,928 Assets £8,881,263
TRUSTEES Rathbone Trust Company Ltd; Henry Farr; Amanda Farr; Barry Davys; Mrs P. K. Myles.
OTHER INFORMATION In 2013/14 grants were given to 105 organisations.
HOW TO APPLY Apply in writing to the correspondent. Applications are considered in March and September/November.
WHO TO APPLY TO John Thompson, Correspondent, 6A The Almshouses, Mansfield Road, Daybrook, Nottingham NG5 6BW Tel. 0115 966 1222 email thomasfarrch@btconnect.com

## ■ The Farthing Trust
CC NO 268066    ESTABLISHED 1974
WHERE FUNDING CAN BE GIVEN UK and overseas.
WHO CAN BENEFIT Individuals and charitable organisations, most of which are personally known to the trustees.
WHAT IS FUNDED General charitable purposes, with a focus on: the advancement of religion; education; health; human rights; the reconciliation and promotion of religious and racial harmony; equality and diversity.
TYPE OF GRANT One-off and recurring grants.
SAMPLE GRANTS During the year grants were broken down into the following categories: UK Churches (£122,000); Christ's Servants (£33,000); Overseas Christian Causes (£20,500); Education (£20,000); UK Christian Causes (£18,000); Local (£9,000); Overseas (£8,000); UK General (£2,300); Individuals.
FINANCES Year 2013/14 Income £52,970 Grants £235,345 Grants to organisations £234,445 Assets £2,467,272
TRUSTEES C. H. Martin; Mrs E. Martin; Mrs J. Martin; Mrs A. White.
HOW TO APPLY Applications and enquiries should be made in writing to the correspondent. Applicants, and any others requesting information, will only receive a response if an sae is enclosed. Most beneficiaries are known to the trustees personally or through their acquaintances, though applications from other organisations are considered.
WHO TO APPLY TO Joy Martin, Correspondent, PO Box 277, Cambridge CB7 9DE email jmartin@bt.co.uk

## ■ The Fassnidge Memorial Trust
CC NO 303078    ESTABLISHED 1963
WHERE FUNDING CAN BE GIVEN London borough of Hillingdon, especially the former urban district of Uxbridge.
WHO CAN BENEFIT Individuals and organisations benefitting children, older people, parents and children, carers, people with disabilities, people disadvantaged by poverty, and victims of domestic violence.
WHAT IS FUNDED Welfare of older people and families, particularly charities working in the fields of care in the community, day centres and meals provision.
WHAT IS NOT FUNDED People or organisations outside the London borough of Hillingdon.
TYPE OF GRANT Small one-off grants and start-up costs. Funding of one year or less will be considered.
SAMPLE GRANTS Previous beneficiaries have included: 60+Fair; Sipson Community Association; and Hillingdon Homelessness Comfort Fund.
FINANCES Year 2013/14 Income £55,175 Grants £5,308 Grants to organisations £5,308 Assets £743,424
TRUSTEES Andrew Retter; David Routledge; David Herriott; Richard Walker; Peter Curling; Peter Ryerson; David Yarrow; George Cooper; Judith Cooper; Tony Burles; John Morgan.
HOW TO APPLY Apply in writing to the correspondent.
WHO TO APPLY TO Paul Cowan, 119 Cannonbury Avenue, Pinner, Middlesex HA5 1TR Tel. 01753 901700 email kfcommunityhall@gmail.com

## ■ The February Foundation
CC NO 1113064    ESTABLISHED 2006
WHERE FUNDING CAN BE GIVEN UK.
WHO CAN BENEFIT Charitable organisations and institutions.
WHAT IS FUNDED The foundation will consider the following organisations for the receipt of grants, equity investment or loans: charities for the benefit of persons who are making an effort to improve their lives; charities for the benefit of persons no longer physically or mentally able to help themselves; charities which protect the environment; charities offering formal education resulting in recognised qualifications; small or minority charities where small grants will have a significant impact; companies where the acquisition of equity would be in line with the foundation's investment policy.
WHAT IS NOT FUNDED Child care; Citizens Advice; community centres; higher education; housing associations; individuals; medical research; minibuses; NHS trusts; non-departmental government bodies; overseas projects; primary or secondary education; Scouts, Guides, Brownies, Cubs and similar organisations; single-faith organisations; sports clubs, unless for people with mental or physical disabilities; village halls; youth centres.
TYPE OF GRANT One-off grants for capital and revenue costs. Loans are also considered.
RANGE OF GRANTS Up to £5,000.
FINANCES Year 2013/14 Income £16,438,141 Grants £1,450,464 Grants to organisations £1,450,464 Assets £1,011,223
TRUSTEE James Carleton.
OTHER INFORMATION In 2013/14 there were 98 grants made to 86 organisations.
HOW TO APPLY 'The February Foundation makes grants to selected charities. It monitors and supports the effective management of grants made. The foundation is focused on managing its current commitments, although applications from some charities are still being accepted. … Email applications are preferred. Send details and budget of the proposed project, how many people would benefit, how those benefits might be measured (not just financially), and what the estimated cost of raising funds for the project is. It is important to include in your email application full accounts for your most recent completed financial year, and, if your accounts

do not contain it, what your total fundraising costs annually are. Note that hardcopy applications take significantly longer to process than email applications. Do not send DVDs, CDs, glossy brochures or other additional information. It normally takes 12 weeks from application to applicants being informed of the trustees' decision. There are no application deadlines as trustees make grant decisions on a monthly basis. **Note that less than 5% of all applications are successful.**'

**WHO TO APPLY TO** Richard Pierce-Saunderson, Chief Executive, Spring Cottage, Church Street, Stradbroke, Suffolk IP21 5HT *Tel.* 01379 388200 *email* rps@thefebruaryfoundation.org *Website* www.thefebruaryfoundation.org

## ■ Federation of Jewish Relief Organisations

**CC NO** 250006   **ESTABLISHED** 1919
**WHERE FUNDING CAN BE GIVEN** Mainly Israel.
**WHO CAN BENEFIT** Jewish organisations.
**WHAT IS FUNDED** Relief of Jewish victims of war and persecution; help wherever Jewish need exists.
**SAMPLE GRANTS** Norwood (£10,000).
**FINANCES** *Year* 2013/14 *Income* £36,290 *Grants* £44,485 *Grants to organisations* £44,485 *Assets* £192,773
**TRUSTEES** Alfred Garfield; Angela Lando.
**OTHER INFORMATION** Founded in 1919 to assist victims of war and persecution in Europe and the Eastern Bloc. Since 1948 it has been concerned mainly in Israel with the rehabilitation, clothing, feeding and education of children of immigrant families.
**HOW TO APPLY** Apply in writing to the correspondent.
**WHO TO APPLY TO** Angela Lando, Honorary Secretary and Trustee, HRS Danescroft Avenue, Hendon, London NW4 2NA *Tel.* 020 8457 9169 *email* fjro@btinternet.com

## ■ The John Feeney Charitable Bequest

**CC NO** 214486   **ESTABLISHED** 1906
**WHERE FUNDING CAN BE GIVEN** Birmingham.
**WHO CAN BENEFIT** Charitable organisations benefitting the Birmingham area. Normally only applications from registered charities will be considered.
**WHAT IS FUNDED** Benefit of public charities in Birmingham; promotion of art in Birmingham; acquisition and maintenance of open spaces near Birmingham. The trustees look to give grants to organisations where they feel that the grants, whatever size, will have a significant impact.
**WHAT IS NOT FUNDED** Individuals; causes which do not directly benefit the Birmingham area or Birmingham charitable organisations; organisations which have political objectives, or could be considered as denominational and promoting religion.
**TYPE OF GRANT** One-off; project costs; capital costs.
**RANGE OF GRANTS** Generally £500–£2,000.
**SAMPLE GRANTS** Ex Cathedra (£21,000); Moor Pool Heritage Trust (£10,000); City of Birmingham Symphony Orchestra (£9,900); Birmingham Bach Choir (£6,500); Birmingham Repertory Theatre, Craftspace and Elmhurst Ballet School Trust (£3,000 each); Friends of Cotteridge Park, Ikon Gallery Limited and Orchestra Of The Swan (£2,000 each); Birmingham Pen Trade Heritage (£1,500); Birmingham Children's Hospital Charities, DanceXchange and Women and Theatre (£1,000 each); Ackers Adventure (£500).
**FINANCES** *Year* 2014 *Income* £75,684 *Grants* £98,082 *Grants to organisations* £90,682 *Assets* £1,648,444
**TRUSTEES** John Smith; Hugh Carslake; Charles King-Farlow, Chair; Geoffrey Oakley; Merryn Ford Lloyd; Anouk Perinpanayagam; William Southall; Sally Luton; Lucy Reid; Catherine Organ; Deirdre Figueiredo; Andrew Spittle.
**OTHER INFORMATION** Grants totalling £7,400 were given to individuals through the Feeney Fellowships scheme for local arts practitioners.
**HOW TO APPLY** Application forms are available from the trust's website, along with guidelines and criteria. Forms should be completed and returned by post or email it with a supporting letter and other documents to the correspondent. Applications should be received by 31 March each year and are best made between January and March. Applications are normally acknowledged and successful applicants will usually be notified by June following the trustee meeting, which takes place once a year.
**WHO TO APPLY TO** Amanda Cadman, Secretary, 55 Wychall Lane, Birmingham B38 8TB *Tel.* 0121 624 3865 *email* secretary@feeneytrust.org.uk *Website* www.feeneytrust.org.uk

## ■ The George Fentham Birmingham Charity

**CC NO** 214487   **ESTABLISHED** 1907
**WHERE FUNDING CAN BE GIVEN** City of Birmingham.
**WHO CAN BENEFIT** Individuals and organisations benefitting young adults and people disadvantaged by poverty.
**WHAT IS FUNDED** Social welfare and education.
**WHAT IS NOT FUNDED** Only registered charities are supported. No grants are given towards salary costs. West Midlands organisations outside the city of Birmingham are not eligible.
**RANGE OF GRANTS** £1,000–£5,000.
**SAMPLE GRANTS** Marie Curie Cancer Care (£5,000); Children with Cystic Fibrosis Dream Holidays (£4,500); Birmingham Federation of Clubs for Young People (£4,000); The Children's Heart Foundation (£3,000); Vitalise (£2,500); Friends of Victoria School and Orchestra of the Swan (£2,000 each); Relate – Birmingham (£1,500); Beanstalk (£1,300); and Mama Enterprises (£1,100).
**FINANCES** *Year* 2013 *Income* £196,133 *Grants* £171,852 *Grants to organisations* £152,912 *Assets* £6,077,240
**TRUSTEES** Jean Turner; Diana Duggan; John Bower; Derek Ridgway; Margaret Martin; Martin Holocombe; Barry Earp; Abdulhamid Malik; Margaret Flynn; Eluned Jones.
**OTHER INFORMATION** Grants were made to 63 organisations totalling £153,000 and to nine individuals totalling £19,000.
**HOW TO APPLY** Application forms are available from the correspondent or to download from the website, where criteria and guidelines are also posted. General grants are made in April and October, while education grants are made from September to April.
**WHO TO APPLY TO** Anne Holmes, Correspondent, c/o Veale Wasbrough Vizards LLP, Second Floor, 3 Bindley Place, Birmingham B1 2JB *Tel.* 0121 227 3700 *email* george.fentham@vwv.co.uk *Website* www.georgefenthamcharity.org.uk

## ■ The A. M. Fenton Trust

**CC NO** 270353　**ESTABLISHED** 1975

**WHERE FUNDING CAN BE GIVEN** UK, preference for North Yorkshire, and overseas.

**WHO CAN BENEFIT** Registered charities.

**WHAT IS FUNDED** General charitable purposes with preference towards health, medical, disability and young people.

**WHAT IS NOT FUNDED** The trust is unlikely to support local appeals, unless they are close to where the trust is based.

**TYPE OF GRANT** Mostly one-off.

**RANGE OF GRANTS** £100–£20,000

**SAMPLE GRANTS** Yorkshire County Cricket Club Charitable Youth Trust (£20,000); Hipperholme Grammar School (£10,000); the Tweed Foundation and Dewsbury League of Friendship (£8,000 each); Horticap, Arthritis Research Council and Police Treatment Centres (£4,000 each); Marie Curie Cancer Care and Epilepsy Research UK (£3,000 each); Every Child and Institute of Medical Engineering (£2,000 each); Crimestoppers Trust, Abandoned Animals Charity and Ability Beyond Disability (£1,000 each); Macmillan Centre Fund and Girl Guides Brighouse (£500 each); and Checkheaton Boxing Academy (£200).

**FINANCES** Year 2013 Income £144,935 Grants £172,785 Grants to organisations £172,785 Assets £5,203,295

**TRUSTEES** James Fenton; C. Fenton.

**HOW TO APPLY** Apply in writing to the correspondent.

**WHO TO APPLY TO** James Fenton, Trustee, 14 Beech Grove, Harrogate HG2 0EX Tel. 01423 504442

## ■ The Allan and Nesta Ferguson Charitable Settlement

**CC NO** 275487　**ESTABLISHED** 1977

**WHERE FUNDING CAN BE GIVEN** UK and overseas.

**WHO CAN BENEFIT** Registered charities and individuals.

**WHAT IS FUNDED** Education including projects that encompass world peace, overseas aid, arts and culture, human rights, equality, promotion of world peace and development.

**RANGE OF GRANTS** Up to £500,000.

**SAMPLE GRANTS** Coventry University (£500,000); East Africa Cricket Foundation (£30,000); Barnardo's and Help Age International (£25,000); Our Sansar and WWF-UK (£20,000 each); and Centre of the Cell, The Protimos Educational Trust and War on Want (£15,000 each).

**FINANCES** Year 2013 Income £820,667 Grants £2,062,306 Grants to organisations £2,023,606 Assets £28,215,481

**TRUSTEES** Elizabeth Banister; Prof. David Banister; James Richard Tee; Letitia Glaister.

**OTHER INFORMATION** Grants are also made towards the fees of postgraduate students who are in their final year of a postgraduate course, subject to evidence of financial hardship.

**HOW TO APPLY** Application forms are available from the trust's website. The following guidance is given by the foundation: 'When to apply: Applications by charities for small to medium grants (up to a maximum of £50,000) may be submitted at any time and will be considered on a regular basis. Applications for larger grants will be considered at bi-annual meetings held in March and October and applications should be submitted at the very latest in the previous months i.e. February or September. **Please note:** No repeat applications will be considered within three years of the conclusion of the grant term. **How to apply:** We prefer where possible that you complete and submit the on-line application form on [the trust's] website and email it to us. Alternatively you may download and print out the application form, complete it and send it by letter post. Please do not extend the length of the forms, or add any attachments. Applications **MUST NOT** exceed 3 pages. Please use text size 12. Please do not apply for more than one project. All applications by email will be acknowledged and considered by the trustees within 6 to 8 weeks. If you do not hear further, after the acknowledgement, then unfortunately your application has not been successful. If the trustees do decide to award you a grant then they will contact you. No progress reports will be given and no correspondence will be entered into in the meantime.'

**WHO TO APPLY TO** James Tee, Trustee, Stanley Tee Solicitors, High Street, Bishops Stortford, Hertfordshire CM23 2LU Tel. 01279 755200 email lpg@teeslaw.co.uk Website www.fergusontrust.co.uk

## ■ Elizabeth Ferguson Charitable Trust Fund

**SC NO** SC026240　**ESTABLISHED** 1988

**WHERE FUNDING CAN BE GIVEN** UK, with some interest in Scotland.

**WHO CAN BENEFIT** Organisations benefitting children and young people, particularly those who are sick.

**WHAT IS FUNDED** The welfare and well-being of children and young people. Also charities involved in medical research and hospitals where special medical equipment is needed.

**WHAT IS NOT FUNDED** Non-registered charities; overseas causes.

**RANGE OF GRANTS** £250–£10,000

**SAMPLE GRANTS** Govan Initiative and Harmony Row Boys' Club.

**FINANCES** Year 2013/14 Income £332,088 Grants £164,238 Grants to organisations £164,238

**TRUSTEES** Sir Alex Ferguson; Cathy Ferguson; Huw Roberts; Ted Way; Les Dalgarno; Paul Hardman; Jason Ferguson.

**HOW TO APPLY** An application form and guidelines should be requested in writing from the correspondent. The committee meets to consider grants at the end of January and July. Applications should be received by December and June respectively.

**WHO TO APPLY TO** The Trustees, c/o 27 Peregrine Crescent, Droylsden, Manchester M43 7TA

## ■ The Fidelity UK Foundation

**CC NO** 327899　**ESTABLISHED** 1988

**WHERE FUNDING CAN BE GIVEN** Unrestricted, in practice particular preference is given to projects in Kent, Surrey and London. Larger grants may be given in Manchester and Birmingham for organisations with revenue of £1 million or more.

**WHO CAN BENEFIT** Not-for-profit organisations; charities.

**WHAT IS FUNDED** General charitable purposes, giving is primarily allocated for charitable purposes in the following areas: community development, health, arts and culture and education. The trust seeks to support projects undertaken by organisations to increase proficiency, achieve goals and reach long-term self-sufficiency. Most often, funding is given for projects such as capital improvements, technology upgrades, organisational development and planning initiatives.

**WHAT IS NOT FUNDED** Grants are not generally made to: charities that have been in existence for less than three years; sectarian or political organisations; schools, colleges, universities or playgroups; individuals; community centres; sports clubs or general appeals and circulars. Grants are not made for: salaries or general running/core costs; training projects; the replacement of dated or out-of-warranty IT equipment; marketing costs; the promotion of religion; sponsorships or benefit events; university/college fees, research projects or gap year expeditions. Grants will not normally cover the entire cost of a project. Grants will not normally be awarded to an organisation in successive years. Grants are one-off investments; they will not normally be awarded for or across multiple years. Grants are for planned expenditure; they will not normally cover costs incurred prior to application and/or the grant being awarded.

**TYPE OF GRANT** Buildings, capital, IT development, one-off grants to develop infrastructure. Funding for less than one year is considered.

**RANGE OF GRANTS** £1,000–£725,000

**SAMPLE GRANTS** Tate Foundation, The National Trust for Places of Historic Interest or Natural Beauty: Knol (£315,000 each); Kent Community Foundation (£300,000); Young Epilepsy (£250,000); Cancer Research Trust UK (£176,000); Scottish Opera Theatre Royal Limited (£170,000); Livability (£50,000); Rainbow Trust Children's Society (£34,000); Bow Arts Trust (£27,000); Hospice in the Weald (£23,000).

**FINANCES** Year 2013 Income £5,787,053 Grants £5,092,058 Grants to organisations £5,092,058 Assets £154,202,000

**TRUSTEES** Edward Johnson; Barry Bateman; Anthony Bolton; Richard Millar; John Owen; Sally Walden.

**HOW TO APPLY** Apply in writing to the correspondent. Applicants should enclose a summary form (form can be downloaded from the foundation's website) as well as a separate document outlining: organisation history and key achievements and an overview of the organisations forward strategy and key objectives. It should give the following project details: an indication and evidence of the need for the project that requires funding; an outline of the proposed project, and how it fits into the wider strategic plan; the project's objectives and forecast outcomes; an indication of how the project's success will be monitored and evaluated; an implementation plan/timeline; an itemised budget; the fundraising plan, including a list of other actual/potential funders and the status of each request; an indication of what a grant would allow your organisation to achieve, and how a grant will change or improve the long-term potential and sustainability of your organisation. You should also attach the following: a list of the directors and trustees with their backgrounds; the most recently audited annual financial statements and the most recent monthly management accounts. There are no deadlines for submitting grant proposals. All applications will normally receive an initial response within three months. The review process can take up to six months, which should be factored into the applicant's funding plan. The foundation may request additional information or a site visit to better familiarise themselves with the organisation, its management team and the project. The foundation welcomes informal phone calls prior to the submission of a formal application. Applicants for international grants should not use the application form. Instead you should post a brief outline of your organisation and funding proposal. If appropriate the foundation will respond and advise you whether you should make a full application.

**WHO TO APPLY TO** Sian Parry, Correspondent, Oakhill House, 130 Tonbridge Road, Hildenborough, Tonbridge, Kent TN11 9DZ *Tel.* 01732 777364 *Website* www.fidelityukfoundation.org

## ■ The Doris Field Charitable Trust

**CC NO** 328687   **ESTABLISHED** 1990
**WHERE FUNDING CAN BE GIVEN** UK, with a preference for Oxfordshire.
**WHO CAN BENEFIT** Large UK and small local organisations in Oxfordshire.
**WHAT IS FUNDED** Medical; welfare; education; general charitable purposes.
**WHAT IS NOT FUNDED** It is unlikely that grants would be made for salaries, training or higher education costs.
**TYPE OF GRANT** One-off and recurrent.
**RANGE OF GRANTS** Up to £40,000 but generally £500 to £2,000.
**SAMPLE GRANTS** Greenpower (£14,500); Soldiers of Oxfordshire (£10,000); Oxford International Biomedical Centre (£4,000); Oxford Preservation Trust (£2,500); Shipton under Whychwood Cricket Club (£2,000); Defibrillators for Milton and The Royal Blind Society and Defibrillators for Milton (£1,500 each); Clean Slate, Contact the Elderly and Oxfordshire Samaritans (£1,000); and Oxfordshire Play Association and Reading Quest (£500 each).
**FINANCES** Year 2013/14 Income £470,838 Grants £265,791 Grants to organisations £264,791 Assets £10,296,598
**TRUSTEES** John Cole; N. Harper; Wilhelmina Church.
**HOW TO APPLY** According to the trustees' report for 2011/12, 'the trustees receive applications from diverse sources. Each applicant is required, except in exceptional cases, to complete a standard application form and to submit information in support of that application.' Applications are considered three times a year or as and when necessary.
**WHO TO APPLY TO** Helen Fanyinka, Correspondent, Blake Morgan LLP, Seacort, West Way, Oxford OX2 0FB *Tel.* 01865 258088 *email* sue.robins@blakemorgan.co.uk

## ■ Field Family Charitable Trust

**CC NO** 259569   **ESTABLISHED** 1969
**WHERE FUNDING CAN BE GIVEN** West Midlands, Warwickshire, London within the boundaries of the M25.
**WHO CAN BENEFIT** Registered UK charities only.
**WHAT IS FUNDED** The trustees are interested in funding causes within the beneficiary area supporting young people between the ages of 16 and 25 and the elderly. As well as considering applications, the trustees also set aside a small amount of funding for continuing grants to projects of which they have personal experience and which fall within the funding criteria.
**WHAT IS NOT FUNDED** Individuals; charities with an income of greater than £1 million or unrestricted reserves to the value of more than

six months annual expenditure; building projects (though furnishings, equipment, and alterations to existing buildings to comply with health and safety regulations are eligible).

**TYPE OF GRANT** Core costs, one-off, project, research, running costs, recurring costs, salaries and start-up costs. Funding of up to two years will be considered.

**RANGE OF GRANTS** Mostly £1,000–£5,000.

**SAMPLE GRANTS** Ucandoit (£3,500); Our Way Self Advocacy (£3,400); Age UK Merton, Emmaus St Albans, Lifespace Trust, St Cuthbert's Centre and St Thomas's Community Network (£3,000 each); Slade Gardens Community Play Association (£2,900); Warwickshire Association of Youth Clubs (£2,800); The Feast Youth Project (£2,500); Dyscover Ltd, Performances Birmingham Limited and Viznitz Ltd (£2,000 each); icandance (£1,000).

**FINANCES** Year 2013/14 Income £73,522 Grants £37,041 Grants to organisations £37,041 Assets £1,997,758

**TRUSTEES** Judith Steele; Rosalind Bagshaw; Josephine Houston; Thomas Steele; Duncan Bagshaw; Elizabeth Brennan; Louise Saunders.

**OTHER INFORMATION** Formerly known as the Woodlands Trust, the trust changed its name in 2013 to The Field Family Charitable Trust, to avoid confusion with another registered charity known as the Woodland Trust. The trust's objectives and activities remain the same. Grants were awarded to 14 organisations in 2013/14.

**HOW TO APPLY** Applications should be made on an online form available, together with criteria and guidelines, from the website. The trustees meet to consider applications in spring and autumn each year and applications should be submitted at least six weeks before the next meeting, the dates of which are published on the trust's website. Unsuccessful applicants will be informed in writing and may re-apply after two years. Successful grant beneficiaries will not be reconsidered for a period of two years, but repeat funding may be granted. Any queries may be directed to the Trust Administrator via email.

**WHO TO APPLY TO** Jayne Day, Correspondent, c/o PWW Solicitors, 70 St George's Square, London SW1V 3RD Tel. 020 7821 8211 email charities@pwwsolicitors.co.uk Website www.pwwsolicitors.co.uk/charity-grants/9-the-field-family-charitable-trust

■ **The Fifty Fund**

**CC NO** 214422 **ESTABLISHED** 1963

**WHERE FUNDING CAN BE GIVEN** Nottinghamshire and surrounding area.

**WHO CAN BENEFIT** Individuals and organisations benefitting retired people; unemployed people; those in care, fostered and adopted; parents and children; one-parent families; widows and widowers; carers; people with disabilities; and people disadvantaged by poverty.

**WHAT IS FUNDED** Relief of poverty; infrastructure development; charity or voluntary umbrella bodies; advice and information on housing; respite care; various community services.

**WHAT IS NOT FUNDED** Education; expeditions; travel.

**TYPE OF GRANT** Mostly one-off grants for revenue costs and project funding.

**RANGE OF GRANTS** £100–£18,000

**SAMPLE GRANTS** Nottinghamshire Hospice (£10,000); Radford Care Group (£4,800); Hope West (£4,000); Council for Family Care (£3,000); Nottingham Mencap (£2,500) Family Holiday Association (£2,000); Fundays in Nottinghamshire and the Respite Association (£1,000 each); Radford Visiting Scheme (£500); and Wilford Parish Church Luncheon Club (£100).

**FINANCES** Year 2013 Income £282,689 Grants £198,763 Grants to organisations £140,353 Assets £7,899,820

**TRUSTEES** E. Whiles; Edward Randall; Revd Canon George Barrodale; Revd Amanda Cartwright; Richard Bonnello.

**OTHER INFORMATION** Grants to 57 organisations totalled £140,500 and grants to 132 individuals amounted to £58,500.

**HOW TO APPLY** Apply in writing to the correspondent.

**WHO TO APPLY TO** Craig Staten-Spencer, Correspondent, c/o Nelsons Solicitors, Pennine House, 8 Stanford Street, Nottingham NG1 7BQ Tel. 0115 989 5251 email craig.staten-spencer@nelsonslaw.co.uk

■ **Filey Foundation Ltd**

**CC NO** 1148376 **ESTABLISHED** 2012

**WHERE FUNDING CAN BE GIVEN** UK.

**WHO CAN BENEFIT** Charities and community groups

**WHAT IS FUNDED** General charitable purposes; education; social welfare.

**FINANCES** Year 2013/14 Income £176,325 Grants £25,208 Grants to organisations £25,208 Assets £250,192

**TRUSTEES** Charles Englard; Rachel Englard.

**OTHER INFORMATION** A list of beneficiaries was not included in the foundation's set accounts.

**HOW TO APPLY** Apply in writing to the correspondent.

**WHO TO APPLY TO** Charles Englard, Trustee, 73 Bishops Road, Prestwich, Manchester M25 0AS Tel. 0161 795 1999

■ **Dixie Rose Findlay Charitable Trust**

**CC NO** 251661 **ESTABLISHED** 1967

**WHERE FUNDING CAN BE GIVEN** UK.

**WHO CAN BENEFIT** Charitable organisations.

**WHAT IS FUNDED** General charitable purposes with preference to children, seafarers, blindness and multiple sclerosis.

**TYPE OF GRANT** One-off and recurrent.

**RANGE OF GRANTS** £1,000–£6,000

**SAMPLE GRANTS** George's Trust (£3,000); Arrive Alive appeal (£2,500); The Children's Trust, Mercia Therapy Centre and Sunny Days Children Fund (£2,000 each); Ipswich Community Playbus and The Springboard Project (£1,500 each); Child Brain Injury Trust, Seafarers UK and Tiny Tim's Children Centre (£1,000 each).

**FINANCES** Year 2013/14 Income £1,914,791 Grants £92,000 Grants to organisations £92,000 Assets £4,660,025

**TRUSTEE** HSBC. Trust Company (UK) Ltd.

**HOW TO APPLY** Apply in writing to the correspondent.

**WHO TO APPLY TO** S. Hill, Trust Manager, HSBC Trust Company UK Limited, Trust Services, 10th Floor, Norwich House, Nelson Gate, Southampton SO15 1GX Tel. 023 8072 2243

■ **Finnart House School Trust**

**CC NO** 220917 **ESTABLISHED** 1901

**WHERE FUNDING CAN BE GIVEN** Worldwide.

**WHO CAN BENEFIT** Schools and charitable organisations benefitting Jewish children and young people in need of care and/or education.

# Firtree

**WHAT IS FUNDED** Bursaries and scholarships are given to Jewish secondary school pupils and university entrants who are capable of achieving, but would probably not do so because of family and economic pressures. Jewish school welfare funds and charities concerned with helping Jewish children are also assisted.
**TYPE OF GRANT** Buildings, capital, one-off and project.
**RANGE OF GRANTS** £1,000–£5,000
**SAMPLE GRANTS** JFS School (£5,000); Jewish Community Secondary School (£2,000).
**FINANCES** Year 2013/14 Income £177,793 Grants £166,756 Grants to organisations £7,000 Assets £5,075,713
**TRUSTEES** Robert Cohen; Dame Hilary Blume; Anthony Yadgaroff; Linda Paterson; Sue Leifer; Gideon Lyons; Gil Cohen; Mervyn Kaye; Lucy Silver.
**OTHER INFORMATION** In 2013/14 two grants totalling £7,000 were made to organisations and the remainder was spent in supporting individual students.
**HOW TO APPLY** Note the following statement taken from the trust's website: 'If you are a charity (working for Jewish children in need) seeking support, please understand that the major part of Finnart's income goes to fund the Finnart Scholars. If you wish to apply, though realising the chances of success are slim, please check by telephone, email or letter before doing so. If you are a school seeking a hardship fund, please remember that our trust deed restricts our grant giving to Jewish children in need. We may also require evidence of the eligibility of any pupil. We will require a report on how any funds have been dispersed.'
**WHO TO APPLY TO** Sophie Reindorp, Correspondent, The Charities Advisory, Radius Works, Back Lane, London NW3 1HL *Tel.* 07804 854905 *email* info@finnart.org *Website* www.finnart.org

## ■ Firtree Trust

**CC NO** 282239   **ESTABLISHED** 1981
**WHERE FUNDING CAN BE GIVEN** UK and abroad.
**WHO CAN BENEFIT** Christian organisations.
**WHAT IS FUNDED** Religious education and the advancement of the Protestant and Evangelical tenets of the Christian faith.
**TYPE OF GRANT** One-year grants for capital and revenue costs.
**RANGE OF GRANTS** Up to £3,000.
**SAMPLE GRANTS** Harvest Christian Fellowship Trust (£3,000); Open Doors (£2,600); Christians Against Poverty and FEBA (£2,000 each); Sat-7 Trust Ltd (£1,500); Warlingham Methodist Trust (£1,200); Titus Trust (£1,300); Tearfund and United Christian Broadcasters (£1,000 each); and UCCF (£750).
**FINANCES** Year 2013/14 Income £47,513 Grants £26,200 Grants to organisations £17,500 Assets £64,730
**TRUSTEES** Maurice Turner; James Turner; Paul Turner; Elizabeth Turner.
**HOW TO APPLY** Apply in writing to the correspondent.
**WHO TO APPLY TO** James Turner, Trustee, 12 Purley Bury Avenue, Purley, Surrey CR8 1JB *Tel.* 020 8668 1994

## ■ Fisherbeck Charitable Trust

**CC NO** 1107287   **ESTABLISHED** 2004
**WHERE FUNDING CAN BE GIVEN** Worldwide.
**WHO CAN BENEFIT** Registered charities worldwide.
**WHAT IS FUNDED** The advancement of the Christian religion; support for the provision of accommodation for the homeless; the relief of poverty; the advancement of education; conservation of the environment and the preservation of heritage.
**WHAT IS NOT FUNDED** Grants are only made to individuals known to the trust or in exceptional circumstances.
**TYPE OF GRANT** One-off and recurrent.
**RANGE OF GRANTS** Up to £50,000.
**SAMPLE GRANTS** Christian Viewpoint for Men (£45,000); Tear Fund and Urban Saints (£40,000 each); Worthing Churches Homeless Project (£30,000); Breakout Trust, Hope for Lugazi and Youth for Christ (£15,000 each) and Alpha International (£10,000); Smiles (£8,000); and Church Army (£6,000).
**FINANCES** Year 2013/14 Income £339,570 Grants £468,800 Grants to organisations £459,450 Assets £174,979
**TRUSTEES** I. R. Cheal; Mrs J. Cheal; M. Cheal.
**OTHER INFORMATION** £5,300 was also given as a grant to one individual.
**HOW TO APPLY** Apply in writing to the correspondent, although note: 'This is a family run charitable trust. We have a list of charities supported on an annual basis. There is no money available for new applicants – only occasionally, but not very often.'
**WHO TO APPLY TO** Ian Cheal, Trustee, Home Farm House, 63 Ferringham Lane, Ferring, Worthing, West Sussex BN12 5LL *Tel.* 01903 241027 *email* ian@roffeyhomes.com

## ■ The Fishmongers' Company's Charitable Trust

**CC NO** 263690   **ESTABLISHED** 1972
**WHERE FUNDING CAN BE GIVEN** UK; however, this refers to charities whose objects extend throughout England. In practice, mainly the City of London and its adjacent boroughs.
**WHO CAN BENEFIT** Registered charities and individuals (for educational grants only).
**WHAT IS FUNDED** General charitable purposes. In practice, education, relief of poverty and disability, in particular assistance to almshouses, fishery related bodies, environment and heritage.
**WHAT IS NOT FUNDED** Individuals (except for educational purposes).
**RANGE OF GRANTS** Up to £150,000 but generally £1,000–£30,000.
**SAMPLE GRANTS** City and Guilds London Art School (£36,500); New Model School (£33,000); The Marion Richardson School (£13,500); East London Science School (£10,000); Bethnal Green Academy (£7,000); London Youth Rowing (£6,000); National Crimebeat (£3,000); Spitalfields (£2,000); and 12F (Tower Hamlets) DF Air Corps (£1,000).
**FINANCES** Year 2013 Income £2,067,784 Grants £518,936 Grants to organisations £492,480 Assets £23,710,098
**TRUSTEES** The Worshipful Company of Fishmongers; Peter Woodward.
**HOW TO APPLY** Apply in writing to the correspondent. Meetings take place three times a year, in March, June/July and November, and applications should be received a month in advance. No applications are considered within

three years of a previous grant application being successful. Unsuccessful applications are not acknowledged.

**WHO TO APPLY TO** Peter Woodward, Correspondent, The Fishmongers' Company, Fishmongers' Hall, London Bridge, London EC4R 9EL *Tel.* 020 7626 3531 *email* ct@fishhall.org.uk *Website* www.fishhall.org.uk

## ■ Marc Fitch Fund

**CC NO** 313303      **ESTABLISHED** 1956
**WHERE FUNDING CAN BE GIVEN** UK
**WHO CAN BENEFIT** Both individuals and institutions benefitting young adults, research workers and students.
**WHAT IS FUNDED** Publication and research in archaeology, historical geography, history of art and architecture, heraldry, genealogy, surnames, catalogues of and use of archives (especially ecclesiastical) and other antiquarian, archaeological or historical studies. In many cases, the awards enable work to be undertaken, or the results published either in print or on-line form, which would not otherwise be achieved.
**WHAT IS NOT FUNDED** Foreign travel or for research outside the British Isles (unless the circumstances are exceptional); building works; mounting exhibitions; general appeals. No awards are made in connection with vocational or higher education courses or to people reading for higher degrees.
**TYPE OF GRANT** Mainly publication costs and incidental research expenses.
**RANGE OF GRANTS** £300–£5,000
**SAMPLE GRANTS** Yorkshire Archaeological Society (£5,000); Glasgow City Archives (£4,300); Museum of London Archaeology and Watts Gallery (£3,000 each); North Wales Dendro Project (£2,900); Winchester Excavations Committee (£2,500); Folklore Society (£1,000); Norwich Cathedral (£500); Church Monuments Society (£300).
**FINANCES** *Year* 2013/14 *Income* £201,052 *Grants* £93,167 *Grants to organisations* £28,985 *Assets* £6,150,550
**TRUSTEES** David White; Lindsay Allason-Jones; Andrew Howard Murison; Dr Helen Forde; Prof. John Blair; Prof. David Hey; Dr Michael Hall; Bernard Nurse; Christiana Payne.
**HOW TO APPLY** Apply in writing to the correspondent, providing a brief outline of the project. The Council of Management meets twice a year, in spring and autumn, to consider applications. The deadlines for receipt of completed applications and references are 1 March and 1 August. The fund requests that any application enquiries be made well in advance of these deadlines as the application process is likely to take at least a few weeks to complete.
**WHO TO APPLY TO** Christopher Catling, Director, 19 The Avenue, Cirencester, Gloucestershire GL7 1EJ *Tel.* 01285 641108 *email* admin@marcfitchfund.org.uk *Website* www.marcfitchfund.org.uk

## ■ The Fitton Trust

**CC NO** 208758      **ESTABLISHED** 1928
**WHERE FUNDING CAN BE GIVEN** UK.
**WHO CAN BENEFIT** Registered charities only.
**WHAT IS FUNDED** General charitable purposes.
**WHAT IS NOT FUNDED** Individuals.
**RANGE OF GRANTS** Usually £100–£350 with some grants up to £1,000.

**SAMPLE GRANTS** King's Medical Research Trust.
**FINANCES** *Year* 2013/14 *Income* £88,887 *Grants* £81,100 *Grants to organisations* £81,100 *Assets* £1,692,384
**TRUSTEES** Dr Rodney Rivers; Duncan Brand; Emma Lumsden; Katherine Lumsden; Lincoln Rivers; Rosemary Shaw.
**OTHER INFORMATION** Grants were made to 347 organisations in 2013/14.
**HOW TO APPLY** Apply in writing to correspondent. The secretary scrutinises and collates applications in preparation for the trustee meetings. The trustees meet three times each year, usually in April, August and December and they consider all applications.
**WHO TO APPLY TO** The Secretary, PO Box 661, West Broyle, Chichester PO19 9JS

## ■ The Earl Fitzwilliam Charitable Trust

**CC NO** 269388      **ESTABLISHED** 1975
**WHERE FUNDING CAN BE GIVEN** UK, with a preference for areas with historical family connections, chiefly in Cambridgeshire, Northamptonshire and Yorkshire.
**WHO CAN BENEFIT** Registered charities and community groups.
**WHAT IS FUNDED** Preference for charitable projects in areas with historical family connections, chiefly in Cambridgeshire, Northamptonshire and Yorkshire. Particularly charities working in the fields of: accommodation and housing; infrastructure, support and development; Christian outreach; churches; religious umbrella bodies; arts, culture and recreation; health facilities and buildings; cancer research; conservation and environment; schools and colleges; and various community facilities and services.
**WHAT IS NOT FUNDED** Individuals.
**TYPE OF GRANT** Buildings, capital, endowments, one-off, project and research.
**RANGE OF GRANTS** Up to £30,000 but generally £300–£5,000.
**SAMPLE GRANTS** Malton Amenity CIC (£30,000); Peterborough Cathedral Development and Preservation Trust (£20,000); Hunt Servants' Fund (£11,000); Game and Wildlife Conservation Trust (£10,000); St John's Hospice (£5,000); East of England Agricultural Society (£4,000); Countryside Alliance Foundation (£3,000); Deafblind UK (£2,500); Heather Trust (£2,000); Spinal Injuries Association (£1,000); YMCA White Rose (£500); Macmillan Cancer Support (£250).
**FINANCES** *Year* 2013/14 *Income* £189,082 *Grants* £159,487 *Grants to organisations* £159,487 *Assets* £14,067,970
**TRUSTEES** Sir Philip Naylor-Leyland; Lady Isabella Naylor-Leyland.
**OTHER INFORMATION** Grants were made to 76 organisations in 2013/14.
**HOW TO APPLY** Apply in writing to the correspondent. The trustees meet about every three months.
**WHO TO APPLY TO** R. Dalgleish, Secretary to the Trustees, Estate Office, Milton Park, Peterborough PE3 9HD *Tel.* 01733 267740 *email* agent@miltonestate.co.uk

## ■ The Ian Fleming Charitable Trust

**CC NO** 263327  **ESTABLISHED** 1971
**WHERE FUNDING CAN BE GIVEN** UK.
**WHO CAN BENEFIT** Individual musicians and registered charities benefitting medical professionals, research workers and scientists. Support is also given to at risk groups, and people who are disabled, disadvantaged by poverty or socially isolated.
**WHAT IS FUNDED** National charities actively operating for the support, relief and welfare of men, women and children who are disabled or otherwise in need of help, care and attention, and charities actively engaged in research on human diseases; and music education awards under a scheme administered by the Musicians Benevolent Fund and advised by a committee of experts in the field of music.
**WHAT IS NOT FUNDED** Individuals (except under the music education award scheme); purely local charities.
**RANGE OF GRANTS** £1,500
**FINANCES** *Year* 2012/13 *Income* £46,286 *Grants* £30,000 *Grants to organisations* £30,000 *Assets* £1,131,418
**TRUSTEES** Archibald Fleming; A. Isaacs; Gordon Wyllie.
**OTHER INFORMATION** The 2012/13 accounts were the latest available at the time of writing (June 2015).
**HOW TO APPLY** Apply in writing to the correspondent.
**WHO TO APPLY TO** Archibald Fleming, Trustee, Hays Macintyre, 26 Red Lion Square, London WC1R 4AG *Tel.* 020 7969 5500 *email* dmcgowan@haysmacintyre.com

## ■ The Joyce Fletcher Charitable Trust

**CC NO** 297901  **ESTABLISHED** 1987
**WHERE FUNDING CAN BE GIVEN** England, almost entirely south west.
**WHO CAN BENEFIT** England-wide and South West charities with a preference towards young people and those with disabilities.
**WHAT IS FUNDED** Music in the community and in a special needs context; children's welfare; and charities in the south west. Currently main areas of interest are institutions and organisations specialising in music education and performance, special needs education and performance involving music, and charities for children's welfare.
**WHAT IS NOT FUNDED** Grants to individuals and students are exceptionally rare. No support is given for areas which are the responsibility of the local authority. No support is given to purely professional music/arts promotions. No support is given for purely medical research charities.
**TYPE OF GRANT** One-off and recurring expenses; capital and revenue; or new projects.
**RANGE OF GRANTS** £500–£5,000
**SAMPLE GRANTS** Bath Festivals and Welsh National Opera (£5,000 each); Wiltshire Music Centre Trust (£4,000); Buxton Festival (£3,000); Bath Mozartfest, Quartet Community Foundation and Young Classical Artists Trust (£2,000 each); Friends of Music at Wells Cathedral School, Live Wire Theatre Company, Magdalen Environmental Trust (£1,000 each).
**FINANCES** *Year* 2013/14 *Income* £80,665 *Grants* £73,000 *Grants to organisations* £73,000 *Assets* £2,323,784
**TRUSTEES** Robert Fletcher; Stephen Fletcher; Susan Sharp; William Fletcher.

**OTHER INFORMATION** A good proportion are repeat grants, and only eight out of the 34 grants made were new in 203/14.
**HOW TO APPLY** Apply in writing to the correspondent before 1 November each year. Applications are considered in the months of October and November. There are no application forms. Letters should include the purpose for the grant, an indication of the history and viability of the organisation and a summary of accounts. Preliminary telephone calls are accepted. Applications via email will not be acknowledged.
**WHO TO APPLY TO** Robert Fletcher, Trustee, 68 Circus Mews, Bath BA1 2PW *Tel.* 01225 314355 *Website* www.joycefletchercharitabletrust.co.uk

## ■ Florence's Charitable Trust

**CC NO** 265754  **ESTABLISHED** 1973
**WHERE FUNDING CAN BE GIVEN** UK with a preference for Lancashire.
**WHO CAN BENEFIT** Individuals, registered charities and charitable organisations.
**WHAT IS FUNDED** General charitable purposes, especially establishment, maintenance and support of places of education; relief of sickness of infirmity for older people; and relief of poverty of anyone employed or formerly employed in the shoe trade.
**TYPE OF GRANT** One-off grants.
**RANGE OF GRANTS** £50–£30,000
**SAMPLE GRANTS** Pioneer Community Club; Bacup Family Centre; Whitworth Water Ski; Rossendale Search and Rescue; Rossendale United Junior Football Club; North West Air Ambulance; British Heart Foundation; Rochdale Special Needs; Macmillan Cancer Support; Children with AIDS; SENSE; Tenovus; All Black Netball Fund; Sport Relief; Heart of Lancashire appeal.
**FINANCES** *Year* 2013/14 *Income* £52,154 *Grants* £72,746 *Grants to organisations* £72,746 *Assets* £1,053,678
**TRUSTEES** Christopher Harrison; Gordon Dewhirst Low; Bob Uttley; Michael Kelly; Simon Holding; Angela Jepson.
**OTHER INFORMATION** The trust made grants to 66 organisations in 2013/14.
**HOW TO APPLY** Apply in writing only to the correspondent (no telephone calls please).
**WHO TO APPLY TO** Brian Terry, Correspondent, E. Suttons and Sons Ltd, PO Box 2, Bacup OL13 0DT *Tel.* 01706 874961 *email* ajepson@esutton.co.uk

## ■ The Flow Foundation

**CC NO** 328274  **ESTABLISHED** 1989
**WHERE FUNDING CAN BE GIVEN** UK.
**WHO CAN BENEFIT** Registered charities and community groups.
**WHAT IS FUNDED** General charitable purposes.
**RANGE OF GRANTS** Usually up to £20,000.
**SAMPLE GRANTS** Imperial College (£143,000); Westminster School (£15,000); Norwood Ravenswood and The Tate Foundation (£10,000 each); British ORT and Sight Savers (£5,000 each); Families of the Fallen and The British Friends of Haifa University (£2,500 each); and Leuka (£1,000).
**FINANCES** *Year* 2013/14 *Income* £11,248 *Grants* £250,000 *Grants to organisations* £250,000
**TRUSTEES** Nathalie Shashou; Nita Sowerbutts; Harold Woolf; Josiane Woolf.
**HOW TO APPLY** Apply in writing to the correspondent on one sheet of paper only.

WHO TO APPLY TO Nita Sowerbutts, Trustee, Flat 44, Crown Lodge, 12 Elystan Street, London SW3 3PP  Tel. 020 7499 9099

## ■ The Gerald Fogel Charitable Trust

CC NO 1004451        ESTABLISHED 1991
WHERE FUNDING CAN BE GIVEN UK.
WHO CAN BENEFIT Mainly headquarters organisations benefitting: children and older people, those in care, fostered and adopted, Jewish people and homeless people.
WHAT IS FUNDED The advancement of the Jewish religion; synagogues; and cultural and religious teaching. The trust may also fund residential facilities; arts activities; care in the community; hospices; hospitals; cancer research and campaigning on health issues.
WHAT IS NOT FUNDED Individuals; non-registered charities.
TYPE OF GRANT One-off and recurrent.
RANGE OF GRANTS Up to £70,000 but generally £1,000–£5,000.
SAMPLE GRANTS Chai Cancer Care (£71,000 in five grants); Jewish Childs Day (£6,000); Norwood and World Jewish Relief (£5,000 each); British Red Cross (£2,000 in two grants); United Jewish Israel Appeal (£1,600 in three grants); Alzheimer's Research (£1,400 in two grants); Community Security Trust, Magen David Adom and Save the Children Fund (£1,000 each).
FINANCES Year 2013/14 Income £77,139 Grants £103,380 Grants to organisations £103,380 Assets £909,107
TRUSTEES David Fogel; Joseph Fogel; Steven Fogel; Benita Fogel.
OTHER INFORMATION Grants were made to 12 organisations in 2013/14.
HOW TO APPLY Apply in writing to the correspondent.
WHO TO APPLY TO David Truman, Correspondent, Menzies LLP, Lynton House, 7–12 Tavistock Square, London WC1H 9LT  Tel. 020 7387 5868  email dtruman@menzies.co.uk

## ■ The Follett Trust

CC NO 328638        ESTABLISHED 1990
WHERE FUNDING CAN BE GIVEN UK and overseas, with a preference for Stevenage in the UK.
WHO CAN BENEFIT Registered charities; community groups and individuals.
WHAT IS FUNDED Education; individual students in higher education (including theatre); disability and health; trusts for writers and publishers; international relief work.
RANGE OF GRANTS Usually up to £25,000.
SAMPLE GRANTS Their World (£25,000); Canon Collins Educational Trust (£19,000); Impilo Place of Safety (£16,900); Tanzilla Lorenz (£15,600); University College (£13,000); Stevenage Community Trust (£11,000); Donald Woods Foundation (£10,000); Dying in Dignity (£6,000); Springfield House (£5,000); The Samburu Project (£4,000); Tracks Autism and Womankind Worldwide (£1,000 each).
FINANCES Year 2013/14 Income £173,818 Grants £210,837 Grants to organisations £174,972 Assets £61,018
TRUSTEES Brian Mitchell; Ken Follett; Barbara Follett.
OTHER INFORMATION Grants were made to over 32 organisations in 2013/14.
HOW TO APPLY The trust states, 'A high proportion of donees come to the attention of the trustees through personal knowledge and contact rather than by written application. Where the trustees find it impossible to make a donation they rarely respond to the applicant unless a stamped addressed envelope is provided.'
WHO TO APPLY TO Brian Mitchell, Trustee, The Follet Office, Broadlands House, Primett Road, Stevenage, Hertfordshire SG1 3EE  Tel. 01438 810400  email folletttrust@thefollettoffice.com

## ■ The Football Association National Sports Centre Trust

CC NO 265132        ESTABLISHED 1972
WHERE FUNDING CAN BE GIVEN UK.
WHO CAN BENEFIT County football associations, football clubs and other sports associations.
WHAT IS FUNDED The provision, maintenance and improvement of facilities for use in recreational and leisure activities.
WHAT IS NOT FUNDED Individuals.
TYPE OF GRANT One-off grants towards community-based projects.
SAMPLE GRANTS The National Football Centre Limited (£3.8 million).
FINANCES Year 2013/14 Income £8,356 Grants £3,919,177 Grants to organisations £3,919,177 Assets £629,875
TRUSTEES Geoff Thompson; Barry Bright; Raymond Berridge; William Annable; Jack Perks.
HOW TO APPLY Apply in writing to the correspondent.
WHO TO APPLY TO Richard McDermott, Secretary to the Trustees, Wembley National Stadium Ltd, PO Box 1966, London SW1P 9EQ  Tel. 0844 980 8200 ext. 6575  email richard.mcdermott@thefa.com

## ■ The Football Association Youth Trust

CC NO 265131        ESTABLISHED 1972
WHERE FUNDING CAN BE GIVEN UK.
WHO CAN BENEFIT County football associations, schools, universities and other sports associations benefitting young people who play football or other sports.
WHAT IS FUNDED The organisation or provision of facilities which will enable young people under the age of 21 in the UK to play association football or other games and sports including the provision of equipment, lectures, training colleges, playing fields or indoor accommodation.
TYPE OF GRANT One-off.
SAMPLE GRANTS County football associations (£132,000).
FINANCES Year 2013/14 Income £964 Grants £132,197 Grants to organisations £132,197 Assets £116,316
TRUSTEES Raymond Berridge; Barry Bright; Geoff Thompson; Mervyn Leggett; Brian Adshead.
OTHER INFORMATION Grants were made to 41 county football associations in 2013/14.
HOW TO APPLY Apply in writing to the correspondent. Grants are made throughout the year. There are no application forms, but a copy of the most recent accounts should be sent.
WHO TO APPLY TO Richard McDermott, Secretary, Wembley National Stadium Ltd, PO Box 1966, London SW1P 9EQ  Tel. 0844 980 8200 ext. 6575  email richard.mcdermott@thefa.com

## ■ The Football Foundation

**CC NO** 1079309 **ESTABLISHED** 2000
**WHERE FUNDING CAN BE GIVEN** England.
**WHO CAN BENEFIT** Charitable organisations; councils; schools; sports clubs.
**WHAT IS FUNDED** The development of new and refurbished grassroots sports facilities improving the quality and experience of playing sport at the grassroots level to sustain and increase participation and improve general skills levels.
**RANGE OF GRANTS** Up to £620,000.
**SAMPLE GRANTS** CB Hounslow United FC (£622,500); Trinity Christian Centre (£492,500); Everton in the Community (£350,000); Southwark Council (£250,000); Charles Darwin School (£160,000); Lea Rowing Club (£100,000); Teachsport (£70,000); The Ainsdale Sport and Social Club (£66,000); The Avenue Tennis Club (£50,000); Cray Valley Bowls Club (£4,500).
**FINANCES** Year 2013/14 Income £31,398,000 Grants £25,249,000 Grants to organisations £25,249,000 Assets £14,973,000
**TRUSTEES** Richard Scudamore; Roger Burden; Peter McCormick; Richard Caborn; Jonathan Hall; Gary Hoffman; Rona Chester.
**OTHER INFORMATION** See the foundation's website for full details of the current schemes.
**HOW TO APPLY** Applications are submitted online. Detailed guidance notes are available on the website.
**WHO TO APPLY TO** Rupen Shah, Whittington House, 19–30 Alfred Place, London WC1E 7EA Tel. 0845 345 4555 email enquiries@footballfoundation.org.uk Website www.footballfoundation.org.uk

## ■ The Forbes Charitable Foundation

**CC NO** 326476 **ESTABLISHED** 1983
**WHERE FUNDING CAN BE GIVEN** UK.
**WHO CAN BENEFIT** Charitable organisations.
**WHAT IS FUNDED** Welfare causes primarily benefitting people with learning disabilities.
**WHAT IS NOT FUNDED** Support is only given to charitable organisations whose work primarily benefits people with learning disabilities.
**TYPE OF GRANT** Capital and some revenue costs.
**RANGE OF GRANTS** Up to £180,000 but generally £1,000 to £10,000.
**SAMPLE GRANTS** Care Fund Limited (£183,000); Cottage and Rural Enterprises (£35,000); The Lodge Trust (£10,000); Action for Kids, Bedfordshire Garden Carers and Garvald Ltd (£5,000 each); Thrive (£4,000); Open Minds (£3,500); Where Next Association (£2,000); Redwoods Caring Foundation (£1,500); Camberley Mencap (£1,000).
**FINANCES** Year 2013/14 Income £198,347 Grants £357,531 Grants to organisations £357,531 Assets £5,664,513
**TRUSTEES** John Waite; C. Packham; Nicolas Townsend; Ian Johnson; John Williamson; Robert Bunting.
**OTHER INFORMATION** Grants were made to 39 organisations in 2013/14.
**HOW TO APPLY** Apply in writing to the correspondent. Applications should be received close to but no later than the last day of February, June or October. A copy of the latest accounts should be provided along with the application form. Application forms can be obtained from the foundation's website or in writing to the correspondent. Successful applicants will be expected to justify the expenditure of the grant given.
**WHO TO APPLY TO** John Shepherd, Correspondent, PO Box 6256, Nuneaton CV11 9HT Tel. 01455 292881 email info@theforbescharitablefoundation.org Website www.theforbescharitablefoundation.org

## ■ Ford Britain Trust

**CC NO** 269410 **ESTABLISHED** 1975
**WHERE FUNDING CAN BE GIVEN** Local to the areas in close proximity to Ford Motor Company Limited's locations in the UK. These are Essex (including East London), Bridgend, Southampton and Daventry.
**WHO CAN BENEFIT** Registered charities; schools; non-profit organisations.
**WHAT IS FUNDED** Education; the environment; children; disabilities; youth education; projects that benefit the local communities that Ford operates in.
**WHAT IS NOT FUNDED** Major building works; sponsorship or advertising; research; overseas projects; travel; religious projects; political projects; purchase of second hand vehicles; third party fundraising initiatives (exceptions may be made for fundraising initiatives by Ford Motor Company Limited employees and retirees). National charities are assisted rarely and then only when the purpose of their application has specific benefit to communities located in close proximity to Ford locations. Applications for core funding and major building projects are rarely considered. Grants cannot be provided to individuals.
**TYPE OF GRANT** Contributions to capital projects (e.g. refurbishments); capital expenditure items (e.g. furniture/equipment/computers); contributions towards the purchase or leasing of new Ford vehicles (up to a maximum of £2,000); and general funds (small grants up to £250 only).
**RANGE OF GRANTS** Most grants range between £250 and £4,000.
**SAMPLE GRANTS** Malayalee Association of the UK (£3,100); Ashlawn School, Nantymoel Primary School, Pavilion Pirates Preschool (£3,000 each); Belchamps Scout Activity Centre, Havering Citizens Advice, (£2,700 each); Oldcastle Primary School, Thames Tennants and Residents Association (£2,500 each); SNAP (£2,400); and Ian Mikadro Primary School (£2,300).
**FINANCES** Year 2013/14 Income £161,163 Grants £119,060 Grants to organisations £119,060 Assets £338,003
**TRUSTEES** Michael Callaghan; David Russell; Michael Brophy; Dr June-Alison Sealy; Wendy James; Jane Skerry; Paul Bailey; Lara Nicoll.
**OTHER INFORMATION** This is the charitable trust of Ford Motor Company Ltd.
**HOW TO APPLY** Applications can be made in three ways: download the PDF version from the website to print out, complete and return by post to the correspondence address; save the Word version to your computer, complete it electronically and return it by email to fbtrust@ford.com; request a paper copy on 01277 252551 to complete and return by post to the correspondence address. Applications for large grants should include a copy of the organisation's most recent report and accounts. Small grant applications are considered in March, June, September and November and should be submitted by the 1st of each month. Applications for large grants are considered in March and September.

**WHO TO APPLY TO** Gary Smith, Correspondent, Room 1/445, c/o Ford Motor Company Limited, Eagle Way, Brentwood, Essex CM13 3BW *Tel.* 01268 404831 *email* fbtrust@ford.com *Website* www.ford.co.uk/fbtrust

## ■ The Oliver Ford Charitable Trust

**CC NO** 1026551  **ESTABLISHED** 1993
**WHERE FUNDING CAN BE GIVEN** UK.
**WHO CAN BENEFIT** Neighbourhood-based community projects, students and institutions. Children, young persons or adults who have learning disabilities or learning difficulties.
**WHAT IS FUNDED** The trust aims to educate the general public and advance knowledge of the history and techniques of interior decoration, the design of fabrics and other decorative materials and landscape gardening. Charities providing housing, educational or training facilities for children, young persons or adults who have learning disabilities or learning difficulties.
**TYPE OF GRANT** One-off.
**RANGE OF GRANTS** £2,000–£10,000
**SAMPLE GRANTS** Scotts Project Trust (£10,000); L'Arche; Livability; MacIntyre; Martha Trust; Scotts Project Trust (£5,000 each); Norman Laud Association (£4,500); Scottish Autism (£4,000); The Roy Kinnear Charitable Foundation (£2,500).
**FINANCES** *Year* 2013/14 *Income* £102,871 *Grants* £88,537 *Grants to organisations* £56,500 *Assets* £2,659,919
**TRUSTEES** Lady Wakeham; Martin Levy.
**OTHER INFORMATION** Grants were also given to students at the Furniture and History Society (£3,000); the Royal Horticultural Society (£5,000); and the Victoria and Albert Museum (£24,000).
**HOW TO APPLY** Apply in writing to the correspondent. The trustees meet in March and October.
**WHO TO APPLY TO** Matthew Pintus, Correspondent, 20 Cursitor Street, London EC4A 1LT *Tel.* 020 7831 9222 *email* ed.kisby@macfarlanes.com

## ■ Fordeve Limited

**CC NO** 1011612  **ESTABLISHED** 1992
**WHERE FUNDING CAN BE GIVEN** UK.
**WHO CAN BENEFIT** Organisations benefitting Jews, at risk groups and people who are unemployed, disadvantaged by poverty or socially isolated. Support may also be given to people who are disabled, homeless, immigrants or refugees.
**WHAT IS FUNDED** Orthodox Jewish causes.
**SAMPLE GRANTS** The Gertner Charitable Trust; Lubavitch Foundation; the Yom Tov Assistance Fund; the Society of Friends of the Torah; Lolev Charitable Trust; Beth Jacob Grammar School for Girls.
**FINANCES** *Year* 2013/14 *Income* £77,802 *Grants* £85,766 *Grants to organisations* £85,766 *Assets* £642,547
**TRUSTEES** Jeremy Kon; Helen Kon.
**HOW TO APPLY** Apply in writing to the correspondent.
**WHO TO APPLY TO** Jeremy Kon, Trustee, Hallswelle House, 1 Hallswelle Road, London NW11 0DH *Tel.* 020 8209 1535

## ■ The Forest Hill Charitable Trust

**CC NO** 1050862  **ESTABLISHED** 1995
**WHERE FUNDING CAN BE GIVEN** UK and overseas.
**WHO CAN BENEFIT** Organisations and individuals.
**WHAT IS FUNDED** Christian causes.
**RANGE OF GRANTS** Grants usually range between £1,000 and £2,000.
**SAMPLE GRANTS** LiNX (£24,000); Great Parks Chapel (£5,000); Barnabas Fund (£3,000); Christian Blind Mission (£2,000); Christian Vision for Men (£1,500); ChildHope, Hand in Hand, Keychange, Prison Fellowship, Time for Families, (£1,000 each).
**FINANCES** *Year* 2013/14 *Income* £161,478 *Grants* £168,660 *Grants to organisations* £168,660 *Assets* £3,431,070
**TRUSTEES** Horace Francis Pile; Ronald Stanley Pile; Marianne Sylvia Tapper; Michael Thomas; Patricia Jean Pile.
**HOW TO APPLY** The trustees have previously stated that their aim was to maintain regular and consistent support to the charities they are currently supporting. New requests for funding are therefore very unlikely to succeed and unsolicited applications are rarely considered.
**WHO TO APPLY TO** Dr Francis Horace Pile, Trustee, Little Bluff, Treknow, Tintagel, Cornwall PL34 0EP *Tel.* 01840 779405 *email* horacepile@tiscali.co.uk

## ■ The Lady Forester Trust

**CC NO** 241187  **ESTABLISHED** 1979
**WHERE FUNDING CAN BE GIVEN** Shropshire.
**WHO CAN BENEFIT** Primarily, the residents of the Parish of Wenlock and then the inhabitants of the County of Shropshire.
**WHAT IS FUNDED** Relief in sickness; convalescence; disability.
**RANGE OF GRANTS** £1,000–£5,000
**SAMPLE GRANTS** Blind Veterans – Llandudno and Oswestry None Cancer Appeal (£5,000 each); Help for Heroes (£4,000); Home Start – Bridgnorth (£3,000); Age UK Telford and Wrekin and County Air Ambulance (£2,000); Changing Faces (£1,500); Acorns Children's Hospital Trust, Dystonia Society and the Firefighters Charity (£1,000 each).
**FINANCES** *Year* 2013/14 *Income* £152,661 *Grants* £146,729 *Grants to organisations* £87,190 *Assets* £4,994,212
**TRUSTEES** Lady Catherine Forester; The Hon. Alice Stoker; Libby Collinson; John Dugdale; Henry Carpenter; Lord Forester; The Lady Forester; Janette Stewart.
**OTHER INFORMATION** In 2013/14 grants to over 33 organisations totalled £93,500 and grants to 117 individuals totalled £59,500.
**HOW TO APPLY** Trustees meet on a quarterly basis to consider applications and will consider unsolicited applications. Grants for individuals are usually recommended by GPs or social workers. Application should be made in writing to the correspondent.
**WHO TO APPLY TO** Lady Forester, Chair, The Estate Office, Willey, Broseley, Shropshire TF12 5JN *Tel.* 01952 884318

## ■ Forever Manchester (The Community Foundation for Greater Manchester)

**CC NO** 1017504      **ESTABLISHED** 1993

**WHERE FUNDING CAN BE GIVEN** Greater Manchester.

**WHO CAN BENEFIT** Registered charities and small, locally run community or voluntary groups who seek to improve the circumstances in economically and socially excluded areas in Greater Manchester facing disadvantage.

**WHAT IS FUNDED** General charitable purposes; health; welfare; education; people with disabilities; older people; youth and children. Improving the quality of life and helping to build stronger communities across Greater Manchester.

**WHAT IS NOT FUNDED** Organisations and projects outside the Greater Manchester area; large organisations including those with a track record of attracting funding or a turnover of more than £150,000 per annum.

**TYPE OF GRANT** One-off; project. Start-up costs will be considered.

**RANGE OF GRANTS** Mostly under £5,000 but can be up to £40,000, depending on the scheme.

**SAMPLE GRANTS** Association of the friends of Hollingworth Lake; Capoeira Conviver; Cheadle Golf Club; Incredible Education CIC; Mode Rehabilitation; Odd Theatre CIC; Oldham Carnival; Standish Lipreading Society; WAVE Adventure; Women Integration Project.

**FINANCES** *Year* 2013/14 *Income* £3,076,143 *Grants* £1,298,629 *Grants to organisations* £1,298,629 *Assets* £9,643,679

**TRUSTEES** Philp Hogben; Sandra Lindsay; Andrea Harrison; Roushon Ahmed; Rachel Smith; Alan Mackin; Jo Farrell.

**OTHER INFORMATION** Grants were made to 760 organisations in 2013/14.

**HOW TO APPLY** Contact the wards team on 0161 214 0940 to discuss deadline dates, eligibility and criteria and to receive guidelines and an application pack.

**WHO TO APPLY TO** Nick Massey, Chief Executive Officer, 2nd Floor, 8 Hewitt Street, Manchester M15 4GB *Tel.* 0161 214 0940 *email* info@forevermanchester.com *Website* www.forevermanchester.com

## ■ The Forman Hardy Charitable Trust

**CC NO** 1000687      **ESTABLISHED** 1990

**WHERE FUNDING CAN BE GIVEN** Nottinghamshire.

**WHO CAN BENEFIT** Registered charities and community groups.

**WHAT IS FUNDED** The charitable needs of the city of Nottingham and the county of Nottinghamshire.

**RANGE OF GRANTS** £1,000–£10,000

**SAMPLE GRANTS** Hint – Base 51 (£10,000); Aysgarth School (£8,000); Hatch – Barnwell Charitable Trust, Sonagachi Sex Workers School Project, NCCL Galleries of Justice and Midlands Appeal for Sri Lanka (£5,000 each); Opera North Limited and The Jennie Marsh Trust (£2,000 each) and National Schools Symphony Orchestra, Relate Nottinghamshire, St Edmund Hall Oxford Boat Club, The British Forces Foundation and The Play Centre (£1,000 each).

**FINANCES** *Year* 2013/14 *Income* £19,646 *Grants* £65,000 *Grants to organisations* £65,000

**TRUSTEES** Nicholas Forman Hardy; Jane Forman Hardy; Charles Bennion; Canon James Neale.

**HOW TO APPLY** Apply in writing to the correspondent.

**WHO TO APPLY TO** Rachael Sulley, Correspondent, 64 St James's Street, Nottingham NG1 6FJ *Tel.* 0115 950 8580 *email* rachaels@formanhardy.com

## ■ Gwyneth Forrester Trust

**CC NO** 1080921      **ESTABLISHED** 2000

**WHERE FUNDING CAN BE GIVEN** England and Wales.

**WHO CAN BENEFIT** Charitable organisations.

**WHAT IS FUNDED** The trustees support a specific charitable sector each year.

**WHAT IS NOT FUNDED** Individuals.

**TYPE OF GRANT** One-off.

**RANGE OF GRANTS** Up to £60,000.

**SAMPLE GRANTS** CLIC Sargent, Great Ormond Street Children's Hospice, Kids Company, Prince's Trust (£60,000 each); Claire House Children's Hospice (£50,000); Sick Children's Trust (£40,000); Chicks (£35,000); Medical Engineering Resource Unit and Keep Out (£30,000 each); Starche (£25,000).

**FINANCES** *Year* 2013/14 *Income* £491,035 *Grants* £450,000 *Grants to organisations* £450,000 *Assets* £23,044,426

**TRUSTEES** Anthony Smee; Wendy Forrester; Adrian Hollands; Hilary Porter; Melissa Jones.

**OTHER INFORMATION** No information was available on the future focus of the trust's grant-making as 'once the charitable sector is chosen, we research that sector and produce a list of possibles and then contact the individual charities to discuss with them their particular needs and any specific projects they have in hand. These are then discussed and the final grant list is decided'.

**HOW TO APPLY** The trust has previously stated that 'applications for aid cannot be considered'.

**WHO TO APPLY TO** Adrian Hollands, Trustee, 11 Whitecroft Way, Beckenham, Kent BR3 3AQ *Tel.* 020 8228 1185 *email* ah.fe@outlook.com

## ■ The Donald Forrester Trust

**CC NO** 295833      **ESTABLISHED** 1986

**WHERE FUNDING CAN BE GIVEN** UK and overseas.

**WHO CAN BENEFIT** Charities and community groups.

**WHAT IS FUNDED** Charities benefitting animals and birds; blind and deaf people; children and youth; community care and social welfare; culture, heritage and environment; hospices and hospitals; maritime; medical relief and welfare; medical research; older people; physical and mental disability; services and ex-services; overseas.

**WHAT IS NOT FUNDED** Individuals.

**TYPE OF GRANT** One off and recurrent.

**RANGE OF GRANTS** Grants are usually for either £5,000 or £10,000.

**SAMPLE GRANTS** DEC Philippines (£20,000); Action for Hearing Loss, Ahoy Centre, Fanshare, Peace Hospice, Vitalise (£10,000 each); Action on Hearing Loss, Children's Trust, Combat Stress, Eastern Angels, National Churches Trust, Myeloma UK and St Christopher's Hospice (£5,000 each).

**FINANCES** *Year* 2013/14 *Income* £733,482 *Grants* £695,000 *Grants to organisations* £695,000 *Assets* £7,924,938

**TRUSTEES** Anthony Smee; Wendy Forrester; Hilary Porter; Melissa Jones; Adrian Hollands.

**OTHER INFORMATION** Grants were made to 110 organisations in 2013/14.

**HOW TO APPLY** The trust's latest annual report notes that due to an increase in the number of applications received by the trust, 'we prioritise

the awarding of grants to charities we've regularly supported in the past, and there is therefore limited scope to consider other charities. Please note therefore that as an immediate change of policy, no unsolicited grant applications will now be considered, other than from charities we've supported in the past.'
**WHO TO APPLY TO** Adrian Hollands, Trustee, 11 Whitecroft Way, Beckenham, Kent BR3 3AQ *Tel.* 020 8228 1185 *email* ah.fe@outlook.com

## ■ The Anna Rosa Forster Charitable Trust
**CC NO** 1090028     **ESTABLISHED** 1996
**WHERE FUNDING CAN BE GIVEN** Worldwide.
**WHO CAN BENEFIT** Charitable organisations.
**WHAT IS FUNDED** Medical research; animal welfare; famine relief.
**RANGE OF GRANTS** Usually between £2,500 and £3,500.
**SAMPLE GRANTS** Alzheimer's Research Trust, Cancer Research UK; British Red Cross; Farm Africa; Cats Protection League; CARE International UK; Motor Neurone Disease Association; the Donkey Sanctuary; PDSA; RSPCA; International Spinal Research Trust; the World Medical Fund.
**FINANCES** Year 2013/14 Income £91,319 Grants £106,320 Grants to organisations £106,320 Assets £2,354,475
**TRUSTEES** Roger Napier; Andrew Morgan.
**OTHER INFORMATION** The trust divides its income equally between animal welfare, famine relief and medical research.
**HOW TO APPLY** Applications can be made in writing to the correspondent.
**WHO TO APPLY TO** Roger Napier, Trustee, c/o R. W. Napier Solicitors, Floor E, Milburn House, Dean Street, Newcastle upon Tyne NE1 1LF *Tel.* 0191 230 1819 *email* rogerw.napier@gmail.com

## ■ The Fort Foundation
**CC NO** 1028639     **ESTABLISHED** 1993
**WHERE FUNDING CAN BE GIVEN** North east Lancashire.
**WHO CAN BENEFIT** Organisations supporting young people and individuals.
**WHAT IS FUNDED** Education and training of young people.
**WHAT IS NOT FUNDED** Education fees.
**TYPE OF GRANT** One-off.
**RANGE OF GRANTS** Up to £7,200.
**SAMPLE GRANTS** Royal Yachting Association (£7,200); Marine Society and Sea Cadets (£5,700); Holy Trinity Church, Colne and HMS Portland (£5,000 each); Etchells Cowes Fleet (£4,000); Burwain Sailing Club and DecAid (£3,000 each); Ridgewood Community High School (£2,500); Community Foundation for Lancashire (£2,000); Teenage Cancer Trust and the Charlie Wailer Memorial Trust (£1,500); and Pendle Croquet Club, Lancashire Wildlife Trust and University of Central Lancashire (£1,000 each).
**FINANCES** Year 2013/14 Income £308,073 Grants £133,279 Grants to organisations £127,984 Assets £674,443
**TRUSTEES** Edward Fort; Ian Wilson; Susan Friedlander.
**OTHER INFORMATION** £10,000 of the grant total was awarded to individuals.
**HOW TO APPLY** Apply in writing to the correspondent.
**WHO TO APPLY TO** Edward Fort, Correspondent, c/o Fort Vale Engineering Ltd, Calder Vale Park, Simonstone Lane, Simonstone, Burnley BB12 7ND *Tel.* 01282 440000 *email* info@fortvale.com

## ■ The Forte Charitable Trust
**CC NO** 326038     **ESTABLISHED** 1982
**WHERE FUNDING CAN BE GIVEN** UK and overseas.
**WHO CAN BENEFIT** Community-based projects and national organisations and institutions.
**WHAT IS FUNDED** The Roman Catholic faith, Alzheimer's disease and senile dementia.
**FINANCES** Year 2013/14 Income £19,531 Grants £65,000 Grants to organisations £65,000
**TRUSTEES** Sir Rocco Forte; Lowndes Trustee Limited; The Hon Olga Polizzi de Sorrentino.
**OTHER INFORMATION** Information was provided by the trust.
**HOW TO APPLY** Apply in writing to the correspondent.
**WHO TO APPLY TO** Judy Lewendon, Correspondent, Rocco Forte Hotels Ltd, 70 Jermyn Street, London SW1Y 6NY *Tel.* 020 7321 2626 *email* jlewendon@roccofortehotels.com

## ■ The Lord Forte Foundation
**CC NO** 298100     **ESTABLISHED** 1987
**WHERE FUNDING CAN BE GIVEN** UK.
**WHO CAN BENEFIT** Educational establishments.
**WHAT IS FUNDED** Training courses and research in the field of hotel management, catering and the travel and tourism industries.
**TYPE OF GRANT** Up to three years.
**RANGE OF GRANTS** Up to £20,000.
**SAMPLE GRANTS** University of West London and Westminster Kingsway College (£20,000 each); WC General Charity Fund (£10,000); The Wine Guild Charitable Trust (£9,000); Springboard Charitable Trust (£8,300); University of Strathclyde (£3,800); University of Plymouth (£2,800); Evangeline Wells (£3,000).
**FINANCES** Year 2013/14 Income £80,893 Grants £76,770 Grants to organisations £76,770 Assets £2,411,577
**TRUSTEES** Sir Rocco Forte; Nick Scade; Andrew McKenzie; Stephen Mannock; The Hon. Olga Di Sorrentino.
**OTHER INFORMATION** Grants were made to eight educational institutions providing training courses in the hospitality industry.
**HOW TO APPLY** Apply in writing to the correspondent.
**WHO TO APPLY TO** Judy Lewendon, Correspondent, Rocco Forte Hotels Ltd, 70 Jermyn Street, London SW1Y 6NY *email* jlewendon@roccofortehotels.com

## ■ The Four Winds Trust
**CC NO** 262524     **ESTABLISHED** 1971
**WHERE FUNDING CAN BE GIVEN** Worldwide.
**WHO CAN BENEFIT** Registered charities and people working in religion.
**WHAT IS FUNDED** Christian causes and overseas aid, and also grants to retired evangelists and to missionaries and their dependants.
**RANGE OF GRANTS** Up to £5,500.
**SAMPLE GRANTS** Zion Beacon Project (£5,000); South Road Church (£4,000); Farm4Life (£3,500); Counties Evangelistic Work (£3,000); Forest Hill Community Church (£1,000); Paulsgrove Baptist Church (£1,300); Swindon Youth for Christ (£1,100); and St Christopher's Hospice (£1,000).

**FINANCES** Year 2013–14 *Income* £119,820 *Grants* £31,135 *Grants to organisations* £31,135 *Assets* £883,451

**TRUSTEES** Sue Charters; Peter John Charters; Simon Charters; Frances Charters.

**OTHER INFORMATION** The grant total includes grants made to individual evangelists and missionaries totalling £5,250.

**HOW TO APPLY** The trust was set up for purposes in which the trustees have a personal interest and the funds are earmarked for these. Unsolicited requests are unlikely to be considered.

**WHO TO APPLY TO** Simon Charters, Trustee, 64 Station Road, Drayton, Portsmouth PO6 1PJ *email* fourwindstrust1971@gmail.com

---

## ■ The Foyle Foundation

**CC NO** 1081766         **ESTABLISHED** 2000

**WHERE FUNDING CAN BE GIVEN** UK.

**WHO CAN BENEFIT** Registered charities and state schools.

**WHAT IS FUNDED** The following information is taken from the foundation's website: 'The arts – helping to make the arts more accessible by developing new audiences, supporting tours, festivals and arts educational projects; encouraging new work and supporting young and emerging artists; building projects that improve or re-equip existing arts venues (rather than construction of new facilities, although this will not be excluded); projects that reduce overheads or which help generate additional revenue. **Learning** – libraries, museums and archives; special educational needs and learning difficulties; projects that reduce overheads or which help generate additional revenue will also be considered. For state funded schools our main initiative will be The Foyle School Libraries Scheme [special guidance notes are available from the foundation's website]. Dedicated schools catering for those with Special Educational Needs (SEN) may also be supported. Private schools will not generally be supported. Citizenship, esteem-building, training, skills acquisition to aid employment, independent living, early learning projects or playgroups will not generally be considered. **The Small Grants Scheme** is designed to support smaller charities in the UK, especially those working at grass roots and local community level, in any field, across a wide range of activities.'

**WHAT IS NOT FUNDED** Individuals; organisations which are not registered charities; international work; retrospective funding.

**TYPE OF GRANT** Capital, revenue and project funding.

**RANGE OF GRANTS** Up to £250,000.

**SAMPLE GRANTS** Liverpool and Merseyside Theatres Trust Ltd (£250,000); Royal National Theatre (£150,000); Scottish Opera (£125,000); Poetry Society (£80,000); North Music Trust (£30,000); Dance (£22,000); The Barn Theatre Trust (£15,000); Kirklees Theatre Trust (£11,000); Cheviot Primary School (£6,500); Friends of Norden (£5,000).

**FINANCES** Year 2013 *Income* £3,015,445 *Grants* £5,768,800 *Grants to organisations* £576,880 *Assets* £76,501,449

**TRUSTEES** James Korner; Michael Smith; Dr Kathryn Skoyles; Sir Peter Duffell; Roy Amlot.

**OTHER INFORMATION** Grants were made to 381 organisations in 2013/14.

**HOW TO APPLY** The foundation's website states: 'Separate guidelines and application forms are available electronically in Word format for the Main Grants Scheme, Small Grants Scheme and Foyle School Library Scheme. Charities and schools wishing to make an application for funding should download and read the appropriate Guidelines for Applicants before completing and signing the appropriate Application Form and sending this together with the supporting information requested to [the correspondent]. Applications are acknowledged by email or by post within two weeks of receipt. If you do not receive this acknowledgement, please contact The Foundation to confirm safe receipt of your request. Applications are accepted all year round. Except for capital projects, it may take up to four months, occasionally longer, to receive a decision from the Trustees. Please apply well in advance of your funding requirements. Please note for capital projects seeking more than £50,000 the Foundation will now only consider these twice per year in the Spring and Autumn. Therefore it could be six months or more before we take a decision on your project. Guidelines for Applicants and the Application Forms are available in hard copy upon request.'

**WHO TO APPLY TO** David Hall, Chief Executive, Rugby Chambers, 2 Rugby Street, London WC1N 3QU *Tel.* 020 7430 9119 *email* info@foylefoundation.org.uk *Website* www.foylefoundation.org.uk

---

## ■ The Isaac and Freda Frankel Memorial Charitable Trust

**CC NO** 1003732         **ESTABLISHED** 1991

**WHERE FUNDING CAN BE GIVEN** UK and overseas, particularly Israel.

**WHO CAN BENEFIT** Established organisations benefitting children, young adults and people disadvantaged by poverty. People of many different religions and cultures will be funded, but preference is given to Jewish people.

**WHAT IS FUNDED** Jewish charities; medicine and health; education; religion; the relief of poverty.

**WHAT IS NOT FUNDED** No grants are given to individuals or students, for expeditions or scholarships.

**TYPE OF GRANT** One-off and recurrent grants.

**RANGE OF GRANTS** £1,000 or less.

**FINANCES** Year 2012/13 *Income* £26,886 *Grants* £58,526 *Grants to organisations* £58,526 *Assets* £398,286

**TRUSTEES** M. D. Frankel; Geraldine Frankel; J. Steinhaus; J. Silkin.

**OTHER INFORMATION** The 2012/13 accounts were the latest available at the time of writing (June 2015).

**HOW TO APPLY** Apply in writing to the correspondent.

**WHO TO APPLY TO** Montague Frankel, Trustee, 33 Welbeck Street, London W1G 8LX *Tel.* 020 7872 0023 *email* geri120@gmail.com

---

## ■ The Elizabeth Frankland Moore and Star Foundation

**CC NO** 257711         **ESTABLISHED** 1968

**WHERE FUNDING CAN BE GIVEN** UK.

**WHO CAN BENEFIT** Charitable organisations.

**WHAT IS FUNDED** General charitable purposes.

**RANGE OF GRANTS** Up to £25,000.

**SAMPLE GRANTS** Lueka (£25,000); Combat Stress (£15,000); Oasis Children's Venture (£12,500); Homestart UK and The Not Forgotten Association (£10,000 each); Lodging House Mission (£7,500); Teenage Cancer Trust (£5,000); Textile Conservation Fund (£4,000);

Princess Alice Hospice (£2,000); UK Youth (£500).
FINANCES Year 2013/14 Income £291,857 Grants £271,700 Grants to organisations £271,700 Assets £11,005,395
TRUSTEES R. A. Griffiths; Anne Ely; Dr David Spalton; Janine Cameron.
HOW TO APPLY Apply in writing to the correspondent. The trustees meet twice a year.
WHO TO APPLY TO Marianne Neuhoff, Correspondent, Neuhoff and Co, 11 Towcester Road, Whittlebury, Towcester NN12 8XU Tel. 01327 858171

## ■ The Jill Franklin Trust
CC NO 1000175  ESTABLISHED 1988
WHERE FUNDING CAN BE GIVEN UK.
WHO CAN BENEFIT Charitable organisations benefitting: people with disabilities; carers; ex-offenders and those at risk of offending; people with a mental illness; refugees and asylum-seekers.
WHAT IS FUNDED Self-help groups, etc. for people with a mental illness or learning difficulties; holidays for carers to provide respite from their career – this is mainly as a block grant to the Princess Royal Trust for Carers; organisations helping and supporting asylum seekers and refugees coming to the UK; restoration of churches of architectural importance.
WHAT IS NOT FUNDED Appeals for building work; endowment funds; branches of a national organisations, and to the centre itself (unless it is a specific grant, probably for training in the branches); replace the duties of government, local authorities or the NHS; encourage the 'contract culture', particularly where authorities are not funding the contract adequately; religious organisations set up for welfare, education, etc. of whatever religion, unless the service is open to and used by people from all denominations; overseas projects; 'heritage schemes' animal charities; students, nor to any individuals nor for overseas travel; and medical research.
RANGE OF GRANTS Up to £7,000 but generally £500–£1,000.
SAMPLE GRANTS Prisoners Education Trust and Camden City and Islington Bereavement Services (£12,000 each); Princess Royal Trust for Carers (£7,000); Camara (£2,500); City University (£1,800); Arboretum Community Project, Grenfell Centre – Redcar and the Respite Association (£1,000 each).
FINANCES Year 2013/14 Income £70,463 Grants £69,603 Grants to organisations £69,603 Assets £1,702,741
TRUSTEES Sally Franklin; Norman Franklin; Andrew Franklin; Dr Samuel Franklin; Thomas Franklin.
OTHER INFORMATION Grants were made to 69 organisations in 2013/14.
HOW TO APPLY Applications for a church grant should complete the online form on the trust's website. All other applications should be made in writing to the correspondent, enclosing a copy of the latest annual report and accounts and a budget for the project. Organisations based outside the UK should provide the name, address and telephone number of a correspondent or referee in the UK. Unsolicited enquiries are not usually acknowledged.
WHO TO APPLY TO Norman Franklin, Trustee, Flat 5, 17–19 Elsworthy Road, London NW3 3DS Tel. 020 7722 4543 email jft@jill-franklin-trust.org.uk Website www.jill-franklin-trust.org.uk

## ■ The Gordon Fraser Charitable Trust
CC NO 260869  ESTABLISHED 1966
WHERE FUNDING CAN BE GIVEN UK, with a preference for Scotland.
WHO CAN BENEFIT Registered charities only.
WHAT IS FUNDED Children; young people; environment; the arts.
WHAT IS NOT FUNDED Individuals.
RANGE OF GRANTS £100–£13,500, average grant £1,500.
SAMPLE GRANTS National Galleries of Scotland (£9,000); Scottish Opera (£6,500); Royal Scottish National Opera (£4,000); Scottish Ballet (£3,000); Scottish Youth Theatre (£2,000); St Mary's Music School (£1,500); Thrive (£1,000); The Roses Charitable Trust (£800); NSPCC ChildLine (£700); Minimum for Maximum Glasgow Testimony (£600); Marine Conservation Society (£500).
FINANCES Year 2013/14 Income £405,011 Grants £142,000 Grants to organisations £142,000 Assets £3,791,948
TRUSTEES M. A. Moss; W. F. T. Anderson; Sarah Moss; Susannah Rae; Alexander Moss; Alison Priestley.
OTHER INFORMATION Grants were made to 92 organisations in 2013/14.
HOW TO APPLY Apply in writing to the correspondent. Applications are considered in January, April, July and October.
WHO TO APPLY TO Claire Armstrong, Gaidrew Farmhouse, Drymen, Glasgow G63 0DN email georgegeorghiou@mercerhole.co.uk

## ■ The Hugh Fraser Foundation
SC NO SC009303  ESTABLISHED 1960
WHERE FUNDING CAN BE GIVEN UK, especially western or deprived areas of Scotland.
WHO CAN BENEFIT Registered charities working in many different sectors principally hospitals, schools and universities, arts organisations and organisations working with people with disabilities, the underprivileged and older people.
WHAT IS FUNDED Medical facilities and research; relief of poverty and assistance for older and infirm people; education and learning; provision of better opportunities for people who are disadvantaged; music and the arts; encouragement of personal development and training of young people.
WHAT IS NOT FUNDED Grants are only awarded to individuals in exceptional circumstances.
TYPE OF GRANT Capital and revenue grants for up to three years, sometimes longer. Start-up costs.
RANGE OF GRANTS Up to £250,000.
SAMPLE GRANTS Riverside Museum Appeal (£250,000); Inspiring Scotland (£200,000); University of Strathclyde and Beatson Pebble Appeal (£100,000 each); National Museums Scotland (£50,000); and Miss Margaret Kerr Charitable Trust (£40,000).
FINANCES Year 2013/14 Income £2,293,754 Grants £1,511,881 Grants to organisations £1,511,881
TRUSTEES Dr Kenneth Chrystie; Patricia Fraser; Belinda Hanson; Gordon Shearer; Heather Thompson.
OTHER INFORMATION Note: In 2007 the Hugh Fraser Foundation merged with the Emily Fraser Trust, a related charity. As a result the trustees will, in exceptional circumstances, also help individuals and the dependants of individuals who were or are engaged in the drapery and allied trades

463

and the printing, publishing, books and stationery, newspaper and allied trades in the UK.
**HOW TO APPLY** Apply in writing to the correspondent. Applications should also include either a copy of your latest formal accounts if prepared or a copy of your most recent balance sheet, income and expenditure account or bank statement if formal accounts are not prepared. If you are not a registered charity you should also enclose a copy of your constitution or policy statement. The trustees meet quarterly to consider applications in March, June, September and December. Applications should be received early in the preceding month in order to be considered.
**WHO TO APPLY TO** The Trustees, Turcan Connell, Princes Exchange, 1 Earl Grey Street, Edinburgh EH3 9EE *Tel.* 0131 228 8111

### ■ The Joseph Strong Frazer Trust
**CC NO** 235311 **ESTABLISHED** 1939
**WHERE FUNDING CAN BE GIVEN** Unrestricted, in practice, England and Wales.
**WHO CAN BENEFIT** Registered charities only.
**WHAT IS FUNDED** General charitable purposes, with broad interests in the fields of: medical and other research; social welfare; people with disabilities; children; hospitals; education; maritime; youth; religion; wildlife.
**WHAT IS NOT FUNDED** Individuals.
**TYPE OF GRANT** One-off, capital and recurring costs.
**RANGE OF GRANTS** Up to £2,000.
**SAMPLE GRANTS** Addaction, Chance UK, Disabled Living Foundation, Heart Research Fund for Wales, Moorfields Eye Charity, Royal Academy Trust, Spinal Injuries Association, Trinity Hospice, Welsh National Opera (£2,000 each).
**FINANCES** *Year* 2013/14 *Income* £488,726 *Grants* £358,750 *Grants to organisations* £358,750 *Assets* £13,255,796
**TRUSTEES** Sir William A. Reardon Smith, Chair; David A. Cook; R. M. H. Read; William N. H. Reardon Smith; William I. Waites.
**OTHER INFORMATION** Grants were made to 283 organisations in 2013/14.
**HOW TO APPLY** Apply in writing to the correspondent. The trustees meet twice a year, usually in March and September. Application forms are not necessary. It is helpful if applicants are concise in their appeal letters, which must include an sae if acknowledgement is required.
**WHO TO APPLY TO** The Trustees, Joseph Miller and Co, Floor A, Milburn House, Dean Street, Newcastle upon Tyne NE1 1LE *Tel.* 0191 232 8065 *email* jsf@joseph-miller.co.uk

### ■ The Fred and Maureen Charitable Trust
**CC NO** 1153511
**WHERE FUNDING CAN BE GIVEN** England and Wales.
**WHO CAN BENEFIT** Charitable organisations and individuals.
**WHAT IS FUNDED** General charitable purposes.
**SAMPLE GRANTS** Old Warke Dam Project (£290,000); and Muscular Dystrophy Campaign (£5,000).
**FINANCES** *Year* 2013/14 *Income* £303,600 *Grants* £295,200 *Grants to organisations* £295,000 *Assets* £4,795
**TRUSTEES** Fred Done; Lea Done-Jackson; Peter Done; Tim Maher.
**OTHER INFORMATION** A further donation of £200 was made to one individual.

**HOW TO APPLY** Apply in writing to the correspondent.
**WHO TO APPLY TO** Mike Hamilton, Correspondent, The Spectrum, 56–58 Benson Road, Birchwood, Warrington WA3 7PQ *Tel.* 01925 288505

### ■ The Louis and Valerie Freedman Charitable Settlement
**CC NO** 271067 **ESTABLISHED** 1976
**WHERE FUNDING CAN BE GIVEN** UK, especially Buckinghamshire.
**WHO CAN BENEFIT** National and local (Burnham in Buckinghamshire) charities.
**WHAT IS FUNDED** Health; welfare; education.
**WHAT IS NOT FUNDED** Individuals; non-registered charities.
**RANGE OF GRANTS** Usually around £5,000 to £10,000.
**SAMPLE GRANTS** Burnham Health Promotion Trust (£50,000); Headway, Medical Detection Dogs, Philippines typhoon appeal, Street Child Africa and Vitalise (£10,000 each); The Pug Dog Welfare and Rescue Association (£5,000).
**FINANCES** *Year* 2013/14 *Income* £146,406 *Grants* £105,960 *Grants to organisations* £105,960 *Assets* £4,533,954
**TRUSTEES** Francis Hughes; Michael Ferrier.
**OTHER INFORMATION** Grants were made to seven organisations in 2013/14.
**HOW TO APPLY** There is no application form. The following information was obtained from the trustees' report 2011/12: 'The trustees meet periodically (and are also in regular contact) to consider what grants they will make and to review any feedback they have received relating to past donations. The trustees receive many applications for assistance but are normally minded to help those with a link to the Freedman family.'
**WHO TO APPLY TO** Francis Hughes, Trustee, c/o Bridge House, 11 Creek Road, East Molesey, Surrey KT8 9BE *Tel.* 020 8941 4455 *email* francis@hughescollett.co.uk

### ■ The Michael and Clara Freeman Charitable Trust
**CC NO** 1125083 **ESTABLISHED** 2008
**WHERE FUNDING CAN BE GIVEN** UK and overseas.
**WHO CAN BENEFIT** Registered charities and community groups.
**WHAT IS FUNDED** General charitable purposes.
**RANGE OF GRANTS** Up to £16,000 but generally £1,000–£5,000.
**FINANCES** *Year* 2013/14 *Income* £25,753 *Grants* £65,794 *Grants to organisations* £65,794 *Assets* £1,555,001
**TRUSTEES** Michael Freeman; Clara Freeman; Laura Freeman; Edward Freeman.
**OTHER INFORMATION** Grants were made to 20 organisations in 2013/14.
**HOW TO APPLY** Apply in writing to the correspondent.
**WHO TO APPLY TO** Michael Freeman, Trustee, 9 Connaught Square, London W2 2HG

### ■ The Freemasons' Grand Charity
**CC NO** 281942 **ESTABLISHED** 1980
**WHERE FUNDING CAN BE GIVEN** England, Wales and overseas.
**WHO CAN BENEFIT** Registered charities; individuals; hospices.
**WHAT IS FUNDED** Charities benefitting freemasons and their dependants; medical research; youth

opportunities; vulnerable people; hospices; air ambulance services; emergency grants.

**WHAT IS NOT FUNDED** Local charities (i.e. serving an individual city or region) should apply to the provincial grand lodge of the region in which they operate, (these are listed in telephone directories, usually under 'freemasons' or 'masons'). Those not eligible for a grant are: individuals (other than for the relief of 'poor and distressed freemasons and their poor and distressed dependants'); charities that serve an individual region or city, for example, a regional hospital, local church, day centre or primary school; organisations not registered with the Charity Commission, except some exempt charities; activities that are primarily the responsibility of central or local government or some other responsible body; organisations or projects outside England and Wales; animal welfare, the arts or environmental causes; charities with sectarian or political objectives; charities that are deemed to hold funds in excess of their requirements. The Freemasons' Grand Charity does not usually fund individual researchers or university research departments directly. Instead the charity prefers to make grants via a medical charity which is a member of the Association of Medical Research Charities.

**RANGE OF GRANTS** £1,000–250,000

**SAMPLE GRANTS** Institute of Cancer Research (£150,000); Centrepoint (£100,000); Blind Veterans UK (£50,000); Happy Days Children's Charity (£20,000); Manchester Cathedral (£10,000); Cornwall Air Ambulance (£4,000); Earl Mountbatten Hospice (£3,300); Anorexia and Bulimia Care and British Blind Sport (£2,000 each); Scotty's Little Soldiers (£1,000).

**FINANCES** Year 2012/13 Income £13,660,100 Grants £13,360,200 Grants to organisations £13,360,200 Assets £64,489,800

**TRUSTEES** Nigel Buchanan; Sir Stuart Hampson; Peter Griffiths; Christopher Grove; Rod Mitchell; Michael Daws; Roy Skinner; Nigel Pett; Charles Akle; Dr Richard Dunstan; Geoff Tuck; Terry Baker; Dr Kevin Williams; Ryland James; Simon Duckworth; Anthony Wood; Timothy Chapman; His Honour Judge Hone QC; Roger Needham; Alexander Stewart; John Hornblow; Wayne Smith; Guy Elgood; Dennis Hill; Roger Friend; Michael Gooderson; Masonic Charity Trustee Limited.

**PUBLICATIONS** Booklet, Information on Masonic Charities.

**OTHER INFORMATION** Grants were split as follows: Relief Chest Scheme (£6.2 million); Masonic grants (£4.5 million); non-Masonic grants (£2.7 million). The 2012/13 accounts were the latest available at the time of writing.

**HOW TO APPLY** Application forms are available from the charity's office or from its website. This form must be completed in full accompanied by a copy of the latest annual report and full audited accounts; these must be less than 18 months old. Hospice grant applications are made on a separate form, available from either the appropriate provincial grand lodge or the trust's office. Applications may be submitted at any time throughout the year and are considered at meetings held in January, April and July. Acknowledgement of receipt will be made by post. Applications are not accepted for 'emergency grants' which are made as 'the need arises' and at the trustees' discretion.

**WHO TO APPLY TO** Laura Chapman, Chief Executive, Freemasons Hall, 60 Great Queen Street, London WC2B 5AZ Tel. 020 7395 9261 Fax 020 7395 9295 email info@the-grand-charity.org Website www.grandcharity.org

■ **The Charles S. French Charitable Trust**

**CC NO** 206476   **ESTABLISHED** 1959

**WHERE FUNDING CAN BE GIVEN** North-east London and south-west Essex.

**WHO CAN BENEFIT** Registered charities.

**WHAT IS FUNDED** General charitable purposes, including community services and facilities.

**WHAT IS NOT FUNDED** Non-registered charities.

**RANGE OF GRANTS** Usually £1,000–£10,000.

**SAMPLE GRANTS** St Luke's Hospice – Basildon (£14,300); Loughton Youth Project (£9,000); Haven House (£7,200); Essex Boys' and Girls' Club and St Clare's Hospice – Essex (£4,000 each); Age Concern – Havering (£3,000); Army Benevolent Fund (£2,000); Waltham Abbey Youth 2000 (£1,500); Just Different (£1,000); Loughton Ladies Women's Institute Choir (£750); Look Essex – Wickford (£350).

**FINANCES** Year 2013/14 Income £244,400 Grants £191,334 Grants to organisations £191,334 Assets £7,827,789

**TRUSTEES** William Noble; Martin Scarth; Joanna Thomas; Michael Foster.

**OTHER INFORMATION** Grants were made to 115 organisations in 2013/14.

**HOW TO APPLY** Apply in writing to the correspondent, including a copy of the latest accounts. The trustees meet four times a year. The trust invites applications for grants and donations from local charities and these applications are reviewed against the trust's objects, with grants and donations being awarded at the trustee's discretion.

**WHO TO APPLY TO** William Noble, Chair, c/o 169 High Road, Loughton, Essex IG10 4LF Tel. 020 8502 3575 email office@csfct.org.uk Website www.csfct.org.uk

■ **The Anne French Memorial Trust**

**CC NO** 254567   **ESTABLISHED** 1963

**WHERE FUNDING CAN BE GIVEN** Diocese of Norwich (Norfolk and north Suffolk).

**WHO CAN BENEFIT** Christians, clergy and local charities.

**WHAT IS FUNDED** Any charitable purpose in the beneficial area, especially church-related causes.

**TYPE OF GRANT** One-off, project, research and feasibility.

**SAMPLE GRANTS** Norwich Cathedral Library (£15,000); Norfolk Community Foundation (£5,000).

**FINANCES** Year 2013/14 Income £256,415 Grants £160,420 Grants to organisations £121,067 Assets £7,273,977

**TRUSTEE** Lord Bishop of Norwich.

**HOW TO APPLY** The trust states that 'in no circumstances does the Bishop wish to encourage applications for grants.'

**WHO TO APPLY TO** Christopher Dicker, Correspondent, Hill House, Ranworth, Norwich, Norfolk NR13 6AB Tel. 01603 270356 email cdicker@hotmail.co.uk

# Freshfield

*Alphabetical register of grant-making charities*

## ■ The Freshfield Foundation

**CC NO** 1003316 **ESTABLISHED** 1991
**WHERE FUNDING CAN BE GIVEN** UK and overseas.
**WHO CAN BENEFIT** Registered charities.
**WHAT IS FUNDED** Sustainable development; health; education; disaster relief.
**RANGE OF GRANTS** £100,000–£500,000
**SAMPLE GRANTS** Disasters Emergency Committee (£500,000); Citizens Advice (£450,000); Friends of the Earth and Sustrans (£100,000 each).
**FINANCES** Year 2013/14 *Income* £582,997 *Grants* £1,150,000 *Grants to organisations* £1,150,000 *Assets* £6,425,189
**TRUSTEES** Paul Kurthausen; Patrick A. Moores; Elizabeth J. Potter.
**OTHER INFORMATION** Grants were made to four organisations in 2013/14.
**HOW TO APPLY** Apply in writing to the correspondent, although the trust states that 'the process of grant-making starts with the trustees analysing an area of interest, consistent with the charity's aims and objectives, and then proactively looking for charities that they think can make the greatest contribution'. With this in mind, a letter of introduction to your organisation's work may be more appropriate than a formal application for funding.
**WHO TO APPLY TO** Paul Kurthausen, Trustee, BWMacfarlane LLP, Castle Chambers, 43 Castle Street L2 9SH *Tel.* 0151 236 1494 *email* paul.k@bwm.co.uk

## ■ The Freshgate Trust Foundation

**CC NO** 221467 **ESTABLISHED** 1962
**WHERE FUNDING CAN BE GIVEN** Mainly Sheffield and South Yorkshire.
**WHO CAN BENEFIT** Organisations benefitting: people of all ages; actors and entertainment professionals; musicians; textile workers and designers; writers and poets; at risk groups; people disadvantaged by poverty and socially isolated people. Both innovatory and established bodies may be considered.
**WHAT IS FUNDED** Local appeals working in the fields of: education (including travel and training); medical (both psychological and physical); recreation; music and arts; welfare and social care; heritage.
**WHAT IS NOT FUNDED** The trust restricts its grants to UK charitable organisations and does not deal with applications from individuals, national appeals or for church fabric unless used for a wider community purpose. The trust does not fund salaries.
**TYPE OF GRANT** Start-up costs and capital costs. One-off grants.
**RANGE OF GRANTS** Up to £13,000.
**SAMPLE GRANTS** Museums Sheffield (£13,000); St Wilfred's Drop In Day Centre and St Luke's Hospice (£10,000 each); South Yorkshire and Hallamshire Clubs for Young People and Sheffield Family Holiday Fund (£4,000); Sheffield Dial-A-Ride Club (£2,000); City of Sheffield Youth Orchestra (£1,300); Sheffield Wildlife Trust and University of Sheffield Bursary (£1,000 each); Pro Soccer Pumas JFC (£500); and Dore and Totley Day Centre Luncheon Club (£150).
**FINANCES** Year 2013 *Income* £194,342 *Grants* £83,870 *Grants to organisations* £83,870 *Assets* £3,287,260
**TRUSTEES** John Hopkins; Liz Murray; David Stone; Geraldine Russell; Jim Mould; Val Linnemann; Holly Dobson; Usha Fitch; Geoff Marston.
**OTHER INFORMATION** Grants were given to 62 organisations in 2013.
**HOW TO APPLY** Apply in writing to the correspondent, by early February, June and October each year. Applications are not normally acknowledged.
**WHO TO APPLY TO** Jonathan Robinson, Secretary, The Hart Shaw Building, Europa Link, Sheffield Business Park, Sheffield S9 1XU *Tel.* 0114 251 8850

## ■ The Friarsgate Trust

**CC NO** 220762 **ESTABLISHED** 1955
**WHERE FUNDING CAN BE GIVEN** UK, with a strong preference for West Sussex, especially Chichester.
**WHO CAN BENEFIT** Registered charities and community groups especially those already supported by the trust.
**WHAT IS FUNDED** General charitable purposes, especially education and welfare of children and young people and care of people who are elderly or in need.
**WHAT IS NOT FUNDED** Local organisations outside Sussex are unlikely to be supported.
**RANGE OF GRANTS** Up to £5,000 but generally £500–£2,000.
**SAMPLE GRANTS** Smile Support and Care (£5,000); Caudwell Children and RSPB (£2,000); The Queen Alexander Hospital Home (£1,500); Alzheimer's Society and BLESMA (£1,000); Deafblind (£800); The Noise Project (£700); Epilepsy Society and Rotary Club of Chichester (£500 each); Pallant House Gallery (£400).
**FINANCES** Year 2013/14 *Income* £97,868 *Grants* £69,467 *Grants to organisations* £69,467 *Assets* £3,339,943
**TRUSTEES** Alan Colenutt; Vivienne Higgins; Nigel Proctor; Sarah Bain.
**OTHER INFORMATION** Grants were made to 62 organisations in 2013/14.
**HOW TO APPLY** Apply in writing to the correspondent. Applicants are welcome to telephone first to check they fit the trust's criteria.
**WHO TO APPLY TO** Amanda King-Jones, Correspondent, Thomas Edgar House, Friary Lane, Chichester, West Sussex PO19 1UF *Tel.* 01243 786111 *email* friarsgate@thomaseggar.com

## ■ Friends of Boyan Trust

**CC NO** 1114498 **ESTABLISHED** 2006
**WHERE FUNDING CAN BE GIVEN** Worldwide.
**WHO CAN BENEFIT** Orthodox Jews.
**WHAT IS FUNDED** Jewish causes.
**RANGE OF GRANTS** Up to £84,000.
**SAMPLE GRANTS** Gomlei Chesed of Chasidei Boyan (£84,000); Mosdot Tiferet Yisroel Boyan (£31,000); Kimcha De'Pischa Boyan (£21,000); Kimcha De'Pischa Beitar Ilit (£13,000); Chevras Mo'oz Ladol (£12,000); Kolel Avrechim Boyan, Betar Ilit (£6,000); Ezer Mikoidesh Foundation (£2,000); Beis Rizhin Trust (£1,500); and Yad Vochessed (£1,000).
**FINANCES** Year 2013/14 *Income* £431,627 *Grants* £397,317 *Grants to organisations* £397,317 *Assets* £112,372
**TRUSTEES** Jacob Getter; Mordechai Freund; Nathan Kuflik.
**HOW TO APPLY** Apply in writing to the correspondent.
**WHO TO APPLY TO** Jacob Getter, Trustee, 23 Durley Road, London N16 5JW *Tel.* 020 8809 6051

## ■ Friends of Essex Churches Trust

**CC NO** 236033 **ESTABLISHED** 1951

**WHERE FUNDING CAN BE GIVEN** Essex and the boroughs of Waltham Forest, Redbridge, Newham, Barking and Dagenham and Havering.

**WHO CAN BENEFIT** Places of worship of Christian faith.

**WHAT IS FUNDED** Preservation and maintenance of churches in Essex and the boroughs of Waltham Forest, Redbridge, Newham, Barking and Havering.

**WHAT IS NOT FUNDED** New work; annual maintenance; heating systems.

**TYPE OF GRANT** One-off grants to organisations. Building repairs only.

**RANGE OF GRANTS** £1,000–£15,000

**SAMPLE GRANTS** Plaistow Memorial Community Church, St Mary – High Ongar and St Paul – Goodmayes (£10,000 each); St John – Mount Bures (£8,000); St Thomas – Navestock (£5,000); St Nicholas – Elmdon and St Peter and St Paul – Saint Osyth (£4,000 each); St Mary the Virgin – Great Bardfield (£3,000); St Lawrence – Bradfield (£2,000); St Nicholas – Tillingham (£1,000).

**FINANCES** Year 2013 Income £145,842 Grants £91,000 Grants to organisations £91,000 Assets £526,510

**TRUSTEES** Dr James Bettley; Keith Gardner; David Lodge; Canon Harry Marsh; David Lodge; Dr Christopher Starr; Ralph Meloy; Fiona Nelmes; Catherine Hutley; Jill Cole; Sandra Markham.

**OTHER INFORMATION** Grants were made to 18 churches in 2013.

**HOW TO APPLY** Application forms can be requested by contacting the correspondent. Further details, conditions and application requirements are outlined on the trust's website. The grants committee meets quarterly.

**WHO TO APPLY TO** Canon Harry Marsh, Trustee, 5 Vicarage Lane, Great Baddow, Chelmsford CM2 8HY email keith@thegreenwood.me.uk Website www.foect.org.uk

## ■ The Friends of Kent Churches

**CC NO** 207021 **ESTABLISHED** 1950

**WHERE FUNDING CAN BE GIVEN** County of Kent.

**WHO CAN BENEFIT** Churches of architectural merit and historical interest.

**WHAT IS FUNDED** The upkeep of their fabric and the preservation of fixtures of importance.

**WHAT IS NOT FUNDED** Work that has already started; reordering; new extensions; toilets and kitchens; heating; redecorating and rewiring; bells, clocks and organs.

**TYPE OF GRANT** Building.

**RANGE OF GRANTS** £250–£15,000

**SAMPLE GRANTS** St Mary the Virgin – Minster in Thanet and St Peter and Paul – Shorne (£22,500 each); St Mary the Virgin – High Halden (£20,000); St Mildred – Canterbury (£15,000); St John the Baptist (£8,000); St Dunstan – Cranbrook (£5,000); St Faith – Maidstone and St Kippingdon (£3,000); St James – Elmers End (£2,000); All Saints – Graveney (£1,000); Bearstead and Thurman Methodist Church (£300).

**FINANCES** Year 2013 Income £172,689 Grants £158,550 Grants to organisations £158,550 Assets £656,209

**TRUSTEES** Charles Banks; Paul Smallwood; Angela Parish; Leslie Smith; Richard Latham; Jane Boucher; Mary Gibbins; Jane Bird.

**OTHER INFORMATION** Grants were made to 27 churches in 2013.

**HOW TO APPLY** Apply using the application form on the website. Grants are offered twice a year at meetings in January and July. Applications should be sent to the secretary by 1 May or 1 November. There are no formal architectural or financial requirements; however, proposals must be sensible. Applications can also be made for the National Churches Trust Partnership grants, which are available for structural repair projects with a total cost of up to £100,000. Forms and guidance notes can be downloaded from the trust's website. Grants are also distributed on behalf of WREN (Waste Recycling Environmental Limited) for the maintenance, repair and restoration of places of religious worship. More information can be found on the trust's website.

**WHO TO APPLY TO** Jane Bird, Trustee, Parsonage Farm House, Hampstead Lane, Yalding, Maidstone ME18 6HG Tel. 01622 815569 Website www.friendsofkentchurches.co.uk

## ■ Friends of Wiznitz Limited

**CC NO** 255685 **ESTABLISHED** 1948

**WHERE FUNDING CAN BE GIVEN** UK and overseas.

**WHO CAN BENEFIT** Registered charities.

**WHAT IS FUNDED** Jewish education; relief of poverty; advancement of the Jewish religion.

**WHAT IS NOT FUNDED** Non-Jewish causes.

**RANGE OF GRANTS** Up to £300,000.

**SAMPLE GRANTS** Igud Mosdos Wiznitz (£250,000); Zidkat Zadik (£191,500); Lehachzikom Velchachyosom (£56,000); and Ahavat Israel Synagogue (£26,000).

**FINANCES** Year 2013/14 Income £1,517,178 Grants £1,272,970 Grants to organisations £1,272,970 Assets £1,700,913

**TRUSTEES** Heinrich Feldman; Shulom Feldman; Ephraim Gottesfeld; Judah Feldman.

**HOW TO APPLY** Apply in writing to the correspondent.

**WHO TO APPLY TO** E. Gottesfeld, Correspondent, 8 Jessam Avenue, London E5 9DU

## ■ Friends Provident Charitable Foundation

**CC NO** 1087053 **ESTABLISHED** 2002

**WHERE FUNDING CAN BE GIVEN** UK.

**WHO CAN BENEFIT** Groups and organisations working with disadvantaged people.

**WHAT IS FUNDED** Projects that contribute to a more resilient, sustainable and fairer economic system.

**WHAT IS NOT FUNDED** Individual or sole trader applicants; organisations applying on behalf of another; work outside the UK, unless there is a clear link to activity or benefit to people or institutions in the UK; work that is to benefit a narrow group of beneficiaries or which cannot be shared; activities to promote a specific political party; activity that has already happened; general appeals.

**TYPE OF GRANT** Up to five years. Full-project funding, capital costs and core costs.

**RANGE OF GRANTS** £5,000–£170,000

**SAMPLE GRANTS** Transition Network (£169,000); WWF – UK (£155,000); Echo Ventures CIC (£140,000); Share Action (£92,000); Ethex (£75,000); Demos (£56,000); New Economics Foundation (£55,000); Institute of Public Policy Research (£54,500); Clore Social Leadership Programme (£35,000); New Weather Institute and Video Wall (£25,000 each); Radical Routes (£10,000); UKSIF (£5,000).

**FINANCES** Year 2013/14 Income £962,752 Grants £951,989 Grants to organisations £951,989 Assets £1,200,806
**TRUSTEES** Jennifer Barraclough; Hetan Shah; Whitni Thomas; Joycelin Dawes; Jim Gilbourne; Rob Lake; Raj Thamotheram; Joanna Elson; Paul Dickinson; Aphra Sklair.
**OTHER INFORMATION** Grants were made to 14 organisations in 2013/14.
**HOW TO APPLY** Applicants are directed, where possible, to the foundation's website where details of current funding programmes, criteria, guidelines and application process are posted.
**WHO TO APPLY TO** Danielle Palmour, Correspondent, Tower House, Fishergate, York YO10 4UA Tel. 01904 629675 email foundation. enquiries@friendsprovident.co.uk Website www. friendsprovidentfoundation.org

## ■ The Frognal Trust
**CC NO** 244444   **ESTABLISHED** 1964
**WHERE FUNDING CAN BE GIVEN** UK.
**WHO CAN BENEFIT** Registered charities.
**WHAT IS FUNDED** Older people; children; disability; blindness/ophthalmological research; environmental heritage.
**WHAT IS NOT FUNDED** Animal charities; the advancement of religion; charities for the benefit of people outside the UK; educational or research trips; branches of national charities; general appeals; individuals.
**TYPE OF GRANT** Buildings, capital, one-off, research and start-up costs will be considered.
**RANGE OF GRANTS** £200–£3,500
**SAMPLE GRANTS** Action Medical Research, Aireborough Voluntary Services to the Elderly, Canniesburn Research Trust, Elderly Accommodation Counsel and Leeds Society for Deaf and Blind People, Friends of the Elderly, Gloucestershire Disabled Afloat Riverboat Trust, National Rheumatoid Arthritis Society, Royal Liverpool and Broad Green University Hospitals, Samantha Dickson Research Trust, Stubbers Adventure Centre, Wireless for the Bedridden Society and Yorkshire Dales Millennium Project.
**FINANCES** Year 2013/14 Income £85,902 Grants £88,500 Grants to organisations £88,500 Assets £2,425,885
**TRUSTEES** Peter Fraser; Jennifer Fraser; Caroline Philipson-Stow; Matthew Bennett.
**HOW TO APPLY** Apply in writing to the correspondent. Applications should be received by February, May, August and November, for consideration at the trustees' meeting the following month.
**WHO TO APPLY TO** Susan Hickley, Correspondent, Wilson Solicitors LLP, Alexandra House, St John's Street, Salisbury SP1 2SB Tel. 01722 427536 email sue.hickley@wilsonslaw.com

## ■ The Patrick and Helena Frost Foundation
**CC NO** 1005505   **ESTABLISHED** 1991
**WHERE FUNDING CAN BE GIVEN** UK.
**WHO CAN BENEFIT** Registered charities and community groups.
**WHAT IS FUNDED** The relief and welfare of people of small means and the less fortunate members of society, and assistance for small organisations where a considerable amount of self-help and voluntary effort is required.
**WHAT IS NOT FUNDED** Individuals.
**TYPE OF GRANT** One-off.
**RANGE OF GRANTS** £5,000–£10,000

**SAMPLE GRANTS** Ability Net, Bowel and Cancer Research, Dogs for the Disabled (£10,000 each); Macmillan Cancer Support (£7,500); Acorn Christian Foundation, Family Holiday Association, The Medical Foundation for Care of Victims of Torture, REACH and the Yeldall Cristian Charity (£5,000 each).
**FINANCES** Year 2013/14 Income £358,018 Grants £400,000 Grants to organisations £400,000 Assets £11,657,925
**TRUSTEES** Luke Valner; Dominic Tayler; Neil Hendriksen.
**OTHER INFORMATION** Grants were made to 49 organisations in 2013/14.
**HOW TO APPLY** Apply in writing to the correspondent enclosing the last set of audited accounts. The trustees regret that due to the large number of applications they receive, they are unable to acknowledge unsuccessful applications.
**WHO TO APPLY TO** Neil Hendriksen, Correspondent, c/o Trowers and Hamlins LLP, 3 Bunhill Row, London EC1Y 8YZ email asorrell@trowers.com

## ■ Mejer and Gertrude Miriam Frydman Foundation
**CC NO** 262806   **ESTABLISHED** 1971
**WHERE FUNDING CAN BE GIVEN** UK and overseas.
**WHO CAN BENEFIT** Jewish, general charitable purposes, particular favour is given to Jewish charities.
**WHAT IS FUNDED** General charitable purposes, with particular preference towards Jewish causes and charitable organisations.
**WHAT IS NOT FUNDED** Individuals for scholarships or any other purpose.
**RANGE OF GRANTS** Up to £4,000.
**SAMPLE GRANTS** Jewish Care and Norwood Ravenswood (£3,800 each); Friends of Yeshiva OHR Elchanan and UK Toremet (£3,000 each); Chai Cancer Care (£2,500); Kesser Torah (£2,100); North West London Jewish Day School (£2,000); Ben Uri Gallery and Jewish Learning Exchange (£1,800 each); Yeshivat Meharash Engel Radomishl (£1,200); Institute for Higher Rabbinicial Studies (£900); Pe'ylim Yad Leachim and Talia Trust for Children (£500 each).
**FINANCES** Year 2013/14 Income £42,126 Grants £37,650 Grants to organisations £37,650 Assets £82,243
**TRUSTEES** Keith Graham; David Frydman; Gerald Frydman; Louis Frydman.
**OTHER INFORMATION** There were 18 grants made.
**HOW TO APPLY** Applications may be made in writing to the correspondent.
**WHO TO APPLY TO** David Frydman, Trustee, Westbury, 145–157 St John Street, London EC1V 4PY Tel. 020 7253 7272 email keithg@westbury.co.uk

## ■ The Fulmer Charitable Trust
**CC NO** 1070428   **ESTABLISHED** 1998
**WHERE FUNDING CAN BE GIVEN** Worldwide, especially financially developing countries and Wiltshire.
**WHO CAN BENEFIT** Registered charities worldwide.
**WHAT IS FUNDED** General charitable purposes; social welfare; the advancement of education; the advancement of religion; community development.
**WHAT IS NOT FUNDED** Gap year requests.
**RANGE OF GRANTS** £500–£8,000
**SAMPLE GRANTS** The Sequal Trust (£8,000); NSPCC (£5,000); Christian Solidarity Worldwide (£4,000); WaterAid (£3,600); Freedom Matters

and Mercy Corps (£2,000 each); Malaria No More UK (£1,500); Housing for Women (£1,000); Resurge Africa (£800); Wiltshire Racial Equality Council (£500).

**FINANCES** *Year* 2012/13 *Income* £375,421 *Grants* £353,270 *Grants to organisations* £353,270 *Assets* £9,854,802

**TRUSTEES** Caroline Mytum; John Reis; Sally Reis; Ren Philip Bromiley.

**OTHER INFORMATION** Grants were made to 250 organisations in 2012/13. The 2012/13 accounts were the latest available at the time of writing (June 2015).

**HOW TO APPLY** Apply in writing to the correspondent. Very few unsolicited applications are accepted.

**WHO TO APPLY TO** John Reis, Trustee, Estate Office, Street Farm, Compton Bassett, Calne, Wiltshire SN11 8SW *Tel.* 01249 760410

## ■ The Fuserna Foundation General Charitable Trust

**CC NO** 1107895   **ESTABLISHED** 2005
**WHERE FUNDING CAN BE GIVEN** UK and overseas.
**WHO CAN BENEFIT** Charitable organisations.
**WHAT IS FUNDED** General charitable purposes, including education and training; the advancement of health; the relief of poverty; accommodation and housing; the arts; the environment; the armed forces; and human rights.
**WHAT IS NOT FUNDED** Charities with an income over £3 million.
**RANGE OF GRANTS** £5,000–£15,000
**SAMPLE GRANTS** Tandem Befriending Project (£20,000); Immediate Theatre and Lakelands Day Care (£15,000 each); Child Brain Injury Trust (£12,000); Tiverton Market Centre (£10,000); Tuberous Sclerosis Association (£7,000); My Voice London and West Sussex Association for the Blind (£5,000 each); and Support Line and Bag Books (£2,500 each).
**FINANCES** *Year* 2013 *Income* £474 *Grants* £155,444 *Grants to organisations* £155,444
**TRUSTEES** Patrick Maxwell; Ariadne Getty; Louise Creasey.
**HOW TO APPLY** **The foundation is no longer accepting applications with a view to stopping grant-making completely.**
**WHO TO APPLY TO** Louise Creasey, Trustee, 26 Curzon Street, London W1J 7TQ *Tel.* 020 7409 3900 *email* info@fusernafoundation.org *Website* www.fusernafoundation.org

# ■ The G. D. Charitable Trust

**CC NO** 1096101 **ESTABLISHED** 2002
**WHERE FUNDING CAN BE GIVEN** Worldwide.
**WHO CAN BENEFIT** Registered charities.
**WHAT IS FUNDED** Animal welfare; the environment; disability; homelessness.
**WHAT IS NOT FUNDED** Individuals.
**RANGE OF GRANTS** £50,000–£200
**SAMPLE GRANTS** Blue Marine Foundation (£50,000); The Eve Appeal and Save the Children (£6,000); Born Free (£3,000); Hampshire and Isle of Wight Air Ambulance (£2,000); Macmillan Cancer Support (£1,000).
**FINANCES** Year 2013/14 Income £90,781 Grants £68,000 Grants to organisations £68,000 Assets £3,829,672
**TRUSTEES** George Duffield; Alexander Fitzgibbons; Natasha Duffield.
**OTHER INFORMATION** Grants to six organisations were made totalling £68,000.
**HOW TO APPLY** Apply in writing to the correspondent.
**WHO TO APPLY TO** Jonathan Brinsden, Bircham Dyson Bell, 50 Broadway, London SW1H 0BL *Tel.* 020 7227 7000

# ■ G. M. C. Trust

**CC NO** 288418 **ESTABLISHED** 1965
**WHERE FUNDING CAN BE GIVEN** UK, predominantly in the West Midlands.
**WHO CAN BENEFIT** General charitable purposes but organisations benefitting children, young adults and older people are largely supported.
**WHAT IS FUNDED** Areas in and around the West Midlands, general charitable purposes.
**WHAT IS NOT FUNDED** Individuals; local or regional appeals outside the West Midlands; national appeals, except where there are established links.
**TYPE OF GRANT** One-off.
**RANGE OF GRANTS** Potentially up to £20,000, but most grants are lower.
**SAMPLE GRANTS** B-eat – Beat Eating Disorders, Evelina Children's Heart Foundation, Friends of Bourneville Carillon, King's College – Cambridge and Mind (£10,000 each); Listening Books, Peterborough 900 Organ Fund, Sense and UN Women UK (£5,000 each); Institute of Economic Affairs (£1,000); Arden Academy Trust (£800); Amnesty International (£200).
**FINANCES** Year 2013/14 Income £228,059 Grants £113,950 Grants to organisations £113,950 Assets £3,315,401
**TRUSTEES** Bes Cadbury; Sir Adrian Cadbury; M. J. Cadbury; C. E. Fowler-Wright.
**OTHER INFORMATION** Grants were made to 19 organisations in 2013/14.
**HOW TO APPLY** Apply in writing to the correspondent. The trust largely supports projects which come to the attention of its trustees through their special interests and knowledge. General applications for grants are not encouraged.
**WHO TO APPLY TO** Rodney Pitts, Secretary, Flat 4 Fairways, 1240 Warwick Road, Knowle, Solihull B93 9LL *Tel.* 01564 779971 *email* spam@rodneypitts.com

# ■ The Galanthus Trust

**CC NO** 1103538 **ESTABLISHED** 2004
**WHERE FUNDING CAN BE GIVEN** UK and overseas.
**WHO CAN BENEFIT** Registered charities and individuals.
**WHAT IS FUNDED** Medical; financially developing countries; environment; conservation.
**RANGE OF GRANTS** UK and overseas.
**FINANCES** Year 2013/14 Income £3,041 Grants £70,000 Grants to organisations £70,000
**TRUSTEES** S. F. Rogers; Mrs J. M. Rogers.
**HOW TO APPLY** Apply in writing to the correspondent. 'All requests for grants are considered carefully by the trustees. The trustees decide whether to donate and the amount to donate.'
**WHO TO APPLY TO** Juliet Rogers, Trustee, Pile Oak Lodge, Donhead St Andrew, Shaftesbury, Dorset SP7 9EH *Tel.* 07478 29138 *email* galanthustrust@yahoo.co.uk

# ■ The Galbraith Trust

**CC NO** 1086717 **ESTABLISHED** 2001
**WHERE FUNDING CAN BE GIVEN** The administrative area of Lancaster City Council.
**WHO CAN BENEFIT** Charitable organisations. You do not need to be registered but must have charitable objectives.
**WHAT IS FUNDED** General charitable purposes. Priority is given to 'applications which provide social benefit to the most needy of the district'. Appeals which involve 'the purchase of goods or services giving consideration to local and independent traders' are also favoured.
**WHAT IS NOT FUNDED** Individuals.
**RANGE OF GRANTS** Usually £100–£3,000.
**SAMPLE GRANTS Previous beneficiaries have included:** Lancashire Outward Bound Association and Night Owls (£1,500 each); Friendship Centre (£1,000); 1st Heysham Guides and Community Learning Network (£800 each); St Barnabas Housebound Club (£600); Lancaster and Garstang Division Girl Guiding and Stage Struck Youth Theatre (£500 each); Greenfield Court residents Association (£300); Archbishop Hutton After School Fun Club; Bare Necessities Pre-School Playgroup; Bolton-le-Sands Village Hall.
**FINANCES** Year 2013/14 Income £16,335 Grants £50,000 Grants to organisations £50,000
**TRUSTEES** Mark Burrow; Warwick Wilson; Kirsten Gordon; Malcolm Harris; Irene Bowker; Robert Bailey; Peter Crowther; Susan Houseman; Richard Bowker.
**OTHER INFORMATION** The CVS acts as administrator and also provides support to any organisation needing help with their application. Due to low income the 2013/14 accounts were not published by the Charity Commission. The trust had a total expenditure of nearly £55,500 and it is likely that about £50,000 was awarded in grants.
**HOW TO APPLY** Application forms and guidelines are available from the website or can be requested from the correspondent. Where possible appeals should be submitted electronically (to janetcherry@lancastercvs.org.uk) and must include a copy of the most recent annual report and audited/examined accounts as well as a breakdown of costs. The trustees meet quarterly – in March, June, September and December.
**WHO TO APPLY TO** Warwick Wilson, Trustee, c/o Lancaster District CVS, Sulyard St, Lancaster,

Lancaster LA1 1PX *Tel.* 01524 555900
*email* email@lancastercvs.org.uk
*Website* lancastercvs.org.uk/funding/galbraith-trust

## ■ The Gale Family Charity Trust

**CC NO** 289212         **ESTABLISHED** 1984
**WHERE FUNDING CAN BE GIVEN** UK, mainly Bedfordshire.
**WHO CAN BENEFIT** Registered charities, with a preference for Bedfordshire-based charities.
**WHAT IS FUNDED** General charitable purposes with preference to churches and church ministries, as well as community life.
**WHAT IS NOT FUNDED** Grants are rarely given to individuals.
**RANGE OF GRANTS** Up to £20,000.
**SAMPLE GRANTS** Bedford Day Care Hospice (£20,000); Bunyan Meeting Free Church (£17,000); St John's Hospice – Moggerhanger (£10,000); St Paul's Church – Bedford (£7,000); Bedford Garden Carers (£5,000); Cople Lower School and Young People of the Year (£2,000 each); Happy Days and Relate – Bedford (£1,000 each); Pavenham Cricket Club (£500);
**FINANCES** *Year* 2013/14 *Income* £126,073 *Grants* £162,509 *Grants to organisations* £162,509 *Assets* £5,780,901
**TRUSTEES** Anthony Ormerod; John Tyley; Doreen Watson; Warwick Browning; Russell Beard; David Fletcher; Gerry Garner; Alison Phillipson.
**OTHER INFORMATION** Grants were made to 59 organisations in 2013/14.
**HOW TO APPLY** Apply in writing to the correspondent.
**WHO TO APPLY TO** Alistair Law, Correspondent, Northwood House, 138 Bromham Road, Bedford MK40 2QW *Tel.* 01234 354508 *email* alistair.law@garnerassociates.co.uk

## ■ Gamlen Charitable Trust

**CC NO** 327977         **ESTABLISHED** 1988
**WHERE FUNDING CAN BE GIVEN** UK.
**WHO CAN BENEFIT** Organisations benefitting law students and trainee solicitors, as well as those looking to relieve poverty and advance education through music and the arts.
**WHAT IS FUNDED** Legal education; provision of scholarships and bursaries; the relief of poverty; the advancement of education, in particular through music and the arts. In practice the trust funds exclusively law students and trainee solicitors, as well as organisations that aim to relieve poverty and advance education through music and the arts.
**TYPE OF GRANT** Grants for scholarships, bursaries and prizes; mostly recurrent; project funding; capital and core costs.
**RANGE OF GRANTS** Up to £30,000.
**SAMPLE GRANTS** Christ Church – Law Fellowship (£30,000); Newbury Spring Festival and Grange Park Opera (£3,000 each); Watermill Theatre (£2,000); Orpheus Foundation (£1,000).
**FINANCES** *Year* 2013/14 *Income* £389,191 *Grants* £39,000 *Grants to organisations* £39,000 *Assets* £1,843,387
**TRUSTEES** Julian Chadwick; Rodney Stubblefield; Paul Eaton.
**OTHER INFORMATION** Grants were made to five organisations. In 2013/14 the trust had a very high income and total expenditure (£348,000, excluding grants), mainly from the sale and for the purchase of investments, accordingly.
**HOW TO APPLY** The trust has previously stated that unsolicited applications are not accepted, as most funds are already committed.
**WHO TO APPLY TO** Julian Chadwick, Trustee, c/o Thomas Eggar LLP, Newbury House, 20 Kings Road West, Newbury, Berkshire RG14 5XR *Tel.* 01635 571000 *email* julian.chadwick@thomaseggar.com

## ■ The Gamma Trust

**SC NO** SC004330         **ESTABLISHED** 1965
**WHERE FUNDING CAN BE GIVEN** UK, with a possible preference for Scotland.
**WHO CAN BENEFIT** Registered charities.
**WHAT IS FUNDED** General charitable purposes; health; the arts, heritage, culture or science; the relief of those in need by reason of age, ill health, disability, financial hardship or other disadvantage.
**TYPE OF GRANT** Project, research and recurring costs.
**SAMPLE GRANTS** British Red Cross, British Heart Foundation, Cancer Research Campaign and Erskine Hospital.
**FINANCES** *Year* 2013/14 *Income* £55,318 *Grants* £70,000 *Grants to organisations* £70,000
**HOW TO APPLY** Apply in writing to the correspondent for consideration quarterly.
**WHO TO APPLY TO** Fiona Tedford, Trust Team Leader, c/o Mazars CYB Services Limited, 90 St Vincent Street, Glasgow G2 5UB *Tel.* 0141 225 4953 *email* glasgowtrustteam@mazars.co.uk

## ■ The Gannochy Trust

**SC NO** SC003133         **ESTABLISHED** 1937
**WHERE FUNDING CAN BE GIVEN** Scotland with a preference for Tayside, specifically Perth and Kinross.
**WHO CAN BENEFIT** Organisations which meet the OSCR Charity Test.
**WHAT IS FUNDED** The trust's grant-making mission is: 'to make a positive difference for the benefit of people living in Scotland, with a preference for Perth and Kinross'. It has four grant-making themes: inspiring young people; improving the quality of life of the disadvantaged and vulnerable; supporting and developing community amenities; care for the natural and man-made environment.
**WHAT IS NOT FUNDED** General applications; individuals; charities that do not meet the OSCR Charity Test; projects outside Scotland; projects that do not demonstrate an element of self or other funding; commitments over three years; holidays with the exception of those for people with disabilities or disadvantaged people living in Perth and Kinross; animal welfare; schools and recreational facilities unless they can demonstrate sustained community involvement; pre-schools groups; play schemes; PTAs; cancer and health-related charities unless providing palliative care within Perth and Kinross that would not normally receive statutory funding; places of worship unless there is a distinct community benefit; charities re-applying within a year of their previous award; funding which would normally be provided by central or local government; waste disposal; pollution control; renewable energy; political or lobbying purposes; higher or further education establishments unless the project has been initiated by the trustees.

**SAMPLE GRANTS** Pert and Kinross Heritage Trust and Black Watch Museum Trust (£300,000 each); Perth and Kinross Council Living Communities Project (£247,000); Perth and Kinross Countryside Trust (£200,000); Scottish Opera (£150,000); and Friends of the Birks Cinema (£50,000).
**FINANCES** Year 2013/14 Income £6,117,832 Grants £2,111,389 Grants to organisations £2,111,389
**TRUSTEES** Dr James Kynaston, Chair; Mark Webster; Ian Macmillan; Stewart Macleod; Dr John Markland.
**HOW TO APPLY** Application forms can be downloaded from the trust's website. The application form also contains detailed guidance notes. Note that the trust's funding strategy is currently being reviewed and funding has been restricted to the Tayside and Perth and Kinross areas while this is taking place. Organisations based outside Tayside area should contact the trust for further guidance.
**WHO TO APPLY TO** Fiona Russell, Secretary, Kincarrathie House Drive, Pitcullen Crescent, Perth PH2 7HX *Tel.* 01738 620653 *email* admin@gannochytrust.org.uk *Website* www.gannochytrust.org.uk

## ■ The Ganzoni Charitable Trust

**CC NO** 263583   **ESTABLISHED** 1971
**WHERE FUNDING CAN BE GIVEN** Suffolk.
**WHO CAN BENEFIT** Registered charities and community groups.
**WHAT IS FUNDED** General charitable purposes.
**WHAT IS NOT FUNDED** Grants to individuals will not be considered. Applications from outside Suffolk are not normally considered and will not be acknowledged.
**RANGE OF GRANTS** £50–£12,000
**SAMPLE GRANTS** Diocese of St Edmundsbury and Ipswich (£12,000); Burgh PCC and Bentley PCC (£5,000 each); Elizabeth Finn Care (£4,000); The Guildhall Project (£2,500); The Porch Project (£2,000); Young People Taking Action (£1,300); SCOPE and The Salvation Army (£1,000 each); Suffolk Accident Rescue Services (£500).
**FINANCES** Year 2013/14 Income £200,020 Grants £99,345 Grants to organisations £99,345 Assets £3,845,966
**TRUSTEES** Hon. Mary Jill Ganzoni; Hon. Charles Boscawen; Nicholas Ridley; John Pickering
**OTHER INFORMATION** Grants were made to 82 organisations in 2013/14.
**HOW TO APPLY** Apply in writing to the correspondent. Telephone calls are not encouraged. There are no application forms, guidelines or deadlines. No sae is required unless material is to be returned.
**WHO TO APPLY TO** Hon. Charles Boscawen, Trustee, c/o Birketts LLP, 24–26 Museum Street, Ipswich IP1 1HZ *Tel.* 01473 232300 *email* bill-white@birketts.co.uk

## ■ The Worshipful Company of Gardeners of London

**CC NO** 222079   **ESTABLISHED** 1962
**WHERE FUNDING CAN BE GIVEN** Mainly City of London.
**WHO CAN BENEFIT** Registered charities and horticultural organisations.
**WHAT IS FUNDED** The fund mainly supports charitable activities connected with horticulture in all its forms and within the City of London.
**RANGE OF GRANTS** £100–£6,000
**SAMPLE GRANTS** Gardening for the Disabled Trust and London Children's Flower Society (£6,000 each); City and Guilds of London Institution (£5,300); London Gardens Society (£5,000); London in Bloom (£4,000).
**FINANCES** Year 2013/14 Income £86,375 Grants £65,000 Grants to organisations £65,000 Assets £666,965
**TRUSTEES** Norman Chalmers; Dr Stephen Dowbiggin; Rod Petty; Brian Porter; Louise Robinson; Roger Hedgecoe; Nicholas Evans; Stephen Bernhard; Bernard Williams; John Rochford.
**OTHER INFORMATION** Grants were made to five organisations in 2013/14.
**HOW TO APPLY** Apply in writing to the correspondent.
**WHO TO APPLY TO** Trevor Faris, Trustee, 25 Luke Street, London EC2A 4AR *Tel.* 020 7149 6404 *email* paclerk@gardenerscompany.org.uk *Website* www.gardenerscompany.org.uk

## ■ The Samuel Gardner Memorial Trust

**CC NO** 261059   **ESTABLISHED** 1970
**WHERE FUNDING CAN BE GIVEN** Harrow on the Hill.
**WHO CAN BENEFIT** Organisations and charitable groups.
**WHAT IS FUNDED** Music and music education; the arts and heritage; preservation of landscaped public spaces. There is an emphasis on the encouragement of young people.
**WHAT IS NOT FUNDED** Individuals.
**SAMPLE GRANTS** Streetwise Opera (£4,000); National Youth Orchestra of GB (£2,200); Sound Connections (£2,000).
**FINANCES** Year 2013/14 Income £47,585 Grants £55,243 Grants to organisations £55,243 Assets £1,581,363
**TRUSTEES** Timothy Brown; Marion Friend; Ursula Jones; Timothy Lines; John Stenhouse; Nicholas Rampley.
**HOW TO APPLY** The trustees usually meet twice per year, in April and September. All applications for consideration at the April meeting must be submitted by the end of February. All applications for consideration in September must be submitted by the end of July. Late applications will be held over until the next meeting. Applications should be submitted by downloading and completing the application form in full and submitting this by email to the Trust Administrator.
**WHO TO APPLY TO** Graham Cooper, Trust Administrator, Apartment 83, New River Head, 173 Rosebery Avenue, London EC1R 4UP *email* samuelgardnertrust@outlook.com *Website* www.samuelgardnertrust.com

## ■ The Garnett Charitable Trust

**CC NO** 327847   **ESTABLISHED** 1988
**WHERE FUNDING CAN BE GIVEN** South west England and Northern Ireland.
**WHO CAN BENEFIT** Registered charities.
**WHAT IS FUNDED** Animal welfare; environmental issues; education; medical research; welfare; the arts and galleries
**WHAT IS NOT FUNDED** Individuals.
**RANGE OF GRANTS** £5–£10,000
**SAMPLE GRANTS** All Hallows' School – Cranmore, CARE International, Design Museum, Ireland Fund of Great Britain, National Gallery Trust, St Michael's Parish and Save the Children.

FINANCES Year 2013/14 Income £2,288
Grants £40,000 Grants to organisations
£40,000
TRUSTEE Sandra Brown.
HOW TO APPLY No grants are given to unsolicited applications. Most funds are earmarked and speculative applications will not be considered.
WHO TO APPLY TO Sandra Brown, Trustee, c/o Michelmores LLP Solicitors, Broad Quay House, Broad Quay, Bristol BS1 4DJ Tel. 0117 906 9313 email jenny.oneill@michelmores.com

## ■ The Garrick Charitable Trust
CC NO 1071279    ESTABLISHED 1998
WHERE FUNDING CAN BE GIVEN UK.
WHO CAN BENEFIT Registered charities only.
WHAT IS FUNDED Institutions which are seeking to further theatre, literature, dance or music.
WHAT IS NOT FUNDED Drama training or academic studies amateur productions projects outside the UK.
TYPE OF GRANT Up to three years.
RANGE OF GRANTS £1,000–£5,000 but usually £2,500.
SAMPLE GRANTS National Youth Theatre of Great Britain (£5,000); Chroma (£4,000) National English Ballet School (£3,800); Lyric Theatre Hammersmith, Mid Wales Opera and National Student and Drama Festival, Pimlico Opera and Rambert (£2,500 each); Mobious Ensemble and Writers in Peterborough (£1,000 each).
FINANCES Year 2013 Income £86,344
Grants £159,373 Grants to organisations £159,373 Assets £5,225,919
TRUSTEES David Sigall; Sir Stephen Waley-Cohen; Roger Braban; Stephen Aris; Ion Trewin.
OTHER INFORMATION Grants were made to 63 organisations in 2013.
HOW TO APPLY Initial applications are reviewed by the trustees who decide whether or not to send an application form. The trustees meet quarterly. The trust's website states: 'First, please write us a short letter – preferably one, but not more than two, pages, perhaps with a publicity flyer. In your letter please tell us: about your organisation and the project you want us to support how much money you are asking for how your organisation will benefit from a grant what will happen if you do not receive a grant. Occasionally we are able to make an immediate grant, but normally we will then send you a form asking for more detailed information about your request and your organisation. The form also asks you for your most recent accounts and income, including earnings and support in kind. You may wish to include CVs of the people involved in the project, reviews of previous productions or publicity flyers.'
WHO TO APPLY TO The Trustees, Garrick Club, 15 Garrick Street, London WC2E 9AY Tel. 020 7395 4136 email michaelkb@garrickclub.co.uk Website www.garrickclub.co.uk

## ■ Garthgwynion Charities
CC NO 229334    ESTABLISHED 1963
WHERE FUNDING CAN BE GIVEN Primarily the parishes of Isygarreg and Uwchygarreg at Machynlleth, Powys.
WHO CAN BENEFIT Organisations benefitting people who are ill, at-risk groups and people who are disadvantaged by poverty or socially isolated.
WHAT IS FUNDED The main areas of interest are: the leading national charities conducting research into cancer, sight or disorders of the nervous system; community projects or individuals with a Welsh (better still, Mid-Wales) link, having either a social or artistic purpose.
WHAT IS NOT FUNDED Applications by individuals are considered only exceptionally
TYPE OF GRANT Usually one off.
SAMPLE GRANTS Gonville and Caius College – Cambridge; Harrow School; Machynlleth Tabernacle Trust; Powys Eisteddfod; the Tannery Appeal.
FINANCES Year 2013/14 Income £63,027
Grants £77,600 Assets £1,730,043
TRUSTEES Eleanor Lambert; David Owen; Edward Owen.
OTHER INFORMATION Grants were made to ten organisations and two individuals in 2013/14.
HOW TO APPLY Apply in writing to the correspondent.
WHO TO APPLY TO June Baker, 13 Osborne Close, Feltham, Hounslow, London TW13 6SR Tel. 020 8890 0469 email junejjbaker@yahoo.co.uk

## ■ The Gatsby Charitable Foundation
CC NO 251988    ESTABLISHED 1967
WHERE FUNDING CAN BE GIVEN Unrestricted
WHO CAN BENEFIT Registered charities only. Many beneficiary organisations are specialist research institutes.
WHAT IS FUNDED **Plant Science**: to develop basic research in fundamental processes of plant growth and development and molecular plant pathology, to encourage young researchers in the field of plant science in the UK; **Neuroscience**: to support world-class research in the area of neural circuits and behaviour, and in the area of theoretical neuroscience; and to support activities which enhance our understanding in these fields; **Science and Engineering Education** to strengthen science and engineering skills in the UK by developing and enabling innovative programmes and informing national policy; **Africa**: to promote economic development in East Africa that benefits the poor through support to the growth and sustainability of key sectors; **Public Policy** – to support: the Institute for Government as an independent institute available to politicians and the civil service, focused on making government more effective; and the Centre for Cities, which provides practical research and policy advice that helps cities understand how they can succeed economically; **The Arts** – to support the fabric and programming of institutions with which Gatsby's founding family has connections.
WHAT IS NOT FUNDED Generally, the trustees do not make grants in response to unsolicited applications or to individuals.
TYPE OF GRANT One-off and recurring grants.
RANGE OF GRANTS Up to £7 million.
SAMPLE GRANTS Institute for Government (£6.8 million); Sainsbury Laboratory (£4.3 million); Two Blades Foundation (£1.4 million); Backstage Trust (£1 million); Bristol Old Vic (£400,000); Royal Academy of Engineering (£330,000); University of Oxford (£323,000); Centre for Mental Health (£300,000); Sainsbury Management Fellows' Society (£189,000); Media Standards Trust (£175,00); Unionlearn (£98,000); J Sainsbury Veterans Association (£50,000).
FINANCES Year 2013/14 Income £64,065,000
Grants £28,974,710 Grants to organisations £28,974,710 Assets £417,905,000
TRUSTEES Joseph Burns; Sir Andrew Cahn; Judith Portrait.

**OTHER INFORMATION** The trust is one of the Sainsbury Family Charitable Trusts which share a common administration. An application to one is taken as an application to all.
**HOW TO APPLY** Proposals are generally invited by the trustees or initiated at their request. Unsolicited applications are not encouraged and are unlikely to be successful.
**WHO TO APPLY TO** Alan Bookbinder, The Peak, 5 Wilton Road, London SW1V 1AP *Tel.* 020 7410 0330 *email* contact@gatsby.org.uk *Website* www.gatsby.org.uk

## ■ Gatwick Airport Community Trust

**CC NO** 1089683    **ESTABLISHED** 2001
**WHERE FUNDING CAN BE GIVEN** Parts of East and West Sussex, Surrey and Kent but particularly communities directly affected by operations at Gatwick Airport. A map of the area of benefit can be seen on the website.
**WHO CAN BENEFIT** Environmental and community projects in the area of benefit.
**WHAT IS FUNDED** The development of young people; the arts; sporting facilities; environmental improvement and conservation; improvements to community facilities; volunteering, older people and people with disabilities.
**WHAT IS NOT FUNDED** Projects or beneficiaries that are completely or largely outside the area of benefit (less attention is given to applications from areas not directly affected by the airport); recurrent expenditure or running costs, ongoing maintenance or deficits; salaries or training costs, except start-up costs in relation to an additional amenity or service being established that will be self-sustaining thereafter; costs that should be funded from other sources, e.g. public bodies; applications from organisations that have statutory responsibilities such as local authorities, hospitals, schools, unless it is a project that is over and above their core activities; the purchase of land or buildings. Grants will not be made to organisations that are working to make a profit for shareholders, partners or sole owners, nor to individuals. Grants will not normally be made where it is evident that little or no effort has been made to raise funds elsewhere.
**TYPE OF GRANT** The trust favours applications that involve one-off capital or project costs, rather than ongoing maintenance, salaries or training costs.
**RANGE OF GRANTS** £1,000–£5,000
**SAMPLE GRANTS** Home Start Crawley, Horsham and Mid-Sussex and Horley Town Council (£10,000 each).
**FINANCES** Year 2013/14 *Income* £194,447 *Grants* £176,524 *Grants to organisations* £176,524 *Assets* £13,946
**TRUSTEES** Richard Burrett; Michael Roberts; Sally Blake; Ian Revell; Michael Sydney; John Kendall; Eddie Redfern; Julie Ayres; Dorothy Ross-Tomlin.
**OTHER INFORMATION** Grants were made to 148 organisations in 2014.
**HOW TO APPLY** Application forms are available during the period each year when applications are being accepted (see below) by contacting the trust by telephone or writing to: GACT, PO Box 464, Tunbridge Wells, Kent TN2 9PU. Forms can also be downloaded from the website. Applications are invited once a year, usually between January and March. Grants are paid by the end of May. Further information can be found on the trust's website. Telephone queries are welcomed.
**WHO TO APPLY TO** Rosamund Quade, Trust Secretary, c/o Spofforths LLP, Comewell House, North Street, Horsham, West Sussex RH12 1RD *Tel.* 01892 826088 *email* mail@gact.org.uk *Website* www.gact.org.uk

## ■ The Robert Gavron Charitable Trust

**CC NO** 268535    **ESTABLISHED** 1974
**WHERE FUNDING CAN BE GIVEN** Mainly UK.
**WHO CAN BENEFIT** Mainly small charities.
**WHAT IS FUNDED** The principal fields of interest continue to include: health and welfare (including charities for people with disabilities); prisons and prison reform; arts and arts education; education; social policy and research.
**WHAT IS NOT FUNDED** Individuals.
**TYPE OF GRANT** One-off; project; research; recurring cost; and salaries. Funding can be given for up to three years.
**RANGE OF GRANTS** Up to £55,000.
**SAMPLE GRANTS** Arab Israel Children's Tennis Charity (£55,500); British Library and Tricycle Theatre (£50,000 each); Barbados Cricket Association (£40,000); Kidstime (£25,000); House of Illustration (£12,000); Open Channels (£10,000); Prisoners Abroad and Runnymede (£5,000 each); All Ears – Cambodia (£4,300); the British Museum (£3,000).
**FINANCES** Year 2013/14 *Income* £433,345 *Grants* £578,460 *Grants to organisations* £578,460 *Assets* £8,884,849
**TRUSTEES** Sarah Gavron; Charles Corman; Jessica Gavron; Lady Katharine Gavron.
**OTHER INFORMATION** There were 44 grants of over £3,000 made in 2013/14. Grants under £3,000 totalled £39,000.
**HOW TO APPLY** The trustees' report for 2013/14 states the following: 'At present the trust is fully committed to its existing areas of interest. Furthermore, the trustees are unlikely to be able to consider further applications for funding in the current financial climate'
**WHO TO APPLY TO** Yvette Dear, 44 Eagle Street, London WC1R 4FS *Tel.* 020 7400 4300 *email* office@rgct.org.uk

## ■ Jacqueline and Michael Gee Charitable Trust

**CC NO** 1062566    **ESTABLISHED** 1997
**WHERE FUNDING CAN BE GIVEN** UK and overseas.
**WHO CAN BENEFIT** Charitable organisations, with a preference for Jewish groups.
**WHAT IS FUNDED** General charitable purposes including health, education and training, arts and culture and overseas aid.
**RANGE OF GRANTS** Usually up to £10,000.
**SAMPLE GRANTS** The Philip and Nicola Gee Charitable Trust (£10,000); My Israel (£7,000); United Synagogue (£4,100); Skiing with Heroes (£4,000); British Emunah Fund (£3,100); Soho Theatre Company Limited (£2,500); Wigmore Hall Trust (£1,500); Southbank Centre (£1,000); Musicworks (£200); Glyndebourne Arts Trust (£100).
**FINANCES** Year 2013/14 *Income* £113,822 *Grants* £121,175 *Grants to organisations* £121,175 *Assets* £115,620
**TRUSTEES** Michael Gee; Jacqueline Gee.

OTHER INFORMATION Grants were made to 56 organisations in 2013/14.
HOW TO APPLY Apply in writing to the correspondent.
WHO TO APPLY TO Michael Gee, Trustee, Flat 27 Berkeley House, 15 Hay Hill, London W1J 8NS *Tel.* 020 7493 1904

## ■ The Nigel Gee Foundation
CC NO 1151843
WHERE FUNDING CAN BE GIVEN London and Israel.
WHO CAN BENEFIT Registered charities; universities; hospices.
WHAT IS FUNDED General charitable purposes; education and training; the promotion of health; social welfare; arts and culture, particularly choral music; Jewish causes.
RANGE OF GRANTS £500–£10,000
SAMPLE GRANTS ORT UK Foundation (£10,000); Philharmonia Chorus Limited (£5,000); Magen David Adom UK (£4,000); Friends of Yad Sarah and Nightingale Hammerson (£2,500 each); Prostate Cancer UK (£1,500); Leeds International Pianoforte Competition (£1,000); and Ben-Gurion University Foundation (£500).
FINANCES *Year* 2013/14 *Income* £494,328 *Grants* £30,896 *Grants to organisations* £30,896 *Assets* £484,404
TRUSTEES Nigel Gee; Raymond Esdaile; Anthony Bunker.
OTHER INFORMATION Grants were made to nine organisations totalling almost £31,000.
HOW TO APPLY Apply in writing to the correspondent.
WHO TO APPLY TO Raymond Esdaile, Trustee, 172–174 Granville Road, London NW2 2LD *Tel.* 020 8455 9881 *email* raymond@bowers-solicitors.com

## ■ Sir Robert Geffery's Almshouse Trust
CC NO 219153    ESTABLISHED 1973
WHERE FUNDING CAN BE GIVEN UK.
WHO CAN BENEFIT Registered charities only.
WHAT IS FUNDED This charity makes grants for educational activities for children and young people up to the age of 25 from disadvantaged backgrounds. It also gives to specific charitable organisations with which the trustee has an ongoing relationship (e.g. a block grant is made to Housing the Homeless which allocates grants to individuals).
RANGE OF GRANTS £1,000–£25,000
SAMPLE GRANTS MakeBelieve Arts (£26,500); Lyric – Hammersmith (£20,000); St Vincent's Family Project (£15,000); Arkwright Scholarship Trust (£10,000); University of Birmingham (£4,000); Carefree Kids and Mary Hare Foundation (£3,000 each); Ancient Technology Centre (£2,500); South of England Show (£480).
FINANCES *Year* 2013/14 *Income* £1,436,746 *Grants* £393,952 *Grants to organisations* £393,952 *Assets* £24,437,402
TRUSTEE The Ironmongers' Trust Company.
OTHER INFORMATION Grants were made to 75 organisations in 2013/14.
HOW TO APPLY Apply in writing to the correspondent.
WHO TO APPLY TO The Charities Manager, Ironmongers' Hall, Barbican, London EC2Y 8AA *Tel.* 020 7776 2311 *email* helen@ironmongers.org *Website* www.ironmongers.org

## ■ The General Nursing Council for England and Wales Trust
CC NO 288068    ESTABLISHED 1983
WHERE FUNDING CAN BE GIVEN England and Wales.
WHO CAN BENEFIT Universities and other public bodies benefitting nurses.
WHAT IS FUNDED Research into matters directly affecting nursing or the nursing profession.
WHAT IS NOT FUNDED Organisational overheads; purchase of equipment; dissemination costs such as conference attendance.
TYPE OF GRANT One-off or annually towards revenue costs.
RANGE OF GRANTS Up to £40,000.
SAMPLE GRANTS The Florence Nightingale Foundation (£40,000); Royal Marsden NHS Foundation Trust (£19,600); University College London (£19,100); Cardiff University (£18,400); University of Manchester (£16,200).
FINANCES *Year* 2013/14 *Income* £105,169 *Grants* £113,204 *Grants to organisations* £113,204 *Assets* £171,102
TRUSTEES Prof. Kate Gerrish. Prof. Susan Proctor; Prof. Dinah Gould; Prof. Sigsworth.
OTHER INFORMATION Grants were made to five organisations in 2013/14.
HOW TO APPLY Application forms are available to download from the website (www.gnct.org.uk), where criteria and guidelines are also posted. All applications must be submitted in an electronic format (e.g. MS Word or PDF) using the trust's research grant application form and the review process will be undertaken electronically. A call for grant applications with a specified closing date will be advertised via the website and promoted through other avenues.
WHO TO APPLY TO Alan Haddon, Secretary, 83 Victoria Road, Lower Edmonton, London N9 9SU *Tel.* 020 8345 5379 *email* gnct@btinternet.com *Website* www.gnct.org.uk

## ■ The Generations Foundation
CC NO 1110565    ESTABLISHED 2005
WHERE FUNDING CAN BE GIVEN UK, London Borough of Merton and overseas
WHO CAN BENEFIT UK-based causes; local causes in the Borough of Merton and also in financially developing countries.
WHAT IS FUNDED Health; family support; environment; education; hospices; overseas aid; children; people with disabilities.
TYPE OF GRANT Capital costs, full project and unrestricted funding for up to, and in some cases over, three years.
RANGE OF GRANTS Up to £50,000.
SAMPLE GRANTS Regenerate (£41,000); British Red Cross (£31,000); Linden Lodge School (£29,000); Hospices of Hope (£16,000); Small Steps (£15,000); Alive and Kicking (£12,000); Child Aid and Tree Aid (£10,000 each); Dream Holidays (£9,000); Housing for Women (£5,000).
FINANCES *Year* 2013/14 *Income* £1,611 *Grants* £337,000 *Grants to organisations* £337,000
TRUSTEES Robert Finch, Stephen Finch; Rohini Finch.
HOW TO APPLY Apply by email to the correspondent.
WHO TO APPLY TO Cathy Green, Administrator of the Generations Foundation, 36 Marryat Road, Wimbledon, London SW19 5BD *Tel.* 020 3542 6269 *email* admin@rfinch.plus.com *Website* www.generationsct.co.uk

## ■ The Steven Gerrard Foundation

**CC NO** 1140813 **ESTABLISHED** 2011

**WHERE FUNDING CAN BE GIVEN** UK, with a preference for Liverpool, and overseas.

**WHO CAN BENEFIT** Registered charities.

**WHAT IS FUNDED** Children and young people who are in need due to illness, family breakdown, disability, 'involvement in the streets', or who are financially or educationally disadvantaged.

**SAMPLE GRANTS** Alder Hey Children's Hospital (£500,000); Autism Initiatives, Friends of Peterhouse, Friends of Presfield Special School and Rare Breeds Survival Trust (£12,000 each); Wirral Resource Centre and Zoe's Place Baby Hospice (£10,000 each); Split Support Services (£9,500); Brainwave (£7,000).

**FINANCES** Year 2013 Income £1,881,653 Grants £584,523 Grants to organisations £584,523 Assets £832,166

**TRUSTEES** Steven Gerrard; Peter Sterling; Kathryn Taylor; Andrew Sterling.

**OTHER INFORMATION** This foundation was established by the Liverpool FC footballer, Steven Gerrard. Nine grants were made during the year.

**HOW TO APPLY** At the time of writing (June 2015) the website stated: 'We currently have no further information on future grants cycles, as soon as we do the website will be updated accordingly.' See the website for updates.

**WHO TO APPLY TO** The Trustees, Black and Norman Solicitors, 67–71 Coronation Road, Crosby, Liverpool L23 5RE Tel. 0151 931 2777 email info@stevengerrardfoundation.org Website www.stevengerrardfoundation.org

## ■ Get Kids Going

**CC NO** 1063471

**WHERE FUNDING CAN BE GIVEN** UK.

**WHO CAN BENEFIT** Registered charities; national sporting bodies; individuals.

**WHAT IS FUNDED** Sport for people with disabilities up to the age of 26.

**RANGE OF GRANTS** £10,000–£40,000

**SAMPLE GRANTS** GB Disabled Ski Team (£40,000); GB Boccia Team and GB Wheelchair Rugby Team (£20,000 each); Archer David Weir Academy and GB Disabled Sailing Team (£10,000 each).

**FINANCES** Year 2013/14 Income £1,159,938 Grants £125,000 Grants to organisations £100,000 Assets £9,718,729

**TRUSTEES** Lesley Tadgell-Foster; Patti Fordyce; Joyce McIntosh.

**OTHER INFORMATION** Grants were made to five organisations in 2013/14.

**HOW TO APPLY** Email the charity to request an application form.

**WHO TO APPLY TO** Jane Emmerson, 10 King Charles Terrace, Sovereign Close, London E1W 3HL Tel. 020 7481 8110 email info@getkidsgoing.com Website www.getkidsgoing.com

## ■ The David Gibbons Foundation

**CC NO** 1134727 **ESTABLISHED** 2010

**WHERE FUNDING CAN BE GIVEN** Devon, with a preference for East Devon.

**WHO CAN BENEFIT** Registered charities and community groups.

**WHAT IS FUNDED** Health; social welfare; older people.

**RANGE OF GRANTS** £3,000–£5,000

**SAMPLE GRANTS** Motability, North Devon Hospice, Open Door Centre – Exmouth and South Devon College Charitable Trust (£5,000 each); Age UK Tiverton and Mid Devon (£4,500); Cullompton Family Centre and PATH (£4,000 each); City of Exeter YMCA Community (£3,500); Brixington Community Church and EDP Drug and Alcohol Services (£3,000 each).

**FINANCES** Year 2013/14 Income £103,427 Grants £105,636 Grants to organisations £95,600 Assets £2,680,058

**TRUSTEES** Roger Dawe; Dr Miles Joyner; Dr John Frankish; Kerensa Pearson.

**OTHER INFORMATION** Grants were made to 47 organisations and 17 individuals in 2013/14.

**HOW TO APPLY** Application forms can be downloaded from the foundation's website. Application forms should only be submitted by post. All applications should specify the amount requested. Organisations should attach a covering letter on your organisation's letter headed paper explaining briefly why you are applying. Additional information may also be attached but the foundation requests no CDs or DVDs. Only send your latest accounts if they are not available on the Charity Commission website.

**WHO TO APPLY TO** Roger Dawe, Trustee, 14 Fore Street, Budleigh Salterton, Devon EX9 6NG Tel. 01395 445259 email enquiries@gibbonstrusts.org Website www.gibbonstrusts.org

## ■ The Gibbs Charitable Trust

**CC NO** 207997 **ESTABLISHED** 1946

**WHERE FUNDING CAN BE GIVEN** UK with a preference for the south of England and worldwide.

**WHO CAN BENEFIT** Registered charities benefitting Methodists are given particular attention.

**WHAT IS FUNDED** Primarily to support Methodist charities; also areas of social or educational concern. Grants are normally made to projects of which the trustees have personal knowledge. Also supported are international causes and creative arts, especially those which use the arts for personal development.

**WHAT IS NOT FUNDED** Animal charities; individuals; organisations that are not registered charities.

**TYPE OF GRANT** Buildings, capital and project grants will be considered.

**RANGE OF GRANTS** £500–£10,000

**SAMPLE GRANTS** Oxfam: for South Sudan (£8,000); Methodist Homes for the Aged and Theatre Royal – Stratford (£5,000); Stoke Methodist Church and Touch Trust – Cardiff (£1,500 each); George Whitfield Tercentenary, Huntington Methodist Church, Oasis Centre – Cardiff and One25 Bristol (£1,000 each); Burma-Assist and Young Vic (£500).

**FINANCES** Year 2013/14 Income £105,075 Grants £115,250 Grants to organisations £115,250 Assets £2,286,804

**TRUSTEES** Dr James Gibbs; Andrew Gibbs; Celia Gibbs; Elizabeth Gibbs; Dr Jessica Gibbs; Dr John E. Gibbs; Dr John Gibbs; Patience Gibbs; Rebecca Gibbs; William Gibbs; Juliet Gibbs; James Gibbs.

**OTHER INFORMATION** Grants were made to 69 organisations in 2013/14.

**HOW TO APPLY** The trust's website gives the following guidance on applications: 'Apply in writing to the Secretary, at 8 Victoria Square, Bristol BS8 4ET. The Secretary says he and his Trustees are 'more often provided with too much information than too little'. He thinks 'Many applications can be made on two sides of paper. 'The pages should include a covering letter, a brief description of the project and a budget. He says Trustees are interested in the answer to the question: 'Who else have you applied to?' Flyers, etc., may be in addition to the two sides. The Secretary says he is 'not impressed by the use of first class stamps' or by the submission of full sets of audited accounts. To keep administration to a minimum, he only communicates with successful applicants. Applications should be in an easily re-cyclable form. In practice, this means no spring-coil binding. Please use both sides of the page!'

**WHO TO APPLY TO** The Secretary, 8 Victoria Square, Clifton, Bristol BS8 4ET *email* jamesgibbs@btinternet.com *Website* www.gibbstrust.org.uk

## ■ Simon Gibson Charitable Trust

**CC NO** 269501 **ESTABLISHED** 1975
**WHERE FUNDING CAN BE GIVEN** UK, with a preference for East Anglia, South Wales and Hertfordshire.
**WHO CAN BENEFIT** Registered charities and community groups.
**WHAT IS FUNDED** General charitable purposes.
**WHAT IS NOT FUNDED** Individuals.
**TYPE OF GRANT** One-off or recurring, core costs, running costs, project, research, buildings and capital grants. Funding may be given for up to three years.
**RANGE OF GRANTS** £1,000 to £25,000, but most grants fall in the range £3,000 to £5,000.
**SAMPLE GRANTS** Tenovus (£21,000); Ely Cathedral Appeal Fund and National Museum of Wales (£10,000 each); ChildLine, the Epilepsy Society and Isabel Hospice (£5,000 each); Montessori School – Burwell, National Osteoporosis Society and Whizz-Kidz (£3,000 each); Mid Glamorgan Scout Area (£2,000); Cowbridge Music Festival (£1,000).
**FINANCES** Year 2013/14 Income £959,724 Grants £624,200 Grants to organisations £624,200 Assets £16,897,543
**TRUSTEES** Bryan Marsh; Angela Homfray; George Gibson; Deborah Connor; John Homfray.
**OTHER INFORMATION** Grants were made to 131 organisations in 2013/14.
**HOW TO APPLY** 'There are no application forms. Charities applying to the trust should make their application in writing in whatever way they think best presents their cause.' The trust acknowledges all applications but does not enter into correspondence with applicants unless they are awarded a grant. The trustees meet in May and applications should be received by the end of March.
**WHO TO APPLY TO** Bryan Marsh, Trustee, Wild Rose House, Llancarfan, Vale of Glamorgan CF62 3AD *Tel.* 01446 781459 *email* marsh575@btinternet.com

## ■ The G. C. Gibson Charitable Trust

**CC NO** 258710 **ESTABLISHED** 1969
**WHERE FUNDING CAN BE GIVEN** UK
**WHO CAN BENEFIT** Registered charities and community organisations.
**WHAT IS FUNDED** General charitable purposes. In practice, mainly: art, music and education; health, hospices and medical research; community and other social projects; religion.
**WHAT IS NOT FUNDED** Individuals.
**TYPE OF GRANT** Capital, research, running and core costs.
**RANGE OF GRANTS** £1,000–£10,000; mostly £1,000–£3,000.

**SAMPLE GRANTS** Botanical Garden Conservation International and Springfield School (£10,000 each); Kind Edward VII's Hospital (£8,000); The Kiloran Trust (£6,000); Bishopwood PCC and Lamp of Lothian Trust (£2,500 each); Enterprise Education Trust (£2,000); Scripture Union (£1,200); the Royal National Institute of Blind People and the Grateful Society (£1,000 each).
**FINANCES** Year 2013/14 Income £709,846 Grants £566,844 Grants to organisations £566,844 Assets £15,265,527
**TRUSTEES** Anna Dalrymple; Martin Gibson; Jane Gibson; Robert Taylor; Lucy Kelly.
**OTHER INFORMATION** Grants were made to 155 organisations in 2013/14 but only around ten were new applicants.
**HOW TO APPLY** Online applications open in late summer and stay open for two months, usually August and September. Check in case the criteria have been amended to reflect the new funding round. Initial online applications are assessed and the trustees will contact a shortlist of charities to make a full application via email. Trustees will provide this email address – no postal or telephone applications will be considered. 'Charities that have already received support from the trust do not need to re-apply, unless they are specifically invited to, or have a specific appeals they feel we might be interested in supporting. Payments are made in early December in each year and not at any other time of the year. Payments will be made direct to bank accounts.'
**WHO TO APPLY TO** The Trustees, Durnsford Mill House, Mildenhall, Marlborough, Wiltshire SN8 2NG *Tel.* 07773 067014 *email* enquiries@gcgct.org *Website* www.gcgct.org

## ■ The Girdlers' Company Charitable Trust

**CC NO** 328026 **ESTABLISHED** 1988
**WHERE FUNDING CAN BE GIVEN** UK, with a preference for City and East End of London, and Hammersmith and Peckham.
**WHO CAN BENEFIT** Charitable organisations benefitting children, young adults, academics, students and teachers.
**WHAT IS FUNDED** Medicine and health; education; welfare; youth welfare; heritage; environment; humanities; Christian religion.
**WHAT IS NOT FUNDED** Students.
**TYPE OF GRANT** One-off and recurrent; core, revenue, salary and capital costs.
**RANGE OF GRANTS** Mostly up to £10,000.
**SAMPLE GRANTS** Leyton Orient Community Sports Programme (£60,000); London Youth (£40,000); St Giles Trust (£19,000); Royal School of Needlework (£15,000); Crown and Manor Club – Hoxton, Habitat for Humanity – Southwark and Macmillan Cancer Support (£10,000 each); The Oxford Kilburn Club (£8,000); Disabled Sailors Association (£2,000); The Coldstream Guards Charitable Fund (£1,700); ActionAid – Ethiopia and The Urology Foundation (£1,200 each); Bath Institute of Medical Engineering (£1,100); Vitalise, Institute of Economic Affairs, St Mary's Church – Brook and Lynn Athletic Club (£1,000 each); and Jubilate Choir (£500).
**FINANCES** Year 2013/14 Income £260,497 Grants £788,966 Grants to organisations £788,966 Assets £7,189,050
**TRUSTEE** The Girdlers' Company

HOW TO APPLY The focus of the trust's grants is with its principal charities, with whom it has long standing relationships. Applications are not invited for these grants. However, the trust operates an open application process for around £20,000 of its total grant-making. Around 20 awards are made, of approximately £1,000, to charitable organisations in England and Wales where the charity has an annual income less than £1 million. The guidelines advise that the applicant success rate is around 4% and around half of the general grants are awarded outside London. These general grants can cover core costs, salaries or capital costs. Applicants should write to the correspondent on letter headed paper. Exempt charities must provide audited accounts. To be considered for a donation cover each of the following points: the beneficial area [which trustees support] under which a grant is sought; a brief summary of the organisation's background and aims; the specific nature of the request, highlighting the change you wish to bring about; how you will know if you have achieved these changes; your charity registration number. Twice yearly the trustee considers general applications with ten donations of approximately £1,000 being made on each occasion. The closing dates are the last Friday in January and August. Successful applicants are unlikely to be awarded a further donation within the following five years. Successful applicants will be informed in May and December.

WHO TO APPLY TO Brigadier Ian Rees, Girdlers' Hall, Basinghall Avenue, London EC2V 5DD Tel. 020 7638 0488 email clerk@girdlers.co.uk Website www.girdlers.co.uk/html/charitable-giving/the-charitable-trust

## ■ The B. and P. Glasser Charitable Trust

CC NO 326571    ESTABLISHED 1984
WHERE FUNDING CAN BE GIVEN UK and worldwide.
WHO CAN BENEFIT Registered charities and community organisations.
WHAT IS FUNDED Health; disability; Jewish causes; welfare.
WHAT IS NOT FUNDED Individuals; students.
RANGE OF GRANTS £500–£8,500
SAMPLE GRANTS Nightingale House (£8,500); Practical Action (£8,000); Jewish Care (£6,500); Royal National Institute for the Blind (£5,000); Medical Aid – Palestine (£3,000); Blind Veterans UK (£2,500); Fair Trials International (£2,000); Jewish Blind and Disabled (£1,800); The Samaritans (£800); Gurkha Welfare Trust (£500).
FINANCES Year 2012/13 Income £83,319 Grants £80,750 Grants to organisations £80,750 Assets £2,502,176
TRUSTEES James Cullingham; Michael Glasser; John Glasser.
OTHER INFORMATION The 2012/13 accounts were the latest available at the time of writing (June 2015).
HOW TO APPLY Apply in writing to the correspondent. To keep administrative costs to a minimum the trust is unable to reply to unsuccessful applicants.
WHO TO APPLY TO Tejinder Kalsi, Chantrey Vellacott DFK, Russell Square House, 10–12 Russell Square, London WC1B 5LF Tel. 020 7509 9463 email tkalsi@cvdfk.com

## ■ Global Care

CC NO 1054008    ESTABLISHED 1996
WHERE FUNDING CAN BE GIVEN Overseas.
WHO CAN BENEFIT Registered charities.
WHAT IS FUNDED Trustees favour children's charities already supported by them working in the poorest countries and the advancement of Christian education.
FINANCES Year 2013/14 Income £1,004,316 Grants £758,218 Grants to organisations £758,218 Assets £740,115
TRUSTEES Norman Lochead; Margaret Patterson; Raymond Neal; Mark Curran; John Scott; Su Matejtschuk; Revd Keith Parr.
OTHER INFORMATION Trustees continue to support projects they seek themselves therefore applications for new grants will not be considered at this time.
HOW TO APPLY Applications are not recommended. Trustees seek out projects to support, as appropriate, and new grants cannot be considered.
WHO TO APPLY TO John White, Chief Executive Officer, Global Care, 2 Dugdale Road, Coventry CV6 1PB Tel. 024 7660 1800 email info@globalcare.org.uk Website www.globalcare.org.uk

## ■ Global Charities

CC NO 1091657    ESTABLISHED 1978
WHERE FUNDING CAN BE GIVEN Greater London; UK.
WHO CAN BENEFIT Community organisations; registered charities.
WHAT IS FUNDED Projects supporting disadvantaged children and young people; or those with an illness or disability.
WHAT IS NOT FUNDED Each individual branch has specific exclusions; generally, however, the charities will not fund: individual children or families; retrospective funding; statutory funding – funding for schools or health projects that would otherwise be covered by designated statutory funding from the local authority; salaried posts; deficit funding or repayment of loans; medical research; purchase of a minibus; trips abroad; distribution to other organisations; religious activities; political groups; general structural changes to buildings; projects which are part of a larger charity and are not separately constituted; core funding for a national or regional charity.
TYPE OF GRANT Capital; core costs; one-off; project; running costs.
RANGE OF GRANTS Mostly under £10,000. Larger grants are made very occasionally.
SAMPLE GRANTS Prince's Foundation for Children and the Arts (£100,000); Missing People (£61,000); and Impact Initiatives (£25,000); Sixth Sense Theatre (£7,500); Cambourne Youth Partnership (£5,000); Havens Hospices – Essex (£3,000); Bangladeshi Parents Association (£2,100); Howbury Friends (£1,800); and Centrepoint – Hammersmith and Fulham (£1,600).
FINANCES Year 2013/14 Income £4,200,565 Grants £1,465,606 Grants to organisations £1,465,606 Assets £949,819
TRUSTEES Moira Swinbank; Paul Soames; Martin George; Jonathan Norbury; Nigel Atkinson; John McGeough; Gareth Andrewartha; Annabel Sweet; Michael Connole.
OTHER INFORMATION Grants were made to 248 organisations in 2013/14.
HOW TO APPLY Full details regarding the criteria required for consideration for a grant award, template application forms and information on

forthcoming grant award rounds are available through the Charity's website.
**WHO TO APPLY TO** Leah Hayden, Correspondent, 29–30 Leicester Square, London WC2H 7LA *Tel.* 020 7054 8393 *email* charities@thisisglobal.com *Website* www.thisisglobal.com/charities

## ■ Gloucestershire Community Foundation

**CC NO** 900239 **ESTABLISHED** 1989
**WHERE FUNDING CAN BE GIVEN** Gloucestershire.
**WHO CAN BENEFIT** Charitable organisations and social enterprises.
**WHAT IS FUNDED** Combating disadvantage in Gloucestershire.
**TYPE OF GRANT** Revenue and full project funding.
**RANGE OF GRANTS** Up to £5,000.
**SAMPLE GRANTS** Active Impact CIC; The Family Haven; Forest of Dean Stroke Club; Gloucestershire Rape Crisis; Kind George's Field Charity; Listening Post; St James City Farm; The Uplands Care Service; Wiggly Worm.
**FINANCES** *Year* 2013 *Income* £568,636 *Grants* £248,988 *Grants to organisations* £248,988 *Assets* £5,439,873
**TRUSTEES** Jane Winstanley; Dr Christopher Wakeman; Tania Hitchens; Ian Brothwood; Roger Head; Lesley Archer; Richard Graham; Gordon Cole; Terry Standing; Helen Lovatt; Chun Kong; Ian Mean; Marcus Heywood; Tom Frost.
**HOW TO APPLY** Information sheets, guidelines and an application forms are available from the website. Staff are pleased to discuss any potential project applications. The foundation operates other funds and administers a number of grant-making trusts. See its website for up-to-date details.
**WHO TO APPLY TO** Diane Kent, c/o The Manor, Boddington, Cheltenham, Gloucestershire GL51 0TJ *Tel.* 01242 851357 *email* diane.kent@gloucestershirecf.org.uk *Website* www.gloucestershirecf.org.uk

## ■ The Gloucestershire Historic Churches Trust

**CC NO** 1120266 **ESTABLISHED** 1980
**WHERE FUNDING CAN BE GIVEN** Gloucestershire.
**WHO CAN BENEFIT** Churches and chapels.
**WHAT IS FUNDED** GHCT is a charity which raises funds to help places of Christian worship of all denominations with repairs and improvements to the fabric of the buildings and their contents, as well as to their surrounding churchyards.
**WHAT IS NOT FUNDED** Routine maintenance.
**TYPE OF GRANT** One-off, but repeat applications will be considered.
**RANGE OF GRANTS** £300–£15,000, typical grants between £1,000 and £4,000.
**SAMPLE GRANTS** St Michael – Stoke Gifford and St Mary – Newent (£11,000 each); St Peter, Paul and Mary – Westbury-on-Severn (£10,000 each); Mariners Church – Gloucester (£7,000); St Mary de Lode – Gloucester (£6,000); St Agnes – Bristol (£4,000); St Mary – Kingswood (£3,000); St Mary – Bitton (£2,000); St John – Slimbridge (£1,000); Holy Cross – Avening (£300).
**FINANCES** *Year* 2013 *Income* £268,714 *Grants* £120,000 *Grants to organisations* £120,000 *Assets* £1,536,052
**TRUSTEES** David Kingsmill; Philip Kendall; Helen Whitbread; Nicholas Rice; Stephen Langton; Jonathan McKechnie-Jarvis.

**OTHER INFORMATION** Grants were made to 40 churches in 2013/14.
**HOW TO APPLY** Application forms and full guidelines can be downloaded from the trust's website. Completed applications should be returned to the Chair of the Grants Committee, Jonathan MacKechnie Jarvis, 73 Forest View Road, Tuffley, Gloucester GL4 0BY. When an application is received the trust will arrange a meeting at your church to discuss your application and view the proposed work. The committee meets in June and December. Applications should be made by the end of April for the June meeting or by the end of October for the December meeting.
**WHO TO APPLY TO** Jonathan MacKechnie Jarvis, Head of the Grants Committee, 73 Forest View Road, Tuffley, Gloucester GL4 0BY *Tel.* 01285 653164 *email* grants@ghct.org.uk *Website* www.ghct.org.uk

## ■ Worshipful Company of Glovers of London Charitable Trust

**CC NO** 269091 **ESTABLISHED** 1975
**WHERE FUNDING CAN BE GIVEN** UK with a preference for the City of London.
**WHO CAN BENEFIT** Glovers and glove-related projects; general charitable purposes.
**WHAT IS FUNDED** The trust makes grants mainly towards the provision of gloves, or to causes that are related to the City of London.
**RANGE OF GRANTS** Up to £5,000.
**SAMPLE GRANTS** King Edwards School, Witley – bursary (£5,000); Crisis (£2,500); Guildhall School of Music and Drama – bursary (£2,100); Kings College Hospital (£1,600); Church of St Margaret, Lothbury (£1,500); Whitechapel Mission (£1,000).
**FINANCES** *Year* 2013/14 *Income* £58,659 *Grants* £40,216 *Grants to organisations* £40,216 *Assets* £716,258
**TRUSTEE** Worshipful Company of Glovers of London.
**HOW TO APPLY** Apply in writing to the correspondent.
**WHO TO APPLY TO** Monique Hood, Clerk, c/o Knox Cropper and Co., 8–9 Well Court, London EC4M 9DN *email* clerk@thegloverscompany.org

## ■ The GNC Trust

**CC NO** 211533 **ESTABLISHED** 1960
**WHERE FUNDING CAN BE GIVEN** UK, with preferences for Birmingham and Cornwall.
**WHO CAN BENEFIT** Charitable organisations.
**WHAT IS FUNDED** General charitable purposes.
**RANGE OF GRANTS** £1,000–£5,000
**SAMPLE GRANTS** Birmingham Royal Ballet (£6,200 in three grants); Brockenhurst College Charitable Trust (£5,000); Friends of Bournville Carillon (£4,500); Performances Birmingham Limited (£4,000); Cure Leukaemia (£1,300 in two grants); National Trust and University of Birmingham (£1,000 each).
**FINANCES** *Year* 2013 *Income* £38,557 *Grants* £42,412 *Grants to organisations* £42,412 *Assets* £1,049,594
**TRUSTEES** G. Cadbury; Jayne Cadbury; P. Richmond-Watson; I. Williamson.
**OTHER INFORMATION** Grants were made to ten organisations during the year.
**HOW TO APPLY** Apply in writing to the correspondent at any time. There are no application forms and applications are not acknowledged.

**WHO TO APPLY TO** Mrs Paddy Spragg, Correspondent, 41 Sycamore Drive, Hollywood, Birmingham B47 5QX *Tel.* 07976 848390

## ■ The Godinton Charitable Trust

**CC NO** 268321 **ESTABLISHED** 1974
**WHERE FUNDING CAN BE GIVEN** Kent-based organisations are given priority.
**WHO CAN BENEFIT** Registered charities.
**WHAT IS FUNDED** A regular payment to Godinton House Preservation Trust; local general charitable purposes.
**WHAT IS NOT FUNDED** Individuals.
**TYPE OF GRANT** One-off and recurrent.
**RANGE OF GRANTS** Up to £13,000 but generally £500–£2,000.
**SAMPLE GRANTS** Godinton House Preservation Trust (£13,000); The Rifles Officers Fund (£5,000); Wyvern Foundation Trust (£2,000); Great Chart PCC (£1,800); Future Trees, Kent Wildlife Trust and North School Farm (£1,000 each); Ashford Family Nursery, Sands Baby Garden and Weald Garden Preservation Society (£500 each).
**FINANCES** *Year* 2012/13 *Income* £140,960 *Grants* £49,600 *Grants to organisations* £49,600 *Assets* £5,098,603
**TRUSTEES** Hon. Wyndham Plumptre; Hon. Jon D. Leigh-Pemberton; Michael Jennings.
**OTHER INFORMATION** Grants were made to 29 organisations in 2012/13. The 2012/13 accounts were the latest available at the time of writing (June 2015).
**HOW TO APPLY** Apply in writing to the correspondent.
**WHO TO APPLY TO** N. Sandford, Godinton House, Godinton Lane, Ashford, Kent TN23 3BP *Tel.* 01233 632652 *email* office@godintonhouse.co.uk

## ■ The Sydney and Phyllis Goldberg Memorial Charitable Trust

**CC NO** 291835 **ESTABLISHED** 1985
**WHERE FUNDING CAN BE GIVEN** UK.
**WHO CAN BENEFIT** Organisations benefitting, research workers, at risk groups, people with disabilities, and people who are disadvantaged by poverty or socially isolated.
**WHAT IS FUNDED** Medical research; welfare; disability.
**TYPE OF GRANT** One-off, some recurrent.
**RANGE OF GRANTS** Up to £14,000.
**SAMPLE GRANTS** The British Stammering Association, The Dystonia Society, Children with Special Needs Foundation, Children of St Mary's Intensive Care Department, Life Centre, Child Brain Injury Trust, Lisa May Foundation and Matthews Friends (£14,000 each); The Isaac Goldberg Charity Trust (£6,000).
**FINANCES** *Year* 2013/14 *Income* £120,662 *Grants* £120,662 *Grants to organisations* £120,662 *Assets* £3,889,639
**TRUSTEES** Christopher Pexton; Howard Vowles; Michael Church.
**OTHER INFORMATION** Grants were made to nine organisations in 2013/14.
**HOW TO APPLY** Apply in writing to the correspondent. Telephone requests are not appreciated. Applicants are advised to apply towards the end of the calendar year.
**WHO TO APPLY TO** Michael Church, Trustee, Coulthards Mackenzie, 17 Park Street, Camberley, Surrey GU15 3PQ *Tel.* 01276 65470

## ■ The Golden Bottle Trust

**CC NO** 327026 **ESTABLISHED** 1985
**WHERE FUNDING CAN BE GIVEN** Worldwide.
**WHO CAN BENEFIT** Registered charities.
**WHAT IS FUNDED** General charitable purposes with a preference for charities supporting the environment, health, education, religion, the arts and financially developing countries.
**WHAT IS NOT FUNDED** Individuals; organisations that are not registered charities.
**TYPE OF GRANT** One-off and recurring.
**RANGE OF GRANTS** Up to £10,000 with larger grants for charities that the Hoare family have a personal relationship with.
**SAMPLE GRANTS** The Bulldog Trust (£200,000); The Master Charitable Trust (£90,000); The Henry C. Hoare Charitable Trust (£60,000); Intermission Youth Theatre (£40,500); Future for Religious Heritage (£30,000); Ashoka Support Network (£20,000); Buglife and Winchester Cathedral Trust (£20,000 each); Media Trust (£15,000); Skiing with Heroes (£10,500); First Story (£10,000).
**FINANCES** *Year* 2012/13 *Income* £1,343,063 *Grants* £1,377,811 *Grants to organisations* £1,377,811 *Assets* £9,494,137
**TRUSTEES** Hoare Trustees ( H. C. Hoare; Sir D. J. Hoare; R. Q. Hoare; A. S. Hoare; V. E. Hoare; S. M. Hoare; A. S. Hoare)
**OTHER INFORMATION** The 2012/13 accounts were the latest available at the time of writing (June 2015).
**HOW TO APPLY** The trustees do not normally respond to unsolicited approaches.
**WHO TO APPLY TO** The Trustees, C. Hoare and Co, 37 Fleet Street, London EC4P 4DQ *Tel.* 020 7353 4522

## ■ Golden Charitable Trust

**CC NO** 263916 **ESTABLISHED** 1972
**WHERE FUNDING CAN BE GIVEN** UK with a preference for West Sussex.
**WHO CAN BENEFIT** Charitable organisations.
**WHAT IS FUNDED** Preservation; conservation; medical research.
**RANGE OF GRANTS** Up to £250,000, usually between £100–£2,500.
**SAMPLE GRANTS** The London Library (£250,000); the Friends of St Mary's Petworth (£22,000); Westminster Synagogue (£7,000); Friends of Pallant House Gallery and the Langdon Foundation (£2,000 each); the Royal Star and Garter Homes and the Royal School of Needlework (£1,000 each); the Wordsworth Trust, Petworth Film House and the Dermatitis and Allied Diseases Research Trust (£500 each); the National Trust and the Parachute Regimental Association (£100 each); and St Wilfred's Hospice (£50).
**FINANCES** *Year* 2013/14 *Income* £43,411 *Grants* £40,000 *Grants to organisations* £40,000
**TRUSTEES** Sara Solnick; Jeremy Solnick.
**HOW TO APPLY** Apply in writing to the correspondent.
**WHO TO APPLY TO** Lewis Golden, Little Leith Gate, Angel Street, Petworth GU28 0BG *Tel.* 01798 342434 *email* lewisgolden@icloud.com

## ■ The Goldman Sachs Charitable Gift Fund (UK)

**CC NO** 1120148 **ESTABLISHED** 2007
**WHERE FUNDING CAN BE GIVEN** USA and the UK, and well as Canada, France and Hong Kong, although in practice organisations are supported worldwide.
**WHO CAN BENEFIT** Registered charities, schools and universities.
**WHAT IS FUNDED** Education; arts and culture; social welfare; medical.
**SAMPLE GRANTS** Trustees of Princeton University and Trustees of the University of Pennsylvania (£674,000 each); Gilman School Inc (£237,000) Tufts College (£87,500); Cornell University (£54,000); Trustees of Dartmouth College (£35,500); Brown University (£17,000); Wellington College (£15,500); Singapore American School Foundation (£13,500).
**FINANCES** Year 2013/14 Income £660,598 Grants £1,913,972 Grants to organisations £1,913,972 Assets £8,987,394
**TRUSTEES** Robert Katz; Mike Housden; Peter Fahey.
**OTHER INFORMATION** This fund was established by Goldman Sachs International in 2007 as one of the vehicles for its charitable giving. It is also connected to Goldman Sachs Gives.
**HOW TO APPLY** Apply in writing to the correspondent.
**WHO TO APPLY TO** Mike Housden, Trustee, Goldman Sachs International, Peterborough Court, 133 Fleet Street, London EC4A 2BB *Tel.* 020 7774 1000

## ■ Goldman Sachs Gives (UK)

**CC NO** 1123956 **ESTABLISHED** 2008
**WHERE FUNDING CAN BE GIVEN** Worldwide.
**WHO CAN BENEFIT** Registered charities, schools and universities.
**WHAT IS FUNDED** Education; arts and culture; social welfare; medical.
**RANGE OF GRANTS** Up to £1.2 million.
**SAMPLE GRANTS** Greenhouse Schools Project (£1.2 million); Grenada Schools Limited (£1 million); Wellesley College (£636,000); DEEDS Public Charitable Trust (£600,000); The American School in London Foundation UK Limited (£570,000); London School of Economics and Political Science (£559,000).
**FINANCES** Year 2013/14 Income £23,286,425 Grants £17,365,078 Grants to organisations £17,365,078 Assets £83,656,160
**TRUSTEES** Jennifer Evans; Robert Katz; Mike Housden; Peter Fahey; Sally Ann Boyle.
**OTHER INFORMATION** This fund was established by Goldman Sachs International in 2008 as one of the vehicles for its charitable giving. It is also connected to the Goldman Sachs Charitable Gift Fund.
**HOW TO APPLY** Apply in writing to the correspondent.
**WHO TO APPLY TO** Mike Housden, Trustee, Goldman Sachs International, Peterborough Court, 133 Fleet Street, London EC4A 2BB *Tel.* 020 7774 1000

## ■ The Goldsmiths' Arts Trust Fund

**CC NO** 313329 **ESTABLISHED** 1965
**WHERE FUNDING CAN BE GIVEN** UK.
**WHO CAN BENEFIT** Registered charities.
**WHAT IS FUNDED** The arts by the encouragement of the art of design and good craftsmanship.
**RANGE OF GRANTS** £7,000–£34,000
**SAMPLE GRANTS** Goldsmiths' Craft and Design Council (£34,000); New Designers – College Grant (£10,500); British Silver Week (£10,000); City and Guilds (£7,000).
**FINANCES** Year 2013/14 Income £772,259 Grants £91,237 Grants to organisations £61,500 Assets £112,485
**TRUSTEE** The Goldsmiths' Company Trustee.
**HOW TO APPLY** Apply in writing to the correspondent.
**WHO TO APPLY TO** The Trustees, The Goldsmiths' Company, Goldsmiths' Hall, Foster Lane, London EC2V 6BN *Tel.* 020 7606 7010 *email* charity@thegoldsmiths.co.uk *Website* www.thegoldsmiths.co.uk

## ■ The Goldsmiths' Company Charity

**CC NO** 1088699 **ESTABLISHED** 1961
**WHERE FUNDING CAN BE GIVEN** UK, with a special interest in London charities.
**WHO CAN BENEFIT** Registered charities, schools, individuals connected with the trade of goldsmithing, silversmithing and jewellery, and Londoners in need. Grants are made to London-based or national charities, but not to local provincial charities. Where charities are members, branches or affiliates of an association, appeals are accepted from the governing body or head office of that association only. In the case of church restoration, block grants are made to the Historic Churches Preservation Trust and therefore appeals from individual churches will not normally be considered.
**WHAT IS FUNDED** Support of the goldsmiths' craft; education; general charitable purposes (including general welfare, medical welfare, youth, heritage, church, and arts).
**WHAT IS NOT FUNDED** Applications are not normally considered on behalf of medical research; animal welfare; memorials to individuals; overseas projects; individual housing associations; endowment schemes; charities with a turnover of more than £10 million.
**TYPE OF GRANT** Buildings, capital, salaries, core, project, start-up and running costs. Funding is occasionally three year, but usually one-off.
**RANGE OF GRANTS** £500 upwards.
**SAMPLE GRANTS** Goldsmiths' Centre (£1,225,000); R L Glasspool Charity Trust (£25,000); Refugee Council (£10,000); South Yorkshire Police (£8,000); Foundation for Young Musicians (£5,000); Young Enterprise London (£4,500); Blind in Business and DreamArts – Paddington (£3,000 each); The Sunnybank Trust (£2,500); Teen Action – Harringey (£2,000); Cambridge University (£500).
**FINANCES** Year 2013/14 Income £3,554,087 Grants £3,333,021 Grants to organisations £3,333,021 Assets £108,434,490
**TRUSTEE** Goldsmith's Company Trustee
**HOW TO APPLY** Application forms can be downloaded from the website and should be returned to the correspondent along with any additional required information.
**WHO TO APPLY TO** The Charities Administrator, Goldsmiths' Hall, 13 Foster Lane, London EC2V 6BN *Tel.* 020 7606 7010 *email* the.clerk@thegoldsmiths.co.uk *Website* www.thegoldsmiths.co.uk/charities

## ■ The Golf Foundation Limited

CC NO 285917　　ESTABLISHED 1982
WHERE FUNDING CAN BE GIVEN UK
WHO CAN BENEFIT Organisations benefitting children and young people.
WHAT IS FUNDED Golf.
WHAT IS NOT FUNDED Individuals.
SAMPLE GRANTS Golf Roots Centres (£105,000); Schools Sports Partnerships (£102,000); Special Projects (£38,000); Community Golf Coaches (£37,000); Schools – Special Needs (£13,000); Dragon Golf Centres (£4,000); County and Regional Groups (£1,400); and Schools (£200).
FINANCES Year 2013 Income £1,617,400 Grants £241,421 Grants to organisations £241,421 Assets £3,236,952
TRUSTEES Duncan Weir; Nicholas Sladden; Sir Robin Miller; Stephen Proctor; Di Horsley; Deborah Allmey; Charles Harrison; Ian Armitage; Doug Poole; Nigel Evans; Sally Stewart.
HOW TO APPLY Although the foundation states that it chooses its beneficiaries each year, there is a suggestion that unsolicited applications from organisations that share its aims and objectives will be considered. Contact the foundation's representative (listed on the website) in your area for further details on applying for funding.
WHO TO APPLY TO Alan Bough, Finance Manager, The Spinning Wheel, High Street, Hoddesdon, Hertfordshire EN11 8BP Tel. 01992 449830 email admin@golf-foundation.org Website www.golf-foundation.org

## ■ The Golsoncott Foundation

CC NO 1070885　　ESTABLISHED 1998
WHERE FUNDING CAN BE GIVEN UK.
WHO CAN BENEFIT Arts organisations.
WHAT IS FUNDED The trust states its objects as follows: 'to promote, maintain, improve and advance the education of the public in the arts generally and in particular the fine arts and music. The fostering of the practice and appreciation of the arts, especially amongst young people and new audiences, is a further specific objective.'
WHAT IS NOT FUNDED Individuals.
TYPE OF GRANT One-off and some recurring; core costs; salaries; project funding; start-up costs.
RANGE OF GRANTS £300–£5,000
SAMPLE GRANTS National Children's Orchestra (£4,000); Creative – Watchet (£2,100); Marian Consort (£2,000); Jessie's Fund and Live Music Now (£1,500 each); Box of Tricks Theatre and Young Vic (£1,000 each); Delphi Trust (£900); Foundling Museum (£800); Purbeck Arts (£500); Green Stag Theatre (£300).
FINANCES Year 2013/14 Income £73,355 Grants £53,986 Grants to organisations £53,986 Assets £2,261,745
TRUSTEES Penelope Lively; Josephine Lively; Stephen Wick; Dr Harriet Wood.
OTHER INFORMATION Grants were made to 60 organisations in 2013/14.
HOW TO APPLY The trustees meet quarterly to consider applications, in February, May, August and November. Applications, made by hard copy with an email contact address, should be sent to the correspondent by the end of the month preceding the month of the trustees' meeting. They should include the following: 'a clear and concise statement of the project, whether the award sought will be for the whole project or a component part. Is the applicant organisation of charitable status?'; 'evidence that there is a clear benefit to the public, i.e. does the project conform with the declared object of the trust'; 'the amount requested should be specified, or a band indicated. Is this the only source of funding being sought? All other sources of funding should be indicated, including those that have refused funding'; 'if the grant requested is part of the match-funding required by the Heritage Lottery Foundation (HLF) following an award, state the amount of that award and the percentage of match-funding required by the HLF and the completion date'; 'wherever possible an annual report and accounts should accompany the application, as may other supporting information deemed relevant'. According to the website, 'second or further applications will not be considered until a minimum of 12 months has elapsed since determination of the previous application, whether successful or not'.
WHO TO APPLY TO Hal Bishop, Correspondent, 53 St Leonard's Road, Exeter EX2 4LS Tel. 01392 252855 email golsoncott@btinternet.com Website www.golsoncott.org.uk

## ■ Nicholas and Judith Goodison's Charitable Settlement

CC NO 1004124　　ESTABLISHED 1991
WHERE FUNDING CAN BE GIVEN UK.
WHO CAN BENEFIT Registered charities.
WHAT IS FUNDED Arts and arts education.
WHAT IS NOT FUNDED Individuals.
TYPE OF GRANT Recurrent capital grants. One-off grants.
RANGE OF GRANTS Up to £30,000 but generally £250–£5,000.
SAMPLE GRANTS Wigmore Hall (£29,000); National Life Stories (£8,000); Royal Academy (£7,500); Fitzwilliam Museum (£5,300); Courtauld Institute (£5,000); Academy of Ancient Music (£2,500); Tate Foundation (£2,000); Crafts Council (£1,500); NMC Recordings (£1,300); Public Catalogue Foundation (£500); World Monuments Trust (£400) Goldsmiths Charity (£300).
FINANCES Year 2013/14 Income £65,554 Grants £82,870 Grants to organisations £82,870 Assets £1,570,639
TRUSTEES Sir Nicholas Goodison; Judith Goodison; Katharine Goodison.
OTHER INFORMATION Grants were made to 25 organisations in 2013/14.
HOW TO APPLY The trust states that it cannot respond to unsolicited applications.
WHO TO APPLY TO Sir Nicholas Goodison, Trustee, PO Box 2512, London W1A 5ZP email goodisonn2@btinternet.com

## ■ The Goodman Foundation

CC NO 1097231　　ESTABLISHED 2003
WHERE FUNDING CAN BE GIVEN UK and overseas.
WHO CAN BENEFIT Registered charities.
WHAT IS FUNDED General charitable purposes; overseas; social welfare; older people; health; disability.
FINANCES Year 2013/14 Income £10,163,749 Grants £228,891 Grants to organisations £228,891 Assets £34,363,454
TRUSTEES Laurence Goodman; Catherine Goodman; Richard Cracknell; Lesley Tidd; Philip Morgan.
OTHER INFORMATION A list of beneficiaries was not included in the accounts.
HOW TO APPLY Apply in writing to the correspondent.

## The Mike Gooley Trailfinders Charity

**CC NO** 1048993  **ESTABLISHED** 1995
**WHERE FUNDING CAN BE GIVEN** UK.
**WHO CAN BENEFIT** Charitable organisations.
**WHAT IS FUNDED** Medical research; youth community projects and the armed forces.
**WHAT IS NOT FUNDED** Overseas charities; individuals.
**RANGE OF GRANTS** Up to £400,000.
**SAMPLE GRANTS** Alzheimer's Society (£400,000); Prostate Cancer Charity (£100,000); and the Second World War Experience Centre (£40,000).
**FINANCES** Year 2013/14 Income £989,376 Grants £1,139,394 Grants to organisations £1,139,394 Assets £9,863,885
**TRUSTEES** Mark Bannister; Tristan Gooley; Michael Gooley; Bernadette Gooley; Fiona Gooley; Louise Breton.
**OTHER INFORMATION** A list of grants was not included in the charity's recent accounts.
**HOW TO APPLY** Apply in writing to the correspondent.
**WHO TO APPLY TO** Michael Gooley, Trustee, 9 Abingdon Road, London W8 6AH *Tel.* 020 7938 3143 *Website* www.trailfinders.com

## The Gosling Foundation Limited

**CC NO** 326840  **ESTABLISHED** 1962
**WHERE FUNDING CAN BE GIVEN** Worldwide. In practice UK.
**WHO CAN BENEFIT** Registered charities.
**WHAT IS FUNDED** Welfare; the advancement of religion; the advancement of education; general charitable purposes.
**RANGE OF GRANTS** Up to £2 million but typically £1,000–£50,000.
**SAMPLE GRANTS** Royal Collection Trust (£2 million); Duke of Edinburgh Award (£103,000 in three grants); Greater London Fund for the Blind and SSAFA (£50,000 each); HMS Duncan (£25,000); Queen's Chapel of the Savoy (£10,000); Winchester Cathedral Trust (£5,00); British Forces Foundation and BLESMA (£2,000 each); Richmond Mencap (£1,000).
**FINANCES** Year 2013/14 Income £4,452,146 Grants £3,483,291 Grants to organisations £3,483,291 Assets £96,767,757
**TRUSTEES** Rear Admiral Sir Donald Gosling; Sir Ronald Hobson; Hon Cmdr Gosling.
**OTHER INFORMATION** Grants were made to 137 organisations in 2013/14.
**HOW TO APPLY** Apply in writing to the correspondent. The grant-making policies of the foundation are 'regularly reviewed' and currently are: applications should fall within the objects of the charity; there is no minimum limit for any grant; all grants will be approved unanimously. The trustees meet quarterly.
**WHO TO APPLY TO** Anne Yusof, Secretary, 21 Bryanston Street, Marble Arch, London W1H 7PR *Tel.* 020 7495 5599 *email* Anne.Yusof@conprop.co.uk

## The Gould Charitable Trust

**CC NO** 1035453  **ESTABLISHED** 1993
**WHERE FUNDING CAN BE GIVEN** Worldwide.
**WHO CAN BENEFIT** Registered charities only.
**WHAT IS FUNDED** Education and training, with preference towards Jewish organisations and causes.
**WHAT IS NOT FUNDED** Individuals.
**TYPE OF GRANT** Up to three years. Unrestricted funding.
**RANGE OF GRANTS** Up to £20,000.
**SAMPLE GRANTS** UJIA (£31,500); One to One (£3,600); Jewish Women's Aid (£3,000); World Jewish Relief (£2,300); FCED Foundation Philippines (£1,800); Jewish Care (£1,500); Médecins Sans Frontières (£1,000); Royal Free Charity (£600); NSPCC (£400); Notting Hill Housing (£200).
**FINANCES** Year 2013/14 Income £26,760 Grants £58,752 Grants to organisations £58,752 Assets £1,010,364
**TRUSTEES** Jean Gould; Simon Gould; Sidney Gould; Lawrence Gould; Matthew Gould.
**OTHER INFORMATION** Grants were made to 30 organisations in 2013/14.
**HOW TO APPLY** Apply in writing to the correspondent.
**WHO TO APPLY TO** S. Gould, Trustee, Cervantes, Pinner Hill, Pinner HA5 3XU *Tel.* 020 8868 2700 *email* sidney.gould@gmail.com

## The Grace Charitable Trust

**CC NO** 292984  **ESTABLISHED** 1985
**WHERE FUNDING CAN BE GIVEN** UK.
**WHO CAN BENEFIT** Registered charities, including Christian organisations.
**WHAT IS FUNDED** General charitable purposes, Christian, education, medical and social welfare.
**RANGE OF GRANTS** £1,000–£10,000
**SAMPLE GRANTS** Alpha, the International Christian College and Euroevangelism.
**FINANCES** Year 2013/14 Income £394,395 Grants £289,492 Grants to organisations £286,092 Assets £2,153,154
**TRUSTEES** G. Payne; E. Payne; G. Snaith; R. Quayle; M. Mitchell.
**HOW TO APPLY** The trust states: 'Grants are made only to charities known to the settlors and unsolicited applications are, therefore, not considered.'
**WHO TO APPLY TO** Mrs G. Payne, Trustee, Swinford House, Nortons Lane, Great Barrow, Chester CH3 7JZ *Tel.* 01928 740773

## A. B. Grace Trust

**CC NO** 504332  **ESTABLISHED** 1975
**WHERE FUNDING CAN BE GIVEN** Garstang and Preston.
**WHO CAN BENEFIT** Charitable organisations.
**WHAT IS FUNDED** General charitable purposes.
**TYPE OF GRANT** Recurrent.
**RANGE OF GRANTS** £4,000–£5000
**SAMPLE GRANTS** Christ Church – Over Wyresdale, Guide Dogs for the Blind, Leonard Cheshire Disability, RNLI, RSPB, St Helen's Church – Churchtown, St Mary's and St Michael's Church – Bonds, St Peter's Parish Church Church – Scorton, United Reformed Church – Garstang (£4,400 each).
**FINANCES** Year 2013/14 Income £44,989 Grants £44,000 Grants to organisations £44,000 Assets £1,194,518
**TRUSTEES** Tony Blunt; Tom Balmain; Valerie Wilson.
**OTHER INFORMATION** Grants were made to ten organisations in 2013/14.

---

**WHO TO APPLY TO** The Trustees, c/o ABP, Unit 6290, Bishops Court, Solihull Parkway, Birmingham Business Park, Birmingham

HOW TO APPLY 'The charity's trust deed sets out very specifically who are beneficiaries are to be and consequently we are unable to consider any grant applications.'
WHO TO APPLY TO Tony Blunt, Trustee, 31 Yewlands Drive, Garstang, Preston PR3 1JP *Tel.* 01995 604158 *email* abgrace@live.co.uk

### ■ The Graff Foundation

CC NO 1012859　　　ESTABLISHED 1991
WHERE FUNDING CAN BE GIVEN UK and worldwide.
WHO CAN BENEFIT Charitable organisations.
WHAT IS FUNDED General charitable purposes.
TYPE OF GRANT One-off and recurrent.
RANGE OF GRANTS £3,000–£400,000
SAMPLE GRANTS The Leonardo DiCaprio Foundation (£396,500); The Museum of Contemporary Art (£120,500); NSPCC and the Tate Foundation (£5,000 each); the Weizmann Institute UK (£3,000).
FINANCES *Year* 2014 *Income* £687,876 *Grants* £530,252 *Grants to organisations* £530,232 *Assets* £3,964,616
TRUSTEES Laurence Graff; Francois Graff; Anthony Kerman.
OTHER INFORMATION Grants were made to six organisations in 2014.
HOW TO APPLY Apply in writing to the correspondent.
WHO TO APPLY TO Anthony Kerman, c/o Kerman and Co. LLP, 200–203 Strand, London WC2R 1DJ *Tel.* 020 7539 7272

### ■ E. C. Graham Belford Charitable Settlement

CC NO 1014869　　　ESTABLISHED 1991
WHERE FUNDING CAN BE GIVEN Northumberland.
WHO CAN BENEFIT Charitable organisations.
WHAT IS FUNDED General charitable purposes.
RANGE OF GRANTS Up to £10,000.
SAMPLE GRANTS Bell View (Belford) Limited, Berwick Youth Project, Hexham Youth Initiative and Tynedale Hospice at Home (£10,000 each); Breast Cancer Care (£5,000); Woodhorn Charitable Trust (£3,000); Cramlington Voluntary Youth Project, Elizabeth Finn Care and Hospicecare Northumberland (£2,500 each); Calvert Trust and Tomorrow's People (£2,000 each).
FINANCES *Year* 2013/14 *Income* £103,832 *Grants* £90,000 *Grants to organisations* £90,000 *Assets* £6,842,365
TRUSTEES Anthony Thompson; George Hutchinson.
HOW TO APPLY Apply in writing to the correspondent.
WHO TO APPLY TO Anthony Thompson, Trustee, 4 More London Riverside, London SE1 2AU *Tel.* 020 7379 0000

### ■ The Grahame Charitable Foundation Limited

CC NO 1102332　　　ESTABLISHED 1969
WHERE FUNDING CAN BE GIVEN UK and overseas.
WHO CAN BENEFIT Organisations benefitting: children, young adults, older people and Jewish people.
WHAT IS FUNDED The advancement of the Jewish religion; health facilities and buildings, medical studies and research; special schools; cultural and religious teaching; and community services.
WHAT IS NOT FUNDED Individuals.
TYPE OF GRANT Capital, core costs, interest-free loans, one-off, recurring costs and start-up costs. Funding for up to two years may be considered.
RANGE OF GRANTS Up to £45,000.
SAMPLE GRANTS Emunah – The Child Resettlement Fund (£45,000); British Friends of the Shaare Zedek Medical Centre (£35,000); Avraham Bezalel Foundation and Jerusalem College of Technology (£25,000 each); Beis Rizhin Trust, Jewish Care and Ezer Leyoldos (£10,000 each); and Beit Haknesset Caesarea (£7,500).
FINANCES *Year* 2014 *Income* £295,262 *Grants* £285,680 *Grants to organisations* £285,680 *Assets* £1,012,383
TRUSTEES Alan Grahame; J. M. Greenwood.
OTHER INFORMATION Grants were made to ten organisations in 2013/14.
HOW TO APPLY The trustees allocate funds on a long-term basis and therefore have none available for other applicants.
WHO TO APPLY TO Miki Shaw, 5 Spencer Walk, Hampstead High Street, London NW3 1QZ *Tel.* 020 7794 5281

### ■ The Granada Foundation

CC NO 241693　　　ESTABLISHED 1965
WHERE FUNDING CAN BE GIVEN North West England.
WHO CAN BENEFIT Organisations.
WHAT IS FUNDED Arts; sciences; recreation; education.
WHAT IS NOT FUNDED General appeals; individuals; expeditions; overseas travel; youth clubs/community associations.
RANGE OF GRANTS Up to £100,000.
SAMPLE GRANTS Royal Liverpool Philharmonic Society (£75,000); Royal Exchange Theatre and National Museums Liverpool (£25,000 each); Liverpool Biennial (£15,000); Buxton Festival (£6,500); Contact (£4,000); Manchester Camerata (£3,000); Manchester Museum (£2,000); Liverpool Live CIC (£1,000).
FINANCES *Year* 2013/14 *Income* £38,095 *Grants* £231,500 *Grants to organisations* £231,500 *Assets* £3,418,954
TRUSTEES Sir Robert Scott; Philip Ramsbottom; Prof. Jennifer Latto.
OTHER INFORMATION Grants were made to 37 organisations in 2013/14.
HOW TO APPLY The foundation's website states: 'Prospective applicants are advised, in the first instance, to provide a brief outline of the project for which funding is sought by completing a short enquiry form or by telephoning [see 'Who to apply to']. Please note only projects taking place in the **North West of England** will be considered.' Detailed information can be added when the formal application is submitted. Details of the next trustees' meeting will be given when an application form is sent (trustees meet three times a year at irregular intervals). All letters are acknowledged.
WHO TO APPLY TO Irene Langford, PO Box 3430, Chester CH1 9BZ *Tel.* 01244 661867 *email* irene.langford@btconnect.com *Website* www.granadafoundation.org

### ■ Grand Charitable Trust of the Order of Women Freemasons

CC NO 1059151　　　ESTABLISHED 1996
WHERE FUNDING CAN BE GIVEN UK and overseas.
WHO CAN BENEFIT Registered charities.
WHAT IS FUNDED General charitable purposes. This trust donates about half its grant total to causes related to the Order of Women

Freemasons, including individual members and their dependants. The remaining half is donated to external charities.
**RANGE OF GRANTS** Up to £150,000.
**SAMPLE GRANTS** Arrowe Park Hospital; Combat Stress; Diabetes UK; Hearing Dogs for the Deaf; Leukaemia Care; Midlands Air Ambulance; Rainbow Hospice; The Splash Appeal; Willen Hospice – Bletchley.
**FINANCES** Year 2013/14 Income £177,468 Grants £210,304 Grants to organisations £210,304 Assets £720,197
**TRUSTEES** Sylvia Major; Dr Iris Boggia-Black; Margaret Masters; Ms H. Naldrett; Zuzanka Penn; Beryl Daniels.
**HOW TO APPLY** Apply in writing to the correspondent. Applications should be submitted by the end of July each year for consideration by the trustees.
**WHO TO APPLY TO** The Trustees, 27 Pembridge Gardens, London, W2 4EF Tel. 020 7229 2368 Website www.owf.org.uk

## ■ The Grange Farm Centre Trust
**CC NO** 285162  **ESTABLISHED** 1984
**WHERE FUNDING CAN BE GIVEN** The London Metropolitan Police District and Epping Forest.
**WHO CAN BENEFIT** Charitable organisations, including scout groups, etc.
**WHAT IS FUNDED** Recreation and leisure activities.
**WHAT IS NOT FUNDED** No grants are given to individuals and usually no grants are given to applications received from local authorities.
**RANGE OF GRANTS** £550–£20,000
**SAMPLE GRANTS** Clapton Common Boys' Club; Epping Netball Club; Flash Musicals; Isleworth Explorer's Club; London Youth; Kids in Action; Marjorie Collins Centre; Pursuing Independent Paths; Shadwell Basin Outdoor Activity Centre; Woodford Parish Church Memorial Church.
**FINANCES** Year 2013/14 Income £333,338 Grants £88,998 Grants to organisations £88,998 Assets £12,772,579
**TRUSTEES** Michael Tomkins; Alex Pelican; Roger Neville; Charles Scrutton; Penny Smith; Peter Minoletti; Trevor Johnson; Robert Church; Margaret McEwen.
**HOW TO APPLY** Apply in writing to the correspondent giving a brief outline of what the grant will be used for. After initial consideration that the application falls within both the area of benefit and the objects of the trust, an application form will be sent to the applicant for completion which will then be considered in greater detail by the trustees.
**WHO TO APPLY TO** Nicholas Gadsby, Clerk, c/o 181 High Street, Epping, Essex CM16 4BQ Tel. 01992 578642 email info@grangefarmcentre.co.uk Website www.grangefarmcentre.co.uk

## ■ Grantham Yorke Trust
**CC NO** 228466  **ESTABLISHED** 1975
**WHERE FUNDING CAN BE GIVEN** The (old) West Midlands metropolitan county area.
**WHO CAN BENEFIT** Registered charities; youth organisations; individuals.
**WHAT IS FUNDED** Education, including providing outfits, clothing, tools, instruments, equipment or books to help such people on leaving school, university and so on, to prepare for, or enter a profession or trade; social welfare.
**WHAT IS NOT FUNDED** People aged 25 or over.
**RANGE OF GRANTS** Generally £50–£5,000.
**SAMPLE GRANTS** Walsall Street Teams (£5,000), Barnardo's (£5,000), Holy Trinity Community Project (£3,750), E R Mason Youth Centre (£3,500), New Testament Church of God – The Rock (£3,000), Support Help and Advice for Relatives of Prisoners (£3,000), St Francis Youth and Community Centre (£2,500).
**FINANCES** Year 2013/14 Income £249,278 Grants £183,042 Grants to organisations £169,490 Assets £6,839,861
**TRUSTEES** Howard Belton; Peter Jones; Tim Clarke; Fred Rattley; Philip Smiglarski, Chair; Barbara Welton; Revd Pamela Ogilvie; Marian Webb; Sue Butler.
**OTHER INFORMATION** Grants were made to 78 organisations and 38 individuals in 2013/14.
**HOW TO APPLY** Apply in writing to the correspondent. The trustees meet four times a year, in March, June, September and December.
**WHO TO APPLY TO** Christine Norgrove, Appeals Clerk, C/o SGH Martineau Solicitors, No. 1 Colmore Square, Birmingham B4 6AA Tel. 0800 763 1000 email christine.norgrove@sghmartineau.com

## ■ GrantScape
**CC NO** 1102249  **ESTABLISHED** 2004
**WHERE FUNDING CAN BE GIVEN** UK, check the website for specific areas in which programmes operate.
**WHO CAN BENEFIT** Registered charities; community organisations; councils.
**WHAT IS FUNDED** Environmental and community-based projects.
**WHAT IS NOT FUNDED** Each programme has slightly different exclusions, consult the fund listing on the website.
**RANGE OF GRANTS** £500–£60,000
**SAMPLE GRANTS** Caring for Life (£60,000); Leeds City Council (£45,000); Keystone Youth Centre (£23,000); Butterfly Conservation (£20,000); Warboys Parish Council (£10,000); East Kent Mencap (£7,500); Friends of Kettering Library (£6,800) Penysarn Village Hall (£5,000); Alverdiscott Community Hall (£3,400); Eastchurch Cricket Club (£1,200); Amlwch Town Juniors Football Club (£500).
**FINANCES** Year 2013/14 Income £1,709,963 Grants £1,307,193 Grants to organisations £1,307,193 Assets £2,029,174
**TRUSTEES** Christopher Preist; Anthony Cox; Mohammed Saddiq; David Bramley; Michael Clarke; Philippa Lyons.
**OTHER INFORMATION** Grantscape manage grant programmes on behalf of other organisations. Grants were made to 92 organisations in 2013/14.
**HOW TO APPLY** Applications are made via the charity's website.
**WHO TO APPLY TO** Mr S. Hargreaves, Office E, Whitsundoles, Broughton Road, Salford, Milton Keynes MK17 8BU Tel. 01908 247630 email helpdesk@grantscape.org.uk Website www.grantscape.org.uk

## ■ The J. G. Graves Charitable Trust
**CC NO** 207481  **ESTABLISHED** 1930
**WHERE FUNDING CAN BE GIVEN** Mainly Sheffield.
**WHO CAN BENEFIT** Registered charities.
**WHAT IS FUNDED** The provision of parks and open spaces; libraries and art galleries; advancement of education; general benefit of people who are sick or poor; and such other charitable purposes as the trustees see fit. The income is

mainly applied to local (Sheffield) charities for capital purposes rather than running costs.
**WHAT IS NOT FUNDED** Grants are generally not made to or for the benefit of individuals.
**TYPE OF GRANT** Mainly for capital and one-off for start-ups. Some for running costs.
**RANGE OF GRANTS** Up to £5,000.
**SAMPLE GRANTS** St Luke's Hospice (£5,000); Sheffield Industrial Museums Trust and Women of Steel (£3,000 each); Christ Church – Pitsmoor, Galvanize – Sheffield, St Wilfrid's Centre (£2,000 each); Chelsea Park Access, Clubs for Young People, EDT and Sage Greenfingers (£1,500 each).
**FINANCES** Year 2013 Income £185,897 Grants £89,325 Grants to organisations £89,325 Assets £4,655,716
**TRUSTEES** Dona Womack; John Bramah; Dr Derek Cullen; Richard Graves; Peter Price; Peter Clarkson; Cllr Jacqueline Drayton; Liz Frost; Hugh Grayson; Roderick Plews.
**OTHER INFORMATION** Grants were made to 20 organisations in 2013/14.
**HOW TO APPLY** Apply in writing to the correspondent, to reach the secretary by 31 March, 30 June, 30 September or 31 December. Applications should indicate whether the applicant is a registered charity, include audited accounts and include a statement giving such up-to-date information as is available with regard to the income and any commitments the organisation has.
**WHO TO APPLY TO** Craig Burton, Correspondent, BDO UK, 2nd Floor, Fountain Precinct, Balm Green, Sheffield S1 2JA Tel. 0114 276 7992 email craig.burton@bdo.co.uk

## ■ The Gray Trust
**CC NO** 210914 **ESTABLISHED** 1962
**WHERE FUNDING CAN BE GIVEN** Nottinghamshire, especially Linby and Southall.
**WHO CAN BENEFIT** Organisations benefitting older people, retired people, ex-service and service people, and people who are disadvantaged by poverty or disability.
**WHAT IS FUNDED** General charitable purposes, primarily for the benefit of older people, charitable purposes in the parishes of Linby and Papplewick and the surrounding area, and to provide sheltered accommodation for older people in Sherwood House and cottages.
**WHAT IS NOT FUNDED** Individuals; applications from outside Nottinghamshire.
**RANGE OF GRANTS** Up to £5,000 but generally £500–£1,000.
**SAMPLE GRANTS** Friends of the Elderly (£77,000); Age UK Limited (£5,000); Caudwell Children, Listening Books, St John's Day Centre for the Elderly, St Paul's Strelley PCC (£1,000 each); Carewatch in Nottingham, the Ear Foundation and Nottinghamshire Historic Churches Trust (£500 each); Action on Hearing Loss (£300).
**FINANCES** Year 2013/14 Income £44,651 Grants £100,364 Grants to organisations £100,364 Assets £5,409,710
**TRUSTEES** Claire Hardstaff; Bella St Clair Harlow; Richard Pannell; Revd Can. Keith Turner; Kirstin Thompson.
**OTHER INFORMATION** Grants were made to 31 organisations in 2014/15.
**HOW TO APPLY** Apply in writing to the correspondent by letter of application together with most recent accounts.

**WHO TO APPLY TO** Nigel Lindley, Trust Co-ordinator, Smith Cooper LLP, 2 Lace Market Square, Nottingham NG1 1PB Tel. 0115 945 4300 email nigel.lindley@smithcooper.co.uk

## ■ The Gordon Gray Trust
**CC NO** 213935 **ESTABLISHED** 1967
**WHERE FUNDING CAN BE GIVEN** England with a preference for Gloucestershire and Worcestershire.
**WHO CAN BENEFIT** Registered charities.
**WHAT IS FUNDED** General charitable purposes including medical, children, older people and environmental.
**WHAT IS NOT FUNDED** Individuals.
**RANGE OF GRANTS** £50 to £12,000.
**SAMPLE GRANTS** Avon Navigation Trust (£12,000); British Heart Foundation and Diabetes UK (£3,000 each); Worcestershire Breast Unit Campaign, Royal Medical Benevolent Fund, Keswick Mountain Rescue Team and NSPCC (£2,000 each); Friends of the Lake District (£1,500); Riders for Health, Samaritans (Cheltenham and District) and Great Oaks Dean Forest Hospice (£1000 each); Tewkesbury and District Choral Society (£750); First Newent Scout Group and Gloucestershire Wildlife Trust (£500 each); and Gloucestershire Historic Churches Trust (£50).
**FINANCES** Year 2013/14 Income £33,763 Grants £99,100 Grants to organisations £99,100 Assets £3,026,378
**TRUSTEES** Dr B. Gray; Mrs S. Watson-Armstrong; Mr C. Wilder; Miss R. Holmes; Mr E. Roberts; Mrs M. Gray.
**OTHER INFORMATION** Grants were made to 56 organisations in 2013/14.
**HOW TO APPLY** Apply in writing to the correspondent.
**WHO TO APPLY TO** Mrs M. Gray, Clerk to the Trustees, Grange Farm, Main Road, Bredon, Tewkesbury, Gloucestershire GL20 7EL

## ■ The Great Britain Sasakawa Foundation
**CC NO** 290766 **ESTABLISHED** 1985
**WHERE FUNDING CAN BE GIVEN** UK and Japan.
**WHO CAN BENEFIT** Voluntary, educational and cultural organisations and registered charities benefitting citizens of UK and Japan. Emphasis on younger people and on projects benefitting groups of people rather than individuals.
**WHAT IS FUNDED** Advancement of the education of the citizens of the UK and Japan in each other's institutions, people, history, language, culture, and society and in each other's intellectual, artistic and economic life. Research, exchanges, seminars, courses, publications and cultural events may all be funded. The foundation has a special scheme for joint research in medicine and health (the Butterfield Awards).
**WHAT IS NOT FUNDED** Individuals; retrospective funding; the construction, conservation or maintenance of land and buildings; student fees or travel in connection with study for a qualification; consumables; salaries.
**TYPE OF GRANT** Mainly one-off; also project and research, maximum term three years. No funding for core-costs.
**RANGE OF GRANTS** £750–£30,000
**SAMPLE GRANTS** Robert Gordon University (£5,000); Cardiff University (£4,000); Workers Educational Association (£3,500); Desford Colliery Band and the Henry Moore Institute (£3,000 each);

National Media Museum (£2,500); The Karate Centre and Tate Liverpool (£2,000 each); Action for Japan UK (£1,500); Pro Art and Co (£800).
**FINANCES** Year 2013 Income £762,168 Grants £675,000 Grants to organisations £675,000 Assets £25,949,581
**TRUSTEES** Michael French; Sir John Boyd; Ambassador Hiroaki Fuji; The Earl of St Andrews; Prof. David Cope; Tatsua Tanami; Joanna Pitman; Prof. Yuichi Hosoya; Ambassador Mutsuyoshi; Prof. Yorkio Kawaguchi; Prof. Janet Hunter.
**OTHER INFORMATION** The foundation is rarely able to consider grants for the total cost of any project and encourages applicants to seek additional support from other donors.
**HOW TO APPLY** Application forms are available from the website and should be returned by email. The awards committee meets in London in March, May and November. Applications should be received by 15 December, 31 March and 15 September. Awards meetings in Tokyo are held in April and October, with applications to be submitted by the end of February and September.
**WHO TO APPLY TO** Stephen McEnally, Chief Executive, Dilke House, 1 Malet Street, London WC1E 7JN Tel. 020 7436 9042 email grants@gbsf.org.uk Website www.gbsf.org.uk

■ **The Great Stone Bridge Trust of Edenbridge**
**CC NO** 224309  **ESTABLISHED** 1964
**WHERE FUNDING CAN BE GIVEN** The parish of Edenbridge, Kent.
**WHO CAN BENEFIT** Organisations, and individuals under 25 for educational purposes.
**WHAT IS FUNDED** General charitable purposes including a wide range of sporting, religious, charitable, educational and social activities.
**TYPE OF GRANT** Some recurrent.
**FINANCES** Year 2013/14 Income £106,620 Grants £62,314 Grants to organisations £59,900 Assets £3,545,589
**TRUSTEES** Richard Davison; Roy Cunningham; Dennis Leigh; Giles Jackman; John Hodson; Christine Burges; Mary Elliot; Clive Pearman; Cllr Peter Deans; Ben Brownless; Dr Spear.
**OTHER INFORMATION** Grants were made to 27 organisations and to five individuals in 2013/14.
**HOW TO APPLY** Apply in writing to the correspondent.
**WHO TO APPLY TO** William Ross, Correspondent, 8 Church Lane, East Grinstead, West Sussex RH19 3BA Tel. 01342 323687 email mross-pearless@btconnect.com

■ **The Great Torrington Town Lands Charity**
**CC NO** 202801  **ESTABLISHED** 1971
**WHERE FUNDING CAN BE GIVEN** Great Torrington, Devon.
**WHO CAN BENEFIT** Individuals and organisations, including clubs, societies and churches.
**WHAT IS FUNDED** Social welfare; general charitable purposes.
**RANGE OF GRANTS** Up to £15,000.
**SAMPLE GRANTS** Plough Arts Centre (£15,000); North Devon Hospice (£2,500).
**FINANCES** Year 2012/13 Income £266,545 Grants £57,011 Grants to organisations £57,011 Assets £6,413,648
**TRUSTEES** Richard Rumbold; Brian Davies; Elaine Norridge; Alan Stacey; Brian Nash; Steven Blake; Trevor Sutton; Elaine Weeks; Sharon Lambert; Toni Batty; Harold Martin; Zoe Fordham-Moore; Nicola Buckey; David Cobbledick.
**OTHER INFORMATION** The 2012/13 accounts were the latest available at the time of writing (June 2015).
**HOW TO APPLY** Apply in writing to the correspondent.
**WHO TO APPLY TO** Ian Newman, Correspondent, 25 South Street, Torrington, Devon EX38 8AA Tel. 01805 623517 email greattorringtoncharities@btconnect.com

■ **The Kenneth and Susan Green Charitable Foundation**
**CC NO** 1147248  **ESTABLISHED** 2012
**WHERE FUNDING CAN BE GIVEN** UK.
**WHO CAN BENEFIT** Charitable organisations.
**WHAT IS FUNDED** General charitable purposes; social welfare; education; health; the arts.
**WHAT IS NOT FUNDED** Individuals.
**FINANCES** Year 2014 Income £1,110,505 Grants £1,630,796 Grants to organisations £1,630,796 Assets £1,630,796
**TRUSTEES** Kenneth Green; Philip Stokes; Susan Green.
**HOW TO APPLY** Apply in writing to the correspondent.
**WHO TO APPLY TO** Philip Stokes, Trustee, c/o Kenneth Green Associates, Hill House, Monument Hill, Weybridge, Surrey KT13 8RX Tel. 01932 827060

■ **The Green Hall Foundation (formerly known as the Constance Green Foundation)**
**CC NO** 270775  **ESTABLISHED** 1976
**WHERE FUNDING CAN BE GIVEN** England, with a preference for West Yorkshire.
**WHO CAN BENEFIT** Registered charities and hospices.
**WHAT IS FUNDED** Social welfare; medicine; health; community projects; general charitable purposes.
**WHAT IS NOT FUNDED** Individuals.
**TYPE OF GRANT** Capital, special project, buildings and one-off funding of one year or less.
**RANGE OF GRANTS** £1,000–£10,000
**SAMPLE GRANTS** Ellen MacArthur Cancer Trust (£10,000); Leonard Cheshire Disability, Livability and Orbis (£5,000 each); Lifelites, Motability, Zoe's Place Baby Hospice (£3,000); FareShare Yorkshire (£2,000); Contact the Elderly and Mercy Ships UK (£1,000 each).
**FINANCES** Year 2013/14 Income £2,334,053 Grants £337,000 Grants to organisations £337,000 Assets £10,416,375
**TRUSTEES** Margaret Hall; Sue Collinson; Nigel Hall; Peter Morgan; Charlotte Footer.
**OTHER INFORMATION** Grants were made to 99 organisations in 2013/14.
**HOW TO APPLY** Applications should be made through the foundation's website. New applicants will have to create a login and will then be directed to the online application form.
**WHO TO APPLY TO** S. Hall, Centenary House, La Grande Route de Saint-Pierre, St Peter, Jersey JE3 7AY Tel. 01534 487757 email greenhallfoundation@fcmtrust.com Website www.greenhallfoundation.org

## ■ The Green Room Charitable Trust

**CC NO** 1134766  **ESTABLISHED** 2010
**WHERE FUNDING CAN BE GIVEN** Not defined. In practice, UK.
**WHO CAN BENEFIT** Charitable organisations.
**WHAT IS FUNDED** Environmental causes.
**FINANCES** Year 2012/13 Income £1,303,459 Grants £30,660 Grants to organisations £30,660 Assets £1,919,364
**TRUSTEES** Tom Prickett; Dino Morra; Andrew Ferry.
**HOW TO APPLY** Apply in writing to the correspondent via email.
**WHO TO APPLY TO** Tom Prickett, Trustee, 28 Ballingdon Road, London SW11 6AJ Tel. 020 3602 9247 email thegreenroomct@yahoo.co.uk

## ■ Philip and Judith Green Trust

**CC NO** 1109933  **ESTABLISHED** 2005
**WHERE FUNDING CAN BE GIVEN** UK and Africa.
**WHO CAN BENEFIT** Registered charities.
**WHAT IS FUNDED** Christian and missionary work.
**RANGE OF GRANTS** Up to £150,000 but generally £1,000–£10,000.
**SAMPLE GRANTS** Hope Through Action (£150,000); Philharmonia Trust (£35,000); Christian Aid and Protimos Education Trust (£10,000 each); Sentebale (£7,000); Inherit your Rights (£5,000); Society for Promoting Christian Knowledge (£2,500); Pioneers UK (£1,500); Greyfriars Mission (£1,100); Mission Aviation (£1,000).
**FINANCES** Year 2013/14 Income £146,216 Grants £348,374 Grants to organisations £348,374 Assets £11,586
**TRUSTEES** Philip Green; Judith Green.
**OTHER INFORMATION** Grants were made to 19 organisations in 2013/14.
**HOW TO APPLY** Apply in writing to the correspondent.
**WHO TO APPLY TO** Philip Green, Trustee, Marchfield, Flowers Hill, Pangbourne, Berkshire RG8 7BD Tel. 0118 984 5935 email philipngreen@me.com

## ■ Greenham Common Community Trust Limited

**CC NO** 1062762  **ESTABLISHED** 1997
**WHERE FUNDING CAN BE GIVEN** Newbury and the surrounding areas, northern edges of North Hampshire, West Berkshire.
**WHO CAN BENEFIT** Charitable organisations and individuals.
**WHAT IS FUNDED** Arts; community; education; health; nature and conservation; sport; youth disability; disadvantage/equality; older people.
**WHAT IS NOT FUNDED** Grants are only made within the trust's geographical area of operation.
**TYPE OF GRANT** One-off grants and specific projects, but grant delivery on a year-by year basis can be considered. Grants to both individuals and organisations.
**RANGE OF GRANTS** £250–£15,000
**SAMPLE GRANTS** Corn Exchange Newbury Trust (£15,000); Newbury College (£8,000); Life Education Centres (£4,400); Community Christmas (£3,000); Newbury Baptist Church (£2,500); Highclere Parish Council Bellringers Association (£2,400); Hungerford Literary Festival (£1,500); Wessex Children's Hospice Trust (£1,000); St Nicholas Performing Arts Project (£360); West Berkshire Minority Ethnic Forum (£250).
**FINANCES** Year 2013/14 Income £6,992,948 Grants £2,342,170 Grants to organisations £2,342,170 Assets £50,402,258
**TRUSTEES** Sir Peter Michael; David Bailey; Graham Mather; Malcolm Morris; Dr Paul Bryant; Julian Cazalet; Charles Brims; Biddy Hayward; Victoria Fishburn.
**HOW TO APPLY** By registering and making an application online at the portal www.findmeagrant.org. A hard copy of application form can be requested or any other assistance obtained by calling Melissa Elliott on 01635 817445 or email melissa@greenham-common-trust.co.uk. If you are applying for funding for a major project (over £75,000) it is suggested that you contact the chief executive, Chris Boulton on 01635 817444 to discuss it further.
**WHO TO APPLY TO** Stuart Tagg, Secretary and Chief Executive, Liberty House, The Enterprise Centre, Greenham Business Park, Newbury, Berkshire RG19 6HS Tel. 01635 817444 email chris@greenham-common-trust.co.uk Website www.greenham-common-trust.co.uk

## ■ The Greggs Foundation (formerly Greggs Trust)

**CC NO** 296590  **ESTABLISHED** 1987
**WHERE FUNDING CAN BE GIVEN** UK, with a preference for the north east of England, and in the regional divisions of Greggs plc.
**WHO CAN BENEFIT** Charitable organisations and individuals.
**WHAT IS FUNDED** Projects in the fields of the arts, the environment, conservation, education and health will be considered so long as they have a social welfare focus and/or are located in areas of deprivation.
**WHAT IS NOT FUNDED** Major grants are not made to: animal charities; friends of associations; branches or federations of national charities; larger organisations with a greater capacity to fundraise; uniformed groups such as scouts, guides and sea cadets; and sports clubs and associations. They are also not made for: overseas travel; curricular activities that take place during the school day; religious promotion; research grants; repayment of loans; purchase of vehicles; unspecified running costs; equipment for hospitals; and major capital projects Hardship fund grants are not made for: unspecified costs; repayment of loans; bankruptcy petition fees; holidays; funeral expenses; medical equipment; and computer equipment. Regional grants are not made for: ongoing running costs; contributions towards larger projects/fundraising appeals; animal charities; friends of associations; uniformed groups such as scouts, guides and sea cadets; sports clubs and associations; overseas travel; curricular activities that take place during the school day; religious promotion; research grants; repayment of loans; purchase of vehicles; medical equipment; major capital projects; and sponsorship of events or activities.
**TYPE OF GRANT** Core costs, running costs, project, start-up costs, recurring costs, salaries, one-off. Funding may be given for up to three years.
**SAMPLE GRANTS** Benwell Young People's Development Group and North East Special Needs Network (£45,000 each); the Hextol Foundation (£31,000); Eastlea Community

Centre (£28,000); Forward Assist and Lynemouth Trust (£25,000 each); Making A Difference (£21,000); Resource Project and Shiney Advice (£15,000 each); Redesign 4 U Ltd (£10,000); Safe @ Last (£9,000); Teesside Homeless Action Group (£5,000); St Andrew's Hospice and Survivors in Transition (£4,000); (£3,000); the Gladiator Programme, RDA Glasgow and Woodlands Community Development Trust (£2,000 each); the Phoenix Detached Youth Project and Sunderland Gateway (£1,500 each); Ashington Joint Welfare Scheme, Baby Buttercup Community Interest Company and Southlands School (£1,000 each).
**FINANCES** Year 2013 Income £1,833,649 Grants £1,537,678 Grants to organisations £1,537,678 Assets £11,193,981
**TRUSTEES** Andrew Davison; Kate Welch; Annemarie Norman; Fiona Nicholson; Richard Hutton; Tony Rowson; Nigel Murray; Roisin Currie; Karen Wilkinson-Bell.
**HOW TO APPLY** Each grants programme has its own criteria, guidelines and application process, all of which are available to view on the website. Applications from small community-led organisations and self-help groups are more likely to be successful than those from larger and well-staffed organisations and those that have greater fundraising capacity.
**WHO TO APPLY TO** David Carnaffan, Grants Manager, Greggs plc, Fernwood House, Clayton Road, Jesmond, Newcastle upon Tyne NE2 1TL Tel. 0191 212 7626 email greggsfoundation@greggs.co.uk Website www.greggsfoundation.org.uk

■ **The Gretna Charitable Trust**
**CC NO** 1020533    **ESTABLISHED** 1993
**WHERE FUNDING CAN BE GIVEN** UK, with a preference for Hertfordshire and London.
**WHO CAN BENEFIT** Registered charities.
**WHAT IS FUNDED** General charitable purposes.
**WHAT IS NOT FUNDED** Salaries or administration costs.
**TYPE OF GRANT** Ongoing and one-off. Seedcorn grants or grants for specific needs.
**RANGE OF GRANTS** Up to £20,000 but typically £500–£5,000.
**SAMPLE GRANTS** Royal Engineers Museum (£20,000); British Australia Society and Collect a Medal (£5,000 each); Garden Museum – Lambeth and The Scout Association (£2,000 each); Mensah Recovery Support Agency (£1,500); Charlie Waller Memorial Trust and The Globe Theatre (£1,000 each); Haileybury Youth Club and World Sight Foundation (£500 each).
**FINANCES** Year 2013/14 Income £120,171 Grants £77,800 Grants to organisations £77,800 Assets £2,331,188
**TRUSTEES** Richard Walduck; Susan Walduck; Alexander Walduck; Colin Bowles.
**OTHER INFORMATION** Grants were made to 41 organisations in 2013/14.
**HOW TO APPLY** This trust does not encourage applications.
**WHO TO APPLY TO** Richard Walduck, Trustee, Lower Woodside House, Lower Woodside, Hatfield AL9 6DJ email awalduck@imperialhotels.co.uk

■ **The Greys Charitable Trust**
**CC NO** 1103717    **ESTABLISHED** 2004
**WHERE FUNDING CAN BE GIVEN** UK and locally in Oxfordshire.
**WHO CAN BENEFIT** Charitable organisations.
**WHAT IS FUNDED** Church and historical preservation projects; the arts.
**SAMPLE GRANTS** The National Trust (£13,200 in two grants); Brighton College (£11,500 in two grants); Trinity College, Oxford (£10,000); Indo-Myanmar Conservation (£3,500); Oxfordshire Historic Churches (£3,000); Vincent's Club – Oxford (£1,000).
**FINANCES** Year 2013/14 Income £29,667 Grants £53,200 Grants to organisations £53,200 Assets £1,109,769
**TRUSTEES** Jacob Brunner; Timothy Brunner.
**OTHER INFORMATION** In 2013/14 ten grants were made to eight organisations.
**HOW TO APPLY** Apply in writing to the correspondent. The trustees usually meet twice a year.
**WHO TO APPLY TO** The Trustees, Flat 3, 2 Inverness Gardens, London W8 4RN Tel. 020 7727 6297 email p.roberts@robco.uk.com

■ **The Grimmitt Trust**
**CC NO** 801975    **ESTABLISHED** 1989
**WHERE FUNDING CAN BE GIVEN** Worldwide, locally Birmingham and the surrounding areas.
**WHO CAN BENEFIT** Charities; charitable organisations; individuals.
**WHAT IS FUNDED** Community development; children and youth; culture; education; medical; older people; overseas aid.
**TYPE OF GRANT** One-off, grants of up to three years.
**RANGE OF GRANTS** Up to £15,000 but mostly less than £2,500.
**SAMPLE GRANTS** King Edwards School Birmingham Trust, Methodist Relief and Development Fund and the Ackers (£10,000 each); Aston University and the Ironbridge Gorge Museum (£5,000 each); Allens Croft Project, Dream Makers and the Royal Institution (£3,000 each); and Action Centres UK, Prince's Trust and Wellington Methodist Church Centre (£2,500 each).
**FINANCES** Year 2013/14 Income £297,468 Grants £313,605 Grants to organisations £313,605 Assets £7,792,341
**TRUSTEES** Sue Day; Leon Murray; David Owen; Tim Welch; Jenny Dickins; Sarah Wilkey; Phil Smith; Trevor Jones.
**OTHER INFORMATION** In 2013/14 grants were made to 273 organisations and individuals.
**HOW TO APPLY** Applicants should contact the secretary who will advise on the best way to design a grant request and to ensure that all the necessary information is included. The trustees meet three times a year to consider applications. Applicants must demonstrate that their project and the grant received is used in line with the trust's objectives.
**WHO TO APPLY TO** Vanessa Welch, 151B All Saints Road, Kings Heath, Birmingham B14 6AT Tel. 0121 251 2951 email admin@grimmitt-trust.org.uk

■ **The Grocers' Charity**
**CC NO** 255230    **ESTABLISHED** 1968
**WHERE FUNDING CAN BE GIVEN** UK.
**WHO CAN BENEFIT** Registered charities only.
**WHAT IS FUNDED** The charity's charitable aims are broad-ranging, encompassing education, the

church, the relief of poverty, medicine, support for the arts, heritage, the elderly, young people and those with disabilities. Grants to churches, schools and other educational organisations are given to bodies with close links to the charity. Other categories are open for applications.

**WHAT IS NOT FUNDED** Support is rarely given to the following unless there is a specific or long-standing connection with the Grocers' Company: places of worship; educational establishments; hospices; charities whose beneficiaries are overseas; non-UK-registered charities; charities with a turnover of over £500,000; individuals.

**TYPE OF GRANT** Both capital and revenue projects. Non-recurring grants of limited size. Core costs, one-off, running costs and salaries will be considered. Funding may be given for up to one year.

**RANGE OF GRANTS** £1,000–£200,000

**SAMPLE GRANTS** Oundle School (£185,000); Motor Neurone Disease (£40,000); Only Connect (£26,000); Peterborough Cathedral Development and Preservation Trust (£10,000); VSO (£7,500); St John the Baptist – Stone (£7,000); Reed's School (£6,600); Royal College of Art (£6,000); St Paul's Cathedral Foundation Fabric Fund (£5,000); National Theatre (£3,000); Ulysses Trust, Bush Theatre and National Osteoporosis Society (£2,000 each); New Forest Disability Information Service (£1,250); and Royal London Society for Blind People (£1,100).

**FINANCES** Year 2013/14 Income £561,550 Grants £627,438 Grants to organisations £627,438 Assets £15,671,490

**TRUSTEES** The Grocers' Trust Company Limited

**OTHER INFORMATION** Grants were made to 120 organisations in 2013/14.

**HOW TO APPLY** Applications for grants can be considered from UK-registered charities only and must comply with current guidelines, including restrictions, as detailed in the Grocers' Charity Annual Review and on the Grocers' Company website: www.grocershall.co.uk. Applicants should complete the online enquiry form on the charity's website. 'Do not send any further information at this stage. We will review your enquiry and contact you if we wish to take your application further. We regret we are unable to acknowledge receipt of enquiries.' Applications are considered three to four times a year. Unsolicited applications are not accepted for the major grants programme: to apply for a Major Grant you must be supported by a member of the Grocers' Company and fit the criteria decided by the committee each year. Do not contact the Grocers' Charity directly and note the Grocers' Company are unable to provide details of members of the Company.

**WHO TO APPLY TO** Michael Griffin, Grocers' Hall, Princes Street, London EC2R 8AD *Tel.* 020 7606 3113 *email* enquiries@grocershall.co.uk *Website* www.grocershall.co.uk

## ■ The M. and R. Gross Charities Limited

**CC NO** 251888    **ESTABLISHED** 1967

**WHERE FUNDING CAN BE GIVEN** UK and overseas.

**WHO CAN BENEFIT** Jewish organisations.

**WHAT IS FUNDED** Organisations supporting the Orthodox Jewish religion and Jewish education.

**SAMPLE GRANTS** Atlas Memorial Limited; United Talmudical Associates Limited, a grant-making organisation which distributes smaller grants made by the trust; Chevras Tsedokoh Limited;

Kolel Shomrei Hachomoth; Telz Talmudical Academy; Talmud Torah Trust; Gevurah Ari Torah Academy Trust; Friends of Yeshivas Brisk; Beis Ruchel Building Fund; Beth Hamedresh Satmar Trust; Kehal Chareidim Trust; Daas Sholem; Craven Walk Beis Hamedrash; Union of Orthodox Hebrew Congregations; and Yetev Lev Jerusalem.

**FINANCES** Year 2013/14 Income £6,844,708 Grants £3,629,710 Grants to organisations £3,629,710 Assets £32,530,594

**TRUSTEES** Rifka Gross; Sarah Padwa; Michael Saberski; Leonard Lerner.

**OTHER INFORMATION** A recent list of grants was not available.

**HOW TO APPLY** Apply in writing to the organisation. Applications are assessed on a weekly basis and many of the smaller grants are dealt with through a grant-making agency, United Talmudical Associates Limited.

**WHO TO APPLY TO** Rifka Gross, Cohen Arnold and Co., New Burlington House, 1075 Finchley Road, London NW11 0PU *Tel.* 020 8731 0777 *email* mail@cohenarnold.com

## ■ The GRP Charitable Trust

**CC NO** 255733    **ESTABLISHED** 1968

**WHERE FUNDING CAN BE GIVEN** UK.

**WHO CAN BENEFIT** Organisations already known to the trust.

**WHAT IS FUNDED** Jewish causes; general charitable purposes.

**WHAT IS NOT FUNDED** Individuals.

**RANGE OF GRANTS** Up to £100,000.

**SAMPLE GRANTS** Oxford Centre for Hebrew and Jewish Studies (£102,000); The Wallace Collection (£75,000); Jerusalem Foundation (£31,000); Traditional Alternatives Foundation (£25,000); Magen David Adom – UK and United Jewish Israel Appeal (£10,000 each); Anglo Jewish Association and Trinity College (£5,000 each); Thames Diamond Jubilee (£3,000); Alexandra Wylie Tower Foundation, Royal British Legion and Simon Marks Jewish Primary School Trust (£1,000 each); Chicken Shed Theatre Company (£500); Spotlight Appeal (£200); and King Edward VII Hospital Sister Agnes (£100).

**FINANCES** Year 2013/14 Income £201,508 Grants £206,395 Grants to organisations £206,395 Assets £5,610,463

**TRUSTEE** Kleinwort Benson Trustees Ltd.

**OTHER INFORMATION** The GRP of the title is George Richard Pinto, a London banker who established the trust.

**HOW TO APPLY** Apply in writing to the correspondent. The trustees meet annually in March.

**WHO TO APPLY TO** The Secretary, 14 St George Street, London W1S 1FE *Tel.* 020 3207 7091

## ■ N. and R. Grunbaum Charitable Trust

**CC NO** 1068524    **ESTABLISHED** 1998

**WHERE FUNDING CAN BE GIVEN** UK and Israel.

**WHO CAN BENEFIT** Registered charities.

**WHAT IS FUNDED** Relief of poverty and the advancement of Jewish education and the Jewish religion.

**FINANCES** Year 2013/14 Income £44,229 Grants £44,228 Grants to organisations £44,228 Assets £1,397

**TRUSTEES** Norman Grunbaum; Rosella Grunbaum; David Grunbaum.

**HOW TO APPLY** Apply in writing to the correspondent.

WHO TO APPLY TO Norman Grunbaum, Trustee, 7 Northdene Gardens, London N15 6LX *Tel.* 020 8800 9974 *email* charity@thegreentrees.co.uk

## ■ The Bishop of Guildford's Foundation

CC NO 1017385　　ESTABLISHED 1993
WHERE FUNDING CAN BE GIVEN Diocese of Guildford.
WHO CAN BENEFIT Voluntary and community groups who are linked with a church or faith community, or engaged in a project working in partnership with a church or faith community. Organisations don't have to be registered charities but do have to have a constitution or set of rules, and a bank account, or be supported by an organisation that has these.
WHAT IS FUNDED Community projects. The purpose of the foundation's grants programme is to support projects and partnerships through which church or faith linked groups meet local needs or get involved in community development and regeneration. Priority will be given to projects and partnerships which build communities' own capacity to meet local needs, especially in relation to those who are excluded or vulnerable.
WHAT IS NOT FUNDED Individuals; capital costs; projects which have already occurred.
TYPE OF GRANT Small grants, usually up to £2,000 and larger strategic grants, usually up to £10,000. Applications for funding for more than one year can be considered, especially where this enables projects to apply for other funding.
RANGE OF GRANTS £500–£6,000
SAMPLE GRANTS The Cellar Care (£5,800); Cobham Area Foodbank, Guilford Diocesan Board of Finance Mentoring Project (£5,000 each); Trinity Trust Team (£3,600); Stoneleigh Youth Project (£3,500); East to West and Molesey Community Church Trust and Molesey Community Church Trust (£2,500); Camberley Frontline Benefit and Debt Advice Service (£1,800); Generation Church – West Ewell and St Mary's Church – Camberley (£1,000 each); Ruxley Church (£600); Special Families Support Group (£300).
FINANCES *Year* 2013/14　*Income* £91,664　*Grants* £38,080　*Grants to organisations* £38,080　*Assets* £45,670
TRUSTEES Canon Chris Rich; Geoffrey Riggs; Hugh Bryant; Michael Gibson; Right Revd Andrew Watson.
OTHER INFORMATION Grants were made to 14 organisations in 2013/14.
HOW TO APPLY 'Grantmaking by the Bishop of Guildford's Foundation is done through the Community Foundation for Surrey (CFS), an independent charitable trust which is part of the national network of Community Foundations.' Criteria is available to download on The Bishop of Guildford's Foundation's website. Applicants should contact CFS on 01483 409230 or go to its website: www.cfsurrey.org.uk/
WHO TO APPLY TO Stephen Marriott, Diocesan Secretary, 11 Woodway, Guilford, Surrey GU1 2TF *Tel.* 01483 538818 *email* info@bgf.org.uk *Website* www.bgf.org.uk

## ■ The Guildry Incorporation of Perth

SC NO SC008072　　ESTABLISHED 1210
WHERE FUNDING CAN BE GIVEN Perth, Guildtown and surrounding areas.
WHO CAN BENEFIT Charities; community organisations; members of the Guildry; residents of Perth and surrounding area who are in need.
WHAT IS FUNDED The main purpose of the trust is to provide support for its members and their families. Charitable donations are also made to local causes at the discretion of the committee.
WHAT IS NOT FUNDED Any appeals outside Perth.
SAMPLE GRANTS Family Mediation; Guildtown Community Association; Perth Access Cars; Perthshire Rugby Club; The Diabetes Research Campaign.
FINANCES *Year* 2013/14　*Income* £185,808　*Grants* £200,000　*Grants to organisations* £200,000
TRUSTEES Gordon Bannerman; Michael Norval; Alastair Anderson; Alexander Sneddon; Ian Nicol; Rae Pattillo; Alistair Barn; Louis Flood; Dr Ronald McDougall.
OTHER INFORMATION There were no full accounts available; therefore the grant total represents the amount likely to have been awarded to organisations and individuals during the year.
HOW TO APPLY Apply in writing to the correspondent. 'Requests for charitable donations may be made to the Guildry by members and close members of their family. Additionally, any other individuals living in, or organisations located in, either Perth or Guildtown, may apply for a donation.' The trust meets to consider grants on the last Tuesday of every month.
WHO TO APPLY TO Lorna Peacock, Secretary, 42 George Street, Perth, Perthshire PH1 5JL *Tel.* 01738 623195 *email* guildryperth@btconnect.com *Website* www.perthguildry.org.uk

## ■ The Walter Guinness Charitable Trust

CC NO 205375　　ESTABLISHED 1961
WHERE FUNDING CAN BE GIVEN UK with a preference for Wiltshire and overseas.
WHO CAN BENEFIT Registered charities and community groups.
WHAT IS FUNDED The trust is unlikely to be able to support anything it is not already in touch with, but would be interested to hear from charities concerned with research, education, communities and ecology.
WHAT IS NOT FUNDED Individuals.
TYPE OF GRANT Normally one-off.
RANGE OF GRANTS Grants from less than £1,000–£10,000.
SAMPLE GRANTS Marie Curie Cancer Care and the National Trust (£5,000 each); Hunt Servants' Fund (£4,000); Macmillan Cancer Support (£3,000); Bi Polar UK, Enham and SCOPE (£2,000 each); British Red Cross, Well Child, Wessex Counselling Service and Wiltshire Mind (£1,000 each).
FINANCES *Year* 2013/14　*Income* £187,273　*Grants* £151,795　*Grants to organisations* £151,795　*Assets* £7,746,445
TRUSTEES Hon. F. B. Guinness; Hon. Mrs R. Mulji; Hon. Catriona Guinness.
HOW TO APPLY Apply in writing to the correspondent. Replies are only sent when there is a positive decision. Initial telephone calls are not possible.

There are no application forms, guidelines or deadlines. No sae is required.
**who to apply to** The Trustees, Biddesden House, Andover, Hampshire SP11 9DN
email WGuinnessCT@tmf-group.com

## ■ The Gunter Charitable Trust

**cc no** 268346  **established** 1974
**where funding can be given** UK.
**who can benefit** Local and UK organisations.
**what is funded** General charitable purposes including medical and wildlife causes in the UK.
**what is not funded** No support is given for unsolicited applications.
**range of grants** Typically up to £20,000.
**sample grants** Practical Action (£9,000); Leeds Community Foundation (£7,500); The Medical Foundation for the Care of Victims of Torture (£7,000); The Toybox Charity (£3,500); The Spitz Charitable Trust (£3,000); Sustrans (£2,000); Hearts and Minds Ltd (£1,700); WaterAid (£1,000); Voluntary Service Overseas (£700); Woodland Trust (£500); Royal National Mission for Deep Sea Fishermen (£350).
**finances** Year 2013/14 Income £115,291 Grants £83,522 Grants to organisations £83,522 Assets £2,529,575
**trustees** James de Cardonnel Findlay; Geoffrey Worrall.
**other information** In 2013/14 grants were made to 54 organisations.
**how to apply** Applications are considered by the trustees twice a year. No unsolicited applications are accepted.
**who to apply to** The Trustees, c/o Forsters LLP, 31 Hill Street, London W1J 5LS Tel. 020 7863 8333

## ■ The Gur Trust

**cc no** 283423  **established** 1961
**where funding can be given** Worldwide.
**who can benefit** Individuals and organisations benefitting children, young adults, students and Jewish people.
**what is funded** Advancement of education and the Orthodox Jewish religion.
**sample grants** Beis Yaacov Casidic Seminary, Beth Yaacov Town, Bnei Emes Institutes, Central Charity Fund, Gur Talmudical College, Kollel Arad, Yeshiva Lezeirim, Pri Gidulim, Maala and Mifal Gevura Shecehessed.
**finances** Year 2013/14 Income £43,140 Grants £50,000 Grants to organisations £50,000
**trustees** Sheldon Morgenstern; David Cymerman; Shaye Traube.
**how to apply** Apply in writing to the correspondent. The trust has previously stated that: 'Funds are raised by the trustees. All calls for help are carefully considered and help is given according to circumstances and funds then available.'
**who to apply to** Sheldon Morgenstern, 206 High Road, London N15 4NP Tel. 020 8801 6038

## ■ The Gurney Charitable Trust

**cc no** 1080803  **established** 2000
**where funding can be given** England with a preference for Sussex, Gloucestershire, Buckinghamshire and Cumbria.
**who can benefit** Registered charities and community groups.
**what is funded** General charitable purposes.

**range of grants** £500–£7,000
**sample grants** Evelina Children's Hospice Appeal and Friends of East Sussex Hospices (£6,500 each); Wildfowl and Wetlands Trust (£3,500); Abbles Army, Calibre Audio Library, Off the Fence, Polka Theatre, Thomley Activity Centre and the Woodland Trust Surrey (£1,000 each); Northern Fells Group (£500).
**finances** Year 2013/14 Income £36,560 Grants £59,000 Grants to organisations £59,000 Assets £1,173,859
**trustees** Margaret Gurney; Dr Michael Gurney; Adrian Gurney; Matthew Gibson.
**other information** Grants were made to 35 organisations in 2013/14.
**how to apply** Apply in writing to the correspondent.
**who to apply to** Dr Michael Gurney, Trustee, The Hundred House, Pound Lane, Framfield, Nr Uckfield, East Sussex TN22 5RU Tel. 01825 890377 email drmichaelgurney@btinternet.com

## ■ Dr Guthrie's Association

**sc no** SC009302  **established** 1986
**where funding can be given** Scotland, with a preference for Edinburgh.
**who can benefit** Not-for-profit organisations benefitting disadvantaged children and young people under 22 years of age.
**what is funded** The care and welfare of young people.
**what is not funded** Individuals, or in support of: projects of an environmental nature; mainstream activities and statutory requirements of schools, universities and hospitals; large-scale building projects; historic restoration; retrospective funding.
**range of grants** £250–£2,000
**sample grants** Abernethy Trust, Citylife Ministries Ltd, City Youth Café, Glasgow City Mission, Happy Days Children's Charity, Reality Adventure Works in Scotland, Riptide Music Studios, Tall Ships Youth Trust, Turning Point Scotland and Visibility (£1,000 each); ChildLine Scotland (£750); Red School Youth Centre (£700); and Bibles for Children (£500).
**finances** Year 2013/14 Income £44,674 Grants £80,000 Grants to organisations £80,000
**trustees** J. M. P. Galbraith, Chair; Mrs S. Crane; Mrs R. Derby; P. J. Derby; Mrs A. M. G. Hepburn; Ms E. Marquis.
**how to apply** Applications are considered by the trustees three times a year (approximately) in February, June and October.
**who to apply to** Grant Administrator, Exchange Place, 3 Semple Street, Edinburgh email drguthrie@tiscali.co.uk

## ■ The H. and M. Charitable Trust

**CC NO** 272391 **ESTABLISHED** 1976
**WHERE FUNDING CAN BE GIVEN** UK, with some preference for Kent.
**WHO CAN BENEFIT** Charities concerned with the advancement of education and the relief of poverty. Seafaring in the UK, with some preference for Kent.
**WHAT IS FUNDED** 'Resources are committed on a regular annual basis to organisations who have come to rely upon [the trust] for their funding.'
**SAMPLE GRANTS** Arethusa Venture Centre, Fairbridge – Kent, Guide Dogs for the Blind, Hand in Gillingham, Jubilee Sailing Trust, Kent Air Ambulance, North London Hospice, RSPCA, Royal Engineers Association, Royal National Lifeboat Association and Royal Star and Garter Home.
**FINANCES** Year 2013 Income £918 Grants £85,000 Grants to organisations £85,000
**TRUSTEES** David Harris; Pamela Lister; John Lister.
**HOW TO APPLY** Unsolicited applications will not be successful.
**WHO TO APPLY TO** David Harris, Trustee, Lilac Cottage, Highwood Hill, London NW7 4HD Tel. 020 8906 3767 email david@brooksgreen.com

## ■ H. and T. Clients Charitable Trust

**CC NO** 1104345 **ESTABLISHED** 2004
**WHERE FUNDING CAN BE GIVEN** England and Wales.
**WHO CAN BENEFIT** Charities and community groups.
**WHAT IS FUNDED** General charitable purposes.
**FINANCES** Year 2013/14 Income £83,432 Grants £106,975 Grants to organisations £106,975 Assets £67,165
**TRUSTEES** Hugh Lask; Ronnie Harris; Neville Newman; Charlotte Harris.
**HOW TO APPLY** Apply in writing to the correspondent.
**WHO TO APPLY TO** Hugh Lask, Trustee, 64 New Cavendish Street, London W1G 8TB Tel. 020 7467 6300

## ■ H. C. D. Memorial Fund

**CC NO** 1044956 **ESTABLISHED** 1995
**WHERE FUNDING CAN BE GIVEN** Worldwide.
**WHO CAN BENEFIT** Organisations benefitting the environment and people who are in need. Especially, people disadvantaged by poverty, education or ill health and people with disabilities.
**WHAT IS FUNDED** Health, education, community, environment, development aid abroad, and other social and educational work in the UK and the Republic of Ireland.
**WHAT IS NOT FUNDED** Evangelism or missionary work; individuals; nationwide emergency appeals; animal, cancer and children's charities; gap year funding.
**TYPE OF GRANT** Can be one-off or recurring, including core costs, buildings and start-up costs. Funding may be given for up to three years.
**RANGE OF GRANTS** Up to £66,000 but typically £5,000–£25,000.
**SAMPLE GRANTS** San Carlos Hospital – Mexico (£66,000), Northumbria Coalition Against Crime and Recycle Africa (£30,000 each); Borderlands UK, Green Alliance and SOFA Project (£20,000 each); Campaign for Better Transport (£15,000); Resurgo Trust (£11,500); Devon and Cornwall Refugees, FareShare and Friends First (£10,000); Southover Counselling (£8,000); Kahaila Reflex (£5,000).
**FINANCES** Year 2013/14 Income £801,207 Grants £800,500 Grants to organisations £189,500 Assets £593,597
**TRUSTEES** Nicholas Debenham, Chair; Bill Flinn; Harriet Lear; Joanna Lear; Jeremy Debenham; Susannah Drummond.
**OTHER INFORMATION** Grants were made to 13 organisations in the UK and to 30 organisations overseas.
**HOW TO APPLY** Apply in writing to the correspondent, although note that the trust has a preference for seeking out its own projects and only very rarely responds to general appeals. 'Unsolicited applications are not encouraged. They are acknowledged, but extremely rarely receive a positive response. No telephone enquiries, please.'
**WHO TO APPLY TO** Suky Drummond, 24 Fern Avenue, Jesmond, Newcastle upon Tyne NE2 2QT Tel. 0191 281 4228 email hcdmemorialfund@gmail.com

## ■ The Hackney Parochial Charities

**CC NO** 219876 **ESTABLISHED** 1904
**WHERE FUNDING CAN BE GIVEN** The London Borough of Hackney.
**WHO CAN BENEFIT** Organisations benefitting children, young adults and people disadvantaged by poverty may be considered. Community organisations can also benefit.
**WHAT IS FUNDED** Community and education projects which benefit people in Hackney who are poor.
**TYPE OF GRANT** One-off and recurrent.
**RANGE OF GRANTS** Up to £8,000.
**SAMPLE GRANTS** The Parish of St John at Hackney (£15,000); Frampton Park Baptist Church (£6,000); Dover Sholem (£5,000); CCHF All About Kids (£4,800); St Michael – London Fields (£4,200); Hackney Doorways (£4,000); Salvation Army (£3,200); S Pinter Youth Project (£3,000).
**FINANCES** Year 2013/14 Income £249,999 Grants £122,091 Grants to organisations £100,000 Assets £5,713,644
**TRUSTEES** Mary Cannon; Cllr. Geoff Taylor; Father Rob Wickham; Peter Ottino; Nicola Baboneau; Cllr Chris Kennedy; Vastiana Belfon.
**OTHER INFORMATION** Grants under £2,500 totalled £57,000.
**HOW TO APPLY** Apply in writing to the correspondent. The trustees will consider written applications for grants and project funding from individuals and organisations that are in line with the charity's objectives and are within the area of benefit at their discretion.
**WHO TO APPLY TO** The Trustees, The Trust Partnership, 6 Trull Farm Buildings, Trull, Tetbury, Gloucestershire GL8 8SQ Tel. 01285 841900 email office@thetrustpartnership.com

## The Hadfield Trust

**CC NO** 1067491     **ESTABLISHED** 1998
**WHERE FUNDING CAN BE GIVEN** Cumbria.
**WHO CAN BENEFIT** Registered charities and community groups.
**WHAT IS FUNDED** Youth and employment; social needs; older people; arts; environment.
**WHAT IS NOT FUNDED** Applicants from outside the county of Cumbria; individuals; any form of sponsorship; religious bodies; political organisations; pressure groups; feasibility studies; schools seeking specialist status; where funding from statutory bodies is, or should be available; any form of memorial; return applicants less than two years after a successful application.
**TYPE OF GRANT** Capital projects preferred; buildings will be considered and funding is generally for one year or less.
**RANGE OF GRANTS** £200–£6,500
**SAMPLE GRANTS** Hospice at Home – Carlisle and North Lakeland (£5,000); Cumbria Military Museum and Flimby ARLFC (£3,000 each); Cumbria Wheelchair Sports Club and Sports Driving (£2,500 each); Art Gene Ltd and Swathmoor Community Group (£2,000 each); Life Education Cumbria (£1,500); Cumbria Deaf Association (£1,000); Cottage Wood Centre (£500).
**FINANCES** Year 2013/14 Income £293,293 Grants £267,500 Grants to organisations £26,750 Assets £8,604,479
**TRUSTEES** Roy Morris; William Rathbone; Alan Forsyth; Andrew Morris; Andrew Forsyth; Caroline Addison; Michael Hope.
**PUBLICATIONS** A leaflet setting out the aims and objectives of the trust (available on request).
**OTHER INFORMATION** Grants were made to 140 organisations in 2013/14.
**HOW TO APPLY** A completed application form is always required and is available from the trust's website or offices. The completed application form should be sent to the administrator together with a copy of the applicant's most recent accounts to reach the trust not later than the deadline for the relevant meeting. The deadlines are always the 1st of the month preceding that of the trustees' meeting i.e. 1 February, 1 June and 1 October. If the application form gives insufficient space for your project to be described, up to two sheets of A4 paper can be accepted. The policy of the trust is that capital funding is strongly preferred but some revenue requests will be accepted in particular circumstances. If in any doubt about the best way to complete the application form, including the size of the grant to be requested, applicants are strongly advised to telephone the Administrator who will be glad to advise. In reaching their decision the trustees have the benefit of advice from the Advisory Panel which meets some weeks before them to discuss in detail the applications. The Advisory Panel, under the chairship of Alan Forsyth, is made up of people resident in Cumbria and drawn from all parts of the county who have wide experience and knowledge of the charitable sector.
**WHO TO APPLY TO** Michael Hope, Trustee, Greystone House, Kings Meaburn, Penrith CA10 3BU Website www.hadfieldtrust.org.uk

## The Hadley Trust

**CC NO** 1064823     **ESTABLISHED** 1997
**WHERE FUNDING CAN BE GIVEN** UK, especially London.
**WHO CAN BENEFIT** Registered charities; hospices.
**WHAT IS FUNDED** Crime and justice; disability; hospices; medical; social investment; welfare reform; young people. The trust's objects allow it to assist in creating opportunities for people who are disadvantaged as a result of environmental, educational or economic circumstances or physical or other disability to improve their situation, either by direct financial assistance, involvement in project and support work, or research into the causes of and means to alleviate hardship.
**SAMPLE GRANTS** The Centre for Justice Innovation; The New Economics Foundation; Noah's Ark Children's Hospice; Policy Exchange; Prison Reform Trust; Voice.
**FINANCES** Year 2013/14 Income £9,434,025 Grants £2,898,233 Grants to organisations £2,898,233 Assets £121,933,739
**TRUSTEES** Janet Hulme; Philip Hulme; Janet Love; Thomas Hulme; Katherine Prideaux; Sophie Hulme.
**HOW TO APPLY** Apply in writing to the correspondent. However, note that the trust prefers to work with established partners and therefore 'the trust does not take on many new funding commitments. Nevertheless the trustees will always consider and respond to proposals which might enhance the effectiveness of the trust.'
**WHO TO APPLY TO** Carol Biggs, Trust Administrator, Gladsmuir, Hadley Common, Barnet, Hertfordshire EN5 5QE Tel. 020 8447 4577 email carol@hadleytrust.org

## The Hadrian Trust

**CC NO** 272161     **ESTABLISHED** 1976
**WHERE FUNDING CAN BE GIVEN** Within the boundaries of the old counties of Northumberland and Durham, this includes Tyne and Wear and the former county of Cleveland (north of the Tees).
**WHO CAN BENEFIT** Organisations benefitting people of all ages; unemployed people; volunteers; people in care, or who are fostered or adopted; one-parent families; and widows and widowers. Typical grants can be to councils of voluntary service, advice and counselling services, women's projects, youth clubs and schools, charities for people with disabilities, older people, arts and environmental projects, church restoration and block grants for individuals in need.
**WHAT IS FUNDED** Social welfare and other charitable projects within the boundaries of the old counties of Northumberland and Durham (this includes Tyne and Wear). The main headings under which applications are considered are: social welfare; youth; women; older people; people with disabilities; ethnic minorities; the arts; the environment; education and churches.
**WHAT IS NOT FUNDED** General appeals from large UK organisations and smaller bodies working outside the beneficial area are not considered.
**TYPE OF GRANT** Usually one-off for a special project or part of a project. The average grant is £1,000. Buildings, capital, project, research, recurring costs, as well as running costs, salaries and start-up costs will be considered. Funding of up to three years will be considered.
**RANGE OF GRANTS** £500–£5,000
**SAMPLE GRANTS** Young Sinfonia Orchestra (£5,000); Funding Information North East and Marie Curie

Cancer Care (£4,000 each); Newcastle CVS (£3,000).
**FINANCES** Year 2013/14 Income £190,794 Grants £194,000 Grants to organisations £174,000 Assets £5,886,221
**TRUSTEES** Hume Hargreave; John Parker; Pauline Dodgson; Katherine Winskell; Jim Dias; Ian Brown.
**OTHER INFORMATION** Grants were made to 163 organisations and four individuals in 2013/14.
**HOW TO APPLY** Apply in writing to the correspondent. Details of what the application letter must include can be found on the website. Applications are considered at meetings usually held in October, January, April and July each year, or as otherwise required. Eligible applications will be acknowledged and given a date when the application will be considered. Successful applicants will hear within two weeks of the meeting; no further correspondence is sent to unsuccessful applicants. Applications for individuals should be sent to: Greggs Charitable Trust, Fernwood House, Clayton Road, Jesmond, Newcastle upon Tyne NE2 1TL.
**WHO TO APPLY TO** Pauline Dodgson, PO Box 785, Whitley Bay NE26 9DW email enquiries@hadriantrust.co.uk Website www.hadriantrust.co.uk

## ■ The Doris Louise Hailes Charitable Trust

**CC NO** 1134434   **ESTABLISHED** 2010
**WHERE FUNDING CAN BE GIVEN** Undefined, in practice in the UK.
**WHO CAN BENEFIT** Registered charities.
**WHAT IS FUNDED** The advancement of health and saving of lives, disability, and animals.
**SAMPLE GRANTS** PDSA; RSBP; Heart Foundation; Arthritis Society; RNIB; RAF Benevolent Fund.
**FINANCES** Year 2013/14 Income £22,854 Grants £40,000 Grants to organisations £40,000
**TRUSTEE** HSBC. Trust Co (UK) Ltd.
**HOW TO APPLY** Apply in writing to the correspondent.
**WHO TO APPLY TO** HSBC Trust Co (UK) Ltd, Norwich House, 10th Floor, Nelson Gate, Commercial Road, Southampton SO15 1GX Tel. 023 8072 2221

## ■ The Alfred Haines Charitable Trust

**CC NO** 327166   **ESTABLISHED** 1986
**WHERE FUNDING CAN BE GIVEN** Birmingham and West Midlands (including Staffordshire and Warwickshire).
**WHO CAN BENEFIT** Mainly smaller charities.
**WHAT IS FUNDED** Grants were broken down into the following categories: family support and counselling; youth and children's work; humanitarian and overseas aid; medically disadvantaged; care for older people and people with disabilities; support for homeless people; and holidays for disadvantaged children and teenagers.
**WHAT IS NOT FUNDED** Activities which are primarily the responsibility of central or local government or some other responsible body; animal welfare; church buildings – restoration, improvements, renovations or new ones; environmental – conservation and protection of wildlife and landscape; expeditions and overseas trips; hospitals and health centres; individuals, including students (on the rare occasions that individuals are supported, the person has to be recommended by someone known to the trustees and the funding should be of long-term benefit to others); large national charities; it is unusual for the trust to support large national charities even where there is a local project; loans and business finance; medical research projects; overseas appeals; purely evangelistic projects; promotion of any religion other than Christianity; school, universities and colleges. Projects overseas or outside the West Midlands, whether Christian or not, will only be considered where the applicants are known to a trustee or are recommended by someone known to a trustee who has first-hand knowledge of the work.
**TYPE OF GRANT** Generally one-off. Specific projects rather than general running costs.
**RANGE OF GRANTS** Up to £13,000.
**FINANCES** Year 2013/14 Income £28,948 Grants £85,410 Grants to organisations £85,410 Assets £1,122,817
**TRUSTEES** Archie Gilmour; Greg Moss.
**OTHER INFORMATION** Grants were made to 82 organisations in 2013/14.
**HOW TO APPLY** Apply in writing to the trustees. Applications should include: a brief description of the activities of the organisation; details of the project and its overall cost; what funds have already been raised and how the remaining funds are to be raised; a copy of the latest accounts including any associated or parent organisation; any other leaflets or supporting documentation. When considering whether to apply for funding, advice (if needed) can be obtained from the administrator prior to writing. Applicants are advised to consider the exclusion list prior to application.
**WHO TO APPLY TO** The Trustees, Dale Farm, Worcester Lane, Sutton Coldfield B75 5PR Tel. 0121 323 3236 Website www.ahct.org.uk

## ■ E. F. and M. G. Hall Charitable Trust

**CC NO** 256453   **ESTABLISHED** 1968
**WHERE FUNDING CAN BE GIVEN** South east England.
**WHO CAN BENEFIT** Registered charities and community groups.
**WHAT IS FUNDED** General charitable purposes including children, older people, disability, medical charities and churches.
**WHAT IS NOT FUNDED** Individuals.
**TYPE OF GRANT** One-off and recurrent.
**RANGE OF GRANTS** £50–£1,000
**SAMPLE GRANTS** Barnardo's and Guide Dogs for the Blind (£1,100 each); Canterbury Cathedral Trust (£800); Crisis, Marie Curie Cancer Care, the Multiple Sclerosis Society and Worldwide Cancer Research (£700 each); ABF The Soldiers Charity, Christian Aid and PCC Mark Beech (£600 each).
**FINANCES** Year 2013/14 Income £61,319 Grants £33,678 Grants to organisations £33,678 Assets £1,056,195
**TRUSTEES** Anthony Hall; Moira Hall; Ian Hall
**OTHER INFORMATION** Grants were made to 165 organisations in 2013/14.
**HOW TO APPLY** Apply in writing to the correspondent.
**WHO TO APPLY TO** Moira Hall, Trustee, Holmsley House, Holtye Common, Cowden, Edenbridge, Kent TN8 7ED Tel. 01342 850571 email shovelstrode@hotmail.com

## ■ The Edith Winifred Hall Charitable Trust

**CC NO** 1057032   **ESTABLISHED** 1996
**WHERE FUNDING CAN BE GIVEN** UK, with a preference for Northamptonshire.
**WHO CAN BENEFIT** Registered charities.
**WHAT IS FUNDED** General charitable purposes including young people and social welfare.
**RANGE OF GRANTS** Up to £400,000 but typically £3,000–£50,000.
**SAMPLE GRANTS** Youthscape (£410,000); Geddington Village Hall (£50,000); Bunker Consulting Services (£49,000); Chellington Centre (£43,000); Road Victims Trust (£15,000); Keystone Youth Centre (£7,500); Vine Community Trust (£5,200); Northamptonshire Crime Stoppers and St Andrews Harlestone Preservation Trust (£5,000 each); Glapthorn PCC (£3,000).
**FINANCES** *Year* 2013/14 *Income* £46,714 *Grants* £528,537 *Grants to organisations* £528,537 *Assets* £723,200
**TRUSTEES** David Endicott; David Reynolds; Lucie Burgess-Lumsden; Pamela Reynolds.
**OTHER INFORMATION** Grants were made to 11 organisations in 2013/14.
**HOW TO APPLY** Apply in writing to the correspondent.
**WHO TO APPLY TO** David Endicott, Trustee, Spratt Endicott, 52–54 South Bar Street, Banbury OX16 9AB *Tel.* 01295 204000 *email* dendicott@se-law.co.uk

## ■ The Hamamelis Trust

**CC NO** 280938   **ESTABLISHED** 1980
**WHERE FUNDING CAN BE GIVEN** UK, but with a special interest in the Godalming and Surrey areas.
**WHO CAN BENEFIT** UK charities involved in medical research or conservation projects.
**WHAT IS FUNDED** Medical research in the UK; and specific projects for conservation of the countryside in the UK.
**WHAT IS NOT FUNDED** Projects outside the UK; individuals.
**TYPE OF GRANT** Project.
**RANGE OF GRANTS** Up to £10,000 but generally £2,000–£3,000.
**SAMPLE GRANTS** Hambledon Almshouses (£10,000); Godalming Museum (£5,000); the Red Squirrel Survival Trust, the Scottish Seabird Centre and Sussex Wildlife Trust (£3,000 each); Pewley Conservation Volunteers (£2,700); Action on Hearing Loss, Autistica, Cerebra and Sayers Croft Environmental Trust (£2,000 each).
**FINANCES** *Year* 2013/14 *Income* £111,113 *Grants* £95,275 *Grants to organisations* £95,275 *Assets* £3,707,196
**TRUSTEES** Laura Dadswell; Dr A. F. M. Stone; Lucy Mirouze.
**OTHER INFORMATION** Grants were made to 37 organisations in 2013/14.
**HOW TO APPLY** Apply in writing to the correspondent. All applicants are asked to include a short summary of the application along with any published material and references. Unsuccessful appeals will not be acknowledged. Dr Adam Stone, one of the trustees, who is medically qualified, assesses medical applications.
**WHO TO APPLY TO** Mrs L. Dadswell, Trustee, c/o Penningtons Solicitors LLP, Highfield, Brighton Road, Godalming, Surrey GU7 1NS *Tel.* 01483 791800

## ■ Hamilton Wallace Trust

**CC NO** 1052453   **ESTABLISHED** 1996
**WHO CAN BENEFIT** Registered charities.
**WHAT IS FUNDED** General charitable purposes.
**RANGE OF GRANTS** £500 to £2,000.
**SAMPLE GRANTS** LEAP (£2,000); DEMAND, Independent Age, St Luke's Hospice (£1,000); Headway, Pancreatic Cancer UK (£500).
**FINANCES** *Year* 2013/14 *Income* £25,318 *Grants* £25,500 *Grants to organisations* £25,500
**TRUSTEES** Timothy Calder; Peter Phillips.
**OTHER INFORMATION** In 2013/14 grants – the majority of which were to the value of £500 – were made to 36 organisations.
**HOW TO APPLY** Apply in writing to the correspondent. The trustees meet twice a year to consider appeals, usually in November and May, and it would be helpful for any appeals to be received about a month before the meetings. The trust notes on its Charity Commission record that individual letters of appeal are not acknowledged and that only successful applicants are notified.
**WHO TO APPLY TO** Peter Phillips, Trustee, c/o Rubinstein Phillips Lewis LLP, 13 Craven Street, London WC2N 5PB *Tel.* 020 7925 2244 *email* thehamiltonwallacetrust@ruphlaw.co.uk

## ■ Paul Hamlyn Foundation

**CC NO** 1102927   **ESTABLISHED** 1987
**WHERE FUNDING CAN BE GIVEN** UK and India.
**WHO CAN BENEFIT** Registered charities and organisations.
**WHAT IS FUNDED** The foundation aims to address issues of inequality and disadvantage, particularly in relation to children and young people. Its main areas of interest are arts, education and learning in the UK, social justice and local organisations supporting vulnerable groups of people, especially children, in India.
**WHAT IS NOT FUNDED** Individuals or proposals for the benefit of one individual; funding for work that has already started; general circulars/appeals; proposals about property or which are mainly about equipment or other capital items; overseas travel, expeditions, adventure and residential courses; promotion of religion; animal welfare; medical/health/residential or day care; proposals from organisations outside the UK, except under the charity's India programme; proposals that benefit people living outside the UK, except under the India programme. The foundation is unlikely to support: endowments; organisations that want to use the foundation's funding to make grants; websites, publications, seminars unless part of a wider proposal.
**TYPE OF GRANT** Grants are usually one-off, for a specific project or for a specific part of a project, and funding is normally given for one year only.
**RANGE OF GRANTS** Grants vary significantly, but averaged around £100,000 across the Open programmes in 2011/12.
**SAMPLE GRANTS** Musical Futures (£366,000); Hearts and Minds Ltd (£250,000); National Youth Theatre (£200,000); Big Community (£150,000); FACT (£90,000); Museum of East Anglian Life (£49,500); Archaeology Scotland (£24,500); My Voice London (£20,000); Beating Wing Orchestra (£10,000); University of Hull (£3,500).
**FINANCES** *Year* 2013/14 *Income* £17,935,000 *Grants* £22,636,000 *Grants to organisations* £22,636,000 *Assets* £600,146,000

TRUSTEES Lord Claus Moser; Peter Wilson-Smith; Anthony Salz; Lord Anthony Hall; Baroness Estelle Morris; Jane Hamlyn; James Lingwood; Michael Hamlyn; Tom Wylie; Tim Bunting; Baroness Kidron of Angel.

HOW TO APPLY The open grants schemes in the arts, education and learning were closed on 31 October 2014. The foundation is working towards its new grant-making strategy which is due to be announced in spring 2015 at which point new funds will be available. The India programme is still open and applications can be made online. Check the foundation's website for latest developments. A newsletter is also available via the website.

WHO TO APPLY TO Lucy Palfreyman, 5–11 Leeke Street, London WC1X 9HY *Tel.* 020 7812 3450 *email* information@phf.org.uk *Website* www.phf.org.uk

## ■ The Helen Hamlyn Trust

CC NO 1084839   ESTABLISHED 2000

WHERE FUNDING CAN BE GIVEN Worldwide.

WHO CAN BENEFIT Charitable organisations; innovative medium to long-term projects 'which will effect lasting change and improve quality of life'. The trust also supports a number of projects with a design focus which are undertaken by the Helen Hamlyn Centre for Design at the Royal College of Art, London.

WHAT IS FUNDED Medical – 'support innovation in the medical arena'; arts and culture – 'increase access to the arts and support the professional development of artists from the fields of music and the performing arts'; education – 'increase intercultural understanding; provide opportunities for young people to develop new interests and practical skills which will contribute to their education and their future lives and to create opportunities for young offenders to acquire practical skills which will support their personal development for their future lives'; welfare; heritage and conservation in India – 'conserve heritage in India for public access and cultural activities'; international humanitarian affairs – 'support examples of good practice in the humanitarian sector'; 'healthy ageing' – 'provide practical support to enable the elderly to maintain their independence for as long as possible'.

RANGE OF GRANTS £100–£250,000

SAMPLE GRANTS The Helen Hamlyn Centre for Design at the RCA (£250,000); Royal Opera House – Paul Hamlyn First Night (£89,000); Railway Children – through the Big Give Trust (£12,500); International National Trusts Organisation and Pegasus Theatre – Oxford (£10,000 each); Beanstalk (£9,700); RNIB and The Moghissi Laser Trust (£5,000 each); Rushmoor Healthy Living (£4,000); Multiple System Atrophy Trust (£3,000); Garsington Opera (£1,500); Emerge (£1,200); Age UK Lewisham and Southwark and Chickenshed Theatre (£1,000 each); Aquila Way – through The Big Give Trust (£800); Green Pastures (£500); Step Football (£200); The Institute of Cancer Research (£150); Project Malawi (£100).

FINANCES *Year* 2013/14 *Income* £2,514,890 *Grants* £846,412 *Grants to organisations* £846,412 *Assets* £4,253,470

TRUSTEES Lady Hamlyn; Dr Kate Gavron; Dr Shobita Punja; Brendan Cahill; Margaret O'Rorke; Dr Deborah Swallow.

OTHER INFORMATION There were 44 awards made. The grant total includes about £392,500 given through Open Futures Trust.

HOW TO APPLY The trustees have previously noted that 'their energies are focused on the initiation of projects and they do not accept unsolicited applications for major grants'. Appeals for small awards may be directed to the correspondent.

WHO TO APPLY TO John Roche-Kuroda, Director of Finance and Administration, 129 Old Church Street, London SW3 6EB *Tel.* 020 7351 5057 *Fax* 020 7352 3284 *email* john.rochekuroda@helenhamlyntrust.org *Website* www.phf.org.uk/apply-funding

## ■ Sue Hammerson Charitable Trust

CC NO 235196   ESTABLISHED 1957

WHERE FUNDING CAN BE GIVEN UK, with some preference for London.

WHO CAN BENEFIT Charitable organisations. The primary beneficiary is the Lewis W Hammerson Memorial Home.

WHAT IS FUNDED General charitable purposes, with particular emphasis on medical research, health care, education and religious causes. The annual report for 2013/14 notes that there is 'particular consideration to the advancement of medical learning and research and to the relief of sickness and poverty, with first consideration being given to the needs of the Lewis W Hammerson Memorial Home'.

WHAT IS NOT FUNDED Grants are not made to individuals.

RANGE OF GRANTS Mostly around or under £1,000.

SAMPLE GRANTS Lewis W Hammerson Memorial Home (£200,000); and West London Synagogue (£800). In the past awards have also been made to Painter-Stainers Fine Art Fund (£5,200); and Army Benevolent Fund (£2,000).

FINANCES *Year* 2013/14 *Income* £194,306 *Grants* £200,803 *Grants to organisations* £200,803 *Assets* £8,427,249

TRUSTEES Sir Gavin Lightman; David Hammerson; Patricia Beecham; Peter Hammerson; Anthony Bernstein; Anthony Thompson; Rory Hammerson.

OTHER INFORMATION Two grants were awarded during the year. The trust shares some common trustees with the Sue Hammerson Foundation (Charity Commission no. 262580) and the Sue and Lew Hammerson Charitable Trust (Charity Commission no. 1001437).

HOW TO APPLY Applications may be made in writing to the correspondent.

WHO TO APPLY TO The Correspondent, c/o H. W. Fisher and Company, Acre House, 11–15 William Road, London NW1 3ER *Tel.* 020 7388 7000 *email* rwatson@hwfisher.co.uk

## ■ The Hampshire and Islands Historic Churches Trust

CC NO 299633   ESTABLISHED 1988

WHERE FUNDING CAN BE GIVEN Hampshire, Isle of Wight and the Channel Islands.

WHO CAN BENEFIT Churches of all denominations in Hampshire, the Isle of Wight and the Channel Islands.

WHAT IS FUNDED The restoration, preservation, repair, maintenance and improvement of churches, including monuments, fittings and furniture, in the area specified above.

WHAT IS NOT FUNDED No grants are paid in respect of work which has already started before approval is given.

**TYPE OF GRANT** One-off grants and loans. Emergency help can be given.
**RANGE OF GRANTS** £500–£7,500
**SAMPLE GRANTS** North Stoneham and Bassett PCC and St Michael and All Angels PCC (£7,500 each); Kimpton PCC, PCC of East Stratton – All Saints and Southsea – St Simon (£5,000 each); Newport Minster and St Mary's Church Copythor (£4,000 each); Fritham Free Church (£3,000); Andover Bridge Street Methodist Church and Tichborne Churchwardens (£2,000 each); and PCC of Newnham and Others and Stratfield Saye Churchwardens (Corinne Bennett Award) (£500 each).
**FINANCES** Year 2013 Income £80,351 Grants £54,179 Grants to organisations £54,179 Assets £107,673
**TRUSTEES** John Steel; The Ven. Adrian Harbidge; Caroline Edwards; Joan Appleyard; Canon Paul Townsend.
**OTHER INFORMATION** Grants were given to 15 churches and a total of almost £700 was given as a share from the fundraising bike ride. Loans totalled £2,500.
**HOW TO APPLY** Application forms are available to download, together with guidelines and criteria, from the website. The grants committee usually meets in February, June and October.
**WHO TO APPLY TO** Meryl Balchin, Hon. Secretary, c/o Hampshire Record Office, Sussex Street, Winchester, Hampshire SO23 8TH *Tel.* 01962 760230 *email* grants@hihct.org.uk *Website* www.hihct.org.uk

■ **Hampshire and Isle of Wight Community Foundation**
**CC NO** 1100417   **ESTABLISHED** 2002
**WHERE FUNDING CAN BE GIVEN** Hampshire and Isle of Wight.
**WHO CAN BENEFIT** Community groups; voluntary organisations; individuals; social enterprises; CICs. The trustees seek to address the needs of vulnerable and disadvantaged individuals, those suffering from discrimination, social exclusion or poverty, including homeless people.
**WHAT IS FUNDED** General charitable purposes; social welfare; community development. The foundation administers a variety of funds, which may open or close throughout the year. Potential applicants should see the foundation's website for details of funds currently available, or contact the foundation directly. According to the latest accounts, for a second year, the foundation targeted three direct issues identified across the County – unemployment for young people, small grants for small items and families in crisis'. Grants are focused geographically on the areas of greater deprivation with priority given to smaller charities and community groups with turnover of less than £300,000 per annum.
**WHAT IS NOT FUNDED** Public bodies; organisations for the sole benefit of plants or animals; national charities; party political activity; commercial ventures; proselytising activities, such as the active promotion of a specific religion or belief system; bids for major capital projects.
**TYPE OF GRANT** One-off and up to two years; capital and core expenditure; project costs; salaries; unrestricted funding.
**RANGE OF GRANTS** £25–£10,000; average grant was of about £1,800.
**SAMPLE GRANTS** Grants were paid through the following funds: Comic Relief (£160,000); Portsmouth City Community Fund (£72,000); Apprenticeship Fund (£69,000); Winter campaigns (£68,500); Families in Crisis (£48,500); First Wessex Revenue Fund (£40,000); Alderman Joe Dawdson (linked charity) Fund (£30,500); IWCF Community Revenue Fund (£27,000); Penton Trust Grass Roots Fund (£24,000); Doris Campbell Memorial Fund and Monday Charitable Trust Flow Through (£22,500 each); Small Grants Small Items (£6,300). Other grant programmes (under £20,000) totalled £174,500.
**FINANCES** Year 2013/14 Income £2,326,516 Grants £743,855 Grants to organisations £711,725 Assets £9,886,669
**TRUSTEES** Hugh Mason; Michael Woodhall; Jonathan Cheshire; Rebecca Kennelly; Tom Floyd; Miles Brown; William Cuthbert; Richard Hibbert; Jonathan Moseley; Alistair Stoke.
**OTHER INFORMATION** During the year a total of 381 'groups and charities' were awarded. Grants to individuals were given totalling £32,000. By the end of 2014 there were 77 endowment funds under the foundation's management. The foundation had planned to distribute £900,000 in 2015.
**HOW TO APPLY** Application criteria, procedures and deadlines may vary for each of the funds. Full details and separate application forms for each fund which can found on the foundation's website.
**WHO TO APPLY TO** Debbie Charlton, Grants Manager, Dame Mary Fagan House, Chineham Court, Lutyens Close, Basingstoke, Hampshire RG24 8AG *Tel.* 01256 776101 *email* grantsadmin@hantscf.org.uk or hiwcfadmin@hantscf.org.uk *Website* www.hantscf.org.uk

■ **The Hampstead Wells and Campden Trust**
**CC NO** 1094611   **ESTABLISHED** 1971
**WHERE FUNDING CAN BE GIVEN** The former metropolitan borough of Hampstead; organisations covering a wider area but whose activities benefit Hampstead residents among others may also apply.
**WHO CAN BENEFIT** Charitable organisations; voluntary groups; community projects; individuals (assisted via an agency); pensioners in need.
**WHAT IS FUNDED** General charitable purposes and community needs, specifically the relief of poverty, health and disability causes, disadvantaged communities and special needs groups.
**WHAT IS NOT FUNDED** General fundraising appeals; work which does not directly benefit people within the specific area; the payment of rates or taxes, fines, school or course fees, or in principle where statutory bodies have the responsibility to help; individuals directly (appeals must be made via a constituted local group). Multi-year grants are not currently given.
**TYPE OF GRANT** One-off; up to one year; running expenditure; occasionally capital costs; core funding; project expenditure.
**RANGE OF GRANTS** Up to £20,000; mainly smaller grants up to £1,000.
**SAMPLE GRANTS** Camden Community Law Centre (£20,000); Kingsgate Community Association (£12,500); Caris Camden C4WS Homeless Project (£12,000); The Community Association for West Hampstead and West Hampstead Women's Centre (£10,000 each); Hampstead Community Centre (£9,400); St Mary's Community Charitable Trust (£7,500); Learning

Development (£6,800); CancerKin (£5,000); KIDS (£4,000); Friendship Works (£2,000); Hampstead Parish Church 2014 Schools Project (£1,500); Children's Country Holiday Fund (£1,000). Grants below £1,000 totalled over £27,500.

**FINANCES** Year 2013/14 Income £553,941 Grants £508,118 Grants to organisations £230,753 Assets £16,420,961

**TRUSTEES** Linda Chung; Dr Diana Dick; Geoffrey Berridge; Gaynor Bassey; Alistair Voaden; Dr Christina Williams; Denis Finning; Francoise Findlay; Gaynor Humphreys Mike Bieber; Revd Stephen Tucker; Angela Mason; Charles Perrin; Tulip Siddiq.

**OTHER INFORMATION** In 2013/14 a total of 155 grants were given to organisations (including 102 grants made to the Mary Ward Centre 'to enable clients from the trust's area of benefit to obtain essential medical evidence to enforce their legal rights') and a total of 3,197 individuals received support totalling £202,000. There were 97 pensioners receiving payments (totalling £75,500). Most organisational grants were for under £1,000 (124 awards). The trust supports individuals permanently resident in the area of benefit who are in severe hardship, provides kitchen and home starter packs, Christmas hampers and offers pensions to older people in need. See the website for details.

**HOW TO APPLY** Application forms are available to download, together with full criteria and guidelines, from the trust's website. Appeals may be made at any time and must include: the budget of the project as well as the organisation; details of the project; most recent accounts; if applying for funding for a post, a job description. The trustees meet eight times a year, but requests for smaller grants (under £1,000) can be fast-tracked and dealt with within one month. Requests for small awards can be made using the application form or sending a letter giving the details of: the work to be supported; its costs; what has been raised so far and how; type and number of beneficiaries; links to the area of benefit; information about your organisation/group; your suitability to run and manage the work.

**WHO TO APPLY TO** Sheila Taylor, Director and Clerk to the Trustees, 62 Rosslyn Hill, London NW3 1ND Tel. 020 7435 1570 Fax 020 7435 1571 email grant@hwct.co.uk Website www.hwct.org.uk

■ **Hampton Fuel Allotment**

**CC NO** 211756   **ESTABLISHED** 1811
**WHERE FUNDING CAN BE GIVEN** Richmond upon Thames (Hampton, Hampton Hill, Hampton Wick, Teddington, Twickenham, Whitton).
**WHO CAN BENEFIT** Charitable bodies; community groups; voluntary organisations; individuals.
**WHAT IS FUNDED** Primarily grants towards fuel costs and essential equipment to individuals; assistance to not-for-profit organisations which support those in need, especially people with disabilities, suffering from illness, social isolation or other disadvantage. A wide range of general charitable causes are assisted.
**WHAT IS NOT FUNDED** Individuals for private and post-compulsory education; adaptations or building alterations for individuals; holidays (except in cases of severe medical need); home decoration, carpeting or central heating; anything which is the responsibility of a statutory body; national general charitable appeals; animal welfare; advancement of religion and religious groups, unless they offer a non-religious service to the community; commercial and business activities; endowment appeals; projects of a political nature; retrospective revenue or capital grants; organisations whose free reserves exceed 12 months' running costs; non-charitable social enterprises.

**TYPE OF GRANT** One-off grants; loans; other funding.
**RANGE OF GRANTS** £400–£75,000
**SAMPLE GRANTS** St Augustine's Community Care Trust – Homelink (£75,000); Age UK Richmond upon Thames (£50,000); Richmond Borough Mind (£30,000); The Mulberry Centre (£23,000); Alzheimer's Society South West London Branch (£16,000); London Wildlife Trust (£15,000); Orange Tree Theatre (£12,000); Addiction Support And Care Agency (£11,500); Richmond Carers Centre (£11,000); Otakar Kraus Music Trust (£10,000); Three Wings Trust (£6,300); Art and Soul and Silverfit Ltd (£5,000 each); Spear Housing Association Ltd (£4,500); Octagon Art Club (£3,100); POD Charitable Trust (£2,400); Richmond upon Thames Performing Arts Festival (£1,500); Richmond Talking Newspaper (£500); Ethnic Minorities Advocacy Group (£400).

**FINANCES** Year 2013/14 Income £2,042,927 Grants £1,645,944 Grants to organisations £899,370 Assets £53,096,842
**TRUSTEES** Revd Derek Winterburn; Dr James Brockbank; Dr Jane Young; Stuart Leamy; Jonathan Cardy; Paula Williams; Richard Montgomery; Hilary Hart; Clive Beaumont; Derek Terrington; Victoria Reid.
**OTHER INFORMATION** A total of £746,500 was given in grants to individuals (1,755 fuel grants and 202 for essential equipment and furniture). There were 72 organisational grants made. Support is also given to pupils in their penultimate or final year at junior school towards school journeys.
**HOW TO APPLY** The charity states: 'Once you have determined that you are likely to meet our funding criteria, please contact the [correspondent] to discuss your funding request, or preferably send a brief outline by email.' Following this the charity will arrange an assessment visit to your organisation and guide you in submitting your application. Application forms can be found on the charity's website along with detailed guidelines. Individual Grants and General Grants panels meet at least six times a year.
**WHO TO APPLY TO** David White, Clerk to the Trustees, 15 High Street, Hampton, Middlesex TW12 2SA Tel. 020 8941 7866 email david@hfac.co.uk Website www.hfac.co.uk

■ **The W. A. Handley Charitable Trust**

**CC NO** 230435   **ESTABLISHED** 1963
**WHERE FUNDING CAN BE GIVEN** North East of England and Cumbria.
**WHO CAN BENEFIT** Registered charities only.
**WHAT IS FUNDED** General charitable purposes with preference for the alleviation of distress, crisis funding, pump-priming finance and operating expenses.
**WHAT IS NOT FUNDED** Individuals; unregistered charities; awards are not normally made outside the area of benefit.
**TYPE OF GRANT** Regular payments and one-off grants.
**RANGE OF GRANTS** £500–£10,000

**SAMPLE GRANTS** Beneficiaries of *regular* grants included: Northumberland Association of Clubs for Young People (£6,000); St Oswald's Hospice (£2,600); Tiny Lives (£2,500); Duke of Edinburgh Award, Literary and Philosophical Society, Mental Health Matters, SHELTER North East Housing Aid Centre and Youth for Christ North East (£1,000 each); and Breakthrough Breast Cancer (£500). Beneficiaries of *one-off* grants included: Haskel and Percy Park Youth Trust (£10,000); Durham County Credit Union (£6,000); Hexham Abbey WW1 Reflection Service, Newcastle Healthcare Breast Cancer Appeal and Tynemouth Volunteer Life Brigade (£5,000 each); Royal British Legion, Rothbury (£3,000); National Centre for Children's Books (£2,000); St Mary's Church, Holy Island (£1,000); and Middlesbrough and Teesside Philanthropic Foundation (£500).
**FINANCES** Year 2013/14 Income £312,574 Grants £303,350 Grants to organisations £303,350 Assets £9,218,151
**TRUSTEES** William Dryden; Anthony Glenton; David Irvin; David Milligan.
**OTHER INFORMATION** Grants were made to 135 organisations.
**HOW TO APPLY** Applications should be made in writing to the correspondent, quoting the applicant's official charity number and providing full back-up information. Our research suggests that grants are made quarterly – in March, June, September and December.
**WHO TO APPLY TO** David Milligan, Trustee, c/o Ryecroft Glenton, 32 Portland Terrace, Newcastle upon Tyne NE2 1QP *Tel.* 0191 281 1292 *email* davidmilligan@ryecroft-glenton.co.uk

## ■ The Kathleen Hannay Memorial Charity
**CC NO** 299600  **ESTABLISHED** 1988
**WHERE FUNDING CAN BE GIVEN** UK and worldwide.
**WHO CAN BENEFIT** Registered charities; churches; hospitals; universities and schools; social enterprises.
**WHAT IS FUNDED** General charitable purposes, including health, social welfare, religious causes, education, arts and culture and environmental protection or improvement.
**WHAT IS NOT FUNDED** Grants are not made to individuals or non-registered charities.
**TYPE OF GRANT** One-off and recurrent grants for capital and revenue costs; unrestricted funding.
**RANGE OF GRANTS** Up to £50,000.
**SAMPLE GRANTS** Save the Children (£50,000); Sheffield Out of School Network (£35,000); Children's Burn Trust (£33,000); and Fleming Wyfold Art Foundation (£30,000). Other grants under £30,000 totalled £210,500 but were not listed.
**FINANCES** Year 2013/14 Income £284,218 Grants £358,500 Grants to organisations £358,500 Assets £11,932,953
**TRUSTEES** Simon Weil; Christian Ward; Jonathan Weil; Laura Watkins.
**OTHER INFORMATION** There were 33 awards made.
**HOW TO APPLY** Applications may be made in writing to the correspondent. The trustees' annual report for 2013/14 states that 'the trustees consider and approve grants annually and although many are made to the same charities each year none are promised or guaranteed'.
**WHO TO APPLY TO** The Trustees, c/o R. F. Trustee Co. Ltd, 15 Suffolk Street, London SW1Y 4HG *Tel.* 020 7036 5685 *email* charities@rftrustee.com

## ■ The Doughty Hanson Charitable Foundation
**CC NO** 1080755  **ESTABLISHED** 2000
**WHERE FUNDING CAN BE GIVEN** UK and overseas.
**WHO CAN BENEFIT** Registered charities and individuals.
**WHAT IS FUNDED** The relief of poverty distress and suffering, advancing education and appreciation in the arts and science, furthering religious work and other charitable purposes in any part of the world.
**RANGE OF GRANTS** £1,000–£20,000
**SAMPLE GRANTS** MediCinema (£20,000); the Snowdon Award Scheme (£15,500); Elizabeth Finn Care (£14,000); the Sick Children's Trust, Brainwave and Canine Partners (£10,000 each); Cancer Research UK (£6,500); Prostate Cancer UK, Brake and the Parkinson's Disease Society (£5,000 each); Listening Books (£3,000); Children's Heart Federation (£2,500); and Coeliac UK (£1,000).
**FINANCES** Year 2013 Income £266,201 Grants £271,926 Grants to organisations £271,926 Assets £4,223
**TRUSTEES** Richard Hanson; Stephen Marquardt; Richard Lund; Graeme Stening.
**OTHER INFORMATION** This foundation is the charitable giving arm of Doughty Hanson & Co., an independent private equity fund manager.
**HOW TO APPLY** Apply in writing to the correspondent – the grants committee meets about four times a year. Only successful applicants receive a response.
**WHO TO APPLY TO** Julie Foreman, Secretary, PO Box 31064, London SW1Y 5ZP

## ■ The Haramead Trust
**CC NO** 1047416  **ESTABLISHED** 1995
**WHERE FUNDING CAN BE GIVEN** Worldwide, in practice, financially developing countries, UK and Ireland and locally in the East Midlands.
**WHO CAN BENEFIT** Registered charities; individuals and families in need of direct assistance.
**WHAT IS FUNDED** Relief in need; health and disability; children and young people; education; disadvantaged individuals. Causes supported include children's charities, social and medical assistance, homelessness and educational needs.
**TYPE OF GRANT** Capital and core support, building/renovation, equipment, vehicles and project support for up to three years.
**RANGE OF GRANTS** Up to £210,000.
**SAMPLE GRANTS** Christian Aid (£210,000); British Red Cross (£100,000); Leicestershire and Rutland Community (£50,000); Intercare (£30,000); Action Aid, Leicestershire Cares, Let the Children Live! and Warning Zone (£20,000 each); and Practical Action (£15,000); Dogs for Disabled, Laura Centre, Peter Le Marchant Trust and Project Trust (£10,000 each). The accounts further specify that 'donations less than £1,000 and more than £4,999' totalled £110,000 and 'donations less than £5,000' totalled £7.600.
**FINANCES** Year 2013/14 Income £751,934 Grants £784,844 Grants to organisations £784,844 Assets £104,383
**TRUSTEES** David Tams; Michael Linnett; Robert Smith; Winifred Linnett; Simon Astil; Revd Joseph Mullen; Victoria Duddles.
**OTHER INFORMATION** During the year grants were made to 49 organisations (following 940 applications). The trustees may visit funded projects, both in the UK and overseas, for monitoring purposes or to assess projects/

organisations for future grants. Travel and administration costs are borne by the settlor; only audit costs are met by the trust. Awards were split as follows: developing world (£401,000); East Midlands (£206,000); and UK and Ireland (£178,000).

HOW TO APPLY Applications may be made in writing to the correspondent, providing relevant financial details of your organisation. The trustees meet every couple of months and may visit funded projects for monitoring purposes or to assess for future grants. All appeals are acknowledged.

WHO TO APPLY TO Michael Linnett, Trustee, Park House, Park Hill, Gaddesby, Leicestershire LE7 4WH *email* harameadtrust@aol.com

### ■ Miss K. M. Harbinson's Charitable Trust

WHERE FUNDING CAN BE GIVEN UK and financially developing countries.

WHO CAN BENEFIT Development organisations; individuals.

WHAT IS FUNDED General charitable purposes and in particular, international development; education; health; agriculture; conservation; natural environment; occasionally arts.

TYPE OF GRANT Capital and core costs; project funding.

RANGE OF GRANTS £1,000–£9,000

SAMPLE GRANTS **Previous beneficiaries have included:** ActionAid; Breadline Africa; British Red Cross; Care Britain; Ethopiaid Intermediate Technology; Marie Stopes International; Oxfam; Romanian Orphanage Trust; Sight Savers International; UNICEF; Worldwide Fund for Nature.

FINANCES *Grants* £125,000 *Grants to organisations* £125,000

TRUSTEES A. Maguire; G. L. Harbinson; R. Harbinson.

OTHER INFORMATION There was very little information available on the trust; we have tried contacting the correspondent via email, but have not received a response. In the past grants have totalled around £100,000–£150,000.

HOW TO APPLY Applications may be made in writing to the correspondent.

WHO TO APPLY TO The Secretary, c/o Miller, Becket and Jackson, 190 St Vincent Street, Glasgow G2 5SP *Tel.* 0141 204 2833 *Fax* 0141 248 7185 *email* mail@millerbj.co.uk

### ■ Harbo Charities Limited

CC NO 282262   ESTABLISHED 1981

WHERE FUNDING CAN BE GIVEN UK and overseas.

WHO CAN BENEFIT Orthodox Jewish charitable organisations.

WHAT IS FUNDED General charitable purposes; Jewish causes; education; religion; relief in need; health and disability. Organisations that offer: 'financial support to the poor'; 'provision of basic necessities to the poor'; 'relief of sickness and disabilities'; 'Jewish education and places of worship for the Jewish community'.

SAMPLE GRANTS **Previous beneficiaries have included:** Beis Chinuch Lebonos Girls School; Beth Rochel d'Satmar; Bobov Trust; Chevras Maoz Ladol; Craven Walk Charitable Trust; Edgware Yeshiva Trust; Keren Yesomim; Kollel Shomrei HaChomoth; Tevini Limited; Tomchei Shabbos; Yad Eliezer; Yesode Ha Torah School; Yeshiva Chachmay Tsorpha.

FINANCES *Year* 2013/14 *Income* £85,380 *Grants* £104,397 *Grants to organisations* £104,397 *Assets* £735,393

TRUSTEES Harold Gluck; Barbara Stern.

OTHER INFORMATION A list of beneficiaries was not included within the latest set of accounts.

HOW TO APPLY Applications may be made in writing to the correspondent. The annual report for 2013/14 states that 'the trustees are approached for donations by a wide variety of charitable institutions operating all over England (and also abroad)' – all requests are considered.

WHO TO APPLY TO Barbara Stern, Trustee, 13 Fairholt Road, London N16 5EW *Tel.* 020 8731 0777

### ■ The Harborne Parish Lands Charity

CC NO 219031   ESTABLISHED 1699

WHERE FUNDING CAN BE GIVEN The ancient parish of Harborne (12 parishes including Harborne, Smethwick and parts of Quinton and Bearwood).

WHO CAN BENEFIT Individuals in need; established organisations aiding people living within the parish.

WHAT IS FUNDED Support to local residents in need; social welfare; community causes; health; accommodation and housing. The charity has adopted the following grant priorities: food and household goods distribution; debt awareness and money management support; people with mental ill health; core funding support for organisations working with disadvantaged groups who are impacted by local and national funding reductions. The accounts state: 'The charity will continue to deliver its in-house individual grant programme, however the remit will be extended to include those in work and also in poverty. The charity will seek additional referral agencies to enable access to this emergent group.'

WHAT IS NOT FUNDED Applications from individuals directly (any appeal must be made through a recognised referral agency).

TYPE OF GRANT Buildings; capital; core costs; interest-free loans; one-off and up to one year; projects; running costs; salaries; start-up costs; unrestricted funding.

RANGE OF GRANTS £400–£17,000

SAMPLE GRANTS Cares Sandwell (£17,000); St Boniface (£15,000); Universal Church of Jesus Christ (£14,300); Birmingham St Mary's Hospice, Cerebral Palsy Midlands and Sandwell Young Care (£10,000 each); Brushstrokes (£9,600); Bearwood Chapel Trust and North Smethwick Development Trust (£8,500 each); Quinborne Community Association (£6,000); Focus Birmingham (£5,000); African French Speaking Community Support (£2,100); Birmingham Samaritans (£2,000); Smethwick Mini Muslims (£1,500); Cottage Crafts (£400).

FINANCES *Year* 2013/14 *Income* £1,274,581 *Grants* £278,923 *Grants to organisations* £218,456 *Assets* £15,035,081

TRUSTEES Cllr Roger Horton; Michael Lloyd; Rachel Silber; Frank Wayt; Nigel Thompson; Geoff Hewitt; Buddhi Chetiyawardana; David Jeffery; Kerry Bolister; Linda Horton; Vic Silvester.

OTHER INFORMATION In 2013/14 a total of £48,000 was given to 98 individuals. There were 29 awards to organisations. The charity also provides almshouse accommodation. For 2015/16 the charity had a budget of

£270,000, with £215,000 for organisations and £55,000 to individuals. The accounts noted that 'efforts will be made to increase this'.

**HOW TO APPLY** Application forms can be requested from the correspondent via email or phone. They should be returned along with a copy of the latest annual report and accounts. An exact map of the beneficial area can be obtained from the charity's website and should be consulted before an appeal is made. Up-to-date submission deadlines are listed online, under 'News' section. Grants from organisations are considered twice a year in September and April. Individual applications are approved weekly.

**WHO TO APPLY TO** Sharon Murphy, Grants Officer, 109 Court Oak Road, Harborne, Birmingham B17 9AA *Tel.* 0121 426 1600 *Fax* 0121 428 2267 *email* sharon.murphy@hplc.org.uk or info@hplc.org.uk *Website* www.hplc.org.uk

## ■ The Harbour Charitable Trust

**CC NO** 234268  **ESTABLISHED** 1962
**WHERE FUNDING CAN BE GIVEN** UK.
**WHO CAN BENEFIT** Organisations benefitting children, young adults and students, also older people. Support may also be given to teachers and governesses, medical professionals, research workers, parents and children and one-parent families.
**WHAT IS FUNDED** Childcare, education and training, the arts, healthcare and other charitable purposes.
**WHAT IS NOT FUNDED** Grants are given to registered charities only.
**SAMPLE GRANTS** Grants were made in the following categories: promotion of the arts (£19,300); religious and inter-faith (£8,200); aged care (£2,500); healthcare (£1,000); and other donations (£400).
**FINANCES** *Year* 2013/14 *Income* £150,320 *Grants* £31,348 *Grants to organisations* £31,348 *Assets* £4,522,285
**TRUSTEES** Zena Sandra Blackman; Tamar Eisenstat; Barbara Brenda Green; Elaine Knobil.
**HOW TO APPLY** Apply in writing to the correspondent.
**WHO TO APPLY TO** Ali Alidina, Correspondent, Barbican House, 80 Coleman Street, Moorgate, London EC2R 5BJ *email* ali.alidina@bfca.eu

## ■ The Harbour Foundation

**CC NO** 264927  **ESTABLISHED** 1970
**WHERE FUNDING CAN BE GIVEN** Worldwide.
**WHO CAN BENEFIT** Organisations and individuals.
**WHAT IS FUNDED** General charitable purposes, especially relief of poverty, refugees and homeless people, education and research and musical training. The foundation has a postgraduate assistance programme 'available to impoverished postgraduate students for science degrees at the Hebrew University of Jerusalem, named in memory of Bert and Fay Harbour'.
**RANGE OF GRANTS** Up to £200,000.
**SAMPLE GRANTS** A list of beneficiaries was not included within the accounts; however, awards were made in the following categories: education (£426,500); social organisation (£81,000); music (£75,000); religious bodies (£45,000); medical (£41,000); relief (£23,000). **Previous beneficiaries have included:** Royal College of Music – London; and the Tel Aviv Foundation – Israel (£15,000 each).

**FINANCES** *Year* 2013/14 *Income* £1,412,179 *Grants* £691,629 *Grants to organisations* £691,629 *Assets* £43,668,761
**TRUSTEES** Rex Harbour; Susan Harbour; Dr Daniel Harbour; Edmond Harbour.
**OTHER INFORMATION** In 2013/14 there were 74 grants made. About £643,000 of the overall total was given to UK-registered charities. The annual report for 2013/14 notes that 'there is increasing emphasis on grants benefitting charitable activities carried out worldwide'.
**HOW TO APPLY** Applications can be made in writing to the correspondent. Our research suggests they need to be received by February, as the trustees normally meet in March.
**WHO TO APPLY TO** The Trustees, 1 Red Place, London W1K 6PL *Tel.* 020 7456 8180

## ■ The Harding Trust

**CC NO** 328182  **ESTABLISHED** 1989
**WHERE FUNDING CAN BE GIVEN** Mainly, but not exclusively, north Staffordshire and surrounding areas.
**WHO CAN BENEFIT** Charitable organisations, theatres, festivals, public concerts, also hospices. Both amateur and professional organisations are supported.
**WHAT IS FUNDED** Charities supported are in most cases connected with music, arts and culture; however, local welfare charities and hospices are also given support.
**TYPE OF GRANT** One-off and recurrent.
**RANGE OF GRANTS** £1,000–£35,000.
**SAMPLE GRANTS** Stoke-on-Trent Festival (£35,000); Harding Trust Piano Recitals (£20,000); Malvern Theatres Trust (£10,000); English Chamber Orchestra, European Union Chamber Orchestra and Royal Philharmonic Orchestra (£6,000 each); Cloner Farm Music Trust (£3,500); Patrons Victoria Hall Organ (£3,000); Midlands Air Ambulance (£2,000); Douglas Macmillan Hospice (£1,500); Bilston Operatic and British Red Cross Society (£1,000 each); Lichfield Festival (£750); and Uttoxeter Choral Society (£500).
**FINANCES** *Year* 2013/14 *Income* £153,572 *Grants* £121,750 *Grants to organisations* £121,750 *Assets* £4,276,912
**TRUSTEES** Geoffrey Snow; Geoffrey Wall; John Fowell; Michael Lloyd.
**OTHER INFORMATION** Grants were made to 26 organisations.
**HOW TO APPLY** Apply in writing to the correspondent. Our research suggests that the trustees meet annually in spring/early summer. Accounts are needed for recurrent applications.
**WHO TO APPLY TO** Peter O'Rourke, Correspondent, Horton House, Exchange Flags, Liverpool L2 3YL *Tel.* 0151 600 3000 *email* peter.o'rourke@brabners.com

## ■ William Harding's Charity

**CC NO** 310619  **ESTABLISHED** 1978
**WHERE FUNDING CAN BE GIVEN** Aylesbury in Buckinghamshire.
**WHO CAN BENEFIT** Individuals and organisations residing and benefitting the population of Aylesbury.
**WHAT IS FUNDED** To assist young people in education, including at an individual level, by providing scholarships, maintenance allowances, travel awards and grants for equipment. At a wider level, grants are made to the LEA for Aylesbury schools to fund equipment

in addition to that which can be provided by the authority. The charity also provides relief in need and for the general benefit of Aylesbury residents.
**WHAT IS NOT FUNDED** People and organisations not based in Aylesbury Town.
**TYPE OF GRANT** One-off and capital costs.
**RANGE OF GRANTS** £250–£15,000 (organisations).
**SAMPLE GRANTS** Previous beneficiaries have included: Aylesbury Project Community Interest Company (£15,000); QPAC (£12,000); Aylesbury Youth Action (£10,000); Youth Concern Aylesbury (£7,000); Community Impact Bucks (£5,000); Monday Contact Club and SPACE (£4,000 each); Buckingham St Youth Club and 14th Vale of Aylesbury Sea Scout (£2,500 each); Aylesbury Centre National Trust (£1,300); Sir Henry Floyd Grammar School (£800).
**FINANCES** Year 2013 Income £887,083 Grants £396,000 Grants to organisations £296,000
**TRUSTEES** Les Sheldon; Anne Brooker; Freda Roberts; Bernard Griffin; Penni Thorne; Roger Evans; William Chapple; Lennard Wakelam; Susan Hewitt.
**OTHER INFORMATION** Full accounts were not available to view at the time of writing. On average about 40% of the overall expenditure is directed at supporting institutions (we estimated this to be about £296,000) and grants to individuals usually fluctuate around £100,000 each year. Further expenditure is also allocated towards the maintenance of the almshouses. Grants are normally given in the following categories: schools and other educational establishments; general benefits/relief in need; travel for clubs/societies/groups; youth groups; equipment and tools for young people.
**HOW TO APPLY** Applications may be made in writing to the correspondent. The trustees meet on a regular basis to consider and determine applications for charitable assistance. The charity's record on the Charity Commission's links to the charity's website; however, it did not seem to function at the time of writing.
**WHO TO APPLY TO** John Leggett, Correspondent, 14 Bourbon Street, Aylesbury, Buckinghamshire HP20 2RS Tel. 01296 318501 email doudjag@pandclip.co.uk

■ **The Hare of Steep Charitable Trust (HOST)**
**CC NO** 297308 **ESTABLISHED** 1987
**WHERE FUNDING CAN BE GIVEN** UK, with preference for the south of England, especially Petersfield and East Hampshire.
**WHO CAN BENEFIT** Registered charities only.
**WHAT IS FUNDED** Charities which benefit the community, in particular the advancement of social, cultural, medical, educational and religious projects.
**TYPE OF GRANT** Mainly annual contributions but one-off grants are made for special projects.
**RANGE OF GRANTS** £250–£3,000
**SAMPLE GRANTS** East Hants Citizens Advice (£3,000). In the past grants have been made to: Alzheimer's Disease Society; Arthritis and Rheumatism Council – Petersfield; British Heart Foundation; Rainbow House Trust; SSAFA.
**FINANCES** Year 2013/14 Income £69,249 Grants £50,750 Grants to organisations £50,750 Assets £128,080

**TRUSTEES** S. M. Fowler; Brigadier P. L. F. Baillon; J. R. F. Fowler; S. E. R. Johnson-Hill; Stephanie Grenfell.
**OTHER INFORMATION** Grants were made to 35 organisations.
**HOW TO APPLY** The trust has previously stated that 'the trustees already support as many charities as they could wish. Unsolicited requests are not acknowledged.'
**WHO TO APPLY TO** S. M. Fowler, Hon. Secretary, 31A Monks Orchard, Petersfield, Hampshire GU32 2JD Tel. 01730 267953 email jrffowler@aol.com

■ **The Harebell Centenary Fund**
**CC NO** 1003552 **ESTABLISHED** 1991
**WHERE FUNDING CAN BE GIVEN** UK.
**WHO CAN BENEFIT** Charitable organisations benefitting children, older people, people who have a disability and animals.
**WHAT IS FUNDED** General charitable purposes; education; medical research; animal welfare. This includes charities working in the fields of health, medical studies and research (particularly neurological and neurosurgical research, motor neurone disease and multiple sclerosis), conservation, heritage, special needs education and holidays and outings.
**WHAT IS NOT FUNDED** Individuals.
**TYPE OF GRANT** One-off awards for core costs, research, recurring expenditure, running costs and funding for one year or less will be considered.
**RANGE OF GRANTS** Up to £7,000.
**SAMPLE GRANTS** Canine Partners for Independence, Children's Air Ambulance, Dyslexia Research Trust, Helen House Hospice, Nordoff-Robbins Music School, Mayhew Animal Home, The Blue Cross and The Tabor Centre (£7,000 each); Crathie School (£4,000); and The Seeing Dogs Alliance (£3,500).
**FINANCES** Year 2013 Income £183,534 Grants £147,879 Grants to organisations £147,879 Assets £6,410,948
**TRUSTEES** Michael Goodbody; Penelope Chapman; Angela Fossick.
**OTHER INFORMATION** There were 22 grants made.
**HOW TO APPLY** Applications can be made in writing to the correspondent. Our research suggests that the trustees meet every six months to consider awards. Unsolicited applications are not requested, as the trustees prefer to make donations to charities whose work they have come across through their own research.
**WHO TO APPLY TO** Penelope Chapman, Trustee, 50 Broadway, Westminster, London SW1H 0BL Tel. 020 7227 7000 email pennychapman@bdb-law.co.uk

■ **The Hargrave Foundation**
**CC NO** 1106524 **ESTABLISHED** 2004
**WHERE FUNDING CAN BE GIVEN** Worldwide.
**WHO CAN BENEFIT** Charitable organisations and individuals.
**WHAT IS FUNDED** Research; social welfare; general charitable purposes.
**WHAT IS NOT FUNDED** Applications from adult or gap year students are not normally considered.
**SAMPLE GRANTS** The Academy of Ideas Ltd and Journalism Education Ltd (£10,000 each).
**FINANCES** Year 2013/14 Income £104,185 Grants £76,755 Grants to organisations £76,755 Assets £3,481,796

TRUSTEES Stephen Hargrave; Dominic Moseley; Adam Parkin.

OTHER INFORMATION Eight grants were made to institutions during the year. In addition to the two grants noted above, grants to 'Others' amounted to a further £57,000.

HOW TO APPLY The trustees do not normally consider unsolicited applications and do not reply to unsolicited correspondence.

WHO TO APPLY TO Stephen Hargrave, Trustee, 47 Lambs Conduit Street, London WC1N 3NG email stephen.hargrave@btinternet.com

## ■ The Harpur Trust

CC NO 1066861   ESTABLISHED 1566

WHERE FUNDING CAN BE GIVEN Borough of Bedford and the surrounding area. There is a helpful facility on the website to check your postcode eligibility.

WHO CAN BENEFIT Community groups, schools, individuals (under education object), and organisations. Particularly children and young adults, people with additional support needs, older people, and people disadvantaged by poverty.

WHAT IS FUNDED Education; social welfare; facilities for recreation and other leisure-time occupations; people who are sick, in hardship or distress; homelessness; child and adolescent mental health. The charity has a Responsive Programme – awarding about £500,000 each year in the areas of education, relief and recreation – and Themed Grants programmes – awarding another approximately £500,000 on topics of particular interest (which still fit within the three objects). The three new programmes are Transitions (for projects which provide preparation, bridges and support for people undergoing difficult life transitions), Resilience or Psychological Fitness (helping residents manage and cope with traumatic changes positively, learning to adapt and prosper despite setbacks) and Isolation (projects which reduce loneliness and lack of social networks amongst the most vulnerable residents. The trust in particular welcomes applications which address these priority areas.

WHAT IS NOT FUNDED Commercial ventures; any project that relates primarily to the promotion of any religion; projects that do not benefit the residents of the borough of Bedford; costs already incurred; trips, except in very limited circumstances (contact the grants manager for specific guidance); services which are the responsibility of the local authority.

TYPE OF GRANT Capital and core funding; equipment; start-up and project costs; salaries; running expenditure; one-off and multi-year grants (but not for repeat funding for the same project activities).

RANGE OF GRANTS £1,300–£100,000; usually up to £5,000 or between £10,000 and £20,000 (often split over several years).

SAMPLE GRANTS Bedford Citizens Housing Association (£100,000); FACES Bedford (£90,000); The Bedford Academy (£80,000); Tibbs Dementia Foundation (£62,500); Bedford Music In Detention (£30,000); YMCA Bedfordshire (£22,500); 21st Century Education Trust (£17,500); ProgressAbility.org (£14,500); Bedfordshire Refugee and Asylum Seeker Support (£11,800); Families United Network (£11,200); Bedford Creative Arts (£6,500); Cople Lower School (£5,000); St Christopher's Fellowship (£4,000); The Prince's Trust (£3,800); Kempston Community Theatre (£1,300).

FINANCES Year 2013/14 Income £55,270,000 Grants £1,068,000 Grants to organisations £979,968 Assets £130,044,000

TRUSTEES David Palfreyman; David Wilson; Rae Levene; Michael Womack; Ian McEwen; Philip Wallace; Anthony Nutt; Justin Phillimore; Susan Clark; Tina Beddoes; Prof. Stephen Mayson; Hugh Stewart; Sally Peck; David Dixon; Prof. Kate Jacques; Dr Jennifer Till; Dr Anne Egan; Cllr Randolph Charles; Rhian Castell; Linbert Spencer; Prof. Seamus Higson.

OTHER INFORMATION Grants, awards and prizes were distributed as follows: relief – £583,000; education – £441,000; recreation – £44,000. Grants to individuals totalled about £95,000, including two grants to individuals, college and bursary programmes and school uniform grants. The website specifies that awards were made to 39 organisations and 20 individuals. The latter is generally given 'to adults who are returning to education in order to improve their employment prospects'. The trust also runs its own independent schools, co-sponsors, with Bedford College, the new Bedford Academy and maintains almshouses.

HOW TO APPLY Prior to making formal appeal or even preliminary proposal applicants are strongly advised to call the trust and discuss their needs. Applications can be made online on the trust's website but **only after** you have been invited to do so. Full guidance and specific deadlines for each stage of the application are also found on the website.

WHO TO APPLY TO Lucy Bardner, Grants Manager, Princeton Court, Pilgrim Centre, Brickhill Drive, Bedford MK41 7PZ Tel. 01234 369500 Fax 01234 369505 email grants@harpur-trust.org.uk Website www.bedfordcharity.org.uk

## ■ The Harris Charity

CC NO 526206   ESTABLISHED 1883

WHERE FUNDING CAN BE GIVEN Lancashire, with a preference for the City of Preston (formally the borough of Preston).

WHO CAN BENEFIT Charities benefitting individuals, children and young people under 25, in the Lancashire area.

WHAT IS FUNDED Children and young people.

WHAT IS NOT FUNDED The charity cannot help with the relief of rates, taxes or other public funds.

TYPE OF GRANT Capital projects and provision of equipment are preferred.

RANGE OF GRANTS £30 to £4,000.

FINANCES Year 2013/14 Income £123,334 Grants £86,838 Grants to organisations £82,886 Assets £3,701,576

TRUSTEES William Huck; Edwin Booth; Dr Anthony Andrews; Timothy Scott; Stanley Smith; Simon Huck; Keith Mellalieu; Audrey Scott; Nicola Fielden; Peter Metcalf; Revd Peter Hamborg; Jennifer Coulston-Hermann.

OTHER INFORMATION Grants to individuals totalled about £4,000.

HOW TO APPLY Application forms are available to download from the charity's website, where criteria and guidelines are also posted. completed applications should be returned to the correspondent enclosing an sae. The website notes: 'Applications from charities must indicate the official registration number as issued by the Charity Commission. Also, the Trustees will require to see evidence from the Chief Inspector of Taxes, Claims Branch, as to exempt charity status from Income Tax.' The trustees invite applications in the local press in March and September every year. Application deadlines are 31 March and 30 September. Successful applicants are notified in July and January respectively following the closing date each year. Each request for a grant must be made on an official application form.

**WHO TO APPLY TO** David Ingram, Secretary, c/o Moore and Smalley, Richard House, 9 Winckley Square, Preston, Lancashire PR1 3HP *Tel.* 01772 821021 *email* harrischarity@mooreandsmalley.co.uk *Website* www.theharrischarity.co.uk

## ■ The Harris Family Charitable Trust

**CC NO** 1064394     **ESTABLISHED** 1997
**WHERE FUNDING CAN BE GIVEN** UK.
**WHO CAN BENEFIT** Charitable organisations.
**WHAT IS FUNDED** Health issues and the alleviation of sickness.
**FINANCES** *Year* 2013/14 *Income* £59,280 *Grants* £118,974 *Grants to organisations* £118,974 *Assets* £1,843,672
**TRUSTEES** Ronnie Harris; Loretta Harris; Charlotte Harris; Sophie Harris; Toby Harris.
**HOW TO APPLY** According to the annual report for 2013/14, the trust 'invites applications for funding of projects through various sources' and 'the applications are reviewed by the trustees that they are in accordance with the charity's objectives'.
**WHO TO APPLY TO** Ronnie Harris, Trustee, 64 New Cavendish Street, London W1G 8TB *Tel.* 020 7467 6300

## ■ The Edith Lilian Harrison 2000 Foundation

**CC NO** 1085651     **ESTABLISHED** 2000
**WHO CAN BENEFIT** Registered charities.
**WHAT IS FUNDED** General charitable purposes.
**TYPE OF GRANT** One-off grants for three years or more.
**RANGE OF GRANTS** £1,500–£55,000
**SAMPLE GRANTS** Salisbury District Hospital CT Scanner Appeal (£55,000); Salisbury Hospice (£25,000); St John's Church Redhill (£20,000); MERU (£15,000); Alzheimer's Society (East Surrey Branch), Guide Dogs for the Blind, Music Alive, NSPCC, The Mission to Seafarers and The Salvation Army (£10,000 each); and Rotary Club of Salisbury (£1,500).
**FINANCES** *Year* 2013/14 *Income* £92,108 *Grants* £246,500 *Grants to organisations* £246,500 *Assets* £2,543,357
**TRUSTEES** Geoffrey Peyer; Clive Andrews; Paul Bradley.
**OTHER INFORMATION** There were 18 grants made to organisations.
**HOW TO APPLY** Apply in writing to the correspondent. The trustees meet every six months. Applications for grants are normally considered and dealt with in November.
**WHO TO APPLY TO** Paul Bradley, Trustee, TWM Solicitors LLP, 40 West Street, Reigate RH2 9BT *Tel.* 01737 221212 *email* paul.bradley@twmsolicitors.com

## ■ The Peter Harrison Foundation

**CC NO** 1076579     **ESTABLISHED** 1999
**WHERE FUNDING CAN BE GIVEN** UK; South East England.
**WHO CAN BENEFIT** Registered charities; community amateur sports clubs; friendly or provident societies; organisations in Scotland and Northern Ireland recognised by the HM Revenue and Customs; local branches of national charities if they have either a separate legal constitution or the endorsement of their national head office.
**WHAT IS FUNDED** Charitable activities that concentrate on people with disabilities, children and young people and disadvantaged individuals and demonstrate an existing high level of community involvement and are well planned. Awards are made through two funds: Opportunities through Sport (nationwide) – mainly one-off awards for capital projects and sporting activities aimed at catering skills development and confidence building of people with disabilities and disadvantaged individuals as well as young people at risk of crime, truancy or addiction; Special Needs and care Programme for Children and Young People (South East England (excluding London and Greater London) – Berkshire, Buckinghamshire, Hampshire, Isle of Wight, Kent, Oxfordshire, Surrey, East Sussex and West Sussex) – Two other funds (Opportunities through Education and awards made at the trustees' discretion) do not invite applications and eligible causes are selected by the trustees.
**WHAT IS NOT FUNDED** General appeals; retrospective funding; individuals; other grant-making bodies to make grants on the foundation's behalf; projects that replace statutory funding; projects that are the responsibility of the central or local government; holidays in the UK or abroad and expeditions; outdoor activity projects, such as camping or outward bound expeditions; overseas projects; projects solely for the promotion of religion.
**TYPE OF GRANT** Capital and core costs; salaries; project expenditure; one-off and up to three years.
**RANGE OF GRANTS** Up to £333,000.
**SAMPLE GRANTS** Young Epilepsy (£333,000); Loughborough University (£200,000); Woodlarks Camp Site Trust (£45,000); Boccia England (£37,500); Farney Close School (£35,000); The Greenbank Project (£33,000); Panathlon (£30,000); Disabled Waterski and Wakeboard Association (£20,000).
**FINANCES** *Year* 2013/14 *Income* £2,642,326 *Grants* £2,483,189 *Grants to organisations* £2,483,189 *Assets* £45,955,969
**TRUSTEES** Sir Peter Harrison; Julia Harrison-Lee; Peter Lee; Nicholas Harrison.
**OTHER INFORMATION** Awards through Opportunities through Sport programme totalled £533,000, and through Special Needs and Care for Children and Young People – £588,000. Educational support to Reigate Grammar School totalled over £1 million and the trustees' discretionary awards were given totalling £380,500.
**HOW TO APPLY** There is a two stage application process – initial enquiry (form available online) to determine whether your project would interest the foundation, and full application (applicants successful in the first stage will be sent one). There is no application deadline but you may only apply to one of the programmes at any time. Be aware that the foundation receives a large number of applications and it may

sometimes take up to two months for an initial enquiry form to be considered. The website notes: 'The Foundation receives many more requests for funding than we are able to support and we regret that we have to turn down many good proposals, even though they meet our criteria.' If you have received a grant you may re-apply after three years (from the date of the final grant payment); if you were unsuccessful you may try again in one year (from the date of the previous rejection).

WHO TO APPLY TO Julia Caines, Operations Executive, Foundation House, 42–48 London Road, Reigate, Surrey RH2 9QQ *Tel.* 01737 228000 *Fax* 01737 228001 *email* enquiries@peterharrisonfoundation.org *Website* www.peterharrisonfoundation.org

..................................................................

### ■ The Hartley Charitable Trust
CC NO 800968   ESTABLISHED 1989
WHERE FUNDING CAN BE GIVEN UK and overseas.
WHO CAN BENEFIT Charitable organisations.
WHAT IS FUNDED General charitable purposes.
WHAT IS NOT FUNDED No grants are awarded to individuals.
TYPE OF GRANT One-off and recurrent grants for core costs, capital expenditure, projects, research and salaries. Awards can be made for one year or less.
RANGE OF GRANTS £5,000–£30,000
SAMPLE GRANTS Alzheimer's Society (£30,000); Open Arms Malawi (£7,000); and Celtic Storm – Cornwall Powerchair Football and Senior Volunteer Network Trust (£5,000 each).
FINANCES *Year* 2013/14 *Income* £65,978 *Grants* £47,000 *Grants to organisations* £47,000 *Assets* £1,948,046
TRUSTEES Richard Hartley; Jane Hartley; Peta Hyland.
HOW TO APPLY In August 2011 the trust told us: 'We are fully committed for four to five years. It would be better if you indicated this in your publications and website, as organisations and individuals are wasting money in putting applications to us.'
WHO TO APPLY TO Richard Hartley, Trustee, 6 Throstle Nest Drive, Harrogate, Yorkshire HG2 9PB *Tel.* 01423 525100 *email* hartleycharitabletrust@hotmail.com

..................................................................

### ■ The Alfred And Peggy Harvey Charitable Trust
CC NO 1095855   ESTABLISHED 2003
WHERE FUNDING CAN BE GIVEN UK, with a strong preference for Kent, Surrey and South East London.
WHO CAN BENEFIT Charitable organisations in the counties of Kent, Surrey and South East London.
WHAT IS FUNDED Care and financial support for the elderly, children and young people with disabilities or living in difficult socio-economic circumstances, blind and deaf people and funding of medical and surgical studies and research.
WHAT IS NOT FUNDED Charitable organisations in Kent, Surrey and South East London only.
RANGE OF GRANTS £1,000–£10,000
SAMPLE GRANTS In the past grant recipients have included: Action for Kids; Child Victims of Crime; Children's Country Holiday Fund; Country Holidays For Inner City Kids; E-Learning Foundation; Happy Days; Hope UK; Kidscape;

Lighthouse Educational Scheme; and Macular Disease Society.
FINANCES *Year* 2013/14 *Income* £11,676 *Grants* £173,000 *Grants to organisations* £173,000
TRUSTEES Kevin Custis; Colin Russell; John Duncan.
HOW TO APPLY Applications may be made in writing to the correspondent.
WHO TO APPLY TO Colin Russell, Trustee, c/o Manches LLP, Aldwych House, 81 Aldwych, London WC2B 4RP *Tel.* 020 7404 4433

..................................................................

### ■ Edward Harvist Trust (The Harvist Estate)
CC NO 211970   ESTABLISHED 1994
WHERE FUNDING CAN BE GIVEN The London boroughs of Barnet, Brent, Camden, Harrow and the City of Westminster.
WHO CAN BENEFIT Registered charities supporting people within the beneficial area.
WHAT IS FUNDED General charitable purposes, relief of sickness, support to educational institutions.
TYPE OF GRANT One-off awards for capital costs.
RANGE OF GRANTS £1,000–£5,000
FINANCES *Year* 2013/14 *Income* £309,319 *Grants* £263,863 *Grants to organisations* £263,863 *Assets* £8,571,032
TRUSTEES Ilan Jacobs; Howard Bluston; Angela Harvey; Shafique Choudhary; Graham Old.
OTHER INFORMATION Income is distributed to the local authorities in proportion to the length of the Edgware Road passing through their area. In 2013/14 this was as follows: London borough of Barnet – (31%) £82,000; London borough of Brent – (28%) £73,000; City of Westminster – (25%) £66,000; London borough of Camden – (11%) £28,000; London borough of Harrow – (6%) £14,800.
HOW TO APPLY Apply in writing to the relevant local authority. Do not write to the correspondent. There may be slightly different criteria and application procedures imposed by the five local authorities.
WHO TO APPLY TO Ian Talbot, Correspondent, London Borough of Harrow, Finance Department, PO Box 21, Civic Centre, Harrow HA1 2UJ *Tel.* 020 8424 1450 *email* treasurymanagement@harrow.gov.uk

..................................................................

### ■ The Hasluck Charitable Trust
CC NO 1115323   ESTABLISHED 2006
WHERE FUNDING CAN BE GIVEN UK.
WHO CAN BENEFIT Charities helping children and young people, people with disabilities, older people and disadvantaged individuals.
WHAT IS FUNDED A wide range of charitable purposes, including health, welfare, disability, young and older people and overseas aid.
WHAT IS NOT FUNDED Individuals.
TYPE OF GRANT One-off; funding is unrestricted.
RANGE OF GRANTS Around £1,000.
FINANCES *Year* 2013/14 *Income* £122,330 *Grants* £82,000 *Grants to organisations* £82,000 *Assets* £1,465,524
TRUSTEES Matthew Wakefield; John Billing.
OTHER INFORMATION Half of the income received by the trust is equally allocated to eight charities (Barnardo's, International Fund for Animal Welfare, Macmillan Cancer Relief, Mrs R. H. Hotblack's Michelham Priory Endowment Fund, the Riding for the Disabled Association, RNLI, RSPB and Scope), which are of particular interest to the settlor. The

remainder is distributed at the trustees' discretion. During the year 51 awards were made.

**HOW TO APPLY** Apply in writing to the correspondent. Grants are generally distributed in January and July, although consideration is given to appeals received at other times of the year. The trust has previously stated that it 'asks applicants not to send copies of their accounts as these can be viewed online'. Only successful applicants are acknowledged.

**WHO TO APPLY TO** John Billing, Trustee, Rathbone Trust Company Limited, 4th Floor, 1 Curzon Street, London W1J 5FB *Tel.* 020 7399 0447 *email* john.billing@rathbones.com

## ■ The Hathaway Trust

**CC NO** 1064086  **ESTABLISHED** 1997
**WHERE FUNDING CAN BE GIVEN** UK and overseas, with a preference for Manchester.
**WHO CAN BENEFIT** Registered charities; individuals; Jewish institutions.
**WHAT IS FUNDED** General charitable purposes, including the relief of poverty, particularly amongst older individuals, the advancement of education, medical assistance, provision of interest-free loans, the advancement of religion and general community benefit. Support is mainly given for Jewish organisations and causes.
**TYPE OF GRANT** One-off and recurrent grants; interest-free loans.
**RANGE OF GRANTS** Up to £13,500.
**SAMPLE GRANTS** Tomchei Shabbos Manchester (£13,500); Yeshivas Shaarei Torah (£3,300); Sayser (£3,000); Asser Bishvil (£2,800); Purim Fund (£2,500); Ahavas Tzedoko Vochessed, Chesed L'Yisroel and Manchester Swallow (£1,800 each); Prestwich Beth Hamedresh (£1,600); Meleches Machsheves (£1,500); Manchester Hachnosas Kallah (£1,000). 'Other grants' (presumably under £1,000) totalled £21,500.
**FINANCES** Year 2013/14 Income £83,951 Grants £55,943 Grants to organisations £55,943 Assets £82,683
**TRUSTEES** Norman Younger; Miriam Younger; Rabbi Stuart Schwalbe; Jonathan Roitenbarg.
**OTHER INFORMATION** During the year, the trust became involved in a variety of new projects and activities aimed at youths in the area of Greater Manchester 'who have yet to find their place in society'. The aim being to help them realize their potential, develop their skills and capabilities to participate and contribute to society.
**HOW TO APPLY** The trustees have stated previously that they have adopted a proactive approach to funding and now only fund projects with which they have a personal connection, therefore unsolicited requests will not be considered.
**WHO TO APPLY TO** The Trustees, 12 Hereford Drive, Prestwich, Manchester M25 0JA

## ■ The Maurice Hatter Foundation

**CC NO** 298119  **ESTABLISHED** 1987
**WHERE FUNDING CAN BE GIVEN** UK and overseas.
**WHO CAN BENEFIT** Registered charities and educational bodies, particularly those with Jewish links.
**WHAT IS FUNDED** Jewish causes, general charitable purposes, international policy research, culture, environment, medical research and education.
**TYPE OF GRANT** Grants, often recurring; loans.

**RANGE OF GRANTS** £2,000–£250,000
**SAMPLE GRANTS** South of England Foundation (Charlton Athletic Community Trust) (£250,000); British Friends of Haifa University (£186,000); University College Hospital Charity Fund (Hatter Cardiovascular Institute) (£141,000); Jewish Leadership Council and UCL Development Fund (£100,000 each); World ORT (£79,000); Israel National Therapeutic Riding Association (£70,000); Covenant and Conversation Trust (£30,000); Prostate Cancer UK (£15,000); Henry Jackson Society (£12,000); Train for Employment and UJIA (£10,000 each); World Jewish Relief (£5,000); and Kol Nidre Appeal (£2,000).
**FINANCES** Year 2013/14 Income £2,905,268 Grants £1,372,173 Grants to organisations £1,372,173 Assets £7,066,860
**TRUSTEES** Ivor Connick; Richard Hatter; Maurice Hatter; Fausto Furlotti.
**HOW TO APPLY** Our research indicates that unsolicited applications will not be considered.
**WHO TO APPLY TO** Smith and Williamson, Correspondent, Smith and Williamson, 1 Bishops Wharf, Walnut Tree Close, Guildford, Surrey GU1 4RA *Tel.* 01483 407100

## ■ The M. A. Hawe Settlement

**CC NO** 327827  **ESTABLISHED** 1988
**WHERE FUNDING CAN BE GIVEN** Lancashire with a preference for the Fylde coastal area.
**WHO CAN BENEFIT** Organisations and schemes in Lancashire benefitting people of all ages, women, at-risk groups, and children who have an illness or disability, people who are socially isolated, homeless or disadvantaged by poverty.
**WHAT IS FUNDED** General charitable purposes, welfare of older people, education, women, children, disability, homelessness, social welfare.
**TYPE OF GRANT** One-off, some recurrent.
**RANGE OF GRANTS** Generally up to £2,500; mostly £500.
**SAMPLE GRANTS** The main beneficiary was Kensington House Trust (£155,000). Other beneficiaries were: Nigam – Cancer charity (£2,500); Barrow and Meakin (£1,000 each); Holy Cross Church and Soup Kitchen (£900); and Father Burns, Father Johnston, Father Dunstan Cooper, Father Gribbens, Mrs M Eastham and Turner (£500 each).
**FINANCES** Year 2013/14 Income £59,125 Grants £165,072 Grants to organisations £163,858 Assets £3,010,648
**TRUSTEES** Marc Hawe; G. Hawe.
**OTHER INFORMATION** The charity's annual report for 2013/14 states: 'The settlement is committed to the support of the Kensington Foundation to which 99% of the grants (by value) made in this year have gone.' Grants to individuals totalled £1,200.
**HOW TO APPLY** Apply in writing to the correspondent.
**WHO TO APPLY TO** Marc Hawe, Trustee, 94 Park View Road, Lytham St Annes, Lancashire FY8 4JF *Tel.* 01253 796888 *email* kensingtontrust@aol.com

## ■ The Hawthorne Charitable Trust

**CC NO** 233921  **ESTABLISHED** 1964
**WHERE FUNDING CAN BE GIVEN** UK, especially Hereford and Worcester.
**WHO CAN BENEFIT** Registered charities benefitting young people and older people, medical

professionals and people disadvantaged by poverty as well as the general public.

**WHAT IS FUNDED** The trustees make donations, generally on an annual basis, to a large number of charities mainly concerned with the care of young people and older people, the relief of pain, sickness and poverty, the advancement of medical research, particularly into the various forms of cancer, research into animal health, the arts, disability and heritage.

**WHAT IS NOT FUNDED** Our research suggests that grants are given to registered charities only. No grants can be made to individuals.

**TYPE OF GRANT** Often recurring.

**RANGE OF GRANTS** £500–£5,000

**SAMPLE GRANTS** Philippines Disaster Fund (£5,000); St Andrew's Club (£3,000); Animal Health Trust, Canine Partners for Independence, Combat Stress, Malvern Festival Theatre Trust Limited and The Salvation Army (£2,500 each); Almshouses Association, Battersea Dogs and Cats Home, Demand, Different Strokes and Midland Air Ambulance (£2,000 each); Acorn Children's Hospice Trust, Crossroads Association, Festival Housing Group, Perennial Gardeners' Royal Benevolent Society and Worcester Cathedral (£1,000 each); and Friends of Public Gardens (£500).

**FINANCES** Year 2013/14 Income £188,516 Grants £138,000 Grants to organisations £138,000 Assets £8,091,513

**TRUSTEES** Alexandra Berington; Richard White; Roger Jackson Clark; Thomas Berington.

**OTHER INFORMATION** There were 70 grants made.

**HOW TO APPLY** Apply in writing to the correspondent. Our research indicates that up-to-date accounts should be included and applications should be received by October for consideration in November.

**WHO TO APPLY TO** Evaline Sarbout, Correspondent, c/o Baker Tilly, 25 Farringdon Street, London EC4A 4AB Tel. 020 3201 8298 email dave.boswell@bakertilly.co.uk

■ **The Dorothy Hay-Bolton Charitable Trust**

**CC NO** 1010438   **ESTABLISHED** 1992

**WHERE FUNDING CAN BE GIVEN** UK, with a preference for the South East of England. Overseas aid is also available.

**WHO CAN BENEFIT** Charities working with people who are blind or deaf, particularly children, young people and older people.

**WHAT IS FUNDED** Welfare causes, children and young people, older people, disability causes and advancement of health.

**WHAT IS NOT FUNDED** The trust does not generally give to individuals.

**TYPE OF GRANT** One-off and ongoing.

**RANGE OF GRANTS** £1,000–£5,000

**SAMPLE GRANTS** In the past grants have been made to: Action for Blind People; British Blind Sport; East Kent Cycling Club; East Sussex Association for the Blind; Esther Benjamin's Trust; Eyeless Trust; Hearing Dogs for the Deaf; the Seeing Ear; Sussex Lantern; and Telephones for the Blind.

**FINANCES** Year 2013/14 Income £22,634 Grants £67,000 Grants to organisations £67,000

**TRUSTEES** Brian Carter; Clare Jeffries.

**HOW TO APPLY** Apply in writing to the correspondent.

**WHO TO APPLY TO** Brian Carter, Trustee, Reeves and Co LLP, 24 Chiswell Street, London EC1Y 4YX Tel. 020 7382 1820 email brian.carter@reeves.co.uk

■ **The Charles Hayward Foundation**

**CC NO** 1078969   **ESTABLISHED** 1961

**WHERE FUNDING CAN BE GIVEN** Unrestricted, in practice mainly UK with some overseas funding (Commonwealth countries of Africa).

**WHO CAN BENEFIT** Registered charities.

**WHAT IS FUNDED** Capital costs and funding of projects which are: preventative or provide early intervention; developmental or innovative; promote or continue good practice; respond to a well-researched and clear need; and demonstrate value for money and have a good understanding of short-term effects and long-term impact of the intervention they propose. Priority areas are criminal justice, heritage and conservation, overseas and older people.

**WHAT IS NOT FUNDED** The website notes that generally funding is not given for the following purposes: endowments; general appeals; grant-making charities; individuals; loan and deficits; retrospectively (costs already incurred prior to receiving a decision from the foundation); running costs. Note that individual categories may have their own additional exclusions – see category-specific guidelines.

**TYPE OF GRANT** Capital and project funding.

**RANGE OF GRANTS** £100–£30,000

**SAMPLE GRANTS** Salisbury Museum (£30,000); Youth at Risk, Hertfordshire (£25,000); Lodge Hill Centre (£20,000); Blue Sky Development and Regeneration (£18,900); Women's Rape and Sexual Abuse Centre (£14,000); Busoga Trust, London (£12,700); Edinburgh Garden Partners and William Morris Gallery (£10,000 each); Children on the Edge (£5,000); Teso Development Trust (£4,000); Cornwall Hospital Broadcasting Network (£2,000); Deptford Action Group for the Elderly (£1,500); Ladywell Neighbourhood Network (£1,300); Gurkha Welfare Trust, Salisbury (£500); and Kidney Research Aid Fund, London (£100).

**FINANCES** Year 2013 Income £1,391,002 Grants £1,091,976 Grants to organisations £1,091,976 Assets £56,528,364

**TRUSTEES** Julia Chamberlain; Jack Hayward; Susan Heath; Nikolas van Leuven; Brian Insch; Alexander Heath; Caroline Donald.

**OTHER INFORMATION** A total of 139 awards were made.

**HOW TO APPLY** Full guidelines and an application form are available on the very informative foundation's website. Note that the foundation currently does not accept applications by e-mail. The main grant programme has a two stage process – in stage one the grants committee selects applications on a quarterly basis to recommend to the trustees; in stage two recommended applications are considered at the trustees' meetings, usually held in February, April, July and November. The small grant programme is a rolling grant programme and applications are considered every two to three months. Previous recipients or unsuccessful charities should wait two years before making a new application. Applicants should not re-apply with the same project.

**WHO TO APPLY TO** Dorothy Napierala, Correspondent, Hayward House, 45 Harrington Gardens, London

SW7 4JU *Tel.* 020 7370 7063 or 020 7370 7067 *email* dorothy@charleshaywardfoundation.org.uk *Website* www.charleshaywardfoundation.org.uk

## ■ Headley-Pitt Charitable Trust

**CC NO** 252023   **ESTABLISHED** 1955
**WHERE FUNDING CAN BE GIVEN** Mainly Ashford, Kent.
**WHO CAN BENEFIT** Older people and those in need.
**WHAT IS FUNDED** Quaker projects. The trust also administers ten bungalows for the benefit of older people in the community.
**WHAT IS NOT FUNDED** Sport or animal projects.
**TYPE OF GRANT** One-off.
**RANGE OF GRANTS** Up to £2,000.
**FINANCES** *Year* 2013/14 *Income* £68,000 *Grants* £73,324 *Grants to organisations* £46,912 *Assets* £2,456,918
**TRUSTEES** Christopher Pitt; Roger Pitt; Jon Pitt; Stella Pitt.
**OTHER INFORMATION** During the year the trust made 110 donations (£26,500) to individuals, principally to assist with cases of poverty or the expenses of education. The trust made a further 134 donations (£47,000) to organisations.
**HOW TO APPLY** Apply in writing to the correspondent.
**WHO TO APPLY TO** Thelma Pitt, Correspondent, Old Mill Cottage, Ulley Road, Kennington, Ashford, Kent TN24 9HX *email* thelma.pitt@headley.co.uk

## ■ The Headley Trust

**CC NO** 266620   **ESTABLISHED** 1973
**WHERE FUNDING CAN BE GIVEN** UK and overseas.
**WHO CAN BENEFIT** 'Registered charities or activities with clearly defined charitable purposes'. The trust prefers to support innovative schemes that can be successfully replicated or become self-sustaining.
**WHAT IS FUNDED Arts and heritage, UK:** museums, for revenue costs or for the purchase of exceptionally important artefacts; conservation projects of the industrial and maritime heritage; archaeological projects; projects to encourage rural crafts and heritage maintenance skills; applied arts and crafts (especially ceramics); repair work to the fabric of cathedrals and large ecclesiastical buildings of exceptional architectural merit (pre-18th century); repair and restoration to the fabric (including windows) of medieval parish churches (or pre-16th century churches of exceptional architectural merit) in rural, sparsely populated or less prosperous villages. **Arts and heritage, overseas:** conservation projects of outstanding artistic or architectural importance; particularly the restoration of buildings, statuary or paintings, primarily in South Eastern Europe. **Health and Social Welfare:** housing for older people and independent living; improvement of older people's quality of life in residential homes; people suffering from dementia; carers; access for people with disabilities; family support, including pre-schoolchildren and parenting education; occasional research projects on medical conditions. **Disability:** small grants for aids for people with varying disabilities, channelled through appropriate charities, agencies and local authorities, including specially adapted computer systems, communication aids, wheelchairs, electric scooters and stair-lifts. **Development:** in the sub-Saharan Anglophone Africa and Ethiopia, including water and sanitation, environment (sustainable energy, farming, forestry), education and literacy, healthcare and emergency appeals. **Education:** bursaries for graduate and postgraduate courses in music and dance and apprenticeships and training in craft skills, including conservation (principally to British students).
**WHAT IS NOT FUNDED** Individuals; educational fees; expeditions; under the Cathedrals Programme modern amenities, organ repair/restoration and choral scholarships are not normally eligible; under The Parish Churches Programme urban churches, construction or refurbishment of church halls, kitchen facilities or other modern amenities, except toilets and disability access are not funded; under the Education support grants are rarely made for secondary education, except for exceptional pupils recommended by the specialist schools for music and dance training.
**TYPE OF GRANT** One-off; capital, core and project costs; over three years or less.
**RANGE OF GRANTS** £7,500–£1 million.
**SAMPLE GRANTS** Auckland Castle Trust (£1 million); British Museum Development Trust (£105,000); Care and Repair (£90,000); National Museums Liverpool (£80,000); Cafe Africa Trust (£70,000); African Wildlife Foundation, Age UK County Durham and Southwark Cathedral (£60,000 each); Carlisle Cathedral Development Trust (£50,000); Bridport Area Development Trust, Heritage Without Borders, Holocaust Centre, Marriage Foundation and Village Water (£40,000 each); Busoga Trust and Ufton Court Educational Trust (£30,000 each); Dundee Heritage Trust and Grandparents Plus (£25,000 each); University of Lincoln (£21,000); Young Musicians Symphony Orchestra (£20,000); British Institute at Ankara, Bournemouth University and Roman Baths (£15,000 each); International Trust for Croatian Monuments and Solent Steam Packet Limited (£10,000 each); Ely Museum and Royal School of Church Music (£8,000 each); Saffron Walden Museum (£7,500).
**FINANCES** *Year* 2013/14 *Income* £2,235,000 *Grants* £5,446,779 *Grants to organisations* £5,446,779 *Assets* £72,178,000
**TRUSTEES** Lady Susan Sainsbury; Judith Portrait; Timothy Sainsbury; Sir Timothy Sainsbury; Camilla Sainsbury; Amanda McCrystal.
**OTHER INFORMATION** The trust is one of the Sainsbury Family Charitable Trust, which share a common administration – application to one is considered as an application to all and directed to the most appropriate. During the year a total of 250 grants were approved. The grant total refers to the figure stated as 'total grants payable' in the accounts.
**HOW TO APPLY** According to the website, the trust 'will consider suitable proposals, so long as they demonstrably and closely fit the specific areas of interest'. The website reminds: 'However, it should be understood that the majority of unsolicited proposals are unsuccessful.' Suitable applications to the trust can be sent by post to the correspondent with a description (strictly up to two pages) of the proposed project, including: your charitable aims and objectives; most recent annual income and expenditure (not a full set of accounts); current financial position; details of why the project is needed, who it will benefit and in what way; the breakdown of costs, any money raised so far, and how the balance will be acquired. All applications are acknowledged and only successful appeals will hear from the trust within the following eight weeks.

# Health

WHO TO APPLY TO Alan Bookbinder, Director, The Sainsbury Family Charitable Trusts, The Peak, 5 Wilton Road, London SW1V 1AP *Tel.* 020 7410 0330 *Fax* 020 7410 0332 *email* info@sfct.org.uk *Website* www.sfct.org.uk

## ■ The Health Foundation

CC NO 286967 ESTABLISHED 1983
WHERE FUNDING CAN BE GIVEN Unrestricted.
WHO CAN BENEFIT Research organisations; educational institutions; NHS bodies; charities; individuals.
WHAT IS FUNDED Improving the quality of healthcare.
TYPE OF GRANT Typically project grants for up to three years.
SAMPLE GRANTS Academy of Medical Sciences (£1.7 million in three grants); The Scottish Funding Council (£500,000); Royal College of Paediatrics and Child Health (£450,000); University of Dundee and University of Leeds (£280,000); King's College London (£202,000); NHS Ayrshire and Arran (£175,000); Imperial College Healthcare NHS Trust (£164,000 in three grants); Western Health and Social Care Trust (£150,000).
FINANCES *Year* 2013 *Income* £14,405,000 *Grants* £13,819,000 *Grants to organisations* £13,819,000 *Assets* £785,939,000
TRUSTEES Sir Alan Langlands; Sir David Dalton; Murray Easton; Margaret Goose; Martyn Hole; Branwen Jeffries; Prof. Deirdre Kelly; Bridget McIntyre; Prof. Andrew Morris; Melloney Poole; David Zahn.
OTHER INFORMATION 171 awards were made during the year. As well as grants made directly, the foundation delivered 'third party support' directly to award holders, amounting to £1.3 million.
HOW TO APPLY Each programme is subject to its own criteria. The details of current programmes can be found on the foundation's website.
WHO TO APPLY TO Programmes team, 90 Long Acre, London WC2E 9RA *Tel.* 020 7257 8000 *Fax* 020 7257 8001 *email* info@health.org.uk *Website* www.health.org.uk

## ■ May Hearnshaw Charitable Trust (May Hearnshaw's Charity)

CC NO 1008638 ESTABLISHED 1992
WHERE FUNDING CAN BE GIVEN UK, particularly South Yorkshire, North Nottinghamshire, Derbyshire, East Lancashire or Cheshire areas.
WHO CAN BENEFIT Nationwide registered charities and local charities in the South Yorkshire, North Nottinghamshire, Derbyshire, East Lancashire or Cheshire areas.
WHAT IS FUNDED General charitable purposes, education, relief of poverty and sickness, health and disability causes and social welfare.
WHAT IS NOT FUNDED Our research suggests that appeals received direct from individuals are not normally considered.
TYPE OF GRANT Our research indicates that one-off grants can be given up to three years. Support for buildings, core costs, research, recurring costs, running costs and salaries can be considered.
RANGE OF GRANTS Usually £500–£3,000, but up to £25,000.
SAMPLE GRANTS St Wilfrid's Centre (£25,000); Brains Trust (£8,000); Meadowhead Community Learning Trust (£3,500); Oundle School Mencap Holidays and Survivors of Bereavement (£2,500 each); Sheffield Samaritans (£2,100); Macmillan Cancer – Sheffield (£2,000 each); Sheffield Sea Cadets, St Luke's Hospice and Whirlow Hall Farm (£1,000 each); Brathay Trust, Buxton festival, Church Army and Wildlife Trust (£500 each).
FINANCES *Year* 2013/14 *Income* £77,647 *Grants* £56,600 *Grants to organisations* £56,600 *Assets* £2,194,208
TRUSTEES Marjorie West; Michael Ferreday; Richard Law; William Munro; Nicholas Wolstenholme.
OTHER INFORMATION A total of 19 organisations received support.
HOW TO APPLY Applications may be made in writing to the correspondent. According to our research the trustees usually meet three times a year when they decide on and make major grants to charitable organisations but may decide to make grants at any time.
WHO TO APPLY TO Michael Ferreday, Trustee, Barber Harrison and Platt, 2 Rutland Park, Sheffield S10 2PD *Tel.* 0114 266 7171 *email* chris.hardwick@bhp.co.uk

## ■ Heart of England Community Foundation

CC NO 1117345 ESTABLISHED 1995
WHERE FUNDING CAN BE GIVEN Coventry, Solihull and Warwickshire.
WHO CAN BENEFIT Community-based groups and activities benefitting a wide range of social circumstances; unregistered but charitable organisations.
WHAT IS FUNDED A wide range of general charitable purposes, including education, employment, disadvantaged and socially excluded individuals, health causes, volunteering, arts and culture, sport and recreation, crime prevention, relief of poverty and a range of other local community causes.
WHAT IS NOT FUNDED Statutory organisations; individuals (although a scheme is being developed to assist people with learning difficulties or disabilities); projects which have already started (although new, distinct elements of existing project may be assisted); statutory provision; activities that promote religious activity; activities that are not socially inclusive; organisations with a turnover of over £100,000 excluding restricted funding; grant-making bodies; mainstream activities of schools and colleges; medical research; animal welfare; political activities; organisations with substantial reserves; general and major fundraising appeals; continuation funding. The foundation does not usually provide part-funding, preferring to be the majority funder. Only one grant will be given to an organisation in any one year from the foundation.
TYPE OF GRANT Project costs, events, materials and equipment.
RANGE OF GRANTS £100–£11,500
SAMPLE GRANTS Beneficiaries have included: Coventry Somali Women's Network (£11,500); Hub @ Blackwell (£10,700); Positive Youth Foundation (£10,000); Friendship Project (£6,000 in two grants); The Open Theatre Company Ltd (£5,000); Support Sport Ltd (£4,500); Write Here Write Now Chic (£3,000); The Friends of Kingsbury Water Park and Pop Up Communities CIC (£2,000 each); Kingshurst Arts Space (£1,500); Lower Ford Street Baptist Church and The Blossomfield Club (£1,000 each); Asperger's United and Welford Junior Football Club (£700 each); Pinley Over 60s Group (£900); Whitley Junior FC (£600).

FINANCES *Year* 2013/14 *Income* £1,320,921 *Grants* £519,353 *Grants to organisations* £519,353 *Assets* £5,203,952
TRUSTEES Amrik Bhabra; Sally Carrick; Brian Clifford; Susan Ong; John Taylor; Paul Belfield; Derek Cake; Philip Ewing; Michelle Vincent; Lucie Byron; Philip Pemble; Sir Nicholas Cadbury.
OTHER INFORMATION Only one grant will be given to an organisation in any one year from the foundation. The foundation will not part-fund large projects and 'would anticipate being the majority funder'. During the year there were 160 projects supported. The average grant was about £3,250.
HOW TO APPLY Before making a formal application you should contact the Grants Team for an informal chat at 02476 883262. Applications should be made by completing an online form. All applicants will hear the outcome of their application within 12 weeks.
WHO TO APPLY TO Tina Costelo, Correspondent, c/o PSA Peugeot Citroen, Torrington Avenue, Tile Hill, Coventry CV4 9AP *Tel.* 024 7688 3260 or 02476 883297 *email* info@heartofenglandcf.co.uk *Website* www.heartofenglandcf.co.uk

■ **Heart Research UK**
CC NO 1044821          ESTABLISHED 1967
WHERE FUNDING CAN BE GIVEN UK.
WHO CAN BENEFIT Community groups; voluntary organisations; educational and medical institutions; people involved in medical research.
WHAT IS FUNDED Medical research and 'lifestyle interventions' focusing on heart disease in the UK. The charity has recently expanded its activities to focus on children. Currently the following programmes operate: Translational Research Project Grants (up to £150,000); Novel and Emerging Technologies Grants (up to £250,000); Aortic Fellowship at Liverpool Heart and Chest Hospital; Masterclass series; Heart Research UK Healthy Heart Grants (up to £5,000 or £10,000 'to UK community groups for innovative projects that encourage and inspire people to lead heart-healthy lifestyles through being active, eating a heart-healthy diet and not smoking'); SUBWAY®/HRUK Healthy Heart Grants (a minimum of nine regional grants each year 'for heart-focused community projects').
WHAT IS NOT FUNDED Government organisations; local authority groups.
TYPE OF GRANT One-off and recurrent (medical research grants usually of up to three years).
RANGE OF GRANTS Up to £250,000 for research and up to £10,000 for local projects.
SAMPLE GRANTS King's College London (£289,500 in two grants); Imperial College London (£125,000); University of Sheffield (£99,000); King's College London and St Thomas Hospital (£93,000); Simplyhealth Grant and University of Exeter (£50,000 each); Leeds General Infirmary (£18,000); Society for Cardiothoracic Surgery (£15,000); Beat It and The Kitchen Healthy Hearts (£10,000 each); Well Hearts (£9,400); Heart of a Gladiator (£8,300); Healthy Hearts for Kids (£7,500); Get Onside 4 a Healthy Heart (£6,100); Babies and Toddlers Healthy Heart Start (£2,200); Healthy Heart @ Caffe West (£2,000).
FINANCES *Year* 2013 *Income* £1,916,423 *Grants* £1,137,637 *Grants to organisations* £1,137,637 *Assets* £3,332,744
TRUSTEES Keith Loudon; Richard Hemsley; Christine Mortimer; Dr David Dickinson; Heather Stewart;
Kevin Watterson; Anthony Knight; Antony Oxley; Paul Rogerson; Dr Catherine Dickinson; Anthony Kilner; Paul Smith; Richard Brown; Peter Braidley.
OTHER INFORMATION Grant total consists of £942,000 in medical research grants and £195,500 in Healthy Heart grants. The annual report for 2013 states that the charity is 'funding 30 medical research projects in 20 centres across the UK'. In 2014 the charity had planned to 'increase spending to substantially more than £1 million on high quality medical projects and continue helping more people live healthier, happier, longer lives'.
HOW TO APPLY Application forms, full guidelines and up to date deadlines for each programme can be found on the charity's website or requested from the correspondent.
WHO TO APPLY TO Michael Clark, Treasurer and Company Secretary, Suite 12D, Joseph's Well, Hanover Walk, Leeds LS3 1AB *Tel.* 0113 234 7474 *Fax* 0113 297 6208 *email* mail@heartresearch.org.uk or grants@heartresearch.org.uk *Website* www.heartresearch.org.uk

■ **The Heathcoat Trust**
CC NO 203367          ESTABLISHED 1945
WHERE FUNDING CAN BE GIVEN Local causes in and around Tiverton, Devon.
WHO CAN BENEFIT Local organisations to Tiverton and national charities working on projects in that area; individual grants to employees and pensioners (and their dependants) of the Heathcoat group of companies.
WHAT IS FUNDED Relief of poverty; social welfare; education and training; health causes; children and young people; older people; local causes.
TYPE OF GRANT Recurring and one-off.
RANGE OF GRANTS Mainly under £1,000.
SAMPLE GRANTS Tiverton Market Centre (£30,000); Twyford Trust (£14,000); Old Heathcoat School Community Centre (£12,100); Cruys Morchard Parish Hall (£10,000); St Andrew's Church, Collumpton (£5,000); Tiverton District Scouts Executive Committee (£3,800); Bampton Heritage and Visitors Centre, Exmoor Search and Rescue Team, Moorhayes Community Association and St Michael and All Angels Community Hall, Bampton (£2,000 each); Willand Rovers Football Club (£1,600); Cornwall Hospice Care, Listening Books, Tiverton Guide HQ Management and Tiverton Swimming Club (£1,000 each).
FINANCES *Year* 2013/14 *Income* £563,201 *Grants* £751,306 *Grants to organisations* £159,825 *Assets* £19,848,788
TRUSTEES Mark Drysdale; Ian Heathcoat-Amory; John Stanley Smith; Susan Westlake.
OTHER INFORMATION There were 154 grants to organisations.
HOW TO APPLY Applications should be made writing to the correspondent giving as much relevant information as possible. The trustees meet regularly to consider applications for grants. There are application forms for certain education grants.
WHO TO APPLY TO C. J. Twose, Secretary, The Factory, Tiverton, Devon EX16 5LL *Tel.* 01884 254949 *email* heathcoattrust@heathcoat.co.uk *Website* www.heathcoat.co.uk

# Heathside

## ■ The Heathside Charitable Trust

**CC NO** 326959   **ESTABLISHED** 1985
**WHERE FUNDING CAN BE GIVEN** UK.
**WHO CAN BENEFIT** Charitable organisations, especially Jewish groups.
**WHAT IS FUNDED** General charitable purposes; Jewish causes
**RANGE OF GRANTS** £1,000–£141,000
**SAMPLE GRANTS Previous beneficiaries have included:** Joint Jewish Charitable Trust (£141,000); Jewish Education Defence Trust and Community Security Trust (£25,000 each); Jewish Care (£15,000); British Friends of Jaffa Institute, GRET and Motivation (£10,000 each); Babes in Arms; CancerKin; Holocaust Educational Trust; First Cheque 2000; Jewish Museum; King Solomon High School; Marie Curie Cancer Care; Royal London Institute; Royal National Theatre; Weitzmann Institute.
**FINANCES** Year 2013 Income £328,670 Grants £317,411 Grants to organisations £317,411 Assets £2,776,425
**TRUSTEES** Harry Solomon; Judith Solomon; Geoffrey Jayson; Louise Jacobs; Daniel Solomon; Juliet Solomon.
**OTHER INFORMATION** In recent years, a list of grants has not been included within the trust's annual accounts.
**HOW TO APPLY** Applications can be made in writing to the correspondent, at any time. The trustees generally meet four times a year.
**WHO TO APPLY TO** Harry Solomon, Trustee, 32 Hampstead High Street, London NW3 1QD Tel. 020 7431 7739

## ■ The Charlotte Heber-Percy Charitable Trust

**CC NO** 284387   **ESTABLISHED** 1981
**WHERE FUNDING CAN BE GIVEN** Worldwide.
**WHO CAN BENEFIT** Charitable organisations.
**WHAT IS FUNDED** General charitable purposes; animal welfare; the environment; medical and health; overseas aid; education; children and young people; the arts.
**WHAT IS NOT FUNDED** Grants are not made to individuals.
**TYPE OF GRANT** Small, one-off grants.
**RANGE OF GRANTS** £500–£20,000
**SAMPLE GRANTS** Elizabeth Finn Care (£20,000); The Grateful Society (£15,000 in two grants); Garsington Opera at Wormsley, The Royal Ballet School and The University of Cape Town (£10,000 each); Friends of Aphrodisias Trust (£6,000); Canine Partners for Independence, Friends of Priestley Smith School, Independent Age, Norfolk Community Foundation, St James' Church – Longborough and The Brooke Hospital for Animals (£5,000 each); Skiing with Heroes and The Adventure Farm Trust (£3,000 each); NSPCC and SSAFA (£2,000 each); Great Western Air Ambulance (£1,000); and Friends of Amasango (£500).
**FINANCES** Year 2013/14 Income £276,201 Grants £255,500 Grants to organisations £255,500 Assets £7,173,274
**TRUSTEES** Joanna Prest; Charlotte Heber-Percy.
**OTHER INFORMATION** There were 48 grants made.
**HOW TO APPLY** The trustees meet on an ad hoc basis to consider applications. Applications should be made in writing to the correspondent.
**WHO TO APPLY TO** Linda Cousins, Correspondent, Rathbone Trust Company Limited, 1 Curzon Street, London W1J 5FB Tel. 020 7399 0820 email linda.cousins@rathbones.com

## ■ The Percy Hedley 1990 Charitable Trust

**CC NO** 1000033   **ESTABLISHED** 1990
**WHERE FUNDING CAN BE GIVEN** UK with a preference for Northumberland and Tyne and Wear.
**WHO CAN BENEFIT** Charitable organisations, hospices and educational establishments.
**WHAT IS FUNDED** General charitable purposes.
**TYPE OF GRANT** One-off and ongoing.
**RANGE OF GRANTS** £250–£3,000; most grants are for £500.
**SAMPLE GRANTS** Central Newcastle High School GDST Bursary Fund, Newcastle Royal Grammar School and The Percy Hedley Foundation (Bursary Fund) (£3,000 each); People's Theatre Arts Trust (£1,500); Anaphylaxis Campaign, Jesmond Library, Marie Curie Conrad House, Samaritans and St Oswald's Hospice (£1,000); Alzheimer's Research Trust British Blind Sport, Combat Stress, Newcastle Dog and Cat Shelter and Woodland Trust (£500 each).
**FINANCES** Year 2013/14 Income £49,760 Grants £40,250 Grants to organisations £40,250 Assets £1,590,907
**TRUSTEES** John Armstrong; Bill Meikle; Fiona Ruffman.
**OTHER INFORMATION** Grants were given to 55 organisations.
**HOW TO APPLY** Applications may be made in writing to the correspondent. Trustees normally meet twice a year. The trust has stated 'we are happy to receive succinct applications. A financial statement can be welcome, but full annual report accounts are too much.'
**WHO TO APPLY TO** John Armstrong, Trustee, 10 Castleton Close, Newcastle upon Tyne NE2 2HF Tel. 0191 281 5953 email contact. phct@gmail.com

## ■ The Hedley Denton Charitable Trust

**CC NO** 1060725   **ESTABLISHED** 1996
**WHERE FUNDING CAN BE GIVEN** UK with a preference for North East England.
**WHO CAN BENEFIT** Charitable organisations, including those operating overseas.
**WHAT IS FUNDED** General charitable purposes.
**RANGE OF GRANTS** £250–£1,000
**SAMPLE GRANTS** North East Promenaders Against Cancer (£2,000); Opera North and Tyneside North (£1,000 each); Age UK, Centrepoint, Combat Stress, Fisherman's Mission, Headway, Mind, Samaritans of Northumbria and Stepney Bank Stables (£500 each).
**FINANCES** Year 2013/14 Income £50,558 Grants £33,500 Grants to organisations £32,750 Assets £1,158,621
**TRUSTEES** Iain Nicholson; Dorothy Wild; Charles Watts; Charles Nicholson.
**OTHER INFORMATION** Grants totalling £750 were made to individuals during the year.
**HOW TO APPLY** Apply in writing to the correspondent. Applications are considered twice during the year and should be received before either the end of April or October.
**WHO TO APPLY TO** Iain Nicholson, Trustee, c/o Iain Nicholson and Co, 5 West Road, Ponteland, Newcastle upon Tyne NE20 9ST Tel. 01661 823863 email law@iainnicholson.co.uk

### ■ Hedley Foundation Limited (The Hedley Foundation)

**CC NO** 262933     **ESTABLISHED** 1971
**WHERE FUNDING CAN BE GIVEN** UK.
**WHO CAN BENEFIT** Registered charities benefitting young people, particularly those in risk groups, individuals with disabilities or terminal illness, and young carers. Local community projects can be assisted.
**WHAT IS FUNDED** Children and young people; individuals at risk; disability and terminal illnesses; outdoor activities; sports and recreation; education and training.
**WHAT IS NOT FUNDED** Organisations which are not UK-registered charities; individuals directly; churches and cathedrals; exclusive charities (which only help people from specific groupings); appeals for general funding, salaries, deficit, core revenue costs, transport funding; appeals for building or refurbishment projects; national or very large appeals.
**TYPE OF GRANT** Mostly one-off grants for specific projects. A limited number of recurring grants for up to three years.
**RANGE OF GRANTS** £1,000–£15,000; average grant is of £3,000.
**SAMPLE GRANTS** Acquired Aphasia Trust; Appledore Community Hall; Bluebell Railway Trust; Braintree Youth Project; Carers Support Merton; Cornwall Blind and Partially Sighted Association; East Anglian Air Ambulance; Frontline Trust; Happy Days Children's Charity; Hornimans Adventure Playground; Kirkwood Hospice; London Symphony Orchestra; MENCAP – Watford; Northern Ireland Hospice; Pinda Kai Do School of Martial Arts; Rainbow Trust; Sensory Trust; Special Olympics; Sunshine Playschool; Vision Care for Homeless People; and Wildwood Trust.
**FINANCES** Year 2013/14 Income £1,369,435 Grants £961,927 Grants to organisations £961,927 Assets £30,554,396
**TRUSTEES** George Broke; John Rodwell; Lorna Stuttaford; Patrick Holcroft; Lt Col Peter Chamberlin; Angus Fanshawe; Lt Col Andrew Ford; David Byam-Cook.
**OTHER INFORMATION** There were 357 awards made.
**HOW TO APPLY** Applications must be made using the application form available from the foundation's website and include a copy of the most recent set of accounts. The trustees usually meet in February, March, May, July, September and November (for exact and most up-to-date deadlines see the website). The applicants are asked to submit the forms (completed in typescript) via post (emailed applications are not considered) at least three weeks before the date of the meeting. Note that the foundation is unable to return any enclosures that are sent in with applications. All applications will be acknowledged, but, in the case of those shortlisted, not until after they have been considered by the trustees. The foundation receives many more applications than it can fund and urges that applicants should not be surprised, or too disappointed, if they are unsuccessful.
**WHO TO APPLY TO** Mary Kitto, Company Secretary, 1–3 College Hill, London EC4R 2RA Tel. 020 7489 8076 email mkitto@hedleyfoundation.org.uk Website www.hedleyfoundation.org.uk

### ■ The H. J. Heinz Company Limited Charitable Trust

**CC NO** 326254     **ESTABLISHED** 1982
**WHERE FUNDING CAN BE GIVEN** UK.
**WHO CAN BENEFIT** Organisations benefitting children and young adults, at-risk groups, people disadvantaged by poverty and socially isolated people.
**WHAT IS FUNDED** The trust typically supports medicine, welfare, education (food technology and nutrition in particular), conservation, community relations and the arts. UK bodies are more likely to be favoured than local groups unless local applicants operate in the immediate vicinity of the company's main operating locations.
**WHAT IS NOT FUNDED** Individuals. Requests for political or denominational causes or for advertising are not considered.
**TYPE OF GRANT** One-off.
**RANGE OF GRANTS** Up to £5,000.
**SAMPLE GRANTS** Foundation for The Study of Infant Deaths, Children's Sunshine Home, Community Albums, Wigan Stars Nelson's Journey and Hope House Children's Hospice (£5,000 each).
**FINANCES** Year 2013 Income £3,595 Grants £25,000 Grants to organisations £25,000
**TRUSTEES** Drue Heinz; Simon Cowdroy; Nigel Dickie; Chris Humphries; Kelly Barker; P. Jones; S. Digby; C. Winter.
**HOW TO APPLY** Apply in writing to the address below, no follow-up telephone calls. Applications are considered once or twice a year. Applicants, whether successful or unsuccessful, are informed of the trustees' decisions.
**WHO TO APPLY TO** Ms Kelly Barker, Trustee, H. J. Heinz Manufacturing UK Ltd, Hayes Park South Building, Hayes End Road, Hayes, Middlesex UB4 8AL Tel. 020 8848 2346 email charitable.trust@uk.hjheinz.com Website www.heinz.co.uk/en/Our-Company/Sustainability/Economic-Sustainability

### ■ The Michael Heller Charitable Foundation

**CC NO** 327832     **ESTABLISHED** 1988
**WHERE FUNDING CAN BE GIVEN** Worldwide.
**WHO CAN BENEFIT** Organisations benefitting academics, medical professionals, research workers, scientists, students and teachers.
**WHAT IS FUNDED** Medical, scientific and educational research as well as humanitarian support.
**WHAT IS NOT FUNDED** No support is available for individuals.
**RANGE OF GRANTS** £5,000–£100,000
**SAMPLE GRANTS** Support was given in the following areas: Education (£688,000); Research (£72,500); and Humanitarian (£68,500).
**FINANCES** Year 2013/14 Income £250,000 Grants £229,500 Grants to organisations £229,500 Assets £3,972,466
**TRUSTEES** Morven Heller; Michael Heller; W. S. Trustee Company Ltd.
**OTHER INFORMATION** A list of beneficiaries was not provided in the trust's accounts.
**HOW TO APPLY** Applications can be made in writing to the correspondent.
**WHO TO APPLY TO** Michael Heller, Trustee, 24 Bruton Place, London W1J 6NE Tel. 020 7415 5000

## ■ The Simon Heller Charitable Settlement

**CC NO** 265405   **ESTABLISHED** 1972
**WHERE FUNDING CAN BE GIVEN** Worldwide.
**WHO CAN BENEFIT** Organisations benefitting academics, medical professionals, research workers, scientists, students and teachers as well as people in need.
**WHAT IS FUNDED** Medical, scientific and educational research as well as humanitarian support worldwide. In the past Jewish causes have also been supported.
**WHAT IS NOT FUNDED** No grants can be made to individuals.
**SAMPLE GRANTS** Previous beneficiaries have included: Institute for Jewish Policy Research (£35,000); Jewish Care (£30,000); Aish Hatora (£15,000 in two grants), Spiro Institute (£13,000), Scopus (£12,000 in two grants); and Chief Rabbinate Charitable Trust (£10,000).
**FINANCES** Year 2013/14 Income £352,479 Grants £316,571 Grants to organisations £316,571 Assets £8,313,426
**TRUSTEES** Michael Heller; Morven Heller; W. S. Trustee Company Limited.
**OTHER INFORMATION** The accounts for 2013/14 state: 'The trustees consider that as this is a private charitable trust to which no public funds have been contributed, the disclosure requirements relating to grants in excess of £1,000 do not apply as the inclusion of such information would, in certain circumstances, be likely to prejudice the furtherance of the purposes of the charitable trust or recipient.'
**HOW TO APPLY** Applications can be made in writing to the correspondent.
**WHO TO APPLY TO** Michael Heller, Trustee, 24 Bruton Place, London W1J 6NE Tel. 020 7415 5000

## ■ Help for Health

**CC NO** 1091814   **ESTABLISHED** 2002
**WHERE FUNDING CAN BE GIVEN** Within the boundaries of East Yorkshire, City of Kingston upon Hull, and both North and North East Lincolnshire.
**WHO CAN BENEFIT** Registered charities; medical and research bodies.
**WHAT IS FUNDED** Healthcare provision (including facilities and equipment); medical research; medical education.
**WHAT IS NOT FUNDED** Individuals.
**SAMPLE GRANTS** Lindsey Lodge Hospice (£30,000); Dove House Hospice (£23,500); Yorkshire Air Ambulance (£10,000). Other grants under £3,500 totalled £4,500.
**FINANCES** Year 2013/14 Income £62,491 Grants £67,990 Grants to organisations £67,990 Assets £4,162,383
**TRUSTEES** Julie Bielby; Prof. Peter Lee; Stuart Smith; Andrew Mould; Andrew Milner; Richard Field; Dawn Mitchell.
**HOW TO APPLY** Application forms and full guidelines are available to download from the charity's website. They should be submitted by post or email. The trustees meet bi-monthly.
**WHO TO APPLY TO** Andrew Mould, Trustee, c/o Baker Tilly, 2 Humber Quays, Wellington Street West, Hull HU1 2BN Tel. 01482 607200 email info@helphealth.org.uk Website www.helphealth.org.uk

## ■ Help the Homeless Limited

**CC NO** 271988   **ESTABLISHED** 1975
**WHERE FUNDING CAN BE GIVEN** UK.
**WHO CAN BENEFIT** Small/medium-sized or new registered charities with a turnover of less than £1 million a year. Grants to larger charities are considered if the project is suitably innovative and it is only possible for a large organisation to develop it.
**WHAT IS FUNDED** Projects which assist individuals in their return to mainstream society, rather than simply offer shelter or other forms of sustenance.
**WHAT IS NOT FUNDED** Charities with substantial funds; individuals.
**TYPE OF GRANT** One-off grants for capital costs.
**RANGE OF GRANTS** Normally up to £5,000. Trustees will also consider applications for larger pump priming grants for major and innovative projects.
**SAMPLE GRANTS** Ace of Clubs, London and DENS, Hemel Hempstead (£5,000 each); Catching Lives, Canterbury (£4,900); Normad Opening Doors, Sheffield and South Tyneside Churches KEY project (£3,000 each); The Bridge, East Midlands (£2,500); Lee Oasis, London and Trinity Winchester (£2,000 each); Barnabas Safe and Sound, Newcastle (£1,700); Beacon House, Colchester (£1,000); The Hope Centre, St Helens (£600); Cardboard Citizens, Whitechapel (£500).
**FINANCES** Year 2013/14 Income £70,002 Grants £71,673 Grants to organisations £71,673 Assets £1,350,848
**TRUSTEES** Francis Bergin; Trevor Cookson; Terry Rogers; Peter Fullerton; Jon Rose; Stuart Holmes.
**OTHER INFORMATION** Grants were made to 30 organisations.
**HOW TO APPLY** Application forms can be downloaded from the charity's website. Applicants should 'clearly describe the aims and structure of their organisation, their future plans and specific details of how any grant money will be spent' as well as provide the latest available audited accounts. The quarterly deadlines for applications each year are: 15 March, 15 June, 15 September and 15 December. Repeat applications can be made no earlier than two years after the receipt of a decision of the previous application.
**WHO TO APPLY TO** Terry Kenny, Secretary, 6th Floor, 248 Tottenham Court Road, London W1T 7QZ email hth@help-the-homeless.org.uk Website www.help-the-homeless.org.uk

## ■ The Helping Foundation

**CC NO** 1104484   **ESTABLISHED** 2004
**WHERE FUNDING CAN BE GIVEN** Mainly in Greater Manchester, also Greater London.
**WHO CAN BENEFIT** Jewish religious and educational institutions; registered charities.
**WHAT IS FUNDED** The advancement of education according to the tenets of the Orthodox Jewish Faith; the advancement of the Orthodox Jewish Religion and the relief of poverty amongst the elderly or persons in need, hardship or distress in the Jewish Community.
**TYPE OF GRANT** Recurrent grants; interest free loans.
**RANGE OF GRANTS** Mostly up to around £50,000.
**SAMPLE GRANTS** British Friends of Ezrat Yisrael Kiryat Sefer (£2.5 million) and RNH Synagogue and College Ltd (£475,000). Previous beneficiaries have also included: Asser Bishvil Foundation (£2 million); British Friends of Ezrat Yisrael (£670,000); Notzar Chesed (£236,500);

New Rachmistrivka Synagogue Trust (£201,000); TTT (£198,500); Emuno Educational Centre (£163,000); United Talmudical Associates (£160,000); BCG CT (£105,000); Friends for the Centre for Torah Education Centre (£57,000); Tomchei Shabbos Manchester (£30,000); Gateshead Kollel (£20,000); Beis Naduorna (£10,000); Law of Truth (£5,500).
**FINANCES** Year 2013 Income £35,616,320 Grants £6,625,467 Grants to organisations £6,625,467 Assets £104,903,445
**TRUSTEES** Rachel Weis; Rabbi Weis; David Neuwirth; Benny Stone.
**OTHER INFORMATION** A full list of beneficiaries was not included within the accounts. The trust gave £6.6 million in grants and also spent a further £38,500 in Mikvah costs (the upkeep of ritual baths).
**HOW TO APPLY** Applications may be made in writing to the correspondent.
**WHO TO APPLY TO** Benny Stone, Secretary, Flat 1, Allandale Court, Waterpark Road, Salford M7 4JN Tel. 01617 40116

## ■ The Hemby Charitable Trust
**CC NO** 1073028 **ESTABLISHED** 1998
**WHERE FUNDING CAN BE GIVEN** Merseyside and Wirral.
**WHO CAN BENEFIT** Charitable organisations – ideally registered charities or those applying to become one. However, any properly constituted body with charitable objectives can apply.
**WHAT IS FUNDED** Social needs, community facilities and services, youth and employment, schools and colleges, help for older people, health, the arts, culture and recreation, the environment and church buildings.
**WHAT IS NOT FUNDED** The following is not given: funds to applicants from outside Merseyside and Wirral; support to individuals; any form of sponsorship; help to religious bodies and places of worship – unless there is significant community use; support to political organisations and pressure groups; assistance where funding from statutory bodies is, or should be available; support to schools seeking specialist status; funds to return applicants less than two years after a successful application; and any form of memorial.
**TYPE OF GRANT** Capital grants.
**RANGE OF GRANTS** £250–£10,000
**SAMPLE GRANTS** Emmaus Merseyside and LCVS (Thrive at 5) (£25,000 each); Roy Castle Lung Cancer Foundation (£7,000); Liverpool Lighthouse and St John's PTFA (£3,000 each); Arkwright Scholarships, Hone Steer Southport and Formby, Park St Youth and Community Club and Zoe's Place Baby Hospice (£2,000 each); Wallasey Sea Cadets (£1,500); Liverpool Centre for Arts and Development, Shoestring and The Black E (£1,000 each); Merseyside Dance Initiative and Sefton Extra (£500 each); and Northern Club Hockey Section (£300).
**FINANCES** Year 2013/14 Income £106,298 Grants £156,916 Grants to organisations £156,916 Assets £2,763,792
**TRUSTEES** Andrew Morris; Roy Morris; Caroline Tod; David Fairclough; Stuart Keppie.
**OTHER INFORMATION** Grants were distributed to 81 organisations in 2013/14.
**HOW TO APPLY** Applications can be made using a form available from the trust's website or the correspondent. Completed application forms should be returned to the correspondent together with a copy of the most recent accounts. The deadlines for submission of applications are normally on the 15th of February, June and October. Applications are not acknowledged, but the applicants are welcome to email or telephone the correspondent to check if it has been received. The website advises potential applicants to get in touch via phone if unsure how to complete the application form (including the size of the grant to be requested). An alternative contact is Val Hewitt at 17 Foxdale Close, Oxton, Prenton, Wirral, CH43 1XW (tel: 0151 652 1714; email: val.hewitti@ntlworld.com).
**WHO TO APPLY TO** Tom Evans, Secretary, c/o Rathbone Investment Management Ltd, Port of Liverpool Building, Pier Head, Liverpool L3 1NW Tel. 07503 319182 email adminathembytrust@talktalk.net Website hembytrust.org.uk

## ■ The Christina Mary Hendrie Trust for Scottish and Canadian Charities
**SC NO** SC014514 **ESTABLISHED** 1975
**WHERE FUNDING CAN BE GIVEN** Scotland and Canada.
**WHO CAN BENEFIT** Charities operating in Scotland and Canada and benefitting young people and older people.
**WHAT IS FUNDED** Charities connected with young people (up to 21 years of age) and older people (over the age of 65). There is a particular interest in hospices and war veterans.
**WHAT IS NOT FUNDED** Grants are not given to individuals, 'except through the channels of another charity and only then rarely'.
**TYPE OF GRANT** Up to one year.
**RANGE OF GRANTS** £1,000–£30,000; average award of £7,500.
**SAMPLE GRANTS** Tailor Ed Foundation (£30,000); Camphill Blair Drummond (£20,000); Crossroads caring Scotland (£16,500); Rape and Abuse Line (£15,000); Prison Phoenix Trust (£10,000); Whizz-Kidz (£8,500); Mooreland's Community Services and Royal British Legion (£5,000 each); Lothian Autistic Society (£3,000); and Epilepsy Scotland (£1,000).
**FINANCES** Year 2013/14 Income £121,287 Grants £298,000 Grants to organisations £298,000
**TRUSTEES** Charles Cox; John Scott-Moncrieff; Anthony Cox; Mary-Rose Grieve; Andrew Desson; Caron Hughes; Laura Cox; Laura Irwin.
**HOW TO APPLY** Application forms can be downloaded from the trust's website and once completed should be returned by post or email (preferably). The trustees meet in March and October and applications should be made no later than 15 February and 15 September, respectively. Applications are acknowledged via email.
**WHO TO APPLY TO** Alan Sharp, Secretary, 1 Rutland Court, Edinburgh EH3 8EY Tel. 0131 270 7700 email alan.sharp@andersonstrathern.co.uk Website www.christinamaryhendrietrust.com

## ■ Henley Educational Trust
**CC NO** 309237 **ESTABLISHED** 1604
**WHERE FUNDING CAN BE GIVEN** Henley-on-Thames and the parishes of Bix and Rotherfield Greys in Oxfordshire and Remenham in Berkshire only.
**WHO CAN BENEFIT** Individuals under the age of 25 and organisations concerned with the education of or activities involving such people. State-maintained schools, colleges, youth and sports clubs in the area defined are eligible.

**WHAT IS FUNDED** Grants are given to alleviate financial hardship, to support particular educational initiatives and courses and to help meet the cost of educational visits, books and equipment at a local school or college.

**WHAT IS NOT FUNDED** Individual applicants must be under 25 years of age, and must either be resident in the area defined above or have attended a state-maintained school in the area for at least two years.

**TYPE OF GRANT** According to our research, mainly one-off grants for core and capital support and project funding are available.

**RANGE OF GRANTS** £100–£20,000

**SAMPLE GRANTS** Nomad (£21,000); Gillotts Academy (£15,500); Henley Cricket Club (£6,000); Henley College and Trinity (£5,500 each); Sacred Heart (£3,500); Henley Youth Festival and Schools Music project – 2014 (£3,000 each); Badgemore (£1,400); Henley Guides (£500); Crazies Hill (£400); and Upper Thames Rowing Club (£140).

**FINANCES** Year 2013/14 Income £142,292 Grants £96,259 Grants to organisations £79,199 Assets £3,289,335

**TRUSTEES** Amanda Heath; Stephan Gawrysiak; Colin Homent; William Hamilton; Marjorie Hall; William Parrish; Maureen Smith; Rosalind Whittaker; Revd Canon Martyn Griffiths; Elizabeth Hodgkin; Martin Akehurst.

**OTHER INFORMATION** There were 20 grants to organisations, 87 individual awards and two grants through the specific prize funds.

**HOW TO APPLY** Apply on a form available to download from the website, where criteria and guidelines are also posted. Completed applications should be returned to the correspondent by post. The trustees meet six times a year – in January, March, May, June, September and November.

**WHO TO APPLY TO** Claire Brown, Clerk to the Trustees, Syringa Cottage, Horsepond Road, Gallowstree Common, Reading, Berkshire RG4 9BP *Tel.* 0118 972 4575 *email* henleyeducationalcharity@hotmail.co.uk *Website* www.henleyeducationaltrust.com

## ■ Philip Sydney Henman Deceased Will Trust (Philip Henman Trust)

**CC NO** 1054707  **ESTABLISHED** 1986
**WHERE FUNDING CAN BE GIVEN** Worldwide.

**WHO CAN BENEFIT** UK-registered charities concerned with long term overseas development, particularly charities working with young children in financially developing countries.

**WHAT IS FUNDED** Grants are aimed at established major UK-registered charity (normally defined as having an income of over £100,000 per annum). The funding from the trust should be important to the project, normally accounting for between 20% and 80% of the total project budget. The project should be partly funded by other sources, voluntary work and central office administration costs can be counted as other source funding.

**WHAT IS NOT FUNDED** Ongoing concerns; one-off grants or projects attending to urgent medical need or other types of emergency.

**TYPE OF GRANT** Partnership grants for three to five years (projects must start and finish within five years). One-off grants are not available.

**RANGE OF GRANTS** Up to around £5,000 per year; a maximum of 25,000 over the course of the project.

**SAMPLE GRANTS** Disasters Emergency Committee (£7,500); Advantage Africa, Child in Need India, Global Giving UK, SWAN, The Point Foundation and Wherever the Need (£5,000 each); Childreach International and The United Kingdom Committee for UNICEF (£4,900); International Children's Trust and Phase Worldwide (£4,500); Impact Foundation (£4,600); St Eanswythe's Church (£2,200).

**FINANCES** Year 2013/14 Income £69,770 Grants £63,751 Grants to organisations £63,751 Assets £2,150,633

**TRUSTEES** David Clark; Jason Duffey; Andrew Clark.

**OTHER INFORMATION** A total of 19 organisations benefitted.

**HOW TO APPLY** Applications are only considered once a year – the deadline is always 10 September. Applications are no longer accepted by post. Use the online form available on the trust's website.

**WHO TO APPLY TO** Andrew Clark, Trustee, 71 High Street, Linton, Cambridge CB21 4HS *Tel.* 01223 890331 *email* info@pht.org.uk *Website* www.pht.org.uk

## ■ The G. D. Herbert Charitable Trust

**CC NO** 295998  **ESTABLISHED** 1986
**WHERE FUNDING CAN BE GIVEN** UK.
**WHO CAN BENEFIT** Registered charities.

**WHAT IS FUNDED** The trust supports general charitable purposes, but particularly medicine, health, social welfare and environmental resources. It mainly gives regular grants to a set list of charities, with a few one-off grants given each year, in the areas of health and welfare only.

**TYPE OF GRANT** Mainly recurrent, also some one-off awards.

**RANGE OF GRANTS** Up to £2,700.

**SAMPLE GRANTS** Catch 22, Disability Rights UK, Friends of the Elderly, Marie Curie Cancer Care, Prostate Cancer UK, Shelter, The Abbeyfield Society and The Woodland Trust (£2,700 each); Barnardo's, Children with Cancer, Royal Brompton and Harefield Hospitals Charity and The Salvation Army (£1,500 each); and Ogbourne St George PCC and Wiltshire Wildlife Trust (£600 each).

**FINANCES** Year 2013/14 Income £56,116 Grants £69,300 Grants to organisations £69,300 Assets £2,092,265

**TRUSTEES** Michael Beaumont; Judith Cuxson.

**OTHER INFORMATION** There were 25 'regular donations' and four 'special awards'.

**HOW TO APPLY** Applications can be made in writing to the correspondent. No applications are invited other than from those charities currently supported by the trust. The trustees review donations at their annual meeting in February/March annually and may make some adjustments.

**WHO TO APPLY TO** M. J. Byrne, Correspondent, Veale Wasbrough Vizards, Barnards Inn, 86 Fetter Lane, London EC4A 1AD *Tel.* 020 7405 1234 *email* mbyrne@vwv.co.uk

## ■ Herefordshire Community Foundation

**CC NO** 1094935  **ESTABLISHED** 2002
**WHERE FUNDING CAN BE GIVEN** Herefordshire.
**WHO CAN BENEFIT** Registered charities; community and voluntary groups; individuals.
**WHAT IS FUNDED** A wide range of general charitable purposes.

RANGE OF GRANTS Generally £1,000–£5,000.
SAMPLE GRANTS Herefordshire Cider Museum (£10,900); City of Herford Swimming Club and Wye Amateur Boxing Club (£3,100 each); and Camden Art Centre, Herefordshire Mencap and The Basement Trust (£2,000 each).
FINANCES Year 2013/14 Income £1,765,885 Grants £90,919 Grants to organisations £90,919 Assets £3,410,513
TRUSTEES Nat Hone; Will Lindesay; Raymond Hunter; Wilma Gilmour; David Snow; Sally Pettiper; Shelagh Wynn; Oliver Cooke.
OTHER INFORMATION The majority of grants are for less than £1,000.
HOW TO APPLY HCF administers a number of different funds, including Comic/Sport Relief, ESF Community Grants and PCT Small Schemes. These all have their specific application processes and criteria and the forms are available to download from the website. Applications for under £1,000 can also be made in writing to the foundation and must include the following information: contact details, what is the grant to be used for and when, a budget/costs and why the grant is needed. Initial telephone calls are welcome.
WHO TO APPLY TO David Barclay, Director, The Fred Bulmer Centre, Wall Street, Hereford HR4 9HP Tel. 01432 272550 email dave.barclay@herefordshire-cf.co.uk or info@herefordshirefoundation.org Website herefordshirecommunityfoundation.org

■ **The Herefordshire Historic Churches Trust**

CC NO 511181    ESTABLISHED 1954
WHERE FUNDING CAN BE GIVEN Old county of Herefordshire.
WHO CAN BENEFIT Churches of all denominations.
WHAT IS FUNDED The restoration, preservation, repair, maintenance and improvement of churches, their contents and their churchyards in Herefordshire.
WHAT IS NOT FUNDED Our research suggests that grants cannot be given for general maintenance of lighting, heating, decoration or furnishings.
TYPE OF GRANT One-off awards for capital and core costs, project funding; loans are also available.
RANGE OF GRANTS £500–£10,000
SAMPLE GRANTS Kingsland and Lyonshall (£10,000 each); St Francis Xavier (£8,000); Almeley (£7,000); Tarrington (£5,000); Abbeydore, Leinthall Starkes and Pipe Aston (£3,000 each); Wigmore (£1,200); and Marstow (£600).
FINANCES Year 2013 Income £74,009 Grants £80,000 Grants to organisations £80,000 Assets £802,632
TRUSTEES Susanna McFarlane; David Furnival; James Devereux; Robin Peers; Canon Patrick Benson; Simon Arbuthnott; Ali Jones; Jill Gallimore; Adam Darnley.
OTHER INFORMATION Grants are given up to the value of 10% of the trust's asset value.
HOW TO APPLY Apply in writing to the correspondent. Informal contact can also be made via email. Deadlines for applications are normally 15 March and 15 September.
WHO TO APPLY TO David Furnival, Treasurer, The Wood House Farm, Staplow, Ledbury, Herefordshire HR8 1NP Tel. 01531 641955 email david.furnival13@btinternet.com Website www.hhct.co.uk

■ **The Heritage of London Trust Limited**

CC NO 280272    ESTABLISHED 1980
WHERE FUNDING CAN BE GIVEN All 33 London boroughs.
WHO CAN BENEFIT Listed architectural, historic or heritage buildings in London.
WHAT IS FUNDED The restoration of buildings of architectural importance. Grants are mainly given for skilled restoration of notable features of listed buildings, generally (though not exclusively) external work. Examples of buildings assisted are churches, community centres, almshouses, theatres, hospitals, museums and educational establishments.
WHAT IS NOT FUNDED Buildings in private ownership that are not open or available for public use and enjoyment, roof replacements or repairs, restoration schemes where the work has already been completed or general maintenance or repairs.
TYPE OF GRANT One-off restoration grants.
RANGE OF GRANTS £2,000–£5,000
SAMPLE GRANTS Wilton's Music Hall, Grace's Alley, Tower Hamlets (£5,000); National Theatre, Lambeth (£4,000); Crystal Palace Subway, Southwark and St John on Bethnal Green, Tower Hamlets (£3,500 each); Garden Museum, Lambeth and Lauderdale House, Camden (£2,000 each); St Thomas's Church, Islington (£1,000); and CricketGreen School, Merton (£700).
FINANCES Year 2013/14 Income £110,459 Grants £50,932 Grants to organisations £32,520 Assets £416,042
TRUSTEES Nicholas Bell; Denise Jones; Alec Forshaw; Michael Hoare; John Fishburn; Geoffrey Hunter; Edward Benyon; Philip Davies; Emily Arnold; Jamie Cayzer-Colvin, Caroline Egremont; Nicholas Collins.
PUBLICATIONS Map: Historic Buildings in Covent Garden.
HOW TO APPLY Eligible applicants should phone or e-mail the office to discuss their restoration project. Following that an application form can be downloaded from the trust's website and returned by post. The website also provides full criteria, guidelines and application deadlines. The trustees meet three times a year, currently in January, June and October.
WHO TO APPLY TO Sophie Martin, Assistant Director, 34 Grosvenor Gardens, London SW1W 0DH Tel. 020 7730 9472 email sophie@heritageoflondon.com or info@heritageoflondon.com Website www.heritageoflondon.com

■ **The Hertfordshire Community Foundation**

CC NO 299438    ESTABLISHED 1988
WHERE FUNDING CAN BE GIVEN Hertfordshire and its immediate neighbourhood.
WHO CAN BENEFIT Organisations which benefit local people; small or less well-known community groups; less 'popular' causes that often find it extremely difficult to obtain funds elsewhere. Preference for organisations with an income of £100,000 or less and projects were £5,000 would make a significant impact. Applicants do not have to be registered charities but must be a properly constituted group carrying out legally charitable work.
WHAT IS FUNDED Work of local charities and voluntary groups for the benefit of the community, with the following particular

517

concerns: disadvantaged children and families; developing young people; access to education, training and employment; the needs of older people; other community needs.

**WHAT IS NOT FUNDED** Political groups; animal welfare; projects that are solely environmental; statutory agencies; medical research; religious activities. Individuals are supported only in very specific situations through selected funds.

**TYPE OF GRANT** Project grants for a specific purpose; start-up costs; capital expenditure; development funding; running costs; training; staff costs; equipment; new initiatives; generally up to three years; one-off events are not preferred.

**RANGE OF GRANTS** Small grants: up to £1,000; large grants: up to £5,000 (average award is for £2,000–£3,000).

**SAMPLE GRANTS** The latest accounts did not list beneficiaries. **Previous beneficiaries have included:** Age Concern Hertfordshire; Alzheimer's Disease Society; Broxbourne and East Hertfordshire Credit Union; Citizens Advice – Hertfordshire; Dacorum Indian Society; Grandparents' Association; Hertfordshire Area Rape Crisis and Sexual Abuse Centre; Hertfordshire PASS; Neomari Beadcraft Training Services; Satsang Manda; Hitchin Town Bowls Club.

**FINANCES** Year 2013/14 Income £1,480,860 Grants £730,544 Grants to organisations £667,893 Assets £8,083,151

**TRUSTEES** David Fryer; James Williams; Michael Master; Gerald Corbett; Penny Williams; John Palmer; Jo Connell; Henry Hibbert; Cllr Teresa Heritage; Simon Tilley; Maggie Turner.

**OTHER INFORMATION** For further information on the grant programmes currently available consult the foundation's website. According to the annual report for 2013/14, 'the foundation is now managing 90 funds in total'. During the year a total of 538 grants were distributed – 153 to organisations and 385 to individuals. Individual awards totalled £62,500.

**HOW TO APPLY** Details of application procedure for each of the funds currently available can be found online. If you are not sure which fund to apply to, you can fill in an expression of interest form and be advised by the foundation. An initial telephone call or e-mail to check eligibility is also welcome.

**WHO TO APPLY TO** The Grants Team, Foundation House, 2–4 Forum Place, Off Fiddlebridge Lane, Hatfield, Hertfordshire AL10 0RN *Tel.* 01707 251351 *email* office@hertscf.org.uk or grants@hertscf.org.uk *Website* www.hertscf.org.uk

■ **Hesed Trust**

**CC NO** 1000489 **ESTABLISHED** 1990
**WHERE FUNDING CAN BE GIVEN** UK and overseas.
**WHO CAN BENEFIT** Christian charities benefitting children, young adults, older people, clergy, students, Christians and evangelists or involved in Christian work overseas.
**WHAT IS FUNDED** Christian charitable purposes. The trust will consider funding the advancement of religion and the Free Church umbrella bodies.
**TYPE OF GRANT** One-off grants, for one year or less.
**RANGE OF GRANTS** £600–£10,000
**SAMPLE GRANTS** Nation Changers and Sports Chaplaincy (£10,000 each); Ministries without Borders (£2,800); All Nations Church (£24,000); Blackpool Church and City Church Coventry (£10,000 each); and Covenant Life Church Leicester (£700). Other unspecified charities received the remaining £1,900.

**FINANCES** Year 2013/14 Income £132,316 Grants £183,880 Grants to organisations £25,399 Assets £29,904
**TRUSTEES** Ronald Eagle; Glyn Rawlings; Charles Smith.
**OTHER INFORMATION** Grants were also given to eight individuals.
**HOW TO APPLY** Applications may be made in writing to the correspondent.
**WHO TO APPLY TO** Glyn Rawlings, Trustee, 14 Chiltern Avenue, Cosby, Leicester LE9 1UF *Tel.* 0116 286 2990 *email* glynrawlings@btopenworld.com

■ **The Hesslewood Children's Trust (Hull Seamen's and General Orphanage)**

**CC NO** 529804 **ESTABLISHED** 1982
**WHERE FUNDING CAN BE GIVEN** East Yorkshire and North Lincolnshire.
**WHO CAN BENEFIT** Individuals and organisations benefitting children and young adults under the age of 24. Support can be given to people in care, individuals who are fostered or adopted; people with disabilities; those disadvantaged by poverty; ex-offenders and people at risk of offending; homeless people; people living in both rural and urban areas; socially isolated people; and victims of abuse and crime.
**WHAT IS FUNDED** Assistance to young individuals in need and to support youth organisations for holidays. Particularly supported are charities working in the fields of education, housing and accommodation, and arts, culture and recreation.
**WHAT IS NOT FUNDED** No grants are given to benefit people over the age of 24 will be made. Building work or salaries are not funded.
**TYPE OF GRANT** One-off grants for up to one year.
**RANGE OF GRANTS** £100–£10,000
**SAMPLE GRANTS** Hull University (£10,000); Hollybank Trust (£2,000); Cat Zero, Holy Trinity Church, Marfleet Primary School and Walker St Child Contact Centre (£1,000 each); Family action North Lines and The Parish of St John Newland (£500 each); and Skateopia – Driffield (£300).
**FINANCES** Year 2013/14 Income £88,131 Grants £72,333 Grants to organisations £34,304 Assets £2,779,636
**TRUSTEES** Ross Allenby; Colin Andrews; Dudley Moore; Gaynel Munn; Dr David Nicholas; Dr Christopher Woodyatt; Revd Timothy Boyns; David Turner; Philip Evans. Capt. Philip Watts; Ray Mann.
**HOW TO APPLY** Our research suggests that applications should be made on a form available from the correspondent, with a telephone number if possible. The trustees meet to consider applications at least three times a year. No replies are given to ineligible organisations. This trust has informed us that it promotes its work through its own avenues, receiving more applications than it can support.
**WHO TO APPLY TO** R. E. Booth, Secretary, 1 Canada Drive, Cherry Burton, Beverley, North Humberside, East Yorkshire HU17 7RQ *Tel.* 01946 550474 *email* detaylor@duttonmoore.co.uk

## ■ Hexham and Newcastle Diocesan Trust (1947)

**CC NO** 235686 **ESTABLISHED** 1867
**WHERE FUNDING CAN BE GIVEN** Diocese of Hexham and Newcastle; overseas.
**WHO CAN BENEFIT** Roman Catholic organisations; projects with a Catholic ethos; churches; educational establishments; clergy.
**WHAT IS FUNDED** 'Promotion of the Roman Catholic faith, by supporting clergy in their work, by providing pastoral work in parishes and in local communities, by providing life-long Christian education in parishes and voluntary-aided schools, and by preserving and investing in a property infrastructure'; relief in need; overseas aid.
**TYPE OF GRANT** One-off and recurring; core costs; salaries; capital expenditure.
**RANGE OF GRANTS** Up to £203,000.
**SAMPLE GRANTS Previous beneficiaries have included:** CAFOD Development and emergency aid (£203,000); Papal Visit (£119,000); National Catholic Fund (£86,000); Catholic Education Service (£46,000); Holy Places (£28,000); Sick and Retired Priests NBF (£25,000); Apostleship of the Sea (£21,000); Day for Life (£13,000); Peter's Pence (£20,000); Day for Life (£13,000).
**FINANCES** Year 2013/14 Income £0 Grants £0 Grants to organisations £0
**TRUSTEES** Seamus Cunningham; Revd James O'Keefe; Revd Martin Stempczyk; Revd Christopher Jackson; Revd John Butters.
**OTHER INFORMATION Note**: This year the trust had no expenditure; however, charitable giving in the previous four years averages at £29.5 million per annum. The trust remains active on the Charity Commission's records; therefore we maintain its entry, as substantial funding may be renewed in the coming years.
**HOW TO APPLY** Further details should be requested from the correspondent. The latest available accounts (2011/12) note the following grant-making policy: 'Each year the Bishop, assisted by guidance from the Catholic Bishops' Conference of England and Wales, decides which organisations will benefit from special collections to be taken in the parishes. At a local level, parish priests and their finance committees decide which additional causes they will support to further the work of the Church, by means of special appeals. The amounts raised from such appeals and paid over to charities are sometimes supplemented from general offertory income, where this is approved by the parish priest and the parish finance committee.'
**WHO TO APPLY TO** Kathleen Smith, Secretary, St Cuthberts House, West Road, Newcastle upon Tyne NE15 7PY *Tel.* 0191 243 3300 *email* office@rcdhn.org.uk or financial.secretary@diocesehn.org.uk *Website* rcdhn.org.uk

## ■ P. and C. Hickinbotham Charitable Trust

**CC NO** 216432 **ESTABLISHED** 1947
**WHERE FUNDING CAN BE GIVEN** UK, with a preference for Leicestershire and Rutland.
**WHO CAN BENEFIT** Registered charities; universities; schools; hospices and other organisations, particularly Quakers or Quaker related. Charities in Leicester and Rutland, also North Wales and Northern Ireland, are favoured.
**WHAT IS FUNDED** General charitable purposes; social welfare; disability and health; substance abuse; disadvantaged and vulnerable groups; children and young people; women; education; the arts; environment.
**WHAT IS NOT FUNDED** No grants are made to individuals applying for bursary-type assistance, to large UK charities (unless for a specific local project) or for general running costs.
**TYPE OF GRANT** Usually one-off grants for equipment, premises, renovation and start-up costs.
**RANGE OF GRANTS** Up to £15,000, but generally under £1,000.
**SAMPLE GRANTS** The University of Leicester (£15,000); Age UK Leicestershire and Rutland (£10,000); Leicester Charity Link (£5,000); YWCA Monaghan (£4,800); Belgrave Playhouse (£1,300); and Barnardo's, Leicestershire Parents Group of Diabetes UK, Leicester Rape Crisis, Pen Green Centre, Simon Community, The Lullaby Trust and Wygglesden and Queen Elizabeth I College (£1,000 each).
**FINANCES** Year 2013/14 Income £72,091 Grants £86,560 Grants to organisations £86,560 Assets £3,784,424
**TRUSTEES** Catherine Hickinbotham; Roger Hickinbotham; Anna Steiger; Rachel Hickinbotham; Charlotte Palmer; Frances Hickinbotham.
**OTHER INFORMATION** Donations under £1,000 totalled £33,500.
**HOW TO APPLY** Applications can be made in writing to the correspondent, giving the following details: a full postal address, a contact email address, details of any applicable website, a contact telephone number, charity registration number and instructions as to who any cheque should be made payable to as well as a brief outline of the purpose of the grant. Replies are not sent to unsuccessful applicants. Successful applicants are usually contacted within 12 weeks.
**WHO TO APPLY TO** Roger Hickinbotham, Trustee, 9 Windmill Way, Lyddington, Oakham, Leicestershire LE15 9LY *Tel.* 01572 821236 *email* roger@hickinbothamtrust.org.uk or rogerhick@gmail.com *Website* www.hickinbothamtrust.org.uk

## ■ The Alan Edward Higgs Charity

**CC NO** 509367 **ESTABLISHED** 1979
**WHERE FUNDING CAN BE GIVEN** Within 25 miles of the centre of Coventry only.
**WHO CAN BENEFIT** Local bodies and national organisations benefitting young people either directly, through their family, or through the provision of facilities or services to the community.
**WHAT IS FUNDED** General charitable purposes; child welfare; underprivileged children.
**WHAT IS NOT FUNDED** Grants from individuals or for the funding of services usually provided by statutory services, medical research, travel outside the UK or evangelical or worship activities are not normally accepted.
**TYPE OF GRANT** One-off capital for buildings and equipment; will consider both core and revenue funding of projects.
**RANGE OF GRANTS** Typically £500–£30,000.
**FINANCES** Year 2013/14 Income £808,131 Grants £155,235 Grants to organisations £155,235 Assets £17,291,095
**TRUSTEES** Marilyn Knatchbull-Hugessen; Paul Harris; Rowley Higgs; Emily Barlow.

519

OTHER INFORMATION During 2013/14 there were three grants awarded. The average grant was of about £57,000.
HOW TO APPLY Applications should be made in writing to the clerk, providing: details about your charity (background and present activities) and charity number (if registered); the specific purpose for which the grant is sought; the amount required and the budget of the project; a copy of the latest audited accounts and annual report; details of any other support received or applied for; a description of how the grant would be applied; a copy of the organisation's policy that ensures the protection of young or vulnerable people and a clear description of how it is implemented and monitored. The charity asks to avoid sending paper where online copies can be provided. The website states: 'The Trustees meet regularly through the year. They receive a large number of applications for support and do not respond unless they have decided to give support.'
WHO TO APPLY TO Peter Knatchbull-Hugessen, Clerk, Ricoh Arena Ltd, Phoenix Way, Coventry CV6 6GE *Tel.* 024 7622 1311 *email* clerk@higgscharity.org.uk *Website* www.higgscharity.org.uk

## ■ Highcroft Charitable Trust
CC NO 272684   ESTABLISHED 1975
WHERE FUNDING CAN BE GIVEN UK and overseas.
WHO CAN BENEFIT Educational and charitable organisations benefitting Jewish people, especially people disadvantaged by poverty, promoting education and/or the Jewish faith.
WHAT IS FUNDED The advancement and study of the Jewish faith and the study of the Torah. The relief of poverty and advancement of education among people of the Jewish faith.
RANGE OF GRANTS £150–£5,000
SAMPLE GRANTS Previously grants have been made to: Friends of Beer Miriam, Institute For Higher Rabbinic Studies and Kollel Ohr Yechiel (£5,000 each); Kollel Chibas Yerushalayim (£4,200); Craven Walk Charity Trust (£2,500); London Friends of Kamenitzer (£2,000); Hachzakas Torah Vachesed Charity (£1,900); Amutat Shaarei Harama, Beis Yaacov High School and Tashbar Manchester (£1,000 each); Belt Haknesset Kehilat Yaacov (£700); and British Friends of College Technology and Delamere Forest School (£100 each).
FINANCES Year 2013/14 Income £75,632 Grants £58,471 Grants to organisations £58,471 Assets £223,194
TRUSTEES Rabbi Richard Fischer; Sarah Fischer.
HOW TO APPLY Apply in writing to the correspondent.
WHO TO APPLY TO Rabbi Richard Fischer, Trustee, 15 Highcroft Gardens, London NW11 0LY *email* fisher@brijnet.org

## ■ The Hilden Charitable Fund
CC NO 232591   ESTABLISHED 1963
WHERE FUNDING CAN BE GIVEN UK and financially developing countries.
WHO CAN BENEFIT Community causes; CICs; charities; voluntary organisations; NGOs; social enterprises; educational establishments (schools – for project but not core funding). In the UK most grant aid is directed to registered charities and overseas projects will normally work with a UK charity partner or show relevant local legal status. Preference is given to smaller organisations rather than large national charities. Scottish charities are only funded through a block grant to the Foundation Scotland (formerly known as Scottish Community Foundation) which is then distributed to the sector.
WHAT IS FUNDED In the UK: homelessness; asylum seekers and refugees; penal affairs; community initiatives for disadvantaged young people (aged 16–25) – 'programmes that are helping these young people in the job market, with advice, training, volunteering and work placement schemes'. Overseas: community development; education; health. Special preference for projects which focus on the needs and potential of girls and women. The charity favours causes which attract less funding.
WHAT IS NOT FUNDED Individuals; well-established causes; overseas grants concentrate on development aid in preference to disaster relief.
TYPE OF GRANT Capital and core costs; salaries; recurring funding; project and general running costs; unrestricted expenditure; funding for over one year.
RANGE OF GRANTS Up to £10,000; average grant is of £5,000.
SAMPLE GRANTS Foundation Scotland (£36,500); Tanzania Development Trust – Tanzania (£16,000); Joint Council for the Welfare of Immigrants – London (£15,000); Children of Choba – Tanzania (£11,000); The Guild of Psychotherapists – South London (£7,000); Bristol Refugee Rights, Children of the Mekong – Cambodia, FareShare Yorkshire, Hope Nottingham and Women's Work (Derbyshire) Ltd (£5,000 each); The Gap Project – Broadstairs (£3,600); Free the Way – Seaham (£3,000); Student Volunteering Cardiff (£2,500); People in Need Ministries – India (£2,000). Through Special Playschemes a total of £22,500 was awarded in 24 grants of £1,500 or less.
FINANCES Year 2013/14 Income £435,261 Grants £430,920 Grants to organisations £430,920 Assets £12,647,994
TRUSTEES C. S. L. Rampton; A. J. M. Rampton; Prof. D. S. Rampton; Prof. C. H. Rodeck; J. R. A. Rampton; Prof. M. B. H. Rampton; Maggie Baxter; Elizabeth Rodeck; E. Rampton; E. J. Rodeck; Samia Khatun; Jonathan Branch.
OTHER INFORMATION The charity also has a small budget to help community groups run summer play schemes for disadvantaged communities, preferably where children from refugee families and people of different ethnic backgrounds are involved. More detailed criteria and application guidelines are given on the charity's' website. During the year a total of 97 grants were awarded.
HOW TO APPLY Applications have to be made using an application form, available from the website. Note that while the appeal should be concise (up to two sides of A4), supporting documentation is essential (most recent annual report and independently inspected accounts as well as projected income and expenditure for the current financial year). The forms should be submitted via post. Be clear in your application form about when the proposed work is to commence, and give the relevant timetable. Applicants from the UK applying for funds for their project partners must complete both the UK application form and the overseas partner profile form. Potential applicants in Scotland should contact the Foundation Scotland (formerly known as Scottish Community Foundation) at 22 Calton Road, Edinburgh EH8 8DP (tel: 0131 524 0300; website: www.foundationscotland.org.uk).

**WHO TO APPLY TO** Rodney Hedley, Secretary, 34 North End Road, London W14 0SH *Tel.* 020 7603 1525 *Fax* 020 7603 1525 *email* hildencharity@hotmail.com *Website* www.hildencharitablefund.org.uk

## ■ The Derek Hill Foundation

**CC NO** 801590     **ESTABLISHED** 1989
**WHERE FUNDING CAN BE GIVEN** UK.
**WHO CAN BENEFIT** Organisations and individuals.
**WHAT IS FUNDED** The promotion of arts and culture.
**TYPE OF GRANT** Bursaries and art related travel costs.
**RANGE OF GRANTS** £500–£10,000
**SAMPLE GRANTS** The London Magazine (£10,000); British School at Rome (£9,200); Agenda Magazine and Letter and Commemorative Arts Trust (£5,000 each); Fulham Opera (£3,000); Art Fund and Llanfyllin Music Festival (£2,000 each); Royal Academy of Music and Royal Northern College of Music (£1,500 each); and Coventry Cathedral (£500).
**FINANCES** *Year* 2013/14 *Income* £48,004 *Grants* £89,642 *Grants to organisations* £57,960 *Assets* £1,508,831
**TRUSTEES** Lord Armstrong of Ilminster; Josephine Batterham; Earl of Gowrie; Ian Paterson; Rathbone Trust Company Limited.
**OTHER INFORMATION** Grants to 15 individuals totalled about £32,000. There were 25 awards to organisations.
**HOW TO APPLY** Apply in writing to the correspondent.
**WHO TO APPLY TO** Trevor Harris, Correspondent, Rathbone Trust Company Limited, 1 Curzon Street, London W1J 5FB *Tel.* 020 7399 0000

## ■ The Hillingdon Community Trust

**CC NO** 1098235     **ESTABLISHED** 2003
**WHERE FUNDING CAN BE GIVEN** The London Borough of Hillingdon: Botwell; Pinkwell; Heathrow Villages; Townfield; West Drayton; Yiewsley.
**WHO CAN BENEFIT** 'Properly constituted voluntary bodies' community organisations; for larger awards preference may be given to registered charities. It is less likely that a grant will be made to a corporate body other than on a matched funding basis.
**WHAT IS FUNDED** Community projects; social welfare; relief of poverty; economic development; conservation of environment and heritage; unemployment; adult education and training; safety and crime prevention; economic development.
**WHAT IS NOT FUNDED** Individuals; public bodies or projects that should be funded by public funds (projects by voluntary bodies that will be partially financed by public bodies are considered); religious bodies except for ancillary activities which meet one of the priorities); organisations that have already received funding in respect of a completed project; work that has already started; political parties or lobbying; non-charitable activities.
**TYPE OF GRANT** One-off or recurrent; capital funding; project costs; development or strategic funding; volunteer expenses; reasonable overheads relating to a project.
**RANGE OF GRANTS** £800–£43,500; Small Grants: £500–£7,500; Main Grants: over £7,500.
**SAMPLE GRANTS** HACS (£43,500); Bell Farm (£35,000); The Rosedale Hewens Academy Trust (£25,000); Cranford Good Neighbours (£15,000); AGE UK-Hillingdon (£14,900); Hillingdon Mind (£14,500 in two grants); West London Somaliland Community (£14,000 in two awards); Green Corridor (£7,500); Kashif Siddiqi Foundation (£6,400); 1st Harmondsworth Scout Group (£4,000); Friends of St Mary's Harmondsworth (£1,700); Brunel University (£800).
**FINANCES** *Year* 2013/14 *Income* £1,042,351 *Grants* £622,109 *Grants to organisations* £622,109 *Assets* £1,838,877
**TRUSTEES** Isabel King; Prof. Ian Campbell; Davinder Sandhumr; Keith Wallis; Carole Jones; Matthew Gorman; Michael Gibson; Jasvir Jassal; Clive Gee; Christopher Geake; Jack Taylor; Peter Money.
**OTHER INFORMATION** In 2013/14 a total of 60 grants were approved – 27 main grants (£581,000) and 33 small grants (£164,000). The grant total represents the sum after deduction of £123,000 defined as 'withdrawn grants previous years'.
**HOW TO APPLY** Application forms and detailed guidelines for both schemes are provided on the trust's website. Remember that Main Grants programme has a two-stage application process and organisations successful in the initial consideration will be invited to complete a full application form. Applicants are welcome to approach the trust prior to submitting a formal application. Awards are considered every second month – see the website for up-to-date deadlines.
**WHO TO APPLY TO** Kathleen Healy, Company Secretary and Trust Director, Barra Hall, Wood end, Green Road, Hayes, Middlesex UB3 2SA *Tel.* 020 8581 1676 *email* info@hillingdoncommunitytrust.org.uk *Website* www.hillingdoncommunitytrust.org.uk

## ■ The Hillingdon Partnership Trust

**CC NO** 284668     **ESTABLISHED** 1982
**WHERE FUNDING CAN BE GIVEN** The London borough of Hillingdon.
**WHO CAN BENEFIT** Organisations benefitting people of all ages, at risk groups, people disadvantaged by poverty and socially isolated people.
**WHAT IS FUNDED** The trust aims: to build links between the local community and the business sector to secure funding for community initiatives and projects; to relieve people resident in Hillingdon who are sick, have disabilities, older people, those in poverty or in other social and economic circumstances; to provide, or assist in providing, equipment and facilities not normally provided by the local authority for the purpose of advancing education or relieving people in need.
**TYPE OF GRANT** Channelling of in-kind gifts or coverage of associated expenses.
**SAMPLE GRANTS** Support given included: recycled furniture and equipment to community groups (£14,000); Hillingdon's Schools Books of the Year literacy and numeracy project (£12,000); and holiday hampers for shelter and residential care homes (£10,000).
**FINANCES** *Year* 2013/14 *Income* £148,263 *Grants* £144,420 *Grants to organisations* £37,325 *Assets* £17,399
**TRUSTEES** Albert Kanjee; Prof. Heinz Wolff; James Crowe; Michael Wisdom; Nicholas Smith; Air Cmdr Paul Thomas; John Watts; David Routledge; Peter O'Reilly; Robert Brightwell; Miranda Clarke; Prof. Ian Campbell; Tony Woodbridge.
**OTHER INFORMATION** The annual report for 2013/14 states that 'the trust was not established to be a grant-making body ... [rather] it channels

**521**

appeals to its business supporters on behalf of needy organisations and, exceptionally, individuals, and [its] business partners may then provide funds for an applicant'. Occasionally, the purchase and delivery can be arranged and covered.

**HOW TO APPLY** Application forms are available from the correspondent.

**WHO TO APPLY TO** John Matthews, Chief Executive Officer, Room 22–25, Building 219, Epsom Square, Eastern Business Park, London Heathrow Airport, Hillingdon, Middlesex TW6 2BW *Tel.* 020 8897 3611 *email* johnmatthewshpt@lineone.net

## ■ R. G. Hills Charitable Trust

**CC NO** 1008914   **ESTABLISHED** 1982
**WHERE FUNDING CAN BE GIVEN** UK and overseas.
**WHO CAN BENEFIT** Local and national registered charities.
**WHAT IS FUNDED** General charitable purposes, with some preference for the fields of health, poverty and education.
**RANGE OF GRANTS** £1,000–£2,500
**SAMPLE GRANTS** Canterbury Cathedral Trust and Disasters Emergency Committee – Philippines Earthquake (£3,000 each); Leprosy Mission, Respite Association, Royal Society for the Protection of Bird and Vitalise (£2,500 each); Hope for Tomorrow (£1,900); Age UK – Herne Bay (£1,500); Battle of Britain Memorial Trust (£1,300); and School Aid UK (£1,000).
**FINANCES** Year 2013/14 Income £105,621 Grants £70,000 Grants to organisations £70,000 Assets £3,327,430
**TRUSTEES** David Pentin; Harvey Barrett.
**OTHER INFORMATION** There were 35 grants made.
**HOW TO APPLY** Applications can be made in writing to the correspondent.
**WHO TO APPLY TO** Harvey Barrett, Trustee, Furley Page, 39–40 St Margaret's Street, Canterbury, Kent CT1 2TX *Tel.* 01227 763939

## ■ Hinchley Charitable Trust

**CC NO** 1108412   **ESTABLISHED** 1973
**WHERE FUNDING CAN BE GIVEN** UK and overseas.
**WHO CAN BENEFIT** Registered or recognised charities; mainly evangelical Christian organisations, including Christian youth organisations and Christian organisations in local communities.
**WHAT IS FUNDED** General charitable purposes, with particular reference to evangelical Christian work. Grants are made in the following five main categories: Christian and other charitable work in local communities (25%); Christian bodies engaged in holistic mission (20%); Christian leadership training (20%); Christian work among young people (20%); Christian bodies at work in the public sphere (15%).
**TYPE OF GRANT** One-off or recurring; usually for projects, but capital and core costs are considered.
**RANGE OF GRANTS** £2,000–£15,000
**SAMPLE GRANTS** Willowfield Parish Community Association (£15,000); A Rocha, Faith2Share and London Institute for Contemporary Christianity (£10,000 each); Centre Pioneer Learning and Elim Church – Huddersfield (£8,000 each); Crisis (£7,500). Awards of under £5,000 totalled £59,500.
**FINANCES** Year 2013/14 Income £162,863 Grants £163,127 Grants to organisations £163,127 Assets £3,162,437

**TRUSTEES** Prof. Brian Stanley; John Levick; Mark Hobbs; Roger Northcott; Rebecca Stanley.
**OTHER INFORMATION** According to the annual report for 2013/14, 'the trustees are particularly keen to support smaller charities where a grant can make a significant difference to the work of the charity'. During the year 25 organisations benefitted.
**HOW TO APPLY** The trust states that 'the trustees adopt a proactive approach to grant-making meaning unsolicited applications are usually unable to be supported'.
**WHO TO APPLY TO** Emma Northcott, Company Secretary, 10 Coplow Terrace, Coplow Street, Birmingham B16 0DQ *Tel.* 0121 455 6632

## ■ The Lady Hind Trust (Lilian Frances Hind Bequest)

**CC NO** 208877   **ESTABLISHED** 1951
**WHERE FUNDING CAN BE GIVEN** UK; in practice mainly Nottinghamshire and Norfolk.
**WHO CAN BENEFIT** Registered and exempt charities; churches; groups and clubs; educational establishments; hospices.
**WHAT IS FUNDED** General charitable purposes, particularly social welfare and health and disability; churches; education; arts and culture; environment and heritage; accommodation; community groups and clubs.
**WHAT IS NOT FUNDED** Individuals.
**TYPE OF GRANT** Core, capital and project support; salaries; in practice unrestricted funding.
**RANGE OF GRANTS** Up to £20,000; mostly under £5,000.
**SAMPLE GRANTS** Nelson's Journey (£20,000); Bromley House Library and National Crimebeat (£10,000 each); Norfolk Community Foundation (£8,500); Lincolnshire and Nottinghamshire Air Ambulance, NSPCC – Nottinghamshire and Oliver Hind Youth Club (£7,500 each); Incest and Sexual Abuse Survivors (£7,000); Partnership Council (£6,000); Framework Knitters Museum, Nottinghamshire Farming and Wildlife and Trent Rivers Trust (£5,000 each); Norfolk Deaf Association (£3,000); Dad's Army Museum – Thetford and The Ear Foundation (£2,500 each); Charles Burrell Museum, Open Youth Trust and Rainbow's Children's Hospice (£2,000 each); Young Potential (East Midlands) Ltd (£1,500); British Association for Adoption and Fostering, Carousel Under Fives Group and The Guide Dogs for the Blind Association (£1,000 each).
**FINANCES** Year 2013 Income £426,478 Grants £502,646 Grants to organisations £502,646 Assets £13,804,483
**TRUSTEES** Charles Barratt; Tim Farr; Nigel Savory; John Pears.
**OTHER INFORMATION** There 169 awards made.
**HOW TO APPLY** Applications should be made in writing to the correspondent at least one month in advance of the trustee meetings, which are usually held in March, July and November. Applicants should also provide their latest set of accounts. Unsuccessful applicants are not notified. The annual report for 2013 states that 'the trustees consider all written applications made to them by charitable organisations'.
**WHO TO APPLY TO** John Thompson, Correspondent, c/o Shakespeares Solicitors, Park House, Friar Lane, Nottingham NG1 6DN *Tel.* 01476 552429 *email* ladyhind@btinternet.com

## ■ The Hinduja Foundation

**CC NO** 802756   **ESTABLISHED** 1989
**WHERE FUNDING CAN BE GIVEN** Worldwide.
**WHO CAN BENEFIT** Registered charities.
**WHAT IS FUNDED** Health, education, relief of poverty, hunger and sickness, medicine, arts and culture, social, economic and international development-related research.
**RANGE OF GRANTS** £100–£33,000
**SAMPLE GRANTS** Francis Holland School Trust (£33,000); International Society for Krishna Consciousness (£12,400 in six donations); BAPS Swaminarayan Sanstha (£10,000 in two donations); The Lily Foundation and UCL Malcolm Grant Scholarship (£5,000 each); Siri Guru Singh Sabha (£2,000 in two donations); The Stroke Association (£200); Help the Aged (£140); and Comic Relief (£100).
**FINANCES** Year 2013/14 Income £91,500 Grants £93,023 Grants to organisations £93,023 Assets £73,754
**TRUSTEES** Srichand Hinduja; Gopichand Hinduja; Prakash Hinduja; Shanu Hinduja.
**HOW TO APPLY** Apply in writing to the correspondent.
**WHO TO APPLY TO** Michael Urwick, Correspondent, New Zealand House, 80 Haymarket, London SW1Y 4TE *email* foundation@hindujagroup.com

## ■ Stuart Hine Trust

**CC NO** 326941   **ESTABLISHED** 1985
**WHERE FUNDING CAN BE GIVEN** UK and overseas.
**WHO CAN BENEFIT** Evangelical Christian organisations, churches and missionary societies. Organisations supported by Stuart Hine during his lifetime or by the trustees since his death are favoured.
**WHAT IS FUNDED** Evangelical Christianity; missionary work.
**TYPE OF GRANT** One-off or ongoing.
**RANGE OF GRANTS** £1,000–£5,000
**SAMPLE GRANTS** Wycliffe Bible Translators (£149,000); and other unnamed institutions (£101,500).
**FINANCES** Year 2013/14 Income £250,846 Grants £250,458 Grants to organisations £250,458 Assets £236,266
**TRUSTEES** Raymond Bodkin; Amelia Gardner; Jonathan Juby; Roland Slater; Leonard Chipping; Melanie Churchyard.
**PUBLICATIONS** A booklet: *How Great Thou Art! – The Inspiring Story of Stuart K. Hine and the Making of a Classic Christian Hymn.* This will be published in the near future.
**OTHER INFORMATION** The trust receives its income mainly from the royalties from the hymn 'How Great Thou Art' (he words of this hymn were written by the late Stuart K. Hine).
**HOW TO APPLY** The trust has stated that 'unsolicited requests for funds will not be considered', as grants are normally made to the same people or organisations year after year, in accordance with the testator's wishes. The trustees maintain contact with all people and organisations supported.
**WHO TO APPLY TO** Raymond Bodkin, Trustee, 23 Derwent Close, Hailsham, East Sussex BN27 3DA *Tel.* 01323 843948 *email* ray.bodkin@talktalk.net

## ■ The Hinrichsen Foundation

**CC NO** 272389   **ESTABLISHED** 1976
**WHERE FUNDING CAN BE GIVEN** UK.
**WHO CAN BENEFIT** Organisations and individuals.
**WHAT IS FUNDED** Assisting contemporary composition and its performance, and musicological research. See the website for more information.
**WHAT IS NOT FUNDED** The purchase of musical instruments or equipment, including the electronic or computer variety; retrospective grants. Degree courses, as a general rule, are not funded.
**TYPE OF GRANT** Usually one-off project funding. Larger-scale funding over a period of time, initially up to three years, is also given through the 'New Initiatives' scheme.
**RANGE OF GRANTS** Mostly £1,000 to £5,000, occasionally larger.
**SAMPLE GRANTS** Huddersfield Contemporary Music Festival and Tête à Tête (£10,000 each); Birmingham Contemporary Music Group (£5,000); Vale of Glamorgan Festival (£4,000); Orpheus Centre (£3,000); Museum of Music History (£2,000); Cheltenham Festival (£1,500); Exeter Festival Chorus and School of Advanced Study – University of London (£1,000 each); London Bach Society (£800).
**FINANCES** Year 2013 Income £6,295,851 Grants £75,200 Grants to organisations £74,200 Assets £1,360,623
**TRUSTEES** Professor Jonathan Cross; Keith Potter; Dr Linda Hirst; Professor Stephen Walsh; Patric Standford; Paul Strang; Tim Berg; Tabby Estell; Eleanor Gussman; Ed McKeon; Mark Bromley; Philip Meaden.
**OTHER INFORMATION** The grant total refers to those approved during the year. Total grants approved for individuals during the year amounted to £1,000.
**HOW TO APPLY** Apply on a form that can be downloaded from the foundation's website. See the website for applications deadlines and a helpful page on 'further guidance'.
**WHO TO APPLY TO** The Secretary, 2–6 Baches Street, London N1 6DN *email* hinrichsen.foundation@editionpeters.com *Website* www.hinrichsenfoundation.org.uk

## ■ The Hintze Family Charity Foundation

**CC NO** 1101842   **ESTABLISHED** 2003
**WHERE FUNDING CAN BE GIVEN** England and Wales, particularly the Diocese of Southwark; overseas.
**WHO CAN BENEFIT** Registered charities; churches; museums, galleries; libraries and other cultural bodies; educational establishments.
**WHAT IS FUNDED** Access to museums, libraries and art galleries; arts and culture; Christian faith; the relief of sickness and people with terminal illnesses; education and the provision of resources and equipment for schools, colleges and universities; other charitable purposes.
**TYPE OF GRANT** One-off and multi-year; capital and revenue funding; salaries; core costs; projects; start-up costs; unrestricted funding.
**RANGE OF GRANTS** Up to £1.2 million.
**SAMPLE GRANTS** Christ Church College (£1.2 million); University of South Wales and University of Sydney (£543,000 each); Royal Navy and Royal Marines Association (£500,000); Royal National Theatre (£250,000); The Prince's Foundation for Building (£200,000); The International Theological Institute (£194,000). Only grants of £50,000 or more were listed in the accounts.

**FINANCES** Year 2013 Income £1,167,387 Grants £3,092,281 Grants to organisations £3,092,281 Assets £1,771,089
**TRUSTEES** Brian Hannon; Sir Michael Hintze; Sir Michael Peat; Adam Sorab; Jonathan Hellewell; Duncan Baxter.
**OTHER INFORMATION** A total of 32 awards were allocated as follows: education – core (£3.4 million); education – cultural (£362,500); religion (£206,000); health (£30,000). The grant total excludes an award of £500,000 (an underwriting no longer required) and a commitment of £422,000 (no longer required) which were both returned during the year. The accounts had some awards listed in Australian dollars; we have used the conversion rate applicable at the time of writing.
**HOW TO APPLY** The foundation offers the following application guidance in its latest accounts: 'The Foundation invites applications for grants from charities which further the objectives of the Foundation. No specific format is required for applications. Applications and potential donations identified by the Chief Executive and the trustees are considered at trustees' meetings.'
**WHO TO APPLY TO** Jeremy Herridge, Secretary, 5th Floor, 33 Chester Street, London SW1X 7BL Tel. 020 7201 6900 email enquiries@hfcf.org.uk

■ **The Hiscox Foundation**
CC NO 327635    ESTABLISHED 1987
**WHERE FUNDING CAN BE GIVEN** Worldwide.
**WHO CAN BENEFIT** Registered charities or individuals, mainly those with which a member of staff of the Hiscox Group is involved.
**WHAT IS FUNDED** General charitable purposes, especially education, medical science, the arts, independent living for older people and other disadvantaged or vulnerable individuals.
**TYPE OF GRANT** Usually one-off.
**RANGE OF GRANTS** £50–£4,000
**SAMPLE GRANTS** Whitechapel Gallery (£25,000); Leukaemia and Lymphoma Research, Royal British Legion and Walking With The Wounded (£5,000 each); Almshouse Association (£2,500); Action for Children and Cancer Research (£1,300 each); Battersea Summer Scheme, Friends of Elverstoke Prison, Hepworth Wakefield Museum and Pimlico opera (£1,000 each); St John Ambulance and Urology Foundation (£500 each); Disasters Emergency Committee (£400); Ability Bow and Movember (£250 each); and Hospice of St Francis (£50).
**FINANCES** Year 2013/14 Income £674,640 Grants £100,410 Grants to organisations £100,410 Assets £5,500,994
**TRUSTEES** Alexander Foster; Robert Hiscox; Rory Barker; Andrew Nix; Amanda Brown.
**OTHER INFORMATION** There were 84 awards made.
**HOW TO APPLY** Our research suggests that the foundation does not accept unsolicited applications.
**WHO TO APPLY TO** Peresha McKenzie, Correspondent, c/o Hiscox Underwriting Ltd, 1 Great St Helen's, London EC3A 6HX Tel. 020 7448 6011

■ **Hitchin Educational Foundation**
CC NO 311024    ESTABLISHED 1965
**WHERE FUNDING CAN BE GIVEN** In practice Hertfordshire.
**WHO CAN BENEFIT** Individuals and local organisations benefitting children, young adults and students under the age of 25 years. Regular support is given to three local schools.
**WHAT IS FUNDED** The advancement of education and training.
**WHAT IS NOT FUNDED** Support is not given for second degrees or the purchase of certain books. Grants are restricted to residents in the Hitchin area and students attending Hitchin secondary schools.
**TYPE OF GRANT** One-off awards and recurrent payments to specified schools.
**RANGE OF GRANTS** £300–£15,000
**FINANCES** Year 2013/14 Income £98,159 Grants £77,740 Grants to organisations £77,740 Assets £1,344,700
**TRUSTEES** Bernard Lovewell; Nigel Brook; C. Minton; Revd M. Roden; Morag Norgan; D. Chapallaz; Sarah Wren; Derrick Ashley; David Leal-Bennett; Allison Ashley; Anthony Buckland; Roy Shakespeare-Smith; Frank Carr.
**OTHER INFORMATION** Our research indicates that applicants must have lived in Hitchin or attended a Hitchin school for at least two years.
**HOW TO APPLY** Application forms can be obtained from the correspondent. The governors meet three or four times a year.
**WHO TO APPLY TO** Brian Frederick, Clerk to the Governors, 33 Birch Close, Broom, Biggleswade SG18 9NR Tel. 01767 313892 email bfred@rmplc.co.uk

■ **The Henry C. Hoare Charitable Trust**
CC NO 1088669    ESTABLISHED 2001
**WHERE FUNDING CAN BE GIVEN** UK.
**WHO CAN BENEFIT** Charitable organisations.
**WHAT IS FUNDED** A range of general charitable purposes. The accounts state: 'In general, the trust supports those causes where the grant made is meaningful to the recipient.'
**TYPE OF GRANT** One-off, irregular and annual awards.
**RANGE OF GRANTS** Up to £11,000.
**SAMPLE GRANTS** **Beneficiaries of £5,000 or more included**: Transform Drug Policy Foundation (£11,000); Future Trees Trust, Leaping Frogs Kindergarten, Prospect Burma, The Brain Tumour Charity and Trinity College Appeal (£10,000 each); Wiltshire Wildlife Trust (£6,000); Burma Campaign UK; The Amber Foundation; The March Foundation and Tree Aid (£5,000 each).
**FINANCES** Year 2012/13 Income £231,549 Grants £119,800 Grants to organisations £119,800 Assets £4,431,547
**TRUSTEES** Henry Hoare; Hoare Trustees.
**OTHER INFORMATION** Awards were made in the following categories: education (£30,000); health (£25,500); environmental protection and improvement (£25,000); citizenship and community development (£19,000); young people, age, ill health, disability and financial hardship (£11,500); animal welfare (£4,800); arts (£4,000); public policy (£300). At the time of writing (June 2015) this was the latest information available.
**HOW TO APPLY** Applications may be made in writing to the correspondent. The trustees meet once a year. However, note the following stated in the accounts: 'The Trustees seldom grant funds to unsolicited requests for donations.'
**WHO TO APPLY TO** The Trustees, C. Hoare and Co., 37 Fleet Street, London EC4P 4DQ Tel. 020 7353 4522

## ■ The Hobson Charity Limited

**CC NO** 326839 **ESTABLISHED** 1985

**WHERE FUNDING CAN BE GIVEN** UK.

**WHO CAN BENEFIT** Registered charities only, including ones benefitting children, older people, disadvantaged individuals, those in poverty, also environment and animals.

**WHAT IS FUNDED** A wide range of general charitable purposes, including social welfare, education, religious activities, relief of poverty, armed forces, arts, culture and heritage, animal welfare, environment and conservation and community causes.

**WHAT IS NOT FUNDED** Individuals (except in exceptional circumstances).

**TYPE OF GRANT** One-off and recurrent.

**RANGE OF GRANTS** £1,000–£150,000

**SAMPLE GRANTS** Royal Foundation of Duke and Duchess of Cambridge and Prince Harry (£150,000); SSAFA (£50,000); Police Foundation (£30,000); Action on Addiction (£26,500); Rekindle (£25,000); Pulborough Medical (£20,000); St Michael's Hospice (£15,000); North London Hospice (£12,000); Wells Cathedral Choristers Trust, Royal Ballet School and Royal National Orthopaedic Hospital Appeal (£10,000 each); RAF Museum Hendon (£6,000); Mayhew Animal Home and Trinity Sailing Foundation (£5,000 each); Horse Rangers Association (£4,000); Mill Hill Preservation Society (£3,000); Fishing for Heroes, Greatwood Charity for Racehorses and Red Squirrel Survival Trust (£2,000 each); Beverley Community Life (£1,500); Haliburton Highlands Health Services Foundation (£1,300); Arkwright Society and International Programme for Ethics, Public Health and Human Rights (£1,000 each).

**FINANCES** Year 2013/14 Income £16,489,520 Grants £950,220 Grants to organisations £950,220 Assets £48,016,286

**TRUSTEES** Rear Admiral Sir Donald Gosling; Deborah Hobson; Lady Hobson; Jennifer Richardson; Sir Ronald Hobson.

**OTHER INFORMATION** There were a total of 88 awards made. Out of the total grant commitment, £316,000 'falls due for payment in future'. The annual report for 2013/14 states that the trustees had aimed to distribute approximately £2 million in grants; however, due to 'fewer applications for donations received by the trustees compared to previous years, total distributions were less than intended'. The trustees intended to distribute about £1.5 million in 2015.

**HOW TO APPLY** Applications should be made in writing to the correspondent. The trustees meet quarterly.

**WHO TO APPLY TO** Deborah Hobson, Secretary, 21 Bryanston Street, Marble Arch, London W1H 7AB *Tel.* 020 7495 5599 *email* Charity@LewisGolden.com

## ■ Hockerill Educational Foundation

**CC NO** 311018 **ESTABLISHED** 1977

**WHERE FUNDING CAN BE GIVEN** UK, with a preference for the dioceses of Chelmsford and St Albans.

**WHO CAN BENEFIT** Individuals; religious bodies; church educational projects; organisations and corporate bodies 'associated with education on Christian principles' benefitting young adults, older people, academics, students, teachers and educational support staff, Christians and the Church of England.

**WHAT IS FUNDED** The foundation makes grants in the field of education in three main areas: individual grants to support the education and training of teachers; research, development and support grants to organisations in the field of religious education; grants to develop the church's educational work, especially in the dioceses of Chelmsford and St Albans. According to the website, 'the trustees would expect any activity, project or research they support to be likely to be of real benefit to Religious Education and/or the Church's educational work' with preference given to 'imaginative new projects which will enhance the Church's contribution to higher and further education and/or promote aspects of Religious Education in schools'.

**WHAT IS NOT FUNDED** General appeals; 'bricks and mortar' building projects; purposes that are the clear responsibility of another body.

**TYPE OF GRANT** Recurrent for up to three years (occasionally a maximum of five years), subject to satisfactory progress reports.

**RANGE OF GRANTS** £50–£95,000

**SAMPLE GRANTS** Chelmsford Diocesan Board of Education (£95,000); St Mark's College – Audley End and RE Council for England and Wales (£10,000 each); National Institute for Christian Education Research and STEP (£5,000 each); Culham St Gabriel's 3forRE scheme (£3,000); Hockerill NATRE Prize for Innovation in RE Teaching (£300); Bath Spa University (£50).

**FINANCES** Year 2013/14 Income £214,022 Grants £313,970 Grants to organisations £245,570 Assets £6,563,382

**TRUSTEES** H. Potter; Jonathan Reynolds; The Venerable Elwin Cockett; Lesley Barlow; Revd Richard Atkinson; Colin Bird; Canon Harry Marsh; Revd John Wraw; Janet Scott; Revd Tim Elbourne; Jonathan Longstaff; Raymond Slade; Revd Dr Alan Smith; Revd Stephen Cottrell.

**OTHER INFORMATION** During the year 106 individuals benefitted from awards totalling £69,500. Generally about two thirds of the annual grant expenditure is allocated to the church's educational work, in the two dioceses and the remainder to institutional and individual grants. Awards are made both in the UK and overseas and the annual report for 2013/14 states that foundation is 'actively seeking a new overseas partner'.

**HOW TO APPLY** Apply on a form available to download from the website. Applications should include some official documentation, such as the most recent annual report and accounts, which clearly show the status, objects and ideals of the organisation and its financial position, and an sae. They should be submitted by 31 March each year. Grants are usually awarded between July and September.

**WHO TO APPLY TO** Derek Humphrey, Secretary, 3 The Swallows, Harlow, Essex CM17 0AR *Tel.* 01279 420855 *email* info@hockerillfoundation.org.uk *Website* www.hockerillfoundation.org.uk

## ■ The Sir Julian Hodge Charitable Trust

**CC NO** 234848 **ESTABLISHED** 1964

**WHERE FUNDING CAN BE GIVEN** UK.

**WHO CAN BENEFIT** Registered charities; medical institutions; educational and religious establishments.

**WHAT IS FUNDED** General charitable purposes, especially medical causes and research (particularly into cancer, polio, tuberculosis and diseases of children), the advancement of

education, religious causes and the relief of older people and individuals with disabilities.
**WHAT IS NOT FUNDED** Individuals; companies.
**TYPE OF GRANT** Generally one-off.
**RANGE OF GRANTS** £1,000–£4,000
**SAMPLE GRANTS** Young enterprise (£4,000); British Limbless Ex-servicemen's Association (£3,000); West of England MS Society (£2,500); Canine P for Independence, Dogs for Disabled and Parish Church of Caerphilly Church Council (£2,000 each); Coventry University and Fire Fighters (£1,500 each); Age Cymru, Alchemy Syndrome UK Support Group, British Polio Fellowship, Calibre Audio Library, Edinburgh Young Carers, Shine Cymru and St David's Church (£1,000 each).
**FINANCES** Year 2012/13 Income £67,079 Grants £67,000 Grants to organisations £67,000 Assets £1,368,711
**TRUSTEES** Jonathan Hodge; Derrek Jones.
**OTHER INFORMATION** At the time of writing (June 2015) this was the latest information available. Support was allocated as follows: medical (£28,000 in 20 awards); other (£26,500 in 19 awards); educational (£6,500 in three awards); religious (£6,000 in four awards).
**HOW TO APPLY** Applications can be made in writing to the correspondent. The latest accounts note the following: 'The trust invites applications for grants from charitable institutions who submit a summary of their proposals in a specific format.'
**WHO TO APPLY TO** Jonathan Hodge, Trustee, 31 Windsor Place, Cardiff CF10 3UR *Tel.* 029 2078 7674

■ **The Jane Hodge Foundation**
**CC NO** 216053     **ESTABLISHED** 1962
**WHERE FUNDING CAN BE GIVEN** UK and overseas, with a preference for Wales.
**WHO CAN BENEFIT** Registered charities or exempt organisations with charitable objectives.
**WHAT IS FUNDED** Medical care and research, especially local hospices, children's care, tuberculosis, poliomyelitis and cancer related research; education (mainly related to business and economics studies); religion; other charitable purposes.
**WHAT IS NOT FUNDED** Individuals.
**TYPE OF GRANT** One-off and up to three years; our research suggests that loans may also be available.
**RANGE OF GRANTS** Up to £139,000.
**SAMPLE GRANTS** Cardiff University (£139,000 in three grants); Royal Welsh College of Music and Drama (£80,000); George Thomas Hospice (£50,000); Tenovus (£30,000); Catholic Church In Jersey (£25,000); Jersey Hospice Care and Ty Hafen – The Children's Hospice (£10,000 each); Race Equality First (£7,000); Council for Education In World Citizenship (£6,000); Adoption UK, Plan Int UK and Shelter Cymru (£5,000 each); Diocese of Portsmouth (£4,000); Bath institute of Medical Engineering and Bedwellty Agricultural Society (£3,000 each). Other grants totalled £267,500.
**FINANCES** Year 2012/13 Income £1,097,783 Grants £569,650 Grants to organisations £569,650 Assets £31,109,459
**TRUSTEES** Derrek Jones; Ian Davies; Jonathan Hodge; Adrian Piper; Karen Hodge; Keith James; Alun Bowen.
**OTHER INFORMATION** The latest accounts note: 'The trustees will continue to encourage applications for grants from charities whose objectives are in accordance with the aims and objectives of the Foundation. Particular emphasis will be given to supporting medical research, especially in the field of cancer prevention, to funding educational posts and projects relating to business and economics and to supporting projects undertaken by religious and other local charities.' There were 220 grants awarded. Support was allocated as follows: education (£391,000); medical (£255,000); other (£126,500); religion (£97,000). At the time of writing (June 2015) this was the latest information available.
**HOW TO APPLY** Applications may be made in writing to the correspondent. The latest annual report states: 'The Trustees invite applications for grants from charitable institutions who submit a summary of their proposals in a specified format.' Appeals are considered at regular meetings of the trustees.
**WHO TO APPLY TO** Jonathan Hodge, Trustee, 31 Windsor Place, Cardiff CF10 3UR *Tel.* 029 2078 7693 *email* info@janehodgefoundation.co.uk

■ **The J. G. Hogg Charitable Trust**
**CC NO** 299042     **ESTABLISHED** 1987
**WHERE FUNDING CAN BE GIVEN** UK and overseas.
**WHO CAN BENEFIT** Registered charities.
**WHAT IS FUNDED** General charitable purposes; preference for social welfare; humanitarian causes; wild and domestic animal welfare.
**WHAT IS NOT FUNDED** Individuals.
**RANGE OF GRANTS** £100–£5,000
**SAMPLE GRANTS** Brenchley Bell Restoration Appeal (£5,000); A21 Campaign, Breakthrough Breast Cancer, Hop Skip and Jump and NCN Orphanage in Sierra Leone (£100 each).
**FINANCES** Year 2012/13 Income £398,278 Grants £5,500 Grants to organisations £5,500
**TRUSTEES** Sarah Houldsworth; Joanna Turvey.
**OTHER INFORMATION** At the time of writing (June 2015) this was the latest information available – 2013/14 accounts were overdue. Note that, although the latest grants' figure is very low, the charitable expenditure seems to exceed £100,000 every second year. During the year five awards were made.
**HOW TO APPLY** Applications may be made in writing to the correspondent. The annual report for 2012/13 states that 'to keep administration costs to a minimum, the trustees are unable to reply to unsuccessful applicants'.
**WHO TO APPLY TO** J. E. Strike, Chantrey Vellacott DFK, Russell Square House, 10 -12 Russell Square, London WC1B 5LF *Tel.* 020 7509 9000 *email* cjones@cvdfk.com

■ **The Holden Charitable Trust**
**CC NO** 264185     **ESTABLISHED** 1972
**WHERE FUNDING CAN BE GIVEN** UK, with a preference for the Manchester area.
**WHO CAN BENEFIT** Orthodox Jewish charities; organisations benefitting Jewish people, including children, young adults and students.
**WHAT IS FUNDED** Jewish causes with some emphasis on the advancement of education and Jewish faith.
**SAMPLE GRANTS** Previous beneficiaries have included: Broom Foundation (£59,000); Ohel Bnei Yaakob (£50,000); Ohr Yerushalayim Synagogue (£33,000); Friends of Beis Eliyahu Trust (£24,000); the FED (£7,500); King David's School (£5,000).

FINANCES Year 2013/14 Income £479,066 Grants £382,535 Grants to organisations £382,535 Assets £909,302
TRUSTEES David Lopian; Marian Lopian; Michael Lopian.
OTHER INFORMATION A list of beneficiaries was not included in the latest accounts but the trust stated that grants were made 'to a number of institutions which carry out activities such as providing Orthodox Jewish education or other activities which advance Jewish religion in accordance with the Orthodox Jewish faith'.
HOW TO APPLY Applications may be made in writing to the correspondent.
WHO TO APPLY TO The Trustees, c/o Lopian Gross Barnett and Co., 6th Floor, Cardinal House, 20 St Mary Parsonage, Manchester M3 2LG Tel. 0161 832 8721 email david.lopian@lopiangb.co.uk

## ■ The Hollands-Warren Fund

CC NO 279747    ESTABLISHED 1977
WHERE FUNDING CAN BE GIVEN Maidstone, Kent.
WHO CAN BENEFIT Individuals and organisations providing medical and nursing care.
WHAT IS FUNDED Temporary medical and nursing services and/or domestic help for residents.
RANGE OF GRANTS Up to £43,000.
FINANCES Year 2013/14 Income £67,687 Grants £105,550 Grants to organisations £105,550 Assets £2,577,409
TRUSTEES Anthony Palmer; Kim Harrington; Daniel Bell.
OTHER INFORMATION There were three grants made.
HOW TO APPLY Applications can be made in writing to the correspondent.
WHO TO APPLY TO Kim Harrington, Trustee, c/o Brachers Solicitors, Somerfield House, 57–59 London Road, Maidstone, Kent ME16 8JH Tel. 01622 690691 email kimharrington@brachers.co.uk

## ■ The Hollick Family Charitable Trust

CC NO 1060228    ESTABLISHED 1997
WHERE FUNDING CAN BE GIVEN UK and overseas.
WHO CAN BENEFIT Registered charities.
WHAT IS FUNDED A wide range of general charitable purposes.
TYPE OF GRANT One-off and recurrent.
RANGE OF GRANTS Up to £15,000.
FINANCES Year 2013/14 Income £658,127 Grants £128,456 Grants to organisations £128,456 Assets £2,841,028
TRUSTEES Caroline Kemp; Georgina Hollick; David Beech; Abigail Benoliel; Sue Hollick; Clive Hollick; Jane Kemp.
OTHER INFORMATION There were 42 awards made. UK grants under £1,000 totalled £5,900.
HOW TO APPLY Applications can be made in writing to the correspondent. The trustees meet at least twice a year.
WHO TO APPLY TO David Beech, Trustee, c/o Peter Bryan and Co, Foxglove House, 166 Piccadilly, London W1J 9EF Tel. 020 7493 4932 email peterbryanco@btinternet.com

## ■ The Holliday Foundation

CC NO 1089931    ESTABLISHED 2002
WHERE FUNDING CAN BE GIVEN Mainly UK.
WHO CAN BENEFIT Organisations and individuals.
WHAT IS FUNDED General charitable purposes, with particular interest in children and young people and in assisting individuals to better themselves.
RANGE OF GRANTS £1,000–£10,000
SAMPLE GRANTS Previous beneficiaries have included: National Centre for Young People with Epilepsy and Training for Life (£10,000 each); Charsfield Recreation Ground and Help the Hospices (£5,000 each); Sparkes Homes Sri Lanka (£2,500); The East Anglian Academy (£1,200); and The Newbury Spring Festival (£1,000).
FINANCES Year 2013/14 Income £16,051 Grants £60,320 Grants to organisations £60,320
TRUSTEES David William; James Garrett; James Cave; Antony Wilson; Jane Garrett; Huw Llewellyn.
OTHER INFORMATION Our research suggests that the trustees review requests for grants and may request further information or visit applicants before deciding whether to make a payment. The trustees will follow up the use of grants where relevant.
HOW TO APPLY Applications can be made in writing to the correspondent. The trustees normally meet at least four times a year.
WHO TO APPLY TO Linda Wasfi, Correspondent, Salisbury Partners LLP, 25 Hill Street, London W1J 5LW Tel. 020 7016 6700 Fax 020 7016 6710 email linda.wasfi@salisburypartners.co.uk

## ■ The Dorothy Holmes Charitable Trust

CC NO 237213    ESTABLISHED 1964
WHERE FUNDING CAN BE GIVEN UK, with a preference for Dorset.
WHO CAN BENEFIT UK-registered charities benefitting: young adults and older people; people who are sick; clergy; ex-service and service people; legal professionals; unemployed people; volunteers; parents and children; one-parent families; widows and widowers; at risk groups; carers; and people with disabilities.
WHAT IS FUNDED Charities working in the fields of advice and information on housing; emergency and short-term housing; residential facilities; respite and sheltered accommodation; information technology and computers; civil society development; support of voluntary and community organisations; health professional bodies; and religion will be considered. Support is also given to healthcare; hospices and hospitals; cancer research; church buildings; heritage; secondary schools and special schools; counselling on social issues; and income support and maintenance.
WHAT IS NOT FUNDED Only applications from registered charities will be considered.
TYPE OF GRANT Generally one-off grants for unrestricted purposes.
RANGE OF GRANTS Normally up to £6,000.
SAMPLE GRANTS Previous beneficiaries have included: Wallingford School (£6,000); Children in Touch, Crisis and Christmas and RNLI (£5,000 each); Hyman Cen Foundation (£4,000); Army Benevolent Fund (£3,000); Action on Elder Abuse and Clic Sargent Cancer Fund (£2,000 each); National Autistic Society and Raleigh International (£1,000 each); and

Royal Free Hospital Retirement Fellowship (£300).

FINANCES Year 2013/14 Income £17,902 Grants £65,000 Grants to organisations £65,000

TRUSTEES Dr Susan Roberts; Margaret Cody; James Roberts.

HOW TO APPLY Applications can be made in writing to the correspondent. Our research suggests that they should be submitted, preferably, in January – March period each year.

WHO TO APPLY TO Michael Kennedy, Correspondent, Smallfield Cody and Co, 5 Harley Place, Harley Street, London W1G 8QD *Tel.* 020 7631 4574 *email* meac@smallfieldcody.co.uk

## ■ The Holst Foundation

CC NO 283668    ESTABLISHED 1981

WHERE FUNDING CAN BE GIVEN Worldwide, but mainly UK.

WHO CAN BENEFIT Mainly musical organisations; individuals; educational establishments; festivals.

WHAT IS FUNDED The promotion of new music as well as public appreciation of the musical works of Gustav and Imogen Holst and to encourage the study and practice of music. The foundation has been awarding funds almost exclusively for the performance of music by living composers. Note that with the expiry of the majority of the copyrights in Holst's music at the end of 2004 the foundation had adopted a policy of distributing funds from capital as well as income and had aimed to maintain its previous grants policy for at least ten years (i.e. until 2014). It should be anticipated that charitable giving might be modest and limited to established beneficiaries. The annual report for 2013/14 states: 'Although the level of other grants will continue to be reduced in future, substantial one-off support was given this year to a number of performing groups with the aim of helping their long term future. This policy will be maintained as long as it is feasible, and the Grants Advisory Committee will keep in mind the most expeditious way to employ the declining funds available to the Foundation.'

WHAT IS NOT FUNDED The recordings or works of Holst that are already well supported; capital projects; individuals for educational purposes, research, travel, purchase of instruments, equipment or publications; the commissioning of new works, although help is sometimes available for the copying and rehearsal costs of works receiving first performances or festivals (other than Aldeburgh) or orchestras or other large organisations.

TYPE OF GRANT Project funding; core and start-up costs; one-off.

RANGE OF GRANTS Usually up to £30,000.

SAMPLE GRANTS NMC Recordings (£120,000); Royal Philharmonic Society (£4,000); Aldeburgh Music and Spitalfields Festival (£2,500 each); London Festival of Contemporary Church Music (£1,500); Birmingham Conservatoire (£1,300); Britten Sinfonia, Huddersfield Contemporary Music Festival and Music Theatre Wales (£1,000 each). Grants below £1,000 totalled 12,900.

FINANCES Year 2013/14 Income £268,980 Grants £152,120 Grants to organisations £152,120 Assets £1,017,124

TRUSTEES Andrew Clements; Prof. Arnold Whittall; Peter Carter; Bayan Northcott; Noel Periton; Julian Anderson.

OTHER INFORMATION During the year there were 37 awards made.

HOW TO APPLY The foundation's website states the following: 'The Foundation was from its inception funded by royalties from the estate of Gustav Holst; these largely ceased when the major copyrights expired at the end of 2004. Consequently most grant-giving activities came to an end in 2014, and applications are no longer accepted. The annual grant to NMC Recordings, which was created under the auspices of the Foundation in 1988, has also been discontinued. The Foundation hopes to be able to continue to fund selected projects on a limited basis, but this will be at the discretion of the Music Committee and not subject to application.' The Foundation continues to administer the estates of both Gustav and Imogen Holst, and any enquiries about its past and present activities may be sent to the correspondent.

WHO TO APPLY TO The Grants Administrator, 43 Alderbrook Road, London SW12 8AD *Tel.* 020 8673 4215 (messages only) *email* holst@dpmail.co.uk *Website* www.holstfoundation.org

## ■ P. H. Holt Foundation

CC NO 1113708    ESTABLISHED 1955

WHERE FUNDING CAN BE GIVEN UK, principally Merseyside.

WHO CAN BENEFIT Wherever possible, grants are paid to or through registered charities; preference for smaller grass roots organisations that find it difficult to attract funds.

WHAT IS FUNDED General charitable purposes; some preference for original work or work of special excellence. Your work should satisfy at least one of the following criteria: 'create opportunities for people to contribute to their local communities; break down barriers preventing people taking control of their lives; widen access to education; increase engagement in the arts for disadvantaged and isolated groups; encourages care of the natural and built environment'.

WHAT IS NOT FUNDED CICs; social enterprise; local branches of national charities; charities operating outside Merseyside; every day running costs and core salaries; recurrent funding; general fundraising appeals; statutory or retrospective funding; academic or medical research; sponsorship, including sports events; holidays, holiday centres or outings and overseas travel; religious and political causes; national charities; vehicles and minibuses.

TYPE OF GRANT Generally one-off or part of a recurrent relationship.

RANGE OF GRANTS Up to £10,000; mostly under £5,000.

SAMPLE GRANTS Grants were made in the following categories: education and social welfare (about £44,500 each); community development and participation (£22,500); arts (£10,500); heritage (£6,800). A full list of grants was not included in the latest account; however, the website gives some examples of grant recipients. **Beneficiaries have included**: Emmaus Merseyside (£15,000); Imagine If Trust (£14,000); Old Roan Baptist Church (£10,000); Apex Trust (£9,000); Rampworx (£6,500); Hearing Dogs for Deaf People and Mencap (£5,000 each); Hope Street Ltd (£4,300); Center 43 (£4,200); Rotters Community Composting (£3,000); Wirral Community Narrowboat Trust (£2,000); Church

Housing Trust (£1,500); Stick'n'Steps (£1,200); 20 Stories High and Involve Northwest (£1,000 each); Tall Ships Youth Trust (£200).

**FINANCES** Year 2013/14 Income £280,582 Grants £128,345 Grants to organisations £128,345 Assets £15,549,640

**TRUSTEES** Martin Cooke; Ian Matthews; Nikki Eastwood; Ken Ravenscroft; Neil Kemsley; Paige Earlam; Anthony Hannay; Elspeth Christie.

**OTHER INFORMATION** During the year a total of 43 organisations were supported. The foundation has a linked charity – The Holt Education Trust Fund (Charity Commission no. 113708–2) – through which individuals are supported (76 students awarded over £20,000 in 2013/14).

**HOW TO APPLY** Application forms can be accessed on the foundation's website and should be returned by email together with a copy of your latest annual report and accounts. The website notes: 'If you wish to discuss your proposal with us before submitting, you are welcome to contact the office for an initial conversation.' The trustees meet four times a year and the deadlines are the first of February, May, August and November. Organisations outside Merseyside are only supported occasionally, the annual report for 2013/14 states that 'but this programme is s response to specific circumstances, and is not open to applications'. Decisions are made within three to four months following the deadline. You can re-apply again after 12 months following the decision.

**WHO TO APPLY TO** Anne Edwards, Trust Administrator, 151 Dale Street, Liverpool L2 2AH Tel. 0151 237 2663 email administrator@phholtfoundation.org.uk Website www.phholtfoundation.org.uk

## ■ The Edward Holt Trust

**CC NO** 224741      **ESTABLISHED** 1955
**WHERE FUNDING CAN BE GIVEN** Mainly Greater Manchester.
**WHO CAN BENEFIT** Registered charities, hospitals.
**WHAT IS FUNDED** Primarily the maintenance of a block of ten flats in Didsbury, Manchester, for retired people. Support to ill health causes, older people and those who are disadvantaged. Preference to charities which the trustees have special interest in, knowledge of or association with, including cancer, neurological and ageing research.
**TYPE OF GRANT** Project funding, core costs, salaries, research. Funding is available for up to three years.
**SAMPLE GRANTS** Christie Hospital (£90,000); Didsbury Good Neighbours (£27,500); and Age Concern (£10,000).
**FINANCES** Year 2013/14 Income £209,386 Grants £127,500 Grants to organisations £127,500 Assets £7,910,233
**TRUSTEES** David Tully; Angela Roden; Richard Kershaw; Mike Fry; Anne Williams; Michael Prior.
**HOW TO APPLY** Applications should be made in writing to the correspondent. Note that in the past the trust has stated that unsolicited appeals are not accepted.
**WHO TO APPLY TO** Bryan Peak, Secretary, 22 Ashworth Park, Knutsford, Cheshire WA16 9DE Tel. 01565 651086 email edwardholt@btinternet.com Website www.edwardholttrust.btck.co.uk

## ■ The Holywood Trust

**SC NO** SC009942      **ESTABLISHED** 1981
**WHERE FUNDING CAN BE GIVEN** Dumfries and Galloway.
**WHO CAN BENEFIT** Organisations working with and providing opportunities for young people, especially those experiencing mental, physical or social disadvantage; individuals directly. Organisations should be appropriately constituted and demonstrate a commitment to equal opportunities.
**WHAT IS FUNDED** Activities and opportunities for young people (primarily aged 15–25); youth and sporting clubs; cultural activities; provision of equipment; group development activities; residential trips; programmes for activities for young people; cultural venues or arts programmes. Support is given to individual applicants, including vulnerable children under the age of 15, especially socially or physically disadvantaged or those who have an exceptional talent.
**TYPE OF GRANT** One-off; capital and core costs; recurring funding (usually limited to three years); salaries; project costs.
**RANGE OF GRANTS** £10–£50,000
**SAMPLE GRANTS** Recent beneficiaries have included: Aberlour Child Care Trust; Alcohol and Drugs Support South West Scotland; Annan Youth Cycling Club; Centre Stage Youth Theatre; Cruse Bereavement Care Scotland; Dumfries and Galloway Arts Festival; Dumfries and Galloway Council; Dumfries and Galloway Multicultural Association; Dumfries and Galloway Youthbank; Finding Albert; Independent Living Support; Lochthorn Youth Centre; Lockerbie Eight Ball Pool Club; Outside the Box; Royal Botanic Garden Edinburgh at Logan; Scottish Ballet; Spring Fling Open Studios; Stewartry Community Sports Club; The Bunbary Banter Theatre Group; The Prince's Trust Scotland; Victim Support; Wigtown Festival Company; Xcel Project; Youth Alive Dumfries and Galloway.
**FINANCES** Year 2013/14 Income £2,128,656 Grants £1,490,917 Grants to organisations £1,490,917
**TRUSTEES** Valerie McElroy; Charles Jencks; Clara Weatherall; Ben Weatherall; John Jencks.
**OTHER INFORMATION** In 2013/14 the trust had a total expenditure of £1.85 million, out of which 'grants and donations' totalled nearly £1.5 million. According to the website, 'the trust is particularly interested in helping to fill gaps in provision, and to support innovative ideas'.
**HOW TO APPLY** Application forms are available from the charity's website or the correspondent, together with full criteria and guidelines. Organisations may submit appeals electronically but will have to provide hard signed copies of supporting documents. The trustees meet every three months (exact dates are published on the website), but appeals for £2,5000 or less can be made at any time and are considered at monthly meetings. Such applications may take up to four or six weeks to proceed.
**WHO TO APPLY TO** Richard Lye, Trust Administrator, Hestan House, Crichton Business Park, Bankend Road, Dumfries DG1 4TA Tel. 01387 269176 Fax 01387 269175 email funds@holywood-trust.org.uk Website www.holywood-trust.org.uk

# Homelands

## ■ The Homelands Charitable Trust

**CC NO** 214322  **ESTABLISHED** 1962
**WHERE FUNDING CAN BE GIVEN** UK.
**WHO CAN BENEFIT** Registered charities benefitting children, particularly people in risk groups or those who are victims of abuse or domestic violence. Support may also be given to clergy, medical professionals and medical research work.
**WHAT IS FUNDED** General charitable purposes; General Conference of the New Church; medical research; care and protection of children; hospices.
**RANGE OF GRANTS** £1,000–£5,000
**SAMPLE GRANTS** Previous beneficiaries have included: General Conference of the New Church (£68,000); Broadfield Memorial Fund (£15,000); New Church College (£11,000); Bournemouth Society (£10,000); Jubilee Sailing Trust, Manic Depression Fellowship and National Children's Homes (£2,400 each); and the Attic Charity – Youth Project, Bikeability, Eyeless Trust and Pestalozzi (£1,600 each).
**FINANCES** Year 2013/14 Income £296,087 Grants £285,250 Grants to organisations £285,250 Assets £8,075,973
**TRUSTEES** Nigel Armstrong; Revd Clifford Curry; Robert Curry.
**OTHER INFORMATION** There was no list of beneficiary organisations available. The annual report for 2013/14 states that support will remain biased towards: General Conference of the New Church; medical research; care and protection of children; and hospices, including those for children.
**HOW TO APPLY** Applications can be made in writing to the correspondent.
**WHO TO APPLY TO** Nigel Armstrong, Trustee, c/o Alliotts, 4th Floor, Imperial House, 15 Kingsway, London WC2B 6UN *Tel.* 020 7240 9971

## ■ The Homestead Charitable Trust

**CC NO** 293979  **ESTABLISHED** 1986
**WHERE FUNDING CAN BE GIVEN** UK.
**WHO CAN BENEFIT** Individuals and organisations.
**WHAT IS FUNDED** General charitable purposes, including medical, health, social welfare, animal welfare, environment, Christianity and the arts.
**TYPE OF GRANT** One-off.
**RANGE OF GRANTS** £100–£10,000
**SAMPLE GRANTS** British Heart Foundation and Joseph Banks Project (£10,000 each); County History Trust, Mildmay Hospice and Meningitis Research (£5,000 each); Epilepsy Society and Leonard Cheshire Disability Fund (£2,000 each); Breast Cancer Care, Butterfly Hospital and RSPB (£1,000 each); Carmelite Mission (£500); and WaterAid (£100).
**FINANCES** Year 2013/14 Income £87,518 Grants £88,628 Grants to organisations £88,128 Assets £5,250,031
**TRUSTEE** Nina Bracewell-Smith.
**OTHER INFORMATION** There were 33 awards made. One individual received a grant totalling £500.
**HOW TO APPLY** Applications can be made in writing to the correspondent.
**WHO TO APPLY TO** Nina Bracewell-Smith, Trustee, Flat 7, Clarence Gate Gardens, Glentworth Street, London NW1 6AY

## ■ The Mary Homfray Charitable Trust

**CC NO** 273564  **ESTABLISHED** 1977
**WHERE FUNDING CAN BE GIVEN** Mainly Wales.
**WHO CAN BENEFIT** Registered charities.
**WHAT IS FUNDED** General charitable purposes.
**WHAT IS NOT FUNDED** Charities outside Wales are not assisted.
**TYPE OF GRANT** One-off and recurrent.
**RANGE OF GRANTS** Up to £5,000.
**FINANCES** Year 2013/14 Income £544,236 Grants £46,000 Grants to organisations £46,000 Assets £2,142,635
**TRUSTEES** Matthew Homfray; Mary Homfray; Josephine Homfray.
**OTHER INFORMATION** Grants were made to 17 organisations.
**HOW TO APPLY** Apply in writing to the correspondent. Applications should be made towards the end of the year, for consideration at the trustees' annual meeting in February or March each year.
**WHO TO APPLY TO** Josephine Homfray, Trustee, c/o Deloitte PCS Ltd, 5 Callaghan Square, Cardiff CF10 5BT *Tel.* 029 2046 0000 *Fax* 029 2026 4444 *email* jdeacy@deloitte.co.uk

## ■ Sir Harold Hood's Charitable Trust

**CC NO** 225870  **ESTABLISHED** 1962
**WHERE FUNDING CAN BE GIVEN** Worldwide.
**WHO CAN BENEFIT** Roman Catholic registered charities and churches.
**WHAT IS FUNDED** Charities dealing with the advancement of the Roman Catholic faith through religious buildings, religious umbrella bodies and other Roman Catholic organisations. A wide range of causes can be assisted within this framework.
**WHAT IS NOT FUNDED** Individuals.
**TYPE OF GRANT** One-off core and capital costs; project expenditure; salaries; unrestricted funding.
**RANGE OF GRANTS** £500–£40,000
**SAMPLE GRANTS** Craig Lodge Trust (£40,000); St Richards Reynolds Catholic Church (£25,000); Royal Navy RC Chaplaincy Trust – Portsmouth (£17,000); Philippines Emergency (£16,000); Westminster Cathedral (£15,000); Venerable English College – Rome (£12,000); Maryvale Institute – Birmingham (£10,000); Apostleship of the Sea (£6,000); Our Lady of Lourdes (£4,000); Centre for Research and Development in Catholic Education (£3,000); Loyola Jesuit (£2,000); Young Alive Zimbabwe (£1,500); St Joseph's Scout Group (£1,000); Network for a Better World (£500
**FINANCES** Year 2013/14 Income £913,952 Grants £692,468 Grants to organisations £692,468 Assets £33,322,803
**TRUSTEES** Dom Hood; Lord Nicholas True; Lady True; Margaret Hood; Christian Elwes.
**OTHER INFORMATION** In 2013/14 a total of 99 awards were given.
**HOW TO APPLY** Applications may be made in writing to the correspondent. The trustees meet once a year to consider applications, usually in November.
**WHO TO APPLY TO** Margaret Hood, Trustee, Haysmacintyre, 26 Red Lion Square WC1R 4AG *email* nlandsman@haysmacintyre.com

## ■ The Hoover Foundation

**CC NO** 200274  **ESTABLISHED** 1961

**WHERE FUNDING CAN BE GIVEN** UK, but with a special interest in South Wales, Glasgow and Bolton.

**WHO CAN BENEFIT** UK-registered charities, universities and small local charities working in South Wales, Glasgow and Bolton. There is a preference for organisations benefitting young adults and students.

**WHAT IS FUNDED** Wide range of charities including education (mainly supported through grants to universities, normally for research in the engineering subjects), welfare, medical research and small local charities.

**WHAT IS NOT FUNDED** The trustees do not make grants to individuals, including students.

**RANGE OF GRANTS** Up to £10,000.

**SAMPLE GRANTS** Beating Blood Disorders, The Cure Parkinson's Trust and Genesis Breast Cancer Prevention (£30,000 each); Derian House Children's Hospice and Welsh Young Consumer (£3,000 each); and Lord Mayor's Charity Appeal Liverpool (£1,000).

**FINANCES** Year 2013/14  Income £82,716  Grants £138,426  Grants to organisations £138,426  Assets £3,133,855

**TRUSTEES** David Lunt; Alberto Bertali; Robert Mudie; Matthew Given.

**OTHER INFORMATION** The Hoover Foundation is the corporate charity of Hoover Limited.

**HOW TO APPLY** Apply in writing to the correspondent.

**WHO TO APPLY TO** Susan Whetter, Correspondent, Hoover Candy Group, Pentrebach, Merthyr Tydfil, Mid Glamorgan CF48 4TU  Tel. 01685 725530  email susan.whetter@hoovercandy.com

## ■ Hope for Youth (NI)

**CC NO** 264843  **ESTABLISHED** 1972

**WHERE FUNDING CAN BE GIVEN** Northern Ireland.

**WHO CAN BENEFIT** Cross-community projects; integrated schools; community playgroups; play buses; youth clubs; women's groups; holiday schemes; and other projects benefitting children and young adults.

**WHAT IS FUNDED** Projects that give disadvantaged 11- to 18-year-olds in Northern Ireland the opportunity to work together on practical projects that foster teamwork, creativity and personal development, especially within the arts or in the great outdoors. Areas of education, the arts, dance, music, media, sport and recreation are favoured.

**WHAT IS NOT FUNDED** The following are not supported: individuals; salaries (project coordinator's fees may be covered); large capital expenditure and building costs; national organisations; publication of research (unless the output is a result of young people's collaborative work); projects outside the island of Ireland; working solely for the welfare of people with physically or mental disabilities, or drug or alcohol related projects; and playgroups or mother and toddler groups.

**TYPE OF GRANT** One-off or recurrent awards given once a year.

**RANGE OF GRANTS** £5,000–£10,000

**SAMPLE GRANTS** Previous beneficiaries have included: Music Theatre for Youth, Youth Initiatives, Appletree Childcare, Careers 'N' Kids, Drumaness Cross Community Playgroup, Old Library Trust, Significance Women's Initiative, St Vincent de Paul, The Diamond Centre.

**FINANCES** Year 2013  Income £136,332  Grants £2,620  Grants to organisations £2,620  Assets £136,947

**TRUSTEES** Dr Miriam McCarthy; Viscount Gough; Judy Lindsay; Julia Corkey; John Montgomery; John Andrews; Daphne Montgomery; Viscount John Crichton; Jonathan Shillington; Emma McCausland; Anthony Jackson; Noel Lamb; Gareth Quinn; Vanne Campbell.

**HOW TO APPLY** Applications are invited on the charity's website where forms and guidelines are available. Applicants are asked to provide a summary of their proposed activities, a profile of their users and financial information. The trustees meet four or five times a year and receive many more applications than can be accepted.

**WHO TO APPLY TO** Karen Hughes, Correspondent, c/o Cherton Enterprise Ltd, Unit 8, Belmont Business Park, 232–240 Belmont Road, Belfast BT4 2AW  Tel. 028 9076 9966  email karen.hughes@cherton.co.uk  Website www.hopeforyouthni.com

## ■ The Hope Trust

**SC NO** SC000987  **ESTABLISHED** 1912

**WHERE FUNDING CAN BE GIVEN** Worldwide, with a preference for Scotland.

**WHO CAN BENEFIT** Christian individuals and organisations; Church of England; evangelists; Methodists; Quakers; Unitarians; people with a substance addiction or organisations helping such individuals.

**WHAT IS FUNDED** The provision of education and the distribution of literature to combat the misuse and effects of drink and drugs and to promote the principles of Reformed Churches; the advancement of the Christian religion, Anglican bodies, Free Church, rehabilitation centres and health education.

**WHAT IS NOT FUNDED** Grants are not made to gap year students, scholarship schemes or the refurbishment of property. Awards to individuals are not made with the exception of PhD students of theology studying at Scottish universities.

**TYPE OF GRANT** One-off grants, largely for unrestricted purposes.

**RANGE OF GRANTS** £1,000–£5,000

**SAMPLE GRANTS** Previous beneficiaries have included: Church of Scotland Priority Areas Fund; Feed the Minds; National Bible Society for Scotland; Waldensian Mission Aid; and World Alliance of Reformed Churches.

**FINANCES** Year 2013  Income £249,900  Grants £250,000  Grants to organisations £250,000

**OTHER INFORMATION** The trust awards about 25 grants each year.

**HOW TO APPLY** Applications can be made in writing to the correspondent. Our research indicates that the trustees normally meet to consider applications in June and December; therefore applications should be submitted by mid-May or mid-November each year. Informal contact is welcomed by phone.

**WHO TO APPLY TO** The Secretary, Drummond Miller LLP, Glenorchy House, 20 Union Street, Edinburgh EH1 3LR  Tel. 0131 226 5151  Fax 0131 225 2608  email reception@drummond-miller.co.uk

## ■ Hopmarket Charity

**CC NO** 244569  **ESTABLISHED** 1964
**WHERE FUNDING CAN BE GIVEN** The city of Worcester.
**WHO CAN BENEFIT** Organisations helping people in need.
**WHAT IS FUNDED** Individuals in need by reason of age, social or financial circumstances.
**WHAT IS NOT FUNDED** Grants are not made to, or on behalf of, individuals.
**RANGE OF GRANTS** £3,000–£15,000
**FINANCES** Year 2013/14 Income £176,245 Grants £90,030 Grants to organisations £90,030 Assets £1,058,584
**TRUSTEES** Dr D. A. Tibbutt; Joy Squires; Josephine Hodges; Robert Rowden; Gareth Jones; Allah Ditta; Roger Berry; Geoffery Williams; Dr Adrian Gregson; Derek Prodger; Liz Smith; Aubrey Tarbuck; Lucy Hodgson; Simon Geraghty; Simon Cronin; Roger Knight; Stephen Hodgson; Paul Denham; Andy Roberts; Patricia Agar; Alan Amos; Douglas Wilkinson; Marc Bayliss; Michael Whitehouse; Jabba Riaz; David Wilkinson; Ken Carpenter; Matthew Lamb; Chris Mitchell; George Squires; Christine Cawthorne; Richard Boorn; Lynn Denham; Neil Laurenson; Richard Udall.
**OTHER INFORMATION** There were 15 grants made.
**HOW TO APPLY** Applications should be made to the Treasurer on a standard application form, available from the correspondent. Applicants should provide details of the project to be assisted as well as financial information about their organisation. Our research suggests that submissions should be made by the beginning of January or August for consideration in March or September respectively.
**WHO TO APPLY TO** Claire Chaplin, Correspondent, c/o Worcester City Council, Orchard House, Farrier Street, Worchester WR1 3BB *Tel.* 01905 722005 *email* claire.chaplin@worcester.gov.uk

## ■ The Horizon Foundation

**CC NO** 1118455  **ESTABLISHED** 2007
**WHERE FUNDING CAN BE GIVEN** Worldwide.
**WHO CAN BENEFIT** Registered charities; educational establishments.
**WHAT IS FUNDED** General charitable purposes; education; women; children and young people.
**TYPE OF GRANT** One-off or recurrent.
**SAMPLE GRANTS** UWC Atlantic College (£98,000); Eton College (£25,000); Rugby School (£23,000); University of London (£15,300); The Hotchkiss School (£12,000); Medical Aid for Palestinians (£10,000); Maastricht University (£7,500); Oakford Estates (£2,000).
**FINANCES** Year 2013/14 Income £510,775 Grants £285,296 Grants to organisations £285,296 Assets £308,517
**TRUSTEES** Kirkland Smulders; Patrick Smulders; Coutts & Co.
**OTHER INFORMATION** There were 12 awards made in 2013/14.
**HOW TO APPLY** Applications should be made in writing to the correspondent and are considered regularly.
**WHO TO APPLY TO** The Trustees, c/o Coutts & Co, 440 The Strand, London WC2R 0QS *Tel.* 020 7663 6814 or 020 7663 6825 *email* couttscharities@coutts.com

## ■ The Antony Hornby Charitable Trust

**CC NO** 263285  **ESTABLISHED** 1971
**WHERE FUNDING CAN BE GIVEN** Unrestricted with a preference for London and the Home Counties.
**WHO CAN BENEFIT** Registered charities.
**WHAT IS FUNDED** General charitable purposes, in particular supporting charities involved in medicine, education, social welfare and the arts.
**WHAT IS NOT FUNDED** Individuals and non-registered charities.
**RANGE OF GRANTS** £100–£1,500
**SAMPLE GRANTS** Reed's School (£5,000); Whizz-Kidz (£2,000); Museum of London and Pro-Action Hertfordshire (£1,500); Alzheimer's Disease Society, Cystic Fibrosis Research Trust, Isabel Hospice, National Art Collection – The Art Fund, The Stroke Association and Tring Park School for Performing Arts (£1,000 each); British Heart Foundation and Wessex Chalk Stream and Rivers Trust (£750 each); Greenhouse Schools Project, Help for Heroes and Youth Talk (£500 each).
**FINANCES** Year 2013/14 Income £46,189 Grants £41,115 Grants to organisations £41,115 Assets £1,425,203
**TRUSTEES** Marie Antoinette Hall; Mark Antony Loveday; Michael Wentworth-Stanley; Jane Wentworth-Stanley.
**OTHER INFORMATION** Grants were awarded to 42 organisations in 2013/14. The grant total includes £23,000 that was distributed via Charities Aid Foundation.
**HOW TO APPLY** The trust has previously stated that it is fully committed and does not usually add new names to its list of beneficiaries unless it is a charity known to the trustees, or a very special appeal.
**WHO TO APPLY TO** Paul Langdon, Saffrey Champness, Lion House, 72–75 Red Lion Street, London WC1R 4GB *Tel.* 020 7841 4000

## ■ The Horne Foundation

**CC NO** 283751  **ESTABLISHED** 1981
**WHERE FUNDING CAN BE GIVEN** UK, mainly Northamptonshire and Oxfordshire.
**WHO CAN BENEFIT** Local organisations benefitting young adults, children and older people, especially those disadvantaged by poverty; occasionally national appeals; bursaries for individual students.
**WHAT IS FUNDED** Predominantly large grants towards major educational projects that involve new buildings and regular smaller donations to local projects in the Northampton and Oxfordshire area and student bursaries for higher education through Northampton schools.
**WHAT IS NOT FUNDED** The foundation prefers organisations without religious affiliation.
**TYPE OF GRANT** Capital and project grants; student bursaries.
**RANGE OF GRANTS** £1,000–£10,000
**SAMPLE GRANTS** Crisis UK Christmas and Northamptonshire Association of Youth Clubs Octopus Project (£10,000 each); Daventry Contact (£1,200).
**FINANCES** Year 2013/14 Income £185,808 Grants £202,200 Grants to organisations £21,200 Assets £7,192,643
**TRUSTEES** Julie Davenport; Ros Harwood; Tina Horne.
**OTHER INFORMATION** In 2013/14 grants were given to one national appeal, two local organisations and 91 individual students (grants given to

students were in the form of bursaries for higher education through Northampton schools).
**HOW TO APPLY** Applications can be made in writing to the correspondent at any time.
**WHO TO APPLY TO** R. Harwood, Secretary, PO Box 6165, Newbury RG14 9FY *email* hornefoundation@googlemail.com

■ **The Thomas J. Horne Memorial Trust**

**CC NO** 1010625 **ESTABLISHED** 1992
**WHERE FUNDING CAN BE GIVEN** UK and overseas, especially financially developing countries.
**WHO CAN BENEFIT** Charities; hospices; charitable projects.
**WHAT IS FUNDED** The vast majority of support is given to hospices, particularly children's hospices, and related charities. Organisations helping homeless people, individuals with disabilities and aiding self-help groups in financially developing countries are also assisted.
**RANGE OF GRANTS** £1,000–£25,000
**SAMPLE GRANTS** DEC Philippines Typhoon Appeal (£25,000); World Medical Fund (£20,000); Demelza House Children's Hospice and St Andrew's Hospice – Grimsby (£10,000 each); Pepper Foundation – Berkhamsted (£7,500); St Nicholas Hospice – Bury St Edmunds (£6,000); Excellent Development, I Can, St Giles Trust and Woodlands Hospice – Liverpool (£5,000 each); Amber Trust and Kent MS Therapy Centre (£2,500 each); Winfield Trust – Tunbridge Wells (£1,000).
**FINANCES** *Year* 2013/14 *Income* £528,543 *Grants* £677,935 *Grants to organisations* £677,935 *Assets* £6,709,677
**TRUSTEES** Jeff Horne; Jon Horne; Emma Horne.
**OTHER INFORMATION** Grants were made to 118 organisations.
**HOW TO APPLY** The correspondent has confirmed that unsolicited requests are still not accepted. To save your and the trustees time the trust asks not to send unsolicited requests – 'We only slightly amend our list of grantees each year, and even with that request we still receive very many unsolicited applications.'
**WHO TO APPLY TO** Jeff Horne, Trustee, Kingsdown, Warmlake Road, Chart Sutton, Maidstone, Kent ME17 3RP *Tel.* 01622 842638 *email* cc@horne-trust.org.uk

■ **The Worshipful Company of Horners' Charitable Trusts**

**CC NO** 292204 **ESTABLISHED** 1985
**WHERE FUNDING CAN BE GIVEN** Mainly in London.
**WHO CAN BENEFIT** Registered charities, educational establishments and individuals.
**WHAT IS FUNDED** General charitable purposes; education; the provision of scholarships and bursaries; and health and disability causes.
**TYPE OF GRANT** One-off and recurrent.
**RANGE OF GRANTS** Generally £2,000–£4,000.
**SAMPLE GRANTS** Salters Horners Advanced Physics (£45,000); Behcets Syndrome (£19,000); Polymer Study Tours (£10,000); London Centre for Cerebral Palsy and West London Day Centre (£5,000 each); Whizz-Kidz (£2,500); Guildhall School Trust (£2,000); Merlin Syria Appeal (£1,300); London Metropolitan Exhibition, Macmillan Nurses and Royal College of Art (£1,000 each).
**FINANCES** *Year* 2013 *Income* £136,886 *Grants* £149,308 *Grants to organisations* £149,308 *Assets* £2,553,832
**TRUSTEES** Newton Grant; Colin Richards; Keith Pinker; Jack Bunyer; Dr Brian Ridgewell; Anthony Layard; Martin Muirhead; Dr David Giachardi; Alison Gill.
**HOW TO APPLY** Applications and enquiries should be addressed to the correspondent, specifying what the funding is needed for.
**WHO TO APPLY TO** Jonathan Mead, Clerk, c/o The Worshipful Company of Horners, 12 Coltsfoot Close, Ixworth, Suffolk IP31 2NJ *email* clerk@horners.org.uk *Website* www.horners.org.uk

■ **The Hornsey Parochial Charities**

**CC NO** 229410 **ESTABLISHED** 1890
**WHERE FUNDING CAN BE GIVEN** Ancient parish of Hornsey in part of the London boroughs of Hackney and Haringey.
**WHO CAN BENEFIT** Individuals and organisations benefitting people disadvantaged by poverty, ill health or age. Schools, community and youth organisations can be supported.
**WHAT IS FUNDED** Relief of poverty amongst local residents and also assistance with educational needs of young people under the age of 25. Financial assistance is granted to individuals and local organisations through bursaries, maintenance allowances, clothing, instruments and books.
**WHAT IS NOT FUNDED** Residential qualification is needed (must have lived in ancient parish of Hornsey for at least a year). Commitment is not made to continuous grants.
**RANGE OF GRANTS** £650–£1,388 (relief of poverty) and £600–£1,200 (education).
**FINANCES** *Year* 2013 *Income* £105,744 *Grants* £86,227 *Grants to organisations* £50,000 *Assets* £3,308,313
**TRUSTEES** Peter Kenyon; Ann Jones; Barbara Simon; Eddie Griffith; John Hudson; Revd Patrick Henderson; Vivienne Manheim; Revd Bruce Batstone; Ann Gillespie; Carol O'Brien; Katy Jones; Paula Lanning; Greg Gordon.
**OTHER INFORMATION** A total of 147 awards were made to individuals and organisations. The average grant for organisations was £1,388 (education) and £1,200 (relief of poverty). The Charities are now registered with the Charity Commission (registered numbers 229410 and 312810), and consist of two funds, one for those in need and one for education.
**HOW TO APPLY** Apply on a form available to download, together with criteria and guidelines, from the charities' website. Initial enquiries by e-mail are welcome. The trustees normally meet in March, May, September and November.
**WHO TO APPLY TO** Lorraine Fincham, Clerk to the Trustees, PO Box 22985, London N10 3XB *Tel.* 020 8352 1601 *Fax* 020 8352 1601 *email* hornseypc@blueyonder.co.uk *Website* www.hornseycharities.com

■ **Hospice UK (formerly known as Help the Hospices)**

**CC NO** 1014851/ SCO41112 **ESTABLISHED** 1984
**WHERE FUNDING CAN BE GIVEN** Throughout the UK and overseas.
**WHO CAN BENEFIT** Hospices and other institutions (individuals or organisations) involved with hospice care in the UK

**WHAT IS FUNDED** Grant programmes vary, visit the website for up-to-date details of open and forthcoming programmes.
**TYPE OF GRANT** One-off and recurrent.
**RANGE OF GRANTS** Generally under £1,000.
**SAMPLE GRANTS** Previous beneficiaries have included: St Luke's Hospice (£78,000); St Giles Hospice (£51,000); St Catherine's Hospice (£49,000); Rowcroft – Torbay and S Devon Hospice (£30,000); Farleigh Hospice (£7,000); Children's Hospice Association Scotland (£5,000); Richard House Children's Hospice (£2,000).
**FINANCES** Year 2013/14 Income £66,533,000 Grants £63,224,000 Grants to organisations £63,224,000 Assets £4,867,000
**TRUSTEES** Lord Howard of Lympne; Peter Holliday; Paul Dyer; Bay Green; Andrew Ryde; Patrick Beasley; Christine Heginbotham; Francis Bourne; Christine Gibbons; Stephen Greenhalgh; Julia Delaney.
**OTHER INFORMATION** There were 516 grants to organisations.
**HOW TO APPLY** The website provides guidelines for each programme and clear information on application procedures and deadlines. Depending on the programme, application forms can be downloaded or completed through the online application system.
**WHO TO APPLY TO** Grants Team, 34–44 Britannia Street, London WC1X 9JG *Tel.* 020 7520 8200 *email* grants@hospiceuk.org *Website* www.hospiceuk.org

## ■ The Hospital of God at Greatham

**CC NO** 1123540        **ESTABLISHED** 1973
**WHERE FUNDING CAN BE GIVEN** The ancient diocese of Durham (Hartlepool, Stockton, Darlington, County Durham, Sunderland, Gateshead, South Tyneside, North Tyneside, Newcastle upon Tyne and Northumberland).
**WHO CAN BENEFIT** Charities and voluntary organisations 'working in lower profile areas of work that reach people who are on the edges of society' individuals.
**WHAT IS FUNDED** Local initiatives aimed at disadvantaged people; social care; community causes. Preference is given to work that 'enhances the ability of the individual or the community to achieve self-determination, directly benefits people who are disadvantaged, demonstrates evidence of the need for the project for which a grant is sought, and shows the ability of the applicant organisation to deliver the service'. According to the website, 'examples of recent grants include support for organisations that work with asylum seekers, prisoner's families and people with drug problems'.
**WHAT IS NOT FUNDED** Capital works or appeals; education, travel and adventure projects; training and conferences; feasibility studies; medical equipment and related projects; organisations that do not have a base in the North East.
**TYPE OF GRANT** One-off and up to three years; core funding; running costs; salaries.
**RANGE OF GRANTS** £1,000–£3,500; up to £5,000.
**SAMPLE GRANTS** Westgate Baptist Church (£3,500); Samaritans Northumbria, The Moses Project – Stockton on Tees and Veterans At Ease (£2,000 each); THRIVE (£1,300); Riverside Community Health Project, Sailors Children's Society, St Cuthberts Hospice, St Margaret's Centre, Stroke North East and Teesdale Disability Access Forum (£1,000 each).
**FINANCES** Year 2012/13 Income £4,029,518 Grants £98,885 Grants to organisations £98,885 Assets £39,740,137
**TRUSTEES** Peter Shields; The Ven. Ian Jagger; John de Martino; John Allen; Stephen Croft; The Ven. Geoffrey Miller; Michael Poole; Philippa Sinclair; Chris Dickinson; Mike Taylerson; Annette Nylund.
**OTHER INFORMATION** The charity also provides care and housing services. During the year it had a total charitable expenditure of £3.6 million. The grant total consists of: grants to voluntary organisations (£84,500); Bishop of Durham Discretionary Fund (£8,000); Newcastle Diocese Discretionary Fund (£6,000); other (£370). During the year a total of 65 grants were made to 63 organisations. At the time of writing (June 2015) this was the latest information available.
**HOW TO APPLY** Applications have to be made in writing to the correspondent (email appeals are **not** accepted). Appeals should not exceed two sides of A4 and must include the following: description of the organisation; description of the project; how it is to be delivered; evidence of need for the project; amount requested and how it is to be spent; a copy of the latest annual report and accounts. Potential applicants are welcome to contact the correspondent for an informal discussion before applying. The Grants Committee meets three times a year – in January, June and September.
**WHO TO APPLY TO** David Granath, Director, The Estate Office, Greatham, Hartlepool TS25 2HS *Tel.* 01429 870247 *Fax* 01429 871469 *email* david.granath@hospitalofgod.org.uk *Website* www.hospitalofgod.org.uk

## ■ The Hospital Saturday Fund

**CC NO** 1123381        **ESTABLISHED** 1987
**WHERE FUNDING CAN BE GIVEN** UK, the Republic of Ireland, the Channel Islands and the Isle of Man.
**WHO CAN BENEFIT** Registered health charities – hospitals, hospices, clinics, medically-associated charities and welfare organisations providing health services; individuals. Organisations must be registered with the Charity Commission or regionally appropriate body (outside England and Wales).
**WHAT IS FUNDED** Medical causes; health care; research; specialist equipment; welfare needs and scholarships to individuals.
**WHAT IS NOT FUNDED** Projects outside the UK, Isle of Man, Channel Islands and Republic of Ireland; unregistered organisations; organisations carrying out non-medically related activities.
**TYPE OF GRANT** Medical capital projects; medical care; research; support of medical training; grants for running costs are also considered; awards are mainly one-off.
**RANGE OF GRANTS** Up to £10,000; mostly £2,000.
**SAMPLE GRANTS** Beneficiaries have included: Leonard Cheshire Disability and London's Air Ambulance (£10,000 each); St Richard's Hospice (£2,000); Arthritis Research; British Liver Trust; Child Bereavement UK; Christopher's Hospice – South-East London; Down's Heart Group; Positive Action on Cancer; The Lullaby Trust; The Mental Health Foundation; Treloar's; Whizz-Kidz.
**FINANCES** Year 2013/14 Income £25,730,247 Grants £740,753 Grants to organisations £693,399 Assets £26,061,514
**TRUSTEES** John Greenwood; Jane Laidlaw Dalton; Michael Boyle; John Randel; David Thomas; Christopher Bottomley; Pauline Lee.

OTHER INFORMATION In 2014 about £47,500 was given to 61 individuals. Support to individuals includes equipment, medical aids, treatment and home adaptations – appeals must be made through a medically-related third party. Grants were made to 274 organisations.

HOW TO APPLY Applications should be made using an online system on the charity's website. The Grant Making Committee meets quarterly. For the application submission dates consult the website – these vary depending on the size of grant but are generally in January, June, August and October. Those without internet access can write to the correspondent detailing the scope of the request (specific project or running costs and details), the amount requested, a copy of the organisation's annual report and accounts, registration number and the correct wording for a cheque, should your grant application be successful.

WHO TO APPLY TO Paul Jackson, Chief Executive, 24 Upper Ground, London SE1 9PD *Tel.* 020 7202 1365 (charity enquiries only) *Fax* 020 7928 0446 *email* charity@hsf.eu.com

## ■ The Sir Joseph Hotung Charitable Settlement

CC NO 1082710  ESTABLISHED 2000
WHERE FUNDING CAN BE GIVEN Worldwide.
WHO CAN BENEFIT Charitable organisations.
WHAT IS FUNDED Mainly medical, educational and cultural sectors.
TYPE OF GRANT Often recurrent.
SAMPLE GRANTS Oxford University Mansfield College – Institute of Human Rights (£750,000); CAABU (£115,000); School of Oriental and African Studies (£61,500); St Jude Childcare Centre (£5,000); St George's Hospital Medical School (£3,900); Spinal Research (£1,100); Reform Club Charitable Trust (£1,000).
FINANCES *Year* 2013/14 *Income* £1,058,754 *Grants* £929,885 *Grants to organisations* £929,885 *Assets* £946,210
TRUSTEES Sir Joseph Hotung; Sir Robert Boyd; Victoria Dicks; Peter Painton.
OTHER INFORMATION The trust tends to support a small number of organisations, often on a regular basis. During 2013/14 seven awards were given.
HOW TO APPLY The trust has previously stated that 'the trustees have their own areas of interest and do not respond to unsolicited applications'.
WHO TO APPLY TO Sir Joseph Hotung, Trustee, c/o HSBC Private Bank Ltd, 78 St James's Street, London, SWIA 1JB *email* henry.painton@blueyonder.co.uk

## ■ House of Industry Estate

CC NO 257079  ESTABLISHED 1968
WHERE FUNDING CAN BE GIVEN The borough of North Bedfordshire.
WHO CAN BENEFIT People who are in need and local organisations helping such individuals.
WHAT IS FUNDED General charitable purposes.
WHAT IS NOT FUNDED Funds are not given in relief of taxes or other public funds. No recurrent grants are given. In exceptional cases people otherwise eligible but resident immediately outside the borough or living within it temporarily can be treated as if resident in the area of benefit. Capital expenditure cannot include works to land or property. Retrospective funding is not given.

TYPE OF GRANT One-off capital grants or core revenue funding.
RANGE OF GRANTS Up to £25,000.
SAMPLE GRANTS **Previous beneficiaries have included:** Bedford Community Rights; Bedfordshire Garden Carers; Bedford Pilgrims Housing Association; Kempston Summer School; and King's Arms Project.
FINANCES *Year* 2013/14 *Income* £234,415 *Grants* £177,115 *Grants to organisations* £177,115 *Assets* £4,316,438
TRUSTEES Colleen Atkins; Tim Hill; Sue Oliver; David Sawyer; Tom Wootton; Stephen Moon; Charles Royden.
OTHER INFORMATION Grants are also made to organisations to make direct payments to individuals.
HOW TO APPLY Applications should be made in writing to the correspondent, providing details on your organisation's activities in the local area and financial position, including full details of the policy on reserves. Full guidelines and criteria can be requested form the correspondent.
WHO TO APPLY TO Assistant CEO and Chief Finance Officer, Bedford Borough Council, Borough Hall, Cauldwell Street, Bedford MK42 9AP *Tel.* 01234 267422

## ■ The Reta Lila Howard Foundation

CC NO 1041634  ESTABLISHED 1994
WHERE FUNDING CAN BE GIVEN UK and the Republic of Ireland.
WHO CAN BENEFIT Organisations benefitting children up to the age of 16; arts and educational institutions.
WHAT IS FUNDED Innovative projects that benefit children and projects concerned with the education of young people or to ameliorate their physical and emotional environment; arts; environment.
WHAT IS NOT FUNDED Individuals; organisations which are not registered charities; operating expenses; budget deficits; (sole) capital projects; annual charitable appeals; general endowment fund; fundraising drives or events; conferences; student aid.
RANGE OF GRANTS £10,000 £70,000
SAMPLE GRANTS **Previous beneficiaries have included:** Countryside Education Trust (£70,000); Barnardo's (£68,500); Civitas (£60,000); The Tree Council (£53,000); Farms for City Children (£40,000); Children's Hospice Association Scotland (£35,000); Teach First (£30,000); New Forest Museum and Library (£20,000); The Bridge End Community Centre (£15,000); Bibles for Children (£10,000).
FINANCES *Year* 2013/14 *Income* £73,947 *Grants* £360,000 *Grants to organisations* £360,000 *Assets* £17,229,327
TRUSTEES Alannah Weston; Charles Burnett; Garfield Mitchell; Christian Bauta; Melissa Murdoch; Tamara Rebanks; Sarah Eidson; Mark Mitchell; Geordie Dalglish.
OTHER INFORMATION A list of beneficiaries was not included within the latest annual report and accounts.
HOW TO APPLY The foundation has previously stated that it does not accept unsolicited applications, since the trustees seek out and support projects they are interested in.

WHO TO APPLY TO The Company Secretary, c/o Jamestown Investments Limited, 4 Felstead Gardens, Ferry Street, London E14 3BS *Tel.* 020 7537 1118 *email* jamestown@btinternet.com

## ■ The Daniel Howard Trust

CC NO 267173 ESTABLISHED 1974
WHERE FUNDING CAN BE GIVEN UK and Israel.
WHO CAN BENEFIT Registered charities, with focus on organisations helping Jewish people.
WHAT IS FUNDED Culture; education; environment; social welfare; Jewish causes. Ongoing support is provided for the Daniel Amichai Education Centre and the Israel Philharmonic Orchestra (both in Israel).
WHAT IS NOT FUNDED Non-registered charities; individuals.
TYPE OF GRANT One-off and recurrent.
RANGE OF GRANTS £500–£2.4 million.
SAMPLE GRANTS Previous beneficiaries have included: The Spero Foundation (£2.4 million); Friends of Daniel for Rowing association (£40,500); Israel Family Therapy Advancement Fund (£20,000); Council for a Beautiful Israel (£10,000); Ringling Museum of Art (£9,600); Israel Philharmonic (£6,400); Israeli Opera Friends Association (£2,500); The Weizmann Institute (£1,400); Marie Selby Botanical Gardens (£600); Schonfeld Square Foundation (£500).
FINANCES Year 2012/13 *Income* £31,109 *Grants* £155,000 *Grants to organisations* £155,000
TRUSTEES Shirley Porter; Linda Streit; Steven Porter; Brian Padgett; Andrew Peggie.
OTHER INFORMATION At the time of writing (June 2015) this was the latest information available. The trust has not submitted its accounts for the past two years. Based on previous giving patterns it is likely that grants have totalled around £155,000.
HOW TO APPLY Applications need to be made in writing to the correspondent. All appeals are considered at the trustees' regular meetings.
WHO TO APPLY TO Sarah Hunt, c/o Principle Capital, 63 Grosvenor Street, London W1K 3JG *Tel.* 020 7499 1957

## ■ James T. Howat Charitable Trust

SC NO SC000201 ESTABLISHED 1989
WHERE FUNDING CAN BE GIVEN Scotland, in particular west Scotland and Glasgow.
WHO CAN BENEFIT Charitable organisations, including universities, cultural bodies and institutions caring for people who are sick; local community organisations and groups; individuals.
WHAT IS FUNDED General charitable purposes, particularly those favoured by the settlor; community services; special needs education; social welfare voluntary and community organisations and volunteers.
WHAT IS NOT FUNDED Medical electives; second or further qualifications; payment of school fees; costs incurred at tertiary educational establishments.
TYPE OF GRANT Core costs; one-off; projects; research; running expenditure; start-up costs; educational support to individuals.
RANGE OF GRANTS £100–£10,000
SAMPLE GRANTS Previous beneficiaries have included: Crossroads (Scotland) Care Attendance Scheme and East Park Home for Inform Children, Royal Blind Asylum and School,

University of Glasgow and University of Strathclyde.
FINANCES Year 2013/14 *Income* £284,753 *Grants* £186,750 *Grants to organisations* £186,750
TRUSTEES Gordon Wyllie; Christine Howat.
OTHER INFORMATION Grants were made totalling nearly £187,000, which includes both organisations and individuals.
HOW TO APPLY Applications may be made in writing to the correspondent, providing: a summary of your request (no longer than one side of A4) backed up as necessary with schedules; a copy of the latest accounts and/or business plan; break down of costs and financial needs (where possible); information on what effect the grant will have; details of other grants applied for or awarded; evidence that the project will help its beneficiaries and that they are involved in the decision making. Generally appeals should be business-like and clearly demonstrated workability and potential impact. Unsuccessful applicants are not acknowledged due to the large number of applications received. The trustees meet to consider grants in March, June, September and December and applications should be received in the preceding month.
WHO TO APPLY TO The Trustees, c/o Harper Macleod LLP, The Ca'd'Oro, 45 Gordon Street, Glasgow G1 3PE

## ■ The Hudson Foundation

CC NO 280332 ESTABLISHED 1980
WHERE FUNDING CAN BE GIVEN UK, with a preference for the Wisbech area.
WHO CAN BENEFIT Charitable bodies; hospices; local community organisations.
WHAT IS FUNDED General charitable purpose, especially the relief of people who are older or infirm.
TYPE OF GRANT Capital projects are preferred over revenue expenditure.
RANGE OF GRANTS £500–£27,000
SAMPLE GRANTS Wisbech Grammar School (£27,000); National Trust (£25,000); Methodist Homes for the Aged (£13,900); Wisbech Angles Theatre (£10,700); Wisbech Swimming Club (£10,000); Norfolk Hospice Tapping House, Sue Ryder and Wisbech and Fenland Museum (£5,000 each); Leverington Primary Academy (£4,000); Wildfowl and Wetlands Trust (£3,300); Wisbech Sea Cadets (£2,000); Camsight and Motability UK (£500 each).
FINANCES Year 2013/14 *Income* £995,072 *Grants* £112,080 *Grants to organisations* £112,080 *Assets* £2,215,366
TRUSTEES David Ball; Stephen Layton; Edward Newling; Stephen Hutchinson.
OTHER INFORMATION There were 13 awards made.
HOW TO APPLY Applications should be made in writing to the correspondent. The trustees meet quarterly.
WHO TO APPLY TO David Ball, Trustee, 1–3 York Row, Wisbech, Cambridgeshire PE13 1EA *Tel.* 01945 461456 *email* davidwball@hotmail.co.uk

## ■ The Huggard Charitable Trust

CC NO 327501 ESTABLISHED 1987
WHERE FUNDING CAN BE GIVEN UK, with a preference for South Wales.
WHO CAN BENEFIT Organisations benefitting older people, people who have a disability or illness and those in poverty.

**WHAT IS FUNDED** Advancement of religion, the relief of poverty, health and disability, welfare of older people.
**TYPE OF GRANT** Ongoing support.
**RANGE OF GRANTS** Up to £30,000; generally under £1,000.
**SAMPLE GRANTS** Amelia Methodist Trust, Vale of Glamorgan (£31,000); other donations under £5,000 (£29,000); Whitton Rosser Trust, Vale of Glamorgan (£8,000); and Huggard, Cardiff (£5,000).
**FINANCES** Year 2013/14 Income £44,901 Grants £72,540 Grants to organisations £72,540 Assets £1,678,658
**TRUSTEES** Anne Helme; Stephen Thomas; Anne Chiplen.
**HOW TO APPLY** The trustees are not inviting applications for funds; they support a list of charities provided by their founder.
**WHO TO APPLY TO** Stephen Thomas, Trustee, 25 Harvey Crescent, Aberavon, Port Talbot SA12 6DF Tel. 01639 681539

## ■ The Hull and East Riding Charitable Trust

**CC NO** 516866    **ESTABLISHED** 1985
**WHERE FUNDING CAN BE GIVEN** Hull and the East Riding of Yorkshire.
**WHO CAN BENEFIT** 'Registered charities or for charitable purposes', with a possible preference for organisations working with children and young people, medical and disability causes and social welfare.
**WHAT IS FUNDED** A range of general charitable purposes.
**WHAT IS NOT FUNDED** Individuals; organisations or causes of a political nature; educational causes; religious purposes (requests for maintenance of significant religious buildings may be considered). If a donation has been made the trustees would not expect to receive a further request from the recipient in the immediate future.
**TYPE OF GRANT** The trust prefers to fund the capital costs of a project, but will consider funding revenue costs over a limited period of time.
**RANGE OF GRANTS** £100–£10,000
**SAMPLE GRANTS** Dove House Love You 2 Appeal and The No Way Trust Ltd (£10,000 each); Barnardo's (£5,000); TeachFirst (£3,900); Autism Plus and Whizz-Kidz (£3,000 each); RNIB (£2,000); Friends of the Elderly and Kingstown Radio (£1,500 each); East Riding Voluntary Action (£1,300); Maxi Fun Club, Narcolepsy UK and Yorkshire Clubs for Young People (£1,000 each); Hull and District Diabetes Support and Positive Changes (£500 each); Open Doors Hull Project (£200); Anne Williams re Glyn – CISV (£100).
**FINANCES** Year 2013/14 Income £189,827 Grants £205,407 Grants to organisations £205,407 Assets £6,542,582
**TRUSTEES** Kate Field; Mary Barker; Adrian Horsley.
**OTHER INFORMATION** There were 118 awards made.
**HOW TO APPLY** Apply in writing to the correspondent via post or email including all relevant information, such as communication details; a brief history and development of the organisation, charity and company numbers, information regarding the project for which funding is requested (including costs), strategy for securing funding, the description of how the grant will benefit of the local people, and future viability of the project. National organisations applying give details of historic activity providing specific benefit for Hull and/or East Riding residents. The trust's website states that 'initial telephone enquiries can be made – if necessary, a message can be left for future response'. The trustees meet twice a year – early in May and November. Appeals should be submitted by 20 April 20 October, respectively.
**WHO TO APPLY TO** John Barnes, Secretary, Greenmeades, Kemp Road, Swanland, North Ferriby, East Yorkshire HU14 3LY Tel. 01482 634664 email john.barnes@herct.org.uk Website hullandeastridingtrust.org.uk

## ■ Hulme Trust Estates (Educational)

**CC NO** 532297    **ESTABLISHED** 1964
**WHERE FUNDING CAN BE GIVEN** Greater Manchester.
**WHO CAN BENEFIT** Educational establishments. According to previous accounts, 'all beneficiaries are higher educational establishments, all of which are registered charities'
**WHAT IS FUNDED** This charity supports educational establishments in the Greater Manchester area. There are named beneficiaries which receive fixed, non-discretionary percentages of income, while a small percentage is distributed by the schools committee on a discretionary basis.
**TYPE OF GRANT** Set percentage to named beneficiaries and discretionary awards.
**SAMPLE GRANTS Most recent previous beneficiaries have included**: Brasenose College (£88,500); Manchester University (£44,000); William Hulmes Grammar School (£25,000); Bury Grammar School, Hulme Grammar School Oldham and William Hulmes Grammar School (£5,500 each); Manchester HS for Girls (£4,600); Manchester Grammar School (£900); Schools Committee has awarded £29,500.
**FINANCES** Year 2014 Income £197,716 Grants £250,000 Grants to organisations £250,000
**TRUSTEES** David Claxton; Thomas Hoyle; Ian Thompson; Alan Bowman; Peter Sidwell; Philip Parker; Ian Rankin; Sarah Newman.
**OTHER INFORMATION** At the time of writing (June 2015) full accounts for 2014 were not yet published by the Charity Commission. Based on the patterns of previous giving it is likely that grants totalled about £250,000.
**HOW TO APPLY** Applications may be made in writing to the correspondent.
**WHO TO APPLY TO** Jonathan Aldersley, Secretary, c/o Butcher and Barlow, 3 Royal Mews, Gadbrook Park, Northwich, Cheshire CW9 7UD Tel. 01606 334309

## ■ Human Relief Foundation

**CC NO** 1126281    **ESTABLISHED** 1995
**WHERE FUNDING CAN BE GIVEN** Conflict and disaster areas worldwide, including Somalia, Ethiopia, Chechnya, Bosnia, Kosovo, Kashmir, Pakistan, India, Bangladesh, Afghanistan and Palestine; emergency relief anywhere in the world.
**WHO CAN BENEFIT** Organisations benefitting at risk groups, carers, people with disabilities, those disadvantaged by poverty, refugees, victims of famine, man-made or natural disasters and war; medical professionals, scientists, volunteers involved in humanitarian projects may be supported.

**WHAT IS FUNDED** Humanitarian help; emergency aid; relief of poverty; education; health; infrastructure support and development.
**WHAT IS NOT FUNDED** Individuals; medical expenses; tutors or examination fees.
**SAMPLE GRANTS** Previous beneficiaries have included: Darfur Health Clinics; Elrahma Charity Trust; Isakhel Hospital Pakistan; Islamic Trust; Muslim Aid; Qatar Charitable Society; Red Crescent UAE; Saudi Arabia – Muslim World League; Well Project – Iraq.
**FINANCES** Year 2013 Income £3,952,093 Grants £215,031 Grants to organisations £215,031 Assets £2,026,376
**TRUSTEES** Dr Haytham Al-Khaffaf; Wael Musabbeh; Dr Nooh Al-Kaddo; Dr Haitham Al-Rawi; Mohanned Rahman.
**OTHER INFORMATION** A list of recent beneficiaries was not included in the accounts. The majority of the foundation's charitable expenditure consists of direct activities with only a part of it being grant-making.
**HOW TO APPLY** Applications may be made in writing to the correspondent.
**WHO TO APPLY TO** Mohanned Rahman, Trustee, PO Box 194, Bradford, West Yorkshire BD7 1YW Tel. 01274 392727 Fax 01274 739992 email donate@hrf.org.uk Website www.hrf.org.uk

..........................................................

### ■ The Humanitarian Trust

**CC NO** 208575    **ESTABLISHED** 1946
**WHERE FUNDING CAN BE GIVEN** Worldwide, largely Israel.
**WHO CAN BENEFIT** Organisations; individuals; educational institutions.
**WHAT IS FUNDED** General charitable purposes; education; health; social welfare; Jewish causes. British citizens under the age of 30 can receive student grants of £200 each.
**TYPE OF GRANT** One-off student grants and long-term awards to organisations.
**RANGE OF GRANTS** Usually £1,000–£5,000.
**SAMPLE GRANTS** Friends of Hebrew University of Jerusalem – H.T. Fellowship and M. Gunsbourg Memorial Scholarships (£25,000 each); New Israel Fund (£12,000); Jerusalem Foundation (£8,000); Olive Tree Programme – City University (£6,000); Etz Hayyim Synagogue, Jewish Literary Trust and University of Southampton (£5,000 each); The British Shalom-Salaam Trust (£4,000); Institute for Jewish Policy Research – Child Poverty in British Jewry (£2,500); Nightingale Hammerson (£2,000); Kids N' Action (£1,000); University of Cambridge (£750); and London School of Economics, Tommy's The Baby Charity and Wolfson College (£500 each).
**FINANCES** Year 2013/14 Income £185,670 Grants £158,698 Grants to organisations £158,698 Assets £4,894,194
**TRUSTEES** Antony Lerman; Jacques Gunsbourg; Pierre Halban; Emmanuelle Gunsbourg-Kasavi.
**OTHER INFORMATION** There were a total of 39 grants made.
**HOW TO APPLY** The annual report and accounts note that 'the trust does not accept any unsolicited applications from charities due to the ongoing relationship that it has with a number of organisations' nevertheless 'the trust occasionally invites charities to send in applications for consideration at board meeting'. In such instances applications should be made in writing to the correspondent, including an annual report and accounts, projected budgets and future plans. The trustees' meetings are normally in March and October. Our research suggests that less than 10% of grants are given to new applicants.
**WHO TO APPLY TO** Prism the Gift Fund, 20 Gloucester Place, London W1U 8HA Tel. 020 7486 7760 Fax 020 7224 2744 email info@prismthegiftfund.co.uk Website thehumanitariantrust.yolasite.com

..........................................................

### ■ The Michael and Shirley Hunt Charitable Trust

**CC NO** 1063418    **ESTABLISHED** 1997
**WHERE FUNDING CAN BE GIVEN** UK and overseas.
**WHO CAN BENEFIT** Prisoners and/or their families, and people charged with criminal offences and held in custody. Also, animals which are unwanted, sick or ill-treated.
**WHAT IS FUNDED** Prisoners rehabilitation, welfare of prisoners' families, citizenship, animal welfare, general charitable causes, overseas aid.
**WHAT IS NOT FUNDED** Grants for capital projects, overheads, support costs, fines, bail, legal costs, rent deposits and so on.
**TYPE OF GRANT** One-off.
**RANGE OF GRANTS** £50–£10,000
**SAMPLE GRANTS** DEC Philippines Typhoon Appeal (£7,500); Marlets Hospice (£6,000); HM Prison Dartmoor and Smile Support and Care (£5,000 each); Miracles to Believe in (£3,800); Church Housing Trust (£2,500); Hope Rescue, New Bridge, and SOFA Project (£2,000 each); and Animal Aid, Dogs Friends and Prison Fellowship (£1,000 each).
**FINANCES** Year 2013/14 Income £278,731 Grants £80,822 Grants to organisations £66,710 Assets £6,000,953
**TRUSTEES** Wanda Baker; Chester Hunt; Shirley Hunt; Deborah Jenkins; Kathy Mayberry.
**OTHER INFORMATION** Grants to 206 individuals (under the 'prisoners' category) totalled £14,000. There were 37 organisational grants.
**HOW TO APPLY** All applications have to be made in writing. Applications are considered upon receipt and formal meetings are held as necessary, at least once a year.
**WHO TO APPLY TO** Deborah Jenkins, Trustee, Ansty House, Henfield Road, Small Dole, Henfield, West Sussex BN5 9XH Tel. 01903 817116

..........................................................

### ■ The Albert Hunt Trust

**CC NO** 277318    **ESTABLISHED** 1979
**WHERE FUNDING CAN BE GIVEN** UK.
**WHO CAN BENEFIT** Registered charities that 'are actively engaged in [their] field of work' which fits the trust's funding criteria.
**WHAT IS FUNDED** Health and medical causes; disadvantaged and vulnerable individuals; social welfare. Projects that 'enhance the physical and mental welfare of individuals, or group of individuals'.
**WHAT IS NOT FUNDED** 'Research or the diagnosis and treatment of specific medical conditions' overseas work.
**TYPE OF GRANT** One-off; capital and core costs; projects; unrestricted funding.
**RANGE OF GRANTS** Up to £50,000; most grants £1,000–£2,000.
**SAMPLE GRANTS** Corbenic Camphill Community (£50,000); Autism Wessex, Greenwich and Bexley Community Hospice and Queen Victoria Seamen's Rest (£25,000 each); Bolton Lads and Girls Club (£13,000); The Hospice of St Francis (£11,000); Avalon School and

Bedfordshire Housing Link (£10,000 each); Puzzle Centre (£9,000); Home-Start (£6,000); Bedford Daycare Hospice, Colchester Hospitals Charity and Prior's Court Foundation (£5,000 each); Camphill Blair Drummond, Medical Engineering Resource Unit and West London Churches Homeless Concern (£3,000 each); Mind – Maidstone (£2,500); Action for Children, The Air Ambulance Service, Cares For Kids Breakfast Club and YMCA – Exeter (£2,000 each); Oak Tree Farm (£1,400); Age UK-Isle of Wight, Age UK – Suffolk, Daylight Christian Prison Trust, Dogs for the Disabled and The Family Haven (£1,000 each); Children and Families Voluntary Sector Forum and Gaddum Centre (£500 each).

**FINANCES** Year 2013/14 Income £1,687,499 Grants £2,134,750 Grants to organisations £2,134,750 Assets £53,488,139

**TRUSTEES** Breda McGuire; Coutts & Co.

**OTHER INFORMATION** Grants were made to 819 institutions. Administration costs totalled £130,500.

**HOW TO APPLY** Applications should be made in writing to the correspondent by letter containing the following: aims and objectives of the charity; nature of appeal; total target if for a specific project; contributions received against target; registered charity number; any other relevant factors. Appeals are considered on a monthly basis. The trust has previously stated that no unsolicited correspondence will be acknowledged unless an application receives favourable consideration.

**WHO TO APPLY TO** The Director, Tax Trust and Estate Planning, c/o Coutts & Co., Tax Trust and Estate Planning, 440 Strand, London WC2R 0QS Tel. 020 7663 6825

## ■ The Hunter Foundation

**SC NO** SC027532  **ESTABLISHED** 1998

**WHERE FUNDING CAN BE GIVEN** UK and overseas.

**WHO CAN BENEFIT** Charitable organisations, schools and universities, social enterprises.

**WHAT IS FUNDED** Educational initiatives aimed largely at children, relief of poverty and community development. Focus in the UK is to invest in national educational programmes that challenge the system-wide issues which prevent children from achieving their potential. Overseas the focus is on investing in holistic developments that embed solutions within communities and countries, again with education being central.

**TYPE OF GRANT** Strategic partnership.

**RANGE OF GRANTS** Above £50,000.

**SAMPLE GRANTS** The foundation's website states – 'we do not distinguish between funding partners and programme partners as far as we see it we are all in this together, either as funders or programme deliverers'. Partners include: University of Strathclyde; The Prince's Scottish Youth Business Trust; Cash for Kids; STV Appeal; BBC Children in Need; Comic Relief; Clinton Foundation; Ethel Mutharika Maternity Hospital; Unicef; Hunter Scholars; Programme; and Entrepreneurial Spark.

**FINANCES** Year 2013/14 Income £1,257,340 Grants £197,887 Grants to organisations £198,200

**TRUSTEES** Vartan Gregorian; Marion Hunter; Tom Hunter, Chair; Jim McMahon; Ewan Hunter.

**HOW TO APPLY** The foundation has previously stated that it is 'pro-active' and does not seek applications. However, in response to our regular survey the foundation indicated that unsolicited applications are considered, so we repeat previous guidance from the foundation on how to make an approach: 'The Hunter Foundation proactively sources programmes for investment, or works with partners to develop new programmes where a gap or clear need is identified. As such it is very rare indeed for THF to fund unsolicited bids; however, if you wish to apply please complete a maximum two page summary outlining how your project fits with our aims and objectives and email it to info@thehunterfoundation.co.uk. This summary should include: summary of project; impact of project; any independent evaluation undertaken of your project/programme; if this is a local programme how it could be scaled to become a national programme; current sources of funding; and funding sought from the Hunter Foundation. Please note: we do not have a large staff and thus we will not consider meetings in advance of this information being provided. If your project appears to be of initial interest, we will then contact you to discuss this further.'

**WHO TO APPLY TO** Tom Hunter, Chair, Marathon House, Olympic Business Park, Drybridge Road, Dundonald, Ayrshire KA2 9AE email info@thehunterfoundation.co.uk Website www.thehunterfoundation.co.uk

## ■ Miss Agnes H. Hunter's Trust

**SC NO** SC004843  **ESTABLISHED** 1954

**WHERE FUNDING CAN BE GIVEN** Projects operating in Scotland.

**WHO CAN BENEFIT** Registered charities. The website specifies: 'The Trustees are inclined to give support to medium and small charities though this does not exclude larger charities where the project is central to the core work of the Trust and where this is not being provided by smaller charities.'

**WHAT IS FUNDED** Health and disability, especially blind and visually impaired people, cancer, arthritis, individuals with physical or mental problems and learning difficulties; social welfare; education, training and employment, especially for disadvantaged individuals; development projects for young people over the age of 13. The trust is particularly looking to support projects advancing the self-management skills of disadvantaged individuals.

**WHAT IS NOT FUNDED** Organisations that are not formally recognised as charities; organisations under the control of the UK or Scottish Government; projects which are primarily intended to promote political or religious beliefs; individuals (including students); expeditions, overseas travel or international projects; projects outside Scotland; general appeals or circulars (including contributions to endowment funds); statutory requirements of local authorities, hospitals, schools, universities and colleges; clinical work within hospitals; animal welfare; the breeding and training of assistance/guide dogs for people who are blind or have disabilities; the bricks and mortar aspect of capital projects; initiatives focused on sports, the arts or the environment, except where the subject is being used as a vehicle to engage with one of the trust's core policy groups; normal youth club activities. According to the website, medical research and hospices will **no longer** be funded.

**TYPE OF GRANT** One-off and recurrent; capital and core costs; project funding; salaries.

**RANGE OF GRANTS** £1,600–£23,000; Main Grants start at £4,000; Small grants are up to £4,000 (the programme is very limited).

**SAMPLE GRANTS** Visibility (£23,000); Institute of Cancer Research (£15,000); Sense Scotland (£14,000); Loanhead Community Learning Association and Waverley Care (£10,000 each); Bethany Christian Trust and Fly Cup Catering (£9,000 each); Lanarkshire Ace (£8,600); Move On (£8,000); Conservation Volunteers (£7,700); Roy Castle Lung Cancer Foundation (£7,500); Breast Cancer Care Scotland (£7,000); St Andrew's Hospice (£5,200); Aberlour, Alcohol Focus Scotland, British Red Cross and Living Paintings (£5,000 each); Revive MS Support (£3,400); Speakability (£3,200); The Tree Club (£2,900); Bag Books (£2,700); Music in Hospitals Scotland (£2,500); Doorway Accessible Software Trust (£1,600).
**FINANCES** Year 2013/14 Income £758,216 Grants £328,293 Grants to organisations £328,293 Assets £16,386,296
**TRUSTEES** Andrew Gray; Walter Thompson; Neil Paterson; Alison Campbell.
**OTHER INFORMATION** During the year 50 grants were approved in the following categories: Education and Training/Youth Development (£92,500 – 14 awards); Mental Health and Learning Disability (£78,000 – 14 awards); Blind and Visually Impaired (£67,000 – seven awards); Arthritis and Cancer – Care (£37,500 – seven awards); Physical Disability and Illness (£32,000 – six awards); Arthritis and Cancer – Research (£25,000 – two awards).
**HOW TO APPLY** The trustees 'encourage all potential applicants to refer to the trust's website as the trust is unable to consider applications unless all information requested on the website is provided'. Applications should be made in writing to the correspondent, providing: a brief description of the organisation's history, background, aims and activities; a full description of the project requiring funding (how the need for this work has been identified, difference or changes that the project will make, activities/services to be carried out to achieve these changes, projected means of monitoring and evaluating the work, income and expenditure budget for the project, proposed timetable for the project). In addition hard copies of the latest annual report and accounts are required. Main Grants are considered twice a year, in June and November (deadlines are normally a couple of months before). Small Grants are decided on an ongoing basis.
**WHO TO APPLY TO** Jane Paterson, Grants Administrator, c/o Pagan Osborne Ltd, Clarendon House, 116 George Street, Edinburgh EH2 4LH *Tel.* 0131 538 5496 *email* grants@agneshunter.org.uk *Website* www.agneshunter.org.uk

■ **The Huntingdon Foundation Limited**
**CC NO** 286504 **ESTABLISHED** 1984
**WHERE FUNDING CAN BE GIVEN** Mainly UK, some giving in the US.
**WHO CAN BENEFIT** Organisations benefitting Jewish people; Jewish schools.
**WHAT IS FUNDED** Jewish causes; education and training.
**WHAT IS NOT FUNDED** Our research indicates that grants are not normally made to individuals.
**RANGE OF GRANTS** About £1,000–£60,000.
**SAMPLE GRANTS** Bnos Beis Yaakov Primary School Limited; King Solomon School; Noam Primary School; and Yavneh College. In addition the trustees have supported 'numerous other Jewish educational institutions'.
**FINANCES** Year 2013/14 Income £605,873 Grants £199,287 Grants to organisations £199,287 Assets £11,676,693
**TRUSTEES** Benjamin Perl; Dr Shoshanna Perl; Jonathan Perl; Joseph Perl; Rachel Jeidel; Naomi Tsorotzkin.
**OTHER INFORMATION** The accounts do not list the amounts given to individual recipient organisations.
**HOW TO APPLY** Applications can be made in writing to the correspondent. The trustees meet several times a year.
**WHO TO APPLY TO** Benjamin Perl, Trustee, 8 Goodyers Gardens, London NW4 2HD *Tel.* 020 8202 2282

■ **Huntingdon Freemen's Trust**
**CC NO** 1044573 **ESTABLISHED** 1993
**WHERE FUNDING CAN BE GIVEN** Huntingdon, including Oxmoor, Hartford, Sapley, Stukeley Meadows and Hinchingbrooke Park (the area covered by PE postcode).
**WHO CAN BENEFIT** Local individuals and organisations.
**WHAT IS FUNDED** Relief in need (including sickness and healthcare provision); provision of pensions; educational needs; and recreational needs.
**WHAT IS NOT FUNDED** Applications from outside the boundaries of Huntingdon (the adjoining parishes, such as The Stukeleys, Godmanchester, Houghton and Wyton, Kings Ripton, Brampton and so on) are not supported. The trust cannot cover services that the government or local councils are supposed to provide, but can supplement them.
**RANGE OF GRANTS** £1,000–£75,000
**SAMPLE GRANTS** 'Significant individual projects' included: student grants for accommodation (£124,500); Huntingdon Gymnastics Club (£50,000); schools grants (£34,500); Natural High – support to youth project (£30,000); Disability Huntingdonshire – DISH (£5,000); Christmas meals/trips for elderly people (£1,400). In addition to the grants made during the year the following awards totalling £160,000 were also contributed (from 'larger grants' budget): Huntingdon Methodist Church (£75,000); Woodlands Centre, Hinchingbooke Hospital (£50,000); Natural High (£35,000).
**FINANCES** Year 2013/14 Income £438,646 Grants £518,209 Grants to organisations £393,658 Assets £15,807,968
**TRUSTEES** Edward Bocking; John Hough; Jonathan Hampstead; Ann Beevor; Brian Bradshaw; Laine Kadic; Michael Shellens.
**OTHER INFORMATION** The trust can also provide specialised equipment on long term loan.
**HOW TO APPLY** Application forms can be downloaded from the trust's website. Individual applications can be made in writing to the correspondent. Applications are considered at monthly meetings. The trust states – 'We are always open to suggestions of how we could provide more help, so if you have an idea drop in for a chat!'
**WHO TO APPLY TO** Ruth Black, Grants Officer, 37 High Street, Huntingdon, Cambridgeshire PE29 3AQ *Tel.* 01480 414909 *email* info@huntingdonfreemen.org.uk *Website* www.huntingdonfreemen.org.uk

## ■ Hurdale Charity Limited

CC NO 276997  ESTABLISHED 1978
WHERE FUNDING CAN BE GIVEN Worldwide.
WHO CAN BENEFIT Charitable organisations benefitting Jewish people and promoting the Orthodox Jewish way of life.
WHAT IS FUNDED Advancement of Jewish religion; relief of poverty; education; medical causes.
TYPE OF GRANT One-off and recurring.
RANGE OF GRANTS Up to £205,000.
SAMPLE GRANTS Fountain of Chesed Limited (£205,000); Harofeh Donations Limited (£188,000); Moundfield Charities Limited (£185,000); Springfield Trust Limited (£170,000).
FINANCES Year 2013/14 Income £1,192,266 Grants £1,208,800 Grants to organisations £1,208,800 Assets £17,281,343
TRUSTEES Pinkas Oestreicher; David Oestreicher; Abraham Oestreicher; Jacob Oestreicher; Benjamin Oestreicher.
OTHER INFORMATION A full list of beneficiaries was not included in the accounts; however, under the 'Related party transactions' organisations which share common trustees with the charity and receive support were listed.
HOW TO APPLY Applications may be made in writing to the correspondent.
WHO TO APPLY TO Abraham Oestreicher, Trustee, 162 Osbaldeston Road, London N16 6NJ email ao@petley.plus.com

## ■ The Hutton Foundation

CC NO 1106521  ESTABLISHED 2004
WHERE FUNDING CAN BE GIVEN UK and overseas.
WHO CAN BENEFIT Charitable organisations.
WHAT IS FUNDED General charitable purposes, particularly Christian causes; health.
SAMPLE GRANTS International Theological Institute (£70,000); and Emmanuel College (£7,400) – both received grants in previous years. Other donations totalled £38,000.
FINANCES Year 2013 Income £127,600 Grants £115,482 Grants to organisations £115,482 Assets £1,664,424
TRUSTEES Graham Hutton; Amanda Hutton; Richard Hutton; James Hutton; Helen Hutton.
HOW TO APPLY Unsolicited applications are not supported. Those interested in learning more about the foundation are encouraged to contact the correspondent.
WHO TO APPLY TO Jackie Hart, Secretary and Treasurer, Hutton Collins Partners LLP, 50 Pall Mall, London SW1Y 5JH Tel. 020 7004 7000 Fax 020 7004 7001 email jackie.hart@huttoncollins.com Website www.huttoncollins.com/about-us/hutton-collins-foundation

## ■ The Nani Huyu Charitable Trust

CC NO 1082868  ESTABLISHED 2000
WHERE FUNDING CAN BE GIVEN UK, but there is a strong preference for causes within 50 miles of Bristol (the old Avon area).
WHO CAN BENEFIT Mainly small local charities; charitable organisations.
WHAT IS FUNDED General charitable purposes; social welfare. The latest annual report states: 'We give in the main to charities whose primary object is to help people who are under privileged, disadvantaged, suffering or ill; young people in matters of accommodation or training; and old people requiring assistance or medical care at the end of their lives.'
WHAT IS NOT FUNDED National charities.
TYPE OF GRANT Capital and revenue costs; one-off and up to one year.
RANGE OF GRANTS £2,000–£13,000
SAMPLE GRANTS Crossroads, Rainbow, Southside Family Project and Womankind (£13,000 each); Jessie May Trust (£11,000); FareShare South West and Young Bristol (£10,000 each); Fairbridge West (£8,000); The Harbour (£5,000); The Family Centre Deaf and Bristol Meditation (£4,000 each); Blenheim Scouts (£3,000); Quartet and Young and Free (£2,000 each).
FINANCES Year 2012/13 Income £169,819 Grants £157,000 Grants to organisations £157,000 Assets £4,864,860
TRUSTEES Ben Whitmore; Charles Thatcher; Maureen Whitmore; Susan Webb.
OTHER INFORMATION At the time of writing (June 2015) this was the latest information available. There were 21 awards made.
HOW TO APPLY Applications may be made in writing to the correspondent.
WHO TO APPLY TO Maureen Whitmore, Trustee, Rusling House, Butcombe, Bristol BS40 7XQ Tel. 01275 474433 email maureensimonwhitmore@btinternet.com

## ■ The P. Y. N. and B. Hyams Trust

CC NO 268129  ESTABLISHED 1974
WHERE FUNDING CAN BE GIVEN Worldwide.
WHO CAN BENEFIT Charitable organisations, especially those benefitting Jewish people.
WHAT IS FUNDED General charitable purposes; Jewish causes.
FINANCES Year 2013/14 Income £61,467 Grants £45,870 Grants to organisations £45,870 Assets £1,026,666
TRUSTEES Miriam Hyams; David Levy; Naresh Shah.
HOW TO APPLY Applications may be made in writing to the correspondent, but note, the trust has previously stated that funds are fully committed and unsolicited applications are not welcome.
WHO TO APPLY TO Naresh Shah, Trustee, Lubbock Fine, Paternoster House, 3rd Floor, 65 St Paul's Churchyard, London EC4M 8AB Tel. 020 7490 7766

## ■ Hyde Charitable Trust (Youth Plus)

CC NO 289888  ESTABLISHED 1984
WHERE FUNDING CAN BE GIVEN The areas in which the Hyde Group operates (currently Buckinghamshire, Cambridgeshire, Greater London, Essex, Hampshire, Kent, Lincolnshire, Norfolk, Northamptonshire; Surrey and Sussex).
WHO CAN BENEFIT Schools and registered charities operating in Hyde Group areas; organisations providing services to residents of Hyde Housing Association and other Hyde Group members.
WHAT IS FUNDED Residents of Hyde Housing Association and other Hyde Group members; disadvantaged children and young people; community projects. The trust supports residents in emergencies and extreme financial need and for training and employment needs, has schemes awarding funds to local young people for community projects and personal development, and helps local groups and organisations for community projects. Schemes to young individuals, including Hyde Youth Bank and Do More! Grants for Young People; schemes for residents include Jobs and Training

# Hyde

Bursary and Home Essentials Fund; schemes to groups and organisations include Cash4Communities fund (awarding up to £500 for projects) and Innovations Fund ('to deliver innovative projects and activities developed jointly with Hyde Plus').

**WHAT IS NOT FUNDED** Unsolicited applications; projects outside Hyde operating area (areas outside the South East of England); sporting, social or fundraising events; medical research, hospices, residential homes for the elderly; any other projects which the trustees deem to fall outside the main criteria.

**SAMPLE GRANTS** Grants were allocated through the following programmes: Vulnerable People – Helping Hands (£80,000); Activities Communities (£71,000); Youth Plus (£60,000); Digital Inclusion (£46,000); Jobs Plus (£45,000); Young Pride Awards (£23,000); Financial Inclusion (£20,000); Navi Learning Fund (£18,000); Matrix – Other (£8,000); Welfare Reform (£4,000).

**FINANCES** Year 2013/14 Income £295,000 Grants £375,000 Grants to organisations £375,000 Assets £7,425,000

**TRUSTEES** Baroness Falkner Of Margravine; Geron Walker; Jonathan Prichard; Michelle Walcott; Ronald Brooks; Andrew Moncreiff; Christopher Carlisle; Charles O'Hanlon.

**OTHER INFORMATION** The grant total includes grants made through all schemes to individuals and organisations.

**HOW TO APPLY** The trust has informed us that 'because the funding available is limited and targeted at Hyde residents the trust does not encourage unsolicited applications'. Awards through Innovations Fund are made **by invitation** only and must be supported by a member of staff.

**WHO TO APPLY TO** John Edwards, Secretary, Hyde Housing Association, 30 Park Street, London SE1 9EQ *Tel.* 020 3207 2762 *email* hydeplus@hyde-housing.co.uk *Website* www.hyde-housing.co.uk/hydeplus

## ■ IBM United Kingdom Trust
**CC NO** 290462   **ESTABLISHED** 1984
**WHERE FUNDING CAN BE GIVEN** UK, Europe, Middle East and Africa.
**WHO CAN BENEFIT** The trust gives preference to organisations concerned with people disadvantaged by poverty and/or at risk of digital exclusion.
**WHAT IS FUNDED** The focus areas for IBM's community investment are the strategic and innovative use of Information and Communication Technology (ICT) in education and training and the promotion of digital inclusion, with the broad objective of raising standards of achievement. Most activity is within the compulsory education phase. The vast majority of IBM's community investment is delivered through specific programmes initiated and developed by IBM in partnership with organisations with appropriate professional expertise.
**WHAT IS NOT FUNDED** The trust does not provide core funding or contribute to appeals for building projects, religious or sectarian organisations, animal charities, individuals (including students), overseas activities or expeditions, recreational and sports clubs, appeals by third parties on behalf of charities or individuals. The company does not currently offer full-time secondments of employees to voluntary organisations.
**TYPE OF GRANT** Equipment and programme costs.
**FINANCES** Year 2013 Income £1,891,000 Grants £1,728,000 Grants to organisations £1,728,000 Assets £3,826,000
**TRUSTEES** Brendan Dineen; Prof. Derek Bell; Jonathan Batty; Anne Wolfe; Naomi Hill.
**OTHER INFORMATION** Specific details of beneficiaries are not listed in the accounts, although information is given there on the IBM programmes and initiatives which the trust supports.
**HOW TO APPLY** Very few unsolicited requests are considered. If requests are submitted then these should be by email or in writing and include a brief resumé of the aims of the organisation and a detail of what assistance is required. Those considering making an application are advised to telephone first for advice.
**WHO TO APPLY TO** Mark Wakefield, Trust Manager, IBM United Kingdom Limited, 76/78 Upper Ground, South Bank, London SE1 9PZ Tel. 020 7202 3608 email wakefim@uk.ibm.com

## ■ Ibrahim Foundation Ltd
**CC NO** 1149438/SC043491**ESTABLISHED** 2012
**WHERE FUNDING CAN BE GIVEN** UK and overseas.
**WHO CAN BENEFIT** Registered charities; educational institutions; community projects.
**WHAT IS FUNDED** General charitable purposes; social welfare; health; education. Specific current projects concern development projects overseas, children and young people and the Scotland Institute, a think tank also founded by Dr Ibrahim in 2012.
**TYPE OF GRANT** Capital, core and project costs.
**SAMPLE GRANTS** Purifi (£301,000); Asia Pacific Children's Fund; Scotland Institute; SOLAS Foundation.
**FINANCES** Year 2013/14 Income £281,285 Grants £250,517 Grants to organisations £250,517 Assets £72
**TRUSTEES** Dr Azeem Ibrahim; Adeel Ibrahim; Aadil Butt.
**OTHER INFORMATION** It would appear that currently support is given to projects already assisted and chosen by Dr Ibrahim.
**HOW TO APPLY** Initial contact can be made via the foundation's website, although potential applicants should note that most funding is likely to go to projects and organisations with which the foundation and Dr Ibrahim already have an involvement.
**WHO TO APPLY TO** Dr Azeem Ibrahim, Trustee, 18 Little Street, Glasgow G3 8DQ Tel. 0141 416 1991 email info@ibrahimfoundation.com Website www.ibrahimfoundation.com

## ■ The Idlewild Trust
**CC NO** 268124   **ESTABLISHED** 1974
**WHERE FUNDING CAN BE GIVEN** UK.
**WHO CAN BENEFIT** Registered charities only; museums, galleries and other venues concerned with the visual arts and crafts; educational institutions.
**WHAT IS FUNDED** Performing and fine arts; culture; restoration and conservation; education; preservation of buildings and items of historical interest or national importance.
**WHAT IS NOT FUNDED** Work which has been completed; individuals; new work within churches, such as heating systems, annexes, facilities; community-based projects or festivals largely involving and attracting people in the immediate area; education work unless it is within the fine arts (performing or visual arts); education work with pre-school or primary school aged children; endowment or deficit funding; nationwide appeals by large charities; appeals where all or most of the recipients live outside the UK; appeals whose sole or main purpose is to make grants from funds collected; projects based in the Channel Islands or Isle of Man.
**TYPE OF GRANT** Projects, buildings, refurbishment, capital work, exhibition costs, event and performance expenditure and research.
**RANGE OF GRANTS** Up to £5,000.
**SAMPLE GRANTS** Ashmolean Museum (£3,500); Coventry Cathedral, Scottish Opera, Sing For Pleasure, The British Library and The Friends of the William Morris Gallery (£3,000 each); Textile Conservation Foundation (£2,900); The Cotswold Canals Trust (£2,500); City Of London Festival (£2,000); Berkshire Maestros (£1,500); Crafts Study Centre (£1,000).
**FINANCES** Year 2013 Income £181,105 Grants £133,990 Grants to organisations £133,990 Assets £5,252,036
**TRUSTEES** Jonathan Ouvry; Tony Ford; Dr Tessa Murdoch; Helen McCabe; John Gittens; Tessa Mayhew.
**OTHER INFORMATION** There were 56 grants awarded.
**HOW TO APPLY** The trust now uses an online application process. Potential applicants are welcome to telephone the trust to discuss their application and confirm eligibility (Mon, Tue and Wed 9am–3pm – but check the website for specific dates when the office is closed). The trustees meet twice a year usually in May and November – exact dates and deadlines are published on the website. The trust will check your Charity Commission record to see if your

543

charity's annual returns and accounts are up-to-date. The outcome of the application is communicated within a fortnight of the trustees' meeting. Grants will not be awarded to any one charity more frequently than every two years. Unsuccessful applicants can re-apply immediately.

**WHO TO APPLY TO** Rachel Oglethorpe, Director, Unit 1A, Taylors Yard, 67 Alderbrook Street, London SW12 8AD *Tel.* 020 8772 3155 *email* info@idlewildtrust.org.uk *Website* www.idlewildtrust.org.uk

## ■ The Iliffe Family Charitable Trust

**CC NO** 273437  **ESTABLISHED** 1977
**WHERE FUNDING CAN BE GIVEN** Worldwide.
**WHO CAN BENEFIT** The majority of donations are made to charities already known to the trustees. Thereafter, preference is given to charities in which the trust has a special interest.
**WHAT IS FUNDED** General charitable purposes; health and disability; medical; heritage and conservation; education.
**WHAT IS NOT FUNDED** Grants are not made to individuals and rarely to non-registered charities.
**RANGE OF GRANTS** £500–£20,000
**FINANCES** Year 2013/14 Income £49,692 Grants £128,090 Grants to organisations £128,090 Assets £1,347,948
**TRUSTEES** Lord Iliffe; Edward Iliffe; Catherine Fleming.
**OTHER INFORMATION** There were 32 awards made.
**HOW TO APPLY** Applications can be made in writing to the correspondent. Only successful applications will be acknowledged. Grants are considered at ad hoc meetings of the trustees, held throughout the year.
**WHO TO APPLY TO** Catherine Fleming, Trustee, Barn Close, Burnt Hill, Yattendon, Berkshire RG18 0UX *Tel.* 01635 203929 *email* ifct@yattendon.co.uk

## ■ Impetus – The Private Equity Foundation (Impetus – PEF)

**CC NO** 1152262  **ESTABLISHED** 2013
**WHERE FUNDING CAN BE GIVEN** UK.
**WHO CAN BENEFIT** Registered charities and social enterprises.
**WHAT IS FUNDED** Funding, management support from the investment team and specialist expertise from pro bono professionals for organisations supporting disadvantaged people particularly children, young people and families.
**TYPE OF GRANT** Development and strategic funding along with management and pro bono support.
**RANGE OF GRANTS** £500,000–£1 million.
**SAMPLE GRANTS** Place2Be (£516,000); Tomorrow's People (£418,000); Skill Force (£282,000); Workingrite (£240,000); Street League (£179,000); Blue Sky (£129,000); Prison Radio Association, Resurgo and Ripplez (£100,000 each); Unitas (£50,000); Education Endowment Fund (£42,000); Oxpip (£25,000); Social Economy Alliance (£15,000); Millennium Kids (£6,500); FRC Group and Kainos Community (£5,000 each).
**FINANCES** Year 2013 Income £15,539,456 Grants £3,272,276 Grants to organisations £3,272,376 Assets £14,669,699
**TRUSTEES** Louise Elson; Johannes Huth; Lionel Assant; Marc Boughton; Stephen Dawson; Craig Dearden-Phillips; Charles Green; Carl Parker; Karl Petersen; Nathaniel Sloane; Hanneke Smits; Nikos Stathopoulos; Prof. Becky Francis; Caroline Mason.
**OTHER INFORMATION** The foundation was formed from the merger of the Impetus Trust and Private Equity Foundation. Out of the overall grant total awards to research organisations totalled £72,000.
**HOW TO APPLY** The foundation's website states that it does not accept unsolicited applications and instead work through referrals from trusted partners who know its investment model. Once a potential charity has been identified, it will undergo a screening process to determine eligibility for the portfolio.
**WHO TO APPLY TO** The Trustees, 138 Eversholt Street, London NW1 1BU *Tel.* 020 3474 1000 *email* info@impetus-pef.org.uk *Website* impetus-pef.org.uk

## ■ Incommunities Foundation

**CC NO** 1152959  **ESTABLISHED** 2013
**WHERE FUNDING CAN BE GIVEN** Currently in the Bradford district.
**WHO CAN BENEFIT** Local organisations and projects.
**WHAT IS FUNDED** General charitable purposes, particularly unemployment, education and training and activities for young people. Help can also be given towards: health; relief of poverty; accommodation and housing; arts and culture; science; heritage; sports and recreation; environment and conservation; economic and community development.
**SAMPLE GRANTS** A detailed list of beneficiaries was not included within the annual report and accounts for 2013/14; however, it was specified that grants went to: other employment initiatives (£451,000); community based enterprises (£232,000); employment advisors (£220,000); Locally Grown – Work Where You Live (£218,000); other young people involvement activities (£94,000); play facilities and other amenities (£72,000); sports coaching (£48,000); community cohesion and resident involvement (£13,000). Support was distributed as follows: Incommunities (£1.1 million); other (£136,000); Bradford Council (£50,000); Sporting Chance (£48,000).
**FINANCES** Year 2013/14 Income £1,405,000 Grants £1,348,000 Grants to organisations £1,348,000 Assets £27,000
**TRUSTEES** Neera Tyagi; Martin Smith; Alison Herbert; David Kennedy; Elizabeth Weatherill.
**OTHER INFORMATION** Funding is given to both internally operated activities and external requests. During the year support given has included: the foundation's Locally Grown initiative which 'has Incommunities' Group as lead partner working with a number of other local organisations to support and help develop people who have business ideas' Get More From Life team to 'provide employment advice, mentoring and support for Incommunities tenants and other residents of Bradford' Your Sporting Chance to help 'young people in danger of getting into trouble or who are already known to the Police' The Brad Factor – an established performance and music event in Bradford.
**HOW TO APPLY** Applications may be made in writing to the correspondent.
**WHO TO APPLY TO** Peter Newbould, Secretary, Incommunities Group Limited, The Quays, Victoria Street, Shipley, West Yorkshire BD17 7BN *Tel.* 01274 254000 *email* enquiry@incommunities.co.uk *Website* www.incommunities.co.uk

## ■ The Indigo Trust

**CC NO** 1075920   **ESTABLISHED** 1999

**WHERE FUNDING CAN BE GIVEN** Primarily Africa, some support in the UK.

**WHO CAN BENEFIT** Organisations using technology to improve equality in Africa.

**WHAT IS FUNDED** Technology-driven projects which focus on innovation, transparency and citizen empowerment. Development can be in any sector, including the health, education, human rights and agricultural spheres.

**WHAT IS NOT FUNDED** No support is given for infrastructure, general equipment costs or generic ICT training. Indigo does accept unsolicited proposals for our overseas work.

**RANGE OF GRANTS** £4,000–£45,000

**SAMPLE GRANTS** Copenhagen Youth Project (£45,000); Institute for Philanthropy (£40,000); Hypercube Technology Trust (Zimbabwe) and iLab Liberia (Liberia) (£30,000 each); Publish What You Fund (£25,000); Integrity Action (West and Central Africa) (£13,000); Hive Colab (Uganda) (£10,000); Hut Space (Ghana) (£5,100); Holborn Community Association (£5,500); Albert Kennedy Trust, Choir with No Name and Trussell Trust (£3,000 each); and University College London – Constitution Unit (£4,100).

**FINANCES** Year 2013/14 Income £1,415,301 Grants £742,729 Grants to organisations £742,729 Assets £8,963,059

**TRUSTEES** Dominic Flynn; Francesca Perrin; William Perrin.

**OTHER INFORMATION** There were a total of 48 awards made with 14% of grants going to UK-based organisations.

**HOW TO APPLY** Indigo does accept unsolicited proposals for UK grants, but 'in line with its commitment to transparency, however, it felt it necessary to publish the details of who and what it funds'. Funds are available for projects overseas, mainly in Africa. According to the website the following guidelines apply for proposals: 'the applicant should be operating wholly or partly in at least one African country or else specifically seeking to benefit those who do work and live in Africa'; 'they must be implementing or hoping to implement a technology-driven project or seeking to raise the profile/efficiency of technology as a development tool in Africa'; 'technology must be integrated into a well-devised project, which will have a social impact'; 'the project must be well researched and tackling an unmet need'; 'any technology used must be appropriate, i.e. available and usable by the target population'; 'projects ought to be sustainable, replicable and/or scalable'; 'there should be a robust evaluation mechanism in place that enables the impact of the project to be measured'; 'any organisation must be willing to be transparent and open about their work, unless security concerns mean that such openness would present a credible risk of harm to people involved in the project'; 'we generally only provide approximately £10,000 to projects. The project budget can be higher, although it's very unlikely that we would be able to cover the full cost.' There is a 'soft spot' for the following: 'local organisations (or strong collaboration with local organisations)'; 'open source projects'; 'small organisations (with a budget of less than £500,000)'; 'interoperable solutions'; 'two way interactivity'; 'innovation'. The trust 'actively encourages collaboration and, in addition to acting as funders, sees one of its key roles as making connections between grantees, other organisations and funders'. Applicants with eligible projects should contact the trust to discuss their proposal. A suitable project proposal can be submitted directly but applicants are requested to keep it brief – two to four sides of A4 where possible. A proposal should contain: 'brief background information on your organisation, the country/countries it operates in, approximate size etc.'; 'if appropriate, an overview of the project for which you are seeking funding, including details of the technology involved, the numbers/types of people it aims to reach, current status etc.'; 'a statement of need, i.e. what problem does this project address'; 'a rough budget for the project'; 'details of how you will evaluate and monitor the project including Milestones or Objectives'; 'any other information, which you think we should know or may be helpful, such as details of partners you'll be working with'. The trust welcomes contact to discuss applications or to answer any questions you may have about applying or eligibility.

**WHO TO APPLY TO** Alan Bookbinder, Director, The Peak, 5 Wilton Road, London SW1V 1AP Tel. 020 7410 7037 Fax 020 7410 0332 email info@sfct.org.uk, loren.treisman@sfct.org.uk or matthew.oreilly@sfct.org.uk Website indigotrust.org.uk

## ■ The Ingram Trust

**CC NO** 1040194   **ESTABLISHED** 1994

**WHERE FUNDING CAN BE GIVEN** UK and overseas, with a local preference for Surrey.

**WHO CAN BENEFIT** Established registered charities only; local organisations in Surrey.

**WHAT IS FUNDED** General charitable purposes. The trust prefers to support specific projects including special services and equipment. It will support major UK charities together with some local ones in the county of Surrey. Normally the policy is to support a limited number of charities, but with a longer-term commitment to each.

**WHAT IS NOT FUNDED** Non-registered charities; individuals; charities specialising in overseas aid (except those dedicated to encouraging self-help and providing more permanent solutions to problems); animal charities (except those concerned with wildlife conservation).

**RANGE OF GRANTS** £1,000–£241,500

**SAMPLE GRANTS** WWF – UK (£241,500); The Royal National Theatre (£206,500); Shelter (£60,000); Almeida Theatre Company Limited and NSPCC (£35,000 each); Young Epilepsy (£30,000); UNICEF UK (£25,000); Countryside Learning (£20,000); The Woodland Trust (£15,000); Pimlico Opera (£12,000); Everychild, Surrey Care Trust and The Princess Alice Hospice (£10,000 each); Cherry Trees – Respite Care (£5,000); The Panathlon Foundation (£1,000).

**FINANCES** Year 2013/14 Income £70,178 Grants £982,334 Grants to organisations £982,334 Assets £10,282,006

**TRUSTEES** Christopher Ingram; Clare Maurice; Janet Ingram; Jonathan Ingram; Sally Ingram.

**OTHER INFORMATION** The trustees prefer to make larger grants to few charities. During the year there were 29 awards made.

**HOW TO APPLY** Applications may be made in writing to the correspondent, although the trust states that it receives far more worthy applications than it is able to support.

**WHO TO APPLY TO** Joan Major, Correspondent, Ground Floor, 22 Chancery Lane, London WC2A 1LS *email* theingramtrust@nqpllp.com

## ■ The Inlight Trust

**CC NO** 236782      **ESTABLISHED** 1957
**WHERE FUNDING CAN BE GIVEN** UK.
**WHO CAN BENEFIT** Registered charities benefitting people from many different religions.
**WHAT IS FUNDED** Donations are made on a non-denominational basis to charities providing valuable contributions to spiritual development and charities concerned with spiritual healing and spiritual growth through religious retreats.
**WHAT IS NOT FUNDED** Individuals, including students; organisations which are not registered charities; general appeals from large national organisations; grants are seldom available for church buildings.
**TYPE OF GRANT** Usually one-off for a specific project or part of a project. Bursary schemes eligible. Core funding and/or salaries are rarely considered.
**RANGE OF GRANTS** £1,000–£32,000
**SAMPLE GRANTS** The Rokpa Trust (£106,000 in four grants); The White Eagle Lodge (£40,000 in two grants); Rochdale Zen Retreat (£20,000 in two grants); Great Ocean Dharma Refuge (£15,000); Nagarjuna Buddhist Centre and Wells Cathedral Chorister Trust (£10,000 each); Lendrick Trust, The Meditation Centre and The White Eagle Publishing Trust (£5,000 each); Bibles for Children (£1,000).
**FINANCES** *Year* 2013/14 *Income* £304,720 *Grants* £217,000 *Grants to organisations* £217,000 *Assets* £7,764,831
**TRUSTEES** Wendy Collett; Judy Hayward; Sharon Knight; Sir Thomas Lucas; Roger Ross.
**OTHER INFORMATION** There were 15 grants made to ten organisations. The average grant was about £14,500.
**HOW TO APPLY** Applications should be made in writing to the correspondent, including details of the need, the intended project to meet it, an outline of budget, the most recent available annual accounts of the organisation, and a copy of your trust deed or your entry on the Charity Commission register. The trustees meet four times a year. Only applications from eligible bodies are acknowledged and only successful applicants are informed.
**WHO TO APPLY TO** Clare Pegden, Correspondent, PO Box 2, Liss, Hampshire GU33 6YP *Tel.* 07970 540015 *email* inlight.trust01@ntlworld.com

## ■ The Inman Charity

**CC NO** 261366      **ESTABLISHED** 1970
**WHERE FUNDING CAN BE GIVEN** UK.
**WHO CAN BENEFIT** A wide range of UK-registered charities; hospices. The charity also makes a regular payment (£20,000 per annum) to the Victor Inman Bursary Fund at Uppingham School of which the settlor had been a lifelong supporter.
**WHAT IS FUNDED** General charitable purposes; medical causes; social welfare; disability; older people; hospices; armed forces.
**WHAT IS NOT FUNDED** Individuals; young children and infants; maintenance of local buildings (such as, churches and village halls); animal welfare; wildlife and environmental conservation; religious charities.
**RANGE OF GRANTS** Most grants are for £5,000 or less.
**SAMPLE GRANTS** : Inman Charity Undergraduate Dental Research Award – King's College London (£30,000 over five years); Victor Inman Bursary Fund at Uppingham School (£20,000); Inman Chanty Medical Research Fund – King's College London (£18,000 over three years); DEC Philippines Typhoon Appeal (£10,000); University of Surrey (£6,000); Contact the Elderly and Institute of Cancer Research (£5,000 each); Ovarian Cancer Action (£4,500); Community Network and Montage Theatre Arts (£3,500 each); Isabel Hospice and Voluntary Action Broxtowe (£3,000 each); Alabare Christian Care and Support and Missing People (£2,000 each).
**FINANCES** *Year* 2013 *Income* £166,195 *Grants* £330,000 *Grants to organisations* £330,000 *Assets* £5,115,149
**TRUSTEES** A. L. Walker; Belinda Strother; Neil Wingerath; Prof. John Langdon; Michael Mathews; Inman Charity Trustees Ltd.
**OTHER INFORMATION** Grants were made to 66 organisations, including the annual commitment to the Victor Inman Bursary Fund. There is around £300,000 available for distribution each year.
**HOW TO APPLY** All applications should be made in writing to the correspondent. They should include: a copy of your latest annual report and audited accounts; registered number, aims and objectives of your charity; nature of the appeal and the amount required; total target, contributions received against it and the timing for completion; any other relevant factors. The directors meet in April and October each year and applications should be received by the end of February and August, respectively. Only successful applicants will be contacted.
**WHO TO APPLY TO** Neil Wingerath, Trustee, BM Box 2831, London WC1N 3XX *Website* www.inmancharity.org

## ■ Inner London Magistrates Court's Poor Box and Feeder Charity

**CC NO** 1046214      **ESTABLISHED** 1995
**WHERE FUNDING CAN BE GIVEN** Inner London.
**WHO CAN BENEFIT** Individuals and organisations.
**WHAT IS FUNDED** Social welfare; relief of need, hardship or distress.
**WHAT IS NOT FUNDED** Direct relief of rates, taxes or other public funds.
**RANGE OF GRANTS** Usually £250 to £15,000.
**SAMPLE GRANTS** St Mungo's and The Passage (£6,000 each); Inner London Probation Services – Prisoners' Family and Friends and St Giles Trust (£5,000 each); West London Day Centre (£4,000); Spitalfields Crypt Trust (£3,000); 999 Club and Thames Reach (£2,000 each).
**FINANCES** *Year* 2013/14 *Income* £46,323 *Grants* £47,397 *Grants to organisations* £47,397 *Assets* £4,025,341
**TRUSTEES** Jane Richardson; Kevin Griffiths; Quentin Purdy; Howard Riddle; Richard Kozak; Nicholas Evans.
**OTHER INFORMATION** In 2013/14 grants were given to 12 organisations.
**HOW TO APPLY** Applications can be made in writing to the correspondent. The trustees meet at least three times a year.
**WHO TO APPLY TO** Paula Carter, Correspondent, City Of Westminster Court, 7th Floor 65 Romney Street, London SW1P 3RD *Tel.* 020 7805 1132 *email* ilmcpbf@btinternet.com

*Alphabetical register of grant-making charities* — **International**

## ■ The Innocent Foundation

**CC NO** 1104289 **ESTABLISHED** 2004

**WHERE FUNDING CAN BE GIVEN** Worldwide, including South Asia, Africa, Bolivia, Honduras and the UK.

**WHO CAN BENEFIT** Community based projects and non-government organisations in the financially developing countries where the Innocent Drinks company sources fruit. Organisations must generally be UK-registered or have UK representation to receive funds.

**WHAT IS FUNDED** Projects which seek to address world hunger and enable people dependent on subsistence agriculture to build sustainable futures. Support is available through: Seed Funding – grants of up to £30,000 to help get new sustainable agriculture projects off the ground which will help 'communities in countries categorised as 'serious', 'alarming' or 'extremely alarming' on the Global Hunger Index to grow enough to feed and support themselves' Local Food Poverty – 'grants to charities who provide healthy, nutritious food to children, families and young people in food poverty in the UK' Breakthrough Development – support for innovative, untested ideas 'to find new models that will become the gold standard to address hunger issues' Emergency Hunger Relief – helping get food to people quickly in a humanitarian crisis.

**WHAT IS NOT FUNDED** Individuals.

**TYPE OF GRANT** Most funds are allocated in three year partnerships; some one-off projects.

**RANGE OF GRANTS** £7,000–£200,000

**SAMPLE GRANTS** The Clinton Foundation (£200,000); Action Against Hunger (£129,500); World Food Programme (£70,000 in two grants); Kids Company (£45,000 in two grants); Send a Cow (£39,000 in two grants); Jeevika Trust (£25,000 in two grants); ADD (£16,000); Practical Action (£9,800); Pragya UK (£7,100).

**FINANCES** Year 2013/14 Income £1,011,088 Grants £646,702 Grants to organisations £646,702 Assets £2,666,826

**TRUSTEES** Adam Balon; Jon Wright; Richard Reed; Christina Archer; Alison Wilson; Douglas Lamont.

**OTHER INFORMATION** The Innocent Foundation was set up by Innocent Drinks in 2004. Each year the company gives at least 10% of its profits to charity, the majority to the foundation. The foundation has detailed criteria for Seed Funding and is due to provide detailed criteria for Local Food Poverty online. During the year grants were distributed to 22 projects (including three emergency relief donations).

**HOW TO APPLY** In the first instance get in touch with the correspondent via an online form, email, phone or post, providing the following: your and your organisation's name; registered charity number; your email address; your organisations website (if applicable); statement of which funding you are applying for; a summary of your project (no more than 200 words), including how you set up the project, your long term aims and what you would use the money for.

**WHO TO APPLY TO** Kate Franks, Manager, Fruit Towers, 342 Ladbroke Grove, London W10 5BU *Tel.* 020 3235 0443 or 0207 993 3311 *email* kate.franks@innocentfoundation.org *Website* www.innocentfoundation.org

## ■ The International Bankers Charitable Trust (The Worshipful Company of International Bankers)

**CC NO** 1087630 **ESTABLISHED** 2001

**WHERE FUNDING CAN BE GIVEN** UK, with preference for inner London.

**WHO CAN BENEFIT** Registered charities only.

**WHAT IS FUNDED** Activities in educational and financial literacy. According to the website, 'the company will seek to promote recruitment and development of employees in the financial services industry with particular emphasis on those younger people in the immediate area of the city who would not normally be able to aspire to a city job.' The latest accounts note: 'The core focus of the Trust remains on providing support for education and financial literacy, with a particular emphasis on strengthening the links between the City and the communities which surround it.' There is also a Small Donations Fund (SDF) which 'enables small, timely donations of as low as a £100 to be made without need for specific prior approval from the Court of the Trustee'.

**WHAT IS NOT FUNDED** Large projects towards which any contribution from the company would have limited impact; general appeals or circulars; replacement of statutory funds; salaries; counselling; course fees for professionals; medical research; fundraising events and sponsorship; responses to requests for charitable aid.

**TYPE OF GRANT** Specific projects to cover either a significant proportion of the cost or an identified element of it; long-term funding of scholarships and/or bursaries.

**RANGE OF GRANTS** Typically up to £1,000; 'larger awards considered where funding can make a clear difference in accordance with Company aims'.

**SAMPLE GRANTS** The Brokerage Citylink Grant (£45,000); City of London School for Boys (£6,700); City of London School for Girls (£5,000); University Academic Prizes (£4,800); Cess Business School (£3,200); Reed's School (£2,000); Business Challenge (£1,200). Further 13 awards of £1,000 or less totalled £2,900.

**FINANCES** Year 2012/13 Income £171,304 Grants £95,515 Grants to organisations £95,515 Assets £905,938

**TRUSTEE** The Worshipful Company of International Bankers.

**OTHER INFORMATION** The website notes: 'As a representative of the major commercial activity in the City, banking and financial services, the Company combines the traditions of the City Livery Companies with a modern outlook on the financial services sector. With more than 700 members, drawn from over 250 companies and institutions and with almost 50 nationalities represented, the Company has a truly international character.' The total of grants includes £82,500 given through unrestricted funds, £7,900 through Past Masters Fund and £5,000 through KC Wu Fund (support to foreign students and young professionals). There were 23 separate awards made. The trust also awards prizes and supports the company employees' volunteering efforts. At the time of writing (June 2015) this was the latest information available.

**HOW TO APPLY** Application forms can be downloaded from the trust's website. Previous grant recipients must wait at least two years (from the

*Think carefully about every application. Is it justified?*

547

date the original grant was awarded) before re-applying.
WHO TO APPLY TO Nicholas Westgarth, Clerk, 3rd Floor, 12 Austin Friars, London EC2N 2HE *Tel.* 020 7374 0212 *Fax* 020 7374 0207 *email* clerk@internationalbankers.co.uk *Website* internationalbankers.org.uk

■ **Interserve Employee Foundation**
CC NO 1145338   ESTABLISHED 2011
WHERE FUNDING CAN BE GIVEN UK; worldwide
WHO CAN BENEFIT Grants are provided to employee nominated charities twice a year.
WHAT IS FUNDED General charitable purposes; disaster relief; education/training; social welfare.
FINANCES *Year* 2013 *Income* £91,366 *Grants* £75,029 *Grants to organisations* £75,029 *Assets* £8,181
TRUSTEES Hugh Johnson; Bob Vince; Jeremy Mead; Stephen Harland; Isa Buencamino; Heather Key; Mark Judge; Sarah Archer; Lianne Lawson; Graham Thwaites; Tony Sanders.
HOW TO APPLY Apply in writing to the correspondent.
WHO TO APPLY TO Heather Key, Trustee, 90 Kidmore Road, Caversham, Reading RG4 7NA *Tel.* 0118 932 0123 *email* Info.foundation@interserve.com *Website* www.interserve.com/about-us/interserve-employee-foundation

■ **The Inverforth Charitable Trust (ICT)**
CC NO 274132   ESTABLISHED 1977
WHERE FUNDING CAN BE GIVEN UK.
WHO CAN BENEFIT Registered charities only.
WHAT IS FUNDED General charitable purposes; health causes; education of young people; arts; military and international support.
TYPE OF GRANT Long-term awards.
RANGE OF GRANTS £500–£4,000
SAMPLE GRANTS Art Fund, Asthma UK, Childhood First, Help for Heroes, Help the Hospices, Ludgrove School Foundation, MS Society, National Youth Orchestra, St John's Hospice, St Mungo's and Trinity Hospice (£4,000 each); and Kids (£500).
FINANCES *Year* 2013 *Income* £35,365 *Grants* £44,500 *Grants to organisations* £44,500 *Assets* £3,714,013
TRUSTEES Lord Inverforth; Jonathan Kane; Elizabeth Inverforth.
OTHER INFORMATION Each year 12 core charities are supported.
HOW TO APPLY Applications should be made in writing to the trustees. The trust asks applicants to provide concise applications. The trustees normally meet in March, June, September and November/early December.
WHO TO APPLY TO Clarinda Kane, Secretary and Treasurer, PO Box 6, 47–49 Chelsea Manor Street, London SW3 5RZ

■ **Investream Charitable Trust**
CC NO 1097052   ESTABLISHED 2003
WHERE FUNDING CAN BE GIVEN Worldwide; largely in the UK and Israel.
WHO CAN BENEFIT Registered charities; educational establishments.
WHAT IS FUNDED Jewish causes; education; social welfare; medical purposes; relief of poverty; care for older people; community needs. The main focus area for the trust is the relief of poverty; however, other charitable causes are also assisted.
RANGE OF GRANTS Up to £164,000.
SAMPLE GRANTS Moreshet Hatorah Ltd (£164,000); Menorah High School for Girls (£159,500); British Friends of Tikva Odessa (£150,000); Cosmon (Belz) Limited (£110,000); Israel Central Committee for Taharas Hamishpacha (£61,000); Beis Yaakov Primary School Foundation (£55,000); Train For Employment Limited (£45,000); Dover Shalom Community Trust (£40,000); Project Seed (£37,000); Chana Charitable Trust (£30,000).
FINANCES *Year* 2013/14 *Income* £1,300,044 *Grants* £1,209,500 *Grants to organisations* £1,209,500 *Assets* £96,141
TRUSTEES Mark Morris; Graham Morris.
HOW TO APPLY Applications may be made in writing to the correspondent.
WHO TO APPLY TO The Trustees, Investream Ltd, 38 Wigmore Street, London W1U 2RU *Tel.* 020 7486 2800

■ **The Ireland Fund of Great Britain**
CC NO 327889   ESTABLISHED 1988
WHERE FUNDING CAN BE GIVEN The Republic of Ireland; throughout Great Britain.
WHO CAN BENEFIT Organisations benefitting people of Irish descent and other vulnerable or disadvantaged individuals; institutions promoting Irish culture and arts.
WHAT IS FUNDED Marginalised people in society, such as homeless people; survivors of institutional abuse; vulnerable and/or older Irish people; projects that tackle loneliness and isolation; social, cultural or educational activities and projects that help young people.
WHAT IS NOT FUNDED Organisations based outside England, Scotland or Wales (although there are worldwide branches of The Ireland Funds); general appeals – assistance must be sought for clearly specified purposes; individuals; tuition or student fees; medical costs; purchase of buildings or land; construction or refurbishment projects; events; debt; retrospective costs or salary costs. CICs cannot be assisted until they have three years' audited accounts available for inspection.
RANGE OF GRANTS £500–£45,000
SAMPLE GRANTS Celtic FC Foundation (£45,000); Southwark Irish Pensioners Project (£29,000); University of Limerick Foundation (£22,000); The Holy Child Killiney Building Appeal (£16,900); Console (£15,400); Coventry Irish Centre (£10,000); Irish Diaspora Foundation (£9,700); Lismore Music Festival (£7,200); The Maya Centre (£2,500); Personal Support Unit Liverpool and Women's Information and Support Project (£1,000 each); Breast Cancer Ireland (£500).
FINANCES *Year* 2013/14 *Income* £389,830 *Grants* £216,253 *Grants to organisations* £216,253 *Assets* £534,833
TRUSTEES Seamus McGarry; Michael Casey; Ruairi Conneely; Zach Webb; Eileen Kelliher; Rory Godson; Garrett Hayes; Kieran McLoughlin.
OTHER INFORMATION Grants were made to 22 organisations. Awards are made through the Small Grants Round (up to £10,000 in the island of Ireland only) and through Flagship Grant Round.
HOW TO APPLY Application forms are available on the charity's website. Applicants must also attach a copy of their audited accounts and can only submit one application per organisation per

year. The trustees meet quarterly. For current deadlines for each of the rounds see the website.

**WHO TO APPLY TO** Sean Henderson, Correspondent, 2nd Floor, Wigglesworth House, 69 Southwark Bridge Road, London SE1 9HH *Tel.* 020 7940 9858 *email* shenderson@irlfunds.org *Website* www.irelandfund.org

## ■ Irish Youth Foundation (UK) Ltd (incorporating The Lawlor Foundation)

**CC NO** 328265     **ESTABLISHED** 1989
**WHERE FUNDING CAN BE GIVEN** UK.
**WHO CAN BENEFIT** Community organisations working directly with young Irish people.
**WHAT IS FUNDED** Projects benefitting young Irish people or enhancing their personal and social development, especially if they are disadvantaged or in need. A wide range of projects are supported which include: training/counselling; drug rehabilitation; advice/advocacy; youth work; family support; homelessness; educational, cultural and social activities; cross-community initiatives; travellers and disability.
**WHAT IS NOT FUNDED** Projects for people over 25 (in northern Ireland) and over 30 (in England, Scotland and Wales); general appeals; large/national charities; academic research; alleviating deficits already incurred; individuals (except for university students applying under Lawlor Foundation Education programme); capital bids; overseas travel; multiple applications from a single organisation.
**TYPE OF GRANT** Programme development grants; seed funding; core costs and salaries; awards to upgrade premises and/or equipment; small grants.
**RANGE OF GRANTS** Up to £5,000 in Northern Ireland; £2,500–£12,000 in England, Scotland and Wales.
**SAMPLE GRANTS** Irish Community Care – Merseyside (£9,500); Construction Youth Trust (£7,000); Artillery Youth Centre – Belfast and Luton Irish Forum (£4,000 each); Willowfield Parish Community Association – Belfast (£3,400); St Cecilia's College, Derry and The Brandon Centre – London (£3,000 each); Birmingham TradFest (£2,500); The Emerald Centre – Leicester (£2,000); Woodlands Pre School Centre – Donemana (£1,900); Conradh na Gaeilge Glaschú (The Gaelic League Glasgow) (£1,300); Irish Arts Foundation – Leeds (£1,000); Felling Irish Association – Gateshead (£500).
**FINANCES** *Year* 2013 *Income* £271,573 *Grants* £196,990 *Grants to organisations* £196,990 *Assets* £2,482,326
**TRUSTEES** John Dwyer; John O'Neill; Virginia Lawlor; June Trimble; Richard Corrigan; Ciara Brett; Cecilia Gallagher.
**OTHER INFORMATION** Irish Youth Foundation (UK) Ltd merged with the Lawlor Foundation in 2005. The work of the Lawlor Foundation towards the advancement of education in Northern Ireland continues with support for Irish students and educational organisations. The latest annual report and accounts for 2013 did not provide a list of beneficiaries; however, 2014 grant recipients were listed online.
**HOW TO APPLY** Applications are assessed on an annual basis and application forms are only available during the annual round either on the website or by request. The foundation's website states: 'Application forms are available during December with a submission deadline at the end of January, and grant awards are made the following May/June. Unsolicited applications at other times during the year are not accepted.' Applications are assessed on the following requirements: need; continuity; track record/evaluation; disadvantaged young people; innovativeness; funding sources; budgetary control. Faxed or emailed applications are not considered.
**WHO TO APPLY TO** Linda Tanner, Head of Operations, The Irish Cultural Centre, 26–28 Hammersmith Grove, Hammersmith, London W6 7HA *Tel.* 020 8748 9640 *email* linda@iyf.org.uk *Website* www.iyf.org.uk

## ■ The Ironmongers' Foundation

**CC NO** 219153–10     **ESTABLISHED** 1964
**WHERE FUNDING CAN BE GIVEN** UK, with some preference for inner London.
**WHO CAN BENEFIT** Registered charities; schools and other educational establishments; churches; projects related to steel and iron work.
**WHAT IS FUNDED** Education, particularly of young people; iron and steel industry and art work; conservation and heritage; Projects that 'provide opportunities for disadvantaged children and young people to fulfil their potential' the promotion of the craft of ironwork; the provision of support 'primarily for the conservation of historic ironwork or the creation of new decorative iron or steel work' (other restoration projects or projects benefitting private individuals are not supported).
**WHAT IS NOT FUNDED** Large projects towards which any contribution from the Company would have limited impact; general appeals or circulars; replacement of statutory funds; general running costs (a reasonable proportion of overheads will be accepted as part of project costs); counselling and therapy; course fees for professionals; medical research; fundraising events and sponsorship; retrospective appeals and projects starting before the date of the relevant Committee meeting; building work; holidays.
**TYPE OF GRANT** Capital costs; projects expenditure; salaries; one-off awards or longer term (over one year) projects, subject to a satisfactory evaluation of progress at the end of each year.
**RANGE OF GRANTS** £500–£15,700
**SAMPLE GRANTS** National Trust (£15,700); Christ's Hospital (£11,500); Arkwright Scholarship Trust (£10,000); Baltic Centre (£6,800); St Mary's Primary School (£6,500); University of Birmingham and University of Manchester (£4,000 each); Friends of Pittville (£2,800); Sheriffs and Recorder's Fund (£2,000); Victoria and Albert Museum (£1,000); South of England Show (£500); City of London Police Widows and Orphans' Fund (£300).
**FINANCES** *Year* 2013/14 *Income* £175,406 *Grants* £156,681 *Grants to organisations* £156,681 *Assets* £2,556,520
**TRUSTEE** The Ironmongers' Trust Company.
**OTHER INFORMATION** Financial information relates to the foundation specifically, although recipients of grants from the Ironmongers' Foundation were not listed specifically. The accounts give details of all beneficiaries receiving grants from all the funds of Sir Robert Geffery's Almshouse Trust which we have used in the sample. Charitable activities supported through each of the fund may slightly vary but broadly cover the areas of education, steel and iron work, provision of almshouses and relief in need. For

more details on other funds see the Ironmongers' Company's website.

**HOW TO APPLY Organisations:** Applications should be made using the 'Grant Application Summary Sheet' (available to download on the website) which needs to be returned together with a description of the project (no more than three A4 pages typed on both sides). The Appeals Committee meets twice a year in March and October; therefore applications should be received by 31 December and 31 July, respectively. Applications are **not** accepted by e-mail. The company asks to enclose a copy of your most recent audited accounts if they are not available from the Charity Commission's website. **Iron:** Applications should be made in writing the correspondent including full details of the project. The website states that it is expected that 'any conservation of historic ironwork to follow the National Heritage Ironwork Group's Conservation Principles (see www.nhig.org.uk)' – applications should confirm that your project will meet these standards. The Company's Iron Committee meets in May (applications should be received by 31 March). **Note:** See the website for full details of information required to include in your application.

**WHO TO APPLY TO** Helen Sant, Charities Manager, Ironmongers' Hall, Barbican, London EC2Y 8AA *Tel.* 020 7776 2311 *Fax* 020 7600 3519 *email* helen@ironmongers.org *Website* www.ironhall.co.uk

## ■ The Charles Irving Charitable Trust

**CC NO** 297712    **ESTABLISHED** 1987
**WHERE FUNDING CAN BE GIVEN** Mainly Gloucestershire.
**WHO CAN BENEFIT** Charitable organisations; individuals.
**WHAT IS FUNDED** Relief in need; social welfare. Priority is given to projects which benefit those 'disadvantaged by poverty, or by physical or mental ability'; however, support is also given to older people, homeless individuals, young people, local community projects, victim support, resettlement of offenders and 'other causes with which the settlor, Sir Charles Irving DL, was associated during his lifetime' or 'projects with which the settlor's name may be linked'.
**WHAT IS NOT FUNDED** Ongoing grants; research; expeditions; computers or other equipment (unless benefitting people with disabilities); causes outside the county of Gloucester except for the few organisations with which Sir Charles was associated and which are already known to the Trustees.
**TYPE OF GRANT** One-off; mainly capital projects, although the trustees 'may look for evidence that consideration has been given to onward revenue funding' project costs.
**RANGE OF GRANTS** Mostly in the range of £50–£500; larger grants are sometimes made.
**SAMPLE GRANTS Beneficiaries of £1,000 or more included**: Motability (£3,000); New Bridge (£2,500); Leonard Cheshire Disability, Listening Books and Prisoners' Advice Service (£2,000 each); Blind Veterans UK, Cheltenham Animal Shelter and YMCA Cheltenham (£1,800 each); Cotswold Care Hospice (£1,600); Abbeyfield Society and Dogs for the Disabled (£1,500 each); St Dunstan's (£1,400); Whizz-Kidz (£1,300); Vitalise (£1,100).

**FINANCES** *Year* 2012/13 *Income* £76,166 *Grants* £72,848 *Grants to organisations* £72,848 *Assets* £2,076,142
**TRUSTEES** Tony Hilder; J. E. Lane; D. J. Oldham; Peter Shephard.
**OTHER INFORMATION** At the time of writing (June 2015) this was the latest information available. Support was distributed as follows: people with disabilities (£29,000); community (£27,000); resettlement of offenders (£5,300); homelessness and older people (£4,300 each); mental health (£2,800); victim support (£500). Most grants (55 awards) were in the range of £50–£500. There is an annual award scheme which allows the trustees to 'identify suitable and deserving causes to which they may be able to award a more substantial sum'. According to the latest report, 'regrettably the trustees were unable, after exploring a number of avenues, to find a suitable project or applicant and therefore no annual award was made'. The trustees were 'looking towards identifying a suitable recipient' for the future awards.
**HOW TO APPLY** The latest annual report states: 'The Trustees welcome applications by letter, giving details of the proposed project, its total cost and the amount if any already raised or promised from other sources. Other information such as a budget and details of the number of people expected to benefit will also be helpful.'
**WHO TO APPLY TO** J. E. Lane, Secretary, PO Box 868, Cheltenham, Gloucestershire GL53 9WZ *Tel.* 01242 234848

## ■ The J. Isaacs Charitable Trust

**CC NO** 1059865    **ESTABLISHED** 1996
**WHERE FUNDING CAN BE GIVEN** England and Wales.
**WHO CAN BENEFIT** Charitable organisations.
**WHAT IS FUNDED** General charitable purposes, particularly care for children, education, older people, tolerance in the community, healthcare, the arts and sports.
**RANGE OF GRANTS** Up to £100,000.
**SAMPLE GRANTS** Beneficiaries have included: Jewish Care (£200,000); the Jewish Museum London (£100,000); Community Security Trust (£75,000); Greenhouse Schools Project (£25,000); Policy Exchange Ltd (£15,000); UCLH Fund (£7,500); UK Jewish Film (£5,000); Royal National Theatre (£1,000). Most recently – Prince's Foundation for Children and the Arts, Greenhouse Schools project, Skiers Trust and Action Against Cancer.
**FINANCES** *Year* 2013/14 *Income* £45,943 *Grants* £471,250 *Grants to organisations* £471,250 *Assets* £14,582,874
**TRUSTEES** Jeremy Isaacs: Joanne Isaacs; Helen Eastick; Vincent Isaacs.
**HOW TO APPLY** Applications can be made in writing to the correspondent.
**WHO TO APPLY TO** The Trustees, JRJ Group, 61 Conduit Street, London W1S 2GB *Tel.* 020 7220 2305 *Fax* 020 7220 2339 *email* enquiries@jrjgroup.com

## ■ The Isle of Anglesey Charitable Trust

**CC NO** 1000818    **ESTABLISHED** 1990
**WHERE FUNDING CAN BE GIVEN** The Isle of Anglesey only.
**WHO CAN BENEFIT** Organisations in Anglesey.

**WHAT IS FUNDED** General charitable purposes; community causes; sports; projects benefitting local people.
**WHAT IS NOT FUNDED** Individuals; projects based outside Anglesey.
**TYPE OF GRANT** One-off and recurring.
**RANGE OF GRANTS** £1,000–£215,000; normally up to £6,000.
**SAMPLE GRANTS** Isle of Anglesey County Council – Oriel Ynys Môn (£215,000); Penysarn Village Hall (£6,000); Cemaes Bay Football Club (£4,300); Amlwch Memorial Hall and Newry Community Centre (£3,400 each); Pritchard Jones Hall (£2,400); Menai Bridge War Memorial Community Centre (£1,900); Community Centre Brynsiencyn (£1,600); Llangoed and Penmon Community Council (£1,300); Talwrn Village Hall (£1,200).
**FINANCES** Year 2013/14 Income £500,435 Grants £328,565 Grants to organisations £328,565 Assets £18,863,093
**TRUSTEE** Isle of Anglesey County Council.
**OTHER INFORMATION** There were 47 awards made to 44 organisations. Only awards above £1,000 were listed. The trust's accounts provide information as to the distribution of its income to various organisations in Anglesey; however, it is not possible to ascertain from the accounts whether any of the grants awarded are used to subsidise the county council by providing facilities and/or services which should be provided by the local authority.
**HOW TO APPLY** Application forms can be requested from the correspondent, following advertisements in the local press in February. The trust considers applications once a year and 'will take details of any prospective applicants during the year, but application forms are sent out annually in February'.
**WHO TO APPLY TO** Gareth Roberts, Vice Chair, Head of Function (Resources), Isle of Anglesey County Council, County Offices, Llangefni, Anglesey LL77 7TW *Tel.* 01248 752610 *email* garethjroberts@anglesey.gov.uk

## ■ The ITF Seafarers Trust

**CC NO** 281936    **ESTABLISHED** 1981
**WHERE FUNDING CAN BE GIVEN** Worldwide.
**WHO CAN BENEFIT** Seafarers, their families and dependants; organisations catering for seafarers' welfare, including welfare agencies, religious bodies, independent missions and trade unions. Applicants should have a proven record of dealing with seafarers' welfare.
**WHAT IS FUNDED** General welfare of seafarers of all nations, their families and dependants.
**WHAT IS NOT FUNDED** The following are not likely to be supported: 'maintenance of buildings and vehicles; wages and other personnel costs; retrospective funding for completed projects; deficits which have already been incurred; projects which promote particular religious beliefs; recurring costs'. Note that 'grants are intended to be additional to and not a substitute for other financial support currently made available from government, other charity or funding body, church or other public bodies'.
**TYPE OF GRANT** Buildings; vehicles; capital and core costs; one-off expenditure; project grants; training and education support.
**RANGE OF GRANTS** Small grants – up to £75,000; large grants – over £75,000.
**SAMPLE GRANTS** Hunter Workers Rehab (£75,000); Global Maritime Ministries (£72,000); Singapore Organization of Seamen (£50,000); World Maritime University Malmo (£34,500); Stella Maris' Friends (£26,000); The Mission to Seafarers (£20,000); AoS Tarragona (£18,300); Adonai Seafarers' Fellowship (£15,000); Space Coast Seafarers' Ministry (£14,000); Association les amis de marins (£6,800); Seafarers' House (£4,000).
**FINANCES** Year 2013 Income £7,721,407 Grants £638,567 Grants to organisations £638,567 Assets £28,357,726
**TRUSTEES** Paddy Crumlin; Dave Heindel; Stephen Cotton; Lars Lindgren; Brian Orrell; Abdulgani Serang.
**OTHER INFORMATION** Organisations which have already received a number of grants over a short time period may find it more difficult to apply successfully for further support. Note that 'the decrease in grant expenditure was largely due to the restrictions placed on grant-giving during 2013 as part of the ongoing strategic review' normally awards total over £1 million each year.
**HOW TO APPLY** Applications have to be made online on the trust's website, where full criteria and guidelines are also available. Applications must be supported by an ITF affiliated seafarers' or dockers' trade union. The trustees' meetings are normally held in January–March, June–July and October–November each year. Requests for small grants (up to £75,000) may take about two to six months to proceed and for large grants (over £75,000) the process can last 3–12 months.
**WHO TO APPLY TO** Theresa Broome, Correspondent, ITF House, 49–60 Borough Road, London SE1 1DR *Tel.* 020 7403 2733 *Fax* 020 7357 7871 *email* trust@itf.org.uk *Website* www.itfglobal.org/seafarers-trust

### ■ The J. and J. Benevolent Foundation

**cc no** 1146602   **established** 2012
**where funding can be given** Throughout the UK.
**who can benefit** Charitable organisations; Jewish places of worship; individuals in need.
**what is funded** General charitable purposes; relief of poverty; health and disability; education; Orthodox Jewish faith. Support has been given in basic necessities and financial support to poor people, help to individuals with illness or disability, Jewish education and assisting the Jewish community.
**finances** Year 2013/14 Income £150,000 Grants £165,517 Grants to organisations £165,517 Assets £149,568
**trustees** Joseph Adler; Judi Adler.
**how to apply** Applications can be made in writing to the correspondent.
**who to apply to** Joseph Adler, Trustee, 46 Woodville Road, London NW11 9TN Tel. 020 8731 0777 email mail@cohenarnold.com

### ■ The J. and J. Charitable Trust

**cc no** 1065660   **established** 1997
**where funding can be given** UK.
**who can benefit** Registered charities; individuals; schools and universities; hospitals and hospices.
**what is funded** General charitable purposes; health causes; work with children and young people; Jewish causes.
**range of grants** Usually up to £10,000.
**sample grants** Covenant and Conversation Trust (£25,000); Jewish Care (£10,200); Save the Children (£10,000); Ambitious about Autism, Myeloma UK and TTK Greenhouse Ltd (£5,000 each); Western Marble Arch Synagogue (£2,200); University of Warwick (£2,000); Technion UK (£1,500); Great Ormond Street Hospital and Harefield Hospital (£1,000 each); Child Bereavement Trust and Friends of Yad Sarah (£500 each); and British Friends of ORT (£240).
**finances** Year 2013/14 Income £162,554 Grants £97,476 Grants to organisations £97,476 Assets £97,200
**trustees** Jahnene Green; Jonathan Green.
**other information** Jonathan Green is a former Goldman Sachs trader and co-founder of London hedge fund GLG. During the year 24 awards were made.
**how to apply** Applications can be made in writing to the correspondent.
**who to apply to** Leon Angel, Correspondent, Hazlems Fenton LLP, Palladium House, 1–4 Argyll Street, London W1F 7LD Tel. 020 7437 7666 Fax 020 7734 0644 email info@hazlemsfenton.com

### ■ The J. A. R. Charitable Trust

**cc no** 248418   **established** 1966
**where funding can be given** Worldwide.
**who can benefit** Organisations benefitting older people, students, Roman Catholics, missionaries, and people disadvantaged by poverty.
**what is funded** Roman Catholic causes; education for people under 30; relief in need (the provision of food, clothing and accommodation) for people in need over 55.
**what is not funded** The trust does not normally support a charity unless it is known to the trustees and it does not support individuals.
**type of grant** One-off and recurring.
**range of grants** £1,000–£10,000
**sample grants** The Ordinariate of Our Lady of Walsingham (£10,000); Saint Colmcilles Catholic Church South Africa (£5,000); Oxford Oratory (£4,000); Catholic Children's Society Brentwood and Liverpool Archdiocesan Youth Pilgrimage (£3,000 each); Anchor House, Little Sisters of the Poor and Youth 2000 (£2,000 each); and Tongabezi Trust School (£1,000).
**finances** Year 2013/14 Income £111,366 Grants £75,000 Grants to organisations £75,000 Assets £2,751,704
**trustees** Philip Noble; Revd William Young; Revd Paschal Ryan.
**other information** There were 26 awards made.
**how to apply** According to the annual report for 2013/14, the trustees 'identify projects and organisations they wish to support and so the charity does not make grants to people or organisations who apply speculatively'. It is further noted that there is 'a policy of not responding to any correspondence unless it relates to grants it has agreed to make or to the general management of the charity'.
**who to apply to** Philip Noble, Trustee, Hunters, 9 New Square, London WC2A 3QN Tel. 020 7412 0050 email gt@hunters-solicitors.co.uk

### ■ The J. J. Charitable Trust

**cc no** 1015792   **established** 1992
**where funding can be given** UK and overseas.
**who can benefit** Registered charities or activities with clearly defined charitable purposes.
**what is funded** Literacy – 'to improve the effectiveness of literacy teaching in primary and secondary education for children with learning difficulties including dyslexia, and for ex-offenders or those at risk of offending'; sustainable lifestyles – 'creative approaches that visualise a sustainable future in positive ways, innovative enterprise and economic models that support sustainable lifestyles and the role of the media in communicating about sustainability'; environment projects overseas – 'especially community-based agriculture initiatives, which aim to help people help themselves in an environmentally sustainable way'.
**what is not funded** Individuals; educational fees; expeditions.
**type of grant** Seed funding; project grants.
**range of grants** £1,700–£225,000
**sample grants** Young Enterprise (£225,000); British Academy of Film and Television Awards – BAFTA (£123,000); Leon Foundation (£75,000); Gaia Foundation (£60,000); Royal Society of Arts (£31,500); Haven Distribution (£24,000); Salisbury Festival Ltd (£20,000); Climate News Network (£14,000); National Energy Foundation (£10,000); Tellus Mater (£5,500); Climate Change Collaboration (£5,000); Low Carbon Community Network (£1,700).
**finances** Year 2013/14 Income £1,229,913 Grants £1,149,772 Grants to organisations £1,149,772 Assets £37,147,886

**TRUSTEES** John Sainsbury; Mark Sainsbury; Judith Portrait; Lucy Guard.
**OTHER INFORMATION** The trust is one of the Sainsbury Family Charitable Trusts, all of which share a joint administration but work autonomously as an independent legal entity. An application to one is taken as an application to all. The trust states: 'Proposals are generally invited by the Trustees or initiated at their request. Unsolicited applications are discouraged and are unlikely to be successful, unless they are closely aligned to the Trust's areas of interest.'
**HOW TO APPLY** Applications should be made in writing via post including a description (strictly no more than two pages) of the proposed project. You should provide: details of your organisation (charitable aims and objectives, most recent annual income and expenditure and current financial position); what is needed for the project and who it will benefit; breakdown of costs, and any other sources of funding. Do not include any accounts or additional brochures. If you are successful you should hear from the trust within eight weeks of the acknowledgement. Unsuccessful appeals are not notified. A single application will be considered for support by all the trusts in the group, provided it fits the objectives. Note that the trust's website states that, although it may consider unsolicited requests the majority of such are unsuccessful.
**WHO TO APPLY TO** Alan Bookbinder, Director, The Peak, 5 Wilton Road, London SW1V 1AP *Tel.* 020 7410 0330 *Fax* 020 7410 0332 *email* info@sfct.org.uk *Website* www.sfct.org.uk

■ **The JRSST Charitable Trust**
**CC NO** 247498   **ESTABLISHED** 1955
**WHERE FUNDING CAN BE GIVEN** UK.
**WHO CAN BENEFIT** Organisations or individuals undertaking research or action in fields which relate directly to the non-charitable work of the Joseph Rowntree Reform Trust Ltd. Academics and research workers may benefit.
**WHAT IS FUNDED** The trust works in close association with the Joseph Rowntree Reform Trust Ltd, which is a non-charitable trust of which all the trustees of The JRSST Charitable Trust are directors, in supporting the development of an increasingly democratic and socially just UK.
**WHAT IS NOT FUNDED** Student grants are not funded.
**TYPE OF GRANT** Specific finance in particular fields of interest to the trust. One-off awards and grants up to one year.
**RANGE OF GRANTS** Up to £40,000.
**SAMPLE GRANTS** Privacy International (£40,000); Full Fact (£27,500); Intergenerational Justice Project (£18,800); Politically Engaged Young Friends (£2,300); and Democratic Audit (£32).
**FINANCES** Year 2013 *Income* £112,372 *Grants* £96,073 *Grants to organisations* £94,948 *Assets* £3,320,727
**TRUSTEES** Christine Day; Dr Christopher Greenfield; Amanda Cormack; Peadar Cremin; Sarah Brinton; Andrew Neal; Alison Goldsworthy; Nick Harvey.
**OTHER INFORMATION** There were 23 awards made paid to organisations.
**HOW TO APPLY** The website states that unsolicited appeals are not accepted. Our research indicates that suitable proposals may be submitted to the Grants and Projects Adviser via email, including a short outline of the proposal and the amount required. Applications for small grants of up to £5,000 are considered at any time. The deadline for grants over £5,000 is four to five weeks before the trustees' meeting, held quarterly. All applications should be received before 12 noon on the deadline day. There is an online application process for proposals to the Joseph Rowntree Reform Trust Ltd.
**WHO TO APPLY TO** Tina Walker, Secretary, The Garden House, Water End, York YO30 6WQ *Tel.* 01904 625744 *Fax* 01904 651502 *email* info@jrrt.org.uk *Website* www.jrrt.org.uk

■ **The Jabbs Foundation**
**CC NO** 1128402   **ESTABLISHED** 2009
**WHERE FUNDING CAN BE GIVEN** UK and overseas.
**WHO CAN BENEFIT** Registered charities; universities; educational and research institutions; projects lead by medics of international reputation and standing; major university hospitals.
**WHAT IS FUNDED** General charitable purposes. Current focus is on: medical research; education (including arts); enhancing family and community relationships in the West Midlands; 'support to vulnerable members of society and organisations which aim to prevent people entering the criminal justice system'. The latest annual report states: 'The trustees do not intend to restrict the broad objects as set out in the trust deed but in the next 12 months are likely to continue to prioritise grants in the above 4 areas. In addition, a fifth area is likely to be added, namely research into trees and forests in the UK and related educational opportunities.'
**SAMPLE GRANTS** A list of beneficiaries was not included in the accounts; however, it was specified that grants went 'to fund medical research projects including plasma cell dyscrasias, acute rheumatic fever and heart disease and a small grants programme to innovative early stage research projects'. In addition awards were paid to 'an organisation supporting vulnerable women to provide a case worker and a fund targeted at smaller organisations in Birmingham and the Black Country that aim to provide positive experiences and support to young people vulnerable to entering the criminal justice system'. A grant of £100,000 was agreed to a leading UK charity specialising in relationship counselling. The foundation also states that he grants totalling £145,000 have been awarded to the Birmingham Medical Research Expeditionary Society.
**FINANCES** Year 2012/13 *Income* £2,625,687 *Grants* £152,994 *Grants to organisations* £152,994 *Assets* £2,717,023
**TRUSTEES** Robin Daniels; Dr Alexander Wright; Ruth Keighley.
**OTHER INFORMATION** At the time of writing (June 2015) this was the latest information available. The grant total includes £133,000 to charitable institutions and £20,000 to academic institutions.
**HOW TO APPLY** Applications may be made in writing to the correspondent.
**WHO TO APPLY TO** The Trustees, PO Box 16067, Harborne, Birmingham, West Midlands B32 9GP *Tel.* 0121 428 2593

## ■ C. Richard Jackson Charitable Trust

**CC NO** 1073442 **ESTABLISHED** 1999
**WHERE FUNDING CAN BE GIVEN** England and Wales.
**WHO CAN BENEFIT** Registered charities.
**WHAT IS FUNDED** General charitable purposes, particularly disadvantaged children and young people, and individuals with life limiting disorders
**RANGE OF GRANTS** Typically £5,000 or less.
**SAMPLE GRANTS** The Prince's Trust (£48,500); St Michael's Hospice (£8,100); British Heart Foundation (£6,200); The Laura Crane Youth Cancer Trust (£6,000); Prince of Wales Hospice (£3,600); Macmillan Cancer Support (£250); The York Early Music Foundation (£50); and Cleveland Alzheimer's Residential Centre and Rehabilitation for Addicted Prisoners Trust (£25 each).
**FINANCES** Year 2013/14 Income £75,720 Grants £76,044 Grants to organisations £76,044 Assets £25,897
**TRUSTEES** Charles Jackson; Jeremy Jackson; Lucy Crack.
**OTHER INFORMATION** There were 17 awards made.
**HOW TO APPLY** Applications can be made in writing to the correspondent.
**WHO TO APPLY TO** Charles Jackson, Trustee, Loftus Hill, Ferrensby, Knaresborough, North Yorkshire HG5 9JT *Tel.* 01423 520232 *email* agk@crjholdings.co.uk

## ■ The Jacobs Charitable Trust

**CC NO** 264942 **ESTABLISHED** 1972
**WHERE FUNDING CAN BE GIVEN** UK and the USA.
**WHO CAN BENEFIT** Registered charities; community groups.
**WHAT IS FUNDED** Jewish causes; the arts.
**RANGE OF GRANTS** Up to £43,000.
**SAMPLE GRANTS** St Jude Childcare Centres India (£43,000); Central Synagogue (£15,000); Friends of Yad Sarah (£2,500).
**FINANCES** Year 2013/14 Income £53,721 Grants £60,435 Grants to organisations £60,435 Assets £60,991
**TRUSTEES** Simon Jacobs; Nicola Jacobs-Schlesinger.
**OTHER INFORMATION** There were three awards made.
**HOW TO APPLY** Applications may be made in writing to the correspondent.
**WHO TO APPLY TO** Alison Meek, Correspondent, c/o Harcus Sinclair, 3 Lincoln's Inn Fields, London WC2A 3AA *Tel.* 020 7242 9700 *email* charity.correspondence@bo.co.uk

## ■ The Ruth and Lionel Jacobson Trust (Second Fund) No 2

**CC NO** 326665 **ESTABLISHED** 1984
**WHERE FUNDING CAN BE GIVEN** UK, with a preference for North East England.
**WHO CAN BENEFIT** Registered charities benefitting people of all ages, medical professionals, parents and children, people with disabilities, people who are sick, homeless people, refugees and victims of famine.
**WHAT IS FUNDED** General charitable purposes; Jewish causes; education, health and disability; medical research; relief in need.
**WHAT IS NOT FUNDED** Grants are not made for individuals. Only registered charities will be supported.
**TYPE OF GRANT** One-off and regular grants; project support; research. Funding is available for one year or less.
**RANGE OF GRANTS** £50–£15,000
**FINANCES** Year 2013/14 Income £65,990 Grants £41,140 Grants to organisations £41,140 Assets £1,602,658
**TRUSTEES** Anne Jacobson; Malcolm Jacobson.
**OTHER INFORMATION** There were 11 awards made.
**HOW TO APPLY** Applications can be made in writing to the correspondent, providing an sae. Applications are considered every other month.
**WHO TO APPLY TO** Malcolm Jacobson, Trustee, 14 The Grainger Suite, Dobson House, Regent Centre, Gosforth, Newcastle upon Tyne NE3 3PF *email* mjacobson2006@gmail.com

## ■ Jaffe Family Relief Fund

**CC NO** 208560 **ESTABLISHED** 1970
**WHERE FUNDING CAN BE GIVEN** UK.
**WHO CAN BENEFIT** Registered charities.
**WHAT IS FUNDED** Relief of poverty.
**WHAT IS NOT FUNDED** Grants are not made to charities for anything which is not direct relief of poverty in UK.
**RANGE OF GRANTS** Under £1,000.
**SAMPLE GRANTS** Previously grants have been made to the following organisations: Bryson House; Camden Charities; Catholic Children's Society; Central Family Service Units; Providence Row; SSAFA Forces Help; West London Action for Children; and West London Family Service Unit.
**FINANCES** Year 2013/14 Income £49,422 Grants £45,708 Grants to organisations £2,500 Assets £1,311,122
**TRUSTEES** James Reinlieb; Dr Robin Jacobson; Dr Gillian Haworth.
**OTHER INFORMATION** The primary objective of the trust is to assist the descendants of David Joseph Jaffe and their families.
**HOW TO APPLY** Unsolicited applications are not normally considered. The trust has stated the following – funds are unlikely to allow us to add to the list of beneficiaries. The annual report notes that 'in practice the bulk of the income is distributed to family rather than charities'.
**WHO TO APPLY TO** Dr Robin Jacobson, Trustee, 24 Manor Way, Beckenham, Kent BR3 3LJ *email* jfrf751@gmail.com

## ■ John James Bristol Foundation

**CC NO** 288417 **ESTABLISHED** 1983
**WHERE FUNDING CAN BE GIVEN** Bristol.
**WHO CAN BENEFIT** Charitable bodies and schools that can clearly show that they are benefitting Bristol residents.
**WHAT IS FUNDED** Key focus areas are: education; health; older people.
**WHAT IS NOT FUNDED** Individuals.
**TYPE OF GRANT** Capital and core costs; unrestricted funding.
**RANGE OF GRANTS** Up to £100,000.
**SAMPLE GRANTS** Teenage Cancer Trust (£100,000); University of Bristol – Bowel Cancer Research (£12,000); Age UK Bristol (£10,000); Huntington's Disease Association (£8,800); Care and Repair – West of England (£7,000); Fairfield High School and InterAct Reading Service (£5,000 each); The Rotary Club of Bristol (£3,600); Merchants' Academy Primary School (£3,500); Drake Music South West (£3,400); Bristol Grammar School and Senior Citizens Liaison Team (£2,000 each); Bristol

Children's Help Society (£1,500); The Canynges Society (£1,000).

**FINANCES** Year 2013/14 Income £2,289,833 Grants £1,997,729 Grants to organisations £1,997,729 Assets £62,573,093

**TRUSTEES** Joan Johnson; David Johnson; Elizabeth Chambers; John Evans; Andrew Jardine; Andrew Webley; Dr John Haworth; Peter Goodwin.

**OTHER INFORMATION** Grants of £1,000 or less totalled about £56,500.

**HOW TO APPLY** The trustees meet quarterly in February, May, August and November to consider appeals received by the 15th of January, April, July and October, respectively. There is no formal application form and appeals must be submitted by post, to Julia Norton, Chief Executive of the foundation. Appeals should be no more than two sides of A4. All appeal applications are acknowledged, stating the month in which the appeal will be considered by the trustees.

**WHO TO APPLY TO** Domina Fisher, Grants Co-ordinator, 7 Clyde Road, Redland, Bristol BS6 6RG Tel. 0117 923 9444 Fax 0117 923 9470 email info@johnjames.org.uk Website www.johnjames.org.uk

## ■ The Susan and Stephen James Charitable Settlement

**CC NO** 801622  **ESTABLISHED** 1988
**WHERE FUNDING CAN BE GIVEN** UK.
**WHO CAN BENEFIT** Registered charities; Jewish organisations.
**WHAT IS FUNDED** General charitable purposes; health; education; Jewish focus.
**TYPE OF GRANT** Capital and other costs; generally unrestricted funding.
**RANGE OF GRANTS** £100–£24,000
**SAMPLE GRANTS** Norwood (£23,500); Community Security Trust (£12,500); Jewish Care (£10,500); Chai Cancer Care (£10,300); British Friends of Yad Sarah (£10,000); Holocaust Education Trust (£5,000); Heart Cells Foundation (£3,800); Kol Nidre Appeal (£2,500); United Synagogue (£1,900); Lifelites (£1,000); WIZO UK (£500); and Macmillan Cancer Support (£100).
**FINANCES** Year 2013 Income £113,564 Grants £105,692 Grants to organisations £105,692 Assets £97,344
**TRUSTEES** Stephen James; Susan James.
**OTHER INFORMATION** In 2013 grants were given to 26 organisations.
**HOW TO APPLY** Applications can be made in writing to the correspondent, although the charity has previously stated that unsolicited applications are not generally considered.
**WHO TO APPLY TO** Stephen James, Trustee, 4 Turner Drive, London NW11 6TX Tel. 020 7486 5838

## ■ The James Trust

**CC NO** 800774  **ESTABLISHED** 1989
**WHERE FUNDING CAN BE GIVEN** UK and overseas.
**WHO CAN BENEFIT** Churches, organisations and individuals. Principally Christian institutions benefitting Christians, young adults, older people, people disadvantaged by poverty, disaster victims, and refugees.
**WHAT IS FUNDED** Support is primarily to Christian causes, the advancement of the Christian religion and Anglican diocesan and Free Church umbrella bodies.

**WHAT IS NOT FUNDED** No grants are given to individuals not personally known to the trustees.
**TYPE OF GRANT** One-off grants; capital, core and projects cots; recurring costs; salaries; start-up costs. Funding is available for up to three years.
**RANGE OF GRANTS** Usually up to £10,000.
**SAMPLE GRANTS** Above Bar Church; Food for the Hungry; Highfield Church; and Tearfund.
**FINANCES** Year 2013/14 Income £64,236 Grants £43,363 Grants to organisations £43,363 Assets £63,876
**TRUSTEES** Richard Todd; George Blue.
**OTHER INFORMATION** Grants were made in the following categories: organisations working in UK (£14,400); churches and church organisations (£13,700); organisations working overseas (£7,900); and development and relief work (£7,400).
**HOW TO APPLY** Applications may be made in writing to the correspondent; however, unsolicited applications are not acknowledged. Phone calls are welcome before an application is submitted. The trustees meet twice a year.
**WHO TO APPLY TO** Richard Todd, Trustee, 27 Radway Road, Southampton, Hampshire SO15 7PL Tel. 023 8078 8249 email r.j.todd@btopenworld.com

## ■ The Jarman Charitable Trust

**CC NO** 239198  **ESTABLISHED** 1964
**WHERE FUNDING CAN BE GIVEN** Birmingham and the surrounding district.
**WHO CAN BENEFIT** Organisations benefitting children, young adults, older people, one-parent families, at-risk groups, homeless people and so on.
**WHAT IS FUNDED** Welfare work, church building extension schemes and general social services in the Birmingham district. This includes convalescent homes, hospices, hospitals, nursing homes, rehabilitation centres, cancer research, community centres and village halls, day centres, holidays and outings, youth work and play schemes.
**WHAT IS NOT FUNDED** There is a preference for registered charities. Grants are not made to individuals.
**TYPE OF GRANT** Annual donations and one-off payments.
**RANGE OF GRANTS** Grants range from £50 to £275.
**SAMPLE GRANTS** **Previous beneficiaries have included:** Coventry Day Centre for the Homeless; Friendship Project for Children; St Anne's Hostel for Men; St Paul's Church; Samaritans – Birmingham; Shakespeare Hospice and Victim Support – East Birmingham.
**FINANCES** Year 2013/14 Income £43,180 Grants £37,954 Grants to organisations £37,954 Assets £1,047,756
**TRUSTEES** Dr Geoffrey Jarman; Susan Chilton; Ilfra Jarman.
**OTHER INFORMATION** Grants were awarded to 169 organisations.
**HOW TO APPLY** The trustees meet in spring and autumn. Our research suggests that applications should be made in writing to the correspondent by the first week in February or the first week in September. The trust does not invite telephone calls and will not acknowledge applications even if an sae is enclosed. Accounts and/or budgets should be included.
**WHO TO APPLY TO** Susan Chilton, Trustee, 52 Lee Crescent, Edgbaston, Birmingham, West Midlands B15 2BJ Tel. 0121 247 2622 email jarmanct@hotmail.com

## John Jarrold Trust

**CC NO** 242029 **ESTABLISHED** 1965
**WHERE FUNDING CAN BE GIVEN** UK and overseas, but mostly Norwich and Norfolk.
**WHO CAN BENEFIT** Charities; churches; hospitals and hospices; educational establishments; social enterprises and charitable companies.
**WHAT IS FUNDED** Social welfare and community causes; arts; education; medical and health; churches and historic buildings; the environment; overseas aid in financially developing countries. Special attention is given to education and research in natural sciences.
**WHAT IS NOT FUNDED** Individual education programmes are not normally supported and the trust will not generally contribute to core costs. Currently gap year projects are not assisted either. In financially developing countries the trust has long-standing relationships with several charities which operate overseas and does not accept applications from new charities unless there is some specific connection to Norwich and Norfolk.
**TYPE OF GRANT** One-off.
**RANGE OF GRANTS** Usually up to £5,000.
**SAMPLE GRANTS** Norfolk Churches Trust (£4,500); Norfolk and Norwich Festival 2014 (£3,000); Arkwright Scholarship and UEA Bone and Joint Appeal (£2,000 each); Age UK Norwich, Alzheimer's Society, Norfolk and Norwich University Hospital, Norwich Puppet Theatre and Voluntary Norfolk (£1,000 each); Meningitis Trust, Norfolk Homemakers, Norwich Philharmonic Society, Pregnancy Choices Norfolk, Stepping Stones and Red Balloon Learner Centre (£500 each); RSPB – Wild About Norfolk (£250); and Rotary Club of Norwich St Edmund (£150).
**FINANCES** Year 2013/14 Income £80,084 Grants £66,261 Grants to organisations £66,261 Assets £2,467,819
**TRUSTEES** Caroline Jarrold; Joan Jarrold; Juliet Jarrold; Peter Jarrold; Richard Jarrold; Antony Jarrold; Waltraud Jarrold; Charles Jarrold.
**OTHER INFORMATION** There were 95 grants made.
**HOW TO APPLY** There is no formal application form and applications should be made in writing to the correspondent, essential details of the project, financial information and providing a set of accounts (where available) as well as giving your email address and details of the account to which any cheques should be made payable if the application is successful. The trustees meet in January and June; therefore applications should be submitted by the end of November and April respectively. Grants of up to £250 can be made between meetings. Only successful applicants are acknowledged.
**WHO TO APPLY TO** Caroline Jarrold, Secretary, Jarrold and Sons Ltd, St James Works, 12–20 Whitefriars, Norwich NR3 1SH Tel. 01603 677360 email caroline.jarrold@jarrold.com Website www.johnjarroldtrust.org.uk

## Jay Education Trust

**CC NO** 1116458 **ESTABLISHED** 2006
**WHERE FUNDING CAN BE GIVEN** Worldwide.
**WHO CAN BENEFIT** Jewish organisations; educational and religious establishments.
**WHAT IS FUNDED** 'The relief of poverty in the Jewish Community worldwide; the advancement of religious education according to the beliefs and values of the Jewish faith worldwide; any charitable purpose at the discretion of the trustees for the benefit of the community.'
**RANGE OF GRANTS** £1,000–£276,500
**SAMPLE GRANTS** The list of grant recipients was not included in the accounts. **Previous beneficiaries have included:** Chevras Mo'oz Ladol (£276,500); Amud Hachesed Trust (£13,000); Notzar Chesed (£10,000); Centre for Torah Education Trust (£5,500); Chaba Kollel and Yeshiva Torah Chaim (£5,000 each); Khal Bais Shmiel (£2,700); Zichron Efraim Orphans Fund (£2,000); Beis Trana (£1,000).
**FINANCES** Year 2013/14 Income £1,055,128 Grants £15,675 Grants to organisations £15,675 Assets £1,503,676
**TRUSTEES** Rabbi Alfred Schechter; Gabriel Gluck; Shlomo Stauber.
**OTHER INFORMATION** No individual grants were made during the year. The annual report for 2013/14 states that 'the application of the funds is by way of grants to either institutions or individuals and is almost always to institutions'. Note that the amount awarded in grants in 2013/14 is much lower than usual. In the previous four years on average about £317,000 was given annually. The trust has very high investment management costs. In 2013/14 these totalled £528,500. In previous years governance costs have also exceeded grants made.
**HOW TO APPLY** Applications can be made in writing to the correspondent.
**WHO TO APPLY TO** Rabbi Alfred Schechter, Trustee, 37 Filey Avenue, London N16 6JL

## JCA Charitable Foundation

**CC NO** 207031 **ESTABLISHED** 1891
**WHERE FUNDING CAN BE GIVEN** Israel.
**WHO CAN BENEFIT** Projects benefitting Jewish people, particularly in rural areas.
**WHAT IS FUNDED** The foundation helps the development of new settlements in Israel, the Kibbutzim and Moshavim, contributes to the resettlement of Jewish people in need, fosters viable agricultural and rural life to support them, and encourages other trusts and foundations to join it in partnership to fulfil its ideals. Assistance is given for development projects, especially in the fields of education, research and agriculture. The work of the foundation is mainly concentrated in rural areas in Israel.
**WHAT IS NOT FUNDED** Individual students' tuition fees in Israel or elsewhere.
**TYPE OF GRANT** Loans, grants and feasibility studies. Funding may be given for one year or less.
**RANGE OF GRANTS** £1,900–£67,500
**SAMPLE GRANTS** Dead Sea and Arava Science Center (£67,500); Ben-Gurion University of the Negev (£61,500); Tel Hai Academic College (£55,500); Ben Dor Nurseries and Miga (£22,000); Central Arava Development and Construction Company (£17,900); Ofanim Mobile Labs (£9,400); Manor-Cabri Association (£4,700); The Fund for Innovative Teaching (£3,700); Association for the Advancement of citizens on the Eshkol Region (£1,900).
**FINANCES** Year 2013 Income £407,000 Grants £575,000 Grants to organisations £575,000 Assets £33,255,000
**TRUSTEES** Dr Ariela Brickner; Prof. Yona Chen; Isaac Lidor; Baron Alain Philippson; Beatrice Jouan; Hana Smouha; Jacques Capelluto; Mark Sebba; Sir Stephen Cohen; Peter Lawrence; Dr Mordechai Cohen; Jacques-Martin Philippson; Marc Vellay; Geoffrey Gestetner; Doron Weiss; Alan Philipp.
**OTHER INFORMATION** Grants were paid in US dollars – we have used conversion rates available at the

time of writing. Awards were given to 34 organisations.
**HOW TO APPLY** Full proposals should be sent to the office in Israel. For further information contact the correspondent.
**WHO TO APPLY TO** Tim Martin, Secretary, c/o The Victoria Palace Theatre, Victoria Street, London SW1E 5EA *Tel.* 020 7828 0600 *email* thejcafoundation@aol.com *Website* www.ica-is.org.il

## ■ Jeffrey Charitable Trust
**SC NO** SC015990     **ESTABLISHED** 1972
**WHERE FUNDING CAN BE GIVEN** Scotland and elsewhere.
**WHO CAN BENEFIT** Organisations benefitting seafarers and fishermen, volunteers, and people in care, or who are fostered or adopted.
**WHAT IS FUNDED** Primarily this trust is concerned with medical research and helping carer organisations. It also considers: holiday and respite accommodation; health; conservation; independent and special schools; tertiary, higher and special needs education; community facilities and transport; and emergency care for refugees and their families.
**WHAT IS NOT FUNDED** Animal-related charities, medical electives and projects eligible for statutory support are not considered.
**TYPE OF GRANT** One-off and recurring grants are most commonly made for capital, buildings, core costs, endowment, project, research, running costs, salaries and start-up costs. Funding is available for up to three years.
**RANGE OF GRANTS** £250–£20,000; typically awards are of £1,000–£1,500.
**SAMPLE GRANTS** Arthritis Care in Scotland; Bethany Christian Trust; Breast Cancer Care Scotland; British Heart Foundation; Bobath Scotland; Canniesburn Research Trust; Daisy Chain Trust; Epilepsy Scotland; Impstart Trust; Nangchen Children's Trust; Morrison's Academy Foundation; Sailors' Families Society; Tullochan Trust; University of Dundee – Breast Cancer Imaging Research; and Whizz-Kidz Scotland.
**FINANCES** *Year* 2013/14 *Income* £63,586 *Grants* £80,000 *Grants to organisations* £80,000
**TRUSTEES** R. B. A. Bolton; R. S. Waddell; Mrs M. E. Bolton; Dr A. C. MacCuish.
**HOW TO APPLY** Applications can be made in writing to the correspondent, although due to continuing support to long-term projects and anticipated repeat grants to other organisations, new requests for assistance are unlikely to be successful.
**WHO TO APPLY TO** Robert Bolton, Correspondent, 29 Comrie Street, Crieff, Perthshire PH7 4BD *Tel.* 01764 652274 *Fax* 01764 653999 *email* mail@gandfsols.co.uk

## ■ Rees Jeffreys Road Fund
**CC NO** 217771     **ESTABLISHED** 1950
**WHERE FUNDING CAN BE GIVEN** UK.
**WHO CAN BENEFIT** Universities; research bodies; academic staff and students; proposals for roadside projects. The charity favours 'projects which lie outside the scope of other funders such as government agencies and research councils'. Normally projects are part-funded; therefore collaborative funding is particularly welcome.
**WHAT IS FUNDED** Education and research in transport; projects that improve the roadside environment for motorists and other road users. The trustees will consider funding lectureships and postgraduate bursaries over an academic year; research projects; physical roadside projects; transport and alternative transport. Only subjects directly related with road and transportation are considered.
**WHAT IS NOT FUNDED** Environmental projects not related to roads and transport; individual works for cycle tracks; works of only local application; operational and administrative staff costs are rarely considered.
**TYPE OF GRANT** One-off; capital costs; projects; bursaries; research; lectureships; some salaries; in some cases running costs and endowments.
**RANGE OF GRANTS** Up to £34,000.
**SAMPLE GRANTS** A full list of beneficiaries was not included in the accounts; however, the charity's website lists some projects supported during the year. **Beneficiaries included**: PACTS (£34,000 in two grants); Independent Transport Commission (£25,000); Aston University (£18,000). Previously support has also been given to: Road Safety Foundation (£20,000); Social Research Associates and Surrey Fire and Rescue Service (£10,000 each); University of Birmingham (£5,700); Department of Transport (£5,000). Each year the charity also provides financial support to schemes submitted by the Wildlife Trust. In 2014 six schemes totalling about £28,500 were successful.
**FINANCES** *Year* 2014 *Income* £21,543 *Grants* £286,839 *Grants to organisations* £212,930 *Assets* £7,201,539
**TRUSTEES** Martin Shaw; David Bayliss; Prof. Stephen Glaister; Ann Frye; Anthony Depledge; David Hutchinson; Michael McDonald; Mary Lewis; David Tarrant.
**OTHER INFORMATION** The annual report for 2014 states that in 2014 the trustees 'adopted a more pro-active approach by commissioning a major research project looking ahead to 2040'. The grant total consisted of: research and other projects (£138,500); educational bursaries and support for universities (£122,500); roadside rests and land adjoining (£25,500). Awards to organisations totalled £213,000 and to individuals – £74,000.
**HOW TO APPLY** Applications should be made in writing to the correspondent (no more than three A4 pages) including the following: the purpose for which funding is sought (including objects, relevance, the proposed methodology of the project and the names of the principal participants); expected costs by category and project timetable; evidence of the willingness of other parties (where the project requires their contribution or participation) to get involved; appropriate evidence of the applicant's in-depth knowledge of the subject of the application and their familiarity with previous work in the field. All necessary supporting material and a digital version of the application should also be submitted. Appeals can be made at any time and the trustees meet five times a year (see the website for up-to-date meeting dates). The deadline for submission of applications or other agenda items is normally a fortnight before the meeting. Informal contact prior to submitting a formal application is welcomed.
**WHO TO APPLY TO** Brian Smith, Secretary, Merriewood, Horsell Park, Woking, Surrey GU21 4LW *Tel.* 01483 750758 *email* briansmith@reesjeffreys.org *Website* www.reesjeffreys.co.uk

## ■ Nick Jenkins Foundation

**CC NO** 1135565      **ESTABLISHED** 2010

**WHERE FUNDING CAN BE GIVEN** UK and overseas, including India and Ethiopia.

**WHO CAN BENEFIT** A wide range of charitable organisations.

**WHAT IS FUNDED** General charitable purposes.

**RANGE OF GRANTS** £500–£25,000

**SAMPLE GRANTS Previous beneficiaries have included:** The Prince's Trust, Opportunity International UK and Give a Future (£25,000 each); Molecular Oncology and Cell Cycle Chantelle Fund and Virgin Unite (£20,000 each); Shivia Microfinance (£15,000); Afghanistan Trust, Marie Curie Cancer Care and Turning Point Trust (£2,000 each); Red Squirrel Survival Trust (£1,000); University of Birmingham (£500).

**FINANCES** Year 2013/14 Income £11,271 Grants £270,000 Grants to organisations £270,000

**TRUSTEES** Rosemary Rafferty; Alison Jenkins; Nicholas Jenkins.

**OTHER INFORMATION** The latest accounts were not required to be filed with the Charity Commission due to low income; however, generally almost all of the charitable expenditure is distributed in grants. There is usually about ten awards made annually.

**HOW TO APPLY** The foundation 'actively seeks projects to fund and does not accept unsolicited applications for grants'.

**WHO TO APPLY TO** Nicholas Jenkins, Trustee, Bapton Manor, Bapton, Warminster, Wiltshire BA12 0SB *email* admin@njenkins.com

## ■ The Jenour Foundation

**CC NO** 256637      **ESTABLISHED** 1968

**WHERE FUNDING CAN BE GIVEN** UK, with a special interest in Wales.

**WHO CAN BENEFIT** Registered charities only. Both UK charities and local charities in Wales are supported.

**WHAT IS FUNDED** General charitable purposes, including health causes, medical research, young people, arts and culture and animal welfare.

**WHAT IS NOT FUNDED** Registered charities only.

**TYPE OF GRANT** Capital projects.

**RANGE OF GRANTS** Usually up to £10,000.

**SAMPLE GRANTS** Army Benevolent Fund (£10,000); Atlantic College and Cancer Research Wales (£9,000 each); British Heart Foundation (£7,000); Barnardo's (£5,000); Marie Curie Hospice – Penarth (£4,500); Vision in Wales (Wales Council for the Blind) (£4,000); Salvation Army and St John Ambulance in Wales (£3,500 each); Samaritans (£2,500); Welsh Sinfonia (£1,000); Tall Ships Youth Trust (£750); and Society for Welfare of Horses and Ponies (£500).

**FINANCES** Year 2013/14 Income £126,994 Grants £124,250 Grants to organisations £124,250 Assets £3,605,708

**TRUSTEES** David Jones; Peter Phillips; James Zorab.

**OTHER INFORMATION** There were 37 grants awarded.

**HOW TO APPLY** Applications should be made in writing to the correspondent. The awards are normally made in February. The annual report for 2013/14 informs that 'correspondence is not entered unless it relates to donations that the foundation has agreed to make'.

**WHO TO APPLY TO** Jacqueline Deacy, Correspondent, Deloitte PCS Ltd, 5 Callaghan Square, Cardiff CF10 5BT *Tel.* 029 2026 4391 *Fax* 029 2026 4444

## ■ The Jephcott Charitable Trust

**CC NO** 240915      **ESTABLISHED** 1965

**WHERE FUNDING CAN BE GIVEN** Worldwide.

**WHO CAN BENEFIT** Charitable organisations worldwide struggling to get started or raise funds from other sources. Note that the trustees prefer to support UK charities that are delivering benefit overseas rather than supporting overseas charities.

**WHAT IS FUNDED** Funding priorities are: population control – support for schemes, particularly educational ones, which help to control excessive growth in population; natural environment – projects involved in conserving the natural environment (except animal welfare or heritage sites or buildings); education – projects will be considered benefitting people of all ages and backgrounds, including formal education, vocational skills to enhance the possibility of employment, development of computer skills, health awareness or distance learning; and healthcare projects (except those that require long-term funding).

**WHAT IS NOT FUNDED** Support is not given to: organisations whose administrative expenses form more than 15% of their annual income; individuals; animal welfare; heritage and buildings; retrospective expenditure. Projects which require long-term funding are not normally considered.

**TYPE OF GRANT** Awards are aimed to help with start-up costs or make a significant step forward. Project and capital costs are favoured, rather than running costs. One-off donations to get many projects started are preferred to supporting fewer projects or charities over a long period.

**RANGE OF GRANTS** £2,000–£10,000; in exceptional cases up to £20,000.

**SAMPLE GRANTS** Street Child (£13,800); Catherine Bullen Foundation, Makhad Trust and Zisize (£10,000 each); Community Action (£9,400); Supporting Dalit Children (£7,100); Helenic Hope (£7,000); Small Steps Foundation (£6,500); Alive and Kicking (£6,000); and Jo Warrington Foundation (£4,500).

**FINANCES** Year 2013/14 Income £127,757 Grants £90,382 Grants to organisations £90,382 Assets £5,757,249

**TRUSTEES** Anthony North; Keith Morgan; Mary Jephcott; Mark Jephcott; Dr David Thomas; James Parker.

**OTHER INFORMATION** Awards were given to 14 projects: two for the public benefit of health; seven for education; four for environmental relief; and one for both health and education.

**HOW TO APPLY** Full and detailed guidelines and application forms can be downloaded from the trust's website. The trustees meet in April and October each year. If your application is ineligible you will be told so within a few weeks of your application. Successful applicants will hear from the trust shortly after the meeting. The website notes: 'Each year we receive many more applications than we can fund. We have to reject many applications which are eligible under our guidelines but are of a lower priority.'

**WHO TO APPLY TO** Dr Felicity Gibling, Secretary to the Trustees, The Threshing Barn, Ford, Kingsbridge, Devon TQ7 2LN *email* jct@adep.

eclipse.co.uk *Website* www.jephcottcharitabletrust.org.uk

## ■ The Jerusalem Trust

**CC NO** 285696      **ESTABLISHED** 1982
**WHERE FUNDING CAN BE GIVEN** Worldwide.
**WHO CAN BENEFIT** Organisations working for the promotion of Christianity; churches; educational establishments.
**WHAT IS FUNDED** Christian Evangelism and relief work overseas – 'the provision of support for indigenous training centres and the provision of Christian literature in Central and Eastern Europe and Anglophone sub-Saharan Africa' Christian media – 'projects that promote Christianity as well as training and networking projects for Christians working professionally in, or considering a career in, the media' Christian education – 'the development of Christian curriculum resource materials for schools in RE and across the curriculum, the recruitment and development of Christian teachers in all subjects, and adult lay Christian training and education' Christian art; Evangelism and Christian mission in the UK – 'particularly Christian projects that develop new ways of working with children and young people; church planting and evangelistic projects, including those that undertake Christian work with prisoners, ex-prisoners and their families'.
**WHAT IS NOT FUNDED** Building or repair work for churches; individuals; educational fees; expeditions.
**RANGE OF GRANTS** Up to £416,500.
**SAMPLE GRANTS** Jerusalem Productions Ltd (£416,500); Catholic Agency for Overseas Development (£278,500); Association of Church College Trusts (£200,000); National Society for Promoting Religious Education (£174,000); Youth for Christ in Britain (£120,000); Church and Media Network (£70,000); University of York (£60,000); Church Army (£51,000); Aid to the Church in Need, Eye Church Development Campaign and Salisbury Cathedral (£20,000 each); Christian Education Movement (£92,000); Liverpool Hope University (£15,000); Acts 29 (£10,000); Haven Kilmacolm (£7,500).
**FINANCES** Year 2013/14 *Income* £2,590,000 *Grants* £4,081,000 *Grants to organisations* £4,081,000 *Assets* £87,824,000
**TRUSTEES** Sir Timothy Sainsbury; Lady Susan Sainsbury; Hartley Booth; Phillida Goad; Dr Peter Frankopan; Melanie Townsend.
**OTHER INFORMATION** This trust is one of the Sainsbury Family Charitable Trusts, all of which share a joint administration but work autonomously as an independent legal entity yet have a common approach to grant-making. There were a total of 156 awards made. About £123,000 was given in smaller grants across all categories.
**HOW TO APPLY** The website states that while the trust 'will consider suitable proposals, so long as they demonstrably and closely fit their specific areas of interest', 'it should be understood that the majority of unsolicited proposals are unsuccessful'. Applications should be made in writing via post including a description (strictly no more than two pages) of the proposed project. You should provide: details of your organisation (charitable aims and objectives, most recent annual income and expenditure and current financial position); what is needed for the project and who it will benefit; breakdown of costs, and any other sources of funding. Do not include any accounts or additional brochures. A single application will be considered for support by all the trusts in the group. If you are successful you should hear from the trust within eight weeks of the acknowledgement. Unsuccessful appeals are not notified.
**WHO TO APPLY TO** Alan Bookbinder, Director, The Peak, 5 Wilton Road, London SW1V 1AP *Tel.* 020 7410 0330 *Fax* 020 7410 0332 *email* jerusalemtrust@sfct.org.uk *Website* www.sfct.org.uk

## ■ The Jerwood Charitable Foundation

**CC NO** 1074036      **ESTABLISHED** 1999
**WHERE FUNDING CAN BE GIVEN** UK only.
**WHO CAN BENEFIT** Organisations benefitting young adults, actors, artists, musicians, research workers, writers, dancers and choreographers, directors, producers and film makers.
**WHAT IS FUNDED** Project and programme support across the arts throughout the UK. The foundation host an open grants programme as well as proactively funding the Jerwood Visual Arts series of events.
**WHAT IS NOT FUNDED** Study or tuition fees, or course fees for individuals, or associated living expenses, travel or accommodation costs; building or capital costs (including purchase of equipment); general rehearsal, touring, production or staging costs for performances or exhibitions; grants towards the purchase of musical instruments; informal education or community participation projects; education or participation projects for those who have not yet left formal education; projects which will happen outside the United Kingdom; projects which support artists who are not resident in the United Kingdom; projects in the fields of religion or sport; animal rights or welfare appeals; general fundraising appeals; appeals to establish endowment funds for other charities; medical research; social welfare; retrospective awards or funding for retrospective activity; environmental or conservation projects; medical or mental health projects; non-arts based projects. The foundation may, where there are very exceptional circumstances, decide to waive an exclusion.
**TYPE OF GRANT** Project support; principally one-off for a project cycle but can be recurrent as a part of a partnership.
**RANGE OF GRANTS** Small grants of £5,000–£10,000; large grants generally £10,000–£50,000; but up to £100,000.
**SAMPLE GRANTS** Jerwood Space – Jerwood Visual Arts (£63,500); Glyndebourne – Jerwood Chorus Development Scheme (£60,000); Arvon Foundation (£54,500); London Sinfonietta (£40,000); Battersea Arts Centre (£32,500); Gate Theatre (£28,000); The Opera Group (£18,200); Camden People's Theatre, Work Together and Young Vic (£10,000 each); Art Licks (£7,500); Gateshead International Festival of Theatre 2013 (£7,000); Chris Goode and Company (£5,000). For more examples of the foundation's current projects see the website.
**FINANCES** Year 2013 *Income* £1,212,116 *Grants* £1,335,525 *Grants to organisations* £1,180,688 *Assets* £27,577,272
**TRUSTEES** Katharine Goodison; Rupert Tyler; Juliane Wharton; Timothy Eyles; Thomas Grieve; Phyllida Earle; Anthony Palmer; Lucy Ash; Philippa Hogan-Hern.

**OTHER INFORMATION** Grants to individuals totalled £155,000. During the year a total of 46 project grants were given.

**HOW TO APPLY** Initial applications should include: a short proposal, not more than two sides of A4, outlining a description of the organisation's aims or a short biography for individuals, and a description of the specific project for which funding is sought and the opportunity it seeks to fulfil; a detailed budget for the project, identifying administrative, management and central costs details of funding already in place for the project, including any other trusts or sources which are being or have been approached for funds; and, if funding is not in place, details of how the applicant plans to secure the remaining funding. The trustees may decide to contact the applicants for further information including: details of the management and staffing structure, including trustees; and the most recent annual report and audited accounts of the organisation, together with current management accounts if relevant to the project. However, the trust asks that this information is **not** sent unless it is requested. Applications may be made online via the website. Alternatively applicants can send proposals by post. The foundation may wish to enter into discussions and/or correspondence with the applicant which may result in modification and/or development of the project or scheme. Any such discussion or correspondence will not commit the foundation to funding that application. Applications are assessed throughout the year. Successful applicants will be invited to report to the foundation at the completion of their project and to provide photographs of the work or project supported. As the foundation receives a large number of applications, it is not always possible to have preliminary meetings to discuss possible support before a written application is made.

**WHO TO APPLY TO** Shonagh Manson, Director, 171 Union Street, Bankside, London SE1 0LN *Tel.* 020 7261 0279 *email* info@jerwood.org *Website* www.jerwoodcharitablefoundation.org

## ■ Jewish Child's Day (JCD)

**CC NO** 209266  **ESTABLISHED** 1947
**WHERE FUNDING CAN BE GIVEN** Worldwide. In practice, mainly Israel, UK, Argentina and Eastern Europe.
**WHO CAN BENEFIT** Registered charities providing equipment or services of direct benefit to Jewish children (up to the age of 18).
**WHAT IS FUNDED** Charitable purposes of direct benefit to Jewish children who are disadvantaged, suffering or in need of special care.
**WHAT IS NOT FUNDED** Individuals; capital expenditure; general services and running costs; building or maintenance of property; staff salaries.
**TYPE OF GRANT** One-off and recurring for specific projects only.
**RANGE OF GRANTS** Generally £500–£5,000.
**SAMPLE GRANTS** Bayis Sheli (£28,000); The Boy's Clubhouse (£6,000); Seeach Sod (£5,300); Orr Shalom and Step by Step (£5,000 each); The Therapeutic Riding Centre of Israel (£4,400); Shema (£4,100); Amit (£4,000); Shutaf and Teens United (£3,000 each); Zion Orphanage (£2,600); Etgarim (£2,500); Nig Brothers Big Sisters of Israel (£2,000); The Friendship Circle (£1,200); Number One (£1,000).

**FINANCES** *Year* 2013/14 *Income* £905,709 *Grants* £572,295 *Grants to organisations* £572,295 *Assets* £633,813
**TRUSTEES** June Jacobs; Joy Moss; Stephen Moss; Virginia Campus; Frankie Epstein; Susie Olins; David Collins; Amanda Ingram; Gaby Lazarus; Dee Lahane; Charles Spungin.
**OTHER INFORMATION** Unrestricted grants were given to 108 organisations totalling £370,500. Further £202,000 was given in restricted grants. The charity's website notes that although in the main Jewish children are the beneficiaries, this should not exclude non-Jewish children.
**HOW TO APPLY** To apply for a grant contact the correspondent to discuss in the first instance. Applications must be supported by audited accounts in English or with the main heading translated into English. and provide a breakdown of items and related costs that are being applied for. Applications should be submitted by 31 December, 30 April and 31 August for consideration in March, June and October, respectively. Organisations with dedicated UK fundraising operations must disclose this in the application.
**WHO TO APPLY TO** Natasha Brookner, Grants and Events Coordinator, 5th Floor, 707 High Road, North Finchley, London N12 0BT *Tel.* 020 8446 8804 *email* natasha.brookner@jcd.uk.com *Website* www.jcd.uk.com

## ■ The Jewish Youth Fund (JYF)

**CC NO** 251902  **ESTABLISHED** 1937
**WHERE FUNDING CAN BE GIVEN** UK.
**WHO CAN BENEFIT** Jewish youth clubs, organisations, centres, movements, groups and so on.
**WHAT IS FUNDED** Jewish youth work projects, equipment and premises.
**WHAT IS NOT FUNDED** Grants are not made in response to general appeals and to individuals. Formal education is not supported. Running costs are not normally covered.
**TYPE OF GRANT** Grants for projects and equipment. Loans may be offered towards the cost of building. The charity can provide start-up costs as well as subsequent funding.
**RANGE OF GRANTS** Generally, £1,000–£10,000.
**SAMPLE GRANTS** B'nai B'rith Foundation – also known as UJS Hillel (£22,500); Jewish Lads' and Girls' Brigade (£15,000); Bnei Akiva (£11,000); Step by Step (£10,000); Maccabi GB (£8,000); London Jewish Family Centre (£4,300); Gateway Action Salford Sports Club (£3,000); London Jewish Cultural Centre (£2,500); and The Boys' Clubhouse (£1,400).
**FINANCES** *Year* 2013/14 *Income* £70,795 *Grants* £107,025 *Grants to organisations* £107,025 *Assets* £3,572,444
**TRUSTEES** Philippa Strauss; Adam Rose; Ruth Morris; Jonathan Morris; David Goldberg; Elliot Simberg; Stephen Spitz; David Brown.
**OTHER INFORMATION** There were 18 organisations supported.
**HOW TO APPLY** Applications can be made on a form available from the correspondent. Applicants should enclose a copy of the latest accounts and an annual report. For the most up-to-date submission deadline consult the charity's website.
**WHO TO APPLY TO** Julia Samuel, Secretary, Third Floor, 24 Chiswell Street, London EC1Y 4YX *Tel.* 07469 980761 *email* info@jyf.org.uk *Website* www.jyf.org.uk

## ■ The Joffe Charitable Trust

**CC NO** 270299    **ESTABLISHED** 1968

**WHERE FUNDING CAN BE GIVEN** Overseas, primarily Anglophone, sub-Saharan Africa.

**WHO CAN BENEFIT** Normally UK-registered charities (or equivalent organisations in other countries) with good quality leadership, clear objectives and realistic project budgets. Preference may be given to organisations which find it hard to obtain funding from other sources and the trust's contribution will make a real difference. The trustees have an ongoing relationship with a considerable number of charities.

**WHAT IS FUNDED** Alleviation of poverty (poverty for this purpose could include some forms of suffering, such as mental or physical disability and lack of education); community and economic development; protection/advancement of human rights.

**WHAT IS NOT FUNDED** One-off projects (unless they show a very clear strategic purpose nor work that primarily delivers basic services to poor people); emergency relief; individuals; the arts; conflict resolution; formal academic education; micro credit; work primarily in the field of HIV/AIDS; physical infrastructure; large charities with income of over £5 million per year.

**TYPE OF GRANT** Grants and loans for up to three years; core costs; salaries.

**RANGE OF GRANTS** Around £5,000–£40,000.

**SAMPLE GRANTS** ADIDEP – Kenya (£99,000); Videre Est Credere (£65,000); Tax Justice Network (£61,000); Charities Aid Foundation and Global Poverty Project UK (£40,000 each); Oxfam (£35,000); International Centre for Social Franchising (£30,000); Centre for Global Development and Transparency International (£25,000 each); Beyond Violence (£23,00); People First Impact Method (£15,000); Business and Human Rights Business Resources (£12,500).

**FINANCES** Year 2013/14 Income £308,678 Grants £1,119,625 Grants to organisations £1,119,625 Assets £10,719,996

**TRUSTEES** Lord Joel Joffe; Lady Vanetta Joffe; Mark Poston; Alex Jacobs; Myles Wickstead.

**OTHER INFORMATION** There were 23 major awards made with grants below £10,000 totalling about £92,500.

**HOW TO APPLY** Appeals should be made in writing to the correspondent.

**WHO TO APPLY TO** Lord Joel Joffe, Trustee, Liddington Manor, 35 The Street, Liddington, Swindon SN4 0HD Tel. 01793 790203 email joffetrust@lidmanor.co.uk Website www.joffecharitabletrust.org

## ■ The Elton John Aids Foundation (EJAF)

**CC NO** 1017336    **ESTABLISHED** 1993

**WHERE FUNDING CAN BE GIVEN** EJAF (London) only makes grants in Europe, Asia and Africa. New York-based sister organisation supports causes in Americas and Caribbean. For a full list of specific eligible countries for each grant programme see the foundation's website.

**WHO CAN BENEFIT** Registered charities.

**WHAT IS FUNDED** The provision of focused and sustainable funding to frontline programmes that help alleviate the physical, emotional and financial hardship of those living with, affected by or at risk of HIV/AIDS, and their families. Grants are available in two categories: Key Vulnerable Populations (Pioneer Grants and Flagship Grants) and Large Scale and Grass Roots Initiatives (Support Grants and Robert Key Memorial Fund awards). For specific eligibility criteria and application details see the website.

**WHAT IS NOT FUNDED** Individuals; academic or pure medical research; conferences; repatriation costs; retrospective funding.

**TYPE OF GRANT** Specific projects; one-off and running costs; salaries; operational research; up to five years; unrestricted funding.

**RANGE OF GRANTS** £1,100–£350,000

**SAMPLE GRANTS** Comic Relief (£350,000); Ukraine Street Children (£176,000); Fair Play – Tackling HIV in Ukraine (£80,000); Life Ball – Funds to support programmes for those at risk in Eastern Europe (£52,000); Summer camps for children living with HIV in Lesotho (£50,500); Reducing HIV infection in the UK (£29,000); Paediatric Palliative Care in Zambia (£4,500); Elena Franchuk ANTIAIDS Foundation and Victor Pinchuk Foundation (£1,100).

**FINANCES** Year 2013 Income £7,136,999 Grants £5,675,149 Grants to organisations £5,675,149 Assets £27,141,648

**TRUSTEES** Anne Aslett; David Furnish; Sir Elton John; Johnny Bergius; Rafi Manoukian; Scott Campbell; Iain Abrahams; Graham Norton.

**HOW TO APPLY** Eligible applicants are invited to submit an online 'Concept Note' (accepted throughout the year). The website warns that 'speculative applications by email cannot be accepted and all such applications will not be reviewed'. The foundation 'aims to respond to all Concept Note applications within six weeks, with those that are successful invited to submit a full application'.

**WHO TO APPLY TO** Anne Aslett, Trustee, 1 Blythe Road, London W14 0HG Tel. 020 7603 9996 Fax 020 7348 4848 email grants@ejaf.com Website www.ejaf.com

## ■ Lillie Johnson Charitable Trust

**CC NO** 326761    **ESTABLISHED** 1985

**WHERE FUNDING CAN BE GIVEN** UK, with some preference for the West Midlands.

**WHO CAN BENEFIT** Charities concerned with children, young people and medical causes.

**WHAT IS FUNDED** General charitable purposes; children, young people, people who are blind or deaf; medical causes.

**WHAT IS NOT FUNDED** In practice, individuals are not supported.

**RANGE OF GRANTS** Up to £45,000. Most grants are under £1,000.

**SAMPLE GRANTS** LEC – Worcester (£45,000); West House School (£10,000); Birmingham Youth Theatre and Prince's Trust (£4,000 each); Acorns Hospice (£3,000); Rotary Club of Edgbaston, Shelter Box and Zoe's Place (£2,000 each); Hearts of England Association and Lord Mayors Charity (£1,500 each); and British Red Cross, Gurkha Welfare Trust, International Dance Festival and National Institute for Conductive Education (£1,000 each). Grants under £1,000 totalled £64,500.

**FINANCES** Year 2013/14 Income £215,245 Grants £209,072 Grants to organisations £209,072 Assets £6,322,979

**TRUSTEES** Victor Lyttle; Peter Adams; John Desmond; Verena Adams.

**OTHER INFORMATION** There were 201 awards made, including 137 grants under £1,000.

**HOW TO APPLY** Applications are only considered from charities which are traditionally supported by the trust. The trust stated that it is inundated with applications it cannot support and feels obliged to respond to all of these.

**WHO TO APPLY TO** John Desmond, Trustee, Heathcote House, 39 Rodbourne Road, Harborne, Birmingham B17 0PN *Tel.* 0121 472 1279 *email* john.w.desmond@googlemail.com

## ■ The Johnson Foundation

**CC NO** 518660  **ESTABLISHED** 1987
**WHERE FUNDING CAN BE GIVEN** City of Liverpool and Merseyside area.
**WHO CAN BENEFIT** Registered charities; community care organisations; educational bodies.
**WHAT IS FUNDED** General charitable purposes; education; health causes; relief of poverty; children and families.
**WHAT IS NOT FUNDED** Grants are not normally given to individuals.
**TYPE OF GRANT** One-off or up to two years. Recurrent cost, project and research grants can be covered.
**RANGE OF GRANTS** Usually £1,000–£5,000.
**SAMPLE GRANTS** University of Liverpool – Head and Neck Cancer Research (£60,000); Thrive @ Five(£25,000); Birkenhead School (£20,000); Community Link Services (£16,000); New Brighton Junior Rugby Development (£10,000); Tomorrow's Women (£6,500); Contact the Elderly (£5,200); Bedford Drive School and Emmaus Merseyside (£5,000 each); Tranmere in the Community (£3,600); St Vincent de Paul Society (£2,500); Friends of Gilbrook Special School (£1,200); and Alzheimer's Society, Help the Heroes and West Wirral Scout and Guides Gang Show (£1,000 each).
**FINANCES** *Year* 2013/14 *Income* £152,231 *Grants* £216,674 *Grants to organisations* £216,674 *Assets* £3,340,168
**TRUSTEES** Christopher Johnson; Peter Johnson.
**OTHER INFORMATION** During the year 32 organisations received grants. The foundation favours small organisations unable to afford professional fund raisers.
**HOW TO APPLY** Applications can be made in writing to the correspondent. The trustees meet monthly.
**WHO TO APPLY TO** Margaret Johnstone, Trust Administrator, c/o Park Group plc, 1 Valley Road, Birkenhead, Wirral CH41 7ED *Tel.* 0151 653 1700 *email* margaret.johnstone@parkgroup.co.uk

## ■ The Johnnie Johnson Trust

**CC NO** 200351  **ESTABLISHED** 1961
**WHERE FUNDING CAN BE GIVEN** UK, with a preference for the West Midlands.
**WHO CAN BENEFIT** Organisations providing or supporting children and young people activities – charities, youth clubs, groups, sports centres and other community bodies.
**WHAT IS FUNDED** Children and young people, particularly those with disability or disadvantaged; education and training; water sports.
**WHAT IS NOT FUNDED** Individual applicants are not assisted.
**TYPE OF GRANT** Normally one-off, for equipment or other specific purposes.
**RANGE OF GRANTS** £500–£26,000
**SAMPLE GRANTS** Docklands Sailing and Watersports Centre (£26,000); Boys2Men (£15,000); Morning Star Trust (£10,000); Birmingham Children's Hospital (£5,800); Enterprise Sailing Trust (£5,000); Action For Kids (£3,000); Happy Days (£2,000); Mad Hatter's Tea Party (£1,000); and 1st Shirley Scouts (£500).

**FINANCES** *Year* 2013 *Income* £121,874 *Grants* £101,476 *Grants to organisations* £101,476 *Assets* £4,138,211
**TRUSTEES** Jane Fordham; Peter Johnson; Victor Johnson; G. W. Ballard; Katherine Cross; Christopher Johnson.
**OTHER INFORMATION** In 2013 grants were given to 19 organisations.
**HOW TO APPLY** Applications may be made in writing to the correspondent.
**WHO TO APPLY TO** Christopher Jackson, Correspondent, 49 Mason Road, Redditch, Worcestershire B97 5DT *Tel.* 01527 544722

## ■ The Johnson Wax Ltd Charitable Trust

**CC NO** 200332  **ESTABLISHED** 1961
**WHERE FUNDING CAN BE GIVEN** Areas surrounding S. C. Johnson's sites; local neighbourhood in Frimley Green, Surrey.
**WHO CAN BENEFIT** Local charities; not-for-profit organisations; educational establishments.
**WHAT IS FUNDED** General charitable purposes; social welfare; disadvantaged individuals; older people; children; education and training; employment; the environment; health and disability; the arts; local community needs.
**WHAT IS NOT FUNDED** Individuals.
**SAMPLE GRANTS** A list of beneficiaries was not included in the latest accounts; however, awards were distributed as follows: health related charities (£55,000); local community (£44,000); education (£39,000); Giving Back scheme (£34,000); environment (£17,600); arts and sports (£11,200). In addition £9,500 was paid through employee matched funding and £26,000 was spent for the annual employee volunteering day (June Community Day) – these costs are included within 'grant funding of activities' in the latest accounts.
**FINANCES** *Year* 2012/13 *Income* £153,886 *Grants* £236,326 *Grants to organisations* £236,326 *Assets* £5,195
**TRUSTEES** Faye Gilbert; Trevor Jessett.
**OTHER INFORMATION** At the time of writing (June 2015) this was the latest information available. The accounts note that 'it is the corporate commitment of S. C. Johnson to make charitable donations to the community of each country in which it conducts its business'.
**HOW TO APPLY** Applications may be made in writing to the correspondent, specifying the amount requested and what it is needed for, details of how the grant will benefit a broad cross-section of the Frimley Green community and how a clear social need will be met within it.
**WHO TO APPLY TO** Faye Gilbert, Trustee, S. C. Johnson Ltd, Frimley Green Road, Frimley, Camberley, Surrey GU16 7AJ *email* givinguk@scj.com

## ■ The Joicey Trust

**CC NO** 244679  **ESTABLISHED** 1965
**WHERE FUNDING CAN BE GIVEN** Unrestricted, but in practice the county of Northumberland, the old metropolitan county of Tyne and Wear and eastern Scottish Borders.
**WHO CAN BENEFIT** Registered charities operating in Northumberland and Tyne and Wear or groups with a specific project within the area defined above. The trust will consider funding organisations benefitting people of all ages, socially or economically disadvantaged

individuals, people with disabilities or health problems as well as the general public.

**WHAT IS FUNDED** The trust considers funding a very wide range of activities, including: residential facilities and services; infrastructure, technical support and development; charity or voluntary umbrella bodies; religious buildings; music, dance and theatre; healthcare; conservation; education and training; and various community facilities and services. UK-wide appeals are not normally supported unless there is specific evidence of activity benefitting the local area.

**WHAT IS NOT FUNDED** Medical research is not supported. Applications from charities registered outside the beneficial area and whose gross incoming resources exceed £1 million are not assisted either. Grants are not generally made to individuals, except under specific circumstances where local residents are sponsored by a charity for an international development project (see more details on the charity's website). The website notes: 'With the exception of core funding, the applicant may not incur expense in relation to the application before the decision of the Trustees has been notified to the applicant – normally within 2 weeks of the meeting.'

**TYPE OF GRANT** One-off for capital and revenue projects, with some preference for discrete projects over running costs. Start-up costs, buildings, core costs and salaries can be covered.

**RANGE OF GRANTS** Up to £5,000 with very occasional larger grants.

**SAMPLE GRANTS** Greggs Foundation (£10,000); Heaton Methodist Church (£6,000); Alnwick District Playhouse Trust, Girl Guiding in North Tyneside and St John's Church – Chevington (£5,000 each); Together Newcastle (£4,000); Action Funding, Brainbox and Disability North (£3,000 each); Daybreak Centres and Friends of the North Pennines (£2,500 each); National Youth Choirs of Great Britain (£2,000); Heartbeat (£1,500); North Country Leisure – Alnwick Rugby Football Club (£1,000); The East Durham Employability Trust (£800); Narcolepsy UK (£500); Go Kids Go – Wheelchair Skills Workshop (£400); and East Bedlington Community Centre (£250).

**FINANCES** Year 2013/14 Income £330,460 Grants £261,000 Grants to organisations £261,000 Assets £7,731,149

**TRUSTEES** R. H. Dickinson; Lord Joicey; Lady Joicey; Andrew Joicey; K. J. Dawson.

**OTHER INFORMATION** In 2013/14 grants were given to 147 organisations.

**HOW TO APPLY** A formal application should preferably be obtained in writing to the correspondent; however, written submissions will be accepted via post or email as well. The trustees' meetings are normally held in January/February and June/July – applications should be received not later than the end of November and May respectively. Applications will need to include supporting documents, such as annual report and accounts and details and budget of project requiring support. The trust welcomes email enquiries before submitting a full application.

**WHO TO APPLY TO** Andrew Bassett, Appeals Secretary, One Trinity, Broad Chare, Newcastle upon Tyne NE1 2HF *Tel.* 0191 279 9662 *email* appeals@thejoiceytrust.org.uk *Website* www.thejoiceytrust.org.uk

■ **The Jones 1986 Charitable Trust**

**CC NO** 327176      **ESTABLISHED** 1986

**WHERE FUNDING CAN BE GIVEN** UK, mostly Nottinghamshire.

**WHO CAN BENEFIT** Charities; local community organisations.

**WHAT IS FUNDED** People with disabilities; welfare of older people; welfare of younger people; medical research; health causes; education; other purposes beneficial to the community.

**WHAT IS NOT FUNDED** Grants are not made to individuals.

**TYPE OF GRANT** Awards are considered for both capital and/or revenue projects as long as each project appears viable.

**RANGE OF GRANTS** Up to around £100,000, but mostly between £4,000 and £25,000.

**SAMPLE GRANTS** The Ruddington Framework Knitters' Museum (£101,500); Dr Powell's Department – Clinical Immunology Research (£75,000); Rainbows (£70,000); Kirkby Community Advice Centre and Riding for the Disabled – Highland Group (£25,000 each); National Head Injuries Association – Headway (£24,000); Fun Days – Shepherd School, Greater Nottingham Groundwork Trust and Young Epilepsy (£10,000 each); Radford Care Group (£8,000); Family Care Nottingham and St John's Day Care Centre for the Elderly (£4,000 each); Nottinghamshire Royal Society for the Blind (£2,000); Shine (£1,400); and Meningitis Trust (£1,000).

**FINANCES** Year 2013/14 Income £697,867 Grants £572,400 Grants to organisations £572,400 Assets £20,113,209

**TRUSTEES** Robert Heason; John Pears.

**OTHER INFORMATION** A total of 37 organisations were supported during the year.

**HOW TO APPLY** Applications may be made in writing to the correspondent. The trust invites applications for grants by advertising in specialist press.

**WHO TO APPLY TO** David Lindley, Correspondent, Smith Cooper LLP, 2 Lace Market Square, Nottingham NG1 1PB *Tel.* 0115 945 4300

■ **The Dezna Robins Jones Charitable Foundation**

**CC NO** 1104252      **ESTABLISHED** 2004

**WHERE FUNDING CAN BE GIVEN** Preference for South Wales.

**WHO CAN BENEFIT** Charitable organisations, hospitals, hospices and educational institutions.

**WHAT IS FUNDED** Medical causes; art; sports; education.

**SAMPLE GRANTS** Previous beneficiaries have included: University Hospital Wales (£88,000); Neil Boobyer Rugby Solutions Limited (£56,000); Performance Arts Education (£54,000); Tredegar Band and St John's School Porthcawl (£50,000 each); Cory Band (£42,000); St David's Hospice and Save the Children Fund (£5,000 each); Maggie's Cancer Care Centre (£2,000); and Cancer Information and Support Services (£1,000).

**FINANCES** Year 2013/14 Income £4,683 Grants £286,000 Grants to organisations £286,000

**TRUSTEES** Bernard Jones; Louise Boobyer; Alexia Cooke.

**OTHER INFORMATION** The foundation states that in recent years main support has been given to medical charities.

**HOW TO APPLY** Applications can be made in writing to the correspondent. The trustees meet at least twice a year.

**563**

**WHO TO APPLY TO** Bernard Jones, Trustee, Greenacres, Laleston, Bridgend CF32 0HN *Tel.* 01656 768584 *email* bernard-jones@btconnect.com

### ■ The Marjorie and Geoffrey Jones Charitable Trust

**CC NO** 1051031  **ESTABLISHED** 1995
**WHERE FUNDING CAN BE GIVEN** UK, with preference for south west of England.
**WHO CAN BENEFIT** Registered charities.
**WHAT IS FUNDED** General charitable purposes, including health and disability, families, arts and culture and environment.
**WHAT IS NOT FUNDED** Grants are not made to individuals.
**RANGE OF GRANTS** £1,000–£5,000
**SAMPLE GRANTS Previous beneficiaries have included:** Torquay Child Contact Centre (£5,000); Children and Families in Grief (£4,000); British Wireless for the Blind Fund, Devon Wildlife Trust and Parkinson's UK (£3,000 each); Epilepsy Society (£2,500); Changing Faces and The Sailors' Families Society (£2,000 each); and 66 Route Youth Trust, Double Elephant Print Workshop and Home-Start Torbay (£1,000 each).
**FINANCES** *Year* 2013/14 *Income* £23,651 *Grants* £67,000 *Grants to organisations* £67,000
**TRUSTEES** Nigel Wollen; William Boughey; Philip Kay; Katrina Vollentine.
**OTHER INFORMATION** The trust has previously stated that grants are principally made charities operating within Torbay, Devon and the South West.
**HOW TO APPLY** Applications can be made in writing to the correspondent. The trustees normally meet two to four times a year to consider awards.
**WHO TO APPLY TO** Karyna Squibb, Correspondent, Wollen Michelmore, Carlton House, 30 The Terrace, Torquay, Devon TQ1 1BS *Tel.* 01803 213251 *Fax* 01803 296871 *email* karyna.squibb@wollenmichelmore.co.uk

### ■ The Muriel Jones Foundation

**CC NO** 1135107  **ESTABLISHED** 2010
**WHERE FUNDING CAN BE GIVEN** UK and overseas.
**WHO CAN BENEFIT** Registered charities.
**WHAT IS FUNDED** General charitable purposes.
**RANGE OF GRANTS** £200–£400,000
**SAMPLE GRANTS** Médecins Sans Frontières (£400,000); Crossflow (£181,000); Anti-Slavery International (£150,000); Animals Asia Foundation (£100,000); Frome Development (£70,000); Bath Cats and Dogs Home (£50,000); Mama Upendo Children's Trust (£45,000); FareShare (£30,000); Celtic Charity Fund (£26,500); Lancashire Foundation (£15,000); Down's Syndrome Diamond Foundation (£2,000); Spinal Muscular Atrophy (£200).
**FINANCES** *Year* 2013/14 *Income* £4,879,384 *Grants* £1,682,911 *Grants to organisations* £1,682,911 *Assets* £8,709,670
**TRUSTEES** Richard Brindle; Katie Brindle; Coutts & Co.
**OTHER INFORMATION** In 2013/14 a total of 39 grants were given to 21 organisations.
**HOW TO APPLY** Applications may be made in writing to the correspondent.

**WHO TO APPLY TO** The Trustees, Coutts & Co., 440 Strand, London WC2R 0QS *Tel.* 020 7663 6825 *email* couttscharities@coutts.com

### ■ The Jordan Charitable Foundation

**CC NO** 1051507  **ESTABLISHED** 1995
**WHERE FUNDING CAN BE GIVEN** UK national charities; Herefordshire, in particular Hereford; Sutherland – Scotland.
**WHO CAN BENEFIT** UK national charities; local charities and community groups in Herefordshire and Sutherland – Scotland.
**WHAT IS FUNDED** General charitable purposes, especially medical equipment, medical research, older people, people with disabilities (including children), animal welfare and maintenance of Hereford Cathedral.
**TYPE OF GRANT** One-off or recurrent; capital and core costs; unrestricted funding.
**RANGE OF GRANTS** £1,000–£50,000; mostly £5,000 or £10,000.
**SAMPLE GRANTS** Extra Care Charitable Trust (£30,000); Brooke Hospital for Animals, Canine Partners For Independence and The Special Air Service Regimental Association (£10,000 each); Sutherland Schools Pipe Band – Golspie (£8,000); Atlantic Salmon Trust, British Red Cross, National Trust for Scotland; The Salvation Army and Wildfowl and Wetlands Trust (£5,000 each); Children's Hospice Association – Scotland and International Animal Rescue (£2,000 each); Queen Elizabeth Castle of May Trust (£1,000).
**FINANCES** *Year* 2013 *Income* £1,020,071 *Grants* £325,000 *Grants to organisations* £350,000 *Assets* £48,961,171
**TRUSTEES** Sir George Russell; Ralph Stockwell; Christopher Bliss; Anthony Brierley; Snowport Ltd; Parkdove Ltd.
**OTHER INFORMATION** In 2013 a total of 47 awards were made. Around 80% of funding was given to organisations working throughout the UK, 17% in Hereford and 3% in Sutherland.
**HOW TO APPLY** Applications may be made in writing to the correspondent. The trustees meet four times a year.
**WHO TO APPLY TO** Ralph Stockwell, Trustee, c/o Rawlinson and Hunter, 8th Floor, 6 New Street Square, New Fetter Lane, London EC4A 3AQ *Tel.* 020 7842 2000 *email* jordan@rawlinson-hunter.com

### ■ The Joron Charitable Trust

**CC NO** 1062547  **ESTABLISHED** 1997
**WHERE FUNDING CAN BE GIVEN** UK.
**WHO CAN BENEFIT** Registered charities.
**WHAT IS FUNDED** General charitable purposes; Jewish causes; education; medical research.
**TYPE OF GRANT** Generally one-off.
**RANGE OF GRANTS** £1,000–£185,000
**SAMPLE GRANTS** The Wilderness Foundation (£185,000); Carers Trust (£25,000); ACVV Central (£4,500); and Cancer Research UK, Devon Air Ambulance, Jamie Proctor Foundation and Maggie Keswick Jenks (£1,000 each).
**FINANCES** *Year* 2013/14 *Income* £175,027 *Grants* £218,613 *Grants to organisations* £218,613 *Assets* £44,168
**TRUSTEES** Bruce Jarvis; Joseph Jarvis; Sandra Jarvis; Juliet Jarvis.
**OTHER INFORMATION** During the year seven grants were made.

**HOW TO APPLY** Applications may be made in writing to the correspondent. The annual report and accounts for 2013/14 state that there is no formal grant procedure.
**WHO TO APPLY TO** Bruce Jarvis, Trustee, Ravensale Ltd, 115 Wembley Commercial Centre, East Lane, North Wembley, Middlesex HA9 7UR *Tel.* 020 8908 4655 *email* ravensale100@btconnect.com

## ■ The J. E. Joseph Charitable Fund

**CC NO** 209058           **ESTABLISHED** 1946
**WHERE FUNDING CAN BE GIVEN** London, Manchester, Israel and India.
**WHO CAN BENEFIT** Jewish community organisations, especially those catering for people who are socially disadvantaged and young people.
**WHAT IS FUNDED** Jewish causes, including health, relief of poverty, education and religion.
**WHAT IS NOT FUNDED** Grants are not normally made to individuals (in exceptional circumstances support may be provided where there is potential for benefit for the whole community). The charity no longer supports large national charities with significant income. Capital projects are not generally supported.
**TYPE OF GRANT** Outright cash grants frequently on an annual basis. Our research suggests that very occasional loans may be made.
**RANGE OF GRANTS** £500–£10,000
**SAMPLE GRANTS** The Future Generation Fund (£10,000); Sir Jacob Sassoon Charity Trust (£8,500); University Jewish Chaplaincy Board (£7,000); Edinburgh House – Home for Elderly (£6,000); Jerusalem Conservatory Hassadna and Morasha Primary School (£5,000 each); Ezra U'Marpeh and Pardes Institute of Jewish Studies (£4,000 each); Spanish and Portuguese Synagogue Hebrew Classes (£3,000); and Jewish Deaf Association and TAL – Torah, Action, Life (£2,000 each).
**FINANCES** Year 2013/14 Income £142,913 Grants £120,500 Grants to organisations £120,500 Assets £4,958,989
**TRUSTEES** Susan Kendal; John Corre; Abe Simon; Peter Sheldon; Edward Mocatta; Robert Shemtob; Mark Sabah.
**HOW TO APPLY** Applications may be made in writing to the correspondent, including a copy of the latest accounts. The trustees respond to all applications which are first vetted by the secretary. The charity has stated in the annual report for 2013/14: 'As in previous years the Trust received far more applications that it can support from its limited funds. However, the Trust does try, if possible, to respond favourably to one or two new applications per year.'
**WHO TO APPLY TO** Roger Leon, Secretary, 10 Compass Close, Edgware, Middlesex HA8 8HU *Tel.* 020 8958 0126 *email* roger.leon@btinternet.com

## ■ The Lady Eileen Joseph Foundation

**CC NO** 327549           **ESTABLISHED** 1987
**WHERE FUNDING CAN BE GIVEN** UK.
**WHO CAN BENEFIT** Mainly UK organisations benefitting at-risk groups and people who are disadvantaged by poverty or social exclusion.
**WHAT IS FUNDED** General charitable purposes; disadvantaged people; relief of poverty; social isolation; at risk groups; welfare; medical causes.

**TYPE OF GRANT** One-off.
**RANGE OF GRANTS** Up to £10,000.
**SAMPLE GRANTS** Previous beneficiaries have included: Second Chance (£7,500); Coldstream Guards Association (£6,500); Alzheimer's Research Trust and Friends of the Home Physiotherapy Service (£5,000 each); Havens Hospices (£4,500); Ellenor Foundation and Queen Alexandra Hospital (£3,000 each); Independent Age and Wellbeing of Women (£2,000 each); and Cystic Fibrosis Trust, Foundation for the Prevention of Blindness and Action for Kids (£1,000 each).
**FINANCES** Year 2013/14 Income £7,752 Grants £50,000 Grants to organisations £50,000
**TRUSTEES** Judith Sawdy; Thurlstan Simpson; Gael Simpson.
**HOW TO APPLY** The trust has previously stated that unsolicited requests will not be considered.
**WHO TO APPLY TO** Thurlstan Simpson, Trustee, Colbrans Farm, Cow Lane, Laughton, Lewes BN8 6BZ *email* joe@colbrans.co.uk

## ■ The Josephs Family Charitable Trust

**CC NO** 1054016         **ESTABLISHED** 1996
**WHERE FUNDING CAN BE GIVEN** UK.
**WHO CAN BENEFIT** Local and national Jewish charities.
**WHAT IS FUNDED** Jewish causes; medical research; children; general charitable purposes.
**RANGE OF GRANTS** Mostly £100 or less.
**SAMPLE GRANTS** Previous beneficiaries have included: United Jewish Israel Appeal (£5,000), Gatehead Academy (£3,000), Kollel Nechovas Israel (£1,000); Ms Society (£500), Law of Truth College Talmudical College (£350), Foodlife Line, Norwood Challenges and St Oswald's College (£100 each).
**FINANCES** Year 2013/14 Income £12,011 Grants £26,000 Grants to organisations £26,000
**TRUSTEES** Anthony Josephs; Kate Ison; Howard Gold.
**HOW TO APPLY** Applications may be made in writing to the correspondent.
**WHO TO APPLY TO** John Josephs, Treasurer, 55 Moor Court, Newcastle upon Tyne NE3 4DY *Tel.* 0191 285 1912

## ■ The Josh Charitable Trust

**CC NO** 1107060         **ESTABLISHED** 2004
**WHERE FUNDING CAN BE GIVEN** UK, Israel and Australia.
**WHO CAN BENEFIT** Registered charities.
**WHAT IS FUNDED** General charitable purposes.
**FINANCES** Year 2013/14 Income £30,391 Grants £29,598 Grants to organisations £29,598 Assets £5,993
**TRUSTEES** Joel Cope; Shoshana Cope.
**OTHER INFORMATION** There were 23 grants made to 'worthy causes'.
**HOW TO APPLY** Applications can be made in writing to the correspondent.
**WHO TO APPLY TO** The Trustees, 1 Lancaster Drive, Prestwich, Manchester M25 0HZ *Tel.* 07973 196025 *email* nopublicaddress@gmail.com

■ **The Cyril and Eve Jumbo Charitable Trust**

CC NO 1097209   ESTABLISHED 2003
WHERE FUNDING CAN BE GIVEN Worldwide.
WHO CAN BENEFIT Charitable organisations.
WHAT IS FUNDED General charitable purposes; overseas aid. Our research suggest that these include: fresh water projects; projects that deal with grass roots and front line action, and that set up sustainable, ongoing projects so that people can increase their independence and create their own livelihoods; and projects that help children (particularly those in countries recovering from war and trauma), older people and people with disabilities/special needs.
RANGE OF GRANTS £500–£12,500
SAMPLE GRANTS Whatever the Need (£12,500); Lubavitch of Edgware and Morasha Jewish Primary School (£10,000 each); Help the Hospices (£5,800); Promise (£3,500); Forest Schools Camp (£3,000); South Hampstead Synagogue (£1,000); Teenage Cancer Trust (£650); and Leatherhead Drama Festival (£500).
FINANCES Year 2013/14 Income £113,739 Grants £75,350 Grants to organisations £75,350 Assets £1,928,053
TRUSTEES Geoffrey Margolis; Rafiq Hayat; Kayla Justice.
OTHER INFORMATION The trust made 25 awards during the year.
HOW TO APPLY Applications should be made in writing to the trustees, including full details of the charity. The trustees meet on a regular basis to consider applications. Unsuccessful applications are not always acknowledged.
WHO TO APPLY TO Edward Engulu, Chief Accountant, Mumbo Jumbo World, 48 Great Marlborough Street, London W1F 7BB Tel. 020 7437 0879 email charity@mjw13.com Website mjw13.com

■ **Anton Jurgens Charitable Trust**

CC NO 259885   ESTABLISHED 1969
WHERE FUNDING CAN BE GIVEN UK, with a preference for the south east of England.
WHO CAN BENEFIT UK-registered charities; youth organisations, centres, clubs and institutions; community organisations; day centres and nurseries; general welfare organisations.
WHAT IS FUNDED General charitable purposes; social welfare; health; children and young people; vulnerable people.
TYPE OF GRANT Generally one-off.
RANGE OF GRANTS Mainly £1,000–£10,000.
SAMPLE GRANTS Malaika Kids (£35,000); The Respite Association (£8,000); Innovative Foundation (£5,000); The Honeypot Children's Charity and Trinity Winchester (£4,000 each); YMCA (£3,500); ActiviTeens, Essex Boys' and Girls' Club and Heathrow Special Needs Farm (£3,000 each); Pecan (£2,000); Greenfingers, My Life My Choice and West Chadsmoor Family Centre Ltd (£1,000 each); and Parachute Regiment (£750).
FINANCES Year 2013/14 Income £270,348 Grants £236,750 Grants to organisations £236,750 Assets £8,019,294
TRUSTEES Eric Deckers; Maria Edge-Jurgens; Frans Jurgens; Steven Jurgens; Paul Beek; Frans Tilman.
OTHER INFORMATION There were a total of 61 awards made.
HOW TO APPLY Applications may be made in writing to the correspondent. The trustees generally meet twice a year in June and October. Note that they do not enter into correspondence concerning grant applications beyond notifying successful applicants.
WHO TO APPLY TO Maria Edge-Jurgens, Trustee, Saffery Champness, Lion House, 72–75 Red Lion Street, London WC1R 4GB Tel. 020 7841 4000 email info@saffery.com

■ **Jusaca Charitable Trust**

CC NO 1012966   ESTABLISHED 1992
WHERE FUNDING CAN BE GIVEN UK and overseas; Israel.
WHO CAN BENEFIT Charitable organisations.
WHAT IS FUNDED General charitable purposes; Jewish causes; health; arts and heritage; education; research; religion; community development; housing.
TYPE OF GRANT Mainly recurrent.
RANGE OF GRANTS Generally £1,000–£5,000.
SAMPLE GRANTS No information available.
FINANCES Year 2013/14 Income £120,804 Grants £218,424 Grants to organisations £218,242 Assets £1,394,759
TRUSTEES Donald Franklin; Sara Emanuel; Diana Franklin; Carolyn Emanuel; Maurice Emanuel; Rachel Paul; Ralph Emanuel.
OTHER INFORMATION The trust aims to distribute at least 50% of donations to Jewish charities in the UK, overseas and Israel, and of the remainder about 40% to be donation to charities operating in the UK and about 60% outside the UK. The majority of grants are given to the same organisations each year in order to provide a long term stream of funding. During the year grants were made to 91 organisations, of these 57 awards exceeded £1,000.
HOW TO APPLY Grants are made at the discretion of the trustees. Unsolicited applications are not encouraged.
WHO TO APPLY TO Sara Emanuel, Trustee, 17 Ashburnham Grove, London SE10 8UH

# K

## ■ The Bernard Kahn Charitable Trust
CC NO 249130          ESTABLISHED 1965
WHERE FUNDING CAN BE GIVEN UK and Israel.
WHO CAN BENEFIT Organisations benefitting Jewish people, especially children and young adults, people disadvantaged by poverty; educational and religious bodies.
WHAT IS FUNDED Relief of poverty and the advancement of education and religion within the Jewish community.
WHAT IS NOT FUNDED Jewish causes only.
RANGE OF GRANTS £600–£35,000
SAMPLE GRANTS Achisomoch Aid Company Ltd (£35,000); Marbeh Torah Trust and Orthodox Council of Jerusalem Limited (£20,000 each); Friends of Be'er Miriam and Society of Friends of the Torah Ltd (£10,000 each); Plant Memorial Fund (£1,500); Toras Chaim (£600).
FINANCES Year 2012/13 Income £41,491 Grants £97,060 Grants to organisations £97,060 Assets £1,527,231
TRUSTEES Shalom Fuehrer; Yaacov Zvi Kahn.
OTHER INFORMATION Grants were made to seven organisations. At the time of writing (June 2015) this was the latest information available – 2013/14 accounts were overdue.
HOW TO APPLY Applications may be made in writing to the correspondent.
WHO TO APPLY TO Yaacov Zvi Kahn, Trustee, 24 Elmcroft Avenue, London NW11 0RR

## ■ The Stanley Kalms Foundation
CC NO 328368          ESTABLISHED 1989
WHERE FUNDING CAN BE GIVEN UK and overseas.
WHO CAN BENEFIT Organisations and individuals involved with Orthodox Jewish education in the UK and Israel, the arts, medicine and other secular and religious programmes.
WHAT IS FUNDED Encouragement of Orthodox Jewish education in the UK and Israel, particularly by providing scholarships, fellowships and research grant; arts; medicine.
TYPE OF GRANT One-off; research; project grants; bursaries and scholarships.
RANGE OF GRANTS Up to £100,000.
SAMPLE GRANTS **Previous beneficiaries have included:** Henry Jackson Society (£100,000); Buckingham University (£25,000); Centre for Social Justice and Oxford Centre for Hebrew and Jewish Studies (£10,000 each); Friends of Melabev (£7,500); and Anglo Israel Association and Dixons City Academy (£5,000 each).
FINANCES Year 2013/14 Income £14,632 Grants £230,000 Grants to organisations £230,000
TRUSTEES Stanley Kalms; Pamela Kalms; Stephen Kalms.
HOW TO APPLY Applications may be made in writing to the correspondent, but note that most of the trust's funds are committed to projects supported for a number of years.
WHO TO APPLY TO Steve Russell, Correspondent, Steve Russell And Associates, Paddock Hill House, Sacombe Green, Ware, Hertfordshire SG12 0JH Tel. 01438 365804 email steve. russell@srandassociates.co.uk

## ■ Karaviotis Foundation (The J. M. K. Charitable Trust)
CC NO 274576          ESTABLISHED 1977
WHERE FUNDING CAN BE GIVEN Worldwide.
WHO CAN BENEFIT Registered charities only, benefitting the appreciation of art and music, also assisting religious organisations to help relations with other faiths.
WHAT IS FUNDED General charitable purposes; arts and music (particularly); Jewish causes; health and medical research.
RANGE OF GRANTS £100–£17,000
SAMPLE GRANTS Royal Academy of Music – Scholarship (£15,000); Salzburg Festival (£7,000); English Touring Opera (£5,100); Les Azuriales Opera Trust (£4,500); Cancer Research UK (£2,600); Central British Fund for World Jewish Relief (£1,200); The Pharos Trust (£900); and Friends of the Royal Academy (£130).
FINANCES Year 2013/14 Income £69,022 Grants £50,757 Grants to organisations £50,757 Assets £2,289,495
TRUSTEES Jill Karaviotis; Joseph Karaviotis.
OTHER INFORMATION There were 21 awards made.
HOW TO APPLY Unsolicited applications will not be considered.
WHO TO APPLY TO The Trustees, c/o Saffery Champness, Lion House, 72–75 Red Lion Street, London WC1R 4GB Tel. 020 7841 4000

## ■ The Boris Karloff Charitable Foundation
CC NO 326898          ESTABLISHED 1985
WHERE FUNDING CAN BE GIVEN Worldwide.
WHO CAN BENEFIT UK-wide and local charities benefitting actors, musicians, people disadvantaged by mental or physical illness and young cricketers.
WHAT IS FUNDED Performing arts; cricket.
WHAT IS NOT FUNDED Grants are not made for individuals, charities with large resources or organisations the activities of which do not relate to performing arts or cricket.
RANGE OF GRANTS £500–£12,600
SAMPLE GRANTS Young Vic (£12,600); Surrey County Cricket Board (£10,000); RADA – Boris Karloff Scholarship Fund, Royal Theatrical Fund and Scene and Heard (£5,000 each); Southwark Playhouse Theatre Company (£2,500); Arts Insight and Theatre Haymarket (£1,000 each); and Friary Guildford Brass Band and Inside Intelligence (£500 each).
FINANCES Year 2013/14 Income £60,238 Grants £72,600 Grants to organisations £72,600 Assets £2,437,522
TRUSTEES James Fairclough; Carole Fairclough; Bernard Coleman; Owen Lewis.
OTHER INFORMATION There were 24 awards made.
HOW TO APPLY Applications can be made in writing to the correspondent.
WHO TO APPLY TO Andrew Studd, Correspondent, Russell Cooke Solicitors, 2 Putney Hill, London SW15 6AB Tel. 020 8789 9111 Fax 020 8780 1194

## ■ The Ian Karten Charitable Trust
CC NO 281721          ESTABLISHED 1980
WHERE FUNDING CAN BE GIVEN UK and Israel, with some local interest in Surrey and London.
WHO CAN BENEFIT CTEC Centres promoting digital inclusion for people with disabilities; educational

institutions for scholarship and bursary support; Jewish organisations.
**WHAT IS FUNDED** Currently the main focus is placed on: 'improving the quality of life and independence of people with severe physical, sensory, cognitive disability or mental health problems by providing Centres for Computer-aided Training, Education and Communication (CTEC Centres)'; 'the support of higher education by funding studentships for postgraduate studies and research at selected universities in the UK' – awards mainly given through the educational institutions. Small number of grants are also made to aid Jewish causes.
**WHAT IS NOT FUNDED** Individuals.
**TYPE OF GRANT** Project costs; up to two years; one-off or recurrent awards to charities; scholarship and bursary support.
**RANGE OF GRANTS** £500–£90,000
**SAMPLE GRANTS** CTEC Centres – 19 grants totalling £400,000 Ono University – Israel (£50,500); Shalava – Israel (£50,000); Chimes – Israel (£49,500); Stockport CP (£25,000); Homefield College (£23,500); QAC Birmingham (£12,200); IsrALS (£7,200); Orchardville Society – Belfast (£1,700). *Large grants – nine grants totalling £56,000* Southampton Karten Outreach (£50,000); Jewish Care (£1,500); World Jewish Relief and Yad Vashem UK Foundation (£1,000 each); UJIA Foundation for Education (£700); Anne Frank Educational Trust, Institute for Jewish Policy Research, Surrey Care Trust (£500 each). *Scholarships – eight institutional grants totalling £146,000* Southampton University Bursaries (£90,000); The Woolf Institute for Abrahamic Faith (£20,000); AJA (£18,000); Southampton University (£10,000); University College London (£4,000).
**FINANCES** *Year* 2013/14 *Income* £152,017 *Grants* £632,500 *Grants to organisations* £632,500 *Assets* £12,904,685
**TRUSTEES** Timothy Simon; Angela Hobbs; David Fullerton; Anthony Davis.
**OTHER INFORMATION** The grant total includes £146,000 given to educational establishments for scholarships and bursaries.
**HOW TO APPLY** The trust currently only considers grants to charities supported in the past. Grants are no longer being made for new CTEC centres. The trustees meet every six months to review the accounts and to discuss any proposed donations, scholarships and bursaries
**WHO TO APPLY TO** Timothy Simon, Trustee, The Mill House, PO Box 386, Lymington SO41 1BD *Tel.* 01590 681345 *Fax* 01483 222420 *email* kartentrust@aol.com *Website* www.karten-network.org.uk

### ■ The Kasner Charitable Trust
**CC NO** 267510  **ESTABLISHED** 1974
**WHERE FUNDING CAN BE GIVEN** UK and Israel.
**WHO CAN BENEFIT** Charities and organisations benefitting Jewish people.
**WHAT IS FUNDED** General charitable purposes with focus on Jewish causes.
**TYPE OF GRANT** Small awards to a few hundred organisations each year.
**RANGE OF GRANTS** Up to £10,000; mainly small grants of up to £500.
**SAMPLE GRANTS** *Previous beneficiaries have included:* British Committee for Israel and United Jewish Appeal (£10,000 each); Gevurath Ari Academy Trust (£5,000); Gateshead Talmudical College (£1,600); Friends of Ohel Sarah (£1,200); Bais Hamedrash Bais Avraham (£1,100); United Synagogue (£800); British Friends of Zaka (£400); Torah Trust (£300); WIZO UK and Yeshivat Zichron Dovid (£100 each); Animal Rescue Foundation and WaterAid (£10 each).
**FINANCES** *Grants* £95,000 *Grants to organisations* £95,000
**TRUSTEES** Judith Erlich; Baruch Erlich; Josef Kasner.
**OTHER INFORMATION** At the time of writing (June 2015) this was the latest information available; the trust has not submitted its accounts since 2011/12. We maintain the entry as the trust remains active on the Charity Commission's record and has been awarding on average around £95,000 annually.
**HOW TO APPLY** Applications can be made in writing to the correspondent. The trust states that it 'receives grant applications from a number of client organisations, and every application is considered by the board of trustees in relation to pre agreed parameters' and 'gives grants to most of the organisations that apply'.
**WHO TO APPLY TO** Josef Kasner, Trustee, 1A Gresham Gardens, London NW11 8NX *Tel.* 020 8455 7830

### ■ The Kass Charitable Trust (KCT)
**CC NO** 1006296  **ESTABLISHED** 1991
**WHERE FUNDING CAN BE GIVEN** UK.
**WHO CAN BENEFIT** Charitable organisations. In the past some support has been available to individuals.
**WHAT IS FUNDED** Social welfare; education; health and medical research; nursing facilities; disadvantaged individuals; Jewish faith and community causes.
**TYPE OF GRANT** One-off; unrestricted funding.
**RANGE OF GRANTS** Usually small, under £500.
**FINANCES** *Year* 2013/14 *Income* £44,280 *Grants* £42,226 *Grants to organisations* £42,226 *Assets* £2,274
**TRUSTEES** David Kass; Shulamith Sandler.
**OTHER INFORMATION** The latest set of accounts had no information of grant beneficiaries.
**HOW TO APPLY** Applications may be made in writing to the correspondent.
**WHO TO APPLY TO** David Kass, Trustee, 37 Sherwood Road, London NW4 1AE *email* dkass@vintange.co.uk

### ■ The Michael and Ilse Katz Foundation
**CC NO** 263726  **ESTABLISHED** 1971
**WHERE FUNDING CAN BE GIVEN** UK and overseas.
**WHO CAN BENEFIT** International and UK schemes and organisations benefitting Jewish people, at risk groups or people who are disadvantaged by poverty or socially isolated.
**WHAT IS FUNDED** Primarily Jewish organisations. Health/disability and welfare causes are also supported. Medical and age support is particularly considered.
**TYPE OF GRANT** One-off and recurring.
**RANGE OF GRANTS** £500–£15,000
**SAMPLE GRANTS** Fight for Sight (£15,000); Jewish Care (£12,000); Community Security Trust and Norwood Children and Families First (£6,000 each); Bournemouth Symphony Orchestra (£4,500); Hannah Levy House Trust, Jewish Blind and Disabled Association and The Worshipful Company of Butchers (£2,000 each); Magen David Adorn UK (£1,500); British Ex-Services Wheelchair Sports Association,

Holidays for Heroes Jersey and Whizz-Kidz (£1,000 each); Blind Veterans UK – St Dunstan's (£500).
FINANCES Year 2013/14 Income £95,734 Grants £83,600 Grants to organisations £83,600 Assets £2,654,394
TRUSTEES Norris Gilbert; Osman Azis.
OTHER INFORMATION At least 30 organisations benefitted and no grants were made to individuals during the year. Sundry grants under £1,000 totalled £4,100.
HOW TO APPLY Applications may be made in writing to the correspondent.
WHO TO APPLY TO Osman Azis, Trustee, Counting House, Trelill, Bodmin PL30 3HZ Tel. 01208 851814 email osmanazis@btconnect.com

## ■ C. S. Kaufman Charitable Trust
CC NO 253194     ESTABLISHED 1967
WHERE FUNDING CAN BE GIVEN UK.
WHO CAN BENEFIT Organisations benefitting Jewish people.
WHAT IS FUNDED Jewish causes; promotion of Jewish faith; education.
TYPE OF GRANT One-off or recurrent.
RANGE OF GRANTS Generally up to £30,000.
SAMPLE GRANTS Merkaz Hatora Belz Machnovke (£21,000); Keren Gemillas Chesed Fund (£15,800 in two grants); Jewish Teachers' Training College (£7,600 in three grants); British Friend of Keren Gemilus Chessed Fund (£7,000); Kollel Schare Schlomo and T.T. Family Relief (£5,000 each); The Shaarei Torah Trust (£1,000); Gateshead Hebrew Congregation (£400); Institution of Higher Rabbinical Studies (£100); and Gateshead Hazolo (£25).
FINANCES Year 2013/14 Income £81,564 Grants £69,667 Grants to organisations £69,667 Assets £463,369
TRUSTEES Israel Kaufman; Simon Kaufman; J. Kaufman; L. Kaufman.
OTHER INFORMATION There were 28 awards made, with some organisations receiving more than one grant during the year.
HOW TO APPLY Applications may be made in writing to the correspondent.
WHO TO APPLY TO The Trustees, Ernst & Young LLP, Citygate, St James Boulevard, Newcastle upon Tyne NE1 4JD Tel. 0191 247 2500

## ■ The Kelly Family Charitable Trust
CC NO 1102440     ESTABLISHED 2004
WHERE FUNDING CAN BE GIVEN UK, there may be some preference for Scotland.
WHO CAN BENEFIT Registered charities that support and encourage family welfare and cohesion; small local organisations. Preference is given to charities whose income is below £500,000 but larger charities with pioneering pilot projects will also be considered.
WHAT IS FUNDED Initiatives that seek to tackle family problems and strengthen family bonds; social inclusion of families with children at risk and marginalised by poverty and discrimination. The accounts state: 'The Trust has decided to prioritise its funding in favour of charities whose activities involve all or most family members in initiatives that support and encourage the family to work as a cohesive unit in tackling problems that face one or more of its members. The overall objective is to reinforce the potential benefit and support that family members as a unit can give to each other.' The following areas are currently in focus: Abuse ('sexual abuse, physical abuse, domestic violence, alcohol abuse, drug abuse and any other form of threat to integrity of the family unit'); Prison Support ('early intervention to avoid the fracture of the family unit'). Applications are welcomed from sports and health-related charities and particularly from relatively new organisations to help them become established.
WHAT IS NOT FUNDED Non-registered charities; grants directly to individuals; national charities (only regional projects will be considered); general appeals; organisations with specific religious or political agendas.
TYPE OF GRANT One-off and up to three years; capital and revenue grants; core funding; set-up costs; projects; salaries.
RANGE OF GRANTS Generally £1,000–£5,000; higher amounts may be considered.
SAMPLE GRANTS A list of beneficiaries was not included in the accounts; however, the website gives some examples of grant recipients.
Beneficiaries have included: Circle; Families Outside; Families Talking; Homelink Family Support; Homestart Teesside; Moira Anderson Foundation; MOSAC; Parent to Parent Dundee; Quaker Social Action; Westminster Befriend a Family.
FINANCES Year 2013/14 Income £126,187 Grants £130,724 Grants to organisations £130,724 Assets £2,864,623
TRUSTEES Annie Kelly; Brian Mattingley; Jenny Kelly; Sheldon Cordell; Michael Field; Kayleigh Wiggins.
OTHER INFORMATION The accounts note that 'the trust has implemented a policy of distributing up to £65,000 per round until the monetary resources have steadied after the recent financial crisis'.
HOW TO APPLY Application forms can be downloaded from the trust's website. They should be returned by email along with a copy of the latest annual accounts (where available). Grants are awarded twice a year and appeals must be submitted by 1 March and 1 September. The trustees will ask for more detail for those applications that pass the initial screening and may visit the projects they wish to support.
WHO TO APPLY TO Stuart Armstrong, Correspondent, 8 Mansfield Place, Edinburgh EH3 6NB Tel. 0131 315 4879 email s.armstrong@kfct.org Website www.kfct.org.uk

## ■ Kelsick's Educational Foundation
CC NO 526956     ESTABLISHED 1723
WHERE FUNDING CAN BE GIVEN Lakes parish (Ambleside, Grasmere, Langdale and part of Troutbeck); any surplus income may be applied in Patterdale Ward and former county of Westmoreland.
WHO CAN BENEFIT Individuals under 25 years of age; organisations benefitting such people; schools (namely Ambleside, Grasmere and Langdale); local groups and clubs for young people.
WHAT IS FUNDED Educational needs of individuals under the age of 25; school activities such as educational visits, field trips, music lessons., reading resources and items of necessary equipment; support for academic courses and apprenticeships, including equipment costs. The website notes: 'The Trustees are aware of funding requirements with particular reference to

pupils' Special Educational Needs, which is an area of increasing demand.'

**WHAT IS NOT FUNDED** Holidays; course items without receipts.

**TYPE OF GRANT** Capital and project support; one-off or for longer than three years.

**RANGE OF GRANTS** £2,000–£54,000

**SAMPLE GRANTS** Grasmere Primary School (£54,000); Ambleside Primary School (£50,000); Langdale Primary School (£46,000); Ambleside Toddlers and Playgroup (£2,000). Support has also been given to: Ambleside Badminton Club; Ambleside Basketball Club; Ambleside Cricket Club; Ambleside Football Club; Ambleside Rugby Club; also Brownies, Cubs and Scouts.

**FINANCES** Year 2013/14 Income £374,258 Grants £230,704 Grants to organisations £152,399 Assets £7,056,227

**TRUSTEES** Peter Jackson; Linda Dixon; Leslie Johnson; Nigel Hutchinson; John Halstead; Angela Renouf; Norman Tyson; Reginald Curphey; Nicholas Martin; Revd Tim Ball; Margaret Weaver; Mark Blackburn.

**OTHER INFORMATION** A total of £78,500 was given to individuals and £152,500 to organisations.

**HOW TO APPLY** Application forms for individuals are available from the foundation's website or otherwise can be requested from the correspondent. Grants are considered in February, May, August and November and appeals should be received by 31 January, 30 April, 31 July, 31 October, respectively.

**WHO TO APPLY** Peter Frost, Clerk to the Trustees, The Kelsick Centre, St Mary's Lane, Ambleside, Cumbria LA22 9DG *Tel.* 01539 431289 *Fax* 01539 431292 *email* john@kelsick.plus.com *Website* www.kelsick.org.uk

## ■ The Kay Kendall Leukaemia Fund

**CC NO** 290772      **ESTABLISHED** 1984

**WHERE FUNDING CAN BE GIVEN** UK.

**WHO CAN BENEFIT** UK and non-UK organisations (for work based primarily in the UK); institutions conducting research into leukaemia or related diseases; patient care and support centres. Preference may be given 'to support first class research in centres of excellence'.

**WHAT IS FUNDED** Medical research into and treatment of leukaemia or related diseases.

**WHAT IS NOT FUNDED** Circular appeals for general support; project grant applications submitted simultaneously to other funding bodies; clinical trials.

**TYPE OF GRANT** Research funding; capital costs; equipment; clinical support; fellowships; project grants for up to three years.

**RANGE OF GRANTS** £50,000–£1 million.

**SAMPLE GRANTS** University of Cambridge (£1 million); Christie Charitable Fund (£245,000); Cambridge Institute for Medical Research (£204,500 in three grants); University of Southampton School of Medicine (£96,500 in two separate grants); Plymouth Citizens Advice (£74,500); Wellcome Trust Sanger Institute (£72,000); Royal Cornwall Hospital NHS Trust (£63,500); University of Southampton (£61,000); Stars Appeal (£50,000).

**FINANCES** Year 2013/14 Income £742,000 Grants £3,202,125 Grants to organisations £3,202,125 Assets £24,755,000

**TRUSTEES** Judith Portrait; Timothy Sainsbury; Charles Metcalfe.

**OTHER INFORMATION** The charity is one of the Sainsbury Family Charitable Trusts which share a common administration. An application to one is taken as an application to all and directed to the most suitable. The annual report for 2013/14 states that the trustees are 'planning to spend in total about £4.1 million per annum; £2.8 million on scientific research grants and £1.3 million on its patient care programme'. During the year £1.88 million was given on research grants, £501,500 in KKLF fellowships and £821,000 in patient care awards.

**HOW TO APPLY** Application forms are available from the correspondent. They should include a research proposal for project grants (aims, background, plan of investigation and justification for budget) which should be three to five single-spaced pages (excluding references, costings, and CVs). Applications should be submitted by email in addition to providing a hard copy with original signatures. Awards are normally considered in May and October and applications should be received by the end of February and mid-July, respectively. Note that Patient Care and Scientific Research programmes are separate – further details on each can be obtained from the trust. A preliminary letter or telephone call to determine eligibility would be helpful. Note that the trustees 'take a proactive approach towards patient care grant-making and proposals are generally invited by the trustees or initiated at their request'.

**WHO TO APPLY TO** Alan Bookbinder, Director, The Peak, 5 Wilton Road, London SW1V 1AP *Tel.* 020 7410 0330 *email* info@kklf.org.uk *Website* www.kklf.org.uk

## ■ William Kendall's Charity (Wax Chandlers' Company)

**CC NO** 228361      **ESTABLISHED** 1559

**WHERE FUNDING CAN BE GIVEN** Greater London and the London borough of Bexley.

**WHO CAN BENEFIT** Charitable organisations in Greater London working for relief of need and any charitable organisations in Bexley.

**WHAT IS FUNDED** Most donations are for relief of need in London.

**WHAT IS NOT FUNDED** Grants are not normally made to: large charities; charities whose accounts disclose substantial reserves; or non-registered charities. Grants are not made to: individuals; replace cuts in funding made by local authorities or others; schemes or activities which would be regarded as relieving central or local government of their statutory responsibilities; or cover deficits already incurred.

**TYPE OF GRANT** One-off or recurring.

**RANGE OF GRANTS** £500–£25,000, typical grant £5,000.

**SAMPLE GRANTS** Leap (£25,000); Westside School (£15,200); Guildhall School of Music and Drama (£5,000); Gardening Leave (£2,500); Bexley Beavers, Bexley Crossroads Care, Bexley Cruse Bereavement Care, Keats Community Organics, Re-Instate Ltd and Spitalfields Music Festival (£2,000 each); St Paul's Church (£1,900); Howbury Tumblers (£1,400); and British Polio Fellowship (£500).

**FINANCES** Year 2013/14 Income £78,816 Grants £72,515 Grants to organisations £72,515 Assets £3,729,062

**TRUSTEES** Peter Tompkins; Gavyn Arthur; David Jefferies; Heather Hawker; Dr Jonathan Munday; Neil Denison; Dr Colin Kolbert; Graeme Marrs;

John Chambers; John Sleeman; Dick Blaxland; Tim Maile; Fianne Stanford; Dr Andrew Mair; Quentin Humberstone; Arthur Davey; Joan Beavington; The Worshipful Company Of Wax Chandlers.

**OTHER INFORMATION** A total of 18 institutions received grants.

**HOW TO APPLY** The charity undertakes its own research and does not respond to unsolicited applications to Greater London fund or Persons in need fund. Bexley fund is administered by Bexley Voluntary Services Council (tel: 020 8304 0911).

**WHO TO APPLY TO** Georgina Brown, Clerk, Wax Chandlers' Hall, 6 Gresham Street, London EC2V 7AD *Tel.* 020 7606 3591 *Fax* 020 7600 5462 *email* clerk@waxchandlers.org.uk *Website* www.waxchandlers.org.uk/charity

■ **John Thomas Kennedy Charitable Foundation**

**CC NO** 1082421    **ESTABLISHED** 2000
**WHERE FUNDING CAN BE GIVEN** UK and overseas.
**WHO CAN BENEFIT** Charitable organisations.
**WHAT IS FUNDED** General charitable purposes.
**WHAT IS NOT FUNDED** Grants are not made to individuals.
**RANGE OF GRANTS** £500–£10,000
**SAMPLE GRANTS** MA Fathers (£10,000); Community Services Volunteers (£6,200); Acorn Treatment Abstinence Focus Services and The Diocese of Killala (£5,000 each); British Red Cross (£2,500); Forever Manchester (£1,000); and Destination Florida, Retrack and RNLI (£500 each).
**FINANCES** *Year* 2013 *Income* £139,500 *Grants* £45,700 *Grants to organisations* £45,700 *Assets* £1,539,577
**TRUSTEES** John Kennedy; Veronica Kennedy.
**OTHER INFORMATION** In 2013 a total of 14 grants were awarded.
**HOW TO APPLY** Applications can be made in writing to the correspondent.
**WHO TO APPLY TO** Keith Taylor, Correspondent, Reedham House, 31 King Street West, Manchester M3 2PJ *Tel.* 0161 834 2574 *email* lgouldman@fft.co.uk

■ **The Kennedy Charitable Foundation**

**CC NO** 1052001    **ESTABLISHED** 1995
**WHERE FUNDING CAN BE GIVEN** Unrestricted, but mainly Ireland with a preference for County Mayo and County Sligo.
**WHO CAN BENEFIT** Registered charities and charitable organisations.
**WHAT IS FUNDED** General charitable causes; Roman Catholic faith.
**RANGE OF GRANTS** £400–£42,000; mainly under £5,000.
**SAMPLE GRANTS** Knock Shrine (£42,000); Diocese of Killala (£13,100); Council for the West of Ireland (£4,200); Cornerstone (£4,000); SMA Fathers and Little Sisters of the Poor (£3,000 each); Archdiocese of Cardiff (£2,500); Irish Abroad (£2,000); Hope House – Foxford, Meningitis Research Foundation and Newman Institute (£1,700 each); Diocese of Hexham and Newcastle, Image and NeuroMuscular Centre (£1,000 each); Irish Emigrant Liaison Committee (£800); Children's Adventure Farm Trust (£500); and Irish Heart Foundation (£400).

**FINANCES** *Year* 2013/14 *Income* £116,356 *Grants* £112,778 *Grants to organisations* £112,778 *Assets* £71,599
**TRUSTEES** John Kennedy; Kathleen Kennedy; Joe Kennedy; Patrick Kennedy; Anna Kelly.
**OTHER INFORMATION** There were 37 awards made.
**HOW TO APPLY** The foundation has previously stated unsolicited applications are not accepted.
**WHO TO APPLY TO** The Trustees, 12th Floor, Bank House, Charlotte Street, Manchester M1 4ET

■ **The Kennel Club Charitable Trust**

**CC NO** 327802    **ESTABLISHED** 1988
**WHERE FUNDING CAN BE GIVEN** UK.
**WHO CAN BENEFIT** Registered charities; associations; re-homing societies; universities and other research bodies benefitting dogs; research workers and vets; people with disabilities, blind or deaf individuals where dogs are involved (in support of human beings).
**WHAT IS FUNDED** Science – research into diseases and other health conditions in dogs; support – the training of dogs to help humans; welfare – the rescue and re-homing of dogs which need help.
**WHAT IS NOT FUNDED** Generally, applications purely for building costs or requests from individuals or from organisations whose concern is not predominantly with the dog do not receive favourable attention. Grants are rarely made to organisations having a political reason. Veterinary nurses can apply to the British Veterinary Nursing Association where bursaries are available.
**TYPE OF GRANT** One-off and recurring for set periods (subject to a satisfactory annual review and report of progress); capital, core and project costs.
**RANGE OF GRANTS** £250–£292,500
**SAMPLE GRANTS** Animal Health Trust (£292,500 in two grants); University of Cambridge (£25,000); University of Bristol (£22,500 in two grants); Support Dogs (£24,000); Royal (Dick) School of Veterinary Studies (£20,000); The Mayhew Animal Rescue Home (£15,000); Rotherham Dog Rescue (£8,000); Guide Dogs for the Blind Association (£6,300); Devon GSD Rescue and Southern Counties German Shepherd Rescue (£5,000 each); Friends for Life (£4,500); Newcastle Dog and Cat Shelter (£2,800); Animal Rescue Cymru (£2,000); University of Nottingham (£700); Cocker Spaniel Breed Council (£250).
**FINANCES** *Year* 2013/14 *Income* £1,179,774 *Grants* £863,461 *Grants to organisations* £863,461 *Assets* £2,912,735
**TRUSTEES** Michael Townsend; Bill King; Steven Dean; Michael Herrtage; John Spurling; Jennifer Fairhall.
**OTHER INFORMATION** Grants were divided into: scientific and research project grants – £536,000 (including £122,000 from restricted funds) to 17 bodies; educational and other grants – £327,500 (including £21,000 from restricted funds) given to 53 bodies. Animal Health Trust remains the main grant recipient. According to the annual report for 2013/14, the trustees have confirmed further £1.55 million over the next five years to be provided to.
**HOW TO APPLY** Applications should be made in writing to the correspondent providing the latest accounts (and registered charity number, if applicable) and clearly stating the details of the costs for which you are requesting funding, for what purpose and over what period of time. The trust further details: 'On the Application Form,

please tell us about your Rescue's activities, such as how many dogs you re-home in a typical year, what support you receive from your breed clubs (and whether you have asked them for any), how many paid staff you have (if any).' The trustees meet four times a year.

**WHO TO APPLY TO** Doug Holford, 1–5 Clarges Street, Piccadilly, London W1J 8AB *Tel.* 01296 318 540 *Fax* 01296 318 540 *email* dholford@the-kennel-club.org.uk *Website* www.thekennelclub.org.uk/charitabletrust

## ■ Kent Community Foundation

**CC NO** 1084361 **ESTABLISHED** 2001
**WHERE FUNDING CAN BE GIVEN** Principally the County of Kent and the Borough of Medway; UK and elsewhere.
**WHO CAN BENEFIT** Local charities, community groups and voluntary organisations and individuals. The website notes: 'You do not have to be a registered charity to apply for a grant; however the work you ask us to support must be legally charitable and your group must be constituted.'
**WHAT IS FUNDED** A wide range of general charitable needs and community projects aimed at improving the quality of life for people in Kent. The foundation administers a number of funds established by individuals, families and organisations. In addition it has its own general fund which enables the trustees to support voluntary groups which fall outside the stated criteria of these funds.
**TYPE OF GRANT** Core, capital and project expenditure; one-off and recurrent.
**RANGE OF GRANTS** £100–£600,000; mostly under £5,000.
**SAMPLE GRANTS** A list of beneficiaries was not included in the accounts; however, awards were made as follows: children and young people (27%); people with health issues (11%); carers and people with disabilities (10% each); older people (8%); disadvantaged or poor people (7%); Local residents (5%); learning difficulties, people with mental health issues and people who have offended (4% each); NEET, adults and families (2% each); women (1%).
**FINANCES** *Year* 2013/14 *Income* £7,031,255 *Grants* £5,864,739 *Grants to organisations* £5,864,739 *Assets* £12,294,572
**TRUSTEES** Arthur Gulland; Sarah Hohler; Bella Colgrain; Peter Williams; Ann West; Tim Bull; Vicki Jessel; Georgina Warne.
**OTHER INFORMATION** As with all community foundations, there are a number of donor advised funds managed on behalf of individuals, families and charitable trusts. Grant schemes tend to change frequently; therefore consult the foundation's website for details of current programmes and their up-to-date deadlines.
**HOW TO APPLY** Further information on applications to each of the funds currently available can be found online or obtained from the Grants Team via the contacts given.
**WHO TO APPLY TO** Carol Lynch, CEO and Company Secretary, 23 Evegate Park Barn, Evegate, Smeeth, Ashford, Kent TN25 6SX *Tel.* 01303 814150 *email* admin@kentcf.org.uk *Website* www.kentcf.org.uk

## ■ The Nancy Kenyon Charitable Trust

**CC NO** 265359 **ESTABLISHED** 1972
**WHERE FUNDING CAN BE GIVEN** Throughout the UK.
**WHO CAN BENEFIT** Registered charities only.
**WHAT IS FUNDED** General charitable purposes. Primarily for people and causes known to the trustees.
**TYPE OF GRANT** One-off and recurrent.
**RANGE OF GRANTS** £100–£10,500
**SAMPLE GRANTS** Nancy Oldfield Trust (£10,500); One More Child (£5,000); St Nicholas Church, Ashchurch (£3,500); Church Mission Society, Earls Court Community Project, The Good Shepherd Project and The Nehemiah Project (£2,000 each); Cheltenham Open Door (£1,500); Emthonjeni Trust, Star College, The Family Haven and TS Warrior (£1,000 each); and Cromer Food Bank and Waveney Food Bank (£500 each).
**FINANCES** *Year* 2013/14 *Income* £65,969 *Grants* £49,102 *Grants to organisations* £44,000 *Assets* £1,720,691
**TRUSTEES** Lucy Phipps; Maureen Kenyon; Christopher Kenyon; Sally Kenyon; Peter Kenyon; Kieron Kenyon.
**OTHER INFORMATION** A total of 22 organisations received grants.
**HOW TO APPLY** Applications can be made in writing to the correspondent at any time. Our research notes that applications for causes not known to the trustees are considered annually in December.
**WHO TO APPLY TO** Alison Smith, Correspondent, c/o Brook Financial Management Ltd, Meads Barn, Ashwell Business Park, Ilminster, Somerset TA19 9DX *Tel.* 01460 259852

## ■ Keren Association Limited

**CC NO** 313119 **ESTABLISHED** 1961
**WHERE FUNDING CAN BE GIVEN** UK and overseas, including Israel, USA and Belgium.
**WHO CAN BENEFIT** Charitable organisations benefitting Jewish people, especially children and young adults; religious and educational establishments.
**WHAT IS FUNDED** General charitable purposes; Jewish causes; the advancement of education; the provision of religious instruction and training in traditional Judaism; relief in need.
**SAMPLE GRANTS** Previous beneficiaries have included: Beis Aharon Trust; British Heart Foundation; Clwk Yaakov; Friends of Arad; Friends of Beis Yaakov; Kupat Gmach Vezer Nlsui; Lomdei Tom h Belz Machnovke; Yeshivah Belz Machnovke; Yeshivat Lomdei Torah; Yetev Lev Jerusalem.
**FINANCES** *Year* 2013/14 *Income* £13,150,227 *Grants* £11,463,915 *Grants to organisations* £11,463,915 *Assets* £38,023,959
**TRUSTEES** S. Englander; H. Z. Weiss; E. Englander; N. Weiss; Jacob Englander; Pinkus Englander; S. Z. Englander.
**OTHER INFORMATION** A list of grant recipients was not included in the accounts.
**HOW TO APPLY** Applications may be made in writing to the correspondent. The annual report for 2013/14 states that 'the trustees consider all requests which they receive and make donations based on the level of funds available'.
**WHO TO APPLY TO** S. Englander, Trustee, 136 Clapton Common, London E5 9AG

## ■ E. and E. Kernkraut Charities Limited

**CC NO** 275636  **ESTABLISHED** 1978
**WHERE FUNDING CAN BE GIVEN** Worldwide.
**WHO CAN BENEFIT** Charitable organisations; Jewish institutions.
**WHAT IS FUNDED** General charitable purposes; Jewish causes; education; religion.
**FINANCES** Year 2013/14 Income £792,148 Grants £883,680 Grants to organisations £883,680 Assets £6,271,536
**TRUSTEES** Eli Kernkraut; Esther Kernkraut; Joseph Kernkraut; Jacob Kernkraut.
**OTHER INFORMATION** Beneficiaries were not listed within the annual report and accounts for 2013/14.
**HOW TO APPLY** Applications may be made in writing to the correspondent.
**WHO TO APPLY TO** Eli Kernkraut, Trustee, The Knoll, Fountayne Road, London N16 7EA Tel. 020 8806 7947 email mail@cohenarnold.com

## ■ The Peter Kershaw Trust

**CC NO** 268934  **ESTABLISHED** 1974
**WHERE FUNDING CAN BE GIVEN** Greater Manchester and north Cheshire.
**WHO CAN BENEFIT** Medical or registered charitable organisations; educational establishments, normally located in Greater Manchester or north Cheshire; hospitals for medical research; churches for social welfare support.
**WHAT IS FUNDED** Social welfare; medical research, especially in the field of oncology; educational bursaries.
**WHAT IS NOT FUNDED** Individuals; building projects; loans; new building work (but payments for fitting out of specialist premises may be made); long term commitments (award may be paid for up to three years).
**TYPE OF GRANT** Capital or core costs; research; salaries; start-up funding; one-off or up to three years; unrestricted funding.
**RANGE OF GRANTS** Up to £60,000.
**SAMPLE GRANTS** The Christie Hospital (£60,000); Mosses Centre (£16,000); Enthusiasm Trust and Reach Out (£15,000 each); Ivy Church (£12,500); Stonehouse Gang (£10,000); Cheadle Hulme School (£6,000); Withington Girls' School (£5,900); Factory Youth Zone (£5,000); Manchester Deaf Centre (£3,500); Ladybarn Community Association and Walthew House (£2,000 each); Age Concern – Wigan and Fatima Women's Association (£1,000 each); Stockport Grammar School (£700); ECHG The Beeches and Royal British Legion (£250).
**FINANCES** Year 2013/14 Income £206,142 Grants £230,003 Grants to organisations £230,003 Assets £6,340,020
**TRUSTEES** David Tully; Margaret Rushbrooke; Richard Kershaw; Rosemary Adams; Tim Page.
**OTHER INFORMATION** The support was allocated between: social welfare institutions (£137,000); memorial bursary (£58,500); school bursaries (£35,000). There were 47 grants made.
**HOW TO APPLY** Applications should be made in writing to the correspondent **by post**. However, note that the trust is always oversubscribed. The trustees normally meet twice a year in May and November (for specific dates consult the website) to consider recommendations for grant aid which is disbursed in June and December, respectively. The website states: 'All applications will be acknowledged – please avoid the use of 'Signed for' delivery as there is not always someone available to accept the delivery.' According to the annual report for 2013/14, applications for social welfare grants and medical research 'must give an outline of the organisation and the project for which financial assistance is being sought, together with budgetary forecasts and a copy of the latest financial accounts'.
**WHO TO APPLY TO** Bryan Peak, Secretary to the Trustees, 22 Ashworth Park, Knutsford, Cheshire WA16 9DE Tel. 01565 651086 email pkershawtrust@btinternet.com Website www.peterkershawtrust.org

## ■ Keswick Hall Charity

**CC NO** 311246  **ESTABLISHED** 1968
**WHERE FUNDING CAN BE GIVEN** UK and overseas; in practice within East Anglia; however, the accounts for 2013/14 state that 'with the diminishing resource centre availability throughout the UK, this geographical area is continuing to expand nationally and also internationally'.
**WHO CAN BENEFIT** Educational establishments; religious bodies; University of East Anglia – its teachers and students (especially student teachers); corporate organisations, especially in the dioceses of Ely – Norwich and St Edmundsbury and Ipswich.
**WHAT IS FUNDED** 'Advancing the understanding and knowledge of religious education by promoting and supporting students, teachers, researchers and charitable institutions engaged in the teaching of religious education at all levels primary, secondary, further and higher education.' The trustees have stated that they give priority to their own initiatives. Research and development grants are also available.
**WHAT IS NOT FUNDED** Buildings; courses in pastoral work or courses which are purely for personal interest; retrospective appeals (if an application is received from a student who has already started a course, but has not yet completed it, the application will not be regarded as a retrospective).
**TYPE OF GRANT** Capital and core costs; salaries; project funding.
**RANGE OF GRANTS** Generally up to £10,000.
**SAMPLE GRANTS** REQM/Eastern Region Advisers (£15,000); Norwich Diocesan Board of Finance (£15,000); 24/7 Prayer (£4,000); RE Council (£3,000); Fountain of Life (£2,500); University of East Anglia (£2,200); Highgate Infants School (£500).
**FINANCES** Year 2013/14 Income £182,634 Grants £126,463 Grants to organisations £52,344 Assets £3,747,803
**TRUSTEES** Andy Mash; Revd Dr Patrick Richmond; David Hicks; David Briggs; David Broom; Doreen Bartlett; Jane Sheat; Peter Maxwell; Tricia Pritchard; Jan Munt.
**OTHER INFORMATION** During the year awards to individuals totalled £63,000, to institutions – £27,500, and further £25,000 was given in grants for Cathedrals Labyrinth Project. In addition £11,000 was paid through Simon Pettitt Memorial Scholarship.
**HOW TO APPLY** Grant applications should be received by the end of May and must be made online at the Keswick Hall Charity website. Appeals are considered in June. Preliminary approaches for advice about applications are welcome by email.
**WHO TO APPLY TO** Malcolm Green, Executive Officer, PO Box 307, Woodbridge IP13 6WL Tel. 07760 433409 email admin@keswickhalltrust.org.uk Website www.keswickhalltrust.org.uk

# Kettering

## ■ The Kettering and District Charitable Medical Trust

**CC NO** 277063     **ESTABLISHED** 1979
**WHERE FUNDING CAN BE GIVEN** Kettering and surrounding district.
**WHO CAN BENEFIT** Hospitals, hospices and community organisations.
**WHAT IS FUNDED** Healthcare; medical equipment.
**WHAT IS NOT FUNDED** Grants are not made to individuals.
**TYPE OF GRANT** Grants for equipment.
**RANGE OF GRANTS** Up to £22,000.
**SAMPLE GRANTS** Previous beneficiaries have included: Kettering General – Patient Monitors (£22,000); Kettering General – Refractor (£9,000); Rothwell and Desborough Surgery – Dermatoscopes (£5,000); Summerdale Medical Centre – ECG Machine (£2,000); Weavers Medical Centre – Dermatoscopes (£1,800); Dryland Surgery – Hydraulic Couches (£1,300); BRA Group – Tattoo Machine (£1,000); and Burton Latimer Medical Centre – Pulse Oximeters (£600).
**FINANCES** Year 2013 Income £10,430 Grants £131,929 Grants to organisations £131,929
**TRUSTEES** Robert Smith; Gareth Ogden; Martin Hill.
**HOW TO APPLY** Applications can be made in writing to the correspondent. The trustees normally meet twice a year.
**WHO TO APPLY TO** Gareth Ogden, Trustee, 73 Windermere Road, Kettering, Northamptonshire NN16 8UF

## ■ The Ursula Keyes Trust

**CC NO** 517200     **ESTABLISHED** 1985
**WHERE FUNDING CAN BE GIVEN** Cheshire, particularly Chester.
**WHO CAN BENEFIT** Charitable organisations; individuals; medical and social care institutions.
**WHAT IS FUNDED** General charitable purposes, particularly health and medical causes and social care. According to the website: 'A wide range of causes are supported, including cultural and leisure projects, particularly when matched by other fundraising efforts. Funds are mainly directed at the cost of capital projects and equipment rather than as a source of funding for on-going running costs or salaries. National charities are also considered for support if there is a clear link to a local beneficiary.'
**WHAT IS NOT FUNDED** Students; political groups.
**TYPE OF GRANT** Capital and project costs.
**RANGE OF GRANTS** Up to £25,000.
**SAMPLE GRANTS** The Baby Grow Appeal and The Queens School (£25,000 each); Countess of Chester NHS Hospital (£15,000); Deeside Ramblers FC (£10,000); Claire House (£7,100); Upton by Chester High School (£5,000); Anthony Nolan Trust (£3,500); Overleigh St Mary Church of England School (£3,100); Blind Veterans UK and Guide Dogs for the Blind (£2,000 each); Chester Mystery Plays (£1,500).
**FINANCES** Year 2013 Income £297,331 Grants £168,144 Grants to organisations £129,166 Assets £4,692,789
**TRUSTEES** Euan Elliott; J. F. Kane; J. R. Leaman; Harold Shaw; John Brimelow; Dr Ian Russell; Dr Peter Reid.
**OTHER INFORMATION** In 2013 a total of £39,000 was given to individuals. There were at least 20 grants to organisations (awards under £1,000 totalled £2,900).

**HOW TO APPLY** Applications can be made in writing to the correspondent, including a form available to download from the website. Appeals are considered at the trustees' quarterly meetings, in January, April, July and October (for exact dates see the website) – they should reach the trustees at least a month before the meeting.
**WHO TO APPLY TO** Dot Lawless, c/o Baker Tilly, The Steam Mill Business Centre, Steam Mill Street, Chester, Cheshire CH3 5AN Tel. 01244 505100 Fax 01244 505101 Website www.ursula-keyes-trust.org.uk

## ■ The Robert Kiln Charitable Trust

**CC NO** 262756     **ESTABLISHED** 1970
**WHERE FUNDING CAN BE GIVEN** UK, with a special interest in Hertfordshire and Bedfordshire; occasionally overseas.
**WHO CAN BENEFIT** Universities; small charitable organisations; museums.
**WHAT IS FUNDED** General charitable purposes with a particular focus on archaeology, history, heritage, environment and conservation.
**WHAT IS NOT FUNDED** Individuals; large national appeals; churches; schools; artistic projects (for example, theatre groups).
**TYPE OF GRANT** Usually one-off grants or instalments for particular projects.
**RANGE OF GRANTS** £25–£2,500; generally about £500.
**SAMPLE GRANTS** Hertford Symphony Orchestra – Children's concert (£3,500); Museum of London – Excavate London Project (£2,100); Bournemouth University – Swash Channel Wreck and University of Sheffield – Viking Camp (£2,000 each); Friends of Corhampton Church and Manchester Museum – Whitworth Park Exhibition (£1,500 each); Bournemouth University – Lyndsay Myers Fieldwork, Society of Antiquaries of Scotland and University of Worcester – Lower Wye Valley Research (£1,000 each).
**FINANCES** Year 2013/14 Income £52,372 Grants £45,531 Grants to organisations £45,531 Assets £933,311
**TRUSTEES** Dr Nicholas Akers; Janet Akers; Barbara Kiln; Stephen Kiln.
**OTHER INFORMATION** Grants were made to 67 organisations. The trust has stated: 'Most of the income is allocated to regular beneficiaries, where relationship has been built up over many years (55%). The trustees are keen to support new projects, particularly those from small local organisations. The trustees support many charities where they have a particular interest.' Note that a common applicants' mistake is to request large amounts of support – see the range within which grants are normally given.
**HOW TO APPLY** Applications can be made in writing to the correspondent, providing as much information as seems relevant and, if possible, including the costings and details of any other support available. Funds are normally distributed within one month of receiving applications, subject to funds being available. The trust does not acknowledge receipt of applications unless an sae is enclosed.
**WHO TO APPLY TO** Sarah Howell, Secretary to the Trustees, 15A Bull Plain, Hertford SG14 1DX Tel. 01992 554962 email robertkilntrust@btconnect.com

## ■ The King Henry VIII Endowed Trust – Warwick

**CC NO** 232862  **ESTABLISHED** 1964
**WHERE FUNDING CAN BE GIVEN** The former borough of Warwick only.
**WHO CAN BENEFIT** Churches; educational establishments; charitable organisations; hospitals; social enterprises; individuals.
**WHAT IS FUNDED** General charitable purposes. Note that charitable expenditure is allocated in following proportions: 50% to the historic Anglican Churches in Warwick; 30% to Kings Schools in Warwick; 20% to the town (including organisations for general charitable causes).
**WHAT IS NOT FUNDED** Projects outside the beneficial area; retrospective grants. The website notes that 'the trustees have only limited powers to make grants for projects for which central or local government has a financial responsibility'.
**RANGE OF GRANTS** Up to £42,000.
**SAMPLE GRANTS** Central England Rehabilitation Unit (£42,000); Warwick Apprenticing Charities (£30,000); Aylesford School (£26,500); Myton School (£15,500); Chase Meadow Community Centre (£7,400); Woodloes Senior Citizens Association (£3,800); West End Senior Citizens Club (£1,700); Domestic Abuse Counselling Service and Warwick Horticultural Society (£1,000 each).
**FINANCES** Year 2013 Income £1,368,199 Grants £1,075,791 Grants to organisations £1,073,641 Assets £27,643,323
**TRUSTEES** Neil Thurley; Gerry Guest; Stephen Copley; Paul Jackson; Rupert Griffiths; Kathryn Parr; John Edwards; Ian Furlong; Revd David Brown; Michael Peachey; Marie Ashe.
**OTHER INFORMATION** According to the application guidelines, the trust will not normally provide grants for 'regular annual revenue expenditure but it is prepared to consider assisting the start-up of a project by providing instalment funding for a period not exceeding three years'. A total of over £1 million was given to: church (£549,500); Warwick Independent Schools Foundation (£337,000); beneficiaries in the town of Warwick (£189,000). Out of the latter, nearly £187,000 was given to local organisations. Two awards were made to individuals totalling £2,200. Town Share' awards were given to 30 organisations with 60% of all grants awarded benefitting local schools or young people.
**HOW TO APPLY** Application forms are available to download from the trust's website or can be requested from the correspondent. They should be returned by post or email. There are detailed guidelines and criteria, available from the trust's website. The trustees consider grants quarterly, in March and June (appeals should be received at the beginning of the month) and September and December (requests should be received by mid-August and November, respectively). The outcome of your application is normally communicated within a week following a meeting. In the case of an emergency, applications may be fast-tracked (provided such urgency is made clear on the application).
**WHO TO APPLY TO** Jonathan Wassall, Clerk and Receiver, 12 High Street, Warwick CV34 4AP *Tel.* 01926 495533 *email* jwassall@kinghenryviii.org.uk *Website* www.kinghenryviii.org.uk

## ■ The King/Cullimore Charitable Trust

**CC NO** 1074928  **ESTABLISHED** 1999
**WHERE FUNDING CAN BE GIVEN** Worldwide.
**WHO CAN BENEFIT** Charitable organisations.
**WHAT IS FUNDED** General charitable purposes.
**TYPE OF GRANT** Capital, core and start-up costs; unrestricted funding; generally one-off.
**RANGE OF GRANTS** £5,000–£2,000
**SAMPLE GRANTS** Bucks Community Foundation (£200,000); Alexander Devine (£100,000); Green Finger (£50,000); Chilterns MS Centre (£30,000); Blond McIndoe Research (£15,000); Plat Kenya (£11,100); Duke of Edinburgh Award (£10,000); Sussex Snowdrop Trust (£5,000)
**FINANCES** Year 2013/14 Income £416,349 Grants £481,050 Grants to organisations £481,050 Assets £7,333,840
**TRUSTEES** Peter Cullimore; Alastair McKechnie; Christopher Gardner; Richard Davies; Jill Pye.
**OTHER INFORMATION** In 2013/14 there were 14 awards made.
**HOW TO APPLY** Applications can be made in writing to the correspondent.
**WHO TO APPLY TO** Peter Cullimore, Trustee, 52 Ledborough Lane, Beaconsfield, Buckinghamshire HP9 2DF *Tel.* 01494 678811 *email* mail@petercullimore.co.uk

## ■ Kingdom Way Trust (formerly known as Sugarworld Trust)

**CC NO** 1139646  **ESTABLISHED** 2011
**WHERE FUNDING CAN BE GIVEN** Worldwide, some preference may be given to Eastbourne area in East Sussex.
**WHO CAN BENEFIT** Registered charities; organisations offering help to disadvantaged, marginalised and vulnerable individuals, such as night shelters.
**WHAT IS FUNDED** General charitable purposes, with a Christian focus; homeless and marginalised people.
**TYPE OF GRANT** Running costs; funds for distribution; project funding.
**RANGE OF GRANTS** Usually under £5,000.
**SAMPLE GRANTS** ROC Eastbourne (£2,000); eight local churches received grants totalling £4,000. In the past grants have been made to E D and F Man Relief Fund (£75,000); and The Salvation Army to fund shelters for homeless people (£5,000).
**FINANCES** Year 2013/14 Income £92,127 Grants £6,000 Grants to organisations £6,000 Assets £406,351
**TRUSTEES** David Barratt; Revd William Lovatt; Brian Arnott; William Owen.
**OTHER INFORMATION** This is the charitable hand of the Sugarworld company.
**HOW TO APPLY** Applications can be made in writing to the correspondent.
**WHO TO APPLY TO** David Barratt, Trustee, Chantry House, 22 Upperton House, Eastbourne, East Sussex BN21 1BF *Tel.* 01323 470807 *email* david@sugarworld.eu

## ■ The Kingsbury Charity

**CC NO** 205797  **ESTABLISHED** 1986
**WHERE FUNDING CAN BE GIVEN** Ancient parish of Kingsbury
**WHO CAN BENEFIT** Older people in need; people who are ill.

**WHAT IS FUNDED** Organisations in the ancient parish of Kingsbury.
**FINANCES** Year 2013 Income £380,232 Grants £75,050 Grants to organisations £75,050 Assets £10,594,094
**TRUSTEES** Valerie Pope; Julia Day; Rose Peacock; Terence Hopkins; Revd Natasha Woodward.
**HOW TO APPLY** Apply in writing to the correspondent
**WHO TO APPLY TO** Philomena Hughes, Hon Secretary, 29 Bowater Close, London NW9 0XD Tel. 020 8205 9712

## ■ The Mary Kinross Charitable Trust

**CC NO** 212206 **ESTABLISHED** 1957
**WHERE FUNDING CAN BE GIVEN** UK.
**WHO CAN BENEFIT** Registered charities benefitting research workers, people in prison or leaving prison, young people and people disadvantaged by poverty.
**WHAT IS FUNDED** General charitable purposes. Donations confined to projects which the trust promotes and manages, particularly in the areas of medical research, to benefit the communities of which trustees have direct knowledge: youth, mental health and penal affairs. Grants made under the heading of youth are often made with crime prevention in mind.
**WHAT IS NOT FUNDED** Individuals.
**TYPE OF GRANT** Capital projects; core costs; one-off or recurring; unrestricted funding.
**RANGE OF GRANTS** £500–£81,000
**SAMPLE GRANTS** Department of Oncology – University of Oxford (£81,000); Royal College of Surgeons of England (£50,000); Barry and Martin's Trust (£35,000); Bipolar UK, Greenhouse and Hepatitis C Trust (£30,000 each); KeepOut – The Crime Diversion Scheme (£20,000); Penumbra and Oxford Concert Party (£15,000 each); Growing Well, Housing for Women and Restore Support Network (£10,000 each); Birmingham Citizens Advice (£9,000); Prisoners' Penfriends and The Buzz Project (£5,000 each); Birmingham Samaritans (£3,000); The Bach Players (£2,500); The Royal Scottish Academy (£2,200); Prison Radio Association (£2,000); Moseley Community Development Trust (£1,700); Consensus Action on Salt and Health (£1,500); Glasgow Play-Resource Association and The Hardman Trust (£1,000 each); Dogs Trust (£500).
**FINANCES** Year 2013/14 Income £803,369 Grants £761,160 Grants to organisations £761,160 Assets £35,100,521
**TRUSTEES** Elizabeth Shields; Fiona Adams; Dr Neil Cross; Jonathan Haw; Gordon Hague; Elizabeth Barber.
**OTHER INFORMATION** There were 47 grants made totalling about £703,500, of which 26 were for more than £10,000 and 21 smaller grants (totalling £58,000).
**HOW TO APPLY** 'Because the trustees have no office staff and work from home, they prefer dealing with written correspondence rather than telephone calls from applicants soliciting funds.' Note: unsolicited applications to this trust are very unlikely to be successful. The majority of new grants are recommended by the chair and the secretary who can authorise small grants of up to £25,000. Other grants are discussed and agreed at trustee meetings.
**WHO TO APPLY TO** Fiona Adams, Trustee, 36 Grove Avenue, Moseley, Birmingham B13 9RY email marykinrossct@gmail.com

## ■ Kirkley Poor's Land Estate

**CC NO** 210177 **ESTABLISHED** 1976
**WHERE FUNDING CAN BE GIVEN** The parish of Kirkley and the former borough of Lowestoft.
**WHO CAN BENEFIT** Individuals and organisations.
**WHAT IS FUNDED** Social welfare; health and disability. The trust administers a grocery voucher scheme enabling people of pensionable age in Kirkley to receive a grant each winter to purchase groceries. Grants are also made to support local residents undertaking their first university degree.
**WHAT IS NOT FUNDED** The annual report and accounts for 2013/14 state: 'It is a general policy of the Trustees not to make grants to well-known charities but to limit its assistance to small local charities and organisations who find raising funds more difficult.'
**TYPE OF GRANT** Generally one-off.
**RANGE OF GRANTS** Up to around £5,000.
**SAMPLE GRANTS** Salvation Army Lowestoft South Corps (£5,300); Lowestoft College (£3,800); Catalyst Waveney Counselling Service (£3,000); 4 C's Counselling and Lowestoft Sixth Form College (£2,500 each); St Elizabeth Hospice (£1,500); and Kirkley Business Association, Lowestoft Shopmobility and Norfolk Community Foundation (£1,000 each).
**FINANCES** Year 2013/14 Income £88,041 Grants £60,371 Grants to organisations £35,500 Assets £2,093,666
**TRUSTEES** Yvonne Cherry; Jennifer Van Pelt; Michael Cook; Ralph Castleton; Elaine High; Revd Andrew White; June Ford; Andrew Shepherd.
**OTHER INFORMATION** Individual students received awards totalling £5,500 and a further sum of £19,500 was distributed through the mid-winter grocery voucher scheme.
**HOW TO APPLY** Applications may be made in writing to the correspondent. The trustees normally meet two to three times a year. The boundaries of the beneficial area are outlined on the charity's website.
**WHO TO APPLY TO** Lucy Walker, Clerk, 4 Station Road, Lowestoft NR32 4QF Tel. 01502 514964 email kirkleypoors@gmail.com Website kirkleypoorslandestate.co.uk

## ■ The Richard Kirkman Trust

**CC NO** 327972 **ESTABLISHED** 1988
**WHERE FUNDING CAN BE GIVEN** UK, with a preference for Hampshire.
**WHO CAN BENEFIT** Registered charities and individuals.
**WHAT IS FUNDED** General charitable purposes. Our research indicates that the trustees have been considering financing various plans for alleviating drug addiction.
**RANGE OF GRANTS** £2,500–£10,000
**SAMPLE GRANTS** Wulfris Educational Foundation (£10,000); British Limbless Ex-Servicemen and Rose Road Association (£4,000 each); Southampton Rotary Club Trust Fund (£3,000); Southampton Society for the Blind, Stroke Association and Wessex Cancer Trust (£2,000 each); and Haemophilia Society (£1,500).
**FINANCES** Year 2013/14 Income £59,740 Grants £44,940 Grants to organisations £28,500 Assets £1,794,984
**TRUSTEES** David Hoare; Michael Howson-Green; Brian Baxendale; M. A. Howson-Green.
**OTHER INFORMATION** Grants of £1,000 or more were given to eight organisations totalling £28,500. Further £16,400 was distributed in 28 grants between individuals and organisations.

**HOW TO APPLY** Our research suggests that the trust carries out its own research for beneficiaries and does not respond to applications by post or telephone.

**WHO TO APPLY TO** Michael Howson-Green, Trustee, Ashton House, 12 The Central Precinct, Winchester Road, Chandler's Ford, Eastleigh, Hampshire SO53 2GB *Tel.* 023 8027 4555 *email* ashton.house@btconnect.com

## ■ Kirschel Foundation

**CC NO** 1067672 **ESTABLISHED** 1998
**WHERE FUNDING CAN BE GIVEN** UK.
**WHO CAN BENEFIT** Registered charities.
**WHAT IS FUNDED** The trust states that its aims and objectives are 'to provide benefits to underprivileged persons, who may be either disabled or lacking resources'. In practice, this mostly includes Jewish organisations.
**RANGE OF GRANTS** £1,500–£84,500
**SAMPLE GRANTS** Ahavat Shalom Charity Fund (£84,500); Jewish Learning Exchange (£40,000); Gateshead Academy for Torah Studies and British Friends of Tikva Odessa (£20,000 each); Rays of Sunshine (£16,300); Gabrielle's Angel Foundation (£15,000); The Israel Film Festival London (£12,600); Amy Winehouse (£12,000); Chai Cancer Care (£10,500); Daliad (£10,000); Centrepoint Soho (£7,000); Friends of Lvov and Jewish Leadership Council (£5,000 each); Jewish Child Day (£3,000); Havenpoint (£1,500).
**FINANCES** *Year* 2013/14 *Income* £625,312 *Grants* £514,626 *Grants to organisations* £514,626 *Assets* £33,894
**TRUSTEES** Laurence Kirschel; Ian Lipman; Steven Pinshaw.
**OTHER INFORMATION** Grants of less than £1,000 totalled about £14,200. In addition to the grant total, about £118,500 was spent for policy, campaigning and research purposes.
**HOW TO APPLY** Appeals may be made writing to the correspondent.
**WHO TO APPLY TO** Steven Pinshaw, Trustee, 26 Soho Square, London W1D 4NU *Tel.* 020 7437 4372

## ■ Robert Kitchin (Saddlers' Company)

**CC NO** 211169 **ESTABLISHED** 1891
**WHERE FUNDING CAN BE GIVEN** City of London and its contiguous boroughs.
**WHO CAN BENEFIT** Educational establishments; charitable organisations.
**WHAT IS FUNDED** General charitable purposes; education; rights and equality; community and economic development.
**RANGE OF GRANTS** £500–£68,000
**SAMPLE GRANTS** City University London (£68,500); St Ethelburga's Centre for Reconciliation and Peace (£20,500); Army Cadet Force (£4,200); Hadlow College Equestrian Skills Centre (£4,000); London Symphony Orchestra (£3,000); Guildhall School Development Fund (£1,400); and the City of London School, the City of London School for Girls, the City of London Freemen's School and Reed's School (£750 each).
**FINANCES** *Year* 2013/14 *Income* £145,811 *Grants* £140,573 *Grants to organisations* £140,573 *Assets* £3,634,959
**TRUSTEES** Campbell Pulley; D. J. Serrell-Watts; David Hardy; David Snowden; Hugh Dyson-Laurie; Iain Pulley; Jonathan Godrich; Michael Laurie; Peter Laurie; Peter Lewis; Tim Satchell; William Dyson-Laurie; Mark Farma; Paul Farmar; Petronella Jameson; Nicholas Mason; Charles Barclay; John Robinson; Hugh Thomas; James Welch; Mark Maffey; Lucy Atherton.
**OTHER INFORMATION** Each year the charity gives a fixed percentage to two organisations – City University receives 50% of net income, while St Ethelburga's Centre for Reconciliation and Peace receives 15% of net income. The remaining 35% is distributed at the discretion of the trustees.
**HOW TO APPLY** Applications can be made in writing to the correspondent; however, note that the discretionary element of the charity's income is generally fully committed each year and the trustees are unable to respond to applications. The annual report for 2013/14 notes: 'The Trustees seek, either through established contacts such as the City University London or by direct contact with the education departments of the City of London's contiguous boroughs or by appeals received direct from other relevant bodies, details of projects that fall within the objectives of the Charity and which, as such, the Trustees could consider for funding.'
**WHO TO APPLY TO** The Clerk to the Trustees, Saddlers' Company, Saddlers' Hall, 40 Gutter Lane, London EC2V 6BR *Tel.* 020 7726 8661 *email* clerk@saddlersco.co.uk *Website* www.saddlersco.co.uk

## ■ The Ernest Kleinwort Charitable Trust

**CC NO** 229665 **ESTABLISHED** 1963
**WHERE FUNDING CAN BE GIVEN** UK, mainly Sussex; overseas.
**WHO CAN BENEFIT** Registered charities, preference for those operating in Sussex across a range of fields and environmental or wildlife organisations.
**WHAT IS FUNDED** Wildlife and environmental conservation; family planning; care of older and young people; disability, general social welfare; hospices; medical research; other charitable causes.
**WHAT IS NOT FUNDED** Large national charities having substantial fundraising potential, income from legacies and or endowment income; organisations not registered as charities or those that have been registered for less than a year; pre-school groups; out of school play schemes including pre-school and holiday schemes; projects which promote a particular religion; charities not funded by any other charity; very small and narrowly specialised activities; local authorities; individuals or charities applying on behalf of individuals; general requests for donations; expeditions or overseas travel; campaigning organisations; charities whose main aim is to raise funds for other charities; charities with substantial cash reserves.
**TYPE OF GRANT** Start-up and capital costs; ongoing expenses; conditionally renewable grants for up to three years may be agreed on occasions.
**RANGE OF GRANTS** £100–£150,000; mostly for £10,000 or less.
**SAMPLE GRANTS** WWF UK (£150,000); Tusk Trust (£125,000); River Trust (£70,000); St Catherine's Hospice (£42,500); Interact Worldwide (£35,000); Guildcare (£30,000); London Metropolitan University (£20,000); Mark Davies Injured Riders Fund (£15,500);

Springboard Project (£10,000); Born Free Foundation (£5,000); Youthnet UK Limited (£4,000); Sarah Lee Trust (£3,800); Meningitis Trust (£2,000); Music in Hospitals (£1,500); Royal Air Force Benevolent Fund (£600); Quintessentially Foundation (£250); Skiing with Heroes (£100).

**FINANCES** Year 2013/14 Income £1,761,550 Grants £1,629,759 Grants to organisations £1,629,759 Assets £55,621,113

**TRUSTEES** Alexander Kleinwort; Marina Kleinwort; Sir Richard Kleinwort; Edmund Christopher; Lord Chandos; Charlie Mayhew; Kleinwort Benson Trustees Ltd.

**OTHER INFORMATION** During the year a total of 186 appeals were supported.

**HOW TO APPLY** Apply in writing to the correspondent via post. Applications should be no longer than two A4 sides, incorporate a short (half page) summary, include a detailed budget for the project and provide most recent audited accounts (any significant surplus or deficit of income needs to be explained). Applicants must also complete and include an Accounts Summary form, which is available on the trust's website. Full details of what information is required for applications are given online. You can re-apply after 12 months from the date of your last application. Generally only successful applicants are notified – 'if you have not heard from [the trust] within five months, it is likely that your application has not been successful'. Appeals are considered approximately every four months (bigger grants over £10,000 are decided twice a year).

**WHO TO APPLY TO** Scott Rice, Trust Officer, Kleinwort Benson Trustees Ltd, 14 St George Street, London W1S 1FE Tel. 020 3207 7337 email ekctadmin@kleinwortbenson.com Website www.ekct.org.uk

■ **The Marina Kleinwort Charitable Trust**

**CC NO** 1081825 **ESTABLISHED** 2000

**WHERE FUNDING CAN BE GIVEN** UK.

**WHO CAN BENEFIT** Arts organisations.

**WHAT IS FUNDED** The trust's current policy is to support arts projects.

**WHAT IS NOT FUNDED** The trustees do not normally respond favourably to appeals from individuals, nor to those unconnected with the arts.

**RANGE OF GRANTS** £1,000–£25,000

**SAMPLE GRANTS** A list of grant recipients was not included in the accounts. **Previous beneficiaries have included:** Rambert Dance Company (£25,000); LAMDA (£5,000); The Art Room and The Old Vic Theatre Trust (£4,000 each); Notting Hill Churches (£3,500); Endymion Ensemble (£3,000); Almeida Theatre (£2,700); Opera Brava (£2,500); Polka Theatre (£2,000).

**FINANCES** Year 2013/14 Income £51,646 Grants £21,646 Grants to organisations £21,646 Assets £1,503,298

**TRUSTEES** Marina Kleinwort; David Robinson; Tessa Bremmer.

**OTHER INFORMATION** Note that in 2013/14 the total of grants was lower than usual. In the previous four years grants have totalled on average about £54,500 each year. Around 14 organisations are supported annually.

**HOW TO APPLY** Applications have to be made in writing to the correspondent, providing a copy of the most recent annual report and financial statements. Only successful applications are notified of the decision.

**WHO TO APPLY TO** Scott Rice, Trust Officer, c/o Kleinwort Benson Trustees Ltd, 14 St George Street, London W1S 1FE Tel. 020 3207 7337 email scott.rice@kleinwortbenson.com

■ **The Sir James Knott Trust**

**CC NO** 1001363 **ESTABLISHED** 1990

**WHERE FUNDING CAN BE GIVEN** Tyne and Wear, Northumberland, County Durham inclusive of Hartlepool but exclusive of Darlington, Stockton-on-Tees, Middlesbrough, Redcar and Cleveland.

**WHO CAN BENEFIT** Registered charities only (unregistered organisations can be assisted through a local CVS); community projects in the local area.

**WHAT IS FUNDED** A wide range of general charitable causes, with special consideration for charitable activities known to have been of particular interest to Sir James Knott, including military and maritime organisations, youth clubs, projects to help older people and education and training. Support is given for the welfare of people who are disadvantaged, homeless people, young or older individuals, people with disabilities, to advance education and training, medical care, historic buildings, the environment, music and the arts and to seafarers' and services' charities.

**WHAT IS NOT FUNDED** Individuals; the replacement of funding withdrawn by local authorities; organisations that do not have an identifiable project within the beneficial area.

**TYPE OF GRANT** One-off; capital and core costs; salaries; start-up expenditure.

**RANGE OF GRANTS** Up to £50,000.

**SAMPLE GRANTS** Auckland Castle Trust (£50,000); Durham University (£25,000); Tyne Housing Association (£20,000); Northumberland Clubs for Young People (£12,000); High Sheriff of Northumberland (£10,000); Newcastle Council for Voluntary Service (£6,000); Age UK North Tyneside and Glendale Agricultural Society (£5,000 each); Young Asian Voices (£4,100); Baltic Centre for Contemporary Art and Rising Sun Farm Trust Ltd (£4,000 each); Caudwell Children (£3,900); Royal Voluntary Service, Sea Cadets-Ashington and Wildfowl and Wetlands Trust (£3,000 each); Cruse Bereavement Care-Tyneside Branch, Durham Wildlife Trust and Royal Shakespeare Company (£2,000 each); Sir James Knott Memorial Flats (£1,200).

**FINANCES** Year 2013/14 Income £1,530,268 Grants £1,213,192 Grants to organisations £1,213,192 Assets £43,805,726

**TRUSTEES** Prof. Oliver James; John Cresswell; Sarah Riddell; Ben Speke.

**OTHER INFORMATION** In 2013/14 a total of 345 grants were made. Applications for awards below £1,000 (or in exceptional circumstances for larger amounts) can be considered between the trustees' meetings.

**HOW TO APPLY** Applications need to be writing to the correspondent, giving a description of the need and providing all the relevant supporting information regarding your organisation as well as a copy of the latest annual report and accounts (see the website for an extensive list of details which the trust expects to find in your appeal. The trustees normally meet in spring, summer and autumn. Applications need to be submitted at least three months before a grant is required (see the website for specific deadlines). Applicants may re-apply again in 18 months following a receipt of grant; unsuccessful applicants can try again in 12 months. The trust welcomes initial enquires by

phone or email and 'endeavours to acknowledge all applications'.
WHO TO APPLY TO Vivien Stapeley, Trust Secretary, 16–18 Hood Street, Newcastle upon Tyne NE1 6JQ *Tel.* 0191 230 4016 *email* info@knott-trust.co.uk *Website* www.knott-trust.co.uk

## ■ The Kobler Trust
CC NO 275237  ESTABLISHED 1963
WHERE FUNDING CAN BE GIVEN UK.
WHO CAN BENEFIT Registered charities.
WHAT IS FUNDED General charitable purposes; the arts; Jewish causes; health and disability.
WHAT IS NOT FUNDED Grants to individuals are only given in exceptional circumstances.
TYPE OF GRANT Generally no restrictions. Awards vary from small grants on a one-off basis for a specific project to a continuing relationship.
RANGE OF GRANTS £250–£25,000
SAMPLE GRANTS Welsh National Opera (£25,000); UIK Jewish Film Limited (£5,000); Arkwright Scholarship (£4,000); Jewish Blind and Disabled (£2,000); Music in Hospitals (£800); Jewish Care (£600); Jumbulance Trust and Skills Factory (£500 each); Merseyside Thursday Club (£350); Wheel Power (£300); and Hospicecare Northumberland, Netherfield Association and Teenager Cancer Trust (£250 each).
FINANCES *Year* 2013/14 *Income* £96,839 *Grants* £65,760 *Grants to organisations* £65,760 *Assets* £3,193,084
TRUSTEES Andrew Stone; Antoine Xuereb; Joel Israelsohn; Joanne Evans.
OTHER INFORMATION There were 43 awards made during the year.
HOW TO APPLY Applications should be made in writing to the correspondent and incorporate full details of the charity for which funding is requested. The trustees meet two to three times a year. Acknowledgements are not generally sent out to unsuccessful applicants.
WHO TO APPLY TO The Trustees, c/o Lewis Silkin LLP, 10 Clifford's Inn Passage, London EC4A 1BL *Tel.* 020 7074 8000 *email* info@lewissilkin.com

## ■ The Kohn Foundation
CC NO 1003951  ESTABLISHED 1991
WHERE FUNDING CAN BE GIVEN UK and overseas.
WHO CAN BENEFIT Registered charities; Jewish organisations.
WHAT IS FUNDED Scientific and medical projects; arts, particularly music; education; Jewish religion; relief of poverty; people with an illness or disability, especially mental health issues; other charitable causes.
RANGE OF GRANTS Up to £160,000.
SAMPLE GRANTS Jesus College Oxford (£252,000); Royal Academy of Music (£163,500); The Royal Society (£35,000); Chai Cancer Care (£20,000); Imperial College (£15,000); Jewish Care and Monteverdi Trust (£10,000 each); Foundation for Liver Research (£5,900); Chess in Schools and Communities (£5,000); Wigmore Hall Trust (£2,200); Service to the Aged (£1,800); United Synagogue (£1,200); North West London Jewish Day School (£1,000).
FINANCES *Year* 2013 *Income* £374,122 *Grants* £696,305 *Grants to organisations* £696,305 *Assets* £897,523
TRUSTEES Sir Ralph Kohn, Chair; Lady Zahava Kohn; Anthony Forwood.

OTHER INFORMATION In 2013 there were 92 grant recipients. Other unlisted awards under £1,000 totalled £14,500 across all three categories.
HOW TO APPLY Applications can be made in writing to the correspondent.
WHO TO APPLY TO Sir Ralph Kohn, Trustee, 14 Harley Street, London W1G 9PQ

## ■ Kollel and Co. Limited
CC NO 1077180  ESTABLISHED 1999
WHERE FUNDING CAN BE GIVEN Worldwide.
WHO CAN BENEFIT Charitable organisations with Jewish focus.
WHAT IS FUNDED Jewish causes; relief of poverty; religious activities and education; medical needs; general charitable purposes.
TYPE OF GRANT Building; equipment; project costs.
RANGE OF GRANTS Up to £66,000.
SAMPLE GRANTS Ezer V'hatzolah (£66,000); Congregation Beth Hamadrash Vyoil Moshe D'Satmar (£97,000). Previously grants have also been made to: Hadras Kodesh Trust and Shaarei Chesed – London (£33,500 each); Inspirations (£28,500); Chochmas Shloime Chasidi Talmud Torah Jerusalem (£25,000).
FINANCES *Year* 2013/14 *Income* £338,651 *Grants* £337,778 *Grants to organisations* £337,778 *Assets* £2,277,401
TRUSTEES Simon Low; Joseph Lipschitz; Zwi Rothschild.
OTHER INFORMATION The annual report and accounts for 2013/14 only list the largest beneficiaries.
HOW TO APPLY According to the annual report for 2013/14, 'grants are made upon application by the charity concerned ... in amounts thought appropriate by the directors/trustees'.
WHO TO APPLY TO Simon Low, Trustee, 7 Overlea Road, London E5 9BG *Tel.* 020 8806 1570

## ■ The KPMG Foundation
CC NO 1086518  ESTABLISHED 2000
WHERE FUNDING CAN BE GIVEN England, Scotland and Wales.
WHO CAN BENEFIT Registered charities.
WHAT IS FUNDED Children and young people in or leaving care; children and young people in disadvantaged families; refugees; young offenders; people lacking educational and employment opportunities.
TYPE OF GRANT Project grants.
RANGE OF GRANTS £10,000–£421,500
SAMPLE GRANTS The Fostering Network (£421,500); Education Endowment Foundation (£70,000); Working Chance (£37,000); Luton Churches Educational Trust (£25,000); Shaftesbury Young People – Siblings United (£20,000); Dance United (£18,500); Strathclyde University – The Jeely Piece Programme (£15,000); and Watts Gallery (£10,000).
FINANCES *Year* 2013/14 *Income* £557,049 *Grants* £617,062 *Grants to organisations* £617,062 *Assets* £6,300,400
TRUSTEES Lisa Harker; Gerry Acher; Surinder Arora; Claire Le Masurier; Robin Cartwright; Peter Sherratt; Simon Collins; Marianne Fallon.
OTHER INFORMATION There were eight awards made in 2013/14.
HOW TO APPLY According to the website, the director and advisor to the foundation 'actively seek projects to support and therefore do not accept any unsolicited applications'. The trustees can also make referrals to the director of the foundation.

## ■ The Kreditor Charitable Trust

**CC NO** 292649   **ESTABLISHED** 1985

**WHERE FUNDING CAN BE GIVEN** UK and overseas, with a preference for London and North East England.

**WHO CAN BENEFIT** Charitable bodies; Jewish organisations; UK welfare organisations benefiting Jewish people, especially those disadvantaged by poverty or social isolation.

**WHAT IS FUNDED** Mainly advancement of religion in accordance with the Orthodox Jewish Faith; education; social and medical welfare; with focus on Jewish causes; other charitable causes.

**SAMPLE GRANTS** *Previous beneficiaries have included:* Academy for Rabbinical Research; British Diabetic Association; British Friends of Israel War Disabled; Fordeve Ltd, Jerusalem Ladies' Society; Jewish Care; Jewish Marriage Council; Kosher Meals on Wheels; London Academy of Jewish Studies; NW London Talmudical College; Ravenswood; RNID; UNICEF UK.

**FINANCES** *Year* 2012/13 *Income* £99,899 *Grants* £58,215 *Grants to organisations* £58,215 *Assets* £43,418

**TRUSTEES** Paul Kreditor; Merle Kreditor; Sharon Kreditor.

**OTHER INFORMATION** At the time of writing (June 2015) this was the latest information available – 2013/14 accounts were overdue. Note that charitable expenditure varies and in the previous years has exceeded £100,000.

**HOW TO APPLY** Applications may be made in writing to the correspondent.

**WHO TO APPLY TO** Paul Kreditor, Trustee, Hallswelle House, 1 Hallswelle Road, London NW11 0DH

**WHO TO APPLY TO** Jo Clunie, Director, KPMG LLP, 15 Canada Square, Canary Wharf, London E14 5GL *Tel.* 020 7311 8039 *email* kpmgfoundation@kpmg.co.uk or jo.clunie@kpmgfoundation.co.uk *Website* www.kpmg.com/uk/en/about/aboutkpmg/kpmgfoundation

## ■ The Kreitman Foundation

**CC NO** 269046   **ESTABLISHED** 1975

**WHERE FUNDING CAN BE GIVEN** UK.

**WHO CAN BENEFIT** Registered charities or charitable organisations which are exempt from charitable registration, benefitting children, young adults and older people, people who have disabilities and people disadvantaged by poverty.

**WHAT IS FUNDED** General charitable purposes, particularly education, health, sports and social welfare.

**WHAT IS NOT FUNDED** Grants are not normally made to individuals.

**TYPE OF GRANT** Generally specific project costs.

**RANGE OF GRANTS** £200–£18,500

**SAMPLE GRANTS** UK Friends of AWIS (£18,500); Maccabi GB (£10,000); Institute of Cancer Research (£5,000); DBTRAF – The Dick Bridgeman TRA Foundation, Myeloma UK and The Friends of Daniel for Rowing (£1,000 each); The Dedanists' Foundation (£500); and The Stroke Association (£200).

**FINANCES** *Year* 2013/14 *Income* £91,464 *Grants* £37,200 *Grants to organisations* £37,200 *Assets* £4,424,622

**TRUSTEES** Jill Luck-Hille; Peter Luck-Hille; Gareth Morgan.

**OTHER INFORMATION** During the year eight grants were made.

**HOW TO APPLY** Applications may be made in writing to the correspondent. The trustees seem to have a list of regular beneficiaries and it may be unlikely that any new applications will be successful.

**WHO TO APPLY TO** The Trustees, Citroen Wells, Devonshire House, 1 Devonshire Street, London W1W 5DR *email* jonathan.prevezer@citroenwells.co.uk

## ■ The Neil Kreitman Foundation

**CC NO** 267171   **ESTABLISHED** 1974

**WHERE FUNDING CAN BE GIVEN** Worldwide.

**WHO CAN BENEFIT** Registered charities or exempt organisations with charitable objectives.

**WHAT IS FUNDED** General charitable purposes, mainly the areas of arts and culture, education, health and social welfare.

**WHAT IS NOT FUNDED** Individuals.

**TYPE OF GRANT** Primarily general funds; some small capital grants or core costs.

**RANGE OF GRANTS** £1,000–£114,500

**SAMPLE GRANTS** The Ancient India and Iran Trust (£114,500); Independent Shakespeare Co. (£75,000); Médecins Sans Frontières (£31,000); International Campaign for Tibet (£18,700); University of Oxford Development Trust Fund (£13,700); Beatrice Wood Centre for the Arts (£10,100); The Royal Numismatic Society (£4,200); Siddhartha School Project (£5,200); School of Oriental and African Studies (£1,000).

**FINANCES** *Year* 2013/14 *Income* £616,219 *Grants* £618,521 *Grants to organisations* £618,521 *Assets* £25,069,577

**TRUSTEES** Neil Kreitman; Gordon Smith.

**OTHER INFORMATION** Financial figures are given in dollars in the foundation's accounts; we have used the conversion rate applicable at the time of writing. A total of 23 awards were allocated as follows: arts and culture (£494,000); health and welfare (£80,500); education (£44,500).

**HOW TO APPLY** Applications can be made in writing to the correspondent.

**WHO TO APPLY TO** Gordon Smith, Trustee, c/o Citroen Wells and Partners, Devonshire House, 1 Devonshire Street, London W1W 5DR *Tel.* 020 7304 2000

## ■ The Heinz, Anna and Carol Kroch Foundation (HACKF)

**CC NO** 207622   **ESTABLISHED** 1962

**WHERE FUNDING CAN BE GIVEN** UK.

**WHO CAN BENEFIT** Individuals with chronic illnesses or disabilities; people who are disadvantaged by poverty; homeless people; victims of abuse and domestic violence; organisations supporting such individuals.

**WHAT IS FUNDED** The foundation exists to support people who have suffered injustice or financial disadvantage and relieve hardship amongst people with medical conditions.

**WHAT IS NOT FUNDED** Grants are not made to students or for holidays. Overseas applications or projects are not considered. The foundation has stated that research or project grants are not normally awarded.

**RANGE OF GRANTS** Generally under £1,000.

**SAMPLE GRANTS** *Previous beneficiaries have included:* Bath Institute of Medical Engineering; Brainwave; Breakthrough Breast Cancer; Eyeless

Trust; Northern Friends of ARMS; VISCERAL; and University College London.
**FINANCES** *Year* 2013/14 *Income* £190,257 *Grants* £87,335 *Grants to organisations* £87,335 *Assets* £6,296,270
**TRUSTEES** John Seagrim; Margaret Cottam; Dr Amatsia Kashti; Daniel Lang; Xavier Lang; Christopher Rushbrook; Annabel Page; Heather Astle.
**OTHER INFORMATION** There were 668 grants made to individuals and organisations. Further £57,500 was spent in support costs, mainly employment.
**HOW TO APPLY** Appeals are considered monthly. Applications on behalf of individuals must be submitted through a recognised body, such as social services, GP/consultant, Citizens Advice or local authorities. Applications receive a reply where an sae is included.
**WHO TO APPLY TO** Beena Astle, Correspondent, PO Box 327, Hampton TW12 9DD *Tel.* 020 8979 0609 *email* hakf50@hotmail.com

## ■ Kupath Gemach Chaim Bechesed Viznitz Trust

**CC NO** 1110323   **ESTABLISHED** 2005
**WHERE FUNDING CAN BE GIVEN** UK and overseas, including Israel.
**WHO CAN BENEFIT** Registered charities; individuals.
**WHAT IS FUNDED** Relief of the poor, sick, feeble and frail throughout the world and in particular, but not exclusively, amongst members of the Jewish faith; the advancement of the Orthodox Jewish faith; the advancement of the Orthodox Jewish religious education.
**TYPE OF GRANT** Grants; interest free loans.
**SAMPLE GRANTS** Kupas Hachesed (£13,200); Kollel Imrei Boruch (£11,600). No further beneficiaries were given, but awards were distributed as follows: education (£51,000); relief of poverty (£28,500); religion (£18,400).
**FINANCES** *Year* 2013/14 *Income* £410,590 *Grants* £381,107 *Grants to organisations* £98,026 *Assets* £29,632
**TRUSTEES** Israel Kahan; Saul Weiss; Alexander Pifko.
**OTHER INFORMATION** During the year a further £283,000 was granted to individuals in need.
**HOW TO APPLY** Applications may be made in writing to the correspondent.
**WHO TO APPLY TO** Saul Weiss, Trustee, 171 Kyverdale Road, London N16 6PS *Tel.* 020 8442 9604 or 0781 125 3203

## ■ The Kyte Charitable Trust

**CC NO** 1035886   **ESTABLISHED** 1994
**WHERE FUNDING CAN BE GIVEN** UK and overseas.
**WHO CAN BENEFIT** Primarily organisations that benefit the Jewish community.
**WHAT IS FUNDED** General charitable purposes with Jewish focus; education; health; sports; community causes; children and young people.
**RANGE OF GRANTS** £1,000–£27,500
**SAMPLE GRANTS** Recreational Trust (£160,000); Jewish Care (£27,500); Jewish Community Secondary School (£20,000); Norwood Ravenswood (£15,600); Maccabi GB (£11,600); Presidents Club (£6,300); Nightingale House (£5,300); United Synagogue (£2,300); Chabbad UK (£1,300); Union of Jewish Students (£1,000).
**FINANCES** *Year* 2013/14 *Income* £379,586 *Grants* £284,358 *Grants to organisations* £284,358 *Assets* £153,584

**TRUSTEES** David Kyte; Tracey Kyte; James Kyte; Ilana Kyte.
**OTHER INFORMATION** A total of 13 organisations benefitted.
**HOW TO APPLY** Appeals may be addressed in writing to the correspondent.
**WHO TO APPLY TO** David Kyte, Trustee, Business Design Centre, 52 Upper Street, London N1 0QH *Tel.* 020 7704 7791

# Ladbrokes in the Community Charitable Trust

CC NO 1101804  ESTABLISHED 2003
WHERE FUNDING CAN BE GIVEN UK (communities in which the shops and businesses of Ladbrokes Betting and Gaming Ltd or Ladbrokes eGaming Limited operate).
WHO CAN BENEFIT Registered charities and community groups.
WHAT IS FUNDED General; health; education; community projects.
SAMPLE GRANTS Barnardo's; Bobby Moore Fund; Cancer Research UK; Child Victims of Crime; Haven House Children's Hospice; NSPCC; Prostate Cancer UK; the Responsible Gambling Trust.
FINANCES Year 2013 Income £515,000 Grants £421,806 Grants to organisations £421,806 Assets £277,827
TRUSTEES Michael O'Kane; Susan Harley; Jan Kunicki; Elaine Moran.
HOW TO APPLY In the first instance, the support of a local shop should be secured in raising funds on behalf of a cause. The grants committee meets monthly to consider applications.
WHO TO APPLY TO Michael O'Kane, Trustee, Ladbrokes plc, Imperial House, Imperial Drive, Harrow, Middlesex HA2 7JW Tel. 020 8515 5611 email claire.simpkin@ladbrokes.co.uk

# The K. P. Ladd Charitable Trust

CC NO 1091493  ESTABLISHED 2002
WHERE FUNDING CAN BE GIVEN UK and overseas.
WHO CAN BENEFIT Churches; charitable organisations involved in religious activities; missionary work.
WHAT IS FUNDED Christian causes; missionaries; overseas aid.
TYPE OF GRANT One off unrestricted funding, including core costs, capital costs, project funding and salaries.
RANGE OF GRANTS £2,000–£25,000
SAMPLE GRANTS London Institute for Contemporary Christianity (£25,000); Hope in Tottenham and Kepplewray Trust (£6,000 each); Amnos Ministries, Cross Pollinate and Volunteers Outreach Working Calverton (£5,000); Wycliffe Bible Translators (£4,000); London City Mission, Salvation Army and Tonbridge Parish Church (£3,000 each); and Church Army, Livability and SOS Bosnia (£2,000 each).
FINANCES Year 2013/14 Income £151,577 Grants £81,500 Grants to organisations £81,500 Assets £1,942,241
TRUSTEES Rosemary Anne-Ladd; Brian Ladd; Kenneth Ladd; Ian Creswick.
OTHER INFORMATION Grants were given to 19 organisations.
HOW TO APPLY The trust has stated that it 'is fully committed and does not reply to unsolicited requests'. The trustees select charities known to them personally.
WHO TO APPLY TO Brian Ladd, Trustee, 34 St Mary's Avenue, Northwood, Middlesex HA6 3AZ email brian.ladd@licc.org.uk

# John Laing Charitable Trust

CC NO 236852  ESTABLISHED 1962
WHERE FUNDING CAN BE GIVEN UK.
WHO CAN BENEFIT Existing and former employees of John Laing plc who are in need; registered charities; in exceptional circumstances not-for-profit organisations.
WHAT IS FUNDED More recently the trust has concentrated its support on charities which support the following main themes: education; community regeneration; young people; homelessness, with a particular emphasis on day centres.
WHAT IS NOT FUNDED Individuals (other than to Laing employees and/or their dependants); animal charities; organisations based outside the UK.
TYPE OF GRANT Usually one-off, but a small number are supported for an agreed period, often up to three years.
RANGE OF GRANTS £2,000–£424,500; normally £250–£25,000.
SAMPLE GRANTS Atlantic College (£424,500); The Reading Agency (£95,000); National Literacy Trust (£60,000); Homeless Link (£50,000); Young Enterprise (£30,000); Hertfordshire Groundworks and Victim Support (£25,000 each); Place2Be (£20,000); Springboard for Children (£15,000); Church Action on Poverty (£10,000); Scarborough Homeless and the Neuroblastoma Society (£5,000 each); Legacy Rainbow House (£3,500); Liverpool Lighthouse (£2,500); The Paddington Academy (£2,000).
FINANCES Year 2013 Income £1,810,000 Grants £2,071,000 Grants to organisations £1,410,000 Assets £55,598,000
TRUSTEES Christopher Laing; Sir Martin Laing; Lynette Krige; Christopher Waples; Daniel Partridge.
OTHER INFORMATION During the year about £1.4 million was given to over 50 organisations and £661,000 was distributed to about 492 individuals who were either current or former employees of John Laing plc. There are also other four charities set up by the Laing family and administered at the same address – for more information see: www.laingfamilytrusts.org.uk.
HOW TO APPLY The website states: 'In November 2013, the Trustees of John Laing Charitable Trust addressed the Trust's proactive approach to its grant giving. Consequently, the Trust made the decision that uninvited applications will no longer be processed.' If you wish to register your charity for future consideration you need to ensure your eligibility and, provided you meet the criteria, fill in a registration form which can be returned via post or email (JLCTRegistration@laing.com). The trust asks to 'kindly assume your charity has not been chosen' if you do not hear back.
WHO TO APPLY TO Jenny Impey, Trust Director, 33 Bunns Lane, Mill Hill, London NW7 2DX Tel. 020 7901 3307 email jenny.impey@laing.com Website www.laing.com

# Maurice and Hilda Laing Charitable Trust

CC NO 1058109  ESTABLISHED 1996
WHERE FUNDING CAN BE GIVEN UK and overseas.
WHO CAN BENEFIT UK-registered charities.
WHAT IS FUNDED Christian religion; relief of poverty. In practice, grants by the trust fall into three main categories: Advancement of the Christian Religion – to promote Christian faith and values through evangelistic, educational, ministerial

and media activities at home and overseas; Relief of Poverty in the UK – to express Christian faith through practical action to help people in need, for example, people with disabilities, homeless individuals, those in ill health, young and older people or people who have offended; Relief of Poverty Overseas – to relieve poverty overseas, with a particular emphasis on helping children who are vulnerable or at risk, advancement of education of women, the quality of health care, HIV/AIDS help and education of children in Africa. In most cases these grants to overseas projects are made through UK-registered charities which are expected to monitor and evaluate the projects on behalf of the trust, providing progress reports at agreed intervals.

**WHAT IS NOT FUNDED** General appeals or circulars; campaigning or lobbying activities; umbrella, second tier or grant-making organisations; professional associations or projects for the training of professionals; feasibility studies and social research; individual sponsorship requirements; grants to individuals for educational, medical or travel purposes including gap year projects and overseas exchange programmes; summer activities for children/young people or after-school clubs; state maintained or independent schools other than those for pupils with special educational needs; uniformed groups such as Scouts and Guides; costs of staging one-off events, festivals or conferences; animal welfare; core running costs of hospices, counselling projects and other local organisations; church restoration or repair (including organs and bells). While ongoing cost of sustaining core activities is not funded, reasonable level of management costs to cover project overheads, including some employment costs, can be covered.

**TYPE OF GRANT** Usually one-off for capital project funding; project costs; some project related core expenditure.

**RANGE OF GRANTS** £5,000–£1 million.

**SAMPLE GRANTS** The Lambeth Trust (£1 million); Friends of the Belarusian Children's Hospice UK (£250,000); The Lighthouse Group (£65,000); Christians Against Poverty (£50,000); Mildmay Mission Hospital (£40,000); Fegans Child and Family Care (£36,000 in three awards); Alton Castle Catholic youth Retreat Centre and Sue Ryder Care (£25,000 each); BMS World Mission (£15,000); Mission to Seafarers, Strategies for Hope Trust, Village Water and Workaid (£10,000 each); Chance for Childhood (£7,500); Coventry Cathedral Development Trust (£6,000); The Living Room and Yeldall Christian Centres (£5,000 each).

**FINANCES** Year 2014 Income £1,328,466 Grants £4,311,097 Grants to organisations £4,311,097 Assets £31,543,004

**TRUSTEES** Andrea Currie; Peter Harper; Simon Martle; Paul van den Bosch; Ewan Harper; Charles Laing; Stephen Ludlow.

**OTHER INFORMATION** This is one of the Laing family trusts. During the year a total of 142 awards were made. Our research indicates that in 2006 the trustees made the decision to work towards winding up the trust by 2020. As such, there will be a controlled increase in the level of future grant expenditure. The trustees are making a number of significant investments to a small number of organisations that they will proactively invite to apply. Charities can still apply for the small grants programme.

**HOW TO APPLY** An application to any of the four charities is considered by all and directed to the most appropriate one. Appeals should be made by post (3–4 pages long) providing the following: contact details; confirmation of charitable status; charitable aims and objectives; details of the project (including costs, fundraising strategy, timing and monitoring arrangements); a copy of most recent accounts and annual report; an sae; covering letter on the charity's headed paper; any other supporting information, if appropriate. The trustees meet four times a year to consider the award of grants of over £10,000. Decisions on smaller grants are made on an ongoing basis. Bear in mind that 'fewer than 50% of unsolicited applications to the trusts are successful'. Applicants should wait at least 12–18 months before re-applying following an unsuccessful application.

**WHO TO APPLY TO** Elizabeth Harley, Trusts Director, 33 Bunns Lane, Mill Hill, London NW7 2DX Tel. 020 8238 8890 email info@laingfamilytrusts.org.uk Website www.laingfamilytrusts.org.uk/maurice_hilda_laing.html

■ **Christopher Laing Foundation**

**CC NO** 278460      **ESTABLISHED** 1979
**WHERE FUNDING CAN BE GIVEN** UK.
**WHO CAN BENEFIT** Registered charities.
**WHAT IS FUNDED** General charitable purposes; arts and culture; sports; environment; health and disability causes. Particular preference for organisations supporting adults with disabilities.
**WHAT IS NOT FUNDED** Donations are only made to registered charities.
**TYPE OF GRANT** Our research indicates that grants may be recurrent and one-off, given for capital and core costs, projects, seed and feasibility funding. Loans may be given.
**RANGE OF GRANTS** £1,000–£75,000
**SAMPLE GRANTS** Livability (£75,000); The Silver Line (£60,000); Greenhouse Schools Project, Fields in Trust – National Playing Fields Association and The Lord's Taverners (£35,000 each); RNLI (£27,000 in two grants); Cure Parkinson's Trust, Global Action Plan and The Duke of Edinburgh's Award (£10,000 each); The Henley Festival Trust (£5,000); Fulham Palace Trust (£3,000); and St Albans and Harpenden Stroke Club, (£1,000).
**FINANCES** Year 2013/14 Income £1,581,141 Grants £368,000 Grants to organisations £368,000 Assets £9,045,302
**TRUSTEES** Christopher Laing; Diana Laing; Peter Jackson; John Keeble; Michael Laing.
**OTHER INFORMATION** There were 17 grants made. During the year the income was boosted with a £1.2 million legacy from The Kirkby Laing Will Trust.
**HOW TO APPLY** Applications may be made in writing to the correspondent. The annual report for 2013/14 noted that 'an enormous and increasing number of requests for donations are received and unfortunately only a small proportion of these requests can be fulfilled'.
**WHO TO APPLY TO** Vince Cheshire, Correspondent, c/o TMF Management (UK) Ltd, 400 Capability Green, Luton, Bedfordshire LU1 3AE Tel. 01582 439200 email claing_charity@tmf-group.com

■ **The David Laing Foundation**

**CC NO** 278462      **ESTABLISHED** 1979
**WHERE FUNDING CAN BE GIVEN** Worldwide, with a preference for the East Midlands and the south of England.

**WHO CAN BENEFIT** Organisations benefitting children, including those who are in care, fostered or adopted; one-parent families; and people who have disabilities.
**WHAT IS FUNDED** General charitable purposes, with a focus on young people, disability and the arts.
**WHAT IS NOT FUNDED** Individuals.
**TYPE OF GRANT** One-off; capital costs; some charities are closely associated with the foundation and would benefit more frequently.
**RANGE OF GRANTS** Up to £45,500.
**SAMPLE GRANTS** Northamptonshire Community Foundation (£45,500); Northamptonshire Association of Youth Clubs and The Hertfordshire Community Foundation (£21,000 each); Oundle Music Trust (£20,000 each); Sue Ryder (£12,300); Crusader Community Boats and Thorpe Hall (£10,000 each); Living Room (£7,000).
**FINANCES** Year 2013/14 Income £1,500,587 Grants £292,663 Grants to organisations £292,663 Assets £5,727,772
**TRUSTEES** David Laing; Stuart Lewis; Frances Laing; Francis Barlow.
**OTHER INFORMATION** The latest accounts for 2013/14 only list beneficiaries receiving over £5,000. Previous information has shown the foundation to make large grants to a wide and varied number of organisations as well as donating smaller grants through Charities Aid Foundation. The latest annual report for 2013/14 notes that the trustees 'propose to maintain the breadth and diversity of giving, and to concentrate spending resources to meet local demands and needs'.
**HOW TO APPLY** Applications may be made in writing to the correspondent.
**WHO TO APPLY TO** David Laing, Trustee, The Manor House, Grafton Underwood, Kettering, Northamptonshire NN14 3AA email david@david-laing.co.uk

## ■ The Kirby Laing Foundation

**CC NO** 264299  **ESTABLISHED** 1972
**WHERE FUNDING CAN BE GIVEN** Unrestricted, but mainly UK.
**WHO CAN BENEFIT** Registered charities benefitting disadvantaged sections of the community, including people with disabilities or mental illness, those in poverty and socially isolated people; UK and overseas mission societies.
**WHAT IS FUNDED** General charitable purposes; arts and culture; health causes and medical research; social welfare; Christian religion; young people; education; overseas aid.
**WHAT IS NOT FUNDED** General appeals or circulars; campaigning or lobbying activities; umbrella, second tier or grant-making organisations; professional associations or projects for the training of professionals; feasibility studies and social research; individual sponsorship requirements; grants to individuals for educational, medical or travel purposes including gap year projects and overseas exchange programmes; summer activities for children/young people or after-school clubs; state maintained or independent schools other than those for pupils with special educational needs; uniformed groups such as Scouts and Guides; costs of staging one-off events, festivals or conferences; animal welfare; core running costs of hospices, counselling projects and other local organisations; church restoration or repair (including organs and bells). While ongoing cost of sustaining core activities is not funded, reasonable level of management costs to cover project overheads, including some employment costs, can be covered.
**TYPE OF GRANT** Capital or project funding is preferred over revenue funding.
**RANGE OF GRANTS** Up to £600,000.
**SAMPLE GRANTS** University of Oxford (£600,000); University of Gloucestershire (£500,000); Imperial War Museums and Leicester Cathedral (£100,000 each); Age UK (£50,000); House of Illustration (£25,000); Federation of British Artists (£20,000); University of Wales Bangor (£15,000); Marie Curie Cancer Care, The Leprosy Mission and Youth for Christ (£10,000 each); Southbank Sinfonia (£7,000); Whizz-Kidz (£6,000); Raleigh International and Resurge Africa (£5,000 each).
**FINANCES** Year 2013 Income £1,856,408 Grants £2,336,435 Grants to organisations £2,336,435 Assets £51,069,703
**TRUSTEES** David Laing; Simon Webley; Revd Charles Burch; Dr Frederick Lewis.
**OTHER INFORMATION** Our research indicates that charities can apply for grants of up to £5,000 while anything over this amount is by invitation only. According to the latest annual report for 2013, the trustees 'have indicated that they expect to wind up the foundation over a period of five to seven years and are in the process of implementing a strategy to achieve this'. During the year awards were given to 99 organisations (including 27 awards through Charities Aid Foundation totalling £50,000).
**HOW TO APPLY** An application to any of the four charities is considered by all and directed to the most appropriate one. Appeals should be made **by post** (3–4 pages long) providing the following: contact details; confirmation of charitable status; charitable aims and objectives; details of the project (including costs, fundraising strategy, timing and monitoring arrangements); a copy of most recent accounts and annual report; an sae; covering letter on the charity's headed paper; any other supporting information, if appropriate. The trustees meet four times a year to consider the award of grants of over £10,000. Decisions on smaller grants are made on an ongoing basis. Bear in mind that 'fewer than 50% of unsolicited applications to the trusts are successful'. Applicants should wait at least 12–18 months before re-applying following an unsuccessful application.
**WHO TO APPLY TO** Elizabeth Harley, Trusts Director, 33 Bunns Lane, Mill Hill, London NW7 2DX Tel. 020 8238 8890 Website www.laingfamilytrusts.org.uk

## ■ The Martin Laing Foundation

**CC NO** 278461  **ESTABLISHED** 1979
**WHERE FUNDING CAN BE GIVEN** UK and worldwide, particularly Malta and Thailand, and Norfolk-based projects.
**WHO CAN BENEFIT** Registered charities.
**WHAT IS FUNDED** General charitable purposes; environment and conservation; young and older people.
**WHAT IS NOT FUNDED** General appeals or circulars; campaigning or lobbying activities; umbrella, second tier or grant-making organisations; professional associations or projects for the training of professionals; feasibility studies and social research; individual sponsorship requirements; grants to individuals for educational, medical or travel purposes including gap year projects and overseas exchange programmes; summer activities for children/young people or after-school clubs;

state maintained or independent schools other than those for pupils with special educational needs; uniformed groups such as scouts and guides; costs of staging one-off events, festivals or conferences; animal welfare; core running costs of hospices, counselling projects and other local organisations; church restoration or repair (including organs and bells).

**TYPE OF GRANT** One-off awards for capital costs or one-off/recurrent project grants.

**RANGE OF GRANTS** £250–£15,000

**SAMPLE GRANTS** Norfolk Wildlife Trust (£15,000); Anthony Nolan, Diocese In Europe, Macmillan Cancer Support, Students' Education Trust and WWF-UK (£10,000 each); Welsh National Opera (£8,000); John Laing Charitable Trust (£7,500); Diabetes UK, Prince's Trust and The Pushkin Trust (£5,000 each); Hertfordshire Heritage Fund (£3,000); Flimkien ghal Ambient Ahjar (£2,600); The Ekklesia Project (£2,000); Bristol Aero Collection Trust, The Ware Museum Trust and Young People's Trust far the Environment (£1,000 each); The African Conservation Foundation (£250).

**FINANCES** Year 2013/14 Income £1,556,007 Grants £172,842 Grants to organisations £172,842 Assets £8,389,453

**TRUSTEES** Edward Laing; Sir Martin Laing; Lady Laing; Nicholas Gregory; Colin Fletcher; Alexandra Gregory; Graham Sillett.

**OTHER INFORMATION** This is one of the Laing family trusts. Detailed information on this and other charities can be found on the website. There were 46 awards made (including 29 through Charities Aid Foundation).

**HOW TO APPLY** The Laing Family Trusts are administered and co-ordinated centrally; therefore an application to one is considered for all funds. Applications should be made **by post** providing a concise proposal (3–4 pages) giving your contact details, confirmation of charitable status, overview of charity's objectives and aims, information and costings of the project to be supported and a copy of most recent accounts, an sae and covering letter on the charity's headed paper (any other supporting information can also be provided). Applications can be submitted at any time (they are not acknowledged) and the trustees normally meet at quarterly intervals. You should here the outcome within four months. If you were unsuccessful you should wait about 12–18 months before re-applying. The website states: 'Potential applicants should note that very few unsolicited approaches to this Foundation are successful.'

**WHO TO APPLY TO** Elizabeth Harley, Trusts Director, 33 Bunns Lane, London NW7 2DX *Tel.* 020 8238 8890 *email* info@laingfamilytrusts.org.uk *Website* www.laingfamilytrusts.org.uk

...........................................................

## ■ The Beatrice Laing Trust

**CC NO** 211884    **ESTABLISHED** 1952
**WHERE FUNDING CAN BE GIVEN** UK and overseas.
**WHO CAN BENEFIT** Mainly registered charities. Grants to overseas projects are normally made through a registered UK charity.
**WHAT IS FUNDED** Relief of poverty; advancement of the evangelical Christian faith; social welfare; disadvantaged individuals; education, training and development of young people; employment; older people; homeless individuals; those with physical, mental or learning difficulties; former armed forces personnel; people who have offended; small-scale development projects overseas; direct health services (rather than medical research). A very small number of individuals are supported, mostly retired missionaries who were known to the founders and who receive an annual grant.

**WHAT IS NOT FUNDED** General appeals or circulars; campaigning or lobbying activities; umbrella, second tier or grant-making organisations; professional associations or projects for the training of professionals; feasibility studies and social research; individual sponsorship requirements; grants to individuals for educational, medical or travel purposes including gap year projects and overseas exchange programmes; summer activities for children/young people or after-school clubs; state maintained or independent schools other than those for pupils with special educational needs; uniformed groups such as Scouts and Guides; costs of staging one-off events, festivals or conferences; animal welfare; core running costs of hospices, counselling projects and other local organisations; church restoration or repair (including organs and bells).

**TYPE OF GRANT** Mainly one-off, capital costs; one-off or recurrent project expenditure.

**RANGE OF GRANTS** Mostly £500–£5,000.

**SAMPLE GRANTS** Queen Alexandra College (£50,000); Smile Support and Care (£30,000); Simeon Care for the Elderly and The PACE Centre (£25,000 each); African Vision Malawi (£15,000); Peace Hospice Care (£10,000); Trust for Oxfordshire's Environment (£8,000); SENSE International (£6,500); Action Mental Health, Freedom from Torture and Housing for Women (£5,000 each); Village Water (£4,100); Hendon Sea Training Corps (£4,000); West London Churches Homeless Concern (£3,000); Operation Youth Quake (£2,500); Pevensey Senior Support Group (£2,000); Disability Action Yorkshire and Friends of Woodlands (£1,000 each); Aberlour Child Care Trust (£500); International Gospel Church (£150).

**FINANCES** Year 2013/14 Income £2,553,397 Grants £1,405,400 Grants to organisations £1,405,400 Assets £55,379,712

**TRUSTEES** Christopher Laing; Sir Martin Laing; David Laing; Charles Laing; Paula Blacker; Alex Gregory.

**OTHER INFORMATION** This is one of the Laing family trusts. During the year grants were made to 239 organisations. In addition to the trust's own funds, the trustees are invited to make nominations to the grants committee of the J W Laing Trust, for donations totalling 20% of that trust's income up to a maximum of £400,000 per annum. These funds are used to support the advancement of the evangelical Christian faith through projects of new church building or extension or church mission activities and in 2013/14 totalled £440,500 given in 115 grants.

**HOW TO APPLY** An application to any of the four charities is considered by all and directed to the most appropriate one. Appeals should be made **by post** (3–4 pages long) providing the following: contact details; confirmation of charitable status; charitable aims and objectives; details of the project (including costs, fundraising strategy, timing and monitoring arrangements); a copy of most recent accounts and annual report; an sae; covering letter on the charity's headed paper; any other supporting information, if appropriate. The trustees meet four times a year to consider the award of grants of over £10,000. Decisions on smaller grants are made on an ongoing basis. Bear in mind that 'fewer than 50% of unsolicited applications to the trusts are successful'. Applicants should wait at

least 12–18 months before re-applying following an unsuccessful application.
**WHO TO APPLY TO** Elizabeth Harley, Trusts Director, c/o Laing Family Trusts, 33 Bunns Lane, Mill Hill, London NW7 2DX *Tel.* 020 8238 8890 *email* info@laingfamilytrusts.org.uk *Website* www.laingfamilytrusts.org.uk

## ■ The Lambert Charitable Trust

**CC NO** 257803 **ESTABLISHED** 1969
**WHERE FUNDING CAN BE GIVEN** UK and Israel.
**WHO CAN BENEFIT** Charitable organisations. Preference can be given to the Greater London area and organisations helping people of Jewish faith.
**WHAT IS FUNDED** Health; social welfare; education and training; children and young people; homes for older people; health and disability; Jewish causes.
**TYPE OF GRANT** One-off and recurrent.
**RANGE OF GRANTS** £250–£15,000
**SAMPLE GRANTS** Jewish Care (£15,000); Medical Engineering Resource Unit and Ro-Ro Sailing Project (£4,500 each); Action on Addiction (£4,000); Dreamstore (£3,000); 999 Group, Anne Frank Trust, Freedom from Torture, Integrated Neurological Services, London Symphony Orchestra and Quaker Social Action (£2,000 each); War Memorials Trust (£1,000); and Ponevez Yeshivah Israel (£250).
**FINANCES** *Year* 2013/14 *Income* £75,274 *Grants* £62,250 *Grants to organisations* £62,250 *Assets* £3,242,735
**TRUSTEES** Maurice Lambert; Prof. Harold Lambert; Jane Lambert; Oliver Lambert; David Wells.
**OTHER INFORMATION** There were a total of 24 awards made.
**HOW TO APPLY** Applications may be made in writing to the correspondent.
**WHO TO APPLY TO** George Georghiou, Correspondent, Mercer and Hole, 72 London Road, St Albans, Hertfordshire AL1 1NS *Tel.* 01727 869141

## ■ Community Foundation for Lancashire (Former)

**CC NO** 1123229 **ESTABLISHED** 2005
**WHERE FUNDING CAN BE GIVEN** Lancashire, Blackburn with Darwen, and Blackpool.
**WHO CAN BENEFIT** Registered charities; community groups; individuals.
**WHAT IS FUNDED** General charitable purposes; community development; social welfare; health; relief of poverty.
**SAMPLE GRANTS** Grants were distributed through the funds including: Big Local Papers (£239,500); Comic Relief (£50,500); Pennine Lancashire Youth Enterprise Fund (£26,000); Lancaster Foundation (£22,500); WO Street Fund (£16,000); Lancaster Council Fund (£11,100); Lancashire 100 Fund (£9,400); Surviving Winter Fund (£4,800); and Mark McQueen Foundation (£3,000).
**FINANCES** *Year* 2013/14 *Income* £497,722 *Grants* £388,821 *Grants to organisations* £388,821 *Assets* £2,984,045
**TRUSTEES** Arthur Roberts; Wendy Swift; David McDonnell.
**OTHER INFORMATION** During the year the foundation supported 89 projects and activities.
**HOW TO APPLY** All funds available, together with the criteria, priorities and application forms and deadlines are detailed on the foundation's website.

**WHO TO APPLY TO** Sue Langfeld, Correspondent, Third Floor, Stanley Building, 43 Hanover Street, Liverpool L1 3DN *Tel.* 0151 232 2444 *email* applications@cflm.email *Website* www.lancsfoundation.org.uk

## ■ Community Foundations for Lancashire and Merseyside

**CC NO** 1068887 **ESTABLISHED** 1998
**WHERE FUNDING CAN BE GIVEN** Merseyside and Lancashire.
**WHO CAN BENEFIT** Charitable organisations.
**WHAT IS FUNDED** A wide range of general charitable purposes; community causes; development and regeneration. The foundation manages funds on behalf of parent donors. Funding priorities will vary considerably depending on the requirements of these donors.
**WHAT IS NOT FUNDED** Each fund administered by the trust has separate guidelines and exclusionary criteria which are available directly from the trust's website. As a general rule the foundation will not fund: 'public sector organisations or those controlled wholly or in part, such as local authority or primary care trust; commercial ventures; purchase/maintenance of vehicles; activities that will have already taken place before the grant is offered; politically connected or exclusively religious activities; projects for personal profit; organisations that are set up for the benefit of animals or plants environmental groups that work with animals or environment such as city farms are acceptable; groups comprising just one family; statutory organisations or work that is their responsibility; debts and other liabilities; reclaimable VAT.' Note that if you are applying to more than one fund at the same time it should be for either a different project or different costs of the same project.
**TYPE OF GRANT** Core costs, salaries, capital expenditure and project, start-up and development funding.
**RANGE OF GRANTS** £250–£10,000
**SAMPLE GRANTS** A list of beneficiaries was not included in the accounts. **Previous beneficiaries have included:** dot-art Schools; Fire Support Network; Halton Voluntary Action; Jo Jo Mind and Body; Liverpool Academy of Art; Liverpool Greenbank Wheelchair Basketball Club; The Zero Centre; and Twin Vision
**FINANCES** *Year* 2013/14 *Income* £2,199,030 *Grants* £1,379,971 *Grants to organisations* £1,332,033 *Assets* £7,942,091
**TRUSTEES** Abi Pointing; Arthur Roberts; William Bowley; David McDonnell; Andrew Myers; Wendy Swift; Chris Bliss.
**OTHER INFORMATION** The funds may open and close regularly; therefore it would not be practicable to list these here and applicants are advised to visit the website to see the most up to date information. During the year there were a further 43 grants totalling almost £48,000 awarded to individuals.
**HOW TO APPLY** Most of the foundation's funds can now be applied for online using a standard form (supporting documents will need to be provided within seven days, preferably electronically). Forms for the other funds are also available online. Once you have submitted the form the foundation will determine which fund the proposal meets. The foundation has a membership scheme available which keeps members up to date on the latest grant schemes. The deadlines will vary according to

the programmes. Applications must include the following documents: constitution of the organisation; latest accounts or income and expenditure sheet; bank statement; relevant safeguarding policies (where applicable). Unless your organisation has received a grant from the foundation in the last 12 months you *must* submit these documents, otherwise your application will not be considered. Full guidelines and application forms for individual funds are available from the foundation's website. General enquiries can be directed to info@cflm.email.

**WHO TO APPLY TO** Sue Langfeld, Operations Director, Third Floor, Stanley Building, 43 Hanover Street, Liverpool L1 3DN *Tel.* 0151 232 2444 *Fax* 0151 232 2445 *email* applications@cflm.email *Website* www.cfmerseyside.org.uk

### ■ Lancashire Environmental Fund Limited

**CC NO** 1074983 **ESTABLISHED** 1998
**WHERE FUNDING CAN BE GIVEN** Lancashire (excluding unitary authority, district of Blackpool and Blackburn).
**WHO CAN BENEFIT** Not-for-profit organisations; registered charities; voluntary groups; parish councils; community groups; applications for a Main Grant will only be accepted from organisations registered with Entrust as an Environmental Body.
**WHAT IS FUNDED** Providing and maintaining public amenities and parks, within ten miles of a landfill site, when the work benefits the natural social or built environment; the provision, conservation, restoration or enhancement of a natural habitat, maintenance or recovery of a species within ten miles of a landfill site; restoring and repairing buildings which are for religious worship, or architectural or historical interest within ten miles of a landfill site.
**WHAT IS NOT FUNDED** Core cost of an organisation; retrospective funding; projects in school grounds; allotment or food growing projects; car parks and public conveniences; recycling projects; projects within the unitary authority districts of Blackpool and Blackburn.
**TYPE OF GRANT** One-off and recurrent capital costs.
**RANGE OF GRANTS** £2,800–£30,000
**FINANCES** *Year* 2014 *Income* £1,073,148 *Grants* £992,312 *Grants to organisations* £992,312 *Assets* £1,669,225
**TRUSTEES** David Tattersall; Cllr Janice Hanson; Roger Hardman; Geraint Rees.
**OTHER INFORMATION** Grants were awarded to 45 projects. Note that 'the fund does not normally consider applications for 100% funding therefore, support from other grant sources is welcome'.
**HOW TO APPLY** Detailed and helpful guidance notes and application forms for each funding strand are available from the correspondent or may be downloaded from the fund's website. Institutional applications are invited to submit a summary of their proposals in a specified format – the Expression of Interest form. Applications are reviewed against specific criteria. The trustees meet quarterly in January, May, July and October (specific dates are given on the website). All applicants will be notified of the outcome and successful request will receive a formal grant offer letter outlining the terms and conditions of the award. Staff are willing to have informal discussions before an application is made. Potential applicants are strongly advised to visit the website and view the guidelines before contacting the fund. Further guidance on the Landfill Communities Fund can be received from the regulatory body Entrust at www.entrust.org.uk or 01926 488 300.

**WHO TO APPLY TO** Andy Rowett, Fund Manager, The Barn, Berkeley Drive, Bamber Bridge, Preston PR5 6BY *Tel.* 01772 317247 *Fax* 01772 628849 *email* andyrowett@lancsenvfund.org.uk *Website* www.lancsenvfund.org.uk

### ■ Duchy of Lancaster Benevolent Fund

**CC NO** 1026752 **ESTABLISHED** 1993
**WHERE FUNDING CAN BE GIVEN** The county palatine of Lancaster (Lancashire, Greater Manchester and Merseyside), and elsewhere in the country where the Duchy of Lancaster has historical links, such as land interests and church livings.
**WHO CAN BENEFIT** Individuals and a wide range of organisations.
**WHAT IS FUNDED** General charitable causes; young people; education; health and disability; older people; community help; religion.
**TYPE OF GRANT** Mainly one-off grants for specific projects. Recurrent grants occasionally given.
**RANGE OF GRANTS** £1,000–£18,000, generally under £5,000.
**SAMPLE GRANTS** Lancaster University bursary fund (£18,000); Creative Support – The Space Centre and Lancashire Infantry Museum – The Somme Room Project (£15,000 each); Independence at Home (£10,000); Message Trust, Safenet Domestic Abuse Service, The Fusiliers Museum, The Monastery Gorton and The Prince's Countryside Fund (£5,000 each); Salford Cathedral (£4,000); Dunsop Bridge Village Hall (£2,800); Champion Bowland (£2,400); and British Red Cross, Countryside Learning, Merseyside Polonia, Mossley Hill Athletics/Cricket Club and The Rotary Club of Crosby (£1,000 each).
**FINANCES** *Year* 2013/14 *Income* £388,315 *Grants* £387,615 *Grants to organisations* £387,615 *Assets* £11,676,001
**TRUSTEES** Warren Smith; Charles Shuttleworth; Alan Reid; Lorna Muirhead; Chris Adcock; David Borrow; Alastair Norris; Robert Miles.
**OTHER INFORMATION** In 2013/14 a total of 351 grants were made, including five grants to individuals totalling £700.
**HOW TO APPLY** Applications need to be made in writing to the appropriate lieutenancy office (see below), at any time. Applications should be by letter, including as much information as possible. All applications are acknowledged. **Lancashire lieutenancy**: County Hall, Preston, Lancashire LPRI 8XJ. **Greater Manchester lieutenancy**: Gaddum House, 6 Great Jackson Street, Manchester M15 4AX. **Merseyside lieutenancy**: PO Box 144, Royal & Sun Alliance Building, New Hall Place, Old Hall Street, Liverpool L69 3EN. Other grants are administered at the general office in London.
**WHO TO APPLY TO** Timothy Crow, Secretary, 1 Lancaster Place, Strand, London WC2E 7ED *Tel.* 020 7269 1700 *email* info@duchyoflancaster.co.uk *Website* www.duchyoflancaster.org.uk

## ■ Lancaster Foundation

**CC NO** 1066850 **ESTABLISHED** 1997

**WHERE FUNDING CAN BE GIVEN** UK and Africa, with a local interest in Clitheroe.

**WHO CAN BENEFIT** Christian based registered charities only. In practice support is given to charities personally known to the trustees.

**WHAT IS FUNDED** Christian causes; missionary work; activities for young people and community engagement; disadvantaged people. Practical projects addressing poverty and social issues, with underlying a Christian ethos.

**TYPE OF GRANT** One-off or recurrent.

**RANGE OF GRANTS** Up to £665,000.

**SAMPLE GRANTS** The Grand at Clitheroe (£655,000); Mission Aviation Fellowship (£437,000); Mary's Meals (£159,000); Shekinah Trust (£100,000); Saltmine Trust (£96,000); Sparrow Ministries (£85,000); Betel of Britain (£60,000); Make Jesus Known (£30,000); Urban Saints (£10,000); Cross Pollinate (£8,500); Medair Chad (£3,000); Philippines Trust (£2,500); Bible Society, Mayor of Clitheroe Welfare Fund and Inspire Arts (£1,000 each).

**FINANCES** Year 2013/14 Income £2,721,350 Grants £2,416,217 Grants to organisations £2,416,217 Assets £51,909,520

**TRUSTEES** Rosemary Lancaster; Dr John Lancaster; Steven Lancaster; Julie Broadhurst.

**OTHER INFORMATION** There were 42 awards made.

**HOW TO APPLY** The foundation's annual report for 2013/14 states: 'Although many applications are received, the administrative structure of the charity does not allow for the consideration of unsolicited requests for grant funding.'

**WHO TO APPLY TO** Rosemary Lancaster, Trustee, c/o Text House, 152 Bawdlands, Clitheroe, Lancashire BB7 2LA *Tel.* 01200 444404 *email* martin.wigley@jones-harris.co.uk

## ■ LandAid Charitable Trust (Land Aid)

**CC NO** 295157 **ESTABLISHED** 1986

**WHERE FUNDING CAN BE GIVEN** UK.

**WHO CAN BENEFIT** Registered charitable organisations working in the UK.

**WHAT IS FUNDED** Disadvantaged children and young people; homelessness; relief of need; education; employment and training. Pro bono support is also available.

**WHAT IS NOT FUNDED** Individuals; projects benefitting people over the age of 25; organisations whose primary purpose is a museum, gallery, library, exhibition centre or heritage attraction; individual churches, cathedrals (unless being used for purposes other than religious) and other historic buildings; individual schools, colleges, universities or other educational establishments. The following are not normally funded: rent for a premises; the purchase of property or buildings; work on premises where the lease is less than seven years; retrospective funding; work to provide office space for charity staff; the purchase/lease of vehicles; purchase/lease of IT equipment; projects outside the UK; health, medicine and medical conditions, including drug and alcohol addiction; specific projects for people with disabilities; animal welfare or projects concerning the protection of single species; expeditions and research projects; individuals volunteering overseas; conferences, cultural festivals, exhibitions and events; endowments.

**TYPE OF GRANT** One-off; project funding; capital costs; salaries; full or part-funding.

**RANGE OF GRANTS** £10,000–£110,000

**SAMPLE GRANTS** Community Housing Advocacy Project (£110,000); Community Links (£80,000); Young Persons Advisory Service (£75,000); Manor and castle Development Trust (£67,500); Cothrom Limited (£40,000); Fuse Youth Cafe Glasgow (£30,000); St Andrew's Club (£28,500); Jericho Foundation (£23,000); Circle Sports (£20,000); Kinetic Foundation (£15,000); Performances Birmingham (£10,000).

**FINANCES** Year 2013/14 Income £1,781,529 Grants £1,190,695 Grants to organisations £1,190,695 Assets £524,908

**TRUSTEES** Robert Bould; Michael Slade; Suzanne Avery; Elizabeth Peace; David Taylor; Lynette Lackey; Timothy Roberts; Robert Noel; Alistair Elliott; Jenny Buck; David Erwin; Mark Reynolds; Craig McWilliam.

**OTHER INFORMATION** Out of the overall grant total £63,000 was restricted project funding (co-investment) given to specific charity projects – The Redevco Foundation (£23,000) and EGRO (£40,000). A total of 25 charities were awarded, ten of these having been funded by LandAid in previous years. The application guidelines state that 'LandAid expects to award up to seven charities grants of average £100,000 in 2015/16, and also to award up to a further seven grants of average £100,000 in 2016/17'.

**HOW TO APPLY** Organisations should apply online through the charity's website. Detailed guidelines and up-to-date submission dates are also available there (most recently the deadline was October with awards decided by the end of December). Supporting documentation, including a copy of the latest annual report and financial statements, is normally required. The charity states: 'Because of the large number of applications we expect to receive, we are sorry that we are not able to provide individual feedback on unsuccessful applications.'

**WHO TO APPLY TO** Paul Morrish, Chief Executive, St Albans House, 5th Floor, 57–59 Haymarket, London SW1Y 4QX *Tel.* 020 3102 7190 *email* enquiries@landaid.org *Website* www.landaid.org

## ■ The Jack Lane Charitable Trust

**CC NO** 1091675 **ESTABLISHED** 2002

**WHERE FUNDING CAN BE GIVEN** Gloucestershire (south) and Wiltshire (north).

**WHO CAN BENEFIT** Registered charities and individuals.

**WHAT IS FUNDED** General charitable purposes, particularly children and young people and individuals with disabilities.

**WHAT IS NOT FUNDED** Large national appeals are not funded.

**TYPE OF GRANT** Grants for specific projects rather than general running expenses. Small awards can be made in urgent cases through the Chair's Discretionary Fund.

**RANGE OF GRANTS** Up to £2,000; occasionally larger awards over two years.

**FINANCES** Year 2013/14 Income £60,195 Grants £52,890 Grants to organisations £52,010 Assets £2,191,647

**TRUSTEES** Jim Toogood; David Crampton; Martin Wright; Richard White; Timothy Newman; Christine MacLachlan; Sarah Priday.

**OTHER INFORMATION** There were a total of 64 grants made, including three to individuals totalling around £900.

**HOW TO APPLY** Applications forms are available to download from the trust's website and can be returned via email or post. The trustees meet quarterly to consider requests. It will help to briefly explain how the grant will be used and what steps have been taken so far to raise funds. The latest set of accounts is also requested.

**WHO TO APPLY TO** Emma Walker, Clerk to the Trustees, Agriculture House, 12 High Street, Wotton-under-Edge, Gloucestershire GL12 7DB *email* admin@jacklane.co.uk *Website* www.jacklane.co.uk

## ■ The Allen Lane Foundation

**CC NO** 248031  **ESTABLISHED** 1966

**WHERE FUNDING CAN BE GIVEN** UK, except projects where the beneficiaries of the work all live in London.

**WHO CAN BENEFIT** Organisations (not necessarily registered charities) whose work is with groups who may be perceived as unpopular. Beneficiaries of your work should include a significant proportion of, for example, asylum seekers and refugees, LGBT communities, Roma and travellers, people who have offended, older people, people experiencing mental health problems and people experiencing violence or abuse.

**WHAT IS FUNDED** Work aimed at making a lasting difference, reducing isolation, stigma and discrimination and encouraging and enabling unpopular groups to share in the life of the whole community. Provision of advice or information; advocacy; arts activities where the primary purpose is therapeutic or social; befriending or mentoring; mediation or conflict resolution; practical work, such as gardening or recycling, which benefits both the provider and the recipient; self-help groups; social activities or drop in centres; strengthening the rights of particular groups and enabling their views and experiences to be heard by policy-makers; research and education aimed at changing public attitudes or policy; work aimed at combatting stigma or discrimination; work developing practical alternatives to violence.

**WHAT IS NOT FUNDED** Academic research; addiction, alcohol or drug abuse; animal welfare or animal rights; arts or cultural or language projects or festivals; children and young people or families; endowments or contributions to other grant-making bodies; health and healthcare; holidays or holiday playschemes, day trips or outings; housing; hospices and medical research; individuals; museums or galleries; overseas travel; particular medical conditions or disorders; physical or learning disabilities; private and/or mainstream education; promotion of sectarian religion; publications; property purchase, building or refurbishment; refugee community groups working with single nationalities; restoration or conservation of historic buildings or sites; sports and recreation; therapy, e.g. counselling; vehicle purchase; work the trustees believe is rightly the responsibility of the state; work outside the UK; work which will already have taken place before a grant is agreed; work by local organisations with an income of more than £100,000 per annum; those working over a wider area with an income of more than £250,000; organisations which receive funding (directly or indirectly) from commercial sources where conflicts of interest for the organisation and its work are likely to arise.

**TYPE OF GRANT** One-off and for up to three years; start-up costs; core or project expenditure; volunteers or participants expenses; venue hire; part-time or sessional staffing costs; training and development expenses.

**RANGE OF GRANTS** Usually £500–£15,000; the average grant size most recently was just over £5,900.

**SAMPLE GRANTS** Witness Confident (£15,000); African Social Health Agency (£12,000); Coventry Peace House (£11,400); Oasis Cardiff (£10,100); Cowran Training (£10,000); Centre for Criminal Appeals and Yarl's Wood Befrienders (£9,000 each); FareShare Yorkshire (£8,000); Centrepoint Christian Church (£9,000); Age Concern Sir Gar (£5,000); Make a Difference Tavistock (£4,000); Bourne Wellbeing Group and Cardiff Refugee and Asylum Welcome (£3,000 each); Northern Ireland Committee for Refugees and Asylum Seekers (£2,000); High Tide Poets (£1,000); Gateway Church (£600); Goal (Getting Older Adults Online) Community Support Group (£500).

**FINANCES** Year 2013/14 *Income* £642,929 *Grants* £761,589 *Grants to organisations* £761,589 *Assets* £19,438,142

**TRUSTEES** Zoe Teale; Guy Dehn; Juliet Walker; Fredrica Teale; Margaret Hyde; Philip Walsh.

**PUBLICATIONS** Every year the foundation hosts a lecture in memory of Sir Allen Lane, the texts of which are published on the foundation's website.

**OTHER INFORMATION** According to the website, 'the foundation is particularly interested in unusual, imaginative or pioneering projects which have perhaps not yet caught the public imagination'. It receives about nine applications for every one that is successful. In 2013/14 a total of 132 grants were committed.

**HOW TO APPLY** There are no formal application forms, but there is a short Registration Form, available from the website, which should accompany the application. Your appeal should give basic information and be no more than four sides of A4 (the project budget may be on extra pages). You will need to include the latest annual report and accounts (if applicable) and the budget for the whole organisation (as well as the project) for the current year. Full details of what information is required for application are listed online. There are no closing dates. You will hear back from the foundation in about two weeks to be asked for more information or hear whether your appeal will be considered. Processing an application and making a grant usually takes between two and six months. The foundation reminds that 'you can always contact its office for advice' and asks that 'all applications should be made to the foundation's office and **not** sent to individual trustees'. If you have received an award or were refused you should a year before re-applying.

**WHO TO APPLY TO** Gill Aconley, Grants Officer, 90 The Mount, York YO24 1AR *Tel.* 01904 613223 *Fax* 01904 613133 *email* info@allenlane.org.uk *Website* www.allenlane.org.uk

## ■ Langdale Trust

**CC NO** 215317  **ESTABLISHED** 1960

**WHERE FUNDING CAN BE GIVEN** UK, with some preference towards Birmingham.

**WHO CAN BENEFIT** Registered charities.

**WHAT IS FUNDED** General charitable purposes, including health causes, environment and conservation, young people, older individuals

and social welfare, especially work with Christian ethos.
WHAT IS NOT FUNDED Individuals.
TYPE OF GRANT Capital projects are preferred over ongoing running costs; one-off.
RANGE OF GRANTS £1,000–£6,000
SAMPLE GRANTS Mountain Rescue and The Scout Association (£6,000 each); Black Country Foodbank (£5,000); Barnardo's (£4,000); Dodford Children's Holiday Farm, The Leprosy Mission, Tree Aid and Woodland Trust (£3,000 each); Galapagos Conservation Trust and Tall Ships Youth Trust (£2,000 each); South Devon Steiner School and The Migraine Trust (£1,000 each).
FINANCES Year 2012/13 Income £143,224 Grants £116,000 Grants to organisations £116,000 Assets £4,398,001
TRUSTEES Timothy Wilson; Theresa Wilson; Jethro Elvin.
OTHER INFORMATION Grants were made to 35 organisations. At the time of writing (June 2015) this was the latest information available. The latest accounts note that 'possibilities of two projects, namely a woodland purchase and a bursary/sponsorship for training in forestry/woodland management are being explored and will be reviewed in the near future'.
HOW TO APPLY Applications should be made in writing to the correspondent. They are considered in or around June with successful applicants being notified in November.
WHO TO APPLY TO Jaime Parkes, c/o Veale Wasbrough Vizards LLP, Second Floor, 3 Brindley Place, Birmingham B1 2JB *Tel.* 0121 227 3705

## ■ Langley Charitable Trust
CC NO 280104  ESTABLISHED 1980
WHERE FUNDING CAN BE GIVEN UK and worldwide, with a preference for the West Midlands.
WHO CAN BENEFIT Individuals and organisations, Christian groups and activities.
WHAT IS FUNDED Christian causes; at risk groups; people disadvantaged by poverty, social or economic circumstances or ill health.
WHAT IS NOT FUNDED According to the annual report for 2013, the trust 'does not support projects that do not directly benefit or help people'.
RANGE OF GRANTS £250–£20,000
SAMPLE GRANTS Youth for Christ (£20,000); Foundation for Underachieving and Dyslexia (£5,000); Devonshire Junior School (£3,500); and Coton Green Church (£250).
FINANCES Year 2013 Income £353,471 Grants £25,750 Grants to organisations £25,750 Assets £4,187,373
TRUSTEES John Gilmour; Sylvia Gilmour.
OTHER INFORMATION Grants were awarded to four organisations. Note that charitable expenditure varies each year and in the past five years on average around £640,000 was given in grants annually, including major awards to Northamptonshire Association of Youth Clubs.
HOW TO APPLY All applications need to be made in writing to the correspondent. The trustees meet on a regular basis to consider awards. The annual report also reminds that a reply from the trust will only be received where the trustees require further information. No telephone calls or correspondence will be entered into concerning any proposed or declined applications.
WHO TO APPLY TO John Gilmour, Trustee, Wheatmoor Farm, 301 Tamworth Road, Sutton Coldfield, West Midlands B75 6JP *Tel.* 0121 308 0165

## ■ The Langtree Trust
CC NO 232924  ESTABLISHED 1963
WHERE FUNDING CAN BE GIVEN In practice Gloucestershire.
WHO CAN BENEFIT Organisations benefitting the local community; church appeals; occasionally to individuals if such grants result in direct benefit to the community.
WHAT IS FUNDED General charitable purposes. Priority can be given to historical or religious heritage causes, cultural development of the county, youth groups and activities, also people who have disabilities or are disadvantaged. The arts have a lower priority.
WHAT IS NOT FUNDED No grants are given in response to general appeals from large UK organisations, for educational purposes and political or sectarian causes.
TYPE OF GRANT Usually one-off for a specific project.
RANGE OF GRANTS £50–£1,000
FINANCES Year 2013/14 Income £127,425 Grants £39,440 Grants to organisations £39,440 Assets £1,485,768
TRUSTEES Ann Shepherd; Katherine Bertram; Paul Haslam; Dr Richard Way; Sally Birch; Mike Page; Will Conway.
OTHER INFORMATION There were 106 grants awarded during the year.
HOW TO APPLY Applications should be made in writing to the correspondent giving a simple, clear statement of the need with the costs of the project, what funding has so far been achieved and/or a recent copy of the annual accounts. Expensive, extensive, glossy appeal brochures are not appreciated. The trustees meet four or five times a year to decide the grant allocation. In exceptional circumstances a grant may be made between meetings. Note that the address is a postal address and the accountants cannot answer any telephone queries.
WHO TO APPLY TO Katherine Bertram, Secretary, c/o Sutton Dipple Accountants Ltd, 8 Wheelwright's Corner, Old Market, Nailsworth, Stroud, Gloucestershire GL6 0DB *Tel.* 01453 833060 *Fax* 01453 833070 *email* info@suttondipple.co.uk

## ■ The LankellyChase Foundation
CC NO 1107583  ESTABLISHED 2005
WHERE FUNDING CAN BE GIVEN UK.
WHO CAN BENEFIT Charities; non-charitable organisations, provided the work itself has charitable purposes and there is no private benefit to non-charitable interests; individual consultants; private companies.
WHAT IS FUNDED The charity is reviewing its grants process and will have new guidelines in September 2015. The following information relates to grant-making prior to any updates. 'Change that will transform the quality of life of people who face severe and multiple disadvantage'. Homelessness; substance misuse; mental and physical illness; extreme poverty; violence and abuse.
WHAT IS NOT FUNDED Work that is focused **exclusively** on a particular health condition, disability issues, imprisonment and/or prisoner resettlement or issues affecting asylum seekers. The website states: 'Our focus is always on people who are experiencing a combination of severe social harms, and we are therefore very unlikely to fund work that is about a single issue, such as mental illness alone.'

Note that previous exclusion of London based projects has been dropped.

**TYPE OF GRANT** Core costs; revenue; project expenditure; up to three years; research; campaigning; unrestricted funding.

**RANGE OF GRANTS** £5,000–£500,000

**SAMPLE GRANTS** Kirckman Concert Society (£500,000); Making Every Adult Matter (£280,500); Wandsworth Community Empowerment Network (£200,000); Advice UK (£168,000); The Disabilities Trust (£150,000); WomenCentre Limited (£130,000); Cornwall Voluntary Sector Forum (£125,000); Can Cook Community Interest Company (£50,000); The Centre for Social Justice (£18,000); Griffins Society (£15,000); Edinburgh Cyrenians and Together Working for Wellbeing (£10,000 each); Black Mental Health UK Ltd (£5,000).

**FINANCES** Year 2013/14 Income £3,864,287 Grants £3,446,201 Grants to organisations £3,446,201 Assets £129,771,092

**TRUSTEES** Peter Latchford; Marion Janner; Andrew Robinson; Morag Burnett; Paul Cheng; Hilary Berg; Dame Suzi Leather; Martin Clarke; Robert Duffy; Jane Millar; Simon Tucker; Jacob Hayman.

**OTHER INFORMATION** The LankellyChase Foundation is the amalgamation of two grant-making trusts, the Lankelly Foundation and the Chase Charity. Grants were made in the following categories: Promoting Change Network (£2.8 million); other (£500,000); annual grants (£70,000); investment readiness grants (£50,000); research and policy (£46,000); race equality in mental health (£23,000); practitioner studentships (£15,000). The foundation is involved in grant-making, special initiatives (see the website) and commissioned policy and research. In 2013 the foundation introduced new grants process (which now is once again changing). The annual report for 2013/14 states that during that year 'the foundation's grant-making was still in transition and the process ... had not been fully implemented'.

**HOW TO APPLY** Note the following information from the website: 'Over the summer [2015] we will be reviewing our grants process, with new guidelines to be introduced in September 2015. Therefore, proposals submitted after 5th June 2015 cannot be put forward to our trustees. If you have a proposal you would like to submit after this date, please keep an eye on our website for news of when the new guidelines become available; however during this period you are welcome to contact us by email or phone to discuss your project ideas.' The foundation is eager to hear from those who 'think their project (large or small, short or lengthy, new or existing) can help it towards its mission' but urges to read the Theory of Change (outlined online) before applying.

**WHO TO APPLY TO** Sara Longmuir, Company Secretary, First Floor Greenworks, Dog and Duck Yard, Princeton Street, London WC1R 4BH Tel. 020 3747 9930 email grants@lankellychase.org.uk Website www.lankellychase.org.uk

## ■ The R. J. Larg Family Charitable Trust

**SC NO** SC004946   **ESTABLISHED** 1970

**WHERE FUNDING CAN BE GIVEN** Scotland, particularly Dundee, County of Angus, occasionally Tayside and North East Fife areas.

**WHO CAN BENEFIT** Charitable organisations benefiting children, young adults, students, people with disabilities or those with medical condition. Funding may also be given to churches, conservation, respite care, hospices, MS and neurological research, also youth organisations, including university students associations.

**WHAT IS FUNDED** Grants are made for cancer research, other medical and disability causes, arts and culture, amateur music, care in the community and other community facilities, relief of poverty, religious causes and community or citizenship development. Other charitable purposes can also be considered.

**WHAT IS NOT FUNDED** Grants are not available for individuals.

**TYPE OF GRANT** Generally one-off, some recurring. Our research suggests that buildings, core costs, running costs, salaries and start-up costs may be considered. Funding can normally be given for up to two years.

**RANGE OF GRANTS** £250–£5,000; typically about £1,000–£2,000.

**SAMPLE GRANTS Previous beneficiaries have included:** Cruse Bereavement Care Scotland; Dundee City Council; High School Dundee; Home Start – Dundee; Macmillan Cancer Relief Dundee; Sense Scotland Children's Hospice; University of Dundee; V&A Museum of Design – Dundee; and Whitehall Theatre Trust.

**FINANCES** Year 2013/14 Income £149,564 Grants £200,000 Grants to organisations £200,000

**TRUSTEES** R. Gibson; D. Brand; S. Stewart.

**OTHER INFORMATION** Preference is given to local charities without a high public profile.

**HOW TO APPLY** Applications can be made in writing to the correspondent. The trustees normally meet in February and August to consider grants.

**WHO TO APPLY TO** The Trustees, c/o Thorntons Law LLP, Whitehall House, Yeaman Shore, Dundee DD1 4BJ Tel. 01382 229111 Fax 01382 202288 email dundee@thorntons-law.co.uk

## ■ Largsmount Ltd

**CC NO** 280509   **ESTABLISHED** 1979

**WHERE FUNDING CAN BE GIVEN** UK and overseas, including Israel.

**WHO CAN BENEFIT** Educational and religious institutions; organisations set up to provide for the people in need. Mainly Orthodox Jewish charities.

**WHAT IS FUNDED** Jewish causes; advancement of the Orthodox Jewish religion and education.

**FINANCES** Year 2013 Income £682,493 Grants £196,075 Grants to organisations £196,075 Assets £4,463,413

**TRUSTEES** Z. M. Kaufman; Simon Kaufman; Naomi Kaufman.

**OTHER INFORMATION** A list of grants was not included in the accounts, although previously the M Y A Charitable Trust, a connected charity, has been the largest beneficiary every year.

**HOW TO APPLY** Applications may be made in writing to the correspondent.

**WHO TO APPLY TO** Simon Kaufman, Trustee, 50 Keswick Street, Gateshead NE8 1TQ Tel. 0191 490 0140

## ■ The Lark Trust

**CC NO** 327982   **ESTABLISHED** 1988

**WHERE FUNDING CAN BE GIVEN** Bristol.

**WHO CAN BENEFIT** Registered charities benefitting people of all ages.

**WHAT IS FUNDED** Support in the areas of counselling, psychotherapy, education and the arts.
**WHAT IS NOT FUNDED** Individuals.
**TYPE OF GRANT** Generally one-off.
**RANGE OF GRANTS** £500 to £3,000.
**SAMPLE GRANTS** The Greenhouse Bristol (£3,000); The Bridge Foundation, Bristol and District Tranquiliser Project and Weston Hospicecare (£2,000 each); Brushstrokes (£1,500); MS Therapy Centre and Relate Avon (£1,000 each); Milton Keynes Gallery (£750); Cruse Bereavement Care (£500); Tall Ships Youth Trust (£400).
**FINANCES** Year 2013/14 Income £47,122 Grants £46,825 Grants to organisations £46,825 Assets £1,649,335
**TRUSTEES** George Tute; Malcolm Tute.
**OTHER INFORMATION** Grants were awarded to 29 organisations during the year.
**HOW TO APPLY** Apply in writing to the correspondent, who will check eligibility and then send a form which must be completed. The trustees do not accept information from charities wishing to build a relationship with them. Applications should be received by the end of January for consideration in March.
**WHO TO APPLY TO** Alice Meason, c/o Quartet Community Foundation, Royal Oak House, Royal Oak Avenue, Bristol BS1 4AH *Tel.* 0117 989 7700

..........................................................

## ■ Laslett's (Hinton) Charity

**CC NO** 233696  **ESTABLISHED** 1879
**WHERE FUNDING CAN BE GIVEN** Worcestershire and the surrounding area.
**WHO CAN BENEFIT** Churches; hospitals; hospices; charitable organisations benefitting children, older people, clergy and those in poverty.
**WHAT IS FUNDED** Church repairs; people who are poor; provision of homes for older people; educating children; relief of sickness; general charitable purposes.
**SAMPLE GRANTS** Laslett's (Almshouse) Charity (£88,000). Further awards were made to a number of other unspecified charities (£20,500).
**FINANCES** Year 2013 Income £417,307 Grants £109,128 Grants to organisations £109,128 Assets £15,481,332
**TRUSTEES** T. J. Bridges; M. Jones; E. A. Pugh-Cook; J. V. Panter; Douglas Dale; A. P. Baxter; A. E. Lodge; Peter Hughes; G. T. Newman; Michael Tarver; Colin Anstey.
**OTHER INFORMATION** As the charity is providing almshouse accommodation, this requires substantial amounts and grant-making to other causes is adjusted accordingly.
**HOW TO APPLY** Applications may be made in writing to the correspondent. The trustees meet quarterly to consider awards.
**WHO TO APPLY TO** Stephen Inman, Clark to the Trustees, Kateryn Heywood House, Berkeley Court, The Foregate, Worcester WR1 3QG *Tel.* 01905 317117 *email* admin@lasletts.org.uk

..........................................................

## ■ Laufer Charitable Trust

**CC NO** 275375  **ESTABLISHED** 1961
**WHERE FUNDING CAN BE GIVEN** Worldwide.
**WHO CAN BENEFIT** Registered charities.
**WHAT IS FUNDED** General charitable purposes, mostly with Jewish focus.
**WHAT IS NOT FUNDED** Grants cannot be given to individuals, as grants are only made to registered charities.
**TYPE OF GRANT** Our research suggests that recurrent core costs for up to one year can be covered.
**FINANCES** Year 2013/14 Income £54,418 Grants £14,720 Grants to organisations £14,720 Assets £965,191
**TRUSTEES** Stanley Laufer; Della Laufer; Simon Goulden; Rowland Aarons; Mark Hoffman.
**OTHER INFORMATION** As this is a small charity, new beneficiaries are only considered in exceptional circumstances as the income is already allocated for some years to come.
**HOW TO APPLY** New beneficiaries are only considered by the trust in exceptional circumstances, as the trustees seek to maintain support for an existing group of charities. In view of this it is suggested that no applications are made.
**WHO TO APPLY TO** Rowland Aarons, Trustee, 342 Regents Park Road, London N3 2LJ *Tel.* 020 8343 1660 *email* stanleylaufer@gmail.com

..........................................................

## ■ The Lauffer Family Charitable Foundation

**CC NO** 251115  **ESTABLISHED** 1965
**WHERE FUNDING CAN BE GIVEN** Commonwealth countries; Israel; USA.
**WHO CAN BENEFIT** Charitable organisations; Jewish charities.
**WHAT IS FUNDED** General charitable purposes, including education, religious activities, environment, medical healthcare, social welfare, children and families and recreation and culture; focus on Jewish causes.
**WHAT IS NOT FUNDED** Individuals.
**TYPE OF GRANT** Start-up costs; recurrent funding for up to five years.
**RANGE OF GRANTS** Up to £19,500.
**SAMPLE GRANTS** Jewish Learning Exchange (£19,500 in four grants); Ponevez Institution Bnei Brak (£16,000); University Jewish Chaplaincy (£10,000); Hasmonean High School (£8,300 in three grants); Bridge Lane Beth Hamidrash (£8,000 in four grants); Chicken Shed Theatre Trust (£7,400 in three grants); United Joint Israel Appeal (£7,000 in three grants); Spiro Ark (£5,000); British Friends of Shvut Ami (£4,000); University of Cambridge (£3,000); Chickensoup Shelter (£1,500); Jewish Care (£1,300 in three grants); Aspire (£1,200 in two grants); Nightingale – Home for Aged Jews (£1,000). Awards below £1,000 totalled over £20,500.
**FINANCES** Year 2013/14 Income £172,777 Grants £277,482 Grants to organisations £277,482 Assets £5,728,157
**TRUSTEES** Jonathan Lauffer; Robin Lauffer; Gideon Lauffer.
**OTHER INFORMATION** During 2013/14 a total of 203 grants were made.
**HOW TO APPLY** Applications may be made in writing to the correspondent and are generally considered once a year.
**WHO TO APPLY TO** The Trustees, c/o Clayton Stark and Co, 5th Floor, Charles House, 108–110 Finchley Road, London NW3 5JJ *Tel.* 020 7431 4200 *email* jonathanlauffer13@gmail.com

## ■ Mrs F. B. Laurence Charitable Trust
**CC NO** 296548  **ESTABLISHED** 1976
**WHERE FUNDING CAN BE GIVEN** UK and overseas.
**WHO CAN BENEFIT** UK-registered charities, particularly organisations benefitting ex-service and service people, retired people, unemployed people and disadvantaged members of society within the UK or overseas to whom the UK owes a duty of care.
**WHAT IS FUNDED** General charitable purposes; social welfare; accommodation and housing; community facilities and activities; protection of environment and wildlife; health and disability; older people; vulnerable and disadvantaged individuals; justice and human rights; service and ex-service men and women; special schools and special needs education and literacy.
**WHAT IS NOT FUNDED** Individuals are not supported. Our research indicates that the following applications are unlikely to be considered: appeals for endowment or sponsorship; overseas projects, unless overseen by the charity's own fieldworkers; maintenance of buildings or landscape; provision of work or materials that are the responsibility of the state; where administration expenses, in all their guises, are considered by the trustees to be excessive; or where the fundraising costs in the preceding year have not resulted in an increase in the succeeding years donations in excess of these costs.
**TYPE OF GRANT** Generally one-off awards for core costs, project expenses and start-up costs. Funding is for one year or less.
**RANGE OF GRANTS** Up to £4,000.
**SAMPLE GRANTS** Halow Project and Disaster Emergency Committee Philippines Typhoon Appeal (£4,000 each); Heaton Ellis Trust and Pancreatic Cancer UK (£2,500 each); Action on Postpartum Psychosis, Cystic Fibrosis Trust, NSPCC, Walking with Giants Foundation and Woodland Heritage (£2,000 each); and Carers, Combat Stress, MENCAP, Seafarers UK and Seeing Dogs Alliance (£1,500 each).
**FINANCES** Year 2013/14 Income £98,308 Grants £87,000 Grants to organisations £87,000 Assets £2,568,474
**TRUSTEES** Caroline Fry; Camilla Carr; Elizabeth Lyle.
**OTHER INFORMATION** There were at least 28 awards made with further smaller grants of £1,000 or less totalling £31,000.
**HOW TO APPLY** Applications may be made in writing to the correspondent, including the latest set of accounts. Only registered charities will be considered. According to our research, applications should be no more than two sides of A4 and should include the following information: who you are; what you do; what distinguishes your work from others in your field; where applicable describe the project that the money you are asking for is going towards and include a business plan/budget; what funds have already been raised and how; how much you are seeking from the trust; and how you intend to measure the potential benefits of your project or work as a whole. The trustees meet twice a year.
**WHO TO APPLY TO** The Trustees, BM Box 2082, London WC1N 3XX

## ■ The Kathleen Laurence Trust
**CC NO** 296461  **ESTABLISHED** 1987
**WHERE FUNDING CAN BE GIVEN** UK.
**WHO CAN BENEFIT** Charitable organisations with specific projects and events.
**WHAT IS FUNDED** General charitable purposes, especially health causes. The trust particularly favours smaller organisations and those raising funds for specific requirements, such as medical research, associations connected with disability and learning difficulties, organisations helping people who are sick, older people and children.
**WHAT IS NOT FUNDED** Running costs; management expenses; individuals.
**TYPE OF GRANT** One-off and recurrent; project funding.
**RANGE OF GRANTS** £750–£40,000
**SAMPLE GRANTS** Most recent beneficiaries have included: Action on Elder Abuse; Bag Books; Battersea Cats and Dogs Home; Cancer Research UK; Dr Bell's Family Centre; Fulmerston Christian Fellowship; Go Kids Go; Helix Art; Macmillan Cancer Support; NSPCC; Special Needs Adventure Playground; The Horder Centre; Tiny Tickers.
**FINANCES** Year 2014/15 Income £225,909 Grants £190,000 Grants to organisations £190,000
**TRUSTEE** Coutts & Co.
**OTHER INFORMATION** At the time of writing (June 2015) the latest accounts for 2014/15 were not published by the Charity Commission. It is likely that grants totalled about £190,000. About 60 awards are made each year.
**HOW TO APPLY** Applications may be made in writing to the correspondent. The trustees usually meet in January and June.
**WHO TO APPLY TO** The Trust Manager, c/o Coutts & Co., Trustee Department, 440 Strand, London WC2R 0QS Tel. 020 7663 6825 email couttscharities@coutts.com

## ■ The Law Society Charity
**CC NO** 268736  **ESTABLISHED** 1974
**WHERE FUNDING CAN BE GIVEN** Worldwide.
**WHO CAN BENEFIT** Organisations protecting people's legal rights and lawyers' welfare as well as law related projects from charities without an identifiable legal connection.
**WHAT IS FUNDED** Law, legal education and access to justice. This includes: charitable educational purposes for lawyers and would-be lawyers; legal research; promotion of an increased understanding of the law; promotion of human rights and charities concerned with the provision of advice, counselling, mediation services connected with the law; welfare directly/indirectly of solicitors, trainee solicitors and other legal and Law Society staff and their families.
**WHAT IS NOT FUNDED** Support is not provided to: charities falling outside the fields of human rights, legal education and access to justice, such as medical charities; individual students seeking help with their studies; and locally-based bodies, such as law centres or Citizens' Advice Bureaux.
**TYPE OF GRANT** One-off or spread over two-three years.
**RANGE OF GRANTS** £5,000–£15,000
**SAMPLE GRANTS** Diyarbakir Bar Association (£16,000); Peace Brigades International and Personal Support Unit (£15,000 each); Caravan Columbia (£12,500); Jubilee Action (£12,100);

Bail for Immigration Detainees (£10,000); Prisoners Abroad and Prisoners' Advice Service (£7,500 each); University of Cape Town (£7,000); Book Aid International (£6,600); Law Centres Network (£6,000); and Detention Advice Service (£5,000).
**FINANCES** Year 2013/14 Income £29,331 Grants £135,238 Grants to organisations £135,238 Assets £555,956
**TRUSTEE** The Law Society Trustees Ltd.
**OTHER INFORMATION** The charity's website states: 'We may regard your asking for a very large amount as an indication that the project and your hopes for funding it are unrealistic, and reject it on that basis.'
**HOW TO APPLY** Application forms are available from the website. Requests are considered at quarterly trustees' meetings, usually held in April, July, September and December with precise dates available on the website. Note that applications should be received four weeks before the date of the meeting. Feedback on unsuccessful applications may be available on request.
**WHO TO APPLY TO** Andrew Dobson, Company Secretary, 110–113 Chancery Lane, London WC2A 1PL *Tel.* 020 7316 5597 *email* lawsocietycharity@lawsociety.org.uk *Website* www.lawsociety.org.uk

## ■ The Edgar E. Lawley Foundation

**CC NO** 201589   **ESTABLISHED** 1961
**WHERE FUNDING CAN BE GIVEN** UK, with a preference for the West Midlands.
**WHO CAN BENEFIT** Registered charities; charitable organisations; hospitals and hospices; schools and universities.
**WHAT IS FUNDED** General charitable purposes; education in arts, commerce and industry; health and disability; medical care and research; older people; children and young people; community causes.
**WHAT IS NOT FUNDED** Appeals from and on behalf of individuals are not considered.
**TYPE OF GRANT** One-off and generally unrestricted funding.
**RANGE OF GRANTS** About £1,500 on average.
**SAMPLE GRANTS** Acorns Children's Hospice; Bag Books; Breast Cancer Campaign; Chris Westwood Charity; Focus Birmingham; Helen and Douglas House; Mildmay Mission Hospital; Shakespeare Hospice; Research Institute for Older People; Redditch Association for the Blind; Scope; Wheelpower; and Working Class Movement Library. Exact amounts given were not listed in the accounts.
**FINANCES** Year 2013/14 Income £195,900 Grants £192,000 Grants to organisations £192,000 Assets £4,370,794
**TRUSTEES** John Cooke; Gillian Hilton; Philip Cooke; Frank Jackson.
**OTHER INFORMATION** There were 128 awards made during the year.
**HOW TO APPLY** Summary grant application forms can be downloaded from the foundation's website and should be returned to the correspondent between 1 August and 31 October, preferably by email. Applicants should outline the reasons for the grant request and the amount of grant being sought. Any supporting information that adds to the strength of the application can be included. The trustees make grant decisions in January. The foundation regrets that it is not possible, unless a stamped addressed envelope has been provided, to communicate with unsuccessful applicants and the fact that a grant has not been received by the end of January indicates that it has not been possible to fund it. The foundation receives about 800 requests per year but can only address about 130 of them.
**WHO TO APPLY TO** Frank Jackson, Trustee, PO Box 456, Esher KT10 1DP *Tel.* 01372 805760 *email* edgarelawley@gmail.com *Website* www.edgarelawleyfoundation.org.uk

## ■ The Herd Lawson and Muriel Lawson Charitable Trust

**CC NO** 1113220   **ESTABLISHED** 1975
**WHERE FUNDING CAN BE GIVEN** Mainly Cumbria.
**WHO CAN BENEFIT** Charitable organisations.
**WHAT IS FUNDED** This trust supports a number of named organisations receiving grants each year and also organisations benefitting older people in need, particularly those who are members of evangelical or Christian Brethren churches.
**RANGE OF GRANTS** £500–£21,000
**SAMPLE GRANTS** British Red Cross Society and WWF – UK (£21,000 each); Christian Workers Relief Fund (£15,000); West Cumbria Hospice (£7,000); Ambleside Baptist Church and Hospice of St Mary of Furness (£4,500 each); Spring Mount Fellowship (£3,000); Ambleside Welfare Charity (£2,500); Cross Roads Care Cumbria (£2,000); Gospel Hall – Bowness on Windermere; Independent Age and Sandhills Lane Christian Brethren Church (£1,000 each); and Heron Corn Mill Project (£500).
**FINANCES** Year 2013/14 Income £221,784 Grants £84,000 Grants to organisations £84,000 Assets £1,839,458
**TRUSTEES** John Scott; Peter Matthews; Robert Barker; Brian Herd.
**OTHER INFORMATION** There were 13 awards made during the year.
**HOW TO APPLY** The trust receives more applications than it can deal with and does not seek further unsolicited appeals. The trust has previously informed us that 'the trustees have established a number of charities to whom they make grants each year and they very rarely make any donations to other charities.'
**WHO TO APPLY TO** John Scott, Trustee, The Estate Office, 14 Church Street, Ambleside, Cumbria LA22 0BT *Tel.* 01539 434758 *email* derekscott@ignetics.co.uk

## ■ Lawson Beckman Charitable Trust

**CC NO** 261378   **ESTABLISHED** 1970
**WHERE FUNDING CAN BE GIVEN** UK and overseas.
**WHO CAN BENEFIT** Charitable organisations; according to our research, often headquarter organisations or major bodies.
**WHAT IS FUNDED** General charitable causes; relief of poverty; Jewish causes; social welfare; education; the arts.
**WHAT IS NOT FUNDED** Grants are not made to individuals.
**TYPE OF GRANT** One-off and recurrent.
**RANGE OF GRANTS** £500–£12,500
**SAMPLE GRANTS** Norwood Ravenswood (£12,500); Chai Lifeline Cancer Care and World Jewish Relief (£5,000 each); The Du Boisson Dance Foundation and United Jewish Israel Appeal – UJIA (£3,000 each); Friends of Yad Sarah and The Prince's Teaching Institute (£2,000 each); The Anne Frank Trust UK and The Jerusalem

Foundation (£1,000 each); and Youth Aliyah Child Rescue (£500).
**FINANCES** Year 2013/14 *Income* £91,259 *Grants* £49,735 *Grants to organisations* £49,735 *Assets* £4,575,559
**TRUSTEES** Melvin Lawson; Lynton Stock; Francis Katz.
**OTHER INFORMATION** Grants were made to 14 organisations.
**HOW TO APPLY** Applications can be made in writing to the correspondent.
**WHO TO APPLY TO** Melvin Lawson, Trustee, A. Beckman plc, PO Box 1ED, London W1A 1ED *Tel.* 020 7637 8412 *email* june@abplc.co.uk

■ **The Raymond and Blanche Lawson Charitable Trust**
**CC NO** 281269 **ESTABLISHED** 1980
**WHERE FUNDING CAN BE GIVEN** UK, with an interest in Kent and East Sussex and West Sussex.
**WHO CAN BENEFIT** Charitable organisations benefitting children, young adults, older people, people with disabilities and those within the armed forces. Preference is given to local organisations.
**WHAT IS FUNDED** According to the annual report, 'the trustees have adopted a policy in the main of giving support to organisations that fall into the following categories: local voluntary organisations; care in the community; local hospices; preservation of buildings; assistance for people with disabilities; support to armed forces and benevolent funds.
**WHAT IS NOT FUNDED** Individuals.
**TYPE OF GRANT** One-of and up to one year; projects; research.
**RANGE OF GRANTS** £500–£6,000; typically £1,000–£2,000.
**SAMPLE GRANTS** The Caldecott Foundation (£6,000); Payment to Flood Victims (£5,000); Dyslexia Action (£2,800); Crisis, Heart of Kent Hospice and Young Lives Foundation (£2,500 each); Church Army, Martha Trust and Sue Ryder Care (£2,000 each); Childhood First, Guide Dogs, Missing People and Vitalise (£1,000 each); Almshouse Association, Great Ormond Street Hospital Charity and St John's School PTA (£500 each).
**FINANCES** Year 2013/14 *Income* £148,386 *Grants* £105,750 *Grants to organisations* £105,750 *Assets* £5,394,249
**TRUSTEES** Philip Thomas; Sarah Hill.
**OTHER INFORMATION** Grants were made to 76 organisations.
**HOW TO APPLY** Applications can be made in writing to the correspondent.
**WHO TO APPLY TO** The Trustees, 28 Barden Road, Tonbridge, Kent TN9 1TX *Tel.* 01732 352183 *email* philip.thomas@worrinlawson.co.uk

■ **The Mason Le Page Charitable Trust**
**CC NO** 1054589 **ESTABLISHED** 1996
**WHERE FUNDING CAN BE GIVEN** London area.
**WHO CAN BENEFIT** Organisations benefitting people with cancer; medical research; hospitals; hospices.
**WHAT IS FUNDED** Health causes, especially related to cancer research and care.
**WHAT IS NOT FUNDED** Individuals.
**TYPE OF GRANT** One-off; capital costs.
**RANGE OF GRANTS** £500–£5,000

**SAMPLE GRANTS** Previous beneficiaries have included: London Chest Hospital and Multiple Sclerosis Society (£5,000 each); Cancer BACUP and Dermatrust (£3,000 each); Harlington Hospice Middlesex and Royal Hospital for Neuro-disability (£2,000 each); The Peaceful Place (£1,500); Sergeant Cancer Care Children (£1,200); CLIC Sargent (£500).
**FINANCES** Year 2012/13 *Income* £15,533 *Grants* £55,000 *Grants to organisations* £55,000
**TRUSTEES** David Morgan; Andrew Stebbings.
**OTHER INFORMATION** At the time of writing (June 2015) this was the latest information available – 2013/14 accounts were overdue and 2012/13 accounts were not required to be published due to low income. It is likely that grants totalled about £55,000.
**HOW TO APPLY** Applications may be made in writing to the correspondent.
**WHO TO APPLY TO** Andrew Stebbings, Charity Manager, c/o Pemberton Greenish LLP, 45 Cadogan Gardens, London SW3 2TB *Tel.* 020 7591 3333 *email* charitymanager@pglaw.co.uk

■ **The Leach Fourteenth Trust**
**CC NO** 204844 **ESTABLISHED** 1961
**WHERE FUNDING CAN BE GIVEN** UK, with some preference for South West England.
**WHO CAN BENEFIT** Registered charities; medical institutions.
**WHAT IS FUNDED** General charitable purposes with a preference towards medicine, health, disability and conservation.
**WHAT IS NOT FUNDED** Only registered charities based in the UK are supported.
**TYPE OF GRANT** Buildings; capital and core costs; one-off; project grants; research; running costs; recurring expenditure; salaries; start-up costs; for more than three years.
**RANGE OF GRANTS** £500–£5,000
**SAMPLE GRANTS** The Country Trust – Suffolk (£5,000); Hope and Homes for Children (£4,000); Plan International UK (£3,500); Deafblind UK (£3,000); Salvation Army and Woodland Trust – FTT (£2,500 each); Age UK; Pancreatic Cancer UK and The Princess Royal Trust for Carers (£1,500 each); Action Medical Research, Carers Trust, Child Hope, Multiple Sclerosis Society, The Friends of Michael Sobell House, The Rainbow Centre and War on Want (£1,000 each); Dorothy House Foundation and Douglas Bader Foundation (£500 each). Grants under £1,000 totalled £6,000.
**FINANCES** Year 2012/13 *Income* £104,045 *Grants* £105,200 *Grants to organisations* £105,200 *Assets* £3,161,022
**TRUSTEES** Roger Murray-Leach; Judith Murray-Nash; Guy Ward; John Henderson; Tamsin Murray-Leach; Grant Nash; Richard Moore.
**OTHER INFORMATION** During the year 73 organisations benefitted. At the time of writing (June 2015) this was the latest information available – accounts for 2013/14 were overdue at the Charity Commission.
**HOW TO APPLY** Applications may be made in writing to the correspondent.
**WHO TO APPLY TO** Guy Ward, Trustee, Bathurst House, 86 Micklegate, York YO1 6LQ *Tel.* 01904 628551 *email* info@barronyork.co.uk

## ■ The David Lean Foundation

**CC NO** 1067074 **ESTABLISHED** 1997
**WHERE FUNDING CAN BE GIVEN** UK.
**WHO CAN BENEFIT** Charitable organisations; educational establishments.
**WHAT IS FUNDED** Promotion and advancement of education and to cultivate and improve public taste in the visual arts, particularly in the field of film production, including screenplay writing, film direction and editing.
**WHAT IS NOT FUNDED** Individual scholarships or other grants.
**TYPE OF GRANT** One-off and recurrent grants.
**RANGE OF GRANTS** £7,000–£89,500
**SAMPLE GRANTS** National Film and Television School (£89,500); British Film Institute (£68,000); British Academy of Film and Television (£56,500); Royal Academy of Arts (£42,000); Film Club UK (£9,500); British Kinematograph S and T Society (£7,000).
**FINANCES** Year 2013 Income £260,778 Grants £272,379 Grants to organisations £272,379 Assets £914,462
**TRUSTEES** Anthony Reeves; Stefan Breitenstein.
**OTHER INFORMATION** A total of six organisations benefitted in 2013.
**HOW TO APPLY** Scholarship grants for students attending the National Film and Television School, Royal Holloway or Leighton Park School, are normally only awarded on the recommendation of the course provider with the trustees. Other applications for grants that would meet the aims of the foundation are invited in writing, enclosing full details of the project and including financial information and two references. Progress reports should be provided when required. The foundation has a website; however, it did not seem to be functioning at the time of writing.
**WHO TO APPLY TO** The Trustees, The Bradshaws, Oaken, Codsall, Stoke-on-Trent WV8 2HU Tel. 01902 754024 email aareeves@davidleanfoundation.com

## ■ The Leathersellers' Company Charitable Fund

**CC NO** 278072 **ESTABLISHED** 1979
**WHERE FUNDING CAN BE GIVEN** UK, particularly Greater London.
**WHO CAN BENEFIT** Registered charities; educational establishments; individuals.
**WHAT IS FUNDED** Charities associated with the Leathersellers' Company, the leather and hide trades, education in leather technology and caring for the welfare of poor and sick former workers in the industry and their dependants. Charities working for the benefit of people in London in the following priority areas: education; disability; children and young people; relief of need.
**TYPE OF GRANT** One-off and multi-year grants up to four years; core costs; project expenditure; development.
**RANGE OF GRANTS** Up to £75,000; small grants – up to £3,000, normally £500–£1,500.
**SAMPLE GRANTS** Leathersellers' Federation of Schools (£75,000); University of Northampton (£60,000); St Catherine's College (£30,000); Fight for Peace – UK (£25,000); London Youth Support Trust and Museum of Leathercraft (£20,000 each); London College of Fashion (£18,000); Beatbullying, Changing Faces, Greenhouse, Live Music Now and The Urology Foundation (£15,000 each). Awards of under £15,000 totalled £743,000.
**FINANCES** Year 2013/14 Income £1,585,000 Grants £1,684,000 Grants to organisations £1,513,000 Assets £50,894,000
**TRUSTEES** The Leathersellers' Company; David Santa-Olalla.
**OTHER INFORMATION** There were 303 grants awarded, including 77 to individuals totalling £171,000 and 226 to charities totalling £1.5 million – 110 single grants (£291,000) and 116 multi-year awards (£1.2 million). Most awards were given towards education (27%), disability (17%) and leather associated (11%) causes. The charity also supports British students through Education Awards and maintains almshouses.
**HOW TO APPLY** Application forms can be accessed online from the charity's website. Small grants are fast-tracked (should be decided within six weeks following an application). Application process for the main grants programme can take up to nine months – the Charities Grants Committee meets three times a year to consider applications (initial assessment takes place within about six weeks). Only one application per organisation can be made in any year. If a charity is in receipt of a multi-year grants or a large single year grant cannot apply for another grant until four years has passed.
**WHO TO APPLY TO** Geoffrey Russell-Jones, Charities and Education Officer, 21 Garlick Hill, London EC4V 2AU Tel. 020 7330 1444 Fax 020 7330 1445 email enquires@leathersellers.co.uk or grussell-jones@leathersellers.co.uk Website www.leathersellers.co.uk

## ■ The Leche Trust

**CC NO** 225659 **ESTABLISHED** 1963
**WHERE FUNDING CAN BE GIVEN** UK.
**WHO CAN BENEFIT** Individuals and charitable organisations; historical buildings and objects; museums and galleries; churches; schools, colleges and universities; concerts and festivals.
**WHAT IS FUNDED** Preservation and conservation of art and architecture, churches and historic collections, preference is given to objects of the Georgian period or earlier; performing arts, particularly music, dance and drama; education. There is also a programme supporting overseas PhD students.
**WHAT IS NOT FUNDED** General education projects; community and outreach projects; domestic or overseas social welfare; schools or school buildings; individual students (except overseas PhD students); projects promoting religion; natural environment or wildlife projects; medicine; and expeditions. The trust is not likely to support the same organisation in two consecutive financial years. The website also notes that 'applications in respect of projects that are the subject of major Heritage Lottery Fund bids must have secured Stage 2 funding before consideration by the trustees'.
**TYPE OF GRANT** One-off projects and capital costs, not recurring expenditure.
**RANGE OF GRANTS** £1,000–£5,000
**SAMPLE GRANTS** British School at Rome, St Paul's Cathedral and Winchester Cathedral (£5,000 each); The Charterhouse in the City of London (£4,800); Turner's House Trust (£4,500); City and Guilds Art School and St Laurence Church in Ludlow (£4,000 each); Royal Academy of Art (£3,500); Ashmolean Museum and St Luke with Holy Trinity – Charlton (£3,000 each); Museum of Childhood at Bethnal Green and The Holburne Museum (£2,500 each); St Mary's Church –

Avington and Yorkshire Sculpture Park (£2,000 each); Amherst Heritage Trust (£1,500); Church of St John and St Mary – Higham (£1,300); and Zoological Society of London (£1,000).
**FINANCES** Year 2013/14 Income £94,840 Grants £215,658 Grants to organisations £188,158 Assets £6,385,748
**TRUSTEES** Martin Williams; Simon Wethered; Anne Greenstock; Ariane Bankes; Caroline Laing; Thomas Howard; Robin Dhar.
**OTHER INFORMATION** There was a total of 81 awards made, including 13 student grants.
**HOW TO APPLY** There is no formal application form and requests should be addressed in writing to the correspondent via post only. They should include relevant supporting documents and budgets for the project. The trustees meet three times a year, in February, June and October; applications need to be received the month before. Unsuccessful applications will be notified within two weeks; however, eligible for consideration applicants will not be contacted until the final selection is made to be forward for the trustees' consideration. **Overseas PhD Student Programme**: Applicants can receive an application from the correspondent. It should be completed by both the student and their tutor.
**WHO TO APPLY TO** Rosemary Ewles, Grants Director, 105 Greenway Avenue, London E17 3QL Tel. 020 3233 0023 email info@lechetrust.org Website www.lechetrust.org

## ■ The Arnold Lee Charitable Trust
**CC NO** 264437  **ESTABLISHED** 1972
**WHERE FUNDING CAN BE GIVEN** UK.
**WHO CAN BENEFIT** Established charities of high repute; mainly organisations linked to the Jewish community.
**WHAT IS FUNDED** General charitable purposes; Jewish causes; education; health.
**WHAT IS NOT FUNDED** Grants are rarely made to individuals.
**RANGE OF GRANTS** Up to £25,000.
**SAMPLE GRANTS** Aish Hatorah (£25,000); DALAID (£19,000); Project Seed (£17,000); Yesodey Hatorah Schools (£16,000); Mesila UK (£12,500); Community Security Trust (£6,000); Western Marble Arch Synagogue (£4,900); and The Institute of Jewish Studies (£3,000). All the remaining awards were for £5,000 or less.
**FINANCES** Year 2013/14 Income £65,661 Grants £176,718 Grants to organisations £176,718 Assets £1,757,092
**TRUSTEES** Edward Lee; Alan Lee.
**OTHER INFORMATION** A list of beneficiaries was not available; however, the trust listed the six largest recipients and another two charities.
**HOW TO APPLY** Applications may be made in writing to the correspondent.
**WHO TO APPLY TO** The Trustees, Hazlems Fenton LLP, Palladium House, 1–4 Argyll Street, London W1F 7LD Tel. 020 7437 7666 email PetronellaEvans@princetonplc.com

## ■ The William Leech Charity
**CC NO** 265491  **ESTABLISHED** 1972
**WHERE FUNDING CAN BE GIVEN** Northumberland, Tyne and Wear, Durham and overseas.
**WHO CAN BENEFIT** Registered charities. Preference for organisations which have: a high proportion of the work undertaken by voluntary, unpaid workers; a close connection to the Settlor, or with districts in which William Leech (Builders) Ltd, built houses during the time when the Settlor was active in business; an active Christian involvement; projects in deprived areas for the benefit of local people, especially those which encourage people to help themselves; been doing practical, new work and putting new ideas into action.
**WHAT IS FUNDED** **The Main Fund:** General charitable purposes, including: community welfare, medical research and healthcare; projects for young people; sports; homelessness and unemployment; education and training; historic buildings and churches; maritime, armed forces charities; disability.
**The Lady Leech Fund:** Overseas projects focusing primarily on the medical, educational and environmental needs of children in underdeveloped countries, which usually have links with the North East of England; also emergency aid in response to natural disasters.
**Volunteer Support:** Grants of £500–£1,000 to assist volunteers in small registered charities, where at least two thirds of the charitable work (excluding administration and fundraising) is done by volunteers.
**WHAT IS NOT FUNDED** Community care centres and similar (exceptionally, those in remote country areas may be supported); running expenses of youth clubs (as opposed to capital projects); running expenses of churches (this includes normal repairs, but churches engaged in social work, or using their buildings largely for 'outside' purposes, may be supported); sport; the arts; individuals or students; organisations which have been supported in the last 12 months (it would be exceptional to support an organisation in two successive years, unless support had been confirmed in advance); holidays, travel, outings; minibuses (unless over 10,000 miles a year is expected); schools; housing associations; salaries; replacement of statutory funding.
**TYPE OF GRANT** One-off and recurring grants; interest-free loans (often to churches to allow them to get on with the building work, avoiding inflation costs); running costs; capital costs.
**RANGE OF GRANTS** £250–£105,500; most grants are for £1,000 or less; the maximum loan is usually £10,000 or 10% of the project cost.
**SAMPLE GRANTS** Seahorse Xf96 Project Newcastle University (£105,500); People's Kitchen (£11,000); Talbot House School and The Peru Mission (£10,000 each); Allendale Creative Artists Community (£6,000); Hospice Care North Northumberland (£5,000); Cramlington Voluntary Youth Project (£2,800); Sacred Heart Church Boldon (£2,200); Action for Children, CAFOD Philippines Haiyan Appeal and Mityana Community Development Foundation (£2,000 each); Tall Ships Youth Trust (£1,500); 2 Youth Zone (£1,000); East Bedlington Community Centre, Evening Chronicle Sunshine Fund and Macmillan Cancer Support – NS Trek from Katmandu to Everest (£500 each); Handicapped Children's Action Group (£400); Break Through Breast Cancer (£250).
**FINANCES** Year 2013/14 Income £467,740 Grants £252,443 Grants to organisations £252,443 Assets £15,778,322
**TRUSTEES** N. Sherlock; David Stabler; Adrian Gifford; Roy Leech; Barry Wallace; Richard Leech; Revd Prof. David Wilkinson; Marc Richard; Prof. Patrick Chinnery.
**OTHER INFORMATION** The trustees allocate approximately one third of the Main Fund's income to medical research undertaken by the University of Newcastle upon Tyne (£105,500 in 2013/14). During the year 72 grants were awarded (mostly in Northumberland), including

ten grants given through The Lady Leech Fund to charities working overseas (a total of £32,000). It is further noted in the accounts that 'a significant amount was 'distributed to medical care projects, initiatives to assist homelessness projects and the maintenance of churches'.

HOW TO APPLY The website notes that the trustees 'accept applications in the short form of a letter, rather than expecting the completion of a complicated application form, which may seem daunting to some applicants'. Appeals must include: registered charity address; a description of the project, who it will help, and any evidence which will support the need for this particular project; how much the project will cost, capital and revenue, with an indication of the amounts involved; how much the charity has raised so far, and where it expects to find the balance; the type of support sought; i.e. small grant, multiple grant, loan, etc.; how much does it cost to run the charity each year, including how much of the revenue is spent on salaries and employees, where the revenue come from, how many paid workers and volunteers there are. Low priority applications can be submitted using an online form, while grant requests for up to £1,000 and loan requests for up to £10,000 should signed and submitted in writing to the correspondent (if your charity has a letterhead, printing the letter onto this will aid the application). Applications to the Lady Leech Fund should also detail the connection between the project overseas and the North East England. To request volunteer support applicants should send a one page letter detailing: the organisation's name and charity registration number; name and address of a correspondent; project aims, progress, funds raised to date, how much is needed and for what; number of paid workers, total annual salary cost, total annual administration overheads and how many unpaid volunteers there are.

WHO TO APPLY TO Kathleen Smith, Secretary, Saville Chambers, 5 North Street, Newcastle upon Tyne NE1 8DF Tel. 0191 243 3300 email enquiries@williamleechcharity.org.uk Website www.williamleechcharity.org.uk

## ■ The Lord Mayor of Leeds Appeal Fund

CC NO 512441   ESTABLISHED 1982
WHERE FUNDING CAN BE GIVEN Leeds.
WHO CAN BENEFIT The charities selected by the lord mayor during her/his year of office.
WHAT IS FUNDED Charitable causes.
SAMPLE GRANTS Paediatric Intensive Care Unit Trust – Leeds General Infirmary (£61,100); Crohn's and Colitis UK (£38,200); Kashmir Orphan Relief Trust (£1,000); Voluntary Action Leeds (£50).
FINANCES Year 2012/13 Income £44,472 Grants £100,420 Grants to organisations £100,420 Assets £448
TRUSTEES The Lord Mayor of Leeds; Thomas Riordan; Gerald Harper; Brian Cleasby; Neil Buckley.
OTHER INFORMATION At the time of writing (June 2015) these were the latest accounts available.
HOW TO APPLY The fund does not accept unsolicited applications.
WHO TO APPLY TO Thomas Riordan, Secretary, Leeds City Council, Civic Hall, Leeds LS1 1JF Tel. 0113 247 4283 email paul.gilmartin@leeds.gov.uk

## ■ Leeds Building Society Charitable Foundation

CC NO 1074429   ESTABLISHED 1999
WHERE FUNDING CAN BE GIVEN Areas where one of the 67 society's branches are located.
WHO CAN BENEFIT Registered charities or groups affiliated to registered charities.
WHAT IS FUNDED General charitable purposes; community projects focusing on social welfare and relief in need; vulnerable people and disadvantaged individuals.
WHAT IS NOT FUNDED The foundation is unlikely to support: the restoration or upgrading of building, including churches; environmental charities (unless there is a benefit to a disadvantaged community); administration equipment, such as IT equipment for charity's own use. Support cannot be given for: running costs; projects with religious, political or military purposes; overseas charities or projects; individuals, including sponsorship of individuals; animal welfare projects; and medical research. Church projects will be considered only where they involve community outreach and benefit (such as supporting homeless people or disadvantaged families).
TYPE OF GRANT One-off awards for capital projects.
RANGE OF GRANTS £250–£1,000
SAMPLE GRANTS Mencap (£3,300).
FINANCES Year 2013 Income £120,303 Grants £129,554 Grants to organisations £129,554 Assets £2,148
TRUSTEES Peter Chadwick; Ann Shelton; Robert Wade; Gary Brook; Martin Richardson; Michael Garnett; Gary Hetherington.
OTHER INFORMATION During the year 164 grants were made. No grants were given over £1,500, apart from one grant given to Mencap for £3,300. A list of beneficiaries was not included within the annual report and accounts for 2013.
HOW TO APPLY Applications have to be made in writing to the correspondent, including the following information: the name of your organisation; the name of the project and brief information about its work; a contact name, address and phone number; the registered charity number; details of what the donation would be used for; who would benefit from the donation; your nearest Leeds Building Society branch (the branch can also forward the application for you). All applications are acknowledged, following the trustees' meetings, which are held quarterly, in March, June, September and November. The foundation is unable to consider applications if support has been provided in the last two years. The foundation operates independently of Leeds Building Society and so local branch staff are unable to answer questions about the foundation. Contact the foundation directly for further information.
WHO TO APPLY TO Sally Smith, Reward Manager, Leeds Building Society, 105 Albion Street, Leeds, West Yorkshire LS1 5AS Tel. 0113 216 7596 Website www.leedsbuildingsociety.co.uk/your-society/about-us/charitable-foundation

### ■ Leicester and Leicestershire Historic Churches Preservation Trust (Leicestershire Historic Churches Trust)

CC NO 233476  ESTABLISHED 1964
WHERE FUNDING CAN BE GIVEN Leicester and Leicestershire.
WHO CAN BENEFIT Churches and chapels.
WHAT IS FUNDED The 'preservation, repair, maintenance, improvement, upkeep, beautification and reconstruction of churches ... and of monuments, fittings, fixtures, stained glass, furniture, ornaments and chattels in such churches, and of the churchyard belonging to such churches'.
WHAT IS NOT FUNDED Our research indicates that grants are not made for: electrical work; disability access; reordering of the interior; redecorating; toilets or kitchen facilities; extensions; school or other ancillary buildings.
TYPE OF GRANT One-off awards for building, renovation and associated expenses.
FINANCES Year 2013/14 Income £46,798 Grants £35,850 Grants to organisations £35,850 Assets £246,457
TRUSTEES Mark Dunkley; David Knowles; Barrie Byford; Janet Arthur; John Hemes; Revd Fabian Radcliffe; James Ireland; Revd Timothy Stevens; Michael Taylor.
HOW TO APPLY Applications should be made using a 'Grant Application Form' obtainable from the correspondent. The trustees meet in March and October to consider applications (they should be submitted a month in advance). Churches and chapels have three years in which to claim the support once a grant has been awarded.
WHO TO APPLY TO Janet Arthur, Trustee, 20 Gumley Road, Smeeton Westerby, Leicester LE8 0LT Tel. 0116 279 3995 email chair@lhct.org.uk Website www.lhct.org.uk

### ■ Leicestershire, Leicester and Rutland Community Foundation

CC NO 1135322  ESTABLISHED 2002
WHERE FUNDING CAN BE GIVEN Leicestershire, Leicester and Rutland.
WHO CAN BENEFIT Charities and community groups with some preference for smaller groups. The foundation's annual report for 2013/14 states that 'all groups of any size with a basic constitution and a bank account in the group's name are eligible to apply'.
WHAT IS FUNDED A wide range of charitable purposes; community development; local projects.
WHAT IS NOT FUNDED Individuals are not supported, but groups can be helped.
TYPE OF GRANT One-off, running and project costs.
RANGE OF GRANTS Mostly around and under £1,000 but can be up to £30,000.
SAMPLE GRANTS The Bridge Homelessness to Hope (£29,000); Leicester Masaya Link Group (£20,000); Age UK Leicester Shire and Rutland and The Old School Barlestone (£15,000 each); Woodgate Residents Association (£12,500); The Cooke e-Learning Foundation (£5,600); Kaine Management Group (£3,500); Pablo's Horse Sanctuary (£2,500); Bottesford Football Club (£2,000); Go-Ahead Youth, Heart of the Forest Festival, St Egelwin's Church Scalford and The Meadows Community Group (£1,000 each); 4Ward Strokes Leicester (£500); Endeavour Club of Desford (£140); and Rutland Food Bank (£30).

FINANCES Year 2013/14 Income £1,293,779 Grants £481,175 Grants to organisations £481,175 Assets £1,946,895
TRUSTEES Mary Chesterton; Steven White; John Strange; James Kirkpatrick; Rick Moore; Ivan Trevor; Joan Stephens; Justine Flack; Stuart Dawkins; Sean Tizzard; Trevor Shaw; Judith Golboy.
OTHER INFORMATION Grants were given to 194 organisations.
HOW TO APPLY Details of funds open for applications are available online. The foundation welcomes enquiries prior to the submission of formal applications either via phone or email. The application process differs depending on the scheme applied for with some schemes using online application forms and others using more traditional paper based forms. The annual report states that 'grants are given on a monthly basis, to enable prompt response'.
WHO TO APPLY TO Hannah Stevens, Funds Co-ordinator, 3 Wycliffe Street, Leicester LE1 5LR Tel. 0116 262 4916 email grants@llrcommunityfoundation.org.uk or hannah.stevens@llrcommunityfoundation.org.uk Website www.llrcommunityfoundation.org.uk

### ■ P Leigh-Bramwell Trust 'E'

CC NO 267333  ESTABLISHED 1973
WHERE FUNDING CAN BE GIVEN UK, with a preference for Bolton.
WHO CAN BENEFIT Registered charities and charitable organisations; schools and universities; hospices; churches. The trust has specific regular allocations, with limited opportunity to add further charities.
WHAT IS FUNDED General charitable purposes. Support is particularly given to Methodist causes and Bolton-based organisations.
WHAT IS NOT FUNDED Grants are not made to individuals.
TYPE OF GRANT Mainly recurrent grants to established beneficiaries.
RANGE OF GRANTS £500–£30,000; most awards are of £1,000–£2,000.
SAMPLE GRANTS North Bolton Methodist Mission (£30,000); The Methodist Church – Bolton Circuit (£11,000); Rivington Parish Church (£6,200); DEC – Philippines Typhoon Appeal and Fet-Lor Youth Club (£5,000 each); Barnes Methodist Church and Octagon Theatre Trust (£2,500 each); Ulverston Inshore Rescue, Save the Children and Trinity Hospice (£2,000 each); Institute of Cancer Research, The Salvation Army and The Samaritans (£1,000 each); and ChildLine North West and Bolton YMCA (£500 each).
FINANCES Year 2013/14 Income £1,180,466 Grants £121,688 Grants to organisations £121,688 Assets £3,368,772
TRUSTEES Jennifer Mitchell; Brian Leigh-Bramwell.
OTHER INFORMATION The trust made 48 awards, including six charities additional to the list of regular beneficiaries.
HOW TO APPLY Applications may be made in writing to the correspondent; however, our research suggests that there is only a small amount of funds available for unsolicited applications and therefore success is unlikely.
WHO TO APPLY TO L. Cooper, Secretary, Suite 2E, Atria, Spa Road, Bolton BL1 4AG Tel. 01204 364656 email carol.spoor@leighbrothers.com

## ■ The Kennedy Leigh Charitable Trust

**CC NO** 288293   **ESTABLISHED** 1983
**WHERE FUNDING CAN BE GIVEN** UK and overseas, including Israel.
**WHO CAN BENEFIT** Registered charities only.
**WHAT IS FUNDED** 'Projects and causes which will improve and enrich the lives of all parts of society, not least those of the young, the needy, the disadvantaged and the underprivileged'. The trust's objects require three-quarters of its grant-making funds to be distributed to charitable institutions within Israel, with the remainder being distributed in the UK and elsewhere.
**WHAT IS NOT FUNDED** Individuals.
**TYPE OF GRANT** Capital and core costs; usually up to three years, with the possibility of renewal.
**RANGE OF GRANTS** Up to £27,500.
**SAMPLE GRANTS** Chai-Lifeline (£27,500); Yadid la Chinuch (£25,000); British Friends of the Hebrew University and T'Lalim (£20,000 each); Jewish Association for the Mentally Ill (£17,500); Yemin Orde (£16,000); Eliya, Jewish Care and Norwood Ravenswood (£10,000 each); The Israel Family Planning Association (£8,500); Oxford Centre for Hebrew and Jewish Studies (£5,000); other awards totalled £2,300.
**FINANCES** Year 2013/14 Income £448,485 Grants £218,217 Grants to organisations £218,217 Assets £20,053,250
**TRUSTEES** Anthony Foux; Geoffrey Goldkorn; Angela Sorkin; Alexander Sorkin; Carole Berman; Benjamin Goldkorn.
**OTHER INFORMATION** In 2013/14 there were 17 grants made.
**HOW TO APPLY** The annual report for 2013/14 notes: 'The funds available for distribution outside of Israel are all but committed for the foreseeable future to several UK charities. The Trustees are therefore unable to consider applications for funding from charitable organisations outside of Israel at this time.'
**WHO TO APPLY TO** Naomi Shoffman, Correspondent, ORT House, 126 Albert Street, London NW1 7NE  *Tel.* 020 7267 6500

## ■ Morris Leigh Foundation

**CC NO** 280695   **ESTABLISHED** 1980
**WHERE FUNDING CAN BE GIVEN** UK and overseas.
**WHO CAN BENEFIT** Charitable organisations, with a strong preference for Jewish organisations with interests abroad, especially Israel.
**WHAT IS FUNDED** General charitable purposes with focus on Jewish faith, including the arts and humanities, education, culture and welfare causes.
**RANGE OF GRANTS** £1,000–£15,000
**SAMPLE GRANTS** Institute of Jewish Policy Research (£15,000); JCC Donations Account (£10,000); Jerusalem Foundation (£7,500); and Nightingale House (£5,000).
**FINANCES** Year 2013/14 Income £39,402 Grants £37,500 Grants to organisations £37,500 Assets £1,696,920
**TRUSTEES** Martin Paisner; Howard Leigh.
**OTHER INFORMATION** There were four grants made in 2013/14.
**HOW TO APPLY** Applications may be made in writing to the correspondent.
**WHO TO APPLY TO** Tina Grant-Brook, Correspondent, 40 Portland Place, London W1B 1NB  *Tel.* 020 7908 6000

## ■ The Leigh Trust

**CC NO** 275372   **ESTABLISHED** 1976
**WHERE FUNDING CAN BE GIVEN** UK and overseas.
**WHO CAN BENEFIT** Charitable organisations benefitting disadvantaged and vulnerable people of any age, including children and young adults, older people, individuals out of work, volunteers, people in care, fostered or adopted individuals, ethnic groups, individuals at risk groups, people who have offended or are at risk of offending, refugees, asylum seekers, socially isolated people, victims of abuse and crime and people with substance abuse problems.
**WHAT IS FUNDED** The current priority of the trust is helping drug and alcohol rehabilitation, criminal justice, asylum seekers, racial equality and education. Awards can be made to support legal services, voluntary and community activities, volunteering, health counselling, support and self-help groups, social counselling, crime prevention and rehabilitation schemes, international rights of the individual, advice and information on social issues and similar causes.
**WHAT IS NOT FUNDED** The trust does not make grants to individuals.
**TYPE OF GRANT** Our research suggests that one-off or recurrent grants can be given for buildings, capital and core costs, projects, salaries and start-up costs. Funding is available for up to three years.
**RANGE OF GRANTS** £200–£6,000
**FINANCES** Year 2013/14 Income £104,110 Grants £119,700 Grants to organisations £119,700 Assets £3,213,686
**TRUSTEES** David Bernstein; Caroline Moorehead.
**HOW TO APPLY** Organisations applying for grants must provide their most recent audited accounts, a registered charity number, a cash flow statement for the next 12 months, and a stamped addressed envelope. Applicants should state clearly on one side of A4 what their charity does and what they are requesting funding for. They should provide a detailed budget and show other sources of funding for the project.
**WHO TO APPLY TO** The Trustees, Begbies Chartered Accountants, Epworth House, 25 City Road, London EC1Y 1AR  *Tel.* 020 7628 5801 *Fax* 020 7628 0390  *email* admin@begbiesaccountants.co.uk

## ■ The Lennox and Wyfold Foundation

**CC NO** 1080198   **ESTABLISHED** 2000
**WHERE FUNDING CAN BE GIVEN** UK and overseas, including Africa, India and Russia.
**WHO CAN BENEFIT** Registered charities.
**WHAT IS FUNDED** General charitable purposes.
**TYPE OF GRANT** Unrestricted funding, including core and capital costs and project expenditure.
**RANGE OF GRANTS** Up to £27,000.
**SAMPLE GRANTS** The Maggie's Cancer Caring Centres Trust – Oxon (£27,000); Maggie's Cancer Caring Centres (£25,000); and Contented Dementia, Friends of Bucklebury C of E School and Royal Scots Dragoon Guards (£20,000 each). There were 89 further donations of £15,000 or under totalling almost £350,000. **Previous beneficiaries have included:** Breakthrough Breast Cancer; Absolute Return for Kids; RNIB; Deafblind UK; Amber Foundation; Tusk Trust; Elephant Family; St George's Chapel – Windsor; Bucklebury Memorial Hall; Chipping Norton Theatre and Friends Trust; Gloucestershire Air Ambulance;

Mary Hare Foundation; and Reform Research Trust.
**FINANCES** Year 2013/14 Income £658,842 Grants £461,750 Grants to organisations £461,750 Assets £37,425,842
**TRUSTEES** Adam Fleming; Christopher Fleming; Caroline Wilmot-Sitwell.
**OTHER INFORMATION** A total of 94 awards were made during the year, including 89 grants of £15,000 or less.
**HOW TO APPLY** Applications may be made in writing to the correspondent. The trustees meet twice a year to discuss applications each of which is reviewed on its own personal merit.
**WHO TO APPLY TO** P. Caruana, Correspondent, RF Trustee Co Limited, 15 Suffolk Street, London SW1Y 4HG Tel. 020 7036 5685 email charities@rftrustee.com

## ■ The Erica Leonard Trust
**CC NO** 291627  **ESTABLISHED** 1985
**WHERE FUNDING CAN BE GIVEN** Mainly Surrey and occasionally overseas.
**WHO CAN BENEFIT** Registered charities only.
**WHAT IS FUNDED** General charitable purposes.
**RANGE OF GRANTS** Most grants are for £1,000 or less.
**SAMPLE GRANTS** Previous beneficiaries have included: Phoenix Trust (£9,000); Wells for India (£4,000); Leonard Trust (£2,000); The Meath Epilepsy Trust, Kensington Philharmonica Orchestra Trust, International Refugee Trust and Haslemere Educational Museum (£1,000 each); Macmillan Cancer Support, Christian Solidarity World Wide and Rainbow Trust (£750 each); Marie Curie Cancer Care (£500); Coundon Care Centre Charity (£250); Prisoners Fellowship (£200).
**FINANCES** Year 2013/14 Income £19,340 Grants £38,000 Grants to organisations £38,000
**TRUSTEES** Richard Grey; Richard Beeston; Andrew Lodge.
**HOW TO APPLY** Apply in writing to the correspondent.
**WHO TO APPLY TO** Richard Grey, Trustee, Old Farmhouse, Farnham Road, Elstead, Goldaming, Surrey GU8 6DB Tel. 01252 702230 email rcegrey@aol.com

## ■ The Mark Leonard Trust
**CC NO** 1040323  **ESTABLISHED** 1994
**WHERE FUNDING CAN BE GIVEN** Worldwide, but mainly UK.
**WHO CAN BENEFIT** 'Registered charities or activities with clearly defined charitable purposes' educational establishments.
**WHAT IS FUNDED** 'Sustainable agriculture and food; tackling climate change, energy efficiency and renewable energy; youth work that supports the rehabilitation of young people involved in anti-social or criminal activities, and helps remove the barriers to social inclusion.' Also general charitable causes.
**WHAT IS NOT FUNDED** Individuals; educational fees; expeditions.
**TYPE OF GRANT** One-off and multi-year grants; capital costs.
**RANGE OF GRANTS** £1,200–£304,000
**SAMPLE GRANTS** Just for Kids Law (£304,100); Sustainable Restaurant Association (£194,500 in five grants); Leon Foundation (£75,000 in two grants); Canterbury Cast Trust (£39,000); City University (£36,000); Royal Society of Arts (£31,500); Climate News Network (£14,000); University of Leeds (£6,700); Flying Seagull Project (£5,900); UK Green Building Council (£4,300); Aldeburgh Food and Drink Festival Ltd (£2,500); Low Carbon Community Network (£1,700); Badgers Bridge Forest School (£1,200).
**FINANCES** Year 2013/14 Income £1,408,509 Grants £951,191 Grants to organisations £951,191 Assets £16,749,413
**TRUSTEES** Zivi Sainsbury; Judith Portrait; John Sainsbury; Mark Sainsbury.
**OTHER INFORMATION** This is one of The Sainsbury family trusts, which share administration. A single application will be considered for support by all the charities in the group. During the year a total of 37 grants were approved (some payable over more than one year) totalling over £1.2 million. The figure we used refers to grants paid in the year. Awards were paid as follows: environment (£731,500); youth work (£143,000); climate change collaboration (£53,000); general (£23,500).
**HOW TO APPLY** The website notes: 'The trustees do not accept unsolicited proposals. Their grant-making focuses on a small portfolio of charities which receive sustained support over an extended period.' It is further reminded in the accounts: 'Unsolicited applications are discouraged and are unlikely to be successful.'
**WHO TO APPLY TO** Alan Bookbinder, Director, Sainsbury Family Charitable Trusts, The Peak, 5 Wilton Road, London SW1V 1AP Tel. 020 7410 0330 Fax 020 7410 0332 email info@sfct.org.uk Website www.sfct.org.uk

## ■ The Leverhulme Trade Charities Trust
**CC NO** 288404  **ESTABLISHED** 1983
**WHERE FUNDING CAN BE GIVEN** UK.
**WHO CAN BENEFIT** Charities connected with and benefitting commercial travellers, grocers or chemists, and their dependants, especially those disadvantaged by poverty; benevolent societies; educational institutions.
**WHAT IS FUNDED** Social welfare; education and training; research.
**WHAT IS NOT FUNDED** Capital grants; general appeals; individual grants are only made through charitable organisations.
**TYPE OF GRANT** One-off and recurrent grants.
**SAMPLE GRANTS** Commercial Travellers' Benevolent Institution (£338,000); Provision Trade Benevolent Institution (£21,000).
**FINANCES** Year 2014 Income £2,227,000 Grants £1,789,000 Grants to organisations £1,789,000 Assets £61,815,000
**TRUSTEES** Sir Iain Anderson; Niall Fitzgerald; Patrick Cescau; Dr Ashok Ganguly; Paul Polman.
**OTHER INFORMATION** Grants to institutions were made totalling £359,000 in grants for benevolence. A further £1.4 million was given to institutions for undergraduate bursaries and £360,000 for postgraduate bursaries.
**HOW TO APPLY** Applications for bursaries need to be made using an online application system on the trust's website (deadlines are in November and March for undergraduate and October for postgraduate funding). Applications from eligible institutions on behalf of qualifying individuals need to be made in writing to the correspondent.
**WHO TO APPLY TO** Paul Read, Secretary, 1 Pemberton Row, London EC4A 3BG Tel. 020 7042 9881 Fax 020 7042 9889 email pdread@leverhulme.ac.uk Website www.leverhulme-trade.org.uk

## ■ The Leverhulme Trust

**CC NO** 288371　　**ESTABLISHED** 1925
**WHERE FUNDING CAN BE GIVEN** Generally unrestricted, excluding USA.
**WHO CAN BENEFIT** Educational establishments; research bodies; registered charities; individuals.
**WHAT IS FUNDED** Funding across academic disciplines; support to talented individuals in the arts, humanities, sciences and social sciences for research and professional training; substantial grants for original research; fellowships for researchers at every stage of their career; grants for international collaboration and travel; support for the fine and performing arts. The trust notes that 'as far as possible, it takes a non-utilitarian and academy-focused approach to funding'.
**WHAT IS NOT FUNDED** Core funding or overheads for institutions (a proportion of overheads may be recovered through the Charity Research Support Fund); individual items of equipment over £1,000; sites, buildings or other capital expenditure; support for the organisation of conferences or workshops, which are not directly associated with International Networks, Early Career Fellowships, Visiting Fellowships or Philip Leverhulme Prizes; contributions to appeals; endowments; a shortfall resulting from a withdrawal of or deficiency in public finance; UK student fees where these are not associated with an application for Research Project Grants, Research Programme Grants, the Arts Scholarships, or with a nomination for a Philip Leverhulme Prize; research where advocacy is an explicit component; research aimed principally at an immediate commercial application; proposals in which the balance between assembling a data bank or database and the related subsequent research is heavily inclined to the former. Continuing activities, established research groups or teams and proposals from established groups working on subjects, areas and themes where the Research Councils have a significant interest are unlikely to be supported. The trust 'is keen to avoid assuming the role of "funder of last resort"'. If you are unsure about your eligibility do not hesitate to contact the trust prior to applying.
**TYPE OF GRANT** One-off; projects; research; running costs; salaries.
**RANGE OF GRANTS** Depends on the scheme and can be up to £1 million a year.
**SAMPLE GRANTS** University of Cambridge (£5.5 million in 46 grants); University of Nottingham (£4.7 million in 17 grants); Durham University (£3.9 million in 18 grants); University of Glasgow (£2.3 million in 11 grants); British Academy (£1.8 million in two grants); University of Southampton (£1.8 million in 13 grants); London School of Economics and Political Science (£1.6 million in eight grants); Open University (£1.4 million in six grants); University of Huddersfield (£1.3 million in three grants); Swansea University (£766,000 in five grants); School of Oriental and African Studies (£750,000 in nine grants); Newcastle University (£517,000 in five grants). Grants below £500,000 to 40 individuals and 51 institutions totalled £6.7 million.
**FINANCES** Year 2014 Income £78,794,000 Grants £85,387,000 Grants to organisations £85,387,000 Assets £2,143,755
**TRUSTEES** Sir Ian Anderson; Patrick Cescau; Niall Fitzgerald; Dr Ashok Ganguly; Paul Polman.
**OTHER INFORMATION Note**: In 2014 the trustees transferred all the assets, liabilities and undertakings of the trust to a newly formed CIO (Charity Commission no. 1159154) which carries the same name and objects as the trust. We have used the former trust's accounts as the new entity has not produced any yet. During the year a total of 644 grants were awarded, including to 40 individuals. The grant total includes both organisations and individuals (institutional awards amount to at least over £78 million).
**HOW TO APPLY** Each programme, scholarship and award has its own individual application deadlines and procedures. Full details and guidelines for each scheme are available from the trust directly or via its website. Consult the full contact details on the trust's website to determine which person is the most suitable to approach. In assessing appeals the trustees evaluate the project's originality, importance, significance and merit. Cross-disciplinary projects may be favoured.
**WHO TO APPLY TO** Paul Read, 1 Pemberton Row, London EC4A 3BG *Tel.* 020 7042 9888 *Fax* 020 7042 9889 *email* pread@leverhulme.ac.uk *Website* www.leverhulme.ac.uk

## ■ Lord Leverhulme's Charitable Trust

**CC NO** 212431　　**ESTABLISHED** 1957
**WHERE FUNDING CAN BE GIVEN** UK, especially Cheshire, Merseyside and Lancashire.
**WHO CAN BENEFIT** Registered and exempt charities. Preference is given to Cheshire, Merseyside, Lancashire and surrounding areas and those charities that have been supported by the settlor or are favoured by the Leverhulme family members.
**WHAT IS FUNDED** General charitable purposes; environment and animal welfare; education; the arts; health and disability; young people; religious causes; community purposes.
**TYPE OF GRANT** Recurrent, one-off and capital expenditure.
**RANGE OF GRANTS** Up to £200,000.
**SAMPLE GRANTS** Liverpool Heart and Chest Hospital (£100,000 in five grants); York Minster Fund (£100,000 in one grant); Animal Health Trust (£51,000 in two grants); Claire House and Royal College of Surgeons (£50,000 each); Moreton Hall School Science Block (£25,000); Prince's Youth Trust (£21,500 in two grants); and Highland Hospice (£20,000). Smaller donations were not listed.
**FINANCES** Year 2013/14 Income £653,887 Grants £723,749 Grants to organisations £723,749 Assets £31,341,406
**TRUSTEES** Algernon Heber-Percy; Anthony Hannay; Henry Wilson.
**HOW TO APPLY** The trust states in its annual report: 'Priority is given [...] to applications from Cheshire, Merseyside and South Lancashire and the charities supported by the settlor in his lifetime. Others who do not meet those criteria should not apply without prior invitation but should, on a single sheet, state briefly their aims and apply fully only on being asked to do so. A handful of charities have heeded this warning and telephoned our administrator but the continuing volume of applications from charities which plainly do not meet the stated criteria suggests that many applicants do not concern themselves with their target's policies. Generally, the trustees do not acknowledge receipt of applications or notify unsuccessful

applicants in order to minimise management expense.'
**WHO TO APPLY TO** Lynne Loxley, Correspondent, Leverhulme Estate Office, Hesketh Grange, Manor Road, Thornton Hough, Wirral CH63 1JD *Tel.* 0151 336 4828 *Fax* 0151 353 0265 *email* lynne.loxley@leverhulmeestates.co.uk

## ■ Joseph Levy Charitable Foundation

**CC NO** 245592      **ESTABLISHED** 1965
**WHERE FUNDING CAN BE GIVEN** UK and Israel.
**WHO CAN BENEFIT** Registered charities benefitting children and young people, older people, working with health causes or medical research.
**WHAT IS FUNDED** General charitable purposes; young people; older people; arts, culture and sports; health; medical research; community care; social welfare.
**WHAT IS NOT FUNDED** Individuals; large appeals.
**TYPE OF GRANT** Project costs; capital and core costs; research; salaries; start-up costs; up to and over three years.
**RANGE OF GRANTS** £1,000–£54,500
**SAMPLE GRANTS** Dementia UK (£54,500 – not required during the year); Creative Future and Friends of Israel Education Fund (£15,000 each); Community Security Trust (£10,000); Oxford Centre for Hebrew Jewish Studies (£5,000 – not required during the year); Stroke Association (£4,000); Cystic Fibrosis Trust (£1,500); Awards for Young Musicians, Lifelites and Sussex Wildlife Trust (£1,000 each).
**FINANCES** Year 2013/14 *Income* £808,316 *Grants* £91,834 *Grants to organisations* £91,834 *Assets* £18,292,959
**TRUSTEES** Jane Jason; Peter Levy; Melanie Levy; Claudia Giat; James Jason.
**OTHER INFORMATION** In 2013/14 a total of ten grants were paid. Further grants were approved for distribution in the coming three years. Support costs totalled £190,000 and governance – further £28,500.
**HOW TO APPLY** The foundation's website states: 'The Trustees wish to inform you that due to current commitments, the Foundation is no longer able to accept unsolicited applications.' Should there be a change in the policy it will be announced on the website.
**WHO TO APPLY TO** Roland Gyallay-Pap, Grants Administrator, 1st Floor, 1 Bell Street, London NW1 5BY *Tel.* 020 7616 1200 *Fax* 020 7616 1206 *email* info@jlf.org.uk *Website* www.jlf.org.uk

## ■ David and Ruth Lewis Family Charitable Trust

**CC NO** 259892      **ESTABLISHED** 1962
**WHERE FUNDING CAN BE GIVEN** UK and Israel.
**WHO CAN BENEFIT** Charitable bodies and research institutions.
**WHAT IS FUNDED** 'Virtually every generally accepted charitable object' health causes; medical research, particularly into possible treatments for cancer; Jewish community work; educational funding, support for older people; children and social care; poverty and disaster relief.
**WHAT IS NOT FUNDED** Grants are not made to individuals (unless in exceptional circumstances).
**TYPE OF GRANT** Potentially up to three years but mostly one-off.
**RANGE OF GRANTS** Up to £250,000.

**SAMPLE GRANTS** Institute of Cancer Research (£250,000); Jewish Care (£67,000); Cambridge University Hospital (£65,000); United Jewish Israel Appeal (£55,000); British Friends of Ezer Mizion (£50,000); The Anna Freud Centre (£36,000); Norwood (£35,000); Jewish Leadership Council (£30,000); Save The Children and The Pares Centre for Peace (£20,000 each); and The Jaffa Institute (£18,000).
**FINANCES** Year 2013/14 *Income* £1,764,162 *Grants* £856,091 *Grants to organisations* £856,091 *Assets* £11,214,666
**TRUSTEES** Julian Lewis; Deborah Lewis; Benjamin Lewis; Simon Lewis.
**OTHER INFORMATION** Grants of £17,500 or less totalled about £159,000. Major grants were given to 13 organisations.
**HOW TO APPLY** Applications may be made in writing to the correspondent.
**WHO TO APPLY TO** The Secretary, Chelsea House, West Gate, Ealing, London W5 1DR *Tel.* 020 8991 4502

## ■ The John Spedan Lewis Foundation

**CC NO** 240473      **ESTABLISHED** 1964
**WHERE FUNDING CAN BE GIVEN** UK.
**WHO CAN BENEFIT** Charitable organisations; educational institutions. The focus is on applications for small projects connected with the natural sciences and of educational nature, particularly benefitting, children, young adults and research workers.
**WHAT IS FUNDED** Natural sciences, particularly horticulture, ornithology, entomology, environmental education, conservation and associated educational and research projects – areas of particular interests to John Spedan Lewis, the founder of John Lewis Partnership. The trustees will also consider applications from organisations for imaginative and original educational projects aimed at developing serious interest and evident talent, particularly among young people. Funding is also given to a small number of PhD research projects on specific topics chosen by the trustees and to selected universities and research institutes.
**WHAT IS NOT FUNDED** Support is not normally made to local branches of national organisations, to cover salaries, medical research, welfare projects, building works or overseas expeditions. Unsolicited applications for PhD funding from individuals, universities or research institutes are not considered.
**TYPE OF GRANT** Mostly one-off donations for project and capital expenditure. Salaries are not normally funded.
**RANGE OF GRANTS** £500–£7,000
**SAMPLE GRANTS** Severn Rivers Trust (£6,000); Chelsea Physic Garden Company (£5,000); Nottingham Trent University Trust Fund (£4,600); Northumberland Wildlife Trust Limited (£4,500); Organisation Cetacea – ORCA (£4,000); Hertfordshire and Middlesex Wildlife Trust Limited (£3,900); Gloucestershire Wildlife Trust (£3,700); Portland Bird Observatory and Field Centre (£3,300).
**FINANCES** Year 2013/14 *Income* £59,454 *Grants* £65,096 *Grants to organisations* £65,096 *Assets* £2,536,583
**TRUSTEES** Charlie Mayfield; David Jones; Dr Vaughan Southgate; Dr John David; Gerrard Keogh-Peters.

**OTHER INFORMATION** The foundation made nine awards to organisations and two individual grants (multi-year awards for research purposes at the Durrell Institute of Conservation and Ecology and University of Kent totalling £30,000).
**HOW TO APPLY** Applications may be made in writing to the correspondent providing the latest annual report and set of accounts and a budget for the proposed project.
**WHO TO APPLY TO** Bridget Chamberlain, Secretary, Partnership House, Carlisle Place, London SW1P 1BX *Tel.* 020 7592 6121 *email* jslf@johnlewis.co.uk

■ **The Sir Edward Lewis Foundation**
**CC NO** 264475   **ESTABLISHED** 1972
**WHERE FUNDING CAN BE GIVEN** UK and overseas, with a preference for Surrey.
**WHO CAN BENEFIT** Registered charities.
**WHAT IS FUNDED** General charitable purposes. According to the annual report for 2013/14, 'the trustees have adopted a practice to make donations to a number of charities who receive payments from the foundation on a regular annual basis; however new appeals are reviewed and donations are allocated accordingly'.
**WHAT IS NOT FUNDED** Individuals. Grants are generally only given to charities, projects or people known to the trustees.
**TYPE OF GRANT** Unrestricted, including core and capital costs, salaries and project funding.
**RANGE OF GRANTS** £500–£35,000; mostly under £2,000.
**SAMPLE GRANTS** Ridgegate Homes and The Arnold Foundation for Rugby School (£35,000 each); Arthritis Research UK (£15,000); Children's Trust Tadworth, Gurkha Welfare Trust and St Anthony's Hospital (£5,000 each); Marie Curie Cancer Care (£4,000); Ophthalmic Aid to Eastern Europe (£3,000); Afghan Connection, Edward Lloyd Trust, Royal British Legion and Wildlife Aid (£2,000); Shipwrecked Fishermans Society (£1,500); City Chamber Choir, SSAFA and War Memorials Trust (£1,000 each); Royal National Institute of the Blind and Uphill Ski Club (£500 each).
**FINANCES** *Year* 2013/14 *Income* £270,896 *Grants* £265,500 *Grants to organisations* £265,500 *Assets* £9,043,504
**TRUSTEES** Richard Lewis; Mark Harris; Christine Lewis; Sarah Dorin.
**OTHER INFORMATION** The trustees prefer to support charities known personally to them and those favoured by the settlor. During the year a total of 99 awards were made. Small awards (under £5,000) totalled £130,500.
**HOW TO APPLY** Applications should be made in writing to the correspondent. The trustees meet every six months, in May and December.
**WHO TO APPLY TO** Darren Wing, Rawlinson and Hunter, The Lower Mill, Kingston Road, Ewell, Surrey KT17 2AE *Tel.* 020 7842 2000 *email* lewis.foundation@rawlinson-hunter.com

■ **John Lewis Partnership General Community Fund**
**CC NO** 209128   **ESTABLISHED** 1961
**WHERE FUNDING CAN BE GIVEN** UK.
**WHO CAN BENEFIT** UK and local registered charities, benefitting children and young adults, at risk groups, people who are sick or who have disabilities, people disadvantaged by poverty and those who are socially isolated; medical professionals and research workers may be considered.
**WHAT IS FUNDED** Welfare; music; arts; education; environment; community causes; young people; relief of poverty.
**WHAT IS NOT FUNDED** Loans; sponsorship; religious, ethnic or political groups; advertising; individuals; third-party fundraising.
**TYPE OF GRANT** One-off and recurring.
**RANGE OF GRANTS** £500–£150,000
**SAMPLE GRANTS** The British Red Cross Society (£150,000); Retail Trust (£50,000); Teenage Cancer Trust (£32,500); Bipolar UK Ltd (£19,000); Welsh Air Ambulance Charitable Trust (£11,400); Carers UK (£8,700); Scope (£6,900); Fishing for Forces, Guernsey Extreme Sports Association LBG and Pimlico Family Workshop Toy Library (£5,000 each); New Sussex Opera and The Windsor Festival Society Limited (£2,000 each); Lingfield Silver Band (£1,200); The Music Makers and The Waverley Singers (£1,000 each); London Conducting Workshop (£750); Springfield Infant School and Nursery (£500).
**FINANCES** *Year* 2013/14 *Income* £672,129 *Grants* £672,129 *Grants to organisations* £672,129
**TRUSTEES** Catherine Houchin; Charlie Mayfield; Mark Price; Ian Hiscock; Derek Bond.
**OTHER INFORMATION** In 2013/14 grants were awarded to 114 organisations. The website states: 'The Partnership favours charities local to the communities where we operate or in which Partners are personally involved.' The charity's record on the Charity Commission's website notes that it 'allocates approximately £1 million per annum for charitable purposes'.
**HOW TO APPLY** The charity provided the following information: 'If you have a cause you think we could support, contact the Waitrose champion for community giving at your local branch (www.waitrose.com) or the John Lewis Community Liaison Coordinator at your local branch (www.johnlewis.com). As we are contacted by so many organisations throughout the year, we cannot always give you a swift reply, but we will reply as soon as possible if we can help.'
**WHO TO APPLY TO** The Correspondent, Partnership House, Carlisle Place, London SW1P 1BX *Website* www.johnlewispartnership.co.uk

■ **The Lewis Ward Trust**
**CC NO** 1100891   **ESTABLISHED** 2003
**WHERE FUNDING CAN BE GIVEN** UK and overseas
**WHO CAN BENEFIT** Registered charities.
**WHAT IS FUNDED** Children, particularly those with special needs or disabilities, are deprived or terminally ill or are lacking adequate nutrition and education.
**RANGE OF GRANTS** Generally £1,000.
**FINANCES** *Year* 2013/14 *Income* £28,840 *Grants* £39,000 *Grants to organisations* £39,000 *Assets* £25,689
**TRUSTEES** Margaret Waugh; Revd Gareth Jones (Chair); Kevin Ward; Stephanie Cheetham; Bernard Cheetham.
**OTHER INFORMATION** A list of beneficiaries was not available.
**HOW TO APPLY** Apply in writing to the correspondent. 'The trustees meet twice a year, when appeals for grants are considered and depending on

monies available, donations are sent to those organisations it is felt are in greatest need.'
**WHO TO APPLY TO** Margaret Waugh, Trustee, 2 Abraham Court, Lutton Close, Oswestry SY11 2TH *Tel.* 01691 688892

## ■ LHR Airport Communities Trust

**CC NO** 1058617    **ESTABLISHED** 1996
**WHERE FUNDING CAN BE GIVEN** Communities local to Heathrow Airport Holdings Group's four UK airports; Aberdeen, Glasgow, Heathrow and Southampton.
**WHO CAN BENEFIT** National/international charities, delivering projects in or involving people from the communities local to Heathrow Airport Holdings Group's airports; locally-based charitable organisations; schools and local authorities delivering community projects; grassroots community groups and organisations; local grant-makers; national/international charities in support of staff fundraising activity.
**WHAT IS FUNDED** The trust was established to help communities, primarily those around BAA Limited airports, meet the challenges of the 21st Century. Through their grants they aim to create learning opportunities for young people and so raise their aspirations, break down barriers to employment through skills development, help protect the environment and support airport staff active in the community.
**WHAT IS NOT FUNDED** Applications which benefit individuals only, whether or not they meet the other criteria, will fail. No support is given for religious or political projects. Grants will not be made to nationally based organisations unless the direct benefit will be felt locally and the other criteria are satisfied. The trust does not support general running costs or staff costs.
**RANGE OF GRANTS** Up to £150,000.
**SAMPLE GRANTS** Groundwork South Trust Limited (£147,000) Eastleigh Youth Trust (£50,000); Kibbleworks (£38,000); the Challenge Network (£25,000); Volunteer Centre Hounslow (£12,600); Friends of the River Crane (£6,400); Houston Playpark Improvement Group (£2,500); the Conservation Volunteers (£2,000); Hamble Sea Scouts, Mackie Academy School Fund (£1,000 each); Tonic Music for Mental Health and Woodlands Primary School (£500 each).
**FINANCES** *Year* 2013 *Income* £930,974 *Grants* £1,025,855 *Grants to organisations* £1,025,855 *Assets* £775,268
**TRUSTEES** Mary Francis; Alison Moore; Alan Coates; Matthew Gorman; Clare Harbord; Punham Karbanda; Steve Ronald; Christine Rawlings.
**OTHER INFORMATION** In 2013 grants were given to 243 organisations.
**HOW TO APPLY** Each airport runs its own community fund. Application forms, criteria and guidelines, for the four funds, are available to download on the website. Before making a formal grant application, email a summary of your proposal to your local community fund representative, or the correspondent, so that they can give guidance. The trustees meet four times a year to assess applications over £5,000. Each local panel meets at least three times a year to consider applications under £5,000.
**WHO TO APPLY TO** Caroline Nicholls, Director, LHR Airports Limited, The Compass Centre, Nelson Road, Hounslow, Middlesex TW6 2GW *Tel.* 07836 342495 *email* communitiestrust@heathrow.com *Website* www.baacommunitiestrust.com

## ■ Liberum Foundation

**CC NO** 1137475    **ESTABLISHED** 2010
**WHERE FUNDING CAN BE GIVEN** UK, with preference for London.
**WHO CAN BENEFIT** Organisations; individuals.
**WHAT IS FUNDED** General charitable purposes, including education and training, relief of poverty, sports, recreation and well-being and community and economic development; all with a focus on disadvantaged young people.
**WHAT IS NOT FUNDED** Adult health; hospitals; animals; older people; the armed services; housing; heritage; environment; and religion.
**RANGE OF GRANTS** £400–£50,000
**SAMPLE GRANTS** School Home Support and St Giles Trust (£50,000 each); Arrival Education (£20,000); Just Different (£5,200); 999 Club (£1,000); Help for Heroes (£400).
**FINANCES** *Year* 2013 *Income* £73,344 *Grants* £126,661 *Grants to organisations* £126,661 *Assets* £55,274
**TRUSTEES** Carolyn Doherty; Antony Scawthorn; Timothy Mayo; Nina Dixon; Mary-Jane Clarke.
**OTHER INFORMATION** During the year a total of six awards were made. The majority of the funds available are used to fund specific projects with two of the three main charities supported. According to the annual report for 2013, the trustees' plans for 2014 included 'considering more sustainable funding opportunities which may include social enterprises'.
**HOW TO APPLY** Applications may be made in writing to the correspondent.
**WHO TO APPLY TO** Anthony Scawthorn, Trustee, Ropemaker Place, Level 12, 25 Ropemaker Street, London EC2Y 9LY *Tel.* 020 3100 2000 *email* info@liberumfoundation.com *Website* www.liberum.com/about-liberum/the-liberum-foundation

## ■ Lifeline 4 Kids (Handicapped Children's Aid Committee)

**CC NO** 200050    **ESTABLISHED** 1961
**WHERE FUNDING CAN BE GIVEN** Worldwide.
**WHO CAN BENEFIT** Organisations and bodies supporting children with disabilities (up to the age of 18), including hospitals, hospices, respite care homes, support centres, special schools, social workers and so on; individuals and their families.
**WHAT IS FUNDED** Promotion of the welfare of children with disabilities and special needs; the provision of equipment and services. The charity states that support ranges 'from sophisticated medical requirements to emergency welfare help to individual families'.
**WHAT IS NOT FUNDED** Building projects; garden works; research grants; fridges or washing machines (unless for medical needs); ovens or cookers; salaries; carpets or floor covering; clothing and shoes (unless specialist); childcare costs; transport costs; tuition/school lessons or fees; driving lessons; recreational activities; holidays. Requests for iPads can be awarded only if they satisfy specific requirements – the charity notes that they are inundated with applications for these.
**TYPE OF GRANT** Money for the purchase of equipment. Note that cash grants are **not** given and the purchase is undertaken on behalf of beneficiaries.
**SAMPLE GRANTS** The latest accounts do not give details of specific beneficiaries; however, the website gives some examples of grant recipients. **Beneficiaries have included**:

Mapledown School – Cricklewood; Mapledown School – High Wycombe Bucks; Orcadia Creative Learning Centre – Edinburgh; Save a Child's Heart; South West Scorpions; St Michael's Hospital Bristol; Swiss Cottage SEN School – London; The Living Paintings; The Seashell Trust; Vernon House School – London.

**FINANCES** Year 2013 Income £58,283 Grants £116,589 Grants to organisations £116,589 Assets £335,986

**TRUSTEES** Roger Adelman; Paul Maurice; Beverley Emden; Roberta Harris; Irving Millman; Jeffrey Bonn.

**OTHER INFORMATION** Note: This charity does not administer cash grants. The website states: 'We have in the past helped equip hospital neonatal units with the latest incubators, infusion pumps and ultrasonic monitors amongst other life saving equipment although today our main activity is to help the individual child.' The grant total includes both organisations and individuals.

**HOW TO APPLY** To receive an application form (specify whether via email or post is preferred) you should send an email to appeals@lifeline4kids.org outlining: a specific requirement and its cost; brief factual information about the child (name, DOB, health condition and contact details). Applications from organisations need to give their name and contact details as well as specify the number of children that are likely to benefit, their age group and details of specific requirements together with costs. Full applications are discussed and decided upon at monthly meetings; however, emergency and welfare appeals can be dealt as soon as they come in. The charity asks not to be phoned unless you are in an emergency, as there is not enough staff to deal with calls.

**WHO TO APPLY TO** Roger Adelman, Trustee, 215 West End Lane, West Hampstead, London NW6 1XJ Tel. 020 7794 1661 Fax 020 8459 8826 email appeals@lifeline4kids.org or rda@lifeline4kids.org Website www.lifeline4kids.org

## ■ The Limbourne Trust

**CC NO** 1113796     **ESTABLISHED** 2006
**WHERE FUNDING CAN BE GIVEN** UK and overseas.
**WHO CAN BENEFIT** Charitable organisations; community projects.
**WHAT IS FUNDED** Environment and sustainability; conservation; community projects; disadvantaged people; advancement of education; protection of health; relief of poverty and distress; the arts; other charitable causes.
**RANGE OF GRANTS** £3,000–£10,000
**SAMPLE GRANTS** CHICKS, Farms for City Children and Jubilee Selling Trust (£10,000 each); BEAT (£9,000); Voluntary Action Maidstone/The V team (£7,500); Friends of Sunera Foundation and I Made This (£6,000 each); Bridewell Organic Gardens, Hope and Homes for Children and Excelsior Trust (£5,000 each); Cairdeas/Palliative Care Works (£3,600); and Buckingham Emergency Food Appeal and Listening Books (£3,000 each).
**FINANCES** Year 2013/14 Income £105,660 Grants £98,150 Grants to organisations £98,150 Assets £2,812,048
**TRUSTEES** Elisabeth Thistlethwayte; Katharine Thistlethwayte; Jocelyn Magnus; Dr Andrew Eastaugh.
**OTHER INFORMATION** Grants were made to 16 organisations.

**HOW TO APPLY** The annual report for 2013/14 states: 'The trustees will seek to identify those projects where the greatest and widest benefit can be attained, and usually will only consider written applications and, where necessary, make further enquiries.'
**WHO TO APPLY TO** Elisabeth Thistlethwayte, Trustee, Downs Farm, Homersfield, Harleston IP20 0NS email lizzie_wayte@hotmail.com

## ■ Limoges Charitable Trust

**CC NO** 1016178     **ESTABLISHED** 1991
**WHERE FUNDING CAN BE GIVEN** UK, with a preference for Birmingham.
**WHO CAN BENEFIT** Registered charities.
**WHAT IS FUNDED** General charitable purposes, including health, heritage and community purposes, animals, young people and nautical causes.
**RANGE OF GRANTS** Up to £10,000; most grants under £1,500.
**SAMPLE GRANTS** Birmingham Museum and Art Gallery (£9,300); City of Birmingham Symphony Orchestra, Edward's Trust, Moseley Community Development Trust and Town Hall Symphony Hall (£5,000 each); Hollytrees Animal Rescue Trust (£3,700); Pershore Abbey PCC (£2,300); Birmingham St Mary's Hospice and Elgar Birthplace Trust (£2,000 each); and Lansallos PCC (£1,600).
**FINANCES** Year 2013/14 Income £489,982 Grants £75,874 Grants to organisations £75,874 Assets £1,078,554
**TRUSTEES** Mike Dyer; Judy Dyke; Andrew Milner.
**OTHER INFORMATION** During the year 63 organisations were supported.
**HOW TO APPLY** Applications may be made in writing to the correspondent. The trustees usually meet four times a year to consider appeals.
**WHO TO APPLY TO** Judy Dyke, Trustee, c/o Tyndallwoods Solicitors, 29 Woodbourne Road, Edgbaston, Birmingham B17 8BY Tel. 0121 693 2222 Fax 0121 693 0844 email jdyke@tyndallwoods.co.uk

## ■ The Linbury Trust

**CC NO** 287077     **ESTABLISHED** 1973
**WHERE FUNDING CAN BE GIVEN** Worldwide.
**WHO CAN BENEFIT** Charitable organisations; museums and galleries; educational institutions.
**WHAT IS FUNDED** Arts; education – promoting the study of history, support for organisations that work with those suffering from poor literacy skills or dyslexia and education in the arts; museums and heritage – generally large museums with major development projects; environment – supporting the arts; social welfare – organisations that work with people who are socially excluded and disadvantaged particularly work with young people to reduce or prevent offending; overseas – particularly medical causes in Palestine and scholarship and bursary programmes in South Africa.
**WHAT IS NOT FUNDED** Individuals; educational fees; expeditions.
**TYPE OF GRANT** Running and capital costs; project expenditure.
**RANGE OF GRANTS** Up to £3.4 million.
**SAMPLE GRANTS** British Museum (£3.4 million); Tate Britain (£1 million); Stonehenge (£250,000); Holburne Museum of Art (£131,000); Ashden, Bletchley Park Trust and New Schools Network (£100,000 each); Salisbury and South Wiltshire Museum (£75,000); Marine Society and Sea

Cadets (£62,500); Bodleian Library, Federation of British Artists, Landlife and SMA Trust (£50,000 each); British School at Rome (£49,000); Black Cultural Archives, KeepOut, Pegasus Theatre, The Priory Church of St Bartholomew the Great, University of Bristol and Worldwide Volunteering for Young People (amounts not specified).

**FINANCES** Year 2013/14 Income £8,784,000 Grants £7,221,000 Grants to organisations £7,221,000 Assets £152,540,000

**TRUSTEES** John Sainsbury; Anya Sainsbury; Martin Jacomb; James Spooner.

**OTHER INFORMATION** The trust is one of the Sainsbury family trusts which share a joint administration but work autonomously as independent legal entities. A single application to The Sainsbury Family Charitable Trust is considered for support by all the trusts in the group. A total of 68 organisations were supported during the year.

**HOW TO APPLY** The Linbury trust, as a rule, does not consider unsolicited appeals. The annual report for 2013/14 states: 'The Trustees take a proactive approach towards grant-making; accordingly, unsolicited applications are not usually successful.' Note that a single application to The Sainsbury Family Charitable Trust is considered for support by all the trusts in the group. See further details on The Sainsbury Family Charitable Trust's website.

**WHO TO APPLY TO** Alan Bookbinder, Director, The Peak, 5 Wilton Road, London SW1V 1AP Tel. 020 7410 0330 Fax 020 7410 0332 Website www.linburytrust.org.uk

■ **Lincolnshire Churches Trust**

**CC NO** 509021   **ESTABLISHED** 1952

**WHERE FUNDING CAN BE GIVEN** Lincolnshire.

**WHO CAN BENEFIT** The annual report states that support is given for: 'Christian churches generally of any denomination within the Anglican diocese of Lincoln, being at least 100 years old, needing repairs aimed at excluding wind and weather, achieving safety and security.'

**WHAT IS FUNDED** Preservation, repair and maintenance of churches and monuments, fittings, fixtures, stained glass, furniture, ornament, bells or chattels in such churches within the Anglican diocese of Lincoln. According to the accounts, 'the trustees limit the award of grants to subject of greatest need'.

**WHAT IS NOT FUNDED** Requirements relating to ritual, heating, lighting; repairs to gravestones.

**TYPE OF GRANT** One-off grants for capital costs.

**RANGE OF GRANTS** £1,000–£5,000

**SAMPLE GRANTS** Grantham – St Wulfrum (£5,000); Bloxholme St Mary, Edenham – St Michael and All Angels and Welton le Marsh – St Martin (£4,000 each); Lutton, St Nicholas (£3,000); Raithby – St Peter (£2,400); Coleby – All Saints (£1,500).

**FINANCES** Year 2014 Income £60,947 Grants £43,400 Grants to organisations £43,400 Assets £476,731

**TRUSTEES** Nevile Camamile; Baroness Jane Willoughby de Eresby; David Lawrence; Revd Clifford Knowles; Jeffrey Couzens; Graham Cook; Anthony Worth; Henrietta Reeve; Linda Lord; Mona Dickinson; Nicholas Ridley; Peter Milnes; Jane Ford; Geoffrey Horsfall; The Lord Bishop Of Lincoln; William Cracroft-Eley; Julie Robinson.

**OTHER INFORMATION** There were 14 awards made.

**HOW TO APPLY** Applications may be made in writing to the correspondent.

**WHO TO APPLY TO** Linda Lord, Trustee, c/o Streets Chartered Accountants, Tower House, Lucy Tower Street, Lincoln LN1 1XW Tel. 01522 551200

■ **Lincolnshire Community Foundation**

**CC NO** 1092328   **ESTABLISHED** 2002

**WHERE FUNDING CAN BE GIVEN** Lincolnshire.

**WHO CAN BENEFIT** Organisations supporting people in Lincolnshire.

**WHAT IS FUNDED** General charitable purposes.

**TYPE OF GRANT** One-off and up to three years funding.

**SAMPLE GRANTS Previous beneficiaries have included:** Sleaford Town Council (£5,900); South Holland Radio (£5,100); Technology Strategy Board (£4,900); Cross Sector Solutions (£1,500); Bracebridge (£990).

**FINANCES** Year 2013/14 Income £2,890,204 Grants £872,734 Grants to organisations £872,734 Assets £5,365,343

**TRUSTEES** Richard Ferens; Stephen Cousins; David Close; Jean Burton; Margaret Serna; Dr Cheryle Berry; Jane Hiles; Paul Scott; Lizzie Milligan-Manby; Lesley Chester.

**HOW TO APPLY** Visit the foundation's website for details of current grant schemes. Application forms can be downloaded from the foundation's website or requested by phone.

**WHO TO APPLY TO** Sue Fortune, Grants Manager, 4 Mill House, Moneys Yard, Carre Street, Sleaford, Lincolnshire NG34 7TW Tel. 01529 305825 email lincolnshirecf@btconnect.com Website www.lincolnshirecf.co.uk

■ **The Lind Trust**

**CC NO** 803174   **ESTABLISHED** 1990

**WHERE FUNDING CAN BE GIVEN** UK, particularly Norwich and Norfolk.

**WHO CAN BENEFIT** Churches; charities and charitable organisations; individuals. Beneficiaries should normally be based in Norfolk.

**WHAT IS FUNDED** Development of young people; social action; community and Christian service. Christian causes and youth work are a priority.

**TYPE OF GRANT** Generally one-off.

**RANGE OF GRANTS** Average grant under £1,000.

**SAMPLE GRANTS** The Open Youth Trust (£199,000); and other charities not listed. The trustees are working with the Today's Lifestyle Church to help it become self-sufficient, providing donations of £10,000 a month (to a total of £110,000).

**FINANCES** Year 2013/14 Income £2,015,032 Grants £537,632 Grants to organisations £537,632 Assets £23,497,789

**TRUSTEES** Leslie Brown; Dr Graham Dacre; Gavin Wilcock; Julia Dacre; Samuel Dacre.

**HOW TO APPLY** Applications can be made in writing to the correspondent at any time. However, the trust commits most of its funds in advance, giving the remainder to eligible applicants as received.

**WHO TO APPLY TO** Gavin Wilcock, Trustee, Drayton Hall, Hall Lane, Drayton, Norwich, Norfolk NR8 6DP email accounts@dacrepropertyholdings.com

## ■ Lindale Educational Foundation
**CC NO** 282758   **ESTABLISHED** 1981
**WHERE FUNDING CAN BE GIVEN** UK and overseas.
**WHO CAN BENEFIT** Roman Catholic institutions; charitable organisations benefitting children, young adults and students.
**WHAT IS FUNDED** The promotion of the Roman Catholic religion; the advancement of education in accordance with Christian principles and ideals within the Roman Catholic tradition. This includes: training priests; improvement and maintenance of places of worship; improvement and maintenance of university halls or halls of residence; courses camps, study centres, meetings, conferences and seminars; the provision of grants, scholarships, loans or donations the pursuit of education or research by individuals or groups of students. Most grants are already allocated to specific charities.
**WHAT IS NOT FUNDED** Individuals.
**TYPE OF GRANT** One-off and recurrent; capital and revenue costs.
**RANGE OF GRANTS** £1,000–£24,500
**SAMPLE GRANTS** Netherhall Educational Association Centre (£24,500 in three grants); Thornycroft Hall (£22,000 in three grants); Hazelwood House (£3,300 in two grants); Charity Siddington Trust Limited (£1,300); SFL-Stiftung (£1,000).
**FINANCES** Year 2013/14   Income £65,400   Grants £51,900   Grants to organisations £51,900   Assets £39,198
**TRUSTEES** Dawliffe Hall Educational Foundation; Greygarth Association; Netherhall Educational Association.
**OTHER INFORMATION** A total of five organisations received ten grants.
**HOW TO APPLY** Applications may be made in writing to the correspondent, but note that most funds are already committed.
**WHO TO APPLY TO** Jack Valero, 6 Orme Court, London W2 4RL   *Tel.* 020 7243 9417

## ■ The Linden Charitable Trust
**CC NO** 326788   **ESTABLISHED** 1985
**WHERE FUNDING CAN BE GIVEN** UK, with a preference for West Yorkshire.
**WHO CAN BENEFIT** Registered charities; arts organisations.
**WHAT IS FUNDED** The trust's current policy is to benefit 'charities specialising in cancer relief and research, those particularly involved with hospices, those involved in arts and also a wider range of charities based in and around Leeds, West Yorkshire'. The trustees have agreed to make a regular donation to Leeds international Pianoforte Competition of £10,000 per year.
**WHAT IS NOT FUNDED** Grants are not made to individuals.
**RANGE OF GRANTS** £500–£10,000
**SAMPLE GRANTS** Leeds International Pianoforte Competition (£10,000); Martin House and Yorkshire Air Ambulance (£5,000 each); Caring for Life, Leeds Lieder, Mary Wood Trust and St George's Crypt (£3,000 each); Emma Maltby Memorial, Guide Dogs for the Blind, Henshaw Society for Blind, Leeds Art Collection, RNLI, St Michael's Hospice and Yorkshire Ladies Council of Education (£2,000 each); Emmaus Leeds, Leonard Cheshire Disability and Yorkshire Sculpture Park (£1,000 each); and Sports Relief and Theodora Children's Charity (£500 each).
**FINANCES** Year 2013/14   Income £62,292   Grants £94,500   Grants to organisations £94,500   Assets £2,572,680
**TRUSTEES** Margaret Pearson; Gerald Holbrook; John Swales; Robert Swales.
**OTHER INFORMATION** The trust made 49 awards during the year.
**HOW TO APPLY** Applications can be made in writing to the correspondent. The trustees meet two or three times a year to discuss the awards. Decisions could also be made in between the meetings.
**WHO TO APPLY TO** The Trustees, Baker Tilly Tax and Accounting Ltd, 2 Whitehall Quay, Leeds, West Yorkshire LS1 4HG

## ■ Lindenleaf Charitable Trust
**CC NO** 1124672   **ESTABLISHED** 2008
**WHERE FUNDING CAN BE GIVEN** UK and overseas.
**WHO CAN BENEFIT** Registered charities.
**WHAT IS FUNDED** General charitable purposes, with a particular focus on community development and poverty.
**SAMPLE GRANTS** Previous beneficiaries have included: BEAT; Build It; Camfed; Concern Worldwide; IntoUniversity; and Shannon Trust.
**FINANCES** Year 2013/14   Income £1   Grants £25,000   Grants to organisations £25,000
**TRUSTEES** Henry Charles; Paul Greatbatch; Elizabeth Haycox; Thomas Howells; Helen Norton.
**OTHER INFORMATION** Beneficiaries are typically organisations working to strengthen communities through the relief of poverty or the promotion of social inclusion or other community projects.
**HOW TO APPLY** Applications can be made in writing to the correspondent.
**WHO TO APPLY TO** Paul Greatbatch, Trustee, 344 Fulham Road, London SW10 9UH   *Tel.* 020 7376 4321   *email* paul_greatbatch@hotmail.com

## ■ The Enid Linder Foundation
**CC NO** 267509   **ESTABLISHED** 1974
**WHERE FUNDING CAN BE GIVEN** UK.
**WHO CAN BENEFIT** UK-registered charities or organisations with exempt status, benefitting children, older people and people with disabilities; universities and teaching hospitals; schools and other educational establishments.
**WHAT IS FUNDED** Medicine – to fund research, education and capital projects related to all areas of medicine through grants to selected medical universities, institutions and charities; arts – to fund projects which aim to develop and encourage individual and group talent in musical, theatre and illustrative art; general – to make donations to projects through other registered UK charities which support and care for the benefit of the public as a whole.
**WHAT IS NOT FUNDED** Projects outside the UK; individuals or individual research or study.
**TYPE OF GRANT** Mainly one-off.
**RANGE OF GRANTS** £2,000–£120,000; generally about £10,000.
**SAMPLE GRANTS** Royal College of Surgeons – Fellowships (£120,000); Royal College of Surgeons – Surgical Trials Unit (£105,000); Bath University (£38,000); Médecins Sans Frontières (£30,000); Neuromuscular Centre (£15,000); St Christopher's Hospice (£12,500); Help for Heroes (£11,000); WheelPower (£10,000); Helen and Douglas House (£9,000);

The Stroke Association (£7,000); ABF The Soldiers Charity, Macmillan Cancer Support and WaterAid (£6,000 each).
**FINANCES** Year 2013/14 Income £557,603 Grants £783,980 Grants to organisations £781,980 Assets £14,827,692
**TRUSTEES** Jack Ladeveze; Audrey Ladeveze; Michael Butler; Carole Cook; Jonathan Fountain.
**OTHER INFORMATION** The grant total includes about £116,500 in elective and hardship grants to university medical schools. During the year 39 awards were made, including one individual (£2,000).
**HOW TO APPLY** Apply using the online form on the foundation's website. The deadline is 1 January for the March trustee meeting and 1 September for the December meeting. Grants are be made in April and January. The annual report for 2013/14 states: 'Unsolicited applications are accepted, but the Trustees do receive a very high number of grant applications which, in line with their grant making policy, are mostly unsuccessful.'
**WHO TO APPLY TO** Martin Pollock, Secretary, c/o Moore Stephens LLP, 150 Aldersgate Street, London EC1A 4AB Tel. 020 7334 9191 Fax 020 7651 1953 email enidlinderfoundation@moorestephens.com Website www.enidlinderfoundation.com

## ■ The Ruth and Stuart Lipton Charitable Trust

**CC NO** 266741   **ESTABLISHED** 1973
**WHERE FUNDING CAN BE GIVEN** UK and overseas, with some preference for London.
**WHO CAN BENEFIT** Charitable organisations. Preference can be given to those benefitting Jewish people.
**WHAT IS FUNDED** General charitable purposes, including health, education and arts; Jewish causes.
**WHAT IS NOT FUNDED** Grants are not made to individuals.
**RANGE OF GRANTS** £50–£12,500
**SAMPLE GRANTS** United Jewish Israel Appeal (£12,500); The Royal Opera House Foundation (£8,700); Nightingale (£5,800); Prostate Cancer UK (£5,400); Western Marble Arch Synagogue (£4,400); Barbican Centre Trust (£3,500); Schools Around The World (£2,500); Jewish Bereavement Counselling Service and St John's Hospice (£200 each); Land Aid Charitable Trust (£100); The Kensington and Chelsea Foundation (£75); and Jewish Women's Aid (£50).
**FINANCES** Year 2013/14 Income £55,236 Grants £61,227 Grants to organisations £61,227 Assets £646,463
**TRUSTEES** Stuart Lipton; Ruth Lipton; Neil Benson.
**OTHER INFORMATION** There is no minimum limit for any grant and all grants must be approved unanimously by the trustees. During the year 18 awards were paid.
**HOW TO APPLY** Applications can be made in writing to the correspondent.
**WHO TO APPLY TO** Neil Benson, Trustee, c/o Lewis Golden and Co, 40 Queen Ann Street, London W1G 9EL Tel. 020 7580 7313 email charity@lewisgolden.com

## ■ The Lister Charitable Trust

**CC NO** 288730   **ESTABLISHED** 1981
**WHERE FUNDING CAN BE GIVEN** UK and overseas.
**WHO CAN BENEFIT** Registered charities which work with young people.
**WHAT IS FUNDED** General charitable purposes; children and young people; environment conservation; health.
**WHAT IS NOT FUNDED** Individuals, including students; general appeals from large UK organisations; smaller bodies working in areas outside the trust's criteria.
**TYPE OF GRANT** Usually one-off for specific project or part of a project given for up to one year. Core funding and/or salaries rarely considered.
**SAMPLE GRANTS** Project Medishare (£75,000); Romanian Children's Relief (£29,500); The Stroke-Association (£20,000); Wildlife Media (£19,000); Home Start Ashford (£10,000); Mount Carmel Hotel and Place 2 Be (£5,000 each); Association Ivan Patzaichin (£4,400).
**FINANCES** Year 2013/14 Income £104,194 Grants £186,018 Grants to organisations £186,018 Assets £5,397,031
**TRUSTEES** Noel Lister; Penny Horne; Sylvia Lister; John Barnsley.
**OTHER INFORMATION** Grants were made to 12 organisations.
**HOW TO APPLY** Applications may be made in writing to the correspondent. They should include clear details of the need the intended project is designed to meet and an outline budget. Only applications from eligible bodies are acknowledged, when further information may be requested. The trustees meet quarterly to consider appeals.
**WHO TO APPLY TO** Nicholas Yellowlees, Correspondent, 44 Welbeck Street, London W1G 8DY Tel. 020 7486 0800 email info@apperleylimited.co.uk

## ■ The Frank Litchfield Charitable Trust

**CC NO** 1038943   **ESTABLISHED** 1994
**WHERE FUNDING CAN BE GIVEN** Mostly in and around Cambridge.
**WHO CAN BENEFIT** Charitable organisations and projects. The trust aims to assist 'direct good'.
**WHAT IS FUNDED** General charitable purposes, particularly health and disability causes, helping disadvantaged and vulnerable people, older people and children and young people. Our research also suggests that support can be given to relieve distress of those involved in agriculture.
**WHAT IS NOT FUNDED** Campaigning and similar expenditure is not considered of direct benefit and therefore is unlikely to be assisted.
**TYPE OF GRANT** Capital and core cost, projects delivering 'direct good'.
**RANGE OF GRANTS** £500–£5,000
**SAMPLE GRANTS** Headway (£5,000); Tom's Trust (£4,000); Blind Veterans UK, Carers Trust, Happy Days and RNLI (£3,000 each); Camtrust and The Ear Foundation (£2,500 each); Riding for the Disabled and Survivors of Bereavement by Suicide (£2,000 each); The Migraine Trust and The Stained Glass Museum (£1,000 each); and St Clare Hospice (£500).
**FINANCES** Year 2013/14 Income £66,403 Grants £61,500 Grants to organisations £61,500 Assets £2,140,350
**TRUSTEES** Michael Womack; David Chater; Michael Hamilton.

OTHER INFORMATION The trust made 25 awards in 2013/14.
HOW TO APPLY Applications may be made in writing to the correspondent. Note that the trust receives more applications each year than it is able to fund.
WHO TO APPLY TO Michael Womack, Trustee, 12 De Freville Avenue, Cambridge CB4 1HR
*Tel.* 01223 358012 *email* womack@btinternet.com

## ■ The Charles Littlewood Hill Trust

CC NO 286350  ESTABLISHED 1978
WHERE FUNDING CAN BE GIVEN UK, with a preference for Nottinghamshire and Norfolk.
WHO CAN BENEFIT Charitable organisations; educational establishments; churches; community organisations.
WHAT IS FUNDED General charitable causes; social welfare; health and disability; armed forces; environment; education; religious activities; arts and culture.
WHAT IS NOT FUNDED Individuals; grants are seldom made for repairs of parish churches outside Nottinghamshire.
TYPE OF GRANT In practice unrestricted funding, including capital and core costs. Applications for starter finance are encouraged but grants are seldom made to endowment or capital funds.
RANGE OF GRANTS £1,000–£10,000; usually £5,000 or less.
SAMPLE GRANTS St Mary's Church – Nottingham (£10,000); Norfolk Community Foundation and The Norfolk Churches Trust (£7,500 each); ABF The Soldiers Charity – Nottinghamshire (£6,000); The Churches Conservation Trust (£6,500); POW Nottingham Ltd (£4,000); Norfolk Eating Disorders Association (£3,000); Camphill – Blair Drummond and Music in Country Churches (£2,500 each); Barnardo's, Groundwork Greater Nottingham, Southwell Music Festival and The Arkwright Scholarships (£2,000 each); Asthma UK, Flitcham C of E Primary School, Leeway Domestic Violence and Abuse Services, Nottingham Sea Cadets, Ovarian Cancer Action, The Conservation Volunteers, The Rifles Care for Casualties Appeal and Trees for Cities (£1,000 each).
FINANCES *Year* 2013 *Income* £203,973 *Grants* £175,500 *Grants to organisations* £175,500 *Assets* £4,484,058
TRUSTEES Charles Barratt; Tim Farr; Nigel Savory; John Pears.
OTHER INFORMATION There were over 76 awards made.
HOW TO APPLY Applications have to be made in writing to the correspondent, including the latest set of audited accounts, at least one month before trustees' meetings in March, July and November. Unsuccessful applicants will not be notified.
WHO TO APPLY TO John Thompson, Correspondent, Po Box 10454, Nottingham NG5 0HQ
*Tel.* 01476 552429 *email* charles.hill@btinternet.com

## ■ The Second Joseph Aaron Littman Foundation

CC NO 201892  ESTABLISHED 1961
WHERE FUNDING CAN BE GIVEN UK.
WHO CAN BENEFIT Registered charities only; educational, medical and religious bodies.
WHAT IS FUNDED General charitable purposes, with a special focus on Jewish causes, as well as academic and medical research and relief of poverty.
WHAT IS NOT FUNDED Individuals.
TYPE OF GRANT One-off and recurrent; core costs.
RANGE OF GRANTS Usually below £10,000.
SAMPLE GRANTS The Littman Library of Jewish Civilisation (£196,000); Lubavitch Senior Girls School (£6,000); Coronary Flow Trust and The Jerusalem Expressive Therapy Centre – Misholim (£5,000 each); Westminster Synagogue (£4,900); Leo Baeck College UK (£3,000); Holocaust Educational Trust and University College London (£2,000 each); Fight for Sight and Institute of Polish Jewish Studies (£1,000 each). Awards below £1,000 totalled £11,000.
FINANCES *Year* 2012/13 *Income* £226,048 *Grants* £249,891 *Grants to organisations* £249,891 *Assets* £5,551,043
TRUSTEES Robert Littman; Glenn Hurstfield; C. Littman.
OTHER INFORMATION At the time of writing (June 2015) this was the latest information available – 2013/14 accounts were overdue at the Charity Commission. The foundation provides continuing substantial support to the Littman Library and distributes smaller grants to other charities.
HOW TO APPLY Applications may be made in writing to the correspondent.
WHO TO APPLY TO Robert Littman, Trustee, Manor Farm, Mill Lane, Charlton Mackrell, Somerton, Somerset TA11 7BQ

## ■ The George John and Sheilah Livanos Charitable Trust

CC NO 1002279  ESTABLISHED 1985
WHERE FUNDING CAN BE GIVEN UK.
WHO CAN BENEFIT Registered charities; hospitals; hospices.
WHAT IS FUNDED General charitable purposes; health; disability; medical charities; maritime charities.
WHAT IS NOT FUNDED Individuals; non-registered charities.
TYPE OF GRANT One-off and recurring; capital grants.
RANGE OF GRANTS £500–£50,000
SAMPLE GRANTS Dorothy Kerin Trust (£50,000); Ekklesia Project Fakenham (£24,000); Bowel Disease Research Foundation (£10,300); Contact The Elderly (£7,500); Age UK, Disasters Emergency Committee and The Hospital of St Cross (£5,000 each); The Dystonia Society (£3,000); Barnardo's and St Mungo's (£2,500 each); Changing Faces, South East Cancer Help Centre and Stroke Association (£2,000 each); Tunbridge Wells Talking Newspaper Association (£500).
FINANCES *Year* 2013 *Income* £89,523 *Grants* £157,800 *Grants to organisations* £157,800 *Assets* £1,886,890
TRUSTEES Philip Harris; Timothy Cripps; Anthony Holmes.
OTHER INFORMATION There were 23 grants made.
HOW TO APPLY The annual report for 2013 states: 'Unsolicited applications are accepted, but the Trustees do receive a very high number of grant applications which, in line with the Trustees' grant making policy, are mostly unsuccessful. The Trustees prefer to make donations to charities whose work they have researched and which is in accordance with the aims and objectives of the Charity for the year.'

WHO TO APPLY TO Philip Harris, Trustee, Jeffrey Green Russell Solicitors, Waverley House, 7–12 Noel Street, London W1F 8GQ *Tel.* 020 7339 7000

## ■ Liverpool Charity and Voluntary Services (LCVS)

CC NO 223485     ESTABLISHED 1970
WHERE FUNDING CAN BE GIVEN Merseyside only.
WHO CAN BENEFIT Registered charities.
WHAT IS FUNDED General charitable purposes. The trustees prefer 'to make relatively modest grants to a wide number of applicants rather than large grants to a small number of applicants'.
WHAT IS NOT FUNDED Non-registered charities; individuals. Applications from charities in successive years are not viewed favourably as are large building appeals or revenue expenditure. Specific exclusions may apply for different funds.
TYPE OF GRANT Capital costs; equipment funding.
FINANCES *Year* 2013/14 *Income* £3,900,611 *Grants* £2,280,763 *Grants to organisations* £2,280,763 *Assets* £7,393,999
TRUSTEES Charles Feeny; Roger Morris; Prof. Hilary Russell; Christine Reeves; Heather Akehurst; Adeyinka Olushonde; Perminda Bal; Caroline Clark; Deborah Shackleton.
OTHER INFORMATION The charity acts in a similar manner to a community foundation, administering the giving of much smaller charitable trusts. The trustees prefer 'to make relatively modest grants to a wide number of applicants rather than large grants to a small number of applicants'. Grants were made as follows: UW Giving – distributed by Charities Aid Foundation in accordance with individual donors' direct instructions (£2.2 million); Liverpool and Merseyside Charities Funds (£4,000).
HOW TO APPLY Application forms are available to download, together with criteria and guidelines, from the charity's website. Grants are considered in the annual meeting, in June. Applications should be received by May.
WHO TO APPLY TO The Grants Team, 151 Dale Street, Liverpool L2 2AH *Tel.* 0151 227 5177 *email* info@lcvs.org.uk *Website* www.lcvs.org.uk

## ■ Jack Livingstone Charitable Trust

CC NO 263473     ESTABLISHED 1971
WHERE FUNDING CAN BE GIVEN UK and worldwide, with a preference for Manchester area.
WHO CAN BENEFIT Registered charities. Preference is given to organisations benefitting Jewish people, at risk groups, and people who are ill, disadvantaged by poverty or socially isolated.
WHAT IS FUNDED General charitable purposes; Jewish causes.
TYPE OF GRANT One-off and recurrent.
RANGE OF GRANTS Up to £50,000; generally under £10,000.
SAMPLE GRANTS The Jerusalem Foundation (£50,000); Federation of Jewish Services (£30,000); Rainsough Charitable Trust (£11,000); Manchester Jewish Museum (£10,000); South Manchester Synagogue (£6,600); Community Security Trust (£6,000); UK Toremet (£5,500); AISH UK (£5,000); LCCC Foundation (£2,500); and North Cheshire Jewish Nursery, Project Seed and Southport New Synagogue (£1,000 each). Grants of less than £1,000 totalled about £10,700.
FINANCES *Year* 2013/14 *Income* £89,217 *Grants* £143,790 *Grants to organisations* £143,790 *Assets* £2,128,697
TRUSTEES Janice Livingstone; Terence Livingstone; Brian White.
OTHER INFORMATION Grants of less than £1,000 totalled £10,700.
HOW TO APPLY Our research indicates that the trust does not respond to unsolicited applications.
WHO TO APPLY TO Janice Livingstone, Trustee, Westholme, The Springs, Bowdon, Altringham, Cheshire WA14 3JH *Tel.* 0161 928 3232 *email* jackandjan@btinternet.com

## ■ The Elaine and Angus Lloyd Charitable Trust

CC NO 237250     ESTABLISHED 1964
WHERE FUNDING CAN BE GIVEN UK, with a preference for Surrey, Kent and the South of England.
WHO CAN BENEFIT Individuals; local, regional and UK-wide organisations.
WHAT IS FUNDED A range of general charitable purposes; health and disability; individuals' education; children and young adults; at risk groups; people disadvantaged by poverty; socially isolated people.
TYPE OF GRANT Recurrent and one-off, some may be paid quarterly.
RANGE OF GRANTS Up to £20,000. Mostly around £1,000–£2,000.
SAMPLE GRANTS What on Earth Foundation (£10,000); Positive Initiative Trust (£7,500); Pitstop (£4,500); Brighton and Hove Parents and Children's Group (£3,500); Grace Community Church (£3,000); Monday to Wednesday Club (£2,300); Rhema Religious and Charitable Trust (£2,200); Diabetes UK (£2,000); Martha Trust (£1,500); and Central London Samaritans, Mo Farrar Foundation, St Clements Church Sandwich and Umbrella Centre of Herne Bay (£1,000 each). Grants of less than £1,000 totalled over £20,000.
FINANCES *Year* 2013/14 *Income* £103,590 *Grants* £98,300 *Grants to organisations* £93,650 *Assets* £3,004,563
TRUSTEES Angus Lloyd; John Gordon; James Lloyd; Philippa Smith; Virginia Best; Christopher Lloyd; Michael Craig-Cooper; Revd Richard Lloyd.
OTHER INFORMATION Five grants were given to individuals and 80 to organisations. Grants under £1,000 totalled over £20,000.
HOW TO APPLY Applications may be made in writing to the correspondent. The trustees meet regularly to consider grants.
WHO TO APPLY TO Ross Badger, 3rd Floor, North Side, Dukes Court, 32 Duke Street, St James's, London SW1Y 6DF *Tel.* 020 7930 7797 *email* ross.badger@hhllp.co.uk

## ■ The Charles Lloyd Foundation

CC NO 235225     ESTABLISHED 1964
WHERE FUNDING CAN BE GIVEN The Roman Catholic Dioceses of Menevia and Wrexham.
WHO CAN BENEFIT Roman Catholic charities.
WHAT IS FUNDED The upkeep of Roman Catholic churches, houses, convents and monasteries; the advancement of religion; the promotion and advancement of music, either religious or secular.
TYPE OF GRANT One-off.

# Lloyd's

**SAMPLE GRANTS** Burry Port (£30,500); Barmouth Catholic Church (£5,800); St Mair – Machynlleth (£2,500).
**FINANCES** Year 2013/14 Income £46,522 Grants £38,780 Grants to organisations £38,780 Assets £1,483,632
**TRUSTEES** Richard Thorn; Patrick Walters; Vincent Ryan; Steven Davies.
**OTHER INFORMATION** Three grants were made during the year.
**HOW TO APPLY** Apply in writing to the correspondent before the project starts. Four copies of the following: income and expenditure pages of the latest financial return; plans and estimates; and what finances the parish can contribute.
**WHO TO APPLY TO** Vincent Ryan, Trustee, 8–10 Grosvenor Road, Wrexham LL11 1BU Tel. 01978 291000 email susanelder@allingtonhughes.co.uk

## ■ Lloyd's Charities Trust

**CC NO** 207232  **ESTABLISHED** 1953
**WHERE FUNDING CAN BE GIVEN** UK, with particular interest in East London.
**WHO CAN BENEFIT** Charitable organisations.
**WHAT IS FUNDED** General charitable purposes, with a specific interest in education, training, employment and enterprise.
**WHAT IS NOT FUNDED** Organisations that are not registered charities or non-UK-registered charities (except at the occasional discretion of trustees); political parties or lobbying organisations; local charities outside London; mainstream schools, PTAs and educational establishments; grant-making bodies to make grants on their behalf; animal welfare causes, zoos, animal rescue; the promotion of religion or other beliefs; individuals, including student grants, bursaries, medical costs or financial assistance; sponsorship of events or individuals including taking tables at gala dinners; advertising including in brochures for charitable events; costs associated with expeditions; retrospective funding for work that has already taken place; military causes (see Lloyd's Patriotic Fund for support for military welfare charities); arts, culture or heritage charities; outward bound courses and adventure experiences; conferences, cultural festivals, exhibitions and events; churches, cathedrals and other historic buildings.
**SAMPLE GRANTS** The Prince's Trust (£75,000); and Bromley By Bow Centre (£50,000).
**FINANCES** Year 2013 Income £1,117,291 Grants £628,079 Grants to organisations £628,079 Assets £1,658,329
**TRUSTEES** John Spencer; Lawrence Holder; Iain Wilson; Rupert Atkin; Graham Clarke; Chris Harman; Vicky Mirfin; Neil Smith; Victoria Carter.
**HOW TO APPLY** Lloyd's Charities Trust makes ad hoc donations; however, the majority of funds are committed to supporting the partnership charities the trust works with. The trust has previously stated that as funds are committed over a three-year period 'it is unable to respond positively to the numerous appeals we receive'.
**WHO TO APPLY TO** Suzanna Nagle, Secretary, Lloyd's of London, Lloyd's Building, 1 Lime Street, London EC3M 7HA Tel. 020 7327 6144 email suzanna.nagle@lloyds.com Website www.lloyds.com/lct

## ■ Lloyds Bank Foundation for England and Wales

**CC NO** 327114  **ESTABLISHED** 1986
**WHERE FUNDING CAN BE GIVEN** England and Wales.
**WHO CAN BENEFIT** Registered charities benefitting people with disabilities or otherwise disadvantaged individuals.
**WHAT IS FUNDED** Education and training and social and community needs.
**WHAT IS NOT FUNDED** The foundation does not fund the following types of organisations and work: *Organisations:* organisations that are **not** registered charities; second or third tier organisations (unless there is evidence of direct benefit to disadvantaged people); charities that mainly work overseas; charities that mainly give funds to other charities, individuals or other organisations; hospitals, hospices or medical centres; rescue services; schools, colleges and universities; *Types of work:* activities which a statutory body is responsible for; capital projects, appeals, refurbishments; environmental work, expeditions and overseas travel; funding to promote religion; holidays or trips; loans or business finance; medical research, funding for medical equipment or medical treatments; sponsorship or funding towards a marketing appeal or fundraising activities; work with animals or to promote animal welfare.
**TYPE OF GRANT** One-off for a specific project, core funding, two or three year funding. Also capital, recurring costs, running costs and salaries.
**RANGE OF GRANTS** £500–£250,000
**SAMPLE GRANTS** Hackney CVS (£250,000); Age Concern in Cornwall and The Isles of Scilly (£188,000); Working With Men (WWM) (£38,000); Norfolk Community Law Service and Sexual Abuse and Rape Advice Centre (£30,000 each); Rainbow Services and Greenwich Mencap (£28,000 each); CVS Tamworth (£27,000); Burnley and Pendle Citizens Advice (£22,000); Mind in West Cumbria (£20,000); Hodan Somali Community (£19,000); Broxlow Youth Homelessness (£18,000); Pakistan Association Liverpool (£15,000); Down's Syndrome Association (£12,000); Halton Disability Advice and Appeals Centre (£14,000); Children and Families in Grief (£8,000).
**FINANCES** Year 2013 Income £26,758,000 Grants £21,167,000 Grants to organisations £21,167,000 Assets £45,544,000
**TRUSTEES** Paul Farmer; Dame Denise Platt; Prof. Ian Diamond; Rob Devey; Hilary Armstrong; Carolyn Fairbairn; Sir Clive Booth; Philip Grant; Mohammad Naeem; Prof. Patricia Broadfoot; Helen Edwards; Catherine Kehoe.
**OTHER INFORMATION** There were 841 awards made.
**HOW TO APPLY** Refer to the foundation's website for current information.
**WHO TO APPLY TO** Paul Streets, Correspondent, Pentagon House, 52–54 Southwark Street, London SE1 1UN Tel. 020 7378 4601 email enquiries@lloydstsbfoundations.org.uk Website www.lloydstsbfoundations.org.uk

## ■ Lloyds Bank Foundation for Northern Ireland

**IR NO** XN72216  **ESTABLISHED** 1986
**WHERE FUNDING CAN BE GIVEN** Northern Ireland.
**WHO CAN BENEFIT** Charities registered with HM Revenue and Customs, benefitting children, young adults, older people, volunteers and people who are unemployed, homeless, living in

rural communities, disabled or disadvantaged by poverty.

**WHAT IS FUNDED** Underfunded voluntary organisations which enable people who have a disability and people who are disadvantaged through social and economic circumstances, to make a contribution to the community. The trustees regret that, as the funds available are limited, they cannot support all fields of voluntary and charitable activity. The two main objectives to which funds are allocated are: (a) social and community needs; (b) education and training. For full details of the foundation's funding objectives go to the website.

**WHAT IS NOT FUNDED** Grants are not usually given for: organisations that are not recognised as a charity by HM Revenue and Customs; organisations which have an income of more than £1 million in the previous year's accounts; individuals, including students; animal welfare; environmental projects including those that deal with geographic and scenic issues – however, the trustees may consider projects that improve the living conditions of disadvantaged individuals and groups; activities that are normally the responsibility of central or local government or some other responsible body; schools, universities and colleges (except for projects specifically to benefit students with special needs); hospitals and medical centres; sponsorship or marketing appeals; fabric appeals for places of worship; promotion of religion; activities that collect funds for subsequent redistribution to others; endowment funds; fundraising events or activities; corporate affiliation or membership of a charity; loans or business finance; expeditions or overseas travel; construction of and extension to buildings; salary or training costs for the pre-school sector. Note: organisations must have a total income of less than £250,000 to be eligible to apply to the Standard Grant Programme. Organisations which do not charge a nominal fee for activities are less likely to be funded.

**TYPE OF GRANT** Capital; core costs; one-off; project; recurring costs; salaries; start-up costs; usually one-off, but support for two years or more is considered.

**RANGE OF GRANTS** Normally a maximum of £5,000, but larger amounts are considered.

**SAMPLE GRANTS** Aisling Centre (£5,000); Arts for All (£4,000); Age Concern Causeway (£4,000); Belfast Interface Project (£3,000); Hillstown Rural Community Group (£2,500); Newtown Butler Playgroup, the Oxygen Therapy Centre (£1,500 each); Meigh Community Pre-School (£1,000); the Open Door Centre (£600); Green Elves Playgroup (£500).

**FINANCES** *Year* 2013 *Income* £1,900,000 *Grants* £2,200,000 *Grants to organisations* £2,200,000 *Assets* £2,100,000

**TRUSTEES** Tony Reynolds; Paddy Bailie; Angela Colhoun; Brian Scott; Hugh Donnelly; Carmel McGukian; Lord Leitch; Janet Leckey; Jim McCooe; Janine Donnelly; Robert Agnew; Sandara Kelso-Robb.

**OTHER INFORMATION** There were 527 awards made.

**HOW TO APPLY** Applications can be made using the online application form. Once registered you will receive a username and password which you can use to access the online grants portal and view and apply for open programmes. Applicants are welcome to contact the foundation or make an appointment to discuss an application. As part of the assessment process the foundation may contact or visit the applicant. If you have not heard from the foundation within four weeks

contact them. Guidelines, advice on completing the form, supporting document checklist and monitoring factsheets are all available from the website.

**WHO TO APPLY TO** Sandara Kelso-Robb, Executive Director, Lloyds Bank, 2nd Floor, 14 Cromac Place, Gasworks, Belfast BT7 2JB *Tel.* 028 9032 3000 *email* info@lloydstsbfoundationni.org *Website* www.lloydstsbfoundationni.org

## ■ Lloyds Bank Foundation for the Channel Islands

**CC NO** 327113   **ESTABLISHED** 1986
**WHERE FUNDING CAN BE GIVEN** The Channel Islands.
**WHO CAN BENEFIT** Organisations benefitting children and young people; older people; volunteers; at risk groups; people who are unemployed, carers, disabled, disadvantaged by poverty or homeless; and victims of abuse and domestic violence.

**WHAT IS FUNDED** The main aims of the foundation are to assist disadvantaged and disabled people and to promote social and community welfare within the Channel Islands. A wide range of activities are supported, and the following examples are meant as a guide only: advice services – addictions (particularly substance misuse rehabilitation), bereavement, counselling, emergency and rescue services, family support, helplines, homelessness, housing, parenting; community relations – crime prevention (particularly activities involving young people), mediation, promotion of volunteering, rehabilitation of offenders, victim support, vulnerable young people; community facilities and services – after school clubs, community centres, family centres, older people's clubs, play schemes, transport, youth organisations; cultural enrichment – improving participation in and access to the arts and national heritage; activities with an educational focus for all ages; improvements to buildings of historic or architectural value which increase their benefit to the community; projects which have a strong focus on benefit to people and the social environment; people with disabilities – advocacy, carers, day centres, information and advice, sheltered accommodation, transport; promotion of health – day care, information and advice, mental health, holistic medicine, home nursing, hospices. The trustees will, on an exceptional basis, also fund research projects in health related areas. The foundation also supports people of all ages in education and training, particularly activities which enhance learning opportunities for those with disabilities or who are disadvantaged.

**WHAT IS NOT FUNDED** Organisations which are not recognised charities; activities which are primarily the responsibility of the Insular authorities in the Islands or some other responsible body; activities which collect funds to give to other charities, individuals or other organisations; animal welfare; corporate subscription or membership of a charity; endowment funds; environment – conserving and protecting plants and animals, geography and scenery; expeditions or overseas travel; fabric appeals for places of worship; fundraising events or activities; hospitals and medical centres (except for projects which are clearly additional to statutory responsibilities); individuals, including students; loans or business finance; promotion of religion; schools and colleges (except for projects that will benefit students with disabilities and are clearly additional to statutory responsibilities); sponsorship or marketing appeals; international appeals – trustees may from time to time consider a limited number of applications from UK-registered charities working abroad.

**TYPE OF GRANT** Depends on merit, but usually one-off for a specific project, operational costs, salaries and start-up costs; for up to three years.

**RANGE OF GRANTS** £1,000–£110,000

**SAMPLE GRANTS** Drug Concern (£105,000); Shelter Trust Jersey (£75,000); Autism Jersey (£73,000); Guernsey Youth LBG (£66,000); the Antoine Trust (£40,000); Creative Learning in Prison (£25,000); St Breland Youth Project (£10,000); Jubilee Sailing Trust Jersey (£7,000); Music in Hospitals (£5,000); Helping Wings Guernsey (£1,000).

**FINANCES** Year 2013 Income £1,117,291 Grants £881,296 Grants to organisations £881,296 Assets £1,658,329

**TRUSTEES** John Bootham; Dr John Ferguson; Patricia Tumelty; Sarah Bamford; Simon Howitt; Andrew Dann; Michael Starkey; Timothy Cooke; Kathryn Le Quesne.

**HOW TO APPLY** Applications are only accepted on the foundation's own form which should be submitted with an income tax letter of exemption, latest audited accounts, a copy of a bank statement and a job description (if salary funding is requested). The form and guidelines are available from its website or from the foundation's office in Jersey and can be returned at any time. They must be returned by post as the foundation does not accept forms that have been emailed or faxed. All applications are reviewed on a continual basis. The trustees meet three times a year to approve donations in March, July and November and deadlines are usually the middle of the preceding month. Decision-making processes can therefore take up to four months. Applications up to £5,000 are normally assessed within one month and all applicants are informed of the outcome of their application. Applicants are encouraged to discuss their project with one of the foundation's staff before completing an application form. This will help ensure that your project is within its criteria and that you are applying for an appropriate amount. You will also be informed of when you should hear a decision.

**WHO TO APPLY TO** John Hutchins, Executive Director, Lloyds Bank, PO Box 160, 25 New Street, St Helier Jersey JE4 8RG *Tel.* 01534 845889 *email* John.Hutchins@lloydsbankfoundation.org.uk *Website* www.lloydsbankfoundationci.org.uk

## ■ Lloyds TSB Foundation for Scotland

**SC NO** SC009481 **ESTABLISHED** 1986
**WHERE FUNDING CAN BE GIVEN** Scotland and overseas.
**WHO CAN BENEFIT** Charities registered in Scotland only; grassroots organisations providing support to the Scottish community and enabling people, primarily those disadvantaged and in need, to become active members of society and improve their quality of life.
**WHAT IS FUNDED** Disadvantaged individuals; families; social isolation; marginalised people; substance abuse; disability and health; older people; homelessness; equality and rights; development of young people. The foundation's current main programmes are Henry Duncan Awards (for charities with an income of £500,000 or less) and the Partnership Drugs Initiative (focusing on children and young people). It also provides Capacity Building support (in partnership with Evaluation Support Scotland) and manages the International Small Grants Programme on behalf of the Scottish Government ('to support projects that help some of the world's poorest countries and fit within the Scottish Government's International Development Policy) and the Recovery Initiative Fund on behalf of the Scottish Recovery Consortium. There is also the Time of Your Life programme 'to support charities operating in West Lothian to deliver innovative preventative approaches with people aged 50 to 70 to help them get as much out of life for as long as possible'.

**WHAT IS NOT FUNDED** Charities with an income of more than £500,000 per annum; activities which are not clearly focused on working with disadvantaged people; organisations which are not formally recognised as charities in Scotland; individuals, including students; animal welfare; initiatives that are focused on sport, the arts or the environment, except where the subject is being used as a vehicle to engage with disadvantaged groups to increase life skills; conservation and protection of flora and fauna; mainstream activities and statutory requirements of hospitals and medical centres, schools, universities and colleges; sponsorship or marketing appeals; establishment/ preservation of endowment funds; contributions to funds for subsequent grant-making to other organisations and/or individuals; expeditions or overseas travel; major capital appeals/building projects; historic restoration/historic publications; retrospective funding; promotion of religion/church fabric appeals.

**TYPE OF GRANT** One-off; up to one year under Henry Duncan Awards and up to three years under the Partnership Drugs Initiative; revenue and capital funding; core activities; running costs; projects; salaries; start-up expenditure; feasibility studies, research.

**RANGE OF GRANTS** £5,000–£6,000 on average.

**SAMPLE GRANTS** Healthy n Happy Community Development Trust (£61,000); Barnardo's (£58,000); Alternatives West Dunbartonshire CDS (£57,500); Addaction and Oban Youth Cafe Project Ltd (£50,000 each); Befriend a Child (£42,500); Children 1st (£27,500); East Lothian Young Carers Ltd (£17,900); Community Law Advice Network (£8,000); Family Mediation Tayside and Fife, Hidden Gardens Trust and Home-Start Dundee (£6,000 each); YMCA Edinburgh (£5,400); Fischy Limited (£5,200); Monifieth Befriending Scheme (£5,000); Avenue Confidential (£4,900); We Step Together (£4,500); Krazy Kat Theatre Company; Kincardine and Deeside Befriending and Send-It Fulfilment Solutions Ltd (£4,000 each); Supporting Children in Learning for Life (£3,000); Inverclyde Autistic Support Group (£2,700); People First – Fraserburgh (£2,500); Russian Centre in Scotland – Haven (£2,400); Dunoon Link Club (£2,200); People and Agencies of Cowal Coming Together (£1,500); Adults with Learning Difficulties Holiday Fund (£1,400); Blind Activities Support Events (£1,000); CAIR Scotland (£230).

**FINANCES** Year 2013 Income £1,057,000 Grants £2,191,000 Grants to organisations £2,191,000 Assets £7,661,000

**TRUSTEES** Charles Abram; Prof. Sir John Arbuthnott; Joy Barlow; Trevor Civval; Tom Halpin; Jacqui Low; Jane Mackie; David Urch.

**OTHER INFORMATION** The vast majority of the foundation's income comes from government funding. A total of 327 awards were allocated as follows: Partnership Drugs Initiative (£900,000); Henry Duncan Awards (£893,000); Standard Grant Scheme (£250,000); Recovery Initiative Fund (£80,000); Time of Your Life (£48,000); Capacity Building Grant Scheme (£20,000). 'Grants approved' totalled £2.7 million and 'awards paid' – £2.2 million.

**HOW TO APPLY** Application forms, complete with comprehensive guidance notes, are available from the foundation's website or the correspondent. They must be returned by post. There is a two-stage application process for the Partnership Drugs Initiative Awards and you will need to work with your local Alcohol and Drug Partnership to complete an initial outline application. If you need assistance with your application or are unsure about anything do not hesitate to get in touch with the foundation. Before re-applying to Henry Duncan Awards you should wait at least one year (for the Partnership Drugs Initiative this may vary). The trustees normally meet in February, April, June, August, October, and December each year and there is a three month period between the submission deadline and a decision being taken. For up-to-date deadlines see the website. Charities with an annual income of less than £25,000 and looking for less than £2,500 can use a special 'small grants' application form for Henry Duncan Awards.

**WHO TO APPLY TO** Connie Williamson, Grants Manager, Riverside House, 502 Gorgie Road, Edinburgh EH11 3AF *Tel.* 0131 444 4020 *Fax* 0131 444 4099 *email* On an online form *Website* www.ltsbfoundationforscotland.org.uk

## ■ Localtrent Ltd

**CC NO** 326329      **ESTABLISHED** 1982
**WHERE FUNDING CAN BE GIVEN** UK, with some preference for Manchester.
**WHO CAN BENEFIT** Charities and educational or religious institutions.
**WHAT IS FUNDED** Advancement of the Orthodox Jewish faith. The trustees will consider applications from organisations concerned with Orthodox Jewish faith education and also the relief of poverty.
**SAMPLE GRANTS** Chasdei Yoel (£39,500); The Bersam Trust (£6,000); and Kol Yom Trust (£4,500).
**FINANCES** *Year* 2013/14 *Income* £334,113 *Grants* £218,028 *Grants to organisations* £218,028 *Assets* £976,051
**TRUSTEES** Hyman Weiss; Mina Weiss; Philip Weiss; Zisel Weiss; Bernardin Weiss; Yocheved Weiss.
**HOW TO APPLY** Applications may be made in writing to the correspondent.
**WHO TO APPLY TO** A. Kahan, Correspondent, Lopian Gross Barnett and Co, 6th Floor, Cardinal House, 20 St Mary's Parsonage, Manchester M3 2LG *Tel.* 0161 832 8721

## ■ The Locker Foundation

**CC NO** 264180      **ESTABLISHED** 1972
**WHERE FUNDING CAN BE GIVEN** UK and overseas.
**WHO CAN BENEFIT** Jewish charities; synagogues; educational establishments.
**WHAT IS FUNDED** General charitable purposes with preference for the welfare of people who are ill and those with disabilities and the teaching of the Jewish religion.

**RANGE OF GRANTS** £1,500–£20,000
**SAMPLE GRANTS** Kahal Chassidim Bobov (£64,000); Nightingale House (£52,000); Birmingham Synagogue and Chai Cancer Care (£25,000 each); Aleh Charitable Foundation (£20,000); Beit Halochem and Ezer Mizion (£17,000); Kisharon and Langdon Foundation (£16,000); Laniado Hospital (£12,000); Camp Simcha (£7,500); Jewish Lads and Girls Brigade, Jewish Museum and (£5,000 each); Zionist Federation (£1,500); Tree of Hope (£1,000); and Lincolnsfield Children's Centre (£700).
**FINANCES** *Year* 2013/14 *Income* £689,283 *Grants* £472,638 *Grants to organisations* £472,638 *Assets* £5,934,395
**TRUSTEES** Susanna Segal; Irving Carter; Malcolm Carter.
**HOW TO APPLY** Applications may be made in writing to the correspondent. Decisions must be made by a unanimous agreement by the trustees.
**WHO TO APPLY TO** Irving Carter, Trustee, 9 Neville Drive, London N2 0QS *Tel.* 020 8455 9280 *email* brian@levyscharteredaccountants.co.uk

## ■ Loftus Charitable Trust

**CC NO** 297664      **ESTABLISHED** 1987
**WHERE FUNDING CAN BE GIVEN** UK and overseas.
**WHO CAN BENEFIT** Jewish organisations; religious and educational institutions.
**WHAT IS FUNDED** Jewish causes; relief of poverty; health and disability; education; religion.
**RANGE OF GRANTS** Up to £500,000.
**SAMPLE GRANTS** Jewish Care (£500,000); Chabad Lubavitch UK (£30,000); Kisharon and Norwood Ravenswood (£20,000 each); United Synagogue (£10,900); British Friend of Tikva Odessa (£10,000); Chai Cancer Care (£7,000); One Family UK and The Jewish Leadership Council (£5,000 each); Chief Rabbinate Trust (£3,000); Finchley Jewish Primary School Trust (£2,500). Awards of £2,500 or less across all categories totalled about £32,500.
**FINANCES** *Year* 2013/14 *Income* £862,500 *Grants* £719,240 *Grants to organisations* £719,240 *Assets* £161,058
**TRUSTEES** Andrew Loftus; Anthony Loftus; Richard Loftus.
**OTHER INFORMATION** There were 105 awards made.
**HOW TO APPLY** The trustees prefer to invite applications rather than considering unsolicited applications. The annual report for 2013/14 states: 'The trustees meet regularly to consider what grants they will make and to review any feedback they have received. Nominations for grants are elicited by formal and informal means. The trustees travel widely in the UK and abroad and use knowledge gained to support the objects of the Trust and to inform grant making. Though the trustees make some grants with no formal application, they normally ask invited organisations to submit a formal application saying how the funds would be used and what would be achieved. The trustees have a policy, which is communicated to all beneficiaries, that they make grants with no guarantees of future funding.'
**WHO TO APPLY TO** Anthony Loftus, Trustee, 55 Blandford Street, Marylebone, London W1U 7HW *Tel.* 020 7604 5900 *email* post@rhodesandrhodes.com

## ■ The Lolev Charitable Trust

**CC NO** 326249 **ESTABLISHED** 1982
**WHERE FUNDING CAN BE GIVEN** UK; Hackney and the surrounding area.
**WHO CAN BENEFIT** Individuals and organisations.
**WHAT IS FUNDED** Orthodox Jewish causes; education; religion; health and disability.
**TYPE OF GRANT** General running costs.
**SAMPLE GRANTS** A list of beneficiaries was not included; however, awards were made in the following categories: religious education (£167,000); poor and needy (£122,500); medical (£26,000); schools – including repairs (£16,500).
**FINANCES** Year 2013 Income £4,310,849 Grants £4,325,596 Grants to organisations £332,181 Assets £14,494
**TRUSTEES** Abraham Tager; Eve Tager; Michael Tager.
**OTHER INFORMATION** The majority of awards were given to individuals (£3.9 million).
**HOW TO APPLY** Applications may be made in writing to the correspondent. The annual report for 2013/14 states: 'Applications by individuals must be accompanied by a letter of recommendation by the applicant's minister or other known religious leader. In the case of applications by charities the collecting agent's references are verified by special agency, unless known to the trustees. Assistance is given according to circumstances and available finance.'
**WHO TO APPLY TO** Abraham Tager, Trustee, 14A Gilda Crescent, London N16 6JP *Tel.* 020 8806 3457

## ■ The Joyce Lomax Bullock Charitable Trust

**CC NO** 1109911 **ESTABLISHED** 2005
**WHERE FUNDING CAN BE GIVEN** Worldwide.
**WHO CAN BENEFIT** Registered charities. There appears to be a set list of organisations supported each year.
**WHAT IS FUNDED** General charitable purposes.
**SAMPLE GRANTS** Age UK; Cancer Research UK; Guide Dogs For The Blind; IWK Health Centre Foundation; Perennial; RAF Benevolent Fund; Royal Commonwealth Society; The National Trust; and The Royal British Legion. Each received two grants totalling £7,250.
**FINANCES** Year 2013/14 Income £1,351,513 Grants £65,250 Grants to organisations £65,250 Assets £3,131,062
**TRUSTEE** HSBC. Trust Company (UK) Limited.
**OTHER INFORMATION** There were a total of 18 awards made to nine organisations.
**HOW TO APPLY** Applications may be made in writing to the correspondent; however, note that 'grants are awarded at the discretion of the trustee but are generally in accordance with a letter of wishes provided by the late Joyce Lomax Bullock'. This seems to dictate that a set list of charities are awarded grants each year.
**WHO TO APPLY TO** C. Stroud, Trust Manager, HSBC Trust Company UK Limited, 10th Floor, Norwich House, Nelson Gate, Commercial Road, Southampton SO15 1GX *Tel.* 023 8072 3344

## ■ The Trust for London

**CC NO** 205629 **ESTABLISHED** 2004
**WHERE FUNDING CAN BE GIVEN** The Metropolitan Police District of London and the City of London.
**WHO CAN BENEFIT** Voluntary, community and other not-for-profit organisations; registered charities; bodies providing advice, information and advocacy; educational and training institutions; new initiatives; shelters and re-settlement homes; CICs and social enterprises. While most recipients are registered charities this is not a requirement. Priority is given to smaller and medium-sized organisations with an income of under £1 million.
**WHAT IS FUNDED The Central Fund:** Work that aims reduce poverty and inequality and bring about policy changes relating to discrimination, isolation, violence and improving people's quality of life. Current priorities (for the 2013–2017 period) are: employment; advice; social justice; violence.
**Exceptional Grants:** The website states: 'We may occasionally fund work to tackle poverty and inequality which falls outside our priorities. Organisations will need to demonstrate clearly how the work is exceptional or how your organisation is developing genuinely innovative approaches to address these issues; or that an exceptional need has arisen. You will need to speak to us if you wish to apply under this heading. Generally we will only make a few grants under this category each year.'
**Strategic Legal Fund for Vulnerable Young Migrants:** The fund 'makes small, one-off grants to voluntary organisations and private law firms to undertake pre-litigation research or to intervene in existing court cases'.
**WHAT IS NOT FUNDED** Proposals which do not benefit Londoners; direct replacement or subsidising of statutory funding (including contracts); work that is the primary responsibility of statutory funders, such as local and central government and health authorities; individuals; appeals on behalf of individuals; mainstream educational activity, including schools; medical purposes, including hospitals and hospices; the promotion of religion; umbrella bodies seeking to distribute grants on behalf of the charity; work that has already taken place; general appeals; large capital appeals (including buildings and minibuses); from applicants who have been rejected by the charity in the last six months. The foundation is unlikely to support proposals: from large national charities which enjoy widespread support; for work that takes place in schools during school hours; where organisations have significant unrestricted reserves, including those that are designated (generally up to six months expenditure is normally acceptable); where organisations are in serious financial deficit.
**TYPE OF GRANT** Core and management costs; capital expenditure; work that aims to change policy; one-off and multi-year funding; unrestricted; contracts.
**RANGE OF GRANTS** £7,500–£240,000
**SAMPLE GRANTS** London Citizens (£240,000); Inquest Charitable Trust (£150,000); Child Poverty Action Group (£136,000); Migrants Resource Centre (£102,000); Manor Gardens Centre (£101,500); Detention Advice Service (£90,000); Maternity Action (£87,000); Sustain: The Alliance for Better Food and Farming (£80,000); Survivors UK (£76,000); Harrow Law Centre (£72,000); Camden Federation for Private Tenants Ltd and Employability Forum (£70,000 each); Family and Childcare Trust (£65,000); Global Action Plan (£64,000); Family Rights Group, Greenwich Community Law Centre and Leap Confronting Conflict (£60,000 each); Migraine Trust (£58,000); Anti-Slavery International and Asylum Support Appeals Project (£50,000 each); Heart n Soul and Street Talk (£45,000 each); Southall Community

Alliance (£32,000); Camden Lesbian, Gay, Bisexual and Transgender Forum (£30,000); Black Training and Enterprise Group and Help Somalia Foundation (£25,000 each); Oromo Relief Association (£22,000); African Women Group, London Hazards Centre and Solace Women's Aid (£20,000 each); Employability Forum (£7,500). Most recent projects funded can be found on the charity's website.

**FINANCES** Year 2013 Income £9,090,334 Grants £11,176,181 Grants to organisations £11,176,181 Assets £264,373,274

**TRUSTEE** Trust for London Trustee Board.

**OTHER INFORMATION** The charity is made up of three funds: The Central Fund 'which aims to tackle poverty and inequality'; The City Church Fund 'for the advancement of religion'; The Trust for London Common Investment Fund 'to pool the investments of the other two funds'. The grant total consists of £6.7 million given through The Central Fund and £4.4 million through The City Churches Fund. Grants were allocated as follows: social justice (23%); advice (22%); employment (19%); violence (13%); small groups (9%); trust's initiatives (7%); Strategic Legal Fund (4%); exceptional cases (2%); Trustee Distribution fund (1%). It is intended to continue 'making fewer but larger grants with the intention that those grants have more impact'. About 130 groups are funded each year.

**HOW TO APPLY** Applications must be made using an online form. There are three deadlines – 4 February, 28 May and 8 October. The charity's website gives full details and extensive guidelines. These should cover all possible areas but if you are unclear about something do not hesitate to get in touch with the charity via phone. The consideration process can take approximately four and a half months from the closing date for successful applicants. Unsuccessful applicants can re-apply after 12 months following the rejection. There is a different application process for Strategic Legal Fund for Vulnerable Young Migrants.

**WHO TO APPLY TO** Mubin Haq, Director of Policy and Grants, 6–9 Middle Street, London EC1A 7PH Tel. 020 7606 6145 Fax 020 7600 1866 email info@trustforlondon.org.uk Website www.trustforlondon.org.uk

■ **London Catalyst**
**CC NO** 1066739   **ESTABLISHED** 1872
**WHERE FUNDING CAN BE GIVEN** Greater London, within the boundaries of the M25.
**WHO CAN BENEFIT** Charities and non-profit organisations; hospitals, homes and medical charities outside the NHS who are also registered charities; NHS hospitals throughout London; social work teams; individuals in need.
**WHAT IS FUNDED** Health inequalities and community projects in areas of social deprivation; relief of poverty; improvement of health and well-being of local people; raising awareness of the needs of people who are in poverty and suffer from illnesses.
**WHAT IS NOT FUNDED** General appeals; charities with an income over £1 million; hospitals and homes within the NHS (except Samaritan Grants); hospital league of friends for NHS and independent hospitals; government departments; profitable organisations.
**TYPE OF GRANT** Small awards; 'any reasonable and appropriate project cost, including salaries, training, volunteer expenses, management, supervision and evaluation costs; limited 'catalytic' project related grants are favoured.

**RANGE OF GRANTS** £200–£8,000

**SAMPLE GRANTS** Havering Citizens Advice and The Spires Centre (£8,000 each); KMEWO (£6,000); Faiths Together in Lambeth (£3,500); Home Start Havering and Newham Food Bank (£3,000 each); Camden Traumatic Stress Clinic (£2,500); Hackney Migrant Centre (£2,000); Carers Lewisham, Norwood and St Christopher's Hospice (£1,500 each); Brampton and Harefield Hospital (£1,300); Alternatives Trust and Barons Court Project (£1,000 each); Alone In London (£800); King George's Hospital SW Team (£500); Island Advice Centre (£400); Elderly SW Team Northwick Park (£200).

**FINANCES** Year 2013 Income £378,226 Grants £349,905 Grants to organisations £349,905 Assets £12,254,414

**TRUSTEES** Dr Steve Mowle; Yoke Wan Hopkins; Zoe Cam; Revd Adrian McKenna-Whyte; Margaret Elliott; Dr Muhammad Bari; Dr Ruth Kosmin; Andrew Davidson.

**OTHER INFORMATION** There were 138 awards to organisations and projects.

**HOW TO APPLY** Application forms and helpful guidance can be downloaded from the charity's website or requested by phone or letter. Applications and other grant enquiries are acceptable via email. All applications are reviewed against eligibility criteria and then considered by the grants scrutiny committee before presenting to the trustees for approval. The trustees meet every three months, normally in February, June, September and December. Application should be received six weeks in advance to a meeting. The Grants Administrator of the charity is Ian Baker.

**WHO TO APPLY TO** Susan Hickey, Secretary of Peabody Trust, c/o The Peabody Trust, Minster Court, 45–47 Westminster Bridge Road, London SE1 7JB Tel. 020 7021 4204 email london.catalyst@peabody.org.uk Website www.londoncatalyst.org.uk

■ **The London Community Foundation (formerly Capital Community Foundation)**
**CC NO** 1091263   **ESTABLISHED** 2002
**WHERE FUNDING CAN BE GIVEN** The London boroughs including the City of London.
**WHO CAN BENEFIT** Charities and community groups which do not attract mass public support with a priority for community based projects and small and medium-sized organisations; registered charities; social enterprises; CICs; companies limited by guarantee without share capital; faith groups; tenants and residents organisations; Friends of Schools; PTAs.
**WHAT IS FUNDED** A wide range of community causes, including environmental groups, employment schemes, mentoring for young people, homeless shelters, day centres for older people, activities supporting particularly disadvantaged and marginalised communities, tackling challenging issues, such as domestic violence or honour killing, relief of poverty, homelessness and social isolation.
**WHAT IS NOT FUNDED** Political groups; overseas trips; statutory organisations; activities which promote religion (faith groups can be assisted). Specific criteria may apply for different funds.
**TYPE OF GRANT** Unrestricted funding, including capital and core costs, feasibility studies, project, running costs, salaries and start-up costs; one-off or up to two years;.
**RANGE OF GRANTS** £500–£141,500

**SAMPLE GRANTS** City Gateway (£141,500); Out of the Dark (£20,000); Advocacy for older people in Greenwich (£19,900); The Choir with no name and The Connection at St Martin's (£15,000 each); Haringey Migrant Support Centre (£10,000); Big Barn CIC and Bromley Gypsy Traveller Project (£5,000 each); Birmingham Playcare Network (£3,700); African Women's Group (£3,600); Kingston Bereavement Service and Lewisham ArtHouse Ltd (£2,500 each); Sing London (£2,200); Society for the advancement of Black Arts (£1,800); Friends of Norwood park and Holland Town Residents Association (£500 each).

**FINANCES** Year 2013/14 Income £7,930,000 Grants £4,332,000 Grants to organisations £4,172,000 Assets £18,688,000

**TRUSTEES** Gaynor Humphreys; William Moore; Sanjay Mazumder; Juliet Wedderburn; Martin Richards; Davina Judelson; Francis Salway; Jesse Zigmund; Nicholas Reid; Paul Cattermull; Clive Cutbill; Christopher Samuel; Rosanna Machado.

**OTHER INFORMATION** The foundation manages and distributes funds on behalf of several donors, including companies, individuals and government programmes and is able to offer a number of grant programmes which cover different areas and types of activity. During the year a total of 1059 awards were made, including 507 to organisations and 552 to individuals (£160,000). In April 2012 North West London Community Foundation merged with LCF and in February 2013 East London Community Foundation decided to close its operations and transferred some of its assets to LCF.

**HOW TO APPLY** As the foundation offers funds on behalf of different donors, you may apply to each and every programme for which your group is eligible. The criteria will vary for each grant programme, so be sure to read the guidance carefully. The foundation notes: 'We endeavour to provide support to groups prior to the submission of applications. Organisations are encouraged to telephone LCF before making an application to discuss the most appropriate programmes for them and to discuss their project and their application. General guidance is given on the suitability of their project to individual funds and advice is given on how to put together an application.' The foundation looks for the following in an application: demonstration of need; sound governance; sound financial management; sound project planning; good partnership working; strong capacity and ability to deliver. Application forms, guidance notes and deadlines specific to each programme are available from the foundation and/or its website.

**WHO TO APPLY TO** Megan Chidlow, Finance and Operations Director, Unit 7, Piano House, 9 Brighton Terrace, London SW9 8DJ *Tel.* 020 7582 5117 *Fax* 020 7582 4020 *email* info@londoncf.org.uk *Website* www.londoncf.org.uk

## ■ London Housing Foundation Ltd (LHF)

**CC NO** 270178 **ESTABLISHED** 1975
**WHERE FUNDING CAN BE GIVEN** Principally, albeit not exclusively, Greater London.
**WHO CAN BENEFIT** Voluntary bodies; charities; housing and social care organisations. Projects 'must help people who are, have been, or are at risk of becoming homeless'.
**WHAT IS FUNDED** Homelessness, especially around criminal justice, health and employment, training and volunteering initiatives. Currently particular interest is on 'projects that look at health and how we can work more closely within the criminal justice system', priority is also given to 'projects looking at migration and destitution, or employment' as well as 'proposals dealing with the use of volunteering, or the prevention of homelessness'.
**TYPE OF GRANT** Capital and revenue costs; project funding; research.
**RANGE OF GRANTS** £3,500–£117,000
**SAMPLE GRANTS** De Paul International (£117,000); Islington Law Centre and Lambeth Law Centre (£30,000 each); South London YMCA (£27,500); Women in Prison (£23,500); Homeless Link (£20,000); Emmaus (£17,500); Hestia (£14,200); St Basil's (£11,300); Providence Row (£10,700); Housing Justice (£10,000); William Wilberforce Trust (£9,000); St Martins (£3,500).
**FINANCES** Year 2013/14 Income £614,152 Grants £522,706 Grants to organisations £522,706 Assets £16,033,333
**TRUSTEES** Simon Dow; Ian Brady; Donald Wood; John Stebbing; Jeremy Swain; Derek Joseph; Clare Miller; Eleanor Stringer; Victoria Rayner.
**OTHER INFORMATION** There were 20 awards made, which are loosely categorised as: organisational strengthening programme (£201,500); Criminal Justice System interface (£159,500); agency support (£133,000); research and special grants (£28,500). Further £60,500 was spent on projects. It is noted by the trustees in their annual report that 'it is likely that the concentration on grants rather than projects which is emphasised in the 2013/14 accounts will continue'.
**HOW TO APPLY** Applicants are asked to complete a short application on the foundation's website detailing their project idea. The foundation will then follow this up with the applicant.
**WHO TO APPLY TO** Jane Woolley, Charity Administrator, Tempus Wharf, 29A Bermondsey Wall West, London SE16 4SA *Tel.* 020 7934 0177 *Fax* 020 7934 0179 *email* info@lhf.org.uk or jane.woolley@lhf.org.uk *Website* www.lhf.org.uk

## ■ The London Law Trust

**CC NO** 1115266 **ESTABLISHED** 1968
**WHERE FUNDING CAN BE GIVEN** UK.
**WHO CAN BENEFIT** Educational and research institutions.
**WHAT IS FUNDED** The London Law Trust Medal, in association with Kings College London (annual fellowships are awarded for research in medicine or dentistry which is designed to impact on patient care); development of leadership qualities in young people (through the British Exploring Society). Note the following: 'The London Law Trust has entered into arrangements for funding medical research and leadership development programmes which are being run in conjunction with other institutions. As for the foreseeable future the Trust will be applying all of its available funds on these programmes, it regrets that it is no longer able to accept any new applications for grants.'
**WHAT IS NOT FUNDED** Applications from individuals, including students, are ineligible.
**SAMPLE GRANTS** King's College London (£112,500); and British Exploring Society (£73,500).

**FINANCES** Year 2013/14 Income £173,630 Grants £234,000 Grants to organisations £234,000 Assets £4,794,934
**TRUSTEES** Prof. Anthony Mellows; Roger Pellant; Michael Hobbs; Ian Gainsford.
**OTHER INFORMATION** In 2015–18 period the trustees have agreed to provide up to £80,000 per annum to King's College London in relation to The London Law Trust Medal and will continue supporting the British Exploring Society.
**HOW TO APPLY** Applications for new grants are not accepted for the foreseeable future.
**WHO TO APPLY TO** Matthew Yates, Correspondent, Hunters, 9 New Square, Lincoln's Inn, London WC2A 3QN Tel. 020 7412 0050 email londonlawtrust@hunters-solicitors.co.uk Website www.thelondonlawtrust.org

## ■ London Legal Support Trust (LLST)

**CC NO** 1101906  **ESTABLISHED** 2004
**WHERE FUNDING CAN BE GIVEN** London and the Home Counties.
**WHO CAN BENEFIT** 'Voluntary sector legal agencies in London and the Home Counties that employ solicitors or retain the services of solicitors as volunteers to provide free legal advice to poor or disadvantaged members the public' and network organisations that support such agencies.
**WHAT IS FUNDED** Legal services and projects that encourage or provide co-operation between voluntary sector legal agencies and volunteers from private practice; crisis intervention to 'keep the doors open' when funding cuts threaten the closure of a voluntary sector legal agency and when the trustees consider that short term funding may lead to sustainable recovery; one-off capital support to increase the capacity of an agency to deliver its service; creation of new social welfare legal and pro bono provision in London and the Home Counties.
**WHAT IS NOT FUNDED** Non-charitable activity; applications for general advice as opposed to specialist legal advice.
**TYPE OF GRANT** Small, one-off grants; core grant and support through Centres of Excellence scheme; facilities to raise funds at LLST events.
**RANGE OF GRANTS** £25–£42,500
**SAMPLE GRANTS** Surrey Law Centre (£42,500); The Royal Courts of Justice Advice Bureau (£28,500); South West London Law Centres (£26,500); Plumstead Law Centre (£15,000); Paddington Law Centre (£10,500); Working Families (£10,000); Public Concern at Work (£6,800); Luton Citizens Advice and Notre Dame Refugee Centre (£2,100 each); Prisoners Advice Service (£2,000); Youth Legal Resource Centre (£400); Money Advice Community Support (£350); The University of Kent Law Clinic (£90); South Westminster Legal Advice Centre (£25).
**FINANCES** Year 2013/14 Income £785,928 Grants £549,815 Grants to organisations £549,815 Assets £94,312
**TRUSTEES** Richard Dyton; Julian Clark; Marc Sosnow; Peter Gardner; Graham Huntley; Steve Hynes; Joy Julien; Jeremy Thomas; John Dunlop; Emma Turnbull; Amanda Illing; Jessica Clark; George Bacon; Rodger Pressland; Alistair Woodland.
**OTHER INFORMATION** There were 99 awards made.
**HOW TO APPLY** Application forms for Small Grants can be downloaded from the trust's website together with criteria and guidelines. The deadline is 25 June (in 2015) and after that at the end of October. If you would like to participate in the Centres of Excellence scheme get in touch with the trust and ask to be added to the waiting list. The process is explained in detail on the website.
**WHO TO APPLY TO** Robert Nightingale, Chief Executive, 40 Alexandra Road, Epsom, Surrey KT17 4BT Tel. 020 3088 3656 email chair@londonlegalsupporttrust.org.uk Website londonlegalsupporttrust.org.uk

## ■ The London Marathon Charitable Trust Limited

**CC NO** 283813  **ESTABLISHED** 1982
**WHERE FUNDING CAN BE GIVEN** London and any area where London Marathon stages an event (South Northamptonshire, Aylesbury Vale and Surrey).
**WHO CAN BENEFIT** Organisations involved with sports, recreation and leisure; educational establishments; local groups; clubs; charities.
**WHAT IS FUNDED** 'Provision of facilities for recreation and leisure activities within the London Boroughs and City of London area and other areas where the subsidiary entities stage events'. Any sport recognised by Sport England can be assisted. Grants have been made towards: the establishment of play areas and nature trails; improvements to existing leisure facilities; provision of MUGAs (Multi Use Games Areas); to various rowing organisations to provide new accommodation and boats.
**WHAT IS NOT FUNDED** 'Closed' clubs, unless the facility is available for regular public use; recurring or revenue costs; individuals.
**TYPE OF GRANT** One-off.
**RANGE OF GRANTS** £7,100–£2.2 million.
**SAMPLE GRANTS** London 2012 Legacy Stadia – Reserve (£2.2 million); City of Westminster – Marylebone Green Playground (£150,000); RB Greenwich – Hornfair park (£70,000); LB Camden – Talacre Community Sports Centre (£66,500); City of London – Golden Lane Estates (£27,000); Capel Parish Council (£23,000); Tolworth Gymnastics Club (£10,000); LB Lambeth – Kangley Bridge Road (£8,000); Challengers (£7,100).
**FINANCES** Year 2013/14 Income £4,181,473 Grants £4,736,495 Grants to organisations £4,736,495 Assets £13,261,218
**TRUSTEES** John Austin; John Disley; Sir Rodney Walker; John Bryant; Simon Cooper; John Spurlin; Ruth Dombey; Peter King; Charles Johnston; Edmond Warner; Charles Reed; Alan Pascoe.
**OTHER INFORMATION** The trust has no connection to the fundraising efforts of the individuals involved in the race, who raise over £40 million each year for their chosen good causes. The accounts note that there were more than £5 million available for allocation in 2014. The charity also spent £2.6 million on staff costs during the year.
**HOW TO APPLY** Application forms are available from the correspondent. The annual report and accounts for 2013/14 state that 'the trustees meet once a year to consider applications and are invariably oversubscribed'. The meeting is usually held at the end of August.
**WHO TO APPLY TO** Sarah Ridley, Chief Grants Officer/Secretary, Marathon House, 115 Southwark Street, London SE1 0JF Tel. 020 7902 0200 email lmct@ffleach.co.uk

## ■ The William and Katherine Longman Trust

**CC NO** 800785  **ESTABLISHED** 1988
**WHERE FUNDING CAN BE GIVEN** UK.
**WHO CAN BENEFIT** Registered charities.
**WHAT IS FUNDED** General charitable purposes.
**WHAT IS NOT FUNDED** Grants are only made to registered charities.
**TYPE OF GRANT** One-off and recurrent.
**RANGE OF GRANTS** £1,000–£30,000
**SAMPLE GRANTS** Mizpah Trust (£70,000); and Chelsea Arts Club (£20,000). Previous beneficiaries have also included: Vanessa Grant Trust (£30,000); Chelsea Festival and World Child Cancer Fund (£20,000 each); Care (£12,000); Hope Education Trust and RADA (£10,000 each); Action for ME (£5,000); The Children's Society (£4,500); Age Concern – Kensington and Chelsea (£3,500); RSPCA – Harmsworth Hospital (£3,000); St Mungo's (£2,500); and Prisoners Abroad (£1,000).
**FINANCES** Year 2013/14 Income £64,482 Grants £285,000 Grants to organisations £285,000 Assets £2,977,877
**TRUSTEES** William Harriman; Alan Bell.
**HOW TO APPLY** The trustees believe in taking a proactive approach in deciding which charities to support and it is their policy not to respond to unsolicited appeals.
**WHO TO APPLY TO** Grainne Feeney, Correspondent, Charles Russell LLP, 5 Fleet Place, London EC4M 7RD Tel. 020 7203 5196 email grainne.feeney@crsblaw.com

## ■ The Lord's Taverners

**CC NO** 306054  **ESTABLISHED** 1950
**WHERE FUNDING CAN BE GIVEN** Unrestricted; in practice, UK.
**WHO CAN BENEFIT** Cricket clubs affiliated to a National Governing Body; individual schools; groups; other organisations directly involved in the organisation of youth cricket and other sports, including rugby, tennis, squash, basketball and boccia, and which have a genuine need for assistance.
**WHAT IS FUNDED** Disability and disadvantaged cricket programmes; disability programmes and Play Spaces for young people with disabilities and special needs; Fun Days for pupils with disabilities and their carers at venues across the UK; the provision of minibuses; specially-adapted sporting equipment, sports wheelchairs, sensory and soft play and outdoor play equipment; high-quality sports kit for socially-deprived communities; support to Fields in Trust; delivery, management and support of inner city, disability and other youth sports activities and competitions; supporting the installation of non-turf pitches to increase the opportunities for young people to play and donation of hundreds of cricket equipment bags to communities, clubs and school teams across the UK; pathways for young people into employment, education and training and other positive activities including mainstream cricket.
**WHAT IS NOT FUNDED** See specific details for each of the programmes.
**SAMPLE GRANTS** A list of beneficiaries was not included in the annual report and accounts.
**FINANCES** Year 2013/14 Income £5,461,186 Grants £2,032,275 Grants to organisations £2,032,275 Assets £8,962,043
**TRUSTEES** Martin Smith; John Ayling; Robert Powell; Sally Surridge; Christine Colbeck; Roger Smith;

Richard White; Bob Bevan; Ruth Fitzsimons; Christopher Cowdrey.
**HOW TO APPLY** The trustees meet at least quarterly. All applications must be presented on the appropriate application forms – see the grant-making section for further information on separate programmes. Application forms with detailed application instructions are available from the charity's website or the correspondent.
**WHO TO APPLY TO** Charlotte Brooks, Grants Executive, 90 Chancery Lane, London WC2A 1EU Tel. 020 7025 0016 email charlotte.brooks@lordstaverners.org Website www.lordstaverners.org

## ■ The Loseley and Guildway Charitable Trust

**CC NO** 267178  **ESTABLISHED** 1973
**WHERE FUNDING CAN BE GIVEN** UK and overseas, particularly Surrey and surrounding counties.
**WHO CAN BENEFIT** Registered charities, charitable associations, trusts, societies and corporations benefitting people with various disabilities and terminal illness, children and victims of natural disasters.
**WHAT IS FUNDED** Compassionate causes, mainly local or causes with which various members of the More-Molyneux family and trustees are associated. General charitable purposes, including health and disability.
**WHAT IS NOT FUNDED** Grants are not made to non-registered charities.
**RANGE OF GRANTS** Up to £7,500.
**SAMPLE GRANTS** Disability Challengers (£7,500); Shooting Star Chase (£7,000); Stroke Association (£3,000); Marie Curie (£2,500); British Legion and Seafarers UK (£2,000 each); and Alt Society, Cherry Trees, Epilepsy Society, Gurkha Welfare, Life Train Trust, Motor Neurone Disease, RABI and RNLI (£1,000 each).
**FINANCES** Year 2013/14 Income £67,349 Grants £50,276 Grants to organisations £50,276 Assets £1,298,185
**TRUSTEES** Michael More-Molyneux; Susan More-Molyneux; Alexander More-Molyneux; Sophia More-Molyneux.
**OTHER INFORMATION** The trust states that 'the major part of the available funds tend to be distributed locally to charitable institutions which the trustees consider to be particularly worthy of support'. The annual grant total includes about £16,800 in awards of less than £1,000.
**HOW TO APPLY** Applications may be made in writing to the correspondent. The trustees meet in February, May and September to consider applications; however, due to commitments, new applications for any causes are unlikely to be successful.
**WHO TO APPLY TO** Helen O'Dwyer, Secretary, The Estate Offices, Loseley Park, Guildford, Surrey GU3 1HS Tel. 01483 405114 email charities@loseleypark.co.uk Website www.loseleypark.co.uk/charities

## ■ The Lotus Foundation

**CC NO** 1070111  **ESTABLISHED** 1998
**WHERE FUNDING CAN BE GIVEN** UK, especially London and Surrey; overseas.
**WHO CAN BENEFIT** Established or newly-formed charities.
**WHAT IS FUNDED** Social welfare; children and families; women; community causes; animal

protection; addiction recovery; homelessness; education.
**TYPE OF GRANT** One-off and recurrent.
**RANGE OF GRANTS** £1,000–£25,000
**SAMPLE GRANTS** British Red Cross and WaterAid (£25,000 each); T B Alert (£20,000); RNIB (£10,000); The Dame Vera Lynn Trust (£5,900); Operation Smile and WWF (£5,000 each); Chicken Shed and Hopes, Garden House School and Homes for Children (£2,500 each); St Joseph's School (£1,500); Alone in London and Save the Rhino (£1,000 each).
**FINANCES** Year 2013 *Income* £254,197 *Grants* £322,348 *Grants to organisations* £322,328 *Assets* £19,010
**TRUSTEES** Barbara Starkey; Richard Starkey; Emma Turner.
**OTHER INFORMATION** There were 46 awards.
**HOW TO APPLY** Applications may be made in writing to the correspondent, giving a brief outline of the work, the amount required and project/programme to benefit. The trustees prefer applications which are simple and economically prepared rather than glossy 'prestige' and mail sorted brochures. However, our research indicates that in order to reduce administration costs and concentrate the efforts on the charitable work at hand, unsolicited requests will no longer be acknowledged by the foundation.
**WHO TO APPLY TO** Barbara Starkey, Trustee, c/o Startling Music Ltd, 90 Jermyn Street, London SW1Y 6JD *Tel.* 020 7930 5133 *email* info@lotusfoundation.com *Website* www.lotusfoundation.com

## ■ The Lower Green Foundation
**CC NO** 1137862   **ESTABLISHED** 2010
**WHERE FUNDING CAN BE GIVEN** Worldwide.
**WHO CAN BENEFIT** Organisations and individuals.
**WHAT IS FUNDED** General charitable purposes. Future priorities include: education for young people; youth apprenticeship schemes; and medical research. The annual report for 2013/14 states: 'Grant requests from charities that focus on students, and particularly those that provide apprenticeship opportunities, are expected to be prioritised in the coming year.'
**RANGE OF GRANTS** £1,000–£60,000
**SAMPLE GRANTS** Youth and Philanthropy Initiative (£60,000); First Give and The Prince's Trust (£25,000 each); Motivation (£20,000); Tick Tock Club (£15,000); Bumley Breakfast Clubs (£12,000); Free The Children and The Pelican Trust (£10,000 each); The Lullaby Trust (£3,000); and Pret Foundation (£1,300).
**FINANCES** Year 2013/14 *Income* £627,441 *Grants* £181,257 *Grants to organisations* £181,257 *Assets* £861,371
**TRUSTEES** Laurence Billett; Marina Sajitz; Sinclair Beecham.
**OTHER INFORMATION** In 2013/14 a total of ten grants were made.
**HOW TO APPLY** Applications could be made in writing to the correspondent.
**WHO TO APPLY TO** Pam Henness, Correspondent, 10–14 Old Church Street, London SW3 5DQ *email* info@lowergreen.com

## ■ The Lowy Mitchell Foundation
**CC NO** 1094430   **ESTABLISHED** 2002
**WHERE FUNDING CAN BE GIVEN** Worldwide.
**WHO CAN BENEFIT** Charitable organisations, chosen at the trustees' discretion.

**WHAT IS FUNDED** General charitable purposes; Jewish causes.
**WHAT IS NOT FUNDED** Religious campaigning is not funded.
**RANGE OF GRANTS** £100–£20,000
**SAMPLE GRANTS** Portobello Media (£20,000); Community Security Trust (£10,000); UK Jewish Film Festival (£5,000); Help for Heroes (£2,000); The Amos Bursary (£1,500); National Theatre (£1,250); Batsheva Dance Company (£1,000); and Pratham UK and Jewish Community Centre (£150 each).
**FINANCES** Year 2013/14 *Income* £5,382 *Grants* £63,000 *Grants to organisations* £63,000
**TRUSTEES** Parry Mitchell; Hannah Mitchell; Amanda Delew; Julia Weiner.
**OTHER INFORMATION** In 2013/14 the foundation had a total expenditure of over £73,000. The grant total is an estimate based on previous research.
**HOW TO APPLY** Applications may be made in writing to the correspondent. The foundation has previously stated that normally only a few awards can be made each year.
**WHO TO APPLY TO** Hannah Mitchell, Correspondent, 3 Elm Row, London NW3 1AA *Tel.* 020 7431 1534 *email* jtrent@hwfisher.co.uk

## ■ The C. L. Loyd Charitable Trust
**CC NO** 265076   **ESTABLISHED** 1973
**WHERE FUNDING CAN BE GIVEN** UK, there may be some preference for local causes in Oxfordshire.
**WHO CAN BENEFIT** National charities and local organisations known or associated to the trustees, benefitting at risk groups, and people with disabilities, those disadvantaged by poverty or socially isolated people.
**WHAT IS FUNDED** General charitable purposes; local causes; health and disability; welfare charities; animal welfare; education; arts and culture.
**WHAT IS NOT FUNDED** Support is not available to individuals or for medical research.
**TYPE OF GRANT** One-off and recurrent.
**RANGE OF GRANTS** Up to £55,000; mostly under £1,000.
**SAMPLE GRANTS** County Buildings Protection Trust (£55,000); The Mobility Trust (£10,000); and Ardington and Lockinge PCC (£8,000); Friends of the Ashmolean Museum and Racing Welfare (£500 each); Royal Agricultural Benevolent Institute (£300); Eton College Fund (£250); Art Collections Fund National, British Sporting Artists and Walpole Society (£100 each); Animal Health Trust and Berkshire Archaeological Society (£50 each); Dean and Chapter – Oxford Cathedral (£20); National Childbirth Trust (£10); and Royal Wilts Yeomanry £5).
**FINANCES** Year 2013/14 *Income* £88,061 *Grants* £63,555 *Grants to organisations* £63,555 *Assets* £2,721,237
**TRUSTEES** Thomas Loyd; Alexandra Loyd.
**OTHER INFORMATION** Other grants of less than £1,000 amounted to £10,000.
**HOW TO APPLY** Applications can be made in writing to the correspondent. Grants are made several times each month.
**WHO TO APPLY TO** Thomas Loyd, Trustee, The Lockinge Estate Office, Ardington, Wantage OX12 8PP *Tel.* 01235 833200

# ■ LSA Charitable Trust

**CC NO** 803671 **ESTABLISHED** 1989
**WHERE FUNDING CAN BE GIVEN** UK.
**WHO CAN BENEFIT** Individuals and institutions working in agricultural and horticultural education and research. Former tenants and employees of the former Land Settlement Association Ltd, who are in need.
**WHAT IS FUNDED** Advancement of horticultural and agricultural education and research. Grants are also made for the relief of poverty for former members, employees and tenants of the Land Settlement Association Limited.
**SAMPLE GRANTS** The Plunkett Foundation (£20,000).
**FINANCES** Year 2013/14 Income £219,915 Grants £39,507 Grants to organisations £20,150 Assets £91,145
**TRUSTEES** G. W. Richards, Chair; Prof. P. Hadley; C. F. Woodhouse; Dr S. P. Thornton-Wood.
**OTHER INFORMATION** In 2013/14 grants totalling £19,400 were made to individuals in need, included in the overall grant total. A grant of £20,000 was made to The Plunkett Foundation. The trustees also resolved to enter into two partnerships: firstly with The Plunkett Foundation, which will receive around £20,000 per year for five years, towards a co-operative horticultural enterprise; secondly with East Malling Research/University of Reading, which will receive around £25,000 per year for three years, towards a plant breeding project.
**HOW TO APPLY** The trust is currently not accepting applications for grants from organisations. The trust's website states the following: 'the trust has recently reviewed its activities, and (alongside its continuing concern for poverty relief) has initiated a longer-term partnership basis to its funding. As a consequence, the Trust is not currently considering applications for small grants.' Grants to individuals for the relief of poverty are made through the Royal Agricultural Benevolent Institution.
**WHO TO APPLY TO** Cheryl Boyce, c/o Farrer and Co, 66 Lincoln's Inn Fields, London WC2A 3LH *Tel.* 020 3375 7000 *email* secretarialservices@farrer.co.uk *Website* lsact.wordpress.com

# ■ The Marie Helen Luen Charitable Trust

**CC NO** 291012 **ESTABLISHED** 1984
**WHERE FUNDING CAN BE GIVEN** Worldwide. Our research indicates that there may be some preference for Wimbledon.
**WHO CAN BENEFIT** Charitable organisations and individuals.
**WHAT IS FUNDED** Social welfare; education; health and disability, particularly cancer relief; homelessness; the relief of hardship, pain and suffering. Grants are also given to relieve poverty and social disadvantage in financially developing countries.
**RANGE OF GRANTS** £1,000–£10,000
**SAMPLE GRANTS** Macmillan Cancer Relief (£10,000); Marie Curie Cancer Care (£6,000); Alzheimer's Society (£2,000); and Crisis, Mpemba Orphanage – Malawi, Paul D'Aria Cancer, Prostate Cancer Research Centre, Smile Train, St Mungo's, Trinity Hospice and WaterAid (£1,000 each). In addition the trust provided funding for educational grants to students in India – 50% of 287 separate grants to assist with paying school fees in conjunction with The Joshi Foundation totalling £7,500.
**FINANCES** Year 2013 Income £44,208 Grants £43,000 Grants to organisations £43,000 Assets £1,229,078
**TRUSTEES** Richard Littleton; Nushi Kassam; Jyoti Joshi.
**OTHER INFORMATION** There were 23 awards made during the year.
**HOW TO APPLY** Applications can be made writing to the correspondent.
**WHO TO APPLY TO** Richard Littleton, Trustee, Littleton, Apartment 221, 21–33 Worple Road, London SW19 4BH *Tel.* 020 8949 6962 *email* richard@esppos.com

# ■ Robert Luff Foundation Ltd

**CC NO** 273810 **ESTABLISHED** 1977
**WHERE FUNDING CAN BE GIVEN** UK.
**WHO CAN BENEFIT** Medical research charities.
**WHAT IS FUNDED** Medical research, especially into Cystic Fibrosis.
**TYPE OF GRANT** Support to selected organisations; one-off where funds left; research.
**RANGE OF GRANTS** Up to £100,000.
**SAMPLE GRANTS** Cystic Fibrosis Trust and ESPA Research (£100,000 each); Bowel Disease Research Foundation and Royal Brompton Hospital (£80,000 each); Asthma UK, Alzheimer's Research UK and Sheffield Teaching Hospital (£50,000 each); Gordon Highlanders (£45,000); Myotubular Trust (£40,000); Bath Institute for Rheumatic Diseases (£25,000); The Inspire Foundation (£22,500); Foundation for Circulatory Health (£20,000); Midlands Air Ambulance (£10,000); Calvert Trust (£7,500); Norman Laud Association (£5,000). Awards under £5,000 totalled £22,500.
**FINANCES** Year 2013/14 Income £386,021 Grants £940,110 Grants to organisations £940,110 Assets £28,976,803
**TRUSTEES** Jean Tomlinson; Richard Price; Sir Robert Johnson; Revd Matthew Tomlinson; Melanie Condon; Brian Nicholson; Lady Ruth Bodey.
**OTHER INFORMATION** There were 29 awards made.
**HOW TO APPLY** The foundation makes its own decisions about what causes to support. It has previously stated that 'outside applications are not considered, or replied to'.
**WHO TO APPLY TO** Richard Price, Secretary, Waters Edge, Ferry Lane, Moulsford, Wallingford, Oxfordshire OX10 9JF *email* rpjprice@gmail.com

# ■ The Henry Lumley Charitable Trust

**CC NO** 1079480 **ESTABLISHED** 2000
**WHERE FUNDING CAN BE GIVEN** UK and overseas.
**WHO CAN BENEFIT** Registered charities and individuals.
**WHAT IS FUNDED** General charitable purposes, with a preference towards medicine, education and the relief of poverty.
**TYPE OF GRANT** Grants of up to three years for capital and core expenditure or project costs.
**RANGE OF GRANTS** £2,000–£15,000
**SAMPLE GRANTS** Royal College of Surgeons (£15,000); Stroke Association (£5,000); Action on Addiction, Blond McIndoe Laboratories – University of Manchester, Diabetes UK and Spinal Research Trust (£4,000 each); Action Medical Research, Army Benevolent Fund, Dystonia Society, Outward Bound Trust, Ovarian Cancer Action, Prostate Cancer Charity, Royal British Legion, Surrey Boys' Club and WOW (Wellbeing of Women) (£2,500 each); and St

Paul's Cathedral Foundation and Young Epilepsy (£2,000 each).
**FINANCES** Year 2013/14 Income £93,372 Grants £126,000 Grants to organisations £126,000 Assets £3,456,755
**TRUSTEES** Henry Lumley; Peter Lumley; Robert Lumley; James Porter.
**HOW TO APPLY** Applications can be made in writing to the correspondent.
**WHO TO APPLY TO** Peter Lumley, Trustee, c/o Lutine Leisure Ltd, Windlesham Golf Club, Bagshot, Surrey GU19 5HY Tel. 01276 472273

## ■ Paul Lunn-Rockliffe Charitable Trust

**CC NO** 264119    **ESTABLISHED** 1972
**WHERE FUNDING CAN BE GIVEN** UK, with a preference for Hampshire.
**WHO CAN BENEFIT** Charitable organisations. Preference is given to smaller and locally based charities and those which may be known to the trustees, or members of their family.
**WHAT IS FUNDED** The trust makes grants in the following categories: older people; children; disability; education and students; family; mission: people in need, individuals with drug addiction, homeless and unemployed people; people who have offended, radio/mission; financially developing countries; young people; one-off emergency aid; and 'others'. Each year the trustees allocate a proportion of the funds for donation to be applied to charities not previously supported and for special one-off causes.
**WHAT IS NOT FUNDED** The trustees will not fund individuals, for example, student expenses or travel grants. The repair and maintenance of historic buildings are also excluded.
**TYPE OF GRANT** Our research suggests that core costs, one-off and start-up costs may be covered. Funding for more than three years will be considered.
**RANGE OF GRANTS** Most grants are for £1,000.
**SAMPLE GRANTS** Afghan Connection, Bible Society, Carroll Youth Centre, Christians Against Poverty, Community of Holy Fire – Zimbabwe children, Friends of the Family, Hull and East Riding Institute for the Blind, Neema Craft UK, Parish of St George Hanworth, People International, Prison Fellowship, Sobell House Hospice Charity, The Door of Hope and Winchester Live at Home Scheme (£1,000 each); and Armed Forces Christian Union and Consequences (£500 each).
**FINANCES** Year 2013/14 Income £77,490 Grants £35,500 Grants to organisations £35,500 Assets £1,745,307
**TRUSTEES** Jacqueline Lunn-Rockliffe; James Lunn-Rockliffe; Bryan Boult; Lucy Tomkins.
**OTHER INFORMATION** Grants were made to 37 organisations.
**HOW TO APPLY** Applications can be made in writing to the correspondent. The trust will generally only reply to written correspondence if an sae has been included.
**WHO TO APPLY TO** James Lunn-Rockliffe, Trustee, 6A Barnes Close, Winchester, Hampshire SO23 9QX email plrcharitabletrust@gmail.com

## ■ C. F. Lunoe Trust Fund

**CC NO** 214850    **ESTABLISHED** 1960
**WHERE FUNDING CAN BE GIVEN** UK.
**WHO CAN BENEFIT** Universities; charities; ex-employees (and their dependants) of Norwest Holst Group Ltd.
**WHAT IS FUNDED** Relief in need; education, training and research in the construction industry.
**RANGE OF GRANTS** £4,000–£34,500
**SAMPLE GRANTS** I.C.E QUEST Fund (£34,500); University of Leeds (£11,000); The Danish Church in London (£4,000).
**FINANCES** Year 2013/14 Income £77,259 Grants £124,230 Grants to organisations £105,500 Assets £1,733,139
**TRUSTEES** Peter Lunoe; John Henke; Alexandra Coghill; John Jefkins; John Dodson; Trevor Parks.
**OTHER INFORMATION** Support was allocated as follows: grants (£89,500); payments to beneficiaries (£18,700); donations (£16,000). The accounts for 2013/14 state that 'the charity did not approve or pay any grants in the year' to individuals but supported eight individuals in the year (we take 'payments to beneficiaries' to account for individual support and deduct this amount from the grant total).
**HOW TO APPLY** Applications may be made in writing to the correspondent. However, the majority of the charity's funds go to organisations already known to the trustees and as a result new applications are unlikely to be successful.
**WHO TO APPLY TO** John Dodson, Trustee, 78 Cassiobury Drive, Watford, Hertfordshire WD17 3AQ Tel. 01923 232502

## ■ The Ruth and Jack Lunzer Charitable Trust

**CC NO** 276201    **ESTABLISHED** 1978
**WHERE FUNDING CAN BE GIVEN** UK.
**WHO CAN BENEFIT** Organisations benefitting children, young adults and students; educational and arts establishments; other charitable bodies.
**WHAT IS FUNDED** General charitable purposes; Jewish causes; children and young adults; education; the arts.
**TYPE OF GRANT** Mainly recurrent.
**RANGE OF GRANTS** £100–£4,000
**SAMPLE GRANTS** Kahal Chassidim Bobov (£5,000); Chai Cancer Care (£4,000); Moreshet Hatorah (£3,000); Community Security Trust (£1,500); Golders Green Beth Hamedrash Congregation (£1,400); Heart Cells Foundation and Ner-Yisrael Education Trust (£500 each); Kisharon (£200); and Drugsline-Chabad, Laniado Hospital UK and Magen David Adorn UK (£100 each).
**FINANCES** Year 2013/14 Income £27,000 Grants £22,925 Grants to organisations £22,925 Assets £549,320
**TRUSTEES** Jack Lunzer; Martin Paisner.
**HOW TO APPLY** Applications have to be made in writing to the correspondent, providing full details of your organisation. Requests are considered on a regular basis. Note that unsuccessful applicants are not acknowledged.
**WHO TO APPLY TO** Martin Paisner, Trustee, c/o Berwin Leighton Paisner, Adelaide House, London Bridge, London EC4R 9HA Tel. 020 7760 1000 email martin.paisner@blplaw.com

## ■ Lord and Lady Lurgan Trust

**CC NO** 297046  **ESTABLISHED** 1987

**WHERE FUNDING CAN BE GIVEN** England (largely London), Northern Ireland and South Africa.

**WHO CAN BENEFIT** Registered charities; educational establishments; hospices.

**WHAT IS FUNDED** The trust's Charity Commission record specifies the following: 'Music and the encouragement of young musicians is a key activity. Other grants in England and Northern Ireland are mainly to medical causes with an emphasis on research and medical conditions affecting older people the care of people suffering from cancer, including support for hospices and disability, particularly deafness.'

**WHAT IS NOT FUNDED** Support is not given for organisations in Scotland. Grants to individuals or for expeditions are not made either. It is unlikely that the trust will be able to help with core costs and it is unable to respond to emergency appeals.

**TYPE OF GRANT** One-off and recurrent awards for specific projects, up to one year.

**RANGE OF GRANTS** £1,000–£5,000

**SAMPLE GRANTS Previous beneficiaries have included:** Deafblind UK; English National Opera; Greater Shankhill Business Forum; Help the Aged; Isabel Hospice; Johannesburg Children's Home; King's College London; Macmillan Cancer Relief; Oesophageal Patients Association; Queen's University – Belfast; Royal College of Music; St Joseph's Hospice; South African Federation for Mental Health; The Pushkin Trust; Ulster Youth Choir; and WaterAid.

**FINANCES** Year 2013/14 Income £21,918 Grants £82,500 Grants to organisations £82,500

**TRUSTEES** Simon Ladd; Andrew Stebbings; Diana Graves; Brendan Beder.

**OTHER INFORMATION** Grants are awarded twice a year totalling approximately £80,000 annually. The grant total is estimated based on the patterns of previous giving, as the accounts were not required to be filed with the Charity Commission. About three quarters of the overall grant total is given in the UK with the remainder awarded in South Africa.

**HOW TO APPLY** Application forms can be downloaded from the trust's website and should be returned preferably by email. Read the grant policy on the website before completing the form. The trustees meet twice a year, in December and July. The deadline for the December meeting is 31 October and for the July meeting – 31 May. Applications must also include: the latest signed and audited accounts; a budget for the financial year in which the project falls, separating income which relates to the project; the budget for the project; and details about any other funding received or pending.

**WHO TO APPLY TO** Andrew Stebbings, Trustee, 45 Cadogan Gardens, London SW3 2AQ Tel. 020 7591 3333 Fax 020 7591 3412 email charitymanager@pglaw.co.uk Website www.lurgantrust.org

## ■ The Lyndhurst Trust

**CC NO** 235252  **ESTABLISHED** 1964

**WHERE FUNDING CAN BE GIVEN** UK and overseas, with preferences for disadvantaged areas in North East England.

**WHO CAN BENEFIT** Christian organisations.

**WHAT IS FUNDED** Bodies connected with the propagation of the gospel or the promotion of the Christian religion; distribution of bibles and other Christian religious works; support for Christian missions in the UK and abroad; support to the clergy; maintenance of churches and chapels of any Christian denomination; work with disadvantaged people in society applying the Christian ethos; promoting awareness of the Christian gospel in those areas of the world where people are prevented from hearing it through the normal channels of communication. The accounts note: 'Agencies operating in difficult circumstances are given special consideration. The trustees have continued their policy of making funds available to the disadvantaged in the United Kingdom. In addition, the trustees have given special consideration to charities involved in supporting the members of the persecuted church around the world. Churches in the north east of England have been given continued support due to the particular needs of the communities where they are operating.'

**WHAT IS NOT FUNDED** Individuals; buildings.

**RANGE OF GRANTS** £500–£12,000

**SAMPLE GRANTS** A full list of beneficiaries was not included in the accounts; however, it was specified that £5,000 was made to St Luke's Church. **Previous beneficiaries have included:** Sowing Seeds (£12,000); Junction 42 (£5,000); Lydia's House, St Luke's Church and Friends International (£3,000 each); Ichthus Christian Fellowship, Newcastle Chaplaincy and St Barnabas Church (£2,000 each); Eden North East and Healing on the Streets (£1,000 each); Action Foundation, Blue Sky Trust and Trinity Church – Gosforth (£500 each).

**FINANCES** Year 2013 Income £37,033 Grants £100,000 Grants to organisations £100,000 Assets £1,357,074

**TRUSTEES** Revd Dr Robert Ward; Jane Hinton; Ben Hinton; Sally Tan.

**OTHER INFORMATION** Support was allocated as follows: North East England (£41,000); overseas relief (£22,000); the rest of the UK (£21,000); overseas mission (£16,000).

**HOW TO APPLY** Applications may be made in writing to the correspondent.

**WHO TO APPLY TO** The Trustees, PO Box 615, North Shields NE29 1AP

## ■ The Lynn Foundation

**CC NO** 326944  **ESTABLISHED** 1985

**WHERE FUNDING CAN BE GIVEN** UK and overseas.

**WHO CAN BENEFIT** Registered charities; institutions benefitting musicians, textile workers and designers, and other artists, organisations benefitting older people and people with disabilities; hospices.

**WHAT IS FUNDED** General charitable causes, particularly people with disabilities, music and other arts, sponsorship of young people, medical research and hospices. Our research suggests that Masonic charities are also assisted.

**TYPE OF GRANT** One-off grants for core, capital and project support. Loans are also made. In practice unrestricted funding.

**RANGE OF GRANTS** In 2013/14 the average grant was £583.

**SAMPLE GRANTS** Grants were given in the following areas, even though a list of beneficiaries was snot included in the accounts: children with disabilities; adults with disabilities; arts; hospices; young people sponsorship; medical research; music; and sundry.

Alphabetical register of grant-making charities — **Lyons**

**FINANCES** Year 2013/14 Income £329,392 Grants £258,400 Grants to organisations £258,400 Assets £6,018,204
**TRUSTEES** Guy Parsons; Ian Fair; John Emmett; Philip Parsons; John Sykes.
**OTHER INFORMATION** A total of 443 awards were made during the year. The foundation's Charity Commission record notes that it awards about 500 grants to individuals and organisations.
**HOW TO APPLY** Applications can be made in writing to the correspondent.
**WHO TO APPLY TO** Guy Parsons, Trustee, 17 Lewes Road, Haywards Heath, West Sussex RH17 7SP *Tel.* 01444 454773 *email* thelynnfoundation@yahoo.com

■ **John Lyon's Charity**

CC NO 237725     ESTABLISHED 1578
**WHERE FUNDING CAN BE GIVEN** The London boroughs of Barnet, Brent, Camden, City of London, City of Westminster, Ealing, Hammersmith and Fulham, Harrow and Kensington and Chelsea.
**WHO CAN BENEFIT** Registered charities and organisations with automatic charitable status working with children and young people; schools; local authorities; exempt charities; churches; national organisations benefitting the defined area.
**WHAT IS FUNDED** Education and training; arts and culture; sport and recreation; activities for young people; disability and counselling services; other projects and services aimed at improving the lives of children and young people in the charity's beneficial area.
**WHAT IS NOT FUNDED** Individuals; national organisations with no track of delivery in the area of benefit; not-for-profit organisations that are not registered charities; housing associations; faith schools with a closed admissions policy; schools that have not yet been inspected by Ofsted; hospitals, hospices or Clinical Commissioning Groups; to cover statutory obligations; general charitable appeals, unless of specific benefit to children and young people in the beneficial area; to provide for lobbying or campaigning; to undertake research, unless it is designed to lead directly to the advancement of practical activities in the community; endowment funds; to help with mother tongue teaching; to help with feasibility studies; to cover medical care, including rehabilitation, and resources; to replace statutory funding; to provide for telephone helplines; to cover overnight school journeys or trips abroad; to provide capital for educational institutions; to help with IT equipment; to provide bursaries for higher education; programmes which fall under PHSE (Personal, Health, Social and Economic Education); environmental projects, conservation and therapeutic gardens; to provide core costs for umbrella bodies or second tier organisations; registered charities that have applied on behalf of organisations that are not registered with the Charity Commission; to promote religion or politics; fund advice and information services; housing associations.
**TYPE OF GRANT** Capital and revenue costs, salaries, buildings and refurbishments, equipment and project expenditure for up to three years. One award per organisation at a time.
**RANGE OF GRANTS** Up to £250,000.
**SAMPLE GRANTS** Anna Freud Centre (£150,000 over three years); Brent Play Association (£60,000); DreamArts and St Andrew's Club (£40,000 each); Revitalise (£32,000); English National Ballet (£30,000); Youth Music Theatre (£25,000); The Big House Theatre Company (£24,000); Cricket Foundation, Egalitarian Trust and Wide Horizons Outdoor Education Trust (£20,000 each); Institute of Physics (£18,000); Chance for Children and Westminster Bangladeshi Welfare Trust (£10,000 each); Asia House (£7,300); Envision (£7,000).
**FINANCES** Year 2013/14 Income £7,246,000 Grants £6,823,000 Grants to organisations £6,823,000 Assets £307,416,000
**TRUSTEE** The Governors of the John Lyon School, Harrow.
**OTHER INFORMATION** During the year a total of 162 new grants were approved. The largest proportion of funding is given for 'education and learning' (16%).
**HOW TO APPLY** The Main Grants Fund

**Stage One – Initial Proposal**
Write to the correspondent at any time with the following information: 'a summary of the main purpose of the project'; 'details of the overall amount requested'; 'the timescale of your project'; 'some indication of how funds from the charity would be allocated'. The trust has produced guidelines on how best to write the initial proposal which can be accessed on the website. The trustees meet to decide awards three times a year in March, June and November.
**Stage Two – Application Form**
If your Initial Proposal is assessed positively, you will be advised whether you will need to complete an application form and informed on when your application form must be returned.
**Small Grants Fund:** There is no application form for this fund – you should send an initial proposal letter and if more information is required the Grants Team will request it.
**School Explorer Fund:** Application forms can be downloaded from the charity's website and submitted at any time. Applications should include: 'a completed application form signed by the Headteacher and the relevant department head or classroom teacher'; 'details of your annual Arts activities, how much these cost and how they are currently funded'; 'the relevant section of your School Improvement Plan'; 'your latest Ofsted inspection results'. Note that it takes at least six months for the application process to be completed. The grants committee meets at least three times a year
**WHO TO APPLY TO** Cathryn Pender, Grants Director, The Grants Office, 45 Cadogan Gardens, London SW3 2TB *Tel.* 020 7591 3330 *Fax* 020 7591 3412 *email* info@johnlyonscharity.org.uk *Website* www.johnlyonscharity.org.uk

■ **The Lyons Charitable Trust**

CC NO 1045650     ESTABLISHED 1995
**WHERE FUNDING CAN BE GIVEN** UK.
**WHO CAN BENEFIT** Registered charities.
**WHAT IS FUNDED** Health and disability; medical research; animals; children; education and training.
**TYPE OF GRANT** Recurrent.
**RANGE OF GRANTS** £4,000–£12,000
**SAMPLE GRANTS** Helen and Douglas House (£12,000); Streetsmart (£10,000); Macmillan Cancer Support, St Thomas Hospital and The Royal Marsden Hospital (£8,000 each); CLIC Sargent (£5,000); and Curwen Print Study Centre (£4,000).

**FINANCES** Year 2013/14 Income £36,046 Grants £55,000 Grants to organisations £55,000 Assets £909,195
**TRUSTEES** Gareth Read; Jonathan Gibbon; Robin Worby; Michael Gibbon.
**OTHER INFORMATION** Historically, the same charities are supported each year. A total of seven grants were given in 2013/14.
**HOW TO APPLY** The annual report for 2013/14 states that 'the trustees have decided that the most effective method of applying the charity's resources is to make distributions to known charitable organisations'. The trust will therefore not be considering any new applications for the foreseeable future.
**WHO TO APPLY TO** Michael Gibbon, Chair, Nicholas House, River Front, Enfield, Middlesex EN1 3FG Tel. 07804 854905 email hibidge@gmail.com

## ■ The Sir Jack Lyons Charitable Trust

**CC NO** 212148      **ESTABLISHED** 1960
**WHERE FUNDING CAN BE GIVEN** UK and Israel.
**WHO CAN BENEFIT** Charitable organisations benefitting children and young people, people in performing arts, particularly musicians, students, at risk groups, people disadvantaged by poverty and those who are socially isolated; Jewish charities; educational establishments; projects for young people.
**WHAT IS FUNDED** Jewish causes; performing arts, especially music; education; humanitarian causes, particularly in Israel.
**WHAT IS NOT FUNDED** Grants are not made to individuals.
**TYPE OF GRANT** Mainly recurrent.
**RANGE OF GRANTS** £1,500–£65,000
**SAMPLE GRANTS** Banff Centre (£70,500); Federation CJA – Youth Futures in Beer Sheva (£65,000); Jerusalem Foundation – Rachel Karwan Centre (£26,000); Yezreel Valley College (£12,300); Federation CJA – Na'eh Youth Centre (£6,100); Jewish Institute of Music (£5,100); Rubinstein Foundation (£3,000); and University of York – Celebration Prize (£1,500).
**FINANCES** Year 2013/14 Income £120,905 Grants £323,998 Grants to organisations £323,998 Assets £3,023,168
**TRUSTEES** Mortimer Friedman; Paul Mitchell; David Lyons; Belinda Lyons-Newman.
**OTHER INFORMATION** The trust made seven grants in 2013/14.
**HOW TO APPLY** Applications may be made in writing to the correspondent; however, note that in the past the trust has stated that 'in the light of increased pressure for funds, unsolicited appeals are less welcome and would waste much time and money for applicants who were looking for funds which were not available.'
**WHO TO APPLY TO** Paul Mitchell, Gresham House, 5–7 St Paul's Street, Leeds LS1 2JG Tel. 01332 976789 email paul.mitchell@sagars.co.uk

## ■ Sylvanus Lysons Charity

**CC NO** 202939      **ESTABLISHED** 1980
**WHERE FUNDING CAN BE GIVEN** Diocese of Gloucester.
**WHO CAN BENEFIT** Individuals; organisations; religious bodies; widows of clergy; Church of England.
**WHAT IS FUNDED** Religious and charitable work in the areas of young people, families, community causes, music, disadvantaged individuals, relief in need for widows, clergy and other people. According to the annual report, 'the trustees have pursued a policy of giving assistance to establish projects within the charity's purposes and to support them through the initial years before they can become self-funding'.
**WHAT IS NOT FUNDED** The latest accounts state: 'The Trustees' policy at present is not to make grants towards the cost of repairs of churches or other buildings, other than in exceptional circumstances.'
**TYPE OF GRANT** One-off and recurrent.
**RANGE OF GRANTS** £300–£30,000
**SAMPLE GRANTS** St Michael's – Cornerstone (£30,000); Gloucester Cathedral Youth Choir and Gloucester Diocese Clergy Conference (£20,000 each); Allsaints Academy Cheltenham (£19,000); CURVE (£16,000); Holy Apostles Cheltenham (£12,000); Youth Trip (£6,200); Three Choirs Festival (£5,000); Gloucester Diocese Clergy Leadership Training (£2,400); Ashchurch PCC St Nicholas (£800); The King's School Bursaries (£300).
**FINANCES** Year 2012/13 Income £344,061 Grants £261,541 Grants to organisations £236,453 Assets £9,605,055
**TRUSTEES** Bernard Day; G. V. Doswell; Revd Anne Spargo; The Ven. Robert Springett; Revd Canon Stephen Bowen.
**OTHER INFORMATION** At the time of writing (June 2015) this was the latest information available. During the year a total of 35 grants were made to organisations and 60 to individuals. Support was classified as follows: youth work (£104,000); courses and training (£33,500); children and family work (£31,000); other (£27,500); choirs and music and grants in aid to clergy, widows and others (£25,000 each); work with disadvantaged children and individuals (£12,000); street pastors (£3,900).
**HOW TO APPLY** Applications can be made in writing to the correspondent.
**WHO TO APPLY TO** A. Holloway, c/o Rowberry Morris Solicitors, Morroway House, Station Road, Gloucester GL1 1DW Tel. 01452 301903

■ **M. and C. Trust**
CC NO 265391   ESTABLISHED 1973
WHERE FUNDING CAN BE GIVEN UK.
WHO CAN BENEFIT Mainly Jewish organisations; educational establishments; health institutions.
WHAT IS FUNDED General charitable purposes; Jewish causes; social welfare; health and disability; disadvantaged people. The trust's primary objects are people of Jewish faith and welfare needs.
WHAT IS NOT FUNDED Grants are not made to individuals.
TYPE OF GRANT One-off and recurrent grants.
RANGE OF GRANTS £2,500–£20,000
SAMPLE GRANTS Jerusalem Foundation, Jewish Care, Norwood and One Voice Europe (£20,000 each); British Heart Foundation, Oasis of Peace and World Jewish Relief (£10,000 each); London Jewish Cultural Centre (£8,000); Nightingale Hammerson (£7,500); Carers Trust and Helen and Douglas House (£7,000 each); Ambitious About Autism, Deafblind UK, Jewish Women's Aid and WaveLength (£5,000 each); Break (£4,000); Chickenshed Theatre Company (£3,000); and Action For Kids and Homestart Camden (£2,500 each).
FINANCES Year 2013/14 Income £120,697 Grants £144,500 Grants to organisations £144,500 Assets £4,546,217
TRUSTEES Rachel Lebus; Kate Bernstein; Elizabeth Marks; Victoria Fairley.
OTHER INFORMATION During the year 29 grants were made. Further £50,000 was agreed for payment in 2014/15.
HOW TO APPLY Applications may be made in writing to the correspondent.
WHO TO APPLY TO Helen Price, Correspondent, c/o Mercer and Hole Trustees Limited, Gloucester House, 72 London Road, St Albans, Hertfordshire AL1 1NS Tel. 01727 869141 email helenprice@mercerhole.co.uk

■ **The M. K. Charitable Trust**
CC NO 260439   ESTABLISHED 1966
WHERE FUNDING CAN BE GIVEN Unrestricted, in practice mainly UK.
WHO CAN BENEFIT Orthodox Jewish organisations.
WHAT IS FUNDED General charitable purposes; Jewish causes; education; religion; health and disability; relief of poverty.
SAMPLE GRANTS In 2013/14 grants were made for: 'financial support to the poor; provision of basic necessities to the poor; relief of sickness and disabilities; Jewish education and places of worship for the Jewish community'. The annual report and accounts did not list any further details of grant recipients.
FINANCES Year 2013/14 Income £977,158 Grants £321,496 Grants to organisations £321,496 Assets £8,867,199
TRUSTEES A. Piller; D. Katz; Simon Kaufman; Z. Kaufman.
HOW TO APPLY Applications can be made in writing to the correspondent. The trust accepts applications for grants from representatives of Orthodox Jewish charities, which are reviewed by the trustees on a regular basis.

WHO TO APPLY TO Simon Kaufman, Trustee, 50 Keswick Street, Gateshead, Tyne and Wear NE8 1TQ Tel. 0191 490 0140

■ **The Madeline Mabey Trust**
CC NO 326450   ESTABLISHED 1983
WHERE FUNDING CAN BE GIVEN UK and overseas, particularly Asia.
WHO CAN BENEFIT Registered charities, including UK and international bodies.
WHAT IS FUNDED Children's welfare and education; medical research; humanitarian aid worldwide.
WHAT IS NOT FUNDED Individuals.
SAMPLE GRANTS Previous beneficiaries have included: Barnardo's; Cancer Research UK; Disasters Emergency Committee; Help for Heroes; Education Engineering Trust; Great Ormond Street Children's Hospital; Save the Children; UNICEF.
FINANCES Year 2013/14 Income £223,032 Grants £232,730 Grants to organisations £232,730 Assets £164,443
TRUSTEES Alan Daliday; Bridget Nelson; Joanna Singeisen.
OTHER INFORMATION Grants were made to 93 organisations. A list of beneficiaries was unavailable.
HOW TO APPLY The annual report for 2013/14 notes: 'The Trust favours identifying organisations itself, although it is willing to consider applications for grants.' Only successful appeals are acknowledged.
WHO TO APPLY TO Joanna Singeisen, Trustee, Madeline Mabey Trust, Woodview, Tolcarne Road, Beacon, Camborne, Cornwall TR14 9AB Tel. 01209 710304 email J.Singeisen@Mabey. co.uk Website www.mabeygroup.co.uk/about/ heritage/the-madeline-mabey-trust

■ **The E. M. MacAndrew Trust**
CC NO 290736   ESTABLISHED 1984
WHERE FUNDING CAN BE GIVEN UK.
WHO CAN BENEFIT Charitable organisations; medical and welfare charities.
WHAT IS FUNDED General charitable purposes; health causes; relief of poverty; education; arts and culture; community causes. The main focus is on medical and social welfare causes.
RANGE OF GRANTS £1,000–£6,000
SAMPLE GRANTS British Red Cross (£6,000 in two grants); Bucks Community Foundation and MK Community Foundation (£4,000 in two donations each); Thames Valley Partnership (£3,000); Medical Detection Dogs (£2,000 in two awards); and ABF The Soldiers' Charity, Beds Garden Carers Appeal, Canine Partners, Hope Asia, National Association of Almshouses, Royal Voluntary Society and Thames Valley Air Ambulance (£1,000 each).
FINANCES Year 2013/4 Income £52,277 Grants £47,000 Grants to organisations £47,000 Assets £1,290,760
TRUSTEES Amanda Nicholson; John Nicholson; Sally Grant; Verity Nicholson.
HOW TO APPLY The trust has informed us that they do not respond to any unsolicited applications under any circumstances, as they prefer to make their own decisions as to which charities to support.
WHO TO APPLY TO James Thornton, Correspondent, J. P. Thornton and Co., The Old Dairy, Adstockfields, Adstock, Buckingham MK18 2JE Tel. 01296 714886 Fax 01296 714711 email jpt@jptco.co.uk

## The Macdonald-Buchanan Charitable Trust

**CC NO** 209994  **ESTABLISHED** 1952

**WHERE FUNDING CAN BE GIVEN** UK, with a slight preference for Northamptonshire.

**WHO CAN BENEFIT** Registered charities, with a small preference for those benefitting Northamptonshire.

**WHAT IS FUNDED** A wide range of general charitable purposes, including health and disability, animal welfare, armed forces, children and young people, older people and religious causes.

**WHAT IS NOT FUNDED** Grants are not made to individuals or for campaigning purposes.

**TYPE OF GRANT** Mainly recurrent, up to one year towards capital expenditure.

**RANGE OF GRANTS** £30–£15,000

**SAMPLE GRANTS** Carriceo Charitable Trust and The Orrin Charitable Trust (£15,000 each); National Horseracing Museum (£3,500); All Saints Church – Cottesbrook (£2,000); Brooke Hospital for Sick Animals, Racing Welfare, Royal National Lifeboat Institute and The Scots Guards Charitable Fund (£1,200 each); The Royal Star and Garter Homes (£900); Gurkha Welfare Trust (£700); Asthma UK, Church of England Children's Society, Hearing Dogs for the Deaf, Help for Heroes, King George's Fund for Sailors, Royal Agricultural Benevolent Fund and WWF UK (£500 each); The Institute of Cancer Research (£400); Queen Elizabeth Foundation (£100); Litchfield Cathedral (£50); and Pytchley Hunt Limited (£30).

**FINANCES** Year 2013 Income £145,603 Grants £114,280 Grants to organisations £114,280 Assets £3,783,409

**TRUSTEES** Alastair Macdonald-Buchanan; Capt. John Macdonald-Buchanan; Mary Philipson; AJ. Macdonald-Buchanan; Joanna Lascelles; Hugh Macdonald-Buchanan.

**OTHER INFORMATION** During the year a total of 147 awards were made, the majority of which were for £500 or less.

**HOW TO APPLY** Applications may be made in writing to the correspondent and are generally considered once a year. Only successful applicants are notified. The annual report for 2013 states that the 'current policy is to make regular payments to a number of national and local charities with which they have long established connections' nevertheless there is a proportion of income reserved 'to make ad hoc substantial donations when approached for funding from those charities with which [the trustees] are more closely involved'.

**WHO TO APPLY TO** Linda Cousins, Correspondent, Rathbone Trust Co Ltd, 1 Curzon Street, London W1J 5FB *Tel.* 020 7399 0820 *email* linda.cousins@rathbone.com

## The R. S. Macdonald Charitable Trust

**SC NO** SC012710  **ESTABLISHED** 1978

**WHERE FUNDING CAN BE GIVEN** Scotland.

**WHO CAN BENEFIT** Charitable organisations and research institutions working in Scotland.

**WHAT IS FUNDED** Individuals suffering from neurological conditions; people who are blind or have a visual impairment; welfare of children (under the age of 18), especially who have been or are in danger of being abused physically, sexually or mentally; animal welfare. There are six charities specifically named in the trust deed (Capability Scotland, Children 1st, Guide Dogs for the Blind, Royal Blind, RNLI, and Scottish SPCA). The trust offers: small grants (up to £10,000 decided on an ongoing basis); main grants (over £10,000 decided twice a year – in March and September); medical research grants (accounts for about 20% of annual awards).

**WHAT IS NOT FUNDED** Non-registered charities; individuals; charitable organisations that cannot demonstrate that they are delivering benefit in Scotland.

**TYPE OF GRANT** One-off and recurring costs; capital and revenue funding; salaries; project expenditure; research (universities – seedcorn or unrestricted funding; charities – specific research projects that have already been through a peer review assessment process).

**RANGE OF GRANTS** £1,500–£53,500; average grants are for about £30,000.

**SAMPLE GRANTS** The trust's website gives details of recent projects supported. **Beneficiaries included**: Alzheimer Scotland (£53,500); University of Glasgow (£50,000); University of Edinburgh Development Trust (£50,000 in two grants); University of St Andrews (£35,000); Visualise Scotland (£30,500); Brook Scotland (£30,000); Action for Children Scotland (£21,000); Stirling Family Support Services (£20,000); Artlink Edinburgh and the Lothians (£16,100); Forget-Me-Not Club (£15,000); Nordoff-Robbins Music Therapy in Scotland (£10,300); Outfit-Moray (£10,000); Calibre Audio Library (£8,000); Garvald Glenesk (£6,300); Dundee Blind and Partially Sighted Society and Scottish Greyhound Sanctuary (£5,000 each); Go Kids Go (£4,000); A-T Society (£1,500).

**FINANCES** Year 2013/14 Income £1,735,251 Grants £1,792,334 Grants to organisations £1,792,334

**TRUSTEES** Richard Austin; Tricia Donald; Moira McCaig; Fiona Patrick; Bruce Rigby.

**OTHER INFORMATION** The website states: 'We aim to distribute up to £2 million annually through our grants programmes and are also keen to assist beneficiary charities with non-financial support.'

**HOW TO APPLY** Applications should be made using an online system on the trust's website. Appeals must also include details of the proposed project and a copy of the latest accounts. There are different deadlines (or no deadline for small grants), depending on the purpose of the grant and the type of organisation applying, but they all fall in March or September (see the website for details). The trust asks to contact the correspondent for an early discussion before making an application for a medical research grant. Decisions on main grants are made at the trustee meetings at the end of May and November.

**WHO TO APPLY TO** Douglas Hamilton, Director, 21 Rutland Square, Edinburgh EH1 2BB *Tel.* 0131 228 4681 *email* dhamilton@rsmacdonald.com *Website* www.rsmacdonald.com

## The Mackay and Brewer Charitable Trust

**CC NO** 1072666  **ESTABLISHED** 1998

**WHERE FUNDING CAN BE GIVEN** UK.

**WHO CAN BENEFIT** Charitable organisations.

**WHAT IS FUNDED** General charitable purposes, including health and disability causes and animal welfare.

**TYPE OF GRANT** One-off or recurrent.

**RANGE OF GRANTS** In 2013/14 two grants totalling £7,275.
**SAMPLE GRANTS** Hampshire Association for the Care of the Blind; Macmillan Cancer Trust; Marie Curie Cancer Care; National Trust for Scotland; Open Doors; PDSA; St John Ambulance for Wales; The National Trust for Scotland; and The Salvation Army. Each beneficiary received two grants totalling £7,275.
**FINANCES** Year 2013/14 Income £1,218,021 Grants £58,200 Grants to organisations £58,200 Assets £2,818,410
**TRUSTEE** HSBC. Trust Company UK. Limited.
**OTHER INFORMATION** During the year 16 grants were made to eight organisations (two awards each).
**HOW TO APPLY** Applications may be made in writing to the correspondent.
**WHO TO APPLY TO** Christopher Stroud, Trust Manager, Trust Services, 10th Floor, Norwich House, Nelson Gate, Commercial Road, Southampton SO15 1GX *Tel.* 023 8072 3344

## ■ The Mackintosh Foundation

**CC NO** 327751   **ESTABLISHED** 1988
**WHERE FUNDING CAN BE GIVEN** Worldwide; in practice mainly UK.
**WHO CAN BENEFIT** Registered charities; educational establishments; hospitals; individuals.
**WHAT IS FUNDED** Preference for theatre and the performing arts; education; young and older people; medicine, especially cancer and HIV/AIDS; homelessness; community projects; conservation projects and the protection of natural environment; refugees; other charitable purposes.
**WHAT IS NOT FUNDED** Religious or political activities; individuals are discouraged (apart from the foundation's drama award and some exceptions).
**TYPE OF GRANT** Capital costs; schools' core costs; project expenditure; recurring costs up to three years.
**RANGE OF GRANTS** Up to £75,000; most grants £1,000–£5,000.
**SAMPLE GRANTS** Chichester Festival Theatre (£125,000); Disasters Emergency Committee (£75,000); Kids Company (£41,000); Buzz Project (£30,000); Taunton Theatre Association (£25,000); Macmillan Cancer Support (£16,000); Royal Welsh College of Music and Drama (£15,000); European Union Youth Orchestra and State Library of Victoria Foundation (£10,000 each); National Youth Theatre of Great Britain (£7,500); Horatio's Garden, Marefat Education Centre, Motivation Charitable Trust, National Student Drama Festival Ltd and Prostate Cancer Charity (£5,000 each). Other grants totalled about £197,500.
**FINANCES** Year 2013/14 Income £56,157 Grants £660,302 Grants to organisations £660,302 Assets £8,445,528
**TRUSTEES** Sir Cameron Mackintosh; Nicholas Mackintosh; Nicholas Allott; Robert Noble; Bart Peerless; Thomas Schonberg; F. Richard Pappas.
**OTHER INFORMATION** A total of 189 grants were made to organisations. There were four individual beneficiaries (amount granted was not specified).
**HOW TO APPLY** Applications should be made in writing to the correspondent, outlining details of the organisation, the project for which funding is required and a breakdown of the costs involved. Supporting documents should be kept to a minimum and an sae enclosed (if materials are to be returned). The trustees meet in May and October in plenary session, but a grants committee meets weekly to consider smaller grants. The foundation responds to all applications in writing and the process normally takes between four and six weeks.
**WHO TO APPLY TO** Richard Nibb, Secretary, 1 Bedford Square, London WC1B 3RB *Tel.* 020 7637 8866 *email* info@camack.co.uk

## ■ The MacRobert Trust

**SC NO** SC031346   **ESTABLISHED** 1943
**WHERE FUNDING CAN BE GIVEN** UK, with a preference for Scotland.
**WHO CAN BENEFIT** Registered charities; organisations benefitting children, young adults and older people, ex-service and service people, seafarers and fishermen, volunteers, people in arts, at risk groups, carers, people with disabilities and those disadvantaged by poverty or socially isolation.
**WHAT IS FUNDED** General charitable purposes. Six core themes are: armed forces services and seafarers; education and training; children and young people; science, engineering and technology; agriculture and horticulture; Tarland and the local area needs.
**WHAT IS NOT FUNDED** Organisations based or beneficiaries resident outside the UK; individuals (except through the trust's own training schemes); general or mailshot appeals; political organisations; religious organisations; retrospective applications; student bodies as opposed to universities; departments within a university unless the appeal gains the support of, and is channelled through, the Principal; fee-paying schools (except through the trust's own Educational Grants Scheme for children who are at, or need to attend, a Scottish independent secondary school); expeditions, except through the auspices of recognised bodies such as the British Exploring Society; community and village halls other than those in Tarland and the local area; pre-school groups, after-school clubs or school PTAs except where they lie in the local area; hospices, except where they lie in the local area.
**TYPE OF GRANT** Core costs; project expenditure; capital costs; buildings; feasibility studies; research; recurring and running costs; salaries; unrestricted funding; one-off and for up to three years.
**RANGE OF GRANTS** Mostly £5,000–£10,000; small donations of up to £1,000 can be made in urgent cases.
**SAMPLE GRANTS** Inspiring Scotland and University of St Andrews (£50,000 each); The Robert Gordon University (£30,000); Sir Oswald Stoll Foundation (£20,000); Wilderness Foundation UK (£10,000); The Royal Institution of Great Britain (£9,100); Blue Sky Development and Regeneration (£7,000); Association for Citizenship Teaching, Oakleaf Enterprise and Toe in the Water (£5,000 each); The Royal Forestry Society (£4,000); Happy Days Children's Charity and Northern Ireland Cancer Fund for Children (£2,000 each); Go Kids and The Royal Aero Club Trust (£1,000 each); SSAFA – Aberdeen Branch (£600); Textile Conservation Foundation (£500); Riding for the Disabled (£40); Advocacy North East (£10).
**FINANCES** Year 2013/14 Income £2,868,338 Grants £573,519 Grants to organisations £573,519 Assets £81,349,740

**TRUSTEES** S. Campbell; C. D. Crole; K. Davis; J. D. Fowlie; C. W. Pagan; J. C. Swan; J. H. Strickland; P. J. Hughesdon; C. Stevenson.

**OTHER INFORMATION** The trust runs a Horticultural Training Scheme (primarily based at Douneside) and can make grants for deserving pupils in independent Scottish secondary schools (and also pupils at two English schools – Oundle and Cranleigh – which were attended by Lady MacRobert's sons). It also provides The MacRobert Award in engineering, The MacRobert Prize to one graduating officer cadet at the Royal Air Force College – Cranwell, The Lady MacRobert Trophy to the North East Scotland Air Training Corps (ATC) squadron, and offers MacRobert Trust flying scholarship operated by the Air League and sponsors Scottish farming scholarships on a trial basis through the Nuffield Farming Scholarship Trust. In 2013/14 awards totalling £25,500 to ten separate schools on behalf of 12 pupils were made. In addition to the grants paid in the year, a total of about £376,500 was committed for payment in a later year and around £152,500 was paid in grants committed in previous years. During the year there were 82 awards made (56 new appeals supported).

**HOW TO APPLY** Application forms and full guidelines can be downloaded from the trust's website, although applications **must** be posted. The trustees meet twice a year, usually in March and October/November. All applicants receive a written acknowledgement of receipt and a reply whether or not they have been successful. To be considered, applications must be received for the March meeting by 31 October previously and for the October meeting by 31 May previously. According to the website: 'Unsuccessful applicants must wait for at least one year from the time of being notified before re-applying. Successful applicants must wait for at least two years from the time of receiving a donation before re-applying. When a multi-year donation has been awarded, the time bar applies from the date of the final instalment. Withdrawn applications do not normally face a time bar.' The trust stresses the importance of including an informative covering letter; completing *all* sections of the application form and asks that applicants maintain a process of dialogue with the trust: 'We deal with many hundreds of worthy applications each year. If we have to chase you for information, you will understand that our interest might wane.'

**WHO TO APPLY TO** Rear Admiral Chris Hockley, Chief Executive Office, Cromar, Tarland, Aboyne, Aberdeenshire AB34 4UD *Tel.* 01339 881444 *email* vicky@themacroberttrust.org.uk *Website* www.themacroberttrust.org.uk

■ **The Mactaggart Third Fund**

**SC NO** SC014285    **ESTABLISHED** 1969
**WHERE FUNDING CAN BE GIVEN** UK and overseas.
**WHO CAN BENEFIT** Charitable organisations.
**WHAT IS FUNDED** A wide range of general charitable purposes, including relief of poverty, health, education, religion, community development, citizen participation, arts and culture, sports, human rights, environment, animal welfare and disadvantaged individuals.
**RANGE OF GRANTS** £100–£31,500; most grants up to £5,000.
**SAMPLE GRANTS** Friends of the Environment (£31,500); Bahamas National Trust (£22,000); Port Ellen Station (£18,800); Kipp New York Inc. (£15,000); The Real Experience (£10,000); Islay Gaelic Choir (£8,900); Above the Clouds (£5,000); Hearing Dogs for Deaf People (£4,100); Medical Aid for Palestinians (£3,000); Wolvercote Young People's Club (£2,800); Great Ormond Children's Hospital (£1,000); Weiner Library (£500); Royal Marsden Cancer Charity (£100).
**FINANCES** *Year* 2013/14  *Income* £576,998  *Grants* £391,005  *Grants to organisations* £391,005  *Assets* £14,258,197
**TRUSTEES** Sandy Mactaggart; Robert Gore; Fiona Mactaggart; Andrew Mactaggart; Sir John Mactaggart.
**OTHER INFORMATION** According to the website the charity aims to award about £250,000 in grants each year. In 2013/14 a total of 138 grants were made.
**HOW TO APPLY** The website notes: 'The Trustees have decided to take a proactive approach to their grant-making. Their present policy is to make grants to those charities whose aims they support and who they believe have demonstrated excellence in their achievements. **Please note the fund does not accept unsolicited applications.**'
**WHO TO APPLY TO** The Trustees, 2 Babmaes Street, London SW1Y 6HD *Website* www.mactaggartthirdfund.org

■ **The Ian Mactaggart Trust (The Mactaggart Second Fund)**

**SC NO** SC012502    **ESTABLISHED** 1969
**WHERE FUNDING CAN BE GIVEN** UK and overseas; there may be some preference for Scotland.
**WHO CAN BENEFIT** Charitable organisations.
**WHAT IS FUNDED** The trust supports a wide range of activities, including education and training, arts and culture and the relief of people who are poor, sick, in need or have disabilities.
**RANGE OF GRANTS** £25–£70,500
**SAMPLE GRANTS** Port Ellen Station (£70,500); Robin Hood Foundation (£47,500); Battersea Arts Centre (£40,000); Oxfordshire Community Foundation (£19,500); Kipp New York Inc. (£15,000); Stagecoach Charitable Trust (£8,000); The Promise (£7,000); Tate Foundation (£5,000); East Harlem Tutorial Program (£4,300); British Tinnitus Association (£3,500); Phoenix Group For Deaf Children (£1,000); Humanitas (£750); Malawi Project 2014 (£500); CHL Charity 0099 (£25).
**FINANCES** *Year* 2013/14  *Income* £576,767  *Grants* £377,950  *Grants to organisations* £377,950  *Assets* £10,965,125
**TRUSTEES** Sir John Mactaggart; Philip Mactaggart; Jane Mactaggart; Fiona Mactaggart; Lady Caroline Mactaggart; Leora Armstrong.
**OTHER INFORMATION** The website states: 'The Trust aims to make grants of circa £200,000 each year.' During the year 102 grants were made.
**HOW TO APPLY** According to the annual report for 2013/14, the trustees 'have decided to take a proactive approach to their grant-making' and 'their present policy is to make grants to those charities whose aims they support and who they believe have demonstrated excellence in their achievements'. Accordingly the trust does not accept unsolicited applications.
**WHO TO APPLY TO** The Trustees, 2 Babmaes Street, London SW1Y 6HD *Website* www.ianmactaggarttrust.org/index.htm

## ■ James Madison Trust

**CC NO** 1084835　　**ESTABLISHED** 2000
**WHERE FUNDING CAN BE GIVEN** UK.
**WHO CAN BENEFIT** Charities; educational institutions; research projects.
**WHAT IS FUNDED** The trust defines its objects as the support and promotion of 'studies of federal government whether within or among states and of related subjects, including the processes that may lead towards the establishment of such government, and to support or promote education and dissemination of knowledge of these subjects'.
**TYPE OF GRANT** Research; seminars; conferences; studies; publications.
**RANGE OF GRANTS** £3,500–£155,000
**SAMPLE GRANTS Previous beneficiaries have included:** Federal Trust; London Metropolitan University; University of Cardiff; University of Edinburgh; University of Kent; University of Middlesex; Unlock Democracy. Our research also notes that the following specific projects have been supported: Additional Constitutionalism; Autonomy Website; Book of Federal Studies 06; Centre for Federal Studies; Climate Change Research; Comparative Devolution; European Foreign and Security Policy; Federal Trust Projects; Regions of England; Welsh Papers.
**TRUSTEES** Robert Emerson; Ernest Wistrich; John Pinder; John Bishop; Richard Corbett.
**OTHER INFORMATION** Information given by the University of Kent website notes that one of the main purposes of the trust has been to support the Centre for Federal Studies at the university and providing funding for academic activities and postgraduate master's and doctoral programmes. At the time of writing (June 2015) this was the latest information available; the trust has not submitted its accounts to the Charity Commission since 2011/12. In the past about £141,500 on average has been spent on charitable expenditure. The charity has remains active on the Charity Commission's records and maintains the potential to give; therefore we maintain the entry.
**HOW TO APPLY** Applications may be made in writing to the correspondent.
**WHO TO APPLY TO** David Grace, 68 Furnham Road, Chard TA20 1AP *Tel.* 01460 67368

## ■ The Magdalen and Lasher Charity (General Fund)

**CC NO** 211415　　**ESTABLISHED** 1951
**WHERE FUNDING CAN BE GIVEN** In or around the borough of Hastings.
**WHO CAN BENEFIT** Individuals; pensioners; charitable organisations helping those in need; educational establishments.
**WHAT IS FUNDED** Pensions for older people in Hastings; education; health care; facilities and buildings; community services; relief of poverty.
**WHAT IS NOT FUNDED** Debt repayment; mini buses.
**TYPE OF GRANT** One-off for one year or less.
**FINANCES** *Year* 2013/14 *Income* £1,882,911 *Grants* £114,193 *Grants to organisations* £24,030 *Assets* £13,431,864
**TRUSTEES** Keith Donaldson; Gareth Bendon; Ian Steel; Jenny Blackburn; Michael Foster; Clive Galbraith; Susan Parsons; John Hodges; Revd Robert Featherstone; Sue Phillips; Yvonne Hardman; Dawn Poole; Ann Wing; Nicola Harris; Joy Waite.
**OTHER INFORMATION** In 2013/14 pensions totalled about £65,000. Out of the overall amount of 'grants in aid' around £28,000 was given to other individuals. There were 26 organisational awards.
**HOW TO APPLY** Application forms are available from the correspondent. Guidelines and criteria are available to view on the charity's website.
**WHO TO APPLY TO** Gill Adamson, Correspondent, 132 High Street, Hastings, East Sussex TN34 3ET *Tel.* 01424 452646 *email* mlc@oldhastingshouse.co.uk *Website* www.magdalenandlasher.co.uk

## ■ The Magen Charitable Trust

**CC NO** 326535　　**ESTABLISHED** 1984
**WHERE FUNDING CAN BE GIVEN** UK.
**WHO CAN BENEFIT** Registered charities, especially Jewish organisations.
**WHAT IS FUNDED** Relief of poverty; education; religious activities; Jewish focus.
**WHAT IS NOT FUNDED** Grant contracts.
**SAMPLE GRANTS Previous beneficiaries have included:** Manchester Yeshiva Kollel; Talmud Educational Trust; Bnos Yisroel School; Mesifta Tiferes Yisroel.
**FINANCES** *Year* 2013/14 *Income* £193,049 *Grants* £156,904 *Grants to organisations* £156,904 *Assets* £1,498,061
**TRUSTEES** Jacob Halpern; Rosa Halpern.
**OTHER INFORMATION** A full list of beneficiaries was not included within the accounts.
**HOW TO APPLY** Applications may be made in writing to the correspondent.
**WHO TO APPLY TO** The Trustees, New Riverside, 439 Lower Broughton, Salford M7 2FX *Tel.* 0161 792 2626 *email* sy@seyo.co.uk

## ■ The Mageni Trust

**CC NO** 1070732　　**ESTABLISHED** 1998
**WHERE FUNDING CAN BE GIVEN** UK.
**WHO CAN BENEFIT** Arts organisations; registered charities.
**WHAT IS FUNDED** A wide range of general charitable purposes; arts.
**WHAT IS NOT FUNDED** Individuals.
**TYPE OF GRANT** One-off and recurrent.
**RANGE OF GRANTS** Up to £10,000.
**FINANCES** *Year* 2013/14 *Income* £18,417 *Grants* £1,000,000 *Grants to organisations* £1,000,000
**TRUSTEES** Garfield Collins; Gillian Collins; Alex Collins; Tom Collins.
**OTHER INFORMATION** Due to low income accounts were not required to be filed with the Charity Commission. In 2013/14 the trust had an unusually high expenditure.
**HOW TO APPLY** Unsolicited applications are not considered.
**WHO TO APPLY TO** Garfield Collins, Trustee, Leslie Cottage, The Promenade, Pevensey Bay, East Sussex BN24 6HE *Tel.* 01323 460770 *email* garfcollins@gmail.com

## ■ The Brian Maguire Charitable Trust

**CC NO** 1091978　　**ESTABLISHED** 2002
**WHERE FUNDING CAN BE GIVEN** UK, with some preference for the south of England.
**WHO CAN BENEFIT** Charitable organisations; hospices; care centres; community projects.
**WHAT IS FUNDED** General charitable purposes.
**RANGE OF GRANTS** Mostly £300–£5,000.

**SAMPLE GRANTS** The Great Steward of Scotland's Dumfries House Trust (£2 million); Camphill and Watford Palace Theatre (£5,000 each); Bowel Disease Research and British Lung Foundation (£3,000 each); Leukaemia and Lymphoma Research, Scottish Autism and The Cure Parkinson's Trust (£2,000 each); Mercy Ships, Royal National Lifeboat Institution, The British Red Cross and West Norfolk RSPCA Rehoming Centre (£1,000 each); Watford Foodbank (£500); Jordan's Music Club and Watford Philharmonic (£300 each).
**FINANCES** Year 2013/14 Income £71,187 Grants £2,047,500 Grants to organisations £2,047,500 Assets £348,568
**TRUSTEES** Margaret Maguire; Martin Bennett; Burges Salmon Trustees Limited.
**OTHER INFORMATION** In 2013/14 grants were given to 33 organisations, including a major grant of £2 million to The Great Steward of Scotland's Dumfries House Trust. Bear in mind that this year's expenditure is unusually high.
**HOW TO APPLY** Applications can be made in writing to the correspondent. The annual report for 2013/14 notes: 'The trustees review applications for donations received from time to time. These applications are considered by the trustees and donations are made based on the merits of the applications.'
**WHO TO APPLY TO** Charles Calcraft, Correspondent, c/o Burges Salmon LLP, 1 Glass Wharf, Bristol BS2 0ZX Tel. 0117 939 2000

## ■ The Mahavir Trust
**CC NO** 298551        **ESTABLISHED** 1988
**WHERE FUNDING CAN BE GIVEN** UK and overseas.
**WHO CAN BENEFIT** Registered charities; individuals; other charitable organisations, including social enterprises and hospitals.
**WHAT IS FUNDED** General charitable purposes, particularly Jain religion; education; animal welfare and vegetarianism; social welfare and relief of poverty; overseas aid; medical causes.
**TYPE OF GRANT** One-off, unrestricted funding.
**RANGE OF GRANTS** Up to £12,300.
**SAMPLE GRANTS** Raj Saubhag Satsang Mandal India (£12,300); Jain Social Group (£7,000); Samast Mahajan (£6,600); Jain Vishva Bharti (£800); Young Indian Vegetarians (£300); Crisis (£250); Tusk Trust (£150); Barbara Bus Fund and Country Air Ambulance Trust (£100 each); Greenpeace (£20).
**FINANCES** Year 2013/14 Income £159,189 Grants £43,701 Grants to organisations £43,543 Assets £572,758
**TRUSTEES** Jay Mehta; Nemish Mehta; Pravinchandra Mehta; Pushpa Mehta; Sheena Sabharwal; Kumar Mehta; Sangita Mehta.
**OTHER INFORMATION** A total of about £160 was given to individuals. There were 39 organisational grants made.
**HOW TO APPLY** Applications may be made in writing to the correspondent. The trustees meet three or four times a year to consider applications.
**WHO TO APPLY TO** Jay Mehta, Trustee, 10 Walled Garden Court, Hampton Road, Stanmore HA7 3GE Tel. 020 8950 6505 email mahavirtrust@googlemail.com

## ■ Malbin Trust
**CC NO** 1045174        **ESTABLISHED** 1995
**WHERE FUNDING CAN BE GIVEN** Worldwide.
**WHO CAN BENEFIT** Charitable organisations; individuals.
**WHAT IS FUNDED** General charitable purposes; Jewish causes, including in the areas of social welfare, health and education.
**SAMPLE GRANTS** A list of beneficiaries was not included in the latest accounts, which state that 'donations represent support for families following childbirth and other charitable activities as per the Charity's object clause'. Previously £10,000 has been given to Chasidei Belz Institutions.
**FINANCES** Year 2012/13 Income £42,310 Grants £52,104 Grants to organisations £52,104 Assets £564,290
**TRUSTEES** Benjamin Leitner; Jehuda Waldman; Margaret Leitner.
**OTHER INFORMATION** At the time of writing (June 2015) this was the latest information available – 2013/14 accounts were overdue.
**HOW TO APPLY** Applications may be made in writing to the correspondent.
**WHO TO APPLY TO** Benjamin Leitner, Trustee, 8 Cheltenham Crescent, Salford M7 4FP Tel. 0161 792 7343 email charities@haffhoff.co.uk

## ■ The Mallinckrodt Foundation
**CC NO** 1058011        **ESTABLISHED** 1996
**WHERE FUNDING CAN BE GIVEN** Worldwide.
**WHO CAN BENEFIT** Registered charities and charitable organisations.
**WHAT IS FUNDED** General charitable purposes.
**RANGE OF GRANTS** £1,000–£855,500
**SAMPLE GRANTS** Washington University St Louis (£855,500); Vatican Library – Rome (£63,000); Historic Royal Places – Hanoverian Accession Tercentenary Celebrations (£25,000); Kennedy School of Government – Harvard (£16,100); Woolf Institute (£10,000); Three Faiths Forum (£5,000); Blackfriars Hall – Oxford (£3,500); Lambeth Partnership and National Association of Almshouses (£2,000 each); Help the Hospices – in Memory of Anne, Duchess of Norfolk (£1,000).
**FINANCES** Year 2013/14 Income £1,007,255 Grants £1,039,936 Grants to organisations £1,039,936 Assets £3,876,318
**TRUSTEES** Charmaine von Mallinckrodt; G. W. Mallinckrodt; Claire Howard; Edward Mallinckrodt; Philip Mallinckrodt.
**OTHER INFORMATION** In 2013/14 grants were given to 17 organisations.
**HOW TO APPLY** Note that the foundation does not welcome unsolicited appeals and 'does not make grants to people or organisations that apply speculatively'. The annual report for 2013/14 states: 'The Trustees travel widely in the UK and abroad and use the knowledge gained to support the work of the Foundation and to inform their grant-making activities.'
**WHO TO APPLY TO** Sally Yates, Correspondent, 81 Rivington Street, London EC2A 3AY

## ■ Man Group plc Charitable Trust
**CC NO** 275386        **ESTABLISHED** 1978
**WHERE FUNDING CAN BE GIVEN** UK and overseas, with some preference for London.
**WHO CAN BENEFIT** Registered charities; voluntary organisations.
**WHAT IS FUNDED** General charitable purposes with some preference for causes near to or linked to the business of Man Group plc.
**WHAT IS NOT FUNDED** Large national charities; charities who use outside fundraising organisations; charities whose administration

costs are thought to be excessive; animal charities; applicants who have applied within the previous 12 months; requests that directly replace statutory funding; individuals (unless under a sponsorship scheme); endowment funds; charities where the main purpose is to promote religious beliefs.
RANGE OF GRANTS £3,000–£100,000
SAMPLE GRANTS Eaves (£100,000); XLP, School-Home Support, National Numeracy Trust, The Passage, MapAction (£50,000 each); Changing Faces (£40,000); Inspire! (£30,000); Community Links, 999 Club (£25,000 each); Ocean Youth Trust South (£15,000); City of London School (£6,500).
FINANCES Year 2013 Income £55,523 Grants £1,061,878 Grants to organisations £1,061,878 Assets £2,254,641
TRUSTEES Murray Steel; Jasveer Singh; David Kingsley; Colin Bettison.
OTHER INFORMATION Grants were made to 24 organisations in 2013.
HOW TO APPLY Grants are provided on an invitation to bid basis or through negotiated partnerships with selected charities The trust has stated that it cannot commit to responding to organisations making unsolicited applications. See the trust's website for criteria.
WHO TO APPLY TO Lisa Clarke, Trust Manager, Man Group plc, Riverbank House, 2 Swan Lane, London EC4R 3AD Tel. 020 7144 1000 email charitable.trust@man.com Website www.man.com/GB/man-charitable-trust

### ■ The Manackerman Charitable Trust
CC NO 326147    ESTABLISHED 1982
WHERE FUNDING CAN BE GIVEN UK, with some preference for Manchester.
WHO CAN BENEFIT Jewish organisations; educational institutions.
WHAT IS FUNDED Education; religion; relief of poverty; focus on Jewish causes.
SAMPLE GRANTS **Previous beneficiaries have included:** Heathlands (£3,200); TTT Charity (£2,500); Manchester Jewish Federation (£2,000); M.B. Foundation (£1,400); Reshet (£1,250); British Friends of New Synagogue Netanya and Child Resettlement Fund (£1,000 each).
FINANCES Year 2013/14 Income £31,151 Grants £70,830 Grants to organisations £70,830 Assets £576,127
TRUSTEES Jonathan Marks; Vanessa Marks; Michael Hammelburger.
OTHER INFORMATION A list of beneficiaries was not included within the annual report and accounts.
HOW TO APPLY Applications should be made in writing to the correspondent. The annual report for 2013/14 states that the 'the charity receives many applications for grants, both by mail and verbally'.
WHO TO APPLY TO Jonathan Marks, Trustee, 3 Park Lane, Salford M7 4HT Tel. 0161 832 3434

### ■ Manchester Airport Community Trust Fund
CC NO 1071703    ESTABLISHED 1997
WHERE FUNDING CAN BE GIVEN The area which is most affected by Manchester Airport. This includes Stockport, Manchester, Trafford, Tameside, Cheshire East and Cheshire West and Chester.
WHO CAN BENEFIT Charitable organisations.
WHAT IS FUNDED Projects which: encourage tree planting; afforestation; landscaping; other environmental improvements or heritage conservation; promote social welfare through recreation, sport and leisure; provide better appreciation of the natural and urban environment.
WHAT IS NOT FUNDED Individuals.
RANGE OF GRANTS £100–£3,500
SAMPLE GRANTS Henbury Millennium Green Trust (£3,300); Community Spirit, Mersey Valley Sports Club and Toft Cricket Club (£3,000 each); Chorlton Arts Festival (£2,800); 162 (Stockport) Squadron ATC (£2,500); Agricultural and Rural Centre CIC and Knutsford Cricket Club (£2,000 each); High Legh Bowling Club and Peel Hall Moatwatch (£1,000 each); Penny Lane Party and Trafford Basketball Club (£800 each); Bowling Green Hotel Bowling Club (£400); Goostrey Parish Archive (£250); Inspire (£120).
FINANCES Year 2013/14 Income £163,761 Grants £139,812 Grants to organisations £139,812 Assets £75,405
TRUSTEES Cllr Paul Andrews; Cllr John Pantall; Cllr Don Stockton; Cllr Malcolm Byram; Michael Whetton; Wendy Sinfield; John Twigg; Bill Fairfoull.
OTHER INFORMATION Grants to 71 charitable organisations were made totalling £140,000.
HOW TO APPLY Application forms can be found on the charity's website and must be submitted online. Successful applicants are encouraged to promote their grant through the local media, and in their own newsletters and publications.
WHO TO APPLY TO Ruth Flatman, Correspondent, Manchester Airport plc, 5 Rutland Drive, Weaverham, Northwich, Cheshire CW8 3JF Tel. 0161 489 5833 email trust.fund@manairport.co.uk Website www.manchesterairport.co.uk

### ■ The Manchester Guardian Society Charitable Trust
CC NO 515341    ESTABLISHED 1984
WHERE FUNDING CAN BE GIVEN Greater Manchester.
WHO CAN BENEFIT Preference is usually shown to smaller charities and community organisations.
WHAT IS FUNDED General charitable purposes, especially children and young people, ill health and disability, older people, disadvantaged individuals, education, the arts and community causes. The emphasis is very much on support in the Greater Manchester area.
WHAT IS NOT FUNDED Individuals.
TYPE OF GRANT Primarily small, one-off awards for capital projects and core costs.
RANGE OF GRANTS £500–£7,500
SAMPLE GRANTS Wood Street Mission (£7,500); EMERGE 3RS – FareShare Community Food Network (£3,000); Willow Wood Hospice (£2,500); Birtle and Rochdale Riding for Special Needs, Survivors of Bereavement by Suicide and The Indian Association Manchester (£2,000 each); Genesis Breast Cancer Prevention (£1,500); Police Community Clubs for Great Britain and Signpost Stockport for Carers (£1,000 each); 23rd Stretford St Matthews Victoria Scout Group and Gatley Festival (£750 each); Levenshulme Personal 8 Community History Group (£600); Chelwood Foodbank Trust, Children With Cystic Fibrosis Dream Holidays, Kids Care and Mayor of Tameside Charity Appeal (£500 each).

FINANCES Year 2013/14 Income £75,872
Grants £84,690 Grants to organisations
£84,690 Assets £4,336,024
TRUSTEES Warren Smith; Lorraine Worsley;
K. Hardinge; Vivien Carter; Diane Hawkins;
K. Ahmed; P. Lochery; Dr D. Burton; Sharman
Birtles; Shauna Dixon.
OTHER INFORMATION In 2013/14 grants were given to 68 organisations.
HOW TO APPLY Application forms are available from the correspondent and are normally considered on the first Monday of March, June, September and December. Requests should arrive 14 days before these dates. The trustees do not welcome repeat applications within two years.
WHO TO APPLY TO Joseph Swift, Clerk to the Trustees, c/o Addleshaw Goddard LLP, 100 Barbirolli Square, Manchester M2 3AB Tel. 0161 934 6190 email joe.swift@addleshawgoddard.com

## ■ Lord Mayor of Manchester's Charity Appeal Trust

CC NO 1066972  ESTABLISHED 1997
WHERE FUNDING CAN BE GIVEN The City of Manchester.
WHO CAN BENEFIT Charities, community groups, organisations and individuals in the City of Manchester. Organisations that do not have access to a professional fundraiser and experience difficulty in attracting funding from other sources are favoured.
WHAT IS FUNDED The charity's aim is to 'improve the lives, aspirations and life chances of Manchester people. Help develop stronger communities by encouraging more citizens to be active in working together to strengthen their community.' In particular, the trust favours projects that are: run by local volunteers to improve disadvantaged communities; encourage involvement of local residents in the planning and delivery of activities; and promote voluntary participation, social inclusion, community involvement and self-help. Applications for individuals must be nominated by a sponsor or third party.
WHAT IS NOT FUNDED Organisations trading for profit or intending to redistribute funds; major capital requests, i.e. building and construction work; replacement or enhancement of statutory provision; academic or medical research and equipment; requests whose primary purpose is to promote religious or political beliefs; retrospective funding; sponsorship or fundraising events unless profits are to be put back into the organisation; local branches of national charities unless locally managed, financially autonomous and not in receipt of financial support from the national body; staff salaries and ongoing costs of established projects e.g. rent, utilities; services for individual benefit such as private counselling, professional legal advice, personal therapy, further education courses and private tuition; fees or payments where individual members of the applicant organisation will benefit; multiple applications for one project; applications from one group for the same project within three years; projects that are funded by Manchester City Council through mainstream budgets; parties for annual events which are part of the community calendar; animal based charities; organisations with an annual income greater than £100,000.
TYPE OF GRANT One-off; project funding.

RANGE OF GRANTS £500–£5,000
SAMPLE GRANTS Mellor Country House (£4,900); Association of Ukrainians in Great Britain (£2,400); The Golden Voices Community Choir and Whalley Range Cricket and Lawn Tennis Club (£2,000 each); Gorton Monastery and Ladybarn Community Association (£1,200 each); Art with Heart (£1,100); College of the Third Age (£1,000); Fallowfield Healthy Living Group and MS Society – Manchester Branch (£500).
FINANCES Year 2013/14 Income £162,442
Grants £54,181 Grants to organisations
£54,181 Assets £857,902
TRUSTEES Arthur Burden; Howard Bernstein; Richard Paver; William Egerton; Lady Mayoress of Manchester; Lord Mayor of Manchester; Chair of the Fundraising Committee; Deputy Executive Member for Children's Services; Ian Perry.
OTHER INFORMATION The grant total includes £25,800 for the purpose of a family holiday programme.
HOW TO APPLY Applications should be made by email or post using a form which is provided on the trust's website, along with guidance notes. Trustee meetings take place four times each year and the deadlines are posted on the trust's website.
WHO TO APPLY TO Kate Lane, We Love MCR Charity, Lord Mayor's Office, Room 412, Level 4, Town Hall, Manchester M60 2LA Tel. 0161 234 3229 email welovemcrcharity@manchester.gov.uk Website www.welovemcrcharity.org

## ■ The Manifold Charitable Trust

CC NO 229501  ESTABLISHED 1962
WHERE FUNDING CAN BE GIVEN UK.
WHO CAN BENEFIT Registered charities only.
WHAT IS FUNDED General charitable purposes; education and training; historic buildings; environmental conservation. The trust has previously focused much attention on the preservation of churches; however, following the death in 2007 of its founder, Sir John Smith, the trust is now allocating most of its grants for educational purposes. The trust still makes grants to the Historic Churches Preservation Trust for onward distribution to churches; however, it would seem that the amount has been reduced in previous years.
WHAT IS NOT FUNDED Individuals; applications for improvements to churches as this is covered by a block grant to the Historic Churches Preservation Trust.
TYPE OF GRANT One-off and recurring capital costs.
RANGE OF GRANTS Most awards £1,000 or less.
SAMPLE GRANTS Eton College (£428,000). Previous recipients have included: Askham PCC; Berkshire Medical Heritage Centre; Brompton Ralph PCC; Gislingham PCC; Historic Churches Preservation Trust; Household Cavalry Museum Trust; Imperial College; Maidenhead Heritage Trust; Morrab Library; Richmond Building Preservation Society; Thames Hospice Care; Westray Heritage Trust.
FINANCES Year 2013 Income £596,353
Grants £476,394 Grants to organisations
£476,394 Assets £8,694,116
TRUSTEE The Manifold Trustee Company Limited.
OTHER INFORMATION Out of the grant total almost £428,000 was given to Eton College. The accounts note that the trustees 'considered that none of the remaining grants that were made were material'. There were 44 awards made.
HOW TO APPLY The latest annual report for 2013 states that since 31 January 2013 the trustee

will no longer consider unsolicited applications from third parties.
**WHO TO APPLY TO** Helen Niven, Studio Cottage, Windsor Great Park, Windsor, Berkshire SL4 2HP *email* themanifoldtrust@gmail.com

## ■ The W. M. Mann Foundation
**SC NO** SC010111  **ESTABLISHED** 1992
**WHERE FUNDING CAN BE GIVEN** Mainly Scotland but UK-wide organisations may be assisted.
**WHO CAN BENEFIT** Charitable organisations; universities.
**WHAT IS FUNDED** General charitable purposes, including arts, education, music, medical causes and sports; disadvantaged individuals.
**WHAT IS NOT FUNDED** Individuals.
**TYPE OF GRANT** Unrestricted funding.
**RANGE OF GRANTS** £150–£25,000
**SAMPLE GRANTS** GAWMT (£25,000); Scottish Opera (£10,000); Glasgow School of Art and Maggie's centre (£5,000 each); TronTheatre (£3,000); Scottish Ballet (£2,500); Teenage Cancer Trust (£1,500); The National Trust of Scotland (£1,300); Blind Veterans UK, Dundee Women's Aid, Jewish Care Scotland and Whizz-Kidz (£1,000 each); ABF The Soldier's Charity and Peebleshire Youth (£800); St Andrew's First Aid (£600); Inverclyde Foodbank and Scottish Refuge Council (£500 each); Scottish Spina Bifida (£150).
**FINANCES** *Year* 2013/14 *Income* £224,146 *Grants* £148,500 *Grants to organisations* £148,500 *Assets* £5,159,914
**TRUSTEES** W. M. Mann; B. M. Mann; A. W. Mann; S. P. Hutcheon.
**OTHER INFORMATION** In 2013/14 awards were made to 82 organisations.
**HOW TO APPLY** Applications may be made in writing to the correspondent providing the latest set of annual report and accounts.
**WHO TO APPLY TO** The Trustees, 201 Bath Street, Glasgow G2 4HZ *Tel.* 0141 248 4936 *Fax* 0141 221 2976 *email* mail@wmmanngroup.co.uk

## ■ R. W. Mann Trust
**CC NO** 1095699  **ESTABLISHED** 1959
**WHERE FUNDING CAN BE GIVEN** In practice, grants are all confined to organisations in Tyne and Wear, with a preference for North Tyneside, South Northumberland and East Newcastle.
**WHO CAN BENEFIT** Community activities, educational establishments, local groups or local branches of national charities addressing local needs and benefitting people, including children and young adults, older people, families, people with disabilities, those disadvantaged by poverty or social exclusion.
**WHAT IS FUNDED** A wide range of general charitable purposes; social welfare; health causes; children and young people; disability; older individuals; voluntary sector, including charity and umbrella bodies; other local community causes.
**WHAT IS NOT FUNDED** 'The trust will not support: 'large well-established national charities'; 'individuals'; 'church buildings except where they are used for community groups'; 'projects or groups which can attract public funds or which appeal to Community Fund grants or national charitable trusts or other sources except if there is a particular part of the project which other sources would be unlikely to fund';

'deficits already incurred or to replace statutory funding'.
**TYPE OF GRANT** Recurrent expenditure, capital or one-off costs; core costs, feasibility studies, interest-free loans, project funding and salaries up to two years will be considered; in practice, unrestricted funding.
**RANGE OF GRANTS** Average grant of £1,000; awards can range between £100 and £10,000.
**SAMPLE GRANTS** Northumberland Clubs for Young People (£6,000); Meadow Well Connected (£5,000); Community and Voluntary Action Blyth Valley and Whitley Bay Young People's Centre (£2,000 each); Phoenix Detached Youth Project (£1,700); 8th Blyth Sea Scout Group, Families in Care, Independent Advocacy North Tyneside, Ocean Youth Trust N. E and St Mary's Church – Holywell (£1,000 each); Forces Support and North Northumberland Amateur Boxing and Fitness Club (£500 each); Springfield Community Association (£450); The Literary and Philosophical Society of Newcastle (£350); Artichoke Trust and Durham University (£250 each); T S Comus (£60).
**FINANCES** *Year* 2013/14 *Income* £70,373 *Grants* £144,098 *Grants to organisations* £144,098 *Assets* £2,400,148
**TRUSTEES** Judith Hamilton; Guy Javens; Monica Heath.
**OTHER INFORMATION** Organisations in the wider Tyne and Wear, Durham and Northumberland areas may only be supported for very exceptional projects. During the year the trust made 158 awards to 137 organisations.
**HOW TO APPLY** Applications have to be made in writing to the correspondent – the trust kindly asks to provide an addressed envelope (no need to include any stamps – the trust is 'very happy to pay for this'). Email applications can also be made, provided they do not exceed four pages. Phone or, preferably, email enquiries are encouraged prior to formal application. Applicants asking for awards of up to £2,000 will normally hear back from the trust within two weeks and for larger amounts – within six weeks. If you are unsuccessful you can re-apply within six months.
**WHO TO APPLY TO** John Hamilton, Secretary, PO Box 119, Gosforth, Newcastle upon Tyne NE3 4WF *Tel.* 0191 284 2158 *email* john.hamilton@onyx.octacon.co.uk *Website* www.rwmanntrust.org.uk

## ■ The Manoukian Charitable Foundation
**CC NO** 1084065  **ESTABLISHED** 2000
**WHERE FUNDING CAN BE GIVEN** Worldwide.
**WHO CAN BENEFIT** Registered charities, particularly those working on educational and cultural projects or helping people in poverty, illness or suffering.
**WHAT IS FUNDED** General charitable purposes, particularly social welfare, education, medical causes and arts and culture in relation to the 'Armenian matters'.
**RANGE OF GRANTS** £3,000–£156,500
**SAMPLE GRANTS** Action Innocence (£156,500); The Lyla Nsouli Foundation (£60,000); Give a Child a Toy (£30,000); Mission Enfance (£8,000); Our Lady of Lebanon Church (£3,000).
**FINANCES** *Year* 2013 *Income* £362,814 *Grants* £281,585 *Grants to organisations* £257,585 *Assets* £3,042
**TRUSTEES** Tamar Manoukian; Anthony Bunker; Steven Press; Dr Armen Sarkissian.

# Maranatha

*Alphabetical register of grant-making charities*

OTHER INFORMATION There were five awards made, broken down into: social services and relief; medical research and care; other. Individual grants 'for religious, cultural and educational purposes' totalled £24,000. The foundation 'will consider providing assistance to projects that may be partly funded by others if this will enable the project to proceed'.

HOW TO APPLY The annual report for 2013 states: 'Requests for grants are received from the general public and charitable and other organisations through their knowledge of the activities of the foundation and through personal contacts of the settlor and the trustees.' The trustees meet at least once per year.

WHO TO APPLY TO Anthony Bunker, Trustee, c/o Berwin Leighton Paisner, Adelaide House, London Bridge, London EC4R 9HA *Tel.* 020 7760 1000

## ■ Maranatha Christian Trust

CC NO 265323     ESTABLISHED 1972
WHERE FUNDING CAN BE GIVEN UK and overseas.
WHO CAN BENEFIT Christian organisations and individuals.
WHAT IS FUNDED General charitable purposes; Christian causes; relief of poverty; education of young people. Focus is on people involved in 'professing the Christian religion or working to promote such religion'.
RANGE OF GRANTS £1,000–£5,000
SAMPLE GRANTS **Previous beneficiaries have included:** CARE (£5,000); Concordis International (£2,500); Café Africa Trust and Stewards Trust (£2,000 each); Intercontinental Church Society and International Health Partners (£1,000 each).
FINANCES *Year* 2013/14 *Income* £15,678 *Grants* £318,000 *Grants to organisations* £318,000
TRUSTEES Alan Bell; Lyndon Bowring; Viscount Crispin Brentford.
OTHER INFORMATION Accounts were not required to be filed with the Charity Commission – the grant total is estimated based on previous patterns of giving (on average about 91% of overall expenditure is given in grants). In the past support has mainly been given to a number of repeat beneficiaries supported on an annual basis.
HOW TO APPLY Applications may be made in writing to the correspondent; however, it would appear that the trust mainly supports the same charities each year.
WHO TO APPLY TO The Secretary, 208 Cooden Drive, Bexhill-On-Sea TN39 3AH *email* maranathachristiantrust@outlook.com

## ■ Marbeh Torah Trust

CC NO 292491     ESTABLISHED 1985
WHERE FUNDING CAN BE GIVEN UK and overseas, particularly Israel.
WHO CAN BENEFIT Jewish charitable organisations, especially educational establishments.
WHAT IS FUNDED Furtherance of Orthodox Jewish religious education and relief of poverty.
TYPE OF GRANT One-off and recurrent costs; interest free loans.
RANGE OF GRANTS £2,400–£152,500
SAMPLE GRANTS Yeshiva Marbeh Torah (£152,500); Yad Gershon (£31,500); Beis Meir (£18,000); Kollel Shaarei Shlomo (£12,000); Chazon Avraham Yitzchak (£10,000); Torah Bezalel (£6,000); Mishkenos Yaakov (£4,000); Beis Dovid (£3,500); Masoret Hatorah (£2,400).
FINANCES *Year* 2013 *Income* £244,950 *Grants* £239,950 *Grants to organisations* £239,950 *Assets* £4,071,000
TRUSTEES Jacob Elzas; Moishe Elzas; Simone Elzas.
OTHER INFORMATION The annual report for 2013/14 notes that charitable giving was directed at religious education. There were nine awards made.
HOW TO APPLY Applications may be made in writing to the correspondent.
WHO TO APPLY TO Moishe Elzas, Trustee, 116 Castlewood Road, London N15 6BE

## ■ The Marcela Trust

CC NO 1127514     ESTABLISHED 2009
WHERE FUNDING CAN BE GIVEN UK.
WHO CAN BENEFIT Registered charities; research institutions.
WHAT IS FUNDED General charitable purposes, especially environment and animals and medical research and care.
TYPE OF GRANT Research grants; capital projects.
RANGE OF GRANTS £1,500–£35,000
SAMPLE GRANTS Fauna and Flora International (£35,000); Make a Wish Foundation (£1,500). According to the accounts for 2013/14, 'post year ended', the trust also awarded three further grants: Nuffield Orthopaedic Canoe Appeal (£1.5 million); Fauna and Flora International (£400,000); Society of Portrait Sculptors (£7,500).
FINANCES *Year* 2013/14 *Income* £5,208,908 *Grants* £36,500 *Grants to organisations* £36,500 *Assets* £75,256,573
TRUSTEES Brian Groves; Dawn Rose; Dr Martin Lenz; Mark Spragg; Jeanette Franklin; Paul Hotham.
OTHER INFORMATION There were two awards made. Note that both the income and the overall charitable expenditure vary each year and in the past five years have averaged at £14.6 million and £327,000, respectively.
HOW TO APPLY Applications may be made in writing to the correspondent, although potential applicants should be aware that grant recipients may be pre-determined by the directors of OMC Investments Limited.
WHO TO APPLY TO Jeanette Franklin, Trustee, Woodcote House, 4 Monks Close, Dorchester on Thames, Oxon OX10 7JA *Tel.* 01865 343802

## ■ The Marchig Animal Welfare Trust

CC NO 802133/SC038057 ESTABLISHED 1989
WHERE FUNDING CAN BE GIVEN Worldwide.
WHO CAN BENEFIT Organisations and individuals that make positive contributions in protecting animals and promoting and encouraging practical work in preventing animal cruelty and suffering.
WHAT IS FUNDED Animal welfare. Projects supported by the trust have included: spay/neuter programmes; alternatives to the use of animals in research; poster campaigns; anti-poaching programmes; establishment of veterinary hospitals, clinics and animal sanctuaries; food, equipment and care to relieve the suffering of animals; education in the field of animal welfare. There are no restrictions on the geographical area of work, types of grants or potential applicants, but all applications must

be related to animal welfare and be of direct benefit to animals.

**WHAT IS NOT FUNDED** Applications failing to meet the trust's criteria; expeditions; activities that are not totally animal welfare related; educational studies or other courses; salaries; support of conferences and meetings.

**TYPE OF GRANT** Based on project.

**RANGE OF GRANTS** Based on project.

**SAMPLE GRANTS** Most recent beneficiaries included: Animals Asia Foundation – Hong Kong; Blue Cross of India; Frendicoes Society for the Eradication of Cruelty to Animals – India; People's Dispensary for Sick Animals – UK; Worldwide Veterinary Service – UK.

**FINANCES** Year 2013 Income £8,433,388 Grants £913,992 Grants to organisations £913,992 Assets £25,351,687

**TRUSTEES** Colin Moor; Les Ward; Dr Jerzy Mlotkiewicz; Alastair Keatinge; Janice McLoughlin.

**OTHER INFORMATION** In addition to making grants the trust also makes The Jeanne Marchig Awards. These awards, which take the form of a financial donation in support of the winner's animal welfare work, are given in either of the following two categories: the development of an alternative method to the use of animals in experimental procedures and the practical implementation of such an alternative resulting in a significant reduction in the number of animals used in experimental procedures; practical work in the field of animal welfare resulting in significant improvements for animals either nationally or internationally. The annual report and accounts did not list grant recipients; however, the most recent grantees are specified on the trust's website.

**HOW TO APPLY** Application forms are available from the trust's website or the correspondent and should be returned via post or email along with the most recent accounts and annual report. Enquiries regarding applications should be addressed to applications@marchigtrust.org. Applications are accepted throughout the year and all of them are acknowledged – the trust requests applicants to be patient and do not contact to ascertain when a decision will be made. You can re-apply after one year following the initial application. Note that applicants are expected to also have applied to other organisation for financial support for the project.

**WHO TO APPLY TO** Alastair Keatinge, Trustee, Caledonian Exchange, 10A Canning Street, Edinburgh EH3 8HE Tel. 0131 656 5746 email info@marchigtrust.org Website www.marchigtrust.org

## ■ The Stella and Alexander Margulies Charitable Trust

**CC NO** 220441  **ESTABLISHED** 1970

**WHERE FUNDING CAN BE GIVEN** UK and overseas.

**WHO CAN BENEFIT** Charitable organisations, particularly benefitting Jewish people.

**WHAT IS FUNDED** General charitable purposes, including health, social welfare and the arts; Jewish causes.

**RANGE OF GRANTS** Generally £200–£5,000; up to £250,000.

**SAMPLE GRANTS** Jerusalem Foundation (£250,000); Shaare Zedek (£117,500); Royal Opera House Foundation (£25,000); Queen Elizabeth Diamond Jubilee Trust (£10,000); Barbican Centre Trust (£5,000); Nightingale Hammerson (£2,000); Chief Rabbinate Trust and Community Security Trust (£1,800 each); Jewish Community Secondary School (£1,500); B'nai B'rith Hillel Foundation and Shalom Foundation of the Zionist Federation of GB (£1,000 each); Lolev Charitable Trust (£680); Enfield Centre for Natural Health (£200).

**FINANCES** Year 2013/14 Income £167,328 Grants £420,605 Grants to organisations £420,605 Assets £8,410,095

**TRUSTEES** Martin Paisner; Sir Stuart Lipton; Alexander Sorkin; Marcus Margulies; Leslie Michaels.

**OTHER INFORMATION** During the year a total of 15 awards were made.

**HOW TO APPLY** Applications may be made in writing to the correspondent.

**WHO TO APPLY TO** Leslie Michaels, Trustee, 34 Dover Street, London W1S 4NG

## ■ Mariapolis Limited

**CC NO** 257912  **ESTABLISHED** 1968

**WHERE FUNDING CAN BE GIVEN** UK and overseas.

**WHO CAN BENEFIT** Organisations and individuals.

**WHAT IS FUNDED** Christian ecumenism; young people; families; education; relief in need. The annual report for 2013/14 notes that 'the charity's grant-making policy and procedures depend on decisions made in consultation with both the members responsible for the Movement in Britain and with those responsible for each local house'. Overseas contributions are made in consultations with headquarters in Rome (PAMOM). Internal projects by and within the movement are prioritised and in addition, financial support is sometimes given to close relatives of community members who are in need.

**RANGE OF GRANTS** £850–£200,000

**SAMPLE GRANTS** Pia Associazione Maschile Opera di Maria – PAMOM (£200,000 in quarterly payments); Focolare Brazil (£85,000); family welfare grants (£2,900); Anglican Priests Training Fund (£850).

**FINANCES** Year 2013/14 Income £770,815 Grants £288,968 Grants to organisations £288,698 Assets £3,070,381

**TRUSTEES** Francis Johnson; Carlo Poggi; Paul Gateshill.

**OTHER INFORMATION** The charity promotes the international Focolare Movement in the UK, and grant-making is only one area of its work. It works towards a united world and its activities focus on peace and co-operation. It has a related interest in ecumenism and also in overseas development. Activities include organising conferences and courses, and publishing books and magazines.

**HOW TO APPLY** Applications may be made in writing to the correspondent.

**WHO TO APPLY TO** Rumold Van Geffen, Secretary/Treasurer, 57 Twyford Avenue, London W3 9PZ Tel. 020 8992 7666 email rumold1949@gmail.com

## ■ Market Harborough and The Bowdens Charity

**CC NO** 1041958  **ESTABLISHED** 1994

**WHERE FUNDING CAN BE GIVEN** The parishes of Market Harborough, Great Bowden and Little Bowden.

**WHO CAN BENEFIT** Charitable organisations; individuals; charitable status is 'helpful, but by no means essential'.

**WHAT IS FUNDED** A wide range of large and small community projects, covering the areas of: amateur sports; arts; education; environment; heritage; social and medical welfare; other community needs. Individuals are given relief-in-need grants and support towards education and training.

**WHAT IS NOT FUNDED** Sporting projects; replacement of statutory funding. Only in exceptional cases the trustees may provide relief-in-need grants to persons who are resident immediately outside the area of benefit.

**TYPE OF GRANT** One-off; capital expenditure; sometimes core, running costs.

**RANGE OF GRANTS** Up to £103,000; small grants up to £15,000.

**SAMPLE GRANTS** Market Harborough RUFC (£103,000); Harborough Evangelical Church (£50,000); Harborough Youth And Community Trust (£24,000); Harborough Christian Counselling Service (£18,500); St Joseph's Catholic Voluntary Academy (£11,000); Leicestershire, Leicester and Rutland Headway (£3,000); Great Bowden Recital Trust (£1,600); HomeStart South Leicestershire (£1,500); Vitalise (£1,100). Awards of under £1,000 totalled £10,500.

**FINANCES** Year 2013 Income £658,730 Grants £353,505 Grants to organisations £258,586 Assets £17,897,763

**TRUSTEES** Janice Hefford; Ian Wells; Mark Stamp; Adrian Trotter; George Stamp; John Clare; Tim Banks; Joan Williams; Paul Beardsmore; David Battersby; Dr Julie Jones; Lennie Rhodes; Guy Hartopp; Angela Allington; William Jones.

**OTHER INFORMATION** The charity maintains almshouses and allotments. Funds are also provided for the maintenance and repair of the parish church of Great Bowden (£37,500 in 2013). Grants to 71 individuals totalled £57,500. There were 29 organisational awards. Note the following stated in the application guidelines: '... grant aiding of one project does not set a precedent – indeed possibly the reverse if the first facility fulfils the identified public need.'

**HOW TO APPLY** Applications have to be made using an application form, which is available from the correspondent or the website. Full criteria and guidelines are also available there. Note that appeals for major awards require further details and supplementary documentation. Potential applicants are welcome to contact the correspondent directly for further guidance. Appeals can also be addressed to the Secretary to the Charity – Miss J A Edwards.

**WHO TO APPLY TO** James Jacobs, Steward, 10 Fairfield Road, Market Harborough, Leicestershire LE16 9QQ Tel. 01858 419128 email admin@mhbcharity.co.uk Website www.mhbcharity.co.uk

## ■ The Michael Marks Charitable Trust

**CC NO** 248136 **ESTABLISHED** 1966
**WHERE FUNDING CAN BE GIVEN** UK and overseas.
**WHO CAN BENEFIT** Registered charities; galleries and museums; educational institutions.
**WHAT IS FUNDED** Arts and culture; environment; conservation.
**WHAT IS NOT FUNDED** Grants are given to registered charities only. Awards are not made to individuals or profit-making organisations.
**RANGE OF GRANTS** Generally £500–£25,000.

**SAMPLE GRANTS** Ashmolean Museum Oxford University (£95,000); Wordsworth Trust (£19,000); Dulwich Picture Gallery (£10,000); St Pancras Community Trust (£7,000); Furniture History Society, Marine Conservation Society and National Library of Scotland (£5,000 each); Harvard Centre of Hellenic Studies, London Wildlife Trust and Royal Society of Literature (£3,000 each); Canal and River Trust (£2,000); Greek Archaeological Committee – UK (£500).

**FINANCES** Year 2013/14 Income £209,366 Grants £160,216 Grants to organisations £160,216 Assets £6,541,703

**TRUSTEES** Lady Marina Marks; Prof. Sir Christopher White; Noel Annesley.

**HOW TO APPLY** Applications should be made in writing to the correspondent and include audited accounts, information on other bodies approached and details of funding obtained. The trustees meet twice a year, usually in January and July, to consider applications. Requests will not receive a response unless they have been successful.

**WHO TO APPLY TO** Lady Marina Marks, 5 Elm Tree Road, London NW8 9JY Tel. 020 7286 4633 email michaelmarkscharitabletrust@hotmail.co.uk

## ■ The Marks Family Foundation

**CC NO** 1137014 **ESTABLISHED** 2010
**WHERE FUNDING CAN BE GIVEN** UK.
**WHO CAN BENEFIT** Charitable organisation, including those working with children and young people and older people.
**WHAT IS FUNDED** General charitable purposes, with a preference for health, arts and culture and older people or young individuals; Jewish causes.
**TYPE OF GRANT** Usually one-off, unrestricted grants; also loans.
**RANGE OF GRANTS** £300–£15,200

**SAMPLE GRANTS** Orchestra of the Age of Enlightenment (£15,200); Jewish Care (£12,500); Royal National Theatre and Royal Philharmonic Society (£10,000 each); Weizmann Institute (£5,000); West London Synagogue (£3,300); Royal Opera House Foundation (£2,700); St Gabriel's Church (£500); Kids Company (£300).

**FINANCES** Year 2013/14 Income £126,652 Grants £60,212 Grants to organisations £60,212 Assets £220,016

**TRUSTEES** David Marks; Selina Marks; James Marks; Dr Daniel Marks.

**OTHER INFORMATION** The settlor of the foundation, David Marks, is a partner in Apax Partners LLP private equity investment group and also a trustee of the Apax Foundation and the R and S Cohen Foundation. During the year there were 11 awards made.

**HOW TO APPLY** The annual report for 2013/14 states the following: 'The Trustees remain concerned about the volume of unsolicited approaches from other charities and the expenditure incurred by these charities in making these submissions. Accordingly, the Trustees have adopted a policy of only considering the making of grants to charitable organisations with which the Trustees have personal contact and will not respond to these unsolicited requests in the hope that this will dissuade such charities from incurring unnecessary expenditure.'

**WHO TO APPLY TO** David Marks, Trustee, 10 Green Street, London W1K 6RP email dmarkstax@aol.com

## ■ The Ann and David Marks Foundation

**CC NO** 326303 **ESTABLISHED** 1983
**WHERE FUNDING CAN BE GIVEN** Worldwide, with a preference for Manchester.
**WHO CAN BENEFIT** Jewish organisations; registered charities; educational institutions.
**WHAT IS FUNDED** General charitable purposes, including social welfare, health and education; Jewish causes; humanitarian aid.
**TYPE OF GRANT** One-off and up to three years; capital and core costs; project funding.
**RANGE OF GRANTS** Under £1,000 on average.
**SAMPLE GRANTS** According to the latest accounts, 'it is not the policy of the trustees to disclose individual donations'; however, it is noted major donations included Morasha Jewish Primary Trust School (£10,000) and UJIA (£2,800).
**FINANCES** Year 2014 Income £68,150 Grants £36,505 Grants to organisations £36,505 Assets £632,817
**TRUSTEES** A. H. Marks; A. M. Marks; G. E. Marks; David Marks; Marcelle Palmer.
**OTHER INFORMATION** The foundation's total charitable expenditure in the past five years has totalled about £44,500 on average.
**HOW TO APPLY** The annual report for 2014 states: 'The Foundation envisages continuing to support Charities known to the Trustees and feels that this will absorb its available funds for the foreseeable future. For this reason the Trustees do not welcome unsolicited applications.'
**WHO TO APPLY TO** David Marks, Trustee, c/o Mutley Properties Ltd, Mutley House, 1 Ambassador Place, Stockport Road, Altrincham WA15 8DB *Tel.* 0161 941 3183 *email* davidmarks@mutleyproperties.co.uk

## ■ The Hilda and Samuel Marks Foundation

**CC NO** 245208 **ESTABLISHED** 1965
**WHERE FUNDING CAN BE GIVEN** Worldwide; in practice the UK and Israel.
**WHO CAN BENEFIT** Charitable organisations.
**WHAT IS FUNDED** General charitable purposes; Jewish causes; relief in need; health; education; religion; community causes.
**WHAT IS NOT FUNDED** Individuals.
**TYPE OF GRANT** Buildings and other capital costs; core costs; project expenditure; start-up costs.
**SAMPLE GRANTS** A full list of beneficiaries was unavailable, as 'the trustees do not feel it appropriate, as a general rule, to comment on individual donations'; however, it was specified that beneficiaries included ALYN Paediatric and Adolescent Rehabilitation Centre (£37,500) and Child Settlement Fund – Emunah (£25,000). Grants were divided between: health (£96,500 – 41.6%); community/education (£70,000 – 30.2%); welfare (£65,500 – 28.2%).
**FINANCES** Year 2013/14 Income £150,394 Grants £232,239 Grants to organisations £232,239 Assets £3,292,200
**TRUSTEES** David Marks; Hilda Marks; Rochelle Selby.
**OTHER INFORMATION** The grant total was divided between UK charities (£97,000) and Israel-based organisations (£122,500).
**HOW TO APPLY** The trust primarily supports projects known to the trustees and its funds are fully committed. Therefore unsolicited applications are not being sought. The annual report for 2013/14 states: 'As stated in previous reports the Trustees are not minded to consider unsolicited applications as it feels its current policy of supporting organisations over a long period means that extra funds to permit such donations will not be available if unsolicited applications were to be encouraged.'
**WHO TO APPLY TO** David Marks, Trustee, 1 Ambassador Place, Stockport Road, Altrincham, Cheshire WA15 8DB *Tel.* 0161 941 3183 *email* davidmarks@mutleyproperties.co.uk

## ■ J. P. Marland Charitable Trust

**CC NO** 1049350 **ESTABLISHED** 1995
**WHERE FUNDING CAN BE GIVEN** UK and USA.
**WHO CAN BENEFIT** Registered charities (UK); non-profit organisations (USA); individuals.
**WHAT IS FUNDED** General charitable purposes, including arts, sports, medical causes, teaching and community needs. According to the annual report for 2013/14, 'the trustees remain committed to making donations to those charities that they consider to be of value and assistance to their particular field of expertise'.
**TYPE OF GRANT** One-off and up to one year; capital costs; project funding.
**RANGE OF GRANTS** Up to £20,000.
**SAMPLE GRANTS** The Churchill Centre – UK (£20,000); The Rugby Football Foundation All Schools Programme (£10,000); The Stars Appeal Breast Cancer Unit Campaign (£5,000); The Guggenheim UK Charitable Trust (£4,500); The Salisbury Museum (£3,000); Beanstalk and Chalke Valley History Trust (£2,000 each). Other awards totalled £5,100.
**FINANCES** Year 2013/14 Income £80,578 Grants £51,620 Grants to organisations £51,620 Assets £686,130
**TRUSTEES** Lord Jonathan Marland; Lady Penelope Marland; Carol Law; Marcus Marland; Hugo Marland.
**OTHER INFORMATION** A total of 18 grants were given to institutions, in the following categories: medical/teaching/community (£36,500); sports (£10,000); arts (£5,000).
**HOW TO APPLY** The trust has previously informed us that unsolicited appeals are not welcomed.
**WHO TO APPLY TO** Lord Jonathan Marland, Trustee, Odstock Manor, Odstock, Salisbury SP5 4JA *Tel.* 01722 329781

## ■ Marmot Charitable Trust

**CC NO** 1106619 **ESTABLISHED** 2004
**WHERE FUNDING CAN BE GIVEN** Worldwide.
**WHO CAN BENEFIT** 'Green' organisations; educational institutions; environmental and peace projects.
**WHAT IS FUNDED** The trust is interested in 'funding green initiatives that are working towards a sustainable future, and peace and security that are seeking to reduce international conflict including by the eventual elimination of nuclear weapons'.
**TYPE OF GRANT** Project and core costs can be covered.
**RANGE OF GRANTS** £650–£16,000
**SAMPLE GRANTS** British American Security Information Council (£16,000); People and Planet – Fossil Free UK Campaign (£10,000); Forum for the Future – The Positive Deviant Website (£8,500); School of Oriental and African Studies – Disarmament Project (£8,000); Network for Social Change (£4,000); War on Want – From Money to Metals website (£3,000); Building Bridges for Peace (£2,000); Greening the Village (£650).

**FINANCES** Year 2013/14 Income £105,710 Grants £64,419 Grants to organisations £64,419 Assets £3,591,851
**TRUSTEES** Bevis Gillett; Jonathan Gillett; Jeanni Barlow.
**OTHER INFORMATION** There were 14 awards made with the average grant being £4,600.
**HOW TO APPLY** The trust has informed us directly that they do not accept unsolicited applications.
**WHO TO APPLY TO** Bevis Gillet, Secretary, c/o BM Marmot, London WC1N 3XX email marmot.trust@gmail.com

## ■ The Marr-Munning Trust

**CC NO** 1153007  **ESTABLISHED** 1970
**WHERE FUNDING CAN BE GIVEN** Worldwide, mainly financially developing countries (in the Indian Subcontinent, South-East Asia and Sub-Saharan Africa).
**WHO CAN BENEFIT** Charitable organisations and NGOs anywhere in the world working on projects in the area of benefit, helping refugees, people disadvantaged by poverty or social circumstances and victims of famine, war and man-made or natural disasters.
**WHAT IS FUNDED** Overseas aid projects aimed at addressing poverty and suffering in financially developing countries, particularly those likely to improve educational of children and training of poor and disadvantaged adults.
**WHAT IS NOT FUNDED** Individuals; work taking place outside the defined beneficial area; retrospective funding.
**TYPE OF GRANT** Recurrent and one-off.
**RANGE OF GRANTS** Up to £23,000.
**SAMPLE GRANTS** Marr Munning Ashram (£23,000); Children's Future International (£20,000); Tools for Self Reliance (£18,000); A Second Chance (£16,000); United Movement to End Child Soldiering (£15,000); Forever Angels UK (£10,000); Magoola Primary School (£9,400); AbleChildAfrica and Children in Crisis (£4,000 each); Phulki (£2,000); The University of St Cyril and Methodius – Skopje and World Child Cancer (£1,000 each).
**FINANCES** Year 2013/14 Income £12,428,846 Grants £330,090 Grants to organisations £330,090 Assets £12,202,155
**TRUSTEES** Glen Barnham; Pierre Thomas; Dr Geetha Oommen; Marianne Elliott; William Perfect; Hur Hassnain; Adeyemi Oyewumi; Samantha Mardell; Khaled Daair.
**OTHER INFORMATION** The trust's website notes: 'On 1st October 2013 a new charitable company established by our trustees took over the assets, liabilities and activities of the unincorporated charity the Marr-Munning Trust (registered number 261786).' The new Charity Commission number of the trust is 1153007. The trust makes grants totalling around £300,000 annually. During 2013/14 a total of £171,000 was made in new grants – to support education for children (£126,500) and livelihood training for adults (£50,500) – with the remainder including those made by the unincorporated charity prior to the date of transfer.
**HOW TO APPLY** Grants are made once a year, in September. Application forms are available on the trust's website and should be returned via email by 30 June. The trust no longer accepts applications not made on their application form. Applicants must submit the following supporting documentation: a copy of the organisation's most recent audited accounts; a copy of the governing document; if an NGO or charitable organisation based outside the UK, a copy of your registration certificate; any further documentation about your organisation is optional. If you supply an email address the trust will acknowledge receipt of your application. Unsuccessful applicants are not informed. The trust has produced very detailed and helpful guidelines for applicants which can be accessed online.
**WHO TO APPLY TO** James Fitzpatrick, Director, 9 Madeley Road, Ealing, London W5 2LA Tel. 020 8998 7747 Fax 020 8998 9593 email info@marrmunningtrust.org.uk Website www.marrmunningtrust.org.uk

## ■ The Michael Marsh Charitable Trust

**CC NO** 220473  **ESTABLISHED** 1958
**WHERE FUNDING CAN BE GIVEN** Birmingham, Staffordshire, Worcestershire, Warwickshire, Coventry, Wolverhampton and associated towns in the Black Country.
**WHO CAN BENEFIT** Organisations benefitting children and young people, older people, at risk groups and people with disabilities and those disadvantaged by poverty or socially isolation; health and welfare charities; community-based organisations.
**WHAT IS FUNDED** General charitable purposes; children and young people; older people; education and training; relief in need; disability; religious activities.
**WHAT IS NOT FUNDED** Animals; entertainment charities; grants to individuals are only given through charitable institutions on their behalf; replacement of statutory funding; running costs are not normally supported.
**TYPE OF GRANT** Generally recurrent; grants subject to remaining project funding found by the charity.
**RANGE OF GRANTS** £500–£10,000
**SAMPLE GRANTS** City of Birmingham Symphony Orchestra (£10,000); Birmingham Royal Ball and West Midlands CARE Team (£5,000); Tipton Youth Project (£3,000); Aston University Engineering Academy (£2,500); Momentum and The Salvation Army (£2,000 each); The Extra Care Charitable Trust (£1,900); The Douglas Bader Foundation (£1,500); The Walled Garden Project (£1,400); Age UK Sandwell, Dogs Trust and The Anaphylaxis Campaign (£1,000 each); Royal Air Forces Association (£900); Carrs Lane Counselling Centre (£800); Listening Books and The PBC Foundation (UIZ) Ltd (500 each).
**FINANCES** Year 2013/14 Income £133,818 Grants £163,656 Grants to organisations £163,656 Assets £4,076,131
**TRUSTEES** Peter Barber; Susan Bennett; Lee Nuttall.
**OTHER INFORMATION** There were 87 awards given. The trust states that it aims 'to make a roughly equal division of funds between charities concerned with old people, children, the disabled, the poor and educational needs'. Grants to specific projects for locally based smaller charities are favoured but larger projects may be considered.
**HOW TO APPLY** Applications may be made in writing to the correspondent. The trustees normally meet in June and December, considering all applications received in the preceding six months. However, they will consider on an ad-hoc basis any requests that they consider should not be retained until their next scheduled meeting.

WHO TO APPLY TO The Trustees, c/o Mills and Reeve, 78–84 Colmore Row, Birmingham B3 2AB *Tel.* 0870 600 0011 *Fax* 0121 200 3028 *email* marsh.charity@mills-reeve.com

## ■ The Marsh Christian Trust

CC NO 284470   ESTABLISHED 1981
WHERE FUNDING CAN BE GIVEN UK.
WHO CAN BENEFIT Registered charities, 'experienced in their chosen field of work'.
WHAT IS FUNDED General charitable purposes, with a preference towards social welfare, environmental causes and animal welfare, health care and medical research, education and training, arts and heritage, also overseas appeals.
WHAT IS NOT FUNDED Individuals; building work; individual restoration projects; single projects; sponsorship proposals; individual churches; individual hospices or hospitals.
TYPE OF GRANT Long-term core funding.
RANGE OF GRANTS £250–£4,000; for new applications at the lower end of this scale.
FINANCES *Year* 2013/14 *Income* £731,734 *Grants* £225,492 *Grants to organisations* £148,225 *Assets* £8,778,518
TRUSTEES Brian Marsh; Natalie Marsh; Lorraine Ryan; Antonia Marsh; Camilla Kenyon; Charles Micklewright; Nicholas Carter.
OTHER INFORMATION The trust also maintains the Marsh Awards Scheme – to recognise individual and group achievements in the charity sector. The grant total includes over £77,000 given in Marshal Awards and over £148,000 in grants. There were about 400 grants and awards made in 2013/14. Grant-making support costs totalled about £119,000, including £110,500 in staff costs and £8,500 in 'other costs'.
HOW TO APPLY Applications can be made in writing to the correspondent at any time. Requests should be one or two sides of A4 and include a copy of the most recent set of accounts. The annual report for 2013/14 states that 'every effort is made to reply to each appeal received whether it is successful or not'.
WHO TO APPLY TO Brian Marsh, Trustee, 2nd Floor, 36 Broadway, London SW1H 0BH *Tel.* 020 7233 3112 *email* reeves@bpmarsh.co.uk

## ■ Charity of John Marshall (Marshall's Charity)

CC NO 206780   ESTABLISHED 1627
WHERE FUNDING CAN BE GIVEN England and Wales with preference for Kent, Surrey, Lincolnshire and Southwark.
WHO CAN BENEFIT Anglican parish churches and cathedrals only.
WHAT IS FUNDED Support for parsonage buildings throughout England and Wales; help with the upkeep of Anglican churches and cathedrals in Kent, Surrey and Lincolnshire (as the counties were defined in 1855), support for the parish of Christ Church in Southwark; awards for educational purposes to Marshall's Educational Foundation (4% of the expenditure).
WHAT IS NOT FUNDED Churches
Applicants who have received a grant from the charity within the past three years; churches outside the counties of Kent, Surrey and Lincolnshire, as defined in 1855; churches of denominations other than Anglican; professional fees; works outside the footprint of the church, such as church halls, external meeting rooms and facilities, church grounds and boundary walls and fences; redecoration; bells; organs; clock; monuments; brasses; stained glass.
**Parsonages:** Applications from individual clergy or other denominations – appeals should be made by applications from the relevant Diocesan Parsonage Board.
TYPE OF GRANT Building and other capital works; loans.
RANGE OF GRANTS Grants to churches usually £3,000–£5,000; awards to parsonages usually up to £4,000.
SAMPLE GRANTS Beneficiaries have included: Christ Church – Clapham and St Mark's – Kennington (£6,000 each); St John the Evangelist – Kingsdown, St Peter – East Stockwith and The Beheading of St John the Baptist – Doddington (£5,000 each); St Mary – West Butterwick (£4,000); St Andrew – Hannah cum Hagnaby with Markby (£3,500); St Nicholas – Deeping and St Saviour – Westgate-on-Sea (£1,000 each).
FINANCES *Year* 2014 *Income* £1,074,586 *Grants* £577,743 *Grants to organisations* £577,743 *Assets* £17,994,263
TRUSTEES Antony Guthrie; Colin Bird; Stephen Clark; William Eason; Anthea Nicholson; Georgina Isaac; John Heawood; Revd Jonathan Rust; Surbhi Malhotra; Lesley Bosman; Charles Ledsam; Alastair Moss; Ruth Martin.
OTHER INFORMATION During the year a total of 147 awards were made to parsonages (£381,500) and a total of 27 to churches (£145,500). The annual report and accounts did not list the beneficiaries; however, 2013 grant recipients were available on the charity's website.
HOW TO APPLY Application forms can be downloaded from the charity's website and can be returned via post, fax or email to the correspondent at any time. The Grants Committee meets three times each year (for exact dates see the website). Additional documents, such as Mission Action Plan, recent church newsletter or parish magazines may be included.
WHO TO APPLY TO Catherine Dawkins, Clerk to the Trustees, Marshall House, 66 Newcomen Street, London SE1 1YT *Tel.* 020 7407 2979 *Fax* 020 7403 3969 *email* grantoffice@marshalls.org.uk *Website* www.marshalls.org.uk

## ■ Charlotte Marshall Charitable Trust

CC NO 211941   ESTABLISHED 1962
WHERE FUNDING CAN BE GIVEN UK.
WHO CAN BENEFIT Registered charities; educational institutions benefitting Roman Catholics, children, young adults and students.
WHAT IS FUNDED Two thirds of the trust's income can be allocated to support educational, religious and other charitable purposes for Roman Catholics and the remainder can be distributed at the trustees' discretion.
WHAT IS NOT FUNDED Grants are not made to individuals.
RANGE OF GRANTS £500–£8,000
SAMPLE GRANTS St Richard's Catholic College (£8,000); Sacred Heart Catholic Primary School (£6,500); Pestalozzi International Village Trust (£5,000); The Sara Lee Trust (£2,700); St Radhals Hospice and West End Churches (£2,000 each); Kent Association for the Blind (£1,700); Army Cadet Force Association, Chestnut Tree House, Happy Days Children's Charity and Piers Road New Communities Centre Association (£1,000 each); Women At

The Well (£800); Beanstalk (£700); Contact The Elderly (£600); JustDifferent (£500).
**FINANCES** Year 2013/14 Income £76,378 Grants £73,590 Grants to organisations £73,590 Assets £520,355
**TRUSTEES** Elizabeth Cosgrave; Joseph Cosgrave; Kevin Page; John Russell; Rachel Cosgrave.
**OTHER INFORMATION** Out of the grant total about £49,000 went to Roman Catholic charitable institutions. There were 45 awards made.
**HOW TO APPLY** Applications should be made by completing a Trust Application Form with a formal request for funds. The trustees consider appeals at their spring meeting, usually around March. Our research suggests that completed forms should be returned in advance to the meeting – by 31 December.
**WHO TO APPLY TO** The Trustees, Sidney Little Road, Churchfields Industrial Estate, St Leonards-on-Sea, East Sussex TN38 9PU Tel. 01424 856655 email hannahh@marshall-tufflex.com

## ■ D. G. Marshall of Cambridge Trust

**CC NO** 286468 **ESTABLISHED** 1982
**WHERE FUNDING CAN BE GIVEN** Predominantly Cambridge and Cambridgeshire.
**WHO CAN BENEFIT** Community projects, local appeals and local charities benefitting people with disabilities and people disadvantaged by poverty.
**WHAT IS FUNDED** Education and training; social welfare; aviation; disability; health; children and young people.
**RANGE OF GRANTS** £250–£10,000
**SAMPLE GRANTS** SOS Children (£10,000); American Air Museum and Arthur Rank Hospice Charity (£5,000 each); Arkwright Scholarship Trust (£4,000); Battle of Britain Memorial Trust (£2,500); the Avenues Youth Project and Ely Cathedral Restoration Trust (£1,500 each); CLIC Sargent and East Anglian Children's Hospice (£1,000 each); Institute of Economic Affairs and Teversham Baptist Church (£500 each); Rainbows Children's Hospice and Sheffield Children's Hospital (£250 each).
**FINANCES** Year 2013/14 Income £217,956 Grants £65,050 Grants to organisations £65,050 Assets £1,657,264
**TRUSTEES** Jonathan Barker; Bill Dastur; Michael Marshall; Robert Marshall.
**OTHER INFORMATION** 40 grants were made totalling £65,000.
**HOW TO APPLY** The charity will consider all applications, providing they are consistent with the objectives of the charity.
**WHO TO APPLY TO** Sarah Moynihan, Company Secretary, Marshall of Cambridge (Holdings) Ltd, Control Building, The Airport, Newmarket Road, Cambridgeshire CB5 8RY Tel. 01223 373273 email sjm@marcamb.co.uk

## ■ The Marshgate Charitable Settlement

**CC NO** 1081645 **ESTABLISHED** 2000
**WHERE FUNDING CAN BE GIVEN** UK and overseas.
**WHO CAN BENEFIT** Charitable organisations; Christian charities.
**WHAT IS FUNDED** Christian work; education; medical purposes; children and young people.
**RANGE OF GRANTS** £200–£38,000; usually about £1,000.

**SAMPLE GRANTS** Highmoor Spring Charitable Trust (£38,000); Wings Like Eagles (£10,000); CARE (£8,500); Inter Health, Karis Kids, Stewardship, Tearfund and The Cans Trust (£2,000 each); Chaplaincy Plus, Cystic Fibrosis Trust and The Godolphin and Latymer School (£1,000 each); The Ffald-y-Brenin Trust (£500); Watson and Oxfordshire VCH Trust (£200 each).
**FINANCES** Year 2013/14 Income £17 Grants £8,000 Grants to organisations £8,000
**TRUSTEES** Clifford Hampton; Marjorie Hampton; Rachel Ambler.
**OTHER INFORMATION** Due to low income accounts were not required to be filed with the Charity Commission. In 2013/14 the charity had a total expenditure of £8,500. **Note**: Charitable giving varies each year and in the past five years has totalled around £41,500 on average.
**HOW TO APPLY** Applications may be made in writing to the correspondent.
**WHO TO APPLY TO** Clifford Hampton, Trustee, Highmoor Hall, Henley-on-Thames, Oxfordshire RG9 5DH Tel. 01491 641543

## ■ Sir George Martin Trust

**CC NO** 223554 **ESTABLISHED** 1956
**WHERE FUNDING CAN BE GIVEN** North and West Yorkshire.
**WHO CAN BENEFIT** Registered charities; churches; educational establishments; hospices; museums. Organisation or project must have a 'Yorkshire angle'.
**WHAT IS FUNDED** General charitable purposes, including countryside, environment, 'green' issues, children and young people, church appeals, health causes and hospices, music and other arts, culture, older people, education and social welfare.
**WHAT IS NOT FUNDED** Restoration schemes of church roofs, spires, etc.; applications from overseas; individuals in the area of music and arts; playgroups; any area of education where there is state funding; applications in the old Yorkshire coalfield; university or college appeals, nor appeals from individuals seeking grants for university fees, postgraduate courses, or other courses; overseas seminars or exchange visits by individuals or groups; medical appeals of a capital or revenue nature; medical research projects.
**TYPE OF GRANT** Grants for capital rather than revenue projects; usually one-off.
**RANGE OF GRANTS** Usually £100–£3,000 with some larger grants.
**SAMPLE GRANTS** Harrogate International Festival, Haworth Church Restoration, Henshaw Society for the Blind, Forget Me Not Trust, Marrick Priory, Sea Cadet Corps Leeds, Square Chapel Centre for the Arts, Wakefield Cathedral and Woodhouse Grove School (larger, unspecified grants); St Jemma's Hospice (£3,000); Woodlands Trust (£2,500); Friends of Middleton Park (£2,300); Leeds Woman's Aid (£1,500); Dial a Ride Scarborough and Methodist Home for the Aged (£1,000 each); Older Wiser Local Seniors (£500); Tall Ships Youth Trust (£270).
**FINANCES** Year 2013/14 Income £125,149 Grants £171,459 Grants to organisations £171,459 Assets £7,096,876
**TRUSTEES** David Coates, Chair; Martin Bethel; Roger Marshall; Paul Taylor; Marjorie Martin; Morven Whyte.
**OTHER INFORMATION** There were 121 awards made. The trust states that it 'prefers to make grants available for capital rather than revenue projects, and is reluctant to give to general

running costs, or areas previously supported by state funds'. The trust states that grants are not normally repeated to any charity in any one year and the maximum number of consecutive grants is usually three. One-off giving policy is preferred.

HOW TO APPLY Application forms can be requested via email or phone from the correspondent. It should be returned via post along with a statement of no more than two pages outlining your proposal and a copy of your latest set of accounts. You should also specify the amount required and whether any other funding has been secured. The trustees meet in March, July and November each year to consider applications. The website notes: 'If an application meets the trust's initial criteria, our secretary will be in touch to arrange a visit to the project prior to the next trustees meeting taking place. Each application will then be reviewed by our five trustees and successful applications will be told following the meeting. Unsuccessful applicants will not be informed because of increased cost of postage.'

WHO TO APPLY TO Carla Marshall, Trust Manager, 6 Firs Avenue, Harrogate, North Yorkshire HG2 9HA *Tel.* 01423 810222 *email* info@sirgeorgemartintrust.org.uk *Website* www.sirgeorgemartintrust.org.uk

## ■ John Martin's Charity

CC NO 527473    ESTABLISHED 1714
WHERE FUNDING CAN BE GIVEN Evesham and 'certain surrounding villages' only.
WHO CAN BENEFIT Individuals and charitable or voluntary organisations and schools benefitting the residents of Evesham.
WHAT IS FUNDED Religious support – to assist the Vicars and Parochial Church Councils within the town of Evesham; relief in need – to assist individuals and organisations within the town of Evesham who are in conditions of need, hardship and distress; promotion of education – to promote education to persons who are or have a parent residing within the town of Evesham and to provide benefits to schools within Evesham; health – to support people with chronic health problems and other related health issues.
WHAT IS NOT FUNDED Payment of rates or taxes; replacement of statutory benefits.
TYPE OF GRANT One-off capital costs, general expenditure and project costs.
RANGE OF GRANTS £500–£30,000
SAMPLE GRANTS Evesham Volunteer Centre (£30,000); St Richards Hospice (£20,000); South Worcestershire Citizens Advice (£11,800); Prince Henry's High School (£10,900); Hampton First School (£9,000); Acquired Aphasia Trust and Pathways to Recovery (£5,000 each); Life Education Centre (£4,200); Acorns Children's' Hospice (£3,000); Church Conservation Trust (£1,500); Youth Music Festival (£500).
FINANCES Year 2013/14 Income £824,508 Grants £619,309 Grants to organisations £229,227 Assets £21,241,000
TRUSTEES Nigel Lamb; John Smith; Richard Emson; Cyril Scorse; Revd Andrew Spurr; Diana Raphael; Josephine Sandalls; Joyce Turner; Julie Westlake; John Wilson; Revd Mark Binney; Catherine Evans; Gabrielle Falkiner.
OTHER INFORMATION A total of £390,000 was granted to individuals. Grants were made to 40 organisations.

HOW TO APPLY Application forms can be accessed from the charity's website. Applicants should also provide: their latest annual accounts, the latest bank statement showing the current balance and the name of the organisation; relevant literature about the organisation (such as leaflets or flyers); details of any other funds secured or applied to. Informal contact prior to submitting the application is welcome. Note that the charity receives more requests than it can support. Awards are considered every quarter and applications should be received by 1 March, 1 June, 1 September or 20 November.

WHO TO APPLY TO John Daniels, Clerk to the Trustees, 16 Queen's Road, Evesham, Worcestershire WR11 4JN *Tel.* 01386 765440 *email* enquiries@johnmartins.org.uk *Website* www.johnmartins.org.uk

## ■ The Dan Maskell Tennis Trust

CC NO 1133589
WHERE FUNDING CAN BE GIVEN Throughout the UK.
WHO CAN BENEFIT Individuals; disability groups and programmes; tennis clubs; associations; schools.
WHAT IS FUNDED Disability; amateur sports.
WHAT IS NOT FUNDED 'Luxury' items, such as electrical equipment (for example, videos), clothing or individual transport costs.
TYPE OF GRANT The purchase of wheelchairs, tennis equipment and grants for coaching.
SAMPLE GRANTS **Previous beneficiaries have included:** Lee Valley Tennis Centre (five general wheelchairs); Deaf Kids project (sound tennis ball and coaching); local authority and specialist school (tennis equipment bags).
FINANCES Year 2013 Income £71,935 Grants £59,736 Grants to organisations £59,736 Assets £572,738
TRUSTEES Lilas Davison; Ian Peacock; John Tucker; Sue Wolstenholme; John James; Robin Maskell-Charlton; Tony Hughes; Noel McShane; Robert McCowen.
OTHER INFORMATION During the year, 65 grants applications were approved. This supported the purchase of 23 individual tennis wheelchairs, 43 general tennis wheelchairs for separate groups and three tennis equipment bags. 27 other grants were also made for a range purposes, including to individuals.
HOW TO APPLY Application forms are available from the trust's website. The trustees meet at least three times a year. The dates of meetings and application submission deadlines (which usually fall in the preceding month) are listed on the website. It is requested that applicants provide as much information as possible and include details of the cost for each item or facility. The guidelines also note: 'Before applying for assistance, you are advised to consult The Tennis Foundation and/or your local County Tennis Association'.
WHO TO APPLY TO The Correspondent, c/o Sport Wins, PO Box 238, Tadworth KT20 5WT *Tel.* 01737 831707 *email* danmaskell@sportwins.co.uk *Website* www.danmaskelltennistrust.org.uk

# The Mason Porter Charitable Trust

**CC NO** 255545     **ESTABLISHED** 1968
**WHERE FUNDING CAN BE GIVEN** UK.
**WHO CAN BENEFIT** Grants are made only to charities known to the settlor.
**WHAT IS FUNDED** General charitable purposes, particularly Christian causes.
**RANGE OF GRANTS** Up to £16,000.
**SAMPLE GRANTS** Just Care (£16,000); Pharmacist Support (£12,000); Abernethy Trust and Cliff College (£10,000 each); Proclaim Trust (£8,000); ECG Trust – Burslem Methodist (£4,000); New Creations (£3,000); Youth for Christ (£2,500); St Luke's Methodist Church (£2,200); More than Gold 2014, Share Jesus International and Wirral Hospice – St John's (£2,000 each); Methodist Evangelicals Together (£1,000). Other awards totalled £13,400.
**FINANCES** Year 2013/14 Income £117,620 Grants £88,057 Grants to organisations £88,057 Assets £1,911,201
**TRUSTEE** Liverpool Charity and Voluntary Services.
**HOW TO APPLY** The trust has informed us that, as this is a personal trust, 'grants are only made to charities already known to the settlor'. The accounts confirm that 'unsolicited applications are therefore not considered'.
**WHO TO APPLY TO** Liverpool Charity and Voluntary Services, Trustee, 151 Dale Street, Liverpool L2 2AH *Tel.* 0151 227 5177

# The Nancie Massey Charitable Trust

**SC NO** SC008977     **ESTABLISHED** 1989
**WHERE FUNDING CAN BE GIVEN** Scotland, particularly Edinburgh and Leith.
**WHO CAN BENEFIT** Registered charities.
**WHAT IS FUNDED** Older people; children and young adults; medical research; education; science; heritage and the arts.
**WHAT IS NOT FUNDED** Individuals.
**TYPE OF GRANT** Capital and core costs; salaries; one-off or recurrent; unrestricted funding.
**RANGE OF GRANTS** Up to £60,000; generally £500–£2,000.
**SAMPLE GRANTS** Royal Lyceum (£60,000); Royal College of Surgeons (£20,000); minor grants totalling £147,000. Previously grants have also been made to National Museums of Scotland Charitable Trust (£100,000); St Columba's Hospice and Tenovus Scotland (£28,000 each); Marie Curie (£27,000).
**FINANCES** Year 2013/14 Income £271,779 Grants £226,980 Grants to organisations £226,980 Assets £7,159,816
**TRUSTEES** Gavin Morton; M. F. Sinclair; E. Wilson.
**HOW TO APPLY** Our research suggests that application forms can be requested by writing to the correspondent. The trustees normally meet three times a year in February, June and October and applications should be received a month in advance. Applicants need to set out what the grant is to be used for, how it will benefit recipients of the grant and how the outcomes are measured.
**WHO TO APPLY TO** Gavin Morton, Trustee, c/o Chiene and Tait LLP, Cairn House, 61 Dublin Street, Edinburgh EH3 6NL *Tel.* 0131 558 5800 *Fax* 0131 558 5899 *email* jgm@chiene.co.uk

# The Mathew Trust

**SC NO** SC016284     **ESTABLISHED** 1935
**WHERE FUNDING CAN BE GIVEN** City of Dundee; Angus; Perth and Kinross; Fife.
**WHO CAN BENEFIT** Registered charities; educational establishments; social enterprises; individuals.
**WHAT IS FUNDED** Adult education; vocational and professional training; relief of poverty by providing assistance in the recruitment of people who are unemployed, or who are likely to become unemployed in the near future.
**WHAT IS NOT FUNDED** Replacement of statutory funding.
**TYPE OF GRANT** One-off and recurrent up to five years (monitored on an annual basis); capital and revenue costs; salaries; project funding.
**RANGE OF GRANTS** £500–£50,000
**SAMPLE GRANTS** Dundee University Medical School and Ninewells Cancer Campaign (£50,000 each); Scottish Enterprise Incubator Units (£47,500); Carolina House Trust (£25,000); Grey Lodge Settlement (£15,000); Check In Works (£5,000); Salvation Army Furniture Project (£4,800); Helm Training (£4,000); Enterprise Education Trust (£1,300); Tall Ships Youth Trust (£600); Deaf Action £500).
**FINANCES** Year 2013/14 Income £262,024 Grants £213,744 Grants to organisations £210,944 Assets £8,128,298
**TRUSTEES** Joyce Matthew; Alan McLeod; Alexander McDonald; Peter Howie; The Lord Provost of the City of Dundee.
**OTHER INFORMATION** During the year 13 grants were given to organisations and seven to individuals to help fund overseas placements totalling £2,800.
**HOW TO APPLY** Applications may be made in writing to the correspondent. Appeals are generally considered every two months.
**WHO TO APPLY TO** Sheena Gibson, Correspondent, c/o Henderson Loggie, The Vision Building, 20 Greenmarket, Dundee DD1 4QB *Tel.* 01382 200055 *Fax* 01382 221240 *email* shg@hlca.co.uk

# The Matliwala Family Charitable Trust

**CC NO** 1012756     **ESTABLISHED** 1992
**WHERE FUNDING CAN BE GIVEN** UK and overseas, especially Bharuch – India.
**WHO CAN BENEFIT** Charitable organisations.
**WHAT IS FUNDED** The advancement of education for pupils at Matliwala School of Baruch in Gujarat – India, including assisting with the provision of equipment and facilities; advancement of the Islamic religion; relief of sickness and poverty; advancement of education.
**RANGE OF GRANTS** £150–£270,000
**SAMPLE GRANTS** A full list of beneficiaries was not included within the latest accounts. Grants were given as follows: Masjid-E-Salam (£270,000); Matliwala Relief Trust (£152,000); education (overseas) (£61,500); Matliwala Education Society (£33,000); The Matliwala Darul Aloom Charitable Trust – UK (£29,500); relief of poverty – overseas (£1,000); education – UK (£150).
**FINANCES** Year 2013/14 Income £546,550 Grants £546,616 Grants to organisations £546,616 Assets £4,614,151
**TRUSTEES** Ayub Bux; Yousuf Bux; Abdul Patel; Usman Salya; Fatima Ismail.
**HOW TO APPLY** Applications may be made in writing to the correspondent. The trustees meet monthly to assess grant applications and

approve awards. The annual report for 2013/14 states: 'The charity welcomes applications for grants from all quarters and these are assessed by the trustees on their individual merits. Awards are given according to the individual needs of the applicant, depending on the funds available.'

**WHO TO APPLY TO** Ayub Bux, Trustee, 9 Brookview, Fulwood, Preston PR2 8FG *Tel.* 01772 706501

## ■ The Matt 6.3 Charitable Trust

**CC NO** 1069985      **ESTABLISHED** 1998
**WHERE FUNDING CAN BE GIVEN** UK.
**WHO CAN BENEFIT** Christian organisations; evangelical societies; individuals.
**WHAT IS FUNDED** General charitable purposes; Christian causes.
**TYPE OF GRANT** One-off awards, including help towards core and start-up costs.
**SAMPLE GRANTS** Christian Centre (Humberside) Limited (£51,000).
**FINANCES** *Year* 2013/14 *Income* £111,023 *Grants* £56,025 *Grants to organisations* £56,025 *Assets* £4,381,773
**TRUSTEES** Doris Dibdin; Christine Barnett.
**OTHER INFORMATION** There were four beneficiaries; however, the only one listed was Christian Centre (Humberside) Limited.
**HOW TO APPLY** The trustees' report for 2013/14 states the following: 'Due to the fact that the charity's income is largely unpredictable, the trustees have adopted a policy of maximising the reserves in order to provide ongoing funding in future years for the organisations they wish to support.'
**WHO TO APPLY TO** Ian Davey, Secretary, Progress House, Progress Park, Cupola Way, Off Normanby Road, Scunthorpe DN15 9YJ *Tel.* 01724 863666 *email* iandavey@tpdibdin.com

## ■ The Violet Mauray Charitable Trust

**CC NO** 1001716      **ESTABLISHED** 1990
**WHERE FUNDING CAN BE GIVEN** UK.
**WHO CAN BENEFIT** Registered charities; Jewish organisations.
**WHAT IS FUNDED** A range of general charitable purposes; Jewish causes; medical causes.
**WHAT IS NOT FUNDED** Grants are not made to individuals.
**TYPE OF GRANT** One-off project grants.
**RANGE OF GRANTS** Usually £750–£5,000.
**SAMPLE GRANTS** Kids Company (£10,000); Teach First (£6,500); Deafness Research, Greenhouse Schools Project and Straight Talking (£3,000 each); Excellent Development (£2,000); British Institute for Brain-injured Children, Help for Heroes and National Animal Welfare Trust (£1,000 each); Nightingale Hammerson (£500); Stillbirth and Neonatal Death Society (£250).
**FINANCES** *Year* 2013/14 *Income* £53,722 *Grants* £53,000 *Grants to organisations* £53,000 *Assets* £2,046,873
**TRUSTEES** Robert Stephany; John Stephany; Alison Karlin.
**OTHER INFORMATION** Grants were made to 23 organisations.
**HOW TO APPLY** Applications may be made in writing to the correspondent. Grants are made on an ad hoc basis.
**WHO TO APPLY TO** John Stephany, Trustee, 9 Bentinck Street, London W1U 2EL *Tel.* 020 7935 0982

## ■ Mayfair Charities Ltd

**CC NO** 255281      **ESTABLISHED** 1968
**WHERE FUNDING CAN BE GIVEN** UK and overseas.
**WHO CAN BENEFIT** Registered charities benefitting Orthodox Jews, particularly children and young adults; educational institutions; religious organisations.
**WHAT IS FUNDED** Orthodox Jewish faith; religion; education; relief of poverty; social welfare in the Jewish community.
**TYPE OF GRANT** One-off awards for capital and running costs.
**RANGE OF GRANTS** Typically £500–£2,500; occasionally large donations.
**SAMPLE GRANTS** **Previous beneficiaries have included:** Beth Jacob Grammar School For Girls Limited (over £1 million) and Regent Charities Limited (£40,000); Beis Aharon Trust; Chaye Olam Institute; Chevras Maoz Ladal; Comet Charities Ltd; Congregation Ichud Chasidim; Edgware Foundation; Ezer Mikodesh Foundation; Gateshead Jewish Teachers Training College; Heritage House; Kiryat Sanz Jerusalem; Kollel Chibas Yerushalayim; Friends of Bobov; Merkaz Lechinuch Torani; Mesivta Letzeirim; Ohr Akiva Institute; PAL Charitable Trust; Regent Charities Ltd; Talmud Torah Zichron Gavriel; Woodstock Sinclair Trust; Yesodei Hatorah School.
**FINANCES** *Year* 2013/14 *Income* £4,394,000 *Grants* £4,328,000 *Grants to organisations* £4,328,000 *Assets* £100,358,000
**TRUSTEES** Benzion Freshwater; D. Davis; Solomon Freshwater; Richard Fischer.
**OTHER INFORMATION** Grants were made to over 450 organisations; however, a recent list of beneficiaries was unavailable. The grant total includes £150,000 given in non-monetary donations – the provision of facilities to Beth Jacob Grammar School for Girls Limited.
**HOW TO APPLY** Applications may be made in writing to the correspondent.
**WHO TO APPLY TO** Benzion Freshwater, Trustee, Freshwater Group of Companies, Freshwater House, 158–162 Shaftesbury Avenue, London WC2H 8HR *Tel.* 020 7836 1555

## ■ The Mayfield Valley Arts Trust

**CC NO** 327665      **ESTABLISHED** 1988
**WHERE FUNDING CAN BE GIVEN** Unrestricted, but with a special interest in Sheffield and South Yorkshire.
**WHO CAN BENEFIT** Charities supporting new and emerging artists; institutions supporting music education, including special needs schools.
**WHAT IS FUNDED** The arts; music education, especially chamber music.
**WHAT IS NOT FUNDED** Our research notes the trust previously stating that 'it will not be involved in the education of individual students nor will it provide grants to individual students; it will not be involved in the provision of musical instruments for individuals, schools or organisations'.
**TYPE OF GRANT** Up to three years for core costs.
**RANGE OF GRANTS** £45,000–£5,000
**SAMPLE GRANTS** Wigmore Hall (£45,000); York Early Music Foundation and Live Music Now (£30,000 each); Music in the Round (£18,000); Prussia Cove (£10,000).

**FINANCES** Year 2013/14 Income £120,335 Grants £133,000 Grants to organisations £133,000 Assets £2,421,521

**TRUSTEES** David Brown; David Whelton; John Rider; Anthony Thornton; Priscilla Thornton; James Thornton.

**OTHER INFORMATION** Grants were made to five organisations.

**HOW TO APPLY** The trust has previously stated that unsolicited applications are not considered. It has also noted that funding is normally considered on a three-year cycle, the next review being summer 2016 – if your organisation meets the criteria you should submit a summary request at that time.

**WHO TO APPLY TO** James Thornton, Trustee, 12 Abbots Way, Abbotswood, Ballasalla, Isle of Man IM9 3EQ email jamesthornton@manx.net

## ■ Mazars Charitable Trust
**CC NO** 1150459    **ESTABLISHED** 2012
**WHERE FUNDING CAN BE GIVEN** UK and Ireland.
**WHO CAN BENEFIT** Registered charities and voluntary organisations.
**WHAT IS FUNDED** General charitable purposes. Support is normally only given to projects which are nominated to the management committee by the partners and staff of Mazars (chartered accountants).
**TYPE OF GRANT** Single strategic projects; one-off; research; building; and capital costs. Funding is for one year or less.
**RANGE OF GRANTS** £1,000–£25,000
**SAMPLE GRANTS** The Prince's Trust (£26,000); Viva (£15,000); The Heal Project (£12,500); Swindon Christian Community Projects (£10,000); Kids Company (£7,500); St Andrew's Hospice (£5,200); CCHF All About Kids (£3,000); RealLondon Mentoring CIC (£2,000); Diabetes UK (£1,600); the British Heart Foundation (£1,300).
**FINANCES** Year 2013/14 Income £525,141 Grants £283,232 Grants to organisations £283,232 Assets £275,333
**TRUSTEES** Bob Neate; David Evans; Phil Verity; Alan Edwards.
**HOW TO APPLY** Charities cannot apply directly for funding but, rather, are nominated by Mazars partners and employees. Unsolicited applications will receive no response.
**WHO TO APPLY TO** Simon Pettit, Mazars LLP, The Pinnacle, 160 Midsummer Boulevard, Milton Keynes MK9 1FF Tel. 020 7063 4000 Website www.mazars.co.uk/Home/About-us/Corporate-Responsibility/Charities

## ■ The Robert McAlpine Foundation
**CC NO** 226646    **ESTABLISHED** 1963
**WHERE FUNDING CAN BE GIVEN** UK.
**WHO CAN BENEFIT** Registered charities; schools; hospices; hospitals.
**WHAT IS FUNDED** General charitable purposes; medical research; social welfare; children with disabilities; older people.
**WHAT IS NOT FUNDED** Overheads; individuals.
**TYPE OF GRANT** Capital costs and unrestricted funding, one-off and up to one year.
**RANGE OF GRANTS** Up to £100,000. Average grants between £10,000 and £15,000.
**SAMPLE GRANTS** Previous beneficiaries have included: Age Concern, Community Self Build Agency, DENS Action Against Homelessness, Downside Fisher Youth Club, Ewing Foundation, the Golden Oldies, Grateful Society, James Hopkins Trust, Merchants Academy Withywood, National Benevolent Fund for the Aged, National Eye Research Centre, Prostate UK, Royal Marsden NHS Trust, St John's Youth Centre and the Towers School and 6th Form Centre.
**FINANCES** Year 2013/14 Income £862,072 Grants £728,000 Grants to organisations £728,000 Assets £15,535,533
**TRUSTEES** Adrian McAlpine; Cullum McAlpine; The Hon David McAlpine; Kenneth McAlpine.
**OTHER INFORMATION** Grants paid during 2013/14 totalled £728,000.
**HOW TO APPLY** Applications can be made in writing to the correspondent at any time. Applications are considered annually, normally in November.
**WHO TO APPLY TO** Brian Arter, Correspondent, Sir Robert McAlpine Ltd, Eaton Court, Maylands Avenue, Hemel Hempstead, Hertfordshire HP2 7TR Tel. 01442 233444 email b.arter@sir-robert-mcalpine.com

## ■ McGreevy No 5 Settlement
**CC NO** 280666    **ESTABLISHED** 1979
**WHERE FUNDING CAN BE GIVEN** UK, with some preference for the Bristol and Bath area.
**WHO CAN BENEFIT** Registered charities.
**WHAT IS FUNDED** General charitable purposes; children and young people; health causes.
**WHAT IS NOT FUNDED** Support cannot be given for individuals.
**RANGE OF GRANTS** £1,000–£25,000
**SAMPLE GRANTS** NSPCC (£25,000); Bath Preservation Trust, Parkinson's UK and The Stroke Association (£5,000 each); Elias Ashmole Trust (£1,000).
**FINANCES** Year 2013/14 Income £57,858 Grants £41,000 Grants to organisations £41,000 Assets £2,525,409
**TRUSTEES** Avon Executor and Trustee Co. Ltd; Anthony McGreevy; Elise McGreevy-Harris; Katrina Paterson.
**OTHER INFORMATION** The trust made a total of five grants during the year.
**HOW TO APPLY** Applications may be made in writing to the correspondent.
**WHO TO APPLY TO** Karen Ganson, Trust Administrator, Yew Court, Riverview Road, Pangbourne, Reading RG8 7AU Tel. 0117 905 4000 email elise139@aol.com

## ■ D. D. McPhail Charitable Settlement
**CC NO** 267588    **ESTABLISHED** 1974
**WHERE FUNDING CAN BE GIVEN** UK.
**WHO CAN BENEFIT** Registered charities; hospices; educational institutions and research centres; organisations benefitting people who are older, young people and those with disabilities.
**WHAT IS FUNDED** Medical research; health care; disability, causes; children and young people; older people.
**TYPE OF GRANT** Mainly recurrent awards for projects, services and research.
**RANGE OF GRANTS** Mostly £2,000–£10,000.
**SAMPLE GRANTS** The University of Nottingham (£100,000 in four awards); Parents for the Early Intervention of Autism in Children – PEACH (£29,500); Amy and Friends – Cockayne Syndrome Support, Cure Parkinson's Trust, Snowdrop for Brain Injured Children and The Woodhouse Centre (£2,000 each).

FINANCES Year 2013/14 Income £321,107 Grants £134,250 Grants to organisations £134,250 Assets £9,619,809
TRUSTEES Julia Noble; Catherine Charles-Jones; Christopher Yates; Tariq Kazi; Michael Craig; Mary Meeks; Olivia Hancock.
OTHER INFORMATION Grants were made to seven organisations, including a major research award in quarterly payments, ongoing contribution and five smaller grants. The charity has had some ongoing funding commitments.
HOW TO APPLY The charity's administrator is Mrs Sheila Watson. The annual report for 2013/14 states the following: 'Trustees identify potential projects for assessment by the Executive Director. The Trust makes no commitment to respond to unsolicited applications. There have also been ongoing smaller grants to causes supported by the Trustees.'
WHO TO APPLY TO Katharine Moss, Executive Director, PO Box 285, Pinner, Middlesex HA5 3FB Tel. 020 8429 2354 email director. ddmcphail@gmail.com

■ **The Medlock Charitable Trust**
CC NO 326927    ESTABLISHED 1985
WHERE FUNDING CAN BE GIVEN Principally, but not exclusively, City of Bath and the Borough of Boston.
WHO CAN BENEFIT Registered charities; educational establishments; local community charities in any part of the country.
WHAT IS FUNDED General charitable purposes, especially education, medicine, research and social services for the benefit of the local community.
WHAT IS NOT FUNDED Individuals; students.
TYPE OF GRANT One-off or multi-year awards; capital and revenue costs; start-up; unrestricted funding.
RANGE OF GRANTS £600–£255,000; mainly under £15,000.
SAMPLE GRANTS Holburne Museum (£255,000 over five years); The University of Bath (£250,000 over five years); The Boshier-Hinton Foundation (£180,000); Quartet Community Foundation (£100,000); Mentoring Plus Ltd (£45,000); The Bath Preservation Trust (£37,500); Friends of the Royal United Hospital and SSAFA – Somerset (£25,000 each); Bath and District Samaritans (£11,000); Boston Food Bank, Castle Primary School, The Louth Living Well Project and Zion United Church (£10,000 each); King Edward's School, Bath (£6,100); Bristol Debt Advice Centre (£5,000); Cruse Bereavement Care – Boston and District (£4,000); Avon Riding Centre for the Disabled Limited, St Luke's Church and The Willow Trust (£2,000 each); Bath Natural History Society, Police and Crime Commissioner for Avon and Somerset and The Canynges Society (£1,000 each); The Park Community Centre Ltd (£800); The Golden-Oldies Charity (£600).
FINANCES Year 2013/14 Income £384,144 Grants £1,972,694 Grants to organisations £1,972,694 Assets £29,457,668
TRUSTEES Jacqueline Medlock; David Medlock; Mark Goodman.
OTHER INFORMATION During the year 178 awards were made the majority of which was for under £15,000 (158 awards).
HOW TO APPLY Applications can be made in writing to the correspondent. Note that 'the trustees have identified the City of Bath and the borough of Boston as the principal but not exclusive areas in which the charity is and will be proactive', although during the year many applications for assistance are also received from many diverse areas in the United Kingdom which are all considered sympathetically. The trustees meet on a regular basis.
WHO TO APPLY TO David Medlock, Trustee, 7 Old Track, Limpley Stoke, Bath BA3 6JY

■ **Melodor Limited**
CC NO 260972    ESTABLISHED 1970
WHERE FUNDING CAN BE GIVEN UK and overseas.
WHO CAN BENEFIT Orthodox Jewish institutions.
WHAT IS FUNDED General charitable purposes, especially education and religion, with focus on Jewish causes; relief of poverty; health; the advancement of Orthodox Jewish faith.
TYPE OF GRANT One-off grants and loans.
RANGE OF GRANTS Up to £30,000.
SAMPLE GRANTS Previous beneficiaries have included: Beis Minchas Yitzhok; Beis Rochel; Beth Hamedrash Hachodosh; Chasdei Yoel; Delman Charitable Trust; Dushinsky Trust; Friends of Viznitz; Kollel Chelkas Yakov; Ovois Ubonim; Talmud Torah Education Trust; The Centre for Torah Education Trust; Yeshivas Ohel Shimon; Yetev Lev.
FINANCES Year 2013/14 Income £169,432 Grants £170,417 Grants to organisations £170,417 Assets £597,142
TRUSTEES Hyman Weiss; Philip Weiss; Zisel Weiss; Pinchas Neumann; Yocheved Weiss; Eli Neumann; Esther Henry; Henry Neumann; Janet Bleier; Maurice Neumann; Miriam Friedlander; Rebecca Delange; Rivka Ollech; Rivka Rabinowitz; Pesha Kohn; Yehoshua Weiss.
HOW TO APPLY The trust's accounts for 2013/14 state: 'The governors receive many applications for grants, mainly by mail, but also verbally. Each application is considered against the criteria established by the charity. Although the charity does not advertise, it is well known within its community and there are many requests received for grants.'
WHO TO APPLY TO Bernardin Weiss, Correspondent, 10 Cubley Road, Salford M7 4GN Tel. 0161 720 6188

■ **The Melow Charitable Trust**
CC NO 275454    ESTABLISHED 1978
WHERE FUNDING CAN BE GIVEN UK and overseas.
WHO CAN BENEFIT Mainly Jewish charities.
WHAT IS FUNDED Jewish causes; the relief of poverty; the advancement of religion and religious education.
RANGE OF GRANTS Up to £314,000.
SAMPLE GRANTS Previous beneficiaries have included: Ezer V'Hatzalah Ltd (£314,000); Lolev Charitable Trust (£265,000); Friends of Kollel Samtar (Antwerp) Ltd (£107,000); Asser Bishvil Foundation (£100,000); United Talmudical Associates Ltd (£64,500); Beis Rochel D'Satmar Girls School (£62,000); Rehabilitation Trust (£57,500).
FINANCES Grants £1,200,000 Grants to organisations £1,200,000
TRUSTEES Miriam Spitz; Esther Weiser.
OTHER INFORMATION At the time of writing (June 2015) the latest available information was for 2011/12 – the trust has not submitted its accounts since. As the trust remains on the Charity Commission's record and has been providing substantial funding, we maintain this entry. In the previous four years charitable expenditure has totalled about £1.2 million on

average. In the past support has been allocated to: general purposes (£391,500); education (£185,500); religious institutions (£96,500); cemetery (£75,000); people in need (£43,000); talmudical colleges (£27,500); synagogues (£25,000); publication of religious books (£24,500); relief of poverty (£10,900); community organisation (£500); integrated school (£250); Mother and Baby Home (£200).
**HOW TO APPLY** Applications may be mad in writing to the correspondent.
**WHO TO APPLY TO** J. I. Low, 21 Warwick Grove, London E5 9HX *Tel.* 020 8806 1549

## ■ Menuchar Limited
**CC NO** 262782 **ESTABLISHED** 1971
**WHERE FUNDING CAN BE GIVEN** UK.
**WHO CAN BENEFIT** Jewish organisations; religious establishments.
**WHAT IS FUNDED** Advancement of religion in accordance with the Orthodox Jewish faith and relief of people in need.
**WHAT IS NOT FUNDED** Non-registered charities; individuals.
**TYPE OF GRANT** Primarily one-off.
**FINANCES** Year 2013/14 *Income* £421,826 *Grants* £412,797 *Grants to organisations* £412,797 *Assets* £160,907
**TRUSTEES** Norman Bude; Gail Bude.
**OTHER INFORMATION** A list of beneficiaries was not included in the accounts; however, they did state that grants went to religious organisations.
**HOW TO APPLY** Applications can be made in writing to the correspondent.
**WHO TO APPLY TO** The Trustees, c/o Barry Flack and Co Limited, The Brentano Suite, Prospect House, 2 Athenaeum Road, London N20 9AE *Tel.* 020 8369 5170 *email* barry@barryflack.com

## ■ Mercaz Torah Vechesed Limited
**CC NO** 1109212 **ESTABLISHED** 2005
**WHERE FUNDING CAN BE GIVEN** Worldwide.
**WHO CAN BENEFIT** Charitable organisations and individuals.
**WHAT IS FUNDED** The advancement of the Orthodox Jewish faith, Orthodox Jewish religious education, and the relief of poverty and infirmity amongst members of the Orthodox Jewish community.
**FINANCES** Year 2013/14 *Income* £856,579 *Grants* £902,514 *Grants to organisations* £902,514 *Assets* £1,117
**TRUSTEES** Joseph Ostreicher; Mordche Rand.
**HOW TO APPLY** Application may be made in writing to the correspondent.
**WHO TO APPLY TO** Joseph Ostreicher, Secretary, 28 Braydon Road, London N16 6QB *Tel.* 020 8880 5366 *email* umarpeh@gmail.com

## ■ The Brian Mercer Charitable Trust
**CC NO** 1076925 **ESTABLISHED** 1999
**WHERE FUNDING CAN BE GIVEN** Worldwide.
**WHO CAN BENEFIT** Charitable organisations.
**WHAT IS FUNDED** Promotion of medical and scientific research and treatment for people with visual impairment and liver diseases; visual arts, especially in the North West.
**TYPE OF GRANT** Mainly recurrent.
**RANGE OF GRANTS** £900–£90,000
**SAMPLE GRANTS** Lancashire Teaching Hospital NHS, Tameside Hospital NHS and Warrington and Halton Hospital NHS (£90,000 each); Blackburn Youth Zone (£85,000); Drugs for Neglected Diseases, Fight for Sight and University of Liverpool (£50,000 each); Manchester Royal Eye Hospital (£30,000); Sculpture Residency in Pietrasanta (£21,500); Médecins Sans Frontières (£20,000); Arkwright Scholarship Trust (£14,500); Age Concern (£10,000); British Art Medal Society (£8,000); Blackburn College, Blackpool Sixth Form College, Lancaster Girls Grammar School and Ripley St Thomas Lancaster (£2,500 each); Tallships Youth Trust (£900).
**FINANCES** Year 2013/14 *Income* £850,438 *Grants* £710,833 *Grants to organisations* £710,833 *Assets* £25,755,013
**TRUSTEES** Christine Clancy; Kenneth Merrill; Roger Duckworth; Mary Clitheroe.
**OTHER INFORMATION** There were 29 awards made. The expenditure is normally distributed in the following proportions: eyesight (30%); liver (30%); arts (20%); other (20%).
**HOW TO APPLY** The trust encourages grant applications via email. They should be received at least four weeks before the trustees' meeting, the exact dates of which are listed online. The trustees meet twice a year, currently in May and October.
**WHO TO APPLY TO** J. M. Adams, Correspondent, c/o Beever and Struthers, Central Buildings, Richmond Terrace, Blackburn BB1 7AP *Tel.* 01254 686600 *Fax* 01254 682483 *email* info@brianmercercharitabletrust.org *Website* www.brianmercercharitabletrust.org

## ■ The Mercers' Charitable Foundation
**CC NO** 326340 **ESTABLISHED** 1982
**WHERE FUNDING CAN BE GIVEN** UK, with a strong preference for London and the West Midlands.
**WHO CAN BENEFIT** Registered charities; charities exempt from registration; maintained schools; churches; graded buildings.
**WHAT IS FUNDED** General welfare; education; heritage and arts; advancement of Christian religion; older and young people. Recently there has been a particular focus on excellence in education and a current focus on work to reduce offending.
**WHAT IS NOT FUNDED** Specific exclusions apply in each of the categories – make sure you read these before applying. Generally the following are not funded: animal welfare charities; endowment appeals; loans or business finance; sponsorship or marketing appeals and fundraising events; campaigning work and projects that are primarily political; activities that are the responsibility of the local, health or education authority or other similar body; activities that have already taken place; organisations that are themselves principally grant-makers; general or mailshot appeals. Capital projects are not funded under Education Grants and otherwise restricted to 'appeals that are within the last 20% of their target'.
**TYPE OF GRANT** Building; other capital grants (with certain restrictions); feasibility studies; one-off grants; project costs; research grants; recurring costs; start-up funding; for up to three years; unrestricted funding.
**RANGE OF GRANTS** Up to £470,000.

SAMPLE GRANTS St Paul's School (£470,000); Gresham College (£344,000); College of Richard Collyer (£165,000); Dauntsey's School (£150,000); Hexham Abbey (£21,500); Startuponline (£20,000); British Library and National Churches Trust (£18,000 each); Play Association Hammersmith and Fulham (£15,000) First Step (£14,200); Young Enterprise London (£12,500); Drive Forward Foundation (£12,300); Textile Conservation Foundation (£12,000); Hexham Abbey and Sandwell Academy (£10,000 each); Royal National Children's Foundation (£6,000). Other 199 grants of under £10,000 totalled over £684,000.

FINANCES Year 2013/14 Income £7,813,000 Grants £2,872,451 Grants to organisations £2,867,171 Assets £15,145,000

TRUSTEE The Mercers' Company.

OTHER INFORMATION The annual report for 2013/14 states: 'The Trustee is undertaking a review of its philanthropic strategy across the four main areas of support (education, welfare, Christian faith and heritage). The intention is to establish a high level framework with clear priorities and for the specialist committees to develop detailed programmes. The Trustee is keen to see its grants used to unlock additional funding from other sources and opportunities to do this will be actively sought.' During the year 24 awards were given to individuals totalling about £5,300.

HOW TO APPLY Applications can be made online via the foundation's website. In addition applicants are required to post or email the most recent statutory report and accounts (produced not later than ten months after the end of the financial year) and a copy of the organisation's bank statement, dated within the last three months. Only one application in three years can be considered from any organisation. Applications must also include a project plan for the funding proposal. Grants officers are happy to give advice by telephone or email, although most information will be covered online. Application deadlines will depend on the category but appeals should generally be submitted four to six weeks in advance. Requests will be acknowledged within ten working days. **Note**: This trust is under the trusteeship of the Mercers' Company and one application to the Company is an application to all its trusts, including the Charity of Sir Richard Whittington and the Earl of Northampton's Charity. There are specific email and phone contact details for Grant Officers working in the areas of welfare, education, religion and heritage and arts (find these online) – enquiries should be directed to an appropriate correspondent.

WHO TO APPLY TO The Grants Officer, The Mercers' Company, Mercers' Hall, Ironmonger Lane, London EC2V 8HE Tel. 020 7726 4991 email info@mercers.co.uk Website www.mercers.co.uk

■ **Merchant Navy Welfare Board**

CC NO 212799, SC039669 ESTABLISHED 1962
WHERE FUNDING CAN BE GIVEN UK and overseas.
WHO CAN BENEFIT Organisations that help or represent seafarers; merchant navy; sailors.
WHAT IS FUNDED The charity makes grants to over 40 of constituent members and maintains 15 Port Welfare Committees to support the welfare and well-being of sailors and their families. It also raises awareness of issues affecting the welfare of merchant seafarers, fishers and their dependants.

WHAT IS NOT FUNDED Funding is not available retrospectively. Although grants are not made to individuals, other than in emergency, the charity act as a 'clearing house' for those seeking assistance from other maritime charities.

TYPE OF GRANT Capital projects, evaluation studies and start-up costs.

RANGE OF GRANTS £3,200–£58,500

SAMPLE GRANTS Fishermen's Mission – repairs and refurbishment (£58,500 in three awards); Vehicle Replacement Fund – annual contribution (£42,000); Sailors' Children's Society – towards replacement mobile holiday home for dependent families (£30,000); Nautilus Welfare Fund – Mariners' Park – provision of Wi-Fi for residents and demolition of three houses and provision of three wet rooms (£25,000 in two awards); Apostleship of the Sea – towards new drop in centre and its refurbishment (£9,500 in two awards); Maritime Charities Group – annual contribution (£5,000); Seaham Seafarers' Centre – new heating system (£4,600); Lighthouse Mission – Stanley, Falkland Islands – contribution to refurbishment (£3,200).

FINANCES Year 2014 Income £731,959 Grants £250,360 Grants to organisations £250,360 Assets £14,325,229

TRUSTEES Anthony Dickinson; Commodore Barry Bryant; Timothy Springett; Stephen Todd; Graham Lane; Robert Jones; Deanne Thomas; Revd Kenneth Peters; Michael Jess; Capt. Andrew Cassels; Mark Carden; David Colclough; Commodore Malcolm Williams; Alexander Campbell.

PUBLICATIONS Port Information Leaflets, 'Remembering those left behind' and Arrested and detained Vessels and Abandoned Seafarers – A guide to Who Does What'

OTHER INFORMATION There were 27 grants made which were distributed amongst 18 organisations.

HOW TO APPLY Application forms are available to download from the charity's website and can be returned by email. Applicants seeking grants over £5,000 should submit their latest annual report and accounts and those applying for amounts over £25,000 a five-year business plan as well. The charity is open to enquiries regarding the application process. The trustees meet to consider applications in March, May, July and November (requests for larger grants of over £10,000 must be submitted by 1 September). Applications should contain the following information: a demonstration of need which highlights the direct benefit to seafarers; a summary of the organisations reserves policy, stating whether the policy is to reduce, maintain or increase reserves and why that policy is appropriate; and whether or not the organisation is able to reclaim VAT. Capital grants will only be paid on proof of expenditure or the submission of a valid invoice.

WHO TO APPLY TO Capt. David Parsons, Chief Executive, 8 Cumberland Place, Southampton SO15 2BH Tel. 023 8033 7799 Fax 023 8063 4444 email enquiries@mnwb.org.uk Website www.mnwb.org

**Merchant**

## ■ The Merchant Taylors' Company Charities Fund

**CC NO** 1069124  **ESTABLISHED** 1941

**WHERE FUNDING CAN BE GIVEN** UK, especially inner London and the boroughs of Lewisham, Southwark, Tower Hamlets and Hackney and their environs.

**WHO CAN BENEFIT** Organisations benefitting children, older people, artists, medical professionals, those suffering from substance abuse, carers, people with disabilities and homeless people.

**WHAT IS FUNDED** General charitable purposes, including the relief of poverty, health and disability, education and training and religious causes. Other areas that can be considered include the arts, social care and community development, disability, older people, medical studies and research, addiction, homelessness and children, with priority for special needs. While grants are largely focused on London, they can exceptionally be made for national work, especially where it benefits members or ex-members of the forces or has some connection to tailoring or clothing.

**WHAT IS NOT FUNDED** Grants are not made for: 'bricks and mortar' appeals; although the trustees will consider contributing to the fitting out or refurbishment of new or existing buildings; medical research, although the charity provides administrative services to a third-party trust with a small reactive capacity in this area, to which such applications may be referred; funds for 'on-granting' to third-party charities or individuals; generalised appeals; and very large charities, except occasionally in support of localised work in the trustees' geographical area of interest'.

**TYPE OF GRANT** One-off grants or three-year tapering grants. The charity states that 'applications for 'seed' funding are particularly welcome' and preference is also given to funding discrete projects with defined outcomes.

**RANGE OF GRANTS** Mostly £5,000–£15,000.

**SAMPLE GRANTS** Jubilee Sailing Trust (£25,000); Cricket for Change, Skillforce and Tailors' Benevolent Institute (£10,000 each); Guildhall School of Music and Drama (£6,000); Addaction and St Saviour's and St Olave's School (£5,000 each); Hackney Deanery (£4,500); Corporation of Sons of the Clergy and St Helen's Church – Bishopsgate (£2,000 each); St Helen's School and St Paul's Cathedral Choir School (£1,000 each); John Harrison Prize (£600); Brandram Road Community Centre Association (£300).

**FINANCES** Year 2013/14 Income £193,994 Grants £123,850 Grants to organisations £123,850 Assets £758,212

**TRUSTEES** Johny Armstrong; Duncan Eggar; Peter Magill; Simon Bass; Rupert Bull.

**OTHER INFORMATION** The Merchant Taylors' Company also administers the Charities for the Infirm (Charity Commission no. 214266) and the Charities for the Poor (Charity Commission no. 214267). There may be ad hoc grants towards the educational expenses of individuals in tertiary and higher education (which may include field trips) but these are usually restricted to people who have attended one among the Merchant Taylors' family of schools or those who have a connection with the company.

**HOW TO APPLY** According to the website, at present awards are restricted at present to charities nominated by the Livery Committee. Applications may only be made with the support of a member of the Merchant Taylors' Company or by invitation.

**WHO TO APPLY TO** David Atkinson, Charities Officer, Merchant Taylor's Hall, 30 Threadneedle Street, London EC2R 8JB Tel. 020 7450 4447 email datkinson@merchant-taylors.co.uk Website www.merchanttaylors.co.uk

## ■ The Merchant Venturers' Charity

**CC NO** 264302  **ESTABLISHED** 1972

**WHERE FUNDING CAN BE GIVEN** Greater Bristol area (not just the city).

**WHO CAN BENEFIT** Local and regional organisations; local branches of national organisations; some individuals. Some preference to organisations benefitting young or older people and disadvantaged individuals.

**WHAT IS FUNDED** Social needs (care of older people, homelessness, poverty or the prevention of crime); young people (training outside educational establishments, character development and employment prospects); education ( primary, secondary and tertiary education, particularly in relation to the Merchants family of schools or other greater Bristol educational activities and initiatives ); social enterprise; health care; culture and arts; projects in Bristol, preferably associated with the Merchant Venturers' Society's spheres of interest and benefitting Bristol and its economic development. Generally any charitable purpose which enhances the quality of life for local people.

**WHAT IS NOT FUNDED** Statutory organisations or the direct replacement of statutory funding; projects that take place before an application can be considered; activities that are intended to raise funds for other organisations. 'Grants are unlikely to be made towards the cost of an existing salaried position'.

**TYPE OF GRANT** One-off and some recurrent; capital and core costs; project expenditure.

**RANGE OF GRANTS** Generally up to £5,000.

**SAMPLE GRANTS** Bristol University MVSE Schools Project (£30,000); Clifton Down Charitable Trust (£29,000); Bristol Initiative Charitable Trust (£10,500); Amos Vale Cemetery (£10,000); Teach First (£8,800); Hartcliffe Club (£6,000); Hillfields Park Baptist Church (£5,000). Awards of under £5,000 totalled about £62,500.

**FINANCES** Year 2013 Income £323,979 Grants £151,933 Grants to organisations £151,188 Assets £7,227,109

**TRUSTEES** David Marsh; Francis Greenacre; John Savage; Anthony Brown; Stephen Parsons; Christopher Curling; Cullum McAlpine; Richard Morris; Charles Clarke; Nicholas Bacon; Peter Rilett; Charles Griffiths; Timothy Ross; Alastair Currie; Robert Davis; Gillian Camm.

**OTHER INFORMATION** Grants were broken down as follows: Community and social (£119,000) and Education (£33,000). During the over £700 was paid to individuals.

**HOW TO APPLY** Application forms and detailed guidelines are accessible on the charity's website. Once completed they can be returned via email. Re-applications may be made in three years following the award of a previous grant. Grant Giving Committees meet a number of times each year, generally in January, May and September. The deadline for the submission of applications to each committee is the 25th of the preceding month. The outcome will be known within six weeks following the meeting.

**WHO TO APPLY TO** Richard Morris, Treasurer, c/o The Society of Merchant Venturers, Merchants' Hall,

The Promenade, Clifton, Bristol BS8 3NH
*Tel.* 0117 973 8058  *Fax* 0117 973 5884
*email* enquiries@merchantventurers.com
*Website* www.merchantventurers.com

## ■ The Merchants' House of Glasgow

**SC NO** SC008900   **ESTABLISHED** 1605
**WHERE FUNDING CAN BE GIVEN** Glasgow area and the west of Scotland.
**WHO CAN BENEFIT** Charities registered in Scotland, benefitting seamen, pensioners and young people (aged 10 to 30) in full-time education; educational institutions.
**WHAT IS FUNDED** General charitable purposes; relief of poverty; health and disability; older people; young people; the arts; education. Support can be made to: 'organisations providing care and assistance to people with disabilities, older people, people who are terminally ill and people who have been socially deprived; organisations providing for the care, advancement and rehabilitation of young people; universities, colleges of further education and schools; organisations connected with the arts, including music, theatre and the visual arts; and institutions that are connected with and represented by the Merchants' House'.
**WHAT IS NOT FUNDED** The charity will not, unless in exceptional circumstances, make grants to: individuals; churches other than Glasgow Cathedral; organisations that have received support in the two years preceding an application; charities, the objects of which are identical to those of the House, namely the award of pensions and/or precepts to individuals); charities which principally operate outside the Glasgow and West of Scotland area.
**TYPE OF GRANT** Capital projects.
**RANGE OF GRANTS** Up to £4,000.
**SAMPLE GRANTS** Previous beneficiaries have included: Erskine; East Park Home; Guide Dogs for the Blind; Citizens Theatre; Greater Glasgow Scout Council; Princess Royal Maternity Unit; Scottish Opera; The Boys' Brigade Glasgow Battalion.
**FINANCES** *Year* 2013 *Income* £2,034,202 *Grants* £429,802 *Grants to organisations* £429,802
**TRUSTEE** The Directors.
**HOW TO APPLY** Application forms can be accessed from the charity's website or submitted online. Applications must be accompanied with the latest copy of audited accounts and any other supporting documentation informing about the organisation's principal activities. The website states: 'It is rare that a month passes without fresh appeals being made to the House. All are carefully considered and assistance given to the best of the House's ability. There is no doubt that, were unlimited funds available, the scope is there for increased benevolence by grants to Institutions ... and others whom the Directors have regretfully had to reject.'
**WHO TO APPLY TO** The Directors, 7 West George Street, Glasgow G2 1BA *Tel.* 0141 221 8272 *Fax* 0141 226 2275 *email* theoffice@merchantshouse.org.uk *Website* www.merchantshouse.org.uk

## ■ Mercury Phoenix Trust

**CC NO** 1013768   **ESTABLISHED** 1992
**WHERE FUNDING CAN BE GIVEN** Worldwide.
**WHO CAN BENEFIT** Registered charities benefitting people with AIDS and HIV.
**WHAT IS FUNDED** Relief of poverty, sickness and distress of people affected by AIDS and HIV and the raising of awareness of the illness throughout the world.
**WHAT IS NOT FUNDED** Funding is not given for individuals or travel costs.
**TYPE OF GRANT** One-off, capital, project and running costs.
**RANGE OF GRANTS** £750–£15,000
**SAMPLE GRANTS** Christian Aid (£15,000); Restless Development (£12,900); Community Oriented Rehab (£11,100); Victory Rural Development Society (£6,600); Kaloko Trust UK (£8,000); Kerti Praja Foundation (£5,500); Socio Educational and Rural Development Society (£3,900); Urunji Childcare Trust (£1,500); Positive East (£1,000); DHIVERSE (£750).
**FINANCES** *Year* 2013/14 *Income* £755,279 *Grants* £177,243 *Grants to organisations* £177,243 *Assets* £1,544,548
**TRUSTEES** Brian May; Henry Beach; Mary Austin; Roger Taylor.
**OTHER INFORMATION** Many of grants were given to organisations benefitting people in Africa and Asia.
**HOW TO APPLY** Application forms are available from the trust upon request via email. In addition to a completed application form, the trust requires the following documents: a budget; registration certificate; audited accounts for the last financial year; constitution or memorandum and articles of association; annual report; and equal opportunities policy.
**WHO TO APPLY TO** Peter Chant, Correspondent, 22 Cottage Offices, The River Wing, Latimer Park, Latimer, Chesham, Buckinghamshire HP5 1TU *Tel.* 01494 766799 *email* mercuryphoenixtrust@idrec.com *Website* www.mercuryphoenixtrust.com

## ■ The Merlin Magic Wand Children's Charity

**CC NO** 1124081   **ESTABLISHED** 2008
**WHERE FUNDING CAN BE GIVEN** Worldwide, within travelling distance of a Merlin Entertainments attraction.
**WHO CAN BENEFIT** Travel grants are made to seriously ill, disadvantaged or disabled children and families to visit Merlin Entertainments attractions. Outreach projects under the Taking the Magic to the Children scheme are for organisations local to the Merlin Entertainment attractions.
**WHAT IS FUNDED** The charity arranges days out at Merlin Entertainments attractions for seriously ill, disabled and disadvantaged children, as well as outreach projects with local organisations benefitting such children.
**FINANCES** *Year* 2014 *Income* £571,114 *Grants* £197,387 *Grants to organisations* £197,387 *Assets* £352,801
**TRUSTEE** Andrew Carr; Adrian Mahon; Colin Armstrong
**OTHER INFORMATION** In 2014, travel grants totalled £40,500 and outreach projects totalled £156,900.
**HOW TO APPLY** Applications can be made online. See the charity's website for further information.
**WHO TO APPLY TO** Unit 5–6, Silverglade Business Park, Leatherhead Road, Chessington, Surrey

KT9 2QL  *Tel.* 01372 751374  *email* admin@merlinsmagicwand.org  *Website* www.merlinsmagicwand.org

### ■ The Mersey Docks and Harbour Company Charitable Fund

**CC NO** 206913   **ESTABLISHED** 1811
**WHERE FUNDING CAN BE GIVEN** Merseyside.
**WHO CAN BENEFIT** Registered charities on Merseyside.
**WHAT IS FUNDED** The relief of people who are sick, disabled and retired in the dock service or the families of those who were killed in service; and to benefit charities in the town or port of Liverpool.
**RANGE OF GRANTS** £25–£24,000
**SAMPLE GRANTS** Community Foundation for Merseyside (£15,500); Liverpool Seafarer's Centre (£10,500); RNLI (£5,000); Plaza Community Cinema (£3,000); Farm Africa and North West Air Ambulance (£1,000 each); Brain Tumour Research (£500); North West Cancer Research (£100).
**FINANCES** Year 2013  Income £40,122  Grants £38,510  Grants to organisations £38,510  Assets £13,654
**TRUSTEES** Gary Hodgson; Mark Whitworth; Ian Charnock.
**OTHER INFORMATION** The charity had an income of £40,000, which was wholly donated by The Mersey Docks and Harbour Company Limited.
**HOW TO APPLY** Applications may be made in writing to the correspondent.
**WHO TO APPLY TO** Caroline Gill, Correspondent, The Mersey Docks and Harbour Company Limited, Maritime Centre, Port of Liverpool, Liverpool L21 1LA  *Tel.* 0151 949 6349

### ■ The Tony Metherell Charitable Trust

**CC NO** 1046899   **ESTABLISHED** 1992
**WHERE FUNDING CAN BE GIVEN** UK. Our research indicates that the trust has a particular preference for Hertfordshire and Worcestershire.
**WHO CAN BENEFIT** Organisations.
**WHAT IS FUNDED** General charitable purposes; however, our research suggests that in the past grants have been made for hospices and cancer-related causes, and for the care and welfare of people who are older or who have disabilities.
**WHAT IS NOT FUNDED** Overseas causes.
**RANGE OF GRANTS** Usually up to £5,000.
**SAMPLE GRANTS** Previous beneficiaries have included: H Hospice (£2,800).
**FINANCES** Year 2013/14  Income £16,124  Grants £40,000  Grants to organisations £40,000
**TRUSTEES** Jemma Eadie; Kate Cooper.
**OTHER INFORMATION** Due to its low income, the trust was not required to submit its accounts to the Charity Commission. In 2013/14 the trust had a total expenditure of £42,000. We have estimated the grant total stated above.
**HOW TO APPLY** Apply in writing to the correspondent.
**WHO TO APPLY TO** Jemma Eadie, Trustee, North End Farm, North End, Newbury, Berkshire RG20 0BE

### ■ The Metropolitan Masonic Charity

**CC NO** 1081205   **ESTABLISHED** 2000
**WHERE FUNDING CAN BE GIVEN** Mainly London, but not exclusively.
**WHO CAN BENEFIT** Individuals and organisations (non-masonic charities), mainly within the area of London.
**WHAT IS FUNDED** General charitable purposes, with particular, albeit not exclusive, focus on the relief of need, poverty or distress and advancement of education.
**TYPE OF GRANT** One-off grants; sponsorship or undertaking of a research. Long-term relationships can be established.
**RANGE OF GRANTS** Normally £100–£6,000.
**SAMPLE GRANTS** Norwood Charity (£8,800); Kings College Hospital and RMBI (£6,000 each); Centrepoint Soho, King Edward VII's Hospital, Lambeth Summer Projects Trust and The Wellchild Trust (£5,000) each); Music First (£4,000); Employment Resource Centre and Tall Ships Youth Trust (£3,000 each); St John's Youth Centre (£2,500); Care in Mind, Drop-in Bereavement Centre, Just Different and Royal London Society for Young Blind Children (£2,000 each).
**FINANCES** Year 2013/14  Income £562,049  Grants £95,243  Grants to organisations £95,243  Assets £1,619,900
**TRUSTEES** Rex Thorne; Robert Corp-Reader; Brian de Neut; Quentin Humberstone; Augustus Ullstein.
**OTHER INFORMATION** In previous years the charity has also been providing particular support to a major project each year. During 2013/14 there were 23 awards made.
**HOW TO APPLY** Applications may be made in writing to the correspondent.
**WHO TO APPLY TO** The Correspondent, 60 Great Queen Street, London WC2B 5AZ  *Tel.* 020 7539 2930  *email* c.hunt@metgl.com

### ■ T. and J. Meyer Family Foundation Limited

**CC NO** 1087507   **ESTABLISHED** 2001
**WHERE FUNDING CAN BE GIVEN** UK and overseas.
**WHO CAN BENEFIT** Charitable organisations.
**WHAT IS FUNDED** The primary focus of the foundation is on education, healthcare and the environment. The criteria for charities are: organisations which alleviate the suffering of humanity through health, education and environment; organisations with extremely high correlation between what is gifted and what the beneficiary receives; organisations who struggle to raise funds either because either they are new, their size or their access to funds is constrained; and organisations who promote long-term effective sustainable solutions.
**RANGE OF GRANTS** £3,000–£139,000
**SAMPLE GRANTS** Royal Marsden Cancer Charity (£139,000); Partners in Health (£124,500); Angkor Hospital for Children (£31,000); Heifer International (£15,600); Temwa (£12,000); Friends of The Citizens Foundation (£10,500); Street Child (£9,700); Riders for Health (£4,900); Tonic (£3,100).
**FINANCES** Year 2013  Income £398,568  Grants £468,029  Grants to organisations £468,029  Assets £16,390,245
**TRUSTEES** Jane Meyer; Annabelle Ahouiyek; Quinn Meyer; Ian Meyer; Miranda Spackman.
**OTHER INFORMATION** During the year the foundation made 17 grants.

652

**HOW TO APPLY** The foundation does not accept unsolicited applications. The trustees meet four times a year.
**WHO TO APPLY TO** Timothy Meyer, Company Secretary, 3 Kendrick Mews, London SW7 3HG *email* info@tjmff.org

## ■ The Mickel Fund
**SC NO** SC003266      **ESTABLISHED** 1970
**WHERE FUNDING CAN BE GIVEN** UK, with a preference for Scotland.
**WHO CAN BENEFIT** Voluntary organisations and charitable groups benefitting people of all ages, especially at risk groups. The charity prefers local charities but does give to organisations throughout the UK.
**WHAT IS FUNDED** Education; relief of poverty; health and disability; arts, culture and heritage; sports. The following categories are funded: older people; animal welfare; cancer care; cancer research; children and young people; education/outreach; hospices; housing and homelessness; injuries; medical assistance; music/culture; medical research; veterans; world wide appeal based projects. Major Grants are available to Scottish charities or homeless charities for large-scale local projects; Annual Grants are made to one charity per each of the above categories.
**WHAT IS NOT FUNDED** Events, such as conferences, seminars and exhibitions; fee charging residential home, nurseries and care facilities; fundraising events; loans or repayments of loans – other than through the hardship fund; religious promotion; replacement of statutory funds; schools other than pre-school and after school clubs activities promoting parental and community involvement.
**TYPE OF GRANT** One-off and recurrent; risky and new projects; ongoing work; core funding; salaries; general running costs; capital grants; building or equipment expenditure.
**RANGE OF GRANTS** Major grants – £5,000–£10,000; Annual Grants – £500–£2,000; Hardship Grants – £50–£500.
**SAMPLE GRANTS** Addaction; Arthritis Research UK; Befriend a Child; Bowel Cancer UK; Butterfly Trust; Community Resource Network Scotland; Douglas Bader Foundation; Dyslexia Action Glasgow Learning Centre; Edinburgh Headway; Hand on Heart; Hearts and Minds; Home Link Family Support; Kidney Kids Scotland; Lifelites; Lung Ha Theatre Company; Macular Society; Motability; National Library of Scotland; RAF Benevolent Fund; Riding for the Disabled; Scottish Association for Mental Health; The Back Up Trust; The Outward Bound Trust; The Rock Trust.
**FINANCES** Year 2013/14 *Income* £151,379 *Grants* £150,000 *Grants to organisations* £150,000
**TRUSTEES** Mairi Mickel; Bruce Mickel; Finlay Mickel; Alan Hartley; Oliver Bassi.
**OTHER INFORMATION** About £100,000 is donated annually. The charity had an overall expenditure of £158,000 in 2013/14; therefore it is likely that grants totalled at about £150,000. The charity also provides free of charge 'value engineering' services for building projects, delivered by one of the charity's trustees.
**HOW TO APPLY** Application forms are available from the charity's website, which should be returned to the charity upon completion. A helpful checklist of requirements and eligibility criteria are also given online. Remember to include a copy of your most recent audited accounts and annual report and a budget for the year as well as the project. The outcome of your application is communicated within two months of the trustees' meeting (they are held in March and September) and awards are paid in March and/or December. The deadline for appeals is normally mid-February and mid-August. Phone and email enquiries are welcome prior to application.
**WHO TO APPLY TO** Lindsay McColl, Trust Administrator, 1 Atlantic Quay, 1 Robertson Avenue, Glasgow G2 8JB *Tel.* 0141 242 7528 *email* admin@mickelfund.org.uk *Website* www.mickelfund.org.uk

## ■ The Mickleham Trust
**CC NO** 1048337      **ESTABLISHED** 1995
**WHERE FUNDING CAN BE GIVEN** UK, with a preference for Norfolk.
**WHO CAN BENEFIT** Registered charities that provide welfare assistance directly to the beneficiaries.
**WHAT IS FUNDED** The relief for the abused and disadvantaged people, particularly children and young people and blind individuals.
**TYPE OF GRANT** Mainly recurrent.
**RANGE OF GRANTS** £100–£52,000; mostly for or around £1,000.
**SAMPLE GRANTS** NNUH Dementia Support Workers (£52,000); Mildmay (£25,000); Livability (£10,000); Barnardo's, Mercy Ships and Motability for Norfolk (£5,000); Listening Books and National Institute for Conductive Education (£2,000 each); Children's Heart Federation, Jubilee Family Centre, Nancy Oldfield Trust, National Association of Almshouses, Opening Doors, Salvation Army and Well Spring Family Centre (£1,000 each).
**FINANCES** Year 2013/14 *Income* £265,742 *Grants* £195,914 *Grants to organisations* £195,914 *Assets* £5,816,541
**TRUSTEES** Philip Norton; Revd Sheila Nunney; Anne Richardson.
**OTHER INFORMATION** Grants were made to 81 organisations.
**HOW TO APPLY** Applications may be made in writing to the correspondent.
**WHO TO APPLY TO** Philip Norton, Trustee, c/o Hansells Solicitors and Financial Advisers, 13–14 The Close, Norwich NR1 4DS *Tel.* 01603 615731 *email* philipnorton@hansells.co.uk

## ■ The Gerald Micklem Charitable Trust
**CC NO** 802583      **ESTABLISHED** 1988
**WHERE FUNDING CAN BE GIVEN** UK; East Hampshire and West Sussex.
**WHO CAN BENEFIT** UK-registered charities 'working either on a national basis, or specifically in Hampshire or West Sussex' in the preferred fields.
**WHAT IS FUNDED** According to the annual report for 2013/14 'the organisations in which the trustees are most interested are those working on a national basis in the following areas': disability; blindness and deafness; medical conditions affecting both adults and children; medical research; people with learning disabilities; children and young people, particularly the disadvantaged; and environment and wildlife.
**WHAT IS NOT FUNDED** The trust does not make grants to, or enter into sponsorship arrangements with,

individuals. Grants are not made to organisations that are not UK-registered charities. The annual report for 2013/14 notes that 'the trustees have not formally excluded any category of charitable activity, but they have established some funding priorities'. The trust is 'unlikely to support the regional work of such charities in locations outside Hampshire and West Sussex or charities working only in other areas of the UK'. The following areas fall outside the trust's current funding priorities: drug/alcohol abuse and counselling; local community groups; museums, galleries and heritage; performing arts and cultural organisations; churches; and overseas aid. It is noted that 'the trustees are prepared to fund core costs as well as capital projects, but are unlikely to provide initial funding for new established organisations'.

**TYPE OF GRANT** One-off and recurrent for capital, core and project costs.

**RANGE OF GRANTS** £1,000–£6,000; generally £3,000–£4,000.

**SAMPLE GRANTS** Self Unlimited (£60,000); The Golf Foundation (£20,000); Penny Brohn Cancer Care (£10,000); The Stroke Association (£7,500); The Rosemary Foundation (£6,000); Contact the Elderly, Friends of Butser Ancient Farm, Over the Wall, The Rowans Hospice and Whizz-Kidz (£5,000 each); Scottish Disability Golf Partnership (£3,000); Rogbonko Village School Trust (£2,500).

**FINANCES** Year 2013 Income £241,745 Grants £226,000 Grants to organisations £226,000 Assets £1,250,335

**TRUSTEES** Susan Shone; Joanna Scott-Dalgleish; Helen Ratcliffe.

**OTHER INFORMATION** During the year a total of 31 awards were made.

**HOW TO APPLY** There is no formal application form and applications should be made in writing to the correspondent by letter – *not by e-mail*. Applicants also have to provide a copy of their latest annual report and accounts. Enquiries prior to any application may be made by e-mail. The trustees usually consider awards in January/February; therefore they ask to submit your requests 'towards the end of a calendar year so that the information they contain is most up to date when considered', preferably as late as possible. Be careful though, as the appeals are not carried forward and should be with the trustees by 31 December. The website informs: 'The trustees receive a very substantial number of appeals each year. It is not their practice to acknowledge appeals, and they prefer not to enter into correspondence with applicants other than those to whom grants are being made or from whom further information is required. Only successful applicants are notified of the outcome of their application.' The annual report for 2013/14 confirms that the trustees 'receive a large number of appeals each year, but they have tended to make (without commitment) recurring grants to several charities as well as one-off grants to some charities newly selected each year'.

**WHO TO APPLY TO** Susan Shone, Trustee, Bolinge Hill Farm, Buriton, Petersfield, Hampshire GU31 4NN *Tel.* 01730 264207 *email* mail@geraldmicklemct.org.uk *Website* www.geraldmicklemct.org.uk

■ **The Masonic Province of Middlesex Charitable Trust (Middlesex Masonic Charity)**

**CC NO** 1064406    **ESTABLISHED** 1997

**WHERE FUNDING CAN BE GIVEN** Province of Middlesex.

**WHO CAN BENEFIT** Generally charities should be registered; both masonic charities and non-masonic charities are assisted; causes and charities in Middlesex, or with strong Middlesex connections.

**WHAT IS FUNDED** General charitable purposes; relief of poverty and assistance towards the education of freemasons and their families. The annual report states: 'The Trustees expect that, in the main, the funds of the MMC will be used to support objects of Provincial Charity, be they non-Masonic charities operating in the former County of Middlesex area or charities enjoying special connections with Middlesex Freemasonry.'

**TYPE OF GRANT** One-off; capital costs; project funding.

**RANGE OF GRANTS** £400–£25,000

**SAMPLE GRANTS** Royal Masonic Trust for Girls and Boys 2020 Festival (£25,000); Paul Strickland Scanner Centre (£10,400); Brunel University Progeria Project and St Mark's Hospital Foundation – Northwick Park (£10,000 each); Grangewood School (£7,000); Bear Rails Scout Campsite, Noah's Ark Children's Hospice and RAFT Mount Vernon Hospital (£5,000 each); Province of Middlesex Winter Wonderland and St Luke's Hospice (£2,900 each); Citizens Advice Enfield (£2,700); Connect Foundation – Cathja Project (£2,500); Young Enterprise (£1,400); Handicapped Children's Action Group (£900); Harrow District Masonic Centre (£600); The Wish Centre (£400).

**FINANCES** Year 2013/14 Income £72,954 Grants £91,646 Grants to organisations £91,646 Assets £2,014,018

**TRUSTEES** David Yeaman; Stephen Ramsay; Jonathan Markham Gollow; Adrian Howorth; Peter Gledhill.

**OTHER INFORMATION** In 2013/14 grants were given to 16 organisations. About 70% of grants went to non-masonic charities.

**HOW TO APPLY** Application forms are available from the correspondent or the Provincial Office. Lodges, chapters or individuals will normally apply on behalf of a charity by completing the form and providing supporting information and copies of two years' audited accounts; however, direct applications may also be considered. The charity will also accept appeals made on the Universal Application Form, available from the Provincial website and submitted to the Provincial Charity Awareness Committee. Requests for individual support should be made in the first instance to the Provincial Grand Almoner.

**WHO TO APPLY TO** Peter Gledhill, Secretary, 85 Fakenham Way, Owlsmoor, Sandhurst, Berkshire GU47 0YS *Tel.* 01344 777077 *email* peter.gledhill@btinternet.com *Website* pglm.org.uk/charity/charities-middlesex-charities

■ **Middlesex Sports Foundation**

**CC NO** 1119091    **ESTABLISHED** 2007

**WHERE FUNDING CAN BE GIVEN** UK.

**WHO CAN BENEFIT** Organisations benefitting children and young people, people with disabilities, injured sportsmen and sportswomen and other disadvantaged individuals.

**WHAT IS FUNDED** Social welfare of children and young people, people with disabilities, disadvantaged individuals; community participation; all with focus on sports and recreation.

**RANGE OF GRANTS** Up to £12,500; mostly for £1,500–£2,000.

**SAMPLE GRANTS** GB Wheelchair Rugby (£12,500); Bristol Children's Help Society (£3,500); British Blind Support, Frenford Clubs, Porchlight, West Coast Crash Wheelchair Rugby and Wheelyboat Trust (£2,000 each); Bede Housing Association, Brent Centre for Young People and Youth Worx (£1,500 each).

**FINANCES** Year 2013/14 Income £48,679 Grants £49,500 Grants to organisations £49,500 Assets £1,674,875

**TRUSTEES** Howard Walters; Rhidian Jones; Julian Tregoning; Gareth Rees; Dr Colin Crosby; Robert Udwin; Paul Astbury.

**OTHER INFORMATION** No grants were made to individuals and a total of 20 awards to organisations in 2013/14.

**HOW TO APPLY** Applications may be made in writing to the correspondent.

**WHO TO APPLY TO** Paul Astbury, Trustee, 32 Kneller Gardens, Isleworth, Middlesex TW7 7NW Tel. 020 8898 5372 email paulastbury@uk2.net

■ **Millennium Stadium Charitable Trust (Ymddiriedolaeth Elusennol Stadiwm y Mileniwm)**

**CC NO** 1086596    **ESTABLISHED** 2001
**WHERE FUNDING CAN BE GIVEN** Wales.
**WHO CAN BENEFIT** Not-for-profit organisations; charitable bodies; voluntary groups working with local authorities; local groups; environmental entities. You do not need to be a registered charity as long as you are non-profit and properly constituted. Priority is given to organisations serving groups and communities suffering from the greatest disadvantage and those affected by social, cultural or economic barriers.

**WHAT IS FUNDED** The trust seeks 'to improve the quality of life of people who live and work in Wales', particularly through the promotion education, history, language and culture, especially for those who face disadvantage or discrimination. Grants are made in four programme areas: sport; the arts; the environment; the community. The trust is keen to help young people learn more about their country via exchange programmes and has made provision to support youth exchange schemes which fall in to any of the funding categories of the trust.

**WHAT IS NOT FUNDED** Projects outside Wales; day-to-day running costs; projects that seek to redistribute grant funds for the benefit of third party organisations; payments of debts/ overdrafts; retrospective requests; requests from individuals; payment to profit making organisations; local authorities; local authority schools (separately constituted organisations, such as PTAs and After School Clubs, are considered).

**TYPE OF GRANT** Project costs; capital expenditure.

**RANGE OF GRANTS** Regional – up to £7,500; local – up to £2,500.

**SAMPLE GRANTS** The latest accounts did not list grant recipients. **Previous beneficiaries have included:** Cardiff Foodbank; City of Cardiff (Melingriffith) Band-Youth and Beginners Group; Caudwell Children; Cefn Cribwr RFC; Fir Tree Community-Get Fit and Have Fun; Liberty in the Community; Minging to Blinging – The Scrap Yard Voluntary Organisation; South Gwent Children's Foundation; Take Part Community Group; The Bridge to Cross Charitable Trust.

**FINANCES** Year 2013/14 Income £290,624 Grants £229,624 Grants to organisations £197,155 Assets £165,043

**TRUSTEES** Ian Davies; Martin Davies; John Lloyd-Jones; Gerallt Hughes; Russell Goodway; Paul Glaze; Louise Prynne; Linda Pepper; Andrew Walker; John Rawlins; William Jones; Cllr Peter Bradbury.

**OTHER INFORMATION** In 2013/14 grants were awarded to organisations in every local authority in Wales. The grant total included £197,000 in 'grants to institutions' and £32,500 in 'donations'. The trust's income is generated through a levy on every ticket purchased for public events at the Millennium Stadium.

**HOW TO APPLY** The trustees meet twice a year to consider awards. The deadline dates can be found on the charity's website (most recent deadlines were in March and November), along with full guidelines and application forms. Appeals should be submitted electronically as Word Document (supporting documents may be sent in PDF format) at applications@millenniumstadiumtrust.org.uk. Paper applications are no longer accepted (if you cannot attach the document to an email, a memory stick containing the documents can be posted to the trust). Submissions are not acknowledged unless specifically asked; however, you will be notified if your appeal is ineligible due to incomplete details. Repeat applications can be made only after three years have passed.

**WHO TO APPLY TO** Sarah Fox, Trust Administrator, c/o Fox SE Consultancy, Suite 1, 4 Bessemer Road, Cardiff CF11 8BA Tel. 029 2002 2143 email info@millenniumstadiumtrust.org.uk Website www.millenniumstadiumtrust.co.uk

■ **Hugh and Mary Miller Bequest Trust**

**SC NO** SC014950    **ESTABLISHED** 1976
**WHERE FUNDING CAN BE GIVEN** Mainly Scotland.
**WHO CAN BENEFIT** Registered charities. The trust supports disability causes, with the same 18 organisations receiving the majority of funding each year.

**WHAT IS FUNDED** General charitable purposes; disability; health.

**WHAT IS NOT FUNDED** Non-registered charities; individuals.

**TYPE OF GRANT** Capital including buildings; core costs; project expenditure; research; recurring costs; salaries; for more than three years.

**RANGE OF GRANTS** £1,000–£5,000

**FINANCES** Year 2013/14 Income £119,481 Grants £90,000 Grants to organisations £90,000

**TRUSTEES** G. R. G. Graham; H. C. Davidson.

**OTHER INFORMATION** Our research indicates that grants are made to regular beneficiaries totalling around £90,000 each year.

**HOW TO APPLY** The trust has previously stated that its funds are fully committed.

## ■ The Ronald Miller Foundation

**SC NO** SC008798  **ESTABLISHED** 1979

**WHO TO APPLY TO** Charities and Third Sector Team, c/o Maclay Murray and Spens LLP, 1 George Square, Glasgow G2 1AL *Tel.* 0330 222 0050 *Fax* 0330 222 0053 *email* andrew.biggart@mms.co.uk

**WHERE FUNDING CAN BE GIVEN** Scotland, especially Glasgow and other parts of the UK.

**WHO CAN BENEFIT** Charities benefitting children and young adults, students, at risk groups, people with disabilities, those disadvantaged by poverty and socially isolated people.

**WHAT IS FUNDED** General charitable purposes; arts, social welfare, education, environment and health have all been supported.

**WHAT IS NOT FUNDED** Individuals.

**RANGE OF GRANTS** £500–£2,000

**FINANCES** Year 2013/14 *Income* £190,304 *Grants* £150,000 *Grants to organisations* £150,000

**TRUSTEES** C. Fleming-Brown; G. R. G. Graham; J. Simpson; G. F. R. Fleming-Brown.

**HOW TO APPLY** Applications may be made in writing to the correspondent.

**WHO TO APPLY TO** Charities and Third Sector Team, Maclay Murray and Spens LLP, 151 St Vincent Street, Glasgow G2 5NJ *Tel.* 0330 222 0050 *Fax* 0330 222 0053

## ■ The Millfield House Foundation (MHF)

**CC NO** 271180  **ESTABLISHED** 1976

**WHERE FUNDING CAN BE GIVEN** North East England (Northumberland, Tyne and Wear, Durham and Tees Valley).

**WHO CAN BENEFIT** Voluntary agencies; other organisations with charitable objectives working with socially and economically disadvantaged people; bodies undertaking policy research and advocacy should have close links with or voluntary or community organisations in the region. The foundation will support national as well as local bodies, provided that projects are based in the North East (includes regional and sub-regional projects; projects which are locally based may be considered so long as they are of wider benefit).

**WHAT IS FUNDED** Social and economic inequality; 'projects that inform discussion and influence public policy, with the aim of empowering communities and reducing social deprivation' with the 'emphasis on tackling the causes of poverty and other social ills rather than alleviating the symptoms'. The foundation mainly invites a limited number of policy-focused organisations to become its strategic partners. It aims to develop the capacity and policy skills of the North East voluntary sector through placements with established organisations. Note that the Open Grants programme is no longer accepting unsolicited applications.

**WHAT IS NOT FUNDED** Straightforward service provision; mainline university research; party political activity; community development; educational work; projects that are eligible for support elsewhere.

**TYPE OF GRANT** Project funding; advocacy; campaigning; project related core costs; for over three years.

**RANGE OF GRANTS** Generally £5,000–£30,000.

**SAMPLE GRANTS** Voluntary Organisations Network North East (£105,000); Institute for Public Policy Research (£35,000); Regional Refugee Forum North East (£32,000); Durham University Institute for Local Governance (£27,500); Tyneside Mind (£21,000); Centrepoint SOHO (£20,000); Association of Charitable Foundations and Centris Limited (£2,000 each).

**FINANCES** Year 2013/14 *Income* £171,197 *Grants* £305,707 *Grants to organisations* £305,707 *Assets* £5,824,216

**TRUSTEES** Stephen McClelland; Jane Streather; Sheila Spencer; Peter Deans; Betty Weallans; Rhiannon Bearne; Toby Lowe; Robert Williamson; Andrew Curry.

**PUBLICATIONS** Report: 'Funding Policy Change for a Better Society in the North East of England', 1996–2004, available in PDF version.

**OTHER INFORMATION** About five to ten awards are made each year (in 2013/14 a total of 11 awards to organisations). This foundation was removed from the Charity Commission register on 17/07/2015 and its funds have been transferred to a new charity: the Millfield House Foundation (1) (Charity Commission no. 1158914). The information given here still applies to the new body.

**HOW TO APPLY** According to the website, 'as of February 2015 the trustees do not accept unsolicited applications'. The foundation's grant programme is now closed and it will concentrate on working with strategic partners and running the fellowship scheme.

**WHO TO APPLY TO** Fiona Ellis, Trust Manager, Brunswick House, Whaelton, Morpeth, Northumberland NE61 3UZ *Tel.* 07500 057825 or 01670 775485 *email* fiona.ellis@mhfdn.org.uk *Website* www.mhfdn.org.uk

## ■ The Millfield Trust

**CC NO** 262406  **ESTABLISHED** 1971

**WHERE FUNDING CAN BE GIVEN** UK and overseas.

**WHO CAN BENEFIT** Charitable and religious organisations; individuals; missionary societies.

**WHAT IS FUNDED** Religious or other charitable work; missionary work; relief in need. Preference is given to charities of which the trust has special interest, knowledge or association. Funds are normally fully allocated or committed.

**TYPE OF GRANT** Unrestricted.

**RANGE OF GRANTS** £100–£12,500

**SAMPLE GRANTS** Gideons International (£12,500); Gospel Mission to South America (£10,000); Ashbury Evangelical Free Church (£4,100); Mission to Europe (£3,000); Armonia (UK) Trust, Crosslinks and Revival (£2,000 each); Scripture Union (£1,800); Christ Mission Fellowship (£1,500); Send a Cow and Tear Fund (£1,100 each). Other awards of under £1,000 totalled about £29,000.

**FINANCES** Year 2013/14 *Income* £81,648 *Grants* £82,500 *Grants to organisations* £81,000 *Assets* £181,463

**TRUSTEES** Andrew Bunce; David Bunce; Philip Bunce; Stephen Bunce; Rita Bunce.

**OTHER INFORMATION** The awards were given as follows: charitable and religious institutions (£81,000); individual evangelist and missionaries (£1,400); and pensioners and widows (£100). Awards under £1,000 totalled about £29,000.

**HOW TO APPLY** Unsolicited applications are not replied to. The trust has stated: 'Most of the organisations and individuals we support are ones in which we have a personal interest and have supported for many years.'

WHO TO APPLY TO David Bunce, Trustee, Millfield House, Bell Lane, Liddington, Swindon, Wiltshire SN4 0HE  Tel. 01793 790181  email millfield@liddington.myzen.co.uk

■ **The Millichope Foundation**

CC NO 282357    ESTABLISHED 1981

WHERE FUNDING CAN BE GIVEN UK, especially the West Midlands and Shropshire; occasionally worldwide.

WHO CAN BENEFIT Registered charities; some international organisations.

WHAT IS FUNDED Arts and culture, heritage, environment and conservation in the UK; conservation projects worldwide; disaster relief; specifically within Shropshire for general charitable purposes.

WHAT IS NOT FUNDED Individuals; non-registered charities.

TYPE OF GRANT Normally an annual commitment for a period of five years.

RANGE OF GRANTS £100–£20,000

SAMPLE GRANTS Fauna and Flora International (£20,000); Oxfam (£13,000); Brazilian Atlantic Rainforest Trust and Shropshire Historic Churches Trust (£10,000 each); Médecins Sans Frontières (£8,000); Save The Children UK (£5,000); Pentabus Theatre (£3,000); Taking Part (£2,500); Age UK – Ludlow and Childhood First (£1,000 each); Music in Hospitals (£750); Ludlow Festival (£500); Girlguiding UK (£250); Rowing4Research (£200); Isle of Jura Development Trust (£100).

FINANCES Year 2013/14 Income £441,636 Grants £281,795 Grants to organisations £281,795 Assets £7,802,041

TRUSTEES Bridget Marshall; Sarah Bury; Lindsay Bury; Frank Bury; H. M. Horne.

OTHER INFORMATION There were 130 awards made.

HOW TO APPLY Applications can be made in writing to the correspondent. The trustees meet several times a year to consider grants.

WHO TO APPLY TO Sarah Bury, Trustee, The Old Rectory, Tugford, Craven Arms, Shropshire SY7 9HS  Tel. 01584 841234  email sarah@millichope.com

■ **The Mills Charity**

CC NO 207259    ESTABLISHED 1981

WHERE FUNDING CAN BE GIVEN Framlingham and the surrounding district.

WHO CAN BENEFIT Charitable organisations and local individuals.

WHAT IS FUNDED General charitable purposes; health and disability; activities for children and young people; social welfare. Separate funds also operate for the benefit of the residents of the almshouses and the upkeep of the facilities.

TYPE OF GRANT Often costs of repairs or refurbishment of facilities.

RANGE OF GRANTS Up to £50,000.

SAMPLE GRANTS The Mills Educational Foundation (£50,000); Framlingham Scout and Guide Hut (£5,000); Framlingham Medical Practice (£2,500); Disability Advice Service (£2,100); Kettleburgh Village Hall – Roof (£1,000); Debenham Girls' Group (£200).

FINANCES Year 2013/14 Income £199,833 Grants £68,222 Grants to organisations £60,826 Assets £7,674,536

TRUSTEES Howard Wright; Martin Kelleway; Dr Charles Wright; Persephone Booth; Revd Mike Vipond; Nick Corke; Robert Snell; Gillian Self.

OTHER INFORMATION Six grants were made to organisations. A total of about £7,400 was also given to individuals.

HOW TO APPLY Applications may be made in writing to the correspondent. The charity appears to have a website (ww.themillscharity.co.uk); however, at the time of writing (June 2015) the facility was not functioning.

WHO TO APPLY TO Deborah Stace, Correspondent, 45 Saxmundham Road, Framlingham, Woodbridge, Suffolk IP13 9BZ  Tel. 01728 724370  email info@themillscharity.co.uk

■ **The Millward Charitable Trust**

CC NO 328564    ESTABLISHED 1989

WHERE FUNDING CAN BE GIVEN UK and overseas.

WHO CAN BENEFIT Charitable organisations.

WHAT IS FUNDED General charitable purposes; social welfare; performing arts; medical research; animal welfare.

TYPE OF GRANT One-off or recurrent grants.

RANGE OF GRANTS £500–£36,000

SAMPLE GRANTS Birds Eye View (£36,000 in three grants); City of Birmingham Symphony Orchestra and CORD Sudan Appeal (£10,000 each); Birmingham Contemporary Music (£7,000 in two grants); Music in the Round (£6,500); All Saints Church and Leamington Music (£5,000 each); Prison Fellowship (£3,000); Council of Christians and Jews (£2,000); Age UK, Divine Healing Church of Christ and Hope for Malawi (£1,000 each); Coventry University (£500).

FINANCES Year 2013/14 Income £53,521 Grants £128,486 Grants to organisations £128,486 Assets £2,038,193

TRUSTEES Maurice Millward; Sheila Millward; John Hulse.

OTHER INFORMATION There were 35 awards made.

HOW TO APPLY Applications may be made in writing to the correspondent. The annual report for 2013/14 notes that 'the trustees meet regularly to consider and approve the making of grants in line with the charity's objects'.

WHO TO APPLY TO John Hulse, Trustee, c/o Burgis and Bullock, 2 Chapel Court, Holly Walk, Leamington Spa, Warwickshire CV32 4YS  Tel. 01926 451000  email john.hulse@burgisbullock.com

■ **The Clare Milne Trust**

CC NO 1084733    ESTABLISHED 1999

WHERE FUNDING CAN BE GIVEN The south west of England; in practice Devon and Cornwall.

WHO CAN BENEFIT Voluntary and community groups providing services, facilities or equipment to people with disabilities; smaller, 'well-run, hands-on' charities; local projects.

WHAT IS FUNDED Disability projects, especially those for adults in the south west of England, mainly in Devon and Cornwall. Preference is given to small and well-run local and regional charities with strong support from volunteers and with only modest expenditure on fundraising and administration.

WHAT IS NOT FUNDED Individuals; national charities are not normally supported.

TYPE OF GRANT Generally a partial contribution towards total cost of a project; one-off awards towards capital or core funding; salaries.

RANGE OF GRANTS Typically £1,000–£25,000.

SAMPLE GRANTS Headway Devon (£60,000); Dawlish Gardens Trust (£25,000); Mobility Trust (£20,000); Active 8 (£15,000); Devon County Association for the Blind (£13,000); Anchorage

Trust (£11,200); Headway Somerset and Saltstone Caring (£10,000 each); Penreath Ltd (£7,200); Horticultural Therapy Trust (£6,000); Blurt Foundation and Listening Books (£5,000 each); Accessible Coach Holidays (£3,000); Difficulties (£2,000); Rest Haven (£1,600); Breathe Easy Teignmouth (£1,100); Happy Days (£1,000).

**FINANCES** Year 2013/14 Income £748,692 Grants £832,010 Grants to organisations £832,010 Assets £21,078,881

**TRUSTEES** Michael Brown; Lucie Nottingham; Tim Robinson; Margaret Rogers; Nigel Urwin; Christine Channing.

**OTHER INFORMATION** There were 103 awards made.

**HOW TO APPLY** Application forms can be downloaded from the trust's website. They should be returned to the correspondent along with covering letter (on your letterhead), details regarding your proposal (up to two sides of A4) and a budget for the project. Detailed guidelines are available online. The trustees usually meet four times a year and to save unnecessary administration only applications which fit the trust's criteria will be responded to.

**WHO TO APPLY TO** Kim Lyons, Secretary, c/o Lee Bolton Monier-Williams Solicitors, 1 The Sanctuary, Westminster, London SW1P 3JT Tel. 020 7960 7173 email milnetrust@hotmail.co.uk Website www.claremilnetrust.com

## ■ Milton Keynes Community Foundation Limited

**CC NO** 295107 **ESTABLISHED** 1987

**WHERE FUNDING CAN BE GIVEN** Milton Keynes Unitary Authority.

**WHO CAN BENEFIT** Community groups; CICs; social enterprises; non-profit organisations; faith bodies; sports clubs; parish councils; local registered charities; organisations people of all ages, at risk groups, carers, people with disabilities, those disadvantaged by poverty, homeless people, victims of abuse, crime and domestic violence and other local people in need.

**WHAT IS FUNDED** The foundation's main priority is to help those in the Milton Keynes Council area who miss out because of poverty, ill health, disability or disadvantage. It also supports important initiatives in the spheres of the arts and leisure. As with all community foundations grant schemes can change frequently – for full details of the foundation's current grant programmes and their deadlines consult the website.

**WHAT IS NOT FUNDED** Statutory obligations (schools, local authority, hospitals, etc.); retrospective funding; profit-making enterprises; the promotion of a religion; medical research or treatment; applications in which one or more signatory has been convicted of a crime involving fraud or theft; animal welfare.

**TYPE OF GRANT** Revenue costs; capital expenditure; project grants; limited multi-year funding.

**RANGE OF GRANTS** Micro Grants up to £200–£300; Small Grants up to £1,500; Community Grants up to £5,000; Extraordinary Grants may also be granted.

**SAMPLE GRANTS** MK Christian Foundation (£30,000 in two grants); MK YMCA (£10,000); Blind Veterans UK and Community Development and Training CIC (£5,000 each); Disaster May Erupt Productions (£4,100); Wolverton 175 Working Group (£3,500); Milton Keynes Gymnastics Ltd (£3,400); Winter Night Shelter MK (£3,000 in two grants); Tattenhoe Youth Football Club (£2,200); Milton Keynes Cenotaph Trust and Woughton Community Council (£1,500 each); York House Centre (£400); Crosslinks Centre (£300); 1st Broughton Brownies (£100).

**FINANCES** Year 2013/14 Income £9,068,282 Grants £513,909 Grants to organisations £489,449 Assets £16,888,179

**TRUSTEES** Michael Murray; Francesca Skelton; Judith Hooper; Peter Selvey; Peter Kara; Richard Brown; Roger Kitchen; Steven Norrish; Jane Matthews; Fola Komolafe; Philip Butler; John Moffoot; Stephen Harris; Lawrence Revill; Melanie Beck.

**OTHER INFORMATION** In 2013/14 the foundation helped 164 organisations in order to support 196 projects. In addition three grants were awarded to individuals within the local arts community, five grants to local musicians and five grants to individuals as part of its sports bursary programme. Grants to individuals totalled £24,500. The foundation also provides bursaries in a number of areas, including arts and crafts, sports, music and engineering. In addition £223,000 given through Local Giving – 'nationwide project local voluntary organisations with the opportunity to create a web page and use this to raise funds for their group'.

**HOW TO APPLY** Applicants are strongly advised to speak to the Grants Team prior to submitting a formal request. Application forms and detailed guidelines can be found on the foundation's website. New applicants can apply for Micro Grant (beneficiaries should live in the new Eastern Expansion area of Broughton Gate and Brooklands – no deadline) or Small Grant (deadline – last Friday each month) and, if successful, can request other awards – Community Grant (deadlines are in March, May, August and October) or, under special circumstances, Extraordinary Grant. The grants committee meets five times a year.

**WHO TO APPLY TO** The Grants Team, Acorn House, 381 Midsummer Boulevard, Central Milton Keynes MK9 3HP Tel. 01908 690276 Fax 01908 233635 email applications@mkcommunityfoundation.co.uk Website www.mkcommunityfoundation.co.uk

## ■ The Edgar Milward Charity

**CC NO** 281018 **ESTABLISHED** 1980

**WHERE FUNDING CAN BE GIVEN** UK and overseas; with a particular interest in Reading.

**WHO CAN BENEFIT** Charitable organisations; educational and religious institutions. In practice causes known to the trustees, particularly those supported by the settlor.

**WHAT IS FUNDED** Support is distributed in the following manner: one-half for the furtherance of the Christian religion within the UK and throughout the world; four-tenths for general charitable purposes; one-tenth for educational purposes within a 15-mile radius of the Civic Centre in Reading. The trustees currently have an established interest in a range of charities. Few new charities will be added to this list.

**TYPE OF GRANT** One-off or up to three years; capital and core costs; salaries.

**RANGE OF GRANTS** Up to £5,000.

**SAMPLE GRANTS** Connect4Life (£5,000); Bible Society and Evangelical Alliance (£1,500 each); Addington School Association, Bibles for Children, Global Outreach, Greyfriars Missionary Trust, The Barnabas Fund, University of Oxford Development Trust and Youth for Christ (£1,000 each).

FINANCES Year 2013/14 Income £51,059 Grants £40,400 Grants to organisations £39,200 Assets £1,402,180

TRUSTEES J. C. Austin; J. S. Milward; Alec Fogwill; S. M. W. Fogwill; M. V. Roberts; Fiona Palethorpe.

OTHER INFORMATION A total of 19 grants of less than £1,000 were made at the trustees' discretion totalling £8,100. There were four awards totalling £1,200 given to individuals.

HOW TO APPLY The annual report for 2013/14 states that 'unsolicited applications are not normally considered'.

WHO TO APPLY TO Fiona Palethorpe, Secretary and Treasurer, 19A Cotterstock Road, Oundle, Peterborough PE8 5HA *Tel.* 01832 270055 *email* edgarmilwardcharity@btinternet.com

## ■ The Peter Minet Trust

CC NO 259963          ESTABLISHED 1969

WHERE FUNDING CAN BE GIVEN Mainly south east London boroughs, particularly Lambeth and Southwark.

WHO CAN BENEFIT UK-registered charities and UK publicly exempt charities helping individuals in need, including children and young people, homeless people, single parents, people who have offended and other disadvantaged individuals; health and disability charities; cultural and community projects; play schemes; youth clubs; sport programmes.

WHAT IS FUNDED General charitable causes, including social welfare, children and young people, health causes, people with disabilities, community and cultural projects, the arts, sports and individuals who are disadvantaged or in need.

WHAT IS NOT FUNDED Individuals; national appeals by large charities; overseas appeals; CICs or social enterprises; parochial appeals outside the inner boroughs of South East London; appeals whose sole purpose is to make grants from collected funds; those who have received a grant in the previous 18 months; and research.

TYPE OF GRANT Main grants of up to £5,000 or small grants of up to £500.

RANGE OF GRANTS Up to £5,000.

SAMPLE GRANTS Slade Gardens Community Paly Association and Springfield Community Flat (£5,000 each); Leonard Cheshire Disability (£4,900); FareShare, Futures Theatre Company and Lambeth Law Centre (£4,000 each); The Healthy Living Club (£3,900); Garden Museum, London Music Masters and Woodgrange Baptist Church (£3,000 each); Springboard for Children and The Ebony Horse Club (£2,000 each); Southbank Centre (£1,300); Vauxhall Gardens Community Centre and Voluntary Services Lewisham (£500 each); 16th Bermondsey Scout Group (£400).

FINANCES Year 2013/14 Income £204,934 Grants £171,069 Grants to organisations £171,069 Assets £5,285,227

TRUSTEES John South; Paula Jones; Rodney Luff; Linda Cleverly; Simon Hebditch.

OTHER INFORMATION During the year the trust awarded 65 grants (following 207 appeals), which included 14 awards given as small grants.

HOW TO APPLY Applications should be made using an online application process on the trust's website. There are also application guidelines which should be carefully read prior to applying, as they contain terms and conditions introduced in February 2014. Main grants are awarded in February, June and October and applications should be submitted approximately two months beforehand. See the website for exact dates. Applications for small grants can be made at any time and a decision will be communicated within four weeks. The office is open Monday, Tuesday and Wednesday 9am-3pm. The trust states: 'If you have any queries about our online application process, please contact the office .... We want to help.'

WHO TO APPLY TO Rachel Oglethorpe, Director, 1A Taylors Yard, 67 Alderbrook Road, London SW12 8AD *Tel.* 020 8772 3155 *email* info@peterminet.org.uk *Website* www.peterminet.org.uk

## ■ Minge's Gift and the Pooled Trusts

CC NO 266073          ESTABLISHED 1972

WHERE FUNDING CAN BE GIVEN UK, with some preference for the City of London.

WHO CAN BENEFIT Registered charities; educational establishments; hospitals; churches; organisations associated with the shoe and leather trade.

WHAT IS FUNDED General charitable purposes; medical causes; disability; education and training; disadvantage individuals; fashion and shoemaking industries. There is a strong focus on supporting education in the shoe and leather industry. In addition support is generally given to blind and other disadvantaged people, Army Reserves and cadet forces, local churches and assisting the charitable aspects of the work of the City of London. Help is directed at educational and medical establishments with which the company has developed long term relationships, ex-service organisations and charities connected with the footwear, fabric and leather trades.

TYPE OF GRANT Grants of up to, and in some cases over, three years; core costs; projects; research; recurring costs; start-up costs may be considered.

RANGE OF GRANTS £250–£18,900

SAMPLE GRANTS University of the Arts – London (£18,900); University of Northampton (£17,000); Guildhall School of Music and Drama (£14,000); Urswick School, Hackney (£13,100); Leukaemia and Lymphoma Research (£8,000); Capel Manor College (£6,500); Victoria and Albert Museum (£5,000); Lord Mayor's Fund (£4,400); City University Music Department and Soldiers, Sailors, Airmen and Families Association (£1,500 each); St Dunstan-in-the-West Church (£1,000); Royal British Legion (£350); City of London – Guildhall Library and Sheriffs' and Recorder's Fund (£250 each).

FINANCES Year 2013/14 Income £287,774 Grants £164,579 Grants to organisations £144,899 Assets £3,364,874

TRUSTEES Lance Shaw; John Rubinstein; Jeremy Blanford.

OTHER INFORMATION In 2013/14 a total of £19,700 was given to individuals (£9,000 from Minge's Gift and £10,700 from Pooled Trusts). There were 35 awards to organisations.

HOW TO APPLY Applications may be made in writing to the correspondent.

WHO TO APPLY TO John Miller, Secretary, The Worshipful Company of Cordwainers, Clothworkers Hall, Dunster Court, Mincing Lane, London EC3R 7AH *Tel.* 020 7929 1121 *Fax* 020 7929 1124 *email* office@cordwainers.org *Website* www.cordwainers.org

## ■ Minton Charitable Trust
**CC NO** 1112106 **ESTABLISHED** 2005
**WHERE FUNDING CAN BE GIVEN** UK.
**WHO CAN BENEFIT** Organisations and individuals.
**WHAT IS FUNDED** According to the annual report for 2013/14, the objectives are 'the advancement and promotion of the education of the public through the provision of, or assisting with, the provision of facilities, support, education, advice and financial assistance.'
**TYPE OF GRANT** Capital and project funding.
**RANGE OF GRANTS** On average £20,000–£25,000.
**SAMPLE GRANTS** St Giles Trust (£100,000).
**FINANCES** Year 2013/14 Income £151,544 Grants £100,000 Grants to organisations £100,000 Assets £792,183
**TRUSTEES** Sir Anthony Greener; Richard Edmunds; Lady Audrey Greener.
**OTHER INFORMATION** In 2013/14 the whole of the grant total was paid to St Giles Trust. In the past some awards have also been made to other beneficiaries.
**HOW TO APPLY** Applications may be made in writing to the correspondent. Bear in mind that the main and sometimes the only beneficiary is St Giles Trust, of which Sir Anthony Greener is also a trustee.
**WHO TO APPLY TO** Sir Anthony Greener, Trustee, Dores Hill, North Sydmonton, Newbury RG20 9AF email greenera@mintontrust.com

## ■ The Mirianog Trust
**CC NO** 1091397 **ESTABLISHED** 2002
**WHERE FUNDING CAN BE GIVEN** UK and overseas.
**WHO CAN BENEFIT** Charitable organisations.
**WHAT IS FUNDED** General charitable purposes. Currently the trustees give preference to: the relief of poverty; overseas aid and famine relief; accommodation and housing; environment, conservation and heritage.
**TYPE OF GRANT** Capital and start-up costs; salaries; unrestricted funding; up to two years.
**RANGE OF GRANTS** £300–£5,000
**SAMPLE GRANTS** DEC Syria (£5,000); Action for ME, Butterwick Hospice and Excellent (£2,000 each); Bereavement by Suicide, Church Housing Trust and Deafblind (£1,000 each); Durham Food Bank (£300). Parts of the list of beneficiaries were missing.
**FINANCES** Year 2013/14 Income £43,752 Grants £56,500 Grants to organisations £56,500 Assets £706,083
**TRUSTEES** Canon William Broad; Daphne Broad; Elizabeth Jeary.
**OTHER INFORMATION** The published accounts were missing pages; therefore it is not clear what amount out of the overall expenditure of about £65,500 was given in grants. Generally about 86% is given in grant awards and it is likely that about £56,500 was distributed.
**HOW TO APPLY** Applications must be made in writing to the correspondent. The trustees consider awards twice each year.
**WHO TO APPLY TO** Canon William Broad, Trustee, Moorcote, Thornley, Tow Law, Bishop Auckland DL13 4NU Tel. 01388 731350 email bill@billbroad.wanadoo.co.uk

## ■ The Laurence Misener Charitable Trust
**CC NO** 283460 **ESTABLISHED** 1981
**WHERE FUNDING CAN BE GIVEN** UK.
**WHO CAN BENEFIT** Charitable organisations. There is a tendency to benefit those charities in which the settlor was interested.
**WHAT IS FUNDED** General charitable purposes, including health, education, armed forces charities, organisations working with people with disabilities and Jewish causes.
**RANGE OF GRANTS** £5,000–£25,000
**SAMPLE GRANTS** Multiple Sclerosis Society of Great Britain and Northern Ireland and Seafarers UK (£25,000 each); Cassel Hospital Families Centre Appeal, Fight for Sight, Great Ormond Street Children's Hospital Fund and Royal National Lifeboat Institution (£20,000 each); Imperial War Museum Development Trust (£15,000); St Peter and St James Home and Hospice (£10,000); Jews' Temporary Shelter (£8,000); Elimination of Leukaemia Fund and World Jewish Relief (£7,000 each); Nightingale House (£5,000).
**FINANCES** Year 2013/14 Income £116,663 Grants £249,000 Grants to organisations £249,000 Assets £2,838,256
**TRUSTEES** Jillian Legane; Capt. George Swaine.
**OTHER INFORMATION** There were 17 awards made.
**HOW TO APPLY** Applications can be made in writing to the correspondent. Note the following taken from the annual report for 2013/14: 'The Trustees receive a considerable number of requests for donations and grants each year but have a policy to restrict donations approved to those charities which in their view would have been approved by the Settlor himself, or fall under the heading of approved charitable purposes ….'
**WHO TO APPLY TO** David Lyons, Correspondent, c/o Leonard Jones and Co, 1 Printing Yard House, London E2 7PR Tel. 020 7739 8790 email enquiries@leonardjones.co.uk

## ■ The Mishcon Family Charitable Trust
**CC NO** 213165 **ESTABLISHED** 1961
**WHERE FUNDING CAN BE GIVEN** UK.
**WHO CAN BENEFIT** Registered charities, particularly Jewish organisations.
**WHAT IS FUNDED** General charitable purposes; Jewish causes; social welfare; health and disability; children and young people. Within the limited funds available each application is considered on its merits with preference given to applications for the relief of poverty from recognised organisations.
**TYPE OF GRANT** One-off project and other, generally unrestricted, awards.
**RANGE OF GRANTS** £50–£33,500
**SAMPLE GRANTS** United Jewish Israel Appeal – UJIA (£33,500); United Synagogue and University College of London (£5,000 each); Board of Deputies Charitable Foundation (£3,500); Norwood (£2,500); Cystic Fibrosis Trust (£1,500); British Friends of Migdal Ohr (£1,000); De Montfort University (£500); London Legal Support Trust (£250); Weizmann Institute (£200); Women and Children First (£150); UNICEF (£100); Action Aid, British Heart Foundation and Friends of Rachashei Lev (£50 each).

FINANCES Year 2013/14 Income £65,730
Grants £87,526 Grants to organisations £87,526 Assets £1,931,300
TRUSTEES Jane Landau; Peter Mishcon; Russell Mishcon.
OTHER INFORMATION There were 91 grants awarded.
HOW TO APPLY Applications may be made in writing to the correspondent.
WHO TO APPLY TO George Georghiou, Correspondent, c/o Mercer and Hole, 72 London Road, St Albans AL1 1NS Tel. 01727 869141

## ■ The Misselbrook Trust

CC NO 327928 ESTABLISHED 1988
WHERE FUNDING CAN BE GIVEN UK, with a preference for the Hampshire area.
WHO CAN BENEFIT Registered charities.
WHAT IS FUNDED General charitable purposes.
TYPE OF GRANT One-off and recurrent.
RANGE OF GRANTS Most grants are for £1,000 or less.
SAMPLE GRANTS Streetscene (£50,000); Enham Trust (£2,000); Leukaemia Busters and Marwell Wildlife (£1,000 each).
FINANCES Year 2013/14 Income £53,005
Grants £108,600 Grants to organisations £108,600 Assets £1,175,078
TRUSTEES David Hoar; Michael Howson-Green; Brian Baxendale; M. A. Howson-Green.
OTHER INFORMATION During the year a total of 153 awards were made. Grants of £1,000 or less were made to 149 organisations and totalled around £54,500.
HOW TO APPLY Applications can be made in writing to the correspondent
WHO TO APPLY TO David Hoare, Trustee, Ashton House, 12 The Central Precinct, Winchester Road, Chandler's Ford, Eastleigh, Hampshire SO53 2GB Tel. 023 8027 4555 email ashton.house@btconnect.com

## ■ The Brian Mitchell Charitable Settlement

CC NO 1003817 ESTABLISHED 1989
WHERE FUNDING CAN BE GIVEN UK.
WHO CAN BENEFIT Charitable organisations, largely registered charities; schools; churches; hospices.
WHAT IS FUNDED General charitable purposes, especially arts and education; medical care and research; social welfare; international support.
RANGE OF GRANTS Up to £25,000.
SAMPLE GRANTS Glyndebourne Festival Society (£25,000); Shakespeare's Globe Theatre and The Skinners School (£15,000 each); Macmillan Nurses (£12,500); British Red Cross (£12,000); Disaster Emergency Committee (£10,000); Romanian Orphanage (£8,600); Hospice on the Weald and Myeloma UK (£7,500 each); Canterbury Cathedral, Child Hope, The Royal Institution and The Trussell Trust (£5,000 each). Other awards totalled over £61,000 but were not listed.
FINANCES Year 2013/14 Income £230,886
Grants £219,208 Grants to organisations £219,208 Assets £2,228,992
TRUSTEES Brian Mitchell; Andy Buss; John Andrews; Michael Conlon; Fraser Reavell.
OTHER INFORMATION In 2013/14 about half of all grants went to supporting arts and education. There were 45 grants made, about one third of these were given to charities with which the charity has established ongoing relationships.

HOW TO APPLY Applications may be made in writing to the correspondent, although note that the charity has identified several regular beneficiaries.
WHO TO APPLY TO Brian Mitchell, Trustee, Round Oak, Old Station Road, Wadhurst, East Sussex TN5 6TZ Tel. 01892 782072 email brnmitchell3@googlemail.com

## ■ The Esmé Mitchell Trust

IR NO XN48053 ESTABLISHED 1965
WHERE FUNDING CAN BE GIVEN Ireland, but mainly Northern Ireland.
WHO CAN BENEFIT Organisations involved in the arts and cultural activities.
WHAT IS FUNDED General charitable purposes with a particular interest in cultural and artistic objects. Part of the trust fund is only available to assist certain heritage bodies as set out in Schedule 3 to the Capital Transfer Act 1984.
WHAT IS NOT FUNDED Individuals.
TYPE OF GRANT Generally unrestricted; on occasions grants have been given over a period of two to three years but generally no long-term commitments are entered.
RANGE OF GRANTS No restrictions.
TRUSTEES P. J. Rankin; F. Jay-O'Boyle; R. P. Blakiston-Houston.
OTHER INFORMATION The trust makes grants totalling around £120,000 a year. There was no further information available.
HOW TO APPLY The trustees meet about five or six times a year. Guidelines for applicants are available upon request from the trust.
WHO TO APPLY TO Lisa Smyth, Cleaver Fulton Rankin Ltd Solicitors, 50 Bedford Street, Belfast BT2 7FW Tel. 028 9024 3141 email info@cfrlaw.co.uk

## ■ Keren Mitzvah Trust

CC NO 1041948 ESTABLISHED 1994
WHERE FUNDING CAN BE GIVEN UK.
WHO CAN BENEFIT Individuals and registered charities, particularly Jewish organisations.
WHAT IS FUNDED General charitable purposes; Jewish causes; relief of poverty; religious activities; education; health.
TYPE OF GRANT One-off and recurrent.
RANGE OF GRANTS Up to £19,000.
SAMPLE GRANTS Camp Simcha (£19,000); Torah and Chesed (£14,600); Good Deed Foundation (£10,300); Cosmon Belz and Natlas Trust (£10,000 each); The Sunderland Kollel (£5,500); Noam Primary School, Beis Nadvorne and Woodstock Sinclair Trust (£5,000 each).
FINANCES Year 2013/14 Income £131,041
Grants £146,958 Grants to organisations £146,958 Assets £36,096
TRUSTEES Manny Weiss; Alan McCormack; Neil Bradley.
OTHER INFORMATION Grants under £5,000 totalled about £46,500.
HOW TO APPLY The trust has previously stated that the trustees generally support their own personal charities.
WHO TO APPLY TO Naomi Crowther, Correspondent, 1 Manchester Square, London W1U 3AB

## ■ The Mizpah Trust

**CC NO** 287231     **ESTABLISHED** 1983
**WHERE FUNDING CAN BE GIVEN** UK and overseas.
**WHO CAN BENEFIT** Registered charities and individuals.
**WHAT IS FUNDED** Relief of poverty, overseas aid and famine relief, Christian causes.
**TYPE OF GRANT** One-off and recurrent.
**RANGE OF GRANTS** Awards range from £50 to 60,000, although most grants are of around £1,000.
**SAMPLE GRANTS Previous beneficiaries have included:** The Vanessa Grant Trust (£60,000); CURE International (£10,000); CARE and World Vision (£5,000 each); Micah Trust (£4,000); Friends of St Andrews (£1,500); The Stewards Trust, The Wilberforce Trust and The Saville Foundation (£1,000 each).
**FINANCES** Year 2013/14 Income £137,952 Grants £140,200 Grants to organisations £134,950 Assets £24,623
**TRUSTEES** Alan Bell; Julia Bell.
**OTHER INFORMATION** Grants to individuals were made totalling £5,300.
**HOW TO APPLY** Unsolicited applications are not invited. The trust proactively distributes funds and does not responded to enquiries and requests for funding.
**WHO TO APPLY TO** Alan Bell, Trustee, Foresters House, Humbly Grove, South Warnborough, Hook, Hampshire RG29 1RY *email* alancobell@gmail.com

## ■ Mobbs Memorial Trust Ltd

**CC NO** 202478     **ESTABLISHED** 1963
**WHERE FUNDING CAN BE GIVEN** Stoke Poges and district within a 35-mile radius of St Giles' Church.
**WHO CAN BENEFIT** Charitable organisations benefitting: people of all ages; ex-service and service people; volunteers; unemployed; those in care, fostered and adopted; parents and children; at-risk groups; people with disabilities; those disadvantaged by poverty; ex-offenders and those at risk of offending; homeless people; those living in rural areas; socially isolated people; victims of abuse, crime and domestic violence and so on.
**WHAT IS FUNDED** St Giles' Church and other charitable purposes including: almshouses; sheltered accommodation; community development; support to voluntary and community organisations; combined and community arts; sports and recreation; health causes; conservation and environment; schools and colleges; and community facilities and services.
**WHAT IS NOT FUNDED** The following applications are not normally supported: from or for individuals or private companies; from national charitable organisations unless a specific need arises with the local area; that should be funded by national or local government; and for running costs, apart from exceptional cases within a four-mile radius of Stoke Poges.
**TYPE OF GRANT** Grants for buildings, equipment and projects. Funding is given for up to three years.
**RANGE OF GRANTS** £500–£10,000
**SAMPLE GRANTS** St Mary's Church, Farnham (£10,000); YMCA Reading (£5,700); Chiltern MS Centre (£5,400); Chesham Cricket Club and Rivertime Boat Trust (£5,000 each); Wycombe High School (£4,700); Action 4 Youth (£3,500); Deafax (£3,200); Stoke Poges Old People's Christmas Fund and Stoke Poges PCC Account (St Giles) (£2,500 each); BACAB (£600); Stoke Poges Flower Fund and Stoke Poges Horticultural Society (£200 each).
**FINANCES** Year 2013/14 Income £71,756 Grants £56,652 Grants to organisations £55,794 Assets £2,701,616
**TRUSTEES** Sandra Greenslade; Chris Mobbs; Dr Charles Mobbs; Michael Mobbs; Alexandra Mobbs.
**OTHER INFORMATION** Grants were made to 17 organisations.
**HOW TO APPLY** Applications can be made in writing to the correspondent. Applications can either be posted or emailed. The trustees meet quarterly, normally in March, June, September and December.
**WHO TO APPLY TO** Dr Charles Mobbs, Chair, Cypress Cottage, 89 St John's Road, Newport, Isle of Wight PO30 1LS *email* applications@mobbsmemorialtrust.com or charlesmobbs@mobbsmemorialtrust.com *Website* www.mobbsmemorialtrust.com

## ■ The Modiano Charitable Trust

**CC NO** 328372     **ESTABLISHED** 1989
**WHERE FUNDING CAN BE GIVEN** UK and overseas.
**WHO CAN BENEFIT** Charitable organisations and educational institutions, with some preference for Jewish groups.
**WHAT IS FUNDED** The arts, Jewish causes, education, the relief of poverty, particularly amongst unemployed people/those in risk of unemployment and people who need help caring for themselves.
**TYPE OF GRANT** One-off and recurrent awards.
**RANGE OF GRANTS** £50–£20,000
**SAMPLE GRANTS Previous beneficiaries have included:** Philharmonic Orchestra (£20,000); the Weiznam Institute Foundation £10,000); DEC Haiti Appeal, St Paul's School and UJIA (£5,000 each); World Jewish Relief (£4,000); Life Action Trust (£3,500); CCJ and The Holocaust Educational Trust (£2,500 each); YMCA and the Reform Research Trust (1,000 each); and British Forces Association, Jewish Association for the Mentally Ill (JAMI) The St John of Jerusalem Eye Hospital (£100 each).
**FINANCES** Year 2013/14 Income £200,000 Grants £64,250 Grants to organisations £64,250 Assets £220,991
**TRUSTEES** Laurence Modiano; Barbara Modiano; Michael Modiano.
**HOW TO APPLY** Applications can be made in writing to the correspondent
**WHO TO APPLY TO** Michael Modiano, Trustee, Broad Street House, 55 Old Broad Street, London EC2M 1RX *Tel.* 020 7012 0000

## ■ Mole Charitable Trust

**CC NO** 281452     **ESTABLISHED** 1980
**WHERE FUNDING CAN BE GIVEN** UK, with a preference for Manchester.
**WHO CAN BENEFIT** Individuals, registered charities and institutions benefitting children, young adults, Jews and people disadvantaged by poverty.
**WHAT IS FUNDED** Jewish causes, educational purposes and the relief of poverty.
**RANGE OF GRANTS** £1,000–£60,000
**SAMPLE GRANTS Previous beneficiaries have included:** Three Pillars Charity (£60,000); Manchester Jewish Grammar School (£26,000); Chasdei Yoel Charitable Trust and United Talmudical Associates Limited (£20,000 each);

Binoh of Manchester (£6,000); Beis Ruchel Girls School (£3,000); Manchester Jewish Federation (£2,500); and Our Kids (£1,000).
FINANCES Year 2013/14 Income £73,397 Grants £140,544 Grants to organisations £140,544 Assets £2,275,543
TRUSTEES Martin Gross; Leah Pearl Gross.
OTHER INFORMATION A total of £79,000 went to religious institutions and charitable organisations and around £62,000 to educational institutions.
HOW TO APPLY Unsolicited applications are not accepted. The annual report and accounts for 2013/14 state: 'The trustees receive many applications for grants, mainly personal contact, but also verbally. Each application is considered against the criteria established by the Charity. Although the Charity does not advertise, it is well known within its community and there are many requests received for grants.'
WHO TO APPLY TO Martin Gross, Trustee, 2 Okeover Road, Salford M7 4JX Tel. 0161 832 8721 email martin.gross@lopiangb.co.uk

## ■ The Monatrea Charitable Trust
CC NO 1131897    ESTABLISHED 2009
WHERE FUNDING CAN BE GIVEN UK.
WHO CAN BENEFIT Registered charities.
WHAT IS FUNDED General charitable purposes.
RANGE OF GRANTS £500–£41,500
SAMPLE GRANTS Previous beneficiaries have included: Africa Conservation; Children Welfare Home; Dr Ambrosoli Memorial Health Care Centre; Family Action; Pregnancy Sickness Support; Prisoners' Advice Service; Roses Charitable Trust; Samata Hospital; Samata Samaj; South Central Youth.
FINANCES Year 2013/14 Income £87,949 Grants £72,500 Grants to organisations £72,500
TRUSTEES Patrick Vernon; Mary Vernon; Coutts & Co.
OTHER INFORMATION At the time of writing (June 2015) full accounts for 2014/15 were not yet published by the Charity Commission. Based on the patterns of previous giving it is likely that grants totalled about £72,500. On average about nine awards are made annually.
HOW TO APPLY The Charity Commission's record notes that 'unsolicited appeals will not be accepted'.
WHO TO APPLY TO The Trustees, c/o Coutts & Co., 440 Strand, London WC2R 0QS Tel. 020 7663 6838 email couttscharities@coutts.com

## ■ Monmouthshire County Council Welsh Church Act Fund
CC NO 507094    ESTABLISHED 1996
WHERE FUNDING CAN BE GIVEN Blaenau Gwent, Caerphilly, Monmouthshire, the City of Newport and Torfaen.
WHO CAN BENEFIT Organisations and individuals, including students, groups at risk, people who are disadvantaged by poverty, socially isolation, ill health and disaster victims.
WHAT IS FUNDED Education, health and disability causes, relief of poverty, older people, medical and social research, probation, social and recreational causes, libraries, museums and art galleries, protection of historic buildings relating to Wales, places of worship and burial grounds, also emergencies and disasters.
TYPE OF GRANT Capital or revenue purposes, also provision, upkeep and repair of religious buildings and community halls.
RANGE OF GRANTS Generally up to £1,000.
SAMPLE GRANTS Previous beneficiaries included: Bridges Community Centre; North Wales Society for the Blind; Parish Church Llandogo; Parish Church Llangybi; St David's Foundation Hospice Care.
FINANCES Year 2013/14 Income £166,021 Grants £130,217 Grants to organisations £129,617 Assets £4,658,456
TRUSTEE Monmouthshire County Council.
OTHER INFORMATION Grants totalling £600 were also made to individuals for educational purposes.
HOW TO APPLY Our research suggests that applications should be made on a form available from the correspondent which must be signed by a county/city councillor. They are normally considered in March, June, September and December.
WHO TO APPLY TO Joy Robson, Head of Finance, Monmouthshire County Council, Innovation House, PO Box 106, Magor, Caldicot NP26 9AN Tel. 01633 644657 email davejarrett@monmouthshire.gov.uk

## ■ The Montague Thompson Coon Charitable Trust
CC NO 294096    ESTABLISHED 1986
WHERE FUNDING CAN BE GIVEN UK.
WHO CAN BENEFIT Children with muscular diseases, medical research, environment.
WHAT IS FUNDED Relief of sickness in children with muscular dystrophy and/or other muscular diseases, carrying out and provide for research into infant diseases and advancing the education of the public in the study of ecology and wildlife.
WHAT IS NOT FUNDED Individuals.
SAMPLE GRANTS Muscular Dystrophy Group (£15,000); Portland Bird Observatory and Field Centre (£10,000); Keech Hospice Care and Nancy Oldfield Trust (£5,000 each); Caring for Life (£4,000); Springhead Trust (£3,000).
FINANCES Year 2013/14 Income £30,544 Grants £54,010 Grants to organisations £54,010 Assets £907,582
TRUSTEES Peter Clarke, Chair; John Lister; Philippa Blake-Roberts.
HOW TO APPLY Apply in writing to the correspondent.
WHO TO APPLY TO Philippa Blake-Roberts, Trustee, Old Rectory, Church Lane, Colton, Norwich NR9 5DE Tel. 07766 072592 email johnplister@hotmail.com

## ■ The Monument Trust
CC NO 242575    ESTABLISHED 1965
WHERE FUNDING CAN BE GIVEN Unrestricted; in practice the UK, South Africa, USA
WHO CAN BENEFIT 'Registered charities or activities with clearly defined charitable purposes'.
WHAT IS FUNDED General charitable purposes; arts and heritage – arts, architectural and environmental projects of national or regional importance, including galleries, museums, and historic houses and gardens, with particular attention paid to 'cultural projects which will make a major contribution to improving economically depressed areas' health and community care -'substantial HIV/AIDS projects in the UK and Africa, social exclusion, the sexual health of young people, and hospices'

social development; criminal justice – including prisoners' resettlement and alternatives to custody, also homelessness'.

**WHAT IS NOT FUNDED** Individuals; educational fees; expeditions.

**TYPE OF GRANT** Core, capital and project costs.

**RANGE OF GRANTS** Up to £4 million; mostly under £500,000.

**SAMPLE GRANTS** Prince's Drawing School (£4 million); Christ Church – Spitalfields (£2.7 million); Lyric Opera of Chicago and Parkinson's UK (£1 million each); National Maritime Museum – Greenwich (£350,000); Burlington Magazine and Midhurst Youth Centre Trust (£300,000 each); African Solutions to African Problems (£293,000); University of Cambridge – Judge Business School (£270,000); Bipolar UK (£225,000); Canine Partners (£200,000); Royal Horticultural Society and Young Women's Trust (£150,000 each); Charles Rennie Mackintosh Society (£140,000); Positive Prison, Positive Futures (£135,000); Youth Music Theatre UK (£120,000); Fine Cell Work (£99,000); Lodge Hill Centre and The Horse Course (£60,000 each); Aldeburgh Music (£45,000); Home-Start Crave (£40,000); FutureFirst (£25,000); Edinburgh International Festival (£20,000); Temple Newsam House (£14,000); Wheelyboat Trust (£10,900). Grants under £10,000 under all the categories totalled around £132,500.

**FINANCES** Year 2013/14 Income £4,440,000 Grants £35,158,000 Grants to organisations £35,158,000 Assets £137,693,000

**TRUSTEES** Stewart Grimshaw; Linda Heathcoat-Amory; Charles Cator.

**OTHER INFORMATION** The annual report for 2013/14 notes that 'the trustees continue to support a number of arts projects of national or regional importance' and 'in other areas they prefer to help prove new ideas or methods that can be replicated widely and where possible become self-sustaining.' The trust makes substantial grants in excess of the trust's income, which can then be funded using the trust's expendable endowment. In the Arts and Heritage category significant appeals are particularly welcome.

**HOW TO APPLY** The website notes that the trust 'will consider suitable proposals, so long as they demonstrably and closely fit their specific areas of interest'. It is further reminded that 'it should be understood that the majority of unsolicited proposals are unsuccessful'. Eligible proposals can be sent via post to the correspondent including the following: details of your organisation – charitable aims and objectives, most recent annual income and expenditure, current financial position (do not send a full set of accounts); information on the project requiring funding – why it is needed, who will benefit and in what way; breakdown of costs – any money raised so far and how the balance will be achieved. Refrain from sending any other supporting materials. All applications are acknowledged and candidates for support are informed within eight weeks of the acknowledgement. If you have not heard from the trust by then assume you have been unsuccessful. Note that a single application will be considered for support by all the trusts in the group.

**WHO TO APPLY TO** Alan Bookbinder, Director, The Peak, 5 Wilton Road, London SW1V 1AP *Tel.* 020 7410 0330 *Fax* 020 7410 0332 *email* info@sfct.org.uk *Website* www.sfct.org.uk

## ■ The Moonpig Foundation

**CC NO** 1136686  **ESTABLISHED** 2010

**WHERE FUNDING CAN BE GIVEN** Worldwide; Southwark and Guernsey; current focus on Uganda.

**WHO CAN BENEFIT** Charitable organisations.

**WHAT IS FUNDED** The accounts for 2013/14 list the following three aims of the foundation: to support the sustainable improvements in the lives of the most impoverished people in the world; to support the local community in Southwark, where the Moonpig head office is based and in Guernsey where the production facility is located; and to encourage awareness of social issues among the Moonpig employees and encourage them to support the foundation through fundraising or volunteering time. For the past few years support has mainly been given to World Vision to support development projects in Uganda.

**SAMPLE GRANTS** World Vision – Ntwetwe project (£139,500).

**FINANCES** Year 2013/14 Income £152,887 Grants £139,500 Grants to organisations £139,500 Assets £31,766

**TRUSTEES** Iain Martin; Paul Lantsbury; Nicholas Jenkins.

**OTHER INFORMATION** The Moonpig Foundation will match any money raised for charity by a Moonpig employee up to a limit of £5,000 in any financial year per employee.

**HOW TO APPLY** The annual report and accounts state: 'The Moonpig Foundation actively seeks projects to fund and does not accept unsolicited applications for grants.'

**WHO TO APPLY TO** Nicholas Jenkins, Trustee, Bapton Manor, Bapton, Warminster, Wiltshire BA12 0SB *email* accounts@moonpig.com

## ■ The George A. Moore Foundation

**CC NO** 262107  **ESTABLISHED** 1970

**WHERE FUNDING CAN BE GIVEN** Principally Yorkshire and the Isle of Man.

**WHO CAN BENEFIT** Charitable and voluntary organisations.

**WHAT IS FUNDED** The trustees select causes and projects from the applications received during the year and also independently research and identify specific objectives where they wish to direct assistance. The type of grants made can vary quite widely from one year to another and care is taken to maintain a rough parity among the various fields covered so that one sphere of activity does not benefit unduly at the expense of another. Areas which are not or cannot be covered by official sources can be favoured.

**WHAT IS NOT FUNDED** Individuals; courses of study; expeditions and overseas travel; holidays; for purposes outside the UK. Local appeals for UK charities will only be considered if in the area of interest. Because of present long-term commitments, the foundation is not prepared to consider appeals for religious property or institutions.

**TYPE OF GRANT** Grants are generally non-recurrent and the foundation is reluctant to contribute to revenue appeals.

**RANGE OF GRANTS** Up to £50,000; mostly under £1,000.

**SAMPLE GRANTS** Boston Charitable Foundation (£50,000); Macmillan (£20,000 each); Caring for Life – Crag house Farm and St Helen's Church (£10,000 each); Horizon Life Training (£3,800); Arthritis Research UK and Sustrans (£3,000 each); Boys' and Girls' Club – Hunslet (£2,500); Association of Wheelchair Children,

Marine Conversation Society and Survivors of Bereavement by Suicide (£1,000 each); Children's Heart Surgery Fund, Horlicap – Bluecoat Wood Nurseries and The West Yorkshire Forget Me Not Trust (£500 each); Sulby and District Rifle Club (£100).
**FINANCES** Year 2013/14 Income £335,643 Grants £191,673 Grants to organisations £191,673 Assets £6,876,634
**TRUSTEES** George Moore; Elizabeth Moore; Jonathan Moore; Paul Turner.
**OTHER INFORMATION** There were 72 awards made. The Charity consists of one general fund (unrestricted) and one expendable endowment fund.
**HOW TO APPLY** Applications have to be made in writing to the correspondent – note that trustees *do not* favour applications via email and appreciate formal style of requests. There are no formal guidelines or application forms issued. Applications should be received by the middle of the month prior to the meeting. The meetings are held four times a year, in March, June, September and December and all applicants are notified of the outcome following the meeting.
**WHO TO APPLY TO** Angela James, Chief Administrator, The Stables, Bilton Hall, Bilton-in-Ainsty, York YO26 7NP *Tel.* 01423 359446 *email* info@gamf.org.uk *Website* www.gamf.org.uk

## ■ The Henry Moore Foundation

**CC NO** 271370 **ESTABLISHED** 1977
**WHERE FUNDING CAN BE GIVEN** UK and overseas.
**WHO CAN BENEFIT** Not-for-profit institutions; arts organisations; educational bodies.
**WHAT IS FUNDED** Grants are awarded 'to a wide range of projects and organisations with a strong sculptural component' or the involvement of the works of Henry Moore in the five main categories: new projects (exhibitions; exhibition catalogues; commissions; up to £20,000); collections (acquisitions; conservation; cataloguing; display; up to £20,000); research and development (long-term research up to £20,000 and small research grants for research on the history and interpretation of sculpture up to £2,500); fellowships (postdoctoral research fellowships and artist residencies up to £6,000); conferences, lectures and publications (up to £5,000)'.
**WHAT IS NOT FUNDED** Revenue expenditure; individuals (except fellowships); retrospective funding; no grant (or part of any grant) may be used to pay any fee or to provide any other benefit to any individual who is a trustee of the foundation.
**TYPE OF GRANT** One-off and longer term funding; publication; research; development; collections; exhibitions; fellowships; conferences and lectures.
**RANGE OF GRANTS** Up to £20,000, depending on grant category.
**SAMPLE GRANTS** The most recent projects supported are listed on the foundation's website.
**Beneficiaries included**: Art Gallery of Ontario (£12,000); The Whitworth – University of Manchester and Yorkshire Sculpture Park/The Hepworth Wakefield (£10,000 each); The Hepworth Wakefield (£7,000); University of Greenwich Gallery – London (£6,000); Catalogue Cooper Gallery, Duncan of Jordanstone College of Art – Dundee and Haus der Kunst – Munchen (£5,000 each); Situations – Bristol (£4,000); Lux – London and Vivid Projects – Birmingham (£3,000 each); CIRCA Projects – Newcastle (£2,500); S1 Artspace – Sheffield (£2,000); University of Stirling (£1,300); University of York (£1,000).
**FINANCES** Year 2013/14 Income £2,349,092 Grants £562,195 Grants to organisations £520,195 Assets £99,926,096
**TRUSTEES** Henry Channon; Laure Genillard; Nigel Carrington; David Wilson; Celia Clear; Peter Weinand; Anne Wagner; Charles Asprey; William Edgerly; Antony Griffiths.
**PUBLICATIONS** The Henry Moore Foundation Review.
**OTHER INFORMATION** According to the website: 'The foundation was founded by the artist in 1977 to encourage public appreciation of the visual arts, and in particular the works of Henry Moore. Its main responsibilities are preserving Moore's legacy at his home in Hertfordshire and through exhibitions worldwide; funding exhibitions and research at the Henry Moore Institute in Leeds; and awarding grants to arts organisations in the UK and abroad.' There were 94 grants were paid in the following categories: exhibitions and new projects (67 awards totalling £426,500); conferences, publications and workshops (18 awards totalling £45,000); fellowship (£42,000); research (6 awards totalling £38,000); collections (£10,600). Note that in 2013/14 the foundation approved grants totalling around £540,500; the above amounts, given as stated in the accounts, 'include brought forward and carried forward details and only include grants notified to recipients in advance of the year end and hence do not correlate directly to the grants approved in the year'. Direct charitable costs to the foundation totalled over £2,7 million, which includes grants, curatorial costs and exhibitions, sculpture studies, estate and visitor services, marketing and works of art acquired. The website notes that in 2014/15 it was aimed to award £500,000.
**HOW TO APPLY** There is an online application form which can be found on the foundation's website. Appeals are considered at quarterly meetings (for latest deadlines see the website). It is advised to apply well in advance (at least six months) to the project start date as funds cannot be paid for retrospective projects. The outcome of your application will be communicated by letter. Our research suggests that applicants should also advise the foundation if it is envisaged that any trustee will have an interest in the project for which a grant is sought, as instances where conflict of interest may occur will not be funded. Organisations may include supporting material with their application and this will be returned if requested.
**WHO TO APPLY TO** Lesley Wake, Chief Operating Officer, Dane Tree House, Perry Green, Much Hadham, Hertfordshire SG10 6EE *Tel.* 01279 843333 *email* admin@henry-moore.org *Website* www.henry-moore.org

## ■ John Moores Foundation (JMF)

**CC NO** 253481 **ESTABLISHED** 1963
**WHERE FUNDING CAN BE GIVEN** Merseyside (including Ellesmere Port, Halton and Skelmersdale) and Northern Ireland.
**WHO CAN BENEFIT** Voluntary organisations; community groups; charities; social enterprises; CICs; other charitable organisations benefitting people who are marginalised and socially, educationally, physically, economically, culturally, geographically or otherwise disadvantaged individuals. Preference is given

# Morel

for 'small, grass-roots and volunteer driven organisations and new rather than long-established groups'. The foundation states: 'We are particularly interested in supporting those groups that find it more than usually difficult to raise money.' Our research suggests that international relief organisations can also be supported, but only organisations proactively selected by the trustees rather than applicants.

**WHAT IS FUNDED** Grass roots community groups; black and minority ethnic organisations; women including girls; second chance learning; advice and information to alleviate poverty; support and training for voluntary organisations; support projects which aim to counter racism, sexism or discrimination of any kind; projects which aim to break down barriers, to encourage co-operation and joint working between different community and voluntary groups and across local boundaries; local trust-building initiatives where there may be tensions or misunderstandings within or between communities. And, in Merseyside only: people with disabilities; carers; refugees; homeless people; family support; young people. And, in Northern Ireland only, promotion of Equal Opportunities.

**WHAT IS NOT FUNDED** Individuals; projects that are not substantially influenced by their target beneficiaries; national or regional organisations or groups based outside the area even where some of the service users come from Merseyside or Northern Ireland; statutory bodies or work previously done by them; mainstream education (schools, colleges, universities); faith-based projects exclusively for members of that faith, or for the promotion of religion; capital building costs; festivals, carnivals and fetes; medicine; holidays and expeditions; gifts, parties, etc.; conferences; sport; vehicles; animal charities; arts, crafts, heritage, or local history projects; conservation and environmental projects; employment and enterprise schemes; academic or medical research; Credit Unions – except for the training of management committee members or the development of a new business plan; uniformed groups (e.g. scouts, cadets, majorettes); sponsorship, advertising or fundraising events; In NI also children and young people – except under eligible headings, and playgroups, except those which directly address marginalisation and focus on real social disadvantage. The foundation states that 'applications may be refused where we feel that the organisation concerned is already well funded or has excessive reserves'.

**TYPE OF GRANT** One-off and up to three years; projects; equipment; start-up costs; running expenditure; volunteer expenses; help towards education and training costs; venue and travel expenses.

**RANGE OF GRANTS** £100–£50,000; generally up to £5,000.

**SAMPLE GRANTS** A list grant recipients did not seem to be within the accounts. **Previous beneficiaries have included:** Wirral Resource Centre and Toy Library (£11,000); The Debt Advice Network (£10,000); Granby Somali Women's Group (£7,500); Wirral Holistic Care Services (£4,800); Support for Asylum Seekers (3,800); Church Road Neighbourhood Resource Centre (£3,000); Women's Enterprise Breakthrough (£2,500); Kirkby Senior Collaborative (£1,200); Southport Access for Everyone (£1,000); Stella Marks Social Enterprise (£650); Ardoyne Association and Foyle Sign Language Centre (£5,000 each); Omagh Independent Advice Services and Dialogue for Diversity (£4,500 each);

Community Focus Learning (£3,300); Loup Women's Group (£3,200); Roundabout Playgroup (£2,000); Belfast Butterfly Club (£1,800).

**FINANCES** Year 2013/14 Income £818,672 Grants £635,646 Grants to organisations £635,646 Assets £25,304,217

**TRUSTEES** Barnaby Moores; Kevin Moores; Nicola Eastwood; Alison Navarro; Christina Mee.

**OTHER INFORMATION** Overseas and one-off exceptional grants are not open to unsolicited applications. Merseyside is 'the first concern of the trustees' with about 60–75% of grants given there. One-off exceptional grants 'are rare and unspecific and are to causes that interest trustees'. The foundation prefers to give smaller grants to a larger number of projects. During the year a total of 233 applications were received (149 in Merseyside, 68 in NI and 16 from other areas) and 133 grants paid. The accounts state that 'the foundation aims to maintain its annual grant-giving at approximately £700,000'.

**HOW TO APPLY** There are slight differences between the application procedures and criteria for Merseyside and Northern Ireland (see the website for full details). Read the eligibility criteria carefully. If you are unsure, or if you would like to discuss your application before submitting it, telephone the foundation staff who will be happy to advise you. Applications should be made by letter (no more than four A4 sides) accompanied by a completed application form, which is available from the foundation's Merseyside and Northern Ireland offices and can be requested via email or phone. All appeals are acknowledged. The trustees meet five or six times a year in Merseyside and four times a year in NI to decide grants and an awards may take about three or four months in Merseyside and four or five months in NI to proceed. Applicants are welcome to contact the office to find out at which meeting their application will be considered. Unsuccessful applicants are advised to wait at least four months before re-applying.

**WHO TO APPLY TO** Phil Godfrey, Grants Director, 7th Floor, Gostins Building, 32–36 Hanover Street, Liverpool L1 4LN *Tel.* 0151 707 6077 *email* info@johnmooresfoundation.com *Website* www.jmf.org.uk

## ■ The Morel Charitable Trust (The Morel Trust)

**CC NO** 268943  **ESTABLISHED** 1972

**WHERE FUNDING CAN BE GIVEN** UK and financially developing countries.

**WHO CAN BENEFIT** Grants are normally made to projects of which the trustees have personal knowledge. Organisations benefitting people disadvantaged by poverty are prioritised, but those benefitting volunteers, people living in inner-city areas and victims of famine will be considered.

**WHAT IS FUNDED** The arts, particularly drama; organisations working for improved race relations; inner-city projects and projects in financially developing countries. Charities working in the fields of arts, culture and recreation; health; conservation and environment; education and training; and social care and development.

**WHAT IS NOT FUNDED** Individuals.

**TYPE OF GRANT** Projects grants.

**RANGE OF GRANTS** Usually £500–£5,000.

**SAMPLE GRANTS** Oxfam (£5,000); British Red Cross and LUCAS (University of Leeds) (£4,000 each); Fair Trade and Medical Aid for Palestinians (£3,000 each); Afrika Eye, Amnesty International, Pump Aid, Tree Aid and Wells for India (£2,000 each); Children in Crisis, John Wesley's Chapel and Manchester University (Museum) (£1,000 each); Fischy Music, Glamorgan House and Kidz Club Leeds (£500 each).
**FINANCES** Year 2013/14 Income £56,092 Grants £75,020 Grants to organisations £75,020 Assets £1,438,252
**TRUSTEES** Benjamin Gibbs; Dr James Gibbs; Dr Emily Parry; Simon Gibbs; Dr Thomas Gibbs; William Gibbs; Abigail Keane.
**OTHER INFORMATION** Projects supported are usually connected with places that the trustees have lived and worked, including the cities of Bristol, Leeds, Brecon and London and the countries of Ghana, Zambia, Malawi and the Solomon Islands. During the year 46 grants were awarded.
**HOW TO APPLY** Apply in writing to the correspondent. The trustees normally meet three times a year to consider applications (most recently in January, April and August).
**WHO TO APPLY TO** Simon Gibbs, Trustee, 34 Durand Gardens, London SW9 0PP *Tel.* 020 7582 6901 *email* simoned.gibbs@yahoo.co.uk

## ■ The Morgan Charitable Foundation

**CC NO** 283128     **ESTABLISHED** 1981
**WHERE FUNDING CAN BE GIVEN** UK.
**WHO CAN BENEFIT** Registered charities and institutions benefitting at risk groups and people who are disadvantaged by poverty or socially isolated.
**WHAT IS FUNDED** General charitable purposes; social welfare; health; Jewish causes; disadvantaged and socially isolated individuals. The trustees are primarily interested in social welfare causes. It has been noted in the accounts: 'The directors of the trustee maintain a list of charitable organisations which they regularly support and the list is reviewed half yearly at the directors' meeting.'
**WHAT IS NOT FUNDED** Individuals.
**TYPE OF GRANT** Capital and core costs; projects; unrestricted funding.
**RANGE OF GRANTS** £1,000–£6,000
**SAMPLE GRANTS** Most recent beneficiaries have included: Magen David Adorn (£6,000); Chai Cancer Care and In Kind Direct Charity (£4,000 each); Jewish Blind and Disabled, Jewish Care and Spanish and Portuguese Jews Congregation Charity (£3,000 each); Duke of Edinburgh Award, Limmud, Macmillan Cancer Support and The Royal Star and Garter Homes (£2,000 each); Family Planning Association, Sabin Foundation Europe and The Hinuch Trust (£1,000 each).
**FINANCES** Year 2013 Income £90,287 Grants £69,500 Grants to organisations £69,500
**TRUSTEES** Leslie Morgan; Carmen Gleen; Nelly Morgan; Ronnie Morgan; Molly Morgan.
**OTHER INFORMATION** At the time of writing (June 2015) this was the latest information available and full accounts for 2013/14 were not yet published by the Charity Commission. Based on the patterns of previous giving it is likely that grants totalled about £69,500. On average about 30 awards are made each year. Each year the annual reports note that the trustees 'hope to increase grants and donations in future years'.
**HOW TO APPLY** Applications have to be made in writing to the correspondent, providing a copy of the latest annual report and accounts. The trustees meet twice a year, usually in April and October. The foundation requests not to receive telephone enquiries.
**WHO TO APPLY TO** The Trustees, PO Box 57749, London NW11 1FD *Tel.* 07968 827709

## ■ The Morgan Foundation

**CC NO** 1087056     **ESTABLISHED** 2001
**WHERE FUNDING CAN BE GIVEN** North Wales, Merseyside, West Cheshire and North Shropshire.
**WHO CAN BENEFIT** Small to medium sized organisations; registered charities; organisations 'which are pursuing charitable causes and where aims and objectives are not-for-profit'. Preference is given to 'hands on' organisations with a high volunteer input. The website states: 'We are particularly keen to support those who have already begun to make an impact, but need a helping hand to expand their work and increase their effectiveness.' Generally an organisation must have been in existence for a minimum of two years.
**WHAT IS FUNDED** General charitable causes, with preference for health and disability, social welfare, children and young people, families and older or socially isolated individuals.
**WHAT IS NOT FUNDED** Animal welfare; arts/heritage; conservation/environment; expeditions and overseas travel; general fundraising appeals; individual and sports sponsorship; large national charities; mainstream education; promotion of specific religions; retrospective funding; local branches of national charities which are based within the remit area, or programmes delivered locally by organisations working on a national basis are not generally supported.
**TYPE OF GRANT** One-off; capital grants; start-up project costs; ongoing running expenses; projects; multi-year revenue grants for core funding; minibuses.
**RANGE OF GRANTS** £50–£500,000
**SAMPLE GRANTS** OnSide (£500,000); Wolves Aid (£300,000); Knights Community Singers (£60,500); Canal Boat Adventure (£60,000); Activate Arts (£50,000); Daffodils and Ferries Family Groups (£45,000 each); Age Integration (£37,500); Wirral (Taiko) Dragons (£36,000); New Belve Youth and Community Centre (£24,500); Rme-Vamp CIC (£19,800); Open Door Project (£17,500); Amy and Friends (£10,000); Friends Unite Newfield (£5,000); Bilbrook Youth FC (£2,000); Cancer Research (£200); Everyday Hero (£50).
**FINANCES** Year 2013/14 Income £1,165,741 Grants £2,266,197 Grants to organisations £2,266,197 Assets £13,331,713
**TRUSTEES** Stephen Morgan, Chair; Vincent Fairclough; Jennie Daly; Rhiannon Walker; Ashley Lewis.
**OTHER INFORMATION** During the year a total of 86 awards were made. The foundation also makes Morgan Foundation Entrepreneur Awards 'to recognise and support entrepreneurial spirit in fledgling businesses, young entrepreneurs, in the third sector and in individuals who have achieved against all odds'. Through Smiley Bus Awards minibuses are provided to eligible organisations to be shared with other supported groups in the community.

HOW TO APPLY Prior to making a formal appeal you should call the foundation for an informal chat. Once your eligibility has been discussed and approved you will be provided a form and asked to give some details about your organisation, your funding needs (including details and costings of a project, if you already have one) and a copy of the most recent annual report and accounts. All applications are acknowledged and all charities and projects visited before a grant is approved. The trustees meet regularly throughout the year but it may take up to six months for the process to be completed. It is suggested that unsuccessful applicants wait a year before re-applying.

WHO TO APPLY TO Jane Harris, Foundation Administrator, PO Box 3517, Chester CH1 9ET *Tel.* 01829 782800 *Fax* 01829 782223 *email* contact@morganfoundation.co.uk *Website* www.morganfoundation.co.uk

## ■ Morgan Stanley International Foundation

CC NO 1042671     ESTABLISHED 1994
WHERE FUNDING CAN BE GIVEN London boroughs of Tower Hamlets and Newham; Glasgow and overseas.
WHO CAN BENEFIT Charitable organisations, hospitals and community based initiatives.
WHAT IS FUNDED The principal objective of the foundation is to make a sustainable impact to children's welfare in disadvantaged communities across Europe, the Middle East and Africa (EMEA). Focusing primarily on child health and education, the foundation works in partnership with charitable organisations to direct funding and utilise expertise of Morgan Stanley employees to benefit the communities in which the firm operates.
WHAT IS NOT FUNDED 'The foundation does not make contributions to organisations that fall within the following criteria: organisations which are not registered as a non-profit organisation with the appropriate regulatory agencies in their country (unless a state funded school); national or international charities which do not operate in the regions we are located; political or religious organisations, 'pressure groups' or individuals outside the firm who are seeking sponsorship either for themselves (e.g. to help pay for education) or for onward transmission to a charitable organisation; programmes that do not include opportunities for employee volunteer engagement.'
RANGE OF GRANTS £2,500–£160,000
SAMPLE GRANTS Kids Company (£116,000); Great Ormond Street Hospital (£78,000); Community Links and East End Community Foundation (£52,000 each); Action For Children (£40,000); UK Career Academy Foundation (£32,000); Pilotlight (£28,000); Tower Hamlets Summer University (£25,000); Gyermeketkeztetesi Alapitvany (£24,000); Tower Hamlets Education Business Partnership (£20,000); Reliable Cancer Therapies (£14,000); Movember Europe (£12,700); Envision (£10,000); Refuge (£4,000); the Kiltwalk and Wildhearts (£2,500 each).
FINANCES Year 2013 *Income* £1,341,573 *Grants* £1,700,247 *Grants to organisations* £1,700,247 *Assets* £1,478,087
TRUSTEES Clare Woodman; Hanns Seibold; Maryann McMahon; Stephen Souchon; Malcolm Bryant; Stephen Mavin; Fergus O'Sullivan; Sue Watts;

Oliver Stuart; Kamal Jabre; Gordon Fraser; Matthew Ostrower.
HOW TO APPLY The foundation gives the following details on making an initial approach for funding: 'Morgan Stanley International Foundation takes a proactive approach to grant-making and therefore does not accept unsolicited proposals. If you think your organisation is a match for the criteria . . . send an email to: communityaffairslondon@morganstanley.com. You will then be sent the guidelines and if your organisation is successful in the first stage of application, you will be invited to complete a full proposal. Grant applications are considered quarterly and the trustees are senior representatives from across the firm's divisions.'
WHO TO APPLY TO Anish Shah, Vice President, Morgan Stanley and Co. International plc, 20 Bank Street, London E14 4AD *Tel.* 020 7425 1302 *email* communityaffairslondon@morganstanley.com *Website* www.morganstanley.com/globalcitizen/msif_guidelines.html

## ■ The Diana and Allan Morgenthau Charitable Trust

CC NO 1062180     ESTABLISHED 1997
WHERE FUNDING CAN BE GIVEN Worldwide.
WHO CAN BENEFIT Charitable organisations, with a particular interest in Jewish groups.
WHAT IS FUNDED General charitable purposes; Jewish causes; education; the arts; relief of poverty; medical causes; overseas aid.
RANGE OF GRANTS Up to £30,000.
SAMPLE GRANTS Previous beneficiaries have included: Belsize Square Synagogue (£30,000); The Central British Fund for World Jewish Relief (£18,000); The British Friends of the Jaffa Institute (£10,000); Marie Curie Cancer Care (£5,000); Holocaust Educational Trust (£4,000); Tricycle Theatre Company (£1,700); Lifelites (£1,500); Tate Foundation (£1,300); Queens' College Cambridge (£800); Grange Park Opera (£500); All Dogs Matter (£300); The Royal Marsden Hospital (£250); The Royal Free Hampstead Charities and Walk the Walk Worldwide (£150 each).
FINANCES Year 2013/14 *Income* £93,764 *Grants* £102,030 *Grants to organisations* £93,030 *Assets* £20,191
TRUSTEES Allan Morgenthau; Diana Morgenthau.
OTHER INFORMATION On average about 9% of the overall total is also given to individuals each year; based on this we estimate that about £9,000 went to individuals.
HOW TO APPLY Applications may be made in writing to the correspondent.
WHO TO APPLY TO Allan Morgenthau, Trustee, Flat 27, Berkeley House, 15 Hay Hill, London W1J 8NS *Tel.* 020 7493 1904 *email* des@baginskycohen.com

## ■ The Oliver Morland Charitable Trust

CC NO 1076213     ESTABLISHED 1999
WHERE FUNDING CAN BE GIVEN UK.
WHO CAN BENEFIT Registered charities usually chosen through personal knowledge of the trustees.
WHAT IS FUNDED Most of the funds are given to Quaker projects or Quaker-related causes.

**WHAT IS NOT FUNDED** Individuals.

**TYPE OF GRANT** Our research suggests that grants are given for core, capital and project support for up to three years.

**RANGE OF GRANTS** Up to £30,000, although most grants range between £500 and £3,000.

**SAMPLE GRANTS** **Previous beneficiaries have included:** Quaker Peace and Service (£32,500); Quaker Home Service – Children and Young People (£16,000); Woodbrooke Bursary Fund (£6,000); Pakistan Environmental Protection Foundation (£3,000); Refugee Council (£2,000); Capetown Quaker Peace Centre (£1,500); Medical Aid for Palestine (£1,000); Friends Housing Bursary Trust and Quaker Tapestry (£500 each); Brooke Animal Hospital (£300).

**FINANCES** Year 2013/14 Income £17,149 Grants £81,000 Grants to organisations £81,000

**TRUSTEES** Charlotte Jones; Priscilla Khan; Kate Lovell; Jennifer Pittard; Simon Pittard; Joseph Rutter; Simon Rutter.

**OTHER INFORMATION** Due to low income accounts were not required to be filed with the Charity Commission.

**HOW TO APPLY** The trust has previously stated the following: 'Most of our grants are for continuing support of existing beneficiaries (approximately 90%) so there is little left for responding to new appeals. We receive unsolicited applications at the rate of 6 or 7 each week, 99% are not even considered.' The Charity Commission's record notes that 'at present there is very little scope for helping new applications especially if they are beyond the West Country'.

**WHO TO APPLY TO** Joseph Rutter, Trustee, Thomas House, Stower Row, Shaftesbury, Dorset SP7 0QW Tel. 01747 853524 email jorutter@tiscali.co.uk

## ■ The Miles Morland Foundation

**CC NO** 1150755

**WHERE FUNDING CAN BE GIVEN** UK and Africa.

**WHO CAN BENEFIT** Charitable organisations and individuals.

**WHAT IS FUNDED** General charitable purposes; education and training; arts and heritage; human rights. The website states that: 'The MMF's main purpose is to support things that don't get enough support in Africa; its key interests lie in the areas of culture and education. It also supports some organisations that fight against torture and other forms of illegal state bullying.'

**RANGE OF GRANTS** £3,000–£56,000

**SAMPLE GRANTS** African Ceremonies Inc. (£56,000); Book Buzz Foundation (£40,000); African Gifted Foundation and African 95 (£25,000 each); Niger Delta Art Project (£20,000); Friends of Guy's Marsh Prison (£14,000); Mind, Tate Foundation and Flaura and Fauna International (£10,000 each); UK Youth and Young Vic (£5,000 each); The African Street Writer (£3,200).

**FINANCES** Year 2013/14 Income £432,746 Grants £388,056 Grants to organisations £334,056 Assets £10,357

**TRUSTEES** The Hon. Alice Bragg; Cornelie Ferguson; Kate Gozzi; Miles Morland.

**OTHER INFORMATION** Grants to 25 organisations totalled £334,000, £168,000 of which was given to support UK organisations. Scholarships were also made to individuals totalling £54,000.

**HOW TO APPLY** Apply in writing to the correspondent. The website states: 'If you would like to pass on information about an African educational or cultural initiative that deserves support, please e-mail the Miles Morland Foundation at MMF@milesmorlandfoundation.com. Please note that we know there are a million good causes in the world which deserve support. Please do not seek that support from the MMF unless it falls within the areas noted above as we will not have the time to review it.'

**WHO TO APPLY TO** Miles Morland, Trustee, 29 Chelsea Wharf, London SW10 0QJ Tel. 020 7349 5030 email mmf@blakman.com Website www.milesmorlandfoundation.com

## ■ S. C. and M. E. Morland's Charitable Trust

**CC NO** 201645 **ESTABLISHED** 1957

**WHERE FUNDING CAN BE GIVEN** UK.

**WHO CAN BENEFIT** Quaker, local and national registered charities which have a strong social bias and some UK-based international charities.

**WHAT IS FUNDED** Support to Quaker charities and others which the trustees have special interest in, knowledge of or association with, including religious groups, relief of poverty and ill health, promotion of peace and development overseas.

**WHAT IS NOT FUNDED** Animal welfare; individuals; medical research.

**RANGE OF GRANTS** Almost all less than £1,000 each.

**SAMPLE GRANTS** Britain Yearly Meeting (£9,000).

**FINANCES** Year 2013/14 Income £38,965 Grants £42,500 Grants to organisations £42,500 Assets £999,873

**TRUSTEES** Janet Morland; David Boyd; Victoria Morland; Rebecca Morland; Rachel Boyd.

**OTHER INFORMATION** The trust generally makes grants to charities it has supported on a long term basis but each year this list is reviewed and new charities may be added. During the year, 37 grants were made to organisations. Grants of £1,000 or less amounted to £33,500.

**HOW TO APPLY** Apply in writing to the correspondent. The trustees meet two times a year to make grants, in March and December. Applications should be submitted in the month before each meeting.

**WHO TO APPLY TO** Victoria Morland, Trustee, 14 Fairmont Terrace, Sherborne DT9 3JS email scandmemtrust@gmail.com

## ■ The Morris Charitable Trust

**CC NO** 802290 **ESTABLISHED** 1989

**WHERE FUNDING CAN BE GIVEN** UK, with a preference for Islington; overseas.

**WHO CAN BENEFIT** National, international and local community charities; community projects

**WHAT IS FUNDED** General charitable purposes, including education, community support and development, health and disability, placing particular emphasis on alleviating social hardship and deprivation. There is a preference for supporting causes within the borough of Islington.

**WHAT IS NOT FUNDED** Grants are not made for individuals and for annual, recurring running costs of organisations. Repeat donations cannot be made within 12 months.

**TYPE OF GRANT** One-off project and capital grants for one year or less are priorities.

**RANGE OF GRANTS** Generally up to £7,500; the majority of grants are under £1,000.

**669**

FINANCES Year 2013/14 Income £96,403 Grants £94,041 Grants to organisations £94,041 Assets £234,788
TRUSTEES Paul Morris; Jack Morris; Alan Stenning; Dominic Jones; Gerald Morris; Linda Morris.
PUBLICATIONS Information pamphlet.
OTHER INFORMATION A list of beneficiaries was not included within the accounts for 2013/14.
HOW TO APPLY Applications should be made on a form available from the trust or downloadable from its website. The completed form should be returned together with any supporting documentation and a copy of your latest annual report and accounts.
WHO TO APPLY TO Jack Morris, Trustee, c/o Management Office, The Business Design Centre, 52 Upper Street, Islington Green, London N1 0QH Tel. 020 7359 3535 Fax 020 7226 0590 email info@morrischaritabletrust.com Website www.morrischaritabletrust.com

## ■ The Willie and Mabel Morris Charitable Trust

CC NO 280554   ESTABLISHED 1980
WHERE FUNDING CAN BE GIVEN UK.
WHO CAN BENEFIT Registered charities, particularly those related to healthcare causes.
WHAT IS FUNDED General charitable purposes, particularly medical causes in the areas of cancer, heart trouble, spasticity, arthritis and rheumatism.
WHAT IS NOT FUNDED Grants are not made for individuals or non-registered charities.
RANGE OF GRANTS £50–£5,000
SAMPLE GRANTS Arthritis Research UK, British Liver Trust and Teenage Cancer Trust (£5,000 each); Association for International Cancer Research, Cardiac Risk in the Young and National Rheumatoid Arthritis Society (£2,500 each); Jennifer Trust (£1,000); Nettlebed Surgery Medical Trust (£700); Willow Foundation (£300); Wadebridge Food Bank (£200); Weavers Company Benevolent Fund (£100).
FINANCES Year 2013/14 Income £120,045 Grants £95,200 Grants to organisations £95,200 Assets £4,125,886
TRUSTEES Suzanne Marriott; Michael Macfadyen; Peter Tether; Angela Tether; Andrew Tether; Alan Bryant; Verity Tether.
OTHER INFORMATION There were 103 awards made during the year. The annual report and accounts for 2013/14 specify that 79% of donations (£75,000) went to medical charities. Out of this figure 42% (£31,500) of donation related to specific-illness related charities: £18,500 (25%) to cancer; £7,500 (10%) to arthritis and rheumatism; £3,000 (4%) to heart trouble; and £2,500 (3%) to spasticity.
HOW TO APPLY According to the annual report, 'trustees meet annually to review applications for funding, investment performance, income levels and the financial statements'. In between the meetings applications are also considered by the trustees.
WHO TO APPLY TO Angela Tether, 41 Field Lane, Letchworth Garden City, Hertfordshire SG6 3LD Tel. 01462 480583

## ■ The Peter Morrison Charitable Foundation

CC NO 277202   ESTABLISHED 1978
WHERE FUNDING CAN BE GIVEN UK.
WHO CAN BENEFIT About 60 registered charities have been supported annually, including organisations benefitting at risk groups, people who are disadvantaged by poverty and social isolation, animals, religious causes and education.
WHAT IS FUNDED A wide range of charitable causes can be assisted.
RANGE OF GRANTS £50–£10,000
SAMPLE GRANTS In the past support has been given to: Hawk Conservancy Trust Ltd (£10,300); London Philharmonic Orchestra (£7,600); World Jewish Relief (£3,000); Alzheimer's Society and The Donkey Sanctuary (£1,000 each); Royal British Legion (£200); Nightingale House (£100).
FINANCES Year 2013/14 Income £21,902 Grants £40,000 Grants to organisations £40,000
TRUSTEES Ian Morrison; Maxwell Morrison; Louise Greenhill; Jane Morrison.
OTHER INFORMATION Due to low income accounts were not required to be filed with the Charity Commission.
HOW TO APPLY Apply in writing to the correspondent.
WHO TO APPLY TO J. Payne, Begbies Chartered Accountants, 9 Bonhill Street, London EC2A 4DJ Tel. 020 7628 5801 email admin@begbiesaccountants.co.uk

## ■ G. M. Morrison Charitable Trust

CC NO 261380   ESTABLISHED 1970
WHERE FUNDING CAN BE GIVEN UK.
WHO CAN BENEFIT Registered charities only.
WHAT IS FUNDED A wide variety of activities in the social welfare, medical and education/training fields. The trustees give priority to those charities already supported. Very few charities are added to the list each year.
WHAT IS NOT FUNDED Individuals; charities not registered in the UK; retrospective applications; schemes or activities which are generally regarded as the responsibility of statutory authorities; commercial or business activities; short-term projects; or one-off capital grants (except for emergency appeals).
TYPE OF GRANT Mostly recurrent annual awards for core costs.
RANGE OF GRANTS £675 to £4,000. In 2013/14 the average grant was £912.
SAMPLE GRANTS British Red Cross – Typhoon Haiyan and The Somerset Community Foundation (£4,000 each); Royal College of Surgeons (£2,500); International Medical Corps UK, Royal Society of Arts Endowment Fund and Shelterbox (£2,200 each); Oxfam Syrian Appeal (£2,000); Age UK and University of Cambridge (£1,400 each); Psychiatry Research Trust, Royal Academy of Music and St Luke's Hospital for the Clergy (£1,200 each); Child in Need India, Deptford Action Group for the Elderly and Refugee Council Day Centre (£1,100 each); Help the Hospices, Mental Health Foundation, Family Holiday Association and WaterAid (£1,000 each); Catch 22 and Contact the Elderly (£900 each); The Bipolar Organisation and Missionaries of Africa (£800 each); Elizabeth Finn Care, Royal British Legion and Salmon Youth Centre (£700 each).

FINANCES Year 2013/14 Income £326,386
Grants £208,875 Grants to organisations
£208,875 Assets £116,003,797

TRUSTEES N. Smith; Anthony Cornick; Jane Hunt; Elizabeth Morrison.

OTHER INFORMATION In 2013/14 the trust made 229 grants.

HOW TO APPLY The trust's annual report for 2013/14 states: 'Beneficiaries of grants are normally selected on the basis of the personal knowledge and recommendation of a trustee. The Trust's grant making policy is, however, to support the recipient of grants on a long term recurring basis. The scope of its giving is determined only by the extent of its resources, and is not otherwise restricted. The trustees have decided that for the present, new applications for grants will only be considered in the most exceptional circumstances, any spare income will be allocated to increasing the grants made to charities currently receiving support. In the future this policy will of course be subject to periodic review. Applicants understanding this policy who nevertheless wish to apply for a grant should write to the [correspondent].' Note that applications are not acknowledged and awards are normally made in January each year. Grants are monitored by assessment of annual reports and accounts.

WHO TO APPLY TO Anthony Cornick, Trustee, c/o Currey and Co, 21 Buckingham Gate, London SW1E 6LS Tel. 020 7802 2700 email gen@curreyandco.co.uk

## ■ The Moshal Charitable Trust

CC NO 284448   ESTABLISHED 1981

WHERE FUNDING CAN BE GIVEN UK.

WHO CAN BENEFIT Charitable organisations and educational establishments.

WHAT IS FUNDED General charitable purposes, particularly Jewish causes.

SAMPLE GRANTS The trust's accounts are routinely basic; therefore no sample grants were available for 2013/14.

FINANCES Year 2013/14 Income £112,292
Grants £78,688 Grants to organisations £78,688 Assets £381,755

TRUSTEES David Halpern; Lea Halpern.

HOW TO APPLY Applications may be made in writing to the correspondent.

WHO TO APPLY TO Sefton Yodaiken, Correspondent, 40A Bury New Road, Prestwich, Manchester M25 0LD email sy@seyo.co.uk

## ■ Vyoel Moshe Charitable Trust

CC NO 327054   ESTABLISHED 1986

WHERE FUNDING CAN BE GIVEN UK and overseas, including Israel, USA and Europe.

WHO CAN BENEFIT Registered charities; religious bodies; individuals.

WHAT IS FUNDED Education; religion; relief of poverty; with focus on Jewish causes. According to the latest accounts, 'institutions are worldwide and are assisted with financial grants over and above of what is available to them locally'. Awards to individuals are given 'to financially deprived families, at Jewish holiday times and other special occasions'.

RANGE OF GRANTS Generally £7,500–£25,000.

SAMPLE GRANTS Tov V'chesed (£60,000); Toldos Aharon (£25,000); Chesed Leavrohom, Chinuch Jerusalem Mishkanos Haroyim, Rabbinical Kolel Nachlas Moshe, Toldos Aharon Beis Shemes

and UTA of Monsey (£20,000 each). Awards under £20,000 totalled £837,000.

FINANCES Year 2013/14 Income £953,905
Grants £1,041,800 Grants to organisations £971,800 Assets £175,737

TRUSTEES Jacob Frankel; Berish Berger; S. Seidenfeld.

OTHER INFORMATION There were 50 organisational awards in 2013/14. Support was allocated as follows: Israel (£510,000); USA (£74,500); Europe (£27,500); UK (£7,500). Grants were given in the following categories: education (£619,500); poor and needy (£245,000); advancement of religion (£107,500); individuals (£70,000). Grants to religious bodies ranged from £10,000 to £20,000 and included grants to synagogues and for the preservation of graves.

HOW TO APPLY Applications can be made in writing to the correspondent. The accounts, however, state: 'In general the trustees select the institutions to be supported according to their personal knowledge of work of the institution. Any application is carefully considered and help given according to circumstances and funds then available. Applications by individuals must be accompanied by a letter of recommendation by the applicant's minister or other known religious leader.'

WHO TO APPLY TO Sholem Cik, Trustee, 2–4 Chardmore Road, London N16 6HX

## ■ The Moshulu Charitable Trust

CC NO 1071479   ESTABLISHED 1998

WHERE FUNDING CAN BE GIVEN UK.

WHO CAN BENEFIT Charitable organisations and individuals involved in humanitarian or evangelical work.

WHAT IS FUNDED Humanitarian and evangelical causes.

TYPE OF GRANT 'Modest grants'.

RANGE OF GRANTS Generally £100–£10,000.

SAMPLE GRANTS Previous beneficiaries have included: Tanzania (almost £57,000); SWYM (£9,200); Christ Church (£6,900); Tear Fund (£4,800); Care for the Family (£2,400); Seaway Trust (£2,000); Open Door Centre (£1,200); Partnership UK (£1,000); Vineyard Christian Fellowship (£200).

FINANCES Year 2013/14 Income £36,883
Grants £42,000 Grants to organisations £42,000

TRUSTEES Henry Fulls; D. M. Fulls; G. N. Fulls; S. M. Fulls; G. F. Symons.

OTHER INFORMATION Due to low income accounts were not required to be filed with the Charity Commission.

HOW TO APPLY Apply in writing to the correspondent.

WHO TO APPLY TO Henry Fulls, Trustee, Devonshire Road, Heathpark, Honiton, Devon EX14 1SD Tel. 01404 540770 email henry.fulls@moshulu.co.uk

## ■ Brian and Jill Moss Charitable Trust

CC NO 1084664   ESTABLISHED 2000

WHERE FUNDING CAN BE GIVEN Worldwide.

WHO CAN BENEFIT Registered charities only.

WHAT IS FUNDED Jewish causes, healthcare.

WHAT IS NOT FUNDED Donations are made to registered charities only.

TYPE OF GRANT Capital projects and towards 'ordinary charity expenditure'.

SAMPLE GRANTS **Previous beneficiaries have included:** Cancer Bacup, Chai Cancer Care; Holocaust Centre; Israel Folk Dance Institute; Jewish Association for the Mentally Ill; Jewish Care; Jewish Museum; Magen David Adom UK; Myeloma UK; National Jewish Chaplaincy Board; Norwood; Operation Wheelchairs; United Jewish Israel Appeal; Prostate Cancer Charitable Trust; United Synagogue-Tribe, WIZO UK; World Jewish Relief.

FINANCES Year 2013/14 Income £219,939 Grants £179,000 Grants to organisations £179,000 Assets £3,711,054

TRUSTEES Brian Peter Moss; Jill Moss; David Paul Moss; Sarah Levy.

HOW TO APPLY Apply in writing to the correspondent. Applications are considered as they are received and the trustees will make donations throughout the year.

WHO TO APPLY TO Private Client Services, c/o Deloitte LLP, 5 Callaghan Square, Cardiff CF10 5BT Tel. 029 2026 4391

## ■ The Moss Family Charitable Trust

CC NO 327529 ESTABLISHED 1987

WHERE FUNDING CAN BE GIVEN England and Wales.

WHO CAN BENEFIT Mainly Jewish organisations.

WHAT IS FUNDED General charitable purposes with preference given to Jewish causes.

WHAT IS NOT FUNDED Music or the arts.

RANGE OF GRANTS Usually £100–£8,000.

SAMPLE GRANTS **Previous beneficiaries have included:** The Children's Charity; Hammerson House; Jewish Child's Day; Norwood; Presidents Club; West London Synagogue.

FINANCES Year 2013/14 Income £115,014 Grants £123,981 Grants to organisations £123,981 Assets £4,150

TRUSTEES Stephen Moss; Roger Moss; Virginia Campus.

HOW TO APPLY Apply in writing to the correspondent. Our research indicates that the trust is unlikely to respond to unsolicited applications.

WHO TO APPLY TO K. Sage, Correspondent, 28 Bolton Street, Mayfair, London W1J 8BP Tel. 020 7491 5108 email kevinsage@grosvenorsecurities.com

## ■ Mosselson Charitable Trust

CC NO 266517 ESTABLISHED 1974

WHERE FUNDING CAN BE GIVEN UK.

WHO CAN BENEFIT Charitable organisations.

WHAT IS FUNDED Education; medicine and medical research; women and children's support and welfare; religion; social welfare.

SAMPLE GRANTS Beneficiaries have included: ChildLine; Holocaust Education Trust; Jewish Women's Week; Family Housing Association; Nightingale House; Shaare Zedek Medical Centre.

FINANCES Year 2012/13 Income £492,889 Grants £105,706 Grants to organisations £105,706 Assets £2,618,101

TRUSTEES Dennis Mosselson; Marian Mosselson.

OTHER INFORMATION At the time of writing (June 2015) these were the latest accounts available for the trust. The trust's 2012/13 annual report states that its long-term goal is to establish a Student Scholarship Programme at graduate level to provide financial assistance in various fields of study, with an emphasis on higher education.

HOW TO APPLY Apply in writing to the correspondent.

WHO TO APPLY TO Dennis Mosselson, Trustee, Denmoss House, 10 Greenland Street, London NW1 0ND Tel. 020 7428 1929

## ■ Mothercare Group Foundation

CC NO 1104386 ESTABLISHED 2004

WHERE FUNDING CAN BE GIVEN UK and worldwide.

WHO CAN BENEFIT Health and well-being of children and their mothers.

WHAT IS FUNDED Registered charities and research organisations that promote the general well-being of children and their mothers; offering them the very best chance of good health, education, well-being and a secure start in life. Specifically, the foundation welcomes applications from registered charities and research organisations associated with the following criteria: ensuring the good health and well-being of mums-to-be, new mums and their children; special baby-care needs and premature births; other parenting initiatives relating to family well-being.

WHAT IS NOT FUNDED No response to circular appeals. Support is not given to: animal welfare, appeals from individuals, the arts, older people, environment/heritage, religious appeals, political appeals, or sport.

SAMPLE GRANTS **Previous beneficiaries have included:** Anthony Nolan Trust, the Healing Foundation, KIDS, Meningitis Research Foundation, PHG Foundation, Wellbeing of Women, Wellchild and University of Bristol.

FINANCES Year 2013/14 Income £44,455 Grants £0 Grants to organisations £0 Assets £65,814

TRUSTEES Lynne Medini; Tim Ashby.

HOW TO APPLY Apply in writing to the correspondent. Requests for donations will only be considered when made in writing on the application form that can be printed from the company's website. Applications are considered on a quarterly basis. Unsolicited appeals are unlikely to be successful.

WHO TO APPLY TO Lynne Medini, Trustee, Mothercare plc, Cherry Tree Road, Watford, Hertfordshire WD24 6SH Tel. 01923 206186 Website www.mothercareplc.com/charity

## ■ Moto in the Community

CC NO 1111147 ESTABLISHED 2005

WHERE FUNDING CAN BE GIVEN Communities local to the 57 Moto service areas around the UK (details of stations can be found on the website).

WHO CAN BENEFIT Community groups and charities.

WHAT IS FUNDED Community development and road safety.

WHAT IS NOT FUNDED The promotion of religion or politics; overseas applications.

RANGE OF GRANTS There is no fixed minimum or maximum amount for grants.

SAMPLE GRANTS Help for Heroes (£189,000); The Bewbush Academy (£2,000); Padbury Preschool (£1,800); Hanging Heaton School (£1,200); Rotary Club of Flitwick (£1,000); Darton College (£750); Rotary Club of South Cotswolds (£500); Hospice at Home (£400); Moto Leigh West (£100).

FINANCES Year 2013 Income £478,677 Grants £218,322 Grants to organisations £211,472 Assets £447,089

TRUSTEES Brian Lotts; Christopher Rogers; Brian Larkin; Helen Budd; Malcolm Plowes; Ashleigh

Lewis; Ian Kernighan; Jon Shore; Nicholas Brokes; Gene MacDonald; Julie Sturgess; Coral Brodie; Guy Latchem; Gavin Sanders; Brynn Hewitt.

**OTHER INFORMATION** 27 community grants totalling £22,500 were made during the year, along with one major grant to Moto's Charity of the Year, Help for Heroes. A further £6,900 was paid in nine benevolent grants in support of Moto employees and their dependants facing hardship. The charity runs an 'Adopted Schools' scheme, by which individual Moto sites partner and support a local school in their area.

**HOW TO APPLY** Organisations interested in becoming a local community partner should email their information to motocharity@talking360.com, stating the Moto service area to which they would like to apply. The application should state details of your organisation's long and short-term objectives, as well as how Moto staff can work with you. Partnerships run from 1 January to 31 December and applications are accepted throughout the year. You may be invited to present information on your charity to Moto staff. If you wish to discuss the community partner scheme, you may contact Moto in the Community by email (motocharity@talking360.com) or by telephone (01525 714 467). Further guidelines are available from the website.

**WHO TO APPLY TO** Suzanne Hollinshead, Moto Hospitality Limited, Toddington Service Area, Junction 12 M1 Southbound, Toddington, Bedfordshire LU5 6HR *Tel.* 01525 878500 *email* motocharity@moto-way.co.uk *Website* www.motointhecommunity.co.uk

## ■ British Motor Sports Training Trust

**CC NO** 273828  **ESTABLISHED** 1977
**WHERE FUNDING CAN BE GIVEN** UK
**WHO CAN BENEFIT** Organisations involved with motor sports.
**WHAT IS FUNDED** Education and training in techniques to prevent and reduce the incidence and severity of accidents in motor sports.
**RANGE OF GRANTS** From around £1,000 to £16,000.
**SAMPLE GRANTS** British Motorsport Marshals Club (£15,900); ATLS Lister (£11,500); Association of Motorsport Recovery Operators (£10,100); British Automobile Racing Club (£8,700); Solway Car Club and West of Scotland Kart Club (£5,000 each); Association of Motorsport Recovery Operators (£3,800); Bo'ness Hillclimb Revival (£3,000); Sarnia Rescue (£2,400); Association of Eastern Motor Clubs (£2,100); Kirby Lonsdale Motor Club (£1,300); Trent Valley Cart Club (£1,100).
**FINANCES** *Year* 2014 *Income* £206,358 *Grants* £218,782 *Grants to organisations* £218,782 *Assets* £4,172,318
**TRUSTEES** Alan Gow; Nicky Moffitt; Rob Jones; Anthony Andrews; Rt Hon the Lord Rooker; Nick Bunting.
**OTHER INFORMATION** During the year, £148,000 was given in grants towards training programmes and equipment and a further £71,000 in rescue development grants.
**HOW TO APPLY** Apply in writing to the correspondent.
**WHO TO APPLY TO** Allan Dean-Lewis, Secretary, Motor Sport House, Riverside Park, Colnbrook, Berkshire SL3 0HG *Tel.* 01753 765000 *Website* www.msauk.org

## ■ J. P. Moulton Charitable Foundation

**CC NO** 1109891  **ESTABLISHED** 2005
**WHERE FUNDING CAN BE GIVEN** UK
**WHO CAN BENEFIT** Registered charities; research institutions; universities; hospitals and hospices.
**WHAT IS FUNDED** Medical research and care; education and training; counselling; community service projects; the general relief of suffering.
**TYPE OF GRANT** One-off and recurrent.
**RANGE OF GRANTS** Up to £190,000.
**SAMPLE GRANTS** Great Ormond Street Hospital (£188,000); University of Manchester (£143,000); King's College London (£131,500); University College London (£128,500); Leukaemia and Lymphoma (£79,000); UCL Malcolm Grant Scholarship (£50,000); Myasthenia Gravis Association (£39,000); Guys and St Thomas Charity (£13,200); Hospice in the Weald (£10,000); The Connection at St Martin in the Field (£5,000); Allergy UK (£2,000); Macmillan Cancer Support (£1,000); Beat and Changing Faces (£500 each); Charity Staff Foundation and Sovereign Art Foundation – Guernsey (£250).
**FINANCES** *Year* 2013 *Income* £26,419 *Grants* £795,418 *Grants to organisations* £795,418 *Assets* £1,265,791
**TRUSTEES** Jon Moulton; Spencer Moulton; Sara Everett.
**HOW TO APPLY** Apply in writing to the correspondent.
**WHO TO APPLY TO** Jon Moulton, Trustee, c/o Better Capital LLP, 39–41 Charing Cross Road, London WC2H 0AR *Tel.* 020 7440 0860

## ■ The Mount Everest Foundation

**CC NO** 208206  **ESTABLISHED** 1955
**WHERE FUNDING CAN BE GIVEN** The majority of expedition members must come from Great Britain or New Zealand.
**WHO CAN BENEFIT** Expeditions.
**WHAT IS FUNDED** The exploration of, and scientific work in, the world's mountain regions.
**WHAT IS NOT FUNDED** Our research indicates that youth, training and commercial expeditions are not eligible. Retrospective grants are never given.
**TYPE OF GRANT** Project.
**RANGE OF GRANTS** £1,000 to £6,900
**FINANCES** *Year* 2013/14 *Income* £115,400 *Grants* £61,400 *Grants to organisations* £61,400 *Assets* £1,401,000
**TRUSTEES** Doug Scott; Dr Andy Hodson; Luke Hughes; Sqn Ldr Colin Scott; Alasdair McLeod; Dr Mike Smith; John Porter; Peter Holden; Sash Tusa.
**PUBLICATIONS** A map of Central Asia has been produced in collaboration with the Royal Geographical Society.
**OTHER INFORMATION** Grants were made for 29 expeditions during the year, totalling £58,400. A further £3,000 was given to the Alpine Journal.
**HOW TO APPLY** Application forms, guidelines and criteria are available to download from the website and should be returned to the correspondent by email. Deadlines for receipt of completed application forms are 30 September and 31 January, to be considered in November and March respectively. One or more members of the expedition may be asked to attend an interview with the Screening Committee in London.

**WHO TO APPLY TO** Glyn Hughes, Hon Secretary, 73 Church Street, Chesham, Bucks HP5 1HY *Tel.* 01494 792073 *email* glynhughes@waitrose.com *Website* www.mef.org.uk

## ■ The Edwina Mountbatten and Leonora Children's Foundation (formerly The Edwina Mountbatten Trust)

**CC NO** 228166 **ESTABLISHED** 1960
**WHERE FUNDING CAN BE GIVEN** UK and overseas.
**WHO CAN BENEFIT** Registered charities; hospitals; hospices.
**WHAT IS FUNDED** Save the Children; expansion of the work of the Order of St John; nursing; primary research into causes of paediatric cancer; the support of nurses caring for children with cancer.
**WHAT IS NOT FUNDED** Research; individual nurses working in the UK for further professional training.
**TYPE OF GRANT** Project grants.
**RANGE OF GRANTS** £3,000 to £40,000
**SAMPLE GRANTS** Save the Children (£40,000); Rainbow Trust and St John of Jerusalem Eye Hospital (£35,000 each); Teenage Cancer Trust (£25,000); Brecknock Hospice (£20,000); Gift of Sight (£10,000); InterCare Medical Aid for Africa and Ripple Africa (£5,000 each); World Child Cancer (£3,000).
**FINANCES** *Year* 2014 *Income* £204,498 *Grants* £173,000 *Grants to organisations* £173,000 *Assets* £5,769,606
**TRUSTEES** Countess Mountbatten of Burma; Hon. Alexandra Knatchbull; Peter Mimpriss; Dame Mary Fagan; Lady Brabourne; Myrddin Rees; Sir Evelyn de Rothschild.
**OTHER INFORMATION** Nine organisations were supported during the year.
**HOW TO APPLY** Details of how to apply for grants can be obtained from the foundation's Secretary. The trustees meet once a year, generally in September/October.
**WHO TO APPLY TO** John Moss, Secretary, Estate Office, Broadlands, Romsey, Hampshire SO51 9ZE *Tel.* 01794 529750

## ■ Mrs Waterhouse Charitable Trust (formerly known as the Houghton Dunn Charitable Trust)

**CC NO** 261685 **ESTABLISHED** 1967
**WHERE FUNDING CAN BE GIVEN** UK, with an interest in north west England and particularly the Lancashire area.
**WHO CAN BENEFIT** Registered charities only.
**WHAT IS FUNDED** General charitable purposes, and particularly the areas of medicine, health, community welfare, environment and wildlife, and churches and heritage.
**WHAT IS NOT FUNDED** Individuals.
**SAMPLE GRANTS** Previous beneficiaries have included: AMEND, Arthritis Research Campaign, Cancer BACUP, Cancer Research UK, Christie Hospital NHS Trust, East Lancashire Hospice Fund, Lancashire Wildlife Trust, Marie Curie Cancer Care, Macmillan Cancer Relief, National Eczema Society, National Trust Lake District Appeal and National Youth Orchestra.
**FINANCES** *Year* 2013/14 *Income* £306,283 *Grants* £302,000 *Grants to organisations* £302,000 *Assets* £7,579,960
**TRUSTEES** Alistair Houghton Dunn; Richard Houghton Dunn.
**OTHER INFORMATION** During the year, 26 charities were supported. Of the grant total, charities based in the North West received £125,000, with a further £45,000 awarded to national charities with North West-based projects.
**HOW TO APPLY** Apply in writing to the correspondent.
**WHO TO APPLY TO** Mark Dunn, Correspondent, Carlton Place, 28–32 Greenwood Street, Altrincham WA14 1RZ *email* markdunnamalg@btconnect.com

## ■ The MSE Charity

**CC NO** 1121320 **ESTABLISHED** 2007
**WHERE FUNDING CAN BE GIVEN** UK
**WHO CAN BENEFIT** Projects and organisations aiming to eradicate financial illiteracy through self-development or innovative projects. There is a preference for small to medium-sized organisations with an annual income of less than £500,000.
**WHAT IS FUNDED** Financial literacy; money management education; debt avoidance.
**WHAT IS NOT FUNDED** Projects which only provide debt advice/management; core funding for an organisation; capital equipment such as laptops, projectors or other electronics is not normally funded.
**TYPE OF GRANT** Full project cost recovery.
**RANGE OF GRANTS** Up to £5,000.
**SAMPLE GRANTS** Chesterfield and North East Derbyshire Credit Union/Chesterfield Citizens Advice, Nairn Citizens Advice and Saffron Lane Neighbourhood Council (£5,000 each); Ponthafren Association (£4,700); Warm Hut UK (£4,600); Family Matters York – York Community Family Trust (£4,100); Nottingham Women's Centre (£3,900); Southwark Muslim Women's Association (£1,200).
**FINANCES** *Year* 2013/14 *Income* £86,356 *Grants* £91,303 *Grants to organisations* £91,303 *Assets* £159,520
**TRUSTEES** Tony Tesciuba; John Hewison; Katie Birkett; Vanessa Bissessur; Teej Dew.
**HOW TO APPLY** Applications must be made via the online application form. There are extensive criteria listed on the website, along with guidance notes which can be downloaded. The charity is open to applications for a month three times a year, usually January, May and September; check the website for upcoming deadlines. The application round will close either after a month or once 40 completed applications have been received, whichever is the earlier. After a provisional eligibility check the application will be given to the Grant Approval Panel, which meets three times a year. Only one application will be accepted from an organisation within a two year period. Funding can only be given to constituted groups. If your group is not constituted, contact the Operations Manager (stuart@msecharity.org), who can put you in touch with people who can help. If you have a project you consider to be special that fits the charity's educational aims but does not fall within the criteria listed on the website, submit the online form and then write directly via email to the Operations Manager, who will bring it to the attention of the trustees.
**WHO TO APPLY TO** The Operations Manager, PO Box 240, Gatley, Cheadle SK8 4XT *email* stuart@msecharity.com *Website* www.msecharity.com

## ■ The Mugdock Children's Trust

**SC NO** SC006001 **ESTABLISHED** 1920
**WHERE FUNDING CAN BE GIVEN** Scotland.
**WHO CAN BENEFIT** Charities benefitting children up to the age of around 14 who are ill or have disabilities.
**WHAT IS FUNDED** 'Poor children from Glasgow or other districts of Scotland who are in need of convalescent treatment for sickness or any other disability; organisations of a charitable nature whose objects either consist of or include the provision in Scotland of rehabilitation, recreation or education for children convalescing or still suffering from the effects of illness, injury or disability; organisations of a charitable nature whose objects either consist of or include the provision in Scotland of accommodation or facilities for children who are in need of care or assistance.'
**RANGE OF GRANTS** Usually around £500 to £6,000.
**SAMPLE GRANTS Previous beneficiaries have included:** Abercorn School; Ark Trust; Barnardo's; Camphill Foundation; Cancer and Leukaemia in Childhood; Children First; Children's Heart Federation; Glasgow Children's Holiday Playscheme; Hopscotch Holidays Ltd; Sense; Sighthill Youth Centre; Stepping Stones for Families; Wanderers Youth Club and West Scotland Deaf Children's Society.
**FINANCES** Year 2013/14 Income £54,984 Grants £60,000 Grants to organisations £60,000
**TRUSTEES** Graham A. Philips; Rosamund Blair; Moira Bruce; Dr Anne Cowan; Joyce Duguid; Avril Meighan; Alastair J. Struthers; Christine Brown; James Morris.
**OTHER INFORMATION** In 2013/14 the trust had a total expenditure of £63,000.
**HOW TO APPLY** Application forms are available from the correspondent. The trustees meet in March and November.
**WHO TO APPLY TO** Mrs J. Simpson, Secretary, Wylie and Bisset Accountants, 168 Bath Street, Glasgow G2 4TP *Tel.* 0141 566 7000

## ■ The Mulberry Trust

**CC NO** 263296 **ESTABLISHED** 1971
**WHERE FUNDING CAN BE GIVEN** UK, with an interest in Essex.
**WHO CAN BENEFIT** Charitable organisations; hospices.
**WHAT IS FUNDED** General charitable purposes, particularly: education and research; people who are disadvantaged; parenting, the family and children's work; health; the Christian church and leadership; community and the environment; debt relief and counselling; homelessness; the arts; older people.
**WHAT IS NOT FUNDED** Individuals.
**RANGE OF GRANTS** Up to £75,000. The majority of grants are of around £5,000 or less.
**SAMPLE GRANTS** Red Balloon of the Air (£75,000); NSPCC (£46,000); Prison Dialogue (£35,000); Harlow Parochial Church Council – St Mary's Church (£29,000); Harlow Citizens Advice (£25,000); Shelter – Essex (£20,000); National Theatre (£15,000); Grandparents Plus (£10,000); Disability Challenges (£7,800); The Lambeth Partnership (£6,000); Home Start Uttlesford (£5,000); InterAct Reading Service (£4,000); St Francis Hospice (£3,000); King George's Fund for Sailors and Williams Syndrome Foundation (£1,000 each).
**FINANCES** Year 2013/14 Income £162,679 Grants £723,254 Grants to organisations £723,254 Assets £4,620,411
**TRUSTEES** Ann Marks; Charles Woodhouse; Timothy Marks; Chris Marks; Rupert Marks; William Marks.
**OTHER INFORMATION** During the year, grants were made to 80 organisations.
**HOW TO APPLY** The trust has previously stated that it 'will not, as a matter of policy, consider applications which are unsolicited'.
**WHO TO APPLY TO** Cheryl Boyce, Farrer and Co, 66 Lincoln's Inn Fields, London WC2A 3LH *Tel.* 020 3375 7000 *email* secretarialservices@farrer.co.uk

## ■ Frederick Mulder Charitable Trust (formerly the Prairie Trust)

**CC NO** 296019 **ESTABLISHED** 1987
**WHERE FUNDING CAN BE GIVEN** Worldwide.
**WHO CAN BENEFIT** Charitable organisations.
**WHAT IS FUNDED** Social change philanthropy; climate change; global poverty.
**TYPE OF GRANT** One-off and recurrent grants of up to two years.
**RANGE OF GRANTS** Generally £2,500 to £30,000.
**SAMPLE GRANTS** The Funding Network (£159,500); Academics Stand Against Poverty and Just for Kids Law (£30,000 each); Playback Theatre Southwest (£27,000); Greenpeace Environmental Trust (£25,000); Results Educational Fund (£15,200); Oxfam Enterprise Development (£10,000); Human Rights Watch (£9,600); Global Education Platform (£8,900); Institute for Philanthropy (£6,300); Peace Brigades International (£5,000); Sheila McKechnie Foundation (£2,500).
**FINANCES** Year 2013/14 Income £229,473 Grants £472,358 Grants to organisations £472,358 Assets £7,287,307
**TRUSTEES** Dr Frederick Mulder; Hannah Mulder; Robin Bowman; Rhodes Pinto.
**OTHER INFORMATION** The trust supports many small social change organisations around the world through The Funding Network, which was founded by Frederick Mulder.
**HOW TO APPLY** The trust does not accept unsolicited applications or enquiries, but rather is proactive in identifying organisations and individuals within its areas of interest.
**WHO TO APPLY TO** Emma Bianchi, Correspondent, 83 Belsize Park Gardens, London NW3 4NJ *Tel.* 020 7722 9628 *email* emma@frederickmulderfoundation.org.uk *Website* www.frederickmulderfoundation.org.uk

## ■ The Edith Murphy Foundation

**CC NO** 1026062 **ESTABLISHED** 1993
**WHERE FUNDING CAN BE GIVEN** UK, with a preference for Leicestershire and the East Midlands.
**WHO CAN BENEFIT** Mainly national charities and organisations based in Leicestershire and the East Midlands.
**WHAT IS FUNDED** Support has been given to organisations working to benefit people who are young, older, disabled, homeless or sick, as well as to animal charities.
**WHAT IS NOT FUNDED** Individuals.
**TYPE OF GRANT** One-off and recurrent.
**RANGE OF GRANTS** Up to £50,000. Most grants are between £500 and £5,000.
**SAMPLE GRANTS** NSPCC (£50,000); Build IT International (£40,000); Leicester Cathedral

(£25,000); PDSA (£24,500 in two grants); Cancer Research UK (£24,000); Scropton Riding for Disabled (£16,500); Healing Little Hearts and National Forest Charitable Trust (£15,000); Age UK, East Anglian Air Services, Guide Dogs and Leicester Children's Holiday Centre (£10,000 each).

**FINANCES** Year 2013/14 Income £834,358 Grants £1,044,404 Grants to organisations £1,044,404 Assets £32,557,988

**TRUSTEES** David Tams; Pamela Breakwell; Christopher Blakesley; Richard Adkinson.

**OTHER INFORMATION** During the year, 186 grants were made to organisations. Grants of less than £10,000 each totalled £540,000.

**HOW TO APPLY** Applications should be made in writing to the correspondent. Email applications are not accepted and enquiries by email are discouraged.

**WHO TO APPLY TO** Richard Adkinson, Trustee, c/o Crane and Walton, 113–117 London Road, Leicester LE2 0RG *Tel.* 0116 255 1901 *email* richard.adkinson@btinternet.com *Website* www.edithmurphy.co.uk

## ■ Murphy-Neumann Charity Company Limited

**CC NO** 229555  **ESTABLISHED** 1963
**WHERE FUNDING CAN BE GIVEN** UK
**WHO CAN BENEFIT** Registered charities only.
**WHAT IS FUNDED** The charity has three main objects: to support projects aimed at helping those in society who suffer economic or social disadvantages or hardship arising from disability and/or social exclusion; to assist those working to alleviate chronic illness and disabling disease; to help fund research into medical conditions (particularly among the very young and the elderly) for which there is not yet a cure.
**WHAT IS NOT FUNDED** Individuals, or non-registered charities.
**TYPE OF GRANT** One-off and recurrent grants for general costs (large charities) and specific projects (smaller organisations).
**RANGE OF GRANTS** £500–£2,500
**SAMPLE GRANTS** Argus Appeal (£2,000); Acorn Villages Ltd (£1,500); The Haemophilia Society (£1,250); North London Hospice (£1,000); Scope (£750); The Research Institute for the Care of Older People (£500).
**FINANCES** Year 2013/14 Income £75,925 Grants £56,250 Grants to organisations £56,250 Assets £1,760,072
**TRUSTEES** Mark Lockett; Paula Christopher; Marcus Richman.
**OTHER INFORMATION** The majority of grants fall within the £750–£2,000 range.
**HOW TO APPLY** Apply in writing to the correspondent, in a letter outlining the purpose of the required charitable donation. Telephone calls are not welcome. There are no application forms, guidelines or deadlines. No sae is required. Grants are usually given in November and December. Printed grant criteria is available on request.
**WHO TO APPLY TO** Mark Lockett, Trustee, Hayling Cottage, Upper Street, Stratford St Mary, Colchester, Essex CO7 6JW *Tel.* 01206 323685 *email* mncc@keme.co.uk

## ■ The John R. Murray Charitable Trust

**CC NO** 1100199  **ESTABLISHED** 2003
**WHERE FUNDING CAN BE GIVEN** UK.
**WHO CAN BENEFIT** Registered charities.
**WHAT IS FUNDED** Arts and literature (although not strictly limited to such areas) and where the award of a grant will have an immediate and tangible benefit to the recipient in question.
**RANGE OF GRANTS** Between £100 and £40,000, though grants are occasionally made.
**SAMPLE GRANTS** National Library of Scotland (£150,000); Jane Austen Memorial Trust (£100,000); River Lea Tidal Mill Trust (£40,000); Sir John Soane's Museum (£35,000); Smile, Support and Care and Tate Gallery (£30,000); Council for Assisting Refugee Academics (£20,500); Gainsborough House Society, Linnean Society and St Mungo's Community Housing Association (£15,000 each); Nottingham Trent University, Scott Polar Research Institute and Trailblazers Mentoring (£10,000 each); Host UK (£5,000); Prison Fellowship (£4,500); Balliol College (£2,000); DEC Philippines Typhoon Appeal (£1,000); King's College London (£500); Art Fund (£100).
**FINANCES** Year 2013 Income £918,822 Grants £2,113,266 Grants to organisations £2,113,266 Assets £25,617,773
**TRUSTEES** John Murray; Virginia Murray; Hallam Murray; John Grey Murray; Charles Grey Murray.
**OTHER INFORMATION** A total of 49 grants were made during the year. One major grant of £1.15 million to the Abbotsford Trust accounted for more than half of the grant total.
**HOW TO APPLY** The trustees will not consider unsolicited applications for grants.
**WHO TO APPLY TO** John Murray, Trustee, 50 Albemarle Street, London W1S 4BD *Tel.* 020 7493 4361

## ■ The Music Sales Charitable Trust

**CC NO** 1014942  **ESTABLISHED** 1992
**WHERE FUNDING CAN BE GIVEN** UK, but mostly Bury St Edmunds and London.
**WHO CAN BENEFIT** Registered charities.
**WHAT IS FUNDED** General charitable purposes, including: health; arts and culture; education and training; religion; overseas and famine relief; disability; children and young people.
**WHAT IS NOT FUNDED** Individuals.
**RANGE OF GRANTS** Mostly up to £5,000.
**SAMPLE GRANTS** East Anglian Children's Hospice (£8,000 in two grants); Bury St Edmunds Borough Council – Festival (£6,500); Bury Bach Society, St Nicholas Hospice Care and Westminster Synagogue (£5,000).
**FINANCES** Year 2013 Income £100,738 Grants £95,738 Grants to organisations £95,739 Assets £218,639
**TRUSTEES** Christopher Butler; Ian Morgan; Robert Wise; David Rockberger; Mildred Wise; A. Latham; M. Wise; Jane Richardson.
**HOW TO APPLY** Apply in writing to the correspondent. The trustees meet quarterly, usually in March, June, September and December.
**WHO TO APPLY TO** Neville Wignall, Clerk, Music Sales Ltd, Dettingen Way, Bury St Edmunds, Suffolk IP33 3YB *Tel.* 01284 702600 *email* neville.wignall@musicsales.co.uk

## ■ Muslim Hands

**CC NO** 1105056 **ESTABLISHED** 1993
**WHERE FUNDING CAN BE GIVEN** Overseas.
**WHO CAN BENEFIT** Organisations benefitting people disadvantaged by poverty and victims of man-made or natural disasters and war.
**WHAT IS FUNDED** The relief of poverty through: education; emergency relief; environment; health; the relief of hunger; livelihoods; care of orphans; and the provision of clean drinking water.
**SAMPLE GRANTS** Grants were given for the following purposes: General (£3 million); Orphans (£2.6 million); Emergency aid (£842,500); Food (£811,000); Safe water (£504,000); Education (£309,500); Health (£225,000); Masjid (£59,500); Shelter (£3,600)
**FINANCES** Year 2013 Income £14,212,504 Grants £8,354,594 Grants to organisations £8,354,594 Assets £9,832,750
**TRUSTEES** Musharaf Hussain; Syed Lakhte Hassanain; Mohammad Amin-Ul Hasanat Shah; Saffi Ullah; Sahibzada Ghulam Jeelani; Muhammad Arshad Jamil.
**OTHER INFORMATION** Of the grant total, at least £6.2 million was disbursed to various Muslim Hands partner organisations in a number of different countries.
**HOW TO APPLY** Apply in writing to the correspondent.
**WHO TO APPLY TO** Asad Minhas, 148–164 Gregory Boulevard, Nottingham NG7 5JE Tel. 0115 911 7222 email mail@muslimhands.org.uk Website www.muslimhands.org.uk

## ■ The Mutual Trust Group

**CC NO** 1039300 **ESTABLISHED** 1994
**WHERE FUNDING CAN BE GIVEN** UK.
**WHO CAN BENEFIT** Organisations.
**WHAT IS FUNDED** Orthodox Jewish education and the relief of poverty.
**SAMPLE GRANTS** Yeshivas Kesser Hatalmud (£264,500); Yeshivas Shaar Hashamayim (£93,500); 'Various other' (£29,500)
**FINANCES** Year 2013 Income £352,527 Grants £387,374 Grants to organisations £387,374 Assets £107,767
**TRUSTEES** Rabbi Benzion Weitz; Michael Weitz; Adrian Weisz.
**HOW TO APPLY** Apply in writing to the correspondent.
**WHO TO APPLY TO** Rabbi Benzion Weitz, Trustee, 12 Dunstan Road, London NW11 8AA Tel. 020 8458 7549

## ■ MW (CL) Foundation

**CC NO** 1134917 **ESTABLISHED** 2010
**WHERE FUNDING CAN BE GIVEN** Worldwide, with preference for the UK.
**WHO CAN BENEFIT** Charitable organisations and education providers.
**WHAT IS FUNDED** Projects which promote education, the relief of poverty and the advancement of the Orthodox Jewish faith.
**RANGE OF GRANTS** From £1,000 to £70,000.
**SAMPLE GRANTS** Previous beneficiaries have included: Achisomoch (£70,000); Zichron Mordechai and Devorah Weiz Foundation (£14,000); Keren Shabbos, N W London Communal Mikvah Ltd and W S T Charity Ltd (£10,000 each); Tiferes High School, The Boys ClubHouse, SEED and Rabbi Zvi Kushalevski (£5,000 each); Sunderland Talmudical College, London Academy of Jewish Studies and Beis Minchat Yitschok Trust (£1,000 each).
**FINANCES** Year 2012/13 Income £211,176 Grants £133,572 Grants to organisations £133,572 Assets £2,771,308
**TRUSTEES** Hilary Olsberg; Vivienne Lewin.
**OTHER INFORMATION** The foundation is closely linked with the MW (RH) Foundation, MW (GK) Foundation and MW (HO) Foundation and shares the same charitable objectives. At the time of writing (June 2015) these were the latest accounts available for the foundation.
**HOW TO APPLY** Apply in writing to the correspondent.
**WHO TO APPLY TO** Vivienne Lewin, Trustee, 38 Princes Park Avenue, London NW11 0JT

## ■ MW (GK) Foundation

**CC NO** 1134916 **ESTABLISHED** 2010
**WHERE FUNDING CAN BE GIVEN** Worldwide, with preference for the UK.
**WHO CAN BENEFIT** Charitable organisations and education providers.
**WHAT IS FUNDED** Projects which promote education, the relief of poverty and the advancement of the Orthodox Jewish faith.
**RANGE OF GRANTS** From £1,000 to £80,000.
**SAMPLE GRANTS** Previous beneficiaries have included: Mercaz Hatorah Belz Machnovke (£80,500); Yad Vochessed (£25,500); Beis Ahron Trust (£16,000); Friends of Dorog (£6,500); Gateshead Talmudical College (£2,000); Chasdei Yoel, Kollel Shoimre Haachomos, Toimche Shaabos (£1,000 each).
**FINANCES** Year 2012/13 Income £229,261 Grants £189,200 Grants to organisations £189,200 Assets £2,748,516
**TRUSTEES** Shlomo Klein; Gella Klein.
**OTHER INFORMATION** The foundation was initially known as the Weisz Children Foundation and is closely linked with the MW (CL) Foundation, MW (RH) Foundation and MW (HO) Foundation. At the time of writing (June 2015) these were the latest accounts available for the foundation.
**HOW TO APPLY** Apply in writing to the correspondent.
**WHO TO APPLY TO** Gella Klein, Trustee, 15 Brantwood Road, Salford M7 4EN

## ■ MW (HO) Foundation

**CC NO** 1134919 **ESTABLISHED** 2010
**WHERE FUNDING CAN BE GIVEN** Worldwide, with a preference for the UK.
**WHO CAN BENEFIT** Charitable organisations and education providers.
**WHAT IS FUNDED** Projects which promote education, the relief of poverty and the advancement of the Orthodox Jewish faith.
**RANGE OF GRANTS** From £1,000 to £55,000.
**SAMPLE GRANTS** Shekel (£55,000); Asser Bishvil Foundation (£37,500); M H Trust (£17,500); Chomel Dalim (£8,500); Three Pillars (£6,500); Beis Chaya Rochel (£3,000); Shemays (£1,000).
**FINANCES** Year 2012/13 Income £252,798 Grants £211,740 Grants to organisations £211,740 Assets £3,178,381
**TRUSTEES** Hilary Olsberg; Rosalind Halpern.
**OTHER INFORMATION** The foundation was initially known as the Meir Weisz Foundation and is closely linked with the MW (CL) Foundation, MW (GK) Foundation and MW (RH) Foundation. At the time of writing (June 2015) these were the latest accounts available for the foundation.
**HOW TO APPLY** Apply in writing to the correspondent.
**WHO TO APPLY TO** David Olsberg, Trustee, 2b Mather Avenue, Prestwich, Manchester M25 0LA

## ■ MW (RH) Foundation

**CC NO** 1134918   **ESTABLISHED** 2010
**WHERE FUNDING CAN BE GIVEN** Worldwide, with a preference for the UK.
**WHO CAN BENEFIT** Charitable organisations and education providers.
**WHAT IS FUNDED** Projects which promote education, the relief of poverty and the advancement of the Orthodox Jewish faith.
**SAMPLE GRANTS** Asser Bishvil Foundation (£53,500); Beis Ruchel School (£28,500); Telz Academy Trust (£18,000); Meir Hatorah (£13,500); Lowcost Ltd (£10,000); Friends of Boyan, Y A M F (£5,000 each); Format Charitable Trust, Merkaz Mosdos Belz, Tomchei Shaabos Manchester (£1,000 each).
**FINANCES** Year 2012/13 Income £281,799 Grants £209,470 Grants to organisations £209,470 Assets £2,642,872
**TRUSTEES** Rosalind Halpern; Jacob Halpern.
**OTHER INFORMATION** This foundation was initially known as the Deborah Weisz Foundation and is closely linked with the MW (CL) Foundation, MW (GK) Foundation and MW (HO) Foundation. At the time of writing (June 2015) these were the latest accounts available for the foundation.
**HOW TO APPLY** Apply in writing to the correspondent.
**WHO TO APPLY TO** Jacob Halpern, Trustee, 29 Waterpark Road, Salford M7 4FT

## ■ MYA Charitable Trust

**CC NO** 299642   **ESTABLISHED** 1987
**WHERE FUNDING CAN BE GIVEN** Worldwide.
**WHO CAN BENEFIT** Organisations and individuals.
**WHAT IS FUNDED** Orthodox Jewish causes, including religious education and the relief of poverty.
**SAMPLE GRANTS Previous beneficiaries have included:** Beis Rochel; Bikur Cholim D'Satmar Trust; Keren Mitzvah Trust; Keren Zedoko Vochesed; KZF; London Friends of Kamenitzer Yeshiva; Ma'os Yesomim Charitable Trust; Wlodowa Charity Rehabilitation Trust; ZSV Trust.
**FINANCES** Year 2013/14 Income £245,295 Grants £575,477 Grants to organisations £561,564 Assets £1,396,142
**TRUSTEES** Myer Rothfeld; Eve Rothfeld; Hannah Schraiber; Joseph Pfeffer.
**OTHER INFORMATION** Grants account for £177,500 of the total awarded to organisations. The remaining £384,000 (referred to in the accounts as an 'Investment donation') we have taken to represent investment shares donated to an organisation by the trust. During the year, individuals received £13,900 in eight grants.
**HOW TO APPLY** Apply in writing to the correspondent.
**WHO TO APPLY TO** Myer Rothfeld, Trustee, Medcar House, 149a Stamford Hill, London N16 5LL Tel. 020 8800 3582

## ■ MYR Charitable Trust

**CC NO** 1104406   **ESTABLISHED** 2004
**WHERE FUNDING CAN BE GIVEN** Israel, USA and England.
**WHO CAN BENEFIT** Jewish organisations.
**WHAT IS FUNDED** Advancement of the Orthodox Jewish religion, relief of sickness and poverty of recognised members of said faith.
**SAMPLE GRANTS Previous beneficiaries have included:** Cong Beth Joseph; HP Charitable Trust; UTA; Gateshead Jewish Boarding School; Keren Eretz Yisroel; SCT Sunderland and GJLC.
**FINANCES** Year 2013 Income £119,146 Grants £25,965 Grants to organisations £25,965 Assets £1,157,436
**TRUSTEES** Z. M. Kaufman; Simon Kaufman; Arthur Zonszajn; Joseph Kaufman.
**OTHER INFORMATION** A list of beneficiaries was not included in the accounts; however, there is a separate publication titled MYR Charitable Trust – Schedule of Charitable Donations, which is available from the correspondent for a fee.
**HOW TO APPLY** Apply in writing to the correspondent. The trustees consider all the requests they receive and make donations based on the level of funds available.
**WHO TO APPLY TO** Z. M. Kaufman, Trustee, 50 Keswick Street, Gateshead, Tyne and Wear NE8 1TQ

## ■ The Janet Nash Charitable Settlement

**CC NO** 326880    **ESTABLISHED** 1985
**WHERE FUNDING CAN BE GIVEN** UK.
**WHO CAN BENEFIT** Organisations and individuals.
**WHAT IS FUNDED** Medical causes; health.
**TYPE OF GRANT** Recurrent.
**SAMPLE GRANTS** The Get A-Head Charitable Trust (£45,000); Dyslexia Institute (£4,000); Birmingham Children's Hospital and Pilgrim Bandits (£1,000 each). One grant of £500 was awarded to an unnamed beneficiary.
**FINANCES** Year 2013/14 Income £550,032 Grants £581,117 Grants to organisations £51,500 Assets £105,449
**TRUSTEES** Ronald Gulliver; Mark Stephen Jacobs; Charlotte Emma Westall.
**OTHER INFORMATION** Grants were made to five organisations totalling £51,500. Grants to 31 individuals totalled £529,500 for medical purposes (£489,500) and hardship relief (£40,000).
**HOW TO APPLY** There is absolutely no response to unsolicited applications. The trustees have previously stated: 'The charity does not, repeat not, ever, consider any applications for benefit from the public'. Furthermore, that: 'Our existing charitable commitments more than use up our potential funds and were found personally by the trustees themselves, never as a result of applications from third parties'.
**WHO TO APPLY TO** Ronald Gulliver, Trustee, Valentine Barn, Shutford Road, North Newington, Oxfordshire OX15 6AN
email JanetNashCharitableSettlement@hotmail.com

## ■ The National Art Collections Fund

**CC NO** 209174    **ESTABLISHED** 1903
**WHERE FUNDING CAN BE GIVEN** UK.
**WHO CAN BENEFIT** Public museums, galleries, historic houses, libraries and archives that are: open for at least half the week for at least six months a year; are fully or provisionally accredited under the Arts Council Scheme.
**WHAT IS FUNDED** For the purchase of works of art and other objects of artistic interest, dating from antiquity to the present day.
**WHAT IS NOT FUNDED** Objects primarily of social-historical interest, scientific or technological material, or letters, manuscripts or archival material with limited aesthetic inscription; objects which are unavailable for viewing by an Art Fund representative; other costs associated with acquisitions such as valuation costs, framing and display, the conservation and restoration of works, transport and storage costs, temporary or permanent exhibitions and digitisation projects; objects already purchased or for which a financial commitment or commitment to purchase has already been made by the applicant; applications from individuals, artists' groups, commercial organisations, hospitals, places of worship, schools or institutions of higher education; touring costs (though the fund may occasionally look for specific strategic opportunities within its network of museums. Though the fund does not accept unsolicited applications for this, it accepts phone calls to discuss it); education or community projects; salary costs (though administrative costs may be supported as part of an application to the Jonathan Ruffer Curatorial Grants Programme); art or art history students at any level; capital projects of any kind.
**TYPE OF GRANT** One-off grants.
**RANGE OF GRANTS** There is no fixed upper or lower limit to the size of grant the committee may offer. There are main grants and small grants schemes.
**SAMPLE GRANTS** Tate, in partnership with other organisations (£629,000); British Museum (£208,500); Bodleian Library (£200,000); British Museum and Wiltshire Heritage Museum (£150,000); Birmingham Museums Trust (£109,500); Lancashire County Council Museums (£33,000); Scottish National Gallery (£25,000); Norwich Castle Museum and Art Gallery (£7,000); Scarborough Art Gallery (£5,000); Nottingham Castle Museum and Art Gallery (£3,800); Jersey Heritage Museum (£1,300); Cartoon Museum (£800).
**FINANCES** Year 2013 Income £10,558,000 Grants £4,357,000 Grants to organisations £4,357,000 Assets £40,974,000
**TRUSTEES** Lord Smith of Finsbury; Jeremy Palmer; Caroline Butler; Richard Calvocoressi; Richard Deacon; Dame Liz Forgan; Philippa Glanville; Prof. Chris Gosden; Antony Griffiths; Alastair Laing; James Lingwood; Jonathan Marsden; Sally Osman; Marcia Pointon; Axel Rüger; Prof. Deborah Swallow; Prof. Lisa Tickner; Michael Wilson; Christopher Lloyd.
**OTHER INFORMATION** Individual UK curators, scholars and researchers may apply for funding to enable travel or other activities which may 'extend and develop their curatorial expertise, collections-based knowledge and art historical interests'. There is a separate grants programme for this (Jonathan Ruffer Curatorial Grants Programme). See the website for details.
**HOW TO APPLY** In the first instance, applicants should call Penny Bull, Programmes Manager (020 7225 4815) to discuss potential acquisitions before beginning an online application. There are extensive guidelines available to download from the website.
**WHO TO APPLY TO** Penny Bull, Programmes Manager (Acquisitions), 2 Granary Square, King's Cross, London N1C 4BH Tel. 020 7225 4800 Fax 020 7225 4848 email programmes@artfund.org Website www.artfund.org

## ■ The National Churches Trust (formerly the Historic Churches Preservation Trust with the Incorporated Church Building Society)

**CC NO** 1119845    **ESTABLISHED** 1953
**WHERE FUNDING CAN BE GIVEN** UK, Isle of Man and the Channel Islands.
**WHO CAN BENEFIT** Christian churches of architectural, historical or community importance used by denominations that are members of Churches Together in Britain and Ireland.
**WHAT IS FUNDED** To assist, with grants and loans, the efforts of congregations to carry out essential repairs to the fabric of historic churches and improve their general facilities

# National

e.g. accessible toilets, kitchens and meeting rooms. The trust has also been working with WREN (Waste Recycling Environmental Ltd) to administer grants on their behalf to churches sited within a ten-mile radius of a landfill site operated by Waste Recycling Group.

**WHAT IS NOT FUNDED** Ancillary buildings and structures; bells and organs (repairs and new); internal furnishings, fixtures and fittings; clocks; monument restoration; heating or lighting; reordering; projects where work has already begun; the construction of new places of worship; applications that have previously been unsuccessful.

**TYPE OF GRANT** Capital costs.

**SAMPLE GRANTS Previous beneficiaries have included:** St Botoloph, Boston (£50,000) St Vincent, Caythorpe, St Michael and the Holy Angels, West Bromwich and St Wilfred, Halton (£40,000 each); Dunlop Parish Church, Dunlop (£35,000); North Shields Baptist Church (£20,000); St David, Llanddewi Aberarth (£10,000); and St John the Baptist, Little Maplestead (£5,000).

**FINANCES** Year 2013 Income £1,664,869 Grants £1,138,028 Grants to organisations £1,138,028 Assets £4,358,034

**TRUSTEES** Luke March; Alastair Hunter; Richard Carr-Archer; Rt Revd Nicholas Holtam; Andrew Day; Jennie Page; John Drew; Peter Readman.

**PUBLICATIONS** 'Keeping Churches Alive – a brief history of the Trust' available directly from the trust or to download from the website.

**OTHER INFORMATION** In 2008 the Charity Commission appointed the National Churches Trust (NCT) as the sole trustee of the Historic Churches Preservation Trust (HCPT) and also granted a 'uniting direction'. Consequently, the NCT and HCPT are treated as a single charity for administrative, accounting and regulatory purposes. They will, however, remain legally distinct so that the HCPT will operate as restricted funds within the NCT. A similar process is envisaged for the Incorporated Church Building Society (ICBS), which has been managed by the HCPT since 1983. In 2013 the trust was involved in making or recommending 139 grant offers.

**HOW TO APPLY** Community and repair applications can be made via the online form on the website and both applications begin with an eligibility quiz. Applications for the Partnership Grants Programme, which must be made through a local Church trust, a list of which can be found on the trust's website.

**WHO TO APPLY TO** Alison Pollard, Grants and Local Trusts Manager, 7 Tufton Street, London SW1P 3QB Tel. 020 7222 0605 Fax 020 7227 1939 email info@nationalchurchestrust.org Website www.nationalchurchestrust.org

## ■ National Committee of the Women's World Day of Prayer for England and Wales and Northern Ireland (formerly known as Women's World Day of Prayer)

**CC NO** 233242     **ESTABLISHED** 1932
**WHERE FUNDING CAN BE GIVEN** UK and worldwide.
**WHO CAN BENEFIT** Charitable organisations.
**WHAT IS FUNDED** Promotion of the Christian faith.
**WHAT IS NOT FUNDED** Individuals.
**TYPE OF GRANT** Mostly one-off, project grants.
**RANGE OF GRANTS** £200 to £20,000.

**SAMPLE GRANTS** Christian Aid – Ebola Crisis (£20,000); Feed the Minds (£10,000); CAFOD (£6,000); Arab World Ministries, Bible Society Northern Ireland and Christian Aid – Syria Appeal (£5,000 each); Mission to Deep Sea Fishermen – Scripture scheme (£3,000); London City Mission and World Day of Prayer European Committee (£2,000 each); Fellowship of Reconciliation and Peace – Wales (£500); Welsh Council on Alcohol and Drugs (£200).

**FINANCES** Year 2014 Income £547,382 Grants £320,960 Grants to organisations £320,960 Assets £398,892

**TRUSTEES** Margaret Pickford; Mimi Barton; Kathleen Skinner.

**OTHER INFORMATION** Project grants are made to organisations supporting only one project and they should not re-apply within three years. Larger organisations involved with a number of projects or which operate internationally may apply for grants in consecutive years so long as each grants serves a different project and country.

**HOW TO APPLY** Application forms can be obtained by the WWDP office.

**WHO TO APPLY TO** Mary Judd, Correspondent, Commercial Road, Tunbridge Wells TN1 2RR Tel. 01892 541411 Fax 01892 541745 email office@wwdp.org.uk Website www.wwdp.org.uk

## ■ The National Express Foundation

**CC NO** 1148231     **ESTABLISHED** 2012
**WHERE FUNDING CAN BE GIVEN** West Midlands and South Essex or East London within five miles of the c2c rail line.
**WHO CAN BENEFIT** Community groups and educational institutions.
**WHAT IS FUNDED** General charitable purposes, social welfare, education, sport, children and young people.
**RANGE OF GRANTS** Up to £30,000.
**SAMPLE GRANTS** Newman University (£30,000 over three years); South Essex College of Further and Higher Education and Walsall College (£20,000 each over two years); Disability Resource Centre, Birmingham, Olio Youth Hub, and Theatre Royal Stratford East (£5,000 each); Changing Our Lives, Sport 4 Life and Voluntary Action Coventry (£2,500 each).

**FINANCES** Year 2013 Income £200,183 Grants £65,000 Grants to organisations £65,000

**TRUSTEES** Anthony Vigor; Denise Rossiter; John Fraser; Lesley Dorrington; Madi Pilgrim; Shabana Mahmood MP.

**OTHER INFORMATION** The foundation made grants of £35,000 to ten community groups and the first annual instalments totalling £30,000 to three educational institutions. At the time of writing (June 2015) the latest accounts were not available from the Charity Commission.

**HOW TO APPLY** Applications are required to provide the following information: background to the organisation, membership and funding; evidence of constitution and independent bank account; description of what the funding would be used for; explanation of how the proposed project would benefit the community; timescale and process for delivering the project; proposals for promoting the link with the foundation; plans to evaluate and quantify the benefits. Applicants are asked to indicate what size of grant they are seeking, and explain what they could deliver for the level of grant applied for. The trustees plan to award more small grants (up to a maximum of £5,000) than large grants (up to maximum £10,000). The trustees may choose to support an organisation but offer a smaller amount than has been requested, so it would help if applicants can show what they would deliver for different levels of funding. While the trustees did not set restrictions on how the funding would be applied, they were seeking evidence of innovation in the how projects will be delivered. We will also want to ensure the successful project benefits the maximum number of children and young people in the community it serves.'

**WHO TO APPLY TO** The Trustees, National Express Group plc, National Express House, Digbeth, Birmingham B5 6DD *Tel.* 0121 460 8423 *email* foundation@nationalexpress.com *Website* nationalexpressgroup.com/foundation

## ■ The National Hockey Foundation
**CC NO** 1015550    **ESTABLISHED** 1992
**WHERE FUNDING CAN BE GIVEN** England.
**WHO CAN BENEFIT** Organisations benefitting people under the age of 21.
**WHAT IS FUNDED** The development of sport at youth level; particularly but not exclusively hockey.
**WHAT IS NOT FUNDED** General donations (grants are only awarded for specific projects); individuals; projects solely supporting elite athletes; fundraising events; award sponsorship; projects outside England; projects that do not provide lasting benefits or are not sustainable; projects where the foundation's impact will not make an impact. Grants are not usually awarded where the primary funding is to support the payment of salaries or for more than 50% of the total cost of a project.
**TYPE OF GRANT** Funding or part-funding for specific projects, on either a one-off basis or over a maximum of three years.
**RANGE OF GRANTS** Usually between £10,000 and £75,000.
**SAMPLE GRANTS** Leeds Adel HC and Penzance HC (£50,000 each); Stony Stratford LTC and Taunton Vale SC (£40,000 each); MK Rowing Club and Olney Colts FC (£20,000 each); Sport Milton Keynes (£15,000); Ravenstone Parish Council (£9,000).
**FINANCES** *Year* 2013/14 *Income* £99,508 *Grants* £200,860 *Grants to organisations* £200,860 *Assets* £2,231,172
**TRUSTEES** David Laing; David Darling; A. Dransfield; Janet Baker; David Billson; John Cove; John Waters; Michael Fulwood; Benjamin Rea.
**OTHER INFORMATION** Eight grants totalling £244,000 were made during the year; two of these were returned to the foundation.
**HOW TO APPLY** Application forms are available to download, together with criteria and guidelines, from the website. Application forms must be complete in order to be considered. If you are unsure as to your project's eligibility, you may ask the trustees by completing a Grant Indication Form, which will allow the foundation to determine your application's suitability without you initially having to complete a full application form.
**WHO TO APPLY TO** David Billson, Secretary and Chair, 9 Hamlet Green, Northampton, Northants NN5 7AR *Tel.* 01604 589720 *email* nathockfoundation@btinternet.com *Website* www.thenationalhockeyfoundation.com

## ■ The National Manuscripts Conservation Trust
**CC NO** 802796    **ESTABLISHED** 1990
**WHERE FUNDING CAN BE GIVEN** UK.
**WHO CAN BENEFIT** Record offices; libraries; other publically funded institutions; owners of manuscript material conditionally exempt from capital taxation or owned by a charitable trust.
**WHAT IS FUNDED** Conservation of manuscripts, documents and archives.
**WHAT IS NOT FUNDED** Institutions directly funded by government; public records within the meaning of the Public Records Acts; the official archives of the applying institution or authority (though older records may qualify for consideration); loan collections (see website for exceptions); photographic material; audio-visual material; printed material; capital costs; equipment; digitisation (if the primary aim is to increase access to manuscripts). Funding towards the costs of arranging and listing manuscripts is usually only given for making summary lists or inventories as the first stage of conservation.
**TYPE OF GRANT** Grants cover the cost of repair, binding and other preservation measures including reprography; the costs of conservation by commercial conservation studios or the salaries and related expenses of staff specially employed and expendable materials required for the project; VAT on project costs (if the applicant is unable to reclaim VAT).
**RANGE OF GRANTS** Most grants range between £2,000 and £10,000.
**SAMPLE GRANTS** Northamptonshire Archives Service (£25,500); London Metropolitan Archives (£25,000); Worcestershire Archives (£15,100); Glasgow University Library (£10,900); Society of Antiquaries of Newcastle upon Tyne (£10,300); Oxford – Christ Church Library, Southampton University Library and Winchester Cathedral Library (£10,000 each); Edinburgh University Library (£9,500); Flintshire Record Office (£9,000); Archives and Records Council Wales (£7,100); East London Mosque Trust (£4,000); Pembrokeshire Archives (£3,600); Denbighshire Archives (£1,600); West Dunbartonshire Archives (£1,400).
**FINANCES** *Year* 2013 *Income* £164,559 *Grants* £174,279 *Grants to organisations* £174,279 *Assets* £2,147,779
**TRUSTEES** Lord Egremont; Dr Bernard Naylor; Charles Sebag-Montefiore; Dr Norman James; Caroline Checkley-Scott.
**HOW TO APPLY** Application forms are available to download from the website, along with guidance notes. The deadlines are usually 1 April and 1 October, check the website for the deadlines and full details of how to apply.
**WHO TO APPLY TO** Nell Hoare, Secretary, PO Box 4291, Reading, Berkshire RG8 9JA *Tel.* 01491 598083 *email* info@nmct.org.uk *Website* www.nmct.co.uk

## ■ The Nationwide Foundation
**CC NO** 1065552    **ESTABLISHED** 1997
**WHERE FUNDING CAN BE GIVEN** UK.
**WHO CAN BENEFIT** Charitable organisations.
**WHAT IS FUNDED** Bringing empty properties back into use as homes for people in need; improving the living conditions of tenants in private rented sector homes; supporting the development of alternative, scalable housing models to provide more affordable housing.
**WHAT IS NOT FUNDED** Charities with 'unrestricted reserves' which exceed 50% of annual

expenditure, as shown in their accounts; charities which are in significant debt as shown in their accounts; promotion of religion or politics; charities which have been declined by the foundation within the last 12 months; applications which do not comply with the foundation's funding criteria/guidelines.
**TYPE OF GRANT** Project, capital and revenue costs.
**RANGE OF GRANTS** £1,000 to £200,000.
**SAMPLE GRANTS** Generation Rent (£198,000); GIPSIL (£140,000); Changing Lives (£128,000); Freebridge Community Housing (£96,000); LATCH and Canopy Housing (£56,000 each); Big Issue Invest (£39,000); National CLT Network (£28,000); Sliced Bread (£6,900); DAH Added Value (£1,300).
**FINANCES** Year 2013/14 Income £726,567 Grants £956,799 Grants to organisations £956,799 Assets £1,646,241
**TRUSTEES** Michael Coppack; Benedict Stimson; Christopher Rhodes; Fiona Ellis; Graeme Hughes; Juliet Cockram; Sarah Mitchell; Bryce Glover; John Taylor; Antonia Bance.
**OTHER INFORMATION** Nationwide Building Society also donated services to the foundation totalling £83,000, which represented the provision of office space, technology, legal and accountancy support.
**HOW TO APPLY** The foundation's website states that 'funding is only available for projects where alternative scalable models can provide more affordable homes, however there is not an open grant programme. If you think you have a project that might fit with our strategy, please contact us to discuss further.'
**WHO TO APPLY TO** Lorna Mackie, Grants Officer, Nationwide Building Society, Nationwide House, Pipers Way, Swindon SN38 2SN *Tel.* 01793 655113 *email* enquiries@nationwidefoundation.org.uk *Website* www.nationwidefoundation.org.uk

■ **The Nazareth Trust Fund**
**CC NO** 210503　　**ESTABLISHED** 1956
**WHERE FUNDING CAN BE GIVEN** UK and financially developing countries.
**WHO CAN BENEFIT** Young adults, Christian missionaries and victims of famine, war, and man-made or natural disasters – both individually and through registered institutions.
**WHAT IS FUNDED** Churches, Christian missionaries, Christian youth work, and overseas aid. Grants are only made to people or causes known personally to the trustees.
**WHAT IS NOT FUNDED** Individuals not known to the trustees.
**TYPE OF GRANT** Grants for up to one year.
**RANGE OF GRANTS** £100–£8,000. Typically under £1,000.
**SAMPLE GRANTS** Harnham Free Church (£18,200 in 14 grants); IREF (£4,500 in two grants); Crusaders and Durham Rd Baptist Church (£1,000 each); London School of Theology (£400); Tear Fund (£200); Salvation Army (£100).
**FINANCES** Year 2013/14 Income £80,174 Grants £41,000 Grants to organisations £40,000 Assets £30,121
**TRUSTEES** Dr Robert Hunt; Revd David Hunt; Philip Hunt; Eileen Hunt; Elma Hunt; Nicola Hunt.
**OTHER INFORMATION** Grants to organisations usually total around £40,000 and to individuals about £1,000–£2,000.
**HOW TO APPLY** Our research notes that the fund only gives to people known to the trustees personally. Unsolicited applications are unsuccessful.
**WHO TO APPLY TO** Dr Robert Hunt, Trustee, Barrowpoint, 18 Millennium Close, Salisbury, Wiltshire SP2 8TB *Tel.* 01722 349322 *email* rwghunt@uwclub.net

■ **The NDL Foundation**
**CC NO** 1133508　　**ESTABLISHED** 2010
**WHERE FUNDING CAN BE GIVEN** Worldwide
**WHO CAN BENEFIT** Registered charities.
**WHAT IS FUNDED** General charitable purposes, including education, medicine and the arts.
**SAMPLE GRANTS** **Previous beneficiaries have included:** Women for Women International (UK) (£42,000); Tumaini Education Trust (£23,000); Kids (£6,000); Swiss Cottage School and Myschoolpulse (£5,000 each); Royal Opera House (£2,500); NSPCC (£2,000); Cancer Research UK (£1,500); Children in Crisis (£1,250); and The Butler Trust (£500).
**FINANCES** Year 2013/14 Income £825 Grants £116,500 Grants to organisations £116,500
**TRUSTEES** Sylviane Destribats; Laura Destribats; Frank Destribats; Diane Destribats.
**OTHER INFORMATION** In 2013/14 the foundation had an income of £825 and a total expenditure of £121,000. Due to its low income, the foundation was not required to submit its accounts to the Charity Commission.
**HOW TO APPLY** Apply in writing to the correspondent.
**WHO TO APPLY TO** Sylviane Destribats, Trustee, 8 Bolton Gardens Mews, London SW10 9LW *email* mai.brown@blickrothenberg.com

■ **The Worshipful Company of Needlemakers' Charitable Fund**
**CC NO** 288646　　**ESTABLISHED** 1952
**WHERE FUNDING CAN BE GIVEN** London.
**WHO CAN BENEFIT** Organisations, including those associated with the needle-making industry, the City of London, and the Lord Mayor's, the Master's and the Chaplain's chosen charities.
**WHAT IS FUNDED** Education; religion; social welfare; general charitable purposes.
**RANGE OF GRANTS** From £100 to £6,000.
**SAMPLE GRANTS** Bishop of Woolwich Discretionary Trust (£6,000); Royal School of Needlework (£5,000); Old Palace School and Royal College of Nursing Foundation (£3,000 each); Guildhall School of Music and Drama (£2,100); Lord Mayor's Charity Appeal (£2,000); Sheriff's and Recorder's Fund (£1,500); St Paul's Cathedral Trust and Victoria and Albert Museum (£500 each); The Royal Masonic School for Girls – Rickmansworth (£100).
**FINANCES** Year 2012/13 Income £90,803 Grants £47,500 Grants to organisations £47,500 Assets £1,822,299
**TRUSTEE** Worshipful Company of Needlemakers.
**OTHER INFORMATION** At the time of writing (June 2015) the fund's 2012/13 accounts were the latest available.
**HOW TO APPLY** Apply in writing to the correspondent, but the trust has stated that it tends to support the same charities each year, so unsolicited applications are unlikely to be successful.
**WHO TO APPLY TO** Philip Grant, Clerk, PO Box 3682, Windsor SL4 3WR *Tel.* 01753 860690 *email* needlemakers.clerk@yahoo.com *Website* www.needlemakers.org.uk

## ■ The Neighbourly Charitable Trust

**CC NO** 258488  **ESTABLISHED** 1969
**WHERE FUNDING CAN BE GIVEN** Bedfordshire and Hertfordshire
**WHO CAN BENEFIT** Organisations benefitting people with disabilities.
**WHAT IS FUNDED** General and leisure/adventure trips for people with disabilities.
**WHAT IS NOT FUNDED** National charities (except occasionally a local branch) or individuals.
**RANGE OF GRANTS** Usually £100–£1,500 with some larger grants.
**SAMPLE GRANTS** Happy Days Children's Charity and Whizz-Kidz (£1,200 each); ActOne Artbase and Music in Hospitals (£1,000 each); Sunnyside Rural Trust and The Hospice of St Francis (£800 each); Farming for All (£750); RDA Gassedon Place (£500); Children's Heart Foundation and Brittle Bone Society (£400 each).
**FINANCES** Year 2013/14 Income £69,353 Grants £36,800 Grants to organisations £36,800 Assets £2,644,447
**TRUSTEES** John Sell; Emma Simpson; Jane Wade.
**OTHER INFORMATION** Grants were made to 49 organisations during the year.
**HOW TO APPLY** Apply in writing to the correspondent, for consideration at trustees' meetings twice a year.
**WHO TO APPLY TO** Sharon Long, Secretary, 8–10 Upper Marlborough Road, St Albans, Hertfordshire AL1 3UR *Tel.* 01727 843603 *email* admin@iplltd.co.uk

## ■ The James Neill Trust Fund

**CC NO** 503203  **ESTABLISHED** 1974
**WHERE FUNDING CAN BE GIVEN** Sheffield and its immediate surroundings.
**WHO CAN BENEFIT** Voluntary organisations.
**WHAT IS FUNDED** Voluntary work for the benefit of people in the area specified above.
**WHAT IS NOT FUNDED** Only rarely are grants given to unconnected individuals.
**TYPE OF GRANT** Ongoing support for established organisations and one-off grants to meet start-up costs or unexpected expenses.
**RANGE OF GRANTS** Up to £5,000.
**SAMPLE GRANTS** **Regular grants:** South Yorkshire and Hallamshire Clubs for Young People (£1,500); St Luke's Hospice (£1,500); Voluntary Action Sheffield (£1,500); Cruse Bereavement Care Sheffield Branch (£750); Whirlow Hall Farm Trust (£750); British Red Cross – South Yorkshire (£300). **One-off grants:** St Luke's Hospice – Capital Appeal (£5,000); FareShare South Yorkshire (£1,300); St Wilfred's Centre (£1,000); Manor Community Transport (£750); Home-Start Sheffield (£500); Listening Books (£300)
**FINANCES** Year 2013/14 Income £47,595 Grants £41,729 Grants to organisations £34,600 Assets £1,346,379
**TRUSTEES** Sir Hugh Neill; G. Peel; Lady Neill; N. Peel; A. Staniforth; J. Neill.
**OTHER INFORMATION** During the year, James Neill Pensioners received £7,100 in support.
**HOW TO APPLY** Apply in writing to the correspondent in time for the application to arrive in the month of July.
**WHO TO APPLY TO** Lady Neill, Trustee, Barn Cottage, Lindrick Common, Worksop, Nottinghamshire S81 8BA *Tel.* 01909 562806 *email* neillcharities@me.com

## ■ Nemoral Ltd

**CC NO** 262270  **ESTABLISHED** 1971
**WHERE FUNDING CAN BE GIVEN** Worldwide.
**WHO CAN BENEFIT** Jewish organisations.
**WHAT IS FUNDED** Jewish religion; Jewish religious education; the relief of poverty in the Jewish community.
**TYPE OF GRANT** One-off, recurring, capital and, occasionally, loans.
**FINANCES** Year 2013 Income £174,606 Grants £198,000 Grants to organisations £198,000 Assets £2,203,164
**TRUSTEES** Ellis Moore; Rivka Gross; Michael Saberski.
**OTHER INFORMATION** A list of grant beneficiaries was not included in the charity's accounts.
**HOW TO APPLY** Apply in writing to the correspondent.
**WHO TO APPLY TO** The Trustees, c/o Cohen Arnold and Co., New Burlington House, 1075 Finchley Road, London NW11 0PU *Tel.* 020 8731 0777

## ■ Ner Foundation

**CC NO** 1104866  **ESTABLISHED** 2004
**WHERE FUNDING CAN BE GIVEN** UK and Israel.
**WHO CAN BENEFIT** Orthodox Jewish organisations, community projects, schools, yeshivos and seminaries. People of the Jewish faith who are older or in need.
**WHAT IS FUNDED** Advancement of the Orthodox Jewish religion and education and the relief of poverty amongst Jewish people.
**FINANCES** Year 2013/14 Income £240,405 Grants £149,670 Grants to organisations £149,670 Assets £562,198
**TRUSTEES** Arnold Henry; Henry Neumann; Esther Henry.
**OTHER INFORMATION** In 2013/14 grants were distributed in the following categories: Relief of poverty (£81,000); Schools (£25,000); Community projects (£23,000); Grants under £1,000 (£13,300); Yeshivos and seminaries (£4,300). No grants were made for religious purposes or to individuals during the year.
**HOW TO APPLY** Apply in writing to the correspondent.
**WHO TO APPLY TO** Arnold Henry, Trustee, 309 Bury New Road, Salford, Manchester M7 2YN

## ■ Nesswall Ltd

**CC NO** 283600  **ESTABLISHED** 1981
**WHERE FUNDING CAN BE GIVEN** UK and overseas.
**WHO CAN BENEFIT** Orthodox Jewish organisations.
**WHAT IS FUNDED** Orthodox Jewish causes, including education and relief in need.
**SAMPLE GRANTS** **Previous beneficiaries have included:** Friends of Horim Establishments, Torah Vochesed L'Ezra Vesaad and Emunah Education Centre.
**FINANCES** Year 2013/14 Income £76,200 Grants £71,875 Grants to organisations £71,875 Assets £602,546
**TRUSTEES** R. Teitelbaum; H. Wahrhaftig.
**HOW TO APPLY** Apply in writing to the correspondent, at any time.
**WHO TO APPLY TO** R. Teitelbaum, Secretary, 28 Overlea Road, London E5 9BG

## ■ Network for Social Change

**CC NO** 295237  **ESTABLISHED** 1986
**WHERE FUNDING CAN BE GIVEN** UK and overseas.
**WHO CAN BENEFIT** Charitable projects and organisations.

**WHAT IS FUNDED** The Network for Social Change is a group of individuals who provide funding for 'progressive social change, particularly in the areas of justice, peace and the environment'. Projects which display innovation, are highly-leveraged and/or difficult to fund are favoured and the group looks to address the root causes of issues, rather than the symptoms.
**WHAT IS NOT FUNDED** Disaster appeals; most types of building; direct contributions to political parties.
**RANGE OF GRANTS** Up to £170,500.
**SAMPLE GRANTS** STAR – Student Action for Refugees (£170,500); The Joseph Rowntree Charitable Trust (£140,500); Oxford Research Group (£90,000); Transparency International UK (£20,000); Prison Reform Trust (£16,500); Children Unite (£15,000); University of Exeter (£12,800); Centre for Criminal Appeals (£11,000); Searchlight Educational Trust (£10,000).
**FINANCES** Year 2013/14 Income £1,255,355 Grants £1,271,601 Grants to organisations £1,271,601 Assets £193,708
**TRUSTEES** Carolyn Hayman; Patrick Boase; Anne Robbins; Ruth Rosselson; Giles Wright; Stuart Field.
**HOW TO APPLY** The network chooses the projects it wishes to support and does not accept unsolicited applications. However, the network is conscious that the policy of only accepting applications brought by its members could limit the range of worthwhile projects it could fund. To address this, the network has set up a 'Project Noticeboard' (accessed via the network's website) to allow outside organisations to post a summary of a project for which they are seeking funding. Members of the network can then access the noticeboard and, if interested, contact the organisation for further information with a view to future sponsorship. Projects are deleted from the noticeboard after about six months. Only 1–2% of project noticeboard entries result in sponsorship and funding.
**WHO TO APPLY TO** Tish McCrory, Correspondent, BM 2063, London WC1N 3XX *Tel.* 01647 61106 *email* thenetwork@gn.apc.org *Website* thenetworkforsocialchange.org.uk

## ■ The New Appeals Organisation for the City and County of Nottingham

**CC NO** 502196                **ESTABLISHED** 1973
**WHERE FUNDING CAN BE GIVEN** Nottinghamshire.
**WHO CAN BENEFIT** Individuals and local organisations, including schools and hospitals.
**WHAT IS FUNDED** Help for local people who are in need and are unable to obtain assistance from any other source.
**WHAT IS NOT FUNDED** Appeals to cover debts, arrears, building expenses or educational expenses are not normally considered.
**TYPE OF GRANT** One-off.
**SAMPLE GRANTS** Previous beneficiaries have included: Oakfield School (£4,400); Rosehill School (£1,600); Bells Lane and Aspley Tenants and Residents Association (£1,000); Highbury Hospital Ward Redwood 2 (£750); Robert Shaw School (£500); Muslim Women's Organisation (£250); and Nottingham Central Women's Aid (£200).
**FINANCES** Year 2013/14 Income £122,826 Grants £69,000 Grants to organisations £69,000

**TRUSTEES** Phillip Everett; Paula McLaren; Gareth Davis; Kevin Hyland; Christopher Bossart; Lisa Hyland; Margot Tighe.
**OTHER INFORMATION** Grants were made to support both organisations and individuals. At the time of writing (June 2015) the charity's 2013/14 annual report and accounts had been received by the Charity Commission but were not yet available to view.
**HOW TO APPLY** Apply in writing to the correspondent. An initial telephone call from the applicant is welcome.
**WHO TO APPLY TO** Philip Everett, Grant Secretary, c/o 4 Rise Court, Hamilton Road, Sherwood Rise, Nottingham NG5 1EU *Tel.* 0115 960 9644 *email* enquiries@newappeals.org.uk *Website* www.newappeals.org

## ■ Newby Trust Limited

**CC NO** 227151                **ESTABLISHED** 1938
**WHERE FUNDING CAN BE GIVEN** UK.
**WHO CAN BENEFIT** Registered charities; individuals.
**WHAT IS FUNDED** Education; health; social welfare. Each year, there is also a 'special category' which falls under one of these headings.
**WHAT IS NOT FUNDED** Statutory bodies; large national charities enjoying widespread support; organisations not registered with the Charity Commission; exhibitions, conferences or events; individuals volunteering overseas; promotion of religion; work outside the UK; large capital appeals; endowment appeals.
**TYPE OF GRANT** Usually one-off for part of a project. Buildings, capital, core costs and salaries may be considered.
**RANGE OF GRANTS** Usually between £500 and £10,000.
**SAMPLE GRANTS** IntoUniversity and Treloar College (£10,000 each); Villiers Park Educational Trust (£8,400); Museum of London Primary Learning Programme (£5,700); Royal School of Needlework and Sistema England (£5,000 each); Future Talent (£4,000).
**FINANCES** Year 2013/14 Income £453,532 Grants £293,119 Grants to organisations £245,994 Assets £18,302,511
**TRUSTEES** Shirley Reed; Susan Charlton; David Charlton; Duncan Reed; Ben Gooder; Anna Foxell; Evelyn Bentley; Nigel Callaghan.
**OTHER INFORMATION** 355 welfare grants totalling £47,000 were paid to organisations on behalf of individuals.
**HOW TO APPLY** In general, unsolicited applications are not accepted. Charities that fall within the 'special category', however, may send an introductory email to the Company Secretary (info@newby-trust.org.uk).
**WHO TO APPLY TO** Annabel Grout, Company Secretary, Hill Farm, Froxfield, Petersfield, Hampshire GU32 1BQ *email* info@newby-trust.org.uk *Website* www.newby-trust.org.uk

## ■ The Newcomen Collett Foundation

**CC NO** 312804                **ESTABLISHED** 1988
**WHERE FUNDING CAN BE GIVEN** London Borough of Southwark.
**WHO CAN BENEFIT** Schools; colleges; organisations; individuals.
**WHAT IS FUNDED** Education of young people under 25 years of age including: equipment; extra curricula activities; organisations providing educational opportunities to schools and

colleges (visiting theatre groups or musicians, for example).
**WHAT IS NOT FUNDED** Capital expenditure; rent; salaries; administration costs; retrospective grants.
**TYPE OF GRANT** One-off.
**RANGE OF GRANTS** Usually up to £1,000, occasionally more.
**SAMPLE GRANTS** The major grants beneficiaries, listed in the accounts, were: Heber Primary School (£2,400); Goodrich Primary School (£2,100); Oliver Goldsmith Primary School (£2,000); Camelot Primary School (£1,600); St Mary Magdalene Church of England Primary School (£1,500); Rambert and St Joseph's Catholic Junior School (£1,400 each); Hollington Youth Centre, KIDS and Lambeth and Southwark Primary Schools Football (£1,200 each); Sacred Heart RC School and St Saviour's and St Olave's School (£1,100 each).
**FINANCES** Year 2013/14 Income £404,626 Grants £73,436 Assets £3,019,066
**TRUSTEES** Richard Edwards; Dame Sylvia Morris; John Spencer; Robin Lovell; Andrew Covell; Robert Ashdown; Alexander Leiffheidt; Helen Cockerill; Michael Ibbott; Clare Clark; Janet Goodland; Peter MacFarlane.
**OTHER INFORMATION** The foundation only has £100,000 to distribute in grants each year so is unlikely to fully support a project. The involvement of other grant-making organisations is often required. The majority of grants are of less than £1,000. Most organisations may not apply for more than one grant in any twelve month period. See the guidelines for details of exceptions.
**HOW TO APPLY** Application forms are available to download, together with criteria and guidelines, from the website. The governors consider requests four times a year. The closing dates for applications are listed on the website.
**WHO TO APPLY TO** Catherine Dawkins, Clerk to the Governors, Marshall House, 66 Newcomen Street, London Bridge, London SE1 1YT Fax 020 7403 3969 email grantoffice@newcomencollett.org.uk Website www.newcomencollett.org.uk

■ **The Frances and Augustus Newman Foundation**
**CC NO** 277964  **ESTABLISHED** 1978
**WHERE FUNDING CAN BE GIVEN** UK.
**WHO CAN BENEFIT** Mainly medical professionals, academic institutions and major research centres.
**WHAT IS FUNDED** Mainly, but not exclusively, funding for medical research projects and equipment including fellowships of the Royal College of Surgeons.
**WHAT IS NOT FUNDED** Applications are not normally accepted from overseas. Requests from other charities seeking funds to supplement their own general funds to support medical research in a particular field are seldom supported.
**TYPE OF GRANT** Mainly one-off. Research and salaries will also be considered. Funding may be given for up to three years.
**RANGE OF GRANTS** £1,000–£100,000
**SAMPLE GRANTS** University of Cambridge (£100,000 for the Next Generation Fellowship); Royal College of Surgeons (£62,000 in two grants; one of £55,000 for Mr J Saunders, the other of £6,800 for the War, Art and Surgery Exhibition); Institute of Cancer Research (£50,500 for Tumour Profiling Unit); UCL (£30,000 for Mr T R Kurzawinski); Stroke Association (£25,500); Royal National Orthopaedic Hospital (£15,000 for Children's and Young People's Ward equipment); Help for Heroes (£2,000 for bike ride).
**FINANCES** Year 2013/14 Income £542,299 Grants £284,925 Grants to organisations £284,925 Assets £13,415,473
**TRUSTEES** David Sweetnam; Lord Hugh Rathcavan; John Williams; Stephen Cannon.
**HOW TO APPLY** Applications should include a detailed protocol and costing and be sent to the correspondent. They may then be peer-reviewed. The trustees meet in June and December each year and applications must be received at the latest by the end of April or October respectively. The foundation awards for surgical research fellowships should be addressed to the Royal College of Surgeons of England at 35–43 Lincoln's Inn Fields, London WC2A 3PE, which evaluates each application.
**WHO TO APPLY TO** Hazel Palfreyman, Correspondent, c/o Baker Tilly Chartered Accountants, Hartwell House, 55–61 Victoria Street, Bristol BS1 6AD Tel. 0117 945 2000 email hazel.palfreyman@bakertilly.co.uk

■ **Newpier Charity Ltd**
**CC NO** 293686  **ESTABLISHED** 1985
**WHERE FUNDING CAN BE GIVEN** UK and Israel.
**WHO CAN BENEFIT** Jewish organisations.
**WHAT IS FUNDED** Advancement of the Orthodox Jewish faith; the relief of poverty; general charitable purposes.
**SAMPLE GRANTS Previous beneficiaries have included:** BML Benityashvut; Friends of Biala; Gateshead Yeshiva; KID; Mesdos Wiznitz; SOFT (for redistribution to other charities).
**FINANCES** Year 2012/13 Income £1,006,577 Grants £723,293 Grants to organisations £723,293 Assets £2,867,888
**TRUSTEES** Charles Margulies; Helen Knopfler; Rachel Margulies.
**OTHER INFORMATION** At the time of writing (June 2015) the charity's 2013/14 accounts were overdue at the Charity Commission. The latest accounts available were those from the 2012/13 financial year.
**HOW TO APPLY** Apply in writing to the correspondent.
**WHO TO APPLY TO** Charles Margulies, Trustee, 186 Lordship Road, London N16 5ES Tel. 020 8802 4449

■ **Alderman Newton's Educational Foundation**
**CC NO** 527881  **ESTABLISHED** 1983
**WHERE FUNDING CAN BE GIVEN** Diocese of Leicester.
**WHO CAN BENEFIT** Maintained Church of England or other maintained schools within the City of Leicester, or any other Church of England school within the Diocese of Leicester.
**WHAT IS FUNDED** Projects that would not normally be funded by the local education authority.
**WHAT IS NOT FUNDED** Equipment or costs that would normally be met from the school budget set by the local education authority.
**TYPE OF GRANT** One-off and recurrent. Project funding.
**FINANCES** Year 2013/14 Income £153,704 Grants £111,361 Grants to organisations £57,536 Assets £4,116,151
**TRUSTEES** Michael Chamberlain; Canon Derek Goodman; Patricia Mounfield; Madan Kallow;

The Revd Canon Peter Taylor; Canon Barry Naylor; Cllr Malcolm Unsworth; Cheryl Pharoah; Dr Richard Harries; Charles Franks; Keith Jones; Wendy Martin; The Revd Canon Philip O'Reilly.
**HOW TO APPLY** An application form and guidelines are available from the correspondent or to download from the Leicester Charity Link website. Applications may be made at any time.
**WHO TO APPLY TO** The Clerk to the Governors, Leicester Charity Link, 20a Millstone Lane, Leicester LE1 5JN *Tel.* 0116 222 2200 *email* info@charity-link.org *Website* www.charity-link.org/trust-administration/trusts-we-support/alderman-newtons-educational-foundation

## ■ The NFU Mutual Charitable Trust
**CC NO** 1073064    **ESTABLISHED** 1998
**WHERE FUNDING CAN BE GIVEN** UK
**WHO CAN BENEFIT** Charitable organisations and individuals.
**WHAT IS FUNDED** Agriculture, rural development and insurance, including education, the relief of poverty, social welfare and research. Focus on initiatives that will have a significant impact on rural communities.
**RANGE OF GRANTS** £47,000 to £1,000.
**SAMPLE GRANTS** Farming and Countryside Education, FACE (£47,000); the National Federation of Young Farmers Clubs (£30,000); Addington Fund and Royal Agricultural Benevolent Institution (£20,000 each); Royal Highland Education Trust (£15,500); Rural Support (£12,500); Farming Community Network and Shakespeare Hospice at Home Service (£10,000 each); Henry Plumb Foundation, Isle of Man Agricultural Benevolent Trust and Ulster Open Farm Weekend (£5,000 each); Yorkshire Rural Support Network (£2,000); Children's Country Holiday Fund and Isle of Man Federation of Young Farmers Club (£1,000 each).
**FINANCES** *Year* 2013 *Income* £258,401 *Grants* £249,010 *Grants to organisations* £249,010 *Assets* £264,106
**TRUSTEES** Lord Curry of Kirkharle; Stephen James; Lindsay Sinclair; Sir Ian Grant; Richard Percy; Richard Butler; Nigel Miller; Ian Marshall; Meurig Raymond.
**OTHER INFORMATION** Grants totalled £249,000 and were made to 21 charitable organisations.
**HOW TO APPLY** Apply in writing to the correspondent either via post or email. According to the website, applications should include details of 'the project, initiative or organisation for which funding is sought; an indication of the amount of the donation requested; any business plans; details of any other funding sought and or obtained; any recognition which would be given to the trust in recognition of its support; and confirmation of whether or not the applicant is a registered charity'.
**WHO TO APPLY TO** James Creechan, Secretary to the Trustees, The National Farmers Union Mutual Insurance Society Limited, Tiddington Road, Stratford-upon-Avon, Warwickshire CV37 7BJ *Tel.* 01789 204211 *email* nfu_mutual_charitable_trust@nfumutual.co.uk *Website* www.nfumutual.co.uk/company-information/charitable-trust

## ■ The Chevras Ezras Nitzrochim Trust
**CC NO** 275352    **ESTABLISHED** 1978
**WHERE FUNDING CAN BE GIVEN** There is a preference for Greater London, though help is also given further afield.
**WHO CAN BENEFIT** Organisations benefitting Jewish people.
**WHAT IS FUNDED** The trust's objects are stated as: 'the relief of the poor, needy and sick and the advancement of Jewish Religious Education'.
**SAMPLE GRANTS** Lolev Trust (£5,900); Edupoor Ltd (£3,900); Care All Ltd (£2,700).
**FINANCES** *Year* 2013 *Income* £258,777 *Grants* £262,187 *Grants to organisations* £36,713 *Assets* £3,445
**TRUSTEES** Kurt Stern; Hertz Kahan; Moshe Rottenberg.
**OTHER INFORMATION** A further £225,500 was given in grants to individuals and families.
**HOW TO APPLY** Apply in writing to the correspondent.
**WHO TO APPLY TO** Hertz Kahan, Trustee, 53 Heathland Road, London N16 5PQ

## ■ NJD Charitable Trust
**CC NO** 1109146    **ESTABLISHED** 2005
**WHERE FUNDING CAN BE GIVEN** UK and Israel.
**WHO CAN BENEFIT** Organisations and individuals.
**WHAT IS FUNDED** The relief of poverty and hardship of members of the Jewish faith; the advancement of Jewish religion through Jewish education.
**SAMPLE GRANTS** **Previous beneficiaries have included:** Jewish Care (£15,000); UJIA (£10,000); Jewish Leadership Council (£7,500); Community Security Trust (£6,600); Holocaust Educational Trust (£5,000).
**FINANCES** *Year* 2012/13 *Income* £142 *Grants* £64,000 *Grants to organisations* £64,000
**TRUSTEES** Nathalie Dwek; Jean Glaskie; Jacob Wolf; Alexander Dwek.
**OTHER INFORMATION** At the time of writing (June 2015) these were the latest figures available for the trust. Due to its low income during the year, the trust was not required to submit its accounts to the Charity Commission. The trust had a total expenditure of £64,500.
**HOW TO APPLY** Apply in writing to the correspondent.
**WHO TO APPLY TO** Alan Dawson, Trust Administrator, St Bride's House, 10 Salisbury Square, London EC4Y 8EH *Tel.* 020 7842 7306 *email* info@igpinvest.com

## ■ Alice Noakes Memorial Charitable Trust
**CC NO** 1039663    **ESTABLISHED** 1994
**WHERE FUNDING CAN BE GIVEN** UK.
**WHO CAN BENEFIT** Organisations and individuals.
**WHAT IS FUNDED** Research, teaching, treatment and care relating to animal welfare.
**RANGE OF GRANTS** £500–£20,000
**SAMPLE GRANTS** University of Cambridge – Residency (£20,000); Animal Health Trust (£12,500); Writtle Agricultural College – Bursary (£12,000); RSPCA – Danaher Animal Home (£10,000); Fauna and Flora International (£1,000); The Gambia Horse and Donkey Trust and Greyhound Rescue (£500 each).
**FINANCES** *Year* 2013/14 *Income* £100,816 *Grants* £66,000 *Grants to organisations* £62,000 *Assets* £2,453,912

TRUSTEES David Whipps; J. Simpson; Spencer Bayer; Jeremy Hulme; Robert Ferdinando.
OTHER INFORMATION The 2013/14 grants to two individuals totalled £4,000. The trustees set no minimum or maximum level of grant, though the majority appear to be of £500.
HOW TO APPLY 'Applications for grants fitting the trust's objectives should be sent to the trustees at the charity's registered office.' The trustees meet twice a year.
WHO TO APPLY TO The Trustees, c/o Holmes and Hills, Bocking End, Braintree, Essex CM7 9AJ *Tel.* 01376 320456

## ■ Nominet Charitable Foundation
CC NO 1125735　　ESTABLISHED 2008
WHERE FUNDING CAN BE GIVEN UK and overseas.
WHO CAN BENEFIT Mainly UK-based initiatives.
WHAT IS FUNDED Digital technology to address social issues in the UK. There are various funding programmes run by the foundation.
WHAT IS NOT FUNDED Hardware infrastructure projects or software procurement projects, e.g. a project to equip a school with PCs, or to install Wi-Fi for a community; website improvements where no new functional or service delivery innovations are delivered; website development unless the project and organisation delivers against one of the foundation's areas of focus and meets its funding guidelines; organisational running costs per se. Political parties and lobbying parties cannot be funded. The website also states: 'If you simply want to add digital to existing services in order to make them more efficient or cost-effective, we are not the funder for you.'
RANGE OF GRANTS Up to £250,000.
SAMPLE GRANTS NESTA (£250,000); The Memory Box Network Ltd (£160,000); Safer London Foundation (£120,000); The Camden Future First Network Ltd (£110,000); Digital Youth Academy (£100,000); FutureGov (£60,000); GlobalGiving UK (£56,500); Disability Rocks and Family Innovation Zone (£51,000).
FINANCES *Year* 2013/14 *Income* £6,067,351 *Grants* £4,261,310 *Grants to organisations* £4,261,310 *Assets* £6,859,120
TRUSTEES Dr Clive Grace; Bill Liao; Sebastien Lahtinen; Nora Nanayakkara.
OTHER INFORMATION In 2013/14 grants of less than £50,000 totalled £1.5 million.
HOW TO APPLY Funding programmes change regularly. The details of current programmes can be found on the website, along with extensive guidelines. There is a two-stage online application process. Stage 1 requires you to submit a video of no more than three minutes in length, in which you should describe the key features of your project and what you hope to achieve. Those applicants whose projects the foundation thinks align closely with its aims and objectives will be invited to complete the second stage of the application process, which is also online. At Stage 2 you will be asked to provide more detail about your initiative, including a project budget and plan.
WHO TO APPLY TO Vicki Hearn, Director, Nominet Trust, Minerva House, Edmund Halley Road, Oxford OX4 4DQ *Tel.* 01865 334000 *Fax* 01865 332314 *email* enquiries@nominettrust.org.uk *Website* www.nominettrust.org.uk

## ■ The Noon Foundation
CC NO 1053654　　ESTABLISHED 1995
WHERE FUNDING CAN BE GIVEN UK.
WHO CAN BENEFIT Charitable organisations.
WHAT IS FUNDED Education; the relief of poverty and sickness; the alleviation of racial discrimination.
RANGE OF GRANTS £50–£56,000
SAMPLE GRANTS **Previous beneficiaries have included:** Birkbeck University of London; Breast Cancer Care; Coexistence Trust; Garsington Opera; Horizon Medical; London School of Economics; Oxfam; Macmillan Cancer Support; Marie Curie Cancer Care; Muslim Aid; Wellbeing.
FINANCES *Year* 2013 *Income* £7,421 *Grants* £355,000 *Grants to organisations* £355,000
TRUSTEES Lord Noon; Akbar Shirazi; Zeenat Harnal; Michael Jepson; Anthony Robinson; Zarmin Noon Sekhon.
OTHER INFORMATION Due to its low income, the foundation was not required to submit its accounts to the Charity Commission.
HOW TO APPLY Our research indicates that all applications and queries should be made by e-mail.
WHO TO APPLY TO The Trustees, 25 Queen Anne's Gate, St James's Park, London SW1H 9BU *Tel.* 020 7654 1600 *email* grants@noongroup.co.uk

## ■ Norfolk Community Foundation
CC NO 1110817　　ESTABLISHED 2004
WHERE FUNDING CAN BE GIVEN Norfolk.
WHO CAN BENEFIT Constituted community and voluntary organisations which look to benefit the needs of the local community.
WHAT IS FUNDED Charitable purposes that benefit people living in the county of Norfolk. All funds administered by the foundation look to address disadvantage and social need, and to improve quality of life, particularly for Norfolk's most vulnerable and marginalised people.
WHAT IS NOT FUNDED According to the application guidelines, which were available on the foundation's website, exclusions are as follows: projects benefitting people outside the stated area of benefit; individuals for their personal needs; retrospective grants; direct replacement of statutory funding; organisations controlled by public sector bodies; the purchase of equipment that will become the property of a statutory body; improvements to land or buildings owned by a statutory body (except parish/town councils); improvements to land or buildings where the grant applicant does not have a legal interest in the land/building; projects where the grant award cannot be spent within the stated grant term (typically 12 months); medical research and equipment; sports projects (unless there is strong evidence of disadvantage or clear evidence of the project addressing social inclusion/ community cohesion). The foundation would not expect to fund applications from groups wanting to attend sporting events; arts projects (unless there is strong evidence that the project is addressing disadvantage and that those taking part are gaining new and useful life skills). The foundation is very unlikely to fund professional performance fees; environmental projects (the foundation usually expects to see strong benefits for people not just the environment); religious or political causes or political lobbying; commercial ventures; general appeals; sponsorship; animal welfare (unless the project benefits people); travel or

expeditions abroad for individuals and groups; organisations raising funds to redistribute to other causes; projects that do not directly contribute to community activity (for example, street decorations, displays or furniture, war memorials or renovations to historic buildings or monuments). This list is not exhaustive and exists simply to provide guidance on activities that would usually be considered unsuitable for funding.

**TYPE OF GRANT** One-off and one-year long projects.

**RANGE OF GRANTS** Grants are usually in the range of £2,000 to £5,000.

**SAMPLE GRANTS** Aylsham Town Council (£100,000); Beetley and East Bilney Village Hall (£99,000); Sheringham Little Theatre (£66,000); Burgh St Peter Village Hall (£57,000); Christian Fellowship Norwich (£50,500); Palling Volunteer Rescue Service (£9,900); 6 Youth Council (£5,000); Catch 22 (£4,000); Neatishead Community Gym (£3,900); Road to Recovery (£3,700); The Conservation Volunteers (£2,000); Dereham Community Support Centre (£1,700); Go Kids Go (£1,500); Total Ensemble Theatre Company (£1,000).

**FINANCES** Year 2013 Income £7,009,927 Grants £4,161,094 Grants to organisations £4,130,964 Assets £11,115,680

**TRUSTEES** Charles Barratt; Jackie Higham; Frank Eliel; Iain Mawson; David White; Bolton Agnew; Martin Webster; Tim Seeley; Jo Pearson; Virginia Edgecombe; Caroline Money; Mary Rudd.

**OTHER INFORMATION** During 2013, the foundation administered more than 100 funds on behalf of individuals and organisations. 493 community groups and other organisations were supported. 82 individuals also received grants totalling £30,000.

**HOW TO APPLY** Each fund has details of how to apply on the its webpage. Application processes usually take place online and require the completion of a Part A, Part B and the submission of appropriate supporting documents. Assistance with any part of the application process, including if you are unable to complete an online form, can be given by the Grants Team, contactable by email (grants@norfolkfoundation.com) or by telephone (01603 623 958).

**WHO TO APPLY TO** Grants Team, St James Mill, Whitefriars, Norwich NR3 1TN Tel. 01603 623958 Fax 01603 230034 email info@norfolkfoundation.com Website www.norfolkfoundation.com

## ■ Normalyn Charitable Trust

**CC NO** 1077985   **ESTABLISHED** 1999

**WHERE FUNDING CAN BE GIVEN** UK.

**WHO CAN BENEFIT** Registered charities.

**WHAT IS FUNDED** General charitable purposes, mainly Jewish causes.

**WHAT IS NOT FUNDED** Non-registered charities.

**TYPE OF GRANT** One-off.

**RANGE OF GRANTS** Our research indicates that the average grant range is £1,001–£5,000.

**SAMPLE GRANTS** United Synagogue (£21,500); Finchley Jewish Primary School Trust (£8,500); Community Security Trust (£6,000); City of London School Trust (£4,500); Norwood (£2,500); Chana Charitable Trust, Teach First and UK Jewish Film Festival (£1,000 each).

**FINANCES** Year 2013/14 Income £22,575 Grants £20,000 Grants to organisations £20,000

**TRUSTEES** Daniel Dover; Jeremy Newman; Judith Newman.

**OTHER INFORMATION** In 2013/14 the trust had a total expenditure of £20,500. Due to its low income, the foundation was not required to submit its accounts to the Charity Commission.

**HOW TO APPLY** The trust does not accept unsolicited applications.

**WHO TO APPLY TO** Jeremy Newman, Trustee, 26 Allandale Avenue, London N3 3PJ

## ■ The Norman Family Charitable Trust

**CC NO** 277616   **ESTABLISHED** 1979

**WHERE FUNDING CAN BE GIVEN** Primarily Cornwall, Devon and southern and western Somerset

**WHO CAN BENEFIT** Registered charities only, preferably smaller, local charities. National charities are only supported for projects helping the area of benefit.

**WHAT IS FUNDED** General charitable purposes, including: medical, including medical research; sport and leisure; community projects; youth; blind, deaf and physically handicapped; children's welfare; animals, environment and conservation; homelessness and social welfare; forces, ex-forces and emergency services; older people; mental health and learning disabilities; crime prevention, rehabilitation and addictions; employment and skills training.

**WHAT IS NOT FUNDED** Organisations which use live animals for experimental or research purposes; the maintenance or repair of religious buildings; projects outside the UK. Individuals are not supported directly.

**TYPE OF GRANT** One-off, project, research and start-up costs will be considered.

**RANGE OF GRANTS** Up to £20,000. Most grants are of £5,000 or less.

**SAMPLE GRANTS** Warm Wish Group – St Peter's Primary School Budleigh (£20,000); National Trust (£15,000); Hospiscare Exeter and North Devon Hospice (£10,000 each); Children's Hospice South West – Cornwall, East Budleigh Community Shop, Shelter-box, Sports Aid South West, St Peter's School Cafe and St Petrocks (£5,000 each); Budleigh Community Youth Trust, Prince's Trust and Sir Francis Chichester (£4,000 each); Woodbury Village Hall (£3,000); Abbeyfield Society Exmouth, Kingfisher Award Scheme and RABI (£2,500 each).

**FINANCES** Year 2013/14 Income £445,343 Grants £335,400 Grants to organisations £332,400 Assets £8,594,121

**TRUSTEES** Roger Dawe, Chair; Margaret Evans; Michael Saunders; Margaret Webb; Catherine Houghton; Sarah Gillingham.

**OTHER INFORMATION** Organisations received 342 grants during the year. A further three grants, totalling £3,000 were paid to individuals for purposes relating to sport and leisure.

**HOW TO APPLY** Applications can be made using the online form, or by downloading the form, completing it and sending via post. The trustees meet in March, June, September and December to consider grants over £5,000. A subcommittee meets every six to eight weeks to deal with applications for less than £5,000. Meeting dates can be found on the website. Applications are not accepted via email. The trust's website notes that it has recently supported six organisations working to help young people from the South West: BSES Expeditions; Sports Aid South West; Sir Francis Chichester Trust; The Prince's Trust; Lord Lieutenant's Trust Fund for the Youth of Cornwall; and Trinity Sailing Trust. Rather than

applying to The Norman Family Charitable Trust, these organisations can be contacted, mentioning the trust's name.
**WHO TO APPLY TO** The Trustees, 14 Fore Street, Budleigh Salterton, Devon EX9 6NG *Tel.* 01395 446699 *email* info@nfct.org *Website* www.nfct.org

## ■ The Normanby Charitable Trust
**CC NO** 252102   **ESTABLISHED** 1966
**WHERE FUNDING CAN BE GIVEN** UK, with a special interest in North Yorkshire and north east England.
**WHO CAN BENEFIT** Registered charities.
**WHAT IS FUNDED** General charitable purposes, particularly arts, culture, heritage and social welfare.
**WHAT IS NOT FUNDED** Non-UK charities. Grants to individuals are only made exceptionally.
**RANGE OF GRANTS** £500 to £20,000.
**SAMPLE GRANTS** Garden Museum (£20,000); Green Howards Museum (£15,000); The Music Pool and The Postgate Parishes (£10,000 each); Seachange Community Trust (£8,500); Fryup Cricket Club (£5,000); Great North Air Ambulance and Whitby Dag (£3,000); British Wireless for the Blind Fund and Children's Cross Country Holidays Fund (£2,000 each); St Matthews Church (£1,500); Crisis UK, Relate and St Hilda's Playgroup (£1,000); Tall Ships Youth Trust (£600); Deafblind UK, Eskdale Festival of the Arts, Panathlon and Staithes Village Memorial Hall (£500 each).
**FINANCES** *Year* 2013/14 *Income* £309,026 *Grants* £123,000 *Grants to organisations* £123,000 *Assets* £11,197,905
**TRUSTEES** The Marquis of Normanby; The Dowager Marchioness of Normanby; Lady Lepel Kornicki; Lady Evelyn Buchan; Lady Peronel Cruz; Lady Henrietta Burridge.
**HOW TO APPLY** Apply in writing to the correspondent. The trustees meet two or three times a year to award grants, although there are no regular dates. Note that only successful applications are acknowledged.
**WHO TO APPLY TO** The Marquis of Normanby, Trustee, 52 Tite Street, London Sw3 4JA *email* nct@normanby.org

## ■ North West Cancer Research (Incorporating Clatterbridge Cancer Research CCR)
**CC NO** 519357
**WHERE FUNDING CAN BE GIVEN** North West of England and North and Mid Wales.
**WHO CAN BENEFIT** Those carrying out cancer research in the North West of England and North and Mid Wales.
**WHAT IS FUNDED** Fundamental research into the causes of all forms of cancers, the mechanisms by which they arrive and their effects. Grants are given across three main areas: Basic; Translational; and Preventative.
**WHAT IS NOT FUNDED** Resubmissions of applications are not accepted within 12 months unless invited by the committee.
**SAMPLE GRANTS** Bangor University; Lancaster University; University of Liverpool.
**FINANCES** *Year* 2012/13 *Income* £1,747,512 *Grants* £1,565,292 *Grants to organisations* £1,565,292 *Assets* £9,434,057
**TRUSTEES** Andrew Rennison; Tony Bagnall; Beryl Lloyd Powell MBE; Olive Lily Cutts; Kate Cowie; Sir Ian Thomas Gilmore; John Cadwaladr Lewys-Lloyd; William Michael Barton; Patricia Mann; Helen Elizabeth Dring; Shiela Tulloch Gill; David Balfour Smith; Michael Stuart Potts; Nigel Stuart Lanceley; Geoff Greenwood; Geoffrey William Stewart; Michael Georgeson; Barbara Smith; Joan Pettitt; David Leach; Francis Margaret Leigh Street; Peter Webster Somerfield; Doreen Sands; Olivia Elizabeth Ley; Wendy Hadwin.
**OTHER INFORMATION** Formerly known as Clatterbridge Cancer Research (CCR), the charity in its current set-up was formed on 1 November 2012 when CCR merged with the North West Cancer Research Fund (NSCRF). At the time of writing (June 2015) the 2012/13 accounts were the latest available at the time of writing. The charity finances research at the University of Liverpool, Lancaster University and Bangor University in grants ranging from £750,000 to £1 million annually. Usually around 30 projects, with an average annual value of £50,000 each, are in progress at any one time.
**HOW TO APPLY** At the time of writing, the charity's website stated that its application process was under review; however, the guidelines noted were as follows: Applications should be made in writing and be no more than 2,000 words. Relevant papers in press or submitted should be included as an appendix and, where possible, be no longer than five pages in total. They should be submitted in time for one of two deadline dates, 1 April or 1 October, for consideration by the North West Cancer Research Scientific Committee around eight weeks later. One original copy of your application should be sent to Dominique Hare, North West Cancer Research, NWCR Centre, 200 London Road, Liverpool, L3 9TA and, additionally, a copy should be sent in PDF form by email to research@nwcr.org. Refer to the website before beginning an application to be sure of any alterations to the application process.
**WHO TO APPLY TO** Erika Lomas, Finance Officer, North West Cancer Research, North West Cancer Research Centre, 200 London Road, Liverpool L3 9TA *Tel.* 0151 709 2919 *Fax* 0151 708 7997 *email* info@nwcr.org *Website* www.nwcr.org

## ■ The Northampton Municipal Church Charities
**CC NO** 259593   **ESTABLISHED** 1969
**WHERE FUNDING CAN BE GIVEN** The borough of Northampton.
**WHO CAN BENEFIT** Organisations and individuals.
**WHAT IS FUNDED** Relief in need.
**TYPE OF GRANT** One-off and recurrent.
**RANGE OF GRANTS** For organisations, usually between £1,000 and £30,000.
**SAMPLE GRANTS** **Previous beneficiaries have included:** Nene Valley CFR (£18,000); Emmanuel Church (£8,700); Mount Pleasant Baptist Church (£5,000); Northampton Hope Centre (£3,000); Motor Neurone Disease and Broadmead Money Advice Centre (£2,500 each); Crime to Christ (£2,000); Deafblind UK and Listening Books (£1,500 each); and Tools for Self Reliance and Samaritans (£1,000 each).
**FINANCES** *Year* 2013/14 *Income* £274,903 *Grants* £110,000 *Grants to organisations* £55,000
**TRUSTEES** Richard Pestell; Eileen Beeby; Keith Davidson; Ronald Gates; Ruth Hampson; Brian

**689**

May; Clive Fowler; Terrence O'Connor; Linda Davitt; Phil Larratt; Brian Sargeant.

**OTHER INFORMATION** Grants are made to individuals and pensioners, and vouchers are distributed at Christmas. The charity also runs an almshouse in Northampton, made up of 17 one-bedroomed flats. At the time of writing (June 2015) the charity's 2013/14 accounts had been submitted to the Charity Commission but were not yet available to view. The grant total above is an estimate based on the average amount given in grants in the three years for which accounts were available to view.

**HOW TO APPLY** The charity has previously stated: 'Institutions or individuals can apply for funding of projects or for grants. Individuals must be in need and an application form containing their financial details has to be completed. Representatives of institutions attend Trustees meetings and the organisation or project must benefit persons in need in the Borough of Northampton.'

**WHO TO APPLY TO** Clerk to the Trustees, Wilson Browne Solicitors, 4 Grange Park Court, Roman Way, Grange Park, Northampton NN4 5EA *Tel.* 01604 876697 *email* jforsyth@wilsonbrowne.co.uk

## ■ Northamptonshire Community Foundation

**CC NO** 1094646    **ESTABLISHED** 2001
**WHERE FUNDING CAN BE GIVEN** Northamptonshire.
**WHO CAN BENEFIT** Registered charities; local organisations.
**WHAT IS FUNDED** Community-based action benefitting Northamptonshire's most disadvantaged residents. Child poverty, unemployment, homelessness, domestic violence and social exclusion are just some of the areas where the foundation looks to make a difference.
**WHAT IS NOT FUNDED** General exclusions include: general and major fundraising appeals; direct replacement of statutory and public funding; work that is a statutory responsibility; schools (except friends organisations) and parish councils; organisations aiming to convert people to any kind of religious or political belief; medical research and equipment; projects operating outside Northamptonshire; animal welfare; large national charities (except for local branches serving local people); work already completed; non-charitable work; projects that will redistribute the funding (with the exception of Surviving Winter grants). Each individual fund is subject to its own criteria and exclusions.
**RANGE OF GRANTS** Generally up to £10,000. The majority of grants are of less than £5,000.
**SAMPLE GRANTS** Abington House of Fun and Blackthorn Good Neighbours (£10,000 each); St James and Dallington Youth Club (£9,200); Northamptonshire YMCA (£7,800); Mawsley Villagers Association and Shout Youth Theatre (£5,000); Northampton and District Citizens Advice (£4,000); Northamptonshire Carers (£3,000); Northampton Food Bank (£2,500); Oundle Badminton Club (£1,500); Rushden Pensioners Forum (£900); Peterborough Cathedral Development and Preservation Trust (£250); Daventry Vineyard Church (£200).
**FINANCES** *Year* 2013/14 *Income* £1,430,869 *Grants* £657,193 *Grants to organisations* £657,193 *Assets* £3,541,205
**TRUSTEES** Sandra Bell; Paul Southworth; Alan Maskell; John Bruce; Robert Tomkinson; Guy Schanschieff; Anne Burnett; Sally Robinson; David Knight; John Griffiths-Elsden; James Shepherd-Cross.
**OTHER INFORMATION** One loan of £48,500 was also made during the year.
**HOW TO APPLY** Application forms for each funding programme can be downloaded from the foundation's website, where criteria and guidelines are also posted. If you require support choosing the best fund for you or any support relating to the applications process, contact the grants team.
**WHO TO APPLY TO** Victoria Miles, Chief Executive, c/o Royal and Derngate, 19 Guildhall Road, Northampton NN1 1DP *Tel.* 01604 230033 *Fax* 01604 636303 *email* enquiries@ncf.com *Website* www.ncf.uk.com

## ■ The Community Foundation for Northern Ireland

**IR NO** XN45242    **ESTABLISHED** 1979
**WHERE FUNDING CAN BE GIVEN** Northern Ireland and the six border counties of the Republic of Ireland.
**WHO CAN BENEFIT** Community groups; voluntary organisations.
**WHAT IS FUNDED** Community development in Northern Ireland.
**WHAT IS NOT FUNDED** General applications are not accepted. See the website for open funds, which each have their own criteria and exclusions.
**TYPE OF GRANT** One-off and reoccurring.
**RANGE OF GRANTS** Generally between £1,000 and £5,000.
**SAMPLE GRANTS** Shopmobility Belfast (£50,000); Aghyaran Development Association CIC (£25,000); Ulster Historical Foundation (£14,100); Leafair Community Association (£6,000); Fountain Dance Association (£4,500); Link Community Association Women's Group (£2,900); Youth Initiatives (£1,000); Holywood and District Community Council (£500); Friends of Arvalee School (£200).
**FINANCES** *Year* 2012/13 *Income* £7,664,835 *Grants* £990,168 *Grants to organisations* £990,168 *Assets* £12,151,540
**TRUSTEES** Tony McCusker; Les Allamby; Fred Bass; Geraldine Donaghy; Brian Dougherty; Rosalie Flanagan; Niamh Goggin; Colin Stutt; John Healy; Bernadette Lavery; Joe McKnight; Carmel O'Connor; Dawn Purvis.
**PUBLICATIONS** Various policy briefs, funder's briefs and models of best practice available on the website.
**OTHER INFORMATION** At the time of writing (June 2015) the 2012/13 accounts were the latest available. During the year 322 grants were awarded. As with any community foundation, funds open and close periodically. See the website for details of currently open funds.
**HOW TO APPLY** Applications to any of the funds are made through the same online process. The foundation will match the application with the most suitable fund. There are comprehensive guidelines available on the website for applications. A turnaround time of 12 weeks should be allowed for all applications. There are two parts to the application process: Part A – complete the short online form to answer the questions about the project, beneficiaries and budget and Part B – you will be given a unique link to your own application form in an email along with guidelines on completing it. This part must be printed off and signed by two members of the organisation. Both parts should then be

posted to the foundation together with the following documentation: a copy of the governing document; a copy of the most recent accounts or income and expenditure statement; a list of the management committee members and their contact details; a recent original bank statement for the organisation's bank account. The foundation will normally only fund groups located in Northern Ireland; however, some funds will make grants in the Republic as well. Applicants should check the fund specifications. Applications are assessed by the foundation's staff and recommendations are considered by the trustee's grants subcommittee. Successful applicants will be required to submit both qualitative and quantitative monitoring information for the benefit of both the grant holder and the foundation.

**WHO TO APPLY TO** Grants Team, Community House, Citylink Business Park, Albert Street, Belfast BT12 4HQ *Tel.* 028 9024 5927 *Fax* 028 7137 1565 *email* info@communityfoundationni.org *Website* www.communityfoundationni.org

■ **The Northern Rock Foundation**

**CC NO** 1063906     **ESTABLISHED** 1997
**WHERE FUNDING CAN BE GIVEN** Cumbria, Northumberland, Tyne and Wear, County Durham and the Tees Valley.
**WHO CAN BENEFIT** Organisations.
**WHAT IS FUNDED** Tackling disadvantage and improving quality of life.
**TYPE OF GRANT** Capital, core or project funding and for up to three or more years (sometimes renewable after that).
**RANGE OF GRANTS** Typically up to £250,000.
**SAMPLE GRANTS** Beneficiaries in previous years have included: Centrepoint County Durham (£218,500); Newcastle Law Centre (£163,000); African Community Advice North East (£86,000); Addaction (£30,000); Cumbria Reducing Offending Partnership Trust (£9,000); University of Sunderland (£6,800); Rape and Sexual Abuse Counselling Centre – Darlington and Co Durham (£5,000); Kidsafe UK (£4,700); Liverpool John Moores University (£2,500).
**FINANCES** *Year* 2013 *Income* £912,000 *Grants* £7,298,000 *Grants to organisations* £7,298,000 *Assets* £23,347,000
**TRUSTEES** Alastair Balls; Sir David Chapman; David Faulkner; Dr Tony Henfrey; Frank Nicholson; Dr Mo O'Toole.
**OTHER INFORMATION** Following discussions between the foundation and Virgin Money, which now owns Northern Rock plc, in April 2014, it was announced that Virgin Money would commit no further funding. A document titled 'History of the Northern Rock Foundation', which is available to download from the website, states: 'In May 2014 Virgin Money then offered the Foundation £1 million per year for five years, on condition that this was matched by the Foundation raising £3 million per year from the private sector locally. This was considered very seriously by the Foundation's trustees. Virgin Money and Northern Rock Foundation together looked at many different ways in which this offer could help to generate an income for the Foundation including reviewing the current funding environment and canvassing views from private, public and voluntary sector bodies. Eventually it was concluded that, given the existing charitable commitments and links with other local funders of many other businesses in the region, this was not a viable option for the foundation.'

**HOW TO APPLY** The website states: 'The Foundation has now closed its grant programmes and is no longer accepting applications. Trustees are preparing for the likely closure of the Foundation, probably within eighteen months from January 2015.'
**WHO TO APPLY TO** Penny Wilkinson, Chief Executive, The Old Chapel, Woodbine Road, Gosforth, Newcastle upon Tyne NE3 1DD *Tel.* 0191 284 8412 *Fax* 0191 284 8413 *email* generaloffice@nr-foundation.org.uk *Website* www.nr-foundation.org.uk

■ **The Northmoor Trust**

**CC NO** 256818     **ESTABLISHED** 1968
**WHERE FUNDING CAN BE GIVEN** UK
**WHO CAN BENEFIT** Registered charities.
**WHAT IS FUNDED** The direct or indirect relief of poverty, hardship or distress.
**WHAT IS NOT FUNDED** Individuals; religion; medicine; the arts; general appeals. Grants are only made to organisations of which one or more of the trustees has direct personal knowledge.
**TYPE OF GRANT** One-off and recurrent.
**RANGE OF GRANTS** Five grants of £10,000 were given.
**SAMPLE GRANTS** Family Friends, Fight for Change, Prisoners' Advice Service, Tower Hamlets Friends and Neighbours and WISH (£10,000 each).
**FINANCES** *Year* 2013/14 *Income* £58,468 *Grants* £50,000 *Grants to organisations* £50,000 *Assets* £1,569,781
**TRUSTEES** Viscount Runciman; Dame Ruth Runciman; Frances Bennett; Cathy Eastburn.
**OTHER INFORMATION** There were five grants recipients during the year.
**HOW TO APPLY** Apply in writing to the correspondent, including the latest accounts and annual report, a list of the main sources of funding and a budget for the current year including details of other grant applications made. For first time applicants, a general description of aims and achievements to date and an outline of plans for future development. Applications should arrive by mid-February for preliminary consideration in March, decisions are made in May. Applicants may be visited or asked to provide additional information for the May meeting.
**WHO TO APPLY TO** Hilary Edwards, Secretary, 44 Clifton Hill, London NW8 0QG *Tel.* 020 7372 0698

■ **The Northumberland Village Homes Trust**

**CC NO** 225429     **ESTABLISHED** 1880
**WHERE FUNDING CAN BE GIVEN** North East England.
**WHO CAN BENEFIT** Organisations.
**WHAT IS FUNDED** The relief of poverty, distress and sickness among children and young persons under the age of 21 years, and the promotion of their education and training. There is a preference for those resident in Northumberland, Durham, Tyne and Wear and Cleveland.
**WHAT IS NOT FUNDED** Gap year projects; medical purposes.
**RANGE OF GRANTS** Mostly between £1,000 and £5,000.
**SAMPLE GRANTS** Barnardo's (£7,000); Evening Chronicle Sunshine Fund (£5,000); Macmillan Tyneside Young Carers and Northumberland

Clubs for Young People (£2,500 each); Tynedale Hospice at Home; Cramlington Voluntary Youth Project and Wallsend Boys' Club (£1,000 each); Contact a Family (£750); REACT (£500).

**FINANCES** *Year* 2013/14 *Income* £57,455 *Grants* £41,325 *Grants to organisations* £41,325 *Assets* £1,490,556

**TRUSTEES** Claire Macalpine; Lord Gisborough; Eileen Savage; Diana Barkes; Richard Savage.

**OTHER INFORMATION** 19 grants were made during the year.

**HOW TO APPLY** Our research suggests that applications should be made by 30 September for consideration in November. Applications should be in writing and state: whether the applicant is an individual, private charity or registered charity; the objects (if a charity); the amount required and what it is for; and any other sources of funding.

**WHO TO APPLY TO** Richard Savage, Trustee, c/o Lambert Taylor and Gregory Solicitors, Robson House, 4 Middle Street, Corbridge NE45 5AT *Tel.* 01434 632505 *email* corbridge@lambert-taylor-gregory.co.uk

## ■ The Northwood Charitable Trust

**SC NO** SC014487   **ESTABLISHED** 1972

**WHERE FUNDING CAN BE GIVEN** Scotland, especially Dundee and Tayside.

**WHO CAN BENEFIT** Registered charities.

**WHAT IS FUNDED** General charitable purposes. In the past, grants have been given to a university and to medical and educational projects.

**TYPE OF GRANT** One-off and recurring grants.

**SAMPLE GRANTS Previous beneficiaries have included:** Brittle Bone Society; Couple Counselling Tayside; Dundee Age Concern; Dundee Samaritans; Dundee Repertory Theatre; Macmillan Cancer Relief Scotland; Tayside Association for the Deaf; Tayside Medical Projects; Tayside Orthopaedic and Rehabilitation Technology.

**FINANCES** *Year* 2013/14 *Income* £2,565,581 *Grants* £2,500,000 *Grants to organisations* £2,500,000

**TRUSTEES** Brian Harold Thomson; Andrew Francis Thomson; Lewis Murray Thomson.

**OTHER INFORMATION** The grant total is an estimate based upon previous years.

**HOW TO APPLY** The trust has previously stated that funds are fully committed and that no applications will be considered or acknowledged.

**WHO TO APPLY TO** Brian McKernie, Secretary, c/o William Thomson and Sons, 22 Meadowside, Dundee DD1 1LN *Tel.* 01382 201534

## ■ The Norton Foundation

**CC NO** 702638   **ESTABLISHED** 1990

**WHERE FUNDING CAN BE GIVEN** Mainly Birmingham, Coventry, Solihull and the county of Warwickshire.

**WHO CAN BENEFIT** Children and young people up to the age of 25 who are in need due to disadvantage. The foundation's website defines this as: those who are 'in care or in need of rehabilitation, lapsing into delinquency, suffering from maltreatment or neglect, or whose potential is not yet realised due to circumstances beyond their control'.

**WHAT IS FUNDED** Grants to support vocational development, entry to employment, establishing a home, provision of equipment and personal development.

**TYPE OF GRANT** One-off capital grants and smaller recurring grants. Unrestricted funding.

**RANGE OF GRANTS** Up to £5,000 for organisations. A one-off capital grants of £100,000 every five years.

**SAMPLE GRANTS** Trailblazers Mentoring (£4,500 in two grants); All Saints Youth Project, Canal and River Trust and Prisoners' Education Trust (£2,000 each); Birmingham Royal Ballet, Blue Orange Arts Ltd and Children with Cystic Fibrosis Dream Holidays (£1,500); St Gabriel's Centre (£1,250); Acorns Children's Hospice (£1,200); Kids (£1,000).

**FINANCES** *Year* 2013/14 *Income* £154,408 *Grants* £88,621 *Grants to organisations* £54,820 *Assets* £4,937,925

**TRUSTEES** Jane Gaynor; Parminder Singh Birdi; Alan Bailey; Graham Suggett; Brian Lewis; Michael Bailey; Sarah Henderson; Richard Perkins; Richard Hurley; Bob Meacham; Louise Sewell; Wendy Carrington.

**OTHER INFORMATION** During the year, a total of 44 grants were made to organisations. £34,000 was given in 161 grants to individuals.

**HOW TO APPLY** Application forms are available with guidance notes from foundation's website. Applications from organisations are normally processed by the trustees at their quarterly meetings.

**WHO TO APPLY TO** The Correspondent, PO Box 10282, Redditch, Worcestershire B97 9ZA *Tel.* 01527 544446 *email* correspondent@nortonfoundation.org *Website* www.nortonfoundation.org

## ■ The Norton Rose Charitable Foundation

**CC NO** 1102142   **ESTABLISHED** 2004

**WHERE FUNDING CAN BE GIVEN** Worldwide.

**WHO CAN BENEFIT** Registered charities and organisations conducting charitable activities worldwide.

**WHAT IS FUNDED** Social welfare; medical; education; disaster relief.

**RANGE OF GRANTS** Up to £100,000.

**SAMPLE GRANTS** Barretstown (£100,000) and The Capital Community Foundation (£52,000).

**FINANCES** *Year* 2013/14 *Income* £597,989 *Grants* £337,928 *Grants to organisations* £337,928 *Assets* £438,895

**TRUSTEES** Simon Cox; Patrick Farrell; Glenn Hall; Campbell Steedman.

**OTHER INFORMATION** Organisations were awarded 37 grants during the year which were distributed as follows: social welfare (£263,500); education (£30,500); medical (£27,500); other (£16,700).

**HOW TO APPLY** The 2013/14 annual report states: 'In many cases, the charities we support are those we have supported in the past, but new charities are considered at all the regular Trustee meetings. The Trustees also meet on an ad hoc basis to consider specific urgent requests such as the support of major disaster relief appeals.'

**WHO TO APPLY TO** Patrick Farrell, Secretary, 3 More London Riverside, London SE1 2AQ *Tel.* 020 7283 6000 *Website* www.nortonrose.com

## ■ The Norwich Town Close Estate Charity

**CC NO** 235678   **ESTABLISHED** 1892
**WHERE FUNDING CAN BE GIVEN** Within a 20-mile radius of the Guildhall of the city of Norwich.
**WHO CAN BENEFIT** Only charities based in the area specified will be supported.
**WHAT IS FUNDED** Education.
**WHAT IS NOT FUNDED** Individuals who are not Freemen (or dependants of Freemen) of the city of Norwich; charities more than 20 miles from Norwich; or charities which are not educational. Revenue funding for educational charities is not generally given.
**TYPE OF GRANT** Buildings, capital, one-off and project. Funding for up to one year will be considered.
**RANGE OF GRANTS** £500–£35,000
**SAMPLE GRANTS** Theatre Royal (Norwich) Trust Ltd (£200,000); University of East Anglia (£100,000); Morley Church of England VA Primary School (£10,000); CAST and Norfolk and Norwich Film Theatre (£5,000); Jubilee Family Centre (£4,700); Farming and Countryside Education (£4,000); The Forum Trust (£3,000); Young Norfolk Arts Festival (£2,000); Norfolk Record Study (£400).
**FINANCES** Year 2013/14 Income £879,658 Grants £747,323 Grants to organisations £565,599 Assets £22,145,550
**TRUSTEES** David Fullman; John Rushmer; Michael Quinton; Brenda Ferris; Geoffrey Loades; Philip Blanchflower; Nigel Back; Jeanette Southgate; Robert Self; Pamela Scutter; Brenda Arthur; Heather Tyrrell; David Barber; John Symonds; Owen Gibbs; Stuart Lamb.
**OTHER INFORMATION** There are close links with Norwich Consolidated Charities and Anguish's Educational Foundation. They share their administration processes and collaborate on grant-making.
**HOW TO APPLY** After a preliminary enquiry, apply in writing to the clerk. When submitting an application the following points should be borne in mind: brevity is a virtue – if too much written material is submitted there is a risk that it may not all be assimilated; the trustees like to have details of any other financial support secured; an indication should be given of the amount that is being sought and also how that figure is arrived at; the trustees will not reimburse expenditure already incurred; nor, generally speaking will the trustees pay running costs, e.g. salaries.
**WHO TO APPLY TO** David Walker, Clerk, 1 Woolgate Court, St Benedict's Street, Norwich NR2 4AP Tel. 01603 621023 email david.walker@norwichcharitabletrusts.org.uk Website www.norwichcharitabletrusts.org.uk

## ■ The Norwood and Newton Settlement

**CC NO** 234964   **ESTABLISHED** 1952
**WHERE FUNDING CAN BE GIVEN** England and Wales.
**WHO CAN BENEFIT** Methodist and other mainline Free Churches. Occasionally, small charities in the east London/Essex.
**WHAT IS FUNDED** Capital building projects.
**WHAT IS NOT FUNDED** General running costs; staffing costs; equipment; repairs or maintenance. The trustees do not normally fund the ongoing work of a charity and only in exceptional circumstances will they consider an appeal where an application for National Lottery funding has been made or contemplated.
**TYPE OF GRANT** One-off capital grants.
**RANGE OF GRANTS** £3,000–£20,000
**SAMPLE GRANTS** Markyate Baptist Church – Herts and Trinity Methodist Church – East Grinstead, Sussex (£20,000 each); Battle Methodist Church – Sussex, Elim Plymouth Christian Centre and Harold Hill Evangelical Free Church – Romford (£15,000 each); Stratford-upon-Avon Methodist Church and Greetland and Lindwell Methodist Church (£10,000 each); Burscough Methodist Church – Lancs and Winchester Road Methodist Church – London E4 (£7,500 each); Trinity Methodist Church – Woodhouse, Sheffield (£5,000); Carlton in Lindrick Methodist Church – Sheffield and Stithians Methodist Church – Cornwall (£3,000).
**FINANCES** Year 2013/14 Income £346,738 Grants £258,000 Grants to organisations £258,000 Assets £8,651,803
**TRUSTEES** David Holland; Alan Gray; Stella Holland; Susan Newsom; Roger Lynch.
**OTHER INFORMATION** There were 30 grants made during the year. Of these grants, 21 were given to Methodist churches building new premises or making improvements to their existing premises.
**HOW TO APPLY** Apply in writing to the correspondent. In normal circumstances, an applicant is sent either a refusal or an application form inviting further information within a few days. Once satisfactory information is received, applications are considered by the trustees at quarterly meetings. Applicants are kept informed of the trustees' timescale at all times.
**WHO TO APPLY TO** David Holland, Trustee, 126 Beauly Way, Romford, Essex RM1 4XL Tel. 01708 723670 email norwoodandnewton@btinternet.com

## ■ The Notgrove Trust

**CC NO** 278692   **ESTABLISHED** 1979
**WHERE FUNDING CAN BE GIVEN** Gloucestershire.
**WHO CAN BENEFIT** Local organisations or those of special interest to the trustees.
**WHAT IS FUNDED** Any local charities can be considered.
**WHAT IS NOT FUNDED** Individuals or medical research.
**TYPE OF GRANT** Except in special circumstances, single donations only will be considered.
**RANGE OF GRANTS** £1,000 to £10,000.
**SAMPLE GRANTS** Cold Aston Church of England Primary School (£10,000); The Cotswold School Association and Notgrove PCC (£7,000 each); Dean and Chapter of Gloucester Cathedral, Disabled Sailors Association and The Mary Rose Trust (£5,000 each); Furniture Recycling Project (£4,000); Cheltenham Housing Aid Centre, Home Start Cotswolds and The Forgiveness Project (£3,000 each); Midlands Air Ambulance Charity (£2,000); Notgrove Village Hall Trust and The Guiting Festival (£1,000 each).
**FINANCES** Year 2013/14 Income £181,656 Grants £159,500 Grants to organisations £159,500 Assets £6,484,028
**TRUSTEES** David Acland; Elizabeth Acland; Harry Acland; Diana Acland.
**OTHER INFORMATION** Grants can be broken down into the following categories: other national and general payments (£50,000); local charities and hospices (£40,000); youth and education (£40,000); religious organisations (£17,500); the arts and museums (£12,000).
**HOW TO APPLY** Applications are considered from Gloucestershire charities or from an

# Nottingham

organisation having an established connection with the trustees. Applicants should include a copy of their latest accounts. Speculative appeals from outside Gloucestershire are strongly discouraged and unlikely to get a positive response. Past donations to charities outside Gloucestershire should not be taken as an indication of likely future support. The trust has stated telephone calls are unwelcome and due to a lack of clerical support, unsuccessful appeals will not be acknowledged.

**WHO TO APPLY TO** David Acland, Trustee, Elmbank Farmhouse, Cold Aston, Cheltenham, Gloucestershire GL54 3BJ *Tel.* 01451 810652

## ■ The Nottingham General Dispensary

**CC NO** 228149     **ESTABLISHED** 1963
**WHERE FUNDING CAN BE GIVEN** Nottingham and Nottinghamshire.
**WHO CAN BENEFIT** Individuals or other organisations.
**WHAT IS FUNDED** The alleviation of need or aid in recovery through the provision of items and services not readily available from ordinary channels. Charities working in the fields of: respite; professional bodies; councils for voluntary service; and health will be considered.
**TYPE OF GRANT** One-off awards are preferred. Capital, project and recurring costs. Funding for up to three years will be considered.
**RANGE OF GRANTS** Mostly under £1,000.
**SAMPLE GRANTS Previous beneficiaries have included:** Vitalise Skylarks (£1,500); Transplant Sport UK, Spinal Injuries Association, Sign Help and Life Education Centres (£1,000 each); Listening Books (£900); Painful Bladder Group and Bilborough Carers Support Group (£800 each); CAKE Carers (£750); Rushcliffe Stroke Survivors Group (£710); Asian Fathers Special Needs Support Group (£645); Deafblind UK and Peter Le Marchant Trust (£500 each); Bereavement Keyworth (£350); Heartline Association (£260).
**FINANCES** *Year* 2013/14 *Income* £44,438 *Grants* £36,500
**TRUSTEES** Andy Roylance; David Levell; Pauline Johnston; William Bendall; Dr Stanley Harris; Alan Hopwood.
**OTHER INFORMATION** At the time of writing (June 2015) the charity had submitted its 2013/14 accounts to the Charity Commission, but they were not yet available to view. During the year, the charity had a total expenditure of £54,500. The grant total above is an estimate based on amounts spent in previous years. We have taken into account the charity's management and administration costs, which average around £18,000 each year. It would appear, based on previous years, that the majority of grants are for the direct benefit of individuals.
**HOW TO APPLY** Organisations should apply in writing and provide a copy of their most recent annual accounts.
**WHO TO APPLY TO** Nigel Cullen, Clerk to the Trustees, Freeth Cartwright LLP, Cumberland Court, 80 Mount Street, Nottingham NG1 6HR *Tel.* 0115 901 5558 *email* anna.chandler@freeths.co.uk

## ■ Nottinghamshire Community Foundation

**CC NO** 1069538     **ESTABLISHED** 1998
**WHERE FUNDING CAN BE GIVEN** Nottinghamshire.
**WHO CAN BENEFIT** Voluntary and community groups.
**WHAT IS FUNDED** The charity aims to promote good health and social conditions amongst all communities within the County of Nottinghamshire.
**SAMPLE GRANTS Previous beneficiaries have included:** Grassroots Nottinghamshire (£134,000); Fair Share Trust (£77,000); One Nottingham (£59,000); Active at 60 (£33,000); Winter Surviving Appeal (£8,000); Keepmoat (£2,500).
**FINANCES** *Year* 2013/14 *Income* £478,505 *Grants* £419,785 *Grants to organisations* £419,785 *Assets* £2,037,904
**TRUSTEES** Christopher Hughes; Frances Walker; Philip Marsh; Kevin Price; Simon Tipping; Paul Bacon; Amanda Farr; Diana Meale; Veronica Pickering; Nikki Weston.
**OTHER INFORMATION** The community foundation approved 131 applications from groups during the year.
**HOW TO APPLY** Refer to the website for full details on the criteria and application processes of the various funds currently being administered by the foundation.
**WHO TO APPLY TO** Nina Dauban, Chief Executive, Pine House B, Southwell Road West, Rainworth, Mansfield, Nottinghamshire NG21 0HJ *Tel.* 01623 620202 *Fax* 01623 620204 *email* enquiries@nottscf.org.uk *Website* www.nottscf.org.uk

## ■ The Nottinghamshire Historic Churches Trust

**CC NO** 518335     **ESTABLISHED** 1985
**WHERE FUNDING CAN BE GIVEN** Nottinghamshire and the Diocese of Sandwell and Nottingham.
**WHO CAN BENEFIT** Churches and chapels.
**WHAT IS FUNDED** The maintenance of churches and chapels.
**WHAT IS NOT FUNDED** Grants are not normally given for works of modernisations, alterations or improvements. This includes: works of routine maintenance (repainting doors, non-specialist cleaning); new buildings, extensions, meeting rooms; disability access projects; coffee areas, sinks, new furniture; routine decoration (unless needing to use some specialist materials); routine electrical work (new switches, lights, cables for new installations); repair of modern furniture, fittings, fixtures; overhead projector screens, sound systems, etc.; new bells; new bell frames entirely for new bells. Grants cannot be made for repairs carried out before the application has been made or, usually, for works begun before the outcome of the application is known.
**RANGE OF GRANTS** Up to £5,000.
**SAMPLE GRANTS Examples of work for which grants have been approved have included:** re-wiring; specialist cleaning of masonry and memorial; re-hanging of bells with new fittings; the restoration of a roof with sand case lead; the replacement of a wooden Sanctuary floor; general repairs and drainage.
**FINANCES** *Year* 2013/14 *Income* £51,332 *Grants* £77,600 *Grants to organisations* £77,600 *Assets* £222,007
**TRUSTEES** Dr Jennifer Alexander; David Atkins; Graham Beaumont; Prof. John Beckett; Richard

Brackenbury; Dr Christopher Brooke; Richard Craven-Smith-Milnes; Keith Goodman; Peter Hoare; Prof. Michael Jones; Anthony Marriott; Jennifer Mellors; Edward Nall; Andrew Paris; Graeme Renton; Malcolm Stacey; Revd Canon Keith Turner.

**HOW TO APPLY** Grant application forms along with guidance notes and details of deadlines are available to download from the trust's website. Alternatively, a paper application form can be obtained from the correspondent.

**WHO TO APPLY TO** Margaret Lowe, Grants Administrator, 1 Gayhurst Green, Park Lane, Old Basford, Nottingham NG6 0LZ *email* info.nhct@gmail.com *Website* nottshistoricchurchtrust.org.uk

## ■ The Nuffield Foundation

**CC NO** 206601         **ESTABLISHED** 1943
**WHERE FUNDING CAN BE GIVEN** UK; southern and eastern Africa.
**WHO CAN BENEFIT** Universities; independent research institutions; voluntary sector organisations.
**WHAT IS FUNDED** Research and innovation through the following seven programmes: Children and Families; Early Years Education and Childcare; Economic Advantage and Disadvantage; Education; Finances of Ageing; Law in Society; Open Door.
**WHAT IS NOT FUNDED** Running costs of voluntary bodies, the continuing provision of a service, or any general appeal for pooled funding; capital or building costs, although grants for equipment are allowed when they are part of a project that is otherwise acceptable; solely for purchase of equipment (including computers); grants simply to support or attend conferences or seminars; projects that could be considered by a government department, a Research Council or a more appropriate charity; the establishment of Chairs, or other permanent academic posts; projects led by individuals unaffiliated to an organisation; the production of films or videos, or for exhibitions; school fees, higher education/university fees, or a gap year project; requests for funding for financial help from or on behalf of individuals in distress; projects led by schools, undergraduates, masters students or work towards a PhD; animal rights or welfare; the arts; conservation, heritage or environmental projects; housing; medical, health or health services research; museums, buildings or capital costs; religion; sports and recreation.
**TYPE OF GRANT** One-off grants for projects.
**SAMPLE GRANTS** The five largest contributions were: University of Oxford (£3.1 million); University College London (£2.7 million); University of Edinburgh (£2.1 million); University of Warwick (£1.8 million); University of Glasgow (£1.76 million).
**FINANCES** *Year* 2013 *Income* £17,232,000 *Grants* £23,671,269 *Grants to organisations* £23,671,269 *Assets* £261,002,000
**TRUSTEES** Prof. Genevra Richardson; Lord Krebs; Prof. Sir David Watson; Prof. David Rhind; Dr Colette Bowe; Prof. James Banks; Prof. Terrie Moffitt.
**OTHER INFORMATION** Many of the funding programmes have individual funding criteria and guidelines which are not listed here. Consult the trust's excellent website before applying.
**HOW TO APPLY** The application process is the same for all of the research and innovation grant programmes. The foundation publishes the extensive 'Grants for Research and Innovation Guide for Applicants', which is available to download from the website, and should be read by any potential applicant. The first stage is to submit an outline application which must be accompanied by a front page summary sheet. This is available to download from the website. If your proposal is taken forward to be considered by the trustees, you will be invited to submit a full application. The trustees meet three times a year to consider applications, in March, July and November. Deadlines for these meetings are four months before for outline applications then two months before for full applications; exact deadlines are available on the website. The contacts for the seven programmes are: Children and Families – Alison Rees; Early Years Education and Childcare – Alison Rees; Economic Advantage and Disadvantage – Alexandra Cornish; Education – Kim Woodruff; Finances of Ageing – Alexandra Cornish; Law in Society – Alison Rees; Open Door – Alexandra Cornish. Applicants for the Nuffield Research Placements should contact their regional co-ordinator, a list of which can be found on the website.
**WHO TO APPLY TO** James Brooke Turner, Finance Director, 28 Bedford Square, London WC1B 3JS *Tel.* 020 7631 0566 *Fax* 020 7232 4877 *email* info@nuffieldfoundation.org *Website* www.nuffieldfoundation.org

## ■ O&G Schreiber Charitable Trust

cc no 1073263
where funding can be given UK.
who can benefit Orthodox Jewish charities.
what is funded General charitable purposes; Orthodox Judaism.
finances Year 2013 Income £173,866 Grants £212,145 Grants to organisations £212,145 Assets £1,053,644
trustees Osias Schreiber; Gyta Schreiber.
how to apply Apply in writing to the correspondent. 'The charity accepts applications for grants from representatives of Orthodox Jewish charities, which are reviewed by the trustees on a regular basis.'
who to apply to Osias Schreiber, Trustee, 34 Jessam Avenue, London E5 9DU Tel. 020 8806 1842

## ■ The Father O'Mahoney Memorial Trust

cc no 1039288          established 1993
where funding can be given Worldwide.
who can benefit Organisations; individuals.
what is funded Medical and educational projects in financially developing countries.
what is not funded Gap year projects; causes benefitting the UK.
range of grants Depends on finances; usually up to £5,000.
sample grants African Mission (£6,000 in two grants); Uganda Development (£3,000); Street Child Africa (£2,000); Computer Aid and Microloan Foundation, Freedom from Torture and Let the Children Live (£1,000 each).
finances Year 2013/14 Income £37,267 Grants £40,563 Grants to organisations £40,563 Assets £77,114
trustees Christopher Carney-Smith; Creina Hearn; Don Maclean; Michael Moran; Revd Gerard Murray; Maureen Jennings; Brenda Carney; Hugh Smith.
how to apply Apply in writing to the correspondent. The trustees meet every two months to consider applications.
who to apply to Hugh Smith, Our Lady of the Wayside Church, 566 Stratford Road, Shirley, Solihull, West Midlands B90 4AY email trust@olwayside.fsnet.co.uk

## ■ The Sir Peter O'Sullevan Charitable Trust

cc no 1078889          established 2000
where funding can be given Worldwide.
who can benefit Charitable organisations.
what is funded Animal welfare.
type of grant Recurrent.
sample grants Blue Cross, Brooke Hospital for Animals, Compassion in World Farming, the Racing Welfare Charities and the Thoroughbred Rehabilitation Centre, World Horse Welfare (£30,000 each).
finances Year 2013/14 Income £297,590 Grants £180,000 Grants to organisations £180,000 Assets £35,606
trustees Christopher Spence; Sir Peter O'Sullevan; Nigel Payne; Geoffrey Hughes; Michael Dillon; John McManus; Michael Kerr-Dineen.
how to apply Apply in writing to the correspondent although applications are very unlikely to be successful as the trust supports the same six charities every year.
who to apply to Nigel Payne, Trustee, The Old School, Bolventor, Launceston, Cornwall PL15 7TS Tel. 01566 880292 email nigel@earthsummit.demon.co.uk Website www.thevoiceofracing.com

## ■ The Oakdale Trust

cc no 218827          established 1950
where funding can be given UK, mainly Wales and overseas.
who can benefit UK-based and registered charities; voluntary groups.
what is funded Social and community projects based in Wales; medical support groups in Wales; UK-based medical research projects; environmental conservation projects in Wales; the arts (where there is a Welsh connection); UK-based and registered charities working in financially developing countries; penal reform.
what is not funded Individuals; holiday schemes; sport activities; expeditions.
type of grant Project and core funding.
range of grants Between £250 and £2,000. The average grant is £750.
sample grants AVA – Against Violence and Abuse and People First Impact Method (£10,000); Concern Universal (£7,000); Friends of Children in Romania (£5,000); Swansea University (£3,000); Eco Centre Wales, Narberth Museum, Rhayader YMCA and St David's Church – Howey (£2,000 each); Arthritis Care and Howard League for Penal Reform (£1,500 each); Children in Crisis, Montgomeryshire Wildlife Trust, Network for Africa and Speakeasy Advice Centre (£1,000 each); Blind Veterans UK, Cardiff Refugee and Asylum Seeker Welcome, Noddfa Community Project and Plantlife Cymru (£500 each); Showcase Performing Arts Association (£250); Swallow Laryngectomee Club (£50).
finances Year 2013/14 Income £314,184 Grants £166,950 Grants to organisations £166,950 Assets £10,229,138
trustees Rupert Cadbury; Bruce Cadbury; Olivia Tatton-Brown; Dr Rebecca Cadbury.
other information Repeat applications are not normally accepted within a two year period.
how to apply Applications can be made in any format, including via the online application form or by post or email using the downloadable application form from the website. The trustees meet twice a year, in April and October, to consider applications. Full guidelines, including closing dates for applications, are published on the website. The trust states that it will accept telephone calls; however, messages should not be left on the answerphone as this is for private use only.
who to apply to Rupert Cadbury, Correspondent and Trustee, Tansor House, Tansor, Oundle, Peterborough PE8 5HS Tel. 01832 226386 email oakdale@tanh.co.uk Website www.oakdaletrust.org.uk

## ■ The Oakley Charitable Trust

**CC NO** 233041 **ESTABLISHED** 1963
**WHERE FUNDING CAN BE GIVEN** UK, but with a strong preference for the Midlands and Jersey.
**WHO CAN BENEFIT** Registered charities.
**WHAT IS FUNDED** Welfare, health, education, the arts, conservation and animal welfare.
**WHAT IS NOT FUNDED** Individuals; non-registered charities.
**TYPE OF GRANT** One-off, core costs, project, research, recurring costs and buildings. Funding is available for one year or less.
**RANGE OF GRANTS** £50–£2,000
**SAMPLE GRANTS** Birmingham Royal Ballet, Dogs Trust (£2,000 each); Dyslexia Action (£1,000); Scope and Whizz-Kidz (£500 each); UK Youth (£250); Emily Jordan Foundation (£50).
**FINANCES** Year 2013/14 Income £75,898 Grants £60,800 Grants to organisations £60,800 Assets £2,364,142
**TRUSTEES** Christine Airey; Geoffrey Oakley; Simon Sharp.
**HOW TO APPLY** Apply in writing to the correspondent. Trustees usually meet in March, July and November. The trust has previously stated: 'We receive a large number of applications from many charities operating in the same or very similar areas, e.g. specific cancer research/ youth work etc. Our policy is to only support one such charity in a particular field. Due to a very high number of unsolicited applications we only respond to successful applicants.'
**WHO TO APPLY TO** Geoffrey M. W. Oakley, Trustee, St Mary's Close, 10 St Mary's Road, Harborne, Birmingham B17 0HA Tel. 0121 427 7150

## ■ The Oakmoor Charitable Trust

**CC NO** 258516 **ESTABLISHED** 1969
**WHERE FUNDING CAN BE GIVEN** UK.
**WHO CAN BENEFIT** Registered charities.
**WHAT IS FUNDED** General charitable purposes.
**WHAT IS NOT FUNDED** Individuals.
**RANGE OF GRANTS** Up to £10,000.
**SAMPLE GRANTS** Marine Society and Sea Cadets (£8,000 in two payments); Save Britain's Heritage (£5,000); National Gallery Trust (£2,500); St Peter's Church – Winchester and The Soldiers Charity (£1,000 each); English Heritage (£750); Alzheimer's Research UK, Furniture History Society and Hampshire Air Ambulance (£500 each); Royal Opera House Foundation (£400).
**FINANCES** Year 2013/14 Income £28,694 Grants £25,250 Grants to organisations £25,250 Assets £1,246,463
**TRUSTEES** Rathbone Trust Company Ltd; Peter Andreae; Rosemary Andreae.
**OTHER INFORMATION** Grants were made to 19 organisations during the year.
**HOW TO APPLY** The trust has previously stated that it does not respond to unsolicited applications.
**WHO TO APPLY TO** The Correspondent, Rathbone Trust Company Limited, Rathbone Trust Company Limited, 4th Floor, 1 Curzon Street, London W1J 5FB Tel. 020 7399 0807

## ■ The Odin Charitable Trust

**CC NO** 1027521 **ESTABLISHED** 1993
**WHERE FUNDING CAN BE GIVEN** UK.
**WHO CAN BENEFIT** Registered charities.
**WHAT IS FUNDED** General charitable purposes with preference for: the arts; care for people who are disadvantaged or have disabilities; hospices; homeless people, prisoners' families, refugees, Roma and 'tribal groups'; research into false memories and dyslexia.
**WHAT IS NOT FUNDED** Individuals.
**RANGE OF GRANTS** Usually between £1,000 and £5,000.
**SAMPLE GRANTS** Style Acre (£15,000 in three grants); Bath Recital Artists' Trust (£10,500 in three grants); Amber Trust, Children's Adventure Farm Trust and Independent Age (£9,000 each in three grants); Interact Reading Service and Northampton Hope Centre (£7,500 each in three grants); Charity Search and Derby TOC-H Children's Camp (£6,000 in three grants); Firebird Theatre (£3,000 in three grants); Crossroads Care North Somerset (£2,500); Beds Garden Carers (£1,500); Art and Power, Brighton and Hove Unemployed Workers Centre, Housing for Women and Norfolk Association for the Disabled (£1,000 each); Help Counselling Services (£500).
**FINANCES** Year 2013/14 Income £463,956 Grants £288,000 Grants to organisations £288,000 Assets £6,442,442
**TRUSTEES** Susan Scotford; A. H. Palmer; Donna Kelly; Pia C. Cherry.
**HOW TO APPLY** Applications should be submitted in the form of a letter or email and contain the following information: aims and objectives of the charity; nature of the appeal; total target, if for a specific project; registered charity number; any other relevant factors. Letters should be accompanied by a set of the charitable organisation's latest report and full accounts and should be addressed to the correspondent.
**WHO TO APPLY TO** Susan Scotford, Trustee, PO Box 1898, Bradford-on-Avon, Wiltshire BA15 1YS Tel. 020 7465 4300 email aanother@phb.co.uk

## ■ The Ofenheim Charitable Trust

**CC NO** 286525 **ESTABLISHED** 1983
**WHERE FUNDING CAN BE GIVEN** Worldwide, in practice UK with some preference for East Sussex.
**WHO CAN BENEFIT** Registered charities. The annual report states that 'the trustees' policy has been to provide regular support for a number of charities and to respond to one-off appeals to bodies where they have some knowledge. It continues to be their policy to support charities in East Sussex because of the founder's association with that area.'
**WHAT IS FUNDED** General charitable purposes, particularly: health; welfare; the arts, animals; the environment.
**WHAT IS NOT FUNDED** Individuals.
**TYPE OF GRANT** Mainly recurring grants, but one-off donations are also made.
**RANGE OF GRANTS** Between £2,500 and £50,000; however, the vast majority of grants were of £5,500 or less.
**SAMPLE GRANTS** DEC Philippines Typhoon Appeal (£50,000); Trinity – Laban Conservatoire of Music and Dance (£13,000); Save the Children Fund and Scope (£12,000 each); National Art Collections Fund, National Council of YMCA and Saint Mungo's (£10,000 each); Game Conservancy Trust, Glyndebourne Arts Trust and NSPCC (£5,500 each); WWF – UK and National Youth Choirs of Great Britain (£5,000 each); Centrepoint – Soho, Shipston Home Nursing and Sisters of the Sacred Heart of Jesus and Mary (£3,300 each); All Saints Church Margaret Street, Barn Owl Trust, Battersea Summer Scheme, Home Start UK, Royal Academy of Music and Sir John Soane's Museum (£2,500 each).

FINANCES Year 2013/14 Income £381,201 Grants £434,800 Grants to organisations £434,800 Assets £13,839,738
TRUSTEES Roger Clark; Rory McLeod; Alexander Clark; Fiona Byrd.
OTHER INFORMATION 69 organisations were supported in 2013/14. No organisation received more than one grant during the year.
HOW TO APPLY Apply in writing to the correspondent.
WHO TO APPLY TO The Trustees, Baker Tilly, The Pinnacle, 170 Midsummer Boulevard, Milton Keynes MK9 1BP Tel. 01908 687800

## ■ The Ogle Christian Trust
CC NO 1061458   ESTABLISHED 1938
WHERE FUNDING CAN BE GIVEN Worldwide.
WHO CAN BENEFIT Registered charities.
WHAT IS FUNDED The advancement of the Christian faith; the relief of poverty, hardship and distress. The annual report and accounts for 2013 state: 'In practice, funds are mainly directed to new initiatives in evangelism world-wide, support of missionary enterprises, Bible student training, help to retired missionary workers and to famine and relief organisations.'
WHAT IS NOT FUNDED Applications from individuals are discouraged; those granted require accreditation by a sponsoring organisation. Grants are rarely made for building projects. Funding will not be given in response to general appeals from large national organisations or towards salaries.
TYPE OF GRANT Normally short-term commitments. About half of grants go to regularly-supported organisations.
RANGE OF GRANTS Mostly between £1,000 and £6,000.
SAMPLE GRANTS OM UK (£48,000); 3P Ministries (£10,000); MEM (£8,000); Haryana Church (£6,000); Langham Partnership (£3,000); Make Jesus Known (£2,000); Caring for Life (£1,000); Beachy Head Chaplaincy Trust and Oak Hill College (£500).
FINANCES Year 2013 Income £133,848 Grants £200,600 Grants to organisations £174,500 Assets £2,644,377
TRUSTEES Fiona Putley; Ronald Goodenough; Stephen Proctor; Lynne Quanrud; Dr David Harley; Dr Carol Walker.
OTHER INFORMATION During the year, 49 grants were made to individuals totalling £26,000.
HOW TO APPLY Apply in writing to the correspondent, accompanied by documentary support and an sae. Our research suggests that trustees meet in May and November, but applications can be made at any time.
WHO TO APPLY TO Fiona Putley, Trustee, 43 Woolstone Road, Forest Hill, London SE23 2TR Tel. 020 8699 1036

## ■ Oglesby Charitable Trust
CC NO 1026669   ESTABLISHED 1992
WHERE FUNDING CAN BE GIVEN The North West of England.
WHO CAN BENEFIT Registered charities.
WHAT IS FUNDED Artistic development; educational grants and building projects; environmental improvement projects; improving the life and welfare of people who are underprivileged; medical aid and research.
WHAT IS NOT FUNDED Non-registered charities; activities with the purpose of redistributing collected funds to other charities; animal charities; charities mainly operating outside the UK; church and all building fabric materials; conferences; continuing running costs of an organisation; costs of employing fundraisers; expeditions; general sports, unless there is an association with a disadvantaged group; holidays; individuals; loans or business finance; charities promoting religion; routine staff training; sponsorship and marketing appeals.
RANGE OF GRANTS Usually between £5,000–£20,000. Small grants of less than £1,000 are distributed through the Acorn Fund.
SAMPLE GRANTS Beneficiaries have included: Action for Kids, Alcohol Drug Abstinence Service, Centre for Alternative Technology, Cheadle Hulme School, Cheetham's School, Fairbridge – Family Contact Line, Halle Youth Orchestra, Manchester City Art Gallery, Manchester University Arts and Drama, Motor Neurone Disease, National Asthma Campaign, National Library For The Blind, Stroke Research and Whitworth Art Gallery.
FINANCES Year 2012/13 Income £1,285,940 Grants £942,760 Grants to organisations £942,760 Assets £1,621,390
TRUSTEES Jean Oglesby; Michael Oglesby; Bob Kitson; Kate Vokes; Jane Oglesby; Chris Oglesby; Peter Renshaw.
OTHER INFORMATION The trust also has a small grants programme, the Acorn Fund, which is administered by Forever Manchester: www.forevermanchester.com. In 2012/13 the trust gave £12,500 for redistribution through the fund. In 2012/13 more than 60 organisations received support. At the time of writing (June 2015) these were the latest accounts available for the trust.
HOW TO APPLY Unsolicited applications are not acknowledged.
WHO TO APPLY TO PO Box 336, Altrincham, Cheshire WA14 3XD email oglesbycharitabletrust@bruntwood.co.uk Website www.oglesbycharitabletrust.co.uk

## ■ Oizer Charitable Trust
CC NO 1014399   ESTABLISHED 1992
WHERE FUNDING CAN BE GIVEN UK with a preference to Greater Manchester.
WHO CAN BENEFIT Jewish organisations.
WHAT IS FUNDED 'Worthy' causes within the Jewish community, particularly the provision of Orthodox Jewish education and the advancement of the Jewish religion according to the Orthodox Jewish faith.
SAMPLE GRANTS B'nos Yisroel (£2,000); Academy for Talmudical Research (£1,250).
FINANCES Year 2012/13 Income £1,080,651 Grants £301,742 Grants to organisations £301,742 Assets £2,184,387
TRUSTEES Joshua Halpern; Cindy Halpern.
OTHER INFORMATION At the time of writing (June 2015) the 2013/14 accounts were overdue at the Charity Commission. The 2012/13 accounts were the latest available for the trust.
HOW TO APPLY Apply in writing to the correspondent. The annual report and accounts for 2012/13 state: 'The trustees have identified a number of Orthodox Jewish charities which profess and teach the principles of traditional Judaism or which carry out activities which advance religion in accordance with the Orthodox Jewish faith. Grants are given on application to the trustees by these or similar charities.'
WHO TO APPLY TO Joshua Halpern, Trustee, Lopian Gross Barnett and Co, 6th Floor, Cardinal House, 20 St Mary's Parsonage, Manchester M3 2LG Tel. 0161 832 8721

## ■ Old Possum's Practical Trust

**CC NO** 328558     **ESTABLISHED** 1990
**WHERE FUNDING CAN BE GIVEN** UK.
**WHO CAN BENEFIT** Registered charities and individuals of all ages.
**WHAT IS FUNDED** Literary, artistic, musical and theatrical projects; people who have a disability; people who are disadvantaged.
**WHAT IS NOT FUNDED** Activities or projects already completed; capital building projects; personal training and education e.g. tuition or living costs for college or university; projects outside the UK; medical care or resources; feasibility studies; national charities having substantial amounts of potential funding likely from other sources.
**RANGE OF GRANTS** Mainly £500–£5,000.
**SAMPLE GRANTS** High Tide (£82,000); First Story (£40,000); St Stephen's Church (£25,000); The Book Trade Charity, The National Theatre and Shakespeare School Festival (£10,000 each); The Bodleian Libraries – Seamus Heaney Memorial (£7,000); The Abyss Theatre School – Lucifer Saved (£5,000); Refugee Council (£4,000); Friends of Little Gidding – Eliot Festival (£3,000); MK Community Foundation (£500).
**FINANCES** Year 2013/14 Income £8,627,363 Grants £247,650 Grants to organisations £246,650 Assets £14,966,811
**TRUSTEES** Judith Hooper; Deidre Simpson; Clare Reihill.
**OTHER INFORMATION** This trust was established by Valerie Eliot in 1990, 25 years after her husband T S Eliot's death. One grant of £1,000 was made to an individual during the year (for research purposes) and the trust also gifted miniatures worth £65,000 to the V&A Museum.
**HOW TO APPLY** Applications can only be made online through the trust's website. The trustees meet regularly to consider applications but state in the latest accounts that: 'the emphasis will be on continued support of those institutions and individuals who have received support in the past. Unfortunately we have to disappoint the great majority of applicants who nevertheless continue to send appeal letters The Trustees do not welcome telephone calls or emails from applicants soliciting funds'. To keep administration costs to a minimum the trust does not give reasons for unsuccessful applications or allow applicants to appeal a decision.
**WHO TO APPLY TO** The Trustees, PO Box 5701, Milton Keynes MK9 2WZ email generalenquiry@old-possums-practical-trust.org.uk Website www.old-possums-practical-trust.org.uk

## ■ The John Oldacre Foundation

**CC NO** 284960     **ESTABLISHED** 1981
**WHERE FUNDING CAN BE GIVEN** UK.
**WHO CAN BENEFIT** Universities, agricultural colleges and innovative projects benefitting students and research workers.
**WHAT IS FUNDED** Research and education in agricultural sciences.
**WHAT IS NOT FUNDED** Tuition fees.
**TYPE OF GRANT** One-off, recurrent, feasibility, project, research and funding of up to three years will be considered.
**RANGE OF GRANTS** Up to £52,000.
**SAMPLE GRANTS** University of Bristol (£52,000); Harper Adams (£46,500 in two grants); Royal Agricultural College (£30,000 in two grants); Oxford University (£25,000); University of Exeter (£20,500); Reading University (£19,700); NIAB (£14,900); Nuffield Farming Trust (£11,000); Hertfordshire University (£5,000).
**FINANCES** Year 2013/14 Income £144,152 Grants £224,713 Grants to organisations £224,713 Assets £8,893,689
**TRUSTEES** Henry Shouler; Stephen Charnock; Ian Bonnett.
**OTHER INFORMATION** A total of 11 grants were made to nine organisations during the year.
**HOW TO APPLY** Apply in writing to the correspondent stating how the funds would be used and what would be achieved.
**WHO TO APPLY TO** Stephen Charnock, Trustee, 35 Broadwater Close, Burwood park, Walton-on-Thames KT12 5DD

## ■ The Olga Charitable Trust

**CC NO** 277925     **ESTABLISHED** 1979
**WHERE FUNDING CAN BE GIVEN** UK and overseas.
**WHO CAN BENEFIT** National organisations benefitting children, young adults, at risk groups, people disadvantaged by poverty, socially isolated people and carers.
**WHAT IS FUNDED** Health and welfare, youth organisations, children's welfare, carers' organisations.
**WHAT IS NOT FUNDED** Grants are only made to charities of which the trustees have a direct knowledge or personal involvement.
**RANGE OF GRANTS** £30–£5,000
**SAMPLE GRANTS** Miracles (£5,100); British Red Cross (£5,000); King Edward VII Hospital (£2,000); Palpa Trust (£1,100); Fitzwilliam Museum (£1,000); St James's Church Piccadilly (£750); University of St Andrews (£300); Royal Society for the Arts (£160); Ranfurly Charitable Services (£30).
**FINANCES** Year 2013/14 Income £43,367 Grants £38,710 Grants to organisations £38,710 Assets £1,039,591
**TRUSTEES** HRH. Princess Alexandra; James Robert Bruce Ogilvy.
**HOW TO APPLY** See 'What is not funded'.
**WHO TO APPLY TO** Adam Broke, Accountant, Fleet Place House, 2 Fleet Place, London EC4M 7RF Tel. 020 7236 2601 email simoncoggins@mercerhole.co.uk

## ■ Open Gate

**CC NO** 1081701     **ESTABLISHED** 2000
**WHERE FUNDING CAN BE GIVEN** UK and overseas. In the UK, support is concentrated on the North Midlands area.
**WHO CAN BENEFIT** Charitable organisations.
**WHAT IS FUNDED** Grassroots environmental, technological and educational projects to benefit small communities; social welfare; disadvantage; disability. Schemes promoting social equality and self-sufficiency are particularly favoured.
**WHAT IS NOT FUNDED** Individuals; overseas-based charities.
**TYPE OF GRANT** Project grants for up to three years. Capital grants, core costs, full project funding. Unrestricted.
**RANGE OF GRANTS** £500–£9,500
**SAMPLE GRANTS** Uganda Development Services (£9,500); Whirlow Hall Farm Trust (£5,500); Highfield Happy Hens (£5,000); Farm Africa and WaterAid (£3,500 each); Latin American Foundation for the Future and Tree for Cities (£3,000); Buttle UK, CAFOD, Practical Action and Sheffield General Cemetery Trust (£2,500);

Impact Foundation (£2,100); Inkersall Allotments and Sheffield Alcohol Support Service (£2,000); The Children's Adventure Farm Trust and Sight Support Derbyshire (£1,300); The CAIRN Trust, Listening Books and Responding to Conflict (£1,000 each); Quakers Community Farm (£800); Enrych (£500).

**FINANCES** Year 2013/14 Income £70,565 Grants £216,992 Grants to organisations £216,992 Assets £1,337,628

**TRUSTEES** Mary Wiltshire; Ned Wiltshire; John Wiltshire; Jane Methuen; Tom Wiltshire; Alice Taylor; Lesley Williamson.

**OTHER INFORMATION** During the year, 104 organisations received support.

**HOW TO APPLY** Applications should be submitted via post or email. The website states that 'there is no specific format for applications. However an application should include details of project costs as well as outcomes.' Applications cannot be made via email, post only. Quarterly meetings are usually held in January, April, July and October. Applications need to be received six weeks in advance of the meetings.

**WHO TO APPLY TO** Mary Wiltshire, Trustee, Brownhouse Farm, Ashleyhay, Wirksworth, Matlock, Derbyshire DE4 4AH Tel. 01629 822018 email opengate@w3z.co.uk Website www.opengatetrust.org.uk

## ■ The O'Sullivan Family Charitable Trust

**CC NO** 1123757 **ESTABLISHED** 2008
**WHERE FUNDING CAN BE GIVEN** In practice, the UK.
**WHO CAN BENEFIT** Organisations.
**WHAT IS FUNDED** The care of people who have disabilities; children and young people; education; genetic research.
**RANGE OF GRANTS** Up to £20,000.
**SAMPLE GRANTS** Rose Road and The Brickworks (£20,000 each); Duke of Edinburgh Award (£15,000); University of Southampton (£12,000); Shepherds Down School (£10,300); Stroke Association (£7,000); Canine Partners, Designability, Hope and Homes and Whizz-Kidz (£5,000 each); Painters Company Charities (£4,500); Listening Books and Winchester Cathedral Trust (£3,000 each); Combat Stress and Hursley Park Cricket Club (£2,000 each); 4 Youth and London Wheelchair Rugby Club (£1,000 each); Walk for Walk (£500); Multiple Sclerosis Trust (£250).
**FINANCES** Year 2013/14 Income £661,049 Grants £399,716 Grants to organisations £399,716 Assets £5,506,908
**TRUSTEES** Diana O'Sullivan; Finian O'Sullivan; Emily O'Sullivan; Sophie O'Sullivan; Tessa O'Sullivan.
**OTHER INFORMATION** One grant of £202,000 to Smile Support and Care accounted for much of the grant total.
**HOW TO APPLY** Apply in writing to the correspondent.
**WHO TO APPLY TO** Diana O'Sullivan, Trustee, 36 Edge Street, London W8 7PN

## ■ The Ouseley Trust

**CC NO** 527519 **ESTABLISHED** 1989
**WHERE FUNDING CAN BE GIVEN** England, Wales and Ireland.
**WHO CAN BENEFIT** Cathedrals; choirs; parish churches; choir schools; children who are members of choirs of recognised choral foundations.
**WHAT IS FUNDED** Projects that promote and maintain to a high standard the choral services of the Church of England, the Church in Wales or the Church of Ireland. Support is given for: courses for individuals or groups; endowment grants; choir school fees; purchase of liturgical music; innovative projects that will directly further the trust's objects.
**WHAT IS NOT FUNDED** Building projects; the making of records; the purchase of furniture or liturgical objects; the repair of organs; the purchase of pianos and other instruments; the design or acquisition of robes; or tours or visits.
**RANGE OF GRANTS** Up to £50,000. For fees, £5,000 maximum.
**FINANCES** Year 2013 Income £259,415 Grants £92,050 Grants to organisations £92,050 Assets £4,457,332
**TRUSTEES** Dr Christopher Robinson; Canon Richard White; Adam Ridley; Dr Stephen Darlington; Canon Martin Pickering; Dr John Rutter; Gillian Perkins; Dean Boyling; Canon Paul Mason; Timothy Byram-Wigfield; Adrian Barlow; Dr Jo Spreadbury.
**OTHER INFORMATION** Grants were awarded for the following purposes: Fees (£57,500); Endowments (£30,500); Other (£2,000); Music (£1,900).
**HOW TO APPLY** Applications must be submitted on the trust's official application form, which is available from the correspondent, by an institution (not an individual). The trust advises potential applicants to consider the application questions and guidelines sections listed on its website before a form is requested. The trustees meet to consider applications twice a year, usually in March and October and the closing date for applications is 28 February and 30 June respectively. Successful applicants are not normally awarded further grants within a two year period.
**WHO TO APPLY TO** Martin Williams, Clerk, PO Box 281, Stamford, Lincolnshire PE9 9BU Tel. 01780 752266 email ouseleytrust@btinternet.com Website www.ouseleytrust.org.uk

## ■ The Owen Family Trust

**CC NO** 251975 **ESTABLISHED** 1967
**WHERE FUNDING CAN BE GIVEN** UK, with a preference for West Midlands.
**WHO CAN BENEFIT** Schools (independent and church), Christian youth centres, churches, community associations, national organisations, and people with Alzheimer's disease, cancer and strokes.
**WHAT IS FUNDED** Mainly support for projects known personally by the trustees. Christian outreach projects are supported, with consideration also given to the arts, conservation, cancer research, Christian education, church and related community buildings.
**WHAT IS NOT FUNDED** The trust has stated 'No grants are given to individuals unless part of a charitable organisation'.
**TYPE OF GRANT** Buildings, capital, and recurring costs will be considered. Funding may be given for more than three years.
**RANGE OF GRANTS** The majority of grants are in the range of £1,000 to £5,000.
**SAMPLE GRANTS** Seven Valley Railway Charitable Trust (£50,000); Frontier Youth Trust (£5,350); Birmingham Federation of Clubs for Young People and St Peter's Church Little Aston (£3,000 each); Josiah Spears Benevolent Fund (£2,200); Bishop Vesey Grammar School and St Giles Hospice (£2,000 each); Bardsey Island

Trust (£1,700); Midland Arts Centre, British Youth for Christ and Kids UK (£1,000 each).
**FINANCES** Year 2013/14 Income £61,317 Grants £128,725 Grants to organisations £128,725 Assets £1,078,317
**TRUSTEES** Grace Jenkins; David Owen.
**OTHER INFORMATION** During the year, the trust awarded one large grant of £50,000 and 13 grants of £1,000 or less totalled £10,500.
**HOW TO APPLY** Apply in writing to the correspondent including annual report, budget for project and general information regarding the application. Organisations need to be a registered charity; however, an 'umbrella' body which would hold funds would be acceptable. Only a small number of grants can be given each year and unsuccessful applications are not acknowledged unless an sae is enclosed. The trustees meet quarterly.
**WHO TO APPLY TO** David Owen, Trustee, C/o Rubery Owen Holdings Limited, PO Box 10, Wednesbury WS10 8JD Tel. 0121 526 3131 email david.owen@ruberyowen.com

## ■ Oxfam (GB)

**CC NO** 202918   **ESTABLISHED** 1958
**WHERE FUNDING CAN BE GIVEN** Africa, Asia, Caribbean, Central America, Eastern Europe, countries of the former Soviet Union, Great Britain, Middle East, South America.
**WHO CAN BENEFIT** Oxfam works with local, national and international partner organisations which share its goals of overcoming poverty and injustice.
**WHAT IS FUNDED** The charity focuses its work on six goals: civil and political rights; women's rights; disaster relief; food supplies; better access to natural resources; and better funding for basic services, such as health or education. In the UK, it runs a poverty programme.
**WHAT IS NOT FUNDED** Work that falls outside Oxfam's charitable or geographical remit; work through governments or government agencies; projects that include the teaching of religion in their proposal; individuals; requests submitted by a second party on behalf of another; requests from UK-based organisations for projects overseas.
**RANGE OF GRANTS** The average grant per project was £50,000, though some were considerably larger.
**SAMPLE GRANTS** Kachin Baptist Convention (£1.65 million); Humanitarian Initiative Just Relief Aid (£1.2 million); Save the Children – UK (£1.1 million); International Organisation for Migration (£1 million); National Association for Vocational Training and Social Services (£502,000); Action Contre la Faim (£445,000); Practical Action (£377,000); Hydraulique Sans Frontières (£294,000); CARE Deustchland Luxemburg (£274,000); United Nations Children's Fund (£229,000); Village Water Zambia (£220,000); Vétérinaires Sans Frontières – Dierenartsen Zonder Grenzen Belgium (£205,000).
**FINANCES** Year 2013/14 Income £389,100,000 Grants £67,400,000 Grants to organisations £67,400,000 Assets £75,100,000
**TRUSTEES** Katy Steward; Patricia Zipfel; Rajiv Joshi; Marjorie Scardino; James Darcy; Keren Brown; David Pitt-Watson; Nkoyo Toyo; Gavin MacNeill Stewart; Stephen Walton; Ruth Ruderham; Kul Chandra Gautam.
**OTHER INFORMATION** In 2013/14 there were 1,337 grants made to 881 organisations.
**HOW TO APPLY** A brief project proposal should be sent to the Oxfam team in the appropriate country, the details of which are noted on the website. At the time of writing, the website stated that unsolicited requests for funding from the UK Poverty Programme were not being accepted.
**WHO TO APPLY TO** Joss Saunders, 2700 John Smith Drive, Oxford Business Park South, Oxford OX4 2JY Tel. 0870 333 2444 email enquiries@oxfam.org.uk Website www.oxfam.org.uk

## ■ City of Oxford Charity

**CC NO** 239151   **ESTABLISHED** 2004
**WHERE FUNDING CAN BE GIVEN** The city of Oxford only.
**WHO CAN BENEFIT** Schools; colleges; organisations; individuals.
**WHAT IS FUNDED** Grants are mainly given to individuals for the relief of need and sickness, and for educational purposes. Schools may apply, for children whose parents are on a low income or income support, for 35% of the full cost of a school trip.
**FINANCES** Year 2014 Income £360,545 Grants £91,949 Grants to organisations £91,949 Assets £5,514,560
**TRUSTEES** Robin Birch; Tony Woodward; John Gould; Jean Fooks; Dr Jason Tomes; Dr Richard Whittington; Michael Lancashire; Ben Lloyd-Shogbesan; Roger Smith; Dr Alan Bogg; Ivan Coulter; Gillian Sanders; Graham Jones; Steve Curran; Catherine Hilliard; Susan Mortimer; Kathleen O'Shea.
**OTHER INFORMATION** In addition to grant-making, the charity also runs almshouses situated in St Clements – Oxford and provides grants for their upkeep.
**HOW TO APPLY** An application form is available to download from the charity's website.
**WHO TO APPLY TO** David Wright, Clerk, 11 Davenant Road, Oxford OX2 8BT Tel. 01865 247161 email enquiries@oxfordcitycharities.fsnet.co.uk Website www.oxfordcitycharities.org

## ■ Oxfordshire Community Foundation

**CC NO** 1151621   **ESTABLISHED** 1995
**WHERE FUNDING CAN BE GIVEN** Oxfordshire.
**WHO CAN BENEFIT** Community-based non-profit organisations constituted in Oxfordshire.
**WHAT IS FUNDED** Local community initiatives benefitting residents of Oxfordshire of all 'ages, ethnicities and abilities'.
**WHAT IS NOT FUNDED** Refer to the foundation's website for exclusions specific to each fund.
**TYPE OF GRANT** One-off; capital costs; core costs; salaries; start-up costs. One-year, start-up awards for projects, training and equipment. Unrestricted funding.
**RANGE OF GRANTS** Generally between £500 and £5,000.
**SAMPLE GRANTS** Oxford Homeless Pathways (£7,500); Leys Youth Programme and Sport for Streets (£5,000 each); Farmability (£3,000); Aspire (£1,900)
**FINANCES** Year 2013/14 Income £922,982 Grants £205,713 Grants to organisations £205,713 Assets £3,275,285
**TRUSTEES** Lady Stephanie North; Colin Alexander; Glyn Benson; Ian Lenagan; Nigel Williams; Anna Moon; Prof. Ann Buchanan; Jane Wates; David Astor; Amanda Phillips.

# Oxfordshire

**OTHER INFORMATION** 123 organisations received funding during the year.

**HOW TO APPLY** Refer to the foundation's website for full details of how to apply to the various programmes currently being administered.

**WHO TO APPLY TO** Grants Manager, Oxfordshire Community Foundation, 3 Woodin's Way, Oxford OX1 1HD  *Tel.* 01865 798666  *email* ocf@oxfordshire.org  *Website* www.oxfordshire.org

## ■ The P. F. Charitable Trust

**CC NO** 220124  **ESTABLISHED** 1951
**WHERE FUNDING CAN BE GIVEN** Unrestricted. In practice UK with local interests in Oxfordshire and Scotland.
**WHO CAN BENEFIT** Voluntary organisations and charitable groups.
**WHAT IS FUNDED** General charitable purposes.
**WHAT IS NOT FUNDED** Individuals; non-registered charities.
**TYPE OF GRANT** One-off and recurring; buildings; core costs; project; research; running costs. Funding may be given for up to three years.
**RANGE OF GRANTS** Mainly up to £50,000.
**SAMPLE GRANTS** Foundation Scotland and Soldiers of Oxfordshire Trust (£110,000 each); Eton College Appeal (£100,000); Healing Foundation, Helen and Douglas House, Institute of Cancer Research, Marie Curie Cancer Care, Oxfordshire Community Foundation, Oxfordshire Historic Churches Trust, Prior's Court Foundation (£50,000 each).
**FINANCES** Year 2013/14 Income £3,205,038 Grants £2,541,160 Grants to organisations £2,541,160 Assets £103,673,640
**TRUSTEES** Robert Fleming; Philip Fleming; Rory Fleming.
**OTHER INFORMATION** Grants of less than £50,000 each totalled £1.9 million.
**HOW TO APPLY** Apply in writing to the correspondent. Trustees usually meet monthly to consider applications and approve grants. Scottish organisations working in the areas disability, health, youth work, older people, children, families and homelessness, may also apply through Foundation Scotland's 'Express Grants' programme. More information is available from the website: www.foundationscotland.org.uk/programmes/pf-charitable-trust.
**WHO TO APPLY TO** The Secretary, c/o Fleming Family and Partners, 15 Suffolk Street, London SW1Y 4HG *Tel.* 020 7036 5685 *email* charities@rftrustee.com

## ■ The Paget Charitable Trust

**CC NO** 327402  **ESTABLISHED** 1986
**WHERE FUNDING CAN BE GIVEN** Worldwide, with an interest in Loughborough.
**WHO CAN BENEFIT** Normally only UK-registered charities.
**WHAT IS FUNDED** Sheer need is paramount, and, in practice, nothing else can be considered. There is a preference for the unglamorous, for maximum achievement with minimal resources. Priorities include financially developing countries, deprived children, old age, 'green' projects, and animal welfare. The trust does sometimes give ongoing support, thus leaving fewer funds for new applicants.
**WHAT IS NOT FUNDED** The trust states that 'sheer need is paramount, in practice, nothing else is considered'. Grants are only given to registered UK charities. Overseas projects can only be funded via UK charities; no money can be sent directly overseas. The trust does not support individuals (including students), projects for people with mental disabilities, medical research or AIDS/HIV projects.
**RANGE OF GRANTS** £500–£4,000
**SAMPLE GRANTS** Oxfam and RABI (£4,000); Tibet Relief Fund of UK (£3,300); Farms for City Children and the Soil Association (£3,000 each); Freedom from Torture, Hospice of the Valleys and Red Cross (£2,000 each); Community of the Holy Fire, Deafblind UK, International Refugee Trust, Student's Education Trust, and Wells for India (£1,000 each); Clinical Science Foundation, Family Care, Headway – Leicestershire and Rutland, HospiceCare North Northumberland, Leicestershire Charity Link, Moon Bear Rescue, St Andrew's Evangelical Mission, and The Gorilla Organisation (£500 each).
**FINANCES** Year 2013/14 Income £205,981 Grants £152,025 Grants to organisations £152,025 Assets £10,594,606
**TRUSTEES** Joanna Herbert-Stepney; Vivienne Matravers.
**OTHER INFORMATION** The full registered name of the trust is The Joanna Herbert-Stepney Charitable Settlement. During the year, 151 charities were supported.
**HOW TO APPLY** Apply in writing to the correspondent; there is no application form. The trustees meet in spring and autumn. The trust regrets that it cannot respond to all applications.
**WHO TO APPLY TO** Joanna Herbert-Stepney, Trustee, Old Village Stores, Dippenhall Street, Crondall, Farnham, Surrey GU10 5NZ *Tel.* 01252 850253

## ■ Eleanor Palmer Trust

**CC NO** 220857  **ESTABLISHED** 1558
**WHERE FUNDING CAN BE GIVEN** Former urban districts of Barnet and East Barnet.
**WHO CAN BENEFIT** Organisations and individuals.
**WHAT IS FUNDED** Relief in need.
**WHAT IS NOT FUNDED** Purposes other than relief-in-need; capital costs.
**TYPE OF GRANT** One-off, funding up to three years will be considered.
**FINANCES** Year 2013/14 Income £1,586,100 Grants £62,536 Grants to organisations £44,415 Assets £4,580,896
**TRUSTEE** Eleanor Palmer Trustee Limited.
**OTHER INFORMATION** Grants were distributed as follows: amenities for and grants for residents: £13,500; grants for relief in need: £48,000; lunch club for residents £800. Grants to individuals totalled £17,400. The trust also runs 75 sheltered flats and bungalows and a residential home.
**HOW TO APPLY** Application forms are usually available to download from the website; however, at the time of writing (June 2015) the trust's website was under construction. Refer to the website for updates.
**WHO TO APPLY TO** Fred Park, Clerk to the Trustees, 106b Wood Street, Barnet, Hertfordshire EN5 4BY *Tel.* 020 8441 3222 *email* info@eleanorpalmertrust.org.uk *Website* www.eleanorpalmertrust.org.uk

## ■ The Panacea Charitable Trust (formerly The Panacea Society)

**CC NO** 227530  **ESTABLISHED** 1926
**WHERE FUNDING CAN BE GIVEN** UK, with a strong preference for Bedford and its immediate region.

**WHO CAN BENEFIT** Christian organisations; universities; registered charities.
**WHAT IS FUNDED** Research, scholarships and conferences in the field of historical theology, in particular: Prophecy; the Book of Revelation; The Second Coming of Christ; Jewish Apocalyptic literature and Christian Theology and Millennialism and Christian millenarian movements. Poverty, sickness and social related grants are made through the Bedfordshire and Luton Community Foundation and Community and Voluntary Services Bedfordshire.
**WHAT IS NOT FUNDED** Political parties or lobbying; pressure groups which support commercial ventures; replacement of statutory funding; non-charitable activities.
**SAMPLE GRANTS** Bedford Project (£168,000); Bedford and Luton Community Foundation (£100,000); Goldsmith's College – Hessayon Research Project (£75,000); Gray Research Sponsorship (£15,000); Bunyan Meeting Church (£2,000).
**FINANCES** Year 2013 Income £533,752 Grants £358,224 Grants to organisations £358,224 Assets £26,739,072
**TRUSTEES** Prof. Christopher Rowland; Charles Monsell; Gordon Allan; Dr Justin Meggitt.
**OTHER INFORMATION** The Bedford Project supported by the charity refers to the development of the buildings that have 'formed the cultural and historical core of the former Panacea Society as a learning and visitor resource'.
**HOW TO APPLY** The charity's annual report and accounts state: 'From time to time research funding is made available by the trustees and applicants are invited to apply for grants to study and research specifically defined topics. The scheme is advertised in the national press, and on the charity's website. Grant awards are made after initial assessment, interview, and review of all applications received. In the past the charity also awarded small grants to certain qualifying doctoral scholars upon review of their research proposal. This scheme has now ceased.' Grants for purposes relating to poverty, sickness and social purposes are administered through the Bedfordshire and Luton Community Foundation (www.blcf.org.uk).
**WHO TO APPLY TO** David McLynn, Executive Officer, 14 Albany Road, Bedford MK40 3PH Tel. 01234 359737 email admin@panacea-society.org Website www.panacea-society.org

## ■ Panahpur

**CC NO** 1130367 **ESTABLISHED** 1911
**WHERE FUNDING CAN BE GIVEN** UK and overseas.
**WHO CAN BENEFIT** Christian charities and individuals, especially Christian missionary organisations.
**WHAT IS FUNDED** Social investment.
**RANGE OF GRANTS** For organisations, £2,000 to £24,500.
**SAMPLE GRANTS** Mission Now Cambodia (£24,500); Concern (£11,500); Xmedia (£4,700); Cinnamon Network (£2,000).
**FINANCES** Year 2012/13 Income £130,364 Grants £50,226 Grants to organisations £50,226 Assets £5,107,925
**TRUSTEES** Paul East; Andrew Perry; Larissa Rwakasiisi; Laurence East; Andrew Matheson; Liz Satow; Judith Houston; Daniel Brewer.
**OTHER INFORMATION** At the time of writing (June 2015) the 2012/13 accounts were the latest available. During the year, grants to individuals amounted to £7,400. The charity also had support costs of £321,500.

**HOW TO APPLY** The trustees do their own research and do not respond to unsolicited applications.
**WHO TO APPLY TO** James Perry, 84 High Street, Tonbridge, Kent TN9 1AP Website www.panahpur.org

## ■ The Panton Trust

**CC NO** 292910 **ESTABLISHED** 1983
**WHERE FUNDING CAN BE GIVEN** UK and overseas.
**WHO CAN BENEFIT** Worldwide organisations concerned with animal wildlife; UK: the environment.
**WHAT IS FUNDED** The trust states that it is 'concerned with any animal or animals or with wildlife in any part of the world, or with the environment of the UK or any part thereof. The trustees consider applications from a wide variety of sources and favour smaller charities which do not have the same capacity for large-scale fundraising as major charities in this field'.
**TYPE OF GRANT** Project costs; one-off; recurrent.
**RANGE OF GRANTS** Up to £5,000.
**SAMPLE GRANTS** St Tiggywinkles Wildlife Hospital and Whale and Dolphin Conservation Society (£5,000 each); Emmanuel College – Cambridge and Zoological Society (£2,000 each); Galapagos Conservation Trust, Moon Bear Rescue, Sunshine Club, and Wroxton Duck Fund (£1,000 each).
**FINANCES** Year 2013/14 Income £60,954 Grants £38,050 Grants to organisations £38,050 Assets £211,342
**TRUSTEES** L. M. Slavin; R. Craig.
**OTHER INFORMATION** Grants under £1,000 totalled £12,000.
**HOW TO APPLY** Apply in writing to the correspondent.
**WHO TO APPLY TO** Laurence Slavin, Trustee, Ramsay House, 18 Vera Avenue, Grange Park, London N12 1RA Tel. 020 8370 7700

## ■ The James Pantyfedwen Foundation

**CC NO** 1069598 **ESTABLISHED** 1998
**WHERE FUNDING CAN BE GIVEN** Wales.
**WHO CAN BENEFIT** Churches; Sunday schools; religious charities; other registered charities; local eisteddfodau; postgraduate students.
**WHAT IS FUNDED** For the benefit of Welsh people, the advancement of religion, education, the arts and agriculture and other charitable purposes. Support is given in three main areas: to individual churches for the improvement and repair of fabric; to local eisteddfodau; to postgraduate students, especially in the area of research.
**WHAT IS NOT FUNDED** Salaries; general revenue costs. Exclusions vary according to the type of grant being applied for. See the appropriate guideline document on the website for details.
**TYPE OF GRANT** One-off, capital costs.
**RANGE OF GRANTS** Generally £1,000–£5,000, larger grants may be given in special cases. The maximum grant to any eisteddfod is £500.
**SAMPLE GRANTS** Young Life International (£13,800); Living Room – Cardiff (£13,100); Eisteddfodau Cylch y Bro (£10,200); St David's Uniting Church – Pontypridd (£8,000); Dewi Sant – Cardiff (£4,000); National Eisteddfod (£3,000); The Gate Arts and Community Centre (£2,500); Baptist Union of Wales and Coleg y Bala (£2,000 each); South Gwent Children's Foundation and United Reformed Church in

Wales (£1,000); Cwm Community Action Group – Penmachno (£750); St Edwards – Roath, Cardiff (£500).
**FINANCES** Year 2013/14 Income £539,116 Grants £360,026 Grants to organisations £360,026 Assets £14,936,074
**TRUSTEES** Gwerfyl Pierce Jones; William Phillips; Ken Richards; Emrys Jones; Roy Sharp; Cr Rhidian Griffiths; Geraint Jones; Revd Alun Evans; Prof. Derec Morgan; David Lewis; Dr Eryn White; Wyn Jones; Gwenan Creunant.
**HOW TO APPLY** Guidelines for student, local eisteddfodau and churches applications can be found on the website and should be carefully considered before an application is made. Application forms for grants to local eisteddfodau and students may be downloaded from the website; however, churches wishing to make an application must contact the foundation to obtain a form. The trustees meet three times a year to consider applications.
**WHO TO APPLY TO** Richard Morgan, Executive Secretary, Pantyfedwen, 9 Market Street, Aberystwyth SY23 1DL Tel. 01970 612806 Fax 01970 612806 email pantyfedwen@btinternet.com Website www.jamespantyfedwenfoundation.org.uk

## ■ The Paphitis Charitable Trust
**CC NO** 1112721    **ESTABLISHED** 2005
**WHERE FUNDING CAN BE GIVEN** UK and overseas.
**WHO CAN BENEFIT** Charitable organisations.
**WHAT IS FUNDED** Education and sport; relief of poverty; care in the community; general charitable purposes. There appears to be a particular interest in children's and medical charities.
**RANGE OF GRANTS** Usually up to £1,000.
**SAMPLE GRANTS** Children with Cancer (£20,000); Ashmole Academy and The Fence Club (£1,000 each); The Royal Marsden Cancer Charity and Theirworld (£500 each); World Jewish Relief (£400); Birmingham Children's Hospital and Maggie's Cancer Caring Centres (£250 each); Limbless Association and Meningitis Now (£200 each); Association of Rizokarpasso (£100); Cancer Research UK (£50).
**FINANCES** Year 2013/14 Income £61,159 Grants £32,465 Grants to organisations £32,465 Assets £67,566
**TRUSTEES** Malcolm Cooke; Richard Towner; Kypros Kyprianou; Ann Mantz; Ian Childs.
**OTHER INFORMATION** This trust was set up by the entrepreneur Theo Paphitis. During the year, 41 donations were made.
**HOW TO APPLY** Apply in writing to the correspondent.
**WHO TO APPLY TO** Ann Mantz, Trustee, 2nd Floor, 22–24 Worple Road, London SW19 4DD Tel. 020 8971 9890

## ■ The Paragon Trust
**CC NO** 278348    **ESTABLISHED** 1979
**WHERE FUNDING CAN BE GIVEN** UK and overseas.
**WHO CAN BENEFIT** Charities and occasionally certain individuals but only those known to the trustees.
**WHAT IS FUNDED** General charitable purposes.
**TYPE OF GRANT** The majority of donations are standing orders.
**RANGE OF GRANTS** £100 to £6,000.
**SAMPLE GRANTS** Compassion in World Farming (£6,000); Lawrence's Roundabout Well Appeal (£3,000); King's College Chapel (£2,000); Bipolar UK, Combat Stress, Great St Mary's Church, National Trust and St Wilfred's Hospice (£1,000 each); Raystede Centre for Animal Welfare (£800); Canine Partners and Rwanda Aid (£500 each); Womankind Worldwide (£300); YMCA (£100).
**FINANCES** Year 2013/14 Income £87,177 Grants £87,520 Grants to organisations £87,520 Assets £2,253,857
**TRUSTEES** The Revd Canon Ronald Coppin; Lucy Whistler; Philip Cunningham; Dr Fiona Cornish; Patricia Russell; Kathleen Larter.
**HOW TO APPLY** The trust states that it does not respond to unsolicited applications; all beneficiaries 'are known personally to the trustees and no attention is paid to appeal literature, which is discarded on receipt. Fundraisers are therefore urged to save resources by not sending literature.'
**WHO TO APPLY TO** Stuart Goodbody, c/o Thomson Snell and Passmore Solicitors, 3 Lonsdale Gardens, Tunbridge Wells, Kent TN1 1NX Tel. 01892 510000

## ■ The Park Charitable Trust
**CC NO** 1095541    **ESTABLISHED** 2003
**WHERE FUNDING CAN BE GIVEN** UK.
**WHO CAN BENEFIT** Charitable organisations and hospitals.
**WHAT IS FUNDED** Jewish religion and education, and the relief of poverty amongst Jewish people. People who are suffering from cancer or heart conditions and hospitals.
**FINANCES** Year 2013/14 Income £2,357,643 Grants £243,463 Grants to organisations £243,463 Assets £1,981,055
**TRUSTEES** David Hammelburger; Martina Hammelburger; Eli Pine.
**HOW TO APPLY** Apply in writing to the correspondent.
**WHO TO APPLY TO** Eli Pine, Trustee, 69 Singleton Road, Salford M7 4LX

## ■ The Park House Charitable Trust
**CC NO** 1077677    **ESTABLISHED** 1999
**WHERE FUNDING CAN BE GIVEN** UK and overseas, with a preference for the Midlands, particularly Coventry and Warwickshire.
**WHO CAN BENEFIT** Charitable organisations.
**WHAT IS FUNDED** Education; social welfare; ecclesiastical causes; medical purposes.
**WHAT IS NOT FUNDED** Individuals.
**TYPE OF GRANT** Normally one-off for general funds.
**RANGE OF GRANTS** £1,000–£200,000
**SAMPLE GRANTS** Scottish International Relief (£200,000); St Joseph and The Helpers Charity, UK (£150,000); St Anne's Church, Wappenbury (£80,000); Friends of the Holy Land (£50,000); CAFOD (£25,000); Aid to the Church in Need (£20,000); Mary Vale Institute and Médecins Sans Frontières (£15,000 each); African Child Trust, Heart of England Community Foundation and St John of Jerusalem Eye Hospital (£10,000 each); Smile Train and Warwickshire and Northamptonshire Air Ambulance (£5,000 each); Daylight Christian Prison Trust (£4,000); African Mission, Bibles for Children, Tiny Tim's Children's Centre and West London Churches Homeless (£3,000 each); Birmingham Medjugorje Centre (£1,000).
**FINANCES** Year 2013 Income £955,638 Grants £935,000 Grants to organisations £935,000 Assets £1,685,066
**TRUSTEES** Margaret Bailey; Niall Bailey; Paul Bailey.
**OTHER INFORMATION** Grants were distributed for the following purposes: social welfare (£686,000);

ecclesiastical (£193,000); medical (£33,000); education (£23,000).
HOW TO APPLY Apply in writing to the correspondent. The trust has previously stated that it does not expect to have surplus funds available to meet the majority of applications.
WHO TO APPLY TO Paul Varney, Correspondent, Dafferns LLP, One Eastwood, Harry Weston Road, Binley Business Park, Coventry CV3 2UB *Tel.* 024 7622 1046

## ■ The Samuel and Freda Parkinson Charitable Trust

CC NO 327749   ESTABLISHED 1987
WHERE FUNDING CAN BE GIVEN UK.
WHO CAN BENEFIT Registered charities specified by the founder of the trust.
WHAT IS FUNDED General charitable purposes.
RANGE OF GRANTS £5,000–£25,000
SAMPLE GRANTS The Leonard Cheshire Foundation (£26,000); The Salvation Army (£25,000); The Church Army and RNLI (£15,000 each); Animal Welfare and RSPCA (£5,000 each); Animal Rescue Cumbria (£4,000). Animal Concern, another regular beneficiary, did not receive a donation during the year.
FINANCES Year 2012/13 Income £111,262 Grants £95,000 Grants to organisations £95,000 Assets £3,300,096
TRUSTEES John Crompton; Judith Todd; Michael Fletcher.
OTHER INFORMATION The trust supports the same eight beneficiaries each year, although for varying amounts. At the time of writing (June 2015) these were the latest accounts available for the trust.
HOW TO APPLY The founder of this charity restricted the list of potential beneficiaries to named charities of his choice and accordingly the trustees do not have discretion to include further beneficiaries, although they do have complete discretion within the stated beneficiary list.
WHO TO APPLY TO Trust Administrator, c/o Thomson Hayton Winkley, Regent House, 25 Crescent Road, Windermere, Cumbria LA23 1BJ *Tel.* 01539 446585 *email* info@thwlegal.co.uk

## ■ Miss M. E. Swinton Paterson's Charitable Trust

SC NO SC004835   ESTABLISHED 1989
WHERE FUNDING CAN BE GIVEN Scotland.
WHO CAN BENEFIT Organisations benefitting Christians, children and young people, the elderly, those in need due to financial hardship and Church of Scotland.
WHAT IS FUNDED Support to the Church of Scotland and other Christian groups in the maintenance of church buildings and in their work with young people, the elderly and disadvantaged people.
WHAT IS NOT FUNDED Individuals; students.
RANGE OF GRANTS £500–£1,000
SAMPLE GRANTS **Previous beneficiaries have included:** L'Arche Edinburgh Community; Livingstone Baptist Church; Lloyd Morris Congregational Church; Haddington West Parish Church; Acorn Christian Centre; Stranraer YMCA; Care for the Family; Boys' and Girls' Clubs of Scotland; Fresh Start; Friends of the Elms; Iona Community; Edinburgh Young Carers' Project; Epilepsy Scotland; Stoneykirk Parish Church; Scotland Yard Adventure Centre; Atholl Centre;

Scottish Crusaders; Disablement Income Group Scotland; Artlink.
FINANCES Year 2013/14 Income £52,410 Grants £57,000 Grants to organisations £57,000
TRUSTEE No information was available.
HOW TO APPLY Apply in writing to the correspondent. The trustees normally meet once a year in July to consider grants.
WHO TO APPLY TO The Trustees, Lindsays' Solicitors, Caledonian Exchange, 19A Canning Street, Edinburgh EH3 8HE *Tel.* 0131 229 1212 *Fax* 0131 229 5611 *email* edinburgh@lindsays.co.uk

## ■ The Patrick Charitable Trust

CC NO 213849   ESTABLISHED 1962
WHERE FUNDING CAN BE GIVEN UK, with a special interest in the West Midlands
WHO CAN BENEFIT Registered charities.
WHAT IS FUNDED General charitable purposes.
WHAT IS NOT FUNDED Individuals.
TYPE OF GRANT One-off or recurrent.
RANGE OF GRANTS £100 to £25,000. Usually below £10,000.
SAMPLE GRANTS **Beneficiaries of donations paid in 2013/14:** Macmillan Cancer Support (£5,000); Action Centres UK Ltd – Pioneer Centre Cleobury Mortimer, Children's Hospice South West, The Mary Stevens Hospice, Motor Neurone Disease Association, The Primrose Hospice – Bromsgrove, and Prodh – Druid's Heath (£1,000 each). Beneficiaries of designated donations in 2014/15: Birmingham Royal Ballet (£25,000); Performances Birmingham Ltd, Marie Curie Hospice – West Midlands, Royal Shakespeare Company and The Stonehouse Gang (£10,000 each); Birmingham Hippodrome Theatre Trust (£6,000); The Belgrade Theatre, Elmhurst School for Dance and The National Trust (£5,000 each).
FINANCES Year 2013/14 Income £102,139 Grants £98,400 Grants to organisations £98,400 Assets £6,998,061
TRUSTEES Joseph Alexander Patrick; Mary Patrick; Heather Cole; William Bond-Williams; Graham Wem.
HOW TO APPLY Apply in writing to the correspondent at any time. The trust endeavours to reply to all applications with a decision.
WHO TO APPLY TO Joseph Alexander Patrick, Trustee, The Lakeside Centre, 180 Lifford Lane, Birmingham B30 3NU *Tel.* 0121 486 3399 *email* thepatricktrust@aol.com

## ■ The Jack Patston Charitable Trust

CC NO 701658   ESTABLISHED 1989
WHERE FUNDING CAN BE GIVEN Preferably Leicestershire and Cambridgeshire.
WHO CAN BENEFIT Charitable organisations, including rural churches.
WHAT IS FUNDED Preservation of wildlife and the environment, advancement of religion and preservation of rural church fabric.
WHAT IS NOT FUNDED Individuals.
TYPE OF GRANT Single payments.
RANGE OF GRANTS Up to £3,000.
SAMPLE GRANTS Peterborough 900 (Peterborough Cathedral) (£5,000); Train a Priest Fund (£3,500); St James' Church, Castle Bytham and Sue Ryder Care – Thorpe Hall (£3,000 each); Derbyshire, Leicestershire and Rutland Air

Ambulance, St Peter's Church, Horninghold and All Saints Church, Buckworth (£2,500 each); East Anglia's Children's Hospices, Bat Conservation Trust and Deafblind UK (£2,000 each); Bumblebee Conservation Trust and Emmaus Leicestershire and Rutland (£1,500 each); Sense (£1,250); St James' Church, Waresley (£1,000).
FINANCES Year 2013/14 Income £108,215 Grants £89,750 Grants to organisations £89,750 Assets £4,748,054
TRUSTEES Allan Veasey; Charles Applegate; Stephen Knipe.
OTHER INFORMATION In 2013/14 grants were made to 41 organisations.
HOW TO APPLY Apply in writing to the correspondent.
WHO TO APPLY TO Charles Applegate, Trustee, Buckles Solicitors LLP, Grant House, 101 Bourges Boulevard, Peterborough PE1 1NG *Tel.* 01733 888888 *email* charles.applegate@buckles-law.co.uk

## ■ Ambika Paul Foundation
CC NO 276127          ESTABLISHED 1978
WHERE FUNDING CAN BE GIVEN Mainly UK and India.
WHO CAN BENEFIT Large organisations, registered charities, colleges and universities benefitting children, young adults and students.
WHAT IS FUNDED Main areas of interest are young people and education.
WHAT IS NOT FUNDED Applications from individuals, including students, are mainly ineligible. Funding for scholarships is made directly to colleges/universities, not to individuals. Expeditions are not funded.
RANGE OF GRANTS Usually £100–£5,000.
SAMPLE GRANTS Where the Need (£5,000); Women's India Association (£2,500); Bharatiya Vidya Bhavan (£1,000); Duchenne Children's Trust (£5000) Metropolitan Police Hindu Association and Rajender (£250 each); Cancer Research (£200); Shooting Star Chase Hospice (£100); and PiggyBankKids (£25).
FINANCES Year 2013/14 Income £589,484 Grants £15,500 Grants to organisations £15,500 Assets £9,592,517
TRUSTEES Lord Paul of Marylebone; Lady Aruna Paul; Hon. Angad Paul; Hon. Anjli Paul; Hon. Ambar Paul; Hon. Akash Paul.
OTHER INFORMATION A large proportion of the foundation's income comes from the Caparo Group which is wholly owned by the Paul family.
HOW TO APPLY Apply in to the trustees at the correspondence address. Acknowledgements are sent if an sae is enclosed. However, the trust has no paid employees and the enormous number of requests it receives creates administrative difficulties.
WHO TO APPLY TO Lord Paul of Marylebone, Trustee, Caparo Group, Caparo House, 103 Baker Street, London W1U 6LN *Tel.* 020 7486 1417 *email* georgina.mason@caparo.com

## ■ The Payne Charitable Trust
CC NO 241816          ESTABLISHED 1965
WHERE FUNDING CAN BE GIVEN Wales, West Midlands, Cumbria and India.
WHO CAN BENEFIT Missionaries, churches, and people engaged in the propagation of the Christian gospel.
WHAT IS FUNDED Religious and charitable objects. The main area of interest is the support of evangelical Christians in the promotion and proclamation of the Christian gospel.
WHAT IS NOT FUNDED Grants are not made for repairs to church buildings or towards education.
TYPE OF GRANT One-off grants and loans; capital and core support.
RANGE OF GRANTS Up to £30,000.
SAMPLE GRANTS **Previous beneficiaries have included:** Andrew League Trust; Biblica; Crusaders; Heart Cry for Wales; Jericho Foundation; Street Pastors.
FINANCES Year 2013/14 Income £19,506 Grants £37,000 Grants to organisations £37,000
TRUSTEES Eric Payne; John Payne.
OTHER INFORMATION Due to the large number of applications, some considerable time can elapse before communication can be sent.
HOW TO APPLY Applications can be made in writing to the correspondent. They should be submitted between 1 January and 21 March only, for grants made from the following 1 May. The trustees regret that they cannot support many of the deserving organisations that apply for a grant. Due to the large number of applications, some considerable time can elapse before communication can be sent.
WHO TO APPLY TO John Payne, Trustee, Fourwinds, Copthorn Road, Colwyn Bay LL28 5YP *Tel.* 01492 532393 *email* john@copthornehouse.com

## ■ The Harry Payne Fund (formerly The Harry Payne Trust)
CC NO 231063          ESTABLISHED 1939
WHERE FUNDING CAN BE GIVEN Birmingham and the immediately surrounding areas of the West Midlands, including the Black Country, Coventry, Warwickshire and parts of Worcestershire and Staffordshire.
WHO CAN BENEFIT Registered charities and CICs, though other non-profit organisations may also be considered as long as they have a constitution and produce accounts. Giving is restricted to organisations with an income of less than £500,000.
WHAT IS FUNDED Social welfare and smaller causes. This includes organisations working in the following areas: older people; victims, offenders and their families; arts, particularly projects aimed at people who are unemployed, disadvantaged or disabled; local environmental projects; marriage/ relationship help and advice; pregnancy advice; sexual health education; carers; disability; community projects, particularly those aimed at improving quality of life in deprived areas; young families; homelessness; poverty, particularly food poverty; local conservation projects; peace organisations; faith organisations (generally for specific projects); inter-faith understanding; training, education and care of children and adults with disabilities; the integration of ethnic minority groups; social inclusion; community care projects; drug and alcohol abuse; holidays for children who are disadvantaged or have disabilities; education, particularly for people who are disadvantaged or have disabilities (but not for maintenance grants).
WHAT IS NOT FUNDED General fundraising appeals; individuals; the promotion of religious causes; research; animal welfare; political activities; mainstream activities of schools and colleges; or sports clubs (except when aimed at addressing disadvantage).
TYPE OF GRANT Specific projects and general running costs.

RANGE OF GRANTS £250–£1,000
SAMPLE GRANTS Bethel Heath and Healing Network (£1,000); Birmingham Law Centre (£750); Cotteridge Church Day Centre and Relate Birmingham (£500 each); Trinity Housing Resource Centre (£300); Handicapped Children's Action Group (£250).
FINANCES Year 2013/14 Income £62,427 Grants £55,660 Grants to organisations £55,660 Assets £1,475,400
TRUSTEES Duncan Cadbury; Robert King; Fiona Adams; Valerie Dub; Fred Rattley; Donald Payne; Joseph Devlin; Kate Hazlewood.
HOW TO APPLY An application form is available to download from the Heart of England Community Foundation website. Your application should be restricted to no more than two sides of A4 and should be returned to the Grants Team along with a copy of your organisation's latest annual report and accounts and latest bank statement. Applicants will be notified of a decision within 16 weeks of submission of a completed application form.
WHO TO APPLY TO The Grants Team, The Heart of England Community Foundation, c/o PSA Peugeot Citroen, Torrington Avenue, Tile Hill, Coventry CV4 9AP *Tel.* 024 7688 3262 *email* info@heartofenglandcf.co.uk *Website* www.heartofenglandcf.co.uk/index.php/grant/harry-payne-fund

## ■ The Peacock Charitable Trust

CC NO 257655 ESTABLISHED 1968
WHERE FUNDING CAN BE GIVEN UK with a possible preference for London and the south of England
WHO CAN BENEFIT Registered charities.
WHAT IS FUNDED Charities which the trustees have special knowledge of, interest in, or association with, particularly medical research, disability, young people and social welfare.
WHAT IS NOT FUNDED No donations are made to individuals and only in rare cases are additions made to the list of charities already being supported.
TYPE OF GRANT Capital, project and some recurring.
RANGE OF GRANTS £1,500–£105,000
SAMPLE GRANTS The Prince's Youth Business Trust (£103,000); Cancer Research UK (£95,000); The Neuro-disability Research Trust (£63,000); The Jubilee Sailing Trust and St Wilfred's Hospice (£50,000 each); Queen Elizabeth's Foundation for the Disabled (£37,000); Royal Society for the Protection of Birds (£16,200); St John Ambulance and UK Youth (£11,000 each); Sightsavers (£9,000); Wimbledon Guild of Social Welfare (£6,000); Prisoner's Education Trust and The National Trust (£5,000 each); Disabled Living Foundation (£4,000).
FINANCES Year 2013/14 Income £594,788 Grants £1,355,800 Grants to organisations £1,355,800 Assets £44,068,571
TRUSTEES Charles Peacock; Bettine Bond; Dr Clare Sellors.
OTHER INFORMATION Of the grant total, only £51,000 was given to new applicants.
HOW TO APPLY Apply in writing to the correspondent. The trustees meet three times a year with representatives from the Charities Aid Foundation (CAF) to decide on the grants to be made. The trust makes a lot of recurring grants therefore new applications are unlikely to be successful.
WHO TO APPLY TO The Correspondent, c/o Charities Aid Foundation, Kings Hill, West Malling, Kent ME19 4TA *Tel.* 01732 520081 *email* mtheodorou@cafonline.org

## ■ The Susanna Peake Charitable Trust

CC NO 283462 ESTABLISHED 1981
WHERE FUNDING CAN BE GIVEN UK, with a preference for the South West of England, particularly Gloucestershire
WHO CAN BENEFIT Registered charities.
WHAT IS FUNDED General charitable purposes.
WHAT IS NOT FUNDED Individuals.
TYPE OF GRANT Usually one-off grants.
RANGE OF GRANTS £250 to £5,000.
SAMPLE GRANTS Chipping Norton Theatre and Friend's Trust, Friends of Longborough School, King Edward VII's Hospital and North Cotswold Volunteers (£5,000 each); St James Church Longborough (£4,000); RDA – Knightsbridge Group and Speech, Language and Hearing Centre (£3,000 each); Book Aid International, Calibre Audio Library, Carers Gloucestershire, Farm Africa, Home Start – Bristol, Independence at Home, North Cotswold Food Bank and Tree Aid (£2,000 each); Listening Books (£1,500); Cotswold Villagers Old People's Housing Association (£1,000); Brain Research Trust and The National Lobster Hatchery (£500 each); Shipston Home Nursing (£250).
FINANCES Year 2013/14 Income £183,863 Grants £121,750 Grants to organisations £121,750 Assets £6,548,258
TRUSTEES Susanna Peake; David Peake.
OTHER INFORMATION During the year, 55 organisations received support.
HOW TO APPLY Apply in writing to the correspondent. The trustees meet on a frequent, ad hoc basis to consider applications.
WHO TO APPLY TO Rathbone Trust Company Limited, 1 Curzon Street, London W1J 5FB *Tel.* 020 7399 0820 *email* linda.cousins@rathbones.com

## ■ The David Pearlman Charitable Foundation

CC NO 287009 ESTABLISHED 1983
WHERE FUNDING CAN BE GIVEN UK.
WHO CAN BENEFIT Jewish organisations.
WHAT IS FUNDED Jewish religion and education; general charitable purposes.
SAMPLE GRANTS **Previous beneficiaries have included:** British Friends of Igud Hakolelim B'Yerushalayim (£60,000); Lolev Charitable Trust (£30,000); Jewish Care (£16,000); Chevras Mo'oz Ladol (£15,000); Norwood (£12,000); the Duke of Edinburgh Trust (£7,000); Community Security Trust (£6,000); Life's 4 Living Trust Ltd (£6,400); Children Number One Foundation (£3,750); the Variety Club Children's Charity (£2,750); London Academy of Jewish Studies (£1,500); Jewish Music Institute and United Jewish Israel Appeal (£1,000).
FINANCES Year 2013/14 Income £1,390,741 Grants £482,806 Grants to organisations £482,806 Assets £3,728,318
TRUSTEES Michael Goldberger; Stuart Appleman; David Pearlman; Jonathan Hager.
HOW TO APPLY Apply in writing to the correspondent.
WHO TO APPLY TO Michael Goldberger, Secretary, New Burlington House, 1075 Finchley Road, London NW11 0PU *Tel.* 020 8731 0777

*Alphabetical register of grant-making charities* **Peel**

## ■ The Pears Family Charitable Foundation

**CC NO** 1009195  **ESTABLISHED** 1991
**WHERE FUNDING CAN BE GIVEN** Worldwide.
**WHO CAN BENEFIT** Charitable organisations.
**WHAT IS FUNDED** The foundation invests in five main areas: identity, community and citizenship in the UK; Jewish contribution to society; education on genocide; Israel as a global citizen; and exploring philanthropy.
**TYPE OF GRANT** Core, project and capital costs.
**RANGE OF GRANTS** Up to £1.75 million.
**SAMPLE GRANTS** Imperial War Museum (£1.75 million); Institute of Education and The Queen Elizabeth Diamond Jubilee Trust (£500,000 each); Carers Trust (£400,000); Tevel B'Tzedek (£336,000); The Hebrew University of Jerusalem (£284,000); The National Holocaust Centre and Museum and The Scout Association (£200,000 each); Institute for Jewish Policy Research (£175,000); Norwood and Scope (£150,000 each); UK Jewish Film (£118,500); Hand in Hand: Centre for Jewish-Arab Education in Israel (£100,500); British Council and Youth Philanthropy Education (£100,000).
**FINANCES** Year 2013/14 *Income* £10,630,598 *Grants* £12,404,276 *Grants to organisations* £12,404,276 *Assets* £18,176,697
**TRUSTEES** Trevor Pears; Mark Pears; David Pears.
**OTHER INFORMATION** During the year, 302 grants of more than £1,000 were made to organisations.
**HOW TO APPLY** The website states: 'We do our own research to identify appropriate delivery partners and do not accept unsolicited proposals for projects or organisational funding.'
**WHO TO APPLY TO** The Trustees, Clive House, 2 Old Brewery Mews, London NW3 1PZ *Tel.* 020 7433 3333 *email* contact@pearsfoundation.org.uk *Website* www.pearsfoundation.org.uk

## ■ Rosanna Pearson's 1987 Charity Trust

**CC NO** 297210  **ESTABLISHED** 1987
**WHERE FUNDING CAN BE GIVEN** UK and overseas, with a preference for Oxfordshire and West Sussex.
**WHO CAN BENEFIT** Registered charities only.
**WHAT IS FUNDED** General charitable purposes; education and training; the promotion of health; overseas aid; the environment; economic and community development.
**WHAT IS NOT FUNDED** Individuals or non-registered charities.
**SAMPLE GRANTS** Charities Aid Foundation, Disaster Emergencies Committee – Haiti Appeal, Pearson Taylor Trust and Resonance FM.
**FINANCES** Year 2013/14 *Income* £11,853 *Grants* £80,000 *Grants to organisations* £80,000
**TRUSTEE** The Cowdray Trust Ltd.
**OTHER INFORMATION** The 2013/14 accounts had been received at the Charity Commission but were unavailable to view.
**HOW TO APPLY** Apply in writing to the correspondent. Acknowledgements are not sent to unsuccessful applicants.
**WHO TO APPLY TO** Anina Cheng, Trust Administrator, Swan House, 17–19 Stratford Place, London W1C 1BQ *email* charity@mfs.co.uk

## ■ The Pedmore Sporting Club Trust Fund

**CC NO** 263907  **ESTABLISHED** 1973
**WHERE FUNDING CAN BE GIVEN** West Midlands.
**WHO CAN BENEFIT** Registered charities and individuals.
**WHAT IS FUNDED** Relief in need; general charitable purposes.
**WHAT IS NOT FUNDED** Running costs; salaries.
**RANGE OF GRANTS** £150 to £10,000.
**SAMPLE GRANTS** Previous beneficiaries have included: Ladies Fighting Breast Cancer (£10,000); Mary Stevens Hospice (£5,000); Stambermlll Scouts (£4,000); Creating Chances Trust (£3,000); Stourbridge Citizens Advice (£3,400); Riding for the Disabled (£2,500); Glasshouse College, Stourbridge (£2,000); Midland Air Ambulance (£1,000); Birmingham Children's Hospital (£500); and Dodford Children's Farm (£150).
**FINANCES** Year 2014 *Income* £41,500 *Grants* £32,422 *Grants to organisations* £32,422
**TRUSTEES** Mr R. Herman-Smith; Mr R. Williams; Mr T. Hickman; Mr J. Price; Paul Pioli; John Whitehouse.
**OTHER INFORMATION** At the time of writing (June 2015) the charity's annual return for 2014 had been submitted to the Charity Commission; however, its accounts had not yet been received. In previous years, grants have accounted for the entirety of the charity's total expenditure. The grant total above also includes any grants which may have been made to individuals. The charity's website was not active at the time of writing.
**HOW TO APPLY** Apply to the correspondent in writing or by email. Our research suggests that trustees meet to consider grants in January, May, September and November and typically will consider 30–40 applications.
**WHO TO APPLY TO** Alan Nicklin, Secretary, Pedmore Sporting Club Trust, Nicklin and Co, Church Court, Stourbridge Road, Halesowen B63 3TT *email* psclub@pedmorehouse.co.uk *Website* www.pedmoresportingclub.co.uk

## ■ The Dowager Countess Eleanor Peel Trust

**CC NO** 214684  **ESTABLISHED** 1951
**WHERE FUNDING CAN BE GIVEN** Worldwide in practice UK, with a preference for Lancashire (especially Lancaster and District), Cumbria, Greater Manchester, Cheshire and Merseyside.
**WHO CAN BENEFIT** Registered charities; universities.
**WHAT IS FUNDED** Charities working to support older people; charities working to support people who face disadvantage through no fault of their own (e.g. people who have disabilities or who are sick, homeless, suffering from mental health issues, victims of disasters, or ex-services); medical care and research, particularly benefitting older people; various charities specified in the trust deed.
**WHAT IS NOT FUNDED** Charities substantially under the control of central or local government; charities primarily devoted to children; individuals, except for medical research grants and annual travelling fellowship awards.
**TYPE OF GRANT** The trust prefers to support projects rather than running costs.
**RANGE OF GRANTS** Mostly between £1,000 and £10,000.

*Have you read* How to use the DGMT *on page xiii?*

**709**

**SAMPLE GRANTS** University of Salford – Institute of Dementia (£300,000); University of Cumbria – Faculty of Health and Science (£136,000); Peel Studentship Trust – University of Lancaster (£50,000); British Red Cross (£20,000); Lancaster University (£19,500); University of Leicester (£15,000); Macmillan Cancer Support and Treetops Hospice Trust (£10,000 each); Manchester Personal Support Unit and Queen Alexandra Home (£5,000 each); The Rossendale Trust (£3,500); Calibra Audio Library (£2,500); Sight Advise South Lakes (£1,500);

**FINANCES** Year 2013/14 Income £596,577 Grants £804,448 Grants to organisations £744,448 Assets £17,501,564

**TRUSTEES** Prof. Sir Robert Boyd; John Parkinson; Michael Parkinson; Prof. Richard Ramsden; Prof. Margaret Pearson; Julius Manduell.

**OTHER INFORMATION** During the year, grants were made to 40 organisations. Grants to individuals through The Peel and Rothwell Jackson Postgraduate Travelling Scholarship amounted to £60,000.

**HOW TO APPLY** The trustees apply the following criteria in making grants: 1. There is no geographical limitation on applications; however, applications from charities in the 'preferred Locations' of Lancashire (especially Lancaster and District), Cumbria, Greater Manchester, Cheshire and Merseyside will receive preference over applications from other geographical areas; 2. The trustees focus on small to medium sized charities where grants will make a difference. Applications from large well-funded charities (with income in excess of £2.5 million per annum) will normally be rejected, unless the project is a capital project; 3. The trustees aim to support fewer charities with larger average grants (£5,000 or more); 4. The trustees' preference is to support capital projects or project driven applications and not running costs, although the trustees are flexible to take account of the needs of smaller charities (with an income of up to £2.5 million) which operate in its preferred locations. The trustees will consider supporting revenue projects and running costs in addition to capital projects for charities in this category. The trustees scrutinise the financial position of all applicants, and those with income accounts showing substantial surpluses are unlikely to be supported; 5. The trustees do make grants to disaster appeals which are considered on a case by case basis. The trustees feel it is important to know the charities to which grants are or may be awarded. Therefore, they will arrange to visit the charity and/or arrange for the charity to make a presentation to a trustees' meeting from time to time. Applications for grants along with the required supporting information, should be forwarded by post or email. The following information is required: a general outline of the reasons for the application; the amount of the grant applied for; the latest annual report and audited accounts; if the application is for a major capital project, details of the cost of the project along with information of funds already in hand or pledged. *Applications for Medical Research Grants*: applications for medical research grants will be categorised as appropriate either for a 'minor grant' (£10,000 or less) or a 'major grant' (up to £50,000 per year for a defined research project for one to three years). Applications to be considered for major grants are assessed en-bloc annually at the trustee's meeting in March. Applications are competitive and will be met from funds set aside for this purpose. The following additional information is required: aims, objectives and direction of the research project; the institution where the research will be carried out and by whom (principal researchers); an outline of costs and of funding required for the project and details of any funds already in hand. A brief (but not too technical) annual report on the progress of projects receiving major grants will be requested from the research team. *Minor medical grants:* these grants are for sums up to a maximum of £10,000 and are usually for areas such as 'pilot study costs' or equipment. Applications for Minor Grants are considered at each of the trustees' meeting which are ordinarily held in March, July and November each year. Grant application form for both the General and Medical research grant funding schemes can be downloaded from the website.

**WHO TO APPLY TO** Michelle Bertenshaw, Secretary, Hill Dickinson LLP, 50 Fountain Street, Manchester M2 2AS *Tel.* 0161 838 4977 *email* secretary@peeltrust.com *Website* www.peeltrust.com

──────────────────────────────────────

■ **The Pell Charitable Trust**

**CC NO** 1135398 **ESTABLISHED** 2010
**WHERE FUNDING CAN BE GIVEN** UK.
**WHO CAN BENEFIT** Registered charities.
**WHAT IS FUNDED** General charitable purposes, with a preference for the arts, particularly music.
**WHAT IS NOT FUNDED** Individuals.
**RANGE OF GRANTS** Usually up to around £16,000.
**SAMPLE GRANTS Previous beneficiaries have included:** Royal National Theatre; British Red Cross; Duke of Edinburgh's Awards; Welsh National Opera; Royal Opera House Foundation; Caudwell Children; Donmar Warehouse Projects; Wylye Valley Disabled Children Riding; Almeida Theatre; English National Opera; London Fund for Young Musicians.
**FINANCES** Year 2014/15 Income £47,875 Grants £44,000 Grants to organisations £44,000
**TRUSTEES** Marian Pell; Gordon Pell; Nicholas Pell; Coutts & Co.
**OTHER INFORMATION** At the time of writing (June 2015) the trust's 2013/14 and 2014/15 accounts had each been submitted to the Charity Commission, but were not yet available to view. The grant total above is an estimate based on amounts given in previous years.
**HOW TO APPLY** Apply in writing to the correspondent.
**WHO TO APPLY TO** Coutts & Co, Trustee Dept, Coutts & Co, 440 Strand, London WC2R 0QS *Tel.* 020 7663 6825 *email* couttscharities@coutts.com

──────────────────────────────────────

■ **The Peltz Trust**

**CC NO** 1002302 **ESTABLISHED** 1991
**WHERE FUNDING CAN BE GIVEN** UK and Israel.
**WHO CAN BENEFIT** Charitable organisations.
**WHAT IS FUNDED** Education; health; arts; Jewish causes; economic and community development.
**RANGE OF GRANTS** In previous years, grants have generally ranged from £1,000–£20,000.
**SAMPLE GRANTS Previous beneficiaries have included:** Birkbeck College (£50,000); British Technion Society (£21,000); Central Synagogue General Charities Fund (£13,000); Norwood Ravencourt (£10,000); City of London School, UK Friends of Magen David Adom, One Family and United Jewish Israel Appeal (£5,000 each); Nightingale House (£2,500); AISH Hatorah UK

Ltd (£1,500); Willow Foundation (£1,000); Mousetrap Theatre Projects (£500).
**FINANCES** *Year* 2013/14 *Income* £6,775 *Grants* £185,000 *Grants to organisations* £185,000
**TRUSTEE** Prism the Gift Fund.
**OTHER INFORMATION** Due to its low income, the trust was not required to submit its accounts for the year to the Charity Commission.
**HOW TO APPLY** Apply in writing to the correspondent. The trustees meet at irregular intervals during the year to consider appeals from appropriate organisations.
**WHO TO APPLY TO** Anna Josse, Correspondent, 20 Gloucester Place, London W1U 8HA *Tel.* 020 7486 7760

## ■ The Pennycress Trust
**CC NO** 261536  **ESTABLISHED** 1970
**WHERE FUNDING CAN BE GIVEN** UK and worldwide, with a preference for Cheshire and Norfolk.
**WHO CAN BENEFIT** Smaller charities, and especially those based in Cheshire and Norfolk, with some donations to national organisations
**WHAT IS FUNDED** General charitable purposes. Support is given to a restricted list of registered charities only in the fields of: arts and cultural heritage; education; infrastructure, support and development; science and technology; community facilities; campaigning on health and social issues; health care and advocacy; medical studies and research; and animal welfare.
**WHAT IS NOT FUNDED** Individuals.
**TYPE OF GRANT** Recurrent and one-off.
**RANGE OF GRANTS** Usually £100–£500.
**SAMPLE GRANTS** **Previous beneficiaries have included:** All Saints' Church – Beeston Regis, Brain Research Trust, Brighton and Hove Parents' and Children's Group, British Red Cross, Crusaid, Depaul Trust, Elimination of Leukaemia Fund, Eyeless Trust, Genesis Appeal, Help the Aged, Matthew Project, RUKBA, St Peter's – Eaton Square Appeal, Salvation Army, Tibet Relief Fund, West Suffolk Headway, Women's Link and Youth Federation.
**FINANCES** *Year* 2013/14 *Income* £77,738 *Grants* £68,300 *Grants to organisations* £68,300 *Assets* £2,363,837
**TRUSTEES** Lady Aline Cholmondeley; Lady Rose Cholmondeley; Anthony Baker; C. G. Cholmondeley.
**OTHER INFORMATION** Occasionally larger grants may be made. During the year individual, one-off donations of £1,000, £1,500 and £2,000 were given.
**HOW TO APPLY** Apply in writing to the correspondent. The trustees meet regularly. The trust does not have an application form and a simple letter is sufficient. Telephone applications are not accepted.
**WHO TO APPLY TO** Doreen Howells, Secretary to the Trustees, Flat D, 15 Millman Street, London WC1N 3EP *Tel.* 020 7404 0145 *email* howellsdoreen@gmail.com

## ■ People's Postcode Trust
**SC NO** SC040387  **ESTABLISHED** 2009
**WHERE FUNDING CAN BE GIVEN** Scotland, Wales and England.
**WHO CAN BENEFIT** Registered charities; constituted community organisations.
**WHAT IS FUNDED** The trust distributes funding through two main channels: Small Grants Programme – registered charities, SCIOs, constituted community or voluntary groups, social enterprises, community interest companies (CICs), non-profit organisations and sports clubs can apply for funding for projects up to 12 months in length (6 months in Wales) which aim to advance community development or citizenship. Dream Fund – registered charities in England, Scotland and Wales can apply for up to £750,000 towards a project lasting 24 months that 'they always dreamed of but never had the opportunity to bring to life'. The project must look to advance one of the following: participation in sports; community development; environmental protection; health; human rights; the prevention of poverty, distress and sickness. **Note:** The Dream Fund is no longer administered through People's Postcode Trust. Awards are now made through the Postcode Dream Trust (OSCR no. SC044911).
**TYPE OF GRANT** Project funding.
**RANGE OF GRANTS** £500 to £20,000 (£10,000 in Wales) for Small Grants Programme. Up to £750,000 for Dream Fund grants.
**SAMPLE GRANTS** Dream Fund: Hazeldene Horticulture (£98,500); The Biospheric Project (£91,000); The Bee Project (£86,000); Moray Firth Coastal Classroom (£74,000). Small Grants Programme: Blind Life in Durham; Community treeCycle; Surfers Against Sewage; Thistle Foundation; Yorkshire Air Ambulance Charity.
**FINANCES** *Year* 2013 *Income* £8,395,394 *Grants* £1,678,149 *Grants to organisations* £1,678,149 *Assets* £261,160
**TRUSTEES** Lawson Muncaster; Mike Pratt; Judy Hills; Rob Flett.
**OTHER INFORMATION** During the year, 202 projects received funding from the trust. Organisations wishing to apply for funding of more than £2,000 must be a registered charity.
**HOW TO APPLY** Apply via the appropriate online application form. The dates of funding rounds differ depending on the region and the programme. More details, including guidance notes to download, are available from the website.
**WHO TO APPLY TO** Grants Officer, 76 George Street, Edinburgh EH2 3BU *Tel.* 0131 555 7287 *email* info@postcodetrust.org.uk *Website* www.postcodetrust.org.uk

## ■ The Performing Right Society Foundation
**CC NO** 1080837  **ESTABLISHED** 2000
**WHERE FUNDING CAN BE GIVEN** UK.
**WHO CAN BENEFIT** Registered charities; companies limited by guarantee; individuals and sole traders; CICs; non-music organisations such as local authorities and museums.
**WHAT IS FUNDED** The creation and performance of outstanding new music in any genre; the development of artists; inspiring audiences. This may include funding towards: touring; recording; PR and marketing; commissions of new music by creators in the UK; exciting community projects; music creator residencies; live programmes featuring UK music.
**WHAT IS NOT FUNDED** Companies limited by shares; projects that contain no element of live performance; technological development if it does not contain a significant aspect of new music creation; the purchase of vans and cars; bursaries, tuition/education costs, or scholarships; capital projects (for example, building work); any project raising funds for

another charity; buying equipment; building a studio; organisations or projects that have been running for less than 18 months and musicians that do not have a track record of at least 18 months; retrospective activity; activity that falls before the foundation's decision date; organisations based outside the UK; artists and music creators based outside the UK; British artists who are no longer permanent residents of the UK; international tours/recording internationally; radio stations/broadcasting costs; start-up companies or labels; a roster of artists on a record label; people who are in full-time education; people who are younger than 18, unless represent by an adult who has a valid DBS check; non-UK residents.

**TYPE OF GRANT** Usually one-year funding for revenue costs.

**RANGE OF GRANTS** For first-time applicants, up to £5,000.

**SAMPLE GRANTS** Aldeburgh Music; Cambridge Folk Festival; Glasgow Improvisers Orchestra; Mahogany Opera Group; Sound City (Liverpool) Ltd; Theatre Cryptic; Wales Millennium Centre.

**FINANCES** *Year* 2013 *Income* £2,249,912 *Grants* £2,114,497 *Grants to organisations* £1,839,612 *Assets* £340,520

**TRUSTEES** Prof. Edward Gregson; Simon Platz; Baroness Estelle Morris; Sally Millest; Paulette Long; Mick Leeson; Stephen McNeff; Royce Bell; Ameet Shah; Vanessa Swann; John Reid; Richard King.

**OTHER INFORMATION** A list of grant recipients was not included in the accounts. However, details of previously funded projects are available on the foundation's website, though without information on the individual grant awards. The information in this entry refers to the foundation's 'open funding', which accounted for around £1 million of the grant total in 2013/14. Details of other funds operated by the foundation can be found on the website. During the year, 240 organisations and groups received funding from the foundation. Grants to 68 individuals amounted to £275,000.

**HOW TO APPLY** Apply via the foundation's website. The application is a two-stage process. At Stage 1, you are asked to provide two examples of music and a brief description of your project. The foundation stresses that the most common reason applications are unsuccessful at the stage is because of eligibility and competition. Applicants must, therefore, refer to the guideline documents, which are available from the website, before an application is started. Those applicants who are successful at Stage 1 will be invited to continue with the second part of the application process. Returning applicants should contact the foundation before making an application.

**WHO TO APPLY TO** Fiona Harvey, Operations Director, 2 Pancras Square, London N1C 4AG *Tel.* 020 7306 4233 *email* info@prsformusicfoundation.com *Website* www.prsformusicfoundation.com

## ■ B. E. Perl Charitable Trust

**CC NO** 282847        **ESTABLISHED** 1981
**WHERE FUNDING CAN BE GIVEN** Barnet, Bournemouth, Brent, Hackney and Israel.
**WHO CAN BENEFIT** Jewish organisations, particularly schools.
**WHAT IS FUNDED** The advancement of education in, and the religion of, the Orthodox Jewish faith and other general charitable purposes.
**SAMPLE GRANTS** Hasmonean High School; JNF; Society of Friends of the Torah; Yavenh College.

**FINANCES** *Year* 2012/13 *Income* £1,960,147 *Grants* £127,754 *Grants to organisations* £127,754 *Assets* £16,588,375
**TRUSTEES** Benjamin Perl, Chair; Dr Shoshanna Perl; Jonathan Perl; Joseph Perl; Naomi Sorotzkin; Rachel Jeidal.
**OTHER INFORMATION** Note the following statement taken from the trust's 2012/13 annual report and accounts: 'The Trustees have considered and approved plans for the establishment of a major educational project in the UK. It is anticipated that the cost of this project will be in the order of £5,000,000 and it is the intentions of the Trustees to accumulate this amount over the next 10 years. During the year an amount of £500,000 (2012–£500,000) was transferred to the Educational Reserve in order to fund this project.' At the time of writing (June 2015) the trust's 2013/14 accounts were overdue at the Charity Commission. The 2012/13 accounts were the latest available.
**HOW TO APPLY** Apply in writing to the correspondent.
**WHO TO APPLY TO** Benjamin Perl, Trustee, Foframe House, 35–37 Brent Street, Hendon, London NW4 2EF

## ■ The Personal Assurance Charitable Trust

**CC NO** 1023274        **ESTABLISHED** 1993
**WHERE FUNDING CAN BE GIVEN** Mainly UK with a preference for the Milton Keynes area, overseas considered.
**WHO CAN BENEFIT** Registered charities and occasionally individuals.
**WHAT IS FUNDED** General charitable purposes, social welfare, health.
**WHAT IS NOT FUNDED** Grants are rarely made to individuals.
**RANGE OF GRANTS** £1,000 to £5,000. Occasionally larger.
**SAMPLE GRANTS** St John Ambulance School Competition (£24,000); Movember and the Retail Trust (£5,000 each); MK Christmas Day Party for the Elderly (£4,500); Little Lives Appeal and Transaid (£3,600 each); Unite the Union (£3,000); British Heart Foundation and Hospitality Action Charity (£2,200 each); TNT Wooden Spoon, Tree of Hope and Shelf Pre-School (£1,000 each).
**FINANCES** *Year* 2013 *Income* £100,536 *Grants* £72,461 *Grants to organisations* £72,461 *Assets* £155,233
**TRUSTEES** Michael Dugdale; Philip Yates; Sarah Mace.
**OTHER INFORMATION** Grants were made totalling almost £73,000. Donations under £1,000 totalled £11,000.
**HOW TO APPLY** Apply in writing to the correspondent.
**WHO TO APPLY TO** Sarah Mace, Trustee, Personal Group Holdings plc, John Ormond House, 899 Silbury Boulevard, Milton Keynes MK9 3XL *email* sarah.mace@personal-group.com

## ■ The Persson Charitable Trust (formerly Highmoore Hall Charitable Trust)

**CC NO** 289027        **ESTABLISHED** 1984
**WHERE FUNDING CAN BE GIVEN** UK and overseas.
**WHO CAN BENEFIT** Registered Christian mission societies and relief agencies.
**WHAT IS FUNDED** Christians; at risk groups; victims of famine, man-made and natural disasters and war.

**WHAT IS NOT FUNDED** Non-registered charities.
**TYPE OF GRANT** Mainly recurrent.
**SAMPLE GRANTS Previous beneficiaries have included:** Bible Reading Fellowship (£111,000); Tearfund – Christian Relief (£55,000); All Nations Christian College (£12,000); Christian Solidarity Worldwide (£10,000).
**FINANCES** *Year* 2013/14 *Income* £41,494 *Grants* £362,662 *Grants to organisations* £362,662 *Assets* £182,432
**TRUSTEES** Paul Persson; Andrew Persson; John Persson; Ann Persson.
**HOW TO APPLY** The trust states that it does not respond to unsolicited applications. Telephone calls are not welcome.
**WHO TO APPLY TO** Paul Persson, Trustee, Long Meadow, Dark Lane, Chearsley, Aylesbury, Buckinghamshire HP18 0DA *email* Paul@paulpersson.co.uk

## ■ The Persula Foundation

**CC NO** 1044174     **ESTABLISHED** 1994
**WHERE FUNDING CAN BE GIVEN** Predominantly UK; overseas grants are given, but this is rare.
**WHO CAN BENEFIT** Mainly small registered charities benefitting at risk groups, people who are socially isolated, disadvantaged by poverty or homeless, people with cancer or disabilities, including visual impairment, deafness, spinal injuries and multiple sclerosis, and animals.
**WHAT IS FUNDED** Original and unique projects of national benefit in the areas of homelessness, disability, and human and animal welfare.
**WHAT IS NOT FUNDED** Grants cannot be given for buildings, individuals or core funding.
**TYPE OF GRANT** Up to two years.
**RANGE OF GRANTS** Up to £65,000.
**SAMPLE GRANTS** ACTS 435 (£65,000); Compassion in World Farming (£40,000); Animal Aid (£30,000); RSPCA (£27,000); League Against Cruel Sports (£25,000).
**FINANCES** *Year* 2013/14 *Income* £881,961 *Grants* £845,349 *Grants to organisations* £845,349 *Assets* £80,495
**TRUSTEES** Hanna Oppenheim; Julian Richer; David Robinson; Rosie Richer; Robert Rosenthal; Jonathan Levy.
**HOW TO APPLY** Apply in writing to the correspondent. The charity considers applications from a variety of charitable organisations for funding. Applications are reviewed and levels of grants payable are decided upon by the trustees.
**WHO TO APPLY TO** Teresa Chapman, Secretary to the Trustees, Richer Sounds plc, Gallery Court, Hankey Place, London SE1 4BB *Tel.* 020 7551 5343 *email* info@persula.org

## ■ The Jack Petchey Foundation

**CC NO** 1076886     **ESTABLISHED** 1999
**WHERE FUNDING CAN BE GIVEN** Greater London and Essex.
**WHO CAN BENEFIT** Registered charities and organisations; individuals.
**WHAT IS FUNDED** Support for young people aged between 11 and 25 through various programmes.
**WHAT IS NOT FUNDED** The foundation will not accept applications: from private schools; from profit making companies; that directly replace statutory funding; from individuals or for the benefit of one individual (unless under the Individual Grants for Volunteering); for work that has already taken place; which do not directly benefit people in the UK; for medical research; for animal welfare; for endowment funds; that are part of general appeals or circulars; building or major refurbishment projects; conferences and seminars; projects where the main purpose is to promote religious beliefs.
**RANGE OF GRANTS** £200 to £578,000.
**SAMPLE GRANTS** Speakers Trust (£578,000); Royal Academy of Dance (£547,000); East London University Technical College (£112,000); The Panathlon Foundation (£81,000); Metropolitan Police Volunteer Cadets (£33,000); Young Enterprise London (£18,000); Girlguiding Croydon (£17,400).
**FINANCES** *Year* 2013 *Income* £7,242,279 *Grants* £5,197,648 *Grants to organisations* £5,197,648 *Assets* £47,074
**TRUSTEE** Jack Petchey Foundation Company.
**HOW TO APPLY** Application details for each of the grant programmes can be found on the website.
**WHO TO APPLY TO** Gemma Dunbar, Head of Grants, Exchange House, 13–14 Clements Court, Clements Lane, Ilford, Essex. IG1 2QY *Tel.* 020 8252 8000 *Fax* 020 8477 1088 *email* mail@jackpetcheyfoundation.org.uk *Website* www.jackpetcheyfoundation.org.uk

## ■ The Petplan Charitable Trust

**CC NO** 1032907     **ESTABLISHED** 1994
**WHERE FUNDING CAN BE GIVEN** UK.
**WHO CAN BENEFIT** Animal charities and organisations benefitting students, research workers and veterinarians.
**WHAT IS FUNDED** Veterinary research; veterinary studies; animal welfare; education in animal welfare. Help is limited to dogs, cats, rabbits and horses only, those being the animals insured by Pet Plan.
**WHAT IS NOT FUNDED** Individuals; non-registered charities; studies involving invasive procedures or experimental animals.
**TYPE OF GRANT** Project funding (excluding overheads); capital costs.
**RANGE OF GRANTS** Scientific grants: £9,800 to £77,000. Welfare and education grants: £300 to £10,000.
**SAMPLE GRANTS** Royal Veterinary College (£168,000 in four grants); Animal Health Trust (£58,000 in three grants); University of Glasgow (£40,500); Dogs for the Disabled (£10,000); University of Bristol (£9,800); Mane Chance Sanctuary and Rabbit Residence Rescue (£7,500 each); Cats Protection Gloucester (£6,000); University of Glasgow (£5,200); Save the Dogs (£4,000); ASAP Cat Rescue (£2,500); Guernsey SPCA (£300).
**FINANCES** *Year* 2013 *Income* £706,872 *Grants* £451,038 *Grants to organisations* £451,038 *Assets* £597,059
**TRUSTEES** John Bower; Clarissa Baldwin; David Simpson; Patsy Bloom; Ted Chandler; Peter Laurie; Kathryn Willis; Jamie Crittall; Gary Davess.
**OTHER INFORMATION** During the year, £301,500 was paid in scientific grants and a further £149,500 in grants for welfare and education.
**HOW TO APPLY** The dates of application rounds vary depending on the type of grant being applied for. See the website for more details.
**WHO TO APPLY TO** Catherine Bourg, Trust Administrator, Great West House GW2, Great West Road, Brentford, Middlesex TW8 9EG *Tel.* 020 8580 8013 *email* catherine.bourg@allianz.co.uk *Website* www.petplantrust.org

## ■ The Pharsalia Charitable Trust

**CC NO** 1120402  **ESTABLISHED** 2007
**WHERE FUNDING CAN BE GIVEN** Oxford region.
**WHO CAN BENEFIT** Registered charities.
**WHAT IS FUNDED** General charitable purposes, particularly the relief of sickness.
**RANGE OF GRANTS** Generally between £250 to £12,000.
**SAMPLE GRANTS** Macmillan Cancer Support (£12,000); The Lee Smith Foundation (£8,500); Age UK Oxfordshire (£5,000); DEC Philippines Typhoon Appeal (£2,000); Blind Veterans (£1,000); Happy Days (£750); Narcolepsy (£500); Pilgrims Hospices (£250).
**FINANCES** Year 2013/14 Income £101,031 Grants £152,300 Grants to organisations £152,300 Assets £2,503,682
**TRUSTEES** Nigel Stirling Blackwell; Christina Blackwell; Trudy Sainsbury.
**OTHER INFORMATION** There were two larger grants made to organisations during the year. These were to ORH Charitable Funds (£72,000) and The Abingdon Bridge (£25,000).
**HOW TO APPLY** Apply in writing to the correspondent.
**WHO TO APPLY TO** Trudy Sainsbury, Trustee, The Ham, Ickleton Road, Wantage, Oxfordshire OX12 9JA *Tel.* 01235 426524

## ■ The Phillips and Rubens Charitable Trust

**CC NO** 260378  **ESTABLISHED** 1970
**WHERE FUNDING CAN BE GIVEN** UK.
**WHO CAN BENEFIT** Registered charities, mostly Jewish organisations.
**WHAT IS FUNDED** Jewish causes; medical and ancillary services (including medical research); education; disability; older people; poverty; sheltered accommodation; development of the arts.
**TYPE OF GRANT** Recurrent and one-off.
**RANGE OF GRANTS** Up to £80,000, though the vast majority of grants were of less than £10,000.
**SAMPLE GRANTS** The Phillips Family Charitable Trust (£80,000); Charities Aid Foundation (£40,000); The Jerusalem Foundation (£36,000); United Jewish Israel Appeal (£28,000); Community Security Trust and Holocaust Educational Trust (£10,000 each); British Friends of the Jaffa Institute (£6,000); Jewish Care (£5,600); Jewish Community Secondary School – JCoSS (£5,100); Nightingale Hammerson and The Jewish Leadership Council (£5,000 each); Shaare Zedek UK (£2,500).
**FINANCES** Year 2013/14 Income £419,908 Grants £306,167 Grants to organisations £306,167 Assets £9,746,034
**TRUSTEES** Michael Phillips; Ruth Phillips; Martin Paisner; Paul Phillips; Gary Phillips; Carolyn Mishon.
**OTHER INFORMATION** Donations of less than £2,500 amounted to £22,500. The Phillips and Rubens Charitable Trust is connected to The Phillips Family Charitable Trust (Charity Commission no. 279120) through common trustees.
**HOW TO APPLY** Apply in writing to the correspondent at any time, although the trust has stated that the majority of grants are to beneficiaries they already support.
**WHO TO APPLY TO** Michael Phillips, Trustee, 67–69 George Street, London W1U 8LT *email* psphillips@aol.com

## ■ The Phillips Charitable Trust

**CC NO** 1057019  **ESTABLISHED** 1995
**WHERE FUNDING CAN BE GIVEN** UK, with a preference for the Midlands, and particularly Northamptonshire.
**WHO CAN BENEFIT** Registered charities.
**WHAT IS FUNDED** Seafarers, animal husbandry and welfare, and smaller one-off national or local projects. Also, the RNLI, The National Trust and The National Trust in Scotland.
**TYPE OF GRANT** One-off and recurrent.
**RANGE OF GRANTS** £350–£42,500
**SAMPLE GRANTS** Northgates Arts College (£42,500); Sportsaid Eastern (£10,000); Serve (£5,000); Hearing Dogs for the Deaf (£3,000); Childhood First (£2,500); Asthma Relief and Ro-Ro Sailing Project (£2,000 each); Extra Care (£1,200); Sailors' Children's Society (£1,000); Hen Welfare (£350).
**FINANCES** Year 2013/14 Income £77,519 Grants £86,700 Grants to organisations £86,700 Assets £2,764,206
**TRUSTEES** John Ford; Michael Percival; Philip Saunderson; S. G. Schanschieff; Anne Marrum.
**OTHER INFORMATION** In 2013/14 a total of 16 organisations received grants. Most grants were in the range of £1,000 to £5,000.
**HOW TO APPLY** Apply in writing to the correspondent.
**WHO TO APPLY TO** Gill Evans, Clerk to the Trustees, 4 Brixworth Road, Spratton, Northamptonshire NN6 8HH *Tel.* 01604 842431 *email* gill_evans@btopenworld.com

## ■ The Phillips Family Charitable Trust

**CC NO** 279120  **ESTABLISHED** 1979
**WHERE FUNDING CAN BE GIVEN** UK.
**WHO CAN BENEFIT** Registered charities only.
**WHAT IS FUNDED** General charitable purposes, mainly Jewish organisations and those concerned with education, the care of people who have disabilities or are older, poverty, or the development of the arts, for example.
**TYPE OF GRANT** Grants are given for core, capital and project support.
**RANGE OF GRANTS** Up to £5,000 per grant.
**SAMPLE GRANTS** Holocaust Educational Trust (£10,000, two payments); Forum for Jewish Leadership (£8,500, five payments); Community Security Trust (£5,200, two payments); London School of Jewish Studies (£5,000, two payments); London Jewish Cultural Centre (£3,000); March of the Living (UK) Ltd (£2,000); Nightingale Hammerson and ORT UK Foundation (£1,500 each); The American Jewish Joint Distribution Committee (UK) Trust and Peace of Mind (£1,000 each).
**FINANCES** Year 2013/14 Income £80,000 Grants £85,495 Grants to organisations £85,495 Assets £18,288
**TRUSTEES** Michael Phillips; Ruth Phillips; Martin Paisner; Paul Phillips; Gary Phillips.
**OTHER INFORMATION** During the year, 84 grants were made.
**HOW TO APPLY** Apply in writing to the correspondent. Note that the trust has previously informed us that there is not much scope for new beneficiaries.
**WHO TO APPLY TO** Paul Phillips, Trustee, 67–69 George Street, London W1U 8LT *Tel.* 020 7487 5757 *email* psphillipsbsh@aol.com

## ■ The David Pickford Charitable Foundation

**CC NO** 243437 **ESTABLISHED** 1965
**WHERE FUNDING CAN BE GIVEN** UK (with a preference for Kent and London) and overseas.
**WHO CAN BENEFIT** Mainly, but not solely, young people particularly young people with special needs, and Christian evangelism.
**WHAT IS FUNDED** Mainly Christian youth work, including the support of a residential Christian youth centre in Kent for those in the 15 to 25 age group and other similar activities.
**WHAT IS NOT FUNDED** Individuals; building projects.
**TYPE OF GRANT** One-off and recurrent.
**RANGE OF GRANTS** Usually £250 to £5,000.
**SAMPLE GRANTS Previous beneficiaries have included:** CARE; Chaucer Trust; Oasis Trust; Brighter Future and Pastor Training international; Toybox; Alpha International, Flow Romania and Mersham Parish Church; Compassion; Samaritans and Lionhart.
**FINANCES** *Year* 2013/14 *Income* £20,861 *Grants* £35,000 *Grants to organisations* £35,000
**TRUSTEES** Charles Pickford; Elizabeth Pettersen.
**OTHER INFORMATION** In 2013/14 the foundation had a total expenditure of £45,500. Due to its low income, the foundation was not required to submit its accounts for the year to the Charity Commission.
**HOW TO APPLY** Apply in writing to the correspondent. The deadline for applications is November. Applications will not be acknowledged. The correspondent states: 'It is our general policy only to give to charities to whom we are personally known'. Unsolicited applications are rarely funded. Those falling outside the criteria mentioned above will be ignored.
**WHO TO APPLY TO** Elizabeth Pettersen, Trustee, Benover House, Rectory Lane, Saltwood, Hythe, Kent CT21 4QA *Tel.* 01303 268322

## ■ The Bernard Piggott Charitable Trust

**CC NO** 1154724 **ESTABLISHED** 1970
**WHERE FUNDING CAN BE GIVEN** North Wales and Birmingham.
**WHO CAN BENEFIT** Registered charities mainly in the City of Birmingham and North Wales, also some national charities with projects in these areas.
**WHAT IS FUNDED** Church of England; Church of Wales; education; medical charities, both care and research; drama and theatre; children and young people.
**WHAT IS NOT FUNDED** Individuals. Grants are not repeated within two-and-a-half years.
**TYPE OF GRANT** Usually one-off capital grants.
**RANGE OF GRANTS** Usually £500 to £1,500.
**SAMPLE GRANTS** Hope House Children's Hospice (£2,000); Bro Ardudwy Church Hall and The Beaumaris Leisure Centre (£1,500 each); All Saints Youth Project – Kings Heath and Cerebral Palsy Midlands (£1,000 each); Independence at Home and National Youth Advocacy Service (£750 each); Clybiau Plant Cymru Kids Club (£600); British Wireless for the Blind (£500); Parish of Llanrug (£300).
**FINANCES** *Year* 2013/14 *Income* £1,517,354 *Grants* £35,633 *Grants to organisations* £35,633 *Assets* £1,447,250
**TRUSTEES** Mark Painter; Derek Lea; Nigel Lea; Richard Easton; Venerable Paul Davies.
**OTHER INFORMATION** The unusually large income figure is due to a transfer of funds from Bernard Piggott Trust (£1.4 million).
**HOW TO APPLY** Applications should be in writing to the secretary including annual accounts and details of the specific project including running costs and so on. They are considered at meetings held on a half-yearly basis in May and November. General policy is not to consider any further grant to the same institution within the next two years.
**WHO TO APPLY TO** Jenny Whitworth, Secretary, 4 Streetsbrook Road, Shirley, Solihull, West Midlands B90 3PL *email* jenny@whitworth4.plus.com

## ■ The Pilgrim Trust

**CC NO** 206602 **ESTABLISHED** 1930
**WHERE FUNDING CAN BE GIVEN** UK (this does not include the Channel Islands or the Isle of Man).
**WHO CAN BENEFIT** UK-registered charities; organisations exempt from registration; recognised public bodies; registered friendly societies.
**WHAT IS FUNDED** Preservation and scholarship – the preservation of historical buildings, monuments and collections; improving access to collections; and supporting projects that promote awareness through making collections more available or by supporting academic research. Social welfare – breaking 'cycles of dependency' and developing a sense of social inclusion amongst the most disadvantaged and marginalised groups in the UK.
**WHAT IS NOT FUNDED** Individuals; non UK-registered charities or charities registered in the Channel Islands or the Isle of Man; CICs or social enterprises; projects based outside the United Kingdom; projects where the work has already been completed or where contracts have already been awarded; projects with a capital cost exceeding £5 million are not usually considered; projects seeking to replace statutory funding from central or local government; general appeals or circulars; projects for the commissioning of new art works; organisations seeking publishing production costs; projects seeking to develop new facilities within a church or the re-ordering of churches or places of worship for wider community use; social welfare projects falling outside the trustees' current priorities; arts and drama projects, except if they can demonstrate clearly that they are linked to goals within the trust's priorities; one-off short-term interventions; youth or sports clubs; travel or adventure projects; community centres; children's playgroups; organisations seeking funding for trips overseas or outward bound courses; organisations seeking funding for educational purposes; one-off events such as exhibitions, festivals, seminars, conferences, or theatrical or musical productions.
**TYPE OF GRANT** Revenue costs, such as salaries and overheads; project costs; the costs of initial 'exploratory work' for organisations wishing to preserve important buildings/monuments, etc.; capital costs where the total cost does not exceed £5 million.
**RANGE OF GRANTS** Small grants of less than £5,000 and main grants of over £5,000.
**SAMPLE GRANTS** Brighton's Women's Centre (£38,000); Fitzwilliam Museum – Cambridge (£30,000); University of Exeter (£19,500); Jamie Roddick Restoration Trust (£15,000); Holy Island of Lindisfarne Community Development (£10,000); Vivat Trust (£6,200);

Hope Church Parochial Council (£4,300); Trustees of Our Lady's High School Memorial Chapel (£2,000).

**FINANCES** Year 2013 Income £1,886,604 Grants £1,704,909 Grants to organisations £1,704,909 Assets £59,790,998

**TRUSTEES** Sir Mark Jones; Michael Baughan; Prof. Sir Colin Blakemore; James Fergusson; Tim Knox; Sir Alan Moses; Kevin Pakenham; John Podmore; Paul Richards; Lady Riddell; Sarah Staniforth.

**OTHER INFORMATION** The trust makes annual block grants for the repair of fabric in historic churches and towards the conservations of churches' historic contents. For details on where to apply for this funding, see the website. Of the amount payable in grants during the year, £1.1 million was for Preservation and Scholarship, and the remaining £578,500 for social welfare.

**HOW TO APPLY** The trust strongly recommends that potential applicants at first read the trust's funding guidelines and guidance notes, which are available from its website. It your project falls within the trust's current funding priorities, then the online Stage 1 application form may be submitted. If you are successful at Stage 1, you will then be invited to submit a Stage 2 application.

**WHO TO APPLY TO** Georgina Nayler, Director, 55a Catherine Place, London SW1E 6DY Tel. 020 7834 6510 email info@thepilgrimtrust.org.uk Website www.thepilgrimtrust.org.uk

## ■ The Elise Pilkington Charitable Trust

**CC NO** 278332 **ESTABLISHED** 1979
**WHERE FUNDING CAN BE GIVEN** UK and overseas.
**WHO CAN BENEFIT** Registered charities.
**WHAT IS FUNDED** The prevention of cruelty to equine animals including welfare, research and medical projects, and equine education projects; older people.
**WHAT IS NOT FUNDED** Ongoing running costs (such as salaries).
**TYPE OF GRANT** Capital project costs.
**SAMPLE GRANTS** The Horse Trust (£25,500); World Horse Welfare (£25,000); The Brooke (£18,000); Bristol University and Horses for Homes (£15,000 each); Gambia Horse and Donkey Trust (£14,900); Age International – Syria (£10,200); Abbeyfield Reading (£5,500); St Peter's and St James Hospice (£4,000); Greenwich and Bexley Hospice (£3,000); Age UK Exeter (£2,000); Windsor Horse Rangers (£1,300); Independent Age (£1,000).
**FINANCES** Year 2013/14 Income £79,857 Grants £180,703 Grants to organisations £180,703 Assets £3,172,685
**TRUSTEES** Caroline Doulton, Chair; Tara Economakis; Revd Rob Merchant; Helen Timpany.
**OTHER INFORMATION** During the year, ten grants totalling £130,500 were made to equine charities, and a further £61,000 was paid in 18 grants to organisations working with older people. Usually, equine welfare grants are only considered for members of the National Equine Welfare Council (NEWC) or organisations proactively working towards membership.
**HOW TO APPLY** Specific guidance notes on how to make an application are available on the trust's website. The trustees meet twice a year to review applications, usually in April and October.

Successful applicants will not be considered within three years of receiving a grant.
**WHO TO APPLY TO** Kenton Lawton, Trust Administrator, Ridgecot, Lewes Road, Horsted Keynes, Haywards Heath, West Sussex RH17 7DY Tel. 01825 790304 email kenton.lawton@btinternet.com Website elisepilkingtontrust.org.uk

## ■ The Pilkington Charities Fund

**CC NO** 225911 **ESTABLISHED** 1964
**WHERE FUNDING CAN BE GIVEN** Worldwide, in practice mainly UK with a preference for Merseyside.
**WHO CAN BENEFIT** Registered charities.
**WHAT IS FUNDED** General charitable purposes including health; social welfare; people with disabilities; older people; young people; and victims of natural disaster or war.
**WHAT IS NOT FUNDED** Non-registered charities; individuals.
**TYPE OF GRANT** Capital (including buildings), core costs, one-off, project, research, recurring costs. Funding for more than three years will be considered.
**RANGE OF GRANTS** Up to £10,000, although exceptional large grants are made.
**SAMPLE GRANTS** C and A Pilkington Trust Fund (£75,000); Target Ovarian Cancer (£15,000); Age UK – Mid Mersey, Foundation for the Prevention of Blindness, Oxfam and Shelter (£10,000 each); Countess of Chester Hospital, Home Start – St Helens and Old Swan Youth Club (£5,000 each); Children's Trust, Claire House, Fairbridge, Mencap Liverpool, Parkhaven Trust and Toxteth Town Hall Community Resource Centre (£3,000 each); Asylum Link Merseyside, Bag Books, Group B Strep Support, The New Belve and Spinal Injuries Association (£2,000 each); Perthes Association (£1,000).
**FINANCES** Year 2013/14 Income £833,912 Grants £522,500 Grants to organisations £522,500 Assets £23,269,033
**TRUSTEES** Neil Pilkington Jones; Jennifer Jones; Arnold Philip Pilkington; Eleanor Jones.
**HOW TO APPLY** Apply in writing to the correspondent. Applications should include charity registration number, a copy of the latest accounts and details of the project for which support is sought. Grants are awarded twice a year, in November and April.
**WHO TO APPLY TO** Sarah Nicklin, Correspondent, Rathbones, Port of Liverpool Building, Pier Head, Liverpool L3 1NW Tel. 0151 236 6666 email sarah.nicklin@rathbones.com

## ■ The Austin and Hope Pilkington Trust

**CC NO** 255274 **ESTABLISHED** 1967
**WHERE FUNDING CAN BE GIVEN** Unrestricted, but see 'What is not funded'.
**WHO CAN BENEFIT** Registered charities only. National projects are preferred to those with a local remit.
**WHAT IS FUNDED** The trust has a three-year cycle of funding: 2015 – Community, medical (non-research), medical research (mental health); 2016 – Children, young people; 2017 – Music and the arts, older people. These categories are then repeated in a three-year rotation.
**WHAT IS NOT FUNDED** Overseas projects; capital appeals; schools; village halls; minibuses; Shopmobility; charities involved with religion (including the repair of church fabric); churches,

even those used by community groups; charities involved with animals; individuals (including individuals going overseas for a charitable organisation); students; scouts, guides, cubs, brownies; sea cadets; holidays; individual hospices (though national organisations may apply).

**TYPE OF GRANT** Grants are usually awarded for one year only.

**RANGE OF GRANTS** Grants are usually between £1,000 and £3,000, with the majority being £1,000. Exceptionally, grants of up to £10,000 are made, but these are usually for medical research projects.

**SAMPLE GRANTS** Bounce Back Foundation, The Door Youth Project, National Association of Clubs for Young People and St Mary's-Le-Bow Young Homeless Project (£3,000 each); Havering Women's Aid, Riverside Housing Association Charitable Trust, Skidz The Wycombe Motor Project Ltd and Tower Hamlets Parents Centre (£1,000 each).

**FINANCES** Year 2013/14 Income £301,136 Grants £316,686 Grants to organisations £316,686 Assets £10,493,298

**TRUSTEES** Jennifer Jones; Debbie Nelson; Penny Shankar; Eleanor Stride.

**OTHER INFORMATION** 181 grants were made during the year. The trust also gave £31,500 to Purcell School as part of its ongoing annual support of funding a music scholarship. National projects are preferred, rather than those with a local remit, and grants are rarely awarded to local projects unknown to the trustees.

**HOW TO APPLY** The trust prefers to receive applications via the online form on its website; however, hard copies of the application form are available for anyone who is unable to complete it online. Postal applications are not accepted. Grants are made twice a year and applications are subject to closing dates, the details of which can be seen on the website.

**WHO TO APPLY TO** Karen Frank, Correspondent, PO Box 124, Stroud, Gloucestershire GL6 7YB email admin@austin-hope-pilkington.org.uk Website www.austin-hope-pilkington.org.uk

## ■ The Sir Harry Pilkington Trust Fund

**CC NO** 206740  **ESTABLISHED** 1962
**WHERE FUNDING CAN BE GIVEN** Merseyside and St Helens.
**WHO CAN BENEFIT** Charitable organisations.
**WHAT IS FUNDED** General charitable purposes with a preference for arts and culture, youth work and health and social welfare.
**RANGE OF GRANTS** Usually between £1,000 and £3,000.
**SAMPLE GRANTS** Liverpool Charity and Voluntary Services (£160,000); Theatre Royal St Helens (£5,000).
**FINANCES** Year 2013/14 Income £172,810 Grants £165,000 Grants to organisations £165,000 Assets £5,778,257
**TRUSTEE** Liverpool Charity and Voluntary Services.
**HOW TO APPLY** Apply writing to the correspondent. Our research indicates that an initial phone call to discuss the proposal is welcomed.
**WHO TO APPLY TO** The Trustees, Liverpool Charity And Voluntary Services, 151 Dale Street, Liverpool L2 2AH Tel. 0151 227 5177

## ■ Estate of the Late Colonel W. W. Pilkington Will Trusts – The General Charity Fund

**CC NO** 234710  **ESTABLISHED** 1964
**WHERE FUNDING CAN BE GIVEN** UK, with a preference for Merseyside.
**WHO CAN BENEFIT** Registered charities only, including hospitals, universities and social enterprises.
**WHAT IS FUNDED** Medical causes; arts; social welfare; drug abuse; international and environmental charities.
**WHAT IS NOT FUNDED** Non-registered charities; building projects; individuals.
**TYPE OF GRANT** One-off and recurrent; capital and core costs; salaries; project funding; start-up costs.
**RANGE OF GRANTS** £750–£2,000
**SAMPLE GRANTS** Crisis Skylight Merseyside, Epilepsy Research UK, Narconon, Prisoners' Education Trust and Royal Liverpool Philharmonic (£2,000 each); Armonico Consort, Bipolar UK, British Forces Foundation and The Comedy Trust (£1,000 each); St Helens Choral Society and St Helens Youth Brass Band (£750 each).
**FINANCES** Year 2013/14 Income £76,523 Grants £40,250 Grants to organisations £40,250 Assets £2,150,953
**TRUSTEES** Arnold Pilkington; Jennifer Jones; Neil Jones; Eleanor Jones.
**OTHER INFORMATION** There were 27 awards made, broken down as follows: medical charities and welfare and drug-related charities (£15,000 each); arts (£10,300).
**HOW TO APPLY** Applications may be made in writing to the correspondent, outlining a clear statement of need and including most recent accounts.
**WHO TO APPLY TO** Sarah Nicklin, Correspondent, c/o Rathbones, Port of Liverpool Building, Pier Head, Liverpool L3 1NW Tel. 0151 236 6666

## ■ Miss A. M. Pilkington's Charitable Trust

**SC NO** SC000282  **ESTABLISHED** 1972
**WHERE FUNDING CAN BE GIVEN** UK, with a preference for Scotland.
**WHO CAN BENEFIT** Registered charities.
**WHAT IS FUNDED** General charitable purposes.
**WHAT IS NOT FUNDED** Overseas projects; political appeals.
**RANGE OF GRANTS** £500–£1,500
**FINANCES** Year 2013/14 Income £127,773 Grants £140,000 Grants to organisations £140,000
**TRUSTEE** No information was available.
**OTHER INFORMATION** The grant total is an approximate amount based on previous years.
**HOW TO APPLY** The trustees have previously stated that, regrettably, they are unable to make grants to new applicants since they already have 'more than enough causes to support'.
**WHO TO APPLY TO** The Clerk, Carters Chartered Accountants, Pentland House, Saltire Centre, Glenrothes, Fife KY6 2AH

## ■ The DLA Piper Charitable Trust

**CC NO** 327280  **ESTABLISHED** 1986
**WHERE FUNDING CAN BE GIVEN** UK.
**WHO CAN BENEFIT** Registered charities.
**WHAT IS FUNDED** General charitable purposes, but mainly medical research and social welfare.
**WHAT IS NOT FUNDED** Individuals.

**TYPE OF GRANT** Mainly single donations.
**RANGE OF GRANTS** Up to £7,500.
**SAMPLE GRANTS** UNICEF (£10,500, two grants); The Bereavement Trust (£8,500, three grants); Leukaemia Research (£7,500); Net4Kids and United Way Romania (£5,000 each); Lymphoma Association (£2,500); Parkinson's UK Ltd (£1,750); Cancer Research and London Legal Support (£1,500 each); Neuroblastoma Alliance UK and St Hilda's East Community Centre (£1,000 each); The Prince's Trust (£1,000, two grants).
**FINANCES** Year 2013/14 Income £50,085 Grants £82,547 Grants to organisations £82,547 Assets £33,267
**TRUSTEES** Nigel Knowles; Philip Rooney; Sean Mahon.
**OTHER INFORMATION** During the year, 52 grants were made. Of these, 31 were of less than £1,000.
**HOW TO APPLY** Apply in writing to the correspondent, for consideration four times a year. Applications from members, partners and employees of DLA Piper for grants in support of charities are encouraged.
**WHO TO APPLY TO** Godfrey Smallman, Secretary, Wrigleys Solicitors LLP, Fountain Precinct, Balm Green, Sheffield S1 2JA email godfrey.smallman@wrigleys.co.uk

## ■ The Platinum Trust

**CC NO** 328570 **ESTABLISHED** 1990
**WHERE FUNDING CAN BE GIVEN** UK.
**WHO CAN BENEFIT** Charities benefitting people with disabilities.
**WHAT IS FUNDED** The relief of children with special needs and adults with mental or physical disabilities 'requiring special attention'.
**WHAT IS NOT FUNDED** Services run by statutory or public bodies; appeals from mental-health organisations; medical research/treatment or equipment; mobility aids/wheelchairs; community transport/disability transport schemes; holidays/exchanges/holiday play schemes; special-needs playgroups; toy and leisure libraries; special Olympic and Paralympics groups; sports and recreation clubs for people with disabilities; residential care/ sheltered housing/respite care; carers; conservation schemes/city farms/horticultural therapy; sheltered or supported employment/ community business/social firms; purchase/ construction/repair of buildings; and conductive education/other special educational programmes.
**RANGE OF GRANTS** Usually £5,000–£45,000.
**SAMPLE GRANTS Previous beneficiaries have included:** United Kingdom Disabled People's Council (£32,500); Centre for Studies on Inclusive Education and Disability, Pregnancy and Parenthood International (£30,000 each); Parents for Inclusion (£27,000); Alliance for Inclusive Education and Independent Panel for Special Education Advice (£20,000 each); Crescent Support Group and Vassal Centre Trust (£15,000 each); Disabled Parents Network (£10,000); Worldwide Volunteering (£5,000); Earthworks and The Cambridge Foundation (£2,500).
**FINANCES** Year 2013/14 Income £16,144 Grants £3,000 Grants to organisations £3,000
**TRUSTEES** Georgios Panayiotou; Stephen Marks; Christopher Organ.
**OTHER INFORMATION** Due to its low income, the trust was not required to submit its accounts for 2013/14 to the Charity Commission. In previous years, support costs and governance costs have accounted for around £44,000 of the trust's total expenditure. We took this figure into consideration when making our estimate for grants made in 2013/14.
**HOW TO APPLY** The trust does not accept unsolicited applications; all future grants will be allocated by the trustees to groups they have already made links with.
**WHO TO APPLY TO** The Secretary, Sedley Richard Laurence Voulters, 89 New Bond Street, London W1S 1DA Tel. 020 7079 8814

## ■ G. S. Plaut Charitable Trust Limited

**CC NO** 261469 **ESTABLISHED** 1970
**WHERE FUNDING CAN BE GIVEN** Mainly in the UK.
**WHO CAN BENEFIT** Voluntary organisations and charitable groups only.
**WHAT IS FUNDED** General charitable purposes including medical care and research, young people, people who have disabilities, military veterans and Jewish organisations.
**WHAT IS NOT FUNDED** Individuals; repeat applications.
**TYPE OF GRANT** One-off and recurrent grants to organisations.
**RANGE OF GRANTS** Between £1,000 and £4,000.
**SAMPLE GRANTS** British Eye Research Foundation (£4,000); British Retinitis Pigmentosa Society (£3,000); Veterans Aid (£2,500); Anglo Jewish Association and Country Holidays for Inner City Kids – CHICKS (both £2,000); The Gurkha Welfare Trust (£1,000).
**FINANCES** Year 2013/14 Income £59,653 Grants £44,500 Grants to organisations £44,500 Assets £1,644,675
**TRUSTEES** A. D. Wrapson; T. A. Warburg; W. E. Murfett; B. A. Sprinz; R. E. Liebeschuetz; Dr J. D. Hall.
**HOW TO APPLY** Apply in writing to the correspondent. Trustees usually meet twice a year and only successful applications are acknowledged.
**WHO TO APPLY TO** Dr Richard Speirs, Secretary, 39 Bay Road, Wormit, Newport-on-Tay, Fife DD6 8LW email GSPCTrust@gmail.com

## ■ Polden-Puckham Charitable Foundation

**CC NO** 1003024 **ESTABLISHED** 1970
**WHERE FUNDING CAN BE GIVEN** UK and overseas.
**WHO CAN BENEFIT** Registered charities; organisations or projects that are not registered, as long as they can show a UK-registered charity is able to receive funds on their behalf. Particular consideration is given to small pioneering headquarters organisations.
**WHAT IS FUNDED** Grants are made under two categories: Peace and Sustainable Security – the development of methods for peaceful resolution of violent conflicts, and addressing their underlying causes; and Environmental Sustainability – addressing the pressures and conditions risking global environmental breakdown. The foundation states on its website: 'We only support practical projects when they are clearly of a pioneering nature, with potential for influencing UK national policy.'
**WHAT IS NOT FUNDED** Large organisations; organisations based outside the UK (unless they are linked with a UK-registered charity and doing work of international focus); work outside the UK (unless it is of international focus); individuals; travel bursaries (including overseas placements and expeditions); study; academic

research; capital projects; community or local practical projects (except innovative projects with a broad scope); environmental/ecological conservation; international agencies and overseas appeals; general appeals; human rights work (unless it relates to peace and environmental sustainability); community mediation and crime related work.

**TYPE OF GRANT** Project funding for up to three years.

**RANGE OF GRANTS** Normally between £5,000 and £15,000.

**SAMPLE GRANTS Previous beneficiaries have included:** European Leadership network (£40,000); Quaker United Nations Office (£22,000); British American Security Information Council (£20,000); Carbon Tracker Initiative (£15,000); Protect the Local Globally (£11,000); Localise West Midlands and SpinWatch (£10,000); Campaign Against Arms trade (£9,000); Mines and Communities (£6,000); Oil Depletion Analysis Centre (£5,000); UK Without Incineration Network (£4,000); and Environmental Funders Network (£2,000).

**FINANCES** Year 2013/14 Income £536,396 Grants £427,000 Grants to organisations £427,000

**TRUSTEES** Harriet Gillett; Bevis Gillett; Stephen Pittam; Angela Seay; Jonathan Gillett.

**OTHER INFORMATION** At the time of writing (June 2015) the foundation's 2013/14 accounts had been submitted to the Charity Commission but were not yet available to view. The grant total above is an estimate based on amounts declared in the accounts of previous years.

**HOW TO APPLY** Application forms and guidance notes can be downloaded from the foundation's website and must be submitted via email. Applicants are also asked to submit their latest set of audited accounts and an annual report, preferably via email. The foundation is happy to provide brief feedback on applications one week after the trustees have made a decision. The trustees meet twice a year in spring and in autumn. Application deadline dates are posted on the website.

**WHO TO APPLY TO** Bryn Higgs, Executive Secretary, BM PPCF, London WC1N 3XX *email* ppcf@polden-puckham.org.uk *Website* www.polden-puckham.org.uk

■ **The George and Esme Pollitzer Charitable Settlement**

**CC NO** 212631 **ESTABLISHED** 1960

**WHERE FUNDING CAN BE GIVEN** UK.

**WHO CAN BENEFIT** Registered charities.

**WHAT IS FUNDED** General charitable purposes. The charity's accounts separate giving into the following categories: parenting, the family and children's work; armed forces; homelessness; disabled and elderly; education; the arts; the community and environment; Jewish faith; health and medical research; and other material grants.

**RANGE OF GRANTS** Usually £2,000 each.

**SAMPLE GRANTS** Calibre Audible Library, The Clink Charity, Fine Cell Works and The Royal Hospital for Neuro-disability (£5,000 each); Barnardo's, The Big Issue, Centrepoint, Combat Stress, Crimestoppers, Fair Trials International, Fight for Sight, Gingerbread, The Holocaust Centre, In Harmony Sistema England, Independent Age, Jewish Blind and Disabled, Kew Foundation, Marie Curie Cancer Care, Mencap, Nightingale House, Personal Support Unit, Seafarers UK, SSAFA (£2,000 each).

**FINANCES** Year 2013/14 Income £127,629 Grants £180,000 Grants to organisations £180,000 Assets £3,574,694

**TRUSTEES** Jeremy Barnes; Richard Pollitzer; Catherine Charles.

**OTHER INFORMATION** During the year, 84 grants were made. All except four of these were of £2,000.

**HOW TO APPLY** Apply in writing to the correspondent.

**WHO TO APPLY TO** Lucy Parrock, Manager – Tax and Trust, Saffery Champness, St Catherine's Court, Berkeley Place, Clifton, Bristol BS8 1BQ *Tel.* 0117 915 1617

■ **The Pollywally Charitable Trust**

**CC NO** 1107513 **ESTABLISHED** 2005

**WHERE FUNDING CAN BE GIVEN** UK.

**WHO CAN BENEFIT** Jewish institutions of primary, secondary and further education and organisations caring for the poor and sick.

**WHAT IS FUNDED** Jewish causes; education; social welfare; sickness.

**RANGE OF GRANTS** Up to £21,000.

**SAMPLE GRANTS** The BSD Charitable Trust (£21,000); Ezer Bekovoid Limited (£9,200); The Edgware Foundation (£4,400).

**FINANCES** Year 2013/14 Income £38,962 Grants £37,690 Grants to organisations £37,690 Assets £20,774

**TRUSTEES** Jeremy Waller; Jeremy Pollins; Sarah Waller; Stephany Pollins.

**HOW TO APPLY** Apply in writing to the correspondent.

**WHO TO APPLY TO** Jeremy Waller, Trustee, Premier House, 8th Floor, c/o Waller Pollins Ltd, 112 Station Road, Edgware HA8 7BJ *Tel.* 020 8238 5858 *email* jwaller@wallerpollins.com

■ **The Polonsky Foundation**

**CC NO** 291143 **ESTABLISHED** 1985

**WHERE FUNDING CAN BE GIVEN** UK, Israel and the USA

**WHO CAN BENEFIT** Primarily universities and arts or educational institutions.

**WHAT IS FUNDED** Higher education (humanities and social sciences); medical research; the arts; the study and resolution of human conflict.

**RANGE OF GRANTS** From £250.

**SAMPLE GRANTS** The Van Leer Institute (£5.25 million); Theatre for New Audiences Inc. (£1.2 million); University of Oxford (£360,000); British Library (£250,000); University of Cambridge (£125,000); Oxford Centre for Jewish and Hebrew Studies (£92,500); New York Public Library (£55,000); Aldenham School (£24,500); Three Faiths Forum (£18,700); Royal College of Music (£13,000); Duke of Edinburgh's Award International Foundation (£12,500); Tel Chai College (£2,100); North London Hospice (£1,250); Food Lifeline Trust (£250).

**FINANCES** Year 2013/14 Income £636,311 Grants £7,831,835 Grants to organisations £7,831,835 Assets £28,829,805

**TRUSTEES** Dr Georgette Bennett; Dr Leonard Polonsky; Marc Polonsky.

**OTHER INFORMATION** During the year, 26 organisations received support.

**HOW TO APPLY** Apply in writing to the correspondent.

**WHO TO APPLY TO** The Trustees, 8 Park Crescent, London W1B 1PG *Tel.* 07785 246923

## ■ The Ponton House Trust

**SC NO** SC021716   **ESTABLISHED** 1993

**WHERE FUNDING CAN BE GIVEN** Edinburgh and Lothians area.

**WHO CAN BENEFIT** Established national and regional voluntary organisations; small local organisations.

**WHAT IS FUNDED** Vulnerable and disadvantaged young people.

**WHAT IS NOT FUNDED** At the time of writing, the trust stated on its website that it does 'not currently fund ongoing services over time'.

**TYPE OF GRANT** One-off.

**RANGE OF GRANTS** Usually between £1,000 and £3,000.

**SAMPLE GRANTS Previous beneficiaries have included:** Edinburgh Voluntary Organisations Trust (£9,000), for onward distribution to individuals; Bethany Christian Trust and Lothian Autistic Society (£1,500 each); Garvald Training Centre, Venture Scotland, Circle, Children 1st and Partners for Advocacy (£1,000); Rock Trust (£900); Maggie's Cancer Caring Centres (£750).

**FINANCES** Year 2013/14 Income £48,438 Grants £40,000 Grants to organisations £40,000

**TRUSTEES** Revd John Munro; Shulah Allan; Patrick Edwardson; Ian Boardman; Jim Verth; David Jack; Jane Sturgeon.

**OTHER INFORMATION** The trust's website states that annually around £40,000 is distributed in grants. Around 25% of funding is given to Edinburgh Voluntary Organisations' Trust (EVOT), which makes grants to individual young people who are in need.

**HOW TO APPLY** Application forms are available from the trust's website, where full guidelines are also given.

**WHO TO APPLY TO** David Reith, Secretary, c/o Lindsays WS, Caledonian Exchange, 19A Canning Street, Edinburgh EH3 8HE *Tel.* 0131 656 5658 *email* info@pontonhouse.org.uk *Website* www.pontonhouse.org.uk

## ■ The Popocatepetl Trust

**CC NO** 1133690   **ESTABLISHED** 2010

**WHERE FUNDING CAN BE GIVEN** UK and worldwide

**WHO CAN BENEFIT** Registered charities.

**WHAT IS FUNDED** Grants are given to UK charities that in turn support projects involving the advancement of education of children and adults worldwide with an emphasis on seriously disadvantaged communities in financially developing countries.

**SAMPLE GRANTS Previous beneficiaries have included:** Izara Khom Loi Trust (£35,000); The Thai Children's Trust (£27,000); The Students Education Trust (£10,000); Karen Hill Tribes Trust (£8,000); and The International Children's Trust, Prospect Burma and Children on the Edge (£6,400 each).

**FINANCES** Year 2013/14 Income £7,981 Grants £85,000 Grants to organisations £85,000

**TRUSTEES** Eleanor Broad; Grania Bryceson; Elizabeth Delliere; Monique Surridge; David Williams.

**HOW TO APPLY** Apply in writing to the correspondent

**WHO TO APPLY TO** Elizabeth Deliere, Longview, 7 Clumps Road, Lower Bourne, Farnham, Surrey GU13 3HF *Tel.* 01252 794238

## ■ Edith and Ferdinand Porjes Charitable Trust

**CC NO** 274012   **ESTABLISHED** 1973

**WHERE FUNDING CAN BE GIVEN** UK and overseas.

**WHO CAN BENEFIT** Jewish organisations; registered charities.

**WHAT IS FUNDED** General charitable purposes, particularly Jewish causes.

**SAMPLE GRANTS** The London School of Jewish Studies (£30,000); International Institute for Jewish Genealogy and Paul Jacobi Centre (£8,100); Camp Simcha (£7,500).

**FINANCES** Year 2013/14 Income £42,986 Grants £45,557 Grants to organisations £45,557 Assets £1,501,313

**TRUSTEES** Martin Paisner; Anthony Rosenfelder; Howard Stanton.

**HOW TO APPLY** Apply in writing to the correspondent.

**WHO TO APPLY TO** Martin Paisner, Trustee, Berwin Leighton Paisner, Adelaide House, London Bridge, London EC4R 9HA *Tel.* 020 7760 1000

## ■ The John Porter Charitable Trust

**CC NO** 267170   **ESTABLISHED** 1974

**WHERE FUNDING CAN BE GIVEN** Worldwide, but mainly UK and Israel.

**WHO CAN BENEFIT** Registered and exempt charities.

**WHAT IS FUNDED** Education; culture; environment; health; welfare.

**WHAT IS NOT FUNDED** Individuals.

**SAMPLE GRANTS** JP Charitable Foundation (£9.8 million); Oxford Centre for Hebrew and Jewish Studies (£10,000 in two grants); The Guild of the Dome Association (£8,100); University of Oxford (£5,000); Friends of the Mariinsky Theatre (£800); Marie Curie Cancer Care (£100).

**FINANCES** Year 2012/13 Income £173,021 Grants £9,821,823 Grants to organisations £9,821,823 Assets £728,302

**TRUSTEES** John Porter; Prof. Baroness Susan Greenfield; Brian Padgett.

**OTHER INFORMATION** At the time of writing (June 2015) the trust's 2013/14 accounts were overdue at the Charity Commission. The latest accounts available were those from 2012/13. The trust made grants to five organisations during the year. There was one major grant to JP Charitable Foundation, a Swiss charity which shares a common trustee with the trust.

**HOW TO APPLY** Apply in writing to the correspondent.

**WHO TO APPLY TO** The Trustees, c/o Blink Rothenberg LLP, 16 Great Queen Street, Covent Garden, London WC2B 5AH *Tel.* 020 7544 8863 *email* robin.marks@blickrothenberg.com

## ■ The Porter Foundation

**CC NO** 261194   **ESTABLISHED** 1970

**WHERE FUNDING CAN BE GIVEN** Israel and the UK.

**WHO CAN BENEFIT** Registered charities; organisations with charitable objects which are exempt from registration.

**WHAT IS FUNDED** In practice: research into environmental issues; improving community relations within Israel; care of older people; improving access to the arts.

**WHAT IS NOT FUNDED** Individuals; general appeals such as direct mail circulars; charities which redistribute funds to other charities; third-party organisations raising money on behalf of other charities; grants to cover general running costs.

**TYPE OF GRANT** Usually project-based and capital grants.

SAMPLE GRANTS Maccabi World Union (£3,300); Mote Marine Laboratory and The John and Mable Ringling Museum of Art (£3,250 each); Musicians of Tomorrow (£2,000); Tel Aviv University Trust (£1,000).
FINANCES Year 2013/14 Income £162,223 Grants £14,765 Grants to organisations £14,765 Assets £5,427,442
TRUSTEES Albert Castle; Dame Shirley Porter; Steven Porter; Prof. Sir Walter Bodmer; John Porter; Linda Streit.
OTHER INFORMATION The foundation has taken the decision to reduce the number of smaller grants distributed in favour of supporting a small number of major capital projects in Israel and the UK. A limited number of small-scale community awards are still given, usually to organisations with which the foundation already has links. The following is stated on its Charity Commission record: 'The foundation continues to support the Porter School of Environmental Studies at Tel Aviv University. In the UK, the foundation continues to support access to the arts by funding Porter galleries, and the foundation has a continuing commitment to the Victoria and Albert Museum.' During the year, seven payments of less than £1,000 each were made totalling £2,000.
HOW TO APPLY An initial letter summarising your application, together with basic costings and background details on your organisation, such as the annual report and accounts, should be sent to the director. Speculative approaches containing expensive publicity material are not encouraged. If your proposal falls within the foundation's current funding criteria you may be contacted for further information, including perhaps a visit from the foundation staff. There is no need to fill out an application form. Applications fulfilling the criteria will be considered by the trustees, who meet three times a year, usually in March, July and November. You will hear shortly after the meeting whether your application has been successful. Unfortunately, it is not possible to acknowledge all unsolicited applications (unless a stamped, addressed envelope is enclosed). If you do not hear from the foundation, you can assume that your application has been unsuccessful. Due to limits on funds available, some excellent projects may have to be refused a grant. In such a case the trustees may invite the applicant to re-apply in a future financial year, without giving a commitment to fund.
WHO TO APPLY TO Sarah Hunt, Silex Administration S.A., 63 Grosvenor Street, London W1K 3JG Tel. 020 7499 1957 email Sarah.Hunt@princapital.com

■ Porticus UK
CC NO 1069245    ESTABLISHED 1998
WHERE FUNDING CAN BE GIVEN England, Scotland and Wales.
WHO CAN BENEFIT Registered charities.
WHAT IS FUNDED The charity has four main programme areas. Education – focusing on: formation, relationships, moral development, values, virtue and ethics; enabling early-years bonding, attachment and cognitive development; improving the involvement of marginalised people in education; leadership development. Society – focusing on: strengthening families; approaches to social concerns; enabling offenders and ex-offenders to positively contribute to society; restorative justice. Faith – focusing on: using Catholic social teaching to address contemporary issues; promoting interfaith engagement; strengthening leadership and governance in the Roman Catholic Church; advancing lay formation. Care – focusing on: strengthening relationships to combat isolation; considering the issues of an aging society; developing intergenerational activities; addressing multiple disadvantage and exclusion.
WHAT IS NOT FUNDED Non-registered charities; individuals; retrospective, crisis or emergency funding; major capital or building restoration projects; applications for the purchase of buildings or land; equipment; one-off conferences or events; travel overseas; endowment appeals. High-profile appeals capable of attracting other funding are not normally considered.
TYPE OF GRANT Core or project costs, including staff salaries or overheads.
RANGE OF GRANTS Most grants exceed £10,000.
TRUSTEES Louise Adams; Mark Brenninkmeyer; Stephen Brenninkmeyer; Bert Brenninkmeyer.
OTHER INFORMATION Porticus UK is not in itself a grant-maker – it advises and assesses grants on behalf of several foundations in the Netherlands, including Stichting Porticus. In 2013 the charity assessed 356 applications resulting in 151 new grants. Our research indicates that total funds available amount to around £4 million each year. Organisations based in Northern Ireland and the Republic of Ireland will be referred to the charity's partner trust in Dublin, the St Stephen's Green Trust.
HOW TO APPLY Application forms are available to download from the website, where a helpful list of FAQs can also be found. If you are unsure as to whether your organisation or project is eligible, contact the charity for further advice.
WHO TO APPLY TO Jane Leek, Michelin House, Fourth Floor, 81 Fulham Road, London SW3 6RD Tel. 020 7024 3503 email porticusuk@porticus.com Website www.porticusuk.com

■ The Portishead Nautical Trust
CC NO 228876    ESTABLISHED 1964
WHERE FUNDING CAN BE GIVEN Bristol and North Somerset.
WHO CAN BENEFIT Organisations and young people.
WHAT IS FUNDED Specific projects helping young people under the age of 25 who are disadvantaged.
WHAT IS NOT FUNDED Further education costs of non-disadvantaged people.
TYPE OF GRANT One-off, project, recurring costs and running costs will be considered. Funding may be given for up to three years.
RANGE OF GRANTS £600 to £20,000.
SAMPLE GRANTS Dyslexia Action (£20,000); Portishead Youth Centre (£10,000); Bristol Children's Help Society (£2,000); ACTA Community Theatre and Room 13 Hareclive (£1,500 each); Keynsham and District Mencap Society and Life Education Centre (£1,000 each); Tall Ships Youth Trust (£900); Happy Days Children's Charity (£600).
FINANCES Year 2013/14 Income £87,510 Grants £56,820 Grants to organisations £49,078 Assets £2,030,744
TRUSTEES Tean Kirby; Stephen Gillingham; M. Cruse; S. Haysom; Colin Crossman; Iris Perry; Dr Gerwyn Owen; Wendy Bryant; Peter Dingley-Brown.
OTHER INFORMATION Most grants to organisations were between £1,000 and £2,000. In 2013/14 grants to individuals totalled £7,700.
HOW TO APPLY Apply in writing to the correspondent.

**721**

WHO TO APPLY TO Liz Knight, Secretary, 108 High Street, Portishead, Bristol BS20 6AJ
*Tel.* 01275 847463
*email* portisheadnauticaltrust@gmail.com

## ■ The Portrack Charitable Trust

CC NO 266120　　　ESTABLISHED 1973
WHERE FUNDING CAN BE GIVEN UK, with some preference for Scotland.
WHO CAN BENEFIT Registered charitable organisations.
WHAT IS FUNDED General charitable purposes.
WHAT IS NOT FUNDED Grants are not given to individuals.
RANGE OF GRANTS Usually £1,000 to £2,000, occasionally more.
SAMPLE GRANTS Maggie's Cancer Centres (£35,000); Medical Aid Palestinians (£4,000); Dumfries and Galloway Health Board (£2,500); Civil Liberties Trust, Just For Kids Law, Princess Royal Trust for Carers, Royal College of Physicians, Scottish Historic Buildings, St John's and St Elizabeth's Hospice, The Woodland Trust, UCL Development, and University of Glasgow (£2,000 each); V&A Museum of Design Dundee (£1,000).
FINANCES Year 2013/14 Income £124,942 Grants £78,500 Grants to organisations £78,500 Assets £5,328,262
TRUSTEES Charles Jencks; Lily Jencks; John Jencks.
OTHER INFORMATION In 2013/14 a total of 22 organisations received funding. The majority of grants were of £2,000.
HOW TO APPLY Apply in writing to the correspondent. The trust notes on its Charity Commission record that it is only administered part-time and, as a result, may take some time to acknowledge an application. Applications are considered in June and December.
WHO TO APPLY TO Lucy Dare, Correspondent, 1 Northampton Row, London EC1R 0JZ
*email* portrackcharitabletrust@gmail.com

## ■ The J. E. Posnansky Charitable Trust

CC NO 210416　　　ESTABLISHED 1962
WHERE FUNDING CAN BE GIVEN Worldwide, in practice mainly UK.
WHO CAN BENEFIT Charitable organisations.
WHAT IS FUNDED Jewish charities, health, social welfare, humanitarian causes, general charitable purposes.
WHAT IS NOT FUNDED Individuals.
TYPE OF GRANT One-off.
RANGE OF GRANTS £250 to £20,000.
SAMPLE GRANTS Magen David Adom UK and UJIA (£20,000 each); WIZO UK (£15,000); Friends of Alyn (£12,800); Jewish Care (£7,500); British Technion Society and World Jewish Relief (£5,000); Macmillan Cancer Relief (£3,000); Action Aid, The Art Room, Norwood and WaterAid (£2,500); Lyric Theatre Hammersmith Ltd (£2,000); British Limbless Ex Servicemen, Terence Higgins Trust, Toynbee Hall and Farm Africa (£1,000 each); The Samaritans (£750); Kisharon Day School Charity Trust and St Martin's in the Fields Christmas Appeal Fund (£500 each); The Dystonia Society (£250).
FINANCES Year 2013/14 Income £103,631 Grants £128,750 Grants to organisations £128,750 Assets £3,876,404
TRUSTEES Gillian Raffles; Anthony Posnansky; Peter Mishcon; Emma Feather; N. S. Posnansky.

OTHER INFORMATION Grants were made to 40 organisations and most were of between £500 and £5,000.
HOW TO APPLY Unsolicited applications will not be considered.
WHO TO APPLY TO Mr N. S. Posnansky, Trustee, c/o Sobell Rhodes LLP, Monument House, 215 Marsh Road, Pinner, Middlesex HA5 5NE
*Tel.* 020 8429 8800

## ■ The Mary Potter Convent Hospital Trust

CC NO 1078525　　　ESTABLISHED 1999
WHERE FUNDING CAN BE GIVEN Nottinghamshire.
WHO CAN BENEFIT Organisations and individuals.
WHAT IS FUNDED Relief of medical and health problems.
WHAT IS NOT FUNDED Non-registered charities; capital/building costs.
TYPE OF GRANT Mainly one-off grants, but payments over two or three years may be considered.
SAMPLE GRANTS Motor Neurone Disease Association (£9,000); Age UK Nottingham and Nottinghamshire, Alzheimer's Society, Cornwater Clubs, Headway, Mary Magdalene Foundation, Radford Visiting Centre (£3,000 each).
FINANCES Year 2013/14 Income £96,863 Grants £72,635 Grants to organisations £56,683 Assets £3,181,496
TRUSTEES Jimmy Pell; Dr J. P. Curran; Chris Bain; Jo Stevenson; Sister Jeanette Connell; Sister Anne Haugh; Mervyn Jones; Martin Witherspoon; Shaun Finn; Aidan Goulding; Godfrey Archer.
HOW TO APPLY Apply in writing to the correspondent. Unsuccessful applicants will not be notified.
WHO TO APPLY TO Martin Witherspoon, Secretary to the Trustees, c/o Massers Solicitors, Rossell House, Tudor Square, West Bridgford, Nottingham NG2 6BT *Tel.* 0115 851 1603
*email* martinw@massers.co.uk

## ■ The David and Elaine Potter Foundation

CC NO 1078217　　　ESTABLISHED 1999
WHERE FUNDING CAN BE GIVEN UK and overseas, particularly sub-Saharan Africa.
WHO CAN BENEFIT Registered charities and educational institutions.
WHAT IS FUNDED Education, particularly projects supporting economic and social well-being in sub-Saharan Africa; civil society, including human rights, governance, anti-corruption, law and legal assistance; social research. More details can be found on the foundation's website.
WHAT IS NOT FUNDED Individuals; CICs; retrospective costs; full economic costs for universities; political organisations; clinical trials; religious organisations that only work for the benefit of members of their own religion; clinical trials.
TYPE OF GRANT Project funding up to a maximum of five years. Joint funding with other grant-makers. Grants for general core costs may also be considered.
RANGE OF GRANTS £500–£150,000
SAMPLE GRANTS Oxford University – Magdalene College Library (£500,000); Ikamva Youth (£106,000); Human Rights Watch (£62,000); Reprieve (£60,000); Bingham Centre for the Rule of Law (£55,000); Global Witness (£50,000); Philharmonia Orchestra Trust Ltd (£45,000); Centre of Investigative Journalism (£40,000); Justice Programme Pakistan

(£31,500); Alive and Kicking UK (£30,000); Community Action and Performa (£25,000 each); Foundation for Women and Soho Theatre (£5,000 each); University of Westminster (£750).
**FINANCES** Year 2013 Income £400,123 Grants £1,598,829 Grants to organisations £1,598,829 Assets £19,366,020
**TRUSTEES** Michael S. Polonsky; Michael Langley; Dr David Potter; Elaine Potter; Samuel Potter.
**OTHER INFORMATION** In 2014 the foundation revised its remit and now focuses its funding on the three areas noted above. Grants were distributed for the following purposes: education (£1.06 million); human rights (£273,500); arts (£100,500); other (£55,000); governance (£50,000); community (£30,000); health (£25,000).
**HOW TO APPLY** Applications are by invitation only unsolicited applications are not accepted. The website states: 'If you think your work may fit our remit you should email us to discuss your potential eligibility and whether it is something that we may potentially fund. Please do not send written correspondence.'
**WHO TO APPLY TO** Ben Stewart, Director, 6 Hamilton Close, London NW8 8QY Tel. 020 7289 3911 Fax 020 7286 3699 email info@potterfoundation.com Website www.potterfoundation.com

## ■ The Praebendo Charitable Foundation
**CC NO** 1137426    **ESTABLISHED** 2010
**WHERE FUNDING CAN BE GIVEN** England, Scotland and Wales.
**WHO CAN BENEFIT** Organisations supporting children and young people; older people; people with disabilities, other charities and the general public/mankind and individuals.
**WHAT IS FUNDED** Education/training; advancement of health or saving of lives; people with disabilities; the prevention or relief of poverty; and religious activities.
**FINANCES** Year 2012/13 Income £10,068 Grants £30,000 Grants to organisations £30,000
**TRUSTEES** Susan Christmas; Helen Leech.
**OTHER INFORMATION** Accounts for 2012/13, the latest dates available at the time of writing were not published due to the low income of the charity. Grant total has been estimated based on the total expenditure of £48,350 and the grant total in previous years.
**HOW TO APPLY** Apply in writing to the correspondent.
**WHO TO APPLY TO** Helen Leech, Correspondent and Trustee, Drift House, First Drift, Wothorpe, Stamford, Lincolnshire PE9 3JL Tel. 01780 489082

## ■ The W. L. Pratt Charitable Trust
**CC NO** 256907    **ESTABLISHED** 1968
**WHERE FUNDING CAN BE GIVEN** UK, with a particular focus on York, and overseas.
**WHO CAN BENEFIT** Charitable organisations.
**WHAT IS FUNDED** In the UK: to support religious and social objectives with priority for York and district, including health and community services. Overseas: to help financially developing countries by assisting in food production and relief of famine and disease.

**WHAT IS NOT FUNDED** Individuals. Grants for the upkeep and preservation of buildings are restricted.
**RANGE OF GRANTS** £250 to £5,000.
**SAMPLE GRANTS** York Diocesan Board of Finance (£5,000); York Minster Development Campaign (£5,000); Wilberforce Trust (£3,000); St Leonard's Hospice (£2,300); Christian Aid (£2,200); Sight Savers International (£2,200); Barnardo's (£1,100); SSAFA (£500); WaterAid (£250).
**FINANCES** Year 2013/14 Income £53,095 Grants £55,800 Grants to organisations £55,800 Assets £1,838,509
**TRUSTEES** Christopher Goodway; Christopher Tetley; John Pratt.
**OTHER INFORMATION** In 2013/14 the trust made 52 grants, 27 of which were of £500 or less. The charity's trustees meet on an annual basis to consider its grant-making activities. Most of the trust's available income fund is distributed following this meeting but further grants may be made at other times where there are special circumstances.
**HOW TO APPLY** Apply in writing to the correspondent. Applications will not be acknowledged unless an sae is supplied. Telephone applications are not accepted.
**WHO TO APPLY TO** Christopher Goodway, Trustee, c/o Grays, Duncombe Place, York YO1 7DY Tel. 01904 634771 email christophergoodway@grayssolicitors.co.uk

## ■ The Premier League Charitable Fund
**CC NO** 1137208    **ESTABLISHED** 2010
**WHERE FUNDING CAN BE GIVEN** England and Wales.
**WHO CAN BENEFIT** Organisations, particularly those 'from the community arm of professional football clubs'.
**WHAT IS FUNDED** General charitable purposes, particularly community-based activities for young people who are from disadvantaged groups or backgrounds. The fund supports projects that fit one or more of the following themes: community cohesion – fulfilling potential; education – encouraging achievement; health – enhancing well-being; sports participation – success through sport.
**RANGE OF GRANTS** £2,000 to £270,000.
**FINANCES** Year 2013/14 Income £14,737,534 Grants £13,486,395 Grants to organisations £13,486,395 Assets £9,033,357
**TRUSTEES** William Bush; David Barnes; Thomas Finn.
**OTHER INFORMATION** During the year, 631 grants were made. The annual report states that 216 new grants were made to community club organisations and two other organisations via a range of grant programmes.
**HOW TO APPLY** Apply in writing to the correspondent.
**WHO TO APPLY TO** Monica Golding, Head of Premier League Charitable Fund, The F. A. Premier League, 30 Gloucester Place, London W1U 8PL Tel. 020 7864 9000 email plcf@premierleague.com Website www.premierleague.com/en-gb

## ■ Premierquote Ltd
**CC NO** 801957    **ESTABLISHED** 1985
**WHERE FUNDING CAN BE GIVEN** Worldwide.
**WHO CAN BENEFIT** Jewish organisations and schools.
**WHAT IS FUNDED** The advancement of the Orthodox Jewish faith; the relief of poverty.

**SAMPLE GRANTS** Previous beneficiaries have included: Achisomoch, Belz Yeshiva Trust, Beth Jacob Grammar School for Girls Ltd, British Friends of Shuvu, Friends of Ohel Moshe, Friends of Senet Wiznitz, Friends of the United Institutions of Arad, Kehal Chasidel Bobov, Meadowgold Limited, Menorah Primary School, North West London Communal Mikvah and Torah Vedaas Primary School.

**FINANCES** Year 2013/14 Income £877,115 Grants £403,335 Grants to organisations £403,335 Assets £7,856,011

**TRUSTEES** David Last; Henry Last; Leah Last; Morris Wiesenfeld.

**OTHER INFORMATION** Grants of £1,000 or more totalled £356,000 and grants of less £1,000, a further £45,500.

**HOW TO APPLY** Apply in writing to the correspondent.

**WHO TO APPLY TO** David Last, Trustee, 18 Green Walk, London NW4 2AJ Tel. 020 7247 8376

## ■ Premishlaner Charitable Trust

**CC NO** 1046945    **ESTABLISHED** 1995

**WHERE FUNDING CAN BE GIVEN** UK and worldwide.

**WHO CAN BENEFIT** Jewish people and people disadvantaged by poverty.

**WHAT IS FUNDED** The advancement of Orthodox Jewish education and the advancement of the religion of the Jewish faith in accordance with the Orthodox practice.

**SAMPLE GRANTS** Wlodowa Charity and Rehabilitation Trust (£41,000); Chen Vochessed Vrachamim (£21,500); C.M.L. and J and R Charitable Trust (£10,000 each); Before Trust, Ezer VeHatzolah Ltd; Mifal Tzedoko Vochesed, Society of Friends of the Torah, U.T.A. and Satmar Nursery Trust (£5,000 each).

**FINANCES** Year 2013/14 Income £140,905 Grants £166,706 Grants to organisations £166,706 Assets £371,592

**TRUSTEES** C. Freudenberger; C. M. Margulies.

**OTHER INFORMATION** Donations of less than £5,000 totalled £54,000.

**HOW TO APPLY** Apply in writing to the correspondent.

**WHO TO APPLY TO** C. M. Margulies, Trustee, 186 Lordship Road, London N16 5ES Tel. 020 8802 4449

## ■ The William Price Charitable Trust

**CC NO** 307319    **ESTABLISHED** 1989

**WHERE FUNDING CAN BE GIVEN** Fareham's town parishes of St Peter and St Paul, Holy Trinity with St Columba and St John the Evangelist. Note this area is that of the Fareham town parishes and not the borough of Fareham.

**WHO CAN BENEFIT** Schools; colleges; churches; individuals under the age of 25.

**WHAT IS FUNDED** Schools for educational benefits not normally provided by the local education authority, and individuals for help with fees, travel, outfits, clothing, books and so on. There is an emphasis supporting subjects and activities that 'enrich quality of life and widen horizons, encourage participation and appreciation of the arts, develop good citizenship and encourage help in the community and local environment.'

**WHAT IS NOT FUNDED** Grants cannot be given to persons who live outside the area of the Fareham town parishes or to any organisation or establishment other than those outlined in this entry.

**RANGE OF GRANTS** £2,000 to £12,000.

**SAMPLE GRANTS** Cams Hill (£12,250); Henry Cort College (£12,000); Fareham Welfare Trust (£10,000); Harrison Primary School (£9,000); Fareham College (£7,000); Wicor Primary School (£6,500); Redlands Primary School (£5,300); Ranvilles Infant School (£3,500); Heathfield School (£2,000); Holy Trinity, St Columba, St John Evangelist and St Peter and St Paul churches (approx. £2,000 each).

**FINANCES** Year 2013/14 Income £199,127 Grants £126,721 Grants to organisations £111,061 Assets £6,717,662

**TRUSTEE** William Price Trust Company.

**OTHER INFORMATION** The trust makes an annual payment to Fareham Welfare Trust.

**HOW TO APPLY** On the appropriate form available to download from the website. The trustees prefer applications to be made through a school or college though applications from individuals are also accepted, especially from those in further education. Major grants for educational purposes are considered by the Grants Committee on a six-monthly basis with closing dates for applications on 1 March and 1 September. Smaller 'hardship' grants for individuals are considered at any time and are usually made through their school or college.

**WHO TO APPLY TO** Dr Christopher Thomas, Company Secretary and Clerk, 24 Cuckoo Lane, Stubbington, Fareham, Hampshire PO14 3PF Tel. 01329 663685 email mazchris@tiscali.co.uk Website www.pricestrust.org.uk

## ■ Sir John Priestman Charity Trust

**CC NO** 209397    **ESTABLISHED** 1931

**WHERE FUNDING CAN BE GIVEN** The County of Durham and, in particular, the County Borough of Sunderland. In relation to Church of England grants, the County of York is also eligible.

**WHO CAN BENEFIT** Charitable organisations; churches; schools.

**WHAT IS FUNDED** General charitable purposes for the benefit of residents of County Durham and, in particular, of the County Borough of Sunderland. Also, the building, maintenance and furnishing of Church of England churches, mission halls and schools, and the relief of Church of England ministers and their dependants who are in need, in the counties of Durham and York.

**WHAT IS NOT FUNDED** Organisations operating outside charity's beneficial area.

**TYPE OF GRANT** The trustees support a number of charities by way of regular annual grants, but otherwise the trustees' aim where possible is to award grants for specific projects as opposed to general running costs.

**RANGE OF GRANTS** From £400 to £14,000.

**SAMPLE GRANTS** Outward Bound Trust (£14,000); St Margaret's Church – Hawes (£12,000); St James the Great Church – Romanby (£10,000); Butterwick Hospice Centre and University of Sunderland Development Trust (£7,500 each); Durham High School (£6,500); Durham Association of Clubs for Young People (£5,500); Age UK Sunderland and Southwick and Monkwearmouth Community Transport (£3,000 each); Northumbria Deaf Mission (£2,500); Farrington Detached Football Club (£2,000); Corporation of the Sons of the Clergy and Durham Wildlife Trust (£1,500 each); Church of St Peter the Apostle – Byers Green (£500); Handicapped Children's Action Group) (£400).

**FINANCES** Year 2013 Income £380,936 Grants £403,118 Grants to organisations £403,118 Assets £11,731,793

TRUSTEES Peter Taylor; Richard Farr; Timothy Norton; Anthony Coates; Thomas Greenwell.
OTHER INFORMATION Only in special circumstances grants are awarded outside the specified geographical area or to individuals. A number of charities are supported by way of annual grants.
HOW TO APPLY Apply in writing to the correspondent. As the previous system entry notes, the trustees meet quarterly, usually in January, April, July and October. Our research indicates that applications should include clear details of the need the project is designed to meet plus estimates, where appropriate, and details of amounts subscribed to date.
WHO TO APPLY TO The Trustees, McKenzie Bell, 19 John Street, Sunderland, Tyne and Wear SR1 1JG *Tel.* 0191 567 4857

## ■ The Primrose Trust
CC NO 800049     ESTABLISHED 1986
WHERE FUNDING CAN BE GIVEN UK.
WHO CAN BENEFIT Registered charities.
WHAT IS FUNDED General charitable purposes.
WHAT IS NOT FUNDED Grants are given to registered charities only.
RANGE OF GRANTS £5,000 to £40,000.
SAMPLE GRANTS Animals Asia (£40,000); Badgers Trust (£30,000); Animal Health Trust (£20,000); British Hen Welfare Trust (£15,000); Retirement Home for Battery Hens (£12,000); Secret World Wildlife (£5,000).
FINANCES *Year* 2013/14 *Income* £153,135 *Grants* £122,000 *Grants to organisations* £122,000 *Assets* £4,238,648
TRUSTEES Malcolm Clark; Susan Boyes-Korkis.
OTHER INFORMATION In 2013/14 six organisations were supported.
HOW TO APPLY Apply in writing to the correspondent and include a copy of your organisation's most recent accounts. The trust does not wish to receive telephone calls.
WHO TO APPLY TO Jacqueline Deacy, Correspondent, Deloitte LLP, 5 Callaghan Square, Cardiff CF10 5BT *Tel.* 029 2026 4388 *email* jdeacy@deloitte.co.uk

## ■ The Prince of Wales's Charitable Foundation
CC NO 1127255     ESTABLISHED 1979
WHERE FUNDING CAN BE GIVEN UK and overseas.
WHO CAN BENEFIT Registered charities that have been active for at least two years.
WHAT IS FUNDED Mainly causes in which the Prince of Wales has a particular interest. This has recently included: arts and culture; education and young people; conservation and heritage; environmental sustainability; community support; health and hospices; religion; emergency relief; and the welfare of service personnel. Applications are particularly welcomed from small, grassroots organisations based in the UK, which look to make a difference for people and their communities.
WHAT IS NOT FUNDED Individuals; public bodies; organisations whose main activity is to distribute grants to other organisations; organisations wishing to deliver projects similar to those of any of The Prince's Charities; organisations whose annual income exceeds £1 million; organisations with political interests or affiliations; capital expenditure (with the exception of community-based, religion-related and heritage restoration projects); sponsorship.
TYPE OF GRANT One-off grants for capital or core expenditure.
RANGE OF GRANTS Typically up to £5,000, though larger grants are also made.
SAMPLE GRANTS The Great Steward of Scotland's Dumfries House Trust (£702,000); The Soil Association (£500,000); The Prince's Foundation for Building Community (£285,000); Children and the Arts (£273,000); The Prince's Drawing School (£211,000); GCHQ (£100,000); The Prince of Wales Foundation (£75,000); The Prince's Countryside Fund (£50,000); The Prince's School of Traditional Arts (£49,000); ARTTA and PRIME (£30,000 each); Prince's Charities Australia and Prince's Charities Canada (£25,000 each); The College of Medicine (£20,000); The Aid to the Church in Need, BITC BERG Emergency Fund, Exeter Cathedral, Navdanya Trust and St Catherine Foundation (£10,000 each).
FINANCES *Year* 2013/14 *Income* £10,603,000 *Grants* £2,701,256 *Grants to organisations* £2,701,256 *Assets* £11,058,000
TRUSTEES John Varley; Sir Michael Rake; William James; Dame Amelia Fawcett; Kenneth Brockington Wilson.
OTHER INFORMATION The foundation operates two grants programmes: Major Grants and Small Grants. The Major Grants programme does not accept unsolicited applications. In the year 19 major grants of £10,000 or more were made, many of them to other Prince of Wales charities. These amounted to more than £2.4 million. Grants of less than £10,000 totalled £276,000.
HOW TO APPLY Fill out the online eligibility form in the first instance which will give you access to the full online application form, should you be eligible. Unsolicited applications are not accepted for the Major Grants programme.
WHO TO APPLY TO David Hutson, The Prince of Wales's Office, Clarence House, St James's, London SW1A 1BA *email* yvonne.abbaopoku@royal.gsx.gov.uk *Website* www.princeofwalescharitablefoundation.org.uk

## ■ Princess Anne's Charities
CC NO 277814     ESTABLISHED 1979
WHERE FUNDING CAN BE GIVEN UK.
WHO CAN BENEFIT Registered charities, mainly those in which Princess Anne has a particular interest.
WHAT IS FUNDED Social welfare; medical research; children and youth; environment and wildlife; armed forces; general charitable purposes.
WHAT IS NOT FUNDED Individuals.
TYPE OF GRANT Project, capital and revenue funding. Loans and contracts may also be issued.
SAMPLE GRANTS **Previous beneficiaries have included:** Butler Trust, the Canal Museum Trust Cranfield Trust, Dogs Trust, Dorothy House Foundation, Durrell Wildlife Conservation Trust, the Evelina Children's Hospital Appeal, Farms for City Children, Farrer and Co Charitable Trust, Fire Services National Benevolent Fund, the Home Farm Trust, Intensive Care Society and International League for the Protection of Horses.
FINANCES *Year* 2013/14 *Income* £154,495 *Grants* £124,525 *Grants to organisations* £124,525 *Assets* £5,816,867
TRUSTEES The Hon. Mark Bridges; Brian Hammond; Vice Admiral Sir Tim Laurence.
OTHER INFORMATION Grants were made to 36 charities in 2013/14.
HOW TO APPLY The trust has previously stated that the trustees generally make awards only to

those charities of which the Princess is Patron. Other appeals are considered on a case by case basis, but only very few are successful.
**WHO TO APPLY TO** Capt. Nick Wright, Buckingham Palace, London SW1A 1AA *Tel.* 020 7024 4199 *email* nick.wright@royal.gsx.gov.uk

■ **Prison Service Charity Fund**
CC NO 801678    ESTABLISHED 1989
**WHERE FUNDING CAN BE GIVEN** England and Wales.
**WHO CAN BENEFIT** Charitable organisations and individuals.
**WHAT IS FUNDED** The trust supports the efforts of prison service staff who are fundraising to provide organisations and individuals with medical treatment or equipment
**RANGE OF GRANTS** Usually up to £2,000, most grants are for less than £1,000.
**SAMPLE GRANTS** Previous beneficiaries have included: Leeds Prison Charity Fund (£2,000); The Twins Appeal and the David Cross Appeal (£1,600 each); Five Charity Appeal, The Alfie Gough Trust and Steps to America Appeal (£1,000 each); Help for Heroes (£750); Chadsgrove Special School (£670); Claire House Children's Hospice and Prostate Cancer Charity (£600 each); Neurofibromatosis Association; Woodlands Hospice (£500); MS Society (£300); and Lymphoma and Leukaemia Association (£220).
**FINANCES** *Year* 2013 *Income* £160,360 *Grants* £101,075 *Grants to organisations* £101,075
**TRUSTEES** Nevill Joseph, Chair; Paul Ashes; John Goldsworthy; Peter McFall; Catherine Smith; Ken Wingfield; John White; Bob Howard.
**OTHER INFORMATION** During the year, the charity received 195 appeals from staff at 51 establishments.
**HOW TO APPLY** Applications are only accepted from members of prison service staff. Outside applications are not accepted.
**WHO TO APPLY TO** Bob Howard, Secretary, 15 Merepark Drive,, Southport PR9 9FB *Tel.* 01995 604997 *email* bob@pscf.co.uk *Website* www.prisonservicecharityfund.co.uk

■ **The Privy Purse Charitable Trust**
CC NO 296079    ESTABLISHED 1987
**WHERE FUNDING CAN BE GIVEN** UK and overseas.
**WHO CAN BENEFIT** The annual report states: 'The main aims of the trustees are to make grants to charities of which The Queen is patron and to support ecclesiastical establishments associated with The Queen and to make contributions in the event of either national or international disasters.'
**WHAT IS FUNDED** General charitable purposes; disaster relief.
**RANGE OF GRANTS** Most grants are usually up to £1,000.
**SAMPLE GRANTS** Chapel Royal – St James's Palace (£85,500); Chapel Royal – Hampton Court Palace (£62,500); Sandringham Group of Parishes (£54,000); Chapel Royal – Windsor Great Park (£21,000); British Red Cross – Philippines Typhoon and The Choral Foundation (£10,000 each).
**FINANCES** *Year* 2013/14 *Income* £602,332 *Grants* £619,312 *Grants to organisations* £619,312 *Assets* £3,018,212
**TRUSTEES** Michael Stevens; Sir Alan Reid; The Right Hon. Sir Christopher Geidt.

**HOW TO APPLY** The trust makes donations to a wide variety of charities, but does not respond to unsolicited applications.
**WHO TO APPLY TO** Michael Stevens, Trustee, Buckingham Palace, London SW1A 1AA *Tel.* 020 7930 4832 *email* mike.stevens@royal.gsx.gov.uk

■ **The Puebla Charitable Trust**
CC NO 290055    ESTABLISHED 1984
**WHERE FUNDING CAN BE GIVEN** Worldwide.
**WHO CAN BENEFIT** Organisations.
**WHAT IS FUNDED** The trust's support is currently limited to charities which assist the poorest sections of the population or are involved in community development work in Britain or overseas.
**WHAT IS NOT FUNDED** Capital projects, religious institutions, research or institutions for people with disabilities. Individuals are not supported and no scholarships are given.
**TYPE OF GRANT** Up to three years.
**SAMPLE GRANTS** Survivors Fund (£75,000).
**FINANCES** *Year* 2013/14 *Income* £97,618 *Grants* £75,000 *Grants to organisations* £75,000 *Assets* £2,563,433
**TRUSTEES** Justin Phipps; Martin Strutt.
**OTHER INFORMATION** The trust made one three year grant commitment during the year.
**HOW TO APPLY** Apply in writing to the correspondent. The trustees usually meet in July. The trust is unable to acknowledge applications.
**WHO TO APPLY TO** The Secretary, Ensors, Cardinal House, 46 St Nicholas Street, Ipswich IP1 1TT *Tel.* 01473 220022

■ **The Puri Foundation**
CC NO 327854    ESTABLISHED 1988
**WHERE FUNDING CAN BE GIVEN** UK (mainly the Nottingham area), India and Nepal.
**WHO CAN BENEFIT** Registered charities; universities; schools; hospitals; individuals.
**WHAT IS FUNDED** The relief of need, hardship or distress; the advancement of education; the provision of facilities for recreation. There is a particular focus on young people.
**WHAT IS NOT FUNDED** Holidays.
**RANGE OF GRANTS** From £25.
**SAMPLE GRANTS** The Puri Foundation for Education in India (£227,000); Global Human Rights (£18,300); National Hindu Student Forum (£15,000); City University London (£8,300); Hindu Temple (£5,400); Black Men Achievers Award (£1,000); Nottingham Asian Arts Council (£500); Nottingham University (£100); Framework (£25).
**FINANCES** *Year* 2013/14 *Income* £345,106 *Grants* £284,232 *Grants to organisations* £280,843 *Assets* £3,196,314
**TRUSTEES** Nathu Puri; Anil Puri; Mary McGowan.
**OTHER INFORMATION** Grants were distributed for the following purposes: education and cultural (£263,500); human rights (£18,300); general support (£2,600). One major grant was made to The Puri Foundation for Education in India, which was also founded by Nathu Puri.
**HOW TO APPLY** Apply in writing to the correspondent.
**WHO TO APPLY TO** Nathu Puri, Trustee, Environment House, 6 Union Road, Nottingham NG3 1FH *Tel.* 0115 901 3000 *Website* www.purico.co.uk/charitable_functions

## ■ The PwC Foundation

CC NO 1144124   ESTABLISHED 2011
WHERE FUNDING CAN BE GIVEN UK.
WHO CAN BENEFIT Charitable organisations.
WHAT IS FUNDED Sustainable development, social inclusion, education and training, healthcare, the environment.
WHAT IS NOT FUNDED Political organisations, lobbying groups, animal rights groups or religious bodies.
RANGE OF GRANTS £10,000–£103,000
SAMPLE GRANTS Wellbeing of Women (£103,000); Teach First (£90,000); School for Entrepreneurs (£86,000); Beyond Food Foundation (£71,000); Groundwork (£50,000); The Shakespeare Globe Trust (£45,000); Alzheimer's Society (£23,000); LandAid and PRIME (£10,000 each).
FINANCES Year 2013/14 Income £1,190,157 Grants £1,029,236 Grants to organisations £1,029,236 Assets £201,193
TRUSTEES Neil Sherlock; Gaenor Bagley; Kevin Ellis; David Adair.
OTHER INFORMATION The PwC Foundation is the corporate charity of PricewaterhouseCoopers LLP (PwC).
HOW TO APPLY The following was taken from the PwC Foundation's website: 'the distribution of funds donated to the foundation are decided by the foundation trustees taking into account the voting preferences of our people'.
WHO TO APPLY TO Sean Good, Correspondent, PricewaterhouseCoopers LLP, 1 Embankment Place, London WC2N 6RH Tel. 07764 902846 email sean.good@uk.pwc.com Website www.pwc.co.uk/corporate-sustainability/the-pwc-foundation.jhtml

## ■ Mr and Mrs J. A. Pye's Charitable Settlement

CC NO 242677   ESTABLISHED 1965
WHERE FUNDING CAN BE GIVEN Mainly Oxfordshire and the
WHO CAN BENEFIT Organisations. The trustees prefer to support under-funded charities in their fields of interest.
WHAT IS FUNDED General charitable purposes at the trustees' discretion. The charity's website states that the following areas are of a particular interest: Environmental – 'This subject particularly deals with organic farming matters, conservation generally and health-related matters such as pollution research and some wildlife protection' Adult health and care – 'Especially causes supporting the following; post-natal depression, schizophrenia, mental health generally and research into the main causes of early death' Children's health and care – 'For physical, mental and learning disabilities, respite breaks, etc.' Youth organisations – 'Particularly projects encouraging self-reliance or dealing with social deprivation' Education – 'Nursery, Primary, Secondary or Higher/Institutions (not individuals)' Heritage and the arts – 'Under this category, the Trustees will consider applications relating to heritage and the arts generally'.
WHAT IS NOT FUNDED Individuals; non-registered organisations; animal welfare; the promotion of religion.
TYPE OF GRANT One-off, core costs, projects, research, recurring, running and start-up costs, and salaries. Capital costs may be considered. Funding may be given for up to or more than three years. Also interest-free loans.
RANGE OF GRANTS £250–£135,000

SAMPLE GRANTS Music @ Oxford (£96,000); Organic Research Centre (£75,000); Harris Manchester College (£30,000); Children with AIDS Charity (£24,000); ORH Children's Hospital Fund (£20,000); The Story Museum (£11,000); Oxford Brookes University Rowing Club (£10,000); The Oxford Victoria County History Trust (£5,000); Oxford Playhouse (£4,300); Brent Centre for Young People (£3,000); Friends of Dorchester Abbey (£2,000); The British Forces Foundation, Leonard Cheshire Disability and Oxford Youth Workers (£1,000 each); Create Arts (£800); Green Pastures (£750).
FINANCES Year 2013 Income £495,240 Grants £508,010 Grants to organisations £508,010 Assets £11,749,727
TRUSTEES Simon Stubbings; David S. Tallon; Patrick Mulcare.
OTHER INFORMATION During the year, 141 grants were given and one new loan of £10,000 was made.
HOW TO APPLY All applications should be sent to the administrative office (and not to individual trustees). There is a list of essential information which must be submitted listed on the website. Applicants are invited to apply via email. They are reviewed on a continual basis and are considered at quarterly trustees' meetings. Therefore, it may be four months before a decision is made. All applicants are notified of their outcome. The charity notes that telephone calls are usually counter-productive.
WHO TO APPLY TO David S. Tallon, Trustee, c/o Mercer and Hole Chartered Accountants, Gloucester House, 72 London Road, St Albans, Hertfordshire AL1 1NS Tel. 01727 869141 email pyecharitablesettlement@mercerhole.co.uk Website www.pyecharitablesettlement.org

## ■ The Pyne Charitable Trust

CC NO 1105357   ESTABLISHED 2004
WHERE FUNDING CAN BE GIVEN UK and overseas.
WHO CAN BENEFIT Organisations and individuals.
WHAT IS FUNDED Christian causes, general charitable purposes.
SAMPLE GRANTS Good Shepherd Mission (£35,000); GrowTH (£7,500); NSPCC (£500).
FINANCES Year 2013 Income £52,500 Grants £43,000 Grants to organisations £43,000 Assets £9,922
TRUSTEES Michael Brennan; Pauline Brennan; Mike Mitchell.
OTHER INFORMATION During the year, a one-off donation was made to GrowTH to support its night shelter in Tower Hamlets. No grants were made to individuals.
HOW TO APPLY Ongoing support appears to be given to projects selected by the trustees.
WHO TO APPLY TO Pauline Brennan, Secretary, 26 Tredegar Square, London E3 5AG email home@mpbrennan.fsnet.co.uk

# Quartet

## ■ Quartet Community Foundation (formerly the Greater Bristol Foundation)

**CC NO** 1080418  **ESTABLISHED** 1987
**WHERE FUNDING CAN BE GIVEN** West England – Bristol, North Somerset, South Gloucestershire, Bath and North East Somerset.
**WHO CAN BENEFIT** Priority is given to small, local charities and voluntary groups, though national charities with a 'significant' local presence may apply if funding will benefit local people.
**WHAT IS FUNDED** The foundation's website states that, through its grant-making, it looks to: 'help people who are most disadvantaged and isolated; encourage people to get involved in improving their own community; give people opportunities others take for granted; respond to the needs and concerns of people living in local communities'.
**RANGE OF GRANTS** Grants ranged from £30 to £67,000. The average grant was of just under £3,400.
**SAMPLE GRANTS** Fredericks Foundation (£130,000); Park Community Centre Ltd (£107,500 in four grants); Creative Youth Network (£49,000 in two grants); Social Enterprise Works (£45,000); Bristol Refugee Rights (£35,500); University of Bristol (£35,000); Bristol Mind (£30,000); Yate Town Council (£23,000 in two grants); Cowden Care Farm (£20,000); Emmaus Bristol and FareShare South West (£15,000 each); North Bristol Advice Centre (£10,000); Playing Out CIC (£9,800); Cross Roads Care Essex (£7,500); Pucklechurch Parish Council (£5,900); St Richard's Hospice (£5,700); Mencap Keynsham and District and Pyramid Youth Club (£5,000 each).
**FINANCES** Year 2013/14 Income £3,524,262 Grants £2,961,893 Grants to organisations £2,961,893 Assets £22,041,954
**TRUSTEES** John Cullum; Jane Moss; Hilary Neal; David Harvey; Christopher Sharp; Lesley Freed; Julian Telling; Trevor Leonard; Becky Small; Merlyn Ipinson-Fleming; Robert Bourns; Annie Kilvington; Nick Baker; Pat Meehan.
**OTHER INFORMATION** The foundation manages a range of funds each with their own priorities, criteria and closing dates as well as its own programme, the Express Programme which makes grants of up to £2,000. During the year, 883 grants were made through 28 programmes.
**HOW TO APPLY** Applicants should refer to the fund's website for details on how to apply to each grants programme. The funding team can be contacted for any help or advice concerning grants applications.
**WHO TO APPLY TO** Grants Team, Royal Oak House, Royal Oak Avenue, Bristol BS1 4GB *Tel.* 0117 989 7700 *Fax* 0117 989 7701 *email* applications@quartetcf.org.uk *Website* www.quartetcf.org.uk

## ■ The Queen Anne's Gate Foundation

**CC NO** 1108903  **ESTABLISHED** 2005
**WHERE FUNDING CAN BE GIVEN** UK and overseas, mainly Asia.
**WHO CAN BENEFIT** Charitable organisations.
**WHAT IS FUNDED** There is a focus on educational, medical and rehabilitative charities and those working with underprivileged areas of society, particularly in the UK and Asia.
**RANGE OF GRANTS** Between £2,000 and £33,000.
**SAMPLE GRANTS** Sri Aurobindo Society (£33,000); The Hong Kong Polytechnic University and The Marylebone Project (£30,000); Families for Children, The Citizens Foundation and The Poppy Factory (£25,000 each); Indochina Starfish Foundation (£21,500); CAADA – Co-ordinated Action Against Domestic Abuse (£20,000); Christian Friends of Korea (£18,000); English National Opera (£17,400); Aanchal Women's Aid (£15,000); City of Exeter YMCA Community Projects (£10,000); Burma Education Partnership (£6,000); The Aquila Trust – Mid-Wales Music Fund, The Playing Field Legacy and Two Moors Festival (£5,000 each); Families for Children – University costs funding (£4,500); Love and Care International UK (£2,000).
**FINANCES** Year 2013/14 Income £50,669 Grants £287,522 Grants to organisations £287,522 Assets £1,956,105
**TRUSTEES** Nicholas Allan; Jonathan Boyer; Roger Wortley.
**OTHER INFORMATION** Grants were given in the following areas: education (£154,000); general welfare (£118,000); children's welfare (£25,000); environment (£9,500 in one grant which was later returned to the foundation).
**HOW TO APPLY** Apply in writing to the correspondent. The trustees meet twice a year.
**WHO TO APPLY TO** Jonathan Wortley, Willcox Lewis LLP, The Old Coach House, Sunnyside, Bergh Apton, Norwich NR15 1DD *Tel.* 01508 480100

## ■ Queen Mary's Roehampton Trust

**CC NO** 211715  **ESTABLISHED** 1928
**WHERE FUNDING CAN BE GIVEN** UK.
**WHO CAN BENEFIT** Organisations.
**WHAT IS FUNDED** The reception, accommodation, treatment or aftercare of ex-service people who were disabled during their service and their dependants. Also, medical or surgical research associated to the needs of people who have disabilities and served in the armed forces.
**WHAT IS NOT FUNDED** Individuals.
**TYPE OF GRANT** Annual recurring and one-off. Also capital and project. Funding may be given for up to two years.
**RANGE OF GRANTS** £2,000 to £40,000.
**SAMPLE GRANTS** The Soldiers' Charity (Army Benevolent Fund) (£40,000); Broughton House and SSAFA (£35,000 each); British Limbless Ex-Servicemen's Association, and the Royal Naval Benevolent Trust (£30,000 each); Combat Stress and Veterans Aid (£20,000 each); British Ex-Services Wheelchair Sports Association and Queen Alexandra Hospital Home (£15,000 each); Gurkha Welfare Trust (£12,000); Canine Partners and Royal Navy and Royal Marines Children's Fund (£7,000 each); Deafblind UK and National Gulf Veterans and Families Association (£5,000 each); Association of Jewish Ex-Service Men and Women (£2,000).

**FINANCES** Year 2013/14 Income £553,271 Grants £544,500 Grants to organisations £544,500 Assets £13,677,533
**TRUSTEES** Lieutenant Col. Simon Brewis; Cathy Walker; James Macnamara; Dr Gordon Paterson; Colin Green; Col. Paul Cummings; Cdr Stephen Farringdon; Beverley Davies; Debbie Bowles; Stephen Coltman; Sir Barry Thornton.
**HOW TO APPLY** On a standard application form available from the correspondent. Representatives of the trust may visit beneficiary organisations.
**WHO TO APPLY TO** Col. Stephen Rowland-Jones, Clerk to the Trustees, 2 Sovereign Close, Quidhampton, Salisbury, Wiltshire SP2 9ES Tel. 01722 501413 email qmrt@hotmail.co.uk

## ■ The Queen's Silver Jubilee Trust

**CC NO** 272373    **ESTABLISHED** 1976
**WHERE FUNDING CAN BE GIVEN** UK.
**WHO CAN BENEFIT** Registered charities.
**WHAT IS FUNDED** Young people, particularly in the areas of their education, employment, collaboration and the development of their confidence, mental health and well-being.
**WHAT IS NOT FUNDED** Non-registered charities; individuals.
**TYPE OF GRANT** One-off and recurring.
**SAMPLE GRANTS** OnSide North West (£1.01 million); Camfed and The Prince's Trust (£1 million each); Create Arts Limited (£480,000); Carers Trust (£400,000); Sentebale, Teenage Cancer Trust and Youth United (£300,000 each); City Year (£274,000); IntoUni (£130,000); Prince's Charities Canada (£75,000); Campaign for Youth Social Action (£50,000); Windsor Festival (£30,000).
**FINANCES** Year 2013/14 Income £243,000 Grants £5,348,922 Grants to organisations £5,348,922 Assets £30,484,000
**TRUSTEES** Rt Hon. Christopher Geidt; Sir Alan Reid; Peter Mimpriss; Michael Marks; Sir Trevor McDonald; Sandra Robertson; Christopher Coombe.
**OTHER INFORMATION** The trust is aiming to spend-out its funds by 2020.
**HOW TO APPLY** The trust states the following on its website: 'As a rule, we do not accept unsolicited applications. We seek out ambitious, well-managed charities, with proven results, that put our core purpose at the heart of what they do: to help young people help others.'
**WHO TO APPLY TO** Anne Threlkeld, Correspondent, Buckingham Palace, London SW1A 1AA Tel. 020 7024 4165 email anne.threlkeld@royal.gsx.gov.uk Website www.queenstrust.org.uk

## ■ Quercus Trust

**CC NO** 1039205    **ESTABLISHED** 1993
**WHERE FUNDING CAN BE GIVEN** UK.
**WHO CAN BENEFIT** Established organisations; registered charities; individuals.
**WHAT IS FUNDED** The arts.
**RANGE OF GRANTS** £850 to £349,000.
**SAMPLE GRANTS** The Royal Opera House Foundation (£349,000); English National Ballet (£200,000); Hofesh Shechter Company (£50,000); Sadler's Wells Trust (£30,000); Mindful Films (£23,000); Dance United (£20,000); Alexander Whitley Dance Company (£15,000); British Lymphology Society (£5,000); Tate Foundation (£900).

**FINANCES** Year 2013/14 Income £87,571 Grants £1,030,316 Grants to organisations £692,816 Assets £2,901,829
**TRUSTEES** Lady Angela Bernstein; Kate Bernstein.
**HOW TO APPLY** Unsolicited applications are not welcomed by the trustees.
**WHO TO APPLY TO** Helen Price, Correspondent, Gloucester House, 72 London Road, St Albans, Hertfordshire AL1 1NS Tel. 01727 869141 email helenprice@mercerhole.co.uk

## ■ Quothquan Trust

**CC NO** 1110647    **ESTABLISHED** 2004
**WHERE FUNDING CAN BE GIVEN** Birmingham and surrounding area, West Midlands.
**WHO CAN BENEFIT** Christian organisations and individuals.
**WHAT IS FUNDED** Promotion of Christian faith through specific projects and initiatives aimed at relieving the poverty and sickness, assisting the elderly, the ill, the socially and economically disadvantaged, advancement of religious education.
**WHAT IS NOT FUNDED** Causes that do not promote Christianity as part of their ethos; activities which are generally the responsibility of the state; animal welfare; church buildings; environmental causes; expeditions and overseas trips; hospitals, hospices and health centres; large national charities or local projects run by them; loans and business finance; medical research projects; overseas appeals; religions other than Christianity; schools, universities and colleges; projects that have had applications previously turned down by the trust; charities supported by The Alfred Haines Charitable Trust. The trust does not usually support individuals whose work is not well-known to the trustees.
**TYPE OF GRANT** Grants are generally made on a one-off basis with an exception to the regular monthly grants.
**RANGE OF GRANTS** £50 to £300.
**SAMPLE GRANTS** A list of specific beneficiaries was not included in the annual accounts.
**FINANCES** Year 2013 Income £268,934 Grants £326,141 Grants to organisations £278,050 Assets £2,837,529
**TRUSTEES** Archie Gilmour; Janet Gilmour.
**OTHER INFORMATION** Grants totalling £48,000 were made to 38 individuals. Quothquan Trust shares support staff with The Alfred Haines Charitable Trust.
**HOW TO APPLY** Apply writing to the correspondent. See the website for guidelines and criteria. Applications by email are not accepted. Unsuccessful applicants are not notified and do not receive feedback or details.
**WHO TO APPLY TO** Archie Gilmour, Trustee, Dale Farm, Worcester Lane, Four Oaks, Sutton Coldfield B75 5PR Tel. 0121 323 3236 Website www.quothquantrust.org.uk

## ■ R. J. M. Charitable Trust

CC NO 288336  ESTABLISHED 1983
WHERE FUNDING CAN BE GIVEN UK and worldwide.
WHO CAN BENEFIT Organisations; synagogues.
WHAT IS FUNDED Mainly Jewish causes.
RANGE OF GRANTS £50–£100,000
SAMPLE GRANTS **Previous beneficiaries have included:** One to One (£10,000); Yeshun (£8,000); North Salford Synagogue (£7,400); South Manchester Synagogue (£5,000); Manchester Jewish Philanthropic (£3,000); Manchester Kellel (£2,000); Navas Chesed, OHR Elcharan and Sunderland Talmund (£1,000); British Friends Masat Moshe (£560); British Friends Israel War (£250); and Crisis (£20).
FINANCES Year 2013/14 Income £957 Grants £200,000 Grants to organisations £200,000
TRUSTEES Joshua Rowe; Michelle Rowe.
OTHER INFORMATION Due to its low income, the trust was not required to submit its accounts to the Charity Commission. During the year, it had a total expenditure of £201,000.
HOW TO APPLY Apply in writing to the correspondent.
WHO TO APPLY TO Joshua Rowe, Trustee, 84 Upper Park Road, Salford M7 4JA Tel. 0161 720 8787 email JR@broomwell.com

## ■ R. S. Charitable Trust

CC NO 1053660  ESTABLISHED 1996
WHERE FUNDING CAN BE GIVEN UK.
WHO CAN BENEFIT Registered charities.
WHAT IS FUNDED Jewish causes; social welfare.
SAMPLE GRANTS **Previous beneficiaries have included:** British Friends of Tshernobil, Forty Ltd, NRST, Society of Friends of the Torah, Talmud Hochschule, Viznitz, Yeshiva Horomo and Yeshivas Luzern.
FINANCES Year 2013/14 Income £419,511 Grants £182,904 Grants to organisations £182,904 Assets £2,432,648
TRUSTEES Harvey Freudenberger; Michelle Freudenberger; Stuart Freudenberger; Max Freudenberger.
HOW TO APPLY Apply in writing to the correspondent.
WHO TO APPLY TO Max Freudenberger, Trustee, 138 Stamford Hill, London N16 6QT

## ■ The RVW Trust

CC NO 1066977  ESTABLISHED 1958
WHERE FUNDING CAN BE GIVEN UK.
WHO CAN BENEFIT Organisations and individuals, particularly composers, musicians and music students.
WHAT IS FUNDED The trust's current priority grant-making areas (at the time of writing) are listed on the website: '1.1 Assistance to British composers who have not yet achieved a broad national or international reputation; 1.2 Assistance towards the performance and recording of music by neglected or currently unfashionable 20th and 21st century British composers, including performances by societies and at festivals, which include works by such composers in their programmes; 1.3 Support for National organisations which promote public knowledge and appreciation of 20th and 21st century British music; 1.4 Occasional support for education projects in the field of music which are connected with public performance of music which qualifies under 1.1 and 1.2. Education projects for children will only be considered for funding if the primary purpose is the performance of new or recent British music; 1.5 Support for postgraduate students of composition taking first master's degrees at British intuitions.'
WHAT IS NOT FUNDED Concerts, concert series or concert tours which do not include music by 20th and 21st century British composers; concerts for which income from box office receipts, together with support from other organisations, is forecast to amount to less than half of the estimated expenditure; commissions purely for youth or children's ensembles; grants for musicals, rock or pop music, ethnic music, jazz or dance music or multi-media and theatrical events in which music is not the primary art form; 'workshops' with no planned public performance; grants to organisations directly administered by local or other public authorities; grants to managing agents and commercial promoters; vocal or instrumental tuition; the making, purchase or repair of musical instruments, computer or multi-media equipment; the construction or restoration of buildings. The trust does not support projects relating to the work of Ralph Vaughan Williams. Requests for commission fees are only considered if there is, at least, a second performance of any new work planned. Concerts by university and conservatoire orchestras and ensembles are only considered for support in the most exceptional of circumstances.
RANGE OF GRANTS Up to £10,000.
SAMPLE GRANTS Park Lane Group (£10,000); Huddersfield Contemporary Music Festival (£9,000); Cheltenham Music Festival (£6,000); Edinburgh Quartet, Onyx Brass and Royal opera House Foundation (£2,000 each); City of Cambridge Brass Band and Piatti Quartet (£1,500 each); City of London Sinfonia (£1,000).
FINANCES Year 2014 Income £352,187 Grants £194,384 Grants to organisations £194,384 Assets £1,924,254
TRUSTEES Sir John Manduell; Hugh Cobbe; Lord Armstrong; Anthony Burton; Jeremy Roberts; Andrew Johnston; Prof. Nicola Lefanu; Sally Groves; Musicians Benevolent Fund.
OTHER INFORMATION The recipients of the 40 largest grants are listed in the annual report and accounts. Other, smaller grants totalled £119,000. The grant total includes those made to individuals.
HOW TO APPLY Apply in writing to the correspondent. Extensive guidelines are available from the website and should be read before an application is started. If you have any doubts as to the eligibility of your application, contact the trust in the first instance.
WHO TO APPLY TO Hannah Vlček, Secretary, 7–11 Britannia Street, London WC1X 9JS Tel. 020 7239 9139 email info@rvwtrust.org.uk Website www.rvwtrust.org.uk

## ■ The Monica Rabagliati Charitable Trust

CC NO 1086368   ESTABLISHED 2001
WHERE FUNDING CAN BE GIVEN UK.
WHO CAN BENEFIT Charitable organisations. Small/medium sized organisations are prioritised.
WHAT IS FUNDED Whilst keeping a general scope, the trust primarily supports 'organisations that focus on the alleviation of child suffering and deprivation'.
RANGE OF GRANTS £1,000–£10,000
SAMPLE GRANTS Inner Temple Scholarships and Outward Bound Trust (£10,000 each); Home-Start Lambeth (£5,000); Victoria Cross (£3,000); Bletchley Park Trust (£2,000); Childhood First (£1,500); Happy Days Children's Charity (£1,000).
FINANCES Year 2013/14 Income £43,945 Grants £43,000 Grants to organisations £43,000 Assets £1,891,080
TRUSTEES S. G. Hambros Trust Company Limited; Robert McLean.
HOW TO APPLY Application forms are available to download from the website. Applications are considered twice a year.
WHO TO APPLY TO Rachel Iles, Director, S. G. Hambros Trust Company Limited, Norfolk House, 31 St James's Square, London SW1Y 4JR *Tel.* 020 7597 3065 *Website* www.rabagliati.org.uk

## ■ Rachel Charitable Trust

CC NO 276441   ESTABLISHED 1978
WHERE FUNDING CAN BE GIVEN UK.
WHO CAN BENEFIT Charitable organisations, mostly Jewish groups.
WHAT IS FUNDED General charitable purposes, in practice, mainly Jewish organisations.
SAMPLE GRANTS **Previous beneficiaries have included:** British Friends of Shuut Ami, Children's Hospital Trust Fund, Cometville Limited, Encounter – Jewish Outreach Network, Choshen Mishpat Centre, Gertner Charitable Trust, Hertsmere Jewish Primary School, Jewish Learning Exchange, London Millennium Bikeathon, Manchester Jewish Grammar School, Project Seed, Shaarei Zedek Hospital, Shomrei Hachomot Jerusalem, Yeshiva Ohel Shimon Trust, Yeshiva Shaarei Torah Manchester.
FINANCES Year 2013/14 Income £6,935,250 Grants £3,047,040 Grants to organisations £3,047,040 Assets £5,463,964
TRUSTEES Leopold Noe; Susan Noe; Simon Kanter.
OTHER INFORMATION A separate list of beneficiary organisations can be purchased from the correspondent.
HOW TO APPLY Apply in writing to the correspondent.
WHO TO APPLY TO Robert Chalk, Secretary, F. & C. Reit Asset Management, 5 Wigmore Street, London W1U 1PB *Tel.* 020 7016 3549

## ■ The Racing Foundation

CC NO 1145297   ESTABLISHED 2012
WHERE FUNDING CAN BE GIVEN UK
WHO CAN BENEFIT Charities associated with the UK horse racing and thoroughbred breeding industry. This may include: registered charities; unregistered charities with an annual income of less than £5,000; and charities regulated by another body, such as universities. Organisations that do not work exclusively within the horse racing and thoroughbred breeding industry may be supported if their work is 'of exceptional quality and can be shown to directly impact industry participants'.
WHAT IS FUNDED Social welfare; training and education; racehorse welfare; equine science research, heritage and culture.
WHAT IS NOT FUNDED Work that does not benefit the horse racing and thoroughbred breeding industry in the UK; individuals or causes which will benefit one person; costs of staffing primarily associated with fundraising; religion; gambling addiction work (unless it specifically focuses on participants within the horse racing and thoroughbred industry; retrospective funding; work that is not legally charitable.
TYPE OF GRANT Project costs; core costs; capital projects. This may include funding for overheads and salaries (except for roles primarily associated with fundraising). Multi-year grants, usually up to three years, are considered.
SAMPLE GRANTS New Astley Club (£150,000); National Horseracing Museum (£65,000); University of Edinburgh and University of Glasgow (£60,000 each); Royal Veterinary College (£40,000); Injured Jockeys Fund (£30,000); British Racing School (£24,500); Home Ex-Racehorses Organisation Scheme (£10,000); Thoroughbred Rehabilitation Centre (£8,900); Moorcroft Racehorse Welfare Centre (£3,000).
FINANCES Year 2013 Income £9,461,729 Grants £619,633 Grants to organisations £619,633 Assets £29,805,546
TRUSTEES Roger Weatherby; Kirsten Rausing; Sir Ian Good.
HOW TO APPLY For **all grants applications apart from those for equine science research** there is a two-stage process. Applicants should submit a first stage application using the online form, providing basic details about their organisation. They should also upload their charity's most recent annual report and accounts as well as a short proposal of no more than 600 words. Applicants successful at the first stage will be invited to submit a second stage application. Guidelines, along with dates of application deadlines, are available from the website. For **equine science research applications**, the website states: 'The Racing Foundation works in partnership with the Horserace Betting Levy Board (HBLB) to administer and assess grant applications for equine science research. To make an application, you will need to register as a user of the HBLB's equine grants system. Once registered you will be able to build and submit a grant application form. To ensure that your application is considered for Racing Foundation funding you will need to mark the relevant box on the application summary. Once submitted, your application will be administered by the HBLB's equine grants team. It will be scrutinised by a number of external peer reviewers and evaluated by the HBLB's Veterinary Advisory Committee. The final funding decision will be made by the Racing Foundation's trustees.' A link for the online application system along with application deadline dates and further guidance can be found on the website. For further information, contact Annie Dodd, Grants Manager at the Levy Board on 020 7333 0043 ext. 73 or email equine.grants@hblb.org.uk.
WHO TO APPLY TO Chris Mills, Executive Officer, 75 High Holborn, London WC1V 6LS *Tel.* 0300 321 1873 *email* chris.mills@racingfoundation.co.uk *Website* www.racingfoundation.co.uk

## ■ Racing Welfare

**CC NO** 1084042 **ESTABLISHED** 2000
**WHERE FUNDING CAN BE GIVEN** UK.
**WHO CAN BENEFIT** Organisations that offer services to people who work in, or are retired from, the horse racing industry.
**WHAT IS FUNDED** The welfare of people who work/ have worked in the horse racing industry.
**RANGE OF GRANTS** Up to around £50,000.
**SAMPLE GRANTS** Sports Chaplaincy Offering Resources and Encouragement (SCORE) (£53,000); New Astley Club (£30,000); and British Racing School (£24,000).
**FINANCES** Year 2013 Income £1,490,000 Grants £274,000 Grants to organisations £107,000 Assets £12,553,000
**TRUSTEES** Joey Newton; Baroness Anne Mallalieu; Christopher Foster; Gary Middlebrook; Gavin MacEchern; Nicky Lyon; John Maxse; Simon Clarke; Patrick Russell; Morag Gray.
**OTHER INFORMATION** During the year, grants were awarded to individuals totalling £167,000. The three beneficiary organisations appear to have had a long-standing relationship with the charity.
**HOW TO APPLY** Apply in writing to the correspondent.
**WHO TO APPLY TO** Jan Byrd, Management Accountant, Robin McAlpine House, 20b Park Lane, Newmarket, Suffolk CB8 8QD Tel. 01638 560763 Fax 01638 565240 email info@racingwelfare.co.uk Website www.racingwelfare.co.uk

## ■ The Mr and Mrs Philip Rackham Charitable Trust

**CC NO** 1013844 **ESTABLISHED** 1992
**WHERE FUNDING CAN BE GIVEN** Norfolk.
**WHO CAN BENEFIT** Registered charities
**WHAT IS FUNDED** General charitable purposes.
**WHAT IS NOT FUNDED** Individuals.
**RANGE OF GRANTS** Up to £6,000 but typically £500–£1,000.
**SAMPLE GRANTS** Nelson's Journey and Papworth Hospital Charity (£5,000 each); Samaritans – Norwich (£2,500); The Addington Fund, East Anglian Air Ambulance, Eating Matters and Pregnancy Choices Norfolk (£1,000 each); Aylsham Care Trust, Motor Neurone Disease Association and Suffolk Family Carers (£500 each).
**FINANCES** Year 2012/13 Income £46,213 Grants £35,000 Grants to organisations £35,000 Assets £1,355,706
**TRUSTEES** Neil Sparrow; Charles Barratt; Ann Rush.
**OTHER INFORMATION** The 2012/13 accounts were the latest available at the time of writing. Grants were awarded to 34 organisations during the year.
**HOW TO APPLY** Apply writing to the correspondent.
**WHO TO APPLY TO** Neil Sparrow, Trustee, c/ Birketts LLP, Kingfisher House, 1 Gilders Way, Norwich NR3 1UB Tel. 01603 232300 Fax 01603 230533

## ■ Richard Radcliffe Charitable Trust

**CC NO** 1068930 **ESTABLISHED** 1998
**WHERE FUNDING CAN BE GIVEN** UK.
**WHO CAN BENEFIT** Local and national charitable organisations.
**WHAT IS FUNDED** Organisations supporting: young people to have a better start in life (e.g. by facilitating technical training); people who have a physical disability; people who are severely deaf and blind; hospice care for people who are terminally ill; and nature conservancy.
**TYPE OF GRANT** Mainly recurrent.
**RANGE OF GRANTS** Between £1,000 and £6,000.
**SAMPLE GRANTS** Willen Hospice (£6,000); St Mungo's and St Barnabas Hospice (£4,000 each); Demand Design and Manufacture for Disability and Sense (£3,000 each); Project Street Life (£2,000); Dorset Mind (£1,000).
**FINANCES** Year 2012/13 Income £55,569 Grants £80,000 Grants to organisations £80,000 Assets £1,860,749
**TRUSTEES** Adrian Bell; Penelope Radcliffe; Dr Paul Radcliffe.
**OTHER INFORMATION** At the time of writing (June 2015) these were the latest accounts available for the trust.
**HOW TO APPLY** Apply in writing to the correspondent.
**WHO TO APPLY TO** Dr Paul Radcliffe, Trustee, Boycott House, Welsh Lane, Stowe, Buckingham MK18 5DJ Tel. 01280 813352

## ■ The Radcliffe Trust

**CC NO** 209212 **ESTABLISHED** 1714
**WHERE FUNDING CAN BE GIVEN** UK.
**WHO CAN BENEFIT** Registered or exempt charities; organisations and projects benefitting musicians and those involved in the crafts.
**WHAT IS FUNDED** Grants are made in the areas of music, heritage and crafts. The following information was taken from the trust's helpful website. Music scheme: 'The Radcliffe Trust supports classical music performance and training especially chamber music, composition and music education. Particular interests within music education are music for children and adults with special needs, youth orchestras and projects at secondary and higher levels, including academic research.' Heritage and crafts scheme: 'The Radcliffe Trust supports the development of the skills, knowledge and experience that underpin the UK's traditional cultural heritage and crafts sectors. This includes support for: craft and conservation training; practical projects, particularly those that include a strong training element; strategic and capacity-building projects which demonstrate clear benefits to the sector; Special Needs projects whose emphasis is on skills development. However, the Trust remains committed to flexible, open and inclusive grant-giving and will consider other projects, should they fall broadly within its remit. The Radcliffe Trust wishes to promote standards of excellence through all its support.'
**WHAT IS NOT FUNDED** Retrospective grants; general appeals; endowment funds. Music scheme: operating costs; competitions; capital projects. Heritage and crafts scheme: conference fees or associated costs; projects whose sole or primary aim is about nature conservation; projects that are primarily social or therapeutic in nature.
**RANGE OF GRANTS** Mostly £1,000–£5,000.
**SAMPLE GRANTS** Church Buildings Council (£22,500); University of York (£10,000); Bible Society (£5,000); St Mary's Cathedral Workshop (£3,500); Live Music Now (£3,000); Fitzwilliam Museum (£2,000); British Institute at Ankara (£1,500); Richmond Music Trust (£1,000); Wildlife Trust – South West (£400).
**FINANCES** Year 2013/14 Income £615,083 Grants £422,217 Grants to organisations £422,217 Assets £17,749,079

**TRUSTEES** Felix Warnock; Sir Henry Aubrey-Fletcher; Christopher Butcher; Mary Ann Sieghart; Timothy Wilson; Ellen Schroder; Richard Morrison.

**OTHER INFORMATION** Grants were distributed for the following purposes: music (£153,500); heritage and crafts (£153,000); tercentenary (£113,500); miscellaneous (£2,100).

**HOW TO APPLY** The trustees meet twice yearly to oversee the charity's activities and to make decisions on grants. The trust works with specialist advisers in each of its main sectors of activity: Mrs Sally Carter, Music Adviser and Ms Carole Milner, Heritage and Crafts Adviser. There is also a Music Panel and a Heritage and Crafts Committee which each meet twice a year to consider applications. The day-to-day running of the trust's financial and administrative affairs and processing of grant applications is undertaken by the Trust Partnership. It is advisable to submit an application well in advance of the deadline: Music deadline – 31 January for the June Trustee meeting; 31 August for the December trustee meeting; Heritage and Crafts deadline – 31 January for the June trustee meeting; 31 July for the December trustee meeting. Applications may now only be submitted via the online application form. Visit the trust's website for further details of its schemes.

**WHO TO APPLY TO** Julia Thorne, Correspondent, 6 Trull Farm Buildings, Tetbury, Gloucestershire GL8 8SQ *Tel.* 01285 841900 *email* radcliffe@thetrustpartnership.com *Website* www.theradcliffetrust.org

## ■ The Bishop Radford Trust

**CC NO** 1113562  **ESTABLISHED** 2006

**WHERE FUNDING CAN BE GIVEN** UK.

**WHO CAN BENEFIT** Organisations whose work is conducted according to the doctrines and principles of the Church of England, including churches.

**WHAT IS FUNDED** Church-related projects; the education of priests, future priests and church workers; support of church ministry.

**RANGE OF GRANTS** £500 to £125,000. Most grants were of £15,000 or less.

**SAMPLE GRANTS** Friends of the Anglican Communion Fund (£125,000); Bible Reading Fellowship (£41,500); International Needs (£40,000); Exeter College – Oxford and World Vision (£30,000 each); SAT-7 Trust (£25,000); Viva Network (£20,000); Community of the Resurrection – Mirfield and Wakefield Cathedral (£15,000 each); Arthur Rank Centre and Christian Responsibility in Public Affairs (£10,000); The Quiet Garden Trust (£7,500); Coffee Tots and Wakefield Diocese (£5,000 each); The St Peter and St James Charitable Trust Hospice – Lewes (£1,000); St Mary the Virgin – Goldington (£500).

**FINANCES** *Year* 2013/14 *Income* £845,215 *Grants* £483,879 *Grants to organisations* £483,879 *Assets* £8,989,895

**TRUSTEES** Stephen Green; Janian Green; Suzannah O'Brien; Ruth Dare.

**OTHER INFORMATION** Grants were given for the following purposes: church-related projects (£349,500 in 19 grants); support of church ministry (£109,500 in eight grants); education of priests and other church workers (£25,000 in two grants).

**HOW TO APPLY** Apply in writing to the correspondent.

**WHO TO APPLY TO** Mr D. Marks, Correspondent, Devonshire House, 1 Devonshire Street, London W1W 5DR *Tel.* 020 7304 2000 *email* thebishopradfordtrust@ntlworld.com

## ■ The Ragdoll Foundation

**CC NO** 1078998  **ESTABLISHED** 2000

**WHERE FUNDING CAN BE GIVEN** UK and worldwide.

**WHO CAN BENEFIT** Projects that involve children during their early years, although appropriate projects for older children will be considered.

**WHAT IS FUNDED** Arts projects which develop the power of imaginative responses in children.

**WHAT IS NOT FUNDED** Replacement of statutory funding; work that has already started or will have been completed whilst the application is being considered; promotion of religion; animal welfare charities; vehicles, emergency relief work; general fundraising or marketing appeals; open ended funding arrangements; loans or business advice; charities which are in serious deficit; holidays; any large capital, endowment or widely distributed appeal; specialist schools; school fees for people over 17 years of age; gap year funds.

**FINANCES** *Year* 2013/14 *Income* £2,320,910 *Grants* £0 *Grants to organisations* £0 *Assets* £2,327,645

**TRUSTEES** Katherine Wood; Peter Hollingsworth; Peter Thornton; Anne Wood; Carole Thomson; Regis Cochefert.

**OTHER INFORMATION** The foundation's website states that its philosophy can be summed up using the following quotation from Sylvia Ashton-Warner's book *Teacher*: 'I see the mind of a five-year-old as a volcano with two vents; destructiveness and creativeness. And I can see that to the extent that we widen the creative channel, we atrophy the destructive one'.

**HOW TO APPLY** At the time of writing, the foundation's website stated that it was closed for applications in 2014–2015, during which period it was undergoing a review. Further information on when the application process will reopen will be posted on the website.

**WHO TO APPLY TO** Karen Newell, Development Co-ordinator, 9 Timothy's Bridge Road, Stratford Enterprise Park, Stratford-upon-Avon, Warwickshire CV37 9NQ *Tel.* 01789 404100 *email* info@ragdollfoundation.org.uk *Website* www.ragdollfoundation.org.uk

## ■ The Rainford Trust

**CC NO** 266157  **ESTABLISHED** 1973

**WHERE FUNDING CAN BE GIVEN** Worldwide, with a preference for areas in which Pilkington plc has works and offices, especially St Helens and Merseyside.

**WHO CAN BENEFIT** Charitable and voluntary organisations; individuals.

**WHAT IS FUNDED** The trust's charitable purposes include the relief of poverty, older people, people who are sick, people who have a disability, and people who are unemployed. Support is also given for the advancement of education including the arts, and other purposes such as environmental and conservation projects which have a wide benefit for the community.

**WHAT IS NOT FUNDED** Our research indicates that funding for the arts is restricted to St Helens only. Applications from individuals for grants for educational purposes will be considered only

from applicants who are normally resident in St Helens.
**RANGE OF GRANTS** Mostly between £500 and £2,000, occasionally higher.
**SAMPLE GRANTS** Willowbrook Hospice (£60,000); Clonter Opera (£14,700); The Citadel Arts Centre (£10,000); DEC Philippines Appeal (£5,000); The John Fawcett Foundation UK (£3,000); Rainforest Concern (£2,100); St Helens Open Art Exhibition (£1,900); Lupus UK (£1,500); Breat Cancer Care, National Association for the Relief of Apnoea and The No-Way Trust (£1,000 each) The Friends of Clinkham Wood, Moss Bank and Carr Mill, International Otter Survival Fund and St Aidens Church of England Primary School (£500 each).
**FINANCES** Year 2013/14 Income £229,427 Grants £210,474 Grants to organisations £210,474 Assets £8,726,800
**TRUSTEES** Lady Pilkington; Dr Frances Graham; Annabel Moseley; Hector Pilkington; David Pilkington; Simon Pilkington; Louisa Walker; Dr Clarissa Pilkington; John Pilkington; Andrew Pilkington.
**OTHER INFORMATION** During the year, 82 grants were made by the trust.
**HOW TO APPLY** Application forms are available from the correspondent. Applications should be accompanied by a copy of the latest accounts and cost data on projects for which funding is sought. Applicants may apply at any time. Trustees normally meet in November, March and July. A sub-appeals committee meets about ten times a year and they can either refuse, grant or pass on an application to the trustees.
**WHO TO APPLY TO** William Simm, Executive Officer, c/o Pilkington Group Ltd, Prescot Road, St Helens, Merseyside WA10 3TT Tel. 01744 20574 email rainfordtrust@btconnect.com

■ **The Joseph and Lena Randall Charitable Trust**
**CC NO** 255035　　　**ESTABLISHED** 1967
**WHERE FUNDING CAN BE GIVEN** Worldwide.
**WHO CAN BENEFIT** Registered charities (mainly headquarters organisations).
**WHAT IS FUNDED** Regular support to a selection of preferred charities working to alleviate poverty and hardship, particularly amongst minorities, and initiatives providing medical, educational and cultural facilities.
**WHAT IS NOT FUNDED** See 'How to apply'.
**SAMPLE GRANTS Previous beneficiaries have included:** Cancer Research UK, Community Security Trust, Diabetes UK, Downe House 21st Century Appeal, Holocaust Educational Trust, Jewish Care, Jewish Deaf Association, LPO, LSE Foundation, Motor Neurone Disease Association, ROH Foundation and Transplant Trust.
**FINANCES** Year 2013/14 Income £73,511 Grants £96,146 Grants to organisations £96,146 Assets £2,070,733
**TRUSTEE** Rofrano Trustee Services Ltd.
**HOW TO APPLY** The 2013/14 annual report and accounts stated: 'The Trustee received many appeals during the year, and a number of new charities have received the benefit of our philanthropy for the first time. All appeals are vetted but we desist from replying in the case of circular letters, not individually signed, appeals from individuals that are not accredited and where letters are sent insufficiently franked.'
**WHO TO APPLY TO** Mr David Anthony Randall, Correspondent, Europa Residence, Place des Moulins, Monte-Carlo, Monaco MC98 000 Tel. 00377 9350 0382 email rofrano.jlrct@hotmail.fr

■ **The Rank Foundation Limited**
**CC NO** 276976　　　**ESTABLISHED** 1953
**WHERE FUNDING CAN BE GIVEN** UK.
**WHO CAN BENEFIT** Registered charities. Applications for grants from the Small Appeals programme are only accepted from those charities with an annual income of less than £500,000.
**WHAT IS FUNDED** The foundation concentrates its grant-making on: encouraging and developing leadership amongst young people; supporting disadvantaged young people and those frail or lonely through old age or disability; and promoting the understanding of Christianity from a perspective that respects those of all faiths and those of none. There are four funding streams: Youth Projects; Community Care Projects; Special Projects and Small Appeals. Unsolicited applications are now only accepted for grants from the Small Appeals stream towards projects costed at less than £1 million. There are two types of grants made: the Small Appeals Capital Grant, towards capital costs such as building work or the purchase of equipment; and the Small Appeals Short Break Application towards a short term activity such as a holiday for disadvantaged young people.
**WHAT IS NOT FUNDED** Non-registered charities. Appeals from individuals or appeals from registered charities on behalf of named individuals will not be considered; neither will appeals from overseas or from UK-based organisations where the object of the appeal is overseas. In an endeavour to contain the calls made upon the foundation to a realistic level, the directors have continued with their policy of not, in general, making grants to projects involved with: agriculture and farming; cathedrals and churches (except where community facilities form an integral part of the appeal); cultural projects; advocacy services; university/school building and bursary funds; medical research. Unsolicited appeals are extremely unlikely to attract a grant for salaries, general running costs or major capital projects.
**TYPE OF GRANT** Small grants are largely one-off.
**RANGE OF GRANTS** Grants from the Small Appeals programme do not exceed £7,500.
**SAMPLE GRANTS** Help the Hospices (£100,000); Winston Churchill Memorial Trust (£82,000); Youth Work in Sport (£66,000); City Year London (£50,000); Oban Youth Cafe (£36,500); Banbury Youth Housing (£31,000); Mersey Youth Support Trust, Royal British Legion Industries and Women's Aid – Berks and Bucks (£30,000 each); Belfast Activity Centre (£28,500); Wellingborough Youth Project (£28,000); Deaf Hill Ward, Greenbank Community Church and Prisoners Abroad (£25,000 each).
**FINANCES** Year 2013 Income £2,275,000 Grants £7,380,000 Grants to organisations £7,380,000 Assets £214,725,000
**TRUSTEES** Lord St Aldwyn; James Cave; Andrew Cowan; Mark Davies; Joey Newton; Lucinda Onslow; Lord Shuttleworth; Hon. Caroline Twiston-Davies; Johanna Ropner; Rose Fitzpatrick; Daniel Simon; Nicholas Buxton; Jason Chaffer; William Wyatt; Andrew Fleming.
**HOW TO APPLY** Unsolicited applications are only accepted for grants from the 'Small Appeals' funding stream. Two online application forms are available: the Small Appeals Capital Grant

Application and the Small Appeals Short Break Application. Further criteria and guidelines are available from on the foundation's website.

**WHO TO APPLY TO** Rosamond McNulty, Grants Administrator, 12 Warwick Square, London SW1V 2AA *Tel.* 020 7834 7731 *email* rosamond.mcnulty@rankfoundation.co.uk *Website* www.rankfoundation.com

## ■ The Joseph Rank Trust

**CC NO** 1093844      **ESTABLISHED** 1929
**WHERE FUNDING CAN BE GIVEN** Unrestricted. In practice, UK.
**WHO CAN BENEFIT** Registered charities.
**WHAT IS FUNDED** The adaptation of Methodist Church properties with a view to providing improved facilities for use both by the church itself and in its work in the community in which it is based. Projects that demonstrate a Christian approach to the practical, educational and spiritual needs of people
**WHAT IS NOT FUNDED** Delayed church maintenance (e.g. roof repairs); purchase of or restoration of stained glass or church bells; loans; overseas projects; organ appeals; completed capital projects; the repayment of loans; individuals; educational bursaries; medical research; gap years; book publishing; intern placements; audio and sound equipment; the benefit of the hospice movement; individual hospices; social enterprises that have no charitable status; the provision of musical instruments; CICs; organisations registered under the Industrial and Provident Societies Act 1965; the benefit of named individuals.
**TYPE OF GRANT** One-off and recurring.
**RANGE OF GRANTS** £5,000 to £50,000.
**SAMPLE GRANTS** The Museum of Methodism (£50,000); Arun Community Church (£48,000); 24–7 Prayer and Caring for Life (£45,000 each); The Big House – Belfast (£39,000); Christian Medical Fellowship and Parity for Disability (£30,000 each); Sir William Powell'£50,000s Almshouses (£25,000); The Torch Trust for the Blind (£16,000); Prison and Hospital Chaplaincy Committee and St Nicholas – Poplar (£10,000 each); SEARCH – Hull and St Michael's Youth Project – Hull (£6,000 each); Hexham Trinity Methodist Church (£9,000); Lurgan High Street Methodist Church (£5,000).
**FINANCES** *Year* 2013 *Income* £2,620,000 *Grants* £2,381,940 *Grants to organisations* £2,381,940 *Assets* £82,881,000
**TRUSTEES** The Revd David Cruise; Revd Darren Holland; Revd Carole Holmes; The Very Revd John Irvine; Gay Moon; James Rank; Tony Reddall; Michael Shortt; Sue Warner.
**HOW TO APPLY** Ongoing commitments, combined with the fact that the trustees are taking an increasingly active role in identifying projects to support, means that uncommitted funds are limited. The website states: 'Unsolicited appeals are selected for consideration by the Trustees that demonstrate, in their view, a Christian approach to the practical, educational and spiritual needs of people.' If applicants consider that their work might fall within the areas of interest of the trust the following basic information is required: charity name and charity registration number; an outline of the project for which funding is sought; a budget and costings for the life time of the project; details of the amount already raised, or irrevocably committed, towards the target; full details of grant applications made to other external funders; details of the amount committed from your own resources; and the contact name, email and telephone number. Copies of your organisation's most recent monthly management accounts and most recent audited annual report and accounts must be enclosed. The essential details of a project must be set out on no more than two sides of A4 paper, with more detailed information being presented in the form of appendices. Applications must be sent in hard copy and not by email. Applications from Methodist churches require further information, which is detailed on the website. The trustees usually meet quarterly. All appeals are acknowledged and applicants are advised that if they do not receive a reply by a specified date it has not been possible for the trustees to make a grant.
**WHO TO APPLY TO** Dr John Higgs, Secretary, Worth Corner, Turners Hill Road, Crawley RH10 7SL *Tel.* 01293 873947 *email* secretary@ranktrust.org *Website* www.ranktrust.org

## ■ Ranworth Trust

**CC NO** 292633      **ESTABLISHED** 1985
**WHERE FUNDING CAN BE GIVEN** UK and financially developing countries, with a preference for East Norfolk.
**WHO CAN BENEFIT** Registered charities.
**WHAT IS FUNDED** Local charities promoting care and education of the community in East Norfolk; national charities working in the area of medical research into curable illnesses; and international charities with a 'long term commitment in providing technological initiative and support'.
**WHAT IS NOT FUNDED** Non-registered charities.
**RANGE OF GRANTS** £1,000 to £50,000.
**SAMPLE GRANTS** Jubilee Sailing Trust (£50,000); Practical Action (£15,000); Cancer Research UK and WaterAid (£12,000 each); Sightsavers (£10,000); Acle High School (£9,800); Hope and Homes for Children and Norfolk Wildlife Trust (£5,000 each); IBBTC Portsmouth (£4,000); East Anglia's Children's Hospices (£3,500); Ranworth Parochial Church Council (£2,500); Coeliac Society (£2,000); East Anglian Arts Foundation and Hearing Dogs for Deaf People (£1,000 each).
**FINANCES** *Year* 2013/14 *Income* £178,191 *Grants* £185,300 *Grants to organisations* £185,300 *Assets* £4,715,294
**TRUSTEES** The Hon. Jacquetta Cator; Charles Cator; Mark Cator.
**OTHER INFORMATION** In 2010 a grant of £350,000 was given to Norfolk Community Foundation to establish 'The Ranworth Grassroots Fund'. The aim of the fund is to support a wide range of charitable, voluntary and community activities across Norfolk.
**HOW TO APPLY** At the time of writing (May 2015), the trust's website stated: 'The trustees are not considering any new applications until 2016'. Refer to the website for updates.
**WHO TO APPLY TO** Jacquetta Cator, Trustee, The Old House, Ranworth, Norwich NR13 6HS *Website* www.ranworthtrust.org.uk

## ■ The Rashbass Family Trust

**CC NO** 1135961      **ESTABLISHED** 2010
**WHERE FUNDING CAN BE GIVEN** Undefined. In practice the Barnet district of London.
**WHO CAN BENEFIT** Organisations and individuals.
**WHAT IS FUNDED** General charitable purposes, with a focus on poverty, education, religion, health and

**735**

the relief in need of people who are disadvantaged.
**SAMPLE GRANTS** A list of specific beneficiaries was not included in the trust's annual report and accounts.
**FINANCES** Year 2013/14 Income £214,049 Grants £218,515 Grants to organisations £218,515 Assets £64,494
**TRUSTEES** Jacqueline Rashbass; Andrew Rashbass.
**OTHER INFORMATION** All grants in 2013/14 were made to organisations for the following causes: health (£101,000); religion (£91,000); education (£19,100); relief in need (£3,100); poverty (£2,900); other (£1,700).
**HOW TO APPLY** Apply in writing to the correspondent.
**WHO TO APPLY TO** Jacqueline Rashbass, Trustee, 17 Wykeham Road, London NW4 2TB Tel. 07974 151494 email jacqueline@rashbass.com

## ■ The Ratcliff Foundation
**CC NO** 222441    **ESTABLISHED** 1959
**WHERE FUNDING CAN BE GIVEN** UK, with a preference for local charities in the Midlands and North Wales.
**WHO CAN BENEFIT** Any organisation that has charitable status for tax purposes.
**WHAT IS FUNDED** General charitable purposes.
**WHAT IS NOT FUNDED** Individuals.
**RANGE OF GRANTS** £2,000–£10,000, though most are for £5,000 or less.
**SAMPLE GRANTS** Bletchley Park Trust and Cancer Research UK – Kemerton Branch (£10,000 each); St David's Hospice (£6,000); Cancer Prevention and Education Society and the Multiple Births Foundation (£5,500); Birmingham Boys' and Girls' Union – Woodlands Adventure (£4,500 each); Harbury Village Hall Development Trust (£3,600); St Nicholas Church – Kemerton (£2,500); Birmingham and Black Country Wildlife Trust, Manor Green Primary School Fund Trust and The Prince's Trust (£3,000 each); Avoncroft Museum of Historic Buildings, Colwyn Choral Society, Home Start UK and the Soil Association (£2,000 each).
**FINANCES** Year 2013/14 Income £216,338 Grants £201,200 Grants to organisations £201,200 Assets £3,791,300
**TRUSTEES** David Ratcliff, Chair; Edward Ratcliff; Carolyn Ratcliff; Gillian Thorpe; Michael Fea; Christopher Gupwell.
**HOW TO APPLY** Apply in writing to the correspondent.
**WHO TO APPLY TO** Christopher Gupwell, Secretary and Trustee, Woodlands, Earls Common Road, Stock Green, Redditch B96 6TB Tel. 01386 792116 email chris.gupwell@btinternet.com

## ■ The E. L. Rathbone Charitable Trust
**CC NO** 233240    **ESTABLISHED** 1921
**WHERE FUNDING CAN BE GIVEN** UK, with a strong preference for Merseyside.
**WHO CAN BENEFIT** Registered charities. Preference is given to charities that the trust has special interest in, knowledge of, or association with.
**WHAT IS FUNDED** General charitable purposes.
**WHAT IS NOT FUNDED** Individuals seeking support for second degrees.
**RANGE OF GRANTS** £650–£10,200. The majority of grants are of up to £2,000.
**SAMPLE GRANTS** Sheila Kay Fund (£10,200); Bootle YMCA Youth Centre – Park Street and Families Fighting for Justice (£2,000 each); Home-Start Liverpool (£1,500); Halebank Youth Club (£1,200); Orrell Park and District Community Association and Wirral Toy Library (£1,000 each); Pull Up A Chair Productions (£750).
**FINANCES** Year 2013/14 Income £80,969 Grants £72,940 Grants to organisations £72,940 Assets £2,298,814
**TRUSTEES** Susan Rathbone; Caroline Rathbone; R. S. Rathbone; Megan Rathbone.
**OTHER INFORMATION** Grants were made to 44 organisations during the year. Grants may also be made in support of individuals.
**HOW TO APPLY** Apply in writing to the correspondent.
**WHO TO APPLY TO** Liese Van Alwon, Secretary, 546 Warrington Road, Rainhill, Prescot, Merseyside L35 4LZ Tel. 0151 430 7914 email elrathbonetrust@gmail.com

## ■ The Eleanor Rathbone Charitable Trust
**CC NO** 233241    **ESTABLISHED** 1947
**WHERE FUNDING CAN BE GIVEN** UK, with the major allocation for Merseyside; also international projects (Africa, the Indian Sub-Continent, plus exceptionally Iraq and Palestine).
**WHO CAN BENEFIT** Organisations benefitting general charitable projects in Merseyside; women; and unpopular and neglected causes.
**WHAT IS FUNDED** (1) Merseyside: charities and projects which are based in or delivered in Merseyside (particularly the more deprived areas) and meet the funding priorities. (2) Holiday Fund: small grants for holidays and outings provided by charities helping disadvantaged children and adults from Merseyside. (3) National: charities and projects which meet the priorities and have a nationwide reach. (4) International: projects in sub-Saharan Africa, the Indian sub-continent and exceptionally Iran, Palestine and Haiti. Projects must be sponsored and monitored by a UK-registered charity and do one or more of the following: benefit women or orphaned children; demonstrate local involvement in scoping and delivery; aim to repair the damage in countries recently ravaged by international or civil war; deliver clean water and sanitation.
**WHAT IS NOT FUNDED** Activities which are the responsibility of a statutory body; individuals; medical research; gap year projects; lobbying or campaigning organisations; organisations that primarily exist to promote a religion, church or sect; local charities based outside Merseyside.
**TYPE OF GRANT** Most donations are on a one-off basis, although requests for commitments over two or more years are considered.
**RANGE OF GRANTS** £100–£5,000 for Merseyside charities, £1,000 to £3,000 for national and international charities. Occasionally higher.
**SAMPLE GRANTS** Asylum Link Merseyside; British Red Cross; Dream Holidays; FareShare; Gingerbread; Merseyside Domestic Violence Service; Old Swan Youth Club; Reprieve; Sahir House; Street Child Africa; Tate Liverpool; The Whitechapel Centre; Tomorrow's Women Wirral; World in Need.
**FINANCES** Year 2013/14 Income £303,641 Grants £387,827 Grants to organisations £387,827 Assets £9,116,473
**TRUSTEES** William Rathbone; Jenny Rathbone; Andrew Rathbone; Angela Morgan; Mark Rathbone.

**OTHER INFORMATION** During the year, 49% of the grant total was awarded to Merseyside-based charities.

**HOW TO APPLY** Applications should be made using the online form, additional supporting documents are listed on the website and should be sent by post. Receipt of applications and unsuccessful applications are not usually acknowledged, though applicants may request acknowledgement by email. Applications are accepted at any time and are considered at trustees' meetings held three times a year.

**WHO TO APPLY TO** Liese van Alwon, Correspondent, 546 Warrington Road, Rainhill, Merseyside L35 4LZ *Tel.* 0151 430 7914 *email* eleanorrathbonetrust@gmail.com *Website* www.eleanorrathbonetrust.org.uk

## ■ The Sigrid Rausing Trust

**CC NO** 1046769   **ESTABLISHED** 1995
**WHERE FUNDING CAN BE GIVEN** UK and overseas.
**WHO CAN BENEFIT** Charitable or voluntary organisations.
**WHAT IS FUNDED** Advocacy, research and litigation; detention, torture and death penalty; human rights defenders; free expression; transitional justice; women's rights; LGBTI rights; xenophobia and intolerance; transparency and accountability.
**WHAT IS NOT FUNDED** Individuals; faith-based groups.
**TYPE OF GRANT** One-year grants; multi-year grants.
**SAMPLE GRANTS** African Centre for Justice and Peace Studies; Coalition for Sexual and Bodily Rights in Muslim Societies; Human Rights First; International Consortium of Investigative Journalists; Liberty; Mesoamerican Initiative for Women Human Rights Defenders; PINK Armenia; Refugee Action; Reporters Without Borders; Reprieve; Sisma Mujer; Stonewall; University of Cape Town Legal Clinic; University of York.
**FINANCES** *Year* 2013 *Income* £23,680,665 *Grants* £19,187,000 *Grants to organisations* £19,187,000 *Assets* £7,442,729
**TRUSTEES** Dr Sigrid Rausing; Andrew Puddephatt; Geoff Budlender; Jonathan Cooper; Margo Picken.
**OTHER INFORMATION** Main grants accounted for £19.1 million of the grant total and smaller grants a further £85,000.
**HOW TO APPLY** The trust does not accept unsolicited applications for funding, but rather invites applications from organisations that it has proactively identified. The trust's website does, however, offer the following advice: If you have not been invited to apply, but wish to let the trust know about your work, you can send an email describing your organisation to research@srtrust.org. Emails are reviewed regularly. Programme directors occasionally look for new organisations in particular areas. In the event of this, details are posted on the 'application process' page on the trust's website.
**WHO TO APPLY TO** Sheetal Patel, Correspondent, 12 Penzance Place, London W11 4PA *Tel.* 020 7313 7727 *email* info@srtrust.org *Website* www.sigrid-rausing-trust.org

## ■ The Ravensdale Trust

**CC NO** 265165   **ESTABLISHED** 1973
**WHERE FUNDING CAN BE GIVEN** Merseyside, particularly St Helens.
**WHO CAN BENEFIT** Registered charities.
**WHAT IS FUNDED** General charitable causes, particularly young people, older people and disadvantaged groups.
**WHAT IS NOT FUNDED** Individuals.
**TYPE OF GRANT** One-off and recurrent.
**RANGE OF GRANTS** Generally between £1,000 and £3,000, though larger grants are occasionally made from the trust's capital.
**SAMPLE GRANTS** Willowbrook Hospice (£50,000); Royal Liverpool Philharmonic (£25,000); Friends of Fairfield (£10,000); United Reformed Church St Helens (£3,000); Liverpool Hope University (£2,500); Arena Options Ltd, St Helens Girl Guide Association, Two Rivers Festival – Birkenhead School, and YMCA St Helens (£2,000 each); Brainwave, Care and Respite Support Services, National Museums Liverpool and Venture Arts (£1,000 each); NW Legal Support Trust (£500).
**FINANCES** *Year* 2013/14 *Income* £66,124 *Grants* £208,684 *Grants to organisations* £208,684 *Assets* £1,266,757
**TRUSTEES** Jane Fagan; Mark Feeny; Karen Toseland.
**HOW TO APPLY** Apply in writing to the correspondent. There is no application form and no acknowledgement of applications is made. Grants are usually paid in May and October.
**WHO TO APPLY TO** Jane Fagan, Trustee, c/o Brabners Chaffe Street, Horton House, Exchange Flags, Liverpool L2 3YL *Tel.* 0151 600 3000 *email* jane.fagan@brabners.com

## ■ The Rayden Charitable Trust

**CC NO** 294446   **ESTABLISHED** 1985
**WHERE FUNDING CAN BE GIVEN** UK.
**WHO CAN BENEFIT** Jewish organisations.
**WHAT IS FUNDED** The advancement of the Orthodox Jewish faith; the relief of poverty; general charitable purposes.
**SAMPLE GRANTS** **Previous beneficiaries have included:** NWJDS (£7,000); Or Chadash (£6,500); Yesodey Hatorah (£3,000); Holocaust Education and Jewish Care (£2,500); Central London Mikveh and CTN Jewish Life (£1,000 each).
**FINANCES** *Year* 2013/14 *Income* £31,030 *Grants* £28,890 *Grants to organisations* £28,890 *Assets* £423
**TRUSTEES** Clive Rayden; Paul Rayden.
**HOW TO APPLY** Apply in writing to the correspondent.
**WHO TO APPLY TO** The Trustees, c/o Beavis Morgan LLP, 82 St John Street, London EC1M 4JN *Tel.* 020 7417 0417 *email* clive.rayden@rcpgroup.co.uk

## ■ The Roger Raymond Charitable Trust

**CC NO** 262217   **ESTABLISHED** 1971
**WHERE FUNDING CAN BE GIVEN** UK (and very occasionally large, well-known overseas organisations).
**WHO CAN BENEFIT** Mainly headquarters of organisations. Overseas grants are generally only made to large, well-known organisations (such as Sight Savers International and UNICEF).
**WHAT IS FUNDED** General charitable purposes.
**TYPE OF GRANT** One-off and recurrent.
**RANGE OF GRANTS** Up to £4,200.
**SAMPLE GRANTS** Bloxham School (£142,500); Tring Park School (£4,300); African Child Trust and Nanyuki Children's Home Charitable Trust (£2,000 each); RNLI (£1,300).

FINANCES Year 2013/14 Income £517,162 Grants £158,395 Grants to organisations £158,395 Assets £12,635,819
TRUSTEES Russell Pullen; Michael Raymond; Alisdair Kruger Thomson.
OTHER INFORMATION The majority of support given each year by the trust is to Bloxham School. During the year, grants of less than £1,200 totalled £6,200.
HOW TO APPLY The trust has stated that applications are considered throughout the year, although funds are not always available.
WHO TO APPLY TO Russell Pullen, Trustee, Suttondene, 17 The South Border, Purley, Surrey CR8 3LL Tel. 020 8660 9133 email russell@pullen.cix.co.uk

## ■ The Rayne Foundation
CC NO 216291         ESTABLISHED 1962
WHERE FUNDING CAN BE GIVEN UK.
WHO CAN BENEFIT Registered charities.
WHAT IS FUNDED Health and medicine; education; social welfare; the arts. Under these four headings the foundation encourages applications which apply to its evolving list of areas of special interest: art in deprived communities; developing numeracy skills; improved quality of life for older people; improved palliative care in the community. If your work does not fit into one of these areas but it fits with the foundation's guiding principles then you may still submit an application.
WHAT IS NOT FUNDED Individuals; organisations operating outside the UK; programmes that have already been completed; repayment of debts; organisations that have applied within the last 12 months; funding for endowments; general appeals.
TYPE OF GRANT Salaries and all types of project costs plus a reasonable contribution to overheads (there is no fixed percentage); general running or core costs (normally for a maximum of three years); capital costs of buildings and equipment (unless specifically stated in certain sectors); 'seed corn' projects which are likely to attract other funding, if successful.
RANGE OF GRANTS Up to £75,000. The average grant was £21,500.
SAMPLE GRANTS Previous beneficiaries have included: Kenilworth Children's Centre and Nursery School (£60,000); Emmaus UK (£50,000); Leap Confronting Conflict (£40,000); Turner Contemporary (£30,000); Youth Dementia UK (£21,000); Pro Contact Expert Services (£15,000); ArtsEkta (£12,000); Stonewall Equality Limited (£10,000); London International Festival of Theatre (£5,000); North Derbyshire Stroke Support Group (£4,000); and Dance Umbrella (£3,000).
FINANCES Year 2013/14 Grants £1,268,073 Grants to organisations £1,268,073 Assets £95,660,382
TRUSTEES Hon Robert Rayne; Lord Moser; Lady Jane Rayne; Prof. Dame Margaret Turner-Warwick; Prof. Sir Anthony Newman Taylor; Hon. Natasha Rayne; Sir Emyr Jones Parry.
OTHER INFORMATION In 2013/14 from 766 applications received 59 were successful.
HOW TO APPLY Applying for a grant is a two-stage process, which usually takes around three to four months to complete but may take longer. At Stage One the application form, which is available to download from the website, should be completed and submitted by email to applications@raynefoundation.org.uk. An automatic email acknowledgment will be sent and you will receive a decision within one month, also by email. If it is not possible for you to submit the application by email, you should contact the correspondent by telephone. Unfortunately, the foundation cannot provide feedback at this stage. Applicants who are successful at Stage One will be invited to submit a Stage Two application within one month. Trustees usually meet quarterly.
WHO TO APPLY TO Morin Carew, Grants Administrator, 100 George Street, London W1U 8NU Tel. 020 7487 9656 email info@raynefoundation.org.uk Website www.raynefoundation.org.uk

## ■ The Rayne Trust
CC NO 207392         ESTABLISHED 1958
WHERE FUNDING CAN BE GIVEN UK and Israel.
WHO CAN BENEFIT Registered charities.
WHAT IS FUNDED Grants are made in Israel to address Jewish-Arab relations and towards improving the mental health of people who are disadvantaged. UK organisations which of a particular interest to a trustee and are approved by the trust are also supported.
SAMPLE GRANTS Malvern College (£100,000); JW3 – Jewish Community Centre London and World Jewish Relief (£50,000 each); Chicken Shed Theatre Trust (£25,000); Hadassah Medical Hospital (£20,000); MEET – Middle East Education through Technology, Oak Haven Hospice Trust and University of Southampton (£10,000 each); Jerusalem Intercultural Centre (£8,100).
FINANCES Year 2013/14 Income £808,395 Grants £492,842 Grants to organisations £492,842 Assets £30,296,236
TRUSTEES Lady Jane Rayne; Robert Rayne; Damian Rayne.
OTHER INFORMATION Grants to UK organisations amounted to £367,500, and to organisations in Israel £125,500.
HOW TO APPLY It would appear that only organisations based in Israel can apply directly for a grant from the trust. UK-based organisations can, however, apply to The Rayne Foundation (Charity Commission no. 216291), an associated but distinct charity, which has its own areas of interest. More information can be found in the foundation's entry and on its website.
WHO TO APPLY TO The Trustees, 100 George Street, London W1U 8NU email info@raynefoundation.org.uk Website www.raynefoundation.org.uk/our-work

## ■ The John Rayner Charitable Trust
CC NO 802363         ESTABLISHED 1989
WHERE FUNDING CAN BE GIVEN England, with some preference for Merseyside and Wiltshire.
WHO CAN BENEFIT Registered charities. There is a preference for small charities in the UK to receive the largest donations.
WHAT IS FUNDED General charitable purposes, including health and disability causes, children and older people, community projects, carers, work with young people, medical research and development and the arts. The annual report for 2013/14 notes that grants 'are often made to medical and medical research charities'.

**WHAT IS NOT FUNDED** Individuals; non-registered charities.
**TYPE OF GRANT** One-off and recurrent grants; capital and core cost; unrestricted funding.
**RANGE OF GRANTS** Up to £3,000.
**SAMPLE GRANTS** Marie Curie Cancer Care, Motability, Surrey University – Faculty of Medical Science and WheelPower (£3,000 each); Carers Trust, Combat Stress and Only Connect (£2,000 each); Dressability, Swindon Sea Cadet Unit and Wiltshire Bobby Van Trust (£1,000 each).
**FINANCES** Year 2013/14 Income £25,792 Grants £40,000 Grants to organisations £40,000 Assets £849,505
**TRUSTEES** Juliet Wilkinson; Dr Jonathan Rayner; Louise McNeilage.
**OTHER INFORMATION** The accounts note: 'The trustees feel that the smaller charities with a lower public profile will often benefit from grants of £1,000 to £3,000 more than the larger well-known and supported charities.' There were 17 awards, broken down as follows: general (£12,000); children (£10,000); disability and medical (£9,000 each).
**HOW TO APPLY** Applications may be made in writing to the correspondent by 31 January each year. The trustees meet to allocate donations in February/March. Only successful applicants will be contacted. Email applications are **not** accepted.
**WHO TO APPLY TO** Juliet Wilkinson, Trustee, Manor Farmhouse, Church Street, Great Bedwyn, Marlborough, Wiltshire SN8 3PE *Tel.* 01672 870362 *email* raynertrust@hotmail.co.uk

## ■ The Sir James Reckitt Charity
**CC NO** 225356   **ESTABLISHED** 1921
**WHERE FUNDING CAN BE GIVEN** Hull and the East Riding of Yorkshire, UK and, occasionally, Red Cross or Quaker work overseas.
**WHO CAN BENEFIT** Community-based groups and projects within the city of Hull and the county of East Yorkshire; Quaker organisations; national and regional charities whose work is of a social, medical, educational or environmental nature, particularly if this benefits Hull or East Yorkshire. Also: individuals and groups from Hull or East Yorkshire seeking experience through voluntary work abroad, residential visits, scouting, guiding or sail training; individuals and families resident in Hull or East Yorkshire who are in need and who are supported by an agency such as social services (these cases are dealt with by the Consortium of Grant Giving Trusts (Hull and East Yorkshire) of which the charity is a member).
**WHAT IS FUNDED** General charitable purposes, focusing on: children and young people; education; older people; environment; medical causes; and social work. There is a particular preference for causes benefitting the areas of Kingston upon Hull, the East Riding of Yorkshire and the people who live there, and Quaker causes.
**WHAT IS NOT FUNDED** Grants are normally made only to registered charities. Local organisations outside the Hull area are not supported, unless their work has regional implications. Grants are not normally made to individuals other than Quakers and residents of Hull and the East Riding of Yorkshire. Support is not given to causes of a warlike or political nature. No replacement of statutory funding or activities which collect funds to be passed on to other organisations, charities or individuals.
**TYPE OF GRANT** Start-up and core costs; purchase of equipment and materials; building improvements; training costs; project development costs.
**RANGE OF GRANTS** The majority of grants are between £500 and £5,000 though larger applications may be considered, especially for organisations with which the foundation already has links.
**SAMPLE GRANTS** Britain Yearly Meeting (£60,000 in three grants); North Humberside Hospice – Dove House (£40,000 in three grants); Sidcot School (£39,500 in three grants); The Retreat – York (£27,000 in two grants); Woodbrooke Quaker Study Centre (£15,000); Friends of the Dyslexia Institute (£8,000); KIDS Yorkshire and Humber (£7,500 in two grants); RAPT Rehabilitation of Addicted Prisoners Trust (£6,000); Hull and E R Institute for the Blind (£5,500); Age UK Hull (£5,000); Farm Africa (£4,000); Bath Institute of Medical Engineering (£3,500); Bricknell Live at Home Scheme and Canine Partners for Independence (£3,000 each); Field Studies Council (£2,500); Duke of Edinburgh Award Schem – Hull, Hull Children's Adventure Society, Hull Rape Crisis and Sexual Abuse and Independent Panel for Special Education (£2,000 each).
**FINANCES** Year 2013 Income £1,263,455 Grants £1,318,047 Grants to organisations £1,236,087 Assets £35,237,419
**TRUSTEES** William Upton; James Holt; Robert Gibson; Caroline Jennings; Philip Holt; Robin Upton; Sarah Craven; Charles Maxted; Simon James Upton; Simon Edward Upton; James Marshall; Edward Upton; Rebecca Holt; Dr Karina Upton; Andrew Palfreman; James Atherton.
**PUBLICATIONS** A History of the Sir James Reckitt Charity 1921–1979 by B N Reckitt; A History of the Sir James Reckitt Charity 1921–1999 by G M Atherton.
**OTHER INFORMATION** Each year, more than 50% of the charity's grant-making is distributed for the benefit of Kingston upon Hull, the East Riding of Yorkshire and their inhabitants. In 2013/14 289 grants were made to individuals totalling £82,000 for social welfare purposes. During the year, 91 grants of less than £2,000 were made amounting to £84,500.
**HOW TO APPLY** Apply in writing to the correspondent. The application should include the following key points: the name and address of your organisation; telephone number and email address; the nature of your organisation; its structure, aims, who it serves, and its links with other agencies and networks; the project or funding need – what is the grant to be used for and who will benefit from it; when the funding is required – the date of the project or event; the bank account payee name of your organisation; any links to the Hull and East Yorkshire region, or the Quakers (which together are the charity's funding priorities); a copy of your latest annual report and accounts or equivalent. Applications are measured against the charity's guidelines and decisions are taken at a twice-yearly meeting of trustees in May and October. Applications should be submitted by 31 March and 30 September respectively.
**WHO TO APPLY TO** James McGlashan, Correspondent, 7 Derrymore Road, Willerby, Hull, East Yorkshire HU10 6ES *Tel.* 01482 655861 *email* charity@thesirjamesreckittcharity.org.uk *Website* www.thesirjamesreckittcharity.org.uk

## ■ Eva Reckitt Trust Fund

**CC NO** 210563     **ESTABLISHED** 1940
**WHERE FUNDING CAN BE GIVEN** UK and overseas.
**WHO CAN BENEFIT** Charitable organisations.
**WHAT IS FUNDED** Social welfare; relief in need; victims of war and refugees; education and training; research of problems affecting poor people; homelessness; disadvantaged or oppressed people; overseas aid. The charity 'provides grants worldwide to movements who work for the education and betterment of the poor, undertake research into problems of the poor, provide relief of poverty and distress amongst persons who suffer as the result of international or industrial unrest, political or legal injustice, tyranny, oppression or persecution or who provide encouragement for the betterment and welfare of the poor'.
**WHAT IS NOT FUNDED** Individuals (although individual cases may be supported through other charities which are able to monitor the use of the funds).
**RANGE OF GRANTS** £500–£3,000
**SAMPLE GRANTS** Centrepoint (£3,000); Seed (£2,900); Navjyoti India Foundation (£2,500); Assnable Association (£2,000); Helen Bamber Foundation (£1,500); Children of the Andes and St John of Jerusalem Eye Hospital Group (£1,000 each); ActionAid (£800); Erinmope Management Committee (£500).
**FINANCES** Year 2013 Income £42,478 Grants £35,692 Grants to organisations £35,692 Assets £718,889
**TRUSTEES** Anna Bunney; Meg Whittaker; David Birch; Diana Holliday.
**OTHER INFORMATION** There were 33 grants awarded.
**HOW TO APPLY** Applications may be made in writing to the correspondent.
**WHO TO APPLY TO** David Birch, Trustee, 44 Hambidge Lane, Lechlade, Gloucestershire GL7 3BL email eva.reckitt.trust@gmail.com

## ■ Red Hill Charitable Trust

**CC NO** 307891     **ESTABLISHED** 1997
**WHERE FUNDING CAN BE GIVEN** South East England is defined as East Anglia, London and Home Counties west to Hampshire.
**WHO CAN BENEFIT** Charitable organisations.
**WHAT IS FUNDED** The education and training/access to education and training of children and young people under the age of 25 who have emotional and behavioural problems.
**WHAT IS NOT FUNDED** Individuals; research projects (generally); causes relating to medical need or social deprivation.
**TYPE OF GRANT** The trustees can only commit to making grants for a year at a time.
**RANGE OF GRANTS** Generally £1,000–£5,000.
**SAMPLE GRANTS** Hampshire Autistic Society (£6,300); Crossroads Care West Kent (£5,600); The Matthew Project (£5,000); Homewood School (£4,000); Arts Depot Trust (£3,300); Young Vic Theatre (£3,200); Youth and Families (£3,000); See Saw (£2,500); Music Well (£2,000); Tall Ships (£1,500); Fordingbridge Infant School (£700).
**FINANCES** Year 2013/14 Income £66,632 Grants £86,546 Grants to organisations £86,546 Assets £2,844,301
**TRUSTEES** Antony Bunting; Dr David Wilson; Kevin Hall; Will Mather; Bernard Head; Roger Barton; Bob Law; John Moore; Michael Startup; Jenny Whittle.
**HOW TO APPLY** Application forms are available from the trust's website, which should be completed and emailed to the trust. The trustees hold meetings twice yearly, in early March and early October. Applications should reach the correspondent at the beginning of the previous month to be sure of being considered.
**WHO TO APPLY TO** The Clerk to the Trustees, 3 Thurnham Oast, Aldington Lane, Thurnham, Kent ME14 3LL email clerk@redhilltrust.org Website www.redhilltrust.org

## ■ The C. A. Redfern Charitable Foundation

**CC NO** 299918     **ESTABLISHED** 1989
**WHERE FUNDING CAN BE GIVEN** UK.
**WHO CAN BENEFIT** Registered UK charities.
**WHAT IS FUNDED** General charitable purposes, with some preference for those concerned with health and welfare.
**WHAT IS NOT FUNDED** Building works; individuals.
**TYPE OF GRANT** Core costs, one-off, project and research. Funding is available for one year or less.
**RANGE OF GRANTS** £1,000 to £30,000, though all but two grants were in the £1,000 to £5,000 range.
**SAMPLE GRANTS** South Bucks Riding for the Disabled (£30,000); White Ensign (£10,000); Canine Partners for Independence, Mousetrap Foundation for the Arts, St Luke's Primary School, The Depaul Trust and Westminster School Research Trust (£5,000 each); British Limbless Ex-Servicemen's Association and Great Ormond Street (£4,000); Epilepsy Research UK, St Christopher's Hospice, The Rainbow Trust and Youth Sport (£3,000 each); BEN, Croydon Youth Information and Counselling Service – Croydon Drop In, Emmaus, Shirley Neighbourhood Care Scheme and The Latch Project (£2,000 each); Herefordshire Red Cross, Institute of Hepatology and The Woodland Trust (£1,000 each).
**FINANCES** Year 2013/14 Income £273,925 Grants £201,000 Grants to organisations £201,000 Assets £4,786,856
**TRUSTEES** William Maclaren; David Redfern; Simon Ward; Julian Heslop.
**HOW TO APPLY** The trustees meet regularly to discuss the making of grants but do not invite unsolicited grant applications.
**WHO TO APPLY TO** The Correspondent, PricewaterhouseCoopers, One Reading Central, 23 Forbury Road, Reading RG1 3JH Tel. 0118 938 3128

## ■ The Reed Foundation

**CC NO** 264728     **ESTABLISHED** 1972
**WHERE FUNDING CAN BE GIVEN** UK and financially developing countries.
**WHO CAN BENEFIT** Charitable organisations.
**WHAT IS FUNDED** General charitable purposes including the arts, environment, overseas, animal welfare, women and children.
**SAMPLE GRANTS** Fauna and Flora International (£31,500); Cool Earth Action (£30,000); Friends of the Earth (£24,500); Birmingham Royal Ballet (£20,000); English National Opera (£17,400); East Neuk Festival (£10,000); Havne House Children's Hospice (£9,000); International Fund for Animal Welfare (£5,500); Freedom Matters (£5,000); Helping the Burmese Delta (£3,000); Greyhound Rescue West of England (£1,500); ChildAid to Russia and the Republics (£1,000); Generation Rwanda – UK (£200).

FINANCES Year 2013 Income £672,295
Grants £1,080,663 Grants to organisations £1,080,663 Assets £13,514,017
TRUSTEES Alec Reed; James Reed; Richard Reed; Alex Chapman.
HOW TO APPLY The foundation has stated that it does not respond to unsolicited applications.
WHO TO APPLY TO Sir Alec Reed, Trustee, First Floor, The Peak, 5 Wilton Road SW1V 1AN Tel. 020 7201 9980 email reed.foundation@reed.co.uk

## ■ Richard Reeve's Foundation

CC NO 1136337   ESTABLISHED 1928
WHERE FUNDING CAN BE GIVEN Camden, City of London and Islington.
WHO CAN BENEFIT Local organisations; charities; schools; individuals.
WHAT IS FUNDED The education and training of people who are disadvantaged. The themes for the foundation's grant-making in 2014/15 are improving literacy and numeracy; preparation for work; and protection and development.
WHAT IS NOT FUNDED Building costs; independent school fees; furniture/household goods; school meals; holidays; school outings; replacement of statutory funding.
TYPE OF GRANT Up to three years. Capital costs, full project funding and core costs.
RANGE OF GRANTS £2,800 to £60,000.
SAMPLE GRANTS Pakeman Primary School (£60,000); Camden Centre for Learning (£34,000); Hungerford Primary School (£30,000); Unlocking Potential – Hugh Myddelton School (£21,000); Torriano Junior School (£20,500); Camden Toy Libraries (£16,300); The Pirate Ship (£15,000); Christ's Hospital £10,500).
FINANCES Year 2013/14 Income £486,919 Grants £278,015 Grants to organisations £210,469 Assets £23,494,946
TRUSTEES Billy Dove; Mavis Hughesdon; John Tickle; Sylvan Dewing; Sarah Betteley; Michael Bennett; Cllr Charlynne Pullen; Mark Jessett; Shannon Farrington; Nigel Thomson; Revd David Ingall; Gerald Rothwell; Lorna Russell.
OTHER INFORMATION During the year, grants to individuals totalled £67,500. They were mostly paid through the foundation's partner organisations, which included City and Islington College, City University and Westminster Kingsway.
HOW TO APPLY At the time of writing (May 2015), the foundation's website stated: 'We are not inviting new applications at this time as we are committed to working with partners in delivering long-term projects that will have a lasting benefit for those assisted by them. We have several applicants under consideration already.'
WHO TO APPLY TO Shirley Scott, Secretary, 13 Elliott's Place, London N1 8HX Tel. 020 7726 4230 email enquiries@richardreevesfoundation.org.uk Website www.richardreevesfoundation.org.uk

## ■ The Rest Harrow Trust

CC NO 238042   ESTABLISHED 1964
WHERE FUNDING CAN BE GIVEN UK.
WHO CAN BENEFIT Registered charities.
WHAT IS FUNDED General charitable purposes, with a focus on medical and relief of poverty charities. Jewish organisations appear to be of a particular interest to the trustees.
WHAT IS NOT FUNDED Non-registered charities; individuals.

TYPE OF GRANT Occasionally one-off for part or all of a particular project.
RANGE OF GRANTS £100–£2,000. The majority of grants were under £500 each.
SAMPLE GRANTS Nightingale Hammerson (£2,000); Jewish Care (£1,000); Institute of Cancer Research and Willow Trust (£500 each); Crisis (£200); Centrepoint (£100).
FINANCES Year 2013/14 Income £69,733 Grants £45,300 Grants to organisations £45,300 Assets £997,255
TRUSTEES Janet Bloch; Dominic Flynn; Judith Portrait.
OTHER INFORMATION Grants are usually made to national bodies rather than local branches, or local groups.
HOW TO APPLY Apply in writing to the correspondent. Applications are considered quarterly. Only submissions from eligible bodies are acknowledged.
WHO TO APPLY TO Judith Portrait, c/o Portrait Solicitors, 21 Whitefriars Street, London EC4Y 8JJ email sarah.hovil@portraitsolicitors.com

## ■ Reuben Foundation

CC NO 1094130   ESTABLISHED 2002
WHERE FUNDING CAN BE GIVEN UK and overseas, with a focus on Israel and the United States.
WHO CAN BENEFIT Organisations, including universities and Jewish organisations.
WHAT IS FUNDED Healthcare; education; general charitable purposes.
RANGE OF GRANTS Up to £600,000.
SAMPLE GRANTS Lyric Theatre (£600,000); Oxford University (£337,500); Nancy Reuben Primary School and University College London (£300,000 each); ARK (£120,000); British Film Institute (£100,000); Mayo Clinic (£30,000); Community Security Trust (£25,000); Impact Scholarships (£20,500); Jewish Care, Leaders Magazine, Norwood Foundation and Princess Royal Trust for Carers (£10,000 each); 'others' (£7,000).
FINANCES Year 2013 Income £3,848,726 Grants £1,454,708 Grants to organisations £1,378,149 Assets £77,316,647
TRUSTEES Richard Stone; Simon Reuben; Malcolm Turner; Annie Benjamin; Patrick O'Driscoll; James Reuben; Dana Reuben.
OTHER INFORMATION During the year, £76,500 was paid in 16 grants to individuals. The foundation supports a number of scholarship initiatives including the Reuben Scholarship programme alongside the University of Oxford, University College London, ARK Schools and the University of Cambridge.
HOW TO APPLY The foundation's website states that applications for grants are made by invitation only.
WHO TO APPLY TO Patrick O'Driscoll, Trustee, 4th Floor, Millbank Tower, 21–24 Millbank, London SW1P 4PQ Tel. 020 7802 5000 Fax 020 7802 5002 email contact@reubenfoundation.com Website www.reubenfoundation.com

## ■ The Rhododendron Trust

CC NO 267192   ESTABLISHED 1974
WHERE FUNDING CAN BE GIVEN UK and overseas.
WHO CAN BENEFIT Registered charities.
WHAT IS FUNDED Overseas charities, UK social welfare charities and UK cultural charities.
WHAT IS NOT FUNDED Individuals, for example, on gap year projects with another charity; local

branches of national societies; restoration work on individual churches and other buildings (the trust works through larger bodies to do this); medical or academic research; or missionary charities.
**TYPE OF GRANT** Preferably project-based.
**RANGE OF GRANTS** £500 or £1,000 each.
**SAMPLE GRANTS** British Red Cross, Cambodia Trust, Farm Africa (£1,000 each); Book Aid International, Historic Chapels Trust, National Autistic Society (£500 each).
**FINANCES** Year 2013/14 Income £66,496 Grants £52,000 Grants to organisations £52,000 Assets £1,723,568
**TRUSTEES** Sarah Ray; Sarah Oliver; Elizabeth Baldwin; Wendy Anderson.
**HOW TO APPLY** Apply in writing to the correspondent at any time. Guidelines are noted on the website. Applicants will be informed within about a month if they have been unsuccessful. If you receive no response within this time frame, then your application has been added to a long list of possible grants. This list will be considered by Grants Officers and trustees in February or March. Following this, you will either receive a cheque or will be notified that you have been unsuccessful.
**WHO TO APPLY TO** The Grants Officer, 6 Bridge Street, Richmond, North Yorkshire DL10 4RW Website www.rhododendron-trust.org.uk

## ■ The Rhondda Cynon Taff Welsh Church Acts Fund

**CC NO** 506658   **ESTABLISHED** 1977
**WHERE FUNDING CAN BE GIVEN** Rhondda Cynon Taff, Bridgend and Merthyr Tydfil County Borough Councils, i.e. the former county of Mid Glamorgan, with the exception of Rhymney Valley which is now outside the area of benefit.
**WHO CAN BENEFIT** Church-based and other organisations.
**WHAT IS FUNDED** Church-based organisations, young people and medical, cultural, recreational and general charitable causes.
**WHAT IS NOT FUNDED** Students; individuals (though individual cases of relief in sickness will be referred to the Council's Community and Children's Services Group); clubs with a liquor licence; projects operating outside the area of benefit; normal running expenses.
**TYPE OF GRANT** Project funding (excluding normal running expenses).
**RANGE OF GRANTS** Up to £10,000.
**SAMPLE GRANTS** Bethel Newydd Chapel, Cefn Cribwr Community Association and Brynna Community Centre Management Committee (£10,000 each); Trecynon Free Library and Institute (£9,900); Ely Valley Miners Welfare Association – Tonyrefail (£9,500); St Barnabas Church – Gilfach Goch (£5,000); Llynfi Valley Credit Union (£4,400); Dowlais Male Voice Choir – Merthyr Tydfil (£3,900); Bridgend Food Bank (£3,000); Georgetown Boys' and Girls' Club – Merthyr Tydfil (£2,500); Llynfi Valley River Care (£2,000).
**FINANCES** Year 2013/14 Income £340,142 Grants £356,324 Grants to organisations £356,324 Assets £11,406,000
**TRUSTEE** Rhondda Cynon Taff County Borough Council.
**OTHER INFORMATION** Grants of more than £2,000 require a minimum of 50% match funding from non-Welsh Church Fund sources. Those grants which are structural in nature are only considered where a professional assessment for the necessary works has been made. Organisations received 81 grants during the year, of which 48 were of £2,000 or more totalling £302,500, and 33 grants, totalling £53,500, were of less than £2,000.
**HOW TO APPLY** The annual report states: 'Recommendations for grant awards are made by officers in an Assessment Round Report, which is considered at special meetings approximately six times a year.'
**WHO TO APPLY TO** George Sheldrick, Local Government Officer, Rhondda Cynon Taff Council, Accounts Section, Council Offices, Bronwydd, Porth CF39 9DL Tel. 01443 680373 email george.p.sheldrick@rctcbc.gov.uk

## ■ Daisie Rich Trust

**CC NO** 236706   **ESTABLISHED** 1964
**WHERE FUNDING CAN BE GIVEN** UK, with a strong preference for the Isle of Wight.
**WHO CAN BENEFIT** Organisations and individuals (particularly former employees, or their spouses, of Upward and Rich Limited).
**WHAT IS FUNDED** General charitable purposes.
**TYPE OF GRANT** Mostly recurrent.
**RANGE OF GRANTS** £300–£5,500
**SAMPLE GRANTS** Isle of Wight Foodbank (£5,500); Hampshire and Isle of Wight Air Ambulance and UKSA (£5,000 each); Carisbrooke Castle Museum (£4,000); Oakfield Primary School, Shanklin Theatre and Shanklin Voluntary Youth and Community Centre (£2,000 each); Isle of Wight SCOPE, Isle of Wight Youth Trust and Meningitis Now (£1,000 each); People's Dispensary for Sick Animals and People's Trust for Endangered Species – Briddlesford Woods (£750 each); YMCA Young Carers Project (£500); Fernhill Bat Survey (£300).
**FINANCES** Year 2013/14 Income £169,618 Grants £137,420 Grants to organisations £106,930 Assets £3,436,830
**TRUSTEES** Adrian Medley, Chair; Ann Medley; Maurice Flux; David Longford; James Woodward Attrill.
**OTHER INFORMATION** There were nine new beneficiary organisations during the year. Grants to individuals totalled £30,500, of which £28,500 was given to former employees of Upward and Rich Limited.
**HOW TO APPLY** Contact the correspondent for an application form. The trustees hold regular meetings to decide on grant applications and are assisted by information gathered by the administrator.
**WHO TO APPLY TO** Lyn Mitchell, Correspondent, The Hawthorns, Main Road, Arreton, Newport, Isle of Wight PO30 3AD Tel. 07866 449855 email daisierich@yahoo.co.uk

## ■ The Sir Cliff Richard Charitable Trust

**CC NO** 1096412   **ESTABLISHED** 1969
**WHERE FUNDING CAN BE GIVEN** UK and overseas.
**WHO CAN BENEFIT** Registered charities only, benefitting a broad spectrum of people, including: children, adults and young people; Baptists, Methodists, Anglicans and Evangelists; people who have disabilities or a medical condition.
**WHAT IS FUNDED** Smaller, grass-roots projects are often preferred, for general charitable purposes that reflect the support, Christian commitment and interest of Sir Cliff Richard including:

special schools, special needs education and vocational training; community centres, village halls, playgrounds and play schemes; care in the community and community transport; respite care and care for carers; cancer, MS and neurological research; Christian education and outreach; missionaries and evangelicals; and animal homes and welfare.

**WHAT IS NOT FUNDED** Capital building projects; church repairs and renovations; individuals.

**TYPE OF GRANT** Usually small one-off sums for operational needs.

**RANGE OF GRANTS** Up to £3,500.

**SAMPLE GRANTS** Genesis Trust (£3,500); Freddie Krivine Foundation (£3,250); Arts Centre Group (£2,500); Chickenshed Theatre Trust and Depaul Nightstop UK (£2,000 each).

**FINANCES** Year 2013/14 Income £52,055 Grants £93,180 Grants to organisations £93,180 Assets £168,070

**TRUSTEES** William Latham; Malcolm Smith; Sir Cliff Richard.

**OTHER INFORMATION** Smaller grants of less than £2,000 were made totalling £80,000.

**HOW TO APPLY** Applications should be from registered charities only, in writing, and for one-off needs. All applications are acknowledged. Grants are usually made quarterly in January, April, July and October.

**WHO TO APPLY TO** William Latham, Trustee, Harley House, 94 Hare Lane, Claygate, Esher, Surrey KT10 0RB *Tel.* 01372 467752 *email* general@cliffrichard.org

--------

## ■ The Clive Richards Charity

**CC NO** 327155     **ESTABLISHED** 1986

**WHERE FUNDING CAN BE GIVEN** UK, with a preference for Herefordshire.

**WHO CAN BENEFIT** Organisations, including churches and schools, and individuals.

**WHAT IS FUNDED** General charitable purposes, though there is a preference for schools, churches, the arts and individuals who have disabilities.

**TYPE OF GRANT** One-off, project and buildings. Interest-free loans are considered. Grants may be for up to two years.

**RANGE OF GRANTS** The majority were of £10,000 or less. A number of larger grants were also made.

**SAMPLE GRANTS** St Michael's Hospice (£1 million); SS Great Britain (£644,500); Bishop Vesey's Grammar School (£222,000); Catholic Trust for England and Wales (£150,000); National Maritime Museum (£100,000); Blackmarston School (£56,000); Mary Rose Appeal (£10,000); Welsh National Opera (£5,300); St Joseph's Church (£4,100); Hereford Police Male Voice Choir (£2,500); Guide Dogs for the Blind (£2,000); St Kentigern's Hospice (£1,200); Huntingdon Disease Association (£1,000).

**FINANCES** Year 2013/14 Income £1,979,392 Grants £2,143,953 Grants to organisations £2,143,953 Assets £272,483

**TRUSTEES** Peter Henry; Clive Richards; Sylvia Richards; Peter Dines.

**OTHER INFORMATION** Grants of less than £1,000 totalled £23,500.

**HOW TO APPLY** Apply in writing to the correspondent. The trustees meet monthly to consider applications. The charity has previously stated that, due to its resources being almost fully committed, it is extremely selective in accepting any requests for funding.

**WHO TO APPLY TO** Peter Henry, Trustee, Lower Hope, Ullingswick, Herefordshire HR1 3JF *Tel.* 01432 820557 *email* peter@crco.co.uk

## ■ The Violet M. Richards Charity

**CC NO** 273928     **ESTABLISHED** 1977

**WHERE FUNDING CAN BE GIVEN** UK, with a preference for East Sussex, particularly Crowborough.

**WHO CAN BENEFIT** Organisations benefitting: older people; medical professionals; researchers; medical students; and people with a medical condition.

**WHAT IS FUNDED** The charity's objects are the relief of ill health and older age, the advancement of medical education and research (particularly regarding geriatric problems) and homes and other facilities for older people and people in ill health. The trustees' 2013/14 annual report states that rather than focusing on long term medical research projects, they currently have a more flexible approach, allowing individual trustees to nominate causes in the spirit of the trust's founder.

**WHAT IS NOT FUNDED** Individuals.

**RANGE OF GRANTS** £5,000–£20,000

**SAMPLE GRANTS** British Liver Trust and Macular Society (£20,000 each); Marie Curie Cancer Care (£19,000); Juvenile Diabetes Research Foundation Ltd (£15,000); Arthritis Research UK, Brain Research Trust, Brain Tumour UK, The Inspire Foundation and The Stroke Association (£10,000 each); Lee Smith Foundation (£6,000); CORE and Southampton Hospital Charity (£5,000).

**FINANCES** Year 2013/14 Income £172,756 Grants £140,000 Grants to organisations £140,000 Assets £2,060,417

**TRUSTEES** Mrs E. H. Hill; G. R. Andersen; C. A. Hicks; Mrs M. Burt; Dr J. Clements.

**OTHER INFORMATION** Grants were made to 12 organisations in 2013/14.

**HOW TO APPLY** Apply in writing to the correspondent; however, the trust states in its accounts that the trustees 'prefer to be proactive with charities of their own choice, rather than reactive to external applications.' Only successful applications are acknowledged and external applications are unlikely to be successful and are therefore discouraged.

**WHO TO APPLY TO** Mr Charles Hicks, Secretary, c/o Wedlake Bell, 52 Bedford Row, London WC1R 4LR *Tel.* 020 7395 3155 *email* chicks@wedlakebell.com

--------

## ■ The Richmond Parish Lands Charity

**CC NO** 200069     **ESTABLISHED** 1786

**WHERE FUNDING CAN BE GIVEN** Richmond, Kew, Ham, North Sheen, East Sheen, Petersham and Mortlake. (the TW9, TW10 and SW14 postcode areas).

**WHO CAN BENEFIT** Charities; voluntary organisations; individuals.

**WHAT IS FUNDED** The main purposes of the charity are: the support of people who are older or in need; the care of people who are ill or facing hardship; the provision of recreational facilities and support for leisure activities; the promotion of education and assisting people to take up courses and training; other charitable purposes. All for the benefit of residents of the foundation's area of benefit. Strategic priorities are reviewed periodically.

**WHAT IS NOT FUNDED** Projects and organisations located outside the benefit area, unless it can be demonstrated that a substantial number of residents from the benefit area will gain from their work. UK charities (even if based in the

**743**

benefit area), except for that part of their work which caters specifically for the area.

**TYPE OF GRANT** One-off and recurring; core costs; project funding; strategic funding.

**SAMPLE GRANTS** Kew and Ham Sports Association (£90,000); Citizens Advice (£53,500 in two grants); SPEAR (£32,500); 2nd Mortlake Scout Group and Me Too and Co (£30,000 each); Richmond Volunteer Police Cadets (£25,000); Richmond Users Independent Living (£22,000 in two grants); Alzheimer's Society (£16,300 in two grants); Richmond Foodbank (£15,000); Mortlake Community Association (£10,600); LBRuT Arts Service (£8,100); Richmond Carers (£5,300); Friends of Meadlands School (£3,000); Library and Information Service (£1,500); Community Mental Health Team (£500); CAYSH Housing Project (£250).

**FINANCES** Year 2013/14 Income £1,860,587 Grants £1,324,874 Grants to organisations £1,058,072 Assets £85,715,223

**TRUSTEES** Rosalind Sweeting; Ashley Casson; Rita Biddulph; Lisa Blakemore; Roger Clark; Paul Cole; Rosie Dalzell; Ian Durant; Kate Ellis; Susan Goddard; Gill Moffett; Time Sketchley; Paul Velluet.

**OTHER INFORMATION** The figure for organisational grants includes £34,500 given to schools in child poverty grants. During the year, welfare grants were made to individuals totalling £267,000. At the time of writing, 39 local charities were receiving regular funding from the charity, amounting annually to more than £400,000 in support of core operational activities. The Mayor of Richmond upon Thames is an ex officio trustee of the charity.

**HOW TO APPLY** There are separate application forms and guidelines available on the website for the various types of grants. Be sure to complete each section and to provide the required documents.

**WHO TO APPLY TO** Jonathan Monckton, Director, The Vestry House, 21 Paradise Road, Richmond, Surrey TW9 1SA Tel. 020 8948 5701 Fax 020 8332 6792 email grants@rplc.org.uk Website www.rplc.org.uk

## ■ Ridgesave Limited

**CC NO** 288020  **ESTABLISHED** 1983
**WHERE FUNDING CAN BE GIVEN** UK and overseas.
**WHO CAN BENEFIT** Individuals and organisations benefitting Jewish people and those disadvantaged by poverty.
**WHAT IS FUNDED** The advancement of the Jewish religion, education and the provision of philanthropic aid to those in need.
**SAMPLE GRANTS Previous beneficiaries have included:** All in Together Girls, Ateres Yeshua Charitable Trust, British Friends of Rinat Aharon, Chanoch Lenaar, My Dream Time, Square Foundation Ltd and Side by Side.
**FINANCES** Year 2013/14 Income £406,093 Grants £2,353,465 Grants to organisations £2,353,465 Assets £321,735
**TRUSTEES** Zelda Weiss; Joseph Weiss; E. Englander.
**OTHER INFORMATION** No grants list was available.
**HOW TO APPLY** Apply in writing to the correspondent. 'The trustees consider all requests they receive and make donation based on the level of funds available.'
**WHO TO APPLY TO** Zelda Weiss, Trustee, Ridgesave Limited, 141b Upper Clapton Road, London E5 9DB email mail@cohenarnold.com

## ■ The Sir John Ritblat Family Foundation

**CC NO** 262463  **ESTABLISHED** 1971
**WHERE FUNDING CAN BE GIVEN** UK.
**WHO CAN BENEFIT** Charitable organisations, with some preference for Jewish and arts groups.
**WHAT IS FUNDED** General charitable purposes.
**WHAT IS NOT FUNDED** Individuals.
**SAMPLE GRANTS Previous beneficiaries have included:** Henry Jackson Society (£25,000); Jewish Care (£11,000); Hertford House Trust and The Outward Bound Trust (£10,000 each); The Wallace Collection (£5,500); Weizmann UK (£4,300); Mayor of London's Fund for Young Musicians (£4,000); Central Synagogue (£2,600); Weizmann Institute and Museum of London (£2,000); The Art Fund (£1,500); The Board of Deputies of British Jews and Open Europe (£1,000 each); Tate Foundation (£850); and Zoë's Place – Baby Hospice (£125).
**FINANCES** Year 2013/14 Income £107,551 Grants £140,000 Grants to organisations £140,000
**TRUSTEES** Sir John Ritblat; N. S. J. Ritblat; C. B. Wagman; J. W. J. Ritblat.
**OTHER INFORMATION** At the time of writing (June 2015) the foundation's 2013/14 accounts had been received by the Charity Commission but were not yet available to view. The grant total above is an estimate.
**HOW TO APPLY** The trust has previously stated that its funds are fully committed.
**WHO TO APPLY TO** The Clerk, c/o Baker Tilly, The Pinnacle, 170 Midsummer Boulevard, Milton Keynes, Buckinghamshire MK9 1BP Tel. 01908 687800

## ■ The River Farm Foundation

**CC NO** 1113109  **ESTABLISHED** 2006
**WHERE FUNDING CAN BE GIVEN** UK and overseas.
**WHO CAN BENEFIT** Organisations.
**WHAT IS FUNDED** Health; social welfare; children's welfare; education; environment.
**RANGE OF GRANTS** £3,000 to £50,000. All but two grants were of £10,000 or less.
**SAMPLE GRANTS** The Busoga Trust (£50,000); Centrepoint Soho (£15,000); Helen and Douglas House, The Prince's Trust, The University of Oxford – St Edmund Hall and the NSPCC (£10,000 each); Shelter (£9,000); The Woodland Trust and Worcestershire Breast Unit (£8,000 each); Sightsavers (£5,000); Royal British Legion (£3,000).
**FINANCES** Year 2013/14 Income £143,096 Grants £138,000 Grants to organisations £138,000 Assets £33,686,194
**TRUSTEES** Mark Haworth; Nigel Langstaff; Deborah Fisher.
**OTHER INFORMATION** Support was given to 11 organisations during the year.
**HOW TO APPLY** Apply in writing to the correspondent. The trustees meet at least twice a year to review applications made and consider grant-making.
**WHO TO APPLY TO** Deborah Fisher, Trustee, The Old Coach House, Sunnyside, Bergh Apton, Norwich NR15 1DD Tel. 01508 480100 email info@willcoxlewis.co.uk

## ■ The River Trust

**CC NO** 275843    **ESTABLISHED** 1977
**WHERE FUNDING CAN BE GIVEN** UK, with a preference for Sussex.
**WHO CAN BENEFIT** Organisations.
**WHAT IS FUNDED** The advancement of the Evangelical Christian faith.
**WHAT IS NOT FUNDED** Individuals; repairs of church fabric; funding towards capital expenditure.
**TYPE OF GRANT** Certain charities are supported for more than one year.
**RANGE OF GRANTS** Between £500 and £6,100.
**SAMPLE GRANTS** Care Trust (£6,100); Care for the Family (£5,700); Chasah Trust (£5,500); Scripture Union (£2,500); Ashburnham Christian Trust – ACT (£2,100); Bible Society (£1,500); Release International (£1,000); Christians Against Poverty and Kidz Klub Brighton and Hove (£500 each).
**FINANCES** Year 2012/13 Income £90,230 Grants £90,778 Grants to organisations £90,778 Assets £687,470
**TRUSTEES** Kleinwort Benson Trustees Ltd; Davina Irwin-Clark.
**OTHER INFORMATION** At the time of writing (June 2015) these were the latest accounts available for the trust.
**HOW TO APPLY** Apply in writing to the correspondent. It is unusual for unsolicited appeals to be successful. Only successful applicants are notified of the trustees' decision. Some charities are supported for more than one year, although no commitment is usually given to the recipients.
**WHO TO APPLY TO** The Trustees, Kleinwort Benson Trustees Ltd, 14 St George Street, London W1S 1FE Tel. 020 3207 7041 email katie.styles@kleinwortbenson.com

## ■ Rivers Foundation

**CC NO** 1078545    **ESTABLISHED** 1999
**WHERE FUNDING CAN BE GIVEN** UK and overseas.
**WHO CAN BENEFIT** Charitable organisations.
**WHAT IS FUNDED** General charitable purposes, especially 'educational projects in the UK and abroad whether it is in terms of actual buildings, educational materials or paying for children's education'. It also supports community projects and arts and culture and 'seeks welfare projects to support via small charities with well targeted schemes'.
**TYPE OF GRANT** One-off and recurring grants; running costs.
**RANGE OF GRANTS** £800–£22,000
**SAMPLE GRANTS** **Beneficiaries were**: Rona Sailing Project (£22,000); Operation Smile (£20,000); Fly Navy Heritage Trust (£16,100); Mathari (£9,500); MASK and Switchback (£5,000 each); Forest Philharmonic (£3,000); Jungle Aid (£2,000); Bench Mark and SES (£800 each).
**FINANCES** Year 2013/14 Income £70,361 Grants £84,108 Grants to organisations £84,108 Assets £786,613
**TRUSTEES** Alan Rivers; Keith Constable; Christine Bolton; Cass Chapman; Susan Rivers.
**OTHER INFORMATION** Awards were made to ten organisations. Note that at the year end the foundation had also offered conditional grants to eight organisations totalling around £74,500.
**HOW TO APPLY** Applications may be made in writing to the correspondent.
**WHO TO APPLY TO** Keri Jenkin, 190A Campden Hill Road, Kensington, London W8 7TH email ajrultra@btinternet.com

## ■ Rix-Thompson-Rothenberg Foundation

**CC NO** 285368    **ESTABLISHED** 1982
**WHERE FUNDING CAN BE GIVEN** UK.
**WHO CAN BENEFIT** Registered charities working with or to support people with learning (intellectual) disabilities and their families.
**WHAT IS FUNDED** The care, education, training, development and leisure activities of people with learning disabilities. A special emphasis is given to grants that will enhance opportunity and lifestyle.
**WHAT IS NOT FUNDED** Applications for specific learning details.
**RANGE OF GRANTS** £2,500 to £6,500.
**SAMPLE GRANTS** My Life My Choice (£6,500); CSIE (£6,000); Accessible Arts and Media, Keynsham and District Mencap, PMLD Link, St Edmunds Arts Trust, Scottish Storytelling Centre, Shape London and Thumbs Up Club (£5,000 each); Everybody Dancing (£4,700); PAMIS (£4,500); Norman Laud Association, SASBAH and Watford Mencap (£4,000 each); Ingleby Foundation (£3,700); Leeds Leider (£2,500).
**FINANCES** Year 2013 Income £128,405 Grants £101,070 Grants to organisations £98,170 Assets £1,462,832
**TRUSTEES** Lord Rix; David Rothenberg; Loretto Lambe; Fred Heddell; Barrie Davis; Jonathan Rix; Brian Baldock; Suzanne Marriott.
**OTHER INFORMATION** During the year, grants were made to 22 organisations. Grants to individuals from the Care fund totalled £2,900.
**HOW TO APPLY** Applicants must complete an application form and provide a copy of their latest audited accounts. In the first instance the applicant should discuss the proposed work either by telephone, email or letter to the administrator, a minimum of four months in advance of a board meeting. Grants are considered in June and December.
**WHO TO APPLY TO** The Correspondent, RTR Administrative Office, White Top Research Unit, Springfield House, 15/16 Springfield, University of Dundee, Dundee D1 4JE email P-RTR@dundee.ac.uk

## ■ Thomas Roberts Trust

**CC NO** 1067235    **ESTABLISHED** 1997
**WHERE FUNDING CAN BE GIVEN** UK.
**WHO CAN BENEFIT** Organisations working in the areas of medical support and research (particularly in relation to cancer), and the care and welfare of older, disadvantaged and sick people. Employees and former employees of the Thomas Roberts Group Companies
**WHAT IS FUNDED** Medical care and research (particularly in relation to cancer), and the care and welfare of older people, people who are ill, disadvantaged or who have a disability.
**RANGE OF GRANTS** Most grants are of between £500 and £2,500.
**SAMPLE GRANTS** Cancer Research UK (£8,300); Marie Curie Cancer Care (£2,500); Institute of Cancer Research (£2,000); The National Brain Appeal (£1,000); Winchester Churches Nightshelter (£750); Vitalise (£500).
**FINANCES** Year 2013/14 Income £38,528 Grants £48,875 Grants to organisations £46,200 Assets £1,104,620
**TRUSTEES** Gillian Hemmings; Richard Gammage; James Roberts.
**OTHER INFORMATION** £2,700 was given in grants to ex-employees of the Thomas Roberts group of companies.

**HOW TO APPLY** Apply in writing to the correspondent. Applicants are required to provide a summary of their proposals to the trustees, explaining how the funds would be used and what would be achieved.

**WHO TO APPLY TO** James Roberts, Trustee, Sheridan House, 40–43 Jewry Street, Winchester, Hampshire SO23 8RY *Tel.* 01962 843211 *email* trtust@thomasroberts.co.uk

..........................................................

## ■ The Robertson Trust

**SC NO** SC002970     **ESTABLISHED** 1961
**WHERE FUNDING CAN BE GIVEN** Scotland.
**WHO CAN BENEFIT** Registered charities only.
**WHAT IS FUNDED** General charitable purposes. The trust has seven main priority areas: alcohol misuse; care; community arts; community sports; criminal justice; education and training; and health. Applications are also considered for: preservation of the environment; strengthening local communities; heritage, culture and science; animal welfare; and saving lives.
**WHAT IS NOT FUNDED** Individuals; CICs limited by shares; non-registered charities; CICs not recognised by the CIC Regulator; projects primarily for political or religious purposes; general appeals and circulars including endowment fund contributions; local charities outside Scotland; organisations/projects whose primary aim is to provide a generic counselling service; projects which are primarily research-based; organisations/projects whose primary aim is to provide information or advice; generic employment and training projects; core revenue costs for mainstream playgroups, nurseries, schools and after-school groups where there is no element of disadvantage; individual students or organisations for personal study, travel or expeditions in the UK or abroad; applications for community projects from Housing Associations; capital costs of memorials/statues; capital costs of providing disability access in order to meet statutory requirements; one-off events, festivals or conferences where there is no wider community engagement; the purchase of buildings and/or land.
**TYPE OF GRANT** One-off grants; grants up to three years; revenue costs; capital costs; core costs; project costs.
**RANGE OF GRANTS** £500 to £1 million. There is no maximum or minimum amount, though grants for revenue costs are rarely awarded outside the range of £500 to £15,000. Capital donations are usually to a maximum of 10% of total capital costs.
**SAMPLE GRANTS** Lloyds TSB Foundation PDI (£1 million); Dundee Museums Foundation (£500,000); Clydesdale Community Initiative (£200,000); Encompass Counselling and Support (£96,000); Medical Foundation for the Care of Victims of Torture (£60,000); Anthony Nolan Trust (£45,000); Scottish Borders Disability Sports Group (£42,000); Enterprise Childcare (£37,500); Church of St John the Evangelist, Fife Animal Trust and St Margaret's Hospice (£20,000 each); Drugs Initiative Group (£18,000); Crichton Carbon Centre and Tayside Council on Alcohol (£17,000 each); Speyside Community Car Share Scheme (£15,000); Prison Fellowship Scotland (£14,000); Making Music Scotland (£5,500); Hopscotch Theatre Company (£5,000); Doorway Accessible Software Trust (£1,000); Eday Heritage Centre Association (£750); Scottish Wheelchair Dance Association – New Wheelies Falkirk Group (£500).
**FINANCES** *Year* 2013/14 *Income* £18,578,000 *Grants* £16,592,200 *Grants to organisations* £16,592,200 *Assets* £351,493,000
**TRUSTEES** Dame Barbara Kelly; Shonaig Macpherson; Judy Cromarty; Sandy Cumming; Mark Laing; Heather Lamont; David Stevenson; Andrew Walls.
**OTHER INFORMATION** During the year, Main Awards and Small Awards together accounted for £12.2 million of the grant total. The average amount for Main Awards was £36,000, and for Small Awards the average amount was £10,000. Applicants should refer to the trust's excellent website.
**HOW TO APPLY** Applicants are advised to read the guidelines available from the trust's website. For Main Awards and Small Awards an application form, an organisation information sheet and a revenue or capital budget form can be downloaded from the website and should be completed and returned to the trust along with a copy of your most recent independently audited accounts. The trust advises that for other applications – for Continuation Awards, Enterprise Awards and Major Capital awards – applicants should at first contact a member of the Assessment Team. Enquiries regarding new applications should be sent to enquiries@therobertsontrust.org.uk. Enquiries from existing grant-holders should be sent to assessment@therobertsontrust.org.uk.
**WHO TO APPLY TO** Lesley Macdonald, Assessment Manager, 152 Bath Street, Glasgow G2 4TB *Tel.* 0141 353 7300 *Fax* 0141 353 7301 *email* enquiries@therobertsontrust.org.uk *Website* www.therobertsontrust.org.uk

..........................................................

## ■ Edwin George Robinson Charitable Trust

**CC NO** 1068763     **ESTABLISHED** 1998
**WHERE FUNDING CAN BE GIVEN** UK.
**WHO CAN BENEFIT** Medical research organisations.
**WHAT IS FUNDED** The trustees favour applications from smaller organisations for specific research projects.
**WHAT IS NOT FUNDED** Individuals or for general running costs for small local organisations.
**RANGE OF GRANTS** Mostly £500–£6,500.
**SAMPLE GRANTS** Previous beneficiaries have included: Action for Medical Research; Bath Institute of Medical Engineering; Brainwave; Cure Parkinson's; Diabetes Research; Holly Lodge Centre; Marie Curie Cancer Care; Ness Foundation; Salvation Army
**FINANCES** *Year* 2013/14 *Income* £12,147 *Grants* £39,000 *Grants to organisations* £39,000
**TRUSTEES** Edwin Robinson; Susan Robinson.
**OTHER INFORMATION** Annual return was received by the Charity Commission but accounts were not required due to low income.
**HOW TO APPLY** Apply in writing to the correspondent.
**WHO TO APPLY TO** Edwin Robinson, Trustee, 71 Manor Road South, Esher, Surrey KT10 0QB *Tel.* 020 8398 6845 *email* marlin@waitrose.com

..........................................................

## ■ Robyn Charitable Trust

**CC NO** 327645     **ESTABLISHED** 1988
**WHERE FUNDING CAN BE GIVEN** UK and overseas.
**WHO CAN BENEFIT** Organisations.
**WHAT IS FUNDED** The welfare of children, particularly the relief of need and education.

**WHAT IS NOT FUNDED** Individuals.
**SAMPLE GRANTS Previous beneficiaries have included:** One to One Children's Fund, The Purcell School, Variety Club, The Honeypot Charity, Malawi Against Aids and Teenage Cancer Trust.
**FINANCES** Year 2013/14 Income £33,840 Grants £164,716 Grants to organisations £164,716 Assets £27,040
**TRUSTEES** Malcolm Webber; Mark Knopfler; Ronnie Harris.
**HOW TO APPLY** Apply in writing to the correspondent.
**WHO TO APPLY TO** Malcolm Webber, Trustee, c/o Harris and Trotter, 64 New Cavendish Street, London W1G 8TB Tel. 020 7467 6300

## ■ The Rochester Bridge Trust

**CC NO** 207100    **ESTABLISHED** 1399
**WHERE FUNDING CAN BE GIVEN** Kent.
**WHO CAN BENEFIT** Charitable bodies.
**WHAT IS FUNDED** At the time of writing, the trust was not inviting new applications for grants; however, it states the following on its website: 'When grants are again available, the programme will reflect the Trust's own history, values, and activities.' Grants have previously been given for projects that link in with the trust's core activities including: education, conservation and research in the areas of bridge engineering, Kent history and Kent agriculture; and repair, conservation or restoration of features of historical importance in listed buildings.
**WHAT IS NOT FUNDED** Individuals; funding for revenue; pet-care charities or general animal charities; the purchase of vehicles or trailers (apart from heritage vehicles) nor for office equipment, including IT equipment and furniture, that supports the running of an organisation rather than being available directly for the beneficiaries of a charity or contributing directly to a charity's objectives; grants towards construction, improvement, refurbishment or other projects associated with community centres, village halls, parish halls, club or association buildings, sports pitches or mainstream schools or colleges; individual mainstream schools and colleges, whether funded by the private, state, faith or charitable sectors, except for projects aimed at promoting interest and learning in the fields of civil engineering, history of Rochester, history of the River Medway, or agriculture (these projects are actively encouraged); nursing or care homes and childcare nurseries, except those providing support to people with severe disabilities and/or seriously disadvantaged children; routine maintenance work to any type of building; general grants to major projects where its contribution would be a very small proportion of the total required (e.g. less than 10%).
**TYPE OF GRANT** Capital costs including equipment, buildings and one-off awards.
**FINANCES** Year 2013/14 Income £3,487,348 Grants £49,544 Grants to organisations £49,544 Assets £89,020,814
**TRUSTEES** John Spence; Paul Oldham; Russell Race; Richard Thornby; Anne Logan; Paul Harriott; Alan Jarrett; Russell Cooper; Peter Homewood; Philip Filmer; Raymond Harris; Bryan Sweetland.
**OTHER INFORMATION** During the year, 13 grants were awarded.
**HOW TO APPLY** At the time of writing, the trust was not inviting new applications. Refer to the website for updates of grants programmes.

**WHO TO APPLY TO** Mrs S.E.P. Threader, Bridge Clerk, The Bridge Chamber, 5 Esplanade, Rochester, Kent ME1 1QE Tel. 01634 846706/843457 Fax 01634 840125 email bridgeclerk@rbt.org.uk Website www.rbt.org.uk

## ■ The Rock Foundation

**CC NO** 294775    **ESTABLISHED** 1986
**WHERE FUNDING CAN BE GIVEN** Worldwide.
**WHO CAN BENEFIT** Charitable organisations, especially those which are built upon a clear biblical basis and which, in most instances, receive little or no publicity.
**WHAT IS FUNDED** Christian ministries and other charitable work.
**WHAT IS NOT FUNDED** The foundation does not respond to unsolicited applications.
**RANGE OF GRANTS** Most grants are of less than £5,000.
**SAMPLE GRANTS** St Helen's Partnership (£47,500); 1–2–1 (£24,500); Lahore Evangelical Ministries (£19,800); Crosslinks (£19,500); Christchurch Kensington (£11,400); Proclamation Trust (£8,600); Equipo Impacto and Harare Central Baptist Church (£8,000 each); I Serve Africa (Ghana) Trust (£7,100); Africa Inland Mission (£7,000); Eclisa (£6,000); Relite Africa Trust (£5,000). The remaining grants were all of less than £5,000.
**FINANCES** Year 2013/14 Income £459,589 Grants £280,198 Grants to organisations £195,377 Assets £334,346
**TRUSTEES** Richard Borgonon; Andrew Green; Kevin Locock; Jane Borgonon; Colin Spreckley; Peter Butler; Penelope Borgonon; Camilla Borgonon.
**OTHER INFORMATION** During the year, 34 grants were made to organisations. A further 33 grants to individuals totalled £85,000.
**HOW TO APPLY** The foundation has stated: 'the trust identifies its beneficiaries through its own networks, choosing to support organisations it has a working relationship with. This allows the trust to verify that the organisation is doing excellent work in a sensible manner in a way which cannot be conveyed from a written application. As such, all appeals from charities the foundation do not find through their own research are simply thrown in the bin. If an sae is included in an application, it will merely end up in the foundation's waste-paper bin rather than a post box.' The foundation does not respond to unsolicited applications.
**WHO TO APPLY TO** Richard Borgonon, Trustee, Park Green Cottage, Barhatch Road, Cranleigh, Surrey GU6 7DJ Tel. 01483 274556 email flemlock@btinternet.com

## ■ The Roddick Foundation

**CC NO** 1061372    **ESTABLISHED** 1997
**WHERE FUNDING CAN BE GIVEN** Worldwide.
**WHO CAN BENEFIT** Charitable organisations.
**WHAT IS FUNDED** Human rights; poverty; social justice; environmental; humanitarian; medical/health; education; media; arts and culture.
**WHAT IS NOT FUNDED** The foundation has previously stated that it is 'particularly not interested in the following: funding anything related to sport; funding fundraising events or conferences; and sponsorship of any kind'.
**RANGE OF GRANTS** Up to £300,000.
**SAMPLE GRANTS** Christian Aid (£200,000); Body and Soul (£100,000); Community Futures Collective (£92,500); Greenpeace Environmental Trust (£85,000); The Hepatitis C Trust, Navdanya

Trust and Winston's Wish (£50,000 each); Shine Trust (£31,000); The Chicken Shed Theatre Trust and Whalefest (£25,000 each); The Restart Project (£20,000); Community Action Fund for Women in Africa (£15,400); Buglife and Inside Time New Bridge (£15,000 each); Campaign Academy and Dirty Beach (£10,000 each); Community Environmental Council (£6,600); UC Santa Barbara Foundation (£6,100); The Freedom Theatre (£3,000).

**FINANCES** Year 2013/14 Income £585,569 Grants £1,565,242 Grants to organisations £1,550,242 Assets £19,236,097

**TRUSTEES** Justine Roddick; Samantha Roddick; Gordon Roddick; Tina Schlieske.

**OTHER INFORMATION** Two grants were made to individuals during the year, totalling £15,000.

**HOW TO APPLY** Unsolicited applications are not accepted.

**WHO TO APPLY TO** Karen Smith, Unit H, The Old Bakery, Golden Square, Petworth, West Sussex GU28 0AP Tel. 01798 344362 email info@theroddickfoundation.org Website www.theroddickfoundation.org

## ■ The Rofeh Trust

**CC NO** 1077682  **ESTABLISHED** 1999
**WHERE FUNDING CAN BE GIVEN** Worldwide.
**WHO CAN BENEFIT** Charitable organisations.
**WHAT IS FUNDED** General charitable purposes, with a possible preference for Jewish causes.
**FINANCES** Year 2013/14 Income £69,423 Grants £58,259 Grants to organisations £58,259 Assets £958,984
**TRUSTEES** Martin Dunitz; Ruth Dunitz; Vivian Wineman; Henry Eder.
**HOW TO APPLY** Apply in writing to the correspondent.
**WHO TO APPLY TO** Martin Dunitz, 44 Southway, London NW11 6SA

## ■ Rokach Family Charitable Trust

**CC NO** 284007  **ESTABLISHED** 1981
**WHERE FUNDING CAN BE GIVEN** Israel and UK.
**WHO CAN BENEFIT** Jewish organisations.
**WHAT IS FUNDED** Advancement of the Jewish religion; education and training; medical purposes; health; general charitable purposes.
**SAMPLE GRANTS** Holdville Ltd (£1.8 million); Moreshet Hatorah Ltd (£55,500); TTMH (£24,000); Cosmon Belz Ltd (£13,200); Beis Yaakov School and Mercaz Torah V'Chesed (£6,000 each); Torah 5759 Ltd (£5,500); B.S.S. Seminary (£5,000); W.S.T. (£3,500); Comet Charity Ltd (£2,500); SOFT and Gateshead School (£2,100); Sassov Beis Hamedrash (£1,000).
**FINANCES** Year 2012/13 Income £254,030 Grants £1,945,809 Grants to organisations £1,945,809 Assets £873,578
**TRUSTEES** Norman Rokach; Helen Rokach; Esther Hoffman; Miriam Feingold; Anita Gefilhaus; Mrs N. Brenig.
**OTHER INFORMATION** Accounts are consistently late when submitted to the Charity Commission. At the time of writing (June 2015) the accounts for 2013/14 were overdue. The latest accounts available were those for the 2012/13 financial year, during which time investment management costs amounted to £136,500. The donations expenditure during the year were unusually large. This was due to the largest contribution (£1.8 million), which represents a net donation in respect of investment properties transferred to Holdville Ltd. Norman and Helen Rokach are

trustees of this charitable company. During 2012/13 'numerous' smaller donations totalled £24,000.

**HOW TO APPLY** Apply in writing to the correspondent.
**WHO TO APPLY TO** The Trustees, Purcells Chartered Accountants, 4 Quex Road, London NW6 4PJ Tel. 020 7328 3272

## ■ The Helen Roll Charitable Trust

**CC NO** 299108  **ESTABLISHED** 1988
**WHERE FUNDING CAN BE GIVEN** UK.
**WHO CAN BENEFIT** Registered charities only, including universities, schools, colleges, research institutions, groups helping disadvantaged people, theatres, animal welfare charities, and environmental and wildlife organisations.
**WHAT IS FUNDED** General charitable purposes, particularly: education, especially higher education; libraries and museums; the arts; health and animal welfare.
**WHAT IS NOT FUNDED** No support is given for individuals or non-registered charities.
**TYPE OF GRANT** Generally one-off for specific projects, but within a framework of charities whose work is known to the trustees.
**RANGE OF GRANTS** £1,000 to £15,000.
**SAMPLE GRANTS** Home Farm Trust (£15,000); Pembroke College Oxford and West Oxfordshire's Citizens Advice (£10,000 each); Purcell School, Sick Children's Trust and Trinity Laban Conservatoire of Music and Dance (£6,000 each); Canine Partners (£4,500); Oxford University Bodleian Libraries and St Nicholas Hospice, Bury St Edmunds (£4,000); Medical Detection Dogs (£3,000); Perthes Association and UCanDoIT (£2,000 each); Compassionate Friends (£1,500); React and Root and Branch (£1,000 each).
**FINANCES** Year 2013/14 Income £53,885 Grants £123,500 Grants to organisations £123,500 Assets £1,528,075
**TRUSTEES** Christine Chapman; Christine Reid; Patrick Stopford; Paul Strang; Frank Williamson; Jennifer Williamson; Peter Williamson; Stephen Williamson.
**OTHER INFORMATION** The charity aims to distribute about £120,000 each year between around 30 charities. The trustees work with the charities and often continue to make grants over a longer period of time. Because of this, there is only capacity for one or two new grants recipients each year.
**HOW TO APPLY** Apply in writing to the correspondent during the first fortnight in February. Applications should be kept short, ideally on one sheet of A4. Further material will then be requested from those who are short-listed. The trustees normally make their distributions in March. Applications by email are welcomed.
**WHO TO APPLY TO** The Trustees, c/o Wenn Townsend Accountants, 30 St Giles, Oxford OX1 3LE Tel. 01865 559900 email helen.roll@aol.co.uk

## ■ The Sir James Roll Charitable Trust

**CC NO** 1064963  **ESTABLISHED** 1997
**WHERE FUNDING CAN BE GIVEN** UK.
**WHO CAN BENEFIT** Registered charities.
**WHAT IS FUNDED** Mainly: the promotion of mutual tolerance, commonality and cordiality in major world religions; the furtherance of access to computer technology as a teaching medium at primary school levels; the promotion of

improved access to computer technology in community-based projects other than political parties or local government; the funding of projects aimed at early identification of specific learning disorders; and any other charitable projects as the trustees see fit.
**RANGE OF GRANTS** £500–£10,000, although most grants are between £500 and £1,000.
**SAMPLE GRANTS** DEC Philippines Typhoon Appeal (£10,000); Crisis (£5,000); Action for Prisoners' Families, Ambitious About Autism, Beating Bowel Cancer, Children in Crisis, Fair Trials International, Handicapped Children's' Action Group, Housing for Women, and Pancreatic Cancer UK (£1,000 each); Basildon Community Resource Centre, Cerebral Palsy Care Kent, Headway – East Kent Group, Keepout – The Crime Diversion Scheme, Kent Air Ambulance, Meningitis Research Foundation, St Mary-le-Bow Young Homeless Project, Tower Hamlets Mission, and Wavelength Charity Limited (£500 each).
**FINANCES** Year 2013/14 Income £210,962 Grants £140,500 Grants to organisations £140,500 Assets £4,818,368
**TRUSTEES** Nicholas Wharton; Brian Elvy; Jonathan Liddiard.
**HOW TO APPLY** Apply in writing to the correspondent.
**WHO TO APPLY TO** Nicholas Wharton, Trustee, 5 New Road Avenue, Chatham, Kent ME4 6AR Tel. 01634 830111 email sirjamesroll@winch-winch.co.uk

## ■ The Gerald Ronson Foundation

**CC NO** 1111728    **ESTABLISHED** 2005
**WHERE FUNDING CAN BE GIVEN** UK and overseas.
**WHO CAN BENEFIT** Registered charities.
**WHAT IS FUNDED** General charitable activities with a preference for Jewish causes.
**RANGE OF GRANTS** Generally up to £20,000 though occasionally larger grants are made.
**SAMPLE GRANTS** Jewish Care (£100,500); Great Ormond Street, King Solomon High School and RNIB (£50,000); The Royal Opera House Foundation (£33,500); Action for Stammering Children (£26,000); Global Warming Policy Federation (£12,500); One Family UK and Presidents Club Charitable Trust (£10,000 each); Manchester United Foundation and World Jewish Relief (£5,000 each); Holocaust Educational Trust (£3,000); Jewish Music Institute (£1,000); Lubavitch Scotland (£500); North London Hospice (£250).
**FINANCES** Year 2013 Income £1,463,543 Grants £866,745 Grants to organisations £866,745 Assets £11,798,118
**TRUSTEES** Gerald Ronson, Chair; Dame Gail Ronson; Alan Goldman; Jonathan Goldstein; Lisa Ronson; Nicole Ronson Allalouf; Hayley Ronson.
**OTHER INFORMATION** Some of the beneficiaries during the year were charities with which the trustees have direct connections.
**HOW TO APPLY** Apply in writing to the correspondent. 'The trust generally makes donations on a quarterly basis in March, June, September and December. In the interim periods, the Chair's Action Committee deals with urgent requests for donations which are approved by the trustees at the quarterly meetings.'
**WHO TO APPLY TO** Jeremy Trent, Secretary, H. W. Fisher and Company, Acre House, 11–15 William Road, London NW1 3ER Tel. 020 7388 7000 email jtrent@hwfisher.co.uk

## ■ Mrs L. D. Rope Third Charitable Settlement

**CC NO** 290533    **ESTABLISHED** 1984
**WHERE FUNDING CAN BE GIVEN** UK and overseas, with a particular interest in Suffolk.
**WHO CAN BENEFIT** For unsolicited applications, charities who work at grassroots level within their community, generally small in size, that are little catered for from other sources, or those that are based in particularly deprived areas. Charities with a large and committed volunteer base and those that have relatively low administration costs, in terms of staff salaries.
**WHAT IS FUNDED** Relief of poverty; advancement of education; advancement of religion; general charitable purposes.
**WHAT IS NOT FUNDED** Overseas projects; national charities; requests for core funding; buildings; medical research/health care (outside the beneficial area); schools (outside the beneficial area); environmental charities and animal welfare; the arts; matched funding; repayment of debts for individuals.
**TYPE OF GRANT** For unsolicited requests, grants are usually one-off and small scale. Funding is given for one year or less.
**RANGE OF GRANTS** Generally £100 to £2,000.
**SAMPLE GRANTS** St Peter and All Souls RC Church – Peterborough (£150,000); Cafod (£40,000); Leiston, Saxmundham and District Citizens Advice (£24,000); ISCU – Ipswich and Suffolk Credit Union (£18,000); St Stephen's Hospital – Uganda (£15,000); St Mary's RC Primary School (£12,200); St Vincent's Family Project (£7,500); Oak Meadow Children's Play Project (£7,000).
**FINANCES** Year 2013/14 Income £1,416,703 Grants £1,163,336 Grants to organisations £768,514 Assets £57,733,251
**TRUSTEES** Crispin Rope; Jeremy Heal; Ellen Jolly; Catherine Scott; Paul Jolly.
**OTHER INFORMATION** The charity has a very informative annual report and accounts. Of total amount given to organisations, £418,500 was awarded in unsolicited grants and £350,000 in grants initiated by the charity.
**HOW TO APPLY** Send a concise letter (preferably one side of A4) explaining the main details of your request. Always send your most recent accounts and a budgeted breakdown of the sum you are looking to raise. The charity will also need to know whether you have applied to other funding sources and whether you have been successful elsewhere. Your application should say who your trustees are and include a daytime telephone number.
**WHO TO APPLY TO** Crispin Rope, Trustee, Crag Farm, Boyton, Near Woodbridge, Suffolk IP12 3LH Tel. 01473 333288 email ropetrust@lucyhouse.org.uk

## ■ The Rosca Trust

**CC NO** 259907    **ESTABLISHED** 1966
**WHERE FUNDING CAN BE GIVEN** The boroughs of Southend-on-Sea, Castle Point and Rochford District Council only.
**WHO CAN BENEFIT** Registered charities.
**WHAT IS FUNDED** Support for young or older people or people with disabilities in the area of benefit.
**WHAT IS NOT FUNDED** Grants are not given outside the beneficial area or to individuals.
**RANGE OF GRANTS** Mainly £500 to £5,000.
**SAMPLE GRANTS** Livability (£7,000); Southend Mind and Southend YMCA (£5,000 each); Headway, Essex (£4,000); Trust Links (£3,500); SOS Domestic Abuse (£2,500); Dial Southend and

Great Wakering Sea Scout Group (£2,000 each); Achievement Through Football (£1,200); Happy Days (£1,100); Brentwood Catholic Children's Society (£1,000); Centre Place Family and Nursery and Southend East and West Divisions of the Girl Guides (£500 each).
**FINANCES** Year 2013/14 Income £130,015 Grants £120,825 Grants to organisations £120,825 Assets £662,557
**TRUSTEES** Ken Crowe; Nigel Gayner; Christopher Bailey; Daphne Powell; Maureen Sarling.
**OTHER INFORMATION** There was one grant of more than £5,000 awarded during the year (£7,000 to Livability).
**HOW TO APPLY** Apply in writing to the correspondent. Applications are reviewed three times a year, usually in January, April and September. An sae is appreciated. Preliminary telephone calls are considered unnecessary.
**WHO TO APPLY TO** Ken Crowe, Trustee, 19 Avenue Terrace, Westcliff-on-Sea, Essex SS0 7PL Tel. 01702 307840 email kenbarcrowe@blueyonder.co.uk

## ■ The Rose Foundation
**CC NO** 274875  **ESTABLISHED** 1977
**WHERE FUNDING CAN BE GIVEN** London area.
**WHO CAN BENEFIT** Registered charities and exempt bodies.
**WHAT IS FUNDED** Small building projects where the cost is of less than £200,000. This could be a general refurbishment or a specific project. With extensive experience with projects of this size, the trustees are often able to contribute advice and recommendations, in both the design and construction phases, in addition to their donation.
**WHAT IS NOT FUNDED** The purchase of equipment; the purchase of a building or site; seed money required to draw-up plans; fees in general. The trustees do not like to support projects already completed or give funds which will be banked 'indefinitely', so require projects to either commence within the first eight months of the year following approval or to have been started and still be ongoing during this period.
**TYPE OF GRANT** Part-funding building projects.
**RANGE OF GRANTS** Typically between £5,000 and £10,000.
**SAMPLE GRANTS** St John Ambulance (£484,000); New Amsterdam Charitable Foundation (£72,000); British Film Institute (£10,000); Jewish Care (£7,600); Cancer Research UK (£7,000); All Souls Church of England Primary School and British Museum (£5,000); Kings College London (£2,500).
**FINANCES** Year 2012/13 Income £915,514 Grants £862,190 Grants to organisations £862,190 Assets £25,782,954
**TRUSTEES** Martin Rose; Alan Rose; John Rose; Paul Rose.
**OTHER INFORMATION** At the time of writing (June 2015) the foundation's 2012/13 accounts were the latest available.
**HOW TO APPLY** Apply in writing to the correspondent including details of the organisation and the registered charity number, together with the nature and probable approximate cost of the scheme and its anticipated start and completion dates. The trustees commit to projects for the following year at their annual June meeting. Applications can be submitted any time between 1 July and 31 March for projects taking place the year after (e.g. between July 2015 and March 2016 for projects in 2017). There are detailed guidelines on the website.

**WHO TO APPLY TO** Martin Rose, Trustee, 28 Crawford Street, London W1H 1LN Tel. 020 7262 1155 Website www.rosefoundation.co.uk

## ■ The Cecil Rosen Foundation
**CC NO** 247425  **ESTABLISHED** 1966
**WHERE FUNDING CAN BE GIVEN** UK.
**WHO CAN BENEFIT** Organisations.
**WHAT IS FUNDED** Jewish causes; disability, including people who are blind.
**WHAT IS NOT FUNDED** Individuals.
**SAMPLE GRANTS** The Jewish Blind and Physically Handicapped Society (£140,000).
**FINANCES** Year 2013/14 Income £511,127 Grants £337,895 Grants to organisations £337,895 Assets £7,984,746
**TRUSTEES** Malcolm Ozin; John Hart; Peter Silverman.
**OTHER INFORMATION** Only one grant beneficiary was listed in the accounts.
**HOW TO APPLY** The correspondent has previously stated that 'no new applications can be considered'. Unsuccessful applications are not acknowledged.
**WHO TO APPLY TO** Malcolm Ozin, Trustee, 35 Langstone Way, Mill Hill East, London NW7 1GT Tel. 020 8346 8940

## ■ Rosetrees Trust
**CC NO** 298582  **ESTABLISHED** 1987
**WHERE FUNDING CAN BE GIVEN** In practice Great Britain (England, Scotland, and Wales).
**WHO CAN BENEFIT** Independent vetted medical research projects, especially if departmentally backed and peer reviewed. The vast majority of grants are made through university and medical schools.
**WHAT IS FUNDED** Medical research only.
**WHAT IS NOT FUNDED** Overheads; equipment or capital; conferences; travel and accommodation; technology transfer; tuition fees; projects outside England, Scotland and Wales; researchers at pre-PhD level; PhD studentships that have already started; research into illnesses that only affect a small number of people in the UK; basic research with no translation vision; psychology or social research.
**TYPE OF GRANT** Project and research funding for up to three years will be considered. Seed corn funding for a preliminary or pilot report is also available.
**RANGE OF GRANTS** Usually between £5,000 and £20,000.
**SAMPLE GRANTS** UCL and Royal Free (£873,500); Imperial College London (£183,000); Hebrew University Jerusalem (£133,500); Kings College London (£148,000); The Royal College of Surgeons (£268,000); University of Cambridge (£131,500); Barts and Queen Mary (£109,000); University of Oxford (£98,500); Institute of Cancer Research (£93,500); University of Southampton (£35,000).
**FINANCES** Year 2013/14 Income £20,501,972 Grants £2,646,422 Grants to organisations £2,646,422 Assets £36,227,744
**TRUSTEES** Richard Ross; Clive Winkler; James Bloom; Lee Mesnick.
**OTHER INFORMATION** During the year, 'Other centres' received £412,000 and 'Other' medical research grants totalled £161,500.
**HOW TO APPLY** Application forms and guidelines are available to download from the website. The is a separate application form and set of criteria for PhD applications. The trust states the following on its website: 'We ask you to complete the

form as concisely as possible but with enough detail for us to understand what your research is about this is best achieved by answering in simple lay terms.' Forms should be returned by email to rmiller@rosetreestrust.co.uk along with the following documentation: a more detailed technical report of no more than five pages (in scientific language for peer reviewer); a CV, of no more than two pages, for the project supervisor and researcher; an outline justification of the costs requested; a list of the highest impact/most relevant publications for the project supervisor and researcher (if applicable); a short covering letter; a reference (if the researcher is a PhD student or a post doc). For those wishing to submit a cancer-related application, the trust notes the following on its website: 'Due to the large number of applications Rosetrees is currently receiving, we will have to be extremely selective in terms of the projects we can consider and very few will receive support. Only those that score top (grade 1 – top 5%) peer review scores will be considered, so bear this in mind before deciding to submit an application.'

**WHO TO APPLY TO** Sam Howard, Chief Executive, Russell House, 140 High Street, Edgware, Middlesex HA8 7LW *Tel.* 020 8952 1414 *email* showard@rosetreestrust.co.uk *Website* www.rosetreestrust.co.uk

## ■ The Rothermere Foundation

**CC NO** 314125 **ESTABLISHED** 1964
**WHERE FUNDING CAN BE GIVEN** UK.
**WHO CAN BENEFIT** Registered charities; individual graduates of the Memorial University of Newfoundland.
**WHAT IS FUNDED** Establishment and maintenance of 'Rothermere Scholarships' to be awarded to graduates of the Memorial University of Newfoundland to enable them to undertake further periods of study in the UK; general charitable causes.
**RANGE OF GRANTS** Mostly up to £10,000.
**SAMPLE GRANTS** The Black Stork Charity (£100,000); Harmsworth Professorship (£62,000); National History Museum and Shakespeare North (£25,000 each); Wellbeing of Women (£15,000); London Symphony Orchestra (£6,500); New Schools Network and St Bride's Church (£5,000 each); Julia's House Hospice (£4,500); Corfu Animal Rescue Establishment (£3,000); Royal College of Music (£2,000); The Cherubim Music Trust (£1,500); The Public Catalogue (£1,000); Andover Young Carers (£500); Daylesford Church (£300); The Independent Museum – Salisbury (£250).
**FINANCES** *Year* 2013/14 *Income* £973,024 *Grants* £491,050 *Grants to organisations* £386,911 *Assets* £39,961,781
**TRUSTEES** Rt Hon. Viscount Rothermere; Viscountess Rothermere; Vyvyan Harmsworth; John Hemingway.
**OTHER INFORMATION** Payments made during the year included two grants to individuals totalling £13,100 and a further £91,000 in fellowship grants to three fellows. The foundation also provides accommodation for the Oxford Professor Scholarship, to a cost of £43,500 in 2013/14.
**HOW TO APPLY** Apply in writing to the correspondent. The trustees meet twice a year to consider grant applications.
**WHO TO APPLY TO** Vyvyan Harmsworth, Secretary, Beech Court, Canterbury Road, Challock, Ashford, Kent TN25 4DJ *Tel.* 01233 740641

## ■ The Rothley Trust

**CC NO** 219849 **ESTABLISHED** 1959
**WHERE FUNDING CAN BE GIVEN** Northumberland, North and South Tyneside, Newcastle upon Tyne, Gateshead and the former counties of Cleveland and Durham (including Darlington) and Cleveland.
**WHO CAN BENEFIT** Registered charities; CICs; voluntary groups (these must be properly constituted and must find a registered charity to act as a cheque handler).
**WHAT IS FUNDED** Children and young people; disability; community; education; energy saving projects; ex-services people; world in need. In-need appeals arising only from the area of benefit will be considered.
**WHAT IS NOT FUNDED** Further education; the repair of buildings solely used for worship; religious purposes; arts, heritage or science; amateur sport; human rights, conflict resolution or reconciliation (except family mediation); environmental protection or improvement; animal welfare; residents associations; parish councils; University of the Third Age.
**TYPE OF GRANT** Mainly one-off donations towards specific projects and not running costs. Start-up costs, buildings, equipment, resources and capital grants will be considered.
**RANGE OF GRANTS** Typically around £300.
**SAMPLE GRANTS** Citizens Advice Newcastle upon Tyne and Macmillan Cancer Support (£7,500 each); The Toby Henderson Trust (£5,000); Combat Stress (£3,750); Community Action Northumberland and Consett Churches Detached Youth Project (£3,500 each); Greggs Foundation – Hardship Fund, Newcastle upon Tyne and St John Ambulance – Northumbria (£3,000 each); Army Cadet Force Association, Brathay Hall Trust – Cumbria and Newcastle upon Tyne Council for Voluntary Service (£2,000) each.
**FINANCES** *Year* 2013/14 *Income* £243,398 *Grants* £267,800 *Grants to organisations* £246,100 *Assets* £7,033,419
**TRUSTEES** Dr Angus Armstrong; Alice Brunton; Julia Brown; Anne Galbraith; Mark Bridgeman; Gerard Salvin; Hume Hargreave; David Holborn.
**OTHER INFORMATION** Grants of less than £2,000 totalled £174,000 and a further £21,500 was given in grants to individuals.
**HOW TO APPLY** Apply in writing to the correspondent including a copy of latest accounts/annual reports and an sae. Full details can be found at the trust's website where criteria, guidelines and closing dates for applications are posted.
**WHO TO APPLY TO** Gillian Allsopp, Trust Secretary, Mea House, Ellison Place, Newcastle upon Tyne NE1 8XS *Tel.* 0191 232 7783 *email* mail@rothleytrust.co.uk *Website* www.rothleytrust.org.uk

## ■ The Roughley Charitable Trust

**CC NO** 264037 **ESTABLISHED** 1972
**WHERE FUNDING CAN BE GIVEN** Birmingham area (excluding Wolverhampton, Coventry, Worcester and the Black Country towns).
**WHO CAN BENEFIT** Registered local charities with an annual turnover of less than £1 million. Our research indicates that funds are mostly committed to projects known to the trustees.
**WHAT IS FUNDED** Community work (including church-based projects); social welfare; health and well-being; education; arts and leisure; heritage; and environment (particularly environmental improvement and green projects).

**WHAT IS NOT FUNDED** Projects in Sandwell, Solihull, Wolverhampton and Walsall; Birmingham-based medical charities; church fabric appeals; CICs; social enterprises; church-based projects which essentially teaching religion; animal charities; national charities, unless the local branch has its own Charity Commission number and accounts.
**RANGE OF GRANTS** Mostly £500 to £3,000. Larger grants to projects where trustees have special knowledge.
**SAMPLE GRANTS** Hope Projects West Midlands (£20,000); Appropriate Technology Asia and Christian Aid (£15,000 each); Birmingham Settlement, Emmaus UK and RaPt (£10,000 each); Birmingham Centre for Arts Therapies and Martineau Gardens (£5,000); St Mark's Day Centre Kingstanding and West Midlands Quaker Peace Process (£2,500 each); E. R. Mason Youth Centre Ladywood, Home Start Sutton Coldfield and Women and Theatre (£2,000 each); Banner Theatre, Birmingham Care Group, Birmingham Pen Trade Heritage Association, Birmingham Talking Newspaper, Community Environment Trust and St Gabriel's Centre (£1,000 each); South Sudanese East Bank Community Association (£500).
**FINANCES** Year 2013/14 Income £274,747 Grants £169,000 Grants to organisations £169,000 Assets £5,964,598
**TRUSTEES** John Smith; Martin Smith; Verity Owen; Victor Thomas; Rebecca McIntyre; Rachel Richards; Benjamin Newton.
**OTHER INFORMATION** Priority is given to small and medium-sized organisations.
**HOW TO APPLY** Applications should be made online via the trust's website, where the trust's criteria and guidelines are also available. Applications are accepted between 1 April and 1 October each year, for a grants meeting which takes place in November.
**WHO TO APPLY TO** John Smith, Trustee, 90 Somerset Road, Edgbaston, Birmingham B15 2PP email correspondent@roughleytrust.org.uk Website www.roughleytrust.org.uk

## ■ Mrs Gladys Row Fogo Charitable Trust
**SC NO** SC009685  **ESTABLISHED** 1970
**WHERE FUNDING CAN BE GIVEN** Edinburgh, Lothians and Dunblane.
**WHO CAN BENEFIT** Research workers and people with neurological diseases, but other medical research and charitable purposes are considered.
**WHAT IS FUNDED** Medical research, particularly in the field of neuroscience; also to local charity projects and to small charities mostly in Central Scotland.
**WHAT IS NOT FUNDED** Individuals.
**TYPE OF GRANT** One-off.
**RANGE OF GRANTS** Usually £1,000 to £8,000.
**SAMPLE GRANTS Previous beneficiaries have included:** SHEFC Brain Imaging Research Centre (£187,000); Macmillan Cancer Relief (£8,000); RNLI (£6,000); Alzheimer Scotland Action on Dementia, Age Concern and Salvation Army (£5,000 each); Multiple Sclerosis Society, Muscular Dystrophy Campaign and The Wishbone Trust (£4,500 each); Drum Riding for the Disabled, Invalids at Home and Stobhill Kidney Patient's Association (£4,000 each); The Sandpiper Trust £3,500; Erskine Hospital and Cancer Support Scotland – Tak Tent (£3,000).

**FINANCES** Year 2013/14 Income £150,050 Grants £410,000 Grants to organisations £410,000
**TRUSTEES** E. J. Cuthbertson; A. W. Waddell; Dr C. Brough.
**OTHER INFORMATION** In 2013/14 the trust had a total expenditure of £425,000, which is unusually high compared to previous years for which figures were available. Expenditure is usually in the region of £80,000 or less.
**HOW TO APPLY** Apply in writing to the trustees. The trustees meet once a year to consider applications, usually in September.
**WHO TO APPLY TO** The Trustees, c/o Brodies LLP Solicitors, 15 Atholl Crescent, Edinburgh EH3 8HA Tel. 0131 228 3777 Fax 0131 228 3878 email Mailbox@brodies.co.uk

## ■ Rowanville Ltd
**CC NO** 267278  **ESTABLISHED** 1973
**WHERE FUNDING CAN BE GIVEN** UK and Israel.
**WHO CAN BENEFIT** Organisations.
**WHAT IS FUNDED** The advancement of the Orthodox Jewish faith.
**RANGE OF GRANTS** Up to £50,000.
**SAMPLE GRANTS** Friends of Beis Yisrael Trust (£36,000); Achisomoch Aid Co (£34,500); Beis Hamedrash Chovevei Torah (£26,000); Yesamach Levov Trust (£24,000); LTC Trust Co (£20,000); Beis Yaakov Primary School (£16,200); The Noam Primary School Ltd (£11,000); The Telz Talmudical Academy and Talmud Torah Trust (£10,000); Phone and Learn (£8,000); Sarah Moseret Food Trust (£7,200); Hasmonean High School (£3,000); Jewish Learning Exchange (£1,500); Institute for Higher Rabbinical Studies and Jewish Rescue and Relief Committee (£1,000 each); Jewish Care (£600); Child Re-settlement (£300).
**FINANCES** Year 2013/14 Income £1,126,289 Grants £700,168 Grants to organisations £700,168 Assets £6,339,964
**TRUSTEES** Joseph Pearlman; Ruth Pearlman; Montague Frankel.
**OTHER INFORMATION** The charity's subsidiary charity, Sylvella Charity Ltd, supports Menorah Grammar School through the provision of free accommodation and, during the year, donated £70,500 in budgetary support. The school also received a grant of £50,500 from the main charity.
**HOW TO APPLY** The charity has previously stated that applications are unlikely to be successful unless one of the trustees has prior personal knowledge of the cause, as this charity's funds are already very heavily committed.
**WHO TO APPLY TO** Joseph Pearlman, Trustee, 8 Highfield Gardens, London NW11 9HB Tel. 020 8458 9266

## ■ The Rowland Family Foundation
**CC NO** 1111177  **ESTABLISHED** 2005
**WHERE FUNDING CAN BE GIVEN** UK and overseas, with a preference for England and Wales.
**WHO CAN BENEFIT** Charitable organisations.
**WHAT IS FUNDED** People with disabilities; children; older people. There is a focus on children who are disadvantaged.
**SAMPLE GRANTS** Chailey Heritage (£25,000); Barncancerfonden and Bevan Trust (£10,000).
**FINANCES** Year 2013/14 Income £471,161 Grants £45,000 Grants to organisations £45,000 Assets £5,956,878
**TRUSTEES** Angela Rowland; Prudence Dawes.

HOW TO APPLY Apply in writing to the correspondent.
WHO TO APPLY TO Lucy Gibson, Correspondent, Harcus Sinclair, 3 Lincoln's Inn Fields, London WC2A 3AA  Tel. 020 7242 9700  email lucy.gibson@harcus-sinclair.co.uk

## ■ The Rowlands Trust

CC NO 1062148    ESTABLISHED 1997
WHERE FUNDING CAN BE GIVEN West and South Midlands, including Hereford and Worcester, Gloucester, South Shropshire and Birmingham.
WHO CAN BENEFIT Organisations, including schools, churches and hospices.
WHAT IS FUNDED Medical and scientific research; people who are sick, poor or who have a disability; older people; music; the arts; the environment; the maintenance and restoration of Anglican church buildings.
WHAT IS NOT FUNDED Individuals; animal charities; annual running costs.
TYPE OF GRANT One-off, capital expenditure including buildings, project and research.
RANGE OF GRANTS Mostly between £500 and £10,000, occasionally larger.
SAMPLE GRANTS Worcestershire Acute Hospitals NHS Trust – Islet Research (£140,000); CTC Kinghurst Academy (£15,000); Baverstock Academy (£12,000); Library of Birmingham Development Trust and St Michael's Hospice (£10,000 each); Pershore Baptist Church (£7,500); Cavell Nurses Trust, Cotswold Canals Trust and Hereford Cathedral Perpetual Trust (£5,000 each); Black Country Food Bank (£2,500); Ironbridge Brass Band Festival (£2,000); Shakespeare Schools Festival (£1,800); Birmingham Citizens Advice and Birmingham and Solihull Women's Aid (£1,000 each); Sutton Coldfield YMCA (£500).
FINANCES Year 2013  Income £215,059  Grants £492,300  Grants to organisations £492,300  Assets £5,467,759
TRUSTEES Felicity Burman; Gary Barber; Timothy Jessop; Diana Crabtree.
HOW TO APPLY Application forms are available from the correspondent and are the preferred means by which to apply. Completed forms should be returned with a copy of the most recent accounts. The trustees meet to consider grants four times a year.
WHO TO APPLY TO Amandip Dhillon, c/o Mills and Reeve, 78–84 Colmore Row, Birmingham B3 2AB  Tel. 0121 456 8308  email amandip.dhillon@mills-reeve.com

## ■ The Joseph Rowntree Charitable Trust

CC NO 210037    ESTABLISHED 1904
WHERE FUNDING CAN BE GIVEN Unrestricted, in practice mainly UK.
WHO CAN BENEFIT Registered charities; voluntary organisations; charitable groups; individuals.
WHAT IS FUNDED The trust's current funding priorities are: Peace and Security; Power and Accountability; Rights and Justice; Sustainable Future; and Northern Ireland. Guidelines for each of the funding areas can be found on the website.
WHAT IS NOT FUNDED Generally, the trust will not fund: larger, older national charities with an established base of supporters and substantial levels of reserves; statutory bodies; for-profit organisations; medical research; academic research, unless this is an integral part of policy and campaigning work that is central to JRCT's funding priority areas; building, buying or repairing buildings; business development or job creation schemes; service provision, including the provision of care, training or support services; housing and homelessness; the arts, except where the project is specifically linked to the trust's issues of interest; individuals who are seeking funding for relief-in-need purposes, travel or adventure projects, or for educational bursaries; general appeals; work which is, or in the recent past has been, funded by statutory sources; work that has been already undertaken; local or national work outside the UK. Further specific exclusions are included for individual programmes and information on these can be found on the trust's website. Within its areas of interest, the trust makes grants to a range of organisations and to individuals. It is not necessary to be a registered charity to apply to the trust; however, only work that is defined as being charitable by UK law may be supported.
TYPE OF GRANT Single and multi-year funding for core and project costs.
SAMPLE GRANTS British American Security Information Council – BASIC (£200,000); Institute of Race Relations (£112,500); British Muslims for Secular Democracy and Northern Ireland Women's European Platform (£100,000 each); European Leadership Network (£90,000); Women for Refugee Women (£50,000); Travellers Aid Trust (£29,000); NATO Watch (£20,000); The Ecumenical Council for Corporate Responsibility (£15,000); Holywood Transition Town Ltd (£11,000); Public Concern at Work (£10,000); Quaker Service (£1,500).
FINANCES Year 2013  Income £4,917,000  Grants £6,806,000  Grants to organisations £6,806,000  Assets £177,282,000
TRUSTEES Margaret Bryan, Chair; Peter Coltman; Jenny Amery; Linda Batten; Helen Carmichael; Michael Eccles; Stan Lee; Emily Miles; Susan Seymour; Hannah Torkington; Imran Tyabji.
OTHER INFORMATION The Joseph Rowntree Charitable Trust is a Quaker trust and the value base of the trustees, as of the founder Joseph Rowntree (1836–1925), reflects the religious convictions of the Society of Friends. From 414 applications received during the year, the trust made 107 grants. The ten largest grants accounted for 23% of the total.
HOW TO APPLY Only online applications are accepted. Those sent by post, email or fax are not considered. The online form must be submitted and you should have the following information ready: a narrative proposal; budgets; accounts; (for non-registered charities) your organisation's governing document; information on your organisation's policies (equal opportunities and sustainability), should you have any. The closing dates of funding rounds are listed on the website.
WHO TO APPLY TO Nick Perks, Trust Secretary, The Garden House, Water End, York YO30 6WQ  Tel. 01904 627810  email enquiries@jrct.org.uk  Website www.jrct.org.uk

## ■ The Joseph Rowntree Foundation

CC NO 210169    ESTABLISHED 1904
WHERE FUNDING CAN BE GIVEN JRF works across the UK.
WHO CAN BENEFIT Organisations carrying out social science research.

# Rowntree

**WHAT IS FUNDED** This is not a conventional grant-making foundation. Working together with Joseph Rowntree Housing Trust, JRF researches the root causes of social problems and developing solutions, with the aim of achieving social change in the UK. The foundation's strategic aims have been shaped by its historic legacy from the Rowntrees as reforming businessmen at work, social change in the places they were part of, and progress by the people whose prospects they helped to shape. During 2015–17 the foundation's work will take on four themes (Partnerships, Diversity, Power and Digital), and will focus on the following strategic aims: Individuals and relationships; The places where people live; and Work and worth. See the website for further details on the foundation's current areas of funding.

**WHAT IS NOT FUNDED** Unsolicited proposals; educational bursaries or sponsorship for individuals for research or further education and training courses; proposals that do not have the potential to make a difference to policy or practice in the UK; projects outside the topics within the current priorities; development projects that are not innovative; development projects from which no general lessons can be drawn; general appeals e.g. from national charities; core or revenue funding, including grants for buildings or equipment; conferences and other events; websites or publications unless they are linked with work that the foundation is already supporting; grants to replace withdrawn or expired statutory funding, or to make up deficits already incurred; grants or sponsorship for individuals.

**TYPE OF GRANT** Project and research. Funding can be given for up to two years.

**FINANCES** Year 2014 Income £8,747,000 Grants £6,000,000 Grants to organisations £6,000,000 Assets £316,164,000

**TRUSTEES** Maureen Loffill; Don Brand; Graham Millar; Prof. Dianne Willcocks; Jas Bains; Steven Burkeman; Tony Stoller; Dame Mavis McDonald; Gillian Ashmore; Will Haire; Karamjit Singh.

**PUBLICATIONS** Findings – short briefing papers summarising the main findings of projects in the Research and Development Programme; Special Reports designed to present research results with clarity and impact.

**OTHER INFORMATION** Through the York Committee, grants, usually between £100 and £5,000, are made to organisations to help improve the quality of life of people in York. Particular regard is given to organisations working to benefit people affected by poverty and disadvantage. Priority is given to applications which fall within the foundation's 2015–17 strategic objectives.

**HOW TO APPLY** The foundation does not respond to unsolicited applications. Instead, it issues 'calls for proposals' and invites submissions to them. Detailed information on all current funding areas and how to make an application is available from the foundation's website. The York Committee has its own application guidelines and form, which are also available from the foundation's website.

**WHO TO APPLY TO** Julia Unwin, Chief Executive, The Homestead, 40 Water End, York YO30 6WP Tel. 01904 629241 Fax 01904 620072 email info@jrf.org.uk Website www.jrf.org.uk

## ■ Joseph Rowntree Reform Trust Limited

**ESTABLISHED** 1904

**WHERE FUNDING CAN BE GIVEN** UK.

**WHO CAN BENEFIT** Individuals, organisations and groups.

**WHAT IS FUNDED** Political, campaigning and lobbying purposes. The trust seeks to bring around political change, democratic reform and to defend civil liberties. It has the following aims: to correct imbalances of power; to strengthen the hand of individuals, groups and organisations striving for reform; to address the underlying causes of weakness and injustice in the body politic; to foster creative intervention by anticipating and brokering change within the body politic; to help to correct the financial imbalance between the major parties; to assist political liberals from all the major parties in the UK to promote new liberal ideas and policies.

**WHAT IS NOT FUNDED** The trust is not a registered charity and does not fund: unsolicited applications from registered charities or for work which may be funded from charitable sources; campaigns outside the UK; local campaigns without national impact; general appeals; academic research; work which the trust believes should be funded from statutory sources, or which has been in the recent past; legal fees; administrative or other core costs of party organisations; personal support of individuals in need; educational bursaries; travel and adventure projects; the construction, purchase or repair of properties; business development or job creation.

**TYPE OF GRANT** Full project funding.

**RANGE OF GRANTS** £100 to £325,000.

**SAMPLE GRANTS** Liberal Democrats (£325,000); Association of Liberal Democrat Councillors (£70,500); Open Rights Group (£50,500); Corporate Watch (£25,000); Black Mental Health UK (£17,200); Women Against Rape (£14,300); Campaign Against Arms Trade (£5,000); Alliance for Choice Northern Ireland (£4,200); Peace and Neutrality Alliance (£600); A7 Action Group (£250).

**FINANCES** Year 2013 Grants £878,838 Grants to organisations £878,838 Assets £33,939,163

**TRUSTEES** Dr Christopher Greenfield, Chair; Tina Day; Mandy Cormack; Dr Peadar Cremin; Alison Goldsworthy; Andrew Neal; Sal Brinton; Nick Harvey.

**PUBLICATIONS** The trust produces a range of reports, all of which are available on its website.

**OTHER INFORMATION** The trust is not a charity and therefore pays tax on its income. The trust budgets £1 million each year for grants.

**HOW TO APPLY** Applicants should email a one to two page outline of their proposal to the correspondent as soon as possible or, for amounts exceeding £7,500, no later than one week before the deadline for full applications. Proposals will be assessed and feedback sent within three working days. If your proposal has been approved, you will be invited to submit a full application. There are detailed guidelines on how to write and submit both a proposal and full application on the website. We would suggest that these are read thoroughly before either stage of the application process is begun. Applications for amounts of more than £7,500 are subject to deadlines, which are listed on the website, and are considered at quarterly Directors' meetings in March, July, October and December. Specific deadline dates can be found on the website. Applications for amounts of less than £7,500 can be submitted at any time apart

from in weeks where there is a deadline for larger applications.
WHO TO APPLY TO Tina Walker, Trust Secretary, The Garden House, Water End, York YO30 6WQ *Tel.* 01904 625744 *Fax* 01904 651502 *email* info@jrrt.org.uk *Website* www.jrrt.org.uk

## ■ Royal Artillery Charitable Fund

CC NO 210202          ESTABLISHED 1964
WHERE FUNDING CAN BE GIVEN UK and overseas.
WHO CAN BENEFIT Service charities.
WHAT IS FUNDED The welfare of all ranks of the Royal Artillery and the relief and assistance of any past or present members, living or deceased, their dependants and families who are in need of such assistance by way of poverty, illness or disability.
RANGE OF GRANTS From £200 to £64,500.
SAMPLE GRANTS Regiments and Batteries and Royal Artillery Sports (£64,500 each); Army Benevolent Fund (£55,000); RAA Grants (£33,000); Gunner Magazine (£18,000); King Edward VII Hospital (£2,800); Veterans Aid (£2,000); Army Widows' Association (£200).
FINANCES *Year* 2013 *Income* £1,243,932 *Grants* £929,791 *Grants to organisations* £246,086 *Assets* £16,091,498
TRUSTEES Maj. Gen. John Milne; C. Fletcher-Wood; Col. Alan Jolley; Maj. Anthony Richards; Maj. Andrew Dines; Brig. David Radcliffe; Maj. James Leighton; Col. William Prior; Col. Michael Kelly; Col. Nicholas Pond; Jeremy Bennett; Col. John Collinge.
OTHER INFORMATION A further £683,500 was given in welfare grants to individuals.
HOW TO APPLY Apply in writing to the correspondent.
WHO TO APPLY TO Lt. Col. Ian Vere Nicoll, General Secretary, Artillery House, Royal Artillery House, Larkhill, Wiltshire SP4 8QT *Tel.* 01980 634309 *email* rarhq-racf-welfare-mailbox@mod.uk *Website* www.theraa.co.uk/how-can-we-help/ra-charitable-fund

## ■ Royal British Legion

CC NO 219279          ESTABLISHED 1921
WHERE FUNDING CAN BE GIVEN UK, excluding Scotland. Grants in Scotland are made by Poppyscotland.
WHO CAN BENEFIT Charitable organisations that have been operating as a charity for at least two years.
WHAT IS FUNDED Projects and services benefitting serving and ex-service personnel and/or their families not already provided by the Royal British Legion and in line with its funding priorities, which are: employment and training; support for families; homelessness and outreach.
WHAT IS NOT FUNDED Commercial ventures (social clubs, for example); statutory services; service units and military wives choirs; commemoration, memorials, monuments or war cemeteries; projects that duplicate services provided by the Legion. Applications for funding exceeding £20,000 for any form of building work are not normally considered unless there are exceptional circumstances.
TYPE OF GRANT One-off and recurring costs.
RANGE OF GRANTS The maximum amount for any single award is £20,000, applications for smaller amounts are encouraged.
SAMPLE GRANTS The Officer's Association (£1.76 million); Citizens Advice Scotland (£382,000, made through Poppyscotland); Imperial College of Science, Technology and Medicine (£173,000).
FINANCES *Year* 2013/14 *Income* £133,472,000 *Grants* £14,262,000 *Grants to organisations* £3,201,000 *Assets* £286,275,000
TRUSTEES Bill Parkin; Terry Whittles; Adrian Burn; John Crisford; Denise Edgar; Martyn Tighe; Anthony MacAuley; Maj. General David Jolliffe; Vice Admiral Peter Wilkinson; Col. Neil Salisbury; Lt. Col. Joe Falzon; Jason Coward; Colin Kemp; Philip Moore; Marilyn Humphrey; Catherine Quinn; Lt. Col. David Whimpenny.
OTHER INFORMATION Grant-making is only a small part of the Royal British Legion's work. During the year, it had a direct charitable expenditure of £76.5 million, of which almost half was spent on the provision of community welfare services. As part of its support for service and ex-service personnel, the Legion also makes welfare grants to individuals. In 2013/14 these totalled more than £11 million.
HOW TO APPLY The application process has two stages. Stage One involves the completion of a brief expression of interest form, which should be returned to the External Grants Officer (externalgrants@britishlegion.org.uk). Applicants that are successful at the first stage will be invited to complete a Stage Two application form to be considered by the Grants Panel. The Stage One application form is available to download from the website along with guidelines.
WHO TO APPLY TO External Grants Officer, Haig House, 199 Borough High Street, London SE1 1AA *Tel.* 020 3207 2138 *email* info@britishlegion.org.uk *Website* www.britishlegion.org.uk

## ■ Royal Docks Trust (London)

CC NO 1045057          ESTABLISHED 1995
WHERE FUNDING CAN BE GIVEN Part of the London Borough of Newham.
WHO CAN BENEFIT The trust supports the community in that part of the London borough of Newham that lies to the south of the London – Tilbury Trunk Road (A13) known as Newham Way.
WHAT IS FUNDED General charitable purposes. Areas of specific interest are: educational and vocational training; recreational and leisure-time activities; the advancement of public education in the arts; general improvement of the physical and social environment; relief of poverty and sickness; housing for people with disabilities or who are otherwise in need; preservation of buildings of historical or architectural significance.
WHAT IS NOT FUNDED Individuals; general appeals; revenue, top-up or retrospective funding are not given through the minor grants programme.
RANGE OF GRANTS Up to £28,500.
SAMPLE GRANTS Ascension Eagles Cheerleaders, Community Links ASTA Centre and Royal Docks Learning and Activity Centre (£28,500); West Silvertown Village Community Foundation (£20,000); Ascension Community Trust – Garden Cafe (£17,200); Newham All Stars Sports Academy (£11,100); Women United (£2,200); Newham Riding School and Association and St Luke's Youth Club Summer Playscheme (£1,500 each); Newham Action Against Domestic Violence (£1,000); The Drop-in Bereavement Centre (£600); Beckton Table Tennis Club (£500); England Netball (£300).
FINANCES *Year* 2013/14 *Income* £299,712 *Grants* £201,319 *Grants to organisations* £201,319 *Assets* £7,416,912

TRUSTEES Eric Sorensen; Richard Gooding; Stephen Nicholas; Sid Keys; Alan Taylor; Ken Wilson; Cherry Patel; Dennis James; Amanda Williams; Robert Heaton; Kayar Raghavan; Cllr Forhad Hussain; Cllr Patrick Murphy.
OTHER INFORMATION Smaller grants of less than £1,000 each were also made to local groups.
HOW TO APPLY The trust partners the London Borough of Newham, which administers the grants programmes. For the annual grants programmes, a broad timetable has been noted on the website: 'June to September – agree priorities/criteria and an indicative level of funding for the forthcoming year; October to December – invite applications via open advertisement and contact with existing recipients of grant aid and voluntary organisations known to LBN/trust; December to January – assessment of applications received, LBN inter-departmental liaison, liaison with other funding bodies and discussions with applicants; January to March – determination of funding for the forthcoming year and approval of applications.' Application forms for the minor grants programme, which is subject to its own criteria, may be downloaded from the trust's website.
WHO TO APPLY TO Stephen Collins, Community Support Unit, Building 1000, Dockside Road, London E16 2QU *Tel.* 020 8430 2433 *email* stephen.collins@newham.gov.uk *Website* www.royaldockstrust.org.uk

## ■ Royal Masonic Trust for Girls and Boys

CC NO 285836  ESTABLISHED 1982
WHERE FUNDING CAN BE GIVEN England and Wales.
WHO CAN BENEFIT Registered charities. Grants are also given to individual children/grandchildren of freemasons.
WHAT IS FUNDED Non-masonic charities can currently apply to the Stepping Stones scheme which gives grants to charities and programmes working to alleviate poverty and improve educational outcomes among children and young people who are extremely disadvantaged and are facing financial hardship.
WHAT IS NOT FUNDED General contributions to capital or building projects.
TYPE OF GRANT Funding or part-funding for specific programmes or initiatives and one-off/specific overhead costs.
RANGE OF GRANTS Up to a maximum of £20,000 for one year and up to £30,000 over two years.
SAMPLE GRANTS Aspire; British Exploring Society; Child Victims of Crime; Family Support Work; Home-Start Sutton; National Autistic Society; SkillForce; White Lodge Centre; Young Lives Foundation and Youth at Risk.
FINANCES Year 2013 *Income* £5,400,000 *Grants* £6,449,000 *Grants to organisations* £318,000 *Assets* £156,676,000
TRUSTEE Council members appointed by a resolution of a General Court.
OTHER INFORMATION Around 15 grants are given through the Stepping Stones scheme each year, two or three of which are maximum grants. During the year, non-Masonic donations amounted to £515,000, of which £218,000 was awarded to Lifelites, £100,000 to other non-Masonic charities, and £197,000 in choral bursaries to individuals. There was a further £5.5 million paid to individuals connected with Freemasonry and £393,000 through the TalentAid scheme.

HOW TO APPLY To apply to the Stepping Stones scheme, submit a one page initial enquiry to steppingstones@rmtgb.org or by post to Oliver Carrington, Policy Advisor. Your enquiry should include: the charity's registration number; its main area of work; the amount of funding requested; and a description of the programme or project, including its location. If your enquiry fits the aims and requirements of the scheme, a full application form will be sent out. Initial enquiries and completed applications are each subject to deadlines, the dates of which are available from the website.
WHO TO APPLY TO Leslie Hutchinson, Chief Executive, Freemasons' Hall, 60 Great Queen Street, London WC2B 5AZ *Tel.* 020 7405 2644 *Fax* 020 7831 4094 *email* info@rmtgb.org *Website* www.rmtgb.org

## ■ The Royal Victoria Hall Foundation

CC NO 211246  ESTABLISHED 1891
WHERE FUNDING CAN BE GIVEN Greater London.
WHO CAN BENEFIT Professional theatre groups (including youth and children's theatre).
WHAT IS FUNDED Encouragement of organisations devoted to the development of and education in theatrical pursuits, infrastructure and technical support, opera and theatre.
WHAT IS NOT FUNDED Projects that relate exclusively to music e.g. a song or a musical recital; dance which is not within a theatrical context; projects that are wholly concerned with drama training or education or the academic study of dramatic performance; amateur dramatic projects; administrative running costs of an organisation; individuals seeking funds for personal tuition.
TYPE OF GRANT Funding of theatre equipment, feasibility studies, production costs, disability and educational access.
RANGE OF GRANTS £500–£1,000
SAMPLE GRANTS Fanshen, Finger in the Pie, Greenwich and Docklands International Festival and Just Jones (£1,000 each); Omnibus (£950); Acting Touring Company and Metta Theatre (£750 each); Belarus Free Theatre, Damont Productions, Emergency Exit Arts and Instant Classic (£500 each).
FINANCES Year 2013/14 *Income* £68,537 *Grants* £47,450 *Grants to organisations* £47,450 *Assets* £1,567,465
TRUSTEES David Collier; Margaret Colgan; Gerald Lidstone; Vivienne Rochester; Brian Daniels; Katie Lancaster; Peader Kirk; Paul Gane; Patricia Myers.
OTHER INFORMATION Grants were made to 36 organisations totalling £47,500. Eleven students from London drama schools received the Lilian Baylis award; each were awarded £1,500.
HOW TO APPLY The following information is taken from the foundation's website. 'If you feel that your project conforms to the criteria for grants, you need to send an application that will consist of: a covering letter outlining the project. This should be on company letter head, showing clearly the company's postal address, email address, and name and telephone number of contact. This is very important as, if a grant is made, the cheque will be made out in the company name. Please state in the first paragraph what you are applying for, how much you are asking for, the date and the venue of the project; a detailed description of the project's artistic content; full CVs of the people

involved in the project; a clear budget that outlines all expenditure and all expected income, including (but not exclusively) earnings, sponsorship and support in-kind; your company's most recent accounts; a clear statement of how much money you are asking the foundation to grant your project and the consequences of your not being given this amount. All the above must be included for the proper consideration of your project. If any part is not submitted we will automatically return your application. Please feel free to send in any supporting documentation such as reviews of previous projects or publicity flyers. All applications should be sent to the Clerk by email (with attachments, not links to file download sites) and by post (not registered or recorded delivery) by 5.30pm on the last working Friday in February for consideration at the April meeting, and by 5.30pm on the last working Friday of August for consideration at the October meeting. Applications for April must be for projects happening between May and October and applications for October must be for projects happening between November and April.'

**WHO TO APPLY TO** Carol Cooper, Correspondent, 111 Green Street, Sunbury-on-Thames TW16 6QX *Tel.* 01932 782341 *email* contact@rvhf.org *Website* www.rvhf.org

## ■ The Rubin Foundation

**CC NO** 327062  **ESTABLISHED** 1986
**WHERE FUNDING CAN BE GIVEN** UK and overseas.
**WHO CAN BENEFIT** Organisations.
**WHAT IS FUNDED** Jewish organisations; the arts; general charitable purposes.
**RANGE OF GRANTS** Up to around £50,000.
**SAMPLE GRANTS Previous beneficiaries have included:** Chai Lifeline Cancer Care (£50,500); The Prince's Trust (£50,000); West London Synagogue and the International Business Leaders' Forum (£25,000 each); Parliamentary Committee against Anti-Semitism Foundation (£15,000); The Prince's Foundation for Children and The Arts and the Roundhouse Trust (£10,000 each); Chickenshed Theatre Company (£6,000); Cherie Blair Foundation for Women (£3,000); Footwear Benevolent Society (£2,000); the Politics and Economic Research Trust (£1,000).
**FINANCES** *Year* 2013/14 *Income* £7,407 *Grants* £575,000 *Grants to organisations* £575,000
**TRUSTEES** Alison Mosheim; Angela Rubin; Robert Rubin; Andrew Rubin; Carolyn Rubin.
**OTHER INFORMATION** Due to its low income, the foundation was not required to submit its accounts for 2013/14 to the Charity Commission.
**HOW TO APPLY** The foundation has previously stated that 'grants are only given to people related to our business', such as charities known to members of the Rubin family and those associated with Pentland Group Ltd. Unsolicited applications are very unlikely to succeed.
**WHO TO APPLY TO** The Trustees, The Pentland Centre, Lakeside House, Squires Lane, Finchley, London N3 2QL *Tel.* 020 8346 2600 *email* amcmillan@pentland.com

## ■ William Arthur Rudd Memorial Trust

**CC NO** 326495  **ESTABLISHED** 1983
**WHERE FUNDING CAN BE GIVEN** UK and Spain.
**WHO CAN BENEFIT** Registered charities in the UK and certain Spanish charities.
**WHAT IS FUNDED** General charitable purposes. The latest accounts note that 'the trustees may have regard to the wishes of the settlor as expressed from time to time in writing'.
**TYPE OF GRANT** Generally one-off; unrestricted funding.
**RANGE OF GRANTS** £1,000–£5,000
**SAMPLE GRANTS** Unfortunately beneficiaries were not specified in the latest accounts.
**FINANCES** *Year* 2013 *Income* £39,013 *Grants* £36,500 *Grants to organisations* £36,500 *Assets* £866,051
**TRUSTEES** Alexandra Sarkis; David Smyth; Robert Maples.
**HOW TO APPLY** Applications can be made in writing to the correspondent. The accounts note that 'as the objects of the charity are not linked to any specific areas of charitable activity, the trustees receive a large number of applications for donations'. Requests are reviewed at the annual meeting.
**WHO TO APPLY TO** Alexandra Sarkis, Trustee, 12 South Square, Gray's Inn, London WC1R 5HH *Tel.* 020 7405 8932 *email* mail@mmandm.co.uk

## ■ The Rufford Foundation (formerly The Rufford Small Grants Foundation)

**CC NO** 1117270  **ESTABLISHED** 2006
**WHERE FUNDING CAN BE GIVEN** Worldwide.
**WHO CAN BENEFIT** Individuals and small groups in financially developing countries.
**WHAT IS FUNDED** Nature/biodiversity conservation projects and pilot programmes.
**WHAT IS NOT FUNDED** Projects in developed countries; pure research with no obvious conservation benefit; expeditions; attending conferences or seminars.
**TYPE OF GRANT** Small-scale and pilot project funding.
**RANGE OF GRANTS** Rufford Small Grants are the entry-level funding and these are for up to £5,000.
**SAMPLE GRANTS** See the foundation's annual report and accounts for a detailed list of beneficiaries, broken down by the stage of grant received.
**FINANCES** *Year* 2013/14 *Income* £3,656,366 *Grants* £3,568,249 *Grants to organisations* £3,568,249 *Assets* £100,013,390
**TRUSTEES** John Laing; Elizabeth Brunwin; Hugo Edwards; Sarah Barbour; Robert Reilly.
**OTHER INFORMATION** There are five different stages of grants, which may be given in sequence, beginning with a Rufford Small Grant. The grant total displayed also includes funding awarded to individuals.
**HOW TO APPLY** Applications should be completed online on the foundation's website, where criteria and guidelines are also posted. Applications are considered on a rolling basis, there is no deadline.
**WHO TO APPLY TO** Josh Cole, Grants Director, 6th Floor, 248 Tottenham Court Road, London W1T 7QZ *Tel.* 020 7436 8604 *email* josh@rufford.org *Website* www.rufford.org

# Rugby

## ■ The Rugby Group Benevolent Fund Limited

**CC NO** 265669    **ESTABLISHED** 1973

**WHERE FUNDING CAN BE GIVEN** Barrington (Cambridgeshire); Chinnor (Oxfordshire); Kensworth (Bedfordshire); Lewes (Sussex); Rochester (Kent); Rugby and Southam (Warwickshire); South Ferriby (North Lincolnshire); and Tilbury (Essex).

**WHO CAN BENEFIT** Organisations with charitable objectives.

**WHAT IS FUNDED** Charitable causes in communities where employees and ex-employees of Rugby Group Limited and their dependants live.

**WHAT IS NOT FUNDED** Organisations operating outside the areas of benefit; support is not normally given for day-to-day revenue costs.

**TYPE OF GRANT** Capital costs for specific projects.

**RANGE OF GRANTS** Up to £30,000.

**SAMPLE GRANTS** Hope 4 (Rugby) Ltd (£30,000); Futures Unlocked (£16,000); Long Itchington Cricket Club and Stockton FC and CC (£15,000 each); Chinnor Village Hall and Warwickshire and Northants Air Ambulance (£10,000 each); New Bilton Community Association (£7,500); Marton Museum of County Bygones (£5,000); Harlton Church Bells Fund (£3,000); Marie Curie Cancer Care (£2,000); Rugby Disability Forum, Rugby Foster Care Association and Rugby Children's Contact Centre (£1,000 each).

**FINANCES** Year 2014 Income £71,788 Grants £275,666 Grants to organisations £226,932 Assets £2,553,985

**TRUSTEES** Graham Fuller; Ian Southcott; Chris Coates; Norman Jones; Nigel Appleyard; Jim Wootten; Geoff Thomas.

**OTHER INFORMATION** This fund was established in 1955 with the aim of supporting employees and former employees of Rugby Group Limited, and their dependants. The Rugby Group is now a part of CEMEX UK, a global cement manufacturer but the fund has kept its independence and is managed by a group of employees and former employees. During the year, 48 grants were made to organisations, of which 18 grants, amounting to £4,700, were of less than £1,000. Grants to individuals totalled £48,500.

**HOW TO APPLY** At the time of writing, the 'Applying' page on the fund's website stated that an initial expression of interest form and a full application form would soon be available. The page also lists guidelines.

**WHO TO APPLY TO** Daphne Murray, Secretary, Cemex House, Coldharbour Lane, Thorpe, Egham, Surrey TW20 8TD *Tel.* 01932 583181 *email* info@rugbygroupbenevolentfund.org.uk *Website* www.rugbygroupbenevolentfund.org.uk

## ■ The Russell Trust

**SC NO** SC004424    **ESTABLISHED** 1985

**WHERE FUNDING CAN BE GIVEN** UK, especially Scotland.

**WHO CAN BENEFIT** Registered charities.

**WHAT IS FUNDED** General charitable purposes.

**WHAT IS NOT FUNDED** Only registered charities or organisations with charitable status are supported.

**TYPE OF GRANT** One-off, unrestricted grants, particularly to pump-prime new projects.

**RANGE OF GRANTS** Usually in the range of £250–£2,000. Three or four larger grants of £20,000 may be awarded annually.

**SAMPLE GRANTS** No grants list was available, but donations were broken down as follows: youth work; health and welfare; education; local; music and the arts; church; preservation/conservation; archaeology; St Andrew's University.

**FINANCES** Year 2013–14 Income £5,918 Grants £150,000 Grants to organisations £150,000

**TRUSTEES** Fred Bowden; Cecilia Croal; Graeme Crombie; David Erdal; Don Munro; Iona Russell; Alan Scott; C. A. G. Parr.

**HOW TO APPLY** Application forms are available from the correspondent. A statement of accounts must be supplied. The trustees meet quarterly, although decisions on the allocation of grants are made more regularly.

**WHO TO APPLY TO** Iona Russell, Administrator and Trustee, Markinch, Glenrothes, Fife KY7 6PB *Tel.* 01592 753311 *email* russelltrust@trg.co.uk

## ■ Ryklow Charitable Trust 1992

**CC NO** 1010122    **ESTABLISHED** 1992

**WHERE FUNDING CAN BE GIVEN** UK and overseas, with a preference for the East Midlands.

**WHO CAN BENEFIT** Organisations, generally small or start-up charities; individuals.

**WHAT IS FUNDED** Projects in financially developing countries, particularly those which are intended to be self-sustaining or concerned with education; help for vulnerable families, minorities and the prevention of abuse or exploitation of children and young people; conservation of natural species, landscape and resources; projects benefitting the local community in Belper, Derbyshire.

**WHAT IS NOT FUNDED** Only organisations which are UK-registered, have a UK sponsor, or are affiliated to a UK-registered charity will be considered.

**RANGE OF GRANTS** Usually £500 to £3,000.

**SAMPLE GRANTS** Field Row Unitarian Chapel, Belper; Safe and Sound.

**FINANCES** Year 2013/14 Income £19,115 Grants £80,000 Grants to organisations £80,000

**TRUSTEES** Andrew Williamson; Ernest Cannings; Philip Hanson; Sheila Taylor.

**OTHER INFORMATION** In 2013/14 the trust had a total expenditure of £96,500. Due to its low income, the trust was not required to submit its accounts for the year to the Charity Commission.

**HOW TO APPLY** The trust no longer accepts unsolicited applications. The trustees actively seek out charities which they invite to apply.

**WHO TO APPLY TO** Stephen Marshall, c/o Robinsons Solicitors, 10–11 St James Court, Friar Gate, Derby DE1 1BT *Tel.* 01332 291431 *email* stephen.marshall@robinsons-solicitors.co.uk

## ■ The J. S. and E. C. Rymer Charitable Trust

**CC NO** 267493    **ESTABLISHED** 1974

**WHERE FUNDING CAN BE GIVEN** East Yorkshire.

**WHO CAN BENEFIT** Organisations; individuals.

**WHAT IS FUNDED** General charitable purposes.

**WHAT IS NOT FUNDED** Causes outside East Yorkshire.

**SAMPLE GRANTS** Recipients have included local churches, community healthcare and a regional branch of the NSPCC.

**FINANCES** *Year* 2013/14 *Income* £78,232 *Grants* £63,952 *Grants to organisations* £63,952

**TRUSTEES** Carol Rymer; Timothy Rymer; Giles Brand.

**OTHER INFORMATION** At the time of writing (June 2015) the trust's accounts for 2013/14 had been submitted to the Charity Commission but were not yet available to view. In previous years, donations have accounted for the entirety of the trust's total expenditure.

**HOW TO APPLY** Apply in writing to the correspondent.

**WHO TO APPLY TO** Beverley Gibson, Southburn Offices, Southburn, Driffield, East Yorkshire YO25 9ED *Tel.* 01377 227785

## ■ S. F. Foundation
CC NO 1105843   ESTABLISHED 2004
WHERE FUNDING CAN BE GIVEN Worldwide.
WHO CAN BENEFIT Jewish organisations.
WHAT IS FUNDED The foundation gives grants towards the 'advancement and furtherance of the Jewish religion and Jewish religious education and the alleviation of poverty amongst the Jewish community throughout the world.'
FINANCES Year 2013/14 Income £6,999,305 Grants £3,149,203 Grants to organisations £3,149,203 Assets £25,225,925
TRUSTEES Hannah Jacob; Rivka Niederman; Miriam Schrieber.
HOW TO APPLY The foundation's annual report states: 'The charity accepts applications for grants from representatives of various charities, which are reviewed by the trustees on a regular basis.'
WHO TO APPLY TO Rivka Niederman, Secretary, 143 Upper Clapton Road, London E5 9DB Tel. 020 8802 5492 email sffoundation143@gmail.com

## ■ The Michael Sacher Charitable Trust (formerly known as the Jeremy and John Sacher Charitable Trust)
CC NO 206321   ESTABLISHED 1957
WHERE FUNDING CAN BE GIVEN UK and Israel.
WHO CAN BENEFIT Registered charities, with a preference for Jewish organisations.
WHAT IS FUNDED General charitable purposes, including arts, culture and heritage, medical and disability causes, community and welfare, education, science and technology, children and young people and religion.
WHAT IS NOT FUNDED Individuals.
RANGE OF GRANTS £100–£20,000
SAMPLE GRANTS The International Centre for the Study of Radicalisation and Political Violence (£20,000); The Royal Opera House Foundation (£15,400); The Airborne Initiative Trust (£15,000); Camden Citizens Advice Service Limited and Chicken Shed Theatre (£5,000 each); Anglo-Israel Association and The Honeypot Children's Charity (£1,000 each); Dementia UK and Dorset Child and Family Counselling Trust (£250 each).
FINANCES Year 2013/14 Income £149,242 Grants £73,413 Grants to organisations £73,413 Assets £5,725,103
TRUSTEES John Sacher; Jeremy Sacher; Rosalind Sacher; Elisabeth Sacher.
OTHER INFORMATION During the year, 21 grants were made to organisations.
HOW TO APPLY Apply in writing to the correspondent at any time.
WHO TO APPLY TO The Trustees, c/o H. W. Fisher and Co., Acre House, 11–15 William Road, London NW1 3ER Tel. 020 7388 7000 email johnsacher@clara.co.uk

## ■ The Michael Harry Sacher Trust
CC NO 288973   ESTABLISHED 1984
WHERE FUNDING CAN BE GIVEN UK and overseas.
WHO CAN BENEFIT Registered charities.
WHAT IS FUNDED General charitable purposes with a preference for organisations working in the areas of arts and culture, health, community and welfare, children and young people, overseas aid and Jewish religious organisations.
WHAT IS NOT FUNDED Individuals; organisations which are not registered charities.
RANGE OF GRANTS £250–£30,000
SAMPLE GRANTS Royal Opera House Foundation (£25,000, two grants); Punchdrunk (£13,500, three grants); John and Jeremy Sacher Charitable Trust (£5,500); British Friends of the Hebrew University of Jerusalem, Harrow Multiple Sclerosis Therapy Centre and Royal Academy of Arts (£5,000 each); Chabad Lubavitch UK, Community Security Trust and Nightingale Hammerson (£2,500 each); Norwood Ravenswood (£2,000); World Jewish Relief (£2,000, two grants); Cancer Research UK, Magen David Adom UK Westminster Synagogue and The Wiener Library (£1,000 each); United Synagogue (£850); Rays of Sunshine (£750); The Colonel's Fund Grenadier Guards (£500).
FINANCES Year 2013/14 Income £69,747 Grants £83,126 Grants to organisations £83,126 Assets £2,398,649
TRUSTEES Nicola Sacher; Michael Sacher.
HOW TO APPLY Apply in writing to the correspondent. Requests are generally only considered if they are from organisations that are personally known to the trustees.
WHO TO APPLY TO The Trustees, c/o H. W. Fisher and Co, Acre House, 11–15 William Road, London NW1 3ER Tel. 020 7388 7000

## ■ Raymond and Beverly Sackler 1988 Foundation
CC NO 327864   ESTABLISHED 1988
WHERE FUNDING CAN BE GIVEN UK and overseas, namely Israel.
WHO CAN BENEFIT The foundation has a list of regular beneficiaries.
WHAT IS FUNDED The arts; science; medical research.
TYPE OF GRANT Annual grants.
SAMPLE GRANTS Yale University; Weill Cornell Medical College; and University College London – Cancer Centre.
FINANCES Year 2013 Income £0 Grants £300,000 Grants to organisations £300,000
TRUSTEES Christopher Mitchell; Dr Raymond Sackler; Jonathan Sackler; R. Smith; Dr Richard Sackler; Ake Wikstrom; Antony Mattessich.
OTHER INFORMATION Formerly known as The Raymond and Beverley Sackler Foundation. In 2013/14 the foundation had a total expenditure of £303,500.
HOW TO APPLY Unsolicited applications are not invited.
WHO TO APPLY TO Christopher Mitchell, Trustee, 9th Floor, New Zealand House, 80 Haymarket, London SW1Y 4TQ Tel. 020 7930 4944

## ■ The Sackler Trust
CC NO 1132097   ESTABLISHED 1988
WHERE FUNDING CAN BE GIVEN England, Wales and Scotland.
WHO CAN BENEFIT Generally larger institutions.

**WHAT IS FUNDED** Arts and culture; science; medical research.
**TYPE OF GRANT** Some recurring; others one-off.
**RANGE OF GRANTS** Up to £1 million, though most grants were of less than £100,000.
**SAMPLE GRANTS** Dulwich Picture Gallery and Glasgow University (£1 million each); The Serpentine Gallery (£500,000); Royal Hospital for Neuro-disability and St Peter's College – Oxford (£250,000 each); LAMDA (£160,000); Salisbury World and City and Guilds Art School (£150,000 each); Médecins Sans Frontières and Historic Royal Palaces (£100,000 each).
**FINANCES** Year 2013 Income £13,387,046 Grants £4,267,493 Grants to organisations £4,267,493 Assets £59,722,960
**TRUSTEES** Dame Theresa Sackler; Peter Stormonth Darling; Christopher Mitchell; Raymond Smith; Marissa Sackler; Sophia Dalrymple; Michael Sackler; Marianne Mitchell.
**OTHER INFORMATION** In 2013 a total of 38 'miscellaneous' grants of less than £100,000 accounted for £607,500 of the grant total. The grant total during the year was unusually high compared with any previous year (2012: £443,500; 2011: £127,000; 2010: £203,000).
**HOW TO APPLY** Apply in writing to the correspondent.
**WHO TO APPLY TO** Christopher Mitchell, Trustee, 9th Floor, New Zealand House, 80 Haymarket, London SW1Y 4TQ Tel. 020 7930 4944

## ■ The Ruzin Sadagora Trust

**CC NO** 285475 **ESTABLISHED** 1982
**WHERE FUNDING CAN BE GIVEN** UK and Israel.
**WHO CAN BENEFIT** Jewish organisations.
**WHAT IS FUNDED** The upkeep and activities of the Ruzin Sadagora Synagogue in London; other associated Sadagora institutions; other Jewish causes.
**SAMPLE GRANTS Previous beneficiaries have included:** Beth Israel Ruzin Sadagora (£196,000); Friends of Ruzin Sadagora (£180,000); Beth Kaknesset Ohr Yisroel (£91,600); Mosdos Sadigur (£40,000); Yeshivas Torah Temimah (£9,000); Chevras Moaz Lodol (£6,500); Pardes House (£2,000).
**FINANCES** Year 2012/13 Income £370,930 Grants £206,000 Grants to organisations £206,000 Assets £526,367
**TRUSTEES** Rabbi Israel Moshe Friedman; Sara Friedman.
**OTHER INFORMATION** The trust's accounts are consistently submitted late to the Charity Commission. At the time of writing (June 2015) the accounts for 2013/14 were overdue. The latest accounts available were from the 2012/13 financial year.
**HOW TO APPLY** Apply in writing to the correspondent.
**WHO TO APPLY TO** Rabbi Israel Moshe Friedman, Trustee, 269 Golders Green Road, London NW11 9JJ Tel. 020 8806 9514

## ■ The Saddlers' Company Charitable Fund

**CC NO** 261962 **ESTABLISHED** 1970
**WHERE FUNDING CAN BE GIVEN** UK.
**WHO CAN BENEFIT** Registered charities and institutions.
**WHAT IS FUNDED** Grants are made by the company in the following categories: education; support for people with disabilities and young people who are disadvantaged; charities benefitting people who are in need, hardship or distress; armed and uniformed services; equestrian charities; the church; British saddlery and leathercraft trades; City of London; general charitable activities.
**TYPE OF GRANT** Usually one-off for one year.
**RANGE OF GRANTS** Up to around £30,000.
**SAMPLE GRANTS** Saddlers' Scholarship and Bursaries at Alleyn's School (£130,000); Riding for the Disabled Association (£30,000); British Horse Society (£27,000); Leather Conservation Centre (£6,000); Nottingham Trent University (£3,900); Lord Mayor's Appeal (£3,000); Blandford Youth Trust (£2,500); Museum of Leathercraft (£2,000); Lucy's Days Out, Stepney Community Trust, St Christopher's Hospice and Tiny Tim's Children's Centre (£1,500 each); Independent Age (£1,250); World Horse Welfare (£1,100); Firefighters Charity Fund, Guy Fox History Project Ltd, Royal Naval Benevolent Trust and St Paul's Cathedral (£1,000 each).
**FINANCES** Year 2013/14 Income £459,276 Grants £409,328 Grants to organisations £409,328 Assets £11,784,336
**TRUSTEES** Jonathan Godrich; Campbell Pulley; DJ. Serrell-Watts; David Hardy; Hugh Dyson-Laurie; Iain Pulley; Michael Laurie; Peter Laurie; Peter Lewis; Tim Satchell; Mark Farmar; David Snowden; Paul Farmar; Nicholas Mason; Charles Barclay; John Robinson; Petronella Jameson; Hugh Thomas; James Welch; William Dyson-Laurie; The Hon Mark Maffey; Lucy Atherton.
**OTHER INFORMATION** The grant total includes funding given to individuals for social welfare and educational purposes. Whilst the majority of grants were made from general funds, within The Saddlers' Company Charitable Fund are the R M Sturdy Trust and the M E Priestly Fund. Criteria and applications processes for all of the funds managed by the Company are available from the website.
**HOW TO APPLY** The company now operates an online application form, which is accessible from the website.
**WHO TO APPLY TO** Clerk to the Saddlers' Company, Saddlers' Hall, 40 Gutter Lane, London EC2V 6BR Tel. 020 7726 8661 Fax 020 7600 0386 email clerk@saddlersco.co.uk Website www.saddlersco.co.uk

## ■ Erach and Roshan Sadri Foundation

**CC NO** 1110736 **ESTABLISHED** 2005
**WHERE FUNDING CAN BE GIVEN** Worldwide.
**WHO CAN BENEFIT** Registered charities; community groups; religious institutions; individuals.
**WHAT IS FUNDED** The main objects of the foundation are: providing financial assistance for education and welfare purposes; relieving poverty by alleviating homelessness; and assisting members of the Zoroastrian religious faith.
**WHAT IS NOT FUNDED** Applications are unlikely to be successful if they: involve animal welfare or heritage; are a general appeal from large UK organisations.
**TYPE OF GRANT** One-off grants for project costs.
**RANGE OF GRANTS** Up to around £25,000.
**SAMPLE GRANTS** British Armed Forces Foundation (£28,000); On Course (£22,000); Children's Trust (£15,000); Honeypot (£10,000); Jessie May (£8,000); REACT (£2,000).
**FINANCES** Year 2013/14 Income £31,393 Grants £434,151 Grants to organisations £432,651 Assets £2,878,210

**TRUSTEES** Margaret Lynch; Darius Sarosh; Sammy Bhiwandiwalla.

**OTHER INFORMATION** Grants were awarded to 53 organisations and two individuals for the following purposes: education and welfare (£351,500); homelessness (£47,500); Zoroastrian (£26,000); general charitable purposes (£9,000).

**HOW TO APPLY** An online application form and extensive guidelines are available on the website, along with closing dates. The website notes that applications are not accepted unless: your organisation has successfully applied for funding from ERSF before; or an ERSF trustee or the Administrator has asked you, either in person or in writing, to submit an application form with their recommendation. Unsuccessful applicants should not re-apply.

**WHO TO APPLY TO** Mark Cann, Administrator, 10A The High Street, Pewsey, Wiltshire SN9 5AQ *Tel.* 01672 569131 *email* markcann@ersf.org.uk *Website* www.ersf.org.uk

## ■ The Saga Charitable Trust

**CC NO** 291991 **ESTABLISHED** 1985
**WHERE FUNDING CAN BE GIVEN** Financially developing countries.
**WHO CAN BENEFIT** Charitable organisations and projects.
**WHAT IS FUNDED** Community projects in financially developing countries that provide education, training, healthcare and income generation.
**WHAT IS NOT FUNDED** Individuals.
**TYPE OF GRANT** Capital costs; full project funding; core costs. One-off, up to three years.
**RANGE OF GRANTS** £1,700–£21,000
**SAMPLE GRANTS** Swim Vietnam (£21,000); the Butterfly Tree, Zambia (£15,000); Kalela Primary School, Kenya and Mikoroshoni Primary School, Kenya (£12,000 each); Centre for Early Childhood Development, South Africa and the Civil Association for Conservation of the Peruvian Amazon Environment, Peru (£9,300 each); This Life Cambodia, Cambodia (£6,100); Philippines Community Fund, the Philippines and Tears of Hope, Namibia (£4,200 each); Himaljyoti Community School, Nepal (£1,700).
**FINANCES** Year 2013/14 Income £242,054 Grants £105,937 Grants to organisations £105,937 Assets £460,394
**TRUSTEES** Makala Thomas; James Duguid; Andrew Stringer; Helen Adamson; Timothy Pethick.
**OTHER INFORMATION** Donations from staff and customers totalled £123,000. Grants were made totalling £106,000.
**HOW TO APPLY** Apply in writing to the correspondent. Applications are accepted at any time throughout the year. Grants are decided at regular meetings by the trustees where applications are considered for various types of funding. Funding proposals should include the following information: outline and objectives of the project; who will benefit and how; resources required and timeframe; management and sustainability of the project; how funds will be managed and accounted for; and three years of the organisation's financial accounts.
**WHO TO APPLY TO** John Billingham, Trust Manager, Saga plc, Enbrook Park, Sandgate High Street, Sandgate, Folkestone CT20 3SE *Tel.* 01303 774421 *email* john.billingham@saga.co.uk *Website* www.sagacharitabletrust.org

## ■ The Jean Sainsbury Animal Welfare Trust

**CC NO** 326358 **ESTABLISHED** 1982
**WHERE FUNDING CAN BE GIVEN** UK and overseas.
**WHO CAN BENEFIT** UK registered national and international animal welfare charities.
**WHAT IS FUNDED** Projects concerned with animal welfare and wildlife.
**WHAT IS NOT FUNDED** The trust's website states that it will not normally support the following: 'charities registered outside the UK; charities offering sanctuary to animals, with no effort to re-home, foster or rehabilitate unless endangered species; applications from individuals; charities that do not have a realistic destruction policy for animals that cannot be given a reasonable quality of life; charities with available reserves equal to more than one year's expenditure will not qualify for consideration unless it can be demonstrated that reserves are being held for a designated project; charities that spend more than a reasonable proportion of their annual income on administration or cannot justify their costs per animal helped; and veterinary schools, unless the money can be seen to be directly benefiting the type of animals the Trust would want to support e.g. welfare-related or low-cost first opinion vet treatment projects.'
**TYPE OF GRANT** Capital; buildings; campaigning; core costs; project; running and recurring costs. Funding for up to one year is available.
**RANGE OF GRANTS** £1,000–£10,000
**SAMPLE GRANTS** RSPCA, Blackpool and North Lancs (£25,000); Waggy Tails Rescue (£20,000); Second Chances (£15,000); The Society for the Welfare of Horses, Worldwide Veterinary Service and Ponies and Lluest Horse and Pony Trust (£10,000 each); Hope Rescue and Munlochy Animal Aid (£8,000 each); Nowzad Dogs, Rottweiler Welfare and Animal Welfare of Luxor (£5,000 each); Animal Aid (£3,000); Greyhound Welfare and Rescue and British Divers Marine Life Rescue (£1,000 each); German Shepherd RRR and Eastbourne Bird Aid (£500 each); Lord Whiskey Sanctuary Fund (£300).
**FINANCES** Year 2013 Income £5,049,962 Grants £412,350 Grants to organisations £412,350 Assets £18,339,186
**TRUSTEES** Colin Russell; Gillian Tarlington; James Keliher; Mark Spurdens; Valerie Pike; Michelle Allen; Adele Sparrow.
**OTHER INFORMATION** The grant total comprised of £369,000 given to charities working in the UK and £43,000 to UK charities working overseas.
**HOW TO APPLY** Application forms are available from the correspondent or to download from the trust's website. Applicants should complete and return nine copies of the form, their latest set of audited accounts and any other information which may be relevant to the application. Note: the trust requests that you do not send originals as these cannot be returned. There are three trustees' meetings every year, usually in March, July and November and applications should be submitted by 15 January, 1 May and 1 September respectively. Further application information and policy guidelines are available by visiting the website. The trust encourages charities to maintain contact with it and is also pleased to receive updates on charities' plans and activities. Repeat applications from charities are supported.

*Alphabetical register of grant-making charities*                                                                                                          **St**

WHO TO APPLY TO Madeleine Orchard, Correspondent, PO Box 469, London W14 8PJ *Tel.* 020 7602 7948 *email* orchardjswelfare@gmail.com *Website* jeansainsburyanimalwelfare.org.uk

■ **The Alan and Babette Sainsbury Charitable Fund**

CC NO 292930   ESTABLISHED 1953
WHERE FUNDING CAN BE GIVEN UK and overseas.
WHO CAN BENEFIT Registered charities and research institutes.
WHAT IS FUNDED Projects in the following fields: civil liberties; scientific and medical research; work with young people; overseas projects; general charitable purposes.
WHAT IS NOT FUNDED Support is not given to individuals, or for educational fees and expeditions.
TYPE OF GRANT One-off and ongoing; core costs; capital, project and running costs.
RANGE OF GRANTS £5,000–£150,000
SAMPLE GRANTS Juvenile Diabetes Research Foundation (£100,000); Freedom from Torture (£30,000); Blue Elephant Theatre and Baobab Centre for Young Survivors in Exile (£25,000 each); Blackfriars Settlement and Ovalhouse (£20,000 each); Anglo-Israel Association (£14,000); Toucan Employment, OneVoice Europe and Prisoners of Conscience (£10,000 each); National Commission on Forced Marriage (£7,500); Kampala Music School and Inspire at St Peter's (£5,000 each); Phoenix Arch School (£1,400).
FINANCES *Year* 2013/14 *Income* £469,075 *Grants* £346,650 *Grants to organisations* £346,650 *Assets* £14,876,805
TRUSTEES Judith Portrait; Timothy Sainsbury; John Sainsbury; Lindsey Anderson.
HOW TO APPLY The charity's website states that it 'will consider proposals, so long as they demonstrably and closely fit their specific areas of interest. However, it should be understood that the majority of unsolicited proposals are unsuccessful.' Applications should be sent via post with a description of the proposed project covering the organisation, the project requiring funding and a breakdown of costs. Supplementary documentation such as books, brochures, DVDs, annual reports or accounts are not needed. Applicants who do not hear from the charity within eight weeks should assume that their application has been unsuccessful.
WHO TO APPLY TO Alan Bookbinder, Head of the Sainsbury Family Charitable Trusts, The Peak, 5 Wilton Road, London SW1V 1AP *Tel.* 020 7410 0330 *email* info@sfct.org.uk *Website* www.sfct.org.uk

■ **The Sainsbury Family Charitable Trusts**

WHO CAN BENEFIT Registered charities and institutions.
WHAT IS FUNDED See the entries for the individuals trusts.
WHAT IS NOT FUNDED No grants are normally given to individuals by many of the trusts (though a number of them fund bursary schemes and the like operated by other organisations). Grants are not made for educational fees or expeditions.

OTHER INFORMATION The trusts are: The Ashden Trust; The Gatsby Charitable Foundation; The Kay Kendall Leukaemia Fund; The Linbury Trust; The True Colours Trust; The Woodward Charitable Trust; The Indigo Trust; The Alan and Babette Sainsbury Charitable Fund; The Glass-House Trust; The Headley Trust; The Jerusalem Trust; The JJ Charitable Trust; The Mark Leonard Trust; The Monument Trust; The Staples Trust; The Tedworth Charitable Trust; The Three Guineas Trust. See the individual trust entries for grants totals.
HOW TO APPLY The website states: 'Please do not send more than one application. It will be considered by all relevant trusts. The trusts only fund registered charities or activities with clearly defined charitable purposes. The trustees take an active role in their grant-making, employing a range of specialist staff and advisers to research their areas of interest and bring forward suitable proposals. Many of the trusts work closely with their chosen beneficiaries over a long period to achieve particular objectives. It should therefore be understood that the majority of unsolicited proposals we receive will be unsuccessful. As a rule the Gatsby, Glass-House, Linbury, Staples and Tedworth trusts do not consider unsolicited proposals. The other trusts will consider exceptional proposals which fit closely their specific areas of interest. There are no application forms, except in a small number of clearly defined areas: the Woodward Charitable Trust; the Kay Kendall Leukaemia Fund; the Headley Museums Archaeological Acquisition Fund. Applications to all other trusts should be sent by post, with a description (strictly no more than two pages please, as any more is unlikely to be read) of the proposed project, covering: the organisation – explaining its charitable aims and objectives, and giving its most recent annual income and expenditure, and current financial position – please do not send a full set of accounts; the project requiring funding – why it is needed, who will benefit and in what way; the funding – breakdown of costs, any money raised so far, and how the balance will be raised. At this stage please do not send supporting books, brochures, DVDs, annual reports or accounts. All applications will receive our standard acknowledgement letter. If your proposal is a candidate for support from one of the trusts, you will hear from us within 8 weeks of the acknowledgement. Applicants who do not hear from us within this time must assume they have been unsuccessful.'
WHO TO APPLY TO Alan Bookbinder, Director, The Peak, 5 Wilton Road, London SW1V 1AP *Tel.* 020 7410 0330 *Fax* 020 7410 0332 *Website* www.sfct.org.uk

■ **The St Hilda's Trust**
CC NO 500962   ESTABLISHED 1904
WHERE FUNDING CAN BE GIVEN The diocese of Newcastle (Newcastle upon Tyne, North Tyneside and Northumberland).
WHO CAN BENEFIT Deprived communities of the diocese of Newcastle (Newcastle upon Tyne, North Tyneside and Northumberland), with extra focus on children and young people.
WHAT IS FUNDED General charitable purposes, particularly social welfare.
WHAT IS NOT FUNDED Beneficiaries outside the trust's operational area.
RANGE OF GRANTS £1,000–£5,000
SAMPLE GRANTS A list of beneficiaries was not included in the latest set of accounts.

**763**

FINANCES *Year* 2013 *Income* £73,046 *Grants* £58,278 *Grants to organisations* £58,278 *Assets* £1,751,265
TRUSTEES Revd Canon Craig; Rosemary Nicholson; Revd Martin Wharton; Dr Margaret Wilkinson; Neil Brockbank; David Welsh.
OTHER INFORMATION A list of beneficiaries was not published.
HOW TO APPLY Apply in writing to the correspondent.
WHO TO APPLY TO Josie Pinnegar, Correspondent, Newcastle Diocesan Board of Finance, Church House, St John's Terrace, North Shields, Tyne and Wear NE29 6HS *Tel.* 0191 270 4100 *email* j.pinnegar@newcastle.anglican.org

## ■ St James's Trust Settlement

CC NO 280455    ESTABLISHED 1980
WHERE FUNDING CAN BE GIVEN UK and USA.
WHO CAN BENEFIT Registered charities.
WHAT IS FUNDED General charitable purposes; education and training; the promotion of health; arts and culture; economic and community development; children and young people; people with disabilities.
WHAT IS NOT FUNDED Individuals.
TYPE OF GRANT Core costs; one-off; project; research; recurring costs; salaries; start-up costs. Funding is for up to three years.
SAMPLE GRANTS Homeopathy Action Trust (£40,000); CARIS and Highbury Vale Blackstock Trust (£20,000 each).
FINANCES *Year* 2013/14 *Income* £124,232 *Grants* £340,223 *Grants to organisations* £340,223 *Assets* £3,088,045
TRUSTEES Jane Wells; Cathy Ingram; Simon Taffler.
OTHER INFORMATION Grants were made during the year totalling £340,000, which included £37,000 to three organisations in the UK and £80,000 to 31 organisations in the USA.
HOW TO APPLY The trust states that it 'does not seek unsolicited applications for grants and, without paid staff, are unable to respond to such applications'.
WHO TO APPLY TO The Trustees, c/o Begbies Accountants, Epworth House, 25 City Road, London EC1Y 1AR *email* janeiwells@gmail.com

## ■ St James's Place Foundation

CC NO 1144606    ESTABLISHED 1994
WHERE FUNDING CAN BE GIVEN In practice mainly UK.
WHO CAN BENEFIT Registered and special needs schools.
WHAT IS FUNDED The foundation's main themes are: cherishing the children; combatting cancer; supporting hospices.
WHAT IS NOT FUNDED The foundation has a policy of not considering an application from any charity within two years of receiving a previous application. The foundation does not provide support for: charities with reserves of over 50% of income; administrative costs; activities primarily the responsibility of statutory agencies; replacement of lost statutory funding; research; events; advertising; holidays; sponsorship; contributions to large capital appeals; single faith charities; social and economic deprivation; charities that are raising funds on behalf of another charity.
TYPE OF GRANT One-off; up to three years.
SAMPLE GRANTS National Star College (£162,000); Brainwave and Leeds Rugby Foundation (£99,000 each); Worldwide Volunteering (£90,000); Winston's Wish (£85,000); the Rose Road Association (£84,000); the Ear Foundation (£74,000); AfriKids (£66,000); British Association for Adoption and Fostering (£65,000); Action for Kids (£50,000); Action for Brazil's Children Trust (£46,000); Jamie's Farm (£45,000); East London Advanced Technology Training (£34,000); Impact Initiatives (£23,000); Castlehaven Community (£10,000); Vauxhall City Farm Riding Therapy Centre (£9,900); and Gaddum Centre (£2,500).
FINANCES *Year* 2013 *Income* £5,378,666 *Grants* £4,893,994 *Grants to organisations* £4,893,994 *Assets* £427,139
TRUSTEES David Bellamy; Ian Gascoigne; Malcolm Cooper-Smith; Hugh Gladman; Andrew Croft; David Lamb; Michael Wilson.
HOW TO APPLY Applications can be made online via the foundation's website. The following information is given on the foundation's website. 'The foundation is only able to consider applications from UK registered charities as well as Special Needs Schools in the UK. We accept applications from national, regional and local charities operating in England, Scotland, Wales and Northern Ireland. Important note: we do not accept unsolicited applications from charities operating overseas. The Small Grants Programme is available to smaller UK registered charities working nationally, regionally or locally in the UK with an annual income of up to £750,000. The amount applied for should be up to a maximum of £10,000 in any two-year rolling period. If an applicant is unsuccessful then a period of twelve months must elapse before re-applying. If you believe that your application falls within the funding policy of the foundation, you are welcome to apply. There are no deadlines or closing dates. Small Grants are considered on receipt and in rotation. The whole procedure can take between four to six months (sometimes longer if many applications are received) so it is advisable to apply in good time if funds are required for a certain date. Each application is considered on its merits based on the information provided in the online application form and the due diligence carried out by the foundation team. We will acknowledge receipt of your application by email. Applications for a Small Grant will normally receive a visit from a representative of the foundation, who will subsequently report to the trustees. Following the trustees' decision, successful applicants will be notified. **Supporting Hospices:** the foundation is proud to support hospices in the United Kingdom. However, we do not currently invite applications from individual hospices. Instead we will be working with Help the Hospices, the umbrella organisation supporting independent hospices in the UK, who will distribute funds to hospices on our behalf.' For more information, visit the Help the Hospices website: www.helpthehospices.org.uk. **Major Grants Programme:** the foundation's Major Grants Programme remains closed to unsolicited applications. Please check the foundation's website for up-to-date information.'
WHO TO APPLY TO Mark Longbottom, Foundation Manager, St James's Place plc, St James's Place House, 1 Tetbury Road, Cirencester GL7 1FP *Tel.* 01285 878562 *email* mark.longbottom@sjp.co.uk *Website* www.sjpfoundation.co.uk

## ■ Sir Walter St John's Educational Charity

**CC NO** 312690  **ESTABLISHED** 1992

**WHERE FUNDING CAN BE GIVEN** The boroughs of Wandsworth and Lambeth, with a preference for Battersea.

**WHO CAN BENEFIT** Individuals; organisations benefitting children and young persons under the age of 25 years residing in the London Boroughs of Wandsworth or Lambeth and in need of financial assistance. Particular preference is given to those residing in the former Metropolitan Borough of Battersea. Grants are awarded both to individuals and local schools, colleges, youth clubs, and voluntary and community organisations. Priority is given to activities benefitting disadvantaged children.

**WHAT IS FUNDED** Promotion of education and training of children and young persons under the age of 25 years who are resident in the London Boroughs of Wandsworth or Lambeth and who are in need of financial assistance. The charity gives priority to those activities that benefit the following groups of local children and young people: living in areas of particular social disadvantage; young refugees and asylum seekers; young carers; children and young people with disabilities; children in and leaving state care. The charity also plays a proactive role in supporting the development of new educational initiatives and projects, curriculum enrichment programmes, play schemes and workshops. Individual grants are primarily made to students undertaking Further Education courses.

**WHAT IS NOT FUNDED** School pupils under 16 and full-time students on university degree courses are not normally supported; individual student grants do not usually cover the cost of a computer or laptop; funding only available to cover expenditure (e.g. registration fees, travel, books or equipment) necessary for attendance on the validated, approved or recognised course; maintenance grants are not available.

**TYPE OF GRANT** One-off and up to three year strategic grants to organisations; individual grants.

**RANGE OF GRANTS** Up to £1,000 for educational grants. Up to £30,000 per year for strategic grants.

**SAMPLE GRANTS** Katherine Low Settlement (£97,880); South Thames College (£7,000); 4 All-Building Community in West Dulwich, Battersea Summer Scheme, Doddington and Rollo Community Association, Triangle Adventure Playground Association (£1,000 each).

**FINANCES** Year 2013/14 Income £151,898 Grants £111,240 Grants to organisations £106,240 Assets £4,172,200

**TRUSTEES** Daphne Daytes; Peter Dyson; John O'Malley; Sarah Rackham; Colonel Julian Radcliffe; Jenny Scribbins; Cllr Sheldon Wilkie; Barry Fairbank; Godfrey Allen; Colonel Martin Stratton; Michael Bates; Canon Simon Butler; Cllr Ademamola Aminu; Wendy Speck; Rosemary Summerfield.

**OTHER INFORMATION** Organisations can apply for small education grants of up to £1,000, or strategic grants of up to £30,000 for up to three years.

**HOW TO APPLY** Further details for both organisations and individuals can be obtained and applications discussed with the charity's manager Susan Perry by email (manager@swsjcharity.org.uk) or phone (020 7498 8878). After initial discussion, an application form will be sent to eligible organisations or individuals. Full application guidelines and grant criteria are available on the charity's website. **Organisations:** Organisations will be asked to provide latest audited accounts where possible. The Grants Committee usually meets four times a year. Applications must be received at least six weeks before the proposed start date of the project. Full details and eligibility criteria can be found on the charity's website. **Individuals:** Application form must be completed after the initial approach. Applicants must be able to provide evidence that they have a good prospect of successfully completing the course on which they are being supported. Full details and eligibility criteria can be found on the charity's website.

**WHO TO APPLY TO** Susan Perry, Manager, Office 1A, Culvert House, Culvert Road, London SW11 5DH *Tel.* 020 7498 8878 *email* manager@swsjcharity.org.uk *Website* www.swsjcharity.org.uk

## ■ The St Laurence Relief In Need Trust

**CC NO** 205043  **ESTABLISHED** 1962

**WHERE FUNDING CAN BE GIVEN** The ancient parish of St Laurence, then the borough of Reading.

**WHO CAN BENEFIT** Residents and charitable organisations of the ancient parish of St Laurence in Reading and, thereafter, in the county borough of Reading.

**WHAT IS FUNDED** Residents who are in conditions of need, hardship or distress; children and young people; older people; people with disabilities.

**WHAT IS NOT FUNDED** Individuals outside the ancient parish of St Laurence, Reading or the county borough of Reading, even when supported by social services or similar agencies.

**TYPE OF GRANT** One-off.

**SAMPLE GRANTS** A list of beneficiaries was not available.

**FINANCES** Year 2013 Income £59,481 Grants £45,334 Grants to organisations £43,934 Assets £137,057

**TRUSTEES** Patricia Thomas; Cllr Rosemary Williams; Revd Canon Christopher Russell; Lorraine Briffitt; Stewart Hotston; Nicholas Burrows; and Dr Rachel Macleod

**OTHER INFORMATION** During the year 33 organisations shared £44,000 and seven individuals received grants totalling £1,400.

**HOW TO APPLY** Apply in writing to the correspondent. The trustees meet twice a year. Informal contact via email is welcomed before an application is submitted.

**WHO TO APPLY TO** Jason Pyke, Trust Administrator, c/o Vale and West, 26 Queen Victoria Street, Reading RG1 1TG *Tel.* 0118 957 3238 *email* mail@valewest.com

## ■ St Luke's College Foundation

**CC NO** 306606  **ESTABLISHED** 1977

**WHERE FUNDING CAN BE GIVEN** UK, with some preference for Exeter and Truro.

**WHO CAN BENEFIT** Individuals; universities, colleges and other institutions operating at university level.

**WHAT IS FUNDED** *Corporate* awards are made to universities and similar institutions to enable them to develop or enhance their provision in these fields, which can be granted for up to three years. *Personal* awards are made to support individuals following university-level studies or research in theology and religious education, or who are undertaking research which will lead to a masters' degree or PHD. *Major awards* are occasionally made to a small number of larger corporate awards to enhance the capacity of universities and other institutions working in the fields of theology and RE.

**WHAT IS NOT FUNDED** Funding is not available for building work or to provide bursaries for institutions to administer. Schools are not supported directly (although support is given to teachers who are taking eligible studies). Grants are not normally made for periods in excess of three years.

**TYPE OF GRANT** Grants can be made for periods of up to three years.

**RANGE OF GRANTS** £1,000–£5,000

**SAMPLE GRANTS** Exeter Diocesan Board of Education (£47,000); Diocese of Truro and Culham St Gabriel's Trust (£5,000); Anglican Consultative Council (£3,000); University of Exeter (£2,000); and South West Youth Ministries (£650).

**FINANCES** *Year* 2013/14 *Income* £1,136,452 *Grants* £124,039 *Grants to organisations* £124,039 *Assets* £5,305,265

**TRUSTEES** The Very Revd Dr Jonathan Draper; Prof. Mark Overton; Prof. Grace Davie; Philip Mantell; Dr Michael Wykes; David Cain; Alice Hutchings; Dick Powell; Revd Dr David Rake; Dr Karen Stockham; Revd Canon Alan Bashforth; Bishop Robert Atwell.

**OTHER INFORMATION** Grants were made totalling £124,000, which were broken down as £52,000 for major awards and £72,000 in personal and corporate awards.

**HOW TO APPLY** From 1 January each year, applicants can request an application pack from the correspondent. Applications are considered once a year and should be received by 1 May for grants starting in September.

**WHO TO APPLY TO** Dr David Benzie, Director, 15 St Maryhaye, Tavistock, Devon PL19 8LR *Tel.* 01822 613143 *email* director@st-lukes-foundation.org.uk *Website* www.st-lukes-foundation.org.uk

■ **St Michael's and All Saints' Charities Relief Branch (The Church Houses Relief in Need Charity)**

**CC NO** 202750          **ESTABLISHED** 1980
**WHERE FUNDING CAN BE GIVEN** City of Oxford.
**WHO CAN BENEFIT** Charitable organisations, with an interest in Christian groups.
**WHAT IS FUNDED** Health and welfare.
**WHAT IS NOT FUNDED** Individuals are very rarely supported.
**TYPE OF GRANT** One-off and recurrent.
**RANGE OF GRANTS** £500–£10,000
**SAMPLE GRANTS** Donnington Doorstep Family Centre (£10,000); Cutteslowe Community Foundation, Leys CDI Clockhouse, Wolvercote Young People's Club (£5,000 each); Crisis Skylight Oxford, Create (Arts ) Ltd, Church of the Holy Family (£3,000 each); Spinal Injuries Association (£1,000); CLIC Sargent Cancer Care for Children and Jellicoe Community (£500 each).
**FINANCES** *Year* 2013 *Income* £69,566 *Grants* £40,300 *Grants to organisations* £40,300 *Assets* £1,723,131
**TRUSTEES** Patrick Beavis; Michael Lear; Lord Krebs; Ruth Loseby; Prudence Dailey; Robert Earl; Samia Shibli; The Very Revd Robert Wilkes;

Simon Stubbings; Prof. Henry Woudhuysen; The Ven. Martin Gorick.

**OTHER INFORMATION** Fewer grants were made this year as, contrary to previous years, no donation was received from the Church branch of the charity.

**HOW TO APPLY** Apply in writing to the correspondent. The trustees take a proactive approach to seeking out potential recipients, looking for a clearly stated purpose and evidence of good management for achieving outcomes.

**WHO TO APPLY TO** Rupert Sheppard, Correspondent, St Michael's Church Centre, Cornmarket, Oxford, Oxfordshire OX1 3EY *Tel.* 01865 255772 *email* rupert.sheppard@smng.org.uk

■ **St Monica Trust (formerly known as St Monica Trust Community Fund)**

**CC NO** 202151          **ESTABLISHED** 1962
**WHERE FUNDING CAN BE GIVEN** Bristol and the surrounding areas.
**WHO CAN BENEFIT** Organisations; individuals and families.
**WHAT IS FUNDED** Support for people who have physical disabilities or long term physical health problems. At the time of writing (June 2015) the fund's giving had two themes: 'Reducing Loneliness and Isolation for Older People' and 'Better Outcomes for People With Dementia and their Carers'.
**WHAT IS NOT FUNDED** Buildings; building adaptations; minibus purchases.
**TYPE OF GRANT** Capital items; running costs.
**SAMPLE GRANTS** **Previous beneficiaries have included:** Citizen's Advice Bureau (£9,800); St Peter's Hospice, Headway Bristol and Motor Neurone Disease Association (£7,500 each); IT Help@Home (£5,000); the New Place (£3,900); Bristol and Avon Chinese Women's Group (£2,000); Bath Institute of Medical Engineering (£1,500); and Western Active Stroke Group (£1,000).
**FINANCES** *Year* 2013 *Income* £24,569,000 *Grants* £372,928 *Grants to organisations* £128,402 *Assets* £232,807,000
**TRUSTEE** St Monica Trustee Company Ltd.
**OTHER INFORMATION** The trust runs retirement villages in Bristol and North Somerset which offer sheltered accommodation, nursing homes and dementia care homes to older people. It makes grants in support of the local community through the Community Fund. Grants are made to individuals in the form of one-off grants for emergency items as well as short-term monthly payments. It also funds Linkage, an initiative helping to provide services and support to improve the well-being of older people in the community. During the year, 18 organisations were supported. Gifts, short term grants and annuities to at least 552 individuals totalled £244,500 and expenditure on Linkage amounted to a further £64,500.
**HOW TO APPLY** For more information, contact the Community Fund Team on 0117 949 4003 or by email community.fund@stmonicatrust.org.uk.
**WHO TO APPLY TO** Robert Whetton, Head of Finance, Cote Lane, Bristol BS9 3UN *Tel.* 0117 949 4000 *email* info@stmonicatrust.org.uk *Website* www.stmonicatrust.org.uk

## ■ St Peter's Saltley Trust

**CC NO** 528915  **ESTABLISHED** 1980
**WHERE FUNDING CAN BE GIVEN** The dioceses of Worcester, Hereford, Lichfield, Birmingham and Coventry.
**WHO CAN BENEFIT** Charitable organisations; schools; colleges; individuals.
**WHAT IS FUNDED** Christianity; theological education.
**WHAT IS NOT FUNDED** The trust is unable to fund: 'subsidies for the existing, ongoing work of an organisation; capital costs (e.g., building renovations, ongoing staff salaries); and individual students undertaking programmes of study merely for their own purposes.'
**RANGE OF GRANTS** Up to £8,500.
**SAMPLE GRANTS** Queen's Foundation (£8,400); Mission Apprentice Scheme (£7,600); Arthur Rank Centre (£6,900); Restore (£6,700); WMCFEC Development (£6,500); Close the Gap Project (£3,400); and North Warwickshire and Hinckley College (£150).
**FINANCES** Year 2013/14 Income £135,163 Grants £55,349 Grants to organisations £55,349 Assets £3,078,123
**TRUSTEES** David Urquhart; The Ven. Hayward Osborne; Gordon Thornhill; Rt Revd Jonathan Gledhill; Dr Peter Kent; Canon Robert Jones; Colin Hopkins; Rt Revd Dr John Inge; Canon Paul Wilson; Philip Hereford; Dr Paula Gooder; Kathleen Kimber; Rt Revd Christopher Cocksworth; Jill Stolberg; Rt Revd Richard Frith.
**HOW TO APPLY** Full criteria and guidelines are available on the trust's website. The trust states that: 'If you are interested to explore how we might work with you, please contact us for a further conversation.'
**WHO TO APPLY TO** Lin Brown, Bursar and Clerk to Trustees, Gray's Court, 3 Nursery Road, Edgbaston, Birmingham B15 3JX *Tel.* 0121 427 6800 *email* bursar@saltleytrust.org.uk *Website* www.saltleytrust.org.uk

## ■ Saint Sarkis Charity Trust

**CC NO** 215352  **ESTABLISHED** 1954
**WHERE FUNDING CAN BE GIVEN** UK and overseas.
**WHO CAN BENEFIT** Smaller registered charities benefitting Armenians in the UK and/or overseas, as well as offenders and their relatives.
**WHAT IS FUNDED** Primarily charitable objectives with an Armenian connection including Armenian religious buildings; other small charities developing innovative projects to support prisoners in the UK. The trust funds the Armenian Church of Saint Sarkis in London and the Gulbenkian Library at the Armenian Patriarchate in Jerusalem on an annual basis.
**WHAT IS NOT FUNDED** The trust does not give grants to: individual applicants; organisations that are not registered charities; and registered charities outside the UK, unless the project benefits the Armenian community in the UK and/or overseas. The trust does not fund: general appeals; core costs or salaries; projects concerning substance abuse; or medical research.
**TYPE OF GRANT** Mainly confined to one-off project grants.
**RANGE OF GRANTS** £1,600–£71,000
**SAMPLE GRANTS** Armenian Church of St Sarkis (£54,000); Gulbenkian Library at the Armenian Patriarchate in Jerusalem (£18,100 plus £20,500 in related fees); Centre for Armenian Information and Advice (£16,000); London Armenian Poor Relief (£8,500); Friends of Armenia (£5,300); London Armenian Opera (£4,000); Armenian Institute (£1,800); Tekeyan Trust (£1,000).
**FINANCES** Year 2013/14 Income £276,410 Grants £481,860 Grants to organisations £481,860 Assets £8,724,832
**TRUSTEES** Martin Essayan; Paul Gulbenkian; Rita Vartoukian; Robert Todd; Alec D'Janoeff.
**OTHER INFORMATION** The grant total includes an exceptional grant of £322,500 to the Armenian Church of St Sarkis for renovation works.
**HOW TO APPLY** Apply in writing to the correspondent. There is no standard application form so applicants should write a covering letter including: an explanation of the exact purpose of the grant; how much is needed, with details of how the budget has been arrived at; details of any other sources of income (firm commitments and those still being explored); the charity registration number; the latest annual report and audited accounts; and any plans for monitoring and evaluating the work. **Note: The trust is no longer accepting unsolicited applications for prisoner support projects.** Refer to the trust's website for current information.
**WHO TO APPLY TO** Tartevik Sargsyan, Secretary to the Trustees, 50 Hoxton Square, London N1 6PB *Tel.* 020 7012 1408 *email* info@saintsarkis.org.uk *Website* www.saintsarkis.org.uk

## ■ The Saintbury Trust

**CC NO** 326790  **ESTABLISHED** 1985
**WHERE FUNDING CAN BE GIVEN** West Midlands and Warwickshire (which the trust considers to be post code areas B, CV, DY, WS and WV), Worcestershire, Herefordshire and Gloucestershire (post code areas WR, HR and GL).
**WHO CAN BENEFIT** Registered charities.
**WHAT IS FUNDED** General charitable purposes; social welfare; older people; the environment; arts and culture; the promotion of health; education and training.
**WHAT IS NOT FUNDED** Individuals; sponsorship; scouts, guides, sea cadets and similar organisations; village halls; local churches; religious charities; cold-calling national charities or local branches of national charities; animal charities; grants rarely given for start-up or general running costs. Note: we have been informed that the Herefordshire area (HR postcodes) is not eligible.
**RANGE OF GRANTS** £1,000–£50,000
**SAMPLE GRANTS** Birmingham Boys' and Girls' Union (£50,000); Midlands Arts Centre (£35,000); The Green Howards Regimental Museum (£16,000); Alzheimer's Research Trust (£15,000); Birmingham Children's Hospital Charities and Wildfowl and Wetlands Trust (£10,000 each); The Amber Foundation (£6,000); Henry Doubleday Research Association (£3,000); Foodcycle and Shipston Home Nursing (£2,000 each); Hill Close Gardens Trust and The Gordon Russell Trust (£1,000 each).
**FINANCES** Year 2013 Income £3,254,769 Grants £332,000 Grants to organisations £332,000 Assets £10,313,906
**TRUSTEES** Victoria Houghton; Anita Bhalla; Anne Thomas; Harry Forrester; Amanda Atkinson-Willes; Jane Lewis; Cerian Brogan.
**OTHER INFORMATION** In 2013 the trust had an income of £3.3 million, a significant increase from 2012 (£222,000). This was due to income derived from The Bryant Trust (Charity Commission no. 501450) and the estate of the

# Salamander

*Alphabetical register of grant-making charities*

late Alan Bryant, a settlor of The Saintbury Trust.
**HOW TO APPLY** Application forms are available to download on the trust's website. Completed applications should be returned via post to the correspondent accompanied by a short letter and the latest set of accounts.
**WHO TO APPLY TO** Jane Lewis, Trustee, PO Box 464, Dorking, Surrey RH4 9AF *email* saintburytrust@btinternet.com *Website* www.thesaintburytrust.co.uk

## ■ The Salamander Charitable Trust

**CC NO** 273657  **ESTABLISHED** 1977
**WHERE FUNDING CAN BE GIVEN** UK.
**WHO CAN BENEFIT** Registered charities.
**WHAT IS FUNDED** General charitable purposes; education and training; the promotion of health; people with disabilities; social welfare; overseas aid; accommodation and housing; Christianity; arts and culture; the environment and animals; children and young people; older people.
**RANGE OF GRANTS** £250–£2,500, generally £1,000 or less.
**SAMPLE GRANTS** SAT-7 Trust; All Nations Christian College; All Saints in Branksome Park; Birmingham Christian College; Christian Aid; Churches Commission on overseas students; FEBA Radio; International Christian College; London Bible College; Middle East Media, Moorland College; St James PCC in Poole; SAMS; Trinity College; Wycliffe Bible Translators.
**FINANCES** *Year* 2013 *Income* £73,046 *Grants* £58,278 *Grants to organisations* £58,278 *Assets* £1,751,265
**TRUSTEES** S. Douglas; Alison Hardwick; Philip Douglas.
**OTHER INFORMATION** Grants were made to 100 organisations.
**HOW TO APPLY** The trust's income is fully allocated each year, mainly to regular beneficiaries. The trustees do not wish to receive any further new requests.
**WHO TO APPLY TO** Catharine Douglas, Correspondent, The Old Rectory, 5 Stamford Road, South Luffenham, Oakham, Leicestershire LE15 8NT *email* info@geens.co.uk

## ■ The Andrew Salvesen Charitable Trust

**SC NO** SC008000  **ESTABLISHED** 1989
**WHERE FUNDING CAN BE GIVEN** Scotland.
**WHO CAN BENEFIT** Organisations.
**WHAT IS FUNDED** Education; disability; health, including medical research; social welfare; the arts and heritage.
**WHAT IS NOT FUNDED** Individuals.
**SAMPLE GRANTS** **Previous beneficiaries have included:** Bield Housing Trust; William Higgins Marathon Account; Multiple Sclerosis Society in Scotland; Royal Zoological Society of Scotland; Sail Training Association; Scottish Down's Syndrome Association; Sick Kids Appeal.
**FINANCES** *Year* 2013/14 *Income* £755,379 *Grants* £350,000 *Grants to organisations* £350,000
**TRUSTEES** A. Salvesen; K. Turner; V. Lall.
**OTHER INFORMATION** In 2013/14 the trust had a total expenditure of £385,000. The grant total stated above is an estimate.
**HOW TO APPLY** The trustees only support organisations known to them through their personal contacts. The trust has previously stated that all applications sent to them are 'thrown in the bin'.
**WHO TO APPLY TO** The Trustees, c/o Bell Ingram, 17 Albert Street, Aberdeen AB25 1XX *Tel.* 01224 621300 *Fax* 01224 634666 *email* aberdeen@bellingram.co.uk

## ■ Sam and Bella Sebba Charitable Trust (formerly The Samuel Sebba Charitable Trust)

**CC NO** 253351  **ESTABLISHED** 1967
**WHERE FUNDING CAN BE GIVEN** UK and Israel.
**WHO CAN BENEFIT** Charitable bodies with a preference for Jewish organisations.
**WHAT IS FUNDED** The trust looks to improve the quality of life of people across a broad range of activities. Key areas in the UK are palliative care, refugees, Jewish education and welfare. In Israel there is a focus on environment, human rights and social justice, disability and at-risk youth.
**WHAT IS NOT FUNDED** Individuals.
**RANGE OF GRANTS** Up to £100,000.
**SAMPLE GRANTS** Green Environment Fund – GEF (£238,500); London School of Jewish Studies (£106,000); Ronen-Aid for Special Needs (£100,500); Rosh Pinah Primary School (£75,000); Association for Civil Rights in Israel – ACRI (£64,500); Freedom of Information Movement (£53,000); Friends of Bait Ham (£41,000); Together for Short Lives (£35,000); Israel Bicycle Association (£27,500); Van Leer Institute ((£27,000); St Oswald's Hospice (£22,500); Community Security Trust and Jewish Women's Aid (£20,000 each); London Philharmonic Orchestra, University of Kent and Wigmore Hall Trust (£15,000).
**FINANCES** *Year* 2013/14 *Income* £1,201,013 *Grants* £3,093,119 *Grants to organisations* £3,093,119 *Assets* £59,090,664
**TRUSTEES** Leigh Sebba; Victor Klein; Yoav Tangir; Odelia Sebba; Tamsin Doyle.
**OTHER INFORMATION** 120 grants were made to organisations during the year, of which 40, totalling £351,500, were of less than £15,000.
**HOW TO APPLY** Organisations applying must provide proof of need, they must forward the most recent audited accounts, a registered charity number, and most importantly a cash flow statement for the next 12 months. All applications should have an sae enclosed. It is also important that the actual request for funds must be concise and preferably summarised on one side of A4. The trustees meet at least three times a year. Note that, due to ongoing support to organisations already known to the trust, new applications are unlikely to be successful, with the annual report for 2013/14 stating: 'The trustees expect to limit the number of new grantees during the next two years.'
**WHO TO APPLY TO** David Lerner, Chief Executive, 25–26 Enford Street, London W1H 1DW *Tel.* 020 7723 6028

## ■ Coral Samuel Charitable Trust

**CC NO** 239677  **ESTABLISHED** 1962
**WHERE FUNDING CAN BE GIVEN** UK.
**WHO CAN BENEFIT** Registered charities only.
**WHAT IS FUNDED** General charitable purposes, with a preference for educational, cultural and socially supportive charities. Grants are made in the following categories: medical/socially supportive; cultural; educational; animal welfare.

WHAT IS NOT FUNDED Grants are only made to registered charities.
RANGE OF GRANTS £250–£25,000
SAMPLE GRANTS English National Opera (£25,000); National Portrait Gallery (£18,000); Southbank Centre (£10,000); The Art Fund (£6,000); Keep Britain Tidy (£5,000); Jubilee Sailing Trust, RNLI, The Royal Horticultural Society, Wiltshire Air Ambulance (£5,000 each); Friends of Bolham School, London Youth Support Trust, Royal British Legion, Royal Veterinary College (£1,000 each).
FINANCES Year 2013/14 Income £108,510 Grants £289,680 Grants to organisations £289,680 Assets £4,907,528
TRUSTEES Coral Samuel; Peter Fineman; Sarah Fineman.
OTHER INFORMATION Grants were made to 41 organisations in 2013/14.
HOW TO APPLY Apply in writing to the correspondent.
WHO TO APPLY TO Coral Samuel, Trustee, c/o Smith and Williamson, 25 Moorgate, London EC2R 6AY Tel. 020 7131 4376

## ■ The M. J. Samuel Charitable Trust

CC NO 327013    ESTABLISHED 1985
WHERE FUNDING CAN BE GIVEN UK and overseas.
WHO CAN BENEFIT Charitable organisations.
WHAT IS FUNDED The trust supports a wide range of causes, many of them Jewish, as well as environmental causes, child welfare and health.
WHAT IS NOT FUNDED Individuals.
TYPE OF GRANT Core costs; project; research. Funding of up to two years will be considered.
RANGE OF GRANTS £100–£100,000
SAMPLE GRANTS The Game and Wildlife Conservation Trust (£30,000); Oxfam (£25,000); Fact Check (£15,000); Spey Foundation (£10,000); Dress for Success London (£3,000); Osteoporosis Society (£2,000); Kindwood College Appeal (£1,500); Mells Church of England School and The Anna Freud Centre (£1,000 each).
FINANCES Year 2013/14 Income £111,160 Grants £259,305 Grants to organisations £259,305 Assets £3,877,395
TRUSTEES Hon. Michael Samuel; Hon. Julia A. Samuel; Viscount Bearsted.
OTHER INFORMATION In addition 13 other donations were made to institutions of less than £1,000 each, totalling £5,100.
HOW TO APPLY Apply in writing to the correspondent. The trustees have regular contact during the year to consider recommendations for, and make final decisions on, the awarding of grants.
WHO TO APPLY TO Lindsay Sutton, Secretary, Mells Park, Mells, Frome, Somerset BA11 3QB Tel. 020 7402 0602 email lindsay@mellspark.com

## ■ The Basil Samuel Charitable Trust

CC NO 206579    ESTABLISHED 1959
WHERE FUNDING CAN BE GIVEN UK and worldwide.
WHO CAN BENEFIT Registered charities.
WHAT IS FUNDED General charitable purposes; education and training; the promotion of health; people with disabilities; arts and culture; the environment and animals; children and young people; older people.
WHAT IS NOT FUNDED Registered charities only.
TYPE OF GRANT One-off and recurring.
RANGE OF GRANTS £1,000–£100,000
SAMPLE GRANTS The Old Vic Theatre (£50,000); Macmillan Cancer Support (£37,500); Westminster Abbey Foundation (£30,000); Mary Rose Trust (£25,000); English National Opera and Royal Albert Hall (£20,000 each); Chai Lifeline Cancer Care and Institute of Historical Research (£10,000 each); Motability and Wiltshire Air Ambulance (£5,000 each); Police Rehabilitation Trust and War Memorial Trust (£1,000 each).
FINANCES Year 2013/14 Income £239,392 Grants £355,500 Grants to organisations £355,500 Assets £9,560,997
TRUSTEES Coral Samuel; Richard Peskin.
HOW TO APPLY Apply in writing to the correspondent. The trustees meet on a formal basis annually and regularly on an informal basis to discuss proposals for individual donations.
WHO TO APPLY TO The Trustees, c/o Smith and Williamson, 25 Moorgate, London EC2R 6AY Tel. 020 7131 4376

## ■ The Peter Samuel Charitable Trust

CC NO 269065    ESTABLISHED 1975
WHERE FUNDING CAN BE GIVEN UK, with some preference for local organisations in South Berkshire, Highlands of Scotland and East Somerset.
WHO CAN BENEFIT Registered charities.
WHAT IS FUNDED Health; welfare; conservation; Jewish care in the UK.
WHAT IS NOT FUNDED Purely local charities outside Berkshire; individuals.
TYPE OF GRANT Single and annual donations.
RANGE OF GRANTS Generally £200–£6,000. A grant of £30,000 was also made to Full Fact Organisation.
SAMPLE GRANTS Full Fact Organisation (£30,000); Child Bereavement Trust (£6,000); Game and Wildlife Conservation Trust (£5,000); Cancer Research (£3,000); Jewish Care (£2,500); Community Security Trust (£2,000); Action on Hearing Loss, Air Ambulance Trust, Bletchley Park Trust, Place2Be (£1,000 each); Berkshire, Buckinghamshire and Oxfordshire Wildlife Trust (£200 each).
FINANCES Year 2013/14 Income £123,490 Grants £75,450 Grants to organisations £75,450 Assets £4,554,403
TRUSTEES Hon. Viscount Bearsted; Hon. Michael Samuel.
OTHER INFORMATION The Hon Michael Samuel is also a trustee of: Col. Wilfred Horatio Micholls Deceased Charitable Trust Fund (Charity Commission no. 267472); The Hon. A G Samuel Charitable Trust (Charity Commission no. 1090481); The M J Samuel Charitable Trust (Charity Commission no. 327013); The Peter Samuel Royal Free Fund (Charity Commission no. 200049).
HOW TO APPLY Apply in writing to the correspondent. The trustees meet twice-yearly.
WHO TO APPLY TO Jenny Dance, Correspondent, The Estate Office, Farley Hall, Castle Road, Farley Hill, Reading, Berkshire RG7 1UL Tel. 0118 973 0047 email pa@farleyfarms.co.uk

## ■ The Samworth Foundation

**CC NO** 265647  **ESTABLISHED** 1973
**WHERE FUNDING CAN BE GIVEN** UK and Africa.
**WHO CAN BENEFIT** Registered charities only.
**WHAT IS FUNDED** The social and educational needs of children and young people, particularly 'those most neglected and vulnerable'. There has been a focus on child trafficking, anti-slavery and exploitation in the UK and Africa. The trustees have also expanded their core strategy to introduce different targeted areas, notably environmental and conservation issues.
**WHAT IS NOT FUNDED** Individuals.
**SAMPLE GRANTS** University of Leicester (£1 million); Uppingham School (£250,000); St Martins Cathedral Properties (£100,000); International Justice Mission UK – Kenya (£52,500); The Children's Society (£32,500); The Green Alliance Trust (£20,000); The Institute of Family Business (£15,000); Community Heartbeat Trust (£4,000); St James the Greater Church (£1,000).
**FINANCES** Year 2013/14 Income £1,689,514 Grants £2,326,909 Grants to organisations £2,326,909 Assets £15,704,616
**TRUSTEES** Bob Dowson; Alison Price; Viccy Stott.
**OTHER INFORMATION** A total of 72 grants were made during the year. Out of these 27 were of less than £1,000 each and totalled £6,500.
**HOW TO APPLY** The foundation's grant-making policy is to support a limited number of causes known to the trustees. Unsolicited applications are not normally considered.
**WHO TO APPLY TO** Wendy Bateman, c/o Samworth Brothers (Holdings) Ltd, Chetwode House, 1 Samworth Way, Melton Mowbray, Leicestershire LE13 1GA Tel. 01664 414500 email wendy.bateman@chetwodehouse.com

## ■ The Sandhu Charitable Foundation

**CC NO** 1114236  **ESTABLISHED** 2006
**WHERE FUNDING CAN BE GIVEN** Worldwide.
**WHO CAN BENEFIT** Charitable organisations.
**WHAT IS FUNDED** General charitable purposes; education and training; the promotion of health; social welfare; overseas aid; arts and culture; religious activities; economic and community development; armed forces; human rights; children and young people; older people; people with disabilities.
**TYPE OF GRANT** One-off.
**RANGE OF GRANTS** £1,000–£35,000
**SAMPLE GRANTS** Variety – The Children's Charity (£35,000); Anne Frank Trust UK (£25,000); Latymer Foundation (£20,000); CASS Business School (£15,000); Helena Kennedy Foundation and ORBIS (£10,000 each); Epilepsy Research UK (£6,000); Richard House Children's Hospice and Stroke Association (£5,000 each); Leukaemia and Lymphoma Research and Mums for Babas (£1,000 each).
**FINANCES** Year 2013/14 Income £414,928 Grants £300,000 Grants to organisations £300,000 Assets £5,211,298
**TRUSTEES** Bim Sandhu; Sean Carey.
**OTHER INFORMATION** The trustees made grants to 18 charities totalling £300,000.
**HOW TO APPLY** The charity supports individual charities or charitable causes, mainly on a single donation basis, which the trustees identify.
**WHO TO APPLY TO** The Trustees, First Floor, Santon House, 53–55 Uxbridge Road, Ealing, London W5 5SA Tel. 020 3478 3900 email nsteele@thesantongroup.com Website thesantongroup.com/charity/the-sandhu-charitable-foundation

## ■ The Sandra Charitable Trust

**CC NO** 327492  **ESTABLISHED** 1987
**WHERE FUNDING CAN BE GIVEN** Not defined, in practice UK with slight preference for south east England.
**WHO CAN BENEFIT** Charitable organisations and nurses.
**WHAT IS FUNDED** Animal welfare and research; environmental protection; relief of poverty; development of young people.
**WHAT IS NOT FUNDED** Individuals other than nurses.
**TYPE OF GRANT** One-off and recurring.
**RANGE OF GRANTS** Typically £5,000 or less.
**SAMPLE GRANTS** Kids (£40,000); Scope (£35,000); Arundel Castle Cricket Foundation (£25,000); The Old Vic (£8,000); St Wilfrid's Hospice (£6,700); Riding for the Disabled Association and St Mary-le-Bow Young Homeless Charity (£3,000 each); Freshwater Habitats Trust and Music in Hospitals (£2,000 each); Plantlife (£1,000).
**FINANCES** Year 2013/14 Income £502,916 Grants £505,009 Grants to organisations £407,950 Assets £19,344,820
**TRUSTEES** Richard Moore; Michael Macfadyen; Lucy Forsyth; Francis Moore.
**OTHER INFORMATION** Three grants of less than £1,000 each were awarded to organisations totalling £1,500. A total of 147 grants to individuals totalled £100,000.
**HOW TO APPLY** The trust's 2014 annual report states that 'unsolicited applications are not requested, as the trustees prefer to support charities whose work they have researched ... the trustees receives a very high number of grant applications which are mostly unsuccessful'.
**WHO TO APPLY TO** Martin Pollock, Secretary, c/o Moore Stephens, 150 Aldersgate Street, London EC1A 4AB Tel. 020 7334 9191 Fax 020 7248 3408 email martin.pollock@moorestephens.com

## ■ The Sands Family Trust

**CC NO** 1136909  **ESTABLISHED** 2010
**WHERE FUNDING CAN BE GIVEN** UK and overseas.
**WHO CAN BENEFIT** Organisations and individuals.
**WHAT IS FUNDED** General charitable purposes. Support is given particularly for the advancement of education, the relief of poverty and the encouragement of performing arts.
**RANGE OF GRANTS** £1,000–£25,000
**SAMPLE GRANTS** United World Colleges (£24,500); The Roundhouse Trust (£4,400); Big House Theatre Company (£9,500); First Story (£4,500); Standard Chartered Disaster Fund (£10,000); Save the Children (£10,000).
**FINANCES** Year 2013/14 Income £318,797 Grants £74,950 Grants to organisations £74,950 Assets £1,116,821
**TRUSTEES** Cripps Trust Corporation Ltd; Betsy Tobin; Peter Sands.
**HOW TO APPLY** Apply in writing to the correspondent.
**WHO TO APPLY TO** The Correspondent, Cripps Harries Hall LLP, Wallside House, 12 Mount Ephraim Road, Tunbridge Wells, Kent TN1 1EG Tel. 01892 515121 email nikki.image@cripps.co.uk

*Alphabetical register of grant-making charities*

# Saunders

## ■ Santander UK Foundation Limited

**CC NO** 803655  **ESTABLISHED** 1990
**WHERE FUNDING CAN BE GIVEN** UK.
**WHO CAN BENEFIT** Registered, excepted or exempt charities. Industrial and Provident societies can only be supported if they are founded under charitable, not membership, rules.
**WHAT IS FUNDED** The Santander Foundation has two grants programmes to help disadvantaged people in the UK: *Community Plus* provides grants of up to £5,000. The scheme is open to small local UK charities or local projects of national charities with funding available to cover salaries, equipment or materials and *Central Fund* offers grants of up to £10,000. The scheme is open to charities and Credit Unions anywhere in the UK for projects related to education, training or financial capability.
**WHAT IS NOT FUNDED** Statutory duties; part of a major capital appeal; a specific individual (this includes gap year funding, overseas travel, medical treatment or holidays); lobbying or political parties; the benefit of a single religious or single ethnic group; causes outside the UK; gaining specialist school status; commercial sponsorship or fundraising events, conferences or advertising.
**TYPE OF GRANT** All funding is for one-off donations. Grants are available to buy tangible items, such as equipment or training materials. Grants are also available to fund project costs, such as sessional worker fees, salaries, room hire or other costs incurred in the delivery of the charitable priorities.
**RANGE OF GRANTS** Usually up to £10,000.
**SAMPLE GRANTS** Teens and Toddlers (£25,000); Action for Blind People, Association of Charitable Foundations, BASIC, Disability Resource Centre, Family Tree Wirral, Manchester Carers Centre, Norfolk Rural Community Council, Shine Project, Sign Health and Stop Abuse For Everyone (£10,000 each).
**FINANCES** Year 2013 Income £5,803,253 Grants £5,928,173 Grants to organisations £5,928,173 Assets £13,027,547
**TRUSTEES** Lord Terence Burns; Steven Williams; Simon Lloyd; Jennifer Scardino; Angela Wakelin; Sue Wills; Keith Moore.
**HOW TO APPLY** The following guidance on making an application is given on the foundation's website. 'We have made applying to us as straightforward as possible and do not use an application form. We operate a rolling programme, with no deadlines for applications. Download and print off the grant application cover sheet which you can use as a checklist as you put together your application [available from the foundation's website]. You need to write us a letter on the headed notepaper of your charity which should include your registered charity number or whatever is appropriate for your charitable status. The letter should include the following: how much you are asking for?; what will this pay for? Include a simple budget detailing the main costs; how will disadvantaged people directly benefit? Include an estimate of the long term difference this grant will make; how does this meet one or both of our charitable priorities?; if the funding is for an existing project, tell us how our funding fits your funding strategy and what the project has achieved so far; if the funding is for a new project, tell us how you identified the need for this piece of work; If you are asking for revenue funding for salaries or running costs tell us what your funding strategy is to replace this funding at the end of our grant; if applicable, which other funders are you applying to? Make sure the letter is signed by two people, one of whom must be a trustee of the charity. If it helps explain what your project will do, you may want to include a flyer, newsletter or other sample training material that is produced for the beneficiaries. Please do **not** include: annual reports and accounts; DVDs or CDs; business plan or constitution; any other bulky items, plastic binders or covers. If you want confirmation that we have received your application, please enclose a self-addressed postcard or envelope with your application letter. We will post this to you when we open your application. If you do not receive any other correspondence from us within six weeks then you should assume that your application has been unsuccessful. We regret that due to the very high volume of requests received, we do not notify unsuccessful applicants or offer feedback on why your application has not been successful. We regret that we cannot accept online or emailed applications.'
**WHO TO APPLY TO** Alan Eagle, Foundation Manager, Santander UK plc, Santander House, 201 Grafton Gate East, Milton Keynes MK9 1AN *Tel.* 01908 343224 *email* grants@santander.co.uk *Website* www.santanderfoundation.org.uk

## ■ The Sants Charitable Trust

**CC NO** 1078555  **ESTABLISHED** 1999
**WHERE FUNDING CAN BE GIVEN** Oxfordshire.
**WHO CAN BENEFIT** Charitable organisations.
**WHAT IS FUNDED** Education and training; the promotion of health; social welfare; Christianity; economic and community development; children and young people.
**RANGE OF GRANTS** £300–£60,000
**SAMPLE GRANTS** Darmouth College (£18,500); Holy Trinity Brompton and Hope Corner Community Church (£6,000 each); Pegasus Theatre Trust and Harry Mahon Cancer Research Trust (£5,000 each); Garsington Opera (£3,000); Trinity College Boat Club (£1,000); CPRE Oxfordshire (£500); Buckinghamshire Foundation (£100).
**FINANCES** Year 2013/14 Income £40,446 Grants £52,213 Grants to organisations £52,213 Assets £1,207,522
**TRUSTEES** Caroline Sants; Hector Hepburn Sants; John Ovens; Alexander Sants; Edward Sants.
**OTHER INFORMATION** The trust gave grants to 13 organisations.
**HOW TO APPLY** Apply in writing to the correspondent.
**WHO TO APPLY TO** The Trustees, 17 Bradmore Road, Oxford OX2 6QP *Tel.* 01865 310813 *email* santscharitabletrust@gmail.com

## ■ The Peter Saunders Trust

**CC NO** 1108153  **ESTABLISHED** 2005
**WHERE FUNDING CAN BE GIVEN** Wales, particularly South Meirionnydd.
**WHO CAN BENEFIT** Charities; community groups; individuals.
**WHAT IS FUNDED** General charitable purposes; amateur sport; economic and community development.
**TYPE OF GRANT** One-off and recurrent.
**RANGE OF GRANTS** Up to £20,000.
**SAMPLE GRANTS** There was no information available.

*Think carefully about every application. Is it justified?*

**Scarfe**

FINANCES Year 2013/14 Income £1,045 Grants £40,000 Grants to organisations £40,000
TRUSTEES Lynda Bennett; Peter Saunders; Theresa Hartland; Keith Bartlett; Ieuan Saunders.
HOW TO APPLY The trust's website has stated that: 'The trust is taking a break now and not considering any new applications at this time. A review is being made of not only the impact of the work of the trust to date, but also its strategy for the future and the impact the trust might have in new areas.'
WHO TO APPLY TO Peter Saunders, Trustee, c/o The Sure Chill Company, Pendre, Tywyn, Gwynedd LL36 9LW Tel. 01654 713939 email enquiries@petersaunderstrust.co.uk Website www.petersaunderstrust.co.uk

■ **The Scarfe Charitable Trust**
CC NO 275535    ESTABLISHED 1978
WHERE FUNDING CAN BE GIVEN UK, with an emphasis on Suffolk.
WHO CAN BENEFIT Individuals and organisations working in the fields of arts, music, medical research and the environment.
WHAT IS FUNDED This trust funds a wide range of projects, such as: conservation; environmental interests; medical research; hospices; youth groups; arts and arts facilities; churches; religious ancillary buildings; art galleries and cultural centres; libraries and museums; theatres and opera houses.
TYPE OF GRANT Capital and core costs; one-off; projects; research; recurring and running costs. Funding is normally for one year or less.
RANGE OF GRANTS £50–£10,000
SAMPLE GRANTS Aldeburgh Music (£10,000); Ipswich School (£3,333); Operation Wallacea (£1,200); Sue Ryder, Suffolk Wildlife Trust (£1,000 each); Listening Books (£900); Deafblind UK (£800); All Saints Laxfield, Bedfield PCC, St Peter's Nowton (£750 each); Gurkha Welfare Trust, Shakespeare Schools Festival (£600 each); Age UK Suffolk, Dance East, Scope (£500 each); Friends of the Royal Academy (£90).
FINANCES Year 2013/14 Income £72,002 Grants £57,458 Grants to organisations £57,458 Assets £1,461,475
TRUSTEES Sean McTernan; Eric Maule; John McCarthy.
OTHER INFORMATION Many grants are under £1,000.
HOW TO APPLY Apply in writing to the correspondent by post or email. The trustees meet quarterly to consider applications.
WHO TO APPLY TO Eric Maule, Trustee, Salix House, Falkenham, Ipswich, Suffolk IP10 0QY Tel. 01728 627929 email ericmaule@hotmail.com

■ **The Schapira Charitable Trust**
CC NO 328435    ESTABLISHED 1989
WHERE FUNDING CAN BE GIVEN UK.
WHO CAN BENEFIT Jewish organisations; other organisations.
WHAT IS FUNDED Jewish charitable purposes; health and education generally.
RANGE OF GRANTS £250–£215,000
SAMPLE GRANTS Keren Association Limited (£215,000); Friends of Achlezer Ared (£109,500); British Friends of Mosdos Tchernobel (£57,000); Chevras Mo'oz Ladol (£19,500); Slabodka Yeshiva (£11,300); Friends of Ramolh Jerusalem FORJ (£8,000); Sameach (£5,000); Yesamach Levav Trust (£2,500); Lolev Charitable Trust (£500); Yom Tov Assistance Fund (£250).
FINANCES Year 2013 Income £244,928 Grants £747,145 Grants to organisations £747,145 Assets £5,048,495
TRUSTEES Isaac Schapira; Michael Neuberger; Suzanne Schapira.
HOW TO APPLY Apply in writing to the correspondent.
WHO TO APPLY TO Isaac Schapira, Trustee, 2 Dancastle Court, 14 Arcadia Avenue, Finchley, London N3 2JU Tel. 020 8371 0381 email londonoffice@istrad.com

■ **The Annie Schiff Charitable Trust**
CC NO 265401    ESTABLISHED 1973
WHERE FUNDING CAN BE GIVEN UK and overseas.
WHO CAN BENEFIT Orthodox Jewish institutions supporting religious, educational and relief of poverty aims.
WHAT IS FUNDED The relief of poverty generally and payment to needy individuals of the Jewish faith, for the advancement of education and religion.
WHAT IS NOT FUNDED Individuals; non-recognised institutions.
RANGE OF GRANTS £400–£22,000
SAMPLE GRANTS Previous beneficiaries have included: Friends of Beis Yisrael Trust and Menorah Grammar School Trust (£15,000 each); Elanore Limited (£10,000); WST Charity Limited (£8,000); Friends of Ohel Moshe (£6,000); Tifres High School, EMET and Yesamech Levav Trust (£5,000 each); North West Separdish Synagogue (£3,000); British Friends of Nadvorne (£1,500); Golders Charitable Trust (£1,100); Beth Jacob Grammar School for Girls Limited (£1,000); Ezra U'Marpeh (£500).
FINANCES Year 2014/15 Income £81,399 Grants £89,122 Grants to organisations £89,122 Assets £92,565
TRUSTEES Joseph Pearlman; Ruth Pearlman.
OTHER INFORMATION There were no details of beneficiaries for 2014/15.
HOW TO APPLY Apply in writing to the correspondent. Grants are generally made only to registered charities.
WHO TO APPLY TO Joseph Pearlman, Trustee, 8 Highfield Gardens, London NW11 9HB Tel. 020 8458 9266

■ **The Schmidt-Bodner Charitable Trust**
CC NO 283014    ESTABLISHED 1981
WHERE FUNDING CAN BE GIVEN UK and overseas
WHO CAN BENEFIT Jewish organisations; other registered charities.
WHAT IS FUNDED General charitable purposes; Jewish causes.
RANGE OF GRANTS £2,500–£21,000
SAMPLE GRANTS World Jewish Relief (£21,000); Jewish Care, Prince's Trust and Prostate Cancer UK (£10,000 each); Holocaust Educational Trust (£7,500); British ORT (£5,000); Maccabi GB (£2,500).
FINANCES Year 2013/14 Income £55,903 Grants £99,000 Grants to organisations £99,000 Assets £2,144,990
TRUSTEES Martin Paisner; Daniel Dover; Harvey Rosenblatt.
OTHER INFORMATION Grants were made to 12 organisations totalling £99,000.

**HOW TO APPLY** Applications can be made in writing to the correspondent. 'All applications received are considered by the trustees on their own merit for suitability of funding.'
**WHO TO APPLY TO** Harvey Rosenblatt, Trustee, 16 Caenwood Court, Hampstead Lane, London N6 4RU *Tel.* 07711 005151 *email* charity.correspondence@bdo.co.uk

## ■ The Schreib Trust

**CC NO** 275240 **ESTABLISHED** 1977
**WHERE FUNDING CAN BE GIVEN** UK.
**WHO CAN BENEFIT** Jewish organisations.
**WHAT IS FUNDED** General charitable purposes, in practice Jewish causes.
**RANGE OF GRANTS** Around £500–£80,000.
**SAMPLE GRANTS Previous beneficiaries have included:** Lolev; Yad Eliezer; Ponovitz; Craven Walk Charity Trust; Shaar Hatalmud; Beis Rochel; Beth Jacob Building Fund; Toiras Chesed; Oneg Shabbos.
**FINANCES** *Year* 2013/14 *Income* £498,407 *Grants* £242,789 *Grants to organisations* £242,789 *Assets* £415,335
**TRUSTEES** Abraham Green; Jacob Schreiber; Irene Schreiber; Rivka Niederman.
**OTHER INFORMATION** A list of beneficiaries was not provided by the trust in its annual report.
**HOW TO APPLY** Apply in writing to the correspondent.
**WHO TO APPLY TO** Rivka Niederman, Trustee, 147 Stamford Hill, London N16 5LG *Tel.* 020 8802 5492

## ■ The Schreiber Charitable Trust

**CC NO** 264735 **ESTABLISHED** 1972
**WHERE FUNDING CAN BE GIVEN** UK.
**WHO CAN BENEFIT** Registered charities.
**WHAT IS FUNDED** Jewish causes; education and training; social welfare; the promotion of health.
**RANGE OF GRANTS** £100–£50,000
**SAMPLE GRANTS Previous beneficiaries have included:** Friends of Rabbinical College Kol Tora; Jerusalem Foundation; SOFT; Gateshead Talmudical College; Dalaid Limited; Aish Hatorah UK Limited.
**FINANCES** *Year* 2013/14 *Income* £121,689 *Grants* £165,226 *Grants to organisations* £165,226 *Assets* £3,728,767
**TRUSTEES** Graham Morris; David Schreiber; Sara Schreiber.
**HOW TO APPLY** The trust states in its accounts for 2013/14 that the trustees 'regularly appraise new opportunities for direct charitable expenditure and actively seek suitable causes to reduce the unrestricted fund to the appropriate level'.
**WHO TO APPLY TO** Graham Morris, Trustee, Schreiber Holdings Ltd, 3 Brent Cross Gardens, London NW4 3RJ *Tel.* 020 8457 6500 *email* graham@schreibers.com

## ■ Schroder Charity Trust

**CC NO** 214050 **ESTABLISHED** 1944
**WHERE FUNDING CAN BE GIVEN** Worldwide, in practice mainly UK.
**WHO CAN BENEFIT** Registered charities.
**WHAT IS FUNDED** General charitable purposes; the promotion of health; social welfare; children and young people; education and training; community and economic development; overseas aid; arts and culture; the environment.
**WHAT IS NOT FUNDED** Individuals.

**TYPE OF GRANT** One-off and recurring.
**RANGE OF GRANTS** Up to £5,000.
**SAMPLE GRANTS** DEC – Philippines typhoon and The Wallace Collection (£5,000 each); Friends of the Elderly, Prostate Cancer Research Centre and Royal Horticultural Society (£3,000 each); St Boswells Public Hall Appeal and Women's Royal Voluntary Service (£2,500 each); Camden Arts Centre, Dame Vera Lynn Trust and Gingerbread (£2,000 each); British Schools Exploring Society and Project Hara Ethiopia (£1,500 each); Giving World (£1,000); Beanstalk (£600); Silversmiths and Jewellers Charity (£500); Royal Chapel Windsor (£400).
**FINANCES** *Year* 2013/14 *Income* £277,600 *Grants* £204,342 *Grants to organisations* £204,342 *Assets* £11,594,026
**TRUSTEES** Bruno Schroder; T. Schroder; Charmaine Von Mallinckrodt; Claire Fitzalan Howard; Leonie Fane; John Schroder.
**OTHER INFORMATION** Grants were made to 116 organisations totalling £204,000. All grants were for £5,000 or less.
**HOW TO APPLY** Apply in writing to the correspondent. Applicants should briefly state their case and enclose a copy of their latest accounts or annual review.
**WHO TO APPLY TO** Sally Yates, Correspondent, 81 Rivington Street, London EC2A 3AY *email* charities@schroderfoundation.com

## ■ The Schuster Charitable Trust

**CC NO** 234580 **ESTABLISHED** 1964
**WHERE FUNDING CAN BE GIVEN** UK, with a particular interest in Oxfordshire.
**WHO CAN BENEFIT** Charitable and voluntary organisations.
**WHAT IS FUNDED** General charitable purposes.
**WHAT IS NOT FUNDED** Individuals.
**SAMPLE GRANTS** Worton Parish Council (£3,500); Marie Curie Cancer Care and Hope and Homes for Children (£2,500 each); Asthma Relief, Carers Trust, Dogs for the Disabled, Keepout, Tree of Hope and Young Dementia (£1,000 each); Hook Norton Community Library and Narcolepsy UK (£500 each).
**FINANCES** *Year* 2013/14 *Income* £45,214 *Grants* £46,001 *Grants to organisations* £46,001 *Assets* £62,516
**TRUSTEES** Joanna Clarke; Richard Schuster; Peter Schuster.
**HOW TO APPLY** Apply in writing to the correspondent, for consideration at meetings twice a year in June and December. No reply is given if an sae is not included.
**WHO TO APPLY TO** Joanna Clarke, Trustee, New House Farm, Nether Worton, Chipping Norton, Oxon OX7 7AX *email* sct@netherworton.com

## ■ Foundation Scotland

**SC NO** SC022910 **ESTABLISHED** 1995
**WHERE FUNDING CAN BE GIVEN** Scotland.
**WHO CAN BENEFIT** Small organisations helping to build and sustain local communities.
**WHAT IS FUNDED** There are two broad programmes, under which there are a range of different funds. Express grants (up to £2,000) – grants are made to groups across a wide spectrum of social welfare and community development activities. Community Benefit Funds – there are a variety of programmes which benefit people in specific areas of Scotland. Each has different grant levels, deadline dates and decision

making practices. A list of local programmes is available on the foundation's website.

**WHAT IS NOT FUNDED** The following are not normally funded under express grants: individuals or groups which do not have a constitution; groups other than not-for-profit groups; groups whose grant request is for the advancement of religion or a political party (the foundation won't fund grant requests to support the core activities of religious or political groups); the purchase of second hand vehicles; trips abroad; the repayment of loans, payment of debts, or other retrospective funding; payments towards areas generally understood to be the responsibility of statutory authorities; groups who will then distribute the funds as grants or bursaries; applications that are for the sole benefit to flora and fauna. Applicants are invited to demonstrate the direct benefit to the local community and/or service users in cases where the grant application is concerned with flora and fauna; projects which do not benefit people in Scotland.

**TYPE OF GRANT** Capital and revenue costs; full project funding.

**RANGE OF GRANTS** Usually between £250 and £5,000 – occasionally larger grants are made.

**SAMPLE GRANTS** Beattock Hall Committee (£63,000); Nith Valley Leaf Trust (£35,000); Cockburnspath Village Hall Committee (£2,500); Hawkhill Community Association (£2,000); Bridge of Earn Institute (£1,600); Crook of Devon Village Hall (£1,500); Dundee Woodcraft Folk and the Volunteer Tutors Organisation (£1,000 each); Coldingham Society (£600); Blackford Festive Lights (£500).

**FINANCES** Year 2013/14 Income £11,304,000 Grants £8,477,000 Grants to organisations £8,477,000

**TRUSTEES** Bob Benson; Gillian Donald; Beth Edberg; Colin Liddell; Ian McAteer; Jimmy McCulloch; John Naylor; Ella Simpson; Lady Emily Stair; Tom Ward.

**HOW TO APPLY** The foundation has a comprehensive website with details of the grant schemes currently being administered. Organisations are welcome to contact the grants team to discuss their funding needs before making any application. The trustees meet at least four times a year.

**WHO TO APPLY TO** Alice Dansey-Wright, Programmes Administrator, Empire House, 131 West Nile Street, Glasgow G1 2RX *Tel.* 0141 341 4960 *email* grants@foundationscotland.org.uk *Website* www.foundationscotland.org.uk

## ■ The Francis C. Scott Charitable Trust

**CC NO** 232131     **ESTABLISHED** 1963

**WHERE FUNDING CAN BE GIVEN** Cumbria and north Lancashire (comprising the towns of Lancaster, Morecambe, Heysham and Carnforth).

**WHO CAN BENEFIT** Mostly registered charities addressing the needs of 0- to 21-year-olds in the most deprived communities of Cumbria and north Lancashire. Organisations who are pursuing charitable objectives and have not-for-profit aims/constitution may be considered. Applications from national organisations will only be considered if the beneficiaries and project workers are based within the beneficial area.

**WHAT IS FUNDED** There is an emphasis on community services, support and development for youth organisations, family support services and community development projects.

**WHAT IS NOT FUNDED** Individuals; statutory organisations; national charities without a local base/project; charities with substantial unrestricted reserves; medical/health establishments; schools/educational establishments; infrastructure organisations/second-tier bodies; projects principally benefitting people outside Cumbria/north Lancashire; retrospective funding; expeditions or overseas travel; the promotion of religion; animal welfare. The trustees prefer to fund small to medium-sized organisations and it is therefore unlikely they will support applications from charities with a turnover in excess of £1 million.

**TYPE OF GRANT** Most grants are multi-year revenue grants (for salaries and running costs); capital projects that make a tangible difference to a local community are also supported.

**RANGE OF GRANTS** Up to £275,000.

**SAMPLE GRANTS** Whitehaven Community Trust (£60,000); Whitehaven Foyer (£50,000); Safety Net Advice 8 Support Centre – Carlisle (£20,000); Walney Community Trust (£18,000); Aspatria Dreamscheme, Cumbria Starting Point and Self-Injury Support in North Cumbria (£15,000 each); Distington Club for Young People (£10,000); Leonard Cheshire North West (£7,500); University of Cumbria (£5,000); New Rainbow Pre School (£4,000); Child and Family Connect (£2,000); Egremont Amenity Committee (£1,000).

**FINANCES** Year 2013 Income £755,250 Grants £833,530 Grants to organisations £833,530 Assets £30,680,182

**TRUSTEES** Donald Shore; Susan Bagot; Clare Spedding; Alexander Scott; Madeleine Scott; Joanna Plumptre; Melanie Wotherspoon; Malcolm Tillyer; Revd John Bannister; Carol Ostermeyer; Steven Swallow.

**OTHER INFORMATION** Applicants should refer to the trust's website which is very comprehensive and covers all aspects of the grant-making process.

**HOW TO APPLY** The trust is always pleased to hear from charities that need help. If an organisation thinks that it may come within the trust's criteria it is encouraged to contact the director for an informal discussion before making an application. Application forms are available to download from the trust's website or can be requested by phone, email or post. Applications should be completed and returned with the latest set of accounts (via email or post). Applications for over £4,000 should be submitted at least four weeks before the trustee's meetings in late February, June, October and November. Check the website for the latest deadlines. Applications for grants of less than £4,000 will be considered at small grants meetings every three to four weeks. It is also worth noting that charities should not apply to both the Frieda Scott and Francis C Scott Charitable Trusts at the same time.

**WHO TO APPLY TO** Chris Batten, Director, Stricklandgate House, 92 Stricklandgate, Kendal, Cumbria LA9 4PU *Tel.* 01539 742608 *email* info@fcsct.org.uk *Website* www.fcsct.org.uk

## ■ The Frieda Scott Charitable Trust

**CC NO** 221593     **ESTABLISHED** 1962

**WHERE FUNDING CAN BE GIVEN** Old county of Westmorland and the area covered by South Lakeland District Council.

**WHO CAN BENEFIT** Small local charities; parish halls; youth groups; occasionally locally based work of larger charities.

**WHAT IS FUNDED** A very wide range of registered charities concerned with social welfare, community projects, the upkeep of village halls and voluntary sector infrastructure support and development.

**WHAT IS NOT FUNDED** Individuals; retrospective funding; parish councils; health establishments; schools or educational establishments; places of worship or promoting religion; environmental causes; multi-year grants (except for start-ups); animal charities; wildlife or heritage causes; gardens or allotments (unless addressing disadvantage); property buying (other than in exceptional circumstances); sporting activity; museums and art galleries; national charities (with exceptions made for branches operating in the beneficial area).Applications are not considered if they are from outside the beneficial area.

**TYPE OF GRANT** Capital costs, including buildings; core costs; one-off; project; research; recurring and running costs; salaries; start-up costs. The Trustees are unwilling to commit to funding more than one year at any one time.

**RANGE OF GRANTS** Usually £200–£10,000.

**SAMPLE GRANTS** Bendrigg Trust (£50,000); Springfield House – Building Development (£60,000); Cumbria Drug and Alcohol Service (£12,000); Growing Well, Ulverston Inshore Rescue (£10,000 each); Kent Estuary Youth Work Project (£6,000); South Lakeland Carers Association (£5,000 each); Cumbria DeafVision, Samaritans – Lancaster and District (£3,500 each); Sedburgh People's Hall (£2,500); Cumbria South Girl Guides Association (£1,500); Casterton Village Hall (£1,000); Milnthorpe Community Playgroup (£500).

**FINANCES** Year 2013/14 Income £305,851 Grants £295,358 Grants to organisations £295,358 Assets £8,896,775

**TRUSTEES** Sally Barker; Richard Brownson; Stuart Fairclough; Claire Hensman; Philip Hoyle; Margaret Wilson; Vanda Lambton; Hugo Pring; Samantha Scott; Peter Smith.

**OTHER INFORMATION** A total of 53 organisations were given grants in 2013/14.

**HOW TO APPLY** An application form is available from the correspondent, or from the trust's website, which should be returned by email or post with the latest set of audited accounts. Potential applicants are welcome to ring for an informal discussion before submitting an application. Applications are considered at meetings in March, June, September and December and should be sent to the Grants Coordinator at least a month beforehand. Grants of less than £3,500 are considered by the small grants committee in between main trustee meetings. Further advice and information about the grant process is available on the trust's website. Note: the trust asks that charities do not apply to both the Frieda Scott and Francis C Scott Charitable Trusts at the same time. If unsure, contact the trust for further guidance. Previous applicants, whether successful or not, are advised to wait for a year before applying to the trust again.

**WHO TO APPLY TO** Naomi Brown, Secretary, Stricklandgate House, 92 Stricklandgate, Kendal, Cumbria LA9 4PU Tel. 01539 742608 email info@fcsct.org.uk Website www.friedascott.org.uk

## ■ Sir Samuel Scott of Yews Trust

**CC NO** 220878 **ESTABLISHED** 1951

**WHERE FUNDING CAN BE GIVEN** UK.

**WHO CAN BENEFIT** Medical research bodies benefitting medical professionals and research workers.

**WHAT IS FUNDED** Medical research.

**WHAT IS NOT FUNDED** Core funding; purely clinical work; individuals (although research by an individual may be funded if sponsored by a registered charity through which the application is made); research leading to higher degrees (unless the departmental head concerned certifies that the work is of real scientific importance); medical students' elective periods; or expeditions (unless involving an element of genuine medical research).

**TYPE OF GRANT** One-off; project.

**RANGE OF GRANTS** Usually £1,000–£10,000.

**SAMPLE GRANTS** Gray Institute at the University of Oxford (£111,000); Multiple Sclerosis Society, University of Surrey and Wellbeing of Women (£10,000 each); Alzheimer's Society, Breast Cancer Campaign and Meningitis Trust (£5,000 each); Roy Castle Lung Cancer Foundation (£4,000); Bowel and Cancer Research and Scat Bone Cancer Trust (£2,000 each); Genesis Breast Cancer Prevention and University of Bournemouth (£1,000 each).

**FINANCES** Year 2013/14 Income £123,669 Grants £192,000 Grants to organisations £192,000 Assets £6,218,685

**TRUSTEES** Edward Perks; Hermione Stanford; Lady Phoebe Scott.

**OTHER INFORMATION** Grants were made to 21 organisations totalling £192,000. As in previous years, the largest grants was made to the Gray Institute at the University of Oxford (£111,000).

**HOW TO APPLY** Applications can be made in writing to the correspondent. Trustees hold their half-yearly meetings in April and October and applications have to be submitted two months before. There are no special forms, but applicants should give the following information: the nature and purpose of the research project or programme; the names, qualifications and present posts of the scientists involved; reference to any published results of their previous research; details of present funding; and if possible, the budget for the next 12 months or other convenient period. All applications are acknowledged and both successful and unsuccessful applicants are notified after each meeting of the trustees. No telephone calls.

**WHO TO APPLY TO** The Trustees, c/o Currey and Co, 21 Buckingham Gate, London SW1E 6LS Tel. 020 7802 2700

## ■ The Sir James and Lady Scott Trust

**CC NO** 231324 **ESTABLISHED** 1907

**WHERE FUNDING CAN BE GIVEN** The borough and district of Bolton.

**WHO CAN BENEFIT** Only registered charities or not-for-profit organisations that are in the process of becoming a charity, will be considered.

**WHAT IS FUNDED** The trust gives priority to projects which help disadvantaged people or communities in Bolton. These have included projects which help older people or people with disabilities, children and young people and ethnic minority groups. It has also indicated on its website that it will consider applications from arts organisations, especially for projects that would benefit the community or improve access or involvement for disadvantaged people. Grants and pensions are also made to former employees of the family of the Settlor who are in need.

**WHAT IS NOT FUNDED** Individuals; church restoration; medical causes; expeditions or scholarships.

**TYPE OF GRANT** Capital costs; core costs; full project funding; salaries. Up to three years.

**RANGE OF GRANTS** Up to £3,000.

**SAMPLE GRANTS** Special Needs Under Fives Support (£2,800); Bolton Wanderers Community Trust (£2,500); Bolton STEPS (£2,000); Bolton Lads and Girls Club and Bolton Kidz2gether (£1,500 each); Beanstalk (£1,200); JIGSAW CVS (£1,000); Rotary Club of Westhoughton (£700); Bolton Deane and Derby Cricket and Social Club (£500).

**FINANCES** Year 2013/14 Income £45,922 Grants £33,323 Grants to organisations £18,900 Assets £2,811,240

**TRUSTEES** Madeleine Scott; Christopher Scott; William Swan.

**OTHER INFORMATION** Payments made to former employees of members of the family of the settlor totalled £17,400.

**HOW TO APPLY** Applications are considered at trustees' meetings which are held in April, August and December. The deadline for applications is four weeks before each meeting. Applications can be downloaded from the trust's website or a paper version can be requested by contacting the correspondent. Completed application forms should be returned either via email or post. An initial telephone call is welcomed.

**WHO TO APPLY TO** Chris Batten, Secretary, Stricklandgate House, 92 Stricklandgate, Kendal, Cumbria LA9 4PU *Tel.* 01539 742608 *email* info@fcsct.org.uk *Website* www.sjlst.org.uk

........................................................

■ **Scottish Coal Industry Special Welfare Fund**

**SC NO** SC001200    **ESTABLISHED** 1932

**WHERE FUNDING CAN BE GIVEN** Scotland.

**WHO CAN BENEFIT** People who are or have been employed in the mining industry and their families.

**WHAT IS FUNDED** The fund was set up to improve the quality of life of people employed in the mining industry and their families. It supports individuals in need and also the provision of recreational facilities, youth clubs and courses.

**SAMPLE GRANTS** Details were not available.

**FINANCES** Year 2013/14 Income £50,406 Grants £90,000 Grants to organisations £90,000

**TRUSTEES** Keith Jones, Chair; William Menzies; Robert McGill.

**OTHER INFORMATION** The fund's website contains only basic information, and that potential applicants should check it for further details on recent beneficiaries and other information as it develops. Total expenditure for 2013/14 was £135,000. In the absence of further information we have estimated the grant total as £90,000.

**HOW TO APPLY** Apply in writing to the correspondent. Applications should include as much information as possible to enable the trustees to respond swiftly. The application's link to the coal mining industry must be highlighted. The trustees meet quarterly to consider grant requests. Applicants are welcome to contact the trust for further information.

**WHO TO APPLY TO** Ian McAlpine, Secretary, c/o CISWO, Second Floor, 50 Hopetoun Street, Bathgate, West Lothian EH48 4EU *Tel.* 01506 635550 *Fax* 01506 631555 *email* ian.mcalpine@ciswo.org.uk *Website* www.sciswf.org.uk

........................................................

■ **The Scottish Power Energy People Trust**

**SC NO** SC036980    **ESTABLISHED** 2005

**WHERE FUNDING CAN BE GIVEN** UK.

**WHO CAN BENEFIT** Charitable organisations.

**WHAT IS FUNDED** Fuel poverty; social welfare; energy efficiency.

**WHAT IS NOT FUNDED** Individuals.

**RANGE OF GRANTS** £20,000–£40,000

**SAMPLE GRANTS** Heely City Farm (£40,000); LESS (£39,500); Doorway (£38,500); Action for Children – Perthshire Families Service partnership project (£30,500); Quarries Homeless Energy Action Project (£23,500); Family Link Stockport (£22,000); Northern Oak Credit Union (£20,000).

**FINANCES** Year 2013 Income £452,943 Grants £1,000,000 Grants to organisations £1,000,000

**TRUSTEES** Ann Loughrey, Secretary; Norman Kerr, Chair; Douglas McLaren; Joan Fraser; Neil Hartwell; Dr Bill Sheldrick; Alan Hughes; Peter Sumby.

**OTHER INFORMATION** Established by Scottish Power in 2005, the trust has distributed over £12.6 million to projects run by grass roots organisations that help people who are on low incomes, live in poor housing or suffer ill health.

**HOW TO APPLY** Applications can be made on an online form on the trust's website. The trustees meet to consider applications three times a year, in March, July and November. Applications should be submitted at least seven weeks prior to the date of the meeting (exact dates available on the site). However, early applications are advised as only 30 applications will be considered at each meeting, with additional applications received being carried over to the next meeting. The following guidelines are available on the trust's website: 'All projects must address fuel poverty explicitly. Tackling fuel poverty must be the primary purpose of the project (not just as an add on). Project applications must identify how the outcomes and outputs of a project will reduce fuel poverty and how a project will meet the trust objectives. Each application should demonstrate how many people will be helped as a direct result of the project. Please note that we will only accept one application per organisation at each trustee meeting. All applicants should create a link to their organisation's latest annual audited accounts and confirm any previous applications to the trust. This information should be updated in the **Project Controls** section of the application. Charity registration number must be included in application, if not it will be rejected.' The trust also cautions that funding is made on the condition that overheads or administration costs associated with a project do not exceed 12.5% of the total funding requested. In special circumstances the trustees may make an exception to this condition provided a valid reason is supplied. Applicants will be notified within two weeks of the trustee meeting and unsuccessful applicants may re-apply only after six months. Successful applicants may re-apply for further funding either six months after the initial funding has expired, or on completion of the project – whichever happens first. Grants are usually made in annual instalments with 10% of the annual total retained by the trust pending receipt of a satisfactory annual report on the progress or completion of the project which the trust states is to 'encourage transparency and responsible reporting'. More details on reporting requirements are available on the trust's site.

WHO TO APPLY TO Kirsteen Lappin, Account Manager, Scottish Power Energy Retail Ltd, Cathcart Business Park, 44 Spean Street, Glasgow G44 4BE *Tel.* 0141 614 4480 *email* SPEnergyPeopleTrust@ScottishPower.com *Website* www.energypeopletrust.com

## ■ The Scottish Power Foundation

**SC NO** SC043862  **ESTABLISHED** 2013

**WHERE FUNDING CAN BE GIVEN** UK.

**WHO CAN BENEFIT** Registered charities and non-profit organisations.

**WHAT IS FUNDED** General charitable purposes.

**WHAT IS NOT FUNDED** Organisations that are not registered charities or non-profit; general appeals and circulars including contributions to endowment funds; local charities whose work takes place outside the United Kingdom; medical research; individuals or support organisations for travel or for expeditions, whether in the United Kingdom or abroad; projects which are primarily or exclusively intended to promote political or religious beliefs; second or third tier organisations (unless there is evidence of direct benefit to disadvantaged people); sponsorship or funding towards a marketing appeal or fundraising activities.

**SAMPLE GRANTS** Action for Achievement; Children's University Scotland; Clwyd Theatre Cymru; Duke of Edinburgh's Award; Loch Lomond and The Trossachs Countryside Trust; National Theatre for Scotland; Northern Lights; O Ddrws i Ddrws; Outward Bound; the Scottish Youth Hostels Association.

**FINANCES** *Year* 2013 *Income* £191,850 *Grants* £60,000 *Grants to organisations* £60,000

**TRUSTEES** Mike Thornton; Elaine Bowker; Sarah Mistry; Mike Thornton; Keith Anderson; Ann Loughrey.

**HOW TO APPLY** The foundation will be inviting applications for projects commencing in 2016 in the summer of 2015. Check the website for the latest information. Applications should be made using the application form which will be available to download from the website during the next application period. Applications should be submitted via email along with: a copy of your most recent annual report and accounts (note that these should have been independently examined or audited); an initial high level project plan with key milestones.

**WHO TO APPLY TO** María Elena Sanz Arcas, Secretary, 1 Atlantic Quay, Robertson Street, Glasgow G2 8SP *Tel.* 0800 027 0072 *email* scottishpowerfoundation@scottishpower. com *Website* www.scottishpower.com/pages/ the_scottishpower_foundation.asp

## ■ The Scouloudi Foundation

**CC NO** 205685  **ESTABLISHED** 1962

**WHERE FUNDING CAN BE GIVEN** UK charities working domestically or overseas.

**WHO CAN BENEFIT** The Institute of Historical Research, University of London, for publications, research and fellowships ('Historical Awards'); registered charities in the fields of: older people; children and young people; environment; famine relief and overseas aid; disability; the humanities (archaeology, art, history, libraries, museums and records); medicine, health and hospices; social welfare; welfare of armed forces and sailors.

**WHAT IS FUNDED** Education and training; the promotion of health; people with disabilities; social welfare; overseas aid; arts and culture; the environment; children and young people; older people.

**WHAT IS NOT FUNDED** Individuals; welfare activities of a purely local nature; loans.

**TYPE OF GRANT** There are three categories of grant: an annual donation for historical research and fellowships to the Institute of Historical Research at the University of London; recurring grants to a regular list of charities; 'special donations' which are one-off grants, usually in connection with capital projects.

**RANGE OF GRANTS** Typically £1,000–£2,000.

**SAMPLE GRANTS** University of London – Institute of Historical Research (£95,000); British Red Cross Disaster Fund (£10,000); Art Fund, Brain Research Trust, British Kidney Patient Association, Cathedral Camps, Canine Partners, Centrepoint, Find Your Feet, Friends of the Elderly, Independence at Home, Kiloran Trust, Landmark Trust, London Record Society, Mental Health Foundation, RAFT, Royal British Legion, Royal Sailor's Rests, SCOPE, Shooting Star Chase, The Conservation Volunteers and Vision Aid Overseas (£1,250 each).

**FINANCES** *Year* 2013/14 *Income* £239,438 *Grants* £199,111 *Grants to organisations* £199,111 *Assets* £6,543,141

**TRUSTEES** Sarah Baxter; David Marnham; James Sewell.

**HOW TO APPLY** Only Historical grants are open to application. Copies of the regulations and application forms for 'Historical Awards' can be obtained from: The Secretary, The Scouloudi Foundation Historical Awards Committee, c/o Institute of Historical Research, University of London, Senate House, Malet Street, London WC1E 7HU.

**WHO TO APPLY TO** The Trustees, c/o Haysmacintyre, 26 Red Lion Square, London WC1R 4AG *Tel.* 020 7969 5500 *email* pholden@ haysmacintyre.com

## ■ The SDL Foundation

**CC NO** 1127138  **ESTABLISHED** 2008

**WHERE FUNDING CAN BE GIVEN** Worldwide.

**WHO CAN BENEFIT** Charitable organisations.

**WHAT IS FUNDED** Social welfare; community and economic development; education and training.

**WHAT IS NOT FUNDED** No grants will be given to causes where trustees or SDL employees would directly benefit. The foundation will also not support political or discriminatory activities; or those appeals that are recognised as being large or well-known.

**RANGE OF GRANTS** £350–£43,000

**SAMPLE GRANTS** Gua Africa, Sudan (£43,000); Village Water, Zambia (£25,000); Hatua Likoni, Kenya (£20,000); Bead For Life, Uganda

(£13,000); Able Children Africa, Kenya Food for the Hungry UK, Kenya and St Wilfrid's, UK (£10,000 each); Stichting Miramundo, Honduras (£8,700); PRIDE, Ethiopia (£6,400); Niall Mellon Township Fund, Kenya (£3,400); Translators Without Borders (£1,600); Operation Sack Lunch, USA (£350).

**FINANCES** Year 2013 Income £261,196 Grants £159,538 Grants to organisations £159,538 Assets £332,442

**TRUSTEES** Mark Lancaster; Alastair Gordon; Dominic Kinnon; Michelle Wilson.

**OTHER INFORMATION** The SDL Foundation is the corporate charity of SDL plc, which provides software for language translation and interpretation services.

**HOW TO APPLY** Only causes supported and sponsored by SDL employees will be considered by the SDL Foundation. Contact the foundation by email for further information on how to request the support of staff and application procedures.

**WHO TO APPLY TO** Alastair Gordon, Trustee, SDL plc, 64 Castelnau, London SW13 9EX email SDLFoundation@sdl.com Website www.sdl.com/en/about-us/charity

## ■ Seafarers UK (King George's Fund for Sailors)

**CC NO** 226446  **ESTABLISHED** 1917
**WHERE FUNDING CAN BE GIVEN** UK and Commonwealth.
**WHO CAN BENEFIT** Specialist maritime charities and organisations, often small local organisations.
**WHAT IS FUNDED** Projects, services or activities that support seafarers, ex-seafarers and their dependants who are facing hardship. Also, activities run by maritime youth organisations with the aim of promoting careers at sea. The charity has four broad programme priorities: older seafarers over the usual age of retirement and their dependants; working age seafarers who are working at sea, former seafarers under the age of retirement and Merchant Navy cadets and trainees; families and dependants of current or former seafarers who are of working age; and young people in maritime youth groups with a focus on those considering or pursuing a career at sea.
**WHAT IS NOT FUNDED** The fund does not make grants directly to individuals but rather helps other organisations which do this. Grants requests for the following are generally not considered: sailing or youth clubs (funding for youth organisations is directed at those that can demonstrate a clear link between their activities and young people choosing or beginning a career at sea); marine societies and sea cadets – individual units (the promotion of sailing or youth work are, by themselves, activities not currently supported by the charity); the promotion of religious beliefs; political/campaigning organisations; sea rescue/lifeboat services. Grants are not awarded for: activities which are the legal obligation of the state; endowments; loans or interest payments; fundraising activities for your organisation or any other group or activity; contingency costs; PR/marketing costs.
**TYPE OF GRANT** Project costs; revenue costs, such as staff salaries or general running costs; some capital costs (though substantial capital funding is unlikely).
**RANGE OF GRANTS** From £1,000 to £240,000.

**SAMPLE GRANTS** Fishermen's Mission (£236,500); Shipwrecked Fishermen and Mariners' Royal Benevolent Society (£194,500); Mission to Seafarers – UK (£150,000); Marine Society and Sea Cadets (£130,000); Maritime Piracy Humanitarian Response Programme (£72,000); Royal Liverpool Seamen's Orphans Institution (£40,000); Queen Alexandra Hospital Home (£25,000); Age UK – Wirral (£16,700); Community Housing and Therapy (£5,000); Maritime Volunteer Service (£2,000); University of Hull (£1,000).

**FINANCES** Year 2014 Income £2,719,000 Grants £2,484,870 Grants to organisations £2,484,870 Assets £39,792,000

**TRUSTEES** Mark Carden; Capt. David Parsons; Michael Acland; Christian Marr; Simon Rivett-Carnac; Alderman The Lord Mountevans; Mark Dickinson; Vice Admiral Peter Wilkinson; Capt. Roger Barker; Dyan Sterling; Surgeon Commodore Peter Buxton; Tom Cadman; Jeremy Monroe; Evelyn Strouts; Duncan Bain.

**OTHER INFORMATION** In 2014 the charity receive 117 grants applications, of which 23 were rejected. A total of 93 grants were made to 70 organisations, out of which 19 were new beneficiaries.

**HOW TO APPLY** There are guidelines available to download from the website, which applicants are strongly advised to read before an application is started. If you are unsure about the eligibility of your project or to which grants programme you should apply, the grants team may be contacted by telephone or by email (grants@seafarers-uk.org). Applications should be made via the online applications system at any time. The trustees meet to consider applications four times a year. In addition to the Seafarers UK grants programme, there is also a Merchant Navy Fund grants programme, which exclusively supports organisations working to benefit those who have served in the Merchant Navy. There is a separate application form and set of guidelines for this fund, which are available to download from the website.

**WHO TO APPLY TO** Dennis Treleaven, Director of Grants and External Operations, 8 Hatherley Street, London SW1P 2YY Tel. 020 7932 0000 Fax 020 7932 0095 email dennis.treleaven@seafarers-uk.org Website www.seafarers-uk.org

## ■ The Searchlight Electric Charitable Trust

**CC NO** 801644  **ESTABLISHED** 1988
**WHERE FUNDING CAN BE GIVEN** UK, with a preference for Manchester and the surrounding areas.
**WHO CAN BENEFIT** Registered charities.
**WHAT IS FUNDED** General charitable purposes; Jewish causes.
**WHAT IS NOT FUNDED** Individuals.
**SAMPLE GRANTS** Previous beneficiaries have included: Bnei Akiva Sefer Torah; Chabad Vilna; CST; Guide Dogs for the Blind; Heathlands; Langdon College; Lubavitch Manchester; Manchester Eruv Committee; Nightingales; Reshet and the Purim Fund; Sense; The Federation; UJIA; Young Israel Synagogue.
**FINANCES** Year 2013/14 Income £163,917 Grants £115,556 Grants to organisations £115,556 Assets £1,210,042
**TRUSTEES** Morris Hamburger; David Hamburger; Herzl Hamburger; Daniel Hamburger.
**HOW TO APPLY** Apply in writing to the correspondent.

**WHO TO APPLY TO** David Hamburger, Trustee, 21 Brantwood Road, Salford M7 4EN *Tel.* 0161 203 3300

## ■ The Seedfield Trust

**CC NO** 283463     **ESTABLISHED** 1981
**WHERE FUNDING CAN BE GIVEN** Worldwide.
**WHO CAN BENEFIT** Registered charities benefitting: Christians; evangelists; victims of famine, man-made and natural disasters and war; people disadvantaged by poverty; retired clergy; missionaries.
**WHAT IS FUNDED** The trust's aims are: to support the preaching and teaching of the Christian faith throughout the world, including publication and distribution of Scripture, Christian literature and audio-visual aids; to assist in the relief of hardship and poverty, including retired ministers and missionaries.
**TYPE OF GRANT** The trust rarely makes grants towards core funding or for activities that may require funding over a number of years, preferring to make one-off project grants.
**RANGE OF GRANTS** Up to £10,000; typically £1,000–2,000.
**SAMPLE GRANTS** Overseas Missionary Fellowship (£8,000); European Christian Mission – Britain (£6,100); International Nepal Fellowship (£4,000); Keswick Ministries, Leprosy Mission – India (£2,000 each); Church Urban fund, DEC Philippines Typhoon appeal, Prison Fellowship, Youth for Christ (£1,000 each); Open Air Campaigners and Prospects (£500 each).
**FINANCES** *Year* 2013 *Income* £112,680 *Grants* £109,950 *Grants to organisations* £109,450 *Assets* £2,727,471
**TRUSTEES** Paul Vipond; Keith Buckler; David Ryan; Janet Buckler; Valerie James; Eric Proudfoot.
**HOW TO APPLY** Apply in writing to the correspondent, for consideration by the trustees who meet twice each year. Applicants should enclose a stamped addressed envelope for acknowledgement.
**WHO TO APPLY TO** Janet Buckler, Trustee, 3 Woodland Vale, Lakeside, Ulverston, Cumbria LA12 8DR *Tel.* 01539 530359

## ■ Leslie Sell Charitable Trust

**CC NO** 258699     **ESTABLISHED** 1969
**WHERE FUNDING CAN BE GIVEN** UK.
**WHO CAN BENEFIT** Scout and Guide associations and individuals.
**WHAT IS FUNDED** Assistance for Scout and Guide associations.
**WHAT IS NOT FUNDED** The project or trip must be part of the Scouting or Guiding movement. The trust cannot award grants within three months of an event date or the date of departure for a trip.
**TYPE OF GRANT** Usually one-off payments for a small project, such as building repair works, transport, trips, events or equipment.
**RANGE OF GRANTS** Up to £5,000.
**SAMPLE GRANTS** Details were not available.
**FINANCES** *Year* 2013/14 *Income* £128,927 *Grants* £99,113 *Grants to organisations* £99,113 *Assets* £3,528,240
**TRUSTEES** Mary Wiltshire; Adrian Sell; Nicola Coggins.
**HOW TO APPLY** Applications should be made with an application form (available from the trust's website) accompanied by a letter on official notepaper. The trust provides guidance for applicants on its website. Applications should include clear details of the project or purpose for which funds are required, together with an estimate of total costs and details of any funds raised by the group or individual for the project. The trust states that: 'Applications are usually treated sympathetically provided they are connected to the Scouting or Guide movement'. The trustees meet to review applications once per month throughout the year. The trustees are unable to consider applications for a trip or event date within three months of submission date. Applications to the Peter Sell Annual Award usually have to be submitted by the end of September. See the trust's website for full guidelines and future deadlines.
**WHO TO APPLY TO** Sharon Long, Secretary, 1st Floor, 8–10 Upper Marlborough Road, St Albans, Hertfordshire AL1 3UR *Tel.* 01727 843603 *Fax* 01727 847118 *email* admin@iplltd.co.uk *Website* www.lesliesellct.org.uk

## ■ Sellata Ltd

**CC NO** 285429     **ESTABLISHED** 1980
**WHERE FUNDING CAN BE GIVEN** UK.
**WHO CAN BENEFIT** Charitable organisations.
**WHAT IS FUNDED** The advancement of religion; the relief of poverty.
**SAMPLE GRANTS** A list of beneficiaries was not available.
**FINANCES** *Year* 2013/14 *Income* £354,404 *Grants* £174,176 *Grants to organisations* £174,176 *Assets* £413,368
**TRUSTEES** Eliezer Benedikt; Nechy Benedikt; Pinchas Benedikt; Joseph Stern.
**OTHER INFORMATION** A list of beneficiaries was not available.
**HOW TO APPLY** Apply in writing to the correspondent.
**WHO TO APPLY TO** Eliezer Benedikt, Trustee, 29 Fountayne Road, London N16 7EA *email* management@abarisltd.co.uk

## ■ SEM Charitable Trust

**CC NO** 265831     **ESTABLISHED** 1973
**WHERE FUNDING CAN BE GIVEN** USA.
**WHO CAN BENEFIT** Specialist organisations working on climate change.
**WHAT IS FUNDED** The trust makes grants to specialist organisations working on climate change. It has previously supported special educational needs and community development, but changed its focus in April 2015.
**SAMPLE GRANTS** Natal Society for Arts (£30,000); Tafta (£4,000); National Deaf Children's Society (£2,500); Bet Shalom, Warrington Youth Club, St Josephs' Specialist School (£2,000 each); Breast Cancer Haven, Disabled Living Foundation, Dogs Trust, Mayrick Bennett Children's Centre, Room to Read (£1,000 each); Activities for Children with Special Needs (£500).
**FINANCES** *Year* 2013/14 *Income* £125,874 *Grants* £179,500 *Grants to organisations* £179,500 *Assets* £876,718
**TRUSTEES** Sarah Radomir; Michael Radomir; David Wolmark.
**OTHER INFORMATION** The beneficiaries listed received grants under the trust's previous focus of special education and community development. The trust changed its focus in April 2015.
**HOW TO APPLY** The trustees advise against making an application for a grant unless invited to do so by the trust.
**WHO TO APPLY TO** Michael Radomir, Trustees, Flat 10, Salamander Court, 135 York Way, London N7 9LG *Tel.* 07771 756065

## ■ The Seneca Trust

**CC NO** 1137147   **ESTABLISHED** 2010
**WHERE FUNDING CAN BE GIVEN** UK.
**WHO CAN BENEFIT** Charitable organisations.
**WHAT IS FUNDED** Education and training; the promotion of health; people with disabilities; social welfare; accommodation and housing; children and young people; Jewish causes.
**SAMPLE GRANTS** Scope (£60,000); One to One (£11,300); Kisharon and WaterAid (£5,000 each); Roundhouse (£4,400); Learning Disabilities Resources (£3,000); Norwood and World Jewish Relief (£1,000 each).
**FINANCES** Year 2013 Income £186,902 Grants £82,500 Grants to organisations £82,500 Assets £125,685
**TRUSTEES** Tatjana May; Adam Sweidan; Natalie Wade.
**OTHER INFORMATION** The settlors of the trust are Kevin Gundle, co-founder of Aurum Funds Limited and also a trustee of Absolute Return for Kids (ARK), and his wife Deborah, who amongst other things has been involved in publishing and film production – her most recent venture is NetBuddy, an online resource offering tips, help and advice for parents and carers of children with learning disabilities.
**HOW TO APPLY** Apply in writing to the correspondent.
**WHO TO APPLY TO** Natalie Wade, Trustee, Ixworth House, 37 Ixworth Place, London SW3 3QH *Tel.* 020 7589 1130

## ■ SF Group Charitable Fund for Disabled People

**CC NO** 1104927   **ESTABLISHED** 2004
**WHERE FUNDING CAN BE GIVEN** East and West Midlands.
**WHO CAN BENEFIT** Individuals; organisations; national and local charities.
**WHAT IS FUNDED** Individuals with disabilities and organisations that provide care for those with physical or mental disabilities.
**WHAT IS NOT FUNDED** The trustees will not award grants to cover: education course fees; debts or reimbursements; nursing or residential home fees; funeral or removal expenses; driving lessons; major home improvements; therapies such as swimming with dolphins or hyperbaric therapy; deposits for housing, vehicles and loads; alternative therapies. The Trustees are unlikely to award grants for salaries, transport costs, iPads and laptops.
**TYPE OF GRANT** Small, one-off grants.
**RANGE OF GRANTS** Up to a maximum of £5,000.
**SAMPLE GRANTS Previous beneficiaries have included:** Acorns Children's Hospice (£5,000 part-funding for a specialist nurse); Green Acres Day Centre (£4,100 for a walking frame); and Willow Wood Day Centre (£2,900 for a combined hoist).
**FINANCES** Year 2013 Income £108,161 Grants £68,672 Grants to organisations £68,672 Assets £230,338
**TRUSTEES** Mrs Warwick; R. Yong.
**OTHER INFORMATION** The fund can help pay for specific items or services which will make a 'positive difference' to the quality of life of individuals or groups. The majority of grants are around £1,000. The grant total includes awards to both individuals and organisations.
**HOW TO APPLY** Initial applications can be made by filling in a short application form. This can be done online at the website, or by completing and posting the form, which can also be requested by phone or email. The Fund Manager will contact potential recipients within two weeks of receiving applications to discuss requests in more detail. Successful grants generally take 6–12 weeks to be awarded. Grants may be awarded for holidays if under £1,000, based in the UK and tailored to the specific needs of the beneficiary. Applications for holiday grants should be made 6–12 months in advance.
**WHO TO APPLY TO** Brenda Yong, Fund Manager, 4 Millennium Way West, Phoenix Park, Nottingham NG8 6AS *email* brenda.yong@sfcharity.co.uk *Website* www.sfcharity.co.uk

## ■ The Cyril Shack Trust

**CC NO** 264270   **ESTABLISHED** 1972
**WHERE FUNDING CAN BE GIVEN** UK.
**WHO CAN BENEFIT** Voluntary organisations and charitable groups only.
**WHAT IS FUNDED** General charitable purposes, with a preference for Jewish organisations.
**TYPE OF GRANT** Capital; recurring.
**SAMPLE GRANTS** No grants list was available. **Previous beneficiaries have included:** Finchley Road Synagogue, Nightingale House and St John's Wood Synagogue.
**FINANCES** Year 2012/13 Income £101,499 Grants £130,708 Grants to organisations £130,708 Assets £664,644
**TRUSTEES** Jonathan Shack; Cyril Shack.
**HOW TO APPLY** Apply in writing to the correspondent.
**WHO TO APPLY TO** The Clerk, c/o Lubbock Fine Chartered Accountants, Paternoster House, 65 St Paul's Churchyard, London EC4M 8AB *Tel.* 020 7490 7766

## ■ The Jean Shanks Foundation

**CC NO** 293108   **ESTABLISHED** 1985
**WHERE FUNDING CAN BE GIVEN** UK.
**WHO CAN BENEFIT** Medical research institutions, i.e. medical schools, medical Royal Colleges and similar bodies.
**WHAT IS FUNDED** Health, particularly medical research; education and training.
**WHAT IS NOT FUNDED** Financial hardship.
**TYPE OF GRANT** Scholarships; research – up to three years.
**RANGE OF GRANTS** £5,000–£70,000
**SAMPLE GRANTS** Pathological Society of Great Britain and Ireland (£28,500); University of Cambridge and University of Oxford (£21,000 each); Queen Mary – University of London (£18,000); Brighton and Sussex Medical School, University of Hull and University of Liverpool (£9,000); University of Aberdeen and University of Edinburgh (£5,500).
**FINANCES** Year 2013/14 Income £401,287 Grants £282,065 Grants to organisations £282,065 Assets £20,051,435
**TRUSTEES** Prof. Sir Nicholas Wright; Prof. Sir James Underwood; Eric Rothbarth; Alistair Jones; Prof. Andrew Carr; Dr Julian Axe; Prof. Adrienne Flanagan.
**OTHER INFORMATION** Grants were made to 26 institutions totalling £282,000.
**HOW TO APPLY** Apply in writing to the correspondent. Note: full grant guidelines are available on the foundation's website.
**WHO TO APPLY TO** Paula Price-Davies, Correspondent, Peppard Cottage, Peppard Common, Henley On Thames, Oxfordshire RG9 5LB *Tel.* 01491 628232 *email* administrator@jeanshanksfoundation.org *Website* www.jeanshanksfoundation.org

## ■ The Shanley Charitable Trust

**CC NO** 1103323 **ESTABLISHED** 2003
**WHERE FUNDING CAN BE GIVEN** Worldwide.
**WHO CAN BENEFIT** Recognised international charities.
**WHAT IS FUNDED** Relief of poverty.
**SAMPLE GRANTS** World Vision UK (£70,000); SOS Children (£60,000); WaterAid (£50,000); DEC Philippines Appeal (£40,000); DEC Syria Appeal and Practical Action (£10,000 each).
**FINANCES** Year 2013/14 Income £86,983 Grants £240,000 Grants to organisations £240,000 Assets £3,549,436
**TRUSTEES** Roger Lander; Steve Atkins; C. Shanley.
**OTHER INFORMATION** Grants were made to six organisations totalling £240,000.
**HOW TO APPLY** Apply in writing to the correspondent.
**WHO TO APPLY TO** Steve Atkins, Trustee, Knowles Benning Solicitors, 32 High Street, Shefford SG17 5DG Tel. 01462 814824

## ■ The Shanti Charitable Trust

**CC NO** 1064813 **ESTABLISHED** 1997
**WHERE FUNDING CAN BE GIVEN** UK, with preference for West Yorkshire, and overseas (especially Nepal).
**WHO CAN BENEFIT** Charitable organisations.
**WHAT IS FUNDED** General charitable purposes; Christian causes; health; international development.
**WHAT IS NOT FUNDED** Gap year students; political or animal welfare causes.
**TYPE OF GRANT** One-off and up to three years; capital and revenue funding.
**RANGE OF GRANTS** £500–£12,500
**SAMPLE GRANTS** Ear Aid – Nepal (£12,500); INF Camps (£10,500); St John's Church (£9,500); Prabhav (£8,000); Development Associates International (£5,500); CMS and World Outreach (£500 each).
**FINANCES** Year 2013/14 Income £46,902 Grants £48,750 Grants to organisations £48,750 Assets £138,339
**TRUSTEES** Barbara Gill; Andrew Gill; Ross Hyett.
**OTHER INFORMATION** There were eight awards granted.
**HOW TO APPLY** Applications may be made in writing to the correspondent; however, note that the trust has stated the following that the 'most beneficiaries are those the trustees already have contact with'.
**WHO TO APPLY TO** Barbara Gill, Trustee, Parkside, Littlemoor, Queensbury, Bradford, West Yorkshire BD13 1DB email catherine.webster@bakertilly.co.uk

## ■ ShareGift (The Orr Mackintosh Foundation)

**CC NO** 1052686 **ESTABLISHED** 1995
**WHERE FUNDING CAN BE GIVEN** UK.
**WHO CAN BENEFIT** UK-registered charities.
**WHAT IS FUNDED** General charitable purposes, guided by the wishes of the donors of shares, from where its income derives.
**WHAT IS NOT FUNDED** Non-UK-registered charities.
**RANGE OF GRANTS** Up to £60,000.
**SAMPLE GRANTS** Macmillan Cancer Support (£60,000); Hospice in the Weald (£55,000); Cancer Research UK (£50,000); Send a Cow and Practical Action Limited (£30,000 each); Arthritis Research UK and Berkshire Community Foundation (£25,000 each); Blind Veterans UK and Youth Music (£10,000).
**FINANCES** Year 2013/14 Income £3,624,165 Grants £1,540,750 Grants to organisations £1,540,750 Assets £2,022,225
**TRUSTEES** Stephen Scott; Paul Killik; John Roundhill; Susan Swabey.
**HOW TO APPLY** Applications for funding are not accepted and no response will be made to charities that send inappropriate applications. ShareGift's trustees choose to support UK-registered charities which reflect the broad range of charities which are of interest to the people and organisations that help to create the charity's income by donating their unwanted shares, or by supporting the charity's operation in other practical ways. However, charities wishing to receive a donation from ShareGift's trustees can increase their chances of doing so by encouraging their supporters to donate unwanted shares to ShareGift and to make a note of their charitable interests when so doing, using the regular donation form provided by ShareGift. In addition, ShareGift is willing to use its extensive experience of share giving philanthropically to help charities which wish to start receiving gifts of shares themselves. Charities are, therefore, welcome to contact ShareGift to discuss this further. ShareGift advises that, as basic training on share giving is now available elsewhere, charities wishing to benefit from their advice should ensure that they have first researched share giving generally and put some thought into how their charity intends to initiate and run a share giving appeal or strategy. Further information on this and other issues is available on the charity's website.
**WHO TO APPLY TO** Lady Mackintosh, 2nd Floor, 17 Carlton House Terrace, London SW1Y 5AH Tel. 020 7930 3737 email help@sharegift.org.uk Website www.sharegift.org

## ■ The Shears Foundation

**CC NO** 1049907 **ESTABLISHED** 1994
**WHERE FUNDING CAN BE GIVEN** Generally in, or for the benefit of, the North East of England. Some consideration is also given to projects from other regions of the UK or those acting nationally.
**WHO CAN BENEFIT** Registered charities only.
**WHAT IS FUNDED** Community development, environment, sustainable development, health, social welfare, culture – all with a focus on education and raising awareness.
**WHAT IS NOT FUNDED** Domestic animal welfare; religious organisations.
**RANGE OF GRANTS** Up to £100,000.
**SAMPLE GRANTS** Community Foundation – Linden Fund (£100,000); Community Foundation – Local Environmental Action Fund and Royal College of Surgeons in England (£50,000 each); Westacre Arts Foundation and Worldwide Fund for Nature (£40,000 each); Bradford Grammar School (£31,500); English National Opera (£30,000).
**FINANCES** Year 2013/14 Income £510,052 Grants £719,550 Grants to organisations £719,550 Assets £14,194,750
**TRUSTEES** Peter Shears; Lyn Shears; Patricia Shears; G. Lyall; Bruce Warnes; Mark Horner.
**OTHER INFORMATION** Grants of under £25,000 each amounted to £194,500. In total, 32 grants were made during the year.
**HOW TO APPLY** Apply in writing to the correspondent.
**WHO TO APPLY TO** Trevor Halliday Shears, Trustee, c/o The Community Foundation, 156 Pilgrim Road, Newcastle upon Tyne NE1 6SU

## ■ The Sheepdrove Trust

CC NO 328369   ESTABLISHED 1989
WHERE FUNDING CAN BE GIVEN UK, but especially north Lambeth, London, where applicable.
WHO CAN BENEFIT Registered charities only.
WHAT IS FUNDED General charitable purposes, particularly sustainability, biodiversity, organic farming, educational research and spiritual care.
TYPE OF GRANT One-off and recurrent.
SAMPLE GRANTS University of the Arts London (£75,000); Garden Organic (£60,000); Newcastle University (£55,000); Videre (£15,000); Care4Cats Ibiza, Compassion in World Farming and Motor Neurone Disease (£10,000 each); Darlington Hall Trust (£8,000); Alzheimer's Society and Dage (£5,000 each); Seed Food and Farming Conference (£600).
FINANCES Year 2013 Income £488,216 Grants £509,358 Grants to organisations £509,358 Assets £19,991,389
TRUSTEES Barnabas Kindersley; Juliet Kindersley; Peter Kindersley; Harriet Treuille; Anabel Kindersley.
HOW TO APPLY Apply in writing to the correspondent.
WHO TO APPLY TO Juliet Kindersley, Trustee, Sheepdrove Farmhouse, Sheepdrove Organic Farm, Lambourn, Berkshire RG17 7UN Tel. 01488 674726

## ■ The Sheffield and District Hospital Services Charitable Fund

CC NO 246057   ESTABLISHED 1965
WHERE FUNDING CAN BE GIVEN Mostly South Yorkshire, also UK.
WHO CAN BENEFIT NHS hospitals and trusts; registered charities.
WHAT IS FUNDED Medical equipment; general charitable purposes.
RANGE OF GRANTS Up to £100,000.
SAMPLE GRANTS Weston Park Sheffield Teaching Hospitals NHS Foundation Trust (£58,000); Action Space Mobile (£50,000); British Transplant Games (£41,000); Anthony Nolan Cancer Charity (£26,000); Leonard Cheshire Disability Association (£20,000); Paces (£15,000); Headway Brain Injury Association (£10,000); Blind Veterans UK (£4,000); Within Reach (£3,000); Sheffield Children's Hospital Charity (£1,200).
FINANCES Year 2013/14 Income £555,983 Grants £1,055,764 Grants to organisations £1,055,764 Assets £385,987
TRUSTEES Graham Moore; David Whitney; Dr Catherine Ryan.
HOW TO APPLY Apply in writing to the correspondent.
WHO TO APPLY TO Graham Moore, Secretary, Westfield House, 87 Division Street, Sheffield S1 1HT Tel. 0114 250 2339 email charity@westfieldhealth.com Website www.westfieldhealth.com

## ■ The Sheldon Trust

CC NO 242328   ESTABLISHED 1965
WHERE FUNDING CAN BE GIVEN West Midlands.
WHO CAN BENEFIT Registered charities.
WHAT IS FUNDED The relief of poverty and distress in society, concentrating on community projects. Aftercare, hospice at home, respite care, self-help and support groups, and rehabilitation centres are also considered. Facilities for people who are disadvantaged or have disabilities, particularly for young people aged 16–25 who are not in training, education or employment. Encouragement of local voluntary groups, recreational facilities, young people, community, rehabilitation for drugs, alcohol and solvent abuse, religion, older people, mental health and learning difficulties.
WHAT IS NOT FUNDED Charities with an annual income of over £1 million and/or free unrestricted reserves to the value of more than six months of their annual expenditure.
SAMPLE GRANTS Acacia Family Support (£15,000); Grapevine Coventry and Warwickshire and Where Next Association (£12,000 each); Bearwood Chapel Trust and Bethel Health and Healing Network (£10,000 each); Ackers Adventure, Cutting Edge Theatre and The No Way Trust Limited (£5,000 each); Street Teams and Wolverhampton Amateur Boxing Club (£4,000 each); The Excelsior Trust (£2,500); Children with Cystic Fibrosis Dream Holidays (£1,500); Bethany Christian Fellowship (£850); Birmingham City Mission (£600).
FINANCES Year 2013/14 Income £229,551 Grants £207,266 Grants to organisations £207,226 Assets £5,157,397
TRUSTEES Revd Roger Bidnell; Andrew Bidnell; John England; Rachel Beatton; Ruth Gibbins; Paul England.
OTHER INFORMATION Grants were made to 44 organisations totalling £207,000.
HOW TO APPLY Applications should be submitted online, via the website. Holiday applications differ from the other schemes. Application forms are made available online. For more information and guidance visit the trust's website.
WHO TO APPLY TO Jayne Day, Correspondent, Pothecary Witham Weld, 70 St George's Square, London SW1V 3RD Tel. 020 7821 8211 email charities@pwwsolicitors.co.uk Website www.pwwsolicitors.co.uk/charity-grants/8-the-sheldon-trust

## ■ The Patricia and Donald Shepherd Charitable Trust

CC NO 272788   ESTABLISHED 1973
WHERE FUNDING CAN BE GIVEN UK, with strong preference for York and North Yorkshire.
WHO CAN BENEFIT Charitable organisations.
WHAT IS FUNDED A wide range of general charitable purposes, including social welfare, health, animal welfare, the arts, young people, disability, education, the elderly. 'The trust has established a policy of making a large number of regular small grants over a wide range of organisations.'
WHAT IS NOT FUNDED Individuals.
TYPE OF GRANT Project funding; capital costs; one-off; recurrent.
RANGE OF GRANTS £100–£5,000; typically £100–£500.
SAMPLE GRANTS The Bar Convent Heritage Project (£30,000); University of York (£7,000); Action Aid (£2,000); Chapter House Choir, Heart Research UK and York Mind (£1,500 each); Disability Rocks, Scarborough YMCA and Yorkshire Air Ambulance (£1,000 each); The Gurkha Welfare Trust (£800); St Michael's Hospice (£650); Age UK Knaresborough, Dogs Trust, Joseph Rowntree Theatre, Listening Books, ME Association and York Ebor District Scouts (£500 each); St John Baptist Bishop Monkton (£400); Blagdon Park Cricket Club and Oaklands Preschool (£300 each); Prostate Cancer UK (£200).

FINANCES Year 2013/14 Income £154,173 Grants £157,404 Grants to organisations £157,404 Assets £2,911,561
TRUSTEES Sara Dickson; David Dickson; Sylvia Shepherd; Lucy Dickson; Sophie Dickson.
OTHER INFORMATION Grants were made to 186 organisations in 2013/14.
HOW TO APPLY Apply in writing to the correspondent. The trustees meet frequently. Applications should include details of the need to be met, achievements and a copy of the latest accounts.
WHO TO APPLY TO The Trustees, 5 Cherry Lane, Dringhouses, York YO24 1QH

■ **The Sylvia and Colin Shepherd Charitable Trust**
CC NO 272948                ESTABLISHED 1973
WHERE FUNDING CAN BE GIVEN Worldwide but particularly the north of England.
WHO CAN BENEFIT Mainly local organisations – particularly those in the north of England.
WHAT IS FUNDED General charitable purposes. Favour is given to local charities or charities with which the trustees have personal knowledge of, interest in or association with, particularly those supporting young people.
WHAT IS NOT FUNDED Individuals, unless they are part of a charitable group, or for local authorities.
TYPE OF GRANT Mainly one-off.
RANGE OF GRANTS Up to £10,000. Most grants below £1,000.
SAMPLE GRANTS Grants of £1,000 or more were made to: Yorkshire Air Museum (£12,000); Special Boat Service Association (£10,000).
FINANCES Year 2013/14 Income £151,351 Grants £58,800 Grants to organisations £58,800 Assets £653,414
TRUSTEES Patricia Shepherd; Iain Robertson; Jane Robertson; Michael Shepherd; Christine Shepherd; Patrick Shepherd; Joseph Shepherd; Rory Robertson; Annabel Robertson.
OTHER INFORMATION Grants were made to 122 charitable organisations. Details were not available of the beneficiaries of grants smaller than £1,000.
HOW TO APPLY Apply in writing to the correspondent. The trustees review and respond to all applications.
WHO TO APPLY TO Sara Dickson, Trustee, Arabesque House, Monks Cross Drive, Huntington, York YO32 9GW

■ **The Archie Sherman Cardiff Foundation**
CC NO 272225                ESTABLISHED 1976
WHERE FUNDING CAN BE GIVEN UK, Canada, Australia, New Zealand, Pakistan, Sri Lanka, South Africa, India, Israel, USA and other parts of the British Commonwealth.
WHO CAN BENEFIT Charitable organisations.
WHAT IS FUNDED Health; overseas aid; community; education and training; preference for Jewish causes.
WHAT IS NOT FUNDED Individuals.
RANGE OF GRANTS Up to £50,000.
SAMPLE GRANTS Jewish Child's Day (£30,000); The Merephdi Foundation – Rabin Medical Center (£22,000); UK Toremet Limited – Israel Tennis Association (£15,500); Yad Vashem – UK Foundation (£10,000).
FINANCES Year 2013/14 Income £106,565 Grants £77,670 Grants to organisations £77,670 Assets £2,078,016
TRUSTEE Rothschild Trust Corporation Ltd.
HOW TO APPLY Apply in writing to the correspondent.
WHO TO APPLY TO The Trustees, Rothschild Trust Corp Ltd, New Court, St Swithin's Lane, London EC4P 4DU Tel. 020 7280 5000

■ **The Archie Sherman Charitable Trust**
CC NO 256893                ESTABLISHED 1967
WHERE FUNDING CAN BE GIVEN UK and Israel.
WHO CAN BENEFIT Charitable organisations.
WHAT IS FUNDED Most grants are to Jewish organisations. Other causes supported are the arts, education, health, welfare and overseas aid.
TYPE OF GRANT Capital costs; buildings; project expenditure. Funding may be given for more than three years.
RANGE OF GRANTS Up to £400,000.
SAMPLE GRANTS Youth Aliyah – Child Rescue (£416,000); The Rosalyn and Nicholas Springer Charitable Trust (£125,000); The Royal Opera House Foundation (£53,500); UK Friends of IDC (£52,000); Jewish Care (£37,500); The London Jewish Cultural Centre (£26,000); Community Security Trust (£15,000); Galila Charitable Trust (£13,000); The Ear Foundation (£1,900); The British Friends of the Jaffa Institute (£1,000).
FINANCES Year 2013/14 Income £1,426,830 Grants £1,049,924 Grants to organisations £1,049,924 Assets £21,176,285
TRUSTEES Michael Gee; Allan Morgenthau; Eric Charles; Rhona Freedman.
HOW TO APPLY Apply in writing to the correspondent.
WHO TO APPLY TO Michael Gee, Trustee, 274A Kentish Town Road, London NW5 2AA Tel. 020 7493 1904 email trust@sherman.co.uk

■ **The R. C. Sherriff Rosebriars Trust**
CC NO 272527                ESTABLISHED 1976
WHERE FUNDING CAN BE GIVEN The borough of Elmbridge.
WHO CAN BENEFIT Local individuals for art training bursaries (short courses only) and local amateur and professional organisations planning arts activities of a developmental nature.
WHAT IS FUNDED The trust is primarily concerned with arts development projects and funds charities, schools and constituted organisations working with one or more art form for the benefit of members of the local community, especially where a professional artist is involved. It has funded projects concerned with music, dance, drama, visual arts, crafts, literature, film and new media.
WHAT IS NOT FUNDED The trust's guidelines, which are available on its website, state that it does not fund: 'arts activities or events taking place outside Elmbridge (except in the case of attendance at training courses/development opportunities for individuals); activities that are not arts-related; fundraising events, e.g. special performances in aid of a local charity; activities that provide no potential benefit to the public; activities which have already taken place; goods or services that have been bought or ordered before receiving an offer letter; commercial ventures which could recoup their costs from their profits (other than underwriting grants for

performances); costs that are already covered by other funding; core costs i.e. ongoing overheads such as salaries, insurance, maintenance budgets for equipment or buildings; and higher education courses, long-term vocational training e.g. drama school, or ongoing training programmes (e.g. piano lessons, regular dance classes).'

**TYPE OF GRANT** Capital costs; one-off; event underwriting; projects; school funds. Funding of up to three years will be considered.

**RANGE OF GRANTS** £180–£12,000; typical grant £1,000.

**SAMPLE GRANTS** Riverhouse (£12,000); Elmbridge Community Link (£2,500); Ember Sports Club and Cleves School (£2,000 each); Music in Hospitals and Molesey Youth Centre (£1,800 each); The Medicine Garden and Churches Together (£1,500 each); and WWAOS and A Capella Singers (£1,000 each).

**FINANCES** Year 2013 Income £186,193 Grants £47,750 Grants to organisations £47,750 Assets £3,948,057

**TRUSTEES** Nigel Cooper; James Vickers; Tannia Shipley; Shweta Kapadia; Barry Cheyne; Wendy Smithers; Elizabeth Cooper; Ruth Lyon; Brian Nathan; Frank Renton.

**PUBLICATIONS** Arts Focus

**OTHER INFORMATION** Project grants are unlikely to exceed £1,500, while underwriting grants are unlikely to exceed £1,000 and grants to individuals are unlikely to exceed £500. It is expected that applicants find approximately 50% of the funding needed from other sources, except for underwriting grants. The grant total includes awards to both organisations and individuals.

**HOW TO APPLY** Application forms can be downloaded from the website or obtained from the trust office. Application deadlines, grant decision dates and full grant guidelines are also available. The trustees meet four times a year to consider applications. Applicants are advised to discuss their proposals and check their eligibility, with the Director, in advance. The website will also give information on past and current projects and successful applications.

**WHO TO APPLY TO** Dean Blanchard, Treasurer, Civic Offices, High Street, Esher, Surrey KT10 9SD Tel. 01372 474140 email arts@rcsherrifftrust.org.uk Website www.rcsherrifftrust.org.uk

## ■ The Shetland Charitable Trust

**SC NO** SC027025  **ESTABLISHED** 1976

**WHERE FUNDING CAN BE GIVEN** Shetland only.

**WHO CAN BENEFIT** Self-help and voluntary organisations benefitting the inhabitants of Shetland.

**WHAT IS FUNDED** Social care and welfare; arts, culture, sport and recreation; the environment, natural history and heritage.

**WHAT IS NOT FUNDED** Funds can only be used to benefit the inhabitants of Shetland.

**TYPE OF GRANT** Project; one-off; capital, running and recurring costs; agricultural ten-year loan scheme.

**RANGE OF GRANTS** Up to £2.5 million.

**SAMPLE GRANTS** Shetland Recreational Trust (£2.5 million); Shetland Amenity Trust (£1 million); Shetland Arts Development Agency (£700,000); COPE Limited (£155,000); Shetland Churches Council Trust (£54,000); Royal Voluntary Service (£47,500); The Swan Trust (£44,500); Festival Grants (£30,000); Disability Shetland Recreation Club (£12,500).

**FINANCES** Year 2013/14 Income £8,534,000 Grants £9,436,000 Grants to organisations £9,436,000 Assets £231,112,000

**TRUSTEES** Bobby Hunter; Jonathan Wills; Malcolm Bell; Andrew Cooper; Allison Duncan; Robert Henderson; Tom Macintyre; Peter Malcolmson; Andrea Manson; Keith Massey; Tom Morton; Ian Napier; Drew Ratter; James Smith; Amanda Westlake.

**HOW TO APPLY** Applications are only accepted from Shetland-based charities. The trustees meet every two months. The trust has different contact points for different categories of grant: arts grants, development grants, senior citizens club grants and support grants – contact Michael Duncan on 01595 743828; and social assistance grants – contact the duty social worker on 01595 744 400.

**WHO TO APPLY TO** Michael Duncan, 22–24 North Road, Lerwick, Shetland ZE1 0NQ Tel. 01595 744994 email mail@shetlandcharitabletrust.co.uk Website www.shetlandcharitabletrust.co.uk

## ■ SHINE (Support and Help in Education)

**CC NO** 1082777  **ESTABLISHED** 1999

**WHERE FUNDING CAN BE GIVEN** Greater London and Manchester.

**WHO CAN BENEFIT** Charitable organisations.

**WHAT IS FUNDED** Educational projects helping children and young people aged between 6 and 18 who are disadvantaged to fulfil their academic potential. Programmes currently include after-school lessons, complementary Saturday lessons and literacy, numeracy and study support sessions. Details of the SHINE's programme can be found on the website.

**WHAT IS NOT FUNDED** Individuals; bursaries or student fees of any kind; direct replacement of statutory funding; programmes where the aim is primarily the personal development of young people rather than raising academic achievements; short term or one-off projects; programmes narrowly targeted at specific beneficiary groups (with some exceptions); parenting programmes – those focusing primarily on the parent rather than the child; activities promoting particular political or religious beliefs; projects taking place outside Greater London or Manchester (except for SHINE's Serious Fun strand, Let Teachers SHINE and projects that are replicating on a national scale).

**TYPE OF GRANT** Start-up costs; pilots; core costs; staff posts; development or replication of projects. Most grants last for two or three years.

**RANGE OF GRANTS** Most grants are in excess of £20,000.

**SAMPLE GRANTS** East Manchester Academy and Lambeth Academy (£104,000 each); Marner Primary School and St James' Primary School (£87,000 each); Sebright Primary School (£20,000); Clapham and Larkhall School (£15,000); Highgate School (£8,100); Bromley High School (£4,700).

**FINANCES** Year 2013/14 Income £2,262,159 Grants £1,811,752 Grants to organisations £1,811,752 Assets £5,583,401

**TRUSTEES** David Blood; Mark Heffernan; Henry Bedford; Gavin Boyle; Mark Ferguson; Cameron Ogden; Dr Krutika Pau; Natasha Pope; Richard Rothwell; Stephen Shields; Bridget Walsh; Dr Caroline Whalley; Terence O'Neill; Ann Mroz.

**OTHER INFORMATION** The grant total above refers to grants awarded during the year. The charity funded 92 projects in its portfolio in the 2013/14 academic year, benefitting 13,500 children. 14 grants were made through the Let Teachers SHINE competition for teachers with innovative ideas for the academic attainment of disadvantaged children.

**HOW TO APPLY** Potential applicants must first check the charity's website for current information of the programmes available. There is also a helpful list of funding FAQs. Following this, the grants team can be contacted by email (info@shinetrust.org.uk) or by telephone (0208 393 1880).

**WHO TO APPLY TO** Paul Carbury, Chief Executive, 1 Cheam Road, Ewell Village, Surrey KT17 1SP *Tel.* 020 8393 1880 *email* info@shinetrust.org.uk *Website* www.shinetrust.org.uk

## ■ The Barnett and Sylvia Shine No 2 Charitable Trust

**CC NO** 281821    **ESTABLISHED** 1980
**WHERE FUNDING CAN BE GIVEN** UK and overseas.
**WHO CAN BENEFIT** Registered charities.
**WHAT IS FUNDED** General charitable purposes, with a preference for older people and people with disabilities.
**WHAT IS NOT FUNDED** Individuals.
**TYPE OF GRANT** Usually one-off.
**RANGE OF GRANTS** £2,000–£10,000
**SAMPLE GRANTS** IPPF (£10,000); Sight Savers International (£5,000); Send a Cow to Africa (£3,000); and British Shalom-Salaam Trust and The Samaritans (£2,000 each).
**FINANCES** *Year* 2013/14 *Income* £44,042 *Grants* £22,000 *Grants to organisations* £22,000 *Assets* £1,433,933
**TRUSTEES** Martin Paisner; Barbara Grahame; Prof. Rodney Grahame.
**OTHER INFORMATION** Grants were made to five organisations totalling £22,000.
**HOW TO APPLY** Apply in writing to the correspondent. The trustees consider applications at formal and informal meetings.
**WHO TO APPLY TO** Martin Paisner, Trustee, Berwin Leiton Paisner, Adelaide House, London Bridge, London EC4R 9HA *Tel.* 020 7760 1000

## ■ The Bassil Shippam and Alsford Trust

**CC NO** 256996    **ESTABLISHED** 1967
**WHERE FUNDING CAN BE GIVEN** UK, with a preference for West Sussex.
**WHO CAN BENEFIT** Charitable organisations.
**WHAT IS FUNDED** Medical research; education and training; the arts; social welfare; children and young people; Christianity.
**TYPE OF GRANT** Capital grants for up to three years.
**RANGE OF GRANTS** Mostly under £1,000.
**SAMPLE GRANTS** Outset Youth Action South West Sussex (£6,000); St Wilfrid's Hospice (£5,000); Christian Care Association (£4,000); Newell Centre Association (£3,600); West Sussex County Council Voluntary Fund (£2,000); Sussex Probation Service (£1,600).
**FINANCES** *Year* 2013/14 *Income* £158,749 *Grants* £148,101 *Grants to organisations* £144,801 *Assets* £4,323,488
**TRUSTEES** Christopher Doman; John Shippam; Molly Hanwell; Susan Trayler; Richard Tayler; Stanley Young; Simon Macfarlane; Janet Bailey.
**OTHER INFORMATION** Grants were also made to individuals totalling £3,300.

**HOW TO APPLY** The accounts for 2013/14 state that the trust 'invites applications for funding to be made to the Trustees in writing together with a summary of their proposals; applications made by organisations should submit a copy of any reports, accounts or forecasts. Applications are reviewed by a panel of Trustees.'
**WHO TO APPLY TO** The Trustees, Thomas Eggar House, Friary Lane, Chichester, West Sussex PO19 1UF *Tel.* 01243 786111 *email* shippam@thomaseggar.com

## ■ The Shipwrights' Company Charitable Fund

**CC NO** 262043    **ESTABLISHED** 1971
**WHERE FUNDING CAN BE GIVEN** UK.
**WHO CAN BENEFIT** Individuals and organisations with a maritime connection. Emphasis is given to those benefitting young people, church work and the City.
**WHAT IS FUNDED** Maritime training, sailors' welfare and maritime heritage. Churches and Anglican bodies are also supported.
**WHAT IS NOT FUNDED** Any application without a clear maritime connection.
**TYPE OF GRANT** Annual donations; general donations; outdoor activity bursaries; buildings; capital and core costs; one-off; projects; start-up costs. Funding for one year or less will be considered.
**RANGE OF GRANTS** Mainly £500–£5,000.
**SAMPLE GRANTS** Tall Ships Youth Trust (£20,000 for bursaries); Thames Shipwright (£13,000); George Green's School (£3,000); Dinghies for Disabled (£1,500); Venture Trust (£1,000); Clyde Maritime Project (£500); Sheriffs' and Recorder's Fund (£200).
**FINANCES** *Year* 2013/14 *Income* £285,298 *Grants* £79,834 *Grants to organisations* £79,834 *Assets* £36,711,161
**TRUSTEES** The Worshipful Company of Shipwrights; M. S. Robinson; The Rt Hon the Lord Clarke of Stone-cum-Ebony; Deputy D. G. F. Barrow; Rear Admiral Sir Jeremy de Halpert; A. F. Smith
**OTHER INFORMATION** Many beneficiaries are supported on a regular basis.
**HOW TO APPLY** Applications to be made by post or email to the correspondent. Applications from organisations should if possible be accompanied by the latest accounts and report. Application forms and further guidelines are available from the trust's website. Applications are considered in February, June and November.
**WHO TO APPLY TO** The Clerk, Ironmongers' Hall, Shaftesbury Place, Barbican, London EC2Y 8AA *Tel.* 020 7606 2376 *Fax* 020 7600 8117 *email* clerk@shipwrights.co.uk *Website* www.shipwrights.co.uk

## ■ The Shirley Foundation

**CC NO** 1097135    **ESTABLISHED** 1996
**WHERE FUNDING CAN BE GIVEN** Unrestricted, in practice, mainly UK.
**WHO CAN BENEFIT** Registered charities and research institutions.
**WHAT IS FUNDED** The main areas of interest are information technology and autism (not excluding Asperger's Syndrome) which occasionally extend to learning disabilities in general. The foundation's mission is 'the facilitation and support of pioneering projects with strategic impact in the field of autism spectrum disorders, with particular emphasis on medical research'.

**WHAT IS NOT FUNDED** Individuals; non-autism-specific work. The foundation does not make political donations.
**TYPE OF GRANT** Capital and revenue grants; full project funding.
**RANGE OF GRANTS** Up to £100,000.
**SAMPLE GRANTS** Autistica (£100,000) University of Oxford – Project on Autism (£72,500).
**FINANCES** Year 2013/14 Income £39,734 Grants £192,500 Grants to organisations £172,500 Assets £1,794,491
**TRUSTEES** Michael MacFadyen; Anne Menzies; Prof. Eve Johnstone; Dame Stephanie Shirley.
**HOW TO APPLY** 'Trustees meet twice yearly but applications for support are received throughout the year. Only those within the foundation's Mission are considered; applicants are reminded that projects should be innovative in nature with the potential to have a strategic impact in the field of Autism Spectrum Disorders. Research proposals should be aimed ultimately at determining causes of autism. Researchers should refer to the 'Guidance: Application for a medical research grant' downloadable [from the foundation's website]. In the first instance a simple letter with outline proposal should be sent to Dame Stephanie Shirley at the registered address or emailed.'
**WHO TO APPLY TO** Dame Stephanie Shirley, Trustee, Videcom House, Newtown Road, Henley-on-Thames, Oxfordshire RG9 1HG *Tel.* 01491 848500 *email* steve@steveshirley.com *Website* www.steveshirley.com/tsf

■ **Shlomo Memorial Fund Limited**
**CC NO** 278973    **ESTABLISHED** 1980
**WHERE FUNDING CAN BE GIVEN** Unrestricted.
**WHO CAN BENEFIT** Organisations benefitting Jewish people.
**WHAT IS FUNDED** General charitable purposes, including the advancement of the Jewish religion and the relief of poverty.
**SAMPLE GRANTS** Previous beneficiaries have included: Amud Haolam, Nachlat Haleviim, Torah Umesorah, Beit Hillel, ZSV Charities, Layesharim Tehilla, British Friends of Tashbar Chazon Ish, Chazon Ish, Mei Menuchos, Mor Uketsio, Shoshanat Hoamakim, Millennium Trust, and Talmud Torah Zichron Meir.
**FINANCES** Year 2012/13 Income £7,476,950 Grants £1,227,490 Grants to organisations £1,227,490 Assets £45,527,440
**TRUSTEES** Amichai Toporowitz; Hezkel Toporowitz; Eliyah Kleineman; Channe Lopian; Chaim Kaufman; Meir Sullam.
**OTHER INFORMATION** At the time of writing (June 2015) the 2012/13 accounts were the most recent available for the charity.
**HOW TO APPLY** Apply in writing to the correspondent.
**WHO TO APPLY TO** Channe Lopian, Secretary, Cohen Arnold and Co., New Burlington House, 1075 Finchley Road, London NW10 0PU *Tel.* 020 8731 0777 *email* info@olnato.com

■ **The Shoe Zone Trust**
**CC NO** 1112972    **ESTABLISHED** 2005
**WHERE FUNDING CAN BE GIVEN** Preference for Leicestershire and Rutland and for certain charities operating in the Philippines and other countries.
**WHO CAN BENEFIT** Organisations benefitting children and young people.
**WHAT IS FUNDED** The objects of the charity are to make grants and donations to other charities to relieve the financial hardship and poverty and/or advancement of education, mainly for children and young persons under the age of 18 particularly in Leicestershire and Rutland and for certain charities operating in the Philippines.
**RANGE OF GRANTS** £25–£49,000
**SAMPLE GRANTS** Shepherd of the Hills, Philippines (£39,000); Ministries Without Borders (£11,000); Amantani Boarding Houses (£10,000); CRLC (£7,000); Rotary Club of Melton Mowbray Philippines Tsunami Appeal (£2,500); Footwear Friends (£1,000). Donations of £250 and under totalled £2,000.
**FINANCES** Year 2014 Income £133,651 Grants £72,534 Grants to organisations £72,534 Assets £140,070
**TRUSTEES** Michael Smith; John Smith; Anthony Smith.
**OTHER INFORMATION** Donations of £250 and under totalled £2,000.
**HOW TO APPLY** Apply in writing to the correspondent.
**WHO TO APPLY TO** Michael Smith, Trustee, Shoe Zone Retail Ltd, Haramead Business Centre, Humberstone Road, Leicester LE1 2LH *Tel.* 0116 222 3007 *Website* www.shoezone.com/ShoeZoneTrust

■ **The J. A. Shone Memorial Trust**
**CC NO** 270104    **ESTABLISHED** 1974
**WHERE FUNDING CAN BE GIVEN** Mainly Merseyside.
**WHO CAN BENEFIT** Registered charities known to the trustees.
**WHAT IS FUNDED** Christian and local causes in Merseyside and mission work overseas.
**RANGE OF GRANTS** Usually up to £10,000.
**SAMPLE GRANTS** St Andrew the Great Ministry, Toxteth Tabernacle Baptist Church and UCCF The Christian Unions (£5,000 each); Mission Aviation Fellowship (£3,000); Royal Liverpool Philharmonic Society and Titus Trust (£2,500 each); and Wirral Ark (£1,000).
**FINANCES** Year 2013/14 Income £40,712 Grants £33,000 Grants to organisations £33,000 Assets £833,478
**TRUSTEES** Anthony Shone; James Stileman; Emma Crowe; Liverpool Charity and Voluntary Services.
**HOW TO APPLY** The trust does not respond to unsolicited applications.
**WHO TO APPLY TO** The Trustees, Liverpool Charity and Voluntary Services, 151 Dale Street, Liverpool L2 2AH *Tel.* 0151 227 5177

■ **The Barbara A. Shuttleworth Memorial Trust**
**CC NO** 1016117    **ESTABLISHED** 1992
**WHERE FUNDING CAN BE GIVEN** UK, with a preference for West Yorkshire.
**WHO CAN BENEFIT** Organisations benefitting people with disabilities.
**WHAT IS FUNDED** Charities working with people who have disabilities, particularly causes associated with children. Grants are given especially for equipment and premises with lasting benefits, but holidays and outings, training courses, and other needs are also considered.
**TYPE OF GRANT** Capital grants.
**SAMPLE GRANTS** BIME and Muir Maxwell (£2,500); Headstart Babies and The Daisy Garland (£1,500 each); Live Music Now (£750); Alstrom Syndrome UK and Caudwell Children (£1,000); Asthma Relief, Dream Holidays, Kirkwood Hospice, Lydgate Special School, Motability and The Fire Fighters Charity (£500 each); British

Wireless for the Blind (£400); Starlight Children's Foundation (£100).
FINANCES *Year* 2013/14 *Income* £23,665 *Grants* £36,668 *Grants to organisations* £36,668 *Assets* £516,340
TRUSTEES John Baty, Chair; Barbara Shuttleworth; John Eaton; William Fenton.
OTHER INFORMATION Grants were made to 55 organisations in 2013/14.
HOW TO APPLY Apply in writing to the correspondent.
WHO TO APPLY TO John Baty, Chair, Baty Casson Long, 23 Moorhead Terrace, Shipley BD18 4LB *Tel.* 01274 584946 *email* baty@btinternet.com

## ■ The Mary Elizabeth Siebel Charity

CC NO 1001255  ESTABLISHED 1990
WHERE FUNDING CAN BE GIVEN Within a 12-mile radius of Newark Town Hall.
WHO CAN BENEFIT Individuals and organisations benefitting older people who are ill, have disabilities or who are disadvantaged by poverty, and their carers.
WHAT IS FUNDED Hospice at home, respite care for carers and care in the community. Preference is given to assisting people who wish to live independently in their own homes.
TYPE OF GRANT Flexible, but one-off grants preferred for buildings, capital and core costs.
SAMPLE GRANTS Crossroads Care North Notts (£7,500).
FINANCES *Year* 2013/14 *Income* £111,436 *Grants* £81,000 *Grants to organisations* £7,500 *Assets* £2,759,875
TRUSTEES P. Blatherwick; D. McKenny; R. White; A. Austin; S. Watson; J. Moore.
OTHER INFORMATION The grant total includes £74,000 given to individuals.
HOW TO APPLY Apply in writing to the correspondent, requesting an application form. The trustees meet every couple of months to discuss applications.
WHO TO APPLY TO Frances Kelly, Correspondent, 3 Middlegate, Newark, Nottinghamshire NG24 1AQ *Tel.* 01636 671881 *email* fck@tallents.co.uk

## ■ David and Jennifer Sieff Charitable Trust

CC NO 206329  ESTABLISHED 1970
WHERE FUNDING CAN BE GIVEN UK.
WHO CAN BENEFIT Registered charities.
WHAT IS FUNDED General charitable purposes; community care services; arts and culture; children and young people; people with disabilities; the promotion of health; education and training; science and technology; Jewish causes; animal welfare.
WHAT IS NOT FUNDED Individuals.
RANGE OF GRANTS £50–£27,000
SAMPLE GRANTS Community Security Trust (£27,000); The Southbank Centre (£12,500); The Tavistock Trust for Aphasia (£10,000); Windsor Greys Jubilee Appeal and British ORT (£5,000 each); Refugee and The Koestler Trust (£2,000 each); Moorcroft Racehorse Welfare Centre (£1,200); Jewish Care, Royal College of Music, Royal National Theatre and Royal Opera House Foundation (£1,000 each); Trinity Hospice and Wiltshire Air Ambulance (£250 each); British Heart Foundation and British Red Cross (£100 each); and Royal British Legion (£50).
FINANCES *Year* 2013/14 *Income* £30,169 *Grants* £111,000 *Grants to organisations* £111,000 *Assets* £528,798
TRUSTEES Sir David Sieff; Lady Jennifer Sieff; Lord Wolfson Of Sunningdale.
OTHER INFORMATION In 2013/14 grants were given to 67 organisations.
HOW TO APPLY Apply in writing to the correspondent.
WHO TO APPLY TO The Trustees, H. W. Fisher and Company, Acre House, 11–15 William Road, London NW1 3ER *Tel.* 020 7388 7000 *email* info@hwfisher.co.uk

## ■ Silver Family Charitable Trust

CC NO 1152141
WHERE FUNDING CAN BE GIVEN UK.
WHO CAN BENEFIT Charitable organisations and individuals.
WHAT IS FUNDED General charitable purposes.
SAMPLE GRANTS A list of beneficiaries was not available.
FINANCES *Year* 2013/14 *Income* £140,000 *Grants* £62,000 *Grants to organisations* £62,000
TRUSTEES Rebecca Silver; Simon Silver.
OTHER INFORMATION It is estimated that grants totalled around £62,000.
HOW TO APPLY Applications can be made in writing to the correspondent.
WHO TO APPLY TO Simon Silver, Trustee, 49 Hamilton Terrace, London NW8 9RG *Tel.* 020 7467 6300

## ■ The Simmons & Simmons Charitable Foundation

CC NO 1129643  ESTABLISHED 2009
WHERE FUNDING CAN BE GIVEN London, with a preference for the City of London and Tower Hamlets.
WHO CAN BENEFIT Registered charities.
WHAT IS FUNDED Social welfare; education and training; access to justice and legal aid.
RANGE OF GRANTS Up to £10,000.
SAMPLE GRANTS Battersea Legal Advice Centre (£36,000); Bingham Centre for the Rule of Law (£15,000); Spitalfields Music, Five Talents UK and London Mozart Platers (£10,000 each); and Room to Read and Fair Trials (£5,000 each).
FINANCES *Year* 2013/14 *Income* £167,991 *Grants* £148,620 *Grants to organisations* £148,620 *Assets* £182,060
TRUSTEES Richard Dyton; Fiona Loughrey; Colin Passmore; Michele Anahory.
HOW TO APPLY Application forms are available to download from the firm's website.
WHO TO APPLY TO The Trustees, Simmons & Simmons LLP, Citypoint, 1 Ropemaker Street, London EC2Y 9SS *Tel.* 020 7628 2020 *email* corporate.responsibility@simmons-simmons.com *Website* www.simmons-simmons.com

## ■ The Huntly and Margery Sinclair Charitable Trust

CC NO 235939  ESTABLISHED 1964
WHERE FUNDING CAN BE GIVEN UK.
WHO CAN BENEFIT Generally registered charities.
WHAT IS FUNDED General charitable purposes.
RANGE OF GRANTS Up to £10,000.
SAMPLE GRANTS Rendcomb College (£10,000); Injured Jockeys Fund (£5,000); Cheltenham County Race Day (£3,000); Lawrence Nursing

Home Trust and Spelsbury P.C.C (£2,000 each); Medical Detection Dogs, Elkstone Parish Church and Myloma UK (£1,000 each); Helen and Douglas House, P.D.S.A and A.B.F The Soldiers Charity (£500 each).

FINANCES Year 2013/14 Income £53,942 Grants £45,000 Grants to organisations £45,000 Assets £1,549,115

TRUSTEES John Floyd; Hugh Sherbrooke; Linda Singer.

OTHER INFORMATION Grants totalled £45,000 during the year.

HOW TO APPLY Unsolicited applications are rarely successful and due to the high number such requests the trust is not able to respond to them or return any printed materials supplied.

WHO TO APPLY TO Wilfrid Vernor-Miles, Correspondent, Hunters, 9 New Square, Lincoln's Inn, London WC2A 3QN Tel. 020 7412 0050 email wvm@hunters-solicitors.co.uk

## ■ The Sino-British Fellowship Trust

CC NO 313669     ESTABLISHED 1948

WHERE FUNDING CAN BE GIVEN UK and China.

WHO CAN BENEFIT Institutions benefitting individual postgraduate students.

WHAT IS FUNDED Scholarships to Chinese citizens to enable them to pursue their studies in Britain. Grants to British citizens in China to educate/train Chinese citizens in any art, science or profession.

TYPE OF GRANT Fees; fares; allowances.

RANGE OF GRANTS Up to around £50,000.

SAMPLE GRANTS Royal Society (£90,000); University of Birmingham (£45,500); Great Britain China Educational Trust (£22,500); Kingston University (£13,500); Needham Research Institute (£4,800); British Library (£3,100).

FINANCES Year 2013 Income £439,671 Grants £431,939 Grants to organisations £357,425 Assets £14,856,734

TRUSTEES Dr Jeremy Langton; Lady Pamela Youde; Anne Ely; Prof. Sir Brian Heap; Prof. Hugh Baker; Peter Ely; Ling Thompson; Prof. Wayne Luk; Dr Frances Wood.

OTHER INFORMATION A total of £432,000 was made in grants, which included £284,500 to organisations in the UK, with the remainder awarded as individual scholarships and to overseas organisations.

HOW TO APPLY Apply on a form available by writing to the correspondence address.

WHO TO APPLY TO Anne Ely, Trustee, Flat 23 Bede House, Manor Fields, London SW15 3LT Tel. 020 8788 6252

## ■ SITA Cornwall Trust Limited

CC NO 1127288     ESTABLISHED 2008

WHERE FUNDING CAN BE GIVEN Cornwall, within a ten-mile radius of a landfill site – a map and a distance calculator are provided on the trust's website.

WHO CAN BENEFIT Community organisations; churches.

WHAT IS FUNDED Projects that provide social and environmental benefits to communities in Cornwall. In particular, projects that fulfil one of the following objectives: bringing land back into use; reducing or preventing pollution; public parks and amenities; buildings and structures; promoting biodiversity. Priority is given to projects benefitting communities local to landfill sites and projects that are community driven.

WHAT IS NOT FUNDED Grants are not given to applicants that have received a grant within the last three years. Funding applications for solar panels will only be considered where there is a clear need for replacement of an existing heating system which is no longer serviceable or if it is part of a wider amenity project in which it makes sense to make such improvements whilst other work is being undertaken. See the trust's website for full criteria.

TYPE OF GRANT Project costs; capital costs; one-off.

RANGE OF GRANTS Up to £100,000. Mostly under £30,000.

SAMPLE GRANTS Previous beneficiaries have included: Wendron Football Club (£50,000); Hayle and District Bowling Club (£35,000); Forder Community Hall (£25,000); Callington Bowling Club (£18,000); Mary Newman's Cottage (£11,500); and Breage Toddlers Kingdom (£5,000).

FINANCES Year 2013/14 Income £1,095,480 Grants £564,421 Grants to organisations £564,421 Assets £1,555,116

TRUSTEES George Hocking; Richard Thomas; Paul Brinsley; Lee Rouse; Philip Rudin; Betty Hale.

OTHER INFORMATION A total of 35 grants were awarded in 2013/14.

HOW TO APPLY Application forms are available to download on the trust's website, along with a detailed list of criteria and application guidelines, which applicants should use to check that their project is eligible. The trust states that 'if you require further information, clarification or have any questions contact the office, and we will be able to answer all your queries.'

WHO TO APPLY TO Wendy Reading, Unit 1 Ashleigh Meadow, Tregondale, Menheniot, Liskeard, Cornwall PL14 3RG Tel. 01579 346816 email wendyreading@btconnect.com Website www.sitacornwalltrust.co.uk

## ■ Six Point Foundation

CC NO 1143324     ESTABLISHED 2012

WHERE FUNDING CAN BE GIVEN UK.

WHO CAN BENEFIT Organisations benefitting Holocaust survivors and Jewish refugees.

WHAT IS FUNDED Projects that will improve health and well-being.

WHAT IS NOT FUNDED The foundation will not fund the following: projects that do not benefit UK resident Jewish Holocaust survivors and refugees from Nazism who are in challenging economic circumstances; Holocaust education projects; general appeals; applications from organisations outside the UK; applications that benefit people living outside the UK; organisations to use funding to make grants; websites, publications or seminars, unless part of a wider project; market or academic research unless part of a wider activity; and work that has already started: the foundation makes grants for the next phase(s) of survivors' and refugees' lives rather than pay for goods, services or activity that has already taken place.

TYPE OF GRANT Usually project costs.

RANGE OF GRANTS Up to £30,000.

SAMPLE GRANTS London Jewish Cultural Centre (£100,000); Holocaust Survivors Friendship Association (£90,000); Selig Court (£84,000); Leeds Jewish Housing Association (£75,000); Reach Out UK (£60,000); Merseyside Jewish Community Care (£40,000); Ezra U'Marpeh (£25,000); and Bikur Cholim (£15,000).

FINANCES Year 2013–14 Income £387,255 Grants £1,111,026 Grants to organisations £871,052 Assets £3,142,519

TRUSTEES Frank Harding; Susan Grant; Vivienne Woolf; Julian Challis; Nigel Raine; Lionel Curry; Joanna Lassman.

OTHER INFORMATION This foundation aims to spend out in the near future. There were an additional 176 grants given to 104 individuals for welfare purposes totalling £240,000 in 2013/14.

HOW TO APPLY The following information was taken from the foundation's guidelines which are available on its website: 'Please call us on 020 3372 8881 to discuss the application before submitting an application. A site visit is also normally required. If we decide during the telephone conversation that it would be a good idea to apply, please download the application form from our website, complete it and return it to us with a detailed budget (Excel document), a copy of the organisation's most recent annual accounts (unless these are available on the Charity Commission website) and a scan of the signed declaration by email to info@sixpointfoundation.org.uk. If the organisation does not have the ability to scan the signed declaration then we will need a copy of it by post addressed to: Six Point Foundation, 25–26 Enford Street, London W1H 1DW. Small grants are processed within 4 weeks of applying, although we aim for a faster turnaround of 1–2 weeks. This is providing the application is thoroughly completed, answering and anticipating all questions about the grant request.'

WHO TO APPLY TO Susan Cohen, Executive Director, 25–26 Enford Street, London W1H 1DW Tel. 020 3372 8881 email info@sixpointfoundation.org.uk Website www.sixpointfoundation.org.uk

## ■ The Skelton Bounty

CC NO 219370   ESTABLISHED 1934
WHERE FUNDING CAN BE GIVEN Lancashire (as it existed in 1934).

WHO CAN BENEFIT Registered charities benefitting young and older people, carers and people with disabilities.

WHAT IS FUNDED Restricted to Lancashire charities (not national ones unless operating in Lancashire from a permanent establishment within the county predominantly for the benefit of residents from that county) assisting young people, elderly people, carers and people with disabilities.

WHAT IS NOT FUNDED Grants are not usually given to large building appeals or revenue expenditure. Grants are not made to individuals.

TYPE OF GRANT Capital expenditure preferred.

RANGE OF GRANTS Up to £8,500. Grants typically £1,000–£3,000.

SAMPLE GRANTS Blackpool Carers Centre Ltd (£3,400); KIND (£3,000); Nightsafe Limited (£2,500); Liverpool and Merseyside Theatre Trust, National Youth Advocacy Service (£2,000 each); Lesbian and Gay Foundation (£1,250); Rossendale and Pendle Mountain Rescue (£1,500); Lancashire Wildlife Trust, Neuromuscular Centre, Tall Ships Youth Trust (£1,000 each).

FINANCES Year 2013/14 Income £105,357 Grants £86,947 Grants to organisations £86,947 Assets £2,559,926

TRUSTEES Patricia Wilson; Dennis Mendoros; Jacqueline Lundy; Dame Lorna Muirhead; Roger Morris; Caroline Reynolds; Robert Hough; Mark Hedley.

OTHER INFORMATION In 2013/14 grants were given to 39 organisations. Most grants are £1,000–£3,000.

HOW TO APPLY Applications should be made on a form available from the correspondent. Requests for application forms should be made as soon as possible after 1 January each year. The completed form should be returned before 31 March immediately following. Applications received after this date will not be considered. The trustees meet annually in July, with successful applicants receiving their grant cheques in late July/early August. Applications should include the charitable registration number of the organisation, or, where appropriate, a letter confirming charitable status. See www.lcvs.org.uk/help-with-money for further details. The trustees prefer to fund grants of a capital nature. Applications from charities in successive years are not viewed favourably.

WHO TO APPLY TO The Trustees, c/o Liverpool Charity and Voluntary Services, 151 Dale street, Liverpool L2 2AH

## ■ The Charles Skey Charitable Trust

CC NO 277697   ESTABLISHED 1979
WHERE FUNDING CAN BE GIVEN UK.

WHO CAN BENEFIT Organisations which the trustees have come across from their own research.

WHAT IS FUNDED General charitable purposes.

TYPE OF GRANT Grants are given on a one-off and recurring basis for core and capital support.

RANGE OF GRANTS £500–£525,000

SAMPLE GRANTS Imperial War Museum Foundation (£525,000); Crosslinks (£100,000); Brasenose College Oxford (£40,000); Alzheimer's Society (£10,000); Princess Alice Hospice; Almeida Projects (£5,000); Camphill Village Trust (£4,000); PumpAid (£3,500); Starlight Children's Foundation (£2,500); Cricket Foundation – Chance to Shine (£2,000); The Soldiers' Charity (£1,000); 2nd Ryde Sea Scouts (£500).

FINANCES Year 2013/14 Income £261,543 Grants £893,500 Grants to organisations £893,500 Assets £12,351,594

TRUSTEES Christopher Berkeley; John Leggett; Revd James Leggett; David Berkeley; Edward Berkeley; James Carleton.

HOW TO APPLY The trust has previously stated that no written or telephoned requests for support will be entertained.

WHO TO APPLY TO John Leggett, Trustee, Flint House, Park Homer Road, Colehill, Wimborne, Dorset BH21 2SP Tel. 01202 882180

## ■ Skinners' Company Lady Neville Charity

CC NO 277174   ESTABLISHED 1978
WHERE FUNDING CAN BE GIVEN UK.

WHO CAN BENEFIT Registered charities with less than four full-time paid staff or equivalent.

WHAT IS FUNDED This charity will consider funding: activities for people with disabilities; the environment; improving the facilities or quality of life for deprived neighbourhoods; performing and visual arts.

WHAT IS NOT FUNDED Organisations working in similar areas as the Skinners' Company and its other charities. These include: schools, education and vocational training; care of older people and sheltered housing; individuals; organisations which are not registered charities working in the UK; organisations with more than four full-time paid staff.

**TYPE OF GRANT** Items of non-recurring expenditure (e.g. equipment, building works or events).

**SAMPLE GRANTS** Details were not available.

**FINANCES** Year 2013/14 Income £40,221 Grants £36,968 Grants to organisations £36,958 Assets £2,583,892

**TRUSTEE** The Worshipful Company of Skinners.

**PUBLICATIONS** Guidelines on Grant Making leaflet is available.

**HOW TO APPLY** Apply in writing to the correspondent enclosing a copy of the latest audited accounts and annual report. Applications need to be received in March and September, for consideration in May and November. Successful applicants will hear the outcome and be sent a cheque in early January and late June. Note, in order to keep administrative costs to a minimum, applications are not acknowledged nor are unsuccessful applicants informed. Organisations that receive a grant from the charity may not re-apply until three years have elapsed.

**WHO TO APPLY TO** The Trustees, Skinners' Hall, 8 Dowgate Hill, London EC4R 2SP Tel. 020 7236 5629 email charitiesadmin@skinners.org.uk Website www.skinnershall.co.uk

## ■ Skipton Building Society Charitable Foundation

**CC NO** 1079538 **ESTABLISHED** 2000

**WHERE FUNDING CAN BE GIVEN** England and Wales.

**WHO CAN BENEFIT** Registered charitable organisations.

**WHAT IS FUNDED** General charitable purposes with particular priority to the charities that benefit children, through education and/or welfare, or older people and their care.

**WHAT IS NOT FUNDED** Running costs; salaries; expenses, research or equipment to be used for administration; causes which serve only a specific sector of the community on religious, ethnic or political grounds; funds for activities outside the UK; activities or equipment for mainstream schools, youth groups or government funded bodies; charities which have unsuccessfully applied for a grant within the last two years; charities without at least one year of published accounts covering a 12 month period. Full criteria can be found on the foundation's website.

**TYPE OF GRANT** Direct donations.

**RANGE OF GRANTS** £500–£10,000; normally not exceeding £5,000.

**SAMPLE GRANTS** Children's Heart Foundation – London (£3,500); Shopmobility – Aberdeen, Troop Aid – Solihull (£3,000 each); Down's Syndrome Training and Support – Bingley (£2,000); Leeds Women's Aid (£1,500); Age Concern Dundee, Play Away – Skipton, Vauxhall City Farm – Luton (£1,000 each); Caring Together – Leeds (£650); Breathing Space – Northallerton (£250).

**FINANCES** Year 2013/14 Income £120,939 Grants £120,278 Grants to organisations £120,278 Assets £65,543

**TRUSTEES** Richard Twigg; Lord Hope of Thornes; Ethne Bannister; Richard Robinson; Rachel Ramsden; Kitty North.

**HOW TO APPLY** Written application forms can be found on foundation's website and should be returned together with enclosed organisation's latest two years' annual accounts, a specific breakdown of how the donation will be used and an explanation of the benefit to its recipients.

**WHO TO APPLY TO** John Gibson, Secretary, The Bailey, Skipton, North Yorkshire BD23 1DN Fax 01756 705000 email john.gibson@skipton.co.uk Website www.skiptoncharitablefoundation.co.uk

## ■ The John Slater Foundation

**CC NO** 231145 **ESTABLISHED** 1963

**WHERE FUNDING CAN BE GIVEN** UK, with a strong preference for the north west of England especially West Lancashire.

**WHO CAN BENEFIT** Registered charities.

**WHAT IS FUNDED** General charitable purposes, with preference for medical causes, animal welfare, education, young people.

**WHAT IS NOT FUNDED** Individuals.

**RANGE OF GRANTS** £500–£11,000

**SAMPLE GRANTS** Bury Grammar School for Girls, Manchester High School for Girls (£10,500 each); Adlington Community Centre, Verona Association (£6,000 each); Wellspring (£4,500); Catholic Blind Institute, PDSA (£2,500); Red Squirrel Survival Trust (£2,000); Lancashire Boys' and Girls' Club (£1,000); Freshfield Animal Rescue (£750); Rebecca Owen Spinal Trust (£500).

**FINANCES** Year 2013/14 Income £1,870,851 Grants £112,636 Grants to organisations £112,636 Assets £4,550,009

**TRUSTEE** HSBC. Trust Company (UK) Ltd.

**OTHER INFORMATION** In 2013/14 a total of 48 grants were made to 30 organisations.

**HOW TO APPLY** The foundation's website states: 'The foundation is presently fully committed to its programme of giving and unfortunately is not able to receive any further new requests of any nature at this time. Should this situation change an appropriate announcement will be made on [the foundation's] website.'

**WHO TO APPLY TO** Richard Thompson, Trust Manager, HSBC Trust Company UK Limited, 10th Floor, Norwich House, Nelson Gate, Commercial Road, Southampton SO15 1GX Tel. 023 8072 2225 Website johnslaterfoundation.org.uk

## ■ The Slaughter and May Charitable Trust

**CC NO** 1082765 **ESTABLISHED** 2000

**WHERE FUNDING CAN BE GIVEN** Mainly local to the Slaughter and May offices in Islington and close to Tower Hamlets and Hackney.

**WHO CAN BENEFIT** Local community, educational and legal professional charities.

**WHAT IS FUNDED** Legal, educational and community projects.

**SAMPLE GRANTS** National Literacy Trust (£53,000); the Access Project (£49,000); Islington Law Centre (£35,000); Legal Advice Centre Bethnal Green and Seeing is Believing (£15,000 each); London Symphony Orchestra (£10,000); CLEFT and RCJ Advice Bureau (£5,000 each); Marie Curie Cancer Care (£2,000); and Royal National Institute for the Blind and Unisex (£1,000 each).

**FINANCES** Year 2013/14 Income £342,030 Grants £337,180 Grants to organisations £337,180 Assets -£36,735

TRUSTEE Slaughter and May Trust Ltd.
HOW TO APPLY The trust's 2013/14 annual report states that it 'makes annual grants at its discretion to a small number of specific charitable causes and does not generally accept unsolicited funding applications'.
WHO TO APPLY TO Kate Hursthouse, Corporate Responsibility Manager, Slaughter and May (Trust Limited), 1 Bunhill Row, London EC1Y 8YY *Tel.* 020 7090 3433 *email* corporateresponsibility@slaughterandmay.com *Website* www.slaughterandmay.com

## ■ Sloane Robinson Foundation

CC NO 1068286  ESTABLISHED 1998
WHERE FUNDING CAN BE GIVEN England and Wales.
WHO CAN BENEFIT Universities; individuals.
WHAT IS FUNDED Advancement of the education of the public through development of long term relationships with academic institutions as well as financial support to private individuals.
WHAT IS NOT FUNDED Undergraduate level, funding fellowships and professorships at universities and places of higher education for both teaching and research grants should not be focused on religion, social sciences and languages; funding of overseas programmes should be focused on the studies in which the country concerned offers better courses (e.g. Chinese history in China); only in exceptional circumstances funding will be provided for the provision of sporting facilities.
TYPE OF GRANT Grants to institutions on an ongoing relationship basis; grants to private individuals.
RANGE OF GRANTS £10,000–£168,000
SAMPLE GRANTS Rugby School (£167,500); Keble College – Oxford (£56,000); Lincoln College – Oxford (£54,000); Oxford University (£10,000).
FINANCES *Year* 2013/14 *Income* £192,204 *Grants* £394,321 *Grants to organisations* £287,169 *Assets* £13,185,616
TRUSTEES Michael Willcox; Hugh Sloane; George Robinson.
HOW TO APPLY Direct written communication with the correspondent. The foundation is very selective in grant-making process, therefore only successful candidates will be notified.
WHO TO APPLY TO Michael Willcox, Trustee, The Old Coach House, Sunnyside, Bergh Apton, Norwich NR15 1DD *Tel.* 01508 480100 *email* info@willcoxlewis.co.uk

## ■ Rita and David Slowe Charitable Trust

CC NO 1048209  ESTABLISHED 1995
WHERE FUNDING CAN BE GIVEN UK and overseas.
WHO CAN BENEFIT Registered charities.
WHAT IS FUNDED General charitable purposes.
WHAT IS NOT FUNDED Individuals.
RANGE OF GRANTS £5,000–£13,000
SAMPLE GRANTS Big Issue Foundation, Books Abroad, Computer Aid International, Crisis, Excellent Development, HERA, Re-cycle, Shelter (£15,000 each).
FINANCES *Year* 2013/14 *Income* £284,674 *Grants* £120,000 *Grants to organisations* £120,000 *Assets* £1,485,977
TRUSTEES Elizabeth Slowe; Graham Weinberg; Jonathan Slowe; Lilian Slowe; Robert Slowe.
HOW TO APPLY Applications may be made in writing to the correspondent.

WHO TO APPLY TO Robert Slowe, Trustee, 32 Hampstead High Street, London NW3 1JQ *Tel.* 020 7435 7800 *email* graham.weinberg@mhllp.co.uk

## ■ Ruth Smart Foundation

CC NO 1080021  ESTABLISHED 2000
WHERE FUNDING CAN BE GIVEN Worldwide.
WHO CAN BENEFIT Registered charities and charitable organisations.
WHAT IS FUNDED Relief of animal suffering.
TYPE OF GRANT One-off.
RANGE OF GRANTS £960–£13,000
SAMPLE GRANTS Fauna and Flora International (£13,000); Monterey County SPCA (£12,800); San Francisco Zoo (£4,500); London Wetland Centre, Reef Conservation Mauritius (£1,000 each); Belize Zoo (£960).
FINANCES *Year* 2013 *Income* £148,990 *Grants* £104,076 *Grants to organisations* £104,076 *Assets* £4,644,976
TRUSTEES Wilfrid Vernor-Miles; John Crosfield Vernor-Miles; Paul Williams.
OTHER INFORMATION Many of the beneficiaries are supported year after year, particularly where trustees are informed of the benefits of foundation funds from previous grants.
HOW TO APPLY Applications should be made in writing to the correspondent. The annual report for 2013 states: 'The trustees support a number of charities on a regular basis and in practice finds that their income is fully committed and there is little, if any, surplus income available for distribution in response to unsolicited appeals.'
WHO TO APPLY TO The Trustees, c/o Hunters Solicitors, 9 New Square, Lincoln's Inn, London WC2A 3QN

## ■ The SMB Charitable Trust

CC NO 263814  ESTABLISHED 1962
WHERE FUNDING CAN BE GIVEN UK and overseas.
WHO CAN BENEFIT Charitable organisations.
WHAT IS FUNDED General charitable purposes; Christian causes; social welfare; overseas aid; the environment; education and training; medical research.
WHAT IS NOT FUNDED Individuals.
TYPE OF GRANT One-off awards, project grants and recurring costs are prioritised. Also considered are building and other capital grants, funding for core and running costs, funding for salaries and start-up costs.
RANGE OF GRANTS Up to £4,000.
SAMPLE GRANTS London City Mission (£4,000); Barnabas Fund, British Red Cross and Interserve (£3,000 each); All Nations Christian College, Bible Society and Christian Aid – Philippines (£2,500 each); Africa Education Trust, Agape and Cameo Aid (£1,000 each); Bible Society Egypt and Junction 12 (£500 each); Happy Now (£150).
FINANCES *Year* 2013/14 *Income* £392,370 *Grants* £250,750 *Grants to organisations* £250,750 *Assets* £9,425,409
TRUSTEES Eric Anstead; Philip Stanford; Jeremy Anstead; Barbara O'Driscoll; Claire Swarbrick.
OTHER INFORMATION Grants were made to 180 organisations totalling £251,000.
HOW TO APPLY Apply in writing to the correspondent, including the aims and principal activities of the applicant, the current financial position and details of any special projects for which funding is sought. Application forms are not used.

Trustees normally meet in March, June, September and December and applications should be received before the beginning of the month in which meetings are held. Because of the volume of appeals received, unsuccessful applicants will only receive a reply if they enclose an sae. However, unsuccessful applicants are welcome to re-apply.

**WHO TO APPLY TO** Barbara O'Driscoll, Trustee, 15 Wilman Road, Tunbridge Wells TN4 9AJ *Tel.* 01892 537301 *email* smbcharitabletrust@googlemail.com

## ■ The Mrs Smith and Mount Trust

**CC NO** 1009718   **ESTABLISHED** 1992
**WHERE FUNDING CAN BE GIVEN** Norfolk, Suffolk, Cambridgeshire, Hertfordshire, Essex, Kent, Surrey and London.
**WHO CAN BENEFIT** Charitable organisations.
**WHAT IS FUNDED** Mental health; people with disabilities; homeless people; community and economic development.
**WHAT IS NOT FUNDED** Individuals; general counselling; charities with an income of over £1 million and/or free unrestricted reserves to the value of more than six months of the applicant organisations and annual expenditure.
**TYPE OF GRANT** One-off and continuing revenue grants are considered. Funding is up to three years.
**RANGE OF GRANTS** £1,000–£7,000
**SAMPLE GRANTS** Kingston Bereavement Service (£8,000); Jubilee Family Centre (£6,000); Disasters Emergency Committee, Mind in Camden and Petals (£5,000 each); Sydenham Garden (£4,000); Southend Mencap and Springfield Community Flat (£3,000 each); Hub Community Project (£1,000).
**FINANCES** *Year* 2013/14 *Income* £241,455 *Grants* £232,800 *Grants to organisations* £232,800 *Assets* £7,021,945
**TRUSTEES** Richard Fowler; Gillian Gorell Barnes; Timothy Buckland Warren; Lisa Weaks; Richard McCadden; James Walker.
**OTHER INFORMATION** Grants were made to 48 organisations totalling £233,000.
**HOW TO APPLY** All applications must be submitted using the online application form which can be downloaded from the website, where full guidelines and criteria are also available to view. The trustees meet three times per year in March, July and November and application forms and supporting documentation must reach the trust's offices by the end of January, May and September respectively.
**WHO TO APPLY TO** Jayne Day, Correspondent, c/o Pothecary Witham Weld Solicitors, 70 St George's Square, London SW1V 3RD *Tel.* 020 7821 8211 *email* charities@pwwsolicitors.co.uk *Website* www.pwwsolicitors.co.uk/charity-grants/7-the-mrs-smith-and-mount-trust

## ■ The DS Smith Charitable Foundation

**CC NO** 1142817   **ESTABLISHED** 2011
**WHERE FUNDING CAN BE GIVEN** England and Wales.
**WHO CAN BENEFIT** Registered charities and voluntary organisations.
**WHAT IS FUNDED** Education and training; conservation.
**RANGE OF GRANTS** £3,000–£42,000
**SAMPLE GRANTS** D'Artgens (£42,000); Arkwright Scholarship Trust (£30,000); In Kind Direct (£30,000); Heart Research UK (£8,400); Royal Institution (£5,000); CHAS and IT Schools Africa (£3,200 each).
**FINANCES** *Year* 2013/14 *Income* £82,631 *Grants* £149,212 *Grants to organisations* £149,212 *Assets* £2,700,919
**TRUSTEES** Anne Steele; Rachel Stevens; Nicholas Feaviour; Mark Greenwood.
**HOW TO APPLY** Application forms are available from the foundation's website.
**WHO TO APPLY TO** Rachel Stevens Trustee, 7th Floor, 350 Euston Road, London NW1 3AX *Tel.* 020 7756 1823 *email* charitablefoundation@dssmith.com *Website* www.dssmith.com/company/sustainability/social-responsibility/charitable-trust

## ■ The N. Smith Charitable Settlement

**CC NO** 276660   **ESTABLISHED** 1978
**WHERE FUNDING CAN BE GIVEN** Worldwide.
**WHO CAN BENEFIT** Registered charities.
**WHAT IS FUNDED** General charitable purposes, including social work, medical research, education, environment/animals, the arts and overseas aid.
**WHAT IS NOT FUNDED** Grants are only made to registered charities and not to individuals.
**RANGE OF GRANTS** £500–£8,000
**SAMPLE GRANTS** Disasters Emergency Committee (£7,500); CAFOD (£1,500); Arthritis Research Campaign, Dundee Women's Aid, Great Ormond Street Children's Hospital, Marine Conservation Society, South Bank Sinfonia, Street Child Africa (£1,000 each); Liverpool Lighthouse, Multiple Sclerosis Therapy Centre (£800); Opera North, RSPB, Scope, Warrington Youth Club Ltd (£500); Medlock and Tame Valley Conservation Association (£250).
**FINANCES** *Year* 2013/14 *Income* £193,968 *Grants* £151,250 *Grants to organisations* £151,250 *Assets* £4,888,761
**TRUSTEES** Anne Merricks; John Williams-Rigby; Graham Wardle; Janet Adam.
**OTHER INFORMATION** Most grants are for under £2,000.
**HOW TO APPLY** Apply in writing to the correspondent. The trustees meet twice a year.
**WHO TO APPLY TO** Sue Darlington, Secretary, Linder Myers, Phoenix House, 45 Cross Street, Manchester M2 4JF *Tel.* 0161 832 6972 *email* sue.darlington@lindermyers.co.uk

## ■ The Smith Charitable Trust

**CC NO** 288570   **ESTABLISHED** 1983
**WHERE FUNDING CAN BE GIVEN** UK and overseas.
**WHO CAN BENEFIT** Registered charities, usually large, well-known UK organisations, which are on a list of regular beneficiaries.
**WHAT IS FUNDED** General charitable purposes, particularly health.
**WHAT IS NOT FUNDED** Animal charities; individuals.
**RANGE OF GRANTS** £3,000–£12,000
**SAMPLE GRANTS** Sue Ryder Care (£6,400); Macmillan Cancer Support and Royal National Lifeboat Institution (£4,300 each); Action for Children (£3,200); Artists' General Benevolent Institution, Scope, Mind and The Marine Society and Sea Cadets (£2,100 each).
**FINANCES** *Year* 2012/13 *Income* £122,454 *Grants* £46,241 *Grants to organisations* £46,241 *Assets* £7,599,526

TRUSTEES A. G. F. Fuller; P. A. Sheils; R. I. Turner; R. J. Weetch.

OTHER INFORMATION Grants were awarded to 23 organisations in 2012/13. At the time of writing (June 2015) this was the latest information available.

HOW TO APPLY Unsolicited applications are not considered.

WHO TO APPLY TO Paul Shiels, Trustee, c/o Moon Beever Solicitors, 24–25 Bloomsbury Square, London WC1A 2PL *Tel.* 020 7637 0661 *email* psheils@moonbeever.com

## ■ The Henry Smith Charity

CC NO 230102      ESTABLISHED 1628

WHERE FUNDING CAN BE GIVEN UK. Specific local programmes in east and west Sussex, Hampshire, Kent, Gloucestershire, Leicestershire, Suffolk and Surrey.

WHO CAN BENEFIT Charitable organisations.

WHAT IS FUNDED Hospitals, hospices and other forms of residential care or provision of health care for those who are sick or in need and for other institutions providing medical assistance for those in financial need; the relief of poor, aged or sick persons and their spouses, widows, widowers and dependants; the relief of poor, aged or sick members of the clergy and their spouses, widows, widowers and dependants; the relief, rehabilitation and training of people with disabilities, including ex-Servicemen and war widows; medical research; the promotion of moral welfare or social service.

WHAT IS NOT FUNDED General appeals; local authorities or work usually considered a statutory responsibility; schools, colleges or universities, except for independent special schools for pupils with disabilities or special educational needs; counselling projects; pre-school projects; community transport organisations or services; projects that promote religion; capital appeals for places of worship; organisations that do not provide direct services to clients (such as umbrella, second tier or grant-making organisations); Organisations with liquid reserves covering more than 12 months' expenditure; arts projects, unless able to evidence therapeutic or rehabilitative benefits to: older people, people with disabilities, vulnerable groups, prisoners, or young people experiencing educational, social and economic disadvantage (such as young people in, or leaving, care); education projects, except those able to evidence practical and rehabilitative benefits to: people with disabilities, prisoners, or young people experiencing educational, social and economic disadvantage; leisure, recreation or play activities, unless they: are specifically for people with disabilities, are able to evidence a significant rehabilitative benefit to people with mental health problems, or significantly improve opportunities and maximise the potential of young people who experience educational, social and economic disadvantage; one-off events (such as festivals, conferences, exhibitions and community events); the core work of Citizens Advice; projects that solely provide legal advice; running costs of hospices; feasibility studies; professional associations, or training for professionals; organisations that do not have charitable aims (such as companies limited by shares and commercial companies); start-up costs, organisations that do not yet have a track record of service delivery, or that have not yet produced accounts; individuals, or organisations applying on their behalf; projects taking place or benefitting people outside the UK; overseas trips; residential holidays (except those that qualify under the charity's Holiday Grants scheme); heritage or environmental conservation projects; social research; campaigning or lobbying projects, or general awareness raising work; projects where the main focus is website development or maintenance; IT equipment (unless related to a member of staff the charity is also being asked to fund); capital projects that are solely to meet the requirements of the Disability Discrimination Act; capital costs towards the purchase or adaptation of a vehicle; organisations that have applied to us unsuccessfully within the previous 12 months; pilot projects are not currently a high priority. If you are seeking funds for a pilot project, be aware you must be able to provide strong evidence from other work that has already been delivered to support the case for funding. You must also provide clear evidence that there is a need to develop a pilot; organisations with an income of over £5 million are rarely funded. If your organisation has income of over £5 million you would need to very clearly demonstrate that your organisation is best placed to deliver the work and that you are unable to source the funding elsewhere.

TYPE OF GRANT Capital and revenue; one-off grants and recurrent grants for up to three years.

RANGE OF GRANTS Small grants: £500–£10,000; Large grants: over £10,000.

SAMPLE GRANTS Co-ordinated Action Against Domestic Abuse (£200,000); Action Medical Research (£120,000); Advocacy in Greenwich (£80,000); Access All Areas (£64,500); Womankind (£33,500); Diversity (£16,000); Helping Hands Community Trust (£10,000); Relate – West Surrey (£5,000); Canonbury School Foundation (£2,500); Gilbrook School (£2,000).

FINANCES *Year* 2013 *Income* £10,621,000 *Grants* £27,069,000 *Grants to organisations* £25,939,000 *Assets* £792,489,000

TRUSTEES Gracia McGrath; Carola Irvine; Sir Richard Thompson; James Hambro; Anna Scott; Merlyn Lowther; Noel Manns; Diana Barran; Marilyn Gallyer; Mark Newton; Patrick Maxwell; Tristan Drake; Miko Giedroyc; James Hordern; Vivienne Dews; Piers Feilden; Emir Fesal; Revd Pail Hackwood.

OTHER INFORMATION Grants to organisations totalled £26 million and grants to individuals totalled £1.1 million. There were 308 awards made during the year.

HOW TO APPLY The following was taken from the charity's website: 'Each of our grant programmes has a slightly different application and assessment process. You will find information about how to make your application in the guidelines for each type of grant. Most of our grants require you to complete an application form. We strongly recommend that you download and read the guidelines of the relevant grant programme carefully before you start your application. It is important that you follow our guidance on how to apply. Guidelines and application forms for each programme can be downloaded from the Grant Programmes section of the website and can be found at the bottom of the relevant sub-page. Please ensure you send us all the supporting documents we ask you to include with your application. Incomplete applications may be returned unread. **PLEASE NOTE** we **DO NOT, UNDER ANY CIRCUMSTANCES**, make grants in response to applications received in the form of general appeals or mail shots.'

**WHO TO APPLY TO** Richard Hopgood, Director, 6th Floor, 65–68 Leadenhall Street, London EC3A 2AD *Tel.* 020 7264 4970 *Website* www.henrysmithcharity.org.uk

## ■ The WH Smith Group Charitable Trust

**CC NO** 1013782 **ESTABLISHED** 1992

**WHERE FUNDING CAN BE GIVEN** UK.

**WHO CAN BENEFIT** Charities and educational establishments in which of WH Smith staff are directly involved.

**WHAT IS FUNDED** General charitable purposes, including medical causes and education. The funds raised by employees are given to employee nominated charities with the remainder used to provide grants to charitable organisations with which members of staff are directly involved (our research suggests that this constitutes one third of the expenditure).

**RANGE OF GRANTS** Up to £55,000.

**SAMPLE GRANTS** National Literacy Trust (£54,500); WH Smith Promotions Ltd (£20,000); WH Smith High Street Limited (£9,800); Diabetes UK and Parkinson's Disease Society of the UK (£1,800 each); Macmillan Cancer Support (£2,800); Children in Need (£1,500); Friends of Newark Academy (£1,300); Savernake Forest Scouts Group, The University of Nottingham and Wiltshire Air Ambulance (£1,000 each).

**FINANCES** *Year* 2013 *Income* £117,621 *Grants* £123,544 *Grants to organisations* £123,544 *Assets* £90,142

**TRUSTEES** Faye Sherman; Anthony Lawrence; Sarah Heath; Adrian Mansfield; Natalie Davidson; Chris Welch; Paul Green.

**OTHER INFORMATION** During the year grants of £1,000 or more were made to 22 organisations. Smaller awards totalled about £14,500.

**HOW TO APPLY** Due to the proactive nature of the trust, applying for a grant directly would be fruitless.

**WHO TO APPLY TO** The Secretary, W. H. Smith Ltd, Greenbridge Road, Swindon SN3 3JE *Tel.* 01793 616161 *Website* www.whsmithplc.co.uk/corporate_responsibility/whsmith_trust

## ■ The Stanley Smith UK Horticultural Trust

**CC NO** 261925 **ESTABLISHED** 1970

**WHERE FUNDING CAN BE GIVEN** UK and overseas.

**WHO CAN BENEFIT** Grants are made to individuals or to institutions benefitting botany and horticulture.

**WHAT IS FUNDED** Grants are made to individual projects which involve the advancement of amenity horticulture and horticultural education. In the past, assistance has been given to: the creation, preservation and development of gardens to which the public is admitted; the cultivation and wider distribution of plants derived by breeding or by collection from the wild, to research; to the publication of books with a direct bearing on horticulture.

**WHAT IS NOT FUNDED** Grants are not made for projects in commercial horticulture (crop production) or agriculture, nor are they made to support students taking academic or diploma courses of any kind, although educational institutions are supported.

**TYPE OF GRANT** Capital (including buildings); core costs; feasibility studies; interest-free loans; one-off; research; start-up costs. Grants are normally made as a contribution to cover the costs of identified projects. In exceptional cases grants are made over a three-year period.

**RANGE OF GRANTS** Grants range from £250 to £5,000; typically £3,000–£4,000.

**SAMPLE GRANTS** Chelsea Physic Garden, Rhododendrons of Subgenus Vireya (£5,000 each); Publication of a book on Aerangis (£4,000); Hexham Abbey (£2,500); Lancashire Age UK (£2,000); Waterloo School – Sierra Leone, Bristol Zoo Gardens (£1,000 each); St John's Primary School – Rowlands Castle (£400).

**FINANCES** *Year* 2013/14 *Income* £129,305 *Grants* £128,870 *Grants to organisations* £128,870 *Assets* £3,653,342

**TRUSTEES** Alexander de Brye; Christopher Brickell; Lady Jane Renfrew; John Simmons; Phillip Rodney Sykes; Edward Reed; Dr John David.

**OTHER INFORMATION** The total grants figure includes a scholarship worth £31,000 which was awarded to the English Heritage Historic and Botanic Garden Training Programme.

**HOW TO APPLY** Apply by post or email to the correspondent. *Guidelines for Applicants* are available from the trust and can be obtained from their website. The director is willing to give advice on how applications should be presented. The factors which are taken into account when assessing an application include: the horticultural value of the project; whether similar projects exist (or are in development) within the UK and abroad; the trust's need to maintain a balance of support across all the areas of horticulture covered by its objectives; the trust's need to maintain a balance of smaller and larger grants; the views of experts who may occasionally be consulted Grants are awarded twice a year, in April and October. To be considered in the spring allocation, applications should reach the director before 15 February of each year; for the autumn allocation the equivalent date is 15 August. Potential recipients are advised to get their applications in early.

**WHO TO APPLY TO** Dr David Rae, Director, Royal Botanic Garden, 20 Inverleith Row, Edinburgh EH3 5LR *Tel.* 0131 248 2905 *Fax* 0131 248 2903 *email* d.rae@rbge.org.uk *Website* www.grantsforhorticulturists.org.uk/Smith.html

## ■ Philip Smith's Charitable Trust

**CC NO** 1003751 **ESTABLISHED** 1991

**WHERE FUNDING CAN BE GIVEN** UK with a preference for Gloucestershire.

**WHO CAN BENEFIT** Local and national registered charities.

**WHAT IS FUNDED** The trust makes grants mainly in the fields of welfare, the environment, older people, children and the armed forces.

**RANGE OF GRANTS** £100–£10,000

**SAMPLE GRANTS Previous beneficiaries have included:** Save the Children (£10,000); League of Friends of Moreton-in-Marsh Hospital and the Gamekeepers Welfare Charitable Trust (£5,000 each); St James PCC Chipping Campden (£4,000); The Salvation Army (£2,500); the Army Benevolent Fund and Church Urban Fund (£1,000 each).

**FINANCES** *Year* 2013/14 *Income* £23,007 *Grants* £110,000 *Grants to organisations* £110,000

**TRUSTEES** Hon. Philip Smith; Mary Smith.

**OTHER INFORMATION** Grant total was estimated based on expenditure in previous years as the trust's annual accounts were not required on the Charity Commission website in 2013/14. Expenditure in 2013/14 totalled £129,000.

**HOW TO APPLY** Apply in writing to the correspondent. The trustees have stated that they meet regularly to consider all requests for grants and that a lack of response can be taken to indicate that the trust does not wish to contribute to an appeal.

**WHO TO APPLY TO** Helen D'Monte, Bircham Dyson Bell, 50 Broadway, London SW1H 0BL *Tel.* 020 7783 3685 *email* helendmonte@bdb-law.co.uk

■ **The R. C. Snelling Charitable Trust**

**CC NO** 1074776   **ESTABLISHED** 1999

**WHERE FUNDING CAN BE GIVEN** Within a 30-mile radius of the village of Blofield in Norfolk.

**WHO CAN BENEFIT** Charitable organisations.

**WHAT IS FUNDED** General charitable purposes; education and training; the promotion of health; people with disabilities; social welfare; accommodation and housing; Christianity; the environment and animals.

**WHAT IS NOT FUNDED** Salaries; sponsorship for more than one year; general appeals where the need could be met several times over by grantors; national appeals; continued assistance with running costs.

**TYPE OF GRANT** One-off.

**RANGE OF GRANTS** Usually £250–£3,500.

**SAMPLE GRANTS** Friends of Drayton Junior School (£3,500); Christian Police Association and Christians Against Poverty (£3,000 each); Lighthouse Attleborough (£2,000); Norwich door to Door, Family Life Centre and East Norwich Youth Project (£1,000 each); Hingham Pre School Playgroup (£750); North Breckland Youth for Christ (£500); Sewell Toy Library (£250).

**FINANCES** Year 2013/14 Income £1,960,020 Grants £45,386 Grants to organisations £45,386 Assets £3,303,919

**TRUSTEES** Philip Buttinger; Rowland Cogman; Toby Wise; Nigel Savory; Stephan Phillips; Colin Jacobs; Samuel Barratt.

**OTHER INFORMATION** Grants to 31 organisations totalled £45,000.

**HOW TO APPLY** An online application form can be completed from the company's website. The trust is happy to receive queries via email.

**WHO TO APPLY TO** Rowland Cogman, Trustee, R. C. Snelling Ltd, Laundry Lane, Blofield Heath, Norwich NR13 4SQ *Tel.* 01603 711737 *email* trust@snellings.co.uk *Website* www.snellings.co.uk/charitable-trust.aspx

■ **The Sobell Foundation**

**CC NO** 274369   **ESTABLISHED** 1977

**WHERE FUNDING CAN BE GIVEN** England and Wales, Israel and the Commonwealth of Independent States.

**WHO CAN BENEFIT** Small national or local registered charities or charities that hold an Certificate of Exemption from the Inland Revenue. Overseas charities must be able to provide the details of a UK-registered charity through which funding can be channelled on their behalf.

**WHAT IS FUNDED** The foundation's website states that the trustees aim 'to achieve a reasonable spread' between Jewish and non-Jewish charities working in the following areas: medical care and treatment, including respite care and hospices; care for adults and children who have physical and mental disabilities; education and training for adults and children with physical and learning disabilities; care and support of older people and children; homelessness. In Israel only, the foundation also funds: immigrant absorption; co-existence projects; higher education.

**WHAT IS NOT FUNDED** Individuals; organisations that have applied to the foundation within the past year. Applications from large national charities which have wide support are unlikely to be considered.

**TYPE OF GRANT** One-off; capita; project; running costs; buildings; core and recurring costs. Funding may be given for up to and over three years.

**RANGE OF GRANTS** Previously between £400 and £300,000.

**SAMPLE GRANTS** Details were not available.

**FINANCES** Year 2013/14 Income £2,100,201 Grants £4,133,938 Grants to organisations £4,133,938 Assets £68,245,798

**TRUSTEES** Susan Lacroix; Roger Lewis; Andrea Scouller.

**OTHER INFORMATION** A total of 472 grants were paid during the year, of which 58 ranged between £20,000 and £50,000. Three grants were in excess of £50,000.

**HOW TO APPLY** Application forms are available to download from the website and should be completed and returned to the foundation by post. The following information from your organisation should be enclosed: the current year's summary income and expenditure budget; the most recent annual report; and the most recent set of accounts. Applications should not be returned by email. The foundation notes that it will write with the result of your application as soon as possible, though this may take up to several months. Applicants, successful or otherwise, may only re-apply to the foundation after 12 months.

**WHO TO APPLY TO** Penny Newton, Correspondent, PO Box 2137, Shepton Mallet, Somerset BA4 6YA *Tel.* 01749 813135 *email* enquiries@sobellfoundation.org.uk *Website* www.sobellfoundation.org.uk

■ **Social Business Trust (Scale-Up)**

**CC NO** 1136151   **ESTABLISHED** 2010

**WHERE FUNDING CAN BE GIVEN** Organisations must be based predominantly in the UK.

**WHO CAN BENEFIT** Social enterprises.

**WHAT IS FUNDED** General charitable purposes. The trust outlines its unique approach on its website: 'We believe there are a number of social enterprises capable of scaling up their operations on a regional and national level and we have a clear and ambitious goal: to help transform the impact of social enterprises and thereby improve the lives of over a million of the UK's most disadvantaged people.' See the website for more information of the trust's work.

**WHAT IS NOT FUNDED** Any organisation not meeting the trust's selection criteria.

**TYPE OF GRANT** Cash grants and in-kind services. Support usually provided instalments each being conditional upon achievement of certain milestones.

**SAMPLE GRANTS** The beneficiaries were: Shakespeare Schools Festival (£738,000); The Challenge Network (£643,000); London Early Years Foundation (£605,500); The Reader Organisation (£245,000); Young Advisors (£98,000); Fashion Enter (£73,500); Challenge Partners (£69,500); Bikeworks (£49,000);

Inspiring Futures Foundation (£38,500); Moneyline (£31,500). The amounts listed include in-kind as well as cash contributions.

**FINANCES** Year 2013/14 Income £3,303,562 Grants £464,464 Grants to organisations £464,464 Assets £586,456

**TRUSTEES** Damon Buffini; Paul Armstrong; Simon Milton; Jonathan Myers; Tim Curry; Alan Hirzel.

**OTHER INFORMATION** The grant total above accounts for cash grants only. In total during the year, the trust contributed £2.6 million to organisations, £2.1 million of which was through the provision of in-kind services. The trust notes on its website that it may take up to seven months to complete the full process to investment.

**HOW TO APPLY** The trust's website provides its selection criteria; however, if unsure, applicants are welcome to contact the correspondent directly. To be eligible the organisation: should be registered as a charity or demonstrate a clear charitable purpose, such as a community interest company (CIC); must have annual revenue in excess of £1.5 million, including a significant proportion of earned income (income that is not grants or donations); needs to have at least one year's audited trading accounts; a minimum of 1,000 people per year must benefit, directly or indirectly, from the organisation's goods or services; needs to be based predominantly in the UK; must not have strong political or religious links. Written communication to the trust must include a one-page covering letter; a summary of *no more than four pages* outlining who you are and what you do, your growth strategy and where you think Social Business Trust can help you most; your organisation's latest audited accounts. As an appendix, a business plan or three to five year strategic plan may be included. Within your four page summary, you may also wish to include: growth objectives; financial projections for the next three years, separating earned income from grants and donations; measurement of your current social impact and how this will grow; the key members of your management team. The trust aims to respond within ten working days to confirm the receipt of application and review it within six weeks. Successful applicants are contacted to obtain further details and unsuccessful applicants are informed in writing. Successful applications have to go through an initial review stage with the investment manager, alongside other applications and the approved applicants are invited to work with the core team to present their application to the investment committee to receive the final approval.

**WHO TO APPLY TO** Adele Blakebrough, Chief Executive, First Floor, 13 St Swithin's Lane, London EC4N 8AL *Tel.* 020 3011 0770 *email* info@socialbusinesstrust.org *Website* www.socialbusinesstrust.org

■ **Sodexo Foundation**

**CC NO** 1110266    **ESTABLISHED** 2005
**WHERE FUNDING CAN BE GIVEN** UK and Ireland.
**WHO CAN BENEFIT** Charitable organisations.
**WHAT IS FUNDED** Education and training; health; community and economic development; social welfare.
**RANGE OF GRANTS** £1,500–£120,000
**SAMPLE GRANTS** FareShare (£120,000); SSAFA Forces Help (£60,000); Scouts Association (£40,000); The Prince's Trust (£38,000); Community Foundation of Ireland (£25,000); Trees for Life (£8,400); Providence Row (£7,500); Queen Alexandra Hospital (£6,000); and CCHF All About Kids (£1,500).

**FINANCES** Year 2013 Income £488,316 Grants £413,173 Grants to organisations £413,713 Assets £52,861

**TRUSTEES** Phil Hooper; Harbhajan Singh Brar; Rebecca Symon; David Mulcahy; Gareth John; Margot Slattery; Debra White.

**OTHER INFORMATION** The Sodexo Foundation is the corporate charity of the food services and facilities management company, Sodexo Ltd.

**HOW TO APPLY** Applications may be made in writing to the correspondent. Application forms can be downloaded from the foundation's website.

**WHO TO APPLY TO** Edwina Hughes, Corporate Responsibility Manager, Sodexo Ltd, 1 Southampton Row, London WC1B 5HA *email* stophunger@sodexo.com *Website* uk.sodexo.com/uken/corporate-responsibility/local-communities/local-communities.aspx

■ **Solev Co Ltd**

**CC NO** 254623    **ESTABLISHED** 1967
**WHERE FUNDING CAN BE GIVEN** UK and Israel.
**WHO CAN BENEFIT** Individuals and organisations benefitting Jewish people.
**WHAT IS FUNDED** Jewish causes, principally education and training, the promotion of health, social welfare, children and young people and older people.
**RANGE OF GRANTS** £1,000–£5,000
**SAMPLE GRANTS** **Previous beneficiaries have included:** Dina Perelman Trust Ltd (£100,000); Songdale Ltd (£40,000); Society of Friends of the Torah (£3,900); Finchley Road Synagogue (£2,300); NW London Talmudical College (£1,500); Yesodey Hatorah School (£700); and Gateshead Talmudical College (£400).
**FINANCES** Year 2013/14 Income £475,921 Grants £325,979 Grants to organisations £325,979 Assets £5,885,182
**TRUSTEES** Romie Tager; Chaim Frommer; Joseph Tager Simon Tager.
**OTHER INFORMATION** No information on grant beneficiaries has been included in the charity's accounts in recent years.
**HOW TO APPLY** Apply in writing to the correspondent.
**WHO TO APPLY TO** Roger Tager, Correspondent, 1 Spaniards Park, Columbas Drive, London NW3 7JD *Tel.* 020 7420 9500

■ **The Solo Charitable Settlement**

**CC NO** 326444    **ESTABLISHED** 1983
**WHERE FUNDING CAN BE GIVEN** UK and Israel.
**WHO CAN BENEFIT** Organisations benefitting children and young people, people with disabilities, older people and the Jewish community.
**WHAT IS FUNDED** General charitable purposes; education and training; the promotion of health; social welfare; arts and culture.
**RANGE OF GRANTS** Between £500 and £12,000.
**SAMPLE GRANTS** Jewish Care (£11,500); Community Security Trust (£9,000); Norwood Ravenswood (£7,500); Jewish Leadership Council, Beth Shalom Holocaust Centre and Nightingale House (£5,000 each); Holocaust Centre (£3,000); Shelter Box and Kol Nidre Appeal (£1,000 each); and President's Club Charitable Trust (£500).
**FINANCES** Year 2013/14 Income £228,669 Grants £70,330 Grants to organisations £70,330 Assets £6,177,821

**TRUSTEES** Edna Goldstein; Peter Goldstein; Dean Goldstein; Jamie Goldstein; Paul Goldstein; Tammy Ward.
**OTHER INFORMATION** Grants were made to 21 organisations totalling £70,500.
**HOW TO APPLY** Apply in writing to the correspondent.
**WHO TO APPLY TO** The Trustees, c/o Gallaghers Accountants, Titchfield House, 2nd Floor, 69–85 Tabernacle Street, London EC2A 4RR *Tel.* 020 7490 7774 *email* info@gallaghers.co.uk

---

## ■ David Solomons Charitable Trust

**CC NO** 297275      **ESTABLISHED** 1986
**WHERE FUNDING CAN BE GIVEN** UK.
**WHO CAN BENEFIT** UK and local charitable organisations benefitting people who have learning difficulties and their carers.
**WHAT IS FUNDED** Research into, or the treatment and care of, people with mental disabilities.
**WHAT IS NOT FUNDED** Individuals.
**TYPE OF GRANT** One-off; project grants; salaries. Administrative expenses and large building projects are not usually funded, although grants can be made towards furnishing or equipping rooms.
**RANGE OF GRANTS** Generally up to £2,000.
**SAMPLE GRANTS** Down's Syndrome Association (£8,000); The Sunnybank Trust (£2,500 in total); St Loyes Foundation, Martha Trust (£2,000 each); Out of the Darkness Theatre Company, Lothian Autistic Society, Toucan Employment (£1,000 each); Follow Your Dreams, Independence South West, Relate, The Garden Science Trust (£500 each).
**FINANCES** *Year* 2013/14 *Income* £136,703 *Grants* £95,030 *Grants to organisations* £95,030 *Assets* £2,591,317
**TRUSTEES** Michael Chamberlayne; John Drewitt; Jeremy Rutter; Dr Richard Solomons; Dr Leila Cooke; Diana Huntingford.
**OTHER INFORMATION** Down's Syndrome Association is funded every year.
**HOW TO APPLY** The trustees have stated that they conduct their own research into potential applicants.
**WHO TO APPLY TO** Graeme Crosby, Correspondent, Jasmine Cottage, 11 Lower Road, Breachwood Green, Hitchin, Hertfordshire SG4 8NS *Tel.* 01438 833254 *email* g.crosby@waitrose.com

---

## ■ Somerset Churches Trust

**CC NO** 1055840      **ESTABLISHED** 1996
**WHERE FUNDING CAN BE GIVEN** The historic county of Somerset.
**WHO CAN BENEFIT** Churches and chapels.
**WHAT IS FUNDED** The repair of churches and chapels, which are open for worship in Somerset.
**WHAT IS NOT FUNDED** Basic maintenance; the repair or provision of bells, decorations, ornaments, lighting, heating, organs and boundary walls; churchyard maintenance; alterations, extensions or re-ordering schemes other than to allow for wider community use as noted above; retrospective grants.
**TYPE OF GRANT** Eligible expenditure and capital grants.
**RANGE OF GRANTS** Up to £10,000.
**SAMPLE GRANTS** St Peter and St Paul – Wincanton (£7,500); St Mary the Virgin – North Petherton (£5,000); Holy Cross – Midlezoy (£3,000); St Benedict's – Glastonbury and St Mary – Stanton Drew (£2,000 each); St Mary – Wambrook (£1,000); St James – Chillington (£500).
**FINANCES** *Year* 2013/14 *Income* £55,193 *Grants* £42,000 *Grants to organisations* £42,000 *Assets* £101,032
**TRUSTEES** Hugh Playfair; Paul Heal; Jennifer Beazley; David Sisson; John Wood; Christopher Hawkings; The Ven. John Read; Angela Waddell Dudley; William Newsom; Lindsey Shaw-Miller.
**PUBLICATIONS** 'Jewels of Somerset' – Stained Glass in parish churches from 1830 was published in 2012.
**OTHER INFORMATION** Grants during the year totalled £42,000 and were given to 19 churches.
**HOW TO APPLY** The trust's website states that: 'Applications should be made on the Trust's application form, which can be obtained from the Grants Secretary or downloaded from the website. When completed, it should be returned to the Grant's Secretary, together with the documents requested. An independent Architect or Surveyor will assess the application for eligibility and quality. The Trust's Area Representative will visit the church or chapel before reporting to the Trustees. The Trustees meet four times a year (normally in January, April, July & October) and will adjudicate the application presented.'
**WHO TO APPLY TO** Paul Heal, Trustee, Culberry Farm, Kennel Lane, East Pennard, Shepton Mallet BA4 6TT *Tel.* 07802 869081 *email* somersetchurchestrust@gmail.com *Website* www.somersetchurchestrust.org

---

## ■ Songdale Ltd

**CC NO** 286075      **ESTABLISHED** 1961
**WHERE FUNDING CAN BE GIVEN** UK and Israel.
**WHO CAN BENEFIT** People of the Orthodox Jewish faith.
**WHAT IS FUNDED** Jewish causes; social welfare; education and training.
**SAMPLE GRANTS** A list of grant beneficiaries was not included in the accounts but previously grants have been given to: Cosmon Belz Ltd, Kollel Belz, BFOT, Ezras Yisroel, Forty Limited, Darkei Ovois, Germach Veholachto, Keren Nedunnia Lchasanim, Belz Nursery and Bais Chinuch.
**FINANCES** *Year* 2013/14 *Income* £196,089 *Grants* £201,597 *Grants to organisations* £201,597 *Assets* £2,398,255
**TRUSTEES** Yechiel Grosskopf; Myer Grosskopf; Malka Grosskopf.
**HOW TO APPLY** Apply in writing to the correspondent.
**WHO TO APPLY TO** Yechiel Grosskopf, Trustee, New Burlington House, 1075 Finchley Road, London NW11 0PU *Tel.* 020 8806 5010

---

## ■ The E. C. Sosnow Charitable Trust

**CC NO** 273578      **ESTABLISHED** 1977
**WHERE FUNDING CAN BE GIVEN** UK and overseas.
**WHO CAN BENEFIT** Charitable organisations.
**WHAT IS FUNDED** Mainly education and the arts, as well as social welfare and healthcare; emergency relief; Judaism.
**WHAT IS NOT FUNDED** Individuals.
**TYPE OF GRANT** One-off.
**RANGE OF GRANTS** £200–£5,500
**SAMPLE GRANTS** Friends of Ascent (£10,000); London School of Economics and Political Science and African Education Trust (£5,000 each); Mental Health Foundation, Holocaust Educational Trust and RNIB (£3,000 each);

Jewish Care and Techinion UK (£2,000 each); Israel Philharmonic Orchestra (£1,000); Friends of Ohel Sarah (£500); Save the Children and MSF UK (£250 each).
**FINANCES** *Year* 2013/14 *Income* £63,696 *Grants* £66,200 *Grants to organisations* £66,200 *Assets* £2,126,540
**TRUSTEES** Elias Fattal; Fiona Fattal; Alexandra Fattal; Richard Fattal.
**OTHER INFORMATION** Grants were made to 23 organisations totalling £66,000.
**HOW TO APPLY** Appeals can be made in writing to the correspondent.
**WHO TO APPLY TO** The Trustees, c/o Bourner Bullock, Sovereign House, 212–224 Shaftesbury Avenue, London WC2H 8HQ *Tel.* 020 7240 5821

## ■ The Souter Charitable Trust
**SC NO** SC029998 **ESTABLISHED** 1991
**WHERE FUNDING CAN BE GIVEN** UK, but with a preference for Scotland; overseas.
**WHO CAN BENEFIT** Grants are given to a variety of organisations supporting: people of all ages; people who are in care, fostered or adopted individuals; Christians; evangelists; carers; people disadvantaged by poverty; refugees; victims of famine, man-made or natural disasters or war.
**WHAT IS FUNDED** Relief of human suffering, particularly projects with a Christian emphasis.
**WHAT IS NOT FUNDED** The trust tend not to get involved with research or capital funding are more likely to provide a contribution towards the revenue costs of a project. Grants are generally given to charitable organisations and not to individuals.
**TYPE OF GRANT** One-off and recurring grants.
**RANGE OF GRANTS** Mostly £1,000 or less.
**SAMPLE GRANTS** Against Malaria Foundation; Bethany Christian Trust; Claypotts Trust; Chest Heart and Stroke Scotland; Christians Against Poverty; Mary's Meals; Oasis Trust; Tearfund; Vine Trust.
**FINANCES** *Year* 2013/14 *Income* £9,086,151 *Grants* £9,992,882 *Grants to organisations* £9,992,882
**TRUSTEES** Brian Souter; Betty Souter; Ann Allen.
**HOW TO APPLY** Apply in writing to the correspondent. Keep applications brief and no more than two sides of A4 paper: if appropriate, send audited accounts, but do not send brochures, business plans, dads and so on. The trust states that it will request more information if necessary. The trustees meet every two months or so, and all applications will be acknowledged in due course, whether successful or not. A stamped addressed envelope would be appreciated. Subsequent applications should not be made within a year of the initial submission.
**WHO TO APPLY TO** Dion Judd, Correspondent, PO Box 7412, Perth PH1 5YX *Tel.* 01738 450408 *email* enquiries@soutercharitabletrust.org.uk *Website* www.soutercharitabletrust.org.uk

## ■ The South Square Trust
**CC NO** 278960 **ESTABLISHED** 1979
**WHERE FUNDING CAN BE GIVEN** UK.
**WHO CAN BENEFIT** Registered charities; educational institutions; individuals.
**WHAT IS FUNDED** Annual income is allocated in awards to individuals for educational purposes, specifically help with tuition fees but living expenses will be considered for courses as specified above. Donations are also considered to registered charities working in fields of older people, medical research and equipment, support groups, community groups, horticulture, green issues and other projects connected with the fine and applied arts.
**WHAT IS NOT FUNDED** Building projects; salaries; individuals wishing to start up a business; individuals under 18; expeditions; travel; courses outside the UK; short courses; courses not connected with fine and applied arts.
**TYPE OF GRANT** Registered charities: single donations to assist with specific projects, one-off expenses, core costs and research. Individual students: funding may be given for the duration of a course, for up to three years, payable in three term instalments to help with tuition fees or living expenses.
**RANGE OF GRANTS** Individuals: £500–£1,500; charities: £300–£2,000.
**SAMPLE GRANTS** St Paul's Art School (£23,000); Chichester Cathedral Choral Fund (£18,000); Cure Parkinson's Trust (£5,000); World Child Cancer (£1,500).
**FINANCES** *Year* 2013/14 *Income* £208,264 *Grants* £134,000 *Grants to organisations* £97,500 *Assets* £4,237,978
**TRUSTEES** Stephen Baldock; Christopher Grimwade; Paul Harriman; Andrew Blessley; Richard Inglis.
**OTHER INFORMATION** Grants were made totalling £134,000, of which £96,500 went to 30 organisations and £36,500 to individuals. Governance costs totalled £24,500.
**HOW TO APPLY** Apply in writing to the correspondent with details about your charity and the reason for requesting funding. Note, however, that the trust is not accepting applications until after July 2015 – check the trust's website for up-to-date information.
**WHO TO APPLY TO** Nicola Chrimes, Clerk to the Trustees, PO Box 169, Lewes, East Sussex BN7 9FB *Tel.* 01825 872264 *Website* www.southsquaretrust.org.uk

## ■ The W. F. Southall Trust
**CC NO** 218371 **ESTABLISHED** 1937
**WHERE FUNDING CAN BE GIVEN** UK and overseas.
**WHO CAN BENEFIT** Registered charities, especially imaginative new grassroots initiatives and smaller charities where funding will make a significant difference.
**WHAT IS FUNDED** Work of the Society of Friends; peace-making and conflict resolution; alcohol or drug abuse and penal affairs; environmental action; homelessness; community action; overseas development.
**WHAT IS NOT FUNDED** Individuals; large national charities.
**TYPE OF GRANT** Normally one-off payments.
**RANGE OF GRANTS** Up to £55,000; usually £100–£5,000.
**SAMPLE GRANTS** Yearly Meeting – Society of Friends (£55,000); Woodbrooke Quaker Study Centre (£13,000); Oxfam (£9,000); Quaker Congo Partnership, Computer Aid International and Peace Direct (£3,000 each); Responding to Conflict (£2,000).
**FINANCES** *Year* 2013/14 *Income* £279,789 *Grants* £269,225 *Grants to organisations* £269,225 *Assets* £9,410,007
**TRUSTEES** Annette Wallis; Donald Southall; Joanna Engelkamp; Mark Holtom; Claire Greaves; Daphne Maw; Richard Maw; Hannah Engelkamp.
**OTHER INFORMATION** Grants were made to 94 organisations totalling £269,000.

**HOW TO APPLY** Application forms are available from the trust's website. Further guidance on making an application is given as follows: 'When making an application, grant seekers should bear in mind the points below. We expect all applicants to complete the funding application form. Please ensure your application includes details regarding the following: your most recent annual report; projected income and expenditure for the coming year; your reserves; particular features of your costs, e.g. high transport costs in rural areas; details of other funding expected; any significant achievements and/or problems or difficulties; any 'matching funding' arrangements e.g. European Social Fund support; timetable for when the proposed work is to start and finish; applications should be accompanied by a stamped addressed envelope.'

**WHO TO APPLY TO** Margaret Rowntree, Secretary, c/o Rutters Solicitors, 2 Bimport, Shaftesbury, Dorset SP7 8AY *Tel.* 01747 852377 *Fax* 01747 851989 *email* southall@rutterslaw.co.uk *Website* wfsouthalltrust.org.uk

## ■ Southdown Trust

**CC NO** 235583   **ESTABLISHED** 1963
**WHERE FUNDING CAN BE GIVEN** UK.
**WHO CAN BENEFIT** Young people aged 17 to 26 years.
**WHAT IS FUNDED** Grants towards the education of the specified age group.
**RANGE OF GRANTS** Up to £13,000.
**SAMPLE GRANTS** No grants are given towards courses in the following subjects: law, journalism, women's studies, counselling, veterinary studies, computer/IT studies and media studies.
**FINANCES** *Year* 2013/14 *Income* £45,113 *Grants* £73,290 *Grants to organisations* £27,885 *Assets* £1,123,011
**TRUSTEES** Meriel Buxton; John Blades McBeath; Paul Kunz.
**OTHER INFORMATION** In 2013/14 grants to individuals totalled £45,500.
**HOW TO APPLY** Apply in writing to the correspondent.
**WHO TO APPLY TO** Rowlie McBeath, Trustee, Brook House, Sandford Orcas, Sherborne, Dorset DT9 4RP *email* thesouthdowntrust@gmail.com

## ■ R. H. Southern Trust

**CC NO** 1077509   **ESTABLISHED** 1999
**WHERE FUNDING CAN BE GIVEN** England; Wales; Scotland; Republic of Ireland; Australia; Belgium; India.
**WHO CAN BENEFIT** Charitable organisations.
**WHAT IS FUNDED** Education and training; people with disabilities; social welfare; the environment. The trust favours projects where the work is innovative, connected to other disciplines/bodies and has diverse application.
**TYPE OF GRANT** Mainly long term core funding and special projects.
**RANGE OF GRANTS** £1,200–£22,000
**SAMPLE GRANTS** Equal Adventure (£22,000); Motivation (£20,000); Sustainable Food Trust (£12,000); Accord – Just Change and James Gibb Stuart Trust (£10,000 each); Action Village India (£7,500); Corporate Europe Observatory (£5,000); Salt of the Earth (£2,100); Dartington Hall Trust (£1,200).
**FINANCES** *Year* 2013/14 *Income* £88,774 *Grants* £198,602 *Grants to organisations* £152,842 *Assets* £2,449,532

**TRUSTEES** Marion Wells; James Bruges; Rathbone Trust Company Ltd.
**OTHER INFORMATION** A total of 25 grants were made to organisations totalling £153,000. A further £46,000 was given to individuals and business during the year.
**HOW TO APPLY** The trust is not accepting any funding applications as their funds are fully committed for the foreseeable future.
**WHO TO APPLY TO** Marion Wells, Trustee, 23 Sydenham Road, Cotham, Bristol BS6 5SJ *Tel.* 0117 942 5834 *email* marionwells@gmail.com *Website* www.rhsoutherntrust.org.uk

## ■ The Southover Manor General Education Trust

**CC NO** 299593   **ESTABLISHED** 1988
**WHERE FUNDING CAN BE GIVEN** Sussex.
**WHO CAN BENEFIT** Schools; colleges; individuals under the age of 25.
**WHAT IS FUNDED** The trustees support the 'education of boys and girls under 25' by 'the provision of educational and recreational facilities, scholarships and awards and the purchase of books and equipment.'
**WHAT IS NOT FUNDED** No grants for people over 25 years of age. Organisations and individuals outside Sussex are not supported.
**TYPE OF GRANT** Capital costs and projects.
**RANGE OF GRANTS** Up to £20,000.
**SAMPLE GRANTS** Downlands Community School (£14,000); Chailey Heritage, Seaford Head Community College, Young Epilepsy (£10,000 each).
**FINANCES** *Year* 2013/14 *Income* £107,627 *Grants* £104,672 *Grants to organisations* £104,672 *Assets* £2,627,381
**TRUSTEES** Charles Davies-Gilbert; Chloe Teacher; Jennifer Gordon-Lennox; Clare Duffield; John Wakely; John Farmer; Wenda Bradley; Jennie Peel; Claire Pool.
**OTHER INFORMATION** Grants were made to 25 organisations and included money for the following projects: library facilities, including books and furniture; building works; IT and other equipment; playground and playing field equipment; sports equipment; outdoor learning equipment.
**HOW TO APPLY** Apply in writing to the correspondent. The trustees meet twice a year, or more frequently if necessary, to approve grants.
**WHO TO APPLY TO** Mrs J. Foot, The Secretary to the Trustees, Old Vicarage Cottage, Newhaven Road, Iford, Lewes, East Sussex BN7 3PL *email* southovermanor@btinternet.com

## ■ The Sovereign Health Care Charitable Trust

**CC NO** 1079024   **ESTABLISHED** 1955
**WHERE FUNDING CAN BE GIVEN** Bradford and the surrounding area (West Yorkshire).
**WHO CAN BENEFIT** Local charities; voluntary organisations; community groups; national health-related charities that benefit people in the area.
**WHAT IS FUNDED** The health and well-being of people in Bradford. The guidelines, which are available to download from the website, state the following: 'In terms of specific diseases and conditions, the charitable trust gives priority to those that are particularly prevalent in Bradford, especially: heart disease; chest/lung disease; lung cancer; stroke; diabetes; breast cancer;

bowel cancer; prostate cancer; and oral cancer. Other priorities are: hospitals and hospices, disease prevention, healthy lifestyle and health promotion; deprivation, poverty or homelessness; disability; and mental health. The trust will also consider applications concerned with carers and with education and training where it relates to one of the other priority areas.'

**WHAT IS NOT FUNDED** Appeals from local organisations and groups outside the area outside Bradford and West Yorkshire; individuals; sponsorship. The trust states that large medical research initiatives where the trust's contribution would not be significant are unlikely to be a high priority.

**TYPE OF GRANT** Buildings; core costs; one-off grants; projects; research; running costs.

**RANGE OF GRANTS** Grants are usually 'a few thousand pounds at most'. Excluding one exceptional grant, the average grant in 2014 was around £2,700.

**SAMPLE GRANTS** Marie Curie Hospice Bradford (£317,500); Sue Ryder Manorlands Hospice (£20,000); Yorkshire Air Ambulance (£15,000); West Yorkshire Medic Response Team (£10,000); Prostate Cancer UK (£7,500); Shipley Stroke Group (£6,000); Muslim Women's Council (£5,000); St Christopher's Family Project (£4,000); DEC Ebola Crisis Appeal (£3,000); Sharing Voices Bradford (£2,500); Hearing Dogs for Deaf People (£2,000); Fire Fighters Charity (£1,500); Idle Exercisers (£1,000).

**FINANCES** Year 2014 Income £828,174 Grants £782,711 Grants to organisations £782,711 Assets £252,289

**TRUSTEES** Mark Hudson; Michael Austin; Dennis Child; Michael Bower; Russ Piper; Kate Robb-Webb; Robert Dugdale; Stewart Cummings.

**OTHER INFORMATION** A total of 186 grants were made during the year and included one exceptional grant to Marie Curie Bradford Hospice as part of a contribution of nearly £1 million for a building repair and refurbishment.

**HOW TO APPLY** Full guidelines are available to download from the website. The trust states 'The charitable trust is keen not to burden the organisations it supports with too much paper work and jumping through hoops. On the other hand, just sending a newsletter in the hope that this will trigger a cheque in return will not succeed. The trustees needs to know what you do, what you want money for, how much it's going to cost and, when appropriate, how you'll know that the money has made a difference. Facts and figures are important how many people will be helped, for instance. There is no application form; just write to the trust with the appropriate information. We will ask for additional information if we feel it necessary; in these cases, we'll assume that you don't want to proceed with the application if we haven't heard back from you within six weeks. The trustees meet six times a year. From the trust receiving an application to the applicant receiving a cheque (or not) usually takes about two or three months. In the case of disasters and emergencies the trust may be able to act much more quickly. The trust notifies all applicants about the outcome of their request.'

**WHO TO APPLY TO** The Secretary, Sovereign Health Care, Royal Standard House, 26 Manningham Lane, Bradford, West Yorkshire BD1 3DN Tel. 01274 729472 email charity@sovereignhealthcare.co.uk Website www.sovereignhealthcare.co.uk/charitable-trust

## ■ Spar Charitable Fund

**CC NO** 236252　　**ESTABLISHED** 1964
**WHERE FUNDING CAN BE GIVEN** UK.
**WHO CAN BENEFIT** Registered charities, mostly well-known national organisations.
**WHAT IS FUNDED** General charitable purposes, with some preference for projects benefitting young people.
**SAMPLE GRANTS** Spar Benevolent Fund (£65,000); Philippines Appeal (£10,000); NSPCC (£8,500); and Retail Industry (£6,600).
**FINANCES** Year 2013/14 Income £48,616 Grants £90,092 Grants to organisations £90,092 Assets £871,497
**TRUSTEE** The National Guild of Spar Ltd.
**HOW TO APPLY** Appeals may be made in writing to the correspondent.
**WHO TO APPLY TO** Philip Marchant, Correspondent, Spar (UK) Ltd, Hygeia Building, 66–68 College Road, Harrow, Middlesex HA1 1BE Tel. 020 8426 3700 email philip.marchant@spar.co.uk

## ■ Sparks Charity (Sport Aiding Medical Research For Kids)

**CC NO** 1003825　　**ESTABLISHED** 1991
**WHERE FUNDING CAN BE GIVEN** UK.
**WHO CAN BENEFIT** Organisations conducting research at UK hospitals and universities. The charity's website states: 'We wish to foster and promote a culture of collaboration in children's health research and will favour projects where there is a strong partnership of basic scientists with clinical academics/consultants and a clear route to potential clinical application.'
**WHAT IS FUNDED** Medical research to enable children to be born healthy and to stay healthy. As part of its research strategy for 2015 to 2020, the charity has identified two priority areas where targeted investment of its funds could have a beneficial impact on the health of children and pregnant women; these are rare diseases and premature birth. Sparks will also continue to fund research into a wide range of medical conditions affecting children's health including pregnancy and birth, first months of life, infancy and early childhood.
**WHAT IS NOT FUNDED** See the website for details of exclusions applicable to the various grants programmes
**TYPE OF GRANT** Depending on available funds, over the five years of its research strategy, the charity aims to offer project grants, innovation grants, PhD studentships, clinical research training fellowships and programme grants.
**SAMPLE GRANTS** University of Bristol (£297,500 in two grants); St Michael's Hospital – Bristol (£278,000); UCL Institute of Child Health (£202,500 in two grants); Imperial Garden London (£154,000); University of California/Kingston University (£81,000); Brunel University (£30,500 in two grants); Queen Victoria Hospital (£4,600); Manchester University (£1,800 through the Rare Diseases Conference Fund).
**FINANCES** Year 2013/14 Income £4,107,087 Grants £1,441,388 Grants to organisations £1,441,388 Assets £559,991
**TRUSTEES** Roger Uttley; Julian Wilkinson; Jonathon Britton; Guy Gregory; David Orr; Frank van den Bosch; Robert Booker; Martin Jepson; Dr Simon Newell; Timothy Pethybridge; Helen Fridell; Prof. Donald Peebles.
**OTHER INFORMATION** The grant total above refers to new awards made during the year.

**HOW TO APPLY** Guidelines and applications information for the charity's grants programmes can be found on the website.

**WHO TO APPLY TO** Zillah Bingley, Chief Executive, 6th Floor, Westminster Tower, 3 Albert Embankment, London SE1 7SP *Tel.* 020 7091 7750 *email* info@sparks.org.uk *Website* www.sparks.org.uk

## ■ Sparquote Limited

**CC NO** 286232  **ESTABLISHED** 1982
**WHERE FUNDING CAN BE GIVEN** England and Wales.
**WHO CAN BENEFIT** Charitable organisations of Jewish community.
**WHAT IS FUNDED** General charitable purposes, advancement of religion, relief of sickness and poverty, education and training – all with focus on Jewish community.
**TYPE OF GRANT** Grants to organisations.
**RANGE OF GRANTS** Up to £40,000.
**SAMPLE GRANTS** Grant beneficiaries in previous years have included: The Wlodowa Charity and Rehabilitation Trust (£41,000); the Telz Academy Trust (£30,000); British Friends of Mosdos Tchernobyl (£20,000); the Society of Friends of the Torah (£19,000); the Gevurath Ari Torah Trust (£15,000); Beis Nadvorna Charitable Trust (£10,000); the Edgware Foundation and Penshurst Corporation Limited (£5,000 each); Gateshead Institute for Rabbinical Studies (£3,500); Dina Perelman Trust Limited (£1,800); and American Friends (£1,000).
**FINANCES** *Year* 2013/14 *Income* £499,285 *Grants* £526,977 *Grants to organisations* £526,977 *Assets* £5,781,519
**TRUSTEES** David Reichmann; Dov Reichmann; Anne-Mette Reichmann.
**OTHER INFORMATION** A list of beneficiaries for 2013/14 is available upon request.
**HOW TO APPLY** Apply in writing to the correspondent.
**WHO TO APPLY TO** Anne-Mette Reichman, Trustee, Sparquote Limited, Cavendish House, 369 Burnt Oak Broadway, Edgware, Middlesex HA8 4AW

## ■ The Spear Charitable Trust

**CC NO** 1041568  **ESTABLISHED** 1962
**WHERE FUNDING CAN BE GIVEN** UK.
**WHO CAN BENEFIT** Individuals and organisations, particularly employees and former employees of J W Spear and Sons plc, their families and dependants.
**WHAT IS FUNDED** Welfare of employees and former employees of J W Spear and Sons plc, their families and dependants; also general charitable purposes, with some preference for animal welfare, the environment and health.
**WHAT IS NOT FUNDED** Appeals from individuals are not considered.
**SAMPLE GRANTS** The Woodland Trust (£30,000); Slide into Action (£27,000); Leukaemia and Lymphoma Research (£5,000); Blue Card Inc. (£4,000); Barn Owl Trust, National Osteoporosis Society (£2,500); Interact Worldwide, St Mungo's, War Memorials Trust, Wildfowl and Wetlands Trust (£2,000 each); Demelza House Children's Hospice, Re-Cycle (£1,000); International Childcare Trust (£500).
**FINANCES** *Year* 2013 *Income* £176,536 *Grants* £1,200,594 *Grants to organisations* £1,200,594 *Assets* £4,451,174
**TRUSTEES** Philip Harris; Francis Spear; Hazel Spear; Nigel Gooch.

**OTHER INFORMATION** As well as grants to organisations, former employees of J W Spear and Sons plc and their families and dependants received £13,400 in 2013.
**HOW TO APPLY** Apply in writing to the correspondent. The trustees state in their annual report that they will make grants without a formal application, but they encourage organisations to provide feedback on how grants are used. Feedback will be used for monitoring the quality of grants and will form the basis of assessment for any further applications.
**WHO TO APPLY TO** Hazel Spear, Secretary, Roughground House, Beggarmans Lane, Old Hall Green, Ware, Hertfordshire SG11 1HB *Tel.* 01920 823071

## ■ Spears-Stutz Charitable Trust

**CC NO** 225491  **ESTABLISHED** 1964
**WHERE FUNDING CAN BE GIVEN** Worldwide.
**WHO CAN BENEFIT** Registered charities.
**WHAT IS FUNDED** General charitable purposes; relief of poverty; Jewish causes; museums and art organisations.
**RANGE OF GRANTS** £250–£130,000
**SAMPLE GRANTS** West Green Opera House Ltd (£130,000); Opera Rara Ltd (£70,000); Plan UK (£45,000); Historic Royal Palaces (£25,000); Oxfam, Seeing Dogs, Stonewall Equality Ltd, Woman Kind (£10,000 each); Patrick School (£3,500); Birmingham Royal Ballet (£2,000); American Cancer Foundation, WYNC New York Public Radio (£500 each).
**FINANCES** *Year* 2013/14 *Income* £109,129 *Grants* £370,898 *Grants to organisations* £370,898 *Assets* £4,648,667
**TRUSTEES** Glenn Hurstfield; Jonathan Spears.
**OTHER INFORMATION** Grants were made to 23 organisations.
**HOW TO APPLY** Apply in writing to the correspondent.
**WHO TO APPLY TO** The Trustees, c/o Berkeley Law, 4th Floor, 19 Berkeley Street, London W1J 8ED *Tel.* 020 7399 0930

## ■ The Worshipful Company of Spectacle Makers' Charity

**CC NO** 1072172  **ESTABLISHED** 1998
**WHERE FUNDING CAN BE GIVEN** Worldwide.
**WHO CAN BENEFIT** Registered charities.
**WHAT IS FUNDED** Work concerned with visual impairments, with a preference for national or international rather than local causes.
**WHAT IS NOT FUNDED** Individuals.
**TYPE OF GRANT** Specific projects, not general funds.
**SAMPLE GRANTS** British Red Cross; The Treloar Trust; 358 Squadron; Blind in Business; British Blind Sport; BWBF; WCHCP; Lord Mayor's Appeal; Monday Moves; Vision 4 Children; British Council.
**FINANCES** *Year* 2013/14 *Income* £67,059 *Grants* £55,625 *Grants to organisations* £55,625 *Assets* £741,344
**TRUSTEES** Elizabeth Shilling; James Osborne; Nigel Andrew; Michael Rudd; John Breeze; Felicity Harding.
**OTHER INFORMATION** The charity's accounts list a number of grant beneficiaries, without the grant amounts.
**HOW TO APPLY** Apply in writing to the correspondent including details of how the grant will be used, and a copy of the latest audited accounts. Refer to full application guidance on the charity's website. Note: the trustees meet in May and

November, so applications for grants should be received by mid-April and mid-October.
**WHO TO APPLY TO** John Salmon, Clerk, Apothecaries Hall, Blackfriars Lane, London EC4V 6EL *Tel.* 020 7236 2932 *email* clerk@spectaclemakers.com *Website* www.spectaclemakers.com

## ■ The Jessie Spencer Trust
**CC NO** 219289  **ESTABLISHED** 1962
**WHERE FUNDING CAN BE GIVEN** UK, with a preference for Nottinghamshire.
**WHO CAN BENEFIT** Registered charities, with a preference for those in the East Midlands.
**WHAT IS FUNDED** General charitable purposes.
**WHAT IS NOT FUNDED** Grants are rarely made for endowment appeals, loans, sponsorship or fundraising events, campaigning and projects that are primarily political or for the repair of parish churches outside Nottinghamshire. The trust's grant-making policy can be found on its website.
**TYPE OF GRANT** Grants are made towards both capital and revenue expenditure. They can be recurrent for up to ten years.
**RANGE OF GRANTS** Generally £500–£5,000.
**SAMPLE GRANTS** Nottingham Historic Churches Trust (£10,000); Nottingham High School Bursary Fund, Rainbows Children's Hospice (£5,000 each); Alzheimer's Research UK (£2,000); 1st Carlton-in-Lindrick Scout Group, SSAFA (£1,000 each); Deafblind UK, Independent Age, Scope, Starlight Children's Foundation, The Koestler Trust (£500 each).
**FINANCES** *Year* 2013/14 *Income* £141,611 *Grants* £97,675 *Grants to organisations* £97,675 *Assets* £4,149,568
**TRUSTEES** Victor Semmens; B. Mitchell; David Wild; Andrew Tiplady; Helen Lee.
**OTHER INFORMATION** One grant totalling £675 was given to an individual.
**HOW TO APPLY** Apply in writing to the correspondent, including an outline of the project and the latest set of formal accounts. Applications should be received by 20 January, 20 April, 20 July or 20 October each year for consideration at trustee meetings in March, June, September and December respectively. Guidance for applications can be found on the trust's website.
**WHO TO APPLY TO** John Thompson, Correspondent, c/o 4 Walsingham Drive, Corby Glen, Grantham, Lincolnshire NG33 4TA *Tel.* 01476 552429 *email* jessiespencer@btinternet.com *Website* www.jessiespencertrust.org.uk

## ■ The Spero Foundation
**CC NO** 1136810  **ESTABLISHED** 2010
**WHERE FUNDING CAN BE GIVEN** UK and overseas
**WHO CAN BENEFIT** Organisations and individuals.
**WHAT IS FUNDED** General charitable purposes; education and training; health; community development; sports and recreation; arts and heritage.
**SAMPLE GRANTS** Details were not available.
**FINANCES** *Year* 2012/13 *Income* £0 *Grants* £120,000 *Grants to organisations* £120,000
**TRUSTEES** Andrew Peggie; Brian Padgett; Joanna Landau; Eden Landau; Jonathan Emmutt.
**OTHER INFORMATION** Due to the trust's low income in 2012/13, only basic financial information was available from the Charity Commission. The grant total is an estimation based on this information.
**HOW TO APPLY** Apply in writing to the correspondent.
**WHO TO APPLY TO** Sarah Hunt, 63 Grosvenor Street, London W1K 3JG *Tel.* 020 7499 1857

## ■ The Ralph and Irma Sperring Charity
**CC NO** 1048101  **ESTABLISHED** 1995
**WHERE FUNDING CAN BE GIVEN** The parishes situated within a five-mile radius of the church of St John the Baptist, Midsomer Norton.
**WHO CAN BENEFIT** Organisations and individuals in the beneficial area.
**WHAT IS FUNDED** Grants are given to: provide or assist with the provision of residential accommodation; for the relief of people who are older, have disabilities or are in need; assist with the establishment of village halls, recreation grounds, charitable sports grounds and playing fields; further the religious or other charitable work of the Anglican churches in the parishes; support hospitals and their leagues of friends; further education of children and young people at educational institutions.
**SAMPLE GRANTS** Unfortunately, a list of beneficiaries was not available.
**FINANCES** *Year* 2013/14 *Income* £218,232 *Grants* £111,280 *Grants to organisations* £111,280 *Assets* £6,227,419
**TRUSTEES** Revd Christopher Chiplin; Ted Hallam; Sally Blanning; Kenneth Saunders; Noreen Busby; Dr John Haxell.
**HOW TO APPLY** Applications should be made in writing to the correspondent.
**WHO TO APPLY TO** Ted Hallam, Trustee, Thatcher and Hallam Solicitors, Island House, Midsomer Norton, Radstock BA3 2HJ *Tel.* 01761 414646 *email* sperringcharity@gmail.com

## ■ The Spielman Charitable Trust
**CC NO** 278306  **ESTABLISHED** 1979
**WHERE FUNDING CAN BE GIVEN** Bristol and the surrounding area.
**WHO CAN BENEFIT** Charities and voluntary organisations.
**WHAT IS FUNDED** General charitable purposes; children and young people; older people; people with disabilities; arts and culture; social welfare; the promotion of health, especially oncology and palliative care; economic and community development.
**RANGE OF GRANTS** Up to £25,000.
**SAMPLE GRANTS** Royal Welsh College of Music and Drama (£25,000); Bristol Children's Help Society, The Wheels Project and Unseen (£15,000 each); NSPCC (£10,000); The Colston Society and Friends of Bristol Oncology (£5,000 each).
**FINANCES** *Year* 2013/14 *Income* £240,406 *Grants* £237,838 *Grants to organisations* £237,838 *Assets* £5,782,918
**TRUSTEES** C. Moorsom; Karen Hann; P. Cooper.
**OTHER INFORMATION** Donations of less than £5,000 were made to 44 other charities.
**HOW TO APPLY** Apply in writing to the correspondent.
**WHO TO APPLY TO** June Moody, Correspondent, 17 St Augustine's Parade, Bristol BS1 4UL *Tel.* 0117 929 1929 *email* g-s.moody@btconnect.com

## ■ Split Infinitive Trust

**CC NO** 1110380  **ESTABLISHED** 2005
**WHERE FUNDING CAN BE GIVEN** UK, with a preference for Yorkshire.
**WHO CAN BENEFIT** Individuals; projects by companies and organisations with charitable status.
**WHAT IS FUNDED** Arts and arts education; the alleviation of sickness, poverty, hardship and distress.
**WHAT IS NOT FUNDED** Grants for general running costs; projects outside the UK; charities seeking funds for their own grant disbursement. Note that 'repeat grants are rare and although previous recipients are welcome to re-apply, the fact of a previous grant is no guarantee of a future one'.
**TYPE OF GRANT** Grants for up to three years to individuals and to organisations for specific projects.
**RANGE OF GRANTS** Generally between £250 and £750.
**SAMPLE GRANTS** Dark Horse, Interact, Animated objects and MST Productions (£1,000 each).
**FINANCES** Year 2013/14 Income £30,916 Grants £46,237 Grants to organisations £46,237 Assets £65,656
**TRUSTEES** Alan Ayckbourn; Heather Stoney; Paul Allen; Neil Adleman; Katherine Dunn-Mines.
**OTHER INFORMATION** Grants of £1,000 were given to four individuals (the number of individual grants below £1,000 was not specified). The trust generally prefers not to be acknowledged in programmes/brochures/sponsor lists or other materials produced by grant recipients. 'Grants made are solely at the trustees' discretion and correspondence regarding their decisions will not be entered into. The trust does not have full-time staff or a permanent office for a phone line to connect to. Email or post is therefore the easiest route for communication.'
**HOW TO APPLY** Organisations are asked to complete an application form and provide a project plan and a detailed budget breakdown (there is a separate application form and requirements for individuals). Application forms can be found on the trust's website. The trustees meet quarterly, normally at the end of March, June, September and December. The website also states that 'there is no fixed cut-off date but generally any applications received up to the 10th day in the month of a meeting will definitely be able to be considered; later arrivals may be rolled over into the following quarter'.
**WHO TO APPLY TO** Heather Stoney, Trustee, PO BOX 409, Scarborough YO11 9AJ email splitinfin@haydonning.co.uk Website www.splitinfinitivetrust.co.uk

## ■ The Spoore, Merry and Rixman Foundation

**CC NO** 309040  **ESTABLISHED** 1958
**WHERE FUNDING CAN BE GIVEN** The (pre-1974) borough of Maidenhead and the ancient parish of Bray, not the whole of Royal Borough of Windsor and Maidenhead.
**WHO CAN BENEFIT** Charitable organisations and individuals.
**WHAT IS FUNDED** Education and training; arts and culture; children and young people.
**WHAT IS NOT FUNDED** Deals only with the (pre-1974) borough of Maidenhead and the ancient parish of Bray.
**SAMPLE GRANTS** A list of beneficiaries was not included in the latest set of accounts.
**FINANCES** Year 2013 Income £901,905 Grants £297,206 Grants to organisations £137,885 Assets £10,943,058
**TRUSTEES** Grahame Fisher; Ann Redgrave; Dorothy Kemp; Leo Walters; Tony Thomas; David Coppinger; Asghar Majeed; Barbara Wielechowski; Philip Love; The Mayor Of The Royal Borough.
**OTHER INFORMATION** Grants totalled £297,000, of which 56 grants totalling £138,000 were given to organisations and £159,000 to 129 individuals.
**HOW TO APPLY** Application forms are available to download, together with guidelines and criteria, on the foundation's website. Applications are considered in January, April, July and October.
**WHO TO APPLY TO** Helen MacDiarmid, Correspondent, PO Box 4229, Slough SL1 0QZ email clerk@smrfmaidenhead.org Website www.smrfmaidenhead.org.uk

## ■ Sported Foundation

**CC NO** 1123313  **ESTABLISHED** 2008
**WHERE FUNDING CAN BE GIVEN** UK.
**WHO CAN BENEFIT** Community organisations that work with young people, aged between 11 and 25, in disadvantaged areas.
**WHAT IS FUNDED** Sports and social welfare.
**WHAT IS NOT FUNDED** Capital costs, such as building facilities; school based projects.
**RANGE OF GRANTS** Usually up to £10,000, but can be higher.
**SAMPLE GRANTS** The Dracaena Centre Ltd (£25,000); Community Action Through Sport (£16,000); Trelya and Grapevine (£15,000 each); Coventry Boys' Club (£14,000); Salle Ursa Fencing Club (£7,000); Longford Short Football Project (£4,000); and The Grangers Club (£1,500).
**FINANCES** Year 2013 Income £764,164 Grants £1,475,807 Grants to organisations £1,475,807 Assets £3,340,503
**TRUSTEES** Sir Keith Mills; Lady Maureen Mills; Alexander Mills; Richard Powles; Dermot Heffernan; Alan Pascoe; Baroness Susan Campbell; Nigel Keen.
**HOW TO APPLY** Application forms and full criteria and guidelines for each region are available online at the foundation's website.
**WHO TO APPLY TO** Chris Grant, 8th Floor, 20 St James's Street, London SW1A 1ES Tel. 020 7389 1907 email info@sported.org.uk Website www.sported.org.uk

## ■ Rosalyn and Nicholas Springer Charitable Trust

**CC NO** 1062239  **ESTABLISHED** 1997
**WHERE FUNDING CAN BE GIVEN** UK and Israel.
**WHO CAN BENEFIT** Organisations, particularly those supporting Jewish people; individuals.
**WHAT IS FUNDED** The promotion of welfare, education and personal development, particularly amongst the Jewish community. Grants are made in the following categories: medical, health and sickness; education and training; arts and culture; religious activities; relief of poverty; general charitable purposes.
**RANGE OF GRANTS** Up to £25,000, but mostly £1,000 or less.
**SAMPLE GRANTS** WIZO (£10,800); UJIA (£10,000); Jewish Women's Aid (£4,500); Belsize Square Synagogue, Chicken Shed Theatre Trust (£1,500 each); World Jewish Relief (£1,300);

Cystic Fibrosis Trust, Holocaust Education Trust, Prostate Cancer UK (£1,000 each); British Friends of Haifa University, North London Hospice, Philharmonia Orchestra (£500 each); Whizz-Kidz (£250); The Harington Scheme (£100); The Rosalyn and Nicholas Charity (£50).
**FINANCES** Year 2013/14 Income £125,016 Grants £115,162 Grants to organisations £115,162 Assets £40,794
**TRUSTEES** Rosalyn Springer; Nicholas Springer.
**OTHER INFORMATION** Grants were made to 65 organisations.
**HOW TO APPLY** Do not apply to this trust. The trust has previously stated that it only supports organisations it is already in contact with. 99% of unsolicited applications are unsuccessful and because of the volume it receives, the trust is unable to reply to such letters. It would therefore be unadvisable to apply.
**WHO TO APPLY TO** Nicholas Springer, Trustee, 15 Park Village West, London NW1 4AE Tel. 020 7253 7272

## ■ Springrule Limited
**CC NO** 802561   **ESTABLISHED** 1992
**WHERE FUNDING CAN BE GIVEN** England and Wales.
**WHO CAN BENEFIT** Jewish organisations.
**WHAT IS FUNDED** Advancement of the Orthodox Jewish faith and the relief of poverty.
**TYPE OF GRANT** One-off grants to organisations.
**SAMPLE GRANTS Previous beneficiaries have included:** Beis Yaakov Institutions, Friends of Horim and Torah Vechesed (£25,000 each); and Yad Eliezer (£5,000).
**FINANCES** Year 2013/14 Income £69,381 Grants £839,500 Grants to organisations £839,500 Assets -£4,277,495
**TRUSTEES** Malka Jacober; Robert Nevies; Jacque Monderer; Rivka Nevies.
**HOW TO APPLY** Apply in writing to the correspondent.
**WHO TO APPLY TO** R. Nevies, Trustee, 45 Cheyne Walk, London NW4 3QH

## ■ The Spurrell Charitable Trust
**CC NO** 267287   **ESTABLISHED** 1960
**WHERE FUNDING CAN BE GIVEN** UK, with some preference for Norfolk. Overseas.
**WHO CAN BENEFIT** Registered charities.
**WHAT IS FUNDED** General charitable purposes; overseas aid; children and young people; older people; people with disabilities.
**WHAT IS NOT FUNDED** Individuals.
**RANGE OF GRANTS** Up to £7,500, on average around £1,000.
**SAMPLE GRANTS** Merlin (£20,000); Air Ambulance (£7,200); Parkinson's UK (£4,500); Big C Appeal (£2,400); Brain and Spine Foundation, Bessingham PCC and Alzheimer's Research Trust (£1,200 each); Church Urban Fund, Clergy Orphan Corporation and Cued Speech Association UK (£600 each); Felbrigg Village Hall and Sheringham Salvation Army Band (£300 each).
**FINANCES** Year 2013/14 Income £64,575 Grants £91,900 Grants to organisations £91,900 Assets £2,449,462
**TRUSTEES** Ingeburg Spurrell; Martyn Spurrell; Christopher Spurrell.
**HOW TO APPLY** Apply in writing to the correspondent. Trustees consider applications in October of each year.
**WHO TO APPLY TO** Martyn Spurrell, Trustee, 78 Wendover Road, Aylesbury HP21 9NJ Tel. 01296 420113 email spurrelltrust@icloud.com

## ■ The Geoff and Fiona Squire Foundation
**CC NO** 1085553   **ESTABLISHED** 2001
**WHERE FUNDING CAN BE GIVEN** UK.
**WHO CAN BENEFIT** Registered charities.
**WHAT IS FUNDED** General charitable purposes, particularly medicine, education, disability and the welfare and healthcare of children.
**RANGE OF GRANTS** £500–£200,000
**SAMPLE GRANTS** Stars Appeal – Salisbury District Hospital (£200,000); Salisbury Cathedral (£150,000); SENSE (£100,000); Newlife Foundation for Disabled Children (£30,000); Canine Partners (£24,500); Music for Youth (£7,500); Jubilee Sailing Trust (£3,000); Event Mobility Charitable Trust (£500).
**FINANCES** Year 2013/14 Income £190,421 Grants £1,234,904 Grants to organisations £1,234,904 Assets £10,365,464
**TRUSTEES** Geoff Squire; Fiona Squire; B. Peerless.
**OTHER INFORMATION** Grants were made to 31 charities during the year.
**HOW TO APPLY** The trust has previously stated: 'the trustees have in place a well-established donations policy and we do not therefore encourage unsolicited grant applications, not least because they take time and expense to deal with properly.'
**WHO TO APPLY TO** Fiona Squire, Trustee, The Walton Canonry, 69 The Close, Salisbury, Wiltshire SP1 2EN

## ■ The Stanley Foundation Ltd
**CC NO** 206866   **ESTABLISHED** 1962
**WHERE FUNDING CAN BE GIVEN** UK.
**WHO CAN BENEFIT** Charitable organisations.
**WHAT IS FUNDED** Education and training; community and economic development; arts and culture; medical care and research.
**WHAT IS NOT FUNDED** Individuals.
**RANGE OF GRANTS** £250–£40,000
**SAMPLE GRANTS** Rodney Aldridge Charitable Trust (£40,000); Tate Gallery (£15,000); Tusk (£14,000); Kensington and Chelsea Foundation and Newbury and District Agricultural Society (£13,000 each); British School in Rome (£7,000); Multiple Sclerosis Society and Naomi House (£4,000 each); Imperial College and Institute of Contemporary Art (£2,500 each); Afghanaid and Berkshire Churches Trust (£1,000 each); Newbury Spring Festival (£250).
**FINANCES** Year 2013/14 Income £85,804 Grants £252,385 Grants to organisations £252,385 Assets £3,194,907
**TRUSTEES** Elodie Stanley; Nicholas Stanley; Shaun Stanley; John Raymond; Patrick Hall; Georgina Stanley; Stephen Hall; Charles Stanley.
**OTHER INFORMATION** Grants were made to 55 organisations totalling £252,500.
**HOW TO APPLY** Apply in writing to the correspondent.
**WHO TO APPLY TO** Nicholas Stanley, Trustee, N. C. Morris and Co., 1 Montpelier Street, London SW7 1EX email nick@meristan.com

## ■ The Staples Trust
CC NO 1010656  ESTABLISHED 1992
WHERE FUNDING CAN BE GIVEN UK and overseas.
WHO CAN BENEFIT Charities working in the fields of international development, environment and women's issues organisations benefitting victims of abuse and domestic violence.
WHAT IS FUNDED Gender issues (domestic violence, women's rights and gender studies); overseas projects which support the rights of indigenous people; charities defending human rights and civil liberties; The Frankopan Fund – small grants to allow gifted Croatian students to further their studies (there specific priorities and guidelines for this fund, which are available from the website). The trustees also have an interest in supporting local charities in Oxfordshire.
WHAT IS NOT FUNDED Normally, no grants are given to individuals.
TYPE OF GRANT One-off and recurring for up to three years.
SAMPLE GRANTS University of Cambridge – Jesus College (£1 million); Dragon School Trust Ltd (£500,000); Summer Fields School (£100,000); Resurgence (£17,000); Latin American Mining Monitoring Programme – LAMMP, Rights Action and Women's Sport and Fitness Foundation (£15,000 each); Ashden, Esther Benjamins Trust and Royal Society of Literature (£5,000 each); Oxfam (£3,000); University of Rijeka – Academy of Applied Arts (£1,700).
FINANCES Year 2013/14 Income £505,146 Grants £1,727,670 Grants to organisations £1,727,670 Assets £13,091,247
TRUSTEES Jessica Frankopan; Peter Frankopan; James Sainsbury; Judith Portrait.
OTHER INFORMATION The trust is one of the Sainsbury Family Charitable Trusts which share a common administration. The grant total above refers to grants approved in 2013/14. During the year a total of 30 grants were approved in the following categories: General (£1.6 million in ten grants); Human rights – environment (£37,000 in three grants); Human rights – overseas development (£20,000 in two grants); Frankopan Fund (£19,000 in 14 grants); Human rights – gender (£15,000 in one grant).
HOW TO APPLY See the guidance for applicants section in the entry for the Sainsbury Family Charitable Trusts. A single application will be considered for support by all the trusts in the group. However, for this, as for many of the family trusts, 'proposals are generally invited by the trustees or initiated at their request. Unsolicited applications are discouraged and are unlikely to be successful, even if they fall within an area in which the trustees are interested'.
WHO TO APPLY TO Alan Bookbinder, Director, The Peak, 5 Wilton Road, London SW1V 1AP Tel. 020 7410 0330 Fax 020 7410 0332 Website www.sfct.org.uk

## ■ The Star Charitable Trust
CC NO 266695  ESTABLISHED 1974
WHERE FUNDING CAN BE GIVEN UK.
WHO CAN BENEFIT Charitable organisations.
WHAT IS FUNDED General charitable purposes.
SAMPLE GRANTS A list of grants was not available.
FINANCES Year 2013/14 Income £5,165 Grants £40,000 Grants to organisations £40,000
TRUSTEES D. A. Rosen; David Taglight.
OTHER INFORMATION Due to low income the trust was not required to submit its accounts. The trust had an overall expenditure of nearly £45,000 and it is likely that grants amounted to at least £40,000.
HOW TO APPLY Applications may be made in writing to the correspondent.
WHO TO APPLY TO The Trustees, Suite A, 2nd Floor, 15 Kean Street, London WC2B 4AZ email daniel@starcapventures.com

## ■ The Peter Stebbings Memorial Charity
CC NO 274862  ESTABLISHED 1977
WHERE FUNDING CAN BE GIVEN UK, with a preference for London, and financially developing countries.
WHO CAN BENEFIT Registered charities.
WHAT IS FUNDED UK charities are supported in the areas of: medical research and care; social welfare; homelessness; hospices; mental health/counselling; drug and alcohol therapeutic support; offender support; community regeneration; vulnerable families, women and children; the promotion of human rights. Overseas charities are supported in the areas of: education; basic skills and tools; health; sustainability; micro finance; the promotion of human rights.
WHAT IS NOT FUNDED Individuals; large national or international charities; animal welfare; publications and journals (unless as part of a supported project); general appeals; any charity whose beneficiaries are restricted to particular faiths; educational institutions, unless for a particular project the trustees wish to support; arts organisations, unless there is a strong social welfare focus to the work (e.g. community arts projects).
TYPE OF GRANT Project costs, although core costs will be considered for charities known to the trustees.
RANGE OF GRANTS Up to £100,000.
SAMPLE GRANTS Liver Group (£89,500); Royal Marsden Hospital Project (£75,000); The Irene Taylor Trust (£20,000); Community Housing and Therapy – CHT (£15,000); Newborns Vietnam (£12,500); Monte San Martino Trust and Westway Community Transport (£10,000 each); Bishop Simeon Trust and Karuna Trust (£5,000 each); Comrades of Children Overseas – COCO (£2,200).
FINANCES Year 2013/14 Income £246,972 Grants £379,328 Grants to organisations £379,328 Assets £8,983,090
TRUSTEES Andrew Stebbings; Nicholas Cosin; Jennifer Clifford.
OTHER INFORMATION Grants were made to 33 organisations totalling £379,500.
HOW TO APPLY An application form is available from the charity's website.
WHO TO APPLY TO Andrew Stebbings, Trustee, 45 Cadogan Gardens, London SW3 2AQ Tel. 020 7591 3333 email charitymanager@pglaw.co.uk Website peterstebbingsmemorialcharity.org

## ■ The Steel Charitable Trust
CC NO 272384  ESTABLISHED 1976
WHERE FUNDING CAN BE GIVEN Mainly UK with 30% of all grants made to organisations in the Luton and Bedfordshire areas.
WHO CAN BENEFIT Registered charities.
WHAT IS FUNDED General charitable purposes. In practice, the trust focuses on the following five areas: arts and heritage; education;

environment; health; social or economic disadvantage.
**WHAT IS NOT FUNDED** Charities not registered in the UK; expeditions; individuals; political parties; the promotion of religion. Organisations may not re-apply within 12 months.
**TYPE OF GRANT** Mostly one-off grants; capital and other project costs; core costs.
**RANGE OF GRANTS** Mostly £1,000 to £5,000; occasionally larger.
**SAMPLE GRANTS** Youthscape (£100,000); Cancer Research UK (£25,000); The Chelsea Physic Garden Company (£20,000); SSAFA (£15,000); The People's Dispensary for Sick Animals (£10,000); Board of Trustees of the Royal Botanic Garden Edinburgh (£6,000); Twickenham Choral Society (£5,000); Salto Gymnastics Club (£3,000); Autism Bedfordshire and Luton Music Club (£2,500 each); Exmoor Search and Rescue Team, Houghton Regis Baptist Church and Richmond YMCA (£2,000 each); Exeter Hebrew Congregation (£1,000).
**FINANCES** Year 2013/14 Income £1,136,275 Grants £1,090,086 Grants to organisations £1,090,086 Assets £26,025,856
**TRUSTEES** Nicholas Wright; John Childs, Chair; John Maddox; Anthony Hawkins; Wendy Bailey; Dr Mary Briggs; Philip Lawford.
**OTHER INFORMATION** A total of 141 grants were made during the year, of which 130, totalling more than £1 million, were to charities registered in England and Wales.
**HOW TO APPLY** All applicants must complete the online application form. Applications submitted by post will not be considered. There is no deadline for applications and all will be acknowledged. The trustees meet regularly during the year, usually in March, June, September and November. All successful applicants will be notified by email and will be required to provide written confirmation of the details of the project or work for which they are seeking a grant. Payment is then made in the following month. The website also states: 'To comply with the Data Protection Act 1998, applicants are required to consent to the use of personal data supplied by them in the processing and review of their application. This includes transfer to and use by such individuals and organisations as the trust deems appropriate. The trust requires the assurance of the applicant that personal data about any other individual is supplied to the trust with his/her consent. At the point of submitting an online application, applicants are asked to confirm this consent and assurance.'
**WHO TO APPLY TO** Carol Langston, Correspondent, Holme Farm, Fore Street, Bradford, Holsworthy, Devon EX22 7AJ Tel. 01409 281403 email administrator@steelcharitabletrust.org.uk Website www.steelcharitabletrust.org.uk

## ■ The Steinberg Family Charitable Trust
**CC NO** 1045231    **ESTABLISHED** 1995
**WHERE FUNDING CAN BE GIVEN** UK, with a preference for Greater Manchester.
**WHO CAN BENEFIT** Charitable organisations, with a preference for Jewish groups.
**WHAT IS FUNDED** General charitable purposes.
**WHAT IS NOT FUNDED** Registered charities only.
**RANGE OF GRANTS** Generally £150–£20,000.
**SAMPLE GRANTS** Aish (£75,000); Fed, Hathaway Trust, UJIA and World Jewish Relief (£50,000) and Integrated Education Fund (£25,000); SEED (£22,000); and Hale Adult Hebrew Education Trust (£20,000); Centre for Social Justice and Policy Exchange (£15,000); Ascent, Ezer Layeled, Imperial War Museum; MDA Israel, Menachim Begin Heritage Foundation and Yeshiva Bais Yisroel (£10,000 each); Chai Cancer Care and Holocaust Centre (£7,500 each); Hamayon and Hazon Yeshaya (£5,000 each); Henshaw's Society, Jewish Education in Manchester, NATA and Rainbow Trust (£2,500 each); and Prostate Cancer Charity (£1,000).
**FINANCES** Year 2012/13 Income £6,579,671 Grants £1,121,975 Grants to organisations £1,121,975 Assets £29,422,237
**TRUSTEES** Beryl Steinberg; Jonathan Steinberg; Lynne Attias.
**OTHER INFORMATION** The 2012/13 accounts were the latest available at the time of writing (June 2015).
**HOW TO APPLY** Apply in writing to the correspondent on letter-headed paper, including evidence of charitable status, the purpose to which the funds are to be put, evidence of other action taken to fund the project concerned, and the outcome of that action.
**WHO TO APPLY TO** The Trustees, Lime Tree Cottage, 16 Bollingway, Hale, Altrincham WA15 0NZ Tel. 0161 903 8854 email admin@steinberg-trust.co.uk

## ■ The Stephen Barry Charitable Trust
**CC NO** 265056    **ESTABLISHED** 1973
**WHERE FUNDING CAN BE GIVEN** UK and worldwide.
**WHO CAN BENEFIT** Charitable organisations.
**WHAT IS FUNDED** General charitable purposes.
**TYPE OF GRANT** One-off grants to organisations.
**RANGE OF GRANTS** Up to £53,000.
**SAMPLE GRANTS** National Gallery (£53,000); Youth Aliyah (£13,960); Prostate Cancer Research (£5,000); Acts of Hope Charitable Trust, British Museum (£2,000 each); Tate Foundation (£1,200); Age Concern, Freedom from Torture, National Theatre, World Jewish Relief (£500 each); Children in Need, Global Warming Foundation, Médecins Sans Frontières, Mind (£250 each); Royal Marsden Hospital (£150); Kensington Society (£25).
**FINANCES** Year 2013/14 Income £51,605 Grants £92,528 Grants to organisations £92,528 Assets £1,537,786
**TRUSTEES** Nicolas Barry; Oliver Barry; Stephen Barry; Linda Barry, Lucinda Barry.
**OTHER INFORMATION** A total of 35 grants were made.
**HOW TO APPLY** Apply in writing to the correspondent.
**WHO TO APPLY TO** Stephen Barry, Trustee, 19 Newman Street, London W1T 1PF Tel. 020 7580 6696 email sjb@limecourt.com

## ■ C. E. K. Stern Charitable Trust
**CC NO** 1049157    **ESTABLISHED** 1992
**WHERE FUNDING CAN BE GIVEN** UK and overseas, particularly Israel.
**WHO CAN BENEFIT** Orthodox Jewish charities; religious and educational institutions.
**WHAT IS FUNDED** General charitable purposes for the benefit of the Orthodox Jewish people.
**SAMPLE GRANTS** A list of beneficiaries was not included within the accounts.
**FINANCES** Year 2013/14 Income £171,622 Grants £47,980 Grants to organisations £47,980 Assets £911,792
**TRUSTEES** Chaya Stern; Z. M. Kaufman; Zvi Stern.

**HOW TO APPLY** Applications may be made in writing to the correspondent. The latest accounts note: 'The Charity accepts applications for grants from representatives of Orthodox Jewish Charities, which are reviewed by the trustees on a regular basis. The trustees consider requests received and make donations based on level of funds available.'
**WHO TO APPLY TO** Z. M. Kaufman, Trustee, 50 Keswick Street, Gateshead NE8 1TQ

---

## ■ Stevenson Family's Charitable Trust

**CC NO** 327148   **ESTABLISHED** 1986
**WHERE FUNDING CAN BE GIVEN** Worldwide, in practice mainly UK.
**WHO CAN BENEFIT** Registered charities.
**WHAT IS FUNDED** Worldwide, in practice mainly UK.
**WHAT IS NOT FUNDED** Individuals.
**TYPE OF GRANT** One-off and recurring.
**RANGE OF GRANTS** £150–£50,000
**SAMPLE GRANTS** SportsAble (£51,000); University College Oxford (£50,000); Glyndebourne Productions (£20,000); Royal Holloway College and The Royal National Theatre (£10,000 each); Museum of London and Sick Children's Trust (£5,000 each); Royal British Legion and War Memorials Trust (£1,000 each); Salvation Army (£500).
**FINANCES** Year 2013/14 Income £224,124 Grants £265,704 Grants to organisations £265,704 Assets £2,163,368
**TRUSTEES** Lady Stevenson; Sir Hugh Stevenson; Joseph Stevenson.
**OTHER INFORMATION** Grants were made to 51 organisations totalling £266,000.
**HOW TO APPLY** 'No unsolicited applications can be considered as the charity's funds are required to support purposes chosen by the trustees.'
**WHO TO APPLY TO** Sir Hugh Stevenson, Trustee, Old Waterfield, Winkfield Road, Ascot SL5 7LJ email hugh.stevenson@oldwaterfield.com

---

## ■ The Stewards' Company Limited (incorporating the J. W. Laing Trust and the J. W. Laing Biblical Scholarship Trust)

**CC NO** 234558   **ESTABLISHED** 1947
**WHERE FUNDING CAN BE GIVEN** UK and overseas.
**WHO CAN BENEFIT** Organisations involved with training people in religious education. About half the trust's funds are given for work overseas.
**WHAT IS FUNDED** Christian evangelism, especially but not exclusively that of Christian Brethren assemblies. Grants given overseas are made under the following categories: church buildings; scriptures and literature; education and orphanages; education of missionaries' children; national evangelists and missionaries' vehicles. Grants given in the UK are categorised under: church buildings; evangelistic associations; scriptures and literature; teachers and evangelists; children and young people. Substantial funds are also transferred to the Beatrice Laing Trust (see separate entry).
**TYPE OF GRANT** Usually one-off.
**RANGE OF GRANTS** About £15,000–£1 million.
**SAMPLE GRANTS** Echoes of Service (£614,000); Universities and Colleges Christian Fellowship (£400,000); Beatrice Laing Trust (£347,500); Retired Missionary Aid Fund (£225,000); Christian Workers Relief Fund (£175,000); Interlink (£140,000); International Fellowships of Evangelical Students (£110,000).
**FINANCES** Year 2013/14 Income £1,826,325 Grants £6,126,512 Grants to organisations £6,079,548 Assets £134,240,733
**TRUSTEES** Brian Chapman; Alexander McIlhinney; Paul Young; William Adams; William Wood; Andrew Street; Prof. Arthur Williamson; Philip Page; Denis Cooper; Alan Paterson; Glyn Davies; Dr John Burness; Andrew Griffiths; Ian Childs; John Gamble; Philip Symons; Simon Tomlinson; J. Aitken; Keith Bintley.
**OTHER INFORMATION** Grants to individuals totalled £47,000.
**HOW TO APPLY** Apply writing to the correspondent.
**WHO TO APPLY TO** Brian Chapman, 124 Wells Road, Bath BA2 3AH Tel. 01225 427236 email stewardsco@stewards.co.uk

---

## ■ The Andy Stewart Charitable Foundation

**CC NO** 1114802   **ESTABLISHED** 2006
**WHERE FUNDING CAN BE GIVEN** Worldwide.
**WHO CAN BENEFIT** Charitable organisations.
**WHAT IS FUNDED** General charitable purposes; education and training; the promotion of health; people with disabilities; children and young people; horse racing.
**SAMPLE GRANTS** Spinal Injuries (£39,000); Sir Peter O'Sullevan Charitable Trust (£24,000); Best Beginnings and The Haven (£5,000 each); Children's Heart Fund (£3,600); Bob Champion Cancer Trust (£2,000); Cancer Research and Jackson Memorial Hospital (£1,000 each).
**FINANCES** Year 2013 Income £26,167 Grants £100,638 Grants to organisations £100,638 Assets £709,904
**TRUSTEES** Andy Stewart; Mark Stewart; Paul Stewart.
**OTHER INFORMATION** Grants totalled £100,000 during the year.
**HOW TO APPLY** Apply in writing to the correspondent.
**WHO TO APPLY TO** The Trustees, Bridger, 14 Glategny Esplanade, St Peter Port, Guernsey

---

## ■ Sir Halley Stewart Trust

**CC NO** 208491   **ESTABLISHED** 1924
**WHERE FUNDING CAN BE GIVEN** UK and some work in Africa.
**WHO CAN BENEFIT** Charitable organisations and researchers.
**WHAT IS FUNDED** Research; innovative projects; feasibility and pilot studies; development projects in medical, social, educational and religious fields.
**WHAT IS NOT FUNDED** Grants are not usually made for the following: running costs of established organisations; conferences; projects proposed indirectly through other 'umbrella' or large charities; personal education fees or fees for taught courses – unless the proposal comes from a senior researcher who is seeking funds for research which could be undertaken by postgraduate student; completion of a project or PhD initiated by other bodies; educational or 'gap year' projects for young people; climate change issues. Grants are never made for the following: donations to general appeals of any kind; the purchase, erection or conversion of buildings; capital costs; university overhead charges; the completion of a project initiated by other funding bodies.

**TYPE OF GRANT** One-off and project grants. Feasibility studies, research and salaries will also be considered. Funding may be given for up to three years.
**RANGE OF GRANTS** £10,000–£28,000
**SAMPLE GRANTS** TB Alert (£56,000); PACE and Touchstones (£50,000 each); Research Autism (£40,000); University of Oxford (£34,000); Plymouth University (£28,000); Meningitis Research Foundation (£27,000); University of Liverpool (£26,000); Centre for Pioneer Learning (£24,000); World Child Cancer (£22,000); Lively Minds (£20,000).
**FINANCES** Year 2013/14 Income £1,063,000 Grants £796,000 Grants to organisations £796,000 Assets £27,019,000
**TRUSTEES** Joanna Womack; Prof. Phyllida Parsloe; Dr Caroline Berry; Dr Duncan Steward; Lord Stewartby; Prof. John Wyatt; Prof. John Leonard-Jones; Michael Collins; Prof. Philip Whitfield; W. Kirkham; Brian Allpress; Prof. Gordon Wilcock; Caroline Thomas; Theresa Bartlett; Louisa Macantab; Amy Holcroft; Jane Gilliard; Revd Prof. David Wilkinson.
**HOW TO APPLY** Apply via email to the trust secretary. Full details of what should be included in the application can be found in the 'How to Apply' section of the trust's website.
**WHO TO APPLY TO** Nick Chant, Secretary to the Trustees, BM Sir Halley Stewart Trust, London WC1N 3XX Tel. 020 8144 0375 email email@sirhalleystewart.org.uk Website www.sirhalleystewart.org.uk

## ■ The Stewarts Law Foundation

**CC NO** 1136714  **ESTABLISHED** 2010
**WHERE FUNDING CAN BE GIVEN** UK and overseas.
**WHO CAN BENEFIT** Charitable organisations and activities.
**WHAT IS FUNDED** General charitable purposes; prevention or relief of poverty and homelessness; disability organisations; furtherance of the arts; advancement of education; overseas humanitarian agencies and environmental protection.
**RANGE OF GRANTS** £2,000–£25,000
**SAMPLE GRANTS** Access to Justice Foundation (£100,000); Headway and Royal College of Art (£30,000 each); Backup Trust and Wheelpower (£25,000 each); Second Sight and Street Kids International (£20,000 each); The Children's Trust Tadworth (£15,000); Forgot Me Not Children's Hospice and The National Pro Bono Centre (£5,000 each).
**FINANCES** Year 2013/14 Income £520,416 Grants £510,456 Grants to organisations £510,456 Assets £68,316
**TRUSTEES** John Cahill; Bennett Townsend; Stuart Dench; Paul Paxton; James Healy-Pratt; Stephen Foster; Julian Chamberlayne; Daniel Herman; Andrew Dinsmore; Kevin Grealis; Clive Zietman; Jane Colston; Sean Upson; Muiris Lyons; Emma Hatley; Debbie Chism; Helen Ward; Jonathan Sinclair.
**HOW TO APPLY** The annual report for 2013/14 states that: 'Trustees are invited to select from a number of organisations in each of the Foundation's selected Charitable categories, following an internal assessment of the charity against the Foundation's guidelines. The Trustees vote as to whether the grant is approved, and agree the amount and the duration of the grant. A majority vote is needed for the grant to be given. It is not the policy of the Trustees to accept direct applications for funds.'

**WHO TO APPLY TO** John Cahill, Trustee, c/o John Cahill, 5 New Street Square, London EC4A 3BF Tel. 020 7822 8000 email info@stewartslaw.com Website www.stewartslaw.com/the-stewarts-law-foundation.aspx

## ■ The Leonard Laity Stoate Charitable Trust

**CC NO** 221325  **ESTABLISHED** 1950
**WHERE FUNDING CAN BE GIVEN** England and Wales with a preference for the southwest of England, Bristol, Cornwall, Devon, Dorset and Somerset (especially west Somerset).
**WHO CAN BENEFIT** Charitable organisations; Methodist organisations; churches.
**WHAT IS FUNDED** General charitable purposes; the promotion of health; people with disabilities; social welfare; children and young people; economic and community development; the environment; religious activities.
**WHAT IS NOT FUNDED** Individuals unless supported by a registered charity; institutions that are not registered charities or established churches that pay wages or other remuneration (this will rule out most Community Interest Companies); large projects (over £500,000 and/or with more than £250,000 still to raise); general appeals by national charities; grants are not normally given for running expenses of a charity.
**TYPE OF GRANT** Usually one-off for a specific project or part of a project.
**RANGE OF GRANTS** Typically £100–£1,000.
**SAMPLE GRANTS** Elim Plymouth Christian Centre and St Augustine's Church – Southville (£2,000 each); Higher St Budeaux Parish Church – Plymouth and Bideford Bay Surf Life Saving Club (£1,000 each); Taunton Association for the Homeless and Changing Tunes (£500 each); Anchor Society and Grateful Society (£250 each); Women for Women International and New Forest Trust (£100 each).
**FINANCES** Year 2013/14 Income £80,591 Grants £70,350 Grants to organisations £70,350 Assets £2,136,461
**TRUSTEES** Stephen Duckworth; Philip Stoate; Revd Anthony Ward Jones; Dr Christopher Stoate; Dr Pam Stoate; Susan Harnden.
**OTHER INFORMATION** Although the trust does not want to rule out anywhere in England and Wales, it is a comparatively small trust and is forced to be very selective. Therefore, the further an applicant is from the trusts core area the less likely they are to be successful.
**HOW TO APPLY** There is no special application form, but applications should be in writing; neither telephone nor email applications will be entertained. Supply clear details of: the need the intended project is designed to meet; the amount raised so far, with a breakdown of how much has been raised from within the local community and how much from other grant-making bodies or other sources. Also supply where possible: your registered charity number or, for unregistered organisations, a copy of your constitution; accounts or budgets; an e-mail address for follow-up correspondence or application acknowledgement. Whilst applications can be considered at any time, the bulk are decided at the trust's half-yearly meetings in mid-March and September of each year. Thus December to February and June to August are probably the best times to submit applications.
**WHO TO APPLY TO** Philip Stoate, Trustee, 41 Tower Hill, Williton, Tautnton TA4 4JR email charity@

erminea.org.uk *Website* www.stoate-charity.org.uk

## ■ The Stobart Newlands Charitable Trust

**CC NO** 328464 **ESTABLISHED** 1989
**WHERE FUNDING CAN BE GIVEN** UK.
**WHO CAN BENEFIT** Registered charities.
**WHAT IS FUNDED** Christian religious and missionary causes.
**WHAT IS NOT FUNDED** Individuals.
**TYPE OF GRANT** Mainly recurrent.
**RANGE OF GRANTS** Up to £360,000.
**SAMPLE GRANTS** World Vision (£360,000); Mission Aviation Fellowship (£280,000); Operation Mobilisation (£175,000); Caring for Life (£155,000); Moorlands (£80,000); Bible Society and Tear Fund (£35,000 each); Christian Medical Fellowship and CUMNISCU (£20,000 each); Biblica Europe, Trans World Radio and Torch Trust (£10,000 each).
**FINANCES** *Year* 2013 *Income* £1,837,790 *Grants* £1,582,729 *Grants to organisations* £1,582,729 *Assets* £453,426
**TRUSTEES** Ronnie Stobart; Linda Rigg; Peter Stobart; Richard Stobart.
**OTHER INFORMATION** A total of 60 grants were made totalling £1.6 million.
**HOW TO APPLY** Unsolicited applications are most unlikely to be successful.
**WHO TO APPLY TO** Ronnie Stobart, Trustee, J. Stobart and Sons Ltd, Mill Croft, Newlands, Hesket Newmarket, Wigton CA7 8HP *Tel.* 01697 478631

## ■ The Edward Stocks-Massey Bequest Fund

**CC NO** 526516 **ESTABLISHED** 1910
**WHERE FUNDING CAN BE GIVEN** Burnley.
**WHO CAN BENEFIT** Charitable organisations.
**WHAT IS FUNDED** Education and training; arts and culture; amateur sport; economic and community development; science; children and young people.
**RANGE OF GRANTS** £280–£13,000
**SAMPLE GRANTS** Towneley Hall Art Gallery (£12,500); Arts Development Creative Peoples and Places (£3,000); Burnley Music Centre LMS (£2,000); Schools Orchestras and Choirs Trust Fund (£1,500); Friends of the Rose School and The Prince's Trust (£1,000 each); Burnley Youth Theatre (£700); Burnley Belvedere Football Club (£400); and Weavers Triangle Trust (£200).
**FINANCES** *Year* 2013/14 *Income* £36,878 *Grants* £50,500 *Grants to organisations* £50,500 *Assets* £978,655
**TRUSTEES** A. David Knagg; Neil Beecham.
**OTHER INFORMATION** Grants were made to Burnley Borough Council and Lancashire County Council for £15,500 each. A total of £6,000 was paid in scholarship awards. Grants totalled £50,500.
**HOW TO APPLY** Application forms are available from the correspondent.
**WHO TO APPLY TO** Chris Gay, Correspondent, Burnley Borough Council, Burnley Town Hall, Manchester Road, Burnley BB11 9SA *Tel.* 01282 425011 *email* cgay@burnley.gov.uk

## ■ The Stoller Charitable Trust

**CC NO** 285415 **ESTABLISHED** 1982
**WHERE FUNDING CAN BE GIVEN** UK, with a preference for the Greater Manchester area.
**WHO CAN BENEFIT** Established UK charities and local causes.
**WHAT IS FUNDED** General charitable purposes; education and training; the promotion of health; people with disabilities; social welfare; arts and culture; economic and community development.
**WHAT IS NOT FUNDED** Individuals.
**TYPE OF GRANT** Buildings; capital costs; one-off; project grants; research; recurring costs; start-up costs will be considered. Funding may be given for up to three years.
**SAMPLE GRANTS Previous beneficiaries have included:** Bauern Helfen Bauern; Onside North West; Broughton House; Central Manchester Children's Hospitals; Live Music Now; Christie Hospital, Greater Manchester Appeal; Imperial War Museum North; National Memorial Arboretum; Cancer Research UK; Oldham Liaison of Ex-Services Associations; Church Housing Trust; Commandery of John of Gaunt; Mines Advisory Group; Salvation Army; and Windermere Air Show.
**FINANCES** *Year* 2013/14 *Income* £47,505,750 *Grants* £1,418,594 *Grants to organisations* £1,418,594 *Assets* £51,600,581
**TRUSTEES** Roger Gould; Norman Stoller; Sheila Stoller; Andrew Dixon; KSL. Trustees Ltd.
**OTHER INFORMATION** The substantial increase in assets and income is as a result of a donation made of just over £47 million made by Norman Stoller, a trustee, as well as gains on investment and less foreign exchange losses. Grants were made to 91 organisations this year totalling £1.4 million.
**HOW TO APPLY** Apply in writing to the correspondent. Applications need to be received by February, May, August or November. The trustees usually meet in March, June, September and December.
**WHO TO APPLY TO** Alison Ford, Correspondent, Wrigley Partington, Sterling House, 501 Middleton Road, Chadderton, Oldham *Tel.* 0161 622 0222 *email* enquiries@stollercharitabletrust.co.uk

## ■ M. J. C. Stone Charitable Trust

**CC NO** 283920 **ESTABLISHED** 1981
**WHERE FUNDING CAN BE GIVEN** Gloucestershire.
**WHO CAN BENEFIT** UK charities and smaller scale local organisations.
**WHAT IS FUNDED** General charitable purposes; education and training; the promotion of health; social welfare; religious causes; the environment.
**RANGE OF GRANTS** Usually up to £50,000.
**SAMPLE GRANTS Previous beneficiaries have included:** Tennis for Free and the Diamond Jubilee Trust (£100,000 each); Bradfield Foundation (£50,000); Centre for Social Justice (£27,000); Game and Wildlife Trust (£18,000); Countryside Learning (£10,000); University of the Highlands and Islands, Evelina Children's Hospital, National Autistic Society, Wheelpower and the Outward Bound Trust (£5,000 each); Pestalozzi World Trust and Making the Change (£1,000 each).
**FINANCES** *Year* 2013 *Income* £2,389 *Grants* £350,000 *Grants to organisations* £350,000
**TRUSTEES** Louisa Stone; Nicola Farquhar; Michael Stone; Andrew Stone; Charles Stone.

**OTHER INFORMATION** Accounts were not required for 2013.
**HOW TO APPLY** Apply in writing to the correspondent. 'The charitable trust makes grants to core charities on an annual basis. Grants to other charities are made on receipt of applications and after discussions between the trustees.'
**WHO TO APPLY TO** Michael Stone, Trustee, Ozleworth Park, Ozleworth, Wotton-Under-Edge, Gloucestershire GL12 7QA *Tel.* 01453 845591

### ■ The Stone Family Foundation
**CC NO** 1108207        **ESTABLISHED** 2005
**WHERE FUNDING CAN BE GIVEN** Worldwide.
**WHO CAN BENEFIT** Charities and international aid organisations.
**WHAT IS FUNDED** Relief of need or hardship. The foundation's website states that: 'Since September 2010, the foundation's main focus has been on water, sanitation and hygiene (WASH). Our goal is to find and support lasting and effective ways to promote good sanitation, safe water and good hygiene across the world.'
**WHAT IS NOT FUNDED** Individuals.
**RANGE OF GRANTS** Up to £1 million.
**SAMPLE GRANTS** Water and Sanitation for the Urban Poor (£1 million); IDE Cambodia (£706,500); Acumen Fund (£435,000); WaterAid (£398,500); Watershed (£197,500); Rethink (£137,000); Mosaic Clubhouse (£70,000); The Samaritans (£60,000); Into University (£50,000); Star Wards (£10,000).
**FINANCES** *Year* 2013 *Income* £443,628 *Grants* £4,176,197 *Grants to organisations* £4,176,197 *Assets* £42,982,064
**TRUSTEES** Coutts & Co.; John Stone; Charles Edwards.
**OTHER INFORMATION** Loans are also available.
**HOW TO APPLY** The foundation is advised on potential grant recipients by New Philanthropy Capital, and states that it is not looking for new organisations to support at present. Check the foundation's website for up-to-date information.
**WHO TO APPLY TO** The Clerk, Coutts & Co., 440 Strand, London WC2R 0QS *Tel.* 020 7663 6825 *Website* www.thesff.com

### ■ The Samuel Storey Family Charitable Trust
**CC NO** 267684        **ESTABLISHED** 1974
**WHERE FUNDING CAN BE GIVEN** UK, with a preference for Yorkshire.
**WHO CAN BENEFIT** Registered charities.
**WHAT IS FUNDED** General charitable purposes.
**WHAT IS NOT FUNDED** Individuals.
**RANGE OF GRANTS** £25–£25,000; typically less than £1,000.
**SAMPLE GRANTS** Old Malton Church (£1,250); New Schools Network, Pebbles Project, Operation New World (£1,000 each); Gurkha Welfare Trust (£460); Yorkshire Cancer Research (£250); Live Music Now Scotland (£200); Friends of the British Museum (£85); Historic Gardens Foundation (£25).
**FINANCES** *Year* 2013/14 *Income* £184,314 *Grants* £119,388 *Grants to organisations* £119,388 *Assets* £5,691,051
**TRUSTEES** Hon. Sir Richard Storey; Wren Abrahall; Kenelm Storey; Elisabeth Critchley.
**HOW TO APPLY** Apply in writing to the correspondent. The trust informed us that, 'in order to give appropriately, we only really do so to personalised applications'.
**WHO TO APPLY TO** Kenelm Storey, Trustee, 21 Buckingham Gate, London SW1E 6LS *Tel.* 020 7802 2700

### ■ Peter Stormonth Darling Charitable Trust
**CC NO** 1049946        **ESTABLISHED** 1995
**WHERE FUNDING CAN BE GIVEN** UK.
**WHO CAN BENEFIT** Organisations benefitting children, young adults, sportsmen and women and the general public.
**WHAT IS FUNDED** Preference for heritage, education, healthcare and sports facilities.
**WHAT IS NOT FUNDED** Individuals.
**RANGE OF GRANTS** Up to £12,000.
**SAMPLE GRANTS** Friends of East Sussex Hospices, Oxford University – Vincent's Club, Royal Hospital for Neuro-disability (£15,000 each); International Trust for Croatian Monuments, Landmark Trust (£10,000); Imperial College Research (£7,500); National Gallery (£2,500); Taunton School Foundation (£2,000); Bath Festivals, Motor Neurone Disease Association (£1,000 each); Hope and Homes for Children (£1,000); Pacoima Singers (£600); Holburne Museum Trust (£500).
**FINANCES** *Year* 2013 *Income* £88,523 *Grants* £206,800 *Grants to organisations* £206,800 *Assets* £3,651,947
**TRUSTEES** John Rodwell; Peter Darling; Elizabeth Cobb; Arabella Johannes; Christa Taylor.
**OTHER INFORMATION** Grants were made to 36 organisations with the following purposes: heritage (17); education (8); health care or sporting facilities (11).
**HOW TO APPLY** The trustees have stated that they do not respond to unsolicited applications.
**WHO TO APPLY TO** Peter Stormonth Darling, Trustee, Soditic Ltd, 12 Charles II Street, London SW1Y 4QU

### ■ Peter Storrs Trust
**CC NO** 313804        **ESTABLISHED** 1970
**WHERE FUNDING CAN BE GIVEN** UK and worldwide.
**WHO CAN BENEFIT** Registered charities.
**WHAT IS FUNDED** General charitable purposes and the advancement of education.
**WHAT IS NOT FUNDED** Individuals.
**TYPE OF GRANT** One-off and recurring.
**RANGE OF GRANTS** £1,000–£10,500
**SAMPLE GRANTS** ACE UK – Africa (£10,500); Peter House (£5,400); Action for the Church in Need, DEC Philippines Typhoon Appeal (£5,000 each); Aids Orphans of Myanmar (£2,500); RNIB (£3,000); Afghan Connection, Age Concern, Big Brum Theatre, Holy Land Institute for the Deaf, Kids Company, Mind, Sight Savers, St Martin-in-the-Fields Christmas Appeal, (£2,000 each); Cherubim Music Trust, Finsbury and Clerkenwell Volunteers (£1,000 each).
**FINANCES** *Year* 2013/14 *Income* £127,160 *Grants* £118,500 *Grants to organisations* £118,500 *Assets* £3,196,458
**TRUSTEES** Geoffrey Adams; Arthur Curtis; Julie Easton.
**OTHER INFORMATION** Grants were split between recurring (£71,000) and one-off (£47,500). Most grants were for £2,000.
**HOW TO APPLY** Apply in writing to the correspondent. Trustees have stated that applications are considered every three to six months. Note the trustees receive far more applications than it is

able to support, many of which do not meet their criteria.

**WHO TO APPLY TO** The Trustees, c/o Smithfield Accountants, 117 Charterhouse Street, London EC1M 6AA *Tel.* 020 7253 3757 *email* postmaster@smithfield-accountants.co.uk

## ■ The Strangward Trust

**CC NO** 1036494   **ESTABLISHED** 1993

**WHERE FUNDING CAN BE GIVEN** Mainly, Bedfordshire, Cambridgeshire and Northamptonshire.

**WHO CAN BENEFIT** Organisations concerned with people with mental and physical disabilities.

**WHAT IS FUNDED** Funding for care and treatment of people with physical or mental disabilities, including direct help and assistance in the purchase of services and equipment.

**TYPE OF GRANT** One-off; capital; core costs. Funding is for one year or less.

**RANGE OF GRANTS** Rarely over £2,500.

**SAMPLE GRANTS** EACH (£25,000); Nansa (£7,500); HFT and Deafblind UK (£5,000 each); Stepping Stones, Footsteps Foundation and Keech Hospice Care (£2,500 each); and Ladybird Boat Trust and Daventry Health Rehabilitation Trust Limited (£1,000 each).

**FINANCES** *Year* 2013/14 *Income* £802,658 *Grants* £112,050 *Grants to organisations* £112,050 *Assets* £10,294,659

**TRUSTEES** Anne Allured; Ross Jones; Paul Goakes; Clare O'Callaghan.

**HOW TO APPLY** Applications forms are available from the correspondent. Attach a copy of your latest accounts (if relevant) and any other supporting documentation (e.g. copy estimates, medical reports, etc., when applying).The trustees meet twice a year (March and September) to decide upon donations. Applications should be submitted by the end of February and August. The trustees will consider every application submitted to them that meets the criteria of the trust. It is important that applications on behalf of national charities identify a specific need for funding in the geographic area referred to above to be considered. The trustees will consider projects where there is an annual ongoing requirement for funds for period of up to five years. Successful applicants will be expected to keep the trust informed on their projects. Only successful applicants will be notified of the outcome of their application.

**WHO TO APPLY TO** Ross Jones, Trustee, Glebe House, Catworth, Huntingdon, Cambridgeshire PE28 0PA *Tel.* 01832 710171 *email* strangwardtrust@aol.com

## ■ Stratford-upon-Avon Town Trust

**CC NO** 1088521   **ESTABLISHED** 2001

**WHERE FUNDING CAN BE GIVEN** Stratford-upon-Avon.

**WHO CAN BENEFIT** Organisations benefitting people living in the Stratford-upon-Avon council area.

**WHAT IS FUNDED** Welfare and well-being; strengthening communities; young people; poverty; older people.

**WHAT IS NOT FUNDED** Organisations outside Stratford-upon-Avon.

**TYPE OF GRANT** Capital and revenue grants for up to three years.

**RANGE OF GRANTS** Up to £50,000.

**SAMPLE GRANTS** King Edward IV Grammar School (£587,500); Citizens Advice (£136,500); Shakespeare Hospice (£62,000); Warwickshire Police Authority (£43,500); Stratford-upon-Avon School (£30,500); Holy Trinity Church (£4,500).

**FINANCES** *Year* 2013 *Income* £3,413,198 *Grants* £3,051,625 *Grants to organisations* £3,051,625 *Assets* £53,624,979

**TRUSTEES** Carole Taylor; Juliet Short; Ian Fradgley; Clarissa Roberts; Robert Townsend; Joan McFarlane; Richard Lane; Alan Haigh; Julia Lucas; Clive Snowdon; Quentin Wilson.

**HOW TO APPLY** Application forms can be completed via the trust's website. Awards are made on a quarterly basis. The latest application deadlines are listed on the trust's website.

**WHO TO APPLY TO** Helen Munro, Chief Executive, 14 Rother Street, Stratford-upon-Avon, Warwickshire CV32 6LU *Tel.* 01789 207111 *email* admin@stratfordtowntrust.co.uk *Website* www.stratfordtowntrust.co.uk

## ■ The Strawberry Charitable Trust

**CC NO** 1090173   **ESTABLISHED** 2000

**WHERE FUNDING CAN BE GIVEN** Not defined but with a preference for Manchester.

**WHO CAN BENEFIT** Registered charities.

**WHAT IS FUNDED** The relief of poverty and hardship mainly amongst Jewish people and the advancement of the Jewish religion.

**RANGE OF GRANTS** Up to £32,000.

**SAMPLE GRANTS** **Previous beneficiaries have included:** United Jewish Israel Appeal; Community Security Trust; The Fed; Lubavitch South Manchester; King David School; World Jewish Relief; Belz and St John's Wood Synagogue; Action on Addiction; Mew Children's Hospital; and Tickets for Troops.

**FINANCES** *Year* 2013/14 *Income* £0 *Grants* £75,000 *Grants to organisations* £75,000

**TRUSTEES** Emma Myers; Laura Avigdori; Anthony Leon.

**OTHER INFORMATION** The grant total was estimated based on expenditure in previous years, as the 2013/14 accounts were not required to be available on the Charity Commission website. The trust had a total expenditure of £80,500 in this year.

**HOW TO APPLY** Apply in writing to the correspondent.

**WHO TO APPLY TO** Anthony Leon, Trustee, 4 Westfields, Hale, Altrincham WA15 0LL *Tel.* 0161 980 8484 *email* anthonysula@hotmail.com

## ■ The W. O. Street Charitable Foundation

**CC NO** 267127   **ESTABLISHED** 1973

**WHERE FUNDING CAN BE GIVEN** Worldwide. There is a preference for the North West of England and Jersey.

**WHO CAN BENEFIT** Registered charities.

**WHAT IS FUNDED** General charitable purposes; education and training; the promotion of health; social welfare; children and young people; older people; people with disabilities.

**WHAT IS NOT FUNDED** Medical research; animal welfare; overseas projects or charities; individuals.

**TYPE OF GRANT** One-off and recurring grants.

**RANGE OF GRANTS** Generally £1,000 to £15,000.

**SAMPLE GRANTS** W O Street Charitable Foundation (£40,000); Emmott Foundation (£30,000); Community Foundation for Merseyside (£14,600); Cheadle Royal (Industries) Ltd (£10,000); Bolton Wanderers Community Trust (£8,100); Chapel St Community Fund, Early Break and Longton Community Church (£5,000

each); Hope House and Manchester Care (£3,000 each); The Matthew Trust and The Olive Branch – Faith In Action (£1,000 each); Extra Care Charitable Trust (£600).
**FINANCES** Year 2013/14 Income £317,850 Grants £406,349 Grants to organisations £406,349 Assets £16,768,776
**TRUSTEES** Barclays Bank Trust Co. Ltd; Clive Cutbill.
**HOW TO APPLY** Apply in writing to the correspondent. Applications are considered on a quarterly basis, at the end of January, April, July and October.
**WHO TO APPLY TO** The Trust Officer, Barclays Bank Trust Co. Ltd, Barclays UK Trusts, Osborne Court, Gadbrook Park, Rudheath, Cheshire CW9 7UE Tel. 01606 313185 email uktrusts.osbornecourt@barclays.com

## ■ The Strowger Trust
**CC NO** 1152108
**WHERE FUNDING CAN BE GIVEN** UK.
**WHO CAN BENEFIT** Charitable organisations.
**WHAT IS FUNDED** General charitable purposes; the promotion of health; children and young people.
**SAMPLE GRANTS** A list of beneficiaries was not available.
**FINANCES** Year 2013/14 Income £137,151 Grants £40,000 Grants to organisations £40,000 Assets £16,285
**TRUSTEES** Clare Strowger; Darren Strowger.
**OTHER INFORMATION** Grants totalled £40,000. A list of beneficiaries was not provided.
**HOW TO APPLY** Applications may be made in writing to the correspondent.
**WHO TO APPLY TO** Darren Strowger, Trustee, 9 Lower John Street, London W1F 9DZ Tel. 07767 622222

## ■ The Sudborough Foundation
**CC NO** 272323        **ESTABLISHED** 1976
**WHERE FUNDING CAN BE GIVEN** UK, with a preference for Northamptonshire.
**WHO CAN BENEFIT** Educational establishments and other charities.
**WHAT IS FUNDED** Education and training.
**RANGE OF GRANTS** £100–£10,500
**SAMPLE GRANTS** The Gordon Robinson Memorial Trust (£10,500); Abington Park Youth Drop In (£10,000); Home Start Northampton and Northampton Sailability (£5,000 each); Charlie Waller Memorial Trust and Northampton Scouts (£2,000 each); Royal College of Music and The Honourable Society of Lincoln's Inn (£1,500 each); Miriam Hyman Memorial Trust and The Peterborough Development and Preservation Trust (£1,000 each); The Kids Time Foundation (£500); Action Medical Research (£250); and Alzheimer's Society (£100).
**FINANCES** Year 2013/14 Income £38,098 Grants £59,650 Grants to organisations £59,650 Assets £1,475,205
**TRUSTEES** William Reason; Julian Woolfson; Elisabeth Engel; Richard Engel; Simon Powis; Susan Leathem; Rachel Engel; Lady Lowther; Lucy Watson.
**OTHER INFORMATION** Grants were made to 37 organisations totalling £60,000.
**HOW TO APPLY** Apply via a form available from the correspondent.
**WHO TO APPLY TO** Richard Engel, Trustee, 8 Hazelwood Road, Northampton NN1 1LP email chair@sudboroughfoundation.org.uk Website www.sudboroughfoundation.org.uk

## ■ Sueberry Ltd
**CC NO** 256566        **ESTABLISHED** 1968
**WHERE FUNDING CAN BE GIVEN** UK and overseas.
**WHO CAN BENEFIT** Jewish organisations; UK welfare and medical organisations benefitting children and young adults; at risk groups; people who are disadvantaged by poverty or socially isolated people.
**WHAT IS FUNDED** General charitable purposes; medical causes; educational and religious activities.
**SAMPLE GRANTS** A list of beneficiaries was not available.
**FINANCES** Year 2013/14 Income £165,372 Grants £130,975 Grants to organisations £130,975 Assets £99,998
**TRUSTEES** D. S. Davis, Chair; C. Davis; H. Davis; J. Davis; A. D. Davis; S. M. Davis; Y. Davis; A. Davis.
**OTHER INFORMATION** Details of grant beneficiaries were not provided in the trust's accounts.
**HOW TO APPLY** Apply in writing to the correspondent.
**WHO TO APPLY TO** D. S. Davis, Trustee, 18 Clifton Gardens, London N15 6AP Tel. 020 8731 0777 email mail@cohenarnold.com

## ■ Suffolk Community Foundation (formerly The Suffolk Foundation)
**CC NO** 1109453        **ESTABLISHED** 2005
**WHERE FUNDING CAN BE GIVEN** Suffolk.
**WHO CAN BENEFIT** Registered charities; voluntary and community groups.
**WHAT IS FUNDED** The foundation has a range of different funds designed for small community and voluntary groups working to help local people across Suffolk. Each scheme tends to have a different application procedure and size of award. Note: grant schemes can change frequently. Potential applicants are advised to consult the foundation's website for details of current programmes and their deadlines.
**WHAT IS NOT FUNDED** Projects not benefitting people living in Suffolk; grants to individuals or families for personal needs (with the exception of Suffolk Disability Care Fund); direct replacement of statutory obligation and public funding; promotion of religious or political causes; groups with significant financial free reserves; retrospective grants; contribution to endowment fund, payment of deficit funding or repayment of loans; national charities that are not providing clear local benefits; overseas travel or expeditions; sponsored or fundraising events or groups raising funds to redistribute to other causes; medical research and equipment for statutory or private healthcare; start-up funding for a project that is unable to start within nine months; commercial ventures, unless the group is a registered not-for-profit organisation; general appeals; animal welfare, unless the project benefits people (e.g. disability riding schemes); statutory work in educational institutions; fees for professional fundraisers.
**TYPE OF GRANT** One-off grants for capital and revenue costs and full project funding.
**RANGE OF GRANTS** Small grants averaging around £2,000.
**FINANCES** Year 2013/14 Income £4,078,504 Grants £2,028,347 Grants to organisations £2,028,347 Assets £6,451,198
**TRUSTEES** Stephen Fletcher; James Buckle; Claire Horsley; Lady Howes; James Dinwiddy; Very Revd Dr Frances Ward; Sir John Rowland;

Gulshan Kayembe; Nigel Smith; Iain Jamie; Terence Ward; Peter Newnham; Jonathan Agar; Neil Walmsley.
**OTHER INFORMATION** Grants were awarded to 541 organisations.
**HOW TO APPLY** The foundation's website has details of the grant schemes currently being administered and how to apply.
**WHO TO APPLY TO** Julie Rose, Grants Officer, The Old Barn, Peninsula Business Centre, Wherstead, Ipswich, Suffolk IP9 2BB *Tel.* 01473 602602 *email* info@suffolkfoundation.org.uk *Website* suffolkcf.org.uk

## ■ The Suffolk Historic Churches Trust

**CC NO** 267047    **ESTABLISHED** 1973
**WHERE FUNDING CAN BE GIVEN** Suffolk.
**WHO CAN BENEFIT** Churches and chapels.
**WHAT IS FUNDED** Preservation, repair, maintenance, restoration and improvement of churches.
**WHAT IS NOT FUNDED** Furnishings and fittings; churchyard walls; brasses and bells; monuments; organs; redecoration, unless needed as part of an eligible project; new buildings or extensions to existing buildings.
**TYPE OF GRANT** One-off for specific project.
**RANGE OF GRANTS** £50–£7,500
**SAMPLE GRANTS** St Botolph – Burgh (£7,500); St John the Baptist – Metfield, All Saints – Laxfield and St Mary – Newbourne (£6,000 each); St Edmund – Hargrave and St Mary – Bucklesham (£4,000 each); St Peter – Moulton (£3,000); St Matthew – Ipswich and St Peter – Theberton (£2,000 each); All Saints – Hollesley (£1,000); St Mary and St Botolph – Whitton (£500).
**FINANCES** *Year* 2013/14 *Income* £236,592 *Grants* £121,080 *Grants to organisations* £121,080 *Assets* £776,991
**TRUSTEES** Martin Favell; Sir Christopher Howes; Hon Charles Boscawen; Christopher Spicer; Robert Williams; Clive Paine; Revd David Jenkins; Simon Tennent; Patrick Grieve; Celia Stephens; Jonathan Penn; Nicholas Pearson; Edward Bland; Geoffrey Probert; David Guymer King; John Devaux; Frances Torrington.
**OTHER INFORMATION** Grants were awarded to 40 churches and chapels totalling £121,000.
**HOW TO APPLY** Application forms can be downloaded from the trust's website. Grants Committee Meetings are held four times a year and the applications are normally required at least two weeks prior to the meeting.
**WHO TO APPLY TO** David Guymer King, Trustee, Peacock Ridge, Brettenham Road, Buxhall, Stowmarket, Suffolk IP14 3DX *Tel.* 01449 737405 *email* shct@btconnect.com *Website* www.shct.org.uk

## ■ The Alan Sugar Foundation

**CC NO** 294880    **ESTABLISHED** 1986
**WHERE FUNDING CAN BE GIVEN** UK.
**WHO CAN BENEFIT** Registered charities.
**WHAT IS FUNDED** General charitable purposes; Jewish causes; children and young people; older people; people who are socially or economically disadvantaged.
**WHAT IS NOT FUNDED** Individuals; non-registered charities.
**TYPE OF GRANT** One-off and recurring; capital and project costs.
**RANGE OF GRANTS** £500–£200,000

**SAMPLE GRANTS** Jewish Care; Sport Relief; Macmillan Cancer; BBC Children in Need; Prostate Cancer Charitable Fund; Cancer Research UK; and St Michael's Hospice.
**FINANCES** *Year* 2013/14 *Income* £707 *Grants* £230,000 *Grants to organisations* £230,000
**TRUSTEES** Simon Sugar; Lord Sugar; Colin Sandy; Daniel Sugar; Louise Baron.
**OTHER INFORMATION** Unfortunately the accounts were not available to view due to the low income, but it is estimated that grants were made totalling around £230,000.
**HOW TO APPLY This trust states that it does not respond to unsolicited applications.** All projects are initiated by the trustees.
**WHO TO APPLY TO** Colin Sandy, Trustee, Amshold House, Goldings Hill, Loughton, Essex IG10 3RW *Tel.* 020 3225 5560 *email* colin@amsprop.com

## ■ The Bernard Sunley Charitable Foundation

**CC NO** 1109099    **ESTABLISHED** 1960
**WHERE FUNDING CAN BE GIVEN** Unrestricted, in practice England and Wales.
**WHO CAN BENEFIT** Registered charities and Community Amateur Sports Clubs (CASC), particularly those serving rural and isolated communities.
**WHAT IS FUNDED** Grants are given in the following categories: community; education; health; social welfare.
**WHAT IS NOT FUNDED** Individuals; overseas projects; running costs. Applications from organisations that have applied within 12 months previously will be automatically declined.
**TYPE OF GRANT** Capital grants, usually as single payments in a one-year period but sometimes over three years.
**RANGE OF GRANTS** The majority of grants (80%) are small (£5,000 or less). Medium grants (£5,001 to £25,000) and large grants (exceeding £25,000) are also available. Large grants are exceptional.
**SAMPLE GRANTS** Design Museum London (£100,000); Ear Foundation (£70,000); Book Aid International and National Horseracing Museum (£50,000 each); Shannon Trust (£45,000); Stoke Methodist Church (£35,000); Outward Bound Trust (£25,000); Girlguiding Bristol and South Gloucestershire (£15,000); Marigolds Recreation Ground – Essex, Northallerton and the Dales Mencap Society, Teach First and Willen Hospice (£10,000 each); National Museum of the Royal Navy (£7,000); Black Country Food Bank (£3,000); Age UK Mid Devon (£2,000); Hull Youth for Christ (£1,000).
**FINANCES** *Year* 2013/14 *Income* £3,802,000 *Grants* £2,915,949 *Grants to organisations* £2,915,949 *Assets* £98,627,000
**TRUSTEES** Joan Tice; Bella Sunley; Sir Donald Gosling; Dr Brian Martin; Anabel Knight; William Tice; Inigo Paternina.
**OTHER INFORMATION** The grant total above refers to the 480 grants approved during the year.
**HOW TO APPLY** There are guidelines for each of the grant categories on the website, which should be read before an application is started. The foundation prefers to receive applications via the online application form, which is available to access following the completion of a brief eligibility questionnaire. Alternatively, applications may be made in writing to the correspondent containing the following

information: the purpose of the charity and its objectives; the need and purpose of the project including who will benefit and how; the cost of the project including, where appropriate, a breakdown of costs; the amount of money raised and from which sources, as well as how you plan to raise the shortfall; and if applicable, how the running costs of the project will be met once the project is established. Any other documentation you feel will support or explain your appeal may be submitted. Those organisations whose annual income is of less than £25,000 should also enclose their latest approved annual accounts. The foundation acknowledges applications via email so, if possible, an email address should be provided. The foundation aims to reach a decision on applications within three months, though the process may take slightly longer.

**WHO TO APPLY TO** John Rimmington, Director, 20 Berkeley Square, London W1J 6LH *Tel.* 020 7408 2198 *email* office@bernardsunley.org *Website* www.bernardsunley.org

## ■ Community Foundation for Surrey

**CC NO** 1111600   **ESTABLISHED** 2005
**WHERE FUNDING CAN BE GIVEN** Surrey.
**WHO CAN BENEFIT** Charities; local community and voluntary groups; individuals.
**WHAT IS FUNDED** Strengthening communities in Surrey.
**TYPE OF GRANT** Surrey Community Foundation has an ongoing grant programme consisting of a number of funds established by individuals, families, trusts and companies.
**RANGE OF GRANTS** Grants range from £50 to £15,000. The average grant awarded during the year was £3,000.
**FINANCES** *Year* 2013/14 *Income* £2,221,315 *Grants* £736,627 *Grants to organisations* £736,627 *Assets* £8,199,216
**TRUSTEES** David Frank, Chair; Peter Hampson; Bridget Biddell; Simon Whalley; Richard Whittington; Graham Williams; Nigel Gillott; Dr Julie Llewelyn; Julia Grant; Graham Healy; Martin De Forest-Brown.
**OTHER INFORMATION** The grant total above includes grants made to individuals. The foundation has two funds for this purpose, which support people who are disadvantaged to gain employment. In total 248 grants were awarded to community, voluntary groups and individuals during the year.
**HOW TO APPLY** An expression of interest form is available on the funder's website, which all individuals and groups are advised to check for more details as all funds have their own criteria and closing dates. Alternatively, contact the foundation's grants team for more information before beginning an application form.
**WHO TO APPLY TO** Wendy Varcoe, Executive Director, Surrey Community Foundation, 1 Bishops Wharf, Walnut Tree Close, Guildford, Surrey GU1 4RA *Tel.* 01483 409230 *email* info@cfsurrey.org.uk *Website* www.cfsurrey.org.uk

## ■ The Sussex Community Foundation

**CC NO** 1113226   **ESTABLISHED** 2006
**WHERE FUNDING CAN BE GIVEN** East Sussex, West Sussex or Brighton and Hove.
**WHO CAN BENEFIT** Charities and community groups whose work benefits people in East Sussex, West Sussex or Brighton and Hove.
**WHAT IS FUNDED** The foundation is particularly interested in supporting groups that work towards the advancement of education, the protection of good health both mental and physical and the relief of poverty and sickness.
**WHAT IS NOT FUNDED** Statutory organisations or groups seeking to improve statutory assets, for example, friends or Parents groups looking for funds for playgrounds, school equipment, etc.; individuals with the exception of those applying to the Paul Rooney Fund or the Westdene Fund; fundraising activities that will be used to make awards to a third party; major capital appeals; projects whose wider community appeal or benefit is limited.
**RANGE OF GRANTS** Up to £30,000 but mostly £1,000–£5,000.
**SAMPLE GRANTS** Brighton and Hove Community Works (£31,500); Survivors Network Ltd (£25,000); Forward Facing (£15,000); Clocktower Sanctuary (£11,500); Equine Partners CIC and MindOut (£10,000 each); Lunch Positive (£8,000); Sussex Nightstop Plus (£6,000); Here4U and Peer Action (£5,500 each).
**FINANCES** *Year* 2013/14 *Income* £4,539,172 *Grants* £1,316,480 *Grants to organisations* £1,316,480 *Assets* £9,500,966
**TRUSTEES** Pamela Stiles; Neil Hart; Trevor James; Richard Pearson; Elizabeth Bennett; Mike Simpkin; Humphrey Price; Michael Martin; David Allam; Charles Drayson; Consuelo Brooke; Jonica Fox; Margaret Burgess; His Honour Keith Hollis; Julia Carrette.
**OTHER INFORMATION** Grants were awarded to 426 organisations.
**HOW TO APPLY** Application forms and a checklist of supporting documents can be found on the 'how to apply' section of the foundation's website.
**WHO TO APPLY TO** Kevin Richmond, Correspondent, Suite B, Falcon Wharf, Railway Lane, Lewes BN7 2AQ *Tel.* 01273 409440 *email* info@sussexgiving.org.uk *Website* www.sussexgiving.org.uk

## ■ The Sussex Historic Churches Trust

**CC NO** 282159   **ESTABLISHED** 1981
**WHERE FUNDING CAN BE GIVEN** Sussex.
**WHO CAN BENEFIT** Churches of any denomination over 100 years old and of some architectural or historical significance.
**WHAT IS FUNDED** Preservation, repair, maintenance and restoration of churches in Sussex.
**WHAT IS NOT FUNDED** Central heating and electrical maintenance; works to church halls; parish rooms; churchyards; bells; works of decoration and embellishment (except in the case of the restoration and conservation of such works).
**RANGE OF GRANTS** £1,000–£10,000; typical grants £5,000.
**SAMPLE GRANTS** St Nicholas – Itchingfield (£22,000); St Michael – Lewes, St Peter – Upper Beeding (£9,000 each); St Thomas a Beckett – Framfield (£7,000); St Giles – Dallington, St Mary Magdalene – Bolney, Holy Trinity – Poynings

(£5,000 each); St Mary – Apuldram (£4,000); All Hallows – Tillington, St Alban – Frant (£2,500 each).
FINANCES Year 2013 Income £130,341 Grants £88,500 Grants to organisations £88,500 Assets £1,279,488
TRUSTEES Philip Jones; Lady Pamela Wedgwood; John Barkshire; The Ven. Roger Combes; The Ven. Douglas H. McKittrick; Sara Stonor; Christopher Whittick; Graham Pound.
OTHER INFORMATION Grant total includes an unusually large grant of £22,000 to St Nicholas – Itchingfield. This was due to a donation from Spiller Trust.
HOW TO APPLY Applications should be made to the correspondent by post or using the form on the trust's website. *Grant Application Guidance Notes* are available from the trust and can be obtained from its website. These notes state the necessary documents to be submitted, which should outline the work to be done and the financial state of the parish. Potential recipients are expected to have already approached other sources of funding where appropriate, and to have participated in the annual Ride and Stride fundraising event. The trustees meet three times a year, in January, June and October. Applications must be made before work is started, and should be submitted as early as possible. Only in cases of genuine emergency can the grant-making timetable be varied.
WHO TO APPLY TO John Barkshire, Trustee, Denes House, High street, Burwash, Etchingham TN19 7EH *Tel.* 01435 882646 *email* jbarkshire19@gmail.com *Website* www.sussexhistoricchurchestrust.org.uk

■ **The Adrienne and Leslie Sussman Charitable Trust**
CC NO 274955    ESTABLISHED 1977
WHERE FUNDING CAN BE GIVEN Israel.
WHO CAN BENEFIT Registered charities.
WHAT IS FUNDED General charitable purposes; Jewish causes.
SAMPLE GRANTS Previous beneficiaries have included: BF Shvut Ami, Chai – Lifeline and B'nai B'rith Hillel Fund, Child Resettlement, Children and Youth Aliyah, Finchley Synagogue, Jewish Care, Nightingale House, Norwood Ravenswood and Sidney Sussex CLL.
FINANCES Year 2013/14 Income £64,488 Grants £64,130 Grants to organisations £64,130 Assets £2,263,991
TRUSTEES Martin Paisner; Adrienne Sussman; Debra Sussman; Adam Sussman; Neal Sussman.
OTHER INFORMATION A recent list of beneficiaries was not available.
HOW TO APPLY Apply in writing to the correspondent.
WHO TO APPLY TO Adrienne Sussman, Trustee, 25 Tillingbourne Gardens, London N3 3JJ *Tel.* 020 8346 6775

■ **The Sutasoma Trust**
CC NO 803301    ESTABLISHED 1990
WHERE FUNDING CAN BE GIVEN UK and overseas.
WHO CAN BENEFIT Individuals and organisations.
WHAT IS FUNDED Bursaries and support to institutions in the field of social sciences, humanities and humanitarian activities. General grants may also be made.
TYPE OF GRANT Mainly recurrent.

SAMPLE GRANTS Lucy Cavendish College Fellowship (£19,500); Helen Bamber Foundation (£11,000); Yehudi Menuhin School (£10,000); Hadja Ama Refuge (£7,200); Life Begins (£7,000); Yangjakot Day Care Centre Nepal (£6,300); Exceed Worldwide (£3,000); Amnesty International (£2,000); Guildhall School Trust, Lewa Wildlife Conservation and The Welfare Ass (£1,000 each); Room to Heal (£500); Link Community – Kongo Primary (£250).
FINANCES Year 2013/14 Income £97,056 Grants £129,969 Grants to organisations £129,969 Assets £2,753,726
TRUSTEES Dr Angela Hobart; Marcel Burgauer; Jane Lichtenstein; Prof. Bruce Kapferer; Dr Sally Wolfe; Dr Piers Vitebsky.
OTHER INFORMATION The grant total includes grants paid to both individuals and organisations.
HOW TO APPLY Apply in writing to the correspondent. The trustees meet annually.
WHO TO APPLY TO Jane Lichtenstein, Trustee, PO Box 157, Haverhill, Suffolk CB9 1AH *Tel.* 07768 245384 *email* sutasoma.trust@btinternet.com

■ **Sutton Coldfield Charitable Trust**
CC NO 218627    ESTABLISHED 1898
WHERE FUNDING CAN BE GIVEN The former borough of Sutton Coldfield, comprising three electoral wards: New Hall, Vesey and Four Oaks.
WHO CAN BENEFIT Individuals in need and organisations, without restriction, in Sutton Coldfield.
WHAT IS FUNDED Social welfare; education; the arts; religion; health; community development; amateur sport; environmental protection.
WHAT IS NOT FUNDED Individuals; organisations outside the area of benefit, unless the organisations are providing essential services in the area.
TYPE OF GRANT The trustees will consider making grants for buildings, projects, research, start-up costs, and capital and running costs for up to three years or as one-off payments. No cash payments are given – payments are made via invoices or vouchers.
RANGE OF GRANTS Up to £75,000.
SAMPLE GRANTS St Giles Hospice; John Willmott School; Boldmere Swimming Club; New Hall Ward Advisory Board; New Hall Primary School; Holy Trinity (Church of England) Parish Church; Boldmere Methodist Church; Victim Support; Walmley Women's Institute; and Sutton Coldfield Asian Society.
FINANCES Year 2013/14 Income £1,764,345 Grants £1,601,050 Grants to organisations £1,601,050 Assets £48,824,883
TRUSTEES John Gray; Susan Bailey; Jane Rothwell; Rodney Kettel; David Owen; Keith Dudley; Carole Hancox; Cllr Margaret Waddington; Dr S. C. Martin; Malcolm Cornish; A. N. Andrews; Linda Lamb; Andrew Burley; Andrew Morris.
HOW TO APPLY Contact the grants manager on 0121 351 2262 to make an application or to discuss further details.
WHO TO APPLY TO The Grants Manager, Lingard House, Fox Hollies Road, Sutton Coldfield, West Midlands B76 2RJ *Tel.* 0121 351 2262 *email* info@suttoncharitabletrust.org *Website* www.suttoncoldfieldcharitabletrust.com

# Sutton

## ■ The Sutton Trust
**CC NO** 1146244
**WHERE FUNDING CAN BE GIVEN** UK.
**WHO CAN BENEFIT** Educational institutions, and other groups that organise formal education projects or undertake educational research.
**WHAT IS FUNDED** The trust looks to combat educational inequality through a wide range of programmes. See the website for current programmes.
**WHAT IS NOT FUNDED** Individuals; educational tuition fees; sports or arts projects; capital projects (building work, equipment, etc.); expeditions; general appeals; projects based outside the UK. The trust is unable to offer advice to individuals on issues relating to independent schools admissions (including fees, bursaries and scholarships).
**SAMPLE GRANTS Previous beneficiaries have included:** Cambridge University (various projects); Durham University; Feltham School; Snapethorpe Primary School; and Policy Exchange.
**FINANCES** Year 2013/14 Income £3,088,396 Grants £1,817,135 Grants to organisations £1,812,560 Assets £1,165,770
**TRUSTEES** Sir Peter Lampl; David Backinsell; David Hall; Lady Susan Lampl.
**OTHER INFORMATION** A total of 131 grants were made during the year of which 21, amounting to £4,600, were to individuals.
**HOW TO APPLY** The website states: 'The Trust takes a proactive approach to the work it wishes to support and tends to develop programmes itself, and in partnership with relevant organisations. The vast majority of unsolicited proposals we receive are unsuccessful, and we are principally committed to further developing our current programmes. We are however willing to consider exceptional proposals which fit closely with our specific areas of interest. If you feel that your organisation has a programme which fits this criteria, first complete a funding enquiry on the Contact Us page, including a couple of paragraphs describing your idea (unfortunately, due to the number of enquiries we receive, we are not always able to provide individual responses). You may then be asked to submit a brief proposal.'
**WHO TO APPLY TO** Guy Graham, Finance Manager, The Sutton Trust, Ninth Floor, Millbank Tower, 21–24 Millbank, London SW1P 4QP *Tel.* 020 7802 1664 *email* info@suttontrust.com *Website* www.suttontrust.com

## ■ The Suva Foundation Limited
**CC NO** 1077057   **ESTABLISHED** 1999
**WHERE FUNDING CAN BE GIVEN** Unrestricted with a preference for Henley-on-Thames.
**WHO CAN BENEFIT** Charitable organisations.
**WHAT IS FUNDED** General charitable purposes; education and training; the promotion of health; arts and culture.
**SAMPLE GRANTS** River and Rowing Museum Foundation (£25,000); Great Ormond Street Hospital (£13,300); RNIB (£10,000); CLIC Sargent and The Prince's Trust (£5,000 each); The Teenage Wilderness Trust (£2,500); Rotary Club (£200).
**FINANCES** Year 2013/14 Income £207,341 Grants £270,083 Grants to organisations £270,083 Assets £11,517,344
**TRUSTEES** Annabel Nicoll; Paddy Nicoll.
**OTHER INFORMATION** The foundation is a regular supporter of the Langley Academy.

**HOW TO APPLY** This trust does not accept unsolicited applications.
**WHO TO APPLY TO** Cristina Wade, Correspondent, 61 Grosvenor Street, London W1K 3JE *Tel.* 020 3011 1100 *email* admin@61grosvenorstreet.com

## ■ Swan Mountain Trust
**CC NO** 275594   **ESTABLISHED** 1977
**WHERE FUNDING CAN BE GIVEN** UK.
**WHO CAN BENEFIT** Organisations benefitting mental health patients and prisoners, ex-offenders and potential offenders.
**WHAT IS FUNDED** Mental health (not disability) and penal affairs.
**WHAT IS NOT FUNDED** Individuals or for annual holidays; debt repayment; large appeals; causes outside the trust's two main areas of work.
**TYPE OF GRANT** One-off.
**RANGE OF GRANTS** Up to £5,000; however, on average, under £1,000.
**SAMPLE GRANTS** Prisoner Education Trust (£5,000); Sea Sanctuary – Falmouth and Circles UK – London (£2,700); Bradford Family Support Network, Autism Ventures – Liverpool and Reprieve – London (£2,000 each); Trailblazers – London and Life Cycle UK – Bristol (£1,500 each); Open Country – Harrogate and Outreach Community and Residential Services – Manchester (£1,000 each); and Cherry Tree Nursery – Bournemouth (£500).
**FINANCES** Year 2013/14 Income £51,771 Grants £46,435 Grants to organisations £46,435 Assets £1,102,124
**TRUSTEES** Peter Kilgarriff; Dodie Carter; Janet Hargreaves.
**OTHER INFORMATION** Grants were made to 26 organisations totalling £46,500 during the year.
**HOW TO APPLY** The trust's website states that: 'The trustees meet three times a year in February, June and October. Postal applications may be made at anytime to: Jan Hargreaves, 7 Mount Vernon, London, NW3 6QS.'
**WHO TO APPLY TO** Janet Hargreaves, Trustee, 7 Mount Vernon, London NW3 6QS *Tel.* 020 7794 2486 *email* info@swanmountaintrust.org.uk *Website* swanmountaintrust.org.uk

## ■ The Swann-Morton Foundation
**CC NO** 271925   **ESTABLISHED** 1976
**WHO CAN BENEFIT** Students and organisations benefitting children and young people, people with disabilities, people suffering from ill health or those disadvantaged by poverty.
**WHAT IS FUNDED** General charitable purposes; education; health; disability; social welfare; animal welfare.
**WHAT IS NOT FUNDED** Gap years.
**RANGE OF GRANTS** £1,000–£3,500
**SAMPLE GRANTS** Sheffield Children's Hospital and St Luke's Hospice (£3,500 each); and Royal College of Surgeons and Whirlow Farm Trust (£1,000 each).
**FINANCES** Year 2013/14 Income £55,010 Grants £44,250 Grants to organisations £44,250 Assets £112,192
**TRUSTEES** Judith Gilmour; Michael McGinley; George Rodgers.
**OTHER INFORMATION** Grants were made totalling £51,000, including £6,500 for individual student grants and electives.
**HOW TO APPLY** Applications can be made in writing to the correspondent. The foundation's annual report for 2012/13 states that it 'invites

applications for funding of projects from hospitals, charities and students. Applicants are invited to submit a summary of their proposals in a specific format. The applications are reviewed against specific criteria and research objectives which are set by the trustees.'
**WHO TO APPLY TO** Michael Hirst, Director, Swann-Morton Ltd, Owlerton Green, Sheffield S6 2BJ *Tel.* 0114 234 4231

■ **Swansea and Brecon Diocesan Board of Finance Limited**
**CC NO** 249810     **ESTABLISHED** 1967
**WHERE FUNDING CAN BE GIVEN** Diocese of Swansea and Brecon (Neath Port Talbot, Powys and Swansea).
**WHO CAN BENEFIT** Clergy and organisations in the diocese of Swansea and Brecon.
**WHAT IS FUNDED** The majority portion of the board's expenditure is on clergy stipends, emoluments and housing, with the balance being spent on Diocesan activities, grants and administration.
**WHAT IS NOT FUNDED** Applications from outside the diocese.
**TYPE OF GRANT** One-off grants to organisations.
**FINANCES** *Year* 2013 *Income* £3,585,064 *Grants* £149,054 *Grants to organisations* £149,054 *Assets* £4,038,176
**TRUSTEES** Archdeacon Randolph Thomas; Gwyn Lewis; Gillian Knight; Rt Revd John Davies; The Venerable Robert Williams; Clive Rees; Revd Canon Peter Williams; Revd Alan Jevons; Peter Davies; Prof. Peter Townsend; The Revd Canon Janet Russell; Geoffrey Hardy; Richard Tyler.
**OTHER INFORMATION** Grant-making to organisations accounts for only a small part of the charity's activities.
**HOW TO APPLY** The charity does not respond to unsolicited applications.
**WHO TO APPLY TO** Heather Price, Diocesan Centre, Cathedral Close, Brecon, Powys LD3 9DP *Tel.* 01874 623716 *Website* www.churchinwales.org.uk/swanbrec

■ **Swimathon Foundation**
**CC NO** 1123870     **ESTABLISHED** 2008
**WHERE FUNDING CAN BE GIVEN** UK.
**WHO CAN BENEFIT** Community groups, including swimming clubs; older people's organisations; groups for young people; disability groups; other charities.
**WHAT IS FUNDED** Swimming. In particular, the promotion of swimming in local communities.
**WHAT IS NOT FUNDED** Organisations which exist to promote religion itself, and groups where the community must participate in religious services in order to benefit, are not eligible to apply. Hydrotherapy pools are not eligible to apply for a Swimathon Foundation grant if they are not a Swimathon pool and organisations which promote a political party or activity are not eligible to apply. Grants will not be given to cover general essential running or maintenance costs. Organisations that have received a grant in the last twelve months may not apply.
**TYPE OF GRANT** One-off grants.
**RANGE OF GRANTS** Between £300 and £2,500.
**SAMPLE GRANTS** Unusually, the only beneficiary in 2012/13 was the Swimming Trust (£26,500). In the previous year, grants totalling £93,000 were awarded to 28 organisations.
**FINANCES** *Year* 2012/13 *Income* £3,012,206 *Grants* £26,512 *Grants to organisations* £26,512 *Assets* £264,326
**TRUSTEES** Anthony Kendall; Ralph Riley; Philip Stinson; Graham Batterham; Donna Notaro; Deana Radice.
**OTHER INFORMATION** In addition to the grant total, the foundation also spent £2 million supporting charities and organisations involved in swimming. In the previous year, grants totalling £93,000 were awarded to 28 organisations.
**HOW TO APPLY** All applications should be submitted using the online application form which is available, together with criteria and comprehensive guidelines, from the foundation's website (Note: Swimathon is an annual fundraising event): Applicants must be a representative of, or have the support of, a pool participating in Swimathon. Details can be found on the foundation's website. All applications must be submitted using the online form. Applications received by post, fax or email will not be considered. For full details regarding when and how to apply for grants refer to the foundation's website, or contact the foundation by phone or email.
**WHO TO APPLY TO** Nick Bush, c/o Cox Costello and Horne Ltd, Langwood House, 63–81 High Street, Rickmansworth, Hertfordshire WD3 1EQ *Tel.* 01923 771977 *email* info@swimathonfoundation.org *Website* www.swimathonfoundation.org

■ **The John Swire (1989) Charitable Trust**
**CC NO** 802142     **ESTABLISHED** 1989
**WHERE FUNDING CAN BE GIVEN** UK, with some preference for Kent.
**WHO CAN BENEFIT** Charitable organisations; universities; schools.
**WHAT IS FUNDED** General charitable purposes, especially arts, welfare, education, sports, medicine and research.
**RANGE OF GRANTS** Generally £1,000–£100,000.
**SAMPLE GRANTS** St John of Jerusalem Eye Hospital Group (£1.1 million); Riding for the Disabled, Cobbes Meadow (£103,000); Kent Wildlife Trust (£50,000); Catching Lives and Faversham Buildings Preservation Trust (£20,000 each); Carers First and Prior's Court Foundation (£15,000 each); Parkinson's UK, School Home Support Service UK and Stour Music (£5,000 each); Artists' General Benevolent Institution and Pilsdon at Malling Community (£4,000 each); GB Women's Rafting Team, Pilgrims Hospices, RNLI and Mission to Seafarers (£2,500 each); the Alternative Theatre Company Ltd, Canterbury Choral Society, Chatham Historic Dockyard Trust and Essex Wildlife Trust (£1,000 each).
**FINANCES** *Year* 2013 *Income* £1,163,100 *Grants* £1,603,951 *Grants to organisations* £1,603,951 *Assets* £32,266,743
**TRUSTEES** B. Swire; J. Swire; Lady Moira Swire; Michael Cradock Robinson; Sir John Swire.
**OTHER INFORMATION** Grants of less than £1,000 amounted to a total of £20,000.
**HOW TO APPLY** Apply in writing to the correspondent explaining how the funds would be used and what would be achieved.
**WHO TO APPLY TO** Sarah Irving, Correspondent, John Swire & Sons Ltd, Swire House, 59 Buckingham Gate, London SW1E 6AJ *Tel.* 020 7834 7717 *email* Sarah.Irving@jssldn.co.uk

# The Swire Charitable Trust

**CC NO** 270726     **ESTABLISHED** 1976
**WHERE FUNDING CAN BE GIVEN** UK.
**WHO CAN BENEFIT** Regional and UK-wide organisations.
**WHAT IS FUNDED** General charitable purposes, including the armed forces, health, medical research, social welfare, the environment and animal welfare.
**RANGE OF GRANTS** £1,000–£75,000
**SAMPLE GRANTS** Marine Society and Sea Cadets (£50,000); the Air League Trust (£27,000); Bentley Priory, Oracle Cancer Trust and the Norman Trust (£25,000 each); Cancer Vaccine Institute and Monte San Martino Trust (£15,000 each); National Maritime Museum, the Stroke Association and Sightsavers International (£10,000 each); British Lung Foundation, Diabetes UK, English Heritage and Missing People (£5,000 each); Buttle UK, Care for Casualties, Prospect Burma and Target Ovarian Cancer (£2,500 each); and International Fund for Animal Welfare and Westminster Tree Trust (£1,000 each).
**FINANCES** Year 2013 Income £1,100,353 Grants £862,818 Grants to organisations £862,818 Assets £193,128
**TRUSTEES** Sir J. Swire; Sir Adrian Swire; B. N. Swire; J. S. Swire; M. Swire; J. W. J. Hughes-Hallett.
**OTHER INFORMATION** Grants to over 145 organisations totalled £863,000.
**HOW TO APPLY** Apply in writing to the correspondent. Applications are considered throughout the year. The annual report for 2013 states that 'although the trustees make some grants with no formal applications, they normally require organisations to submit a request explaining how the funds could be used and what would be achieved'.
**WHO TO APPLY TO** Sarah Irving, Correspondent, John Swire & Sons Ltd, Swire House, 59 Buckingham Gate, London SW1E 6AJ *Tel.* 020 7834 7717 *email* Sarah.Irving@jssldn.co.uk

# The Hugh and Ruby Sykes Charitable Trust

**CC NO** 327648     **ESTABLISHED** 1987
**WHERE FUNDING CAN BE GIVEN** Principally South Yorkshire, also Derbyshire.
**WHO CAN BENEFIT** Registered charities.
**WHAT IS FUNDED** General charitable purposes.
**WHAT IS NOT FUNDED** Individuals.
**FINANCES** Year 2013/14 Income £129,125 Grants £140,732 Grants to organisations £140,732 Assets £1,838,859
**TRUSTEES** Sir Hugh Sykes; Lady Ruby Sykes.
**OTHER INFORMATION** A list of beneficiaries was not included in the accounts.
**HOW TO APPLY** Apply in writing to the correspondent.
**WHO TO APPLY TO** Brian Evans, Correspondent, Brookfield Manor, Hathersage, Hope Valley S32 1BR *Tel.* 01433 651190 *email* info@brookfieldmanor.com

# The Charles and Elsie Sykes Trust

**CC NO** 206926     **ESTABLISHED** 1954
**WHERE FUNDING CAN BE GIVEN** UK, with a preference for Yorkshire.
**WHO CAN BENEFIT** Registered charities only. Grants are predominantly made to charities based in Yorkshire or to national charities for the benefit of people in Yorkshire. A number of grants are made to charities based in other areas of the country, though these tend to be specialist medical organisations.
**WHAT IS FUNDED** A broad range of causes are supported, including: people who are blind or partially sighted; children and youth; cultural and environmental heritage; people who are deaf, hard of hearing or speech impaired; people with disabilities; education; hospices and hospitals; medical research; medical welfare; mental health and mental disability; welfare of older people; overseas aid; services and ex-services; social and moral welfare; animals and birds.
**WHAT IS NOT FUNDED** Individuals; overseas appeals; not-registered charities. Local organisations not in the north of England, and recently-established charities are unlikely to be successful.
**TYPE OF GRANT** Mostly one-off.
**RANGE OF GRANTS** Up to £25,500.
**SAMPLE GRANTS** Royal Holloway – University of London (£25,500); Next Steps Mental Health Resource Centre – Ryedale (£10,000); Yorkshire Air Ambulance (£7,500); Opera North (£6,000); Bradford Disability Services, Horizon Life Training and Yorkshire Dales Millennium Trust (£5,000 each); Harrogate Citizens Advice (£1,500); Caring for Life (£1,000).
**FINANCES** Year 2013 Income £392,967 Grants £377,825 Grants to organisations £377,825 Assets £14,541,426
**TRUSTEES** John Ward, Chair; Anne Brownlie; Martin Coultas; Michael Garnett; Barry Kay; Dr Michael McEvoy; Peter Rous; Dr Rosemary Livingstone; Sara Buchan.
**OTHER INFORMATION** During the year a total 140 grants were made.
**HOW TO APPLY** Application forms can be downloaded from the website. The form should be completed and then be sent to the trust along with a copy of the organisation's latest accounts, annual report and any other relevant information. It is more favourable for the application if the accounts are current. If a grant is required for a particular project, full details and costings should be provided. Applications from schools, playgroups, cadet forces, scouts, guides, and churches must be for outreach programmes, and not for maintenance projects. Successful applications will receive a donation which may or may not be subject to conditions.
**WHO TO APPLY TO** Judith Long, Secretary, Barber Titleys Solicitors, 6 North Park Road, Harrogate, Yorkshire HG1 5PA *Tel.* 01423 817238 *Fax* 01423 566288 *Website* www.charlesandelsiesykestrust.co.uk

# Sylvia Waddilove Foundation UK

**CC NO** 1118097
**WHERE FUNDING CAN BE GIVEN** UK and overseas.
**WHO CAN BENEFIT** Registered or exempt charities (small charities are favoured, with the exception of those undertaking medical research projects). Individuals undertaking medical research may be supported.
**WHAT IS FUNDED** Projects benefitting of the community and relating to: education, particularly organic farming, animal husbandry, veterinary science, animal welfare and surgery and research into animal surgery, or visual and performing arts; medical research; the relief of disability or illness; the preservation of built environment; accommodation and housing; skills-based training of younger people. The administrator's website details essential and desirable criteria for applications in each

category. Only applications 'that are for the benefit of the community or sizeable groups within the community, and from organisations that will carry out the projects themselves' are accepted.

**WHAT IS NOT FUNDED** Individuals (except medical research projects); requests made within two years of a previous application. Check the eligibility criteria for each area of the foundation's grant-making.

**TYPE OF GRANT** One-off or recurrent; awards may be spread over two or three years.

**RANGE OF GRANTS** £400–£33,000; generally up to £10,000.

**SAMPLE GRANTS** Glasgow Building Preservation Trust, Sir Robert Christopher's Almshouses and The Arvon Foundation (£33,000 each); The Arkwright Society (£25,000); Tara Arts Group Ltd (£6,000); Kidney Research Trust, Square Chapel Trust and The Poltimore House Trust (£5,000 each); Diabetes UK, Heel and Toes Children's Charity and The London Bubble Theatre Company (£4,000 each); The Magdalen Environmental Trust (£3,500); Central Youth Theatre and National Glass Centre (£3,000 each); Yusuf Youth Initiative (£2,000); Outfit Moray (£1,500); South West Community Cycles (£700); Belarus Free Theatre (£500); Riverhouse Barn Arts Centre (£400)

**FINANCES** Year 2013 Income £122,454 Grants £309,770 Grants to organisations £309,770 Assets £3,885,896

**TRUSTEES** Gerald Kidd; Percy Robson; Nadeem Azhar.

**OTHER INFORMATION** The trustees particularly seek innovative projects that are less than five years old. During the year grants were made to 81 organisations.

**HOW TO APPLY** Application forms are available from the administrator's website. If successful, applicants can expect to receive their grant within three months of completing an application. The trustees meet in January, April, July and October. Note that 'the trustees receive a large number of applications and can only open the application dates for a short period of time'.

**WHO TO APPLY TO** The Trustees, c/o Pothecary Witham Weld Solicitors, 70 St George's Square, London SW1V 3RD Tel. 020 7821 8211 email waddilove@pwwsolicitors.co.uk Website www.pwwsolicitors.co.uk/funding-applications/13-the-sylvia-waddilove-foundation-uk

## ■ The Charity of Stella Symons

**CC NO** 259638  **ESTABLISHED** 1968
**WHERE FUNDING CAN BE GIVEN** UK.
**WHO CAN BENEFIT** Registered charities.
**WHAT IS FUNDED** General charitable purposes, with a preference for health, older people, children and young people, and ex-service people.
**WHAT IS NOT FUNDED** Individuals.
**TYPE OF GRANT** Buildings; capital and core costs; one-off; project funding; research; recurring and running costs; salaries; start-up costs. Outright gifts and larger sums on loan on beneficial terms. Funding for up to and over three years will be considered.
**RANGE OF GRANTS** The majority of grants are for £250.
**SAMPLE GRANTS** GOSHCC Isla Cecil Fund (£1,000); Action for Blind People, Child Brain Injury, Douglas Badar Foundation, Endeavour Trust, Forces Support, Hope UK, International Animal Rescue, Julian House, Lupus UK, Missing People, National Tremor Foundation, Pregnancy Choices Norfolk, Secret World Wildlife Rescue, The Feast, Wave Length and Young Aliyah Child Rescue (£250 each).

**FINANCES** Year 2013/14 Income £41,347 Grants £25,650 Grants to organisations £25,650 Assets £2,104,810

**TRUSTEES** Jonathan Bosley; Katherine Willis; Mervyne Mitchell.

**OTHER INFORMATION** Grants totalled £25,500 during the year and were made to 98 organisations.

**HOW TO APPLY** Appeals may be made in writing to the correspondent.

**WHO TO APPLY TO** Jonathan Bosley, Trustee, 20 Mill Street, Shipston-on-Stour, Warwickshire CV36 4AW email stellasymonscharitabletrust@gmail.com

# Tajtelbaum

## ■ The Tajtelbaum Charitable Trust
**CC NO** 273184 **ESTABLISHED** 1974
**WHERE FUNDING CAN BE GIVEN** Mainly UK and Israel.
**WHO CAN BENEFIT** Jewish organisations benefitting children, young adults and students will be considered. Support may be given to older and sick people.
**WHAT IS FUNDED** Support for Orthodox synagogues, education establishments, hospitals and homes for older people.
**RANGE OF GRANTS** £500–£150,000
**SAMPLE GRANTS Previous beneficiaries have included:** United Institutions Arad, Emuno Educational Centre, Ruzin Sadiger Trust, Gur Foundation, Before Trust, Beth Hassidei Gur, Comet Charities Limited, Delharville, Kupat Gemach Trust, Centre for Torah and Chesed, Friends of Nachlat David and Friends of Sanz Institute.
**FINANCES** Year 2012/13 Income £998,749 Grants £356,144 Grants to organisations £356,144 Assets £4,207,726
**TRUSTEES** Ilsa Tajtelbaum; Jacob Tajtelbaum; Emanuel Tajtelbaum; Eli Jaswon; H. Frydenson.
**HOW TO APPLY** Apply in writing to the correspondent.
**WHO TO APPLY TO** Ilsa Tajtelbaum, Trustee, PO Box 33911, London NW9 7ZX

## ■ The Gay and Keith Talbot Trust
**CC NO** 1102192 **ESTABLISHED** 2004
**WHERE FUNDING CAN BE GIVEN** Worldwide.
**WHO CAN BENEFIT** Charities working in financially developing countries.
**WHAT IS FUNDED** General charitable purposes in financially developing countries. The trust currently has a particular focus on funding fistula work and has also in recent years funded projects including medical causes, water projects and human rights. Grants in 2013/14 were distributed between the following causes: fistula work; research and development; general purposes.
**TYPE OF GRANT** One-off and recurring; capital costs; revenue costs; full project funding.
**RANGE OF GRANTS** £100–£50,000
**SAMPLE GRANTS Previous beneficiaries have included:** CAFOD (£50,000, for water projects in Sudan); International Nepal Fellowship (£19,000, for a fistula repair camp); International Refugee Trust (£16,000, for aid in Sudan); Jesuit Missions (£10,000, to support torture victims in Zimbabwe); Medical Missionaries of Mary (£10,000 in total); Impact Foundation (£10,000 in total); Our Lady of Windermere and St Herbert (£500); and Amnesty International (£100).
**FINANCES** Year 2013/14 Income £57,848 Grants £90,668 Grants to organisations £90,668 Assets £76,770
**TRUSTEES** Gay Talbot; Keith Talbot.
**OTHER INFORMATION** Grants in 2013/14 went towards funding fistula work in several countries, surgery for spina bifida in Bangladesh and medical aid in Sudan.
**HOW TO APPLY** Apply in writing to the correspondent.

**WHO TO APPLY TO** Keith Talbot, Chair, Fold Howe, Kentmere, Kendal, Cumbria LA8 9JW Tel. 01539 821504 email rktalbot@yahoo.co.uk

## ■ The Talbot Trusts
**CC NO** 221356 **ESTABLISHED** 1928
**WHERE FUNDING CAN BE GIVEN** Sheffield and immediate surrounding areas.
**WHO CAN BENEFIT** Charitable organisations; healthcare professionals.
**WHAT IS FUNDED** Health; people with disabilities; children and young people; older people.
**WHAT IS NOT FUNDED** Non registered charities; individuals; appeal requests; research; educational costs; fundraising activities; recurrent grants.
**TYPE OF GRANT** One-off; capital and core costs; running costs; salaries; start-up costs. Funding may be given for up to one year.
**RANGE OF GRANTS** Usually £500–£5,500.
**SAMPLE GRANTS** Happy Days (£5,500); Trinity Day Care Trust and Family Action (£4,000 each); The Sick Children's Trust and SHARE Psychotherapy (£2,500 each); Weston Park and Brittle Bone Society (£1,000 each); Ileostomy Association (£500).
**FINANCES** Year 2013/14 Income £92,665 Grants £85,752 Grants to organisations £85,752 Assets £2,235,672
**TRUSTEES** Tim Plant; Dr Brenda Jackson; Godfrey Smallman; Ronald Jones; Jo Frisby; Dr Zackary McMurray.
**HOW TO APPLY** Apply in writing to the correspondent.
**WHO TO APPLY TO** Neil Charlesworth, Correspondent, 11 Russett Court, Maltby, Rotherham S66 8SP Tel. 01709 769022 email ncharlesworth@equitysolutions.org.uk

## ■ The Talbot Village Trust
**CC NO** 249349 **ESTABLISHED** 1867
**WHERE FUNDING CAN BE GIVEN** The boroughs of Bournemouth, Christchurch and Poole; the districts of east Dorset and Purbeck.
**WHO CAN BENEFIT** Community organisations (such as schools, churches, youth clubs, playgroups, etc.).
**WHAT IS FUNDED** Capital projects benefitting young, older or people who, in general, are disadvantaged in the area of benefit.
**WHAT IS NOT FUNDED** Individuals.
**TYPE OF GRANT** Grants and loans. Mainly for capital costs.
**RANGE OF GRANTS** £2,000 to £100,000.
**SAMPLE GRANTS** Bournemouth War Memorial Homes and Broadstone Baptist Church (£100,000 each); Streetwise (£40,500); Bearwood Community Centre (£35,000); St Christopher's Church (£20,000); Church of Lady St Mary – Wareham (£10,000); 1st Lytchett Minster Scout Group (£6,000); St Thomas Community Centre (£3,800); Parish of Our Lady Fatima – Parkstone (£2,000).
**FINANCES** Year 2013 Income £2,146,020 Grants £1,016,027 Grants to organisations £1,016,027 Assets £41,959,192
**TRUSTEES** Christopher Lees, Chair; James Fleming; Sir George Meyrick; Sir Thomas Salt; Russell Rowe; Earl of Shaftesbury.
**OTHER INFORMATION** The grant total above refers to those, both paid and unpaid, that were approved during the year. The trust also provides housing for people who are older, who have a disability and who are in need, including students.

HOW TO APPLY Apply in writing to the correspondent.
WHO TO APPLY TO Gary Cox, Clerk, Dickinson Manser LLP, 5 Parkstone Road, Poole, Dorset BH15 2NL *Tel.* 01202 673071 *email* garycox@dickinsonmanser.co.uk

## ■ The Lady Tangye Charitable Trust

CC NO 1044220 ESTABLISHED 1995
WHERE FUNDING CAN BE GIVEN UK and worldwide, with some preference for the Midlands.
WHO CAN BENEFIT Charitable organisations.
WHAT IS FUNDED General charitable purposes, including Christian and environmental causes.
RANGE OF GRANTS £1,000–£6,000
SAMPLE GRANTS Staffordshire Wildlife Trust (£6,000); Birmingham Boys' and Girls' Union and New Wine Cymru (£4,000 each); RSPB and West Midland Urban Wildlife Trust (£2,000 each); Amnesty International, Crew Trust and Priest's Training Fund (£1,500 each); Big Ideas and Life (£1,000 each).
FINANCES *Year* 2013/14 *Income* £82,597 *Grants* £58,500 *Grants to organisations* £58,500 *Assets* £1,220,733
TRUSTEES Gitta Tangye; Colin Smith; Michael Plaut.
OTHER INFORMATION Grants were made to 29 organisations during the year.
HOW TO APPLY Apply in writing to the correspondent.
WHO TO APPLY TO Colin Ferguson Smith Trustee, 55 Warwick Crest, Arthur Road, Birmingham B15 2LH *Tel.* 0121 454 4698 *email* tobeascertained@tangye.co.uk

## ■ The David Tannen Charitable Trust

CC NO 280392 ESTABLISHED 1974
WHERE FUNDING CAN BE GIVEN Barnet, Hackney, Haringey; Israel.
WHO CAN BENEFIT Charitable organisations; synagogues; schools.
WHAT IS FUNDED Jewish causes; social welfare; education and training.
RANGE OF GRANTS About £1,000–£100,000.
SAMPLE GRANTS **Previous beneficiaries have included:** Cosmon Belz, Gevurath Ari Trust, Telz Academy Trust, Friends of Ohr Elchonon, Beis Ahron Trust, Wlodowa Charity, Chai Cancer Care, Kollel Skver Trust, Centre for Torah Trust, Gateshead Talmudical College, Jewish Women's Aid Trust, Torah 5759 Ltd and YTAF.
FINANCES *Year* 2013/14 *Income* £1,657,135 *Grants* £310,500 *Grants to organisations* £310,500 *Assets* £19,266,826
TRUSTEES David Tannen; Jonathan Miller; Alan Rose.
OTHER INFORMATION A list of beneficiaries was not included in the trust's accounts.
HOW TO APPLY Apply in writing to the correspondent.
WHO TO APPLY TO Jonathan Miller, Trustee, c/o Sutherland House, 70–78 West Hendon Broadway, London NW9 7BT *Tel.* 020 8202 1066

## ■ The Tanner Trust

CC NO 1021175 ESTABLISHED 1993
WHERE FUNDING CAN BE GIVEN UK, with a slight preference for the South of England, and overseas.
WHO CAN BENEFIT Charities; schools; societies; charitable projects.
WHAT IS FUNDED General charitable purposes; the environment; children and young people; the promotion of health; older people; people with disabilities; arts and culture; overseas aid.
WHAT IS NOT FUNDED Individuals.
RANGE OF GRANTS Up to £10,000.
SAMPLE GRANTS Canterbury Cathedral Trust and The Brokerage (£10,000 each); National Trust, Wheal Martyn Trust and World Monument Fund Britain (£7,500 each); Chalke Valley History Festival (£6,000); Admiral Nurses, British Homeopathic Association and British Red Cross (£5,000 each); Help for Heroes, National Churches Trust and Parkinson's Disease Society (£4,000 each); Community Action Nepal, Conservation Foundation, Practical Action and Prison Phoenix Trust (£3,000 each); Poems in the Waiting Room (£2,000); Cornwall Air Ambulance (£1,500); CPRE (£500).
FINANCES *Year* 2013/14 *Income* £402,471 *Grants* £420,000 *Grants to organisations* £420,000 *Assets* £5,412,342
TRUSTEES Alice Williams; Lucie Nottingham.
HOW TO APPLY The trust states that unsolicited applications are, without exception, not considered. Support is only given to charities personally known to the trustees.
WHO TO APPLY TO Celine Lecomte, Correspondent, Blake Lapthorn, Harbour Court, Compass Road, Portsmouth PO6 4ST *Tel.* 023 9222 1122 ext. 552 *email* info@blakemorgan.co.uk

## ■ The Lili Tapper Charitable Foundation

CC NO 268523 ESTABLISHED 1974
WHERE FUNDING CAN BE GIVEN UK.
WHO CAN BENEFIT Organisations benefitting Jewish people.
WHAT IS FUNDED Jewish causes; children and young people; older people; people with disabilities; education and training; arts and culture.
WHAT IS NOT FUNDED Individuals
SAMPLE GRANTS **Previous beneficiaries have included:** UJIA, CST, Manchester Jewish Foundation, Teenage Cancer Trust, Keshet Eilon, Israel Educational Foundation, Chicken Shed Theatre Company and Jewish Representation Council.
FINANCES *Year* 2013/14 *Income* £46,136 *Grants* £67,963 *Grants to organisations* £67,963 *Assets* £3,202,406
TRUSTEES Michael Webber; Dr Jonathan Webber.
OTHER INFORMATION Details of grant beneficiaries were not available for 2013/14.
HOW TO APPLY Apply in writing to the correspondent.
WHO TO APPLY TO Michael Webber, Trustee, Yew Tree Cottage, Artists Lane, Nether Alderley, Macclesfield SK10 4UA *email* tappercharitablefoundation@gmail.com

## ■ The Taurus Foundation

CC NO 1128441 ESTABLISHED 2009
WHERE FUNDING CAN BE GIVEN UK.
WHO CAN BENEFIT Registered charities.
WHAT IS FUNDED General charitable purposes.
SAMPLE GRANTS Beneficiaries in previous years have included: The Purcell School (£28,000); Concordia Foundation, Jewish Care, Just for Kids Law and Norwood Ravenswood (£10,000 each); Core Arts, Hillside Clubhouse and Magic Me (£5,000 each); and Royal Opera House (£2,500).

**FINANCES** Year 2013/14 *Income* £264,567 *Grants* £202,350 *Grants to organisations* £202,350 *Assets* £1,192,349

**TRUSTEES** Denis Felsenstein; Michael Jacobs; Alan Fenton; Anthony Forwood; Priscilla Fenton; Wendy Pollecoff; Carole Cook; Dominic Fenton.

**OTHER INFORMATION** Grants were made to 28 organisations.

**HOW TO APPLY** Grants will not be given for unsolicited applications. The trustees proactively identify organisations that are eligible for funding and contact them with the relevant information to make an application.

**WHO TO APPLY TO** Carole Cook, Trustee, Forsters LLP, 31 Hill Street, London W1J 5LS *Tel.* 020 7863 8333 *email* aclellland@taurus-foundation.org.uk

## ■ The Tay Charitable Trust

**SC NO** SC001004    **ESTABLISHED** 1951

**WHERE FUNDING CAN BE GIVEN** UK, with a preference for Scotland, particularly Dundee.

**WHO CAN BENEFIT** Registered charities.

**WHAT IS FUNDED** General charitable purposes.

**WHAT IS NOT FUNDED** Individuals.

**TYPE OF GRANT** One-off and recurring.

**RANGE OF GRANTS** Up to £5,000.

**SAMPLE GRANTS Previous beneficiaries have included:** V&A at Dundee (£10,000); University of Dundee and Ninewells Cancer Campaign (£5,000 each); Cerebral Palsy Africa (£3,000); Factory Skatepark, John Muir Trust and National Trust for Scotland (£2,000 each); St Giles' Cathedral, Trees for Life, Victim Support Dundee, Changing Faces and Dundee Science Centre (£1,000 each).

**FINANCES** Year 2013/14 *Income* £228,009 *Grants* £220,000 *Grants to organisations* £220,000

**HOW TO APPLY** There is no standard form. Applications should be made in writing to the correspondent, including a financial statement. 'The trustees regret to say they now do not notify applicants who have not succeeded due to the cost of postage.'

**WHO TO APPLY TO** E. Mussen, Correspondent, 6 Douglas Terrace, Broughty Ferry, Dundee DD5 1EA

## ■ C. B. and H. H. Taylor 1984 Trust

**CC NO** 291363    **ESTABLISHED** 1946

**WHERE FUNDING CAN BE GIVEN** West Midlands, Ireland and overseas.

**WHO CAN BENEFIT** Approximately 60% of funds available are currently given to the work and concerns of the Religious Society of Friends. The remaining funds are allocated to those charities in which the trustees have a special interest, particularly in the West Midlands. Applications are encouraged from minority groups and woman-led initiatives.

**WHAT IS FUNDED** The general areas of benefit are: The Religious Society of Friends (Quakers) and other religious denominations; healthcare projects; social welfare (community groups; children and young people; older people; disadvantaged people; people with disabilities; homeless people; housing initiatives; counselling and mediation agencies); education (adult literacy schemes; employment training; youth work); penal affairs (work with offenders and ex-offenders; police projects); the environment and conservation work; the arts; museums and art galleries; music and drama;

Ireland (cross-community health and social welfare projects); UK charities working overseas on long-term development projects.

**WHAT IS NOT FUNDED** Individuals (whether for research, expeditions, educational purposes and so on); local projects or groups outside the West Midlands; or projects concerned with travel or adventure; annual grants for revenue costs.

**TYPE OF GRANT** One-off; sometimes recurrent awards up to three years.

**RANGE OF GRANTS** £500–£45,000

**SAMPLE GRANTS** Britain Yearly Meeting (£45,000); Central England Quakers (£10,500); Ulster Quaker Service (£8,000); Oxfam (£5,000); MEDAIR UK, Médecins Sans Frontières and Unisex UK (£4,000 each); Welfare Association and Down's Heart Group (£3,000 each); Refugee and Migrants Centre, St Giles Trust and United Nations Association (£1,000 each); The Pen Museum, Tipton Youth Project and Straight Talking (£500 each).

**FINANCES** Year 2013/14 *Income* £400,457 *Grants* £345,250 *Grants to organisations* £345,250 *Assets* £11,883,455

**TRUSTEES** Constance Penny; Elizabeth Birmingham; Clare Norton; John Taylor; Thomas Penny; Robert Birmingham; Simon Taylor.

**OTHER INFORMATION** Grants were made to 184 organisations totalling £345,000. Most grants were for £1,000 or less.

**HOW TO APPLY** Apply in writing to the correspondent.

**WHO TO APPLY TO** Clare Norton, Trustee, 266 Malvern Road, Worcester WR2 4PA

## ■ The Connie and Albert Taylor Charitable Trust

**CC NO** 1074785    **ESTABLISHED** 1998

**WHERE FUNDING CAN BE GIVEN** West Midlands.

**WHO CAN BENEFIT** Organisations concerned with medical research, hospices, education and recreation and preservation.

**WHAT IS FUNDED** The trust's objectives are: research into the cure and causes of cancer, blindness and heart disease; provision and maintenance of nursing homes for people who are elderly or unable to look after themselves; provision of maintenance of hospices for people with terminal illnesses; facilities for the education and recreation of children and young people; the preservation, protection and improvements of any amenity or land of beauty, scientific or of horticultural interest and any building of historical, architectural or artistic or scientific interest.

**WHAT IS NOT FUNDED** Individuals.

**TYPE OF GRANT** Project costs; capital costs; salaries; one-off, sometimes up to three years.

**RANGE OF GRANTS** Up to £100,000.

**SAMPLE GRANTS** Birmingham Children's Hospital (£100,000); Donna Louise Children's Hospice (£40,000); Williams Syndrome Foundation (£30,000); Fight for Sight (£25,000); Church of the Holy Angels – Hoar Cross and Footsteps (£10,000 each); Birmingham Boys' and Girls' Union (£6,000); South Stafford Medical Foundation (£3,000);

**FINANCES** Year 2013 *Income* £127,030 *Grants* £448,400 *Grants to organisations* £448,400 *Assets* £5,118,087

**TRUSTEES** Alan Foster; Harry Grundy; Richard Long.

**OTHER INFORMATION** The trustees state in their 2013 annual report that 'at the beginning of 2014 the trustees decided that they would try to work towards bringing the trust to an end, within approximately a five-year time-span. This hopefully will be achieved by working mainly with certain of the charities we have supported over the previous 15 years. There is no particular time frame in which applications may be made and we shall continue to receive them until our funds are exhausted. The short-term effect is that we have very substantially increased our donations and pledges in 2014'. A total of 13 organisations received grants in 2013.

**HOW TO APPLY** Apply in writing to the correspondent. The trustees prefer to receive applications via email. The trust may visit applicants/beneficiaries. Trustees normally meet quarterly to consider grants. Some projects have received long term support from the trustees, but support is rarely given for more than three years and the trustees are unlikely to enter into any long term pledge in future.

**WHO TO APPLY TO** Alan Foster, Trustee, 1 High Street, Lindfield, Haywards Heath, West Sussex RH16 2HG *email* applications@taylortrust.co.uk *Website* www.taylortrust.co.uk

■ **The Taylor Family Foundation**

**CC NO** 1118032  **ESTABLISHED** 2007
**WHERE FUNDING CAN BE GIVEN** UK and overseas, with a preference for London and the south east.
**WHO CAN BENEFIT** Registered charities and statutory bodies.
**WHAT IS FUNDED** Children and young people. The aims of the foundation are 'to help and support children and young people, particularly those from disadvantaged backgrounds, in the areas of education, health, recreation and the performing arts.'
**WHAT IS NOT FUNDED** Individuals.
**TYPE OF GRANT** One-off and recurring grants.
**RANGE OF GRANTS** Up to £500,000 but generally £1,000–£150,000.
**SAMPLE GRANTS** Royal Opera House Foundation (£500,000); Tate Foundation (£260,000); Save the Children Fund (£39,000); The Prince's Trust (£25,000); Médecins Sans Frontières (£15,000); Straight Talking (£10,000); Honey Pot Children's Charity (£7,500); Wimbledon Music Festival (£5,000), REACT (£3,000); St Raphael's Hospice (£1,000).
**FINANCES** *Year* 2013/14 *Income* £1,250,210 *Grants* £1,463,338 *Grants to organisations* £1,463,338 *Assets* £377,559
**TRUSTEES** Ian Taylor; Cristina Taylor; Neville Shepherd.
**HOW TO APPLY** Apply in writing to the correspondent. The trust welcomes written applications and invites charities and relevant organisations to contact them with their report of activities and a copy of their accounts. All applications should be accompanied by an application form which is available to download from the foundation's website.
**WHO TO APPLY TO** Neville Shepherd, Trustee, Hill Place House, 55a High Street, Wimbledon, London SW19 5BA *Tel.* 020 8605 2629 *email* info@thetaylorfamilyfoundation *Website* www.thetaylorfamilyfoundation.co.uk

■ **A. P. Taylor Trust**

**CC NO** 260741  **ESTABLISHED** 1969
**WHERE FUNDING CAN BE GIVEN** The parishes of Hayes and Harlington (as they existed on 9 January 1953).
**WHO CAN BENEFIT** Charitable organisations.
**WHAT IS FUNDED** Medical causes; the arts; sport; children and young people; older people; women.
**WHAT IS NOT FUNDED** The Hayes and Harlington area only.
**RANGE OF GRANTS** The majority of grants are for £500 or less.
**SAMPLE GRANTS** Harlington Hospice Association (£20,000); Barra Hall Community Development Committee (£2,000); Hayes and Harlington Old People's Welfare (£800); Brookside Pretty Asian Ladies Group, Rosedale Park Bowling Club and St Mary's Social Club (£500 each); People First, Harlington Women's Institute and Charville Community Association (£400 each); Dallega Rangers and Girl Guiding Harlington District (£300 each); The Melodics and Hayes Horticultural Society (£250 each); and TOD Ladies Club (£200).
**FINANCES** *Year* 2013/14 *Income* £93,393 *Grants* £51,250 *Grants to organisations* £51,250 *Assets* £1,340,931
**TRUSTEES** Alan Woodhouse; Sean Fitzpatrick; Timothy McCarthy; Peter Chidwick.
**OTHER INFORMATION** Grants were made to 83 organisations totalling £51,500.
**HOW TO APPLY** Application forms are available to download via the trust's website. Completed forms plus a copy of the previous year's accounts should be sent to the trust by 31 January of each year. Grants are distributed in May.
**WHO TO APPLY TO** Sean Fitzpatrick, Trustee, Homleigh, 68 Vine Lane, Uxbridge UB10 0BD *Tel.* 01895 812811 *email* enquiries@aptaylortrust.org.uk *Website* www.aptaylortrust.org.uk

■ **Tearfund**

**CC NO** 265464  **ESTABLISHED** 1968
**WHERE FUNDING CAN BE GIVEN** Worldwide, but mainly financially developing countries.
**WHO CAN BENEFIT** Evangelical Christian organisations which benefit at risk groups; people with disabilities, those disadvantaged by poverty or socially isolated, and victims of famine, man-made or natural disasters and war.
**WHAT IS FUNDED** Evangelical Christian ministry to meet all needs – physical, mental, social and spiritual. Funding is given to partner organisations only.
**TYPE OF GRANT** Project grants; partnerships.
**RANGE OF GRANTS** Smallest £1,000; typical £15,000.
**FINANCES** *Year* 2013/14 *Income* £59,372,000 *Grants* £20,231,000 *Grants to organisations* £20,231,000 *Assets* £24,611,000
**TRUSTEES** Deepak Mahtani; Robert Camp; H. C. Mather; Craig Rowland; Jillian Mills; Julia Ogilvy; Revd Mark Melluish; David Campanale; Jenny Baker; Stephanie Heald; John Shaw.
**PUBLICATIONS** Tear Times.
**HOW TO APPLY** The trust works only with selected partner organisations and therefore they do not accept unsolicited requests or approaches.
**WHO TO APPLY TO** Andrew Slatter, Secretary, 100 Church Road, Teddington, Middlesex TW11 8QE *Tel.* 0845 355 8355 *email* enquiry@tearfund.org *Website* www.tearfund.org

# Tedworth

## ■ The Tedworth Charitable Trust

**CC NO** 328524   **ESTABLISHED** 1990
**WHERE FUNDING CAN BE GIVEN** Unrestricted, but UK in practice.
**WHO CAN BENEFIT** Registered charities.
**WHAT IS FUNDED** Parenting, family welfare and child development; environment and the arts; general charitable purposes.
**WHAT IS NOT FUNDED** Individuals.
**TYPE OF GRANT** One-off and core costs.
**RANGE OF GRANTS** Up to £60,000.
**SAMPLE GRANTS** Home-Start Headquarters UK (£110,000); Resurgence (£70,000); IntoUniversity and Sutton Trust (£30,000 each); Best Beginnings (£20,000); Option Institute (£10,000); Women's Environmental Network (£8,000); The Sainsbury Archive (£1,400).
**FINANCES** Year 2013/14 Income £426,134 Grants £522,505 Grants to organisations £522,505 Assets £11,315,261
**TRUSTEES** Judith Portrait; Timothy Sainsbury; Jessica Sainsbury; Margaret Sainsbury.
**OTHER INFORMATION** The trust is one of the Sainsbury Family Charitable Trusts which share a common administration. An application to one is taken as an application to all.
**HOW TO APPLY** The trust's annual report for 2013/14 stated that: 'Proposals are generally invited by the Trustees or initiated at their request. Unsolicited applications are unlikely to be successful, even if they fall within an area in which the Trustees are interested.'
**WHO TO APPLY TO** Alan Bookbinder, Correspondent, The Peak, 5 Wilton Road, London SW1V 1AP Tel. 020 7410 0330 email info@sfct.org.uk Website www.sfct.org.uk

## ■ Tees Valley Community Foundation

**CC NO** 1111222   **ESTABLISHED** 1988
**WHERE FUNDING CAN BE GIVEN** The former county of Cleveland, being the local authority areas of Hartlepool, Middlesbrough, Redcar and Cleveland and Stockton-On-Tees.
**WHO CAN BENEFIT** Registered charities and constituted community groups benefitting the communities of Hartlepool, Middlesbrough, Redcar and Cleveland or Stockton-on-Tees.
**WHAT IS FUNDED** General charitable purposes. The foundation makes grants from various different funds, each with its own criteria.
**WHAT IS NOT FUNDED** Major fundraising appeals; sponsored events; promotion of religion; retrospective funding; holidays or social outings; existing operating costs, e.g. salaries, rent, overheads; groups with excessive unrestricted or free reserves; groups in serious deficit; replacement of statutory funding; meeting any need which is the responsibility of central or local government; religious or political causes; fabric appeals; or animal welfare. Each fund has separate exclusions which are available on the foundation's website.
**TYPE OF GRANT** Capital or revenue costs.
**RANGE OF GRANTS** Mostly under £12,000.
**SAMPLE GRANTS** Peat Rigg Training Centre Ltd (£20,000); Tees Valley Sport (£10,000); Redcar and Cleveland Mind (£6,000); Tees Valley Support (£5,000); Christian Fellowship Ministry (£3,800); Saltburn Bowls Club (£3,300); Cotham Heritage Group and the Lighthouse Group (£1,000 each); Redcar Academy (£600); Grandparents Together (£500).
**FINANCES** Year 2013/14 Income £1,350,774 Grants £391,533 Grants to organisations £391,533 Assets £12,594,744
**TRUSTEES** Chris Hope, Chair; Brian Beaumont; Rosemary Young; Marjory Houseman; Neil Kenley; Alan Kitching; Keith Robinson; Peter Rowley; Wendy Shepherd; Jeff Taylor; Keith Smith; Eileen Martin.
**OTHER INFORMATION** As with all community foundations grant schemes change frequently. Contact the foundation or check their website for details of current programmes and their deadlines.
**HOW TO APPLY** Application forms are available on the foundation's website. Applicants can received a maximum of £5,000 in any 12 month period from one or a combination of funds.
**WHO TO APPLY TO** Hugh McGouran, Wallace House, Fallon Court, Preston Farm Industrial Estate, Stockton-Tees TS18 3TX Tel. 01642 260860 email info@teesvalleyfoundation.org Website www.teesvalleyfoundation.org

## ■ Tegham Limited

**CC NO** 283066   **ESTABLISHED** 1981
**WHERE FUNDING CAN BE GIVEN** UK.
**WHO CAN BENEFIT** Registered charities.
**WHAT IS FUNDED** Jewish Orthodox faith and the relief of poverty.
**FINANCES** Year 2013/14 Income £472,444 Grants £219,135 Grants to organisations £219,135 Assets £2,413,584
**TRUSTEES** Nizza Fluss; Daniel Fluss.
**OTHER INFORMATION** Details of beneficiaries were not included in the accounts.
**HOW TO APPLY** The trustees have stated previously that the charity has enough causes to support and they do not welcome other applications.
**WHO TO APPLY TO** Nizza Fluss, Trustee, c/o Gerald Kreditor and Co, Hallswelle House, 1 Hallswelle Road, London NW11 0DH email admin@geraldkreditor.co.uk

## ■ The Templeton Goodwill Trust

**SC NO** SC004177   **ESTABLISHED** 1938
**WHERE FUNDING CAN BE GIVEN** Glasgow and the West of Scotland (the Glasgow postal area).
**WHO CAN BENEFIT** Scottish registered charities.
**WHAT IS FUNDED** General charitable purposes. The trust is interested in supporting organisations which help others, particularly those concerned with social welfare, the relief of poverty, health, community development and support of people in need or disadvantage. A wide range of charitable organisations are supported, such as: youth organisations; medical research charities; churches; ex-services' organisations; other organisations concerned with social work and providing caring services for all age groups.
**WHAT IS NOT FUNDED** Support is given to Scottish registered charities only. Individuals are not supported and grants are generally not given to arts or cultural organizations.
**TYPE OF GRANT** Discretionary, both continuing annual sums and one-off support grants.
**RANGE OF GRANTS** £450–£4,600
**SAMPLE GRANTS** **Previous beneficiaries have included:** Girl Guides Association (£6,500); SSAFA (£4,200); Salvation Army and Scout Association (£4,000 each); Scottish Furniture Trades Benevolent Association (£3,300); Cancer Research UK and Marie Curie Memorial Foundation (£2,800 each); Tenovus Scotland (£2,500); Scottish Bible Society (£1,900);

Dyslexia Scotwest (£1,000); The Fishermen's Mission (£700); and Diabetes UK Scotland (£500).

**FINANCES** Year 2013/14 Income £246,286 Grants £100,000 Grants to organisations £100,000

**TRUSTEES** J. H. Millar, Chair; B. Bannerman; W. T. P. Barnstaple; C. Barrowman.

**OTHER INFORMATION** The grant total was estimated based on expenditure in previous years, as the accounts for 2013/14 were not available from the OSCR website. The trust had a total expenditure of £210,500 in 2013/14.

**HOW TO APPLY** Apply in writing to the correspondent, preferably including a copy of accounts. The trustees have previously stated applications should be received by April as the trustees meet once a year, at the end of April or in May. Initial telephone calls are welcome. An sae is required from applicants to receive a reply.

**WHO TO APPLY TO** W. T. P. Barnstaple, Trustee and Administrator, 12 Doon Street, Motherwell ML1 2BN

---

## ■ The Tennis Foundation

**CC NO** 298175  **ESTABLISHED** 1987

**WHERE FUNDING CAN BE GIVEN** UK.

**WHO CAN BENEFIT** County and local authority organisations; clubs; schools; individuals; there is a particular interest in young people, older people and people with a disability.

**WHAT IS FUNDED** The foundation promotes participation in tennis. It categorises its activities as: junior development (including development and support) and places to play (including community and local authority sites); tennis development (including supporting the field team, national associations, county associations and clubs); coaching; education (including schools, colleges, universities and further education colleges); competitions and tennis for people with disabilities which incorporates a performance and development programme for them.

**TYPE OF GRANT** Capital and revenue grants.

**SAMPLE GRANTS** Arete Leisure Limited (£500,000); Tennis Scotland (£36,000). **Previous beneficiaries have included:** Advanced Apprenticeship in Sporting Excellence (£443,000); Win Tennis – High performance centre funding (£300,000); Give it Your Max (£36,000); and Clissold Park Development Fund (£10,000).

**FINANCES** Year 2013/14 Income £14,827,000 Grants £3,008,000 Grants to organisations £2,697,000 Assets £7,639,000

**TRUSTEES** Charles Trippe; Jonathan Lane; Sir Geoffrey Cass; Funke Awoderu; Matthew Stocks; Barry Horne; Ian Hewitt; Jeffrey Hunter; Karen Keohane; Dame Tessa Jowell; Baroness Margaret Ford; Baroness Tanni Grey-Thompson; Martin Corrie.

**OTHER INFORMATION** The financial information covers a 15 month period ending 31 December 2014. Grants to organisations totalled £2.7 million and grants to individuals totalled £311,000.

**HOW TO APPLY** Initial enquiries should be made by telephone.

**WHO TO APPLY TO** Joanna Farquharson, Secretary, National Tennis Centre, 100 Priory Lane, London SW15 5JQ Tel. 0845 872 0522 email info@tennisfoundation.org.uk Website www.tennisfoundation.org.uk

---

## ■ Tesco Charity Trust

**CC NO** 297126  **ESTABLISHED** 1987

**WHERE FUNDING CAN BE GIVEN** Worldwide.

**WHO CAN BENEFIT** International, national and local charitable organisations.

**WHAT IS FUNDED** Education and training; social welfare; health; people with disabilities; children and young people; older people.

**WHAT IS NOT FUNDED** Political organisations; individuals; towards new buildings; other trusts or charities for onward transmission to other charitable organisations.

**TYPE OF GRANT** Generally one-off, or for one year or less.

**RANGE OF GRANTS** £500–£4,000. Grants are also made to larger appeals and ranged from £40,000 to £6 million in 2013/14.

**SAMPLE GRANTS** Diabetes UK (£6 million); Cancer Research UK (£1 million); and Barking Badgers (£40,000). Other donations were made but details of grant allocations were not provided. These included: Age Concern Neath Port Talbot, the Brain Injury Foundation, Hammersmith and Fulham Mencap, Leeds Powerchair Football Club, Multiple Sclerosis UK, Starbeck School, the Stuart Low Trust and Trinity Community Centre.

**FINANCES** Year 2013/14 Income £9,162,000 Grants £8,600,000 Grants to organisations £8,600,000 Assets £807,000

**TRUSTEES** Paul Smythe; Juliet Crisp; Christophe Roussel; Rebecca Shelley; John Scouler; Damian Leeson.

**OTHER INFORMATION** The trust also recycled inkjet cartridges, whose monetary value totalled £153,000.

**HOW TO APPLY** Applications should be made via the trust's website.

**WHO TO APPLY TO** Michelle Cornish, Corporate Responsibility Executive, Tesco plc, 25 Furlong Way, Great Amwell, Near Ware, Hertfordshire SG12 9TE Tel. 01992 644598 email charity.enquiries@uk.tesco.com Website www.tescoplc.com/tescocharitytrust

---

## ■ The C. Paul Thackray General Charitable Trust

**CC NO** 328650  **ESTABLISHED** 1990

**WHERE FUNDING CAN BE GIVEN** UK, with a preference for Yorkshire particularly within a ten-mile radius of Harrogate. Financially developing countries.

**WHO CAN BENEFIT** Registered charities helping people with disabilities, ex-offenders, people suffering from serious illness and their families, substance misusers and victims of domestic violence.

**WHAT IS FUNDED** The trust makes grants to UK-registered charities, with a preference for charities operating in Yorkshire, as well as in financially developing countries. It supports education and training, the promotion of health, conservation and heritage and social welfare.

**RANGE OF GRANTS** £300–£10,000

**SAMPLE GRANTS** The Paul Thackray Heritage Foundation (£10,000); AOG Pentecostal Church (£5,000); Victory Outreach (£3,500); Checkpoint Christian Youth Trust and Macmillan Cancer Support (£1,700 each); Camphill Village Trust (£1,400); Megan Baker House, Birmingham City Mission and Acorns Children's Hospice (£1,150); Royal Lifeboat Institution, SENSE and Sightsavers International (£600 each); and Tom Roberts Adventure Centre and Accessible Arts and Media (£300 each).

**FINANCES** Year 2013/14 Income £40,329 Grants £57,370 Grants to organisations £57,370 Assets £1,199,107
**TRUSTEES** Matthew Wrigley; Paul Thackray; Louise Thackray.
**OTHER INFORMATION** Grants were made to 58 organisations and totalled £57,500.
**HOW TO APPLY** Appeals may be made in writing to the correspondent. The trustees meet on an annual basis to consider applications for grants.
**WHO TO APPLY TO** Matthew Wrigley, Trustee, 19 Cookridge Street, Leeds LS2 3AG Tel. 0113 244 6100 email philip.nelson@wrigleys.co.uk

## ■ Thackray Medical Research Trust
**CC NO** 702896 **ESTABLISHED** 1990
**WHERE FUNDING CAN BE GIVEN** Worldwide.
**WHO CAN BENEFIT** Charitable organisations; university departments; individual researchers.
**WHAT IS FUNDED** Medical research; overseas aid.
**TYPE OF GRANT** 'Pump-priming', start-up or organisational expenses where alternative funding is not available for medical supply organisations.
**SAMPLE GRANTS** Thackray Medical Museum (£202,000).
**FINANCES** Year 2013/14 Income £263,869 Grants £201,800 Grants to organisations £201,800 Assets £6,811,961
**TRUSTEES** Matthew Wrigley; Dr Martin Schweiger; Christin Thackray; William Mathie; John Campbell; Steven Burt; Ian Mallinson.
**OTHER INFORMATION** The trust initiated and supported the establishment of the award-winning Thackray Museum in Leeds, one of the largest medical museums in the world, and continues to support the research resource there.
**HOW TO APPLY** Application forms and guidance notes are available from the trust's website. Applications are usually considered in October and April but may be considered at other times. The closing date for applications is the last day of July and January respectively.
**WHO TO APPLY TO** John Campbell, Trustee, 6 Montagu Way, Wetherby, West Yorkshire LS22 5PZ Tel. 01937 588107 email chair@tmrt.co.uk Website www.tmrt.co.uk

## ■ The Thales Charitable Trust
**CC NO** 1000162 **ESTABLISHED** 1990
**WHERE FUNDING CAN BE GIVEN** UK.
**WHO CAN BENEFIT** Charitable organisations, particularly benefitting young people and people with disabilities.
**WHAT IS FUNDED** General charitable purposes; education and training; technology; health.
**SAMPLE GRANTS** The seven main organisations during the year were: Alzheimer's Society, Arkwright Solicitors, Combat Stress, Engineering UK, Railway Children, RUSI and UK Electronics Skills Foundation. Other beneficiaries included: Children in Need, Hope UK, Jubilee Sailing Trust, QED Foundation and Shaftesbury Young People.
**FINANCES** Year 2013 Income £150,000 Grants £224,225 Grants to organisations £224,225 Assets £60,588
**TRUSTEES** John Howe; Michael Seabrook; Marion Broughton; Markus Leutert.
**OTHER INFORMATION** The trust has stated in its Summary Information Return (SIR) for 2013 that it gave grants to seven main organisations and also gave a further 36 grants to other organisations.
**HOW TO APPLY** Apply in writing to the correspondent. The trust does not generally solicit requests unless for major donations.
**WHO TO APPLY TO** Michael Seabrook, Trustee, Thales Corporate Services Ltd, 2 Dashwood Lang Road, Bourne Business Park, Addlestone, Surrey KT15 2NX Tel. 01932 824800 email mike.seabrook@thalesgroup.com

## ■ The Thistle Trust
**CC NO** 1091327 **ESTABLISHED** 2002
**WHERE FUNDING CAN BE GIVEN** UK.
**WHO CAN BENEFIT** Charitable institutions or projects in the UK.
**WHAT IS FUNDED** The promotion of study and research in the arts; furthering public knowledge and education of art.
**RANGE OF GRANTS** Up to £8,000.
**SAMPLE GRANTS** Chickenshed Theatre (£5,000); Gate Theatre Notting Hill (£2,400); Academy of Sacred Music, V&A Museum of Childhood and Actors Touring Company (£2,000 each); Royal Exchange Theatre (£1,700); National Student Drama Festival and Bush Theatre (£1,500 each); The Lowry (£1,200); and London Song Festival, Manchester Camerata and Bampton Classical Opera (£1,000 each).
**FINANCES** Year 2013/14 Income £44,620 Grants £50,732 Grants to organisations £50,732 Assets £1,244,752
**TRUSTEES** Catherine Trevelyan; Madeleine Kleinwort; Neil Morris; Donald McGilvray; Selina Kleinwort Dabbas.
**OTHER INFORMATION** Grants were made to 34 organisations totalling £51,000 during the year.
**HOW TO APPLY** Applications can be made in writing to the correspondent including most recent report and financial accounts. The trustees meet at least once a year with only successful applicants notified of the trustees' decision.
**WHO TO APPLY TO** Elizabeth Fettes-Neame, Trust Officer, Kleinwort Benson Trustees Ltd, 14 St George Street, London W1S 1FE Tel. 020 3207 7337 email elizabeth.fettes-neame@kleinwortbenson.com

## ■ The Loke Wan Tho Memorial Foundation
**CC NO** 264273 **ESTABLISHED** 1972
**WHERE FUNDING CAN BE GIVEN** UK and overseas, particularly England, Hong Kong and Malaysia.
**WHO CAN BENEFIT** Registered charities only.
**WHAT IS FUNDED** Education and training; the promotion of health; overseas aid; animals and the environment.
**TYPE OF GRANT** One-off.
**RANGE OF GRANTS** £1,000–£24,000
**SAMPLE GRANTS** National History Publications (£24,000); Bowel Disease Research Foundation (£10,000); Sound Seekers (£8,000); International Animal Rescue and Client Earth (£5,000 each); Care for the Wild International (£3,000); Kidney Research UK (£2,000); Africa Education Trust, Birdlife International and Age UK Lancashire (£1,000 each).
**FINANCES** Year 2013/14 Income £142,932 Grants £88,165 Grants to organisations £88,165
**TRUSTEES** Alan Tonkyn; Tanis Tonkyn.
**HOW TO APPLY** Apply in writing to the correspondent.

WHO TO APPLY TO The Trustees, RBC Trust Company (International) Ltd, La Motte Chambers, St Helier, Jersey, Channel Islands JE1 1BJ *Tel.* 01534 602000

## ■ The Thompson Family Charitable Trust

CC NO 326801  ESTABLISHED 1985
WHERE FUNDING CAN BE GIVEN UK.
WHO CAN BENEFIT Registered charities only.
WHAT IS FUNDED General charitable purposes, although the trustees appear to be mostly interested in educational, medical, arts and veterinary organisations, particularly those concerned with horses and horse racing.
WHAT IS NOT FUNDED Individuals.
TYPE OF GRANT The trust makes one-off grants, recurring grants and pledges.
RANGE OF GRANTS From £250.
SAMPLE GRANTS Royal National Theatre (£500,000); East Anglia's Children's Hospices and Great Ormond Street Hospital Children's Charity (£200,000 each); Action on Addiction and Sports Aid Trust (£100,000 each); St Andrew's Primary School (£50,000); Cambridge Women's Aid (£20,000 in two grants); The London Library (£20,000); Training the Teachers of Tomorrow (£5,000); Ealing Lawn Tennis Community Amateur Sports Club (£2,000); Brooke Hospital for Animals (£1,000); British Horseracing Education and Standards Trust (£250).
FINANCES *Year* 2013/14 *Income* £6,714,340 *Grants* £3,486,400 *Grants to organisations* £3,486,400 *Assets* £104,939,980
TRUSTEES David Thompson; Patricia Thompson; Katie Woodward.
OTHER INFORMATION The trust regularly builds up its reserves to enable it to make large donations in the future, for example towards the construction of new medical or educational facilities. 'It is the policy of the charity to hold reserves which will enable [it] to make major donations for capital projects in the near future (for example, to fund the construction and endowment of new medical or educational facilities) and appropriate projects are currently being investigated. ... In addition to such capital projects it is envisaged that grants to other charities will in future be made at a higher annual level than in recent years.'
HOW TO APPLY Apply in writing to the correspondent.
WHO TO APPLY TO Katie Woodward, Trustee, Hillsdown Court, 15 Totteridge Common, London N20 8LR *Tel.* 01608 676789 *email* roy.copus@btinternet.com

## ■ The Len Thomson Charitable Trust

SC NO SC000981  ESTABLISHED 1989
WHERE FUNDING CAN BE GIVEN Scotland, with a preference for Midlothian, particularly Dalkeith.
WHO CAN BENEFIT Charitable organisations.
WHAT IS FUNDED The trust supports young people, local community organisations and medical research.
WHAT IS NOT FUNDED Individuals directly.
RANGE OF GRANTS £1,000–£5,000
SAMPLE GRANTS **Previous beneficiaries have included:** The Edinburgh Sick Kids Friends Foundation (£5,000); Brass in the Park (£3,000); CHAS, Maggie's Centre and Mercy Ships (£2,000 each); and British Red Cross, Lothian Special Olympics, Newtongrange Children's Gala Day, the Princess Royal Trust for Carers and Save the Children Fund (£1,000 each).
FINANCES *Year* 2013/14 *Income* £15,508 *Grants* £40,000 *Grants to organisations* £40,000
TRUSTEES Douglas Connell; Elizabeth Thomson.
OTHER INFORMATION Accounts for 2013/14 were not available. Grant total has been estimated based on previous years and the trust's total expenditure of £50,300 in 2013/14.
HOW TO APPLY The trust does not reply to unsolicited applications.
WHO TO APPLY TO Douglas Connell, Trustee, Turcan Connell WS, Princes Exchange, 1 Earl Grey Street, Edinburgh EH3 9EE *Tel.* 0131 228 8111 *email* dac@turcanconnell.com

## ■ The Sue Thomson Foundation

CC NO 298808  ESTABLISHED 1988
WHERE FUNDING CAN BE GIVEN UK, Sussex, London or Surrey.
WHO CAN BENEFIT Charitable organisations.
WHAT IS FUNDED **Major grants** The principal beneficiary is Christ's Hospital. The foundation nominates one new entrant each year from a needy background to the school, subject to the child meeting Christ's Hospital's own admissions criteria academically, socially and in terms of need. The foundation commits to contributing to the child's costs at a level agreed with Christ's Hospital for as long as each of them remains in the school.
**Regular grants:** It is the policy of the trustees to provide up to 10% of the foundation's available income each year for grants in this category, subject to the foundation's commitments to Christ's Hospital having been satisfied. Charities eligible for consideration for grants at this level include: charities related to Christ's Hospital including the sister school, King Edward's – Witley; UK book trade charities, including the charities of the Worshipful Company of Stationers and Newspaper Makers; suitable grant-making charities selected in recognition of pro bono professional work done for the foundation by its trustees or others; special situations or other applications at the trustees' discretion. Grants in this category may be spread over a period of years.
**Major grants:** It is the policy of the trustees to set aside a further 10% of available income each year for this programme, subject to its commitments in the major and medium categories and other financial needs having been met. Special grants are confined to fund education or welfare projects that aim to help people who are in need and cannot be readily helped by statutory bodies. They are confined to charities in Sussex, Surrey or London.
WHAT IS NOT FUNDED Large, national charities (except Christ's Hospital); individuals, except as part of a specific scheme; research projects; charities concerned with animals; birds; the environment; gardens; historic buildings.
TYPE OF GRANT Major grants which are above £5,000; regular grants which can be from £500 to £5,000; special grants which can be up to £3,000 per year.
RANGE OF GRANTS £1,000–£3,000
SAMPLE GRANTS The Leonard Sainer Legal Education Foundation (£3,000); The Bridewell Foundation (£2,000); Book Trade Benevolent Society (£1,500); Disasters Aid Committee, Henfield Youth Club, The Worshipful Company of

# Thomson

Musicians (£1,000 each); The Stationers' Foundation (£500).

**FINANCES** Year 2013/14 Income £254,425 Grants £122,807 Grants to organisations £97,976 Assets £3,498,363

**TRUSTEES** Susan Mitchell, Chair; Timothy Binnington; Charles Corman; Kathleen Duncan; Susannah Holliman.

**OTHER INFORMATION** The organisational grant total includes a grant of £86,000 to the Christ's Hospital for the student support scheme, but does not include additional grants of £24,831 for students and parents at Christ's Hospital. Grants to other organisations totalled £10,000.

**HOW TO APPLY** Apply in writing to the correspondent. Preliminary telephone or email enquiries are encouraged. Unsolicited applications are not acknowledged, unless accompanied by an sae or an email address. Grant-making policies are published in the annual report and accounts, available from the Charity Commission website, and in relevant charity sector publications when the trustees are able to do so free of charge. This statement of policies is provided to anyone on request.

**WHO TO APPLY TO** Susannah Holliman, Correspondent, Arcadia, 58a Woodland Way, Kingswood, Surrey KT20 6NW
email stfsusannah@aol.com

## ■ Thomson Reuters Foundation

**CC NO** 1082139 **ESTABLISHED** 2000
**WHERE FUNDING CAN BE GIVEN** Worldwide.
**WHO CAN BENEFIT** Charitable organisations.
**WHAT IS FUNDED** General charitable purposes; education and training; humanitarian causes; free speech; women's rights. The foundation's website states: '[The foundation] stands for free, independent journalism, human rights, women's empowerment and the rule of law. We expose corruption worldwide and play a leading role in the global fight against human trafficking. We use the skills, values and expertise of Thomson Reuters to run programmes that trigger real change and empower people around the world, including free legal assistance, journalism and media training, coverage of the world's under-reported stories and the Trust Women Conference. We tackle global issues and achieve lasting impact.'
**SAMPLE GRANTS** Oxford University (£410,000).
**FINANCES** Year 2013 Income £8,371,000 Grants £410,000 Grants to organisations £410,000 Assets £1,886,000
**TRUSTEES** Sir Crispin Tickell; Ken Olisa; Geert Linnebank; Lawton Fitt; David Craig; David Binet; Peter Warwick; Eileen Lynch; Stephen Adler; Susan Martin.
**HOW TO APPLY** The foundation's annual report for 2013 states that: 'Thomson Reuters Foundation does not accept applications for cash grants but focuses on using the skills, values and expertise of Thomson Reuters to run its global programmes. Grants are rarely made and only where they are in line with the foundation's programme objectives or meet the conditions of restricted funds.'
**WHO TO APPLY TO** The Trustees, Thomson Reuters (Reuters Ltd), Thomson Reuters Building, 30 South Colonnade, Canary Wharf, London E14 5EP Tel. 020 7542 4148
email foundation@reuters.com Website www.trust.org

## ■ The Sir Jules Thorn Charitable Trust

**CC NO** 233838 **ESTABLISHED** 1964
**WHERE FUNDING CAN BE GIVEN** UK.
**WHO CAN BENEFIT** Registered charities; universities; NHS hospitals; organisations holding exempt status whose work benefits medical science, medicine or people facing serious illness, disability, disadvantage or adversity.
**WHAT IS FUNDED** Medical research with strong clinical relevance; medicine generally; small grants for humanitarian appeals. Medical research is only funded through universities and recognised NHS research facilities.
**WHAT IS NOT FUNDED** The grants programmes run by the trust have their own guidelines and exclusions. If you would like to determine the eligibility of your organisation to apply for a grant, the trust has a useful 'Which grant programme should I apply for?' guide on its website, which can be completed online.
**TYPE OF GRANT** Medical research projects, usually covering a period of up to five years; one-off donations to other charities.
**SAMPLE GRANTS** University College London/ Moorfield's Eye Hospital and University of Oxford (£5 million each through the trust's 50th Anniversary Award); University of Cambridge (£1.1 million); The National Brain Appeal (£500,000); Addenbrooke's Charitable Trust (£193,000); University of Glasgow (£84,000); Smile Support and Care (£50,000); Bolton Hospice (£50,000); The Whitley Homes Trust (£5,000); Bath Institute of Medical Engineering (£1,500); Edinburgh Young Carers Project (£1,000); Oxfordshire Advocacy and Waterloo Community Counselling (£500 each); Ruddi's Retreat (£300).
**FINANCES** Year 2013 Income £2,438,336 Grants £12,725,159 Grants to organisations £12,725,159 Assets £108,962,762
**TRUSTEES** Elizabeth Charal, Chair; Prof. Sir Ravinder Maini; Sir Bruce McPhail; William Sporborg; John Rhodes; Prof. David Russell-Jones.
**OTHER INFORMATION** The grant total above refers to net commitments made during the year. In 2013 a total of 409 grants were made.
**HOW TO APPLY** There are different applications processes depending on the programme being applied for. The Sir Jules Thorn Award: Applicants should first contact the trust to discuss their proposal before applying. The Sir Jules Thorn PhD Scholarship Programme: Scholarships are available only through medical schools invited to participate. Medically-related donations: An expression of interest form is available to download from the website and should be completed and returned to donations@julesthorntrust.org.uk along with an electronic copy of your organisation's latest Trustees' report and Financial Statements. Ann Rylands small donations programme: The preferred method of application is via the online application form on the trust's website; however, a form can also be downloaded and returned by email. There are detailed guidance notes for all the grants programmes online, which should be read before an application is started.
**WHO TO APPLY TO** David Richings, Director, 24 Manchester Square, London W1U 3TH Tel. 020 7487 5851 Fax 020 7224 3976
email info@julesthorntrust.org.uk Website www.julesthorntrust.org.uk

828

## ■ The Thornton Foundation

**CC NO** 326383  **ESTABLISHED** 1983
**WHERE FUNDING CAN BE GIVEN** UK.
**WHO CAN BENEFIT** Charities which are personally known to the trustees.
**WHAT IS FUNDED** General charitable purposes.
**SAMPLE GRANTS** St Paul's Church Knightsbridge Foundation (£23,500); Campaign to Protect Rural England and Moorfields Eye Hospital (£10,000 each); Helen House and Prisoners of Conscience (£7,000 each); Parachute Regiment Afghanistan Trust, Parkinson's UK and RADA (£5,000 each); Tait Memorial Trust (£3,500); Sense (£1,000).
**FINANCES** Year 2013/14 Income £99,449 Grants £140,640 Grants to organisations £140,640 Assets £4,067,946
**TRUSTEES** Anthony Isaacs; Henry Thornton; Susan Thornton.
**HOW TO APPLY** The trust strongly emphasises that it does not accept unsolicited applications and only organisations that are known to one of the trustees will be considered for support. Any unsolicited applications will not receive a reply.
**WHO TO APPLY TO** Anthony Isaacs, Trustee, Jordans, Eashing, Godalming, Surrey GU7 2QA *Tel.* 01580 713055 *email* danielvalentine@ begbiesaccountants.co.uk

## ■ The Thornton Trust

**CC NO** 205357  **ESTABLISHED** 1962
**WHERE FUNDING CAN BE GIVEN** UK and overseas.
**WHO CAN BENEFIT** Charitable organisations.
**WHAT IS FUNDED** 'The promotion and furthering of education and the Evangelical Christian faith, and assisting in the relief of sickness, suffering and poverty'. The 2013/14 trustees' annual report states: 'Some organisations are involved in all of the activities referred to in the deed, but generally one third in supporting the Christian church, training and associated societies in the UK; a third in Christian missions and relief work overseas; and the balance in education, youth work, medical and other.'
**RANGE OF GRANTS** £50–£15,000
**SAMPLE GRANTS** AIM International (£14,000); Saffron Walden Baptist Church (£11,600); Hereford Community Church (£4,200); CARE – Christian Action Research and Education (£3,000); Middle East Christian Outreach Ltd, Send a Cow (£2,000 each); London School of Theology (£1,500); Christians in Sport, Stort Valley Schools Trust (£1,000 each); Christian Solidarity Worldwide (£750); RAF Benevolent Fund (£300); Greenbelt (£250); Clatterbridge Cancer Charity (£100); Chips (£50).
**FINANCES** Year 2013/14 Income £45,686 Grants £100,850 Grants to organisations £100,850 Assets £844,751
**TRUSTEES** Douglas Thornton; Betty Thornton; James Thornton.
**OTHER INFORMATION** Grants were made to 50 organisations.
**HOW TO APPLY** The trustees identify organisations and projects that they wish to support and have stated that they do not respond to speculative grant applications.
**WHO TO APPLY TO** Douglas Thornton, Trustee, Hunters Cottage, Hunters Yard, Debden Road, Saffron Walden, Essex CB11 4AA *Tel.* 01799 526712

## ■ The Thousandth Man – Richard Burns Charitable Trust (formerly known as The Hammonds Charitable Trust)

**CC NO** 1064028  **ESTABLISHED** 1997
**WHERE FUNDING CAN BE GIVEN** Mainly Birmingham, London, Leeds and Manchester.
**WHO CAN BENEFIT** Registered charities only.
**WHAT IS FUNDED** General charitable purposes, particularly the advancement of health and medical research, children and young people, education and people with disabilities.
**WHAT IS NOT FUNDED** The charity generally supports smaller charities local to the firm's offices.
**RANGE OF GRANTS** Most grants are £250 or below.
**SAMPLE GRANTS** Alzheimer's Society (£2,900); Crohn's and Colitis in Childhood (£2,800); Yorkshire Air Ambulance (£1,500); Disasters Emergency Committee and Star Support and Counselling (£1,000 each); Right to Play UK Limited (£500); SSAFA (£450); St Gemma's Hospice (£300); Lichfield Festival Ltd, Manchester Victoria Baths Trust and Muscular Dystrophy Campaign (£250 each); British Wireless for the Blind Fund, L'Arche, National Kidney Federation, Pancreatic Cancer UK and WaterAid (£200 each); The National Youth Orchestra of Great Britain (£150); The Royal National Lifeboat Institution (£50).
**FINANCES** Year 2013/14 Income £94,413 Grants £56,530 Grants to organisations £56,530 Assets £210,377
**TRUSTEES** John Forrest; Simon Miller; Susan Nickson; Robert Weekes; Robert Elvin; Anne O'Meara.
**OTHER INFORMATION** The Thousandth Man – Richard Burns Charitable Trust was formerly known as The Hammonds Charitable Trust. Grants were made to 171 organisations in 2013/14.
**HOW TO APPLY** Apply in writing to the correspondent. The trustees' 2013/14 annual report states that 'partners and staff of Squire Patton Boggs (UK) LLP are invited to make applications for which charities should be granted payment. The trustees review such requests and if deemed to be in keeping with the charity's purpose, and dependent on available funds, will at their discretion accept such requests. In addition, the trustees have reviewed and made donations in support of over 105 charities which have made unsolicited applications directly to the Trust.'
**WHO TO APPLY TO** Linda Sylvester, Correspondent, Squire Sanders (UK) LLP, Rutland House, 148 Edmund Street, Birmingham B3 2JR *Tel.* 0121 222 3318 *email* linda.sylvester@ squiresanders.com *Website* www.squiresanders.com

## ■ The Three Guineas Trust

**CC NO** 1059652  **ESTABLISHED** 1996
**WHERE FUNDING CAN BE GIVEN** Worldwide, in practice mainly UK.
**WHO CAN BENEFIT** Registered charities or activities with clearly defined charitable purposes.
**WHAT IS FUNDED** Projects in the fields of autism and Asperger Syndrome. Many of the grants made result from research conducted by the trustees and contact with experts working in these fields. The trust prefers to fund projects where people with ASD are included in the decision-making. The 2013/14 annual report also states: 'In 2008 the Trustees extended their grant-making to the field of climate change and its consequences. They made a large grant to the

University of Cambridge to construct a new global economic model of a world free from dependence on carbon. At present this is the only climate change project that Trustees have chosen to support.'

**WHAT IS NOT FUNDED** Individuals; educational fees; expeditions; funding for pure research.

**TYPE OF GRANT** One-off and recurrent.

**RANGE OF GRANTS** The majority of grants are for up to £10,000.

**SAMPLE GRANTS** Sunbeams Play (£255,000); Asperger East Anglia (£159,500); Autism NI (£99,000); Autism Concern (£60,000); Onside Independent Advocacy (£50,500); Friends of Thomas Bewick School (£10,000); Hillingdon Autistic Care and Support (£8,000); National Autistic Society – West Berkshire branch (£5,000); Play Montgomeryshire (£3,000); National Autistic Society – West Cornwall branch (£1,000).

**FINANCES** *Year* 2013/14 *Income* £1,978,135 *Grants* £821,030 *Grants to organisations* £821,030 *Assets* £19,717,119

**TRUSTEES** Clare Sainsbury; Bernard Willis; Dominic Flynn.

**OTHER INFORMATION** The trust is one of the Sainsbury Family Charitable Trusts which share a common administration. An application to one is taken as an application to all. A total of 32 grants were approved during the year.

**HOW TO APPLY** See the guidance for applicants in the entry for the Sainsbury Family Charitable Trusts. A single application will be considered for support by all the trusts in the group. It is noted on the website that the majority of unsolicited proposals are unsuccessful.

**WHO TO APPLY TO** Alan Bookbinder, Director, The Peak, 5 Wilton Road, London SW1V 1AP *Tel.* 020 7410 0330 *Fax* 020 7410 0332 *email* info@sfct.org.uk *Website* www.sfct.org.uk

■ **The Thriplow Charitable Trust**

**CC NO** 1025531        **ESTABLISHED** 1993

**WHERE FUNDING CAN BE GIVEN** Preference for British institutions.

**WHO CAN BENEFIT** Universities; university colleges; other places of learning benefitting young adults and older people, academics, research workers and students.

**WHAT IS FUNDED** Advancement of higher and further education, the promotion of research and the dissemination of the results of such research.

**WHAT IS NOT FUNDED** Grants can only be made to charitable bodies or component parts of charitable bodies. In no circumstances can grants be made to individuals.

**TYPE OF GRANT** Research study funds; research fellowships; certain academic training schemes; computer facilities; building projects related to research.

**RANGE OF GRANTS** Generally £1,000–£5,000.

**SAMPLE GRANTS Previous beneficiaries have included:** Cambridge University Library, Centre of South Asian Studies, Computer Aid International, Fight for Sight, Fitzwilliam Museum, Foundation for Prevention of Blindness, Foundation of Research Students, Hearing Research Trust, Inspire Foundation, Loughborough University, Marie Curie Cancer Care, Royal Botanic Gardens, Royal College of Music, Transplant Trust and University of Reading.

**FINANCES** *Year* 2013/14 *Income* £455,371 *Grants* £94,225 *Grants to organisations* £94,225 *Assets* £4,520,440

**TRUSTEES** Sir Peter Swinnerton-Dyer, Chair; Dr Harriet Crawford; Prof. Christopher Bayly; Sir David Wallace; Dame Jean Thomas; Prof. Robert Mair.

**HOW TO APPLY** There is no application form. A letter of application should specify the purpose for which funds are sought and the costings of the project. It should be indicated whether other applications for funds are pending and, if the funds are to be channelled to an individual or a small group, what degree of supervision over the quality of the work would be exercised by the institution. Trustee meetings are held twice a year – in spring and in autumn.

**WHO TO APPLY TO** Catharine Walston, Secretary, PO Box 225, Royston SG8 1BG *email* cat@walston.demon.co.uk

■ **The Daniel Thwaites Charitable Trust**

**CC NO** 1038097        **ESTABLISHED** 1994

**WHERE FUNDING CAN BE GIVEN** Blackburn.

**WHO CAN BENEFIT** Local charitable organisations.

**WHAT IS FUNDED** General charitable purposes.

**WHAT IS NOT FUNDED** Organisations or activities not usually considered by the trust: national appeals; appeals for large projects where the trust's contributions would not be permanently recognisable (i.e. contributions to building projects or vehicle acquisitions); activities which are primarily the responsibility of central or local government or some other responsible or statutory body; activities which collect funds for subsequent redistribution to other charities or individuals; animal welfare; advertising or membership of other bodies; expeditions or overseas travel; student support or sponsorship; schools, universities and colleges; and sponsorship or marketing appeals.

**SAMPLE GRANTS Previous beneficiaries have included:** Audiotec-Trinity Community Partnership – towards audio equipment; Cardiac Risk in Young – towards a monitor; Green Lane Community Association – towards a digital camera; HARV Outreach Domestic Violence Team – towards a projector; Motability – towards a wheelchair hoist; MS Regional Therapy and Support – towards aromatic oil; Pendle Riding for the Disabled – towards a visit to MEN arena; Read United Reformed Church – towards range style cookware; RNID – towards flashing doorbells; and The Women's Centre – towards refurbishment of its training room.

**FINANCES** *Year* 2013/14 *Income* £0 *Grants* £0 *Grants to organisations* £0

**TRUSTEES** Julie Telford; Joan Halse; Susan Woodward; Julian Markham; Charles Beardmore.

**OTHER INFORMATION** Note that the trust only starts accepting applications from 2015; therefore the latest financial information suggests no financial activity.

**HOW TO APPLY** The trust has stated that it is not accepting applications until at least 2015.

**WHO TO APPLY TO** Susan Woodward, Trustee, Daniel Thwaites plc, PO Box 50, Blackburn BB1 5BU *Tel.* 01254 686868 *email* samwalker@thwaites.co.uk *Website* www.thwaites.co.uk

## ■ The Tinsley Foundation
**CC NO** 1076537  **ESTABLISHED** 1999
**WHERE FUNDING CAN BE GIVEN** UK and overseas.
**WHO CAN BENEFIT** Charitable organisations.
**WHAT IS FUNDED** The foundation will support: charities which promote human rights and democratisation and/or which educate against racism, discrimination and oppression; charities which promote self-help in fighting poverty and homelessness; charities which provide reproductive health education in underdeveloped countries, but specifically excluding charities whose policy is against abortion or birth control.
**RANGE OF GRANTS** £500–£50,000
**SAMPLE GRANTS** Network for Africa (£50,000); Client Earth (£35,000); Article 1 Charitable Trust (£30,000); Peace Brigades International UK and Reprieve (£25,000 each); Hope Not Hate Educational Limited (£20,000); Open Trust (£10,000); Just Fair (£5,000); Anti-Slavery International and Soil Association (£1,000 each); Global Dialogue (£500).
**FINANCES** Year 2013/14 Income £431,780 Grants £238,500 Grants to organisations £238,500 Assets £4,408,411
**TRUSTEES** Henry Tinsley; Rebecca Tinsley; Tim Jones.
**OTHER INFORMATION** The foundation aims to spend at least 5% of its net assets on grants each year. It made 23 grants to organisations totalling £238,500. The foundation also made an investment of £100,000 in the Big Issue Social Enterprise Investment Fund.
**HOW TO APPLY** While the charity welcomes applications from eligible potential grantees, the trustees seek out organisations that will effectively fulfil the foundation's objectives.
**WHO TO APPLY TO** Henry Tinsley, Trustee, 14 St Mary's Street, Stamford, Lincolnshire PE9 2DF *Tel.* 01780 762056 *email* Lesleyedmunds@btconnect.com

## ■ The Tisbury Telegraph Trust
**CC NO** 328595  **ESTABLISHED** 1990
**WHERE FUNDING CAN BE GIVEN** UK and overseas.
**WHO CAN BENEFIT** Registered charities and churches.
**WHAT IS FUNDED** Christianity; overseas aid; the environment; social welfare.
**WHAT IS NOT FUNDED** Individuals – for expeditions or courses.
**TYPE OF GRANT** Core costs; one-off; project; research and running costs will be considered.
**RANGE OF GRANTS** £300–£135,000
**SAMPLE GRANTS** Tear Fund (£134,500); World Vision (£25,000); Helen and Douglas House, Mission without Borders and Interserve (£15,000 each); Christians against Poverty (£7,000); Faith to Share (£6,000); Faith to Share (£6,000); Pecan (£2,000); Bible Society and Traidcraft (£1,000 each); Barnabas Trust (£300).
**FINANCES** Year 2013/14 Income £377,048 Grants £329,910 Grants to organisations £329,910 Assets £238,837
**TRUSTEES** Eleanor Orr; John Davidson; Roger Orr; Alison Davidson; Sonia Phippard; Michael Hartley.
**OTHER INFORMATION** Grants were made to 64 organisations, including churches, totalling £330,000.
**HOW TO APPLY** Apply in writing to the correspondent. However, it is extremely rare that unsolicited applications are successful and the trust does not respond to applicants unless an sae is included.
**WHO TO APPLY TO** Eleanor Orr, Trustee, 35 Kitto Road, Telegraph Hill, London SE14 5TW *email* tisburytelegraphtrust@gmail.com

## ■ The Tobacco Pipe Makers and Tobacco Trade Benevolent Fund
**CC NO** 1135646  **ESTABLISHED** 1961
**WHERE FUNDING CAN BE GIVEN** City of London and Sevenoaks School.
**WHO CAN BENEFIT** Charities and educational establishments benefitting children, young adults, students and people disadvantaged by poverty.
**WHAT IS FUNDED** General charitable purposes. Emphasis on education and training, as well as disadvantaged young people in Inner London.
**TYPE OF GRANT** Ongoing scholarships; annual donations; one-off grants.
**RANGE OF GRANTS** £100–£20,000
**SAMPLE GRANTS** Pembroke Music academy (£20,000); Arundel Castle Cricket Foundation, Guildhall School of Music Awards, Speech and Language Hearing Centre (£10,000 each); Riding for the Disabled Barrow Farm (£6,000); Sheriffs' and Recorder's Fund (£1,000); Corporation of the Sons of the Clergy (£500); Royal British Legion (£100).
**FINANCES** Year 2013/14 Income £391,624 Grants £74,950 Grants to organisations £74,950 Assets £6,196,228
**TRUSTEES** Roger Merton; Stephen Preedy; David Lewis; Fiona Adler; George Lankester; Graham Blashill; David Glynn-Jones; Michael Richards; Nigel Rich.
**OTHER INFORMATION** Many beneficiaries are supported year after year, but the trust also gave one off grants totalling £12,000. The trust also runs a welfare support scheme for individuals with links to the tobacco trade.
**HOW TO APPLY** The trustees have stated that they prefer applications from small charities and organisations that have links, including geographically, to the city of London. Applications should be made in writing to the secretary. The committee meets regularly during the year to review and approve grants.
**WHO TO APPLY TO** Ralph Edmonson, Secretary, 2 Spa Close, Brill, Aylesbury, Buckinghamshire HP18 9RZ *Tel.* 01844 238655 *email* benevolentfund@tobaccolivery.org *Website* www.tobaccocharity.org.uk

## ■ The Tolkien Trust
**CC NO** 1150801  **ESTABLISHED** 1977
**WHERE FUNDING CAN BE GIVEN** UK, with some preference for Oxfordshire; overseas.
**WHO CAN BENEFIT** Registered charities.
**WHAT IS FUNDED** The trust does not publish specific guidelines; however, it notes on its website that it has supported charitable causes worldwide in the following areas: emergency and disaster relief; overseas aid and development; people who are homeless or refugees; healthcare charities, particularly those focused on illnesses associated with childhood or old age, disadvantaged communities and medical research; religious causes promoting peace and reconciliation and work in poor communities; environmental causes; education; the arts.
**WHAT IS NOT FUNDED** Individuals.
**RANGE OF GRANTS** From £3,000 to £240,000.
**SAMPLE GRANTS** Rebuilding Sri Lanka (£240,000); University of Manitoba – Alan Klass Memorial

Fund (£160,000); Bodleian Library (£135,000); Find Your Feet (£40,000); Laguna Blanca School (£3,000).
**FINANCES** Year 2013 Income £1,942,814 Grants £578,000 Grants to organisations £578,000 Assets £28,489,210
**TRUSTEES** Christopher Tolkien; Priscilla Tolkien; Michael Tolkien; Baillie Tolkien.
**OTHER INFORMATION** In May 2013 the Tolkien Trust (Charity Commission no. 273615) ceased to exist, with funds being transferred to create this trust. The grant total above refers to grants expenditure. During the year, support costs totalled £104,000.
**HOW TO APPLY** Unsolicited applications are not accepted; however, the trustees may approach organisations to invite applications, which should be made in writing and submitted by post.
**WHO TO APPLY TO** Cathleen Blackburn, Correspondent, c/o Maier Blackburn LLP, Prama House, 267 Banbury Road, Oxford OX2 7HT Website www.tolkientrust.org

## ■ Tomchei Torah Charitable Trust
**CC NO** 802125   **ESTABLISHED** 1989
**WHERE FUNDING CAN BE GIVEN** Barnet and Hackney.
**WHO CAN BENEFIT** Jewish people and organisations.
**WHAT IS FUNDED** General charitable purposes; social welfare; education and training; Jewish causes.
**RANGE OF GRANTS** Average £5,000.
**SAMPLE GRANTS** Previous beneficiaries have included: Friends of Mir; MST College; Friends of Sanz Institutions; United Talmudical Associates; Ezer North West; Menorah Grammar School; Friends of Torah Ohr; Ruzin Sadagora Trust; Achisomoch Aid Co and Chesed Charity Trust.
**FINANCES** Year 2013/14 Income £208,097 Grants £55,521 Grants to organisations £55,521 Assets £137,724
**TRUSTEES** Israel Kohn; Daniel Netzer; Sandra Kohn.
**HOW TO APPLY** Apply in writing to the correspondent.
**WHO TO APPLY TO** Israel Kohn, Trustee, 36 Cranbourne Gardens, London NW11 0HP Tel. 020 8458 5706 email jerry@familykohn.com

## ■ The Tompkins Foundation
**CC NO** 281405   **ESTABLISHED** 1980
**WHERE FUNDING CAN BE GIVEN** UK, with a preference for specific parishes of Hampstead Norreys in the county of Berkshire and of West Grinstead in the county of West Sussex.
**WHO CAN BENEFIT** Registered charities; including schools; hospitals; churches.
**WHAT IS FUNDED** General charitable purposes; education and training; recreation; religious causes; the promotion of health; children and young people.
**WHAT IS NOT FUNDED** Individuals.
**TYPE OF GRANT** One-off and recurring.
**RANGE OF GRANTS** £500–£50,000
**SAMPLE GRANTS** The Foundation of Nursing Studies (£80,000); Chicken Shed Theatre, The Passage and The Police Foundation (£25,000 each); Great Ormond Street Hospital CC (£21,000); Anna Freud Centre and Place 2 Be (£10,000 each); CTBF Enterprises (£3,500).
**FINANCES** Year 2013/14 Income £337,905 Grants £311,450 Grants to organisations £311,450 Assets £12,116,293
**TRUSTEES** Peter Vaines; Elizabeth Tompkins; Victoria Brenninkmeijer.

**OTHER INFORMATION** Grants were made to 13 organisations totalling £311,500, with ten of the beneficiaries having received donations in the previous year.
**HOW TO APPLY** Apply in writing to the correspondent, although unsolicited applications are unlikely to be successful as the trust has a regular list of charities which receive support.
**WHO TO APPLY TO** The Accountant, 7 Belgrave Square, London SW1X 8PH Tel. 020 7235 9322

## ■ Toras Chesed (London) Trust
**CC NO** 1110653   **ESTABLISHED** 2005
**WHERE FUNDING CAN BE GIVEN** UK.
**WHO CAN BENEFIT** Jewish organisations.
**WHAT IS FUNDED** Jewish causes; education and training; social welfare; children and young people; older people.
**FINANCES** Year 2013/14 Income £356,425 Grants £365,441 Grants to organisations £365,441
**TRUSTEES** Aaron Langberg; Akiva Stern; Simon Stern.
**OTHER INFORMATION** A list of beneficiaries was not provided within the accounts.
**HOW TO APPLY** 'Applications for grants are considered by the trustees and reviewed in depth for final approval.'
**WHO TO APPLY TO** Aaron Langberg, Trustee, 14 Lampard Grove, London N16 6UZ Tel. 020 8806 9589 email ari@toraschesed.co.uk

## ■ The Tory Family Foundation
**CC NO** 326584   **ESTABLISHED** 1984
**WHERE FUNDING CAN BE GIVEN** Worldwide, but principally East Kent.
**WHO CAN BENEFIT** Churches and charitable organisations.
**WHAT IS FUNDED** General charitable purposes; education and training; Christian causes; social welfare; the promotion of health.
**WHAT IS NOT FUNDED** Priority is given to applications from East Kent.
**TYPE OF GRANT** Capital costs; research. The foundation does not usually fund full projects.
**RANGE OF GRANTS** Up to £10,000; mostly £1,000 or less.
**SAMPLE GRANTS** Previous beneficiaries have included: Ashford YMCA, Bletchley Park, Canterbury Cathedral, Concern Worldwide, Deal Festival, Disability Law Service, Folk Rainbow Club, Foresight, Friends of Birzett, Gurkha Welfare, Kent Cancer Trust, Royal British Legion, Uppingham Foundation and Youth Action Wiltshire.
**FINANCES** Year 2013/14 Income £125,662 Grants £81,220 Grants to organisations £81,220 Assets £3,354,133
**TRUSTEES** James Nettlam Tory; Paul Tory; S. Tory; David Callister; Jill Perkins.
**OTHER INFORMATION** Grants were made totalling over £81,000.
**HOW TO APPLY** Apply in writing to the correspondent. To keep costs down, unsuccessful applicants will not be notified.
**WHO TO APPLY TO** Paul Tory, Trustee, The Estate Office, Etchinghill Golf Club, Canterbury Road, Etchinghill, Folkestone CT18 8FA Tel. 01303 862280

*Alphabetical register of grant-making charities* **Towry**

## ■ Tottenham Grammar School Foundation

**CC NO** 312634  **ESTABLISHED** 1989
**WHERE FUNDING CAN BE GIVEN** The borough of Haringey.
**WHO CAN BENEFIT** Individuals under the age of 25 who are resident or have attended a school in the borough; schools; charities; other voluntary organisations working to support such individuals.
**WHAT IS FUNDED** Educational equipment and activities not provided by local authorities.
**WHAT IS NOT FUNDED** Direct delivery of the National Curriculum; the employment of staff; the construction, adaptation, repair and maintenance of buildings; the repair and maintenance of equipment; the provision of computers and other ICT equipment; vehicle purchase; staff training; resources exclusively for parents; the costs of adults attending school trips; people aged 25 or over; people who do not live in the borough of Haringey, unless they attend or have attended a school there.
**SAMPLE GRANTS** Haringey Sports Development Trust (£77,000 in 68 grants); Haringey Music Service (£20,000); Chaverim Youth Organisation (£17,500 in three grants); Haringey Shed Theatre Company (£11,800 in two grants) Coleridge Primary School (£8,000 in three grants); Embrace UK Community Support Centre (£2,000 in two grants); Belmont Junior School (£1,900); Twisted Stocking Theatre (£1,800 in two grants).
**FINANCES** Year 2013/14 Income £489,443 Grants £807,062 Grants to organisations £380,300 Assets £22,839,699
**TRUSTEES** Keith Brown; Terry Clarke; Paul Compton; Roger Knight; Frederick Gruncell; Peter Jones; Graham Kantorowicz; Keith McGuinness; Victoria Phillips; Andrew Krokou; John Fowl.
**OTHER INFORMATION** During the year a total of 65 grants of £1,000 or more were paid to schools and other organisations. In addition, individuals received grants in the form of Somerset Awards totalling £331,500 and other sponsorship and bursaries amounting to £95,500.
**HOW TO APPLY** Application forms are available from the foundation's website. Refer to the website for full criteria and guidelines.
**WHO TO APPLY TO** Graham Chappell, Clerk, PO Box 34098, London N13 5XU *Tel.* 020 8882 2999 *Fax* Available on request *email* info@tgsf.info *Website* tgsf.org.uk

## ■ The Tower Hill Trust

**CC NO** 206225  **ESTABLISHED** 1938
**WHERE FUNDING CAN BE GIVEN** Tower Hill and St Katherine's ward in Tower Hamlets.
**WHO CAN BENEFIT** Community-based organisations and appeals benefitting children and young adults, older people, individuals with disabilities and people disadvantaged by poverty and socially isolation.
**WHAT IS FUNDED** Organisations working to provide and maintain gardens and open spaces, for the provision of leisure and recreation facilities, for the provision of education facilities and for the relief of need or sickness.
**WHAT IS NOT FUNDED** The promotion of religion; medical research and support for medical conditions; retrospective funding; applicants rejected within the previous six months; payment of salaries; individual applications; organisations in serious financial deficit or with significant unrestricted reserves. Full guidelines available on the trust's website.
**TYPE OF GRANT** General costs; capital projects; equipment; building renovation can be considered.
**RANGE OF GRANTS** Generally £300–£25,000.
**SAMPLE GRANTS** Shadwell Community Project (£20,000); Ability Bow (£8,800); Spitalfields City Farm (£7,000); Play Association Tower Hamlets (£6,600); Barbican Centre Trust, Mayor's Music Fund, Suited and Booted (£5,000 each); Connaught Opera (£1,200); Friends of Mile End Park (£1,000).
**FINANCES** Year 2013/14 Income £193,711 Grants £98,825 Grants to organisations £98,825 Assets £5,759,755
**TRUSTEES** Maj. Gen. Geoffrey Field; John Polk; John Burton-Hall; Susan Wood; Kenneth Clunie; Jonathan Solomon; Davina Walter.
**OTHER INFORMATION** Some grants to organisations extend over a number of years. The trust also pays bursaries for two pupils from Tower Hamlets at the City of London School for Girls, which totalled £11,600 in 2013/14.
**HOW TO APPLY** Full application guidelines are available on the trust's website. An initial proposal should be submitted containing the information requested in the application guidelines, along with the most recent signed annual accounts. Trustees will then review all proposals and draw up a shortlist. Applicants who are shortlisted will be contacted by the Grant Officer for further information and the final decisions will be made at the trustees' meeting. Trustees receive more applications than they are able to support. Grant decisions are made at meetings in April, July, October and January, so proposals should be submitted by March, June, September or November respectively. Further details of these dates can be found on the trust's website and funding guidelines.
**WHO TO APPLY TO** Roland Smith, Oxford House, Derbyshire Street, London E2 6HQ *Tel.* 020 7749 1118 *Fax* 020 7377 9822 *email* enquiries@towerhilltrust.org.uk *Website* www.towerhilltrust.org.uk

## ■ The Towry Law Charitable Trust

(also known as the Castle Educational Trust)
**CC NO** 278880  **ESTABLISHED** 1979
**WHERE FUNDING CAN BE GIVEN** UK, with a slight preference for the south of England.
**WHO CAN BENEFIT** Organisations benefitting people of all ages and people with disabilities.
**WHAT IS FUNDED** Education; medical research; social welfare.
**WHAT IS NOT FUNDED** Individuals; bodies which are not UK-registered charities; local branches; associates of UK charities.
**RANGE OF GRANTS** £45–£100,000
**SAMPLE GRANTS** The Prince's Trust (£100,000); Age UK; Berkshire MS Therapy Centre; Birmingham Children's Hospital; Bournemouth Food Bank; Children in Need; DEC Philippines Typhoon Appeal; Guide Dogs for the Blind; Midlands Air Ambulance; Phyllis Tuckwell Hospice; Salvation Army; St George's Crypt; The 4th Bracknell Sea Scout Group; The Stroke Association.
**FINANCES** Year 2013/14 Income £29,804 Grants £127,762 Grants to organisations £127,762 Assets £1,292,592
**TRUSTEES** Andrew Fisher; David Middleton; Alex Rickard; Jill Pinington.

*Have you read* How to use the DGMT *on page xiii?*

**833**

**OTHER INFORMATION** The trust gives a regular donation to the Prince's Trust. Grants were made to 72 organisations in total.
**HOW TO APPLY** The trustees look out for eligible projects in their local communities and have in the past stated that unsolicited applications are not considered. The trustees meet twice a year to make grant decisions.
**WHO TO APPLY TO** Jacqueline Gregory, c/o Towry Group, 6 New Street Square, London EC4A 3BF Tel. 020 7936 7236 email jacqui.gregory@towry.com

## ■ The Toy Trust
**CC NO** 1001634  **ESTABLISHED** 1991
**WHERE FUNDING CAN BE GIVEN** UK.
**WHO CAN BENEFIT** Charitable organisations.
**WHAT IS FUNDED** General charitable purposes; the promotion of health; social welfare; overseas aid; children and young people; people with disabilities.
**SAMPLE GRANTS** Handicapped Children Action Group (£90,000); Disability Africa (£20,500); Christian Aid (£17,500); Samaritans Purse (£7,500); Adventure Projects Trust, Children First Uganda and Ecologia Youth Trust (£5,000 each); CHICKS (£4,000).
**FINANCES** Year 2013 Income £283,060 Grants £305,135 Grants to organisations £305,135 Assets £34,311
**TRUSTEES** Clive Jones; Frank Martin; Kevin Jones; Philip Ratcliffe; British Toy and Hobby Association Ltd.
**OTHER INFORMATION** This trust was registered in 1991 to centralise the giving of the British Toy and Hobby Association.
**HOW TO APPLY** Apply in writing to the correspondent.
**WHO TO APPLY TO** Roland Earl, General Director c/o British Toy and Hobby Association, 80 Camberwell Road, London SE5 0EG Tel. 020 7701 7271 email admin@btha.co.uk Website www.btha.co.uk

## ■ Toyota Manufacturing UK Charitable Trust
**CC NO** 1124678  **ESTABLISHED** 2008
**WHERE FUNDING CAN BE GIVEN** Burnaston (Derbyshire) and Deeside (North Wales).
**WHO CAN BENEFIT** Registered charities and local community groups.
**WHAT IS FUNDED** Children and young people; education; health; the environment.
**RANGE OF GRANTS** Mostly up to £5,000.
**FINANCES** Year 2013 Income £316,464 Grants £160,000 Grants to organisations £160,000
**TRUSTEES** Michael Mitchell; Anthony Walker.
**OTHER INFORMATION** This is the charitable trust of Toyota Motor Manufacturing (UK) Ltd. Income is largely derived from company employees through fundraising activities.
**HOW TO APPLY** Applications may be made in writing to the correspondent.
**WHO TO APPLY TO** Laura Kristiansen, Correspondent, 3 Bretby Fairways, Bretby, Burton-on-Trent, Staffordshire DE15 0QY Tel. 01332 283608 email charitabletrust@toyotauk.com Website www.toyotauk.com/the-toyota-charitable-trust/charitable-trust-overview

## ■ Annie Tranmer Charitable Trust
**CC NO** 1044231  **ESTABLISHED** 1989
**WHERE FUNDING CAN BE GIVEN** UK, particularly Suffolk and adjacent counties.
**WHO CAN BENEFIT** Organisations and individuals.
**WHAT IS FUNDED** General charitable purposes; education and training; the promotion of health; people with disabilities; social welfare; arts and culture; amateur sport; animal welfare; children and young people; older people.
**RANGE OF GRANTS** Up to £129,000.
**SAMPLE GRANTS** East Anglian Air Ambulance (£10,000); Cancer Research UK and Mid Essex Hospital Services NHS Trust – Burns Unit (£5,000 each); St Elizabeth Hospice (£3,000); Action for Children, Age UK Suffolk and Bowel Cancer UK (£2,000 each); Deafblind UK, Independent Age and Lifelites (£1,000 each); Missing People, Motor Neurone Disease and The Cyds Project (£500 each); Ipswich Housing Action Group (£250); Sutton Heath Parish Council (£100).
**FINANCES** Year 2013/14 Income £118,597 Grants £109,632 Grants to organisations £92,958 Assets £3,719,997
**TRUSTEES** John Miller; Valerie Lewis; Nigel Bonham-Carter; Patrick Grieve.
**OTHER INFORMATION** Grants were made totalling £109,500 of which £93,000 was donated to 72 organisations and £6,700 to 23 individuals.
**HOW TO APPLY** The accounts for 2013/14 states that: 'The charity receives applications for funding from institutions and individuals. The trustees review the applications against the objectives of the charity before deciding whether or not to authorise the application and make the grant.'
**WHO TO APPLY TO** Mary Kirby, Correspondent, 51 Bennett Road, Ipswich IP1 5HX Tel. 01473 743694 email mary.kirby@timicomail.co.uk

## ■ The Constance Travis Charitable Trust
**CC NO** 294540  **ESTABLISHED** 1986
**WHERE FUNDING CAN BE GIVEN** UK (national charities only); Northamptonshire (all sectors).
**WHO CAN BENEFIT** UK-wide organisations and local groups in Northamptonshire.
**WHAT IS FUNDED** General charitable purposes.
**WHAT IS NOT FUNDED** Individuals; non-registered charities.
**TYPE OF GRANT** One-off grants for core, capital and project support.
**RANGE OF GRANTS** Up to £30,000.
**SAMPLE GRANTS** Northamptonshire Community Foundation (£1 million); Royal Albert Hall (£50,000); Royal Academy of Music (£28,000); Royal Opera House (£20,000); Northamptonshire Association of Youth Clubs (£15,000); Alzheimer's Research UK and The Brain Research Trust (£10,000 each).
**FINANCES** Year 2014 Income £2,716,570 Grants £1,906,664 Grants to organisations £1,906,664 Assets £99,670,522
**TRUSTEES** Constance Travis; Ernest Travis; Peta Travis; Matthew Travis.
**OTHER INFORMATION** In 2014 a total of 170 grants were made. The trust makes small grants to local groups in Northamptonshire through the Northamptonshire Community Foundation.
**HOW TO APPLY** The trust does not welcome contact prior to application.
**WHO TO APPLY TO** Ernest Travis, Trustee, 86 Drayton Gardens, London SW10 9SB

## ■ The Trefoil Trust (formerly known as Anona Winn Charitable Trust)

**CC NO** 1044101  **ESTABLISHED** 1995
**WHERE FUNDING CAN BE GIVEN** UK.
**WHO CAN BENEFIT** Charitable organisations.
**WHAT IS FUNDED** Health; young people; disability; the arts; armed forces.
**WHAT IS NOT FUNDED** Individuals.
**TYPE OF GRANT** Regular and one-off grants.
**RANGE OF GRANTS** Mostly £1,000–£5,000.
**SAMPLE GRANTS** Charities Aid Foundation (£22,500); DEC Philippines Typhoon Appeal (£10,000); Inter Care (£6,000); Chestnut Tree Hospice (£4,000); Blackpool Merchant Navy Association (£2,500); Childhood Eye Cancer Trust, The Fire Fighters' Charity, Wiltshire Wildlife Trust (£2,000 each); Children in Need (£250); Cirencester Rugby Football Club (£200).
**FINANCES** Year 2013 Income £48,755 Grants £101,450 Grants to organisations £101,450 Assets £1,171,900
**TRUSTEE** Trefoil Trustees Ltd.
**OTHER INFORMATION** Grants to 24 organisations totalled £101,000.
**HOW TO APPLY** Applications should be made in writing to the correspondent and accompanied by the organisation's latest report and full accounts. The trustees usually meet in April and November to decide on distributions.
**WHO TO APPLY TO** Rupert Hughes, Correspondent, New Inn Cottage, Croft Lane, Winstone, Cirencester GL7 7LN *Tel.* 01285 821338

## ■ The Tresillian Trust

**CC NO** 1105826  **ESTABLISHED** 2004
**WHERE FUNDING CAN BE GIVEN** UK and overseas.
**WHO CAN BENEFIT** Charitable organisations.
**WHAT IS FUNDED** Overseas aid and welfare causes. In the UK, community based projects supporting older people and young individuals; in Africa, Asia and South America, projects supporting the education and health of women and children; worldwide – projects dealing with conflict and disaster areas and the environment.
**TYPE OF GRANT** One-off and recurrent grants.
**RANGE OF GRANTS** £10,000–£1,000
**SAMPLE GRANTS** Christian Friends of Korea (£10,000); Human Rights Watch Charitable Trust and World Child Cancer (£5,000 each); Condor Trust (£4,000); Blacksmith Institute and Esther Benjamins Trust (£3,000 each); International Children's Trust and Theatre for Cliange Limited (£2,000 each); and Motivation Charitable Trust (£1,400).
**FINANCES** Year 2013/14 Income £58,239 Grants £83,400 Grants to organisations £83,400 Assets £2,571,189
**TRUSTEES** George Robinson; Michael Willcox; Paul Bate.
**OTHER INFORMATION** Grants were made to 24 organisations.
**HOW TO APPLY** Apply in writing to the correspondent. The annual report for 2013/14 notes that 'the trustees decide on the grants to be paid after careful review of the applications received. This strategy will continue to be implemented for as long as the number of applications remains relatively small.'
**WHO TO APPLY TO** Michael Willcox, Trustee, Old Coach House, Sunnyside, Bergh Apton, Norwich NR15 1DD *Tel.* 01508 480100 *email* info@willcoxlewis.co.uk

## ■ The Triangle Trust (1949) Fund

**CC NO** 222860  **ESTABLISHED** 1949
**WHERE FUNDING CAN BE GIVEN** UK.
**WHO CAN BENEFIT** Charitable organisations.
**WHAT IS FUNDED** Specialist organisations working with carers or the rehabilitation of ex-offenders.
**WHAT IS NOT FUNDED** Overseas charities or projects outside the UK; charities for the promotion of religion; medical research; environmental, wildlife or heritage appeals. Also refer to the trust's eligibility criteria on its website.
**TYPE OF GRANT** One-off; recurring costs; salaries; running costs.
**RANGE OF GRANTS** Up to £40,000.
**SAMPLE GRANTS** Back on Track, Carers Trust and Spark Inside (£40,000 each); Southwark Carers (£35,000); Storybook Dads (£30,000); From Springhill (£20,000); Cumbria Crossroads (£15,000); The Horse Course (£10,000); Young Carers Development Trust (£5,000); Renfrewshire Carers Centre (£3,100).
**FINANCES** Year 2013/14 Income £643,950 Grants £493,238 Grants to organisations £466,338 Assets £18,440,711
**TRUSTEES** Andrew Pitt; Julian Weinberg; Mark Powell; Melanie Burfitt; Bruce Newbigging; Kate Purcell; Helen Moss; Dr James Anderson.
**OTHER INFORMATION** The grant total includes and £27,000 to individuals.
**HOW TO APPLY** The following information was taken from the trust's website: 'The application process is two-stage. The first stage is the completion of the online application form. These are reviewed by the Trustees who are specifically looking for the following: Does the application meet the criteria, i.e. is the organisation's primary purpose to support unpaid carers or the rehabilitation of offenders?; Will the grant make a difference?; Has a development rather than a project grant been applied for?; How will the funding be sustained long term?. All shortlisted applicants (usually about 8–10 organisations) go on to the second stage of the application process which involves a visit from the Triangle Trust. Applicants are invited to present their proposal with full business plan and monitoring and reporting ideas. Trustees consider which proposals most closely meet the criteria of the Development Grant and which are most likely to achieve their expected outcomes and award grants accordingly. All organisations are informed of the outcomes of their application at each stage and written feedback for unsuccessful applications is available on request. Grants for all successful applications are awarded approximately 5 months after the initial closing date.'
**WHO TO APPLY TO** Dr Joanne Knight, Director, Foundation House, 2–4 Forum Place, Fiddlebridge Lane, Hatfield AL10 ORN *Tel.* 01707 707078 *email* info@triangletrust.org.uk *Website* www.triangletrust.org.uk

## ■ The True Colours Trust

**CC NO** 1089893  **ESTABLISHED** 2001
**WHERE FUNDING CAN BE GIVEN** UK and Africa.
**WHO CAN BENEFIT** Registered charities.
**WHAT IS FUNDED** Grant-making is focused in three areas: children and young people with complex disabilities in the UK; palliative care for children and young people in the UK; palliative care in sub-Saharan Africa. The trust also makes small grants to local charities supporting children with

disabilities or life-limiting conditions, their siblings and families.
**WHAT IS NOT FUNDED** Individuals.
**TYPE OF GRANT** One-off and recurring. Local grants tend to be one-off and for capital expenditure.
**RANGE OF GRANTS** Up to £250,000. Small grants up to £10,000.
**SAMPLE GRANTS** Community Service Volunteers (£295,000); Sky Badger (£60,000); St Oswald's Hospice (£24,000); Small Steps (£13,000); TopCats (£10,000); Norfolk Carers Support (£9,700); Music as Therapy International (£9,200); Wirral Toy Library (£7,500); the Children's Trust, Friends of Victoria and LimbPower (£5,000 each).
**FINANCES** Year 2013/14 Income £2,156,290 Grants £2,053,342 Grants to organisations £2,053,342 Assets £10,392,556
**TRUSTEES** Lucy Sainsbury; Dominic Flynn; Bernard Willis; Tim Price.
**HOW TO APPLY** The following information is taken from the trust's website: 'Programme Grants: the trust only funds registered charities or activities with clearly defined charitable purposes. Trustees only consider unsolicited applications for their Small Grants Programmes (UK and Africa) and for their Individual Grants UK programme. Proposals for the trust's other programmes are invited by the trustees or initiated at their request. The trustees are keen to learn more about organisations whose work fits into the categories above but unsolicited applications are not encouraged and are unlikely to be successful. Information about your organisation and project should be sent by post to The True Colours Trust, The Peak, 5 Wilton Road, London SW1P 1AP, please do not send more than 2 pages of A4 covering: the organisation – explaining its charitable aims and objectives, and giving its most recent annual income and expenditure, and current financial position. Please do not send a full set of accounts; the project requiring funding – why it is needed, who will benefit and in what way; the funding – breakdown of costs, any money raised so far, and how the balance will be raised; at this stage please do not send supporting books, brochures, DVDs, annual reports or accounts. All correspondence will be acknowledged by post. If your organisation is a candidate for support, you will hear from us within 12 weeks of the acknowledgement. Applicants who do not hear from us within this time must assume they have been unsuccessful. Small Grants – UK and Africa: the trustees welcome unsolicited applications for their small grants programmes, both in the UK and in Africa. Trustees are keen to make these programmes available to as many organisations as possible; it is therefore unlikely that they will fund any organisation in consecutive years. Small Grants UK: the trustees are committed to supporting a large number of excellent local organisations and projects that work with children with disabilities and their families on a daily basis. This is done through the trust's small grants programme. It provides grants of up to £10,000 to help smaller organisations develop and deliver programmes for children, their siblings and families. It is open to applications at any time. Grants in this category are usually one-off contributions rather than multi-year grants for on-going revenue costs. Please note the following: this programme is for UK organisations and projects only; the programme is unable to provide support to local authorities; trustees are keen to make the grant programme available to as many organisations as possible; it is therefore unlikely that they will fund organisations in consecutive years. Upon submission of your application you will receive an acknowledgement letter or email. If you do not hear from us within twelve weeks of the date of this acknowledgement please accept that the trustees, with regret, have not been able to make a grant in response to your appeal. You will not receive a letter explaining that your application has been unsuccessful. Applications for small grants should be made using our online application form or alternatively you may complete the downloadable version of the form and either return to us by post or email.'
**WHO TO APPLY TO** Alan Bookbinder, Director, The Peak, 5 Wilton Road, London SW1V 1AP Tel. 020 7410 0330 email truecolours@sfct.org.uk Website www.truecolourstrust.org.uk

## ■ Truedene Co. Ltd
**CC NO** 248268 **ESTABLISHED** 1966
**WHERE FUNDING CAN BE GIVEN** UK and overseas.
**WHO CAN BENEFIT** Jewish organisations.
**WHAT IS FUNDED** Jewish religious education; support for Jewish people who are in need.
**RANGE OF GRANTS** Usually between £1,000 and £150,000.
**SAMPLE GRANTS Previous beneficiaries have included:** Beis Rochel D'Satmar Girls School Ltd, British Friends of Tchernobyl, Congregation Paile Yoetz, Cosmon Belz Limited, Friends of Mir, Kolel Shomrei Hachomoth, Mesifta Talmudical College, Mosdos Ramou, Orthodox Council of Jerusalem, Tevini Limited, United Talmudical Associates Limited, VMCT and Yeshivo Horomo Talmudical College.
**FINANCES** Year 2013/14 Income £701,461 Grants £854,000 Grants to organisations £854,000 Assets £7,836,823
**TRUSTEES** Sarah Klein, Chair; Samuel Berger; Solomon Laufer; Sije Berger; Zelda Sternlicht.
**OTHER INFORMATION** No list of grant beneficiaries was included in the accounts.
**HOW TO APPLY** Apply in writing to the correspondent
**WHO TO APPLY TO** The Trustees, Truedene Co. Ltd, Hatton House, 8 Timberwharf Road, London N16 6DB

## ■ The Truemark Trust
**CC NO** 265855 **ESTABLISHED** 1973
**WHERE FUNDING CAN BE GIVEN** UK.
**WHO CAN BENEFIT** Registered charities with preference for small local charities, neighbourhood-based community projects and innovative work with less popular groups.
**WHAT IS FUNDED** 'The relief of all kinds of social distress and disadvantage.'
**WHAT IS NOT FUNDED** Individuals, including students; general appeals; large national charities; churches or church buildings; medical research projects.
**TYPE OF GRANT** Usually one-off for a specific project or part of a project. Core funding and/or salaries are rarely considered.
**RANGE OF GRANTS** Average grant £1,000.
**SAMPLE GRANTS** Pathway Workshop and The Rosemary Foundation (£10,000 each); Barnabus and The Iris Trust (£5,000 each); New Dimensions and Root and Branch (£4,500 each); A World of Girls (£2,500); Arts Together and Beds Garden Carers (£2,000 each); Alternatives Watford and Needham Market Institute and Club (£1,000 each).

*Alphabetical register of grant-making charities* — **Trusthouse**

**FINANCES** Year 2013/14 Income £596,557 Grants £367,500 Grants to organisations £367,500 Assets £19,089,161
**TRUSTEES** Sir Thomas Lucas; Wendy Collett; Sharon Knight; Judy Hayward; Roger Ross.
**HOW TO APPLY** Apply in writing to the correspondent, including the most recent set of accounts, clear details of the need the project is designed to meet and an outline budget. The trustees meet four times a year. Only successful applicants receive a reply.
**WHO TO APPLY TO** Clare Pegden, Correspondent, PO Box 2, Liss, Hampshire GU33 6YP *Tel.* 07970 540015 *email* truemark.trust01@ntlworld.com

----

## ■ Truemart Limited

**CC NO** 1090586    **ESTABLISHED** 1984
**WHERE FUNDING CAN BE GIVEN** UK-wide, with a preference for Greater London.
**WHO CAN BENEFIT** Charitable organisations.
**WHAT IS FUNDED** General charitable purposes; Jewish causes; social welfare.
**FINANCES** Year 2013/14 Income £267,692 Grants £108,440 Grants to organisations £108,440 Assets £167,307
**TRUSTEES** S. Heitner; Ian Heitner.
**OTHER INFORMATION** No list of grant beneficiaries was included in the accounts.
**HOW TO APPLY** Apply in writing to the correspondent.
**WHO TO APPLY TO** S. Heitner, Trustee, 34 The Ridgeway, London NW11 8QS *Tel.* 020 8455 4456

----

## ■ Trumros Limited

**CC NO** 285533    **ESTABLISHED** 1982
**WHERE FUNDING CAN BE GIVEN** UK.
**WHO CAN BENEFIT** Charitable organisations.
**WHAT IS FUNDED** Jewish causes; education and training; social welfare; the promotion of health; children and young people.
**SAMPLE GRANTS Previous beneficiaries have included:** Emuno Educational Centre (£51,000); Before Trust (£32,000); Ichud Mosdos Gur (£31,000); Chevras Mo'oz Ladol (£25,500); Am Ha Chessed (£20,000); Beis Yosef Zvi (£12,500); Gesher Charitable Trust and Ozer Gemillas Chasodim (£10,000 each).
**FINANCES** Year 2013 Income £298,743 Grants £155,720 Grants to organisations £155,720 Assets £91,916
**TRUSTEES** Hannah Hofbauer; Ronald Hofbauer.
**HOW TO APPLY** Apply in writing to the correspondent.
**WHO TO APPLY TO** Ronald Hofbauer, Trustee, 282 Finchley Road, London NW3 7AD *Tel.* 020 7431 3282 *email* r.hofbauer@btconnect.com

----

## ■ The Trusthouse Charitable Foundation

**CC NO** 1063945    **ESTABLISHED** 1997
**WHERE FUNDING CAN BE GIVEN** Unrestricted, but mainly UK.
**WHO CAN BENEFIT** Registered charities and other not-for-profit organisations.
**WHAT IS FUNDED** The foundation has two overarching themes – rural issues and urban deprivation. Within these themes, there are three areas of interest: community support; disability and healthcare; arts, education and heritage. The foundation also runs three-year grants programmes focused on a specific issue of interest to the trustees. At the time of writing (June 2015) the current focus of the programme was young families.
**WHAT IS NOT FUNDED** Individuals; organisations and projects outside the UK; statutory services including schools (unless these are specifically for children with disabilities), prisons, local authority services and NHS hospitals or services; universities and further education colleges; organisations with a total annual income of £5 million or more (except hospices); grant-making organisations; umbrella organisations. The foundation is not currently funding: set-up costs for new organisations; the purchase of computers and other electronic equipment; the creation or maintenance of websites; animal welfare projects; projects with primarily an ecological aim; medical research; feasibility studies; capital appeals for places of worship (unless these are primarily for community use); projects to enable a building to comply with the Disability and Discrimination Act; staff training that is required by a statutory authority or as part of continuing professional development by an industry body; one-off events; PR and raising awareness; salaries of fundraising staff or fundraising initiatives; projects that have the primary concern of producing DVDs or other media. Grants are not given towards hospice running costs. Furthermore the annual report 2013/14 states that, as of 1 July 2013, grants are no longer given in support of unsolicited applications for projects in financially developing countries.
**TYPE OF GRANT** Running costs; one-off grants for capital costs.
**RANGE OF GRANTS** Most grants are of less than £10,000 (Small Grants Scheme). Grants from the Large Grants Scheme range up to £30,000.
**SAMPLE GRANTS** Belfast City Mission and People's Theatre Arts Group (£110,000 each through the Super Grant Programme); Humanitarian Aid Relief Trust – HART (£76,000); South Creake War Memorial Institute and St Luke's Hospice (£30,000 each); Etchingham Trust for Sports and Recreation (£25,000); Enfield Asian Welfare Association Ltd (£15,000); Reader Organisation (£10,800); Reeth and District Community Transport Ltd (£10,000); St George and St Peter's Community Association (£9,000); Chesterfield and North East Derbyshire Credit Union Ltd (£6,000); Sudbury Neighbourhood Centre (£4,500); Doncaster Housing for Young People (£3,500); Omega the National Association for End of Life Care (£2,000); Norfolk Carers Support (£1,000).
**FINANCES** Year 2013/14 Income £1,895,000 Grants £2,108,000 Grants to organisations £2,108,000 Assets £73,601,000
**TRUSTEES** Sir Jeremy Beecham; Baroness Sarah Hogg; The Duke of Marlborough; Anthony Peel; The Hon. Olga Polizzi; Sir Hugh Rossi; Lady Janet Balfour of Burleigh; Sir John Nutting; Howell Harris-Hughes; Revd Rose Hudson-Wilkin; Lady Hamilton.
**OTHER INFORMATION** Of 1,203 applications received by the foundation during the year, 331 grants were made.
**HOW TO APPLY** Application forms are available to download from the foundation's website, accessed following the completion of a brief eligibility questionnaire, which also identifies which type of grant may be most suitable. Application forms should be completed and returned via post along with a budget for the work for which you are applying for support and a copy of your organisation's latest annual accounts. Applications are not currently accepted via email. Detailed guidelines are

available to download from the website. There is a specific section for hospices on the website, where further guidelines and a downloadable application form can be found.
**WHO TO APPLY TO** Judith Leigh, Grants Manager, 6th Floor, 65 Leadenhall Street, London EC3A 2AD *Tel.* 020 7264 4990 *Website* www.trusthousecharitablefoundation.org.uk

..........

## ■ The James Tudor Foundation
**CC NO** 1105916 **ESTABLISHED** 2004
**WHERE FUNDING CAN BE GIVEN** UK and overseas.
**WHO CAN BENEFIT** Institutions and registered charities.
**WHAT IS FUNDED** The foundation has the principal aim of relieving sickness. Its six programme areas are: palliative care; medical research; health education, awards and scholarship; the direct relief of sickness; overseas work for the relief of sickness; activities that, by other means, fulfil the foundation's objects.
**WHAT IS NOT FUNDED** Individuals; overseas organisations; applicants who have applied within the last 12 months; capital projects (building and refurbishment costs); funding that directly replaces, or negatively affects, statutory funding; work that has already taken place; endowments; community development; any sport or recreation use; adventure or residential courses, respite holidays and excursions, expeditions, bursaries or overseas travel; environmental, conservation or heritage causes; animal welfare; sports and recreation. The foundation is unlikely to fund: large national charities with widespread support and local organisations which are part of a wider network. Items of equipment may be funded but applicants whose proposal includes a request for equipment funding should at first contact the foundation.
**TYPE OF GRANT** Project costs. Core costs may also be considered, but generally only for organisations with which the foundation has a longstanding relationship. Grants are usually for one year.
**RANGE OF GRANTS** Up to £50,000; the majority of grants are of £10,000 or less.
**SAMPLE GRANTS** University of Bristol (£67,500 in two grants); University of Nottingham (£50,000); World Health Organisation (£25,000); Children's Hospice South West (£20,000); St Peter's Hospice (£15,000); Changing Faces (£10,000); Cerebral Palsy Plus (£5,000); Womankind (£3,400); African Initiatives (£3,000); Cruse Bereavement Hampshire (£1,800); Mobility Trust (£500).
**FINANCES** *Year* 2013/14 *Income* £968,443 *Grants* £821,918 *Grants to organisations* £821,918 *Assets* £27,297,327
**TRUSTEES** Martin Wren; Richard Esler; Roger Jones; Cedric Nash; Susan Evans.
**OTHER INFORMATION** During the year, the foundation received 219 full written applications, 33 of which came from outline proposals. In total, 89 grants were made to organisations during the year.
**HOW TO APPLY** Potential applicants must at first read the foundation's guidelines and can complete an initial eligibility check, both of which can be found on the website. Organisations that are eligible at this stage can send an outline application along with a coversheet to the foundation and, following this, may be invited to submit a full application. There is a brief guide on how to apply on the website.

**WHO TO APPLY TO** Rod Shaw, Chief Executive, WestPoint, 78 Queens Road, Clifton, Bristol BS8 1QU *Tel.* 0117 985 8715 *Fax* 0117 985 8716 *email* admin@jamestudor.org.uk *Website* www.jamestudor.org.uk

..........

## ■ Tudor Rose Ltd
**CC NO** 800576 **ESTABLISHED** 1987
**WHERE FUNDING CAN BE GIVEN** UK.
**WHO CAN BENEFIT** Registered charities.
**WHAT IS FUNDED** Orthodox Jewish causes; social welfare.
**SAMPLE GRANTS Previous beneficiaries have included:** Lolev Charitable Trust; Woodlands Charity; KTV; Bell Synagogue; Hatzola; Lubavitch Centre; and TCT.
**FINANCES** *Year* 2013/14 *Income* £384,856 *Grants* £824,167 *Grants to organisations* £824,167 *Assets* £3,478,505
**TRUSTEES** Miriam Lehrfield; Aaron Taub.
**OTHER INFORMATION** A list of grant beneficiaries was not included in the accounts.
**HOW TO APPLY** Apply in writing to the correspondent.
**WHO TO APPLY TO** The Trustees, c/o Martin and Heller, 5 North End Road, London NW11 7RJ *email* frank@martin-heller.com

..........

## ■ The Tudor Trust
**CC NO** 1105580 **ESTABLISHED** 1955
**WHERE FUNDING CAN BE GIVEN** UK and sub-Saharan Africa.
**WHO CAN BENEFIT** Registered charities and other charitable organisations.
**WHAT IS FUNDED** Organisations working directly with people who are on the margins of society; a focus on building stronger communities by overcoming isolation and fragmentation and encouraging inclusion, connection and integration; organisations which are embedded in and have developed out of their community – whether the local area or a 'community of interest' high levels of user involvement, and an emphasis on self-help where this is appropriate; work which addresses complex and multi-stranded problems in unusual or imaginative ways; organisations which are thoughtful in their use of resources and which foster community resilience in the face of environmental, economic or social change.
**WHAT IS NOT FUNDED** Individuals, or organisations applying on behalf of individuals; larger charities (both national and local) enjoying widespread support; statutory bodies; hospitals, health authorities or hospices; medical care, medical equipment or medical research; universities, colleges or schools; academic research, scholarships or bursaries; nurseries, playgroups or crèches; one-off holidays, residentials, trips, exhibitions, conferences, events, etc.; animal charities; the promotion of religion; the restoration or conservation of buildings or habitats (where there isn't a strong social welfare focus); work outside the UK. The trust runs a targeted grants programme promoting sustainable agriculture in sub-Saharan Africa. They do not consider unsolicited proposals from groups working overseas; endowment appeals; and work that has already taken place. Applicants are encouraged to call the information team for advice concerning applications.
**TYPE OF GRANT** Capital and revenue grants; core funding.

**RANGE OF GRANTS** There is no minimum or maximum grant.
**SAMPLE GRANTS** Older Women's Cohousing (£1.2 million); Stand Alone (£150,000); Community Action Through Sport (£65,000); Blaze (£45,000); Avon Club for Young People (£30,000); Manor House Agricultural Centre (£15,000); Centre for Complementary Care (£5,000); Young Minds Matter (£2,100); Kawuku Women's Group (£2,000); Fuse Youth Cafe (£1,300).
**FINANCES** Year 2013/14 Income £20,806,000 Grants £19,855,291 Grants to organisations £19,855,291 Assets £231,967,000
**TRUSTEES** James Long; Dr Desmond Graves; Catherine Antcliff; Monica Barlow; Nell Buckler; Louise Collins; Elizabeth Crawshaw; Ben Dunwell; Matt Dunwell; Christopher Graves; Francis Runacres; Vanessa James; Rosalind Dunwell; Any Collins; Carey Buckler.
**OTHER INFORMATION** Excellent annual report and accounts are available from the trust. The trust's website also includes full, clear guidelines for applicants.
**HOW TO APPLY** According to the trust's website, the application process is made up of two stages. A first stage application must include the following: a brief introductory letter; a completed organisation details sheet (available from the funding section of the trust's website); a copy of your most recent annual accounts, and annual report if you produce one; and answers to the following questions, on no more than two sides of A4: what difference do you want to make, and how will your organisation achieve this?; why are you the right organisation to do this work?; how do you know there is a need for your work, and who benefits from the work that you do?; and how would you use funding from Tudor? The proposal should be addressed to the trustees and sent via post. Proposals will be acknowledged within a few days of being received. If the first-stage proposal is successful, applicants will receive an acknowledgement letter plus details about the second-stage of the process. The second stage will be conducted via telephone or a visit. The trust aims to let applicants know within a month whether or not they have progressed to the second stage application. The trust aims to make a decision on most applications three months after progressing to the second stage. Trustees and staff meet every three weeks to consider applications. More information is available on the trust's website.
**WHO TO APPLY TO** Fiona Young, 7 Ladbroke Grove, London W11 3BD Tel. 020 7727 8522 email general@tudortrust.org.uk Website www.tudortrust.org.uk

## ■ The Tufton Charitable Trust
**CC NO** 801479 **ESTABLISHED** 1989
**WHERE FUNDING CAN BE GIVEN** UK.
**WHO CAN BENEFIT** Individuals and charitable organisations.
**WHAT IS FUNDED** Christian activity supporting evangelism.
**WHAT IS NOT FUNDED** Repair or maintenance of buildings.
**TYPE OF GRANT** One-off and project-related costs.
**SAMPLE GRANTS** The Church of England (£83,000); Stowe School Foundation (£60,000); Soul Survivor (£25,000); Off The Fence (£22,000); London Institute of Contemporary Christianity (£20,000); Glyndebourne Productions and Jesus College – Cambridge (£10,000 each); Caritas Foundation of Western Kansas (£9,900); Royal Opera House and The British Library (£5,000 each).
**FINANCES** Year 2013 Income £1,009,173 Grants £255,952 Grants to organisations £255,952 Assets £624,631
**TRUSTEES** Lady Georgina Wates; Sir Christopher Wates; Joseph Lulham; Wates Charitable Trustees Ltd.
**OTHER INFORMATION** Grants were made totalling £256,000 to ten organisations.
**HOW TO APPLY** Apply in writing to the correspondent, including an sae. The trustees meet regularly to review applications.
**WHO TO APPLY TO** The Trustees, Tufton Place, Ewhurst Place, Northiam, East Sussex TN31 6HL

## ■ Tuixen Foundation
**CC NO** 1081124 **ESTABLISHED** 2000
**WHERE FUNDING CAN BE GIVEN** Worldwide, mainly UK.
**WHO CAN BENEFIT** Registered charities; hospitals; schools; other similar charitable organisations.
**WHAT IS FUNDED** Education; health; disability; poverty; children and young people.
**WHAT IS NOT FUNDED** Individuals.
**RANGE OF GRANTS** Up to £175,000.
**SAMPLE GRANTS** Previous beneficiaries have included: Impetus Trust (£175,500); University of Manchester (£100,000); Camfed (£50,000); Chance UK, Facing the World, School Home Support and Street League (£30,000 each); Sports Aid Trust (£25,000); First Step Trust (£20,000); and the Shannon Trust (£10,000).
**FINANCES** Year 2013/14 Income £1,114,551 Grants £826,000 Grants to organisations £826,000 Assets £21,711,793
**TRUSTEES** Peter Englander; Dr Leanda Kroll; Stephen Rosefield; Peter Clements.
**OTHER INFORMATION** A list of grants was not available to view with the current accounts.
**HOW TO APPLY** The foundation has previously stated that 'unsolicited applications are not sought and correspondence will not be entered into'.
**WHO TO APPLY TO** Paul Clements, Trustee, c/o Coutts & Co., 440 Strand, London WC2R 0QS Tel. 020 7649 2903

## ■ The Douglas Turner Trust
**CC NO** 227892 **ESTABLISHED** 1964
**WHERE FUNDING CAN BE GIVEN** UK and overseas; however, in practice, there is a strong preference for Birmingham and the West Midlands.
**WHO CAN BENEFIT** Mainly local registered charities.
**WHAT IS FUNDED** General charitable purposes; people with disabilities; the promotion of health; children and young people; community work; hospices; the environment; arts and heritage; social welfare; overseas aid; medical research.
**WHAT IS NOT FUNDED** Individuals; non-registered charities.
**TYPE OF GRANT** Recurring and one-off awards; capital and core costs.
**RANGE OF GRANTS** £500–£20,000
**SAMPLE GRANTS** Previous beneficiaries have included: St Mary's Hospice Ltd (£18,000); Birmingham Boys' and Girls' Union (£10,000); and WaterAid (£4,000 each).
**FINANCES** Year 2013/14 Income £444,769 Grants £427,000 Grants to organisations £427,000 Assets £16,534,542
**TRUSTEES** David Pearson; Stephen Luing Preedy; John Morland Del Mar; Geoffrey Patterson

Thomas; James Grindall; Peter Millward; Amanda McGeever.

**OTHER INFORMATION** Grants were made to 149 organisations totalling £427,000.

**HOW TO APPLY** The trust's accounts for 2014 state that: 'The Trust does not have a grant application form. Applicant charities are requested to send a letter of no more than two pages describing their appeal to the Trust Administrator at the Grants Office, accompanied by Annual Accounts. Full Appeal Guidelines are available from the Trust Administrator. Applicants are welcome to e-mail or telephone the Trust Administrator. Unsuitable applications are acknowledged within a few days of receipt. All applications presented to the Trustees are acknowledged after the Trustees quarterly meeting at which they are considered.'

**WHO TO APPLY TO** Tim Patrickson, Administrator, 3 Poplar Piece, Inkberrow, Worcester WR7 4JD *Tel.* 01386 792014 *email* timpatrickson@hotmail.co.uk

······················································

### ■ The Florence Turner Trust

**CC NO** 502721      **ESTABLISHED** 1973

**WHERE FUNDING CAN BE GIVEN** UK, but with a strong preference for Leicestershire.

**WHO CAN BENEFIT** Smaller projects are favoured where donations will make a 'quantifiable difference to the recipients rather than favouring large national charities whose income is measured in millions rather than thousands.' Grants are made for the benefit of individuals through a referring agency such as social services, NHS trusts or similar responsible bodies.

**WHAT IS FUNDED** The trust gives to general charitable purposes. Smaller projects are favoured where donations will make a quantifiable difference to individuals. Grants to individuals are made through referral by agencies, such as social services or NHS trusts.

**WHAT IS NOT FUNDED** Individuals for educational purposes.

**SAMPLE GRANTS** Previous beneficiaries have included: Leicester Charity Link (£12,000); Leicester Grammar School – Bursary (£10,000); Age Concern Leicester, Leicester and Leicestershire Historic Churches Preservation Trust and VISTA (£2,400 each); LOROS (£2,000); New Parks Club for Young People (£1,500); and Four Twelve Ministries and Help for Heroes (£1,000 each).

**FINANCES** *Year* 2013/14 *Income* £200,263 *Grants* £117,905 *Grants to organisations* £117,905 *Assets* £6,111,629

**TRUSTEES** Roger Bowder; Katherine Hall; Michael Jones.

**OTHER INFORMATION** Grants totalled £99,000. Support costs were £17,000; auditor's remuneration £3,400 and 'trustees remuneration' was £6,000.

**HOW TO APPLY** Apply in writing to the correspondent. The trustees meet every eight or nine weeks.

**WHO TO APPLY TO** Jenny Coleman, Correspondent, Shakespeares, Two Colton Square, Leicester LE1 1 QH *Tel.* 0116 257 6129 *email* paula.fowle@Shakespeares.co.uk

······················································

### ■ The G. J. W. Turner Trust

**CC NO** 258615      **ESTABLISHED** 1969

**WHERE FUNDING CAN BE GIVEN** Birmingham and the Midlands area.

**WHO CAN BENEFIT** Charitable organisations.

**WHAT IS FUNDED** General charitable purposes.

**RANGE OF GRANTS** Up to £40,000.

**SAMPLE GRANTS** Previous beneficiaries have included: Birmingham St Mary's Hospice and Sunfield Children's Homes (£40,000 each); Birmingham Rathbone Society (£30,000); Victoria School and Shakespeare's Hospice (£15,000 each); Elmhurst Ballet School Bursary Fund and The Diabetic Foot Trust Fund (£10,000 each); Barnardo's, Birmingham Hippodrome, Children's Hand and Arm Surgery, County Air Ambulance and Queen Alexandra College (£5,000 each); Saltley Neighbourhood Pensioner's Centre (£3,000); St Margaret's Church Short Heath (£2,000); and The National Children's Orchestra of Great Britain (£1,000).

**FINANCES** *Year* 2013/14 *Income* £375,925 *Grants* £350,700 *Grants to organisations* £350,700 *Assets* £10,283,119

**TRUSTEES** David Pearson; Andrew Inglis; Hugh Carslake.

**HOW TO APPLY** Apply in writing to the correspondent. The trustees meet annually, usually in July.

**WHO TO APPLY TO** Chrissy Norgrove, Correspondent, c/o SGH Martineau LLP, 1 Colmore Square, Birmingham B4 6AA *Tel.* 0870 763 1000 *email* christine.norgrove@sghmartineau.com

······················································

### ■ TVML Foundation

**CC NO** 1135495      **ESTABLISHED** 2010

**WHERE FUNDING CAN BE GIVEN** UK and overseas, with preference towards Brazil and Israel.

**WHO CAN BENEFIT** Charitable organisations.

**WHAT IS FUNDED** General charitable purposes, particularly education and training and social welfare, as well as children and young people.

**FINANCES** *Year* 2013 *Income* £1,807,163 *Grants* £375,747 *Grants to organisations* £375,747 *Assets* £5,800,974

**TRUSTEES** Vivian Lederman; Marcos Lederman; Marcelo Steuer.

**OTHER INFORMATION** Grants are made to organisations and individuals. A list of grant beneficiaries was not included in the accounts.

**HOW TO APPLY** Apply in writing to the correspondent.

**WHO TO APPLY TO** Tania Lima, Correspondent, 8 Sand Ridge, Ridgewood, Uckfield, East Sussex TN22 5ET

······················································

### ■ Two Ridings Community Foundation

**CC NO** 1084043      **ESTABLISHED** 2000

**WHERE FUNDING CAN BE GIVEN** North and East Yorkshire, York and Hull.

**WHO CAN BENEFIT** Charitable organisations and community groups.

**WHAT IS FUNDED** The foundation manages a number of grant programmes. The website states: 'We encourage applications for activities that: support particularly disadvantaged and marginalised communities; tackle challenging issues; encourage inclusive community activity and participation; respond to their communities' needs; engage people who face discrimination or disadvantage; produce a wide range of benefits and provide good value for money.' Grant schemes change frequently. Consult the foundation's website for details of current programmes.

**WHAT IS NOT FUNDED** Each of the foundation's funding programmes has specific criteria which can be found on the website. Generally, grants are not given to: private businesses; general appeals or sponsorship; national organisations and their affiliates (this does not include locally constituted and managed branches of national or large charities); statutory agencies, including parish councils and schools, in the discharge of their statutory obligations; organisations that have substantial unrestricted funds; previous grant recipients who have outstanding monitoring information. Grants are not given for: advancement of religion; activities solely benefitting animals; overseas holidays or trips; political campaigning; medical research, equipment or treatment; work normally undertaken or funded by statutory bodies; retrospective funding.

**TYPE OF GRANT** See individual programmes.

**RANGE OF GRANTS** Most grants £250–£10,000.

**SAMPLE GRANTS** Butterflies Memory Loss Support Group (£30,00); Leyburn Arts Centre Ltd (£9,400); Clarence Gardens Association Ltd (£8,000); Airmyn Cricket Club (£5,000); Castle Community Network (£4,600); 1st Heworth Scout Group – York (£3,000); North Bransholme Sports Forum (£2,500); Swainby Playing Fields Association (£1,500); Darley Preschool, Hull Northern Social Club and Withernsea Carnival (£1,000 each); Easington Youth Club (£900); Dorchester Parents' Group and Skipton Community Orchestra (£750 each); Rethink Mental Illness – The York Fellowship (£700); Haltomprice Stroke Club and Reedness Over 60 Group (£500 each); Ripon Grammar School (£200).

**FINANCES** Year 2013/14 Income £204,451 Grants £321,264 Grants to organisations £321,264 Assets £2,510,522

**TRUSTEES** Wendy Bundy; Paul Lee; Maureen Macleod; Joe Goodhart; Philip Ingham; Gil Richardson; Richard Fletcher; Hannah Purkis; Tracey Smith.

**OTHER INFORMATION** Grants were awarded to 136 organisations in 2013/14.

**HOW TO APPLY** Application forms for each of the grant programmes can be found on the foundation's website, along with eligibility criteria and guidance notes. Applications are not accepted by email.

**WHO TO APPLY TO** Jackie McCafferty, Programmes Manager, Primrose Hill, Buttercrambe Road, Stamford Bridge, York YO41 1AW *Tel.* 01759 377400 *email* office@trcf.org.uk *Website* www.trcf.org.uk

## ■ Community Foundation Serving Tyne and Wear and Northumberland

**CC NO** 700510    **ESTABLISHED** 1988

**WHERE FUNDING CAN BE GIVEN** Tyne and Wear and Northumberland.

**WHO CAN BENEFIT** Charitable organisations. The foundation is particularly keen to help grassroots community groups and small-to-medium-sized voluntary organisations.

**WHAT IS FUNDED** The funds generally have a specific cause as their individual funding priority, but overall the foundation has social welfare as its predominant cause to support. Projects that help communities and individuals who are disadvantaged because of poverty, poor health or disability are of particular interest.

**WHAT IS NOT FUNDED** Contributions to general appeals or circulars; religious activity which is not for wider public benefit; public bodies to carry out their statutory obligations; activities which solely support animal welfare; activities which have already taken place; grant-making by other organisations.

**TYPE OF GRANT** Mostly single grants, but some grants recurrent for up to three years. Will consider capital, core costs, recurring, running and start-up costs, as well as one-off, feasibility studies and salaries.

**RANGE OF GRANTS** Usually up to £5,000, exceptionally up to £100,000.

**FINANCES** Year 2013/14 Income £7,904,552 Grants £5,130,231 Grants to organisations £5,130,231 Assets £58,549,575

**TRUSTEES** Prof. Drinkwater; Susan Winfield; Ashley Winter; Alastair Conn; Jo Curry; Colin Seccombe; Prof. Charles Harvey; Jane Robinson; John Clough; Fiona Cruickshank; Nick Hall; Geoffrey Hodgson; Sally Young; Sharon Spurling.

**HOW TO APPLY** There is one application form for the general Community Foundation grants and generally, separate forms for the other rolling grants programmes and one-off funds. Funds that support individuals are advertised separately. All of these plus application guidelines are available on the website under the 'apply' section. Some of the programmes have deadlines and some do not; also, programmes change regularly so the trust's website should be checked for the most recent information. If a grant is approved, there are terms and conditions that must be adhered to and a project report is to be submitted. Organisations that are not registered charities can apply to get a grant, but grants can only be distributed for activities that are charitable in law. CICs or other social enterprises with a good business plan can apply for help with start-up or expansion, but help with general running costs is not usually supported. Applicants must provide a copy of the bank statement; a copy of the latest annual accounts; constitution or set of rules; Child Protection or Vulnerable Adult Policy (if applicable); and copies of written estimates or catalogue pages if applying for grants regarding equipment or capital items. Email this information where possible to documents@communityfoundation.org.uk and write the name of the organisation making the application in the subject line of the email. Alternatively, send this information to the correspondent. Mark each of the documents clearly with the name of the organisation making the application.

**WHO TO APPLY TO** Sonia Waugh, Deputy Chief Executive, Cale Cross House, 156 Pilgrim Street, Newcastle upon Tyne NE1 6SU *Tel.* 0191 222 0945 *email* general@communityfoundation.org.uk *Website* www.communityfoundation.org.uk

## ■ Trustees of Tzedakah

**CC NO** 251897    **ESTABLISHED** 1966

**WHERE FUNDING CAN BE GIVEN** Worldwide, in practice UK and Israel.

**WHO CAN BENEFIT** Mainly Jewish religious institutions.

**WHAT IS FUNDED** Jewish causes; education and training; social welfare; children and young people.

**WHAT IS NOT FUNDED** Individuals.

**RANGE OF GRANTS** £25–£35,000

**SAMPLE GRANTS Previous beneficiaries have included:** Hasmonean High School Charitable Trust; Gertner Charitable Trust; Society of Friends of the Torah; Hendon Adath Yisroel Synagogue; Medrash Shmuel Theological College; Torah Temimoh; Willow Foundation;

Tifferes Girls School; Sage Home for the Aged; WIZO; and Torah Movement of Great Britain.

**FINANCES** *Year* 2013/14 *Income* £307,508 *Grants* £333,363 *Grants to organisations* £333,363 *Assets* £218,882

**TRUSTEES** Leonard Finn; Michael Lebrett.

**HOW TO APPLY** This trust states that it does not respond to unsolicited applications.

**WHO TO APPLY TO** Michael Lebrett, Trustee, Brentmead House, Britannia Road, London N12 9RU *Tel.* 020 8446 6767 *email* lfinnco@aol.com

## ■ The Udlington Trust

**CC NO** 1129443  **ESTABLISHED** 2009
**WHERE FUNDING CAN BE GIVEN** UK and overseas.
**WHO CAN BENEFIT** Registered charities.
**WHAT IS FUNDED** General charitable purposes.
**SAMPLE GRANTS** Unfortunately a list of beneficiaries was not available in the trust's accounts.
**FINANCES** Year 2014 Income £100,000 Grants £87,700 Grants to organisations £87,700 Assets £186,463
**TRUSTEES** Bruce Blackledge; Richard Blackledge; Robert Blackledge; Rebecca Blackledge.
**OTHER INFORMATION** In 2014 a total of 27 grants were awarded to eight organisations. A list of beneficiaries was not provided in the trust's accounts.
**HOW TO APPLY** Apply in writing to the correspondent.
**WHO TO APPLY TO** Richard Blackledge, Trustee, Udlington Manor, Isle Lane, Bicton, Shrewsbury, Shropshire SY3 8DY *Tel.* 01743 850270 *email* richard@arrowcounty.com

## ■ UIA Charitable Foundation

**CC NO** 1079982  **ESTABLISHED** 2000
**WHERE FUNDING CAN BE GIVEN** Worldwide.
**WHO CAN BENEFIT** Registered charities.
**WHAT IS FUNDED** Financially developing countries; human rights; social welfare; rehabilitation of offenders; victims of domestic abuse; victims of drug and alcohol addiction.
**WHAT IS NOT FUNDED** The foundation's website states that it will not fund the following: 'work which it believes to be publicly funded; retrospective projects; organisations that have an annual turnover in excess of £500,000 unless the organisation is acting as a conduit for a partner that fulfils the criteria and may find it difficult to obtain access to funding through independent channels; and organisations whose combined grant related support costs and governance costs are greater than 10% of their turnover'.
**RANGE OF GRANTS** £1,500–£20,000
**SAMPLE GRANTS** Hertfordshire Community Foundation (£20,000); Helping Rwanda (£15,000); Computer Aid International – Nicaragua Project, GMB – Colombian Storm Victims, Groundwork Manchester, Salford, Stockport, Tameside and Trafford, Tracks Autism and War on Want – Garment Workers Initiative (£5,000 each); United Kingdom Acquired Brain Injury Forum (£2,000); and GMB – Belize Project (£1,500).
**FINANCES** Year 2014 Income £66,049 Grants £63,514 Grants to organisations £63,514 Assets £0
**TRUSTEE** UIA. Trustees Ltd.
**OTHER INFORMATION** The foundation is a grant-making body established to provide financial support to formally constituted voluntary organisations and small registered charities that help people in need. It is funded entirely by donations from UIA (Insurance) Limited, a mutual insurance company, that is provider of insurances to members of UNISON, UNITE and other trade unions.
**HOW TO APPLY** The foundation is not accepting new applications for funding. Check the foundation's website for current information.
**WHO TO APPLY TO** Jackie White, Correspondent, UIA (Insurance) Ltd, Kings Court, London Road, Stevenage, Hertfordshire SG1 2TP *Tel.* 01438 761761  *Fax* 01438 761762  *email* charitable.foundation@uia.co.uk  *Website* www.uia.co.uk/About-Us/Charitable-foundation

## ■ UKI Charitable Foundation

**CC NO** 1071978  **ESTABLISHED** 1998
**WHERE FUNDING CAN BE GIVEN** UK.
**WHO CAN BENEFIT** Registered charities and individuals.
**WHAT IS FUNDED** General charitable purposes; education training; medical causes, health and sickness; disability; the relief of poverty; religious activities.
**SAMPLE GRANTS** No details were available.
**FINANCES** Year 2013/14 Income £418,328 Grants £28,200 Grants to organisations £28,200 Assets £2,981,603
**TRUSTEES** Jacob Schimmel; Vered Schimmel; Anna Schimmel.
**HOW TO APPLY** Apply in writing to the correspondent.
**WHO TO APPLY TO** Jacob Schimmel, Trustee, Suite 137, Devonshire House, 582 Honeypot Lane, Stanmore, Middlesex HA7 1JS *Tel.* 020 8732 5560  *email* four4charities@gmail.com

## ■ Ulster Garden Villages Ltd

**ESTABLISHED** 1946
**WHERE FUNDING CAN BE GIVEN** Northern Ireland.
**WHO CAN BENEFIT** Organisations.
**WHAT IS FUNDED** The charity primarily supports projects based in Northern Ireland that will have a positive impact there. The main purposes for which funds are distributed are: health; disadvantaged sections of society; young people; culture and heritage; environment. The charity prefers to fund projects that demonstrate active participation and self-help.
**WHAT IS NOT FUNDED** Individuals; organisations whose application is not charitable and with public benefit; activities which are primarily the responsibility of central and local government; the direct replacement of statutory funding; sponsorship or marketing appeals; promotion of religion; expeditions or overseas travel; charities who collect funds for distribution to other charities; retrospective funding. Grants are not usually given for office expenses or administrative staff salaries.
**TYPE OF GRANT** Grants and loans.
**RANGE OF GRANTS** Our research indicates that grants are usually in the region of £1,000 to £5,000, though larger grants may be considered.
**SAMPLE GRANTS** Royal Victoria Hospital – Institute of Vision Science; Royal Victoria Hospital – Percutaneous Aortic Valve Replacement; Belfast City Hospital – the Garden Village Suite; the Northern Ireland Children's Hospice; QUB Foundation Great Hall; Belmont Tower; the Lyric Theatre, Camphill Communities in Northern Ireland; Croft Community; Disability Sport NI; Clifton Nursing Home; Habitat for Humanity Northern Ireland; the Scout Association; Ulster Waterways Group; Rams Island.
**FINANCES** Grants £1,000,000 Grants to organisations £1,000,000
**TRUSTEES** Tony Hopkins; Kevin Baird; Martie Boyd; Drew Crawford; Susan Crowe; Brian Garrett;

Erskine Holmes; Sir Desmond Lorimer; William Webb.
**OTHER INFORMATION** No current financial information was available. Our research indicates that grants have previously totalled around £1 million.
**HOW TO APPLY** Applications must be made using the society's application form. Forms are available to download from the website – where guidelines can also be found – and should be posted or delivered to the office. Applications for amounts exceeding £50,000 require more detail with regards to project rationale, economic appraisal and building proposals, if applicable, should be included. Your organisation's most recent annual report and audited accounts should also be provided, along with evidence of charitable status. The office is normally attended on Tuesday, Wednesday and Thursday between 9am and 1pm.
**WHO TO APPLY TO** The Administration Officer, Forestview, Purdy's Lane, Newtownbreda, Belfast BT8 7AR *Tel.* 028 9049 1111 *Fax* 028 9049 1007 *email* admin@ulstergardenvillages.co.uk *Website* www.ulstergardenvillages.co.uk

## ■ Ulting Overseas Trust

**CC NO** 294397    **ESTABLISHED** 1986
**WHERE FUNDING CAN BE GIVEN** Financially developing countries (mostly, but not exclusively, Asia, Africa and South and Central America).
**WHO CAN BENEFIT** Christian workers in financially developing countries undergoing further training for Christian service.
**WHAT IS FUNDED** Bursaries, normally via grants to Christian theological training institutions or organisations with a training focus, for those in financially developing countries who wish to train for the Christian ministry, or for those who wish to improve their ministry skills. The trust gives priority to the training of students in their home countries or continents.
**WHAT IS NOT FUNDED** Capital projects, such as buildings or library stock; training in subjects other than Biblical, theological and missionary studies.
**TYPE OF GRANT** One-off; bursary support.
**RANGE OF GRANTS** Up to £15,000.
**SAMPLE GRANTS** International Fellowship of Evangelical Students (£15,000); Langham Trust (£13,000); Oxford Centre for Mission Studies (£5,000); Latin Link (£4,000); London School of Theology (£3,000); Alliance Development Fund, Theological College Central Africa (£2,200 each); Bangkok Bible Seminary (£1,850); Operation Mobilisation (£1,200); Surgeons College (£1,000).
**FINANCES** *Year* 2013/14 *Income* £123,861 *Grants* £109,922 *Grants to organisations* £103,122 *Assets* £4,127,025
**TRUSTEES** Tim Warren; Mary Brinkley; Alan Bale; John Heyward; Dr Jean Kessler; Revd Joseph Kapolyo; Nicholas Durlacher; Roger Pearce; Carol Walker; John Whitfield.
**OTHER INFORMATION** There were 32 organisational grants made in the year totalling £103,122 and two further individual grants made totalling £6,800.
**HOW TO APPLY** Apply in writing to the correspondent. Trustees examine each application against strict criteria. Grants are reviewed and awarded on an annual basis.
**WHO TO APPLY TO** Timothy Buckland, Correspondent, Pothecary, Witham Weld, 70 St George's Square, London SW1V 3RD *Tel.* 020 7821 8211

## ■ The Ulverscroft Foundation

**CC NO** 264873    **ESTABLISHED** 1972
**WHERE FUNDING CAN BE GIVEN** Worldwide.
**WHO CAN BENEFIT** Recognised organisations helping people who are visually impaired, for example, libraries, hospitals, clinics, schools, colleges and social and welfare organisations.
**WHAT IS FUNDED** Projects which will have a positive effect on the quality of life of people who have visual impairments (people who are blind or partially sighted) or people who have a print disability.
**WHAT IS NOT FUNDED** Grants are rarely given to individuals. Generally, assistance towards salaries and general running costs are not given, though funding for salaries can be considered if it is for a particular project. The foundation is unable to consider reapplications within a period of 18 months to two years.
**TYPE OF GRANT** Annual for up to and more than three years. Buildings; capital; project and research; one-off and recurring grants.
**RANGE OF GRANTS** Up to £25,000.
**SAMPLE GRANTS** University of Liverpool (£25,000); Eye Disease in Hot Climates 4th edition (£20,000); Sightsavers (£5,000); John Fawcett Foundation UK (£3,600); Intercare (£2,500); Listening Books (£1,500); Braille Chess Association (£1,000).
**FINANCES** *Year* 2012/13 *Income* £11,696,292 *Grants* £167,036 *Grants to organisations* £167,036 *Assets* £20,511,109
**TRUSTEES** John Bush; Peter Carr; Pat Beech; David Owen; Roger Crooks; John Sanford-Smith; Robert Gent.
**OTHER INFORMATION** The foundation controls a trading subsidiary which republishes books in a form accessible by people with partial sight. At the time of writing (June 2015) the 2012/13 accounts were the latest available. A total of 30 grants were approved during the year. Grants of less than £1,000 were given totalling £500.
**HOW TO APPLY** Applications should be made in writing to the correspondent and be as detailed as possible. Details should include those of any current services your organisation provides for visually impaired people, if any, and how your proposed project will be integrated or enhanced. If possible, an estimate of the number of people who use/will use your service should be provided, as well as information of any funding that has already been obtained and the names of other organisations to which you have applied. Organisations are also asked to submit a copy of their latest annual report and accounts. The trustees meet quarterly to consider applications, in January, April, July and October and deadlines for submissions fall on the 15th day of the previous month.
**WHO TO APPLY TO** Joyce Sumner, Secretary, 1 The Green, Bradgate Road, Anstey, Leicester LE7 7FU *Tel.* 0116 236 1595 *Fax* 0116 236 1594 *email* foundation@ulverscroft.co.uk *Website* www.foundation.ulverscroft.com

## ■ The Underwood Trust

**CC NO** 266164    **ESTABLISHED** 1973
**WHERE FUNDING CAN BE GIVEN** UK, particularly Scotland and Wiltshire.
**WHO CAN BENEFIT** UK-registered charities and other official charitable organisations which benefit society nationally or locally, in Scotland and Wiltshire.
**WHAT IS FUNDED** Medicine and health; social welfare; education; the arts; environment and wildlife.

**WHAT IS NOT FUNDED** Individuals directly; political activities; commercial ventures or publications; the purchase of vehicles including minibuses; overseas travel, holidays or expeditions; retrospective grants or loans; direct replacement of statutory funding or activities that are primarily the responsibility of central or local government; large capital, endowment or widely distributed appeals.

**SAMPLE GRANTS** The Merchants House of Glasgow and Restorative Solutions (£1 million each); Chamber Orchestra of Europe (£165,000); Greenpeace Environmental Trust (£100,000); Prospect Hospice (£91,500); Prisoners Abroad (£50,000); Stage One (£30,000); Wiltshire and Berkshire Canal Trust (£20,000); The British Stammering Association and Royal Agricultural Benevolent Institution (£16,500 each).

**FINANCES** Year 2013/14 Income £650,267 Grants £3,101,500 Grants to organisations £3,101,500 Assets £19,708,264

**TRUSTEES** Robin Clark, Chair; Jack Taylor; Briony Wilson; Reg Harvey; Richard Bennison.

**OTHER INFORMATION** The grant total above refers to grants committed during the year.

**HOW TO APPLY** The trust is unable to accept unsolicited applications. All available funds are allocated proactively by the trustees and organisations must not make an application unless invited to do so. Note that the trust is unable to deal with telephone or email enquiries regarding applications.

**WHO TO APPLY TO** Michele Judge, Manager, c/o Tcp Atlantic Square Limited, Fourth Floor South, 35 Portman Square, London W1H 6LR *Tel.* 020 7486 0100 *email* johnd@taylorclark.co.uk *Website* www.theunderwoodtrust.org.uk

## ■ The Union of Orthodox Hebrew Congregation

**CC NO** 249892　　　　**ESTABLISHED** 1966
**WHERE FUNDING CAN BE GIVEN** UK.
**WHO CAN BENEFIT** Charitable organisations.
**WHAT IS FUNDED** Jewish causes.
**SAMPLE GRANTS Previous beneficiaries have included:** Addas Yisoroel Mikva Foundation, Achieve Trust, Atereth Shau, Beis Malka, Beis Shmuel, Belz Nursery, Bnos Yerushaim, Chesed Charity Trust, London Board of Schechita, Mutual Trust, Maoz Ladol, North West London Mikvah, Needy Families and Poor Families Pesach, Society of Friends of the Torah, Talmud Centre Trust and VMCT.

**FINANCES** Year 2013 Income £1,365,169 Grants £734,306 Grants to organisations £734,306 Assets £1,698,533

**TRUSTEES** Rabbi Abraham Pinter; Benzion Freshwater; Chaim Konig.

**OTHER INFORMATION** Grants to organisations totalled £601,500, as well as £38,000 donated to individuals.

**HOW TO APPLY** Apply in writing to the correspondent.

**WHO TO APPLY TO** D. Passey, Correspondent, Landau Morley, Lanmor House, 370–386 High Road, Wembley HA9 6AX *Tel.* 020 8903 5122

## ■ The UNITE Foundation

**CC NO** 1147344　　　　**ESTABLISHED** 2012
**WHERE FUNDING CAN BE GIVEN** UK.
**WHO CAN BENEFIT** Universities; registered charities; individual students.
**WHAT IS FUNDED** Education, training and student scholarships.

**TYPE OF GRANT** Mainly scholarships, but also project grants and support costs.

**FINANCES** Year 2013 Income £500,000 Grants £495,660 Grants to organisations £90,500 Assets £13,283

**TRUSTEES** Sally Quigg; Prof. Stuart Cooper Billingham; Jenny Shaw; Richard Smith; Nicholas Miller; Joe Lister.

**OTHER INFORMATION** This is the charitable foundation of the UNITE Group plc, a manager and developer of student accommodation in the UK. The foundation's three objectives are: to enable access to higher education for young people facing serious disadvantage and/or challenging circumstances; to help young people develop employability skills; to integrate students into local communities. The foundation is also keen to work with universities and other organisations that share its aims and objectives. The grant total includes: £243,000 on student rental payments; £162,000 on student bursaries; and £90,500 on donations to other organisations.

**HOW TO APPLY** Contact the foundation via its website to discuss how you might work with the foundation.

**WHO TO APPLY TO** Jenny Shaw, Trustee, The Core, 40 St Thomas Street, Bristol BS1 6JX *Tel.* 0117 302 7073 *email* info@unitefoundation.co.uk *Website* www.unitefoundation.co.uk

## ■ The United Society for the Propagation of the Gospel

**CC NO** 234518　　　　**ESTABLISHED** 1701
**WHERE FUNDING CAN BE GIVEN** Mainly churches in Africa, West Indies, South Pacific, South America, Pakistan, India, Indian Ocean, Myanmar (Burma), Bangladesh, East Asia.
**WHO CAN BENEFIT** Overseas Anglican provinces and dioceses and churches in communion with the Anglican Church which benefit Christians and other disadvantaged groups.
**WHAT IS FUNDED** The promotion of the Christian religion and related charitable works.
**WHAT IS NOT FUNDED** Direct applications from individuals are not considered.
**TYPE OF GRANT** One-off grants; bursaries; loans.
**SAMPLE GRANTS** Church for the Province of Central Africa (£338,000); Anglican Church of South Africa (£149,000); Anglican Church of Tanzania (£102,000); Church of the Province of West Africa (£83,000); Church of the Province of Indian Ocean (£40,000).

**FINANCES** Year 2013 Income £3,752,000 Grants £1,756,000 Grants to organisations £1,756,000 Assets £43,525,000

**TRUSTEES** Rt Revd Cannon Christopher Chivers; Revd Cannon Richard Bartlett; Revd Dr John Perumbalath; Nigel Wildish; Revd Cannon Christopher Burke; Rt Revd Michael Burrows; Revd Dr Ian Rock; Dr Jane Watkeys; Rt Revd Dr Jacob Ayeebo; Rt Revd Edward Malecdan; Rosemary Kempsell; Dr Joabe Gomes Cavalcanti; Simon Gill; Jacqueline Humphreys; John Chilver.

**OTHER INFORMATION** The charity is now known as United Society.

**HOW TO APPLY** Applications must be submitted by Anglican Archbishops or Bishops to the Finance in Mission Officer.

**WHO TO APPLY TO** The Trustees, Harling House, 47/51 Great Suffolk Street, London SE1 0BS *Tel.* 020 7921 2200 *email* benk@weareus.org.uk *Website* www.weareus.org.uk

**United**

## ■ United Utilities Trust Fund

**CC NO** 1108296    **ESTABLISHED** 2005

**WHERE FUNDING CAN BE GIVEN** The area supplied by United Utilities Water plc (predominantly the north west of England).

**WHO CAN BENEFIT** Mainly individuals, but also organisations.

**WHAT IS FUNDED** Social welfare; money advice; debt counselling; financial literacy.

**WHAT IS NOT FUNDED** Existing projects; charities which appear to us to have sufficient unrestricted or free reserves, or are in serious deficit; projects outside the geographical area; national charities that do not have the facility to accept the funding on a regional basis; grant-making bodies seeking to distribute grants on UUTFs behalf; general appeals, sponsorship and marketing appeals; replacement of existing programmes or statutory funding.

**TYPE OF GRANT** Small one-off donations and larger grants for up to two years.

**RANGE OF GRANTS** Usually up to £30,000.

**SAMPLE GRANTS** Sefton Citizens Advice (£30,000); Salford Mental Health Services (£29,000); Blackburn with Darwen Citizens Advice (£26,500); Fylde Coast Women's Aid (£23,000); and Advocacy in Wirral (£22,000).

**FINANCES** Year 2013/14 Income £7,001,894 Grants £6,240,221 Grants to organisations £329,733 Assets £404,272

**TRUSTEES** Deborah Moreton; Alastair Richards; Simon Dewsnip; Allen Mackie; Carl Smith.

**OTHER INFORMATION** During the year a total of £5.9 million was given to individuals and £330,000 to organisations.

**HOW TO APPLY** At the time of writing (June 2015) the trust was closed to applications from organisations – check the trust's website for current information.

**WHO TO APPLY TO** The Secretary (Auriga Services Limited), Emmanuel Court, 12–14 Mill Street, Sutton Coldfield, B72 1TJ, Tel. 0845 179 1791 email contact@uutf.org.uk Website www.uutf.org.uk

## ■ The Michael Uren Foundation

**CC NO** 1094102    **ESTABLISHED** 2002

**WHERE FUNDING CAN BE GIVEN** UK and overseas.

**WHO CAN BENEFIT** Registered charities.

**WHAT IS FUNDED** General charitable purposes, particularly armed forces, medical research and medical facilities, animal welfare, education and historic buildings. The foundation's restricted fund is designated for grants towards the relief of blind people and for education.

**TYPE OF GRANT** Mainly large project grants.

**RANGE OF GRANTS** £500–£500,000

**SAMPLE GRANTS** King Edward VII Hospital (£5 million); Friends of St Mary's Kenardington (£688,000); The Gurkha Welfare Trust (£570,000); The Royal British Legion (£333,500); The Royal Navy Benevolent Trust (£250,000); International Animal Rescue, Chatham Historic Dockyard Trust, The UK Trust for Nature Conservation in Nepal, (£100,000 each); Imperial College Trust, WAVE Heritage Fund (£60,000 each); HMS Alliance Appeal (£25,000); The Magdalen and Lasher Trust (£22,000); Victoria Cross and George Cross Benevolent Fund, Seafarers UK, Penzance Sea Cadets (£20,000 each); Urology Foundation (£5,000).

**FINANCES** Year 2013/14 Income £4,512,749 Grants £7,373,565 Grants to organisations £7,373,565 Assets £73,519,008

**TRUSTEES** Michael Uren; Anne Gregory-Jones; Janis Bennett; Alastair McDonald.

**OTHER INFORMATION** Grants were made to 16 organisations in 2013/14. Out of these grants seven were made from the restricted fund.

**HOW TO APPLY** Apply in writing to the correspondent.

**WHO TO APPLY TO** Anne Gregory-Jones, Trustee, Haysmacintyre, 26 Red Lion Square, London WC1R 4AG email mpattenden@haysmacintyre.com

## ■ Uxbridge United Welfare Trust

**CC NO** 217066    **ESTABLISHED** 1991

**WHERE FUNDING CAN BE GIVEN** Former urban district of Uxbridge, includes Uxbridge, Hillingdon, Ickenham, Harefield and Cowley.

**WHO CAN BENEFIT** Individuals and local organisations benefitting children, young adults and people disadvantaged by poverty.

**WHAT IS FUNDED** Educational grants for purposes, such as course costs, books, equipment, school uniform, school trips and transport costs. Hardship relief grants for the provision of essential services and goods for those with limited income or in need of financial assistance, as well as the provision of almshouses.

**WHAT IS NOT FUNDED** Projects outside the beneficial area.

**SAMPLE GRANTS** A list of beneficiaries was not available.

**FINANCES** Year 2013 Income £462,831 Grants £150,705 Grants to organisations £150,705 Assets £6,419,958

**TRUSTEES** John Childs; David Routledge; Peter Ryerson; Gerda Driver; Raymond Graham; Duncan Struthers; Susan James; Alan Morris; Dominic Gilham; Beulah East; Nita Kakad.

**OTHER INFORMATION** Grant total includes individuals and organisations. A total of 173 grants were made for welfare and 16 grants for educational purposes.

**HOW TO APPLY** Applications should be made on a form available from the correspondent. Applications are considered at the trustee's monthly meetings. The trust's grant officer may arrange to interview applicants to discuss eligibility. Further information and advice is available on the trust's website.

**WHO TO APPLY TO** Josie Duffy, Grants Officer, Woodbridge House, New Windsor Street, Uxbridge UB8 2TY Tel. 01895 232976 email info@uuwt.org Website www.uuwt.org

## ■ The Vail Foundation

**CC NO** 1089579 **ESTABLISHED** 2001
**WHERE FUNDING CAN BE GIVEN** UK and overseas.
**WHO CAN BENEFIT** Registered charities.
**WHAT IS FUNDED** Jewish causes.
**RANGE OF GRANTS** Up to £500,000.
**SAMPLE GRANTS** KKL Charity (£590,000 in total); United Jewish Israel (£135,000 in total); London School of Jewish Studies (£75,000); Community Security Trust (£50,000); Jewish Volunteering Network and Finchley Jewish Primary School Trust (£30,000 each); Anne Frank Trust UK (£10,000); Kesher – The Learning Connection (£5,000); Israeli Dance Institute (£2,500); Chicken Shed Theatre Trust (£2,000); and Ivan and Rachel Binstock Charity Account (£1,000).
**FINANCES** Year 2012/13 Income £402,996 Grants £1,289,500 Grants to organisations £1,289,500 Assets £7,060,078
**TRUSTEES** Michael Bradfield; Paul Brett; Michael Goldstein.
**OTHER INFORMATION** Grants were awarded to 22 organisations in 2012/13. At the time of writing (June 2015) this was the latest information available.
**HOW TO APPLY** Apply in writing to the correspondent.
**WHO TO APPLY TO** Michael Bradfield, Trustee, 5 Fitzhardinge Street, London W1H 6ED Tel. 020 7317 3000 email mai.brown@blickrothenberg.com

## ■ The Valentine Charitable Trust

**CC NO** 1001782 **ESTABLISHED** 1990
**WHERE FUNDING CAN BE GIVEN** Unrestricted, but mainly Dorset. Financially developing countries.
**WHO CAN BENEFIT** Registered charities in the UK with preference to Dorset and sometimes overseas.
**WHAT IS FUNDED** General charitable purposes, including local charities, charities which historically received small grants from the trust, overseas charities and medical research and hospitals.
**WHAT IS NOT FUNDED** Individuals. The trust would not normally fund appeals for village halls or the fabric of church buildings.
**TYPE OF GRANT** One-off appeals; recurrent grants; core costs; capital costs; matched funding; loan finance.
**RANGE OF GRANTS** Up to £20,000.
**SAMPLE GRANTS** Kajuki Water Project (£25,000); Deafblind UK (£20,000); Bournemouth Symphony Orchestra (£15,000); Youth Action Group (£14,000); Swanage Sea Rowing Club and UNICEF UK (£10,000 each); Fine Cell Work, Honeypot Charity and Wessex Autistic Society (£5,000 each); Bournemouth Citizens Advice and Chernobyl Children in Need (£3,000 each); Huntington's Disease Association and National Coastwatch Institution (£2,500 each); Poole Christian Fellowship (£2,000); Dorset Mind (£1,000); Purbeck Strings (£300).
**FINANCES** Year 2012/13 Income £872,105 Grants £827,125 Grants to organisations £827,125 Assets £29,952,422
**TRUSTEES** Douglas Neville-Jones; Patricia Walker; Peter Leatherdale; Susan Patterson; Roger Gregory; Diana Tory; Sheila Cox; Wing Cdr Donald Jack; Susan Ridley.
**OTHER INFORMATION** Grants were made to 141 organisations in 2012/13. At the time of writing (June 2015) this was the latest information available.
**HOW TO APPLY** Apply in writing to the correspondent. Generally the trustees prefer to only consider applications from applicants with whom they have an established relationship, but they are occasionally able to make grants outside this, particularly for local applicants. All applications will be acknowledged and decisions are made at quarterly trustees' meetings. The trust provides the following guidance about the application process in its annual report: 'The trustees look for value for money. While this concept is difficult to apply in a voluntary sector it can certainly be used on a comparative basis and subjectively. If the trustees have competing applications they will usually decide to support just one of them as they believe that to concentrate the charity's donations is more beneficial than to dilute them. Regular contact with the charities to which donations are made is considered essential. Reports and accounts are also requested from charities which are supported and the trustees consider those at their meetings. The trustees take great comfort from the fact that they employ the policy of only making donations to other charities or similar bodies. However they are not complacent about the need to review all donations made and the objects to which those have been given. The trustees are conscious that, particularly with the smaller and local charities, the community of those working for and with the charity is an important consideration. The trustees regularly review the classifications to which donations have been made so that they can obtain an overview of the charity's donations and assess whether their policies are being implemented in practice. They are conscious that when dealing with individual donations it is easy to lose sight of the overall picture.'
**WHO TO APPLY TO** Douglas Neville-Jones, Trustee, Preston Redman, Hinton House, Hinton Road, Bournemouth BH1 2EN Tel. 01202 292424

## ■ The Valiant Charitable Trust

**CC NO** 1135810 **ESTABLISHED** 2010
**WHERE FUNDING CAN BE GIVEN** UK.
**WHO CAN BENEFIT** Registered charities.
**WHAT IS FUNDED** General charitable purposes, with a preference for organisations working with older people and people with disabilities.
**TYPE OF GRANT** One-off grants, grants paid over a number of years for a larger project.
**RANGE OF GRANTS** £10,000–£500,000
**SAMPLE GRANTS** Keech Hospice Care (£410,000); Motor Neurone Disease Association (£50,000); St Elizabeth's (£40,000).
**FINANCES** Year 2013/14 Income £26,891 Grants £26,891 Grants to organisations £26,891 Assets £1,228,964
**TRUSTEES** Roger Woolfe; Lady Valarie Dixon; Paul Brenham.
**HOW TO APPLY** Apply in writing to the correspondent.
**WHO TO APPLY TO** Roger Woolfe, Trustee, Collyer Bristow Solicitors, 4 Bedford Row, London WC1R 4DF Tel. 020 7242 7363 email roy.jordan@collyerbristow.com

# Van

## ■ The Albert Van Den Bergh Charitable Trust

**CC NO** 296885  **ESTABLISHED** 1987
**WHERE FUNDING CAN BE GIVEN** UK and overseas.
**WHO CAN BENEFIT** Charitable organisations.
**WHAT IS FUNDED** General charitable purposes, particularly medical research and care of older people and children. Grants are distributed in the following categories: cultural charities; conservation; disadvantaged; disability; help in the community; homelessness; hospices; medical research, care and support; outward bound; overseas; servicemen and women; older people; churches; other charities.
**SAMPLE GRANTS Previous beneficiaries have included:** BLISS, Bishop of Guildford's Charity, British Heart Foundation, Counsel and Care for the Elderly, Leukaemia Research Trust, Multiple Sclerosis Society, Parentline Surrey, National Osteoporosis Society, RNID, Riding for the Disabled – Cranleigh Age Concern, SSAFA, St John Ambulance and United Charities Fund – Liberal Jewish Synagogue.
**FINANCES** Year 2013/14 Income £116,594 Grants £284,750 Grants to organisations £284,750 Assets £3,314,451
**TRUSTEES** Jane Hartley; Nicola Glover; Bruce Hopkins.
**OTHER INFORMATION** Grants were made to 80 organisations in 2013/14.
**HOW TO APPLY** Apply in writing to the correspondent, including accounts and budgets.
**WHO TO APPLY TO** Jane Hartley, Trustee, Trevornick Farmhouse, Holywell Bay, Newquay, Cornwall TR8 5PW email jane@trevornick.co.uk

## ■ The Van Neste Foundation

**CC NO** 201951  **ESTABLISHED** 1959
**WHERE FUNDING CAN BE GIVEN** UK (especially the Bristol area) and overseas.
**WHO CAN BENEFIT** Registered charities.
**WHAT IS FUNDED** Currently the main areas of interest are: financially developing countries; older individuals or people with disabilities; advancement of religion; community and 'Christian family life' 'respect for the sanctity and dignity of life'.
**WHAT IS NOT FUNDED** Individuals; large, well-known charities. Applications are only considered from registered charities.
**TYPE OF GRANT** Usually one-off for a specific project or part of a project. Core funding is rarely considered.
**RANGE OF GRANTS** £1,000–£30,000
**SAMPLE GRANTS** CAFOD (£30,000); St Bede's Catholic College, St Gregory's Catholic College Bath (£25,000 each); Rainbow Development in Africa, St Vincent's Southmead (£20,000 each); New Economics Foundation, St Peter's Hospice, Temwa (£10,000 each); Girlguiding Bristol and South Gloucester, MS Therapy Centre (£5,000); Bristol and District Tranquiliser Project (£3,000); Holy Ghost Church – Midsomer Norton, Life Education Bristol, The Daisy Garland (£2,000 each); Artists First (£1,000).
**FINANCES** Year 2013/14 Income £295,724 Grants £312,300 Grants to organisations £312,300 Assets £8,774,621
**TRUSTEES** Martin Appleby; Fergus Lyons; Gerald Walker; Jeremy Lyons; Benedict Appleby; Michael Lyons; Tom Appleby; Joanna Dickens.
**OTHER INFORMATION** Grants were given to 36 organisations.
**HOW TO APPLY** Applications should be in the form of a concise letter setting out the clear objectives to be obtained, which must be charitable. Information must be supplied concerning agreed funding from other sources together with a timetable for achieving the objectives of the appeal and a copy of the latest accounts. The foundation does not normally make grants on a continuing basis. To keep overheads to a minimum, only successful applications are acknowledged. Appeals are considered by the trustees at their meetings in January, June and October.
**WHO TO APPLY TO** Fergus Lyons, Secretary, 15 Alexandra Road, Clifton, Bristol BS8 2DD Tel. 0117 973 5167 email fergus.lyons@virgin.net

## ■ Mrs Maud Van Norden's Charitable Foundation

**CC NO** 210844  **ESTABLISHED** 1962
**WHERE FUNDING CAN BE GIVEN** UK.
**WHO CAN BENEFIT** Registered UK charities only.
**WHAT IS FUNDED** General charitable purposes, particularly aid to younger or older people. Also preservation of the environment and heritage, disability causes and animal welfare.
**WHAT IS NOT FUNDED** Individuals; expeditions; scholarships. The trustees make donations to registered UK charities only.
**TYPE OF GRANT** One-off and research grants.
**RANGE OF GRANTS** Most grants are for £1,500 each.
**SAMPLE GRANTS Previous beneficiaries have included:** Salvation Army (£4,000); Women's Royal Voluntary Service (£3,000); Royal Hospital for Neuro-disability and Crisis UK (£2,500); and Action on Elder Abuse, Humane Slaughter Association, Gurkha Welfare Trust, Calibre Audio Library, The Cure Parkinson's Trust, Police Community Clubs of Great Britain and Princess Alice Hospice (£1,500 each).
**FINANCES** Year 2012/13 Income £41,912 Grants £56,333 Grants to organisations £40,000
**TRUSTEES** Ena Dukler; John Gordon; Elizabeth Humphryes; Neil Wingerath.
**OTHER INFORMATION** The accounts were not published due to the low income of the foundation. The grant total has been estimated based grant total in previous years and the foundation's total expenditure in 2012/13 of £56,000.
**HOW TO APPLY** All appeals should be by letter containing the following: aims and objectives of the charity; nature of the appeal; total target, if for a specific project; contributions received against target; registered charity number; any other factors. Letters should be accompanied by a copy of the applicant's latest reports and accounts.
**WHO TO APPLY TO** The Trustees, BM Box 2367, London WC1N 3XX

## ■ The Vandervell Foundation

**CC NO** 255651  **ESTABLISHED** 1968
**WHERE FUNDING CAN BE GIVEN** UK.
**WHO CAN BENEFIT** Individuals and organisations.
**WHAT IS FUNDED** General charitable purposes. Grants in 2013/14 were distributed for the following purposes: social welfare (44 grants); medical research (27 grants); education (8 grants); performing arts (14 grants); environmental regeneration (5 grants).
**RANGE OF GRANTS** £1,000–£30,000

Alphabetical register of grant-making charities — **Variety**

SAMPLE GRANTS The Big Issue Foundation (£30,000); Prisoners Education Trust (£20,000); Arts Education School Tring Park, British Exploring Society, King's College London School of Medicine (£15,000 each); Cancer Research UK, Weekend Arts College (£10,000); FareShare (£6,000); Tricycle Theatre, London Air Ambulance, St Joseph's Hospice (£5,000 each).
FINANCES Year 2013 Income £286,022 Grants £370,350 Grants to organisations £370,350 Assets £7,382,682
TRUSTEE The Vandervell Foundation Limited Trustee Company.
OTHER INFORMATION There was also one grant to an individual of £350.
HOW TO APPLY Apply in writing to the correspondent. The trustees meet every two months to consider major grant applications; smaller grants are considered more frequently.
WHO TO APPLY TO Valerie Kaye, Correspondent, Hampstead Town Hall Centre, 213 Haverstock Hill, London NW3 4QP Tel. 020 7435 7546

## ■ The Vardy Foundation

CC NO 328415   ESTABLISHED 1987
WHERE FUNDING CAN BE GIVEN UK with a preference for north east England, overseas.
WHO CAN BENEFIT Registered charities and individuals.
WHAT IS FUNDED General charitable purposes, particularly social welfare, young people and Christian causes. Grants are distributed in the following categories: education; religion; welfare; relief in need; the arts.
WHAT IS NOT FUNDED Applications for more than a three year commitment; animal welfare projects; health related charities; projects normally provided by central or local government; individuals (including requests for educational support costs) ( the foundation does award grants to individuals; however, these are likely to already be connected to the foundation or one of the educational institutions that receive funding from the foundation); projects that do not demonstrate an element of self-funding or other funding; contribution to an organisation's healthy reserves or endowments.
TYPE OF GRANT One-off and recurrent, for up to two years.
RANGE OF GRANTS £300–£1.5 million.
SAMPLE GRANTS Safe Families for Children (£625,000); North Music Trust (£250,000); Thana Trust – India (£100,000); EAPE (£94,500); A Way Out (£75,500); Sowing Seeds Ministries (£59,000); Christians Against Poverty (£50,000); Youth For Christ (£50,000); Premier Radio (£40,000); Salvation Army UK (£35,000).
FINANCES Year 2013/14 Income £17,856,159 Grants £2,257,021 Grants to organisations £2,205,072 Assets £38,351,543
TRUSTEES Lady Margaret Vardy; Peter Vardy; Richard Vardy; Sir Peter Vardy; Victoria Vardy.
OTHER INFORMATION Grants were given to 196 organisations. A total of 23 individuals were also given grants totalling £52,000.
HOW TO APPLY Apply in writing to the correspondent. The trustees meet every two months to review grants. Each application is considered against the criteria outlined above.
WHO TO APPLY TO Sir Peter Vardy, Trustee, Venture House, Aykley Heads, Durham DH1 5TS Tel. 0191 374 4744

## ■ The Variety Club Children's Charity

CC NO 209259   ESTABLISHED 1949
WHERE FUNDING CAN BE GIVEN UK.
WHO CAN BENEFIT Hospitals; schools; individuals; charities; other organisations.
WHAT IS FUNDED The welfare of children and young people who are disadvantaged, or have disabilities or are in ill health.
WHAT IS NOT FUNDED Repayment of loans; garden adaptions; cost of a family/wheelchair adapted vehicle; administrative/salary costs; maintenance or ongoing costs; reimbursement of funds already paid out; hire, rental costs or down payments; computers; trips abroad or holiday costs; medical treatment or research; and education/tuition fees.
TYPE OF GRANT One-off and recurring costs. Money and equipment, including coaches, to organisations. Individual children have received money, electric wheelchairs, toys and holidays.
RANGE OF GRANTS Up to £125,000.
SAMPLE GRANTS North Ridge Specialist Support – Manchester (£37,500); Kingsland School – Wakefield, Victoria Education Centre – Poole (£37,000 each); Sandfield Park School – Liverpool (£34,500); Young Epilepsy – Lingfield (£32,000); Drumbeat School and ASD Service (£26,500); Kings College Hospital – London (£25,000); Martin House Children Hospice – Kent (£20,000); Stubbers Adventure Centre – Essex (£7,500); Frederick Holmes School – Hull (£5,000).
FINANCES Year 2013 Income £6,526,337 Grants £2,074,994 Grants to organisations £1,593,924 Assets £3,033,492
TRUSTEES Jarvis Astaire; Raymond Curtis; Stanley Salter; Anthony Harris; Anthony Hatch; Lionel Rosenblatt; Pamela Sinclair; Ronald Nathan; Russell Kahn; Trevor Green; Jonathan Shalit; Laurence Davis; Norman Kaphan; Keith Andrews; Malcolm Brenner; Lloyd Barr; Jason Lewis; Nicholas Shattock; William Sangster; Rodney Natkiel; Jane Kerner; Anthony Blackburn; Neil Sinclair
OTHER INFORMATION A total of just over £83,500 was given in grants of less than £5,000 to organisations. A further £481,000 was made in grants to individuals.
HOW TO APPLY Full information, application guidance and application forms for each of the charity's programmes are available on its website. General application guidelines for the charity's website, at the time of writing (May 2015), include the following: applications can be made by parents, medical professionals, a school or organisation, hospitals and registered charities; applications can be made on behalf of individual children, and must be supported by a letter from an appropriately qualified medical professional, e.g. occupational therapist, physiotherapist or paediatrician; applications can also be made from non-profit making groups and organisations working with children up to, and including, the physical age of 18 years, such as statutory bodies (schools and hospitals), hospices and small registered charities; for wheelchairs, applications can be made from parents, Physiotherapists, Occupational Therapists or the child themselves, providing that there is written agreement in support of the item required from the appropriately qualified professional (i.e., the child's Occupational Therapist or Physiotherapist) who was present at the time of assessment; youth club applications will not be funded for organisations that are not affiliated to a National Youth Organisation quotations for

equipment should accompany an application; organisations are advised to think carefully before submitting a request and Variety will need to be convinced of the high quality and efficiency of your organisation before consideration is given to making a donation. The grants committee meets six times per year; therefore, there is no deadline for applications to be made. In most cases a member of the grants committee will contact you to discuss your application more fully. Notification of the outcome of applications will be by letter, and the decision of the trustees is final.

**WHO TO APPLY TO** Stanley Salter, Trustee, Variety Club House, 93 Bayham Street, London NW1 0AG *email* info@varietyclub.org.uk *Website* www.varietyclub.org.uk

### ■ Veneziana Fund

**CC NO** 1061760     **ESTABLISHED** 1997
**WHERE FUNDING CAN BE GIVEN** Venice and the UK.
**WHO CAN BENEFIT** Charitable organisations working with old buildings or art.
**WHAT IS FUNDED** This charity gives half of its grant total to the Venice in Peril Fund, and in the UK supports the preservation, restoration, repair and maintenance of: buildings originally constructed before 1750; the fixtures and fittings of such buildings; works of art made before 1750 (including the purchase of such items).
**WHAT IS NOT FUNDED** Heating systems; toilets.
**TYPE OF GRANT** One-off, capital grants.
**RANGE OF GRANTS** Up to £2,000.
**SAMPLE GRANTS** Venice in Peril Fund (£30,000); Medway Council, South Newington PCC, The Vivat Trust (£2,000 each); St Mary the Virgin – Cleobury Mortimer (£1,500); Birmingham Cathedral, St James Church – Wigmore (£1,000 each); St Mary the Virgin – Sheering (£900); Blandford Forum Town Council (£800).
**FINANCES** *Year* 2013/14 *Income* £64,976 *Grants* £60,426 *Grants to organisations* £60,426
**TRUSTEES** Peter Boizot MBE; Timothy Warren; Jackie Freeman; Jane Botros.
**OTHER INFORMATION** About 50% of the fund's income is donated to the Venice in Peril Fund every year. A total of 20 grants were given to other organisations. The trust had negative assets in 2013/14.
**HOW TO APPLY** The trustees meet to consider appeals twice a year, in May and December. Applications should be submitted via the fund's online application form. Email confirmation will be given upon receipt of an application, detailing further supporting documents to be sent. The trustees state that before applying to the fund, applicants must have raised two thirds of the total amount required for their project. Further information is available on the fund's website.
**WHO TO APPLY TO** Jayne Day, The Trust Administrator, c/o Pothecary Witham Weld Solicitors, 70 St George's Square, London SW1V 3RD *Tel.* 020 7821 8211 *email* charities@pwwsolicitors.co.uk *Website* www.pwwsolicitors.co.uk

### ■ The William and Patricia Venton Charitable Trust

**CC NO** 1103884     **ESTABLISHED** 2004
**WHERE FUNDING CAN BE GIVEN** UK.
**WHO CAN BENEFIT** Charitable organisations benefitting older people, providing day centre care or working the field of animal welfare.
**WHAT IS FUNDED** Relief in need for older people, particularly day centre provision; the prevention of cruelty and suffering among animals.
**RANGE OF GRANTS** £1,000–£25,000
**SAMPLE GRANTS** Age Concern Northamptonshire (£25,000); Age UK Solihull (£7,000); PDSA – Southampton, Sudbury Neighbourhood Centre – Middlesex, Guild Care (£5,000 each); Battersea Dogs and Cats Home (£2,500); Tyddyn Cat Rescue Centre (£1,000).
**FINANCES** *Year* 2013/14 *Income* £93,769 *Grants* £55,000 *Grants to organisations* £55,000 *Assets* £2,713,191
**TRUSTEES** George Hillman-Liggett; Christopher Saunby; Graham Cudlipp.
**HOW TO APPLY** Apply in writing to the correspondent. Following an initial approach, eligible applicants will be sent the relevant application forms, to be returned with the appropriate documentation and then reviewed by trustees. The trustees favour applications from charities with which the trust's founders had a connection, but all applications meeting the trust's objectives are considered.
**WHO TO APPLY TO** The Trustees, Broadlands Gate, Broadlands Road, Brockenhurst, Hampshire SO42 7SX *Tel.* 01590 623818 *email* johngriffiths@wpventontrust.org.uk

### ■ Roger Vere Foundation

**CC NO** 1077559     **ESTABLISHED** 1999
**WHERE FUNDING CAN BE GIVEN** UK and worldwide, with a special interest in High Wycombe.
**WHO CAN BENEFIT** Charitable organisations.
**WHAT IS FUNDED** The relief of financial hardship in and around, but not restricted to, High Wycombe; advancement of education; advancement of religion; advancement of scientific and medical research; conservation and protection of the natural environment and endangered plants and animals; relief of natural and civil disasters; general charitable purposes.
**RANGE OF GRANTS** Up to £1,000.
**SAMPLE GRANTS Previous beneficiaries have included:** Cord Blood Charity, the Leprosy Mission, Claire House Children's Hospice, Angels International, Signalong Group, Changing Faces, Women's Aid, St John Water Wing, UK Youth and Jubilee Plus.
**FINANCES** *Year* 2013/14 *Income* £116,237 *Grants* £312,293 *Grants to organisations* £312,293 *Assets* £2,974,175
**TRUSTEES** Rosemary Vere, Chair; Marion Lyon; Peter Allen.
**HOW TO APPLY** Apply in writing to the correspondent. The trustees meet regularly to consider requests. The trustees also contact organisations in need of assistance that come to their attention.
**WHO TO APPLY TO** Peter Allen, Trustee, 19 Berwick Road, Marlow, Buckinghamshire SL7 3AR *Tel.* 01628 471702 *email* rogerverefoundation@gmail.co.uk

## ■ Victoria Homes Trust

**IR NO** XN45474    **ESTABLISHED** 1892
**WHERE FUNDING CAN BE GIVEN** Northern Ireland.
**WHO CAN BENEFIT** Registered charities benefitting children and young people under the age of 21.
**WHAT IS FUNDED** The trust supports young people with accommodation, education and training. Funding is given for projects addressing the needs of children and young people, particularly in the areas of homelessness, alcohol and drug abuse and counselling. Short term projects are favoured, where visible outcomes can be seen within 3–12 months, as well as those with 'multiplier' positive effects.
**WHAT IS NOT FUNDED** Projects whose beneficiaries are outside Northern Ireland; projects which do not target the needs of children and young people; projects for which expenditure has already been incurred; applications to support playgroups are discouraged; the trust is unlikely to contribute towards core running costs of charities and voluntary organisations. Grants are given to individuals only in exceptional circumstances.
**TYPE OF GRANT** Project funding, particularly projects with demonstrable short term benefits.
**RANGE OF GRANTS** Usually £500–£2,500.
**SAMPLE GRANTS** Details were not available.
**FINANCES** Grants £40,000 Grants to organisations £40,000
**OTHER INFORMATION** Accounts for the charity were not available. Grant total in previous years has been around £40,000 to £50,000 a year.
**HOW TO APPLY** Application forms are available from the correspondent or from the charity's website. A copy of the most recent audited accounts should be included. Applications should be typed or written in block capital letters using black ink. If the project requires work which involves planning permission, evidence that the permission has been granted should be enclosed. The trust asks that pamphlets or other printed matter should not be sent. The trustees meet twice each year and applications should be received by 30 April or 30 November and all applicants will be informed of the outcome of their application. Applicants should refer to the trust's website for further information.
**WHO TO APPLY TO** Derek Catney, Secretary, 2 Tudor Court, Rochester Road, Belfast BT6 9LB *Tel.* 028 9079 4306 *email* derek.catney@victoriahomestrust.org.uk *Website* www.victoriahomestrust.org.uk

## ■ The Nigel Vinson Charitable Trust

**CC NO** 265077    **ESTABLISHED** 1973
**WHERE FUNDING CAN BE GIVEN** UK, with a preference for north east England.
**WHO CAN BENEFIT** Individuals and organisations.
**WHAT IS FUNDED** General charitable purposes, including economic and community development and citizenship, education, environmental protection, the arts and other causes.
**TYPE OF GRANT** Capital costs (including buildings); one-off; projects; research. Grants are awarded on an annual, irregular or one-off basis.
**RANGE OF GRANTS** Under £500–£100,000.
**SAMPLE GRANTS** Hampden Trust, Institute of Economic Affairs (£100,000 each); Civitas (£75,000); Songbird Survival (£50,000); Amnesty International, Global Warming Policy Foundation (£10,000 each); Berwick Citizens Advice, Christian Institute, Free Society Educational Network, Public Memorials Appeal, Ryedale Festival, Young Britons' Foundation (£5,000 each); Thomas Telford (£2,000).
**FINANCES** Year 2013/14 Income £225,332 Grants £771,705 Grants to organisations £771,705 Assets £10,253,498
**TRUSTEES** Hon. Rowena Cowan; Rt Hon. Lord Vinson of Roddam Dene; Thomas Harris; Hon. Bettina Witheridge; Hon. Antonia Bennett; Elizabeth Passey; Hoare Trustees.
**HOW TO APPLY** Apply in writing to the correspondent. The trustees meet periodically to consider applications for grants, which may range from under £500 to over £25,000. Decisions on smaller grants may be approved by a single trustee, whereas larger grants require the approval of a number of trustees.
**WHO TO APPLY TO** The Trustees, Hoare Trustees, 37 Fleet Street, London EC4P 4DQ *Tel.* 020 7353 4522

## ■ The William and Ellen Vinten Trust

**CC NO** 285758    **ESTABLISHED** 1982
**WHERE FUNDING CAN BE GIVEN** UK, but mostly Bury St Edmunds.
**WHO CAN BENEFIT** Individuals; schools and colleges; industrial firms and companies. There is a strong preference for Bury St Edmunds.
**WHAT IS FUNDED** The trust's main objective is to support initiatives which engage young people in science and technology subjects, with a view to raising attainment and encouraging students to consider careers in industry, engineering and related areas. Other objectives of the trust include supporting the welfare of employees in industry and their families.
**SAMPLE GRANTS** A list of beneficiaries was not available.
**FINANCES** Year 2013/14 Income £63,879 Grants £36,336 Grants to organisations £36,336 Assets £1,578,125
**TRUSTEES** Adrian Williams; David Youngman; Robin Crosher; Igor Wowk; Alan Bonnett; James Guest; Keith Honeyman.
**OTHER INFORMATION** The grant total includes grants made to both individuals and organisations. Grants were given towards education (£30,800) and training (£5,500).
**HOW TO APPLY** Refer to the trust's website for current information. The trustees have previously stated that, as a proactive charity with links to organisations and schools, they do not seek unsolicited applications and that such applications are now so significant in number that the trust has decided not to respond to them.
**WHO TO APPLY TO** David Marriott, Valhalla, School Road, Thurston, Bury St Edmunds, Suffolk IP31 3SY *Tel.* 01359 234494 *email* vinten@vintentrust.org *Website* www.vintentrust.org.uk

## ■ The Vintners' Foundation

**CC NO** 1015212    **ESTABLISHED** 1992
**WHERE FUNDING CAN BE GIVEN** Greater London only.
**WHO CAN BENEFIT** Schools and charitable organisations.
**WHAT IS FUNDED** Primarily the prevention of drug and alcohol abuse and its social consequences. Grants are also made towards education, the services, social welfare for people who are disadvantaged or vulnerable, church and other charities requested by the Company's members.

**WHAT IS NOT FUNDED** Research charities; charities relating to buildings; UK-wide charities.
**TYPE OF GRANT** One-off; ongoing support.
**RANGE OF GRANTS** Up to £5,000.
**SAMPLE GRANTS** The Benevolent – March for Mobility (£50,000); Tower Hamlets Mission (£5,200); Addaction (£5,000); Stepney Greencoat School – Numicon Maths Project (£4,000); Caritas Anchor House, National Memorial Arboretum – Heroes Square paving stone (£3,000 each); Henley River and Rowing Museum, St James Garlickhythe (£2,500 each); KIDS, St Paul's Cathedral, City of London Academy, Youth Clubs Hampshire and Isle of Wight (£1,000 each).
**FINANCES** Year 2013/14 Income £350,418 Grants £103,129 Grants to organisations £103,129 Assets £1,329,455
**TRUSTEES** Michael Cox; Brigadier Jonathan Bourne-May; Anthony Sykes; Rupert Clevely.
**HOW TO APPLY** Apply in writing to the correspondent. The trustees meet four times per year to review grants. Criteria and further information can be viewed on the foundation's website.
**WHO TO APPLY TO** Andrew Ling, Charities Secretary, Vintners' Company, Vintners' Hall, 68ø Upper Thames Street, London EC4V 3BG *Tel.* 020 7236 1863 *email* stephen.freeth@vintershall.co.uk *Website* www.vintnershall.co.uk

### ■ Virgin Atlantic Foundation

**CC NO** 1097580  **ESTABLISHED** 2003
**WHERE FUNDING CAN BE GIVEN** UK and overseas, although in practice mainly China and Kenya.
**WHO CAN BENEFIT** Registered charities working with children and young people.
**WHAT IS FUNDED** Health; social welfare; general charitable purposes.
**RANGE OF GRANTS** £10,000–£643,000
**SAMPLE GRANTS** Free the Children (£643,000); Disaster Emergency Committee (£32,500); Nelson Mandela Children's Fund (£13,500); and Caudwell Children (£10,000).
**FINANCES** Year 2013/14 Income £793,888 Grants £699,199 Grants to organisations £699,199 Assets £4,731,000
**TRUSTEES** Ian de Sousa; Jillian Brady; Thomas Maher; Maria Sebastian; Craig Kreeger; Meigan Terry.
**OTHER INFORMATION** The foundation's income appears to be entirely generated by staff and customers of Virgin Atlantic.
**HOW TO APPLY** Applications can be made in writing to the correspondent, although potential applicant should be aware that currently the foundation's sole charity partner is Feed the Children.
**WHO TO APPLY TO** Ian de Sousa, Virgin Atlantic Airways Ltd, The Office, Manor Royal, Crawley, West Sussex RH10 9NU *Tel.* 01293 747128

### ■ The Virgin Foundation (Virgin Unite)

**CC NO** 297540  **ESTABLISHED** 1987
**WHERE FUNDING CAN BE GIVEN** Worldwide.
**WHO CAN BENEFIT** Organisations; individuals; innovative and entrepreneurial projects.
**WHAT IS FUNDED** Entrepreneurial approaches to social and environmental issues. The three key areas are: Global Leadership Initiatives – 'new collaborations that address gaps in global leadership' Business Innovation – 'across the Virgin family of businesses' The Next Generation of Entrepreneurs – supporting them to 'launch and grow their businesses so that they are sources of good jobs, prosperity and community impact'. Other initiatives 'providing support where it's needed most, for example emergency relief provisions in times of crisis'.
**TYPE OF GRANT** Grants; loans; non-financial support.
**RANGE OF GRANTS** Up to £366,000.
**SAMPLE GRANTS** Elders Foundation (£366,000); Carbon War Room (£312,000); B-Team (£222,000); RE*Generation USA (£156,000); Business as a force for good Canada (£!51,000); Bhubezi (£111,000); Entrepreneurship – including Virgin Unite Entrepreneurs (£91,000); Rural Transport Network (£84,000); Big Change and Business as a force for good Australia (£75,000 each); Pride'n Purpose (£73,000); Business as a force for good Morocco – Eve Branson Foundation (£70,000); Gala Rocks (£45,000); Fistula (£18,000); Emergency Response (£6,000). Other initiatives totalled £221,000.
**FINANCES** Year 2013/14 Income £13,313,000 Grants £1,977,000 Grants to organisations £1,977,000 Assets £17,456,000
**TRUSTEES** Vanessa Branson; Jane Tewson; Holly Branson; Ajaz Ahmed; Peter Norris.
**OTHER INFORMATION** The foundation's income included £5.17 million from Richard Branson's speaking fee donations and support from the Virgin Group totalling 3.46 million. Donations in-kind form the Virgin companies amounted to £880,000. Financial details refer to consolidated accounts of the group, which includes Virgin Unite Trading Ltd, Virgin Unite USA Inc., Virgin Unite (Canada), Virgin Unite Nominees Pty Ltd, Virgin Unite Africa and The Branson Centre of Entrepreneurship – Caribbean. Support can be classified as follows: Global Leadership Initiatives (£945,000); Business Innovation (£720,000); other initiatives (£221,000); Next Generation of Entrepreneurs (£91,000).
**HOW TO APPLY** For further information contact the foundation to see whether your project is suitable for assistance.
**WHO TO APPLY TO** Rosanne Gray, The Battleship Building, 179 Harrow Road, London W2 6NB *email* contact@virginunite.co.uk *Website* www.virginunite.com

### ■ Vision Charity

**CC NO** 1075630  **ESTABLISHED** 1976
**WHERE FUNDING CAN BE GIVEN** UK and overseas.
**WHO CAN BENEFIT** 'Registered institutional charities and other organisations and individuals involved in helping blind, dyslexic or visually impaired children.'
**WHAT IS FUNDED** Welfare of children who are blind, dyslexic or visually impaired.
**TYPE OF GRANT** Funds to purchase equipment, goods or specialist services; rarely cash donations.
**RANGE OF GRANTS** Under £1,000 and up to £30,000.
**SAMPLE GRANTS** The Pace Centre – Aylesbury (£26,000); The Fighting Chance Project – London, Joseph Clarke School – London (£5,000 each)
**FINANCES** Year 2013/14 Income £40,595 Grants £38,414 Grants to organisations £38,414 Assets £138,354
**TRUSTEES** Richard Morgan; William Vestey.
**HOW TO APPLY** A brief summary of the request should be sent to the correspondent. If the request is of interest to the trustees, further details will be requested. If the request has not been acknowledged within three months of submission, the applicant should assume that it

has not been successful. The charity is interested to receive such applications but regrets that it is not able to acknowledge every unsuccessful submission. For current information, refer to the charity's website.
WHO TO APPLY TO Peter Thompson, President, 59 Victoria Road, Surbiton, Surrey KT6 4NQ *Tel.* 01296 655227 *email* peter.thompson@visioncharity.co.uk *Website* www.visioncharity.co.uk

## ■ Vivdale Ltd
CC NO 268505 ESTABLISHED 1974
WHERE FUNDING CAN BE GIVEN UK.
WHO CAN BENEFIT Organisations benefitting Jewish people.
WHAT IS FUNDED The advancement of religion in accordance with the Orthodox Jewish faith and general charitable purposes.
TYPE OF GRANT One-off, one-year grants.
SAMPLE GRANTS **Previous beneficiaries have included:** Achisomach Aid Company Ltd, Beis Soroh Schneirer, Beis Yaakov Town, Beis Yisroel Tel Aviv, Comet Charities Ltd, Friends of Harim Bnei Brak, Jewish Teachers Training College Gateshead, Mosdos Bnei Brak, Torah Vechesed Ashdod and Woodstock Sinclair Trust.
FINANCES *Year* 2013/14 *Income* £147,070 *Grants* £116,545 *Grants to organisations* £116,545 *Assets* £2,434,348
TRUSTEES David Henry Marks; Francesca Sinclair; Loretta Marks.
OTHER INFORMATION No list of grant beneficiaries was included in the accounts.
HOW TO APPLY Apply in writing to the correspondent.
WHO TO APPLY TO David Henry Marks, Trustee, 17 Cheyne Walk, London NW4 3QH *Tel.* 020 8202 9367 *email* aepton@goldwins.co.uk

## ■ The Vodafone Foundation
CC NO 1089625 ESTABLISHED 2002
WHERE FUNDING CAN BE GIVEN UK and overseas (where Vodafone operates).
WHO CAN BENEFIT Registered charities and community groups.
WHAT IS FUNDED General charitable purposes, with a preference for technology, disadvantaged communities, humanitarian crises and disasters.
WHAT IS NOT FUNDED Individuals.
RANGE OF GRANTS £200–£400,000
SAMPLE GRANTS Télécoms Sans Frontières (£400,000); Moyo Tanzania (£398,000); UN World Food Programme (£264,000); Keeping Kids Company (£200,000); Democratic Republic on Congo Charitable Fund (£167,000); Tanzania Charitable Fund (£144,000); Text Santa (£101,000); Vidavo SA (£109,000); DEC Philippines Typhoon Appeal (£93,000); Naomi House (£51,000); Dream Foundation (£4,000); and RSPB (£200).
FINANCES *Year* 2013/14 *Income* £22,026,277 *Grants* £19,529,838 *Grants to organisations* £19,529,838 *Assets* £7,090,802
TRUSTEES Nick Land; Margherita Della Valle; Hatem Dowidar; Elizabeth Filkin; Lord Hastings of Scarisbrick; Jeroen Hoencamp; Matthew Kirk; Francisco Roman; Ronald Schellekens; Helen Lamprell; Mwavita Makamba; Andrew Dunnett.
OTHER INFORMATION During the year, the foundation made grants worldwide totalling £19.6 million, which included over £14.5 million worth of grants to local Vodafone Foundations.
HOW TO APPLY Contact the foundation or see the website for details of all application processes.
WHO TO APPLY TO Andrew Dunnett, Foundation Director, Vodafone Group plc, 1 Kingdom Street, London W2 6BY *email* groupfoundation@vodafone.com *Website* www.vodafone.com/content/index/about/foundation.html

## ■ Volant Charitable Trust
SC NO SC030790 ESTABLISHED 2000
WHERE FUNDING CAN BE GIVEN UK and overseas, with a preference for Scotland.
WHO CAN BENEFIT Organisations benefitting women, children, the relief of poverty, the alleviation of social deprivation and the provision of social benefit to the community.
WHAT IS FUNDED Charitable organisations involved in the support and protection of women, children, relief of poverty and alleviating social deprivation and the provision of social benefit to the community and the public at large; research and teaching related to the treatment, cure and nursing of Multiple Sclerosis and related conditions.
WHAT IS NOT FUNDED Individuals; major capital projects; projects relating to flora and fauna. The trust has not been considering applications for overseas projects, due to their commitments to major disaster appeals, or for projects relating to Multiple Sclerosis, health care or medical research, due to their commitment to research the University of Edinburgh. Check the website for current information.
TYPE OF GRANT One-off and recurrent grants.
RANGE OF GRANTS Up to £100,000.
SAMPLE GRANTS **Previous beneficiaries have included:** Foundation Scotland (£350,000); Médecins Sans Frontières – Congo, Save the Children – Ivory Coast (£100,000 each); The Place2Be (£90,000); The Roses Charitable Trust (£75,000); Women Onto Work (£60,000); and Kids Company (£50,000).
FINANCES *Year* 2013/14 *Income* £3,299,600 *Grants* £4,290,684 *Grants to organisations* £4,290,684
TRUSTEES J. K. Rowling; Dr N. S. Murray; G. C. Smith; R. D. Fulton.
OTHER INFORMATION A list of beneficiaries for 2013/14 was not available.
HOW TO APPLY Applications for funding requests of up to and including £10,000 per annum, for those projects based in Scotland only, are dealt with by the appointed agents, Foundation Scotland (www.foundationscotland.org.uk/programmes/volant.aspx). According to Foundation Scotland's website, 'the fund's primary focus is to support women, children and young people who are at risk and facing social deprivation. Projects must demonstrate a strong focus on supporting women affected by hardship or disadvantage and on tackling the issues they face in order to make a lasting difference to their lives and life chances. There is limited funding available, so only those projects that closely match the above criteria are likely to be considered for support.' Organisations who are currently in receipt of a grant may not apply. Groups that will distribute funds as grants or bursaries to other groups may not apply. An outline of the project using the enquiry form should be sent to grants@foundationscotland.org.uk. Any questions should be directed towards Jane Martin on 0131 524 0301 or jane@foundationscotland.org.uk. All other requests for funding, including applications for over £10,000 per year in Scotland, or for any

projects in the UK, are dealt with via an application form available from the Volant Trust's website. The form should be completed and returned to the trust via post. Applications should not be hand delivered; management at mail boxes are not able to discuss applications and cannot be expected to provide a receipt. The trustees meet twice a year to review applications, in March and September, and successful applicants will be notified immediately after the meeting. Check the website for application deadlines. The trust regrets that it is not able to enter into any communication regarding general enquiries, due to the very large number of applications received.

**WHO TO APPLY TO** Christine Collingwood, Trust Administrator, Box 8, 196 Rose Street, Edinburgh EH2 4AT *email* admin@volanttrust.com *Website* www.volanttrust.com

## ■ Voluntary Action Fund (VAF)

**SC NO** SC035037    **ESTABLISHED** 2003
**WHERE FUNDING CAN BE GIVEN** Scotland.
**WHO CAN BENEFIT** Registered charities and organisations with a constitution and activities that could be considered charitable.
**WHAT IS FUNDED** VAF manages funds that are open to application from eligible groups and organisations. The funding and support VAF provides enables community based organisations to involve volunteers, undertake projects that challenge inequalities and overcome barriers to being involved in community life.
**WHAT IS NOT FUNDED** See the fund's website for details of any individual exclusions for each fund.
**TYPE OF GRANT** Check the individual scheme guidelines.
**RANGE OF GRANTS** Up to £1 million.
**SAMPLE GRANTS** Glasgow Community and Safety Services (£1 million); Lothian and Borders Community Justice Authority (£375,000); Youthlink Scotland – NKBL (£285,000); Rape Crisis Scotland (£260,000); Citizens Theatre (£194,000); Sense over Sectarianism (£161,500); Dundee Women's Aid (£129,000); Shetland Women's Aid (£111,000); Place for Hope – Community Dialogue (£104,500).
**FINANCES** *Year* 2013/14 *Income* £19,252,944 *Grants* £17,580,767 *Grants to organisations* £17,580,767 *Assets* £821,816
**TRUSTEES** Ron Daniel; Dorothy MacLauchlin; Michael Cunningham; Pam Judson; John McDonald; Douglas Guest; Shirley Grieve; Gail Edwards; Andrew Marshall-Roberts; Bridgid Corr; Sid Wales; Caron Hughes; Anne-Marie Riley; Angus Hannah; Graham Leydon; Michael Wilson; Sarah Kersey.
**PUBLICATIONS** Programme evaluations.
**OTHER INFORMATION** In 2013/14 grants were distributed in the following categories: Violence Against Women Programme; Drugs and Community Safety Division; Equality Programme; Volunteering Scotland Grant Scheme.
**HOW TO APPLY** Application forms and guidance notes for open programmes are available on the fund's website. The fund recommends that interested parties contact them to discuss the project before making any application. Funds may open and close so applicants should check the website for the most recent updates. Different funds have different application guidance.
**WHO TO APPLY TO** Keith Wimbles, Chief Executive, Suite 3, Forth House, Burnside Business Court, North Road, Inverkeithing, Fife KY11 1NZ *Tel.* 01383 620780 *Fax* 01383 626314 *email* info@vaf.org.uk *Website* www.voluntaryactionfund.org.uk

## ■ Wade's Charity

**CC NO** 224939 **ESTABLISHED** 1530

**WHERE FUNDING CAN BE GIVEN** Leeds, within the pre-1974 boundary of the city (approximately LS1 to LS17 postcodes).

**WHO CAN BENEFIT** Charities benefitting people of all ages within the beneficiary area, particularly youth organisations and community centres.

**WHAT IS FUNDED** A wide range of activities and projects, all of which must be either the preservation of open space or the provision of facilities for recreation. Projects which are often support include: youth clubs, activities, residential trips and holiday schemes; community facilities and activities; activities and holidays for older people; arts projects; projects working with disadvantaged groups.

**WHAT IS NOT FUNDED** Applications from outside the beneficiary area, i.e. from outside the pre-1974 boundary of the city of Leeds covered roughly by postcodes LS1 to LS17; applications from non-charitable organisations; applications from individuals; applications for church repairs (unless there is proven significant community use); circulars or general appeals from high profile national charities; applications which do not offer benefit within the terms of the trust; applications for activities which are the responsibility of statutory or local authority funding, particularly within health or education; applications to fund salaries.

**TYPE OF GRANT** The majority of grants are given on a one-off basis.

**RANGE OF GRANTS** Average grant around £2,000.

**SAMPLE GRANTS** Better Action For Families, Leeds Children's Charity (£6,000 each); Friends of Middleton Park (£3,000); Leeds Mencap, Leeds Tigers Basketball, Youth Theatres Leeds (£2,500 each); Hyde Park Community Cafe (£2,200); Al Haqq Supplementary School, Leeds Women's Aid (£2,000 each); Richmond Hill Elderly Action (£1,700 each); Live Music Now (£1,600); Sikh Sports (£600); CREATE (£300).

**FINANCES** Year 2014 Income £262,225 Grants £123,365 Grants to organisations £123,365 Assets £6,569,050

**TRUSTEES** Bernard Atha; Susan Reddington; John Tinker; Ann Chadwick; John Roberts; John Stoddart-Scott; Hilary Finnigan; Bruce Smith; Mark Pullan; Nicholas Mercer; John Pike; David Richardson; Nick Rose; Timothy Ward; The Rector of Leeds; The Lord Mayor of Leeds.

**OTHER INFORMATION** The charity also has a small grants programme, operating through Voluntary Action Leeds, which enables small community groups (with an annual income of less than £10,000) who may not be a registered charity to apply for funds of up to £200 towards their administrative costs. In 2014, the charity made 54 larger grants and 20 small grants.

**HOW TO APPLY** Full guidance and current information can be found on the charity's website. Applications should be made in writing to the correspondent, including the following information: the name, address and telephone number of both the applicant and the organisations they are applying on behalf of; registered charity number; an outline of what the organisation does; an outline of the purpose for which the grant is being sought; a copy of the latest signed accounts. All applications will be acknowledged, and those that fulfil at least one of the charity's primary charitable objectives will then be contacted by the Grants Adviser to arrange an appointment to visit the organisation, in order to gain further information and understanding about the project. Applications will then be reviewed by the trustees at a Grants Meeting. All applicants will be notified of the trustees' decision in writing. Grant beneficiaries are asked to submit a report on how the grant has been used, which is considered when reviewing future applications. Further visits may also be made to grant recipients. Grants meetings are usually held in April, July and November, and applications should be received four weeks prior to the meeting date. The charity is happy to discuss ideas before a formal application is made. Applicants may only submit an application once per calendar year. Voluntary Action Leeds advertises the small grants programme in their newsletter and on their website, where an application form can be obtained.

**WHO TO APPLY TO** Kathryn Hodges, Grants Adviser and Administrator, 5 Grimston Park Mews, Grimston Park, Grimston, Tadcaster LS24 9DB Tel. 01937 830295 email wadescharity@btinernet.com Website www.wadescharity.org

## ■ The Scurrah Wainwright Charity

**CC NO** 1002755 **ESTABLISHED** 1991

**WHERE FUNDING CAN BE GIVEN** Preference for Yorkshire, South Africa and Zimbabwe.

**WHO CAN BENEFIT** Charitable organisations.

**WHAT IS FUNDED** The charity 'looks for innovative work in the field of social reform, with a preference for 'root-cause' rather than palliative projects. The charity favours causes which are outside the mainstream and unlikely to receive funding elsewhere.

**WHAT IS NOT FUNDED** Individuals; animal welfare; buildings; medical research or support for individual medical conditions; substitution for Government funding (e.g. in education and health); charities who send unsolicited general appeal letters; activities that have already happened; applicants who do not have a UK bank into which a grant can be paid; applicants who have already applied for a grant, successfully or not, within the last 12 months; large, national charities, unless working specifically in the Yorkshire region and providing local control and access to the grant.

**TYPE OF GRANT** Contributions to core costs. Rarely funds for more than one year.

**RANGE OF GRANTS** Typically £1,000–£5,000, but in 'cases of exceptional merit' larger grants may be awarded.

**SAMPLE GRANTS** Gipton Methodists (£10,600); Public Law Project (£5,000); The Grandparents Association (£4,800); Carbon Trade Watch (£3,000); LGBT Young North West, Out There Supporting Families of Prisoners, The Business Bridge – South Africa, York Mind, Zimbabwe Educational Trust (£2,000 each); Campaign Boot Camp (£1,500); Ryedale Citizens Advice (£1,000); Ottringham Computer Club (£650).

**FINANCES** Year 2013/14 Income £189,504 Grants £99,050 Grants to organisations £99,050 Assets £1,738,195

**TRUSTEES** M. S. Wainwright, Chair; R. R. Bhaskar; H. P. I. Scott; H. A. Wainwright; P. Wainwright; T. M. Wainwright.

**OTHER INFORMATION** 'The Wainwright family runs two trusts, one charitable [The Scurrah Wainwright Charity], one non-charitable [The Andrew Wainwright Reform Trust Ltd]. The trusts are based on the family's traditions of liberal values and support for the socially disempowered. The trustees are all family members, based in West Yorkshire.'

**HOW TO APPLY** Applicants are encouraged to refer to the charity's website, where application forms and further information and guidance are available. The charity advises that before applying applicants should: check that the amount of money requested need falls within the charity's limits; check that the aims meet the charity's criteria; check deadlines: the trustees meet three times a year – in March, July and November – and applications must be submitted by 14 January, 14 May or 14 September respectively. An application should include a completed application form, the most recent audited accounts, and no more than two A4 pages setting out the following: background information about applicant and/or organisation; outline of the project and its aims; plans for practical implementation of the work and a budget; details of any other current funding applications, successful or not. For questions about the application procedure, applicants may contact the administrator, preferably by email. If applicants have not heard from the administrator by the end of the month in which the trustees' meeting was held, it should be assumed that the application was not successful. Grant recipients are expected to provide a report within 12 to 15 months of the grant being awarded.

**WHO TO APPLY TO** Kerry McQuade, Correspondent, 16 Blenheim Street, Hebden Bridge, West Yorkshire HX7 8BU *email* admin@wainwrighttrusts.org.uk *Website* www.wainwrighttrusts.org.uk

## ■ The Wakefield and Tetley Trust

**CC NO** 1121779   **ESTABLISHED** 2008

**WHERE FUNDING CAN BE GIVEN** London boroughs of Tower Hamlets, Southwark and the City of London.

**WHO CAN BENEFIT** Community groups and charities.

**WHAT IS FUNDED** Social welfare and general charitable purposes. Grants are made for projects which benefit 'people who face significant disadvantage and have limited choices and opportunities', breaking down barriers and encouraging social inclusion and community cohesion.

**WHAT IS NOT FUNDED** Individuals; work that has already taken place; applicants already rejected by the trust within the last six months; organisations with significant unrestricted reserves or in serious financial deficit; the promotion of religion; animal welfare charities; statutory bodies and work that is primarily the responsibility of central or local government; health trusts, health authorities and hospices (or any sort of medical equipment or medical research); building restoration or conservation; uniformed youth groups; schools, supplementary schools or vocational training; environmental improvements.

**TYPE OF GRANT** Up to three years for project costs and core costs.

**RANGE OF GRANTS** Grants range from £500 to £65,000 over one year; the average grant awarded in 2009–10 was £7,000.

**SAMPLE GRANTS** All Hallows by the Tower (£49,500); Southwark Daycentre for Asylum Seekers (£10,000); Eclectic Productions (£7,000); Tower Hamlets Parents Centre (£6,000); Bishop Ho Ming Wah Association, Docklands Youth Service, Ernest Foundation and First Love Foundation (£2,500 each); and East London Chinese Community Centre (£1,500).

**FINANCES** *Year* 2014 *Income* £363,255 *Grants* £224,520 *Grants to organisations* £224,520 *Assets* £8,678,342

**TRUSTEES** The Ven. Peter Delaney, Chair; Patrick Kelly; Lady Judy Moody-Stuart; Stuart Morganstein; Clare Murphy; Kenneth Prideaux-Brune; Helal Rahman; Susan Reardon-Smith; Cherry Bushell; Dawn Plimmer.

**OTHER INFORMATION** The grant total includes an annual donation to All Hallows by the Tower. 37 organisations received grants in 2014.

**HOW TO APPLY** In order to be eligible, organisations must: undertake charitable work (not necessarily as a registered charity) benefitting people resident or working in Tower Hamlets and/or Southwark and/or City of London; have a constitution or set of governing rules; have a bank or building society account with two or more named people to sign all cheques, and for which annual accounts for the previous year can be provided (or most recent bank statement if a new organisation). Application guidelines for both grant programmes are available on the trust's website and should be referred to. For the Main Grants programme, an initial proposal should be sent outlining the points required in the guidelines, including details about the organisation, a description of how the grant will be used, the project budget, evidence of the need for the project and supporting documents. Trustees review applications in June, September and December and proposals must be submitted by April, July and October respectively. For Fast Track grants, an application form, which is available from the trust's website, should be completed and returned to the trust. Applications can be made at any time and decisions are generally made within six weeks. Applicants are encouraged to contact the trust's Grant Officer for advice on making an application.

**WHO TO APPLY TO** Elaine Crush, Grant Officer, Oxford House, Derbyshire Street, London E2 6HG *Tel.* 020 7749 1118 *email* enquiries@wakefieldtrust.org.uk *Website* www.wakefieldtrust.org.uk

## ■ Wakeham Trust

**CC NO** 267495   **ESTABLISHED** 1974

**WHERE FUNDING CAN BE GIVEN** UK.

**WHO CAN BENEFIT** Registered charities.

**WHAT IS FUNDED** The trust's website describes its activities as follows: 'We provide grants to help people rebuild their communities. We are particularly interested in neighbourhood projects, community arts projects, projects involving community service by young people, or projects set up by those who are socially excluded. We also support innovative projects to promote excellence in teaching (at any level, from primary schools to universities), though we never support individuals.' Preference is also given to projects which are: small enough that a small grant can make a big difference; new to a local area or not well established; do not employ staff; have the potential to be self-sustaining; are outward looking and help a significant number of people.

**WHAT IS NOT FUNDED** Individuals; large, well-established charities; large capital projects such as towards buildings and transport; staff salaries; academic research posts.
**TYPE OF GRANT** One-off project costs.
**RANGE OF GRANTS** Normally £75–£750.
**SAMPLE GRANTS Previous beneficiaries have included:** a furniture reclamation and delivery enterprise (£500); a group of elderly and disabled volunteers for a children's cafe (£350); New youth club and The Kaiama Community Association (£250 each); Community garden and toy boxes for DHSS offices (£200 each); Martin Youth Bikers (£150); and Community football (£50).
**FINANCES** Year 2012/13 *Income* £23,000 *Grants* £40,000 *Grants to organisations* £40,000
**TRUSTEES** Harold Carter; Barnaby Newbolt; Tess Silkstone.
**OTHER INFORMATION** Accounts for 2013/14 were not available due to the trust's low income this year. Grant total has been estimated based on the trust's total expenditure of £51,000 and grant totals in previous years.
**HOW TO APPLY** At the time of writing (June 2015), the trust's website states that they are not handling new applications at the moment, due to a transition in their administration, but that they will be accepting applications in the future. Applicants should check the website for updated information. Applications can normally be made either by letter or by filling in the online form. The trust prefers online applications. Full guidelines are available on the trust's website. The 2012/13 accounts were the latest available.
**WHO TO APPLY TO** Anina Cheng, Correspondent, Swan House, 17–19 Stratford Place, London W1C 1BQ *Tel.* 020 7907 2100 *Website* www.wakehamtrust.org

........................................................

## ■ The Community Foundation in Wales

**CC NO** 1074655    **ESTABLISHED** 1999
**WHERE FUNDING CAN BE GIVEN** Wales.
**WHO CAN BENEFIT** Local charities, community groups and voluntary organisations that are engaged in strengthening communities and tackling social needs at a local level.
**WHAT IS FUNDED** Grants for projects that strengthen communities in Wales. The foundation focuses on grassroots organisations engaged in addressing local needs. The foundation's grants programmes fall under five core themes: 'enabling young people and promoting education'; 'enterprise and life-long learning'; 'building cohesion and confidence in communities'; 'improving physical and mental health'; 'nurturing heritage and culture'; 'protecting our environment'.
**WHAT IS NOT FUNDED** Each of the grant programmes has specific criteria. However, in general, the foundation is unlikely to fund: large capital projects; national or UK-wide organisations; organisations with an income exceeding £1 million; fundraising costs; projects that promote a certain faith or are exclusively available to those of a certain faith
**RANGE OF GRANTS** The majority of grants awarded are under £5,000.
**FINANCES** Year 2013/14 *Income* £3,465,551 *Grants* £2,169,972 *Grants to organisations* £2,169,972 *Assets* £10,607,450
**TRUSTEES** Janet Lewis-Jones; Michael Westerman; Julian Smith; Frank Learner; Dr Caryl Cresswell; Lulu Burridge; Sheila Maxwell; Thomas Jones; Revd John Davies; Alun Evans; Lloyd Fitzhugh; Kathryn Morris.
**OTHER INFORMATION** The foundation promotes and manages philanthropy, 'awarding grants on behalf of clients, fund holders and donors, which enable local people to achieve inspiring change in their communities'.
**HOW TO APPLY** The foundation manages a number of funds, many with their own individual criteria, and some which relate to specific geographical areas of Wales. Visit the grants page of the foundation's website, where information about each of the funding programmes can be found, along with guidance notes, application forms and deadlines.
**WHO TO APPLY TO** Liza Kellett, St Andrew's House, 24 St Andrew's Crescent, Cardiff CF10 3DD *Tel.* 029 2037 9580 *email* mail@cfiw.org.uk *Website* www.cfiw.org.uk

........................................................

## ■ Wales Council for Voluntary Action

**CC NO** 218093    **ESTABLISHED** 1963
**WHERE FUNDING CAN BE GIVEN** Wales.
**WHO CAN BENEFIT** Registered charities and voluntary organisations only.
**WHAT IS FUNDED** Local community; volunteering; social welfare; environment; regeneration. WCVA represents supports and campaigns for the voluntary sector in Wales and administers a variety of grant programmes; check WCVA's website for up-to-date information on current programmes and deadlines.
**WHAT IS NOT FUNDED** Grants are made to constituted voluntary organisations only. Check the WCVA website for specific exclusions for individual funds.
**TYPE OF GRANT** Capital and core costs; one-off; projects; recurring and running costs; start-up costs.
**RANGE OF GRANTS** Up to and above £1 million, depending on the grant programme.
**SAMPLE GRANTS** Gwent Association of Voluntary Organisations – Gwent (£726,000); Powys Association of Voluntary Organisations (£399,500); Interlink – Rhondda Cynon Taff (£267,000); Torfaen Voluntary Alliance (£204,500); Groundwork North Wales (£150,000); Melin Homes (£98,570); Merthyr Tydfil Institute for the Blind (£72,000); New Economics Foundation (£49,000); Llanelli Women's Aid (£46,000); Community Wellbeing Coaches CIC Ltd (£46,000).
**FINANCES** Year 2013/14 *Income* £23,364,155 *Grants* £11,199,418 *Grants to organisations* £11,199,418 *Assets* £10,199,245
**TRUSTEES** Phillip Avery; Louise Bennett; Pamela Boyd; Daisy Cole; Rocio Cifuentes; Peter Davies; Mike Denman; Walter Dickie; Cherrie Galvin; Paul Glaze; Eirwen Godden; Efa Gruffudd Jones; Catherine Mair Gwynant; Simon Harris; Sioned Hughes; Dilys Jackson; Harri Jones; Helen Jones; John Jones; Liza Kellett; Joy Kent; Judy Leering; Moira Lockitt; Salah Mohamed; Barbara Natasegara; Roy Norris; Catherine O'Sullivan; Martin Pollard; L. Mair Stephens; Anne Stephenson; Hilary Stevens; Fran Targett; Janet Walsh; Catriona Williams; Michael Williams; Thomas Williams; Clive Wolfendale; Pauline Young; Win Griffiths; Margaret Jervis; Eurwen Edwards; Chad Patel.

PUBLICATIONS Guidance notes for applicants available on request. Visit www.wcva.org.uk or call the Helpdesk on 0800 2888 329.
OTHER INFORMATION Grants were made to 541 organisations.
HOW TO APPLY There are separate application forms for each scheme. Contact WCVA on 0800 2888 329, or visit its website, for further information.
WHO TO APPLY TO Tracey Lewis, Secretary, Baltic House, Mount Stuart Square, Cardiff CF10 5FH *Tel.* 0800 288 8329 *email* help@wcva.org.uk *Website* www.wcva.org.uk

## ■ Robert and Felicity Waley-Cohen Charitable Trust

CC NO 272126    ESTABLISHED 1976
WHERE FUNDING CAN BE GIVEN England and Wales, focus on Warwickshire and Oxfordshire.
WHO CAN BENEFIT Charitable organisations.
WHAT IS FUNDED The trust makes grants for general charitable purposes. In particular, 'the trustees have determined to consider applications for and make grants as appropriate to charitable institutions, mainly in Warwickshire and Oxfordshire, with special regard to charities working to promote health, the arts and the welfare of children'.
WHAT IS NOT FUNDED Individuals.
RANGE OF GRANTS £50–£50,000
SAMPLE GRANTS Cancer Research UK (£50,000); Heart of England Community Foundation (£47,500); The Alternative Theatre Company (£14,000); West London Synagogue (£6,200); The Victoria and Albert Museum (£1,000); Plan International (£900); Art Angel Trust (£500); Injured Jockeys Fund, Spinal Research (£250 each); Katharine House Hospice Trust (£120); Greatwood Raceday (£75).
FINANCES *Year* 2013/14 *Income* £84,512 *Grants* £179,137 *Grants to organisations* £179,137 *Assets* £1,948,080
TRUSTEES R. B. Waley-Cohen; Hon F. A. Waley-Cohen.
OTHER INFORMATION Grants were made to 37 organisations in 2013/14.
HOW TO APPLY Apply in writing to the correspondent.
WHO TO APPLY TO Robert Waley-Cohen, Trustee, 18 Gilston Road, London SW10 9SR *Tel.* 020 7244 6022 *email* ccopeman@uptonviva.com

## ■ The Walker Trust

CC NO 215479    ESTABLISHED 1897
WHERE FUNDING CAN BE GIVEN Shropshire.
WHO CAN BENEFIT Individuals and organisations benefitting children and young adults who are in care, fostered and adopted.
WHAT IS FUNDED The trust makes grants in Shropshire to health-related organisations and to organisations and individuals for wide educational purposes.
WHAT IS NOT FUNDED Appeals from outside Shropshire will not be considered or replied to. The trustees generally do not assist students in higher education (due to the assistance available from student finance) apart from in exceptional circumstances, such as disability, or for medical or veterinary courses.
TYPE OF GRANT Funding given up to one year. Part project funding and capital costs.
RANGE OF GRANTS Up to £100,000.
SAMPLE GRANTS New Consultant Maternity Unit – Princess Royal Hospital (£100,000); Moreton Hall School, Tickwood Care Farm (£25,000 each); Oswestry Bone Cancer (£20,000); Shropshire Wildlife (£5,000); Shrewsbury Children's Bookfest (£2,500); Deafblind UK, Firefighters Charity, Shrewsbury Street Pastors (£2,000 each); St Mary's Youth Project (£1,500); Haughton School (£1,200); Albrighton Trust (£500); Blood Pressure UK (£300); St Peter's Primary Bratton (£210).
FINANCES *Year* 2013/14 *Income* £243,754 *Grants* £2,736,642 *Grants to organisations* £217,323 *Assets* £6,125,984
TRUSTEES Algernon Herber-Percy; Caroline Paton-Smith; David Lloyd; Malcolm Pate; Shirley Reynolds; Lady Lydia Forester.
OTHER INFORMATION Grants were awarded to 29 organisations. The grant total also includes grants awarded to individuals totalling £56,319.
HOW TO APPLY Apply in writing to the correspondent. Details of other assistance applied for must be given and, in the case of organisations, the latest annual report and accounts. The trustees meet four times a year, but arrangements can be made for urgent applications to receive consideration between meetings. Individuals receiving larger grants are paid termly subject to reports from university/college at end of previous term.
WHO TO APPLY TO Edward Hewitt, Clerk, 2 Breidden Way, Bayston Hill, Shrewsbury SY3 0LN *Tel.* 01743 873866 *email* edward.hewitt@btinternet.com

## ■ Wallace and Gromit's Children's Foundation

CC NO 1043603    ESTABLISHED 2003
WHERE FUNDING CAN BE GIVEN UK.
WHO CAN BENEFIT Children's hospitals, hospices and healthcare organisations.
WHAT IS FUNDED Wallace and Gromit's Children's Foundation is a national charity raising funds to improve the quality of life for children in hospitals and hospices throughout the UK. Examples of projects which the trustees will fund include: arts, music, play and leisure programmes; facilities to support families of children treated in hospitals or hospices; welcoming and accessible environments; facilities in hospices; promoting education and information programmes; supporting children with physical and emotional difficulties; medical equipment (when it can be shown that funding is not available from statutory sources).
WHAT IS NOT FUNDED Charities not supporting children's healthcare; organisations that are not registered charities; animal, religious or international charities; retrospective funding; organisations that do not work in a hospice or hospital environment; organisations providing away days, holidays or excursions; individuals; funding of clown doctors.
RANGE OF GRANTS £100–£10,000
TRUSTEES I. Hannah; S. Cooper; P. Lord, Chair; J. Moule; N. Park; D. Sproxton; C. Griffiths; M. Norton.
OTHER INFORMATION In April 2014, the Wallace and Gromit Children's Charity merged with The Royal Hospital for Children Bristol Appeal Ltd (otherwise known as Wallace and Gromit's Grand Appeal) to form the Wallace and Gromit's Children's Foundation. Accounts for the year following the merger were not available at the time of writing.
HOW TO APPLY Full guidelines and an application form are available on the charity's website. Applicants are encouraged to check that their

organisation meets the criteria set out in the guidelines before making an application. Applications from organisations working within a hospice or hospital will require a supporting reference from the hospice or hospital. An application form should be completed and sent via email to the correspondent. Supporting documentation may be sent by post, but annual reports and accounts should not be sent unless requested. Grant recipients are required to send a grant report and case study within ten months of receiving a grant. Check the charity's website for current information on grant application deadlines.

**WHO TO APPLY TO** Anna Shepherd, Deputy Director, 24 Upper Maudlin Street, Bristol BS2 8DJ *Tel.* 020 7841 8987 *email* info@wallaceandgromitcharity.org *Website* wallaceandgromitcharity.org

## ■ War on Want

**CC NO** 208724      **ESTABLISHED** 1959
**WHERE FUNDING CAN BE GIVEN** Financially developing countries only.
**WHO CAN BENEFIT** Typically, War on Want directly funds the work of labour organisations and NGOs in financially developing countries, usually trade unions or similar workers' organizations, and women's organisations.
**WHAT IS FUNDED** Overseas development projects that address the root causes of poverty, oppression and injustice in financially developing countries. The charity works towards three charitable objects: to relieve global poverty working in partnership; to promote human rights; to educate the public on the causes of poverty.
**WHAT IS NOT FUNDED** War on Want works with organisations all over the world, including UK, but most of its projects are overseas.
**TYPE OF GRANT** Continuous project funding.
**FINANCES** *Year* 2013/14 *Income* £1,816,009 *Grants* £1,233,432 *Grants to organisations* £1,233,432 *Assets* £2,129,648
**TRUSTEES** Sue Branford; Polly Jones; David Hillman; Mark Luetchford; Guillermo Rogel; Steve Preston; Gaynelle Samuel; Atif Choudhury; Branislava Milosevic; Anna Morser; Tony McMullan; Michael Whithouse; John Neall; Nick Moore.
**PUBLICATIONS** Upfront (a regular newsletter); publications list – covering subjects such as health, women, trade, aid, Asia, Latin America and Africa.
**HOW TO APPLY** Unsolicited applications are not accepted or acknowledged, due to demand and restrictions on time.
**WHO TO APPLY TO** The Executive Director, 44–48 Shepherdess Walk, London N1 7JP *Tel.* 020 7324 5040 *Fax* 020 7324 5041 *email* mailroom@waronwant.org *Website* www.waronwant.org

## ■ Sir Siegmund Warburg's Voluntary Settlement

**CC NO** 286719      **ESTABLISHED** 1983
**WHERE FUNDING CAN BE GIVEN** UK, especially London.
**WHO CAN BENEFIT** Registered charities only.
**WHAT IS FUNDED** The arts.
**WHAT IS NOT FUNDED** Individuals.
**TYPE OF GRANT** Revenue funding and capital projects.
**RANGE OF GRANTS** Up to £250,000.

**SAMPLE GRANTS** National Trust Knole, Victoria and Albert Museum (£200,000 each); Tricycle Theatre (£150,000); Academy of Ancient Music (£125,000); Art Fund (£100,000); Gorton Monastery (£75,000); Dance United, Theatre Royal Plymouth (£50,000); Dulwich Picture Gallery, National Life Stories, Story Museum (£25,000 each); National Youth Orchestra (£20,000); Oxford Lieder Festival, St Bride's Foundation (£5,000 each); St Paul's Girls School (£2,000).
**FINANCES** *Year* 2013/14 *Income* £119,485 *Grants* £1,787,000 *Grants to organisations* £1,787,000 *Assets* £5,773,199
**TRUSTEES** Sir Hugh Stevenson; Doris Wasserman; Dr Michael Harding; Christopher Purvis.
**OTHER INFORMATION** Following the trustees decision to start planning for the eventual wind-down of the trust, they have begun withdrawing larger amounts from the invested portfolio and distributing this in grants.
**HOW TO APPLY** Registered charities only are invited to send applications by email to applications@sswvs.org. Initial applications should be no more than four sides of A4 and should be accompanied by the latest audited accounts. Applications sent by post will not be considered.
**WHO TO APPLY TO** The Trustees, 19 Norland Square, London W11 4PU *email* applications@sswvs.org

## ■ The Ward Blenkinsop Trust

**CC NO** 265449      **ESTABLISHED** 1972
**WHERE FUNDING CAN BE GIVEN** UK, with a special interest in Merseyside and surrounding counties.
**WHO CAN BENEFIT** Charitable organisations.
**WHAT IS FUNDED** General charitable purposes. In the past, the trust has given support for causes including medical research, social welfare, the arts and education.
**WHAT IS NOT FUNDED** Individuals.
**SAMPLE GRANTS Previous beneficiaries have included:** Action on Addiction, BID, Chase Children's Hospice, Clatterbridge Cancer Research, Clod Ensemble, Comic Relief, Depaul Trust, Fairley House, Give Youth a Break, Halton Autistic Family Support Group, Hope HIV, Infertility Network, George Martin Music Foundation, Royal Academy of Dance, St Joseph's Family Centre, Strongbones Children's Charitable Trust, Walk the Walk, Winchester Visitors Group and Wirral Holistic Care Services.
**FINANCES** *Year* 2013/14 *Income* £141,046 *Grants* £128,779 *Grants to organisations* £126,547 *Assets* £1,830,771
**TRUSTEES** Andrew Blenkinsop; Sarah Blenkinsop; Charlotte Blenkinsop; Frances Stormer; Haidee Millin.
**OTHER INFORMATION** Brief accounts available at the Charity Commission. Grants of £2,200 were given to ex-employees of Ward Blenkinsop and Co.
**HOW TO APPLY** Apply in writing to the correspondent.
**WHO TO APPLY TO** Charlotte Blenkinsop, Trustee, PO Box 28840, London SW13 0WZ *Tel.* 020 8878 9975

## ■ The Barbara Ward Children's Foundation

**CC NO** 1089783  **ESTABLISHED** 2001
**WHERE FUNDING CAN BE GIVEN** Mainly UK, some overseas.
**WHO CAN BENEFIT** Registered charities and other institutions.
**WHAT IS FUNDED** Grants are awarded to organisations serving children who are disadvantaged in some respect. Purposes that have previously been funded include: educational projects; holidays; support, care and respite; health and well-being; sport, play and leisure. Grants may also be given to charities supporting adults with learning disabilities.
**WHAT IS NOT FUNDED** Religious charities.
**TYPE OF GRANT** Grants given range from one-off donations to project-related grants that run for two to five years.
**RANGE OF GRANTS** £500–£35,000
**SAMPLE GRANTS** Small Steps (£30,000); WellChild (£26,000); Ambitious about Autism (£15,000); Readwell – Read for Good and Charlton Park School Fund (£10,000 each); Oasis Children's Venture (£9,000); Arts for All (£6,500); CHICKS and Youth Adventure Trust (£5,000 each); Norfolk Carers Support (£4,000); Lincoln College Vacation Project (£3,500); Down Syndrome Training and Support (£1,200); Leyton Sailing Trust and Tall Ships Youth Trust (£600 each).
**FINANCES** Year 2014 Income £519,276 Grants £507,312 Grants to organisations £507,312 Assets £9,646,865
**TRUSTEES** Barbara Ward, Chair; David Bailey; John Banks; Alan Gardner; Kenneth Parker; Brian Walters; Christopher Brown.
**OTHER INFORMATION** Grants were made to 67 organisations in 2014.
**HOW TO APPLY** Apply in writing to the correspondent detailing the purpose for which the grant is requested and including latest annual report and set of audited financial statements. Beneficiaries or applicants may be visited by trustees, who usually meet quarterly to review and award grants. The foundation prefers to make grants to 'financially healthy children's charities where funding is not forthcoming from statutory bodies, where incomes and fund balances are constantly put to good use and where administration overheads are kept to a minimum'.
**WHO TO APPLY TO** Christopher Banks, Trustee, 85 Fleet Street, London EC4 1AE *Tel.* 020 7222 7040 *Fax* 020 7222 6208 *email* info@bwcf.org.uk *Website* www.bwcf.org.uk

## ■ The Waterloo Foundation

**CC NO** 1117535  **ESTABLISHED** 2007
**WHERE FUNDING CAN BE GIVEN** UK, with a preference for Wales, and overseas.
**WHO CAN BENEFIT** Organisations with a charitable purpose, working on childhood development, in financially developing countries, in the field of the environment, and on projects in Wales.
**WHAT IS FUNDED** The foundation gives grants to projects that help globally, particularly focusing on disparity of wealth and opportunity, as well as the unsustainable use of natural resources. The foundation has four grants programmes: world development; the environment; child development; Wales. Potential applicants are encouraged to check the foundation's website for information on the foundation's current priorities within each of these programmes.
**WHAT IS NOT FUNDED** Individuals; the promotion of political or religious causes; general appeals or circulars. Each of the grant programmes has specific criteria and exclusions which can be found on the foundation's website.
**TYPE OF GRANT** Project costs; core costs; salaries; capital costs; one-off and recurrent grants; start-up funding; initial stages as well as ongoing funding.
**RANGE OF GRANTS** Up to £100,000.
**FINANCES** Year 2013 Income £11,534,383 Grants £7,146,135 Grants to organisations £7,146,135 Assets £110,542,782
**TRUSTEES** Heather Stevens; David Stevens; Janet Alexander; Caroline Oakes.
**OTHER INFORMATION** Detailed information about previous beneficiaries is available on the foundation's website. In 2013, 270 grants were made.
**HOW TO APPLY** Application guidelines, criteria and deadlines for each of the grants programmes are available on the foundation's website, which potential applicants are encouraged check before making an application. Applications are welcomed from organisations with a clear charitable purpose. There is no application form and all applications should be submitted by email to applications@waterloofoundation.org.uk. Details of what should be included in the application are specific to each grant programme and can be found on the foundation's website. All applications are reviewed at a first assessment stage, after which ineligible applicants will be informed, while those which are deemed to best meet the foundation's criteria will be contacted by the relevant Fund Manager for further information.
**WHO TO APPLY TO** Janice Matthews, Finance Manager, c/o 46–48 Cardiff Road, Llandaff, Cardiff CF5 2DT *Tel.* 029 2083 8980 *email* info@waterloofoundation.org.uk *Website* www.waterloofoundation.org.uk

## ■ G. R. Waters Charitable Trust 2000

**CC NO** 1091525  **ESTABLISHED** 2000
**WHERE FUNDING CAN BE GIVEN** UK, also North and Central America.
**WHO CAN BENEFIT** Registered charities.
**WHAT IS FUNDED** General charitable purposes.
**TYPE OF GRANT** One-off and recurrent.
**RANGE OF GRANTS** £100–£50,000
**SAMPLE GRANTS** Mandeville School (£50,000); Dream Holidays, React (£10,000 each); ABF The Soldiers' Charity (£5,000); Cancer Vaccine Institute, Derby Toc H Children's Camp, Wessex Children's Hospital Trust, Young Minds (£5,000 each); The Smile Train (£1,000); Turf Club Staff Fund (£500); Loosen Up (£17).
**FINANCES** Year 2013/14 Income £124,542 Grants £96,517 Grants to organisations £96,517 Assets £1,691,546
**TRUSTEES** M. Fenwick; C. Organ.
**OTHER INFORMATION** This trust was registered with the Charity Commission in 2002, replacing Roger Waters 1989 Charitable Trust (Charity Commission number 328574), which transferred its assets to this new trust. (The 2000 in the title refers to when the declaration of trust was made.) Like the former trust, it receives a share of the Pink Floyd's royalties as part of its annual income. It has general

charitable purposes throughout the UK, as well as North and Central America.
**HOW TO APPLY** Apply in writing to the correspondent.
**WHO TO APPLY TO** Michael Lewis, Howard Kennedy LLP, No. 1 London Bridge, London SE1 9BG *Tel.* 020 7344 7676

■ **Wates Family Enterprise Trust**
**CC NO** 1126007    **ESTABLISHED** 2008
**WHERE FUNDING CAN BE GIVEN** UK.
**WHO CAN BENEFIT** Registered charities; schools; universities; social enterprises.
**WHAT IS FUNDED** Education; employment and training; community projects.
**RANGE OF GRANTS** £5,000–£64,000
**SAMPLE GRANTS** Business Class 4 (£64,000); Royal Institute off British Architects (£55,500); Campaign for Youth Social Action (£40,000); Dollywood Imagination Library (£25,000); Barlow Moor Community Centre (£20,000); Walsall Enterprise Hub (£16,000); Institute for Family Business Research Foundation (£15,000); Reform (£10,000); Surrey Fire and Rescue Service (£7,500); Shackleford Cricket Club (£5,000).
**FINANCES** *Year* 2013 *Income* £1,317,759 *Grants* £660,619 *Grants to organisations* £660,619 *Assets* £196,422
**TRUSTEES** Andrew Wates, Chair; James Wates; Paul Wates; Tim Wates; Andy Wates; Michael Wates; Charles Wates; Jonathan Wates.
**OTHER INFORMATION** The trust is the vehicle for the philanthropic and charitable activities of the Wates family, owners of the Wates Group.
**HOW TO APPLY** Unsolicited applications are not considered.
**WHO TO APPLY TO** Brian Wheelwright, Director, Wates House, Station Approach, Leatherhead, Surrey KT22 7SW *Tel.* 01372 861373 *email* director@watesfoundation.org.uk *Website* watesgiving.org.uk

■ **The Wates Foundation**
**CC NO** 247941    **ESTABLISHED** 1966
**WHERE FUNDING CAN BE GIVEN** Berkshire; Bristol, Avon and Somerset; Buckinghamshire; Dorset; Gloucestershire; Middlesex; Nottinghamshire; Oxfordshire; Surrey; Sussex and the Greater London Metropolitan Area as defined by the M25 motorway.
**WHO CAN BENEFIT** Projects with charitable status. Practical projects involving people are preferred especially those benefitting young and disadvantaged people.
**WHAT IS FUNDED** The foundation currently awards grants under the following programmes: building social values; community health; safer communities; life transitions; strengthening the charitable and voluntary sector; education and employment.
**TYPE OF GRANT** Grants may be one-off and for salaries, although buildings, capital, project, research, start-up, core, running and recurring costs will also be considered. Grants are paid over between one and four years.
**RANGE OF GRANTS** Normally up to £50,000.
**SAMPLE GRANTS** Cranfield Trust (£30,000); Arts at the Old Fire Station – Oxford, St Mark's Hospital – London, Irene Taylor Trust – Music in Prisons (£20,000 each); Sulgrave Youth Club – London (£15,800); HALOW – Surrey (£10,000); Royal Philharmonic Orchestra (£8,400); Baale Mane – India (£5,000); St Mary's Nursing Home – Chiswick (£3,000); UK Youth (£2,000); Islington Refugee and Migrant Centre – London, St Matthew's Church, Croydon (£1,000 each).
**FINANCES** *Year* 2013/14 *Income* £392,005 *Grants* £775,601 *Grants to organisations* £775,601 *Assets* £16,481,182
**TRUSTEES** Richard Wates; Kate Minch; William Wates; Jonathan Heynes; Claire Spotwood-Brown; Christopher Wates.
**OTHER INFORMATION** The foundation regularly reviews its activities and programmes – check the foundation's website for current information.
**HOW TO APPLY** Following a review of its grant-making policy in 2011, the Wates Foundation decided to take a new proactive grant-making strategy. 'Wates Family members seek out charities to support, often from within their local community. **Applications are by invitation only. Unsolicited applications will be automatically rejected.**' Check the foundation's website for updates.
**WHO TO APPLY TO** Brian Wheelwright, Director, Wates House, Station Approach, Leatherhead, Surrey KT22 7SW *Tel.* 01372 861000 *Fax* 01372 861252 *email* director@watesfoundation.org.uk *Website* www.watesfoundation.org.uk

■ **Blyth Watson Charitable Trust**
**CC NO** 1071390    **ESTABLISHED** 1997
**WHERE FUNDING CAN BE GIVEN** UK.
**WHO CAN BENEFIT** Charitable organisations.
**WHAT IS FUNDED** The trust dedicates its grant-giving policy in the areas of humanitarian causes based in the UK, and other general charitable purposes.
**TYPE OF GRANT** Mainly one-off; some recurrent; occasional loans.
**RANGE OF GRANTS** £1,000–£5,000
**SAMPLE GRANTS** St-Martin-in-the-Fields Endowment Fund (£10,000 in two grants); Society for the Relief of Distress (£10,000 in two grants); Trinity Hospice (£6,000 in two grants); Bread and Water for Africa (£5,000 in two grants); Cystic Fibrosis and Royal Academy of Music (£3,000 each); UCL Development Fund and Comitato Fiori di Lavanda Onlus (£2,000 each); Cats Protection League and CLIC Sargent (£1,000).
**FINANCES** *Year* 2012/13 *Income* £108,784 *Grants* £67,500 *Grants to organisations* £67,500 *Assets* £3,543,952
**TRUSTEES** Nicholas Brown; Ian McCulloch.
**OTHER INFORMATION** Grants were made to 26 organisations in 2012/13. This was the latest information available at the time of writing (June 2015).
**HOW TO APPLY** Apply in writing to the correspondent. Trustees usually meet twice each year, usually in June and December.
**WHO TO APPLY TO** The Trustees, c/o Bircham Dyson Bell Solicitors, 50 Broadway, Westminster, London SW1H 0BL *Tel.* 020 7227 7000

■ **John Watson's Trust**
**SC NO** SC014004    **ESTABLISHED** 1984
**WHERE FUNDING CAN BE GIVEN** Scotland, with a strong preference for Lothian.
**WHO CAN BENEFIT** Individuals; charitable organisations; ad hoc groups; research bodies. Beneficiaries must be children or young people under 21 years of age, with a physical or learning disability, or who are socially disadvantaged.
**WHAT IS FUNDED** Grants for educational purposes are made for children and young people under the age of 21 with a physical or learning disability or

who are socially disadvantaged. Grants may be made directly to individuals for purposes, such as private tuition, educational travel costs, or equipment. Funding may be given for boarding fees in some circumstances. Grants are also made to organisations to provide educational projects, outings or research benefitting eligible children and young people.

**WHAT IS NOT FUNDED** General appeals; general running costs; salaries.

**TYPE OF GRANT** Equipment; small capital expenditure; tuition; student support; personal equipment (such as special wheelchairs, special typewriters); projects; activities, including travel. One year only, but can be extended.

**RANGE OF GRANTS** Up to £5,000.

**SAMPLE GRANTS** Previous beneficiaries have included: Dunedin School (£5,000); Lothian Special Olympics (£3,500); Craigroyston High School, Nancy Ovens Trust and Scouts Scotland (£2,000 each); Gracemount Primary School and Multicultural Family Base (£1,500 each); and Cosgrove Care, Ferryhill Primary School and Sleep Scotland (£1,000 each).

**FINANCES** Year 2013 Income £190,816 Grants £170,000 Grants to organisations £170,000

**TRUSTEES** Six representatives of the Society of Writers to Her Majesty's Signet; two nominated by the City of Edinburgh Council; one nominated by the Lothian Association of Youth Clubs; one nominated by the Merchant Company Education Board; one co-opted trustee.

**PUBLICATIONS** Background notes and application forms available.

**OTHER INFORMATION** The trust had an expenditure of £205,000 in 2013. No further information was available and so grant total has been estimated.

**HOW TO APPLY** Applications should be made on forms available to download, together with criteria and guidelines, on the trust's website. Queries about applications should be directed to the trust's administrator.

**WHO TO APPLY TO** Laura Campbell, Correspondent, The Signet Library, Parliament Square, Edinburgh EH1 1RF Tel. 0131 225 0658 email lcampbell@wssociety.co.uk Website www.wssociety.co.uk

■ **Waynflete Charitable Trust**

**CC NO** 1068892　　**ESTABLISHED** 1998

**WHERE FUNDING CAN BE GIVEN** UK, with a preference for Lincolnshire.

**WHO CAN BENEFIT** Lincolnshire-based charities and organisations; national charities and organisations where Lincolnshire residents are involved and new individual initiatives.

**WHAT IS FUNDED** General charitable purposes, with particular interest in supporting local charitable organisations in the training of volunteers and staff, running costs or new projects, as well as rural projects which maintain and enhance the local landscape and ecology.

**TYPE OF GRANT** Core costs; capital costs; project costs; staff costs.

**SAMPLE GRANTS** Previous beneficiaries have included: Lincolnshire Blind Society (£6,000); Canine Partners, Lincolnshire and Nottinghamshire Air Ambulance and the Order of St John (£4,000 each); Deaf Blind (£2,500); Action for Kids, Gurka Welfare Trust and Marine Conservation Society (£1,000); Braille Chess Association, Children's Safety Education Foundation and Royal National Lifeboat Fund (£500 each); and Mouth and Foot Painting Artists (£100).

**FINANCES** Year 2014 Income £1,136,125 Grants £247,065 Grants to organisations £247,065 Assets £2,949,749

**TRUSTEES** Michael Worth; Graham Scrimshaw.

**OTHER INFORMATION** Grants were made to 208 organisations in 2014.

**HOW TO APPLY** Applications can be made in writing to the correspondent, or through contact with one of the trust's local Community Champions. Criteria are available to view on the trust's website.

**WHO TO APPLY TO** Michael Worth, Chair, PO Box 9686, Grantham, Lincolnshire NG31 0FJ Tel. 01400 250210 email info@waynfletecharity.com Website www.waynfletecharity.com

■ **Weatherley Charitable Trust**

**CC NO** 1079267　　**ESTABLISHED** 1999

**WHERE FUNDING CAN BE GIVEN** UK.

**WHO CAN BENEFIT** Individuals and organisations.

**WHAT IS FUNDED** General charitable purposes, particularly research into mental and physical illness.

**SAMPLE GRANTS** Details were not available.

**FINANCES** Year 2014 Income £0 Grants £70,000 Grants to organisations £70,000

**TRUSTEES** Christine Weatherley; Richard Weatherley; Neil Weatherley

**OTHER INFORMATION** In 2014 there had been no income for the past four years, suggesting the trust may be spending out. Accounts were not published due to the low income of the trust. Grants were estimated based on the trust's expenditure of £82,000.

**HOW TO APPLY** This trust does not accept unsolicited applications.

**WHO TO APPLY TO** Christine Weatherley, Trustee, Northampton Science Park Ltd, Newton House, Kings Park Road Moulton Park, Northampton NN3 6LG Tel. 01604 821841

■ **The Weavers' Company Benevolent Fund**

**CC NO** 266189　　**ESTABLISHED** 1973

**WHERE FUNDING CAN BE GIVEN** UK.

**WHO CAN BENEFIT** Registered charities; preference to small, community-based groups, rather than larger, established charities. 'To be eligible for funding, local organisations such as those working in a village, estate or small town should normally have an income of less than about £100,000. Those working across the UK should normally have an income of not more than about £250,000.'

**WHAT IS FUNDED** Supporting work with: disadvantaged young people; offenders and ex-offenders, particularly those under 30 years of age. The charity notes: 'We like to encourage new ideas and to fund projects that could inspire similar work in other areas of the country.' Smaller casual grants are also given for general charitable purposes.

**WHAT IS NOT FUNDED** Long-term support; general appeals; sponsorship, marketing or other fundraising activities; endowment funds, bursaries or long-term capital projects; grant-giving charities; retrospective funding for work that has been completed or will be completed while the application is being considered; replacement of statutory funding; building projects (but help may be given for the cost of equipment or furnishings); capital projects to provide access in compliance with the Disability Discrimination Act; personal appeals from individuals; umbrella bodies or large, established organisations; projects in which the charity is collaborating or working in partnership with umbrella bodies or large, established organisations; organisations outside the UK and overseas expeditions or travel; work with children under five years of age; universities or colleges; medical charities or those involved in medical care; organisations of and for people with disabilities; environmental projects; work in promotion of religious or political causes. Applicants must be registered charities, in the process of registering, or qualified as charitable.

**TYPE OF GRANT** Grants may be awarded for up to three years. The trust particularly welcomes applications for pump-priming grants from small community-based organisations where a grant would form a major element of the funding. It prefers to support projects where the charity's grant will be used for an identified purpose. Applications for core funding will be considered, such as general administration and training that enable an organisation to develop and maintain expertise. The trust appreciates the importance of providing ongoing funding for successful projects, which have 'proved their worth'. In exceptional circumstances, the trust may provide emergency or deficit funding for an established organisation. Applicants most likely to be granted emergency funding are charities which the company knows or has previously supported.

**RANGE OF GRANTS** Usually up to £15,000, but applications for smaller amounts are welcomed.

**SAMPLE GRANTS** The Clink Restaurant (£15,000); The Bounce Back Foundation (£12,500); Fine Cell Work, Junction Community Trust and Suited and Booted (£10,000 each); Christchurch Community Project (£9,000); PhotoVoice (£5,000); Prison Reform Trust (£4,000); Globe Community Project and Guildhall School of Music and Drama (£3,000 each); Lord Mayor's Appeal (£2,000); Wickwar Youth Club (£500); Gate Posts Trust and the Octagon Theatre (£250); Channel Swim Relay for Diabetes (£100).

**FINANCES** Year 2013/14 Income £540,579 Grants £562,380 Grants to organisations £562,380 Assets £11,288,902

**TRUSTEE** The Worshipful Company of Weavers.

**OTHER INFORMATION** The grant total includes: major grants totalling £542,500, given to meet the fund's main criteria; smaller casual grants totalling £20,000, which may fall outside the main criteria but are considered to merit a donation by the trustees. Not included in the grant total are grants from the Millennial Fund, which is designated specifically for work with primary schools in areas of social deprivation and family breakdown.

**HOW TO APPLY** Detailed *Guidelines for Applicants* are available from the Weaver's Company website. Application forms can be downloaded from the fund's website, or obtained by post or e-mail. Where possible, applicants will be notified within two weeks whether their initial application has been accepted for further consideration. The grants committee meets in February, June and October of each year. Deadlines are detailed on the website, applications should be received at least ten weeks prior to the meetings. The Charities Officer is happy to answer specific queries about applications.

**WHO TO APPLY TO** Anne Howe, Charities Officer, The Weavers Company, Saddlers' House, Gutter Lane, London EC2V 6BR *Tel.* 020 7606 1155 *Fax* 020 7606 1119 *email* charity@weavers.org.uk *Website* www.weavers.org.uk

## ■ Webb Memorial Trust

**CC NO** 313760     **ESTABLISHED** 1944
**WHERE FUNDING CAN BE GIVEN** Mainly UK.
**WHO CAN BENEFIT** Universities; research bodies; other organisations.
**WHAT IS FUNDED** The trust is set up with the aims of the advancement of education and learning with respect to the history and problem of government and social policy (including socialism, trade unionism and co-operation) in Great Britain and elsewhere by: research; lectures, scholarships and educational grants; such other educational means as the trustees may from time to time approve. Although most of the trust's funding resources (85%) are committed to a designated programme concentrating on poverty and inequality in the UK, applications for grants outside that programme, but focusing on the same issues and reflecting the trust's aims, are considered for the remaining funds (15%).
**WHAT IS NOT FUNDED** Direct party political purposes; individuals, including students.
**RANGE OF GRANTS** £1,000–£100,000
**SAMPLE GRANTS** Centris (£102,500); New Statesman (£29,000); Children North East (£28,000); YouGov (£10,600); TCPA (£9,800); University of Birmingham (£8,500); Compass (£8,400); Edge Hill University (£7,500); Michael Ward Consulting Ltd (£6,600); Teesside University (£4,600); All Party Political Group on Poverty (£4,400); Essay Competition Prizes (£1,500).
**FINANCES** Year 2013/14 Income £32,603 Grants £221,473 Grants to organisations £221,473 Assets £1,154,136
**TRUSTEES** Richard Rawes, Chair; Mike Parker; Richard Fries; Kate Green; Robert Lloyd-Davies; Baroness Dianne Hayter; Mike Gapes; Chris White; Lord John Shipley.
**OTHER INFORMATION** The Webb Memorial Trust was established as a memorial to the socialist pioneer Beatrice Webb. In 2011 the trustees decided to spend down the remaining resources using at least 85% of the budget for a co-ordinated programme leaving a legacy worthy of Beatrice Webb. As such most of its funding resources are committed to a structured programme that will concentrate on the issues of poverty and inequality on the UK. Funding applications outside these programmes may be considered if they reflect the original aims and ambitions of the Webbs.
**HOW TO APPLY** Apply via the online form on the trust's website. Applications by post or email will not be accepted. The trustees meet three to four times a year.
**WHO TO APPLY TO** Mike Parker, Secretary, Crane House, Unit 19 Apex Business Village, Annitsford, Newcastle NE23 7BF *Tel.* 0191 250 1969 *email* webb@cranehouse.eu *Website* www.webbmemorialtrust.org.uk

## ■ The David Webster Charitable Trust
**CC NO** 1055111  **ESTABLISHED** 1995
**WHERE FUNDING CAN BE GIVEN** UK.
**WHO CAN BENEFIT** Charitable organisations.
**WHAT IS FUNDED** General charitable purposes, mainly ecological and broadly environmental projects.
**RANGE OF GRANTS** £500–£100,000
**SAMPLE GRANTS** Bird Life International (£100,000); National Trust Knole Project and South Georgia Heritage Trust (£25,000 each); Bury St Edmund's Heritage Trust and Future Trees Trust (£10,000 each); Bird Life International Canada Delegates (£5,500); National Churches Trust, The National Trust Neptune and Coastline Campaign (£5,000 each); CPRE Norfolk Footpath Campaign and The Merchants House Marlborough (£3,000); Bat Conservation Trust and Norfolk Wherry Trust (£2,000 each).
**FINANCES** Year 2012/13 Income £195,108 Grants £206,100 Grants to organisations £206,100 Assets £3,498,162
**TRUSTEES** Thomas Webster; Nikola Thompson.
**OTHER INFORMATION** Grants were made to 15 organisations in 2012/13. This was the latest information available at the time of writing (June 2015).
**HOW TO APPLY** Apply in writing to the correspondent.
**WHO TO APPLY TO** Nikola Thompson, Trustee, Marshalls, Marshalls Lane, High Cross, Ware, Hertfordshire SG11 1AJ Tel. 01920 462001

## ■ The William Webster Charitable Trust
**CC NO** 259848  **ESTABLISHED** 1969
**WHERE FUNDING CAN BE GIVEN** North East England, principally Northumberland, Tyne and Wear, Durham and Cleveland.
**WHO CAN BENEFIT** Registered charitable organisations in the north east of England.
**WHAT IS FUNDED** General charitable purposes.
**WHAT IS NOT FUNDED** Individuals; non-charitable organisations; core/running costs; salaries.
**TYPE OF GRANT** One-off only, for capital projects.
**RANGE OF GRANTS** £500–£3,000
**SAMPLE GRANTS** Derwenthaugh Boat Station and Hartlepool and District Hospice (£3,000 each); Boys' Brigade – Broomley Grange (£2,500) St Cuthbert's Catholic Church Durham (£2,000); Newcastle Society for Blind People (£1,500); Beanstalk, South Tyneside Football Trust and Tyne and Wear Autistic Society (£1,000 each); Hartlepool Ukulele Group and Heartbeat (£500 each).
**FINANCES** Year 2013/14 Income £86,176 Grants £73,000 Grants to organisations £73,000 Assets £2,309,777
**TRUSTEE** Barclays Bank Trust Company Ltd.
**OTHER INFORMATION** Grants were awarded to 40 organisations in 2013/14.
**HOW TO APPLY** Apply in writing to the correspondent. Applications should include details of the costings of capital projects, of funding already raised, a set of the latest annual accounts and details of the current charity registration. The trustees meet four times each year to approve grants.
**WHO TO APPLY TO** The Trustees, c/o Barclays Bank Trust Co. Ltd, Osborne Court, Gadbrook Park, Rudheath, Cheshire CW9 7UE Tel. 01606 313179

## ■ The Weinstein Foundation
**CC NO** 277779  **ESTABLISHED** 1979
**WHERE FUNDING CAN BE GIVEN** Worldwide.
**WHO CAN BENEFIT** Registered charities.
**WHAT IS FUNDED** General charitable purposes, particularly Jewish causes, medical and welfare causes.
**WHAT IS NOT FUNDED** Individuals.
**TYPE OF GRANT** Recurrent.
**RANGE OF GRANTS** Up to £20,000.
**SAMPLE GRANTS Previous beneficiaries have included:** Chevras Evas Nitzrochim Trust; Friends of Mir; SOFT UK; Chesed Charitable Trust; and Youth Aliyah.
**FINANCES** Year 2013/14 Income £54,143 Grants £67,810 Grants to organisations £67,810 Assets £1,707,762
**TRUSTEES** Stella Weinstein; Michael Weinstein; Philip Weinstein; Lea Anne Newman.
**HOW TO APPLY** Apply in writing to the correspondent.
**WHO TO APPLY TO** Michael Weinstein, Trustee, 32 Fairholme Gardens, Finchley, London N3 3EB Tel. 020 8346 1257 email charity.correspondence@bdo.co.uk

## ■ The James Weir Foundation
**CC NO** 251764  **ESTABLISHED** 1967
**WHERE FUNDING CAN BE GIVEN** UK, with a preference for Ayrshire and Glasgow.
**WHO CAN BENEFIT** Registered charities in the UK, mainly Scottish charities.
**WHAT IS FUNDED** The foundation has general charitable purposes, giving priority to Scottish organisations, especially local charities in Ayrshire and Glasgow.
**WHAT IS NOT FUNDED** Individuals.
**TYPE OF GRANT** One-off and recurrent; capital and core costs.
**RANGE OF GRANTS** Mostly £1,000–£3,000.
**SAMPLE GRANTS** Bag Books, British Stammering Association, Princess Royal Trust for Carers Scotland, Raleigh International and Spinal Injuries Association, Ro-Ro Sailing Project (£3,000 each); Fishing For Heroes, Leuchie House, Survivors of Bereavement by Suicide (£2,000); American Museum in Britain and Mobility Trust (£1,000).
**FINANCES** Year 2013 Income £244,710 Grants £189,000 Grants to organisations £189,000 Assets £7,560,134
**TRUSTEES** Simon Bonham; Elizabeth Bonham; William Ducas.
**OTHER INFORMATION** The following six charities are listed in the trust deed as specific beneficiaries and receive regular donations from the foundation: the Royal Society; the British Science Association; the RAF Benevolent Fund; the Royal College of Surgeons; the Royal College of Physicians; and the University of Strathclyde. Grants were made to 60 additional organisations in 2013.
**HOW TO APPLY** The trust's website states that 'applications should be received by letter with supporting evidence and a copy of the latest annual report. No applications can be received by email. Successful applicants are not able to submit a further application for two years. Unsuccessful applicants will be notified by postcard after the Trustees' meeting has taken place.' Trustees meet twice a year to review applications.
**WHO TO APPLY TO** Louisa Lawson, Secretary, PO Box 72361, London, SW18 9NB, United Kingdom email info@jamesweirfoundation.org Website jamesweirfoundation.org

*Alphabetical register of grant-making charities*  **Welsh**

## ■ The Joir and Kato Weisz Foundation

**CC NO** 1134632  **ESTABLISHED** 2010
**WHERE FUNDING CAN BE GIVEN** Worldwide.
**WHO CAN BENEFIT** Registered charities and individuals.
**WHAT IS FUNDED** General charitable purposes, including Jewish causes.
**RANGE OF GRANTS** Mainly under £10,000.
**SAMPLE GRANTS** Spanish and Portuguese Synagogue (£3,000). A grant of £5,000 was also awarded to one individual.
**FINANCES** *Year* 2012/13 *Income* £25,281 *Grants* £8,000 *Grants to organisations* £3,000 *Assets* £189,282
**TRUSTEES** George Weisz; Gideon Wittenberg; Thomas Kardos.
**OTHER INFORMATION** This was the latest information available at the time of writing (June 2015). The following is taken from the 2012/13 accounts: 'While retaining its general scope, it is intended that the charity will make grants to any individual, group, organisation or institution to provide and assist in the provision of conferences, courses of instruction, exhibitions, lectures and other educational activities.' In 2012/13 the charities income and expenditure was lower than in previous years. The grant total has generally been higher in previous years (£184,000 in 2011/12). Although the foundation makes grants to both organisations and individuals, the amount awarded to either varies with each year.
**HOW TO APPLY** Apply in writing to the correspondent.
**WHO TO APPLY TO** The Trustees, c/o SG Hambros Bank Ltd, Norfolk House, 31 St James's Square, London SW1Y 4JR *Tel.* 020 7597 3000 *email* rachel.iles@sghambros.com

## ■ The Wellcome Trust

**CC NO** 210183  **ESTABLISHED** 1936
**WHERE FUNDING CAN BE GIVEN** UK and overseas.
**WHO CAN BENEFIT** Academic researchers working in health, particularly in the fields of biomedical science, innovations, public engagement, medical humanities and society and ethics.
**WHAT IS FUNDED** The trust is dedicated to improving health, through research and activities in science, humanities, social sciences and public engagement. A wide range of grants are given within the funding areas, which are currently: biomedical science; innovations; public engagement; medical humanities; society and ethics. Grants to individuals are usually given via a university, although small grants for travel or developing public understanding of science may be given directly.
**WHAT IS NOT FUNDED** Specific criteria and exclusions for each funding programme is detailed on the trust's website. However, in general, the trust will not: make grants to other charities where the sole intention is to redistribute the funds; supplement support provided by other funding bodies; award grants to cover expenditure already incurred; consider support for the extension of professional education or experience, nor for the care of patients; fund individuals who are employed by a commercial organisation; fund individuals who are applying for, holding, or employed under a research grant from the tobacco industry.
**TYPE OF GRANT** All types of grant including project grants, programme grants, fellowships, research expenses, travel grants and equipment. Grants may last for more than three years. Check the trust's website for details of each funding programme.
**SAMPLE GRANTS** These figures represent the total amount awarded during the year, and may comprise many grants: University of Oxford (£82.9 million); University of Edinburgh (£35.9 million); King's College London (£25.6 million); Cardiff University (£10.4 million); University of Manchester (£7.3 million); Institute of Cancer Research (£7.1 million); London School of Hygiene and Tropical Medicine (£5.7 million); MRC National Institute for Medical Research (£5.3 million); UK Biobank Ltd (£5 million); Medical Research Council (£4.5 million).
**FINANCES** *Year* 2013/14 *Income* £338,000,000 *Grants* £593,200,000 *Grants to organisations* £593,200,000 *Assets* £16,736,900,000
**TRUSTEES** Sir William Castell; Prof. Dame Kay Davies; Prof. Tobias Bonhoeffer; Prof. Richard Hynes; Baroness Eliza Manningham-Buller; Prof. Peter Rigby; Prof. Anne Johnson; Damon Buffini; Prof. Michael Ferguson; Alan Brown; Prof. Bryan Grenfell.
**PUBLICATIONS** The trust produces various reports and publications, all of which are available from its website.
**OTHER INFORMATION** The Wellcome Trust is one of the world's leading biomedical research charities and is the UK's largest non-governmental source of funds for biomedical research – it is also the UK's largest charity. The trust has a revised strategic plan for 2010–2020. In 2013/14 1044 grants were awarded.
**HOW TO APPLY** The Wellcome Trust is rolling out a new application and grants management system online during 2015, which will eventually replace their previous eGrants system, but at the time of writing (June 2015) the eGrants system is still in operation for certain grants programmes. Applicants must check the trust's website to determine which application system they should use, depending on the grants programme they are applying for. Application forms in Word format are also being replaced. Guidance for each scheme is given on the trust's website, along with deadlines and grant conditions. For further information, applicants may refer to the website or contact the Grants Information Desk, either by emailing gtsupport@wellcome.ac.uk or by telephone.
**WHO TO APPLY TO** Jonathan Best, Grants Operations Manager, Gibbs Building, 215 Euston Road, London NW1 2BE *Tel.* 020 7611 8383 *email* grantenquiries@wellcome.ac.uk *Website* www.wellcome.ac.uk

## ■ Welsh Church Fund – Dyfed area (Carmarthenshire, Ceredigion and Pembrokeshire)

**CC NO** 506583  **ESTABLISHED** 1977
**WHERE FUNDING CAN BE GIVEN** Carmarthenshire, Ceredigion and Pembrokeshire.
**WHO CAN BENEFIT** Individuals; churches; chapels; registered charities.
**WHAT IS FUNDED** Grants are mainly awarded towards the costs of maintaining places of worship. Funding is also given to registered charities which benefit local residents.
**TYPE OF GRANT** One-off and recurrent; project costs; capital costs; core costs.
**RANGE OF GRANTS** Up to £15,000. Average grant around £3,000.

*Have you read* How to use the DGMT *on page xiii?*

**865**

**SAMPLE GRANTS** Carmarthenshire: Ebenezer Baptist Chapel, Gosen Chapel – Llandybie and Penybanc Welfare Association (£3,000 each); Welsh Historic Gardens Trust (£2,900); Engineering Education Scheme Wales (£2,250); and Seren Charity (£1,200). Ceredigion: Capel y Cwm Cwmsychpant (£14,800); Bethel Siliam Baptist Chapel and St Tygwydd Church (£3,300); Musicfest (£2,000); and Small World Theatre (£1,500). Pembrokeshire: Bethseda Baptist Church – Narberth, St David's Church, Clynderwen and St Mary's Church – Haverfordwest (£3,000 each); and St Peter's Church – Goodwick (£2,600).
**FINANCES** Year 2013/14 Income £73,853 Grants £142,560 Grants to organisations £142,560 Assets £5,831,659
**TRUSTEE** Selected members of Carmarthenshire, Ceredigion and Pembrokeshire County Councils.
**OTHER INFORMATION** A total of 47 grants were made across the three counties.
**HOW TO APPLY** Apply in writing to the correspondent.
**WHO TO APPLY TO** Anthony Parnell, Resources Department, Carmarthenshire County Council, County Hall, Carmarthen, Dyfed SA31 1JP Tel. 01267 224180 email communitybureau@carmarthenshire.gov.uk Website www.carmarthenshire.gov.uk

## ■ The Welton Foundation
**CC NO** 245319   **ESTABLISHED** 1965
**WHERE FUNDING CAN BE GIVEN** UK and overseas.
**WHO CAN BENEFIT** Registered charities and organisations with a charitable purpose.
**WHAT IS FUNDED** Principally supports projects in the health and medical fields. Grants for other general charitable purposes are also considered. In 2013/14 grants were distributed for the following purposes: health and medicine; community development; culture and the arts, disability; education and training.
**WHAT IS NOT FUNDED** Grants only to registered charities and organisations with a charitable purpose.
**TYPE OF GRANT** Some recurrent funding and several small and large donations.
**RANGE OF GRANTS** £500–£500,000
**SAMPLE GRANTS** National Heart and Lung Institute (£505,000); Institute of Child Health at Great Ormond Street Children's Hospital (£500,000); Arnold Foundation for Rugby School (£495,000); Young Epilepsy (£250,000); UCL Cancer Institute (£100,000); Autistica (£10,000); The Birmingham Bach Choir (£7,500); British Association for Adoption and Fostering (£5,000); Launchpad – Reading (£3,600); Jumbulance Trust and National Orchestra for All (£3,000 each); Sparks (£2,000); Milson Parochial Church Council (£1,000); Beds Garden Carers (£500).
**FINANCES** Year 2013/14 Income £159,290 Grants £2,302,283 Grants to organisations £2,302,283 Assets £3,004,404
**TRUSTEES** Sir Hugh Stevenson; D. B. Vaughan; Dr Michael Harding.
**OTHER INFORMATION** Grants were made to 25 organisations.
**HOW TO APPLY** Apply in writing to the correspondent.
**WHO TO APPLY TO** The Trustees, Old Waterfield, Winkfield Road, Ascot, Berkshire SL5 7LJ email hugh.stevenson@oldwaterfield.com

## ■ The Wessex Youth Trust
**CC NO** 1076003   **ESTABLISHED** 1999
**WHERE FUNDING CAN BE GIVEN** Worldwide.
**WHO CAN BENEFIT** Registered charities with which the Earl and Countess have a personal interest; in practice, organisations working with children and young people.
**WHAT IS FUNDED** Grants are given to a wide range of projects providing opportunities and support for children and young people up to the age of 21. Funding is generally given for small specific projects, rather than projects for which a number of other funding sources are available. Some preference is given to applications from 'self-help organisations and to charities requiring support to 'prime the pumps' for development and more extensive fund-raising initiatives'.
**WHAT IS NOT FUNDED** Organisations or groups which are not registered as charities or charitable causes; in response to applications by, or for the benefit of, individuals; by means of sponsorship for individuals undertaking fundraising activities on behalf of any charity; to organisations or groups whose main objects are to fund or support other charitable bodies; generally not to charities whose accounts disclose substantial financial resources and which have well established and ample fundraising capabilities; and to charities with religious objectives, political, industrial or commercial appeal.
**TYPE OF GRANT** One-off grants; capital costs; development expenditure; full project funding.
**SAMPLE GRANTS** Caring for Life; Children's Adventure Farm Trust; CF Dream Holidays; Friends of Castledon School; HopScotch Children's Charity; London Air Ambulance; Orcadia Creative Learning Centre; Perth Autism Support; Reading Mencap; Spitalfields Music; Sports4Life; Teens Unite Fighting Cancer.
**FINANCES** Year 2013/14 Income £132,410 Grants £169,499 Grants to organisations £169,499 Assets £536,907
**TRUSTEES** Robert Clinton; Mark Foster-Brown; Mary Poulton; Richard Parry; Kathryn Cavelle; Francesca Schwarzenbach.
**OTHER INFORMATION** Grants were made to 31 organisations in 2013/14. The accounts stated: the Charity Commission has been supplied with details of amounts given to each charity together with an explanation of the reason for the non-disclosure of individual amounts in the financial statements.
**HOW TO APPLY** Applicants must complete an application form which can be downloaded from the trust's website. Completed forms must be submitted by 1 May or 1 November. All of the requested information must be completed on the form rather than on supplementary documents. Clarity of presentation and provision of financial details are among the qualities which impress the trustees. Successful applicants will receive a letter stating that acceptance of funding is conditional on an update report received within six months. Unsuccessful applicants will receive a letter of notification following the trustees' meeting. The trust cannot enter any further communication with applicants.
**WHO TO APPLY TO** Jenny Cannon, Correspondent, Chelwood, Rectory Road, East Carleton, Norwich NR14 8HT Tel. 01508 571230 email j.cannon@wessexyouthtrust.org.uk Website www.wessexyouthtrust.org.uk

## ■ The West Derby Wastelands Charity

**CC NO** 223623 **ESTABLISHED** 1964

**WHERE FUNDING CAN BE GIVEN** The ancient township of West Derby in Liverpool (a map is available on request).

**WHO CAN BENEFIT** Individuals living within the specified area, or charitable organisations benefitting the community within this area. Beneficiaries include young people, older individuals, those in ill health or in financial difficulties, and a wide range of community based activities.

**WHAT IS FUNDED** The charity's aim is to enhance the lives, health, welfare and general well-being of people in the beneficiary area, particularly for the relief of poverty. Grants are given to both individuals in need and to organisations benefitting the local community.

**WHAT IS NOT FUNDED** The trust has previously stated that grants are not given for 'education or maintenance during education'.

**RANGE OF GRANTS** £200–£5,000

**SAMPLE GRANTS** Fairfield Scout Association and St Christopher's Church (£5,000 each); Bradbury Fields (£3,000); Sandfield Park School (£2,700); Derby Saints FC (£1,650); Gardeners Arms Crown Green Bowling Club and Old Swan Youth Club (£1,500 each); Kensington 26th Girls Brigade (£1,250); Merseyside Police – Safer Schools (£1,000); 1913 Knotty Ash Squadron ATC (£600); Independent Age (£500); St Andrew's Community Network (£400).

**FINANCES** Year 2013 Income £52,984 Grants £42,038 Grants to organisations £39,291 Assets £1,818,760

**TRUSTEES** Joan Driscoll; Barry Flynn; John Kerr; Barbara Kerr; Peter North; Barbara Shacklady; Derek Corlett; Barbara Antrobus; Anthony Heath.

**OTHER INFORMATION** The grant total includes £2,700 given to four individuals. Grants were awarded to 24 organisations.

**HOW TO APPLY** Organisations should apply in writing to the correspondent. For individuals, an application form is available on the charity's website. The trustees prefer that applications by individuals are supported by an independent body, such as social services, and all applications must disclose full details of the income and assets of the individual applicant. Further information is available on the charity's website. The Grants Committee meets prior to the quarterly trustee meetings to recommend the grants to be awarded, which are then approved at the meetings of the full board of trustees.

**WHO TO APPLY TO** Lawrence Downey, Secretary, Ripley House, 56 Freshfield Road, Formby, Liverpool L37 3HW Tel. 01704 879330 email lawrence@westderbywastelands.co.uk Website www.westderbywastelands.co.uk

## ■ The Westcroft Trust

**CC NO** 212931 **ESTABLISHED** 1947

**WHERE FUNDING CAN BE GIVEN** Unrestricted, but with a special interest in Shropshire.

**WHO CAN BENEFIT** Registered charities only.

**WHAT IS FUNDED** Currently the trustees have four main areas of interest: 'conflict resolution and human rights including the material needs of the developing world where such enhances international understanding; religious causes, in particular of social outreach, usually of the Society of Friends (Quakers) but also for those originating in Shropshire; development of the voluntary sector in Shropshire; special needs of those with disabilities, primarily in Shropshire.' Medical aid, education and relief work in financially developing countries are supported but mainly through UK agencies; international disasters may be helped in response to public appeals.

**WHAT IS NOT FUNDED** Individuals or for medical electives; sport; the arts (unless specifically for people with disabilities in Shropshire); armed forces charities; requests for sponsorship. Grants are given to registered charities only. Annual grants are withheld if recent accounts are not available or do not satisfy the trustees as to continuing need.

**TYPE OF GRANT** Single or annual with or without specified time limit; one-off and recurrent; research; running costs; start-up funding. Funding for up to and over three years and capital costs will be considered.

**RANGE OF GRANTS** £250–£4,500

**SAMPLE GRANTS** Previous beneficiaries have included: Northern Friends Peace Board (£3,600); British Epilepsy Association (£3,000); Community Council of Shropshire (£1,500); Institute of Orthopaedics (£1,300); Quaker Bolivia Link (£1,100); Disasters Emergency Committee (£1,000); BuildIT International and Bethseda Leprosy Hospital (£750 each); and Tolerance International and Derwen College (£500 each).

**FINANCES** Year 2013/14 Income £113,325 Grants £103,620 Grants to organisations £103,620 Assets £2,508,655

**TRUSTEES** Mary Cadbury; Richard Cadbury; James Cadbury; Erica Cadbury.

**OTHER INFORMATION** The largest donation in 2013/14 was £10,000 to the Britain Yearly Meeting of the Society of Friends. Although a specific list of beneficiaries was not provided, grants were broken down into the following categories: international understanding and overseas aid (£41,000); Quaker activities (£32,500); disabilities, health and special needs (£14,000); development of community groups (£15,500); conservation (£500).

**HOW TO APPLY** Apply in writing to the correspondent. Applications should consist of no more than two pages of A4, clearly stating the aims of the project and how it meets the trust's objectives, as well as the time scale of the project, any funding received so far, and information about the organisation.

**WHO TO APPLY TO** Martin Beardwell, Clerk, 32 Hampton Road, Oswestry, Shropshire SY11 1SJ email westcroft32@btinternet.com

## ■ The Westminster Foundation

**CC NO** 267618 **ESTABLISHED** 1974

**WHERE FUNDING CAN BE GIVEN** Mainly UK, particularly Westminster, Cheshire West and Chester, Rural Lancashire (near the Forest of Bowland) and North West Sunderland. Outside these areas, grants are made through local Community Foundations.

**WHO CAN BENEFIT** Registered charities.

**WHAT IS FUNDED** Social welfare. The foundation is currently focusing its grant-making on issues around poverty in UK, including supporting communities in need, vulnerable groups, building long term resilience and crisis intervention.

**WHAT IS NOT FUNDED** General appeals or letters requesting non-specific donations; organisations that do not have charitable aims (e.g. commercial companies and companies limited by shares); overtly political projects (including party-political and campaigning projects); individuals (or organisations applying on behalf of an individual); student fees/bursaries; projects taking place or benefitting people outside the UK; projects benefitting people outside the foundation's specific geographical criteria; holidays/trips; projects where the main focus is website development or maintenance; start-up costs; entire salary costs; organisations that have applied unsuccessfully within the previous 12 months.

**TYPE OF GRANT** Small, one-off grants; major grants over more than one year; core costs; rents.

**RANGE OF GRANTS** Small grants up to £5,000; Major grants over £5,000. Average grant size £13,250.

**SAMPLE GRANTS** Grants over £20,000 included: Cardinal Hume Centre (£153,500); Forum Housing Association (£79,500); ABF The Soldiers' Charity (£60,000); Alzheimer's Society (£55,500); Habitat et Humanisme (£50,500); Cheshire Community Foundation and Plantlife International (£50,000 each); Farms for City Children (£47,000); Age UK Cheshire and St Vincent's Family Project (£45,500 each); Medical Detection Dogs (£25,000); Debt Advice Network (£20,500).

**FINANCES** Year 2013 Income £2,628,664 Grants £2,120,169 Grants to organisations £2,120,169 Assets £41,912,736

**TRUSTEES** The Duke of Westminster, Chair; Jeremy Newsum; Mark Loveday; Mark Preston.

**OTHER INFORMATION** A total of 160 grants were awarded in 2013.

**HOW TO APPLY** The foundation advises potential applicants to check their eligibility for a grant according to the information on the website. Organisations must be registered with the Charity Commission, or have exclusively charitable objectives, and be working to benefit people in the areas funded by the foundation. Appeals must fall within the criteria of the foundation's current funding programme. Applications should be made online at the foundation's website, where application guidelines are also available.

**WHO TO APPLY TO** Jane Sandars, Director, 70 Grosvenor Street, London W1K 3JP Tel. 020 7408 0988 Fax 020 7312 6244 email westminster.foundation@grosvenor.com Website www.westminsterfoundation.org.uk

...........................................................

# ■ The Garfield Weston Foundation

**CC NO** 230260 **ESTABLISHED** 1958
**WHERE FUNDING CAN BE GIVEN** UK.
**WHO CAN BENEFIT** UK-registered charities; educational establishments; hospitals; housing associations; churches.
**WHAT IS FUNDED** A broad variety of activities in the fields of education, the arts, health (including research), welfare, environment, youth, religion and community. The website states that 'the trustees are especially keen to see applications for core and project costs for charities delivering services directly to beneficiaries, especially in the welfare, youth and community fields, and also in regions of economic disadvantage'. The foundation gives a range of smaller and larger grants, supporting many different organisations, and regularly reviews its aims, objectives and policies, providing up to date information on their website.

**WHAT IS NOT FUNDED** According to the foundation's guidelines, which can be found on its website, the foundation does not fund the areas indicated here: any funding request made within 12 months of the outcome of a previous application, whether a grant was received or not; UK-registered charities only (unless it holds exempt status as a church, educational establishment, hospital or housing corporation); overseas projects; individual applicants, individual research or study including gap year activities, study trips, fundraising expeditions and sponsorship; animal welfare charities; umbrella organisations, as organisations working with beneficiaries at a grassroots level are preferred; one-off events such as galas or festivals, even if for fundraising purposes; specific salaries and positions; however, core operating costs are supported where general salary costs are recognised; funding commitments over several years – grants made are typically for a single year; and organisations who cannot demonstrate significant progress with fundraising.

**TYPE OF GRANT** Capital costs (including buildings); core costs; one-off; research; recurring and running costs; start-up expenditure. Funding is given by means of a single cash donation. Most grants are for a single year, but may be spread over a number of years if the trustees decide this is appropriate.

**RANGE OF GRANTS** Up to £3 million.

**SAMPLE GRANTS** The Foundation and Friends of The Royal Botanic Gardens Kew (£3 million); Westminster Abbey (£2 million); Auckland Castle Trust (£1 million); The Institute of Cancer Research, National Theatre and University of Buckingham (£500,000 each); Bournemouth University, City YMCA London and OnSide North West (£350,000 each); New Schools Network (£300,000); Ely Cathedral, Toynbee Hall, Teenage Cancer Trust and Welsh National Opera (£250,000 each); Tomorrow's People (£222,000); Alzheimer's Society (£200,000); Royal Shakespeare Company (£150,000); The Sutton Trust (£135,000); Manchester Central Library Development Trust and Prisoners Education Trust (£100,000 each); Aquaculture Stewardship Council (£75,000); RJAH Orthopaedic Hospital (£50,000); Age UK Newcastle, Springhill Hospice, The Reader Organisation and YouthAction Northern Ireland (£30,000 each); Albion Street Church, Ashurst Village Hall, Isabel Hospice and Keep Britain Tidy (£20,000 each); Families in Care, The Door Youth Project and The Makaton Charity (£15,000); Fatima Women's Association, Oxford Homeless Pathways, Phoenix Dance Theatre and Wiltshire Mind (£10,000 each); Community Action Norwich (£7,500); Durham Wildlife Trust, Plymouth Sports Academy and St Mary's Church – Mellor (£5,000 each); East Kent Mencap (£3,000); Yerbury Primary School (£3,500); 9th Dartford Scout Group (£2,500); Circular Arts (£1,500); Muscular Dystrophy Campaign (£500); Sailors' Society (£200).

**FINANCES** Year 2013/14 Income £51,790,000 Grants £54,101,297 Grants to organisations £54,101,297 Assets £10,546,570,000

**TRUSTEES** Guy Weston; Jana Khayat; Camilla Dalglish; Catrina Hobhouse; Eliza Mitchell; Galen Weston; George Weston; Sophia Mason; Melissa Murdoch.

**OTHER INFORMATION** In 2013/14 the trust created the Weston Charter, setting out their grant-making approach and commitment to applicants and beneficiaries, which can be viewed on their website. The foundation made 1,991 grants over the year, 1,576 of which were for £20,000 or under and 415 greater than £20,000.

**HOW TO APPLY** Applications can be made using the foundation's online system or in the post by downloading the application form from the website. The foundation's website states that applications are accepted at any time during the year and that there are no formal deadlines for the submission of applications. Full information on criteria and how to complete an application are given in the foundation's guidelines, available from the website or by request. Organisations are unlikely to be funded if they cannot demonstrate significant progress with fundraising, as the trustees generally expect organisations to have raised the majority of their required funds through local or statutory sources. Applicants should allow approximately 14 weeks for a final outcome but acknowledgement of an application will be received by email immediately or within two weeks by post. Where necessary, applicants may be contacted or visited by a trustee or foundation staff member. For major grants (over £100,000), trustees meet eight times each year, and an initial letter should be sent by post outlining the project, objectives, overall cost, current shortfall and time frames. The trust will then be in contact for further discussion. Refer to the foundation's website for further information.

**WHO TO APPLY TO** Philippa Charles, Director, Weston Centre, 10 Grosvenor Street, London W1K 4QY *Tel.* 020 7399 6565 *email* gdarocha@garfieldweston.org *Website* www.garfieldweston.org

## ■ The Barbara Whatmore Charitable Trust

**CC NO** 283336      **ESTABLISHED** 1981
**WHERE FUNDING CAN BE GIVEN** UK.
**WHO CAN BENEFIT** Charitable organisations.
**WHAT IS FUNDED** The trusts objects lie in the following areas: the arts and music; relief of poverty; cultural and heritage projects, particularly in East Anglia. Eligible areas of support include: classical music education; conservation and crafts training; education projects in museums, the theatre and poetry; conservation of historic artefacts and of the natural heritage environment.
**WHAT IS NOT FUNDED** Repair work to the fabric of buildings or structures; the purchase of medical equipment or works of art; choral societies; individuals; organisations without charitable status.
**TYPE OF GRANT** One-off and recurrent.
**RANGE OF GRANTS** Up to £5,000.
**SAMPLE GRANTS** NMC Recordings; City and Guilds of London Art School (£4,000); National Youth Orchestra (£3,500); Textile Conservation Centre (£3,200); Polka Theatre (£2,500); Dartington International Summer School (£2,400); Foundation for Young Musicians (£2,100); Arcola Theatre, Holst Birthplace Museum and Pond Conservation (£2,000); Welsh National Youth Opera (£1,600); Suffolk Owl Sanctuary (£1,000); Southwark Cathedral (£750); Fry Art Gallery (£500); New Lanark Conservation (£250).
**FINANCES** *Year* 2013/14 *Income* £67,321 *Grants* £69,040 *Grants to organisations* £69,040 *Assets* £1,865,088
**TRUSTEES** David Eldridge; Denis Borrow; Gillian Lewis; Luke Gardiner; Patricia Cooke-Yarborough; Sally Carter; Stephen Bate.

**OTHER INFORMATION** Grants were awarded to 33 organisations in 2013/14.
**HOW TO APPLY** Apply in writing to the correspondent.
**WHO TO APPLY TO** Denise Gardiner, Correspondent, 3 Honeyhanger, Hindhead Road, Hindhead GU26 6BA *email* denise@bwct.org

## ■ The Whitaker Charitable Trust

**CC NO** 234491      **ESTABLISHED** 1964
**WHERE FUNDING CAN BE GIVEN** UK, but mostly East Midlands and Scotland.
**WHO CAN BENEFIT** UK-wide organisations and local organisations (registered charities only).
**WHAT IS FUNDED** The trust has general charitable objects, although with stated preferences in the following fields: local charities in Nottinghamshire and the east Midlands; music; agriculture and silviculture; countryside conservation; Scottish charities.
**WHAT IS NOT FUNDED** Individuals.
**RANGE OF GRANTS** £100–£50,000. Most grants under £5,000.
**SAMPLE GRANTS** Atlantic College (£42,000); School of Artisan Food (£18,000); Nottingham University Hospitals Charity and Royal Forestry Society (£15,000 each); Jasmine Trust, Leith School of Art and Opera Education North (£10,000 each); Alzheimer's Research Institute and Nottinghamshire Coalition of Disabled People (£1,000 each); European Squirrel Initiative and Perth Festival of Arts (£500 each); Help for Heroes (£250).
**FINANCES** *Year* 2013/14 *Income* £177,444 *Grants* £189,350 *Grants to organisations* £189,350 *Assets* £8,019,290
**TRUSTEES** David Price; Edward Perks; Lady Elizabeth Whitaker.
**OTHER INFORMATION** Grants were made to 56 organisations in 2013/14.
**HOW TO APPLY** Apply in writing to the correspondent. The trustees meet regularly to review grant applications.
**WHO TO APPLY TO** The Trustees, c/o Currey and Co., 21 Buckingham Gate, London SW1E 6LS *Tel.* 020 7802 2700

## ■ The Colonel W. H. Whitbread Charitable Trust

**CC NO** 210496      **ESTABLISHED** 1953
**WHERE FUNDING CAN BE GIVEN** UK, with an interest in Gloucestershire.
**WHO CAN BENEFIT** Charitable organisations.
**WHAT IS FUNDED** The promotion of education and in particular: the provision of financial assistance towards the maintenance and development of Aldenham School; the creation of Colonel W H Whitbread scholarships or bursaries or prizes to be awarded to pupils at Aldenham School; charitable organisations within Gloucestershire; the preservation, protection and improvement for the public benefit of places of historic interest and natural beauty. The trustees make charitable distributions on an discretionary basis, having reviewed all applications and considered other charities that they wish to benefit. The trustees will only in exceptional circumstances consider grant applications for purposes which fall outside its stated areas of support.
**RANGE OF GRANTS** £500 and upwards.
**SAMPLE GRANTS** **Previous beneficiaries have included:** 1st Queen's Dragon Guards Regimental Trust, Abbey School Tewkesbury,

# White

Army Benevolent Fund, CLIC Sargent, DEC Tsunami Earthquake Appeal, Friends of Alderman Knights School, Gloucestershire Historic Churches Trust, Great Ormond Street Hospital Children's Charity, Household Cavalry Museum Appeal, Hunt Servants' Fund, Queen Mary's Clothing Guild, Royal Hospital Chelsea and St Richard's Hospice.
**FINANCES** Year 2013/14 Income £160,370 Grants £104,900 Grants to organisations £104,900 Assets £9,248,199
**TRUSTEES** H. F. Whitbread; Jeremy Barkes; Rupert Foley.
**OTHER INFORMATION** Grants were awarded to 23 organisations in 2013/14, but no further information about beneficiaries was available.
**HOW TO APPLY** Apply in writing to the correspondent.
**WHO TO APPLY TO** Susan Smith, Correspondent, Fir Tree Cottage, World's End, Sinton Green Tel. 07812 454321 email whwhitbread.trust@googlemail.com

## ■ The Melanie White Foundation Limited

**CC NO** 1077150    **ESTABLISHED** 1999
**WHERE FUNDING CAN BE GIVEN** UK.
**WHO CAN BENEFIT** Charitable organisations.
**WHAT IS FUNDED** General charitable purposes, particularly health, medicine and social welfare.
**SAMPLE GRANTS** Great Ormond Street Hospital (£235,000); Alfred Dunhill Foundation (£25,000); CLIC Sargent (2 grants totalling £7,200); Marina Dalglish Foundation (£5,000); Bowel and Cancer Research (£2,8000); Millfield Development (£2,000); World Food Programme (£500); Ride for Hope (£300); Laureus Sport for Good Foundation and Meningitis Research (£250 each); Movember (£100).
**FINANCES** Year 2013/14 Income £203,359 Grants £284,293 Grants to organisations £284,293 Assets £11,245,089
**TRUSTEES** Melanie White; Andrew White.
**OTHER INFORMATION** Grants were made to 19 organisations in 2013/14. The foundation supports CLIC Sargent on a recurrent basis.
**HOW TO APPLY** This trust does not accept unsolicited applications as the trustees proactively identify beneficiaries.
**WHO TO APPLY TO** Paula Doraisamy, 61 Grosvenor Street, London W1K 3JE Tel. 020 3011 1041 email melaniewhitefoundation@gmail.com

## ■ White Stuff Foundation

**CC NO** 1134754    **ESTABLISHED** 2010
**WHERE FUNDING CAN BE GIVEN** UK.
**WHO CAN BENEFIT** Registered charities, which are local to a White Stuff shop, office, warehouse or manufacturer.
**WHAT IS FUNDED** Projects supporting disadvantaged children and/or young people.
**WHAT IS NOT FUNDED** Grants are only made to partner charities. According to the website, potential partner charities must be registered charities, supporting disadvantaged children or young people (operating at county or local authority level, rather than nationally or internationally), with an annual income of under £1 million. Potential partners must not be political or religious or conflict with the foundation values.
**SAMPLE GRANTS** The Rathbone Society (£76,000); ID Care Trust (£58,000); Wishes 4 Kids (£21,500); Save the Children – Philippines Appeal (£5,000); Valley Kids (£3,100); Brad's Cancer Foundation (£2,500); Trinity Hospice (£2,400); Child Bereavement UK and Lymington Sailability (£2,300 each); Voice of Young People in Care (£2,200); Wallace and Gromit's Grand Appeal and Into University (£2,100 each).
**FINANCES** Year 2013/14 Income £223,916 Grants £300,942 Grants to organisations £300,942 Assets £143,959
**TRUSTEES** Rebecca Kong; Sean Thomas; Victoria Hodges; Louise McGarr; Jeremy Selgal.
**OTHER INFORMATION** The foundation runs a partnering scheme between White Stuff shops and small charities supporting disadvantaged children and young people. 95 charities received grants in 2013/14. Grants below £2,000 totalled £92,000.
**HOW TO APPLY** Application forms are available to download via the foundation's website. Grants are given only to partner charities and unsolicited requests for funding will not be accepted.
**WHO TO APPLY TO** Sally Crane, Foundation Manager, Canterbury Court, 1–3 Brixton Road, London SW9 6DE Tel. 020 7091 8501 email giving@whitestufffoundation.org Website www.whitestuff.com

## ■ The Whitecourt Charitable Trust

**CC NO** 1000012    **ESTABLISHED** 1990
**WHERE FUNDING CAN BE GIVEN** UK and overseas, with a preference for South Yorkshire.
**WHO CAN BENEFIT** Organisations benefitting Christians.
**WHAT IS FUNDED** General charitable purposes. The trustees prefer to support Christian projects, especially near Sheffield.
**WHAT IS NOT FUNDED** Animal or conservation organisations or for campaigning on social issues.
**TYPE OF GRANT** Recurrent; some one-off; capital costs; start-up costs; project funding.
**RANGE OF GRANTS** £25–£10,000
**SAMPLE GRANTS** Christ Church Fulwood (£7,500); Monkton Combe School Bursary Fund (£5,000); Church Mission Society (£2,200); South Yorkshire Community Foundation (£1,100); UCCF (£1,200); St John's College – Nottingham (£1,000); Send a Cow (£300); Sheffield Royal Society for the Blind (£250); Child Aid and Sheffield Cathedral (£150 each); Crisis at Christmas and National Trust (£100 each); Angel Tree Sheffield and Barnardo's (£50).
**FINANCES** Year 2013/14 Income £72,424 Grants £54,955 Grants to organisations £54,955 Assets £644,789
**TRUSTEES** Peter Lee; Gillian Lee; Martin Lee.
**OTHER INFORMATION** Grants were awarded to 164 organisations in 2013/14.
**HOW TO APPLY** Apply in writing to the correspondent. However, the trustees have previously stated that money available for unsolicited applications is limited, due to advance commitments. Many previous beneficiaries receive repeat grants without re-application.
**WHO TO APPLY TO** Gillian Lee, Trustee, 1 Old Fulwood Road, Sheffield S10 3TG Tel. 0114 230 5555 email pwlee@waitrose.com

## ■ A. H. and B. C. Whiteley Charitable Trust

**CC NO** 1002220 **ESTABLISHED** 1990
**WHERE FUNDING CAN BE GIVEN** England, Scotland and Wales, with a special interest in Nottinghamshire.
**WHO CAN BENEFIT** Registered charities and community groups.
**WHAT IS FUNDED** General charitable purposes, particularly those causes based in Nottinghamshire.
**RANGE OF GRANTS** £1,000–£10,000
**SAMPLE GRANTS** Macmillan Cancer Support and YCR Bradford Cancer Appeal (£10,000 each); HomeStart Mansfield and Southwell Minster (£5,000); Nottingham Churches Holding Fund and University of Liverpool (£3,000 each); Salvation Army (£2,000); St Mary's Church (£1,000).
**FINANCES** Year 2013/14 Income £46,466 Grants £38,950 Grants to organisations £38,950 Assets £984,155
**TRUSTEES** Ted Aspley; Keith Clayton.
**OTHER INFORMATION** Grants were made to eight organisations during the year.
**HOW TO APPLY** The trust does not seek applications.
**WHO TO APPLY TO** Ted Aspley, Trustee, Marchant and Co., Regent Chambers, 2A Regent Street, Mansfield NG18 1SW *Tel.* 01623 655111 *email* edgaspley@tiscali.co.uk

## ■ The Norman Whiteley Trust

**CC NO** 226445 **ESTABLISHED** 1963
**WHERE FUNDING CAN BE GIVEN** Worldwide, although in practice mainly Cumbria and Austria.
**WHO CAN BENEFIT** Organisations benefitting Christians and evangelists.
**WHAT IS FUNDED** Evangelical Christian causes primarily. The trust's objects are to fund activities which further the spread of the Gospel, relieving poverty and assisting with education.
**TYPE OF GRANT** One-off and recurrent; capital and core costs; salaries.
**SAMPLE GRANTS** International Aid Trust (£7,800); Pure Creative Arts (£6,800); Luv Preston and St Thomas Church (£3,000 each); Cross Rhythms and Trinity School (£2,000 each); Bibles for Children (£1,500); Parr Street Church (£1,000); UCCF (£750); James Nicholson (£500).
**FINANCES** Year 2013/14 Income £95,994 Grants £46,834 Grants to organisations £46,834 Assets £2,525,200
**TRUSTEES** Pippa Whiteley; Paul Whiteley; Derek Dickson; Jeremy Ratcliff.
**OTHER INFORMATION** A total of 22 grants were made in 2013/14.
**HOW TO APPLY** Apply in writing to the correspondent.
**WHO TO APPLY TO** Mr D. Foster, Bovil Barn, Newbiggin on Lune, Kirkby Stephen, Cumbria CA17 4NT *email* normanwhiteleytrust@gmail.com

## ■ The Whitley Animal Protection Trust

**CC NO** 236746 **ESTABLISHED** 1964
**WHERE FUNDING CAN BE GIVEN** UK and overseas.
**WHO CAN BENEFIT** Registered charities only.
**WHAT IS FUNDED** Animal welfare; conservation.
**WHAT IS NOT FUNDED** Non-registered charities.
**TYPE OF GRANT** Core and project costs; one-off grants, but usually recurring grants that last for several years.
**RANGE OF GRANTS** Generally £1,000–£20,000, although larger grants are also given.
**SAMPLE GRANTS** Whitley Fund for Nature (£145,000); WILDCRU Wildlife Conservation Research Unit (£25,000); Fauna and Flora International (£15,000); Orangutan Foundation (£7,500); Cuan House Wildlife Rescue Centre, Forum for the Future and Rivers and Fisheries Trust of Scotland (£5,000 each); Songbird Survival (£3,000); National Great Dane Rescue (£2,000); The Wye and Usk Foundation and Welsh Dee Trust (£1,000 each).
**FINANCES** Year 2013 Income £361,111 Grants £287,500 Grants to organisations £287,500 Assets £9,591,769
**TRUSTEES** Edward Whitley; Edward Whitley; Jeremy Whitley; Penelope Whitley.
**OTHER INFORMATION** Grants were made to 22 organisations in 2013.
**HOW TO APPLY** The trust has previously stated that: 'the trust honours existing commitments and initiates new ones through its own contacts rather than responding to unsolicited applications.'
**WHO TO APPLY TO** Michael Gwynne, Correspondent, Padmore House, Hall Court, Hall Park Way, Telford TF3 4LX *Tel.* 01952 641651

## ■ The Lionel Wigram Memorial Trust

**CC NO** 800533 **ESTABLISHED** 1988
**WHERE FUNDING CAN BE GIVEN** UK, with a preference for Greater London.
**WHO CAN BENEFIT** Registered charities and voluntary organisations. The trust favours charities with an income of under £500,000, and those run by volunteers, though special projects by larger charities are occasionally supported.
**WHAT IS FUNDED** General charitable purposes. The trustees 'have particular regard to projects which will commemorate the life of Major Lionel Wigram who was killed in action in Italy in 1944'. The trust makes grants to a wide range of organisations in the UK, especially those providing services or support for people who are blind, deaf or have disabilities, people with ill health, or projects benefitting disadvantaged communities. Charities with original ideas are particularly favoured.
**WHAT IS NOT FUNDED** Individuals; building projects; medical research; charities providing a service outside the UK; charities which do not have a three year record.
**TYPE OF GRANT** One-off and recurrent; core costs; salaries; project costs.
**RANGE OF GRANTS** £50–£8,000. Average grant under £1,000.
**SAMPLE GRANTS** U Can Do IT (£32,000 in four grants); Newbury Spring Festival and PHAB (£1,000 each); Home Start Westminster (£500); Dorset Blind Association, East Sussex Hearing Resource Centre, Keynsham and District Mencap, South Hampshire Lifestyle and Wheelchair Dance Sport Association (£400 each); Mary Have Foundation (£250); and British Red Cross (£100).
**FINANCES** Year 2013/14 Income £81,226 Grants £61,966 Grants to organisations £61,966 Assets £686,941
**TRUSTEES** Antony Wigram; Sally Wigram.

OTHER INFORMATION In 2013/14 a total of 89 grants were awarded to 74 organisations. The trust gives regular support to the charity U Can Do IT.

HOW TO APPLY Applications should be made using the form on the trust's website. Grants are awarded in March. Apart from this the trust does not communicate with applicants. Support is often given to charities where the applicants are known by the trustees.

WHO TO APPLY TO Tracy Pernice PA to A. F. Wigram, Highfield House, 4 Woodfall Street, London SW3 4DJ *Tel.* 020 7730 6820 *email* info@lionelwigrammemorialtrust.org *Website* www.lionelwigrammemorialtrust.org

## ■ The Felicity Wilde Charitable Trust

CC NO 264404    ESTABLISHED 1972
WHERE FUNDING CAN BE GIVEN UK.
WHO CAN BENEFIT Registered charities only.
WHAT IS FUNDED Children's charities and medical research, particularly into asthma.
WHAT IS NOT FUNDED Individuals; non-registered charities.
RANGE OF GRANTS £1,000–£10,000. Most grants are for £1,000.
SAMPLE GRANTS Kings College London – Dept. of Respiratory Medicine and Allergy (£10,000); Sparks (£4,000); Asthma UK (£3,000); Caudwell Children, Claire House Children's Hospice, Lothian Autistic Society, Make a Wish Foundation, The Honeypot Charity, The Anthony Nolan Bone Marrow Trust, The Christie Charitable Fund and The National ME Centre (£1,000 each).
FINANCES *Year* 2013/14 *Income* £52,314 *Grants* £67,000 *Grants to organisations* £67,000 *Assets* £37,316
TRUSTEE Barclays Bank Trust Co Ltd.
OTHER INFORMATION Grants were given to 50 organisations in 2013/14.
HOW TO APPLY Apply in writing to the correspondent at any time. Applications are usually considered quarterly.
WHO TO APPLY TO S. Wakefield, Trustee, Barclays Bank Trust Co. Ltd, Osborne Court, Gadbrook Park, Rudheath, Cheshire CW9 7UE *Tel.* 01606 313206

## ■ The Will Charitable Trust

CC NO 801682    ESTABLISHED 1989
WHERE FUNDING CAN BE GIVEN UK.
WHO CAN BENEFIT UK charities benefitting people with sight loss and the prevention and cure of blindness, services for people suffering from cancer and their families and the provision of residential care for people with learning disabilities.
WHAT IS FUNDED Care of and services for blind people, and the prevention and cure of blindness; care of people with learning disabilities, either in a residential care or supported living environment with a wide choice of activities and lifestyle, or providing long-term day/employment activities; care of and services for people suffering from cancer, and their families.
WHAT IS NOT FUNDED Grants are only given to registered or exempt charities, with proven successful track records or, for newer organisations, convincing evidence of ability. 'It is unlikely that applications relating to academic or research projects will be successful. The trustees recognise the importance of research, but lack the resources and expertise required to judge its relevance and value.' No grants are given to individuals or community interest companies. Applications for core costs or ongoing running costs will be funded only in exceptional circumstances and should be discussed with the grants administrator.
TYPE OF GRANT One-off; project costs; occasionally core costs.
RANGE OF GRANTS £5,000–£20,000.
SAMPLE GRANTS **Previous beneficiaries have included:** Bury Hospice and St David's Foundation Hospice Care (£20,000 each); Cam Sight, L'Arche and CLIC Sargent Care for Children (£15,000 each); Weston Hospice Care and West Northumberland Citizens Advice (£12,000 each) County Durham Society for the Blind and FORCE Cancer Charity (£10,000 each); Mousetrap Theatre Projects and Livability (£8,000 each); Music in Hospitals and Talking Newspaper Association of the UK (£5,000 each).
FINANCES *Year* 2013/14 *Income* £732,152 *Grants* £994,900 *Grants to organisations* £994,900 *Assets* £19,348,878
TRUSTEES Alastair McDonald; Rodney Luff; Vanessa Reburn.
OTHER INFORMATION A list of beneficiaries was not provided in the 2013/14 accounts.
HOW TO APPLY The trust's website provides full information and guidance for applicants. Charities of all sizes will be considered and grants vary in amount but generally fall between £5,000 and £20,000. Grants are normally one-off annual grants and charities are welcome to apply in subsequent years, whether successful or not, but will rarely be funded for four consecutive years. Exceptional larger grants are occasionally awarded to charities that the trust has supported for some time. Applicants are strongly advised to read the grants policy and follow the application guidance provided on the trust's website. There is no application form and applications should be made in writing, including an overview of the organisation, a project description, costs, contingency plan, a timetable, annual accounts and any other relevant information. The trust is happy to discuss applications or answer queries, either by telephone or by email to the Grants Administrator at admin@willcharitabletrust.org.uk. Applications for grants for people with learning disabilities or blind people should be submitted between November and 31 January for decision in April and applications for cancer care should be submitted between June and 31 August for decision in November. Successful applicants will be notified by the end of the month in which the grants decision meeting occurs. The trust regrets that it is not able to notify unsuccessful applicants individually due to the high volume of applications. Applicants are advised to submit their applications as early as possible within the specified window and applications will usually be acknowledged within three weeks. Grant beneficiaries are required to submit an update on their project within a year.
WHO TO APPLY TO Christine Dix, Grants Administrator, Haysmacintyre, 26 Red Lion Square, London WC1R 4AG *email* admin@willcharitabletrust.org.uk *Website* willcharitabletrust.org.uk

## ■ The William Barrow's Charity

**CC NO** 307574     **ESTABLISHED** 1965
**WHERE FUNDING CAN BE GIVEN** The parish of Borden, Kent.
**WHO CAN BENEFIT** Residents of Borden – Kent and organisations aiding such individuals.
**WHAT IS FUNDED** The charity distributes its income equally between the Barrows Eleemosynary Charity and Barrows Educational Foundation. Grants from both funds are awarded to individuals, either for the relief of hardship or for educational purposes. The latter fund also supports local schools, one of which is supported each year in accordance with the trust deed. One other school was also supported in 2014.
**WHAT IS NOT FUNDED** Projects outside the parish of Borden.
**FINANCES** Year 2014 Income £242,354 Grants £124,502 Grants to organisations £51,807 Assets £6,712,081
**TRUSTEES** D. Jordan; P. Aspin; S. C. Batt; P. E. Cole; E. G. Doubleday; C. Ford; J. J. Jefferiss; F. J. Lewis; J. M. Scott; R. Suddick.
**OTHER INFORMATION** The grant total includes grants to individuals totalling almost £72,500. Grants were also given to Borden C. E. Primary School and Borden Grammar School, totalling £52,000.
**HOW TO APPLY** Apply in writing to the correspondent. The trustees meet four times each year.
**WHO TO APPLY TO** c/o George Webb Finn, 43 Park Road, Sittingbourne, Kent ME10 1DX Tel. 01795 470556 email stuart@georgewebbfinn.com

## ■ The Charity of William Williams

**CC NO** 202188     **ESTABLISHED** 1621
**WHERE FUNDING CAN BE GIVEN** The ancient parishes of Blandford, Shaftesbury and Sturminster Newton.
**WHO CAN BENEFIT** Primarily individuals who have lived in the beneficiary area for at least one year; local organisations benefitting people in need, children, young adults, at risk groups and people disadvantaged by poverty or social isolation.
**WHAT IS FUNDED** Welfare and education. Grants are primarily given to individuals, either for the relief of hardship or distress, by funding necessary items, services and facilities, or for educational purposes, mainly for higher education or recognised training schemes. Grants are also given to local organisations which benefit local residents and meet the charity's objectives, such as youth groups, community organisations, schools and welfare charities.
**WHAT IS NOT FUNDED** Grants are not given to organisations whose offices are not based within the beneficiary area or whose work does not benefit residents within this area.
**SAMPLE GRANTS** Equilibrium Youth Work Co. (£40,000); Shaftesbury Bowling Club (£4,000); Panda Pre-School and Youth Trust (£3,000 each); Sturminster Newton Boxing Club (£1,500); Blandford Methodist Church (£1,000).
**FINANCES** Year 2013 Income £306,702 Grants £195,120 Grants to organisations £55,558 Assets £7,917,741
**TRUSTEES** Robert Cowley; Richard Prideaux-Brune; Leo Williams; Carole Sharpe; Richard Gillam; Ray Humphries; Haydn White; Joe Rose.
**OTHER INFORMATION** The grant total includes grants of £139,500 given to individuals and £55,500 to organisations.

**HOW TO APPLY** Organisations should apply in writing to the correspondent, stating the reason for which a grant is requested, as well as providing information on the work of the organisation and its benefit for local residents, which may be in the form of a leaflet. Financial details should also be included and trustees may request the latest audited accounts later in the application process. The trustees meet at least four times each year and applicants will be contacted by the steward or a trustee before the application is reviewed at a trustee meeting. Further information and details of the application processes for individual grants can be found on the charity's website.
**WHO TO APPLY TO** Ian Winsor, Steward, Stafford House, 10 Prince of Wales Road, Dorchester, Dorset DT1 1PW Tel. 01305 264573 email enquiries@williamwilliams.org.uk Website www.williamwilliams.org.uk

## ■ The Kay Williams Charitable Foundation

**CC NO** 1047947     **ESTABLISHED** 1995
**WHERE FUNDING CAN BE GIVEN** UK.
**WHO CAN BENEFIT** Registered charities.
**WHAT IS FUNDED** General charitable purposes including medical research, disability causes and animal welfare.
**SAMPLE GRANTS** Teddington Memorial Hospital (£400); Princess Alice Hospital and Priest's Fund (£250 each); The Lord's Taverners – Mickey's Appeal (£200).
**FINANCES** Year 2013/14 Income £0 Grants £75,000 Grants to organisations £75,000
**TRUSTEES** Richard Cantor; Margaret Williams.
**OTHER INFORMATION** The grant total has been estimated based on grant-making in previous years.
**HOW TO APPLY** Apply in writing to the correspondent.
**WHO TO APPLY TO** Richard Cantor, Trustee, BDO LLP, Kings Wharf, 20–30 Kings Road, Reading, Berkshire RG1 3EX Tel. 0118 925 4400

## ■ The Williams Charitable Trust

**CC NO** 1086668     **ESTABLISHED** 2001
**WHERE FUNDING CAN BE GIVEN** UK.
**WHO CAN BENEFIT** Charitable organisations.
**WHAT IS FUNDED** The objects of the trust are 'to support education and training, the advancement of medicine and general charitable purposes.' It often supports theatre projects.
**TYPE OF GRANT** One-off and recurrent grants.
**RANGE OF GRANTS** £500–£25,000
**SAMPLE GRANTS** Donmar Warehouse and The Old Vic (£25,000 each); Alternative Theatre Co (£10,000); Stage One (£7,500); London Firebird Orchestra (£5,000); British Film Institute (£4,500); Make a Difference Trust (£4,000); Multiple System Atrophy Trust and Norwood Charity (£2,000 each); The British Museum (£1,700).
**FINANCES** Year 2013/14 Income £145,531 Grants £122,491 Grants to organisations £122,491 Assets £3,345,447
**TRUSTEES** Stuart Williams; Hilary Williams; Andrew Williams; Matthew Williams; Keith Percival Eyre-Varnier.
**OTHER INFORMATION** 31 grants were awarded in 2013/14, 14 of which were for £1,000 or less.

**HOW TO APPLY** Apply in writing to the correspondent. 'The trustees adopt a proactive approach in seeking worthy causes requiring support.'
**WHO TO APPLY TO** Stuart Williams, Trustee, Flat 85 Capital Wharf, 50 Wapping High Street, London E1W 1LY

## ■ Williams Serendipity Trust

**CC NO** 1114631         **ESTABLISHED** 2006
**WHERE FUNDING CAN BE GIVEN** UK and overseas, with a preference for London.
**WHO CAN BENEFIT** Charitable organisations.
**WHAT IS FUNDED** General charitable purposes; education; social welfare; arts and culture; young people; people with disabilities; older people.
**RANGE OF GRANTS** £100–£500,000
**SAMPLE GRANTS** Uppingham School (£100,000); YMCA England (£25,000); Care for Children (£15,000); Cambs Community Foundation, Pembroke College – Cambridge and West Coast Crash Wheelchair Rugby (£10,000 each); Contact The Elderly Limited, Ecologia Youth Trust and Archway Project (£5,000 each); Eden Project and The Special Yoga Centre (£2,000 each).
**FINANCES** Year 2013 Income £164,335 Grants £279,151 Grants to organisations £279,151 Assets £259,679
**TRUSTEES** Colin Williams; Alexander Williams; Sophie Williams; Gerlinde Williams.
**OTHER INFORMATION** Grants were given to 33 different charities, including educational organisations and the YMCA.
**HOW TO APPLY** Apply in writing to the correspondent. Trustees' meetings are held at least twice each year.
**WHO TO APPLY TO** The Trustees, c/o 4 The Sanctuary, Westminster, London SW1P 3JS

## ■ The HDH Wills 1965 Charitable Trust

**CC NO** 1117747         **ESTABLISHED** 1965
**WHERE FUNDING CAN BE GIVEN** Mainly UK, occasionally overseas.
**WHO CAN BENEFIT** Registered or recognised charities only.
**WHAT IS FUNDED** General charitable purposes. The trust makes grants from two separate funds – the General Fund and the Martin Wills Fund. The general fund is used to make grants for general charitable purposes, whereas the Martin Wills Fund operates on a seven-year funding priority cycle. In years three and four of this seven year cycle particular favour is given to wildlife conservation projects.
**WHAT IS NOT FUNDED** Individuals; charities which have received a grant in the previous eighteen months. Only registered or recognised charities are supported.
**TYPE OF GRANT** One-off grants. Grants may be made towards revenue, capital or project expenditure.
**RANGE OF GRANTS** Grants from the general fund may be up to £5,000 but are typically £100–£1,000. Grants from the Martin Wills Fund are typically £2,000–£25,000.
**SAMPLE GRANTS** Salzburg Global Seminar (£10,000); Sandford St Martin PCC (£3,000); Sandy Gall's Afghanistan Appeal (£1,250); British Institute of Florence; County Air Ambulance Trust – Walsall, Courtauld Institute of Art, Great Ormond Street Children's Hospital – Isla Cecil Brighter Future Fund, Sandford St Martin Parish Hall, Oxfordshire Historic Churches Trust, and Siblings Together (all £1,000 each).
**FINANCES** Year 2013/14 Income £3,244,376 Grants £899,518 Grants to organisations £899,518 Assets £76,086,187
**TRUSTEES** Dr Catherine Wills; John Carson; Lord Victor Killearn; Liell Francklin; Martin Fiennes; Thomas Nelson.
**OTHER INFORMATION** A total of 116 grants were made from the general fund in 2013/14, 107 of which were for under £1,000. A grant of £818,500 was also made to Magdalen College, Oxford, which benefits once in every seven years from the Martin Wills Fund. The trust also manages the Knockando Church Fund for the upkeep of Knockando Church in Morayshire, which received a grant of £9,000 in 2013/14.
**HOW TO APPLY** An online submission form is available from the trust's website. Only one application from a given charity will be considered in any 18-month period. According to the trust's website, 'on application you will be asked to supply the following information: contact name, address, telephone number and email address; organisation's charitable status and charity registration number; brief description of the organisation and its work; the organisation's most recent set of accounts; and a project document containing the following: a description of the project; a budget for the project; how the project will be monitored and evaluated'. As stated on the trust's website, grants from both funds may be made for revenue, capital or project expenditure. While grants for up to £5,000 will be considered from the general fund, the trust seeks to make donations to charities which are small enough in size, or which apply for support for a modest project, to benefit substantially from a donation of £250 or £500. Grants from the general fund are made on a rolling basis so there is no deadline for applications. Grants from the Martin Wills Fund are distributed after the end of each financial year (the trust's financial year runs from 1 April to 31 March) and applications must be received by the trust before the end of the appropriate financial year.
**WHO TO APPLY TO** Sue Trafford, Company Secretary and Administrator, Henley Knapp Barn, Fulwell, Chipping Norton, Oxon OX7 4EN Tel. 01608 678051 email hdhwills@btconnect.com Website www.hdhwills.org

## ■ Dame Violet Wills Charitable Trust

**CC NO** 219485         **ESTABLISHED** 1955
**WHERE FUNDING CAN BE GIVEN** UK and overseas.
**WHO CAN BENEFIT** Registered evangelical Christian charities.
**WHAT IS FUNDED** Evangelical Christian activities.
**WHAT IS NOT FUNDED** Individuals.
**TYPE OF GRANT** One-off and recurrent; capital; core costs; salaries; full-project funding.
**RANGE OF GRANTS** Mainly £500–£5,000.
**SAMPLE GRANTS** WC and SWET Evangelists Fund (£14,000); Echoes of Service – Bristol Missionaries (£1,750); Bristol International Student Centre (£1,600); Bibles for Children and Christian TV Association (£1,000 each); Oxford Centre for Mission Studies (£750); Breadline and Medical Missionary News (£600 each); France Mission Trust and Langham Partnership – Cambodia Project (£500 each); Centre for Christian Muslim Studies (£100).

**FINANCES** Year 2013 Income £74,462 Grants £61,300 Grants to organisations £61,300 Assets £1,924,147
**TRUSTEES** Julian Marsh; Revd Dr Ernest Lucas; Revd Alexander Cooper; Revd Ray Lockhart; Derek Cleave; John Dean; Rosalind Peskett; Janet Persson; Rachel Daws; Revd David Caporn; E. Street; Yme Potjewijd.
**OTHER INFORMATION** Grants were made to 68 organisations.
**HOW TO APPLY** Apply in writing to the correspondent. The trustees meet annually and grants are generally more likely to be made to applicants personally known to one or more of the trustees. The trust operates a system of sponsoring trustees, whereby each trustee is responsible for the support, contact with and monitoring of a number of grant beneficiaries.
**WHO TO APPLY TO** Julian Marsh, Trustee, 3 Cedar Way, Portishead, Bristol BS20 6TT Tel. 01275 848770

## ■ The Dame Violet Wills Will Trust

**CC NO** 262251   **ESTABLISHED** 1965
**WHERE FUNDING CAN BE GIVEN** Bristol and south Devon areas.
**WHO CAN BENEFIT** Registered charities.
**WHAT IS FUNDED** General charitable purposes. Charities with which the trust's founder was concerned during her lifetime are favoured.
**TYPE OF GRANT** One-off grants.
**SAMPLE GRANTS Previous beneficiaries have included:** Amos Vale, Bristol and the Colston Society, Bristol Cathedral Trust, Church of the Good Shepherd, Clifton Gateway Club, Guide Dogs for the Blind, Lord Mamhead Homes, RNLI, Rainbow Centre, Rowcroft Hospice, Samaritans, St Loye's Foundation and WRVS.
**FINANCES** Year 2013/14 Income £113,784 Grants £100,000 Grants to organisations £100,000 Assets £3,109,883
**TRUSTEES** J. Brooks; D. P. L. Howe; T. J. Baines.
**OTHER INFORMATION** A total of 127 grants were made in 2013/14, but no further information about beneficiaries was available.
**HOW TO APPLY** Apply in writing to the correspondent. The trustees meet three or four times per year to consider applications.
**WHO TO APPLY TO** D. P. L. Howe, Trustee, 7 Christchurch Road, Clifton, Bristol BS8 4EE

## ■ The Wilmcote Charitrust

**CC NO** 503837   **ESTABLISHED** 1974
**WHERE FUNDING CAN BE GIVEN** UK and occasionally overseas, with preference for Birmingham and Midlands.
**WHO CAN BENEFIT** Registered charities and voluntary organisations.
**WHAT IS FUNDED** General charitable purposes. In 2014 grants were awarded in the following categories: ex-service charities; medical charities; children's and young person's charities; religious charities; aged charities; general charities.
**TYPE OF GRANT** Many recurrent, some one-off.
**RANGE OF GRANTS** £95–£2,500; mainly around £500.
**SAMPLE GRANTS** Carers Trust and Douglas House (£2,000 each); City of Birmingham Symphony Orchestra Education Programme and Cotswold Canals Trust (£1,000 each); Arthritis Research UK, Birmingham Royal Ballet, Coram, Dogs for the Disabled, Domestic Abuse Counselling, Dream Makers, PDSA, Royal British Legion, Mercia MS Therapy Centre, Red Cross Typhoon Haiyan Appeal, Wilmcote Church Appeal and Young Minds (£500 each); 1st Wilmcote Scout Group, Friends of the Earth Bee Cause and SSAFA (£250 each).
**FINANCES** Year 2013/14 Income £27,410 Grants £75,724 Grants to organisations £75,724 Assets £1,809,924
**TRUSTEES** Carol Worrall; Anabel Murphy; Roseamond Whiteside; Graham Beach.
**OTHER INFORMATION** Grants were awarded to 48 organisations in 2013/14.
**HOW TO APPLY** Apply in writing to the correspondent.
**WHO TO APPLY TO** Carol Worrall Trust Administrator, Warren Chase, Billesley Road, Wilmcote, Stratford-upon-Avon CV37 9XG Tel. 01789 298472 email graham@leighgraham.co.uk

## ■ Sumner Wilson Charitable Trust

**CC NO** 1018852   **ESTABLISHED** 1992
**WHERE FUNDING CAN BE GIVEN** UK.
**WHO CAN BENEFIT** Registered charities.
**WHAT IS FUNDED** General charitable purposes.
**RANGE OF GRANTS** Mostly under £2,000.
**SAMPLE GRANTS** Mental Health Foundation (£101,000); St James's Place Foundation (£71,500); Rainmaker Foundation (£50,000); Young Carers (£30,000); Lewisham Youth Theatre (£13,500); Panathlon Challenge (£8,000); Great Ormond Street Hospital and Oxonian Heart Foundation (£5,000); Poached Rhino and Prostate Cancer Research (£2,500 each).
**FINANCES** Year 2013/14 Income £98,929 Grants £443,643 Grants to organisations £443,643 Assets £6,439,403
**TRUSTEES** Michael Wilson; Amanda Christie; Anne-Marie Challen.
**OTHER INFORMATION** Grants were made to over 20 organisations. Grants for £1,000 or less totalled £24,000.
**HOW TO APPLY** Apply in writing to the correspondent, or to the trustees.
**WHO TO APPLY TO** N. Steinberg, Correspondent, Munslows, 2nd Floor, Manfield House, 1 Southampton Street, London WC2R 0LR Tel. 020 7845 7500 email nathan@munslows.co.uk

## ■ David Wilson Foundation

**CC NO** 1049047   **ESTABLISHED** 1995
**WHERE FUNDING CAN BE GIVEN** UK with a strong preference for the Leicestershire and Rutland area.
**WHO CAN BENEFIT** Primarily organisations which benefit the Leicestershire and Rutland area.
**WHAT IS FUNDED** General charitable purposes, with a preference for youth education and sport, particularly young people wishing to enter the construction industry.
**WHAT IS NOT FUNDED** Political activity; general appeals; one-off events.
**TYPE OF GRANT** Project costs; core costs; salaries; capital expenditure.
**RANGE OF GRANTS** £100–£500,000
**SAMPLE GRANTS** 1st Ibstock Scouts and Jimmy's Cancer Centre (£5,000 each).
**FINANCES** Year 2014 Income £181,365 Grants £10,000 Grants to organisations £10,000 Assets £7,919,720
**TRUSTEES** James Wilson; Thomas Neiland; Laura Wilson; Richard Wilson; Robert Wilson; Sarah Carley.

# Wilson

OTHER INFORMATION The foundation supports only a few local institutions each year. Although grants totalling only £10,000 were awarded in 2013/14, grant totals in previous years have been higher. In 2012, a significant grant of £500,000 was awarded to fund the University of Leicester Cardiovascular Research Centre.

HOW TO APPLY Apply in writing to the correspondent, initially with no more than one side of A4 (250–300 words) detailing the project, the aspects for which support requested and how the project meets the foundation's criteria. Assessments usually take a minimum of three months. Applications are considered from UK-registered charities and may also be considered from schools, universities and public sector organisations. The foundation's website provides further information.

WHO TO APPLY TO John Gillions, Secretary, c/o Fisher Solicitors, 4–8 Kilwardby Street, Ashby-de-la-Zouch, Leicestershire LE65 2FU *Tel.* 01530 412167 *email* john.gillions@fisherslaw.co.uk *Website* www.davidwilsonfoundation.com/Default.aspx

## ■ The Wilson Foundation

CC NO 1074414 ESTABLISHED 1999
WHERE FUNDING CAN BE GIVEN Northamptonshire.
WHO CAN BENEFIT Organisations working with people aged 10 to 21.
WHAT IS FUNDED Young people in Northamptonshire, particularly those facing disadvantage. Grants are given to both organisations and individuals, for a range of projects and purposes, including educational scholarships, youth projects and trips that provide opportunities for character building and where individuals would otherwise not be able to participate.
WHAT IS NOT FUNDED Individuals living outside Northamptonshire.
TYPE OF GRANT Capital costs; recurrent project funding; one-off scholarships; core costs; start-up funding.
RANGE OF GRANTS £100–£20,000
SAMPLE GRANTS Holcot Village Hall Association (£110,000); Longtown Outdoor Educational Centre (£14,300); Oakham School (£8,500); Bunbury ESCA Festival and Prince's Trust (£5,000 each); Kettering Children's Holiday Fund (£3,200 in two grants); Northampton Music Festival (£2,500); Boys' Brigade 7th Northampton (£1,800); Northampton Young Carers (£700); and Northampton General Hospital Circus Starr (£140).
FINANCES Year 2013/14 Income £109,850 Grants £178,570 Grants to organisations £165,070 Assets £5,302,949
TRUSTEES Anthony Hewitt; Giles Wilson; Nicholas Wilson; Fiona Wilson; Adam Welch; Pollyanna Wilson.
OTHER INFORMATION The grant total includes £13,500 that was donated to 38 individuals. Grants were given to 26 organisations. A significant grant was given to Holcot Village Hall for the development of a new youth wing.
HOW TO APPLY Application forms for individuals are available on the trust's website. Organisations should apply in writing to the trustees.
WHO TO APPLY TO Nick Wilson Chair, The Maltings, Tithe Farm, Moulton Road, Holcot, Northamptonshire NN6 9SH *Tel.* 01604 782240 *email* polly@tithefarm.com *Website* www.thewilsonfoundation.co.uk

## ■ J. and J. R. Wilson Trust

SC NO SC007411 ESTABLISHED 1989
WHERE FUNDING CAN BE GIVEN Mainly Scotland, particularly Glasgow and the west coast of Scotland.
WHO CAN BENEFIT Organisations benefitting older people and animals and birds.
WHAT IS FUNDED Grants are given to charitable bodies which are concerned with the care of older people, or the care of both domestic and wild animals and birds.
WHAT IS NOT FUNDED Individuals.
SAMPLE GRANTS Previous beneficiaries have included: Royal Society for the Protection of Birds (£4,500); Cancer Bacup (£4,000); St Margaret's Hospice – Clydebank and SSPCA (£3,000 each); Maggie's Cancer Care – Glasgow and Marine Connection (£2,000 each); Accord Hospice – Paisley, Ardgowan Hospice – Greenock, British Red Cross, Princess Royal Trust for Carers, Royal National Institute of Blind People, Royal Zoological Society Scotland and Trees for Life (£1,000 each).
FINANCES Year 2013/14 Income £138,371 Grants £130,000 Grants to organisations £130,000
TRUSTEES H. M. K. Hopkins; J. G. L. Robinson; K. H. Mackenzie; R. N. C. Douglas; G. I. M. Chapman.
OTHER INFORMATION Accounts were not available from OSCR. Grant total has been estimated based on total expenditure and grant totals in previous years.
HOW TO APPLY Apply in writing to the correspondent.
WHO TO APPLY TO Beth Hamilton, c/o Tho and JW Barty Solicitors, 61 High Street, Dunblane FK15 0EH *Tel.* 01786 822296

## ■ The Community Foundation for Wiltshire and Swindon

CC NO 1123126 ESTABLISHED 1991
WHERE FUNDING CAN BE GIVEN Wiltshire and Swindon only.
WHO CAN BENEFIT Local voluntary and community groups.
WHAT IS FUNDED Supporting communities in Wiltshire and Swindon. The primary focus is on disadvantage, including tackling isolation, investing in young people, improving opportunities for employment and skills development and providing social and recreational opportunities. The foundation manages a number of grant programmes – see the website for details of up-to-date schemes.
WHAT IS NOT FUNDED Projects which duplicate existing local services; statutory organisations, including schools, academies, area boards, town and parish councils and NHS trusts; community interest companies, except for start-up costs; one-off or sponsored events; general large fundraising appeals; the advancement of religion; medical research and equipment; animal welfare; party political activities; projects which have already taken place; replacement of statutory funding; running costs for community area partnerships.
TYPE OF GRANT Projects; core costs; capital grants.
RANGE OF GRANTS Main grants: £750–£10,000 per year for three years. Small grants: £50–£750 on a one-off basis.
SAMPLE GRANTS SMASH Youth Project (£90,000); Open Blue Trust (£18,000); Splash Wiltshire (£15,000); Home-Start Kennet, Relate Mid-Wiltshire and Waste Not Want Not (£14,000 each); Crosspoint – Westbury (£13,500);

Seeds4Success (£13,000); Kandu Arts Sustainable Development and Wiltshire Mind (£10,500); Devizes Opendoor and Help Counselling Services (£10,000 each).

**FINANCES** *Year* 2013/14 *Income* £2,269,943 *Grants* £779,916 *Grants to organisations* £560,006 *Assets* £17,355,393

**TRUSTEES** John Woodget, Chair; Elizabeth Webbe; Emma Gibbons; John Adams; Denise Bentley; Christopher Bromfield; Helen Birchenough; Jason Dalley; Angus Macpherson; Dame Elizabeth Neville; Alison Radevsky; Ram Thiagarajah; Sally Walden; William Wyldbore-Smith; Steve Wall.

**OTHER INFORMATION** In 2013/14 a total of 215 grants were awarded to 157 groups. Grants were also made to 391 individuals, totalling £240,000.

**HOW TO APPLY** Applicants should firstly read the exclusions and funding criteria on the foundation's website. Projects that the foundation will fund include: 'projects where the majority of people who will benefit are disadvantaged; groups working with children where the majority are disadvantaged or have special needs; groups with 12 months or less running costs in unrestricted reserves; groups operating within the county of Wiltshire or the Borough of Swindon; groups with a registered address and/or local voluntary management committee or Board of Trustees in Swindon/Wiltshire; projects starting within 6 months of the grant award and spent within 12 months; core costs and overheads for your organisation; salaries and equipment purchases.' To apply, an initial expression of interest should be made on the foundation's website, including information about income, expenditure, trustees or committee and the purpose for which the grant is requested. Applicants will then be contacted or visited for further information. Applicants will be notified of a decision within four weeks for small grants and within six months for main grants. According to the foundation's annual report, decisions are made by a Grants Panel of up to two trustees, volunteers from the local community, specialists and someone with accountancy or banking background. Decisions are then ratified by the trustees. Applications can be made throughout the year. Monitoring and evaluation reports are usually completed a year after receiving a grant. Check the foundation's website for up-to-date further information. Applicants are encouraged to contact the foundation for support with the application process.

**WHO TO APPLY TO** Heidi Yorke, Grants Programme Director, Sandcliffe House, 21 Northgate Street, Devizes, Wiltshire SN10 1JX *Tel.* 01380 729284 *email* info@wscf.org.uk *Website* wiltshirecf.org.uk

## ■ The Benjamin Winegarten Charitable Trust

**CC NO** 271442   **ESTABLISHED** 1976
**WHERE FUNDING CAN BE GIVEN** UK.
**WHO CAN BENEFIT** Individuals and organisations benefitting Jewish people and people disadvantaged by poverty.
**WHAT IS FUNDED** Relief of poverty and the advancement of Jewish religion and religious education. Grants are also given to individuals in need.
**SAMPLE GRANTS Previous beneficiaries have included:** Heichal HaTorah Institute, the Jewish Educational Trust, the Mechinah School, Merkaz Lechinuch Torani Zichron Ya'akov, Ohr Someach Friends, Or Akiva Community Centre, Yeshivo Hovomo Talmudical College and ZSVT.

**FINANCES** *Year* 2013/14 *Income* £218,015 *Grants* £40,660 *Grants to organisations* £38,160 *Assets* £1,154,243

**TRUSTEES** Benjamin Winegarten; Esther Winegarten.

**OTHER INFORMATION** The grant total in 2013/14 includes £2,500 donated to individuals.

**HOW TO APPLY** Apply in writing to the correspondent.

**WHO TO APPLY TO** Benjamin Winegarten, Trustee, 25 St Andrew's Grove, Stoke Newington, London N16 5NF *Tel.* 020 8800 6669

## ■ The Harold Hyam Wingate Foundation

**CC NO** 264114   **ESTABLISHED** 1960
**WHERE FUNDING CAN BE GIVEN** UK and financially developing countries.
**WHO CAN BENEFIT** Registered charities and organisations working in financially developing countries.
**WHAT IS FUNDED** Jewish life and learning; performing arts; music; education and social exclusion; overseas development; medical research (travel costs).
**WHAT IS NOT FUNDED** Individuals. The foundation will not normally make grants to the general funds of large charitable bodies, wishing instead to focus support on specific projects.
**TYPE OF GRANT** Either one-off or recurrent for a limited period.
**RANGE OF GRANTS** Generally £10,000 or less.
**SAMPLE GRANTS** Queen Mary and Westfield College (£161,500); The Karuna Trust (£22,500); In Harmony Sistema England and Royal Botanic Gardens Kew (£10,000 each); Belarus Free Theatre (£9,500); The Kanga Project (£9,000); Southbank Sinfonia (£6,500); Anne Frank Trust UK and Jewish Care (£6,000 each); FilmClubUK, Place2Be and Tricycle Theatre (£5,000 each); Music in Detention (£2,500); Camden People's Theatre (£2,000); King's College London (£900); The Lea Singers (£500).
**FINANCES** *Year* 2013/14 *Income* £260,418 *Grants* £712,493 *Grants to organisations* £712,493 *Assets* £7,856,814
**TRUSTEES** Roger Wingate; Tony Wingate; Prof. Robert Cassen; Prof. David Wingate; Prof. Jonathon Drori; Daphne Hyman; Emily Kasriel; Dr Richard Wingate.
**OTHER INFORMATION** An additional £31,500 was awarded in individual scholarships in 2013/14. However, the foundation has decided to discontinue its scholarship scheme and no further scholarships will be awarded.
**HOW TO APPLY** Applications should be made using the application form available from the foundation's website, sent with supporting documentation and most recent accounts. Applications are only acknowledged if a stamped addressed envelope is enclosed or if the application is successful. The administrator of the foundation only deals with enquiries by post and it is hoped that the guidelines and examples of previous support for successful applicants, given on the foundation's website, provides sufficient information. There is no email address for the foundation. Trustee meetings are held quarterly and further information on upcoming deadlines can be found on the foundation's website.
**WHO TO APPLY TO** Karen Marshall, Trust Administrator, 2nd Floor, 20–22 Stukeley

Street, London WC2B 5LR *Website* www.wingatefoundation.org.uk

## ■ The Francis Winham Foundation
**CC NO** 278092   **ESTABLISHED** 1979
**WHERE FUNDING CAN BE GIVEN** England.
**WHO CAN BENEFIT** Charitable organisations or exempt charities, benefitting older people.
**WHAT IS FUNDED** Grants for organisations working to improve the quality of life of older people.
**SAMPLE GRANTS** London Clinic (£7 donations totalling £47,000); Capio Nightingale Hospital (£3 donations totalling £26,500); Care and Repair (81 donations totalling £26,500); Age UK (2 donations totalling £17,500); Help the Hospices and Royal Voluntary Service (£10,000 each); Independence at Home (£6,500); Alzheimer's Society and The Royal Star and Garter Home (£5,000 each).
**FINANCES** *Year* 2013/14 *Income* £712,275 *Grants* £412,525 *Grants to organisations* £412,525 *Assets* £2,842,780
**TRUSTEES** Francine Winham; Josephine Winham; Elsa Peters; Desmond Corcoran.
**OTHER INFORMATION** Grants were made to 16 organisations in 2013/14.
**HOW TO APPLY** Apply in writing to the correspondent. The trust regrets it cannot send replies to applications outside its specific field of help for older people.
**WHO TO APPLY TO** Josephine Winham, Trustee, 41 Langton Street, London SW10 0JL *Tel.* 020 7795 1261 *email* francinetrust@btopenworld.com

## ■ The Winton Charitable Foundation
**CC NO** 1110131   **ESTABLISHED** 2005
**WHERE FUNDING CAN BE GIVEN** National and overseas.
**WHO CAN BENEFIT** Academic institutions and other organisations.
**WHAT IS FUNDED** The foundation's objectives are to develop science in the UK and overseas; to further the study of risk and statistics for public benefit; also to award grants for general charitable purposes at the discretion of the trustees.
**SAMPLE GRANTS** Francis Crick Institute (£1.25 million); Absolute Return for Kids – ARK (£50,000); CHICKS (£25,000); Holland Park Opera (£25,000); Fight for Sight (£24,000).
**FINANCES** *Year* 2013 *Income* £1,907,979 *Grants* £1,602,276 *Grants to organisations* £1,602,276 *Assets* £394,961
**TRUSTEES** David Winton; Martin Hunt.
**OTHER INFORMATION** The grant total includes an exceptionally large grant from the restricted fund, in agreement with Cancer Research UK, towards the construction of the Francis Crick Institute, a biomedical research centre. The foundation also provides match funding for Winton Capital employee donations of up to £10,000. The foundation established and maintains a professorship in the public understanding of statistics and risk at the University of Cambridge.
**HOW TO APPLY** Apply in writing to the correspondent.
**WHO TO APPLY TO** Martin Hunt, Trustee, Grove House, 27 Hammersmith Grove, London W6 ONE *email* i.hayhoe@wintoncapital.com *Website* www.wintoncapital.com/AboutUs/Charities

## ■ The James Wise Charitable Trust
**CC NO** 273853   **ESTABLISHED** 1977
**WHERE FUNDING CAN BE GIVEN** UK, but mainly Surrey and Hampshire.
**WHO CAN BENEFIT** Charitable organisations and individuals.
**WHAT IS FUNDED** General charitable purposes, including people with ill health or disability, older people and people who are disadvantaged.
**TYPE OF GRANT** Generally one-off grants.
**RANGE OF GRANTS** Most grants under £1,000.
**SAMPLE GRANTS** St Michael's Hospice North Hants, S Pinter Youth Project (£1,000); Berkshire Multiple Sclerosis Therapy Centre, Listening Books, North London Foodbank, SSAFA and Toynbee Hall (£500 each); Clowns in the Sky (£400); Motability (£350); Headstart 4 Babies and Kingston Carers Network (£300 each); Compassion in World Farming, CSV, Marie Curie Cancer Care and The Rainbow Centre (£250 each); Mencap (£100).
**FINANCES** *Year* 2013/14 *Income* £59,613 *Grants* £28,879 *Grants to organisations* £28,080 *Assets* £2,030,596
**TRUSTEES** Lisa Rabinowitz; Barry Kilburn; Sara Coate.
**OTHER INFORMATION** The grant total includes a grant to one individual totalling £800. Grants were awarded to 65 organisations.
**HOW TO APPLY** Apply in writing to the correspondent.
**WHO TO APPLY TO** Claire Burnett, c/o Marshalls Solicitors, 102 High Street, Godalming, Surrey GU7 1DS *Tel.* 01483 416101 *email* cburnett@marshalls.uk.net

## ■ The Michael and Anna Wix Charitable Trust
**CC NO** 207863   **ESTABLISHED** 1955
**WHERE FUNDING CAN BE GIVEN** UK.
**WHO CAN BENEFIT** Registered charities (mainly UK) benefitting a range of causes including medical research, at risk groups, people with disabilities and people who are disadvantaged by poverty or socially isolated.
**WHAT IS FUNDED** General charitable purposes. A wide range of causes receive funding, including medicine and health, poverty and welfare, older people, disability, education and Jewish causes.
**WHAT IS NOT FUNDED** Individuals are not considered. Grants are generally to national bodies rather than local branches or local groups.
**TYPE OF GRANT** 'Modest semi-regular' donations. Also one-off for part or all of a specific project.
**RANGE OF GRANTS** Mostly for smaller amounts in the range of £100 and £500 each.
**SAMPLE GRANTS** Nightingale Hammerson and Weizmann UK (£6,000 each); Pinhas Rutenberg Educational Trust (£3,000); Jewish Care (£2,000); Alzheimer's Research UK and World Jewish Relief (£1,500 each); Cancer Research UK (£1,000); Age UK (£500); Big Issue Foundation, British Blind Sport, British Friends of Ohel Sarah, Concern Worldwide, Cystic Fibrosis Trust, Multiple Sclerosis Society, Royal Star and Garter Homes, Salvation Army, St John Ambulance, Youth Aliyah (£200 each); Bolton Lads and Girls Club, Fire Fighters Charity, Health Poverty Action, Meningitis UK, Traidcraft (£100 each).
**FINANCES** *Year* 2013/14 *Income* £103,830 *Grants* £88,300 *Grants to organisations* £88,300 *Assets* £1,990,198
**TRUSTEES** Janet Bloch; Dominic Flynn; Judith Portrait.

OTHER INFORMATION Grants were awarded to 343 organisations in 2013/14.
HOW TO APPLY Apply in writing to the trustees. The trustees meet to consider applications twice each year. Only applications from registered charities are acknowledged.
WHO TO APPLY TO Sarah Hovil, Correspondent, c/o Portrait Solicitors, 21 Whitefriars Street, London EC4Y 8JJ *Tel.* 020 7092 6985 *email* sarah.hovil@portraitsolicitors.com

## ■ The Wixamtree Trust

CC NO 210089   ESTABLISHED 1949
WHERE FUNDING CAN BE GIVEN UK and overseas, in practice mainly Bedfordshire.
WHO CAN BENEFIT Local charities and a small number of national charities with a focus on family social issues and some overseas. Applicants must be a registered charity or considered to be charitable in nature by the Inland Revenue.
WHAT IS FUNDED General charitable purposes. Grants are awarded in the following categories: social welfare; environment and conservation; medicine and health; the arts; education; training and employment; sports and leisure; international.
WHAT IS NOT FUNDED Individuals.
TYPE OF GRANT One-off projects; capital and core costs; research.
RANGE OF GRANTS Usually grants between £1,000 and £10,000 with a small number of donations outside this range.
SAMPLE GRANTS Previous beneficiaries have included: British Epilepsy Association; Narcolepsy UK; Keech Hospice Care; Leighton Linslade Homeless Service; Barton Scouts and Guides Headquarters Management Committee; Farms for City Children; Bibles for Children; British Association for Adoption and Fostering (BAAF); Mitalee Youth Association; Oakley Rural Day Care Centre; Bedfordshire African Community Centre; Dunstable and District Citizens Advice; Luton West Indian Community Association; Autism Bedfordshire; Special Needs Out Of School Club in Beds (SNOOSC); Whizz-Kidz; Child Bereavement UK; Road Victims Trust; Westminster College – Cambridge; Bedford Creative Arts; Music First; Bedfordshire Historical Record Society; Bedfordshire Wildlife Rescue; European Squirrel Initiative; Campaign to Protect Rural England (CPRE); Fauna and Flora International; Wheelchair Dance Sport Association (UK); and Sandy Cricket Club.
FINANCES Year 2013/14 *Income* £885,069 *Grants* £799,487 *Grants to organisations* £799,487 *Assets* £26,804,468
TRUSTEES Sir Samuel Whitbread; Lady Whitbread; H. F. Whitbread; Charles Whitbread; Ian Pilkington; Geoff McMullen; Elizabeth Bennett.
OTHER INFORMATION A total of 158 grants were awarded in 2013/14.
HOW TO APPLY Application forms can be downloaded from the website or requested via email or post. The method of submission must be via email if possible: wixamtree@thetrustpartnership.com. The trustees meet four times a year, usually in January, April, July and November. Future meeting dates and application deadlines are listed on the trust's website. Along with the application form, applicants must provide a copy of their latest audited report and accounts. If the organisation is not a charity, then a copy of its constitution must also be provided. Applicants are permitted to provide additional information to support their application if they wish to do so. Successful applicants will be notified within 14 days of the trustees' meeting of the amount that has been approved. Unsuccessful applicants will receive a letter detailing the trustees' decision within seven days of the meeting. Before another application can be submitted, the trust asks previously successful organisations who already hold grants to submit an annual report on how the earlier grant has been used. A separate application form is available for applications from Bedfordshire churches seeking grants for fabric repairs to their buildings, as the trustees have an arrangement with the Beds and Herts Historic Churches Trust (BHHCT) who make decisions on grants in this area according to their expertise. Such applications should be submitted to the BHHCT's administrator, who will arrange a site visit to evaluate the project.
WHO TO APPLY TO Paul Patten, Correspondent, 148 The Grove, West Wickham, Kent BR4 9JZ *Tel.* 020 8777 4140 *email* wixamtree@thetrustpartnership.com *Website* www.wixamtree.org

## ■ The Maurice Wohl Charitable Foundation

CC NO 244519   ESTABLISHED 1965
WHERE FUNDING CAN BE GIVEN UK and Israel.
WHO CAN BENEFIT In practice, Jewish groups and health, welfare and medical organisations. Registered UK charities or recognised not-for-profits outside the UK.
WHAT IS FUNDED Support is given to charitable organisations with emphasis on the following areas: health and medical sciences; welfare within the Jewish community; Jewish education.
WHAT IS NOT FUNDED The trustees do not in general entertain applications for grants for ongoing maintenance projects. The trustees do not administer any schemes for individual awards or scholarships and they do not, therefore, entertain any individual applications for grants.
TYPE OF GRANT One-off grants; grants committed over one to five years.
RANGE OF GRANTS £1,000–£3 million.
SAMPLE GRANTS Jewish Care (£3 million); Birkbeck College – University of London (£1.3 million); Royal College of Surgeons of Edinburgh (£1 million); King Solomon High School (£500,000); Jewish Lads' and Girls' Brigade (£250,000); Train for Employment Limited (£120,000); Camp Simcha (£40,000); London Jewish Cultural Centre (£34,500); Community Security Trust (£35,000); Yad Harav Herzog (£6,000).
FINANCES Year 2013/14 *Income* £2,059,633 *Grants* £8,825,277 *Grants to organisations* £8,825,277 *Assets* £80,287,822
TRUSTEES Ella Latchman; Martin Paisner; Prof. David Latchman; Sir Ian Gainsford; Daniel Dover.
OTHER INFORMATION The foundation is part of the Wohl Legacy, a group of three charitable foundations established by Maurice and Vivienne Wohl.
HOW TO APPLY The website for the Wohl Legacy group states that unsolicited applications will not be accepted, as trustees work with full-time staff to identify suitable projects.
WHO TO APPLY TO Joseph Houri, Secretary, Fitzrovia House, 2nd Floor, 153 - 157 Cleveland Street, London W1T 6QW *Tel.* 020 7383 5111 *email* info@wohl.org.uk *Website* www.wohl.org.uk

# Wolfson

## ■ The Charles Wolfson Charitable Trust

**CC NO** 238043　　**ESTABLISHED** 1960
**WHERE FUNDING CAN BE GIVEN** Unrestricted, mainly UK.
**WHO CAN BENEFIT** Registered charities; hospitals; schools. Particular, but not exclusive regard is given to the Jewish community.
**WHAT IS FUNDED** Medical and scientific research and facilities; education and welfare.
**WHAT IS NOT FUNDED** Individuals.
**TYPE OF GRANT** Mostly capital or fixed-term projects and the provision of rent-free premises. Grants may be made for up to three years.
**RANGE OF GRANTS** Up to £500,000.
**SAMPLE GRANTS** Previous beneficiaries have included: Addenbrookes Charitable Trust and Yavneh College Trust (£500,000 each); Jewish Care (£350,000); Cure Parkinson's Trust (£200,000); Huntingdon Foundation (£125,000); Royal Marsden Cancer Campaign (£50,000); Sir George Pinker Appeal (£30,000); Zoological Society of London (£25,000); Priors Court Foundation (£10,000); Tavistock Trust for Aphasia (£5,000); and the Roundhouse Trust (£1,000).
**FINANCES** Year 2013/14 Income £8,669,345 Grants £4,926,060 Grants to organisations £4,926,060 Assets £190,815,830
**TRUSTEES** Lord Simon Wolfson; Dr Sara Levene; The Hon Andrew Wolfson; Lord David Wolfson.
**OTHER INFORMATION** A list of beneficiaries was not available.
**HOW TO APPLY** Apply in writing to the correspondent.
**WHO TO APPLY TO** Cynthia Crawford, Correspondent, 129 Battenhall Road, Worcester WR5 2BU

## ■ The Wolfson Family Charitable Trust

**CC NO** 228382　　**ESTABLISHED** 1958
**WHERE FUNDING CAN BE GIVEN** Israel and UK.
**WHO CAN BENEFIT** Particularly Jewish groups and Israeli institutions.
**WHAT IS FUNDED** Science and medicine; education; health and disability; arts and humanities.
**WHAT IS NOT FUNDED** Grants are generally only awarded for capital projects to charities or organisations with charitable status. Exclusions, as stated on the trust's website, are as follows: 'grants to individuals or through conduit organisations; overheads, maintenance costs, VAT and professional fees; non-specific appeals (including circulars) and endowment funds; costs of meetings, exhibitions, concerts, expeditions, etc.; the purchase of land or existing buildings (including a building's freehold); film or promotional materials; repayment of loans and projects that have already been completed or will be by the time of award.'
**TYPE OF GRANT** One-off grants for capital costs and equipment.
**RANGE OF GRANTS** Up to £200,000.
**SAMPLE GRANTS** Hadassah University Hospitals and Rambam Health Care Campus (£140,000 each); Soroka University Medical Centre (£110,000); British Israel Research and Academic Exchange Partnership and Israel Museum (£50,000 each); The Fed – Manchester (£30,000); St Antony's College Oxford (£25,000); Garnethill Synagogue (£20,000); Beit Issie Shapiro (£15,000); The Association for Children at Risk (£13,000); London School of Jewish Studies and The Association of the Deaf in Israel (£10,000 each); Variety Israel (£8,000); Reut Sderot (£5,000).
**FINANCES** Year 2013/14 Income £832,000 Grants £1,422,000 Grants to organisations £1,422,000 Assets £33,384,000
**TRUSTEES** Martin Paisner; Sir Ian Gainsford; Sir Bernard Rix; Sir Eric Ash; The Hon Laura Wolfson Townsley; The Hon Janet de Botton; Lord Turnberg; The Hon Elizabeth Wolfson Peltz; Alexandra Wolfson Halamish.
**OTHER INFORMATION** Grants were awarded to 30 organisations in the UK and Israel in 2013/14.
**HOW TO APPLY** According to the trust's website, awards are usually made once or twice a year. Organisations should be charities or have a charitable purpose, generally have an income of above £50,000 and show evidence of long-term financial viability. Within the cultural field, organisations should have a national reputation for excellence. In the area of heritage, there is a particular interest in historic synagogues. Funding is provided for capital projects and applicants should guarantee matched funding. Requests should generally be in the range of £5,000–£25,000. Applications can be made online via the trust's website. Awards for Israeli universities, hospitals and other organisations are made in conjunction with designated programmes and unsolicited applications are generally not accepted in these areas.
**WHO TO APPLY TO** Paul Ramsbottom, Secretary, 8 Queen Anne Street, London W1G 9LD Tel. 020 7323 5730 email grants@wolfson.org.uk Website www.wolfson.org.uk

## ■ The Wolfson Foundation

**CC NO** 206495　　**ESTABLISHED** 1955
**WHERE FUNDING CAN BE GIVEN** Mainly UK, but also Israel.
**WHO CAN BENEFIT** Registered charities and exempt charities (such as universities and schools), benefitting people of all ages.
**WHAT IS FUNDED** Grants are generally given for capital projects 'supporting excellence' in the following areas: science and medicine; arts and humanities; health and disability; education. The foundation's bursary, scholarship and salary programmes are generally not open to application and are run with selected organisations. Grants for university research are awarded through designated programmes. The foundation often works in partnership with other funding bodies.
**WHAT IS NOT FUNDED** The following are ineligible for funding: individuals; overheads, maintenance cost (including for software), VAT and professional fees; VAT and professional fees; non-specific appeals (including circulars) and endowment funds; costs of meetings, exhibitions, concerts, expeditions, etc.; purchasing of land or existing buildings (including a building's freehold); film or promotional materials; repayment of loans; completed projects; and projects where the total cost is below £15,000.
**TYPE OF GRANT** Capital costs; equipment.
**RANGE OF GRANTS** £1,000–£2,000,000
**SAMPLE GRANTS** University of Cambridge – laboratories for high specification imaging (£2 million); Art Fund (£1.5 million); Royal Academy of Arts (£1 million); Birkbeck University – autism research facility (£800,000); Westonbirt Arboretum (£430,000); Jewish Care (£300,000); National Youth Orchestra of Great Britain (£270,000); The

National Gallery (£250,000); University of Birmingham – library (£150,000); Royal College of Psychiatrists (£120,000); Hereford Sixth Form College and Teach First (£100,000 each); Royal Court Theatre (£80,000); Bournemouth School (£50,000); Salisbury Cathedral (£45,000); Woodlands Hospice (£30,000); Action for Deafness (£29,000); Norton Priory Museum and Gardens (£24,000); Ballet Cymru and Oasis Children's Venture (£20,000 each); Channing School (£14,000); St Leonard Church – Shoreditch (£5,000); St Mary's Church – Amersham (£1,000).

FINANCES Year 2013/14 Income £19,765,000 Grants £31,856,000 Grants to organisations £31,856,000 Assets £702,243,000

TRUSTEES Sir David Cannadine; Sir Eric Ash; Lord McColl of Dulwich; Hon Janet de Botton; Hon Laura Wolfson Townsley; Lord Turnberg; Hon Deborah Wolfson Davis; Dame Hermione Lee; Sir Michael Pepper; Dame Jean Thomas; Prof. Sir Peter Ratcliffe.

OTHER INFORMATION The foundation awarded 351 grants in total.

HOW TO APPLY The foundation's website states that 'The Wolfson Foundation has a two stage application process. Details of eligibility and what we fund are contained within the various funding programme pages. Please note that, under some funding programmes, applicants are asked to submit via partner organisations, and so the application process and deadlines may vary from those described here. Such cases are signposted within the relevant programme area pages. We are committed to rigorous assessment in order to fund high quality projects. All applications undergo detailed internal review and assessment by external experts. As such, the time between submission of a stage 1 application and a funding decision on a Stage 2 application will be a minimum of some five months (and may in some cases be substantially longer). As we do not make retrospective grants (i.e. your project will need to be on-going at the time that it is considered by our trustees), it is important to plan carefully the timing of your application. Grants are generally given for capital infrastructure (new build, refurbishment and equipment) supporting excellence in the fields of science and medicine, health & disability, education and the arts and humanities. The large majority of our funding is allocated through open programmes (i.e. programmes which are open for any applicant to apply, albeit within defined eligibility criteria). We also run a small number of closed programmes (i.e. programmes where the particular field being funded is tightly defined and where we work with a number of carefully selected organisations). Generally our capital infrastructure programmes are open programmes and our closed programmes are all bursary, scholarship or salary schemes focussed on people rather than buildings or equipment. We welcome applications under our open programmes but do not accept unsolicited applications under our closed programmes. The foundation is committed to working, where possible, in partnership with other funders and expert bodies. A number of our funding programmes are administered by other organisations and this website provides details of those programmes, including links to the relevant information on how to apply (which is generally via the partner organisation rather than direct to us). By partnership programmes we mean all programmes that are administered and/or co-funded by other organisations.' All stage applications should be submitted online through the foundation's website. For more information visit the website's funding pages. Charities are encouraged to apply only once in a five year period.

WHO TO APPLY TO Paul Ramsbottom, Chief Executive, 8 Queen Anne Street, London W1G 9LD Tel. 020 7323 5730 email grants@wolfson.org.uk Website www.wolfson.org.uk

■ **The James Wood Bequest Fund**

SC NO SC000459    ESTABLISHED 1932

WHERE FUNDING CAN BE GIVEN Glasgow and the 'central belt of Scotland'.

WHO CAN BENEFIT Registered charities.

WHAT IS FUNDED General charitable purposes; Church of Scotland; historic buildings; other registered charities based in Scotland with preference being given to the central belt.

WHAT IS NOT FUNDED Individuals.

TYPE OF GRANT Capital costs; full project funding; one-off.

RANGE OF GRANTS £500–£4,000

SAMPLE GRANTS Previous beneficiaries have included: Society of Friends of Glasgow Cathedral, Scottish Brass Band Association, Shelter Scotland, Children 1st, Princess Royal Trust for Carers, Erskine Hospital and Scottish Spina Bifida Association; Glasgow and West of Scotland Society for the Blind, Mental Health Foundation, Aberlour Child Care Trust, RSPB Scotland, Hopscotch Theatre Company, Reality at Work in Scotland and Sense Scotland.

FINANCES Year 2013/14 Income £75,208 Grants £100,000 Grants to organisations £100,000

TRUSTEES Eric Webster; David Ballantine; Alastair Campbell.

OTHER INFORMATION The accounts for 2013/14 were not available so grant total was estimated based on the trust's total expenditure of £108,000.

HOW TO APPLY Apply in writing to the correspondent, including if possible a copy of the latest accounts, a budget for the project, sources of funding received and other relevant financial information. The trustees meet in January, April, July and October. Applications should be received by the preceding month.

WHO TO APPLY TO David Ballantine, Trustee, Mitchells Roberton Solicitors, George House, 36 North Hanover Street, Glasgow G1 2AD Tel. 0141 552 3422 email darb@mitchells-roberton.co.uk

■ **The Wood Family Trust**

SC NO SC037957    ESTABLISHED 2007

WHERE FUNDING CAN BE GIVEN UK, with a preference for Scotland; Sub-Saharan Africa.

WHO CAN BENEFIT Organisations and individuals.

WHAT IS FUNDED The Wood Family Trust has two clear areas of investment focus: 'Making Markets Work for the Poor Sub Saharan Africa', focusing on long term poverty reduction through trade and employment (anticipated to be 75% of the Trust's overall investment); 'Developing Young People in Scotland', encouraging young people to become enterprising, independent, tolerant and caring members of society (anticipated to be 25% of the overall investment).

SAMPLE GRANTS Grants were made to 146 organisations totalling £2.8 million, which was distributed to organisations with the following purposes: two grants for the purpose of 'making markets work for the poor' (£1.24 million in total); 110 grants for the purpose of 'developing young people in Scotland' (£775,000 in total); 7 'miscellaneous grants' (£747,000 in total); 27 grants for the purpose of 'volunteering overseas' (£58,000 in total).

**FINANCES** Year 2013/14  Income £5,066,000  Grants £2,823,000  Grants to organisations £2,823,000  Assets £121,075

**TRUSTEES** Sir Ian Wood, Chair; Lady Helen Wood; Garreth Wood; Graham Good.

**OTHER INFORMATION** This trust became operational in September 2007. During 2013/14 no grants were awarded to individuals.

**HOW TO APPLY** The trust proactively seeks out beneficiaries rather than inviting open applications. However, the foundation will accept applications 'from individuals and groups, local to the North East of Scotland, who are undertaking an overseas volunteering opportunity' for their Developing Young People in Scotland programme. Contact the trust for further information on how to make an application.

**WHO TO APPLY TO** Ailsa McRae, Correspondent, Blenheim House, Fountainhall Road, Aberdeen AB15 4DT Tel. 01224 619831 email info@woodfamilytrust.org.uk Website www.thewoodfoundation.org.uk

------

## ■ Wooden Spoon Society

**CC NO** 326691    **ESTABLISHED** 1984

**WHERE FUNDING CAN BE GIVEN** UK.

**WHO CAN BENEFIT** Charitable and community organisations that support people under the age of 25 with physical or mental disabilities or social deprivation.

**WHAT IS FUNDED** Capital Projects – with a particular interest in rugby for young people with disabilities and recreational and sporting facilities. Grants are currently awarded for such things as buildings and extensions, equipment and activity aids, sensory rooms/gardens, playgrounds, sports areas, transport and soft play rooms. Community Projects – that support disenfranchised young people back into education, employment or training, or provide opportunities for children and young people with disabilities to engage in rugby and sports activities.

**WHAT IS NOT FUNDED** For capital projects, grants will not be given for salaries, administration costs, professional fees and ongoing overheads. For educational, community or sports programmes, grants will be considered for kit, equipment, salaries and administration costs and there must be a key rugby element to engage children and young people. Applications for minibuses will only be considered where it is shown that funding is not available from other sources and that a minibus would raise awareness of the charity in the area. No grants are given to individuals.

**RANGE OF GRANTS** Usually up to £100,000.

**SAMPLE GRANTS** RFL (£80,000); 999 Club (£58,500); Quarriers Epilepsy Centre (£50,000); Camphill School (£29,000); Claytons Primary School (£23,000); Greenbank Sports Academy (£15,000); Horseworld (£11,000); PACT (£10,000); Printfield Community Project (£6,500); Scottish Spina Bifida Association (£5,000); Our Lady of Walsingham School (£1,000).

**FINANCES** Year 2013/14  Income £3,819,022  Grants £1,905,822  Grants to organisations £1,905,822  Assets £835,283

**TRUSTEES** David Allen; Stephen Bellamy-James; John Gibson; Steuart Howie; Alison Lowe; Fiona Morris; Martin Sanders; Peter Scott; Nigel Timson; Richard Smith; Brian Whitefoot; Mark McCafferty; Adam Mack.

**OTHER INFORMATION** A total of 79 grants were awarded in 2013/14.

**HOW TO APPLY** Application forms, full guidelines and criteria are available to download on the website. For applications regarding Community Projects contact Jai Purewal: jpurewal@woodenspoon.com and for applications regarding Capital Projects contact the correspondent.

**WHO TO APPLY TO** 115–117 Fleet Road, Fleet, Hampshire GU51 3PD Tel. 01252 773720 email projects@woodenspoon.com Website www.woodenspoon.com

------

## ■ The F. Glenister Woodger Trust

**CC NO** 802642    **ESTABLISHED** 1990

**WHERE FUNDING CAN BE GIVEN** West Wittering.

**WHO CAN BENEFIT** Charities and other community organisations.

**WHAT IS FUNDED** General charitable purposes in West Wittering and surrounding areas.

**WHAT IS NOT FUNDED** Individuals.

**TYPE OF GRANT** Capital costs; project funding.

**RANGE OF GRANTS** Up to £165,000.

**SAMPLE GRANTS** Witterings Medical Centre – building adaptation (£192,500); New Park Community and Arts Association (£80,000); Friends of St Richard's Hospital – Eye Clinic (£35,000); East Wittering Community Primary School (£34,000); Chichester Rugby Football Club (£25,000); Fordwater School (£15,000); Manhood Mobility Volunteer Service (£9,000); West Wittering Croquet Club (£3,000); Cruse Chichester and Arun Branches (£2,000); PASCO (£1,000); and Calibre Audio Library (£750).

**FINANCES** Year 2013/14  Income £1,277,472  Grants £397,339  Grants to organisations £397,339  Assets £37,212,659

**TRUSTEES** Richard Shrubb, Chair; Rosamund Champ; William Craven; Stuart Dobbin; Maxine Pickup; Tamaris Thompson.

**OTHER INFORMATION** Grants were given to 14 organisations.

**HOW TO APPLY** Apply in writing to the correspondent. The trustees meet quarterly to review grant applications.

**WHO TO APPLY TO** Richard Shrubb, Chair, Wicks Farm Holiday Park, Redlands Lane, West Wittering, West Sussex PO20 8QE Tel. 01243 513116 email wicks.farm@virgin.net

------

## ■ Woodlands Green Ltd

**CC NO** 277299    **ESTABLISHED** 1979

**WHERE FUNDING CAN BE GIVEN** Worldwide.

**WHO CAN BENEFIT** Organisations benefitting Jewish people.

**WHAT IS FUNDED** The charity's objectives are the advancement of the Orthodox Jewish faith and the relief of poverty.

**WHAT IS NOT FUNDED** Individuals; expeditions or scholarships.

**SAMPLE GRANTS Previous beneficiaries have included:** Achisomoch Aid Co, Beis Soro Schneirer, Friends of Beis Yisroel Trust, Friends of Mir, Friends of Seret Wiznitz, Friends of Toldos Avrohom Yitzchok, JET, Kahal Imrei

Chaim, Oizer Dalim Trust, NWLCM, TYY Square and UTA.
**FINANCES** Year 2013/14 Income £239,315 Grants £180,450 Grants to organisations £180,450 Assets £1,283,496
**TRUSTEES** Daniel Ost; E. Ost; A. Ost; J. A. Ost; A. Hepner.
**OTHER INFORMATION** Grants were made to almost 40 organisations in 2013/14, but a list of beneficiaries was not included in the accounts.
**HOW TO APPLY** Apply in writing to the correspondent.
**WHO TO APPLY TO** Daniel Ost, Trustee, 19 Green Walk, London NW4 2AL Tel. 020 8209 1458

## ■ Woodroffe Benton Foundation
**CC NO** 1075272   **ESTABLISHED** 1988
**WHERE FUNDING CAN BE GIVEN** UK.
**WHO CAN BENEFIT** Any charitable organisation based in the UK is eligible to apply for a grant, as are any educational institutions (schools, universities, etc.) whether or not they have charitable status.
**WHAT IS FUNDED** Grants are given to charitable organisations for: the relief of people in need due to disaster or social or economic circumstances; provision and maintenance of care and accommodation for people who are older or sick; promotion of education, particularly in Derbyshire; conservation, preservation, protection and improvement of the environment, particularly where improving access for members of the public. Grants range from £250–£2,000, so the trustees prefer to support smaller charities where a modest donation could provide greater benefit. Organisations with an income of above £1 million are unlikely to receive funding. The trustees prefer to contribute to core operating costs, but will also consider project funding.
**WHAT IS NOT FUNDED** Individuals; organisations that operate primarily outside the UK or for the benefit of non-UK residents; places of worship seeking funds for restoration or upgrade of facilities; students requesting a grant for tertiary education or a gap year; educational organisations based outside the Derbyshire region – although the trustees may choose to do so; museums, historical or heritage organisations; palliative care; animal welfare organisations whose primary purpose is not conservation of the environment; organisations that have been operating for fewer than 12 months; bodies affiliated to or a local 'branch' of a national organisation, even when registered as a separate charity – if you are unsure whether you would fall within this category, submit a query via the foundation's website.
**TYPE OF GRANT** Core costs and running costs; project costs; one-off; ongoing support; small grants for one year or less.
**RANGE OF GRANTS** Most grants are for less than £2,000.
**SAMPLE GRANTS** Beneficiaries of grants which receive ongoing support included: Community Links (£113,000 in three grants); Ilfield Park Care Home (£22,500 in two grants); Queen Elizabeth's Grammar School (£19,000 in six grants); Action for Stammering Children, Furniture Re-Use Network and Prisoners' Families and Friends Service (£5,000 each); Beauchamp Lodge Settlement (£4,000); Theatre Peckham (£1,500).
**FINANCES** Year 2013 Income £226,697 Grants £355,000 Grants to organisations £355,000 Assets £6,568,910
**TRUSTEES** James Hope, Chair; Philip Miles; Colin Russell; Rita Drew; Peter Foster; Richard Page.
**OTHER INFORMATION** In 2013 a total of 238 grants from the foundation's open small grants programme were awarded to 230 organisations, totalling £355,000. The trust gives ongoing support with larger grants to a number of charities. In 2013 a total of 29 charities received ongoing support, totalling £195,000. The trustees also awarded 27 discretionary grants totalling £15,500.
**HOW TO APPLY** Applications are made via an online form on the foundation's website. The trustees meet quarterly, in the second or third week of January, April, July and October and the deadline for the receipt of applications is approximately five weeks prior to each meeting. Applications are not considered between meetings but any received after the deadline are automatically carried forward. Multiple grants are not usually awarded to the same charity in a 12 month period.
**WHO TO APPLY TO** Alan King, Secretary, 44 Leasway, Wickford, Essex SS12 0HE Tel. 01268 562941 email secretary@woodroffebenton.org.uk Website www.woodroffebenton.org.uk

## ■ The Woodward Charitable Trust
**CC NO** 299963   **ESTABLISHED** 1988
**WHERE FUNDING CAN BE GIVEN** UK.
**WHO CAN BENEFIT** Registered charities. Trustees favour small-scale, locally based initiatives.
**WHAT IS FUNDED** General charitable purposes. Grants are distributed in the following categories: arts; community and social welfare; disability and health; education; environment; summer play schemes. As stated on the trust's website, 'Trustees are interested in helping smaller organisations that offer direct services and those that encourage cross community participation. Any participation by past or current users of the service should be mentioned and is encouraged.'
**WHAT IS NOT FUNDED** Charities whose annual turnover exceeds £300,000; construction projects such as playgrounds, village halls, and disability access; general school appeals including out of hours provision; hospices; medical research; parish facilities; playgroups and pre-school groups; requests for vehicles; individuals in any capacity or educational fees. In addition, for summer play schemes, the trustees will also not fund: trips that are only social (trustees prefer to fund trips that are educational and motivational); overseas projects; playgroups.
**TYPE OF GRANT** Usually one-off. Grants from the trust are awarded as small grants (£100–£5,000), large grants (over £5,000 and only given to charities know to the trustees) or children's summer play scheme grants (£500–1,000). The trustees favour one-off projects but will consider core costs and salaries.
**RANGE OF GRANTS** Up to £30,000. Average grant £1,000–5,000.
**SAMPLE GRANTS** London Academy of Music and Dramatic Art (£100,000); Trialogue Educational Trust (£30,000); Dragon School Trust Ltd (£10,000); Blue Sky Development and Regeneration (£5,000); Cartwheel Arts (£3,000); Cricket Without Boundaries Trust (£2,500); African Caribbean Leukaemia Trust, Broxtowe Youth Homelessness and Burnley Youth Theatre (£2,000 each); Conservation Volunteers (£1,700); Hackney Migrant Centre (£1,500); Listening Ear – Merseyside, Malaria

No More UK, Middle Park Play Scheme and Otesha Project UK (£1,000 each); Maternal OCD and Steppin' Stone – the Porch (£500); Crescent Summer School Project and Sheena Amos Youth Trust (£200 each).

**FINANCES** Year 2013/14 Income £115,221 Grants £337,246 Grants to organisations £337,246 Assets £10,894,857

**TRUSTEES** Camilla Woodward; Rt Hon. Shaun A. Woodward; Judith Portrait.

**OTHER INFORMATION** The trust is one of the Sainsbury Family Charitable Trusts which share a common administration. An application to one is taken as an application to all. The trustees particularly favour small/medium-sized organisations and projects that involve past or current users. 177 grants were made in 2013/14, including one exceptionally large grant to LAMDA for a redevelopment project.

**HOW TO APPLY** Full criteria and guidelines are available from the trust's website, along with application forms, which can also be obtained by email. Potential applicants whose project falls within the criteria are invited to telephone the administrator in advance to discuss the advisability of making an application. Applications should not be longer than one page, and all sections must be answered rather than referring to supplementary material. Accounts should only be included if they are not already available on the Charity Commission website. The project's projected outcomes, beneficiaries and legacy should be made clear. Further advice on how to best complete the form is available on the website. Main grants are allocated following trustees' meetings in January and July each year, with the exception of summer schemes, which are considered in May each year. The website has a useful diary of trustees' meetings and of the cut-off dates for applications. All application forms are assessed on arrival and acknowledged within six to eight weeks. Applicants will be contacted if additional information is required. The trust advises that only around 15% of applicants are successful and the majority of grants are for less than £5,000.

**WHO TO APPLY TO** Karin Hooper, Correspondent, The Peak, 5 Wilton Road, London SW1V 1AP Tel. 020 7410 0330 email contact@woodwardcharitabletrust.org.uk Website www.woodwardcharitabletrust.org.uk

.........................................................

■ **Worcester Municipal Charities**

**CC NO** 205299 **ESTABLISHED** 1836
**WHERE FUNDING CAN BE GIVEN** The city of Worcester.
**WHO CAN BENEFIT** Poorer people, individually or generally, in Worcester City.
**WHAT IS FUNDED** Social welfare and the relief of hardship. Grants are given to local individuals to fund 'essential' items or services. Revenue grants and one-off grants are awarded to local organisations that provide services to help those in need. The Worcester Municipal Exhibitions Foundation.
**WHAT IS NOT FUNDED** Organisations of over 49% of their annual income; individuals, unless all statutory sources have been exhausted, and a referral must be made by a professional, such as Citizens Advice advisor, health visitor or social worker.
**TYPE OF GRANT** Cheque or purchase of an item.
**RANGE OF GRANTS** £1,000–£35,000 for running costs; £100–£100,000 for capital costs; £50–£1,000 for individuals.

**SAMPLE GRANTS** Worcester Citizens Advice and WHABAC (£155,500); Maggs Day Centre (£24,000 total); Worcester Community Trust (£15,000); Armchair (£14,500); Worcester Action for Youth (£12,800); ASHA Women's Centre (£10,000); Headway Worcester Trust (£8,500); Shopmobility (£8,000); Worcester Community Trust (£3,800).

**FINANCES** Year 2014 Income £1,723,189 Grants £552,377 Grants to organisations £252,384 Assets £15,200,473

**TRUSTEES** Paul Griffith, Chair; Margaret Jones; Roger Berry; Jess Bird; Paul Denham; Graham Hughes; Bob Kington; Mel Kirk; Roger Knight; Cliff Lord; Stan Markwell; Sue Osborne; Margaret Panter; Robert Peachey; Ron Rust; George Salmon; Martyn Saunders; Brenda Sheridan; Dr David Tibbutt; Tony Whitcher; Mike Whitehouse.

**OTHER INFORMATION** The grant total includes one-off grants made to individuals totalling £4,000, as well as a constitutional grant of £57,000 to the Worcester Municipal Exhibitions Foundation. The grant total includes only those given from the Worcester Consolidated Municipal Charity, not including those from the Worcester Municipal Exhibitions Foundation.

**HOW TO APPLY** Full guidelines are available on the charity's website, along with an application form which should be sent with accounts and any additional information by email. The grants committee meet on a monthly basis to review grant applications.

**WHO TO APPLY TO** Ian Pugh, Clerk to the Trustees, Kateryn Heywood House, Berkeley Court, The Foregate, Worcester WR1 3QG Tel. 01905 317117 email admin@wmcharities.org.uk

.........................................................

■ **The Worcestershire and Dudley Historic Churches Trust**

**CC NO** 1035156 **ESTABLISHED** 1993
**WHERE FUNDING CAN BE GIVEN** The diocese and county of Worcester.
**WHO CAN BENEFIT** Christian churches.
**WHAT IS FUNDED** Grants for the preservation, repair and improvement of churches in the beneficial area and of the monuments, fittings, furniture and so on of such churches.
**WHAT IS NOT FUNDED** Our research suggests that grants are not available for new building projects, organs or bells.
**RANGE OF GRANTS** £500–£5,000
**SAMPLE GRANTS** St Leonard, Ribbesford (£5,000); St Mary, Stanford-on-Teme, Stourbridge Meeting House and St Nicholas, Earls Croome (£2,500 each); St Mary de Witton, Droitwich (£1,500); St Mary and St Andrew, Knightwick and Holy Trinity, Old Hill (£1,000); and St Giles, Heightington (£500).
**FINANCES** Year 2013/14 Income £25,627 Grants £21,346 Grants to organisations £21,346 Assets £34,767
**TRUSTEES** Tim Bridges; John Davies; Jean Crabbe; Samuel White; Annette Leech; Richard Slawson; Michael Thomas; Andrew Grant; Phillip Jones.
**OTHER INFORMATION** In 2013/14 grants were awarded to eight churches totalling £16,500 (and provisional grants approved to seven churches totalling £7,500). About £4,800 was refunded to churches and chapels from a sponsored cycle ride.
**HOW TO APPLY** Requests for grants should be discussed with the secretary who will advise as to whether the project meets the criteria and provide an application form, if applicable. Decisions on grants are made at the trust's

quarterly meetings and following a visit by a trustee. The annual report and accounts state: 'The grant reservation is normally held for a maximum period of twelve months and payment will only be made following receipt of an architect's interim certificate or an appropriate invoice.'

**WHO TO APPLY TO** John Davies, Secretary, Yarrington's, Alfrick, Worcestershire WR6 5EX *Tel.* 01886 884336 *email* flora.donald@virgin.net *Website* www.worcestershirechurches.blogspot.co.uk

## ■ The Wragge & Co Charitable Trust

**CC NO** 803009      **ESTABLISHED** 1990
**WHERE FUNDING CAN BE GIVEN** Mainly West Midlands.
**WHO CAN BENEFIT** Local and national charities operating in the area.
**WHAT IS FUNDED** General charitable purposes with an interest in health and social welfare.
**WHAT IS NOT FUNDED** Individuals; organisations which are not charities.
**RANGE OF GRANTS** Usually up to £6,000.
**SAMPLE GRANTS** SIFA Fireside (£6,000); Make a Wish (£4,200); University of Birmingham (£3,600); Movember Europe (£2,600); Deptford Action Group for the Elderly (£1,300); Birmingham LGBT and Free@last (£1,000 each); Birmingham Children's Hospital Charity (£900); Ackers Adventure, Asthma Relief and Birmingham City Mission (£500 each); Heart of England Community Foundation (£350); Acorns Children's Hospice, Bag Books and Buttle UK (£250 each); and Rainbow Children's Hospice and Walk the Walk Worldwide (£100 each).
**FINANCES** *Year* 2013/14 *Income* £62,530 *Grants* £67,806 *Grants to organisations* £67,806 *Assets* £42,148
**TRUSTEES** Lee Nuttall; Quentin Poole; Philip Clissitt.
**HOW TO APPLY** Appeals may be made in writing to the correspondent.
**WHO TO APPLY TO** Lee Nuttall, Trustee, Wragge Lawrence Graham & Co. LLP, 2 Snowhill, Birmingham B4 6WR *Tel.* 0121 233 1000

## ■ The Diana Edgson Wright Charitable Trust

**CC NO** 327737      **ESTABLISHED** 1987
**WHERE FUNDING CAN BE GIVEN** UK with some preference for Kent.
**WHO CAN BENEFIT** Registered charities.
**WHAT IS FUNDED** General charitable purposes; animal conservation; social welfare causes.
**RANGE OF GRANTS** £500–£3,000
**SAMPLE GRANTS** Starlight Children's Foundation and The Royal British Legion – Santiago Branch (£3,000 each); Royal National Lifeboat Institution and World Horse Welfare (£2,000 each); The Donkey Sanctuary (£1,500); Cantebury Cathedral Trust, Kent Crimestoppers and Stillbirths and Neonatal Death Charity (£1,000 each); Meningitis Trust and The Sebakwe Black Rhino Trust (£500 each).
**FINANCES** *Year* 2013/14 *Income* £64,886 *Grants* £44,500 *Grants to organisations* £44,500 *Assets* £1,451,531
**TRUSTEES** Robert Moorhead; G. Edgson Wright; Henry Moorhead.
**OTHER INFORMATION** In 2013/14 grants were awarded to 45 organisations.
**HOW TO APPLY** Apply in writing to the correspondent.

**WHO TO APPLY TO** Henry Moorhead, Trustee, c/o Henry Moorhead and Company Solicitors, 2 Stade Street, Hythe, Kent CT21 6BD *Tel.* 01303 262525 *email* henmo4@talktalk.net

## ■ The Matthews Wrightson Charity Trust

**CC NO** 262109      **ESTABLISHED** 1970
**WHERE FUNDING CAN BE GIVEN** UK and some overseas.
**WHO CAN BENEFIT** Smaller charities and individuals undertaking charitable projects.
**WHAT IS FUNDED** Funding is given to organisations for general charitable purposes, with preference towards: young people; disability; social welfare, poverty and homelessness; health; the elderly; Christian causes; rehabilitation; the arts; financially developing countries. Grants are also awarded to individuals undertaking charitable work (including medical elective expenses), particularly if that work is overseas. The trust also funds hardship grants for students at the Royal College of Art.
**WHAT IS NOT FUNDED** Maintenance of the fabric of churches, schools and village halls; personal education of individuals (unless for a charitable purpose, such as medical electives); animal charities; large charities or those with an income greater than £250,000.
**TYPE OF GRANT** Mainly one-off; occasionally recurrent; capital and core costs; salaries; start-up funding.
**RANGE OF GRANTS** Typical grant size is £500, with a few larger grants made to regular beneficiaries.
**SAMPLE GRANTS Previous beneficiaries have included:** Tools for Self-Reliance (£2,400); and the Butler Trust, Childhood First, the Daneford Trust, DEMAND, Live Music Now! New Bridge and Practical Action (£1,200 each). Most other donations, with a few exceptions, were for £400 or £500 each.
**FINANCES** *Year* 2013/14 *Income* £65,057 *Grants* £46,800 *Grants to organisations* £46,800 *Assets* £1,701,454
**TRUSTEES** Isabelle White; Guy Garmondsay Wrightson; Priscilla Wilmot Wrightson; Maria de Broe Ferguson; Robert Partridge.
**OTHER INFORMATION** There were 88 grants made in 2013, including grants to individuals. The largest grant of £8,000 was made to the Royal College of Art, to fund 13 hardship grants. The other causes which received the most funding were youth, overseas aid, disability and the poor and homeless.
**HOW TO APPLY** Applications should be made online to the relevant trustee. A list of trustees and the causes in which they are particularly interested is published on the trust's website, along with a link to an online application form for each person. Applications received are considered by the trustees on a monthly basis. Applicants who wish to be advised of the outcome of their application must include an sae. Successful applicants are advised of the trustees' decision at the earliest opportunity.
**WHO TO APPLY TO** Jon Mills, Correspondent, The Old School House, Church Lane, Easton, Winchester SO21 1EH *Tel.* 0845 241 2574 *email* matthewswrightson@gmail.com *Website* matthewswrightson.org.uk

## ■ Wychdale Ltd

**CC NO** 267447     **ESTABLISHED** 1974
**WHERE FUNDING CAN BE GIVEN** UK and abroad.
**WHO CAN BENEFIT** Jewish organisations and charitable organisations.
**WHAT IS FUNDED** Jewish causes, particularly Jewish education, as well as medicine, relief of poverty and general charitable purposes.
**WHAT IS NOT FUNDED** Non-Jewish organisations are generally not supported.
**SAMPLE GRANTS Previous beneficiaries have included:** M and R Gross Charitable Trust (£50,000); Friends of the Yeshivat Shaar Hashamayim (£43,000); Friends of Beis Abraham (£21,000); and Chevras Machzikei Mesifta and Emuno Education (£20,000 each)
**FINANCES** Year 2013/14 Income £24,512 Grants £300,000 Grants to organisations £300,000
**TRUSTEES** C. D. Schlaff; J. Schlaff; Z. Schlaff.
**OTHER INFORMATION** Accounts were not published by the Charity Commission due to the low income of the charity, so the grant total is estimated based on expenditure and grant total in previous years. Expenditure in 2013/14 was £331,000.
**HOW TO APPLY** Apply in writing to the correspondent.
**WHO TO APPLY TO** Sugarwhite Associates, 5 Windus Road, London N16 6UT

## ■ Wychville Ltd

**CC NO** 267584     **ESTABLISHED** 1973
**WHERE FUNDING CAN BE GIVEN** UK.
**WHO CAN BENEFIT** Charitable organisations, particularly those benefitting people of the Jewish faith.
**WHAT IS FUNDED** The advancement of the Orthodox Jewish faith; education; general charitable purposes.
**SAMPLE GRANTS** No information was available regarding beneficiaries.
**FINANCES** Year 2013/14 Income £340,232 Grants £388,846 Grants to organisations £388,846
**TRUSTEES** S. Englander; E. Englander; B. R. Englander.
**OTHER INFORMATION** The trust had negative assets in 2013/14.
**HOW TO APPLY** Apply in writing to the correspondent. All requests are considered by the trustees.
**WHO TO APPLY TO** S. Englander, Trustee, 44 Leweston Place, London N16 6RH Tel. 020 8802 3948

## ■ The Wyndham Charitable Trust

**CC NO** 259313     **ESTABLISHED** 1969
**WHERE FUNDING CAN BE GIVEN** UK and overseas.
**WHO CAN BENEFIT** Charitable organisations.
**WHAT IS FUNDED** General charitable purposes. The trust's main interest lies with helping to bring about the elimination of modern-day slavery through supporting charities connected with this cause.
**WHAT IS NOT FUNDED** Organisations not known to the trustees; individuals.
**RANGE OF GRANTS** Up to £10,000.
**SAMPLE GRANTS** Anti-Slavery International (£10,000); The Royal College of Surgeons of England (£3,700); Christian Aid (£3,000); Dalit Solidarity Network of the UK and ECPAT UK (£1,500 each); Combat Stress (£1,000); Helen and Douglas House, Kidney Research UK, Marine Conservation Society and Prisoners of Conscience Appeal Fund (£500 each); Centrepoint and Multiple Sclerosis Society (£350 each); Royal British Legion (£100); RGJ Museum Waterloo Appeal (£50).
**FINANCES** Year 2013/14 Income £58,749 Grants £56,410 Grants to organisations £56,410 Assets £7,350
**TRUSTEES** John Gaselee; Juliet Gaselee; David Gaselee; Sarah Gaselee.
**OTHER INFORMATION** Grants were given to 74 organisations.
**HOW TO APPLY** The trust has stated that unsolicited applications are unlikely to be supported and they do not encourage requests.
**WHO TO APPLY TO** John Gaselee, Trustee, 34a Westfield Road, Lymington, Hampshire SO41 3QA email wyndham_ct@yahoo.co.uk Website www.wyndham-ct.org

## ■ The Wyseliot Charitable Trust

**CC NO** 257219     **ESTABLISHED** 1968
**WHERE FUNDING CAN BE GIVEN** UK.
**WHO CAN BENEFIT** Registered charities only.
**WHAT IS FUNDED** Medical causes; arts; social welfare of those in need or disadvantage.
**WHAT IS NOT FUNDED** Individuals; grants are only made to registered charities of national significance.
**TYPE OF GRANT** Recurrent funding; core costs; capital costs; project costs.
**RANGE OF GRANTS** Up to £5,000.
**SAMPLE GRANTS** Royal College of Music (£5,000); Alzheimer's Trust (£4,000); Mind and Street Games (£3,500 each); Cystic Fibrosis Trust (£3,000); The Art Fund (£2,500); Centrepoint Soho and Fare Share (£2,000 each); International Glaucoma Association and Runnymede Trust (£1,500 each).
**FINANCES** Year 2013/14 Income £83,063 Grants £80,500 Grants to organisations £80,500 Assets £1,874,760
**TRUSTEES** Jonathan Rose; Emma Rose; Adam Raphael.
**OTHER INFORMATION** Grants were awarded to 29 organisations in 2013/14.
**HOW TO APPLY** Apply in writing to the correspondent; however, note the trust has previously stated that the many of the same charities are supported each year, with perhaps one or two changes. It is unlikely new charities sending circular appeals will be supported and large UK charities are generally not supported. Currently approximately one application is successful each year.
**WHO TO APPLY TO** Jonathan Rose, Trustee, 17 Chelsea Square, London SW3 6LF email charity@friend-james.co.uk

## ■ The Xerox (UK) Trust
CC NO 284698  ESTABLISHED 1982
WHERE FUNDING CAN BE GIVEN UK.
WHO CAN BENEFIT Usually local or mid-sized organisations benefitting children, young adults, at risk groups, people with disabilities, and people who are disadvantaged by poverty or socially isolated.
WHAT IS FUNDED The advancement of equality of opportunity, working with people with disabilities and those who are disadvantaged or terminally ill; young people.
WHAT IS NOT FUNDED Individuals; religious or political organisations; national bodies.
TYPE OF GRANT One-off grants.
RANGE OF GRANTS £500–£2,500
SAMPLE GRANTS Gobo Theatre Foundation (£2,500); Hertfordshire Multiple Sclerosis Therapy Centre (£2,000); Clapton Common Boys' Club (£1,600); Holidays For Disabled People and Special Needs Adventure Playground (£1,000 each); The Respite Association (£600); and Birmingham Youth Foundation, Debtford Action Group for the Elderly, Mid Sussex Community Support Association and Cerebral Palsy Plus (£500 each).
FINANCES Year 2013 Income £65,213 Grants £5,000 Grants to organisations £5,000
TRUSTEES Francis Mooney; John Edwards; John Hopwood.
HOW TO APPLY Applications can be made in writing to the correspondent, preferably supported by a Xerox employee. Applications are considered in April and October, for payment in June and December respectively.
WHO TO APPLY TO Cheryl Walsh, Trust Secretary, Xerox Ltd, Bridge House, Oxford Road, Uxbridge UB8 1HS Tel. 01895 251133

## ■ Yankov Charitable Trust
CC NO 1106703  ESTABLISHED 2004
WHERE FUNDING CAN BE GIVEN Worldwide.
WHO CAN BENEFIT Jewish organisations.
WHAT IS FUNDED Advancement of the Jewish religion and culture among the Jewish community throughout the world.
SAMPLE GRANTS Previous grant beneficiaries include: European Yarchei Kalloh (£53,000); Keren Machzikei Torah (£23,000); Kollel Tiferes Chaim (£21,000); Agudas Israel Housing Association (£12,000); Ponovez Hachnosos Kalloh (£7,600); Freiman Appeal (£7,200); Beth Jacob Grammar School (£4,000); British Friends of Tiferes Chaim (£3,000); Yeshiva Tzemach Yisroel (£2,000); British Friends of Rinat Ahsron (£1,500); and Yeshivat Givat Shaul (£1,000).
FINANCES Year 2013/14 Income £94,827 Grants £98,005 Grants to organisations £98,005 Assets £91,764
TRUSTEES Jacob Schonberg; Bertha Schonberg; Aryeh Schonberg.
OTHER INFORMATION A list of beneficiaries was unavailable.
HOW TO APPLY Apply in writing to the correspondent.
WHO TO APPLY TO Jacob Schonberg, Trustee, 40 Wellington Avenue, London N15 6AS Tel. 020 3150 1227

## ■ The Yapp Charitable Trust
CC NO 1076803  ESTABLISHED 1999
WHERE FUNDING CAN BE GIVEN England and Wales.
WHO CAN BENEFIT It is the trustees' policy to focus their support on smaller charities (local rather than UK), and to offer grants only in situations where a small grant will make a significant difference. The trust therefore only considers applications from charities whose normal turnover is less than £40,000 in the year of application. Grants are only made to applicants who have charitable status. The trust funds charities to sustain their existing work rather than funding new work or projects.
WHAT IS FUNDED Grants are given to charities supporting the following priority groups: older people; children and young people (aged 5–25); people with physical disabilities, learning disabilities or mental health challenges; social welfare, particularly people trying to overcome life-limiting problems of a social nature (such as addiction, relationship difficulties, abuse or offending); education and learning, particularly adults or children who are educationally disadvantaged. The trust gives priority to work that is unattractive to the general public or unpopular with other funders, particularly when it helps improve the lives of marginalised, disadvantaged or isolated people. Preference is also given to charities that can demonstrate the effective use of volunteers, an element of self-sustainability, if possible, and preventive work aiming to create change through raising awareness and campaigning. Grant-making policies are kept under review – current priorities and exclusions are publicised on the trust's website.

# Yardley

*Alphabetical register of grant-making charities*

**WHAT IS NOT FUNDED** The trust's website states that the trustees cannot fund: charities with a total annual expenditure of more than £40,000; charities that are not registered with the Charity Commission in England and Wales (must have own charity number or be excepted from registration. Industrial Provident Societies and Community Interest Companies are not eligible); work that is based in Scotland and Northern Ireland – funding is given only to charities operating in England or Wales; charities with unrestricted reserves equating to more than 12 months expenditure; branches of national charities (must have own charity number, not a shared national registration); new organisations – must have been operating as a fully constituted organisation for at least three years, even though you may have registered as a charity more recently; new work that has not been occurring for at least a year; new paid posts – even if the work is now being done by volunteers; additional activities, expansion or development plans; special events, trips or outings; capital expenditure – including equipment, buildings, renovations, furnishings, minibuses; work with under-5s; childcare; holidays and holiday centres; core funding of charities that benefit the wider community such as general advice services and community centres unless a significant element of their work focuses on one of the trust's priority groups; bereavement support; debt advice; community safety initiatives; charities raising money to give to another organisation, such as schools, hospitals or other voluntary groups; individuals – including charities raising funds to purchase equipment for or make grants to individuals.

**TYPE OF GRANT** Running costs and salaries only. Grants are usually made for more than one year.

**RANGE OF GRANTS** Grants are normally for a maximum of £3,000 per year. Most grants are for more than one year.

**SAMPLE GRANTS** Bradford Phab Club, Kent Refugee Help and Plymouth Focus (£9,000 each); Basantu Outreach Project (£6,000); The Garden Science Trust (£4,000); Barry Beavers Disabled Swimming Club, Derby Access and Child Contact Centre, New Testament Welfare Association and Pembrokeshire Counselling Service (£3,000 each); Somali Community Advancement Organisation and The Muslim Women's Organisation (£2,000 each); British Yemeni Forum and Twynham Rangers Football Club (£1,500 each).

**FINANCES** Year 2012/13 Income £189,875 Grants £226,250 Grants to organisations £226,250 Assets £5,790,479

**TRUSTEES** Revd Timothy C. Brooke; Ron Lis; Alfred Hill; Jane Fergusson; Andrew Burgen; Lisa Suchet.

**OTHER INFORMATION** The Yapp Welfare Trust (two-thirds share) and The Yapp Education and Research Trust (one-third share) merged in September 1999 to become The Yapp Charitable Trust. In 2012/13 grants were awarded to 45 organisations. The largest amount of funding went to social welfare causes. This was the latest information available at the time of writing (June 2015).

**HOW TO APPLY** Application forms and comprehensive guidance are available on the trust's website and can also be received by post. Potential applicants are advised to read the guidelines on the trust's website and check their eligibility. The trust also encourages applicants to contact the trust by telephone for a preliminary discussion before making an application. Applications are usually acknowledged within two weeks. The trustees meet three times a year to review and award grants. Grant recipients are eligible to re-apply for funding from three months before their grant expires. The trust seeks feedback and progress reports from grant recipients, particularly for grants that are paid over a number of years.

**WHO TO APPLY TO** Joanne Anderson, Correspondent, 8 Leyburn Close, Ouston, Chester le Street DH2 1TD *Tel.* 0191 492 2118 *email* info@yappcharitabletrust.org.uk *Website* www.yappcharitabletrust.org.uk

..................................................................

## ■ The Yardley Great Trust

**CC NO** 216082    **ESTABLISHED** 1355

**WHERE FUNDING CAN BE GIVEN** The ancient parish of Yardley, in the South East of Birmingham, amounting to around one fifth in area of the city.

**WHO CAN BENEFIT** Individuals and organisations benefitting people of all ages in the ancient parish of Yardley in Birmingham.

**WHAT IS FUNDED** Grants are made to individuals in need, hardship or distress for the provision of essentials items which will benefit the individual's quality of life. Grants are also made to organisations for projects which benefit the local community, relieving poverty or other need, particularly support for voluntary and community organisations, community centres and village halls, community transport, day centres, holidays and outings, meals provision and play schemes.

**WHAT IS NOT FUNDED** General appeals from national or regional charities.

**TYPE OF GRANT** Usually one-off; capital costs; core costs; project costs.

**RANGE OF GRANTS** £200–£7,500

**SAMPLE GRANTS** St John the Evangelist Church (£6,200); Coventry Law Centre (£5,500); Narthex Centre (£3,500); St John's Primary School (£3,000); St Richard's Centre (£2,300); Gospel Oak Community Centre and Hall Green Churches Child Contact Centre (£1,500 each); Birmingham and Solihull Women's Aid, Highter's Heath Community School and Spark Alive (£1,000 each); Hallmoor School (£500); and The Friends of Glebe Farm (£200).

**FINANCES** Year 2013 Income £2,329,531 Grants £66,904 Grants to organisations £32,169 Assets £8,511,532

**TRUSTEES** Iris Aylin; Revd Andrew Bullock; Jean Hayes; Joy Holt; Cllr Barbara Jackson; Conrad James; Revd John Ray; Revd John Richards; Keith Rollins; Revd John Self; Revd Paul Leckey; Malcolm Cox; Revd William Sands; Andrew Veitch; Robert Jones; Stewart Stacey; Lydia Gaston.

**OTHER INFORMATION** The grant total includes £32,400 that was disbursed in grants of less than £500 to individuals and £2,500 given to residents of Yardley Great Trust. Twelve organisations received grants. The trust owns six sheltered housing developments and provides care services for older people.

**HOW TO APPLY** Applications from individuals should be via a third party such as Neighbourhood Offices or Citizens Advice and should be submitted online. Applications from organisations should be made in writing to the correspondent and should set out the aims of the project, the beneficiary group and anticipated number of beneficiaries, a business or progress plan for at least the next year and information of other possible sources of funding and other grant application outcomes. According to the annual report, criteria that the trustees consider when awarding grants include: 'the possible benefit to the community; the support enjoyed by the project from the community; the number and likely income of people who might benefit from the project and the proportion of such people who live within the Trust's area of benefit; other possible sources of funding; the likelihood of continued success; other factors which the Trustees, at their sole discretion, consider to be relevant.' The trustees meet monthly (except in August) to consider grant applications. Guidance and further information are available on the trust's website.

**WHO TO APPLY TO** Mrs K. L. Grice, Clerk to the Trustees, 31 Old Brookside, Yardley Fields Road, Stechford, Birmingham B33 8QL *Tel.* 0121 784 7889 *email* enquiries@ygtrust.org.uk *Website* www.ygtrust.org.uk

## ■ The W. Wing Yip and Brothers Foundation

**CC NO** 326999     **ESTABLISHED** 1986
**WHERE FUNDING CAN BE GIVEN** UK, particularly Birmingham, Manchester, Croydon and Cricklewood.
**WHO CAN BENEFIT** Individuals, particularly students of Chinese origin; charitable organisations, particularly those with a Chinese connection.
**WHAT IS FUNDED** Educational grants are given to students of Chinese origin to study in the UK, as well as scholarships for Chinese students to study at Churchill College, Cambridge and for students from this college to study in China. Grants are also made to charitable organisations for a range of general charitable purposes, including community welfare, education, medical research and religious activities.
**TYPE OF GRANT** One-off and recurrent grants; project and capital funding.
**RANGE OF GRANTS** Most under £3,000.
**SAMPLE GRANTS** Churchill College Cambridge (£33,600); Host UK (£3,000); Birmingham Chinese School (£2,000); Chinese Education Cultural Community Centre (£1,500); Confederation of Chinese Business and Riding for the Disabled Association (£1,000 each); Royal British Legion (£300); County Air Ambulance and Headway (£250 each); Motor Neurone Disease Association (£200); Little Sisters of the Poor (£100); World Cancer Research Fund (£50).
**FINANCES** Year 2013/14 Income £194,311 Grants £155,150 Grants to organisations £49,150 Assets £1,486,550
**TRUSTEES** Robert Brittain; Jenny Loynton; Git Ying Yap; Hon Yuen Yap; Brian Win Yip; Woon Wing Yip; Albert Yip.
**OTHER INFORMATION** The grant total includes £106,000 given in bursaries to 63 students.
**HOW TO APPLY** Apply in writing to the correspondent.
**WHO TO APPLY TO** Robert Brittain, Trustee, c/o W. Wing Yip plc, The Wing Yip Centre, 375 Nechells Park Road, Birmingham B7 5NT *Tel.* 0121 327 6618 *email* robert.brittain@wingyip.com *Website* www.wingyip.com/Supporting-our-communities/Wing-Yip-Foundation

## ■ Yorkshire and Clydesdale Bank Foundation

**SC NO** SC039747     **ESTABLISHED** 2008
**WHERE FUNDING CAN BE GIVEN** UK.
**WHO CAN BENEFIT** Young people, older people, people with disabilities, disadvantaged people and communities.
**WHAT IS FUNDED** Health; education; community development; social welfare; sports; the environment; arts and culture; equality and diversity; animal welfare.
**RANGE OF GRANTS** £252,000–£2,000
**SAMPLE GRANTS** Help the Hospices (£252,000); Spirit of the Community Awards (£250,000); Money Advice Trust (£50,000); Business in the Community (£26,000); The Chartered Institute of Bankers in Scotland (£12,000); Charities Aid Foundation (£7,000); and Bank Workers Charity and Yorkshire Business in the Arts (£2,000 each).
**FINANCES** Year 2012/13 Income £713,647 Grants £826,087 Grants to organisations £826,087 Assets £302,000
**TRUSTEES** Douglas Campbell; Lorna Macmillan; David Thorburn.
**OTHER INFORMATION** Grants made totalled £826,000. Donations under £2,000 totalled £201,000. This was the latest information available at the time of writing (June 2015).
**HOW TO APPLY** Apply in writing to the correspondent.
**WHO TO APPLY TO** Graeme Duncan, Assistant Company Secretary, Ground Floor Mezzanine, 30 St Vincent Place, Glasgow G1 2HL *Website* www.cbonline.co.uk/about-clydesdale-bank/community

## ■ Yorkshire Building Society Charitable Foundation

**CC NO** 1069082     **ESTABLISHED** 1998
**WHERE FUNDING CAN BE GIVEN** UK, with a preference for grant-making in branch localities.
**WHO CAN BENEFIT** Charitable organisations and good causes meeting the foundation's criteria.
**WHAT IS FUNDED** General charitable purposes including education and training, health, animal welfare, people with disabilities, children and young people, older people.
**WHAT IS NOT FUNDED** Contributions towards large funds; expenses; fees; salaries; administration; research; sponsorship of individuals or events; religious or political activities; mainstream schools; local or government funded bodies.
**TYPE OF GRANT** Money for specific items.
**RANGE OF GRANTS** Usually around £2,000.
**SAMPLE GRANTS** Age UK (£6,300); RSPCA (£5,900); Norfolk Community Foundation (£5,200); Butterwick Hospice (£4,600); One In A Million (£3,600); Cancer Research UK and Marie Curie Cancer Care (£3,100 each); Hospiscare and Trinity Hospice (£3,000 each); East Anglia Children's Hospice (£2,700); Multiple Sclerosis Society (£2,200); and Five Lamps, Loxwood House and Teesside Homeless (£2,000 each).
**FINANCES** Year 2013 Income £523,905 Grants £528,461 Grants to organisations £528,461 Assets £138,542
**TRUSTEES** Christopher Parrish; Andy Caton; Christopher Faulkner; Richard Brown; Linda Oakes.
**OTHER INFORMATION** Grants totalling £529,000 were made to 2,266 'charities and good causes'. 79% of the 2,266 grants made to good causes that were supported in the financial year were nominated by the society's staff and members,

with the remainder of causes being requests received directly from the charity.

**HOW TO APPLY** Application forms can be downloaded, together with guidelines and criteria, from the society's website. Alternatively, you can apply in your local branch of Yorkshire Building Society. The foundation's accounts for 2013 state the following: 'applications for support are usually made through the submission of a form (which members can obtain from Society branches, agencies and online). In addition, requests are received direct from external applicants. All nominations and requests are reviewed by the administrative personnel of the society who are charged with undertaking support for the charity under the framework agreement as referred to above.'

**WHO TO APPLY TO** Nirmisha Popat, Company Secretary, Yorkshire Building Society, Yorkshire House, Yorkshire Drive, Bradford, West Yorkshire BD5 8LJ *Tel.* 01274 706606 *email* charitable@ybs.co.uk *Website* www.ybs.co.uk/your-society/charity/charitable-foundation/apply.html

■ **The South Yorkshire Community Foundation**

**CC NO** 1140947        **ESTABLISHED** 1986
**WHERE FUNDING CAN BE GIVEN** South Yorkshire wide, with specific reference to Barnsley, Doncaster, Rotherham, Sheffield.
**WHO CAN BENEFIT** Community and voluntary organisations benefitting communities in the beneficiary area, particularly people in poverty or disadvantage.
**WHAT IS FUNDED** General charitable purposes, particularly social welfare. The foundation aims to meet the needs of local communities and improve the lives of local people, particularly people facing economic hardship and barriers to aspiration. A number of grants programmes are administered by the foundation, funding a wide range of organisations supporting communities in South Yorkshire.
**WHAT IS NOT FUNDED** Check the website or contact the foundation for exclusions and criteria relevant to each of their funding programmes. For the foundation's Small Grants programmes, funding is not given for: groups that have substantial unrestricted funds; national charities; activities promoting political or religious beliefs or where people are excluded on political or religious grounds; statutory bodies e.g. schools, local councils, colleges; projects outside South Yorkshire; endowments; projects supporting animals; contributions to large project where the amount requested is less than 20% of total project cost; retrospective funding; consultancy fees or feasibility studies; sponsorship or fundraising events; minibuses or other vehicles; activities for personal profit; grants for IT and associated equipment amounting to over £400.
**TYPE OF GRANT** Capital and core costs; projects; salaries. Grants vary according to each funding programme. The main small grants programme is for amounts under £1,500.
**RANGE OF GRANTS** £100–£50,000. Most grants under £10,000.
**SAMPLE GRANTS** Monk Bretton Cricket Club (£37,500); Business and Education South Yorkshire (£15,000); Barnsley Neighbourhood Watch Liaison Group (£11,500); FareShare Yorkshire and The Children's Hospital Charity (£10,000 each); Music in the Round (£2,000 in total); Rossington Community Carnival Association (£1,500); Age UK Rotherham, Sheffield ME Group and The Conservation Volunteers (£1,000 each); Doncaster Pride (£800); Museums Sheffield (£500 each); Friends of Ruskin Park and Gujarat Association of Barnsley (£350); Brampton Junior Youth Club (£250); I Can Charity (£100).
**FINANCES** *Year* 2012/13 *Income* £1,220,965 *Grants* £632,957 *Grants to organisations* £632,957 *Assets* £9,122,376
**TRUSTEES** Jonathan Hunt, Chair; R. J. Giles Bloomer; Timothy Greenacre; Peter Hollis; Rick Plews; Paul Benington; Frank Carter; Jackie Drayton; Galen Ives; Allan Jackson; Jane Kemp; Jane Marshall; The Earl of Scarborough; Sue Scholey; Maureen Shah; Alan Sherriff; Lady R. Sykes; Tim Reed; William Warrack.
**OTHER INFORMATION** At the time of writing (June 2015) this was the latest information available. A total of 261 grants were made in 2012/13. A list of beneficiaries was provided on the foundation's website.
**HOW TO APPLY** Information and guidelines on each of the foundation's funding programmes are available on the website. Before making an application, potential applicants are strongly advised to contact the grants team by telephone to check the current status of funds, discuss eligibility and receive advice and support on making an application. Stage 1 applications should then be completed online and applicants will be informed within one month whether they have been invited to complete the second stage of applications. Decisions on second stage applications are made by a panel of independent volunteers that meet around every 12 weeks.
**WHO TO APPLY TO** Sue Wragg, Fund Manager, Unit 3 - G1 Building, 6 Leeds Road, Sheffield S9 3TY *Tel.* 0114 242 4294 *email* grants@sycf.org.uk *Website* www.sycf.org.uk

■ **The Yorkshire Dales Millennium Trust**

**CC NO** 1061687        **ESTABLISHED** 1996
**WHERE FUNDING CAN BE GIVEN** The Yorkshire Dales.
**WHO CAN BENEFIT** Voluntary organisations; community groups; farmers and other individuals; Yorkshire Dales National Park Authority; estates; National Trust; parish councils; district councils; English Nature.
**WHAT IS FUNDED** The conservation and regeneration of the natural and built heritage and community life of the Yorkshire Dales, for example, planting new and restoring old woods, the restoration of dry stone walls and field barns, conservation of historical features and community projects.
**SAMPLE GRANTS** Grants were distributed to organisations under the following programmes: YDNPA Sustainable Development Fund (£368,000); Woodland Projects (£77,500); Three Peaks Access Project (£12,800); Settle Riverside (£200).
**FINANCES** *Year* 2013/14 *Income* £1,240,913 *Grants* £458,516 *Grants to organisations* £458,516 *Assets* £442,501
**TRUSTEES** Stephen Macare; Joseph Pearlman; Carl Lis; Colin Speakman; Dorothy Fairburn; David Rees-Jones; Jane Roberts; Peter Charlesworth; David Joy; Thomas Wheelwright; Andrew Campbell; David Shaw; Wendy Hull; Karen Cowley; Christine Leigh.

HOW TO APPLY Check the trust's website for information on any current grant funding programmes.
WHO TO APPLY TO Isobel Hall, Projects and Grants Manager, The Old Post Office, Main Street, Clapham, Lancaster LA2 8DP *Tel.* 01524 251002 *email* info@ydmt.org *Website* www.ydmt.org

## ■ The Yorkshire Historic Churches Trust

CC NO 700639  ESTABLISHED 1988
WHERE FUNDING CAN BE GIVEN Yorkshire (the historic county of Yorkshire before local government reorganisation in 1974).
WHO CAN BENEFIT All Christian churches.
WHAT IS FUNDED The repair, restoration, preservation and maintenance of churches in the area stated above. Priority is given to the main fabric of the church. Lower priority items include bells, monuments, clocks and organs.
WHAT IS NOT FUNDED Improvements of organs and clocks rather than replacements (e.g. manual organ to electronic); heating facilities; disability access facilities; work that has already commenced before the application has been received and acknowledged.
TYPE OF GRANT Capital building grants. Funding of up to three years will be considered.
RANGE OF GRANTS £250–£6,000
SAMPLE GRANTS St Peter – Huddersfield (£5,000); Bullhouse Chapel – Sheffield (£4,000); Hope Baptist Church – Hebden Bridge and St Wilfrid – Monk Fryston (£3,000 each); Ripon Cathedral (£2,500); St Mary – Watton (£1,500); All Hallows – Walkington (£500); and All Souls – Leeds (£400).
FINANCES *Year* 2013 *Income* £149,979 *Grants* £105,650 *Grants to organisations* £105,650 *Assets* £1,020,601
TRUSTEES Prof. Clyde Binfield; Richard Carr-Archer; The Lord Crathorne; Malcolm Warburton; Tom Ramsden; David Quick; Rory Wardroper; John Smith; Peter Johnston; Anthony Hesselwood; Jane Hedley.
OTHER INFORMATION A total of 43 grants were awarded in 2013/14.
HOW TO APPLY Applications should be made in writing to the trust's Grants Secretary. Applicants should be able to demonstrate a good fundraising effort and are expected to have applied to at least five other sources of grants. Decisions on awarding a grant will be delayed until the outcome of applications to major grant bodies are known.
WHO TO APPLY TO Mr J. K. Stamp, Grants Secretary, c/o 11 Ovington Close, Templetown, Consett, Co Durham DH8 7NY *Tel.* 07594 578665 *email* yhctgrants@sky.com *Website* www.yhct.org.uk

## ■ The William Allen Young Charitable Trust

CC NO 283102  ESTABLISHED 1978
WHERE FUNDING CAN BE GIVEN UK, with a preference for South London.
WHO CAN BENEFIT Registered charities.
WHAT IS FUNDED General charitable purposes, with a preference for health and social welfare.
RANGE OF GRANTS £100–£40,000
SAMPLE GRANTS British Embassy British Cemetery Account (£40,000); Halow Project (£25,000); Anti-Slavery International (£20,000); National Brain Appeal (£15,000); Great Ormond Street Hospital Charity (£14,000); Crisis (£10,000); Trinity Hospice (£9,000); Holy Trinity Church Ebernoe (£5,000); Arundel Cricket Foundation and CHICKS (£2,000 each); Diabetes UK, Interact Reading Service, National M.E. Centre and Scope (£1,000 each); Henry Cavendish School (£500); Street Child Africa and Uganda Development Services (£100 each).
FINANCES *Year* 2013/14 *Income* £491,835 *Grants* £563,544 *Grants to organisations* £563,544 *Assets* £31,081,076
TRUSTEES Torquil Sligo-Young; James Young.
OTHER INFORMATION Grants were made to 194 organisations in 2013/14.
HOW TO APPLY The trust has previously stated that all funds are committed and consequently unsolicited applications will not be supported.
WHO TO APPLY TO Torquil Sligo-Young, Trustee, Young and Co.'s Brewery plc, Riverside House, 26 Osiers Road, London SW18 1NH *Tel.* 020 8875 7000 *email* janice.pearce@youngs.co.uk

## ■ The John Kirkhope Young Endowment Fund

SC NO SC002264  ESTABLISHED 1992
WHERE FUNDING CAN BE GIVEN Edinburgh.
WHO CAN BENEFIT Registered charities.
WHAT IS FUNDED Grants are given to support medical and surgical research and research in chemistry as an aid to UK industry. The charity also funds charities which are concerned with the physical well-being of young people in Edinburgh and the treatment of those in ill health.
WHAT IS NOT FUNDED Individuals; non-registered charities.
TYPE OF GRANT One-off; up to one year; core costs; salaries; capital costs; project funding.
RANGE OF GRANTS £500–£2,000
SAMPLE GRANTS **Previous beneficiaries have included:** Alzheimer's Scotland, Kidney Kids Scotland and Tommy's (£2,000 each); Alzheimer's Research Trust, British Institute for Brian Injured Children, Capability Scotland, Maggie's Cancer Caring Centres and Lee Smith Foundation (£1,000 each); Bethany Christian Trust and Fairbridge in Scotland (£1,500 each); and Guide Dogs for the Blind Association, PBC Foundation and Youth Scotland (£500 each).
FINANCES *Year* 2014 *Income* £43,968 *Grants* £50,000 *Grants to organisations* £50,000
TRUSTEES A. J. R. Ferguson; R. J. S. Morton; S. F. J. Judson; D. J. Hamilton.
OTHER INFORMATION The trust had a total expenditure of £58,000 in 2014. Accounts for the year were not available, so the grant total has been estimated based on expenditure.
HOW TO APPLY Apply in writing to the correspondent. The trustees meet to consider grants in the autumn.
WHO TO APPLY TO The Trust Administrator, Quartermile Two, 2 Lister Square, Edinburgh EH3 9GL

## ■ Youth Music (previously known as National Foundation for Youth Music)

CC NO 1075032  ESTABLISHED 1999
WHERE FUNDING CAN BE GIVEN England.
WHO CAN BENEFIT Music organisations; singing groups; nursery schools; nursery departments of large organisations; schools; after-school clubs;

youth groups; recording studios; local authority departments; other organisations providing music-making opportunities to children and young people of any age up to 18.

**WHAT IS FUNDED** Youth Music funds projects that provide musical opportunities and activities for children and young people, working towards greater inclusion of youth in musical activities, across all genres and styles. The fund's four main priorities are: supporting children and young people in challenging circumstances; creating high quality music-making experiences; supporting young people's progression; sharing practice. Grants are awarded from Fund A, B or C, depending on the size of the grant and duration of the project.

**WHAT IS NOT FUNDED** Individuals and sole traders; companies limited by shares or other profit-making organisations; activities that do not mainly take place in England or do not benefit people in England; activities that promote party political or religious beliefs; retrospective funding; significant capital costs such as land, buildings, vehicles, property, refurbishment or landscaping; reserves, loans or interest payments; art forms unrelated to music.

**TYPE OF GRANT** Project duration can be from one year up to three years and longer. Core costs and salaries are funded.

**RANGE OF GRANTS** £2,000–£180,000

**SAMPLE GRANTS** Unitas (£199,000); The Garage (£180,000); Bristol Plays Music (£138,000); Birmingham Youth Offending Service (£115,500); GemArts (£100,000); National Centre for Early Music (£95,000); Winchcombe Secondary School (£20,000 each); Heart'n Soul, New Charter Homes Ltd (£19,000); Percy Community Centre (£16,500); Pre-School Learning Alliance (£13,500); xplorARTS (£7,000).

**FINANCES** Year 2013/14 Income £9,973,009 Grants £9,218,220 Grants to organisations £9,218,220 Assets £1,308,465

**TRUSTEES** Andy Parfitt; Richard Peel; David Poole; Nicholas Cleobury; Sean Gregory; Clive Grant; Constance Agyeman; Timothy Berg; Rafi Gokay

**OTHER INFORMATION** This trust is funded each year by a payment of around £10 million from the National Lottery, channelled through Arts Council England. In 2013/14 grants were given to 165 organisations to support 192 projects.

**HOW TO APPLY** The three funds from which grants are awarded each differ in their funding criteria and application process. Potential applicants are advised to refer to the Youth Music Network website for up-to-date criteria, priorities, guidelines and deadlines. Applications are made online, via the Youth Music Network website.

**WHO TO APPLY TO** Angela Linton, Suites 3–5, Swan Court, 9 Tanner Street, London SE1 3LE Tel. 020 7902 1060 email grants@youthmusic.org.uk Website www.youthmusic.org.uk

## ■ Youth United Foundation

**CC NO** 1147952 **ESTABLISHED** 2012
**WHERE FUNDING CAN BE GIVEN** UK
**WHO CAN BENEFIT** Uniformed youth groups. This charity exists for the benefit of all uniformed youth groups, including: The Scouts Association; Girlguiding UK; St John Ambulance; Army Cadets; Sea Cadets; Boy's Brigade; Girl's Brigade; Volunteer Police Cadets; Fire Cadets; RAF Air Cadets.

**WHAT IS FUNDED** Supporting joint work amongst a network of established national voluntary youth organisations, with a particular focus on increasing access and participation in disadvantaged areas. Grants are awarded to member organisations for a wide range of purposes and are intended to flexible in order to facilitate meeting diverse local needs, whether supporting activities, recruitment, delivery or growth.

**WHAT IS NOT FUNDED** Grants are available to member organisations.

**SAMPLE GRANTS** Beneficiaries included the following Youth United organisations: Emergency Services Cadets, Fire Cadets, St John Ambulance, Reserve Forces and Cadets Association (RFCA), Voluntary Police Cadets, Marine Society and Sea Cadets, The Scout Association, Girlguiding, The Girls' Brigade and The Boys' Brigade.

**FINANCES** Year 2014 Income £5,743,793 Grants £4,607,818 Grants to organisations £4,607,818 Assets £593,073

**TRUSTEES** Susan Lomas; Adam Hale; Martin Coles; Shyama Perera; David Feldman; Roderick Jarman; Paul Stephen.

**OTHER INFORMATION** The foundation has received funding from DCLG, The Queen's Trust, Laing Foundation, Cabinet Office, Youth Social Action Fund and the Libor fines.

**HOW TO APPLY** Organisations wishing to apply for a grant should contact their local branch or the national charity. Youth United has local branches in Wales, Ayrshire, Avon, Cheshire, Derbyshire, Greater Manchester, London and Bedfordshire.

**WHO TO APPLY TO** Rosie Thomas, Director, 202 Lambert Road, London SE1 7JW Tel. 020 7401 7601 email youth.united@yuf.org.uk Website www.youthunited.org.uk

## ■ Zephyr Charitable Trust

**CC NO** 1003234  **ESTABLISHED** 1991
**WHERE FUNDING CAN BE GIVEN** UK and worldwide.
**WHO CAN BENEFIT** Registered charities.
**WHAT IS FUNDED** The trust's grants are particularly targeted towards three areas: enabling lower income communities to be self-sustaining; the protection and improvement of the environment; providing relief and support for those in need, particularly from medical conditions or social or financial disadvantage.
**WHAT IS NOT FUNDED** Individuals; expeditions or scholarships.
**TYPE OF GRANT** Mainly annual 'subscriptions' decided by the trustees.
**RANGE OF GRANTS** Most grants under £5,000.
**SAMPLE GRANTS** Survival International (£50,000); Practical Action (£3,700); Sandema Educational Resource Centre (£3,300); Pesticide Action Network (£3,200); Freedom From Torture and Friends of the Earth Trust (£2,800 each); Womankind (£2,300); Crisis (£2,200); Missing People and Quaker Social Action Group (£2,000 each); Paddington Farm Trust and Tools for Self Reliance (£1,800 each); Action Village India (£1,000).
**FINANCES** Year 2013/14 Income £64,654 Grants £87,700 Grants to organisations £87,700 Assets £1,733,909
**TRUSTEES** Elizabeth Breeze; Marigo Harries; David Baldock; Donald Watson.
**OTHER INFORMATION** Grants were made to 17 organisations in 2013/14.
**HOW TO APPLY** The trustees state in their annual report that unsolicited applications will not be accepted.
**WHO TO APPLY TO** The Trust Administrator, Luminary Finance LLP, PO Box 135, Longfield, Kent DA3 8WF Tel. 01732 822114

## ■ The Marjorie and Arnold Ziff Charitable Foundation

**CC NO** 249368  **ESTABLISHED** 1964
**WHERE FUNDING CAN BE GIVEN** UK, with a preference for Yorkshire, especially Leeds and Harrogate.
**WHO CAN BENEFIT** There are no restrictions regarding which organisations can benefit.
**WHAT IS FUNDED** This foundation likes to support causes that will provide good value for the money donated by benefitting a large number of people, as well as encouraging others to make contributions to the work. This includes a wide variety of schemes that involve the community at many levels, including education, public places, the arts and helping people who are disadvantaged.
**WHAT IS NOT FUNDED** Individuals.
**TYPE OF GRANT** Capital costs and building work are particularly favoured by the trustees.
**RANGE OF GRANTS** £30–£125,000
**SAMPLE GRANTS** United Jewish Israel Appeal (£125,000); Maccabi (£36,000); 70 Days for 70 Years (£35,000); LGI Oncology (£25,000); Lifeline for the Old (£15,000); Leeds Jewish Blind Society (£3,000); Jewish Museum (£2,500); Prostate Cancer UK (£1,400); WaterAid (£400); Wellbeing of Women (£350);
Ronald McDonald House – Bristol (£250); The Anthony Nolan Trust and Variety – the Children's Charity (£100 each); Agape Volunteers (£50); British Red Cross (£30).
**FINANCES** Year 2013/14 Income £961,900 Grants £488,831 Grants to organisations £488,831 Assets £8,845,210
**TRUSTEES** Marjorie Ziff; Michael Ziff; Edward Ziff; Ann Manning.
**OTHER INFORMATION** Grants were awarded to 79 organisations in 2013/14.
**HOW TO APPLY** Apply in writing to the correspondent.
**WHO TO APPLY TO** Debra Evans, Secretary, Town Centre House, The Merrion Centre, Leeds LS2 8LY Tel. 0113 222 1234

## ■ Stephen Zimmerman Charitable Trust

**CC NO** 1038310  **ESTABLISHED** 1994
**WHERE FUNDING CAN BE GIVEN** UK.
**WHO CAN BENEFIT** Charitable organisations; Jewish organisations.
**WHAT IS FUNDED** General charitable purposes, with a preference for Jewish causes.
**SAMPLE GRANTS** **Previous beneficiaries have included:** British ORT, Cancer Research, CIS Development Fund, London Youth, Jewish Association of Business Ethics, Jewish Care, Norwood Ltd, RNIB, United Jewish Israel Appeal and United Synagogue.
**FINANCES** Year 2013/14 Income £37,592 Grants £100,054 Grants to organisations £100,054 Assets £62,984
**TRUSTEES** Laura Zimmerman; Michael Marks; Stephen Zimmerman.
**OTHER INFORMATION** No information about recent beneficiaries was available.
**HOW TO APPLY** The trust does not respond to unsolicited applications.
**WHO TO APPLY TO** Stephen Zimmerman, Trustee, 35 Stormont Road, London N6 4NR Tel. 020 7518 3849 email stephen.zimmerman@mzcapital.co.uk

## ■ The Zochonis Charitable Trust

**CC NO** 274769  **ESTABLISHED** 1978
**WHERE FUNDING CAN BE GIVEN** UK, particularly Greater Manchester, and overseas, particularly Africa.
**WHO CAN BENEFIT** Registered charities only.
**WHAT IS FUNDED** General charitable purposes, with some preference for education and the welfare of children.
**WHAT IS NOT FUNDED** Individuals.
**TYPE OF GRANT** One-off and recurrent.
**RANGE OF GRANTS** £2,000–£300,000
**SAMPLE GRANTS** **Previous beneficiaries have included:** Cancer Research UK, University of Manchester, Manchester High School for Girls, British Red Cross, Breakthrough Breast Cancer, Asthma Relief and National Talking Newspapers and Magazines.
**FINANCES** Year 2013/14 Income £26,377,248 Grants £3,844,770 Grants to organisations £3,844,770 Assets £199,945,588
**TRUSTEES** Christopher Green; Archibald Calder; Paul Milner; Joseph Swift.
**OTHER INFORMATION** A total of 188 grants were made in 2013/14. The trust was established by the late Sir John Zochonis, former head of P Z Cussons plc, the soap and toiletries manufacturer, with shares in the company. About £22 million of this year's income was in

the form of P Z Cussons shares from the estate of Christine Zochonis.
**HOW TO APPLY** Apply in writing to the correspondent.
**WHO TO APPLY TO** Marie Gallagher, Correspondent, Manchester Business Park, 3500 Aviator Way, Manchester M22 5TG *Tel.* 0161 435 1005 *email* enquiries@zochonischaritabletrust.com

## ■ The Zolfo Cooper Foundation

**CC NO** 1134913   **ESTABLISHED** 2010
**WHERE FUNDING CAN BE GIVEN** Not defined. In practice, UK.
**WHO CAN BENEFIT** Registered charities.
**WHAT IS FUNDED** General charitable purposes.
**TYPE OF GRANT** One-off and recurrent grants.
**RANGE OF GRANTS** £1,000–£11,000
**SAMPLE GRANTS** RMHC (£11,900); Dulwich Picture Gallery (£10,000); The Christie (£8,700); Anna Freud Centre and London Music Masters (£5,000 each); International Childcare Trust (£3,000); Cancer Research UK and Movember (£2,500); DEC Philippines Appeal and Meningitis Research Organisation (£2,000 each); Shooting Star Chase (£1,800); NSPCC (£1,700); Sue Ryder Wheatfields Hospice and Belmont Academy (£1,000 each).
**FINANCES** *Year* 2013/14 *Income* £119,183 *Grants* £95,420 *Grants to organisations* £95,420 *Assets* £102,446
**TRUSTEES** Nick Gittings; Anne O'Keefe; Anne-Marie Laing; Alastair Beveridge; Ryan Grant; Luke Hartley.
**OTHER INFORMATION** A total of 125 grants were made in 2013/14. Out of these 101 were for less than £1,000 and totalled £21,000.
**HOW TO APPLY** Apply in writing to the correspondent.
**WHO TO APPLY TO** The Trustees, c/o Zolfo Cooper LLP, 10 Fleet Place, London EC4M 7RB *Tel.* 020 7332 5000 *email* ctompson@alixpartners.com

## ■ Zurich Community Trust (UK) Limited

**CC NO** 266983   **ESTABLISHED** 1973
**WHERE FUNDING CAN BE GIVEN** UK and overseas.
**WHO CAN BENEFIT** Registered charities; voluntary organisations; non-governmental organisations.
**WHAT IS FUNDED** Social welfare, improving quality of life for disadvantaged people; supporting disadvantaged children to become independent.
**WHAT IS NOT FUNDED** Individuals; medical research; statutory organisations including mainstream schools and hospitals, unless exclusively for a special needs group; animal welfare; conservation or environmental projects, unless involving disadvantaged people; political or military organisations; religious organisations; sports clubs, village halls, playgroups and mother and toddler groups, unless for a special needs group; scouts, girl guides, cadets and other similar organisations, unless specifically supporting disadvantaged children; fundraising events including appeals or events for national charities; and advertising or sponsorship connected with charitable activities. For overseas projects the foundation will not fund: disaster relief or emergency work; proposals which show any racial, political or religious bias; individuals; expeditions or study exchanges; medical research; and fundraising events or appeals.
**TYPE OF GRANT** One-off, or partnership grants for three to five years; core costs; project costs; revenues; salaries; seed funding; capital grants.
**RANGE OF GRANTS** Grants tend to range from £100 to £5,000.
**SAMPLE GRANTS** A list of local and overseas grants was not available.
**FINANCES** *Year* 2013 *Income* £3,697,000 *Grants* £2,110,000 *Grants to organisations* £2,110,000 *Assets* £4,293,000
**TRUSTEES** Ian Lovett; Tim Culling; Kay Martin; Gary Shaughnessy; Vinicio Cellerini; Vibhu Sharma; Jonathan Plumtree; Miranda Chalk; Dr Subo Shanmuganathan; Wayne Myslik.
**HOW TO APPLY** In the first instance, visit the trust's website and follow the links to check eligibility and download the guidelines and application forms.
**WHO TO APPLY TO** Pam Webb, Head of Zurich Community Trust (UK) Limited, Zurich Financial Services (UKISA) Ltd, PO Box 1288, Swindon SN1 1FL *Tel.* 01793 502450 *email* pam.webb@zct.org.uk *Website* www.zurich.co.uk/zurichcommunitytrust/home/home.htm

# What else can DSC do for you?

Let us help you to be the best you possibly can be. DSC equips individuals and organisations with expert skills and information to help them provide better services and outcomes for their beneficiaries. With the latest techniques, best practice and funding resources all brought to you by our team of experts, you will not only boost your income but also exceed your expectations.

## Publications

With over 100 titles we produce fundraising directories and research reports, as well as accessible 'how to' guides and best practice handbooks, all to help you help others.

## Training

The voluntary sector's best-selling training – 80 courses covering every type of voluntary sector training.

## In-house Training

All DSC courses are available on your premises, delivered by expert trainers and facilitators. We also offer coaching, consultancy, mentoring and support.

## Conferences and Fairs

DSC conferences are a fantastic way to network with voluntary sector professionals whilst taking part in intensive, practical training workshops.

## Funding Websites

DSC's funding websites provide access to thousands of trusts, grants, statutory funds and corporate donations. You won't get more funders, commentary and analysis anywhere else. Demo our sites free today.

Trust**funding**.org.uk
Government**funding**.org.uk
Company**giving**.org.uk
Grantsfor**individuals**.org.uk

Visit our website today and see what we can do for you:

## www.dsc.org.uk

Or contact us directly:
publications@dsc.org.uk

**@DSC_Charity**
*For top tips and special offers*